Encyclopedia of
North American Railroads

Editorial Board

Encyclopedia of
North American Railroads

Edited by

William D. Middleton,
George M. Smerk,
and Roberta L. Diehl

Indiana University Press

Bloomington and Indianapolis

This book is a publication of

Indiana University Press
601 North Morton Street
Bloomington, Indiana 47404-3797 USA

http://iupress.indiana.edu

Telephone orders   800-842-6796
Fax orders   812-855-7931
Orders by e-mail   iuporder@indiana.edu

The paper used in this publication meets the minimum requirements of American
National Standard for Information Sciences—Permanence of Paper for Printed Library
Materials, ANSI Z39.48-1984.

Manufactured in China

Cataloging information is available from the Library of Congress.

ISBN 978-0-253-34916-3 (cl.)

1   2   3   4   5   12   11   10   09   08   07

Indiana University Press thanks the following sponsors for their generous support
of the *Encyclopedia of North American Railroads*:

The Indiana Rail Road Company

CSX Corporation

The Arthur R. Metz Foundation at the Indiana University Foundation

Mr. and Mrs. John J. Atherton

James W. McClellan

Robert E. McMillan

Contents

Foreword

The United States was the first nation, outside of England, to enthusiastically build railways on a large scale. In fact, it had more iron highways than other countries by about 1860. Almost all of the system was built by private investors, and a good portion of it was built through unsettled territory. To claim that it altered the lives of most Americans is an understatement. It revolutionized the transportation of goods and people and propelled America into the industrial age. Was the rush to mechanize transit a good idea? If you believe that colonizing the vast undeveloped territory of North America quickly and creating of enormous wealth with equal speed were good things, then of course it was the right way to go. If you believe in a more careful, regulated, and conservative exploitation of the natural riches of the New World, then it was not at all a wise plan. However, the wisdom or folly of what was done cannot now be greatly altered, and so it is the purpose of this book to explain what happened rather than pass judgment on the actions of our forefathers.

American historians and thinkers have generally regarded railroads as a positive force. Emerson said, "Railroad iron is a magician's rod in its power to wake the sleeping energies of land and water." It created a revolution in travel, space, and time. Nothing so speeded up travel in the history of mankind as the steam locomotive. Its capital needs created a new business order of unprecedented size and power. The railway was the economic detonator of the nineteenth century, according to British historian Michael Robbins. It was America's first big business, in the opinion of Professor Alfred D. Chandler, Jr. Of course, counterclaims have been made by other economic historians such as Professor Robert Fogel, who contends that highways and canals were capable of performing the same transportation miracles in the nineteenth century. Other critics felt that the railroads' very success led to excesses in cost of service and neglect of safety. As the railroad monopoly of inland transport grew ever stronger by about 1900, so too did the demand for regulation and reform.

While this debate raged on, the railroads took over the transport of every product from the most basic, such as coal and lumber, to the most ephemeral, such as cut flowers and newspapers. There was no product that did not move over steel rails. The local station was the community center. Almost all travelers arrived or departed from it. So, too, did fresh bread, baby chicks, pianos, the U.S. mail, and coffins. The telegraph clicked away with information on world news and the most personal family happenings. This has all changed. The small-town depot is gone, and few items are dropped for local use. The railroad has almost no direct contact with the average citizen. It is now a highly specialized, bulk carrier serving large industries. Yet it remains one of the most efficient in terms of fuel economy and land use.

The railroad's contact with ordinary people was once profound. It economically carried millions of our ancestors in reasonable, if not deluxe, accommodations for just three cents a mile. By 1916, 98 percent of American travelers went by train. Those unhappy with small-town life could board a train for the big city. Major terminals such as Chicago saw a train arrive or depart every four minutes. Friends and family kept in touch easily and cheaply by our once-remarkable passenger train network. Those who wanted to live in the country could commute to work on a suburban train. The personal touch of the iron network was extended by a great array of railroad workers. At the time of World War I the railroad workforce was nearly 2 million strong and represented every imaginable trade, well beyond the familiar locomotive engineers, conductors, and brakemen. Track-repair gangs gave thousands of jobs to unskilled immigrants. Machinists, carpenters, and painters labored in the repair shops. Clerks by the battalion were needed to care for billing and accounting. Women worked in these positions and as station agents. Just about every family had someone with a railroad job. There were so many railroad workers that the federal government established a separate retirement system for them.

The United States once boasted the largest railway system in the world. At 250,000 miles, it was long enough to reach the moon. Some sections of the network were so busy that four main-line tracks were necessary. Every few minutes another train dashed onward to a distant terminal. Much of that mileage has been abandoned. Thousands more miles have been downgraded to low-speed switching service. Employment and rolling numbers have declined considerably, as reflected in the tables appearing elsewhere in this volume. Yet freight traffic is at a record level, showing the inherent efficiency of steel wheels on steel rails to move goods. The productivity of rail transport remains unchallenged.

One educated guess has estimated that 13,000 books have been produced about North American railroads over the past 150 years or so. These include corporate histories of major and minor lines and regional and statewide studies. Hundreds of volumes have been produced about locomotives. Logging railroads are a popular topic. There are biographies of famous and not-so-famous railroad men. We could go on to list more topics covered by past writers. Yet not one of these tomes really summarizes the subject in a very satisfactory manner, and the few that tried to do so are now very out-of-date. The present book was assembled with the ambitious purpose of filling this void. If we are only somewhat successful in that endeavor, the various participants will feel that they have done their duty to record a subject they very much admire.

John H. White, Jr.

Preface

The development of North American railways must be numbered among the most important achievements of the nineteenth century. They provided the fast and efficient overland transportation that permitted settlement of the vast spaces of the central and western territories; enabled development of the country's agricultural and mineral riches and its manufactured goods; created a transcontinental transportation network that helped tie together the widely scattered places of the huge continent; and helped create truly united nations. They were central to the development of the continent, and they would be unsurpassed anywhere in the world.

The story of America's railroads has many facets. Those who built them were people of extraordinary vision, courage, and ingenuity. Technology and operating practice were invented and reinvented over a 175-year period that continues even today, and they brought steady improvement. An early decision to look to private enterprise for the development of railroads promoted a vigorous entrepreneurial spirit for the task. The enormous financial requirements, the governing legal framework, the legislative policies that shaped its growth and the later policies for regulation of the railroads—all made fundamental impacts on the nature of the railroads.

Hundreds of volumes tell the story of North American railroads in many different ways. They consider the railroads' histories and technologies or examine their management, finance, and governmental issues. But in this encyclopedia we have endeavored to paint with a much broader brush, to look at every significant element, in order to give the reader the whole story of the railroads. We hope we have succeeded.

The idea of a North American railroad encyclopedia was first raised in 1998 in discussions between John Gallman, then director of Indiana University Press, and George M. Smerk, professor of transportation at Indiana University and railroad books editor for the press. An encyclopedia, Gallman believed, would contribute to knowledge and understanding and provide a valuable reference work. Acquisitions editor Roberta L. Diehl and William D. Middleton, author of several current Indiana University Press railroad books, were soon brought into early planning. George Smerk and Bill Middleton completed a preliminary outline and summary of the book, while the Press assembled a recommended editorial board, made up of knowledgeable academics, transportation writers, and railroad professionals, and invited them to a productive planning session held at Indianapolis, Indiana, on February 11–13, 2000. The results of this meeting provided what would be the final outline and summary, with some subsequent recommendations from the editors and editorial board members as the work progressed.

Overall editorial direction of the encyclopedia project was initially by George Smerk and Bill Middleton. After her retirement, Bobbi Diehl joined the editorial team in 2002, with the primary task of assuring the editorial quality of the work, seeing that its overall tone and style remained consistent (not an easy job with so many writers involved), and readying the final text for publication. Additional editorial direction of specific areas came from several members of the editorial board. Kevin P. Keefe edited some 140 biographical summaries included in the book, and George H. Drury edited a similar number of railroad profiles and wrote many of them. Richard W. Barsness and George Smerk edited entries in the area of history and development. George Smerk and Bill Middleton combined forces to edit entries concerning railroads in society. Bill Middleton worked with J. Parker Lamb in editing railroad technology and operations entries, and Robert G. Lewis and Middleton handled entries on railroad suppliers. The book has more than 400 entries contributed by more than 100 well-known authors and writers (see the list of contributors).

Support of the encyclopedia from Indiana University Press began with John Gallman until his retirement as director in 2000, followed briefly by Peter-John Leone and, since 2005, by Janet Rabinowitch. Other key supporters of the work have included acquisitions editor Linda Oblack, editorial director Robert J. Sloan, production manager Bernadette Zoss, and former production manager Marian Morgan Ezzell. The completion of this encyclopedia has been aided immeasurably in many other ways by the willing advice and assistance of both individuals and organizations, and we are deeply appreciative of them all.

The Kalmbach Publishing Co., publishers of *Trains* and *Classic Trains* magazines, has provided a variety of assistance, most notably through the use of a substantial number of photographs from the David P. Morgan Memorial Library. Kevin P. Keefe, Kalmbach's vice president, editorial, and Nancy L. Bartol, librarian, have been of particular help. The Association of American Railroads, through Thomas White, director of editorial services, has aided us in a variety of ways, most particularly in helping provide substantial historical railroad statistical data.

John H. White, Jr., in addition to his authorship of the foreword, an essay on railroad technology of the nineteenth century, and a number of individual entries, has provided almost endless advice based on his incomparable knowledge of nineteenth-century railroading. J. W. Swanberg has provided much advice from his long experience in railroad operations. George H. Douglas has assisted in the rich history of railroading's involvement with literature and the performing and visual arts. The late Albert S. Eggerton, Jr., got a start on the important topic of railroad computerization before his untimely death in 2004. David C. Lester picked up the topic and finished it in a first-rate entry and has taken on other topics with equal skill, extending even to the task of finding out where the thrice-moved statue of Southern Railway's president Samuel Spencer had gone. Christopher P. L. Barkan of the University of Illinois's railroad program provided much information about locomotive testing, while Albert J. Reinschmidt at the Transportation Technology Center provided help with both current locomotive testing and TTC's Heavy-Haul program. John Teichmoeller of the Rail-Marine Information Group has been of great help on the rich history of railroad marine undertakings. Father David Brant made available the music and lyrics of two little-known railroad songs. Officers Jim Beach of the Union Pacific and Mary Ann Lorimer of Amtrak provided much information on the current state of railroad policing. Karen Furnweger at Chicago's John G. Shedd Aquarium and Randi Sue Smith, curator at the U.S. Fish & Wildlife Service, provided much information concerning the remarkable fish-car programs. Richard D. Baker and other members of the National Association of Timetable Collectors were helpful in filling in the story of the *Official Guide* and other timetable guides. A number of people were helpful to us in determining the present location and status of many of the railroad monuments, among them Paul W. Schopp on the Camden & Amboy monument, the National Park Service's Dennis Montagna about statues of Grenville Dodge, Gene Hinkle of the UP and Judy Wolf of Wyoming Parks and Resources about the Ames Monument, and George Eichelberger on the Southern's Samuel Spencer statue. The extensive holdings of the University of Virginia Library have aided our research in a number of topics. Nicholas Middleton developed a database for the project, and Andrea Klarman-Middleton located the splendid Mary Cassatt pastel portrait of her brother, Alexander J. Cassatt.

Illustrations for the book are individually credited to their source, and we are grateful to all of them for their help. Particularly helpful have been the Prints and Photographs Division and Photoduplication Service of the Library of Congress, which have provided a number of images. Scott Creasy and the staff of the University of Virginia Health System, Media Services division, have copied a number of rare images, and photographer Stan Kistler also prepared a number of photographs for the book.

Cartographer Tony Howe, aided by reviewers John C. Decker and George H. Drury, completed more than 50 maps that are included in the book. Rick Johnson developed a number of drawings that have helped convey technical issues. Artist Mitchell A. Markovitz painted the dramatic dust-jacket view that well conveys the artist's and the editors' conviction of modern railroading's future. Mark Reutter, editor of the Railway & Locomotive Historical Society's *Railroad History*, together with a distinguished panel of railroad scholars, selected the 130 most notable railroad books listed in appendix D.

Our goal has been to convey a broad understanding of how this remarkable undertaking grew and developed, and how it is likely to continue to develop in the years to come. We hope that you, the reader, will find that this work of many hands will have attained those ambitious goals, and that its errors and omissions are both few in number and inconsequential in nature. And may you also find the *Encyclopedia of North American Railroads* a useful and interesting work.

William D. Middleton
George M. Smerk
Roberta L. Diehl

Encyclopedia of
North American Railroads

Development of North American Railroads

Keith L. Bryant, Jr.

The railroad revolutionized transportation around the world, but nowhere was the impact so widely felt as in North America. Occupying nearly 17 percent of the world's landmass, the continent featured vast, inaccessible interior areas divided by three major mountain ranges. Until iron rails penetrated the interior, it remained largely uninhabited save for nomads and small groups of farmers. Although Euro-American settlers brought wheeled vehicles, horses, cattle, and other domestic animals, they followed trails long established by Native Americans. The indigenous people had discovered passes through the mountains and portages between rivers and lakes, and they navigated the treeless plains guided by the stars, creating pathways followed by Europeans at only an slightly higher rate of speed. Roads for wagons and canals for barges enhanced the movement of people and goods by the early nineteenth century, but residents of the United States, the Republic of Mexico, and the Dominion of Canada traveled no more rapidly or more efficiently than those who had traversed the roads of ancient Rome or the canals of imperial China. The coming of the "iron horse" brought about massive changes in the society and the economy of North America.

From the late 1840s until World War I railroads dominated the transportation of people and goods in most of North America. They opened vast reaches of land to the farmer, and bountiful crops generated food and fiber for domestic consumption and export. The railroad industry also generated demand for iron and steel, wood products, and a host of other manufactured goods. Production of freight and passenger cars and locomotives created major new industries. Small cities became metropolitan giants, and interior crossroad villages became large centers of trade and commerce as the railway enhanced the mobility of people and resources. Low freight rates and passenger fares and ease of access brought immigrants into the interior of the continent. The U.S. population center moved from a point on the Potomac River near Washington, D.C., in 1800 to a site near Athens, Ohio, by 1860. Mining, metalworking, food processing, textile manufacturing, and other industries followed the rail routes, creating employment opportunities for millions. By 1914, with 250,000 miles of railroad, the United States had become the industrial leader of the world as a consequence of this transportation revolution. Much of Canada and portions of Mexico witnessed similar, if less spectacular, transformation. The railroads emerged as the nation's first big businesses and served as models for the organization of other large-scale enterprises. The inherent efficiency of flanged metal wheels rolling on metal rails allowed the railways to displace ox teams, stagecoaches, and river and canal boats to become the premier mode of transportation across the vast reaches of North America.

The Spanish, English, and French explorers and settlers of the sixteenth and seventeenth centuries discovered a continent with narrow coastal plains; high, seemingly impenetrable mountain ranges; vast open plains and arid steppes; widespread forests of huge trees; and a few broad river valleys in portions of the interior. The absence of navigable waterways in many areas, mountain barriers, and waterless wastelands forced settlers to rely on modes of transportation little changed since ancient times. Nevertheless, intrepid colonists established settlements in Mexico, the American Southwest, along the Atlantic Coast, and in the St. Lawrence River valley. These early colonies gave rise to Spanish, French, and English empires in North America. The settlements of the latter grew and expanded at a greater rate, and by the end of the seventeenth century England controlled a territory extending from Canada to the Mississippi River and the Gulf of Mexico. English settlers determined to establish a society replicating that of their homeland, but as in all the colonies, distance from the mother country gave rise to an economy at once decentralized and individualistic.

The British policy of mercantilism and the entrepreneurial spirit of the colonists produced an economy that expanded rapidly from New England south to the coast of Georgia. By the time of the American Revolution in 1776, the colonists exported manufactured goods and agricultural products in large quantities, the latter a primary goal of the mercantile philosophy, but the former anathema to the concept. Restrictions on economic endeavors by the mother country, seemingly high taxes, and limitations on western expansion gave rise to a rebellion that led to the creation of the United States of America. A new nation emerged determined to expand to the west and to

With the coming of the Pacific railroad the Native Americans and the bountiful wildlife would be swept away from the western prairies forever. As the railroad builders headed west for the Pacific, this allegorical vision of the Course of Empire appeared in *Harper's New Monthly Magazine* in June 1867. —Middleton Collection

do so with the support of both the central and state governments.

The Constitution of the new republic organized the 13 states into the largest free-trade zone in the world, but geographic constraints limited economic growth. Historian Henry Adams declared, "No civilized country had yet been required to deal with physical difficulties so serious, nor did experience warrant conviction that such difficulties could be overcome." Nevertheless, coastal commerce linked the major ports of Boston, New York, Philadelphia, Baltimore, Charleston, and Savannah to smaller trading centers, and primitive roads, traversed by pack trains and drovers, reached into the interior. Navigable waterways, notably the Hudson River, provided alternative routes, but the cost of transportation often exceeded the value of the goods, and movement was very slow. A journey north from Philadelphia to Connecticut took five days in good weather, for example, and high stagecoach fares excluded all but the wealthy. Internal improvement schemes won the enthusiastic support of shippers, travelers, and politicians. In 1808 Secretary of the Treasury Albert Gallatin issued a report on roads and canals that called for federal involvement in the creation of a transportation system, but his voice went unheeded.

In the three decades that followed, the federal government completed the Cumberland (National) Road westward to Wheeling, Virginia, and purchased securities in only four canal companies, thus leaving major internal improvement efforts to the states and the cities. Direct subsidies, purchases of securities, donations of rights-of-way, and other benefits led to the construction of primitive roads and turnpikes, short canals around waterfalls, and improved port facilities. In 1817 political leader John C. Calhoun cried out for binding "the Republic together with a perfect system of roads and canals," but alas, nationalists such as Gallatin and Calhoun could not persuade their colleagues in Washington to finance a systematic internal improvements plan. Rather, the states and the port cities embarked on independent projects to bring trade from their hinterlands to the Atlantic Ocean.

States chartered turnpikes and canals to reach from ports westward across coastal plains to the first range of mountains. Between the War of 1812 and the mid-1830s states authorized many such projects; Pennsylvania alone issued charters for 150 turnpikes extending nearly 2,000 miles. Some states owned the roads, and others purchased securities to support the schemes. Urban rivalries led to projects that could not be sustained at profitable levels, and many turnpikes failed. Transporting goods in wagons over plank or log roads proved slow and expensive. The National Road reached Columbus, Ohio, from Cumberland, Maryland, in 1833, but clearly these primitive highways could not sustain a growing economy. As midwestern farmers chanted:

> Hardly jackassable;
> The roads are impassable
> I think those that travel 'em
> Should turn out and gravel 'em.

Emulating the canal booms that had swept Great Britain and western Europe after the end of the Napoleonic Wars, state and local governments turned to waterways to penetrate their hinterlands. Benjamin Franklin and George Washington advocated canals even before the Revolution, and Thomas Jefferson endorsed a canal across New York to link the Hudson River and Lake Erie. Jefferson wrote in 1808: "It is a splendid project and may be executed a century hence. . . . It is a little short of madness to think of it at this day!" Jefferson failed to see the ardor of New Yorkers who spent $8 million to make New York City America's premier port. The opening of the Erie Canal in 1825 prompted other cities along the Atlantic Coast to promote similar projects, but results were mixed.

Canal projects launched by commercial interests in Boston, Philadelphia, Baltimore, and Charleston did not match the success of the Erie Canal. Waterways penetrated the Pennsylvania anthracite coalfields and linked Philadelphia to Pittsburgh with inclined planes used to cross the Allegheny Mountains. The new midwestern states embraced canal transportation, and Ohio and Indiana sank deeply into debt to construct waterways from the Great Lakes to the Ohio River. By 1840, 20 states had spent over $125 million to build 3,000 miles of canals. The canal era brought virtual bankruptcy to Pennsylvania, Ohio, and Indiana. Although canal boats moved slowly and winter saw the waterways frozen and closed, freight rates nonetheless declined and stimulated east-west traffic via the canals and the Great Lakes. North-south traffic on the Ohio and Mississippi river systems remained important, however, until the Civil War.

Even as the canals improved the transit of people and goods, the coming of the steamboat enhanced river traffic on the Hudson, Ohio, and Mississippi rivers. Faster than canal boats or keelboats and with established schedules, the steamboats accelerated the transit of people and freight, but the movement of bulk commodities remained expensive, and the steamboats proved dangerous, with explosions and wrecks commonplace.

By the end of the 1820s American farmers, merchants, industrialists, and travelers sought a safe, fast, efficient, and reliable mode of transportation. The nation's poor roads lacked the sophisticated engineering of the great Roman network, and the Chinese would have ridiculed the crudeness of the country's canals. Once again the United States turned to England for a model, the steam-powered railroad.

The Industrial Revolution in Great Britain generated far more traffic than that nation's road and canal systems could support. British railroads emerged to serve existing markets, particularly to enhance the production of coal and iron ore. Manufacturers in interior trading towns sought outlets to nearby ports and a cheap means to move raw materials from the coast to the rising industrial centers in the Midlands and elsewhere. The steam engine had been fully developed by the early nineteenth century when engineers and investors began to apply the power of that device to move goods over plateways of wooden timbers or rails. George Stephenson and others perfected steam locomotives designed to pull larger loads over "railways" that used wooden rails covered with iron. The application of steam power and the highly efficient use of iron wheels on iron rails led to a rapid expansion of short, unconnected industrial lines into longer and more useful routes 30 or 40 miles in length. Stephenson's engines found their way to numerous lines as he constantly improved the locomotives' power

Among all the internal improvements that preceded the development of railways, none was more successful than the Erie Canal, which linked the Hudson River with the Great Lakes. This drawing from *America Illustrated* (1883) shows a grain boat on the canal. —Middleton Collection

and ability to operate over longer distances. The Stockton & Darlington Railway opened on September 27, 1825, and became the basis for similar lines throughout Great Britain. The era of the modern railway had arrived. British railways by the end of the 1830s operated trunk lines linking mines, factories, ports, trading centers, and cities. Engineers laid out routes that avoided steep grades and designed bridges and viaducts requiring substantial capital expenditures. From the outset, British railways emphasized low operating costs gained by a sophisticated and expensive infrastructure. The Americans familiar with this new transportation system and hugely enthusiastic for its adoption saw the railway as a means to create new markets and open new territories. They emphasized speed of construction with lines built at the lowest possible cost. Perhaps future profits could be reinvested to fully emulate the British carriers, but initial capital outlays had to be kept low.

Americans embraced the railway with an almost unbounded enthusiasm. By 1840 Europe had 1,818 miles of track; the United States had almost 3,000 miles. The North American upstart became the leader in the development of the railway because of the vast distances to be overcome, the ease of incorporation, and the absence of the vested interests and customs that retarded European rail expansion. Although some opposition arose—an Ohio school board proclaimed that the steam railroad was "a device of Satan to lead immortal souls to Hell"—most Americans welcomed the railways, and many invested their savings and supported the promoters of early rail schemes.

Baltimore, Charleston, and Boston envied the rise of the port of New York after the completion of the Erie Canal. Not situated at the mouth of a great river like the Hudson, they turned to the railroad to advance trade into their hinterlands. Pioneering in advocating lengthy railways to the west, Baltimore capitalists constructed the Baltimore & Ohio Railroad, chartered in 1828, across the Alleghenies to tap markets in the Ohio River valley. Charlestonians built a railway west to the Savannah River,

The Mississippi River and its tributaries formed a great water highway for commerce well ahead of the railroads, and one that would give way to the trains only reluctantly. This drawing from *America Illustrated* (1883) shows two steamboats heading down the Mississippi. —Middleton Collection

hoping to divert traffic from its archrival, Savannah, Georgia. Bostonians constructed a railway westward to Albany, New York, on the Hudson River to attract freight bound eastward from the Great Lakes via the Erie Canal. These cities initiated the railroad era.

Beginning of the Railroads

On July 4, 1828, one of the signers of the Declaration of Independence, Charles Carroll, turned the first earth to initiate the Baltimore & Ohio. Later that summer Peter Cooper's *Tom Thumb* experimental steam locomotive lost a race with a horse-powered vehicle, but the iron horse eventually prevailed on the B&O. Construction advanced the Baltimore & Ohio across Maryland and the mountains to Wheeling, Virginia, in 1852. Freight from the Ohio River valley began to flow eastward to the port of Baltimore. In South Carolina, on Christmas Day 1830, the first locomotive built for sale in the United States, the *Best Friend of Charleston*, carried 140 passengers on the first scheduled steam railroad in the country. The 136-mile line from Charleston to Hamburg, South Carolina, opposite Augusta, Georgia, opened in 1833, making it the longest railroad in the world. The success of these pioneer lines produced a boisterous railway fever as every town and city sought to emulate the success of Baltimore, Charleston, and Boston.

Throughout the 1830s railway expansion became a predominant economic pursuit. Of the 26 states in 1840, only 4 lacked railroads. A through route from New York City to Philadelphia opened in 1833, with the English-built locomotive *John Bull* making the trip in seven hours.

Carriers quickly penetrated the regions beyond the Allegheny and Appalachian mountains. Initially most of the mileage could be found in New England and the midatlantic states, but not even the panic of 1837 could stop the inexorable growth of this new transportation artery into the Midwest and the Southeast. Though several midwestern states and many European investors lost money when some railroads entered bankruptcy after 1837, construction continued to expand the burgeoning rail system.

With expansion came technological improvements that led to even greater efficiencies. Americans followed English practices, such as using iron straps or bars fastened to wooden rails that were attached to blocks of stone embedded in the earth. Only 20 to 25 feet long, the iron straps frequently broke loose, curled, and impaled cars as they passed over the break. Robert L. Stevens, an engineer and railroad president, designed an iron T-rail that when spiked to wooden ties or "sleepers" formed a smooth, safe track. The rails and ties rested on crushed stone or gravel that drained moisture from the roadbed. Stevens's design did not deal with the problem of multiplicity of track gauges, that is, the distance between the rails. Gauges varied from carrier to carrier, ranging from a narrow gauge of 3 feet to a wide gauge of 6 feet. While many railroads opted for what became "standard gauge," that is, 4 feet 8½ inches, as in England, most of the longer lines in the South were 5-foot gauge. The absence of uniformity prevented the exchange of cars, resulting in time-consuming transshipments. Individual carriers were still not seen as part of a railroad system.

Locomotives, initially imported from England, grew beyond small iron teapots to larger, more powerful de-

Among the early railroads was the Mohawk & Hudson, which pulled a series of cars resembling stagecoaches over the rails at its inaugural on August 9, 1831. The train made its first trip out on the 17-mile run between Albany and Schenectady in 105 minutes, but the trip back took only 38 minutes. —Jim Harter, *American Railroads of the Nineteenth Century* (Lubbock: Texas Tech University Press, 1998)

signs, especially those of Matthias Baldwin of Philadelphia. A jewelry manufacturer, Baldwin created a large locomotive works that innovated major improvements in locomotives. His success spawned a new industry as other locomotive builders emerged in the Northeast. Locomotives produced by Baldwin and others hauled a growing fleet of more modern equipment. Diminutive freight cars of four wheels grew larger with greater capacity, while passenger cars, simply stagecoaches with iron wheels at first, became larger and enclosed with primitive heating and lighting systems. As the railways expanded, a large and complex supporting network of locomotive and car builders emerged, and the demand for iron, and then steel, enhanced the rise of large-scale metal works.

Trunk Lines

The rapid expansion of the railway system in the 1840s and 1850s not only stimulated industrialization, but also enhanced the rise of interior urban places and the growth of agricultural production. By 1850 the nation had 8,829 miles of railroad constructed at a cost of $310 million. By 1860 over 30,000 miles of line were in operation, with over $1 billion invested. The decade before the Civil War also saw consolidations that created through trunk lines, particularly in the North and Northeast. Although a few carriers, such as the Baltimore & Ohio, had been conceived as single companies, the majority of through trunk lines represented mergers of short, segmented railroad companies. Yet there was no unified system. Only three connections existed between the railways north of the Ohio River and those in the South. Some cities prevented carriers from linking to create jobs for local drayage firms and to force travelers to spend a night waiting for connecting trains. Nevertheless, lines proliferated as private and public capital poured into the hands of promoters and builders.

From the outset of the railroad revolution, funds for construction and subsequent operations flowed from investors and governments at all levels. States, counties, and cities donated rights of way, purchased securities, and granted lands to carriers. Even as citizens acquired stocks and bonds in these often speculative enterprises, governments dictated the routes and operations of the carriers through both direct and indirect subsidies. Liberal state charters allowed some railroads to engage in real estate and banking activities, for example. The federal government reduced the tariff on imported iron to benefit the railroads. Before the Civil War state governments borrowed $90 million to help finance railroad construction. The carriers represented progress and economic growth; no state wished to be left behind.

The granting of lands to railroads by the federal government began before the Civil War with 25 million acres made available. The congressional debate over land grants helped fuel the rise of sectionalism before 1860, as northern and southern representatives fought over the location of the grants. Two basic issues emerged. Should the federal government provide land for the railroads by way of a financial inducement? Most in the Northeast said "no," but southerners and westerners shouted "yes." And what should be the route of the first transcontinental? Southerners said that the eastern terminus should be New Orleans or Memphis; northerners pushed for Chicago or perhaps St. Louis. In 1850 a grant to construct a line from northern Illinois to Mobile, Alabama, established a significant precedent. A 200-foot-wide right of way occupied the middle of a 6-mile-wide grant, the railroad receiving the alternate, even-numbered sections of land on both sides of the track. The railroad could acquire other acreage if land in the grant was already occupied. In turn, the railroad had to transport federal property and troops free, and Congress would establish rates for carrying the mail. Forty-five carriers benefited from federal land grants before the Civil War. But sectional tensions in the 1850s postponed a decision on the route of the first transcontinental railroad.

In 1862 Congress chartered a transcontinental route from Council Bluffs, Iowa, to Sacramento, California, and offered a substantial grant of land, as well as loans and cash subsidies. Congress believed that large-scale settlement of the West would not take place without railroads. The population was sparse or nonexistent in "the Great American Desert"; railroads built in advance of settlement needed subsidies. By 1871 the federal government had granted 175 million acres of land to railroads, though some 35 million acres ultimately were returned. Seventy railroads received land, but four (the Northern Pacific, Atchison, Topeka & Santa Fe, Southern Pacific, and Union Pacific) gained 70 percent of the total. These lands represented 20,000 miles of track, but that number encompassed only 10 percent of the total rail mileage in the nation. Most railroads did not receive such largess.

Land grants and other subsidies gave impetus to the construction of thousands of miles of line and fostered the belief that the carriers would soon pay dividends on their stock and interest on their bonds. Subsidies attracted private investment and encouraged construction across vast, virtually empty lands, especially west of the Mississippi River. Although reduced charges for the federal government ultimately produced a savings of $900 million by 1945, the land grants sparked a debate as to the role of government in the economy, the efficacy of the largess, and the obvious congressional corruption related to several of the grants. Of the total capital absorbed by the nation's railroads, the amount contributed by governments remained very small compared with private investment.

People from all walks of life purchased railroad securities, as did foreign investors captivated by the rise of a transportation system that displaced existing modes. The railroads reduced the cost of shipping and travel, as well as the time involved. Domestic commerce soared as the railways moved both raw materials and finished goods at ever-declining rates. Wagon rates for wheat in the Old Northwest had been 30 cents per ton-mile; by 1860 wheat moved from Chicago to New York by rail at 1.2 cents per ton-mile. The carriers gave impetus to industrialization, the expansion of agriculture, and urbanization, even as the nation fragmented and entered a brutal civil war.

In 1860 through routes connected New York and the Northeast to Chicago, St. Louis, Detroit, and Cincinnati, and a number of carriers joined to provide service from Washington, D.C., south to Atlanta, Charleston, and Memphis. But the railroad lines in the North and the South differed markedly. Northern railroads had achieved some degree of systemization, but those of the South had not. The 11 states that formed the Confederacy in 1861 had only 9,000 miles of railroads, one-third of the national total. Railways of the South were lightly constructed, had few locomotive works or maintenance facilities, and lacked strategic connections, such as from Atlanta to New Orleans. The Civil War proved dramatically the military value of the railroad, and its use tactically and strategically emphasized the backwardness of the southern carriers. Northern railroads moved troops and munitions efficiently, with some companies generating profits for the first time. Neither the federal nor Confederate governments took control of their railroads, but both recognized the value of strategic rail junctions such as Chattanooga and Atlanta, scenes of major battles. At the end of the war in the spring of 1865, the railroads of the South lay in ruins, while leaders of northern railways prepared to send iron rails westward across half the continent to the Pacific Ocean.

The miles of railway in the nation doubled between 1865 and 1873 and doubled again during the next 14 years. The construction of the Central Pacific and Union Pacific railroads dramatized this extraordinary growth. Authorized by the Pacific Railway Act of 1862, the carriers initiated construction westward from Omaha and eastward from Sacramento. Track crews of Irish immigrants and war veterans raced across the plains of Nebraska and Wyoming even as gangs of workers, largely Chinese, blasted a line through the Sierra Nevada and created a right of way across the deserts of Nevada and Utah Territory. At Promontory, Utah, in 1869, the armies of tracklayers met, completing the first transcontinental route. A new era of railroad expansion began. In 1883 the Northern Pacific completed its line from Duluth, Minnesota, to Tacoma, Washington, and the Southern Pacific opened from Los Angeles to New Orleans. Shortly the Atchison, Topeka & Santa Fe operated a system from Chicago to San Diego and Los Angeles. James J. Hill's Great Northern Railway extended to Seattle from St. Paul in 1893, the first transcontinental completed without a federal land grant. Maps of the trans-Mississippi West soon showed a spiderweb of railways expanding into the Great Plains and the Southwest. Other carriers penetrated the interior of California, Oregon, and Washington.

As the railroads spread across the trans-Mississippi West, hundreds of thousands of homesteaders followed. Towns sprang up along the railroads to serve cattle drives coming from Texas, Wyoming, and Montana. Grain elevators rose above the plains to hold the corn and wheat produced from the virgin land. The railroads that held land grants sold farms to settlers lured to the West by the promise of cheap land and bountiful harvests. Scores of towns served as division points for the railroads, and some contained railway facilities such as shops and roundhouses. Train crews, section gangs, and their families joined townspeople in local schools and churches. "Railroad towns" sprang up across the West, replicating similar communities in the East and South. The old concept of "the Great American Desert" disappeared as freight trains laden with wheat, corn, and cattle flowed eastward and returned with finished goods from metropolitan manufacturers. The rising traffic forced the carriers to rebuild the hastily constructed trackage, replace spindly wooden bridges with iron or steel, and purchase additional modern equipment. The rise of the great western railroads served to bring millions of immigrants to the West and generated publicity about the region and the railways that served them. Railroad land agents toured the Midwest, the Northeast, and much of western Europe recruiting farm-

Travelers over the great prairies of the West newly opened by the railroads saw vast herds of wildlife. All too soon, however, their numbers were quickly reduced by the new settlers. This wood engraving, by W. Meason after a drawing by Ernest Griset, showed the wholesale slaughter of buffalo along the Kansas Pacific Railroad. —Library of Congress (Neg. LC-USZ62-44079)

ers, and the carriers circulated millions of pamphlets and brochures lauding the lands of the West. While some exaggerated the climate—a Northern Pacific publication depicted banana trees in North Dakota—the larger message prevailed: the West was a land of great promise.

A Transcontinental System

Even as the transcontinental routes generated even greater interest in the nation's railways, the carriers quietly applied new technologies to their operations. Reconstructed lines in the South and improved railways in the North and West purchased larger and more powerful locomotives. They standardized track gauges to 4 feet 8½ inches so that cars could be exchanged nationally. Interchanging traffic meant uniform couplers, brakes, bills of lading, and classification of products. New bridges across the Ohio, Mississippi, and Missouri rivers enhanced the flow of freight and passengers. Steel rails replaced iron for a smoother, faster, and safer track. New, modern freight cars entered service designed for specific traffic and commodities such as refrigerated meat, petroleum products, and livestock. More apparent to the public were the standardized time zones or "Railroad Time" after November 1883, which became the unofficial national time system. As giant railroads emerged as the nation's first big busi-

nesses, they did what was necessary to operate and control thousands of miles of track, tens of thousands of employees, hundreds of locomotives, and thousands of freight and passenger cars. The railroads created the modern large-scale business structure.

The management of a canal, turnpike, or steamboat had been relatively simple, and these businesses operated not unlike enterprises in fifteenth-century Venice. But the railways required system and order on a vast scale. Operations needed to be direct, scheduled, and safe, extending over great distances. Internal procedures had to be routinized and controls established for accounting, maintenance, and statistics gathering. Modern managers, often civil engineers trained at West Point, developed a bureaucracy to meet these demands. They eschewed European models and established divisions of responsibility based on specific functions using a military model. Vice presidents, general managers, division superintendents, trainmasters, and other officials had clear lines of authority in a complex structure. They required daily detailed reports on operations and devised new accounting procedures and billing systems. The telegraph, and later the telephone, allowed for nearly instant communication, enhancing operating procedures. Young, bright, talented employees joined the carriers, and the best moved up through the ranks. The large industries that emerged after

1870 required a fast, regular, and dependable transportation network even as they adopted the hierarchical managerial structure the railroads created.

The railroads employed 419,000 workers by 1880; the number grew to 1,701,000 by 1916. This army of labor had to meet stringent work rules and accept absolute discipline because of the scope and intricacies of railway operations. Technologically skilled employees faced hard-and-fast work rules in an egalitarian society. Management demanded minute controls that workers found arbitrary, capricious, and against their interests. Too, railway employees labored under horrific working conditions and suffered astronomical accident rates. Link-and-pin couplers required brakemen to drop a metal pin between freight cars, and a slight slip meant the loss of fingers or a hand. Brakemen raced across the roofs of cars to set hand brakes as trains roared along regardless of rain, sleet, or snow. Engineers and firemen on locomotives suffered from boiler explosions and tragic wrecks. Shopmen and yardmen faced similar accidents and unsafe conditions. Four large railroad brotherhoods or unions emerged largely as mutual aid societies offering life and medical insurance. Engineers, conductors, firemen, and trainmen joined together to cope with the vagaries of their occupations. Some railway laborers floated from one carrier to another, creating generations of "boomers."

Labor-management relations deteriorated rapidly in the 1870s as major carriers cut wages while 10- or 12-hour workdays continued. In July 1877 railroad workers launched a strike on the Baltimore & Ohio Railroad after two wage cuts. Violence in Baltimore and Pittsburgh brought federal troops to crush the strike. Other outbreaks of violence led to military intervention, as in the Pullman strike of 1894. When George M. Pullman reduced wages at his car works south of Chicago but maintained the same rents in company housing, his employees struck and were aided by the American Railway Union (ARU) and its members. Federal troops ended not only the strike, but also the efforts of Eugene V. Debs to bring all railroad workers into the ARU. Railroads employed blacklists, labor spies, and other tools to prevent unionization. Yet a constant stream of young workers sought jobs on the carriers, and many families could count two or three generations employed by a single railroad. Railway workers received comparatively high wages and were viewed with respect in their communities.

The accidents and carnage on the railroads forced the companies to adopt modern safety devices and to seek new technologies. Eli H. Janney invented the safety coupler that replaced the dangerous link-and-pin system. George Westinghouse solved the problem of hand-set brakes with an air brake employing compressed air. He also improved railway

The new Pacific Railroad soon brought visitors on a grand tour of the scenic wonders of the West. Here, passengers on a Central Pacific train enjoy the Palisades in Ten-Mile Canyon in Nevada. The drawing was in *Harper's Weekly*, about 1869. —Library of Congress (Neg. LC-USZ62-35456)

signaling systems. In 1893 Congress mandated the use of safety couplers and air brakes, thus standardizing operations and reducing accidents and loss of life. Stronger and heavier steel rails improved operations, as did a manual block signal system that controlled train movement. These operating improvements meant longer, heavier, and faster trains pulled by larger, more powerful locomotives, enabling the railroads to increase profits and reduce rates. But the American public focused less on the improved efficiency of the carriers than on the corruption and greed of many of their promoters, owners, and managers. Wit Ambrose Bierce called these men "railrogues."

The financing of the Central Pacific and Union Pacific railroads produced scandals that rocked the industry for 50 years. The construction firm known as the Crédit Mobilier built the Union Pacific under contracts far in excess of the value of the track received by the carrier. Stock in the construction company, much of it held by the railroad's leaders, was also distributed to members of Congress and even the vice president of the United States. The Crédit Mobilier pocketed an estimated $23 million. Further, the Union Pacific had a capitalization of $110 million, but the road was worth barely half that. "Watered stock," securities issued beyond a railroad's true value, grievously harmed the Union Pacific and other carriers. To gain investments, railroads gave security purchasers bonuses of stock or bonds, hoping that future profits would create real values. But overcapitalization prevented payment of dividends and interest, causing many railroads, particularly in the West and South, to declare bankruptcy well before the coming of the depression of 1893.

"Switched Off." A party of immigrants waited uncertainly at a remote station platform on their journey to a new home in the West. *Harper's Weekly* published the drawing on January 24, 1874. —Library of Congress (Neg. LC-USZ62-42264)

"Solid Train Load of Settlers for Alberta": these settlers arrived by special train from Colorado in March 1914. The party was photographed at Bassano, Alberta, on the prairie east of Calgary. The group settled at nearby Gem, Alberta. —Glenbow Museum (Neg. NA-984-2)

The manipulation of railroad securities by bankers and plungers in the Northeast angered small investors who saw their stocks and bonds fall in value unrelated to the success of the railway. Daniel Drew, Jim Fisk, and Jay Gould manipulated the Erie Railway's securities in the 1860s in a war with the New York Central's Cornelius Vanderbilt that virtually destroyed the Erie. Both sides bribed members of the New York legislature and numerous judges. Of his fight to gain control of the Erie, Vanderbilt declared that it had "learned me it never pays to kick a skunk." The public responded with outrage as revelations of corruption plagued an industry engaged in cutthroat competition that drove rates downward, leading to massive losses each year. As a consequence of the security scandals and rate manipulation by the railroads in the Gilded Age (1865–1895), journalists created the image of the "robber baron," a devious, greedy Wall Street pirate who displayed no interest in operating a railroad for profit or in improving the property, but simply used the carrier's stocks and bonds as vehicles for personal gain. At least, this was the public perception. Jay Gould came to symbolize this image in the popular press, a legacy that continued well into the twentieth century. While Gould's complicity in the Erie Railway scandal is clear, his later control of the Union Pacific and other railroads suggests a different approach. In the 1880s and the early 1890s Gould behaved more like a "captain of industry" as he constantly toured his properties, reinvested profits in major improvements, and sought new indus-

tries in their territories. He labored to create viable, profitable railroads and in the process became a developmental investor rather than a speculator. The picture of Gould and others as "robber barons" never dissipated, however, and was used again and again by detractors of the industry as representative of the behavior of all railroad executives. The image proved particularly advantageous to those demanding lower railroad freight rates, the end of rebating, and governmental control of the carriers.

Regulation

Railroad rates, based largely on the value of the goods carried, fell dramatically in the 1870s and 1880s. Railroads classified freight for the purpose of ratemaking, but cutthroat competition drove many rates lower than benefits from economies of scale. Railroad rates fell faster than the general price level in the period. As more carriers entered markets in the Great Plains and the South, freight rates on wheat and cotton declined by almost 50 percent. Yet farmers considered the rates "sky high" because the price of wheat and other commodities fell almost as dramatically. American farmers now competed with agriculturalists around the world and had no control over the prices of their crops. Farmers typically regarded the railroads as villains. Shippers also complained that rates for short hauls exceeded those for long hauls. In response, railroad managers pointed to their fixed costs and argued that such rates were necessary to obtain an equitable re-

Information as to
AGRICULTURAL SETTLEMENT OPPORTUNITIES
will be supplied on application to
THE CANADIAN PACIFIC RAILWAY
DEPT. OF IMMIGRATION AND COLONIZATION
at
CALGARY, EDMONTON, SASKATOON
WINNIPEG OR MONTREAL

This "Agricultural Settlement Opportunities" poster of 1933 offered information on settlements from the Canadian Pacific Railway's Department of Immigration and Colonization. CPR actively promoted colonization from its beginnings until after World War II. —Canadian Pacific Railway Archives (Neg. A.6198)

turn on investment. Clearly, large shippers not only obtained lower rates than farmers and small business owners, but also, where multiple lines existed, they could move their traffic to cheaper carriers.

When the railroads responded by pooling traffic and profits and granting rebates to large shippers, complaints became a national cacophony. In less than two years Standard Oil Co. received rebates in excess of $10 million, for example. In Illinois, Iowa, Wisconsin, and elsewhere, state regulatory agencies arose to control railroad rates. In 1877 the Supreme Court upheld the so-called Granger laws in *Munn v. Illinois*, but nine years later a more conservative Court revised that position in the Wabash case, ruling that only the federal government could regulate interstate commerce. Ratemaking and control of rebates and other discriminatory practices proved complex, and uninformed or indifferent state legislators and railroad commissioners failed to silence public protests. Journalists noted that politicians, ministers, and community leaders received free passes from the railroads in return

for their support. Although railroad managers believed that freight rates should be "all the traffic will bear," this philosophy seemed rapacious and served only to fuel the fires of discontent.

Even before the Wabash case Congress moved to create a federal railroad regulatory agency, which it did in 1887, the Interstate Commerce Commission (ICC). Authorized to regulate the railroads and to establish rates that were "reasonable and just," the ICC did neither. The language of the law was vague and contradictory. The Interstate Commerce Act simply cartelized the railroads because the commission could not establish maximum rates or stop rebating. Pools ended, but industry traffic associations continued to establish advantageous rates for the carriers. When legal disputes about the commission's power over the carriers reached the Supreme Court, that body ruled for the carriers in 15 of 16 cases between 1887 and 1905. However, the formation of the ICC did begin a shift from a policy of laissez-faire to one of governmental regulation. Although creation of the ICC as a federal regulatory body eventually had a profound impact on the railroad industry, its immediate consequences were far less important than those of the depression of 1893 and the subsequent reorganization of major railroads by investment bankers.

By 1890 the railroads had become the nation's largest business enterprises. Capitalization of $2.5 billion in 1870 had risen to nearly $10 billion in only 20 years. With 166,703 miles of track, the railroads produced gross revenues of $1 billion in 1890. This enormous financial investment could not have been achieved without significant purchases of stocks and bonds by eastern and European investors. The New York Stock Exchange's growth after 1850 had been fueled by railroad securities, and huge issues of stocks and bonds gave rise to the modern investment banking houses. Capital from Great Britain helped construct several major railroads before the Civil War, but by the 1870s English pounds, Dutch guilders, German marks, and French francs in substantial amounts flowed through the investment banks to purchase railway securities. Some railroads, such as the Missouri-Kansas-Texas, soon had European representatives on their boards of directors. Despite the presence of often conservative spokesmen for foreign investors, railroad managers continued to reduce freight rates, construct new and often-duplicative routes, and issue additional securities even as revenues declined and profits disappeared. By the end of the 1880s the industry confronted a financial crisis.

The collapse of rates, traffic, and security values drove dozens of railroads into bankruptcy in the 1890s. Seeking to reorganize their company's finances, railroad managers turned to investment houses in New York, Philadelphia, and Boston. J. Pierpont Morgan, Edward H. Harriman, Kuhn, Loeb, J. and W. Seligman, and others formed new rail corporations, creating regional giants. The Reading Co., Chesapeake & Ohio, and Baltimore & Ohio emerged from bankruptcy with reduced fixed charges and stronger systems. The Atchison, Topeka & Santa Fe Railroad became a major transcontinental with its profitless subsidiaries jettisoned and a new management installed. The Richmond Terminal in the South became the Southern Railway, a regional giant. The investment bankers reduced the railroads' debts and fixed charges and rationalized routes. They also reduced competition.

Seven financial groups soon controlled two-thirds of the nation's rail mileage. These "communities of interest," as Morgan called them, aroused the public's desire for effective regulation. State and federal investigations of railroad security manipulations produced lurid headlines and calls for intervention. Increased operating costs led to higher average rates after 1900, inciting greater hostility. When Harriman and James J. Hill sought to form one giant carrier in the Pacific Northwest through a holding company, Northern Securities Co., President Theodore Roosevelt invoked the Sherman Antitrust Act of 1890, and in 1904 the Supreme Court ordered Northern Securities dissolved. The Progressive Era of reforms that swept the nation after 1900 focused much of its attention on the "abuses" of the railroads, including "tax dodging," poor service, and shabby public facilities.

The attention generated by discriminatory rates, securities manipulation, and other abuses obscured the economic and social contributions the railroads made in the nineteenth century. The rail system made possible the industrialization of a nation that had been primarily a producer of food and fiber. Great cities arose as rail networks facilitated the rapid flow of freight and passengers from region to region. Across the nation, almost all Americans lived within the sound of a locomotive's whistle. As the population of the country approached 100 million, the role of the railroads in creating an industrial giant was obvious to investors, industrialists, business executives, bankers, and many political leaders. The general public saw powerful corporations able to manipulate not only rates, but also governments at all levels. When Frank Norris published the muckraking novel *The Octopus* (1901), readers believed that the story had to be true; the Southern Pacific Railroad controlled California and destroyed farmers in the Central Valley in the absence of competition. Despite their achievements, the railroads entered the twentieth century facing a hostile public demanding a "square deal" in the marketplace. When William Jennings Bryan campaigned for the presidency as the Democratic nominee in 1900 advocating nationalization of the railroads, the carriers were clearly in deep trouble.

Under Roosevelt and Presidents William Howard Taft and Woodrow Wilson, federal regulation of the railroads brought great changes. The Elkins Act of 1903 virtually ended rebating by making both the granting and receiving of a rebate illegal. Other discriminatory practices continued, however. The Hepburn Act of 1906 extended the powers of the ICC over other forms of transportation and, more important, gave it power to establish maximum rates. It also ended the granting of passes. This landmark legislation in federal regulation led to giving the ICC even greater authority under the Mann-Elkins Act of 1910, which placed the burden of proof for higher rates on the carriers. Progressives believed that the com-

The central and western railroads were all engaged in the development of agriculture along their lines. The Great Northern was one of the most active. This car was developed for a 1911 display of farm products from the states along GN lines.
—James J. Hill Library (Neg. LH1883)

Shortly after the Civil War, financiers Jim Fisk, Daniel Drew, Cornelius Vanderbilt, and Jay Gould became involved in the Erie Railroad, with unfortunate results for the railroad. By early 1872 the first three had been forced out, and Gould alone held control of the Erie. But other rivals on the Erie board succeeded in March 1872 in forcing Gould out. Political cartoonist Thomas Nast, in the March 30, 1872, *Harper's Weekly*, celebrated the occasion with this view of "Justice on the Rail—Erie Railroad (Ring) Smash Up," showing Gould and several underlings tumbling off the line. Gould, as usual, came out all right. The news that he was selling out drove up the stock price, and Gould was said to have made more than a million dollars. —Middleton Collection

missioners would act in the best interest of the public; the commissioners, responding to political pressure, saw only a mandate to keep rates low. The Railroad Valuation Act of 1913 sought to examine and expose inflated security values or "watered stock" and establish the "real" value of the railroads for ratemaking purposes. The Adamson Act of 1916 gave operating employees and telegraphers an eight-hour day, increasing labor costs even as it bettered

the lot of many railway workers. Progressives advocated regulation rather than nationalization of the railroads.

Ironically, the Progressive Era regulations inhibited the ability of the railroads to raise capital in a period requiring costly modernization. Investors feared to place their savings in an industry faced with rising costs and lower profits. The carriers sought capital to pay for improvements such as tunnels under the Hudson River in New

York, modern locomotives and cars, new signal systems, and major rebuilding projects to reduce grades and circuitous mileage. Investors cringed as annual railroad wages increased from an average of $567 in 1900 to $880 in 1916. As a consequence of rising costs and lower rates, the operating ratio of the railroads, the ratio of operating expenses to operating revenues, rose to almost 70 percent by 1917. The ICC denied requests for rate increases, and by the start of World War I the nation's railroads faced ominous financial problems.

Circumstances in Canada and Mexico paralleled those in the United States early in the twentieth century, though in many respects the railroads in those two countries had developed quite independently. The railroads north and south of the United States engaged in a lively exchange of freight and passengers with their neighbor, because operating and equipment standards were essentially the same. Other aspects, especially in Canada, differed. Watching nervously as American railways reached its borders, Canada passed the Guarantee Act of 1849, designed to lure British investment for its own railroads. Manifest Destiny rankled Canadians just as it did Mexicans, and the response was feverish railroad construction, so that by the end of the 1850s the Grand Trunk Railway extended westward from Quebec and Portland, Maine, through Montreal and Toronto to Windsor, opposite Detroit. Rising nationalism and fear of American railways invading the Prairie Provinces led to the construction of the first Canadian transcontinental, the Canadian Pacific Railway (CPR). By 1885 the CPR linked Vancouver in British Columbia with eastern Canada. Further expansion by the Grand Trunk established a second transcontinental route, but in the aftermath of World War I that carrier and six others failed, leading the Canadian government to form a giant Crown property, the Canadian National Railways (CN), to absorb the bankrupts. Thus Canada had two major carriers, the privately owned CPR and the CN, property of the government. Not only did they compete with each other, but both also invaded the United States with subsidiaries reaching Chicago from the east and north.

Unlike the Canadian government, the leaders of Mexico from the 1860s to 1911 avidly sought American as well as British capital to build a rail network. Under dictator Porfirio Díaz, American and European investors and promoters joined with Mexican bankers to construct lines radiating from Mexico City. In 1873 a railroad opened to the port of Veracruz; in 1884 the Mexican Central reached El Paso, Texas; and in 1888 the Mexican National offered service to Laredo, Texas. The government of Mexico invested heavily in the latter two carriers and in 1908 formed the National Railways of Mexico, into which these and other lines were merged. By the time of the Mexican Revolution in 1911, the nation had 24,717 kilometers (15,359 miles) of railroad, most of which were later nationalized and made part of the National Railways. Interestingly, after 1900 some U.S. politicians and union leaders advocated either a dual system, as in Canada, or nationalization, as in Mexico, but the closest America would move was for federal control during World War I.

World War I

Railroad mileage in the United States peaked in 1917 even as the nation prepared to enter the Great War. At the same time the industry was financially shackled by the ICC, the railways struggled under tremendous traffic loads. By 1915 railroads operating one-sixth of the national system were in or facing bankruptcy, yet the ICC refused to grant rate increases. Great industrial giants such as United States Steel Corp. and International Harvester poured forth vast shipments, and America's farms and ranches enjoyed unprecedented prosperity and bounteous harvests. An improved rail industry infrastructure tried to cope with these burdens, but rising exports to Europe, particularly in 1916–1917, created massive congestion at eastern ports. General price increases, higher wages, rising taxes, and steady or falling freight rates strapped the carriers, while public ill will was increasing rapidly. The outbreak of war in April 1917 saw 180,000 loaded cars blocked in eastern ports with no place to unload cargoes. The chaos brought traffic to a standstill.

On December 26 President Wilson assumed control of the nation's railroads under the U.S. Railroad Administration (USRA), with William G. McAdoo as director general. McAdoo unified schedules, purchased standardized locomotives and rolling stock, granted wage increases, and by 1920 drove the operating ratio upward from 65.5 percent to a catastrophic 94.3 percent. Federal control of the railroads cost the taxpayers $1.1 billion before the carriers were returned to their owners on March 1, 1920.

While some labor leaders again called for nationalization of the railways, Congress responded to the experiences of World War I with the Transportation Act of 1920. The law provided that the railroads should receive a fair rate of return on their investment, 5.5 percent, but expanded and strengthened the authority of the ICC. That body finally granted a rate increase ranging from 25 to 40 percent. The act encouraged mergers, and several plans were published proposing that strong carriers absorb the weak, but the concepts mostly failed. The ICC did use its new authority to prevent the abandonment of redundant trackage. The Transportation Act of 1920 viewed the transportation system as a de facto railroad monopoly as it existed in the 1890s, with no understanding of the rise of interstate trucking and pipelines, mass ownership of automobiles, the creation of national bus systems, and the rise of incipient airlines. Throughout the 1920s and 1930s competition from other forms of transportation emerged, taking away freight and passenger traffic at an astonishing rate. The railroad industry stood alone as the thoroughly regulated form of transportation in the 1920s.

The Transportation Act of 1920 included the formation of the Railroad Labor Board that received jurisdiction over labor disputes on the carriers to include such issues as wages, working conditions, and grievances. Composed of nine members equally representing the railroads, workers, and the general public, the board frequently sided with the brotherhoods and in 1920 ordered wage increases averaging 22 percent, which cost the carriers $600 million. Despite this action and other favorable labor rulings, relations between the unions and railway management floundered. The railroads laid off nearly 15 percent of their employees in 1921, and some carriers reduced wages. In 1922 railroad shopmen struck, the largest work stoppage in the nation's history. Violence during this strike and others in the 1920s drove a gap between management and labor that was never successfully bridged. In 1926 Congress passed the Railway Labor Act, which established a new mediation board to resolve wage disputes and grievances in an attempt to prevent disruption of rail services, but railroad managers viewed the board as pro-labor in its actions.

Rebuilding the Railroads

The railroads embarked on a program to maximize operating efficiency to counter rising labor costs and competition from trucks and buses. Millions of dollars were invested in locomotives and rolling stock, as well as signaling systems. By the end of the decade centralized traffic control (CTC) began to spread across the rail network. CTC allowed single dispatchers to control train movements over long distances from one location. New passenger equipment and lower fares countered the rise of long-distance bus companies. These efforts only slowed the loss of traffic. The 1920s saw a substantial increase in miles of all-weather highways, which were soon filled with trucks, buses, and private automobiles. Well before the stock market crash of 1929 and the subsequent Great Depression, many railroads faced a bleak financial future.

During the 1930s many of the nation's major railways entered bankruptcy. Carriers in the Midwest and Southwest fell victim to declining agricultural traffic and high fixed costs. A major federal recovery agency, the Reconstruction Finance Corp. (RFC), after 1932 loaned money to some railroads so they could avoid receivership. The RFC also extended loans for new equipment and for line improvements, most notably the electrification of the Pennsylvania Railroad from New York to Washington. Management tried to retain workers on the payrolls even if only half- or quarter-time, but salary and wage reductions could not be avoided. Rail employment peaked in 1920 at 2,076,000, but collapsed to only 991,000 in 1933. Services were reduced on main lines, and many branches saw only one train each day. Some branches were abandoned altogether. Although some of the major carriers

eked out small profits, others saw red ink for nearly a decade.

The one bright spot, the coming of the diesel locomotive, ushered in a new era; indeed, some called it a revolution. The diesel engine, invented in the 1890s by German engineer Rudolf Diesel, had proved its worth as a power source for ships. After developing motor cars powered by gasoline engines, the General Electric Co. (GE) experimented with diesels for railroad locomotion. The GE concept employed a diesel engine powering a generator that supplied electricity to traction motors on the locomotive axles. As early as 1925 GE diesel switching locomotives entered yard service in New York. Some had engines by Ingersoll-Rand with mechanical components by American Locomotive. Ralph Budd, president of the Chicago, Burlington & Quincy Railroad, decided to use diesel engines from General Motors' Electro-Motive Division to power the new stainless-steel *Zephyr* passenger train being built by the E. G. Budd Manufacturing Co. Hoping to regain lost passenger traffic with faster, streamlined trains, in 1933 Budd boldly announced a nonstop test run of the *Zephyr* from Denver to Chicago's Century of Progress exhibition. The *Zephyr* streaked eastward in 13 hours, reaching 112.5 miles per hour at one point and generating a public relations coup. The diesel proved extremely efficient and far cheaper to operate than steam locomotives. The Union Pacific, the Santa Fe, and other carriers quickly ordered diesel-powered streamliners of their own. General Motors soon offered a diesel freight locomotive, and those units began to arrive on the railroads on the eve of World War II. Only the coming of war slowed the dieselization process as the railroads sought to capitalize on the cost savings inherent in diesel power.

World War II

World War II was the finest hour for America's railroads. As Europe fell victim to German aggression in 1939, the nation's rail carriers moved to prevent a recurrence of the chaos and federalization of 1917. Lend-Lease aid and the nation's rearmament efforts generated increased traffic, and operating revenues were the highest since 1930. A favorable operating ratio of 72 percent in 1940 showed the impact of modernization efforts in the 1920s, particularly the growing use of diesel locomotives and new technologies such as CTC. By 1941 the railroads' freight ton-mileage of 475 billion exceeded the peak of World War I by nearly 20 percent. Prosperity returned to the railways as the government created the Transportation Division of the Office of Emergency Management to coordinate operations. The day after the attack on Pearl Harbor, President Franklin D. Roosevelt appointed Joseph B. Eastman to lead the Office of Defense Transportation. With fewer locomotives, cars, and employees than in 1916, America's railroads carried far greater traffic. Freight movement exceeded that of 1918 by 50 percent, while passenger traffic was 25 percent greater. During the war 97 percent of domestic troop movements were by rail, and nearly 90 percent of army and navy supplies moved over the railroads. The efficiency of the carriers astounded federal officials, especially when vast shipments of petroleum shifted from coastal vessels to railroad tank cars after 1941. The railroads handled unprecedented traffic from 1941 to 1945.

These accomplishments were achieved even though over 350,000 railroad employees entered military service. Many railroad workers served in transportation units in Africa, Europe, and Asia. Recruiting women, minorities, and Mexican workers as replacements, the railroads added employees so that in 1945 some 1,420,000 labored on the carriers. Labor disputes continued, but wage concessions prevented nationwide strikes in 1941 and 1943. The railroads prospered during the war despite excess profits taxes. Management paid off debt by retiring bonds and issued modest cash dividends. At the end of the war railroad debt was lower than before 1916. While the federal government had lost more than $1 billion operating the railroads during World War I, between 1942 and 1945 the railroads paid federal taxes of more than $3 million every day. The increase in operating efficiency between the two world wars made the industry's contributions to the war effort possible. When the nation celebrated V-J Day in August 1945, the railroads appeared to be on the cusp of yet another prosperous era. It was not to be.

Prospering from the earnings of the wartime period, the railroads began an intense effort to rebuild the equipment and structures heavily used during the war. Encouraged by the popularity of the new streamlined passenger trains and the enormous use of passenger trains during the war, the railroads embarked upon a costly program of modern new passenger equipment. The diesel locomotive proved itself during the war period, and the railroads quickly set about replacing their steam locomotives. But the railroads' profitable new postwar period never materialized. The railroads, unlike their highway, waterway, and air competitors, were handicapped by excessive regulation and taxation. Massive highway construction encouraged the expansion of private automobile use and buses, and a burgeoning air transport system quickly led to rapidly declining passenger trains, despite all of the railroads' investment. Improved highways, pipelines, and federally funded inland waterways brought heightened competition to the railroads' freight business. Instead of a time of great prosperity, the railroads were in for the fight of their lives.

A Social History of American Railroads

H. Roger Grant

For more than 150 years railroads have had a pronounced impact on the lives of residents of North America. More than any other form of technology, the iron horse literally became an engine for growth and general well-being. By the 1880s the railway age had fully arrived, although expansion continued into the 1920s, especially in Canada. In 1880 U.S. mileage stood at 92,147; a decade later it soared to 163,359, peaking in 1916 at 254,251. In states such as Illinois, Iowa, and Ohio, mileage became so dense that inhabitants of small communities might have two or more carriers, and farm families likely lived within a manageable driving distance to a station.

The earliest expectations of "rail road" proponents mostly materialized. When on October 1, 1833, Elias Horry, president of the South Carolina Canal and Rail-Road Company, addressed an audience in Charleston about the impact of the recent opening of his 136-mile road between Charleston and Hamburg, briefly the world's longest, he hardly misrepresented the railroad of that day or even later. "Our citizens immediately, and correctly saw, that every benefit arising from the system [of railroads], could be extended to every City and Town in the United States, and particularly to those near the Atlantic." Added Horry, "That, by establishing Rail-Roads, so located as to pass into the interior of the several States, every agricultural, commercial, or saleable production could be brought down from remote parts of the Country to these Cities and Towns; and from them, such returns, as the wants of the inhabitants of the interior required, could be forwarded with great dispatch and economy, thereby forming a perfect system of mercantile exchanges, effected in the shortest possible time, and giving life to a most advantageous Commerce."

The impact of the railroad upon the daily lives of Americans can be seen in a variety of ways. This social history arguably is best revealed by exploring the topics of trains, stations, communities, and legacies. Travel by rail left lasting memories. The sight of a train alone could conjure up wonderful dreams about people and places. Similarly, even if train travel were not taken or contemplated, the station for generations served as a locus of community life, and the individuals associated with it were important to nearly everyone. The railroad, too, long affected communities, even their physical appearance. And the legacy of trains has had both a contemporary impact during the railway age and an ongoing one. Whether in literature, music, language, or art, the social history of this often-beloved transport form remains alive.

Trains

The train, with its fascinating and powerful steam locomotive, was much more than an instrument of progress; it was a wonder. In "To a Locomotive in Winter" poet Walt Whitman captured the essence of the common attraction for these mechanical marvels: "Type of modern-emblem of motion and power—pulse of the continent." It took novelist Sherwood Anderson more words to convey a similar message: "There was a passenger train going away into the mysterious West [at Clyde, Ohio] at some twenty minutes after seven in the evenings and, as six o'clock was our universal supper hour, we congregated at the station to see the train arrive, we boys gathering far down the station platform to gape with hungry eyes at the locomotive." Although Anderson pursued a literary career, it is understandable that with the dawn of the railway age the desire to work on or around the iron horse became great. Starry-eyed farm and village lads, often seeking their first regular wage-earning experience, found employment with the local railroad company. Whether they won jobs in train service, machine shops, or country stations, thoughts of being connected to the railway had strong appeal. "Every day that I went to work, I encountered new experiences," remembered a veteran depot agent. "I would always see trains, freight and passenger, something that I never, never, tired of." And he admitted, "Railroading got totally in my blood." Some of the first employees had originally worked for other forms of transport that declined with rail competition. It was not unusual for a steamboat captain to become a locomotive engineer or a stagecoach driver to take the position of train conductor.

The first trains, which were dedicated more to transporting goods than passengers, had at the throttle of the locomotive the most skilled crewman, the engineer, and his hardworking assistant, the fireman, who stoked cord wood (later coal) into the firebox. When not braking, coupling, or uncoupling cars, a head brakeman usually joined them in the cab. The caboose, "crummy," or "way-car" (its name varied from road to road) became home to the conductor or "captain," who commanded the train, and a brakeman or two.

Once the railway passenger train developed beyond the initial primitive locomotive pulling what might be described as stagecoaches on flanged wheels, the typical "consist" also had a similar array of employees. By the 1870s there might be situated directly behind the cab crew an express agent who organized and guarded often-valuable shipments in the baggage or express car. If the train included a U.S. Railway Post Office (RPO) car, which appeared about the same time as express equipment, several RPO employees would be sorting mail en route. In the passenger coaches the conductor, who was officially in charge of the train, worked with several trainmen, who collected tickets, assisted riders, "called" stations, and at stops protected the train with flags or flares. When dining cars became common by the 1880s, there was a complement of stewards, cooks, and waiters. If the train included a dining car, it probably carried one or more sleeping cars with a conductor and porters, the latter nearly always men of color. Porters made beds, served meals, and shined shoes. Some trains might have "news butchers," entrepreneurial lads who sold newspapers, tobacco products, and sundries.

During Prohibition news butchers might unlawfully offer "hooch," and, in fact, other crewmembers might do the same. In the 1920s passengers who traveled through the Midwest could usually purchase the popular "Templeton rye," an illegally distilled liquor produced in the Carroll County, Iowa, village of Templeton. And for years "moonshines" in the mountains of northeastern Georgia maintained a regular "drop" for train crews on the Southern Railway's Charlotte-Atlanta line. These trainmen merely put down their empty canning jars, albeit with cash, and later picked up filled ones of "white lightning" for their own consumption or for resale, perhaps on board a train.

Although American train riders did not confront the rigid class structure of Great Britain, with its first-, second-, and third-class carriages, affluent travelers could purchase luxury accommodations. In the mid-1870s Florence Leslie, wife of the well-to-do publisher of *Frank Leslie's Illustrated Newspaper*, described the resplendent Pullman Hotel car that operated between Chicago, Illinois, and Omaha, Nebraska: "Our *chef*, of ebon color, and proportions suggesting a liberal sampling of the good things he prepares, wears the regulation snow-white apron and cap, and gives us cordial welcome and information. . . . At six the tables are laid for two each, with dainty linen, and the finest of glass and china, and we presently sit down to dinner. Our repast is Delmonican in its nature and style, consisting of soup, fish, *entries*, roast

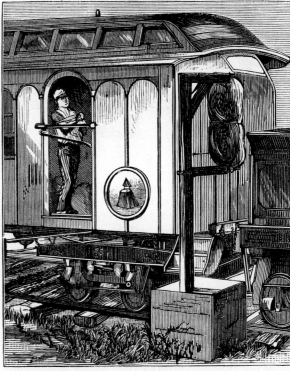

The U.S. mail began using the railroad from an early date, and the Railway Post Office was a marvel of speed and efficiency. Postal clerks sorted the mail even as the car sped through the night (*left*), and the specially designed post catcher made it possible to pick up mail en route even as the train went by without stopping (*right*). —(both) Middleton Collection

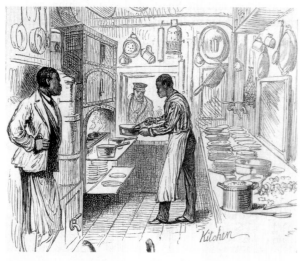

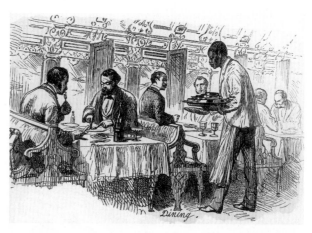

Long-distance travel by rail could be comfortable for those who could afford the best accommodations. The Pullman Palace Car was lavishly furnished and decorated (*top, left*), and the washroom facilities were commodious and well equipped (*top, right*). The tiny kitchen (*bottom, left*) was a marvel of efficiency, and the dining staff could offer a multicourse meal (*bottom, right*). —Middleton Collection; *London Illustrated News*; Union Pacific; *Trains* Magazine Collection

meat and vegetables, followed by the conventional dessert and the essential spoonful of black coffee."

Fine accommodations and food remained available throughout much of the passenger era. Not until jet airplane travel, which burst upon the transportation scene in the late 1950s, did luxury service decline, at times precipitously. When in January 1918 the family of a wealthy Cedar Rapids, Iowa, businessman escaped from a harsh midwestern winter to the sunny warmth of Southern Cal-

ifornia, a daughter vividly recalled the posh service that was part of a first-class Pullman ticket on the *Overland Limited*. "The first day on the train was just as exciting as getting on it. After we had taken turns . . . getting washed up in our small washroom with the shiny nickel-plated wash bowl, . . . a waiter arrived all the way from the dining car, bringing us breakfast on a huge silver tray. . . . [He] spread a white table cloth, unloaded his tray, and soon we were peeking into one covered silver dish after another and filling our plates with hot corn muffins, bacon and jam. Besides that we poured hot cocoa from thermos jugs into our cups, and topped them off with whipped cream. Through the windows we could see flat snow-covered Nebraska. We were on our way!"

In the 1930s trains like the *Overland Limited*, with their heavyweight steel cars, gave way to lightweight, diesel-electric-powered streamliners. The grime produced by most coal-burning locomotives became only a memory, but the quality of service on these fast trains remained high. In the age of streamliners, leading trains, including the *City of San Francisco*, the *Panama Limited*, and the *20th Century Limited*, featured uniformed nurses or similar personnel to assist passengers, particularly the young and the elderly. In the dining cars delicacies such as fresh trout, berries in season, and fancy pastries adorned menus. For the business traveler there might be an onboard barber, secretary, and valet. A few trains boasted a small reading library.

Not all riders received such favorable treatment. For decades literally thousands of main- and branch-line "locals" rattled leisurely along their routes, hauling passengers, mail, and express. Often railroads assigned their oldest, soot-blackened equipment to these runs. When, for example, air-conditioned passenger cars made up the best trains, open windows in these locals provided the only circulating air, allowing cinders, dirt, and smoke to penetrate the coaches.

Nevertheless, these workhorse trains meant much to their patrons. Most of all, they offered a dependable means to travel from their hometowns to destinations both near and far. The usual train crews might become popular with "regulars" and even be honored on special occasions. In the 1930s the Milwaukee Road local that operated between the Iowa cities of Cedar Rapids and Ottumwa, a distance of 89 miles, had employees who became near and dear to the German-American residents of the Amana Colonies. "They would appear [at Christmas time]," fondly recalled a brakeman, "with savory hams, delicious wines, and gifts for the crew."

In the South, or wherever "Jim Crow" laws had been enacted, trains nearly always featured racial segregation. Companies either used a coach partitioned into white and "colored" sections or provided separate cars, with ones assigned to African American riders often being the most decrepit rolling stock. Since train crews (with the possible exception of the locomotive fireman and porters) were white, the feeling of personal closeness between black riders and passenger train employees likely never developed.

Passengers commonly experienced the worst equipment on "mixed" trains, where companies, frequently shortline carriers, found it uneconomical to dispatch separate freight and passenger trains. These runs, designed to haul "hogs and humans," typically consisted of ancient coaches located behind a string of freight cars and not-so-modern locomotives. Stops might be made in rail yards rather than at depot platforms, attesting to management's main desire to serve freight customers. The public might be told that these trains had "service irregular" or "subject to freight connections" or "passenger connections uncertain," and that they operated "Mon., Wed. & Fri. only." Although such consists brought joy to railroad enthusiasts, they usually did not please patrons. Yet for thousands of Americans, "mixed trains" were their only links to the outside world until automobiles and all-weather roads increased their options, and these trains were thus as familiar as the general store and the country church.

Whether the passenger train was a "ballast-scorching" express, a plodding local, or a poky mixed, there were riders who did not usually fuss about what they rode. Indeed, these riders "without tickets" were more likely to "take freights." For decades there were hoards of hoboes or " 'boes" who never paid for rail transportation, especially after the Civil War and on through the Great Depression of the 1930s. These men (and occasionally women and children) sought adventure or a better life down the tracks.

Traveling the "side-door Pullman route" took various forms. Frequently the ticketless rider sat inside an empty boxcar or on a flatcar or squatted on the roof of a freight car. If he actually "rode the rods," this meant placing his "ticket," namely, a thick wooden plank, between the metal support trusses that were once found underneath rail cars and lying horizontally on it. Another alternative was "riding the blinds." The hobo stood in the recessed entryway of a baggage or mail car or coach that was positioned directly behind the locomotive tender or "tank." Occasionally he dared to make the trip on top of a passenger car—called "decking"—or even aboard the tender, hiding in piles of coal. One adventuresome youngster related his exciting, albeit foolhardy, trip with a companion in the late 1890s on the pilot or "cowcatcher" of an Atchison, Topeka & Santa Fe Railway locomotive across the Kansas prairie: "Now the light beam from the headlight, shining on the track, made the rails look like two silver ribbons that were being unreeled out of the darkness ahead of us and swallowed up right under the pilot below us and we went sailing along through the dark and gee, we were getting thrills and chills in turn, one after another."

Railroad companies' attempts to keep hoboes from their trains met with limited success, yet they extended free passage to others. Most full-time railway employees and their immediate families received complimentary passes. If the rider lacked ticket or pass but was a railroad man and carried his paid-up dues receipt to one of the several brotherhoods, a freight or passenger conductor might allow him to ride in a caboose or coach. Before passage of the Elkins Act in 1903, railroads commonly distributed passes to a variety of nonrailroad persons, including clergy, journalists, and politicians, in an effort to create goodwill.

There were other riders who might be closely watched and asked to leave the train or even placed under arrest. Conductors and railroad detectives ("cinder dicks") kept a watchful eye out for confidence men, professional gamblers, and prostitutes. But many of these unsavory individuals understood how to ply their trade in the presence of railroad personnel. One frequent traveler remembered that in the early 1940s two women had a standing reservation for the drawing room of a Pullman car on the *Sunshine Special*, a popular Missouri Pacific Railroad train that operated between St. Louis and Texas destinations. "Business always appeared to be good on the southbound trip," he recalled. "There was never a 'line' to this rolling brothel (which was occupied by one of these entrepreneurs each night), but somehow word would get around to the other sections of the train." Apparently these hookers were not "put off" the train, although surely the crew, including the Pullman conductor, knew what was happening. Perhaps money exchanged hands or sexual favors were bestowed.

In addition to regularly scheduled passenger runs, from their earliest days railroads offered special "excursions." These trains ran as "extras" that flew white flags or at night carried white classification lamps on the locomotive to denote this distinction. Railroad companies promoted virtually any type of public attraction to generate business. On May 20, 1847, Superintendent Charles Minot of the Medford Branch Railroad in Massachusetts announced: "During the whole of the week of the Religious Anniversaries in Boston, commencing on Monday, May 24th, an Extra Train will leave Medford for Boston, every Evening, except on Saturday, at 9 1-2, P.M.; and returning, will leave Boston at 10, P.M." More than a half century later the Minneapolis & St. Louis Railroad distributed a graphically attractive broadside: "VISIT THE LEGISLATURE, SPECIAL TRAIN TO DES MOINES AND RETURN, FRIDAY MARCH 22," advertising an excursion train that would depart Ruthven, Iowa, at 5:45 A.M. and make 22 intermediate stops before arriving in the Iowa capital at 11:13 A.M. Excursionists would reboard in Des Moines for a 6:30 P.M. departure. As late as September 28, 1957, the Wabash Railroad operated a special "Theatre Train" between Decatur, Illinois, and St. Louis, Missouri, for a Saturday matinee performance of a stage production of *My Fair Lady* at Kiel Auditorium. Never overlooking an opportunity for extra passenger business, the Illinois Central Railroad once maintained a tariff for "spectacle" lynchings and public hangings. If such a horrific event were to occur, a local station agent could request a special train or additional coaches on a regularly scheduled run and advertise reduced fares.

Much less ghoulish were organized tours that either used a scheduled train or an occasional extra operation. Beginning in 1880, the Phillips-Judson Company, based in Boston and with offices in other American cities, offered "Personally Conducted Overland Excursions." The firm sold sleeping-car space and provided guides en route and at publicized stops. In 1898, for example, Phillips-Judson arranged an eight-hour layover in Salt Lake City, Utah, providing an escorted tour of "the great Mormon

Temple, the Tabernacle, and the many places of historic interest in the city."

One version of the "organized tour" or special movement was the troop train. Although during the Mexican War between 1846 and 1848 some soldiers and their equipment traveled over rail routes, the Civil War demonstrated that railroads were vital to the military. Armies of both the North and the South moved extensively by rail. In the summer of 1863, for example, the Confederate high command transferred the forces of Gen. James Longstreet from Virginia to northern Georgia (Chickamauga), and in the early fall of 1863 the 11th and 12th Corps of the Union army journeyed from northern Virginia to relieve the Army of the Cumberland at Chattanooga, Tennessee. Both sides pressed into service all types of rolling stock. Soldiers might find themselves riding in boxcars, prompting them to tear off the side boards or even the roof itself for better ventilation and "to see the country." Long after the Civil War troops continued to move by rail. During the Spanish-American War, World War I, World War II, and the Korean Conflict, troop trains were common. As with earlier experiences, soldiers often found their accommodations less than satisfactory. "I believe for many GIs that being herded onboard troop trains during World War II convinced them that they never again would travel by rail," observed one railroad official. "Likely with the troop trains the industry planted some of the seeds that grew eventually into the demise of the intercity passenger service."

Although troop trains occasionally derailed, perhaps engineered by the enemy during the Civil War, wrecks of passenger trains were common, whether with the earliest trains that treaded slowly over spindly iron-strap rails or the later limiteds that sped along "high iron." Before trains customarily traveled faster than 30 or 35 miles an hour, loss of life or serious injury was unlikely; an accident became merely an inconvenience. But when speeds increased, carnage became common in a major mishap. Indeed, speed played a role in America's worst passenger disaster. On July 9, 1918, two Nashville, Chattanooga & St. Louis passenger trains, each running at approximately 50 miles per hour, smashed head-on near Nashville, Tennessee. Rescuers found 101 dead crew members and passengers and scores more who were seriously injured.

Railroad companies made serious attempts to improve safety. Starting in the early twentieth century, the Chicago & North Western Railway launched a safety crusade and in the process coined the famous "Safety-First" slogan, widely emulated by other carriers and industries. But speed of travel served as a major attraction of rail transport; in fact, Americans expected it. They read with pleasure newspaper accounts of the first 100 mph passenger-train run. In May 1893 the New York Central & Hudson River Railroad's *Empire State Express*, pulled by the high-stepping American-type (4-4-0) locomotive 999, reached 112 mph near Crittenden, New York, establishing a world record.

Railroads also claimed newspaper space for nonspeed

events, and these happenings often became part of an individual's memory of trains. It was not uncommon on the day of the funeral of a prominent politician or railroad executive to have trains briefly come to a standstill. On September 19, 1901, the Wabash Railroad (and most others as well) halted their service to commemorate the martyred William McKinley. The trainmaster at Moberly, Missouri, for one, issued this train order: " 'God's will not ours be done.' All trains and Engines will stop for five minutes at two o'clock P.M. [CST] September nineteenth out of respect for memory of President McKinley." At 2 P.M. (CST) on May 31, 1916, the hour of the funeral of James Jerome Hill, founder of the Great Northern Railway, every train on the Hill Lines stopped for five minutes. Passengers on a Northern Pacific train high in the Rocky Mountains, enjoying lunch in the dining car, laid down their cups, glasses, and silverware in silence when the conductor explained the reason for their unscheduled stop.

One of the most touching unscheduled timetable stops in the annals of American railroading honored the "Little Fellow." From the late 1880s until the end of passenger service in 1950, Chicago & North Western train crews on the Watertown-Redfield, South Dakota, branch halted every Memorial Day to place flowers and to pray at a modest grave marker on the lonely prairie. Buried there was a boy, his name forgotten, the son of a construction worker and cook, who had died in a bunk car near Elrod, South Dakota, and was interred at that trackside location. The event vividly revealed the human side of a colossal American industry.

No matter the train or the occasion, a railroad journey surely provided at least one memorable experience. For children it might be a walk through the aisles to a water cooler or toilet; for families it could be dinner in the diner or a more economical home-packed meal of fried chicken, bread-and-butter sandwiches, and cake; for newlyweds it was probably the privacy of a sleeping car; and for the professional traveler or "drummer" it was perhaps the lively after-dinner card game or drink and cigar in the parlor car. Anticipating this special event, travelers customarily wore their Sunday clothes when they boarded a passenger train, and everyone was usually on his or her best behavior.

By the beginning of the twentieth century passenger trains paid calls at more than 125,000 communities in North America, even though some places had only mixed-train service. It was common for citizens who felt that they should have more or better train service to complain to railroad officials and to public officials, usually state railroad commissioners. Some residents might continue to fuss about trains that operated on Sunday, although most criticisms had ended by the Civil War. Still, some roads, usually small ones, cooperated with these diehard Sabbatarians. But as America became more urban and industrial, the issue of trains on Sunday became largely moot, and progress prevailed over tradition.

Stations

In every community the building most closely associated with the railroad was the depot, a tangible manifestation of the modern industrial age. Residents universally viewed the "dee-po" as a vital public place. Whether it occurred in a vibrant metropolis or a peaceful village, train-time excited the residents. "The depot is always a beehive of activity," observed a midwestern businessman shortly after the turn of the twentieth century. "The hustle-bustle, which is America, can be found there." Or as a Pennsylvanian opined, "The rhythms of the railroad be-

A recurrent theme in railroad folklore is the story of a dead child buried alongside the track. This is the "Little Fellow" grave near Elrod, South Dakota, where the crew of a Chicago & North Western train stopped every Memorial Day. —Chicago & North Western, *Trains* Magazine Collection

Trains connected isolated cities and towns with the outside world. This drawing by F. H. Wellington in *The American Railway* (1892) conveys the bustle that went with an expected train. —Middleton Collection

came the rhythms of the town." During the golden age of railways in the first part of the twentieth century John Faulkner, brother of author William Faulkner, noted that in Oxford, Mississippi, "about half the town would meet the train to see who was coming in or leaving." It is no wonder that "station loungers" became as ubiquitous as loafers at the courthouse, general store, or post office. The news they gathered at the depot was fresh and filled with import, and not the worn-out gossip picked up elsewhere. Unquestionably the depot served as a community's gateway to the outside world; no single structure has taken its place after the triumph of the automobile and the airplane.

Depot buildings varied enormously, and the first railroad officials did not fret about depot design or construction. They concentrated on constructing their rights-of-way, bridges, and tracks, acquiring suitable locomotives and rolling stock, and recruiting reliable workers. Rail leaders sought to start operations quickly in order to generate badly needed revenues. Lacking funds, management opted to use available buildings, if possible, for depot-related services. When in May 1830 the infant Baltimore & Ohio reached Ellicott's Mills, Maryland, 13 miles west of its starting point on Pratt Street in Baltimore, the company decided that its passengers could wait in the newly opened Patapsco Hotel near its terminal point. After all, travelers could fend for themselves. This had also been

the plight of stagecoach riders, because operators of stage lines did not usually own their station facilities; rather, proprietors of hotels, stores, and taverns served their patrons. If necessary, travelers made their own arrangements for food and lodging. Yet the B&O felt the need to erect a building in Ellicott's Mills, and it eventually constructed a freight depot that served passengers as well.

Throughout the pre–Civil War period and occasionally thereafter, railroads used existing buildings for their stations. However, carriers preferred to control these trackside structures, and they could more likely do so once their financial health improved. What emerged was the most popular design of all depots, the single-story "combination" station. Such a structure served the needs of a small community. The combination depot provided space for an agent's office (usually located in the center with a protruding bay window that faced the tracks), a freight section, and a passenger waiting room. Variations occurred. It was not uncommon to have a separate waiting room for women and children because of the perceived coarseness of cigar-smoking, tobacco-chewing working-class males. And in Dixie, with the advent of post–Civil War Jim Crow laws, the "colored" waiting room for racial segregation of African Americans became the norm. In larger stations in the South, waiting rooms separated by both race and gender were not uncommon.

An important variation of the combination depot, with or without a ladies or "colored" waiting room, was a structure that provided living quarters for agents and their dependents. Early on, the concept of "living in the depot" developed, largely to satisfy housing shortages in many communities, particularly in raw prairie towns that had only recently emerged at trackside. An agent appreciated the availability of decent housing and the common practice of free rent. The railroad found it advantageous, too. The agent was essentially on call 24 hours a day, seven days a week. "This would insure the practically continuous presence of someone to receive service and emergency messages," correctly noted a railway trade journal. An occupied station also meant that an agent or family member could respond quickly to any crisis, whether to call an officer of the law if a burglar entered (there was concern about break-ins because of cash kept in depot offices and valuable freight and express—beer and whiskey before Prohibition—stored on the premises) or to report a fire to the local volunteer brigade. Also, railroad officials considered married agents "steady" and "reliable," and company housing could attract and keep these preferred employees.

Station agents or "operators," whether they lived in the depot or not, became highly respected community figures. As official representatives of the railroad, they were probably as well known locally as constables, pastors, or physicians. Often wearing a dark cap with a bright STATION AGENT badge, agents met the public when they sold tickets, planned travel itineraries, and reported freight and express shipments. At times they offered for sale newspapers, magazines, and postcards, especially during the picture postcard craze before World War I.

But there was more. Having firsthand knowledge of the cryptic Morse code, agents were the best-informed persons in town. The telegraph carried more than just routine railroad business (train "meets," equipment requests, and switch lists); it transmitted commercial messages from Postal Telegraph, Western Union, or some other firm. "There wasn't any radio in those days," remembered President Harry S Truman. "Those old stationmasters had [telegraph] machines in every station, and when the machines weren't being used to send over railroad information, they'd send news over them." He added, "Out at Grandview [Missouri] we didn't get the Kansas City papers until the next morning, and so if you wanted to find out what was going on, that was the only way you could do it."

Local newspapers relied heavily on the agent's telegraphic skills. As the daughter of a small-town newspaper publisher recalled, "The depot was truly our link with national events, for in those days before radio and television the telegrapher got everything first, including the weather forecast. My father haunted the depot for these forecasts as well as important world events."

The varied services provided by the depot agent-operator are detailed in these autobiographical passages by a Milwaukee Road agent who for more than 50 years served stations in Iowa and South Dakota:

Each half hour 9:30 AM to 2:30 PM the "bosses" of the 7 elevators and 1 flour mill [in Akron, Iowa] came to the men's waiting room, lined up like a bunch of crows on the benches, and waited for the latest grain and livestock quotations sent out of [Sioux City] each half hour. [Sioux City] Western Union XD [long-distance opera-

The telegraph operator ran the small local stations along the line. Operator Minnie L. Beissel ran the Southern Pacific station at Chatsworth, California, in April 1954. —William D. Middleton

tors] interrupted all other biz each half hour. He called no one. Each opr. was expected to be at the wire to get the figures and to OK them in turn, starting with Elk Point [South Dakota] ofc. No one "broke in" on XD. If you missed a figure you got it later from a neighboring agent. How well I recall the grain men stepping out of the waiting room on winter days while I was unloading freight from a passenger train, covered with snow, fingers so cold I couldn't write, and saying, "Hey Kid, it's time for the CND [Commercial News Department]!!"

CND offered all big events. All the local sports had to do was to pass the hat. . . . I got 10% of it for the work. I copied the presidential election of Nov. 1916, the heavyweight prize fight between Jack Johnson and "white hope" Jess Willard [in April 1915]. . . . There wasn't time to copy the World Series except on Sunday PM. Far too much time would be taken from the daily routine.

Elections were bad—the office would be filled with tobacco smoke by 10 PM and by 5 AM the ol' head, or what was left of it, would be swirling. Pieces of yellow paper called "clips," half sheet size went into the typewriter (mill) and when the sheet being written on was jerked out the next sheet would be pulled into writing position in the mill. A couple of happy fellows would stand at each shoulder and often would jerk the paper out when only a line or two had been written, turning to the rest of the "assembled mob" with, " 'Hey, Listen to this! So n so wins in New York!!' " I copied the 1924 election in Mitchell, S.D. . . . By 1928 the first radios were "doing their stuff."

Before widespread use of long-distance telephone calling, individuals who needed to communicate with someone out of town telegraphed. Common messages were death notices, but residents might want to wire for help to fight a fire or to catch a criminal. Agents expected to be awakened at home to send these emergency telegrams. No wonder the agent-telegrapher was "looked up to" by the town boys and admired by many a girl. They became central characters in railroad fiction, which often appeared in widely circulated male-oriented adventure magazines.

Agents were not the only individuals who made the depot a community institution. Larger towns had express agents who occupied depot space. Before 1913, when Congress passed the Parcel Post Act, private express companies operating over most railroads carried all packages. Thus firms such as Adams, American, Great Northern, National, Southern, United States, and Wells Fargo became household names. Still another nonrailroad employee often seen at the depot was the person who had contracted with the U.S. Post Office to pick up and deliver mail. This individual might have the most erratic work schedule in town, meeting trains daily during the day and night and catching sleep when he could. "Hack" or "omnibus" drivers also met trains, regularly transporting salesmen and their sample cases and trunks in handsome horse-drawn vehicles, some of which were brightly colored with side panels adorned with eye-catching landscapes.

Some depots, usually in the larger county-seat communities or at important railroad junctions, contained a small restaurant or lunchroom. Food would be served by "hash slingers" to waiting passengers, railroad personnel, and anyone who needed a meal. The arrival of a passenger train brought a small crowd to the depot, and some would linger for a repast. Such eateries at a minimum usually employed a cook and waitress, though the "cuisine" served varied enormously with the talents of the small staff.

While the typical small-town depot lunchroom rarely deserved any degree of immortality, a different story holds for the Fred Harvey lunchrooms. The Harvey company, launched in the mid-1870s by British immigrant Frederick Henry Harvey, developed a chain of eating establishments in depots or nearby locations (for example, Newton, Kansas, and Williams, Arizona) along the Atchison, Topeka & Santa Fe Railway and that carrier's onetime affiliate, the St. Louis–San Francisco (Frisco) Railway. The Harvey firm came to represent the best in food, cleanliness, and service. The efficiency and courtesy of its waitresses, "Harvey Girls," became legendary and the subject of a hit 1946 Hollywood movie starring Ray Bolger, Judy Garland, John Hodiak, Angela Lansbury, and Marjorie Main.

In large urban terminals travelers expected a wide range of services and specialized employees. These involved food, information, and assistance. Eating accommodations ranged from lunchrooms for low-cost, quick meals to more formal and expensive restaurants, complete with maitre d', head and specialty chefs, and an array of waiters and helpers. Inevitably there was an information booth or room where knowledgeable station employees dispensed train arrival and departure times and locations. By World War I there would likely be an office of the National Travelers' Aid Society. Predictably, the society's bright beacon logo was a comforting sign to the public. Larger stations might have paid attendants to supervise the popular women's lounge. Other employees attended immigrant waiting areas where travelers in a strange land might wash clothes, bathe or shower, or relax in a sanitary and safe environment before resuming their journey. These urban monuments to the railway age had an army of "red caps" who assisted travelers with the luggage and other items and also aided the elderly and very young. Other workers daily handled thousands of pieces of luggage, trunks, and sample cases. Vast urban stations typically provided creature comforts and services, including a beauty salon, barbershop, drugstore, bookstore, and notions shops. Travelers could acquire a manicure, haircut, bottle of painkiller, magazine, or package of writing paper in facilities spacious and often luxurious.

The physical location of the depot contributed to its importance. In some communities, especially those in New England and along the Atlantic Seaboard where settlement preceded railroads, depots might be a distance from the town center. In those places where the existing community hugged a ridge or high point, the rail line

The Travelers' Aid office provided familiar and helpful support. This busy one was located at New York's Grand Central Terminal. —Ed Nowak, Penn Central

might be in a valley, a mile or so from the commercial heart. But if the railroad had preceded town building, the depot was likely to be centrally situated. A. B. Stickney, founder of the 1,500-mile-long Chicago Great Western Railway, argued that the depot should be as prominent as possible, largely so residents would not forget about the road, especially its passenger service. In "T-towns," communities established directly by the railroad or by a town-site affiliate, the depot usually appeared in the most prominent place. Since the track formed the top of the letter "T" and the principal street created the stem, the station was almost always where the town's "main drag" met the railroad. Although these T-towns were usually smaller communities, several capital cities, including Bismarck, North Dakota, Cheyenne, Wyoming, and Lincoln, Nebraska, featured this type of railroad-street relationship with stations at the main intersection.

Because of its prominent location and the availability of this public structure, the depot might serve nonrailroad functions. Local governments, for example, during the formative months or years of communities might be organized in the waiting room and continue to function there until appropriate nonrailroad space could be built. Occasionally schools had their origins in a depot. It was not unusual for church services to occur in the waiting room and for church-related events, including baptisms, weddings, and funerals, to be held there. Groups and societies, too, might temporarily use the facility, perhaps a fraternal lodge such as the Ancient Order of United Workmen or the Knights of Pythias.

For generations most Americans had strong personal memories linked to the depot that likely involved a special event in their lives. It might be meeting the train that brought a loved one or even a new member of the family. They might recall greeting a famous person, such as William Jennings Bryan, "Buffalo Bill" Cody, Eugene V. Debs, Robert Ingersoll, Theodore Roosevelt, or Billy Sunday, or remember watching a special train, perhaps one that carried the circus, a major-league baseball team, or the body of a deceased governor or president. The depot was also the place for farewells, maybe for newlyweds who happily said temporary good-byes when they left on their honeymoon or soldiers who sadly bid farewell to family and friends, perhaps for the last time, on their way to war. There could be raw emotions associated with platform experiences.

Communities

The arrival of the first iron horse was always a joyful event and one worthy of community celebration. A formal gala to welcome the railroad became traditional along newly completed rail lines. One such festivity took place in 1856 at Sterling, Illinois, with completion by the Galena & Chicago Union Rail Road of a line to Chicago. "Simeon Coe furnished a three-year old ox, which was roasted on a primitive arrangement of forked sticks, and then borne in triumph, bedecked with flags and oranges, to an immense arbor of branches near the present Central school," recounted a local historian in 1908. "After the

Train travelers usually carried plenty of baggage. "In a Baggage-room" depicts baggage handling in a large station as illustrated by artist W. C. Broughton for *The American Railway* (1892). —Middleton Collection

banquet, B. F. Taylor, the poet, made a flowery address. The lion of the day was Stephen A. Douglas, who talked to the masses in his own earnest style. . . . Estimates of the multitude ran as high as five thousand."

Once the railroad became established as part of the community, residents wanted to make certain that train service was adequate and that the depot made an attractive entrance, that it was properly equipped, and that it had a competent and public-spirited agent. When problems occurred, letters flooded the general offices of the railroad company. If satisfaction were not forthcoming, complaints were then sent to politicians and state railroad commissioners.

Early in the twentieth century a classic example of a community's unhappiness with a local depot arose in Greenwich, Ohio. Even though its 1,000 inhabitants enjoyed excellent access to railroads (it was located on the Pittsburgh-to-Chicago main line of the B&O, the Cleveland-to-Columbus stem of the New York Central System, and the Akron-to-Delphos line of the Northern Ohio Railroad), deep dissatisfaction developed. The former two roads offered acceptable depot facilities, but the latter decidedly did not. When in 1890 a predecessor company of the Northern Ohio built through Greenwich, it erected a modest building in an inconvenient location. After the Northern Ohio emerged in the late 1890s, it showed even less interest in the community, subsequently removing its agent and permitting the depot structure to fall into disrepair. The company instructed patrons to use either the New London station seven miles to the east or the Plymouth stop nine miles to the west. Residents howled. They depended upon the two daily trains of the Northern Ohio for personal travel to the nearby communities of Cary, Medina, New London, New Washington, and Plymouth and for freight, express, and mail service over the carrier and its strategic connections.

Understandably, Greenwich citizens complained, first to the railroad and then to the Ohio Railroad Commission. In a formal protest filed with the latter in late 1907, they charged that the Northern Ohio provided "an old, dilapidated, abandoned and partly destroyed building" and argued that it should be replaced immediately. The railroad offered a weak response, indicating that it did not need to maintain a depot at a station that it considered to be a "flag stop." But townspeople challenged that position. The attorney for Greenwich told regulators that while the company might use the flag-stop designation in its public timetables, in reality the place was a bona fide regular stop. To prove his contention, a postal worker who for eight years had carried the mails to and from the station twice daily testified that trains always stopped, regardless of its flag-stop status.

In March 1908 the commission sided with the town. It found that the Northern Ohio had treated Greenwich as a regular station stop and ordered that "[t]he defendant should provide a suitable building at said station, and keep the same well lighted for the comfort . . . of its patrons . . . and that some person should be placed in charge thereof to receive and receipt for parcel freight . . . and that such person [should] take care of incoming parcel freight and store the same in the usual and customary way until called for by the owner." Shortly thereafter the company complied. Greenwich received its replacement depot and also a full-time agent.

Railroads usually avoided confrontations with the public. Goodwill was important. Company managers recognized that attractive and smoothly functioning stations kept the public happy and served as a good advertisement. Indeed, stations possessed a certain "marquee" value; happy residents would surely travel and ship over their rails.

One way that railroads improved their public image involved building attractive replacement depots. When communities prospered, likely their original wood-frame structures could no longer accommodate local needs. Roads such as the Burlington, Illinois Central, New Haven, and Santa Fe erected scores of "county-seat" depots, buildings nearly always constructed of brick (stucco was also popular), with commodious waiting rooms and ample office, express, and freight space. The exterior appearance might be significantly enhanced by a hip roof, shed dormers, or other architectural features. Some buildings even received a porte cochère or carriage porch on the public road entrance.

Throughout the country the "depot park" became a familiar feature. Companies, agents, and community-booster groups might alone or collectively build and maintain these public betterments. The name of the community might be spelled out in large block letters, a practical way to show train riders that they had arrived in AKRON, BISMARCK, or ROCK SPRINGS. Trees and benches usually adorned the park grounds, and in season a variety of annuals and perennials bloomed. In the North Dakota capital children from an elementary school planted, watered, and weeded the flowers. "A depot park," recalled a station agent, "really added a nice touch to the entrance to town and it was the subject of much positive comment." But, he added, "you had better be certain that the grass was cut and the weeds pulled!" The depot and the park were part of what landscape historian John R. Stilgoe has aptly called the "metropolitan corridor." When the railroad arrived, not only did the depot adjoin the rails, but a host of structures, mostly commercial facilities, appeared at trackside: factories, power plants, grain elevators, lumber and coal yards, hotels, boardinghouses, restaurants, and other establishments. The rail-

The Richmond, Kentucky, depot became the center of activity with the arrival of the Louisville & Nashville train, bringing a crowd of horse-drawn vehicles and spectators to the scene. —C. U. Williams photograph, Middleton Collection

road corridor often itself became a line of social or racial demarcation, with the poor living "on the wrong side of the tracks." For example, in Springfield, Ohio, there developed a trackside neighborhood that residents called the Levee, which consisted of a row of brothels, gambling houses, and saloons "notorious in the early twentieth century for providing just about anything a man could pay for." The Levee was also home to the city's small African American community. When in 1904 a black man killed a white policeman, a white mob lynched the murderer and then launched a full-scale attack on the Levee, destroying a considerable amount of property.

In "railroad towns," usually division points, maintenance and repair centers, and operating hubs, a distinctive building often appeared near the center of rail activities, the Railroad Y. Beginning in 1872 in Cleveland, Ohio, the Young Men's Christian Association (YMCA) pushed hard to develop a network of hotels that catered specifically to railroaders. By World War I there were nearly 200 of these facilities nationwide, including Ys in such places as Cleburne, Texas, Brewster, Ohio, and New York City. These hotels were nearly always clean and inexpensive. Moreover, they were respectable.

Yet railroad towns, with their large numbers of male residents, often young and single, did support a variety of "sinful" places. If vice crusaders had been unsuccessful in "cleaning up" the community, there would be saloons, pool halls, and "sporting houses" where illicit activities occurred. Often these "dens of iniquity" were found on the other side of the tracks or tucked away near railroad operations or where railroaders lived.

Some railroad communities claimed a special structure, the "railroad hospital," perhaps unique for a town of its size. In the late nineteenth century, spearheaded by the Missouri Pacific Railroad, various carriers decided that it was cheaper and more convenient to operate a hospital facility in strategic locations than to rely exclusively on local physicians and health facilities, if they existed at all. Usually the company and modest deductions from employees' wages financed these medical centers. One railroad hospital cared for all ailments "except venereal diseases, injuries received in fights and brawls or the mentally deficient." Some carriers allowed employees' families and perhaps the general public to use these hospitals, although others cared for railroaders exclusively.

Another part of the metropolitan corridor was the "hobo jungle." All large towns and cities and especially those localities that were on or near a railroad junction likely had one. With a flood of hoboes on the move during hard times, especially in the 1890s and 1930s, and during the annual harvest season (apples, sugarcane, wheat, and the like), these places swelled (and smelled). Although hardly developed to a common plan, the typical jungle was not only near a key railroad artery (unlikely along a branch or shortline) but also close to firewood and water. A good description of the hobo's on-the-road home is found in a rare autobiography of a former 'bo who, with a companion, at the turn of the twentieth century lived during the summer and fall in many jungles. "We all . . . went into the jungles and made us a camp, and we each one would throw in some money and make up a jackpot, then a couple of us would go into the town and buy some groceries, and bring them back to the jungles and cook up a big can of mulligan-stew. . . . We only eat two meals a day, but oh, boy, they sure did taste good. No doubt you wonder what we used for cooking utensils in the jungles. Well in all hobo jungle camps, there is all sorts of tin cans, ranging from the well known tomato cans, up to the big five gallon square oil cans, and the hoboes cut the tops out of these different cans, and used them to cook with, and they also used the big oil cans to boil . . . and wash their clothes. . . . We used to take one of the big square cans and cut it off about two inches from the bottom and use [the bottom part] to fry bacon and eggs and potatoes in, just like a skillet or a frying pan." This 'bo and his friends, however, did not sleep under the stars or in a makeshift shelter: "We would go out into the Northern Pacific train yards where they had many boxcars stored, waiting to be used in the wheat rush, and sleep in a boxcar on a bed of straw that we would fix up for ourselves."

Local residents often sought to eliminate these hobo jungles because they feared the "yeggs," hoboes who stole and robbed. Some communities passed and vigorously enforced antivagrancy ordinances, either arresting these "knights of the road" or forcing them out of town. Yet in 1900 the town of Britt, Iowa, located on the Milwaukee Road and Minneapolis & St. Louis railroads, decided as a publicity stunt to honor the 'bo, sponsoring what has become a popular annual celebration, complete with the crowning of the "king of the hoboes" and plenty of mulligan stew.

Although Britt's town leaders selected an unusual way to connect railroads with civic pride and boosterism, other municipalities sought the same thing in different ways. Communities might pave the street that connected the station with the commercial hub, indicating, of course, that the place was "progressive." Leaders, too, encouraged the opening of a horsecar line or later an electric trolley between the depot and the major local destinations, again in part to show "outsiders" that "live-wires" dominated community life. When picture postcards became a national mania about 1905, boosters made certain that cards depicting the depot or depots and other railroad facilities were readily available. They preferred the smokiest scenes, an indication that prosperity was at hand. Moreover, these civic types encouraged railroad station agents to stock a variety of town images for sale in the depot waiting room, including prominent churches and public buildings.

The presence of a large number of railroad workers often influenced the ethnic and religious composition of a community. When in the 1890s the Chicago Great Western Railway (Maple Leaf Route) relocated its shops from South St. Paul, Minnesota, to Oelwein, Iowa, this quiet Iowa village in Fayette County, strategically situated on the Great Western and a branch line of the Rock Island, changed significantly. Before the arrival of the shops Oelwein was predominantly German, with some English and Scotch-Irish residents. With the large influx of railway workers, a sizable Italian community emerged. Although Oelwein had a German Catholic church, the town soon acquired an Italian Catholic congregation. Oelwein's one-time Protestant majority found itself threatened as the Lutheran, Methodist, and Presbyterian churches became less dominant in community life. The Maple Leaf Route was a "Protestant" road, however, where in order to advance steadily in either train service or in the office force an individual needed to be both a Protestant and a member of the Masonic order. This resulted in a pronounced division in the community between the generally better-paid Protestants and the more modestly compensated Italian Catholics who frequently held menial jobs in the shops and coach yards or worked with section gangs.

Residents of railroad centers (and towns that had a sizable number of railroad workers) nevertheless generally took pride in having such employees as part of the community. There was the obvious economic connection. Like miners, but unlike farmers, railroaders often spent most or all of their better-than-average wages, and this meant business for merchants, tradesmen, and others. This is not to suggest that some railroaders were not savers, especially those with families, but young, single men were considered to be "less thrifty" and more pleasure oriented.

In railroad towns a company employee-sponsored event could well be the community's social event of the year. In the late nineteenth century, for example, the Order of Railway Conductors Ball was unmistakably *the* happening in Moberly, Missouri, an operating and repair hub for the Wabash Railroad. Hegarthy's Opera House became "gayly decorated" for the dinner and dance, and Postlewait's Band of St. Louis provided the "brilliant" music. For the ball held on Washington's Birthday, 1886, "390 took supper and remarked that it was the finest they ever sat down to."

It became common for strong bonds to develop between railroaders and other citizens in railway communities. When strikes erupted—and some bitter disputes occurred in the 1870s, 1890s, and 1920s—workers often received the loyal support of townspeople, especially in smaller places such as Creston, Iowa, or Marshall, Texas. After all, residents knew these men and their families. Positive ties developed through businesses, churches, lodges, schools, and other organizations. The local constabulary likewise was less likely to "bust skulls" or take harsh action against the strikers; again, they knew them, and for a mayor or sheriff there were important political considerations.

The centrality of the railroad and its workers in community life had other ramifications. Newspaper editors featured railroad-related stories on the front pages of their weeklies or dailies. Frequently there would be a

The traveling hobo was once a familiar sight along the railroad. In the June 1899 *Century Illustrated Monthly Magazine*, artist Jay Hambidge depicted a hoboes' camp. —Middleton Collection

"railroad news" column, particularly in operating and shop towns. There might be reports of "railroad gossip," including who boarded and detrained at the station and any rumors or plans for new construction, management changes, or corporate reorganizations. Residents often came up with nicknames for the railroad company itself, whether the "Little Dummy Line" for the Augusta Railroad, "Big Four" for the Cleveland, Cincinnati, Chicago & St. Louis Railroad, the "Louie" for the Minneapolis & St. Louis Railway, or the "Tweetsie" for the East Tennessee & Western North Carolina Railroad. Certain passenger trains also received monikers, usually affectionate. The "Wally Flier" plied a Pennsylvania Railroad branch line in eastern Ohio, and the "Virginia Creeper" was a local on the Chesapeake & Ohio Railway in western Virginia. The public, moreover, had fun with corporate initials. Examples abound. Atchison, Topeka & Santa Fe: "Ate

Tamales & Spit Fire"; Chicago Great Western: "Cinders, Grass & Weeds"; Colorado & Southern: "Cough & Snort"; Houston & Texas Central: "Hoboes & Tin Cans"; Lake Erie & Western: "Leave Early & Walk"; Maryland & Pennsylvania: "Ma & Pa"; Nevada, California & Oregon: "Narrow, Crooked & Ornery"; and Toronto, Hamilton & Buffalo: "To Hell & Back."

While fun could be poked at a particular railroad, citizens realized that they depended heavily on a carrier for their economic livelihood. The railway age made their hometowns less "island communities" than before, allowing them to participate in the larger economy and enhancing their standard of living. By the end of the nineteenth century most neighborhood grocery stores provided customers with an array of formerly exotic items, whether California oranges or Maryland oysters. Necessities, too, entered the community on flanged wheels. Anthracite or "stone coal" from the mines of northeastern Pennsylvania, for example, heated homes and businesses in South Dakota and South Carolina. The Lackawanna brand of fuel became nationally recognized and trusted. Few would deny that the railroad was truly the "magic carpet."

Communities also experienced negative dimensions of an integrated economy. The rise in the 1870s and 1880s of mail-order houses, fostered by a maturing network of rail lines, competed vigorously with Main Street merchants. Montgomery Ward and Sears, Roebuck, leaders in this field, wisely selected goods that small-town and rural customers wanted and by purchasing in volume offered reduced prices even after discounting transportation charges. Residents, too, might experience the collapse of a hometown enterprise—brewery, cigar factory, or flour mill—because large-scale producers could dominate a national or regional market. Railroads, of course, made this unwanted competition possible. Although consumers benefited, others in the community did not, and some lives were ruined or at least altered.

Legacies

Even after a railroad lost its corporate identity, becoming a "fallen flag" carrier, or when a named passenger train disappeared, the collective memory of citizens in a particular place might long recall the nickname or pet moniker. But other, more powerful and important legacies exist. Official place names are an illustration. The number of them is massive and particularly involves counties, towns, and streets.

Although there are few counties in the East and South that bear names of railroad officials, promoters, and surveyors, the opposite is true in the trans-Chicago West, especially where lines preceded settlement. In Minnesota, for example, Pennington County honors Edmund Pennington, who headed the Minneapolis, St. Paul & Sault Ste. Marie Railway, and Stearns County remembers Isaac Ingalls Stearns, who directed surveys for the construction of the Northern Pacific Railroad.

The number of community names with a railroad connection is much greater. When in the 1870s the Eastern Land Association, a town-site company affiliated with the Burlington & Missouri River Railroad in Nebraska, established communities west of Lincoln, they named them in alphabetical order, the so-called alphabet communities: Crete, Dorchester, Exeter, Fairmont, Grafton, Harvard, Inland, Juniata, Kenesaw, and Lowell. Another case can be found in eastern Washington. The village of Oakesdale honors Thomas F. Oakes, an official of the Northern Pacific Railroad; the towns of Endicott and Prescott are named for William Endicott, Jr., and C. H. Prescott, directors of a railroad holding company; and the Starbuck settlement venerates Gen. W. H. Starbuck of the Oregon Railway & Navigation Company, remembered for providing his namesake community with its first church bell. In the South the Georgia Railroad in 1837 created Camak, Cumming (now Burnett), and Dearing, all named for company directors and organizers. A final illustration comes from Texas. Three towns along a Southern Pacific predecessor, the New York, Texas & Mexican Railway, are named Edna, Inez, and Louise, honoring daughters of Count Joseph Telfener, an Italian nobleman, who sponsored the road. Two peculiar town names with railroad origins are found in Iowa. The first is Primghar, seat of O'Brien County. In the early 1870s at a brand-new Illinois Central station, the promoter of what became a neighboring settlement combined the last initials of the first eight people to detrain to create the town name. Colo, located in Story County, was named for the favorite dog of the landowner on which the Chicago & North Western station was built.

Street names with railroad connections are even more common. Irrespective of geography, a "depot" or "railroad" avenue or street can easily be found, especially in smaller communities. In an autobiographical essay Arthur E. Stilwell (he named Port Arthur, Texas, in his own honor), who guided the Kansas City, Pittsburg & Gulf Railway and the Kansas City, Mexico & Orient Railroad, recalled, "The buying of townsites, laying them out, naming the principal streets after the directors of the road or my friends, and booming these newly found communities as desirable places for people to locate, constituted no small part of my work." And railroader Stilwell was not alone with his street-naming efforts.

Even businesses and consumer products might bear a railroad-inspired moniker. One illustration is the impact the fleet of *400* streamliners introduced in the 1930s by the Chicago & North Western Railway had on its midwestern service territory. A number of taverns in the region, but mostly in Wisconsin, carry the *400* moniker in their names. In one case a beer brewed in Waukesha, Wisconsin, capitalized on the *Capitol 400* name. Until the early 1960s the Fox Head Waukesha Corporation, located near the North Western station in Waukesha, brewed "with Waukesha water" Fox Head 400 Beer.

While a beer with a railroad connection likely received

only local advertising, national concerns during the railway age repeatedly exploited knowledge of the railroad to peddle products or services. The Post Cereal Company, for one, in the 1920s creatively used "The Block Signals Are Working" copy to promote sales of Grape Nuts. The text read:

> In some respects, human experience is like railroading. Every moment of the business and social day the block signals are giving right of way to keenness and alertness—while the slow and the heavy wait on the sidetrack for their chance to move forward.
> The ability to "go through" and to "get there" depends much on the poise of body, brain and nerves that comes with correct diet and proper nourishment.

The legacy of the railway age can also be found in a variety of art forms, including painting, photography, literature, poetry, music, and film. Although this connection weakened considerably by the 1950s, it nevertheless continues into the twenty-first century. When the iron horse made its debut, some artists in Europe and America incorporated the railroad into their works. One of the most famous of these early paintings done by an American dates from the mid-1850s when landscape painter George Inness (1825–1894) received a commission from the recently established Delaware, Lackawanna & Western Railroad to show its presence in Scranton, Pennsylvania. Although initially called *The First Roundhouse of the D. L. & W. Railroad at Scranton*, this work by a famous Hudson River school artist became known as *The Lackawanna Valley* and for years has pleased viewers at the National Gallery of Art in Washington, D.C. Inness's work superbly depicts the "machine in the garden," a popular nineteenth-century theme.

Although no painter commemorated the "wedding of the rails" at Promontory, Utah Territory, artists of the period remained interested in the iron horse. Some railroads sent artists into the West, often to create paintings that could adorn corporate advertising, including calendars, promotional folders, and timetables. One who was not commissioned by a railroad was Edward Lamson Henry (1841–1919), a prolific genre painter, who produced several important railroad-inspired works. Likely his best known, painted in 1867, is titled *The 9:45 Accommodation, Stamford, Connecticut* and graphically captures the excitement of "train-time" in this New England town.

While George Inness and Edward Lamson Henry produced only a few important railroad-related paintings, a much different story occurred with lithographs and prints. For more than 70 years America's largest publisher of lithographs, Currier & Ives, offered a variety of colored railroad prints depicting locomotives, trains, stations, and landscape scenes. Nathaniel Currier (1813–1888) and his brother-in-law James Ives (1824–1895) correctly sensed a strong public demand for such images. They sold thousands of lithographs at reasonable prices, thus creating art for "democratic man." Excitement, power, and speed were surely the endearing qualities to the public.

Later artists and illustrators incorporated railroads and railroad themes into their works. When the Ashcan school of American art emerged in the early twentieth century, urban realist painters, including William Glackens, Robert Henri, George Luks, Everett Shinn, and John Sloan, found railroads irresistible. After all, these artists sought to paint "real life," and a gritty steam locomotive or smoky rail yard fit the bill. Charles Burchfield, Edward Hopper, Reginald Marsh, and Charles Sheeler, for example, continued with this realistic approach into the 1930s. Representative of these twentieth-century works are Hopper's *Toward Boston* (1936), *Compartment C, Car 293* (1938), *Approaching a City* (1946), and *Chair Car* (1965). When asked about *Approaching a City*, perhaps his most famous railroad work, Hopper (1882–1967) indicated that he wished to express the emotions one has on a train coming into a strange city: "interest, curiosity, fear."

More recently some artists have exploited the strong public enthusiasm for the rails. In addition to works privately commissioned and for sale through galleries, their railroad art, often meticulously researched, appears on calendars, Christmas cards, stationery, book dust jackets, and other printed forms. Howard Fogg (who died in 1996), Gil Reid, and Ted Rose (who died in 2002) were among this cadre of talented and prodigious specialized artists.

Photography and the railroads emerged about the same time; from the 1840s onward photographers repeatedly aimed their lenses at railroad subjects. Surely one of the most historically significant photographs in American history came in 1869 when Andrew Joseph Russell (1830–1902) captured on glass-plate negatives the golden-spike ceremony at Promontory, Utah. Admittedly, these were staged photographs; few Chinese laborers, for example, were included. Soon after this epochal event Russell's *Great West Illustrated* appeared, containing what became photographic icons of the nineteenth century. For decades carriers hired some of North America's leading professional photographers, including F. Jay Haynes, Alexander Henderson, William Henry Jackson, and William H. Rau, to record their properties and used the images for an array of purposes, ranging from ornately framed photographs hung in depot waiting rooms to eye-pleasing scenes for promotional brochures. Indeed, as early as 1858 the Baltimore & Ohio organized a publicity tour along its western lines (present-day West Virginia), becoming a pioneer in the promotion of its business through the visual arts. The special B&O train included a car designed solely for photographic purposes.

A century after the B&O trip professionals continued this tradition of railroad image making. Likely the best known are the works of O. Winston Link (1914–2001). In the mid-1950s this New York commercial photographer, employed by the Norfolk & Western Railway, captured the final days of steam on this predominantly coal-carrying road. Link gained fame for his striking nighttime photography. A perfectionist, he worked as long as a week at one trackside location arranging scores of flashes for a single picture.

Just as historic paintings and photographs abound, there emerged an extensive variety of literary works that recognized the railway age. Some of America's best writers, including Sherwood Anderson, Willa Cather, William Faulkner, Hamlin Garland, Flannery O'Conner, and Eudora Welty, loved railroads. North Carolinian Thomas Wolfe (1900–1938) claimed to have traveled "between 125,000–150,000 miles by train," and he repeatedly employed railroad scenes. For example, part 2 of *Look Homeward, Angel* (1929) ends with Eugene Gant's first trip to Charleston, South Carolina, without his mother, which involves riding down Saluda grade, near the North Carolina–South Carolina border, the steepest piece of trackage on the Southern Railway: "His mind was bound in the sad lulling magic of the car wheels."

Similar imagery of the rails is repeatedly found in American literary works, and readers instantly recognized the symbolism. In *Sanctuary* (1931) by William Faulkner (1897–1962), where train travel is frequently mentioned, Miss Reba, who operates a "sporting house" in Memphis, tells a not-so-worldly visitor: "Look here, mister, folks what uses this waiting room has got to get on the train now and then."

A host of lesser writers, including Harry Bedwell, E. S. Dellinger, Frank Packard, John Rhodes Sturdy (a Canadian), and Cy Warman, made up the so-called Railroad school. Railroad fiction in North America enjoyed its greatest popularity during the late nineteenth and early twentieth centuries and coincided with the heyday of railroading. Arguably the best known of this genre is Frank Hamilton Spearman (1859–1937), whose books *Held for Orders: Being Stories of Railroad Life* (1901) and *Whispering Smith* (1906) became classics in the field. Short stories with railroad themes appeared in popular magazines, ranging from the *Saturday Evening Post* to *Railroad Man's Magazine*. Others were published as dime novels and similar forms of pulp fiction. The audience for railroad fiction was overwhelmingly male and especially readers who wanted action-packed tales. Railroad workers themselves, both active and retired, avidly consumed this slice of literature.

And there existed railroad titles solely for the youngest audience. Parents and other adults commonly gave boys for birthdays and Christmas such books as the *Ralph* railroad stories by Allen Chapman, a pseudonym used by the Stratemeyer publishing syndicate. This series featured *Ralph of the Roundhouse* (1906), *Ralph in the Switch Tower* (1907), and *Ralph and the Train Wreckers* (1928).

Poetry also has been part of the railroad literary legacy. As with novelists and short-story writers, the rails have inspired the famous and the not-so-famous. The former category includes William Cullen Bryant, Emily Dickinson, Vachel Lindsay, Carl Sandburg, Robert Penn Warren, and Walt Whitman and the latter Dave Etter, Robert Hedin, Howard Nemerov, May Swenson, and Dave Smith. Edna St. Vincent Millay (1892–1950) captured the spirit, penning in *Travel* (1921) these often-quoted lines:

> Yet there isn't a train goes by all day
> But I hear its whistle shrieking. . . .
> Yet there isn't a train I wouldn't take,
> No matter where it's going.

In *The Great Train Robbery* (1903), Edwin S. Porter of the Edison Co. filmed the first movie to present a genuine narrative. It was the first of many films that would involve the railroad in the action. —University of Illinois Library

If poets found railroads appealing, so did musicians. The legacy is as rich as it is diverse. Likely more Americans have been exposed to railroad-related music than to any other art form. "I've Been Workin' on the Railroad" is found in virtually every camp songbook and may be one of the first songs a child learns. For years "Little Red Caboose behind the Train" probably ranked a close second. Indeed, popular culture is ripe with railroad music. Many of these tunes have no known author, for example, "In the Pines," "New River Train," "Nine Hundred Miles," and the "Wabash Cannonball." Some of the melodies can be traced to Irish immigrants who constructed and maintained track. "Paddy on the Railway" is an example. Scores of others came from Tin Pan Alley songsmiths, including "Casey Jones" and "The Lightning Express." A few, too, for example, "The L&N Rag," reflect the ragtime craze that swept America between 1899 and 1917. And numerous songs are part of the blues, bluegrass, and country and western traditions. "John Henry," "Brakeman's Blues," "Train Whistle Blues," "Waiting for a Train," and "The Wreck of Old 97" belong to this genre. The "father of country music," Jimmie Rodgers (1897–1933), had a railroad connection. This Meridian, Mississippi, native, who became known as the "Singing Brakeman," worked as a brakeman for the New Orleans & Northeastern and later as a switchman for the Southern Pacific. Even the pop music field made contributions, such as "On the Atchison, Topeka and the Santa Fe" and "Chattanooga Choo Choo."

There has also existed a long-standing and extensive connection between railroads and the American film industry. Arguably, the first movie designed for entertainment was *The Great Train Robbery*, which the Edison Company produced in 1903. Since trains were exciting and readily available and such a large part of daily American life, other filmmakers exploited them. By the end of the twentieth century hundreds of movies depended upon trains for their story lines, ranging from *Union Pacific* (1939) and *North by Northwest* (1959) to *Planes, Trains and Automobiles* (1987).

Although the appeal of railroad-inspired music and films is widespread, there is also the enormous lure of trains and railroad-related memorabilia to a smaller, more select group, the ubiquitous railroad enthusiasts, generally known as "railfans," who have been active almost since the dawn of the industry. There exists, for example, the diary of a conductor for the Western Railroad of Massachusetts from the 1840s in which entries note new or unusual pieces of rolling stock, much like records meticulously kept by British "trainspotters" from the latter part of the nineteenth century and later.

Alexis de Tocqueville, the French sage who visited the United States during the 1830s, correctly observed that Americans were "joiners." It is understandable, then, that railfan-oriented organizations developed, with the first "formal" group appearing in 1921, the Railway & Locomotive Historical Society. Additional organizations emerged; the largest and best known is the National Railway Historical Society, which dates from 1935. In recent decades scores of railroad-specific historical groups have developed, including the Boston & Maine Historical Society, the Southern Pacific Historical & Technical Society, and the Southern Railway Historical Society. These groups sponsor train rides (often on vintage equipment), hold monthly or annual meetings, publish newsletters, journals, and books, and collect photographs and "railroadiana" (which encompasses lanterns, passes, timetables, dining-car china, bells, whistles, and the like). Railfans remain numerous and active. *Trains*, a monthly magazine with a circulation of about 100,000, dutifully lists fan trips and railroadiana shows.

The ongoing railroad legacy involves another type of enthusiast, the modeler. For generations toy trains have enjoyed great popularity. Even in the antebellum period wood carvers and other artisans made models of locomotives and trains, usually for children. In the late 1860s the Ives Company of Plymouth, Connecticut, started to manufacture a line of metal toy trains. Other firms followed. In the twentieth century the dominant companies were A. C. Gilbert (American Flyer), Lionel, and Marx. Although manufactured key-wind or "windup" and then electric trains were marketed as toys for children, adult males became interested and even obsessed with modeling. While some might be content to buy locomotives and cars off the shelf, many put their trains together from kits supplied by both domestic and foreign manufacturers; others may build from scratch. Although most layouts are found in attics, basements, garages, or some other inside location, recently garden railways, frequently using German-made track and rolling stock, have gained popularity. Since World War II magazines for model train aficionados have flourished. *Model Railroader*, the largest, has more than twice the monthly circulation of *Trains*. And there are modeling and train-collecting clubs and groups. The most important of the latter is the Train Collectors Association, founded in 1954, which has a present membership in excess of 30,000. Hundreds of toy train meets or shows annually take place throughout North America. Finally, there is the popularity of Brio wooden trains and Public Broadcasting's *Thomas the Tank Engine*, all attesting to the public acclaim for railroading.

A person does not have to be joiner, collector, or modeler to be a railfan. It might be merely watching a freight train passing by a crossing, riding occasionally on Amtrak, or reading a book on railroad history that would qualify an individual as an enthusiast. Filmmaker Alfred Hitchcock (1899–1980), for one, loved to read copies of the 1,500-plus-page, two-inch-thick *Official Guide of the Railways*. In fact, he told the publisher, the National Railway Publication Co. of New York City, that if he were stranded on a desert island, the one book that he would like to have was a copy (any year would do) of the *Official Guide*. Until its demise during the era of Amtrak, the *Official Guide* was where a reader could find a complete array of passenger-train schedules and parlor and sleeping-car routes. And the publisher carefully maintained the volume's well-deserved reputation for accuracy. Understandably, railfans seek copies of the *Official Guide* much as philatelists collect old postage stamps.

Another tie to the past since the 1960s has been widespread interest in historic preservation. Indeed, one event that contributed to passage of the National Historic Preservation Act, which became law in October 1966, was the destruction, three years earlier, of the beautiful and much-admired Pennsylvania Station in New York City. In addition to a growing desire to save the past, including structures associated with the railway age, has come government support for preservation, including the Tax Reform Act of 1976 and the Economic Recovery Act of 1981. These measures, coupled with public support, have led to the saving and recycling of hundreds of depots, ranging from Union Station in St. Louis, Missouri, to the former Southern Pacific depot in Goleta, California. Other types of railroad structures have been preserved and restored, including an old Chicago & North Western water tank in Lusk, Wyoming, and the former Southern Railway shops complex in Spencer, North Carolina.

Not only railroad buildings have been preserved, but also former railroad rights of way. As the national railroad mileage began to shrink, at times dramatically, the result of modal competition, corporate mergers, and the like, thousands of miles of abandoned rights of way appeared throughout North America. In the mid-1960s the "rails-to-trails" movement emerged. In 1963 May Watts, a Chicago naturalist, proposed in a letter to the *Chicago Tribune* the constructive reuse of these former rail lines outside the Windy City. "We are human beings. We are able to walk upright on two feet. We need a footpath. Right now there is a chance for Chicago and its suburbs to have a footpath, a long one." Watts's efforts led to creation of the 55-mile Illinois Prairie Path, a 20-year project, and others in the state and nation. Starting in 1986, the Rails-to-Trails Conservancy has done much to sustain this public-interest crusade. By the beginning of the twenty-first century nearly 1,000 of these trails dotted the North American landscape.

Although in recent times the impact of railroads has diminished, it has not ended. Whether it be a catchy railroad song, an active railfan group, or a depot that is now a museum, office, or restaurant, the legacy continues. The railroad has been an integral part of the social fabric of American life.

Technology and Operating Practice in the Nineteenth Century

John H. White, Jr.

Young America was vast and underpopulated. There were few large cities, and over 90 percent of the population were farmers. A gigantic, old-growth forest covered North America from the Atlantic Coast to the Mississippi River valley. Only a few navigable rivers and an erratic maze of animal trails afforded transit. The public clamored for better transportation.

Internal improvement became the single most talked-about domestic policy issue. Elaborate plans were developed for roads, bridges, canals, and river navigation, but there was little capital to finance any of them. America was rich in land and natural resources but cash poor. The federal government backed away repeatedly from major transportation projects, rejecting even the eminently practical Erie Canal scheme. State and local governments stepped in to fill the void, but they, too, had limited resources. A small population could handle only a small tax burden. The private sector was frail and unable to generate the large sums needed to finance a national network for trade and travel. Yet despite the lack of funding, some progress was made in developing an internal transport system.

Roads were constructed by private turnpike companies. A few good roads were built, such as the Lancaster Pike (1795), but in the main, the road network was primitive. Cost was the overriding consideration, and roads were built to minimal standards. Most were little more than dirt pathways through the forest. Travel speeds much over a walk were difficult, and most roads became impassable during spring rains and winter snows. Stagecoaches were slow, costly, and unspeakably uncomfortable. Freight travel barely creaked along. Wagons took 20 days to go from Pittsburgh to Philadelphia, and this over some of the best roads in the nation. Freight charges were so high (20 cents per ton-mile) that long-distance shipments were uneconomical. Some goods were worth far less than the shipping costs. Worse yet, highway transport was the least economical in terms of the ratio of horsepower to the movement of a ton of goods. This is not to say that roads played no important role in early transport or that they were not improved or expanded. They were essential for local transit, and macadam (crushed stone) road surfaces did much to improve their service. Yet highways were clearly not the solution to American transportation needs.

Many felt that the canal was the answer to internal improvements requirements. Canals had proved themselves over the centuries in China and Europe. Many European settlers were familiar with these artificial waterways as a great avenue for transportation. A few small canals were projected during colonial times, but the opening of the Erie Canal from Albany to Buffalo in 1825 set off a canal mania that swept the land. The Erie was a grand success in every respect—its revenue and traffic exceeded even the optimistic levels predicted by its promoters. Other canal advocates projected equally successful results, and some 4,000 miles were constructed over the next few decades. None approached the Erie's success, and some were dismal failures. The canal had one major asset—as a water carrier it could move large loads with very little power (one horse could pull 50 tons) as long as very low speeds of about 2 mph were maintained. (If the speed increases to 4 mph, the resistance of the water goes up by the square of the velocity, and so four, not two, horses are required.)

Canals' advantage, however, was offset by several disadvantages. They were expensive; most cost $30,000 a mile, and in hilly terrain they could cost twice that amount. Canals were simply not well suited to rugged territory. Overcoming changes in elevation required costly locks or inclined planes. Worse yet, they slowed an already languid form of transit to an unacceptably sluggish pace. Passengers, especially American passengers, are in a hurry, and express boats moving along at 4 or 5 mph just did not meet the needs or expectations of their "go-ahead" society. Even freight shippers found the canal deficient. Service was often suspended because of low water in the fall or summer, and northern canals were forced to shut down for months during the winter freeze. The canal was actually only a fair-weather carrier. All things considered, it did not meet America's transport needs either.

Proponents of water transport held up the rivers as a sovereign cure for domestic transit ills. The eastern states were blessed with such waterways as the Connecticut, Hudson, Delaware, and Potomac rivers. The interior was drained by the great Mississippi River system and its many tributaries. Early settlers found the rivers the easy way to go, and many cities were established along their banks. The introduction of steamboats in 1807 greatly improved river travel. Like the canal, river transit enjoyed the power-to-weight advantage of waterborne vessels. But the rivers offered few other advantages. The routing was arbitrary at best, for the river ran as the landscape dictated. While the prevailing traffic pattern was east and west, many of the rivers ran north and south. And the meandering nature of streams added significantly to distances. St. Louis and Cincinnati, for example, are only about 350 miles apart as the crow flies, but by river the distance is about 700 miles. Few rivers in their natural state offered year-round travel. The Ohio was often shut down three months a year because of low water. Freezing during the winter added another three months or so to the embargo. The rivers offered no panacea for the ills of American transport.

In 1830 the public or common-carrier railroad was introduced into the country, and its inherent advantages gained it rapid acceptance. It was superior to all its rivals in answering the basic needs of shippers and travelers. What were some of the fundamental characteristics and qualities of railroad technology that assured success while its rivals failed or could only satisfy a special or limited market?

The railroad could be built in a direct line between major traffic centers, and it worked well in almost any terrain. Low or freezing water did not affect its operation. Except for extreme storms, it was an all-weather system. A blizzard or flood might shut it down for a few days, but most lines could reopen quickly. Its carrying capacity was astonishing; a single rail line could carry the same traffic as multiple highway lanes. In low-cost, bulk carriage it outperformed most canals and was often competitive with other water carriers. A railroad cost about the same per mile to build as a canal, but it ran year-round, rather than eight or nine months out of the year, making it a better investment. Its power-to-load ratio was 20 tons per horse, not as good as a water carrier but better than a highway vehicle at 1 or 2 tons per horse. Speed was a major advantage of the railroads. Pioneer lines could sustain average passenger train speeds of 20 to 25 mph. Stagecoaches did well to maintain a 5 mph schedule. Canals did less well and ranged from 2 to 4 mph. River steamers ran upstream at 10 mph and downstream at 15.

The iron horse was the fleetest of all the travel modes available to our ancestors. Because of its many advantages, the railway became the carrier of choice for nineteenth-century Americans, and the rail network grew at a remarkable pace, as revealed in Table 1.

Imported Technology

Colonial America was a land of imports. Its language, law, customs, and religious beliefs were all brought over by the first settlers. Even everyday foodstuffs, cows, hogs, chickens, carrots, and onions, were imported because they did not exist in North America. It should be no surprise to find that the steam railway also immigrated across the Atlantic.

Its origins are among the many mysteries of history, but some very diminutive mine railways were used in Germany as early as the fourteenth century. Small tramways appeared in Britain during the sixteenth-century reign of Elizabeth I, when Britain was experiencing a fuel crisis. Firewood was becoming scarce, and the country began exploiting the coal deposits of northern England. Most of the fuel went south to major markets such as London by coastal sailboats. Getting the coal to the seacoast was the railway's job. Horse-drawn four-wheeled hopper cars rumbled over wooden rails on shortlines connecting the mines to the ships. It all seems slow, undersized, and primitive, but these curious little tram roads were considered marvels of efficiency at the time of Queen Bess. They grew and prospered and adopted improved techniques. Wooden rails received iron caps to improve durability and reduce friction. Wooden wheels were replaced by ones made from cast iron. The cars were fitted with drop-bottom doors so they could discharge their cargos without manual labor. Whatever their limitations, they succeeded in moving thousands of tons of fuel to market each year.

As coal production progressed, the mines grew deeper and filled with water. Animal-powered pumps were barely able to keep the water level in check for continued mining, and so in 1712 a steam-powered pumping engine was devised by a Devonshire blacksmith named Thomas Newcomen. Improvements in steam technology over the next century led to more compact and powerful engines

Table 1. Growth in U.S. Railroads, 1830–1920

Year	Miles	Ton-Miles (Billions)	Passengers Carried (Millions)	Freight Cars	Passenger Cars	Locomotives	Employees	U.S. Population (Millions)
1830	23							12
1850	9,000	1		30,000	3,000	3,000	18,000	23
1880	93,000	32	280 (est.)	540,000	16,000	17,900	418,000	50
1900	193,000	141	600	1,365,000	34,000	37,600	1,018,000	76
1920	252,000	413	1,269	2,388,000	56,000	68,900	2,076,000	105

Source: Courtesy of J. H. White.

that could be applied to other purposes, including overland travel. And so the locomotive was born in 1804.

Just seven years later a Leeds machinist named Matthew Murray produced a steam railway engine that was more efficient than horses. Such machines required greater support because of their weight, and so iron rails were adopted. More engines were produced, yet all of these developments took place in industrial backwaters and attracted little public attention.

In 1825 the Stockton & Darlington Railway opened with considerable fanfare. The line's premier locomotive drew a train of 21 cars and about 500 passengers past a throng of onlookers who lined the track. The steam railway had gone public in a big way, and the public liked what it saw. More lines were opened, and formerly obscure engineers, such as George Stephenson, became celebrities. Accounts of the wonders of the iron roads and their speedy and powerful steeds traveled around the world. Americans, already greatly excited about internal improvements, flocked to England to witness this new marvel in transportation.

Actually, they were a rather sober crowd of engineers and technicians, who for all their somber and practical demeanor could not help but be impressed and just a little excited by what John Bull had accomplished. It all seemed so advanced and well executed that American engineering appeared antediluvian by comparison. Engines such as the *Rocket* that could race down the track at nearly a mile a minute were viewed with wonder and envy. They looked, took notes, made copies of drawings, and interviewed Stephenson and his colleagues until the Britons were weary of their questions.

William Strickland, an architect, went back to Philadelphia to write a book in 1825 about all that he had seen. A year later another Pennsylvanian, Erskine Hazard, returned to his coal mine at Mauch Chunk determined to build a railway based on what he had observed in England. The 9-mile gravity line opened in May 1827 and was one of the very first railways in the New World. Trains of 14 cars ran downhill to the Lehigh River, where they dumped coal into barges for shipment down the river. Mules pulled the empties back up the hill. In many ways this was not a very impressive railway—obsolete, in fact, when compared to the great civil engineering works then being constructed in England—but it worked very well. Of more consequence, it offered a concrete working model that railroads were practical and economic. It became a destination for tourists and engineers who wanted to see and ride upon this strange new conveyance. The directors of the newly formed Baltimore & Ohio Railroad came in 1827 and went away convinced that their plan for a long-distance rail line was practical. On this very minor key, the railroad era opened in the United States.

American Railroads, 1820–1850

When considering the first decades of American railroading, it is important to visualize the small scale of these early operations. While the modern railroad is built on a superhuman scale, with locomotives, cars, and structures that dwarf the humans around them, the entire physical plant of the pre–Civil War railroad was undersize. Bridges and tracks were lightly built structures. The locomotives and cars were minuscule. Trains were short, often made up of just a few cars.

A second characteristic of equal importance is the cost or investment aspect of early railroads. The lack of capital was a fundamental fact of the economy in pioneer America. When it came time to build a rail line, it was done on the cheap. America simply could not afford to build in the grand manner.

Because economy was the watchword, everything was done to stretch out the available funding to produce the most mileage for the least money. Track was light and flimsy. Stations were small, simple wooden structures. The same was true for bridges. Sometimes ferries were used to avoid the need for large and expensive bridges altogether. Locomotives and cars were specifically designed to work with the sharp curves, steep grades, and inferior track that were all America could afford.

It was very different in Britain. The homeland of the railway was a very rich nation and could afford to do everything on a first-class basis. Its lines were models of civil engineering, built with gentle grades and broad curves. They crossed streams and valleys on great masonry viaducts such as the Romans would have built. Its stations were palaces with great high ceilings encased in costly stone. Constructed to last for the ages, its track was properly called "permanent way." All of this first-class construction would pay off in the long run through lower operation and maintenance costs. But the first costs were huge—a typical English trunk line cost about $180,000 a mile (in part, it must be added, because of high land costs). America's provisional style of railway cost only around $20,000 to $30,000 per mile.

Track and roadbed form the foundation of any railway. The elements of well-constructed track were clearly understood at the beginning of the public railway. These included deep ballast with good drainage, frequent culverts for small streams, substantial bridges for major rivers, easy grades, broad curves, and heavy rail made from the best iron. A few early lines in this country proceeded on such a plan. The Boston & Lowell, for example, was a slavish copy of the Liverpool & Manchester Railway. Everything was executed in a first-class manner. Even the locomotives and cars were faithful copies of their British counterparts. The backers of this particular line were rich, old-line New England titans laden with the wealth generated by the China trade and the textile mills. Pennsylvania's Main Line of Public Works, the combined railroad and canal that connected Philadelphia and Pittsburgh, used the British stone-block ties and chair-rail scheme, but cut back when it came to easy curves or masonry bridges. Yet it had a double track soon after it opened in 1834 and was on the whole a well-executed piece of engineering.

Elsewhere, our ancestors showed a decided preference to cheapen the British track plan. Sharp curves and steep grades became the rule. Ballast was often eliminated—the topsoil was removed, the track structure was set on the subsoil, and a little earth was filled in to hold the ties in place. Wooden culverts and bridges, some of the latter very lightly built, became part of this make-do style of railway building. Even greater economies were realized in the style of rail employed. In a great step backwards Americans reinvented the ancient wood and strap-rail form of track. Iron was very dear, while wood was abundant and cheap. In 1830 British iron makers dominated the world market, and no American producer could compete with them in quality or price. This condition prevailed until 1874, and so most American lines were built with British iron. Even the cost of the transatlantic journey did not undercut Welsh and English iron makers' price advantage.

Strap rail normally measured about ⅝ inch thick by 2½ inches wide by 18 feet long. It weighed about 16 pounds per yard, and about 25 tons was required for one mile of track. Rolled or edge rail, that is, a solid bar of iron often shaped like a girder, generally weighed 40 pounds per yard in this early period, requiring 62 tons of rail for a mile of track. The choice of strap-rail track promised substantial savings, and many roads adopted it.

The straps were spiked to wooden stringers, usually six-inch-square timbers. Very often a longitudinal subsill was used to stiffen the structure. Wooden crossties held the rails in gauge. Altogether, this kind of track used a substantial amount of wood and relatively little iron. Upwards of 3,000 miles of track were built on this plan during the first decades of American railroads. It managed to get many lines rolling and thus, in the short run, was hailed as a success. But in the long run it proved a costly mistake. After a few years of operations the rolling action of the trains caused the ends of the rails to curl and spring up. The uplifted rails caused derailments and in a few cases pierced the undersides of cars as they passed over, threatening passengers with impalement. The actual number of such incidents appears to be rather small, yet one line advertised that its cars had iron plates fastened to their underside to prevent the entry of such unwanted visitors. By the late 1840s the defects of strap-rail track were well understood, and little new construction was done on this plan except for very minor lines. Older main lines converted to some form of T-rail. In 1847 the State of New York passed a law to hasten the conversion and in effect forced lines operating within its boundaries to replace the obsolete flat bars with rails of at least 56 pounds to the yard. Some of the old rail was sent west for use on midwestern pioneers such as the Galena & Chicago Union.

T-rail, sometimes also called H-rail, was devised in

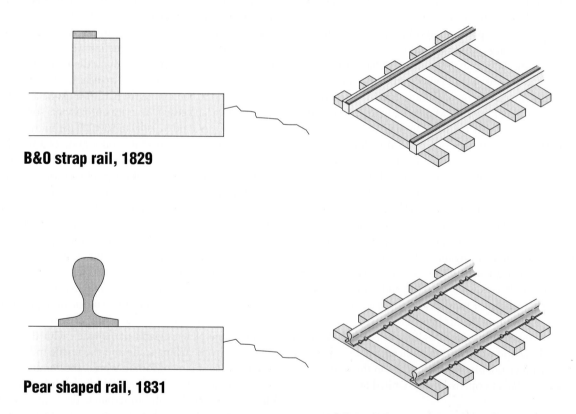

B&O strap rail, 1829

Pear shaped rail, 1831

Early lines used strap rail (*top*), a long metal strip that was screwed down on the wooden rail. This quickly proved inadequate to the task. Another early design was the pear-shaped rail (*bottom*), rolled out of wrought iron, with a flat bottom and pear shaped above the flanges. Developed around 1831, this form of rail was used for several decades until it was superseded by the modern T-rail design. —Rick Johnson

1830 for use on the Camden & Amboy Rail Road in New Jersey. It was at first fastened to stone-block ties. When the supply of stones fell short, the contractors used wooden crossties as a substitute. The temporary track was found superior to the planned form, and so what became a world standard was invented by accident. The flat bottom of the T-rail formed its own seat upon the wooden tie. Hook-headed spikes fastened the rail to the ties. It was so simple, so quickly put together, and so secure that eventually everyone came to adopt it. The shape of the rail proved eminently practical as well—a more rational distribution of the metal has never been found. The head has the mass for support and wear; the stem or web connects the head to the stable flat-bottom base. It is a design marvel. Some engineers advocated bridge rail, which resembled an upside-down U and was moderately popular during the 1840s and 1850s. But the material was poorly arranged. A variant of T-rail was developed that permitted the use of poorer grades of iron and so allowed new lines with meager budgets to open long stretches of track with the minimum investment. It was called pear rail; it much resembled a pear in cross section. The slender profile of T-rail slumped down into a short, fat cousin whose bulky interior often harbored pockets of cinder rather than iron. This inferior rail was popular with speculators intent on fast openings and quick profits. It was made in large quantities by British workers for the American market until around 1865.

Building a railroad started with a survey. Engineers walked or rode horseback over the terrain, seeking the most direct and level route. It was very much a matter of compromise, usually resulting in a more roundabout path than desired to avoid inclines, tunnels, or extended excavations. Cost was always a governing factor. Managers of the line might pray for a dead straight track between Buffalo and Oswego but end up settling for a meandering road to avoid a large hill or a deep valley. Often the best general route was simply to follow a river.

Once a route was selected, surveyors staked out the line in a very exacting manner. Land acquisitions would be under way at the same time. Most public railroads had the power of eminent domain and could condemn property, paying the owners what was adjudged a fair market value. Some land was actually donated to encourage a railway to build across the property, thus providing access that increased property values.

Most railroads hired contractors to actually build the line. Crews would remove trees so that men and horses could set to work removing earth to form a right of way. Black powder was used to uproot very large stumps or demolish big rocks. Horse-drawn scrapers did much of the grading, but men, shovels, and wheelbarrows performed much of the work. Steam-powered shovels and pile drivers were introduced in the 1830s, somewhat easing the arduous labor of workers with mechanical power. Bridge and culvert builders worked hand in hand with the grading crews. After months of heavy labor the line was ready for the track workers, who could usually assemble around two miles of track a day even at this early period.

Stations, engine houses, water tanks, and fueling stations had to be erected before the railroad could begin operations. Typically a railroad was opened in sections, and an initial segment might be in service for several years before the entire line was ready.

Locomotives and Cars, 1830–1850

It was fairly well established by the early 1830s that a ten-ton locomotive was about the right size to pull a paying load over the light track and bridges of America's pioneer lines. A few roads felt that even lighter engines would be adequate, but underweight power units such as the *De Witt Clinton* (1831) were soon abandoned as too feeble for the service requirements. Many early managers believed that good-quality engines could only be obtained in England, but this opinion was reversed by the late 1830s, and the last British engine was imported in 1841. Domestic machinists produced engines well suited to America's serpentine, strap-rail roads. The rigid British plan gave way to a more limber and flexible style of running gear, notable for its small leading wheels that guided the locomotive over rough track and around curves. Higher boiler pressures boosted traction. Thinner boiler plates lowered weight. Both of these features increased the risk of explosion, but American railroaders felt that the hazard was acceptable.

For the first decade six-wheel engines were used for both freight and passenger service. They had a four-wheel leading truck at the head end and a pair of driving wheels at the rear. In 1836 an extra pair of drivers was first added to improve traction. The wheelbase was spread out to distribute the weight over the frail track. Once the suspension problems of the new eight-wheelers were worked out, this became the standard form of locomotive on American railroads. As more power was required, the eight-wheelers increased in size, so that by 1850 they weighed around 20 tons.

During this period, too, the American locomotive became the object of an add-on technology. The basic machinery remained very much on the Stephenson pattern, but Americans could not resist tinkering with the details. Because wood rather than coke or coal was the prevailing fuel, smokestack design went through a dramatic evolution to arrest the abundance of sparks emitted as the engine rattled along on its journey. Dozens of ideas were tried, but most involved a large funnel-shaped top and internal wire screening to kill the sparks.

Much else was needed to reform the locomotive for American operating conditions. Tracks were unfenced, and cattle wandered into the path of approaching trains. Even a large hog could derail a locomotive of the time. Pilots or "cowcatchers" were installed to push animals off the track. Whistles and bells were adopted to warn man and beast of the train's approach. Headlights were adopted starting around 1838 to illuminate the track at night. Their glow also warned approaching trains of their presence. A housing (called a cab) was erected over the rear platform to protect the engine crew from the elements, but this was not a standard feature until almost 1855.

Not all of the pioneer lines began operation with steam locomotives; many opened with horsepower. The B&O experimented with horse-powered treadmill and sail-powered cars, and it commenced operation with horse-propelled trains, as did a number of other lines. Pennsylvania's Main Line of Public Works found horses more economical on short segments of its line and continued their use until 1850. Where steam locomotives were not allowed in the city limits, some trunk lines were forced to use horsepower into the 1870s. A few lines used horses to switch cars into the early twentieth century.

Inclined-plane railways were used even on roads already employing steam locomotives to overcome unusual gradients. Typically, a stationary engine powered a winding drum at the top of the grade, which raised or lowered a heavy rope or cable to lift trains up or down the plane. The major user of such hill climbers was the Allegheny Portage Railroad, part of Pennsylvania's Main Line of Public Works, with no less than ten inclines on its crossing of the Alleghenies. The South Carolina Railroad, the B&O, and the Mohawk & Hudson also depended on inclines. Most were abandoned before 1860, but the Central Railroad of New Jersey operated such a facility until around 1948.

The earliest passenger cars were faithful copies of stagecoaches, a logical, if not inspired, design choice. The city omnibus was next copied; it featured three compartments with side entrances and running boards so the conductor could move from one car to the next. Boxy bodies with end platforms and entrance doors provided a safer arrangement for the trainman's passage. Seats were placed on either side of a center aisle. Most of these pioneer cars carried around 20 passengers and weighed two or three tons. Travelers enjoyed little in the way of heating and lighting; there were no toilets or drinking-water facilities. Yet compared to cramped and rough-riding stagecoaches, these little four-wheelers were paragons of comfort.

Railroad managers soon found that large double-truck or eight-wheel cars offered several advantages. They were much more spacious and so appealed to the public. They rode far better because they eliminated the galloping characteristic of the four-wheelers. And they were actually lighter and cheaper per passenger because so many partitions and ends were eliminated. And so the eight-wheel, center-aisle style of car became the standard in this country by the early 1840s. Improved ventilation, seating, and heating were introduced before the middle of the century. Lighting remained on the stingy side for some time, and many passengers complained about the uneven heat given by the stoves, but in general the coaches were adequate for the short trips typical of the time. There

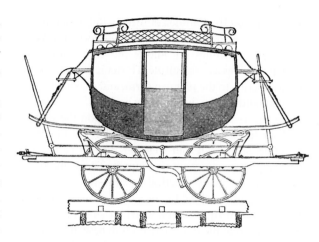

The earliest passenger cars looked not much different from the stagecoaches they replaced. This illustration, from *The American Railway* (1892), shows one of the first cars of the 1831 Mohawk & Hudson Rail Road. —Middleton Collection

were few railroads over 100 miles long before 1850, and when journeys were short, fairly spartan accommodations were acceptable.

Freight cars underwent a similar metamorphosis. Very small four-wheel cars, hardly more than low-sided open wagons with flanged wheels, were used at first. Very much in the British tradition, canvas covers were used to protect fragile cargos. These did not work well in harsh North American winters. The profusion of sparks from wood burners also set the cloth covers on fire. Box bodies were adopted instead, and so America's favorite style of freight car, the boxcar, was much in evidence by 1840. The eight-wheel variety came into being at the same time, and most domestic lines soon adopted this form. Wooden bodies and frames were standard throughout the Victorian age, although a few lines such as the Baltimore & Ohio and the Reading used a sizable number of iron-body coal cars. In general, freight shipment by rail was not a large trade, and freight-car development was equally modest. Specialized cars, such as refrigerators, did not appear in any number until after 1870.

Train Operation, 1830–1850

The number and speed of early trains were limited. Speeds were especially modest where animal power was used. Steam locomotives were capable of fairly high speeds—50 to 60 mph—but the track was hardly up to such rapid running, and so for reasons of safety and repair costs, freights ambled along at 10 mph and passengers rarely exceeded 25 mph. Horse-drawn trains moved even slower, and their progress was hampered by the need to change horses every 10 miles or so. A major stop on the Baltimore & Ohio, just outside the city limits, was named Relay because this was where the teams were changed. The mix of steam- and horse-powered trains was found very dangerous, and so most lines abandoned mixed operations at an early date, at least on their main lines. The Pennsylvania Main Line of Public Works, however, operated as a public highway, and private contractors operated cars over its track at will, as long as they paid the toll. Some used horses, while others employed locomotives. This line opened in 1834 with a single track, and the confusion over who had the right of way was extreme. A second track opened some months later, which improved matters slightly. In March 1836 locomotive and horse-powered trains were scheduled to run at different hours of the day, but confusion and delays continued until the state took over operation of the trains with regular crews in 1844.

During these first decades of railroading many lines operated only a few trains a day. Some had one up and one down passenger train. Freight was scheduled as the traffic required. Busy roads such as the Camden & Amboy offered several trains a day. In 1839 the line carried 1,000 passengers on a busy day. It was a 61-mile-long line with 17 locomotives and 71 passenger cars; during good years it paid dividends of 30 percent to its shareholders.

The ability of early railways to transport trains of great weight was illustrated by the Philadelphia & Reading. By 1842 the Reading ran seven coal trains a day to Port Richmond, its seaport terminal. Each train consisted of 100 to 150 four-wheel coal cars, with each car carrying five tons of coal.

Trains ran on a schedule organized to follow one another at a safe distance. Because most lines were single track, trains were scheduled to meet oncoming trains at a passing siding. Inferior trains (freights, locals, or work trains) would take to the siding so that superior trains (express passenger or mail) could move ahead on the main line. All of this worked well as long as all trains were on time. That happened occasionally, but mechanical failures, fallen trees, snow, rain, or inattentive crews led to delays. And if one train was late, all trains were likely affected. But how could the crews communicate with each other or headquarters about the nature of the delay or their location? They did not and could not, at least not until telegraphic dispatching was introduced in 1851. The crew could sit and wait or proceed ahead until they found the next train. If they moved cautiously with a flagman preceding them, all might go well. They might find the missing train up the line broken down or stopped for some other reason. However, if the opposing train was running fast to make up time, a head-on collision was a likely outcome. Hence engine crews peered ahead looking for smoke on the horizon or listened carefully for a distant whistle. And all would hope and pray that they could stop in time. This made passengers nervous, but no one wanted to sit and wait indefinitely.

Impatient passengers waiting at a depot might urge the station agent to head up the line to see what was holding up a delayed train. If an agent took his handcar to look up the track, he risked life and limb if the missing train should appear suddenly around the next curve. The Chicago & North Western devised a safer method to locate late-running trains. It put a cupola on the station roof and gave the stationmaster a telescope so he could scan the prairies for signs of smoke that signaled an approaching train.

There were few trackside signals at this time. A few depots might have a manual order board, and hand flag and lantern signals were used. Mariners and the military had employed such methods for many generations. Remaining alert and sober was about the best rule for the average trainman to observe. Following schedules carefully and using an accurate watch were other good ways to avoid wrecks. Some railroads issued their own timepieces to make sure workers had a dependable watch. Before 1850 train operations were very much a "seat-of-the-pants" kind of business. Sadly, this remained so for many more generations.

Railroad Technology at Midcentury, 1850s and 1860s

By 1850 the American railway was no longer an infant industry. It had matured into a robust, if not fully developed, national carrier. New England had a fine network of iron highways, and most other regions, save the Far West, were developing basic systems.

America itself was growing quickly in all aspects of national life. In 1848 the United States seized over a million square miles of land from Mexico. Immigration and domestic births were swelling the population by about a third every decade. Industry, banking, and trade seemed to expand each year at a faster pace. Periodic financial panics only slowed the economic expansion temporarily. It was clear that the United States would take its place among the great nations of the world.

Railroad technology was maturing at the same time. Locomotives, cars, track, and bridges—just about every aspect of the physical plant—were getting bigger and more efficient. The locomotive of the 1830s was a trifling four- or six-wheel affair weighing 10 tons and capable of pulling around 200 tons on a level track. By 1850 eight-wheel engines were standard. They weighed 15 or 20 tons and could haul around 500 tons on a level line. New appliances were being added. Cabs to shelter engine crews from the elements were now fairly common. Headlights, bells, whistles, and pilots made the engine safer to operate. Steam gauges, introduced in 1851, added another measure of safety.

Other fundamental features adopted during this period were the wagon-top boiler, the spread leading truck, level cylinders, and the link-motion valve gear. The wagon-top boiler offered generous steam space but simpler construction than the Bury or dome-style boiler formerly favored. The spread or long-wheelbase leading truck gave the engine a smoother guidance system. Level cylinders brought the pistons down on a level with the

center of the driving wheel axles, a more rational and secure position for this hardworking element in the drive train of the engine. The link motion worked the valves and the cylinders in a manner superior to the valve gears formerly used. They were simple and trouble free. They could be quickly shifted from forward to reverse, and they could offer a wide range of cutoffs necessary to the economical use of steam.

Most of these features had become standard by around 1855, and all remained in favor until 1900. Level cylinders and spread trucks remained a standard design feature until the end of steam locomotive production in the 1950s. Wood was abundant in early America and remained the usual locomotive fuel well into the 1850s. Efforts to adopt coal started in this decade as North America's vast coal reserves began to be developed, but progress was slow, and by 1870 only about half the nation's locomotives were coal burners. The conversion gained considerable momentum in the following decade, and by 1880 some 90 percent of U.S. locomotives used coal for fuel. Only a few lines in the South and New England, and industrial lines, continued to burn wood after this time. With an end to wood burning, the funnel-shaped smokestacks that made early American locomotives so distinctive disappeared.

Science was applied to locomotive feedwater service when Venturi's law was put to work. The traditional feedwater pumps used to maintain water levels in boilers had always been a troublesome device. They tended to fail just when most needed and were a constant source of complaint by crew members. A French airship designer, Henri J. Giffard, invented a clever valvelike device that used the principle of speed in overcoming pressure to induce water into the boiler powered by a jet of steam. It was compact and effective. First tried in 1858, it was only reluctantly accepted in railway engineering circles but had become more or less standard by 1890.

Well into the 1860s the eight-wheel locomotive remained the standard wheel arrangement for both freight and passenger service. A typical engine of 1860 would weigh 25 tons and have 16-by-22-inch cylinders and 60-inch-diameter driving wheels. Steam pressure of 110 psi was normal. But much larger engines for freight service were on the way. In 1866 the first 2-8-0 or Consolidation type entered service on the Lehigh Valley Railroad. This 42-ton machine was a giant for the time and yet was able to move over a curving track safely. It rounded curves as sharp as 400 feet in radius and could haul trains of over 2,000 tons on the level. Not all railroads required such powerful engines, but lines moving heavy cargos, such as coal, found them to be a good investment. By 1880 they were in general use on many major U.S. railroads. Even

This woodcut, by A. Hill for the December 19, 1857, *Ballou's Pictorial*, showed a train at Anthony's Nose along the Mohawk River in New York. —Middleton Collection

so, the eight-wheel standard locomotive continued to prevail. Most railroad managers remained convinced that if more powerful engines were needed, the best course was simply to design a larger eight-wheeler.

Less evident than the growth in locomotive size and power was change in the materials used in their construction. Bessemer steel, introduced in 1857, was not widely used at first. Mechanics were suspicious of the new material, but slowly gained enthusiasm for it. In 1860 it was tried for firebox construction and was found to be far more durable than wrought-iron plates then in use, and it was, of course, far cheaper than copper. By 1870 steel fireboxes had become common. Steel driving-wheel tires underwent a similar rapid test and acceptance response. But the same was not true for car and locomotive axles. As late as 1891 only a minority of railroad master mechanics favored steel for this purpose. Others would accept steel axles only when no wrought-iron ones were available. The prejudice against steel axles seemed to center on the variable quality of the steel; wrought iron tended to be more dependable and even in quality. But as wrought-iron production declined by the 1890s, railroads were forced to accept steel axles, and so the old-fashioned iron axle had vanished around the turn of the century.

As the locomotive grew and changed, so did freight and passenger cars. They too grew in size decade by decade. However, the general arrangement and the basic materials of construction remained constant. Wooden double-truck cars with a center aisle, side seats, and end entrances prevailed for passenger cars. A typical coach of the 1850s was just over 40 feet long, seated 56 persons, and weighed 10 tons. The arch roof prevailed until around 1859, when the raised or clerestory roof was introduced. The elevated center section of the roof ran the length of the carbody and was fitted with small windows for additional light and ventilation. It also gave more headroom for gentlemen passengers with top hats. By the mid-1860s the clerestory roof was very nearly standard equipment. Double-acting brakes became common during midcentury, greatly improving the ability to stop a train. All wheels on the car now had brake shoes that were connected to a hand wheel at either end of the car so that the brakes on both trucks could be worked by a single brakeman.

First-class passengers received more attention during this decade. Trips were longer as the rail system reached out to more distant cities, and wealthy travelers were willing to pay extra for the comforts of parlor and sleeping cars. During the 1850s pioneers such as Woodruff, Wagner, and Pullman began operating sleeping cars. More elaborate heating and air-cleaning ventilation systems were installed. Gas lighting was introduced in 1851 for the more deluxe rail vehicles. Coach passengers, however, continued to endure unpleasant conditions: seats were hard and had low backs, candle and oil lamps prevailed, and the heating furnished by iron stoves always seemed to be either too much or too little. Toilets were little more than a seat box that emptied out on the tracks below without benefit of a water flush. Drinking water was supplied by train boys who carried kettles filled with ice water. A common cup or glass was offered to thirsty patrons.

Larger cars were adopted during the 1860s; overall length was now around 52 feet, and weight registered about 18 tons, about twice the weight of a coach built a decade earlier. Some cars were carried by wheels made with compressed paper centers that were quieter than the conventional cast-iron variety. The paper wheels had steel or iron tires. Other technical innovations during this decade included hot-water heating that offered more uniform heat and the air brake that contributed much to railroad safety. The air brake eliminated dependence on brakemen located throughout the train and gave control of stopping the train to the engineer. Air brakes were adopted rather quickly for passenger trains. The need to protect human life was obvious, and relatively few cars were involved. Freight equipment did not see power

The vast majority traveled in the uncomfortable seats of a crowded coach, shown here in the August 1885 *Harper's New Monthly Magazine*. —Middleton Collection

Readers liked to view the modern comforts provided for first-class railroad passengers. This drawing, from a May 1872 article about travel to California in *Harper's New Monthly Magazine*, shows a Pullman Palace Car. —Middleton Collection

brakes until after 1893, when federal law required it. Even so, progress was slow in making this essential improvement to railway safety.

Eight-wheel wooden freight cars were standard by 1850. Most carried 8 to 10 tons and measured between 24 and 28 feet in length. Disc or plate wheels began to replace the old-style spoked variety. The 1860s saw important changes in the style and operation of freight cars as more specialized car types were introduced. The refrigerator car, essentially an insulated boxcar with ice bunkers, appeared. Tank cars for the transport of petroleum and other liquids moved in bulk were introduced. Upright wooden tanks soon gave way to horizontal iron tanks. A few high-capacity flatcars were built to carry very large loads. The caboose, first tried in the mid-1850s, was adopted as an office and shelter for freight-train crews. A few lines built a limited number of iron-bodied cars, but in the main wooden construction prevailed because America's vast forests continued to supply top-grade lumber at low prices.

Fast freight lines began operation in the early 1860s, offering rapid transit over several railroads between major cities for time-sensitive shipments. This scheme ushered in the most important system of freight handling on America's national rail networks. The interchange of freight cars was a cooperative arrangement among all rail lines that allowed cars to move over every connecting line in the nation. Before this interchange system began around 1864, freight was transferred from the cars of one line to the cars of a connecting railroad. The labor, time, and cost of these transfers, known in the shipping business

Dining cars were used by the well-to-do. Most passengers brought a picnic basket or patronized one of the notorious station lunchrooms. This drawing from the *Graphic* (April 14, 1877) shows a man beating a large gong as travelers bolted their 20-minute lunch. —Middleton Collection

Titled "Ten Minutes for Refreshments," a December 2, 1876, woodcut from *Harper's Weekly,* based on a painting by Knut Ekwall, shows passengers during the bedlam of a railroad lunch stop. —Library of Congress (Neg. LC-USZ62-5363)

TECHNOLOGY AND OPERATING PRACTICE IN THE NINETEENTH CENTURY

as the breaking of bulk, were considerable. A single load of grain or lumber might be transferred several times between Baltimore and Chicago under the old system. But with interchange agreements, the same car was accepted by all the roads along the way, and the loaded car passed from one carrier to the next with no breaking of bulk. From this time forward, the freight car became a tramp that wandered around the nation, sometimes not returning to its home railroad for years at a time.

The free-ranging nature of the freight car created repair and control problems for the managers of this growing fleet. In 1867 the Master Car Builders Association was established as the railroads banded together to work out procedures for the repair and management of this freight-car fleet. Standard designs and technology were established gradually over the next several decades. Depreciation schedules and fair costs for specific repairs were created. Ways were devised to find lost cars, because even as large and bulky an item as a boxcar did occasionally disappear. Rail transit was now very much an interstate business.

The growth in locomotives and cars required a corresponding strengthening of track and bridges. Cheap iron rails used during the 1850s proved inferior, and most lasted only from as little as 6 months to 2 years, while good-quality wrought iron would serve from 20 to 25 years. Untreated wood crossties remained the norm during this and succeeding decades, for wood was abundant and cheap. Even so, a few roads attempted to develop long-life ties. The Philadelphia & Reading opened a cre-

osoting plant for this purpose in the 1850s and produced thousands of treated ties for its own use, but no large-scale adoption of treated ties would come until almost 1920.

Henry Bessemer introduced cheap steel in England in 1857, but it several years passed before it received much attention for everyday use. In 1862 the Pennsylvania Railroad began to test steel rails. Three years later the North Chicago Rolling Mill produced the first steel rails in the United States. They proved very durable and less likely to crack during cold weather, a problem with wrought iron. Even so, few main lines used steel rails until the late 1870s.

Engineers found iron bridges a compromise between very durable but expensive stone viaducts and the cheap but short-lived wooden trestles or trusses favored by early railroad builders. The B&O had adopted iron bridges for its main lines in the early 1850s and slowly replaced most of its main-line wooden spans. But the large-scale iron bridges came to the fore with the opening of the great railway bridge across the Ohio River at Steubenville, Ohio, in 1865. More such structures appeared on the Ohio in the next several years at Louisville, Cincinnati, Parkersburg, and Benwood. James Eads's great steel arch bridge across the Mississippi at St. Louis (1874) represented the zenith of this new generation of very large American railway bridges.

Railroad stations began to grow and evolve in the 1850s as well. The great majority of these were plain or

Horses, mules, and men provided most of the hard work for the Pacific Railroad builders. Mormon graders excavated a cut west of the narrows in Weber Canyon, Utah. —*Trains* Magazine Collection

This spectacular crossing of Arizona's Canyon Diablo, 26 miles west of Williams, was the Santa Fe's tallest structure. The iron bridge of tall viaducts and Howe trusses had a height of 222.5 feet and was 560 feet long. The structure was prefabricated in New York and shipped west, where it opened to traffic in 1882. —National Archives

fancy wooden structures meant to serve small communities. Substantial stone and brick edifices were built in major cities at an earlier date. For the most part they served one railroad. But a new concept in station use and design came about in Indianapolis in 1853, when a central Union Station serving every major railroad entering the state capital was completed. Passengers no longer had to find their way across town from one station to another to continue their journey. They got off one train and walked a short distance inside the protective walls of the Union Station to make their connection.

During the mid-nineteenth century the safe operation of trains depended largely upon vigilant train crews. Enginemen were alert and watchful, looking ahead for smoke on the horizon or the glimmer of a distant headlight. Trainmen listened for the rumble of an approaching train or the shriek of a whistle. The new technology of the electric telegraph that became available in 1844 did much to improve the control of train operations and railway safety in general. This simple, low-voltage communication system could send messages hundreds of miles in an instant. It was first tried for train dispatching on the Erie Railway. Trains were no longer like ships lost at sea, for once telegraphs were set up at stations along the line, it was pos-

sible to locate the position of a train by means of reports from the telegraphers. Now that a dispatcher could learn where one of his trains was located, he could begin to work out a plan to reschedule a late train and all other trains affected by its lateness. The telegraph further offered the dispatcher a way to hold or stop trains so that others might pass around them. This was done by using the station telegrapher as an intermediary. The dispatcher would telegraph the agent with instructions; the agent would prepare a written order and pass it along to the crew either by stopping the train or by passing the order to the crew via a hoop as the train slowly passed by. Telegraph dispatching had become common by the mid-1860s.

At the same time a few eastern lines began to install trackside signals at locations where traffic problems demanded them, not just at stations. These were illuminated at night with kerosene lanterns; a clear lens indicated clear or proceed, red indicated stop or danger, and blue indicated caution or proceed slowly. Signals were connected by telegraph, but were manually operated. In 1868 a Yankee inventor, Thomas S. Hall, tested an automatic electric signal that eliminated the fallible human operative and so promised to usher in a new age for railway safety.

Some early railroad men. Artist David Hunter Strother (pseud. Porte Crayon) during an 1858 artists' excursion pictured the Baltimore & Ohio's "model conductor" in the June 1859 *Harper's New Monthly Magazine* (*top, left*). A brakeman (*top, right*) and a locomotive engineer (*bottom*) are shown in the August 1874 *Harper's New Monthly Magazine*. —(all) Middleton Collection

Railroad Technology in the Gilded Age and Beyond, 1870s–1890s

By 1870 railroads dominated American transportation. Steamboats moved over rivers and lakes as before, and stagecoaches rattled along many routes, but the bulk of traffic now went over iron rails. Freight trains moved 93 million tons in 1870, almost double what they had a decade earlier. By 1880 about 290 million tons were transported. To successfully transport this runaway traffic growth, hard-pressed railroad managers demanded ever-larger cars and locomotives. Track and bridges were necessarily strengthened or replaced. More men and ever-larger repair shops were needed as well. Railroads were a true growth industry.

Freight cars developed along a linear pattern, with few changes in basic construction techniques. Heavy floor timber formed the main frame. By the late 1870s these were being strengthened with truss-rod supports. Iron body bolsters replaced the traditional wooden variety on some railroads. Boxcars grew in length and carrying capacity. By the early 1880s 20-ton-capacity cars about 34 feet long had become common. By the middle of the same decade 25- and 30-ton-capacity cars were appearing. The 1890s saw still more of this gradual step-up in size and capacity. But of more consequence was the introduction of pressed-steel parts and more and more iron plates and truss rods in the floor and body framing. In 1897 the first all-steel freight cars joined the fleet, which had grown by this time to over 1 million cars. The superior strength and durability of the steel cars prompted

This drawing from the March 19, 1870, issue of *Harper's Weekly* shows a stranded train somewhere in the snows of the Sierras on the Central Pacific Railroad's first winter of transcontinental operation. —Middleton Collection

their acceptance by all major railroads. By 1905, 45 percent of all new cars were steel or steel framed. The federal Safety Appliance Act of 1893 required the application of air brakes and automatic couplers to all freight cars in interstate service. A dozen years passed, however, before the industry was in compliance with this legislation.

The true genius of American rail freight service was its cheapness. Despite all of the Grangers' complaints, America's pioneer railroads offered the cheapest rates in the world—few other systems came close to their charge of less than one cent a ton-mile. Clearly Americans were doing many things right.

Passenger travel was escalating as well because of a growing population and the spread of settlement through the western states. By 1880 the U.S. census estimated that 280 million annual passengers were carried on domestic rail lines. This traffic demanded not just more rolling stock but increased efforts to move this enormous human cargo safely, and so power brakes (air or vacuum) became standard on passenger trains. By 1876 three-quarters of all passenger cars in the United States were equipped with air brakes. Many of the others had vacuum brakes. At the same time most main-line passenger cars had adopted Miller hook couplers. An even safer design, introduced by Eli Janney in 1873, eventually became the industry standard.

Gas lighting gradually replaced kerosene lamps on the better cars during the 1880s. It provided superior illumination and was somewhat safer than oil lamps. Steam heating came into favor during the same decade. It too offered a safer, more uniform system of heating than did the wood or coal stoves formerly used. It was used mainly on the first-class cars. Vestibules, introduced in 1887, allowed passengers to pass from one car to the next protected from the elements. It also meant that they were less likely to fall off, because the passageway was enclosed. Most cars had vestibules by about 1900, branch-line or commuter cars excepted. But the greatest advance in passenger-car safety did not come until the early twentieth century when the steel car was at last introduced. Talk of such fire- and crash-resistant conveyances had been around for decades, and a number of test models were produced. Even when commercial production began, travelers waited for decades before the majority of American trains were equipped with steel cars.

Even locomotives were marshaled into the safety movement. Air pumps for brakes were carried on the locomotive and powered by steam produced by the engine boilers. Yet few locomotives had any brakes except for a tender brake. Locomotive superintendents were adamant in their belief that brakes belonged on the cars but not on locomotives. But they were forced to relent as passenger-train speeds and weights advanced. In 1888 the Baltimore & Ohio began running 45-minute trains between Washington and Baltimore. These trains averaged 53 mph. At the same time the Pennsylvania Railroad introduced a fast train from Jersey City to Philadelphia that raced along at a 48 mph average. Within a few years the New York Central introduced a fast train to Buffalo that traveled over 400 miles at an average speed of 50 mph. Fast traveling was becoming an everyday event, and so too was the notion of engine brakes. As late as 1885 only a few U.S. locomotives had them, but opinions were changing, and by the end of the decade about 50 percent of locomotives were equipped with brakes.

In other areas less progress was evident. Railway signaling remained nearly stagnant with the telegraph station operator and hand-operated semaphores. Automatic electric signaling had been available since 1870, but only a few roads could be persuaded to adopt it. One notable exception was the Cincinnati Southern, which installed automatic signals along its 300-mile main line in 1891. Yet by 1900 less than 1 percent of the nation's trackage was protected by signals of this type.

Track was a brighter area of railroad engineering in terms of durability and safety. Many old-fashioned track elements began to disappear in the 1870s. Very short rails, generally only 20 feet long, produced too many joints that made a weak track and a rough and noisy ride. Rail lengths grew to 30 feet. The chair-style joint was replaced by fishplates or, as they were sometimes called, angle bars. Cast-iron switch frogs were made obsolete by fabricated or cast-steel frogs. Steel rails overtook the wrought-iron variety in the 1880s. By 1883 the cost of steel rails was less than that of iron, and the new forms overtook the old-style makers' rail. American rail dominated the domestic market, having underpriced the British producers as early as 1874. Railroads gradually gave up their preference for individual designs—there were 300 rail patterns in 1880—and by the late 1890s 60 percent of the new rail was made to the standard designs of the American Society of Civil Engineers.

Conclusion

Americans at first copied the British plan for railways, in some cases in an exact pattern. However, they began to modify and change the ideas of Stephenson and his associates for a cheaper, more flexible system of rail transport. Cheaper was not better; in fact, many of America's pioneer lines were inferior in safety, comfort, and maintenance. But Americans were able to build a very large system quickly by using a lower standard of engineering. For a capital-poor system with a large territory to serve, low-cost track and bridges were a necessity. In time America rebuilt and improved. Starting around 1870, more permanent structures and tracks became more common. Old lines were rebuilt with lower grades, more gentle curves, iron bridges, and, in a few cases, double tracks. By the 1890s the United States was a rich and powerful industrial giant, and its railways reflected its growth and maturity. It had not only one of the largest but one of the best rail systems in the world.

Technology and Operating Practice in the Twentieth Century

William D. Middleton

By the beginning of the twentieth century North American railroads were nearing the end of their geographic growth. Important new routes and even entire railroads would come into being in the first decades of the new century, but the railroads had already become a mature, fully developed industry providing an integrated transportation system that reached virtually every part of the continent. Railroad technology and operating practice were both well developed and largely standardized. The twentieth century proved to be both a time of intense growth in rail traffic and a period in which competing transport modes challenged the railroads' market dominance. Throughout the century and into the next the railroads pursued a quest for the advances in technology and operating practice that could provide the expanded capacity, improved performance, and greater efficiency needed to meet these challenges successfully.

The last half of the nineteenth century had seen the emergence of the United States as the world's greatest industrial power. This tremendous industrial growth paralleled that of the railroads that supported it; the two were interdependent. From the time of the Civil War until the end of the century American manufacturing output had grown fivefold. Coal powered the industrial economy, and by the end of the century coal production had reached some 270 million tons annually, ten times its level at the time of the Civil War. Development of the Bessemer and open-hearth processes transformed steelmaking into a giant industry that produced more than 10 million long tons of steel in 1900. More than 27 million tons of iron ore a year flowed by rail and water from the mines of Minnesota and Michigan's Upper Peninsula to feed the great blast furnaces of the steel mills. Although overtaken by manufacturing as the nation's principal source of income before the end of the century, the output of America's farms almost tripled between the time of the Civil War and 1900, and the products of the nation's forests more than tripled to reach more than 35 billion board feet.

By this time American railroads had grown to an industry of some 259,000 miles of track that was transporting an annual traffic of almost 142 billion freight ton-miles and over 16 billion passenger-miles. In just the decade from 1890 to 1900 freight traffic had nearly dou-

bled, and passenger traffic had grown by a third. As we have seen, the technology of the railroad had evolved in parallel with the increasing demand for capacity and performance. While the typical 4-4-0 American Standard locomotive of the post–Civil War period was capable of an output of perhaps 500 hp and a tractive effort of 10,000 pounds, by 1900 the locomotive builders were delivering 2-8-0 and 4-8-0 freight locomotives capable of an output of as much as 1,500 hp and a tractive effort of close to 50,000 pounds. Together with larger cars, improved couplings, and the development of air brakes, the use of more powerful locomotives had permitted the railroads to more than double the average trainload in just the last two decades of the nineteenth century. By the end of the century some roads were beginning to offer fast freight services for high-value or perishable cargos. Even though such speeds were never seen in regular service, modern 4-4-0 and 4-4-2 passenger locomotives had demonstrated a capability of speeds in excess of 100 mph, while passenger equipment had attained an unprecedented level of luxury and convenience. Wherever warranted by traffic levels, automatic block signaling provided a high standard of safety. Heavier steel rails, improved roadbed standards, and new or rebuilt structures capable of heavier loads provided a fixed plant adequate to transport the railroads' enormous traffic.

Impressive as it was, the capability of American railroads at the beginning of the twentieth century was soon overshadowed by what was to come. American manufacturing output grew more than 70 percent over the next decade and more than tripled by the end of the 1920s. Steel production more than doubled by 1910 and more than doubled again by 1929. The railroads' freight ton-miles very nearly doubled by 1910 and more than tripled by 1929. By the end of the century the railroads were carrying very nearly ten times the freight traffic level of 1900. Until the rise of private automobile travel in the 1920s, passenger traffic grew at an even faster pace, to double the 1900 level by 1910 and almost triple it by 1920, when passenger travel reached a peak of over 47 billion passenger-miles. To accommodate this cornucopia of traffic on a railroad system that had very nearly reached its maximum growth required still greater advances in technology and operating practice. In a period when government regulators resisted efforts to increase rates to allow more adequate earnings, the enormous capital investment needed for this expansion of capacity was not easily found.

The new century soon brought significant advances in motive-power technology. As traffic demand and train size grew, steam locomotives became still larger and more powerful. By the end of the 1890s builders had begun to adopt the use of a wide firebox and swiveling trailing trucks, both measures that allowed a larger firebox and thus a greater capacity to generate steam, while the development of mechanical stokers or, sometimes, the use of oil fuel enabled the burning of more fuel than was possible with a hand-fired coal burner. Larger 2-8-2 Mikado and 4-6-2 Pacific locomotives became commonplace for freight and passenger service, and even larger 2-10-2 and 4-8-2 designs were later developed. The first North American example of the articulated compound locomotive, a design developed in Europe by Swiss engineer Anatole Mallet, appeared on the Baltimore & Ohio in an 0-6-6-0 wheel arrangement in 1904, and the Mallet soon became popular for heavy freight operation in a variety of wheel arrangements. Helping make these larger locomotives feasible was the development of cast-steel frames around 1900, while the introduction of such features as superheaters, feedwater heaters, and boosters enhanced locomotive efficiency.

By 1900, too, an entirely new motive-power technology, electric traction, had come on the scene. Developed for urban street railways in the 1880s, electric power was successfully applied to main-line operation with the 1895 electrification of the Baltimore & Ohio's new Howard Street Tunnel at Baltimore. By the end of the first decade of the twentieth century it had been adopted as well for extensive electrifications of the New York Central, New Haven, Long Island, and Pennsylvania railroads at New York City, and some believed that it would supplant steam power altogether. North American electrification ultimately reached significant dimensions, but it never toppled steam power. Another new motive-power technology, the internal combustion engine, did eventually supplant steam, but its initial application as the power plant for light self-propelled passenger cars gave little hint of the dominant technology it later became.

The rapid development of the American steel industry in the late nineteenth century had made steel an economical material for car building, and by 1900 steel was in increasing use in both freight and passenger equipment. The need for fire-safe equipment for New York's new subway and the tunnels that carried Pennsylvania and Long Island trains under the Hudson and East rivers into Manhattan led to a rapid transition to the construction of all-steel passenger cars, but a shift to all-steel freight-car construction came much more slowly.

The first major electrification was the New York Central & Hudson River's extensive New York terminal and suburban 600-volt system. The first of the new electrics, No. 6000, is seen in a test run at Wyatts Crossing, New York, near Schenectady on November 12, 1904. —Industrial Photo Service (GE Neg. 202241A)

Completed in 1915, the Delaware, Lackawanna & Western's great concrete Tunkhannock Viaduct at Nicholson, Pennsylvania, took 167,000 cubic yards of concrete and was—and still is—the largest concrete structure of its kind in the world. —Nicholson Public Library

Despite the shortage of investment capital created by regulatory control of rates, the early years of the century were a time of heavy investment in fixed plant as the railroads rebuilt their lines and structures for the greater capacity and operating efficiency that were needed to handle growing traffic. Heavier rail and higher standards for track construction allowed higher speeds and heavier axle loads. During the first decade of the century the Pennsylvania—by far the busiest North American railroad—set out to expand its entire main line between New York and Pittsburgh to four tracks. Many railroads now had sufficient earnings to afford improvements to their original routes, which had been built as cheaply and quickly as possible. The Southern Pacific, for example, completed line relocations that eased some of the worst grades on the original transcontinental route through California's Donner Pass, while the 102-mile Lucin Cutoff completed in 1904 carried the SP's main line right across Utah's Great Salt Lake to cut almost 44 miles, 11 full circles of curvature, and 1,515 feet of vertical grade from those of the original line through Promontory, Utah. In 1900 the Great Northern, which had built its original line across

Washington's Cascade Mountains with a tortuous route of eight switchbacks, severe curves, and grades as steep as 4 percent, completed the 2.6-mile Cascade Tunnel that reduced the length of the line by 9 miles, eliminated more than 6 complete circles of curvature, and cut the maximum grade to 2.2 percent. The Delaware, Lackawanna & Western spent more than $25 million between 1908 and 1915 to build the 28.5-mile Lackawanna Cutoff in New Jersey and the 40-mile Summit Cutoff in northeastern Pennsylvania to substantially improve the line and grade on its main line between Hoboken, New Jersey and Buffalo, New York.

Railroad bridge construction was advanced by the development of reinforced-concrete technology and improved alloy steels, enabling the construction of remarkable structures, among them some that still stand as record-breaking spans of their type. The still-unequaled reinforced-concrete Tunkhannock Viaduct at Nicholson, Pennsylvania, was completed in 1915 as part of the Lackawanna's Summit Cutoff. Four great steel bridges completed in 1917 included the Canadian Government Railway's cantilever crossing of the St. Lawrence at Quebec, the New York Connecting Railroad's Hell Gate arch across the East River at New York, the Chesapeaka & Ohio's continuous-truss crossing of the Ohio River at Sciotoville, Ohio, and the Burlington's simple truss crossing of the Ohio at Metropolis, Illinois. The shield tunneling technology developed in the late nineteenth century made possible such difficult underwater tunnels as the Pennsylvania's Hudson and East River tubes at New York, while a new sunken-tube technology that emerged early in the new century enabled the Michigan Central to economically complete a difficult tunnel crossing of the Detroit River between Detroit and Windsor, Ontario.

The early years of the century saw unprecedented investment by the railroads in their passenger facilities as traffic climbed to record levels. Sometimes this was as much to outdo each other in the scale and magnificence of their terminals as it was to serve the needs of the traffic; architectural historian Carroll L. V. Meeks called it the "megalomania" phase of station building. At New York, for example, the Pennsylvania spent some $160 million on all elements of the enormous tunnel and terminal project that brought trains into the splendid new Pennsylvania Station in Manhattan, while the rival New York Central spent some $72 million to electrify its New York lines and to erect the magnificent new Grand Central Terminal.

As the volume of bulk cargos continued to grow, the railroads developed such facilities as mechanized ore and coal docks and grain elevators that efficiently and rapidly transferred huge volumes between railcars and ships. Massive ore docks at the lakehead ports were capable of loading trainloads of iron ore into a lake steamer in a matter of hours, while the enormous Hulett unloading machines that transferred the ore from the steamers to railcars at the other end of the Great Lakes haul could handle 17 tons at a single bite.

While average passenger-train speeds remained relatively low, there was a growing number of fast limited train services in some of the principal, highly competitive corridors. Easily the most notable of these was the New York–Chicago route, where the New York Central and the Pennsylvania provided the finest motive power and rolling stock for their premier trains. As early as 1905 the Pennsylvania was operating its all-Pullman *Pennsylvania Special* between the two cities on an 18-hour schedule, an average speed of over 50 mph for the 908-mile journey. The Central soon responded with an identical schedule for its *20th Century Limited*, which represented an average speed of more than 53 mph over the railroad's longer, 960-mile route.

Freight-train speeds remained low; as late as 1920 their average speed, including all stops, was only 10.3 mph. But by the beginning of the century there was already a growing number of fast freight services, typically operated for high-value or perishable traffic. By the 1920s many of these symbol freights, as they were often called, operated over long distances at terminal-to-terminal averages of 19 or 20 mph. Among particularly fast freights were the New Haven's Boston–New York "fish train," which averaged over 25 mph for its 227-mile run, and the Southern Railway's special trains that moved the Georgia peach crop north from Atlanta to Washington in only 22 hours, a 29 mph average for the 637-mile journey.

The two decades after the Great War were a time of dramatic transformation for the railroads as they were confronted with the rapidly growing competition of automotive transport and the ravages of the Great Depression of the 1930s. The early 1920s saw a significant breakthrough in steam locomotive design, largely through the efforts of Ohio's Lima Locomotive Works that began what came to be called the Super-Power era. Reasoning that locomotives had reached their physical limitations because of clearance and weight restrictions, Lima's William E. Woodward suggested that only internal changes, such as larger and more efficient fireboxes and efficiency-enhancing appliances, would improve steam locomotive performance. An initial application of Woodward's ideas to a redesign of a standard New York Central 2-8-2 Mikado in 1922 produced a locomotive with drawbar horsepower as much as 35 percent greater and the highest boiler efficiency ever attained by a steam locomotive. Lima next developed the A-1, a 2-8-4 locomotive that incorporated even greater technical advances and set new records for boiler and fuel efficiency in tests on the Boston & Albany. The A-1 was widely demonstrated on other eastern and midwestern roads, and Lima and other builders were soon booking orders for Super-Power locomotives in a variety of wheel arrangements that included 4-6-4s, 2-10-4s, 4-8-4s, and several simple articulated wheel arrangements, as well as 2-8-4s. Reflecting the capacity of this new generation of steam power, the tractive effort of the steam locomotives in service on American railroads increased by 40 percent between 1920 and 1940, from an average of 36,365 pounds to almost 51,000 pounds.

Even as this much-improved steam power came on the scene, railroad electrification continued to advance. Between 1915 and 1925 both Norfolk & Western and the Virginian carried out significant heavy-haul electrifications in the coalfields of Virginia and West Virginia. During the same period the Milwaukee Road completed almost 900 track-miles of electrification on its crossings of the Rocky Mountains and the Cascades. Significant suburban electrifications went in on the Canadian Northern at Montreal, the Illinois Central at Chicago, the Lackawanna in northern New Jersey, and the Reading at Philadelphia. The Mexican Railway electrified its steep grade into the Sierra Madre Oriental. In 1915 the Pennsylvania completed a single-phase AC electrification of its Philadelphia suburban service to Paoli that by 1938 grew into a 656-route-mile, 2,150-track-mile electrification—at the time, the greatest in the world.

Internal combustion motor cars from a variety of builders—usually gasoline-electric—had proved successful for branch-line services, and by the early 1920s several

The Pennsylvania Railroad's great Manhattan terminal included new Hudson and East River tunnels and electrification as well as Pennsylvania Station itself, which occupied two full city blocks with space for 11 platforms almost 30 feet below street level. This drawing (*top*) shows the overall arrangement of the station. The main waiting room (*bottom*) had a 150-foot-high ceiling. —(top) *Fortune* Magazine, July 1939; (bottom) Hagley Museum and Library

builders were producing diesel-electric switching locomotives. In 1934 General Motors' Electro-Motive Division, a former gas-electric car supplier, powered the Burlington's new *Zephyr* streamlined passenger train with a diesel-electric power plant. The train was a dramatic success, and a motive-power revolution was soon under way on North American railroads. By the end of the decade diesel power had been widely adopted for streamliner and other premier passenger services, and the first road freight diesel-electric was introduced by the Santa Fe in 1939. Steam locomotive builders continued to develop new Super-Power designs that reached unprecedented levels of performance and efficiency, but the diesel would ultimately win the contest of technologies.

Largely because of the rapid development of paved roads and widespread automobile ownership, railroad passenger traffic began a sharp decline after World War I. From the record level of 1920, passenger traffic on U.S. railroads had fallen by a third, to less than 31.1 billion passenger-miles, by 1929. The Depression only aggravated this trend. By 1932 traffic had dropped to less than 17 billion passenger-miles, little more than half even that of 1929. Unwilling to accept losses of such proportions, the railroads responded with extraordinary innovation to usher in an era of streamlined passenger trains that represented a golden age of overland transport in North America.

Aerodynamic styling, new lightweight materials, air conditioning, a high standard of service amenities, and high-speed schedules characterized the new trains. The Burlington *Zephyr* of 1934 was fabricated from welded stainless steel, while the Union Pacific's contemporary M-10,000 streamliner was built of aluminum. Diesel-electrics were the motive power of choice for the new trains, but several roads developed streamlined steam locomotives, some of which were capable of speeds up to 120 mph. By the end of the decade the Union Pacific and its connections were operating a great *Streamliner* fleet between Chicago and the principal West Coast cities. The Southern Pacific immodestly called its streamlined Los Angeles–San Francisco *Daylight* the "most beautiful train in

the world." Burlington's *Zephyr*s, the Milwaukee Road's *Hiawatha*s, and the Chicago & North Western's *400* fleet served principal destinations on these midwestern roads, and all three competed with each other, and with highways, for traffic in the Chicago–Twin Cities corridor. The two principal competitors in the New York–Chicago market reequipped their premier *20th Century Limited* and *Broadway Limited* with streamlined equipment. New streamlined trains served the Florida vacation market from Chicago and the Northeast.

Well into the 1930s Great Lakes and intercoastal water carriers represented the principal competitors to the railroads for intercity freight traffic, but by the end of the decade this had begun to change. Federal investment in the nation's inland waterways had developed a growing barge-line competition for bulk freight. Far more significant, however, was the impact of highway competition. From 1930 to 1940 the railroads' market share of intercity freight ton-miles declined from over 74 percent to just over 61 percent, while trucks increased their traffic more than threefold to gain a 10 percent market share. Highway transport was more expensive, but offered advantages of speed, reliability, and point-to-point pickup and delivery that the traditional freight train could not match.

There were new efforts to apply intermodal technologies that combined the advantages of highway transport with the long-haul efficiencies of trainload movement. Almost from the beginning of the railway era there had been attempts to develop containers that could be trans-

One of the stars of Super-Power was the Union Pacific's 4-6-6-4 Challenger articulateds. UP bought 105 of them from Alco between 1936 and 1944. Although intended for freight service, they often worked in passenger service as well. Westbound Challenger 3965, built by Alco in 1942, was west of Rock River, Wyoming, with a 59-car extra on June 27, 1950. —William D. Middleton

Eastbound from Denver to Chicago, the bright yellow Union Pacific–Chicago & North Western streamliner *City of Denver* sped through Sterling, Colorado, at a good 70 mph at sunset on May 30, 1938. —R. H. Kindig, *Trains* Magazine Collection

ferred fully loaded between railcars and wagons or boats, avoiding the time-consuming and costly breaking of bulk that was usually required to transfer freight between transport modes. Well before the end of the nineteenth century several lines developed services in which an entire loaded freight wagon was loaded aboard a railcar for shipment. Much of the new experimentation in this area was by electric interurban railways, which developed special cars for rail transportation of highway trailers or systems of large containers that could be easily transferred between trucks and railcars. The most extensive service of this kind operated anywhere before World War II was by the Chicago North Shore & Milwaukee, which began moving highway trailers between Chicago and Milwaukee in what was called "ferry-truck" service in 1926, eventually reaching a peak of more than 18,000 truck trailers annually. Among main-line railroads the New York Central and the Pennsylvania were pioneers. During the 1920s both roads established less-than-carload-lot (LCL) services with large containers that were transshipped between trucks and railcars. In the late 1930s the Chicago Great Western and the New Haven began operating significant "train-ferry" services, transporting highway trailers on standard flatcars. It was well after World War II, however, before intermodal services became a significant part of railroad freight services.

For most elements of railroad freight service, however, the changes in the interwar years were gradual and evolutionary. By every measure operating efficiency showed steady improvement as more efficient and powerful motive power and higher-capacity freight cars entered service. Average freight-train speed, which had stood at only 10.3 mph in 1920, climbed by more than 50 percent to 16.7 mph in 1940. Another significant measure, the average net ton-miles per freight-train hour, nearly doubled, from 7,303 in 1920 to 14,028 in 1940. The average freight car traveled more miles and carried more freight, increasing the average daily ton-miles per car from 498 in 1920 to 664 in 1940.

Signaling and communications saw their greatest advances since the development of the automatic block signal in the decade after World War I. Various systems for automatically stopping a train if it attempted to pass a signal set against it had been developed as far back as 1880, and simple trip-stop devices had been installed on subways and elevated railways as early as the turn of the century. Railroads experimented with a number of these devices over the next two decades, and in 1922 the Interstate Commerce Commission ordered the installation of automatic train control systems on certain divisions of 49 railroads. Out of the continuous-induction system developed to meet this requirement came the ability to provide cab signals that provided an engineman with a continuous indication of track conditions ahead. Still another advance in signaling and train control at about the same time was the development of coded track circuits, which permitted more signal indications than the usual three-aspect signal provided.

Most of the North American railroad system, however, was single-track territory operated under traditional timetable and train-order procedures. The mid-1920s development of centralized traffic control (CTC), under which switches and signals were set by remote control from a central location, greatly increased line capacity over what was possible with traditional train control and dispatching methods. The installation of CTC typically increased the capacity of a single-track line by about half and reduced delays for the issuance of orders or train meets. An initial installation on the Missouri Pacific in 1925 controlled signals and switches on a 50-mile section of single-track line. The New York Central followed with a similar installation in 1927 on 40 miles of single track between Toledo and Berwick, Ohio. Within the next decade entire subdivisions were being operated under CTC control. By 1940 there were more than 2,400 miles of track under CTC control in the United States.

During the same period new technologies brought significant increases to the efficiency and productivity of freight classification yards. The traditional flat classification yards of early railroading had begun to shift by the end of the nineteenth century toward the use of hump yards, which used gravity to assist in the classification of freight cars. A locomotive pushed a train up an incline to the crest of the hump, where the cars were uncoupled to coast down the hump grade to be switched into the appropriate track of the classification yard. Initially, switchmen did this switching manually, but by the turn of the century it was often controlled by a single opera-

tor through the use of electropneumatic machines. Although hump yards greatly increased classification productivity, they were still labor intensive. Large numbers of car riders were required to ride each cut or car down into the classification yard to set the brakes and control the speed of the car.

A major advance in hump-yard technology came in the early 1920s with the development of pneumatic retarders, which provided a way to control car speeds without putting a rider on each car to set the brakes manually. The first installation of pneumatic retarders in North America was in 1924 at the Indiana Harbor Belt's yard at Gibson, Indiana, on the north hump. It eliminated the need for 60 car riders, and *Railway Review* reported that the yard's daily classification productivity had increased from 25 to 43 cars per man. By 1940 some two dozen major U.S. hump yards had been equipped with retarders.

Reflecting the increasing demands imposed by higher speeds and heavier cars and locomotives, the railroads' track structure was steadily upgraded. In 1921 American railroads had just over 37,000 miles of line laid with rail of 100 pounds per yard or more; by 1940 this had grown to almost 130,000 miles.

The unprecedented traffic demands of World War II, as the United States and Canada fought a worldwide war and supplied materiel to allies in both European and

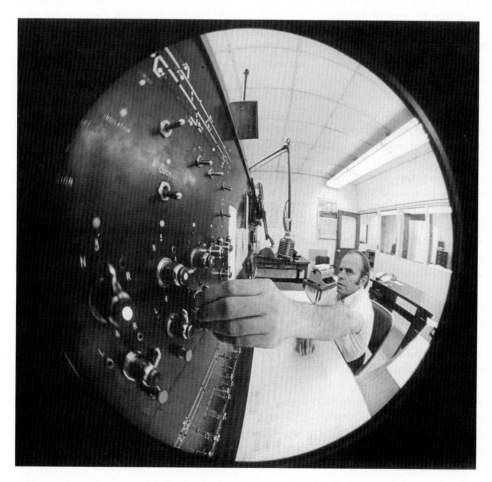

Centralized traffic control (CTC) transformed the way train control was managed and substantially increased line capacity. A Milwaukee Road dispatcher at Milwaukee, Wisconsin, controlled a train movement in 1977.
—Mike Schafer, *Trains* Magazine Collection

Asian theaters, helped accelerate technological change. Production of diesel-electric locomotives was continued throughout the war to increase freight capacity, swelling the ranks of diesel motive power sixfold, from only 510 units in 1939 to more than 3,000 by 1944. Installation of CTC helped increase the capacity of key single-track lines, and by 1945 CTC had grown to cover almost 7,400 track-miles, almost three times the 1940 mileage.

The intense traffic of the wartime years left the railroads with substantial needs for renewal of equipment and plant, but it also left the industry in a much stronger financial position. In the five years after the end of the war U.S. railroads spent more than $3.5 billion to acquire almost 10,600 new locomotives, more than 311,000 new freight cars, and more than 4,300 new passenger cars and to rebuild thousands more. Fixed-plant expenditures reached more than $1.56 billion during the same period. Annual capital spending by U.S. railroads for equipment and for roadway and structures climbed to almost $1.3 billion by 1948 and stayed at or near that level for the next five years.

The transition from steam to diesel-electric motive power that played out in the decade after World War II represented a fundamental shift in railroad technology. By war's end the superior performance and efficiency of internal combustion motive power was evident to all but a few diehard roads, most with heavy coal traffic, and virtually all new motive power built after the end of the war was diesel-electric. From a total of well under 6,000 units in service in 1947, diesel-electric motive power reached a total of almost 20,500 units by 1952, exceeding the number of steam locomotives in service for the first time. The last new reciprocating steam locomotive built for U.S. railroads was a switching locomotive that rolled out of the Norfolk & Western's Roanoke shops in December 1953, and by the end of the decade the steam locomotive had all but vanished from North American railroads. Capable of longer runs and higher availability than the steam power they displaced, and requiring far less frequent servicing and maintenance, diesel-electric locomotives transformed railroad employment and operation. It is no exaggeration to state that diesel-electric motive power was the key technological asset that enabled North American railroads to survive as a viable for-profit industry in the intensely competitive transportation environment that followed World War II.

With the enormously successful example of the Pennsylvania's Depression-era electrification before the industry, there was much talk of expanded electrification in the years after World War II. The development of the ignitron rectifier, which could convert AC power to DC, offered an ability to electrify much more economically from the standard commercial-frequency power grid. This new technology did indeed lead to wide-scale electrification—all of it overseas; North American electrification actually began to decline as diesel-electric power displaced earlier tunnel and smoke-abatement electrifications. For North American railroads that were short of investment capital, diesel-electric motive power offered a better path to improved operating efficiency. Efforts to develop gas-turbine locomotives fared little better.

Convinced by a wartime passenger traffic that had reached the highest levels in the industry's history that there was a bright future for the passenger business, North American railroads lavished unprecedented resources on new streamlined rolling stock in the immediate postwar period. In addition to the customary comforts of first-class Pullman travel, the new trains offered such amenities as reclining-seat coaches, budget "sleeper coaches," and coffee-shop cars to appeal to the economy-minded leisure traveler. Sightseeing dome cars added to the appeal of long rail journeys through the scenic West. The introduction of high-capacity bilevel cars helped increase the efficiency of commuter services.

It proved to be an ill-considered investment. The American automobile industry quickly shifted from wartime production back to automobiles to fill a pent-up American yearning to return to the highways. Road building resumed with a vengeance, and the Interstate Highway Act of 1956 set in motion the construction of an unparalleled national system of grade-separated high-speed superhighways. By 1960 the total U.S. passenger-miles traveled by private autos had reached nearly three times the 1940 level.

If highways were not competition enough for passenger trains, commercial aviation finally came into its own in the postwar decade. Wartime advances in aircraft design had produced a new family of efficient, long-range four-engine transports that quickly revolutionized air transport. From a common-carrier market share of less than 3 percent in 1940, airlines had increased their traffic tenfold by 1950. By the end of another decade, as faster jet aircraft began to come into the commercial fleet, the air carriers were transporting an annual total of almost 34 billion passenger-miles, half again the railroad total.

A few railroads turned to new designs of low-slung, ultralightweight passenger trains they hoped would cut costs, increase speeds, and win passengers back to the rails. None enjoyed significant success, and the passenger train continued a seemingly inexorable decline.

The railroad freight business was in a battle for survival as well. The new interstate highways had proved a boon to the trucking industry, which increased its traffic almost fivefold from 1940 to 1960 to gain a market share of almost 22 percent. Such high-value traffic as express and LCL freight proved particularly vulnerable to highway carriers. Federally supported waterway development and an expanding privately supported pipeline network took steadily larger shares of bulk cargo and petroleum traffic. While the total freight transport market was growing, rail freight ton-miles remained more or less static, constituting a steadily declining market share. The rail share of U.S. intercity freight traffic reached a low point of about 36 percent in 1977 before the decline was halted.

A steady upgrade of freight equipment and operating practice proved far more successful at reversing this decline than had similar efforts to revive the passenger business, but it was a long and difficult process. Diesel-electric motive power hauled longer trains at higher speeds. Improved freight-car trucks and a shift from traditional friction bearings to roller bearings permitted both higher speeds and heavier axle loadings for freight cars and thus the use of higher-capacity equipment. Such productivity measures as average freight-train speed and net ton-miles per freight-train hour showed more or less steady gains. By 1960 the average freight train produced almost 23,900 ton-miles per hour, a productivity gain of 70 percent over the prewar average.

In addition to substantial increases in car capacity, the railroads began to develop a widening range of specialized cars. Designed to handle certain categories of traffic more economically and efficiently, the new cars often helped recapture traffic that had been lost to highway or water carriers. "Damage-free" boxcars, for example, employed cushioned draft gear and better systems for restraining lading to reduce freight loss and damage. There were all-door boxcars for bulky freight; high-cube boxcars for light, bulky freight; and special cars for handling lumber, wood chips, and other commodities with special requirements. High-capacity covered hopper cars for grain and other weather-sensitive bulk cargos became common. A covered hopper celebrity of sorts was the Southern Railway's aluminum Big John of the early 1960s, capable of handling 100 tons of grain or other bulk cargo, which became the centerpiece of the railroad's efforts to gain approval for the lower, barge-competitive rates the high-capacity cars made possible. Mechanical refrigerator cars proved far more reliable than the traditional ice-refrigerated cars and eliminated the need for periodic stops for re-icing. One of the most successful specialized car designs was the trilevel automobile carrier, which so substantially reduced the cost of transporting new automobiles that railroads were able to recapture a major share of a traffic that had gone almost entirely to highway carriers.

Easily the most significant postwar development in rail freight, however, was in the intermodal movement of freight in truck trailers or containers. By the early 1950s the few railroads that had begun to experiment with trailer-on-flatcar (TOFC) "piggyback" services before the war had been joined by a growing number of other lines. This new traffic was typically made up of trailers loaded on standard flatcars from ramps, circus-train style, but specialized gantry cranes, giant forklift trucks, cars, and trailers designed for more efficient loading and unloading were soon available. By the mid-1950s still another technology had appeared in the form of the intermodal container, which could be transported by highway, rail, or ship. The container soon revolutionized ocean shipping, and TOFC and COFC (container-on-flatcar) services became a steadily growing component of North American railroad freight services. In 1955 U.S. railroads reported a modest total of just over 168,000 TOFC/COFC carloadings. Within a decade that figure grew to more than 1 million, and by 1985 it reached almost 5 million. Containers represented a steadily growing share of the traffic, and specially designed double-stack well cars were developed to handle the traffic in fast, dedicated trains. The successful development of TOFC/COFC traffic was a major contributor to the railroads' ability to finally halt a steady decline in freight traffic market share.

Steadily improving track and roadbed standards supported the transition to higher freight-train speeds and higher axle loadings. By the 1950s a growing number of railroads had adopted the use of continuously welded rail in place of jointed rail, a technology that reduced rail maintenance costs and equipment wear and tear, as well as improved ride quality. By 1960 almost 150,000 miles of U.S. railroads—almost two-thirds of the total mileage—were laid with rail weighing 100 pounds per yard or more. Such new construction technologies as welded steel and prestressed concrete came into common use for railroad structures.

In the postwar period several roads carried out major line relocations designed to reduce running times and increase operating efficiencies. In 1952, for example, the Burlington completed the Kansas City Shortcut that cut 22 miles and 136 curves off its Chicago–Kansas City route and reduced the maximum grade from 1.6 to 0.8 percent. In 1967 the Southern Pacific completed one of the largest such projects, the 78-mile Palmdale-Colton Cutoff that bypassed Los Angeles, cutting grades and saving 46 miles and eight complete circles of curvature for through freights moving between SP's San Joaquin Valley, Sunset, and Golden State routes.

The installation of CTC, which had proved very effective in increasing line capacity, accelerated after World War II. By 1950 more than 13,000 miles of U.S. railroads, double the 1945 level, were under CTC control, and this more than doubled again by 1960. Increasingly, radio and the microwave technologies developed during the war were applied to railroad communications. Railroads had been pioneers in the adoption of new types of automatic tabulating machines that had been introduced around the turn of the century, and they quickly moved into the use of the new electronic computers that emerged after the war for various accounting, payroll, inventory management, and other business tasks. Ultimately computers moved into applications in such diverse elements of railroad operations as car tracing, yard automation, dispatching, crew calling, operations simulation, and locomotive control.

During several postwar decades the railroads invested heavily in large modern hump yards, which typically absorbed the work of a number of smaller flat-switched or small hump yards. The application of electronic and emerging computer technologies permitted a steadily increasing level of automation of hump-yard operation. At the same time whole new categories of specialized load-

In the post–World War II period railroads transformed maintenance-of-way with innovative machinery that improved productivity. This modern Jackson 6500 tamping machine, for example, can compact ballast and realign track, using a laser guidance system. It was at work on a section of the Louisville & Nashville near Lowell, Indiana, in 1980. —William D. Middleton

ing equipment and terminal facilities were developed for efficient rail-truck or rail-ship interchange of the rapidly growing TOFC/COFC intermodal traffic.

New operating methods contributed to the efficiency of both passenger and freight operations. In 1959 the Chicago & North Western became the first North American railroad to employ the European concept of push-pull operation, in which a diesel or electric locomotive remained at one end of a train, with operation remotely controlled from a passenger-car cab at the opposite end of the train when the locomotive was at the rear. By eliminating the need to switch locomotives at the end of each run, push-pull operation significantly improved the efficiency of short-haul passenger movements and was widely adopted for commuter services, as well as some intercity services. In freight service radio control permitted the use of motive-power units distributed throughout a long train. Single-commodity unit trains moving, for example, between mine and power plant became increasingly common for such bulk traffic as coal. The increasing operation of interline run-through trains improved the timeliness and reliability of freight services.

Diesel-electric motive power continued to evolve in capacity into the new century. The most powerful diesel-electric locomotives of the immediate post–World War II period had been capable of no more than 1,500 hp from a single diesel engine; by the end of the century units powered by a single engine were rated as high as 6,000 hp. Such advances as steerable and high-adhesion trucks and sophisticated computer controls had significantly advanced diesel-electric efficiency as well. In 1955 diesel lo-

comotives on American railroads produced an average of 184 ton-miles per gallon of fuel consumed; by 2000 efficiency gains had more than doubled locomotive productivity to an average of 396 ton-miles per gallon.

Despite the steadily improving productivity and efficiency of the diesel-electric, however, there was new interest in electrification as freight traffic density continued to trend upward, an interest that took on new urgency with the energy crisis of the early 1970s and the sharp run-up in diesel fuel prices that came with it. Over the next decade more than a dozen railroads initiated electrification studies or at least seriously considered electrification. Several new mine-to-generating-plant coal lines completed during this period were seen as prototypes for this new era of electrification. But once again very little happened. A few more isolated coal lines and a British Columbia Railway coal-hauling branch were electrified. The only main-line electrification was an installation on the Mexican National Railways that never did go into full operation.

As money-losing intercity passenger services faded away, to be replaced by Amtrak in the United States and VIA Rail in Canada, there was a growing interest in high-speed trains for such high-density, intermediate corridors as the Washington–New York–Boston Northeast Corridor. In 1965 the Pennsylvania Railroad, with federal government assistance, launched a high-speed Metroliner program for the New York–Washington corridor, and a few years later innovative gas-turbine-powered, tilting Turbo-Trains entered demonstration service between New York and Boston. After the Amtrak startup in 1971 these efforts evolved into major federal programs that transformed the entire Washington-Boston corridor into a modern, electrically operated high-speed railroad by the end of the century, with Acela Express trains operating at maximum speeds of 150 mph over limited sections of the corridor.

The new national passenger carriers and new public agencies that began operating commuter services brought important advances in the equipment of ordinary passenger services as well. Amtrak experimented with gas-turbine trains and tilting Talgo trainsets of European origin and adopted high-capacity double-deck cars for much of its long-distance network. VIA Rail acquired Canadian-built tilting equipment for many of its eastern Canada services. Passenger-train steam heating systems were phased out in favor of more reliable electrical heating supplied from head-end power units.

Freight rolling stock continued to evolve, with still higher-capacity cars and heavier axle loadings. By 2000 the average U.S. freight-car capacity had reached nearly 93 tons, almost double what it had been in 1929. Significant improvements to freight-car technology included the development of self-steering trucks and devices that helped solve the problems of rocking and rolling or truck "hunting." End-of-train telemetry devices supplied performance information to train crews in the locomotive cab, allowing the elimination of the traditional caboose from almost all freight trains. As conventional air-braking systems were reaching their performance limits with increasing freight-train loadings and operating speeds, new electronically controlled pneumatic (ECP) braking systems were coming into use at the end of the century.

By the end of the century signaling and train control were on the edge of an era of transformation as new communications-based signaling technologies and location systems based upon global positioning satellites (GPS) began coming into use. The application of computers was pervasive in every area of railroad management and operations.

The development of high-speed services and ever-heavier freight-car axle loadings had brought new, higher standards for track systems. Continuous welded rail had become the standard for new or relaid track. By 2000 more than 94 percent of the U.S. rail network was laid with rail of 100 pounds per yard or more. For high-speed and heavy-haul track, concrete ties were taking the place of the timber ties that had served the industry very well from its earliest years. New high-speed turnouts with movable-point frogs were being introduced from Europe.

As North American railroads began a new century, they could look back on a century of extraordinary transformation in technology and operating practice that had brought the industry to levels of capacity, efficiency, and reliability that could hardly have been imagined in 1900. In 2000 U.S. railroad freight traffic reached almost 1,466 billion ton-miles, its highest level ever and more than ten times the 1900 level. And it was done with far fewer locomotives, cars, and railroad workers, and on a 168,535 track-mile railroad plant that had shed more than 90,000 miles of redundant track since 1900. One employee productivity measure suggests just how far the industry had come. In 1929 U.S. railroads generated just 300,000 freight ton-miles per employee. By 2000 that indicator had increased almost 30-fold, to 8.7 million ton-miles per employee.

Building a New Rail System

Don Phillips

World War II was a golden age for America. The world's greatest industrial power and millions of its people had joined with their allies to defeat the greatest military power in history. It was an age of clarity and certainty. America's railroads were tired but proud of their vital contributions. The railroad system had hauled 71 percent of all freight, 90 percent of military freight, and 90 percent of passengers, bending under the load but not breaking. Now the railroads were ready to enjoy the new prosperity of the postwar era.

But much had changed. Americans had resumed their affair with the automobile, and many had seen such new wonders as the German autobahns and jet aircraft. And American industry was ready to shift from its wartime production of bombers to passenger planes, and from assembling jeeps and tanks to building civilian automobiles and trucks. For a period the railroads fought to compete with the new highways and airways, but as the years passed, it seemed to be a losing battle. From 1947 to 1970 the railroads' share of freight ton-miles declined from 54 percent to 35 percent, while truck ton-miles tripled to 16 percent and pipelines doubled to 21 percent. River traffic remained constant at 28 percent. But that did not tell the whole story. Gradually, railroads were relegated to low-value bulk freight such as coal, while trucks and, slowly, planes began to take over the high-value freight. The decline in passenger service was worse, down to a negligible 1 percent.

Railroading in the second half of the twentieth century, in retrospect, can be divided into three eras. The first was the era of decline, when nothing railroads could do seemed to work. Next came railroading's near collapse in the late 1960s and 1970s that frightened the government into action. Finally came the era of recovery, leading now to a better but uncertain future.

The Era of Decline, 1945–1970

In many ways the railroads brought on their own problems in the postwar years. In hindsight, the greatest and most expensive failure of all was the unwise decision to spend many millions of dollars on modernizing passenger-train service. Many railroad officials felt that the passenger business could be profitably retained in the face of competition. After all, passenger trains were far more comfortable and reliable than the piston airplane and faster than the private automobile. The new gleaming streamliners would pack the passengers in and lead to greater expansion.

Railroaders largely underestimated Americans' new attachment to the automobile, and they had not yet dreamed of passenger jet aircraft. Almost everyone overlooked the effect of the war on both aviation technology and availability. Wartime air technology gave aviation a great leap forward in both technology and concrete. The need for accurate bombing led to increasingly sophisticated navigation, radar, and instrument landing systems. New military airports had sprouted around the world, and at war's end many of these airports were anxiously looking for civilian investment. The United States was the Allied country that built the multiengine bombers and transports of World War II, and thousands of planes like the durable C-47s, originally the DC-3, were available as military surplus for a song.

The railroaders also overlooked the fact that the passenger train was often the only way to go during the war. Rationing of rubber and gasoline literally forced Americans to travel by train. After the war, given the choice, a lot of them wanted to drive. And America spent a lot of money for brand-new highways while giving nothing to the railroads. In fact, railroads were treated as a cash cow by local and state governments across the country, often being taxed at a higher rate than other property.

In retrospect, the passenger train never stood a chance. But, for a while, the railroads did not understand what was happening. New streamliners sprang from the erecting floors of Budd, Pullman, and other builders. They were sleek, popular newsmakers, fun to ride and useful. The major railroads spent millions on passenger equipment. Americans rode familiar old names in a new dress such as the *Broadway Limited*, as well as sleek new trains such as the *California Zephyr*, which promised not only transportation but a view. Everyone had to have a streamliner. Passengers who continued to ride fast trains hauled by steam locomotives for a while after the war sometimes did not know that they were hauled by steam. Some of the

At the end of World War II the New York Central ordered 720 new streamlined cars, the largest new fleet anywhere in the United States. One of the products was the new all-coach *Pacemaker* streamliner in New York–Chicago service, seen here westbound at Rensselaer, New York, in May 1949. —William D. Middleton

most beautiful locomotives of the age were streamlined steam engines, such as Southern Pacific's Daylight 4-8-4s. A generation saw the Daylight every week at the opening of the *Superman* black-and-white television series, roaring along as the announcer intoned, "More powerful than a locomotive . . ."

But the fickle public had new love affairs, and the passenger train gradually retreated from the American dream. After hauling about three-quarters of all commercial passenger-miles in 1944, the railroad share sank to 47 percent by 1950 and 29 percent by 1960. The decline was worse than those numbers indicate because burgeoning highway travel is not counted in the statistics.

Some railroads such as the Santa Fe, Great Northern, and Atlantic Coast Line consistently worked to maintain passenger-train quality. Others deliberately provided deteriorating equipment, poor on-time performance, and onboard service that did not merit the name. State public service commissions had firm control over passenger-train discontinuances, often rejecting railroad train-off petitions for political and social reasons, disregarding railroad losses and poor passenger loadings. The best way to force the state to give in to the railroad abandonment petitions was to make the service so poor that almost no one would ride.

During this sad era railroading retreated from the American economic battlefield. A generation of railroad men knew nothing of real growth. They supervised a slow march to the rear of the transportation field. Luckily, the economy was growing rapidly, and there was enough freight to keep railroads running, but generally with economic returns of less than 2 percent. By the end of the 1960s rail freight service was fighting to hold on to economic crumbs, and rail passenger service was in horrible shape. But something new was about to happen.

It is somewhat of an oversimplification, but history now shows that one thing nearly killed railroading after World War II and one thing preserved it long enough to enter its era of recovery. Unbending and outdated government regulation nearly killed it, and General Motors' new diesel engine preserved it.

Regulation has a colorful history. Some historians say that every revolutionary new idea goes through at least three phases. First, it is just a quaint idea that will not amount to much. Next, it is the great salvation for mankind and everyone wants to own it or use it. Then, it becomes far too powerful and must be regulated. In fact, the rail industry was firmly crammed into the third camp by the Hepburn Act in 1906, during the Progressive Era when muckrakers and reformers roamed the land. The Interstate Commerce Commission, which had been all but asleep for years, was given nearly absolute new powers. The rail labor movement also was flexing its new muscles. And in 1917 the railroads were temporarily nationalized. The Transportation Act of 1920 and subsequent legislation in 1933 clamped even firmer controls on railroading.

As the Great Depression was ending, regulation was extended to the growing truck lines in 1935, to the airlines in 1938, and to the waterways in 1940. But there were such exceptions in the legislation that only 39 percent of truck traffic and 13 percent of barge traffic was affected. As the railroads declined, the ICC not only did nothing to help them but also clamped down harder and harder. They could not raise or lower freight rates, abandon track, discontinue a passenger train, or merge with another railroad without ICC approval.

One of the most destructive ICC practices of the era leading up to 1970 was the requirement that freight revenues be used to cross-subsidize passenger losses. The ICC had broad powers in this area because the Transportation Act of 1920 empowered it to control "exit" from any service. The underlying principle behind this power was, basically, that the ICC must protect the public good, and that included effectively requiring a railroad to use its profitable services to subsidize unprofitable ones. By the late 1960s passenger losses on freight revenues had grown so significant and draining for the railroads that the real possibility loomed of liquidation or nationalization, particularly in the Northeast. Criticism of the ICC grew, but no succeeding administration or Congress could reach consensus on what to do about it.

Railroad freight companies made tremendous technical progress during this period, with the spread of computers, centralized traffic control, automated hump yards, and other modernization. But railroads' real savior was the diesel locomotive. And not just any diesel locomotive but the General Motors concept of the diesel, which was the railroad equivalent of one size fits all. General Motors' Electro-Motive Division, the new boy on the block when it entered the business in the late 1930s, simply refused to listen to any railroad chief of motive power who wanted modifications. Any railroad that wanted a GM diesel would take the off-the-shelf version. It could be geared for passenger speeds or freight speeds, but that was the only significant option. This ran totally counter to railroad experience up to that date. In the steam era every locomotive type was custom built, with great differences from railroad to railroad and often within the same railroad.

There was a method to GM's heresy. The diesel was a different animal. It introduced a new word into the vocabulary: "transition." At low speeds the diesel power plant delivered electric current to the traction motors on the axles on an individual basis, called a series connection. Thus a lot of power went to each axle, good for low-

Orange Bowl Queen Carolyn Stroupe, 21, smashed a bottle of orange juice to inaugurate the Chicago & Eastern Illinois Railroad's all-new streamliner *Dixie Land* on the Chicago-Florida run on December 16, 1954. —*Trains* Magazine Collection

speed pull. As speed increased, however, the engine went through transition, switching to deliver the electricity in parallel, much like Christmas tree lights, with all axles connected to the same power wire. This allowed for greater pulling power at higher speeds. (Today, diesels are so powerful that transition is no longer necessary. They all operate in parallel.)

Electro-Motive's diesel salesmen also benefited from the luck of timing. The Santa Fe bought 69 of the new diesel-electric freight locomotives in 1940 just before the war broke out, for use in desert territory where steam locomotives suffered from bad water. By the war's end the Santa Fe engines and others sprinkled here and there across the railroad system had blown away the popular assumption that diesels were lightweight creatures that could not handle the rough-and-tumble of the main line.

Diesels had other advantages. Want more power? Connect together more diesel units controlled by the same engineer. Want to save brake shoes and eliminate wheel-cooling stops on heavy downgrades? Use dynamic brakes. Want a snazzy, good-looking paint style? Just turn it over to GM's styling studio. Most compelling of all, diesels could be operated with far fewer facilities and workers. By 1947, 90 percent of locomotive orders were for diesels.

The steam fraternity fought valiantly, squeezing greater efficiency from the steam engine compared with the tired 1920s-era engines that still mostly ran the railroads. Lima built the last commercial U.S. steam locomotive in 1949, while the N&W kept building steam locomotives until

1953. The end of steam came rapidly, far faster than would have been necessary if railroads simply ran steam to the end of its natural useful life. The last miles were run on Class 1 U.S. railroads in the spring of 1960. Almost in unison, the last few fires were dropped on N&W, Illinois Central, Grand Trunk Western, and Duluth, Missabe & Iron Range. Steam lasted much longer on some short-lines, but 1960 was the last gasp of regular-service steam for the big railroads.

The elimination of steam was devastating for the old railroad towns, such as Altoona, Pennsylvania, Havre, Montana, and Hornell, New York, and for many thousands of skilled laborers. There was no need any more for a boilermaker or a blacksmith. The relationship between rail labor and management had always been combative. In the postwar era labor seemed to be winning. Not only did labor win the right to run firemen on diesel locomotives, a practice that did not even begin to change for decades, but also railroads were very slow in eliminating employees even as freight and passenger service began to erode. The diesel eventually changed all that. Railroads employed 1.4 million people in 1946. By 1962 that number was cut in half to 700,000, and it has continued to sink in the years since.

Railroads changed dramatically between the war and the late 1960s. Centralized traffic control, mechanized roadway maintenance machinery, welded rail, train radio, more efficient diesel locomotives, roller bearings, and other innovations made railroading more efficient and safer, reduced the number of employees, and thereby kept the railroads running a little longer. As for the ICC, railroaders had grown accustomed to its rate and service dictates. It was easier to sell a customer on using your railroad with good liquor and a slap on the back than it was to get into the complicated problems of negotiating rates and service.

In the late 1950s and 1960s a few visionaries found artful and innovative ways to defy the system. One of these was fabled Southern Railway president D. W. Brosnan. Under Brosnan the Southern built dozens of automated hump yards across the system and was the first railroad to mechanize track maintenance. Brosnan was famous for distributing desk signs to all officers each year. One read, "It Can't Be Done," with the "t" crossed out. Another read, "YCSFSOYA." After a period of befuddlement, the meaning was deciphered: "You Can't Sell Freight Sitting on Your Ass." New and sometimes odd-looking railcars began appearing on the Southern. One was a giant car with big round glass portholes all over a slanted roof, designed to haul giant racks of flue-cured tobacco. Another, the Big John covered hopper car, was destined to go down in regulatory history. Defying an ICC order voiding lower Big John rates, Brosnan won a court order overturning the ICC. It was one of the most important regulatory rulings of the second half of the twentieth century.

D. W. "Bill" Brosnan was a man of vision, drive, and leadership who led the Southern Railway in making necessary changes and helped transform the North American railroad industry.
—Southern Railway, *Trains* Magazine Collection

Another visionary was trucker Malcolm McLean. He had an inspiration that almost no one recognized as important to railroads. On April 26, 1956, a beat-up old tub of a ship called the *Ideal X* wheezed out of New York harbor, bound for Houston with 58 shipping containers. McLean had refurbished the old ship to haul truck containers. He was so convinced he was right that he sold his trucking company, necessary under ICC rules prohibiting cross-ownership between modes. A trucker could not own a ship. Like many innovators, McLean was mocked. His old ship was too slow to ever compete with the big guys. What the big guys did not realize for a while was that when the *Ideal X* reached Houston, it could unload its cargo in a day and set sail again. Their ships sat for 10 days or more, unloading pallet by pallet. Speed at sea was almost irrelevant. Speed of loading was of prime economic importance.

Railroads did not catch on to intermodalism for many years, and even then it required many outsiders to force them to innovate. In fact, this became a pattern in the last half of the century, with outsiders dragging the railroads into the modern era. One of those early outsiders was United Parcel Service, today the railroads' largest single shipper. UPS approached the Atlantic Coast Line in 1966 with a problem. It was opening new routes from the Midwest to Florida, but Florida had a serious load imbalance, with 15 times more packages heading to Florida than leaving. No trucker could economically handle such an imbalance. Therefore, UPS persuaded its Teamster drivers that far more jobs would be created in local delivery in Florida if the railroads could get the trailers to Florida. UPS then set a pattern that would benefit railroads far more than they realized. First, it required dedicated "piggyback" trains, rejecting the common practice of hauling trailers on freight trains. Second, it demanded exacting service. In exchange, it would not quibble about rates. Within a short time UPS trains got the attention and pride once reserved for passenger trains.

Major mergers, largely moribund for decades, began picking up steam during this time. The cascade began in 1959 with the merger of the Norfolk & Western with its smaller rival, the Virginian. In 1960 came the merger of the Erie and the Delaware, Lackawanna & Western into the Erie Lackawanna. The Chessie System was formed by a combination of the Chesapeake & Ohio and the Baltimore & Ohio in 1963. The N&W took over the Nickel Plate Road and the Wabash in 1964. The Atlantic Coast Line and the Seaboard Air Line formed the Seaboard Coast Line in 1967. And in 1970 the Burlington Northern was formed from the Great Northern, the Northern Pacific, the Burlington, and the Spokane, Portland & Seattle. But the greatest merger of all, and the most disastrous, was the combination of the Pennsylvania Railroad and the New York Central into the new Penn Central. The Senate Commerce Committee summed up the cascading mergers as a decade of debilitating combinations that started innocently with N&W and Virginian:

That merger unleashed a wave of mergers that did not expire until the entire eastern rail system was completely restructured and the Penn Central, the great house of cards, had been created. The Virginian-N&W merger ended the New York Central's access to the Pocahontas coal territory. With its valuable coal traffic threatened, the New York Central sought protection in a merger with the B&O. Pressed to consider merger, the B&O decided to merge instead in a two-way arrangement with the C&O.

When the C&O and the B&O merged, the N&W was threatened because it gave the C&O access to St. Louis and to transcontinental traffic. To counter this move, the N&W merged with the Nickel Plate and the Wabash railroads, an affiliation that, in a sense, "one-upped" the C&O-B&O since it gave the N&W access not only to St. Louis but to Chicago, Kansas City and Omaha as well. These moves placed the New York Central in even greater jeopardy.

With what it regarded as its more desirable partners having already merged, the NYC finally agreed to join with the Pennsylvania in their ill-fated union. When the Penn Central merger was authorized in 1968, only 10 years had passed since the Virginian-N&W merger, but the entire eastern railroad industry had been restructured.

The *New Yorker* magazine announced the arrival of the new Penn Central in 1966. —© The New Yorker Collection, 1966, Frank Modell. From cartoonbank.com. All rights reserved

The possibility of an NYC-Pennsy merger was first broached in 1957 by PRR chief executive James M. Symes, but the New York Central was more interested in a combination of the NYC, the B&O, and the C&O. However, later in the 1960s a new PRR chairman, Stuart Saunders, again approached the New York Central and its talented new top man, Alfred E. Perlman. Perlman was reluctant, but with everyone else newly merged with someone else, he had no alternative. The dynamic and politically well-connected Saunders fairly forced the merger through the political and regulatory process. The ICC approved it in 1966, but consummation was delayed for two years by a suspicious Justice Department and various lawsuits. With Supreme Court approval, the Penn Central became a reality on February 1, 1968. The few clear-eyed critics were bowled over by the political and legal muscle of Saunders and his soldiers.

With perfect hindsight, it is difficult to understand why Saunders did not run from this overburdened merger. Among other things, the ICC saddled the Penn Central with the New Haven Railroad as a condition of approval. With the bankrupt New Haven came its $24 million per year loss. And Saunders, remarkably, agreed with the 24 railroad brotherhoods involved to guarantee all current employees a job to retirement, plus rehiring 5,000 laid-off workers.

While the ICC dithered for five years considering the merger and the Justice Department challenged in court, Saunders did everything possible to pretend that nothing was wrong. He cut back sharply on maintenance and failed to make needed investments. Unbelievably, the Penn Central actually paid a dividend in 1968 that amounted to 63 percent of reported net income, simply to mask the company's true condition. Losses of $250,000 a day, rather than shrinking toward profits, mounted to $500,000 and then $1 million a day. Then, at the worst of all possible times, a major blizzard struck the East in January and February 1970. And the economy also took a downturn.

The Great Railway Crisis, published in 1976 in limited numbers by the National Academy of Public Administration and now a collector's item, summed up the closing days of the decade this way: "As the late 1960s wore on, actual government policy toward the railroads still consisted of excessive regulation, no promotion, 'muddling through,' and hoping for the best. In a democracy, it often takes a crisis—a war, a depression, urban riots, or a series of bankruptcies—to galvanize action and create the conditions for a decisive breakthrough. The railroad men had been staving off disaster for so long, it began to seem as if they could do so forever. . . . Moreover, so long as there was not a manifest breakdown, any level of performance might be regarded as satisfactory or at least tolerable. But the manifest breakdown soon came."

Disaster and Redemption, 1970–Early 1980s

The 1970s dawned with a railroad problem of epic proportions, but hardly anyone realized it. There was blessed ignorance almost everywhere that cold January, even though what happened would determine the fate of the railroad industry for many decades into the future. Audits by the Penn Central's prestigious accounting firm Peat, Marwick & Mitchell had offered hardly more than a hint of anything amiss. Standard auditing procedures simply did not pick up what was happening—a severe blow to the reputation of the old-line auditing firm. But Congress and the Nixon White House soon began to feel serious heat. To anyone who could slice through the obfuscation and cast a realistic eye over the railroad, nothing was going well at Penn Central.

The first hint came when Saunders approached the new secretary of the Department of Transportation, John Volpe, to say that the severe winter of 1969–1970 had left Penn Central in need of a $50 million loan to tide it over. No private lender would supply the necessary money without a federal guarantee. True, it had been a severe winter. Penn Central, in fact, had actually lost an entire coal train under the snow, and the crew did not remember where it was. Several management trainees were sent out with snowshoes and probes to find it.

Volpe told Saunders that he would talk to Treasury Secretary David Kennedy and others about the loan. He then directed Transportation Under Secretary James Beggs to look into the matter. Beggs had great difficulty getting straight information, but when he did, he was shocked. Penn Central was surviving only on credit. And $50 million was almost a joke. Beggs estimated that the railroad would need at least $200 million or it would soon go bankrupt.

Nixon faced a dilemma. Many of his top administration officials had long-standing business and personal relationships with top Penn Central creditors, and a former Nixon law partner, Robert Guthrie, had been retained by the Penn Central. The administration formulated a bait-and-switch plan in which the Defense Department would supply the $200 million under a twisted interpretation of the Defense Production Act, and the Transportation Department then would repay the Defense Department from new legislation to authorize $750 million in loans to railroads.

This house of cards tumbled when the scheme ran head-on into Wright Patman of Texas, chairman of the House Committee on Banking and Currency. Patman already knew a lot about what was going on. The personally conservative Patman had been angered by a series of documents and photographs, including some nude photographs of female flight attendants aboard the Penn Central private aircraft, taken by top officials—not Saunders, according to Patman aides—who were not exactly thinking about railroad matters.

Word then leaked out about the unbelievably bad state of the largest merger in U.S. history. As a run began on Penn Central stock, and the board fired Saunders and other top officers, there came the largest bankruptcy in U.S. history. The board voted to seek protection under Section 77 of the Bankruptcy Act. On Sunday morning, June 21, Penn Central attorneys went to the home of U.S. District Judge C. William Craft, Jr., to file bankruptcy papers. Penn Central, once the darling of Wall Street, survived as a going concern for 873 days.

Worse, the weather did not improve. Hurricane Agnes came rumbling up the East Coast, doing serious damage to railroad property. In a short time several other storm-damaged railroads were forced into bankruptcy: the Reading, the Lehigh Valley, the Jersey Central, the Boston & Maine, and the Erie Lackawanna. All filed under Section 77, which provides protection from creditors while the railroad reorganizes. However, reorganization cannot drone on forever. The Fifth Amendment to the Constitution says that the government cannot take private property without just compensation. Therefore, a "taking" cannot result in serious erosion of a bankrupt estate while it is being reorganized.

Onto the scene stepped one of the now-legendary figures of the era, Judge John P. Fullam of the U.S. District Court for the Eastern District of Pennsylvania. For the next few years the skillful Fullam kept the heat on the government by repeatedly reminding everyone that a solution would have to come soon or he would be forced to allow the creditors to liquidate the property. This pressure was key to the congressional action that followed.

Congress was very busy with railroad matters for the first few years of the 1970s. It formed Amtrak on May 1, 1971, to take the passenger train's financial burden off sinking freight railroads, too late to be of any help in avoiding the eastern bankruptcies. And in 1973, when it became obvious that a standard reorganization would not work for the Penn Central and other railroads, Congress passed a series of groundbreaking bills that led to revolutionary changes in the federal relationship with railroads. Only the federal takeover of the railroads in World War I was more drastic, and that had been temporary.

In fact, four revolutions hit railroading in the 1970s and early 1980s: the formation of Conrail from the ashes of bankrupt eastern railroading, the formation of a new national passenger-train system, the rise of intermodal freight, and the nearly total deregulation of the railroads. Once again, the American political system proved that often it works decisively only in a crisis.

Onto the 1970s stage stepped a cast of railroaders who would play a major role on the railroad scene for most of the rest of the century. Many of them had been trained on the New York Central in such then-revolutionary practices as marketing, under the legendary Alfred Perlman. They included such men as James Hagen, 38, and James McClellan, 31. McClellan was one of many who had worked for the forward-looking "green team" at New York Central, but left in 1968 when the Pennsylvania Railroad "red team" effectively took over. Hagen, McClellan, and others were attracted to the Federal Railroad administration by FRA Administrator John Ingram, a plainspoken but talented leader. (Ingram later became the last president of the Rock Island Railroad.) Veterans of the political process also rose to the occasion, including John Barnum, the deputy transportation secretary who was the key contact with the Nixon administration, William Loftus of the DOT, who later played a key role in restructuring midwestern railroading, and a number of members of Congress, led by Congressman Brock Adams, a Washington State Democrat.

It became clear to Judge Fullam in early 1973 that the standard reorganization would not work. The broken-down Penn Central was too saddled with excess employees and excess track that the bankruptcy trustees had made no progress in shedding. It was still in the grip of the ICC, state public service commissions, and the unions, none of which would move rapidly enough toward change, if they moved at all.

Early in 1973 the trustees made a desperate move that became a turning point in the crisis. They ordered that crew consists be arbitrarily reduced. In those days train crews were made up of five or six men: an engineer, a fireman, and a head brakeman on the locomotive and a conductor and one or two rear brakemen on the caboose. The unions felt that they had been backed into a corner and had no choice. When the new crew levels were implemented on February 8, they went on strike. The strike lasted only a few hours. By 4 P.M. that day Congress had passed Senate Joint Resolution 59 ordering the strikers back to work. The resolution also put a freeze on crew consists for 90 days, but more important, it ordered the secretary of transportation to submit within 45 days a plan for preserving essential rail services in the Northeast.

It was as if Washington had awakened from a sleep. The railroad crisis was back on the front burner. On March 6 Fullam added even more pressure. He ordered the trustees to come up with either a reorganization plan or a liquidation plan by July 2. Fullam said that it was doubtful that he could properly allow the railroad to continue running past October 1. "It seems clear that the point of unconstitutionality is fast approaching if it has not already arrived," he wrote. Fullam would prove flexible many times during the next few years, as long as he could see solid progress. But repeatedly the judge made clear that his patience was limited.

Complicating this period of history was the Watergate crisis, which also began to unravel in March 1973 and led 17 months later to Nixon's resignation. It is remarkable that during this period of political and constitutional turmoil and its aftermath, the government basically saved the railroad industry.

The process of putting together vital legislation in only five months is itself worthy of a book. But the process proves that when there is a true crisis, Congress is capable of teaming with industry, the courts, the White House, creditors, shippers, and many others to develop solutions. The end result was the Regional Rail Reorganization Act of 1973, known as the 3R Act. Even though many legislators had not even seen a copy, the bill passed the House on December 20 by a vote of 284 to 59 and the Senate on December 21 by 45 to 16. Nixon signed the bill into law on January 2, 1974, saying that while it spent more money than he liked and he did not agree with all aspects of the bill, "[it] represents an appropriate legislative compromise."

The act created a remarkable new organization, the U.S. Railway Assn. The USRA was to be a temporary agency with an unusual set of powers. The government created it, but it was not a government agency. It was not exactly a private agency either because it had many government powers. It was to develop a plan to save the railroad industry, and it could do things that no other entity could have done since early in the century when the government firmly regulated the industry. That included abandoning track throughout the East without the permission of the ICC or any state agency.

Congress wisely limited itself to reviewing the USRA's plan at the end of the process, giving the USRA full freedom to develop its plan without interference. The Nixon administration had only limited powers over the USRA through 3 members on its 11-member board of directors. As *The Great Railway Crisis* described it: "A great deal of money, hope and faith were thereby placed in an organization which did not yet exist, to be run by people not yet hired, to be governed by a board not yet selected, with its operations to be conducted according to policies, methods, rules and regulations, the majority of which had not yet been devised."

The USRA was on a tight schedule. Assuming that the new agency could be organized by early April, it would have only six months to perform the preliminary version of one of the most comprehensive industrial planning efforts in U.S. history. The result was to be the Preliminary System Plan, the last major step before the agency was to present a final plan. Already, preliminary planning was under way in the Federal Railroad Administration, with the process being led by James McClellan and another young analyst, Gerald Davies. Those names would be heard repeatedly over the next few years as they eventually moved to the USRA and to other positions affecting railroad history. The first task of the FRA group, among many other things, was to determine how many miles of track among the 61,184 miles at hand could be abandoned, a potentially dangerous political move. The process became a work of faith because the men worked with only semireliable data. It was clear that some mistakes would be made and the proposed cuts could not be considered final. Working against a tight deadline, they produced what became known as the "orange line report" of 15,575 miles of "potentially excess" line. That was 25 percent of mileage but only 4 percent of rail traffic, a good indication of why Penn Central was in trouble. The orange line report was only one small part of the overall effort, but the question of line abandonments and whether some lines could be saved with state or local subsidies was a continuous public concern even when more important tasks gained no notoriety.

The USRA officially came into existence on February 1, 1974, but weeks of staffing and selection of a board of directors lay ahead. There were no guarantees of jobs after the process was completed and the USRA went out of business. In fact, there were no retirement benefits and certainly no job security. Therefore, the USRA tended to attract just the kind of employees it needed: risk takers who loved a challenge. Seldom have so many of the right people been in the right place at the right time, starting with Chairman Arthur Lewis and President Edward Jordan (later chairman of Conrail). The 11-person board included men from railroading, labor, politics, and government who overcame some natural friction to work amazingly well together—such men as former Pennsylvania governor William Scranton, Rio Grande president Gale Aydelott, and United Transportation Union vice president James Burke.

Three members were from government, including two successive transportation secretaries: Claude Brinegar, an even-tempered man with a corporate background who led the Nixon team during the early stages of the process, and his successor, William T. Coleman, who never really believed in Conrail. By far the most valuable government board member, however, was Deputy Transportation Secretary John Barnum. Few USRA officials worked harder and with more dedication.

At the top of a talented staff were many who later became rail industry leaders. All seemed to understand that they were the gang who would either save the private-sector railroad industry or officiate at its burial. Many worked seven-day weeks for several hundred days without a break. There were colossal blunders, but mostly the staff plunged ahead into brilliant or lucky territory.

McClellan, at first informally, began a practice that proved valuable in zeroing in on issues, the "white paper," in which he spelled out some specific issue in 10 to 30 pages of copy that had the McClellan touch for good writing, clear thinking, wry humor, and weird dreaming. Very quickly the white-paper process was formalized, with McClellan producing a paper just before major decisions were due, increasingly with input and editing by other staff members. With such titles as "The Precarious Condition of American Railroads," "Alternatives for Conrail Operations in the Northeast Corridor," and "Valuation," these white papers became the basis for chapters in the upcoming Preliminary System Plan. During the critical period of late 1974 and early 1975 they became the central theme of staff decisions and board debates.

In late 1974 the deadlines in the planning process were advanced 120 days because of earlier delays in appointment and confirmation of the USRA board. Congress appeared so pleased with the USRA, and so happy it was not doing the dirty work, that it gladly agreed. The USRA staff and board spent much of this time actively debating which form the new rail system would take. Almost everything was on the table, from formation of a giant single eastern railroad system to "controlled liquidation" in which the Penn Central and the other eastern railroads would be divided between other freight railroads, Amtrak, commuter lines, and port authorities.

The USRA was living under a tight requirement. The agency must opt either for a free-enterprise solution or for government ownership and operation. As the work dragged on, it became clear to many in the USRA that nothing they could develop would work. There was a feeling of impending doom. One night, when some of the staffers were having their customary after-work drink in the bar across the street, McClellan and Gary Collins, USRA chief of interstate routes, began doodling on cocktail napkins. The doodling grew more intense. Using one napkin after another, McClellan and Collins drew up a plan under which eastern railroading would be divided under a new Conrail, with chunks such as the Erie Lackawanna and the Reading going to the Chessie and the Norfolk & Western.

Sweeping up the cocktail napkins and striding back to USRA headquarters, McClellan and Collins found that no one had left. As the two laid out the napkins and explained their plan to the others, a sense of excitement grew. This could be the solution. The next morning, in a more sober condition, McClellan and Collins presented the plan to Jordan, who looked at them with some amusement and said, "You mean you had this answer all the time? Why didn't you tell me before?"

The board itself was keenly interested but not quite as enthusiastic when the plan was presented to it on January 17, and it continued to discuss various other options. But in the end it had no choice, given the negative financial analysis of other options. The three-system plan was the solution. Like many "great ideas," this one fell on its face many months later when the Chessie and the N&W, and later the Southern, scoffed at it or simply withdrew or ran into union problems. But it allowed the USRA to honestly report that it had found a plan that would work. It kept the process moving.

Numerous other issues were proceeding simultaneously, including labor negotiations and branch-line abandonment. The period leading up to the Preliminary System Plan on February 26, 1975, became known as a time of sweetness and light, with general cooperation between the USRA and the Transportation Department, and with Congress happy to let the process proceed. Every court decision went in the USRA's favor.

Things changed when the Preliminary System Plan was released, for a variety of reasons, especially when states and local governments saw the potential for massive branch-line abandonments. The complications of the ensuing negotiations and battles have filled whole books, but none of these changed a basic fact: something had to be done. Congress simply had not provided enough money to allow any plan to work. At one time the USRA staff thought that as much as $6 billion would be required. Although this estimate was later cut roughly in half, history showed that this amount was exactly what was spent.

Nonetheless, the estimate was more than three times the amount Congress had planned. This meant that despite the overall complexity of the plan, the debate around the country and in Congress boiled down to two items, branch-line abandonment and how to fund the new railroad. Inside the USRA staff, however, the debate continued over what form the new system should take.

William T. Coleman, a Philadelphia attorney, replaced the mild-mannered Brinegar as U.S. secretary of transportation in the spring of 1975. Sparks flew for the duration of the Conrail debate, with Coleman angrily questioning or attempting to reverse almost every decision, the sole result of which seemed to be that Congress's support for the USRA increased. Barnum later said that he thought it was comical that his position as DOT's "bad guy" suddenly changed to DOT's "good guy" when Coleman arrived.

As the final system plan took shape, it became obvious that new legislation would be required to implement a final plan. It began life as the Railroad Revitalization and Regulatory Reform Act (the 4R Act). And partly because of the nastiness between Coleman and Congress, the original legislation effectively froze the administration out of any meaningful role in the implementation of the new Conrail and the Northeast Corridor, which the legislation removed from Conrail and gave to Amtrak.

At the end of 1975, with the holidays approaching, both houses passed the bill overwhelmingly. But the fireworks were just beginning. Coleman had strongly recommended a veto to President Gerald Ford, and it was uncertain that Congress could override a veto. Senator Vance Hartke (D-Ind.), chairman of the Senate Subcommittee on Surface Transportation, pulled a trick that had never before been pulled in Congress. He had the bill "held at the desk" in the Senate, not giving Ford a chance to veto it but also not allowing it to become law. The idea

was to effectively rewrite parts of the bill in consultation with the White House, then quickly pass it again. That accomplished two things: it gave proponents time to develop a strategy, and it increased pressure on the White House as, day by day, the planned April 1, 1976, formation of Conrail drew closer.

Ford was different from Nixon in many ways. As a former House leader himself, Ford was intimately familiar with the legislative process, and he was kept informed on the progress of the Conrail legislation. Working around Coleman, Hartke cut a deal with Ford and his lieutenants. Congress would work with the Ford administration on a slightly new bill. Since there was animosity between Hartke and Coleman, it was agreed that neither of them would attend the compromise sessions. A final compromise was indeed reached after days of angst-filled negotiations. Ford signed the bill on February 5, 1976.

But at the signing ceremony Coleman got a shock. He learned in a casual conversation with Chessie chairman Hays Watkins that the three-system plan, now including Chessie and the Southern Railway but not the N&W, was close to unraveling. A little-noticed part of the 1973 3R legislation had required organized labor to agree on employee-protection provisions before either railroad could take over any part of the bankrupt eastern railroads, and there was a labor-management stalemate. Coleman swung into action, but he could do little despite his best efforts. At the last minute the three-system plan failed. For good or ill, "big Conrail" was a reality. The final conveyance documents alone were massive, 2,000 separate documents adding up to 30,000 pages, plus huge

The new Conrail that emerged from the wreckage of PC was an unexpected success and ultimately became a merger target for other lines. In August 1986 General Electric C30-7A units powered eastbound and westbound Conrail freights just west of State Line Tunnel on the old Boston & Albany between New York and Massachusetts. —William D. Middleton

numbers of computer printouts and maps. Then, at one minute past midnight on April 1, Conrail was born.

The first day went smoothly, with only one glitch of note. Someone had forgotten to convey a 2.9-mile section of track in northeastern Indiana, suddenly halting the Amtrak train *James Whitcomb Riley*. The passengers were bused the rest of the way while the glitch was corrected.

Final success was still not assured, however, and the remainder of the 1970s was touch-and-go for Conrail. But emerging from the Conrail experience was the solid beginnings of deregulation of the railroads, including the 4R Act of 1976, which was far more than just a piece of legislation to help Conrail. All railroads would be protected from discriminatory taxation, among other things, and the ICC was given tight deadlines for approving or disapproving mergers. And importantly, the 4R Act established the principle that if railway service was mandated in the public service, the public would pay for the service.

While it got little notice among the general public, one of the most important USRA decisions was to designate which properties would be transferred to Conrail and which could be returned to the estate of the bankrupt Penn Central. Making all such decisions was USRA's Victor Hand and his small staff. Hand's decisions could be appealed to top USRA officials, and many were. Some went to court. But he was never overturned. Hand, a well-known photographer, as well as an experienced railroad real estate consultant, impressed many federal judges with his encyclopedic memory of the railroad and his quick and comprehensive reasons why a particular piece of real estate was needed for railroad purposes.

One of Hand's decisions was to keep several valuable pieces of real estate in the Albany, New York, area because they might be needed some day for high-speed passenger-train service. Today, passenger trains run at up to 120 mph on some of his track decisions. In later years, as we will see, his knowledge of this era became a valuable tool in Norfolk Southern's battle with CSX over how to split Conrail.

The Intermodalism Challenge

While the USRA struggled to save eastern railroading and the new Conrail crew struggled to produce profitability, another sea change was approaching the railroad industry in the 1970s. At first timidly, then with outright opposition from many railroaders, and finally with a stubborn push from shippers and railroad dreamers, the intermodal revolution appeared.

"Piggyback" transportation had existed for decades; some of the early efforts could be traced back to the nineteenth century. But as the 1970s dawned, railroading was still on a boxcar standard. UPS was moving some of its trailers on a few special trains, and many freight trains had a few flatcars carrying trucks mixed in with its boxcars and hoppers and tank cars. There were even some all-piggyback trains. The Trailer Train Corp. had been in existence since 1955. But those were the exceptions. Even as

traffic grew, American railroading had only marginal interest in piggyback.

The railroad industry struggled throughout the 1960s to decide what to do with this new beast. Something happened to change boxcar railroading in the 1970s, however. In truth, many things came together, including rail deregulation legislation in 1980, which freed railroading from government interference. And from outside the railroad industry came a constant push for trailer-on-flatcar (TOFC) and container-on-flatcar (COFC) service not just from UPS, but from steamship lines and industries.

But few things made such an impact as the stubborn dedication of two bureaucrats at the Federal Railroad Administration, David DeBoer and Bill Edson, both veterans of the New York Central in the pre–Penn Central era. In combination with some forward-thinking railroaders, these two had a major impact on the future of railroading.

The federal government's entry into intermodalism began in 1971 when Bill Loftus of the FRA called a meeting in Washington to discuss the economic research budget. The budget was a tiny $50,000, which had to be spread across all projects. That left no doubt that there could never be railroad economic research without the active economic cooperation of the railroads, something that was always difficult to obtain. Intermodal research fell to DeBoer.

DeBoer, putting enthusiasm ahead of realism, pushed ahead with a plan to spread true intermodalism to the rail industry. His New York Central experience had taught him how railroading really works; his government experience had taught him that nothing changes easily or overnight, and that who you know is often more important than what you know. He also had Edson, the consummate brilliant numbers man.

One of the most important intermodal projects ever conceived, which set the pattern for the future, was the Illinois Central Gulf–Norfolk & Western "Slingshot" service from Chicago to St. Louis in the mid-1970s. In those prederegulation days, operating this service was not easy under the best of circumstances because it required approval of a slow-moving ICC and some stubborn unions (these trains would be operated with two-man crews and no caboose in an era when unions were fighting to keep the four- and five-man crew).

But in an amazing confluence of events, the federal government firmly backed the concept, with DeBoer and Edson on the scene and pushing enthusiastically. They were not the only two players, of course. Another was George Stern of the Illinois Central Gulf, an intermodal partisan. Throughout railroading were men who dreamed of fast, frequent intermodal trains, although senior management shot them down more often than not. In some ways DeBoer and Edson were merely facilitators for these visionary railroaders.

The first and potentially most damaging hurdle was the ICC, then still powerful but under growing pressure and criticism. Such an interline arrangement would be subject to ICC approval, which could take years. Stern decided to test the ICC first, paying a visit to ICC chairman Virginia Mae Brown, the commission's first woman chairman, known as "Peaches." Brown was noncommittal, but approval came in an amazing two weeks.

The next hurdle was rail labor. A meeting was arranged on January 14, 1975, between ICG officials and union representatives, led by Eugene Abbott, general chairman of the United Transportation Union. Stern later called the meeting at a Holiday Inn in Bloomington, Illinois, "one of the most fateful sessions in railroad history." Stern made the two-man-crew concept as attractive as possible. There would be three trains a day, meaning that employment would be increased, and the crews would be home every night. What was more, they would be paid at a four-day rate for just eight hours work.

Stern later wrote that the 62-year-old Abbott, swilling coffee and popping a nitroglycerine pill for his bad heart, turned introspective. He had presided over 25 years of massive job losses, made worse by an ongoing recession, and his people were demanding to know what he was doing for them. "Gene said he would like to believe he could put his men to work, but how could he trust management? Would management run the new train service for one week right then? If management would run one train for five days right then, even though there was no traffic, he would negotiate and assist in development of the new service." John Lange, ICG's director of labor relations, immediately extended his hand across the table. No one knew if upper rail management or labor rank and file would ever agree, but a historic hurdle had been crossed.

The miracles continued. As expected, almost every cor-

One of the earliest railroads to offer scheduled intermodal service was the Milwaukee Road, which began operating its fast Sprint trains between Chicago and Minneapolis in 1979. Powered by a single unit, a short eastbound Sprint flew through Columbus, Wisconsin, in May 1980. —William D. Middleton

BUILDING A NEW RAIL SYSTEM

porate officer at ICG said, "No way, won't happen; the company cannot invest in such a risky venture." But the negativism did not come from the one man who counted, ICG president Alan Boyd, who had been the country's first transportation secretary and second president of Amtrak. Stern remembers Boyd saying that "if the service was not successful in the first six months, or in the second six months, he would be in favor of giving it a third six months." Equally surprisingly, organized labor also agreed.

The icing on the cake was when Bill Maisch of United Parcel Service agreed on August 7, one week before startup, to buy half of one train. Stern remembered Maisch as saying that "he felt UPS had a stake in the piggyback business and should support innovation whenever and wherever it reasonably could." Thus the Slingshot was born.

Congress, with strong testimony from the ICG, appropriated $6 million for an intermodal demonstration project. There was a price for innovation, however. The FRA ruled that no existing service would qualify for subsidies, leaving ICG out in the cold financially. But the Slingshot service continued nonetheless.

That left DeBoer and his $6 million to go looking for another project. It was not easy. Some routes were not right, and several railroads just were not interested. But a cash-starved Milwaukee Road took the bait for a Chicago–Twin Cities run, much to the consternation of the Chicago & North Western, which earlier had sniffed at a similar idea. The project, called the Sprint, was highly successful, benefiting from a winter of terrible driving conditions and a trucker owner-operator sickout in June 1979. UPS and the Postal Service also jumped on board. The die was cast. Other railroads began to make similar deals. Equipment improved. Various intermodal plans

were tried. But two events catapulted intermodalism to the forefront of the railroad experience.

First, there were two new faces at the Interstate Commerce Commission, beginning in 1978 with Chairman A. Daniel O'Neal. This former Senate staff member dropped a bomb on the old agency, beginning the process of deregulation. At a meeting in 1979 O'Neal announced that the commission had voted to deregulate shipments of perishables by rail. The cumbersome rate bureaus had just seen the beginning of the end. Succeeding O'Neal was Darius Gaskins, who not only was a deregulator but who took over just as Congress passed the Staggers Rail Act of 1980. Gaskins had his marching orders—deregulate, deregulate, deregulate—and he complied with zeal and passion. An early and important decision came on November 19, 1980, when the commission announced deregulation of intermodal traffic. The final order, effective on March 23, 1981, covered all intermodal, both domestic and international. Growth in the intermodal industry has been spectacular since.

The second major event was the emergence of the double-stack car, developed and pushed strongly by two shipping lines. First American President Lines and then Sea Land Services fought not only to use double-stack service but also to own their own fleets. The hero of this era was Don Orris of APL, who all but browbeat the railroad industry into running his double-stack trains and sharing the cost saving with APL. For the rest of the century intermodal became *the* railroad growth business. It was already a slow-growth business, rising to 3 million loadings from almost nothing between 1955 and 1980. But between 1980 and 1990 business doubled to 6 million loadings. By 2000 loadings surpassed 9 million, then

Double-stack container trains were linked with huge post-panamax (too large for the Panama Canal) container ships at enormous intermodal terminals. At the modern Deltaport terminal near Vancouver, British Columbia, opened in 1967, this 170-foot-wide rail-mounted gantry straddles the entire intermodal yard, moving 30 containers an hour. —William D. Middleton

spiked upward to 11 million in 2004. By late 2002 intermodal revenue surpassed coal revenue for the first time. By 2004 intermodal constituted 23 percent of rail revenue, and coal 21.5 percent. And in 2004 intermodal loadings shot up 10.4 percent, while carload traffic increased 2.9 percent.

The Passenger-Train Challenge

While intermodal and other railroad freight business was all but ignored by the public, something much less significant was getting constant attention—rail passenger service. From the point of view of the economy and social usefulness, rail passenger service in America is hardly a yawn. The only exceptions are rail commuter operations in New York and Chicago and intercity rail traffic between New York and Washington. But from the point of view of the public, passenger service *is* railroading. That was true even when the public first deserted the passenger train for the airplane and the automobile. Even if it did not ride, it wanted the trains to run through the old hometown, with the whistle moaning in the night. The ICC seemed to like that moaning whistle too, with its policy of forcing freight revenues to subsidize the "public service" of passenger trains. But it was railroad treasurers who were moaning loudest.

The survival of the passenger train can largely be traced to Lyndon Johnson's effort to win a second term, Stuart Saunders's campaign to win approval of the Penn Central merger, and the well-publicized dreams of a certain northeastern senator. The decision to form Amtrak in 1971 was just one more stop along the way to a passenger train revival, not the passenger train's great salvation.

The passenger train's revival can be traced to May 20, 1962, when freshman senator Claiborne Pell (D-R.I.) made his fabled "megalopolis" speech on the Senate floor. The heart of Pell's speech was a learned discussion of passenger travel in the increasingly crowded Northeast. He suggested a nine-state compact to borrow money at low interest rates to modernize and speed passenger service, organized along the lines of the New York Port Authority. His conclusion was prophetic: "The answer is to divide the railroad system into a public authority that would carry passengers while the existing private companies would continue their more profitable function of hauling freight."

One senator and one speech are not enough, of course, but Pell's timing was excellent. His speech gained an unusual amount of attention, including that of John F. Kennedy and, later, Lyndon Johnson. Kennedy established a White House task force in May 1963 to recommend a coordinated program of development of road, rail, and air facilities between Boston and Washington. The study was completed just a few days before Kennedy's assassination.

Then Johnson suddenly became president and began to realize that he would need votes in the Northeast if a Texan such as he was ever to be elected on his own. What was more, he immediately began a crusade to enact almost every piece of legislation and every idea still pending when Kennedy died. He was amazingly successful, probably more successful than Kennedy would have been.

The White House task force report lay dormant for months, until suddenly it resurfaced in June 1964, just months before the 1964 elections. But Johnson took far grander steps than just a publicity stunt to gain votes. He ordered more detailed studies and, in August, formed the Northeast Corridor Project. Pell played a key role in Johnson's decision making. A year later, on September 30, 1965, Johnson signed into law new Northeast Corridor legislation, saying, "An astronaut can orbit the earth faster than a man on the ground can get from New York to Washington."

The bill authorized only $20 million the first year and $35 million each year thereafter. But Johnson had an ace in the hole. The Pennsylvania Railroad and the New York Central had applied to merge, and there was no way that Stuart Saunders was about to anger Johnson at such a critical time. The only possible answer was "yes, sir." Johnson announced what was already an open secret: the Pennsylvania and the New Haven would purchase new high-speed trains, with the specifications going to the builders within two weeks. And roadbed would be upgraded to handle 125 mph speeds. Saunders gushingly predicted 150 mph speeds within five years, and profitable operations.

The first Metroliner round trip began on January 16, 1969, to rave reviews. By that time the secretly cash-pressed railroad, then successfully merged into the Penn Central, had spent $35 million to improve its roadbed and was investing $21.5 million for the new cars, a substantial amount for the time. The new cars rode roughly. They bounced a lot, and it was sometimes difficult to walk down the aisle. But no one seemed to notice. There was almost a battle at ticket counters to get a seat on the new train. The *New York Times* called patronage "astonishingly good." But even as Saunders beamed at the positive publicity, bankruptcy was slightly more than a year away. With that bankruptcy came the growing realization that railroads could no longer handle the financial burden of the passenger train. Even before the bankruptcy, the railroad industry and Congress had begun to explore ways to ease the crushing burden while still operating passenger trains.

Even the ICC got into the act, recommending on July 16, 1969, that passenger trains receive government subsidies if the railroads were forced to continue operating them. Congressional hearings were held in 1969, but Congress agreed to hold off on legislation until it received the Nixon administration's recommendations. These recommendations arrived on January 18, 1970. Or did they?

Although the Transportation Department announced a proposal called Railpax, with a $40 million grant, the White House the next day disputed the DOT statement. White House press secretary Ronald Ziegler called Railpax "the least-likely" plan to be approved by the White House.

One of the last attempts to modernize passenger rail before the era of federal involvement was the Pennsylvania Railroad's Metroliner New York–Washington high-speed train. By the time the trains were finally ready for regular service, the Pennsylvania had become part of Penn Central. Southbound Metroliner No. 2005 roared through Lanham, Maryland, at a good 120 mph in October 1969. —William D. Middleton

Thereupon began an unusual public debate between Transportation Secretary John Volpe and the White House, followed by silence and no proposed bill. Obviously there was cutthroat disagreement in the administration. Tired of waiting, the Senate Commerce Committee approved a $435 million subsidy bill on March 12, 1970. Only then did the administration agree to compromise.

On May 1 the Senate and the Nixon administration reached a deal, which passed the Senate 78 to 3 just five days later. The House passed its bill by voice vote on October 14, and the Senate almost immediately accepted the House version and sent it to the White House. After a lively internal debate Nixon signed the bill on October 30. The White House at first ordered Volpe to propose a bare skeleton of a system, but after hot public and congressional reaction, a number of other routes were added.

On May 1, 1971, hundreds of passenger trains disappeared all over the country. Nonetheless, there was hope for survival of the passenger train because now the trains would be run by an agency, Amtrak, that really wanted to run trains. Or did it?

There is little doubt that the White House assumed that passengers would continue to desert trains, and within a couple of years Amtrak would simply go away. The first Amtrak president, former General Dynamics Corp. president Roger Lewis, seemed to assume that too. Very little was done for the first year or two to prepare for a revival of passenger service. Whether the lack of action was according to some plan is open to debate.

But passengers began returning to the rails, clearly believing that the government was serious about reviving the passenger train. Some were in for a rude awakening, particularly during summer air-conditioning breakdowns and winter heat fizzles. Most of Amtrak's equipment was old and broken-down and was not being replaced.

The passenger revival put the administration in a quandary. Many insiders knew that designating Amtrak a for-profit corporation was a joke. Also, the legislation contained only $40 million in direct appropriations and $60 million in loans. If passengers had only deserted Amtrak and it had gone out of business, fine. But that did not happen.

For the next few decades Amtrak, Congress, and the White House have put on a morality play resembling the movie *Groundhog Day*, in which the same scene is replayed year after year with slight variations. First, the White House attempts to kill Amtrak, pretending in some form that the lack of profitability makes it a failure. Passenger-advocacy groups such as the National Assn. of Railroad Passengers stage nationwide lobbying campaigns. And Congress simply ignores the White House and gives Amtrak a budget, but it is never quite enough to do the job right. The repeated presidential attempts to kill Amtrak continue, from Democrat Jimmy Carter to Republican George W. Bush.

Meanwhile, Amtrak attracted some top-flight presidents—Boyd, former Illinois Central passenger guru Paul Reistrup, former Southern Railway president W. Graham Claytor, Jr., and nonrailroader Tom Downs. The service gradually improved during this period, and slowly new

Amtrak began to order new equipment in 1973, and double-deck Superliner cars began to equip the company's long-distance western trains in 1979. The *Coast Starlight*, southbound at San Luis Obispo, was equipped with both the new Superliner cars and a new fleet of F40PH diesels in May 1981. —William D. Middleton

For the high-speed Northeast Corridor a new fleet of 125 mph Electro-Motive AEM7 electrics and Budd Co. Amfleet cars became the standard-bearers for Amtrak. Northbound Metroliner schedule 118 was approaching Baltimore in August 1989. —William D. Middleton

equipment was ordered. By the end of the twentieth century Amtrak's locomotive fleet was in its second generation, hundreds of new passenger cars had been put into service, and the original Metroliner had been replaced, first by faster-moving regular trains and then by the flawed but highly popular Acela Express.

But in 1998 a man with a different style assumed the presidency of Amtrak, George Warrington. Abandoning straight talk, Warrington adopted a policy of spin, assuring the White House, Congress, and the public that Amtrak was on its way to better days. There seems little doubt that he believed it for a while, aided by the fact that finances were in such a mess that it was difficult to tell exactly how much Amtrak had in reserves or how much it was really spending. One of the main methods of making the world seem better was to draw down reserves, basically borrowing from future years. Amtrak mortgaged property and equipment in an effort to make it appear that Warrington was asking for less money each year. The charade came to an end when Warrington was forced to go to Transportation Secretary Norman Y. Mineta to ask permission to mortgage Penn Station in New York to prevent a shutdown within weeks.

David Gunn, a longtime passenger and transit and freight railroader with a reputation for bluntness and straight talk, replaced Warrington in 2002. He was nearly his total opposite. Gunn returned to basics: get finances in order, keep accurate financial records, start rebuilding and repairing the deteriorating Northeast Corridor, and, most important, be open and honest with the government. The government was shocked. It would take at least $1.5 billion a year—and growing—to put Amtrak into basic good repair. Even with a new and honest management, the White House made even greater efforts to kill Amtrak. So Amtrak sits year after year in a netherworld, with one branch of the government unable to kill it and another branch unwilling either to let it die or to fund it properly.

While Amtrak floundered year after year, the passenger train made a major comeback in the United States in another guise, as the commuter train. This has long been a fixture in a few American cities, such as New York, Chicago, Boston, and Philadelphia. But in the 1980s and 1990s the commuter train roared onto the scene in many other cities. Some operations were relatively small at first and were even intended to be temporary during highway construction, as in Miami. Some began anew and grew almost too rapidly, as in northern Virginia. Others had been in service for many years at a relatively low level, such as the Maryland commuter trains between Baltimore, Washington, and Brunswick, Maryland. Some were already relatively major systems, such as San Francisco–San Jose, but grew rapidly under government ownership. Others popped out of nowhere and surprised almost everyone, as in Dallas and Fort Worth.

The greatest surprise of all was automobile-clogged Los Angeles, which shocked the transportation world by quickly beginning more than 400 miles of commuter service and then growing into one of the country's major

Beginning with President Ronald Reagan, Amtrak has frequently come under the gun of federal cost cutters, most recently the second George Bush.
—Toles © 2001, The Washington Post. Reprinted with permission of Universal Press Syndicate. All rights reserved

"Great Scott! Now what's happened?"

Bankrupt eastern railroads and their massive losses in commuter railroad services brought the New York area lines to a poor state of repair in the 1960s. —The New Yorker Collection, 1963, Peter Arno. From cartoonbank.com. All rights reserved.

commuter railroad areas. Los Angeles made its move out of congestion desperation, but thousands of commuters have now made it a way of life. As a new century gets under way, the passenger train is thriving in the Northeast Corridor and in big cities, but is an orphan where it began—the long-distance intercity sleeper train.

What, Growth Again? What Do We Do Now?

Late in 1980 Congress passed the single most important railroad legislation of the second half of the twentieth century, the Staggers Rail Act. The word "revolutionary" is often overused, but the Staggers Act was truly revolutionary. By far its most important section was the one allowing long-term secret contracts with shippers. Rates and guarantees no longer had to be open to the public and other shippers. "One size fits all" disappeared from the railroad scene. By 2000, 90 percent of rail traffic moved under contract.

The ICC, still in existence at that time, had gotten the deregulation religion. The Staggers Act had also clipped its wings, severely limiting its powers. Suddenly intermodal freight was free of regulation, able to write long-term contracts and use equipment in any way it saw fit. It seems quaint today that freedom to do business was such a revolutionary concept back then. Freed of artificial restraints, intermodal traffic boomed, particularly double-stack traffic.

A fateful train ride took place in 1989. Mike Haverty, then president of the Santa Fe, invited trucker J. B. Hunt to take a ride on one of his intermodal trains west out of Chicago. Haverty was doing everything he could to persuade the private trucking industry to ship its trailers on the train. Hunt—the old man, the original J. B.—accepted. Haverty still remembers the day. Boarding an office car, the two chatted awhile. At some point after the train reached a steady 70 mph, Haverty and Hunt walked to the front of the office car, where they stood facing the rear container. It rode steady as a rock—no sway, no bounce, no roll. Haverty remembers that Hunt stood and watched silently for a long time. The deal was done. A new era in intermodal transport was born. With Hunt leading the way, other major truckers began joining in. As the twenty-first century dawned, Hunt and many other truckers were such major users of intermodal transportation that they could not return to all-road operation without a huge investment in new trucks. With a chronic driver shortage anyway, the cost of new drivers would skyrocket. By the end of the twentieth century, by far the majority of trucks between California and the Midwest were on rails.

The Staggers Act also made unit grain trains possible when they were most needed. Up to 1980 the ICC routinely forced railroads to break up unit trains when there was a shortage of cars in harvest season and distribute those cars more evenly across the grain-growing Midwest, thus making them extremely inefficient and unable to handle as much traffic as when they were run as unit trains.

An unintended effect of the Staggers Act was the disappearance of station freight agents all over the country. The act dictated that state regulatory laws could not be more strict than, or inconsistent with, federal laws and regulations. That effectively voided state laws requiring agents at many cities and towns. Customer service was consolidated in central call centers, eliminating thousands of local jobs and computerizing many functions that had been handled by a friendly chat between the agent and the shipper. This produced a rough transition for shippers, who often found themselves on the phone with a different person each time.

Railroads were the last of the transportation industries to be deregulated, and for a different reason than the airlines and truck lines. While air and truck deregulation was intended to foster greater competition, rail deregulation was intended to allow railroads to raise rates and to lessen—but not totally remove—federal regulation. Again, Staggers created an unintended consequence. Rates did not go up; they went down. As volume rose steadily, railroads more than

The future of Amtrak's long-distance trains was uncertain, but commuter rail was booming. This was the West Coast Express's new service at Vancouver, British Columbia—opened in 1995—that unloaded afternoon rush-hour passengers at Coquitlam Central in September 1997. —William D. Middleton

made up in volume what they lost by lowering prices and thereby attracting even more volume. Diesel engines also became more efficient, and the average freight car grew larger. As rail employment decreased, employee productivity rose remarkably, from about 2 ton-miles per employee in 1981 to 10 ton-miles in 2003, a 400 percent increase. In addition, locomotive productivity rose 128 percent, track productivity rose 144 percent, and fuel efficiency rose 72 percent.

Between 1981 and 2003 rail freight rates decreased 60 percent, adjusted for inflation, and 29 percent in current dollars. Partly as a result of deregulation, rail market share ended its decline relative to trucks, barges, and pipelines. The lowest rail percentage, measured in terms of ton-miles, was in 1978 at 35.2 percent. By 2003 the rail

share of ton-miles rose to 42 percent. The Staggers Act cannot take full credit for this increase, because coal from the Powder River Basin in Wyoming is partly responsible, but it gets a substantial share. Overall, revenue ton-miles per constant dollar of operating expense rose 178 percent between 1980 and 2003.

Even as railroads modernized and new signal systems became more efficient, the problem of train crew size continued to dog the railroads. Gradually, the fireman began to disappear, beginning in the late 1960s and 1970s, but only on the basis of railroad-by-railroad agreements and usually with costly monetary protection agreements. In 1978 a nationwide agreement was reached allowing crew size to be reduced to three through the use of attrition. In 1985 unions agreed to use attrition to eliminate hostlers, men who moved locomotives around terminals, yards, and service facilities. Railroads insisted that hostlers had not been needed since the steam locomotive disappeared.

In 1991 the crew size issue was settled by a quirk of fate. The railroads and unions had been negotiating new national contract terms for two years and had hammered out all issues except one: health care. True to form, both sides dug in, and the National Mediation Board released the unions to strike. On April 17, 1991, they walked out. As expected, Congress ordered an end to the strike, acting within 17 hours. The idea was that the health care issue would go to a Presidential Emergency Board, which would work out a solution. Congress ordered that whatever the board decided be imposed on everyone involved.

But the board, designated PEB 219, had a surprise for both sides. It also took up other matters. It suggested that the crew consist issue be bargained at the local level, with the final outcome subject to binding arbitration. Within a few months agreements proliferated that allowed elimination of 25,000 jobs. Through-freight jobs could be reduced to two crewmembers. The agreements were a windfall of $200 million a year to railroads.

In the meantime, nontrain craftwork was hit even harder with job losses. The disappearance of the steam locomotive had eliminated many thousands of jobs such as boilermaker and blacksmith, but craft unions had held on as tightly as possible to jobs and the craft rules that would preserve them. But in 1970 work rules were implemented that allowed workers in one craft to be required to perform work in another craft. Shop employment dropped from 345,500 in 1952, one of the last years that major numbers of steam locomotives were operated, to 61,200 in 1984. Shop workers constituted 28 percent of railroad employment in 1952, but dropped to 19 percent in 1984, even though employment in other areas was falling too.

Technology blossomed during the 1980s and 1990s, sometimes in ways that were obvious to the average railroader, such as locomotives filled with microprocessors and new diesel drive technology such as alternating-current-traction motors that can pull at walking speed without slipping, and that will never overheat like DC-traction motors. On some railroads, locomotives can report back to the home maintenance base when something mechanical or electrical is going wrong, even before the crew knows. But there were other important innovations that were not obvious. Welded rail in quarter-mile lengths, and later in continuous welds, gradually covered most main-line and much branch-line track, beginning in the 1960s. As trains grew heavier, rail kept pace with the need for a better, longer-lasting track structure. In the 1980s heavy main-line rail came due for replacement after 750 million gross ton-miles of traffic, but by the end of the 1990s rail was good for 1.7 billion ton-miles.

Concrete ties, once scorned as something for lightweight traffic, began spreading throughout some of the most heavy-duty track in the country as quality and toughness improved. Better ties and more heavy-duty rail allowed greater tonnage per car, providing greater efficiency in moving bulk traffic such as coal. Track-maintenance machinery improved in sophistication.

From the 1960s, when maximum car weight was around 200,000 pounds, standard heavyweight car capacity grew to 286,000 pounds, an increase of 43 percent. Roller bearings and hotbox detectors all but ended burned-out journals that sometimes led to derailments. New trackside detectors now do far more than simply search for overheated wheel journals. They use laser technology to search for wheels showing too much wear, and acoustic detectors to listen to the sound of passing wheel bearings and detect those near failure. Freight-car wheels, which look much as they did 50 years ago, have taken great technological leaps. They are made from different alloys and are shaped differently between the axle and the tire, allowing them to take much greater heat and pounding. Computers basically took over most railroad functions by the end of the twentieth century, from locomotive control to maintenance to billing to dispatching.

The one promising technology still being resisted by railroads is positive train control, a system successfully tested in one form as early as the 1980s, which can stop or slow a train before it runs a signal or approaches another train in unsignaled territory. Railroads say that many of the train control functions developed in the last 20 years have already been deployed. But they also say that the fail-safe anticollision function of positive train control is simply too expensive to be cost effective in preventing the few collisions in today's railroad environment. Inevitably, railroads are taking a chance that one great disaster costing thousands of lives will turn around the concept of cost-effectiveness and lead to serious negative consequences, including possible re-regulation.

Between 1980 and the end of the century a new merger wave washed over railroading, effectively leaving four giant railroads in the United States plus one large Canadian road that pushed deeply into the United States from Canada. Only one merger was rejected by the ICC and its successor the Surface Transportation Board, a combination of the Santa Fe and the Southern Pacific, both of which later merged with others.

At first, the process went well. In fact, the merger of Seaboard Coast Line and the Chessie System into CSX on November 1, 1980, was a model of how to do a merger right. CSX learned a lot from the Penn Central disaster and did everything possible to avoid the same traps. Both railroads harmonized their computer systems in advance and continued to operate separately until all merger details were worked out. Helped by cost cutting and booming export coal traffic, CSX earnings in the first quarter of 1981 rose 59 percent above earnings of the two railroads operating separately a year earlier.

Working defensively against CSX, Norfolk & Western

and the Southern Railway completed their merger on June 1, 1982. The merger of the new Norfolk Southern also went mostly smoothly, although there was an internal battle over which predecessor railroad would control the new company. N&W won that battle when some suspicious dealings by a top Southern official were uncovered. There was little operational disruption, although the new NS did not do as well financially as CSX.

There was then a long quiet period on the major merger front. But in the mid-1990s another major combination did well operationally, if not financially. The Santa Fe and Burlington Northern merged to become the Burlington Northern Santa Fe. BN was supposed to be the acquiring company, but there was never any doubt that the Santa Fe was the big dog on the block. Santa Fe's Rob Krebs took over the new railroad and ran it with absolute control.

So far the merger movement was three for three. Things had gone well, if not perfectly. But the lucky streak ran out big time. On September 11, 1996, the Union Pacific assumed control of the Southern Pacific. One would have thought that Union Pacific would have learned its lessons from the breakdown of a much smaller merger earlier with the Chicago & North Western, a connection for the UP from Omaha to Chicago. But the UP-SP merger seemed to copy the C&NW breakdown in a much bigger way. Arrogantly the Union Pacific moved in, laid off 3,000 employees, and transferred another 3,000. Seeing the handwriting on the rail, a large number of SP managers took buyouts and left. UP managers moved into SP territory to show the weak sister how to do things right. What they did not realize was that the SP managers knew how to cut corners and keep their overcrowded and weak system somehow fluid.

Beginning at Houston, yards became clogged, freight was held out on the main line, and trains backed up for dozens, then hundreds of miles. Crews reached the federal 12-hour limit on duty and were transported to the next terminal for a mandatory rest period. This slowdown cascaded throughout the Southwest and West. Railroad traffic all but ground to a halt. A year later, in early October 1997, as many as 550 trains were stalled on the UP with either no rested crews or no locomotives available. It took almost two years for the UP to return to some semblance of health. Shippers were angry. Railroad workers were angry. Years would be required to ease the bad feelings.

Even as the UP struggled to dig out of its mess, two railroad leaders, John Snow of CSX and David LeVan of Conrail, began quietly talking about a possible merger. CSX had shown no particular interest in Conrail before, and Conrail had used the shield of Pennsylvania's tough takeover protection law to fight off earlier attempts by Norfolk Southern to acquire Conrail, so this came as something of a surprise.

Conrail had become so successful that the government decided to allow it to go fully private in 1987 by selling off all government stock. Conrail was perfectly happy to go private, but not to go to the Norfolk Southern. Despite a $1.3 billion bid, NS was rebuffed. Now, here were Snow and LeVan talking merger a decade later. Why?

There were many reasons, some of which remain locked away in the minds of those secret negotiators. But one of them was that LeVan saw a way to expand Conrail's influence, with LeVan effectively becoming the head of the new railroad. After all, Snow was near retirement, and there was no obvious strong successor at CSX. With CSX, LeVan seemed to assume, the Conrail culture would simply move south. But with a Norfolk Southern takeover, LeVan and his top managers had no chance. NS was deep with outstanding managers, and there was no doubt that Conrail would be quickly absorbed into its culture.

Snow and LeVan hoped that NS would be so stunned by the sudden move that it would crumble in disarray and CSX would at least get the lion's share of Conrail, including all its major main lines. CSX might be forced to give up its own Philadelphia-Baltimore-Chicago line, but that was clearly inferior to the old Pennsylvania and New York Central main lines of Conrail. Snow and LeVan announced the merger proposal early one morning, and the country was stunned. Norfolk Southern was less stunned, for its top officers had begun to pick up hints of something big a few days earlier. For ten days NS headquarters quietly debated the next move. In the end Snow and LeVan were wrong. Norfolk Southern did not wimp out. It came out swinging.

Jim McClellan, who had helped plan Conrail and who had long coveted the railroad, emerged from the internal NS debate as the company's gladiator. NS president David Goode had given him carte blanche, so McClellan hired his own team, fearful that the "gentlemen" at the top of NS would not let the contest get vicious enough. He even hired his own press relations man, former reporter Larry Kaufman. And he called on some of the USRA veterans who had helped plan Conrail and knew almost everything about the railroad and its business and physical plant. These included Victor Hand, whose no-nonsense style was even more direct, and whose memory of the Conrail property and traffic flows was even more encyclopedic, than McClellan's.

Almost immediately there was a falling-out between Snow and LeVan. Snow wanted to offer a compromise, while still keeping the best lines for the new CSX-Conrail. LeVan absolutely refused. He wanted everything. This opened the door for McClellan. Now there would be a real fight.

The bidding began, and Snow's original $60 per share offer began to look small. Up and up it went, passing $100 a share for a railroad that sold for only $13 a share when it went private in 1987. It reached $110, then $115. Snow could not afford to up that bid, but LeVan stubbornly refused to compromise. Finally, Linda Morgan, chairman of the Surface Transportation Board, sent a clear signal: any division of Conrail would have to be fair and equal. She gave LeVan no wiggle room. Rather than lead a new, bigger Conrail, he was forced to watch his prize divided. He left railroading to become a Harley Davidson dealer in Gettysburg.

Both railroads vastly overpaid for Conrail—more than $10 billion—and both had problems absorbing it, although this merger was not nearly as disastrous as Union Pacific's takeover of Southern Pacific. In some ways LeVan had the last laugh; he and the rest of Conrail's shareholders made out just fine. As the 1990s flowed toward a new century, railroads were again a growth in-dustry, and a profitable one. True to form, once railroad management learned a new trick, it worked merely to perfect the trick, rather than watching for the next trend. Branch lines and some main lines were abandoned. Traf-fic was consolidated on the remaining improved main lines. But in the meantime, traffic was going up and up, from 932 million ton-miles in 1980 to 1.6 billion in 2003. Inevitably, the two lines met and crossed. Railroads were not just a growth industry, they were an overcrowded growth industry. And the question for the twenty-first century is whether railroads can learn how to act like a true growth industry.

A

Accidents

Train accidents by most definitions include collisions, derailments, locomotive accidents, and a miscellany of other train-related mishaps such as fires and explosions. The following concentrates on collisions, derailments, and locomotive accidents. Throughout the nineteenth century train accidents occurred by the thousands, but most were small-scale affairs that did little damage and injured no one. The absolute numbers in part reflect the scale of traffic, and so it is usual to express accidents relative to some appropriate size measure such as locomotive-, train-, or car-miles. Such accidents were by no means the major cause of railroad casualties (injuries and fatalities); typically about half of all passenger casualties resulted from train accidents. And while wrecks killed far more workers than they did passengers, even for trainmen they were a comparatively minor source of risk (*see* SAFETY). Most railroad casualties involved trespassers or individuals crossing the tracks at grade. Yet train accidents are more significant than such statistics suggest. A few, remembered to this day, were spectacular. To nineteenth-century Americans they symbolized both the ambiguous power of technology and the need for public regulation.

The history of train accidents broadly divides into four periods. In the early years, through the Civil War, everything about railroads was new, and accidents probably became common, although no statistics exist on their numbers. The period from the 1870s to the beginning of the twentieth century saw an enormous expansion in railroading. It was also littered with spectacular train accidents; the first statistics, gathered by the *Railroad Gazette*, date from 1873. The third period began about 1907. Railroads were no longer expanding as rapidly, and under rising public pressure the carriers undertook major steps to reduce train accidents. The last period, characterized by increased federalization of safety, dates from 1970.

In the Beginning, 1828–1870

The causes of train accidents can be broadly grouped into defects in roadbed or equipment and human failures, although these can sometimes interact, as when bet-ter equipment can prevent human failure. Both causes reflect the state of technology and the economics of railroading. Early railroads involved a large-scale application of a host of novel technologies. The properties of steam and iron were not well understood, and learning involved much trial and error. Moreover, railroads are complex technological and business systems in which each part affects all the others. Train rules, ballast, rail, ties, axles, wheels, brakes, and signals were all new and could interact with each other and with train speed and weight, while changes in any part of the system could adversely affect others.

The novelty and unreliability of early technology resulted in many train wrecks. In America economic conditions during the years of expansion—roughly from 1830 to 1900—led to a system of railroading that was relatively dangerous. Carriers confronted a landscape of vast distances and thin traffic compared with their European counterparts; wages were high and capital scarce, but natural resources such as wood were cheap. Predictably, early American lines were single track with many curves because the carriers tried to avoid expensive cuts and fills. Ballast was scarce, and light rails were poorly spiked. Bridges were made of wood and wheels of cast iron (Europeans soon employed steel), and few lines were fenced. High wages and a constantly expanding demand for labor led American carriers to skimp on inspection and supervision and made enforcement of rules difficult. Thus the strategy was to build cheap and then improve as the traffic warranted, and by the late nineteenth century, as traffic expanded, some American carriers began to lose their distinctive characteristics. But throughout the nineteenth century the American system remained comparatively accident-prone. American carriers were also subject to far fewer safety regulations than their European counterparts. Beginning in the 1840s and 1850s, New York, Connecticut, and a few other states instituted commissions that sometimes inspected roadbeds, but their impact was minor until the 1870s.

The first recorded train accident that resulted in a casualty occurred on the South Carolina Railroad on June 17, 1831, a result of both general ignorance about steam locomotives and poor supervision. The fireman, a slave, irritated with the hiss from the safety valve, tied it down

The earliest serious railroad-crossing accident happened on the Camden & Amboy Rail Road near Burlington, New Jersey, on August 29, 1855, when a backing eight-car Philadelphia–New York "up" train collided with a two-horse carriage. Twenty-three passengers lost their lives. The scene was lithographed by John Collins. —Library of Congress (LC-USZ62-1383)

and was killed in the resulting explosion. The remainder of the 1830s and the 1840s were marked by a sprinkling of accidents with comparatively few casualties. There were more boiler explosions, derailments from broken axles, bridge collapses, and brake failures, and collisions that reflected the haphazard nature of early operating rules. These were merely a warm-up for the 1850s, however. There were 11 major wrecks in 1853 alone; one, a derailment on the New York & New Haven at an open drawbridge at Norwalk, Connecticut, on May 6, resulted in 46 deaths. Three years later, in 1856, a head-on collision on the North Pennsylvania at Camp Hill, Pennsylvania, killed 66.

The sudden appearance of major disasters involving many casualties in the 1850s has been blamed on increasing speed, as well as poor maintenance. Yet overall railroad safety was probably improving during these years. More plausibly the upsurge simply reflected exposure as the 1850s saw far more train-miles and large trains that carried hundreds of people. But whatever the cause, disasters cost the carriers dearly, for courts almost invariably found them liable for passengers' safety. The Norwalk accident, for example, cost the New York & New Haven $253,000—roughly the equivalent of $5.9 million in year 2002 dollars. In response, the carriers experimented with numerous improvements in technology and operating practices. They

were supported in these efforts by a host of individuals and satellite institutions. By the 1850s a technological community had evolved that included inventors, technical societies such as the Franklin Institute and later groups including the regional railroad clubs, and publications such as Henry Varnum Poor's *American Railroad Journal.* Together they improved, evaluated, publicized, and diffused new technology and operating practices.

Research at the Franklin Institute yielded a better understanding of locomotive boiler explosions, while British and German investigations of axle and bridge failures discovered the phenomenon of metal fatigue. Beginning with the Erie in 1851, companies applied the telegraph to control train operations. In the 1860s Ezra Miller developed a coupling and platform for passenger cars that reduced the chance that one car might telescope another during a wreck. A bit later George Westinghouse developed the air brake for passenger equipment. Competition among carriers ensured that both innovations were widely adopted on main lines by the mid-1870s. Regulators also began to shape accident rates about this time. On August 26, 1871, a frightful wreck on the Eastern Railroad at Revere, Massachusetts, killed 29 people. Under the leadership of Charles Francis Adams, the Massachusetts Board of Railroad Commissioners investigated, discovering that the Eastern lacked both air brakes and Miller's platform. Although the commissioners had no regulatory authority, Adams skillfully used public opinion to press for reform.

Steel rails, better ballast and roadbed, and a host of other improvements improved safety and almost invariably increased efficiency as well. But because they improved safety, they sometimes encouraged the carriers to change operating practices in ways that offset some of the safety gain. For example, both Miller's platform and the Westinghouse brake led companies to increase train speed.

The Changing Nature of Train Accidents, 1870–1907

In response to such improvements, accident rates probably declined relative to train-miles between the 1850s and 1870s, although no hard figures are available. In 1873, however, the *Railroad Gazette*, under the editorship of engineer Mathias Forney, began to publish the first reliable statistics of train accidents by cause. As the journal noted, its figures ignored all casualties that resulted from other causes, and they also missed minor train accidents, but they were a reasonably complete list of accidents that resulted in casualties. These data suggest that train accidents declined relative to train-miles during the late nineteenth century and that they changed in composition (Table 1, Figure 1). Derailments declined as the carriers steadily improved roadbed, bridges, and equipment, although they were also subject to major cycles reflecting the ebb and flow of business activity and the introduction of new technologies. Locomotive accidents also fell as suppliers and railroad master mechanics steadily improved designs. Col-

Table 1. Train Accidents, 1873–1900
(Figures are annual averages)

Year	1873–1877	1878–1882	1883–1887	1888–1892	1893–1897	1898–1900
Train-miles*	433	510	565	781	850	914
Total accidents	1,055	1,100	1,347	2,083	1,674	2,438
Total collisions	295	417	548	959	632	1,096
Collisions/train-miles**	0.68	0.82	0.97	1.23	0.74	1.20
Rear coll.	155	275	342	464	264	460
Butting coll.	96	121	174	286	151	235
Other coll.	44	21	32	209	217	401
Total derailments	709	646	725	1,032	914	1,266
Derailments/train-miles**	1.64	1.27	1.29	1.32	1.07	1.39
Derailment causes						
Road defects	149	116	191	175	120	111
Broken rail	71	48	68	49	39	24
Spread rail	31	34	66	47	29	28
Broken bridge	24	27	32	38	21	26
Broken switch	9	3	13	27	18	19
Broken frog	5	2	11	11	7	5
Other	9	2	1	3	6	9
Equipment defects	76	79	108	171	203	289
Broken wheel	22	28	33	40	40	65
Broken axle	32	36	49	56	76	107
Broken truck	10	11	15	28	25	37
Coupling/drawbar	4	1	4	13	23	27
Brake beam fall	3	0	5	16	15	15
Air brake	0	0	0	0	0	8
Other	5	3	2	18	24	30
Operating negligence	97	91	85	124	98	139
Misplaced switch	76	77	69	71	47	48
Derailing switch	0	0	0	0	4	13
Trackmen's neg.	9	5	5	8	7	10
Runaway engine	2	2	2	10	7	18
Open draw	4	3	4	3	4	2
Other	6	4	5	32	29	48
Track obstructions	158	128	157	178	157	130
Animals	48	39	33	53	31	27
Snow or ice	20	13	17	9	12	6
Washout	28	21	21	19	16	19
Landslide	6	7	16	29	26	30
Accidental	38	32	32	21	26	22
Malicious	15	13	30	39	40	21
Other	3	3	8	8	6	5
Other derailments	229	232	184	384	336	597

Source: *Railroad Gazette*, various years.

*Train-miles for 1873–1882 estimated.

**Per million train-miles.

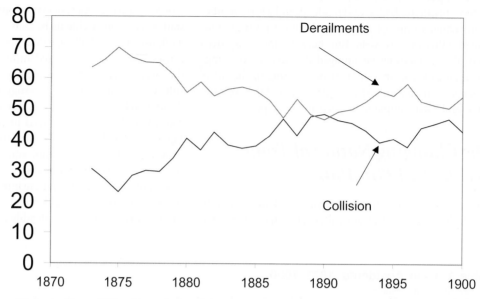

Percent of Accidents

Derailments

Collision

Figure 1. Evolution of Train Accidents, 1873–1900. —*Railroad Gazette*

lisions rose as traffic density increased and the carriers failed to develop the means to prevent human failures.

Both the forces that led to derailments and the carriers' response can be highlighted by a focus on one particular form of derailment: bridge accidents. While the 1853 disaster at Norwalk was the first serious bridge accident, the next quarter century brought a host of fires, washouts, collapses, and derailments that culminated in a collapse on the Lake Shore & Michigan Southern at Ashtabula, Ohio, on December 29, 1876, that killed 81 people. After 1870 the *Gazette*'s data revealed the magnitude of the problem: in the half decade beginning in 1873 American railroads experienced at least 126 bridge failures. The *Gazette*'s data also demonstrate the importance of statistical categories: simply tabulating bridge failures helped make them a public issue.

While European carriers were by no means immune, such wrecks were probably more common on American lines for a number of reasons. One was that American roads were bridge and trestle intensive; either was far cheaper than fills or tunnels. And men with scant knowledge of engineering often constructed early bridges, such as that at Ashtabula. Ignorance and the desire to save money led to bad designs; the truss chords of the Ashtabula Bridge had a factor of safety of about 1.6 when 5 was the minimum accepted by most engineers at the time. But most bridges failed not from faulty designs but rather from design choices that consciously traded safety for economy. While in Europe bridge technology evolved from masonry to riveted iron trusses, most early American bridges were cheap wooden trestles or Howe trusses that were subject to rot and fire unless carefully inspected. The Tariffville, Connecticut, disaster on the Connecticut West-

ern in 1877 (13 killed) and that on the Toledo, Peoria, & Western at Chatsworth, Illinois, in 1887 (82 killed) resulted from rot and fire, respectively. If fire or rot did not get a bridge, flood often did. Grading for approaches was often skimpy, leading to washouts. And as train weight increased, bridges were routinely overloaded, for with interest rates high it was uneconomic to invest in heavy structures.

But the most common reason bridges failed was because they were knocked down by derailed trains, and this too reflected the peculiarities of American construction methods. When the carriers began to build iron truss bridges in the 1850s, they skimped on iron, which was expensive, and assembled them using pins (bolts). These pin-connected American bridges could be factory made and field assembled using comparatively unskilled labor. British builders, by contrast, preferred riveting, which—because it employed skilled labor—was more expensive. But pin-connected bridges were nonredundant structures; knock out any single member, and the bridge might fold up like a hinge. Thus the design of American iron bridges made them particularly likely to collapse when hit by a derailed car at a time when American railroads were peculiarly liable to derailments.

By the 1880s bridge failures had become an expensive embarrassment, and reform was in the air. The American Society of Civil Engineers steadily improved designs, while carriers hired consulting engineers to supervise their builders and improved maintenance and inspection. Journals such as *Engineering News* campaigned for better bridge guards and floors. Disasters led to better state regulation in Massachusetts, New York, Ohio, and Vermont, and individual engineers such as New York's bridge inspector Charles Stowell urged the use of riveting for short bridges. Finally, by the late 1890s cheaper iron and steel led to use of plate girders. Reinforced concrete also made an appearance. Both types of bridges were nearly indestructible. After 1900 public interest in bridge failures disappeared, in part because safety improved, but in part because the Interstate Commerce Commission's accident statistics supplanted those of the *Gazette*, and the ICC kept no data on bridge accidents. Decisions on how to present statistics therefore helped both create the problem of bridge accidents and "solve" it.

Until the early twentieth century other causes of derailment also yielded to the same research, investment, and more careful inspection that reduced bridge accidents; yet over the same period collision risks worsened, despite car-

riers' efforts to standardize signals and their adoption of a standard code of train rules in the 1880s. In large part this reflected the growth of traffic; the journal *Railway Age* pointed out that on a single-track line the opportunity of collision rose as $(N/2)^2 + N - 2$, where N is the number of trains per day. Thus with 10 trains (5 each way) there are 25 potential meets that could yield a head-on collision and 8 potential rear collisions. But double the number of trains to 20, and the number of potential collisions rises from 33 to 118. In addition, as the railroads evolved into great systems, switching and yard work increased, and so did the number of yard collisions. Still, although collision rates rose after the Civil War, there is no evidence that casualty rates to passengers or employees increased.

Rising traffic density was a special problem because until

The "Angola Horror": derailment of the last two cars of the Lake Shore Railroad's *New York Express* at Angola, New York, 21 miles west of Buffalo on December 18, 1867, sent them plunging into Big Sisters Creek. Forty-two passengers died. This lurid drawing is from the January 4, 1868, issue of *Frank Leslie's Illustrated Newspaper.* —Middleton Collection

the twentieth century most American lines operated with the timetable and train-order system, while in Britain use of manual block signals was universal after 1880. The block system divided track into blocks, and no train could enter a previously occupied block. This system, which used space to separate trains, was inherently safer than the American system that separated trains by time. With the American approach, a misread train order, a road breakdown, or a misidentified extra train all might lead to disaster. Such dangers were worsened by differences in signals among carriers, by the difficulty in monitoring trainmen, and by labor turnover that often resulted in inexperienced and hard-to-discipline workers who sometimes ignored train rules. Employees in turn claimed that they violated train rules because they were expected to, to get over the road. Running past a meet to the next siding was winked at as long as no wreck resulted.

Although most collisions, like most derailments, were minor affairs, if conditions were right, disaster might ensue. The head-on wreck on the Baltimore & Ohio at Republic, Ohio, on January 4, 1887, provides an illustration. A freight train with a bad engine stalled on the single-track line to Republic, and the conductor failed to send out a flagman to warn an oncoming passenger train. Because its brakes were obsolete, the passenger train failed to stop in time and plowed into the freight, telescoping several cars and starting a fire from a coal stove that killed 13. As this example suggests, disasters required a confluence of rare events; in the late 1870s only about .36 percent of accidents reported in the *Railroad Gazette* killed as many as 6 people. Still, as train-miles increased, so did the number of collisions. In the 1880s fiery disasters such as Republic led a number of northern states to require steam heating, and by the twentieth century train accidents were an important public issue.

The Campaign against Train Accidents, 1900–1970

In the 1890s, on many lines traffic density began to overwhelm the train-order system. On January 14, 1894, when fog slowed a Lackawanna suburban express near Jersey Meadows, New Jersey, it was rammed by another commuter train that was traveling only three minutes behind it, killing 15. The expansion in traffic between 1897 and World War I saw an upsurge in collisions, but changes in technology also caused derailments to skyrocket. The shift to larger, longer freights increased collisions from break-in-twos and worsened derailments from broken wheels. At the same time rising train weight and deteriorating rail quality resulted in another epidemic of derailments from broken rails.

Public reporting of train accidents to the ICC began in 1901 when Congress passed the Accident Report Act. These first reports, which listed all accidents that did $150 of damage or resulted in a casualty, yielded thousands of train accidents, many of them serious, and contributed to a decade of public clamor. Stunned by its statistics and by accidents such as a head-on collision on the Southern on July 7, 1903, that resulted from a misreading of train orders and killed 23, the ICC requested that Congress grant it broad authority to require block signals and other safety measures. In 1908 Congress passed an Hours of Service Act intended to prevent accidents due to fatigue, and from 1907 to World War I it authorized investigations and held hearings on the need for block signals, steel passenger cars, and other equipment intended to prevent accidents.

The Accident Reports Act of 1910 gave the ICC power to investigate train accidents, and one of its first investigations was of a broken rail that caused a wreck on the Lehigh Valley on August 25, 1911, near Manchester, New York, that killed 28. The wreck reflected a novel form of failure—a transverse fissure—that took nearly 30 years of research to contain. The Locomotive Inspection Act was also passed in 1911, giving the ICC authority to inspect locomotive boilers. The commission also began to collect statistics on locomotive accidents, and as its actions bore fruit, the data reveal a sharp decline in such accidents up to World War I.

The carriers responded to rising accidents and regulatory threats in several ways. They made important changes in labor policies that were motivated in part by the desire to reduce accidents. Physical exams for trainmen spread, administered by company medical services, and hiring practices were centralized. Use of record discipline also increased; it improved morale and reduced suspensions, thereby diminishing the need to hire new men. About 1903 Julius Kruttschnitt of the Southern Pacific instituted unannounced safety inspections, and the practice spread widely. Finally, the Safety First campaign, which began on the Chicago & North Western in 1910 (*see* SAFETY), was motivated partly by the belief that a generalized concern with safety would automatically reduce train accidents as well.

Major carriers also upgraded track and equipment. Working with suppliers and through technical associations such as the Master Car Builders and the American Railway Engineering Assn., they began investigations that lasted for decades and greatly improved rail and wheel quality. They also made massive investments in both manual and automatic block signaling, which rose from about 16 percent of main track in 1901 to 45 percent in 1920. And since the carriers invested where traffic was heaviest, at least 70 percent of passenger-miles were protected by the latter date. The shift to steel passenger cars also reduced casualties when trains wrecked, as occurred on the Pennsylvania on June 16, 1910, near Mount Union, Pennsylvania, when a potentially deadly derailment caused no fatalities. By 1914 about a quarter of all passenger cars were steel or steel frame.

In one surprising development the carriers actually requested increased safety regulation. In 1905 a derailment and collision that led to a dynamite explosion in the Harrisburg, Pennsylvania, yards of the Pennsylvania Railroad killed 23. At the company's behest, the American Railway Assn. (ARA) formed the Bureau for the Safe Transportation of Explosives and Other Dangerous Articles to enforce ARA rules, and in 1908 it successfully lobbied Congress to grant the ICC power to regulate transport of explosives. The commission in turn promptly adopted the ARA's rules as its own and left inspection and enforcement up to the bureau. This rather informal public and private arrangement sharply reduced risks and survived into the 1960s.

The impact of these improvements was masked for a time by the boom associated with World War I. The surge in traffic resulted in some memorable disasters, such as the head-on collision on the Nashville, Chattanooga & St. Louis that killed 101 people on July 9, 1918, near Nashville, Tennessee. In addition, because ICC rules required reporting of all accidents doing $150 of damage, wartime inflation ballooned the reporting of minor accidents.

The Transportation Act of 1920 finally gave the ICC power to require block signals or other safety devices. But accidents such as the rear-end collision at South Byron, New York, on January 12, 1919, where an engineman ran a signal, killing 22, had caused the commission to lose faith in the railroads' ability to make enginemen obey signals. It had fastened instead upon the novel idea of automatic train control. The simplest versions would automatically apply the brakes if the engineman ran a signal, thus preventing an accident, or so it was hoped. In 1922 the ICC ordered all large carriers to implement train control on at least one passenger division. This marked a major advance in federal efforts to control train accidents.

The order proved contentious; when the carriers undertook safety investments, they usually expected efficiency gains as well, but for most lines train control promised costs without efficiency gains. Where, the carriers asked, were funds to come from if the ICC refused to increase rates? And they argued that the benefits of train control could be more cheaply achieved elsewhere. While the order had little impact on safety, it did stimulate the development of train control and cab signals, and some carriers began to install it voluntarily. In 1923 the ICC also began an investigation of power brakes on freight trains that resulted in major improvements that were embodied in the AB brake a decade later. The Signal Inspection Act of 1937, although motivated by the employment worries of signalmen, gave the ICC power to authorize block signals, which it began to employ, usually in response to an accident investigation.

Although these federal controls had comparatively modest effects on train accidents, the interwar decades witnessed steady reduction in accident risks (Figure 2). The main causes were a massive upgrading in track and equipment, technological improvements, and safety-first activities. Locomotive safety improved both as a result of continuing federal inspection and because after 1924 the carriers scrapped thousands of old, dangerous locomotives. The spreading block system continued to reduce collisions, and as employment stabilized in the 1920s and then declined in the 1930s, discipline improved and workers' experience increased. Research by the carriers and their suppliers also reduced derailments, and in the mid-1930s they discovered new methods to produce rails that would not develop transverse fissures. About the same time Elmer Sperry invented a nondestructive detector that could discover these and other

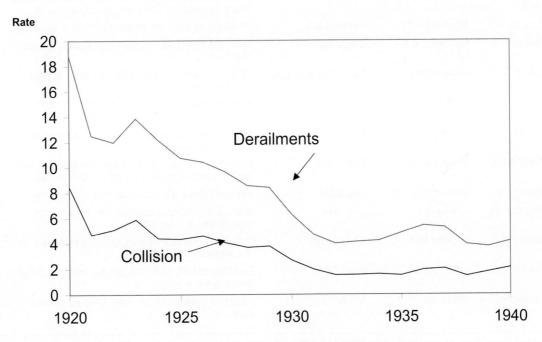

Figure 2. Collisions and Derailments, 1920–1940. —Interstate Commerce Commission

defective rails in track. In the 1930s depressed traffic conditions also contributed to very low accident rates.

Despite this improving record, a sprinkling of disasters from misplaced switches, excessive speed, and track defects marred the record during the interwar years. Broken rails remained a danger, and one caused a major wreck on the Frisco on October 27, 1925, at Victoria, Texas, that killed 21. Sabotage wrecked the Southern Pacific's crack *City of San Francisco* near Harney, Nevada, on August 12, 1939, taking the lives of 24. And 1940 was marred by two disasters—a derailment from excessive speed on the New York Central at Little Falls, New York, that killed 30, and a

head-on collision on the Pennsylvania near Cuyahoga Falls, Ohio, that killed 41.

World War II brought an unprecedented increase in both passenger and freight traffic. Predictably, both collisions and derailments jumped, and with them came a spate of disasters. The most serious was a derailment at Philadelphia resulting from a burned-off axle journal on the Pennsylvania Railroad's *Congressional Limited* on September 6, 1943, that killed 79. Yet the striking feature of the war years is not how much but how little accidents increased. Interwar efficiency gains that resulted in longer, heavier trains allowed the carriers to move more men and

Table 2. Twenty-two Significant Train Accidents, 1831–2000

Date	Place	Road	Description	Killed
1831, June 17	Charleston, S.C.	South Carolina	Boiler explodes, *Best Friend of Charleston;* first recorded train accident.	1
1853, May 6	Norwalk, Conn.	New Haven	Open drawbridge; one of the first large-scale disasters.	46
1856, July 17	Camp Hill, Pa.	North Pennsylvania	Head-on collision exemplifying weaknesses of timetable and train-order system.	66
1871, August 26	Revere, Mass.	Eastern	Rear-end collision; Mass. Commissioners force general improvements in operating practices.	29
1876, December 29	Ashtabula, Ohio	Lake Shore	Bridge collapse; worst accident of nineteenth century begins movement for reform.	81
1887, January 4	Republic, Ohio	Baltimore & Ohio	Head-on collision and fire; Ohio becomes one of several leading states to ban stoves.	13
1894, January 14	Jersey Meadows, N.J.	Lackawanna	Rear-end collision; such accidents from rising traffic density pressure companies to install block signals.	15
1900, April 30	Vaughan, Miss.	Illinois Central	Casey Jones killed.	1
1903, July 7	Rockfish, Va.	Southern	Head-on collision from misread orders; one of many leading ICC to call for mandatory block signals.	23
1903, September 28	Danville, Va.	Southern	Derailment on trestle inspires *Wreck of the Old '97.*	9
1905, May 11	Harrisburg, Pa.	Pennsylvania	Derailment and dynamite explosion lead railroads to request federal regulations for transporting hazardous materials.	23
1910, June 16	Mount Union, Pa.	Pennsylvania	Derailment; no one killed because cars made of steel.	0
1911, August 25	Manchester, N.Y.	Lehigh Valley	Derailment from broken rail due to first reported transverse fissure.	28
1918, July 9	Nashville, Tenn.	Nash., Chat. & St. Louis	Head-on collision from misreading train order; deadliest American wreck.	101
1919, January 12	South Byron, N.Y.	New York Central	Rear-end collision; engineer ran block signal; helped persuade ICC to order automatic train control.	22
1940, July 31	Cuyahoga Falls, Ohio	Pennsylvania	Head-on motor car and freight; passengers killed by fire; worst interwar collision.	41
1943, September 6	Philadelphia, Pa.	Pennsylvania	Derailment of *Congressional Ltd.* from burned journal; worst wartime accident demonstrates need for better journals.	79
1950, February 17	Richmond Hill, N.Y.	Long Island	Rear-end collision when commuter train ignored signals.	79
1950, November 22	Jamaica, N.Y.	Long Island	Rear-end collision when commuter train ran block signal, showing need for train control.	31
1961, January 17	Magnolia, Miss.	Illinois Central	Crossing collision with oil truck causes derailment and fire and emphasizes crossing dangers.	6
1969, September 12	Glendora, Miss.	Illinois Central	Derailment and release of phosgene gas, leading to stricter federal control in 1970.	0
1993, September 22	Mobile, Ala.	Amtrak	Derailment of *Sunset Ltd.* on bridge hit by tug boat and barge.	47

Source: Robert Shaw, "Shaw's All-Time List of Notable Railroad Accidents, 1831–2000." *Railroad History* 184 (Spring 2001): 37–45, and ICC, accident reports.

material with fewer trains, thereby reducing accident exposure, while block signals, better rails, and Safety First all combined to hold down accidents (Table 2).

The postwar years began in 1947 with another major ICC order requiring block signals or some form of train control on many miles of high-speed track. The carriers again claimed that with rate regulation they could not afford the new equipment, and they argued that speed was a poor measure of danger. This fact was illustrated on February 17, 1950, and again on November 22, when two slow-speed wrecks of Long Island commuter trains killed a total of 110 people. The act probably increased the use of train control, but use of block signals remained unchanged; probably the order led some lines to reduce speed or abandon passenger traffic.

The companies themselves were introducing centralized traffic control (CTC) during these years. First developed in the 1930s, it governed a third of all track by 1965. While CTC was motivated by the desire to increase track capacity cheaply, it increased safety as well. A host of other technological changes reduced accident risks during these years. Decades of track research resulted in better rail designs, while use of ultrasound and Magnaflux nondestructive fault detection reduced dangerous flaws in axles and wheels. The spread of train radiotelephones, hotbox and dragging-equipment detectors, and many other improvements also diminished risks.

Federalization of Safety, 1970–

These improvements failed to yield the expected reduction in accidents. As in the 1890s, they were partly offset by sharp increases in freight-car weight, which increased dangers from rail and wheel failure. And by the 1950s many eastern and midwestern lines were in serious financial difficulty, a result of declining traffic, as well as stifling state and federal economic regulation. The result was an epidemic of bankruptcies and mergers. Track and equipment on some lines sharply deteriorated. Corrected for inflation, accident rates per train- or car-mile remained stable into the mid-1960s and thereafter rose, led by roadbed-related derailments. Moreover, as freight cars grew in size and trains became longer, derailments involving hazardous substances became more dangerous to bystanders. Newspapers carried stories of towns that had to be evacuated and of citizens killed by poison gas escaping from derailed freight cars. In one spectacular wreck, on September 12, 1969, an Illinois Central freight derailed near Glendora, Mississippi, releasing phosgene gas and routing 30,000 citizens from their homes, including Senator James Eastland. Such disasters again made railroad accidents a public issue.

Between 1966 and 1970 Congress revamped railroad safety regulation. In 1966 the newly formed Federal Railroad Administration (FRA) was given control over rail safety, and in 1967 the National Transportation Safety Board received power to investigate accidents. In 1970, in response to fears of derailments involving hazardous substances, Congress passed the Federal Railroad Safety Act, which gave the FRA power to regulate track conditions and operating rules. Although FRA practice has been sharply criticized by the General Accounting Office, among other groups, it has established much stricter rules over all aspects of railroad safety. In addition, by the mid-1970s the old system of rate regulation was beginning to crumble, and in 1980 the Staggers Act largely deregulated railroad pricing and service.

Economic deregulation reduced train accidents in two

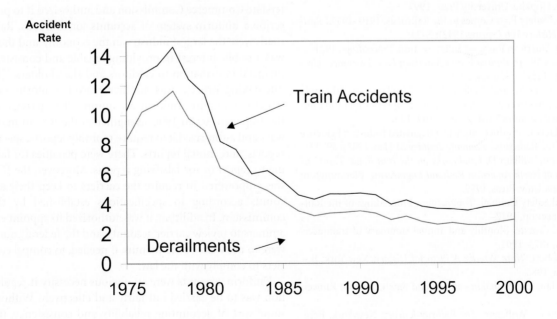

Figure 3. Train Accidents and Derailments, 1975–2000. —Federal Railroad Administration

related ways. First, carriers' improving financial health, along with FRA rules, encouraged better track maintenance. Second, the combination of larger merged carriers that were freer to experiment with unit trains reduced switching, which had always been a fruitful source of accidents. These changes sharply reduced the risks of train accidents (Figure 3). Inflation-adjusted accidents per train-mile fell by half from 1980 to 1986. Disasters have become rare, although they continue to mar the record, as when Amtrak's *Sunset Ltd.* went through a broken bridge near Mobile, Alabama, on September 22, 1993, killing 47. Since the mid-1980s train accident rates have stabilized, but the goal remains, as the FRA puts it, "zero tolerance" for accidents.

—Mark Aldrich

REFERENCES

Aldrich, Mark. "Combating the Collision Horror: The Interstate Commerce Commission and Automatic Train Control." *Technology and Culture* 34, no. 1 (Jan. 1993): 49–77.

———. *Death Rode the Rails: American Railroad Accidents and Safety, 1828–1965*. Baltimore: Johns Hopkins University Press, 2006.

———. "Engineering Success and Disaster: American Railroad Bridges, 1840–1900." *Railroad History* 180 (Spring 1999): 31–72.

———. "The Peril of the Broken Rail: The Carriers, the Steel Companies and Rail Technology, 1900–1945." *Technology and Culture* 40, no. 2 (April 1999): 263–291.

———. "Regulating the Transportation of Hazardous Substances: Railroads and Reform." *Business History Review* 76, no. 2 (Summer 2002): 267–298.

———. "Safe and Suitable Boilers, the Railroads, the Interstate Commerce Commission, and Locomotive Safety, 1900–1945." *Railroad History* 171 (Autumn 1994): 23–44.

———. *Safety First: Technology, Labor, and Business in the Building of American Work Safety, 1870–1939*. Baltimore: Johns Hopkins University Press, 1997.

———. "Safety First Comes to the Railroads, 1910–1939." *Railroad History* 166 (Spring 1992): 5–33.

Assn. of American Railways Safety Section. *Proceedings*, 1921–.

Ely, James W., Jr. *Railroads and American Law*. Lawrence: University Press of Kansas, 2001.

Gasparini, D. A., and Melissa Fields. "Collapse of Ashtabula Bridge on December 29, 1876." *Journal of Performance of Constructed Facilities* 7 (May 1993): 109–125.

Golub, Devra. "Product Safety in a Regulated Industry: Evidence from the Railroads." *Economic Inquiry* 21 (Jan. 1983): 39–52.

Middleton, William D. *Landmarks on the Iron Road: Two Centuries of North American Railroad Engineering*. Bloomington: Indiana Univ. Press, 1999.

National Safety Council. *Transactions*, Proceedings of the Railroad Section, 1912–.

Railroad Gazette. Monthly and annual summary of train accidents, 1873–1901.

Reed, Robert. *Train Wrecks: A Pictorial History*. New York: Bonanza, 1982.

Savage, Ian. *The Economics of Railroad Safety*. Boston: Kluwer, 1998.

Schivelbusch, Wolfgang. *The Railway Journey*. New York: Berg, 1986.

Shaw, Robert B. *Down Brakes: A History of Railroad Accidents, Safety Precautions and Operating Practices in the United States of America*. London: P. R. Macmillan, 1961.

Shaw, Robert B. "Shaw's All-Time List of Notable Railroad Accidents, 1831–2000." *Railroad History* 184 (Spring 2001): 37–45.

Shulman, A. E., and C. E. Taylor. *Analysis of Nine Years of Railroad Accident Data, 1966–1974*. Washington, D.C.: Assn. of American Railroads, 1976.

U.S. Congress. Office of Technology Assessment. *An Evaluation of Railroad Safety*. Washington, D.C.: Government Printing Office, 1978.

U.S. Department of Transportation. Online Digital Special Collections. "ICC Historical Railroad Investigation Reports (1911–1966)." http://specialcollections.tasc.dot.gov/

U.S. Federal Railroad Administration. Office of Safety. http://www.fra.dot.gov/safety/index.html

U.S. Interstate Commerce Commission. *Accident Bulletin*, 1901–1965.

Usselman, Steven. "Air Brakes for Freight Trains: Technological Innovation in the American Railroad Industry, 1869–1900." *Business History Review* 58, no. 1 (Spring 1984): 30–50.

Vance, James E., Jr. *The North American Railroad*. Baltimore: Johns Hopkins University Press, 1995.

Accounting

To understand how an enterprise is maintaining itself financially, it must keep orderly books, set up, track, and audit its financial situation, and analyze its financial status and operating results on a regular basis. Railroad accounting practices are unusual in that, rather than keeping one set of books that reflect their financial status at any given time, railroads (and certain other enterprises, particularly utilities) keep three.

The Act to Regulate Commerce of 1887 created the Interstate Commerce Commission and authorized it to prescribe a uniform system of accounts for railroads. Railroads were the largest industry in the economy, and there was a public interest in providing reliable and consistent financial information to creditors and shareholders. The ratemaking process was another reason; uniform rate structures require uniform accounting. The passage of the Hepburn Act in 1906 strengthened the ICC in many ways and authorized it to require monthly reports, special reports, and annual reports. There were penalties for failing to report or for falsifying reports. Moreover, the ICC was empowered to require the carriers to keep their accounts according to specifications established by the commission. In addition, it was authorized to appoint examiners to review carrier accounts, and the federal courts were to use writs of mandamus, if needed, to compel carriers to comply with the law.

Uniform accounts were an obvious necessity if regulation was to be carried out fairly and effectively. Without some sort of accounting reliability and consistency, the idea of fair rates based on the concept of fair return on fair value (an idea popular in rate regulation until fairly recently) could not be carried out successfully. While each railroad would certainly have its own accounting system, uniformity could only be achieved by government mandate. The ability of investors to make comparisons between railroads would not be possible without a uniform system.

To be useful, a uniform system of accounts must indeed be truly uniform. A second requirement is the separation of carrier business from noncarrier business. If a railroad owned a chain of hotels or restaurants, those businesses would have to be handled as distinct enterprises. Only property used for the purpose of rail transportation could be included in the valuation. Likewise, historically separate accounts had to be kept for passenger and freight service. The regulatory concern was the cross-subsidy of the passenger service by the freight customers.

Throughout most of the twentieth century the regulatory approach prevailed in railroad accounting, and it was not until 1980 that fundamental changes occurred. The Staggers Act, which resulted in partial decontrol of the economic regulation of the railroads, and the Securities and Exchange Commission mandated that railroads use "depreciation accounting" for reporting to shareholders. To further complicate the situation, the Internal Revenue Service was encouraging very short depreciable life to encourage investment through rapid recovery of the invested capital through tax policy. Thus the railroads were in the position of legally maintaining three sets of books; one for regulatory accounting filed with the ICC, now the Surface Transportation Board, a second with the SEC for reporting to shareholders, and a third to the IRS in filing their tax returns.

The debate between government agencies and accounting practitioners focused on two principal issues: depreciation accounting versus betterment accounting, and deferred tax accounting. These same issues apply to public utilities, as well as other asset-intensive industries. To further understand this issue, the definition of a "capital asset" versus a "current expense or expenditure" is helpful. In its simplest terms, a "capital asset" is an expenditure that will benefit a period longer than one year or the current accounting cycle, while an expense is something where the benefit is immediate or, in many cases, is for services rendered in the immediate past, labor being the principal example.

However, railroad accounting has another nuance or complication. A maintenance worker can be performing the same function, for example, working on track, but the accounting treatment can be different if it is a "project" versus "routine maintenance." A project is typically a rehabilitation effort where so much rail, so many ties, and so much ballast are replaced per mile. A project is deemed to be a capital asset because it is presumed that it will offer benefit for a number of years. Routine maintenance is to be expensed in the current period because it is deemed to have no future benefit. Examples of routine maintenance are replacing a tie here and there, tightening bolts, and replacing short sections of typically less than 1,320 feet per section of rail.

Perhaps the most fundamental element in the prescribed accounting system is the distinction between expenditures for capital assets and those operating expenses charged to income. An investment in an asset such as a locomotive should be properly charged to the relevant asset account. Current expenses for carrying out the business of a railroad should be deducted from current revenues that are credited to an income account. In considering assets and their replacement, care must be taken in separating replacement of facilities and betterment of the facilities. The critical point is whether the replacement is in kind or a betterment. In replacing a fixed-block signal system with centralized traffic control, the difference in cost of replacing in kind and the new system is a betterment. Under ICC accounting rules, additions or betterments must be charged to a capital account. When property is retired and is replaced in kind, the ledger value of the retired property is deducted from the property account. The expense for new property installed is allocated to the relevant property account.

The prescribed system must provide an accurate statement of the property account, and the accounts have to show the actual money cost to the carrier. When consideration other than money has been given for property, the monetary value of the consideration at the time of the transaction should be charged to the property account. For accuracy, the property account must show all additions and betterments. Property that is abandoned should be written out of the property account at once.

"Betterment accounting" is focused on whether or not a betterment has taken place. "Depreciation accounting" ignores the betterment assumption; it is based on the assumption that an asset's usefulness or utility will be spread over a period of years, and that the consumption of this asset through its use in the production of income needs to be measured on some ratable basis over its useful life. In the case of the elements of a track structure, those elements are the amount of wear the track structure experiences from passing trains and climate: wet weather, dry rot, or freeze-thaw cycles. The impact on a track structure is geometric as weight and speed of the trains increase. Gross ton-miles are perhaps the most rational basis for calculating these estimates of future useful life.

Depreciation was also a matter of prescription by the ICC. Depreciation is a means of accounting for the using up of materials and equipment. As an item of property is used up or consumed, it is transferred from the balance sheet to the operating statement. The Transportation Act of 1920 charged the ICC to prescribe the types of property for which depreciation was properly included in operating expenses; the commission was also to prescribe the percentage of depreciation to be charged to each variety or class of depreciable property. It took some time for the commission to carry out the congressional requirement. Full compliance did not come until January 1, 1943. The depreciation order of the ICC set out the various classes of property for which depreciation charges should be established. Equipment and virtually all classes of fixed property were included. Items not included as depreciable for regulatory and financial reporting purposes included land, engineering expenses for construction, organization expenses, and legal expenses during construction.

The debate on betterment versus depreciation accounting and deferred tax accounting versus current recognition was prompted by concern over the proper recording of net income in the current period (year). The issue had its origins in the Great Depression. One of the debacles of that depression was the collapse of the conglomerate of utilities and electric interurban railroads assembled by Samuel Insull over the previous three decades. In the aftermath of the collapse and bankruptcy of the Insull empire, the Federal Trade Commission mandated depreciation accounting on the Insull companies, including the Chicago South Shore & South Bend Railroad.

The decision of the FTC was based on its conclusion that depreciation accounting more "fairly presented" the results of operation (income statement) and financial position (balance sheet) of the company. The concern then, and in later decades, was that asset-intensive companies, including railroads and utilities, could manipulate current earnings through timing of capital projects accounted for under betterment accounting. If work was done, expenses in the current year would increase; if work was deferred, expenses would drop, resulting in increased earnings. This basic assumption needs to be placed in the context that railroads are a very cyclical industry, and the accounting impacts of the cycle could be severely affected by the timing of betterment projects.

Of equal concern to some accountants was tax accounting practices. "Current tax accounting" versus "deferred tax accounting" revolves around the question of essentially reporting income taxes on the basis of cash paid versus accruing the tax liability that would ultimately have to be paid over time. Reducing the number of years over which a capital asset could be depreciated for tax purposes increased the deduction that could be taken in a given year, thus reducing the actual taxes paid. A given asset would be depreciated over, say, 5 years for tax purposes; the same asset would be depreciated over, say 25 years for financial accounting purposes. The accounting for the "timing difference" is deferred tax accounting. Despite how much cash is paid for income taxes in a given year, deferred tax accounting reconciles the difference between when the cash was paid for tax purposes versus how the taxes would be recognized for financial accounting purposes.

The balance sheet accounts prescribed by the ICC included "Road and Equipment Property" and "Improvements on Leased Property." "Accumulated Depreciation" is a deduction from the investment accounts named ear-

lier. "Total Transportation Property" is the cost of the assets less the recorded accumulated depreciation. Any investment in noncarrier property in other accounts is shown as "Investments in Affiliated Companies." Cash and materials and supplies are shown as "Current Assets." The liabilities side of the balance sheet shows accounts representing current liabilities, reserves of various types, and deferred credits, "Shareholders Equity, Capital Stock, Capital Surplus, and Retained Income." Another liability item is long-term debt.

In 2004 the regulatory accounting rules were prescribed in Section 49 of the Code of Federal Regulations (CFR) and applied only to Class 1 railroads, not to Class 2 (regional) or Class 3 (shortline) railroads, which are a growing segment of the industry. The separation of freight and passenger costs is essentially moot. Regulatory accounting only plays a role when a shipper is captive to a single railroad and ratemaking is not fully determined by competitive forces. Many such cases involve coal moving to utilities over long distances where one railroad controls the last few miles to the generating station, resulting in a bottleneck, hence the term "bottleneck cases." The other principal application of regulatory accounting is abandonment cases. Entry or exit of railroads by investors or existing railroads is still subject to economic regulation in varying degrees.

—George M. Smerk and Norman Carlson

REFERENCES

Interstate Commerce Commission. *Uniform System of Accounts for Railroad Companies.* Washington, D.C.: U.S. Government Printing Office (regularly updated and reissued).

Locklin, D. Philip. *Economics of Transportation.* 7th ed. Chap. 23. Homewood, Ill.: R. D. Irwin, 1972.

Act to Regulate Commerce (1887). *See* REGULATION

Adams, Charles Francis, Jr. (1835–1915)

Charles Francis Adams, Jr., was a historian, railroad executive, great-grandson of President John Adams, and grandson of President John Quincy Adams. Adams graduated from Harvard in 1856 and quickly became involved in public affairs. He served in the Civil War and was present at the battles of Antietam and Gettysburg. By the war's close he had risen to the brevet rank of brigadier general. After the war he became involved in the railroad industry, which he perceived to be the nation's most important business, but became increasingly troubled by the drift of railroad finance and management.

Adams came to believe that the giant railroad industry was in need of public regulation, and he was the principal impulse behind the Massachusetts Board of Railroad Commissioners, serving as its chairman between 1872 and 1879. But he also believed that regulation should not be heavy-handed and later was less than pleased with the scope of the Interstate Commerce Commission.

As early as 1869, in his article "A Chapter of Erie," published in the *North American Review*, Adams began pointing the finger at various Wall Street freebooters engaged in stock-manipulation schemes, among them Daniel Drew, Jay Gould, Jim Fisk, and Cornelius Vanderbilt. He subsequently published a book with his brother, Henry Adams, called *Chapters of Erie*, a classic of American history, a remarkable account of a dark period in American finance. It is a major early contribution to the effort to control unbridled laissez-faire capitalism and shady financial practices. Adams also wrote other important works, including *Railroads: Their Origins and Problems* (1878) and *Three Episodes in Massachusetts History* (1892). For many years he was president of the Massachusetts Historical Society.

Adams was elected a director of the Union Pacific Railroad and served as president of that railroad between 1884 and 1890. His term there opened with considerable success, but financial problems later forced him to withdraw in favor of his old archenemy Jay Gould—a bitter irony.

Adams was in many ways a typical Boston Brahmin, a patrician figure who believed that men of wealth and privilege owed something to society. In his later life he was a major reformer in the Boston area and was largely responsible for developing the city's parks and parkways. He served for many years as an overseer of Harvard University.

—George H. Douglas

REFERENCE

Kirkland, Edward Chase. *Charles Francis Adams, Jr., 1836–1916: The Patrician at Bay*. Cambridge, Mass.: Harvard Univ. Press, 1965.

Agricultural Development

Between 1850 and 1871 railroad companies received subsidies of federal and state land totaling approximately 180 million acres. In addition, railroads were involved with inducing agricultural settlement on various cutover lands, trying to repopulate abandoned eastern and southern farms, and opening other assorted tracts to agriculture. With so much acreage to liquidate, carriers as grant recipients and real estate agents faced two interwoven challenges from 1850 to the 1930s. Taken as one, the tasks of identifying prospective buyers and coaxing land purchases constituted a major first concern for railroad executives in their role as corporate landholders, but there was another issue that would have far-reaching consequences for both purchasers and sellers. Succeeding agriculturally became the most overriding common interest of pioneers and the carriers who had promoted settlements.

Without sufficient outputs from the new farms, failure would await not only the settlers but also the railroads, which depended upon sufficient traffic to pay off their investments in transportation lines that had preceded other developments across remote stretches in the Great Plains, West, and South. To stimulate profitable farming, railroads between the 1860s and the 1960s thus tried many programs and offered much support to farmers.

Railroad magazine, in a five-part series in 1951, covered land-grant activities by five major carriers. Looking at the Illinois Central, Northern Pacific, Great Northern, Burlington, and Santa Fe railroads, Harriet H. Gross found both similar and diverse ways in which these railroads promoted settlements on pristine lands. Movement to these lands came in most cases not so much as a result of railroad developments as because of the systematic real estate marketing and selling efforts of the lines. To encourage success among land purchasers, these transportation companies then aided settlers with timely agricultural advice, seeds, and purebred livestock. Activities by the Chicago, Burlington & Quincy were typical. It furnished prospective settlers with sample corn and wheat and planted many trees to keep snow from drifting on tracks, prevent erosion, and beautify rural areas. More than any other agency or organization, the Burlington was behind alfalfa growing in Nebraska; its promotion culminated in Nebraska becoming the nation's top grower of the crop. Through its efforts as well, major potato and sugar-beet production occurred across Nebraska, Colorado, Wyoming, and elsewhere. This railroad also promoted the building of silos, a campaign that saved many farmers from being ravaged by droughts of 1934 and 1936. In addition, the Burlington promoted and popularized both drought-resistant sorghums and soil-building crops, and it led campaigns against wheat smut and assisted farmers in wars with grasshoppers. Finally, in 1919 and throughout the following decade CB&Q worked at upgrading Nebraska's dairy herds by sponsoring travel by the state's dairymen to Wisconsin, introducing superior cows and bulls at no charge, and contributing substantially to the organization of the Nebraska Dairy Development Society.

Assistance with adjustment to new lands was an integral part of railroads' developmental programs. In these efforts the Illinois Central was a leader. Beginning in Illinois during the Civil War with efforts to promote the growing of cotton and sugar beets, the IC followed with other projects. In 1865 the railroad subsidized a chemical analysis of Illinois soils, and later it encouraged the development of orchards in downstate Illinois's Little Egypt, the growing of tomatoes in Copiah County, Mississippi, and strawberry production and dairying in Tangipahoa Parish, Louisiana.

West of the Mississippi River, James J. Hill of the Great Northern Railway did much to encourage and develop agriculture. In Minnesota and North Dakota during the 1880s, concerned about an overdependence upon wheat growing, Hill distributed to farmers 7,000 head of livestock, including 800 purebred bulls. To convince farmers of the value of scientific farming, the Empire Builder transported them at reduced rates to the state agricultural experiment station near St. Paul. In the Red River valley he was so certain that draining of land would be useful to cultivation that he challenged the counties by offering to share surveying costs with them. Hill and the Great Northern were also directly involved in several irrigation projects. They were largely responsible for one of the first systems in the Columbia Basin, and several years after Congress had enacted the Newlands Act of 1902 the railroad was active in developing the West Okanogan Irrigation District in north central Washington. In this instance it assisted the district in marketing bonds, and it sent a favorite contractor to build the irrigation works. Moreover, the Great Northern and four other major trans-Mississippi railroads contributed about $125,000 to the National Irrigation Assn., a lobby organization formed in 1899 to ensure passage of a bill for federal assistance to irrigation.

Other carriers were also involved with useful projects. As pioneers were settling their newly acquired land, railroads aided in the removal of stumps by providing dynamite and stump-pulling machinery. In the cutover areas of northern Wisconsin and Minnesota and Michigan's Upper Peninsula, land-clearing trains with equipment and experts appeared to show farmers how their land might yield satisfactory returns. To encourage settlements, the Kansas Pacific during the 1870s distributed seeds to farmers and tested soil for productivity. The Chicago, Burlington & Quincy Railroad gave prairie farmers seedlings, donated alfalfa seed to Nebraska pioneers, sponsored exhibits at agricultural fairs, and for several years beginning in 1895 published the *Corn Belt,* an educational newspaper. In order to provide cuttings at cost to farmers, the Northern Pacific ran a nursery at Fargo, North Dakota.

As development activities grew at railroads, new officers were appointed to handle them. As their workload expanded, several railroads formed distinct departments to handle agricultural development work. During the decade that preceded American involvement in World War I, many railroad corporations began hiring agricultural specialists. Both the Santa Fe and the Rock Island employed their experts in 1910, while the Missouri Pacific, New York Central, and Lehigh Valley added agents the following year. By the spring of 1917 no fewer than 50 major railroad companies had in place development departments of some sort. With rail transportation under federal control during the war years, development programs became inactive, but after the railroads' return to private management in 1920, they resumed. Before the war, colonization and agricultural development had often been inseparable at many trans-Mississippi railroads, but after 1920 most railroads increased their emphasis on industrial development.

Departing from an earlier adversarial relationship with farmers, railroad executives adopted a new strategy in the early 1900s. For more than three decades they had battled farmers' demands, first for federally regulated railroads and then, with the Populists in 1892, for government-owned and operated carriers. Several transportation lead-

The Great Northern's James J. Hill assisted farmers in acquiring thousands of head of livestock. These oxen-drawn farm implements were operated on Hill's own Northcote farm in Minnesota. —James J. Hill Library (Neg. LH1673)

The Great Northern helped develop several early irrigation projects in the Cascade Basin of Washington. This 1903 photograph shows farmworkers in the Cascade Mountain valley in 1903. —James J. Hill Library (Neg. JH481)

ers decided that boosting the production of agricultural goods would serve their companies' interests more than fighting with producers of food and fiber. Beside this goal, there was general agreement that it might be more prudent to have farmers on the side of the business than against it.

Emerging from several carriers almost simultaneously, diverse plans with the common objective of promoting the expansion of agricultural output unfolded. The railroads thus became a part of a strong interest in reforming rural America. The establishment of the Country Life Commission in 1909 by Theodore Roosevelt and such legislation as the Smith-Lever Act of 1914 for rural education and the Smith-Hughes Act of 1917 for vocational agriculture in high schools were associated with a general movement for rural reform. In overall support of this, railroad leaders promoted a simple idea. They reasoned that if they could encourage farmers to increase their output, the volume of freight from and to rural communities would increase significantly. Outbound traffic levels would improve as farmers produced more grain and meat for urban markets, and the net result would be increased disposable income for agriculturists. With growing wealth, their op-

portunities would improve for consuming more manufactures, thereby creating more inbound rail shipments, much of which would be high-rated less-than-carload-lot (LCL) goods.

With motives more financial than altruistic, railroads joined a national reform movement coalesced by a common desire to transform traditional farming into a more modern, productive system. In a desire to link agricultural prosperity to corporate responsibility, Frisco's Frank Anderson interpreted the tie of compatibility with railroads' activities for F. B. Mumford of the University of Missouri's College of Agriculture. The link was a result of the transportation company's attempts at "demonstrating and carrying to the farmer the methods already developed and pronounced as successful by various agricultural agencies." In another example, by confiding that "we [at the Illinois Central] are not in this for philanthropy; we have a selfish motive," J. C. Clair was clear about his company's true interests.

In order to promote commercial agriculture, several railroad executives recognized a need for effective teaching to induce farmers to alter their operations. To discover what might work most effectively required years of trying new approaches. Railroad-sponsored exhibits appeared at local, regional, state, and national expositions. To stimulate improved farming methods, railroads awarded prizes for excellence. The Great Northern's Hill believed in the value of personal rewards. In 1906, for every congressional district in Minnesota and the two Dakotas, he gave cash awards ranging from $75 to $300 for exceptional achievements in agriculture. In 1911 at the American Land and Irrigation Exposition, his prize for the best 100 pounds of wheat was a silver cup worth $1,000.

To promote greater agricultural output along their lines, a number of carriers published farm periodicals. The Baltimore & Ohio distributed *Messenger of Agricultural Development*, while the *Long Island Agronomist* was the Long Island Rail Road's contribution to better farming. The Pennsylvania Railroad issued *Increase the Crop per Acre*, a 112-page guide that included tips for better yields. Several railroads employed agricultural agents to write articles for publication in newspapers and periodicals. In many cases these were simplified distillations of scientific studies published either by the U.S. Department of Agriculture or state agricultural experiment stations.

The demonstration or educational train was the most popular means of reaching farmers. At the end of the nineteenth century Hill's Great Northern pioneered the use of railroad coaches to bring exhibits to rural areas, but Perry G. Holden of Iowa's agricultural college at Ames unintentionally provided the inspiration that resulted in formal links between land-grant institutions and railroads for the purpose of educating farmers with cooperative extension activities. Impressed by the importance Holden had given in a lecture to corn-seed selection, a Rock Island official, working with faculty from the land-grant institution, arranged what was called the Seed Corn Special. On April 18, 1904, it began a 400-mile journey through Iowa, visiting in the process 50 communities in 15 counties and attracting about 3,000 farmers.

This experiment became the prototype for similar efforts by other carriers. Railroads supplied specially outfitted coaches or freight cars, and either land-grant schools or state departments of agriculture assembled materials and livestock for exhibits and furnished staff members to accompany the displays. During 1911 an estimated 939,000 people boarded 62 "agricultural colleges on wheels" and heard 740 lectures.

Since the train stops were brief, neither the lectures given nor the displays viewed on these excursions had much direct impact on agricultural practices. There was value, nevertheless. Demonstration trains solidified in farmers' minds the value of scientific farming and made visitors more receptive to advice from "book" farmers. An estimated 93,000 Missourians waited on railroad platforms in 1911 for the Chief Josephine Special car being moved from town to town by locomotives owned by the state's three major lines, which cooperated in an endeavor to show off a world-record-setting dairy cow. Crowds along the route were rewarded for their patience with ten-minute glimpses of the famous bovine. Bred and raised at the College of Agriculture in Columbia, Chief Josephine and the accompanying professors who spoke along the route about her milk-producing ability might well have deposited some positive impressions about the accomplishments of scientific agriculture. If on this, as well as on the other excursion trains, only handfuls of visitors at each stopover gained one or two useful tips, there would be rapid dissemination through neighborhood networking. Soon after a lesson had proven its value to testers' satisfactions, boasts about results spread from farm to farm.

Like several much larger carriers, the Chicago & Illinois Midland Railway assumed more direct responsibility for agricultural progress and education. Near Havana, Illinois, it operated the company's CIMCO Farm as a model that used the latest scientific developments in crop and livestock management and soil improvement. Spanning more than two decades from November 12, 1932, through July 11, 1953, Trevor L. Jones's results as the railroad's agricultural agent reached farmers through *CIMCO Fortnightly*, a free newsletter. Moreover, WENR radio carried a popular weekly program that Chicago & Illinois Midland sponsored in the late 1920s and 1930s and that featured the railroad's own E. W. "Farmer" Rusk discussing relevant farm topics.

Major railroads operated model farms to demonstrate scientific farming principles. Both the Illinois Central and the New York Central acquired land or worked with owners to show what could be accomplished. The latter railroad owned experimental farms at West Bergen, New Jersey, and Chittenango, New York. In 1912, on the other hand, the IC established a carefully conceived arrangement with owners of 12 40-acre plots in Louisiana and Mississippi. Under contract terms, landowners were required to farm their plots according to IC instructions, plant only IC-provided seeds, and apply proper fertilizers provided by the railroad. For guidance in the two states, the IC turned to Mississippi and Louisiana's land-grant institutions and to three railroad-employed supervisors. The railroad hoped to prove to ordinary farmers what they could gain from diversification and crop rotation. The railroad must have been satisfied with the initial results of these experiments; it expanded the number of plots to 32 and opened work in three additional states.

Several other southern and southwestern lines followed a different approach. H. M. Bainer, a Santa Fe officer, in 1910 rejected suggestions that the railroad establish a central demonstration farm. Bainer maintained that if farmers were not directly involved, the work would be less effective and a waste of Santa Fe resources. His alternative was for the railroad to supply farmers with enough high-quality seeds to sow 10 acres of a crop and to require their adherence to instructions. Most participants of this plan farmed Texas's Panhandle and South Plains.

The Great Northern operated one of the most ambitious demonstration programs. Beginning in 1912, Hill's railroad gave farmers an opportunity to lease 5-acre plots in western Minnesota and in North Dakota for $8 per acre. As part of the deal, the railroad supplied seed and fertilizer. By 1915 there were 987 plots in the program, giving it the reputation of being "the largest private agricultural extension system in the world."

Railroads were also active in soil conservation. To assist farmers in improving yields on acidic soil, several midwestern carriers transported at no charge gondola cars loaded with ground limestone to rights of way near farms. In Missouri between Sedalia and Otterville, the Missouri Pacific, for example, deposited 500 tons during April 1929. These efforts often corresponded with legume and alfalfa campaigns directed by agricultural colleges.

In efforts intended to assist farmers in their transport of produce, grain, and livestock to markets, railroads were active promoters of road improvements. Although the logic behind these campaigns had seemed faultless, the longer-term results were detrimental to railroads. More passable roadways quickly opened up competition from trucks. Statistical data for the transport of livestock to slaughterhouses during the 1920s and 1930s confirm a trend of ever-increasing reliance on motor vehicles.

The most direct effect of railroads on farming came from the introduction of refrigerated cars. Although there had been various experiments and experiences with icing down shipments of beer, dairy products, meat, and produce before and after the Civil War, it was meatpacker Gustavus Swift who initiated large-scale use of refrigera-

tion. Tired of the bulk-weight costs of transporting live beef cattle from Chicago to butchers elsewhere, Swift decided that shipments of dressed meat would offer many advantages. Failing on his own to discover some way to prevent rotting in transit from the Windy City to the East Coast, Swift turned to Boston inventor Andrew J. Chase. After some trial and error, the Bostonian in 1881 offered a plan for the first relatively successful refrigerator car. Using roof hatches at both ends of tightly sealed cars, Chase proposed packing ice in specially designed and protected holding cells or bunkers.

Railroads initially opposed Swift's plans for shipping hung carcasses instead of live cattle and hogs. Opposition also came from East Coast slaughterhouses and butchers and from their customers. Each had a special interest to protect. For eastbound freight carriers, the increased use of refrigerator cars meant a considerable loss of tonnage and unneeded animal loading docks, stalls, and feeding stations. Proprietors of and many local workers at abattoirs and butcher shops suffered as a result of Swift's innovation. Between 1881 and 1900 the packing industries of Chicago and Kansas City expanded at the same time that those in New York and Boston were dwindling. In effect, refrigeration caused a rapid move from local meat operations to Midwest-dominated packers of pork and beef and reliance upon refrigerated railroad boxcars or "reefers" to supply a nation of carnivores.

With poultry, something similar was transpiring. Chicken and other fowl had come to local markets for slaughter and preparation for sale. Before the refrigerator

Open stock cars transported livestock from the farms to the packing plants. In 1920, one of the best years for livestock shipment, U.S. railroads transported 27 million tons of livestock. By the time this much more recent photograph was taken at Peach Springs, Arizona, in May 1972, livestock shipment by rail had all but vanished with a shift to decentralized packing plants and highway carriers. —Joe McMillan, *Trains* Magazine Collection

The development of the railroad refrigerator car transformed the way perishable foods were shipped and vastly improved the American diet. This drawing, from the July 13, 1877, *Railroad Gazette*, shows an early example of the ice-cooled refrigerator car. —Donald Duke Collection

car, poultry literally came fresh from a butcher's chopping block. Then gradually, with reefer improvements, dressed fowl began appearing in such chain grocery stores as A&P. By 1890 Kansas City's poultry-processing plants were already using refrigerated railroad cars to transport 2,500,000 pounds of dressed poultry to scattered markets.

Reefers also increased the consumption of seafood. Before icing-down procedures became common on railroad freight cars, fresh shrimp, for example, were rarely available from northeastern fishmongers. With no means to ship these crustaceans to urban markets, commercial fishermen who trolled the Atlantic Ocean along North Carolina's coastline considered the shellfish nuisances because of their tendency to clog nets.

Without prolonged periods of freezing temperatures, North Carolina, with its generally mild winters, needed more than freight cars capable of holding ice to ship perishable seafood to northern cities. To become a supplier, the state's fishing industry had to have a way to produce ice. Importing ice from northern companies was impractical and expensive. Thus it was not until inexpensive artificial ice

making was perfected that North Carolina shrimp could reach New York City's Fulton Street markets. Because there were no possibilities for shipments before the development and availability of the ammonia-compression system for making ice, rail service had not existed between North Carolina's fishing towns and north-south through lines. A breakthrough came with the completion of the Wilmington, Brunswick & Southern Railroad to Southport in 1914. As a result of WB&S reaching the fishing village, an entrepreneur used the availabilities of a railroad and a fledgling commercial fishing industry to open a firm that specialized in packing and shipping fresh seafood for sale in the North. According to a November 2, 1914, report in the *Southport News*, its first shipment of 300 bushels of iced shrimp had recently left by rail for New York City. With transits of less than 24 hours from Southport to Fulton Street fishmongers and relatively low per pound costs, North Carolina shrimp soon became a popular new addition to New Yorkers' dinner tables. Similar activity occurred in the Northeast with New England lobsters and cod.

In addition, refrigerator cars revolutionized American

This cutaway drawing shows a typical arrangement of refrigerated meat and fowl from a Swift Refrigeration Transportation Co. car. Meatpacker Gustavus Franklin Swift was also the operator of a major refrigerator-car line. —Illinois Historical Survey

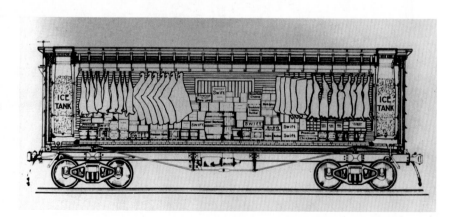

consumption of fruit and vegetables. Areas of the United States with year-round or early growing seasons became important suppliers of produce. Tree-ripened peaches from Georgia, Louisiana strawberries, Washington State apples, and California and Florida citrus had been unknown outside their immediate growing radii. Bananas were exotic and available only in such southern ports as New Orleans and Mobile. Excepting such root vegetables as carrots, beets, potatoes, onions, and turnips, other fresh varieties like lettuce, tomatoes, and squash existed in the diets of most Americans only after summer or fall harvests.

Having no means of transporting fruits and vegetables from the South and West to colder areas of the nation without spoilage, growers had no reason to expand their production. The introduction of reefers changed everything. As an illustration, prosperity in Washington's berry-producing Puyallup Valley followed refrigeration. Before it, the ideal berry-growing conditions of this section of Puget Sound could not be adequately exploited by landowners who wished to take advantage of the region's abundant rainfall and relatively cool summers to develop thriving commercial operations.

Oranges and grapes from California were two other perishables that reached U.S. markets because of refrigeration. The West Coast state produced two main varieties of oranges. The Washington Navel ripens in winter and has a marketing season from November to May. Given its maturity period, this fruit could be transported from California to almost anywhere in the United States without the use of ice. Valencias, on the other hand, begin to ripen in late April or early May and are available until November. Before reefers, these oranges were rarely seen outside California. The first evidence of a shift in preferences occurred in 1918, and by 1926 Valencia oranges were America's favorite variety.

The evolution of the refrigerator car and its components had much to do with its success. Railroad managers learned when and how often to place ice in the hatches. Evidence of how much the industry had discovered about the safe handling of perishable vegetables, fruit, and meat came from years of experiences with grapes. With 90 percent of their production in California by the 1930s and from 29,000 to 36,000 reefer loads being handled annually, officials had gained knowledge about icing requirements. According to the U.S. Department of Agriculture (USDA), there had been only two alternatives available to shippers before July 1932. "Standard refrigeration" was for shipments during warm months. En route to the Atlantic Coast, trains stopped 10 to 12 times at regular icing stations. At each, crews filled the reefers' ice bunkers to capacity. During late autumn and through the winter months, initial icings at departures from warehouses in California would not be supplemented during the trip. But since risks from losses could be high from a warm front, one or more stops for ice replenishment might be necessary.

Builders of reefer cars gained over time a better understanding of how to make them more efficient. They experimented with different kinds of insulation to find those that were most effective under adverse conditions.

Given the seasonal nature of many perishable fruits and vegetables, most railroads preferred outsourcing the operation of refrigerator cars. A large majority of reefers were under the control of specialists or major shippers. The Pacific Fruit Express Co. was the largest independent

This print, dating to about 1937, shows icing of cars at the Fruit Growers Express Co. icing station at Hurt Street in Atlanta, Georgia. —Library of Congress (Neg. LC-USZ62-116753)

operator. Formed in 1906 by the Southern Pacific and the Union Pacific to handle West Coast perishable food, it began with 6,000 yellow-painted reefers. By mid-1955 PFE had almost 39,000 refrigerated cars in service. The Fruit Growers Express Co. dominated the transportation of perishable foodstuffs east of the Mississippi River. Organized on March 18, 1920, as a result of antitrust litigation against the Armour Packing Co., it was a joint effort of the Chicago & Eastern Illinois, the Norfolk & Western, and the New York, New Haven & Hartford railroads.

Whether independently or internally controlled, the operation of reefers was dependent upon icing stations. From the West Coast to the Midwest, the Railway Ice Co. of Newton, Kansas, as supplier to the Santa Fe, was one of the most important operators of icing services because by 1922, 11,751 or 16 percent of Santa Fe's freight cars were refrigerated. The Kansas firm managed ice-replenishment stations from New Mexico to Fort Madison, Iowa. Its plant at Argentine, Kansas, had a daily production capability of 150 tons of ice.

Forewarned of an incoming freight train, icing crews at stations knew how many reefers were on their way. As a locomotive approached, workers were ready, prepared with enough ice to step from icing platforms to reefer roofs to open hatches for the refilling of bunkers as quickly as possible. Speed was essential since every wasted minute reduced the value of perishable cargos. The icing station at Fulton, Kentucky, located at a strategic railroad junction of the Illinois Central and the Louisville & Nashville, became famous for its ability to load the blocks of ice rapidly in Fruit Growers Express reefers carrying bananas and strawberries from New Orleans and other southern depots to the Midwest or the East. The Fulton icing station handled reefers loaded with many different fruits and vegetables, but it became known as the Banana Capital of the United States because of its important relationship to banana shipments.

Using the Fulton ice works, the Illinois Central achieved a milestone in June 1924. Carrying perishable produce from the South, its trains set an average daily miles-covered record of 98.88 miles, thereby breaking its old monthly average of 97.13. That was not all that was being achieved by IC-pulled reefers. Between January 26 and May 12, 1924, the carrier handled 6,146 refrigerated cars on 153 vegetable trains from Baton Rouge to Chicago. An amazing 148 of these arrived in Chicago in time for third-morning deliveries, or in other words, 63.5 hours after their Louisiana departures.

No matter how a refrigerator car is defined or when designation is made for the first iced shipment, reefers underwent steady refinements and improvements. During the first half of the twentieth century the cars built by Fruit Growers Express Co. of Alexandria, Virginia, had a basic design that typified reefers generally. Painted yellow, these cars had steel underframes, galvanized steel roofs, and wood sheathing. Adjustable ice grates along with the bunkers folded to the floor to permit use of the cars for the transport of nonperishable cargos. Ice-holding capacity varied according to the ice's physical description. Transporters preferred chunks to coarse or crushed ice because it thawed more slowly. Ice bunkers held 9,600

Bananas from Central American ships were loaded aboard IC refrigerators cars in New Orleans in the 1950s.
—Illinois Central

pounds of ice, and reefers had cargo capacities of 30.2 tons. As insulation improved, prejudice against metal cars disappeared, and by 1948 Fruit Growers Express replaced ice with mechanical refrigerators, a step long postponed because of uncertainties about the reliability of motor-generated cooling.

From the earliest attempts at shipping fresh food by rail, the task of avoiding excessive spoilage has been a continuous challenge for car designers. Railroads quickly realized that their common wooden boxcars packed down with ice would require basic modifications for heat-sensitive cargos. Changes eventually included everything from improving door latches to better insulation and sealants. In the battle to protect reefer interiors against outdoor heat, car walls, floors, and roofs thickened as layers of wood, paper, cork, sheet metal, and hair felt insulation were added. By the late 1930s the once-standard two-inch thickness of the early 1900s had increased by four or five times. After 1945 such newly developed materials as fiberglass and Styrofoam allowed for the shrinkage of insulation to only four inches. Cars also underwent a transformation as builders slowly began fabricating with different construction materials. In the opinion of John H. White, author of *The Great Yellow Fleet*, reefer cars have been "the most conservative of all American freight cars." Wood frames and bodies did not begin to disappear until 1940. Carmakers only used steel for underframes. In the immediate postwar era both the Illinois Central and the Santa Fe experimented with some new construction concepts. At its Mississippi car shop in McComb, the former carrier produced a reefer with an aluminum body, circulating air fans, fiberglass insulation, electric lighting, collapsing ice bunkers, an underframe with a cushioned draft gear, and antitheft ice hatches. By manufacturing a refrigerator car with a stainless-steel body, the latter railroad, like the Illinois Central with aluminum, did not become a rail industry pacesetter because the initial cost of using standard steel was so much cheaper than the experimental metals. For maintaining coolness, axle-driven fans to augment bunker ices effectively, a feature first tested and shown to work in 1885 by Newton L. Baumgardner, became the basis for better forced-air systems. William Van Dorn was the inventor who did the most work to perfect these. Named Preco fans for the company that marketed them, Van Dorn's device was found on roughly one-third of all reefers less than a decade after its invention. In the early 1950s an electrical drive began supplanting units powered by axle movements.

Long after the icebox had disappeared from American homes, railroads began adopting mechanical refrigeration. Although there were still some cars that required ice as late as 1978, most of the nation's fleet of refrigerated boxcars was now being cooled mechanically. This meant the disappearance of ice crews, plants, and docks. In the final analysis, it was the growing importance of the frozen-food industry with its dependence upon fixed subfreezing temperatures that accounted for icing's de-

mise. Had it not been for this new demand, railroads likely would have continued to use ice. Mechanical units were heavy, required space whether or not there was any need for refrigeration, and demanded maintenance.

By 1950 trucking fruits and vegetables to American markets, in terms of carloads, had almost pulled even to shipping produce by rail. Thereafter, over the next 25 years, the transport of perishable foodstuffs by motor vehicles almost monopolized all such movements to urban distribution points. The advantages of trucks over railroads in the moving of produce to markets were clear to shippers. For one thing, they could easily arrange multiple pickups and deliveries by truck. Generally as well, shipments of produce arrived in better shape because of speedier transits. Of equal importance, road carriers operated with fewer governmental regulations, with the results being rate-assessment flexibility and quicker resolution of damage claims. Then, with the completion of the interstate highway network, trucks were able to cover much greater distances in less time.

Both directly and indirectly, railroads affected American agriculture. There is no way to measure results of many of their programs. At changing agricultural practices and methods, the carriers' earliest direct efforts probably had only minimal impact. It was as a catalyst for change that railroads achieved importance. Through lobbying efforts that supported such developments as the county-agent system and irrigation, railroads contributed to changes in farming. In the final analysis, however, technological and scientific developments were more responsible for the emergence of modern farming than the railroads' efforts. An exception was the refrigerator car. It opened up new areas for food supplies, and it encouraged both the growing and consuming of new foods. Moreover, it permitted northern households to enjoy summer produce throughout the year.

—Dennis S. Nordin

REFERENCES

Gross, Harriet H. "The Land Grant Legend." *Railroad* 55, no. 3 (Aug. 1951): 28–49; 55, no. 4 (Sept. 1951): 64–77; 56, no. 1 (Oct. 1951): 68–79; 56, no. 2 (Nov. 1951): 30–41; 56, no. 3 (Dec. 1951): 40–53.

Scott, Roy V. *Railroad Development Programs in the Twentieth Century*. Ames: Iowa State Univ. Press, 1985.

White, John H. *The Great Yellow Fleet: A History of American Railroad Refrigerator Cars*. San Marino, Calif.: Golden West, 1986.

See also LAND GRANTS.

Air Transportation

Commercial air transportation, one of the twentieth century's great growth industries, developed quite slowly before World War II. Public interest in aviation was high after the first powered controlled flight by Orville and Wilbur Wright in 1903, but industry activity was initially directed toward experimentation, technological improvements, and demonstration flying. Priorities shifted to military aviation during World War I. The federal government spent hundreds of millions of dollars to build several thousand two-seat Curtiss JN-4 "Jennies" and DeHavilland DH-4 aircraft, train pilots, and establish support systems. Airmail service between Washington and New York was launched by the army in May 1918 and soon taken over by the Post Office. Despite accidents and other difficulties, government-operated airmail routes expanded and continued until 1926, when they were gradually transferred to private contractors. To support airmail service, which competed with the railroads, and facilitate the growth of air navigation generally, in the mid-1920s the federal government began to establish beacons, weather and communication facilities, and other navigation aids along airways connecting major cities.

Technological progress continued throughout the 1920s, but no aircraft (including Ford and Fokker trimotor designs) offered the prospect of economically viable passenger service. The survival and growth of air transport companies continued to depend on federal subsidies embedded in airmail contracts. When scandals surfaced in 1934 from the postmaster general's authority to issue noncompetitive contracts and make other major decisions affecting the industry, President Franklin D. Roosevelt and Congress intervened. The shakeout from the scandals included an upheaval in industry structure (including a separation of aircraft manufacturing from air transportation) and the restoration of competitive bid requirements. Carriers that survived the shakeout and gained airmail contracts under the new system had their routes certified under the grandfather clause of the Civil Aeronautics Act of 1938. This statute provided the framework for federal promotion and regulation of civil aviation until 1958.

The most notable aircraft developed during the 1930s was the Douglas DC-3, which entered service in 1936. The DC-3 was developed at the behest of American Airlines, which wanted to provide Pullman-type sleeper service on its 16- to 18-hour transcontinental routes. With a cruising speed of 185 mph and a range of about 1,500 miles, the DC-3 could carry 21 passengers in its daytime configuration and was the first airliner capable of producing a profit for its operators without some form of subsidy. It was so superior to other aircraft that within three years DC-3s carried more than 90 percent of domestic airline traffic. During World War II more than 10,000 military versions of the versatile plane were built, and in 1949 DC-3s still outnumbered newer aircraft types in domestic airline service.

Although air transportation was a glamorous and exciting industry, it was only a peripheral competitor for railroad passenger traffic before World War II. Airlines generated 1.3 billion passenger-miles in 1940, but this constituted only 2.8 percent of common-carrier passenger-miles and 0.4 percent of total U.S. passenger-miles. Private automobiles and intercity buses remained the railroads' principal competitors. The airline industry's future competitive prospects were significantly enhanced and accelerated by wartime aviation developments. Major technological progress occurred in aircraft design and materials, aircraft engines, avionics, communications, and air traffic control. In addition, new airfields were built and existing airports expanded, thousands of pilots and flight engineers were trained, and hundreds of thousands of individuals had their first flight experience.

Air transportation grew so rapidly in the decades after World War II that the competitive battle with other modes did not last long. From 1947 through 1965 airline industry growth averaged nearly 14 percent per year,

In this early 1930s view an air express plane, an REA express truck, and a Rock Island train were linked to offer expedited air express service. —REA Express, *Trains* Magazine Collection

twice the rate of the next growth industry (electric utilities) and almost four times the growth rate (3.7 percent) of the entire economy. Domestic airline passenger-miles exceeded first-class rail service in 1955, intercity bus service in 1956, total rail passenger-miles in 1957, and the total of railroads and buses combined in 1963. International airline traffic manifested similar impressive growth rates. In 1958 airline passengers crossing the North Atlantic for the first time outnumbered those traveling by ship, and the gap widened in each subsequent year.

In 1965 domestic airline traffic totaled 58.1 billion passenger-miles, compared with 23.8 billion for intercity buses and 17.6 billion for the railroads. Eleven years later, in 1976, airline passenger-miles had nearly tripled to 152.3 billion, which constituted 79.5 percent of for-hire intercity passenger traffic. Air transportation completely dominated long-distance business and personal travel, and despite the development of the interstate highway system, airlines provided increasingly serious competition to private automobiles over short and medium distances. In 1976 the average length of haul in trunk-line domestic passenger service was 819 miles.

Several factors contributed to this remarkable postwar success. First, a rapid succession of new aircraft came into service offering greater size, range, speed, and comfort. During the 1950s larger, faster, pressurized long-distance piston aircraft were followed by turboprop planes and by the introduction of long-distance pure jet transports in 1958. In the mid-1960s turboprops and smaller jets revolutionized short- and medium-haul markets, and in the early 1970s wide-body jumbo jets redefined competition on high-density long-distance routes. The succession of new planes attracted passengers from other transport modes and generated entirely new demand. The equipment splurge also boosted carrier productivity and pushed the industry relentlessly toward mass-market transportation. Passenger service continued to generate more than 80 percent of industry revenues, with the balance coming from freight, mail, and express.

U.S. international carriers and domestic trunk lines (the principal domestic carriers) went off federal subsidy in the mid-1950s and for the most part remained profitable until the 1970s. Local-service airlines, which generated about 10 percent of industry revenues and served smaller communities, continued to receive "public service revenues" from the federal government. Despite postwar inflation, airline fares, in real terms, were held steady or even reduced as a result of increased industry efficiency and pricing innovations. "Coach Class" with higher-density seating and fewer frills than first-class service was introduced in 1948, and "Economy Class" in the mid-1950s. A wide variety of other incentive fares were also introduced. "Discount" fares attracted large numbers of budget-conscious travelers, helped fill the rapid growth of scheduled airline seats, and put many low-fare nonscheduled airlines out of business.

The industry's growth and prosperity in the decades after World War II were also due in part to the supportive policies of the Civil Aeronautics Board. CAB decisions involving routes, fares, mergers, and other matters typically sought to limit competition to keep carriers sufficiently profitable to ensure a safe, reliable, and stable air transport industry. However, the CAB could not prevent self-inflicted industry wounds from persistent overcapacity, excessive schedule frequency, and poorly executed mergers.

By the early 1970s air transportation had become a mature industry. Market growth continued, but at slower single-digit rates. In 1999 U.S. scheduled airlines carried 635 million passengers and had operating revenues of $118.2 billion. Important technological progress also continued, especially in the areas of fuel efficiency, engine reliability, avionics, and increased aircraft range. However, the airlines also encountered a succession of unprecedented economic shocks that caused wrenching changes in the industry and turned erratic profitability into financial disaster. The problems included huge increases in jet fuel costs, aircraft hijackings and terrorist attacks, economic deregulation of both air cargo and passenger service, numerous carrier bankruptcies, air traffic controller strikes, and the impact of the Gulf War and September 11, 2001, on airline costs and revenues.

—Richard W. Barsness

REFERENCES

Air Transport Assn. of America. *Annual Report.* Washington, D.C., 1990–2000.

Davies, R. E. G. *Airlines of the United States since 1914.* London: Putnam, 1972.

Harper, Donald V. *Transportation in America: Users, Carriers, Government.* Englewood Cliffs, N.J.: Prentice-Hall, 1978.

Heppenheimer, T. A. *Turbulent Skies: The History of Commercial Aviation.* New York: John Wiley & Sons, 1995.

Szurovy, Geza. *Classic American Airlines.* St. Paul, Minn.: Motorbooks International, 2003.

See also HIGHWAY TRANSPORTATION; WATER TRANSPORTATION.

Alaska Railroad

The discovery of gold in the 1880s and 1890s stimulated settlement in Alaska, bringing with it the need for a railroad from a port to the interior. Alaska's sparse population could not finance the construction of a railroad and furnish enough business to keep it going; it would have to be built by the U.S. government. Congress provided for a railroad as a rider on the bill granting self-government to the territory in 1912.

Two short railroads, one standard gauge and one narrow, were already in operation and were designated the end portions of the new railroad: the Alaska Northern Railway and the Tanana Valley Railroad. In 1902 the Alaska Central Railroad was organized to build a standard-gauge line inland from the port of Seward. The company was reorganized as the Alaska Northern in 1909. In 1915, when the government bought it, its rails reached 71 miles north from Seward to Kern Creek; only the 34-mile stretch from Seward to Sunrise Station was in operation. The narrow-gauge ancestor was the Tanana Valley Railroad, which began operating in 1904. It ran west from Fairbanks to the head of navigation on the Tanana River and northeast from Fairbanks to a gold-mining area. The U.S. government purchased it in 1917 and standard-gauged it in 1923.

The Alaska Railroad Commission proposed a two-pronged railroad running from both Seward and Cordova to Fairbanks. The Copper River & Northwestern Railway, completed in 1911, ran 195 miles from Cordova northeast to copper mines and had proposed a line north to Fairbanks. Political considerations precluded using the Copper River & Northwestern, so the proposal was changed to a single line from Seward to Fairbanks.

Construction of more than 300 miles of railroad to connect the two shortlines began in 1915 at what is now Anchorage, using much of the equipment and many of the men who had just completed the Panama Canal. President Warren G. Harding drove a ceremonial last spike on July 15, 1923, and the railroad was named the Alaska Railroad (ARR).

World War II brought an enormous increase in traffic to the railroad, and military personnel were brought in to operate it and to build a 12-mile spur from Portage through the Chugach Mountains to the ice-free port of Whittier. The U.S. Department of the Interior operated the Alaska Railroad until 1967, when it came under the Federal Railroad Administration, an agency of the newly formed Department of Transportation. The State of Alaska took ownership of the railroad on January 6, 1985.

Much of Alaska's population lives in the area along the 526-mile railroad. ARR's passenger services are aimed largely at tourists, many of whom are traveling to Mt. McKinley National Park. Commuter service at Anchorage is under consideration. The railroad's principal freight commodities are sand and gravel, coal, chemicals, and petroleum.

In 2005 the Alaska Railroad operated 466 miles of main line and 59 miles of branch lines, with a total track ownership of 611 miles. The railroad operated 61 locomotives, 1,643 owned and leased freight cars, and 48 passenger cars, with 754 employees. Traffic in 2005 totaled 471,348 passengers and 8,136,643 tons of freight. Total 2004 revenues were $144 million, and operating expenses of $131.3 million meant a 91 percent operating ratio.

—George H. Drury

REFERENCE

Cohen, Stan. *Rails across the Tundra*. Missoula, Mont.: Pictorial Histories, 1984.

Algoma Central & Hudson Bay Railway

In 1899 the Algoma Central Railway was chartered to build northward from Sault Ste. Marie, Ontario, to bring iron ore and pulpwood out of the wilderness. Two years later the railway ambitiously added "& Hudson Bay" to its corporate name. By 1912 the track reached 165 miles north from Sault Ste. Marie to Hawk Junction, where a branch diverged west to Lake Superior at Michipicoten Harbor. The main line was pushed north, crossing the Canadian Pacific at Franz and the Canadian Northern at Oba. It reached a connection with the National Transcontinental Railway (like Canadian Northern a predecessor of Canadian National Railways) at Hearst, 297 miles from Sault Ste. Marie, in 1914.

In the 1970s, 1980s, and 1990s the Algoma Central was best known for its tourist operations, one-day round trips from Sault Ste. Marie to the Agawa River Canyon, where the railway established a park. In 1965 the company dropped "& Hudson Bay" from its corporate title. In 1990 it became the Algoma Central Corp., with railway, ship, trucking, real estate, and land and forest subsidiaries. It was purchased in January 1995 by the expanding Wisconsin Central.

Affiliated with the Algoma Central in early days was the Algoma Eastern Railway, whose line ran west 87 miles from Sudbury, Ontario, through Drury and Espanola to Manitoulin Island. For more than half its length it paralleled Canadian Pacific Railway's Sudbury–Sault Ste. Marie route. CPR leased the Algoma Eastern in 1930.

—George H. Drury

REFERENCES

Nock, O. S. *Algoma Central Railway*. London: A & C Black, 1975.
Wilson, Dale. *The Algoma Central Railway Story*. Sudbury, Ont.: Nickel Belt Rails, 1984.

Allegheny Portage Railroad

As east-west transportation developed during the first half century of the American nation, the state of Pennsylvania and the city of Philadelphia were aware that the terrain of the state posed a handicap to participation in the commerce of the new western regions. To the north, the state of New York created the first commercially usable western route with the Erie Canal. To the south were projected the National Road and the Baltimore & Ohio Railroad. If no way could be found to overcome Pennsylvania's mountainous terrain, it was likely that the trade of the west would bypass the state.

Studies began in earnest in 1824, and a final plan for the Main Line of Public Works was enacted on March 24, 1828. This was to be a route across the state that was part canal, part railroad. The Columbia Railroad would carry traffic between Philadelphia and Columbia, on the Susquehanna River, while a canal along the Susquehanna and Juniata rivers would link Columbia with Hollidaysburg, on the eastern slope of the Alleghenies. The Allegheny Portage Railroad would take the route over the summit of the Alleghenies between Hollidaysburg and Johnstown. Another canal along the Conemaugh River would complete the route to Pittsburgh.

With the necessity for a rise of 1,400 feet from the Juniata River at Hollidaysburg and a descent of 1,175 feet to the Little Conemaugh at Johnstown, the engineers for the Allegheny Portage Railroad were faced with an unprecedented challenge. The solution was a railroad that employed ten inclined planes, five on each side of the summit. Between the planes were "levels," most of them only about 2 miles in length, though two on the west slope were 4 and 13 miles long, and usually on a slight grade. The overall length was 36.69 miles. The railroad was built with double track. It included the first railroad tunnel in the United States, a 900-foot bore at Staple Bend, near Johnstown.

Construction was started in 1831, and the railroad opened on March 18, 1834, initially as a public highway, with tolls charged for operation of privately owned cars. The inclines were operated by state employees, and for the first 14 months operation on the levels was by horsepower. In May 1835 the state took over the complete operation and began to introduce steam locomotives on some of the levels.

Such a railroad was not very fast. Freight was eventually expedited by an early version of piggyback, with canal boats constructed in sections so they could be disassembled, transported by rail, then reassembled. In fact, freight traveled all the way from Philadelphia to Pittsburgh in these containers. After the operating crews became experienced, passenger cars could travel over the road in about six hours.

The Allegheny Portage Railroad was a unique engineering achievement, but an economic failure. Its operating costs and its rates were so high that in 1839 bulk commodities such as flour could be shipped from Pittsburgh to Philadelphia more economically by water via New Orleans than by the canal-rail route. As early as 1836 appropriations were made for surveys to establish a route not requiring inclined planes. Construction of an alternate route, the New Portage Railroad, began in 1851. The railroad was completed in 1856, but by then the Pennsylvania Railroad had completed a superior competing route over the mountains.

The Pennsylvania had reached the base of the Alleghenies at Hollidaysburg in late 1850, while a line from the west reached Johnstown from Pittsburgh in 1852, connecting with the Allegheny Portage Railroad to create an all-rail route across the state. There was a lack of cooperation between the state and the Pennsylvania. The Portage shut down in wintertime when the canals froze, and it also refused to operate trains at night. The Pennsylvania accelerated the construction of its own route over the mountains, which opened in February 1854, making the Allegheny Portage Railroad obsolete and the New Portage redundant. The state wastefully completed the New Portage. After much negotiation, in 1857 the state sold the entire Main Line of Public Works to the Pennsylvania Railroad. The PRR had no real use for the New Portage and promptly abandoned it, salvaging the rails for use elsewhere.

Shortly after the turn of the twentieth century traffic on the Pennsylvania had increased so that an alternate route over the mountains would be useful. The grade of the New Portage was rehabilitated, track was relaid, and the line became a freight bypass. The route included a curve that was a little brother to the Horseshoe Curve west of Altoona and was named Muleshoe Curve. The Pennsylvania also made use of the west end of the grade of the New Portage near Johnstown.

Some of the west end of the New Portage is still occupied by the former Pennsylvania Railroad main-line tracks (later Conrail, now Norfolk Southern). Conrail abandoned the east end of the New Portage route, including Muleshoe Curve, in 1981.

Today, little can be seen of any of the inclined planes on the western slope, but many are still visible on the eastern slope. The Allegheny Portage Railroad National Historic Site, established by the National Park Service in the 1960s, operates a visitors' center at the Cresson Summit near Gallitzin, which encompasses a reconstructed engine house and a section of incline, and the Lemon House tavern built on the site around 1832. The Staple Bend Tunnel, the first railroad tunnel in the United States, was opened to visitors in 2001.

—Adrian Ettlinger

REFERENCES

Burgess, George H., and Miles C. Kennedy. *Centennial History of the Pennsylvania Railroad Company, 1846–1946*. Philadelphia: Pennsylvania Railroad, 1949.

Gerstner, Franz Anton Ritter von. *Early American Railroads*. Ed. Frederick C. Gamst. Stanford, Calif.: Stanford Univ. Press, 1997 [1842–1843].

Roberts, Solomon W. "Reminiscences of the First Railroad over the Allegheny Mountain." *Bulletin of the Railway and Locomotive Historical Society,* no. 44 (Oct. 1937): 6–23.

Rubin, Julius. *Canal or Railroad? Imitation and Innovation in the Response to the Erie Canal in Philadelphia, Baltimore, and Boston.* Philadelphia: American Philosophical Society, 1961.

Taber, Thomas T., III. *Railroads of Pennsylvania Encyclopedia and Atlas.* Muncy, Pa.: self-published, 1987.

Allen, Horatio (1802–1889)

Horatio Allen was a major figure in the early days of railroading. He was born on May 10, 1802, in Schenectady, New York, and grew up in a family that prized thought and intellectual activity. His father, Dr. Benjamin Allen, was a professor of mathematics at Union College, and his mother, Mary Benedict Allen, was a highly cultured woman. Schenectady stood at the entryway to the Mohawk Valley as it was emerging as the path to the West. At this point in Allen's life, the new Erie Canal was an exciting engineering venture, later to become a corridor for early railway development.

Allen graduated from Columbia College in 1823 with a degree and high honors in mathematics. After a brief detour into law, in 1824 he became a resident engineer for the Chesapeake & Delaware Canal Co., where he was a colleague of Benjamin Wright. When Wright moved on to be chief engineer of the Delaware & Hudson Canal Co., Allen became his assistant engineer.

The D&H canal was built to bring coal from northeastern Pennsylvania to the market in New York City by linking the Delaware River with the Hudson. When Wright left the D&H in 1827, he was replaced by John B. Jervis, who hired Horatio Allen. In planning for the canal, Jervis realized that it would be enormously difficult and costly to build over the mountains and decided that a railway should be built to feed the canal. Jervis commissioned Allen to travel to England to purchase strap iron for rails and four steam locomotives. One locomotive was built by Robert Stephenson of Newcastle, the other three by Foster & Rastrick of Stourbridge.

All four locomotives reached New York City in 1829, but only one Foster Rastrick & Co. engine, dubbed the *Stourbridge Lion,* made it to the D&H canal at Honesdale, for testing and use. Jervis had specified that the four-wheeled locomotives should weigh no more than five tons because of the frail strap iron on wooden stringers that formed the track structure of the railway. The *Stourbridge Lion* weighed in at almost seven tons, but Allen agreed to take the throttle and make a test turn. Allen and the *Lion* chugged off for a run through the woods and back, covering a distance of about three miles. But the locomotive had worked. It was clearly a practical device, but one that had to be modified to meet the low capital input in infrastructure that typified U.S. railways during the early years. The *Stourbridge Lion* was put into storage and then, with wheels removed, came to be used as a stationary boiler to power one of the inclined planes of the D&H.

The South Carolina Railroad Co. planned to build a line between Charleston and Hamburg, South Carolina, and selected steam as the motive power and Allen as its chief engineer. Allen spent the hot months of the year in New York State, where he again worked with Jervis, who was now chief engineer of the Mohawk & Hudson Railroad, a predecessor of the New York Central. Both worked on locomotive designs that could be operated at fairly high speed around the curves and up the steep grades that characterized early U.S. railway lines. To get the South Carolina Railroad up and running, Allen ordered a steam locomotive, the first built in the United States, from the West Point Foundry in New York. It was called the *Best Friend of Charleston* and operated successfully for a time until the fireman, irked by the noise of steam escaping from the safety valve, tied the valve down and precipitated the first locomotive boiler explosion in the United States. Allen resigned from the position in South Carolina in 1834 and moved back to New York. He married and spent three years in Europe with his wife, returning in 1838 to New York to join Jervis in work on the construction of the Croton Aqueduct, a major engineering project to help furnish New York City with a steady supply of water. Allen's engineering ability was challenged in the construction of the High Bridge for the aqueduct over the Harlem River. He devised a method of testing the bridge piles to determine the amount of weight they could bear, a method still in use.

While working on the Croton Aqueduct project, Allen

Horatio Allen. —Middleton Collection

became a consultant to the New York & Erie Railroad; he left the aqueduct project in 1843 and became president of the railroad. Becoming dissatisfied with the demands of raising money for the construction of the railroad, he resigned as president in 1844, but remained in the employ of the New York & Erie as chief engineer. For the reminder of his life Allen was mainly involved in the management of the Novelty Iron Works, which had a factory along the East River in Manhattan. In the middle of the nineteenth century the firm became one of the major suppliers of steam engines and boilers, principally for steamships. Late in his life Allen developed an interest in improving the valve mechanisms of steam engines. Allen was elected president of the American Society of Civil Engineers from 1871 to 1873. He died in East Orange, New Jersey, on December 21, 1889.

—George M. Smerk

REFERENCES

Finch, J. K. *Early Columbia Engineers.* New York: Columbia Univ. Press, 1929.

Frey, Robert L., ed. *Encyclopedia of American Business History and Biography: Railroads in the Nineteenth Century.* New York: Facts on File, 1988.

Alstom Signaling (General Railway Signal Co.)

Alstom Signaling is the successor to the General Railway Signal Co., one of the pioneers and a leader in the development of railway signaling and train control equipment and systems. GRS was incorporated in 1904 from several predecessor firms, each specializing in parts of the general business of railway signaling. One of these predecessor firms, for example, developed and sold low-pressure compressed-air interlocking systems, while others produced mechanical interlocking and electric block signals.

One of three principal GRS predecessors was the Taylor Switch & Signal Co., formed in 1889 and specializing in all-electric interlocking systems with dynamic indications. Taylor's first electric interlocking was installed at Norwood, Ohio, in 1889 at a crossing of the Baltimore & Ohio Southwest Railroad and the Cincinnati Northern Railway. In 1898 it was reorganized into the Taylor-Sargent Signal Co. and became Taylor Signal Co. in 1900.

A second GRS predecessor was formed in 1891 as the Automatic Pneumatic Railway Signal Co. Pneumatic Railway Signal Co. bought the company in 1897, and International Pneumatic Railway Signal Co., which was reorganized two years later as the Pneumatic Signal Co., then acquired the two firms in 1900. As suggested by their names, each of these companies manufactured and sold compressed-air interlocking switches and signals. Although their products were similar, there was usually enough of a difference that each was able to obtain patents. Their consolidation reflected the general trend of American industry toward larger and stronger concentrations. Still another merger in 1904 brought Pneumatic Signal and Taylor Signal together to form the General Railway Signal Co.

General Railway Signal grew again in 1923, when it merged with the Federal Signal Co. GRS now had a complete line of signaling and control systems equipment that it could offer to railroads. Federal Signal itself was the result of a 1913 merger of the former Federal Railway Signal Co., a supplier of electric interlocking systems and automatic block signals for subway and rapid-transit lines formed in 1905, and the American Railway Signal Co., which had been formed in 1904 to manufacture electric semaphore signals, switch locks, highway-crossing alarms, and electric and mechanical interlocking. By this time GRS had developed as a formidable competitor to Union Switch & Signal.

Throughout its history General Railway Signal has been both a major supplier to the railroad industry and a leader in the development of new and improved signaling and train control technology. In 1911, for example, the first absolute permissive block (APB) signaling system developed by GRS engineers went into service on the Toronto, Hamilton & Buffalo Railway between Kinnear and Vinemount, Ontario. In APB operation, when a train leaves double track and enters single track, all opposing signals are set to the stop position. Thus only one train at a time operates on the single track between ends of sidings or ends of double-track sections. This was an important safety improvement over automatic block signaling, in which two trains could occupy a single-track section and be brought to a stop facing each other with opposing signals in the stop position.

A 1922 Interstate Commerce Commission order, under which certain railroads were given an opportunity to show cause why an order should not be entered requiring them to equip all locomotives operating over a specified passenger locomotive division with automatic train stop or train control, generated much activity among the ICC, manufacturers of train control equipment, and the Signal Division of the American Railway Assn. GRS was active in the resulting development of intermittent inductive train control equipment, as well as a continuous system and automatic train stop systems. More than a decade in advance of the ICC order, in fact, GRS had begun work on an intermittent inductive train control system that was installed on the Buffalo, Rochester & Pittsburgh Railway in 1910.

Also during the 1920s GRS contributed a major advance in the efficiency and safety of train operations beyond timetable and train-order systems with its development of centralized traffic control (CTC), which combined automatic block signaling, absolute permissive block signaling, and interlocking systems into a unified system. The invention of GRS engineer Sedgwick N. Wight, the first CTC went into service on June 25, 1927, between Stanley and Berwick, Ohio, on the Ohio Division of the New York Central. From a single machine with a track diagram in front of him, a dispatcher could control all switches and signals in the territory under CTC control. Advances were made in CTC systems so that today most systems are under computer control that includes record keeping of train moves over the entire territory.

Equipment for classification yards became a major product line for GRS through acquisition of the patents and manufacturing rights of the Hannauer electric car retarder in 1925. Improvements were made over the years, adding automatic control of switches leading to the classification tracks. Automatic switching system controls were installed in 1950 at yards of the Illinois Central and Canadian Pacific. Fully automatic retarders and switch controls were developed, and the first installation was at Kirk Yard in Gary, Indiana, on the Elgin, Joliet & Eastern. By the 1970s distributed minicomputer systems were controlling these classification yard functions. The first computers were analog types, later replaced with digital computers. Today, microprocessors rather than large mainframe machines are used extensively for yard controls.

GRS gradually phased out its pneumatic interlocking equipment and concentrated on electric interlocking systems. In 1937 it came up with its eNtrance-eXit machine, with the first installation at Girard Jct., Pennsylvania. With this new concept, the operator pushed a button where a train entered the interlocking plant, then pushed a button where the train would leave the plant. By pressing just two buttons an entire route through an interlocking could be set, with all switches properly positioned and signals cleared. Previously, each switch had to be positioned and then each signal cleared in the route through the interlocking.

In 1964 General Railway Signal and its principal rival, Union Switch & Signal, received a consent order from the Federal Trade Commission (FTC) concerning their competitive practices (*see* UNION SWITCH & SIGNAL CO. for a brief account). The consent agreed by the two firms and the FTC in 1964 also included a requirement that GRS sell all of its assets in Railroad Accessories Corp., a competing manufacturer of railroad signaling equipment controlled by GRS through stock ownership and interlocking directors.

In 1962 GRS and electronic controls manufacturer Edwards were merged into a new company called General Signal Corp. Each firm retained its identity for sales and marketing purposes. By the 1980s federal funds were being provided to assist railroads and transit authorities to provide safety equipment, and there was an interest by European signaling firms to look to the United States as a potential market.

In 1990 the first European train control and signaling firm entered the North American market. Sasib of Bologna,

Italy, a major manufacturer of transportation products and controls, purchased General Railway Signal from General Signal Corp. GRS became Sasib Railway GRS and built a new engineering, administrative, and transportation products manufacturing facility at Rochester, New York. Despite all of the investment by Sasib, by 1998 the firm sold the GRS firm to the French transportation giant GEC Alsthom, now known simply as Alstom. The former General Railway Signal became Alstom Signaling, Inc., which remains a full-line supplier of signaling equipment and controls.

—Robert W. McKnight

REFERENCE

Solomon, Brian. *Railroad Signaling*. St. Paul, Minn.: MBI, 2003.

American Car & Foundry

ACF Industries is the oldest railroad-car-building concern still in operation. Its immediate predecessor, American Car & Foundry Co., was formed in 1899 by the merger of 13 separate builders. The oldest dated to 1840, when a small foundry measuring 24 by 40 feet was built in Berwick, Pennsylvania. The foundry began building railroad cars in 1861 and by 1941 had grown to occupy more than 400 acres, making it the largest car-building facility in the world at that time. The 13 car builders were Buffalo Car Manufacturing Co., Buffalo, New York; Ensign Manufacturing Co., Huntington, West Virginia; Jackson & Woodin Manufacturing Co., Berwick, Pennsylvania; Michigan-Peninsular Car Co., Detroit, Michigan; Minerva Car Co., Minerva, Ohio; Missouri Car & Foundry Co., Madison, Illinois, and St. Louis, Missouri; Murray, Dougal & Co., Milton, Pennsylvania; Niagara Car Wheel Co., Buffalo, New York; Ohio Falls Car Manufacturing Co., Jeffersonville, Indiana; St. Charles Car Co., St. Charles, Missouri; Terre Haute Car & Manufacturing Co., Terre Haute, Indiana; Union Car Co., Depew, New York; and Wells & French Co., Chicago, Illinois.

Later significant acquisitions by AC&F included Bloomsburg Car Manufacturing Co., Bloomsburg, Pennsylvania; Jackson & Sharp Co., Wilmington, Delaware; Common-Sense Bolster Co., Chicago, Illinois; Indiana Car & Foundry Co., Indianapolis, Indiana; Southern Car & Foundry Co., Memphis, Tennessee; J. G. Brill Co., Philadelphia, Pennsylvania; Pacific Car & Foundry Co., Portland, Oregon (1924–1932 only); Hall-Scott Motor Car Co., Berkeley, California; and Fageol Motors Co., Oakland, California. Other companies controlled through the years by AC&F included American Car & Foundry Motor Corp. (buses and truck bodies); Carter Carburetor Co.; W-K-M Valve Co.; and Polymers Corp.

In 1865 AC&F's former Murray, Dougal & Co. plant in Milton, Pennsylvania, built what has been widely credited as the first tank car in the United States. The first all-steel passenger car ever manufactured by a car builder left the assembly line of the Berwick, Pennsylvania, plant in 1904 for New York City's pioneer rapid-transit line, the Interborough Rapid Transit Co.

Aside from supplying railroad equipment, AC&F has manufactured motor coaches, subway cars, trolley cars, automobile carburetors, oil industry valves, and tank trucks. The diversity of the products offered led to a name change in 1954 to ACF Industries, Inc. The railcar division came to be known as American Car & Foundry Division of ACF Industries. Since it was so vast and diverse, AC&F was conscripted to produce large amounts of materiel for both world wars and the Korean War. It was a major producer of the USRA-design freight cars in 1918 and 1919, and during World War II it built 15,224 light army tanks, two-thirds of the entire domestic production for this tank type. AC&F also produced bomb casings, military shells, troop sleeping and hospital cars, tractors, marine landing boats, navy net-layer ships, landing barges, gun mounts, artillery vehicles, field ranges, projectiles, and armor plate, as well as yachts and pleasure craft for a time in the 1920s and 1930s. Regarded by many as the best of the car builders, AC&F was a pioneer of heavy electric arc welding techniques and technology.

Over the past 100 years AC&F has been a leader in the construction of freight and passenger equipment, delivering more than 20,000 orders totaling over 2 million railcars for most North American railroads and shippers and for many customers overseas. AC&F has engineered and built boxcars, flatcars, open-top hoppers, covered hoppers, tank cars, refrigerator cars, stock cars, mine cars, gondolas, intermodal cars, passenger cars, snowplows, and cabooses.

AC&F also entered the locomotive business in 1934 with the diesel-powered, nonarticulated Rebel streamliner built for the Gulf, Mobile & Northern Railroad, followed by the Model 60 gasoline-powered motor cars for the Seaboard Air Line Railway and the popular series of self-propelled, lightweight aluminum Motorailers. In 1949 AC&F constructed the Talgo passenger trainsets for domestic and European customers, powered by a variety of diesel engines. Spanish interests designed the Talgo, and AC&F obtained the marketing rights. The Talgo concept employed a tilt mechanism with a low center of gravity, which allowed higher train speeds. One Talgo trainset with a Fairbanks-Morse diesel engine toured several American railroads to demonstrate the advantages of the new technology, including the New York, New Haven & Hartford, the Delaware, Lackawanna & Western, the Boston & Maine, and the Chicago, Rock Island & Pacific. While the initial North American Talgo concept never really caught on, today's Talgos on Amtrak in the Pacific Northwest are direct descendants of the 1950s Talgos.

During the 1960s, with a reduction in demand for freight cars and the nationwide decline in passenger service, AC&F consolidated to three big plants: Milton, Pennsylvania, dating to 1842; Huntington, West Virginia, dating to 1872; and St. Louis, Missouri, dating to 1876. The Berwick, Pennsylvania, plant closed in 1962 after more than 100 years of car building.

Aside from manufacturing railcars, AC&F operates a lease fleet available to shippers and maintained through a network of full-service repair shops in the United States and Canada, including mobile maintenance units. For many years the Shippers Car Line Division of AC&F was responsible for the leasing of railcars to shippers other than railroads. Shippers Car Line was a small leasing company in Milton, Pennsylvania, which AC&F acquired

In the post–World War II boom in passenger-car construction, American Car & Foundry's St. Charles, Missouri, plant hurried to complete equipment for the 1951 introduction of the Great Northern's streamlined *Empire Builder*. —Bruce Owen Nett, *Trains* Magazine Collection

in 1926. It quickly became the AC&F's main leasing operation. Railcars operating for the Shippers Car Line Division carried SHPX reporting marks. The SHPX reporting mark for AC&F's Shippers Car Line leasing division was among the most common reporting marks during the twentieth century. The Shippers Car Line Division was wrapped into AC&F in the early 1980s. As a historical note, in 1997 AC&F once again began using the SHPX reporting mark on its lease fleet of covered hoppers and tank cars. The mark had not been used on new equipment since 1968, when the ACFX reporting mark replaced it.

Today, AC&F is still an industry-leading manufacturer of tank cars and Center Flow covered hoppers for lease and sale. AC&F has manufacturing facilities for covered hoppers in Huntington, West Virginia, and for tank cars and covered hoppers in Milton, Pennsylvania. AC&F's affiliate, American Railcar Industries, operates manufacturing facilities in Paragould, Arkansas, for covered hoppers and in Marmaduke, Arkansas, for tank cars. ARI also has railcar component manufacturing plants in Jackson, Missouri; Kennett, Missouri; St. Louis, Missouri; and Longview, Texas. Research and Development, located at AC&F's St. Charles, Missouri, headquarters, is the backbone of the manufacturing group. St. Charles also offers complete in-house and over-the-road testing capabilities for railcars. With over 100 years of serving the railroad industry, AC&F is North America's oldest continuously operating manufacturer of railcars.

—Edward S. Kaminski

REFERENCES

Kaminski, Edward S. *American Car & Foundry Company: A Centennial History, 1899–1999.* Wilton, Calif.: Signature Press, 1999.
———. *Tank Cars of American Car & Foundry Company, 1865–1955.* Wilton, Calif.: Signature Press, 2003.

American Locomotive Co. (Alco)

The June 1901 formation of the American Locomotive Co. can be attributed to the Baldwin Locomotive Works, whose dominance of U.S. locomotive building at the turn of the century threatened to become a monopoly. To combat this dominance, eight widely scattered smaller builders joined to create Alco. Arranged in order of total locomotives produced up to 1901, these builders were Schenectady (6,194 locomotives), Brooks (4,114), Rhode Island (3,376), Cooke (2,755), Pittsburgh (2,410), Manchester (1,793), Dickson (1,330), and Richmond (1,035). Alco acquired Rogers (6,261) in 1905. This company was Alco's oldest predecessor, having built locomotives since 1837. In 1904 Alco acquired a Canadian subsidiary that later became the Montreal Locomotive Works.

All ten builders initially continued to function as indi-

The largest component of the American Locomotive Co., formed in 1901 from ten locomotive builders, was the massive 112-acre "Big Shop" of the Schenectady Locomotive Works. —American Locomotive Co., *Trains* Magazine Collection

vidual Alco works, but within a few years Alco closed its obsolete plants, and by 1920 only Schenectady, Brooks, Richmond, and Montreal were building locomotives (plus Cooke for smaller engines). Schenectady had been dominant since Alco's formation, and its "Big Shop" was always the heart of Alco; by 1929 Schenectady had become the only Alco works producing locomotives, other than Montreal.

Alco's plant rationalizations represented sound business strategy and were part of a broad pattern of intra-industry mergers at the turn of the twentieth century. The Alco merger eliminated competition among its predecessors, it provided a large pool of production talent and skilled personnel, and it enabled the introduction of a comprehensive standardization program. The company thwarted the threatened Baldwin monopoly, as illustrated by steam locomotive production totals for the three large locomotive builders from 1901 through 1952. Alco captured 42 percent of the market, with Baldwin second at 34 percent and Lima Locomotive Works a distant third at 5 percent (Lima became a major competitor only from the 1920s on, so its overall total is misleadingly small). Railroad company shops and smaller builders accounted for the remaining 19 percent.

Alco introduced many locomotive innovations and improvements in the early 1900s under Mechanical Engineer (later Chief Consulting Engineer) Francis J. Cole, a Rogers veteran. These developments included the first American compound articulated (1904) and the first 4-8-2 (1911). Compound articulateds used their steam twice for greater efficiency, first in the high-pressure rear cylinders and then in the larger low-pressure front cylinders. To increase starting tractive effort, they could use high-pressure steam in all four cylinders, thus operating in the simple rather than in the compound mode. In 1918 Alco built ten huge compound 2-10-10-2s for the Virginian Railway that developed the highest tractive effort ever achieved by a successful steam locomotive: 176,000 pounds in the simple mode. Their 118-inch boiler diameter and 48-inch-diameter low-pressure cylinders were the largest ever on a locomotive.

A complement to Alco's abilities came from an unlikely source: the Pennsylvania Railroad. The PRR operated its own testing facilities, designed its own locomotives, and built many of them at its shops in Altoona. Most other PRR locomotives came from Baldwin, but nonetheless the Pennsylvania ordered six experimental locomotives from Alco in 1905—a pair each of 2-8-0s, 4-4-2s, and 2-6-2s. These were the first engines on the railroad to have truly massive boilers, and future PRR standard boiler designs owed much to this Alco sextet. In 1907 Alco built the Pennsylvania's first Pacific, an experimental K28, which was the design basis for the PRR's initial 257 K2-class 4-6-2s (there were no K1s).

In 1910 F. J. Cole designed a landmark locomotive: Alco demonstrator 4-6-2 No. 50000, which was the first high-capacity modern Pacific. Freed of any particular railroad's design wishes, Cole was able to include innovative cast-vanadium-steel cylinders and many other weight-reducing improvements, which in turn allowed a very large superheated boiler with outside steam pipes and rationalized proportions of boiler and cylinders—and all this despite staying within the restrictive clearances and weight limits of several railroads. The 50000 was a highly successful demonstrator and became the basis for many other 4-6-2 designs. A heavier version supplied to the Pennsylvania Railroad as an experimental K29 was so successful that it played a large part in the design of the well-known PRR K4s Pacific. However, as remarkable as Cole's No. 50000 was, it was nonetheless an evolutionary rather than a revolutionary locomotive. It incorporated great improvements, but it did not change any basic design concepts.

By the close of World War I, U.S. railroads were looking for even greater power and efficiency than was available from current locomotive designs. Alco's answer was the three-cylinder locomotive, in which an additional center cylinder drove an inside main rod connected to a cranked driver axle. Alco claimed that benefits included reduced crankpin stress and decreased slippage, thus producing more power. Alco sold some three-cylinder locomotives in the 1920s, including 88 unique 4-12-2s for the Union Pacific, but the concept was not successful in the long term, other than for slow-speed service. Three-cylinder locomotives, despite superior initial performance, soon suffered high maintenance costs and failures due to the inaccessibility of their inside machinery and excessive stress on the big end of the inside main rod. Even Alco eventually had to admit that they should be restricted to 35 mph, and none were produced after 1930.

The Lima Locomotive Works of Lima, Ohio, became an increasingly effective competitor to Alco. Lima initially built small conventional locomotives and Shay geared logging locomotives, but it began producing large locomotives in 1913. Author Eric Hirsimaki states that initial efforts to make a transition from small one-of-a-kind orders to large-scale mass production were inefficient, and the company lost money on most orders. Help was needed, so Lima raided the competition by hiring managers from other builders. One of these men was Alco's assistant mechanical engineer, William Woodard, who went over to Lima in 1916.

Woodard led a team of Lima, New York Central, and Franklin Railway Supply engineers who developed the Super-Power concept, as embodied in Lima's demonstrator 2-8-4 No. A-1 of 1925. Much greater boiler capacity was produced by a larger firebox (made possible by a four-wheel trailing truck) and other improvements, while an improved front-end throttle and limited cutoff produced more efficient use of steam.

With Super-Power, horsepower replaced tractive effort as the measure of a locomotive's performance, and the drag freight locomotive was at once obsolete. (A drag freight locomotive could start a heavy train, but it lacked

In the 1920s Alco aggressively marketed its three-cylinder locomotives. Union Pacific liked the idea and bought 88 of them between 1926 and 1930. They were the largest nonarticulated locomotives in the world. The first one, No. 9000, is seen here on Sherman Hill, Wyoming. —J. W. Swanberg Collection

the boiler capacity to move that train at higher speeds.) Lima's A-1 demonstrator was revolutionary rather than evolutionary, and it was the prototype for the modern American steam locomotive. Besides the 2-8-4 wheel arrangement, it spawned 4-6-4s, 4-8-4s, 2-10-4s, and simple articulateds with four-wheel trailing trucks. Woodard and Lima had produced a remarkably efficient locomotive.

Even though Alco had not developed the Super-Power

concept, the company continued to secure substantial orders. The reason was twofold: Lima could not patent the Super-Power idea; and railroad-to-builder loyalty and close personal relationships did not change. Although Lima captured about 20 percent of the market in the 1920s as railroads quickly incorporated the Super-Power concept into their own locomotive designs, more orders still went to Alco and Baldwin. After moving away from three-cylinder designs, Alco soon built Super-Power

Although Lima developed the concept of Super-Power locomotives, both Alco and Baldwin were among the major builders. An early version of Super-Power design was New York Central's legendary 4-6-4 Hudson. Alco built all but 10 of the New York Central's 275 Hudsons between 1927 and 1938. This one is a J-3 class built in 1937. —J. W. Swanberg Collection

2-8-4s and 2-10-4s, among others. An example was the New York Central's legendary 4-6-4 Hudson: although this locomotive was designed by the NYC in accordance with Woodard's principles, Lima built only 10 of the Central's 275 Hudsons; Alco built the rest.

Alco did so well during the prosperous 1920s that Schenectady's production equaled its maximum capacity of 2 locomotives per day. A 1929 order to Alco for 14 Rio Grande 4-8-4s had to be subcontracted to Baldwin's giant Eddystone plant (which could produce six locomotives per day). The company paid extremely high dividends during these years, drawing the ire of financial analysts, yet this policy was necessary in order to attract investment capital to a volatile sector of the capital goods industry. Despite an unsuccessful foray into the automotive business during 1905–1914, Alco again entered other fields in the 1920s, including wheels, springs, pipe, refining equipment, and bridge components. In addition to retaining its controlling interest in the Montreal Locomotive Works, Alco purchased the Railway Steel Spring Co., the Jackson Engineering Corp., and Heat Transfer Products between 1926 and 1930. Alco also maintained a close working relationship with the Superheater Co., and one of the latter firm's founders, Samuel G. Allen, later became an Alco president. These acquisitions, designed to ensure ready access to critical components, tended to reinforce Alco's commitment to steam locomotive manufacturing at a time when diesel locomotive technology showed increasing promise.

In late 1929 the Great Depression struck. Stock market prices collapsed, as did locomotive orders: 1,230 steam locomotives had been ordered from all the builders in 1929, but that number shrank to 382 in 1930, 62 in 1931, 5 in 1932, and 17 in 1933. Lima shut down altogether for three years, while Baldwin declared bankruptcy in 1935. Alco's 1920s diversification policies helped the company avoid a similar fate. These nonlocomotive efforts held up well enough to carry the company through the Depression and into the renewed locomotive orders and boom times leading up to and during World War II.

Alco's nonrail production continued during the war years, together with the production of tanks, tank destroyers, marine boilers, and other military hardware—and over 2,000 locomotives. These locomotives were still mostly steam, and they included the Union Pacific's legendary 4-8-8-4 Big Boys built in 1941 and 1944. The Schenectady plant covered 112 busy acres, and its wartime employment peaked at 10,958 in 1943.

Alco attempted to maintain steam momentum after the war. The brightest hope appeared to lie in the modern dual-service 4-8-4, which had been built in many variations during the conflict (the War Production Board had not enforced strict steam locomotive design standardization during World War II). The 6,000-hp 4-8-4 Niagaras that Alco built in 1945 and 1946 for the New York Central were cited by noted railroad historian E. P. Alexander for attaining "the highest records for mileage and availability of any steam locomotives in the world." Despite representing the best available steam locomotive technology, they could not compete against more efficient postwar

Few would disagree that the 25 Union Pacific 4-8-8-4s built by Alco in 1941 and 1944 represented the pinnacle of American steam locomotives. The record-breaking 772,000-pound locomotive could haul more tonnage faster than any other steam locomotive. Someone chalked the name Big Boy on one of the new engines, and it stuck. Big Boy No. 4021 was eastbound at Rock River, Wyoming, in September 1956. —Stan Kistler

diesels. Schenectady built its last steam locomotive in 1948.

As early as 1903 Alco joined with the Schenectady-based General Electric Co. in the manufacture of electric locomotives under a joint GE-Alco builder's plate. Alco built the mechanical parts—trucks, frames, and bodies—while GE supplied the electrical equipment and controls. An early Alco-GE main-line customer was the New York Central, for which the two builders supplied the initial motive power for the railroad's 1906 New York terminal electrification, while other customers included the Baltimore & Ohio, the Great Northern, the Butte, Anaconda & Pacific, the Mexican Railway, and the Milwaukee Road. Joint Alco-GE production of main-line electric locomotives continued through 1931 and totaled more than 300 units. The two builders also jointly produced a line of light electric locomotives for interurban electric railways through about 1912, when GE moved its Locomotive & Car Equipment Department to a new plant at Erie, Pennsylvania, and began building most of the mechanical components itself. On two occasions during the mid-1920s Alco joined with GE's principal rival, the Westinghouse Electric & Manufacturing Co., to build main-line electrics for the Virginian and Norfolk & Western railways.

Alco had taken an early interest in diesel locomotives, providing the mechanical components for Alco–General Electric–Ingersoll Rand diesel-electrics beginning in 1924. The first of these (Central Railroad of New Jersey 1000) was the first commercially successful diesel-electric locomotive in America. Final assembly was at GE's Erie, Pennsylvania, plant, but in 1928 GE began constructing its own mechanical components at Erie, and Alco then began assembling complete diesel locomotives at Schenectady. That year, using GE electrical components and an Ingersoll-Rand prime mover, Alco built New York Central 1550, the first successful U.S. diesel road locomotive. Railroads typically employed these early diesels only in locations where local smoke-abatement ordinances or the risk of fire precluded the use of steam locomotives. Alco management thus remained committed to steam locomotive production, regarding these early diesels as underpowered, suitable only for niche applications, and unlikely to displace steam locomotives in main-line railroad assignments.

In 1928 Alco purchased the McIntosh & Seymour Co. of Auburn, New York, to produce its own diesel engines, developing the 300-hp Model 330 and the 600-hp Model 531 engines. From 1931 on, Alco offered standard production switchers that used these engines, and Alco 531 engines were also used to power Gulf, Mobile & Northern's *Rebel* lightweight trains of 1935 and 1937. Alco retained a Swiss consulting engineer, Dr. Alfred Buchi, to design a suitable turbocharger, which when applied to the 531 engine resulted in the 900-hp 531T and thus a more powerful switcher.

In 1940 further engine evolution to the 539 and 539T allowed the introduction of standard S-series 660-hp and 1,000-hp switchers, which were so successful that Alco continued to produce them until 1953 and 1961, respectively. In 1939 Alco installed two of the 1,000-hp engines in a new streamlined passenger diesel, the DL-109, with regular production commencing in 1940. In 1941 Alco introduced what is generally considered the first true road switcher, the 1,000-hp RS-1 (this model designation was added later), which the company produced until 1960. In 1940 Alco negotiated a joint-production and sales agreement with General Electric ensuring that GE would not build diesels that exceeded 100 tons for the domestic market. Alco agreed to use only GE electrical equipment, marketing its locomotives as Alco-GE products. Thus at the eve of World War II Alco offered a standard line of diesel switchers and a road switcher, but no road freight diesel model and only a newly developed road passenger locomotive. The company had also relinquished control over the potentially lucrative small-diesel and export-diesel markets, allowing GE the option of using those fields as a test bed for the development of its own manufacturing, marketing, and service capabilities.

The United States entered the war in December 1941, and the War Production Board was established the following month. In April 1942 the WPB assumed direct control of all locomotive manufacture and restricted diesel production to already-proven models, thus freezing the Alco and Electro-Motive Division (EMD) diesel designs for the duration of the war. However, Alco and Baldwin were given a wartime monopoly on the substantial diesel switcher market. This gave a tremendous advantage in road diesel production to EMD, which built almost 1,100-foot road freight diesels throughout the conflict, while Alco had no road freight diesel to offer; its only road diesels produced during the war were a mere 52 DL-109s, almost all of which were dual-service versions for the New Haven Railroad.

These wartime restrictions permitted the development of new locomotive and prime-mover designs for postwar production, enabling Alco to remain a competitive producer. Alco had already authorized in 1940 the development of a new V-type diesel prime mover to compete with EMD's 567 engine. Designated the 241, this new engine was to have a Buchi turbocharger and was to produce 1,000 hp with 12 cylinders and 1,500 hp with 16 cylinders. However, Alco's steam-oriented top management hesitated, and the project lagged; the company did not complete the first 241 engine until March 1944. WPB restrictions did not cause this delay. Alco installed three 241 engines in an A-B-A road freight demonstrator, and this so-called Black Maria locomotive set began road tests in the fall of 1945.

Meanwhile, Alco decided in early 1944 that constant-pressure supercharging (developed by GE) would make possible higher horsepower ratings, but would require major modifications to the 241 engine design. Instead, a mostly new 244 engine design was developed using the

Raymond Loewy's design for Alco's post–World War II diesel locomotive was highly regarded, and never was it shown to better advantage than in the Santa Fe's dramatic red, yellow, black, and silver "warbonnet" livery. This publicity view shows a 6,000-hp, three-unit Alco diesel and 11 streamlined cars in Cajon Pass about 1946. —*Trains* Magazine Collection

same bore and stroke as the 241, and the first 244 engine was built for stationary testing in October 1945. Alco discarded the 241 and instead used the mostly untested 244 engine in a new line of postwar road switcher, road freight, and road passenger locomotives (later dubbed the RS-2, FA-1, and PA-1 respectively). The 244 engine contained serious design flaws, but it remained standard for Alco's U.S. road diesels until 1954. Furthermore, instead of designing its own turbocharger for the 244, Alco adopted a General Electric aviation turbocharger that was unsuitable for railroad service, but was not satisfactorily supplanted until 1952.

In 1946 Alco had 40 percent of the diesel locomotive market, almost equal to EMD's 47 percent, showing that many railroads' loyalty to Alco was strong. However, embarrassing 244 engine failures soon began causing expensive warranty claims, and that loyalty quickly evaporated. By 1954 Alco's market share plummeted to 13 percent, while EMD's share soared to 76 percent. Alco's sales would have been even smaller had it not been for heavy demand during mass dieselization, which caused EMD production backlogs and a resulting diversion of some orders to Alco as a second choice. Alco's managers blamed the WPB for this precipitous decline, but they also pointed to Alco's higher labor costs, EMD's superior marketing skills, and EMD's "traffic reciprocity" (meaning General Motors' alleged threats to ship its freight via a competing carrier if a railroad did not buy EMD diesels—a threat that would seem to have been countered at least until 1953 by Alco partner GE's own freight-shipping leverage).

Most of Alco's difficulties could be explained by the inadequacies of its products. Alco diesels performed well in local services. Some railroads found them satisfactory for road service as well, and Alco diesels far outsold those of rivals Baldwin-Lima-Hamilton and Fairbanks-Morse. But in extremely heavy road freight or passenger service, where locomotives operated at full load for hours at a time under punishing conditions with the minimal maintenance typical of American railroads, Alco's 244-powered locomotives were no match for EMD's 567-powered products.

Alco introduced the 251 diesel engine in 1954, this time after adequate testing, but the initial postwar surge in diesel locomotive orders had subsided. The company would never again enjoy any meaningful domestic market share; by now its orders were often just tokens to ensure that EMD did not become a monopoly. Alco attempted a new round of diversification, changing its name to Alco Products in 1955. The renamed company remained committed to custom-manufactured specialty products, including those in the emerging atomic energy field. Given the nature of its expanded product line, Alco continued to suffer from the same feast-or-famine business cycles that characterized the locomotive industry, and the company divested its unprofitable subsidiaries in 1962 and 1963. Responding to customer complaints about the poor quality of Alco-GE diesels and sensing a market opportunity, GE withdrew from its joint production agreement with Alco in 1953. GE introduced its competing U25B road freight diesel in 1961. The FDL-16 power plant used in the U25B had many problems, but GE soon earned a far better service reputation than Alco; it backed its locomotives while continually improving the FDL-16.

Alco quickly lost its status as the number two locomotive builder, and the introduction of its improved Century Series locomotives in 1963 did not halt the company's decline. At the end of 1964 the Worthington Corp. purchased Alco Products. Worthington in turn merged with the Studebaker Corp. in 1967. Alco's market share sank to 3 percent in 1968, and Studebaker-Worthington terminated locomotive production at Schenectady in January 1969. The Montreal Locomotive Works continued to manufacture diesels to Alco designs, which it purchased from Studebaker-Worthington.

Alco and its constituents built more than 75,000 steam locomotives, and the Schenectady plant produced over 10,000 diesels. Subsidiary Montreal (later Bombardier) produced almost 3,000 diesels, and Alco's export diesel sales were substantial, mostly in the post-244 engine era. In addition, companies in Australia, France, Japan, Romania, Spain, and India continued to manufacture 251-powered locomotives under license (with 251 engine production continuing in India as of 2005).

—J. W. Swanberg

REFERENCES

Bruce, Alfred W. *The Steam Locomotive in America*. New York: W. W. Norton, 1952.

Churella, Albert J. *Success That Didn't Last: Decline and Fall of the American Locomotive Company in the Diesel Locomotive Industry*. Schenectady, N.Y.: Schenectady Heritage Area, City of Schenectady, 2001.

Kirkland, John F. *The Diesel Builders*. Vol. 2. Glendale, Calif.: Interurban, 1989.

Westwood, J. N. *Locomotive Designers in the Age of Steam*. Rutherford, N.J.: Fairleigh Dickinson Univ. Press, 1971.

White, John H., Jr. *A Short History of American Locomotive Builders in the Steam Era*. Washington, D.C.: Bass, 1982.

See also LOCOMOTIVE BUILDERS.

American Short Line and Regional Railroad Assn. (ASLRRA)

A nonprofit trade association, the Washington-based American Short Line and Regional Railroad Assn. (ASLRRA) represents the interests of more than 400 shortline and regional railroads. Its principal activities are monitoring and analyzing legislative and regulatory initiatives for its member railroads and testifying before congressional committees. It also represents its members in their relationships with major railroads, keeps them informed of current activities and opportunities, and has established model programs to help them meet federal requirements for random alcohol and drug testing, engineer certification, environmental regulations, and other issues. Assistance with tariff and rate issues is also available on a fee-for-service basis.

The earliest ASLRRA predecessor was the Short Line Railroad Assn. of the Southeast, formed in 1913 with 22 members in Atlanta, Georgia. By 1916 there were 105 members, and the name was changed to the Short Line Railroad Assn. of the South to reflect a broader membership base. A year later the name was changed again to the American Short Line Railroad Assn., adding members from throughout the continental United States and its possessions. The name was changed once again to the present one in 1998, reflecting the merger of the small railroad organization with the previously separate Regional Railroads of America, established in 1987.

Shortline and regional railroads have been a major growth area for railroads since passage of the Staggers Rail Act of 1980. The Staggers Act gave Class 1 railroads much greater freedom to dispose of lines identified as surplus or unprofitable and encouraged the sale of these lines to new operators. The result has been a transformation of these light-density rail lines from candidates for abandonment into viable new small or regional railroads. Typically, new entrepreneurs offer innovative marketing, flexible and user-friendly service, and lower operating costs. The number of small and regional railroads has more than doubled, from about 220 companies in 1980 to more than 500 today. Today, 50,000 miles of line—29 percent of all U.S. rail mileage—is now operated by non–Class 1 railroads. Regional and small railroads now account for 9 percent of all railroad freight revenue; in 1980 they accounted for only about 2 percent.

A major problem now confronting small and regional railroads is the growing impact of the heavier axle-load standards coming into service on Class 1 railroads, with a 286,000-pound total axle load (as of July 2004) allowed in unrestricted interchange service. In order to handle these heavier cars efficiently, the shortlines typically are confronting the need for costly heavier rail, ties, right of way, ballast, and bridge upgrading. ASLRRA is pursuing a two-part strategy for a solution. The first includes a determination through the Assn. of American Railroads' Transportation Test Center of the technological requirements that will have to be met; the second seeks financial assistance for shortline and regional railroad operators. Some federal funding through the most recent intermodal transportation equity act (TEA-21, 1997) is anticipated, and the association is also pursuing assistance from other federal and state sources.

—William D. Middleton

Ames, Oakes (1804–1873)

Born in Easton, Massachusetts, the son of Oliver Ames, owner of a well-known factory that manufactured shovels, Oakes Ames ended his formal education at the age of 16 in order to enter the factory as a laborer. He soon became familiar with every part of the plant, and upon his father's retirement in 1844 the business was turned over to Oakes and his younger brother Oliver Ames. It prospered as a result of the discovery of gold in California in 1848, the later gold rush in Australia, and the growth of agriculture in the Northwest. It was said that the Ames shovel was "legal tender in every part of the Mississippi Valley."

Active as a Free-Soiler and Republican, Ames was an important member of the executive council of Massachusetts. In 1862 he successfully ran for Congress and held his seat for the remainder of his life. Ames had invested in the Central Pacific and other railroad projects, and he and Oliver were soon drawn into the Union Pacific by vice president Thomas C. Durant with the formation of the Crédit Mobilier, organized to build and finance the UP and to make a lot of money in the process. Oakes Ames was particularly helpful in rounding up financial support for the Crédit Mobilier from bankers, businessmen, and fellow congressmen. Ultimately the Crédit Mobilier split into two factions, one led by Durant and one by Ames. The result was an arrangement under which Oakes Ames would take control of the Crédit Mobilier, while his brother Oliver would become president of the UP.

With some of these arrangements likely to come under question, Ames sold (at a price advantage) a number of shares of the Crédit Mobilier to members of Congress, always maintaining that this was done, not to obtain favors from the House, but only as a cautionary measure to assure noninterference for the UP. "I shall put them where they will do the most good to us," he wrote of the new shares in 1868.

Whatever Ames's intent, the Crédit Mobilier became a scandal that would not go away. There was widespread criticism of the magnitude of the costs charged and profits gained from the Union Pacific. Several years later Oakes Ames was alleged to have misused the company's stocks, and a detailed account of the affair was published in 1872 by the *New York Sun* under the caption "The King of Frauds: How the Crédit Mobilier Bought Its Way into Congress." Ames vigorously defended his actions to an 1872 congressional committee that was investigating the matter, but to no avail. The committee reported that Ames had been "guilty of selling to members of Congress shares of stock in the Crédit Mobilier of America for prices much below the true value of such stock, with intent thereby to influence the votes and decisions of such members in matters to be brought before Congress for action." A recommendation that Ames be expelled from Congress was dropped, but the committee adopted a resolution that it "absolutely condemns the conduct of Oakes Ames." Many defended Ames as being no more than a product of his time in terms of ethical perceptions. Indeed, many congressmen assured him that they had full confidence in his intentions, and Boston businessmen organized a testimonial banquet in his honor. However, broken by the political disgrace, Ames returned to Easton to deal with urgent problems at the firm. His health undermined by the affair, he died there the following year.

—William D. Middleton

REFERENCE

Bain, David Haward. *Empire Express: Building the First Transcontinental Railroad.* New York: Viking, 1999.

Ames, Oliver (1807–1877)

One of six sons and two daughters, Oliver Ames was born at Plymouth, Massachusetts, and studied at North Easton local schools and the Franklin Academy at North Andover. Original plans to take up the law were abandoned because of illness; instead, he went to work in his father's shovel factory. Learning the business from the ground up, Oliver joined his older brother, Oakes Ames, in running the firm after his father retired in 1844.

In 1852 and 1857 Ames was elected to the Massachusetts State Senate, but after that gave up further political service to devote his full attention to business and moneymaking. While the Oliver Ames & Son factory was booming, Oliver joined his brother Oakes in several railroad-building projects and in 1865 was caught up in plans for the Crédit Mobilier scheme to build and finance the Union Pacific. Although involved with the Crédit Mobilier, Ames was not implicated in the later congressional investigation of his brother in 1872.

While Oakes Ames worked with the Crédit Mobilier, Oliver Ames became president of the Union Pacific from 1866 through 1871 and remained on the board of directors until his death. He returned to take on the problems of the shovel business, heading the firm after his brother's death in 1873. Well known in the business and railroad community, Ames served as a director of the Atlantic & Pacific, Kansas Pacific, Denver Pacific, Colorado Central, Old Colony, and other railroads. He died at North Easton in early 1877. In 1883 Oliver Ames and his brother Oakes Ames were commemorated by the enormous truncated pyramid of Wyoming granite that still stands astride the Continental Divide near Sherman, Wyo. (*see* MONUMENTS).

—William D. Middleton

REFERENCES

Bain, David Haward. *Empire Express: Building the First Transcontinental Railroad.* New York: Viking, 1999.
Klein, Maury. *Union Pacific: Birth of a Railroad, 1862–1893.* Garden City, N.Y.: Doubleday, 1987.

Amtrak. *See* NATIONAL RAILROAD PASSENGER CORP.

Andrews's Raid

During the Civil War a bold plan was devised to steal a train in the Confederacy and use it to help destroy part of the rail line between Marietta, Georgia, and Chattanooga, Tennessee. Union general O. M. Mitchel was planning to seize Chattanooga, and, with the Western & Atlantic Railroad from Marietta blocked, the Confederate forces would find it difficult to move in troops and supplies to keep Chattanooga from falling. James J. Andrews, an experienced Union spy who had served under Gen. Don Carlos Buell, worked out the plan with General Mitchel. Once the rail line was made useless, Mitchel would invade Chattanooga. Twenty-one Union soldiers, two of whom were locomotive engineers, volunteered to join with Andrews; all were dressed in southern-style civilian clothes.

Following the plan, the Andrews raiders made their way separately to Marietta, where last-minute plans were laid; on the morning of Saturday, April 12, 1862, the group boarded the morning express train from Marietta to Chattanooga, which was powered by the locomotive named *General*. The train stopped at Big Shanty, Georgia, for breakfast, and at that point the raiders stole the locomotive and several boxcars, with the boxcars used to hold the raiders. Andrews chose Big Shanty because it had no telegraph connection to the rest of the railroad or the rest of the world. The seizure was dangerous because Big Shanty was a Confederate encampment, and many southern soldiers witnessed the event without realizing its significance until too late.

The raiders were armed only with revolvers. To ward off Southerners' suspicions, the story was that they were a special train loaded with powder and ammunition to be used in the defense of Chattanooga. In Andrews's plan, the raiders were to tear up rails and burn several of the wooden bridges along the line. A lack of the proper tools for pulling spikes and tearing up rail was a major hindrance to blocking the line; a steady light rain the whole day made burning the bridges impractical without abundant fuel and time to ignite and destroy the dampened structures.

An unexpected factor was the determination of conductor W. A. Fuller to take back his train after it was stolen. Fuller, accompanied by Anthony Murphy, chief engineer of the railroad's Atlanta shops, began the chase on foot by running after the departing train for a number of miles. At one point Fuller and Murphy employed a handcar for the pursuit, only to be wrecked into a ditch by obstructions placed on the track by the raiders. At Etowah they commandeered the locomotive *Yonah*, which was owned by a local iron works, and steamed after the Andrews raiders. Knowing that there would be opposing trains at Kingston to delay Andrews, Fuller expected to catch up with and fight the raiders at that point. Instead, the opposing trains blocked Fuller until he took the locomotive *Texas* from a local passenger train arriving on the Rome branch of the railroad. Fuller immediately took off after Andrews with the locomotive and tender loaded with Confederate soldiers.

Both trains had to stop to take on water and wood. The

An artist for the *Harper's New Monthly Magazine*'s July 1865 issue depicted the Confederates in hot pursuit of Andrews's raiding party. —Middleton Collection

All members of Andrews's party were captured when they ran out of fuel and were overtaken by their Confederate pursuers.
—Middleton Collection

Andrews train also stopped frequently to cut telegraph wires, attempt to tear up track, and seek opportunities to burn bridges. When they stopped, Andrews's men would also load the boxcars with crossties to be dropped off on the rails in an effort to derail the *Texas* and Fuller's train. As the race drew close and the fuel supply for the *General* ran low, Andrews ordered his men to begin dismantling the boxcars in order to use the wood for fuel and to avoid stopping. From time to time the denuded boxcars were uncoupled and let loose in an effort to thwart Fuller; Fuller ordered the boxcars pushed ahead of the *Texas*, and the chase continued. The pressure of the chase was strong, and Fuller was so close behind that it hindered the raiders in their effort to pull up rail.

As Fuller grew closer to Andrews, Andrews ordered the last boxcar to be set afire and left in the middle of a covered bridge; unfortunately there was not enough time for the dampened bridge to catch fire, and Fuller's train pushed the burning car out of the bridge and deposited it at the nearest siding. Out of fuel and with steam pressure dying, Andrews ordered his men to jump from the *General* and escape individually into the woods; the *General* was put into reverse and began to move toward the *Texas*, but the steam pressure was so low that the Fuller train pushed the *General* to a halt.

All of the Andrews raiders were eventually captured, and eight were put to death as spies, including Andrews. They were the first U.S. soldiers to be awarded the Congressional Medal of Honor. Eight of the prisoners succeeded in escaping, and six others escaped and were recaptured.

Andrews's raid makes an exciting story. Buster Keaton made a classic film about the event called *The General*. In the film Keaton is the engineer of the commandeered locomotive, and it is he who chases it. In the early 1970s the Walt Disney Co. made *The Great Locomotive Chase* with Fess Parker as Andrews and Jeffrey Hunter as Fuller.

—George M. Smerk

REFERENCE

Pittenger, Rev. William. "The Locomotive Chase in Georgia." In *The Century War Series*, vol. 2, ed. Robert Underwood Johnson and Clarence Clough Buel, 709–716. New York: Century, 1884, 1887, 1888.

Ann Arbor Railroad

Construction of a railroad line from Toledo, Ohio, northwest through Ann Arbor to the shore of Lake Michigan at Frankfort, Michigan, 292 miles, took from 1869 to 1893. The construction was not difficult; finances and corporate reorganizations were the problem.

The principal reason for the railroad's existence was to provide a bypass around congested Chicago for through freight by using car ferries across Lake Michigan from Frankfort to Manitowoc and Kewaunee, Wisconsin, and Menominee and Manistique, Michigan. To ensure a friendly connection on the west shore of the lake, in 1911 the Ann Arbor purchased the Manistique & Lake Superior Railroad, which reached from Manistique north to connections with the Lake Superior & Ishpeming and the Duluth, South Shore & Atlantic. Ann Arbor dropped its last passenger train, an all-day, coach-only Toledo-Frankfort train, in 1950, but continued to carry passengers on its ferries across Lake Michigan.

The Ann Arbor spent most of its existence owned or controlled by other railroads. The Detroit, Toledo & Ironton controlled it from 1905 to 1910. The Wabash acquired control of the Ann Arbor in 1925 and by 1930 owned 97 percent of its stock. (The Wabash in turn was controlled by the Pennsylvania Railroad.) The Detroit, Toledo & Ironton, which was owned by the Wabash and the Pennsylvania, purchased the Ann Arbor for the second time in 1963.

The Ann Arbor began to prune its ferry routes in 1968 with the discontinuance of the 100-mile route to Manistique and the abandonment of the Manistique & Lake Superior Railroad (the former Duluth, South Shore & Atlantic was no longer a through route of any consequence). Two years later AA abandoned its 80-mile ferry route to Menominee and the facilities there.

The Ann Arbor declared bankruptcy on October 16, 1973, and ceased operation on April 1, 1976. Conrail operated the Ann Arbor until the State of Michigan purchased the property and arranged for the Michigan Interstate Railway to operate it. The 60-mile ferry route to Kewaunee (and a connection with the Green Bay & Western Railroad) and the 79-mile ferry route to Manitowoc closed in April 1982.

In 1983 operation of the former Ann Arbor was split among three railroads: Michigan Northern from Frankfort to Alma, Tuscola & Saginaw Bay from Alma to Ann Arbor, and Michigan Interstate from Ann Arbor to Toledo. A year later T&SB took over Michigan Northern's portion of the AA. The 23 miles from Thompsonville to Frankfort were subsequently abandoned. A new Ann Arbor company appeared in 1988 to operate the Ann Arbor–Toledo portion of the railroad.

In 1972, the last year before it declared bankruptcy, the Ann Arbor operated a system of 300 route-miles plus 139 miles of car-ferry route, with 15 locomotives, 454 freight and company service cars, 3 car ferries, and 450 employees. Freight traffic totaled over 671 million ton-miles in 1972. Ann Arbor operating revenues totaled $36.4 million in 1972, and the railroad achieved a 93 percent operating ratio.

—George H. Drury

REFERENCE

Riggs, Henry Earle. *The Ann Arbor Railroad 50 Years Ago*. Ann Arbor, Mich.: privately published rept., 1992.

Architecture

Railroad architecture, broadly defined, encompasses all of the structures associated with the operation and the image of the railroads. These are stations (passenger and freight, including head houses and trainsheds), shop and servicing facilities (roundhouses, foundries, mills, factories, and coal and water towers), interlocking and signal towers, office buildings and warehouses, workers' housing, hotels and restaurants, park structures, suburbs, towns, and the trains themselves. Bridges, viaducts, and tunnels—normally considered works of engineering—also qualify.

Stations and Trainsheds

The station building is the most prominent example of railroad architecture. In 1916, the peak year for American railroad track mileage, an estimated 85,000 train stations stood in the United States. By the early 1990s the number had fallen to about 12,000 (Potter 1996, 54). The extant station buildings range from major metropolitan terminals designed as city gateways (e.g., in New York, Chicago, and Los Angeles) and landscaped suburban stations to a wide variety of depots located in medium-size cities, small towns, and rural areas. In many cases these buildings have either been converted to other uses, such as museums, restaurants, and hotels, or stand neglected.

Nationally known architects and landscape architects who did significant work for the railroads were Daniel H. Burnham, Paul Philippe Cret, Frank Furness, McKim, Mead & White, Frederick Law Olmsted, John Russell Pope, Bruce Price, and Henry Hobson Richardson. Some lesser-known but important railroad architects were E. Francis Baldwin, Solon S. Beman, Mary Colter, Cyrus L. W. Eidlitz, Fellheimer & Wagner, Bradford Lee Gilbert, Graham, Anderson, Probst & White, Samuel Huckle, Jr., Kenneth M. Murchison, John R. Niernsee, Peabody & Stearns, Reed & Stem, Lilian J. Rice, Shepley, Rutan & Coolidge, Warren & Wetmore, and the Wilson Brothers. Engineers, largely unnoted beyond their profession, designed many station buildings.

Existing stations in North America represent the major nineteenth- through twenty-first-century architectural styles: Neoclassical, Greek Revival, Italianate, Gothic Revival, Stick style, Shingle style, Romanesque Revival, Beaux Arts, Neoclassical Revival, Mission style, Spanish Colonial Revival, Modernistic, International, and Postmodern. Although these styles tend to succeed one another, there are no clear boundaries between them, and elements of two or more were often combined, particularly in the Victorian era, to create "picturesque eclecticism" (Meeks 1995, ix). (The Victorian era, 1837–1901, when Romantic or Picturesque styles were replacing Neoclassicism, coincided with the coming-of-age of railroads in America.)

The old question in architecture of whether aesthetic considerations or practical needs should predominate in building design was decided by the railroads in favor of the latter for train stations and all of their other buildings. The plan should take precedence over the architectural features of the structure (Berg 1893). The exterior design of the station ought to indicate its main interior functions (Droege 1916). Architectural beauty is secondary to construction and utility (Gilbert 1895). The railroads definitely believed that form followed function.

Berg, in his *Buildings and Structures of American Railroads* (1893), typed terminal (i.e., end-of-the-line) passenger stations as side or head stations, depending on whether they were located at the side of, or across the end of, the tracks. Droege categorized them as through (side) or head (stub) stations. Meeks grouped stations as one-sided, two-sided, and head. New York's Pennsylvania Station is an example of a through station, and Grand Central Terminal of a head station. (Some metropolitan passenger terminals, e.g., Union Station, Washington, D.C., operate as both through and head stations.) As a practical matter, these distinctions are perhaps less useful for classification purposes than location, size, period, and style.

The station functioned as a sheltered connection or conduit between the departing passenger and the train and the arriving passenger and the local destination. This was true whether the building was an open shed or a small enclosed frame building at a flag stop (flag depot or way station), a larger structure designed to handle both freight and passengers in a small town (combination depot), a building located in the angle of two intersecting rail lines (junction station), one of a series of regularly spaced facilities beyond the city line (suburban station), an imposing downtown edifice (metropolitan station), or a complex of buildings in a great city occupying several blocks, serving numerous railroad companies, and offering a full range of services and amenities (terminal depot, union station). Most stations also served the railroad companies as offices for their ticket and freight agents and myriad other employees.

Shelter was a primary concern. This often took the form of a platform shed, usually attached to the station building. In most cases the shed was an integral part of the station: an overhanging eave or roof extension. This added architectural feature sometimes made the buildings more picturesque and handsome than they might otherwise have been. As cities evolved with the railroads and station buildings grew larger, the trainshed began to be treated separately, as a matter of architectural design, from the station building or head house. In time, the shed dominated the station; in fact, at its apogee at the close of the nineteenth century, the shed became the station.

The waiting room was another common element. Small or large, it was heated initially with fireplaces and stoves and furnished with benches and occasionally armchairs or rocking chairs in the bigger stations. Radiators came later with central heating, but sometimes the fireplaces and individual chairs remained, giving the waiting room an atmosphere of comfort and familiarity. There were often separate waiting rooms for men and women. In the South segregated waiting rooms for blacks and whites were customary. (Railroad coaches in the South were segregated also.) Toilet facilities and a baggage or freight room were found in most stations.

Another necessary component was the agent's office, where train movements were monitored and controlled, tickets were sold, and freight was accounted for. This usually had a trackside bay window where the agent's desk and telegraph key were located. Here the agent, acting as the intermediary between the dispatcher and the train crews, could see both ways down the tracks, be in contact with the railroad and the world, and attend to paperwork. Small-town stations additionally served as the news, trade, and social centers in their communities; a train arrival was one of the day's major events.

Railroad companies replaced some of their earlier wooden stations with buildings of brick, stone, concrete, and stucco. Interior finishes tended to be plain: wooden wainscoting and plaster walls. A simple one-story combination depot might consist only of a waiting room and freight or baggage room, divided by the agent's office. Smaller stations frequently had a second floor with living quarters for the agent and his family, especially in remote areas where housing might not be readily available.

Railroad architects and engineers gradually evolved standard designs for the more modest stations (class depots) that could be expanded depending on the needs of the community. However, they tried to vary their appearance. Every 100 miles marked a railroad division in the steam age; the necessarily larger stations at these points also included the railroad's division management offices. Crew facilities at division points could be quite elaborate: the YMCA Branch Building at East Buffalo, New York, had a restaurant, a barber shop, a library and reading room, a game room, classrooms, dormitories, and a nurse's room.

Metropolitan station buildings included the basic service facilities, but on a much grander scale. In addition, they sometimes had stores and restaurants, telephone and telegraph offices, smoking rooms, nurseries, doctors' offices, immigrant waiting rooms (with their own dressing spaces and toilets), baggage and travelers' aid facilities, and even artworks, athletic facilities, and theaters. The larger stations also customarily housed railroad offices.

Metropolitan stations commonly had an axial plan. The central main entrance led to a lobby and then to the rear doorway and the tracks. Perpendicular to this axis, another ran the full width of the station. Corridors on either side of the lobby led to waiting rooms, ticket counters, the restaurant, the baggage room, and other facilities. The railroad offices were often on the upper floors of these stations.

Terminal depots and union stations in the nation's largest cities, capable of handling hundreds of trains and thousands of passengers a day, were huge structures with complex plans, multiple levels, and myriad connections to outside transportation and other services. Concourses between the station buildings and the tracks acted as mixing areas or gathering spaces for crowds. These stations extensively served commuters (the business class), who often included the railroad company's own executives. In their efforts to impress the clientele and compete with rivals, the railroads spared no expense in architectural design or materials. Employing first timber, then brick and stone, iron and steel, they decorated the exteriors of terminals or union stations with classical columns and carved statuary and the interiors with fine marble, hardwood furniture, ironwork, and art glass. The great stations were small cities in themselves, sometimes surrounded by other railroad or affiliated structures such as office buildings and hotels, post offices, and express agencies.

Freight Depots, Towers, Yard Facilities, and Engine Houses

Freight depots (houses, sheds) were in many cases built alongside the passenger facilities, whether they were small stations or big-city terminals. They were as a rule similar in scale and design to the passenger station—one theory being that if the latter burned, the freight depot could be used instead—but with platforms front and back for loading and unloading, wide sliding doors, and few windows. The interiors were commonly open, unobstructed spaces for the movement and storage of freight, with perhaps a small office at one end. The smaller freight depots were set up to handle less-than-carload (LCL) freight (or packages); sorting, storing, and reloading were the general order of business. Terminal freight depots could be plainly utilitarian or visually distinctive, echoing the grander station buildings with clock towers and decoration.

The repair and maintenance facilities needed to support the terminal depots and union stations were normally at some distance, but occasionally close by, as in Washington, D.C., Chicago, and Kansas City. The tracks behind the head houses and trainsheds of the great depots typically formed an hourglass shape as the rail lines converged to a narrow "throat," then spread out again as they approached the station. Shepley, Rutan & Coolidge's Beaux Arts–style South Station, Boston (1898), once the largest and busiest in America, had two levels and loop tracks (unused), the first such arrangement. Directing the trains to the proper tracks on their way in and out of South Station required nine signal bridges and a tower housing an electropneumatic interlocking system with 165 levers to move the switches and set the signals. Such interlocking towers were normally of two stories and had an enclosed ground floor and a heavily fenestrated second

story with a projecting bay similar to the station agent's bay and serving the same purpose of providing an unobstructed view of the tracks. As a rule, an outside stairway climbed to the second floor. Squat, usually square buildings, strictly functional, with reticent architectural decoration, the interlocking towers were nevertheless readily distinguishable by their shape and appearance near stations small and large. These towers are rapidly being phased out and replaced by computer-operated centralized traffic control at remote locations; a few remain, lonely outposts in the railroad landscape.

Signal towers and shanties (the latter sometimes elevated on exposed or covered timber framing) at switches, road crossings, and other hazardous points on the line were smaller and more basic. (The shanties hardly had room for one person.) Yet sometimes even these had roof cresting and other decoration, especially in towns where all railroad structures were expected to present a "neat appearance." A few surpassed this requirement. Frank Furness's signal towers on the Reading Railroad at Wayne Junction, Philadelphia (1881), had cupolas, balconies, and open observation platforms as distinctive as his Wayne Junction station (demolished).

Coaling stations and water tanks were part of the yard facilities for major stations in the age of steam and were spread out at intervals along the entire length of the rail lines. The early coaling stations and water tanks were wooden, elevated on timber trestles, with conical roofs. "Tank town" and "jerkwater town" (so called because the fireman yanked down the nozzle to replenish the boiler) became part of the American vocabulary. The coaling stations evolved into much larger timber or concrete structures that spanned one or more tracks and permitted the locomotives and tenders to pass underneath to take on coal. These more permanent, sometimes-grotesque, structures can still be seen, sentinels from a former age.

Engine houses (usually in the form of roundhouses) were located at terminal and intermediate points on the line to store, service, and repair locomotives. These could be semicircular or completely enclosed, depending on the number of stalls required; their size was dictated by the length of the turntable. They generally had conical or flat roofs. (The roundhouse of the Great Central Railway Depot, Detroit, Michigan, ca. 1850, had a full dome topped by a lantern that would have pleased the most visionary French Neoclassical architect.)

Ventilation was a major consideration. In a conical-roofed roundhouse the whole form acted as an inverted funnel to channel the smoke to a central ventilator at the top. Flat-roofed roundhouses used individual ventilating stacks, positioned directly over the smokestacks of the locomotives when they were in the roundhouse.

In either case the sulfurous engine smoke quickly corroded the iron stacks; terra-cotta or galvanized-metal flues were an improvement. Iron roof trusses and metal roofs of the early engine houses also suffered from the smoke. Therefore, timber trusses and roofs covered with tar, gravel, or slate were substituted. The outer walls of the roundhouse might be timber, corrugated iron, or masonry. Cast-iron lintels, windowsills, and apron panels were employed for protection and fireproofing.

The oldest roundhouse still standing in North America is the Chicago, Burlington & Quincy Railroad's 40-stall, 264-foot-diameter engine house (ca. 1855) at Aurora, Illinois. Its walls are of local limestone; the design and material of the three-hinged steel roof trusses indicate that the roof was replaced around 1900 (restored, transportation center). Engineer Albert Fink's cast-iron-framed engine house (1866) at Martinsburg, West Virginia, and E. Francis Baldwin's 1884 Passenger Car Shop at Mt. Clare in Baltimore, the largest such circular structure ever built, are other extant roundhouses (both for the B&O Railroad).

The B&O's Mt. Clare shops are the oldest and were once one of the largest and most complete railroad shop complexes in America. Included were stables, a forge and machine shop, a blacksmith shop, a bridge shop, and locomotive and car shops. At its height in the 1920s, 3,000 people worked at the 30-acre complex, building and repairing locomotives and passenger and freight cars and producing whatever else the railroad needed, including furniture. The shops closed in the 1970s; most of the structures, dating primarily from the late 1800s, were demolished. These were basically long, two-story brick buildings with pitched roofs, metal floor trusses, timber roof framing, and cast-iron lintels and jamb plates. Many other railroad shop complexes still exist and are in use in the United States; their buildings, comprising basic industrial space, are readily adaptable for other purposes.

Warehouses and Office Buildings

Warehouses for general goods storage or individual commodities such as coffee and tobacco were some of the largest structures the railroads built. These, along with grain elevators, were usually located at rail-sea interchanges. Having mostly served their purposes, they are also readily reusable.

The B&O Railroad's Camden Warehouse in Baltimore (1898–1905), by Baldwin & Pennington, was a vastly expanded version of a small-town freight depot. Eight stories high and built in sections, it grew to be four city blocks long. The freight, from coconuts to refrigerators, moved directly between trucks and railcars through the ground floor or was elevated for storage to the upper levels. The style was commercial Neoclassical Revival; the materials were brick, granite, iron, and yellow pine. The warehouse, looking something like a great train, now serves as the backdrop for Oriole Park at Camden Yards; its tenants include the team's offices, a large architectural firm, and a publisher.

Railroad companies after about 1850 usually maintained their corporate offices in their home cities' station buildings. As the railroads grew in wealth and power and their increasing business became more complex, they began about 1880 to build individual office buildings. Sometimes these were part of a new station, with the office floors located over the lower-level ticket counters and waiting rooms. This trend continued for the next 50 years or so. Several of these railroad office buildings still stand in major cities and have been converted to other uses.

Philadelphia's Reading Terminal (1893), by the Wilson Brothers and Francis H. Kimball, is one of the finest and best known. The head house is an eight-story Second Renaissance Revival–style building with terra-cotta trim and an arcade facing Market Street. It housed the railroad's administrative offices above the train station. (It is now a Marriott Hotel affiliated with the Philadelphia Convention Center.)

D. H. Burnham & Co. in 1903 designed the Pennsylvania Railroad's Pennsylvania Station, Pittsburgh, in a commercial Romanesque style, fronted by a dramatic rotunda, "the world's greatest cab stand." This vehicular concourse functioned as a symbolic city gate and as an "arcaded porch" for the ten-story station and office building. Its sophisticated design and structure fused elements of the Beaux Arts and Neoclassical Revival styles with modern construction techniques. Four broad elliptical vaults framed a coffered pendentive dome; square pavilions, also arched, anchored the four corners. The steel-frame structure was faced with stone and terra-cotta; its interior was richly decorated. A wide-span trainshed in the rear of the station and office building completed the ensemble (trainshed demolished; rotunda restored; head house converted to apartments).

Another Burnham building, the Railway Exchange (1904) on South Michigan Avenue in Chicago, was one of the most successful of the firm's many high-rise office-building projects. Not connected with a station, it was the Santa Fe Railway's Chicago headquarters; several other railroads also had offices there. The 17-story Commercial-style structure, faced with enameled terra-cotta, was later known as the Santa Fe Building (renovated, general office building).

Reed & Stem and Warren & Wetmore, the architects of New York's Grand Central Station, created Detroit's Michigan Central Station, whose Beaux Arts styling closely resembled Grand Central's; both stations opened in 1913. For Detroit, they also designed a 15-story office building behind the station building; it was never fully completed or occupied (station and office building vacant).

Graham, Anderson, Probst & White (successor firm to D. H. Burnham & Co.) designed Union Terminal in Cleveland (1930), for the New York Central and the New York, Chicago & St. Louis (Nickel Plate) railroads and for the Van Sweringen real estate interests. The complex included a 52-story office tower that for a time was the tallest building west of New York City, a hotel, a department store, and three other office buildings, all developed on air rights over the tracks. The terminal itself was buried inside the complex, but there were separate concourses for railroad and rapid-transit lines and four acres of underground stores, restaurants, and other services managed by the Fred Harvey Co. (now Tower City Center, retail and office complex; rapid-transit stop).

As a prelude to their Cincinnati Union Terminal, architects Fellheimer & Wagner designed New York Central Terminal in Buffalo with a 17-story office tower in 1930. The Art Deco station's huge arched entrance (also employed in Cincinnati) and corner tower were reminiscent of Eliel Saarinen's 1914 Helsinki Central Station. The Buffalo terminal's vaulted main concourse was faced with Guastavino tile (vacant). Another notable Art Deco station and office tower is Herman C. Koeppe's 1931 Texas & Pacific Railroad facility in Forth Worth, Texas.

Railroad Suburbs and Towns

The railroads' golden age in America in the last half of the nineteenth century coincided with the rise of the planned suburb. Railroads made commuting faster and more feasible. The Northern Central Railway, between Baltimore and Harrisburg, was organized in 1854. Two years later, developers advertised the Mount Washington Rural Retreat, one of Baltimore's early planned suburbs. They offered country residences within easy commuting distance of the city in a healthy environment "free from the annoyance of city rowdies" (a reference to urban violence during the Know-Nothing age). The early houses in Mount Washington were in the Rural Gothic and Italianate styles popularized by Downing.

Railroad suburbs developed along the main line of the Pennsylvania Railroad and other rail routes serving Philadelphia; in Long Island, Connecticut, and New Jersey surrounding New York; to the north, south, and west of Boston; and around Detroit, Chicago, San Francisco, and virtually every other major American city. No longer did one have to be wealthy to own a country house (in addition to a house in town). Rail commuting and the rising middle class made possible a country house for everyone, with a manicured front lawn, a wide veranda, and a welcoming hearth.

The railroads themselves created towns. In the American West, Southwest, Pacific Northwest, and western Canada, there were few settlements of any size for the early transcontinental routes to serve. Therefore, they promoted their own. Albuquerque, New Mexico (Santa Fe Railway), Cheyenne, Wyoming (Union Pacific Railroad), Billings, Montana, and Tacoma, Washington (both Northern Pacific Railway), were towns planned by the railroad companies that became sizable cities.

A 1910 map of the communities platted along the routes and branch lines of James J. Hill's Great Northern Railway and the Minneapolis, St. Paul & Sault Ste. Marie Railway (the Soo Line), in the vicinity of Minot, North Dakota, reveals a distinct pattern created by the railroads. Large towns are interspersed regularly among strings of villages. At greater intervals occur small cities such as

Devil's Lake and Minot. Surrounding the railroad towns are previously existing communities where post offices were discontinued, reflecting the railroads' mail-carrying capability and the gravitation of the local population to the new centers. This pattern of railroad development still survives, seemingly unaffected by the twentieth-century agents of progress, the automobile and the interstate highway. (Minot is currently served by Amtrak.)

Ignoring the freelance entrepreneurs, the railroads hired their own promoters, local businessmen, to act as agents in establishing and attracting businesses for their new towns. One such agent, a banker who laid out 60 towns along the Great Northern Railway from 1905 to 1912, as a rule sought several lumberyards and two each of banks, general, hardware, and farm machinery stores, plus a drugstore, hotel, print shop, market, restaurant, and livery stable.

Like the small-town stations, the towns, whose lots and streets were of uniform size, assumed standard forms, basically two. One was T-shaped, in which the main business street lay perpendicular to the rail line, the depot, and ancillary structures (silos, feed stores). This form minimized grade crossings and accidents. In the other, the rail line bisected the town, with two business streets paralleling it on either side, separated by the 300-foot railroad right of way. One side typically would have the major businesses; the other, a string of bars and cheap hotels. In the South the rail line often separated the races as well, with poorer, socially less acceptable residents relegated to living "on the wrong side of the tracks." Thousands of American communities still have their Railroad Avenue and Depot Street, though the trains and passengers have largely disappeared.

Signature Styles

Because of the influence of the Spanish heritage, regionalism had its strongest effect on railroad architecture in the West and the Deep South. In California the Spanish Colonial Revival style is evident in the tile roofs, iron grilles, and Baroque decoration of the 1927 Santa Fe station in Claremont, California (train stop) and the Southern Pacific Railroad's 1924 Glendale station (Amtrak stop). This style of station architecture was a deliberate choice by the railroad companies in their attempt to replace the commonplace image of the Wild West with one of a healthy, sunny, settled land and thereby promote their lines.

When these two companies and the Union Pacific Railroad built Los Angeles Union Passenger Terminal in 1939, the architects' committee from the three companies employed the plainer Mission Revival style. The station has a clock tower, a prominent arched, tiled entrance, and Art Deco details. The comfortable Mission-style armchairs in the waiting room give it a domestic appearance and mitigate the station's large scale. Mary Colter designed the Fred Harvey restaurant, the newsstand, and retail and other facilities. Other extant examples of Spanish Colo-

The Los Angeles Union Passenger Terminal (1939) was designed in the Mission Revival style by architects Donald and John Parkinson. With the addition of commuter rail and rapid-transit services, the station is busier today than ever. The exterior (*top*) shows the main entrance, while the interior (*bottom*) shows the main waiting room. —(both) William D. Middleton

nial or Mission Revival train stations, all built between 1907 and 1926, are in San Diego, California; Boise, Idaho; San Antonio, Texas; Mobile, Alabama; and Orlando and West Palm Beach, Florida. Spanish-influenced styles also appeared in the Northeast.

Colter, an architect and interior designer, spent her professional career with the Fred Harvey Co. and its business partner, the Santa Fe Railway. Her designs for stations, hotels, restaurants, and park structures fused elements of the Spanish Colonial and Mission Revival styles with Native American themes. The image of the Southwest that Colter's "travel architecture" expressed was a

In the 1880s Boston architect H. H. Richardson, working with landscape architect Frederick Law Olmsted, designed a series of small stations for the Boston & Albany Railroad with large stone arches and widely overhanging roofs. Two examples are Auburndale (*top*) and Wellesley Hills (*bottom*). —Middleton Collection

major component of the Santa Fe Railway's and the Harvey Co.'s marketing and tourism programs.

Henry Hobson Richardson gave a similar signature appearance to several New England train stations and set a new course for station design other than revivals or "picturesque eclecticism." Richardson's direct, utilitarian approach and powerful forms—massive masonry arches and walls—were eminently suited to the purpose. He designed nine stations for the Boston & Albany Railroad and the 1884 Old Colony Railroad station in Easton, Massachusetts. Typically compact and forceful, its flared roof overhanging the round-arched entrances, the building is both welcoming and protective (museum). Frederick Law Olmsted was the landscape architect. The Richardsonian Romanesque style had a widespread influence on railroad and American architecture. Shepley, Rutan & Coolidge, the successor firm to H. H. Richardson, designed the 1887 New London, Connecticut, Union Station in the same style.

Bruce Price designed and built railroad cars for the Pennsylvania and Boston & Albany railroads. Other architects and industrial designers gave a streamlined, modern look to whole trains. In the 1930s the French Beaux Arts architect Paul Philippe Cret designed locomotives and coaches for the Burlington *Zephyr*s and for several other railroads. Industrial designers Raymond Loewy and Henry Dreyfuss did the same thing, respectively, for the Pennsylvania Railroad's *Broadway Limited* and the New York Central Railroad's *20th Century Limited*. Chicago architects Holabird & Root came up with a sleek Denver ticket office for the Burlington Lines that employed the same stainless-steel panels as the railroad coaches. They also designed a Fred Harvey restaurant in the Kansas City, Missouri, Union Station with murals depicting the city's history.

History

Following the earlier practice of turnpikes and canals, the first railroad stations were in inns, convenient places to sell tickets and use as points of departure. The earliest purpose-built stations were often next to or attached to existing inns. The track customarily ran alongside these structures, under a canopy or shed (or sometimes right through the building), with platforms for handling passengers and freight. Only later, and mainly in metropolitan areas, did the separate station building (head house) and the shelter for passengers and for storing coaches (trainshed) evolve.

The initial railroad stations in the United States were rudimentary in the extreme. For the Baltimore & Ohio Railroad, the nation's pioneer line, carpenter John Ready in 1829 built a temporary shed at Baltimore's Mt. Clare depot from boards salvaged from workmen's shanties. (He also fenced in the yard.)

Architect Jacob Small, Jr., designed a stone freight depot in a very plain Federal style for the B&O Railroad at Ellicotts Mills, 13 miles from Baltimore. B&O contractor John McCartney built it of local gray granite. The station opened in 1832. (It is now America's oldest railroad station and a museum.) A deep roof overhang provided trackside shelter for the passengers, who boarded the trains from a platform extended to the Patapsco Hotel across the street opposite the station, a stagecoach stop on the National Road.

The B&O Railroad's first station in Washington, D.C., occupied a former three-story boardinghouse to which it added a belfry and car shed in 1835. In the Boston & Lowell Railroad's severe 1835 Greek Revival station at Lowell, Massachusetts, the trainshed was part of the building, and the trains passed through it behind a colonnade that formed one side of the structure. (This was known in New England as a "train barn"; one still exists at Lexington, Massachusetts.) The B&O Railroad's first station in Cumberland, Maryland, around the early 1840s, was built next to the Revere House, an inn on the National Road. It was a two-story building; apparently the ticket office (with agent's quarters above) occupied one side and the trainshed, again an integral part of the structure, the other.

American railroad stations of some pretension began to appear about the middle of the nineteenth century. A trio of notable early buildings designed in three different styles by architects reflected their understanding of contemporary trends and indicated the coming High Victorian eclecticism. Thomas Tefft's 1849 Union Station in Providence, Rhode Island, a broad-fronted building with distinctive towers, arcades, and terminating pavilions, was in the German Rundbogenstil (round-arched style); the swept-back arcades screened lateral trainsheds.

Niernsee & Neilson's more compact Calvert Station, Baltimore (1850), was a prototype of the Italianate style (and also of the terminal head house backed by a trainshed). Built for the Baltimore & Susquehanna Railroad,

Calvert Station's Italianate towers flanked a basically Neoclassical structure with a projecting central pavilion; the ensemble fronted an attractive three-bay trainshed whose roof was supported by granite columns and timber and iron Howe trusses. (Niernsee in the 1840s designed prefabricated iron roofs for B&O Railroad stations, engine sheds, and freight houses that were the earliest known composite iron roofs in this country.) Italianate proved so popular for future railroad stations that it became known as the "railroad style." (Both stations have disappeared.)

Joseph F. Kemp's Camden Station in downtown Baltimore for the B&O Railroad (1856–1865) had a Georgian five-part plan: a central building with a tall tower, hyphens, and wings; shorter Italianate towers terminated the extensive facade. An assortment of sheds and engine houses extended out to the rear. The central building's door and window openings were framed in cast iron. Railroads had begun to use this ancient material structurally in bridge and roof trusses, as well as in locomotives and cars.

Camden Station carried a landmark tower and clock, two emblems of the railroad terminal. The main tower, 185 feet high, one of the tallest structures in the city, clearly marked the station's location. The "approved astronomical clock" was crucial to the operation of the railroad, in addition to serving as a convenience for passengers and passersby. Its meridian was relayed daily by telegraph to the 26 operators on the line who set their clocks by it, ensuring standard time over the 380 miles of railroad between Baltimore and the Ohio River. (Camden, the oldest major metropolitan railroad station still standing, was renovated as a sports museum; the exterior has been restored to its 1865 appearance.)

The remaining stations of the mid-nineteenth century exhibit the wide range of eclectic styles popular in the Victorian age. The Philadelphia, Wilmington & Baltimore Railroad's station at Dover, Delaware (ca. 1856), is a classic Greek Temple to which the Pennsylvania Railroad (the PW&B's successor), added an appropriate Neoclassical Revival extension in 1911 (state offices). The architect of the Illinois Central Railroad's 1857 Galena, Illinois, depot chose to decorate his Rundbogenstil station with twin Italianate towers (visitors' center). Starrucca House (1865) at Susquehanna, Pennsylvania (near the Erie Railroad's famed Starrucca Viaduct), combined Romanesque and Gothic Revival themes in its 327-foot-long station-hotel, whose vaulted dining room rises the full 2½-story height of the building. It was later turned into a railroad YMCA and is now a private restaurant.

E. Francis Baldwin's photogenic 1875 station at Point of Rocks, Maryland, is a superb response to the site, located in the cleft of the Y formed by the B&O Railroad's Old Main Line and Metropolitan Branch, which join at the Potomac River. The brick and brownstone junction station, its tower facing Harpers Ferry and the west, is in the High Victorian Gothic style (active Maryland Rail Commuter station).

were the successor firm to the Wilson Brothers, who designed some of the Pennsylvania Railroad's most significant structures (Amtrak service; multimodal transportation center).

Between 1850 and 1950 stations and other railroad structures proliferated and atrophied following the curve of technological development and the fortunes of the railroads as primary means of transportation. Routes and stations multiplied rapidly in the post–Civil War period. Some of the most impressive station buildings and the largest trainsheds of the steam age appeared before 1900.

One reason that many representative examples remain, despite abandonment and redevelopment projects, is that

Built in the High Victorian Gothic style, this B&O station at Point of Rocks, Maryland, designed by E. Francis Baldwin in 1875, remains a well-kept station still in service. —William D. Middleton

Many considered Chicago's Grand Central Station the railroad capital's finest terminal. Architect Solon S. Beman completed the station in 1890. —Photo taken by Kaufmann & Fabry, 1922, Chicago Historical Society (Neg. ICHi 05342)

Some critics felt that Chicago's magnificent Grand Central Station by Solon S. Beman, in the Commercial Romanesque style, with a signature 220-foot-high clock tower and palatial interior, was the finest station in America's railroad capital. The B&O Railroad acquired the building shortly after it was built. When it opened in 1890, Grand Central Station's iron and glass balloon trainshed was second in size only to the 1871 balloon shed at the original Grand Central Terminal, New York. (Both were soon outdone, however, by the Pennsylvania Railroad's new terminal in Jersey City.) Chicago's Grand Central Station and trainshed were torn down in the 1970s.

Richmond's eye-filling Main Street Station (1901), with a red terra-cotta tile roof, is in the French Renaissance style. The union station was shared by the Chesapeake & Ohio Railway and the Seaboard Air Line. It possesses one of the ten or so remaining trainsheds in the United States. The architects, Wilson, Harris & Richards,

the railroads, like the Romans, built for the ages. They used talented designers, good materials, and sound construction techniques. The stations were usually designed by architects, the sheds by engineers, the latter often but not always in the employ of the particular railroad. In several instances company engineers also designed stations. Conversely, architects, who were usually in private practice (but sometimes closely affiliated with railroad companies), seldom were involved in the design of trainsheds. In a few cases, for example, the Wilson Brothers, the designers were both architects and engineers.

G. B. Nicholson, chief engineer of the Alabama Great Southern Railroad, designed a handsome Richardsonian Romanesque brick and stone station with a slate roof, veranda and porte cochère, and women's and men's waiting rooms at Fort Payne, Alabama, in 1891 (depot museum). The chief engineer of the New York Central & Hudson River Railroad also designed stations, as did M. J. Becker, chief engineer of the Pennsylvania Railroad. The latter's Standard Passenger Depot, Class F of the 1880s for the lines west of Pittsburgh was a small frame Stick-style structure with a pitched roof, scrollwork in the gables, and bracketed roof overhangs.

The designs for the Rural Gothic Cottage and the Italian Villa popularized in Andrew Jackson Downing's 1842 *Cottage Residences* were eminently adaptable to small train stations. The little Wayland, Massachusetts, depot built in 1881 by a predecessor to the Boston & Maine Railroad is typical, with its board and batten siding, brackets, covered platform, and agent's bay. The domestic forms were reassuringly familiar, and the verandas and deep roof overhangs provided some of the same security and shelter for the passengers as did the trainsheds of the larger stations (gift shop).

Trainsheds

The large trainsheds were the structural wonders of the age, "the most original and efficient part of railroad architecture," urban "room-streets" (Meeks 1995, 46, 62). The inspiration for many of those built in America was the Midland Railroad's magnificent trainshed at St. Pancras, London, designed by engineer William H. Barlow and completed in 1868. It covered the tracks and platforms with an unprecedented clear span of 240 feet; its cast-iron arches, whose bases were tied together by iron girders under the station floor, met in a slightly pointed Gothic arch. The vast trainshed, heavily glazed and enclosed by glass screens at either end, was "a symphony of structure, steam, and slanting rays of light." It housed the station (the booking office and waiting rooms) and was fortuitously though perfectly integrated with George Gilbert Scott's equally magnificent Gothic Revival St. Pancras Hotel, constructed in 1873 across its front.

St. Pancras (the shed, not the hotel) was the model for New York City's first Grand Central Depot. Constructed for the New York Central & Hudson River Railroad and other lines in 1871, it was America's earliest rail station built on the scale of those in Europe and the country's first major balloon shed. The L-shaped station fronting on 42nd Street, designed by architect John B. Snook, was a mélange of Neoclassical and Second Empire themes. In the crook of the L was the shed, designed by engineer Isaac C. Buckhout. Like St. Pancras, it was framed in metal, with a clear span of 200 feet; wrought-iron tie rods connected the arches of the barrel vault beneath the station floor. The roof, covered with sheet iron and glass, was carried on curved wrought-iron Howe trusses resting on decorative bases of cast iron.

In 1892 a trainshed appeared in Jersey City, across the Hudson River from Manhattan, that eclipsed both Grand Central and St. Pancras. It was built by the New York Central's archrival, the Pennsylvania Railroad. The shed, covering 12 tracks and six platforms with a clear span of 253 feet, was an elliptical vault supported on three-hinged, wrought-iron trusses, their bottom hinges connected by 12-inch I-beams riveted together at butt joints under the tracks. (These heavy members were designed to resist compressive forces from wind and snow loads, as well as the tension forces due to the outward thrust of the arches.) The roof was of metal and glass.

Conrad C. Schneider, a bridge engineer and not an employee of the railroad company, was responsible for the design of the shed, which found a receptive audience with the railroad's officers, who wanted a monumental structure. William H. Brown, the Pennsylvania's chief engineer, was in charge of the remaining station buildings. They were in the familiar L shape: a low-profile head house, a multistory office block, and in front, a smaller version of the large shed, which served as the concourse between the tracks and the ferry slips. The great shed, visible to thousands of ferry passengers between New Jersey and Manhattan, not only symbolized the station as the gateway to the city, it literally was the station (demolished).

This and the other stations in Jersey City and Hoboken comprised what was, in the early twentieth century, the greatest rail-ferry terminal complex in the world. The era also marked the penultimate stage of railroad megalomania when the companies tried to outdo one another—and attract passengers—with the scale and grandeur of their stations.

The first to be built was the Central Railroad of New Jersey's station at Jersey City, erected in 1887. Peabody & Stearns designed the head house and ferry concourse in Rundbogenstil, similar to their Park Square Station, Boston (1874). The trainshed, the largest single-span gable shed (143 feet), was designed by William H. Peddle, the railroad's chief engineer. It had the form of a basilica: a central gable flanked by lower lean-to (shed) roofs, the whole covered with corrugated sheet iron and glass (head house restored; shed demolished).

Next in order of appearance was the Erie Railroad's station of 1888. The Railroad Gothic head house was designed by architect George E. Archer. The trainshed, another central gable flanked by lower roofs, spanned 140 feet. It was the work of C. W. Buchholz, the Erie's chief engineer, and was erected by the Phoenix Bridge Co. (demolished).

The final addition to the train-ferry terminals opposite New York City, the Delaware, Lackawanna & Western Railroad's 1907 Hoboken terminal, spelled the end of the great trainsheds. The waterfront site conditions and the resulting engineering decisions dictated the physical appearance of the terminal complex.

Several previous wooden terminals on the site, beneath which was unstable fill, had burned. Lincoln Bush, the DL&W's chief engineer, wanted to lessen the load on the new foundation of concrete platforms resting on timber pilings and grillage. The head house is therefore a steel-frame structure with reinforced concrete walls; the concrete contains a cinder aggregate to reduce the weight. It is faced with lightweight copper sheathing chosen by the architect, Kenneth M. Murchison, who designed it in the Beaux Arts style. (The 225-foot clock tower has been replaced with a radio antenna.)

Even more innovative was the trainshed: low concrete and glass vaults supported by steel girders, spanning just the distance between platforms with open slots over the center of the track for the engine smoke to escape. Lincoln Bush's invention, through the proliferation of columns, spread the load on the foundation rather than concentrating it under the arch footings, as in the balloon sheds. The Bush design also solved the other major defect of the great sheds, the smoke that tended to collect under the roof rather than being dissipated through the rooftop monitors, corroding the ironwork and resulting in costly maintenance. The Bush shed was employed in Hoboken for the first time; it later became common in a slightly different version as the butterfly shed or platform canopy. (The Hoboken terminal is undergoing a $300 million redevelopment.)

Meanwhile, two very important balloon sheds with head houses had been erected in Philadelphia, both in 1893. The Pennsylvania Railroad's Broad Street Station won the race for the world's largest single-span trainshed, 301 feet; it was designed by Wilson Brothers, architects and engineers. The head house, in Railroad Gothic style, was the work of four architects: Joseph Wilson and Arthur Truscott (1881) and Frank Furness and Allan Evans (1893 reconstruction and addition). The Wilson Brothers and architect Francis H. Kimball designed the nearby Reading Terminal's trainshed, with a 260-foot span, and the handsome nine-story head house. It is the last remaining balloon shed in America (renovated as the Philadelphia Convention Center; located over the Reading Terminal Market).

Engineer George H. Pegram's 1894 trainshed at Union Terminal, St. Louis, the largest to date, also deserves men-

tion. The structure, 606 feet wide and 630 feet long and composed of five separate spans supported by metal trusses of Pegram's design, enclosed 30 tracks and an area of nearly ten acres (station restored, privately owned; mixed use; the trainshed now covers a boat lake; the site was originally a millpond).

Engineers were now in the ascendant. The advent of electric traction facilitated the construction of two of America's greatest stations: New York City's Pennsylvania Station (1910) and Grand Central Terminal (1913); the latter's then-novel development of air rights over Park Avenue transformed the center of Manhattan. These immense public works projects, involving bridges, underwater tunnels, and large-scale buildings, were undertaken by private railroad companies at the zenith of their power and as emblems of that power. They inspired new terminal depots and union stations in other cities, a movement that culminated in the 1930s.

The architectural model for the New York terminals and at least five other union stations was Charles B. Atwood's terminal for the 1893 Chicago World's Fair. Heading the fair's design team were Frederick Law Olmsted, "landscape artist," and Burnham & Root, consulting architects. When John Wellborn Root died in 1891, Daniel H. Burnham named Atwood, a talented New York architect, the fair's designer in chief. The appearance of the monumental "White City" and its Beaux Arts style, due in part to Atwood, influenced American architecture for the next several decades.

Atwood's temporary train station was in turn based on the Baths of Caracalla in Rome (A.D. 216), a building of colossal scale whose bilateral symmetry, axial plan, multiple entrances, and vaulted interiors would typify the great American train stations of the early twentieth century. The major characteristics of Atwood's 1893 Chicago World's Fair station were three large, arched portals, centrally located, and a prominent gabled pavilion above the roofline expressing the vaulted waiting room–concourse within. This form was followed, with minor variations, in Daniel H. Burnham's Union Station, Washington, D.C. (1907); McKim, Mead & White's Pennsylvania Station, New York (1910); Union Station, Worcester, Massachusetts, by Samuel Huckel, Jr. (a Philadelphia architect who had worked on the 1900 reconstruction of the first Grand Central Depot) (1911); Grand Central Terminal, New York, by Reed & Stem and Warren & Wetmore (1913); the same architects' Michigan Central Station, Detroit (1913); Union Station, Kansas City, Missouri, Jarvis Hunt (1914); and Kenneth M. Murchison's Union Terminal, Jacksonville,

"AMERICA'S GRANDEST RAILWAY TERMINAL"
— PENNSYLVANIA RAILROAD —
New Passenger Station, Broad Street, Philadelphia, U.S.A.

Florida (1919). (All these buildings except Pennsylvania Station are extant.)

During the 1920s, mainly because of competition from automobiles, passenger traffic on local (accommodation) trains fell sharply. At the same time long-distance and Pullman patronage was up. The railroads accordingly, in this and the following decade, invested in luxury equipment, high-speed service, and newer and bigger union station buildings. But it proved to be "the sunset mistaken for the sunrise." The railroads shortly entered a decline that, with the exception of the World War II period, has continued up to the present, particularly affecting passenger service.

The last generation of major metropolitan stations constructed in America in the twentieth century includes Union Station, Chicago, by Graham, Anderson, Probst, & White (1925); the same architects' Union Terminal, Cleveland (1930); New York Central Station, Buffalo, Fellheimer & Wagner (successor firm to Reed & Stem) (1930); Union Station, Omaha, Gilbert Stanley Underwood (1931); Union Terminal, Cincinnati, Fellheimer & Wagner, with consulting architect Paul Philippe Cret (1933); the grandiose 30th Street Station, Philadelphia, by Graham, Anderson, Probst & White (1933); and the 1939 Los Angeles Union Passenger Terminal, by H. L. Gilman, J. H. Christie, R. J. Wirth, and consulting architects John and Donald Parkinson. Most of these stations were in the Neoclassical Revival style, then becoming unfashionable; two (Buffalo and Cincinnati) were in the prevailing Modernistic style; and one (Los Angeles), in the Mission Revival style. (All are still standing.) Two of the greatest names in twentieth-century American architecture and modernism, Frank Lloyd Wright and Mies van der Rohe, were not chosen to design stations by conservative railroad officials, who preferred architects who shared their preference for familiar styles.

No metropolitan train stations of note have been built in the United States since the 1930s. Railroad companies in midcentury replaced some of their suburban and other smaller stations with new International-style buildings, functional but spiritless compared with their predecessors. Encouraging signs of a revival in good train station design, if not of a resurgence in train travel itself, occurred in the 1990s on opposite sides of the country in Boston and Solana Beach, California.

In creating a new entrance to Boston's Back Bay Station, architects Kallmann, McKinnell & Wood combined the traditional head house and trainshed in a dramatic abstract version of a barrel vault composed of laminated timber arches screened by a rectangular masonry structure with side walls of glass (Amtrak, commuter, and transit service). Architect Rob Wellington Quigley also chose the barrel vault for his Solana Beach station (actually the form is based on a Quonset hut). Glass end walls and a central roof monitor light the building as in the old trainsheds; the vault, paneled in redwood, is supported by steel arches. The concrete tower is a community landmark.

Station Profiles

Grand Central Terminal (1913), Reed & Stem, Warren & Wetmore, New York, New York

"The Grand Central Terminal is not only a station," said Droege in 1916, "it is a monument, a civic center or, if one will, a city." Grand Central is America's greatest railroad station, not so much because of size—although the total track area and double level of tracks make it the largest railroad terminal in the world—as because of its very successful combination of engineering, architecture, and urban planning. Grand Central Terminal is also historically important as the first completely electrified station (in terms of its operations and interior lighting). Grand Central pioneered the concept of air rights development. Its rescue and restoration (1978–1998) were a landmark in the U.S. preservation movement.

The new Grand Central Terminal was conceived by William J. Wilgus, chief engineer of the New York Central & Hudson River Railroad, in response to a substantial increase in trains and traffic. (The number of passengers at Grand Central doubled from 1890 to 1910.) As a way to increase the station's capacity but not expand the very large site—some 25 city blocks, including the head house, shed, ancillary facilities, and trackage—Wilgus devised a terminal with stacked track levels and loop tracks to turn the trains. This arrangement was possible only with the elimination of steam locomotives, whose smoke and gases were responsible for major problems in the approaches to the station.

In 1902 low visibility due to smoke and steam caused a train to run a signal, resulting in an accident that killed 15 commuters. When, in 1903, the New York legislature outlawed steam locomotives in the approaches to Grand Central, the railroad had already decided to employ electric traction, a relatively new technology. That same year Wilgus presented his plan for a new all-electric, 57-track, double-level terminal to replace the earlier station. A key concept in financing the improvements was the sale of air rights over the area occupied by the shed and open approaches north of the head house that would now be covered. Four architectural firms were asked to submit designs: McKim, Mead & White; Daniel H. Burnham; Samuel Huckel, Jr.; and Reed & Stem.

Stanford White's spectacular scheme called for a 14-story head house and a 60-story office tower from whose peak would rise a 300-foot steam jet illuminated by red floodlights. Reed & Stem's more modest design for a low, wide head house based on Atwood's 1893 Chicago terminal, topped by a slightly narrower office tower, was chosen instead. (Wilgus, who was Charles Reed's brother-in-law, had contributed to the Reed & Stem design.) Their plan included some of the most successful features of the new terminal: the sunken, high-ceilinged, open main concourse; a system of ramps rather than stairways to facilitate a gravity-like flow of passengers from the street into and through the station; the main concourse for long-distance trains and the suburban concourse below it; and the passage of Park Avenue around the station. Immediately north of the building was the three-block Court of Honor, set aside for the first air rights development.

In 1904 the New York architectural firm of Warren & Wetmore was added to the design team. (Whitney Warren, a cousin and personal friend of William K. Vanderbilt, New York Central chairman, had trained at the Ecole des Beaux Arts in Paris and had begun his career with McKim, Mead & White.) While retaining the major features of the Reed-Wilgus plan, Warren redesigned the head house in true Beaux Arts style with coupled columns and a clock and large statuary group atop the main 42nd Street facade. (The office tower was eliminated.)

Construction took ten years. The demolition of some 200 buildings and the use of 500 tons of dynamite to blast loose the underlying Manhattan schist were required before the terminal complex was completed. Removing the trainshed, which contained 1,700 tons of cast and wrought iron, while maintaining railroad service below, was an especially difficult task.

In the meantime, Wilgus resigned in 1907 in a dispute with the company, Charles Reed died in 1911, and Warren & Wetmore immediately signed a new contract with the railroad that made them sole architects. When Grand Central Terminal was finished, Warren & Wetmore generally received credit as the designers. (They still do in some press accounts of the restoration.) Allen Stem, the surviving partner, later sued to collect his firm's design fees and won; Whitney Warren was expelled from the American Institute of Architects. Warren & Wetmore went on to design several nearby air rights structures such as the Biltmore Hotel and other railroad stations elsewhere. In fact, credit for Grand Central Terminal should be divided among William J. Wilgus, developer of the basic concept and engineering plan; Charles Reed, who contributed innovative functional features; and Whitney Warren, largely responsible for the design of the station building.

It is a steel-frame structure, faced with Connecticut granite and Bedford, Indiana, limestone. The sculpture group depicting Mercury, the Roman god of commerce, flanked by Minerva and Hercules, is by Jules Coutan, professor at the Ecole des Beaux Arts. The main concourse, 120 by 275 feet, with an information booth in the center and ticket windows lining one wall, is paved with Tennessee marble; the walls of imitation Caen stone are trimmed with Botticino marble. On the barrel-vaulted ceiling, 125 feet up, is French artist Paul Helleu's painting

A system of sloping ramps instead of stairways facilitated the flow of passengers between the streets and the station, and an extended system of interconnected passages helped make Grand Central Terminal into a "city within a city." This cutaway drawing from the December 7, 1912, *Scientific American* shows the complex system of connections between the streets, railroads, and rapid-transit lines. —Middleton Collection

of the constellations of the zodiac (in reverse order), composed of 2,500 gold-leaf stars on a blue background. In addition to the huge, arched windows, large bronze electric chandeliers light the concourse balconies and the waiting room in front of the station. The lower-level restaurant, the famous Oyster Bar, is vaulted with Guastavino tile.

There were few precedents for a building of the scale and complexity of Grand Central Terminal. Accommodating two levels of moving trains, air rights development on top of them, and the myriad entrances and exits connecting the station to streets, subways, and outside buildings required an intricate structure and a strong one. All of the steel columns are based on solid rock. Three-foot-deep plate girders support the concrete floors in the head house; long-span girders are from seven to ten feet deep. Pratt and Warren trusses hold up the roof and ceiling.

To heat the terminal and provide electricity for its operation, the railroad erected its own power plant and substation. (The powerhouse had four corner towers and resembled a Romanesque church.) To guide the trains in and out, one of the largest and most advanced signal and interlocking systems to date (five interlocking towers) was installed. The total cost for land and terminal was $80 million, nearly double the original estimate.

In 1914, 470 trains and 75,000 passengers used Grand Central Terminal every day; in 1946 it handled 550 trains and 204,000 passengers per day. Besides transportation, "Grand Central City" offered stores, bars and restaurants, a post office, a movie theater, a gymnasium, tennis courts, and an emergency hospital. On either side were the Biltmore and Commodore hotels, both owned by the railroad. The planned Court of Honor north of the head house never materialized, but air rights development proceeded, one of the most important new buildings being the 1931 Waldorf-Astoria Hotel on Park Avenue between 49th and 50th streets.

By the 1950s Grand Central Terminal was in decline. The 1963 construction of the Pan Am Building blocked the vista on Park Avenue to the north. In 1967 the terminal was one of the first buildings designated a landmark by New York City's Landmarks Preservation Commission. That designation and the Penn Central Transportation Co.'s 1968 plans to build a 55-story tower atop the station building instigated a public controversy and a court suit. In deciding the case in favor of the preservationists, the U.S. Supreme Court in 1978 upheld the constitutionality of the city's landmarks law and the right of local governments to protect their historic architecture.

The Metropolitan Transit Authority (MTA) leased the terminal in the 1970s to serve its Metro-North commuter service. (Long-distance trains were later transferred to Penn Station.) In 1998 the MTA completed a $200 million restoration that included structural repairs, exterior and interior restoration, and construction of an eastern stairway in the main concourse (originally planned but never built), providing access to new restaurants on the balcony. New York's Beyer, Blinder, Belle was the restoration architect. (The tennis courts on the third level are still in use.)

Currently 250,000 daily commuters pass through the station, and thousands of other people patronize its more than 100 shops, cafés, and restaurants. A century after its birth, Grand Central Terminal still functions efficiently as a cathedral of transportation and commerce and more than ever as Manhattan's majestic public parlor.

Michigan Central Station (1887), Cyrus L. W. Eidlitz, Kalamazoo, Michigan

Michigan Central Station is a modest-size, midwestern depot by an architect whose stations make a decisive visual impact. Cyrus L. W. Eidlitz (1853–1921) was the son of another architect, Leopold Eidlitz, born in Prague and a major exponent of the German Rundbogenstil. The elder Eidlitz emigrated to America and became a New York architect and also an architectural writer, orator, and philosopher. His American-born son, who studied at Stuttgart's Polytechnic Institute, evidently let his buildings speak for him.

Dearborn Street Station in Chicago (1885), for the Chicago & Western Indiana Railroad, by Eidlitz, built of brick, terra-cotta, and brownstone, was in a straightforward Rundbogenstil. However, the clock tower's Gothic roof and dormers were pure architectural fantasy (office building; original roof and tower demolished). For his Kalamazoo station Eidlitz used the same materials (adding a red tile roof), but a very different approach and combination of styles. The station presents a low, broad profile. Its two-story center portion has heavy stone arches and a steeply pitched roof with towers and dormers. Hyphens linked this building to two smaller dependencies with variable shapes and roofs. Eidlitz thus successfully combined the Richardsonian Romanesque style with the classic villa plan.

In the station proper, men's and women's waiting rooms lay on either side of the hallway leading from the centered main entrance to the ticket office and agent's half-round bay facing the tracks. The small conductor's room on the second floor was reached by a winding staircase. The waiting rooms were finished in quartered oak with paneled ceilings; they had tiled fireplaces and stained-glass windows. One of the wings housed the baggage room and telegraph office; the other, the express office and men's toilet.

The City of Kalamazoo bought the building from the Penn Central in the early 1970s and adapted it to serve as a bus station, as well as a train station. The former station agent's bay is now the newsstand and gift shop (Amtrak stop).

Cyrus L. W. Eidlitz designed this handsome 1887 Michigan Central Station at Kalamazoo, Michigan. Other notable designs by Eidlitz include the Michigan Central's Detroit Station (1883) and Chicago's Dearborn-Street Station (1885). —James D. Dilts

Graver's Station (1883), Frank Furness, Philadelphia, Pennsylvania

Frank Furness was a genius whose brilliant and unique designs, growing out of a boldly conceived fusion of disparate styles, both summarized and surpassed all of America's Victorian architecture. The suburban station at Graver's Lane on the Chestnut Hill line was one of about 125 projects he did for the Reading Railroad. It is a modest but representative example of his work that illustrates two company aims for small-station architecture: the avoidance of monotony in standard designs and attractive landscaping.

In 1879 Franklin B. Gowen, the powerful president of the Reading Railroad (and ruthless prosecutor of the Molly Maguires), hired Furness as the company's official architect. Furness's job, like that of other railroad architects, was to give the stations an identifiable look or image. Furness certainly did that; in fact, his stations looked like no others anywhere. They were, said his biographer, "lively and witty, lighthearted pavilions under complex roofs, hardly different from zoo buildings or gatehouses" (Lewis 2001, 146). They were also idiosyncratic commercial versions of Andrew Jackson Downing's picturesque Italianate villas and rural Gothic cottages whose projecting roofs, verandas, and prominent chimneys expressed domestic comfort. Furness extended his

station roof planes into ample trackside shelters for the passengers; his chimneys indicated the waiting room's warmth and protection from the elements.

Graver's Station is two stops north of Mount Airy, where Gowen had his estate. The projecting roof of Furness's Mount Airy station was trimmed back when the tracks were raised. The only change at Graver's Station appears to be a brief extension and porch added to the south side. The major exterior feature is a three-story tower topped by picturesque dormers that rises over the semicircular agent's bay. Next to this, a broad set of steps descends to the tracks beneath a long shed roof supported by intricate wooden trusswork. The station materials, interwoven in the Queen Anne style, are stone, brick, stucco, wood, and asphalt shingle.

On the street side opposite the tower is a porte cochère. The interior follows the traditional axial plan, this time with the agent's living room and kitchen on one side, and the waiting room and toilets for the passengers on the other. The second-floor bedrooms and tower spaces with their sloping roofs and fairy-tale windows must have delighted the agent's children. The railroads during the High Victorian period invested in landscaping and railroad gardens, before the space around stations was devoted to parking automobiles. The Boston & Albany Railroad hired Frederick Law Olmsted to design station grounds. The subject became part of the landscape architecture curriculum, and in 1905 a comprehensive report on railroad station gardens was issued. The trees, shrubbery, and well-kept lawn surrounding the Graver's Station are still familiar and welcoming signs to the suburban riders of the Reading line (restored, occupied, SEPTA train stop).

Canada, Mexico, and Central America

Major railroad development took place somewhat later in Canada and much later in Mexico and Central America than in the United States. Therefore, the stations and other railroad facilities to the north and south of the United States reflect for the most part later nineteenth-century architectural styles mixed with local design traditions.

The Canadian Pacific Railway, instrumental in the formation of Canada as a nation, also had a great influence on its architecture. In 1883 the CPR decided to build its Montreal station and office building on Dominion Square. To design it, CPR vice president William Van Horne, an amateur artist knowledgeable about architecture, selected New York architect Bruce Price. Price's 1889 Windsor Station, a handsome structure of gray Montreal limestone, was his first building in the Richardsonian Romanesque style. The company was evidently satisfied. "This is an imposing structure," said an 1897 CPR guidebook, "somewhat resembling the keep of a Norman castle. It is a rare combination of elegance, comfort, and architectural beauty . . . a fitting illustration of the enterprise of the road."

Price designed several other buildings for the CPR, including Alberta's 1888 Banff Springs Hotel, spectacularly sited in the Canadian Rockies, in a combination French chateau–Scots Baronial style (thus expressing the two major branches of Canada's cultural heritage); and the Chateauesque Place Viger Station-Hotel (1898) in Montreal. He also designed the first stage of the famous Chateau Frontenac in Quebec City.

Windsor Station was expanded several times. Montreal architect Edward Maxwell designed a wing, built in 1900, that included a new major public entrance; a glass-roofed concourse was added in 1913. Maxwell and his brother William designed CPR hotels in Winnipeg and Calgary and made several additions to the Chateau Frontenac. Windsor Station is a Montreal landmark and one of the great Victorian buildings of Canada (commuter and Metro service).

On the plains halfway across the country, in Winnipeg, Manitoba, the Canadian Northern and Grand Trunk Pacific (later combined in the Canadian National Railways) built a station in 1911 that expressed the city's importance as a rail junction, river port, and wheat center. Warren & Wetmore of Grand Central Terminal fame designed a Neoclassical Revival building whose huge central arch marked the major entrance, which led to a spectacular circular ticket lobby, 90 feet in diameter, covered by a dome and skylight 93 feet high (VIA rail terminal, office building).

The Canadian Pacific and Grand Trunk railways cooperated in building Toronto's monumental Union Station. The product of three architects, Ross & Macdonald, the CPR's Hugh G. Jones, and John M. Lyle, it was Canada's version of New York's 1910 Pennsylvania Station by McKim, Mead & White. (Union Station, Ottawa, 1912, by B. L. Gilbert and Ross & McFarlane, was also quite similar to Pennsylvania Station; it is now a government conference center.) Construction of Toronto's Union Station took 13 years, mainly because of the intervention of

Canadian Pacific vice president William Van Horne selected architect Bruce Price to design the city's handsome Richardsonian Romanesque station and office building at Montreal in 1889. There were later additions to the structure, and Price also designed such notable CPR buildings as the Banff Springs Hotel, the Place Viger Station-Hotel in Montreal, and the first stage of the Chateau Frontenac Hotel in Quebec. —Middleton Collection

Winnipeg, Manitoba, went all the way to New York—the prestigious firm of Warren and Wetmore—for the design of Union Station (1911), its important center of the prairies of western Canada. The Neoclassical Revival building, incorporating a huge central arch, a dome, and a skylight 93 feet high, showed off to advantage in August 1959. —William D. Middleton

World War I. The building was officially opened in 1927, but was not actually completed until 1930. The style was Neoclassical Revival, the scale Roman. The 22 exterior Bedford, Indiana, limestone columns marking the main entrance each stood 40 feet high and weighed 75 tons. The 260-foot-long concourse was paved with Tennessee marble; the vaulted, coffered ceiling, 88 feet high, with Guastavino tile. A tunnel under Front Street connected the station to the Royal York Hotel across the street.

The series of low, 1,200-foot-long trainsheds in the rear were similar to the Bush sheds at Hoboken, New Jersey. Designed by engineer A. R. Ketterson, they consisted of steel columns and trusses, timber roofs, and precast-concrete smoke ducts. The City of Toronto purchased Union Station in 2000 with plans for a $200 million restoration of the building and redevelopment of the space (VIA Rail, GO Transit service).

In Mexico City the Mexican National Railroad's station, general offices, and terminal hotel were illustrated in Bradford L. Gilbert's 1895 article "The Architecture of Railroad Stations" in *Engineering Magazine*. Designed for the Mexico climate, it had a porte cochère, corner clock tower, and flat roof. It appears to be a combination of the Neoclassical and Mission Revival styles. The same railroad's two-story Mission Revival station at Toluca, west of Mexico City, had a pavilion above the main roofline with stepped gables reminiscent of Dutch or Flemish Renaissance architecture. The native stone to build it, said

Gilbert, "was carried on the backs of peons and burros for many miles." Gilbert designed both stations.

—James D. Dilts

REFERENCES

Berg, Walter G. *Buildings and Structures of American Railroads.* New York: Wiley, 1893.

Condit, Carl W. *The Port of New York: A History of the Rail and Terminal System from the Beginnings to Pennsylvania Station.* Chicago: Univ. of Chicago Press, 1980.

Droege, John A. *Passenger Terminals and Trains.* New York: McGraw-Hill, 1916.

Gilbert, Bradford Lee. "The Architecture of Railroad Stations." *The Engineering Magazine,* 1895. www.railroadextra.com/arstat.html

Grow, Lawrence, and Clay Lancaster. *Waiting for the 5:05: Terminal, Station, and Depot in America.* New York: Universe, 1977.

Lewis, Michael J. *Frank Furness: Architecture and the Violent Mind.* New York: Norton, 2001.

Meeks, Carroll L. V. *The Railroad Station: An Architectural History.* New York: Dover, 1995.

Middleton, William D. *Grand Central, the World's Greatest Railway Terminal.* San Marino, Calif.: Golden West, 1978.

Potter, Janet Greenstein. *Great American Railroad Stations.* New York: Wiley, 1996.

Richards, Jeffrey, and John M. Mackenzie. *The Railway Station: A Social History.* Oxford: Oxford Univ. Press, 1986.

Stilgoe, John R. *Metropolitan Corridor: Railroads and the American Scene.* New Haven, Conn.: Yale Univ. Press, 1983.

Argot

Most industries generate an extensive, often-arcane vocabulary—a private argot that is a verbal badge of honor. The more people intensive the industry, the richer its trove of slang. For all its focus on machines and rights of way, railroading was once a hugely human undertaking. Not surprisingly, a vast lexicon of train talk flourished around the steam locomotives, cabooses, passenger trains, towers, and stations that once proliferated and defined this industry. For better or worse, twenty-first-century railroading has lost much of its humanity. With the disappearance of many of the artifacts and practices of the past have gone enormous chunks of specialized language, making a consideration of the argot of railroading largely an exercise in history and nostalgia.

The steam locomotive was the centerpiece of railroading past, so it is unsurprising that it trails behind it a long train of slang. "Iron horse"—a term that is a natural, since the earliest trains were pulled by horses—is probably the best-known slang term for locomotive, though perhaps used more by those outside the industry than by railroaders themselves. (An interesting corollary is "hostler," for a worker who moves and tends engines within a servicing facility; it originally meant a stableman who cared for flesh-and-blood horses when they came off the road.)

Other terms for steam locomotive include teapot, teakettle, or kettle (for small locomotives, after those more diminutive steam producers), goat (for a yard engine), pig, or, most commonly, hog. There are slang terms for diesels as well. Generically, they were sometimes called "growlers." Electro-Motive Division's E- and F-class cab units were "covered wagons," from their shape, and that builder's early high-hood road switchers—GP and SD 7s and 9s—were "Cadillacs." Proving that railroad argot lives on in the twenty-first century is "techno toaster" for late-model GE diesels, particularly the Genesis units.

From "hog" comes "hogger," the most common slang term for locomotive engineer. "Hoghead" and "hog jockey" are variants, as is the more obscure "pig mauler." "Ballast scorcher," "highball artist," and "Casey Jones" (from the most famous of all engineers, who was killed in a wreck) applied particularly to fast runners. "Eagle eye" was complimentary, "throttle-jerker" less so.

Together in the cab with the engineer was his fireman, sometimes called an "ashcat," "bakehead," "coal heaver," "diamond pusher" or "diamond cracker" (coal being black diamonds), "bell-ringer," "smoke," or "smoke agent"—all for obvious reasons. Another common term, "tallowpot," stemmed from the use in the nineteenth century of tallow to lubricate locomotive running gear. The fireman would throw coal in the firebox with what was typically called a "scoop," not a shovel; the slang term was "banjo," for the shape.

The engineer might be "highballing" with the "Johnson bar" (or reverse lever) in the "company notch," that is, set just off center for greatest fuel efficiency (and thus maximum profitability). Alternatively, he might be running in the "brotherhood notch," less effective at getting the locomotive over the road but requiring less work of the fireman. ("Highball," to move ahead, especially at high speed, derives from the now-vanished "ball signals," especially common in New England, that were raised and lowered to control train movements.)

If the engineer has to make a sudden stop, he will "big hole her," or throw the air brakes into emergency. This is also known as "dumping the air" or "wiping the clock," since the air-brake handle, reminiscent of the hand on a clock, would be quickly flung around the "dial" to make an emergency application. This might prevent the train's "going on the ground" (derailing) or even being involved in a "cornfield meet" (head-on collision). "Service application" is the term for routine air-brake use in controlling train speed.

Of course, not only engine crews had slang handles. A switchman was known as a "snake" because of the serpentine S that dominated the membership pins of the Switchmen's Union of North America. If he threw a switch, he would be "bending the iron"—the "iron," of course, being the rails. A related term is "high iron," for main line, where rails are heavier and thus taller than those on secondary lines. A railroad was sometimes called a "streak of rust."

A brakeman was a "shack" or "stinger"—this latter, it is said, from the large B (or bee) on the Brotherhood of Railroad Trainmen's membership pins. He was also sometimes a pinner or pinhead, terms harking back to the days before Janney knuckle couplers when dangerous link-and-pin couplers were used. Early practice also required brakemen to traverse the roof walks atop freight cars to set brakes while a train was in motion; this was known as "decorating." Otherwise the rear-end brakeman rode in the caboose, also known as a hack, buggy, way car, cabin car (on the Pennsylvania Railroad particularly), ambulance, shanty, palace, parlor, chariot, crib, bouncer, doghouse, or crummy—a list dominated by the wry irony common in occupational slang. (Though they may have jokingly derided them, operating crews—as well as train-watchers across the land—were sorry to lose their cabooses when they were replaced by "flashing rear-end devices," which communicate by telemetrics with the engineer. The slang acronym FRED for these boxes is far from affectionate.)

Also in the caboose would be the conductor—"brains" or "skipper," since he was the man in charge of the train, whether freight or passenger. A conductor working a passenger train—known as "cushions" or "varnish" (a term dating from the early period when passenger cars were highly varnished outside as well as in)—might be called a "dude," perhaps reflecting the combination of jovial contempt and envy that freight crews felt for their passenger brethren, whose jobs they viewed as far easier. "Door slammers" was a similarly inspired term for passenger trainmen.

Freight trains were called "rattlers." Fast freights were "redballs" or "hotshots," slow freights with low-priority commodities were "drags," and "way freights" serving local customers were "peddlers."

Railroad policemen are "bulls" or "cinder dicks." Car inspectors are "car knockers," "car tonks," "wheel knockers" (all terms deriving from the practice of tapping on wheels with a hammer to detect flaws), or "car toads" (presumably from the worker's hunched-over posture while inspecting wheels and working under cars). The yardmaster was the "ringmaster," presiding over his busy circus. Unloved by operating crews for putting them "in the hole," or siding, for meets with other trains, a dispatcher was a "delayer" or "detainer." Tower operators or station agents—"brass-pounders," "lightning-slingers," or "Morse-slingers" in the days when communications were by telegraphy rather than telephone—would "OS" trains to the dispatcher, which meant placing them "on (the train) sheet." They would "hoop up" to the train crews on the fly "flimsies," train orders from the "DS" (dispatcher) that they had written or typed on tissue paper, better for making multiple carbon copies.

Employees in all these roles might have to "buck the extra board" or "spare board," meaning work (on a seniority basis) as relief or on extra trains. Most would be part of the "home guard," but a few might be "boomers"—footloose, moving from one region of the country to another as seasonal traffic peaks dictated. Originally, perhaps, they followed boom camps; maybe they were "Boomer's men"—"Boomer" being L. T. Boomer, president in the late nineteenth century of the American Bridge Co., which employed many itinerant workers.

"Gandy dancers" worked on "section gangs" that laid or repaired track. The repetitive motions involved in tamping ballast, lifting rail, and driving spikes no doubt had choreographic aspects; "Gandy" was long thought to derive from the Gandy Manufacturing Co. of Chicago, a railway tool manufacturer, but this etymology has recently been called into question, as no record of such a company appears to exist.

Some railroad-related terms, like a roundhouse curve in baseball and a roundhouse punch in boxing, have entered the mainstream of American speech. A "tank town" is so insignificant that a train would stop there only to take water. Likewise, a "jerkwater" town is one a train sped through, scooping up water on the fly from track pans between the rails. Whether used broadly or only by railroaders, train talk in the age of steam was rich and diverse.

—Karl Zimmermann

REFERENCE

Hubbard, Freeman H. "Lingo of the Rails." *Railroad Magazine* 27, no. 5 (Apr. 1940): 32–55.

Art

Virtually from the industry's beginning, railroading and art have been linked. In 1855, 30-year-old George Inness, an American landscape artist who would become one of the major figures of the Hudson River school, accepted a commission from the Delaware, Lackawanna & Western Railroad, which had been created in 1853 by the consolidation of the Lackawanna & Western and the Delaware & Cobb's Gap, to paint *The Lackawanna Valley*, depicting a train steaming through a pastoral scene with the railroad's new Scranton, Pennsylvania, roundhouse (its first) in the background. Here, in what is generally considered to be the first important American railway painting, and probably the finest of the nineteenth century, the train is seen by most as a comfortable, even romantic, component of the landscape. Immediately afterward Inness painted two oils for the DL&W of the railroad near the Delaware Water Gap, which may have formed a set with the Scranton painting. Again, the train appears as a minor, appropriate part of a spacious landscape.

Thomas Cole, the dean of American landscape artists, had tucked the railway into his *River in the Catskills* (1843) more than a decade before the Inness masterpiece. Cole's train is tiny and partly obliterated by a bridge, but its presence is symbolic of change in the now-agrarian countryside he depicted. In the splendid *Starrucca Viaduct, Pennsylvania* (1865), Jasper Francis Cropsey, another member of the Hudson River school, showed this magnificent bridge in harmony with nature. Not only did Cropsey paint images of trains, he painted on them; in 1869 he decorated an engine for the Brooks Locomotive Works.

The developing West and its railroads fascinated both artists and the public. It was a frequent subject for the colored lithographs published by Currier & Ives. *Westward the Course of Empire Takes Its Way* (1868) by Fanny Frances Palmer is one example.

Inness's *Lackawanna Valley* commission was far from the only time that fine arts—as opposed to the more workaday illustrations on railroad posters, calendars, timetables, brochures, and advertisements—served railroading. The Baltimore & Ohio, the first railroad to promote itself through the visual arts by publishing travel guides and the like, in 1858 ran an excursion for artists and photographers (providing for the latter a coach set up as a darkroom, since the glass-plate negatives of the time had to be developed immediately after exposure). One of the artists aboard was Thomas Prichard Rossiter, whose evocative oil *Opening of the Wilderness* (ca. 1858) admirably met the railroad's request that participants focus not only on the splendor of the landscape but also on the heroic accomplishments of the railroad builders.

In 1871 Thomas Moran, another member of the Hudson River school, went to what the following year would become Yellowstone National Park with the Hayden ex-

The Baltimore & Ohio was the first railroad to promote the visual arts, operating the Baltimore & Ohio Artists' Excursion across the Alleghenies on June 1–5, 1858. This wood engraving, "Ascending the Alleghanies," by David Hunter Strother (pseud. Porte Crayon) depicted the excursion in the June 1859 issue of *Harper's New Monthly Magazine*.
—Middleton Collection

pedition. The result was his epic *Grand Canyon of the Yellowstone* (1872). Though the U.S. Geological Survey officially sponsored this expedition, Jay Cooke, promoter of the Northern Pacific (which later would serve Yellowstone), provided behind-the-scenes finances and muscle.

North of the border, shortly after the completion in 1885 of the Canadian Pacific Railway's transcontinental line, CPR president William C. Van Horne began an ambitious program of inviting distinguished Canadian artists to the Rockies, which the railroad promoted as the "Switzerland of North America," and supporting their residency there—all with the expectation that they would produce dramatic images (which they did) that would entice travelers to visit. Railways in their early years were inspiring artists in Great Britain and Europe as well. J. M. W. Turner in 1844 painted *Rain, Steam and Speed—*

The Great Western Railway, a highly atmospheric oil of a train racing across the Thames on the Maidenhead railway bridge. The French Impressionist Claude Monet in 1877 painted a series of steamy, smoky, evocative oils of *La Gare Saint-Lazare* (*Saint-Lazare Station*). These works focus on the trains themselves and the environment they create, with humans dwarfed or obscured, in contrast with Edouard Manet's *Le chemin de fer* (*The Railway*) of 1873, in which a steamy station provides a background for two figures, presumably a mother and daughter.

Though some of the novelty of railroading had worn off by 1900, trains continued to attract distinguished artists, such as Edward Hopper. Throughout his life Hopper featured trains both inside and out, tracks, and the appurtenances of railroading in some of his finest work—oils and, less notably, etchings. Early in his career Hopper worked for many years as an illustrator, and railroads were a frequent subject there too. Among his notable railroad oils are *Railroad Train* (1908), showing coaches with smoke from the unseen locomotive ahead trailing over them; *Railroad Sunset* (1928), with signal tower and order boards silhouetted in the foreground; and *Dawn in Pennsylvania* (1942), a scene of a deserted station platform. Loneliness, a recurrent theme for Hopper, informs these latter two oils. His first railroad-car interior—*Compartment C, Car 293*, depicting a reading woman bathed in the white light that was a Hopper staple—was painted in 1938. His last, *Chair Car* of 1965, was actually his penultimate work and is freighted with a foreboding of his death.

Contemporaries of Hopper's who were also drawn to trains were realists John Sloan and Reginald Marsh. As a member of the Ashcan school and committed to capturing the gritty reality of New York City in the early years of the twentieth century, Sloan focused on the city's elevated lines, as in *The City from Greenwich Village* (1922). Marsh's interest in railroading was more eclectic, and he tended to set his scenes in the sooty, industrial margins of cities. This is the case with *Tank Cars* (1932), an oil worked primarily in a brown palette. Some of Marsh's best railroad scenes

are etchings, such as *Loco—Going through Oneida* (1930) and *20th Century Limited* (1931).

German-born Otto Kuhler also produced both oils and etchings, and watercolors as well. His oils, such as *Desert Storm* and *Sunrise on Sherman Hill*, often depicted trains on the prairies or in the mountains of the West. He paid special attention to the narrow-gauge lines in Colorado, where he lived his final years. His etchings, which numbered some 250 plates made in the 1920s through 1934, including a series of five he made in 1926 in Baldwin Locomotive Works' Eddystone Shops in Philadelphia; *The Curve* (1928), on the New York Central; *The Rattler* (1929), a spare, snakelike rendition of a freight train (a "rattler" in railroad slang) crossing the Arizona desert; and *Ladies in Waiting* (1932). His final etching was *Hiawatha Nights* (1934), a wintry scene of Chicago, Milwaukee & St. Paul's No. 1, a streamlined 4-4-2 that Kuhler himself had styled for Alco. From that point on, the laborious, painstaking process of etching gave way to his work streamlining both diesel and steam locomotives, which included 4-6-2s for both the Baltimore & Ohio's *Royal Blue* and the Lehigh Valley's *Black Diamond*.

If Cropsey and Kuhler worked for railroads in unusual

Artists captured the wonders of the new technology. A splendid early example was this drawing of the Baltimore & Ohio's Thomas Viaduct, *Viaduct on Baltimore and Washington Railroad,* by artist W. H. Bartlett, engraved by H. Adlard (London, 1838). Visible on the far left is the commemorative granite obelisk erected on completion of the viaduct in 1835. —Middleton Collection

A popular subject for nineteenth-century artists was the Erie Railroad's magnificent Starrucca Viaduct in the Susquehanna Valley (1848), which drew such distinguished artists as Jasper Francis Cropsey and Edwin Whitefield. However, the artist for this atmospheric woodcut of the viaduct from the August 1874 *Harper's New Monthly Magazine* is unknown. —Middleton Collection

ways, many other artists served the industry in a more predictable fashion as illustrators, providing art for calendars, timetables, brochures, and other advertising. Posters, a dramatic medium, never achieved the popularity in the United States that they did abroad or in Canada. Their golden age came shortly after World War I and lasted through the midcentury decades. In Britain the "Big Four" lines—the London, Midland & Scottish, the London & North Eastern, the Great Western Railway, and the Southern Railway—and later British Railway produced huge numbers of holiday posters, mostly idealized scenes with the trains themselves notably absent. Quite different were such European posters as A. M. Cassandre's angular *Nord Express* (1927), which brilliantly expressed speed and stylishness, and Pierre Fix-Masseau's *Côte d'Azur Pullman* (1929).

However, North American railroads did produce some wonderful posters. Notable artists included Gustav Krollmann, who set the Northern Pacific's passenger trains amid the grandeur of the Montana Rockies and Rainier National Park. N. C. Wyeth executed some posters for the Pennsylvania Railroad. The Chicago-area South Shore Line produced a striking series of posters in the 1920s. Canadian Pacific sponsored a splendid array of posters through the decades, featuring all aspects of its tourism empire—hotels and ships as well as trains. Near the end of the run, in the 1940s and 1950s, Peter Ewart produced some memorably strong images.

Many railroads published wall calendars (and some still do, with photographs) to hang in their ticket offices and give to shippers. None were more notable and long running than the calendars issued by rivals New York Central and Pennsylvania Railroad. The Central got the jump in the calendar sweepstakes, beginning in 1922 with paintings by William Harden Foster in three sequential years. His *As the Centuries Pass in the Night* (1923), full of steam, smoke, speed, and the firebox glow, is among the most widely reproduced railroad images. In 1925, working in a similar style, Walter L. Greene took over the NYC calendars with *A National Institution*, once again depicting the *20th Century Limited*. Later, Leslie Ragan (who had been producing outstanding posters for Central since 1929) became its calendar artist of choice, specializing in views along the Hudson River, such as *Empire State Express* (1941). (Along with his work for NYC and other railroads, Ragan painted a fine series of images that the Budd Co. used to promote its stainless-steel passenger trains.)

Harold Brett painted the first two calendars for the Pennsylvania: *Speed and Security*, on the Rockville Bridge over the Susquehanna near Harrisburg, Pennsylvania, which was used in both 1925 and 1926, and *The Broad Way of Commerce* (1927). Grif Teller took over in 1928 with the impressionistic *When the Broad Way Meets the Dawn*, beginning an extraordinary sequence of paintings that lasted (with the exception of four years in the mid-1940s) until Pennsy ended its wall calendar program in

1958. Though Teller considered himself just an illustrator, his 27 PRR calendars, all oils on canvas, represent a remarkable body of work, with *On Time* (1931), a snowy scene of a K4 Pacific rounding a curve, considered by many the pinnacle. More than a decade after his calendar work for the Pennsylvania ended, Teller was discovered by train enthusiasts; he was kept busy for the balance of his life producing roughly 90 railroad paintings for them, most on PRR subjects.

Possibly the most prolific railroad artist was Howard Fogg, who, like Teller, painted both for the industry and the fan. Among his most successful projects were multiple oils for the 1969 Union Pacific monthly calendar marking the centennial of the driving of the golden spike. Earlier he had executed an extensive series of paintings for Alco. Other notable industry commissions—for the Pittsburgh & Lake Erie, Rock Island, Katy, and Boston & Maine— came through John Barriger, an executive with those railroads who became Fogg's close friend. Fogg made over a thousand paintings, watercolors as well as oils, avidly sought by train enthusiasts. They depicted railroads from coast to coast. Many appeared on calendars and Christmas cards.

If Fogg's work was sometimes criticized as too purely illustrative, watercolorist Ted Rose, generally considered the outstanding railroad artist of the late twentieth century, worked in a freer, more emotional style. His evocative images adorned countless magazine and book covers, including that of his own *In the Traces* (2000). When in 1999 the U.S. Postal Service planned a four-stamp issue to honor great railroad streamliners, Rose was chosen to make the paintings. His death in 2002 left the railroad world waiting for the next giant with a paintbrush to emerge.

—Karl Zimmermann

REFERENCES

Danly, Susan, and Leo Marx, eds. *The Railroad in American Art: Representations of Technological Change*. Cambridge, Mass.: MIT Press, 1988.

Goldsborough, Robert, ed. *Great Railroad Paintings*. New York: Peacock Press/Bantam, 1976.

Zega, Michael E., and John E. Gruber. *Travel by Train: The American Railroad Poster, 1870–1950*. Bloomington: Indiana Univ. Press, 2002.

Assn. of American Railroads (AAR)

The Association of American Railroads (AAR) is a trade association that represents the major railroads of the United States, Canada, and Mexico. Members include all Class 1 railroads, major freight lines, major passenger lines, and switching and terminal railroads. Associate members include non–Class 1 railroads and rail industry suppliers. The Washington-based AAR conducts a broad range of activities that include representing the rail industry to Congress, regulatory agencies, and others; developing policy positions and data on a variety of issues; and a broad range of safety and operations activities, with two wholly owned for-profit subsidiaries.

The AAR was formed in 1934, but the railroad industry included a wide variety of earlier organizations. Railroad freight and passenger traffic organizations, for example, were established on regional, state, or local levels to obtain joint arrangements concerning rates and traffic. More comparable with the AAR were those organized for the purpose of securing harmony of practice and policy among the carriers. Some of these were associations of technical officers, such as surgeons, master mechanics, engineers of maintenance-of-way, and accounting officers, while others were made up of administrative officers such as general baggage agents, general passenger agents, railroad superintendents, and other executives. Still others were structured to advocate and promote railroad interests. Among the most important of these earlier associations was the American Railway Assn. (ARA), formed in 1891 as a successor to the General Time Convention, originally formed to deal with interline timetable matters and the organization of Standard Time in 1883. The ARA had members in virtually every railroad and did much to standardize railway methods in all departments. The Assn. of Railway Executives (ARE, 1912) included in its membership the chief executive officers of all large U.S. railroads; its purpose was largely to represent the carriers on matters concerning the federal regulation of railroads. One of the earliest AAR predecessors was the Master Car Builders Assn., established in 1867, organized to develop the freight-car standards needed for compatible interline service. Later organizations were established to similarly develop other areas of technical interest or to represent and advocate railroad interests.

The unification of railroad associations in 1934 came as a result of passage of the federal Rail Transportation Act of 1933. Joseph B. Eastman, the federal coordinator of transportation, was appointed to deal with Depression-era problems affecting railroads and wanted a railroad organization that could speak for the entire industry. Established on October 12, 1934, the new AAR combined the activities of such previous organizations as the ARA, the ARE, the Bureau of Railway Economics, the Railway Treasury Officers' Assn., the Railway Accounting Officers' Assn., the Bureau for the Safe Transportation of Explosives and Other Dangerous Articles, and others.

The AAR's president and chief executive officer is its chief spokesperson at congressional hearings, before regulatory agencies, and at the Department of Transportation, the Surface Transportation Board, and other interested parties, promoting and implementing the policies established by a board of directors named by AAR's membership. Legal, communications, and policy and economic staffs support the development of legislative and other public policy objectives and provide a variety of other information, including forecasts of railroad costs and statistical reports on the operations of U.S. railroads.

The AAR's safety and operations functions cover a broad range of activities concerning the industry's interchange standards. Included are freight-car, car component, and locomotive standards; car-service/car-hire rules; mechanical, track, and infrastructure quality assurance programs; customer, safety and environmental, hazardous-materials, communications, and signals issues; and tank-car safety and design standards. AAR's interests in safety and operations are also supported by a Safety and Operations Management Committee and subordinate committees on risk management, technical services, interline service management, communications, signal and train control and railway technology, and a Network Efficiency Management Committee with subordinate committees on customer service, information technology, asset utilization, transborder issues, and damage prevention.

Transportation Test Center

Originally built and operated by the Federal Railroad Administration in 1971, the Transportation Test Center (TTC) at Pueblo, Colorado, has been operated and maintained by the AAR since 1982. This 52-square-mile center provides a comprehensive intermodal research and test center for a wide range of capabilities for research, development, and testing of transportation and nontransportation systems for both government and private sectors.

TTC's 48 miles of track test all types of rolling stock, track components, and signal and safety devices. Track structure and vehicle performance testing is done for track and service worthiness, life-cycle and component reliability, and ride comfort. Vehicle testing includes studies of safety, performance, propulsion and braking systems, and characterization testing. Test tracks include a 2.7-mile high-tonnage loop; a 14.7-mile high-speed stability and endurance track, including a capability for electric-powered motive power; a 9.1-mile transit track with DC power capability; a 3.5-mile wheel/rail mechanisms track; and a 6.2-mile vehicle-dynamics test track. A major long-range program at TTC has been the Heavy Axleload (HAL) test program carried out on the high-tonnage loop since 1986.

Other TTC capabilities include test laboratories for vibration tests and roll dynamics, a simuloader for full-scale vibration and fatigue testing, a minishaker unit, a traction-motor dynamometer, and a DOT-certified package laboratory. Still other capabilities include rail vehicle dynamic modeling, component testing and development, instrumentation and data-acquisition systems, environmental studies, off-site research and testing services, testing of pro-

cedures for freight damage prevention, hazardous-materials training, Emergency Response Training Center (ERTC), and the Bureau of Explosives (BOE) Field Force, which acts as an information and service group to enhance and maintain safe transportation in the railroad industry.

Railinc

AAR's other subsidiary, Railinc, in Cary, North Carolina, provides information technology services to railroads, equipment owners, shippers, and logistics services. Services include a wide variety of support, for example, car-repair data exchange, car tracking and tracing, damage prevention, railcar accounting, and interline load planning.

—William D. Middleton

REFERENCE

Capabilities: Transportation Technology Center, Inc. Pueblo, Colo.: TTC, ca. 2004.

Atchison, Topeka & Santa Fe Railway

Visionary promoter Cyrus K. Holliday founded the Atchison & Topeka Railroad in Kansas in 1859. It was only four years old when it added "Santa Fe" to its corporate title. It evolved into the 12,000-mile-long Atchison, Topeka & Santa Fe Railway (AT&SF), which by the 1950s was one of America's premier railroads. Holliday predicted that his Sunflower State shortline would ultimately link Kansas with the Pacific Ocean, the Gulf of Mexico, Santa Fe, and even Mexico City. The AT&SF never reached Mexico City, but by 1888 its lines extended west to the Pacific, south to the Gulf, and east to Chicago. Soon one of the largest, and later one of the most profitable, railroads in the nation, the Santa Fe, as it was known to the traveling public, built a network of branches in Kansas, Oklahoma, Texas, New Mexico, Arizona, and California that fed traffic to its main lines. As the Great Plains and the Southwest developed mature economies and became home to some of the country's largest cities, the AT&SF grew as well.

Initially the Atchison, as investors referred to the company, built westward from Topeka, Kansas, to Colorado, winning the first of several land grants. The carrier sought the booming cattle trade as herds moved northward from Texas to Wichita and Dodge City. The Santa Fe recruited farmers to settle in Kansas, particularly Russian farmers who brought winter wheat to the Great Plains. After reaching Pueblo, Colorado, in 1876, construction proceeded north to Denver and south over Raton Pass into New Mexico Territory. An ambitious management drove steel rails across New Mexico and Arizona by acquiring the land grant of the Atlantic & Pacific Railroad.

The Southern Pacific (SP) dominated California's transportation system and blocked the Santa Fe's first efforts to enter the Golden State. Through a connection at Deming, New Mexico, with the SP, a continuous route was formed. Temporarily blocked, the Santa Fe constructed a line south from Benson, Arizona, to Guaymas, Mexico, on the Gulf of California to gain access to the Pacific. The carrier achieved a truce with the SP, and the AT&SF opened its own line to Los Angeles in 1887, thus achieving part of Colonel Holliday's dream. Holliday was a colonel in the free militia (Kansas) and participated in the fighting of 1855–1856 (he later became a brigadier general).

The construction of the Santa Fe to California and its expansion to Texas and Chicago required a vast amount of capital. Investors in Boston, Great Britain, and western Europe provided the requisite sums. A small group of Bostonians controlled the carrier until the early 1890s. They made William Barstow Strong president of the AT&SF in 1877, and this energetic expansion advocate embarked on a major program of growth. Strong believed that the only way to block other railroads from invading the Santa Fe's territory was through constructing new track. He built a line from Kansas City to Chicago and acquired the Gulf, Colorado & Santa Fe, which extended north from Houston and Galveston to Dallas and Fort Worth and into Indian Territory. Strong sent a connecting line south from Kansas into Indian Territory to form a new through line to the Gulf of Mexico and the burgeoning Texas economy. Unfortunately, Strong's vigorous expansion plan included the purchase of the Colorado Midland Railroad and the St. Louis & San Francisco Railway (Frisco), creating an enormous debt. The Santa Fe fell on fiscal hard times, and overexpansion led to bankruptcy in 1893.

In the ensuing reorganization the Santa Fe lost control of the Colorado Midland and the Frisco, as well as some branch lines, but it emerged stronger with its financial obligations substantially reduced—and with a slightly altered name: Atchison, Topeka & Santa Fe Railway. The new board of directors named Edward P. Ripley president in 1895; he held that office until 1919. The conservative Ripley moved to expand the carrier only when a new territory offered traffic potential or where a new, shorter line would lead to operating efficiency. Gradual growth saw the carrier reach San Francisco and build the Coleman Cutoff in western Texas and the Belen Cutoff across central New Mexico to reduce mileage from the Lone Star State to California and to create a low-grade alternative to the line over Raton Pass. Branch lines blanketed parts of the new states of Oklahoma, New Mexico, and Arizona. As Southern California's economy grew and its population soared, Ripley created yet another system of branch lines. Guiding the AT&SF with a firm hand, Ripley led the

carrier to substantial profitability; the Atchison became a darling of Wall Street even as it retained its independence from cartelization.

From its earliest years, the Santa Fe used nonrail interests, often selling its land grants to farmers and investors while purchasing coal mines and other mineral interests and later exploring for petroleum on railway-owned land in California. As cities in the region grew enormously after 1900, the AT&SF purchased extensive urban property for yards, freight terminals, and passenger stations. In 1933 the railway bought the Kirby Lumber Co., which was a major customer on its eastern Texas line.

Ripley also labored to attract industry along the carrier's routes and to encourage scientific farming in the region. From 1900 to 1914 the AT&SF invested millions of dollars in new equipment and locomotives, signaling systems, stations, and other betterments.

Part of the positive reputation built by the Santa Fe came from its widespread passenger service, particularly its trains from Chicago to California. Constantly enhancing the quality of its passenger cars and acquiring larger and faster motive power for that service, the AT&SF became a premier passenger operator. The railway's partner, the Fred Harvey Co., provided excellent meal service, first in depots, then in dining cars, hotels, and resorts. The AT&SF and Fred Harvey contributed mightily to the rise of tourism in the region.

During World War I the Santa Fe, like other railroads, was operated by the U.S. Railroad Administration (USRA) and saw its profits decline even as heavy traffic on the system wore out equipment, rails, and motive power. With the return to private management in 1920, the AT&SF began to prosper once again. Led by President William Benson Storey, the carrier continued to construct branch lines and modernize operations. In 1928 the AT&SF purchased the Kansas City, Mexico & Orient Railroad, which extended from Wichita, Kansas, to the port of Topolobampo, Mexico, but with two long unbuilt gaps in Mexico (Santa Fe soon sold the lines in Mexico).

Faced with rising competition from truck lines and bus operators, Storey formed a bus company and a truck subsidiary to serve smaller communities along the line. The coming of the Dust Bowl and the Great Depression hit the Santa Fe and its territory hard, but the railway survived the vagaries of the national economy and inaugurated a fleet of stainless-steel passenger trains that included the famous *Super Chief* running between Chicago and Los Angeles in less than 40 hours. More important, the diesel locomotive came to the system at the end of the 1930s to revolutionize the Santa Fe's operations.

World War II brought enormous freight and passenger traffic to the carrier, for its territory included many defense plants and military installations. President Fred G. Gurley used profits generated by the war to reduce the company's indebtedness and, when possible, to purchase more diesels and modern steam locomotives. Gurley witnessed the rise of airlines after 1945 and sought to create

From its inception in 1937 until Santa Fe passenger service ended with the formation of Amtrak in 1971, the all-Pullman Chicago–Los Angeles *Super Chief* was the proud standard-bearer of the Santa Fe. The train had just added a dome lounge car in this 1950 view of the eastbound train alongside the red cliffs near the New Mexico–Arizona state line. —Santa Fe, *Trains* Magazine Collection

an air subsidiary, but federal regulators rejected the proposal. Under his leadership the Santa Fe bought more diesel locomotives, streamlined passenger cars, and larger, more efficient freight equipment. Dieselization and the abandonment of some branch lines led to fewer employees, but like other railroads, the Santa Fe had high labor costs and faced a hostile Interstate Commerce Commission (ICC) that rejected most requests for higher rates. When the AT&SF sought to enter St. Louis, the ICC denied that application.

In the 1960s and 1970s the Santa Fe turned to technology in an effort to gain greater efficiency of operations. New signal and communications systems and computers enhanced profits. The AT&SF created unit trains for coal, sulfur, wheat, and other products and promoted trailers and containers on flatcar service. Expedited freight trains moved between Chicago and California at speeds comparable with the *Super Chief*. John S. Reed, who became president in 1967, joined other railway leaders in seeking regulatory relief on issues such as rates, abandonments, and the discontinuance of passenger trains. Although the Santa Fe ended passenger service in many areas, the remaining trains continued to offer premier service.

Recognizing that investors looked at the Santa Fe largely as a railroad and ignored its nonrail assets, and seeking to end the periodic rise and fall of revenues and profits, in 1968 Reed and the board of directors formed a conglomerate, Santa Fe Industries. The new firm held not only the railway, but also subsidiaries in petroleum and mineral production, pipelines, real estate, trucking, lumber, and construction. By the mid-1970s the nonrail activities generated profits nearly equal to those of the railway. Reed recognized that although the Santa Fe con-

tinued to prosper, the nation's railroads faced enormous challenges.

In the last three decades of the twentieth century the management of Santa Fe Industries and the Santa Fe Railway confronted a new transportation environment. The federal government created Amtrak, relieving carriers of their massive financial losses from operating passenger trains. Cries for deregulation led to a series of federal laws opening the transportation marketplace and ultimately to the elimination of the ICC. Massive mergers resulted in the formation of four giant railroad systems, two in the East and two in the West.

Technological changes continued to reduce the number of employees and improve the efficiency of operations. Deregulation led to a vast increase in trailer-on-flatcar and container traffic to include faster freight schedules and contracts to haul trailers for express and highway freight companies. At the same time the Santa Fe sought to maximize its assets through diversification and emphasis on its nonrail holdings, most important, real estate.

Management watched as rail mergers accelerated in the 1960s and 1970s, and it studied acquisition of other carriers, such as the Missouri Pacific and later even Conrail. The ICC thwarted Santa Fe's effort to acquire the Western Pacific. A lengthy, contentious fight with the Union Pacific and the Southern Pacific over the Chicago, Rock Island & Pacific led to the latter's demise as the ICC deliberated for over a decade. The "asset-rich" AT&SF sought to purchase longtime rival Southern Pacific in 1980, but different management styles and personality clashes led the carriers to withdraw their proposal.

When the ever-aggressive Union Pacific moved to acquire the Missouri Pacific and the Western Pacific and later the Missouri-Kansas-Texas and the Chicago & North Western, the Santa Fe found itself surrounded. The Burlington Northern had invaded the Santa Fe's territory in 1980 when it acquired the Frisco. Thus in 1983 Santa Fe Industries leader John J. Schmidt proposed to merge with the Southern Pacific Co., pooling their nonrail assets while asking the ICC for approval to merge the two railways. Not waiting for a response, the carriers began to repaint locomotives and install new crossings, but the ICC cast a resounding "no" vote in 1986. The merged entity, Santa Fe Southern Pacific Corp., was ordered to sell one of the railroads.

Robert D. Krebs, the young, energetic president of SFSP, had come to the corporation from the SP, but he decided to sell that carrier. The Southern Pacific, with 10,000 miles of track and $2.0 billion in revenue, had earned only $40.3 million in 1984, while the 12,000-mile Santa Fe generated profits of $168.8 million from revenues of $1.7 billion. After the merger debacle Santa Fe chairman John J. Schmidt resigned, and John S. Reed returned as temporary chairman. After Krebs became chief executive officer in 1987, he accelerated the sale of nonrail assets or spun off subsidiaries to the stockholders as new entities.

The vast SFSP Corp. property holdings led to rival hostile takeover efforts by two real estate conglomerates, the Henley Group and Olympia & York, and Krebs and Reed responded aggressively. The SFSP Corp. began to purchase its own shares, issued large dividends, transferred the real estate holdings to an investment trust, and sold the Southern Pacific Railroad to the Denver & Rio Grande Western. SFSP continued to sell branch lines, including over 300 miles of track in Southern California, to state and regional transit authorities. Fighting the hostile takeover bids created a $3.7 billion debt, but by early 1990 that had been reduced to $140 million.

The merger movement accelerated across the country as Conrail was divided up by the Norfolk Southern and CSX, and the Union Pacific absorbed C&NW. Surrounded by the UP when the latter moved to acquire the Southern Pacific, the Santa Fe sought a merger partner and in 1993 announced that it would sell SFSP to Burlington Northern for $2.7 billion. But it was "Jonah swallowing the whale," according to Wall Street. Some BN executives accepted early retirement as Krebs and SFSP executives took control of the new company. The ICC approved the acquisition in July 1995, and the following year the Atchison, Topeka & Santa Fe Railway became part of the Burlington Northern & Santa Fe Railway Co. with Krebs as president and chief executive officer. Colonel Holliday's railroad disappeared as an operating entity, but its legacy and mystique continued.

The Atchison, Topeka & Santa Fe Railway remains one of the most storied of America's railroads, with thousands of fans and buffs celebrating its history. Many Americans remember the *Super Chief*, meals by Fred Harvey, warbonnet-painted diesel locomotives, modern steam power, and fast transcontinental freight trains roaring over Raton Pass, along the Belen Cutoff, and across the plains of Kansas, Oklahoma, and Texas. The Santa Fe is an integral part of the history of the Southwest and American railroading.

In 1994, its last year before the merger with Burlington Northern, the Santa Fe operated a system of 8,350 route-miles and 15,075 track-miles, with 1,766 locomotives, 30,321 freight cars, 1,678 company service cars, and 15,323 employees. In 1994 Santa Fe freight traffic totaled 100 billion ton-miles (the predominant commodity was intermodal traffic), operating revenues totaled $2,681 million, and the railroad achieved an 85.3 percent operating ratio.

—Keith L. Bryant, Jr.

REFERENCES

Bryant, Keith L., Jr. *History of the Atchison, Topeka and Santa Fe Railway*. New York: Macmillan, 1974.

Marshall, James. *Santa Fe: The Railroad That Built an Empire*. New York: Random House, 1945.

Atlanta & West Point Rail Road

Through much of their existence the Atlanta & West Point (A&WP) and the Western Railway of Alabama (WRA) were for most purposes a single entity known as the West Point Route. They formed a route from Atlanta, Georgia, through Montgomery to Selma, Alabama—A&WP for 87 miles from Atlanta to West Point, Georgia, right on the Alabama state line, and WRA for 88 miles from there to Montgomery plus the 50-mile Selma Division, from Montgomery to Selma. Neither railroad had any branch lines.

The West Point Route was affiliated with the Georgia Railroad, which ran from Augusta, Georgia, to Atlanta, 171 miles, with branches to Macon, Washington, Athens, and Monroe, Georgia. The Georgia Railroad was the railroad property of the Georgia Railroad & Banking Co., which owned substantial interests in the A&WP and WRA. The company's railroad property was leased to the Louisville & Nashville and the Atlantic Coast Line; those two railroads formed the Georgia Railroad to operate it.

Ownership of the three railroads was complicated; it simplifies matters to think of them as part of the Atlantic Coast Line family (and it resembled a family with lots of first, second, and third cousins and several marriages among them—plus a few nonmarriages). In addition, the three railroads were affiliated with the Central Railroad & Banking Co. of Georgia during the nineteenth century.

Georgia Railroad

The Georgia Railroad was chartered quite early, in 1833. Three years later "& Banking Company" was added to its name. The charter provided exemption from local and state taxation, except for a small tax on net earnings. Its main line from Augusta to Atlanta, Georgia, was constructed between 1835 and 1845 under the direction of engineer J. Edgar Thomson, later chief engineer of the Pennsylvania Railroad. The company acquired stock in the Atlanta & West Point and purchased the Western Railway of Alabama jointly with the Central Railroad & Banking Co. of Georgia (CofG). In 1980 the Georgia Railroad operated 3,329 route-miles, with 35 locomotives, 988 freight cars, 65 company service cars, and 325 employees. Operating revenues totaled $23.5 million, and the railroad achieved a 117.2 percent operating ratio.

Atlanta & West Point

In 1854 the Atlanta & La Grange Rail Road, which had been chartered in 1847, put in operation a line from East Point, Georgia, through La Grange to West Point. Trackage rights on 6 miles of Macon & Western rails brought its trains into Atlanta. The railroad was renamed Atlanta & West Point in 1857. In 1889 the A&WP built its own line from East Point into Atlanta, and 1909 the A&WP and the Central of Georgia, successor to the Macon & Western, agreed to operate the two lines between East Point and Atlanta as paired track—the trains of both roads in one direction on one line and in the other direction on the other.

Western Railway of Alabama

In 1854 the Montgomery Rail Road was organized to build a railroad east from Montgomery, Alabama, to West Point, Georgia. After constructing 32 miles of standard-gauge track (curious, given the universality of 5-foot-gauge track in the South), the company ran out of money. A new company, the Montgomery & West Point Rail Road, took its place in 1843 and completed the line in 1851. It opened a branch from Opelika, Alabama, to Columbus, Georgia, in 1854. The track gauge—3½ inches narrower than the gauge of neighboring railroads—kept the railroad's equipment from straying during the Civil War. The railroad operated through the war, but an attack a few days after Lee's surrender brought operation to a halt. When it was rebuilt in 1866, the track gauge was widened to 5 feet.

In 1870 the Western Rail Road of Alabama, which had a line from Montgomery to Selma, acquired the Montgomery & West Point. Financial health did not follow the growth in size, and in 1875 the Western was sold at foreclosure jointly to the Central Railroad & Banking Co. of Georgia (CofG) and the Georgia Railroad & Banking Co.

The Opelika-Columbus branch was leased to the Columbus & Western in 1881; the line became part of the Central of Georgia later. In 1883 the Western Rail Road of Alabama underwent reorganization and became the Western Railway of Alabama in an effort to untangle some of the leases.

In 1980 the Western Railway of Alabama operated 133 route-miles and 216 track-miles, with 15 locomotives, 428 freight cars, 21 company service cars, and 291 employees. Operating revenues totaled $14.1 million, and the railroad achieved a 91.2 percent operating ratio.

Affiliation with Louisville & Nashville and Atlantic Coast Line

William Wadley, president of the CofG, leased the Georgia Railroad and its interests in the A&WP and WRA in 1881. He assigned the lease jointly to the CofG and the Louisville & Nashville (L&N). The CofG entered receivership in 1892, and its half of the lease passed to the L&N. The L&N was the sole lessee of the West Point Route and the Georgia Railroad for only a short time before assigning the former CofG share of the lease to the Atlantic Coast Line (which in 1902 acquired control of the L&N). However, the CofG continued to own some WRA stock until 1944.

Although firmly in the L&N-ACL camp, the West Point Route for years was the route of the Southern Railway's top train, the New York–New Orleans *Crescent Limited*. Instead of using the Southern Railway's own line from Atlanta to New Orleans, the *Crescent* used the A&WP-WRA route between Atlanta and Montgomery and the Louisville & Nashville between Montgomery and New Orleans. Passenger service on the Georgia Railroad was not nearly as exalted, though until 1964 the night train carried a sleeping car between Atlanta and Wilmington, North Carolina, where Atlantic Coast Line's general offices were located, and in later years its mixed trains—trains carrying freight and passengers—ran until 1983, when the Seaboard System Railroad, successor to Atlantic Coast Line and Louisville & Nashville, bought the Georgia Railroad from the banking company.

In 1982, the last year for which figures are available before the purchase by Seaboard System, the Atlanta & West Point operated a system of 93 route-miles and 184 track-miles, with 11 locomotives, 274 freight cars, 19 company service cars, and 231 employees. Atlanta & West Point operating revenues totaled $8.47 million in 1981, and the railroad achieved a 108.6 percent operating ratio.

—George H. Drury

REFERENCES

Hillyer, William H. "Cotton and a Yankee Build the Georgia Railroad." *Railroad* 50, no. 4 (Jan. 1950): 56–67.
Sadler, Joseph P. "West Point Route." *Trains* 3, no. 8 (June 1942): 8–13.

Atlantic Coast Line Railroad

The Atlantic Coast Line Railroad (ACL) was one of the three strong railroads of the South, along with Louisville & Nashville, which ACL controlled, and the Southern Railway. It carried the majority of Northeast-to-Florida passengers, giving the Miami passengers to the Florida East Coast Railway at Jacksonville but taking west coast passengers to Tampa, St. Petersburg, Sarasota, Fort Myers, and Naples. It participated in most of the Midwest-to-Florida routes to a greater or lesser extent, and ACL's Perry Cutoff, opened in 1928 between Thomasville, Georgia, and Dunnellon, Florida, across the swamps of the northwest part of the Florida Peninsula, shortened the route between the Midwest and the resorts on the west coast of Florida.

By its own proclamation, the Pennsylvania Railroad was the Standard Railroad of the World. ACL advertised itself somewhat more modestly as the Standard Railroad of the South. As befitted a standard railroad, its route between Richmond and Jacksonville was double-tracked and fully signaled, but ACL had two nonstandard characteristics. It considered the Pacific a dual-service engine, and the profile of its main line was such that a 4-6-2 could move long freight trains at good speed. It chose purple for its diesel locomotives and passenger cars (the president of the ACL, Champion McDowell Davis, liked purple).

ACL's oldest ancestor was the Petersburg Railroad, organized in 1830 and opened in 1833 from Petersburg, Virginia, south to the north bank of the Roanoke River at Weldon, North Carolina, about 8 miles south of the state line. The Richmond & Petersburg Railroad made an end-on connection to the Petersburg road in 1838.

Two years later, in 1840, the Wilmington & Raleigh Railroad arrived in Weldon from Wilmington, 161 miles south. The railroad's destination had been the state capital, Raleigh, but there was no interest in a railroad at that point. In 1855 the railroad was renamed Wilmington & Weldon.

Two more railroads were added to the chain. The Wilmington & Manchester Railroad opened a line west from Wilmington into South Carolina in 1853 (no Manchester appears on maps anywhere near the railroad line), and the North Eastern Railroad began service between Florence and Charleston, South Carolina, in 1857.

After the Civil War the five railroads—the Richmond & Petersburg, the Petersburg, the Wilmington & Weldon, the Wilmington & Manchester, and the North Eastern—came under the control of William T. Walters of Baltimore, Maryland. The railroads were collectively known as the Atlantic Coast Line, which was an association of independent railroads. The association acquired several smaller railroads, and between 1885 and 1892 the Wilmington & Weldon built a cutoff from Wilson, North Carolina, through Fayetteville to Pee Dee, South Carolina. The new line was 62 miles shorter than the route through Wilmington, and it became the main route of the Atlantic Coast Line. The holding company that Walters formed in 1889 was renamed the Atlantic Coast Line Co. in 1893.

The ACL name filtered down to the railroads, too. The Richmond & Petersburg merged the Petersburg Railroad in 1898 and was renamed the Atlantic Coast Line Railroad of Virginia. Two years later the ACL of Virginia merged the Norfolk & Carolina (which ran from Norfolk, Virginia, to Tarboro, North Carolina), the Wilmington & Weldon, and the Atlantic Coast Line of South Carolina (which consisted of five railroads between Wilmington and Charleston). The new railroad, the Atlantic Coast Line Railroad, reached from Richmond and Norfolk, Virginia, to Charleston, South Carolina, and Augusta, Georgia.

Plant System

In 1902 Atlantic Coast Line purchased the Plant System, extending the ACL system south and west of Charleston, South Carolina. The Plant System had been assembled by Henry Plant. Before the Civil War, Plant had been superintendent of Adams Express. He organized Southern Express in 1861; it became part of American Railway Express during World War I. Plant began his railroad empire in 1879 by acquiring the Atlantic & Gulf Railroad. Its main line ran from Savannah, Georgia, to Bainbridge, Georgia; a branch diverged south to Live Oak, Florida. Plant reorganized the company as the Savannah, Florida & Western Railway and built three extensions: from Bainbridge to Chattahoochee, Florida, from Waycross to Jacksonville, Florida, and from Live Oak to Gainesville, Florida.

The Plant System absorbed the South Florida Railroad in 1893 (it ran from Sanford to Port Tampa) and the Jacksonville, Tampa & Key West in 1899 (Jacksonville to Sanford). In 1901 it merged the Charleston & Savannah, the Brunswick & Western (which ran from Brunswick, Georgia, through Waycross to Albany, Georgia), and the Alabama Midland (Bainbridge to Montgomery). Also in 1901 the Plant System built a cutoff from Jesup, Georgia, south to Folkston, Georgia, bypassing Waycross and reducing the Savannah-Jacksonville distance by 20 miles.

Charleston & Western Carolina

In 1897 ACL gained control of the Charleston & Western Carolina, which ran from Port Royal, South Carolina (about 65 miles southwest of Charleston), northwest through Augusta, Georgia, to Anderson, Greenville, and Spartanburg, South Carolina. The first part of the road, as far inland as Augusta, had been backed by the Georgia Railroad & Banking Co., but the Central Railroad & Banking Co. (Central of Georgia) got control of the company in 1881.

The C&WC was part of the Atlantic Coast Line family. After 1930 it shared officers with ACL, and, though operated independently, it looked like ACL, with secondhand ACL steam locomotives and, later, silver and purple diesels. ACL's efforts to merge the C&WC were blocked by neighboring railroads for a long time. ACL finally merged the C&WC in 1959. Also part of the ACL family was the Columbia, Newberry & Laurens Railroad, which connected the state capital, Columbia, with the C&WC at Laurens.

Other Railroads

ACL acquired control of the Louisville & Nashville Railroad in 1902. L&N in turn controlled the Nashville, Chattanooga & St. Louis Railway. ACL and L&N jointly leased the Carolina, Clinchfield & Ohio Railway (with which the C&WC connected at Spartanburg) and created the Clinchfield Railroad to operate the CC&O. ACL and L&N also leased the railroad properties of the Georgia Railroad & Banking Co. (which had ties with the Atlanta & West Point and the Western Railway of Alabama) and formed the Georgia Railroad to operate it.

ACL incorporated the Atlanta, Birmingham & Coast Railroad in 1926 to acquire and operate the financially troubled Atlanta, Birmingham & Atlantic Railway. The move gave ACL lines from Waycross to Atlanta and Birmingham. ACL merged the AB&C at the end of 1945.

Streamliners

In late 1939 ACL inaugurated the daily New York–Miami *Champion*, a stainless-steel coach streamliner, using two Atlantic Coast Line trainsets and one from the Florida East Coast Railway. Seaboard Air Line's *Silver Meteor* had already been in operation for ten months. After World War II the *Champion* became two trains, the *East Coast Champion*, to Miami, and the *West Coast Champion*, to St. Petersburg, Tampa, Sarasota, and Naples. The two railroads also competed with winter-season luxury trains: Seaboard's *Orange Blossom Special* and Coast Line's *Florida Special*. The *Florida Special* was the older of the two limiteds. It eventually received streamlined cars and ran until Amtrak took over the nation's passenger trains on May 1, 1971. The *Orange Blossom Special* made its last run in April 1953 and was never given modern streamlined cars.

ACL also participated in the operation of streamliners between Chicago and Florida. Until the mid-1950s three streamliners operated on three routes out of Chicago every three days: the *Dixie Flagler* via the Chicago & Eastern Illinois, the *South Wind* running between Chicago and Louisville on the Pennsylvania Railroad, and Illinois Central's *City of Miami*. No matter which route they used from Chicago, all three reached Florida on Atlantic Coast Line rails.

Merger with Seaboard Air Line

The Seaboard Air Line went pretty much everywhere the Atlantic Coast Line did and was a vigorous competitor. In the late 1950s the two railroads began to study merger, particularly the economies that would result from the elimination of duplicate facilities. They petitioned to merge in 1960. The Interstate Commerce Commission had no history of approving mergers of parallel

railroads and surprised the industry by approving the merger, which took place on July 1, 1967.

In 1966, the last year before the merger with Air Line, Atlantic Coast Line operated a system of 5,743 route-miles and 8,187 track-miles, with 629 locomotives, 361 passenger cars, 31,284 freight cars, 1,116 company service cars, and 11,986 employees. Freight traffic totaled 15,506,252,855 ton-miles in 1967, and phosphate rock (12.3 percent), other stone and rock (11.3 percent), pulpwood (11.3 percent), and coal (7.6 percent) were the principal commodities carried. Passenger traffic totaled 487,465,379 passenger-miles. Atlantic Coast Line operating revenues totaled $215.7 million in 1967, and the railroad achieved a 76.7 percent operating ratio.

—George H. Drury

REFERENCES

Prince, Richard E. *Atlantic Coast Line Railroad: Steam Locomotives, Ships, and History*. N.P.: Richard E. Prince, 1966. Repr., Bloomington: Indiana Univ. Press, 2000.

Turner, Gregg M., and Seth H. Bramson. *The Plant System of Railroads, Steamships and Hotels*. Laurys Station, Pa.: Garrigues House, 2004.

Atterbury, William Wallace (1866–1935)

The 7th son and 12th child of John and Catherine Atterbury, William Atterbury was born in 1866 in New Albany, Indiana, where his father had given up the law to become a Presbyterian home missionary. The family later moved to Detroit, where young Wallace completed a preparatory education in public school. He then attended the Sheffield Scientific School at Yale, receiving a Ph.B. degree in engineering in 1886.

Atterbury soon entered the Pennsylvania Railroad's Altoona, Pennsylvania, shops, completing the railroad's four-year apprentice course in only three years to begin the climb through the PRR's management ranks. In 1889 he was made an assistant road foreman of engines, and by 1892 he was assistant engineer of motive power for the railroad's Northwest System. Just a year later he became the master mechanic at Fort Wayne, Indiana, and by 1896, still only 30 years old, he was superintendent of motive power for PRR's lines east of Pittsburgh. In 1901 he became the Pennsylvania's general superintendent of motive power.

In a 1902 trip over the railroad with President Alexander Cassatt, Atterbury so impressed Cassatt with his knowledge and ideas that he was soon promoted over more senior officers to become the Pennsylvania's general manager of Lines East. He entered the railroad's vice presidential ranks in 1909, becoming in 1912 vice president in charge of operations.

In 1916 Atterbury took on additional responsibilities as president of the American Railway Assn., an Assn. of American Railroads predecessor. He attracted considerable notice for handling railroad movements to the Mexican border for Gen. John J. Pershing's attempt to catch Pancho Villa in 1916, and for preparing the railroads for World War I.

As the United States entered the war, one of the many pressing problems faced by Pershing was the movement of the American Expeditionary Force troops and supplies across France. Pershing asked for the "ablest man in the country" to run the AEF railroads, and Atterbury was given the task. As AEF general director he took over the movement of four French railroads, moving men and supplies from the French ports into the war zone. His success in the war was confirmed when he received the U.S. Distinguished Service Medal, the British Order of the Bath, France's Legion of Honor, and other decorations. Commissioned as a brigadier general, Atterbury was thereafter always called "General" by his colleagues.

Atterbury returned to his post at the Pennsylvania in 1920, helping set up a more efficient regional system and working with the labor problems that emerged after the war. In 1924 Atterbury was named vice president, senior to all other vice presidents, and a year later was named president, succeeding the retiring Samuel Rea.

Atterbury's decade-long presidency proved to be one of the most challenging the railroads would ever see. Improvements in operating efficiencies that Atterbury had begun well before his presidency had brought the PRR's operating ratio down from almost 90 percent in 1921 to the low 70s by the end of the decade. Traffic, which had climbed to new levels through the 1920s, dropped abruptly in the wake of the Great Depression of 1929, and the rapid expansion of motor truck and highway services was a growing problem for the railroad.

Soon after Atterbury took office, the Pennsylvania began the greatest improvement program since the Cassatt era. In 1926 work began on a major reconfiguration of Philadelphia's passenger terminals. A new suburban passenger station was completed in 1930, and the new Thirtieth Street station was opened in 1933. Extensive track and tunnel improvements were made at Baltimore, and a large new passenger terminal at Newark, New Jersey, was opened in 1935.

But by far the largest of the Pennsylvania's improvements carried out under Atterbury's presidency was the greatest railroad electrification ever made in North America. The Pennsylvania already operated extensive DC electrifications on suburban lines in New Jersey and on Long Island, as well as the New York terminal electrification, while a growing network of AC electrics had been developed at Philadelphia. In 1928 and 1929 President Atterbury announced plans that PRR would carry out a $175 million program that would extend AC electrification all the way from New York to Washington, D.C., and on the low-grade line west from Philadelphia to Columbia, Pennsylvania.

William W. Atterbury. —Historical Society of Pennsylvania

With the drastic decline in traffic and railroad earnings that soon followed, one might have expected delays in this ambitious program, or even cancellation of the Pennsylvania's electrification. Instead, Atterbury in 1931 announced plans to accelerate the work, completing in two and a half years what had originally been planned for four years. The reduced traffic level helped accelerate the work, and costs were low and skilled labor plentiful. Through 1931 the Pennsylvania managed to finance the work itself, and it then obtained loans through the federal Reconstruction Finance Corp. and the Public Works Administration to complete it. The new electrics were running between New York and Wilmington in 1933, and electric operation over the entire distance from New York to Washington began early in 1935. In poor health, Atterbury declined reelection to the PRR presidency in April 1935 and died only five months later at his Bryn Mawr, Pennsylvania, home.

—William D. Middleton

REFERENCES

Burgess, George H., and Miles C. Kennedy. *Centennial History of the Pennsylvania Railroad Company, 1846–1946*. Philadelphia: Pennsylvania Railroad, 1949.
National Cyclopaedia of American Biography.

B

Baldwin, Matthias W. (1795–1866)

Matthias Baldwin founded the company that evolved into the Baldwin Locomotive Works, the largest and most successful steam locomotive manufacturer in the world. Born on December 10, 1795, Matthias had a challenging childhood; his family was poor. Although his father, William Baldwin, had owned a prosperous carriage-manufacturing business, he died when Matthias was only four. William left a large estate, but it was poorly managed and soon depleted. Further, Matthias did not enjoy school and looked for other things to pique his interests. He found pleasure in working with mechanical objects and, as a teenager, joined the Woolworth Bros. in Pennsylvania as a jeweler's apprentice. Finding that he was well suited for this work, he joined Fletcher & Gardiner, a Philadelphia jewelry firm, and enjoyed three successful years there. He then went into business for himself and continued making jewelry for several more years.

Baldwin next went into business with David Mason manufacturing machinery for wood engraving and bookbinding. As Baldwin-Mason grew, it required larger facilities and more powerful machinery. Turning to steam power, they attempted unsuccessfully to use several engines manufactured by various companies. Baldwin then decided to try his hand at building a steam engine and was successful. His steam engine attracted tremendous interest from other machinists and resulted in Baldwin-Mason's decision to refocus on the manufacture of steam engines. After continued success in this market, Matthias Baldwin purchased Mason's interest in the firm.

Becoming the president of his own steam-engine-manufacturing company in 1831, Baldwin was well positioned to take advantage of the development of the railroad industry. He began building steam locomotives, which required a move to even larger facilities. The quality of Baldwin locomotives and the efficiency they brought to the industry established Baldwin as the nation's and later the world's leading manufacturer of railroad steam locomotives. Matthias Baldwin became one of the weathiest men in Philadelphia. He remained active at Baldwin until his death in 1866.

—David C. Lester

Matthias W. Baldwin. —*Trains* Magazine Collection

REFERENCES

Brown, John K. *The Baldwin Locomotive Works, 1831–1915.* Baltimore: Johns Hopkins Univ. Press, 1995.

Dolzall, Gary W., and Stephen F. Dolzall. *Diesels from Eddystone: The Story of Baldwin Diesel Locomotives.* Milwaukee, Wis.: Kalmbach, 1984.

Drury, George H. *Guide to North American Steam Locomotives.* Waukesha, Wis.: Kalmbach, 1993.

Frey, Robert L., ed. *Encyclopedia of American Business History and Biography: Railroads in the 19th Century*. New York: Facts on File, 1988.

Baldwin Locomotive Works

Founded in 1831 at the dawn of the railway age, the Baldwin Locomotive Works grew to become the largest producer of railroad locomotives in North America and a significant global exporter. During its 125 years of locomotive production the firm built over 70,000 locomotives—mostly steam but also compressed-air, gasoline, electric, and diesel models. The firm succeeded so well for so long because of its astute management, continuous but conservative innovation, close relations with its railroad customers, and impressive flexibility in production. With these attributes, Baldwin became the dominant firm in the American locomotive industry by 1870. In 1901 the majority of Baldwin's small competitors merged to form the American Locomotive Co. (Alco), a consolidation that achieved rough parity with Baldwin. Baldwin entered its eclipse in the 1930s with the rise of diesel locomotives, a technological revolution that left all the steam builders behind. Its transition to diesels was late and weak, and the firm finally exited the industry in 1956.

The business originated from a general jobbing machine shop founded by Matthias W. Baldwin near Independence Hall in Philadelphia. Baldwin began his career as a jeweler; by 1825 he formed a partnership to make bookbinding tools and cylinders for printing. The business grew, eventually requiring Baldwin to acquire a steam engine to provide power. The model he purchased proved to be inadequate, so he designed his own engine. It proved so efficient that other shops asked Baldwin to build stationary engines for them. Around 1830 railroading was in its infancy, with few steam railroads in England and none in America. But the concept excited much interest in the United States, a large nation in great need of better transport links to the interior of the continent. Sensing this interest, Franklin Peale, proprietor of the Philadelphia Museum, asked Baldwin to design a miniature locomotive as an operating exhibit for the museum. On April 25, 1831, this first Baldwin locomotive made its debut, running on a circular track made of wood covered with iron straps and pulling two small cars that could carry four passengers.

The success of the miniature museum locomotive led to an order for a full-sized locomotive from the Philadelphia, Germantown & Norristown Railroad. Completed in 1832 and christened *Old Ironsides*, it had a horizontal boiler and 54-inch driving wheels and could make 30 mph. This early success placed Baldwin at the front rank of the nascent American locomotive industry. By 1836 Baldwin opened a new, purpose-built locomotive factory on Philadelphia's Broad Street, employing 240 men and capable of making 40 locomotives per year. Over the next 70 years the firm expanded almost continuously on that site. By 1906 it employed over 17,000 men who built 2,666 locomotives that year. The overall history of the firm (1831–1956) divides into four periods.

In its entrepreneurial era (1831–1854) the firm remained very much an extension of its founder. Matthias Baldwin was an innovative mechanic and continuously incorporated his own ideas or novel patents by outsiders. Baldwin's patented flexible-beam freight engines of the

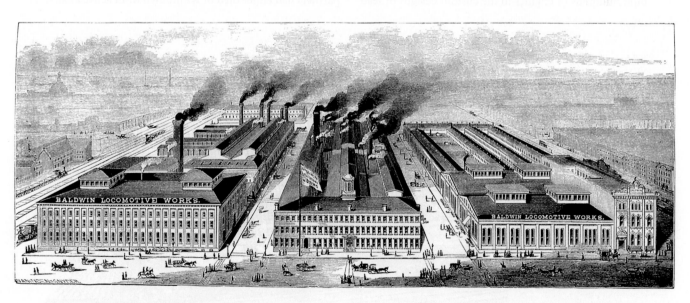

Dating to about 1875, the busy Baldwin Works occupied this 196-acre site in the heart of downtown Philadelphia. Work began on a new Eddystone site on the Delaware River 12 miles south of Philadelphia in 1906. —Jim Harter, *American Railroads of the Nineteenth Century* (Lubbock: Texas Tech University Press, 1998)

early 1840s enjoyed good sales. His experiments in coal burners, feedwater heaters, and variable valve motions were less successful. Such experimentation was common in this early period of locomotive development and appears to have had little effect on sales, up or down. More important to the firm's success was growing demand for motive power nationally, as railways spread across the nation from the Eastern Seaboard to the Mississippi. Notwithstanding a number of new competitors, Baldwin maintained a record of modest growth in this era. But productive efficiency and profits were limited by the continuous design experiments and by the lack of a thoroughgoing managerial staff to oversee operations.

In its collaborative era (1854–1909) the Baldwin company grew to dominate the locomotive industry, pulling decisively ahead of all rivals. Two policies were key to that advance. Management of the firm passed to a series of partners, initially selected by Matthias Baldwin, who broadened and deepened the expertise at the top. Partners William Henszey and William Austin oversaw drafting and designing; Edward Longstreth, Charles Parry, and Samuel Vauclain took charge of production; Edward H. Williams had primary responsibility for sales; and George Burnham and John Converse managed finances. A second collaborative policy entailed close cooperation between the firm and its railway customers. Baldwin developed the capacity to custom-build any kind of engine its customers desired. For example, in 1890 the firm turned out 946 engines in 316 different designs. In this era Baldwin developed many standard designs for specific market segments, including steam streetcars (dummies), light Forney and other mass-transit engines, industrial switchers, standard American types (4-4-0) for passenger service, and Consolidations (2-8-0) to haul freight. Layered onto that design and production virtuosity, the firm also built hundreds of engines to the custom designs of leading main-line carriers, both American and export. Collaborative relationships with customers brought the work in; the partners ensured quality design and efficient production; and collaborative relations with its skilled workforce allowed the firm to build these made-to-order products rapidly—normally under an eight-week schedule.

In this era the firm originated some important design innovations, notably the Vauclain compound (1889) and the two-wheel trailing truck (1893). Some other innovations were less successful: smokebox superheaters (1905), articulated boilers for Mallet compounds (1910), and triple-articulated compound engines (1913). For the most part, Baldwin was not particularly innovative in this era. Yet that proved no real handicap. Railroading had become a steady, conservative business by 1900, concentrating on incremental innovations that boosted freight- and passenger-miles. Baldwin excelled at meeting that challenge.

After 1909 Baldwin moved into a third phase, the Vauclain era, which extended until 1929. The charismatic Samuel Vauclain had joined the company in 1883, becoming its general superintendent in 1886, partner (1896), vice president (1911), president (1919), and chairman (1929). The first departure of the Vauclain era was Baldwin's new plant at Eddystone, just south and west of the Philadelphia city limits. Begun in 1906 at Vauclain's insistence and over the objections of some partners, the new factory finally provided relief from the crowded and improvised conditions at the center-city plant. Over the next 22 years Vauclain created a thoroughly modern facility at Eddystone. By the time of its dedication in 1928, the Eddystone complex included 90 buildings and 26 miles of track spread over nearly 600 acres, with rail connections to three railroads and a deepwater dock for worldwide shipments. With Vauclain's ascendancy as president (1919), his old partners had either died or withdrawn from active affairs.

Baldwin designer Samuel M. Vauclain developed a new compound locomotive design in 1889 that was sold by the hundreds over the next several decades. Norfolk & Western's Ten Wheeler No. 72, built in 1900, incorporated dual crosshead cylinders with a high-pressure cylinder above a low-pressure cylinder on each side.
—*Trains* Magazine Collection

Collaborative management was over; Vauclain steered the firm according to his vision. Eddystone was his monument.

During World War I the Baldwin Works, its Eddystone plant, and Samuel Vauclain made arguably their greatest contributions to history. Baldwin built over 5,500 locomotives, while associated munitions firms at Eddystone produced 6.5 million artillery shells and nearly 2 million rifles. These contributions to Allied victory required the efforts of thousands, yet Vauclain deserves most of the credit. During the war all American main-line railways came under the control of the U.S. Railroad Administration. Under mandate from the USRA, Baldwin designers joined representatives from other locomotive builders and the railways to produce a series of 12 standard designs of freight and passenger engines for use nationally. Baldwin made the first USRA standard, a Mikado (2-8-2) exhibited today at the B&O Railroad Museum in Baltimore.

A commitment to steam power was another hallmark of the Vauclain era at Baldwin. Notable locomotive designs of the period included the famed Cab Forward 4-8-8-2 for the Southern Pacific, which burned oil and had the cab at the front end to alleviate smoke problems for crews in the numerous tunnels on the SP. In 1930 Baldwin produced eleven articulated 2-8-8-4 locomotives for the Northern Pacific, dubbed Yellowstones for the river that paralleled the NP main line. At the time they were the largest steam locomotives ever constructed, pulling trains of 4,000 tons over NP's sawtooth-profile main line between Glendive, Montana, and Mandan, North Dakota. And in 1941 Baldwin claimed the title of world's most powerful steam locomotive ever built with its eight Yellowstones for Minnesota's Duluth, Missabe & Iron Range Railway. The DM&IR engines attained a starting tractive effort of 140,000 pounds and routinely handled 180-car trains of iron ore, weighing more than 19,000 gross tons.

Baldwin entered its fourth era around 1929, a period of decline. The chief nadir came in 1956, when it made its last engine, but the firm continued making other lines of capital goods until its liquidation in 1972. What went wrong? Nearly everything. During the 1920s sales entered a long slide, reflecting the overall decline of American railroading, and Eddystone never ran close to full capacity. So Baldwin made a number of acquisitions to diversify its business and fill excess capacity. Under the Baldwin Group the company included three divisions: the Locomotive & Ordnance Division, the Southwark Division, which built hydraulic machinery, turbines, valves, and equipment, and the Cramp Brass and Iron Foundries Division, which manufactured bronze valves, castings and forgings, and ship propellers. But the firm made these acquisitions in 1929; soon thereafter the Depression hammered all of Baldwin's product lines.

Baldwin also fumbled in making the transition to diesel locomotives. It constructed its first diesel locomotive in 1925, the largest such engine in the United States. Numbered 58501, the locomotive was tested on railroads near Philadelphia, but did not attain the advertised 1,000 hp and was a failure. During the 1930s the Electro-Motive Division of General Motors (EMD) committed vast resources to refine the diesel locomotive, which was gradually gaining acceptance on U.S. railroads in streamlined passenger service and in urban switching roles. Baldwin and its chief competitor, Alco, scarcely perceived the challenge, keeping faith with the steam locomotive. Baldwin's 1935 bankruptcy, the result of the Depression-era sales drought, also signaled its lack of R&D funds. Finally, in 1939 the firm committed itself to building a standard main-line diesel switcher. During World War II, however, the War Production Board placed severe restrictions on locomotive production. In the field of diesel locomotive production, Baldwin and Alco were only allowed to produce locomotives of 660 to 1,000 hp, essentially limiting them to switchers, while EMD could build only its 5,400-hp FT road diesels. This gave EMD a huge advantage over its competitors, since during the war many railroads purchased the EMD road diesels and found them to their liking, while Baldwin and Alco built more steam locomotives and diesel switchers. During the war Baldwin constructed thousands of tanks, ship propellers, and steam locomotives, but only 397 diesel switchers.

In the postwar era Baldwin did indeed produce more diesels, introducing a line of road locomotives in 1945. Its road units were aesthetically pleasing, but never caught on with the railroads. Included among the handsome designs were streamlined diesels such as the 3,000-hp Centipede, named for the numerous wheels that supported the massive carbody. A 1,600-hp road unit styled by Raymond Loewy was dubbed the Sharknose. But neither design was a big seller: only 53 Centipedes and 152 of the Sharknose units were built.

Baldwin had long been associated with Westinghouse Electric in building electric locomotives; Baldwin provided the mechanical components, and Westinghouse supplied the electrical equipment. The two firms built electric locomotives for several main-line electrifications, including some of the Pennsylvania Railroad's celebrated streamlined GG1 locomotives, as well as a series of standardized light electric locomotives that were widely adopted by interurban electric railways.

This long association carried over into the building of diesel locomotives. But by the end of World War II Baldwin was growing dissatisfied with Westinghouse electric transmissions for its diesels and began looking for an alternative. Westinghouse did not want to lose such a major customer, and in 1948 it purchased a minority interest in Baldwin, effectively gaining working control of the company. Westinghouse installed its own management team and eliminated any competition for electrical gear for Baldwin diesels. In 1954 Westinghouse control ended when Baldwin bought back Westinghouse-owned stock. Baldwin then used General Electric electrical apparatus until diesel locomotive production ended.

Unmistakable in appearance were Baldwin's massive articulated Centipede diesels, which were carried on a 2-D+D-2 underframe. Two 1,500-hp diesels and eight traction motors powered the locomotive. Seaboard Air Line was one of the few buyers. Only 54 were sold during 1945–1948.
—*Trains* Magazine Collection

In the late 1940s and early 1950s dieselization of U.S. railroads accelerated, yet Baldwin still cast about for a winning strategy. It clung to steam, for example, building the last conventional steam locomotives made for a U.S. Class 1 railroad: ten 2-6-6-2s for the Chesapeake & Ohio, completed in 1948. The last order for steam locomotives produced in the United States by any of the major locomotive manufacturers came in 1955, when Baldwin completed 50 2-8-2s for the Indian State Railways. In 1950 Baldwin acquired a steam-era competitor, purchasing the Lima Hamilton Corp. to form the Baldwin-Lima-Hamilton (B-L-H) Corp. Lima had been an innovator in building high-horsepower steam locomotives, but had very limited experience building diesel switchers. With this acquisition, Lima was eliminated as a competitor, but Baldwin really wanted Lima for its nonlocomotive products, such as cranes and power shovels. In 1951 B-L-H acquired the Austin-Western Co. of Aurora, Illinois, a builder of power graders, cranes and shovels, and crushing plants. Baldwin was positioning itself to be a leader in providing road-building products, a position that would hold the company in good stead as the 1950s road-building boom progressed.

As steam power production wound down, the standard line of switch engines and road switchers kept Baldwin in the locomotive business. Its three most popular switcher models were the 1,000-hp VO 1000 (1939–1946, 476 locomotives constructed), the 1,000-hp DS-4-4-10 (1947–1951, 446 built), and the 1,200-hp S-12 (1950–1956, 459 examples). Baldwin switchers were definitely rugged and could pull with the best of its competitors' diesel locomotives. But the engines were based on a design from the 1930s, and their Westinghouse electrical gear was expensive to maintain. Baldwin had increasing difficulty competing against EMD and Alco, which were producing more modern engine designs. In the early 1950s annual orders for diesel locomotives began to shrink as North American railroads approached full dieselization. In 1952 U.S. railroads ordered 1,829 diesels, but Baldwin landed orders for only 106 of them. Its other industrial products were on the upswing, but locomotive production was headed down, accounting for only 30 percent of the sales dollars that year. As more and more EMD and Alco diesels rolled across U.S. rail lines, the railroads' familiarity with those locomotives meant that they would prefer those vendors in future orders unless Baldwin offered a clearly superior product. The venerable firm never could produce that superior diesel locomotive, and Baldwin finally halted locomotive production in 1956.

After the completion of locomotive production, most of the Eddystone land was sold. Boeing purchased portions of the plant to construct military helicopters and light-rail vehicles during the 1960s and 1970s. Baldwin-Lima-Hamilton was purchased in 1965 by Armour & Co., which in turn was acquired by Greyhound Corp. in 1970. Greyhound sold off most of Armour's assets, and the various B-L-H product lines were sold off separately. The renewal parts department became the Baldwin-Hamilton Co. in 1971, the last descendant of the original Baldwin Locomotive Works. The statue of founder Matthias W. Baldwin, which had graced the entrance of the Eddystone office building since 1928, now stands at the Railroad Museum of Pennsylvania in Strasburg. Also at the museum are Baldwin's builder's photos, the priceless Broadbent collection.

—**Steve Glischinski and John K. "Jack" Brown**

REFERENCES

Brown, John K. *The Baldwin Locomotive Works, 1831–1915*. Baltimore: Johns Hopkins Univ. Press, 1995.

Dolzall, Gary W., and Stephen F. Dolzall. *Diesels from Eddystone: The Story of Baldwin Diesel Locomotives*. Milwaukee, Wis.: Kalmbach, 1984.

Kirkland, John F. *The Diesel Builders*. Vol. 3, *Baldwin Locomotive Works*. Glendale, Calif.: Interurban, 1994.

Morgan, David P. *Steam's Finest Hour*. Milwaukee, Wis.: Kalmbach, 1959.

Westing, Fred. *The Locomotives That Baldwin Built*. Seattle, Wash.: Superior, 1966.

See also LOCOMOTIVE BUILDERS.

Baltimore & Ohio Railroad

If any railroad can be called the mother of American railroading, it is the Baltimore & Ohio. It was North America's first common-carrier (or public) railroad. It pioneered much railway technology and was the largest, most daring project of its kind in the world when it was established. It was a long-lived corporation, lasting 160 years from 1827 to formal merger into CSX Transportation in 1987.

The B&O's corporate title literally expressed the company's aims. Baltimore bankers and merchants created it on February 28, 1827, to connect their fast-growing port city with the Ohio River, over 300 miles to the west. Railroading was a new and unproven technology, but for the Baltimoreans it was a case more of desperation than of vision. Baltimore's chief commercial rival, New York, had opened the Erie Canal in 1825, a vastly cheaper and easier means of moving goods and people between the port and the western frontiers than the existing turnpikes and (in Baltimore's case) the National Road. Baltimore had no such easy waterway route and was forced to gamble on the new railway technology then being developed in England.

Construction started in Baltimore on July 4, 1828, when Charles Carroll of Carrollton, the last surviving signer of the Declaration of Independence, dedicated the First Stone. After the celebration, though, the company struggled to develop suitable engineering, construction, and equipment technology, inevitably making expensive mistakes. Initially stone was used for bridges and track bed, creating some long-lasting monuments (the 1829 Carrollton Viaduct remains America's oldest surviving railroad bridge) but also draining the company's limited resources. Sharp curves and iron-strap rail precluded English-design steam locomotives, so horses provided the motive power.

Regular train service began on May 24, 1830, over 13 miles between Baltimore and present-day Ellicott City. It was the country's first scheduled rail passenger service. Shortly after, entrepreneur Peter Cooper built his tiny *Tom Thumb* (not so named at the time) to demonstrate a practical locomotive design for the B&O's operating conditions. His concept of a geared two-axle design with vertical boiler soon evolved into the B&O's odd but successful Grasshoppers, a fleet of which was built between 1833 and 1837.

Progress westward was hampered by legal, political, and financial problems. B&O crossed the Potomac at Harpers Ferry (then in Virginia) in 1836 and reached the base of the Alleghenies at Cumberland, Maryland, in 1842. There it hit a jackpot in the form of bituminous coal, which began moving eastward in ever-larger volumes and became the B&O's chief sustenance. The burgeoning bulk coal traffic demanded more mechanical and engineering pioneering to handle such loads, and the B&O developed heavy eight-coupled locomotives (notably designer Ross Winans's ungainly Camels), metal hopper cars, and iron truss bridges of the Fink and Bollman designs.

In the meantime the railroad had built a short branch from Baltimore to Washington, leaving the main line at Relay, west of Baltimore, and crossing the Patapsco River valley on the magnificent multiarch stone Thomas Viaduct. Opened in 1835, the line was Washington's first railroad and became the city's lifeline to the North during the Civil War.

More struggles followed, including political problems with the Commonwealth of Pennsylvania, which controlled the best route across the mountains. The B&O was forced into a difficult route through Virginia (now West Virginia) that included two separate summits reached over 2.2 percent grades—the steepest of any main-line railroad east of the Rockies. Ever afterward the railroad was obsessed with high-tractive-effort locomotive designs and was forever at an economic disadvantage against its competitors.

The B&O achieved its original goal of the Ohio River at Wheeling in January 1853. A branch from Grafton to Parkersburg (which soon became the main line) opened in 1857, giving a connection to Cincinnati and St. Louis via the Marietta & Cincinnati and Ohio & Mississippi railroads. These two lines gradually came under B&O control and were merged as the Baltimore & Ohio Southwestern in 1893.

In 1858 Baltimore banker John W. Garrett ascended to the presidency, inaugurating an autocratic reign that lasted 26 years and shaped the railroad for good and ill forever after. First he had to cope with the Civil War. B&O's Baltimore-Washington branch was the sole rail channel between Washington and the rest of the Union. It remained intact and busy during the entire conflict. B&O's east-west main line was another story; it suffered almost constant closures, damage, and other disruptions; the strategic Potomac River bridge at Harpers Ferry was destroyed several times by both Confederate and Union troops, as well as floods. Other notable losses were the shops at Martinsburg, bridges over the Monongahela, Youghioheny, and Cheat rivers, and the Confederate kidnapping of locomotives and other materials.

Afterward Garrett entered the postwar railroad expansion free-for-all. In 1866 he leased the Central Ohio Railroad, which ran from Bellaire, Ohio (opposite Wheeling), to Columbus via Newark. Using this as his springboard, he leased the Sandusky, Mansfield & Newark in 1869 to Lake Erie at Sandusky, Ohio. In 1874 he built a "branch" to Chicago from this line at Chicago Junction, Ohio, later renamed Willard. In the interim Garrett also managed to breach Pennsylvania, completing the Pittsburgh & Connellsville line from Cumberland to Pittsburgh via the Sand Patch summit in 1871. In 1873 he opened the Metropolitan Branch between Washington and a junction with the original main line at Point of Rocks, Maryland, finally giving the capital a direct route to the West.

Garrett was less successful at entering the South. He obtained control of the former Orange & Alexandria and Manassas Gap railroads (which he reorganized as the Virginia Midland, later to become a key part of the Southern Railway) and also built the Valley Railroad up the Shenandoah Valley toward Salem, Virginia. After 13 years of effort the latter gave up after reaching Lexington, Virginia.

Garrett made several strategic errors that weakened the company and helped put it in a perennial third place among the large eastern trunk lines. By paying out unearned dividends he accumulated a large debt, which in turn limited his ability to expand and upgrade the railroad. He let himself be outmaneuvered by major rivals, particularly the Pennsylvania, which in 1872 broke the B&O's monopoly between Baltimore and Washington and closed off B&O's routes to the South. Nine years later the Pennsylvania shut Garrett out of the Philadelphia and New York markets by acquiring the Philadelphia, Wilmington & Baltimore. Garrett retaliated by building his own Baltimore-Philadelphia line and establishing a route from Philadelphia to New York via the Philadelphia & Reading and Central Railroad of New Jersey. The new route, later advertised as the Royal Blue Line, opened in 1886. At the same time B&O established its own freight beachhead on New York Harbor by acquiring the Staten Island Rapid Transit Railway and extending it to a connection with the Central of New Jersey at Cranford, New Jersey.

Garrett died in 1884, but the B&O continued expanding. In 1892 it completed control of the Pittsburgh & Western, a onetime narrow-gauge line linking Pittsburgh with Akron, Ohio, and with Lake Erie at Painesville, Ohio. It then extended the P&W route west to Chicago Junction (Willard) to form a more direct route between Baltimore and Chicago via Pittsburgh.

Purchase of the Cleveland Terminal & Valley in 1891 and the Cleveland, Lorain & Wheeling in 1900 gave the B&O additional routes to Lake Erie at Cleveland and Lorain, Ohio, as well as access to the coalfields of southeast Ohio. In this period, too, B&O acquired and extended lines into the coal country south of Grafton and Clarksburg, West Virginia.

B&O's final nineteenth-century construction project was among its most famous: the Baltimore Belt Line, connecting its Baltimore terminals with the Philadelphia line (previously trains for Philadelphia and New York had been ferried across Baltimore harbor). Opened in 1895, the costly Belt Line included the 1.4-mile-long Howard Street Tunnel, Mount Royal Station, and the world's first heavy-duty mainline electrification.

By then Garrett's financial sins had caught up with the railroad, and in 1896 it was forced into receivership. Brief as it was (three years), the receivership led to what seemed the end of B&O's world—control in 1901 by the Pennsylvania Railroad.

But it was not the end of the world. Installed as a Pennsylvania puppet, Leonor F. Loree turned out to be B&O's most dynamic and underrated president, realigning and rebuilding vast stretches of main line (including much of the twisting Old Main Line), replacing obsolete bridges, installing modern motive power (including North America's first Mallet articulated), and expanding yards. He also bought the Ohio River Railroad, connecting Wheeling with Huntington and Kenova, West Virginia, as well as a substantial interest in the Reading to secure B&O's New York route.

PRR control also produced a cooperative effort to rebuild and modernize facilities at Washington, allowing B&O to reenter the southeastern freight market. The two railroads jointly built the monumental Washington Union Station (opened in 1907) and were part owners of the huge new Potomac Yard at Alexandria, Virginia (1906).

Loree left in 1904, and in 1906 the Pennsylvania began to divest itself of its B&O stock. B&O's expansion continued under Oscar G. Murray with the lease in 1909 of the Cincinnati, Hamilton & Dayton, a strategic north-south line between Toledo and Cincinnati.

Daniel Willard arrived from the Burlington in 1910 to begin his memorable 31-year presidency. He completed Loree's rebuilding program with the Magnolia Cutoff in 1914, eliminating a bottleneck in the Potomac River valley. He bought the bankrupt Chicago Terminal & Transfer Railroad, which served much of the Chicago switching district, in 1910 and reorganized it as the immensely valuable Baltimore & Ohio Chicago Terminal. In 1916 he purchased the Cincinnati, Hamilton & Dayton outright.

Then Willard proceeded to rebuild the B&O's sagging public image and employee morale. An industry statesman in labor relations, Willard developed cooperative shopwork and traffic solicitation programs on the B&O. His master publicity production was the 1927 Fair of the Iron Horse celebrating the B&O's centenary; afterward Willard shaped a distinctive, if sometimes eccentric, corporate image that survived into the early 1960s.

B&O's last major expansion, a case of unfortunate financial timing, came in the late 1920s and early 1930s. In 1927 it acquired the Cincinnati, Indianapolis & Western, a railroad from Hamilton, Ohio, through Indianapolis to Springfield, Illinois. In the same year, as a defensive measure, it bought control of the paralleling Western Maryland from the Rockefellers. The Interstate Commerce Commission subsequently forced the B&O to place its WM stock in an independent voting trusteeship, where it remained until 1968.

In 1929 B&O purchased the Buffalo, Rochester & Pittsburgh and the Buffalo & Susquehanna as part of a never-realized plan to create a new shortcut freight route between the Midwest and the East Coast. The two lines were absorbed in 1932, giving the B&O access to Buffalo and Rochester, New York, plus some western Pennsylvania coal country. Even less worthwhile was its 1930 purchase of the Chicago & Alton, which it reorganized in 1931 as the Alton Railroad. B&O never merged the Alton but allowed it to lapse into receivership in 1942 and sold it to the Gulf, Mobile & Ohio in 1947.

One positive product of the Depression was the 1934 acquisition of trackage rights over the Pittsburgh & Lake Erie's main line between McKeesport and New Castle Junction, Pennsylvania, so that through passenger and freight trains could use the water-level P&LE route rather

than B&O's own hilly, twisting, and roundabout line through the Pittsburgh area (in 1992 B&O's successor, CSX Transportation, bought the P&LE outright).

The Depression brought another brush with bankruptcy, avoided partly by Reconstruction Finance Corp. loans. Thanks to its latest acquisitions, the B&O reached its all-time peak of 6,396 route-miles (excluding the Alton) in 1936—"Linking 13 Great States with the Nation," as a later slogan told the world.

Daniel Willard retired in 1941 at age 80. The last years of his regime were marked by equipment innovations and numerous technological firsts: the country's first successful air-conditioned cars in 1929, the first fully air-conditioned train in 1931 (the *Columbian*), the first nonarticulated lightweight streamlined passenger trains in 1935, the first diesel passenger road locomotive that same year, the first streamlined production passenger diesels in 1937, and the distinctive wagon-top freight-car and caboose designs.

Traffic declines and financial problems returned after World War II. Dieselization proceeded slowly but was fi-

The pride of the Baltimore & Ohio was its Washington-Chicago *Capitol Limited*, an all-Pullman train offering the only Stratadome dome cars in the East. The westbound train passed through the Potomac River valley near Sandy Point, Maryland, about 1951.
—Baltimore & Ohio, *Trains* Magazine Collection

nally achieved in 1958, the year the well-loved but weak Royal Blue Line passenger services between Baltimore and New York City ceased. The railroad hit a financial nadir in 1961 with an unprecedented $30 million deficit.

By then the postwar merger movement was churning, and partners were being chosen. During 1959 and 1960 the rich Chesapeake & Ohio and the somewhat shaky New York Central both pursued the B&O. The C&O handily won and in 1963 took stock control and began a slow process of integrating management. In 1967 the ICC at last allowed the B&O to exercise its control of the Western Maryland, adding it to the C&O-B&O fold. The C&O, B&O, and WM remained legally separate companies, but by 1972 were being managed as a single unit under the Chessie System marketing name and logo.

As rail mergers metamorphosed into megamergers, the CSX Corp. was created in 1980 to control both the Chessie System railroads and the Seaboard Coast Line (or Family Lines) group of southeastern lines, although the Chessie and Seaboard systems remained separate entities through the mid-1980s. During that time the B&O leased the onetime Rock Island main line between Blue Island and Henry, Illinois, in 1981, and in 1983 it assumed direct operation of the surviving Western Maryland lines through another lease. But the Baltimore & Ohio's legal life finally ended on April 30, 1987, when it was formally merged into the C&O as part of a multistage process to create CSX Transportation.

In 1985, the Baltimore & Ohio operated a system of 5,268 route-miles and 9,999 track-miles, with 879 locomotives, 38,892 freight and company service cars, and 11,102 employees. Freight traffic totaled 25.3 billion ton-miles in 1985, and coal (34 percent), transportation equipment (12 percent), chemical products (6 percent), and petroleum and coal products (6 percent) were its principal traffic sources. Baltimore & Ohio operating revenues totaled $1,022 million in 1985, and the railroad achieved a 111 percent operating ratio.

—Herbert H. Harwood, Jr.

REFERENCES

Dilts, James D. *The Great Road: The Building of the Baltimore and Ohio, the Nation's First Railroad, 1828–1853*. Stanford, Calif.: Stanford Univ. Press, 1993.

Harwood, Herbert H., Jr. *Impossible Challenge II*. Baltimore: Barnard, Roberts, 1994.

Hungerford, Edward. *The Story of the Baltimore & Ohio Railroad, 1827–1927*. New York: G. P. Putnam's Sons, 1928.

Stover, John F. *History of the Baltimore and Ohio Railroad*. West Lafayette, Ind.: Purdue Univ. Press, 1987.

Bamberger Railroad

The strongest and longest lived of a 200-mile chain of interurbans that extended north from Provo, Utah, through the fertile plains west of the Wasatch Mountains to Preston, Idaho, was the middle link, the 36-mile Bamberger Railroad, which connected Utah's two largest cities, Salt Lake City and Ogden. Dissatisfied with the service of the steam railroads, coal-mine operator and later Utah governor Simon Bamberger set out to build a local railroad to better serve its needs. Completed in 1908, the Salt Lake & Ogden Railway was converted from steam to electric power in 1910 and adopted the Bamberger family name in 1917. Passenger traffic between the two cities was vigorous. The railroad created the elaborate Lagoon amusement park near Farmington that was long a major traffic source. In 1923 the Bamberger and the connecting Salt Lake & Utah Railroad built a splendid new terminal opposite Salt Lake City's Temple Square that was among the finest interurban terminals in North America.

With future freight traffic in mind from the beginning, Bamberger built the railroad on private right-of-way, with wide curves and grades that were no steeper than 1.1 percent. Some of the connecting steam railroads established interchange agreements with the Bamberger before World War I, but it was not until 1923 that the railroad was able to establish full interchange arrangements.

A flourishing passenger and freight operation continued through the mid-twentieth century, and the Bamberger's traffic reached record levels during World War II. Rebuilt and modernized original passenger cars were augmented in 1939 by five lightweight, high-speed Bullet cars originally acquired in 1932 by the Fonda, Johnstown & Gloversville Railroad in upstate New York. Secondhand electric locomotives and a diesel-electric locomotive were acquired to help with the booming freight business. During the war years passenger traffic grew to as much as five times its 1939 level, and freight traffic grew to a peak of nine times the prewar level.

The end of the war brought the usual decline in passenger operations. The connecting electric railroads north of Ogden and south of Salt Lake City were both gone by 1947, and the Bamberger's own bus services competed with the trains. Rail passenger service was brought to an abrupt end by two disastrous fires in 1952, and freight service was converted to diesel-electric operation. Freight operation over most of the railroad ended in 1959. A few segments of track in Ogden and Salt Lake City were sold to the Union Pacific and the Denver & Rio Grande Western. In 1957, its last year before abandonment, the Bamberger Railroad operated 37 route-miles and 54 track-miles, with 3 locomotives, 24 freight and company service cars, and 93 employees. Operating revenues totaled $680,000 in 1957.

—William D. Middleton

REFERENCE

Swett, Ira L., ed. *Interurbans of Utah*. Interurbans Special 15. Los Angeles: Interurbans, 1954.

Bangor & Aroostook Railroad

Aroostook is Maine's largest county; its area takes up over one-fifth of the state. In the 1890s Aroostook County was largely forested wilderness or, in the northeast, agricultural land suitable for potatoes. A grant of land from the state induced the European & North American Railway to bend its Bangor–Saint John, New Brunswick, line into Aroostook County for a few miles. Somewhat more useful to county farmers were two narrow-gauge railroads that built west from New Brunswick to Houlton and to Caribou and Presque Isle, but delays caused by transferring freight between standard- and narrow-gauge cars and two crossings of the international boundary pointed up the need for a direct route south within the state of Maine.

The Northern Maine Railroad was incorporated in 1859, but accomplished almost nothing until it was revived briefly in 1887 with the hope that it would be taken over by the Maine Central. The Maine Central, however, was stymied by the Canadian Pacific Railway (CPR), which threatened to divert traffic from the Boston & Maine to the Fitchburg Railroad if B&M encouraged the Maine Central.

In 1891 the Bangor & Aroostook Railroad (BAR) was incorporated. Its starting point was Brownville, on the Canadian Pacific route across the middle of the state (the direct route from Montreal to Saint John); its destinations were Ashland and Caribou in Aroostook County. The legislature protected the new railroad from competing railroads and authorized it to acquire two existing railroads, the Bangor & Piscataquis Railroad and the Bangor & Katahdin Iron Works Railway. The Bangor & Piscataquis was built between 1868 and 1884 from Old Town, 12 miles north of Bangor, north and west to a connection with the Canadian Pacific at Greenville. The Bangor & Katahdin Iron Works ran from Milo, on the B&P, through Brownville to mines and a smelter at Katahdin Iron Works. It opened in 1881 and was leased by the B&P in 1887, the same year it established a connection with the Megantic-Mattawamkeag line that would become part of the Canadian Pacific.

Rails reached Houlton in December 1893 and Caribou in December 1894. At the beginning of 1895 the BAR was operating from Old Town to Greenville and Katahdin Iron Works, and from Brownville to Caribou and Fort Fairfield. The railroad continued to extend its routes: in late 1895 from Oakfield north to Ashland; in 1898 from Old Town to Bangor on trackage rights over the Maine Central; in 1899 to Van Buren; and in 1902 from Ashland to Fort Kent. The most significant construction was a line opened in 1905 from South La Grange to tidewater at Searsport, plus port facilities for handling inbound coal and outbound paper and potatoes and a new connection with the Maine Central west of Bangor at a point named Northern Maine Junction. In 1907 the railroad built a straight, low-grade cutoff north from South La Grange to West Seboeis, bypassing steep grades near Brownville. In 1909 the railroad was granted charters for several more lines, the principal ones being from Van Buren along the St. John River to St. Francis and from Squa Pan to Mapleton. BAR's final piece of construction was a bridge built in 1915 from Van Buren across the St. John River to St. Leonard, New Brunswick, and connections with the National Transcontinental Railway and the International New Brunswick Railway (both would become part of Canadian National Railways).

The Bangor & Aroostook settled down to a stable, profitable existence starting the products of northern Maine—paper, lumber, and potatoes—on their journeys to points beyond Maine's borders. Its red, white, and blue boxcars lettered "State of Maine Products," unique in an era when freight cars were either iron-oxide red or black, advertised the railroad. BAR's passenger trains, two each way each day, carried through coaches and sleeping cars to and from Boston; BAR also operated buses on the region's highways.

In late 1993 ownership of the BAR passed from the Amoskeag Corp., which had owned it since 1969, to a group of New York investors. Within a year the railroad was again sold to Iron Road Railways, a company owning shortline and regional railroads around the United States.

For a number of years Canadian Pacific had tried to lease, sell, or otherwise distance itself from its route from Montreal east to Saint John, New Brunswick. In 1995 BAR and the Irving Group of New Brunswick bought the CPR line, to which Iron Road added several former CPR lines in southern Quebec and northeast Vermont. By 1999 Iron Road was in financial difficulty and BAR was forced into reorganization. In late 2001 Rail World, under the direction of Edward Burkhardt, creator of the Wisconsin Central, led a consortium that purchased BAR.

In 1993, the last year for which information is available, Bangor & Aroostook operated a system of 420 route-miles and 591 track-miles, with 341 employees. The predominant items of freight traffic were paper and forest products.

—George H. Drury

REFERENCE

Angier, Jerry, and Herb Cleaves. *Bangor and Aroostook*. Littleton, Mass.: Flying Yankee, 1986.

Barriger, John W., III (1899–1976)

John W. Barriger III was a consummate railroad executive, thinker, visionary, champion, writer, and enthusiast. Born in Dallas, Texas, on December 3, 1899, he grew up in St. Louis, in the shadow of St. Louis Union Station, and

John W. Barriger. —*Trains* Magazine Collection

began working for the Pennsylvania Railroad during summer vacations while a student at MIT. Upon graduation in 1921 he joined the Pennsy's management training program and served the railroad for seven years as a junior executive. In 1927 he joined Kuhn, Loeb & Co. to work in railroad finance and stayed with the firm for two years. Upon leaving Kuhn, Loeb, he continued on a career path that included a broad range of assignments, but spent comparatively little time in each. Barriger served as president and vice president of several railroads, and his enthusiasm for the industry kept him active until just before his death on December 9, 1976. His last position was as a senior traveling freight agent with the Chicago, Rock Island & Pacific Railway.

Barriger's appearance on the national scene began when he was asked to prepare the Prince Plan, named after a Boston businessman from whom a plan for reorganization of the rail industry had been requested by Franklin D. Roosevelt. Barriger's plan, delivered in May 1933, proposed a consolidation of the industry into eight regional lines. Not surprisingly, the railroads were not eager to embrace national plans that they did not feel served their lines' best interests, and the plan was not adopted. Barriger's delivery of the plan did, however, bring him sufficient notoriety to pave the way to a position working on railroad issues at the Reconstruction Finance Corp. (RFC). In this new position Barriger built

upon his already-strong knowledge of the U.S. railroad industry.

The RFC position, along with several subsequent positions with government and private organizations, resulted in Barriger's development of a basic doctrine that he called "super railroading." The primary notion behind this doctrine was essentially that railroads should be constructed with as little grade and curvature as possible, enabling trains to run at higher speeds, thus delivering better service to the customer. He also believed that the freight agent or salesperson must be given a stronger role in the business in order to solicit business more effectively and to communicate the benefits of super railroading to shippers.

From 1946 to 1952 Barriger served as president of the Chicago, Indianapolis & Louisville, better known as the Monon. He arrived at the Monon with plans to implement his concepts of super railroading on a property that, from an engineering perspective, was not an ideal candidate. Curves, steep grades, and some street running prevented full implementation of super railroading, but Barriger nonetheless made tremendous improvements to the Monon. He improved the railroad's physical plant, purchased diesel locomotives, expanded passenger service, and even introduced paint schemes on locomotives and cars that honored the state's two largest universities—red and gray passenger equipment for Indiana University and black and gold freight equipment for Purdue. Although efforts to renew passenger service made for good public relations, they were not financially successful. Improvements to freight service, however, returned strong results. Monon's operating revenues nearly doubled, and the road returned to profitability during Barriger's tenure.

After leaving the Monon, Barriger served as vice president of the New Haven railroad, then as vice president of the Chicago, Rock Island & Pacific. After limited time in both positions, Barriger was asked to serve as president of the Pittsburgh & Lake Erie Railroad by Alfred E. Perlman, chairman of the New York Central, which controlled the P&LE. This was another opportunity for Barriger to promote his super railroad concepts. The P&LE physical plant, along with the New York Central's emphasis on quality, gave him a platform, and he actively promoted his philosophy during his presidency.

The New York Central had a policy of mandatory retirement at age 65, so Barriger had to leave the Central, but did not retire from railroading. Over the next few years he was a consultant to the St. Louis–San Francisco Railway, president of both the Missouri-Kansas-Texas and the Boston & Maine, and assistant to John Ingram, the administrator of the Federal Railroad Administration (FRA). In 1974 Ingram left the FRA to become president of the Chicago, Rock Island & Pacific and asked Barriger to join him at the Rock Island in 1976 as a senior traveling freight agent. Barriger died in St. Louis on December 9, 1976.

—**David C. Lester**

REFERENCES

Dolzall, Gary W., and Stephen F. Dolzall. *Monon: The Hoosier Line*. Glendale, Calif.: Interurban, 1987. Rev. ed. Bloomington: Indiana Univ. Press, 2002.

Hilton, George W. "John W. Barriger III." In *Railroads in the Age of Regulation, 1900–1980*, ed. Keith L. Bryant, Jr. A volume in *Encyclopedia of American Business History and Biography*, gen. ed. William H. Becker. New York: Bruccoli Clark Layman and Facts on File, 1988.

———. *Monon Route*. Berkeley, Calif.: Howell-North, 1978.

BC Rail

The Pacific Great Eastern Railway (PGE) was chartered in 1912 to be the Vancouver branch of the Grand Trunk Pacific, which was building westward from Winnipeg to the Pacific at Prince Rupert, British Columbia. Initially the PGE built a few miles west and north along the shore from North Vancouver, British Columbia, to Horseshoe Bay, and it acquired the property of a bankrupt company that had built inland a few miles from Squamish, on the shore 28 miles west of Horseshoe Bay.

From the beginning the PGE was subsidized by the province, and in 1918 the province acquired full ownership. In 1921 the line from Squamish reached Quesnel, British Columbia, and it went no farther for 30 years. The line was completely isolated. Ships and car ferries between Vancouver and Squamish were its only connection with the rest of the North American rail network. For a while the PGE intended to connect Horseshoe Bay and Squamish, but in 1928 it abandoned its initial North Vancouver–Horseshoe Bay route. The company was a consistent money-loser.

In the 1950s the Pacific Great Eastern began to expand, not only to connect with other railroads but also to assist the development of northern British Columbia. The track was pushed north 82 miles from Quesnel to a connection with Canadian National's Jasper–Prince Rupert line (the former Grand Trunk Pacific) at Prince George. In 1956 the railway built east along the shore from Squamish to North Vancouver, in the process replacing the 12 miles of track it had abandoned in 1928, and in 1958 it opened an extension north and east from Prince George to Dawson Creek.

The 1970s brought further expansion: north to Fort Nelson in 1971 and northwest toward Dease Lake in 1977. The Tumbler Ridge branch opened in 1983 to serve coal mines near the British Columbia–Alberta border, bringing the railroad to a total of 1,438 miles of track. Tunnel-ventilation considerations on that branch prompted electrification. There were also two name changes: to British Columbia Railway in 1972, then to BC Rail in 1984.

PGE's Squamish-Quesnel passenger train carried a singularly random assortment of secondhand equipment, including former electric interurban sleeping and parlor cars. In its early years PGE offered automobile-on-flatcar service between Lillooet and Shalath because there was no highway. In 1956 equipment was replaced by Budd Rail Diesel Cars, some with kitchenettes, reclining seats, and other amenities for long-distance travel. More recently, the railroad initiated seasonal steam train service to Prince George.

In 1992 BC Rail operated 1,387 route-miles of railroad, with 107 locomotives, 10,090 freight cars, and 12 passenger cars. The principal items of freight traffic were forest products and coal. Declining coal traffic brought an end to electric operation in 2000, and passenger services were ended in 2002. Late in 2003 the Province of British Columbia and Canadian National announced that CN would purchase and merge BC Rail.

—George H. Drury

REFERENCES

Hungry Wolf, Adolf. *Route of the Cariboo: PGE/BC Rail*. Skookumchuck, B.C.: Canadian Caboose, 1994.

Schmidt, Paul. "Splintered Dream." *Trains* 63, no. 4 (Apr. 2003): 46–59.

Bedwell, Harry (1888–1955)

Beginning in the late nineteenth century there was a lively market for popular railroad fiction that continued through World War II before largely vanishing. There were both novels and short stories, the latter often appearing in such popular general magazines as the *Saturday Evening Post*, *McClure's*, *Scribner's*, and *Collier's*. The old *Railroad Man's Magazine*, oriented to the railroad worker and published from 1906 to 1919, was a regular source of railroad fiction. It was revived in 1929 as *Railroad Stories* and, after 1937, as *Railroad Magazine*.

Among *Railroad's* writers in the 1930s and 1940s were E. S. Dellinger, William F. "Bill" Knapke, Gilbert A. Lathrop, and Harry K. McClintock, almost all of them railroad workers. One of the best—and the last—of these writers was Harry Chester Bedwell. Born on a farm near Kellerton, Iowa, in 1888, Bedwell decided early on that he wanted to be a railroad man. He learned telegraphy from the Kellerton station operator and hired out on the Chicago, Burlington & Quincy as an operator in 1905. Bedwell got a sound education in railroad operation during two years as a relief operator working on nearly a dozen different stations in Iowa and Missouri. He became a "boomer" of sorts, moving on to learn mountain railroading on the Denver & Rio Grande Western on Utah stations and then to a long career on the Pacific Electric Railway and Southern Pacific in Southern California.

Still only 20 years old, Bedwell began his long career as a writer in 1908. His first pieces were published in the *Los*

Angeles Times Illustrated Weekly Magazine in 1908 and 1909. His first railroad story was "Campbell's Wedding Race," published in the *Railroad Man's Magazine* in October 1909, immediately followed by a two-part article for *American Magazine* later that year. Bedwell's work appeared in such publications as *Argosy*, *Bluebook Magazine*, *Harper's Weekly*, and *Short Stories*. He wrote frequently for the *Saturday Evening Post*. But Harry Bedwell's most frequent publisher by far was *Railroad Stories*, later *Railroad Magazine*, which published more than 30 of his short stories, novelettes, and articles between 1936 and 1955.

Bedwell's stories were fiction based on fact, often using his own experiences or those of other railroaders. His descriptions conveyed the sense of the place he was writing about, and his characters were believable. Bedwell's readers could look forward to seeing their favorites reappear in his stories. Eddie Sand was a popular carrot-topped boomer telegrapher who bore quite a resemblance to Harry Bedwell himself, or so it was said. Walley Sterling was an often-seen dispatcher or operator, and Hi Wheeler was a boomer brakeman. Buck Barabe was a martinet superintendent, while Salt-and-Molasses Nickerson was the revered railroad president.

Bedwell's writing career lasted through 1955, by which time the market for railroad fiction writing had pretty well ended. All told, Harry Bedwell published some 70 stories or articles. His only novel, *The Boomer: A Story of the Rails*, sold over 100,000 copies in 1942. The *Saturday Evening Post* posthumously published his last story, the novelette "Avalanche Warning," in 1957.

Harry Bedwell worked for his last few years at several SP stations in Oregon, retiring from the railroad in 1955. Injured in an accident while preparing a retirement home with his wife, Lorraine, at Nevada City, California, he died only a few months after his retirement.

—William D. Middleton

REFERENCE

Donovan, Frank P., Jr. *Harry Bedwell: Last of the Great Railroad Story Tellers*. Minneapolis, Minn.: Ross & Haines, 1959.

Beebe, Lucius (1902–1966)

Perhaps no other writer did more to take railroading to a mass audience than Lucius Morris Beebe, a flamboyant writer, photographer, and socialite credited with inventing the railroad book market with his 1938 picture book *High Iron*. He ultimately wrote some 40 books, 27 of them about railroads.

Beebe was born to a prosperous family in Wakefield, Massachusetts, on December 9, 1902. His father, Junius, headed the family's various business interests, among them leather, gas, and banking. Young Lucius spent much of his childhood at the 140-acre Beebe farm, attended several exclusive preparatory schools, then entered Yale in 1923. But his penchant for pranks and troublemaking got in the way, and Yale expelled him. He went on to Harvard, which also suspended him briefly, but he returned to graduate in 1926.

A journalism career beckoned. After working for newspapers in Boston, Beebe joined the *New York Herald Tribune* in 1929 at age 27, and in 1933 he began writing a column for the paper called "This New York," documenting the city's high society. Hardly the impartial journalist, Beebe himself became a central figure in what he termed "café society" and in 1939 was featured on the cover of *Life* magazine in top hat and tails. He frequently made various "best-dressed" lists. He remained on the *Herald Tribune* staff for 21 years.

Beebe found time to become immersed in much of American railroading. An inveterate train rider, especially of the New York Central's *20th Century Limited*, Beebe also established an imposing reputation as a photographer. Armed with a ponderous Speed Graphic camera, he perfected a style of ¾-angle action photography that became a mainstay in his first series of picture books for Appleton-Century, beginning with *High Iron* (1938) and continuing through *Highliners* (1940), *Trains in Transition* (1941), and *Highball* (1945).

Postwar New York lost some of its appeal for Beebe, and in 1950 he moved to Virginia City, Nevada, with his partner and collaborator Charles M. Clegg, himself a notable photographer. In the ensuing decade and a half Beebe (usually with Clegg) published an astonishing array of lavish railroad books, mostly for publisher Howell-North. These volumes included *The Age of Steam* (1957), *Mansions on Rails* (1959), *Mixed Train Daily* (1961), and *Twentieth Century Limited* (1962). They were distinguished not only by Beebe's rich, evocative, ornamental writing style, but also by his skill in choosing photographs. A visionary photo editor, Beebe showcased the early work of numerous masters, including Richard Steinheimer, Philip R. Hastings, Robert Hale, and Jim Shaughnessy.

Beebe flourished in Virginia City, purchasing the dormant *Territorial Enterprise* newspaper and launching it anew in 1952. By 1954 the weekly paper boasted a record circulation. He continued to write for a number of national magazines—among them *Gourmet*, *Esquire*, *Holiday*, and *Playboy*—and in 1960 began writing the column "This Wild West" for the *San Francisco Chronicle*. He and Clegg owned two ostentatious private railroad cars, *Virginia City* and *Gold Coast*. The latter is part of the collection of the California State Railroad Museum.

Beebe continued to produce books at a steady rate and by 1965 was working on a massive two-volume set, *The Trains We Rode*. But his health was failing, and his latest project perhaps became too much for him. Beebe died of a heart attack on February 4, 1966, at his home in Hillsborough, California, with the second volume unfinished. Clegg completed it for Howell-North, giving Beebe's huge audience one more chance to enjoy the work of the man whom historian Walter P. Gray III described as "the last Edwardian gentleman."

—Kevin P. Keefe

REFERENCES

Clegg, Charles, and Duncan Emrich, eds. *The Lucius Beebe Reader*. Garden City, N.Y.: Doubleday, 1967.
Gray, Walter P., III. "The Last Edwardian Gentleman." *Trains* 60, no. 1 (Jan. 2000): 80–81.
Morgan, David P. "Lucius Beebe, 1902–1966." *Trains* 26, no. 6 (Aug. 1965): 4.

Belt Railway of Chicago

In the latter part of the nineteenth century Chicago developed into the railroad center of the United States. As soon as the first few railroads established junctions there, Chicago became a good place for other railroads to connect with them and with each other. It became the principal western terminal of eastern railroads and the principal eastern terminal of western railroads. Its location at the south end of Lake Michigan created a concentration of railroads.

Early on, it was sufficient for the railroads to interchange freight cars at or near the passenger stations in downtown Chicago, but the area and the railroads soon became congested. By 1880 it became desirable to interchange freight cars away from the congestion and the passenger stations of downtown. Several railroads established subsidiaries either solely or in cooperation with other railroads to handle the rapidly increasing freight traffic.

The Belt Division of the Chicago & Western Indiana, a terminal railroad owned by the predecessors of the Chicago & Eastern Illinois, Monon, Erie, Wabash, and Grand Trunk Western, was built between 1880 and 1882. In 1882 it was reincorporated as the Belt Railway Co. of Chicago under the control not of the Chicago & Western Indiana but of C&WI's owners.

The new railroad provided connections between line-haul railroads outside downtown Chicago. A. B. Stickney of the Chicago Great Western Railway designed a circular yard that would serve as a clearinghouse for freight cars. Although only a small part of that yard was built (and with a conventional layout), Clearing Yard was the largest freight yard in the world when it opened in 1902, and one of the first three hump yards in the United States (the other two were on the New York Central at Syracuse, New York, and the Pennsylvania at East Altoona, Pennsylvania).

Several more railroads became owners of the Belt Railway in 1912: the Atchison, Topeka & Santa Fe, the Chesapeake & Ohio, the Chicago, Burlington & Quincy, the Chicago, Rock Island & Pacific, the Illinois Central, the Minneapolis, St. Paul & Sault Ste. Marie (Soo Line), and the Pennsylvania. The Pere Marquette Railway was added to the list in 1924.

The Belt Railway of Chicago still connects with all the line-haul railroads entering Chicago. As railroads merged, the list of owners shrank to the six major railroads of North America: Burlington Northern & Santa Fe, Canadian National, Canadian Pacific, CSX, Norfolk Southern, and Union Pacific. Belt Railway of Chicago operates 28 miles of main-line track and more than 300 miles of switching tracks with 520 employees.

—George H. Drury

REFERENCE

Pinkepank, Jerry A. "Serving Twelve Masters." *Trains* 26, no. 11 (Sept. 1966): 36–46; 26, no. 12 (Oct. 1966): 42–49.

BNSF Railway

BNSF Railway, formerly Burlington Northern & Santa Fe Railway Co., operates the second-largest railroad network in North America, with nearly 33,000 route-miles covering 28 states and two Canadian provinces. The BNSF network covers the western two-thirds of the United States, from major Pacific Northwest and Southern California ports to the Midwest, Southeast, and Southwest, and from the Gulf of Mexico to Canada. BNSF was created on September 22, 1995, by the merger of Burlington Northern, Inc. (parent company of Burlington Northern Railroad), and Santa Fe Pacific Corp. (parent company of the Atchison, Topeka & Santa Fe Railway). The two railroads were formally merged on December 31, 1996.

The largest BNSF predecessor railroad, Burlington Northern, was created on March 2, 1970, through the merger of the Burlington, Great Northern (GN), Northern Pacific (NP), and Spokane, Portland & Seattle railways. In 1980 Burlington Northern merged the 4,674-mile St. Louis–San Francisco (Frisco) into its system, putting many former SLSF managers in executive positions at BN (BN chairman Louis Menk had been president of the Frisco before moving to the CB&Q in 1965). The Frisco acquisition gave BN direct routes from Kansas City and St. Louis to Texas and allowed the consolidation of duplicate facilities in Kansas City and St. Louis. It also allowed BN to tap growing markets in the Southeast with its line from Kansas City through Memphis.

In the 1990s BN looked to the Atchison, Topeka & Santa Fe Railway (Santa Fe) as a potential merger partner. Neighboring Union Pacific had been gobbling up railroads throughout the 1980s and 1990s, and BN felt that it had to merge with another railroad to round out its system and remain competitive. The Santa Fe system, at

8,649 miles, complemented Burlington Northern's. The chief physical asset of the Chicago-based Santa Fe was its magnificent high-speed transcontinental main line, which reached west from Chicago to Kansas City to Los Angeles and the Bay Area. At 2,214 miles, it was the shortest rail route between Chicago and Los Angeles. Other principal Santa Fe routes reached Fort Worth, Denver, and the Texas Gulf Coast.

The Santa Fe had attempted a merger with Southern Pacific in the mid-1980s, but that merger was rebuffed by the Interstate Commerce Commission (ICC) as anticompetitive, since many of the two railroads' lines duplicated one another and would reduce shippers' choices for routing goods. As a result of that merger attempt, both the Santa Fe and Southern Pacific had suffered heavy financial losses. However, by the 1990s the Santa Fe emerged as a strong, profitable railroad. Much of the credit for the turnaround was given to Santa Fe president Robert D. Krebs (who began his railroad career with Southern Pacific). The Santa Fe franchise relied heavily upon intermodal freight traffic, which it carried long distances over the transcontinental main line. Burlington Northern's expertise was in coal. Since passage of the Clean Air Act in 1970, it had become one of the largest transporters of low-sulfur Powder River Basin coal, mined in Wyoming and Montana (in 2001, BNSF's former BN coal lines hauled enough coal to generate nearly 10 percent of U.S. electricity). The merger would be "end to end" with little duplicate trackage, which would alleviate the concerns of the Surface Transportation Board, which had been created in 1995 as the successor to the ICC. It seemed an excellent match.

On June 29, 1994, the BN and Santa Fe boards met separately and approved a merger agreement. However, competitor Union Pacific (UP) intervened when UP chairman Drew Lewis proposed a merger between UP and Santa Fe, offering one-third more money than BN was offering. Many thought that the offer was not serious and was motivated more by a desire to up the ante for BN. However, UP went to court to try to force Santa Fe to deal. BN was forced to increase its purchase offer to approximate Union Pacific's, and Santa Fe stockholders approved the merger with Burlington Northern.

On July 20, 1995, the ICC approved the merger, and on September 22 the railroad's two holding companies, Burlington Northern, Inc., and Santa Fe Pacific Corp., merged to form the Burlington Northern Santa Fe Corp. The new company managed both railroads as one organization until the end of 1996, with both the parent company and the railroad referred to as BNSF. On December 31, 1996, the Atchison, Topeka & Santa Fe Railway merged into Burlington Northern Railroad. BN then changed its name to the Burlington Northern & Santa Fe Railway Co. Krebs became the railroad's first president and CEO.

Immediately after the merger the two railroads began implementation of a new operating plan. In at least three corridors the railroads rerouted traffic to save costs: Denver–Kansas City–Chicago, Denver-Texas, and Chicago–Kansas City–Texas. For example, between Chicago and Houston BN traffic would save 30 miles by consolidating the two railroads' routes, and Santa Fe traffic would save 80 miles. Even though this seems minor, when operating costs such as fuel and train- and locomotive-miles are factored in, the savings can be large. There were also yard consolidations in Kansas City and Amarillo and Fort Worth, Texas. New connections between the two railroads were built at Cameron, Illinois, and connections were upgraded in Amarillo, Bucklin, Missouri, and Olathe, Kansas.

Krebs was a believer in new locomotives and track upgrades, and in 1996, the first full year of merged operations, the company spent almost $1 billion to increase line and terminal capacity and to expand the locomotive and car fleet. The new locomotives wore a handsome new paint scheme that used the "Omaha orange" from the old Great Northern combined with dark green from the Northern Pacific, plus gold pinstriping and the Santa Fe cigar-band logo with the letters "BNSF." The most popular model BNSF ordered was the 4,400-hp General Electric C44-9W; 164 were received between July 1996 and January 1997 as part of the combined railroads' first new locomotive order. More locomotive orders followed, including 426 new units in 1998 and 539 new or rebuilt locomotives in 1999. A number of double-track projects were initiated to improve track capacity, mainly along the former Santa Fe transcontinental main line and along coal lines in Wyoming, some of which were triple-tracked.

One of the larger projects handled by BNSF in its first years was reopening the former Northern Pacific crossing of the Cascade Mountains at Stampede Pass in western Washington State. In April 1996 BNSF announced that it would spend $125 million to rebuild the line, which had been closed since 1983. An additional $40 million would be spent to buy back the 149-mile former NP main line from Kennewick to Cle Elum, Washington, which BN had sold to regional railroad Washington Central in 1986. The reason for reopening the route was to relieve traffic bottlenecks into the Pacific Northwest over the former Great Northern route over Stevens Pass and the former Spokane, Portland & Seattle line along the Columbia River. Both were nearing capacity, and BNSF hoped that Stampede Pass would relieve the congestion. Reconstruction proceeded rapidly during the summer of 1996, with 500 workers working to rebuild the 230 miles of track between Auburn and Kennewick, Washington. To reopen the line, extensive rebuilding of the 1.8-mile Stampede Tunnel was required. Timber snow sheds that once guarded approaches at both ends of the tunnel were gone and had to be replaced. New concrete snow sheds were built, and the tunnel was relined with concrete. On December 7, 1996, an eastbound empty grain train became the first revenue movement over the rebuilt line, giving BNSF a third route across Washington State.

In Kansas City, long a key point for Santa Fe, the company reconstructed the former AT&SF Argentine Yard. The yard occupies 780 acres of land and once had two "humps," one eastbound and one westbound, for sorting and classifying trains. The eastbound hump and yard were taken out of service in early 1996 and the tracks pulled up. A total of 1.2 million cubic yards of earth was moved, and 75 miles of new track were laid. A new hump and an office building were constructed. After 18 months of work and $95 million in improvements, the new yard opened in July 1997. After the new yard opened, the westward classification hump was removed. Included in the work at Argentine were 120 solar-powered switches and 7,000 distributive resistive retarders in the hump yard to control railcar speed.

In September 1996 Union Pacific merged Southern Pacific into its system. As part of an agreement reached with UP before the merger, BNSF was granted trackage or haulage rights over 3,550 miles of SP-UP lines. BNSF also purchased 200 miles of track from the merged company, primarily consisting of former Western Pacific trackage between Bieber and Keddie, California, part of the so-called Inside Gateway route Great Northern and Western Pacific used to compete with SP between the Pacific Northwest and the Bay Area. From Keddie to Oakland, BNSF was granted trackage rights over UP. The intent of the premerger agreement was to preserve two-railroad competition for shippers and eliminate possible opposition from the Surface Transportation Board and BNSF, since it gave the latter the ability to serve every shipper then served jointly by UP and SP.

In 2005 the Burlington Northern Santa Fe operated a system of 32,000 route-miles and 50,000 track miles, with 5,790 locomotives, 81,881 freight cars, 179 passenger commuter cars, and 40,000 employees. Freight traffic totaled 596,575 million revenue ton-miles in 2005, and its four principal commodity groups were coal (19 percent), consumer goods (41 percent), industrial products (23 percent), and agricultural (17 percent). BNSF operating revenues totaled $12,987 million in 2005, with operating expenses of $10,065 million, representing a 78 percent operating ratio. As of January 2005, the company officially became BNSF Railway.

—Steve Glischinski

REFERENCES

Del Grosso, Robert C. *Burlington Northern and Santa Fe 1985 Annual*. Bonners Ferry, Idaho: Great Northern Pacific, 1999.
———. *Burlington Northern Santa Fe 1995 Annual*. La Mirada, Calif.: Four Ways West, 1996.
Glischinski, Steve. *Burlington Northern and Its Heritage*. Andover, N.J.: Andover Junction, 1992.

Bombardier

In the late 1930s, in a small workshop in Valcourt, Quebec (southeast of Montreal, near Sherbrooke), a self-taught inventor named Joseph-Armand Bombardier refined his design for a tracked vehicle capable of traversing snow-covered terrain. Bombardier's B7 snowmobile received patent approval in June 1937; from that unlikely invention rose a company that bore his name and would one day become a global force in the design and construction not just of all-terrain vehicles, but rail and transit locomotives and cars, as well as aircraft.

Founded in 1942 as L'Auto-Neige Bombardier Limitée, the fledgling company concentrated on the production of large multipurpose snowmobiles and all-terrain vehicles for military and commercial use, from personnel carriers, rescue vehicles, and even snowmobile school buses to tractors and tracked vehicles for forestry and other applications in muskeg and difficult terrain. The Ski-Doo, a two-passenger, personal-use snowmobile introduced by Bombardier in 1959, propelled the company's profits and profile to unexpected heights. In 1967 it formally changed its name to Bombardier Ltd. Two years later it went public with stock offerings on the Montreal and Toronto stock exchanges.

In 1974 Bombardier was awarded a contract to construct more than 400 subway cars for the Montreal, Quebec, Metro system. This first foray into the rail-transit field heralded a diversification plan that would lead Bombardier to eventual domination of the North American rail-transit market and to prominence in the locomotive- and railcar-construction business worldwide. To fill the Montreal order, Bombardier established a new facility in La Pocatière, Quebec, on the south shore of the St. Lawrence River, approximately 120 miles east of Quebec City. Twenty years later the 503,000-square-foot plant employs approximately 700 people and has produced thousands of rail transit and passenger cars, from bilevel electric multiple-unit cars (M.U.'s) for Illinois Central's (now Metra) electrified Chicago commuter service to subway cars for the New York City Transit Authority.

Further expanding into the railroad market, Bombardier purchased locomotive builder MLW-Worthington in 1975. The historic works in Montreal's east end were established in 1902 as the Locomotive & Machine Co. of Montreal, Ltd., were acquired by the American Locomotive Co. (Alco) in 1904, and were renamed Montreal Locomotive Works in 1908. After Alco exited the locomotive trade in 1969, MLW continued to build Alco- and MLW-design locomotives for the Canadian and world markets. By the time of the Bombardier acquisition, MLW's stake in the locomotive business was slipping. Bombardier invested in engineering and marketing efforts for MLW's domestic and export locomotive lines, still powered by Alco-design 251 prime movers.

On the domestic front MLW-designed M-series models were replaced by Bombardier HR (High Reliability) models for freight service. For the passenger trade Bombardier offered LRC (Light Rapid Comfortable) trainsets consisting of a low-slung 2,750-hp, Model 251 Alco-design powered locomotive and matching LRC passenger cars built at La Pocatière.

Facing stiff competition from Electro-Motive and General Electric, Bombardier succeeded in selling only small orders of HR412 and HR616 freight locomotives to Canadian National and LRC passenger locomotives and cars to VIA and Amtrak. Sales of MLW-design, Alco-powered export locomotives to countries including Greece, Tanzania, Malawi, Cameroon, Tunisia, Guatemala, and Bangladesh were the mainstay of the Montreal locomotive works during Bombardier's tenure. However, orders were insufficient, and the former MLW plant was closed and sold to GE in 1988.

Meanwhile, Bombardier's passenger-car and transit trade was increasing as it won contracts from passenger haulers and commuter agencies throughout North America. A 1982 order to build 825 R62A-class subway cars for New York City helped Bombardier gain a solid footing in the U.S. marketplace.

In order to meet growing demand, as well as satisfy the domestic content regulations of many U.S. agencies, Bombardier established assembly plants in Barre, Vermont, and Plattsburgh, New York. In addition, a parts plant in the former Alco engine plant in Auburn, New York, manufactures truck frames for cars assembled at Plattsburgh and Barre, as well as parts for Bombardier-built aircraft.

Bolstering its position in the railcar business, Bombardier purchased the passenger-car patents and designs of Pullman-Standard and the Budd Co. in 1987. Shortly thereafter Bombardier won contracts for several orders of passenger cars based on Pullman designs, including Comet commuter coaches for New Jersey Transit and Boston's Massachusetts Bay Transportation Authority (MBTA), along with Horizon intercity cars for Amtrak.

Continuing its expansion and diversification, Bombardier purchased the Canadian assets of the Urban Transit Development Corp. in February 1992. The UTDC acquisition included the headquarters, engineering offices, and light-rail rapid-transit equipment-manufacturing facility at Kingston, Ontario, as well as the passenger-car plant in Thunder Bay, Ontario.

Construction of the Thunder Bay plant (in what was known as the city of Fort William until amalgamation with its twin city of Port Arthur took place in January 1970) was begun in 1912 by the Canadian Car and Foundry Co. of Montreal, Quebec. A downturn in business delayed completion until 1917, but by 1918 the plant had secured orders for 5,000 boxcars for the Canadian Government Railways and 4,000 more for the Canadian Northern. Production peaked at 32 cars per day in May 1918. Other early orders included passenger cars for the Canadian Northern and 450 Hart-Otis dump cars for

the CGR. The Can-Car plant also tried its hand at ship-building in 1918, turning out a dozen minesweepers for the French government, as well as a Canadian-flagged freighter, the *E. D. Kingsley*.

Orders evaporated after World War I, and the plant stood silent until 1937, when it was retooled to produce aircraft. During and after World War II the Fort William plant produced more than 2,400 military aircraft, followed by almost 700 training aircraft, before aircraft production ended early in the 1950s. After World War II the Can-Car plant produced well over 4,000 buses, highway trailers and forestry equipment, and 100 PCC (Presidents' Conference Committee) streetcars for Toronto. British aircraft manufacturer A. V. Roe took over Can-Car in 1957. Avro was in turn taken over by U.K.-based Hawker Siddeley in 1962. The following year the Fort William facility took its first passenger-car order since the PCC cars of 1949: 164 H1-class subway cars, also for the Toronto Transit Commission. The Fort William design, with its extensive use of aluminum, allowed a two-ton weight reduction over earlier cars and gave the H1 the lowest weight/space ratio of any North American rapid-transit vehicle at the time.

On the heels of the TTC order came a deal to supply eight automated six-car trains (based on the H1 design) for Expo 67, the 1967 World's Fair in Montreal. Construction of the Expo Express equipment gave Hawker Siddeley's Fort William plant the distinction of building the first automated mass-transit system in North America.

Since then the plant has become one of North America's leading suppliers of transit vehicles, from subway cars for Toronto and New York's Part Authority Trans-Hudson (PATH) system and cars for Boston's MBTA to Canadian Light Rail Vehicle (CRLV) streetcars for Toronto and articulated streetcars for Santa Clara, California.

The Fort William plant's rebirth as a railcar builder was not limited to rapid-transit equipment. Coincident with the early TTC orders came contracts to supply Canadian National with 25 lightweight, aluminum-bodied, outside-disc-brake-equipped coaches and food-service cars for its new Toronto–Windsor/Sarnia Tempo trains; for final assembly of 150 CN cabooses (whose shells were built at Hawker Siddeley's Trenton, Nova Scotia, works); and to supply the Canadian government with 2 business cars for the governor general. The most significant order, though, was a contract to supply the newly formed Toronto, Ontario, area commuter agency GO Transit with equipment for its 1967 startup.

GO Transit initiated its Toronto Lakeshore commuter service with eight GMD-built GP40TC locomotives and 49 coaches built by Hawker Siddeley–Fort William: 40 94-seat coaches for diesel-hauled push-pull service and 9 self-propelled, Rolls Royce–powered railcars. As GO Transit's ridership and route-mileage expanded, the agency returned for more and more of the distinctive single-level HS coaches, but burgeoning passenger loads demanded another solution. In 1975 the Thunder Bay plant won a GO contract to design and build 80 bilevel commuter cars. In contrast with bilevel cars in use in other North American cities, which were of a "gallery" design with upper-level seating perched in open galleries above the main-floor seats, the new GO cars were to be true double-deckers. Developed in close cooperation with GO Transit personnel, the Hawker Siddeley bilevel commuter car, with control-cab options for push-pull operation and seating capacity for more than 160 passengers, set the standard for commuter equipment throughout North America for decades to come. GO Transit alone has purchased more than 370 Thunder Bay–built bilevels.

The Thunder Bay plant has changed hands, from Hawker Siddeley to UTDC-Lavalin control in the mid-1980s and to Bombardier in 1992, but its GO-inspired bilevel remains one of the most successful and best-selling commuter coach designs in North America. Their design refined over the decades, Thunder Bay–built bilevels have been sold to commuter agencies in U.S. and Canadian cities from coast to coast, including Los Angeles, San Diego, San Francisco–San Jose, and Stockton, California, Seattle, Washington, Miami, Florida, Vancouver, British Columbia, Dallas/Fort Worth, Texas, Virginia–Washington, D.C., and most recently, Montreal, Quebec.

While Thunder Bay concentrates on bilevel production, Bombardier's plants at La Pocatière, Quebec, Barre, Vermont, and Plattsburgh, New York, have produced hundreds of cars for transit agencies throughout North America, including more than 1,800 subway cars for the New York City Transit Authority. In addition, the plants have constructed commuter equipment for rail operators including New Jersey Transit, New York's Metro-North, the Connecticut Department of Transportation, Philadelphia's Southeastern Pennsylvania Transportation Authority (SEPTA), and Boston's MBTA.

In the late 1990s Bombardier and Alstom teamed to design and construct electric locomotives and trainsets for high-speed Acela service on Amtrak's 460-mile Boston–New York–Washington Northeast Corridor. Assembled at Bombardier's Barre and Plattsburgh plants, the Acela equipment includes eight 8,000-hp high-speed HHP-8 locomotives for use with Amfleet cars and 20 Acela trainsets consisting of two electric-powered cars bracketing a six-car consist including first-class and business-class cars, along with a café car. The trains began testing at the Department of Transportation facility near Pueblo, Colorado, in 1999, and revenue Acela service commenced in December 2000. The 150 mph trains cut 90 minutes from the Boston–New York schedules, and Washington–New York travel times have been reduced by 45 minutes.

In addition to its high-profile transit and rail passenger business in the United States and Canada, Bombardier has lesser-known operations in Mexico. Through its Mexican subsidiary, Bombardier-Concarril, S.A. de C.V., the company acquired railway rolling-stock manufacturer Constructora Nacional de Carros de Ferrocarril in 1992 and in 1998 formed a joint venture with Greenbrier to build freight cars in Mexico.

More than just freight cars roll from the shops of Bombardier-Concarril's Ciudad Sahagún shop. Long after the closure of Bombardier's former MLW locomotive plant in Montreal, the company is assembling locomotives for its onetime archrival Electro-Motive. Because of limited capacity at EMD's London, Ontario, locomotive plant, General Motors has contracted Bombardier-Concarril to assemble numerous orders of its SD70M locomotives. Since 1997 Bombardier's Ciudad Sahagún facility has outshopped nearly 1,000 SD70M's for Burlington Northern Santa Fe, Union Pacific, and Mexico's Transportación Ferroviaria Mexicana.

With the acquisition of European firms, Bombardier has become a rail and transit concern with worldwide holdings and activities. Since the 1988 acquisition of Belgian railway equipment manufacturer BN Constructions Ferroviaires et Métalliques S.A., Bombardier has continued to expand in Europe and Asia. ANF-Industrie, the second-largest manufacturer of railway equipment in France, became a Bombardier holding in December 1989, followed by Britain's Procor Engineering, a builder of passenger-car and locomotive carbodies, in November 1990. In 1998 Bombardier acquired German equipment manufacturer Deutsche Waggonbau A.G. and entered a cooperative venture with Canada's Power Corp. and China's Sifang Locomotive & Rolling Stock Works of Quingdao to produce transit equipment.

The May 2001 acquisition of Adtranz, a wholly owned subsidiary of German-based DaimlerChrysler A.G., has been Bombardier's most significant addition to date. A builder of diesel and electric locomotives, high-speed, intercity, and regional trains, and transit equipment, as well as signal and traffic control systems and infrastructure installations, Adtranz came with 22,000 employees and facilities in 19 countries on four continents. The Adtranz acquisition cemented Bombardier's position as a world leader in the design and manufacture of railway locomotives, cars, and transit equipment. Included in the transaction was the famed Henschel locomotive works in Kassel, Germany. Even as Bombardier was negotiating the Adtranz purchase, American locomotives were taking shape on the shop floor in Kassel. Illustrating the global nature of its business, Bombardier delivered the first of 29 Kassel-built ALP46 electrics—based on the design of German Railways' Class 101 locomotives—to New Jersey Transit in October 2001.

In addition to manufacture and design of rail and transit equipment, Bombardier also designs and builds total transit systems and holds service and maintenance contracts with transit agencies and rail passenger operators throughout the world. A long way from its humble beginnings in that Valcourt workshop, Bombardier has become a Montreal-based supplier with approximately 80,000 people in its rail and nonrail businesses in 24 countries throughout the world.

Bombardier rail equipment-manufacturing facilities in North America include the following:

La Pocatière, Quebec: transit vehicles, rail passenger cars
Kingston, Ontario (former UTDC): transit vehicles
Thunder Bay, Ontario (former Can-Car): transit and rail passenger cars
Barre, Vermont: transit vehicles, rail passenger cars, Acela
Plattsburgh, New York: transit vehicles, passenger cars, Acela
Ciudad Sahagún, Mexico: freight cars, EMD locomotive assembly.

—Greg McDonnell

REFERENCE

Burkowski, Gordon. *A History of Can-Car, 1912–1992*. Thunder Bay, Ont.: Bombardier, 1995.

See also LOCOMOTIVE BUILDERS.

Boston & Maine Railroad

The Boston & Maine (B&M) was not so much built as it was assembled, mostly at the end of the nineteenth century, from other railroad systems: the Eastern, Boston & Lowell, Fitchburg, and Connecticut River railroads. The Andover & Wilmington Railroad, the B&M's earliest corporate predecessor, opened in 1836 from Andover, Massachusetts, south to a junction with the Boston & Lowell at Wilmington, about seven miles. Over the next few years the Andover & Wilmington was extended northeast across the southeast portion of New Hampshire to North Berwick, Maine. The railroad companies, one for each state, were consolidated under the name of the New Hampshire company, the Boston & Maine Railroad. At North Berwick the Portland, Saco & Portsmouth Railroad provided a connection to Portland, Maine.

B&M opened its own line from North Wilmington through Reading to Boston in 1845. There followed a boom in railroad construction in eastern Massachusetts as the three principal railroads in the area, B&M, Boston & Lowell, and Eastern (Boston to Portsmouth, New Hampshire, opened in 1840), built branches into each other's territory.

Eastern

The Eastern Railroad opened in 1840 from Boston northeast along the coast to Portsmouth, New Hampshire. Its route was several miles shorter than the Boston & Maine's, but at the expense of a ferry connection across Boston Harbor. In 1854 the Eastern opened a roundabout route to a terminal in Boston proper. The B&M and the Eastern competed vigorously at the south end of the Boston-Portland route; the two roads jointly leased the Portland, Saco & Portsmouth. The Eastern obtained control of the Maine Central Railroad, which ran north and east from Portland. In an attempt to control the Boston-Portland traffic, the Eastern canceled the lease of the PS&P. The Boston & Maine, which carried most of the traffic, built its own line from North Berwick to Portland. The Eastern and the B&M agreed to end the worst of the competition, and in 1883 B&M leased the Eastern and acquired control of the Maine Central.

Boston & Lowell

The Boston & Lowell Railroad opened in 1835 between Boston and the new industrial city of Lowell, Massachusetts, 26 miles north on the Merrimac River. The new railroad could operate all year; the Middlesex Canal, which it replaced, froze in the winter and dried up in the summer.

Soon other railroads reached north from Lowell alongside the Merrimac River to Nashua, Manchester, and Concord, New Hampshire. After a railroad war in the New Hampshire legislature, the Boston & Lowell leased itself to the Boston & Maine in 1887. In 1895 the B&M leased the Concord & Montreal Railroad and became the dominant railroad in New Hampshire.

Fitchburg

The Fitchburg Railroad opened from Boston to Fitchburg, Massachusetts, in 1845. The Vermont & Massachusetts extended the line west from Fitchburg over a range of hills to the Connecticut River near Greenfield, then turned north, reaching Brattleboro, Vermont, in 1850. In 1873 the Fitchburg leased the Vermont & Massachusetts.

As early as 1819 there was a proposal for a canal across northern Massachusetts, using a tunnel to penetrate Hoosac Mountain, which stood between the valleys of the Deerfield and Hoosic rivers. The proposal for a canal later changed to one for a railroad from Boston to the Great Lakes at Oswego or Buffalo, New York. The tunnel was begun in 1851 by the Commonwealth of Massachusetts, which also built the Troy & Greenfield Railroad west from Greenfield to the east portal of the Hoosac Tunnel and a short portion west of the future tunnel.

The Troy & Boston Railroad opened in the early 1850s from Troy, New York, north to the Hoosic River. By 1859 the Troy & Boston, the Southern Vermont (8 miles across the southwest corner of Vermont), and the 7-mile-long western portion of the Troy & Greenfield formed a route from Troy to North Adams, Massachusetts.

As the Hoosac Tunnel neared completion in 1875, two other railroads began construction. The Massachusetts Central was projected west from Boston to a connection with the Troy & Greenfield near the Hoosac Tunnel, and the Boston, Hoosac Tunnel & Western Railroad was to run west from the tunnel to Oswego, New York. They constituted a threat to the Fitchburg, which wanted to control the Hoosac Tunnel. The state would allow that only if the Fitchburg had its own route to the Hudson River. Accordingly, in 1887 the Fitchburg consolidated with the Troy & Boston and the Troy & Greenfield and in 1892 with the Boston, Hoosac Tunnel & Western, which had reached the Mohawk River at Rotterdam, New York. (The Massachusetts Central never became more than a local railroad from Boston to Northampton, Massachusetts.)

In 1899 the New York Central considered leasing either the Boston & Albany or the Fitchburg to reach Boston. When NYC chose the B&A, the Boston & Maine leased the Fitchburg.

Connecticut River

A chain of six railroads ran along the Connecticut River from Springfield, Massachusetts, to the Canadian border at Newport, Vermont. Most were under the control of the Connecticut River Railroad. In 1893, during a brief foray into New England, the Philadelphia & Reading secured control of the Connecticut River Railroad and leased it to the B&M.

By the early twentieth century the B&M had attained its greatest reach, with principal routes radiating from Boston northeast to Portland, Maine, northwest through New Hampshire to the Canadian border, and west to Troy and Schenectady, New York. A route north along the Connecticut River connected with the routes through New Hampshire; the B&M controlled all the railroading in the southern half of Maine and had a strong presence in Vermont. Through much of its territory B&M had secondary and duplicate routes. In 1911 the railroad completed an electrification of its line through the long (4.7 miles) Hoosac Tunnel.

As a passenger carrier, the B&M was isolated by the lack of a rail line through Boston and by its terminal at Troy, a few miles short of Albany. Nevertheless, it operated through trains between New York and the resort areas of Maine (the trains ran through Worcester, Massachusetts, on a route as advantageous for freight as it was seemingly circuitous for passengers), and until 1946 it sent a sleeping car to Chicago via Troy and Albany. It operated an extremely dense network of suburban service in northeastern Massachusetts—even as late as the early 1950s B&M commuter trains connected Boston with towns on at least 15 different routes.

The New Haven, expanding under the leadership of Charles S. Mellen, acquired control of the B&M in 1907. In 1914 the New Haven's B&M stock was placed in the hands of trustees for eventual sale, and that same year B&M sold its Maine Central stock. B&M was placed in receivership in 1916.

After World War I B&M absorbed several of its components, returned several shortlines to independent operation, leased its lines north of Wells River, Vermont, to the Canadian Pacific, and began to abandon some of its weakest redundant branch lines. Floods in 1936 and a hurricane in 1938 brought the abandonment of several more branches.

By the early 1950s the B&M was a modern, efficient railroad. In 1935 the B&M, with the Maine Central, had acquired the stainless-steel diesel-electric streamliner *Flying Yankee*, a near duplicate of the Burlington's pioneer *Zephyr*, and the road was an early convert to diesel-electric motive power, completing the transition to diesel power in 1956. Its Boston commuter services were operated with the largest North American fleet of Budd Rail Diesel Cars. But the B&M's territory was losing its industrial base, and superhighways were under construction everywhere. In 1958 the railroad posted a deficit on its ledgers, and the deficits continued in the following years. By the mid-1960s all interstate passenger service was gone, and the road operated only suburban service subsidized by the Massachusetts Bay Transportation Authority (MBTA).

On March 23, 1970, B&M declared bankruptcy. By the end of the year B&M's trustees had chosen John W. Barriger III to be chief executive officer. Barriger retired at the end of 1972, having made a start at rerailing the B&M. Rather than split the B&M among its connections or ask for its inclusion in Conrail, B&M's trustees decided to reorganize independently. Under the leadership of Alan Dustin, the B&M bought new locomotives and rebuilt its track. It sold the tracks and rolling stock used by its commuter operations to MBTA in 1975, but retained freight rights on those lines and continued to operate the commuter trains for MBTA. In 1982 it purchased several lines in Massachusetts and Connecticut from Conrail.

A revived Boston & Maine was purchased in 1983 by Timothy Mellon's Guilford Transportation Industries, which had bought the Maine Central in 1981 and in 1984 would buy the Delaware & Hudson. Guilford began operating the three railroads as a unified system, selling unprofitable lines, closing redundant yards and shops, and eliminating jobs. Employees went on strike. Guilford leased most of the B&M and the Maine Central to the Springfield Terminal, a shortline subsidiary, to take advantage of work rules. By the end of the twentieth century the B&M consisted principally of a freight route from Portland, Maine, to Mechanicville, New York. Its owner, Guilford Transportation Industries, developed a reputation for independence and bellicosity. The inauguration of Amtrak service between Boston and Portland in 2002 was delayed for more than a decade because of Guilford's intransigence.

In 1981 Boston & Maine operated a system of 1,317 route-miles and 2,122 track-miles, with 151 locomotives, 3,544 freight and company service cars, and 3,146 employees. The principal items of freight traffic were pulp and paper products (25 percent), chemicals and plastics (11 percent), grain-mill products (8 percent), and food products (8 percent). Boston & Maine operating revenues totaled $122 million, and the railroad achieved a 101 percent operating ratio.

—George H. Drury

REFERENCES

Baker, George Pierce. *The Formation of the New England Railroad Systems*. Cambridge, Mass.: Harvard Univ. Press, 1937.

Harlow, Alvin F. *Steelways of New England*. New York: Creative Age Press, 1946.

Kyper, Frank. *Philip Ross Hastings: The Boston & Maine; A Photographic Essay*. Richmond, Vt.: Locomotive & Railway Preservation, 1989.

Neal, R. M. *High Green and the Bark Peelers*. New York: Duell, Sloan & Pearce, 1950.

Brady, James Buchanan "Diamond Jim" (1856–1917)

One of railroading's most colorful tycoons, James Brady was born to an Irish immigrant who kept a saloon in the slums at Cedar and West streets in New York, a block from what would much later be the World Trade Center. Brady received little formal education and left school at age 11 to become a hotel bellboy, where he came into regular contact with the swells and nabobs of New York society and was determined to join their ranks.

The way upward for a half-literate Irish lad was difficult, but he showed tremendous energy. While still a teenager he took a job as a baggageman at the old Grand Central Station and later became a ticket agent at the nearby New York Central station at Spuyten Duyvil. He was noticed by the railroad's general manager, John M. Toucey, who brought Brady into headquarters as a clerk. Before he was out of his teens, Brady was promoted to chief clerk in Toucey's office, where he gained an encyclopedic knowledge of every aspect of railroad operation. He also earned a handsome salary of $50 a month, allowing him to become a young man about town. He spent all of his disposable income on fancy clothes and meals in good restaurants.

In 1879 Charles A. Moore of the railroad supply firm of Manning, Maxwell & Moore was looking for an equipment salesman, and Toucey recommended Brady. While Brady's language was not refined, he had purchased for himself a splendid wardrobe, which helped him get into a railroad president's office. Brady's philosophy was "to make money you have to look like money." Railroads flourished in the coming decade, and in no time at all, working strictly on commission, Brady became Manning, Maxwell & Moore's top salesman.

Brady became a millionaire with great suddenness. In 1888 an Englishman named Sampson Fox, who owned a forging company in Leeds, arrived in America to promote a lightweight all-steel railroad truck that was being used with great success in England. Fox could not get hide-bound railroad executives to give the device a try. He asked Charles Moore for advice, and Moore suggested that this was something Brady could do as a sideline; Brady could sell anything.

Brady took up the idea with the understanding that he would own one-third of the American manufacturing arm, which soon involved a manufacturing plant in Joliet, Illinois. More important, Brady sold the idea to American railroads and made a considerable fortune in the bargain. In time, Brady had large interests in numerous other railroad industries, including Reading Car Wheel Co., Buffalo Car Wheel Co., and Magnus Steel. He also became involved in numerous stock deals, including an attempt to take over the Louisville & Nashville Railroad.

So successful was Brady that he could afford to devote most of his time to high living. He bought racehorses and was an avid theatergoer. While he never smoked or drank, he was a great trencherman. The owner of a prominent New York lobster palace declared that Brady was the "best twenty-five customers he ever had." Brady was known to consume six dozen Lynnhaven oysters at a sitting. One friend joked that Brady liked his steaks smothered in veal cutlets. For dessert he occasionally ate an entire five-pound box of chocolates.

Brady's nickname came from his large jewelry collection—he was said to own at least 30 complete sets. On one occasion Brady displayed an enormous diamond on his shirtfront, which some friend suggested might be a bit gaudy. Brady responded, "Them as has 'em wears 'em." An affable man, he was always showering his friends with gifts. Once when hospitalized he gave a small diamond to every nurse in the hospital. When Brady died in 1917, he left a considerable portion of his fortune to establish the James Buchanan Brady Urological Institute at the Johns Hopkins Medical School, still one of the most famous of its kind in the world.

—George H. Douglas

REFERENCE

Jeffers, H. Paul. *Diamond Jim Brady: Prince of the Gilded Age*. New York: John Wiley & Sons, 2001.

Bridges. *See* CIVIL ENGINEERING

British Columbia Electric Railway

The largest Canadian interurban was the Vancouver-centered British Columbia Electric Railway, which also operated urban streetcar services in Vancouver and Victoria and supplied electric power to much of the province. The earliest section of the line between Vancouver and New Westminster was built in 1891, and by 1913 BCE had completed a system of 125 miles on six routes, including an isolated 22-mile line between Victoria and Deep Cove on Vancouver Island. Most of BCE's lines were long suburban routes serving the Vancouver urban area; a 77-mile interurban line extended east across the Fraser River and through the fertile Fraser Valley area to Chilliwack.

BCE acquired a diverse variety of passenger equipment from Canadian and U.S. builders, as well as cars constructed in its own shops. Three handsome arched-roof, Romanesque-windowed cars built in BCE's own shops in 1911 in honor of a visit by the Duke of Connaught were always identified thereafter as the Connaught Cars. Freight motive power included the typical General Electric and Baldwin-Westinghouse light electric locomotives, as well as three not-so-typical electrics built by Great Britain's Dick Kerr.

BCE's shorter interurban routes radiating from Vancouver transported heavy passenger traffic. By far the busiest was the 12-mile Central Park line, which linked downtown Vancouver with the city of New Westminster. At one time some 60 daily trains were operated over the line, carrying fully half of BCE's 5 million annual interurban passengers.

Freight traffic was always important to British Columbia Electric, which enjoyed close interchange arrangements with the connecting steam railroads. For the long Chilliwack line, freight was more important than passengers. Logs and timber and fruit, vegetables, and milk from the Fraser Valley were among the principal products carried. Oats and hay were among the principal freight items on the line to Lulu Island, south of Vancouver.

Twenty steel cars delivered in 1913 turned out to be the last new equipment ever acquired by BCE, yet the line continued to operate virtually its entire system until well after 1950. The isolated line at Victoria was closed in 1924, but the system otherwise continued almost intact through World War II. BCE began to make plans for motorbus conversions after the war, and the first line to be shut down was the long Fraser Valley line, which ended passenger operation in 1950. The last passenger interurban line to close was an 8-mile route between Marpole and Stevenson in 1958.

Freight service, however, continued to operate over almost the entire BCE system, which was sold to the provincial government and became the British Columbia Hydro & Power Authority in 1961. Diesel-electric power took over the trains, although a couple of electric locomotives continued to switch one yard for a more than a decade. The Fraser Valley line was sold to the Southern Railway of British Columbia in 1988, which now operates 75 miles of main line between New Westminster and Chilliwack and carries more than 50,000 carloads of freight annually. Other remaining portions of the former BCE track have been absorbed by mainline railroads.

—William D. Middleton

REFERENCE

Kelly, Brian, and Daniel Francis. *Transit in British Columbia: The First Hundred Years.* Madeira Park, B.C.: Harbour, 1990.

British Columbia Railway.

See BC RAIL

Brosnan, Dennis William, II (1903–1985)

D. W. "Bill" Brosnan, one of the most influential railroad executives of the mid-twentieth century, was born on a farm near Albany, Georgia. He attended public high school, graduated from Georgia Tech in 1923, and joined Southern Railway in 1926. Brosnan began his career at Southern in the railroad's student apprentice program, which was designed to acquaint bright young college graduates with railroad fundamentals and groom them for careers in management. He spent 12 years progressing through Southern's engineering department before switching to the transportation department as a trainmaster at Oakdale, Tennessee, in 1938, later serving in the same role at Birmingham, Alabama. By the fall of 1938 he was promoted to division superintendent at Selma, Alabama.

Less than two years later, in May 1940, Bill Brosnan transferred to the division superintendent's post at Macon, Georgia, and then was made superintendent at Birmingham in February 1943. By this time he had caught the eye of Vice President for Operations Harry DeButts, who mentored him through subsequent promotions, first as chief engineer, maintenance-of-way and structures, of Western Lines at Cincinnati (in February 1946), then as general manager of Central Lines at Knoxville a year later. When DeButts became Southern's president in 1952, he named Brosnan to succeed him as vice president for operations at the company's headquarters in Washington, D.C.

From this point on, Brosnan transformed Southern from a progressive railroad to a revolutionary one. His vision, nerve, drive, leadership, and ruthlessness pushed Southern to modernize relentlessly. He realized earlier than most that postwar inflation and rising labor costs would overwhelm routine efficiencies if they were left unchecked. His first strategy was to explain to his supervisors that the future of the company lay in their hands. Brosnan promised that if they helped him realize his vision, no supervisor would be laid off, although thousands of rank-and-file jobs would, of necessity, be eliminated.

Brosnan's next strategy was to implement dozens of new processes necessary to maintain and operate the railroad: mechanized track maintenance, centralized diesel locomotive repair, automated freight classification yards, microwave communications, and computerized accounting functions. All used cutting-edge—frequently home-grown—hardware and were largely built or inaugurated with internally generated funds.

By the time Brosnan succeeded DeButts as president in 1962, the number of Southern's employees had shrunk from 37,000 to 18,000. Southern was one of only a handful of railroads to report better financial and operating results in the second half of the 1950s than in the first half.

Although Brosnan's tenure as president was relatively brief (1962–1967), it was remarkable. The hallmarks were the creation of a department to market the railroad's services (a poorly understood concept in the industry at the time) and the triumph of the Big John rate case. Like all railroads, Southern was regulated heavily by the Interstate Commerce Commission (ICC), which in 1960 still set railroad rates high enough to "protect" competing forms of transportation, such as trucks and barges. Under Brosnan, Southern bought aluminum Big John covered hopper cars to transport grain, 100 tons at a time. The efficiencies of using the new cars, compared with the standard 40-foot boxcar, were colossal: Southern filed new rates that were more than 50 percent lower, but increased the railroad's margins.

Competitors cried foul, the ICC held hearings, and Brosnan and the Southern fought back. After four years of deliberation, 13 hearings before federal appellate courts, and two trips to the U.S. Supreme Court, Southern prevailed in 1965. The Big John case was the first domino to fall on the path to railroad deregulation, which occurred (albeit imperfectly) 15 years later.

Among employees, Brosnan was both respected and feared. His capricious firing and rehiring of managers were legendary. He was the master of the stretch goal, demanding new equipment or services in absurdly short time frames. He rarely took "no" for an answer. More often than not, his managers remained loyal and came through for him. His deficiencies in people skills were more than offset by his ability to achieve his visions.

Two of his chief lieutenants were Bob Hamilton and Stanley Crane. Hamilton, a crusty automotive engineer when Brosnan hired him, helped design many of the new machines in the 1950s and in the 1960s organized and ruled Southern's unorthodox but effective marketing department. A career railroader with a superb intellect, Crane rose through Southern's Research & Tests Depart-

ment, designed key processes and equipment, and later became Southern's eighth (and subsequently Conrail's second) president.

Brosnan died on June 14, 1985, in Asheville, North Carolina, at age 82. His contribution to railroading was that he anticipated the trends of the time and adjusted the performance of his company accordingly. Among Southern railway firsts or near firsts on his watch were 100-ton freight cars, unit trains, distributed locomotive power, a scheduled railroad with freight trains running on regular schedules, a marketing department that truly marketed, wireless communication, and computerization—all mainstays today, but rarities when Bill Brosnan began his bold makeover in the early 1950s.

—G. William Schafer

REFERENCE

Morgret, Charles O. *Brosnan: The Railroads' Messiah.* 2 vols. New York: Vantage Press, 1996.

Brunel, Isambard Kingdom (1806–1859)

A British engineer and one of the great early railway pioneers, Isambard Kingdom Brunel was the son of Marc Isambard Brunel, a well-known French engineer working in London. Educated in Paris, Isambard joined his father in London, and the two worked together on the Thames Tunnel, the first to be built using the shield method. The two also worked on what became the accepted design for the Clifton Suspension Bridge in Bristol. The younger Brunel, a man of forceful personality and determined manner, in 1833 won the position of chief engineer of the proposed Great Western Railway between London and Bristol. With the foresight to see that railroads were likely to develop much larger locomotives than then existed, Brunel designed his line to a 7-foot gauge, in contrast to the 4-foot 8½-inch gauge used by George Stephenson for his early common-carrier railroads.

The Great Western Railway eventually built 1,000 miles of track and was completed in 1841. Brunel, who always considered himself a generalist rather than a specialist in engineering, moved on to other major projects. Today he is probably best known for some steamships he designed during the 1840s and 1850s. Hoping to compete vigorously with the Cunard Line, Brunel built three enormous steamships: the *Great Western*, the *Great Britain*, and the *Great Eastern*. Brunel worked on numerous other railway projects and designed tunnels and bridges. His great wrought-iron Royal Albert Bridge at Saltash is regarded as a masterpiece of its kind.

—George H. Douglas

REFERENCE

Rolt, L. T. C. *Isambard Kingdom Brunel*. London: Longmans, Green, 1957.

Bryant, Gridley (1789–1867)

Gridley Bryant, the reputed "inventor" of the "First American Railroad," was not treated kindly by fate in his later years or by recent historians. The originality of his accomplishment in designing the Granite Railway in Quincy, Massachusetts, which opened in 1826, was much exaggerated at the time, and more recently there has been a tendency to disparage both Bryant and the historical significance of his railroad. Yet the fact remains that he was a highly skilled engineer and designer, and his short railway was the first in North America to be successful for its intended purpose over an extended period of time.

Bryant was born in Scituate, Massachusetts, on August 26, 1789. He came from a poor family, and his father died when he was a child. As a young boy, he showed considerable mechanical aptitude and in later life reminisced about being recognized among his playmates as the ideal "chief engineer" for play construction projects such as forts and cabins. His mother apprenticed him to a Boston building contractor, and he quickly showed talent as a builder and manager. In 1808 he was placed in complete charge of his employer's operations, then struck out on his own as a contractor two years later. In 1823 he invented a portable derrick for a bank-building project; the design later came into general use.

For the Granite Railway, Bryant designed and installed North America's first swiveled-truck cars, split-point switches, and turntable. He was widely but questionably credited with having invented these devices; in fact, all had been used in Europe beforehand. It is assumed that Bryant had studied British railway technology; the degree to which he conceived these designs independently is unknown.

In the years after the completion of the Granite Railway, Bryant continued to own and operate the quarry it served. He devoted most of his energy to the quarry and his contracting business, for the most part avoiding involvement in the expansion of the railroad industry. But he was drawn back into railroad matters when he was called upon several times to testify on behalf of railroads defending against patent-infringement suits brought by Ross Winans to enforce Winans's patent for an eight-wheeled swiveled-truck car. This litigation began in 1838 and was not finally settled until 1859, when the Winans patent was invalidated because its claims were ruled to be too broad.

In the last years of Bryant's life business losses placed him in difficult financial circumstances. During that time he received repeated promises of remuneration for the services he had rendered with respect to the Winans patent litigation, but the payments were never forthcoming. He died on June 13, 1867. A son, Gridley James Fox Bryant, who had trained in his father's office, went on to become a prominent and prolific architect and builder responsible for many public buildings in Boston.

—Adrian Ettlinger

REFERENCES

Dictionary of American Biography.

Reed, Roger G. "To Exist for Centuries: Gridley [J. F.] Bryant and the Boston City Hospital." *Old Time New England* 77, no. 266. Boston: Society for the Preservation of New England Antiquities, 1999.

Stuart, Charles B. *Lives and Works of Civil and Military Engineers of America*. New York: D. Van Nostrand, 1871.

Budd Co. (Edward G. Budd Manufacturing Co.)

Edward Gowen Budd (born in Smyrna, Delaware, December 28, 1870; died in Germantown, Pennsylvania, November 30, 1946, aged 75) built one of the nation's leading transportation manufacturing firms. A 1937 *Fortune* magazine profile reported that Budd exhibited "an impatience with the slowness of progress." Even the officers of the Pullman-Standard Car Manufacturing Co., his major rival, concurred, terming him "a go-getter" and praising his competitive ability.

Private, modest, and quiet-spoken, Budd also was something of a showman. Once, in order to demonstrate the strength of his firm's all-steel automobile body, he perched an elephant atop one and challenged his rivals, all of whom produced composite wood and metal car-bodies, to do the same. Of course, they could not.

From childhood Budd exhibited an inclination for the mechanical. At 17 he apprenticed to a local Smyrna machine shop; two years later he hired on with the Philadelphia firm of William Sellers & Co., a leader in the railroad supply sector. By 1895 he had begun experimenting with steel pressings. Budd's biographer, Mark E. Reutter, points out that he was among the first to appreciate the "superior properties of thin pressed steel." Budd found that the new material was both strong and light in weight, in contrast to wood, which, although light in weight, suffered from weakness, and cast iron, which was heavy and brittle.

In 1902 Budd joined Hale & Kilburn Manufacturing Co., makers of railway car seats, as plant superintendent, where he was instrumental in introducing the pressed-steel railway car seat in 1904. The new product proved his first success. Many others followed. From 1904 to 1908 Budd was involved in the design of the revolutionary gasoline-powered self-propelled McKeen railcar. Hale & Kilburn produced the car's innovative all-around exterior steel sheathing, which covered its roof and underbelly in addition to the car sides and was intended to increase crash strength. Still, the McKeen car proved an operational and marketing failure, largely because of problems with the mechanical drive. In 1908 Budd pioneered pressed steel as the interior finish of the first generation of all-steel passenger cars. He subsequently produced the first steel interiors for Pullman's first several thousand steel sleepers.

In 1912 Budd founded his own firm, the Edward G. Budd Manufacturing Co., in Philadelphia with the objective of developing sheet-metal stampings and entering the auto-fabricating business. His new venture made its reputation in the production of steel automobile and truck bodies. Charles Nash, president of General Motors, placed the firm's first order, for bodies for Oakland Touring cars, that same year. John and Horace Dodge soon followed, ordering 5,000 bodies in 1914 and continuing as Budd's best customer through the 1920s.

During World War I Budd began building welded all-steel auto bodies. Until then, manufacturers had used steel plates to reinforce wooden frames. Budd's was the first integral unit. The firm also proved a successful innovator in the closely related product line of steel automotive wheels, produced by subsidiary Budd Wheel Corp., organized in Philadelphia in 1916. This combination of an expanded product line and overall business growth prompted the establishment of a Detroit division in 1925. Indeed, the auto business remained the firm's bread and butter throughout its existence.

Budd focused marketing and advertising strategy on his firm's unique efforts to square "weight with strength in transportation and machinery." In 1926 he introduced an advertising campaign produced by Young & Rubicam and designed to speak directly to the automobile consumer, rather than to manufacturers. The initiative emphasized safety by pointing out that railroads had long ago adopted all-steel construction for safety's sake. Testimonials by experts such as PRR president W. W. Atterbury effectively reinforced copy claims.

The Budd firm maintained a positive outlook in the face of economic contraction. In the fall of 1930 it built the first entirely stainless-steel airplane, an amphibious seaplane that actually flew. A year later, in September 1931, it entered into a licensing agreement with the Michelin Co., a French tire manufacturer, to produce a rubber-tired all-mechanical rail motor car. The first Micheline railcar was completed in February 1932. In 1932–1933 Budd manufactured examples for three domestic clients, Reading, PRR, and Texas & Pacific. While all failed in service, they provided valuable experience in carbody design and the mechanics of self-propulsion for projects to follow.

Edward Budd's interest in the physical properties of stainless steel dates to 1930, when his firm began experiments in the alloy's application to transportation. Alloy steels had been introduced in the mid-1920s. By 1928

Budd had become aware of a "certain family of chromium steels, known as stainless steels." A particular alloy identified as 18-8 demonstrated unusual properties. An alloy of chromium and nickel added to high-grade carbon steel, stainless steel became known for its noncorrosive, low-maintenance qualities and especially for its strength. The new material was also well suited to the precepts of modern design.

Budd introduced the lightweight stainless-steel diesel-powered passenger train on April 9, 1934, the Burlington *Zephyr*. Reutter argues that "the train represented a quantum leap in technology, which badly upset [Budd's] rivals and forced other manufacturers to innovate to keep up with his improvements or perish." Unfortunately for Budd, even though the stream of copies by others that followed proved inferior, the new product registered only a marginal improvement in profitability.

For over a decade Budd cars alone were made of stainless steel, assembled by means of a unique and patented technological breakthrough, the Shotweld process. Invented by the firm's chief engineer, Col. Earl James Wilson Ragsdale, this method of joining stainless steel relied upon electrical adhesion to produce a weld with no discernible joints, no addition of metal, and no smoothing off by grinding. Lasting for only a split second, its process of heat buildup produced a joint stronger than the surrounding metal. (Experience by trial and error had shown that the lengthy heat absorption of conventional welding processes broke down the stainless-steel alloy.) It also proved to be remarkably strong, offering more overall strength with half the weight of its all-steel alternative. Perhaps most important, the alloy's corrosion-free, ever-glistening surface never required paint and attracted passengers like bees to honey.

Budd grew the streamlined passenger-car market with aggressive marketing. In collaboration with Philadelphia architect and designer Paul P. Cret, Budd produced dramatically stylish trains, notably CB&Q's 1936 *Denver Zephyr* and AT&SF's Native American–themed *Super Chief* of 1937. Significantly, Budd sold full trains, not just cars, that it specially designed to meet the defining characteristics of a particular route: market size, railroad operating capacity, scenery, competition. *Trains* magazine editor David P. Morgan credited Colonel Ragsdale as the source of this "militant merchandising."

Nonetheless, many carriers were ambivalent about purchasing Budd's silver cars. In fact, as late as March 1937 New York Central president Frederick E. Williamson and Pennsylvania president Martin W. Clement were negotiating the joint purchase of a single Budd coach to be tested by the companies' engineering staffs. Others ostensibly demurred for reasons of corporate identity, wanting to retain the distinctive paint schemes and corporate colors that travelers had come to associate with their names. PRR's Clement, NYC's Williamson, and even UP's Averell Harriman expressed the desire to maintain their trademark colors.

The Budd Co. developed an entirely new technology for car construction using its Shotweld process for welding stainless steel. This was the rear observation compartment for the radical new *Pioneer Zephyr* of 1934. —Burlington Northern Santa Fe Archives

Beginning in 1936, Budd introduced a long-running advertising campaign intended to address this shared skepticism about the safety and durability of its new designs. Headlines such as "Why is this the Safest form of Travel?" (July 1936) asserted that its cars were stronger, lighter, and safer than any other type of construction. Five years later, advertising copy asked: "Can a Railroad Train be 'TOO SAFE'?" (January 1941). In other ads Budd sought to outmaneuver the railroaders' reticence by advertising over their heads in a direct appeal to consumers—the travelers themselves—as he had first done in 1926.

The intense competition with Pullman and the railroaders' reticence and skeptical dismissal of Budd's new claims furthered the firm's need for aggressive marketing strategies. Stymied by Pullman's use of its monopoly power to undercut his firm's sleeping-car innovations, Budd responded with the concept of the fast and luxurious overnight all-coach train. Imaginatively dubbed Sleeper-Coach service and debuting with Seaboard Air Line's *Silver Meteor* of 1939, the trains proved an effective counter to Pullman's conservative ways. They targeted the Pullman Co.'s prime customer, the overnight-section sleeping-car passenger, while eliminating the contract premium that Pullman charged to each carrier, thereby affording substantially improved operating margins at a time of economic distress.

For all Budd's aggressive innovation, the passenger railcar market remained an opportunity never fully realized. Through 1940 Pullman-Standard continued to maintain its traditional dominance of the market, manufacturing 1,000 lightweight cars to Budd's 300. While Budd's ad agency, N. W. Ayer & Son of Philadelphia, promoted its

Budd aggressively promoted the greater strength and comfort of its new stainless-steel streamliners. "What happens when a Zephyr, traveling at high speed, slams into a snow-drift? Nothing, so far as any passenger can tell!" boasted the car builder. —Michael E. Zega Collection

client's new trains as "the most profitable idea in railroading," the hard realities of the railroad industry's competitive position dictated otherwise.

In the postwar era Budd maintained its stance in the face of rail travelers' shift en masse to other modes. But its achievements proved too little, too late as the huge postwar backlog of orders vanished overnight to be replaced with pessimism. Still, the firm's tradition of innovative leadership continued in response to competitive inroads.

In 1946, anticipating a substantial postwar expansion, Budd leased the sprawling government-owned Red Lion plant at Bustleton, Pennsylvania. Its vast assembly bays provided a stunning contrast to the cramped and antiquated quarters of its first plant, opened in 1915 at North Philadelphia, dwarfing railcar frames being built on the assembly line.

The passenger-car market quickly unraveled: from a war-deferred peak of 2,993 cars ordered in 1945, the number plummeted to just 109 in 1949. Still, it fell to Budd to introduce the era's most popular innovations: producing both the prototype Vista-Dome car (1945) and the bulk of the design's production and introducing enclosed toilets in sleeping-car double bedrooms (1946). Its self-propelled, bidirectional Rail Diesel Car (RDC) of November 1949 introduced streamliner comfort and performance to local and branch-line operations, heretofore neglected, and proved enduringly efficient and reliable, especially as a commuter vehicle.

During the 1950s innovative designs kept the firm in business. The all-room economy sleeper Siesta Coach was introduced in 1953, the same year that *Trains* reported Budd's total output at some 1,600 cars. The year 1956 saw the first sales of the economy sleeper design, newly renamed Slumbercoach, and the double-decker long-distance train, Santa Fe's groundbreaking *El Capitan*. To its credit, the firm energetically promoted the streamliners' profit and loss performance, commissioning industrywide studies by the engineering firm Coverdale & Colpitts throughout the postwar years.

Unfortunately, the firm's most innovative proposals fared poorly and were never brought to market. These included private showers in all multiple-passenger sleeping-car accommodations (1946) and the Pioneer III family of ultralightweight economy passenger-car designs (1956). (Pioneer III saw limited production as an electric multiple-unit commuter coach in 1958.)

Budd's products registered modest overseas sales. By 1954 the firm's advertisements reported that RDCs operated in Australia, Cuba, and Saudi Arabia. During the 1960s, 80 duplex single-room sleepers for Wagons-Lits used Budd patents, and Australia's transcontinental train, the *Indian-Pacific*, received new Budd-licensed equipment late in the decade.

In 1965 Budd was named a partner in the Northeast Corridor project, along with the federal government and the Pennsylvania Railroad. The firm contracted to build the nation's first high-speed passenger trains, the New York–Washington Metroliners. Much delayed, the electrically powered, multiple-unit trains made their first revenue run on January 16, 1969. Their design, albeit without traction motors, subsequently became the model for Amtrak's Amfleet cars of 1977–1980. Ironically, Pullman-Standard's final passenger cars, the Amtrak Superliners of 1977–1980, were modeled on Budd's *El Capitan* design and incorporated Budd's patented all-stainless-steel construction. At the beginning of the twenty-first century Budd's design and construction techniques remained the industry standard.

Long-term profitability problems forced Budd to exit the intercity passenger-car-building business upon the completion of the Amfleet II order of 1981–1982. The firm's transit division, renamed Transit America, continued to operate through 1987, when its patents were acquired by Bombardier Corp. of Canada. Perhaps the strongest testament to the extraordinary resiliency of Budd's product is a contemporary (2004) Amtrak program to refit dining cars built from 1947 to 1958 for service well into the twenty-first century.

—Michael E. Zega

REFERENCES

Budd, Edward G., Jr. *Edward G. Budd, 1870–1946, "Father of the Streamliners," and the Budd Company.* New York: Newcomen Society, 1950.

Dubin, Arthur D. *More Classic Trains.* Milwaukee, Wis.: Kalmbach, 1974.

ICC Pullman-Standard case files, 1946.

New York Times, December 2, 1946.

Pennsylvania Railroad Papers. Hagley Museum and Library, Wilmington, Del.

Pennypacker, Bert. "Budd before the Zephyr." *Trains* 33, no. 6 (April 1973): 24–28.

"Pioneer without Profit." *Fortune*, Feb. 1937, 82–134.

"Pullman Incorporated." *Fortune*, Jan. 1938, 38–102; Feb. 1938, 73–101.

Reutter, Mark. "The Lost Promise of the American Railroad." *Wilson Quarterly* 18, no. 1 (Winter 1994): 10–37.

Staufer, Alvin F., and Bert Pennypacker. *Pennsy Power II: Steam, Diesel, and Electric Locomotives of the Pennsylvania Railroad.* Medina, Ohio: Alvin F. Staufer, 1968. Union Pacific Papers. Omaha.

Burlington Northern & Santa Fe Railway. *See* BNSF RAILWAY

Burlington Northern Railroad

The Burlington Northern Railroad was the product of the 1970 merger of four major railroads: the Chicago,

Burlington & Quincy (CB&Q, Burlington Route), the Great Northern (GN), the Northern Pacific (NP), and the Spokane, Portland & Seattle (SP&S). They were collectively called the Hill Lines because of the influence of Great Northern founder James J. Hill, who at one time controlled both GN and NP, which in turn owned 50 percent each of Burlington and SP&S. At the time Burlington Northern was created in 1970, it was the largest railroad in the United States.

The first effort to unite the railroads took place about 1900. James J. Hill had won a long campaign to control the NP and then went after the CB&Q. E. H. Harriman of the Union Pacific also hoped to gain control of the CB&Q. Rebuffed by Hill, Harriman attempted to achieve his goal indirectly by gaining control of the Northern Pacific. This touched off a long battle, but Harriman was able to gain several seats on the NP and Burlington directorates. Hill then devised a plan to protect his interests in the three railroads and in 1901 established a holding company, Northern Securities Co., to control GN and NP, and through them the Burlington. The U.S. Supreme Court, however, found that Northern Securities violated the Sherman Antitrust Act and eventually scuttled Hill's plan.

Another attempt to unite the railroads occurred in 1925, when the directors of GN, NP, and Burlington agreed to proceed with a merger. The new company was to be called the Great Northern Pacific Railway Co., with the Burlington controlled under stock ownership and the SP&S under lease. On July 28, 1927, a merger application was filed with the Interstate Commerce Commission. Merger opponents were quick to decry the proposal as anticompetitive. In February 1930 the ICC approved the merger with four conditions. Three were minor, but the fourth called for the GN and NP to sell their interest in the CB&Q. Losing the Burlington was unacceptable, and on January 31, 1931, the merger application was withdrawn.

In the 1950s John Budd, president of the Great Northern, and Robert S. Macfarlane, president of the Northern Pacific, determined to try once again to merge their companies. The new system would have over 26,000 miles of railroad line extending from Vancouver, British Columbia, to Galveston, Texas. The benefits of a merger were far-reaching. In many cities GN and NP had duplicate yards, depots, and support facilities. The railroads roughly paralleled one another from St. Paul to Seattle. If all their lines could be brought together, the best routes could be retained and duplicate routes eliminated, with resulting cost savings.

In 1960 the railroads' boards approved the plan. On February 17, 1961, a formal merger application was presented to the ICC, but in 1966 the ICC rejected the proposed merger, citing concerns about loss of competition and jobs. However, in early 1967 the commission agreed to reconsider the case, and late in the year the commissioners reversed their earlier decision and approved the

consolidation. Still, opposition remained from several quarters, and the ICC delayed merger implementation several months.

Finally, the stage was set for the new company to begin operations on May 10, 1968. It would be Burlington Northern, Inc., a name developed by the New York industrial design firm of Lippincott & Margulies to replace the unwieldy Great Northern Pacific & Burlington Lines, which was used in merger applications. However, at virtually the last minute the Department of Justice, which opposed the consolidation, was able to obtain an injunction from Supreme Court chief justice Earl Warren to delay the merger. Late in 1969 the Supreme Court heard arguments from the Department of Justice, which made the case that the merger would eliminate competition and was not in the public interest. On February 2, 1970, the Supreme Court approved the consolidation. Merger day was set for March 2, 1970. John Budd of GN was named chairman, and Louis Menk of the NP was appointed president. The railroad would be based in St. Paul, Minnesota.

The first Burlington Northern freight train, number 97 for Seattle, departed Chicago on March 2, 1970, powered by six GP38 locomotives, all painted in BN's new color, Cascade green. Also painted green for merger day were former CB&Q E8 locomotives 9042 and 9043, which pulled the combined *Afternoon Zephyr*, *Empire Builder*, and *North Coast Limited* passenger train from Chicago to St. Paul. One of the first tasks the BN faced was renumbering and repainting nearly 2,000 locomotives. It took more than seven years.

A main benefit of the BN merger was the elimination of duplicate trackage. The best parts of several of the predecessor lines were combined to create the finest possible route for BN. The merger caused two large construction projects. In the Twin Cities, NP, GN, and CB&Q had scattered yards and engine facilities. BN consolidated the facilities at NP's Northtown Yard in northeast Minneapolis, where in 1971 BN began construction of a modern hump yard, diesel shop, and service facility at a cost of $40 million.

The transcontinental main lines of both Great Northern and Northern Pacific served Spokane. Several options were considered for linking the former GN, NP, and SP&S lines in the city and establishing a single route for through traffic and efficient switching. By June 1970 BN had selected the former NP route through the city center. Ground was broken for the project on March 2, 1971. Nearly 7 miles of new railroad were constructed; ten new bridges had to be built and one bridge raised. In addition, the schedule for the project was tight: an island in the Spokane River occupied by the former Great Northern station was to be the site of Expo '74. The entire project cost $16.2 million and was completed on December 6, 1972, three months ahead of schedule.

Immediately after the merger BN benefited from the proximity of its lines to huge deposits of low-sulfur coal in southern Montana and northern and central Wyoming. The Clean Air Act of 1970 required that companies that burned coal reduce their air-polluting sulfur emissions. The easiest way to comply was to use coal with low sulfur content, such as that found in the coalfields of Montana and Wyoming served by Burlington Northern. Throughout its 25-year history BN's revenues steadily increased from the transportation of Montana and Wyoming coal to markets across the United States. In 1970 BN carried 3 million tons of coal and ran one unit coal train weekly on the average. By 1988 BN was carrying 129 million tons of coal annually. Coal had surpassed grain as its number one commodity. BN's routes were not in condition to carry the heavy coal loads, so huge sums were spent to upgrade them.

BN's single largest coal-related construction project began in 1976: a new line in Wyoming's Powder River Basin. The line would cut as much as 155 miles off the distance some coal trains would travel, allowing coal to reach southern destinations more quickly. The new route extended 116 miles from a mine spur near Gillette south to Orin. In 1972 BN applied to the ICC for authority to build the line. The following year competitor Chicago & North Western also asked for ICC authority to build a line into the area. The commission directed the two carriers to build a joint line rather than parallel lines. After long negotiations BN and C&NW worked out a joint-ownership arrangement, and the ICC approved the start of construction under BN's supervision in 1976. BN ran its first train over the line on November 6, 1979. After a long dispute over financing, the Chicago & North Western began operation over the new line in 1984.

In addition to coal, BN carried large quantities of farm and forest products; they accounted for 44 percent of the railroad's revenues in 1977. Taconite, a form of iron ore, was another important commodity; BN built a $67.4 million taconite-handling facility at the Allouez ore dock near Superior, Wisconsin, to handle storage and transloading from railcars to boats.

Merger with the Frisco

On February 1, 1977, Burlington Northern announced that it was conducting a joint merger feasibility study with the 4,674-mile St. Louis–San Francisco Railway (Frisco). BN chairman Louis Menk had been president of the Frisco before moving to the CB&Q in 1965. A Frisco merger would give BN direct routes from Kansas City and St. Louis to Texas and would allow the consolidation of duplicate facilities in Kansas City and St. Louis. It would also allow BN to tap growing markets in the Southeast. The two companies filed a formal merger application with the ICC on December 28, 1977. On November 21, 1980, the Frisco was merged into BN. Changes in top management of the railroad immediately after the Frisco merger put many former SLSF managers in executive positions at BN.

At this point BN reached its zenith: it was 31,420 miles long, including subsidiaries Fort Worth & Denver and Col-

orado & Southern, making it the largest railroad in the United States. In late November 1980 BN launched a new freight train that connected Portland, Oregon, with Birmingham, Alabama, the longest through freight (3,076 miles) over a single railroad in the United States at the time.

On June 1, 1980, shortly before the Frisco merger, Richard M. Bressler, formerly an executive vice president of Atlantic Richfield, was named president of BN, Inc. He was the first Burlington Northern executive hired from outside the company.

The Burlington Northern had an abundance of assets, and executives decided to form a holding company to manage them. It was incorporated on March 30, 1981, as Burlington Northern Holding Co. On May 14, 1981, this company acquired Burlington Northern, Inc. At the same time, the former Burlington Northern, Inc., changed its name to Burlington Northern Railroad, and the holding company adopted the Burlington Northern, Inc. (BNI) name.

During the 1980s there were corporate restructurings and management changes. Many of the executives from the old railroads were terminated or retired. In 1983 corporate headquarters personnel began moving from BN's traditional home in St. Paul to Fort Worth, Texas. The number of railroad employees shrank from 57,300 in December 1980 to 49,800 by December 1981; by 1990 the count was less than 33,000. BN closed locomotive and car shops and excess yards and eliminated their personnel. Many miles of branch-line track were either abandoned or sold to shortline railroads. While painful, some of the changes and the overall streamlining of the organization in the 1980s helped it survive competitive pressures and increase productivity. However, the manner in which the changes were carried out had an adverse effect on employee morale.

BN was at the forefront of innovative experiments with different types of motive power. It experimented with natural gas as fuel and was the first American railroad to embrace alternating-current (AC) diesel-electric locomotives. Unlike conventional diesel locomotives, which use direct current in their traction motors, AC locomotives feed alternating current to their motors. The chief benefit of the design is lower maintenance costs for traction motors, since they have no brushes or commutators.

In December 1988 Gerald Grinstein, formerly with Western Airlines, became president and CEO of Burlington Northern, Inc. Grinstein took a more cooperative approach on labor issues. On June 3, 1988, BN was again reorganized in a restructuring that kept the railroad as the major component of the holding company, but spun off other properties in a new subsidiary, Burlington Resources, Inc. BR was to function as a holding company for BNI's natural-resource operations, including its holdings in timber, forest products, real estate, coal, oil, and gas and the companies related to them (BN's air freight company was sold in 1982). The move saddled the railroad with billions of dollars in debt to fund BR, which took years to pay down. While BN was consistently profitable, many industry and investor analysts felt that it never lived up to its potential.

Merger with the Santa Fe

In the 1990s BN looked to the Atchison, Topeka & Santa Fe Railway as a potential merger partner. On July 20, 1995, the ICC approved the BN–Santa Fe merger, and on September 22, the two holding companies, Burlington Northern, Inc., and Santa Fe Pacific Corp., merged to form the Burlington Northern Santa Fe Corp. The new company managed both railroads as one organization until the end of 1996, with both the parent company and the railroad referred to as BNSF. On December 31, 1996, the Atchison, Topeka & Santa Fe Railway quietly merged into Burlington Northern Railroad. BN then changed its name to Burlington Northern & Santa Fe Railway Co., and in 2005 to BNSF Railway.

In 1995, its last year before merger with the Santa Fe, Burlington Northern operated a system of 22,200 route-miles and 32,582 track-miles, with 2,574 locomotives, 141 passenger cars (for commuter service at Chicago), 67,421 freight cars, and 30,671 employees. Freight traffic totaled 293.4 billion ton-miles in 1995, and coal (33 percent), farm products (19 percent), foodstuffs (7 percent), and lumber and wood products (10 percent) were its principal traffic sources. Burlington Northern operating revenues totaled $5.4 billion in 1995, and the railroad achieved an 80 percent operating ratio.

—Steve Glischinski

REFERENCES

Glischinski, Steve. *Burlington Northern and Its Heritage.* Andover, N.J.: Andover Junction, 1992.
Hidy, Ralph W., Muriel E. Hidy, and Roy V. Scott, with Don L. Hofsommer. *The Great Northern Railway: A History.* Cambridge, Mass.: Harvard Business School Press, 1988.

See also BNSF Railway.

Burlington Route. *See* Chicago, Burlington & Quincy Railroad

Burnham, George (1817–1912)

Few persons in business are connected with a single firm for 73 years, but this was the case with George Burnham, Sr., who served the Baldwin Locomotive Works for almost three-quarters of a century. His primary role was tending to the financial requirements of the company. A native of Springfield, Massachusetts, Burnham was born on March 11, 1817. He could trace his New England ancestry back to John White, who arrived in the country in 1632. At about the age of 15 he moved to Philadelphia. In the Quaker City he obtained a position as a clerk in the grocery store owned by Simon Colton at Fourth and Market streets, a location then close to the center of business and social activity in the city.

One of the customers in the Colton store was Matthias W. Baldwin, who came to regard the grocery clerk as a bright, ambitious, and energetic young man. Baldwin was a watchmaker and jeweler who had started a machine shop and became interested in the new business of railroads in the 1830s. With experience gained in constructing a stationary steam engine for his machine shop, in 1832 Baldwin built the locomotive *Old Ironsides* for the Philadelphia, Germantown & Norristown Railroad. It was successful, and on that basis he launched the locomotive-building business. His favorable impressions of George Burnham led Baldwin to offer the young man the position of bookkeeper in the new business.

Burnham handled the official correspondence of the firm, but worked mainly in the area of finance; he rose steadily into the upper ranks of management. Baldwin himself was not interested in finance and left such matters in Burnham's hands. Baldwin credited Burnham's competence with keeping the company in operation and successful over many years. The Baldwin Locomotive Works was not incorporated until 1909 and was instead a succession of partnerships. Upon the death of Matthias Baldwin, Burnham became a partner of the successor firm of M. Baird & Co. in 1867. When Baird retired in 1873, Burnham became the senior partner in Burnham, Parry, Williams & Co. Upon Parry's death the firm continued as Burnham, Williams & Co. until the need for greater access to capital led to the incorporation of the Baldwin Locomotive Works in 1909. At first it was privately held, finally becoming a public company in 1911. Burnham was a major shareholder.

Burnham married Anna Hemple in 1843 and had several children. Son George Burnham, Jr., became a member of the Baldwin management team; son William became president of the Standard Steel Co.; daughter Mary was a well-known philanthropist in Philadelphia. During his career George Burnham was active in civic affairs in Philadelphia and was affiliated with the important Committee of 100 and an early member of the prestigious Union League. His passing on December 10, 1912, was the result of general physical breakdown due to advanced age.

—George M. Smerk

REFERENCES

Brown, John K. *The Baldwin Locomotive Works, 1831–1915.* Baltimore: Johns Hopkins Univ. Press, 1995.
Obituary. *Philadelphia Evening Public Ledger,* Dec. 11, 1912.

C

Caltrain. *See* PENINSULA CORRIDOR

JOINT POWERS BOARD

Camden & Amboy Rail Road

The earliest predecessor of the Pennsylvania Railroad, the Camden & Amboy was the first railroad built to connect two major population centers—Philadelphia and New York—rather than to serve the development interests of a single state. It was the first railroad chartered in New Jersey, on February 4, 1830. The charter date was preceded by a bitter struggle in the state legislature between canal proponents and railroad advocates. By way of compromise, the Delaware & Raritan Canal was chartered on the same day. The two companies competed briefly, but became "joint companies" the following year. Such was the acceptance of the need for this railroad that the stock was fully subscribed on the first day of offering, unusual for early railroads.

The Camden & Amboy was the culmination of a dream of Col. John Stevens, an early proponent and operator of steamboats. Stevens had demonstrated an experimental steam locomotive on a circular track on his estate in Hoboken in 1825. His two sons were to be the principals in the Camden & Amboy, with Robert as the president.

The railroad opened for business under horsepower on October 20, 1832, between Bordentown and Hightstown. Its initial route was from Bordentown on the Delaware River to South Amboy on New York Bay, with steamboat connections from Bordentown to Philadelphia and from South Amboy to New York. The line was extended south to Camden in 1834, and a branch was opened to Trenton in 1837 and on to New Brunswick in 1839.

A steam locomotive, the *John Bull*, was imported from England and demonstrated in 1831. It was initially plagued with tracking problems—common for English locomotives on American track, as several early railroads learned—but the addition of a pilot truck solved the problems. Operation with steam power between Bordentown and South Amboy began in September 1833.

The *John Bull* was assembled without drawings or instructions by mechanic Isaac Dripps, who went on, in collaboration with Robert Stevens, to design and build additional locomotives for the railroad. The *John Bull* operated for many years and was donated to the Smithsonian Institution in 1884. It was operated as recently as 1981 on its 150th anniversary. A replica, built in 1940 by the Altoona shops of the Pennsylvania Railroad, runs on occasion at the Pennsylvania State Railroad Museum at Strasburg.

The basic T-rail shape, which later became the standard rail shape used worldwide, was first employed on the Camden & Amboy. The design is said to have been conceived by Robert Stevens while on his way to England, and only with difficulty did he find an English manufacturer willing to produce it. Stevens experimented with a number of designs for roadbed and track as construction proceeded.

One of New Jersey's early unofficial nicknames was the Camden & Amboy State, testifying to the political power of the railroad, at its peak the greatest economic enterprise in the state. This is another first for the Camden & Amboy, anticipating a situation that later prevailed in some other states, where the major railroad was thought by many to own the state legislature.

An infamous aspect of the Camden & Amboy's history was its safety record. An accident on November 11, 1833, caused by a broken axle, caused the first fatality to a revenue passenger on an American railroad. Two persons of note were on that train, former U.S. president John Quincy Adams and Cornelius Vanderbilt. Adams escaped the wreckage unharmed. Vanderbilt was seriously injured, but survived to become one of the titans of the American railroad industry. The end of the Camden & Amboy as an independent entity came in 1867, when it became part of the United New Jersey Railroad & Canal Co.'s group, although it was not formally merged until after the component companies were leased by the Pennsylvania Railroad in 1871.

The New Brunswick–Trenton section of the former Camden & Amboy is now part of Amtrak's high-speed

Northeast Corridor, while the Trenton-Camden segment became a Conrail branch that is now shared by CSX and Norfolk Southern. Passenger service over the line ended in 1962, but was revived in 2003 by NJ Transit as the Southern New Jersey light rail line, called the River Line, with an innovative diesel light-rail service connecting Trenton and Camden.

—Adrian Ettlinger

REFERENCES

Burgess, George H., and Miles C. Kennedy. *Centennial History of the Pennsylvania Railroad Company*, 1846–1946. Philadelphia: Pennsylvania Railroad, 1949.

Cunningham, John T. *Railroads in New Jersey: The Formative Years*. Andover, N.J.: Afton, 1997.

Gerstner, Franz Anton Ritter von. *Early American Railroads*. Ed. Frederick C. Gamst. Stanford, Calif.: Stanford Univ. Press, 1997 [1842–1843].

White, John H., Jr. *The John Bull: 150 Years a Locomotive*. Washington, D.C.: Smithsonian Institution Press, 1981.

Canadian National Railways

Canadian National Railways was assembled under government auspices from five principal components, all in financial difficulty, much like Conrail more than 50 years later. The components, in the order in which they came under government control, were the Intercolonial, National Transcontinental, Canadian Northern, Grand Trunk Pacific, and Grand Trunk railways. The National Transcontinental was the youngest of the railways, the Grand Trunk the oldest.

Grand Trunk Railway

Canada's railway age began in 1832, when several little railways poked southward from Montreal. Soon the growth of the railway system demanded an east-west main line, the Grand Trunk Railway. Chartered in 1852, it was to extend from Trois Pistoles, Quebec, on the south bank of the St. Lawrence River about 140 miles downstream from Quebec City, through Montreal and Toronto to Sarnia, Ontario, across the St. Clair River from Michigan, with branches to Portland, Maine, the nearest seaport, and to Niagara Falls. Since Canadians had bought only 2 percent of its shares, the Grand Trunk was owned in London and was managed well by a succession of capable Britons employing American railroad customs. However, it was abused by its bankers, its builders, and the Canadian government. Construction expenses far exceeded the budget, and winter brought delays and high labor costs.

In 1860 the two-mile Victoria bridge over the St. Lawrence at Montreal opened as the route to reach Trois Pistoles to the east; construction of the bridge almost bankrupted the Grand Trunk. In 1873 a British manager built the costly but vital International Bridge from Fort Erie, Ontario, to Buffalo, New York. In 1875 William H. Vanderbilt invaded southwestern Ontario by buying the Canada Southern, a line from Buffalo to Windsor, and adding it to his Michigan Central system. The Canada Air Line, from near Windsor to Buffalo, was the Trunk's rejoinder, and in 1890 it triumphed by tunneling under the St. Clair River at Sarnia, Ontario, to connect with its previously constructed route across Michigan and Indiana to Chicago. In 1885 the Grand Trunk acquired a half interest in the Central Vermont Railroad, which ran from the Canadian border south of Montreal to New London, Connecticut, and in 1904 it bought the Canada Atlantic Railway from a U.S. lumber baron to connect Montreal with Ottawa, the national capital.

Intercolonial Railway

In 1854 a railroad was extended down the river from Trois Pistoles to Mont Joli, over mountains to the tidewater of Chaleur Bay, keeping a careful distance from the international boundary, then southeast to Halifax. The company was the government-owned Intercolonial Railway. Britain, concerned about the intentions of the United States after the U.S. Civil War, decided to strengthen the Canadian garrison and guaranteed some of the Intercolonial's funding. The ICR has been described as a "clownish" enterprise, principally because of the venality of local politicians and their patronage. Rivals quarreled about which party ought to appoint a station agent or decide on a route deviation. It took World War I to bring respectability to the Intercolonial as it moved troops and cargo to the port of Halifax.

Canadian Northern Railway

Among the contractors that built the Canadian Pacific Railway was Ross, Mackenzie, Holt & Mann. After the completion of the CPR, Donald Mann stayed in the West and brought William Mackenzie from the East in 1898 to build the Canadian Northern Railway as a prairie competitor to the Canadian Pacific. Mann began his railroad at Winnipeg, crossed the Rockies at Yellowhead Pass, the easiest passage across the Continental Divide in North America, and reached the south bank of the Fraser River near Vancouver in 1916. Trackage rights over the Great Northern brought the Canadian Northern into Vancouver proper.

Canadian Northern's grain route to Lake Superior lay along the Minnesota border, and its Duluth, Winnipeg & Pacific subsidiary provided another port for grain at Duluth. Then, in a long sweeping curve to the northeast, the Canadian Northern left the lake and angled southeast to Toronto in 1908, but it did not reach Montreal until 1916.

Grand Trunk Pacific Railway

In 1895 Charles Melville Hays became general manager of the Grand Trunk Railway. Western Canada drew his and Prime Minister Sir Wilfrid Laurier's attention. A third western railway was deemed necessary, to be part of the Grand Trunk, but starting at Winnipeg, 1,000 miles away from the nearest point on the Grand Trunk.

Hays's own ambition coincided with Laurier's hunger for a railway in his list of accomplishments, so the Grand Trunk Pacific Railway was created in 1905 with the customary government loan but no land. It too crested the Rockies at Yellowhead Pass, alongside the Canadian Northern. The new port of Prince Rupert was put on the northern Pacific in 1909, terminus of "the best long railroad in America," arrowing straight across the prairie with towns named in alphabetic order from A to Z. Hays died in 1912 on the *Titanic*.

National Transcontinental Railway

Laurier was defeated at the next election, and Canada now had a third line across the West, but the Grand Trunk Pacific needed a connection east from Winnipeg. The National Transcontinental Railway, the mad finale to Laurier's dream, was formed to build between Winnipeg and Halifax, far to the north of Toronto, Ottawa, and Montreal. It was called the Eastern Division of the Grand Trunk Pacific, which was its reluctant lessor and operator, although it never did connect with GTP.

Building across the barren rock of Quebec and Ontario, NTR's contractors were slow, their estimates were wrong, and many defrauded their client by billing for work not done. The NTR was to cross the St. Lawrence over the ill-fated Quebec Bridge, the world's longest clear-span cantilevered structure. Before the bridge opened in 1917, it crumpled twice, killing 88 men—not the fault of the NTR. Once across the St. Lawrence, the NTR extended east over the tail of the Appalachians on easy grades through central New Brunswick to Moncton, where it joined the Intercolonial Railway.

Canadian National Railways

The Canadian government had two major worries in the second decade of the twentieth century: the Great War and the distress of two railroad companies. The Canadian Northern was a western railroad that had entered eastern Canada, and the Grand Trunk by way of the Grand Trunk Pacific was an eastern railroad that had expanded into western Canada, to the discomfiture of both. Moreover, the Grand Trunk wanted to surrender the National Transcontinental to the government, which refused it.

The Canadian Pacific suggested that the Canadian Northern and Grand Trunk Pacific merge, with rights over CPR in between. This was also urged by the prime minister, but was rejected by Canadians; that government was overthrown at the next election.

In 1916 a royal commission, chaired by the esteemed A. H. Smith of the New York Central, was set up to examine the entire railway situation. As expected, the commission reported overoptimism on the part of the Canadian Northern, which had wanted to buy the Intercolonial. Although Smith advised patience, the Canadian Northern was facing the greatest business failure in Canadian history. Its banker was the Canadian Bank of Commerce. By 1916 the total government involvement in the Canadian Northern, the GTP, the ICR, and the NTR was $712 million, and public ownership became inevitable.

In 1917 the Canadian Bank of Commerce and the owners sold the Canadian Northern to the government of Canada at ten cents on the dollar. Canadian Government Railways then took over the NTR since the GTP could not afford the lease, plus the Intercolonial, which it turned over to the Canadian Northern to manage.

Canadian Government Railways was never incorporated, but its name was replaced by that of Canadian National Railways, with 14,000 miles to its name and D. B. Hanna as its president. Still left outside at that point was the Grand Trunk with its expensive child to the Pacific.

The government assumed financial responsibility for the Grand Trunk in 1920 and set up an arbitration board to judge how much it was worth. The decision was that it was worth nothing; William Howard Taft, acting for the GT, demurred to no avail. Its shares became waste paper, to the rage of the English stockholders.

Canadian National Railways needed a new president. Henry Worth Thornton had been in charge of the Long Island Rail Road and then had been hired by the British Great Eastern Railway, which had similar commuter traffic. He became inspector general of railways during the war, for which he was knighted. He turned down an offer of a job with the Milwaukee Road in favor of the Canadian National at $50,000 a year. Thornton was a genial passenger-oriented magnifico, complete with spats, silver-headed cane, and a winter raccoon coat. He took up his job with high enthusiasm. He bought America's first (two-unit) diesel-electric road locomotive and put the first radio in passenger trains. Under his management CN inaugurated new, faster trains between Montreal and Toronto.

East of Winnipeg, Canadian Northern's line dipped down into the United States, while the National Transcontinental route went straight east. Nakina on the NTR was only 25 miles north of Longlac, a division point on the Canadian Northern. Canadian National Railways built a line connecting the two points and created a new all-Canada route through western Ontario: the Canadian Northern route from Toronto through Capreol to Longlac, the new line to Nakina, and the National Transcontinental line from Nakina to Winnipeg. The new cutoff downgraded the Winnipeg–Port Arthur–Fort William–Longlac portion of the Canadian Northern to secondary status and removed almost all traffic from the middle portion—Nakina to Quebec—of the National Transcontinental.

Thornton had two major passions: the Montreal passenger station and labor relations. GT's sad old Bonaventure Station was to be replaced by a big station on the site of Canadian Northern's little two-track electrified depot. Thornton had dug only a huge hole in midtown Montreal before the Depression stopped the project. He delighted in visiting men at work, especially at night in yards and roundhouses; when he died, the men put up a bronze plaque to him at every big station, unique in America. Thornton spent a lot of money, and when a new government took office, in the finest traditions of the Canadian parliamentary party system, it fired him for extravagance. Sir Henry Thornton never saw his new station finished. He died in 1933.

CN was served by three presidents during World War II, but the prime minister of the day thought them ingrown; the railway was war-wounded as well. Since every director was political, it was no problem for the directors to approve the nomination of Donald Gordon, onetime deputy governor of the Bank of Canada, as president of Canadian National in 1949. Knowing nothing about railways, Gordon demanded to be taught and absorbed facts like a sponge, though not always without argument. He was resented in his attempts to pierce the wall around him and turned out to be rough, noisy, and difficult, even at the annual parliamentary review of CN. Being a banker, he replaced CN's debt with government-owned preference shares, saving $30 million a year in interest. He could not stand the sight of Thornton's 24-acre hole in the middle of Montreal, so he filled the south side of the hole with a 14-track high-platform passenger station (Central Station), a CN office building, and a 1,000-room hotel (the Queen Elizabeth). He arranged a lease with a major developer to fill the remainder of the hole with Place Ville Marie, a luxury underground shopping center and a group of office buildings, including the city's tallest, connected to the hotel and station. Gordon completed dieselization of Canadian National and founded a staff training school at a nearby university. Under his direction CN adopted its prize-winning "wiggly worm" logo and established an imaginative passenger pricing plan. Gordon's labor style was aggressive, and he was thought insensitive to French Canadian values. He left in 1967, having altered nearly everything. He was succeeded by his own trainees.

CN joined in Canada's biggest container terminal in Halifax, offering ocean carriers reduced high-volume inland rates on an Antwerp-Montreal through bill of lading. Subsidiary Grand Trunk Western bought the Detroit, Toledo & Ironton Railroad in 1980 to capture Ford Motor Co. traffic.

In 1993 Paul Tellier, an Oxford-educated senior civil servant, was awarded the CN presidency. He privatized CN by selling 84 million shares at a price of about C$25.

CN bought the Illinois Central Railroad, most especially for its connection with the Kansas City Southern at Jackson, Mississippi, giving a route to Dallas and on to Mexico, important under the North American Free Trade Agreement. It was a benign union: although the IC name and logo have disappeared, Hunter Harrison, the president of IC, became chief operating officer of CN. Burlington Northern Santa Fe considered CN and GTW's hold on the automotive traffic in southwestern Ontario and Michigan and proposed merger with CN. Although the merger was postponed by U.S. authorities, BNSF and CN have coordinated their services.

Under the provisions of the Canada Transportation Act, CN has sold such routes as the old ICR and most of the old Canadian Northern north from Montreal to form shortline railroads. The absurd 1917 Hudson's Bay line has been sold, and so has the once-critical branch to Portland, Maine. The former NTR track east of Nakina has been dismantled. Most export grain now goes west to Pacific ports. The little eastward export grain traffic that remains moves via Toronto to elevators at Quebec City.

Canadian National in 2005 operated a system of 19,200 route-miles and 29,800 track miles in the United States and Canada, with 22,246 employees, and owned or leased equipment of 2,100 locomotives, 107,000 freight cars, and 27 passenger cars. Freight traffic in 2005 totaled 179.7 billion ton-miles of freight, and its commodity groups were petroleum and chemicals (15 percent), metals and minerals (12 percent), forest products (24 percent), coal (5 percent), grain and fertilizers (15 percent), intermodal (18 percent), automotive (7 percent), and other (5 percent). CN operating revenues totaled C$7,240 million in 2005, with operating expenses of C$4,616 million, representing a 63.8 percent operating ratio, the lowest in North America.

—F. H. "Joe" Howard

REFERENCES

Bruce, Harry. *The Pig That Flew: The Battle to Privatize Canadian National.* Vancouver: Douglas & McIntyre, 1997.
MacKay, Donald. *The People's Railway.* Vancouver: Douglas & McIntyre, 1992.
Marsh, D'Arcy. *The Tragedy of Henry Thornton.* Toronto: Macmillan of Canada, 1935.
Stevens, George R. *History of the Canadian National Railways.* New York: Macmillan, 1973.

Canadian Pacific Railway

In 1870 Canada consisted of a few hundred thousand people, most of them living east of Lake Superior. British Columbia was a Crown colony on the Pacific that the prime minister needed to complete the country. However, the West had little use for the East and could easily join the United States. The prime minister promised British Columbia a railway to connect it to the rest of Canada.

First, a route had to be chosen. Nobody had ever explored the 1,000 miles between Winnipeg and the mountains nor the land north of Lake Superior. Most of the latter lay on the Precambrian Shield; what was not solid rock was spongy muskeg. Survey parties set out to explore the land, and many routes were "discovered," but as yet there was no railway to build on one.

In 1870 the St. Paul & Pacific Railroad, 200 miles of rickety track and decrepit equipment, ran from St. Paul toward Winnipeg. In St. Paul lived a one-eyed Canadian adventurer and visionary named James J. Hill. Through study and experience he knew that he wanted the St. Paul & Pacific.

Donald Smith, a Scot and president of the Hudson's Bay Co., wondered if the St. Paul & Pacific could be part of a rail line to British Columbia. Hill recognized in the wealthy Smith the source of the funds he needed to buy the St. Paul line. Smith was prepared to finish the St. Paul & Pacific to the Canadian border to join his own road south from Winnipeg. The St. Paul was bankrupt, but the bonds might be bought, followed by foreclosure. As well, Smith was a director of the Bank of Montreal, of which his cousin, George Stephen, another Scot, was president. Though Stephen knew little about railways, he was captivated by Hill's and Smith's adventure and joined them.

Hill engaged William C. Van Horne, a young superintendent of the Milwaukee Road, to be general manager of the railroad. He brought with him Thomas Shaughnessy, the son of a Milwaukee policeman, and said, "I'm going to the Pacific; send the bills to Shaughnessy." Through a variety of stratagems Shaughnessy kept the creditors at bay for months.

Van Horne was a truly colorful character. An all-night cigar-smoking poker player, he became a gourmand and wine expert, a violinist, a good painter, an amateur geologist, and an authority on Chinese porcelain. He drove the railway to the Pacific in five years, not ten, building his own dynamite factory to get through the Canadian Shield. To find two mountain passes, he hired A. B. Rogers, a profane former U.S. Army major; a chew of tobacco and a seabiscuit were his idea of a surveyor's meal. He found passes through both ranges, and his name stands at the peak of the Selkirks.

The Canadian Pacific Railway was to begin at Callander, Ontario, on Lake Nipissing, 200 miles north of Toronto, and run to the Pacific. Callander, at the end of a Grand Trunk Railway line from Toronto, was no place for a railway terminal, so Canadian Pacific purchased two small railways in order to reach east to Montreal.

Meanwhile, the Northern Pacific Railroad had begun construction of a line from the Great Lakes to Puget Sound. Hill saw that the Canadian Pacific Railway could be an outlet to the Pacific for the St. Paul & Pacific. He hoped that construction north of Lake Superior would be so difficult that the Canadian Pacific would have to detour south of Lake Superior through St. Paul. However, Canada's prime minister was adamant about an all-Canada route. Hill eventually broke with Stephen and Van Horne. Hill's St. Paul & Pacific developed into the Great Northern Railway, and Hill was suspected of wanting to poke into southern British Columbia, which he did, most notably into Vancouver.

In 1885 the last spike of the Canadian Pacific was driven at Craigellachie, British Columbia, by Smith. Scottish for "stand fast," the name Craigellachie recalled the one-word message from Stephen to Smith on one anxious occasion. It is the rallying cry of the Clan Grant (also seen on the Grant's whisky label).

Canadian Pacific was the first railway in North America to superheat its steam locomotives and stood alone in replacing worn-out branch-line power with modern light steam locomotives, a policy that ceased upon the arrival of the diesel. For years Canadian Pacific advertised itself as the world's greatest travel system. Its properties included ships, hotels, and an airline. In 1955 CPR placed in service the *Canadian*, a stainless-steel domed streamliner from Montreal and Toronto to Vancouver. The train quickly became a cruise train, something more than simple transportation, and its reputation continued long after CPR became disenchanted with passenger trains. When VIA Rail Canada, the Crown corporation that took over passenger-train operation in Canada in the late 1970s, moved the *Canadian* to the Canadian National route in 1990, the news media treated the event as the total discontinuance of rail passenger service across Canada.

Crossing the Selkirks, CPR's line had originally traversed Rogers Pass, but too many avalanches and too many fatalities brought the five-mile Connaught Tunnel bypass in 1916. Even so, the line still climbed 1,200 feet in 25 miles. In 1988 that grade was eliminated by nine-mile Mount Macdonald Tunnel, the longest railroad tunnel in the Americas. Eastbound trains continue to use the Connaught Tunnel. West of the Selkirks there is a 1,900-foot drop in the 50 miles into Revelstoke. Electrification of this territory has been studied three times since 1915.

CPR handles a massive flow of metallurgical coal destined for Japan from mines in southern British Columbia in 16,000-ton unit trains, dumped without stopping at the Vancouver coal terminal. Nearly all export coal from British Columbia moves over CPR. Canadian Pacific also moves large quantities of potash and sulfur for export and carries forest products eastward from British Columbia.

Export grain is collected from country elevators and placed among five waterside elevators in the Port of Vancouver. To comprehend grain is to understand the Canadian Pacific. Canada grows far more grain than it eats; the rest is for export. For over 100 years the grain community has been accusing the railway of rapacity and incompetence in the movement to export points. The western politicians listen, and their latest response in a succession of regulations is a cap on revenues and profit. The shippers have demanded shortline access, as if using another railroad company, also regulated, will provide price competition. Nevertheless, this will likely be ordained before long. Rate deregulation is not for grain and probably never will be, but open access is on the horizon.

In recent years Canadian Pacific has sold significant mileage to shortlines and no longer reaches the Atlantic. The Quebec Central lease has been terminated, and the Dominion Atlantic has been sold to Bangor & Aroostook interests.

Like most other railroads, CPR once actively solicited less-than-carload freight traffic. In addition, it owned a major truck line and its own express company. These were folded into CP Transport. CP Rail Intermodal is now the domestic container operator, the first to replace trailers with containers. Minor terminals have been replaced with major terminals in the bigger cities. CPR's containers belong to a North American pool, and CPR moves Triple Crown RoadRailers into Toronto.

CP Rail is a major carrier of ocean containers. East from Vancouver it shares that traffic with Canadian National Railways, but CPR is the dominant carrier of containers west from the Port of Montreal. That port handles more Atlantic Ocean containers than New York, thanks to CP Ship movements. Two-thirds of the westbound containers are destined for Detroit or Chicago, while half of Chicago's exports sail from Montreal.

Canadian Pacific has extensive operations in the United States. These include the former Delaware & Hudson Railway from Montreal to Sunbury, Pennsylvania; the former Soo Line, long a CP subsidiary, from Moose Jaw to Chicago; and the remains of the former Milwaukee Road. CPR is now half-owner of the former Michigan Central Detroit River Tunnel and half the Indiana Harbor Belt Railroad. CPR enters New York City via rights over CSX, bestowed by the U.S. Surface Transportation Board. CPR has eight U.S. border crossings and access to seven border points in Mexico through an alliance with Union Pacific.

The majority of its traffic is centered in the West, which is why CPR's headquarters and officers are now in Calgary. Montreal's Windsor Station, which Van Horne built 100 years ago, is almost deserted; the train-shed area is now a hockey arena, the home of Les Canadiens. The giant Angus locomotive and car shops at Montreal have been demolished, as have most of those in Winnipeg. Repair work is now concentrated at Calgary.

In 1996, Canadian Pacific Railway was merged into Canadian Pacific Limited, along with its ownership of a modest chain of hotels, an ocean carrier, and a coal mine. In 2005 the railway operated a system of 13,626 route-miles in the United States and Canada, with 16,448 employees, and owned or leased 1,655 locomotives and 50,300 freight cars. Freight traffic in 2005 totaled 125.3 billion ton-miles of freight, and its commodity groups were grain (18 percent), coal (17 percent), sulphur and fertilizers (10 percent), forest products (8 percent), industrial and consumer products (13 percent), automotive (7 percent), and intermodal (27 percent). CPR operating revenues totaled C$4,391.6 million in 2005, with operating expenses of C$3,390.2 million, representing a 77.2 percent operating ratio.

—F. H. "Joe" Howard

REFERENCES

Berton, Pierre. *The Last Spike*. Montreal: McClelland & Stewart, 1971.

———. *The National Dream*. Montreal: McClelland & Stewart, 1970.

Gibbon, John Murray. *Steel of Empire*. Indianapolis: Bobbs-Merrill, 1935.

Lavallée, Omer. *Van Horne's Road*. Montreal: Railfare Enterprises, 1974.

Canadian Railways

Although there are significant and ever-increasing similarities between Canada and the United States, there are also many major differences, probably stemming primarily from the manner in which the two countries were formed. While the United States cut its ties with the British Crown in the 1770s and went on its entrepreneurial way, Canada did not. When the steam locomotive made railways possible in the late 1820s and 1830s, British North America was under the control of Britain. What was to become Canada comprised the colonies of Ontario, Quebec, New Brunswick, Nova Scotia, Prince Edward Island, and Newfoundland, while the prairies were part of Rupert's Land. This had been granted to the Hudson's Bay Co. by the English Crown in 1670. On the West Coast European settlement had not yet begun. All major decisions were made in England, which meant that they were made by the government, and, probably because of this, Canadians have proven to be far less entrepreneurial than Americans. In addition, under the colonial system, there was little capital to finance railway development in Canada, and hence nearly all major railroad ventures were financed in the United Kingdom.

At this time nonwinter travel was mainly by canoe or sailing vessel along rivers, lakes, and estuaries, with which the land is well endowed. Roads were practically nonexistent, but a start had been made at building canals to improve waterborne transport. The Lachine Canal, immediately upriver from Montreal, was the first major project and was constructed between 1821 and 1825 to bypass the Lachine Rapids, which formed the head of navigation on the St. Lawrence River. Considerable government money was necessary to complete the venture, which was followed between 1826 and 1832 by the construction of the Rideau Canal between Lake Ontario at Kingston and Bytown (later Ottawa). This was a defensive measure because war with the United States was still thought likely, and the canal was built under the direction of the British Royal Engineers. On the other hand, the Chambly Canal was built between 1833 and 1843 to connect the St. Lawrence with the Hudson River to bypass rapids on the Richelieu River. This was a commercial venture to improve trade with the United States. But the days of widespread water transport were numbered with the invention of the steam locomotive.

Horse-drawn tramways are thought to have been introduced into what was to become Canada around 1720 when a short section was used in connection with the construction of Louisbourg, the fortified town built to protect French interests in Nova Scotia. A tramway was constructed at Pictou, Nova Scotia, in 1818 to haul coal to tidewater, and metal rails, reputedly the first in North America, were introduced on this line in 1829. Other horse-drawn tramways sprang up in various localities, including one at Bytown to haul stone for locks on the Rideau Canal.

George Stephenson's development of the steam locomotive in England made longer-distance rail travel possible, and an export market for engines soon resulted. With its British connections, it is not surprising that Canada's first locomotive was the 0-4-0 *Dorchester* built by Robert Stephenson & Co. in Newcastle, England. It was constructed for the Champlain & St. Lawrence Railroad, which was a shortline, built to a gauge of 4 feet 8½ inches, to avoid the Richelieu River Rapids, southeast of Montreal. The official opening was on July 1, 1836, and service on the 16-mile line began three days later, with the railway acting as a "portage" between the St. Lawrence and Richelieu rivers. The second steam-operated line, the Albion Mines Railway, opened at Stellarton, Nova Scotia, on September 19, 1839, to haul coal to docks on the coast. Three locomotives, built by Hackworth in England and named *Samson, Hercules,* and *John Buddle,* were much superior to the *Dorchester* and marked the first successful use of steam power in Canada. This line was followed by the Montreal & Lachine Railroad, which was another portage line to avoid navigational hazards—these being the Lachine Rapids just west of Montreal. Service commenced on November 19, 1847. But long-distance lines were now possible, and between 1846 and 1853 the St. Lawrence & Atlantic Railway was built between Longueuil, Quebec, and Portland, Maine—the first line between the two countries and important for Quebec because it was now connected to Portland, which was ice-free.

Railway Mania

Ontario and Quebec (Upper and Lower Canada) became the Province of Canada on February 10, 1841, and in 1849 the Legislative Assembly introduced the Guarantee Act, which provided government assistance for railways more than 75 miles long. Under this act, railways were reimbursed by the government for half the interest on their bonds once half the line had been completed. This, coupled with the Municipal Loan Act of 1852, led to a stampede of railway construction; in the decade from 1850 the total length of railways in Ontario increased from just over 60 to 2,000 miles. This was Canada's first period of railway mania, and even the 1851 act under which a gauge of 5 feet 6 inches was adopted for all railways in the province could not quell it. In 1852 the Canadian government announced that it planned to connect Montreal and Toronto by rail. In the event, the broad-gauge railways were converted to standard gauge in the mid-1870s.

On January 27, 1854, the Great Western Railway opened its line from Niagara Falls, Hamilton, and London through to Windsor. It thus offered a bridge, and much shorter, route from New York to Michigan, and this generated considerable traffic for this British- and U.S.-financed company. It competed aggressively, and ultimately unsuccessfully, with the much larger Grand Trunk Railway, which was incorporated on November 10, 1852, to build a line across the Province of Canada and on to Halifax. Headquartered in London, England, it commenced operations by purchasing four short Ontario and Quebec lines, as well as the St. Lawrence & Atlantic Railway in 1853. The bulk of the financing was raised in Britain, and the line from Toronto to Montreal was constructed by a British company that employed many English workers. This section was opened on October 27, 1856, and by the following month the company connected Sarnia with Portland, Maine. Unfortunately, a depression in 1857 caused severe economic grief to both the Grand Trunk and the Great Western railways. In 1861 Sir Edward Watkin, president of the Grand Trunk, came from England and persuaded the government of the Province of Canada to introduce legislation allowing the Grand Trunk to reorganize its debt to the government. His other task on this trip was to determine for the British Colonial Office whether the British North American colonies would be prepared to join together as a confederation.

Confederation

Primarily for economic and defensive reasons, and with the support of the Colonial Office, the Province of Canada (Ontario and Quebec) and Nova Scotia and New Brunswick formed the Dominion of Canada on July 1, 1867. Completion of a railway linking the maritime colonies with the Province of Canada at or near Quebec City was a condition of confederation. A line had been opened between Halifax and Truro, Nova Scotia, by the Nova Scotian government in 1858, and the European & North American Railway commenced service between St. John and Shediac on August 1, 1860. The same year the

Grand Trunk extended its line eastward as far as Rivière du Loup. The Intercolonial Railway was formed to take over the lines in Nova Scotia, and Sir Sandford Fleming was appointed to oversee the surveying and construction of the railway between Rivière du Loup and Truro. The 700-mile line was ready for through service on July 1, 1876, and the Dominion government purchased the Grand Trunk line from Rivière du Loup to Point Levis, Quebec, in 1879. In 1889 the Intercolonial obtained running rights over the Grand Trunk into Montreal, and on March 1, 1898, it commenced through service between Montreal and Halifax. The railway was operated by the Dominion's minister of railways and canals and provided low-cost transportation between Montreal and the Maritimes, assisting considerably in developing this area. In 1919 the Intercolonial Railway became an initial constituent of the Canadian National Railways.

Western Canada was virtually unknown at the time of confederation. The only scientific examination of Rupert's Land had been the Palliser expedition, which, between 1857 and 1860, explored the Canadian route to Winnipeg, the western plains, and the Rocky Mountains. The conclusions were that to construct a route through British North America to Winnipeg would be difficult and costly, and that although there was a triangle of semi-arid country (the Palliser Triangle) along the U.S. border, east of the Rockies, this was surrounded by a fertile belt suitable for agriculture. Of major importance was James Hector's discovery of Kicking Horse Pass in 1858; it enabled the Canadian Pacific Railway to cross the Rockies when the line was built in 1884.

Rupert's Land became part of the Dominion on July 15, 1870, and the eastern portion became the province of Manitoba on the same day. On the West Coast, settlement had begun on Vancouver's Island and on the mainland around the mouth of the Fraser River in the 1840s. These were united as one colony in 1858 under the name of British Columbia, with its capital in Victoria, and joined Canada on July 20, 1871, with the proviso that the Dominion government would within two years commence construction of a railway line—the Pacific Railway—linking the new province with the rest of Canada. The line was supposed to be completed within ten years.

Prince Edward Island was the next province to join the Dominion on July 1, 1873, with the promise from the government to take over and complete the island's railways, which became part of the Intercolonial Railway. This part of the government's plan went well, and the line opened on January 4, 1875. The Pacific Railway, on the other hand, was a severe problem and led to the downfall of Prime Minister John A. Macdonald's Conservative government. In return for funds to bribe voters to elect the Conservatives in the 1872 election, Macdonald awarded Sir Hugh Allan the contract to build the Pacific Railway with government subsidies of $30 million and 50 million acres of land. The opposition Liberals found out what had happened and broke the story on April 2, 1873.

Macdonald's government was forced to resign on October 23, 1873, and the Liberals swept into power in the ensuing election. The new prime minister, Alexander Mackenzie, also supported the Pacific Railway but believed that it should be built without government help. Not surprisingly, in view of the size of the venture, its cost, and construction difficulties that the line faced, Mackenzie met with little success, although construction around Selkirk (Winnipeg) was commenced, and in the 1878 election Macdonald's Conservatives returned to power.

Canadian Pacific Railway

By this time there was pressure from the electorate to ensure that Canada resisted any suspected U.S. move to take over the western portion of the country. The best way to do this was to construct the Pacific Railway as rapidly as possible. To placate British Columbia, which had been promised a transcontinental railway by 1881, the Conservatives contracted with Andrew Onderdonk to construct a line up the Fraser Canyon from Yale, British Columbia, which was commenced on May 14, 1880. Next, on October 21, 1880, a syndicate led by Donald Smith, George Stephen, and James Hill was formed to bid to build the Canadian Pacific Railway. With excellent financial contacts in the United Kingdom and the United States, it was believed that this group offered the best chance of success, and on February 16, 1881, the Canadian Pacific Railway Co. was incorporated. In return for $25 million, 25 million acres of land "fairly fit for settlement," the lines already under construction, and a noncompetition clause for 20 years, the CPR undertook to construct a railway within ten years and to operate it "in perpetuity" from Callendar, Ontario, to Port Moody, British Columbia, following the route surveyed by Sir Sandford Fleming. Paradoxically, the only other location mentioned in the contract was the Yellowhead Pass, west of Jasper, Alberta; if this route had been followed, it would have taken the line over 200 miles north of the U.S. border.

Relatively little main line was built in 1881. To ensure that the construction rate improved, William Cornelius Van Horne was hired as general manager at the beginning of 1882. At that time the end of track was at Oak Lake, Manitoba, 161 miles west of Winnipeg; by the end of the year Van Horne had added 421 miles of main line. At this time the major problem was how the railway was to cross the Selkirk Mountains, west of the Rockies. From its earliest days, it wanted to locate the line as close to the U.S. border as possible. This was never stated; the company referred only to searching for a "better" route.

The Palliser expedition had noted that there were passes in the Rockies south of the Yellowhead Pass that were suitable for railway construction, but that the Selkirks presented a formidable barrier. Maj. A. B. Rogers, a U.S. surveyor, was employed to find a pass through the Selkirks, and he achieved this on July 22, 1882, when the end of track was almost 300 miles west of Winnipeg and heading toward Calgary, Alberta. The railway petitioned the government to allow it to relocate its line from the Yellowhead to the Rogers Pass, and in 1883 this was agreed to, but no subsidies would be paid nor any land grants provided for construction west of Moose Jaw (388 miles west of Winnipeg) until an independent evaluation of the Rogers Pass was made.

The government assigned Sandford Fleming to evaluate the CPR's new route. He had originally surveyed the line through the Yellowhead Pass, and everyone held their collective breaths in August and September 1883 while Fleming reviewed the route. To everyone's surprise he reported that the line was "quite practicable and highly satisfactory." Van Horne had built a farther 300 miles by the time Fleming's report reached Montreal, and the railhead was about to enter the Rocky Mountains. While building the Canadian Pacific Railway was a major gamble, holding out for the southern route was the second-greatest risk taken in constructing the line.

By the end of 1883 the line was laid to just short of the Continental Divide, which marked the boundary between the North West Territories (Alberta) and British Columbia. Construction restarted in May 1884, crossed the Divide at 5,296 feet above sea level, and immediately encountered severe problems. Down the Kicking Horse Canyon it proved impossible to limit the maximum grade to 2.2 percent as called for in the contract, and the government had to give the railway "temporary" permission to adopt a 4.5 percent grade. This steep grade proved to be extremely difficult to work, and in August 1909 the railway opened the Spiral Tunnels, which by doubling the distance to the summit reduced the climb to 2.2 percent.

It took all the 1884 and 1885 construction seasons to build the remaining 169 miles from the Continental Divide to Craigellachie, 28 miles west of Revelstoke—an indication of the difficulties encountered. The climb from Beavermouth, on the Columbia River, over the 20 miles to the summit of the Rogers Pass at 4,300 feet, involved a climb of 1,800 feet, an average of 1.7 percent. The only major construction problem was several deeply incised creeks that had to be bridged, but to maintain the maximum 2.2 percent grade on the western descent to Revelstoke, the line was looped through a total of 2,500 degrees, requiring the construction of extensive wooden trestles. This area is subject to considerable snowfall; over a 16-mile stretch, a total of 31 snow sheds had to be built to protect the track from avalanches. Even with snowshed protection, disasters still occurred, and, in 1916 Canadian Pacific opened the five-mile Connaught Tunnel under the Rogers Pass.

The last spike joining the eastward and westward portions of the main line was driven at Craigellachie on November 7, 1885, by Donald Smith. Van Horne was present. When asked to make a speech, he said, "All I can say is that the work has been well done in every way." In spite of

this declaration, much work remained—mainly upgrading the Onderdonk construction, which was not up to Canadian Pacific standards. The first transcontinental train left Montreal on June 28, 1886, and arrived at Port Moody, on the Pacific Coast, six days later.

In order to provide traffic for the railway, Canadian Pacific's agents chartered seven sailing ships to carry cargos across the Pacific in 1886. The first of these, the *W. B. Flint,* arrived at Port Moody on July 27, 1886, only three weeks after the first train had crossed the continent, with tea for Hamilton, Toronto, and New York. In the first year of operation over 4,000 tons of freight arrived by sea, but it was soon realized that Port Moody was not an ideal seaport. Consequently, the main line was extended 12.2 miles westward to Vancouver, where deepwater enabled direct transfers to be made from oceangoing vessels to the railway. The first train arrived in Vancouver on May 23, 1887, and from June 3, 1889, Canadian Pacific trains operated between the Pacific and from St. John, New Brunswick, on the Atlantic. The railway was now a truly transcontinental system—the first in North America.

Meanwhile, traffic on the prairies was gradually building up. At first, the problem was getting freight to and from a railhead; a horse could only haul a wagon between five and ten miles to the railway if it was to return home that night. Thus only a narrow belt close to the main line was populated at first. As luck would have it, much of this was dry prairie in the Palliser Triangle with little agricultural potential at the time. Branch lines were necessary to serve the homesteaders on the prairies, and the first feeder line was the North Western Coal & Navigation Co.'s 36-inch-gauge track constructed over the 109 miles from Dunmore, near Medicine Hat, to Lethbridge, Alberta. As well as providing a source of freight, the line enabled coal to be hauled to the main line, solving a major problem for Canadian Pacific, as wood was the primary locomotive fuel until then. The narrow-gauge system was extended to serve other centers in southern Alberta and northern Montana. Standard-gauging commenced in the 1890s, and the Canadian portions of the system were acquired by Canadian Pacific in 1897.

The first standard-gauge branch line to be built on the prairies connected Calgary with Edmonton. This opened for traffic on August 23, 1891, and was then extended south of Calgary toward the U.S. border, opening on November 1, 1892. Although operated by Canadian Pacific, the Calgary & Edmonton Railway was nominally independent and was built by a company formed by William Mackenzie and Donald Mann, who were to construct the Canadian Northern Railway. To facilitate construction, the Dominion government granted the railway 6,400 acres of land for every mile of line laid. Gradually, other branch lines were added with similar land grants, and by the beginning of the twentieth century southern Alberta had a relatively extensive system of railways.

Although this was not a consideration at the time it was built, the location of the Canadian Pacific main line took the route through an area of southern Alberta and British Columbia almost totally devoid of mineral resources. The Crow's Nest route was never considered as a location for the transcontinental main line, even though it was known that extensive coal deposits existed on both sides of the provincial border. With James Hill's Great Northern Railway casting covetous eyes northward, Canadian Pacific recognized that it had to protect its southern border. On September 6, 1897, the Dominion government and Canadian Pacific signed the contract for the Crowsnest Line, which authorized the railway to build its line from Lethbridge to Nelson, British Columbia, in return for a grant of C$11,000 per mile (to a maximum of C$3.6 million), as well as land grants. At that time many western Canadians were unhappy with Canadian Pacific's traffic monopoly, and the Crowsnest contract specified that when the line reached Kootenay Lake, freight rates (mainly grain) be reduced on "the main line or any other line throughout Canada owned, leased or operated" by the Canadian Pacific Railway. In addition, the act stated that "no higher rates . . . shall thereafter be charged by the Company." With the benefit of hindsight, one wonders how the railway's lawyers missed that, because it was to cause considerable difficulties for not only the Canadian Pacific but other Canadian railways that were deemed to be covered by the act. The line to Kootenay Landing opened on June 18, 1899, and the rates were reduced.

The Canadian National System

Relations between William Mackenzie and Donald Mann and the Canadian Pacific worsened during the 1890s, culminating with the formation of Mackenzie and Mann's Canadian Northern Railway on January 13, 1899. This marked the beginning of the country's second railway mania; the first 15 years of the twentieth century were marked by building of not one but two more transcontinental railways, financed mainly by government and British money together with government guarantees and land grants. Between 1900 and 1915 Canada's railway mileage increased almost threefold from 17,000 to nearly 50,000 miles. The Canadian Northern Railway rapidly built up a strong prairie network by acquiring shortlines and running rights and, where necessary, constructing track. By 1902 the railway had a line from Winnipeg to Lake Superior, and Mackenzie and Mann were encouraged by the premiers of British Columbia and Ontario to extend the Canadian Northern to the Pacific Coast and the St. Lawrence. Originally, it had been planned to build these extensions only after the railway had 5,000 miles of prairie lines to provide sufficient traffic to warrant a transcontinental system. However, the aggressive Grand Trunk Railway wanted to extend into western Canada and on to the Pacific Coast and tried unsuccessfully to purchase the Canadian Northern system. Although the western Canadian members of the Cabinet supported Mackenzie and Mann, Wilfrid Laurier, the prime minister, pushed through the National Transcontinental Railway Act on October 24, 1903, which provided for the Grand Trunk and the government to build a line connecting Moncton, New Brunswick, with the Pacific. To protect their position, Mackenzie and Mann were forced to build the Canadian Northern into a transcontinental system, and their railhead arrived in Edmonton on November 24, 1905. A line was built around the north shore of Lake Superior to Ottawa, opening in 1908, and the last spike was driven home on January 15, 1915, near Ashcroft, British Columbia. The first passenger train arrived in Vancouver on August 28, 1915, and full service began on the 10,000-mile system the following November. But World War I had broken out, and although traffic had increased, there was insufficient business to support this 10,000-mile system. Moreover, funds from the United Kingdom had dried up, and the flow of immigrants had slowed to a trickle.

As already mentioned, the Grand Trunk Railway, as Ontario's premier line, wanted to extend its influence to the Pacific Coast. After failing to acquire Mackenzie and Mann's Canadian Northern, the Grand Trunk worked with Prime Minister Laurier, and the government passed the National Transcontinental Railway Act providing for the government to build the National Transcontinental Railway from Moncton to Winnipeg, and the Grand Trunk's wholly owned subsidiary, the Grand Trunk Pacific Railway, to construct the line from Winnipeg to Prince Rupert, British Columbia. After completion the government would turn over its portion to the Grand Trunk Pacific for operation. For the first seven years after the turnover, there was to be no charge for the National Transcontinental, and for the following 43 years, the Grand Trunk Pacific would pay 3 percent of the construction cost annually.

Both the Canadian Northern and the Grand Trunk Pacific crossed the Rockies through the Yellowhead Pass, but whereas the former swung south for Vancouver, the Grand Trunk Pacific went northwest to Prince George and reached the Pacific at Prince Rupert. The last-spike ceremony was held in early April 1914 at Finmoore, 93 miles west of Prince George, and service between Winnipeg and Prince Rupert commenced in September 1914. The National Transcontinental was completed in November 1913 and, after considerable upgrading, was declared open on June 1, 1915, but the Grand Trunk Pacific had declined to take over operations of the government railway, as had originally been agreed.

By November Canada had three transcontinental railways, but while the Canadian Pacific had net earnings of $33.6 million in the year to June 30, 1915, neither the Canadian Northern nor the Grand Trunk could cover their expenses. Indeed, the Dominion government had had to provide loans to both the Canadian Northern and the Grand Trunk Pacific in 1914 to enable them to complete their construction and continue operations. In order to prevent a complete collapse of the unprofitable lines, which would cause untold harm to Canada, the

Dominion government, which was primarily responsible for the debacle, had to introduce comprehensive policies to solve the problems. Initially it formed the Canadian Government Railways to operate the National Transcontinental and the Intercolonial Railways on May 1, 1915, and, to investigate the problems fully, in 1916 it appointed what was to become known as the Drayton-Acworth Royal Commission. Under the chairmanship of A. H. Smith, president of the New York Central, the two other members of the commission issued a majority report recommending that the government roll the Canadian Northern, the Grand Trunk, the Grand Trunk Pacific, the Intercolonial, and the National Transcontinental railways into one government-owned system. By cabinet order the Canadian Northern was taken over on November 20, 1918, a new board was appointed, and the Canadian Government Railways was placed under the control of the new board. One month later the cabinet approved the name of Canadian National Railways to identify its railway assets. In February 1919 the Grand Trunk informed the government that it would no longer operate the Grand Trunk Pacific after March 10, and on March 7 the minister of railways became the Grand Trunk Pacific's receiver.

The Canadian National Railway Co. was created on June 6, 1919, and responsibility for the Grand Trunk Pacific was assigned to Canadian National on March 8, 1920. The Grand Trunk Railway was turned over to the government in May 1920, but a board of arbitration had to be appointed to determine the railway's value. The majority decision, given in September 1921, stated that there was no value to either the common or preferred stock, though the minority report stated that the railway was worth $48 million, and it was not until January 19, 1923, that a cabinet order merged the Grand Trunk into the Canadian National. Under the chairmanship and presidency of Sir Henry Thornton, the railway now had to be streamlined and molded into a commercial operation, a process that continued until well after World War II.

The 1920s and 1930s

During the long gestation of the Canadian National system, the Canadian Pacific continued to develop and expand. It took over the Esquimalt & Nanaimo Railway on Vancouver Island in 1905 and built up an extensive fleet of ocean, coastal, and inland vessels. Hotels were built in the mountains and on both coasts, and as early as 1919 its charter was altered to allow the company to operate an airline. Many of its oceangoing ships were requisitioned by the British government because they were registered in the United Kingdom, and during hostilities 14 vessels were lost. After the war several former German ships were acquired, and service across the Atlantic and Pacific soon developed to prewar levels.

Until the 1920s both railways used relatively small steam locomotives to haul their freight and passenger trains. Up to the early 1900s these were mostly 4-4-0s, with heavier 2-8-0s to supply power on mountain grades. The introduction of the superheater allowed both systems to achieve fuel economies, and 4-6-0s and 4-6-2s were introduced as heavier passenger trains were brought into service. During World War I, 2-10-0s were constructed for freight service, and some 2-10-2s were built for heavy freight and pusher service. Competition between the two railways was intense, and while Canadian Pacific thought that the Canadian National system had an unfair advantage with the government's unlimited funds behind it, Canadian Pacific was seen as having benefited from the munificent government of the 1880s.

The 1920s were a period of prairie expansion as both railways constructed branch lines to capture the grain traffic. The two railways could work together, as shown in the June 26, 1929, joint purchase of the 857-mile Northern Alberta Railways, which extended into the wheatlands northwest of Edmonton. But the railways were beginning to feel the competition from trucks and buses. By the end of the decade the first passenger-train withdrawals were taking place when services were not supported by mail contracts.

In an attempt to maintain service without making undue losses, the Canadian Northern had experimented with a self-propelled car in 1918. The most significant railway development, though probably overlooked at the time, was the Canadian National's operation of an oil diesel-electric railcar from Montreal to Vancouver in November 1925. No. 15820 covered the 2,937-mile trip in 67 hours of running time with only 5 hours spent at division points—a feat no steam locomotive could have emulated. This was followed by the introduction of Nos. 9000 and 9001, North America's first diesel-electric locomotives, which were built in 1928 and 1929 by the Canadian Locomotive Co. at Kingston, Ontario. On August 26, 1929, the two units hauled the *International Limited* between Montreal and Toronto. However, this was a one-off experiment; both Canadian Pacific and Canadian National were still steam railways, and while the latter purchased 4-8-2 Mountains for its prime passenger trains, Canadian Pacific designed 4-6-4 Hudsons for its services and 2-10-4 Selkirks for the 262 miles of mountains between Calgary and Revelstoke. To investigate the feasibility of cutting operating costs, Canadian Pacific's Hudson No. 2808 ran the entire 1,251 miles between Fort William and Calgary and back between June 19 and 24. As a result, Canadian Pacific was able to reduce the 17 locomotives used on passenger trains between Montreal and Vancouver to 3 Hudsons as far as Calgary, a Selkirk from Calgary to Revelstoke and a Pacific from Revelstoke to Vancouver.

With the stock market crash of October 1929 and the subsequent Depression, rail traffic fell dramatically, and during the 1930s there was much discussion of the two railways either amalgamating or being amalgamated. Nothing came of this, though there is little doubt that the government catered to Canadian National whenever possible. To rationalize service and to cut competition, from April 2, 1933, Canadian Pacific and Canadian National were allowed under the Canadian National Canadian Pacific Act to pool their passenger traffic between Montreal and Toronto. This agreement remained in place until October 30, 1965.

In 1937 Canadian Pacific acquired its first diesel-electric switcher. Again, this was a one-off venture. Steam locomotives continued to be purchased, now in a semi-streamlined form reflecting the styling in vogue worldwide at that time. The 1930s ended with the Royal Tour of 1939 when King George VI and Queen Elizabeth visited the Dominion and traveled from Quebec to Vancouver on the Canadian Pacific, returning eastbound on the Canadian National. This, the first visit of the reigning monarch to Canada, was highly successful. It is generally accepted that it ensured Canada's unconditional participation in World War II.

The 1940s to the Present

Canada entered World War II on September 10, 1939, and once more made a huge commitment, far greater than its relatively small population would have suggested. The railways were stretched to the limit providing freight and passenger services, and both the Canadian Pacific and Montreal Locomotive Works produced tanks and other ordnance for the military. Canadian Pacific pioneered transatlantic flight as it investigated, organized, and initially operated the ferry service flying U.S.-built aircraft from Canada to the United Kingdom. Both Canadian Pacific and Canadian National ships were requisitioned by the British government, and at the end of hostilities few returned to their respective owners. A few diesel-electric switchers were purchased by both railways during the war. Canadian National purchased 15 Electro-Motive Division (EMD) NW2s in 1941–1942 and 21 Alco S-2s between 1941 and 1946, and Canadian Pacific acquired 29 S-2s between 1943 and 1945. Canadian National received its last new steam locomotive, No. 6079, a U-1-f Mountain 4-8-2, in December 1944 when the steam roster totaled 2,500 steam locomotives. The last steam locomotive built for Canadian Pacific arrived a few years later when T-1-c Selkirk No. 5935 was delivered in March 1949. This was the last of 3,257 steam locomotives owned by Canadian Pacific, of which 1,700 were still in service. Both railways ran their last steam-operated services in 1960.

On April 1, 1949, the British colony of Newfoundland joined Canada as its tenth province, and the Newfoundland Railway became part of Canadian National Railways, adding 800 route-miles to the government system. The 3-foot 6-inch–gauge railway consisted of the 547-mile route across the island from St. John's to Port aux Basques, which had been completed in 1910, and four branch lines.

The sweep of main-line diesel-electrics commenced in 1948 with Canadian National acquiring 28 EMD F3s. Both Canada's major railways experimented with products from the three major diesel builders. Canadian National continued with additional General Motors units, purchasing a further 206 F units from GM Diesel of London, Ontario, between 1951 and 1958 and 105 GP7s and 9s from 1952 to 1959, primarily from EMD. The Canadian Locomotive Co. built Fairbanks-Morse locomotives under license at Kingston, Ontario, and supplied 32 C-Liners to Canadian National between 1952 and 1955. The Montreal Locomotive Works, owned by Alco, between 1955 and 1959 constructed 62 FPA and FPB units for the railway. Canadian Pacific's ordering was equally eclectic, but rather than dieselizing by service, it replaced steam locomotives by area at first and introduced its first diesel-electrics on Vancouver Island in 1948. These were 24 Baldwin diesel road switchers, built in Kingston, followed by three EMD-built E8s delivered in 1949 to take over the main-line passenger service from Montreal to the East Coast. Alco constructed 12 FA1/FB1 units for the railway in 1949, and 47 MLW-built FA/FPA locomotives were purchased between 1950 and 1953. Canadian Pacific then turned to GMD for a total of 83 F units constructed at London between 1950 and 1954. Over the same period both railways were attempting to cut operating costs on branch-line services, and between 1951 and 1958 Canadian Pacific purchased 63 Budd cars, which it named Dayliners. Over roughly the same period Canadian National acquired 52 Budd cars (Railiners), together with 18 trailer cars.

In an attempt to curtail the steady decrease in passenger traffic, both Canadian Pacific and Canadian National introduced new transcontinental trains in 1955 to take advantage of the capabilities of diesel-electric power. Canadian National put the *Super Contintental* into service, taking only 73 hours and 20 minutes for the trip from Montreal to Vancouver—almost identical to No. 15820's elapsed time for the same journey in 1925 but 25 hours faster than in steam days. The Canadian Pacific, going even further to attract passengers, in 1953 ordered 173 stainless-steel passenger cars from the Budd Co. of Philadelphia. Of these, 77 were to be used on a new service from Montreal and Toronto to Vancouver, and the remainder were for Toronto-Montreal and Montreal–St. John trains. A new train, *The Canadian*, was introduced from Montreal-Toronto to Vancouver on April 25, 1955, and was scheduled to take 71 hours and 10 minutes for the 2,881 miles from Montreal to Vancouver—16 hours faster than *The Dominion*, which it supplemented. At first both trains were highly successful, but by 1960 no train could compete with the convenience of the automobile or the speed of jet aircraft. Both railways sought government permission to abandon passenger trains throughout the country. A temporary solution was the government's agreement to pay 80 percent of the railways' losses, but in 1977 a government company, VIA Rail, was formed to take over main-line passenger services.

Freight

The two main Canadian railways have always been prodigious freight haulers, over which the government has exercised considerable control. The Crow's Nest Pass Agreement of 1897 was a contract between the Canadian Pacific Railway and the government that saw the rates reduced on wheat shipments by approximately 15 percent and a similar reduction on inbound settlers' effects. In return for a grant of $3.3 million, the railway agreed to maintain 1897 rates "in perpetuity."

Because of the inflation of World War I and the cutback in immigration, the railway petitioned the government to rescind the rate schedule, and the agreement was suspended. In 1925, however, the Board of Railway Commissioners reinstituted the 1897 rates, and the railways lost considerable amounts on grain handling. By 1981 payments for hauling grain covered only 19 percent of the true cost of the transport. The railways were unable and unprepared to upgrade their fleet of grain cars, and there was considerable debate between the railways, the government, and the farmers and farmers' organizations. This led to the government passing the Western Grain Transportation Act on November 17, 1983, allowing a gradual increase in shipping rates, with the government paying the balance of the shipping costs. In return, the railways agreed to upgrade their systems. After the 1993 federal election the government made a onetime payment to the farmers and eliminated its control of the rates entirely.

Until the elimination of steam, the two main railway lines continued to operate much as usual, with relatively short freight trains being operated as and when necessary. Since every locomotive had to be manned, whenever possible a single locomotive was assigned to a train. With the multiple-unit feature of diesel-electrics, it was possible to have a single crew operate several locomotives, and longer freight trains, running at higher speeds, were now economically attractive. Fewer personnel were required. On August 22, 1950, nearly 126,000 railway workers across the country went on strike. The country was paralyzed, and the government legislated the strikers back to work on August 30. The damage, however, had been done; the rise in long-distance truck competition stems from this work dislocation. To fight this competition, Canadian Pacific introduced an intermodal freight system hauling piggyback road trailers on flatcars between Montreal and Toronto on December 1, 1952. Canadian National introduced a similar system in 1960, and truck trailers riding on flatcars soon became a common sight across the country. Today, freight containers have largely replaced trailers, and both transcontinental lines carry large numbers of standard containers. These are for service within North America and as part of the North American Land Bridge, transporting products between Europe and the Far East.

In 1967 Canadian Pacific's railway assets were renamed CP Rail, a subsidiary of the parent company Canadian Pacific Ltd. The railway experimented with unit trains and on July 11 ran a train carrying 3,700 tons of sulfuric acid from near Sudbury, Ontario, to Sarnia. The following November 16, the railway commenced testing the use of remotely controlled midtrain locomotives in regular freight trains. This enabled power to be spread throughout the train, reducing the risk of drawbar breakages. On one test a train of 178 cars was hauled up the Fraser Canyon. Remote units made it possible for 88-car unit coal trains to be hauled from southeastern British Columbia to tidewater, south of Vancouver. This service began on April 30, 1970, and has grown over the years so that 110-car trains are now operated in this service. Both railways have concentrated on transporting bulk commodities, and today coal, petroleum products, potash, and sulfur constitute the majority of the railways' traffic.

Other relatively recent developments include the opening of the 9.1-mile Mount Macdonald Tunnel on the Canadian Pacific main line on December 12, 1988, in the Selkirk Mountains. The longest tunnel in North America, it reduces the westbound grade to 1.0 percent. Canadian National opened its new tunnel from Sarnia, Ontario, to Port Huron, Michigan, on May 5, 1995. Double-stack containers can be carried through the tunnel.

Changes in government outlook occurred in the 1990s, probably as a result of the trend started by Margaret Thatcher in Britain. Privatization became the policy of the government. On November 17, 1995, Canadian National was privatized, and shares began trading soon afterwards. Under the leadership of Paul Tellier, the company underwent considerable streamlining, began selling off loss-making lines, became profitable, and expanded vigorously. It acquired the Illinois Central Railroad on July 1, 1999, and in December of the same year it was announced that CN Rail and the Burlington Northern Santa Fe would merge to form North American Railways. This caused a furor from the other Class 1 railroads (Union Pacific, Norfolk Southern, CSX and CP Rail), and after a 15-month moratorium imposed by the U.S. Surface Transportation Board, the proposed merger was called off. Unperturbed, CN Rail continued to expand; it acquired Wisconsin Central Transportation on October 9, 2001, and followed this up with the takeover of Great Lakes Transportation on May 10, 2004, and the British Columbia Railway on July 15, 2004. It now operates 19,200 miles of track and has more than 22,000 employees.

CP Rail has also undergone a similar streamlining and expansion. In early 1990 it acquired full ownership of the Soo Line, a company in which it had held a controlling interest since 1890. It purchased the bankrupt Delaware & Hudson Railroad in 1991 to gain access to the northeastern U.S. seaboard, and in 1996 it merged its southern Ontario and Quebec lines with the Delaware & Hudson into the St. Lawrence & Hudson Railway. It arranged running rights to access New York City, and in 1996 it moved its headquarters from Montreal to Calgary. On October 3,

2001, the Canadian Pacific Railway became a stand-alone company. It operates almost 14,000 route-miles of track and employs more than 16,000 workers. Both railways are profitable, and in 2005 CN had an operating ratio (expenses as a percentage of revenues) of 64 percent—a phenomenally good figure. Canadian Pacific's is not as good but still a respectable 71 percent.

—Donald M. Bain

REFERENCES

Berton, Pierre. *The Last Spike*. Montreal: McClelland & Stewart, 1971.

———. *The National Dream*. Montreal: McClelland & Stewart, 1970.

Bruce, Harry. *The Pig That Flew: The Battle to Privatize Canadian National*. Vancouver: Douglas & McIntyre, 1997.

Gibbon, John Murray. *Steel of Empire*. Indianapolis: Bobbs-Merrill, 1935.

Lavallée, Omer. *Van Horne's Road*. Montreal: Railfare Enterprises, 1974.

MacKay, Donald. *The People's Railway*. Vancouver: Douglas & McIntyre, 1992.

Marsh, D'Arcy. *The Tragedy of Henry Thornton*. Toronto: Macmillan of Canada, 1935.

Stevens, George R. *History of the Canadian National Railways*. New York: Macmillan, 1973.

Car Builders

There have been several hundred different railroad-car builders in North America since the earliest railroads. Their history is complicated by mergers, failures, and changes in ownership. Many nineteenth-century builders are particularly obscure, with little known about the full extent of their production. Early car builders fall into two major groups: railroad and contract builders. Some railroads, such as the Philadelphia & Reading, built most of their cars in their own shops until the late 1880s, while others, such as the Central Railroad of New Jersey, relied primarily on contract builders. During the 1900s it also became common for leasing companies, such as the Union Tank Car Co., to build their own cars. The separation of the three types of builders is not always well defined; some railroads and leasing companies do contract building, and some contract shops build cars for lease.

Among the better-known early contract builders were Harlan & Hollingsworth Co., which at first built all kinds of cars but eventually specialized in passenger equipment; Ensign Manufacturing Co., which was primarily a builder of freight cars and became part of American Car & Foundry Co. (AC&F); Murray, Dougal & Co., a builder of freight cars specializing in tank cars that also became part of AC&F; Haskell & Barker Car Co., which was once listed as the largest builder of freight cars; and the Pullman Co., an important builder of both freight and passenger cars.

Many other builders failed to survive and were quickly forgotten. McKee, Fuller & Co., also known as the Lehigh Car, Wheel & Axle Works, of Fullerton, Pennsylvania, was one of these. The company was founded in 1866 to manufacture railroad wheels. About 1879 it started to manufacture freight cars. By the early 1880s business was very good, and cars were built for railroads as distant as Australia. After electric lights were installed to allow a second shift, 1,879 freight cars were produced in the first half of 1882. A few years later weekly capacity was reported to be up to 150 boxcars or 450 coal cars, presumably of the four-wheeled variety. In comparison, actual production by each of the largest twentieth-century car builders averaged about 300 cars a week. As business at McKee, Fuller declined in the late 1880s, an interest in the company was purchased by Lehigh Valley Railroad associates. After that, the Lehigh Valley was the primary customer until the works closed about 1892. Like McKee, Fuller, most of the established builders were located in the East, while the demand for cars and sources for raw materials were moving west. Competition from Pullman's new Chicago works and other western builders was becoming an important factor by the mid-1880s. Over 2,800 freight cars were built by Pullman in 1884, and in 1890 its production increased to over 7,000 cars.

Two extremely large builders dominated the industry in North America for most of the twentieth century. American Car & Foundry was formed in 1899 and was the largest car builder until about 1940. Total twentieth-century production was perhaps 2 million freight and passenger cars. The Pullman-Standard Car Manufacturing Co. overtook American Car & Foundry about 1940 and remained the largest car builder until 1982. During the twentieth century Pullman-Standard and predecessor companies built about 1.5 million freight and passenger cars. After the collapse of Pullman-Standard in the 1980s, Trinity Industries rose to dominance, producing over a quarter of a million freight cars in the last two decades.

The end of the 1800s saw the rise of numerous new car-building companies that specialized in steel cars. The largest of these was the Pressed Steel Car Co., which produced about half a million freight and passenger cars before production ended in 1954. About half a dozen other builders were large enough to produce well over 100,000 cars. The majority of the car builders built fewer than 100,000 cars, and a substantial number produced less than 1,000 cars each.

A few builders concentrated primarily on passenger cars, including Bombardier and the Budd Co. Two other important passenger-car builders were St. Louis Car and Brill. Both built electric railway cars in addition to standard railway cars. Several freight-car builders built passenger cars as well. Following in alphabetical order are summaries of the North American car builders that constructed at least 60,000 cars during the twentieth century.

The Bethlehem Steel Corp. became a freight-car builder when it acquired Midvale Steel Car & Ordinance in 1923. The latter company had acquired Cambria Steel Co. of Johnstown, Pennsylvania, in 1916. Cambria Steel was founded in 1852 as the Cambria Iron Co. and was a manufacturer of iron and steel products, including rolled-steel rail and structural shapes. Its first freight cars were apparently several flatcars and gondola cars for Lackawanna Steel in early 1901, followed by 1,500 drop-bottom gondola cars built for the Philadelphia & Reading in 1901 and 1902. Although the Philadelphia & Reading did not place an additional order until 1907, Johnstown already had orders to build 800 Vanderbilt-design hopper cars for the West Virginia Central & Pittsburg Railway and 10 similar cars for Lackawanna Steel. Starting in 1902, the Pennsylvania Railroad and subsidiaries repeatedly placed substantial orders, as did other railroads. From the very beginning, Cambria Steel concentrated on gondolas, hoppers, and flatcars, which required little wood beyond flooring. Occasional orders for boxcars and covered and tank cars were also filled. Bethlehem Steel also produced car parts and car kits from at least 1936 through 1970.

As more companies shifted from using hopper to gondola cars in unit coal trains, Bethlehem Steel developed the BethGon Coalporter, which went into production in 1978. Prototype aluminum-bodied hopper and gondola cars were introduced in the mid-1980s, and the company name was changed to the Johnstown America Corp. in 1991. Johnstown America currently describes itself as the largest manufacturer of aluminum-bodied cars.

Bethlehem Steel also became a passenger-car builder through acquisition of Harlan & Hollingsworth Co. of Wilmington, Delaware, about 1920. Harlan & Hollingsworth was a well-known builder of first-class passenger cars. It completed the transition to all-steel construction by 1913, but did not make a successful transition into the lightweight passenger-car market. Production ended in 1939. An unsuccessful attempt was made to revitalize Harlan & Hollingsworth as an independent freight-car builder immediately after World War II.

Canadian Car & Foundry Co. was incorporated in November 1909 as a combination of three companies. The Rhodes Curry Co. of Amherst, Nova Scotia, started in 1893 to build both freight and passenger cars. The Canada Car Co. of Turcot, Montreal, Quebec, was opened in 1905 and also built both types of cars. Dominion Car & Foundry of Montreal was associated with American Steel Foundries and opened in 1906 to build freight cars. Canadian Car & Foundry was the largest car builder in Canada until its closure. Canadian Car produced the full range of freight- and passenger-car types, although many tank cars were subcontracted to American Car & Foundry and General American during the 1920s and 1930s. Soon after A. V. Roe gained control over both Canadian Car & Foundry and Eastern Car, it determined that there was insufficient business to support both plants and shut Canadian Car down.

The Chicago, Burlington & Quincy Railroad had car shops at Aurora and Galesburg, Illinois, as well as Havelock and Plattsmouth, Nebraska. After operations at Havelock were expanded in the early 1940s, all new car construction was done there. Production was fairly steady from before the turn of the century until the end in 1969, with a total of over 67,000 cars, which went primarily to CB&Q and its subsidiaries Colorado & Southern and Ft. Worth & Denver City. Among the wide variety of freight cars produced were a large number of covered hopper and refrigerator cars.

The Chicago, Milwaukee, St. Paul & Pacific Railroad, previously the Chicago, Milwaukee & St. Paul Railroad, was an active builder of varied freight cars from at least the 1880s through 1919 and again from 1936 to 1952, primarily at its shops in West Milwaukee, Wisconsin. The Milwaukee's later production was known for adopting welded construction as a standard when other builders were just experimenting with it. The Milwaukee built around 89,000 cars during the twentieth century and also built some lightweight passenger cars of its own design.

The Eastern Car Co. was organized as a subsidiary of the Nova Scotia Steel & Coal Co., later known as the Dominion Steel & Coal Co. Its plant opened in Trenton, Nova Scotia, in 1913. It was acquired by A. V. Roe Ltd. in the late 1950s and became known as Hawker Siddeley Canada Ltd. in 1963. Then the company was acquired by Lavelin in 1987 and became known as the Trenton Works. Acquired by Greenbrier during the 1990s, it is the second-largest car builder in Canada. Early production was varied, although few tank cars were built before Canadian Car & Foundry closed in 1962. Since then, it has been the main producer of tank cars in Canada. Recent production has centered around boxcars and center-beam flatcars used in the paper and lumber industries. There have also been some large orders for covered hopper, intermodal, and auto-rack cars. Since 1995 a large part of its production has gone to U.S. railroads and companies.

General American Transportation Corp. was originally known as the German-American Car Co. from 1902 until 1916 and the General American Tank Car Corp. from 1916 to 1933. General American was an equipment-leasing company that started building cars for its own use in 1907 using plants of Graver Tank & Boiler Works in East Chicago, Indiana, and Warren City Tank & Boiler Works of Warren, Ohio. By 1910 General American had built its own plant in East Chicago. Most of the cars built through 1919 were tank cars. Starting in 1920, General American regularly received large orders for many kinds of freight cars from railroads and private companies. All types except tank cars were generally built at East Chicago. In 1927 tank-car production was moved from Warren to Sharon, Pennsylvania, after General American acquired the Standard Tank Car Co., a major manufacturer of tank cars. Standard Tank started building tank cars about 1916.

General American introduced the revolutionary Airslide covered hopper car in 1953 and continued as a major manufacturer of all kinds of freight cars into the 1960s. After 1968 East Chicago was restricted to building Airslide covered hopper cars until the end in 1984. Tank-car production continued at Sharon until 1984. General American left the freight-car-building business but continued to lease cars, with Trinity Industries, American Car & Foundry, and Union Tank Car supplying whatever new cars were needed.

Greenville Steel Car Co. was located in Greenville, Pennsylvania. As early as 1915 it received orders for some underframes and hopper-car bodies, followed by some scattered orders for new and rebuilt cars. By 1923 Greenville was building dump cars for Clark Car Co. and later (1934) became involved in building covered hoppers for cement. The first boxcars were built in 1936 and were followed by stock cars and flatcars. Greenville became an important producer of 60-foot and 85-foot auto-part boxcars from 1963 through 1978 and continued to build numerous gondola and hopper cars. Production dropped off after the middle of 1982, but some cars were built through 1984, including some aluminum hopper cars for unit coal train service. Greenville was acquired by Trinity Industries in 1986 or 1987, and the plant continued to operate until about November 2000.

Gunderson Brothers Engineering Corp. began building freight cars at its Portland, Oregon, plant in 1960. About 3,600 cars of various types were built there by July 1965, when the company was purchased by the FMC Corp. Shortly after purchasing Gunderson, FMC also built at least 2,520 hopper and covered hopper cars and flatcars at its Charleston, West Virginia, plant from 1966 to 1967. During the 1970s FMC produced mainly boxcars and also covered hopper, rotary coal gondola, wood-chip, and ore cars. By October 1981 the outlook was bleak as it completed its last substantial order, 225 covered hopper cars for North American Car. FMC then filled a series of very small orders, mostly prototype articulated intermodal cars, until late 1984 when it built 75 five-unit articulated intermodal cars for TrailerTrain and 130 rotary coal gondolas for electric utilities. The company was renamed Gunderson, Inc., in April 1985 as large-scale production of five-unit articulated intermodal cars began for a number of customers. Greenbrier was one of the customers and eventually took control of both Gunderson and Trenton Works. In 1987 Gunderson introduced a 73-foot center-beam flatcar for lumber and other building products. It was immediately successful and increased its business substantially. In 1988 it began to build boxcars again after a seven-year break. Some cryogenic refrigerator cars were built from 1990 to 1992. Prototype articulated auto-rack cars were built in 1997, and production began about 1999.

About 1998 Greenbrier and Bombardier formed a joint venture known as Gunderson-Concarril to revitalize the Bombardier Mexico plant, previously Constructora Nacional de Carros de Ferrocarril, in Ciudad Sahagún, Mexico. From 1962 to 1988 the plant had turned out at least 16,000 cars, including about 4,000 for the U.S. market.

Bombardier used the plant to produce 125 gondola cars for the Atchison, Topeka & Santa Fe in 1993. Production under Gunderson-Concarril began in November 1998. By the end of 2000 over 2,500 boxcars, gondola cars, and flatcars were built.

Magor Car Corp. of Clifton, New Jersey, was building freight cars at least as early as 1906, when its name was the Wonhan-Magor Engineering Works. The first cars produced for major railroads were 1,000 steel-frame drop-bottom gondolas built for the U.S. Railroad Administration (USRA) in about 1919 and 1920. Magor had developed an automatic dump car at least as early as 1916 and obtained regular orders for similar cars through the 1950s. In late 1959 Magor started producing a variety of steel and aluminum covered hopper cars for the Southern Railway. The aluminum cars were fairly conventional in design but apparently filled a niche. A large part of Magor's business during the 1960s was aluminum covered hoppers sold to over 18 railroads and private companies. Cars with capacities of 5,325 cubic feet built early in 1965 were the largest in North America at the time. For years Magor was associated with the National Steel Car Corp. In 1964 Magor was sold to Fruehauf, which continued to build cars at Clifton until February 1973. The last orders included several thousand cars built for Penn Central, bringing the grand total to about 36,500 cars.

Merchants Despatch Transportation Corp., later Despatch Shops, Inc., had a unique history. It began as a leasing company, started building its own cars, came under control of the New York Central, and was ultimately turned into a contract shop. The shops were in East Rochester, New York, where it started building boxcars and refrigerator cars for lease at least as early as 1898. Beginning in 1902, it also built cars under contract for half a dozen railroads. On January 1, 1913, Merchants Despatch was sold to the New York Central. Production of various types continued at a steady pace until the last new cars were built in 1970. Total production was over 129,000 freight cars, easily putting this plant in second place among the railroad-car shops. Merchants Despatch also built milk and express cars for use in passenger trains. Another 2,800 freight cars or so were built at other New York Central shops from 1904 to 1968. A few passenger cars were also built at New York Central shops.

Mt. Vernon Car & Manufacturing Co. of Mt. Vernon, Illinois, was organized in 1890. It was a fairly large builder, mostly of wooden cars until 1911. After that, most cars were steel underframe, steel frame or all steel. It built and sold car underframes to railroads and other builders from at least 1914 to 1917. It produced all kinds of freight cars except tank cars. It was acquired by Pressed Steel Car about 1946 and apparently built its last cars in 1954.

National Steel Car Corp., Ltd., was established at Hamilton, Ontario, in 1912 by interests associated with the Magor Car Corp. It was the second-largest car builder in Canada and became the largest after Canadian Car & Foundry shut down about 1962. Production began in 1913 and included passenger as well as freight cars. Although all types of cars were produced, only a few were tank cars. The Hamilton plant continues to build freight cars used primarily in lumber, paper, and intermodal service.

The Norfolk & Western Railway was already active in freight-car building by the 1890s and continued through at least 1990. Well over half the cars were hopper cars, including some for other companies in 1978 and 1979. The remainder were mostly gondola and covered hopper cars as well as a few boxcars, stock and refrigerator cars, and flatcars. Norfolk & Western built all its cars at Roanoke, Virginia, except for several thousand built at Portsmouth, Ohio, and around 1,700 built at the old Virginian shops at Princeton, West Virginia, from 1960 to 1967. About 105,000 cars were built during the twentieth century, making the Norfolk & Western third among the railroad-car builders.

Pacific Car & Foundry Co. was formed in 1917 as the merger of Seattle Car & Foundry Co. of Seattle, Washington, founded in February 1905, and Twohy Brothers Co. of Portland, Oregon, founded in 1910. The main Seattle Car & Foundry plant was opened in Renton, Washington, on February 1, 1908. Production was mostly small local orders for flatcars, but some substantial orders for boxcars were placed by Union Pacific and Southern Pacific in late 1916 and early 1917. The USRA ordered 2,000 boxcars from the merged companies in May 1918. From 1920 through 1931 the company specialized in logging equipment, as well as building 4,804 refrigerator cars for Pacific Fruit Express. A number of boxcars and automobile, stock, and caboose cars were also built for major railroads in the northwestern United States. From 1924 through 1934 Pacific Car & Foundry was owned by American Car & Foundry with little apparent effect on operations. After the Great Depression Pacific Car built increasing numbers of refrigerator cars for a large customer base. Even the Bangor & Aroostook Railroad at the opposite end of

the country placed several orders. Pacific Car occasionally filled boxcar, flatcar, and ore- and caboose-car orders through the mid-1970s. The company name was changed to Paccar, Inc., about 1972. When the demand for refrigerator cars dropped off in the late 1970s, Paccar production shifted more to boxcars and other types of cars. The last order of 100 cars or more was built at Renton early in 1982. Some three-unit articulated intermodal cars were built in 1984 and 1985 before production ended.

Pacific Car acquired International Car Co. in 1975. This company had been building caboose cars in Kenton, Ohio, since 1946 and had emerged as the dominant manufacturer by the early 1960s. From 1977 to 1981, 414 boxcars were built at Kenton as the demand for new boxcars peaked. The last caboose car was built at Kenton in 1981. Caboose cars had become obsolete for the most part, and there was a sufficient supply of surplus cars to meet whatever needs anyone could envision for the next 35 years.

The Pennsylvania Railroad and successors built more cars than any other railroad. Although cars were built at numerous locations, most were built at Altoona, Pennsylvania, and then at the nearby Samuel Rea Shops in Hollidaysburg. About 132,100 cars of all types were built from 1901 to 1967. Another 7,100 or so cars were built at Samuel Rea Shops under Penn Central from 1968 to 1971, and Conrail built about 5,400 cars at the Hollidaysburg Car Shops between 1980 and 1998. The Pennsylvania Railroad also built passenger cars in its shops. It was the most active railroad builder and easily made the transition to building steel cars. Production ended about 1930.

Schoen Pressed Steel Car Co., soon shortened to just Pressed Steel Car Co., was founded with the belief that all-steel cars made from pressed-steel parts would achieve maximum strength with minimum weight. Its first order was for 600 hopper cars for the Pittsburg, Bessemer &

The Pennsylvania Railroad and its successors built more cars than any other builder; most were built at Altoona, Pennsylvania, or the nearby Hollidaysburg shops. This lithograph by T. M. Fowler shows the extensive shops for building and repairing both passenger and freight cars at Altoona in 1895. —Library of Congress (Neg. LC-USZ62-1411)

Lake Erie Railroad built in 1897. Part of the order was built with pressed-steel shapes and the other part with sheet and standard rolled shapes. Use of pressed-steel parts saved 3,000 pounds, clearly proving Schoen's point. Orders for similar cars were soon placed by other railroads. Early production was almost exclusively all-steel gondola and hopper cars. Steel-frame gondola cars and boxcars were built starting in 1900. For the week ending on March 16, 1901, an amazing 106 cars were shipped from McKees Rocks, Pennsylvania, each day on average. A second plant in Allegheny, Pennsylvania, was in operation by December 1901. Pressed Steel Car also sold steel car parts to other builders. In the beginning, Pressed Steel Car had virtually no competition in the steel car market, but by 1903 was facing very serious competition from Standard Steel Car and other companies. Pressed Steel Car started moving away from proprietary designs and using rolled shapes for some parts. It was able to remain in business as a major but less distinguished car builder until about 1950, when the last car was built. Pressed Steel Car was also an important manufacturer of passenger cars between 1903 and 1942. Nearly all were built entirely from steel.

Western Steel Car & Foundry Co. was a Pressed Steel Car subsidiary that was started in 1902 to take over the Hegewisch, Illinois, plant of the Illinois Car & Equipment Co. Illinois Car & Equipment was a fairly substantial builder previously known as the United States Rolling Stock Co. and the United States Car Co. Western Steel retained an independent identity until the mid-1920s. The Hegewisch plant produced mostly wood, steel-underframe, and steel-frame cars and was still active at least as late as 1930.

Sometime in the early 1920s Pressed Steel Car acquired the Koppel Industrial Car & Equipment Co., which had started about 1914. While its principal product under Pressed Steel Car was automatic air dump cars, it also produced 1,300 steel boxcars for the Pennsylvania Railroad in 1924. Pressed Steel Car also acquired the Mt. Vernon Car & Manufacturing Co. (discussed earlier) about April 1946.

The Ralston Steel Car Co. of Columbus, Ohio, developed designs for a combination stock, coal, and boxcar, and a flush-floor drop-bottom gondola car. A prototype of each was built by Pullman early in 1905. The drop doors were hinged along the center sill and dumped to the outside. The general-service gondola-car design helped it get a good start; it soon received orders for 5,000 cars from the Hocking Valley and related railroads. Production started at Columbus in 1906. Ralston continued until 1950, building about 65,600 boxcars, stock, gondola, hopper, and covered hopper cars, and flatcars for many customers. Ralston also sold steel underframes from at least 1907 to 1916.

Thrall Car Manufacturing Co. of Chicago Heights, Illinois, was known as Haffner-Thrall until the late 1940s. Thrall went into business around 1916. Until the 1950s it produced small custom lots of cars, mostly for the U.S.

government or for special service. In 1959 Thrall introduced a new carbon-black car design. From then on, it dominated the market for carbon-black cars, especially after introducing Granuflator-equipped cars about 1967. The variety of cars produced expanded during the 1960s, including some popular 60-foot and 86-foot auto-part boxcars. By 1965 Thrall had increased its share of the flatcar market and had built its first rotary coal gondola car. By the mid-1970s it was a dominant producer of unit coal cars. It built some all-door boxcars in 1967 and again was one of the dominant manufacturers by the early 1970s. Thrall increased production of mill gondola cars around 1974 and introduced a moderately successful covered grain hopper in 1978. In 1983 it introduced a covered hopper for conveying plastic resin, obviously inspired by AC&F's Center Flow. The design sold well, with most going into the Union Tank Car lease fleet. In 1984 Thrall successfully entered the articulated intermodal car market. It was also well situated to profit from a sudden demand for center-beam flatcars, which it had been building since 1977.

By the end of 1984 Thrall had acquired Whitehead & Kales of Detroit, Michigan. Best known for auto racks, it had also built about 1,100 freight cars between 1963 and 1982. Beginning in 1985, Thrall took over Portec, Inc., which was a combination of several companies that started operations during the 1970s and early 1980s, producing a combined total of about 6,000 freight cars. The United-American Car Co. of Cartersville, Georgia, built about 2,000 cars from 1979 to 1984 and was acquired by Thrall about 1985.

After being a very minor freight-car builder for over half a century, Thrall had emerged as possibly the second-largest builder of freight cars and definitely the largest builder of auto racks in North America. Acquisition of Thrall by Trinity Industries was announced in August 2001, excluding the Chicago Heights plant, which had closed about April 2001. Only the Cartersville, Georgia, and Clinton, Illinois, plants were active at that time. The acquisition allowed Trinity to strengthen its position in several types of cars, including coil-steel cars and auto racks for flatcars.

The origins of Trinity Industries, Inc., freight-car production appear to date back to Quick-Car of Fort Worth, Texas, which built some covered hoppers for North American Car in early 1978. Production expanded to include open hopper and tank cars by early 1979. Around this time the Fort Worth plant started building cars for Trinity, which also opened plants in Houston and Longview, Texas, Montgomery, Alabama, and Oklahoma City and Tulsa, Oklahoma. Gondola cars were produced starting in the mid-1980s at yet another plant in Dallas, Texas. Trinity took over Pullman-Standard's Bessemer, Alabama, plant and began building cars there in October 1984. It took over Greenville Steel Car in 1986 or 1987 and Ortner Freight Car in August 1988. Sometime during this period of rapid expansion, perhaps as early as 1982,

Trinity had become the largest freight-car manufacturer in North America. Its product line expanded to include all types of freight cars. Three new plants were opened in Texas at Denton, Saginaw, and Beaumont in the 1990s.

At some point Trinity acquired AMF Beaird, Inc., of Shreveport, Louisiana. AMF Beaird produced tanks and covered hopper bodies that were assembled by North American Car in Texarkana, Arkansas, from at least the early 1960s until 1978. Trinity sold off AMF Beaird in July 1998.

Differential Steel Car of Findlay, Ohio, was a manufacturer of automatic dump cars from around 1940. The name was later changed to Difco, Inc. By the 1990s Difco was building special and heavy-duty flatcars. Trinity Industries acquired Difco by 1998. Covered hopper cars were produced there at least as late as 1999.

About April 1998 Trinity started producing cars at a new plant in Monclova, Mexico. Trinity Industries is also associated with another plant in Mexico that builds tank cars. As previously mentioned, Trinity acquired Thrall Car in August 2001.

The Union Tank Car Co. and General American are the two largest owners and lessors of tank cars in North America. Unlike General American, Union Tank Car was content to purchase cars built to its specifications from contract builders until it started building its own around 1948. Significant outside purchases continued until about 1952. Union Tank Car moved production to East Chicago, Indiana, after acquiring the Graver Tank & Manufacturing Co. in September 1957. Union Tank Car built exclusively tank cars except for some pressure-differential covered hopper cars in the 1960s and early 1970s and about 300 covered hopper grain and plastic resin cars in 1980 and 1981. About 1995 a second plant began production in Sheldon, Texas, near Houston. Union Tank Car has control of Procor Ltd. of Oakville, Ontario, which has produced tank cars since about 1967 and covered hopper cars since about 1975.

—Eric A. Neubauer

REFERENCES

American Engineer & Railroad Journal, various issues.
Epstein, Ralph C. *GATX: A History of the General American Transportation Corporation, 1898–1948.* New York: North River Press, 1948.
Kaminski, Edward S. *The Magor Car Corporation.* Wilton, Calif.: Signature Press, 2000.
Merrilees, Andrew. "The Railway Rolling Stock Industry in Canada." Unpublished, 1963.
White, John H., Jr. *The American Railroad Freight Car.* Baltimore: Johns Hopkins Univ. Press, 1993.
———. *The American Railroad Passenger Car.* Baltimore: Johns Hopkins Univ. Press, 1978.

See also AMERICAN CAR & FOUNDRY; BOMBARDIER; BUDD CO. (EDWARD G. BUDD MANUFACTURING CO.); PULLMAN CO.

Car Ferries. *See* MARINE

OPERATIONS

Car Scheduling

Freight-car scheduling was first developed by the Missouri Pacific Railroad (MoPac) in the mid-1970s. The Federal Railroad Administration (FRA) contributed $5.5 million to the car-scheduling project to mitigate business risk and to encourage car scheduling on other railroads. In return, the MoPac agreed to conduct industry seminars on car scheduling and to make project documents, system design, and source code available to other roads for the cost of reproduction.

Over the years other Class 1 railroads have implemented their own car-scheduling systems. Many of these systems have built on the concepts and design pioneered by the MoPac. The following discussion relates to the car-scheduling system as developed at MoPac and subsequently implemented on the Union Pacific Railroad.

Car scheduling can be defined as the process whereby a car is assigned a "trip plan" as soon as its availability time (industry release, interchange receipt, or hold release) and movement data (waybill or Car Distribution assigned destination) are known. A trip plan defines the sequence of blocks and trains a car is scheduled to move on and the locations where the car will be picked up and set out as it travels from its origin to its destination.

The generation of each move in the trip plan begins by determining the appropriate yard block for the car. Yard blocks tell local personnel how cars should be switched and lined up in the correct order to depart in train blocks on trains. A yard-block definition is based primarily on destination parameters. It may also specify that only cars containing certain commodities and/or coming from certain sources should be assigned to the block. Once a yard block is assigned, car scheduling prepares a list of candidate trains and train blocks that are logical choices to carry the yard block. This list also identifies the setout location for each train block.

Car scheduling assigns each car to the earliest departing candidate train that it can make. A car can make an outbound connection if it is available (based upon interchange receipt, hold release, or industry release time) or is scheduled to be available (based on estimated train arrival time) before cutoff time. Cutoff time is the latest time a car can be available and still be scheduled to depart on the train. It is based on how long it takes to process a car through a terminal and get it on an outbound train.

A key component of the car-scheduling philosophy is that the trip plan remains intact until some overt action triggers a reschedule request. For example, if a car is on an inbound train that has been delayed to the extent that it will be arriving after the cutoff time of its scheduled outbound connection, the trip plan remains intact. The rationale for this approach is that it is still the intent that the connection should be made. The inbound train might make up some time, the outbound train might be delayed, or the situation at the station may be such that the connection can be protected. The car's trip plan will be regenerated based on its current estimated arrival time only if a specific reschedule request is made or if a departure is reported for the connecting train.

Car scheduling involves more than assigning a schedule to individual cars. It provides inquiries to plan work, and it provides reports to monitor for compliance. It provides local operating personnel with working documents that show the portion of the trip plan they need to do their job. A car's next block and train assignment is visible at the yard level on inquiries and work documents such as the advance train consist and switch list. Pickup and setout instructions for blocks and cars are included on crew work orders.

Car scheduling alerts terminal management to situations where corrective action may be required to prevent a car from being mishandled. When the physical makeup of a train is reported, car scheduling alerts terminal management of cars that should be on the train but are missing, cars that are on the wrong train, or cars that are blocked incorrectly. Car scheduling also provides alerts to situations that may require manual intervention, such as when a train may have too many cars scheduled to it.

Car scheduling provides operating officers at all levels the information they require to plan their activities so they can meet their schedule commitments. Some car-scheduling functions make it possible to assess the impact of making a temporary change to the operating plan before that change is actually made. Reports provided by car scheduling include trains scheduled into or out of a yard, the outbound connections to be made by cars on an inbound train, cars scheduled to make an outbound train, and the yard inventory projected for the next 24 hours.

A railroad that incorporates car scheduling into its operating and service strategy can expect more efficient operations and a more reliable transportation product. Car scheduling gives the ability to centrally define, manage, and communicate the operating plan at the car and train levels, provides a computer-accessible definition of the operating plan that can be analyzed and tuned to meet goals for efficiency and levels of service, and provides the basis from which network planning and evaluation tools can be built. For example, the Union Pacific has developed a car-scheduling simulator that replicates the operational car-scheduling system. The simulator can schedule historic or projected traffic using the current or modified operating plan. This simulation capability makes it easier to keep the operating plan consistent with expected changes in service demand.

—Jim Fuller

REFERENCE

Missouri Pacific's Computerized Freight Car Scheduling System: State of the Art Survey. Report No. FRA-OPPD-76-5, April 1976. *System Functional Requirements.* Report No. FRA-OPPD-77-10, July 1977. *Orientation Module.* Report No. FRA-OPPD-80-02, March 1980. *Advanced Systems Study.* Report No. FRA-OPPD-80-04, June 1980. *Evaluation of the MoPac's Freight Car Scheduling System.* Report No. DOT-FR-9077, June 1981.

Carnegie, Andrew (1835–1919)

If any one person epitomized the transformation of the United States from an agricultural country to an industrial power, it was Andrew Carnegie, and the rise of both country and man was inextricably linked to railroads. Carnegie was born in Dunfermline, Scotland. His father, Will Carnegie, was a linen weaver. Machine looms were putting the cottage weavers out of business, and in 1848 the Carnegie family moved to the United States, settling near Pittsburgh, where several relatives already resided. Will was no more successful in the new country than he had been in the old, but Andrew's rise was meteoric, and he was soon supporting the family. His great gifts were his eagerness to learn and his aptitude for recognizing innovations whose time had come.

When he was 14, Andrew's formal schooling ended, and he went to work. His first job of note was in a telegraph office, first as a messenger and then as a telegrapher. There he came to know a young Pennsylvania Railroad executive, Thomas A. Scott, who appreciated Carnegie's qualities and hired him as his personal telegrapher and assistant. During the Civil War Scott went to Washington, D.C., as assistant secretary of war in charge of military transportation; Carnegie accompanied him to help organize the military telegraph system, then returned to Pittsburgh as Scott's successor at the Pennsylvania. In all, he worked 12 years there, and it was a productive time for him in terms of learning managerial skills and the ins and outs of running a railroad. He also made valuable contacts, including J. Edgar Thomson, president of the PRR. Carnegie had purchased his first shares of stock in 1856, and soon his annual income from dividends was outpacing his salary. When the war ended, Carnegie resigned from the Pennsylvania to tend his own interests, which included telegraphy, sleeping cars, and bridge building—particularly railroad bridges. All proved to be extremely remunerative for him. Recognizing the potential profitability of sleeping cars as railroads traveled greater distances, he purchased an interest in the Woodruff Sleeping Car Co. and later parlayed it into part ownership of the Pullman Co.

The telegraph, which made almost instant communication possible, would revolutionize business, and railroad franchises were the key to profitable telegraph companies.

Telegraph wires were strung on the railroad's poles, and the railroad in return had free use of the telegraph. Carnegie's Keystone Telegraph Co. (with secret partners Scott and Thomson and a franchise from the PRR) was soon snapped up by a rival, Pacific & Atlantic Telegraph, which in turn was acquired by Western Union. Carnegie and his friends ended up with an interest in Western Union.

There was a need for replacing the fragile and inadequate wooden bridges of the time with iron and later with steel—and more important, once the war ended, for building new bridges as the railroads expanded. Comprehending this, in 1862 Carnegie took a one-fifth interest in what later became his "pet," Keystone Bridge, where his partners were a veritable who's who of PRR officials.

Major railroad bridges were erected not by the railroads themselves but by separate companies. These sold stocks to finance construction—another opportunity for profit. For several years Carnegie traveled regularly to Europe, selling bonds for his bridge company and various American railroads to European investment houses.

By 1872 Carnegie was turning to the manufacture of steel, something he had learned about in his travels to England. He saw that steel would shortly replace iron for manufacturing rails. Indeed, the Pennsylvania had already started using steel rails in areas of track that saw heavy use. These originally had to be imported from England. But high-quality iron-ore fields had been discovered in Michigan's Upper Peninsula, making U.S. steel production potentially feasible and efficient. Construction started in 1872 on what would be Carnegie Steel; from that point, he pursued his new goal with single-minded dedication. The timing was bad; during the panic of 1873 some 5,000 businesses failed. Carnegie had to sell his Western Union and Pullman stock in order to hang on. It was 1878 before U.S. production was back up to 1872 levels.

Carnegie never lost sight of the fact that steel had potential beyond railroads; his Homestead Works concentrated on the nonrailroad market and greatly increased his total production just at a time when the railroad boom was slowing down. By 1892 he owned three complete steel mills: Edgar Thomson, Homestead, and the just-purchased Duquesne, the most up-to-date steel mill in the world, in addition to Keystone Bridge, Union Iron, and sundry other companies. Regrettably, both Homestead and Duquesne had a history of labor problems, something his other plants had managed to avoid. The infamous Homestead strike of 1892 was precipitated by Carnegie's partner Henry Clay Frick, but Carnegie, who liked to be known as the workingman's friend, could have done much more to avert it. The *St. Louis Post-Dispatch* editorialized, "Ten thousand Carnegie Public Libraries could not compensate the country for the direct and indirect evils resulting from the Homestead lockout." Late in life Carnegie himself wrote, "No pangs remain of any wound received in my business career save that of Homestead."

In 1901 the 65-year-old Carnegie retired after selling his holdings to J. P. Morgan and the newly formed United States Steel Corp. He used the proceeds to fund numerous philanthropic endeavors, including 3,000 Carnegie libraries, 4,100 church organs, the Carnegie Institutes, the Carnegie School of Technology, Carnegie Hall, and much more. He died in 1919, having succeeded in giving much of his wealth away.

—Roberta L. Diehl

REFERENCES

Livesay, Harold C. *Andrew Carnegie and the Rise of Big Business*. 2nd ed. New York: Longman, 2000.
Wall, Joseph Frazier. *Andrew Carnegie*. New York: Oxford Univ. Press, 1970.

Cartier Railway

Port Cartier, Quebec, is located 30 miles west of Sept-Iles and is the southern terminus of the 260-mile Cartier Railway, which hauls iron ore to tidewater from Mont Wright. Construction commenced in 1958 and was completed to Lake Jeannine in 1960, when the first ore began its 190-mile trip south. An 86-mile extension to Mont Wright was built in 1972, and now 18 million metric tonnes of ore are exported annually from this facility in 150-car trains. The Cartier railway is also totally isolated from other railways and is located entirely within Quebec.

—Donald M. Bain

Casement, John S. (1829–1909)

Best known for his work as a railroad contractor in building the Union Pacific Railroad, Jack Casement was a superior tracklayer who was more at home out at the construction site than in his office. He was born in Geneva, New York, on January 19, 1829, to parents who had recently emigrated from the Isle of Man. Like most poor boys, he was put to work at an early age to help support his family. He was laying track on the Michigan Central by the time he was 18. He continued his labors on the Cleveland, Columbus, Cincinnati & Indianapolis, and by about 1850 he was made a foreman. His first contracting job came three years later to ballast track on the Lake Shore Line. Many more jobs followed as his reputation as a track builder grew.

Casement served in the Ohio volunteer infantry during the Civil War and rose to the rank of brigadier general. After the war he returned to railroad contracting. Early in 1866 he signed a contract to lay track for the Union Pa-

John S. Casement. —*Trains* Magazine Collection

cific. Progress on this ambitious project was too slow. Casement's challenge was to speed up the work. The previous contractor completed just 40 miles of track during the first five months of construction; "General Jack" did that much in a week. He built a special construction train that included sleeping and dining cars for the use of the workers.

Casement was on the job every day driving his men to work faster. Other contractors had already graded the line and built the bridges. Casement's firm assembled only the track itself, and the workers assembled it in a most lively fashion. They were laying 3 to 5 miles a day, and on some days, as many as 8 miles were spiked down. The railroad was finished ahead of schedule on May 10, 1869, in large part because of Casement's push and drive.

His reputation attracted many new jobs, but he found time to build a fine home in Painesville, Ohio, where he lived for the rest of his life. He was active in politics as well. He served in the Ohio State Senate and remained a loyal Republican until his last days. He went into semiretirement in the 1890s but reached out for one more big job in 1897, signing a contract with the Costa Rican government to build a 55-mile line to the Pacific from the central highlands.

The task was far more difficult than Casement had anticipated. The jungle, the tropical rains, and diseases were more than the tough old contractor could handle. His normal procedures did not work this time. He had expected to finish the job in two years, but after nearly six years of frustrating labor he had completed only 35 miles of track. That was it. Casement declared that the railroad was finished and returned to Painesville.

Casement remained active until the last weeks of his life. He died of pneumonia at his home on December 13, 1909.

—John H. White, Jr.

REFERENCES

Klein, Maury. *Union Pacific: Birth of a Railroad, 1862–1893.* Garden City, N.Y.: Doubleday, 1987.

White, John H., Jr. "Making Tracks: John Casement's Triumph." *Timeline* (Ohio Historical Society) 18, no. 2 (Mar.–Apr. 2001): 2–17.

Cassatt, Alexander Johnston (1839–1906)

Born in Pittsburgh, Pennsylvania, in 1839, Alexander Cassatt was the son of wealthy parents. His father, Robert Cassatt, was a prominent banker in Pittsburgh and, later, Philadelphia. His younger sister, Mary, became the great Impressionist painter. His father's business took the family to Europe, and Cassatt studied in schools there, including Darmstadt University. He returned to the United States to attend Rensselaer Polytechnic Institute, where he received a degree in civil engineering in 1859.

Alexander J. Cassatt posed in 1888 for this pastel portrait by his younger sister, Mary. Alexander was then 49 and would take the helm of the Pennsylvania a little more than 10 years later, while Mary Cassatt would achieve renown for her Impressionist paintings. —Seattle Art Museum, Gift of Mr. and Mrs. Louis Brechemin, by exchange

Cassatt worked for two years in railroad location in Georgia before joining the Pennsylvania Railroad as a rodman in 1861. His rise through the PRR's engineering and operating ranks was rapid. By 1873 he was general manager of the Lines East of Pittsburgh and Erie, and in 1874 he became the railroad's third vice president in charge of transportation and traffic. What may well have been one of Cassatt's most difficult tasks came when he was called to Pittsburgh to deal with the bloody strike of July 1877. Cassatt gave his attention to preserving railroad property and getting the trains under way, leaving city officers to deal with angry strikers, which led to the tragic outcome. A confrontation between the National Guard and Pennsylvania workers, angry about pay reductions and other changes, left 22 dead, and the resulting riots and fires brought millions in damages to the railroad.

With the retirement of Thomas A. Scott from the Pennsylvania presidency, Cassatt became the railroad's first vice president in 1880.

Cassatt resigned from the company unexpectedly in 1882 at the age of only 42. Some said that he was disappointed over not being elevated to the presidency at the retirement of Scott a few years before. In any event, Cassatt was named a Pennsylvania director a few years later and served in this capacity almost continuously for the rest of his life. Much of his time over the next 17 years was devoted to the breeding of horses. From 1885 until 1899 he served as president of the New York, Philadelphia & Norfolk Railroad.

Alexander Cassatt came to the Pennsylvania's presidency in 1899 as one of several visionary leaders—Samuel Rea and W. W. Atterbury among them—developed by the railroad in the great growth years of the late nineteenth and early twentieth centuries. Beginning in the engineering ranks at an early stage, each moved through increasingly difficult and diverse assignments as they demonstrated the ability to lead the railroad.

Cassatt's election to the presidency upon the death of Frank Thompson came at just the right time for the Pennsylvania. While it proved to be a short one—it lasted only seven years—the Cassatt presidency proved one of the most important and successful in the railroad's history. The PRR and other carriers suffered from the frequently ruthless competition between railroads and their major shippers. Cassatt organized other major railroads to present a unified effort to end rebates and led the fight for the adoption by Congress of the Elkins Amendment in 1903, which gave the Act to Regulate Commerce, or the Interstate Commerce Act, as it was usually known, additional powers to enforce the law against rebaters and rate cutters.

During the first decade of the twentieth century Alexander Cassatt led the Pennsylvania on an extraordinary program of improvement and expansion. By 1906 the railroad had increased its total investment in plant and equipment by almost 150 percent to rebuild the railroad for greater capacity and efficiency. Several thousand miles of new line came into the Pennsylvania fold, most notably the busy Long Island Rail Road at New York. Track grade and curvature were improved, and almost the entire main line from the Hudson River to Pittsburgh was widened to four tracks. A new double-track freight cutoff was extended between Trenton, New Jersey, and Harrisburg. Freight yards and passenger terminals were improved.

Cassatt had long been interested in the problem of an extension of the Pennsylvania across the Hudson River into Manhattan to give the railroad a fully competitive status with the rival New York Central's Grand Central Terminal, and in 1900 he led the Pennsylvania into the greatest of all its improvement projects. New tunnels under the Hudson and East rivers brought Pennsylvania and Long Island Rail Road trains into the splendid new Pennsylvania Station in Manhattan. The Hell Gate Bridge—built jointly with the New York, New Haven & Hartford—linked the Pennsylvania with New England.

Cassatt died on December 28, 1906, at his Haverford home near Philadelphia before the great project was complete. A handsome bronze statue in Penn Station's main waiting room (now at the Railroad Museum of Pennsylvania at Strasburg) celebrated its completion four years later, commemorating the man "whose foresight, courage and ability achieved the extension of the Pennsylvania Railroad System into New York City."

—William D. Middleton

REFERENCES

Burgess, George H., and Miles C. Kennedy. *Centennial History of the Pennsylvania Railroad Company, 1846–1946*. Philadelphia: Pennsylvania Railroad, 1949.
Davis, Patricia T. *End of the Line: Alexander J. Cassatt and the Pennsylvania Railroad*. New York: Neale Watson, 1978.

Cedar Rapids & Iowa City Railway

Opened in 1904, the Cedar Rapids & Iowa City Railway (CR&IC) was a typical electric interurban operating over a 27-mile route between its prosperous namesake cities. Originally planned as a high-speed electric passenger line, the railway soon realized the possibilities in intercity freight traffic and established connections with the trunk-line railroads in the two cities. For just short of 50 years the CR&IC operated a busy passenger service between the two cities. The shortline attracted considerable attention in the early 1930s when it began to operate a subsidiary, Crandic Stages, Inc., in interstate bus service all the way from Chicago to Omaha via Cedar Rapids. The CR&IC gained more attention in 1939 when it acquired six lightweight, high-speed cars from the former Cincinnati &

Lake Erie (they were later augmented by a similar Indiana Railroad car). The fast cars, with a 65 mph balancing speed, operated the 27-mile run in as little as 50 minutes despite nine intermediate stops, and during World War II the interurban transported more than 500,000 passengers annually.

Passenger traffic fell off rapidly after the war and came to an end in 1953. Electric freight operation ended soon afterward. But instead of abandoning the railroad or merging it into a larger one, the CR&IC took advantage of its good industrial connections and trunk-line interchanges to become an extraordinarily successful shortline railroad of its own. In addition to the original Cedar Rapids–Iowa City line, CR&IC has since acquired a former Milwaukee Road branch west of Cedar Rapids and a former Rock Island branch south of Iowa City to more than double its size to 60 miles of main-line track and more than 40 miles of industrial track. A current traffic of more than 90,000 carloads of freight is close to four times what it was in 1952.

—William D. Middleton

REFERENCES

Carlson, Norman, ed. *Iowa Trolleys*. Chicago: Central Electric Railfans' Assn., Bulletin 114, 1975.
Donovan, Frank P., Jr. "Interurbans in Iowa." *Palimpsest* 35, no. 5 (May 1954): 177–212.

Central of Georgia Railway

The South Carolina Railroad began operation between Charleston, South Carolina, and Savannah, Georgia, in 1830. Its purpose was to divert traffic moving down the Savannah River to the port of Charleston. In 1833 Savannah interests organized a railroad to recapture that traffic: the Central Rail Road & Canal Co. Construction got under way in 1835, about the same time the company's name was changed to Central Rail Road & Banking Co. of Georgia (CofG). The company's rails reached Macon in late 1843, and in the next two decades it acquired by purchase or lease branch lines to Augusta and through Milledgeville (which was the capital of Georgia until 1867) to Eatonton.

After the Civil War the CofG began to expand. Lease of the South Western Railroad (the construction of which CofG had financed) in 1869 gave it routes from Macon to Columbus, Fort Gaines, and Albany, Georgia, and Eufala, Alabama. The CofG purchased a Savannah–New York steamship company in 1872 and three years later joined with the Georgia Railroad to buy the Western Rail Road of Alabama. The CofG reached Montgomery, Alabama, in 1879 by acquiring control of the Montgomery & Eufala. In 1881 the CofG was assigned a half interest in a lease of Georgia Railroad and its interests in the Western Rail

Road of Alabama and the Atlanta & West Point by William Wadley, president of the CofG (the Louisville & Nashville was assigned the other half interest in the lease). The CofG built lines northwest from Columbus to Birmingham, Alabama, and north to Chattanooga, Tennessee.

The CofG's attempt to develop a network of routes in South Carolina was thwarted by the State of South Carolina. CofG briefly controlled the Port Royal & Augusta; that railroad became the Charleston & Western Carolina, part of the Atlantic Coast Line system.

By the mid-1880s the CofG was a 2,600-mile railroad that could funnel traffic from Montgomery, Birmingham, and Chattanooga through Columbus and Macon to Savannah. In 1888 it came under control of the Richmond Terminal and was leased to a subsidiary of the Richmond & Danville, a predecessor of the Southern Railway. That era lasted only four years before the CofG entered receivership. The company was reorganized as the Central of Georgia Railway. It included several previous subsidiaries, but it had lost the interests in the lease of the Georgia Railroad and the West Point Route, and it had lost the line to Chattanooga.

At the turn of the century the CofG resumed expansion with the construction of a line southwest from Albany through Dothan to Florala, Alabama, on the Alabama–Florida state line. It recovered the Chattanooga line, which had been operating independently, in 1901, and in 1905 it widened a branch north from Columbus to standard gauge and extended it to a connection with the Atlanta & West Point at Newnan, creating a Columbus-Atlanta route.

The CofG came under the control of E. H. Harriman in 1907. Harriman extended the Illinois Central from Jackson, Tennessee, to Birmingham with 129 miles of trackage rights on Southern, Frisco, and Mobile & Ohio and 80 miles of new railroad. Harriman sold his interest in the CofG to the Illinois Central in 1909.

The CofG of the 1910s and 1920s shared a few officers with Illinois Central, but it was not simply a division of the IC. It had several diverse roles. It was a link in the Midwest-Florida train services operated by the Louisville & Nashville from Cincinnati and the IC from Chicago. It carried freight to and from the port of Savannah. Its main lines and branches covered southwest Georgia and southeast Alabama. It was the principal railroad connecting Savannah, Macon, and Columbus with Atlanta.

When New England's textile mills moved to the South, the CofG lost traffic; much of its traffic had been cotton moving through the port of Savannah. The Depression aggravated matters, and the Central of Georgia entered receivership in 1932.

The CofG was reorganized in 1948, no longer under control of the Illinois Central and without affiliation with the Georgia Railroad and the West Point Route. It purchased the Savannah & Atlanta Railway (S&A) in 1951. The S&A ran from Savannah to Camak, Georgia, 145 miles, and served as the Savannah extension of the Georgia Railroad.

In 1962 the CofG and the S&A consolidated their operations between Savannah and Waynesboro, Georgia, and abandoned part of each company's track between those points.

Several large railroads saw the Central of Georgia as a desirable property. The St. Louis–San Francisco purchased control of the CofG in 1956, subject to the Interstate Commerce Commission's approval, which was not granted. The SLSF was ordered to sell its CofG holdings in 1961. However, the commission approved acquisition of the CofG by the Southern Railway. That took place in 1963. In 1971 the Central of Georgia Railroad was incorporated to merge the Central of Georgia Railway, the Savannah & Atlanta, the Georgia & Florida Railway (a subsidiary of the Southern Railway), and the Wrightsville & Tennille Railroad (a longtime subsidiary of the CofG). Although the Central of Georgia survived on paper, its image and identity were quickly swallowed by the Southern Railway.

In 1970, its last year before merging with the Georgia & Florida, the Savannah & Atlanta, and the Wrightsville & Tennille, the Central of Georgia Railway operated a system of 1,729 route-miles and 2,759 track-miles, with 131 locomotives, 29 passenger cars, 8,002 freight cars, and 1,253 employees. The principal commodities carried were forest products (19.3 percent), stone, clay, and glass (14.5 percent), nonmetallic minerals other than fuel (10.7 percent), coal (9.2 percent), and food and food products (8.2 percent). Passenger traffic totaled 24 million passenger-miles. Central of Georgia Railway operating revenues totaled $34.2 million in 1970, and the railroad achieved a 76 percent operating ratio.

—George H. Drury

REFERENCE

Prince, Richard E. *Central of Georgia Railway and Connecting Lines*. N.p.: Richard E. Prince, 1976.

Central Pacific. *See* PACIFIC RAILROAD; SOUTHERN PACIFIC RAILROAD

Central Railroad Co. of New Jersey

The Elizabethtown & Somerville Railroad was incorporated in 1831, one of several lines chartered to build west from New York City with Easton, Pennsylvania, and the Delaware Water Gap, gateways to the anthracite coal region, as the main objective. It opened from Elizabethport to Elizabeth with horsepower in 1836 and to Plainfield with steam in 1839; it collapsed financially after reaching Somerville in 1842. The company passed into the hands of its chief creditors, the contractors Colkett & Sterns and the iron-importing house of Boorman, Johnston & Co., which formed the Somerville & Easton Railroad with New York capital in 1847. The S&E bought the E&S in 1849 and changed its name to the Central Railroad Co. of New Jersey (CNJ).

The road was completed to a point opposite Easton in 1852. The Lehigh Valley Railroad (1855) and the Delaware, Lackawanna & Western (1856) made the CNJ their tidewater connections, giving it a huge coal traffic and high revenue. The CNJ also backed construction of a line from Allentown to join the Pennsylvania Railroad near Harrisburg (1859) to avoid the breaks of line and gauge in Philadelphia. In 1864 the CNJ was extended eastward to Jersey City, where it created a large terminal on landfill. During the presidency of John Taylor Johnston (1848–1876) the CNJ used its freight income to develop a first-class passenger service and a chain of suburban communities. Farther out, the CNJ served a rich agricultural region, while the High Bridge Branch (1876) linked the iron mines and furnaces of Morris County with the Lehigh Valley.

This enviable situation ended between 1871 and 1875 as the LV, DL&W, and PRR acquired their own routes to New York and withdrew their traffic. The CNJ was forced to lease the Lehigh & Susquehanna in 1871, the only remaining source of coal traffic. The L&S had been built by the Lehigh Coal & Navigation Co. between Easton and Wilkes-Barre between 1837 and 1867. The road climbed south out of Wilkes-Barre via the three Ashley Planes, operated with stationary engines, which were in service until 1948. The CNJ was also forced to join the scramble for coal lands and formed the Lehigh & Wilkes-Barre Coal Co. in 1873. Despite these losses, Johnston continued to extend passenger branches, including the New York & Long Branch Railroad (1875) for the summer beach traffic. Under cutthroat competition, earnings collapsed, Johnston resigned, and the CNJ entered its first bankruptcy (1877–1883).

In 1879 the CNJ acquired the New Jersey Southern Railroad. This line began life as the Raritan & Delaware Bay in 1856, a part of a fanciful scheme for a direct route to Norfolk, Virginia. Instead, it formed a roundabout and illegal link between New York and Philadelphia—illegal because the state had granted the Camden & Amboy exclusive rights to carry passengers by rail between New York and Philadelphia. The company failed, and in 1872 it came under the control of Jay Gould, who tried to develop a New York–Baltimore route with three ferry crossings: Chesapeake Bay, the Delaware River, and New York Bay. The bondholders foreclosed and leased the property to the CNJ, which gained many rural branches and eliminated competition for the Jersey shore resort traffic. The monopoly was short lived, since the PRR forced the CNJ to grant it the use of the New York & Long Branch in 1882 and a full half interest in 1930. Two legacies of the NJS were the line between Bombay Hook and Chestertown on the Delmarva Peninsula, which was sold to the PRR in 1901, and the elegant Sandy Hook Route steamboats that served vacationers and commuters until 1941.

In 1876 the CNJ became the eastern end of the new Bound Brook Route between New York and Philadelphia, which gave it a new strategic purpose. The Bound Brook Route gave the PRR some stiff and speedy competition until the 1920s. It forever linked the CNJ's destiny to that of the Philadelphia & Reading, which acquired the other two-thirds of the Bound Brook Route in 1879 and leased the CNJ from 1883 to 1886. The Reading's collapse precipitated a second CNJ receivership in 1887. A second Reading lease followed in 1892, and the Reading finally secured stock control in 1901. The Reading alliance brought through traffic from the Baltimore & Ohio and New York Central via gateways at Philadelphia, Shippensburg, and Williamsport, Pennsylvania. The B&O's famous Royal Blue Line trains operated over the CNJ from 1890 to 1958. At Easton the CNJ formed part of a route to the Poughkeepsie Bridge. Allentown Yard, built in 1909, became the CNJ's freight hub.

The CNJ enjoyed a high income and main-line traffic density until the Depression. The Lehigh & Wilkes-Barre Coal Co. was sold under antitrust decrees in 1923, a blessing in disguise, since the CNJ used the money for plant modernization, while the anthracite industry continued to decline. Always innovative, the CNJ was the first Class 1 road to purchase a diesel switcher (1925), and its Jersey City–Atlantic City *Blue Comet* of 1929–1941 was one of the first luxury coach trains. After 1930 the fall in coal traffic, extensive suburban service, short hauls, and high terminal costs and taxes combined to throw the CNJ into its third bankruptcy (1939–1949). Dieselization permitted a brief rally, but the recession of 1957 threw the company into a tailspin. Branch lines were pruned, and in 1965 the CNJ and Lehigh Valley consolidated their parallel trackage between Easton and Wilkes-Barre. Deferred maintenance and other economies failed to halt the slide, and a fourth and final bankruptcy followed in March 1967.

Under the State of New Jersey's Aldene Plan, CNJ's suburban service was pared and rerouted to the PRR's Newark station, eliminating the huge Jersey City terminal and ferries. Freight traffic also collapsed, and the CNJ surrendered its Pennsylvania lines to the Lehigh Valley in 1972. Conrail acquired the viable portions of the CNJ in 1976, including Allentown Yard and a network of industrial branches in northern New Jersey. NJ Transit operates the NY&LB and the former CNJ main line between Aldene and High Bridge and has recently opened a light-rail line over former CNJ lines in Jersey City and Bayonne.

In 1974, the last year for which figures are available before Conrail acquired the property, the Central Railroad of New Jersey operated a system of 526 route-miles, with 101 locomotives, 157 passenger cars, 2,232 freight cars, and 1,420 employees. Principal freight traffic sources included nonmetallic minerals other than fuel (16.6 percent), chemicals (14.4 percent), food and food products (10.7 percent), and pulp and paper (9.6 percent). Passenger traffic totaled just over 111.9 million passenger-miles. Central Railroad of New Jersey operating revenues totaled $46.7 million in 1974, and the railroad achieved a 90.3 percent operating ratio.

—Christopher T. Baer

REFERENCES

Baer, Christopher T., William J. Coxey, and Paul W. Schopp. *The Trail of the Blue Comet: A History of the Jersey Central's New Jersey Southern Division*. Palmyra, N.J.: West Jersey Chapter, National Railway Historical Society, 1994.

Cunningham, John T. *Railroads in New Jersey: The Formative Years*. Andover, N.J.: Afton, 1997.

Railroads in the Lehigh River Valley. Rev. ed. Allentown, Pa.: Lehigh Valley Chapter, National Railway Historical Society, 1962.

Central Vermont Railway

A recurring theme in the development of railroads in New England is the desire to create a route between Boston and the Great Lakes. Much of the railroad development in Vermont, New Hampshire, and northern Massachusetts had that as its goal. Impediments to such routes were the range of hills that extends south from the White Mountains through New Hampshire and Massachusetts, the Green Mountains in Vermont and the Berkshire Hills in Massachusetts, Lake Champlain, and the Adirondack Mountains of New York.

In 1849 the Vermont Central Railroad opened a 118-mile line from Windsor, on the Connecticut River, to Burlington, on the shore of Lake Champlain. The railroad followed the White and Winooski river valleys and made a relatively easy crossing of the Green Mountains, which form the spine of Vermont. Within a year there were connecting railroads at both ends that formed a route between Boston and Ogdensburg, New York, on the St. Lawrence River.

At Essex Junction, just short of Burlington, the Vermont Central connected with the Vermont & Canada, which ran north through St. Albans, then across the north end of Lake Champlain to Rouses Point, New York, 59 miles. The Vermont Central leased the Vermont & Canada. At the end of 1854 the Vermont Central found itself unable to pay the rent, and a clause in the lease allowed the Vermont & Canada to take over the Vermont Central.

Despite frequent trips to the courts, the railroads continued to be operated by the same management. The Vermont Central made traffic agreements with the Northern Railroad of New Hampshire (Concord to White River Junction, Vermont) and the Northern Railroad of New York (Rouses Point to Ogdensburg) that effectively shut other neighboring railroads out of the through traffic.

In the 1860s and early 1870s the Vermont Central extended itself down to Long Island Sound at New London, Connecticut, by leasing a series of railroads, including the Rutland. By 1873 it controlled all the railroading in Vermont and reached up the west side of Lake Champlain and west to Ogdensburg (by leasing the Northern Railroad of New York, which later became the Ogdensburg & Lake Champlain). It also had several short branches in southern Quebec. The Vermont Central soon found itself in financial difficulty and spun off the O&LC, the lines up the west side of Lake Champlain, and the Harlem Extension Railroad (Bennington, Vermont, to Chatham, New York). It reorganized as the Central Vermont Railroad.

The situation settled down for a few years. In 1885 the CV came under the control of the Grand Trunk Railway of Canada, and in 1886 it again leased the Ogdensburg & Lake Champlain. In 1896 the Rutland and the O&LC resumed independent operation (the O&LC became part of the Rutland in 1899), and the CV assumed the shape it would have through most of the twentieth century: a line from New London, Connecticut, northwest to the Connecticut River in northern Massachusetts, then north along the river to Brattleboro, Vermont, and from Windsor through White River Junction to the northwest corner of Vermont, with trackage rights on the Boston & Maine from Brattleboro to Windsor.

The CV was again reorganized in 1898 as the Central Vermont Railway, with the Grand Trunk Railway as its majority owner. Control passed to Canadian National Railways in 1923. As a result of severe floods in 1927, the CV underwent a short receivership, during which it trimmed back several branches. After World War II it shut down its New London–New York steamship line. Steam locomotives remained in service relatively late, until 1957.

Canadian National Railways placed its U.S. subsidiaries under the control of the Grand Trunk Corp. in 1971. By the end of the 1970s Central Vermont had regained some autonomy but had also seen much of its traffic disappear as mergers changed the railroad map. In 1983 Central Vermont was offered for sale, but there were no buyers.

During the 1980s the Boston & Maine allowed the track between Brattleboro and Windsor to deteriorate to the point that in 1987 Amtrak suspended its Washington-Montreal *Montrealer*, then used its condemnation powers to take ownership of that segment of the route, which it subsequently conveyed to the Central Vermont. CV rebuilt the track, and the *Montrealer* resumed operation.

CV was again offered for sale in the early 1990s. RailTex, Inc., purchased the railroad and took over its operations on February 4, 1995, as the New England Central

Railroad. In 1990, the last year for which figures are available before the RailTex purchase, the Central Vermont Railway operated a system of 375 route-miles, with 22 locomotives, 223 freight cars, and 208 employees. Central Vermont operating revenues totaled $19.8 million in 1992, and the railroad achieved an 85 percent operating ratio.

—George H. Drury

REFERENCES

Baker, George Pierce. *The Formation of the New England Railroad Systems*. Cambridge, Mass.: Harvard Univ. Press, 1937.
Jones, Robert C. *The Central Vermont Railway*. 6 vols. Silverton, Colo.: Sundance, 1981–1982.

Chapel Cars

An unusual chapter in the annals of American rail history is the story of chapel cars: 13 churches-on-rails that carried the gospel and the sacraments of the church to over 36 states and more than 4,000 towns, mainly west of the Mississippi River, from 1890 to the 1940s. In 1889 Bishop William David Walker of the Episcopal Diocese of North Dakota saw a Russian Orthodox car built to minister to the workers and settlers along the route of the Trans-Siberian Railroad. The bishop raised funds to have the Pullman Palace Car Co. build *The Cathedral Car of North Dakota: Church of the Advent* to bring the sacraments to the far corners of the bishop's vast territory.

Completed in 1890, the 60-foot car featured an elevated transept framing a rose window.

Two Episcopal chapel cars in the Upper Peninsula of northern Michigan operated from 1891 to the early 1900s. These simple reconstructed business cars, likely from the Chicago & North Western Railroad, served where the town or church had been destroyed by forest fires.

The 67-foot *Evangel* was the first of seven American Baptist Publication Society chapel cars built by the Barney & Smith Car Co. of Dayton, Ohio, each featuring a quarter-sawn golden oak chapel with art glass, pews, and organ. To the rear were compact but comfortable living quarters for the missionary and his wife, including berths, office, kitchen, and washroom. *Evangel*, built in 1891 and paid for by wealthy Baptists such as John D. Rockefeller, traveled in Minnesota, North Dakota, Montana, Oregon, Washington, California, Arizona, New Mexico, Arkansas, Kansas, Missouri, Louisiana, Indian Territory (later Oklahoma), Colorado, Nebraska, and Wyoming.

Emmanuel, at 77 feet 8½ inches, was the longest railroad chapel car in service in 1893. This car, its exterior built of Barney & Smith's favorite catalpa wood, featured a brass church bell mounted on the roof. It served in California, Arizona, New Mexico, Oregon, Washington, Nevada, Montana, Idaho, and Colorado.

Glad Tidings, built in 1894, traveled Wisconsin, Iowa, Missouri, Colorado, Wyoming, the Dakotas, Minnesota, Iowa, Nebraska, and Arizona. *Good Will*, built to the same Barney & Smith plan, began its ministry in Texas in 1895 and traveled from the Panhandle to the Mexican border, surviving the great Galveston hurricane of 1900. The car later saw service in Colorado, Utah, Nevada, Idaho, Oregon, and California. *Messenger of Peace*, built in 1898 to the

Baptist missionaries prepare for a service in the chapel car *Emmanuel*, around 1896. —American Baptist Historical Society Archives, from Wilma Rugh Taylor

same basic plan, worked extensively with the Railroad YMCA and in Missouri, Kansas, Colorado, Illinois, West Virginia, Montana, Nevada, California, Oregon, and Washington. *Herald of Hope* (1900), the last wooden chapel car built by Barney & Smith, served mainly east of the Mississippi starting in Michigan, then in Iowa, Illinois, and Ohio, and spent many years in West Virginia working with miners during a period of labor unrest.

Grace was the last chapel car built, in 1915. This 85-foot 6-inch car with Gothic touches and stained-glass window and door trim served in Nevada, California, Colorado, and Wyoming and was the last chapel car to remain in service when it was retired in 1946 after ministering in a defense housing development in Orem, Utah.

At the 1904 St. Louis World's Fair *Messenger of Peace* was seen by Father Francis C. Kelley of the Catholic Extension Society, who said, "If the Baptists can do it, why not the Catholics?" The first Catholic Extension Society car, *St. Anthony*, was a 70-foot 9-inch Wagner sleeping car, reconstructed by the Pullman Palace Co. in 1907 with pews, altar, confessional, stations of the cross, and living quarters for two priests and a porter. The car served mainly in Louisiana, Kansas, South Dakota, Mississippi, Idaho, Washington, and Oregon.

The Catholic Extension Society's *St. Peter* (1912) was the first steel chapel car built by Barney & Smith. The 84-foot 6⅝-inch car featured a Cuban mahogany, Gothic-style interior. *St. Peter* conducted missions in Kansas, Minnesota, Montana, Idaho, Washington, Oregon, and North Carolina. *St. Paul*, built by Barney & Smith in 1915, was paid for by wealthy Dayton lumberman Peter Kuntz, who also donated the funds for *St. Peter*. This beautiful 84-foot 10½-inch chapel car visited towns in Louisiana before being sidetracked in December 1917 by World War I government restrictions on private railroad cars. After serving in North Carolina, Louisiana, Oklahoma, Montana, and Iowa, the car was sent west to be a chapel at the entrances to Glacier and Yellowstone national parks.

Life on the chapel cars was cramped but comfortable, as there was almost anything the missionaries or priests required on board. On the Baptist chapel cars the wives of the missionaries took charge of the housekeeping and cooking, as well as providing the music and working with the women and children who came to the car. Four babies were born to missionary wives during chapel-car service, and in one case, nestled in soft blankets, a baby swung in a hammock between two berths as chapel car *Glad Tidings* rolled through the Iowa countryside. From the lower berth, her mother monitored the arc of the swing with her hand, and her father watched apprehensively from above. But it did not take long for the Charles Herbert Rusts to discover that a chapel car was no place to raise a baby. Because of space limitations and the difficulties of schooling, most of the missionary wives who had children stayed at home with them while their husbands worked with assistants, usually singers, on the cars.

With rare exceptions, the men on the Baptist chapel cars were ordained ministers with college and seminary backgrounds, and several of the wives were also ordained. The American Baptist Publication Society looked for men who had a passion for ministering to railroad workers. Several of them were former railroad workers. It was also an advantage if the men had some experience with fund-raising or church building.

On the Episcopal cars the bishops traveled alone in their diocese, and their stays were brief because their living quarters were very small, and they had their duties at their main cathedrals. Many of the priests who served on the Catholic cars were members of the Congregation of the Most Holy Redeemer, better known as Redemptorists. George Hennessey, a layman and car superintendent, traveled on the chapel cars with a priest and a porter.

The chapel cars were sided at a town for one day to as long as two years, depending on whether the missionaries or priests were conducting a gospel service, offering the sacraments, or helping organize and build a new church (many of the new railroad towns lacked churches). For more than half a century the chapel cars rolled over the rails of America, bringing the church to communities from coast to coast. The first chapel car, *The Cathedral Car of North Dakota: Church of the Advent*, was retired and dismantled at Carrington, North Dakota, in 1901. *Glad Tidings* was dismantled at Flagstaff, Arizona, in 1926 after witnessing to Mexican communities in the state, and the proceeds were used to rebuild a church. *Herald of Hope* was retired in 1935 and dismantled in West Virginia. The Catholic chapel car *St. Anthony* was dismantled at Wishram, Washington, in 1919 after serving as a church, and the *St. Peter* was dismantled at Oxford, North Carolina, in 1953.

Many of the cars survived in some form. One of the upper Michigan cars, a 45-foot open-platform car, later saw service as a gift shop in Negaunee, Michigan, and was then purchased by a private museum in Illinois. In 1924 *Evangel* was incorporated into the structure of the First Baptist Church of Rawlins, Wyoming. *Emmanuel*, retired in 1942, is now being restored at Prairie Village, South Dakota, and is on the National Register of Historic Places. *Good Will*, retired from service at Boyes Hot Springs, Sonoma County, California, in 1938, remains there today in poor condition, stripped of its trucks on private property. *Messenger of Peace* was retired in 1935 and survives in poor condition on the Washington Peninsula. The *St. Paul* was sold to a rail museum in Nevada City, Montana, in 1967, and has been restored. *Grace*, the very last of the chapel cars built, survives today in excellent condition on its original Barney & Smith trucks at the Green Lake Conference Center at Green Lake, Wisconsin, where it is still used for worship and is visited by hundreds each year.

During the time of the chapel-car ministry, the railroad industry was the largest in America. It employed over 873,000 workers, whose jobs and lifestyles led them away from the teachings of the church, but they felt that the chapel cars were made just for them, and by the thou-

Railroad men gather outside chapel car *Emmanuel* after a service about 1900. —Norman T. Taylor Collection

sands they came. One railroad engineer said to a Baptist chapel-car missionary, "I have not been to church in many years, but you have brought the church to me."

—Wilma Rugh Taylor

REFERENCE

Taylor, Wilma Rugh, and Norman Thomas Taylor. *This Train Is Bound for Glory: The Story of America's Chapel Cars.* Valley Forge, Pa.: Judson Press, 1999.

Chesapeake & Ohio Railway

The Chesapeake & Ohio Railway (C&O) developed principally as a coal carrier linking the coalfields of Virginia, West Virginia, and eastern Kentucky with tidewater at Hampton Roads, Virginia. Later acquisitions through merger gave the railroad a link across Indiana with Chicago and a coal route north through Ohio to Lake Erie at Toledo. Merger with the Pere Marquette in 1947 gave it an extensive network of lines in lower Michigan and southern Ontario.

The C&O began as the Louisa Railroad in 1837, carrying farm goods in central Virginia. By 1850 it had expanded east to Richmond and west to Charlottesville and renamed itself the Virginia Central. By 1856 it had reached what is now Clifton Forge, Virginia, at the base of the Alleghenies, having conquered the Blue Ridge through the Blue Ridge Tunnel planned by Claudius Crozet, Virginia's state engineer. Meanwhile, the state chartered another railroad, the Covington & Ohio, to build from Covington, connecting the Virginia Central to the Ohio River. Considerable work had been done on this line when the Civil War intervened.

During the war the Virginia Central was an important supply line for the Confederacy, bringing the agricultural plenty of the Shenandoah Valley to Richmond. It was used tactically to move troops, but it was also heavily damaged; by war's end only a few miles of track near Richmond were in operation.

Lacking local capital and failing to secure backing in Great Britain, southern entrepreneurs turned to Collis P. Huntington. With his backing the railroad was renamed Chesapeake & Ohio in 1868, and in 1869 it pushed its line west through the new state of West Virginia, reaching the Ohio in 1873. Without good western connections the line was unable to survive on local business and entered receivership, emerging in 1878 with a name change: from Chesapeake & Ohio Railroad to Chesapeake & Ohio Railway.

In 1881 a line was built down the peninsula of Virginia to Newport News, opposite Norfolk on Hampton Roads, giving the C&O access to one of the best ice-free ports on the East Coast. In the 1880s coal became the dominant commodity for the C&O as mines opened in southern West Virginia's rich coalfields. Most of the coal the C&O carried moved east to Newport News and thence by coastwise shipping to the northeastern United States.

In the early 1880s the C&O reached Louisville, Kentucky, over the Huntington-controlled Elizabethtown, Lexington & Big Sandy and trackage rights over the Louisville & Nashville. In 1888 the C&O completed its main line along the south bank of the Ohio, crossing the river from Covington, Kentucky, to Cincinnati, opening western connections. In Virginia the C&O bought the Richmond & Alleghany Railroad, which had built a line along the towpath of the old James River & Kanawha Canal. This gave the C&O a line with a gentle downward-sloping gradient to move its coal from Clifton Forge to Richmond and thence to the coast, rather than using the old C&O line over the mountains via Charlottesville. This, combined with the 0.57 percent eastward grade over the Alleghenies, gave the C&O the easiest Appalachian crossing of any railroad.

The C&O was again reorganized, without foreclosure, in 1888, and Huntington lost control to Vanderbilt interests. Melville E. Ingalls, president of the Big Four (the Cleveland, Cincinnati, Chicago & St. Louis), also became president of the C&O.

By the 1890s coal dominated the C&O's traffic, now moving both east and west, with much going to steel mills. During the next 30 years a maze of coal branches was built in West Virginia and eastern Kentucky, and by the end of that era the modern C&O was in place. In 1910 the C&O bought the Chicago, Cincinnati & Louisville, which provided it a line from Cincinnati across Indiana to Chicago. At about the same time controlling interest was obtained in the Hocking Valley Railway of Ohio, which gave the C&O a good road from Columbus to Great Lakes shipping at Toledo. To use this connection for its westbound coal, the Northern Subdivision was built from a point on the Cincinnati Division seven miles west of Russell, Kentucky, across the Ohio River on the massive Sciotoville Bridge (known on the C&O as Limeville Bridge) to a connection with Norfolk & Western at Waverly, Ohio, thence by trackage rights to the HV at Columbus. In 1926 the N&W connection was eliminated with the C&O's construction of the last link between Waverly and Columbus.

By the early 1920s the C&O with its coal traffic was a highly desirable investment, and the Van Sweringen brothers of Cleveland included it in their "Greater Nickel Plate" scheme, which ultimately unraveled in the Depression, but left the C&O as the controlling power in an amalgam of the C&O, the Pere Marquette, the Hocking Valley, and the Erie. The C&O merged the Hocking Valley in 1930. The C&O was so well heeled that it engaged in a massive reengineering of its line in the early 1930s when many other railroads were financially strapped. Traffic fell, but coal was still essential. By World War II the C&O was ready in every aspect, from a superior physical plant maintained at the highest levels to the most modern heavy locomotives and a large fleet of rolling stock.

Although passengers accounted for only about 5 percent of revenues, the C&O always lavished great attention on passenger trains, inaugurating in 1889 a through all-electrically lighted, all-vestibule train between New York (over the Pennsylvania Railroad to Washington) and Cincinnati called the *Fast Flying Virginian*. By the early 1900s a pattern had been established whereby the main-line trains operated from Washington to Cincinnati, with feeder trains connecting Newport News with Charlottesville, Virginia, where through cars were cut in and out of the main-line trains, and at Ashland, Kentucky,

where the same occurred for trains between there and Louisville. In 1930 a new train, the *Sportsman*, was inaugurated on a route between Newport News and Detroit, operating over the newly completed connections in Ohio. The train afforded its coach passengers unrivaled luxury with two-and-one seating in swiveling reclining chairs at no extra fare. In 1932 the C&O introduced what would be its flagship until the end, the *George Washington*. The train was part of the celebration of the bicentennial of Washington's birth, and the C&O claimed him as its first president as well (Washington had been honorary president of the James River Canal, which was taken over by the Richmond & Alleghany, later part of the C&O). The train was made up of refurbished heavyweight cars in C&O's colonial theme, with interior fittings in the Georgian style and cars named for people and places in Washington's life. The *George Washington* was one of the first all-air-conditioned long-distance trains.

During World War II the railway came under the control of Robert R. Young as chairman. Young controlled the remnants of the Van Sweringen empire, and over the next decade he was the dominant force on the C&O, known as the "gadfly of the railroads" for his iconoclastic and progressive views.

Using the C&O as his platform, Young began his crusade to modernize railroads by fixating on passenger service. He introduced innovative new approaches to passenger travel, many of which became standard in railroading and business: credit cards, toll-free telephone ticket ordering, tickets on the train, passenger representatives on the train, low-density seating, lounge space, and other amenities. One innovation that did not stick very long was a no-tipping policy. Young ordered 48 streamlined cars for the *Chessie*, a daylight domeliner planned for service between Washington and Cincinnati. Because of deficits in C&O postwar budgets and steeply declining passenger traffic, the train never entered service.

Other Young innovations included the establishment of a research department, headed by Ken Brown, a former airline official. Among its projects were new ideas in both passenger and freight equipment, which later took form as the New York Central's Train X, the United Aircraft TurboTrain, and Roadrailer.

The Pere Marquette was merged in 1947 and the Nickel Plate was spun off. Under the guidance of Walter Tuohy, whom Young brought on as president in 1948, the C&O prospered in the 1950s and was ready for the merger era, beginning by taking control of the Baltimore & Ohio in 1963. In 1972, under the leadership of Hays Watkins, one of "Young's young men" of the late 1940s, the Chessie System was formed to own the C&O, the B&O, and the Western Maryland. The B&O later absorbed the WM, and in April 1987 the C&O merged with the B&O. Four months later the C&O was merged into CSX Transportation.

The C&O is well remembered for Chessie, the sleeping kitten who was probably the best-known American corporate symbol in the 1935–1950 era. Chessie has graced calendars, timetables, ads, and all manner of souvenirs down to the present day, spending almost a decade in stylized outline as the "C" of Chessie System.

By the early 1900s the C&O's steam locomotives included some of the heaviest and most powerful anywhere. In 1911 the road acquired 2-6-6-2 Mallets and the first 4-8-2 in America, as well as huge 2-8-2s. In 1923 the C&O designed a giant 2-8-8-2 simple articulated for fast freight and heavy coal. For passengers it got some of the heaviest of all Pacifics in the mid-1920s and 4-8-4s in 1935. During World War II the C&O received the giants of steam, the heaviest of all 4-6-4 Hudsons for passengers, 90 all-purpose 2-8-4s, and the incomparable 2-6-6-6 Allegheny type, which recorded both the highest instantaneous and the highest sustained drawbar horsepower of any steam locomotive. The C&O remained firmly in the steam camp as late as 1948. Among Robert R. Young's innovations were three giant steam-turbine-electrics that pulled passenger trains for about a year before the railroad recognized that they were failures. The C&O's first diesels arrived in 1949, and the C&O had completed the transition from steam by October 1956. The railroad's main repair facilities were at Huntington, West Virginia, and Clifton Forge, Virginia. The latter shops were closed under CSX, but Huntington is now one of CSX's three major shop facilities.

In 1972, its last year before it became part of Chessie System, the Chesapeake & Ohio operated a system of 4,994 route-miles and 10,135 track-miles, with 1,030 locomotives, 74,962 freight cars, 1,850 company service cars, and 20,587 employees. Chesapeake & Ohio operating revenues totaled $409.8 million in 1972, and the railroad achieved a 76.1 percent operating ratio.

—Thomas W. Dixon, Jr.

REFERENCE

Turner, Charles W. *Chessie's Road*. Richmond, Va.: Garrett & Massie, 1956.

Chessie System

The Chessie System was never a railroad corporate entity as such. Rather, it was two things: the name of a holding company—Chessie System, Inc.—and the common marketing identity of three separate railroads that the holding company controlled.

In 1963 the Chesapeake & Ohio Railway acquired full stock control of the Baltimore & Ohio Railroad. The two companies retained their separate legal identities, equipment, and properties, however, although they were gradually put under a single management. This process intentionally took several years, during which time the two companies were usually (but awkwardly) referred to as the C&O/B&O system.

In 1972, however, it was decided to create a common marketing image to cover not only the C&O and the B&O, but also the Western Maryland, which was then being brought directly into the fold. (The B&O had owned a controlling interest in the WM since 1927, but had not been allowed to exercise control.) Chessie, the C&O's famous sleeping kitten, used in advertisements since the early 1930s, became the common system name, and a stylized version of the image was adopted for equipment, letterheads, advertising, and other uses. The three railroads remained legally separate, however, and equipment and property still carried their owners' names, as did employees' paychecks. Chessie System, Inc., was formed in 1973 as a holding company that controlled the three railroads as well as other ventures. But the C&O, the B&O, and the WM still remained separate corporations until they were merged into CSX Transportation in 1987.

—Herbert H. Harwood, Jr.

Chevalier, Michel (1806–1879)

Michel Chevalier was one of the first European engineers to study the fledgling U.S. canal and railroad system. He was surely one of the best educated and the most philosophical of these observers. The young French mining engineer was a student and disciple of Claude-Henri Saint-Simon (1760–1825), the French philosopher and social scientist whose socialistic views conflicted with conservative religious and marriage views. Chevalier graduated from the École Polytechnic as a mining engineer but soon established a journal devoted to the teachings of Saint-Simon. This radical publishing venture caused his arrest in 1832, but he was pardoned after a few months. His return to favor appeared complete, for late the next year he was sent by the French government on a mission to report on happenings in the United States.

Chevalier spent two years traveling around the New World, expounding on the beliefs of Saint-Simon and his own views for free trade as he wandered. Chevalier was amazed by the energy and ambition of this youthful giant among nations. He marveled at the great wooden railroad trestle over the Susquehanna River—how could a 6,000-foot-long bridge cost only $130,000? He was impressed by complete railroads costing $24,500 or less per mile and the iceboats that crossed the frozen Delaware River during the winter. The young Frenchman noted, however, that for all the enthusiasm, not a great deal had been finished at the time of his visit. Most railroads were short, and no comprehensive system was completed in any region of the nation. Yet the Erie Canal was up and running and had done much to boost the economy of New York. He was very much encouraged by the freedom to express opinions and to act upon them. Yet like Tocqueville, he feared the oppression of the majority and its possible tyranny over unpopular minorities. Chevalier reported all of this in a series of brilliant letters to a popular French journal. These were collected and reprinted in two volumes published in Paris in 1836. A few years after his return to his homeland Chevalier was appointed professor of political economy at the Collège de France. He was already at work on a second but more technical book on U.S. railroads and canals, *Histoire et description des voies des communications aux Etats-Unis* (published in Paris in 1840–1841).

Chevalier wrote on many other subjects: free trade, the gold standard, the Suez and Panama canals, and the right of France to intervene in Mexico. In 1860 he negotiated a trade agreement between France and England. He also served in the French Senate under Napoleon III.

—John H. White, Jr.

REFERENCES

Chevalier, Michel. *Society, Manners, and Politics in the United States: Letters on North America.* Trans. and ed. John W. Ward. Ithaca, N.Y.: Cornell Univ. Press, 1961.

Manuel, Frank E. *The New World of Henri Saint-Simon.* Cambridge, Mass.: Harvard Univ. Press, 1956.

Nouvelle Biographie Generale, 9–10: 260–265. Paris, 1964.

Chicago, Burlington & Quincy Railroad

The Chicago, Burlington & Quincy Railroad reached from its headquarters city of Chicago through the Midwest to Colorado, Wyoming, and Montana. It extended its reach into New Mexico and across Texas to Galveston through subsidiaries Colorado & Southern and Fort Worth & Denver. It had two nicknames, "Burlington" and "Q." The railroad disappeared in 1970, but its name lived on as the "Burlington" in Burlington Northern (BN) and survives today in the corporate name of the Burlington Northern & Santa Fe Railway.

Burlington was owned by the Great Northern (GN) and the Northern Pacific (NP), each with 48.59 percent. Curiously, CB&Q was larger than its parent companies— 8,430 route-miles at the time of the 1970 BN merger (11,000 miles if subsidiaries Colorado & Southern and Fort Worth & Denver are included), versus 8,263 for GN and 6,682 for NP. GN and NP largely let the Burlington go its own way, with its own Chicago offices and executives throughout its existence. Most of Burlington's business was in the agricultural Midwest, a tough area for a railroad to make a living, but while competing midwestern railroads always seemed to be moving in and out of bankruptcy, the Burlington maintained a strong presence and an excellent physical plant.

The Burlington could trace its heritage back to February 12, 1849, when a group of millers in Aurora, Illinois, obtained a charter to build a 12-mile railroad connecting Aurora with the Galena & Chicago Union Rail Road, a predecessor of the Chicago & North Western. The Aurora Branch Railroad ran its first train on September 2, 1850, between Turner Junction (West Chicago) on the Galena & Chicago Union and Batavia, Illinois. Later the new line obtained trackage rights over the Galena & Chicago Union to operate directly into Chicago.

In 1852 the Aurora Branch changed its name to Chicago & Aurora, and in 1855 the C&A was authorized to change its name again, this time to Chicago, Burlington & Quincy Rail Road. Several consolidations with small railroads followed, and the company became the Chicago, Burlington & Quincy Railroad in 1864, the same year the road reached Chicago via its own line. In the 1860s the Burlington built west to Iowa, Missouri, and Nebraska. On August 23, 1886, the "Q" opened its route to St. Paul and a connection with predecessors of the NP and the GN. In 1895 a line that extended northwest across Nebraska and corners of South Dakota and Wyoming met the NP at Huntley, Montana (Burlington acquired trackage rights over NP rails through Billings to Laurel, Montana).

Acquisition by Great Northern and Northern Pacific

By the end of the nineteenth century James J. Hill had developed a keen interest in acquiring a line to Chicago for his Great Northern Railway. Hill also held NP stock and bonds, so a link to Chicago would benefit both GN and NP. Acquiring the Burlington would give Hill's railroads access not only to Chicago, but also to Kansas City and St. Louis. Hill encountered opposition, though, from E. H. Harriman. Eventually the management of the CB&Q realized that an alliance with Hill would be more politically palatable than one with the Union Pacific, which it essentially paralleled between Omaha and Denver—and the Burlington was already handling the traffic of Hill's railroads. On May 21, 1901, the CB&Q was sold to the NP and the GN. The three railroads were held under the Northern Securities holding company, which planned for their merger. However, the Supreme Court ordered dissolution of Northern Securities under the Sherman Antitrust Act. Eventually Hill was forced to give up control of NP, but ownership of the Burlington remained split between GN and NP for the next 69 years.

In 1908 the Burlington extended its reach from Wyoming and Colorado to the Gulf of Mexico by purchasing control of the Colorado & Southern Railway (C&S) and its subsidiaries the Fort Worth & Denver City Railway (FW&DC) and the Trinity & Brazos Valley Railway (later the Burlington–Rock Island Railroad). The C&S also had 3-foot-gauge lines extending west from

Denver deep into the Rockies. The last of C&S's narrow-gauge track west of Denver was abandoned in 1941, and narrow-gauge operations came to an end in August 1943 with the conversion to standard gauge of a 14-mile branch between Leadville and Climax. It had been isolated from the rest of the C&S after abandonment of the narrow-gauge lines, but it connected with the Denver & Rio Grande Western at Leadville.

Zephyrs *and Diesels*

In the modern era Burlington became an industry innovator, thanks in large part to President Ralph Budd, who left the Great Northern in 1931 to become the seventeenth president of the Burlington. While the country was in the throes of the Great Depression, Budd daringly went ahead with the production of the nation's first diesel-powered streamlined train. In 1933 the Burlington placed an order for the new lightweight train with the E. G. Budd Manufacturing Co. of Philadelphia (there was a distant relationship, but no direct family connection). At the time the order was placed, no decision had yet been made as to its power supply. Budd was approached by H. L. Hamilton, president of Electro-Motive Corp., to see if he would be interested in placing a newly developed two-cycle, eight-cylinder diesel engine in the new train. Ralph Budd embraced the concept, and the diesel revolution that would sweep steam from the railroads of America was born. Budd also was instrumental in naming the new train. In meetings one of Budd's officers had suggested that the name of the train begin with the last word in the dictionary because it would be the "last word" in transportation. When Budd looked up the last words in his dictionary, none of them seemed a good fit, but he remembered some lines from Chaucer's *Canterbury Tales*, in which Zephyrus, the god of the West Wind, typifies renaissance. Budd suggested the name *Zephyr*, which, while not the last word in the dictionary, did begin with the last letter of the alphabet.

The *Zephyr*, built entirely of stainless steel, had three cars, was 196 feet long, carried 70 passengers, and could reach speeds up to 120 mph. It cost almost $200,000. The train left the manufacturer on April 7, 1934, and was turned over to the Burlington on April 17. It was sent on a tour of the eastern part of the country and later several cities in Burlington territory. On May 26, 1934, the train made a nonstop run from Denver to the Century of Progress Exhibition in Chicago in just 14 hours. It then toured the western part of the Burlington system, participated in ceremonies opening the Moffat Tunnel in Colorado, and had the title role in the movie *Silver Streak*. It entered regular service on November 11, 1934, making a daily round trip between Lincoln, Nebraska, and Kansas City. It was an immediate success and became the first of an entire fleet of *Zephyr*s to ride Burlington rails. It was later renamed *Pioneer Zephyr* to distinguish it from others in the fleet.

While the diesel *Zephyr*s were revolutionizing passenger service, the Burlington continued to build its own steam locomotives for freight service, Northern-type locomotives that were classed O5. The first 8 were built by Baldwin in 1930, but CB&Q's West Burlington, Iowa, shops constructed 28 more between 1936 and 1940. One of the 1940-built machines, number 5632, went on to fame pulling steam excursions until 1964, but unfortunately was scrapped in 1976.

Freight diesel power came to the Burlington under Ralph Budd's tenure. Like many railroads, the Burlington first tested diesel switchers in freight service, then leaped headlong into the diesel era with diesel purchases during World War II. Burlington dieselization was essentially complete by 1958. Subsidiary Colorado & Southern holds the distinction of operating the last standard-gauge Class 1 steam locomotive in regular service, keeping 2-8-0 No. 641 in service on the isolated Leadville-Climax branch until October 11, 1962, when it was placed on display.

The Burlington continued to innovate in passenger service with the construction of the first Vista-Dome car in 1945. The Aurora, Illinois, Shops fitted a stainless-steel coach, *Silver Alchemy* (Burlington named nearly all its stainless-steel passenger equipment, almost always beginning the name with *Silver*), with a dome, giving passengers an "engineer's eye view" forward above the roofline, and renamed the car *Silver Dome*. The Budd Co. then began building domes for the railroad. The first regularly dome-equipped train was the 1947 version of the *Twin Zephyrs* between Chicago and Minneapolis. The dome trend spawned by the Burlington spread to other railroads throughout the United States and to Canada.

In 1949 the CB&Q, the Rio Grande, and the Western Pacific inaugurated the *California Zephyr* between Chicago and San Francisco. Vista-Domes were its primary feature, and its schedule was set up not for speed, but for the best scenery along the way. Burlington also participated with its parent roads in moving the dome-equipped NP *North Coast Limited* and GN *Empire Builder* between Chicago and St. Paul.

In 1949 Ralph Budd retired from Burlington service. Vice president of operations Harry C. Murphy succeeded him. A longtime CB&Q employee, he had been one of the crewmen on the *Zephyr*'s record-breaking Denver-Chicago run. Murphy finished Burlington's dieselization, yet had a soft spot in his heart for the steam locomotive and retained two locomotives for a steam excursion program into the 1960s.

Murphy continued to support the passenger business while other railroads began to sour on it, saying, "Take away the passenger train, and a railroad is nothing more than a truck company." During his administration the Burlington completely reequipped the Chicago–Denver–Colorado Springs *Denver Zephyr* in 1956; it was the last all-new passenger train built until the advent of Amtrak. Chicago commuter service saw improvement as well with new stainless-steel double-deck gallery cars. Murphy also oversaw a major piece of railroad construction: Burlington's Kansas City Shortcut, which cut 22 miles off Burlington's Chicago–Kansas City distance.

Merger

Upon Murphy's retirement on October 1, 1965, Louis W. Menk, who had been president of the St. Louis–San Francisco, took Murphy's place as president of the Burlington. At that time Burlington's earnings were sagging—in 1965 the road netted only $16.6 million on earnings of $270 million. Menk was considered a rising star in the industry, but he was also a controversial figure. One of his first acts was to kill Murphy's popular steam excursion program. He made no bones about the fact that many of Burlington's passenger trains were a drain on the railroad's treasury. His tenure was brief: he left the Burlington only a year after he arrived. Since GN and NP owned CB&Q, Menk thought the place to be in the coming Burlington Northern merger was at the head of one of those two roads. When longtime Northern Pacific president Robert S. Macfarlane moved up to chairman of the NP on October 1, 1966, the 48-year-old Menk was brought in to replace him. It was a wise decision: Menk became Burlington Northern's first president in 1970. Replacing him as president of the Burlington was William J. Quinn of the Milwaukee Road, who returned to that railroad after the BN merger. On "M-Day," March 2, 1970, Burlington, GN, NP, and Spokane, Portland & Seattle merged to form Burlington Northern, Inc., and the Chicago, Burlington & Quincy slipped into history.

In 1969, its last year before the Burlington Northern merger, the Burlington operated a system of 8,430 miles, including 4,578 miles of main line and 3,220 branch-line miles. The Burlington owned 629 locomotives and 35,847 freight cars and had 16,374 employees. CB&Q annual passenger traffic, including commuters, totaled 508,005,920 passenger-miles in 1969, while freight traffic reached 23,601,019,000 ton-miles. Principal commodities carried included coal (22.5 percent), farm products (16.4 percent), food products (14.7 percent), nonmetallic minerals (8.1 percent), chemicals (7.5 percent), and stone, clay, and glass (6.2 percent). Burlington operating revenues totaled $299,243,727 in 1969, and the railroad achieved an 80.92 percent operating ratio.

—Steve Glischinski

REFERENCES

Corbin, Bernard G., and Joseph C. Hardy. *The Burlington in Transition.* Red Oak, Iowa: Corbin, 1967.

Martin, Albro. *James J. Hill and the Opening of the Northwest.* New York: Oxford Univ. Press, 1976.

Overton, Richard C. *Burlington Route: A History of the Burlington Lines.* New York: Alfred A. Knopf, 1965.

Wagner, F. Hol. *The Colorado Road.* Denver: Intermountain Chapter, National Railway Historical Society, 1970.

Chicago, Indianapolis & Louisville Railway (Monon Railroad)

In 1847 a railroad company was organized to construct a line north from New Albany, Indiana, across the Ohio River from Louisville, Kentucky. The promoter of the line, James Brooks, named it the New Albany & Salem Rail Road (NA&S), with the thought that the 35-mile distance to Salem was conservative enough to attract investors. The railroad opened to Salem in 1851 and to Bloomington in 1853. The railhead continued to advance and early in 1854 reached Gosport, where work was begun on a branch to Indianapolis, but the company encountered financial difficulty, and work stopped. The roadbed for the branch, only partially graded, was eventually used by the Pennsylvania Railroad.

Brooks went north to do some trading. The Michigan Central Railroad, building from Detroit to Chicago, had reached Michigan City, Indiana, as far as was possible with its Michigan charter. The NA&S's charter allowed it to build anywhere in Indiana. In exchange for a franchise to build to the Illinois state line, Michigan Central bought a block of NA&S stock, providing enough capital to extend NA&S's line from Gosport to Crawfordsville, 170 miles from New Albany. Meanwhile, the NA&S had acquired the Crawfordsville & Wabash, which had built a railroad from Crawfordsville to Lafayette, about 27 miles. The NA&S extended the line north to Michigan City. The south end of the NA&S was hilly and crooked; the line to Michigan City was flat and straight (including a 65-mile stretch without a curve). The northern portion of the NA&S opened in 1853.

The year 1856 brought a drought. Shipments of agricultural commodities along the NA&S were down, as was traffic to and from Ohio River steamboats. The NA&S defaulted on its interest payments and was put in the hands of a receiver in 1858. A reorganization as the Louisville, New Albany & Chicago Railway under New York financier John Jacob Astor was declared illegal. The railroad was again sold at foreclosure to the same investors, and in 1873 it made a second start at being the Louisville, New Albany & Chicago Railway. Because of the reorganization, the railroad lost any chance of using the Michigan Central's line to reach Chicago from Michigan City.

In 1865 the Indianapolis, Delphi & Chicago Railway was incorporated; it was reincorporated in 1872 as part of a proposed line from Chicago to Charleston, South Carolina. In 1877 construction began in the middle by means of a narrow-gauge line between Bradford (soon renamed Monon) and Rensselaer. In 1881 it was taken over by the Chicago & Indianapolis Air Line Railway and converted to standard gauge; that company merged with the Louisville,

New Albany & Chicago in 1883. By then its line had been extended north to a connection with the Chicago & Western Indiana. Arrangements were made for trains to reach Indianapolis using the Indianapolis Union Railway and Louisville on the rails of the Pennsylvania and the Louisville & Nashville.

The company's map consisted of Louisville–Michigan City and Indianapolis-Chicago lines crossing at Monon. It soon adopted the slogan "The Monon Route," and the nickname was soon better known than the official name. In the 1880s the Monon acquired branches from Orleans to French Lick and from Bedford west toward the coalfields of western Indiana. A branch that reached the coalfields was intended to be the beginning of an Indianapolis-Evansville line, but the Wallace Junction–Victoria line was all that was built.

The Monon expanded into Kentucky in 1889 with an agreement to use the Kentucky & Indiana bridge to connect with the Louisville Southern and with construction of branches to Lexington, Kentucky, and to the eastern Kentucky coalfields. However, when Astor died in early 1890, a New Albany shareholder, William L. Breyfogle, managed to unseat the Monon's management and cancel its plans for expansion in Kentucky. In 1897 the Monon underwent reorganization and became the Chicago, Indianapolis & Louisville Railway.

In 1899 J. P. Morgan acquired control of the railroad. In 1902 the Louisville & Nashville and the Southern Railway, both controlled by Morgan, purchased a majority interest in the Monon. The railroad did well enough in the early years of the twentieth century to consider double-tracking the Chicago-Monon line. As a start on that project it acquired a parallel shortline, the Chicago & Wabash Valley, but went no further.

The Monon began to decline in the 1920s. It did not reach the industrial section of Indianapolis, and its principal connection at Indianapolis was the Cincinnati, Hamilton & Dayton Railway (CH&D). The Baltimore & Ohio acquired the CH&D in 1917 for its Cincinnati-Toledo line. The CH&D had just cast off its Hamilton, Ohio–Indianapolis–Springfield, Illinois, route as Cincinnati, Indianapolis & Western, but the Baltimore & Ohio acquired that in 1927. Cincinnati-Chicago traffic that had moved via Indianapolis and the Monon could remain on Baltimore & Ohio rails for the entire distance. As construction activity dropped in the Depression, so did the demand for building stone, which sometimes amounted to almost one-fourth of the Monon's freight traffic. The Louisville & Nashville and the Southern, the Monon's connections at Louisville and its owners, sent much of their Chicago traffic by other routes.

In December 1933 the Monon applied to the Reconstruction Finance Corp. for a loan in order to stave off bankruptcy. The head of the RFC's railroad division, John W. Barriger III, refused the loan. Barriger could see that the Monon needed to completely reorganize its financial structure. On December 30, 1933, the Monon entered bankruptcy. It abandoned weak branches and cut passenger service as much as possible. Its trustees even considered liquidating the road—its route was longer than competing routes, and it was harder to operate. The increased traffic levels of World War II may have been the key to the Monon's survival.

A new Chicago, Indianapolis & Louisville Railway took over the Monon on May 1, 1946. The president of the company was John W. Barriger III. Barriger was an advocate of the straight, fast, flat, multiple-track, heavy-duty "Super Railroad"—everything the Monon was not. Barriger dieselized the road, gave the passenger trains a low-budget revamp with surplus U.S. Army hospital cars, bought freight cars by the hundreds, caught up on 20 years of deferred maintenance, and solicited business. He concentrated line-relocation efforts at the north end of the railroad: a new bridge over the Wabash River and a bypass around a bottomless bog. The south end of the railroad needed to be completely relocated, a task that was as impossible as removing the Monon from the streets in four cities. By 1952 the Monon was in good shape and profitable. During the 1950s the railroad adopted its nickname as its official title.

The Louisville & Nashville reached Chicago in 1969 by buying the eastern half of the Chicago & Eastern Illinois. The Monon suggested merger to the Southern Railway, but the Southern had just upgraded its line to Cincinnati and preferred interchanging Chicago traffic there to acquiring its own line to Chicago. The Louisville & Nashville was more receptive, considering the Monon a useful alternate route with interests in several terminal railroads. It merged the Monon on July 31, 1971. Ownership subsequently passed to Seaboard System and CSX Transportation. By the early 1990s the Michigan City and Indianapolis lines had been abandoned except for short stubs out of Monon. Later a large portion of the Louisville line through Bloomington was also abandoned.

In 1970, its last full year before the Louisville & Nashville merger, the Monon operated a system of 541 route-miles and 794 track-miles, with 44 locomotives, 2,970 freight cars, 93 company service cars, and 930 employees. Predominant freight traffic revenues included coal (13.6 percent), food and food products (10.4 percent), pulp and paper products (10.4 percent), and chemicals (9.7 percent). Monon operating revenues totaled $23.5 million in 1971, and the railroad achieved a 77.8 percent operating ratio.

—George H. Drury

REFERENCES

Dolzall, Gary W., and Stephen F. Dolzall. *Monon: The Hoosier Line.* Rev. ed. Bloomington: Indiana Univ. Press, 2002.

Hilton, George W. *Monon Route.* Berkeley, Calif.: Howell-North, 1978.

Chicago, Milwaukee, St. Paul & Pacific Railroad (Milwaukee Road)

Inhabitants of the Wisconsin Territory began to agitate for internal improvements, preferably railroads, in the mid-1830s. The lead miners of southwestern Wisconsin and a growing farming community needed a better way to get their products to market. In 1847 Milwaukeeans finally chartered Wisconsin's first railroad, the Milwaukee & Waukesha Rail Road, to run west about 20 miles from the Lake Michigan shore. The city and the new state were booming when the charter was revised in 1849 to permit extension all the way to the Mississippi River. Tracklaying began in September 1850 for what was now the Milwaukee & Mississippi Rail Road. Service commenced to Wauwatosa, five miles from Milwaukee, on November 20, 1850, and the line was welcomed to Waukesha on February 25, 1851. The railroad arrived at Madison, the state capital, in 1854 and finally reached the Mississippi at Prairie du Chien in 1857.

In 1852 another railroad, the La Crosse & Milwaukee Rail Road, began building from the north edge of Milwaukee's business district through Horicon, Beaver Dam, and Portage to La Crosse, completing a second rail route from Milwaukee to the Mississippi in 1858. A major feat was construction of the state's first rail tunnel near Tomah.

The panic of 1857 was followed by a complicated series of events involving mortgages, bankruptcies, and sales of these and other early Wisconsin railroads. This brought Alexander Mitchell, a Scotsman and a prominent Milwaukee banker, into a leading role in the formation of what would become The Milwaukee Road. In 1863 Mitchell took the lead in organizing the new Milwaukee & St. Paul Railway, which succeeded the La Crosse & Milwaukee, and set out to unify the railroads of Wisconsin. The Milwaukee & Prairie du Chien, which had succeeded the bankrupt Milwaukee & Mississippi in 1861, was acquired by the Milwaukee & St. Paul late in 1867. With some 820 miles of track, 125 locomotives, almost 2,400 passenger and freight cars, and annual net earnings of more than $2 million, it was one of the largest railroad companies in the Midwest.

Still another new railroad, the Minnesota Central Railway, had built a line between Minneapolis and Owatonna, Minnesota, between 1864 and 1866, while the McGregor Western Railway built northwesterly from what is now Marquette, Iowa, across the Mississippi from Prairie du Chien, to Cresco, Iowa, in 1866. In June 1867 the two roads became one, and less than two months later the combined company was acquired by the Milwaukee & St. Paul. The Owatonna-Cresco gap was quickly filled, creating a through rail route, except for a Mississippi River crossing, from Milwaukee to the Twin Cities.

The Milwaukee & St. Paul reduced the length of its route between Milwaukee and St. Paul by 80 miles in 1872 through acquisition of a railway along the west bank of the Mississippi south from St. Paul to La Crescent, Minnesota (opposite La Crosse), which had been built by a predecessor of the Great Northern Railway. A predecessor of the Chicago & North Western was used between La Crosse and Winona, Minnesota, where it bridged the Mississippi, until the St. Paul (Milwaukee Road was a latter-day byname for the railroad) built its own bridge at North La Crosse in 1876.

In 1873 the M&StP opened a line between Milwaukee and Chicago, and the next year it changed its name to Chicago, Milwaukee & St. Paul. Between 1866 and 1879 the Southern Minnesota Railroad was constructed from La Crescent into Dakota Territory, and the Hastings & Dakota completed a route from Hastings, on the Mississippi 20 miles south of St. Paul, to the Dakota border and then on to Fargo. Both lines were swept into the CM&StP empire in 1880. The Iowa & Dakota Division was completed across the northern tier of the Hawkeye State into Dakota Territory, where it veered southwest to make the railway's first contact with the Missouri river at Running Water on the Nebraska border.

In 1879 the Western Union Railroad, which had been built between 1855 and 1866 from Racine, Wisconsin, to the Mississippi at East Moline, Illinois, entered the St. Paul fold, becoming its Racine & Southwestern Division. The next year the optimistically named Chicago & Pacific was acquired and extended from Byron, Illinois, to meet the Racine & Southwestern Division, giving CM&StP a direct route from Chicago to Savanna, Illinois. Across the Mississippi the railway had already laid steel west from Sabula, Iowa, reaching Marion (immediately north of Cedar Rapids) in 1872. A bridge linking Savanna and Sabula was completed in 1881, and a line across western Iowa from Marion was completed into Council Bluffs a year later.

In 1887 the CM&StP arrived in Kansas City from Cedar Rapids via Ottumwa, completing lines from Chicago to three western gateways: St. Paul, Omaha, and Kansas City. A more direct route to Kansas City was created when the cutoff between Davenport and Ottumwa was opened in 1903.

Most of CM&StP's Wisconsin lines were in the southern portion of that state, but long fingers projected into Michigan's Upper Peninsula: from New Lisbon through Wisconsin Rapids, Wausau, and Merrill, and from Milwaukee through Green Bay. The Wisconsin lines were considerably fleshed out in the last part of the nineteenth century. The original Northern Division was centered at Horicon and reached Oshkosh and Fond du Lac. Madison received a shorter route from Milwaukee and a connection to Portage (for the Twin Cities). The Mineral Point Division comprised lines constructed over a period of 30 years between that historic little city and Janesville. From Wabasha, Minnesota, a pontoon drawbridge on the Mississippi River provided access to Eau Claire in 1882.

There was similar expansion in Iowa, where the St. Paul had more route-miles than in any other state. During the 1870s the line along the west bank of the Mississippi from Clinton through Dubuque to River Junction, Minnesota (opposite La Crosse), was built. Originally under control of the Burlington, it came into the St. Paul camp in 1899. Its 3-foot-gauge Waukon (Iowa) and Preston (Minnesota) branches were widened to standard gauge, but the line from Bellevue to Cascade, Iowa, remained narrow gauge. Sioux City, which had been reached earlier in a roundabout manner by a line extending south from Canton, South Dakota, received a more direct link with Chicago via Manilla, Iowa, in 1887. In 1899 the railway made its way into Des Moines over a former narrow-gauge railroad, the Des Moines Northern & Western, which had been built between 1878 and 1882. CM&StP's other 3-foot-gauge branch, between Wabasha and Zumbrota, Minnesota, was standard-gauged in 1903.

After the death of Alexander Mitchell in 1887, control of the CM&StP drifted away from Milwaukeeans and Scottish banks to Standard Oil and Armour meatpacking interests. The railroad's general offices were moved to Chicago in 1890.

In 1900 the CM&StP was regarded as a blue-chip property; this would unfortunately change markedly during the next quarter century. In 1901 the St. Paul made an arrangement under which its shipments were handled in Northern Pacific trains between St. Paul and Duluth, and in 1925 it exercised its option to run its own trains to Duluth on NP's track.

The CM&StP had received much freight from Great Northern and Northern Pacific for movement from St. Paul to Chicago, but when those two railways acquired the Chicago, Burlington & Quincy in 1901, that valuable source of business dried up. At Council Bluffs the road always received less business from the Union Pacific than did the Chicago & North Western. CM&StP finally decided that it had no choice but to build its own line to the West Coast and in 1905 announced its intent to build from its South Dakota railhead to Puget Sound.

Costing some $234 million, the Milwaukee's Puget Sound Extension was completed in less than three years. Separate construction companies were formed in each of the four states traversed by the extension—North Dakota, Montana, Idaho, and Washington—to carry out the work, and as many as 20,000 men at one time were reported to be engaged in it. From Harlowton to Lombard, Montana, the route followed the Montana Railroad, better known as the Jawbone. The 717-mile section west to Butte, Montana, opened in August 1908, and the entire 1,412-mile extension between Mobridge, South Dakota, and Tacoma was completed with a last-spike ceremony near Garrison, in western Montana, on May 14, 1909, six months before the completion of the Western Pacific, which would be the last "transcontinental" (in railroad terms, "transcontinental" means reaching to the Pacific from the Great Lakes, the Missouri River, or even Salt Lake City). Not until early 1915, however, when the 2¼-mile Snoqualmie Tunnel was completed, did the St. Paul have a permanent crossing of Washington's Cascade Mountains.

Construction subsidiaries used in building the line were consolidated into the Chicago, Milwaukee & Puget Sound, which in turn was fully integrated into the St. Paul in 1912. The railroad expanded its reach in Washington through the acquisition or construction of branches, and Union Pacific trackage rights gave the St. Paul access to Spokane, Washington.

Just a few years later the St. Paul made another bold move with a decision to electrify 647 route-miles of its western extension. It would rank as the longest electrification yet undertaken anywhere in the world. An initial segment completed during 1914–1916 installed 3,000-volt DC catenary over 438 miles of line between Harlowton, Montana, and Avery, Idaho, that included the crossings of the Belt Mountains, the main range of the Rockies, and the Bitter Root Mountains. So successful was this installation that the St. Paul soon decided to add a second section between Othello and Tacoma, Washington, which included the arduous crossings of the Saddle Mountains and the Cascades. This 207-mile section was in full electric operation by 1920. Costing some $23 million, electrification paid off handsomely for the railroad. By 1923 the St. Paul reported net annual savings in operating costs of almost $1.3 million, and a 1925 report showed a net savings of $12.4 million, including allowance for interest and depreciation costs on the electrification investment, from the start of electric operation through 1924.

During 1921 and 1922 the CM&StP advanced into Indiana with the acquisition of the Chicago, Terre Haute & Southeastern Railway and the Chicago, Milwaukee & Gary Railway. The Southeastern reached into the Indiana coalfields near Linton and Dugger (an on-line source of locomotive coal was important—railroads disliked paying other railroads to haul their fuel), and the Gary afforded a link to the CTH&SE that bypassed the congestion of the Chicago area.

In 1925, burdened by the debt-service requirements for the Puget Sound Extension and its electrification, the costs of acquiring the Southeastern and the Gary, and the effects of a general post–World War I decline in business, the CM&StP entered the largest industrial bankruptcy to that time. A new company, the Chicago, Milwaukee, St. Paul & Pacific Railroad, emerged from the reorganization court in mid-January 1928.

Only seven years later, in June 1935, The Milwaukee Road, as it had become known informally, was once again back in the hands of trustees and the federal court. However, Depression and bankruptcy notwithstanding, a positive attitude imbued much of The Milwaukee Road's activities. This was perhaps most evident in its spirited competition with C&NW and CB&Q for Chicago–Twin Cities passenger traffic. For its entry, the Milwaukee ordered streamlined 4-4-2 Atlantic-type locomotives whose 7-foot driving wheels could roll a train at 120 mph and built innovative welded steel cars in its own Milwaukee shops. Just a month before the 1935 bankruptcy the road inaugurated the first of its famed orange and maroon *Hiawatha* streamlined trains. Others followed over the next decade and a half, culminating with the 1947 introduction of the *Olympian Hiawatha* between Chicago and Seattle-Tacoma. The large shops at Milwaukee, under the direction of Karl F. Nystrom, brought construction of all-welded freight and passenger cars to high levels of accomplishment. A fine group of 4-8-4-type steam locomotives were acquired. The transportation needs of World War II produced huge increases in tonnage handled and passengers carried. In late 1945 the road once again came out of reorganization.

A heavy program of postwar modernization was in full swing during the late 1940s. Improved signaling was extended over much of the system, and radio communication began and was steadily expanded. The Truman Bridge across the Missouri at Kansas City was a joint project with the Chicago, Rock Island & Pacific Railroad. Passenger trains were upgraded, and nearly all were assigned streamlined coaches. Dieselization, which had begun in 1940, was completed early in 1956. In October 1955 the Union Pacific's *City* streamliners began using the Milwaukee Road between Council Bluffs, Iowa, and Chicago, replacing Chicago & North Western as the eastern portion of the Overland Route. Unfortunately, an increase in freight volume did not follow the passenger trains.

Herald and reporting marks of a Milwaukee Road wood-framed boxcar were photographed on the Southern Pacific at San Bernardino, California, in March 1943. —Jack Delano photograph, Office of War Information, Library of Congress (Neg. LC-USW3-21560-E)

The *Olympian Hiawatha* was discontinued in May 1961, turning the west end of the Puget Sound Extension into a freight-only backwater, but two years later the long western appendage was in the transportation spotlight when a fast freight train, the *XL Special,* was introduced on a 55-hour schedule from Chicago to Seattle. The eastbound *Thunderhawk* was introduced shortly thereafter; its schedule was almost as fast as that of the *XL Special.* Electric operation ended in Washington in 1972 and in Montana and Idaho two years later. Beginning in 1961, the Milwaukee upgraded its Chicago suburban service with new diesel locomotives and bilevel gallery cars, a process that took several years to complete.

Merger was in the air after World War II as railroads in the overbuilt midwestern states struggled with new competitive realities. Three times during the 1950s and 1960s the Milwaukee and the North Western explored the possibility of combining the two companies. At the same time CMStP&P also considered a merger with the Rock Island. None of these attempts reached fruition, however. In the early 1970s the Milwaukee expanded its reach through trackage rights awarded by the Interstate Commerce Commission as a result of other mergers. In 1971 a condition of the merger that created Burlington Northern gave CMStP&P an entry into Portland, Oregon, from Longview, Washington, over former NP tracks, affording the Milwaukee access not only to that city's industries and harbor but a direct connection with Southern Pacific. Two years later, after a down-to-the-wire ruling by the U.S. Supreme Court, Milwaukee trains began rolling over the former Monon (which had been merged into Louisville & Nashville) between Bedford, Indiana, and Louisville, Kentucky.

In December 1977 such problems as declining traffic, an excess of light-density branch lines, rising costs, and an excess of competition landed the Chicago, Milwaukee, St. Paul & Pacific in bankruptcy court for the third time in the twentieth century. Seven years of tumult and disintegration followed. In the end, two-thirds of the railroad—those portions considered not viable—had been abandoned or sold. Essentially all the lines west of Terry, Montana, were abandoned, together with major portions of secondary main and branch lines elsewhere. The slimmed-down railroad that remained, known informally as Milwaukee II, attracted potential buyers. Grand Trunk Corp., which operated Grand Trunk Western and Duluth, Winnipeg & Pacific, saw it as a link between its lines and as a route to Kansas City. Grand Trunk Corp. and the Milwaukee Road developed a close working relationship, and GTC announced its intention of acquiring the Milwaukee. This provoked the interest of the Chicago & North Western and, somewhat later, the Soo Line. A bidding war ensued, ultimately forcing GTC to drop out of the contest. After much wrangling, the reorganization court decided in February 1985 that Soo Line (and its parent Canadian Pacific) should become the owner of The Milwaukee Road. A new company, Milwaukee Road, Inc., was established as a Soo Line subsidiary until The

Milwaukee Road was fully merged into the Soo Line Railroad on December 31, 1985.

The much-diminished Milwaukee Road by the end of its last year was operating only some 34 percent of the main-line roads that it had operated in 1980. At the end of its last full year of operation in 1984 the railroad was operating only 1,638 miles of its main routes and 1,385 miles of branch routes, with a total operating track ownership of 3,043 miles. Equipment included 323 locomotives, 11,411 freight cars, and 1,492 other rolling stock, and employees totaled 4,846. The Milwaukee's operating revenue for 1984 was $34,335,000.

—Jim Scribbins

REFERENCES

Cary, John W. *The Organization and History of the Chicago, Milwaukee & St. Paul Railway Company*. Milwaukee: Cramer, Aikens & Cramer, 1893.

Derleth, August. *The Milwaukee Road: Its First Hundred Years*. New York: Creative Age, 1948.

Field, Herman H. *History of Milwaukee Railroad, 1892–1940*. Chicago: Privately published, 1940.

Scribbins, Jim. *The Milwaukee Road, 1928–1985*. Forest Park, Ill.: Heimburger House, 2001.

Chicago, Rock Island & Pacific Railroad (Rock Island)

For a doomed railroad, the Chicago, Rock Island & Pacific had a glorious 128-year history. The railroad was rich in character, instrumental in settling the American West, and a pioneer in developing railroad technology. Nonetheless, it was doomed: doomed to have its first business plan dashed; doomed to build the first bridge over the Mississippi River, only to see it rammed and burned after two weeks in service; doomed to overbuild in the dense web of grain-country railroads; doomed to endure several receiverships and ultimately to bankruptcy and dissolution. For all that, large segments of the Rock Island Lines (which grew to serve 14 states) continue to serve as vital transportation links, now in the hands of other railroads.

In 1845 a meeting was convened at Rock Island, Illinois, to discuss creation of a railroad. Led by Judge James Grant, the group envisioned a railroad connecting two waterways, the Illinois and Mississippi rivers, from La Salle in central Illinois to Rock Island on the Mississippi River. After its chartering as the Rock Island & La Salle Railroad, investors were slow to come forward until an experienced railroad man, Henry Farnam, appraised the situation and determined that railroads would not be built for the purpose of connecting canals, but rather to replace them. In 1850 a revised charter was issued for the Chicago & Rock Island Railroad.

Construction began on October 1, 1851, and 375 days later, on October 10, 1852, the locomotive *Rocket*, under the charge of engineer James Lendabarker, hauled a train of six coaches the 38 miles between Chicago's 22nd Street and Joliet, Illinois. Along the way passengers saw depots being built at Blue Island and Mokena, shared the first coach with wood laid in for fuel, and noted that the *Rocket* was operated backwards from Joliet to Chicago because no turning facilities had yet been built.

With plans well under way for construction of the railroad across Illinois to Rock Island (which was accomplished less than two years later), thoughts turned to the wide Mississippi and how to cross it. Incorporation of the Mississippi & Missouri Railroad Co., which would be one of many railroads absorbed into the Rock Island Lines, added to the interest in crossing the Mississippi. The M&M would stretch across Iowa, but without an outlet to the East it would be of limited value.

A charter was granted by the Illinois General Assembly to build a bridge across the river at Rock Island in 1853. This act did not quell unrest between competing river and barge interests. Under pressure from the custodian of an island the bridge would cross on the site of the Rock Island arsenal, Secretary of War Jefferson Davis (later president of the Confederacy) applied for an injunction to prevent the bridge from being built. The railroad prevailed in a U.S. circuit court, and on April 21, 1856, the bridge was opened to traffic.

The first train crossed the 1,528-foot structure, and more followed. Just two weeks later the steamboat *Effie Afton*, moving upstream, somehow faltered 200 feet beyond the bridge. The boat drifted back into the draw pier, and a stove in the boat tipped over. Both boat and bridge were engulfed in flame.

An investigation by another figure who would play a significant role in the Civil War, Abraham Lincoln, led to a final settlement of the heated dispute between steamboat men and railroad men. A pitched legal battle first saw the tide turned against railroad interests when, in 1858, the U.S. district court ruled the bridge "a common and public nuisance" to be removed. On appeal, the U.S. Supreme Court ruled in favor of the railroad, stating, "According to this assumption, no lawful bridge could be built across the Mississippi anywhere. Nor could harbors or rivers be improved; nor could the great facilities to commerce, accomplished by the invention of the railroads, be made available where great rivers had to be crossed."

As the railroad sought to secure its right to cross the river, progress on other fronts continued. Predecessor M&M operated the first train in Iowa from Davenport (across the Mississippi from Rock Island) on November 20, 1855. Under a legislative imperative to reach Iowa City by the end of that year, track construction continued through difficult winter weather, with a dramatic climax as track was laid up to the city's depot at the stroke of midnight on December 31. According to one account the engineer, overcome by emotion, fainted and had to be carried into the depot.

With the essential line of the Chicago & Rock Island completed, expansion assumed a rapid pace through the last part of the nineteenth century. Though the railroad built many of its own lines, much of its system was the result of acquisition or merger—for example, the M&M through Iowa. The M&M itself was composed of more than one railroad consolidation, and when it failed in 1866, it was acquired by the Rock Island in a public sale at the Davenport courthouse on July 9. A month earlier the Chicago & Rock Island had been incorporated in Iowa as the Chicago, Rock Island & Pacific Railroad Co.

With its new property in hand, the CRI&P continued building west across Iowa, connecting with the Union Pacific at Council Bluffs on May 11, 1869, the day after the golden spike was driven at Promontory, Utah. The Rock Island continued to add significant components, and on June 2, 1880, the name of the corporation was changed to Chicago, Rock Island & Pacific Railway Co. The next significant expansion occurred on July 15, 1885, when capital stock of the Burlington, Cedar Rapids & Northern was acquired, adding 850 miles of line, principally in Iowa and reaching northwest to Watertown, South Dakota. In 1891 another major consolidation occurred with acquisition of subsidiary Chicago, Kansas & Nebraska, which reached to Colorado Springs, Colorado, and El Reno, Indian Territory (later Oklahoma).

Many western railroads of the era concluded their names with "& Pacific," though many never made it that far. The Rock Island got as close as it would get on February 1, 1902, when it completed its extension from Liberal, Kansas, to Santa Rosa, New Mexico, connecting with the El Paso & Southwestern system. The inauguration later that year of the *Golden State Limited* passenger train between Chicago and Los Angeles placed the Rock Island in a competition with the shorter, faster route of rival Atchison, Topeka & Santa Fe Railway. The Rock Island ultimately lost that race, as it did many others on both fronts: freight and passenger traffic.

In the early 1900s, however, the managers of the railroad were optimistic. By 1914 the Rock Island system included 8,328 miles of line, and its fleet had grown to 1,678 locomotives, 45,674 freight cars and 1,163 passenger cars.

The optimism was short lived. The Rock Island entered voluntary bankruptcy on April 12, 1915. It emerged two years later, only to be taken under control of the U.S. government on December 28, 1917, along with all other railroads as part of the mobilization for World War I under the U.S. Railroad Administration. The boom of war traffic gave way to the Great Depression, and the Rock Island again entered bankruptcy on June 7, 1933, where it remained for the next 15 years.

Despite being operated in receivership, the Rock Island recorded many achievements during this period. In 1918 the railroad recorded gross revenue in excess of $100 million for the first time, and by 1922 revenue grew to $142 million. But in the depths of the Depression annual revenue dropped more than half, to $71 million in 1932.

In 1936 a new president, J. D. Farrington, identified a path for the Rock Island of "planned progress." His idea was to rebuild and modernize. Early use of diesel locomotives was a hallmark of this strategy—in 1937 the railroad acquired its first diesel switch engines and inaugurated six diesel-powered streamlined *Rocket*s. A later Rock Island executive (and noted president of other railroads), John W. Barriger, later wrote, "The Rock Island was substantially rehabilitated under Farrington but being a penny pincher he limited his plans to the minimum necessities of the present rather than expanded them to the opportunities of the future. . . . Farrington's lack of vision and fiscal courage alienated Southern Pacific and led it to concentrate its interest for an eastern outlet in the Cotton Belt. . . . This was a serious and lasting blow to CRI&P and disadvantaged Union Pacific too."

Profound problems faced by the Rock Island were given a hiatus with the onset of World War II and the record-breaking traffic that resulted. Revenue reached an all-time high of $192 million in 1945 (net income was $21 million).

That managers were perhaps distracted from their railroads' underlying deficiencies can be understood in the statistics for wartime passenger traffic. U.S. railroad passenger volume had reached its previous peak in 1920 when 47 billion passenger-miles were handled, dropping precipitously to 16 billion in 1933 during the Depression. The wartime surge inflated this number to an amazing 88 billion passenger-miles in 1943.

The Rock Island enjoyed its share of this increase and emerged from World War II making plans for continued strong traffic. In 1948 the railroad built a major hump-retarder yard at Armourdale, Kansas, then another such facility the next year at Silvis, Illinois. These facilities, dieselization, advanced signaling systems, including centralized traffic control, and other improvements were made to support the railroad's development of Rocket Freight Service, named in honor of the railroad's first locomotive (*Rocket*). Rocket Freight Service was joined by the glamorous fleet of *Rocket* passenger trains that fanned out across the system.

As the Rock Island struggled to compete with trucks and automobiles using the nation's expanding network of interstate highways in the 1950s and 1960s, its top executives sought a merger to avoid an inevitable decline. This was not the first time mergers had been considered for the railroad. Talks were opened in 1926 with the St. Louis–San Francisco Railway (Frisco), which purchased 183,333 shares of the Rock Island. A planned 1933 merger with the Frisco was projected to save $10 million. Depression-era economics and an antimerger regulatory environment worked to defeat that plan.

By the early 1960s merger was seen as the only viable alternative for the Rock Island. Its top executives engaged in active discussions for merger with Southern Pacific (SP). Henry Crown, a powerful Chicago businessman and major Rock Island investor, prompted this discussion

The Rock Island–Southern Pacific *Golden State Limited*, a competitor with Santa Fe and the Union Pacific for the Chicago–Los Angeles business, was ready to depart from Chicago's LaSalle Street Station in 1946. A year later the Rock Island intended to begin running its new all-streamlined *Golden Rocket* over the route, but its plans fell through. —*Trains* Magazine Collection

as an avenue for SP that would provide entry into Chicago and gain a competitive advantage over rival Union Pacific (UP), among others.

However, UP sought to diffuse or completely block this effort with a counterproposal in 1962 that the Rock Island be split between SP and UP. What followed was a complicated and lengthy set of proceedings before the Interstate Commerce Commission that lasted virtually until the Rock Island declared bankruptcy in 1975 and collapsed in 1980. The inability of the ICC and the involved parties to reach a conclusion symbolized the ills created for the railroad industry by outdated government regulation. There is little doubt that the Rock Island could no longer survive on its own, but the prolonged period of uncertainty and deferred investment in the Rock Island that resulted from the UP merger fiasco was the ultimate undoing of this once-proud railroad.

The Rock Island deteriorated rapidly after the onset of merger discussions. In 1969 the railroad recorded a deficit of $9.3 million, and in its annual report for that year President Jervis Langdon said, "Only massive infusions of cash which Union Pacific stands committed to advance . . . will save the Rock Island." A newspaper clipping from that period reports that the Rock Island was recording one train wreck for every 32 miles of track operated in the state of Iowa.

On September 26, 1979, the ICC declared the Rock Island to be cashless and incapable of continuing rail operations. The Kansas City Terminal Railway (KCT) was designated the operator of the Rock Island. KCT was owned by 12 major railroads and could serve as a neutral party to continue service to Rock Island shippers. Final efforts to salvage the railroad as an entity were unsuccessful, and di-

rected service was officially ended on March 24, 1980, with a wind-down operation that concluded on March 31. Significant portions of the Rock Island were subsequently acquired by other railroads. Many of these lines will continue in operation for the foreseeable future, ensuring that the once-mighty Rock Island will not completely disappear.

In 1978, the last year before its abandonment for which figures are available, the Rock Island operated a system of 7,025 route-miles and 10,468 track-miles, with 660 locomotives, 79 passenger cars, 26,592 freight and company service cars, and 8,280 employees. Freight traffic totaled over 14,866 ton-miles in 1978, and food and food products (18.2 percent), farm products (16.2 percent), nonmetallic minerals (9.5 percent), and chemicals (8.8 percent) were the principal items of traffic. Rock Island's operating revenues totaled $391.6 million in 1978, and the railroad achieved a 104.8 percent operating ratio.

—Bill Fahrenwald

REFERENCE

Hayes, William Edward. *Iron Road to Empire: The History of 100 Years of the Progress and Achievements of the Rock Island Lines.* New York: Simmons-Boardman, 1953.

Chicago & Eastern Illinois Railroad

The main line of the Chicago & Eastern Illinois Railroad ran south from Chicago through Danville, Illinois, to

Evansville, Indiana, where it connected with the Louisville & Nashville, with which (along with several other railroads) it formed the "Dixie Route" for passenger trains between Chicago, Atlanta, and Florida. Indeed, C&EI carried the majority of Florida-bound passengers out of Chicago on such trains as the *Dixie Limited, Dixie Flyer, Dixie Flagler,* and *Dixie Mail.* A branch ran southwest from the main line at Danville through the coalfields of southern Illinois to the Mississippi River, and a branch off that branch reached St. Louis, mostly through trackage rights on the New York Central. No other railroad had more slogans than the C&EI: the Danville Route, the Evansville Route, the Modern Route, the Noiseless Route, the Boulevard of Steel, and the Chicago Line (which could have been used by many railroads).

The C&EI main line between Chicago and Evansville was built by three companies: the Evansville & Illinois, chartered in 1849 and opened from Evansville through Vincennes to Terre Haute in 1854 (by then it was the Evansville & Terre Haute Railway); the Evansville, Terre Haute & Chicago Railroad, chartered in 1869 and opened from Terre Haute to Danville, Illinois, in 1871; and the corporate ancestor of the C&EI, the Chicago, Danville & Vincennes Railroad, which was chartered in 1865 and completed in 1872 between Dolton, Illinois, just south of Chicago, and Danville. The Chicago, Danville & Vincennes defaulted on its debt in 1873 and was sold at foreclosure in 1877 to become the Chicago & Eastern Illinois Railroad. In 1880 it extended itself south from Danville by leasing the Evansville, Terre Haute & Chicago and southwest from Danville by construction. By 1900 it reached the Mississippi River at Thebes, Illinois.

Meanwhile, in 1894 a new Chicago & Eastern Illinois Railroad had been created by consolidating the old C&EI and the Chicago & Indiana Coal Railway. The latter consisted of a line from Momence, Illinois, on the C&EI southeast across the state line, then south to Brazil, Indiana, about 20 miles east-northeast of Terre Haute, and a branch from Goodland, Indiana, northeast to La Crosse, where several branches and secondary lines of other railroads came together. The Chicago & Indiana Coal Railroad had leased the Chicago & West Michigan branch from La Crosse to New Buffalo, Michigan. (The Chicago & West Michigan was a forerunner of the Pere Marquette, which became the Michigan portion of the Chesapeake & Ohio in 1947.)

Between 1894 and 1900 the C&EI purchased several lines that had been leased or that were subsidiaries: the Evansville, Terre Haute & Chicago (Danville to Terre Haute), the Chicago, Paducah & Memphis Railroad (Mt. Vernon to Marion, Illinois), the Eastern Illinois & Mississippi River Railroad (Marion to Thebes), and the Indiana Block Coal Railroad. The C&EI still relied on the Evansville & Terre Haute for the connection from Terre Haute to the Ohio River. The E&TH controlled the Evansville & Indianapolis, which formed a second Evansville–Terre Haute route east of the E&TH's own line and connected with the former Chicago & Indiana Coal Railroad at Brazil, Indiana.

The St. Louis–San Francisco, which was expanding under the leadership of B. F. Yoakum, acquired control of the C&EI in 1902. To create a connection, the C&EI built a line from Findlay to Pana, Illinois, about 20 miles, and acquired trackage rights on the Cleveland, Cincinnati, Chicago & St. Louis Railway (the Big Four, part of the New York Central) for the 85 miles from Pana to St. Louis. About the same time C&EI built a cutoff between Villa Grove and Woodland Junction, Illinois, eliminating a dogleg through Danville (and 20 miles) for Chicago–St. Louis trains (the Findlay-Pana line similarly cut off a right-angle turn at Shelbyville, where C&EI's line to southern Illinois crossed the Big Four, and saved 5 miles).

The C&EI absorbed the Evansville & Terre Haute and the Evansville Belt Railway in 1911, putting a line from Chicago all the way to the Ohio River under its proprietorship. Indeed, with the Evansville & Indianapolis and the Chicago & Indiana Coal Railroad, the C&EI had two lines from the Ohio River at Evansville north to Lake Michigan at Chicago and New Buffalo, Michigan. About the same time the C&EI bought coal mines and coal lands in southern Illinois and Indiana.

The C&EI and its parent, the Frisco, both entered receivership in 1913, and Yoakum's empire collapsed. Shortly after U.S. Railroad Administration (USRA) control ended in 1920, the Chicago & Eastern Illinois Railway was formed to acquire the franchises and properties of the Chicago & Eastern Illinois Railroad, with several exceptions: the coal lands, the former Evansville & Indianapolis (eventually it became part of the Big Four), the former Evansville & Richmond (it became part of the Milwaukee Road's lines in southern Indiana), and the former Chicago & Indiana Coal Railway (which became the Chicago, Attica & Southern Railroad, which went nowhere and had no business).

As a result of a coal strike in 1922, southern Illinois coal became more expensive even as the market for it was shrinking. C&EI's coal traffic declined. The Van Sweringen brothers of Cleveland added the C&EI to their empire in 1928 but did little with it. C&EI entered reorganization.

On December 31, 1940, the Chicago & Eastern Illinois Railroad took over the properties, assets, and business of the Chicago & Eastern Illinois Railway. Among its leaders were John Budd, primarily associated with the Great Northern, and Downing B. Jenks, who would later head the Missouri Pacific. Much of the reorganization plan was the work of John W. Barriger III.

The reorganized C&EI did well in World War II and immediately thereafter. By 1953 a rejuvenated railroad was making record freight profits on revived southern Illinois coal and other traffic. The C&EI was a pioneer in such technical innovations as automatic train control, the Mars light, and trailer-on-flatcar service.

The Missouri Pacific began discussing merger with the

C&EI in 1959. Two years later both the Missouri Pacific and the Louisville & Nashville petitioned the Interstate Commerce Commission for control of the road. The ICC ruled in favor of the Missouri Pacific in 1963 with the requirement that the MP negotiate to sell the Woodland Junction–Evansville line to the L&N. In 1969 the L&N acquired that line plus a half interest in the former C&EI main line from Woodland Junction north to Dolton and half of C&EI's interests in two terminal railroads, the Chicago & Western Indiana and the Belt Railway of Chicago. The Missouri Pacific merged the C&EI in 1976.

In 1975, its last year before the Missouri Pacific merger, Chicago & Eastern Illinois operated a system of 644 route-miles and 1,290 track-miles, with 49 locomotives, 7,210 freight and company service cars, and 1,132 employees. Principal freight traffic sources included coal (15.9 percent), chemicals (11.3 percent), transportation equipment (11.3 percent), and food and food products (7.6 percent). Chicago & Eastern Illinois operating revenues totaled $57.7 million in 1975, and the railroad achieved a 62.6 percent operating ratio.

—George H. Drury

REFERENCES

Anderson, Willard V. "The Century-Old C&EI . . ." *Trains* 9, no. 10 (Aug. 1949): 16–23.
Gregory, William W., and Robert St. Clair. "You Can't Keep a Good Railroad Down." *Trains* 14, no. 12 (Oct. 1954): 18–26.

Chicago & North Western Railway

Chicago's first railroad was the Galena & Chicago Union Rail Road, chartered in 1836 to connect Chicago with Galena, a booming lead-mining town in northwestern Illinois. Construction of the railroad began in 1848, and by 1854 it had reached Freeport, where it met the Illinois Central's original north-south line.

An isolated railroad, built southwest from Fond du Lac, Wisconsin, between 1851 and 1854, and another road built in 1854 from Chicago to Cary, Illinois, consolidated in 1855 as the Chicago, St. Paul & Fond du Lac and extended the Chicago-Cary line to Janesville, Wisconsin, late that year. The company entered bankruptcy in 1857 and was reorganized in 1859 as the Chicago & North Western Railway. That same year it connected the Chicago-Janesville line with the line from Fond du Lac.

By 1864 the Galena ran from Chicago to Fulton, Illinois, on the Mississippi River, and from West Chicago (then known simply as Junction) via Belvidere and Rockford to Freeport. Branches extended north from the Freeport line at Elgin to Richmond, Illinois, and from Belvidere through Beloit and Janesville, Wisconsin, to Madison. The North Western's lines extended from Chicago to Green Bay, Wisconsin, via Janesville and Fond du Lac and from Kenosha, Wisconsin, to Rockford, Illinois. The Galena & Chicago Union and the Chicago & North Western consolidated in 1864, retaining the North Western name. Two years later the new company leased the Chicago & Milwaukee Railroad, which had opened in 1855 between the cities of its name.

Subsidiary companies extended a line westward across Iowa from Clinton through Cedar Rapids to Council Bluffs between 1857 and 1867. Much of the early freight traffic on that line was material to construct the Union Pacific Railroad. A branch that opened in 1868 gave the line a second terminal on the Missouri River at Sioux City, Iowa.

During the early 1870s the C&NW extended a line north from Green Bay into the copper-mining country of Michigan's Upper Peninsula. Between 1871 and 1885 the Milwaukee, Lake Shore & Western was constructed between Milwaukee and Ashland, Wisconsin, on Lake Superior. C&NW acquired that railroad in September 1893.

During that same era subsidiary companies built an extensive network of branches in Minnesota, Iowa, and the Dakota Territory. In 1884 the C&NW purchased the Fremont, Elkhorn & Missouri Valley, which was building westward across northern Nebraska; it remained a separate company until 1903.

The main line across Iowa was double-tracked by 1902, and a new Mississippi crossing was completed at Clinton in 1909. Automatic train control (which arbitrarily stops a train if the engineer disregards signal indications) was completed between Chicago and Council Bluffs in 1928. The Chicago & North Western was almost unique among American railroads in keeping to the left on double track. The most plausible explanation for the practice involves the placement of station buildings when the line was originally built. The North Western's last major construction projects were a second line from Chicago to Milwaukee for freight trains and a belt line around Milwaukee (1908), a main line, the Adams Cutoff, diagonally across Wisconsin from Milwaukee to a connection with the existing Chicago–Twin Cities line at Wyeville, Wisconsin (1911), and a long line south from Nelson, Illinois, through Peoria to a connection with the Litchfield & Madison Railway at Benld (1914).

The Omaha Road

For 90 years the Chicago, St. Paul, Minneapolis & Omaha Railway (the Omaha Road) formed a large portion of the C&NW system. After 1900 or so, there was little visible contrast between the Omaha and the North Western. The most significant difference was that CStPM&O trains, unlike those on its parent road, kept to the right on double track. Most locomotives were twins of their C&NW brothers, with only a different numbering scheme and "CStPM&O" below their cab windows to distinguish them. Passenger crew uniforms carried the Omaha name on their lapels.

The Omaha began as a line built southwest from Mendota, Minnesota, near St. Paul, in 1865, and extended into southwestern Minnesota as the St. Paul & Sioux City. In 1872 the StP&SC reached Sioux City, then continued down the Nebraska side of the Missouri River to Omaha.

Meanwhile, the West Wisconsin Railway began building northwest from Tomah, Wisconsin, on the Milwaukee & St. Paul, to St. Paul, Minnesota. It soon shifted its southern terminal from Tomah to Elroy on the Chicago & North Western's line from Madison, Wisconsin, through La Crosse to southern Minnesota, creating a Chicago-Madison-Elroy–St. Paul route competitive with the Milwaukee & St. Paul. At the same time the North Wisconsin Railway was building a line northeast from Hudson, Wisconsin, toward Ashland and Duluth.

The West Wisconsin entered bankruptcy and was quickly reorganized as the Chicago, St. Paul & Minneapolis Railway in 1878. Two years later it was consolidated with the North Wisconsin as the Chicago, St. Paul, Minneapolis & Omaha; that company soon brought in the St. Paul & Sioux City. In 1882 the C&NW acquired control of the Omaha Road.

The Omaha built a line from Eau Claire to Spooner, Wisconsin, eliminating the dogleg to Hudson for Chicago-Superior-Duluth traffic. It double-tracked and signaled its Elroy-Hudson route between 1900 and 1915. The CStPM&O continued a separate corporate existence through much of the twentieth century, although to all appearances it was just another piece of the Chicago & North Western. The C&NW increased its holdings in the Omaha Road, leased it in 1957, and finally merged it in 1972.

"Route of the 400s"

Passengers long represented a significant component of North Western's traffic, including both an extensive intercity business over its principal routes and branch lines and a heavy commuter traffic at Chicago. The most competitive of its intercity routes was that between Chicago and the Twin Cities, and in the mid-1930s the C&NW went head-to-head with Burlington and The Milwaukee Road in competition for high-speed daytime traffic over the route. In early 1935, while the Burlington and the Milwaukee awaited the completion of new streamliners for the service, the North Western beat them to the starting post by almost four months with the introduction of a new train made up of refurbished standard equipment and powered by steam locomotives modified for extended operation at "over 90 mph" speeds. It operated on a schedule that made it the fastest train in North America and the fastest long-distance train in the world. Dubbed the *400* for its "400 miles in 400 minutes" schedule, the train proved a great success in building Chicago–Twin Cities passenger traffic. New streamlined equipment replaced the conventional equipment in September 1939, and the *400*'s success soon spawned a fleet of *400* streamliners serving principal routes on the entire C&NW system. In 1935 the North Western also became a partner with the Union Pacific in the operation of the first of

The short-lived Chicago & North Western, Union Pacific, and Southern Pacific *Forty Niner* operated an all-Pullman, extra-fare service between Chicago and San Francisco. Inaugurated in 1937, the train operated five round trips per month until 1941. Streamlined C&NW 4-6-4 Hudson No. 4001 headed the westbound *Forty Niner* out of Chicago. —*Trains* Magazine Collection

what would become a celebrated long-distance streamliner fleet operating between Chicago and western points, with the C&NW responsible for the Chicago-Omaha leg.

By the mid-twentieth century the North Western had fallen on hard times. The railroad network of the Midwest put every farmer within a day's drive of a railroad station—by horse and buggy on an unpaved road. The paved highway and the automobile had made that kind of coverage redundant. Good roads created another redundancy: less freight moved by rail, and there was not enough business to divide among a large number of railroads. Seven railroads connected Chicago with Omaha; seven ran between Chicago and Kansas City. Passenger traffic was in a period of steep decline.

After involvement with Chicago Great Western and Minneapolis & St. Louis, Ben W. Heineman became C&NW's chairman in the spring of 1956. Heineman saw that the choice was eat or be eaten and set the C&NW on a course of expansion. C&NW acquired the Litchfield & Madison in 1958, extending its Nelson-Peoria-Benld route into East St. Louis. It strengthened its route map in Minnesota and Iowa by acquiring the Minneapolis & St. Louis in 1960 and the Chicago Great Western in 1968, subsequently abandoning much of the track of both those roads. Also in 1968 C&NW brought erstwhile interurbans Des Moines & Central Iowa and Fort Dodge, Des Moines & Southern into its fold. In 1963 it began efforts to acquire the Chicago, Rock Island & Pacific (as did several other railroads).

A significant accomplishment of the Heineman era was an innovative modernization of the railroad's Chicago commuter service. By the early 1960s the North Western had completed the replacement of its aging commuter coaches with modern air-conditioned bilevel gallery cars and had introduced to North America the concept of push-pull operation. Under this practice a diesel locomotive pulled on outbound trips from Chicago and pushed on the way in, eliminating the cost and inefficiencies of switching locomotives from one end to the other at the end of each run. By 1963 the modernized service was showing a modest net income, something that was virtually unprecedented in the commuter service economics of the time. By the late 1960s Heineman had lost his enthusiasm for railroading and willingly sold the railway to a group conceived and organized in 1970: the North Western Employees Transportation Co., which changed its name to Chicago & North Western Transportation Co. when it purchased the operating assets of the Chicago & North Western Railway in 1972.

Chicago, Rock Island & Pacific entered bankruptcy in 1975 and after further misfortunes was ordered liquidated by a federal court early in 1980. That April C&NW leased the Rock Island's route between the Twin Cities and Kansas City, as well as grain-gathering branches in northwestern Iowa. After successfully fending off both the Soo Line and adverse Iowa public opinion, North Western was able to purchase the former CRI&P trackage in June 1983.

In the early 1970s the North Western became interested in the coal deposits in eastern Wyoming's Powder River Basin. After difficult negotiations, C&NW and Burlington Northern began operation of a new rail line to tap the Powder River Basin. Faced with the seemingly impossible task of financing the reconstruction of its line across northern Nebraska (subsequently largely abandoned), the C&NW built instead another new line to connect with Union Pacific's North Platte Valley line. Unit coal trains started rolling over the new lines in August 1984.

Relations with Union Pacific

During the first half of the twentieth century the North Western was Union Pacific's preferred eastern connection, and a substantial volume of freight and passenger traffic to and from the UP moved between Omaha and Chicago on C&NW rails. An early period of strained relations between the two roads resulted from the C&NW's completion of a long route west across northern Nebraska and central Wyoming to Lander in 1906. Historians disagree about whether C&NW planned a further extension over South Pass and westward to the Pacific that would have competed with UP or was merely reaching for the timber and mineral resources of central Wyoming. A later period of strained relations resulting from deteriorating performance by C&NW caused the UP to suddenly switch its prestigious Streamliner fleet to The Milwaukee Road east of Omaha in 1955.

By the late 1980s the North Western was once again Union Pacific's preferred eastern connection, and UP solidified the relationship by acquiring part ownership of C&NW. After the C&NW became the target of several hostile takeover bids, Union Pacific set out to increase its share of the North Western and merged it in April 1995.

—Jim Scribbins

REFERENCES

Casey, Robert, and W. A. Douglas. *Pioneer Railroad*. New York: Whittlesey House, 1948.

Grant, H. Roger. *The North Western*. DeKalb: Northern Illinois Univ. Press, 1996.

Stennett, William H. *Yesterday and Today*. Chicago: Chicago & North Western Railway, 1910.

Chicago Aurora & Elgin

The Chicago Aurora & Elgin was an interurban-turned-suburban electric railroad from Chicago to cities along the Fox River 40 miles west: Aurora, Batavia, Geneva, and Elgin. It was unusual in that it used third-rail power distribution except in yards and terminals and along streets. Its trains entered Chicago over the rails of a Chicago Transit

Authority elevated. Its demise in 1957 was the consequence of the replacement of the elevated with an expressway. Even though tracks would be restored in the new expressway, the "temporary" decline in ridership when the CA&E cut back its trains on Chicago's west side helped accelerate the interurban's abandonment.

CA&E's main line and Geneva branch closely paralleled and competed with the first 35 miles of Chicago & North Western's line to Omaha. Aurora was well served by the suburban trains of the Chicago, Burlington & Quincy, whose line ran well south of the CA&E. Elgin was the western terminus of suburban service on the Milwaukee Road. Only at Batavia and St. Charles was the electric line without direct competition from steam railroad suburban services, and those two cities were adjacent to Geneva. The CA&E was primarily a passenger carrier, although the line handled a modest freight service in interchange with its connecting steam railroads.

The CA&E began life in 1901 as the Aurora, Elgin & Chicago Railway. Little more than a year after its incorporation it was operating a main line between Aurora and Laramie Avenue in Chicago and a branch to Batavia. In 1903 it opened a branch from Wheaton northwest to Elgin. The AE&C extended its service to Chicago's Loop in 1905 over the rails of the Metropolitan West Side Elevated (the "L"). A year later, in 1906, several streetcar lines in the Fox River valley were consolidated with the AE&C to form the Aurora, Elgin & Chicago Railroad. A subsidiary of the new company built a branch to Geneva. Service on that branch was extended to St. Charles on streetcar tracks.

The company entered receivership in 1919. In 1922 its properties were divided into the Fox River Division, which comprised the streetcar lines in and between the Fox River cities, and the Third Rail Division, the line from Chicago to Aurora, Batavia, Geneva, and Elgin. The Third Rail Division was sold to the Chicago, Aurora & Elgin Railroad, which began operation on July 1, 1922.

Samuel Insull obtained control of the CA&E in 1926. One of his first proposals was for a new route to bypass the local stations and congestion on the main line. It would be much like the Skokie Valley line that Insull's Chicago North Shore & Milwaukee put in service that same year. The Depression, though, killed CA&E's project and threw the company into another receivership.

For lack of sufficient traffic, CA&E replaced rail service to Geneva and St. Charles with buses in 1937. In 1939 it built a new terminal in Aurora and replaced street running there, the last on the CA&E, with new private right of way. The CA&E developed an interesting operating pattern: alternating local trains between Chicago and Wheaton (25 miles from Chicago) with express trains that carried cars for Aurora, Batavia, and Elgin. The expresses were divided and put together at Wheaton.

The receivership that began during the Depression continued until 1946, when the company was reorganized as the Chicago Aurora & Elgin Railway. Postwar prosperity allowed the CA&E to upgrade its lines and order ten new steel cars. However, as the 1950s began, it faced amputation of its main line about six miles west of its Chicago terminal. Federal and state highway administrations, Cook County, and the City of Chicago proposed an expressway along the route of the elevated. The new highway, today's Eisenhower Expressway, I-290, would have rapid-transit tracks in the median. During the several years it took to build the highway, CTA's "L" trains would detour on streetcar tracks in the middle of Van Buren Street. CA&E and CTA established an interchange station at Des Plaines Avenue in 1953. The loss of one-seat service to and from Chicago and the longer running times caused CA&E's business to drop by half in three months.

CA&E struggled on for more than a year before petitioning in 1955 to drop all passenger service. Passenger operation ceased on July 3, 1957 (CA&E's minimal freight service continued until June 9, 1959). CA&E's track and rolling stock were not scrapped immediately. There were proposals to revive the service, using the tracks in the median of the expressway, but CA&E's cars could not fit into the subway at the east end of the new rapid-transit line. Legal abandonment took place on June 10, 1961. Much of CA&E's right of way is now a bicycle trail, the Prairie Path.

—George H. Drury

REFERENCES

Krambles, George, ed. *The Great Third Rail*. Chicago: Central Electric Railfans' Assn., 1961.

Plachno, Larry. *Sunset Lines: The Story of the Chicago, Aurora & Elgin Railroad*. Polo, Ill.: Transportation Trails, 1989.

Chicago Great Western Railway

The Chicago Great Western Railway (CGW) reached all the principal gateways of the upper Midwest and had a reputation for innovation, but it was never considered a strong or important railroad. Shaped by St. Paul capitalist and promoter A. B. Stickney (1840–1916), it appeared late in the era of railroad construction. In the mid-1880s Stickney pushed the moribund Minnesota & Northwestern from St. Paul to Dubuque, Iowa, and by 1888 he had forged a route to Chicago across the hilly country of northwestern Illinois. Soon the hard-driving Stickney reorganized his expanding property as the Chicago, St. Paul & Kansas City and extended it to the Missouri railroad centers of St. Joseph and Kansas City. He completed his "Maple Leaf System" largely through purchasing and leasing connecting trackage and early in the twentieth century by building the Omaha Extension between Fort

Dodge and Council Bluffs, Iowa. The company was reorganized again as the Chicago Great Western Railway in 1892.

While the Stickney road was not always the most direct way between its five principal gateways (Chicago, Kansas City, Omaha, St. Joseph, and the Twin Cities), it nevertheless possessed competitive routes. Stickney saw that future prosperity lay with trunk lines and not with more localized trackage. With access to several strategic centers, the CGW attracted considerable freight and passenger traffic, often by offering bargain rates and swift, dependable service. Although it was constructed through a generally settled region, it reached places that even in the late 1880s had large amounts of goods to transport, yet remained either inadequately served by railroads or not served at all. There were also places where the CGW could spawn new towns. When the road built through western Iowa in 1902 and 1903, for example, its Iowa Townsite Co. created nearly a dozen communities.

Pitted as it was against tough, determined competitors, it is understandable that the CGW revealed an innovative flair. Indeed, much of its history supports the hypothesis that smaller, less entrenched carriers frequently caused changes in industry thinking and practices or at least sparked serious discussions. The innovation most often associated with the company involved its trailer-on-flatcar (TOFC) or "piggyback" service, introduced in 1935, but it is also remembered for its early use of internal combustion motive power, including McKeen cars, continuous welded rail, long freight trains, and radio communication.

The piggyback story warrants attention. In 1935 the CGW's traffic department called management's attention to piggybacking. The property was in receivership (its second since 1907), and additional revenues were essential to a successful reorganization. Officials were impressed with the success of the Chicago North Shore & Milwaukee, a Samuel Insull interurban that for several years had been transporting specially designed truck trailers on modified flatcars. Another Insull property, the Chicago South Shore & South Bend, had also begun a TOFC business. After an encouraging experiment in the summer of 1935, the following year the CGW launched its intermodal operations. Although at first "trailer trains" traveled only between Chicago and the Twin Cities, by the start of World War II they appeared on other parts of the system, with the Chicago–Kansas City route being the most popular. By the mid-1950s the CGW ranked fourth behind the Southern Pacific, the Pennsylvania, and the New Haven (another early piggyback carrier) among carriers providing this service, although as other larger roads entered the field, the CGW position dropped.

Chicago Great Western was not a major passenger carrier. Except for the Minneapolis–Kansas City route, CGW's routes were about the same length as those of its competitors, but even before World War II CGW's service consisted primarily of local trains that converged on the road's hub, Oelwein, Iowa, in the small hours of the morning to exchange through sleeping cars. The Mayo Clinic at Rochester, Minnesota, was a major source of passenger traffic. CGW's last passenger train was a Minneapolis-Omaha train that survived until September 1965 on the strength of mail and express traffic.

The CGW remained independent throughout its existence, but financial control of the railroad passed to several groups and individuals. In the wake of the panic of 1907 Stickney lost out to J. P. Morgan, Sr., and in the 1920s a group of speculators led by Standard Steel Car Co. executive Patrick Joyce took charge. Their Bremo Corp. holding-company scheme failed to work, largely because of the negative impact of the Great Depression. At the end of the 1940s several wealthy investors, the "Kansas City Group," took control of the reorganized CGW (it had emerged from its second bankruptcy in 1941) from the remnants of the Joyce regime. Soon, one of the new owners, William N. Deramus III, assumed the presidency and spearheaded a variety of laborsaving reforms and physical-plant betterments.

By the 1960s the prospects for an independent CGW were not promising. Shareholders, most notably members of the Kansas City Group, wished to protect their investments, and although they contemplated an end-to-end merger with the Soo Line, they decided to accept an attractive offer from Ben W. Heineman of the Chicago & North Western. At the time of the merger, July 1, 1968, the CGW was in excellent physical condition. Its 1,500-mile route map was mostly stem and not branch. It possessed a fleet of modern diesel locomotives and freight cars. However, the Chicago & North Western must have agreed with a comment made in the 1930s by John W. Barriger, head of the Railroad Division of the Reconstruction Finance Corp., who characterized the CGW as "a mountain railroad in a prairie country serving a traffic vacuum." C&NW soon abandoned and dismantled nearly all the former CGW lines.

In 1967, its last year before the Chicago & North Western merger, Chicago Great Western operated a system of 1,411 route-miles and 2,048 track-miles, with 139 locomotives, 3,540 freight and company service cars, and 1,612 employees. Freight traffic totaled just over 2,452 million ton-miles in 1967, and food products (28 percent), lumber (15.9 percent), chemicals (10 percent), and farm products (9.7 percent) were its principal traffic items. Chicago Great Western operating revenues totaled $28.7 million in 1967, and the railroad achieved an 80.8 percent operating ratio.

—H. Roger Grant

REFERENCES

Berk, Gerald. *Alternative Tracks: The Constitution of American Industrial Order, 1865–1917.* Baltimore: Johns Hopkins Univ. Press, 1994.

Grant, H. Roger. *The Corn Belt Route: A History of the Chicago Great Western Railroad Company*. DeKalb: Northern Illinois Univ. Press, 1984.

Chicago North Shore & Milwaukee Railroad

The North Shore Line, as it was generally known, was perhaps the finest interurban electric railway in America. Its earliest predecessor was a modest streetcar line organized in 1891 at Waukegan, Illinois. By 1897 it had become the Chicago & Milwaukee Electric Railway; the new name reflected the expansive plans of its owners. By 1899 the line had been extended southward to Evanston, where it connected with steam railroad trains for Chicago, and in 1904 construction crews began building north toward Milwaukee. This double-track northern extension, built to exceptionally high standards on a virtually straight alignment, laid the foundation for the North Shore's later preeminence among high-speed electric railways. The line reached Milwaukee in October 1908, and the company was soon operating fast Evanston-Milwaukee limited trains that included handsomely appointed parlor-buffet cars, connecting at Chicago with a steam line and, later, the elevated line. By this time, however, the road was in financial trouble and had entered bankruptcy early in 1908. This came to an end in 1916; the company was reorganized as the Chicago North Shore & Milwaukee under the control of Chicago utilities tycoon Samuel Insull.

During the next decade and a half Insull management invested millions of dollars in improvements to track, structures, power supply, and stations. The lack of a direct entry into Chicago was resolved in 1919 when North Shore trains began operating into the Loop over the Insull-controlled elevated system. The line began acquiring a fleet of fast steel interurban cars that reached a total of 146 cars by 1930. The new equipment included parlor-dining cars, and the North Shore was soon operating an expanded schedule of fast limited trains. An extensive network of connecting bus services was developed. Innovative advertising and marketing efforts and enlightened labor relations helped the road win the American Electric Railway Assn.'s Charles A. Coffin gold medal in 1923 "for distinguished contribution to the development of electric transportation."

The line's route through the North Shore suburbs was an impediment to a faster Chicago-Milwaukee service, and the most significant improvement of the Insull era was the construction of a 23-mile, high-speed cutoff through the Skokie Valley west of the original Shore Line route. Trains began operating over the $10 million line in 1926, highlighting one of the best years ever in the North Shore's entire history, when the railroad transported almost 19.5 million passengers, a figure that was not ex-

ceeded until the height of World War II. The new line gave the North Shore a high-speed route over almost the entire distance between Chicago and Milwaukee. New Chicago-Milwaukee timings of only 2 hours 9 minutes won the North Shore *Electric Traction* magazine's annual interurban speed trophy in 1927, and the railroad went on to win it a total of five times in the period of nine years the trophy was awarded, taking permanent possession of the trophy in 1933. In 1935 the British trade journal *Railway Gazette* described the North Shore as "the fastest electric railway service in the world."

The Great Depression brought new financial troubles, and in 1932 the North Shore entered a bankruptcy that lasted 14 years. A paralyzing strike in 1938 shut the line down for 51 days and brought the road close to abandonment. Instead, North Shore management initiated a valiant effort to rebuild its traffic. Existing equipment was improved and refurbished, and two new Electroliner streamlined trains were ordered for Chicago-Milwaukee service. These magnificent articulated trains were the finest equipment of the entire interurban era and offered all the amenities of competing steam railroad streamliners. Capable of 85 mph, the trains set a new standard for high-speed service, operating on schedules that allowed as little as 1 hour 40 minutes for the 87-mile journey despite more than a dozen intermediate stops. In a 1950 test an Electroliner equipped with field shunting for even higher speeds reached a record speed of 111 mph.

North Shore freight service was as innovative as its passenger operation. In addition to an extensive interchange business with connecting steam railroads, the line established a fast merchandise dispatch service in 1917 that provided overnight delivery for express and less-than-carload shipments between Chicago and Milwaukee. Together with Lake Michigan steamship lines and connecting interurbans, the North Shore provided fast freight service to and from points throughout southern Michigan. In 1926 the North Shore introduced some of the first mechanical refrigerator cars and in the same year began the first "piggyback" trailer-on-flatcar service on any U.S. railroad.

World War II brought unprecedented traffic to the North Shore—a record passenger total of almost 28 million in 1945—and enough earnings finally to end its long bankruptcy in 1946. But traffic fell rapidly at war's end, and the line was soon in financial trouble again. The money-losing Shore Line route was closed in 1955. The remainder of the system was soon doing no better, and the North Shore began an effort to abandon all operations. The ICC finally granted the necessary permission, and the last North Shore trains completed their runs early on the morning of January 21, 1963. A year later a 5-mile section of the Skokie Valley line came back to life as the Chicago Transit Authority's Skokie Swift, a high-speed shuttle linked to the "L" at Howard Street.

—**William D. Middleton**

REFERENCES

Interurban to Milwaukee. Chicago: Central Electric Railfans' Assn., Bulletin 106, 1962.

Middleton, William D. *North Shore: America's Fastest Interurban.* San Marino, Calif.: Golden West Books, 1964.

Route of the Electroliners. Chicago: Central Electric Railfans' Assn., Bulletin 107, 1963.

Chicago South Shore & South Bend Railroad (South Shore Line)

Still operating electric passenger service over its original route, the South Shore Line, as it is popularly known, can claim the title of "the last interurban." The line's earliest predecessor, the Chicago & Indiana Air Line Railway, began operating a 3.4-mile streetcar line between East Chicago and Indiana Harbor, Indiana, in 1903. A year later the company was reorganized as the Chicago, Lake Shore & South Bend Railway. Trains were operating between Hammond, Indiana, and South Bend by September 6, 1908. By the following April the Illinois Central had completed the connecting Kensington & Eastern and leased it to the CLS&SB. Trains began operating through to Pullman, Illinois, where Chicago passengers could transfer to or from the IC's suburban trains.

The South Shore was planned for 75 mph operation. With a few exceptions, grades were limited to 0.2 percent, and curvature was held to a 3 degree maximum. For its power supply the South Shore adopted a Westinghouse 6,600-volt, single-phase AC system, with power distributed through an overhead catenary system.

Despite its promising territory and high construction standards, the CLS&SB was not very successful. Through World War I the company's financial performance was among the poorest of any major interurban, and its traffic and earnings began to decline rapidly in the 1920s. By the end of 1924 the road was in disrepair and had accumulated a deficit of over $1.7 million. Abandonment appeared likely. Instead, the stage was set for a dramatic recovery at the hands of Chicago public utilities entrepreneur Samuel Insull, who had begun a move into northern Indiana utilities.

The South Shore was a good addition to Insull's portfolio because of its potential for freight and passenger traffic development. By early 1925 Insull's Midland Utilities Co. had worked out acquisition plans, and in July the new Chicago South Shore & South Bend Railroad took over the property. Work was soon under way to transform the South Shore into one of the finest properties of the interurban era. Track, roadbed, and stations were rebuilt, and the road's troublesome AC electrification was re-placed by a 1,500-volt DC system that matched IC's new suburban electrification, enabling the South Shore to begin operation into downtown Chicago. Orders were placed for a fleet of heavy steel passenger cars that numbered 69 by 1929. Schedules were expanded, and parlor- and dining-car service was added. A connecting bus line was established to provide service into Illinois, Indiana, and Michigan, and in 1927 *Golden Arrow* train-bus service was inaugurated between Chicago and Detroit. Using the enormous traffic base of its utilities companies, the Insull management persuaded connecting steam railroads to establish new interchanges with the South Shore.

In 1929 South Shore passenger and freight traffic reached record levels, and gross revenues were 330 percent over the 1925 level. That year the railroad won the American Electric Railway Assn.'s Charles A. Coffin gold medal "for distinguished contribution to the development of electric transportation." With some trains making the 90-mile run between Chicago and South Bend in as little as 2 hours 5 minutes, the South Shore also won *Electric Traction* magazine's annual interurban speed trophy.

The Great Depression and the plummeting traffic that came with it brought the South Shore into bankruptcy in 1933, but the superb condition of the road enabled it to survive. The bankruptcy ended in 1938, and the interurban went on to transport the greatest traffic in its history during World War II as heavily industrialized northwestern Indiana geared up for wartime production. By 1945 the South Shore's annual passenger volume passed 6 million, almost double that of 1929. To cope with this enormous traffic, the road's innovative Michigan City shops in 1942 had begun to lengthen the steel cars of the Insull era, a program that continued after the war, when many cars got such amenities as air conditioning and large windows. For its booming freight business the road acquired three enormous 273-ton electric locomotives, originally destined for the Soviet Union, and seven former New York Central electrics.

Attracted by the growing freight traffic, the Chesapeake & Ohio acquired control of the line in 1967. Freight profits, however, were more than offset by growing losses from the declining passenger service, and the line's fleet of 50-year-old passenger cars would soon require replacement. The C&O threatened to abandon passenger service, but some public funding began to come from Illinois in 1973, and by 1977 the newly formed Northern Indiana Commuter Transportation District (NICTD) began to provide public support for the Indiana portion of the service. NICTD was able to assemble funding for 44 new stainless-steel multiple-unit (M.U.) cars that arrived in 1982 to replace the old steel cars.

NICTD's hopes to acquire the South Shore were dashed when C&O sold the road to the Venango River Corp. in 1984, but a few years later Venango declared bankruptcy, and in 1990 NICTD acquired ownership of all the South Shore's Indiana passenger facilities and track, while a new freight operator, the Chicago South Shore & South Bend, acquired all freight-only trackage and exclusive freight rights on NICTD track. In addition, the freight carrier acquired ownership of the Kensington & Eastern, with NICTD retaining a perpetual lease of the line.

Improvements financed through NICTD transformed the South Shore once again. Track, stations, and the power supply system were improved and modernized. New stations were built at several points, and in 1992 the South Shore shifted its South Bend terminal to the Michiana Regional Airport. More new M.U. cars were added as traffic grew, reaching a total of 68 cars. Total ridership passed 3.8 million in 2005. NICTD has been studying a West Lake Corridor route from Hammond to either Lowell or Valparaiso, Indiana, on existing rail rights of way that would represent the first expansion of South Shore service since the line was completed in 1908.

—William D. Middleton

REFERENCES

Kaplan, Donald R. *Duneland Electric: South Shore Line in Transition.* Homewood, Ill.: PTJ, 1984.

Middleton, William D. *South Shore: The Last Interurban.* Rev. 2nd ed. Bloomington: Indiana Univ. Press, 1999.

Cincinnati & Lake Erie Railroad

With almost 2,800 miles and with lines operating to every town of 10,000 or more, Ohio had the largest interurban railway network of any state around the time of World War I. Interurbans served the populous cities along Lake Erie from the Pennsylvania border to Toledo and much of the area in central and western Ohio all the way south to Cincinnati. But by the early 1920s much of this interurban system was in financial trouble. The Ohio Electric Railway, which had brought together a number of independent properties in 1907 to create a system of over 600 miles, went bankrupt and broke up the system into separate properties between 1918 and 1921. Many of these, in turn, went bankrupt as well.

Thomas Conway, Jr., a professor of transportation in the University of Pennsylvania's Wharton School of Finance and a specialist in electric railway properties, had moved into the operation of electric railways in the early 1920s. In 1922 Conway had taken control of the Chicago Aurora & Elgin and revived its financial performance with new equipment and improved operations. In 1925 Conway became interested in the opportunities in the failing systems in Ohio. The first line to come under Conway's control, early in 1926, was the badly deteriorated

Cincinnati, Hamilton & Dayton, a 54-mile line from Cincinnati north to Dayton. New financing was obtained, a new power plant and maintenance shop were built, and track was reconstructed to virtually rebuild the railroad. Modern passenger cars and new freight equipment were acquired. Conway then brought the CH&D together with the connecting Indiana Columbus & Eastern and the Lima-Toledo Railroad, effective January 1, 1930, to establish the new Cincinnati & Lake Erie Railroad.

The new railroad was a 269-mile, river-to-lake system that extended from Cincinnati to Toledo, with a single east-west route from Springfield to Columbus. Conway set out to rebuild the balance of the system as he had for the CH&D. Tracks were rebuilt. Even before the C&LE consolidation was complete, Conway had begun to vigorously expand its interurban freight trains through coordinated services with connecting lines. In October 1929, for example, the CH&D began operating a daily freight service between Cincinnati and Cleveland in connection with the Lake Shore Electric.

Before the C&LE began operation, Conway had begun the development of a radically improved interurban car that would help the railroad meet an important new role that he saw in intermediate-distance limited service. Development of the car was in charge of William L. Butler, an engineer who had previously worked with Conway on the development of new cars for the Chicago Aurora & Elgin. Experiments were carried out together with electric suppliers, car builders, and a traction-brake supplier. Orders were placed in 1929, and 20 low-level, high-speed, lightweight cars were delivered from the Cincinnati Car Co. the following year. Built of steel and aluminum and fitted with powerful new traction motors, the cars were capable of sustained speeds in excess of 75 mph.

Conway introduced the new cars with a flurry of publicity. Newspaper people rode the new cars; ten on-line cities displayed them to the public. In a celebrated race staged before a Pathé newsreel camera, one of the cars attained an estimated speed of 97 mph to outdistance an airplane, while another handily beat a racing car between Springfield and Columbus. New high-speed services began running in July 1930. Before the end of the year C&LE high-speed cars were running over the 280 miles between Cincinnati and Detroit, the longest run in interurban history, using the Eastern Michigan–Toledo Railroad between Toledo and Detroit. The new service was widely acclaimed. By August 1930 ticket sales were up by more than 40 percent, and the Big Four Railroad had given up its competing train between Cincinnati and Columbus. Coordinated bus services were linked with the trains.

Despite the attraction of the new cars, Ohio's heavily industrialized economy was hard hit by the Depression, and automobiles steadily took a larger share of the traffic. Pre-C&LE revenues of more than $3 million in 1929 proved to be better than they ever would be for the new company. By 1930 revenue was down to little more than

$2.5 million. By 1932 it had dropped to about $1.6 million, and the C&LE was running huge deficits as its operating ratio hit 124 percent.

In October 1932 the long interurban run between Cincinnati and Detroit was ended when the Eastern Michigan–Toledo interurban abandoned its line. The C&LE went into receivership that year, and service was drastically cut back as the railroad tried to get its costs in line with revenues. The Dayton & Western, which provided an important connection between the C&LE and its Indiana connections, had been operated by the C&LE since 1931. C&LE operation ended in 1936, and the line was taken over by the Indiana Railroad, but early in 1937 the line was closed. The Lake Shore Electric ended its freight service in 1937, eliminating an important connection with the C&LE. The operating revenue continued to decline. The portion of the railroad north from Springfield to Toledo was closed in November 1937, and the balance of C&LE interurban service was shut down on May 31, 1939. The company's bus services took over the interurban lines, and a small streetcar operation at Dayton continued through 1941. C&LE's advanced interurban cars and a few other pieces of equipment went to new owners, and most of them continued to operate into the early 1950s.

—William D. Middleton

REFERENCE

Keenan, Jack. *Cincinnati & Lake Erie Railroad: Ohio's Great Interurban System*. San Marino, Calif.: Golden West, 1974.

Cinema and Railroads

In the 1890s the railroad was the most dramatic form of transportation in existence. It is thus not surprising that when the Lumière brothers opened the first public cinema in Paris in 1895, the first program featured a short film titled *Arrival of a Train at the Ciotat Station*. Seeing a steam engine stopping, one could easily imagine the sound it made, even though the pictures were silent. A short time later, when this program was shown in London, a man with bottled compressed air came down the aisle of the theater as the train approached, causing many viewers to lurch backward in their seats. The motion picture and the steam locomotive seemed to be made for one another.

In the United States Thomas Alva Edison, whose collaborators at his West Orange, New Jersey, laboratory had invented the Kinetoscope in 1889—a device to run strips of celluloid film through a camera—began showing his films in peep shows. Later, developing his own projector, following the practice of the Lumière brothers, he established a production company to make and exhibit "motion pictures" on a screen. He needed subject matter, of course, and it was only natural that many of his early "moving" films consisted of shots of railroad trains. A great many short films on railroad topics were made in the late 1890s, and Edison's photographers were well aware of the melodramatic possibilities of steam engines, trolley cars, wrecks, and so on. More important, however, one of Edison's early photographers, Edwin S. Porter, made in 1903 the first movie to present an entire narrative, and once again the railroad was involved. Titled *The Great Train Robbery* and filmed near Edison's laboratories, on the Lackawanna and Erie railroads, it was not only the first story film of the kind we are familiar with today, it was the first to make use of closeups, cuts, and editing techniques that presented a story line in a filmic way rather than using traditional theatrical acting devices. The film was not much longer than many others of the time (about eight minutes), but a wholly new way of telling stories had been developed.

As the "movies" became an industry, the railroad continued to be a presence. During the silent era trains and other railroad settings appeared in literally hundreds of movies, most of them still worth watching. In a great many the railroad is only a casual presence, but in a goodly number railroad scenes and ambiance are the threads that hold the story together. Obviously, the railroad could hardly be avoided in the new genre of western movies. Train robbers, daring holdups and rescues, and cowboys and Indians invariably meant railroads in the early days, and they were there aplenty. Train holdup themes were used over and over again as vehicles for the big stars of the day. *The Great K & A Train Robbery* of 1921 has the legendary Tom Mix hired to protect his company's trains from holdups, which of course he does.

Railroad's possibilities for melodrama are obvious, and in the first few decades of the twentieth century the movies adapted the works of popular railroad writers to turn out melodramatic plots. A number of stories of Frank H. Spearman were brought to the screen, including *Whispering Smith*, *The Yellow Mail* (made from *Held for Orders*), and *The Love Special* (made from *The Daughter of a Magnate*). But the burgeoning film industry hardly needed to borrow; it was quite capable of coming up with its own material. D. W. Griffith, usually considered the first great film director, used railroad settings for several of his early movies. One of the most successful was *The Lonedale Operator* (1911), starring the beguiling Blanche Sweet as a telegraph operator who outwits some robbers. Griffith brought back the girl telegrapher the following year in *The Girl and Her Trust*. In both of these movies the heroines have to be rescued by their lovers—railroad men—although it hardly seems necessary since Griffith's heroines always seemed quite capable of doing everything themselves.

Interestingly, in the years before World War I not only Griffith but also numerous other directors offered audiences a number of tomboy railroad heroines, who seem

The indefatigable actress Helen Holmes was about to make yet another daring leap in one of the 119 episodes of the 1914 serial *The Hazards of Helen.*
—Kalem Pictures, from George H. Douglas

to have been enormously popular (after 1920 this type seems to have completely disappeared). The movie serial became a staple after 1915, and one studio of the time, Kalem, probably following the success of Griffith's *Lonedale Operator,* produced a series called *The Hazards of Helen,* of which there were an unbelievable 119 episodes filmed between 1914 and 1917. Helen was another lovely tomboy telegraph operator (played by actress Helen Holmes), and there seemed to be nothing on the railroad she could not do; she foiled robberies, prevented embez-

zlements, chased runaway locomotives, prevented derailments and collisions, saved the railroad president from a train crash, and so on. In one episode bandits lock her in a refrigerator car, and she does something few Boy Scouts have ever really done: she starts a fire by rubbing two sticks together. In another she stops a runaway train by pulling a bolt out of a locomotive.

Among the hundreds of silent films involving the railroad, a few were masterpieces—films that have been saved for posterity. One such is certainly *The Iron Horse*

Paramount Pictures' 1937 *Wells Fargo,* in a scene that shows how movies were made. The locomotive was a borrowed B&O replica of the 1837 4-2-0 *Lafayette,* while the engine was run by B&O engineer Herman Oberender and the B&O's well-known public relations man, with cap, Larry Sagle.
—*Trains* Magazine Collection

(1924) by the Irish American director John Ford. This tale of the building of the transcontinental railroad in the 1860s may well be the greatest railroad saga ever filmed. On the comic side, another silent masterpiece is Buster Keaton's *The General*. Although it is an adaptation (and not really historically accurate) of the famous locomotive chase during the Civil War, it would be hard to imagine that there was any silent film (even by Chaplin) that put together sight gags with such ingenuity and finesse. (This story was told again by Disney in 1956 with greater historical accuracy but without much stellar impact.)

Trains continued to provide drama and excitement after the arrival of sound in the late 1920s. Nearly all the major studios had their own collections of old wood-burning locomotives on their back lots—some still do to this day. Everybody knew that the railroads played a significant part in the development of the West, so many sound westerns featured train sequences; in a good number the railroad played a significant role. Among these was *Union Pacific*, Cecil B. DeMille's 1938 attempt to tell the transcontinental railroad story. While not the masterpiece Ford's *Iron Horse* was, it is still a very good movie.

Also worthy of mention in the sound era are *How the West Was Won, 3:10 to Yuma, Jessie James, Bad Day at Black Rock, Canadian Pacific, Last Train from Gun Hill, Man without a Star, Breakheart Pass,* and *The Harvey Girls.* In one of the most famous of all westerns, *High Noon,* it is not the railroad itself but the station, often the center of activities in western towns, that plays an important role in the drama. Regular cutaways to the station clock provide the suspense leading up to the great moment of truth.

Trains have also always been used to excellent effect for comic purposes. In silent films, such as those of Mack Sennett and Hal Roach, they were used repeatedly for gag sequences. But all of the great silent screen comedians used trains. There were wonderful train gags in Harold Lloyd's and Buster Keaton's films (in addition to *The General* there was his *Our Hospitality*). One of the great comic sequences of all time has the lovable Harry Langdon attempting to shave in the crowded men's room of a swaying Pullman car in *The Luck of the Foolish.* But there were excellent comic sequences in many sound films: Laurel and Hardy trying to sleep in the same berth in *Berth Marks,*

The Virginia & Truckee's 4-4-0 No. 11, *Reno,* was purchased by Metro-Goldwin-Mayer for its 1946 film *The Harvey Girls.* Ray Bolger danced on the running board. —*Trains* Magazine Collection

CINEMA AND RAILROADS   **241**

W. C. Fields stepping on and stealing another man's Pullman berth ticket in *Poppy*, and W. C. Fields and Mae West in *My Little Chickadee*. There were the Marx Brothers chopping up railway cars for fuel in *Go West*. There was the hilarious station arrival of the Dictator of Bacteria, Benzino Napolini, in Charlie Chaplin's *The Great Dictator*. Trains could be used for both high and low comedy, as in *The Twentieth Century* with John Barrymore. There was Hal Roach's *Broadway Limited*. And train comedy sequences did not vanish in the last half of the twentieth century. Examples are *Around the World in Eighty Days* and the fabulous sleeping-car scenes in *Some Like It Hot*. *Planes, Trains and Automobiles* (1987) with Steve Martin and John Candy neatly establishes the premise that with all forms of modern transportation, if anything can go wrong it will.

One of the most frequent uses of the railroad in films in sound days was melodrama and suspense. European filmmakers were positively addicted to melodramatic railroad themes. One can think of countless "Orient Express" mysteries and melodramas, spy stories, escapes from Hitler's Germany or from behind the Iron Curtain, and so on. The British ran the gamut from serious drama (*Brief Encounter, The Last Journey, Terminus*) to mystery (*The Lady Vanishes, The Ghost Train*), the sentimental (*The Railway Children*), and the comic (*Oh, Mr. Porter* and *The Titfield Thunderbolt*), all masterpieces of their kind. The French made Zola's great railroad novel *La bête humaine* into a very good movie, but without the relentless power of the book.

In the United States melodramatic uses of the railroad were legion. British-born Alfred Hitchcock, fascinated by trains, had used them for suspense while still in England. Train or station scenes appeared in *The 39 Steps, The Secret Agent, Sabotage,* and *The Lady Vanishes*, all widely seen in the United States. After moving to Hollywood in the late 1930s, Hitchcock (who had memorized American railroad timetables before setting foot on American soil) continued to use train settings to superb advantage in *Saboteur, Shadow of a Doubt, Strangers on a Train, The Wrong Man,* and *North by Northwest*. In this last, Hitchcock's genius for comedy, melodrama, suspense, and understated sex are all on display with numerous railroad episodes.

Many other dramatic movies have important railway sequences. One thinks of *The Train* (1964), an American film dealing with French railway operations during World War II, with star performances by Burt Lancaster and Paul Scofield. There are many others, a few with European settings although the movies are strictly American: *Silver Streak* (made twice, in 1934 and 1976, with entirely different stories), *The Sting, Anna Karenina, The Manchurian Candidate, The Hucksters, Metropolitan, Double Indemnity, Sullivan's Travels, Carrie,* and *From Russia with Love*.

Numerous films have made use of railroad stations or terminals. Such great terminals as Grand Central in New York and the union stations in Chicago and Los Angeles have made literally hundreds of vignette appearances. Occasionally whole movies have been built around great terminals. One such was *Union Station* (1950), in which the entire action takes place at Los Angeles Union Station—so much so that the station itself could not be used and a set had to be built. Other films in which train terminals or stations are of critical importance are *The Clock, Grand Central Murder, Union Depot, Since You Went Away, Anna Karenina, High Noon, 3:10 to Yuma, The Train, In the Heat of the Night, I'll Never Forget Whatshisname,* and *Witness*. Many political films feature back-vestibule goodbyes at train depots, for example, *Abe Lincoln in Illinois* and *All the King's Men*.

Many films have train sequences dealing with subways and elevateds. On the whole, when the subway is more than a fleeting presence, criminality, brutality, or other sinister activities are usually involved. Films in which subways or elevated trains have played a central role are *The Taking of Pelham One, Two, Three; Dutchman; The French Connection; King Kong; The FBI Story; The Liquidator;* and *Dressed to Kill*. Some movies feature musical numbers in subways. One thinks of *Dames* and *On the Town*. A light romantic story with a subway setting is *Practically Yours*. Very occasionally the subway is used for comedy sequences. There is a superb subway comic scene in Woody Allen's *Bananas*. Probably the funniest subway sequence ever filmed is in Harold Lloyd's last silent picture, *Speedy* (1928). This film also has wonderful shots of New York City's old street railways.

It is quite likely that there will always be trains in the movies. The railroad moves along the ground, it goes where people are, and it is exciting.

—George H. Douglas

REFERENCES

Kirby, Lynne. *Parallel Tracks: The Railroad and Silent Cinema.* Durham, N.C.: Duke Univ. Press, 1997.
Walker, John, ed. *Halliwell's Film and Video Guide.* New York: HarperPerennial, 1999.

Circuses and Railroads

In 1825 J. Purdy Brown revolutionized the circus business by introducing the canvas tent, which allowed circuses to set up and take down their shows quickly, perform in large and small cities, stay as long as business warranted, and then pack up and move on. The canvas tent was second in importance only to the next greatest technological innovation: use of the railroad to transport the American circus.

Before railroads, circus and menagerie owners moved their shows via wagons and boats. These wagon shows—sometimes referred to as "trains"—had many components that would eventually become part of the railroad circus, such as cage wagons and baggage wagons. Some grew to a size that rivaled the later railroad shows. When the railroad became an option, many shows quickly adopted the new form of transportation, which gave them the flexibility to go farther and play more cities.

Early American circuses realized the railroad's potential, but the railroad could not handle the specialized movement of the circus if more than one track gauge was involved. Transferring from one gauge to another would necessitate unloading the cars and transporting the equipment to the waiting railroad. During the 1850s and 1860s a typical railroad show could be called a "gilly" show—one using manual labor to transport the show from train to lot in rented wagons. This method solved the problem of getting to the lot; however, it was both labor intensive and expensive.

The first recorded movement of the American circus by rail occurred in 1832, when Charles Bacon and Edward Derious moved parts of their show in Georgia. There were other minor attempts to move shows over the next two decades, but it was during the 1850s that circus owners began to look seriously at rail. In 1851 Stone & Madigan Circus played the Mississippi Valley, using the railroad for many of its moves. Other early railroad users were the Railroad Circus & Crystal Amphitheatre in 1853, Madigan, Myers & Barton's Railroad Circus & Amphitheatre and Den Stone's Original Railroad Circus in 1854, and the Great Western Railroad Circus in 1855. All of these shows were small in comparison with some of the conventional wagon shows, such as Seth B. Howes.

In 1857, using experience gained from previous shows, Gilbert R. Spalding and Charles J. Rogers operated a new show called Spalding & Rogers Railroad Circus on nine custom-built cars. The tour started in Washington, D.C., and traveled through Pennsylvania, New York, Massachusetts, Maine and the British provinces of Canada and into Michigan. To deal with changes in gauge, the show's cars had adjustable axles. Although Spalding & Rogers did not continue to move by rail after this tour, a number of other circuses, including Dan Rice, Howes & Robinson, and Lewis Lent, began doing so. In the 1860s a number of circuses used both methods in the same season.

Just as the railroads aspired to link the eastern portion of the country with the West, circus owners aspired to travel coast to coast. Dan Castello Circus was the first of these: although Castello did not move on the rails the entire distance, he nevertheless used them to reach California by July 1869, only two months after completion of the transcontinental railroad.

The late 1860s and early 1870s saw an increased number of railroad circuses and a corresponding increase in touring. With urban centers becoming larger, circus owners envisioned greater income from larger crowds, but that required grander shows to attract them and bigger tents to accommodate them. In order to cover expenses, circuses not only had to play in cities that could support more ambitious operations, but also had to move more efficiently and faster and make longer jumps. In "Development of the Railroad Circus" Fred Dahlinger, Jr., noted that "of the 31 shows covered in the *Clipper's* 1872 circus special, eight of them announced their intent to travel all or part of the season by rail: 'Many of the largest shows during the coming season will travel almost entirely by railroad, chartering for this purpose special trains, and visiting only the larger cities and towns.'"

W. C. Coup has long been credited with putting the circus on rails. While his was not the first such venture, Coup was the first to organize the labor and equipment to move efficiently from town to town and to convince the railroad that the trains must arrive on time so that the show could give its scheduled performances. In *Sawdust and Spangles* he writes:

> The railroad people were utterly ignorant of our wants, as we ourselves were in the beginning. Frequently . . . the yardmaster would order us to load one car at a time, then switch it away and commence on another. To load a train in this way would have taken us twenty-four hours! Finally, however, system and good order came out of chaos. Once properly launched on our season, we were able to give three performances daily, and quite often made jumps of one hundred miles in one night. The scheme, as I had predicted, completely revolutionized the show business, and has been adopted since, not only in this country, but by the French and English circus proprietors in their travels in Germany.

In 1870 Coup persuaded P. T. Barnum to come out of retirement and join Coup and Castello's circus. On April 10, 1871, Barnum, Coup, and Castello opened their new show, P. T. Barnum's Museum, Menagerie, Caravan, and Hippodrome, in Brooklyn. It was the largest overland circus ever to tour America. During its tour Coup worked with circus agents and the railroads to develop the circus excursion system. Circus agents arranged with the railroads at each town to run special trains into the city on performance day. This proved profitable for both circus and railroad.

On April 18, 1872, the Barnum show, in New Brunswick, New Jersey, made its debut as a railroad show with Pennsylvania Railroad cars on Pennsy rails. The show first leased system cars from the railroads upon whose tracks they were routed, but encountered difficulty; the system cars were differently sized and not designed to haul the specialized circus equipment. The Barnum show was forced to order special railroad cars to suit its needs. In May 1872 the load out in Washington was problematic. Brake wheels were mounted at the end of the flatcars, which were in the way of loading the cars. They prevented the wagons from rolling from car to car; they needed to be removed and remounted. The yardmaster refused to remove the brake wheels and insisted that the show be loaded one car at a time. "I showed him my contract, wherein the company had agreed to remove all brakes, but he still refused, so I finally resorted to strategy," Coup confessed. "I invited him to a restaurant, and while we were absent . . . Baker, the boss canvas-man, wrenched the brakes off, and by the time the yardmaster and I returned the train was almost loaded."

The 1872 show was not the first to transport a circus by rail, nor did it originate the piggyback method of moving wheeled vehicles (a British railway, the Birmingham & Derby Junction, transported horses and carriages as early as 1839). According to Coup, two innovations can be attributed to the 1872 Barnum show, however. It was "the earliest successful attempt to place a complete large overland circus, including all annexes and a parade, on rails and move it daily from date to date"; and it purchased "the first conventional railroad cars built for a circus. The Barnum train was the first which was both circus owned and incorporated the stock and flat cars, which typified the fully developed railroad circus of the next eighty-four years."

For the development of the circus, 1873 was a banner year. With increased attendance and larger tents, a second ring was added for additional performance space. Another innovation at this time was the debut of the flying squadron. A group of men arrived in town a day ahead of the circus to drive the tent stakes. This saved time on setup day. Also in 1873 W. W. Cole New York & New Orleans Circus, a 35-car railroad show, traveled 9,387 miles, earning the distinction of being the first show to play to and from the West Coast entirely by rail.

Over the next ten years the Howes Great London Circus moved on 52 cars, the Forepaugh Circus traveled with 37 cars, and in 1881 "the first fully coordinated combine of railroad cars and circus wagons built for each other was waiting for the W. W. Cole Circus when it returned from Australia. Wagons were dimensioned both for their own loads and for loading on the flats," note Parkinson and Fox (1978).

During the golden age of the circus (from the 1870s to the 1930s) the circus train was as impressive a sight as the tented city and the show itself. Typically in the later years of the golden age the American circus traveled on 30 railcars, with one advance car moving 14 days ahead of the show. Before its arrival, hundreds of towners lined the tracks awaiting the great spectacle. As soon as the trains were spotted or placed in the rail yard, roustabouts (circus laborers) began unloading with the precision of a military unit. Chocks and chains that held the wagons in place were knocked out and unshackled. Steel crossover plates were placed between the gaps of the flatcars, which allowed the wagons to be pulled from flat to flat and eventually to the runs or ramps at the end of the train where the wagons were removed. Chutes were placed in the doors of the stock cars for the unloading of the baggage horses (work horses), elephants, zebras, and camels. Within the hour the first section of the circus train had been unloaded and the work was progressing on the second train. After the evening show began, this same process was repeated in reverse to load the trains.

On August 26, 1880, a deal was struck with the Great London Show of Cooper, Bailey, and Hutchinson and P. T. Barnum to form what would be eventually known as

The arrival of a circus train was as exciting as the performance itself. Teams of horses unloaded the wagons that carried the tents and all the equipment of the show, while the animals, circus performers, and supporting staff disembarked from the cars. —*Trains* Magazine Collection

the Barnum & Bailey Circus, Greatest Show on Earth. In the 1881 season the show moved on 77 cars. However, a rival was on the horizon. In 1884 the Ringling Bros. from Baraboo, Wisconsin, began as a wagon show. By 1890 it too was a railroad circus traveling on 18 cars. Between 1890 and 1896 Ringling expanded to 50 railroad cars and in 1897 pulled ahead by two cars: 57 for Ringling and 55 for Barnum. With the passing of Barnum (1881) and James A. Bailey (1906), the Ringling Brothers bought the Barnum & Bailey circus in 1907, operating the two shows separately until 1919 when they merged into Ringling Bros. and Barnum & Bailey Circus, Greatest Show on Earth. The combined show traveled on 95 cars: 42 flats, 26 stock cars, 24 coaches, and 3 advertising cars. By 1923 it was traveling on 100 cars.

Circus trains were privately owned, which created financial burdens for owners. To move the circus by rail required equipment that needed constant maintenance but generated no income for the show. As a result, between 1872 and 1900 the circus train underwent changes: cars were leased and added to equipment already owned by the shows, and the length of cars increased from 28 feet to 60 feet (the longest in show business); subsequent years saw train length tripling from 1,200 feet to over 3,600 feet.

Moving privately owned cars over railroad lines could be challenging. The rail line supplied the motive power, crews, and tracks. A railroad did not always welcome the circus to its line. Showmen suspected that railroads did not want the extra trouble and disruption of normal activity that hauling a circus entailed. Planning a route for a season depended many times on the railroad lines to be traveled. It might be too expensive to leave one line and switch to another to get to a subsequent performance date. Moreover, switching required transfer charges, switching costs, and car inspections. A circus would play as many towns on the same line as it could to avoid extra expense. The region where they were performing determined the rates for the traveling shows. Rates were calculated according to the number of cars. The charge for shows up to 35 cars was in 5-car increments; for 40 through 110 cars in 10-car increments. Length and load were not factors in determining cost, which is why the circus had cars built to their maximum length. Initially about 30 to 35 feet long, circus cars were 45 to 50 feet by the late 1870s and reached 60 feet by the early 1880s. They were 50 to 100 percent longer than similar system cars and were usually advertised as "double length" to convey grander proportions.

After 1911 circuses began to convert from wooden cars to steel. This change allowed the cars to be built even longer and carry more capacity. By 1927 the cars' length had reached 72 feet with a capacity of 100,000 pounds. Dahlinger notes in *Trains of the Circus, 1872–1956* that more than four dozen different companies furnished show cars, including Barney & Smith Car Co., Mt. Vernon Car Co., Warren Tank Car Co., and Haffner-Thrall Car Co.

The circus on rails reached its zenith in 1911 with 32 shows touring the country. Highlights of the next 18 years included the largest train (Ringling Bros. and Barnum & Bailey, after their merger in 1919, toured with 100 cars in 1923), tents that held more than 10,000 spectators, and circuses that required over 14 acres of land on which to locate their tented cities. But the country was experiencing changes that would lead to the demise of many of the touring shows. In 1927 the talking picture debuted, and movie theaters began competing for Americans' entertainment dollars. In October 1929 the Great Depression swept the country, and circus crowds dwindled. With growing urban congestion, street parades were no longer practical, and vacant land on which to erect large circus tents was less available. Gentry Bros., Christy, Cole, Robbins, Robinson, Sparks, 101 Ranch, and Sells Floto soon folded. By 1933 there were only 3 railroad circuses traveling in America.

The use of private cars on the circus train was limited to show owners and general managers. The staff and top performers lived in staterooms or compartments. Living space for nonstars and the workers was far from spacious. Bunks were two high and two across. Roustabouts lived in sleepers that had three-high bunks and were sweltering in summer.

The circus used railroad equipment that was designed for the specific needs of the show. General equipment consisted of coaches, stock cars, and flatcars. If something had to be transported that could not be accommodated with the general equipment, a car would be constructed. In order to transport an Asian elephant named Tusko for the 1922 season, Al G. Barnes ordered a drop-frame elephant car from the Mt. Vernon Car Manufacturing Co.

Accidents plagued circuses on rails. They were caused by fires, faulty journal boxes, split switches, and human error. Fire was especially feared. In 1898 the Ringling Bros. circus was traveling in Arkansas when the wagon carrying the sacred white elephant caught fire, resulting in the animal's death. The Campbell Bros. Circus had a string of fire disasters starting in 1902 at La Junta, Colorado. In 1903 gasoline was sprayed over the circus train when a chandelier wagon—a car carrying lighting equipment—exploded. In 1904 a stock car burned, killing many performing animals. In 1914 the Ringling Bros. Circus lost 43 empty cars to fire in Cleveland, Ohio. In 1924 Al G. Barnes lost its advance car in a fire at Massillon, Ohio, and later that same year lost 36 performing horses in another fire while traveling in California.

Next to fires, the disasters most greatly feared were collisions and derailments. The worst wreck in circus history occurred in 1918 near Ivanhoe, Indiana, when the Hagenbeck-Wallace first section stopped and was rammed from the rear by an empty troop train heading for Chicago. The troop train passed an automatic block signal set at caution, a red signal, and a flagman behind the circus train. The wooden cars on the circus train were

The huge, lumbering elephants were always an important part of the circus's menagerie. Here they unload from a car of the Ringling Brothers and Barnum & Bailey Combined Show. —C. P. Fox, *Trains* Magazine Collection

illuminated with kerosene lanterns; five of the coaches were consumed by fire. The accident killed 68 people and injured 127.

In the 1930s, as we have seen, many railroad shows either went out of business or converted to truck shows. The 1940s saw a slight upswing in the use of trains moving the circus, but many of the same problems that plagued the circus in the 1920s and 1930s continued to stalk it, with increasing rates and unwarranted charges. The storm clouds became darkest in the 1950s. The Bailey Brothers folded in 1950, and the greatest of all, the Ringling Bros. and Barnum & Bailey Circus, came to a halt in July 1956 in Pittsburgh, Pennsylvania. The following year the Clyde Beatty Circus, the last remaining railroad circus

For almost every year from 1966 through 2003 the Circus World Museum at Baraboo, Wisconsin, brought an annual return to the magic of the circus with a train of circus wagons to Milwaukee or Chicago. On a May 19, 1981, trip from Baraboo to a Memorial Day parade in Chicago the annual train crossed over the Chicago & North Western's Wisconsin River bridge at Merrimac, Wisconsin. —Great Chicago Circus Parade, *Trains* Magazine Collection

touring the country, left the rails. The future looked bleak, not only for rail travel, but also for the circus's survival in general.

The 1957 season saw the Ringling show open in Madison Square Garden. The circus was transported in nine semitrailers, an assortment of trucks, and three balloon-top baggage cars (special cars built to provide extra height for animals) from the Pennsylvania Railroad. The show traveled with this arrangement until 1960, when Ringling Bros. and Barnum & Bailey reemerged as a full railroad show. Under the direction of circus manager Art Concello and his assistant, Lloyd Morgan, Sr., it converted 15 American Car & Foundry coaches, which the circus had purchased from the Army Medical Corps. This new show was a 15-car show, including 8 coaches, 1 elephant car, 1 ring stock car, and 4 tunnel cars.

In 1968 the Ringling/Barnum show was sold to the Feld family of Washington, D.C. In 1969 the circus, under the direction of Irvin Feld, added a second unit. The existing unit (the Red Unit) traveled on 25 cars. The new Blue Unit moved on 20 cars from the Penn Central's *20th Century Limited* and the Rock Island's *Rocket*, which had been discontinued. This new unit also saw the return of the flatcar, which had not been used since 1956.

The 1973 season saw the demise of a custom that probably went back to Coup and Barnum—paying cash for each railroad move. It was proposed by the Ringling show that the railroad invoice the company for each move at the end of the month. The railroad agreed.

Ringling Bros./Barnum & Bailey continues to move two units by rail. The 132nd edition Blue Unit (2003) moved on 38 conventional passengers cars, 4 of them stocks (baggage cars) behind the locomotives on the head end, followed by 2 container flats and 17 piggyback flats on the rear end. The train's 57 cars weighed 4,135 tons and were 5,044 feet long. The 133rd edition Red Unit (2003) moved on 36 conventional passenger cars on the head end, followed by 2 container flats and 18 piggyback flats on the rear end. As in the Blue Unit, 4 of the cars were baggage cars. This 56-car train weighed 4,065 tons and was 4,968 feet long. These are the largest privately owned trains in the world.

Today Feld Entertainment, owners of the Ringling Bros. and Barnum & Bailey Circus, maintains a train-recycling facility in Palmetto, Florida. This facility converts old railroad cars into usable rolling stock for the circus.

For decades, all types of entertainment traveled by rail across the country—circuses, carnivals, operas, melodrama troupes, *Uncle Tom's Cabin* companies, dog and pony shows, theater companies, minstrel shows, Chautauquas, and many others. Today only the Ringling Bros./Barnum & Bailey Circus and the Strates Shows, Inc., carnival travel by rail. How long the tradition will continue is uncertain.

—Lavahn G. Hoh

REFERENCES

Coup, W. C. *Sawdust and Spangles: Stories and Secrets of the Circus.* Chicago: Herbert S. Stone, 1901.

Dahlinger, Fred, Jr. "Development of the Railroad Circus." 4 pts., *Bandwagon* 27, no. 6 (Nov.–Dec. 1983): 6–11; 28, no. 1 (Jan.–Feb. 1984): 16–27; 28, no. 2 (Mar.–Apr. 1984): 28–36; 28, no. 3 (May–June 1984): 29–36.

———. *Show Trains of the 20th Century.* Hudson, Wis.: Iconografix, 2000.

———. *Trains of the Circus, 1872–1956.* Hudson, Wis.: Iconografix, 2000.

Hoh, Lavahn, and William Rough. *Step Right Up! The Adventure of Circus in America.* White Hall, Va.: Betterway, 1990.

Parkinson, Tom, and Charles Philip Fox. *The Circus Moves by Rail.* Newton, N.J.: Carstens, 1978.

Civil Engineering

Location and Construction

Railroad location was often as much art as science. In route location the engineer had to be concerned with both the immediate cost of construction and a line's prospective capacity and operating costs, two objectives that were often mutually exclusive. A line cheaply built to follow existing terrain might have steep grades and sharp curves that would both limit its capacity and create extremely high operating costs. Conversely, a line built with low grades and long radius curves for operating efficiency might require costly cut and fill work, bridging, and tunneling. Most North American railroads built their lines as quickly and cheaply as possible with the intent of later relocating or otherwise improving them. For many, this process has been ongoing.

Engineers typically developed location surveys in three parts. First, a general reconnaissance was carried out to identify which of several prospective routes was most promising. This was followed by a preliminary survey, a more accurate topographic survey of the general route selected. It usually established the maximum grade, determined the best line, and developed a detailed map and other data needed for final location. The last step, a location survey, laid out the plan for a line on the ground, ready for construction.

Few things were more important to the success of a railroad project than the initial reconnaissance. A poorly chosen route could not be easily corrected. A reconnaissance could be relatively easily and accurately done for a planned route between well-defined points, and for which accurate and complete topographical maps were available. But it was a much more difficult process for the pioneer engineers who built the early railroads across the vast western reaches of a North American continent that was often unsettled and largely unexplored.

A reconnaissance was typically done without survey

instruments, using perhaps a compass for direction, an aneroid barometer to measure elevation, and some kind of odometer or pedometer to measure distance. One authority, Willard Beahan, in his *Field Practice of Railway Location* advocated "an experienced saddle-horse, whose speeds at his various gaits have been learned accurately by previous timing," as one way to do this rapidly.

Railroad location through mountainous terrain required a skilled and experienced engineer to balance considerations of elevation, gradient, curvature, and cut and fill issues. Elevation and gradient were critical. The higher a train had to climb to cross a range of hills or mountains, the greater was the energy required to lift it to the summit. The steeper the gradient, the less tonnage a locomotive could pull. The engineer's principal goal was always to locate the lowest possible summit, combined with the best possible gradients on either side of it.

The Baltimore & Ohio built its pioneer line west to the Ohio at a maximum grade of 2.2 percent, later adopted by the Land Grant Acts of 1862 for the Pacific Railroad and other land-grant lines, which specified that "the grades and curves shall not exceed the grades and curves of the Baltimore & Ohio Railroad." Thus 2.2 percent became a maximum grade for the builders of the western railroads.

The principal earlier railroads of the eastern United States and Canada were usually able to do much better across the mountain ranges of the east. The Pennsylvania, for example, built across the Alleghenies with a maximum grade of 1.6 percent on the westbound grade out of Altoona to the summit. The rival New York Central avoided high summits and long grades altogether with its celebrated Water Level Route, which followed the Hudson River and the shore of Lake Erie, but its route between

Table 1. Notable North American Mountain Passes

Name	Date	Mountain Grade	Ruling Grades	Notable Features	Present Status
Western Railroad, Massachusetts	1841	Berkshire Hills	Eastbound grade, 1.5 percent; westbound grade, 1.7 percent.	Springfield-Berkshire line climbed 1,400 feet in 39 miles. Summit cut was as much as 52 feet deep and half a mile long. The Berkshire line was the most extensive line yet built.	In service. Portions of the westbound slope extensively rebuilt, with several original arch bridges still in use.
Pennsylvania Railroad, Pennsylvania	1854	Allegheny Mountains	Westbound grade, 1.8 percent; eastbound grade, 1.0 percent.	To hold the grade to 1.8 percent, the line was built that formed the famous Horseshoe Curve through a 220-degree curve; it once had four tracks.	In service.
Central Pacific, California	1867	Donner Pass, Sierra Nevada	Eastbound grade, 2.0 percent.	Maximum climb over 7,000 feet, with extremely difficult snowstorms. One cut was 63 feet deep and 800 feet long. Fifteen tunnels built.	In service. Some line relocations have been built, but the line follows the same basic alignment.
Mexican Railway, Veracruz, Mexico	1872	Maltrata Incline, Sierra Madre Oriental	Westbound grade, 4.7 percent.	Westbound trains negotiated some of the most difficult anywhere, with many tunnels and grades as sharp as 16.5 degrees.	In the 1980s the Ferrocarril Mexicano rebuilt the westbound line with a longer alignment, reducing maximum grade to 2.5 percent.
Southern Pacific, California	1876	Tehachapi Mountains	Eastbound grade, 2.2 percent.	Westbound (or east) line climbed 2,737 feet and required 17 tunnels. The famous Tehachapi Loop made a complete loop to maintain the 2.2 percent maximum.	In service, with some relocations.
Canadian Pacific, British Columbia	1885	Selkirk Mountains	Eastbound grade, 2.2 percent; westbound grade, 2.2 percent.	Exceedingly difficult pass with a 4,351 feet peak. West slope built an elongated figure-8 loop to hold to 2.2 percent. Extremely heavy snowfall.	In 1916 the pass was replaced with the Connaught Tunnel (9,491 feet), and the peak was reduced by 540 feet. In 1989 CPR built the Mount Macdonald Tunnel (48,304 feet), which reduced the westbound grade to 1.0 percent.
Great Northern, Montana	1893	Rocky Mountains	Westbound grade, 1.8 percent; eastbound grade, 1.0 percent.	The location of Marias Pass at the Continental Divide at only 5,213 feet and without a tunnel, the best of any U.S. northern routes.	In service.
Chihuahua Pacific, Chihuahua and Sinaloa, Mexico	1961	Sierra Madre Occidental	Eastbound grade, 2.5 percent.	The western slope of the line descended from 8,071 feet to tidewater. The line required 86 tunnels, curves as high as 9 degrees, and a complete loop.	In service.

New York and Chicago was more than 70 miles longer than the Pennsylvania's as a result.

The railroads of the West faced far greater challenges as they pushed across the Rockies to the Pacific. Most of the transcontinental lines had to climb to elevations of well over a mile to get across the Continental Divide, and many had grades of 2 percent or more. The highest of them all was the Denver & Rio Grande's crossing of Tennessee Pass in Colorado, which reached an elevation of 10,239 feet and had a maximum grade of 4.0 percent for eastbound traffic.

The lowest U.S. crossing of the Rockies was the Great Northern route through Marias Pass, located by John Stevens, which was at an elevation of only 5,213 feet, with a maximum grade of 1.8 percent, giving the GN a permanent operating advantage over its rivals for traffic to and from the Pacific Northwest. The earlier Northern Pacific crossed the Divide at 5,566 feet in Montana's Mullan Pass, with grades of 2.2 percent in both directions. West of Bozeman the line reached an elevation of 6,328 feet in Homestake, with the same maximum of 2.2 percent for both east and west lines. The Milwaukee Road, the last to build west, had an equally difficult crossing, climbing to 6,347 feet to cross the Divide in Pipestone Pass, where it faced maximum grades of 1.7 percent eastbound and 2.0 percent westbound. Table 1 lists some notable North American mountain passes.

Maintaining reasonable grades in mountainous terrain could be a challenge. Sometimes the engineer could find natural terrain along a ridge or stream that provided a direct route at a satisfactory grade, but more often the slopes were too steep, and the only solution was to reduce the rate of change of elevation by lengthening the line. This was usually accomplished by taking advantage of some topographical feature to introduce a deviation, for example, by running a line up one side of a lateral valley and back down the other, reversing direction with a sweeping curve. Thus was created the Pennsylvania Railroad's celebrated Horseshoe Curve as the railroad climbed the east slope of the Alleghenies above Altoona, Pennsylvania.

Another method was the switchback. Instead of going straight up a slope, the additional length of line required to reduce the gradient was gained by running the line backward and forward up a slope with a zigzag track arrangement. But switchbacks were a time-wasting burden to the operating forces, since a train had to be stopped and reversed every time the line changed direction, and they were seldom employed except as a temporary expedient. One early example was in the construction of the B&O in 1851. To permit trains to continue west to the railhead even before the long Kingwood Tunnel was complete, a series of steep switchbacks was built right across the top of the tunnel alignment. In 1886 the Northern Pacific used a similar arrangement to carry traffic across Stampede Pass in Washington's Cascade Mountains while a long tunnel under the pass was completed. Further north in the Cascades, James J.

This drawing, from *The American Railway* (1892), shows the successive tiers of line at Rocky Point, Colorado, which climbed the Rockies for the Denver, South Park & Pacific Railroad.
—Middleton Collection

Hill's Great Northern operated across Stevens Pass from 1893 to 1900 on a series of switchbacks with 4 percent grades until the first Cascade Tunnel was completed.

Still another alternative was to develop some sort of loop or spiral, in which a line climbed through a complete circle, passing over itself with a tunnel or bridge. Among the best-known North American examples are the Southern Pacific's Tehachapi Loop in California and the Canadian Pacific's spiral tunnels in Kicking Horse Pass, British Columbia. One of the most spectacular of all, however, was the famous Georgetown Loop built by the Union Pacific to reach the Silver Plume mining camp from Georgetown, Colorado. A direct line between the two points would have had to climb 600 feet in 1¼ miles, requiring a gradient of over 9 percent. By building a loop line that reversed itself four times and extended the distance to 4 miles, the railroad was able to reduce the maximum grade to 3 percent.

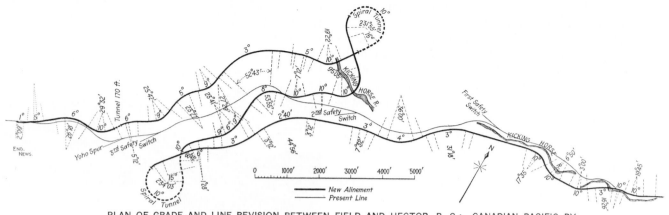

PLAN OF GRADE AND LINE REVISION BETWEEN FIELD AND HECTOR, B. C.; CANADIAN PACIFIC RY.

Present line: Distance, 4.1 miles; Grade, 4.4%
New line: Distance, 8.2 miles; Grade, 2.2%

This drawing, from the January 23, 1908, *Engineering News*, shows how the Canadian Pacific rebuilt its temporary and arduous 4.4 percent line through Kicking Horse Pass in British Columbia. More than 8 miles of new line and two long spiral tunnels were needed to reduce the line's grade to a more manageable 2.2 percent. —Middleton Collection

Climbing to a summit of 4,351 feet, and receiving an average annual snowfall of 40 feet, Canadian Pacific's Rogers Pass in the Selkirks of British Columbia was a difficult passage for the transcontinental trains. CPR built 31 timber snow sheds with an aggregate length of over 5 miles. —Glenbow Museum (Neg. NA-387-21)

Grade, Curvature, and Cut and Fill

Grade

In North American practice, the rate of change in the elevation of a railroad line is typically expressed in feet per mile, or as a percent grade, which represents the change of elevation in 100 feet as a percentage. A 2 percent grade, for example, is one that has a rise of 2 feet in each 100 feet. In English practice, however, the grade is stated in terms of the number of feet in which the grade rises a foot. Thus, a grade of 1 foot in 20 feet in the English system would be the same as a rise of 5 feet in 100, or a 5 percent grade, in the U.S. system.

The steeper the grade, of course, the less tonnage a locomotive can pull, and railroad engineers attempt to limit grades to a maximum that will permit economical operation. Just how much a locomotive of given capacity can haul on a grade, compared with its capacity on level track, is a complex question that involves locomotive adhesion, desired operating speeds, and train resistance.

Main-line railroads usually held their maximum grades to 2 percent or less except under the most severe conditions. Perhaps the steepest grade on any current main-line transcontinental route is the 2.4 percent maximum westbound grade on UP's former Rio Grande line across Soldier Summit in the Wasatch Mountains of Utah, southeast of Provo.

Grades of 4 percent and more were commonplace on the narrow-gauge railroads of Colorado and similar mountain lines elsewhere. The Southern Railway operated a line over Saluda Mountain in North Carolina on a 4.7 percent grade that ranked as the steepest main-line grade anywhere in North America until the line was closed in 2001.

A *ruling grade* is usually established for each segment of line. This is not necessarily the maximum grade on the line, but rather the grade that limits the maximum tonnage a locomotive can haul over the line segment. A long grade, or one on which trains might have to stop and start, for example, can be more restrictive than a short, steeper grade that can be partially overcome by the momentum of a train. In order to maintain the lowest possible ruling grade over a line for reasons of overall operating efficiency, steeper intermediate *pusher* or *helper grades* are sometimes established. At these points helper locomotives are assigned to enable a road engine get the same full-tonnage train over the steeper grade that it can handle unassisted over the balance of the line.

A *compensated grade* represents the combination of an actual grade with an equivalent additional grade representing the greater train resistance of a curved track, as discussed more fully later under curvature. In practice, engineers typically reduce the actual grade on curves in

BNSF and Union Pacific jointly use Cajon Pass to cross over the San Bernardino Mountains between the Mojave Desert and Southern California. An eastward-bound train climbs almost 2,800 feet in 25 miles of 2.2 percent grade between San Bernardino and Summit. Five Santa Fe diesels pulled a 67-car train upgrade past Sullivan's Curve in June 1974. —William D. Middleton

order to maintain a compensated grade equal to the established maximum grade for the line. To avoid an abrupt change in slope as a train moves between line sections on different gradients, engineers usually introduce a parabolic *vertical curve* to provide a smooth transition between the two sections.

Curvature

Railroad curves are typically made up of arcs of a simple circle. In British or metric practice, curves are normally designated by their radius. In North American practice, curvature is usually expressed in degrees, minutes, and seconds of the central angle subtended by a straight line or chord of 100 feet, measured between two points on the curve, rather than by the radius of the curve. Thus the shorter the radius and the sharper the curve, the greater the degree of curvature. A 1-degree curve, for example, has a radius of about 5,730 feet; a 10-degree curve a radius of 573 feet; and a 60-degree curve a radius of only about 95 feet. A rule of thumb is to divide 5,730 by the degree of curvature to obtain the radius in feet.

A curve made up of segments of different degrees of curvature or radii is called a *compound curve*, while a curve in which the direction of curvature changes from one direction to the other is called a *reverse curve*. Railroads normally use *spiral* or *easement* curves to provide a gradual transition and a smoother ride between straight or tangent-line and curved track. A spiral is also used to gradually introduce *superelevation*, a raising of the outer rail in a curve to offset the lateral centrifugal force created as a train passes through a curve at speed.

Operation around curves, in addition to limiting train speeds, also increases the frictional resistance of trains, largely because of the binding of wheels mounted on parallel axles that are not exactly radial to the curve. This is partially offset by slightly widening the track gauge on curves, but a significant resistance remains. In a curved line on a grade, this additional curvature resistance is usually converted to an equivalent grade that, when added to the actual grade, establishes a compensated grade for the section. In practice, engineers usually compensate for grades on curves at a rate of about 0.04 percent grade for each degree of curve. Thus a 5-degree curve on a 2 percent actual grade would add an equivalent grade of 0.2 percent to establish a compensated grade of 2.2 percent for the curved section.

Cut and Fill

The alignment for a line being built over irregular topography rarely coincides with existing ground level. Instead, the line usually falls below or above, requiring some amount of cutting or filling to establish a roadbed at the required level. Excavation, as well as placing and compacting fill material, is expensive work, and still another concern of the location engineer is to plan an alignment that will keep this cut and fill work to a minimum.

However much or little excavation or filling is required, the engineer tries to plan a line so that the required quantities of cut and fill between adjacent sections of line are equal, or "balanced." This balance avoids the cost of either acquiring additional fill or disposing of excess excavated material during construction. Additional fill must be of a suitable material for a roadbed. The greater the distance it is carried, the more expensive the haul material will be. In some cases as much as 2 miles or more might be required, usually at an extra haul rate for each cubic yard for each 100 feet of additional cost. If the required fill cannot be located at a reasonable cost, a road might simply build on timber trestles, either permanently or until such time as the additional grading costs can be afforded.

Once a tentative horizontal and vertical alignment has been established for a line, the engineer can use topographic data and cross sections of the cut or fill sections to compute the volume of cut or fill for each segment of line. This is then developed into a "mass diagram," a graphic representation used to determine the balance of cut and fill and average haul distances. This process might be repeated several times with different grade lines or

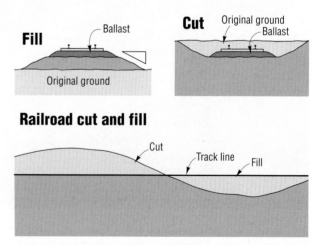

Figure 2. Railroad Cut and Fill. —Rick Johnson

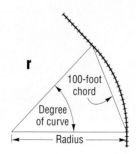

Figure 1. Railroad Curves. —Rick Johnson

alignments until the best possible balance of cut and fill and the most economical haul distances are achieved.

Bridges

Railroad Bridge History

Central to the nineteenth-century era of railroad expansion were the great bridges that carried the rails across the wide rivers and deep valleys of the North American continent. The art of bridge building had been practiced for centuries, but well into the nineteenth century it remained a tedious, empirical process ill suited to the needs of the railroads for quickly built, economical structures. Indeed, it was the railroads that advanced bridge building to a scientific process and laid much of the foundation for the modern profession of civil engineering.

One of the oldest bridge forms was the classical masonry arch, which dated to prehistoric times. The builders of pioneer railroads turned to this for their first major bridges. Notable among these were the Baltimore & Ohio's Carrollton Viaduct (1829) at Baltimore and Thomas Viaduct (1835) at Relay, Maryland; the Boston & Providence's viaduct over the Neponset River (1835) at Canton, Massachusetts; and the New York & Erie's Starrucca Viaduct (1848) near Susquehanna, Pennsylvania.

These large arches were built in place. Temporary timber centering was erected to support each arch until it was complete. Stone was quarried as close to the site as it could be found and then cut and mortared into place. The great strength and durability of these early arches

were evidenced by their long service lives. Many still serve today, carrying loads that could scarcely have been imagined at the time they were built. One, the Canton Viaduct, today even carries Amtrak's Acela Express high-speed trains on the Northeast Corridor.

But building masonry structures was a slow and costly process. Often, too, the multiple piers required were impractical for deep streams and valleys and sometimes acted as barriers to navigation. It soon became evident that other structural forms were needed to provide bridges that could be quickly and cheaply built to keep pace with the growth of the railroad network.

The railroad builders turned first to timber structures. Wood was plentiful, cheap, and easily shaped and worked. Arched timber truss road bridges with spans of as much as 360 feet had been built as early as 1804. In 1830 the B&O engaged Lewis Wernwag, one of the most successful builders of these pioneer timber bridges, to build the first wood-frame railroad bridge in America. This was a 350-foot-long bridge of three arched deck trusses over the Monocacy River in Maryland. Several years later Wernwag built the B&O's first crossing of the Potomac at Harpers Ferry, a seven-span timber structure 830 feet long.

The most common timber bridges, simple "post and stringer" trestles, were economical and practical for the railroads' many short-span bridge requirements. For longer spans there was a wide range of designs for simple, practical trusses of timber construction.

The arched designs used for most early timber bridges were not well suited to most railroad uses, since they re-

The Erie Railroad's 1,040-foot Starrucca Viaduct in northeastern Pennsylvania, completed in 1848, was made of 17 semicircular arches, each spanning 51 feet, and stood 100 feet above the level of Starrucca Creek. Conrail diesels carried a westbound train across the viaduct on August 14, 1985. —Jim Shaughnessy

The Canadian Pacific Railway consumed prodigious quantities of timber to build the transcontinental lines across British Columbia. This high timber trestle and a 100-foot-long Howe timber truss were required to bridge the Nahatlatch River 6 miles north of North Bend, British Columbia, in 1885. —City of Vancouver Archives (Neg. CAN.P.133, N.100)

quired heavy abutments capable of resisting the horizontal thrust of the arches. Moreover, the arch spans made it more difficult to provide the level floor required for tracks. Simple truss bridges, on the other hand, readily provided a level deck and exerted only vertical loads at their supports.

One early design favored by railroad builders was a wood lattice truss patented by Ithiel Town in 1820. This was built with principal horizontal top and bottom sections, or chords, of two or more timber members with a latticework web of planks between them. Most were built as covered bridges, contributing to a remarkable longevity. The design was popular in New England, where more than 100 survived into the twentieth century on Boston & Maine branches.

A much more successful early timber truss design was developed in 1838 by William Howe of Spencer, Massachusetts. The Howe truss was not, strictly speaking, an all-timber design, since it combined heavy top and bottom chords and diagonal members of wood with vertical-tension members of wrought iron. Later simplified, the Howe design soon became the most widely used wooden truss for railroad bridges.

Although wooden railroad bridges remained popular during much of the nineteenth century, bridge designers were beginning to use metal even before the beginning of the railroad era. Typically, these early metal bridges were built of cast or wrought iron. The brittle cast iron was usually used only for members under compressive loads, while the tougher wrought iron was used for tension members.

The first metal railroad bridge in North America was built by Richard B. Osborne, chief engineer for the Philadelphia & Reading, at Manayunk, Pennsylvania, in 1845. This was a 34-foot Howe truss span, in which cast-iron members replaced the usual wooden diagonals and wrought-iron sections were used for the vertical members and the top and bottom chords. One of the trusses from this historic bridge survives today in the Smithsonian Institution's National Museum of American History at Washington, D.C.

The early railroad builders had plenty of other truss designs to choose from for iron bridges. In 1846 Squire Whipple, one of the foremost early bridge engineers, developed the Whipple truss, which was made from cast and wrought iron. At about the same time Boston engineer Thomas W. Pratt and his father, Caleb, designed the Pratt truss, which reversed the web design of the Howe truss to place the diagonal members in tension and the vertical members in compression. One of the most popular truss forms was the Warren truss, first built in 1846 by British engineers James Warren and Willoughby Monzani. This was designed with diagonals that were alternately sloped in opposite directions, one in tension and one in compression. In the original design there were no vertical posts, but these were added in later versions.

Still other popular truss designs were developed by two early B&O engineers. In 1850 Wendell Bollman developed a type of suspension truss that employed cast-iron top and bottom chords, wrought-iron web diagonals, and a system of wrought-iron suspension rods radiating from the top of the end posts. Another type of suspension truss was developed a year later by Albert Fink. Usually built as a deck truss, the Fink design had a top chord and posts of either wood or cast iron; a series of wrought-iron diagonals in tension radiated from the ends to the bottom of each post. The trusses were usually built without a bottom chord, and additional diagonals took the tension normally carried by the chord. The Fink truss was extensively used on the B&O's western extension from Cumberland, Maryland, and was later used for some of the most notable long-span bridges of the time.

Through the middle of the century the design of these bridges remained largely empirical in nature; bridge builders had little to guide them as they tried to cope with steadily increasing locomotive weights and operating speeds. But paralleling the increasing use of metal for bridge construction was the development of scientific methods for the analysis of stresses and the proportioning of members in a bridge structure. The first American engineers to develop a thorough understanding of stress analysis in trusses were Squire Whipple and Herman Haupt, who independently developed and published their theories in 1847 and 1851, respectively.

The work of Whipple, Haupt, and others marked the beginning of an era of scientific bridge analysis and design and a period of great progress in bridge building. In 1859, for example, Albert Fink completed a remarkable bridge over the Green River south of Louisville on the Louisville & Nashville main line. With two truss spans of 180 feet and three of 208 feet, it ranked as the longest iron bridge in America. Fink's record-breaking span length was soon surpassed by crossings of the Ohio River completed over the next two decades. By 1877 Jacob H. Linville had pushed truss spans to a record 517 feet with his design for the main-channel span of a crossing of the Ohio at Cincinnati for the Cincinnati & Southern.

An alternative to the metal truss for long-span bridges was the tubular bridge developed by England's great railroad engineer Robert Stephenson. Instead of iron trusses, this design employed a huge wrought-iron box girder as its principal structural element, with trains passing through the tubular structure. Stephenson had built two of these innovative bridges in Wales when he came to North America to design a similar structure for a Grand Trunk crossing of the St. Lawrence River at Montreal. Completed in 1859, Stephenson's Victoria Bridge included a continuous tubular structure 6,592 feet long that was made up of 24 tubular iron spans of 242 to 247 feet. It served the Grand Trunk for nearly half a century before it was replaced with a more conventional steel truss structure. Although at least one other tubular bridge—at Ste-Anne-de-Bellevue, Quebec—was built for the Grand Trunk, the design never caught on in North America.

These spectacular achievements were not without their price, for failure, frequently with calamitous loss of life, was altogether too common. In the decade between 1870 and 1880, for example, railroad and highway bridges collapsed at a rate of about 40 a year. One particular failure claimed wide public attention: the collapse of the Lake

A typical modern iron truss bridge across the Saco River in Maine on the Portland & Ogdensburg Railroad was pictured in the May 31, 1873, *Scientific American*. Clarke, Reeves & Co. of Phoenixville, Pennsylvania, built the two 185-foot spans at a cost of $20,000. —Middleton Collection

Shore & Michigan Southern's bridge over the deep gorge of Ashtabula Creek at Ashtabula, Ohio, on December 29, 1876. One of two locomotives and all eleven cars of the railroad's *Pacific Express* fell with the bridge, and approximately 90 people died, either in the crash or the holocaust that followed when heating stoves set fire to the splintered wreckage of the wooden cars.

Investigation of this and other failures revealed many shortcomings in bridge-building practice. Frequently, designers had an imperfect understanding of the forces acting on a bridge structure or of the potential dangers against which they had to safeguard their structures. Steadily increasing loads often subjected bridges to stresses for which they had never been designed. Wood was subject to decay and fire, while cast iron was often of uneven quality, brittle, and extremely weak in tension. All too commonly bridges were hastily built by the cheapest means allowable. Quite generally, too, they were designed and built for the railroads by independent bridge companies on a competitive-bid basis.

The conversion of bridge engineering to a more scientific and reliable process was largely completed by roughly 1860–1880. Whipple and Haupt had developed a scientific basis for stress analysis by the mid-1850s. Improved materials and such technical advances as testing of material, a scientific basis for railroad bridge loadings, and comprehensive developments of bridge specification were all important parts of the process.

Over this period metal bridge structures gradually moved from cast iron to wrought iron and then to steel. Cast iron was reasonably strong in compression, but was brittle and prone to fail in tension. Wrought iron was fabricated through an annealing or wrought-iron process that gave the metal a fibrous character, making it stronger than iron, much more ductile, and stronger and more reliable in tension. First used for tension members, it was soon adopted for all parts of a bridge. Finally, steel began to come into use in the 1860s, providing a material of even greater strength, toughness, and reliability.

A major breakthrough was Jacob Linville's development of testing machines that could "test to failure" full-sized bridge members, permitting engineers to accurately determine the properties of materials and the performance of structural members. A natural outgrowth of this new capability was the development of detailed specifications governing the required performance of materials and standards for workmanship and construction. Thomas C. Clarke and Samuel Reeves, partners in a bridge-building firm, developed some of the first bridge specifications in 1871, and the practice was in general use by the end of the decade. Theodore Cooper, who would become one of the leading bridge engineers of the time, developed a specification for the Erie in 1878 that was the most comprehensive yet; it became a model widely used by other roads.

At this time, too, engineers began to develop systems of concentrated loads approximating locomotive and train wheel loadings, which provided a far more accurate basis for the design of individual bridge members. Louis F. G. Bouscaren, chief engineer of the Cincinnati Southern, developed the first one in 1873, and Theodore Cooper later devised an improved system that was almost universally adopted by American railroads.

The converter process for making steel, developed in 1856 by English engineer and inventor Henry Bessemer, led to further advances. Steel possessed greater strength, toughness, and wear resistance than either cast or wrought iron. Within a few decades the Bessemer process had made steel both plentiful and cheap, and it soon was widely used for bridge construction. James Buchanan Eads used steel for the arch sections of his great Mississippi River bridge at St. Louis, completed during 1867–1874, and the first all-steel bridge was erected over the Missouri River at Glasgow, Missouri, in 1879 by the Chicago & Alton. At first, steel was typically used in combination with wrought iron, but by the 1890s bridges were usually being built entirely of steel.

Paralleling the rapid gains of the 1860s and 1870s in the materials and techniques of bridge design and construction were some notable advances in the field of foundation construction. In the early years cofferdams were normally used whenever it was necessary to construct foundations below water level. Typically these were enclosures made of sheet piling driven into the streambed or boxlike structures that were floated into place, sunk to the bottom of the stream, and then pumped out to enable construction of a pier "in the dry." Both the heavy loadings imposed on the cofferdam structure by deep water and the difficulty in pumping water out as water depth and pressure increased limited the practical maximum depth for this method.

An alternative was the pneumatic caisson. In this method excavation was carried out from inside what amounted to an upside-down box from which water was excluded by air pressure. Although it was used in Europe as early as 1850, its first major use in North America was by James Eads during 1869–1871 for the construction of foundations for the St. Louis bridge, where the deepest caisson was sunk to a depth of 136 feet below high-water level. Eads encountered the new problem of caisson disease, which was attributed to too-rapid decompression as workers returned to the surface from the pressurized caissons. Once this problem was solved, the pneumatic caisson method helped make possible many of the great bridges of the late nineteenth and early twentieth centuries.

With the availability of steel, bridge builders successfully pushed truss bridges to still greater span lengths. By 1895 William H. Burr had designed a Big Four bridge over the Ohio River at Louisville that incorporated three truss spans each 547 feet long. Over the next two decades these were eclipsed by spans of 668 feet for the Municipal Bridge over the Mississippi at St. Louis, completed in 1912, and the 723-foot main span of the Paducah & Illinois crossing of the Ohio at Metropolis, Illinois, completed in 1917. But this was just about the practical limit for the length of a simple, single-span truss; the main span of the Metropolis bridge has never been exceeded.

Railroad truss bridges were usually built as simple spans, which spanned between two supports with an independent structure that was easily designed and fabricated. Because a simple truss bridge was incapable of taking any load until the structure was complete, these were usually erected on temporary falsework. Often, when a bridge spanned open water, trusses were assembled elsewhere and floated into position on a barge. But as engineers attempted to cross wider and deeper streams, the erection of these simple truss spans became increasingly difficult. American bridge builders had begun at an early date to seek other structural forms that could provide more economical or practical solutions to the need for long clear spans.

One of the earliest of these to be tried was the suspension bridge, a form that had been in use for centuries. Typically, these used cables or chains, supported by towers and anchored at each end of the span, to carry a suspended roadway; they could be erected without falsework by first building the towers and anchorages, spinning the cables, and then hanging the roadway from the cables. The first railroad suspension bridge was erected across the Niagara River by John A. Roebling during 1851–1855. With a clear span of 821 feet, it was the longest railroad bridge anywhere. But the lack of rigidity characteristic of suspension bridges proved a serious shortcoming for railroad use. On the Niagara bridge it was necessary to severely limit train speeds; no other railroad suspension bridges were ever built in North America.

Another early bridge form that proved much more successful for long-span railroad needs was the metal arch. Cast-iron arches had been built for road bridges in England as early as 1781, but the first metal arch railroad bridge in the United States was Eads's St. Louis Bridge. This was followed by a number of long-span steel arch bridges, culminating in Gustav Lindenthal's record Hell Gate Bridge of 1917 over the East River at New York, with a clear span of 977 feet 6 inches.

The use of arch bridges was generally limited to locations at which the site could provide foundations that could withstand the great horizontal thrust of the arches. A much more versatile structural form for extremely long spans was the cantilever truss bridge, first used in 1869 by German engineer Heinrich Gerber for a crossing of the Main River. In its basic form, the cantilever truss was typically made up of anchor arms at each end that were anchored to piers at the shore end and built continuous with cantilever arms projecting beyond intermediate supporting piers. These two cantilever arms were then joined by a "suspended" or "floating" simple truss span at the center to form the main span of the bridge. With this arrangement, the anchor arms of the bridge counterbalanced the load of the cantilever arms and the suspended span, substantially reducing the maximum bending load at the center of the span and allowing significant material economies.

Although the anchor arms at each end of a cantilever bridge were typically erected on falsework much like a conventional truss bridge, the cantilever arms could be erected without it by building them outward from the supporting piers. The central suspended span was often erected by continuing to build outward from the end of each cantilever arm as a cantilever and then converting the center structure to a simple truss after the two halves were joined. Sometimes, too, the suspended span was as-

This enormous span, more than a mile in length, was completed in 1888 to cross the Hudson River at Poughkeepsie, New York. One of the earliest cantilever bridges in North America, it was the first to be built entirely of steel. The bridge still stands but was idled after a fire in 1974. —Jim Shaughnessy

CIVIL ENGINEERING   **257**

sembled elsewhere, floated into position on barges, and lifted into place.

The first North American cantilever bridge was a Cincinnati Southern crossing of the Kentucky River completed in 1877. Still longer cantilever spans followed, and by 1892 engineers George Shattuck Morison and Alfred Noble had completed a crossing of the Mississippi River at Memphis, Tennessee, with a cantilevered span of 791 feet over the main channel of the river. But by 1917 this and all other cantilever spans were eclipsed by the great Quebec Bridge, with a clear span of 1,800 feet, which remains today the longest cantilever bridge ever built.

Still another bridge form that offered advantages over simple truss spans was the continuous truss, which employed a single truss structure that was continuous over two or more spans. This continuity, much like that of the cantilever, enabled one span to counterbalance the load of an adjacent span, allowing significant economies in material over simple truss structures and making much longer clear spans feasible. Like the cantilever, continuous trusses were easily erected without falsework by the cantilevering method.

Continuous-truss bridges had been built in England as early as 1850. The first in North America was an 1887 Canadian Pacific crossing of the St. Lawrence River near Montreal designed by C. Shaler Smith. However, the form was little used until Gustav Lindenthal completed an enormous bridge across the Ohio River at Sciotoville, Ohio, for the Chesapeake & Ohio in 1917. This led to its adoption for several other major North American bridges.

Still another metal bridge form, used as early as 1847 for a bridge on the Baltimore & Susquehanna, was the plate girder, which was widely employed for spans of moderate length, usually up to around 125 feet. Assembled from structural steel shapes and plates by riveting—and later welding—the plate girder is simply an "I" section of larger size than can be manufactured in a single rolled section.

Late in the nineteenth century there was a modest revival in the use of the masonry arch for railroad bridges, largely because of its permanence and its ability to permit train operation without speed restrictions. During this period both the Pennsylvania and the B&O built a large number of arch bridges, using both stone and Portland cement concrete, largely as a substitute for masonry.

The highest railway bridge in the British Commonwealth, the Canadian Pacific's Lethbridge Viaduct in Alberta was over 1 mile long and stood 314 feet above the Oldman River. It was built as part of CPR's Continental Divide crossing over Crowsnest Pass.
—Canadian Pacific, *Trains* Magazine Collection

There was nothing new about cement. Made by forming a cementing material that was mixed with a mineral aggregate and sufficient water, the cementing material set and bound the mixture into a solid mass of concrete. Plain concrete, however, had very low tensile strength and could be used only in compression.

By the beginning of the twentieth century bridge designers began using Portland cement in combination with structural reinforcing steel to combine concrete for compressive strength and reinforcing bars for tensile strength. The Delaware, Lackawanna & Western was the leading practitioner of reinforced-concrete arch construction, with a number of major structures built between 1908 and 1915 for extensive line relocations in New Jersey and Pennsylvania, most notably the Tunkhannock Viaduct at Nicholson, Pennsylvania, which incorporated 167,000 cubic yards of concrete in a 2,375-foot-long structure that reached a height of 242 feet.

From almost the beginning of the railroad era the conflict between navigation and the railroads' crossing of major waterways required the development of a specialized form of bridge that permitted the passage of water traffic. Probably the earliest drawbridge structure was built across the Charles River at Boston in 1835 by the Boston & Lowell. Built of wooden trusses, this horizontal jackknife span was hinged from a corner at one end. A system of cables radiating from a tower at the hinged end permitted the span to be swung horizontally to a position parallel to the shore to permit passage of water traffic.

A variation, the center-pivoted swing bridge, was developed about 1850 to meet a need for greater openings in major waterway crossings. One of the first important bridges of this type was completed by the Chicago & Rock Island in 1856 for its crossing of the Mississippi between Rock Island, Illinois, and Davenport, Iowa, the first railroad bridge over the Mississippi. For its main channel crossing the Rock Island built a 285-foot truss draw span that turned on a swivel at the center, providing a clear opening of 120 feet on either side for the passage of boats. With its center pier, however, the swing-span bridge presented some obstruction to water traffic, and the position of the span in the open position made it vulnerable to damage from errant vessels. Two other drawbridge designs developed later in the nineteenth century largely eliminated these shortcomings.

The first of these to be used for railroad purposes was the vertical lift bridge, which employs counterweights and a system of cables and sheaves to lift a movable span vertically on towers at each end to clear water traffic. Patented by Squire Whipple and first used for a crossing of the Erie Canal in 1874, the vertical lift bridge became a popular type for railroad use, and lift bridge spans of 300 feet or more have become relatively common. The longest ever built was the 558-foot lift span for a crossing of the Arthur Kill near Elizabeth, New Jersey, completed in 1959 to link the Central of New Jersey with the B&O's Staten Island Rapid Transit.

The other principal type of movable bridge was the bascule bridge, which owed its basic principle to the medieval drawbridge. This employs a span, hinged or pivoted at one end, which can be raised clear of the waterway. This form became feasible for heavy railroad spans late in the nineteenth century with the development of counterweighted bascule spans and the necessary mechanical equipment for raising and lowering them.

Typically, bascule bridges rotate to a vertical position on some sort of roller or trunnion arrangement. Depending upon span requirements, they can be built as either single-leaf spans, opening from one side only, or double-leaf spans, which open from both sides. The largest railroad bascule bridge ever built was a double-leaf bascule erected by the Canadian Pacific in 1941 at a crossing of the ship canal at Sault Ste. Marie, Michigan, which has a clear span of 336 feet.

An unusual approach to the drawbridge problem was the floating bridge used by the Milwaukee Road for crossings of the Mississippi and Missouri rivers. The first of these, completed in 1874 at Prairie du Chien, Wisconsin, provided a crossing of the Mississippi at a point where east and west channels of the river were separated by an intervening island, requiring a structure of some 7,000 feet between the Wisconsin and Iowa shores. The entire structure was built as an ordinary timber pile trestle except for the novel pontoon draw spans in the navigable east and west channels. Each of these was a huge wooden float 6 feet deep, 41 feet wide at the deck level, and 408 feet long. A single track on each pontoon was supported by wooden blocking, arranged so that it could be raised or lowered by hydraulic jacks to accommodate variations between high- and low-water levels of as much as 22 feet. An adjustable truss at each end of the pontoon provided the necessary connection with track on the adjacent trestle. In order to open the span for river traffic, the pontoon was pivoted about one end and was pulled into the open position, parallel to the current flow, by a system of chains powered from a steam engine on the pontoon.

Although the great era of railroad growth and expansion ended early in the twentieth century, the construction of new bridges has continued at a moderate rate, either to replace aging structures with newer and heavier spans or to meet the needs of line relocations. Advances in the materials and techniques of bridge building have made these modern spans quite different from those of an earlier era.

Occasionally, bridge builders have tried entirely new materials. Aluminum was used as early as 1946 in an experimental plate girder bridge that weighed less than half as much as a comparable steel span. The material's high cost, however, precluded its wider adoption for bridge construction. Wood, the oldest bridge-building material of all, has been used experimentally for railroad bridge construction in the entirely new form of glued, laminated fabrication, in which separate boards are bonded together

Table 2. Notable North American Railroad Bridges

Name	Date	Bridge Type and Construction	Overall Dimensions	Principal Spans and Navigational Clearance	Notable Features	Present Status
Baltimore & Ohio, Canton Viaduct, Maryland	1836	Stone arch bridge.	Overall span 704 feet.	Eight elliptical arches, each spanning 58 feet. Roadway 66 feet above water level and 26-foot width for double track.	Structure on a 4.5-degree curve.	In service.
Grand Trunk, St. Lawrence, Quebec	1859	Simple tubular spans of wrought iron.	Overall span length 9,144 feet; total length of truss spans 6,592 feet.	Main spans 24 bridges 242 to 247 feet, and a single center span of 330-feet. Navigation clearance 60 feet.	British design built in England. Except for smaller structures in Canada, no other tubular bridges in North America.	In service. Piers widened and tubular structures replaced by trusses, 1898.
Eads Bridge, Mississippi, St. Louis, Missouri and Illinois	1874	Steel arch bridge.	Overall span length of 2,440 feet (approx.) over east and west stone abutments; total length of arches 1,627 feet.	Two arch spans at 502 feet and a central span of 520 feet. Navigation clearance of not less than 50 feet at mean high water.	First major steel bridge, and first major use of pneumatic piers in North America.	In service. Railroad line inactivated 1974 and restored as MetroLink light rail in 1993.
Cincinnati Southern, Kentucky River, Kentucky.	1877	Cantilever truss spans of wrought iron.	Overall span of 1,138 feet.	Three equal spans of 275 feet used a continuous center truss with a 75-foot extension on either side, supporting simple spans of 300 feet on each side. Main gorge was 275 feet deep.	First major North American span of cantilever construction.	Original structure was replaced in 1911 with a heavier structure and double tracks.
Erie, Kinzua Viaduct, Pennsylvania	1882	Viaduct structure of wrought iron.	Overall span of 2,051 feet.	Structures of 38 feet 6 inches were alternated with 20 spans of 61 feet and 1 of 62 feet. Highest elevation was 301 feet over gorge.	At its erection Kinuza was the highest railway bridge in the world.	Original structure was replaced by a heavier steel structure in 1900. Regular service ended in 1957, and in more recent years a tourist line operated over the line. The structure collapsed in 2003.
Southern Pacific, Lucin Cutoff, Great Salt Lake, Utah	1904	Great Salt Lake crossing of fill and timber trestles.	Total length of 32 miles. Longest 12.7-mile session used section of timber trestle.	Timber trestle built of typical trestle bents with a rock ballast.	The 12.7-mile timber trestle fill was the longest bridge ever built in the United States.	SP has encountered maintenance problems as water has climbed as much as 16 feet. In 1955 the trestle was replaced with earth fill.
Lackawanna, Tunkhannock Creek, Pennsylvania	1915	Reinforced concrete arches.	Overall bridge length of 2,375 feet.	Ten 1,800-foot and two 100-foot structures with a maximum height of 240 feet above creek bed.	Required 167,000 cubic yards of concrete, the largest of its kind ever built.	In service.
New York Connecting, East River, New York	1917	Steel main arch spans, with supporting steel trestles and bridges.	Overall New York Connecting Railroad length of 16,481 feet. Main arch 977 feet 6 inches.	Main arch bridge spans 977 feet 6 inches between bridge centers. Peak of arch is 305 feet above main high water, with a 135-foot navigation clearance.	World's longest railroad arch, with four tracks.	In service.
Canadian Government, St. Lawrence, Quebec	1917	Steel cantilever K trusses for anchor and anchor arms; Baltimore truss for center arm.	Overall bridge length of 3,239 feet. Main cantilever 2,830 feet.	Main cantilever bridge with a 515-foot anchor span at each end and a 1,800-foot main span, with a suspended center span of 640 feet. Navigation clearance 150 feet.	World's longest railroad cantilever. The original bridge failed during construction in 1907. The second bridge was built on the same site.	In service.
Burlington Railroad, Ohio River, Metropolis, Illinois	1917	Steel simple Pratt truss.	Overall bridge length of 5,442 feet. Main trusses 3,251 feet.	Principal span has four Pratt trusses of 551 feet, one of 300 feet, and a main span of 720 feet. Navigation clearance 53 feet at high water.	World's longest simple truss.	In service.
Chesapeake & Ohio, Ohio River, Sciotoville, Ohio	1917	Steel continuous Warren truss.	Overall bridge length of 3,435 feet. Main trusses 1,550 feet.	Principal structure is a 1,550-foot continuous structure divided into two equal spans of 775 feet. Navigation clearance 40 feet at high water.	World's longest railroad continuous truss.	In service.

to form homogenous wood members of much greater size than is possible with sawn timber.

But the greatest advances have been those in the use of the two basic materials of modern bridge building, concrete and steel. The utility of concrete in bridge construction was advanced enormously by the mid-twentieth-century development of prestressing, which places reinforced concrete in a state of permanent compression before any loads are applied. This is done by means of tensioning of high-strength steel wires or rods used as reinforcement. Tensile stresses developed when the structure is loaded are then canceled out by the compressive stresses already developed, permitting the concrete to function only in compression, in which state it is much stronger. Prestressing permits the use of much lighter concrete structures and makes the use of concrete feasible for much longer bridge spans. Railroad use of prestressed concrete has been largely confined to relatively short spans, although a 1,739-foot, seven-span light-rail crossing of the North Saskatchewan River at Edmonton, Alberta, is made up of precast, pretensioned continuous box girders.

Improvements in the metallurgy of steel itself and in the methods of fabrication and erection of steel structures have greatly expanded the usefulness of this basic material. Newer alloy steels have been developed with yield strengths of as much as three times those for ordinary structural carbon steels. Another variation is a corrosion-resistant alloy steel that weathers to a uniform brown color and requires no painting. High-tension bolts or arc welding have almost entirely replaced riveting in the erection of steel structures. Welding, in particular, has helped reduce the dead weight of steel bridges, both by eliminating many of the splice plates required for riveted construction and by avoiding the loss of a part of the cross-sectional area of members necessitated by punching rivet holes.

These new materials and techniques have permitted both improvements to the existing forms of steel bridging and the development of new forms. Robert Stephenson's tubular bridge design of the 1850s, for example, has reappeared in a modern form as the steel box girder, which is simply a large steel box section typically assembled from steel plate and structural shapes by welding. Although it is similar to the plate girder in many of its features, the box girder can be used for considerably longer spans. A notable example is a 4,260-foot crossing of Latah Creek canyon built as part of a Burlington Northern line relocation at Spokane, Washington, during 1971–1972. The bridge employed welded steel box girders 3 feet 6 inches wide and up to 12 feet deep for the 160-foot spans of the main canyon crossing. Table 2 lists some notable North American railroad bridges.

Bridge Forms

Stresses on a bridge member can fall into any one, or several, types of loading on each member of the struc-

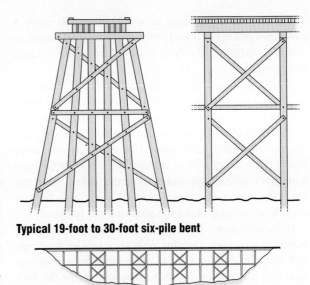

Typical 19-foot to 30-foot six-pile bent

Typical longitudinal bracing

Figure 3. Typical Timber Trestle. —Rick Johnson

ture. The total loading—or stresses—identifies the total load carried on a member. The ability of a structural system to safely carry a load is dependent upon the kind of loading, the characteristics of the material, and the allowable unit stress, usually expressed in allowable stress per square inch.

TRESTLES

Erected in simple spans supported on piers or abutments, beams or girders have long constituted one of the most common forms for short spans. Wood beams were the most common material for early railroad bridge construction, while rolled or built-up iron beams later began to come into use. The ubiquitous *timber trestle* is typically made up of short wooden beams or stringer spans carried on a series of supports called *bents*, which may be made up of either a row of timber piling or framed timber construction. The beams or stringers are carried on transverse top members, or caps, and diagonal and longitudinal sway bracing provides rigidity. Usually, when a trestle exceeds about 30 feet in height, it is constructed as a series of stories, with bent panels placed one on the other.

The timber trestle remains a common form. Frequently in modern practice, however, steel, reinforced-concrete, or prestressed-concrete members are used in place of wood.

ARCHES

The arch has been known since prehistoric times. In its traditional form of stone or brick masonry construction the arch carries its load in a curved structure made up of wedge-shaped segments called *voussoirs*. The central voussoir at the high point, or *crown*, of the arch is called the *keystone*, while those at each end are called *springers*.

These structural members of a masonry arch carry a compression load only and develop a horizontal thrust, as well as a vertical load, which must be carried by the arch abutments.

The Romans were the first to make wide use of the arch as a bridge form in their great masonry bridges and aqueducts. The early stone arch bridges built by American railroads closely followed the construction practices of the Romans nearly 2,000 years earlier. Cut stone voussoirs were laid in place, either with or without a cement mortar, on a temporary wood supporting structure called *centering*. Once the keystone had been placed and the arch became capable of carrying a load, the centering was removed.

In its traditional form the arch bridge was a massive masonry structure, carrying only compressive loadings. But with the development of such modern materials as steel and concrete engineers became able to use the arch for structures of much more ambitious dimensions.

In the most common forms used in steel arch construction, fixed, two-hinged or three-hinged structures are used. A two-hinged arch typically has a hinged design at each end of the arch, while a three-hinged design has an additional hinge at the center of the arch. The fixed arch affords a greater rigidity than the two other types, but is an indeterminate structure that is more difficult to design and subject to heavy stresses that can be induced by temperature changes or foundation movement. Two- and three-hinged arches, while less rigid, are easier to analyze and are less subject to stresses caused by temperature or foundation movement. Steel arches can be further subdivided by the method in which the arch rib is fabricated and the deck supported by the rib. The arch rib may be constructed as a solid member, similar to a plate girder, or may be built with diagonal web members, looking much like a truss, separating the main top and bottom chords with vertical and diagonal members between the top and bottom chord. In what is usually called a spandrel braced arch, a horizontal top chord is usually connected to the arched bottom chord by a system of diagonal bracing.

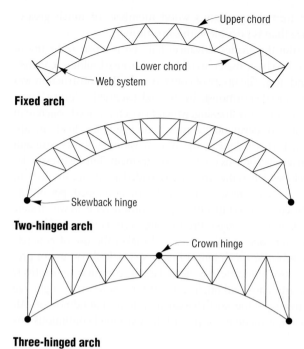

Fixed arch

Two-hinged arch

Three-hinged arch

Figure 5. Principal Steel Arch Forms. —Rick Johnson

As in the circular masonry arch, a steel arch develops both vertical loads and a horizontal thrust at its foundations. Consequently, the choice of an arch bridge is normally limited to situations that offer good foundation conditions.

Unlike masonry arches, which required the use of centering for temporary support of the arch during construction, a steel arch can be erected without falsework either by means of cantilevering the structure outward or by the use of temporary backstays to support the partially completed arch. Primarily in Europe reinforced concrete has been used for railroad arch spans of prodigious dimensions. A concrete arch completed in 1977 on Austria's Tauern line, for example, spans more than 500 feet. Nothing even approaching this scale has been attempted in America, where the most notable concrete bridges have been those of the Lackawanna's pre–World War I line relocations in New Jersey and Pennsylvania, which were distinguished for their great overall size rather than individual span lengths or innovative structural engineering.

TRUSSES

The truss of a bridge is a framework of members, typically designed in some arrangement of triangular patterns, which converts the bending forces of loads on the structure into direct tension or compression loads on the individual members. The principal sections are the longitudinal main trusses, called *chords*, which span the supporting structures and carry the supporting loads. A

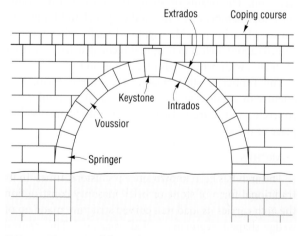

Figure 4. Elements of the Arch. —Rick Johnson

main truss includes two principal top and bottom members, usually horizontal but which may also be inclined, extending the full length of the truss. These are separated by a series of either vertical or inclined members called *web members,* in which the inclined web members are often called *diagonals.* The points at which vertical web members intersect the main chords are called *panel points,* and the area between successive panel points is called a *panel.* In its basic and most common arrangement, in which it is designed to extend over a single span and to deliver only vertical loads to its supports, a truss is called a *simple truss.*

Almost as important as the design of the main truss itself is that of the system of lateral and sway bracing used to tie two main trusses together so that they function as an integral unit and provide resistance to the various lateral loadings to which a bridge is subject, and the floor system that transmits the traffic loading to the main trusses. A *deck truss* span is one in which the floor system is carried by the top chords, and traffic runs on top of the bridge, while a *through truss* span carries the floor system on the bottom chord, and traffic runs through the structure. A short truss span loaded on the bottom chord but too shallow to allow for lateral bracing between the top chords is called a *pony truss.*

The truss did not become an important structural form until the nineteenth century, when engineers developed a wide variety of truss designs to meet the needs of America's expanding railroads. The principal truss forms had largely been developed by the mid-nineteenth century. Only two forms, the Pratt and Warren trusses, remained popular into the twentieth century. In modern practice the Warren truss is often modified by the addition of vertical members at the panel points, while both the Pennsylvania and Baltimore trusses are variations of the Pratt truss, with the addition of substrut and subvertical members. The K-truss, used for long spans, is the only new type of truss adopted for railroad bridges in the twentieth century.

Early iron trusses were usually assembled by bolting, but by the 1860s the assembly of trusses by a combination of riveting and pin connections had become the usual American practice. Built-up iron members were generally fabricated in the bridge builder's shops by riveting, in which driving hot rivets through punched rivet holes connected the metal pieces. These riveted joints derived their strength from a combination of the capacity of the rivet itself to withstand a shearing force between the connected members, and the friction developed between the two members by the contraction of the rivet as it cooled. Erection of a truss on the site, however, was typically accomplished by pin connecting, in which the members were connected by machined iron pins inserted through holes bored in the built-up members or the ends of the iron eyebars used for tension members. This combination of shop fabrication of the parts of a bridge and their erection in the field by pin connections helped make bridge construction fast and simple, and it became the almost universal American practice for much of the nineteenth century. Eventually, however, American engineers went over to the British practice of riveted field connections, which provided a much stiffer structure.

SUSPENSION BRIDGES

Perhaps the most attractive of all long-span bridge forms, the suspension bridge consists of a roadway structure suspended from cables carried on supporting towers. Most nineteenth-century suspension bridges were built with masonry towers. Structural steel has been used for all major spans built since about 1900. The principal structural elements of a suspension bridge are the cables, usually made up of parallel high-tensile steel wires or twisted wire ropes, which span continuously between heavy anchorages at each end of the bridge, assuming a parabolic curve between the anchorages and the towers and between the towers. Vertical suspenders of wire rope hanging from the cables carry the roadway structure. Since its main structural elements—the cables and suspenders—function purely in tension, the suspension bridge is by far the most efficient long-span bridge form in terms of material requirements.

The greatest weakness of early suspension bridges built for railroad use was their relative lack of rigidity. Engineers have since learned how to use heavy stiffening trusses as part of the roadway system to provide adequate stability for long suspension spans. A modern variation is the cable-stayed bridge, in which the bridge deck is supported by a series of cable stays radiating from the tops of the bridge towers. A modern cable-stayed bridge across the Fraser River was completed in 1995 for rail rapid transit at Vancouver, British Columbia.

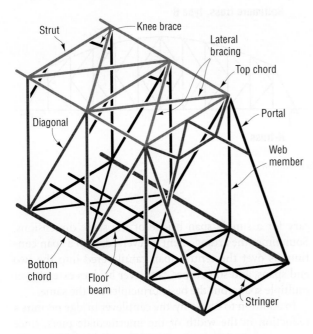

Figure 6. Through Truss Bridge Bracing. —Rick Johnson

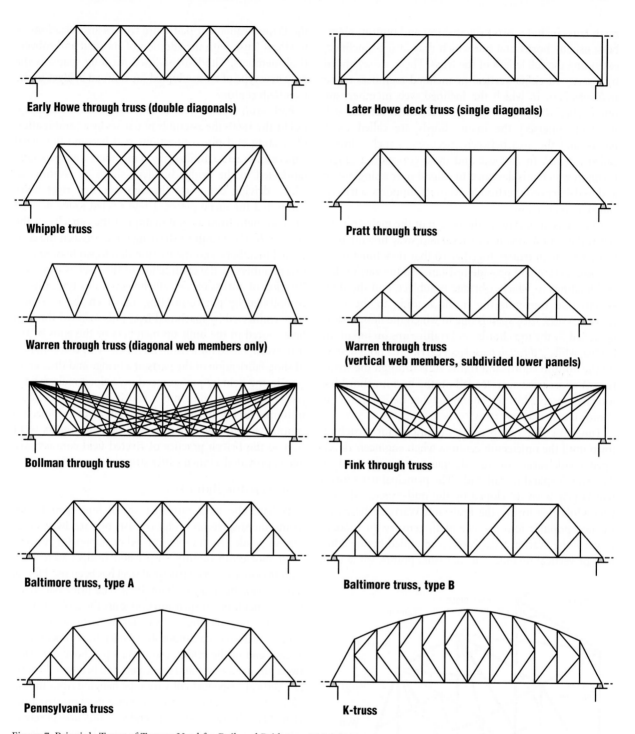

Figure 7. Principle Types of Trusses Used for Railroad Bridges. —Rick Johnson

Cantilever Trusses

In its most common arrangement the cantilever bridge employs counterbalanced end spans, which are cantilevered over intermediate supports to carry a suspended simple truss at the center of the span. The effect of this arrangement is to shorten the required simple truss span and thus reduce the maximum bending stresses, affording a considerable economy in material over that neces-sary for a simple span bridge of the same dimensions. Sometimes the arrangement is reversed, with a span continuous over the central span cantilevered into the two end spans, and sometimes cantilever bridges extend over multiple spans, but the basic principles are the same.

In addition to economy, the cantilever bridge permits a reduction in the width of the intermediate piers, since only one support is required instead of the two that would be necessary with adjacent simple spans. Perhaps

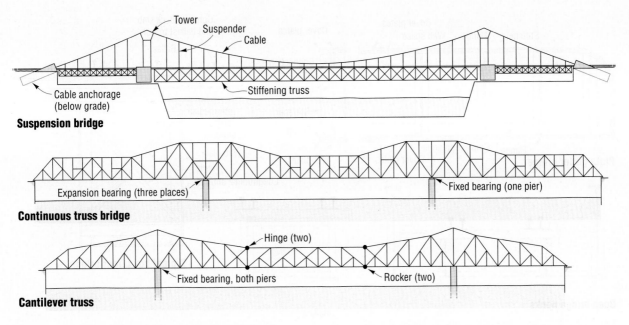

Figure 8. Major Long-Span Bridges. —Rick Johnson

its most important advantage is ease of erection, since the cantilever arms can be built outward without requiring supporting falsework, and the suspended span can either be similarly erected or raised into position in a completed form from below.

CONTINUOUS TRUSSES

Erected as a continuous structure over two or more adjacent spans, the continuous truss affords the same material economies as the cantilever bridge by reducing the maximum bending stresses as compared with simple trusses over the same arrangement of spans. It also provides most of the other advantages of the cantilever, as well as greater rigidity. Since unequal settlement of its foundations can induce significant stresses in the truss members, most engineers consider that a continuous truss should be used only where good foundation conditions are present.

PLATE GIRDERS

Built up from plate steel and structural shapes to form an I-beam section larger than those available as rolled sections, the plate girder is used for spans of moderate length falling between those that can be constructed with rolled beam sections and those for which a truss provides the most economic structure. Generally, plate girders are used for spans of about 50 to 125 feet. Although most frequently employed in railroad practice as a simply supported beam, the plate-girder form can also be used in continuous or cantilevered bridge structures.

A plate girder or box girder provides a structural form that uses the thick horizontal flanges at top and bottom and a vertical web between the top and bottom to carry the shearing stresses. The principal elements of a plate girder are its steel plate web, which gives the required resistance to shearing stresses and separates the top and bottom flanges, and the flanges, which provide the necessary resistance to bending stresses. These flanges are also made of steel plate connected to the web either by structural angles, in the case of riveted construction, or directly by arc welding. Usually a single flange plate runs the full length of the girder, and additional plates, called cover plates, are added to provide additional steel area to resist bending stresses at points where the maximum bending forces occur. Since a plate web is subject to buckling under heavy shearing stresses, an additional characteristic of plate girders is the use of vertical web stiffeners, made of either structural angles or plate steel. These stiffeners are normally spaced more closely near the supports, where shearing stresses are greatest.

Like any beam or truss, a plate girder requires lateral support to prevent buckling under load. Plate girders are typically erected in pairs with a system of cross-bracing to provide the necessary lateral support.

BOX GIRDERS

The box girder is essentially a modern variation of the plate girder, built as a unified structure that is more efficient in material and makes longer span lengths economic. Instead of pairing two plate girders to form a bridge span, the box girder in effect combines them into a single structure. Steel plate webs form the sides of the box section, and a steel plate across the bottom, typically reinforced with structural shapes, forms a single bottom flange. The top flange is similarly formed, but most box-girder designs also use some type of shear connectors to make a concrete deck an integral part of the structure in resisting compressive stresses at the top of the girder. An

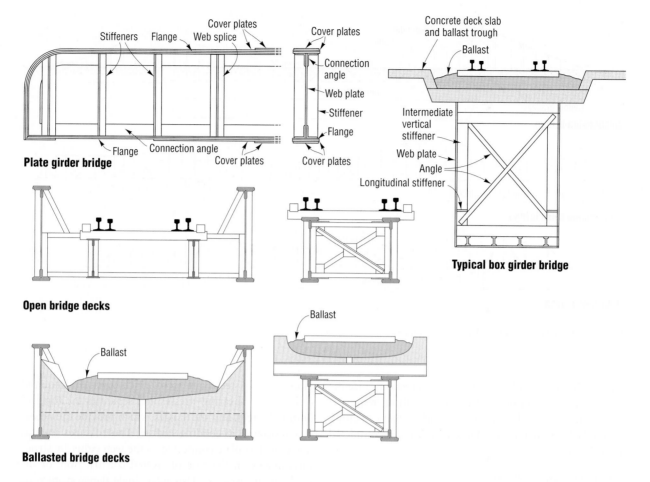

Plate girder bridge

Stiffeners Flange Cover plates Web splice Cover plates

Cover plates

Connection angle

Web plate

Stiffener

Flange

Flange Connection angle Cover plates Cover plates

Open bridge decks

Ballasted bridge decks

Ballast

Ballast

Concrete deck slab and ballast trough

Ballast

Intermediate vertical stiffener

Web plate

Angle

Longitudinal stiffener

Typical box girder bridge

Figure 9. Girder Bridges. —Rick Johnson

internal system of cross-bracing and stiffeners provides a box girder with the necessary stability.

Draw Spans

The earliest type of draw span to come into general use, and still frequently used, is the *swing bridge*, which pivots 90 degrees on a center pier in order to permit water traffic to pass. In the *center-bearing swing bridge* a cross-girder between the trusses rests on a large center bearing that carries the entire weight of the structure when it is open. Balance wheels fastened to the trusses and floor system and running on a circular track keep the structure level. When the bridge is closed, mechanical wedges are driven that raise the ends and transfer a portion of the load from the center bearing to the ends, and the bridge functions as a continuous truss under traffic. A *rim-bearing swing bridge* functions in much the same way except that the structure is supported on a large circular girder, which rotates on conical rollers as the bridge turns. A center pivot carries little or no load.

In its usual form for railroad use, the *lift bridge* consists of a counterweighted movable span that is raised vertically on towers at each end. Steel cables passing over large sheaves at the tops of the towers are used to lift it. Guides

attached to the corners of the lift span fit into vertical tracks on the towers to keep the span in line as it is raised or lowered. The machinery to raise and lower the bridge is typically placed in a machinery house on top of the lift span, but in some recent lift spans synchronous equipment is placed at the top of each tower. The lift span is generally considered the best type of drawbridge where particularly long or heavy spans are required.

The *bascule bridge* is a counterbalanced draw span, pivoted at the end, that is rotated by machinery to a vertical position to allow water traffic to pass. Bascule bridges may open from one or both sides and are called single- or double-leaf bascules, respectively. This form of bridge has attracted much attention from inventors, and a wide variety of systems have been developed for the lifting mechanism.

Bridge Decks and Floors

There are two types of bridge deck in general use. In an *open deck* the rails are spiked directly to timber bridge ties supported directly on the floor system of the bridge superstructure. A *ballasted deck* incorporates some kind of floor to support ballast, which in turn carries a conventional track structure. Floors for ballasted bridge decks

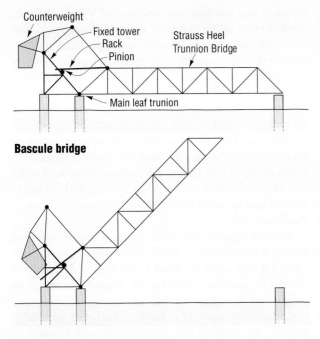

Bascule bridge

Bascule bridge, open

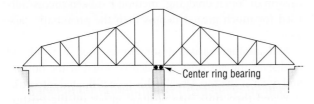

Swing bridge

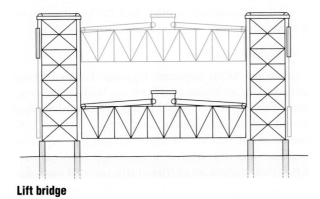

Lift bridge

Figure 10. Draw Spans. —Rick Johnson

are built of timber, steel plates, or a variety of metal or concrete trough sections. A ballasted deck provides a better riding track and helps reduce the noise of a train passing over a structure, although there is greater maintenance cost.

SUBSTRUCTURES AND FOUNDATIONS

No less important than the superstructure of a bridge are the substructure and foundations, which transmit loads from the structure to the underlying soil. Indeed,

such substructure and foundation design considerations as the height of the supporting structure, required channel widths, and depth and difficulty of foundation construction usually have much to do with the determination of span lengths or even the choice of the type of construction for the superstructure.

ABUTMENTS

In addition to carrying the load from the superstructure, the end supporting structure or *abutment* of a bridge usually also serves as a retaining structure for the approach embankment. Thus, in addition to the vertical load and any thrust loading from the superstructure, an abutment must withstand a horizontal pressure from the embankment fill material. There are a number of different types of abutments. All of them have as a common feature the main body section, usually called the *breast*. Probably the most widely used abutment type is the *wing abutment*, which has "wing" walls on either side sloped to conform to the natural slope of the embankment material. In several abutment types the embankment material is allowed to spill around the structure, assuming a natural slope alongside or in front of the abutment.

PIERS

The intermediate supports for a multiple-span bridge are called *piers*. In addition to carrying loads from the superstructure, a pier must also be designed to withstand such forces as the pressure of stream flow or ice. Piers are usually built with curved ends to reduce resistance to water flow, and where rapid stream flow or heavy ice movement is expected, a pointed "cutwater," sometimes with a metal nosing, is often used. For particularly severe ice conditions a pier is sometimes built with a *starling*, a sloped cutwater on which the ice will ride up out of the water and then break from its own weight. One of the most important considerations in the design of any pier

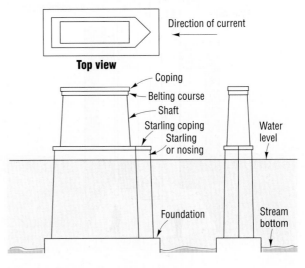

Figure 11. Typical Pier Design. —Rick Johnson

CIVIL ENGINEERING   **267**

in a stream is to assure that it is extended well below the level of any possible "scouring," the erosion of the stream bed by a high-velocity water flow.

Most often, a pier is built in the form of a solid shaft of sufficient length and width to accommodate the required bearings. Wide or particularly large piers are sometimes built in the form of an open portal or frame, or as a series of two or more separate columns.

During the nineteenth century most piers and abutments were built of stone or brick, but plain or reinforced concrete had come into general use by the end of the century. Wood, iron, and later steel have all been widely used for bridge substructures, particularly where high piers are required. In modern practice hollow cylindrical piers of steel or reinforced concrete are sometimes used.

FOUNDATIONS

If rock or other material of sufficient bearing capacity is available, an adequate support for bridge abutments or piers may be provided by means of a spread foundation of sufficient size to distribute the load over the subsurface bearing material. When such material is not available or is at too great a depth for economic construction of a spread foundation, piling is often used. Piles may be of wood, concrete, or metal and are either driven to "refusal," where they reach hard materials and can carry a load much like a column, or act as "friction piles," developing enough frictional resistance from the subsurface material into which they are driven to provide an adequate bearing capacity.

Several methods are in common use for the construction of bridge foundations below water level. At relatively shallow depths the *cofferdam* method has been in use since at least Roman times. The cofferdam is a watertight enclosure built around the construction site to permit ex-

cavation and construction "in the dry." Wood, concrete, or steel sheet piling is usually driven to form the cofferdam. Adequate bracing to resist water pressures must be provided, and pumping is required to clear the site of water.

For deep foundations several types of *caisson* are usually used. The *pneumatic caisson* process uses what is essentially an inverted open box with cutting edges on the lower edges. The caisson is sunk to the required depth by excavation from within the working chamber formed beneath the open box. Compressed air is used to hold water out of the chamber, and air locks are required for workmen to gain access to the chamber or to remove the excavated material.

Another type of caisson is the *open caisson*, which is simply a rectangular or cylindrical section open at both ends. Cutting edges are fitted to the lower edge, and the caisson is sunk into position by a combination of its weight and excavation carried out through the open caisson, usually by means of a clamshell bucket or something similar. By avoiding the complexities and hazards to workmen inherent in the pneumatic process, the open caisson or "open dredging" method has been successfully used for much greater depths than the pneumatic caisson.

Still another variation sometimes used for railroad bridges is the *box caisson*, which is closed at the bottom and open at the top. Usually this type is floated into position and then sunk into position either on the existing bottom, if it is smooth and level, or on an area that has been dredged and cleared for it. Once in place, the caisson is filled with concrete or other material to form the required foundation.

COOPER'S LOADING

Until the 1870s engineers typically designed bridge structures by assuming a uniform live load on the structure. This method provided design loadings that often varied widely from those actually produced by the concentrated axle loads of a heavy locomotive. Beginning with the work of Louis F. G. Bouscaren in 1873, railroads based their designs on a series of concentrated loads that more closely approximated the actual loads imposed by a locomotive. The system developed by bridge engineer Theodore Cooper was soon adopted as a standard loading system by most American railroads.

Cooper's loading assumes a freight train pulled by double-headed 2-8-0 Consolidation-type locomotives of standard dimensions, followed by an indefinite number of freight cars. The axle loadings for the locomotives and a uniform load representing the train vary with the loading standard adopted for a particular line or structure. Cooper's Class E10 loading, for example, is based upon driving-axle loadings of 10,000 pounds for the two Consolidation locomotives and loadings of 5,000 and 6,500 pounds for the locomotive leading truck and tender axles, respectively. The following train is represented by a uni-

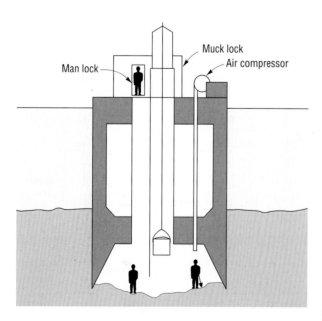

Figure 12. Pneumatic Caisson. —Rick Johnson

Man lock

Muck lock

Air compressor

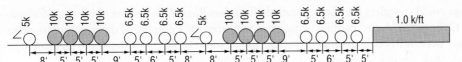

Figure 13. Cooper's Loading.
—Rick Johnson

Axle loading in kips (k)

form load of 1,000 pounds per linear foot of track. These loadings are usually expressed in kips, an engineer's shorthand unit representing 1,000 pounds, rather than in pounds. The standard 2-8-0 provided a good distribution of loads and, with the use of different loading, varied in standards all the way from E10 locomotives with a 10,000-pound loading on each axle to an E90 locomotive at a 90,000-pound axle.

Different standards of loading are then based simply on multiples of this E10 loading. Axle and uniform loadings for a Cooper's E72 loading, for example, are 7.2 times the values for an E10 loading. This makes it possible to compute tables of bending moments (the bending effect, representing force times distance), shears, and floorbeam reactions for an E10 loading that can readily be converted to the correct values for any class of loading by the use of a simple multiplier.

The loading standards for railroad bridge design have steadily increased over the years along with locomotive and train weights. During the 1880s, when Cooper first introduced his loading system, bridges were usually designed for loadings no greater than Cooper's E20. By 1894 Cooper was recommending the use of his E40 loading as a standard, and within another 20 years bridges were commonly being designed for a Cooper's E55 or E60 loading standard. One of the heaviest loading standards ever adopted was used for the Burlington's bridge across the Ohio River at Metropolis, Illinois, which was designed for a live loading of two Cooper's E90 locomotives, followed by a uniform train loading of 7,500 pounds per linear foot of track. For contemporary railroad bridge design the American Railway Engineering Assn. recommends the use of a Cooper's E72 loading for concrete bridges and an E80 loading for steel structures.

Tunneling

The art of tunneling has been practiced since ancient times. Early civilizations built a variety of underground shafts, temples, tombs, aqueducts, and the like, with some early Egyptian subterranean tombs dating as far back as 1500 B.C. The Romans were the greatest early tunnelers of all. One tunnel completed by Emperor Claudius in 52 A.D. to drain a lake east of Rome was 3½ miles long and took 11 years to build.

These early tunnels were built without machinery or explosives. Rock was most often removed by hammer and chisel. The Egyptians used channeling and wedging, a method in which wooden wedges were driven into channels cut into the rock, which was then broken out by the swelling action of the wedges when soaked with water. Still another method was to heat the rock to a very high temperature with fires and then to quench it with water, causing the rock to shatter from the sudden change in temperature. These primitive tunneling methods remained in use until the seventeenth century, when German miners began to drill and blast with gunpowder.

The first railroad tunnels were built in France and England between 1826 and 1830. The first in North America was at Staple Bend along the Conemaugh River on the Allegheny Portage Railroad near Johnstown, Pennsylvania. This was a 901-foot tunnel with an arch section 19 feet high and 20 feet wide that was driven through a slate hill during 1831–1832. The tunnel remained in service less than a quarter century before the entire Portage Railroad was rendered obsolete by completion of the Pennsylvania Railroad's all-rail route across the Alleghenies. The tunnel is still there, however, and is now part of the Allegheny Portage Railroad National Historic Site.

Among other early U.S. railroad tunnels were the Norwich & Worcester's tunnel at Tafts, Connecticut, and the Philadelphia & Reading's Black Rock tunnel near Phoenixville, Pennsylvania, both completed in 1837 and both still in service today. By 1850 some 48 railroad tunnels had been completed in the United States.

These early tunnels were typically driven through hard rock by laboriously drilling holes with hammer and chisel and then blasting with black powder. Removal of the excavated material, or mucking, was usually accomplished by means of horses and wagons or small railcars. Sometimes the surrounding rock was firm and stable enough that no additional support was required, but more often some form of timber or masonry lining was required.

Tunneling done in this way was exceedingly costly and time consuming. In drilling the Virginia Central's Blue Ridge Tunnel at Rockfish Gap, Virginia, which was the longest ever built in North America by hand drilling and black-powder blasting, the tunnelers averaged just 26.5 feet a month at a cost of $114 a foot. Tunnelers using the same primitive methods struggled ineffectually for some 15 years to drill the 4.75-mile Hoosac Tunnel in Massachusetts before the introduction of improved tunneling methods finally brought the project to a close.

The successful completion of the Hoosac and other great tunnels of the late nineteenth century, such as the even longer Mont Cenis, Gotthard, and Arlberg tunnels in Europe, clearly required better methods, and they came in the form of compressed-air rock drills, nitroglycerin, and dynamite that were developed during the 1860s. The new compressed-air drills mounted in batteries on a moving drill jumbo or carriage could complete the blast holes in a fraction of the time required for manual drilling; and the new explosives were nearly half again as effective as black powder, while their smokeless qualities eliminated the problems associated with the toxic fumes from powder.

In traditional tunneling methods the full cross section of larger tunnels, such as those for railroads, was usually not excavated at one time. The most common method of excavation for hard-rock tunnels was the heading-and-bench method. A heading, or drift, was a smaller segment drilled within the cross section of the tunnel. In the heading-and-bench method a heading the full width of the tunnel was driven at the top of the tunnel section, while the lower portion, or bench, was excavated later. Sometimes, too, hard-rock tunnels were driven in a series of headings. Quite commonly, tunnels constructed in this manner would be driven with as many as six to eight sep-

This drawing from *The American Railway* shows the typical timber and strutting used to support a soft-rock tunnel during construction. This temporary support was later replaced with a permanent lining of timber, brick, or concrete. In the foreground are the horses and dump cars used to remove excavated material. —Middleton Collection

arate drifts or headings. This had the advantage of allowing work to proceed at a number of different points along the axis of the tunnel, and it facilitated the placement of timber supports when needed.

Another approach often used for long rock tunnels was the center-heading method, in which a heading or drift at the center of the tunnel cross section was driven through from portal to portal and the tunnel then was enlarged to its full cross section by radial drilling from the center heading. For very long tunnels, a parallel heading was sometimes excavated first to establish a smaller pilot or pioneer tunnel. Transverse headings were then driven over to the main tunnel axis, allowing tunnel excavation to proceed in both directions from several locations. The pilot tunnel was used to transport materials and workers to and from the drilling faces and as a drainage and ventilation tunnel.

When support of the tunnel section was required to prevent caving-in of the tunnel roof or sides, it was usually provided in the form of temporary timbering and strutting, as it was usually called, that was installed in stages as excavation was completed. This temporary support was then replaced by a permanent tunnel lining, sometimes of timber, but more often of brick or later concrete.

Tunnels in soft or loose material required different methods of construction and always required both a temporary supporting structure and some form of permanent tunnel lining. Although small tunnels might be constructed in a single heading, larger railroad tunnels were typically excavated by a variety of combinations of multiple headings, followed by the installation of temporary timber supports and then the construction of permanent masonry or concrete lining.

Most of these soft-ground-tunneling methods took the name of their country of origin. The American method, for example, started with excavation of a top heading at the center, or crown, of the tunnel arch. This was then widened on each side, excavated down each side to the invert level, and finally excavated at the center. In the Austrian method excavation began with a full-height center heading, followed by widening of the tunnel arch to its full width, and then excavation of the lower section at each side of the tunnel. Still other variations were known as the Belgian, English, German, and Italian methods. In every case temporary timbering was installed at each stage of the excavation.

Tunneling under water presented an entirely different set of problems. The combination of hydraulic pressure with the soft or fluid material typically found in streambeds made it impossible to use ordinary methods, and there were few attempts at subaqueous tunneling before the early nineteenth century. The first important underwater tunnel was driven by Marc Isambard Brunel under the Thames River at London beginning in 1825. Brunel designed a novel cast-iron device called a "shield" that supported the soft clay of the riverbed as the excavation progressed. Wood boards in the front of the shield held the material in place. As each section was completed, a permanent brick lining was put in place and the shield moved forward by screw jacks to the next section.

The project proved both difficult and costly and took 18 years to complete, but it did demonstrate for the first time an effective method for underwater tunneling. A second Thames tunnel, completed in 1869 by James Henry Greathead, used a circular iron shield and a segmental cast-iron tunnel lining, which could be bolted in place much more rapidly than a masonry lining. Greathead completed his tunnel in less than a year.

At about the same time a similar tunneling project was being completed at New York by Alfred Ely Beach, a noted inventor and the editor and publisher of *Scientific American*. Beach used a cylindrical shield to drive a short subway under Broadway to demonstrate his design for a pneumatic subway. An important advance of the Beach design was the use of hydraulic rams, rather than screw jacks, to advance the shield.

Another New York tunneling project a few years later introduced the use of compressed air. This was a project to tunnel under the Hudson River developed by DeWitt Clinton Haskin, who had become interested in the use of compressed air caissons for underwater construction after James Eads successfully adopted the technique for the piers of the St. Louis Bridge. In 1874 Haskin patented a tunneling method that eliminated the use of a shield, using only air pressure to keep water out of the tunnel until the permanent lining was installed. The use of air pressure for underwater tunneling was an important advance, but the elimination of the shield was not. Haskin's company struggled for nearly 20 years to finish the tunnel. When another company finally completed the project in 1908, it was with a more conventional shield technology.

By the late nineteenth century these early efforts had formed the basis for a well-developed underwater tunneling technology that combined the use of compressed-air ground support during construction, a movable shield advanced by hydraulic jacks, and a segmental cast-iron tunnel lining. Its first major railroad application was for the Grand Trunk Railway's St. Clair River Tunnel between

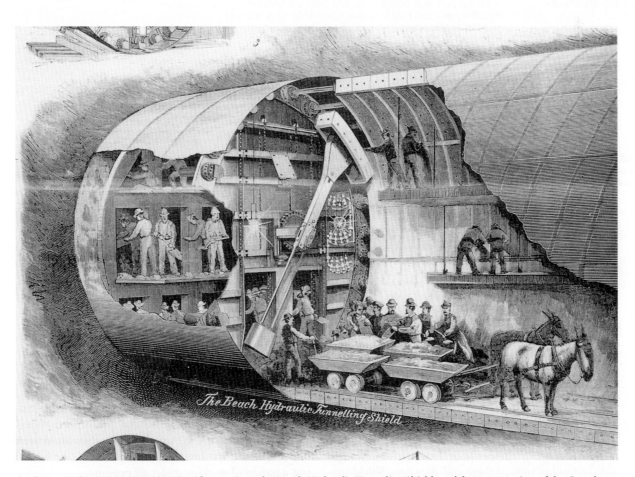

As shown in the August 9, 1890, *Scientific American,* the Beach Hydraulic Tunneling Shield used for construction of the Grand Trunk Railway's St. Clair River Tunnel between Sarnia, Ontario, and Port Huron, Michigan. At left, tunnel workers on three levels excavate material from the face of the shield through door openings. At the center, the shield is moved forward into the tunnel opening by hydraulic jacks. The rotating arm at the center is used to place additional sections of the cast-iron tunnel lining, while tunnel workers place and bolt the sections. Bottom right, mules and cars are used to remove the excavated material. —Middleton Collection

Table 3. Notable North American Tunnels

Name	Date	Construction and Material	Length and Grade	Notable Features	Present Status
Blue Ridge Railroad, Blue Ridge Tunnel, Virginia	1858	Hard-rock and earth tunnel. Built by hand drilling and black-powder blasting.	Tunnel length 4,264 feet. Eastbound grade 1.3 percent.	Longest tunnel ever built in North America with black-powder blasting.	Replaced by new tunnel in 1942.
Troy & Greenfield Railroad, Hoosac Tunnel, Massachusetts	1876	Limestone, gneiss, and slate tunneling. Started with manual drilling and black-powder blasting; work was not completed until development of compressed-air drilling and nitroglycerin blasting	Tunnel length 25,081 feet. Track grade rose to center of the tunnel from each end.	The greatest North American tunneling of the nineteenth century.	In service. Tunnel enlarged in 1998 for 20-foot double-stacks.
Grand Trunk Railroad, St. Clair River Tunnel, Ontario and Michigan	1891	Blue clay covering under St. Clair River. Built by hydraulic tunneling shield.	Tunnel length 6,050 feet. Descending grades from each side at 2.0 percent to the center point.	First major hydraulic shield tunnel.	Tunnel replaced by a larger tunnel in 1995.
Canadian Pacific, Spiral Tunnels, Kicking Horse Pass, British Columbia	1909	Hard-rock and compressed-air drilling and dynamite.	Two spiral tunnels to reduce grade. No. 1 upper tunnel was 3,206 feet with 234 degrees of curve; No. 2 lower tunnel was 2,890 feet with 282 degrees of curve. Eastbound grade is 2.2 percent.	Kicking Horse Pass reduced from a 4.4 percent to a 2.2 percent grade with two complete spiral tunnels.	In service.
Pennsylvania Railroad, Hudson River Tunnels, New York and New Jersey	1910	Hard-rock and compressed-air drilling and dynamite under New Jersey approach. Main Hudson River bore was a fluid material excavated by shield-driven, compressed-air tunneling.	Tunnel length of 2.76 miles from west side of Bergen Hill to 32nd Street and Ninth Avenue. Shield-driven tubes were 6,575 feet. Descending grade from New Jersey 1.3 percent, and the Manhattan descending grade 1.93 percent.	Twin tubes.	In service.
Michigan Central Railroad, Detroit River Tunnel, Ontario and Michigan	1910	Main underwater tunnel was drilled and prefabricated by "trench and tube" tunnel sections, with twin steel section loaded into place and filled with concrete.	Tunnel length was 10,175 feet. "Trench and tube" section under river was 2,620 feet. Eastbound approach 2.0 percent; westbound approach 1.5 percent.	First major use of the "trench and tube" tunneling method, since widely adopted by other tunnel projects.	In service.
Great Northern Railroad, Cascade Tunnel, Washington	1929	Main tunnel largely through granite, with mounted drill carriages and dynamite blasting. A single track was built with a paralleled access tunnel for multiple access.	Tunnel length was 41,152 feet (7.79 miles). The line descending from a westbound grade of 1.565 percent.	This new line was 501 feet lower than the earlier 2.63-mile tunnel and eliminated avalanches. The 7.79-mile tunnel was the longest in North America until Mount Macdonald tunnel was completed in 1989.	In service.
Canadian Pacific, Mount Macdonald, British Columbia	1989	Main tunnel built through hard rock, with conventional drill carriages and blasting on the 4-mile west end. The remainder was built with a tunnel-boring machine followed by conventional drill and blasting to the full size.	Tunnel was 48,304 feet (9.1 miles). The line ascending with a westbound grade of 1.0 percent.	The longest North American tunnel. The line handles westbound coal trains, while the older Connaught Tunnel continues to handle 2.2 percent grade eastbound traffic.	In service.

Sarnia, Ontario, and Port Huron, Michigan, which opened in 1891. Later shield tunneling projects included the Pennsylvania Railroad's Hudson and East River tubes at New York and a number of underwater subway, highway, and utility tunnels there and elsewhere. Shield tunneling was also widely used for other types of soft-ground tunneling, as well as underwater work.

Shield tunneling under water was always an exacting, risky business. A compressed-air "blowout" into the river bottom, which could send water cascading into the tunnel, was an ever-present danger in soft or silty soils. Tunnelers had to enter and leave the pressurized tunnel through air locks, and the length of time they could work under pressure was limited. Caisson disease (the bends) was a hazard of working under air pressure.

An alternate sunken-tube underwater tunneling method was pioneered by the Michigan Central's Detroit River Tunnel completed in 1910 between Windsor, Ontario, and Detroit. A trench was first dredged in the bed of the river along the alignment of the tunnel, and steel tunnel sections fabricated elsewhere were then floated into place over the trench and lowered into position. Using the steel sections as a form, exterior concrete was then placed around the tunnel from a barge above the trench. Once all the tubes and exterior concrete were in place, wooden plugs at the ends of each tube section were removed and the tunnel was lined with concrete. This procedure eliminated much of the dangerous and costly underwater work associated with shield tunneling and has been widely used ever since. The Transbay Tube under San Francisco Bay, completed by Bay Area Rapid Transit in 1969, covered 3.6 miles of sunken-tube sections fabricated elsewhere in a shipyard and sunk in place.

The development of new materials and types of heavy tunneling machinery brought substantial change to tunneling technology during the twentieth century. Some of the most notable projects included the Denver & Salt Lake Railroad's 32,799-foot Moffat Tunnel west of Denver, under the Rocky Mountains, completed in 1928, and the Great Northern's 41,152-foot tunnel under the Cascade Mountains, completed a year later. Recent examples of hard-rock tunneling have included drilling by full-face tunneling, in which the entire tunnel cross section is excavated at one time with the use of high-speed drills mounted on huge track- or rubber-wheel-mounted jumbo frames. Mucking, the removal of excavated material, is done with large mechanized loaders and trucks or mine cars. Prefabricated steel sections have largely taken the place of temporary timber supports. Precast-concrete sections have often been used in place of segmental cast-iron tunnel liners.

The greatest change of all, however, has come through the development of enormous tunnel-boring machines, which place a tunnel lining and excavate as they drive forward. For hard-rock tunnels these machines are typically fitted with a rotating head on which cutting tools are mounted. Hydraulic jacks force the cutting head against the rock face under heavy pressure. Tunneling machines for soft ground are sometimes fitted with some kind of rotating cutter head within a shield. A backhoe type is more effective in some soils.

The idea of these tunneling machines is nothing new. One was tried—and proved a failure—as early as 1852 on the Hoosac Tunnel. A 1914 textbook on tunneling identified no less than 46 patents that had been issued to that time for some sort of tunneling machine. But it was not until relatively recent years that reliable and effective machines were finally developed. Given suitable conditions, they have greatly reduced the time required for tunneling. Portions of the Canadian Pacific's new 9.1-mile Macdonald Tunnel in Rogers Pass, completed in 1989, were drilled by the top-heading-and-bench method, and a tunnel-boring machine drilled the heading. It proved capable of advancing the heading at rates of over 200 feet a day in some of the softer rock encountered.

The Canadian National's new St. Clair River Tunnel, completed in 1995, was drilled with an enormous soft-soil tunnel-boring machine that was fitted with spade-type and ripper teeth and twin disc cutters. The shield was pushed forward by hydraulic cylinders to cut through the clay of the river bottom. Guided by lasers and satellite navigation, the enormous machine advanced under the river averaging 26 feet a day, installing a segmented precast reinforced-concrete tunnel lining as it went.

While drilling has always been the most difficult part of tunneling, tunnel builders have faced other challenges. Whether beneath a river or in the heart of a mountain, water intrusion is almost always a problem; keeping it out in the first place, or draining it, can require some innovative engineering and construction work. Adequate ventilation is a requirement, and the longer the tunnel, the harder it is to achieve. Indeed, the problem of clearing locomotive smoke and gases remained a major barrier to the use of long or underwater tunnels until electric operation became feasible. The problems have become more manageable with diesel motive power, but a long, heavy-traffic tunnel still requires a substantial, high-capacity ventilation system. Table 3 lists some notable North American tunnels.

—William D. Middleton

Adapted with permission from the author's book *Landmarks on the Iron Road* and articles in the December 1999, January 2000, and February 2000 issues of *Railroad Model Craftsman*.

REFERENCES

Allen, C. Frank. *Railroad Curves and Earthwork*. New York: McGraw-Hill, 1931.

Beaver, Patrick. *A History of Tunnels*. Secaucus, N.J.: Citadel, 1972.

Black, Archibald. *The Story of Tunnels*. New York: Whittlesey House, 1937.

Brunton, David W., and John A. Davis. *Modern Tunneling*. New York: John Wiley & Sons, 1914.

Budd, Ralph. "Conquest of the Rockies." *Trains* 7, no. 12 (Oct. 1947): 42–55.

Clarke, Thomas Curtis, et al. *The American Railway*. New York: Charles Scribner's Sons, 1892.

Condit, Carl W. *American Building Art*. 2 vols. New York: Oxford Univ. Press, 1960, 1961.

Covington, Stuart. "Railroad Tunnels." *Trains* 6, no. 7 (May 1946): 11–21.

Crandall, Charles Lee, and Fred Asa Barnes. *Railroad Construction*. New York: McGraw-Hill, 1913.

DeLony, Eric. *Landmark American Bridges*. Boston: Bullfinch, 1993.

Hay, William W. *Railroad Engineering*. New York: John Wiley & Sons, 1982.

Jackson, Donald C. *Great American Bridges and Dams*. Washington, D.C.: Preservation, 1988.

Jacobs, David, and Anthony E. Neville. *Bridges, Canals & Tunnels*. New York: American Heritage, 1968.

Lauchli, Eugene. *Tunneling*. New York: McGraw-Hill, 1915.

Middleton, William D. *Landmarks on the Iron Road: Two Centuries of North American Railroad Engineering*. Bloomington: Indiana Univ. Press, 1999.

Modelski, Andrew M. *Railroad Maps of North America: The First Hundred Years*. Washington, D.C.: Library of Congress, 1984.

Plowden, David. *Bridges: The Spans of North America*. Rev. ed. New York: W. W. Norton, 2002.

Prelini, Charles, with Charles S. Hill. *Tunneling: A Practical Treatise*. New York: D. Van Nostrand, 1901.

Raymond, William G., Henry E. Riggs, and Walter C. Sadler. *Elements of Railroad Engineering*. New York: John Wiley & Sons, 1941.

Richardson, Harold W., and Robert S. Mayo. *Practical Tunnel Driving*. New York: McGraw-Hill, 1941.

Schodek, Daniel L. *Landmarks in American Civil Engineering*. Cambridge, Mass.: MIT Press, 1987.

Vance, James E., Jr. *The North American Railroad*. Baltimore: Johns Hopkins Univ. Press, 1995.

Vogel, Robert M. "Tunnel Engineering—A Museum Treatment." Paper 41, *Bulletin 240: Contributions from the Museum of History and Technology* (Smithsonian Institution) (1964): 203–239.

Webb, Walter Loring. *Railroad Construction: Theory and Practice*. New York: John Wiley & Sons, 1922.

Civil War Railroads

The American Civil War of 1861–1865 was the first major conflict in which railroads played a decisive role in military operations and economic mobilization. Their value was so appreciated by Union and Confederate leaders alike that rail arteries were identified as priority objectives during the four years of exhausting strife.

From the outset the basic resource equation was unequal. With a population of 22.3 million, the North contained 21,973 miles of railroad, 1.3 million industrial workers, and 4 million males of military age. The South had a population of 9.1 million, 9,283 miles of railroad, only 100,000 industrial workers, and 1.14 million potential soldiers and sailors.

In spite of bloody engagements, neither side proved able to inflict war-winning battlefield defeats upon the other. Military realities favored defending forces. Attackers could not mount lengthy campaigns unless they were supplied and reinforced by railroads and/or waterways. With few exceptions, military strategy during the war's final two years centered on a series of large-scale raids against the opposition's supply lines. Railroads and terminal cities were the most lucrative targets.

Northern Railroads in Wartime

Although the North's railroads were handicapped by varying track gauges and inadequate connections at terminal cities, by 1861 they had taken on many features of a true "system" that included four trunk lines ranging westward from the Atlantic Coast (New York Central, Erie, Pennsylvania, and Baltimore & Ohio). Multiple routes extended to Chicago and the Mississippi River. The manufacture of locomotives, freight and passenger cars, and rail was concentrated within states that remained loyal to the Union.

Still suffering from the economic effects of the panic of 1857, rail executives initially feared that wartime disruption would prolong their distress. Instead, business boomed. It was aided by the closure of the Mississippi River to agricultural export trade. River traffic was diverted to rail. Freight and passenger business rose briskly, and lines such as the New York Central and the Pittsburgh, Fort Wayne & Chicago ultimately posted annual freight volumes triple their prewar levels. The Pennsylvania Railroad alone carried 953,397 troops between April 1861 and December 1865.

Surging inflation and labor shortages cut into profits and compounded managers' challenges. Only locomotive engineers and telegraphers were exempt from the draft, but military officials often released other skilled workers to their former employers. Shortages of wood—and workers to cut it—prompted several carriers to begin converting to coal for locomotive fuel.

Although Congress in January 1862 authorized President Abraham Lincoln to seize railroads' property and take control of their employees when the public interest justified it, these powers were used sparingly, generally during specific large-scale movements of soldiers and their equipment. Northern railroads successfully met the needs of the military, commercial freight customers, and civilian passengers throughout the war, although they were nearly overwhelmed on some occasions. Only the southernmost main line, the Baltimore & Ohio through western Maryland, was seriously impaired by Confederate raids. B&O segments between Point of Rocks and Cumberland were disrupted for months at a time.

The Confederacy's Rail System

The South's rail network lagged behind in track quality, traffic density, available rolling stock, and the industrial capability to augment or replace essential equipment. Gauge variations and poor connections between railroads posed even more severe constraints than in the North. With few true trunk lines, the southern rail system in many ways resembled a loosely joined set of local routes. Key lines had been built to link coastal ports with the interior, but the Union's successful blockade of six of the South's ten leading seaports diminished their transportation value.

Even with these deficiencies, the South's railroads were adequate to support military requirements in the war's early stages. As long as the Confederacy's armies avoided catastrophic defeats and refrained from overly ambitious military campaigns northward, its railroads offered a useful network of interior lines to support a strategy that might enable the South to survive on the defensive if it could prolong the conflict until northerners became war weary.

For the most part the South's railroads remained under their owners' control, although compensation for military traffic was paid in Confederate bonds, worthless by war's end. Lacking a sufficient industrial base, rail managers confronted ever-worsening shortages of rolling stock and rail. Branch lines were torn up to provide replacement rail for main-line routes. Wartime inflation and labor shortages were more crippling than in the North. Over time the system's performance deteriorated markedly, and rail bottlenecks in Virginia reached dimensions that sometimes delayed supply trains supporting Gen. Robert E. Lee's forces for as long as 30 days. As invading Union armies wrecked track and captured vital terminal cities, conditions deteriorated even further.

By war's end much of the South's rail mileage was in ruins, along with the region's economy. A measure of relief was provided when the U.S. government sold equipment from the U.S. Military Railroads to southern railroads, but a few main lines were not fully restored until five years after the conflict had ceased.

The U.S. Military Railroads

Congress created the U.S. Military Railroads (USMR) in January 1862 to construct short routes to support the Union army and to operate lines captured in Confederate territory. Daniel C. McCallum, a former Erie Railroad superintendent, was named military director. Veteran railroader Herman Haupt was USMR's chief field operative and troubleshooter through the summer of 1863. An outstanding manager with a prickly personality, Haupt developed two guiding principles: military officers should not interfere with the running of trains, and freight cars were to be loaded and unloaded promptly to avoid their wastage as temporary warehouses. Enforcing these directives often required the intervention of Secretary of War Edwin M. Stanton.

Haupt achieved remarkable feats of rapid track repair and bridge replacement. His crews also were talented railroad wreckers, destroying bridges with a few well-placed powder charges and disabling locomotives by firing a cannon shot through the boiler. The process became so highly organized that 1,000 men could destroy 5 miles of track per day.

McCallum went to Tennessee in December 1863 to repair rail lines between Nashville and Chattanooga. In February 1864 he was placed in charge of military railways in the western region. McCallum's efforts sustained Gen. William T. Sherman's advances to the southeast. As Sherman moved through Georgia and the Carolinas, USMR personnel restored tracks and operations to support his 100,000-man army, which by then was ranging hundreds of miles beyond its sources of supply and reinforcement.

By war's end USMR operated 2,105 miles of railroad and used 419 locomotives and 6,330 freight and troop-hauling cars. The agency had rebuilt 26 miles of bridge structures and had laid or repaired 642 miles of track.

Railroads in Military Operations

Both the Union and the South quickly became adept at moving large troop formations to combat zones by rail,

In June 1862 General McClellan's battered army was obliged to fall back from its encampment at Chickahominy, east of Richmond. The railroads suffered as retreating Union soldiers set fire to trains of ammunition to keep them from falling into Confederate hands. The April 1864 issue of *Harper's New Monthly Magazine* pictured the destruction. —Middleton Collection

In April 1863 Col. B. H. Grierson led some 1,700 Union soldiers south on a daring raid across the full length of Mississippi and as far south as Baton Rouge. The February 1865 *Harper's New Monthly Magazine* pictured the destruction of track and railroad buildings during Grierson's raid. —Middleton Collection

A March 1867 *Harper's Monthly* view of the burnt railroad bridge on the Narrow Passage Creek, in the Shenandoah Valley between Front Royal and Strasburg, suggests that it had been wrecked at least twice. —Middleton Collection

Railroad transportation of troops and supplies proved vital in the conduct of the war. This woodcut from a contemporary periodical shows the arrival of the 16th Regiment of Ohio Volunteers under Colonel Irwine crossing the Baltimore & Ohio's spectacular iron viaduct across the Tray Run, near the Cheat River in western Maryland. —Middleton Collection

beginning with engagements in Virginia and later in the West. In July 1862 Confederate General Braxton Bragg transported about 30,000 soldiers from Tupelo, Mississippi, to Chattanooga, Tennessee, in a week's time—a journey of 776 miles via six different railroads. One year later the Union rushed 25,000 reinforcements from the Army of the Potomac at Washington, D.C., to Chattanooga in about 12 days. The 1,200-mile expedition involved 30 trains carrying troops, baggage, and ten batteries of artillery and their horses.

Early military activity centered in Virginia. Control of that state's railroads, along with the important rail terminal cities of Richmond and Petersburg, was contested in a series of battles and raids that continued throughout the war. The region west of the Appalachian Mountains, however, proved to be the decisive combat zone as the North endeavored to wear down the South's ability to fight.

In 1862 Gen. Ulysses S. Grant struck southward using river transportation through Kentucky and Tennessee, seized control of the navigable waterways, and broke the Memphis & Ohio's rail route from Memphis to northern Kentucky. As Grant continued his southbound march, he increasingly relied upon captured railroads for supplies and reinforcements. Gen. Don Carlos Buell meanwhile

took the industrial and rail center of Nashville, Tennessee. Grant then moved against the rail network of western Tennessee and northern Mississippi, including the Memphis & Charleston—described by one southern leader as "the vertebrae of the Confederacy." Grant captured Corinth, Mississippi, a major railroad hub in this network, but the Confederates repeatedly battled to win back the town.

By the time Grant had placed Vicksburg, Mississippi, under siege in 1863, he led a front-line force of 36,000 soldiers, but another 62,000 Union troops were tied up in rear areas to protect his fragile railroad and river supply lines against incessant raids and sabotage by Confederate guerrillas. During 1863 the Union army also ventured forth to break the railroads of eastern Tennessee, including the East Tennessee & Virginia, which President Lincoln ranked as an objective fully as important as capturing the Confederate capital city of Richmond. The ET&V and its connections served as the primary rail conduit between Virginia and the West. With the fall of Chattanooga and portions of eastern Tennessee, the South suffered a serious logistical reverse.

In February 1864 Grant sent a 21,000-strong contingent east from Vicksburg toward Meridian, Mississippi, another vital rail junction. The capture of Meridian, Grant believed, would cut off all rebel supplies originating in the entire state. The advancing army ruined Jackson and Meridian, destroyed 115 miles of railroad, and demolished 61 bridges.

During the assault on Georgia, General Sherman protected his rail supply line with armed blockhouses at every bridge and infantry units stationed at every depot. As he neared Atlanta, 160 carloads a day were moving by rail from Louisville to the front. In his memoirs the general noted that substituting wagons for rail deliveries would have required more than 36,000 wagons and 220,000 mules (plus the necessary teamsters and forage). It would have been an impossible undertaking in light of the abominable road network available to him.

When Atlanta fell in September 1864, the Confederacy effectively was cut in half, and a critical railroad and manufacturing center was lost to the South. As Sherman proceeded toward the coast, his forces destroyed 200 miles of railroad, including extensive sections of the Georgia Railroad between Atlanta and Augusta and the Central of Georgia from Macon to Savannah. By this time the South's supply system was in a shambles. Sherman's troops then headed north, wreaking havoc upon the tracks of the South Carolina Railroad, the Charlotte & South Carolina, the Wilmington & Weldon, the Wilmington & Manchester, and the North Carolina Railroad.

His army completed its roundabout railroad-supported journey with an invasion of Virginia from the south. General Lee's Army of Northern Virginia now was completely isolated and under unrelenting pressure from Grant's Army of the Potomac, which had captured Richmond. With munitions and other supplies nearly exhausted, Lee was compelled to surrender. The Confederacy collapsed.

—William J. Watt

REFERENCES

Black, Robert C., III. *The Railroads of the Confederacy*. Chapel Hill: Univ. of North Carolina Press, 1970.

Hattaway, Herman, and Archer Jones. *How the North Won*. Urbana: Univ. of Illinois Press, 1983.

Weber, Thomas. *The Northern Railroads in the Civil War*, 1861–1865. Westport, Conn.: Greenwood Press, 1952.

Classification

Classifications of U.S. railroads have been a longstanding requirement of the Interstate Commerce Commission (ICC) or (since 1996) the Surface Transportation Board (STB). Based upon the size and type of railroad, these classifications establish reporting and cost-accounting requirements.

The federal Act to Regulate Commerce of 1887 established the ICC, which authorized a uniform system of accounts for the railroads and required the submission of annual reports. The commission published the first annual report of its *Statistics of Railways in the United States* with the statistics for 1888. For more than 20 years the ICC classified U.S. railroads solely on the basis of operating mileage, with Class 1 representing operating companies of more than 1,000 miles, Class 2 lines from 600 to 1,000 miles, Class 3 lines from 400 to 600 miles, Class 4 lines from 250 to 400 miles, and Class 5 lines for all railroads under 250 miles.

Passage of the Hepburn Act (*see* REGULATION) in 1906 significantly expanded the scope of ICC control over the railroads. Among its provisions, the ICC was able to establish required procedures for a uniform system of accounts and reports. Following this revised system of accounting, the ICC reported annual statistical data under a revised classification system based upon different levels of annual revenues, beginning with the 1911 report of *Statistics of Railways in the United States*. First, line-haul companies, operating trains between terminals and stations, were subdivided by the commission into three categories: railways of Class 1, with annual revenues above $1 million; railways of Class 2, with annual revenues from $100,000 to $1 million; and railways of Class 3, with annual revenues below $100,000. Switching and terminal companies were subdivided from reports for line-haul companies. Beginning with the 1911 annual report, the ICC covered only Class 1 railroads, omitting Class 2 and Class 3 railroads and switching and terminal companies.

After nearly a half century in use without change, the ICC revised the annual revenue classifications for line-haul railroads beginning with the annual report for 1956. Companies with annual revenues of $3 million or more were now Class 1 railroads, while all other line-haul railroads were in Class 2; switching and terminal companies were excluded from the annual reports. Beginning with the 1965 annual reports, the minimum annual revenue for Class 1 railroads became $5 million.

The annual revenue threshold for Class 1 railroads was raised again to a minimum of $10 million beginning with the 1976 annual report. Just two years later, with the 1978 annual reports, the commission's classification of line-haul railroads was modified again, returning to three levels. Companies with $50 million or more in annual operating revenue were now in Class 1; those with revenues from $10 million up to the Class 1 threshold of $50 million were now in Class 2; and those with revenues below $10 million were in Class 3.

In 1982 the ICC began to adjust the threshold for Class 2 railroads annually by restating the 1978 revenue minimum ($50 million) on the basis of inflation, thus raising the 1982 annual threshold to about $82 million. Although Class 2 and Class 3 levels were annually adjusted on the basis of inflation, beginning in 1979 the ICC no longer required either Class 2 or Class 3 financial reports. In order to classify railroads other than Class 1 railroads in a more useful manner, the Assn. of American Railroads (AAR) in 1986 established two new classification categories. Railroads with an annual revenue level between $40 million and the minimum for a Class 1 level, or at least 350 miles of track, became Regional Railroads, while the remainder were categorized as Local or Switching and Terminal Railroads. The lower threshold for Class 2 railroads continued to climb with inflation, reaching a level of $94.4 million in 1990, for example.

The most recent change to the railroad classification structure was made in 1991, when the ICC adjusted the lower threshold of Class 1 railroads to $250 million, adjusted upward annually on the basis of the Railroad Freight Rate Index published by the Bureau of Labor Statistics. By 2000, for example, the lower threshold for Class 1 railroads had climbed to $261.9 million.

The many changes to the ICC, and later STB, definitions of the thresholds of U.S. Class 1 railroads make it difficult to compare statistical data for principal line-haul railroads. However, the combined effects of the historic trends to mergers and the impact of inflation have historically placed the great majority of railroad revenues in the Class 1 category, regardless of exactly how the revenue thresholds were set at any time.

With the new classification of U.S. railroads in 1911, 90 percent or more of total U.S. railroad mileage was shown in Class 1 roads, usually varying from 94 to 96 percent of the total until major changes in the classification structure were made in the 1980s. More important, Class 1 operating revenues typically accounted for about 96 to 99 percent of the total revenues until the mid-1980s.

Since that time the percentage of U.S. railroad lines classified as Class 1 has significantly declined. The new classification for Regional Railroads established in 1986, together with the higher thresholds for Class 1, has moved a number of railroads from Class 1 to a Regional classification. At the same time, Class 1 carriers have sold off a significant mileage of low-density trackage to regional or local carriers or abandoned it. In just the ten years from 1990 to 1999, for example, the total U.S. mileage of Class 1 railroads declined by almost 10 percent from these sell-offs. Total revenues for Class 1 railroads now represent about 91 percent of the total, while Class 1 track mileage is now down to 71 percent.

—William D. Middleton

REFERENCE

Railroad Facts or similar annual publications have been published by the Assn. of American Railroads or predecessor publishers since 1923. These publications provide a comprehensive guide to major indicators of railroad performance. Recent data are available from AAR at www.aar.org.

Classification Yards

The main job of a railroad classification yard, whether it is a handful of tracks in a crowded city or a sprawling hump yard on an open plain, is to build trains and break them down. Often attached are functions such as locomotive servicing and intermodal ramps, but these are sideshows. Railroads are an efficient means of moving products because they consolidate many shipments into a single train. Yet the fundamental process of consolidation can be time consuming and expensive. Cars might roll across desert and plain at 60 mph, but then disappear into yards for 24 hours or more. It was railroading's original problem, and it remains one today.

Individual cars are gathered from shippers' docks, assembled into trains for travel to another yard, and then segregated for delivery to receivers' docks. While no two cars in a train may have the same origin and destination pair, they do travel between common intermediate points. By placing yards at those intermediate points, railroads can run trains built of many cars between the yards and maximize their line-haul advantage.

The classification yard's mission is deceptively simple: create order out of chaos by classifying cars into the right place in the right train at the right time. A train is an ordered assemblage of blocks. A block is a group of cars bound for a common destination. The yard's job is to sort, or classify, cars so that each car is placed in a block on a train that will take it closer to its final destination.

Loose-car railroading is an inherently time-consuming and costly activity. Yet as long as general merchandise traffic exists that cannot be moved in trainload quantities, railroads will have to sort cars in yards. Because carload traffic usually demands a higher rate than bulk or intermodal traffic, its value is sufficient to justify the expense of yards. The challenge for the future, then, is to move cars through the yard as quickly and cost-effectively as possible.

Location of Yards

From the very beginning, the availability and cost of land influenced yard location. Early railroads often started their lines on the urban fringe rather than in downtown areas; in 1827 the Baltimore & Ohio began construction at Mt. Clare rather than central Baltimore. As cities grew and hemmed in the first yards, railroads built large new yards on inexpensive tracts of land far beyond city limits. Surviving yards in urban areas tend to be used only for direct support of local switching or have been converted to intermodal yards.

Today's yards are preferably located at the point of funnels from several main lines; for example, North Platte classifies almost every east-west car moving across Union Pacific except for those moving on the former Southern Pacific Sunset and Golden State routes. With few exceptions, yards are not located in major cities on the East or West Coast because land prices are too high.

Yards are rarely located at interchange gateways either, because railroads do not want to share investments and operational control of joint yards. This is not new: Belt

Railway of Chicago's Clearing Yard sat idle for nearly ten years after completion in 1902 because railroads would not pay the switching fees the Belt levied on its users, even though most of these users were also the Belt's owners. The modern-day equivalent is St. Louis, which railroads avoid because of slow transit times and high switching fees. A major hump yard was proposed for East St. Louis, Illinois, in the 1950s and again in the 1970s; instead of building the new yard, however, carriers preferred to invest within their own systems. New York Central, for instance, upgraded its Big Four Yard in Avon, Indiana (near Indianapolis) in 1960 rather than invest in a shared facility at St. Louis.

In the 1950s computerized controls enabled railroads to increase throughput at hump yards, allowing them to consolidate the work of smaller hump and flat-switching yards to their largest and most strategically located hump yards. For example, New York Central's $14 million automated hump yard in Elkhart, Indiana, which opened in 1958, enabled the railroad to close 11 other yards. Ten years later Penn Central opened a rebuilt yard at Selkirk, New York (the last of New York Central's five electronic hump yards), which absorbed the work done at DeWitt Yard in Syracuse, New York; only fifteen years before, DeWitt and the Pennsylvania's Enola Yard had been the two largest hump yards in the United States.

Mergers accelerated the pattern of yard consolidations. Hamlet, North Carolina, was an ideal place for the Seaboard Air Line to build a hump yard since its main north-south and east-west lines crossed there. But when successor CSX abandoned the Seaboard main line north of Raleigh, North Carolina, in favor of Atlantic Coast Line's parallel route, Hamlet Yard was in the wrong place. Although Hamlet is still a convenient classification point for east-west Atlanta-bound traffic, most north-south traffic today is flat-switched at CSX's Rocky Mount, North Carolina, yard.

Even some of the largest yards have vanished, notably Richmond, Fredericksburg & Potomac's 526-acre Potomac Yard near Washington, D.C. After CSX acquired RF&P, it sent a significant portion of Potomac Yard's work to Rocky Mount. Norfolk Southern's rerouting of north-south traffic from Washington to Hagerstown, Maryland, drastically reduced the number of cars handled at Potomac, while Conrail's deemphasis of north-south movements and the loss of carload traffic to truckers on I-95 meant that no new business was forthcoming. RF&P ended all classification work at Potomac Yard in 1990 and leveled the hump; by the end of 1992 only a handful of run-through tracks remained.

Opened by the Pennsylvania Railroad in 1906, Enola Yard sat at the junction of east-west and north-south PRR main lines near Harrisburg, Pennsylvania, and once held the title of world's largest yard. Under Conrail, which concentrated on long-haul east-west business, Enola became superfluous; its hump was shut down in 1993, and its classification work was divided between Allentown, Pennsylvania, and Conway Yard west of Pittsburgh.

But since NS's 1999 takeover of Conrail, north-south traffic has grown, and hauling cars 100 miles east or 260 miles west of Enola for classification has become costly, time consuming, and contradictory to the operating plan. NS spent $1.9 million to upgrade 31 tracks in Enola Yard, boosting switching capacity from 125 to 600 cars a day. With Enola back on line, the railroad was able to add 4 new trains and abolish 11 others. Presently Norfolk Southern is continuing its program of reinvestment at Enola with the goal of reopening that facility as a hump yard.

However, Enola's 2001 reopening is the exception, not the rule. The number of classification yards, particularly hump yards, is declining: fewer than 70 remain of the 152 such yards operating in 1975. Downtown yards are especially vulnerable because the land they occupy is extremely valuable.

The Evolution of Classification Yards

Two basic types of yards are in use today: flat yards and hump yards. In flat yards, locomotives move cars around; in hump yards, gravity also helps classify cars. Additional obsolete yard types include gravity and poling yards.

Flat Yards

A flat yard consists of little more than a set of parallel tracks interconnected by switches in a ladder arrangement—a switch lead at each end gives access through the ladder to each yard track. Cars can be moved in blocks, or they can be individually sorted. When cars are grouped in blocks, they are typically moved with their air brakes operational to give the engineer better control over the movement. When cars are individually sorted, the air brakes are usually released or "bled off" first.

To classify individual cars, a switch engine kicks the cars, first by accelerating rapidly and then braking hard while a switchman pulls the uncoupling lever. Given momentum and now cut loose, the car rolls into a yard track, slowed only by friction or collision with standing cars. This process, called drilling, is repeated until the engine has sorted an entire cut of cars or train; then it begins anew with the next.

Drilling imparts numerous and often-damaging shocks to cars and cargo unless the locomotive takes each car to a coupling. It usually requires one or more crewmembers on the ground to hand-throw switches and manually uncouple cars. To get a reasonable level of production, work must be done quickly, which is both labor intensive and dangerous to the inattentive or unskilled.

Flat yards are simple to design, inexpensive to build and operate, and versatile. However, they are limited by their inability to classify large numbers of cars efficiently or to build a large number of blocks and are rarely called on to switch more than about 1,000 cars a day. Flat-yard productivity depends more on the number of back-and-forth moves than number of cars handled. A 1960 study found that for each group of cars switched, the first car required an average of 3 minutes, 10 seconds to classify, but only an additional 17 seconds were required for each additional car going into the same track at the same time.

Poling Yards

The major disadvantage of flat switching is the need to repeatedly accelerate and decelerate a whole train in order to impart energy to only the leading few cars. The most direct way to avoid this disadvantage is to move only the leading cars while allowing the rest of the train to remain stationary.

In poling, a locomotive moved on a track parallel to the switching lead, positioning itself behind and slightly to the side of the cut to be moved. Power was transmitted through a pole laterally to the rear of the cut to be moved. Each car had a socket at each corner, known as a "poling pocket," to receive the pole and reduce the chances of slippage or accident. Sometimes a special car, with poles on all four corners, was built to precede the engine.

The pole yard, now obsolete, offered advantages of higher capacity over flat switching. The engine had better control over car speed because it did not have to accelerate a large body of cars, but only the single cut being switched. Since it only had to move a few cars at a time, an engine could provide sufficient speed to a car in a short distance. Car riders were frequently employed in poling yards to control car speed by means of the hand brake.

The poling technique was refined to a point that two cuts could be started at once. Two cuts, coupled, were released from the rest of the train and propelled by a pole on the rear car of the first cut. When the cuts were rolling at a speed proper to the second cut, the coupling between the two cuts was released. The engine again accelerated, moving the first cut far enough ahead of the second to enable throwing of the switches between cuts.

Poling is no longer used in the United States. Although it was superior to flat switching for medium-traffic yards (500 to 1,000 cars per day), gravity switching eventually proved even more advantageous and decidedly safer.

Gravity Yards

To sort even larger numbers of cars efficiently, at an early date railroads began using gravity to assist the switch engine. Yards that took advantage of gravity switching were constructed in Europe as early as 1846. Gravity yards were not hump yards as we think of them today; tracks were built on an incline, so once hand brakes were released, the cars began rolling downhill. Operations were aided by the European practice of mounting hand brakes on the sides of the cars, rather than on the ends, and by uncoupling cars before sorting began.

The European gravity yard did not translate to North American practice. North American freight cars will not work in a gravity yard because of their automatic couplers. When a string of cars with automatic couplers is stretched out, the coupling pins are held so tight that the couplers cannot be released until slack is compressed. Once slack is introduced to loosen the pins, the couplers may reengage unless the uncoupling lever is held up continuously.

Hump Yards

The American solution to allow gravity sorting was the hump yard (Figure 1). By shoving a train to the top of a raised hill, or hump, usually about 30 feet high, cars can be uncoupled just ahead of the hump crest while the couplers remain compressed. At this point the cars are manually uncoupled and allowed to roll by gravity into any one of several dozen classification tracks. A certain minimum distance is needed between cars to facilitate safe switching. Processing rates vary according to the design of each facility, but three to four cars a minute is typical for U.S. yards. This corresponds to a comfortable walking speed for pin pullers who uncouple each car as it crests the hump. The humping operation is considered a success if all cars recouple at speeds not exceeding that of a brisk walk (4 mph), no cars stop short of the coupling point, and cars do not collide or "corner" each other in the track switches.

To accomplish this while maximizing the capacity of the yard requires some means for controlling car speeds and regulating the spacing of cars as they roll through the switches. Two main methods for controlling car speeds are in use today: conventional "clasp" retarders, which slow cars down using friction by squeezing the car wheels, and Dowty retarders, which build up pressure in hydraulic cylinders mounted between the rails as the car wheels roll over them. Yards controlled by "clasp" retarders are also known as "target-shooting" yards, since control is applied only at discrete points, as opposed to Dowty yards, which continuously control car speeds. Target-shooting yards are by far the most common in the United States today, although Dowty yards are gaining increasing acceptance in spite of their higher initial cost.

Unlike flat yards, which are most efficient at switching large cuts of cars that remain together, hump yards work best when cars arrive mixed up. In fact, multiple-car groups cause problems in the automatic retarders used to control speed. Groups of cars accelerate differently than single cars, which can cause the retarder control computer to miscalculate the amount of retarding force needed. Typically, yard managers find it better to hump cars individually, rather than in groups.

The Pennsylvania Railroad was the first to use gravity switching in North America, although it is unclear in which yard it was first used. Droege (1925) says that the first yard was built in 1882 at Huff's Station, near Greens-

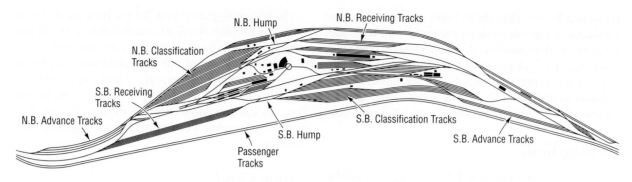

Figure 1. A typical modern hump classification yard is shown in this drawing of the Richmond, Fredericksburg & Potomac's Potomac Yard. —Rick Johnson

burg, Pennsylvania. While some gravity switching might have been done at Huff's on an experimental basis, there is no evidence that a hump yard was ever constructed there. Other sources say that PRR's Honey Pot yard near Wilkes-Barre, Pennsylvania, was first. Droege confirms that humping operations occurred at Honey Pot as early as 1899. In 1902 the Pennsylvania did build a hump yard at Youngwood, Pennsylvania, a few miles south of Huff's on subsidiary South-West Pennsylvania Railway's line to Connellsville, Pennsylvania. Both Honey Pot and Youngwood yards sorted coal cars, for which freight damage claims were not much of an issue.

Railroads soon realized the potential of gravity switching for all types of traffic. To reduce damage to equipment and cargo, workers rode free-rolling cars down the hump, manually setting hand brakes to control the collision speed with standing cars. A significant challenge in rider yards was the need to get the riders back to the hump. If the hump ran out of riders, switching stopped. Hump grades were not as steep as those used today, and yard tracks typically branched off a central ladder: this provided access to all switches without requiring a switchman to cross the tracks, improving safety, and also allowed one switchman to work two switching leads at once, increasing productivity.

Rider humps required a tremendous amount of labor, so in the early twentieth century companies such as Union Switch & Signal and General Railway Signal developed mechanical retarders. Retarders grip each car's wheel flanges and brake it to just the right speed to not couple too fast to standing cars already in its track.

Automated hump yards represented a major step forward in yard productivity, but introduced a new set of operational problems, many of which continue to plague classification yards today. Indiana Harbor Belt, a New York Central subsidiary, was the first to install automatic car retarders at its Gibson, Indiana, yard in 1924. While car riders could adjust speed any time by tightening or loosening hand brakes, automatic clasp retarders only slow cars down at predetermined points. Cars must be released from the retarders at a speed fast enough to clear the switching area, but slow enough to prevent damage when coupling to standing cars in the yard. However, not all cars roll the same, and some of the factors affecting car "rollability" are unpredictable. Loaded cars roll faster than empty cars, and more force is needed to reduce their speed—a performance gap that will only widen as cars continue to get heavier. Wind, temperature, rain, snow, and ice affect not only cars, but also the retarders. Since gradients in older yard tracks were originally designed for friction-bearing cars, the hump grades may be too steep for modern cars; in some yards roller-bearing-equipped cars actually accelerate after passing through the retarders.

Automation required a radical rethinking of yard design. To minimize the likelihood of cars catching up to one another, the distance from the hump to the last bowl-track switch was made as short as possible by redesigning the classification yard in what is known as a balloon-track formation. To assemble trains of more than one block, blocks of cars are flat-switched at the trim end of the yard, pulled out of the classification tracks, and coupled to other blocks in the departure yard.

Most hump yards today are subdivided into three distinct areas with specific functions: the receiving yard, the hump and classification tracks, and the departure yard. Inbound trains arrive in the receiving yard, and the locomotives (and in the past, cabooses) are cut off and moved to their servicing area. The cars are inspected for mechanical defects, and the air is bled from their brake systems, allowing them to roll freely.

As soon as possible, the hump engine (typically a special locomotive that develops high tractive effort at low speeds) reaches into the receiving yard for the former train and shoves it over the hump for gravity classification in the bowl tracks. In this way cars bound for the same destination can be grouped in one classification track and even sorted into proper order (so-called infinite blocking) for ultimate delivery to customers' receiving docks. Most often, each car is cut individually in the humping process and routed from the yardmaster's switch list, which lists each car and the track to which it is headed. Sometime a group of cars all destined for the same yard will be humped together in a group. At the hump summit a yard brakeman or "pin puller" verifies

CLASSIFICATION YARDS

that all car numbers are correct and then pulls the uncoupling lever. In the third area, the departure yard, blocks of cars are pulled from the yard's "trim" end—that is, the opposite end of the classification tracks from the hump—by switch engines and moved into departure tracks. There, air hoses are reconnected, road engines are coupled on, air brakes are charged and tested, and the train receives a final inspection before it departs.

This time-consuming second handling is the limiting factor in yard productivity today and costs more than the first handling at the hump. Two or three trim crews are needed to pull cars from the yard at the rate a single hump crew can put cars into the yard; if the trim crews are working on ladder tracks so close together that they interfere with each other, productivity will drop even further.

Small yards often combine the arrival, classification, and departure yard functions on a single set of tracks, which makes them more flexible than large facilities. But small yards typically rely on flat switching and therefore are not as efficient as larger hump yards for car-by-car sorting.

Yards also provide a broad variety of support functions. They provide space to store empty cars waiting for a new assignment and hold loads awaiting final delivery to a customer's siding. Entire trains can be stored out of the way should a shortage of crews or motive power, congestion, or a disruption on the main line delay their further movement. And because cars and locomotives converge on yards, they are the ideal location for car-repair and locomotive-servicing facilities and train crew accommodations.

Though some U.S. hump yards once classified more than 3,000 cars a day, the increasing weight and length of modern freight cars has cut yard capacity; a typical hump yard now classifies 2,000 to 2,500 cars a day. Conversely, in Europe and South Africa, where small two-axle cars are the norm, some yards can process up to 5,000 cars a day across a single hump.

Blocking Theory

Before 1900 limitations of draft gear and air brakes restricted train sizes. Long trains with the old "straight-air" system experienced violent slack action when brake applications were made; 25 cars were the practical maximum train length. All yards were flat-switched and consisted of just a few tracks. Each yard had the capacity to make classifications only for the next yard up or down the line and local destinations. Trains left the yard several times a day as needed, often once a predetermined number of cars or volume of tonnage had accumulated.

In essence, cars were "bumped along" from yard to yard until they reached their destination. In an era when trains were limited in tonnage to whatever a locomotive could stagger over each subdivision's ruling grades with, the bump-along system was successful because it minimized

cost while maximizing each train's available capacity. Since cars were only bumped along from one yard to the next, and trains left each yard several times a day, yard delays were short. Yet despite the short yard times, overall transit times were irregular because of the erratic tonnage-driven nature of train operations, and because cars were switched so often.

The first wave of hump-yard construction in the United States occurred in the first two decades of the twentieth century. Most of these yards were built in the intensely industrialized, rail-heavy Official Territory (Chicago to the Atlantic Seaboard, north of the Ohio and Potomac rivers), with notable large yards built at Clearing, Illinois, Enola, Pennsylvania, De Witt, New York, and Brunswick, Maryland.

These expensive new hump yards created a dilemma that ultimately led railroads to radically change not just their blocking policies, but their entire method of train operation and management. Historically, local supervisors developed the classification policy that best met the needs of their own division. Hump yards could create systemwide savings, but not as long as classification policy was set division by division. Accordingly, railroad management and control, which previously had been highly regionalized, began to accumulate to the central headquarters in the 1920s.

Two essential approaches to planning the movement of cars were characterized in 1908 by M. L. Byers, chief engineer of the Missouri Pacific Railroad, as *extreme deferment*, where no classification of a car is made until it has arrived at the yard nearest its final destination and is then uncoupled from cars going to yards beyond (the bump-along system), and *extreme anticipation*, where each car is classified at the first possible yard it visits, that yard bringing together all cars bound for the same destination and building trains in blocks arranged by the blocks in the order in which subsequent yards follow (the system often used today because it minimizes the number of times each car is handled). Between these two extremes are an infinite variety of possibilities. Byers realized that the anticipation method required considerably more switching work overall, but would ultimately allow cars to move faster between endpoints if a car's destination was a large city because the anticipation method shifts switching work to outlying yards that have the capacity to handle more cars. The number of switching moves needed at successively smaller yards closer to urban areas was reduced, allowing those yards to operate more efficiently.

Hump yards changed the economics in favor of the anticipation method. Their ability to collect large numbers of cars (compared with a typical small flat-switch yard) made it possible to hold cars until enough were on hand to run them as a solid train. Presorting cars could be done more economically and efficiently at hump yards, and further cost savings could be realized from the reduced switching work at flat yards. Using hump and flat yards together in this fashion is called support blocking.

The major operational change was a switch from deferment classification to anticipation classification, pioneered by the Rock Island in 1923. Traffic growth had pushed the railroad's yards to capacity, and projected growth would soon overwhelm them. The Rock Island then had no hump yards nor funds to build any. Its solution was to study the traffic of its entire network and establish (for the first time) a systemwide car classification policy. The policy set an explicit blocking plan for each yard, along with detailed train schedules and a list of blocks handled by each train. Yards began building trains in a specified order, and train arrivals were spaced for a consistent flow of work. Departing trains were designated by class, from divisional local freights to "main-trackers," or run-through trains, which ran across divisions between major terminals, bypassing intermediate yards with restricted setouts or pickups en route.

Administered from Rock Island headquarters in Chicago, the operating plan achieved dramatic results. Within three years time spent by trains in yards dropped

42 percent. Reliability improved as well. In 1923 only 2 percent of the cars moving between Little Rock and Chicago arrived at their destination within five days; an additional 8 percent arrived on the sixth day. By 1925, 25 percent of the cars arrived within five days and another 26 percent on the sixth day. At Silvis, Illinois, where the number of cars handled increased 15.6 percent between 1923 and 1926, yard engine hours dropped by 11.6 percent. Impressed, other railroads adopted preblocking plans. By the 1950s the anticipation method had become the primary classification policy of most railroads. Nonetheless, the costs of building and operating yards remained high. In 1932 yard operations were directly responsible for 54 percent of total railway cost, and the number of switch engine hours was 50 percent greater than the number of road engine hours.

Although hump yards are still a railroad's most efficient means of classifying carload traffic, they also contribute to car delays. In 1923 the average car traveled only 27.8 miles a day. By 1956 this had improved to 48.3 miles

Southern Pacific's radar-controlled hump classification yard, Englewood Yard in Houston, Texas, was the first of its kind in the Southwest when it opened in 1956. In the foreground are the hump and control tower, followed by a single set of master and six group retarders for the 48 classification tracks. —Bert Brandt & Assoc., *Trains* Magazine Collection

and by 1965 to 51.7 miles. However, average daily mileage for general merchandise cars has not budged much since 1965 and recently dropped because of merger-related problems. In the past, the time and expense of collecting, sorting, and switching cars was simply passed on to customers. But price a shipment too high today, or fail to move a car from point A to point B in a reasonable amount of time, and the business goes to trucks.

Modern Classification Yard Practice

Hump yards today are high-tech wonders with tremendous room and capacity. Union Pacific's Bailey Yard at North Platte, Nebraska, the largest classification yard in the world, occupies 2,850 acres, stretches 8 miles from end to end, contains 315 miles of track, and handles 10,000 cars a day, of which 3,000 are humped. More typical is Norfolk Southern's Conway Yard west of Pittsburgh, Pennsylvania, just under 4 miles in length and covering 568 acres.

The trend toward "anticipatory" preblocking that began in the 1920s has only accelerated in recent years. As train sizes continued to increase, railroads began collecting cars into a block for a whole day rather than just for eight hours to allow the greatest possible number of bypass blocks to be built. Extending the car-collection time was necessary to build blocks and trains of economical size. Reverting to the previous deferment policy to keep cars from sitting in yards for inordinate amounts of time was by then impossible, as *Modern Railroads* explained in July 1973: "Adherence to the old policy would find the yard

being 'gutted' at four-, six-, or eight-hour intervals. Its inventory would then be dumped on the next yard down the line. Congestion would move from one yard to the next with no improvement in service to shippers."

This deliberate, planned increase in dwell time at major yards was considered a reasonable price to pay for the benefit of reduced yard handling overall. Long-haul cars could travel a considerable distance before having to be classified again, and for them overall transit times were reduced. Short-haul traffic did not benefit nearly as much from preblocking, yet the cars were still subject to the same added delays at each major yard. Shippers, fed up with the increase in delivery times, began switching their short-haul traffic to trucks.

By the 1960s many railroads were in perilous financial straits and looked for ways to save money anywhere they could. They returned to a tonnage-actuated operating philosophy, running trains only as needed, while still trying to build complex multiblock trains for bypassing yards. In the 1920s, when simple bump-along blocking was in use, train frequency could be adjusted without much effect on service. Bypass blocking changed that. Now the system depended on a regular schedule of departures, regardless of train length, and yards ran smoothly only when train schedules were strictly adhered to. Thus as frequency dropped, and train service became sporadic, cars missed their connections, and already-lengthy yard delays were further aggravated.

Instead of addressing this inherent conflict between tonnage railroading and scheduled operations, most railroads simply redoubled their efforts to implement more anticipatory blocking. At the same time they reduced their investments in yard facilities. The situation spiraled as railroads scrambled to build smaller blocks while holding cars longer in yards that were chronically congested. Ultimately, the added yard handling cost per car outweighed any benefits of preblocking the traffic.

Most railroads chose to return to some form of scheduled operations, recognizing that the key to better service is not deemphasizing yards. Probably the best example is Canadian National's 1998 implementation of a scheduled operating plan for merchandise and intermodal trains, including a detailed trip plan for every car moving on the system. Trip plans and train schedules are based on seven operating principles, four of which directly pertain to yard handling: minimize dwell time in yards; limit systemwide classifications per car to two whenever possible; concentrate classification work at major terminals; and space train arrivals at yards for a steady workflow.

Key to making CN's system work is a strict adherence to the schedule. That commits the railway to running a train whether or not there are enough cars to justify its cost. Thus to maximize train capacity, CN broke with tradition and now mixes intermodal, carload, and bulk traffic rather than moving each in separate trains. For instance, merchandise trains are filled to tonnage with grain that once moved in unit trains. This allows CN to run more bypass trains to a greater number of destinations. In 2001 on-time performance for carload traffic was over 90 percent; CN now uses 800 fewer locomotives and 22,000 fewer freight cars than previously for about the same amount of business.

New Ideas

New ideas for new yards are abundant. Original—even radical—approaches have been successfully applied on European, Japanese, and South African railroads. North American railroads, by contrast, have made only incremental changes to the design and operation of yards in order to meet narrow, specific goals: reduce costs, add processing capacity, and build more blocks to eliminate intermediate classifications.

One simple way to boost yard capacity is to add another set of retarders. Most hump yards have only two sets: master and group retarders. A third set of tangent-point retarders at the entrance to each classification track enables a higher speed to be maintained through the switching area and reduces the likelihood of cars catching up to one another or being misrouted. Tangent retarders also allow cars to be spaced closer together, increasing hump capacity.

An even better solution is to install Dowty retarders. Named for the British company that first developed them, these look like mushrooms springing up next to the rails. A Dowty retarder consists of a hydraulic piston-and-cylinder so positioned that a wheel flange depresses the piston as the car passes over. A valve in the retarder

slams shut if the car's speed exceeds a preset value, forcing hydraulic fluid through a narrow orifice. That resists the downward pressure of the wheel and slows the car. If the car is moving slower than the preset speed, the valve remains open, so the cylinder compresses without resistance. A closely related design, the spiral retarder, works on the same principle. Spiral retarders are more powerful but also more expensive.

For the highest hump capacity, precisely uniform speeds must be maintained throughout the switching area. A special variation of the Dowty retarder actually speeds the car up for just this purpose. A boost is applied if a car is moving slower than the target speed, a retarding force if a car's speed is too high. Although Dowty retarders are self-contained, boosters require an external power supply. The first boosters, installed at British Rail's Tinsley Yard, used power supplied by hydraulic lines. These lines proved leaky and maintenance-prone and were easily damaged in derailments. A newer design, powered by compressed air, is environmentally friendly and was installed at Spoornet's yard at Sentrarand, South Africa, and at some European yards. The boosters at Sentrarand have been operating successfully for more than two decades, although none have been used in North America.

A critical goal for yards is to eliminate the bottleneck flat switching at the trim end. Herringbones are a special track arrangement for doing just that. These consist of a group of yard tracks constructed in sets of three or more. A central running track is connected to outside classification tracks by means of crossovers. These crossovers divide the outside tracks into "pockets" for receiving and storing blocks of cars. During classification, cars roll down the center running track until they reach the appropriate crossover. At that point, they are diverted into the side-pocket classification track. A car stopper prevents cars from running out the end of each pocket. Once all the cars for the outbound train have been collected, the car stoppers are retracted. A locomotive then backs into the blocks of cars until they are coupled together.

If a train consists of more blocks than the herringbone track has pockets, it may be necessary to double into an additional track to collect the remaining blocks. Although the concept dates at least to 1912, it was strongly advocated in a December 1957 *Trains* article by George Billmeyer ("The Trainmaker: Yard of the Future?"). Herringbones were actually built in 1968 at Koriyama Yard in Japan and in 1975 at Sentrarand. Only the Sentrarand herringbones are still in use today.

In practice, the use of herringbones is not as simple as the design might suggest, which is part of the reason they have not been installed in many yards. A significant difficulty is maintaining proper spacing between cars throughout the entire length of the long central running track. Too much retardation would cause cars to stop short. Too little would either send cars crashing into standing cars or rolling out the far end. Should a fast car catch up to a slower one in front of it, the faster car would be misrouted.

Another drawback is cost. Since the central running track must be kept clear, it cannot be used for classifying cars. Thus to have 200-car holding capacity, nearly 300 cars of track length must be built. Herringbone yards must be equipped with power switches, Dowty retarders, and car stoppers, all of which add to their cost. The only way to justify the enormous capital investment of herringbone tracks is to keep them in constant use building trains, because they are too costly to be used only as storage tracks. This need for rapid turnover is not compatible with the once-a-day train departure policy typical of North American railroad operations. The herringbone yard, in sum, offers only a partial solution to the yard problem.

Another way to process cars faster is to replace the flat switching that takes place at the trim end of today's yards with additional humping. Cars from an inbound train are pulled back from the classification tracks by way of the escape tracks, then onto one of the dual hump-lead tracks, where they are shoved over the hump in the usual fashion. The cars are then repeatedly pulled out of the classification yard and rehumped to sort them behind other cars already in the yard, using a multiple-stage switching technique called triangular sorting. By use of this process, a train composed of several blocks can be assembled so every block is in proper sequence ready for departure. The train is built ready-to-go on a single classification track without the need for a trim-end switcher. A train of as many as six blocks can be built using only three tracks.

—Edwin R. Kraft

© 2002 *Trains* magazine. Used with permission.

How Humping Works

In a target-shooting yard the goal is to release each car at exactly the right speed to safely couple to those cars already standing in the classification tracks. The earliest target-shooting yards ran manually. Beginning in 1964, digital computers became the primary means for monitoring and controlling all yard hardware, as well as keeping track of all the cars in the yard. Modern computer systems are easily capable of tracking 18 or more distinct moving groups of cars. Spacing criteria and speed predictions are updated continuously, and the computer or tower operator addresses situations that could bring about collisions or sorting errors, even on short notice.

The process is perhaps best illustrated by following a car from the hump crest to the coupling point in a typical yard. Figure 2 shows the essential physical features of such a yard. The cars are pushed at a speed of not more than about 2½ mph over the crest of the hump, which may be 20 to 30 feet above the level of the classification or bowl tracks. Just after uncoupling, the car passes between

Figure 2. A typical hump classification yard, with cars descending from the hump crest at left through a scale, master retarder, and group retarders before entering individual classification tracks. —Courtesy of *Trains* magazine

a vertical array of spotlights and photocells, where its height and length are measured. The car passes over a scale as it accelerates through a length of straight track, often called master test section, where the car's rolling characteristics are measured. Either wheel detectors or radar are used to measure the car's travel times over the test section, which permits the process-control computer to calculate an average acceleration for the car. The car's acceleration, combined with the grade of the test section, wind, and other factors, leads to an estimate of its rolling resistance.

By the time the car leaves the master test section, its speed is between about 8 and 15 mph. The car enters the master retarder, where its speed is reduced to a uniform value for all cars, such as 9 mph. The retarder mechanism does this by gripping the wheel flanges with varying degrees of force for controlled periods of time such that the desired exit speed is achieved.

Slow-moving "hump" engines pushed a train of cars over the hump for classification. A Milwaukee Road "cow and calf" humping engine idled in front of the retarder tower at St. Paul's Pigs Eye Yard during shift change in the winter of 1959.
—William D. Middleton

A hump engine made up of two switchers and a yard "slug" pushed the last car and the caboose over the hump at the Southern Railway's automated Spencer Yard in Linwood, North Carolina, in September 1982. —William D. Middleton

An aerial view of the Pennsylvania Railroad's Enola Yard near Harrisburg, Pennsylvania, shows the descent of cars from the westbound hump in the background through the master and group retarders. Two elevated towers visible at the left control the master and group retarders. —Pennsylvania State Archives (Tom Hollyman Aerial Photographs, MG-286, Penn Central Railroad Collection)

Immediately below the master retarder the tracks diverge into groups, each of which has its own test section for measuring rolling resistance and its own group retarder. The track at this stage has curves and a lower grade than the master test section that cause cars to accelerate differently than they did before. The accuracy of the measurement and control processes are critical because the group retarder is the last point of control of speed before the car enters the individual classification tracks, unless a third stage of tangent-point retarders is used further on.

Maintaining consistent performance in target-shooting yards can be a problem, given the constantly changing mix of car types and their mechanical conditions. Temperature variations, wind, rain, and snow all have significant effects on the "rollability" of freight cars. Temperatures below about 20°F substantially increase the bearing friction for both friction and roller bearings, largely because of the increase in viscosity of the lubricants. (However, as cars roll, their bearings warm up, making the rollability of cars often difficult to predict.) The height of the hump is largely dictated by the need to move the "stiffest" car to the

Hydraulic retarders grip the car wheels on either side to slow a descending car to the required speed. This was on a master retarder at the Milwaukee Road's Pigs Eye Yard at St. Paul, Minnesota. —William D. Middleton

A tank car is slowed to the required speed by the master retarder at the Pigs Eye Yard on a snowy night in 1959. —William D. Middleton

end of the farthest track on the coldest day of the year. In practice, one would not make the hump that high, because excess retardation would be required on other days. Thus cars often stall part way down the hump on very cold, windy, or snowy days. Indeed, winds have a major effect on freight cars, particularly empty ones. There have been cases in some yards when lightweight empty cars, such as bulkhead flatcars, have even been blown back toward the crest of the hump or out the opposite end of the yard. Side winds can also have quite unpredictable effects, particularly on curves.

Most gravity-yard computers try to make a correction for the measured wind speed and direction, but this is not always successful. The algorithms take into account the car's height, length, weight, and travel direction, and perhaps other factors. Corrections for wind usually take the form of an additive or subtractive adjustment to the rolling resistance wherever that value is used in a calculation.

Industry groups such as the American Railway Engineering and Maintenance-of-Way Assn. (AREMA), the signal companies that design and equip these yards, and individual railroads have all conducted research into engineering design and operation of gravity retarder yards. For a relatively brief period in the 1970s and 1980s the U.S. Department of Transportation (DOT) sponsored studies of gravity yards, and these both confirmed experi-

ence and yielded greater insights into yard physics and optimization. The area of yard design has also received significant attention internationally, where other hardware practices and standards are in use.

SRI International, Menlo Park, California, carried out one notable study under a contract with the Department of Transportation's Transportation Systems Center (now the John A. Volpe National Transportation Systems Center) at Cambridge, Massachusetts. This study collected data at five hump yards in different regions of the United States. The study focused on providing information and understanding of freight-car rolling resistance distributions, factors affecting car rollability, and rollability measurement methodology. Data for several thousand cars classified at each yard over a period of months were collected and analyzed by various techniques. Since many factors influenced the motion of each car, it was not a trivial problem to connect cause with effect. Nevertheless, some general results did emerge.

The study confirmed the rule that "light cars roll harder than heavy cars." The average 30-ton boxcar had a rolling resistance approximately 54 percent higher than the average 80-ton boxcar.

Gondola cars, flatcars, and tank cars on the average had higher rolling resistances than boxcars. All other types behaved essentially the same as boxcars (of the same weight).

One surprising result was the nearly identical rollability of roller-bearing and friction-bearing cars, although the latter are now rare in the car population. This did not agree with dynamometer measurements on trains and locomotives, or with other studies.

The expected strong dependence of rolling resistance on speed was observed. A linear fit of the form

$$RR = a + bv$$

is adequate until speeds exceed about 15 mph.

A study of the difficult area of wind effects yielded a rule of thumb that the rolling resistance of a car increases by about 0.2 lbs/ton for each 1 foot/second of headwind. As temperatures increase, rolling resistance decreases.

Freight cars and the weather are not the only variables. Yards themselves are not static. Rails wear, grades change, joints loosen, detectors are replaced, and yard management criteria change. The task of keeping the yard "in tune" is never-ending. At the newer yards sufficient statistics are kept for the system to be self-tuning. That is, the software, based on a statistical analysis of recent performance, periodically adjusts the track constants. At many yards, however, this task is carried out manually, and much of it depends on a seat-of-the-pants approach used by experienced railroad personnel.

—Dennis C. Henry

REFERENCES

American Railway Engineering Assn. *Manual for Railway Engineering*, Ch. 14. Chicago: American Railway Engineering Assn., 1976.

Droege, John A. *Freight Terminals and Trains*. New York: McGraw-Hill, 1925.

Henry, D. C. "Some Physics at the Railroad Hump Yard." *Physics Teacher* 20, no. 4 (Apr. 1982).

U.S. Dept. of Transportation. Federal Railroad Administration. *Proceedings of the October 1979 Workshop for Classification Yard Technology: A Status Report on Yard Research*. Report No. FRA/ORD-80/17. May 1980. Also available through the National Technical Information Service, Springfield, Va.

Wong, P. J., et al. *Railroad Classification Yard Technology Manual*. Vol. 3, *Freight Car Rollability*. U.S. Dept. of Transportation, Transportation Systems Center. Contract DOTTSC-1762. July 1981. Available through the National Technical Information Service, Springfield, Va.

Clergy Passes

Starting in the early days of the railroad, religious organizations depended on clergy passes to carry out their charitable duties. Railroads granted clergy passes, either trip or annual, to ministers, missionaries, evangelists, Sisters of Charity, and others engaged exclusively in work of a religious nature. In order to receive passes, a member of the clergy had to go through his denomination or organization, and that organization had to substantiate its position as a nonprofit agency committed only to the propagation of religion.

Traffic managers of the different religious groups had to keep careful records in the issuing of passes to their clergy and forward them on schedule to the railroad companies. For annual passes, forms indicated the railroad used, pass number, times used, and miles traveled. The number and amount of any cash fares also had to be noted. For trip passes, only the record of the railroad and the miles traveled were required.

If persons did not use their annual pass over enough lines, indicate enough miles, or file their records on time, the annual privilege could be denied the next year and would be given to another person or organization that would make better use of it. Similar rules would apply to the use of trip passes. If the trip pass was not used within the day limit, it had to be returned to the railroad before another pass could be issued to that person. Because each railroad had a limit of passes available, there were always more requests than passes that could be issued. As an example of the variety of passes used on one trip, one evangelist received an annual pass No. 15329 from the Southern Pacific, as well as a North Western trip pass No. 132206, Chicago to Omaha and return, and a Union Pacific trip pass No. 187625, Omaha to Seattle and return.

The lines in the less traveled routes, such as those in the northern and northwestern parts of the country, were not as strict about the issuance of passes. In some cases, if the railroad management was sympathetic toward one religious organization or biased against another, it could give special favors or withdraw favors.

Most of the railroads would not grant clergy passes to women, and that included women who were ordained. The Sisters of Charity seemed to be an exception. Although Mrs. C. W. Cutler was a graduate of Kansas Bible Seminary and an ordained minister who helped with her husband's ministry, the Great Northern Railroad refused when her church requested a pass for her. Some passenger associations would grant a half-time pass good on all its lines to anyone who qualified under their definition. Others would only grant passes to those residing within the states traversed by their railroad. Different districts of the same company might have different rules for clergy passes. Edwin Bell, traffic manager of the Northern Baptist Convention, reported his concern over the proper use of clergy passes in 1941. "We are very careful never to abuse our privileges in any way. The railway companies trust us, and we surely want them to continue to do so."

—Wilma Rugh Taylor

REFERENCES

"Clergy Permits." *Dallas Morning News*, June 6, 1898.

Correspondence from Edwin A. Bell and W. G. Brinson, traffic managers for the Northern Baptist Convention to missionaries in service. Files of the American Baptist Historical Society, Valley Forge, Pa.

Clinchfield Railroad

The Clinchfield Railroad was a 277-mile line running north and south across the Blue Ridge Mountains between Elkhorn City, Kentucky, and Spartanburg, South Carolina. It was built between 1905 and 1915, quite late—almost an afterthought to the era of railroad construction—but late enough that it could take advantage of modern construction methods. Its original purpose was to bring coal out of the mountains and hand it over to other railroads for distribution throughout the Southeast, but it became a bridge railroad, carrying automobiles and other manufactured goods south from Michigan and Ohio and fruit and vegetables north from the Southeast.

The idea of such a railroad had been around for much of the 1800s, but the mountains were daunting. They run from northeast to southwest, and a north-south railroad would have to cross numerous ridges and zigzag to find river valleys it could follow. In 1900 the only piece of the future Clinchfield in existence was the Ohio River & Charleston, which consisted of a few miles of track near Johnson City, Tennessee, hundreds of miles from either the Ohio River or Charleston, South Carolina.

In 1905 the South & Western Railroad was incorporated and almost immediately became affiliated with a coal-mining syndicate. In 1908 it was renamed the Carolina, Clinchfield & Ohio Railway; by 1909 it reached from Dante, Virginia, south to Spartanburg, South Carolina. In 1915 it was extended north from Dante to a connection with the Chesapeake & Ohio's Big Sandy District, which ran south from the Ohio River at Ashland, Kentucky. At Spartanburg the CC&O connected with the Charleston & Western Carolina, a subsidiary of the Atlantic Coast Line.

The Atlantic Coast Line and Louisville & Nashville railroads jointly leased the CC&O in 1924 (ACL had controlled the L&N since 1902) and created the Clinchfield Railroad Co., an unincorporated entity, to operate the CC&O. The creation of the Seaboard System at the end of 1982 by the merger of Seaboard Coast Line (itself the product of the merger of Atlantic Coast Line and Seaboard Air Line) and Louisville & Nashville made the existence of the Clinchfield Railroad unnecessary. The Clinchfield became part of the Seaboard System at the beginning of 1983.

The Clinchfield was notable for having no significant branch lines. It was not a major passenger-train operator. In the years before World War II it operated a daily local train the length of its main line. By 1951 that train operated three days a week each way, and it was discontinued in the early 1950s. In 1968 the Clinchfield resurrected a Ten-Wheeler built in 1882 that had been decaying behind the road's shop in Erwin, Tennessee, and operated excursion trains up and down the railroad for several years. The operation was noteworthy because of the apparatus for controlling diesel locomotives from the cab of the steam locomotive. The diesels were necessary because the Ten-Wheeler could pull no more than two steel passenger cars.

In 1982, its last year before the Seaboard System merger, the Clinchfield operated a system of 296 route-miles and 494 track-miles, with 98 locomotives, 5,291 freight and company service cars, and 825 employees. Freight traffic totaled over 4,104 million ton-miles in 1982, and coal (50.2 percent), chemicals (13.3 percent), and stone, clay, and glass (7.8 percent) were its principal traffic items. Clinchfield achieved a 90.8 percent operating ratio in 1982.

—George H. Drury

REFERENCES

Helm, Robert A. *The Clinchfield Railroad in the Coalfields*. Forest, Va.: TLC, 2005.
McBride, H. A. "The Clinchfield Route." *Railroad* 62, no. 3 (Dec. 1953): 16–33.
Shafer, Frank E. "Here Comes Clinchfield!" *Trains* 20, no. 10 (Aug. 1961): 30–39.

Coal and Railroads

Coal is the single most important commodity moved by North American railroads in terms of volume and from the industry's earliest days has been an extremely important source of revenue as well. Early railroads were often built to facilitate the movement of coal (and other minerals) from mines to river docks, ports, or points of consumption to feed America's growing needs for fuel and power. In England, too, the earliest railroads were often constructed to move coal from mines to the cities that sprang up during the Industrial Revolution.

Initially the U.S. coal trade centered on the Richmond Basin in Virginia. Lack of economical transportation, however, limited the growth of this trade, and by the early nineteenth century anthracite coal from Pennsylvania was an increasingly important commodity. Also known as hard coal, anthracite had much higher heat values than bituminous coal. It burned cleaner and therefore was suitable for home heating. Because of its high heat value (BTU content), anthracite was also ideal for smelting ores used in iron and steel production. By the 1830s anthracite was an important fuel both for heating and for powering foundries and other manufactories. In 1853 more than 1,300,000 tons of coal were shipped from Ohio mines. These mines became increasingly important with the arrival of new railroads that made transportation of this valuable fuel more economical. By the turn of the twentieth century important northeastern railroads such as the Reading, Lehigh Valley, and others found anthracite movements into major eastern markets to be their single most important source of revenue.

Railroads were ideal for moving large volumes of coal

Modern coal loading uses large silos such as these for low-sulfur western coal storage near Gillette, Wyoming. The coal is moved by truck and conveyers into the silos and then is loaded into a moving unit train of coal hoppers. This 110-car Burlington Northern train was loaded in about two hours. —Burlington Northern, *Trains* Magazine Collection

and other bulk minerals to markets or ports. First, railroads could serve areas not accessible by water. In addition, because of the nature of minerals such as coal, horse-drawn wagons were extremely expensive for moving such products. Trains moved minerals to distant locations, obviating the need to rely solely on water transportation with its limited geographic reach. Because mining companies could market their coal over much longer distances, vast new business opportunities opened up.

Second, by supplying specialized open-top gondolas and hopper cars to shippers, railroads encouraged the movement of relatively dense products over their lines. The use of specialized equipment for moving coal helped railroads keep costs down by increasing the ratio of net weight to tare weight. During World War I, for example, the average hopper car carried about 50 tons of coal. These freight cars gradually became larger, and 70-ton cars were prevalent during the middle part of the twentieth century. The average coal car carried 109 tons in 2000;

Electrically operated coal-car dumpers used by the New York Central and the Baltimore & Ohio at Toledo, Ohio, were capable of dumping a car per minute of coal destined for Canadian and western U.S. Great Lakes ports. The ship was the *Howard M. Hanna, Jr.,* of Wilmington, Delaware. —Baltimore & Ohio, *Trains* Magazine Collection

This Canadian Pacific coal dock at Fort William (now part of Thunder Bay), Ontario, unloaded coal from Great Lakes ships for rail movement to the west in this early twentieth-century photograph. —Middleton Collection

C. P. R. Coal Docks, Fort William, Ont.

by 2002 cars with a 100- to 115-ton capacity were the norm.

A third reason railroads became the primary means for coal transportation was their own need for this fuel. Railroads used prodigious amounts of coal to operate trains and to fuel their numerous shop facilities and other buildings.

Even into the late twentieth century railroads continued to find ways to move coal more economically. Using specialized freight cars that can hold more than 110 tons of coal, often with aluminum carbodies, the industry has become more efficient. Railroads have also used longer trains with more efficient locomotives as another way to keep costs down. For instance, the Union Pacific is moving trains of up to 135 cars long powered by only three high-horsepower locomotives. These and other efficiencies continue to reduce the cost of moving coal over long distances. Most coal today moves in unit trains, which are dedicated trains that usually move coal from only one mine to one receiver.

Over the past several decades coal markets have shifted, affecting North American railroads in significant ways. Historically, coal moved from mines centered in the Appalachian region and the Midwestern Illinois Basin to major markets. These included electric utilities, steel mills, and the export market. After the U.S. Congress passed the Clean Air Act Amendments in 1970, many electric utilities were given the choice either to scrub higher-sulfur coal or to burn cleaner coal in order to reduce sulfur dioxide and other emissions. Conse-

Growing tonnages of export coal traffic and the development of new "supercolliers" to transport it have required the development of equally large, deep draft piers. Pier No. 6 at Norfolk, Virginia, is 1,636 feet long and 82 feet wide, with a 50-foot draft. The Panamanian collier *Cape Eagle* loaded coal in August 1997. —William D. Middleton

quently, beginning in the 1970s, enormous reserves of very low-sulfur coal were exploited in Wyoming's Powder River Basin. This led to a major shift in coal production from the East and Midwest to the West, ultimately including mines in Montana and Colorado as well. This provided a major benefit to the Burlington Northern Railroad (now Burlington Northern Santa Fe) and subsequently the Union Pacific, because both carriers today serve most of these western mines. Mining in the Midwestern Illinois Basin coalfields declined dramatically during the same period, resulting in a corresponding decline in revenue to several important midwestern railroads.

Western coal is so important that it has encouraged a regional railroad, the Dakota, Minnesota & Eastern, to propose extending a new connection from its line in South Dakota into Wyoming's Powder River Basin as a third competitor to move coal east. The proposed new line would cost more than $1.5 billion.

To illustrate how important coal is today, the United States saw production of more than 1 billion tons of coal in 2000. Approximately 905 million tons of that total, or 88.6 percent, were used to generate electricity. Sixty percent of the electricity in the United States is produced by coal. Railroads handled more than 607 million tons into the electrical generation market in 2000, or 67.1 percent of the utilities' total generation by coal. Other power sources for generation of electricity include nuclear, natural gas, oil, and hydroelectric. Nonutility coal, such as coking coal used in blast furnaces, as well as conventional coal for heating plants and other industrial users, accounted for 116,642,000 tons in 2000, of which the railroad market share was about 54 million tons, or 46 percent.

In 2000, U.S. railroads moved about 27,763,000 total carloads. Of that total, coal accounted for 6,954,000 carloads, or about 25 percent. Those same carloads, however, represented 757.8 million tons, or 43.6 percent of all tons carried by U.S. railroads in 2000.

Another way to look at the importance of coal to railroads is to examine revenue generated. Also in 2000 railroads generated about $36.331 billion of freight revenue. Coal contributed about $7.794 billion, or 21.5 percent of total revenue generated. The next principal category of freight moved by railroads in terms of revenue, chemicals and allied products, by comparison accounted for only $4.68 billion in freight revenue and 1,860,000 carloads.

—Thomas G. Hoback

REFERENCES

EH.Net, www.eh.net/encyclopedia/adams.industry.coal.us.php
Railroad Facts. Association of American Railroads, Oct. 2001.
Other statistics came from the Energy Information Administration (EIA), Office of Coal, Nuclear, Electric and Alternate Fuels published by the U.S. Department of Energy, Washington, DC 20585.

Coffin, J. S. (1861–1935)

Joel S. Coffin was active in the railway supply and locomotive-building industries. He was born on February 17, 1861, in St. Clair County, Michigan. His first job was as a blacksmith's helper. At age 19 he became a machinist's apprentice in the shops of the Chicago & West Michigan Railroad. He later worked as a locomotive engineer and in 1892 joined the Galena Signal Oil Co. He was promoted within the ranks at Galena, then located in northwestern Pennsylvania in the small town of Franklin, and became manager of its mechanical staff in 1896. By 1907 Coffin was a vice president of the Galena company.

In 1902 Coffin organized the Franklin Railway Supply Co. In 1911 he quit his regular job to devote full time to his own company and began to take over or create more new businesses devoted to making appliances for steam locomotives. In May 1910 he organized the American Arch Co. and a month later the Locomotive Superheater Co. He had acquired a valuable business partner by this time, Samuel G. Allen (1870–1956), an attorney who would remain with Franklin until his last days.

In 1916 the two partners purchased and reorganized the Lima Locomotive Works, determined to rebuild it into a major manufacturer of steam locomotives. Their energy and foresight were remarkable. They faced formidable competition in the field from Baldwin Locomotive Works and American Locomotive Co., both well-established firms. The partners wisely hired new talent to jump-start the Lima operation. John E. Dixon, originally with the Brooks Locomotive Works, was made vice president of sales, and William E. Woodard was put in charge of engineering. Within a few years Lima was producing very advanced and successful designs and began to capture a larger portion of new locomotive orders.

Franklin Railway Supply and its various subsidiaries began to produce a greater variety of locomotive appliances: feedwater heaters, booster engines, stokers, power reverses for valve gears, grate shakers, tandem main rods, and even patented lock nuts. One of the most ingenious of these new appliances was the pneumatic fire-door opener. This allowed a fireman to open the firebox door by depressing a foot treadle; thus he could use both hands to control the shovel. The door opener was designed by one of Franklin's more gifted inventors, Albert G. Elvin, who also designed a stoker marketed by Coffin and Allen for several years.

All of these products made the two partners rich. Coffin served on several corporate boards, including that of the Chase National Bank. He clearly had a talent for finance, as well as engineering. He joined many clubs and enjoyed an active social life. He easily relocated to the fashionable New York City suburb of Englewood, New Jersey, and maintained a fancy suite of offices on East 42nd Street. In fact, all the officers of Franklin—including W. E. Woodard—lived in or near Manhattan, and none would consider residence in Lima, Ohio, Franklin,

Pennsylvania, or other such rustic locations in industrial America.

Coffin died on March 11, 1935. Some of his business empire outlived him for nearly half a century. The demise of the steam locomotive in the 1950s brought an end to Franklin, Lima, and several other related enterprises. The Superheater Co. was reorganized as Combustion Engineering in December 1948 and flourished as a producer of giant steam boilers for the electric power industry, but it too fell on hard times and closed by about 1990.

—John H. White, Jr.

REFERENCES

Moody's Industrial Manual, 1955, pp. 2740–2742.
National Cyclopaedia of American Biography.
Who's Who in Railroading, 1940.

Cog, Rack, or Mountain Railways

Ordinary railroads are not capable of working grades much over 5 percent, and most U.S. main lines rarely attempted grades much over 2 percent. Cable-operated inclined planes (*see* INCLINED-PLANE RAILWAYS) and rack railways were used where heavy grades could not be avoided. Most rack railways have a toothed rack placed in the center of the track. A gear or cog powered by the locomotive engages the rack and so pulls the train forward. The cog drive also helps control the train's speed as it descends. Most North American rack lines are, or were, short scenic or tourist railways.

The first rack railway on record was opened in June 1812 near Leeds, England, at the Middleton Colliery (coal mine). It was a nearly level railway, but the mine manager, John Blenkinsop, felt that a positive form of traction was needed, and so he patented a side-of-the-track cog railway propulsion system. The locomotives were designed and built by Matthew Murray of Leeds. The engine weighed only five tons but could pull loads of up to 140 tons at a speed of 3½ mph. The system worked well, and more rack-style engines were built for use elsewhere in Britain and Germany at Murray's machine shop. The Middleton Colliery line was a commercial success and operated its original 1812–1813 locomotives until 1835. Meanwhile, other early British railways decided that conventional adhesion worked well enough for normal operations on comparatively level railways.

The idea of rack propulsion was revived in the United States in 1825 by Col. John Stevens of Hoboken, New Jersey. The rack was placed in the center of a circular track located on Stevens's estate, part of which served as a public garden and amusement park. The small four-wheel steam wagon operated around a 630-foot-long oval track. It was not a toy but a full-size machine with a vertical water-tube boiler. This modest rack railway had little long-term influence but did demonstrate to a doubting American public that steam traction was a practical reality.

The rack was a forgotten technology for another 20 years until it was unexpectedly revived in one of the flattest states in the Union. Indiana's first railroad, the Madison & Indianapolis, made its way northward from the Ohio River, starting in 1837. Ten years later the line opened to the state capital. Most of the route traveled over level territory, but at the southern end, a hill 413 feet high separated Madison's riverfront from a plateau just behind the town. A straight inclined track was completed through the escarpment in 1841. A deep cut held the grade to 5.8 percent. Cars were let down the grade by gravity, but eight horses were needed to pull one car uphill. Traffic over the incline expanded once the railroad reached its northern terminus, and it became clear that a better plan for working the incline was needed. A cable-operated incline was the most obvious solution, but the railroad's master mechanic, Andrew Cathcart, had a better idea. Actually he borrowed the idea of a local resident named William Hoyt for a rack railway proposed in about 1845. But Cathcart greatly improved it, retaining only Hoyt's scheme for a cast-iron rack. In his patent of October 23, 1849, Cathcart proposed a locomotive with four cylinders and a rack-and-pinion drive on a countershaft at the middle of the engine. Two of the cylinders were connected as on a conventional locomotive, but the other two were placed upright and connected to cranks on the end of the countershaft. A small steam cylinder placed on top of the boiler raised or lowered the cogwheel drive to engage or disengage the rack. The rack, made in 3-foot-long cast-iron segments, was fastened to the center of the track. When the rack was disengaged, the locomotive could be operated like a conventional locomotive. The rack and the drive gear were very broad and measured 8 inches wide. The Baldwin Locomotive Works completed an eight-wheel engine on Cathcart's plan in December 1847, almost two years before the patent was granted.

The railway itself was not ready for rack operations until November 1848. Braking was achieved by working the engine in forward motion while backing down the grade so that the cylinders acted as air compressors, and the power thus consumed acted to retard the train's downward travel. A steam brake was used as well. Although the system worked well enough, the engines proved costly to maintain because of all the extra machinery, and their progress up and down the 7,000-foot-long incline could be heard all over town, especially when the cog drive misengaged the rack. Cathcart retired from the M&I about 1855. One of his successors, Reuben Wells, decided that the noisy rack operation was no longer needed and designed a massive 55-ton, 0-10-0T conventional adhesion locomotive that proved equal to the job; the rack system was abandoned in 1868. The big adhesion locomotive is on display at the Children's Museum in Indianapolis.

Just as the southern Indiana rack operation was closing down, a new cog railway was nearing completion in New Hampshire. Like most North American cog lines, this was a scenic railway, built to carry tourists 3 miles up to the peak of Mt. Washington, part of the White Mountain range and the tallest mountain in New England. Sylvester Marsh was a native of the area who had made a fortune in the Chicago grain market. Marsh moved back to New Hampshire in 1865 with plans to build a cog railway up Mt. Washington. He obtained a state charter for the line in 1858 but had difficulty convincing many others that such a line could be constructed. He was told that it would be as easy to build a railway to the moon. Marsh began to mature his plans and obtained three patents in the 1860s for cog railways. In August 1866 he completed a mile-long demonstration track to answer his critics and prove that such a railway was practical. The base station was fairly well up the mountain's lower slope, so the actual climb to the top was only 3,600 feet and not the full 6,288 feet that Mt. Washington rose above sea level. The work was almost finished in October 1868, but early winter storms prevented completion of the last segment of the railroad until the following summer.

The line opened on July 3, 1869, and remains in operation to the present time with the same technology. The rack, made on Marsh's design, was fabricated from angle irons and 1½-inch pins riveted between in the form of a ladder. The pins were placed on 4-inch centers. The engines were also built on a peculiar plan created largely by Marsh. The antique nature of the operation is underscored by the continued use of coal-fired steam locomotives. Reflecting the line's inclined operation, the boilers were tilted. These small four-wheel engines work at a furious pace, but because of a gear drive they move along at only about 3 mph. The braking and propulsion are done through the cogwheel drive. The wheels are loose on the axles and have no brakes. A manually operated drum brake is mounted on the driving-wheel axles. It is useful, but it is more of a parking brake than a service brake. The downward speed of the trains is controlled by the four pistons of the locomotive. The valve gear is set in forward and no steam is admitted to the cylinders; thus the pistons work as an air pump and so slow the progress of the train. The air is pumped into the boiler and is vented slowly into the atmosphere. A small jet of water is let into each cylinder to prevent overheating and to lubricate the pistons. A ratchet wheel on the axles allows the engine to move forward; should it lose power or become disabled, the pawl will stop the engine from rolling down the grade on the upward ascent.

New Hampshire's Mt. Washington Cog Railway has continued to operate behind steam locomotives ever since the line opened in 1869. The 3½-mile railway climbs to an elevation of 6,288 feet. Powered by locomotive No. 3, *Agiocochook*, an upbound train approached the water tank and siding at Waumbek in 1996. —William D. Middleton

Typical of most tourist lines, the Mt. Washington railway does not operate during the winter season. The average grade is 25 percent, and the steepest part of the track is a fearsome 37 percent. Even so, the safety record of the mountain-climbing line was excellent. The railway operated without a single fatality until an accident marred the 1929 celebration of the line's 60th anniversary. The line's original locomotive was refurbished and operated for the occasion. A tooth in the cogwheel broke, causing the cog gear to jump out of the rack rail. Before safety devices could be activated, the locomotive ran away on the steep grade and jumped the tracks at a sharp curve, killing a photographer who had failed to jump when the mishap occurred. The railway's only other fatal accident occurred in September 1967, when 8 were killed and 75 injured when a train ran away because of an open switch at one of the passing sidings.

Another scenic cog railway was built up Green Mountain (now Cadillac Mountain) on Mt. Desert Island on the coast of Maine. The story of its origin is a curious one. A group of tourists were standing at the base of the mountain talking to several young men who had just climbed down its granite slope. They spoke of the wonderful views, especially the view out to sea, from the summit. A stout lady said that she too wanted to see the view and why did not someone build a railway to take her and other less athletic persons up to the top? A young lawyer, Francis H. Clergue, standing nearby, was inspired by the lady's chance remark. When he returned to Bangor, he and several friends incorporated the Green Mountain Railway to make her dream a reality. A survey was started in December 1882, and construction began in the spring of 1883. The line was built as a duplicate of the Mt. Wash-

ington line. The locomotives, rack, and cars were copies of the well-established plan worked out by Marsh and his associates some years earlier. There were a few differences. The new line was just over a mile long. The track was fastened directly to the granite ledge wherever possible, and very little trestlework was necessary. The ascent was 1,270 feet. Opening day was July 1, 1883.

In the first few years the little line was busy, but then traffic fell off. Mt. Desert was still a remote area, and not that many tourists came to visit. The regulars who showed up season after season likely grew a little bored with the view after a few visits. And then there was the tiresome journey by stagecoach and steamer from the island's main town, Bar Harbor. It was only 4½ miles distant, but just far enough to discourage repeat visits. In addition, like all tourist businesses, it was seasonal in nature, and the season was basically the summer months. By 1890 the Green Mountain Railway was operating at a loss. It did not reopen the next year. On January 16, 1893, it was sold for scrap at a sheriff's sale. The two locomotives were later sold to the Mt. Washington line, where both remain in service. However, they have been rebuilt so often that little of the original machines has likely survived.

The most spectacular rack railway in North America runs up Pikes Peak. This great mountain, located near Colorado Springs, Colorado, was named for Gen. Zebulon Pike, who first observed it in 1806. At 14,110 feet above sea level, it is not the tallest in the Rockies, but it stands near the plains and so offers a better view than other peaks more centrally located in the western mountains. On a clear day it is possible to see Kansas from the summit. The grand view made it ideal for a tourist railroad. The first effort to construct such a line in 1883

Unlike its Mt. Washington counterpart, Colorado's Manitou & Pike's Peak Cog Railway keeps up with modern technology for its 8.9-mile journey to the summit of Pikes Peak, 14,100 feet above sea level. A two-car train on its way down to Manitou met an upbound train in the siding at Windy Point in August 1994. —William D. Middleton

failed. Five years later the Manitou & Pike's Peak Railway was organized to build an 8.9-mile-long cog line to the summit. It would be a first-class railway with iron bridges, solid masonry culverts, and the best locomotives and cars available. The Abt system of rack railway was adopted to ensure a safe and smooth journey. Its inventor, Roman Abt, had perfected a staggered-tooth cog system in 1882 that used two or three parallel rack rails. The teeth were tapered, and the teeth of one rail were placed opposite the indent of the opposite rail. The Abt system is now used on about 75 percent of the world's cog railways.

Construction began in September 1889 at the top of Pikes Peak. Nearly 1,000 workers prepared the grading and track. The high altitude caused shortness of breath, and a few men died from heart attacks because of the lack of oxygen. Horses and mules carried rails, ties, and other materials up the mountain packsaddle fashion. The steepest grade was 25 percent; other parts of the line were less steep, but the average grade was 16.6 percent, far steeper than the typical main-line railroad. The lower end of the railroad proved more difficult to build because of the rougher terrain and was costly, as had been expected: half a million dollars. Fortunately the line had a wealthy patron, Z. G. Simmons of Kenosha, Wisconsin, who paid all costs. He and his family controlled the line for over a generation.

The track was finished in October 1890, but trains did not operate to the top until June of the following year. Trips usually took 1 hour and 45 minutes. The average speed was 3 mph. The point was to enjoy the view, not rapid transit. During the steam era five or six trains were run a day. The engines could handle only one car. The cars had large windows to offer as much viewing space as possible. Each car seated 50 passengers in seats that were angled to conform to the average grade of 16 percent. The railway was a fair-weather operation and ran from late spring to late fall.

The Pikes Peak line represents an achievement in railway engineering. It is one of the largest rack lines in the world. It is the highest among scenic railways. The operation has been profitable through the years and remains in private hands. It has always adopted the best and most modern equipment and operating procedures. It began to experiment with internal combustion railcars in 1938. Diesel railcars followed. These proved so successful that steam power was retired in 1958. It is likely the best-maintained railway in the United States. Visitors cannot help but be impressed with the order and cleanliness of the property. The track is perfect, the train crews are in immaculate uniforms, and the cars are spotless inside and out. It presents a remarkable contrast to the smoky and old-fashioned Mt. Washington cog line.

Another North American rack line was built in Mexico in 1896 for the Penoles Mining Co. This narrow-gauge line ran 26 miles (42 kilometers) from the mine to a junction at Berejillo, Durango Province, on the Mexican Central Railroad. It was not a common carrier, but even so, passenger service was provided. On the steeper grade the locomotives operated on the Abt rack system, but a clutch allowed the cogwheel drive to be disengaged so that the engines could be run as conventional locomotives. The Baldwin Locomotive Works provided four locomotives for the Penoles line.

—John H. White, Jr.

REFERENCES

Abbott, Morris W. *The Pike's Peak Cog Road*. San Marino, Calif.: Golden West Books, 1972.

Ackerman, John H. *Mountain-Climbing Trains*. New York: Ives Washburn, 1969.

Kidder, Glen M. *Railway to the Moon: A History of the Unique Mt. Washington Ry.* Littleton, N.H.: Courier, 1969.

Ransome-Wallis, P., ed. *The Concise Encyclopaedia of World Railway Locomotives*. London: Hutchinson, 1959.

Sulzer, Elmer G. "Locomotives for the Madison Hill." *Bulletin of the Railway and Locomotive Historical Society*, no. 123 (Oct. 1970): 23–43.

Worthen, S. S. "Steep but Slow (Mt. Washington Cog Railway)." *Trains* 16, no. 9 (July 1956): 38–42.

Cold War Railroads

Indispensable in World War II, railroads abruptly lost importance in postwar defense planning. At the onset of the Cold War in 1946 only the United States possessed the atomic bomb. It was believed that this nuclear weapons monopoly fundamentally altered the nature of future conflicts. Instead of mass mobilizations of personnel and economic resources, a few long-range bombers delivering atomic payloads would decide the outcome. The number of U.S. armed services personnel on active duty plummeted from 14.4 million in 1945 to 1.6 million by 1950. The development of missiles with intercontinental striking reach only solidified the Pentagon's strategy.

For the first time, Department of Defense (DOD) transportation planners also possessed alternatives. Their postwar inventories included a huge fleet of multiengine transport aircraft able to provide rapid movement of personnel and cargo. Postwar highway improvements enabled military logisticians to expand their usage of trucks. By the 1960s the army's light vehicles and flatbed transporters of tracked equipment regularly traveled interstate highways, although railroads often delivered this equipment from the factory to military installations or from army bases to large training areas such as Fort Irwin, California.

Although railroads continued to carry armored vehicles, jet engines, rocket fuel, artillery shell casings, and low-grade explosives, DOD agencies displayed a clear preference for commercial and military trucks in routine operations. After the Korean War military use of rail passenger service all but disappeared. A 1981 Department of Defense report stated that in future mobilizations passenger trains might be used only in the Northeast Corridor.

Railroads were not an important factor in the Korean War of 1950–1953. At no time did the army have more than 440,000 soldiers deployed in Korea—about 6 percent of its total World War II strength. In the war's early stages troops and equipment were drawn from existing forces in Japan, Okinawa, and Hawaii. Petroleum products accounted for nearly two-thirds of the supply tonnage delivered to the forces in Korea, and nearly all of the petroleum shipments originated at West Coast refineries and pipeline terminals. Rail passenger travel by military personnel temporarily increased during 1952 and 1953 as the army added about 1 million active-duty personnel. The railroads' share of this traffic was easily handled on passenger trains, whose capacity by then far outstripped civilian demand.

Although the Vietnam War resulted in a larger troop commitment than Korea, the buildup was gradual, extending over a five-year period. Total freight ton-miles on the U.S. rail system rose by less than 4 percent during the 1966–1970 period when supply shipments to Vietnam were at their peak.

In light of the 1970s' plague of railroad bankruptcies and route abandonments in the East and Midwest, DOD conducted a five-year research project that led to the 1981 publication *A Study of Rail Lines Important to National Defense*. Working with the Federal Railroad Administration (FRA), Pentagon planners sought to determine if the nation's rail system was adequate to meet peacetime requirements for military freight—especially heavyweight and oversize shipments. DOD defined a core network of 32,422 miles of existing freight railroad main lines, augmented by 5,034 miles of connecting routes to specific military installations. The system was called the Strategic Rail Corridor Network (STRACNET). It was intended to be a planners' tool that, among other purposes, would alert state and federal transportation agencies to those routes that the military deemed important as civilian officials considered abandonment petitions, mergers, and the like.

The report concluded that among roughly 1,000 important defense installations, 350 facilities had access to rail service, but only 216 of these bases actually required it. Bridge and tunnel clearance problems existed at only four points on STRACNET mainline routes. Only 233 miles of the core system failed to meet the department's maintenance criteria. FRA's Class 2 designation, permitting train operations at 25 mph, represented the acceptable minimum, although ratings of Class 3 (40 mph) or higher were preferred.

A defense strategy that by the 1960s had settled upon missile-delivered nuclear warheads ultimately affected the railroads. Worried that a Soviet strike would wipe out its missile silos, the Air Force's Strategic Air Command (SAC) considered the mobile deployment of multiple-warhead MX missiles on trains or trucks. The concept was simple. By the time Soviet intelligence analysts could pinpoint precise locations from satellite data, the targets would have moved. SAC proposed to deploy 50 MX missiles in special excess-dimension boxcars, which would be components of military trainsets normally maintained at enclosures known as "rail garrisons" within air force bases in the western United States. If an alert were sounded, the missiles would scatter upon railroad main lines.

A prototype train was developed and tested in 1990. It consisted of a locomotive, two missile launch cars, two security cars, a control car, and a supply car. The units were designed and painted to be visually indistinguishable from conventional freight trains. The 205,000-pound missiles would be elevated to a vertical launch position for firing. SAC proposed 25 rail garrison trains, but the collapse of the Soviet Union in 1993, coupled with the ratification of two arms-control treaties, effectively ended the Cold War, and with it rail garrisons.

—William J. Watt

REFERENCES

Boldrick, Michael R. "Missile Trains Move Forward." *Trains* 50, no. 11 (Sept. 1990): 25–26.
———. "Missiles on Rails." *Trains* 48, no. 12 (Oct. 1988): 36–40.
Phillips, Don. "An Interstate Rail System—alias STRACNET." *Trains*, Apr. 1982.

Colonization of the West

Before 1850 the U.S. population had only moved as far west as the tier of states east of the Mississippi River. Beyond was the huge expanse of public lands acquired in the Louisiana Purchase of 1803. Subsequent additions increased the public land to tens of millions of acres. Two-thirds of the country was either vacant or only sparsely populated. Government policy was to encourage occupancy of its vast territory all the way to the Pacific Ocean.

By the late 1830s a growing population and the strong desire of many to own their own land pressured moves from the Eastern Seaboard to the seemingly boundless West. To encourage this movement, the U.S. government priced its public lands low; much of it was available for $1.25 an acre. At first there were few takers because of the remoteness of the area in the absence of reliable, inexpensive, easy-to-use transportation.

Anxious to grow, the frontier states encouraged the construction of railroads. Illinois was particularly eager to attract additional population, and through the efforts of Senator Stephen A. Douglas, Congress passed the law in 1850 that allowed grants of public land for the construction of railroads. This modified an earlier law that permitted land grants for the construction of canals.

THE FINEST FARMING LANDS

CORN — COTTON — FRUITS & VEGETABLES

EQUAL TO ANY IN THE WORLD!!!

MAY BE PROCURED

AT FROM $6 TO $12 PER ACRE,

Near Markets, Schools, Railroads, Churches, and all the blessings of Civilization.

1,200,000 Acres in Farms of 40, 80, 120, 160 Acres and upwards; in ILLINOIS, the Garden State of America.

The Illinois Central Railroad Company offer, on LONG CREDIT, the beautiful and fertile PRAIRIE LANDS lying along the whole line of their Railroad, 700 MILES IN LENGTH, upon the most Favorable Terms for enabling Farmers, Manufacturers, Mechanics, and Workingmen, to make for themselves and their families a competency, and a home they can call Their Own.

ILLINOIS

Is about equal in extent to England, with a population of 1,722,666, and a soil capable of supporting 20,000,000. No State in the valley of the Mississippi offers so great an inducement to the settler as the State of Illinois. There is no part of the world where all the conditions of climate and soil so admirably combine to produce those two great staples, Corn and Wheat.

CLIMATE.

Nowhere can the industrious farmer secure such immediate results from his labor as on these deep, rich, loamy soils, cultivated with so much ease. The climate from the extreme southern part of the State to the Terre Haute, Alton and St. Louis Railroad, a distance of nearly 200 miles, is well adapted to Winter

WHEAT, CORN, COTTON, TOBACCO,

Peaches, Pears, Tomatoes, and every variety of fruit and vegetables are grown in great abundance, from which Chicago and other Northern markets are furnished from four to six weeks earlier than their immediate vicinity.

THE ORDINARY YIELD

of Corn is from 50 to 80 bushels per acre. Cattle, Horses, Mules, Sheep and Hogs are raised here at a small cost, and yield large profits. It is believed that no section of country presents greater inducements for Dairy Farming than the Prairies of Illinois, a branch of farming to which but little attention has been paid, and which must yield sure profitable results.

AGRICULTURAL PRODUCTS.

The Agricultural products of Illinois are greater than those of any other State. The Wheat crop of 1861 was estimated at 35,000,000 bushels, while the Corn crop yields not less than 140,000,000 bushels, besides the crop of Oats, Barley, Rye, Buckwheat, Potatoes, Sweet Potatoes, Pump-

kins, Squashes, Flax, Hemp, Peas, Clover, Cabbage, Beets, Tobacco, Sorghum, Grapes, Peaches, Apples, &c., which go to swell the vast aggregate of production in this fertile region. Over Four Million tons of produce were sent out of Illinois during the past year.

CULTIVATION OF COTTON.

The experiments in Cotton culture are of very great promise. Commencing in latitude 39 deg. 30 min. (see Mattoon on the Branch, and Assumption on the Main Line), the Company owns thousands of acres well adapted to the perfection of this fibre. A settler having a family of young children can turn their youthful labor to a most profitable account in the growth and perfection of this plant.

THE ILLINOIS CENTRAL RAILROAD

Traverses the whole length of the State, from the banks of the Mississippi and Lake Michigan to the Ohio. As its name imports, the Railroad runs through the centre of the State, and on either side of the road along its whole length lie the lands offered for sale.

CITIES, TOWNS, MARKETS, DEPOTS.

There are ninety eight Depots on the Company's Railway, giving about one every seven miles. Cities, Towns, and Villages are situated at convenient distances throughout the whole route, where every desirable commodity may be found as readily as in the oldest cities of the Union, and where buyers are to be met for all kinds of farm produce.

EDUCATION.

Mechanics and working men will find the free school system encouraged by the State, and endowed with a large revenue for the support of the schools. Children can live in sight of the school, the college, the church, and grow up with the prosperity of the leading State of the Great Western Empire.

For Prices and Terms of Payment,
ADDRESS LAND COMMISSIONER, Ill. Central R. R. Co., Chicago, Ill.

The first U.S. railroads were generally built in already-settled areas and joined well-established places. Some early lines were built to act as feeders to rivers and canals. To build a railroad in sparsely populated Illinois was risky in the extreme because of the lack of people and freight to move. By 1850, thanks to the Land Grant Act, railroads were to be employed as a force to attract and help settle the men and women who would populate the new frontier.

The Illinois Central Railroad was the first to receive a land grant. There was uncertainty at the time as to whether or not land could be granted directly to a private company, so Congress granted the land to the State of Illinois, which in turn granted it to the Illinois Central Rail-

road. From the beginning it was a bold venture; the proposed railroad would be 700 miles long when completed, the longest railroad in the world. It was to be built north from Cairo at the confluence of the Ohio and Mississippi rivers in the general direction of Rockford, Illinois. At Freeport, Illinois, the line then veered westward and terminated in Dunleith (now East Dubuque) on the banks of the Mississippi, across the river from Dubuque, Iowa. A long branch took off from the main line at Centralia, Illinois, and was built north and east to Chicago on Lake Michigan.

There was a strong incentive for the Illinois Central to do all it could to bring in more people by colonizing the area along the railroad. First, the land in the alternate sec-

The Union Pacific depot at Omaha was a veritable bedlam of men, women, and children immigrants on their way to a new life in the West, as depicted in this wood engraving published in *Frank Leslie's Illustrated Newspaper* around 1877. —Library of Congress (Neg. LC-USZ62-2916)

tions owned by the railroad had to be sold to help generate the capital needed for construction of the railroad. Second, settlers had to be attracted, or there would be no people or goods to move. It was necessary for the Illinois Central and the railroads subsequently constructed in remote areas to establish colonization programs.

To generate business, the colonizing railroads had to promote the richness of the soil and help find minerals that would form the basis of traffic from the mines. To support the population, help had to be given to develop crops both to support the newcomers and to be marketed elsewhere to provide traffic for the railroads to move.

All the railroads with much land to sell and settlers to find adopted much the same approach. A land department was created or a land agent was appointed to attract settlers and to sell the land. Advertising was used in the eastern cities of the United States at first, and then in Great Britain and Europe. Next, agents were assigned to work the eastern United States and Europe (experience proved that ministers and former army men were most effective). In the early 1850s the Illinois Central led the way in advertising for workers to help build the railroad; there was a belief, which proved correct, that many workers would choose to stay and purchase land along the rail line they helped build and where they could see firsthand the richness of the soil.

There were some variations in seeking colonists from abroad. Typically the railroads offered reduced fares to visit the area in which land was for sale. Reduced passenger and freight rates were offered to colonists after purchase of land to move their families and possessions. On some occasions passage was arranged at no cost, including steamship travel across the Atlantic. In almost all cases agents of the railroad would meet the immigrants in Great Britain or Europe or at the port of entry and guide or accompany them to their new homes.

The Northern Pacific and the Great Northern paid special attention to attracting immigrants from Scandinavia in the correct belief that these hardy souls would flourish in the northern-tier states served by the railroads. The Atchison, Topeka & Santa Fe sought to attract Mennonite farmers because of their reputation for agricultural prowess, a skill necessary in the drier land served by that railroad. A large band of German Mennonites living in Russia were anxious to leave because they were about to be forced, against their religious beliefs, to bear arms for the czar. The Santa Fe arranged and paid for all passage and settled the immigrants on a large area of land in Kansas. The $2 million in savings the Mennonites brought with them helped Kansas prosper.

The railroads that sought colonists generally promoted

A large gathering celebrated the departure of a trainload of immigrants for the West. Sponsored by the National Land Co., the German immigrants were departing from St. Louis on their way to Colorado in August 1869. —Library of Congress (Neg. LC-USZ62-744)

On the last leg of their long journey from Europe, immigrants boarded a colonist (third-class) sleeping car on the Canadian Pacific around 1885. —J. Bruce, Canadian Pacific, *Trains* Magazine Collection

In 1902 the Santa Fe offered Colonist Excursions to California at special low fares. The ad shows a farmer, accompanied by his dog, plowing his field with a horse in a blanket with a Santa Fe logo. —Michael E. Zega Collection

the high quality of the lands that were available for sale. Agents set up displays at county and state fairs in the United States, and the Burlington and Northern Pacific helped subsidize the fairs. The Santa Fe set up a notable agricultural exhibition at the centennial celebration and World's Fair in Philadelphia in 1876. The Great Northern, Burlington, and some others outfitted special cars to show the farming possibilities along their lines. These toured the East, South, and Midwest. All the lines published brochures touting land for sale, and all employed strong advertising programs and persuasive agents. The Illinois Central even advertised in Manhattan streetcars.

Understanding that enthusiastic letters from immigrants to those left behind were the best form of promotion, colonizing railroads helped develop better means of farming and introduced varieties of seed and crops that would flourish in the land adjacent to the railroad lines. In treeless Nebraska the Burlington planted hundreds of thousands of trees along its right of way; it also created tree nurseries from which trees were donated to farmers. The Burlington introduced alfalfa as a crop that would do well in a dry climate and also enrich the soil, as well as helping raise healthy cattle. The Burlington introduced potatoes into northwest Nebraska as a good cash crop and encouraged sugar-beet farming in eastern Colorado.

Under the direction of James J. Hill, the empire-building head of the Great Northern, that railroad helped introduce strains of wheat into the northern-tier states that would do well in the harsh climate of the Dakotas and Minnesota. The Great Northern also provided prize-winning cattle and hogs to help farmers breed quality livestock. The Illinois Central hired experts to study the land along its tracks for minerals (the coalfields of southern Illinois were found in this way) and encouraged mining companies to enter the area; the other railroads did

likewise. In Montana the Northern Pacific promoted the use of its land for cattle raising and encouraged ranching. The same was true of the Santa Fe; realizing that New Mexico and Arizona were not suitable for farming, the railroad promoted ranching and grazing.

Supporting the farmers was sensible. Good crops and prosperous farms meant freight to haul in the form of supplies and equipment shipped into the farming regions and crops outbound to markets in the East and elsewhere. The tree growing promoted by the Burlington helped diminish the drifting of snow across its tracks in winter and provided a cash crop of timber for fence posts, crossties, and lumber for buildings. As James Hill noted, when the rail lines proceeded westward, there had to be economic activity behind it to give the railroad the freight traffic it needed to prosper. Profitable operations meant that the railroad could plow back some of its profits to improve the right of way, reduce grades and curvature, and permit the purchase of more powerful and efficient locomotives to reduce the cost of transportation and eventually reduce the rates to encourage even more settlement and more business.

—George M. Smerk

REFERENCES

Gross, Harriet H. "The Land Grant Legend." *Railroad* 55, no. 3 (Aug. 1951): 28–49; 55, no. 4 (Sept. 1951): 64–77; 56, no. 1 (Oct. 1951): 68–79; 56, no. 2 (Nov. 1951): 30–41; 56, no. 3 (Dec. 1951): 40–53.

Holbrook, Stewart H. *The Story of American Railroads*. Chap. 8. New York: Crown, 1947.

Klein, Maury. *Union Pacific: Birth of a Railroad, 1862–1893*. Garden City, N.Y.: Doubleday, 1987.

Riegel, Robert Edgar. *The Story of the Western Railroads: From 1852 through the Reign of the Giants*. Chap. 18. Repr., Lincoln: Univ. of Nebraska Press, 1964.

Stover, John F. *American Railroads*. 2nd ed. Chicago: Univ. of Chicago Press, 1997.

Vance, James E., Jr. *The North American Railroad: Its Origin, Evolution, and Geography*. Baltimore: Johns Hopkins Univ. Press, 1995.

Waters, L. L. *Steel Trails to Santa Fe*. Chap. 7. Lawrence: Univ. of Kansas Press, 1950.

Colorado & Southern Railway

For most of its life the Colorado & Southern was a subsidiary of the Chicago, Burlington & Quincy Railroad, but in the nineteenth century its predecessors were associated with the Union Pacific. Its lines ran north, west, southwest, and southeast from Denver. Its operations included a narrow-gauge division, an electric interurban railway, and a streetcar system.

West from Denver

The Colorado Central Railroad opened a standard-gauge line from Denver to Golden, 16 miles, in 1870. Continuing west from Golden, the Colorado Central opened 3-foot-gauge lines to Black Hawk (20 miles from Golden) in 1872 and Georgetown (34 miles from Golden) in 1877; it extended the Black Hawk line 4 miles and almost 500 feet higher to Central City in 1878. A third rail for narrow-gauge trains was added to the Denver-Golden line in 1879. A 4-mile extension west from Georgetown to Silver Plume required a complete loop, part of it on a trestle, to gain elevation. The railroad intended to tunnel under the Continental Divide and made a start at digging a tunnel, but the project went no further. The Georgetown Loop was abandoned in 1939, but it was reconstructed in the 1970s as part of a tourist railroad.

North from Denver

With assistance from the Union Pacific, the Colorado Central built north from Golden through Boulder, aiming at Julesburg on the UP main line in the northeast corner of the state. Work stopped at Longmont during the panic of 1873. Construction resumed in 1877, but on a route south from Cheyenne, Wyoming. The Union Pacific leased the Colorado Central in 1879.

The line to Julesburg was opened in 1882 as a La Salle–Julesburg route not connected to the rest of the Colorado Central. In 1886 the Colorado Central built a cutoff from Denver to Boulder and three years later abandoned its lines from Golden to Boulder and from Fort Collins to Cheyenne.

However, there was other activity at Cheyenne. In 1886 the Cheyenne & Northern Railway began constructing northward to head off a Chicago & North Western subsidiary that was building west toward Douglas, Wyoming.

The C&NW line reached Douglas unimpeded in 1887. The Cheyenne & Northern line paused for a few years at Wendover, 121 miles from Cheyenne, then was extended to a connection with the C&NW at Orin Junction.

Southwest from Denver

The Denver, South Park & Pacific started building a narrow-gauge railroad southwest from Denver in 1873, but the financial panic that year slowed the construction. In 1880 the line reached Buena Vista, where it connected with the Denver & Rio Grande's Pueblo-Leadville line. To extend its line west to Gunnison, the DSP&P bored the 1,805-foot-long Alpine Tunnel under the Continental Divide.

Jay Gould bought the Denver, South Park & Pacific in 1880 and sold it to the Union Pacific (he controlled the Union Pacific and held a half interest in the Denver & Rio Grande). To reach Leadville, the DSP&P negotiated trackage rights over the Denver & Rio Grande from Buena Vista. The two railroads found themselves in frequent disagreement, despite their affiliation through Gould, so in 1884 the DSP&P built a line from Como to Leadville over Boreas and Fremont passes. The line crossed the Continental Divide twice, but it created a 151-mile Denver-Leadville route that was 20 miles shorter than the old route through Buena Vista and 125 miles shorter than the Denver & Rio Grande's route through Pueblo.

In 1889 the South Park entered receivership and emerged, still under UP control, as the Denver, Leadville & Gunnison Railway. Four years later the UP entered receivership, and in 1895 the DL&G gained its independence as part of the reorganization of the UP.

Southeast from Denver

John Evans, who had been the first governor of Colorado, incorporated the Denver & New Orleans Railroad in 1881 to build a line to Fort Worth, Texas, a destination soon changed to a junction with the Fort Worth & Denver City Railway, which was building northwest from Fort Worth. The Denver & New Orleans looped southeast, then southwest to Pueblo; it also built a 10-mile branch from Manitou Junction west to Colorado Springs.

To build the line onward from Pueblo, the Denver, Texas & Fort Worth was organized. In 1888 it met the advancing Fort Worth & Denver City. In quick succession the Denver, Texas & Fort Worth came under Union Pacific control and acquired the Fort Worth & Denver City and the Denver, Texas & Gulf, which was a reorganization of the Denver & New Orleans.

Consolidation into the Colorado & Southern

In 1890 the Union Pacific formed the Union Pacific, Denver & Gulf to consolidate the Cheyenne & Northern, the Colorado Central, the Denver, Texas & Gulf, and the Denver, Texas & Fort Worth, which formed a route from Orin Junction, Wyoming, south through Denver to the New Mexico–Texas border at Texline. When the Union Pacific went into receivership in 1893, the UPD&G was placed under a separate receiver, Frank Trumbull, who was also receiver of the Denver, Leadville & Gunnison.

In 1898 the Denver, Leadville & Gunnison and all the railroads making up the Union Pacific, Denver & Gulf were sold at foreclosure and consolidated as the Colorado & Southern Railway, except for the La Salle–Julesburg line, which was sold to the Union Pacific. The new C&S arranged with the Santa Fe for joint terminals in Denver, Colorado Springs, and Pueblo and for trackage rights between Denver and Pueblo. It abandoned its own line between Manitou Junction and Pueblo. The C&S owned the Fort Worth & Denver City, but it was necessary for that road to remain a separate entity because of Texas laws.

The boomtown of Cripple Creek caught the attention of the Colorado & Southern. The C&S made plans to extend its former Denver, South Park & Pacific line south to a connection with the Colorado Midland, which entered Cripple Creek from the north, and jointly with the Rio Grande Western it acquired control of the Colorado Midland in 1900. It acquired control of the Colorado Springs & Cripple Creek District Railway in 1905. The mining boom soon subsided. The C&S sold its interest in the Colorado Midland in 1912, and the CS&CCD was abandoned in 1922.

About the same time the Colorado & Southern organized the Denver & Interurban Railroad, which built an electric railway between Denver and Boulder and a streetcar system in Fort Collins. The D&I entered receivership in 1918. The Fort Collins system was sold to the city and continued to operate until 1951; the Denver-Boulder interurban line was abandoned in 1926.

Control by the Burlington

The Great Northern, Northern Pacific, and Chicago, Burlington & Quincy came under common control in 1901. Recognizing that the Colorado & Southern and its Texas subsidiaries could form a route to the Gulf of Mexico for lumber from the Pacific Northwest and grain from the Great Plains, they began to put the pieces of the route together. In 1908 the Chicago, Burlington & Quincy bought control of the C&S and the Fort Worth & Denver City. The two roads were operated as Burlington subsidiaries, with the president of the CB&Q also serving as president of the subsidiaries, but both roads maintained a degree of independence, even after the 1970 merger that created Burlington Northern.

The gaps in the Northwest-to-Gulf route were closed when C&S restored the Fort Collins–Cheyenne line in 1911 and the Burlington built south from Billings, Montana, to connect with the C&S in 1914. Also in 1911 the C&S constructed a new line jointly with the Denver & Rio Grande from Pueblo to Walsenburg, Colorado, and abandoned the former Denver, South Park & Pacific narrow-gauge line west of Buena Vista. Mining was in decline and paved roads were penetrating the Colorado Rockies.

In the 1930s the C&S trimmed back many of its marginal operations. Floods destroyed much of the original Denver & New Orleans line between the outskirts of Denver and Manitou Junction in 1935, and the C&S had no reason to rebuild it; the area along the line was almost totally unpopulated. The C&S abandoned almost all the rest of the South Park—from Denver to Climax—in 1937 and the former Colorado Central lines west of Golden in 1941. The isolated Leadville-Climax line was converted to standard gauge in 1943, ending the C&S's narrow-gauge operations.

Through most of the second half of the twentieth century the Colorado & Southern and Fort Worth & Denver remained something of a backwater of the Burlington system. With the development of the coalfields of Wyoming's Powder River Basin, however, the route from Wyoming down through Denver became a conduit for heavy coal trains moving fuel to the power plants of Texas. The C&S was integrated into Burlington Northern in December 1981, and the Fort Worth & Denver was similarly consolidated into BN just a year later.

Texas Subsidiaries

For years a Texas statute required that railroads operating in Texas have their headquarters there. But for that regulation, the Fort Worth & Denver City would have been folded into the Colorado & Southern in the late 1800s.

The Fort Worth & Denver City began construction northwest from Fort Worth in 1881 and met the Denver, Texas & Fort Worth in 1888. Several subsidiary companies known collectively as the Wichita Valley Lines built into the area southwest of Wichita Falls in the 1890s. The name of the railroad was truncated to Fort Worth & Denver in 1951.

The history of the Dallas-Houston-Galveston line is complicated by several reorganizations and joint ownership. The Trinity & Brazos Valley Railway was chartered in 1902 and began building and assembling a line from Fort Worth and Dallas southeast to Houston and Galveston. In 1905 the Colorado & Southern purchased control of the Trinity & Brazos Valley and a year later sold a half interest in it to the Chicago, Rock Island & Pacific.

There was not enough business to keep the T&BV going—Houston was not yet a boomtown—and the T&BV slipped into a 16-year receivership in 1914. It was reorganized in 1930 as the Burlington–Rock Island Railroad. The Fort Worth & Denver and the Rock Island jointly leased the northern portion of the railroad and began operating it in alternate five-year periods. In 1950 the B-RI's owners made a new joint lease. The B-RI ceased operation, and its two owners began to operate the entire line in alternate five-year periods. The Fort Worth & Denver and the Rock Island purchased the property of the B-RI jointly in 1964 and dissolved the B-RI corporation. When the Rock Island ceased operation in 1980, the Fort Worth & Denver became the sole operator.

In 1980, the last year before the Burlington Northern merger, the Colorado & Southern operated a system of 678 route-miles, with 235 locomotives, 2,329 freight cars, 65 company service cars, and 893 employees. C&S freight traffic totaled 7.2 billion ton-miles in 1980, and coal was by far the predominant commodity. C&S operating revenues totaled $126.2 million in 1980, and the railroad achieved a 96.3 percent operating ratio. The Fort Worth & Denver operated a system of 1,181 route-miles and 1,596 track-miles, with 24 locomotives, 1,443 freight cars, 105 company service cars, and 1,531 employees. Fort Worth & Denver operating revenues totaled $137 million in 1980, and the railroad achieved an 85.8 percent operating ratio.

—George H. Drury

REFERENCE

Wagner, F. Hol. *The Colorado Road*. Denver: Intermountain Chapter, National Railway Historical Society, 1970.

Communities of Interest

Given the appetite for capital possessed by railroads, it was common sense to limit the number of carriers and their competition for freight and passenger traffic and for funds to make necessary capital investments. Consolidation of railroads was a way of solving the problem. There were four means of accomplishing the consolidation. One railroad could purchase another; leases could be used to gain control; and stock holdings were an obvious method. The fourth method, and a surprisingly effective ploy, was communities of interest.

At the turn of the twentieth century some states made it illegal for one railroad to buy out another. However, the same objective could be gained by leasing the desired property. Purchase, of course, means permanent and absolute control, but the purchase usually required the issue of additional securities and additional debt. A lease does not require the issuance of additional securities and allows control at minimum or no cost. Another means of gaining control is to purchase sufficient capital stock to effect control of management. It need not be a majority of shares. The community of interest was achieved by making some of the directors or managers of one railroad company members of the boards of other railroad companies. Under the community of interest, the railroads would not invade each other's territory physically or attempt to solicit traffic in the territory of other railroads.

J. P. Morgan was a master of bringing peace to a difficult and wasteful competitive situation by creating a community of interest. For example, early in the twentieth century there was major infighting between the Union Pacific and Great Northern railroads for control of the Northern Pacific. Also involved was the issue of control of the Chicago, Burlington & Quincy, which was a primary link between Chicago and the Union Pacific at Omaha and the Great Northern and the Northern Pacific at Minneapolis and St. Paul. The Burlington was a major competitor of the Chicago & North Western, which had a close traffic relationship with the New York Central and other rail interests of the Vanderbilt family. Joining in the fray was the Chicago, Milwaukee & St. Paul, which had close relationships with the Pennsylvania Railroad. Morgan was engaged to bring an end to what might have been an expensive fight over control. The potential problem was settled by placing the president of the Great Northern on the board of the Northern Pacific, along with the chairman of the Union Pacific executive committee, a director of the Chicago & North Western, a director of the Milwaukee Road, and a vice president of the Pennsylvania Railroad.

The use of the community of interest became commonplace after 1898 as a way of settling the wasteful corporate warfare that rankled J. P. Morgan. Interlocking directorates were a key. Indeed, a study in 1905 revealed that only 39 individuals as board members controlled all of the railroads between the Mississippi River and the seaport cities on the Atlantic Ocean. Another study in 1912 showed that 34 transportation companies operating in Trunk Line Territory were controlled by 13 men, who also were directors of banking and industrial companies.

There was regulatory ferment in the first decades of the twentieth century, and there was a slowdown of railroad consolidations or communities of interest, triggered in large part by President Theodore Roosevelt and his objection to the creation of Northern Securities, which would have merged the Great Northern, Northern Pacific, and Burlington. The Sherman Antitrust Act was used to prevent creation of Northern Securities. The use of the community of interest did continue, and interlocking directorates were not unusual in the railroad industry. However, the use of rate associations became a powerful and effective means of avoiding destructive competition without the need for ownership or communities of interest.

Public unhappiness with the power of big business has ebbed and flowed over the years, and legislation to prevent combinations in restraint of trade has also been imposed or deposed according to power shifts in government. Interlocking directorates were to a large extent outlawed by the Transportation Act of 1920, but they were not totally abolished. A director serving on the board of more than one railroad required the approval of the Interstate Commerce Commission after showing that neither public nor private interests were harmed by the interlocking board membership.

—George M. Smerk

REFERENCES

Johnson, Emory R. *American Railway Transportation.* Chap. 17. New York: D. Appleton, 1912.

Johnson, Emory R., and Thurman W. Van Metre. *Principles of Railroad Transportation.* Chap. 19. New York: D. Appleton, 1924.

Locklin, D. Philip. *Economics of Transportation.* Chap. 14. Homewood, Ill.: Richard D. Irwin, 1972.

Commuter Railroads

From their beginning in the 1830s, most railroads offered local service or "accommodation" trains, primarily designed to enable country merchants and lawyers to visit urban centers on business, urban capitalists to visit their rural factories and mines, or, to a lesser extent, well-to-do city families to take pleasure trips into the countryside. Wealthy families had long owned country homes as a refuge from the heat and smells of urban summers, but the notion of living year-round in a suburb and traveling to work in a city every day was a later innovation that was tied intimately to the development of rail transportation. It appears to have developed in two waves tied to cycles of great inflation followed by deflation and depression, the first between 1836 and 1846, which saw the development of the "commuted" fare, and the second between 1863 and 1873, which saw the proliferation of planned communities oriented to a railroad station, many of them the work of railroad companies or their promoters.

The terms "commuter" and "commute," which now merely denote a regular journey to work of some distance, derive from the "commuted" or reduced fares introduced by railroad companies to stimulate travel. Instead of payment by the trip, payment was "commuted" into a lump sum for repeated daily travel. The first commuter tickets were usually for a full year or six months and required an up-front payment of $100 or so, this at a time when the average wage was $1 a day. Early commuting was thus an elite affair, but business downturns drove down fares along with other prices, and by 1880 commuting was an option for a large segment of the middle classes. More affordable monthly tickets, the norm today, made their appearance during the Civil War years.

The Boston & Worcester Railroad may have been the first North American railroad to offer commuted fares, in 1838. Initially, most trains ran through the full length of the line, but the railroad began operating regular trains for commuter traffic between Boston and West Newton

Inbound commuters head from their morning trains to their workplace in the city. The Massachusetts Bay Transportation Authority passengers were arriving at South Station, Boston, in October 1997. —William D. Middleton

in 1843. At New York the New Jersey Railroad (predecessor of the Pennsylvania) began offering commuter tickets in 1840, the Morris & Essex (predecessor of the Lackawanna) in 1841, the Long Island Rail Road in 1842, and the Paterson & Hudson River Railroad (predecessor of the Erie) in 1843. The Philadelphia, Wilmington & Baltimore Railroad began offering commuter tickets between Philadelphia and Wilmington in 1844 and out of Baltimore in 1849.

Commuting in the Railway Age

Railroad commuting went hand in hand with suburban real estate development. Sometimes the railroad company entered the land business under its own name and sometimes through subsidiary companies, but the majority of developments were independent endeavors. However, the process was the same. The developer would divide a tract into lots and provide the streets and other infrastructure, and purchasers would engage a builder to put up a house. There were suburbs for every income excepting the lowest. The most exclusive had a number of common features: wide or curving streets, often laid out by a famous landscape architect; designer homes in fashionable styles; ample parks and community facilities; and usually price and legal restrictions to exclude "undesirable" groups. Many nineteenth-century suburbs featured a summer resort hotel that also served to attract would-be buyers. Llewellyn Park, developed on the outskirts of Orange, New Jersey, by Llewellyn S. Haskell in 1853, was one of the first suburbs in the Romantic style.

Most late nineteenth-century suburbs centered on the railroad station, often set in a park or plaza that would be converted into a parking lot after World War II. The typical suburb was designed for walking, so in densely populated areas, stations would average a mile apart. Beyond the areas that had been subdivided into lots were neighborhoods of large estates, and in the "exurban" area past the suburban fringe were even larger estates, horse farms, and country retreats, whose occupants would be driven to the nearest station by carriage or, later, "station wagon."

Despite the concern for exclusivity, wealthy residents required a robust service sector of domestics and tradespeople, none of whom were expected to commute long distance themselves, unlike today. Thus the old suburbs were more of a mosaic than a homogenous sprawl, and communities at various points on the socioeconomic scale might share a common rail line.

Commuting was practically synonymous with the "rush hour," between 8 and 9 A.M. and 5 and 6 P.M. In fact, in the largest cities there were multiple rush hours for blue-collar workers and plant office workers tied to the shift system and the short "banker's hours" of executives in the financial sector. In the nineteenth century the six-day week prevailed in most businesses other than the banks and stock exchanges, and from about 1900 to the late 1940s there was a four-hour "half-holiday" on Saturdays requiring the operation of noontime commuter trains. On all but the lightest-density lines, midday trains were provided for students and shoppers and after-hours service for people working late or staying in town for entertainment.

Railroad commuters moved to familiar rhythms and rituals. Morning and evening papers were obtained from kiosks run by the Union News Co. rather than lock boxes, and friendships grew among seatmates and between commuters and railroad employees. All celebrated the retirements of favorite conductors or "oldest living commuters." Subscription club cars made their appearance in the late 1880s. Some were merely refurbished coaches or lounge cars, while others were specially designed, and most featured individual chairs, card tables, a bar, and, later, air conditioning. The cars were rented to private clubs that one was invited to join. The operation of private club cars was suspended during both world wars and finally halted by public authorities sensitive to charges of elitism in the 1980s. A more democratic version, the bar car, made its appearance after World War II. In New York, Philadelphia, and San Francisco many commuters ended and began their journeys on ferryboats that provided a slow-tempo interlude filled with the sights, sounds, and smells of the harbors, the rhythmic churning of the engines, and the dash from boat to train.

Boston

The Boston region was unusual in that railroad commuting was superimposed over a well-developed and dense pattern of agricultural, manufacturing, and maritime villages, many of them already two centuries old. While perhaps not the first to offer commuted fares, the Boston & Providence was the first to schedule trains leaving the city after business hours on its Dedham line in 1842. It was soon joined by the Boston & Worcester and Boston & Lowell. By 1848 there were said to be no less than 83 commuter stations within 15 miles of Boston, and an estimated one-fifth of Boston's white-collar managerial class lived in the surrounding suburban towns and reached their work by train.

The Boston & Worcester, later part of the Boston & Albany, ran commuter trains as far west as Newton and later Framingham, and such communities as Longwood, Brookline, Wellesley Hills, Wellesley Farms, and Wellesley became handsome suburbs favored by the well-off. During the late nineteenth century the B&A, under the guidance of landscape architect Frederick Law Olmsted and architect Henry Hobson Richardson, created a comprehensive architectural development of the landscape and suburban stations of its "Newton Circuit" line through wealthy Boston suburbs.

By the 1890s the Boston & Providence and the Old Colony Railroad had become parts of the New Haven, operating lines to hundreds of commuting towns in southeastern Massachusetts and Rhode Island. The Old Colony served such communities as Dorchester, Ashmont, West

Quincy, and the Neponset Hills. Here, too, architect Richardson was commissioned to build some extraordinary suburban stations. The most notable of these was his station for the Old Colony at North Easton, built in the 1880s, while a number of commuter stations along the former Boston & Providence possessed attractive masonry structures.

Suburban development of the area to the north came a little later than in other parts of the Boston area, and it was not until the 1880s and 1890s that the railroads began to develop a major suburban traffic. By 1900 all of the northern lines had been absorbed by the Boston & Maine, and the pace of suburbanization was accelerating. The historic towns of Concord, Winchester, Woburn, Salem, and Beverly had begun to attract commuters, and new towns and stations, such as Melrose and Middlesex Falls, and the northwestern towns of Weston, Lincoln, and Concord became popular by 1910.

By 1913 the two downtown Boston terminals at South and North stations were the busiest anywhere in the United States. At South Station some 850 daily New Haven and Boston & Albany trains were handling over 38.4 million arriving or departing passengers annually, most of them commuters. At North Station some 750 daily Boston & Maine trains carried a largely commuter traffic that numbered more than 29.5 million passengers yearly. By 1920, a peak year for Boston commuter trains, the three railroads serving the city were carrying close to a quarter of a million commuters every day. Other cities were growing rapidly, too, and over the last half of the nineteenth century similar commuter rail services were operating in half a dozen of the largest North American urban centers.

New York

At New York City, which by 1830 had surpassed Philadelphia as the national metropolis, enormous population growth helped develop the transportation market. Between 1850 and 1900 the city's population grew almost sevenfold, from a little over half a million to almost 3.5 million.

Paradoxically, the very factors that ensured New York's emergence served to retard or hamper railroad development. The sprawling harbor and long-distance water communications made steamboats a viable alternative into the early twentieth century, even on routes as important as New York to Albany and New York to Boston. Except for the lines entering Manhattan directly from the north, railroads faced a formidable water barrier. Consequently, much early commuting, at least in part, was by steamboat and ferry.

The city's first railroad, the New York & Harlem of 1832, was originally little more than a horsecar line, but by 1841 it crossed into what is now the South Bronx, where Gouverneur Morris laid out the new suburb of Morrisania. On the west side of the Hudson, the New Jersey Railroad opened what later became the Pennsylvania Railroad's main line between Jersey City and Newark, also with horses, in 1834. The first railroad on Long Island, the Brooklyn & Jamaica, opened in 1836.

While most cities have a single, focused center, New York was so large that Manhattan developed two separate office districts about three and a half miles apart. The original Downtown occupied the triangle below Chambers Street with Wall Street at its heart. Around 1900 commercial development leapfrogged to 23rd Street and by 1940 had reached almost to Central Park at 59th Street, creating the Midtown office district and leaving only shipping and financial services Downtown. As a result, most railroads were obliged to maintain both Midtown and Downtown terminals or ferries, and many rail commuters had to transfer to the transit system to reach their destinations in the city.

Likewise, the metropolitan area sustained several secondary centers that were major cities and commuter destinations in their own right, of which the largest were downtown Brooklyn and Newark, New Jersey. Several railroads maintained transfer stations at some distance from the city to route commuters to different destinations within the metropolitan area. Nothing in commuter raildom could compare with Jamaica on the LIRR, where three lines from the city met and diverged again, making "Change at Jamaica!" the watchword for generations of commuters.

The most desirable suburban home sites in Greater New York featured hillside or water views. Those with both, such as both shores of Long Island Sound and the Hudson River, had a special cachet, with the wooded hill country north of Manhattan and the highlands of northwestern New Jersey close behind. The rest of New Jersey and the plains of central and southern Long Island were largely settled by the middle classes. Much of the flat land eventually attracted manufacturing plants, creating blue-collar suburbs as well.

The high price of New York real estate and the sheer size of its commercial center pushed the main commuting zone out to a radius of 30 to 40 miles by the end of the nineteenth century. The exurban zone of estates and farms extended as much as 80 miles in some directions, and by the interwar years there was even substantial commuting from Philadelphia and its northern environs to New York. Many New York artists and writers maintained country homes in Bucks County, Pennsylvania, or eastern Connecticut.

Much early commuting was seasonal, a tradition that persisted on a large scale until World War II in some parts of the region. Wealthy families would move to summer homes, particularly on both shores of Long Island and the north Jersey coast around Long Branch, from which the head of the household would commute to an office in Wall Street or Madison Avenue. Lakewood, New Jersey, 70 miles out, functioned the same way as a winter resort between February and May from the 1880s to the 1930s.

New York was also unusual for its large amount of blue-collar commuting. Many industries and railroad installations in the Jersey Meadowlands just west of the Hudson were accessible only by rail, and many factories located in what had begun as commuter suburbs. During both world wars special trains brought city workers to shipyards and other defense plants in New Jersey and on Long Island. Further complicating the picture were the many racetracks and beaches, such as Rockaway and Coney Island, within the New York City limits, which added their traffic surges to the commuting mix.

By 1900 all the lines serving such prestigious eastern suburbs as Rye, Larchmont, and Greenwich, New York, and Stamford, Westport, and New Canaan, Connecticut, had come under the control of the New York, New Haven & Hartford, successor to the original New York & New Haven of 1848. The four-track main line hosted suburban service as far east as New Haven, from which the Shore Line expresses continued to Boston. Principal branches ran north to Danbury and the Berkshires and to Waterbury.

The New Haven reached New York over the tracks of the pioneer New York & Harlem, which by then had been extended to White Plains and Chatham. During the 1860s "Commodore" Cornelius Vanderbilt united the Harlem, the Hudson River Railroad to Albany, and the New York Central into one of the nation's foremost rail systems, and in 1871 all trains began running into the magnificent Grand Central Depot at 42nd Street. Traffic grew from 130 trains in 1871 to over 500 by 1900, at which time the station was rebuilt and enlarged. A new Grand Central Terminal, with tracks on two underground levels, replaced the old station in 1913. The number of suburban passengers rose from 14.5 million in 1913 to 33.5 million in 1929. All of the principal New York Central and New Haven commuter lines were electrified between 1907 and 1925.

The Harlem line, running up the Bronx River valley through Bronxville and Scarsdale to White Plains, was the New York Central's main suburban line, with reduced service beyond the electrified zone to Brewster, Dover Plains, and Chatham. The Hudson River line through

Riverdale, Yonkers, and Tarrytown to Croton, while serving as the main line to points north and west, had less commuter traffic, in part because of the more rugged topography, with service maintained north of the electrified zone as far as Poughkeepsie. The Hudson shore had been the site of large estates from colonial times to such modern examples as those of the Roosevelts and Vanderbilts at Hyde Park.

The New York Central maintained two lesser commuter routes, both of which ceased operations in 1959. The Putnam Division meandered through small villages in the area between the Hudson and Harlem lines with an electrified branch to Yonkers. On the New Jersey side of the Hudson River, the West Shore Railroad (1884–1885) operated an extensive commuter service to Dumont, New Jersey, and Haverstraw, New York, from a ferry terminal in Weehawken.

Eventually, almost the entire Jersey shore from Jersey City to Weehawken was occupied by railroad facilities, including five big rail-ferry passenger terminals. At first the New Jersey Railroad (the Pennsylvania Railroad after 1871) at Exchange Place, Jersey City, served all the lines running west from the city, but one by one, the tenant roads secured direct access to the waterfront, the Erie at Pavonia Avenue, Jersey City (1861), the Morris & Essex (later the Delaware, Lackawanna & Western) at Hoboken (1863), and the Central Railroad of New Jersey (CNJ) at Communipaw, Jersey City (1864).

The earliest New Jersey commuter line, the future PRR main line, followed the western limit of tidewater navigation through relatively flat country. As a result, the railroad divided towns like Newark, Elizabeth, Rahway, and New Brunswick into residential west sides and industrial east sides on "the wrong side of the tracks." Most PRR commuters were middle and lower middle class. While Menlo Park temporarily attracted Thomas Edison, it failed as a garden suburb and eventually lost its railroad station. The only truly elite suburb on the PRR was Princeton, at the end of a one-mile shuttle line. New York suburban service ended at Trenton, and the New York–Philadelphia expresses also carried many commuters. Although the completion of Pennsylvania Station in 1910 gave the PRR a Manhattan terminal for the first time, commuters were generally excluded until an office district finally developed around the station starting in the late 1920s. The PRR continued to run trains for Wall Street commuters to its old Jersey City terminal until 1961.

The CNJ was the first New Jersey railroad to actively focus on commuter traffic, starting soon after its extension to Jersey City in 1864. Through a subsidiary it developed several suburbs, of which Fanwood was the most prestigious, and was a pioneer in providing club cars and other amenities. The hilly section between Westfield and Plainfield was the most exclusive section on the CNJ main line, with Roselle, Cranford, and Dunellen as solid middle-class communities. Bayonne and Elizabeth were each half commuter suburb and half factory town. Mainline suburban service terminated at Somerville/Raritan, with limited rush-hour service as far west as Hampton.

The CNJ was also a pioneer in developing rail resort traffic to the north Jersey coast by building the New York & Long Branch Railroad in 1875. By 1890 it had acquired a network of lines throughout Monmouth County that became year-round commuter lines by the 1940s. Its popular Sandy Hook steamboats provided an alternate service for summer commuters from exclusive resorts such as Sea Bright, Rumson, West Long Branch, Deal, and Allenhurst via a rail terminal at Atlantic Highlands Pier before World War II. The PRR obtained running rights on the NY&LB in 1882 and eventually took a large share of the commuter business, but the CNJ retained exclusive control of the branches.

At Bound Brook Junction the CNJ connected with the Reading line to Philadelphia, which handled a long-distance commuting business from central New Jersey and the northern suburbs of Philadelphia. In the interwar years the route featured the *Seven O'Klocker* with the private *Seven O'Klocker Klub*, but perhaps the most elegant commuter train on the East Coast was the 1937 Budd streamliner *Crusader* with a café-diner and observation lounge at each end for quick turnarounds. It was joined by the heavyweight streamliner *Wall Street* in 1948.

Although the CNJ was first in the field, the DL&W emerged as the premier commuter line on the Jersey side. The Morris & Essex Railroad's original route through the hills was an operating headache, but the territory offered some of the region's choicest sites for suburban development. The suburban business grew steadily, but without much encouragement from management, which during the nineteenth century was parsimonious and freight oriented and kept the line closed on Sundays. All that changed after 1899, when a new management rebuilt the entire line to first-class standards with elegant concrete and stone stations. Suburban service on the M&E line traversed the more densely developed suburbs of East, West, and South Orange, bucolic Short Hills and Chatham, and the posh satellite towns of Madison and Morristown before terminating at Dover, an old iron-manufacturing center 40 miles from Hoboken. A short branch ran from the west side of Newark to the important suburbs of Bloomfield and Montclair, and a much longer one meandered from Summit through the estate and hunt country to Gladstone. All of these lines were electrified in 1931. The DL&W's freight main line took an easier route, looping to the north through Paterson and joining the M&E line at Denville, east of Dover. The western part of this line served a pleasant hill and lake country and supported a less intensive commuter service that extended beyond the electrified zone to Hackettstown and Washington and on the Sussex Branch to Newton.

The Erie maintained a large suburban service from its Pavonia Avenue ferry terminal in Jersey City, partly overlapping the Lackawanna and covering the territory to the

The Delaware, Lackawanna & Western operated an extensive New York commuter service on its New Jersey lines. Its principal routes were electrified in 1930–1931. An inbound express from Dover to Hoboken made a stop at Convent station in May 1970. —Fred W. Schneider III

north and east. The Paterson & Hudson River Railroad was originally built in the 1830s to reach the manufacturing town of Paterson, and it became part of the Erie main line in the 1850s. One of the first large suburban developments was Rutherford, just west of the Meadowlands. A second area of wealthy suburbs, of which Ridgewood was the most prominent, occupied the area between Paterson and the main suburban terminal at Suffern, New York. A long-distance commuter service continued through Middletown to Port Jervis. Immediately north of Suffern the Erie passed through the Highlands, where a group of wealthy New Yorkers established the exclusive colony of Tuxedo Park, a settlement that gave its name both to the style of dinner jacket first worn there and to a later Erie commuter express. Railroad magnate Edward H. Harriman had his country estate a bit farther north at Arden.

Of the many Erie commuter branches, the Northern ran parallel to the Hudson west of the Palisades through Englewood, New Jersey, to Nyack, New York. The New Jersey & New York ran north from Rutherford through the Pascack Valley to Spring Valley, New York. The Greenwood Lake Branch passed through North Newark, Bloomfield, and northern Montclair and continued north into the lake country northwest of Paterson. Another branch diverged at Croxton to Newark and then ran north along the Passaic River through Belleville and Nutley to rejoin the main line in Paterson.

In 1908–1910 the Hudson and Manhattan Railroad (Port Authority Trans-Hudson or PATH after 1962) built a subway system linking the PRR, Erie, and Lackawanna stations with terminals in lower Manhattan (later the site

of the World Trade Center) and at Herald Square near Penn Station in the Midtown shopping district. Although the "Hudson Tubes" were quicker, many commuters preferred the ferry ride to the crowded trains until the ferries made their final trips in 1967.

Two other New Jersey lines offered modest commuter service. The New York, Susquehanna & Western ran from Jersey City through Paterson and North Hawthorne to Butler. The Lehigh Valley main line avoided formal commuting towns, but the road fielded a single commuter train to South Plainfield and Flemington until the 1940s.

The Long Island Rail Road had been built as a long-distance line through the unpopulated center of the island, and its early management was reluctant to build branches or cater to local passengers. As a result, two rival systems emerged, and in the intense period of competition in the decade after the Civil War the island was overbuilt, with as many as three rival lines serving the same points. By 1881 everything had been consolidated into the LIRR, and even after the removal of much redundant trackage the surviving net was dense enough to evolve into the country's largest commuter rail system. From 1900 to 1966 the LIRR was controlled by the Pennsylvania Railroad, although for most of that time it operated independently.

The LIRR main line offered suburban service as far as Lake Ronkonkoma and Speonk but was less important than what were technically branch lines. The most exclusive communities and the Gold Coast estate country were found along the hilly north shore. Major branches served Great Neck (1866) and Port Washington (1898), Glen

Cove (1868) and Oyster Bay (1889), and Huntington (1867) and Port Jefferson (1873).

The south shore was originally occupied by summer resorts, many of which grew into year-round suburbs, from working-class Coney Island on the west to the exclusive Hamptons and Montauk on the far east. The latter were served by summer parlor-car expresses with names such as *Sunrise Special* and *Cannon Ball*. The main suburban terminal was at Babylon, jumping-off point for the steamers to Fire Island, and the area west of that point filled up with middle-class commuter towns.

The territory just east of the old village of Hempstead, at the convergence of three branch lines, was one of the first to be suburbanized. Alexander T. Stewart, the department store mogul, bought a huge tract of land on the Hempstead Plains in the late 1860s and built the model town of Garden City, as well as his own railroad. LIRR trackage and traffic were dense enough to permit loop operation to both Mineola/Hempstead and the Rockaways.

The original western terminal of the LIRR was located at the Atlantic Avenue ferry in Brooklyn, opposite lower Manhattan. From 1861 to 1877 steam trains were banished from the tracks inside the Brooklyn city limits, and a new ferry terminal was located at Hunters Point in Queens opposite Midtown. Rail service was restored on Atlantic Avenue as far west as Flatbush Avenue in downtown Brooklyn in 1877, from which the majority of the LIRR's commuters could reach the Financial District via the elevated trains on the Brooklyn Bridge, and later by the subway. The LIRR also operated a number of joint services with the Brooklyn Rapid Transit Co., allowing through service between LIRR points and the elevated terminals in Manhattan. Electrified operation between Brooklyn and the Rockaways began in 1905 and was extended to all of the major lines west of Babylon and Mineola by 1926.

The PRR brought the LIRR into Penn Station in 1910, and by 1930 the Long Island accounted for about two-thirds of passengers using the facility. The new upscale communities of Kew Gardens and Forest Hills sprouted on vacant land in Queens to take advantage of the quick travel time to Midtown. From the first, Penn Station was well sited with respect to theaters and department stores, but Brooklyn continued to handle more commuters for many years until the development of adequate subway connections between Penn Station and the rest of the Midtown office district in the 1930s. The LIRR also constructed a station at Hunters Point Avenue in Queens, just a short walk to the Flushing Line subway leading directly to Grand Central.

The LIRR was not only the busiest U.S. commuter line, but also one of great contrasts. Its eastern extremities were all single track running through sparsely populated country. On the west these joined into four- and six-track main lines with the traffic density, high-level platforms, and other characteristics of a rapid-transit system. With

little freight business to offset its growing passenger deficit, the PRR refused to extend further aid in 1949, throwing the road into bankruptcy. It was modernized with state funds and passed into public ownership in 1966, a harbinger of the fate of most commuter rail systems.

Philadelphia

Philadelphia's commercial and financial sectors were already in decline even as the first railroads were being built. Instead, Philadelphia emerged as a great manufacturing center, an agglomeration of neighborhoods anchored by groups of factories in which most people walked to work. The development of rail commuting was further hampered by the fact that the trains halted outside the old city limits, beyond an easy walk to the commercial core. Furthermore, many of the satellite settlements were mill villages or factory towns, such as Manayunk, not the sort of places to attract white-collar commuters.

Philadelphia's first steam railroad, the six-mile Philadelphia, Germantown & Norristown of 1832, ran from the northern outskirts of the city to a long-established village, but its 1854 extension to Chestnut Hill was one of the city's first true commuting lines, serving a district of upper-class country villas. Commuting on the Pennsylvania Railroad's Main Line began with the establishment of the first regular local to Paoli, about 20 miles west of Philadelphia, in 1864. During a line-straightening project in 1869, the PRR was obliged to buy several whole farms about ten miles west of the city, which it subdivided into lots as the village of Bryn Mawr, the first fully planned suburb on the Main Line.

The Philadelphia commuter network had assumed its basic shape by the 1880s. Between 1869 and 1889 all the lines radiating from the city on both sides of the Delaware were absorbed by either the Reading or the PRR. The latter's Broad Street Station (1881) and Reading Terminal (1893) gave each a high-capacity terminus within walking distance of offices and shopping, which themselves had migrated westward. Working clockwise, the PRR operated suburban service to Chester and Wilmington, West Chester via Media and via Paoli, Paoli and Downingtown, Norristown via Bala-Cynwyd, Chestnut Hill, Whitemarsh, and Trenton. The Reading suburban terminals were located at Norristown, Chestnut Hill, Lansdale/Doylestown, Hatboro/New Hope, Newtown, and West Trenton. In addition, both systems maintained New Jersey lines fanning out from ferry terminals at Camden that, while devoted to either agricultural or seashore resort traffic, supported some commuter service: on the PRR to Trenton, Mount Holly/Pemberton, Berlin, and Glassboro, and on the Reading to Williamstown Junction. The Baltimore & Ohio, the last major railroad to arrive in Philadelphia (1886), maintained a meager service to Wilmington and Singerly, Maryland.

The Philadelphia suburban region had a radius of

about 15 miles on average, with a zone of gentlemen's farms, county seats, and small villages beyond. Each of the lines had its own characteristics.

Chestnut Hill was practically synonymous with "old money." The PRR's Henry H. Houston and his son-in-law George Woodward developed the southern side along the PRR starting in 1884, building their own estates and more modest homes and luxury apartments, which they rented to people of good family. North of Chestnut Hill lay the estate country of the White Marsh Valley, home of Edward T. Stotesbury, Philadelphia head of the Drexel-Morgan banking interests.

The PRR Main Line was initially "new money," sprinkled with the estates of the railroad's own executives and other captains of industry. The presence of many elite colleges and boarding schools gave the eastern half of the Main Line a slightly different character from the western and attracted many professionals as the larger estates were subdivided after World War I. The Main Line found its bard in Christopher Morley, author of *Kitty Foyle*, who intoned, "Nothing is so holy as the local to Paoli." Bala and Cynwyd, developed on the ancestral acres of PRR president George B. Roberts, while physically off the Main Line, were culturally and politically part of it.

The PRR's Media line turned a string of old mill villages into modest middle-class suburbs, although the presence of Swarthmore College created another enclave of wealthy professionals between Swarthmore and Media. The land on both banks of the Delaware hosted many fine estates from the days of William Penn onward, but during the nineteenth century most of it was appropriated by heavy industry, and the lines to Wilmington and Trenton featured a few middle-class suburbs interspersed with factory towns. The Philadelphia, Wilmington & Baltimore (PW&B) had relocated its main line from the riverside marshes to wooded high ground between Philadelphia and Chester in 1872. Some elegant suburbs were laid out here, notably Ridley Park, but they never achieved elite status.

North of the city line, in an area dominated by the Reading, lay another cluster of exclusive suburbs. P. A. B. Widener and William L. Elkins, national traction and utility moguls who were even more nouveau than the Main Liners, established their estates and developed the surrounding acres at Elkins Park. It and the adjacent communities of Jenkintown and Abington supplied the bulk of upper-middle-class riders on the Reading's Bethlehem and New York branches, although they lacked the cachet of Chestnut Hill or the Main Line. A bit to the east, at Bryn Athyn, the Pitcairn family (glass, aviation) established an opulent retreat for their fellow Swedenborgians.

Across the Delaware in New Jersey, Haddonfield and Moorestown made the transition from farm villages to prestigious suburbs, while Collingswood on the PRR's Atlantic City line and Wenonah on the Glassboro line were typical of the middle-class communities created by the coming of the railroads.

Because of the generally shorter ride, neither the PRR nor the Reading offered amenities like the subscription club cars or bar cars found at New York. CEOs from the Main Line and Chestnut Hill bluebloods rode the same spartan red multiple-unit (M.U.) cars as the residents of Bridesburg or Chester. Traffic densities and train length were also lower. Likewise, there was less blue-collar commuting than at New York. Both the PRR and the Reading were renowned for their frequent, mile-a-minute service to Atlantic City and other points "down the shore." Like many of the beach services at New York, this encompassed summertime commuting that became year-round after World War II.

The PRR electrified suburban service on the Jersey side to Glassboro and Millville in 1906, and its lines west of the Delaware were electrified between 1915 and 1930. The Reading electrified in 1931 and 1933. As part of its Philadelphia improvements of 1927–1932, the PRR built a separate underground Suburban Station for electric commuter trains topped by an Art Deco office building in 1930. These were the last improvements undertaken by the railroad companies.

Chicago

Chicago's commuter trains developed differently from those of the older eastern cities. There was nothing there before the railroads, and trains and city evolved together. As Chicago grew into America's greatest railroad capital, the rail lines spread into a great iron network that radiated out in every direction from the northbound lines along the western shore of Lake Michigan to the lines that carried the trains around the lake's south shore and east to eastern states. There were only about 350 people living there when the town was incorporated in 1833, and fewer than 30,000 in 1850. By 1890 well over 1 million people lived in Chicago. As the city expanded in every direction, the railroads developed a suburban system that helped populate what would soon become a commuter network second only to New York's. Real estate promotion was a significant factor in developing the new suburban operations, and the term "railroad suburbs" became common for Chicago's fast-growing commuter towns. As at New York, the main commuting zone grew to a radius of 30 to 40 miles, with exurban service extending an equal distance beyond, particularly to the north and northwest. With few exceptions, the suburbs along the lake shore north of the city were the most prestigious, and suburbs decreased in status as one moved counterclockwise to the areas of heavy industry on the southeast.

Chicago's first real suburban line began operating in July 1856 over the main line of the Illinois Central Railroad, then under construction from Chicago south across Illinois. Paul Cornell, a Chicago lawyer and real estate promoter who owned 300 acres of land 6 miles south of the city, had come to the Illinois Central with a proposal that he would sell the railroad 60 acres of the tract if it would agree to establish a railway station named Hyde

On May 10, 1956, the Chicago & North Western's Northwest Line was fully dieselized, and this World War I–era Class E 4-6-2 Pacific No. 1538 was out of work. —Chicago & North Western Railway, *Trains* Magazine Collection

Park and establish daily passenger service. The deal was made, and Hyde Park became the first of many Chicago suburban stations.

Other new communities along the Illinois Central, such as Kenwood, Kensington, South Shore, Riverdale, Harvey, and Homewood, soon followed. Main-line suburban service eventually reached University Park, some 30 miles south of downtown, as well as branches to Blue Island and South Chicago, and it became the busiest of all Chicago suburban routes. So heavy had traffic become that the railroad was obliged to add fifth and sixth tracks between downtown Chicago and Kensington, at 115th Street, in 1885. Obliged by Chicago's Lake Front Ordinance, the Illinois Central electrified its entire suburban system in 1926 and carried out an extensive rebuilding of the system that included elimination of grade crossings and a dedicated suburban right of way over the entire main line from Randolph Street to Richton.

Other lines that opened even earlier than the Illinois Central later evolved into suburban services. Chicago's

first railroad, the Galena & Chicago Union, began operating in 1848 between Chicago and Oak Park and over the next few years was extended further west, while new routes were opened over northwest and northern routes over the next several years. All three lines were consolidated into the Chicago & North Western in 1864, and commuter development began in earnest soon after the Civil War. The first to develop in a major way was the north line along Lake Michigan, reaching such early suburban towns as Lake View, Ravenswood, and Evanston and then extending to Winnetka, Highland Park, and Lake Forest and eventually all the way to Kenosha, Wisconsin. The North Western's Galena line served such early suburban communities as Austin and Oak Park and before the end of the century such more distant places as Elmhurst, Lombard, and Wheaton and as far west as Geneva, some 35 miles from downtown Chicago. The northwest line developed similarly, serving such points as Des Plaines, Arlington Heights, and Barrington, with service eventually extended as far away as Harvard and on a

The Illinois Central Railroad completed one of the most advanced commuter railroads in North America, beginning in 1921 with a massive electrification and terminal improvements program. A southbound train from the IC's downtown Randolph Street suburban terminal headed past the east side of the Chicago Loop between Van Buren Street and Roosevelt Road in June 1966. —William D. Middleton

Hat styles help date this daily rush-hour photograph of the Illinois Central's Chicago suburban service to about 1943. —Library of Congress

branch all the way to Williams Bay, Wisconsin, on Lake Geneva, some 79 miles from Chicago.

Another early start in Chicago rail service was by the Chicago, Rock Island & Pacific, which began running trains between Chicago and Joliet in 1852 and all the way to Rock Island, Illinois, in 1854. A substantial commuter traffic had developed in Englewood, South Englewood, and Blue Island well before the end of the nineteenth century and had reached all the way to Joliet soon after.

A relative latecomer in Chicago commuting was the Chicago, Burlington & Quincy, which did not build its own line between Aurora and Chicago until 1864. The Burlington's suburban trains began operating in 1869, first reaching out as far as Riverside, developed in the late 1860s as a model garden city, with Frederick Law Olmsted and Calvert Vaux brought in as landscape architects. By 1883 trains were operating beyond to La Grange, Hinsdale, and Downers Grove and eventually all the way to Aurora, 38 miles from Chicago.

The Chicago, Milwaukee, St. Paul & Pacific was another latecomer to Chicago commuting, not having completed its line south from Milwaukee to Chicago until 1872. Located between the competing north and northwest North Western lines, the Milwaukee's Milwaukee line developed a relatively modest business to such suburban towns as Morton Grove, Glenview, Northbrook, and Deerfield, while a second line ran west through Elgin.

For a time the three major Chicago electric interurban lines played a leading role in commuter traffic. Both the Chicago Aurora & Elgin and the Chicago North Shore & Milwaukee began operating service into downtown Chicago over the connecting elevated railways relatively early in the twentieth century and remained major suburban carriers through their closure in 1957 and 1963, respectively. Still surviving is the Chicago South Shore & South Bend, which extends around the south end of Lake Michigan to such points as Hammond, East Chicago, Gary, Michigan City, and South Bend in northwest Indiana. Originally the South Shore had provided a connecting service to Illinois Central commuter trains at Kensington until electrification of the Illinois Central in 1926 permitted a direct, one-seat service all the way into downtown Chicago. Still other, less extensive suburban service was operated by the New York Central, Pennsylvania, Chicago & Western Indiana, Chicago & Alton, Wabash, Wisconsin Central, and Chicago Great Western railroads.

San Francisco

West of Chicago only cosmopolitan San Francisco, the financial center for much of the Far West, developed an early commuter rail service. Suburban building sites were almost entirely confined to a narrow band between San Francisco Bay and the foothills of the surrounding mountains, and until the 1930s the region was dependent upon a large fleet of ferries. By 1900 the Southern Pacific Co. controlled most of the steam railroad passenger routes in the Bay Area.

The oldest commuter rail operation west of Chicago was the San Francisco Bay Area's Peninsula line south of San Francisco to San Jose, which began operation in 1864. A modern push-pull train of Caltrain double-decker gallery cars headed south to San Jose near Bay Shore. —William D. Middleton

The only area enjoying direct rail access to San Francisco was the peninsula south of the city, where the San Francisco & San Jose Railroad began operating over a 45-mile route in 1864. The foothills west of the railroad thus became the site of many of the region's most exclusive suburbs.

Even before the San Jose line began operating, mining millionaire Darius Ogden Mills had acquired 1,500 acres of a former Spanish land grant 17 miles south of San Francisco to build a splendid estate called Millbrae. Another wealthy San Franciscan, William Ralston, established an equally fine estate at Belmont, farther south along the peninsula. The towns of Burlingame and neighboring Hillsborough became the homes of the wealthy, the latter in particular being one of the most sought-after addresses in the Bay Area. Farther south, railroad president Leland Stanford acquired a large horse ranch called Palo Alto, where Stanford University opened in 1891, forming the nucleus of another affluent area. SP's San Jose "commute" service increased steadily. Operating under the close oversight of several generations of Southern Pacific chief executives at their Fourth and Townsend and later Market Street headquarters, the trains long enjoyed a reputation for well-run service.

About the same time that the San Jose service began, several short railroads were constructed to ferry landings at Oakland and Alameda on the East Bay shore. In 1869 Oakland became the western terminus of the Central Pacific Railroad's transcontinental line, and in 1882 the company completed a large rail-ferry terminal at Oakland Pier that became the hub for both a frequent local service and long-distance trains running north, south, and east. The first of many local branches opened to the new University of California at Berkeley in 1876. Over the next decade a rival narrow-gauge system developed, centering on Alameda Mole (an earth pier), before being absorbed by the SP system in 1887. By the early 1900s the East Bay was served by a dense network of suburban lines blanketing the area about 10 miles from the ferry terminals.

During 1905 to 1912 the Southern Pacific widened the narrow-gauge lines and installed a new system of electric multiple-unit cars. Even in the steam era the Southern Pacific's East Bay lines resembled an urban rapid-transit line more than a typical commuter service, with much street running, separate tracks, and frequent stops. Their lifespan was also more typical of streetcar systems. The SP's "red electric" survived barely long enough to operate over the bay on the new San Francisco–Oakland Bay Bridge and expired in 1941. Most service was replaced with buses, but two short segments were integrated into the rival Key System rail transit lines, which in turn shut down in 1958.

A third Bay Area commuter service operated from San Francisco to scenic Marin County, north of the Golden Gate. Originally built as a steam-operated narrow-gauge railroad, the North Shore Railroad, later the Northwestern Pacific, by the early 1900s had begun to handle a modest traffic from San Rafael and San Anselmo to a ferry terminal at Sausalito, where transbay ferries completed the journey to and from San Francisco. The line was electrified between 1903 and 1908 and was later converted to standard gauge, and traffic grew as suburban commuters moved to the splendid and peaceful scenery north of the Golden Gate. The train-ferry commuter service ended in 1941, soon after the completion of the Golden Gate Bridge.

Montreal

Montreal, Canada's commercial and financial center, was the only city in the country large enough to sustain an early commuter railroad network. In 1899, less than a decade after the Canadian Pacific Railway had completed its transcontinental railroad between New Brunswick and British Columbia, it began a commuter service from Montreal's Windsor Station. Extending eventually some 40 miles westward over the main line, the line served such pleasant suburbs along the north bank of the St. Lawrence as Montreal West, Dorval, Beaconsfield, and Dorion and Rigaud, just west of the confluence of the Ottawa and St. Lawrence rivers. Other CPR lines extending northwest to Ste. Therese and east across the St. Lawrence to Iberville and Farnham were later discontinued.

Late in 1918 a second major Montreal commuter line began operating with the completion of a new 3.2-mile tunnel under Mt. Royal that gave the Canadian Northern Railway direct access to a downtown Montreal station from the north. The new railroad, operated with electric power, eventually extended some 17 miles northwest to Deux-Montagnes. Just beyond the tunnel's north portal the railroad undertook the development of a planned "model city" of Mt. Royal, which soon became a choice residential area, only a few minutes away from downtown Montreal by electric train. Other CN commuter lines operating parallel to the CPR's route to Rigaud and a line east across the St. Lawrence to St. Lawrence were later discontinued.

By 1900, rail commuting flourished in many other cities. Pittsburgh had an extensive system, and lines operated, among others, at Baltimore-Washington, Buffalo, Cleveland, Cincinnati, Detroit, Harrisburg, Pennsylvania, Milwaukee, and St. Louis. Although it lacked an early commuter railroad service, Los Angeles grew into a major city largely along the electric interurban lines of the Pacific Electric Railway.

Modern Commuter Railroading

Commuter railroading continued to grow well into the twentieth century. By 1913, for example, the Long Island Rail Road was handling more than 9.6 million passengers a year at its Manhattan terminal in the new Penn Station and almost 15.8 million more at its Flatbush Avenue and Long Island City terminals in Brooklyn and Queens. Across the Hudson River the Lackawanna, one of the largest New Jersey commuter roads, was handling 17 million annual passengers through its Hoboken terminal, most of them commuters. During the same year a dozen Chicago railroads handled a daily traffic of more than 123,000 commuters through the city's six terminals. At San Francisco the Southern Pacific's East Bay suburban trains and ferries were carrying more than 19.7 million commuters a year between San Francisco and Oakland, Alameda, and Berkeley, and the Northwestern Pacific was carrying almost 5.4 million more from Marin County.

Much of this growth in commuter traffic was aided early in the century by the new technology of electric traction, which offered improved train performance and greater operating economy for suburban services. Between 1900 and the early 1930s almost all the principal commuter routes at New York and Philadelphia, as well as several major routes at Chicago, San Francisco, and Montreal, were electrified.

But by 1930, under the combined effects of the growing use of the private automobile and the impact of the Great Depression on economic activity, North American commuter railroading had ceased to grow. From a peak level of almost 7 billion passenger-miles in 1929, commuter rail traffic on U.S. railroads declined steadily to a level of less than 4 billion passenger-miles in 1940. The

"I just never imagined they wouldn't finally come up with some form of government aid."

Commuter services on the eastern railroads came close to collapse in the 1960s before government financing became available. The *New Yorker* commented on the situation in April 1965. —© The New Yorker Collection, 1965, James Stevenson. From www.cartoonbank.com. All rights reserved

intense economic activity of the World War II period, together with fuel rationing and automobile shortages, brought a sharp revival in U.S. commuter traffic to a 1947 peak of just over 6 billion passenger-miles. Soon, however, new roads were being built at a record rate, and American commuters quickly returned to their automobiles. By 1962, only 15 years later, U.S. commuter traffic had dropped back to an annual level of only a little more than 4 billion passenger-miles.

Commuter railroading was in trouble for other reasons as well. An uneconomic traffic made up of the daily morning and evening rush hours required the development of peak-period rolling stock, plant, and staff that were only needed during the rush periods. In the years after World War II midday shopping and downtown entertainment traffic declined, and the workweek was shortened from six days to five. Commuter fares had historically been low, and regulatory bodies were reluctant to permit more adequate fares, even though operating costs were climbing. The New York Public Service Commission, to cite one extreme example, froze commutation fares on the Long Island Rail Road for almost 30 years, from 1918 to 1947. The result was that the operation of commuter trains became an increasingly uneconomic service for the main-line railroads. Few of them were willing to make major investments in the business, and the quality of equipment, plant, and service for most commuter services declined from the 1950s onward.

But even as the overall quality of commuter rail service—and ridership—declined, there was a growing recognition of the need for public transportation alternatives to congested roads and highways. The Urban Mass Transportation Act of 1964 was a major development that began a significant flow of federal funding to U.S. transit systems, and local and state governments also began to provide financial support to transit. Commuter rail services shared in this public support and soon began a new era of growth and vitality.

The first major commuter line to move from private ownership to public support was also the largest, the Long Island Rail Road. Hopelessly uneconomic, the Long Island paid its last dividend in 1933 and was bankrupt by 1949. Two disastrous wrecks in 1950 and steadily deteriorating service first brought public support to the Long Island in the 1950s and finally, in 1966, public ownership as a subsidiary of what is now New York's Metropolitan Transportation Authority.

Over the next decade and a half public support became universal for U.S. and Canadian commuter rail services. What began, in many cases, as public assistance for capital or operating costs generally evolved into some form of more direct public agency control and operation of the services. Such major systems as Boston's Massachusetts Bay Transportation Authority (MBTA), New York's Metro-North and Long Island railroads, New Jersey Transit,

Philadelphia's Southeastern Pennsylvania Transportation Authority (SEPTA), Chicago's Northeast Illinois Railroad Corp. (Metra), and San Francisco's Peninsula Corridor Joint Powers Board (Caltrain) now not only operate but also own all or a substantial portion of the systems over which they operate. Others operate much of their service under contract arrangements with the freight railroads that own the fixed plant.

This new era of public involvement has brought with it the strong financial support needed to rehabilitate the fixed plant, acquire new equipment, and improve and expand services, and it has made commuter rail the fastest-growing segment of public transportation for much of the past two decades. While the already-existing systems expanded, entirely new commuter services were being added. Toronto's GO Transit, which opened in 1967, was the first of the new post–World War II commuter lines to operate, eventually reaching a total of eight routes radiating from Toronto. By the end of the twentieth century there were close to a dozen more. Connecticut established a new service along the Northeast Corridor. Maryland developed an extensive service in the region around Washington and Baltimore over three routes, and Virginia established new services over two routes. Florida developed a new Miami–West Palm Peach service. Dallas and Fort Worth joined to open a new line between the two cities. Los Angeles Metrolink services operated over seven routes in four Southern California counties, and San Diego opened a new route between San Diego and Oceanside. In the San Francisco Bay Area commuter trains linked the San Joaquin Valley with San Jose. In the Northwest a new service linked Seattle, Tacoma, and Everett, and a new route operated to suburban points east of Vancouver, British Columbia. Plans were well along for beginning still more commuter lines, including Nashville, Tennessee, Atlanta, Georgia, Salt Lake City, Denver, Colorado, Orlando, Florida, Albuquerque, New Mexico, and Minneapolis. From the 1962 low point of 4 billion passenger-miles, commuter rail had increased by half again by 1982 to reach just over 6 billion annual passenger-miles and had climbed by half again to more than 9.5 billion commuter passenger-miles by the beginning of the twenty-first century.

Operating Commuter Rail

North American commuter rail services have typically been integrated with other railroad operations, sharing track space, stations, and other facilities with long-distance passenger and freight services. On some of the largest commuter carriers separate terminal facilities were developed for the suburban services. New York's Grand Central Terminal, for example, was developed with a separate lower level designed exclusively to handle the throngs of commuters from the New York Central and New Haven commuter services. At Philadelphia the Pennsylvania Railroad developed an entirely separate under-ground Suburban Station with direct connections to the subway system. Alone among North American commuter railroads, the Illinois Central Railroad developed a completely separate fixed plant for its Chicago suburban operation when the service was modernized and electrified in 1926.

Operating practices typically followed traditional railroad standards. Trains operated on timetable schedules, rather than on the headway basis common on rapid-transit lines. And unlike rapid-transit systems, which used a fixed-fare or zone-fare system, with off-train fare collection at stations, commuter lines typically employed a distance-based fare structure, with labor-intensive on-train ticket collection or inspection by the train crew.

The shared use of tracks for both freight and passenger operations introduced still other labor-intensive practices. Because of freight equipment clearance problems, for example, commuter stations were typically built with low-level station platforms, which in turn necessitated a large-enough train crew to handle doors and traps at each entrance and required longer station dwell times compared with what was possible with high-level platforms.

Most of these standard railroad practices carried over into modern commuter rail services, but in recent years innovations in the fixed plant, equipment, and operating practices of commuter rail services have been improving their productivity and efficiency. Wherever possible, many commuter lines are shifting to the use of high-level platforms to speed loading and unloading and more readily meet the needs of disabled passengers. Ticketing and fare collection on commuter rail systems are beginning to shift to more efficient systems, including the European-style barrier-free, proof-of-payment system. The system, which requires possession of a valid ticket or pass, subject to random checks by security staff, has helped reduce the costs of fare collection, while also improving passenger flow at stations by permitting unimpeded entrance and exit.

Commuter rail operators are finding that the market they serve is changing radically from the traditional radial pattern based upon travel between suburban home and downtown employment. Commuter travel is also increasingly intermodal in nature, linked to private automobile or public transportation use at either end of the train trip, and commuter systems are being revised to make these changed journeys more convenient.

Many lines are experiencing growth in "reverse commute" or "suburb-to-suburb" commuting as workers move between inner-city or suburban residence and employment in another suburb. At Philadelphia the completion of the Center City Commuter Tunnel that linked the former Reading Terminal and Suburban Station in 1983 gave SEPTA the ability to through-route a number of its suburban tines, greatly facilitating this new traffic pattern, and a long-planned Cross County Metro "intrasuburban" rail line would link suburban residential and employment centers in Chester and Bucks counties north of

Philadelphia. Chicago has developed similar commuting patterns, and Metra is now planning what it calls the STAR Line, which will install a north-south line in the circumferential Elgin, Joliet & Eastern Railway north from Joliet to Hoffman Estates and then southeast to O'Hare Airport. The line is designed to serve people living and working in the suburbs and will also provide connections with three of Metra's existing radial routes. At the suburban end of systems this means that plenty of parking is needed, and several lines have even built new "cornfield" stations that are not within a suburban community at all, but have plenty of parking and are convenient to the suburban road system.

Much better connections between commuter rail and other transit services are being developed. MBTA's new Southwest Corridor project at Boston, for example, provides direct links at several stations between commuter trains and MBTA bus and rail transit services. The Metropolitan Transportation Agency (AMT) at Montreal operates a new intermodal station at Vendôme that gives Rigaud-line commuter rail passengers direct links with the Montreal Metro and bus services. Both Virginia Railway Express and Maryland Rail Commuter (MARC) have established several similar connections with the Washington Metro, and MARC's Camden Line now has a cross-platform connection with Baltimore's Central Corridor light-rail line at Camden Station. The new Bay Area Rapid Transit (BART) terminal opposite the San Francisco airport has a major transfer point between commuter rail, BART rapid transit, buses, and automobiles at Millbrae.

Commuter Equipment

Historically, there was little difference between the equipment employed for commuter services and that operated in

In 1950 Chicago's commuter lines first began operating double-deck gallery cars, which can typically seat about 159 passengers, and the city's Metra commuter rail line now operates about 1,000 of them. A northbound Milwaukee District train to Fox Lake departed from Union Station in April 1989. —William D. Middleton

other passenger services. A few roads operated steam locomotives that were specially designed for commuter service, but more often the suburban trains were operated with older steam, and later diesel, locomotives stepped down from main-line service. Similarly, passenger cars were often no more than downgraded main-line rolling stock, and even when cars were built new for commuter service, they were usually little more than austere, high-capacity versions of the standard railroad day coach. Only for electrified commuter services, where the multiple-unit (M.U.) car became the preferred equipment standard, was there a distinctive commuter passenger car, but even these were little more than self-propelled electric versions of the standard day coach.

More recently, however, there has been extensive innovation in equipment designed specifically to provide the high capacity, rapid loading and unloading, and laborsaving operation needed for an efficient commuter service. Some of this innovative thinking in equipment goes back as far as 1932, when the Long Island first experimented with high-capacity double-deck passenger cars. The first fully successful move in this direction, however, came in 1950, when the Burlington introduced the first multilevel gallery cars that seated as many as 148 passengers in an 85-foot car. Other Chicago-area commuter lines later adopted the gallery-car design, and Chicago's Metra now operates a fleet of some 1,000 gallery cars. Similar gallery cars have also been acquired for San Francisco's Peninsula Commute Service and Montreal's Rigaud line, and still other secondhand gallery cars are in use on other lines. A few years after Chicago introduced North America's first gallery cars, the Chicago & North Western introduced the European concept of push-pull train operation, which precluded the need to switch locomotives at each end of a run; it has since become the standard for North American commuter operation.

In 1977 Toronto's GO Transit and supplier Hawker Siddeley (now Bombardier) developed a distinctive, aluminum-bodied, bilevel design that seats as many as 162 passengers in an 85-foot car, with two full decks, as well as intermediate-level end decks over the trucks. Two wide doors on each side, placed at the quarter points on the lower level, can empty or load in less then two minutes. GO Transit has since shifted to all bilevel cars, with a current fleet of 341 in push-pull service. The same design has been a popular choice for other new commuter lines: the Canadian-built bilevels now operate on more than half a dozen other lines.

For some of the older eastern commuter lines, restricted clearances precluded the use of most available double-decker car designs as a means of increasing train capacity within the constraints of available platform lengths. Instead, these lines have adopted the use of a 3-2 seating configuration in a single-level car that can typically accommodate as many as 131 passengers in a standard 85-foot car. Many of these cars are equipped with standard platforms at both ends, which can be used with

In 1977 Toronto's GO Transit, together with supplier Hawker Siddeley (now part of Bombardier), developed a new design of bilevel aluminum cars that can seat as many as 162 passengers. The design has proved popular for new commuter rail lines all over North America. This was a GO Transit train at the Old Cummer station on the Richmond Hill line in 1990. —GO Transit

either high- or low-level platforms, or a center door that can be used for high-level platforms. Where all-high-level loading is possible, such designs as the modern single-level cars for the Long Island or Metro-North place wide doors at the quarter points for more efficient loading and unloading.

However, several eastern lines are now operating or planning new designs for double-deck cars as a means to further increase capacity. Confronted by steadily growing traffic, and with a maximum train length limited by station platform lengths, Boston's MBTA in 1989 developed a bilevel-car design that could meet its restricted clearances and would permit passenger loading and unloading from either high- or low-level platforms, needed on the Boston system. Employing 3-2 seating, the big cars seat as many as 185 passengers. Similar bilevel cars for restricted eastern clearances have since been adopted for the Long Island's nonelectric car fleet, Maryland's MARC, and Virginia Railway Express, and bilevel cars are now being planned for New Jersey Transit.

Major technological changes have also been introduced for new versions of the electrified M.U. cars that have long been the mainstay of electrified commuter rail systems. The biggest change is a shift to AC propulsion systems, which promise as much as 20 percent greater energy efficiency, as well as reduced maintenance costs and improved reliability, over those for conventional DC series motor propulsion systems. The key to these modern AC propulsion systems is the use of semiconductor-based inverters to provide a three-phase AC current for three-phase asyn-

chronous traction motors. Other typical technical features include the use of advanced, microprocessor-based control systems that permit onboard vehicle diagnostics, fault monitoring, and reporting capabilities, which can improve reliability and reduce maintenance downtime. Modern semiconductor-based power inverters, which weigh less and reduce maintenance costs, are replacing motor-generator sets for auxiliary power requirements. Typically, M.U. cars are now built as married pairs or even three-car sets to share electrical equipment and other support services. Early examples of these new-technology propulsion systems have included remanufactured Arrow III cars for New Jersey Transit and a new M.U. car fleet for Montreal's Deux-Montagnes line.

Several electrified commuter lines have recently shifted to the use of electric-locomotive-hauled push-pull trains as a more economical alternative to the use of expensive electric M.U. cars. In 1986–1987 both Maryland's MARC and Philadelphia's SEPTA acquired the same 125 mph AEM7 electrics built by Electro-Motive for Amtrak service, and New Jersey Transit acquired a number of similar ABB Traction (now part of Bombardier) ALP-44 units for push-pull service a few years later. More recent commuter electrics have included the acquisition by Maryland's MARC of the same high-speed, 8,000-hp HHL Bombardier/GEC Alstom unit used by Amtrak and a 7,000-hp ALP-46 design built by Bombardier for New Jersey Transit that is similar to locomotives used in Germany and elsewhere in Europe.

In 1956 Electro-Motive and the New Haven came up

with the novel idea of a dual-power locomotive that could operate either as a normal diesel-electric or as a straight electric from the DC third rail in the New York City terminal area, permitting a locomotive-hauled train originating in nonelectric territory to operate into Grand Central Terminal or Penn Station without a change of locomotive. EMD built 60 of these FL9 units that eventually ended up in both Metro-North and Amtrak service. Some of these durable locomotives are still in service, and the same concept has been employed for newer generations of the dual-power commuter locomotive for both Metro-North and the Long Island. General Electric built a dual-power version of its Genesis diesel-electric, and Electro-Motive built a new dual-power design for the Long Island.

Except for the electrified commuter lines in the East and the two electric lines on Chicago's Metra, however, the diesel-electric locomotive is the motive power of choice for most commuter lines. Earlier, diesel-electric power was usually an older unit handed down from main-line service, but these have now largely been supplanted by either new or remanufactured units designed for the frequent starts and stops and high acceleration requirements of commuter operation. Electro-Motive's F40 unit or similar rebuilt units have been widely used. In 1988 Electro-Motive developed the newer 3,000-hp F59PH design to provide enhanced acceleration, deceleration, and braking characteristics to better meet the needs of commuter service, and a more recent F59M streamlined design is now being supplied. The choice of locomotive builders, once limited to GE or Electro-Motive, was widened in 2003 by delivery of 27 new 3,600-hp MP36PH-3S units built by Wabtec Corp. for Chicago's Metra. European supplier Alstom Transport offered still another choice in 2004 with the delivery of 33 of its 4,200-hp PL-42AC diesel-electrics, equipped with Electro-Motive diesels.

In the early 1950s the Budd Rail Diesel Car (RDC) was a popular new idea in passenger equipment. From the time the first RDC prototype went into service in 1949 to the end of RDC production in 1962, nearly 400 of the diesel cars were built, many of them for commuter services. The Boston & Maine was by far the biggest user of the RDC in commuter service, operating virtually all of its Boston services with an RDC fleet that reached more than 100 cars, giving B&M maximum flexibility in using its equipment in what *Railway Age* called "a multiple-unit suburban service without electrification." Central of New Jersey, the New Haven, the Baltimore & Ohio, the Reading, and their successor companies or public authorities were among other significant commuter operators of the RDC. As the original RDCs began to wear out, Budd developed what was planned to be a successor diesel car, the SPV2000, in 1973, but the new car experienced a variety of mechanical problems. Only a few were built, and the aging RDCs gradually went out of service.

Even without a modern car on the market, the concept of a rail diesel car that could more efficiently operate low-density or off-peak commuter services continued to draw interest. In 1996 Dallas Area Rapid Transit (DART) went ahead with old RDCs, completely remanufactured as like-new cars, for its new Trinity Railway Express service between Dallas and Fort Worth, and by 2002 Colorado Railcar Mfg. had built a new federally compliant diesel multiple-unit (DMU) car that was in trial operation all over North America, with a single-level and two bilevel DMUs going into service on Florida's Tri-Rail commuter line. Plans were under way for a DMU service in a Raleigh-Durham corridor in North Carolina. A new concept was diesel light rail (DLR), which uses a diesel-powered light-rail-type vehicle. Already in operation were DLR lines at Ottawa, Ontario, and between Camden and Trenton, New Jersey, with a third under way for a line between Oceanside and Escondido, California. All three lines are using European-built equipment.

—Christopher T. Baer and William D. Middleton,
with additional contributions from
Norman Carlson and Arthur L. Lloyd

REFERENCES

Demoro, Harre W. *Electric Railway Pioneer: Commuting on the Northwestern Pacific, 1903–1941.* Glendale, Calif.: Interurban, 1983.

Dorin, Patrick C. *Commuter Railroads: A Pictorial Review of the Most Traveled Railroads.* Seattle, Wash.: Superior, 1970.

Ford, Robert S. *Red Trains in the East Bay: The History of the Southern Pacific Transbay Train and Ferry System.* Glendale, Calif.: Interurban, 1977.

Grow, Lawrence. *On the 8:02: An Informal History of Commuting by Rail in America.* New York: Mayflower, 1979.

Humphrey, Thomas J., and Norton D. Clark. *Boston's Commuter Rail: Second Section.* Cambridge, Mass.: Boston Street Railway Assn., 1986.

———. *Boston's Commuter Rail: The First 150 Years.* Cambridge, Mass.: Boston Street Railway Assn., 1985.

Lind, Alan R. *Limiteds along the Lakefront: The Illinois Central in Chicago.* Park Forest, Ill.: Transport History Press, 1986.

Nelligan, Tom. *Commuter Trains to Grand Central Terminal.* New York: Quadrant, 1986.

North American Commuter Rail 1994. Pasadena, Calif.: Passenger Train Journal, 1994.

Railway Age. Annual inserts titled *Commuter or Regional Rail Planner's Guides,* Oct. 1988, Oct. 1989, and each Nov. from 1990 to 1999, ed. William D. Middleton; *Passenger Rail Planner's Guide,* each Mar. from 2000 to 2002, ed. William D. Middleton and Julian Wolinsky; in Mar. 2003 and Mar. 2004, edited by Frank Malone; and in Mar. 2005 and Mar. 2006, ed. Greg Gormick.

Rosenbaum, Joel, and Tom Gallo. *NJ Transit Rail Operations.* Piscataway, N.J.: Railpace, 1996.

Williams, Gerry. *Trains, Trolleys & Transit: A Guide to Philadelphia Area Rail Transit.* Piscataway, N.J.: Railpace, 1998.

Competition. *See* AIR

TRANSPORTATION; HIGHWAY

TRANSPORTATION; PIPELINES; WATER

TRANSPORTATION

Computerization

Mechanical and electronic computing shares the stage with electricity, the automobile, telephones, and commercial aviation as twentieth-century innovations that fundamentally affected the structure and operation of the world economy. The U.S. railroad industry was among the pioneers in the implementation of computing technology and often led the way in the quest for its successful application to the solution of business and engineering problems. From the bulky mechanical machines of the early 1900s to today's powerful computers, driven by complex application and operating system software, the railroads continue to benefit from the changes in the continuously evolving hardware and software industries.

In the very early 1900s Herman Hollerith, a Washington, D.C., inventor, joined with Otto E. Braitmayer, a machinist, to form the Tabulating Machine Co. to continue the development and marketing of machines that Hollerith had been working on for several years. Hollerith's system consisted of a special card, along with machines that would read and manipulate the data on the card. The process flow was to take a blank card and insert it into a manual keypunch machine, and a keypunch operator would punch holes in the card that corresponded to the keys struck on the keypunch machine. This process was applied to as many cards as necessary to complete the data entry. Then the cards were entered into other machines, a sorter and a tabulator, to record the data, then perform calculations to produce the results in report format.

Hollerith became interested in developing this technology while working at the U.S. Census Bureau, which worked through a mountain of statistics and calculations every day. As he began to develop and market his new machine, the business community, including several railroads, became interested in applying the technology to their work because they, too, regularly dealt with large quantities of statistics and financial information. To this point, the railroads had been completing this work by hand, which, while relatively accurate and reliable, was painfully slow and tedious. The idea of freeing the time of those who did all this work by hand to enable them to focus on more productive pursuits was very attractive to business and railroad managements.

The Southern was among several railroads that explored the capabilities of the new Hollerith cards and machines for automatic tabulation in accounting work. This early equipment was called the Hollerith Tabulator with Motor Driven Card Feed. —IBM Corporate Archives

In 1906 several railroads, including the Pennsylvania, the New York Central, and the Southern Railway, began using the new Hollerith cards and machines. Since the headquarters of the Southern were in Washington, D.C., also the headquarters of the Tabulating Machine Co., Southern was able to provide a test environment for further development of Hollerith's technology. Tabulating Machine developed an automatic version of the tabulator and installed one in Southern's accounting offices for testing. During the testing phase work was done concurrently on the old manual and the new automatic machines to ensure that they both produced the same results. When the results from the automatic machine did not agree with those from the manual machine, Hollerith and Braitmayer would make the necessary modifications to both machines to ensure correct calculations.

The railroads purchased additional computing equipment from the Tabulating Machine Co. over the next three years and implemented it in more departments that dealt with statistics and calculations. Again, since they were close to Southern's headquarters, Hollerith and Braitmayer were regular visitors to the road's offices as they refined their machines and worked with the railroad to host other businesses that were interested in the technology. In 1911 the assets of the Tabulating Machine Co. were sold to organizations that eventually joined to form the International Business Machines Corp.

During the next 40 years the railroads continued to expand their use of computing technology. The economic and cultural challenges associated with World War I, the Great Depression, and World War II affected the development and adoption of computing technology in various ways. Although the economic crisis of the 1930s slowed business spending significantly, the global military conflicts, as well as the space program, subsequently accelerated research and development.

One historic challenge the railroads faced was keeping track of the whereabouts of their freight cars on foreign lines, as well as foreign-line cars running on their own line. This was, and remains today, critical for the calculation of per diem that the railroads must pay each other for the use of each other's freight cars. Shortly after the end of World War II computing technology was applied to this work,

and it provided enormous improvements by reducing manual effort, as well as increasing the accuracy of freight-car tracking and per diem payments. Recording and input of data for tracking cars and per diem payments was made much more efficient with the introduction of new punch-card equipment, which allowed information that was duplicated for all cars (e.g., basic information needed for all cars in a freight train, regardless of their destination or contents) to be reproduced on multiple cards, so the only punching required was for information specific to each individual car. Once all the punching, sorting, and reading of cards was complete, reports were generated that presented this information in a readable format. These reports were often bound in books for later reference.

As the U.S. economy began its postwar growth in the 1950s, the improved computing technology developed during the war was more readily available to businesses. Mainframe computing was rapidly adopted, and the speed and capabilities of computers were now far beyond anything available before. Furthermore, the railroad industry began to realize that computing technology not only was a tool to provide improved efficiency in completing daily tasks, but was also developing into a strategic competitive weapon. As the railroads began to analyze the movement of traffic over their lines, they learned much about what traffic was moving where, which shippers

By 1955 the Southern had installed an IBM 650 Magnetic Drum Data Processing Machine in its Atlanta offices. Keypunch operator Barbara B. Cox translates data from a waybill and freight bill onto punched cards for the IBM 650. —Southern Railway Historical Assn. Archives at the Southern Museum

TIES

THE SOUTHERN RAILWAY SYSTEM MAGAZINE

January 1957

Southern made further advances in its ability to manage data electronically with its adoption of the advanced IBM 705 Model II, Electronic Data Processing Machine. Southern president Harry A. DeButts (*left*) and IBM vice president L. H. LaMotte celebrated the occasion in December 1956. —Southern Railway, Southern Railway Historical Assn. Archives at the Southern Museum

were generating the most revenue, and which traffic was the most profitable. This information enabled the sales force in the field to better organize its marketing efforts by focusing on new opportunities, as well as to adjust its work with existing shippers to better reflect the importance of that shipper to the railroad. Although early adopters of computing technology enjoyed a brief competitive advantage, it quickly became apparent that implementation of it by all railroads was required for survival.

Significant improvements in data-transfer speed and storage came with the introduction of the magnetic drum, magnetic tape, and disc drives in the 1950s. The familiar punched cards were still run through the card reader, but the data could go directly to the computer for calculation or could be fed to and stored on either drum, tape, or disc. Tapes could feed data to the computer and receive the completed data calculations at high rates of

speed. Further, tapes, drums, and disc drives were much more convenient media for storing large amounts of data than boxes of punched cards.

The development of on-line data input terminals enabled users to feed data directly to the computer without the use of punched cards. In the 1960s Southern Railway employed these terminals, along with long-distance xerography (LDX), to facilitate faster processing of freight-car waybills. Southern equipped stations along the line with LDX scanners, into which the agent would feed actual car waybills, and the waybills would print out on special LDX printers at the railroad's computer center. This network of LDX printers and scanners, which operated much like modern facsimile machines, was linked together by a microwave communication system owned by the railroad. Clerks at the computer center would enter information from the waybill directly into the computer, providing relatively current car movement information

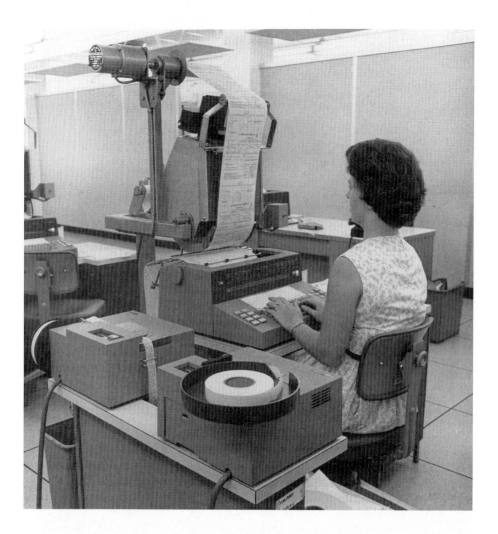

for shippers and railroad managers. This process also provided for faster generation of freight bills, which improved cash flow.

The 1960s saw continued and significant improvement in the maturity and capabilities of computing technology, and the railroads were not only applying it to the traditional accounting, payroll, and traffic analysis tasks, but also to the management of the vast inventory of materials and supplies used, as well as to the operation of the railroad itself. The Missouri Pacific Railroad, for example, initiated a multiyear effort in 1959 to computerize the tracking and management of all supplies. As one must before replacing a manual system with an automated one, a thorough review of the current data and processes was conducted. As the Missouri Pacific worked through its evaluation of the current state, it quickly learned of improvements to be made. For example, the railroad lacked a structured methodology for deciding upon the quantities of particular items to maintain in stock. To this point, warehouse and supply managers had determined the quantity of a particular item to order based on an estimate of what they thought would be needed after reviewing past experience. In addition, the railroad realized that it had a large inventory of materials necessary for supporting a fleet of steam locomotives, which, of course, it

no longer needed. As a result, MoPac developed a well-organized system for cataloging inventory items, as well as assigning reorder points and reorder quantities for each item in the computer. With a more logical method of inventory management in place, MoPac was able to reduce its investment in inventory, increase inventory turnover, and operate on a system that was closer to one of "just in time," all improvements that contributed to the bottom line.

Naturally, the implementation of this system created challenges for the workforce. Managers who were accustomed to ordering items in quantities that they decided upon were now provided order quantities by the new computer system. The implementation of the system on the railroad also required a commensurate adjustment in the behavior of suppliers. With the railroad tightly controlling its inventory, the supplier could no longer count on large orders based on estimates by railroad warehouse managers. In addition to affecting the supplier's shipping strategy, it also forced a more precise view of its own manufacturing and procurement processes in order to avoid incurring large inventory holding costs that had previously been borne by the railroads.

While the railroad industry was using computing technology to support and standardize several business processes in the 1960s, a key area that was ripe for improvement was the system of daily communication between various divisions of the railroad as trains moved over the line and into and out of yards. Although the computer reports that the railroads had previously relied upon for car movements and traffic information were very valuable, they were usually at least a day or two old. With the amount of change that could occur within just a 24-hour period, it became apparent that more timely information was needed in order to effectively run a modern railroad and provide better service to the customer.

In the 1960s the Southern Pacific Railroad, along with Stanford University and IBM, developed a system referred to as Total Operations Process System (TOPS). This system enabled the SP to communicate train and car movements on its lines on a real-time basis so that the operation of terminals throughout the system could be coordinated with the movement of trains over the main line. Introduced on the railroad in 1968, it provided shippers with current information on the progress of their shipments, kept terminals throughout the railroad apprised of train and car movements, and provided other railroads with standards for data interchange should they want to implement their own real-time systems. It was a vast improvement over the older systems in that information on a car's whereabouts was updated instantly on the computer, instead of waiting for the information to be received, then input into a central computer. TOPS also provided SP terminal managers with information on the status of diesel locomotive maintenance, so they could arrange for the servicing needs of any locomotives that were headed to their terminals. As the Southern Pacific continued to work with the system, it found more and more things it could do to improve the operation of the railroad.

When the railroad industry as a whole began to look carefully at the work Southern Pacific had done, the SP formed its own consulting business to provide software and training to railroads around the country, as well as in other parts of the world. Working with the SP, the Burlington Northern, Union Pacific, and Missouri Pacific developed similar systems for their roads, and thus an effort was set in motion to spread this technology throughout the industry.

As the industry worked through the 1970s, a decade that saw much turbulence in railroading, causing many observers to question the ability of the industry to survive in private hands, computer technology continued to be implemented and its use refined in an effort to help the troubled industry. In 1980 the Southern Railway completed the implementation of its own systemwide real-time information system, known as Terminal Information Processing System (TIPS). This was built on the technology that many railroads, including Southern, had developed and implemented during the previous decade.

The daily operation of the railroad is heavily supported by computer systems in many ways. For example, they are used for controlling car routing and speed in hump yards. These systems line the switches and control car speed through the use of retarders and provide significant savings in labor costs and freight damage. Computers also drive centralized traffic control (CTC) on the railroads, which enables main-line crossover switches, interlockings, and block signals all over the railroad to be controlled from a single operations center. In addition, lineside detectors for hotboxes and dragging equipment, which are critical to the safe operation of the railroad, rely on computer technology for operation.

Special railroad cars are equipped with computers and other equipment to evaluate various aspects of railroad operation in order to identify needed improvements. One type of car is used to analyze the track as it travels over the line, to ensure that it is in top shape. Another type is designed to record and evaluate train performance and handling on particular routes. This information provides insight into possible changes needed in the way trains are operated on these routes and is particularly useful for implementing changes that will reduce claims for damaged freight. The information also serves as the basis for simulated runs in the locomotive and train simulators used by the railroads to train locomotive engineers.

Advanced software and hardware support the efforts of managers who are charged with providing tactical direction for the railroad each day. Decision support software is used to help railroaders manage the distribution of locomotives and cars on the line, as well as crew scheduling. Automatic Equipment Identification on cars, read by lineside devices, enables railroads to keep track of all equipment on their systems for more effective management of the car fleet.

An area that benefits significantly from computer technology is operations research. Railroads are able to build computer models that allow them to simulate a variety of train and car movements over the railroad in order to evaluate outcomes and to determine if a change in operations would improve efficiency. This is very helpful for evaluating potential changes in the movement of trains over the railroad main line, as well as in classification yards.

Perhaps one of the most interesting new uses of computing technology in daily railroad operation is the use of handheld devices to remotely control the speed and direction of locomotives in yard movements. Instead of relying on radio and hand-signal communication from the railroader on the ground to the locomotive engineer to direct train movements, the person on the ground actually operates the train with a device that sends a digital signal to a computer on the locomotive, greatly reducing the likelihood of an accident.

The economic deregulation of the railroad industry brought about by the Staggers Act of 1980 required a greater emphasis on the application of computing technology to market and economic research, and today's planners and marketing specialists rely on it more than ever. With greatly expanded marketing freedom, the railroads use computers to evaluate market and pricing activity, as well as to build models that serve as testing grounds for new strategies in a freer regulatory environment. Analysts are also able to use general economic models to evaluate the national and regional economies and incorporate this data in specific railroad economic models to refine the quality of their analysis. More accurate cost analysis obtained through the use of computers enables planners to take advantage of the ratemaking freedom introduced by Staggers to price service in accordance with costs, thereby improving profitability.

The introduction of the personal computer in the early 1980s began a revolution in computing technology. In addition to facilitating tasks that had previously been done on mainframe terminals, the railroads, along with the rest of the business community, could engage the computer in helping with a variety of office tasks, such as word processing, which replaced the typewriter. Spreadsheet programs benefited many bookkeeping and accounting tasks that had previously been produced by the "computer department." Further, new types of storage and retrieval devices, such as hard drives, floppy discs, and compact tapes, permitted easier and faster data transfer from one system to another. Personal computers could also be used as terminals for mainframe computers.

The speed and capability of personal computer hardware and software exploded in the 1980s and 1990s. In addition to the automation of daily office tasks and enhanced communication via electronic mail throughout the railroad, the personal computer provides tremendous support to the railroad's sales force. Using laptops to connect to wireless networks, marketing representatives are able to access real-time information about a variety of issues while visiting customer sites, thereby sharpening the effectiveness of the railroad's overall marketing efforts and customer service. Presentations for internal business meetings, as well as those with customers, are enhanced through the use of software such as Microsoft PowerPoint. Completed presentations can be shown to meeting participants in the form of a slide show and can also be sent via email for follow-up and reference after the meeting.

The introduction of client-server networks brought new levels of speed, flexibility, and effectiveness to users of personal computers. Particularly well suited for large networks, the client-server model enables software applications to be shared across a community of users at a much lower cost per machine. Further, these systems can leverage the use of relational databases employed by the complex software used for large businesses like railroads. Relational databases provide much more efficient storage and retrieval of data and enable the end user to access needed information more quickly. Although many mainframe computing systems still exist in the railroad industry, as they do in other industries, such as banking, the use of the personal computer and the client-server networks that support them continues to grow.

The Internet has also provided a convenient medium for the railroads to share information with shippers, the press, and the general public through their websites. Shippers can log on to the railroad's website to trace shipments and learn about additional services offered by the railroad. The press can access it for earnings information, annual reports, press releases, and executive speeches. The general public can visit it to obtain general information about the railroad, and many websites offer sections that celebrate the history of the line and contain photographs of trains and the more scenic parts of the territory they serve.

The computer is no longer simply a tool that provides information to make the railroad run more efficiently and profitably. The industry is so reliant on computer systems that a computer virus or major system glitch can shut down a railroad. The advanced computers that support modern locomotives, signaling and communication systems, and other operational processes are as critical to the business of running trains as are track, cars, and personnel. Consequently, information technology departments must be more robust and technically savvy than ever to ensure that trains continue to move uninterrupted across the system.

In the future the role of information technology will likely change in ways that are difficult to imagine now. For example, some suggest that trains will one day operate without a human crew. Farfetched, perhaps, but considering what today's railroading would look like to an early twentieth-century railroader, that day may be closer than we think. Easier to envision, however, are enhancements to decision support technology, which will continue to improve resource distribution and use. One example is main-line dispatching systems that interface with terminal planning systems to provide seamless interaction between line and terminal operations, thereby improving the overall operation of the railroad. Systems that support the pacing of trains as they move over the railroad in order to optimize capacity use and conserve fuel are another opportunity for improvement.

The past 100 years have seen an almost unbelievable expansion of the capabilities and availability of computing technology. While the railroad industry has certainly been a beneficiary of this technology on many levels, it has played, and continues to play, a significant role in its development. From the days of Herman Hollerith working on his manual keypunch machines and tabulating equipment through the growth of mainframe computing in midcentury to the implementation of the personal computer and growing commercial use of the Internet, the railroad industry has been an active participant every step of the way. One can safely assume that the implementation of computing technology in the next 100 years will be just as exciting, if not more so.

—David C. Lester

REFERENCES

Ceruzzi, Paul E. *A History of Modern Computing.* Cambridge, Mass.: MIT Press, 1998.

"Knowledge Is Power—To Compete, to Serve Better, to Earn More." *Ties: Southern Railway System Magazine,* Jan. 1957, 4.

Miner, H. Craig. *The Rebirth of the Missouri Pacific, 1956–1983.* College Station: Texas A&M Univ. Press, 1983.

"Modern Business Machines Help Southern in Putting the Finger on Freight Cars." *Ties: Southern Railway System Magazine,* Apr. 1953, 16.

"The More We Know, the Better We Serve." *Ties: Southern Railway System Magazine,* Nov. 1955, 5.

Southern Railway Company Annual Report, 1980.

"The Southern's Part in the Development of Machines That Remember." *Ties: Southern Railway System Magazine,* Nov. 1950, 14.

"This Is Southern Pacific." Special edition of *Southern Pacific Bulletin,* June 1973.

Consolidated Rail Corp. (Conrail)

Conrail was formed on April 1, 1976, from six bankrupt eastern railroads and a seventh that was all but bankrupt. Its gestation was in the years after World War II, when eastern railroads lost much of their traditional traffic in heavy manufactured goods and coal as businesses moved south and west. The construction of the interstate highway system and other highway projects caused railroads to lose their most lucrative traffic to trucks. Growing passenger deficits, inflexible labor arrangements, strict federal regulation, and high terminal costs aggravated the situation. Inability to effectively compete for traffic or manage infrastructure and labor reductions to reflect changing traffic patterns resulted in heavy financial losses.

In 1957 the bankrupt and largely redundant New York, Ontario & Western Railway was abandoned. The liquidation set a frightening precedent: an entire insolvent Class 1 railroad system could disappear. By the late 1950s mergers were seen as a cure-all for the railroads' difficulties. Consolidation was seen as a way to reduce expenses and minimize competition. Most eastern railroads entertained merger proposals, but only a few mergers came about.

In 1960 the Erie Railroad merged with its longtime competitor, the Delaware, Lackawanna & Western, to form Erie Lackawanna. The East's two largest railroads (indeed, the nation's two largest transportation ventures), the Pennsylvania and the New York Central, first discussed merger in 1957, but nothing came of it. However, in 1961, when Norfolk & Western and Nickel Plate were discussing merger, as were Chesapeake & Ohio and Baltimore & Ohio, Pennsylvania and New York Central resumed their discussions. In 1966 the Interstate Commerce Commission approved their merger to create Penn Central, with the caveat that PC include the bankrupt New Haven Railroad. Penn Central was consummated in 1968, and the New Haven was included in 1969.

Although initially viewed favorably, the Penn Central was soon the largest bankruptcy in history. In addition to the problems facing its predecessors, Penn Central suffered from poor integration, infighting, and a serious cash crisis caused in part by overextended credit. Merger provided the tools needed to sort out the fundamental problems faced by the railroads, but created even greater problems. PC's onerous passenger deficit was blamed for a large share of the losses. In response to PC's woes, the federal government created Amtrak in 1971 to relieve American railroads from the responsibility of operating passenger services (when Amtrak was created, Penn Central trains carried approximately half of Amtrak's passengers).

Penn Central continued to lose money. Further, by 1972 financial crisis had afflicted many other eastern railroads. The New Haven had been in bankruptcy since 1961, and the Central Railroad of New Jersey, Reading, Lehigh Valley, and Lehigh & Hudson River had entered bankruptcy more recently. Damage from Hurricane Agnes in June 1972 pushed Erie Lackawanna into bankruptcy.

Eastern railroading was on the verge of collapse, and drastic action was needed. The rail lines were too important to be abandoned, yet the concept of railroad nationalization was despised by government and the industry even though most railroads in the rest of the world were run as government institutions.

A variety of proposals were discussed by Congress, including liquidating Penn Central and parceling out its most profitable routes to the highest bidders while combining the remaining carriers into a single privately run railroad. In 1973 the federal government drafted and passed a congressional plan for government-financed restructuring of the eastern railroads. It was signed into law by President Nixon on January 2, 1974. The Regional Rail Reorganization Act of 1973 (the 3R Act) created the U.S. Railway Association, a nonprofit public-private corporation whose mission was to plan and finance a new company called the Consolidated Rail Corp. (Conrail) that would take over and restructure the lines of the bankrupt carriers.

Detailed studies were made of railroad lines to determine which routes should be included and which should be abandoned or sold to shortline operators. During the planning stage competition for Conrail was considered. It was hoped that Erie Lackawanna and possibly the Reading would become part of the Chessie System to offer competition to Conrail. However, stiff labor-protection provisions in the federal legislation made it impossible for Chessie System to agree to that. As a result, competition in the East was provided by expanding the Delaware & Hudson, one of the few eastern railroads to stay out of Conrail. D&H was given trackage rights over Conrail routes to Buffalo, Harrisburg, Oak Island, New Jersey (Newark), Philadelphia, and Potomac Yard (across the Potomac River from Washington). A serious flaw in the plan was that although D&H was expanded to connect with other railroads, it was given little access to on-line shippers and in the end provided only minimal competition. Boston & Maine, also financially strapped, decided to reorganize independently of Conrail.

As created, Conrail included Penn Central, Erie Lackawanna, Reading, Central Railroad of New Jersey, Lehigh Valley, Lehigh & Hudson River, and the barely solvent Pennsylvania-Reading Seashore Lines. To defuse fears of nationalization, Conrail was set up as a private corporation and not as a federal agency. Its corporate headquarters were in Philadelphia, not in Washington. Stock was distributed to stockholders of the bankrupt railroads, and these stockholders helped in the selection of Conrail's directors. There was a significant caveat: as long as the majority of Conrail's outstanding debt was owed to or guaranteed by the federal government, the government reserved the right to appoint the majority of the company's directors.

It was hoped that Conrail could overcome the problems that had beset its predecessors. However, in its first few years, despite a substantial influx of cash from government loans, Conrail lost money. Three years after its creation Conrail had still not become profitable and continued to require substantial federal subsidy. As a result of Conrail's continued losses and the financial difficulties of the Rock Island and the Milwaukee Road, further action on the part of the government was needed. Conrail executives were among those who lobbied for the deregulation of the railroad industry, which followed similar deregulation of the airline industry. This was accomplished largely through the Staggers Act of 1980, which removed archaic rate regulation and allowed railroads to discontinue unprofitable operations and to set their own rates.

The most significant changes to Conrail occurred under Stanley Crane, retired president of the Southern Railway, who led Conrail from 1981 to 1988. Crane transformed Conrail and returned eastern railroading to profitability, reversing decades of decline. Under Crane, Conrail negotiated labor concessions, drastically cutting the number of employees needed to run the railroad. It continued to trim its network, reducing redundant infrastructure, selling marginal routes to shortlines, and closing unnecessary facilities. Congress was persuaded to free Conrail of suburban passenger obligations, and Conrail's remaining passenger services were conveyed to state agencies. On its inception in 1976 Conrail operated approximately 17,000 route-miles and had 95,700 employees. By 1984 its route mileage had been trimmed to 13,400 and employees to about 39,000. Conrail earned its first net profit in 1981, and three years later it made its largest net profit.

With Conrail profitable, the U.S. Department of Transportation urged the sale of the railroad to the highest bidder. In 1985 Norfolk Southern made an offer for Conrail. Stanley Crane and members of Congress opposed the NS offer, insisting that Conrail was better off as an independent railroad. In 1987 Conrail was made public in the largest stock offering on the New York Stock Exchange at that time. This sale netted the federal government approximately $1.8 billion, thus allowing it to recover roughly one-third of the money it had invested in Conrail over the previous decade. Stanley Crane stepped down in 1988 after Conrail was made public. He was briefly succeeded by Richard D. Sanborn, who died after just a few weeks and was replaced by James Hagen.

In 1994 Conrail resumed merger negotiation with NS in reaction to the announcement of the Burlington Northern–Santa Fe merger. These talks were inconclusive, and in 1995 Conrail offered to buy Cotton Belt from Southern Pacific, which was looking to merge with Union Pacific. This arrangement was rejected, and by the fall of 1996 Conrail began merger negotiations with CSX. This resulted in an immediate counteroffer from Norfolk Southern. In 1997 CSX and NS agreed to divide Conrail and acquired Conrail stock. Control of Conrail by CSX and NS was authorized in June 1998 by the Surface Transportation Board (successor to the ICC), and Conrail operations were officially split between CSX and NS a year later at the end of May 1999.

Conrail Operations

When Conrail began operation on April 1, 1976, it was something less than the sum of its predecessors. Numerous lightly trafficked lines had been omitted from the Conrail system plan. Furthermore, Conrail's primary route structure had allowed for the abandonment or deemphasis of its predecessors' main lines. Most of the Erie Lackawanna west of the Ohio-Pennsylvania state line was abandoned, as was Lehigh Valley's main line from Waverly, New York, to Buffalo.

The Northeast Corridor, consisting of the former New Haven Railroad between Boston and New York and the former Pennsylvania Railroad from New York to Washington and from Philadelphia to Harrisburg, was conveyed to Amtrak. In the Midwest many lines that were perceived as redundant were abandoned or sold. As did Penn Central, in Ohio, Indiana, and Illinois Conrail favored former New York Central routes over former Pennsylvania Railroad routes.

The majority of Conrail's through freight traffic was handled on former Penn Central routes, except along the Northeast Corridor, where former Central of New Jersey, Reading, and Lehigh Valley routes were favored over those of the former Pennsylvania Railroad in order to avoid Amtrak charges and keep former Pennsylvania electrified routes free for passenger operations. As a result of this shift of traffic, and to avoid engine changes, Conrail discontinued its electrified freight operations in 1982.

Conrail used former Penn Central yards to sort most of

its freight traffic. Former New York Central yards at Selkirk, New York (near Albany), De Witt, New York (near Syracuse), Frontier, New York (at Buffalo), Elkhart, Indiana, and Avon (Indianapolis) and former Pennsylvania yards at Conway, Pennsylvania (northwest of Pittsburgh) and Enola, Pennsylvania (near Harrisburg), and terminals in northern New Jersey, Philadelphia, and Baltimore were Conrail's primary facilities. Numerous yards that had once played important roles for predecessor companies such as Reading's Rutherford, Pennsylvania, facility and Erie Lackawanna's yards at Hornell, New York, Meadville, Pennsylvania, and Marion, Ohio, were closed or had their operations greatly reduced. A few non-PC facilities, such as Lehigh Valley's Allentown Yard, remained integral to Conrail operations. Likewise, Conrail closed or sold most of its predecessors' shop facilities and focused its shop work at the former PRR Altoona and Hollidaysburg, Pennsylvania, shops, although in its early years it assigned some work to the former Reading shops at Reading, Pennsylvania, and former EL shops at Meadville, Pennsylvania.

During the 1980s and 1990s Conrail continued to trim its lines and focus on the most profitable aspects of its business. By selling marginally profitable lines to shortlines, Conrail was able to develop greater traffic, because shortlines were often more effective at operating and marketing branch lines than Conrail had been. Conrail invested heavily in its physical plant. Late-era Conrail was characterized by superbly maintained main lines with heavy welded rail, deep ballast, and centralized traffic control. Conrail consolidated its dispatchers at several moderately sized regional dispatcher centers, replacing numerous local dispatching desks.

Conrail became a major intermodal carrier. Its premier intermodal service moved containers and trailers between northern New Jersey and Los Angeles in conjunction with the Atchison, Topeka & Santa Fe Railway.

Conrail's basic through-traffic map formed a large X centered on Berea, Ohio, just west of Cleveland. East of Berea, traffic moved on the former New York Central Water Level Route to and from Boston and New York. West of Berea, Conrail freight moved on the former NYC line to Chicago or on a line pieced together from NYC and PRR lines to St. Louis. A myriad of secondary lines formed a spiderweb over and around the basic X.

The former Erie Lackawanna main lines between northern New Jersey and Buffalo and between Hornell, New York, and Meadville, Pennsylvania (the Southern Tier Route) remained in service at the request of the State of New York, although Hornell-Meadville operations were discontinued after 1990. The Southern Tier Route served as a bypass for the Water Level Route, and from the mid-1980s it handled double-stack container traffic. The former PRR route between Buffalo, Harrisburg, and Perryville, Maryland, was used to bridge through traffic between those points. Pennsylvania Railroad's Fort Wayne route (its principal Pittsburgh-Chicago route) carried moderate traffic as far west as Alliance, Ohio, but was only lightly used west of there. Other secondary main lines, largely of NYC heritage, reached cities in Ohio, Indiana, and Illinois, as well as connecting Syracuse, New York, with Montreal and Columbus, Ohio, with Charleston, West Virginia.

The CSX–Norfolk Southern Split

In 1999 CSX and Norfolk Southern split Conrail between them. CSX's portion consisted primarily of former New York Central routes east of Cleveland and the Cleveland–St. Louis line. Norfolk Southern received the former New York Central between Cleveland and Chicago, the former Pennsylvania Railroad main lines east of Cleveland and Pittsburgh, and former Erie Lackawanna, Reading, Central of New Jersey, and Lehigh Valley routes. The Conrail name continues to exist as Conrail Joint Assets on lines in New Jersey and eastern Pennsylvania jointly operated by CSX and NS. In 1996 Conrail operated a system of 10,543 route-miles and 16,970 track-miles, with 2,006 locomotives and 45,988 freight cars.

—Brian Solomon

REFERENCES

Loving, Rush, Jr. *The Men Who Loved Trains*. Bloomington: Indiana University Press, 2006.
Saunders, Richard. *The Railroad Mergers and the Coming of Conrail*. Westport, Conn.: Greenwood Press, 1978.

Construction Companies

Construction companies existed to facilitate the building of new railroads. Like every other aspect of railroads, their nature and function evolved over time. During the early nineteenth century, when railroad technology was in its infancy, they often served as the vehicle for building a railroad when capital was in short supply, as it usually was. After the Civil War they tended to become a device by which promoters of a new line realized profits on its construction to offset the long wait for a return on the large investment required by any railroad. No new road could produce income until it was completed, and even then it might not generate a profit for years, if at all. The construction company enabled promoters to minimize risk by making money on the building of the line.

The construction company did no actual construction. Rather, it was a financial entity that served as an intermediary between the railroad and the contractors who did the actual work. Contractors had to be paid largely in cash because they had to pay their workers in coin. Laborers were hard to obtain and even harder to keep, which kept wages high. Since costs invariably exceeded estimates, contractors often failed before work was completed, and new arrangements had to be made. Sometimes the railroad itself assumed the contract and put the work under the supervision of its own engineers and officers. More often a construction company would be formed with some or all of the railroad's directors as its owners. In effect, the construction company assumed financial responsibility for building the road. Operating as a separate corporate entity, it issued stock to the controlling directors and select insiders or associates. When the road was completed, the construction company sold it back to the railroad company for a price that included a handsome profit.

Typically the construction company agreed to take payment from the railroad half in cash and half in securities of the road. It used the cash to build a section of the road, then received securities for the rest of the payment due on that section. To build the next section, it used the securities as collateral for loans. If all went well, it repeated this process until the line was completed. By then it hoped to have enough securities left over for a profit and often for control of the road. If problems arose, as they often did, its directors had to raise additional capital for the work, sometimes by pledging their personal credit. The earliest railroads relied on stock subscriptions to build their line, but beyond the populated regions of the East promoters had to resort increasingly to bond issues for the necessary capital.

Construction companies became useful vehicles for paying bills by selling bonds while holding on to enough stock to control the railroad. Honest promoters used this vehicle to limit their liability and overcome the difficulty of raising large amounts of capital for high-risk projects. Less savory promoters found it an ideal way to pile up easy profits by overcharging the railroad for everything. Arthur T. Hadley described the process this way: "To make money out of the building of a railroad, it was only necessary to subscribe the small sum requisite for obtaining a charter, with the right to issue first-mortgage bonds. The original subscribers would then have at their disposal whatever funds the bondholders might furnish. They could pay themselves a good commission for selling the bonds. They could then organize as a construction company, and contract to pay themselves a high price for building the road."

The device was widely practiced in Europe as well. In Germany construction companies were so numerous and so disreputable that calling someone a "constructor" became a supreme insult. In America the practice gained widespread notoriety with the Crédit Mobilier scandal, which broke in September 1872 and led to two congressional investigations. Crédit Mobilier was a construction company formed to build the Union Pacific Railroad. This much-misunderstood scandal first brought to public attention a major issue that would become far more prevalent in the newly emerging corporate era: conflict of interest. The clash of fiduciary responsibilities for men who were directors of both a railroad and its construction company was glaring but not yet widely understood. It drew attention in the case of Crédit Mobilier because two of the key figures, Oakes Ames and James Brooks, were government directors of the Union Pacific (which had a federal charter) and members of Congress, as well as shareholders in the construction company.

Later critics condemned the construction company device harshly. Edward C. Kirkland referred to "the noisome construction companies of a later era." William Z. Ripley declared that such companies invited the issue of excessive securities and observed, "The construction profits were the promoters' cake; in issuing enough stock to leave them a majority of railroad stock thereafter, they were enabled to eat it too." Many construction companies deserved the criticism heaped on them. The Morgan Improvement Co., for example, issued $4 million in securities to build a road that cost only $1.5 million. Some unscrupulous promoters made a career out of such chicanery, using construction companies as vehicles to unload securities of dubious value on unwary investors.

The reputation of construction companies became so bad that the executives of the Wisconsin Central Railroad felt obliged to report that "The officers of the Construction Company . . . were to receive no compensation whatever except their respective salaries, which were fixed in their contract, and they never have, to the best of our knowledge and belief, received in any manner any profits or private gain or advantage, directly or indirectly, from their connection with this work." However much this unsavory reputation was deserved in individual cases, it did not apply universally. Although often used to glean quick profits or to defraud investors, the construction company also served legitimate purposes, most notably, securing large sums of capital and overseeing the construction process.

Construction companies raised capital by selling the railroad's securities to local investors, wealthy individuals, and bankers. As the railroad boom intensified, Europe became a prime market for rail-company securities. Support also came from local, state, and sometimes national governments, which provided subsidies in the form of land grants, bonds, and even donations of materials or supplies. During the 1850s alone, 11 states received more than 22 million acres of land for railroad-construction purposes. Some states and cities authorized loans in the form of bond issues; others advanced funds directly to pay for surveys and other expenses. Many charters forbade railroads to sell their stock at a price below face value, which made it virtually impossible to market. But the road could "sell" it to the construction company at face value, which helped give the latter control of the road. The construction company could also profit from the sale of bonds and often got land for right of way by donation. In many cases, however, bonds had to be sold at a heavy discount.

Finding reliable contractors posed another difficult problem. The early use of small, usually local contractors seldom worked well. Early in railroad history there emerged contracting firms large enough to accept responsibility for building an entire line, often by subletting sections to smaller contractors. One Portland, Maine, contractor agreed in 1849 to build a road for $26,000 per mile, taking its pay half in cash, a quarter in stock, and a quarter in bonds. The road cost twice its estimates. During construction of the Illinois Central the contractors (who were paid half in cash and half in bonds) found the cost of labor and supplies rising while the value of company bonds dropped. Some demanded renegotiated contracts; a few stopped work, forcing the railroad to take it over. The Pacific Railroad of Missouri saw construction grind to a halt when a cholera epidemic decimated the workforce.

The St. Paul & Pacific Railroad offers a good example of the complex relationship between construction and finance. In 1862 the road's president, Edmund Rice, signed a contract with a Brooklyn firm that guaranteed to build 70 miles of road in return for all stock issued on that mileage and cash payments at specified dates set by a schedule geared to earning a land grant. To raise the cash, the St. Paul issued bonds; Rice used some as collateral for short-term loans and also bartered others for rails. When bond sales fell short, the road issued special stock on designated parts of the potential line and offered control of these segments to any party promising to build them.

Predictably, this arrangement led to serious complications and delays. The difficulty of finding reliable contractors, the uncertainty of the financial weather, the shifting costs of labor, rails, and supplies, and often the political pressure generated by raised expectations or direct public investment greatly complicated the building of most railroads. Construction companies could neither predict nor ameliorate all of these problems, but if desired, they could at least promise their stockholders a return on investment in the form of profits from the construction itself. For example, a construction company might amass $2 million in cash from the sale of bonds and land to pay for a railroad that actually cost only $1.5 million. The remaining $500,000 would be divided among the stockholders of the construction company along with any remaining securities in the railroad.

To avoid this fate, the directors of a railroad had to oversee construction carefully and monitor its costs diligently. But when the officers of the two companies were identical, this was not likely to occur. Ripley cites an example of a railroad president paying notes for construction obligations to a construction company of which he was also president. "Then you, as president of the railroad company, are paying yourself as president of the construction company, without the supervision of the treasurer or of any one else, and without any auditing of your accounts?" The president admitted that this was the case. Such cases were made worse by the still-crude accounting practices of the era, which lacked standard or uniform methods for treating the complexities of railroad accounts.

If the railroad failed and went into receivership, the directors holding a majority of its stock might then profit from its reorganization, which usually involved scaling down its funded debt. The losers would be the investors who had bought the road's bonds on which interest was no longer paid during receivership, and whose holdings usually lost value from reorganization. The construction company and its abuses endured into the early twentieth century. It faded only when construction itself slowed, railroads merged into ever-larger systems, and regulation made accounting practices more uniform. However, the practice of overcapitalizing construction through one device or another continued long after the construction company had become a museum relic.

—Maury Klein

REFERENCES

Chandler, Alfred D., Jr., ed. *The Railroads: The Nation's First Big Business.* New York: Harcourt, Brace & World, 1965.

Greenberg, Dolores. *Financiers and Railroads, 1869–1889: A Study of Morton, Bliss & Company.* Newark: Univ. of Delaware Press, 1980.

Hadley, Arthur T. *Railroad Transportation: Its History and Its Laws.* New York: G. P. Putnam's Sons, 1903.

Hidy, Ralph W., Muriel E. Hidy, and Roy V. Scott, with Don L. Hofsommer. *The Great Northern Railway: A History.* Boston: Harvard Business School Press, 1988.

Kirkland, Edward C. *Men, Cities, and Transportation: A Study in New England History, 1820–1900.* Cambridge, Mass.: Harvard Univ. Press, 1948.

Klein, Maury. *Union Pacific: The Birth, 1862–1893.* Garden City, N.Y.: Doubleday, 1987.

Ripley, William Z. *Railroads: Finance & Organization.* New York: Longmans, Green, 1915.

Stover, John F. *History of the Illinois Central Railroad.* New York: Macmillan, 1975.

Cooke, Jay (1821–1905)

Jay Cooke was a descendant of an old (1636) Massachusetts family. He worked as a banker and financier and was largely responsible for the successful funding of the Civil War for the U.S. federal government. Before his birth Cooke's family moved to Connecticut, then to New York State and then to the Western Reserve, where he was born on August 10, 1821, in what became Sandusky, Ohio. Jay Cooke was the second son of Eleutheros and Martha (Carswell) Cooke. The senior Cooke, a lawyer and a leader in his community, was elected to Congress.

An ambitious youth, Jay Cooke got a job as a clerk in a local store. In 1836, at age 15, he found a position in St. Louis, but the firm was ruined in the panic of 1837, and young Cooke soon became a clerk in a canal packet line based in Philadelphia. Shortly thereafter he moved to the bank of E. W. Clark & Co. and pursued a career in banking. He continued to make his home in Philadelphia. He retired from the Clark firm after the panic of 1857; in 1861 he formed his own partnership as Jay Cooke & Co. in Philadelphia.

Meanwhile, in Ohio, Cooke's younger brother, Henry David Cooke, pursued a career in the newspaper business in Columbus and in that role developed an acquaintance and friendship with Governor Salmon Chase. In 1861 Chase was selected by President Abraham Lincoln as secretary of the Treasury and soon developed a close relationship with Jay Cooke. The men worked to assist the federal government in meeting ordinary expenses while raising and equipping a large army. Chase and Cooke met with New York bankers in 1861 shortly after the first battle of Bull Run, and the Associated Banks agreed to advance $50 million to the federal government; this was to be repaid by the sale of Treasury notes bearing interest at the rate of 7.30 percent.

Cooke became skilled at advertising and marketing federal securities. Indeed, a loan of $500 million in 1864 was oversubscribed. William P. Fessenden replaced Chase in 1864, and Cooke, acting as the fiscal agent for the U.S. Treasury, sold $600 million of securities in less than six months.

After the war ended, Cooke developed a large general banking business that began to focus on railroad finances. Of special interest was the project to build a second Pacific railroad, this time following a northern route. Cooke brought his monetary skills to bear on the financing of the Northern Pacific. The proposed railway had its eastern terminus at Duluth, Minnesota, and its western terminus on Puget Sound at Tacoma, Washington. Cooke was especially attracted by the 47-million-acre land grant from the federal government. By the early 1870s the Northern Pacific was completed as far as the Missouri River in the east, and some work had been carried out on the western end of the railroad. There were problems, however. Construction costs were higher than expected, and revenues from early operations were insufficient to allow the Northern Pacific to meet its financial obligations. The railroad slid into bankruptcy. As a consequence, the firm of Jay Cooke & Co. closed its doors on September 18, 1873, which precipitated a general financial panic in the United States that lasted for the remainder of the 1870s.

Because of his service to the nation and the important nature of the rail project that had ruined him, Cooke met with general sympathy and support. He was eventually able to recover his fortune and in time enjoyed a prosperous life. He died on February 16, 1905.

—George M. Smerk

REFERENCES

Brown, Dee. *Hear That Lonesome Whistle Blow.* Chap. 10. New York: Holt, Rinehart & Winston, 1977.

de Borchgrave, Alexandra Villard, and John Cullen. *Villard: The Life and Times of an American Titan.* Chaps. 16, 17. New York: Doubleday, 2001.

Dictionary of American Biography.

Oberholtzer, Ellis Paxson. *Jay Cooke, Financier of the Civil War.* 2 vols. Philadelphia: Jacobs, 1907.

Cooper, Peter (1791–1883)

Railroad historians invariably associate Peter Cooper with *Tom Thumb*, the little steam engine credited as the first American-built locomotive and as the engine that introduced steam power to the pioneering Baltimore & Ohio Railroad. But there was far more to the man. Almost entirely uneducated, Cooper had a native inventive genius, a shrewd business sense, and a restless intellect, all of which led him into a string of successful enterprises and social crusades. *Tom Thumb* (the name actually was given long after it had been scrapped) was but a brief sidelight in these many ventures.

Cooper had already made his first fortune in glue manufacturing in his native New York City when, in 1828, he was lured to Baltimore to be a partner in creating the Canton Co., which planned to develop the city's waterfront. The venture was prompted by the Baltimore & Ohio's incorporation over a year earlier. Cooper also built an ironworks on the Canton tract to produce locomotives and rail for the railroad.

Unfortunately, the B&O's construction standards—which included extremely sharp curves and strap-rail track—precluded using existing English steam locomotive designs. As an expedient, horses powered the railroad's first services in 1830. Cooper volunteered to solve the problem by cobbling together a demonstrator locomotive, combining a tiny cylinder from his glue factory, a short two-axle railroad-car chassis, a vertical homemade firetube boiler, and a geared drive. The locomotive made its first public trip on August 24, 1830. Although the midget was unsuitable for regular service, its basic design eventually set the pattern for the B&O's first generation of steam power.

But Cooper's Baltimore adventure turned out to be short lived; by 1833 he had sold his ironworks and Canton Co. interests without having produced either locomotives or rail. Over the next 20 years he became an innovative leader in the American iron industry. He was a heavy investor in the company that laid the Atlantic cable and was its president for 20 years. He also headed the American Telegraph Co., which at the time controlled over half of the country's telegraph lines. He invented the washing machine, a compressed-air engine, and a variety of other mechanical devices, including attempts at a flying machine.

Cooper also constantly championed the cause of the working class and social reform. As a New York City alderman and civic leader, he led a successful fight for a public schools system and endowed and personally designed Cooper Union (opened in 1859) as a free school for the advanced study of arts and engineering. In 1876, at age 85, he ran as the Greenback Party's presidential candidate. Adding a long life to his other accomplishments, Cooper died on April 4, 1883, at age 92.

—Herbert H. Harwood, Jr.

REFERENCES

Dilts, James D. *The Great Road*. Stanford, Calif.: Stanford Univ. Press, 1993.
Harwood, Herbert H., Jr. *Impossible Challenge II*. Baltimore: Barnard, Roberts, 1994.

Cooper, Theodore (1839–1919)

Civil engineer Theodore Cooper was one of the leaders in the development of improved standards and practices for the design and construction of bridges. The son of a physician, he was born in Cooper's Plain, New York, and graduated in civil engineering from Rensselaer Polytechnic Institute at Troy in 1858. Cooper's early engineering work included surveying for the Troy & Greenfield and the Hoosac Tunnel in Massachusetts before he entered the navy at the end of 1861. After Civil War duty aboard the USS *Chocura,* his service included an assignment as an instructor in steam engineering and in charge of civil engineering work at the Naval Academy and a two-year tour in the South Pacific on the USS *Nyack.*

Cooper's distinguished career in bridge design and construction began in 1872 when he left the navy to work under Capt. James Buchanan Eads in the construction of the St. Louis Bridge. His work on the landmark steel arch bridge was followed by a variety of posts in bridge and structures engineering before he established his own consulting practice at New York in 1879. Cooper in 1878 developed an iron-bridge specification for the Erie Railroad that was the most comprehensive yet used and was adopted by many other railroads. This led to publication in 1884 of his widely used *General Specifications for Iron Railroad Bridges and Viaducts*, which went through seven editions by 1906. Cooper also developed the system of locomotive and train loading for bridge design that bears his name and is still in use today. His *American Railroad Bridges*, published by the American Society of Civil Engineers in 1889, was a widely recognized history of the development of bridge engineering to that time. That publication and an 1879 paper, "The Use of Steel for Bridges," won him the society's Norman Medal.

In 1900 Cooper was appointed consulting engineer for the design and construction of a great cantilever bridge across the St. Lawrence River at Quebec. What was to have been the greatest achievement of his career ended instead in disaster in 1907 when the bridge collapsed during construction with great loss of life. Censured by a royal commission for design and judgment errors, Cooper retired from engineering practice that same year. He died in New York in 1919.

—William D. Middleton

REFERENCES

Dictionary of American Biography.
"Memoir of Theodore Cooper." *Transactions of the American Society of Civil Engineers* 84 (1921): 828–830.
National Cyclopaedia of American Biography.

Costa Rican Railroads

Costa Rica's first railway was a largely American undertaking. American railway builder and engineer Henry Meigs, who had pioneered railways in Chile and Peru, proposed the Atlantic Railway in 1871. Although it was only 100 miles from the Atlantic Coast to the Costa Rican capital at San José, it took the railway builders 19 years to build the 3-foot, 6-inch–gauge line through the jungles of Costa Rica's east coast and up through the rugged valleys of the Cordillera Central to a nearly mile-high crossing of the Continental Divide to reach the capital city. The line's builders imported banana plants and established plantations to help pay for the railway. The enterprise grew into the redoubtable United Fruit Co., which eventually took over ownership of the railway as the Northern Railway Co. of Costa Rica.

A second rail line, built for the Costa Rican government by Ohio railway contractor John S. Casement, began operating between San José and the Pacific coast at Puntarenas in 1910 to complete a 3-foot, 6-inch–gauge route across the Central American isthmus. Initially operated with steam power, the 72-mile line was electrified in 1929, becoming the Ferrocarril Electrico al Pacífico, or Pacific Electric Railway.

The two railways were merged under government ownership in 1977 as the Ferrocarriles de Costa Rica (FECOSA). Foreign loans paid for an extensive rebuilding and electrification of the Atlantic line's principal banana route across the coastal jungle, and FECOSA developed grandiose plans for modernization, expansion, and electrification that would extend the system throughout the country. A new agency, the Instituto Costarricense de Ferrocarriles (Incofer), took over from FECOSA in 1985 and in 1987 added a 155-mile banana line, the Ferrocaril del Sur, to the national system. Instead of modernization, however, Incofer, faced with mounting losses, finally shut down the entire system in 1995. Despite efforts to find a private operator willing to take it over, the system remained closed in 2006.

—William D. Middleton

REFERENCE

Middleton, William D. "Coast to Coast by Narrow Gauge." *Trains* 46, no. 11 (Sept. 1986): 42–48.

Crane, L. Stanley (1915–2003)

Leo Stanley Crane was a career railroader who served as chief executive of two major rail systems: Southern Railway from 1977 to 1980 and Consolidated Rail Corp. (Conrail) from 1981 to 1988. He left Southern at the mandatory retirement age of 65 and immediately went to Conrail as chairman and chief executive officer. Born in Cincinnati, Ohio, on September 7, 1915, Crane moved to Florida after retirement from Conrail, where he died on July 15, 2003.

Stanley Crane's father, Leo Vincent Crane, was an executive at Southern Railway, so Crane naturally considered a railroad career at a relatively early age. After graduating from George Washington University in 1938 with a degree in chemical engineering, he obtained work as a chemist with Southern's test lab in Alexandria, Virginia.

For the next 21 years Crane was promoted to increasingly responsible positions until his appointment as assistant chief mechanical officer in 1959. During these years he worked on testing and refining a variety of materials and equipment used by the railroad. He designed new railcars and modified existing designs. Perhaps one of his more interesting and visible projects was the famous Big John aluminum covered hopper car for use in grain service. It sparked a notable rate case before the Interstate Commerce Commission (ICC), which Southern eventually won.

During Crane's years with Southern the legendary D. William Brosnan, while serving as vice president of operations, began to solicit Crane's help with adopting labor-saving mechanical improvements for many aspects of the railroad's operation. Crane developed a good working relationship with Brosnan, and this continued when Brosnan moved into the presidency of Southern in 1962. Brosnan is credited with implementing significant improvements to the railroad's mechanized equipment and physical plant, and he relied on men like Crane to help him accomplish the transformation of the Southern into a modern, first-class railroad.

Brosnan was an extremely demanding leader, however, and when an opportunity for promotion developed in the early 1960s, Brosnan did not believe that Crane was quite ready for the position. As a result, Crane left Southern to join the Pennsylvania Railroad in 1963, where he served as director of industrial engineering for two years. In 1965, however, Brosnan was able to win back Crane for the Southern by offering him the position of vice president of engineering, in which he was responsible for the railroad's engineering and research departments.

In 1970 W. Graham Claytor assumed the presidency of Southern. Not long afterward Crane was named executive vice president of operations and became an integral part of Claytor's new management team. Claytor's enlightened approach, which included listening to and considering the viewpoints of others and improving relations with both the U.S. Congress and the financial community, impressed Crane. When Claytor retired from Southern in 1976 to serve as Jimmy Carter's secretary of the navy, Crane was elected to the position of president and chief executive officer.

Crane's four years as Southern's chief executive saw the continuation of the more open management style begun by Claytor, as well as a 50 percent increase in operating revenues and a doubling of net income. Southern also built a new major classification yard in Linwood, North Carolina, during this time and continued the practice of investing significant dollars in the maintenance and strengthening of the road's physical plant. Crane also led the railroad's review of potential merger partners, with the most significant focus on the Illinois Central Gulf, which was dropped because the companies could not come to terms, and the Norfolk & Western Railway, with which an agreement was reached to form the Norfolk Southern Corp. in 1982. Although the merger agreement was consummated after Crane left Southern, it was his work that established the foundation for bringing the two companies together. Upon retiring from a 42-year career with the Southern, Crane's greatest challenge and achievement, in the minds of many rail analysts, were still ahead of him.

Although the entire U.S. rail industry experienced tough times during the 1960s and 1970s, the problems were particularly acute among northeastern railroads, in large measure because of the bankruptcy of the Penn Central in 1970. After six years of uncertainty and concern over the future of the Penn Central (which was able to maintain operation only through massive investment by the federal government), as well as the industry as a whole, Conrail was created in 1976 as a private, for-profit corporation, which continued to be supported by the federal government.

Crane, upon his retirement from Southern Railway in 1980, was named chairman and chief executive officer of Conrail. Although the prior leadership of Conrail had begun the process of improving the physical plant, Crane immediately began a program of continued improvements and maintenance to the railroad, along with bringing his proven and considerable leadership skills to the railroad and its management team. Despite these improvements, however, Conrail was still losing big money. In the early 1980s help arrived in the form of two significant pieces of legislation, the Staggers Rail Act of 1980, which provided the U.S. rail industry with greatly expanded economic freedom, and the Northeast Rail Services Act of 1981, which allowed Conrail to modify labor agreements and drop commuter rail service. Crane capitalized on these and other opportunities for improvement immediately. Within one year Conrail began to show a small profit, and net income grew to over $500 million by 1984.

One of the provisions of the Northeast Rail Services Act of 1981 was that the ownership of Conrail was to be transferred to private hands by the end of 1984. The Reagan administration was particularly eager to see this through, and the Department of Transportation identified three investors that it believed were capable of running the railroad, one of which was Norfolk Southern. Crane, on the other hand, believed that a public offering was the best route. The effort to make a public offering eventually prevailed, and it took place in March 1987.

Conrail continued to thrive under private ownership, and Crane retired from Conrail in 1988. After Norfolk Southern again expressed interest in acquiring Conrail in 1996, the ownership of Conrail was divided between CSX Corp. and Norfolk Southern in 1999, after an intense and protracted battle between the two companies. The contributions of L. Stanley Crane to the Southern Railway, which became part of Norfolk Southern, and to Conrail, ownership of which was eventually divided between CSX and NS, were tremendous. The value of his efforts is even more apparent when one considers the significant groundwork he laid during his time with both Southern and Conrail for the Norfolk Southern and CSX operations that exist today.

—David C. Lester

REFERENCES

Davis, Burke. *The Southern Railway: Road of the Innovators.* Chapel Hill: Univ. of North Carolina Press, 1985.

Eggerton, Albert S., Jr. "L. Stanley Crane." In *Railroads in the Age of Regulation, 1900–1980,* ed. Keith L. Bryant, Jr., 99–103. A volume in *Encyclopedia of American Business History and Biography,* gen. ed. William H. Becker. New York: Bruccoli Clark Layman and Facts on File, 1988.

Saunders, Richard, Jr. *Main Lines: Rebirth of the North American Railroads, 1970–2002.* DeKalb: Northern Illinois Univ. Press, 2003.

Crime

Railroad Police

Given the value of cargos and the decentralized nature of railroad operation, crime was a concern in North America from the earliest years of railroading. Although there would have been watchmen or others concerned with property protection at a much earlier date, it was not until the time of the Civil War that a more formal category of railroad police was first employed. In the single decade from 1850 to 1860 railroad miles more than tripled, and transportation problems grew as well. As the

railroads expanded with the towns that followed the new rights of way, they brought with them settlers, speculators, adventure seekers, and drifters and became a prime source for pilferage of freight, parcels, and luggage and other forms of crime.

Even before the formation of their own formal railroad police, the companies had begun to turn to private detectives. The first of these was the celebrated Allan Pinkerton. Born in Scotland in 1819, Pinkerton made a name for himself around Chicago by running down a gang of counterfeiters and moved on to police positions in Cook County and Chicago. Pinkerton next became a special agent for the Post Office Department and then the City of Chicago's first detective. In 1855 he formed Pinkerton's National Detective Agency and was engaged by the Rock Island, the Galena & Chicago Union (later the Chicago & North Western), and the Illinois Central to assist with investigation of labor problems, property thefts, and customer complaints.

The railroad express companies had also become large-scale businesses. Many of these had started as stagecoach services and then moved to the railroads as lines were extended. With large shipments of valuable parcels and cash, they represented a prime target for thieves. The Adams Express Co., in 1858, was the first of the express companies to use Pinkerton's services to investigate disappearances from an express car running between Montgomery, Alabama, and Atlanta, Georgia. Pinkerton quickly rounded up the dishonest express clerk and went on to do regular investigative work for the company. Through his work with Adams Express, Pinkerton in 1861 formed a five-man branch office for a major new client, the Philadelphia, Wilmington & Baltimore (later the Pennsylvania). Using his contacts with the railroad, Pinkerton uncovered a plot to assassinate the newly elected Abraham Lincoln on his trip to Washington. During the Civil War Pinkerton organized systems for obtaining information from the southern states and headed up the establishment of the U.S. Secret Service. After the war he expanded his agency, but remained primarily in the railroad and express business. Allan Pinkerton was joined by his two brothers, William and Robert, and the firm became probably the best known of its kind.

The Baltimore & Ohio had its own railroad police force as early as 1870, and several other roads began to employ their own men by the mid-1870s. Early police officers typically had little in the way of training. "It was the general custom simply to hand the newly appointed man a badge, a revolver and a club, and send him out to work, without further instructions as to the laws or how to enforce them, or even how to make an arrest," commented a later railroad policeman, H. S. Dewhurst. "The nature of the times called for prompt and vigorous action," he continued. "If a railroad detective or special agent could hold his own in the accuracy and quickness with which he could fire a gun in battles with train robbers, he was considered an asset to the railroad."

One of the earliest railroads to establish a better-trained and organized police department was the Grand Trunk Railway, which by 1885 had a systemwide service that was divided into eastern and western lines, each under a chief special agent. Other railroads soon did the same, with officers who were trained and supervised in some kind of organization similar to a municipal police department. Responsibilities were much like those of any police department, with additional emphasis on things like checking freight-car seals, freight claim investigations, or derailment investigations.

An early problem in railroad police work was the attainment of police power. The first statewide official authority for railroad police was established by Pennsylvania in 1865. Similar police powers were established in other states, but in many of them not until well into the twentieth century. Many states had special provisions limiting police authority. In contrast, Canada established its first police act on a federal level in 1860, under which all railway peace officers were sworn in under the Railway Act of Canada. This enabled a police officer to act in and along railroad lines anywhere in Canada. Only recently has a 1996 U.S. public law established a comparable U.S. national authority. It permits a railroad police officer to deal with both local and federal crimes at any location.

Most railroads began establishing trained police officers on a systemwide basis in the late nineteenth or early twentieth centuries. The move paid off. From the peak year for thefts of goods in 1920, which cost railroads more than $12 million, the costs dropped to less than $1 million by 1953. At that time railroad police numbered almost 9,000 in the United States and Canada, serving close to 400 railroads and 225,000 miles of line. As railroads have merged, and the technology available to railroad police has changed, their numbers have decreased to about 1,500.

Modern railroad police face many of the same problems as their early brethren, but are aided by modern equipment such as helicopters and night scopes for surveillance. Often, however, similar equipment can be found in the hands of organized criminals. Railroads still use the traditional flat tin seals with numbers that can identify when a container has been broken, which are checked periodically along a freight shipment, but newer types of seals also provide some kind of locking system. Now being developed are seals that can send notification if broken as they pass through the next available Automatic Equipment Identification (AEI) reporter.

Protection of railroad crews, reduction of vandalism, and work with Operation Lifesaver grade-crossing education teams are among other current activities. Since the September 11, 2001, attacks, particular emphasis has been placed on eliminating trespassing.

Amtrak operates a police force staffed by some 370 sworn peace officers and civilians and deployed systemwide in stations and along the Northeast Corridor. Principal areas of responsibility include the stations, trains, right of way, and maintenance facilities, and vandalism, trespassing, and larcenies are the most significant types of crimes. Amtrak police have federal law enforcement training, and in 1992 they became the first national agency accredited by the Commission on Accreditation of Law Enforcement Agencies. Operations center around the 30th Street Station in Philadelphia, which houses a national communication center and operates such technologies as a mobile commend center, K-9 corps, bicycle patrol units, and a Pennsylvania-based helicopter.

Train Robberies

Armed train robbery began shortly after the Civil War and grew into a uniquely American phenomenon. This is not to say that there were no armed robberies in other countries, but they were highly unusual. In contrast, American train robberies were so numerous over such a long period—they were common for more than 50 years—that the railroads and the express companies were obliged to invest substantial resources to try to cut down their frequency and cost. Postwar economic conditions undoubtedly exacerbated the problem. Unemployed war veterans often turned to crime as a source of income. The expansion of railroads into the sparsely populated West was made to order for holdups, and the increasing volume of gold and other valuables sent by rail made them a rewarding business.

The first armed train robbery was a holdup of the Ohio & Mississippi near Cincinnati on May 5, 1865, but most agree that the perpetrators were Civil War irregulars still active in Kentucky. The first peacetime armed train robbery came in Seymour, Indiana, on October 6, 1866. An Ohio & Mississippi train en route from East St. Louis to Cincinnati carried an Adams Express Co. express car immediately behind the locomotive. As the train left Seymour in the early evening, two masked men climbed on board the end platform of the express car. They then entered, leveled their revolvers at the express messenger, and obtained the keys to the safe. One man then gave a stop signal for the train, and the two vanished into the night after signaling the train to proceed. Before the year was out, two Louisville & Nashville trains had been robbed, in one case of $8,000. Less than a year later another two-man gang carried out a similar robbery of an Ohio & Mississippi train near Seymour. The idea of train robbery had caught on.

Many early train robberies were in midwestern and southern states, but the new form of crime soon spread. The wide-open spaces of the West, which made it easy to evade the law, became particularly popular. But train robbery could happen almost anywhere. On February 15, 1894, two masked men attempted to rob passengers on a Fort Wayne line train within the Chicago city limits shortly after it left a downtown station. The attempt failed; angry passengers and gunshots sent the two men running.

Probably the most common method of train robbery involved the robbers climbing on the forward end of the baggage car, just behind the locomotive, where they could not be seen by either the locomotive crew or the train

A typical nineteenth-century train robbery was this holdup of an express train of the Kansas Pacific Railroad at Muncie, Kansas, on December 8, 1874. Five masked robbers blocked the line for the coming express train and took almost $30,000 in cash and gold dust, as shown in the January 2, 1875, issue of *Harper's Weekly*. —Middleton Collection

crew. They would go forward over the tender to the locomotive, requiring the crew to stop at their planned location, and then would disarm the express messenger to go through safes or mail. If they were unable to get into the car, they would shoot their way in, or after dynamite had become available, would blow up doors and safes. The train was typically stopped at a remote location, making for an easy escape. Some locations were so well suited for train robbery that they were visited repeatedly. Blue Cut, Missouri, a short distance east of Kansas City, was one such location, with what may have been a record four holdups between 1881 and 1897.

Sometimes a train was stopped with barricades or switches at the desired location, or by a derailment. One of the most lethal of these was an 1896 holdup of a Louisville & Nashville passenger train at Cahaba River Bridge, south of Birmingham, Alabama. The rail was displaced on the bridge, the train fell into the river, and 27 crew and passengers were killed. The holdup men then went through cars, robbing the dead and dying.

Only rarely was a train robbed by a single man. Most robbers worked in pairs so that one could guard the train crew while the other dealt with the safe or mails, and a few gangs numbered eight or ten people. Among the most notorious was the James-Younger gang. Between 1873 and 1881 Frank and Jesse James, sometimes with the

Younger brothers, are credited with half a dozen train robberies in Missouri, Kansas, and Iowa. Missouri's Dalton brothers, four of ten who turned to crime, were responsible for at least three major train robberies in Oklahoma. So exercised were the local authorities that a special posse was formed to hunt the gang down. They finally met during a bank robbery at Coffeyville, Kansas, in 1892, and only one Dalton brother survived the shootout.

Among the best known of all train robbers was Robert Leroy Parker, better known as Butch Cassidy. A native of Utah, Cassidy got into crime about 1889 and in 1896 began forming a gang called the Wild Bunch, which engaged in a variety of bank and railroad robberies over the next decade. Cassidy is credited with at least three train robberies in Utah, Wyoming, and Montana. Usually working with Butch was Harry Longabaugh, known as the Sundance Kid. After moving to Argentina, Cassidy continued his life of crime. Reported as killed in a fight with Bolivian soldiers in 1909, Cassidy was also claimed to be living under an assumed name in Washington State, where he died in his old age.

During the 1890s train robbery peaked. In January 1894 *Railway Age* reported that holdups in Missouri (called "the train robbers' state") were happening on almost a weekly basis. There was no shortage of defenses. Building a more secure express car was one. By the 1890s express cars could

Titled *Hands Up,* this woodcut by Alfred Rasmus Sorenson in the Western Engineering Co. of Omaha depicted the great Union Pacific Express robbery. —Library of Congress (Neg. LC-USZ62-39654)

withstand most assaults, unless dynamite was used. In the 1880s the U.S. Post Office even considered building armored cars, but settled for stronger ones. But after a 1924 robbery at Rondout, Illinois (discussed later), the Post Office ordered the construction of bulletproof and gas-proof cars and designed a new postal car with an outside lighting system, special loopholes through which a mail clerk could fire, and a riot gun fired from under the floor.

Railroads and express companies strove repeatedly for tougher penalties against train robbery on a national level, but without success. Their view was that train robbery should be made a capital offense. "Make certain death the penalty of train robbing, whether the crime happens to result in murder or not," wrote Harry P. Robinson, editor and publisher of *Railway Age* during the 1890s, "and the avocation will speedily be abandoned."

In 1898 the Union Pacific's Edward H. Harriman, chairman of the railroad's executive committee, came up with the idea of using horse and rider teams to pursue robbers. Special fast trains could transport the horses and men to the scene of a holdup in an hour or less. Robberies soon decreased on the UP.

While the closing in of the frontier, improved telegraphy, and other changes brought a sharp decline after 1900, train robberies continued for several decades more. The biggest ever, in 1924, was planned by William J. Fahy, a postal in-spector gone wrong. Westbound Chicago, Milwaukee & St. Paul train 57, made up only of mail and express cars and carrying a large Federal Reserve Bank shipment, was stopped by three men just south of Rondout, about 30 miles north of Chicago. Other members of the eight- or nine-member gang were standing by with automobiles. There were 70 mail clerks and guards on the train, and the scene soon became a hail of lead. The train robbers fled in three cars with an estimated $2 million to $3 million. One by one they were rounded up, and almost all the money was recovered.

The train robber was often celebrated in cheap novels and popular songs. Later, one of the first motion pictures by the Edison Co. was *The Great Train Robbery,* and the genre went on for several generations more glamorizing train robberies. It is difficult to assess just how widespread train robbery was, for there seems to be no overall account, but it is safe to say that it was substantial. The most frequently attacked railroads were in the West. Wells, Fargo & Co. had its own private detectives; their chief, James B. Hume, pursued bank robbers for more than a quarter century. Before the train robberies ended, Central Pacific and Southern Pacific had experienced over 50 robberies, more than any other railroad.

—William D. Middleton

REFERENCES

Dewhurst, H. S. *The Railroad Police.* Springfield, Ill.: Charles C. Thomas, 1955.

Patterson, Richard. *Train Robbery: The Birth, Flowering, and Decline of a Notorious Western Enterprise.* Boulder, Colo.: Johnson Books, 1981.

———. *The Train Robbery Era: An Encyclopedic History.* Boulder, Colo.: Pruett, 1991.

Crocker, Charles (1822–1888)

Charles Crocker was born in Troy, New York. He had little formal education and worked for his father, a liquor wholesaler, from an early age. When Crocker was 14, his father went bankrupt, and the family moved to Marshall County, Indiana, in 1836 to start a new life on a farm. Three years later Crocker moved away from home and began to support himself, working as a farmhand, at a sawmill, and at an iron forge. In 1845, having discovered a bed of iron ore in Marshall County, he established his own forge. When gold was discovered in California, he sold the business and traveled with some other young men, including his two younger brothers, by the overland route to the Pacific Coast, where he tried mining for a couple of years, then opened a dry goods store in Sacramento. By 1854 he was one of the most prominent men in the city. He served on the city council and later was elected to the state legislature. Soon afterward he became associated with engineer Theodore Judah and fellow merchants Collis P. Huntington, Mark Hopkins, and Leland Stanford in the building of the Central Pacific Railroad.

Crocker took charge of the actual construction work on the railroad, leaving questions of financing and general policy to his associates. A man of tremendous energy with a talent for supervising, Crocker was well suited to the task. He lived with the workers in the Sierras, constantly on the move as he supervised operations of this vast army of men. When labor became scarce, he hired crews of Chinese workers, who proved hardworking and dependable. By the time of the railroad's completion approximately 80 percent of his 5,000-man workforce was Chinese. Under Crocker, they set records for railroad building that have never been bettered, laying three miles of track per day in the mountains and, one day in Utah—with the deadline looming—an entire 10 miles of track. The railroad was completed on May 10, 1869.

In 1870 Crocker attempted to sell out to the other partners but was ultimately unsuccessful. He left for a time but returned to the company in a largely honorific role. Crocker also had interests in real estate, banking, and industrial properties and irrigation projects throughout California. After the Central Pacific Railroad's success was assured, he built a mansion on San Francisco's Nob Hill

Charles Crocker. —*Trains* Magazine Collection

that was said to have cost $1.5 million (later destroyed in the 1906 fire) and another home in New York City.

Crocker had simple tastes and lived quietly despite his wealth. In 1886 he was seriously injured in a carriage accident in New York City but made a partial recovery. Other health problems, such as diabetes, stemmed from obesity. He died while sojourning at the Southern Pacific's luxurious new Del Monte Lodge on Monterey Bay, survived by his wife, three sons, and a daughter. His fortune was estimated at $40 million.

—Roberta L. Diehl

REFERENCES

Bain, David Haward. *Empire Express: Building the First Transcontinental Railroad.* New York: Viking, 1999.

Dictionary of American Biography.

Lewis, Oscar. *The Big Four.* New York: Alfred A. Knopf, 1938.

See also PACIFIC RAILROAD.

CSX

Among the large North American railroads, CSX has the shortest name but the most complex modern lineage. It is not only one of the largest railroads in North America, but also an international freight transport system.

Complicating the study of its history, several of CSX's primary predecessors were each composed of a number of smaller railroads. Financial interconnections made for a corporate web nearly as complex as CSX's route structure. Unlike the formation of Conrail, which came about very quickly, CSX was created gradually and in effect was the coalescence of many companies over several decades.

CSX Corp. was created in 1980. Its name was derived from the initials C of the Chessie System and S of the Seaboard Coast Line plus an X symbolizing the union of these railroad systems. Before examining the details of modern-day CSX, it is helpful to understand the railroad combinations that led to it. Since the lineage of these predecessors has been covered in detail elsewhere, only the modern transactions are discussed here.

CSX predecessor lines include some of the first railroads in the United States: the Baltimore & Ohio, often cited as the first railroad common carrier, which was chartered in 1827 to link the port of Baltimore with the Ohio River; the Portsmouth & Roanoke Rail Road, a Seaboard Air Line predecessor, which was formed in 1832 to construct a line between Portsmouth, Virginia, and Weldon, North Carolina; and the Louisa Railroad, a predecessor of the Chesapeake & Ohio, which dated from 1836.

Chessie System was a combination of the Chesapeake & Ohio, Baltimore & Ohio, and Western Maryland railroads. Chesapeake & Ohio main lines extended from Newport News, Virginia, and Washington, D.C. (by trackage rights on Southern Railway) across Virginia and West Virginia to Cincinnati and Toledo, Ohio, Chicago, Illinois, and Louisville, Kentucky. In 1947 C&O merged with the Pere Marquette Railway, which it had controlled since 1928, expanding its operations into Michigan and across Ontario to Buffalo, New York. Baltimore & Ohio had fulfilled its original charter by the 1850s and gradually extended its operations westward to Chicago and St. Louis; it also expanded eastward to Philadelphia and built a network of lines to tap coalfields in West Virginia, Pennsylvania, and Ohio. In 1932 B&O acquired the Buffalo, Rochester & Pittsburgh Railway, gaining access to important western New York markets and connections. In 1962 the Interstate Commerce Commission approved C&O control of B&O, and in 1967 it approved C&O-B&O control of the Western Maryland. The Western Maryland had long been partly owned by B&O, and its routes largely paralleled B&O's in western Maryland and West Virginia. Much of the west end of WM was destroyed by floods in 1972, and west of Cherry Run, West Virginia, many WM lines were abandoned or dismembered in favor of B&O's. Chessie System was formed in February 1973; four months later C&O, B&O, and WM became subsidiaries of the new company. Although Chessie System portrayed a common image, the railroad operations remained largely independent. In 1983 B&O took over the remaining operations of WM, and C&O took control of WM property. B&O and C&O identities survived until 1987, when B&O was merged into C&O, then C&O into CSX.

Since the turn of the last century the Atlantic Coast Line had been one of the strongest railroads in the Southeast. Since 1902 it had controlled the Louisville & Nashville Railroad. Jointly with L&N, ACL leased the Carolina, Clinchfield & Ohio Railway, which was operated as the Clinchfield Railroad; ACL and L&N also leased the Georgia Railroad, which in turn controlled the West Point Route (the Western Railway of Alabama and the Atlanta & West Point Rail Road). ACL's own routes connected Richmond and Norfolk, Virginia, with Florida by way of Charleston, South Carolina, and Savannah, Georgia. Secondary lines reached Wilmington, North Carolina, Columbia, South Carolina, Atlanta, Georgia, and Birmingham and Montgomery, Alabama.

The Seaboard Air Line was a weaker railroad with a route structure similar to ACL's. It reached many of the same cities, but its routes generally lay inland through hilly country. Its main north-south routes connected Richmond and Portsmouth with Florida and with Atlanta, Birmingham, and Montgomery. ACL and SAL, which had numerous common points and duplicate lines, began merger discussions in 1958. The two roads merged in 1967 to form the Seaboard Coast Line Railroad. The parent company was Seaboard Coast Line Industries.

Louisville & Nashville's main route ran from its headquarters city of Louisville, Kentucky, through Nashville, Birmingham, Montgomery, and Mobile to New Orleans. Other lines reached out to Cincinnati, Atlanta, St. Louis, Memphis, and the Florida Panhandle. Secondary and branch lines covered much of Kentucky, in particular the coalfields of eastern Kentucky. In 1957 L&N expanded its route structure in Tennessee by merging with the Nashville, Chattanooga & St. Louis Railway, which it had controlled for nearly 70 years. In the 1960s it bought portions of the old Tennessee Central. L&N expanded its operations to Chicago in 1969 when it purchased the eastern portion of the Chicago & Eastern Illinois between Evansville, Indiana, and Woodland, Illinois, and a half interest in the line from Woodland to Chicago from the Missouri Pacific. Two years later it merged with the Monon Railroad, which connected Chicago with Louisville and Indianapolis.

The close relationship between SCL and L&N resulted in a joint marketing strategy called the Family Lines that began in 1972. It included the Clinchfield, the Georgia Railroad, and the West Point Route. Family Lines was not a merger, and the components retained their identities, although locomotives and equipment were painted for Family Lines and lettered for the railroads.

In November 1980 the Chessie System and Seaboard Coast Line Industries merged to become CSX Corp. At that time the railroads retained their independence, and there was no immediate change in marketing or operations to the various railroads under the CSX name. At the end of December 1982 the Seaboard Coast Line Railroad was merged with Louisville & Nashville and some leased lines (including the Clinchfield and the Georgia Railroad) to form the Seaboard System Railroad, effectively cementing the relationship that had existed under the Family Lines name. Chessie System and Seaboard System maintained independent operations during this period.

During 1986 and 1987 CSX Corp. merged the Chessie System and Seaboard System into a single railroad known as CSX Transportation (CSXT). At that time it looked to develop its railroads as part of an intermodal freight transport network and purchased Sea-Land, a large international container-shipping company and CSX's largest intermodal customer. In 1988 it formed CSX-Sea-Land Intermodal (CSLI) to handle intermodal operations. In 1987 the CSXT image began to slowly replace that of predecessor railroads, and gradually over the next 15 years railroad equipment and structures were lettered for CSXT, although it was possible to find locomotives lettered for B&O, C&O, SCL, and L&N into the mid-1990s. Although CSX made minor operational changes to its various properties, until recently the pride of predecessor roads showed through the corporate image. A tower operator on the old Baltimore & Ohio explained, "CSX is what the paycheck says, but the railroad is the B&O."

In the mid-1980s CSX spun off a few of its routes to become shortline and regional railroads. The most significant of these was the Buffalo, Rochester & Pittsburgh routes, which became Genesee & Wyoming's Rochester & Southern in 1986 and Buffalo & Pittsburgh in 1988.

The Richmond, Fredericksburg & Potomac retained its independence until 1991, despite majority ownership by CSX. Objections from the Commonwealth of Virginia had prevented earlier attempts to merge RF&P.

In 1934 B&O began to operate the majority of its traffic through Pittsburgh, Pennsylvania, over Pittsburgh & Lake Erie's river-level route in order to avoid steep grades on B&O's own line. In 1992 CSX bought the P&LE and began to operate it through its Three Rivers subsidiary.

CSX and Conrail

The most significant undertaking of CSX was not the gradual coalescence of its predecessors but the ambitious takeover and split of Conrail operations with Norfolk Southern. Although NS had been wooing Conrail for the better part of a decade, in 1996 Conrail approached CSX as a merger partner, believing that Conrail and CSX were a better match than Conrail and NS. This resulted in an immediate counteroffer from NS. In 1997 CSX and NS agreed to divide Conrail and gained ownership of Conrail stock. Control of Conrail by CSX and Norfolk Southern was authorized by the Surface Transportation Board (successor to the Interstate Commerce Commission) in June 1998, and Conrail operations were officially split between CSX and NS a year later at the end of May 1999.

CSX received approximately 40 percent of Conrail's routes, primarily former New York Central routes east of Cleveland, Ohio, and Conrail's Cleveland–St. Louis line. These routes gave CSXT direct rail access to the New York metropolitan area, Boston, and Montreal. CSXT is now the largest railroad in the East. One of the most lucrative aspects of Conrail had been its east-west intermodal business. Since CSX inherited the old New York Central Water Level Route only east of Berea, Ohio (near Cleveland), it refurbished and expanded the capacity of its former B&O route to Chicago by restoring double track, which had been removed in a cost-cutting exercise a decade earlier. Initially CSX had difficulty integrating Conrail operations and suffered from a variety of operational inefficiencies.

Centralized Dispatching

Shortly after CSX combined its component railroads, it established a computerized dispatching center, the Jacksonville Super Center, at Jacksonville, Florida, to direct operations across its entire system. Union Switch & Signal constructed the dispatching center in 1987, and it went into operation in 1988. Dispatchers work at computerized consoles to direct movements. A track diagram gives dispatchers and managers a sense of the big picture and allows for better planning decisions. Although major dispatching functions are handled from Jacksonville, some CSX lines, such as those of the former Baltimore & Ohio, continued to rely on local control centers in the form of traditional switching towers for the operation of switches and signals. As of early 2003, former Conrail operations were still controlled from Conrail's premerger dispatching centers. In February 2003 CSX contracted with US&S to revamp its dispatching system in preparation for integration with Conrail operations.

Traffic

CSX's complex decentralized route structure involves numerous hubs connecting its various main lines. In addition to CSX's large east-west traffic flow on former NYC, B&O, and C&O routes, CSX moves considerable traffic on the former Seaboard System north-south routes. It operates significant yards at Selkirk, New York (near Albany), Buffalo, New York, Cumberland, Maryland, Willard, Toledo, and Cincinnati, Ohio, Chicago, Illinois, Russell, Louisville, and DeCoursey, Kentucky, Nashville, Tennessee, Hamlet, North Carolina, Atlanta and Waycross, Georgia, Birmingham, Alabama, and Jacksonville, Florida.

CSXT's traffic is divided into four categories: merchandise, intermodal, coal, and automotive. CSXT lists its merchandise traffic in the following major subcategories: chemicals, paper and forest products, phosphates and fertilizer, agricultural products, metals, minerals, foods, and emerging markets. Intermodal traffic has become one of CSXT's most important traffic areas; in recent years intermodal shipments have outnumbered coal movements. In recent years CSXT has made clearance improvements on many of its key routes to allow the movement of double-stack container trains. Coal has traditionally been one of CSXT's most important areas. Its predecessors C&O,

B&O, WM, L&N, and Clinchfield were known as coal railroads. In 2001 CSXT served more than 125 coal mines and more than 100 coal-fired power plants. It transported approximately 1,722,000 carloads of coal over its lines.

Locomotives

Since the mid-1990s CSXT has been one of the foremost proponents of alternating-current-traction technology. It encouraged General Electric to develop diesel locomotives with AC transmission and has placed hundreds of these locomotives in revenue service in all traffic areas. The railroad still operates a large number of older locomotives with direct-current electrical systems but since 1995 has only bought AC diesels and currently operates General Electric AC4400CWs and AC6000CWs and Electro-Motive SD70MACs and SD80MACs (the last acquired from Conrail).

CSX Today

CSX Transportation in 2005 operated a system of 21,357 route-miles, including track under operating contract, lease, or trackage rights, in 23 states and Canada, with 3,788 locomotives, 103,554 freight cars, and 34,000 employees. Freight traffic in 2005 totaled 246.8 billion ton-miles of freight, and its four principal commodity groups were merchandise (50 percent), automotive (10 percent), coal, coke, and iron ore (24 percent), and intermodal (16 percent). CSX operating revenues totaled $8,618 million in 2005, with operating expenses of $7,069 million, representing an 81.3 percent operating ratio.

—Brian Solomon

Cuban Railroads

Lying south of Florida and bounded by the Atlantic, the Caribbean, and the Gulf of Mexico, the island nation of Cuba stretches 780 miles from east to west and anywhere from 19 miles wide in the northwest to 110 miles wide in the southeast. Havana, the capital, is on the north coast of the island near its western end, only 100 miles from Key West, Florida. There are mountains in the center and at each end of the island, but between them are largely fertile lowlands ideal for growing the sugarcane that has made Cuba one of the world's leading sugar exporters.

Railroads have had a long and remarkable influence on the pace and course of Cuba's development since 1837, when the first railroad in the Hispanic world commenced operation. By the middle of the twentieth century Cuba had the highest rail density in Latin America and the seventh highest in the world. Only one-third of the rail system belonged to public carriers; the other two-thirds were private lines, almost all of them owned by sugar producers (see Table 1). Most of the private railroad lines were narrow gauge. The common carriers also had an important role in the sugar industry. Except for a small share held by the Hershey Cuban Railroad, roughly half the common-carrier lines were owned by the United Railways of Havana (hereafter United) and the other half by the Consolidated Railroads of Cuba.

Table 1. The Cuban Railroad System, Mid-Twentieth Century

Company or Type of Carrier	Km. (Miles)	Percentage
Common carriers	5,862 (3,643)	32%
United Railways of Havana	2,719 (1,690)	
Consolidated Railroads of Cuba	2,295 (1,426)	
Hershey Cuban Railroad	176 (109)	
15 other companies, mainly sugar lines, performing common carrier duties as well	672 (418)	
Private lines, mostly performing sugar duties	12,197 (7,579)	68%

Source: Ministry of Communications, Cuba, 1958, as reported in Marrero (1981).

From the Iron Road to the United Railways

At the beginning of the 1830s Cuba was a sparsely populated Spanish colony. Because few rivers were navigable in the dry season, population clustered mostly around harbors. Development of the fertile interior was held back by the high cost and the labor- and animal-intensive nature of road transport. In the early 1830s the Real Junta de Fomento or Royal Development Commission, appointed by the Spanish Crown to foster the island's development, petitioned for funding of feasibility studies and eventual support for the construction of a Camino de Hierro or Iron Road from Havana to the agricultural hub in Güines, 35 miles to the south. Guaranteed by the Spanish Crown, using Havana harbor tax receipts, financed in London, equipped with British engines, and built by American engineers, the railroad dramatically reduced the cost of transport, propelling a rapid increase in the cultivation of sugarcane and the industrialization of sugar production.

The pedigree of the Camino de Hierro's builders is intriguing, for the Junta had contracted with some of the best names in the railroad business: Robert Stephenson for the steam engines and Benjamin Wright, one of the three civil engineers who designed and built the Erie Canal, for the civil engineering work. Wright had little direct involvement in the effort; he brought his son Benjamin and another American civil engineer by the name of Alfred Cruger to do much of the work. Benjamin, Jr., was ineffective, and Cruger essentially took over. The construction records of the Black River Canal make reference to Wright's statement that he had known Cruger for some 30 years and was favorably impressed with Cruger's inclined-plane designs—the use of rail lines as opposed to locks to transport canal barges over large changes in elevation.

Political haggling between the Junta and Cuba's capricious Lieutenant Governor Tacón delayed construction and altered the rail path, introducing some steeper inclines and sharper curves. Operation commenced on November 7, 1837. The British engines that had been ordered before Cruger was fully in charge were a failure from the start. Stephenson had commissioned the construction of the first four engines to John Braithwaite, who sold a number of engines to American railroads. The second batch was built by George and John Rennie, the latter the famed builder of London Bridge, who proved to be a failure as an engine builder. In addition to design problems, the British engines were too heavy and high for the line and had traction problems. None of this would have been a surprise to Cruger. His chief engineer was Ezra Kitchell Dod, who had close family ties to Robert Stevens, founder and owner of the Camden & Amboy Railroad, which had encountered similar problems with Stephenson engines.

In 1837 the U.S. railroad equipment business was in a slump, and Cruger and Dod were able to quickly secure replacement engines from Baldwin, Rogers, and Norris at attractive prices. With the American engines in place, the railroad became profitable. By 1841 the Junta was able to privatize the railroad and then assist with the underwriting of other rail lines east of Havana. One of its next projects was the Matanzas Railroad, another venture in which Cruger participated. Its No. 1 engine, a Norris, Ketchum & Grosvenor 4-2-0 design of 1842, sits today in Havana's railroad museum and is regarded as one of the earliest and most originally preserved engines in the world.

The new owners of the Iron Road renamed it Caminos de Hierro de la Habana, the plural indicating their vision of building a rail network around Havana harbor. Over the next three decades the number of sugar mills and their total production grew severalfold. Ownership of the Caminos eventually passed to London creditors who gradually acquired almost all lines west of Santa Clara, naming the parent company United Railways of Havana. One of the acquired companies, the Ferrocarril del Oeste (Railway of the West, or FCO) had as its hub the Cristina station in Havana, named in 2002 as the site of Cuba's national railroad museum.

By the end of the 1920s virtually all common-carrier mileage in western Cuba was owned by United Railways, the final key acquisition being the Cuban Central Railways, also a British venture, which also had an extensive narrow-gauge network and steam roster serving sugar mills in central Cuba. United Railways' engine roster by 1930 reflected its eclectic origins, with few truly standardized designs. It included quite a number of Belpaire boilered units. Perhaps its most distinctive engines were the light, long-legged 700-series 4-4-0 designs and its small, light 400-series Baldwin and Alco Pacifics, similar to U.S. export engines sold to foreign railroads. With the advent of automobile and truck competition and construction of the Central Highway in the 1920s, United Railways' profitability suffered the most as vehicular traffic made the most inroads in the western part of the island. To compete, Mack AC and ACX buses and J. G. Brill 250 rail buses were acquired. Over the years these were supplemented with secondhand Brill 450s and other gas-electrics, including a Brill 55 lookalike assembled in Cuba from Mack parts. In 1950 the company acquired two Baldwin 800-hp diesel switchers.

At the end of 1952 all assets of United Railways were acquired by the Cuban state, and the new enterprise was named Ferrocarriles Occidentales de Cuba (Western Railroads of Cuba). It proceeded to purchase a number of four-coupled German diesel-hydraulic MAK engines of 600, 850, and 1,000 hp, Budd Rail Diesel Cars (RDCs), French Brissoneau et Lotz 600-hp diesel-electrics, and Uerdingen diesel-hydraulic railcars, as well as surplus heavyweight American passenger cars. In 1965 Occidentales and Consolidated Railroads were merged into one entity, Ferrocarriles de Cuba (FCC), which operates to this day.

The Railroad That Van Horne Built

At the end of the Spanish-American War in 1898, Cuba was in ruins from nearly three decades of almost constant insurrection. To travel across the length of the island, passengers and cargo had a choice of a grueling several-day journey by road or coastal schooner. The eastern part of the island was mired in devastation and poverty. While the idea of a central railroad linking the island had been discussed, Spanish authorities were fearful that it would become a conduit for rebellion. In fact, the only significant eastern railroad was the Military Railroad of La Trocha, linking a series of fortifications in a futile attempt to confine armed insurrection to the east.

In 1900 Sir William C. Van Horne, who had recently resigned as head of the Canadian Pacific, visited Cuba to have a firsthand look at his investment in the Havana Electric Co. There he learned from Lieutenant Governor Leonard Wood, head of the American occupation government, of both the American interest in the construction of a central railroad and the apparent legal impossibility of the project. The Foraker Act, passed by the U.S. Congress in 1900, forbade the granting of land to foreign citizens or companies. Irrevocable land grants had enabled the construction of Canada's and the United States' transcontinental railroads. Land served as collateral for construction and equipment loans; the sale of land fed cash-starved railroad ventures; and the commerce generated by the farmsteads along the right of way made the ventures feasible. Moreover, land grants prevented opportunistic landowners from extorting inflated prices for desirable right of way. To further complicate matters, the U.S. government was in the process of imposing a series of onerous conditions known as the Platt Amendment on the granting of Cuban independence. This aroused Cuban nationalism and a deep distrust of anything American. Van Horne's private correspondence and his biographical account confirm his frustration with General Wood's and later President Roosevelt's disdain for Cuban leaders and lack of vision and tact in their dealings with them.

The Cuba Railroad was built thanks to Van Horne's diplomatic skills, acquired through his experience as an American building the Canadian Pacific, and to his command of every aspect of the railroad business. He took several key steps to make the project a reality. First, he sold subscriptions of preferred stock in the Cuba Co. to a core of wealthy and experienced railroad people, including coal magnate Edward J. Berwind, the Florida East Coast's Henry M. Flagler, the Union Pacific's Edward H. Harriman, the Great Northern's James J. Hill, and Percival Rockefeller. Second, he circumvented the Foraker Act's injunction against concessions of land to Americans by buying much of the land and obtaining the rest (including rights of way over public land such as road crossings) through revocable grants given to La Compañía Cubana. Should construction be completed within an agreed time span, the Cuba Co. would have first rights to purchase the assets of La Compañía Cubana. Third, drawing on his Canadian Pacific experience, he oversaw every aspect of the project. Fourth, he won the support of communities and some recalcitrant landowners by offering, and scrupulously delivering, feeder lines to the railhead, thus opening lands to development.

Two construction crews were engaged, one starting from Santa Clara eastward and the other from Santiago westward. The rail line, scouted by a party of civil engineers in winter 1900–1901, largely followed the watershed, thus avoiding major natural obstacles. Still, there were some tricky sections to the line, and a fair number of bridges. The bridges were prefabricated by the New York Iron & Bridge Co. to Van Horne's specifications and were barged into Cienfuegos and Santiago harbors in sequential order of placement. Less than 18 months from the start of the survey, over 500 miles of main line were completed. The new railroad was named the Cuba Railroad. Scheduled service began on December 1, 1902.

Van Horne failed in one regard. His original plan was to sell land along the right of way to European immigrants. In fact, the Cuba Co. was incorporated as a development company to pursue not only railroading but also activities ranging from tourism to agriculture and international freight. It established experimental farms for a variety of crops, as well as sugar mills of its own. But Van Horne's vision never became reality. Unlike North America, where land was held by the states, Cuba's eastern land was largely privately owned, and a significant portion was concentrated in large holdings. Spanish laws had left land

virtually untaxed, encouraging concentration of property ownership. Van Horne's efforts to secure Washington's support for a change in Cuba's tax laws failed, as did similar initiatives with Cuba's Constitutional Assembly or, after the Republic was instituted, its Congress.

Documentation at the Cuba Co. Archives unequivocally establishes Van Horne's refusal to accept higher-priced offers from land speculators, such as the Cuba Colonization Co. of Detroit, on the grounds that the land was intended for individual settlers. In the end, however, large landholders either formed their own sugar-mill empires or sold to U.S. (and some Cuban) investors who built giant centrals or large-scale sugar-mill complexes fed by huge land extensions. The Braga Brothers Collection provides many insights into the vastness of land holdings and the extensive network of the sugar lines of large-scale sugar producers, such as the Cuba Cane Sugar Co. Even where property did not transfer outright to the centrals, the bargaining power certainly did. This concentration of power and ownership and the social problems of a labor force dependent on a highly seasonal industry were at the root of many of Cuba's social ills.

Notwithstanding this failure, the Cuba Railroad became an agent of progress in many ways. Cuba's income per capita compared favorably with most countries of the region, in no small part because of the production and export trade spurred by the Cuba Railroad. It was unquestionably the island's best-equipped and run railroad. Steam power was purchased primarily from the American Locomotive Co. At the Canadian Pacific Van Horne had objected to the Pullman Co.'s dominance of sleeper-car revenues. Thus he acquired passenger rolling stock from American Car & Foundry and from Jackson & Sharp, using Canadian Pacific designs as the starting point. These two companies and their subsidiaries and the Magor Co. also supplied most of the freight rolling stock. The Cuba Railroad's Garrido Shops in Camagüey were on a par with the best U.S. facilities. The harbor of Antilla in the northeastern part of the island was developed into a freight and passenger terminal, and many improvements were made to the city.

Within just a few years many new towns sprouted along the right of way, with land grants and civil engineering assistance from the Cuba Railroad. At a time when foreign investors in Latin America excluded natives from positions of responsibility, the railroad hired, trained, and promoted Cubans to management positions. In 1924 its chief competitor in the east, the Cuba Northern Railways, was acquired. The resulting company was called Consolidated Railroads of Cuba, a subsidiary of the Cuba Co. Mikado engines, slightly smaller but with the same profile as the U.S. Railroad Administration (USRA) design, were purchased in 1925 and 1945. In 1950–1951 Alco RSC3 and FA2 diesel-electrics, a large batch of Budd RDCs, and a large amount of rolling stock were acquired. In 1954–1955 a total of 51 General Motors G-8 export engines arrived. By the end of the 1990s some of the RDCs still operated as demotored trailers, and most of the G8s were still active, as originally intended, pulling light consists. In 1959, high-speed Fiat rail diesel cars entered Havana-Santiago service.

In 1959 the Cuba Railroad went into dissolution and was nationalized when Cuba's new Revolutionary Government refused to guarantee a number of the railroad's debts. In 1965 Occidentales and Consolidated were fused into a new enterprise, Ferrocarriles de Cuba (FCC), which since then has operated the common-carrier network. A number of the Cuba Railroad's 4-6-0 Ten Wheelers, 2-8-0 Consolidations, and 2-8-2 Mikados were transferred to the Ministerio del Azucar (MINAZ), the sugar ministry. By 1997 reportedly all or nearly all the mainline Ten Wheelers had been scrapped. One Baldwin and one Alco Mikado were rescued from the scrap heap and have been performing sugar duties at the Ifraín Alfonso mill, where they have been a tourist attraction.

Ferrocarriles de Cuba (FCC)

In the 1960s Cuba's economic and political structures moved to the socialist camp. The Soviet Union assisted Cuba in a modernization program to upgrade rail lines, operations, maintenance facilities, and equipment. Most but not all new equipment came from the Soviet Union and Eastern Europe. There were also some imports from France and (early on) from Germany, as well as Argentine-built Fiat rail diesel cars and express coaches. A number of new diesel locomotives built by the Montreal Locomotive Works and secondhand engines of U.S. origin, and even some refurbished Canadian RDCs, have also been acquired. Some 2,500 pieces of freight rolling stock were acquired or built. In 1984 the Havana-Santiago main line and several of the main connecting lines were completely upgraded. With the end of Soviet subsidies and the collapse of the eastern bloc, investment has been on a much more limited scale.

With the cessation of U.S.-Cuba trade, a concerted effort was made to manufacture substitute parts and to manufacture or assemble rolling stock. The first efforts entailed conversions of boxcars (Girón class) and motorbus conversions (Pionero class) and the design and construction of 40-ton hoppers without center sill for use in the sugar industry (Cheo class). In the 1970s Cuban shops designed and built two-axle self-propelled passenger railcars (Caharata class) from Soviet components. These were used on sugar and feeder lines to transport sugar workers. In the 1980s SIME (Empresa Sidero Mecánica) took charge of all railcar production. Taíno-class passenger cars were built in this decade, with capacities ranging up to 88 passengers; some were air-conditioned. Also, a large number of 30-ton sugar hoppers, 50-ton molasses cars, and gondolas were built. New car construction ceased in the 1990s; there are no known plans for resumption. Economic difficulties have aggravated the lack of spare parts, and as a result there is increasing concern about the deteriorating condition of rail service. Nonetheless, Cuban crews have shown a great deal of creativity in keeping the rail system going.

The Hershey Cuban Railroad

Some rail operations blurred the dichotomy between private lines and common carriers. The Cuban Central's narrow-gauge network, for example, served sugar mills in the central part of the island but also carried passengers and general cargo. Some sugar-mill lines, such as the Ferrocarril de Yaguajay, the Juraguá Railroad, the Caracas Railroad, and the Chaparra Railroad, served freight and passenger needs of communities along the right of way.

Cuba's most colorful and scenic dual-purpose railroad was built by the Hershey Chocolate Corp. to supply sugar and sugar by-products to its U.S. chocolate- and candy-manufacturing plants. Its sugar mills and refinery were linked to the eastern part of Havana harbor and the western part of Matanzas harbor by what eventually was named the Hershey Cuban Railroad or Ferrocarril Cubano de Hershey. Fires sparked by steam engines during the dry season brought about electrification of the principal lines between 1918 and 1922. Equipment included typical electric interurban cars built by the J. G. Brill Co. at Philadelphia and the Cincinnati Car Co., and 70-ton General Electric steeple-cab locomotives. Much later the electric locomotives were supplemented by 44-ton and 70-ton GE diesel-electric switchers.

With nationalization of the sugar industry and the rail system, the Hershey operation became a part of MINAZ, as did all the sugar lines. The Hershey line was renamed the Camilo Cienfuegos Division. However, true to its origins, it continues to perform common-carrier duties. After nationalization several of Occidentales' Uerdingen rail diesel cars and one of its Brissoneau diesel-electrics were converted to fully electric operation and transferred to the Hershey/Camilo Cienfuegos system. The system also operates electric coaches converted from heavyweight passenger cars and two much-photographed Brill catenary (1,200-volt) maintenance cars. In 1998 secondhand electric cars purchased from the Cataluña Railway at Barcelona, Spain, replaced most of the aging Brill interurban cars, but the GE steeple cabs soldiered on with a variety of modifications and updates.

Still other Cuban common carriers included the Gibara & Holguín; the Banes Railroad; the Guantánamo & Occidente; the Camagüey & Nuevitas Railroad, which eventually merged with the Cuba Railroad; shortlines such as the Ferrocarril entre Cienfuegos y Santa Clara, which merged with the Cuban Central; the industrial line serving the nickel industry; the spectacularly creative gravity railroad that since the nineteenth century hauled El Cobre's copper ore to the Daiquirí pier near Santiago de Cuba; and the extensive Caibarién & Morón narrow-gauge common-carrier system.

The future was uncertain for Cuba's extensive network of sugar railroads. By 2003 Cuban authorities had announced their intention to close down a number of sugar mills that were no longer viable. The consequences of this for the preservation of a rich and still-extant treasury of steam power are still unfolding, although a number of people in Cuba and abroad are working hard to save as much as possible of what is a valuable legacy of humanity and a rich part of American industrial history. The recently created national railroad museum is a welcome step toward this.

—Luis V. Dominguez and Manuel Diaz Ceballos

REFERENCES

Braga Brothers Collection. George C. Smathers Library, Univ. of Florida, Gainesville.

Cuba Co. Archives. Hornbake Library, Univ. of Maryland, College Park.

Guerra, Ramiro. *Azúcar y población en las Antillas*. Havana: Editorial Lex., 1961.

Knowles, Valerie. *From Telegrapher to Titan: The Life of William C. Van Horne*. Toronto: Dundurn Press, 2004.

Marrero, Leví. *Geografía de Cuba*. Miami: La Moderna Poesía, 1981.

Moreno Fraginals, Manuel. The Sugarmill: *The Socioeconomic Complex of Sugar in Cuba, 1760–1860*. New York: Monthly Review Press, 1976.

Vaughan, Walter. *The Life and Work of Sir William Van Horne*. New York: Century, 1920.

Zanetti, Oscar, and Alejandro García. *Sugar and Railroads: A Cuban History, 1837–1959*. Chapel Hill: Univ. of North Carolina Press, 1998.

D

Debs, Eugene V. (1855–1926)

Five-time Socialist candidate for president, cofounder of the Industrial Workers of the World, and leader of the American Railway Union's 1894 Pullman strike, Eugene V. Debs was a significant figure in the history of organized labor. Debs was born in Terre Haute, Indiana, where he became a locomotive fireman in 1870. Though his railroading career ended four years later, he remained active in the Brotherhood of Locomotive Firemen, becoming its grand secretary and editor of its magazine in 1880. He later came to believe that separate unions for each railroading craft (e.g., firemen, engineers, brakemen, conductors, and so on) were too easily broken by management and therefore founded the American Railway Union, open to all crafts, in 1893.

The ARU enjoyed great early success, chiefly because of Debs's reputation in the labor movement and his skill as an orator and organizer. In less than a year the union had 125 locals and 150,000 members. By early 1894 the ARU had waged a successful 18-day strike against James J. Hill's Great Northern, winning higher wages and establishing itself as a threat in the eyes of management.

The Pullman strike later that year was the ARU's undoing, though it began innocently enough. Wages had been cut by 25 percent at Pullman, without a corresponding cut in the cost of housing in Pullman's company town. Workers were rebuffed in their attempts to have the pay cuts restored and appealed to the ARU for aid.

Debs initially advised against a boycott of Pullman, counseling further negotiations instead. When the company refused to talk, the ARU had little choice but to boycott all trains with Pullman cars. Since many of those trains also handled the U.S. mail, President Cleveland ordered an estimated 12,000 troops to break the strike. Debs was imprisoned for five months, leaving the ARU without leadership. The union never recovered.

A decade later Debs helped found the Industrial Workers of the World (IWW, derisively called the Wobblies), but soon left the union in a disagreement with its militant factions. (Debs was a lifelong pacifist, and his opposition to U.S. involvement in World War I resulted in a three-year prison sentence late in life.)

As a result of his unhappy experience with the ARU, Debs decided that workers' rights would never be secure without political and legal changes, and most of his attention after 1894 was directed to politics. Notwithstanding his lack of electoral victory, Debs was more successful in politics than he had been as a union official. Most of the causes he advocated later became law, including measures to protect the rights to organize and strike.

—Peter A. Hansen

REFERENCE

Ginger, Ray. *The Bending Cross: A Biography of Eugene Victor Debs.* New Brunswick, N.J.: Rutgers Univ. Press, 1949.

Delaware, Lackawanna & Western Railroad

Anthracite—hard coal—was the keystone of the Delaware, Lackawanna & Western from the beginning. The railroad hauled it and, in the age of steam, burned it. The Lackawanna was the Road of Anthracite.

The Lackawanna's operating headquarters were in Scranton, in Pennsylvania's hard-coal region. In 1846 George and Selden Scranton, in partnership with Joseph Platt, contracted to deliver 12,000 tons of T-rail to the New York & Erie. George Scranton then joined in a partnership with the Erie's William Dodge to buy and rebuild the Ithaca & Oswego Railroad. Next, seeking an outlet for the anthracite that lay under the Lackawanna Valley, George Scranton in 1849 acquired the charter for the Liggett's Gap Railway, which had been incorporated 17 years earlier to connect Slocum's Hollow (the original name of the city of Scranton) with the then-proposed NY&E at Great Bend, on the Susquehanna River. In 1851 Scranton's railroad, now called the Lackawanna & Western, did just that. In 1853 the railroad company was consolidated with the Delaware & Cobb's Gap Railroad, which ran from Scranton to the Delaware Water Gap, to create the Delaware, Lackawanna & Western. Further extensions and additions in time created a main line that reached from Hoboken, New Jersey, across the Hudson River from New York City, to Buffalo, on Lake Erie. Branches reached to Utica and Oswego, New York, and Northumberland, Pennsylvania.

The most heroic era in the Lackawanna's history came during the leadership of William H. Truesdale, who was the railroad's president from 1899 to 1925. He spearheaded a massive modernization program that gave the Lackawanna a right of way that was among the best in the country and the shortest route between New York City and Buffalo (396 miles; the Erie's was 425 miles; the New York Central's, 436; and the Lehigh Valley's, 448).

The first step was the completion in 1910 of the New Jersey Cutoff, a 28.5-mile line from Port Morris Junction to Slateford Junction, just across the Delaware River in Pennsylvania. Lincoln Bush was chief engineer for the project. The line across the mountains of western New Jersey included massive Pequest Fill (110 feet high and 3 miles long) and two large viaducts built of reinforced concrete. The Paulins Kill Viaduct at Hainesburg was 1,100 feet long and 115 feet high; the Delaware River Viaduct was 1,450 feet long and 65 feet high.

The New Jersey Cutoff, which cost more than $11 million, was well worth the investment. It shortened the route by 11 miles, decreased the ruling grade from 1.14 to .56 percent, and dramatically reduced curvatures. But it was just the prologue to an even grander project: the 39.6-mile Clark's Summit–Hallstead Cutoff in Pennsylvania, built at a cost of $12 million under the direction of George J. Ray, who had replaced Bush in 1909. The cutoff's centerpiece was the magnificent Tunkhannock Viaduct; 2,375 feet long and 240 feet high, it consists of ten graceful arches of reinforced concrete, each topped with a series of spandrel arches. Theodore Dreiser called it "a new wonder of the world." Martins Creek Viaduct (1,600 feet long, 150 feet high) and 3,630-foot-long Nicholson Tunnel were additional aspects of the cutoff, which reduced the ruling grade from 1.23 percent to .68 percent.

Lackawanna's Hoboken Terminal was opened in 1907. Designed by Kenneth Murchison with Lincoln Bush as engineer, the copper-clad Beaux Arts structure had six ferry slips, from which boats left for Manhattan. (DL&W ran New York City–Hoboken ferry service from 1904 to 1967.) The terminal has been handsomely restored, even to its stained-glass ceiling, and is very much in use today by NJ Transit commuter trains.

For half a century the grandest train to depart from Hoboken Terminal was the Hoboken-Buffalo *Lackawanna Limited*, the railroad's flagship, inaugurated in 1899. The very next year DL&W passenger service gained an advertising icon whose fame outstripped any individual train: Phoebe Snow. To tout the cleanliness of the hard coal that the railroad burned, as well as hauled, the advertising department (with help from illustrator Penrhyn Stanlaus) created a refined, Gibson Girl–like personage clad in

white. Accompanied by a series of clever jingles, dozens in all, her image appeared in Lackawanna's advertising until World War I directives forced the railroad to burn soft coal. An early verse:

> Says Phoebe Snow
> About to go
> Upon a trip to Buffalo,
> "My gown stays white
> From morn 'til night
> Upon the road of anthracite."

The slogan "The Route of Phoebe Snow" appeared on boxcars in 1942, but Phoebe's truly dramatic return came on November 11, 1949, with the inauguration of her eponymous streamliner, the *Phoebe Snow*. Named by President William White, the Hoboken-Buffalo train (with through sleepers to Chicago) was a notable member of the fleet of streamlined passenger trains that appeared across the nation after World War II.

The handsome gray and maroon train survived the Erie-Lackawanna merger, after which it was combined, rerouted, and stripped of its name—which was eventually restored—before being discontinued on November 27, 1966. The last through passenger train to run on former Lackawanna rails was the Chicago-Hoboken *Lake Cities*, an Erie refugee, which rang down the curtain on EL's long-haul passenger service when it was discontinued on January 5, 1970.

Lackawanna's commuter operation from Hoboken Terminal was at least as notable as its long-haul service. The commuter routes began as the Morris & Essex Railroad, opened in 1836. Initially running just from Morristown to Newark, it was eventually extended west to Dover, Hackettstown, and Phillipsburg and east to Hoboken. In 1869 the DL&W acquired the Morris & Essex, along with the Newark & Bloomfield Railroad, an M&E property that became the Lackawanna's Montclair Branch.

Soon after acquiring the M&E, the DL&W built the Boonton Line, a bypass primarily for freight that left the main line at Denville and extended east to Hoboken. The M&E division's commuter operations gained distinction when 68 route-miles were electrified in 1930 and 1931. The project, with dual goals of economy and smoke abatement, included the M&E main line through Morristown to Dover, the Montclair Branch, and the Gladstone Branch (the Boonton Line was never electrified).

General Electric provided all the electrical equipment for the project, including the traction motors for the powered coaches—141 new motor cars built by Pullman. A like number of trailers were created from existing coaches at American Car & Foundry's plant at Berwick, Pennsylvania, on DL&W's Bloomsburg Branch. (Originally the Lackawanna & Bloomsburg Railroad, this line had become part of the DL&W in 1873.) The electrification was a 3,000-volt direct-current operation unique in the United States for multiple-unit (M.U.) service, though the Chicago, Milwaukee, St. Paul & Pacific's main-line electrification, also a GE project, used that voltage.

No less a personage than Thomas A. Edison was at the controls of a train for the ceremonial opening of the electrification. The original motor cars and trailers soldiered on for nearly five decades.

Their contemporaries, Lackawanna's steam locomotives of the period, typically had far shorter lives. DL&W's most unusual locomotives were a fleet of center-cab "camelbacks" (also called Mother Hubbards) that had the wide firebox necessary to burn hard coal. Designed by the Philadelphia & Reading's John E. Wootten, the firebox was too wide to fit between a locomotive's driving wheels and was considered too wide to permit forward vision. In consequence, the engineer sat in a cab that straddled the boiler ahead of the firebox, and the fireman worked under a rudimentary shelter at the rear.

Between 1927 and 1934 the Lackawanna received 55 4-8-4s from American Locomotive Co. The railroad called them Poconos, after the Pennsylvania mountains they crested. The first five were passenger locomotives; most of the Poconos were intended for freight or dual service. The Lackawanna dieselized relatively early, and by the end of 1953 steam was only a memory. In 1954 the Lackawanna and the parallel, competing Erie began to consider cooperation. The initial result was the consolidation of freight facilities at Binghamton and Elmira. In 1956 the Erie moved its passenger trains from its Jersey City terminal to Lackawanna's terminal at Hoboken. Later the two railroads eliminated some duplicate track in western New York.

By the 1950s the market for anthracite had dwindled, and the commodity was no longer the Lackawanna's mainstay. Hurricanes in 1955 damaged Lackawanna's lines, and the railroad posted deficits on its ledgers in 1958 and 1959. The subject of the discussions with the Erie changed from cooperation to merger, and on October 17, 1960, the two railroads merged as the Erie-Lackawanna (the hyphen in the name soon disappeared). After the EL had joined most other eastern railroads in bankruptcy in the 1970s, it was combined with Penn Central, Reading, Lehigh Valley, Jersey Central, Lehigh & Hudson River, and Pennsylvania-Reading Seashore Lines to form Conrail, the government-supported railroad that opened for business in 1976. In 1959, the last year before the merger with Erie, the Lackawanna operated a system of 918 route-miles and 2,174 track-miles, with 223 locomotives, 668 passenger cars, 12,765 freight and company service cars, and 7,981 employees. Freight traffic totaled 3.2 billion ton-miles in 1959, and coal (15 percent), freight forwarder traffic (6 percent), iron and steel products (5 percent), and fresh meat (4 percent) were its principal traffic sources. Lackawanna operating revenues totaled $76.3 million in 1959, and the railroad achieved an 89.6 percent operating ratio.

—Karl Zimmermann

REFERENCE

Casey, Robert J., and W. A. S. Douglas. *The Lackawanna Story.* New York: McGraw-Hill, 1951.

Delaware & Hudson Railroad

The Delaware & Hudson of the middle and late twentieth century was essentially two railroads that met at Albany, New York. D&H's principal passenger route ran from Albany north to Montreal. The daytime *Laurentian* and the overnight *Montreal Limited* operated over the shortest, fastest New York–Montreal line, a route that remained in service until Amtrak took over the nation's passenger trains on May 1, 1971. D&H's principal freight route ran from Mechanicville, New York, southwest to a connection with the Erie (later Erie Lackawanna) at Binghamton, New York, and its major flow of freight traffic was between New England and the West.

The Delaware & Hudson Canal Co. was chartered on April 23, 1823, to build a canal to transport coal from the Delaware Valley at Honesdale, Pennsylvania, to the Hudson River at Rondout, New York, for further shipment down the Hudson to New York City. A gravity railroad with stationary engines and ropes for the uphill portions served the mines near Carbondale, Pennsylvania. The company purchased four steam locomotives in England in 1829. One of them, the *Stourbridge Lion*, was the first steam locomotive to operate in America. It was found to be too heavy for the track, and all four locomotives were stored and left to deteriorate.

Delaware & Hudson increased its coal holdings as the demand for coal grew. In 1863 it proposed a route from Carbondale north to Lanesboro, Pennsylvania, on the Erie Railroad, and in 1866 it contracted with the Albany & Susquehanna Railroad, which had just opened between Albany and Binghamton, for access to the Albany area. D&H contracted with the Erie to build the line from Carbondale to Lanesboro, and in 1870 D&H opened extensions of that line north to Nineveh, New York, on the Albany & Susquehanna and south from Carbondale to Scranton. About the same time, D&H leased the Albany & Susquehanna to keep Jay Gould and Jim Fisk from getting control of it. One complication arose: D&H's gravity lines were built with a track gauge of 4 feet 3 inches, its new lines were standard gauge, and the Albany & Susquehanna was built to the Erie's 6-foot gauge. The gravity lines remained separate until they were closed, and the A&S was converted to standard gauge after lease in 1871.

The following year, seeking further markets for coal, D&H leased the Rensselaer & Saratoga Railroad, which ran north from Albany to the south end of Lake Champlain at Whitehall, New York, and had a network of lines in New York and western Vermont. By 1875 it had completed a line north along the west side of Lake Champlain as far as Montreal, linking the largest cities in the United States and Canada (New York and Montreal).

In 1898 Delaware & Hudson sold the canal to steamboat magnate Thomas Cornell, dropped the word "canal" from its corporate title, and began to broaden its horizons to encompass steamboats and hotels on Lake George and Lake Champlain, iron mines in the Adirondacks, electric interurban and street railways in the Capital District, apple orchards and lime kilns north of Plattsburgh, and expansion of its coal mines in Pennsylvania. The D&H became one of the financially strongest and technologically most advanced U.S. railroads for its size under the presidency of Leonor F. Loree from 1907 until 1938, while still paying dividends through World War I and the early Depression years. In the late 1930s D&H divested itself of many of its nonrailroad subsidiaries.

In the 1940s the use of coal in industry and home heating declined, and moving merchandise became the primary endeavor of the railroad. Several marginal branch lines were abandoned, and most local passenger service was eliminated in the mid-1950s.

By the early 1960s Delaware & Hudson's passenger service had shrunk to two daily trains that primarily served the New York–Montreal market: the daytime *Laurentian* and the overnight *Montreal Limited*. D&H petitioned to discontinue the *Laurentian*, then proposed to substitute Budd Rail Diesel Cars north of Albany, then again petitioned to discontinue the train. The State of New York refused to grant approval. Then two things occurred: Montreal hosted a world's fair in 1967, and D&H came under the management of Frederic C. Dumaine, Jr., who decided to upgrade D&H's passenger trains. As an interim step, D&H leased two dining-lounge cars from the Chesapeake & Ohio and staffed them with waitresses, then purchased passenger cars from the Denver & Rio Grande Western, which had just dropped its Denver–Salt Lake City *Prospector*, and four American Locomotive Co. PA-1 passenger diesels from the Atchison, Topeka & Santa Fe.

D&H's passenger business did not immediately rebound, but the refurbished passenger trains became a focal point for employee pride and a valuable publicity tool—the public usually equates "no passenger trains" with "no trains." The *Laurentian* and the *Montreal Limited* made their last departures on April 30, 1971, on the eve of Amtrak's inception, but in 1974 Amtrak initiated daytime train service—the *Adirondack*—between New York and Montreal using D&H rails north of Albany. The expanded use of trucks and cars on improved highways and industrial migration to the South gradually eroded rail traffic in the Northeast, and railroad mergers and abandonments were necessary for survival. In 1968 the D&H and Erie Lackawanna Railroad joined the Norfolk & Western's subsidiary Dereco in hopes of maintaining adequate traffic volume in the face of the threat of the newly merged giant Penn Central. D&H returned to independence in 1972 when EL declared bankruptcy.

Upon the formation of Conrail in 1976, the D&H realized that it had to extend its system to reach beyond the boundaries of the Conrail territory to maintain its traffic base. While extension was necessary for D&H to survive as an independent railroad, it was expensive. With dwindling traffic, losses were inevitable. Guilford Transportation Industries (GTI) purchased the D&H in 1984 with the aim of incorporating it into a long-proposed New En-

gland system, but after extended labor trouble Guilford placed D&H in bankruptcy in 1988. The Canadian Pacific Railway purchased the D&H in January 1991, and it became part of that company's St. Lawrence & Hudson subsidiary in 1996.

In 1983, the last year before it was purchased by Guilford Transportation Industries, Delaware & Hudson operated 1,581 route-miles with 132 locomotives, 4,341 freight cars, and 328 company service cars. The principal items of freight traffic were chemicals, wood products, paper products, and piggyback and container traffic. The 177-year existence of the oldest continuously operated transportation enterprise in America ended on December 1, 2000, when Canadian Pacific obtained authority from the states of New York and Pennsylvania to eliminate the name and operate the trackage as Canadian Pacific Railway.

—Jim Shaughnessy and George H. Drury

REFERENCES

A Century of Progress (1823–1923). Albany, N.Y.: J. B. Lyon, 1925.
Shaughnessy, Jim. *Delaware & Hudson*. Berkeley, Calif.: Howell-North, 1967. Repr., Syracuse, N.Y.: Syracuse Univ. Press, 1997.
Zimmermann, Karl R. *A Decade of D&H*. Oradell, N.J.: Delford, 1978.

Dennis, Olive W. (1880–1957)

Olive Dennis was among the first women railroad officials, and in an engineering position at that. Born in Thurlow, Pennsylvania, but raised in Baltimore, she was fascinated by structural engineering even as a child. Instead of playing with dolls, she built dollhouses, a trolley car, and, later, a full-size playhouse. After graduating from Goucher College in Baltimore, in 1909 she earned a master's degree in mathematics and astronomy at Columbia University. After teaching mathematics for ten years in Washington, D.C., she earned a civil engineering degree from Cornell University, the second woman to do so.

In 1920 Dennis was hired as a draftsman in the Baltimore & Ohio's bridge engineering department and a year later was appointed to the newly created position of engineer of service, reporting directly to B&O president Daniel Willard. Her first assignment was to ride passenger trains and look for ways to improve the equipment and services. "I was told to get ideas that would make women want to travel on our line. After all," she said, "if women went on it, men would follow." Among her improvements were simplified timetables, improved lighting, reclining seats with footrests, lighter food on diners, and an individually operated window ventilator that allowed fresh air to circulate without a draft—a device she had patented in 1928. In 1930 she helped develop the first railroad air-conditioning installation in the diner *Martha*

Washington and, a year later, in equipment for the first fully air-conditioned train, the B&O's New York–Washington *Columbian.*

Dennis was also charged with creating the famous B&O Blue China patterns, first developed for the railroad's 1927 centenary, subsequently used in B&O dining cars for more than 50 years, and now prized by collectors. To many, however, Olive Dennis's most memorable achievement came after World War II, when she was given full responsibility for both the exterior and interior design of a new Baltimore-Cincinnati daylight streamliner, the *Cincinnatian.* Her assignment included not only the train's completely redesigned heavyweight cars, but also the streamlining applied to its rebuilt P-7–class 4-6-2 steam locomotives. Olive Dennis retired in 1951 and died in Baltimore on November 5, 1957.

—Anne Calhoun

REFERENCES

B&O Railroad Museum Archives, Baltimore, Md.
Who's Who in Railroading. 1949 ed. New York: Simmons-Boardman, 1949.

Denver & Rio Grande Western Railroad

A year after the completion of the first transcontinental railroad, Gen. William Jackson Palmer incorporated the Denver & Rio Grande Railroad to build south from Denver to El Paso. He chose a track gauge of 3 feet. By 1871, a year after it was begun, the D&RG reached the new town of Colorado Springs. In 1872 it was extended farther south to Pueblo, then west to coalfields in the area of Canon City. For several years the D&RG remained a Denver-Pueblo–Canon City operation. Then it remembered that it was supposed to be building to El Paso, Texas, and extended its rails southward from Pueblo to Trinidad, aiming at Raton Pass, a gap in a range of mountains that formed a divide between the Arkansas and Cimarron rivers.

The Atchison, Topeka & Santa Fe was building southwestward toward Santa Fe and also intended to use Raton Pass—and the pass could accommodate only one railroad. On the evening of February 26, 1878, D&RG and AT&SF surveying crews both arrived at El Moro, near Trinidad, on the same train. The D&RG crews went to bed, intending to get an early start in the morning, but the AT&SF crews went right to work and established the Santa Fe's claim to Raton Pass. Later that year D&RG and AT&SF crews both tried to establish a line through the Royal Gorge west of Canon City. The D&RG prevailed, resulting in an agreement that the D&RG would turn west into the Rockies and the Santa Fe would build south to the valley of the Rio Grande and eventually west to the Pacific.

After a year's lease to the AT&SF, the D&RG resumed management of its own affairs in 1879 under the leadership of Palmer and Jay Gould. Its narrow-gauge rails reached Gunnison and Durango in 1881, and that same year it added a third rail, for standard-gauge trains, to its line between Denver and Pueblo.

D&RG continued building westward from Gunnison through Montrose and Grand Junction. In 1883 its rails met those of its affiliate and lessee, the Denver & Rio Grande Western Railway, which had been building southeast from Salt Lake City, creating a continuous narrow-gauge route from Denver to Salt Lake City. About that same time D&RG built a route north from Leadville over Tennessee Pass, at 10,239 feet, the highest point on a standard-gauge main line in North America. The rails followed the Eagle and Grand rivers downstream to Glenwood Springs (the upper portion of the Colorado River was called the Grand River). In 1889 that line reached Rifle; from there to Grand Junction the line was built by the Rio Grande Junction Railway, which was owned jointly by D&RG and the standard-gauge Colorado Midland, which came under the control of the Santa Fe in 1890.

The D&RG continued to add a third rail for standard-gauge trains to its lines, and by 1890 it had standard-gauge track from Denver to Ogden, Utah, via Pueblo, Glenwood Springs, and Grand Junction. It also continued to expand its narrow-gauge network in the mountains west of the Pueblo–Glenwood Springs main line. In 1880 it built a line south from Antonito, Colorado, to Espanola, New Mexico. The Texas, Santa Fe & Northern built north from Santa Fe to Espanola in 1886; the D&RG acquired that company in 1895. In 1890 D&RG built a line from Alamosa north to Salida to connect its two groups of narrow-gauge lines.

The cost of construction of the Western Pacific Railway from Salt Lake City to San Francisco (it opened in 1910) and the lack of on-line traffic sources drove WP into bankruptcy in 1915, and WP dragged along the D&RG, which had backed the construction of the WP. In 1920 the D&RG was sold to interests affiliated with the WP as the Denver & Rio Grande Western Railroad. The D&RGW entered receivership almost immediately. It came out of receivership in 1924 under the ownership of the Missouri Pacific and the Western Pacific, but it carried a load of debt that put it back in trusteeship in 1935. This time, though, the trustees were not eastern bankers but Wilson McCarthy of Salt Lake City and Henry Swan of Denver—local men who understood the railroad.

Denver & Salt Lake Railroad

The city of Denver had long wanted a direct rail route west, but geography hindered that. In the first years of the twentieth century David Moffat pushed the Denver, Northwestern & Pacific Railway west into the mountains and over Rollins Pass (almost 1,500 feet higher than Tennessee Pass, but the DNW&P was not considered a main line). Moffat died in 1911; the railroad was reorganized as the Denver & Salt Lake Railroad in 1912; and the railroad pushed its rails to Craig, Colorado, as far as they would get, in 1913.

The D&SL struggled through receivership and strike. The City of Denver constructed the Moffat Tunnel under the Continental Divide so the D&SL could avoid the 4 percent grades and year-round snows of Rollins Pass and also to bring water to Denver from Colorado's western slope. The tunnel, more than 6 miles long, opened in 1928, but the D&SL was still a railroad to nowhere. Both the D&SL and the D&RGW recognized that at Bond, Colorado, the D&SL was only 40 river-level miles from the D&RGW main line at Dotsero. Both railroads saw that building and owning a connecting line would bring prosperity. The Interstate Commerce Commission (ICC) gave the nod to the D&RGW. The Dotsero Cutoff opened in 1934, and D&RGW acquired trackage rights on the D&SL from Denver to Bond. Denver had its direct route west, and D&RGW's route to Salt Lake City and Ogden was 175 miles shorter. D&RGW began to buy D&SL stock and merged the D&SL on April 11, 1947.

The D&RGW joined with the Burlington and the Western Pacific to operate a Chicago–San Francisco passenger train, the *Exposition Flyer*, in 1939. The *Flyer* was slower than anything operated by the competition (Union Pacific), but it offered (at least westbound) views of the Rockies and California's Feather River Canyon. In 1949 the train received new equipment and a new name: *California Zephyr*. It was still slower than the competition, but it was scheduled through the scenery by day in both directions, and it had Vista-Domes for viewing the scenery. It was more than transportation; it was a land cruise. It was enormously successful.

In the late 1960s, though, Western Pacific petitioned to discontinue its part of the run, and on March 22, 1970, 21 years and 2 days after the *California Zephyr* began operating, WP became freight only and the *California Zephyr* disintegrated into an extension of Burlington Northern's *Nebraska Zephyr*, the Denver-Ogden *Rio Grande Zephyr*, and a connection at Ogden to Southern Pacific's *City of San Francisco*, all operating three times a week. When Amtrak began operating the nation's passenger trains on May 1, 1971, the D&RGW chose to stay out of Amtrak and operated the *Rio Grande Zephyr* between Denver and Salt Lake City. In 1983 D&RGW joined Amtrak, and the triweekly *Rio Grande Zephyr* was replaced by Amtrak's daily three-destination train between Chicago and San Francisco, Los Angeles, and Seattle.

Only two narrow-gauge routes remained in the late 1920s: the original main line from Salida west over Marshall Pass, then south to a connection with the Rio Grande Southern at Ridgway, and from Alamosa to Durango and a second connection with the Rio Grande Southern. From Antonito, Colorado, a branch ran south to Santa Fe, New Mexico; from Durango, branches ran south to Farmington, New Mexico, and north to Silverton. A narrow-gauge line between Salida and Alamosa connected the two routes and with the Rio Grande Southern formed a narrow-gauge circle. The "Chili Line" to Santa Fe was closed in 1942, and the Marshall Pass route was severed in 1949. Abandonments continued, and by the mid-1950s D&RGW's only narrow-gauge route was from Alamosa to Farmington and Silverton. It remained in service until 1967 and was abandoned in 1968. Two portions of the route, Antonito to Chama, New Mexico, and Durango to Silverton, still exist as tourist railroads.

Southern Pacific

Even though coal from mines along the former Denver & Salt Lake route in northwestern Colorado formed an increasing part of D&RGW's traffic, D&RGW's main purpose was to be a bridge route between Denver and Salt Lake City. The Rock Island, which had been a major source of traffic at Denver, ceased operation in 1980. Union Pacific acquired D&RGW's principal connections, the Missouri Pacific and the Western Pacific, in 1982. D&RGW's other western connection, the Southern Pacific, began merger negotiations with Santa Fe. As a condition of that merger, D&RGW asked for SP's lines from Ogden to Roseville, California, and Klamath Falls, Oregon, plus trackage rights to Bakersfield and Oakland. Rio Grande got all that and more by purchasing the Southern Pacific in 1988 after the ICC rejected the SP-AT&SF merger. The new company was called Southern Pacific Lines. Union Pacific purchased Southern Pacific in 1996.

In 1986 the Rio Grande operated a system of 2,248 route-miles and 3,431 track-miles, with 314 locomotives, 9 passenger cars, 10,593 freight and company service cars, and 2,233 employees. Freight traffic totaled 11.1 billion ton-miles in 1986, and coal (36 percent), food products (9 percent), lumber and wood products (9 percent), and transportation equipment (6 percent) representing its principal traffic sources. Rio Grande's operating revenues totaled $285 million in 1986, and the railroad achieved a 75.3 percent operating ratio.

—George H. Drury

REFERENCES

Athearn, Robert G. *Rebel of the Rockies*. New Haven, Conn.: Yale Univ. Press, 1962.

Le Massena, Robert A. *Rio Grande to the Pacific*. Denver: Sundance, 1974.

Department of Transportation

Proposals to create a unified federal transportation agency first emerged during the Great Depression and became more frequent after World War II when the railroads and other sectors of the transportation industry encountered serious problems. However, because many nonrail transport groups and their constituents were apprehensive about their future in a unified policy arena, they lobbied hard to block congressional action or at least retain their traditional independent status. When Congress approved a cabinet-level Department of Transportation (DOT) in October 1966, the legislation provided for the transfer of most federal promotional and safety activities in transportation, but did not include promotional agencies such as the Maritime Administration or independent regulatory commissions such as the Civil Aeronautics Board, Federal Maritime Commission, and Interstate Commerce Commission.

President Lyndon B. Johnson summarized the ultimate objective of the legislation as being "a coordinated transportation system that permits travelers and goods to move conveniently and efficiently from one means of transportation to another, using the best characteristics of each." Transportation coordination has physical, economic, social, and political dimensions, and it was the manifest hope of the president and the Congress that each of these dimensions would benefit from the establishment of DOT.

For example, the range and quality of intermodal connections available to shippers and travelers lagged well behind the level of facilities found within individual modes. Even more compelling was the need for improved coordination of federal economic policies affecting transportation. The "Declaration of National Transportation Policy" in the Transportation Act of 1940 had called for "fair and impartial regulation of all modes of transportation . . . so administered as to recognize and preserve the inherent advantage of each." However, the absence of any specific standards for determining "inherent advantage" had left this goal as far from realization as when it was adopted in 1940. Federal promotional and regulatory policies that evolved over time for individual transport modes were replete with contradictions and conflicts. For example, the railroads labored under excessive regulation at the same time barge operators and some segments of the motor carrier industry enjoyed extensive freedom from regulation.

The creation of DOT also sought to strengthen a president's ability to coordinate transportation policies and programs with macroeconomic goals and national social objectives. For example, until the 1960s urban expressway designs were governed almost solely by the minimum-cost criteria of traditional highway engineering, with little or no concern for the relationship between expressways and other urban problems such as congestion, air pollution, and the physical and economic deterioration of previously viable neighborhoods.

When the Department of Transportation began operations on April 1, 1967, it included some 31 independent or semi-independent programs previously dispersed through-

out seven major federal agencies. The new department, headed by Secretary of Transportation Alan S. Boyd, had 95,000 employees and an annual budget of approximately $6.6 billion. Although DOT's sheer size and potential scope of action were impressive, its organizational structure was quite conservative. For the most part, it reflected the relocation of existing agencies and units (often in identical form) under the umbrella of a new "holding company" called the Department of Transportation. President Johnson's original proposal envisioned a more imaginative structure, but carrier and shipper groups in each mode, plus congressional and other interests, successfully insisted that DOT's organizational structure preserve the identity of most existing transportation agencies and programs. The fiscal 1968 budget authority of DOT's major components spoke volumes about federal transport priorities at the time: Federal Aviation Administration ($915 million); Federal Highway Administration ($5.1 billion); U.S. Coast Guard ($527 million); St. Lawrence Seaway Development Corp. (no new funding); Federal Railroad Administration ($16 million); Urban Mass Transportation Administration ($125 million); National Transportation Safety Board ($4 million); Office of the Secretary ($13 million).

The Department of Transportation has faced a daunting array of policy challenges throughout its history. Broadly stated, these have been to coordinate transportation policy more closely with national goals such as economic growth, efficiency, and environmental quality; improve transport policy and program coordination within the federal government and with state and local governments; clarify and strengthen criteria for federal investment in transportation facilities; enhance technological research and development; and increase safety standards and performance in all modes of transportation. Priorities among these broad goals have changed from time to time because of compelling issues that DOT has chosen or been forced to address and frequent turnover in the agency's top leadership. The typical tenure of a secretary of transportation has been about two years.

From the outset, many of the policy issues confronting DOT have had far-reaching consequences for the nation's transportation system. Fortunately, the leadership and staff of the Office of the Secretary of Transportation (OST) have typically responded with sound analyses and forward-thinking solutions consistent with DOT's broad policy mandate. For example, the Office of the Secretary, in cooperation with the Federal Railroad Administration (FRA), played a key role in designing the legislation that established the National Railroad Passenger Corp. (Amtrak) in 1970 and in federal efforts to deal with the northeast rail service crisis that occurred when Penn Central declared bankruptcy in 1970. The FRA and the Office of the Secretary made DOT a key player in shaping the Regional Rail Reorganization (3R) Act of 1973 and the Railroad Revitalization and Regulatory Reform (4R) Act of 1976, which sought to reverse the industry's physical and financial deterioration and liberalize federal economic regulation.

These urgent measures helped stabilize the railroad industry's immediate circumstances and set the stage for fundamental long-term policy changes in the Staggers Rail Act of 1980. The Staggers Act basically reversed a century of federal economic regulation on the premise that the railroad industry was no longer a monopoly and that free-market forces were the best mechanism to provide lower rates for shippers, lower inflation, reduced energy consumption, and an efficient, healthy rail system. DOT's leadership role in railroad deregulation was consistent with its strong support for deregulation in other modes, and its initiatives to improve railroad safety were matched by similarly successful safety programs in other modes.

The challenges DOT has faced in aviation have been every bit as daunting. A succession of operational, safety, security, and economic crises have plagued the airline industry from the time DOT was established to the present day. Despite these crises, the department has successfully transformed long-term federal aviation policy from promotion and regulation of an infant industry to a self-supporting, market-based environment.

Most of the aviation industry's operational problems have been due to extremely rapid growth. From 1950 to the late 1960s revenue passenger-miles increased nearly 14 percent annually, creating congestion problems on the ground and in the air. Delays at hub airports and in the traffic flow between major destinations were costly for carriers, frustrating for passengers, and worrisome with respect to safety. To provide a long-term solution to the capacity problem, DOT helped shape the Airport and Airway Development and Revenue Acts of 1970. The legislation authorized $11 billion for airport and airway development over the next five years and established a trust fund and airline ticket taxes to pay for the improvements. The new framework proved successful and was subsequently renewed and expanded.

Unfortunately, gradual improvement of the nation's aviation infrastructure did little to improve the human dimensions of the system. Starting in the early 1970s, a protracted struggle developed between the nation's air traffic controllers and the Federal Aviation Administration (FAA). The controllers, represented by an increasingly militant union, the Professional Air Traffic Controllers Organization (PATCO), used work slowdowns, sickouts, and other measures to express their dissatisfaction with increased workloads, outmoded equipment, and heavy-handed FAA management practices. The struggle escalated until August 3, 1981, when some 13,000 PATCO controllers went on strike. The strike was illegal under federal law, and President Ronald Reagan gave the strikers 48 hours to return to work. Only about 10 percent of them did so. The remaining 11,345 were fired by the FAA without redress. DOT then faced the challenge of rebuilding a safe and efficient air traffic control system and developing more effective personnel management systems.

Although aviation safety was a priority responsibility of DOT from the outset, a much more ominous dimension soon appeared. Traditional concerns involving aviation equipment, personnel, and operating procedures were joined in the late 1960s by a wave of international hijackings and terrorist attacks on aircraft. The federal government and the airlines responded with security measures that included sky marshals, electronic screening of passengers, metal detectors, and inspection of carry-on luggage. However, terrorist use of explosives against commercial aircraft and the tragic events of September 11, 2001, have made it clear that aviation security remains a work in progress and a difficult and expensive challenge.

The Department of Transportation also played an important role in other major developments affecting the aviation industry. DOT was responsible for the Supersonic Transport (SST) program until public concern about the economic costs and environmental risks of the project caused Congress to terminate funding in 1971. Air and noise pollution from conventional jets also became an important issue as the nation's jet transport fleet rapidly expanded. Congress responded with noise-abatement legislation, and DOT developed mandatory noise standards the airlines had to meet over time. The nation's airlines did not lament the demise of the SST program because the SST's projected capital and operating costs were horrific. However, noise-abatement standards were another matter. Compliance represented an additional cost for an industry that was already experiencing serious economic problems. Some of the problems were due to sharply higher fuel costs and the economic recessions that followed OPEC oil embargoes in 1973 and 1978. In the end, the industry's urgent need for new, fuel-efficient aircraft also helped resolve the noise compliance issue because new aircraft types were both fuel-efficient and much quieter.

The Airline Deregulation Act of 1978 brought the most fundamental change in federal policy toward the airline industry since the 1930s and set the stage for economic deregulation of the railroad and motor carrier industries two years later. Academic economists, especially Alfred E. Kahn of Cornell University, provided the analytical rationale for deregulation and played a crucial role in transforming CAB regulatory decisions and shaping congressional policy. Economic deregulation of the domestic airline industry removed federal authority over such matters as market entry and exit, service frequency, pricing, and mergers and acquisitions. Advocates of deregulation believed that because the airline industry was mature and inherently competitive, market forces provided the best mechanism to protect the public interest and help carriers adapt to their rapidly changing environment. Congress strongly agreed and passed legislation deregulating air cargo in 1977, a year before deregulation of passenger service. The U.S. government believed that deregulation was equally appropriate for international air service, but DOT's efforts to negotiate open-skies agreements with key European nations made little headway initially. Most foreign nations were extremely reluctant to liberalize bilateral air service agreements with the United States or within their own regions and did not change their views until the 1990s.

Since the 1920s federal expenditures for transportation have been heavily skewed toward the highway industry. Under the framework initiated by the Federal-Aid Road Act (1916), appropriations soon reflected the nation's growing commitment to automobile and truck transportation. Expenditures also increased during the Great Depression as part of the federal government's efforts to stimulate the economy. After a hiatus caused by World War II, road and highway improvements quickly became a priority goal of all levels of government—federal, state, and local. The federal commitment to highway expansion entered a new era with passage of the Federal Aid Highway Act of 1956, which authorized construction of a 40,000-mile interstate highway system and created the Highway Trust Fund based on user charges to finance federal aid programs.

When the Department of Transportation became operational in 1967, the powerful highway lobby (critics called it the Road Gang) was well entrenched. It included motor vehicle manufacturers, petroleum companies, the highway-construction industry, state highway departments, and the federal government's own Bureau of Public Roads, which administered the federal aid programs. However, social values and political circumstances were placing DOT at the forefront of significant changes in highway policy that have continued to the present day. Since the late 1960s a seemingly endless parade of congressional legislation and DOT administrative actions have led to higher motor vehicle and traffic safety standards, reductions in air and noise pollution, less disruptive highway location and design decisions, increased motor vehicle energy efficiency, stricter requirements for transportation of hazardous materials, and growing use of Highway Trust Fund monies for urban mass transit.

—Richard W. Barsness

REFERENCES

Barsness, Richard W. "The Department of Transportation: Concept and Structure." *Western Political Quarterly* 28 (Sept. 1970): 500–515.

———. "Policy Challenges and Objectives of the Department of Transportation." *Quarterly Review of Economics & Business* 9 (1969): 63–76.

Harper, Donald V. *Transportation in America: Users, Carriers, Government.* Englewood Cliffs, N.J.: Prentice-Hall, 1978.

Hazard, John L. *Managing National Transportation Policy.* Westport, Conn.: Eno Foundation for Transportation, 1988.

Heppenheimer, T. A. *Turbulent Skies: The History of Commercial Aviation.* New York: John Wiley & Sons, 1995.

Lewis, Tom. *Divided Highways: Building the Interstate Highways, Transforming American Life.* London: Penguin Books, 1997.

Whitnah, Donald R. *U.S. Department of Transportation: A Reference History.* Westport, Conn.: Greenwood Press, 1998.

Depew, Chauncey M. (1834–1928)

Chauncey M. Depew was one of railroading's great statesmen. Born in Peekskill, New York, Depew went to Yale, read law in an office in his hometown of Peekskill, and was admitted to the bar of the state of New York in 1858. After practicing law for some time he was drawn to politics and served as a Republican representative in the New York State Assembly during 1862–1863. Subsequently he was New York secretary of state in 1864–1865. In 1866 he was offered an ambassadorship, but in his practice of law he had had dealings with Cornelius Vanderbilt, who urged him not to take the position. "Railroads are the career for a young man," said Vanderbilt. "There's nothing in politics." Consequently Depew began a long relationship with the New York Central Railroad.

Depew did not entirely leave politics; indeed, he was a candidate for the presidency in 1888, eventually withdrawing in favor of Benjamin Harrison, who on election offered him the post of secretary of state. Depew refused the position. Depew's association with the New York Central and the Vanderbilt family continued; he was general counsel (1875–1882), vice president (1882–1885), and then president of the railroad (1885–1899). Although he had no practical experience in railroading, Depew's skills

Chauncey M. Depew. —Middleton Collection

in diplomacy, jurisprudence, and administration served the New York Central well as it grew into one of America's greatest railroad companies. In 1899 he retired at the age of 65 but continued as chairman until his death in 1928. But by this time he had been elected to the U.S. Senate and served two terms there (1899–1911).

Depew was the very picture of a statesmanlike railroad president. It was said that during the 1890s he was the best-known American except the president himself. A public orator of the first rank, he was seen everywhere as the ambassador of American capitalism. Depew attended every Republican national convention for 50 years and was nearly always a speaker. H. L. Mencken, who covered national conventions of both parties for decades, insisted that Depew was the only speaker of real wit and intelligence ever heard at these doleful jamborees.

Without much doubt Depew was the most celebrated orator of his day. He was called upon to offer the principal address at the dedication of the Statue of Liberty on October 28, 1886, the dedication of Grant's Tomb in 1897, and the opening of the World's Columbian Exposition in Chicago in 1893. He was also called upon often as a dinner speaker in New York.

—George H. Douglas

REFERENCE

Depew, Chauncey M. *My Memories of Eighty Years*. New York: Scribner's, 1922.

Detroit, Toledo & Ironton Railroad

On the map, the Detroit, Toledo & Ironton made a wide westerly arc from Detroit, Michigan, south to Ironton, almost at the southernmost point of the state of Ohio. The railroad was owned by Henry Ford in the 1920s and thereafter was more or less part of the Pennsylvania Railroad family. The DT&I was not even a minor passenger carrier; by 1941 its passenger service consisted of a mixed train that covered less than a fourth of the road's mileage. DT&I excelled, though, at carrying freight to and from connections with all the east-west railroads.

The Detroit, Toledo & Ironton Railway was created in 1905 by the merger of two bankrupt railroads, the Detroit Southern and the Ohio Southern. The Detroit Southern reached southwest from Detroit to Lima, Ohio. The Ohio Southern's ancestry included a narrow-gauge railroad that was to have been a part of a narrow-gauge system reaching from Toledo to Mexico City.

The new Detroit, Toledo & Ironton wanted to reach Toledo (possibly to fulfill its corporate title) and acquired the Ann Arbor, which reached from Toledo northwest to Frankfort, Michigan. DT&I cast off the Ann Arbor in 1910 and was reorganized in 1914 as the Detroit, Toledo & Ironton Railroad.

In 1920 Henry Ford needed to straighten the channel through which lake freighters reached his new plant at Dearborn, Michigan. A new bridge for the DT&I was necessary, and the management of the DT&I said that they would exchange DT&I bonds for a loan for the money to build the bridge. Ford's response was to purchase the railroad. He instituted a number of unusual labor practices (high wages, white uniforms, no facial hair, time waiting in sidings to be spent polishing the locomotives), electrified 17 miles of the line between Dearborn and Carleton, Michigan, and built a 46-mile cutoff from Dundee, Michigan, to Malinta, Ohio.

Ford sold the DT&I in 1929 to the Pennroad Corp., an affiliate of the Pennsylvania Railroad. In the 1930s DT&I dropped all of its passenger service except a mixed train between Springfield and Jackson, Ohio, and acquired a number of modern steam locomotives for over-the-road service. DT&I dieselized in the late 1940s and early 1950s.

In 1951 Pennroad's stock in the DT&I was purchased by the Pennsylvania Co. (another Pennsylvania Railroad affiliate) and the Wabash Railroad. The Wabash sold its share, 18 percent, to the Pennsylvania Co. in 1965 (the Pennsylvania Co. held 87 percent of the Wabash's stock). Shortly before that (in 1963) DT&I purchased the Ann Arbor Railroad from the Wabash. The Ann Arbor, never robust financially, declared bankruptcy in 1973. The State of Michigan purchased parts of its line; DT&I retained trackage rights into Toledo from the north. When Conrail was formed in 1976, DT&I acquired trackage rights into Cincinnati from Springfield, Ohio.

The Pennsylvania Co., by then a subsidiary of Penn Central, put the DT&I up for sale. Grand Trunk Western, Chessie System, and Norfolk & Western were all interested. The Interstate Commerce Commission gave the nod to the Grand Trunk Western (a subsidiary of Canadian National Railways). The sale was completed on June 24, 1980, and GTW merged the DT&I at the end of 1983.

In the early 1980s the line south of Washington Court House, Ohio, was abandoned piece by piece: first the very southernmost portion, then more of it, to be replaced by trackage rights on Chessie System, then the portion that was made up by those trackage rights. In 1990 GTW sold the Springfield–Washington Court House portion of the line to the Indiana & Ohio Railway and in 1997 sold most of the rest of the line to the I&O, leaving only a short stub out of Detroit under GTW ownership.

In 1980 the Detroit, Toledo & Ironton operated a system of 540 route-miles and 812 track-miles, with 72 locomotives and 3,803 freight and company service cars. Freight traffic totaled 1.5 billion ton-miles in 1980. DT&I operating revenues totaled $74.2 million in 1980, and the railroad achieved a 103.3 percent operating ratio.

—George H. Drury

REFERENCE

Trostel, Scott D. *The Detroit, Toledo & Ironton Railroad: Henry Ford's Railroad*. Fletcher, Ohio: Cam-Tech, 1988.

Diesel, Rudolf (1858–1913)

Rudolf Diesel, inventor of the internal combustion engine that bears his name, did not live to see its use spread to the railroad industry. On trips to the United States in 1904 and 1912 he visited investors who were building stationary diesel engines, and he predicted the locomotive development that came later.

Born in Paris on March 18, 1858, to Bavarian parents, Rudolf Christian Karl Diesel showed an early aptitude for things mechanical. His father, Theodor, owned a leather-working shop. The family lived reasonably well until 1870, when war between France and Prussia forced the Diesels to flee to England. After France surrendered to Prussia in January 1871, they returned to Paris, and Rudolf ultimately went to engineering school in Germany, followed by a job at the Swiss firm Sulzer Maschinenfabrik, where he established his reputation as a promising engineer and inventor.

While helping build and manage a refrigeration plant, Diesel tried unsuccessfully to design an expansion engine using ammonia. About 1890 he decided to use air, which when highly compressed in a cylinder increases in temperature. Oil injected into this hot air would burn spontaneously. Combustion would occur at constant temperature and pressure, and expansion of the gas would drive the piston.

Diesel patented his engine in 1892 and the next year described it in a paper, "The Theory and Design of a Rational Heat Engine." Two German companies, Maschinenfabrik Augsburg and Krupp, Essen, financed its development. The engine was perfected in 1897 and in 1898 was shown at the Munich Exposition. The engine's fuel economy was remarkable, and it ran quietly. Adolphus Busch, the St. Louis brewer, acquired a license in 1897 for $1 million for U.S. and Canadian manufacturing rights to the engine. In 1902 Busch and Joseph Hoadley of the International Power Co. signed a manufacturing agreement, and the resulting venture sold 157 stationary engines—a total of 27,360 horsepower—between 1902 and 1909. Although this initial effort ended in receivership, eventually the Busch–Sulzer Brothers Diesel Engine Co. emerged. (Sulzer had started diesel engine production in 1903.)

In June 1904 Diesel sailed for New York City, briefly stopping at the Diesel Motors of America office at 11 Broadway. He took the train to St. Louis to see Busch and visit the Louisiana Purchase Exposition. His American trip included stops in Denver, Salt Lake City, San Francisco, Yellowstone Park, and Niagara Falls before he returned to Europe in November. Diesel apparently was not involved in an attempt by the International Power Co. to build a diesel-electric locomotive in 1904–1905, but he wrote to Busch in September 1906 suggesting that "some large locomotive factory, for instance, Baldwin in Philadelphia, could undertake the building of the Diesel-Sulzer locomotives."

In 1912, when submarines across the world were using Diesel's engine, the Prussian State Railways set up initial trials of his "thermo-locomotive." Hermann Lemp, a General Electric engineer, was with Diesel at the trials. (Lemp is best known for his invention of a single-lever system replacing separate, complicated throttle and electrical controls.)

About a month later Diesel again traveled to New York and other U.S. cities. "The next great advance in the diesel engine," he said, "would be its adoption for railway locomotives," the *New York Times* reported. "It is certain to take over all the railroads," Diesel told a cub reporter in Fayetteville, Arkansas. "How soon depends mostly on what these monster American railroads do and decide." He attended a ceremony breaking ground for the Busch-Sulzer company's new factory in St. Louis and delivered a lecture to the American Society of Mechanical Engineers in New York City. He struck up a friendship with Thomas Edison, who told Diesel not to eat too much and he would live to be 100.

Illness from overwork in the development period had slowed Diesel, and although his health improved, his finances declined. He died in 1913 at sea after falling from the steamer *Dresden* on his way to a meeting of the Consolidated Diesel Engine Manufacturers in London, ending a brilliant career in a tragic manner.

—John E. Gruber

REFERENCES

Cummins, C. Lyle, Jr. *Diesel's Engine*. Vol. 1, *From Conception to 1918*. Wilsonville, Ore.: Carnot Press, 1993.

Diesel, Eugen. *Diesel, der Mensch, das Werk, das Schicksal*. Hamburg, Germany: Hanseatische Verlagsanstalt, 1937.

Grosser, Morton. *Diesel: The Man and the Engine*. New York: Atheneum, 1978.

New York Times, Apr. 7, 1912; Oct. 2, 1913.

Wilson, Charles Morrow. "I Remember Rudolf Diesel." *Railroad* 68, no. 6 (Oct. 1957): 18–23.

Diesel-Electric Locomotives

Before retracing the evolutionary details of diesel-electric power, we will find it instructive to understand the larger context of this period of railroad history. Even as the steam locomotive was reaching the apex of its development during the decade beginning in 1935, there were major strides in the use of internal combustion power sources, which were inherently more efficient than the reciprocating steam engine, an external combustion device.

It is often overlooked that main-line diesel power did not get its start because steam locomotives could not do the job, but rather because of the public's perception of modernity. The initial push for diesel locomotive development came from Union Pacific and the Burlington Route (CB&Q), which, like all other major passenger carriers, had seen no significant increase in ridership as the nation emerged from the Great Depression. The highway system was expanding because of public works programs, and automobile travel was becoming more popular, thanks to Henry Ford's new mass-production techniques. These two railways wanted to show the nation that a smokeless, brightly painted, diesel-powered streamlined train was the best way to travel cross-country. It was clear that grimy, black steam engines were not in tune with the traveling public's idea of future railroad transportation.

For assistance, UP and CB&Q turned not to the three major builders of steam locomotives (American, Baldwin, and Lima), but to the upstart Electro-Motive Corp., a subsidiary of the industrial giant General Motors. EMC had established a good track record for producing reliable machines, having sold 250 gas-electric motor cars to both large and small railroads since 1924. Thus UP unveiled the aluminum M-10000 in February 1934, and CB&Q its shovel-nosed, stainless-steel *Zephyr* two months later.

These revolutionary passenger trains became the forerunners of a number of self-contained streamlined trains that ushered in the era of main-line diesel power. However, with the success of these "pretty trains," it would be only a few years before independent power units were developed to haul conventional passenger trains, but there was still the widespread belief among operating people that "when heavy work needs to be done, you put a steam engine in front."

The designers at EMC countered that idea when they unveiled the FT model in November 1939. A four-unit set of FTs completed a successful national tour only two months before World War II began. The government's response to wartime conditions was to maximize the production of steam locomotives and limit diesel production to designs already available. This was a wise strategy, but, as the following narratives make clear, it had a profound influence on the development scenario for diesel locomotives. At war's end EMD had produced almost 1,100 FTs and was far ahead of its primary competitor, Alco, which was restricted to switchers and road switchers, although it had produced some successful prewar passenger locomotives.

Diesel locomotives were built using a wide range of truck configurations. To describe these running gears, diesel builders adopted the alphanumeric system that originated with the evolution of straight electric locomotives. In this code unpowered truck axles are given numbers, and power-truck axles are denoted by A, B, C, and D for one to four axles. Most locomotives rode a pair of similar trucks, B-B or C-C, where the hyphen indicates a common frame (the locomotive). In other cases, notably for passenger power, a three-axle power truck was used for a smoother ride at high speed, although the light tonnage suggested the need for only two powered axles. This led to the A1A-A1A configuration. While these three wheel arrangements were the most often used during the early years of diesel evolution, other combinations were occasionally employed. These included B-1, B-2, B-A1A, D-D, and B-B+B-B, where the plus sign indicates a main frame riding on two pairs of B trucks, each pair being connected with a bolster.

—J. Parker Lamb

The Electro-Motive Co. began operation in 1924 as a small supplier of gas-electric cars assembled with components from other manufacturers. Minneapolis & St. Louis car GE-30 was delivered in 1931 with a carbody by the St. Louis Car Co., a Winton gas engine, and General Electric drive equipment. —Middleton Collection

Engine Evolution

At the turn of the twentieth century the spark-ignition engine (known scientifically as an Otto cycle engine) proved itself as a reliable power source for automobiles and trucks. Two decades later it had become robust enough to power gasoline-electric railcars (gas-electrics) that became common during the 1920s as low-cost alternatives to conventional passenger trains. Later spark engines, burning a less volatile (and cheaper) fuel known as "distillate" (similar to kerosene), were also used in early switching locomotives.

Corresponding development of the compression-ignition engine (known as a diesel cycle engine) was considerably slower because it operated with higher temperatures and pressures inside the cylinders. Thus it required more substantial structural materials and was therefore heavier and less attractive for vehicles, where the primary figure of merit was horsepower per pound of vehicle weight. Moreover, the reliability and performance of early diesel engines was poor because they used the same method as spark engines for introducing fuel into the cylinders (a carburetor). It was not until the early 1930s that an effective method of fuel intake to a diesel engine was perfected. Since diesel fuel is much less volatile than gasoline, it was found necessary to inject a small amount of fuel directly into each cylinder, rather than spray fuel into incoming air in a carburetor and pass the mixture into the cylinders. Once this problem was solved, along with the weight problem (by using more modern materials), the efficient diesel engine was ready for big-time railroading (and many other applications).

Another important feature of all internal combustion engines is the number of power strokes made by the piston in one revolution of the crankshaft. High-pressure vapor acts alternately on both sides of a steam-engine piston, producing two power strokes per revolution of the driver (or crankshaft for stationary engines). However, this is not possible for an internal combustion engine where power is produced only during a downward stroke of the piston. Thus one obtains only a single power stroke per revolution of the crankshaft. This operation is known as a "two-stroke cycle," in which the upward stroke is for compression of the air. Ignition occurs near top dead center (TDC), followed by a downward power stroke. It is recognized that this cycle requires special pumps, valves, and piping to introduce air into the cylinder and then exhaust the combustion gas. The common name for this design is "two-cycle."

However, an alternate pattern of operation includes one power stroke over two crankshaft revolutions (or four strokes), defined by these processes. The first downward stroke draws air into the cylinder, the second (upward) compresses it, the third produces power, and the fourth (upward) stroke evacuates the exhaust gases. This is called a "four-stroke cycle," or commonly "four-cycle." Each of these operating patterns, having specific strengths and weaknesses, was successful when applied to locomotive diesel engines. The pioneering Winton model 201A eight-cylinder engine of 1932 was a two-cycle design, as was the famous 567 engine developed by Electro-Motive Corp. In contrast, General Electric's FDL engines of the 1950s were four-cycle machines, as were Alco's designs inherited from McIntosh & Seymour.

Through the last half of the twentieth century each company's basic engine designs were improved constantly to meet the need for more power and greater reliability. The process by which engine designers were able to do this provides insight into the versatility of internal combustion (IC) machines in general and of diesel engines in particular. We must first recognize that the maximum power of any IC engine is determined by three characteristics: compression ratio, total cylinder displacement, and maximum engine speed (in revolutions per minute, or rpm), although a fourth variable, aspiration, can also be a part of the picture. The latter term refers to the method of introducing air into the cylinders. This process is important to performance because greater power is produced when a larger mass of air enters the cylinder before each power stroke.

The designer has three options on aspiration: natural, blower, and supercharger. Natural aspiration employs the suction effect of a downward stroke, while a blower (high-pressure fan) provides a small level of augmentation to the engine's suction. A supercharger (compressor), which can be either gear driven or powered by a turbine operating from hot exhaust gas, provides the most augmentation. As a historical footnote, supercharged aircraft engines saw major development during World War II in order for bombers to fly at higher altitudes (where the air density is low) and thus avoid ground-based artillery.

The engines used by EMC and EMD indicate clearly how power increases were attained over six decades. The Winton 201 design (1934–1939), with a 500-cubic-inch displacement per cylinder, was constructed in 8-, 12-, and 16-cylinder configurations, with the smallest being an in-line arrangement, while the others were 60-degree Vee designs. These operated at 750 rpm with a compression ratio (CR) of 16 and, like most two-cycle engines, used a blower (based on the Roots helical configuration).

The 567 series (indicating cylinder displacement) was introduced in 1938 and was used until 1966. It was based on a 45-degree Vee configuration with a CR of 16 and ran at 800 rpm. In 1953 the 567C model was produced in 6-, 8-, 12-, and 16-cylinder versions with output ranging from 600 hp to 1,750 hp, allowing it to be used in all EMD models. In 1959 a more powerful V-16 version (567D) was available, using a 14.5 CR plus a turbine-driven supercharger, and a speed range of 835–900 rpm. The result was a power output in 1966 of 2,500 hp.

Having stretched this early design to its limit, EMD introduced the 645 series (larger displacement) in late 1965. Running at 900 rpm with a CR of 16, it could produce 1000 hp (8 cylinders), 1,500 hp (12) and 2,000 hp (16) when aspirated with a Roots blower. The turbocharged, 16-cylinder version producing 3,000 hp was EMD's premier design for over 20 years (through the GP/SD40 models). In an attempt to push this design a bit further, EMD offered a 20-cylinder version with turbocharging in 1965. It was capable of 3,600 hp (14.5 CR) and 4,200 hp (16 CR). Because of its extremely long crankshaft, the engine's reliability was poor, and few roads used it.

Another increase in displacement occurred in 1984 when the 710-series engine was introduced. Engine speed was increased to 950 rpm, and all engines were turbocharged. Power output for various sizes was 3,000 hp (12 cylinders), 3,800–4,300 hp (16) and 5,000 hp (20). But again the longest configuration proved to be troublesome, and in 1984, striving to keep pace with its competition, EMD introduced an entirely new 16-cylinder four-cycle turbocharged engine (Model 265H) with a displacement of 1,010 cubic inches. Designed for an output of 6,000 hp, it has not yet been put into production.

While we have used EMD as an example, the General Electric FDL design, a turbocharged four-cycle engine with a displacement of 670 cubic inches and a maximum of 1,050 rpm, was offered in both 12- and 16-cylinder versions (2,250 to 4,400 hp) and has been that company's mainstay since 1959. Moreover, a 5,000-hp V-16 version (960 cubic inches) has been available since 1995.

—J. Parker Lamb

Electrical Details

The early models of diesel-electric power employed low-voltage DC electrical systems similar to those already in use on urban street railways and rapid-transit systems. Direct-current generators and traction motors were relatively light in weight, inexpensive, and trouble free, with performance characteristics well suited to railway service. The DC series motor, so called because its armature and field are wired in series, has long been the most common type of traction motor because of its superior operating characteristics. As the load on the motor increases, the field strength automatically increases, and the result is an increase in torque with a decrease in speed. Consequently, the series motor tends to adjust itself readily to the varying tractive effort required to accelerate and decelerate a train. Moreover, during the starting process motor speed is controlled by resistances, field control, and grouping of motors. This grouping is generally in even numbers of motors—most often four—and, while starting a train, they are transitioned through three types of connecting circuits: full series, series-parallel, and full parallel arrangements. An important operating advantage of electric drive is the use of dynamic braking, which allows traction motors to revert briefly to generators, thus producing extra drag on a moving locomotive. The resulting electric power generated by locomotive inertia is dissipated through air-cooled resistance grids.

Early control systems used mechanical relays and air-actuated switches. Although units with a common manufacturer could usually be run in multiple-unit (M.U.) operation, it was sometimes difficult or impossible to operate diesels of different makes because of the incompatibility of their control systems. Most of these problems had been solved by the early 1950s, and the result was often a lash-up of models from different builders. Eventually the smooth noses of cab units, both passenger and freight, were defaced with M.U. receptacles, so that the units need not be in the lead.

—J. Parker Lamb, with William D. Middleton

The Diesel's First Generation

In 1945, when the push to dieselize began in earnest, this type of motive power had already evolved to its major dimensions. Streamlined or semistreamlined carbodies, similar to passenger-car or electric locomotive designs, were standard for passenger and long-haul freight service, with horsepower in the 1,500 to 2,000 range. Smaller units, generally in the 600- to 1,200-hp range, were designed for switching service, built on simpler platform frames with sheet-metal hoods and operating cabs of utilitarian design. For local freight, involving pickup and delivery switching, a slightly larger, more powerful version of the simple frame-hood-cab construction with a horsepower rating between low-end switchers and large long-distance designs, generally around 1,500 hp, was used. In broad terms, these were the parameters that guided American diesel builders during the first years when internal combustion power set out to supplant steam on the rails.

The very early period of diesel locomotive production engaged a large number of builders, including the three steam locomotive companies that dominated during World War II. These are most conveniently discussed on a company-by-company basis and will be taken up in an order suggested by their later histories. Thus we start with General Motors.

General Motors

When industrial giant GM began to take an interest in the diesel-electric locomotive, it turned to a firm already experienced in diesel power. The Electro-Motive Corp. had been formed in Cleveland in 1922 by an entrepreneurial truck salesman named Harold L. Hamilton. For engineering expertise, he hired a former General Electric railcar mechanic, Richard M. Dilworth. General Electric had abandoned its railcar business during World War I, and Dilworth brought with him whatever he could glean from GE's experience. Hamilton also consulted extensively with Hermann Lemp of GE, who continued to work on electrical and control problems associated with gas- (or diesel-) electric traction even after GE abandoned the business of making gas-electrics. That was the void that Hamilton proposed to fill.

Combining the bright new concept of fluted stainless steel from the Budd Co. and an eight-cylinder Winton diesel-electric locomotive from Electro-Motive, the Chicago, Burlington & Quincy's *Pioneer Zephyr* helped lead the way into railroading's streamliner era. —Library of Congress (LC-USF 344-RA 880-ZB)

There was a back door to converting steam railroads to internal combustion, and it had been opened by the lowly branch-line motor car, or "doodlebug," built by GE as early as 1910. Hamilton's Electro-Motive Corp. set its sights on taking up where GE had left off and selling steam railroads on the economies of the self-propelled passenger car. To supply his first prime movers, Hamilton contracted with Winton Engine Co. for its line of small marine and stationary gasoline engines, initially around 75 hp. Carbodies would come from established builder St. Louis Car. Other parts came from various outside sources, and in February 1924 the first sale was made, a 175-hp gas-electric railcar to the Chicago Great Western.

Through the boom years of the 1920s Electro-Motive rose to dominate its modest niche in the railroad market and ultimately produced 465 Winton-powered gas-electrics and repowered some two dozen built originally by other firms. As business dropped sharply at the onset of the Depression, General Motors sensed opportunity and bought Electro-Motive, keeping its well-respected corporate name. Earlier in the same year (1930) GM had acquired the Winton Engine Co., EMC's sole supplier of gasoline engines. Winton was already working on diesel designs with an eye to rail applications, and that work was given a rapid injection of GM money and engineering talent. Clearly, General

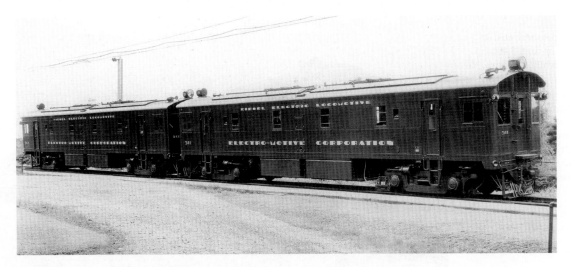

In 1935 Electro-Motive began developing full-size diesel-electric passenger locomotives. The first were these two 1,800-hp units, each powered by two 900-hp Winton diesels. —*Trains* Magazine Collection

Built for the Boston & Maine in November 1941, Electro-Motive's 1,000-hp model NW-2 was a typical EMD switching locomotive. Thousands of these switchers were built in a variety of configurations, usually ranging from 600 to 1,200 hp. —Louis A. Marre Collection

Motors was interested in rail traction, with the diesel engine as its prime mover.

In its ultimate development, the Winton/GM diesel engine, model 201-A, developed 600 hp in its 8-cylinder version, 900 in the 12-cylinder, and 1,200 in the 16-cylinder. Power-to-weight ratio was good, with the 12-cylinder version having 20.5 pounds per horsepower. It powered the Burlington *Pioneer Zephyr* and its descendants, launching the diesel-electric on its journey to dominance.

Good as it was, the Winton/EMC 201-A was not satisfactory for general railroad service. GM set about designing an entirely new engine, retaining the two-cycle operation but essentially starting from scratch. The 16-cylinder 567 engine powered the demonstrator model FT set of

1939, and its successful nationwide demonstration represented the start of serious dieselization of freight operations. By War Production Board order, Electro-Motive Division (which EMC became in 1941) alone produced road freight units during World War II. By the time the other builders were able to enter that field, General Motors held what proved to be an insurmountable lead by virtue of its experience with the FT and, most important, the experience of the railroads that operated them. In the postwar rush to dieselization, EMD had not only the product, but also the production facilities to satisfy demand. A new locomotive plant at La Grange, Illinois, went on line just as the 567 engine was emerging. Established steam builders, saddled with the enormous facili-

EMD demonstrated its first four-unit, 5,400-hp FT freight locomotive, No. 103, in late 1939, and its success all over the United States was key to the railroads' wholesale shift from steam to diesel-electric power. —Electro-Motive Division, *Trains* Magazine Collection

In October 1949 Electro-Motive introduced what it called the General Purpose (GP) unit, nicknamed the "geep." It could function as a switcher, in freight service, and in passenger operation (when fitted with a boiler for train heating). Ultimately this type of hood unit became the dominant form taken by the diesel locomotive in America. Prototype No. 100 was completed at EMD's La Grange, Illinois, plant in October 1949. —Louis A. Marre Collection

ties needed for such production, had to make do with renovated or adapted plants, to their disadvantage.

Between 1945 and 1960 EMD enjoyed as much as 89 percent of the market and was producing 10 units a day at La Grange and a second plant in Cleveland, which was called upon to assist at the peak of the rush to dieselize. Indeed, Cleveland produced 3,600 units between 1948 and 1954. The 10,000th diesel unit was delivered in 1951, the 25,000th in 1962. At the end of World War II there were 38,800 steam locomotives on Class 1 railroads, but by 1962 this number was zero for all practical purposes. Nearly three-quarters of the diesels that replaced steam carried General Motors' builder's plates.

General Electric

As with GM later, General Electric entered the diesel locomotive market early by way of the gas-electric railcar. Indeed, it is credited with producing the first internal combustion railcar in 1904. Its performance was sufficiently promising to lead in 1908 to a car for the Delaware & Hudson. This success led to development of a line of "standard" gas-electric cars launched in 1909. Before closing down the line in 1917, GE managed to build 94 production models and 2 demonstrators. Counted among its customers were both Class 1 steam railroads and shortlines. The experience gained, especially in the area of electric transmission control systems, led directly to GE's diesel locomotive development. In 1913, in the midst of its gas-electric venture, GE built a gas-electric box-cab locomotive for the Minneapolis, St. Paul, Rochester & Dubuque Electric Traction Co., followed by three more for the same operation.

No satisfactory diesel prime mover was available to GE at that period, but by the end of its railcar days GE had a test engine under development. The company's presiding electrical guru was Hermann Lemp, a Swiss engineer who

General Electric sold almost 100 cars before World War I, among them this gas-electric locomotive, which was turned out for the Minneapolis, St. Paul, Rochester & Dubuque Electric Traction Co. in 1913. —Middleton Collection

When GE decided to enter the full-size locomotive market in 1961, the initial dieselization of the steam railroads was already accomplished. What GE was after was the second generation, replacing the first set of diesels then in service. GE entered the market with a 2,500-hp road switcher, part of an export line of "universal" locomotives. This U25-B represented a universal, 2,500-hp unit on two axle B trucks. Two of the U25-B demonstrators are seen here. —Louis A. Marre Collection

had been with GE since 1892. After meeting with Rudolf Diesel during the latter's 1912 visit to the United States, Lemp was convinced that a suitable diesel power plant could be developed for rail application and turned his attention to the electrical side of the locomotive. While he worked on harnessing internal combustion to electric traction, GE's diesel-engine program produced a test unit in 1916 and another in 1917. Unfortunately, these were not promising enough to warrant production. Instead, GE decided to link up with an established engine manufacturer and chose the Ingersoll-Rand Co. (IR), which had been in the engine field long enough to have a variety of production and developmental engines already in hand. A test unit was fielded in 1924 and led to introduction of two

models for switchers, a single-engine 300-hp model and a dual-engine 600 hp. Lacking facilities to construct carbodies, GE entered into a triple alliance with American Locomotive and Ingersoll-Rand. American would construct the carbodies, General Electric the electrical components, and Ingersoll-Rand the prime movers.

The Alco-GE–Ingersoll-Rand consortium of 1925 marked the entry of major American corporations into the diesel-electric locomotive market. However, the market for these machines was hardly significant. In fact, it was minuscule, and the initial applications were in humble niches—mostly terminal and industrial switching. In the six-year span of the three-company consortium, it sold only 49 units, plus 1 assembled in Canada.

Among several early designs for small diesel-electric switchers was Central Railroad of New Jersey boxcab unit No. 1000. Delivered in 1925, the 300-hp, 60-ton locomotive represented a joint venture, with Alco supplying mechanical parts, Ingersoll-Rand the diesel, and General Electric the electrical equipment. The pioneer diesel remained in service until 1957, when it was retired to the B&O Railroad Museum in Baltimore. —General Electric, *Trains* Magazine Collection

Alco pulled out after three years when GE built its own facilities to produce carbodies. At the onset of the Depression GE was in a position to build both the mechanical and electrical portions of locomotives at its Erie, Pennsylvania, works, while Ingersoll-Rand continued to supply prime movers, but for a new line. The earlier box-cab configuration was dropped in favor of single-cab models with one or two diesels housed in close-fitting hoods, thus providing sufficient visibility from the cab to dispense with operating stations at both ends.

Under Depression conditions, GE/IR built and sold only 22 of these standard units, insufficient to justify continuance. Thus GE left the market in 1937, having constructed 119 diesel-electric locomotives. Although the company reentered the locomotive field as a major player some decades later, during the development of first-generation road units General Electric was limited to a minor role of supplying small industrial-size switching locomotives. While the initial tide of dieselization swept over American railroading, the mighty General Electric Co. stood in the shadows.

American Locomotive (Alco)

After Alco withdrew from the GE-IR consortium, the company decided to proceed with diesel locomotive development independently. However, it immediately sought another partner and purchased an established diesel-engine builder, the McIntosh & Seymour Corp. of Auburn, New York. In 1930 M&S was producing a dozen engine models and was able to design a large new one specifically for loco-

motive applications. Alco initially offered a small 300-hp switcher with an existing M&S engine, along with a 600-hp model with the new engine. The market for small units fizzled quickly, but the larger engine sold 24 copies in the depressed market of 1931 to 1935. Thus Alco decided to discontinue production of the small model and improve the large one.

By 1939, with a 1,000-hp engine in production, Alco entered the full-scale market with a line of switchers, road switchers, and passenger units. The road switcher, an elongated yard unit, was a new concept for American railroads, but ideal for the versatile diesel-electric. It could work in yards or on main lines with equal efficiency. A freight cab unit was curtailed by War Production Board restrictions and did not enter the market until 1946, lagging behind General Motors' successful FT model of 1939, which continued production during the war years. That lag and inherent deficiencies in the first postwar prime mover kept Alco in second place, well behind EMD.

With its early models using GE electrical gear, units were marketed under the name Alco-GE, but the latter company terminated the arrangement in 1953, and Alco thereafter was obliged to be self-sufficient in that area as well. GE in fact became a direct competitor with its own line of full-size road locomotives in 1961, and its success eventually forced Alco into third place as a producer and doomed any chance of its long-term success as an American builder.

Alco produced approximately 8,000 diesel locomotives for the domestic market. There was also a sizable export market, including large Mexican orders. In addition, the

Alco's first line of standardized diesel locomotives was the 600-hp switcher, seen here in the newly delivered No. 10 for the Louisville & Nashville in March 1939. The high hood required for the McIntosh & Seymour 6-cylinder in line model 531 was soon replaced by a revised engine that permitted a lower hood. —Louis A. Marre Collection

Montreal Locomotive Works partnership produced about 1,700 units for the Canadian market, plus exports. All told, the Alco family contributed about 12,000 locomotives produced in North America and many thousands more produced by licensees in overseas markets in a life span that is still continuing in some other countries.

Baldwin

The powerful Baldwin company of Philadelphia was the world's largest builder of steam locomotives, but it also constructed many other types of heavy machinery. Thus it is not surprising that Baldwin president Samuel Vauclain and his engineering staff were thinking about diesel-powered locomotives in the mid-1920s when steam power was still king around the world. Indeed, there is evidence that other locomotive builders as well believed that the diesel power plant in some form would eventually replace the steam locomotive because of the inherent advantage in thermodynamic efficiency of an internal combustion design over conventional steam power.

Baldwin's initial efforts in this direction were based on the general belief that a minimum of 1,000 hp was required and that a maximum of 300 pounds of engine weight per horsepower must be met. True to his conviction, Vauclain's company constructed a 1,000-hp road locomotive powered by a Knudsen Motor Co. diesel engine, employing electric transmission, and having a power-to-weight ratio of 275 pounds per horsepower. This 137-ton unit, which bore its Baldwin serial number on its number board (58501), began testing on June 25, 1925. During those tests it successfully handled 2,000-ton coal trains for the Reading Railroad, proving that diesel-electric

Design of Alco's first main-line passenger diesel in 1940 was similar to the slightly earlier Electro-Motive diesels, fitted with six-wheel high-speed trucks and two 6-cylinder turbocharged 539 engines to deliver a total of 2,000 hp per unit. The locomotive's performance proved to be less impressive than Otto Kuhler's exterior design. Only 78 were built, and only the New Haven used very many, operating a total of 60 units in dual freight and passenger service. —J. W. Swanberg Collection

Alco came up with a road switcher diesel that could function as a switcher, a freight engine, or a passenger locomotive. The original RS-1 design incorporated a 1,000-hp diesel switcher on an elongated frame over the road trucks. A short hood behind the cab could include a heating boiler if needed for passenger operation. Developed in 1941, the versatile RS-1 first went to military needs, and many served on the Trans-Iranian Railway and in the Soviet Union. One of the first put to civilian use was this 1944 version for the Chicago & North Western. —*Trains* Magazine Collection

traction of sufficient size and power was more than theoretically possible. As an experiment, the locomotive was not offered for sale and was not duplicated, primarily because of shortcomings in the diesel-engine design. But it had made Vauclain's point: this new type of motive power could be built, and it would work.

With the appearance of improved diesel-engine designs in the early 1930s, Baldwin began to think more seriously about its earlier experimental unit and, like Alco and General Motors, purchased an established engine builder, the De La Vergne Engine Co., in 1931. By the late 1930s the company was ready to enter the market and, again like Alco, began in 1939 with a line of standardized units consisting of 660-hp and 1,000-hp switchers. Unfor-

Alco's postwar passenger diesel was the stylish PA-1 engine, which used six-wheel, high-speed trucks and powered the locomotive by a single 16-cylinder Model 244 engine, unlike the rival EMD passenger units, which used two 1,000-hp diesels. Although its styling was a favorite of railroad enthusiasts, its sales were disappointing. The very first model, dubbed *Spirit of 1776*, is seen here at the head end of the U.S. Freedom Tour at the Peoria Union Station in July 1948. —Louis A. Marre Collection

The Baldwin Locomotive Works was an early experimenter with diesel-electric locomotives and began producing a line of standardized VO switchers in 1939. It built almost 2,000 of these sturdy units by the time production ended in 1956. This 1,000-hp VO type was built for the Burlington in 1943.
—Louis A. Marre Collection

tunately for road-unit development, diesel locomotive production was frozen to existing models by the government early in World War II, effectively locking both Baldwin and Alco out of that market for the duration.

By 1946 Baldwin had a new prime mover available and began to market road freight and passenger units. Like Alco, it found the established lead of General Motors all but insurmountable. Acquisition of the Lima-Hamilton Corp. in 1950 removed the smallest competitor from the field, but had little impact on design or marketing of the subsequent Baldwin-Lima-Hamilton label. Baldwin suffered from its lack of a modern production facility, making do with a small portion of its enormous steam-era facility in Eddystone, Pennsylvania. It was peculiarly unable to standardize

in the full sense, constantly tinkering with models that might thus differ in details from unit to unit, much less from order to order, of ostensibly identical models.

Were it not for the sustained purchases of the Pennsylvania Railroad, which served the Eddystone complex, Baldwin would not have survived as long as it did. The Pennsylvania completed its initial dieselization in 1956, and Baldwin left the business soon thereafter. In its span from 1939 to the close of production, it contributed just over 3,200 diesel locomotives to its market, including a modest level of export business, notably to France and its colonies, in the immediate postwar period. Though it had been Samuel Vauclain's opinion that the diesel would ultimately supplant the steam locomotive, his company was

Baldwin frequently went its own way in both its diesel wheel arrangements and visual styles. One design that never caught on was Baldwin's monstrous Centipede locomotive, made up of two semipermanently coupled 2-D+D-2 units powered by four diesel engines and rated at 6,000 hp. Only 54 single units were sold. —Louis A. Marre Collection

While visually distinctive with their "shark-nose" cab-unit design, Baldwin's B-B road freight diesels followed the typical mechanical design of other builders. Demonstrator 6001 and a cabless booster are shown on the Wabash at Des Moines, Iowa, in May 1950. —Louis A. Marre Collection

unable to capture that market when it came about. However, its postwar prime-mover design proved durable, and overseas licensees continued to produce locomotives with Baldwin power plants for at least 20 years after the Eddystone Works closed.

Lima

The smallest of the traditional steam builders was Lima, named for its Ohio hometown. In the waning years of the steam era Lima enjoyed a reputation as a designer

Steam locomotive builder Lima Locomotive Works made a late entry into diesel-electric production by merging with diesel-engine builder Hamilton. The first Lima-Hamilton diesels came out in 1949. Scarcely a year later the firm was merged with Baldwin, and by 1951 Lima production ended. Lima produced a few road switcher and transfer locomotives, but by far its largest production was for diesel switchers. Wabash 400 was a 1,000-hp version of a series of standard designs that ranged from 750- to 1,200-hp units. —Louis A. Marre Collection

of advanced technology and high production quality. The company reluctantly entered the diesel era and followed the lead of its larger competitors in that it forged a relationship with an established diesel-engine builder rather than undertake an original design. Lima aligned itself with the Hamilton Engine Co., likewise named for its Ohio location. Lima-Hamilton offered a modest line of switcher, light road switcher, and heavy transfer locomotives, commencing production in May 1949, precisely coincident with shipment of its final steam locomotive.

Lima's corporate history dates to 1869, but neither longevity nor reputation allowed it to survive in the postwar diesel locomotive market. After delivering just 174 diesel units, it was subsumed by industrial giant Baldwin, which became Baldwin-Lima-Hamilton from 1951. None of Lima's designs were produced under the new name, and the association with Hamilton Engine was dropped in favor of Baldwin's established line of its own designs. For all its impact on steam development, Lima's impact on the course of American dieselization was insignificant.

Fairbanks, Morse & Co.

For sheer antiquity, Fairbanks, Morse & Co. cannot be surpassed. Its ancestry goes back to 1830, when Erastus and Thaddeus Fairbanks commenced operations in the mechanical scale trade. Over time the Fairbanks family acquired a partner, becoming Fairbanks, Morse & Co. in 1866. Growing into a diversified machinery company put FM into contact with the expanding railroad industry, and it became a supplier of scales, track equipment, pumps, tiny gasoline locomotives for maintenance chores, prefabricated coaling towers, and other equipment. When the diesel locomotive became commercially attractive, FM found itself in the full-size locomotive market almost by serendipity. During the 1930s the U.S. Navy supported diesel-engine development from a number of entities, including Winton and FM. To FM fell the prize of designing a new configuration for the diesel engine.

Known as the opposed-piston model, each of its power cylinders contained two pistons driving crankshafts on both bottom and top of the engine. For the navy this was an ideal design because it maximized the power produced for a given volume of space in a small vessel such as a submarine. Although troublesome cylinder heads were eliminated in this configuration, it was necessary to include elaborate gear trains in order to drive a single shaft. The Navy liked the O-P engines, and by 1944 FM was in a position to enter the railroad market in a big way.

At first a line of switchers was all that could be managed, because FM lacked production space at its Beloit, Wisconsin, engine plant for manufacture of road locomotive carbodies. This handicap was bridged by a contract with General Electric, whose Erie, Pennsylvania, works was able to accommodate larger units. After 111 units had been sold under this arrangement, FM's Beloit Works had been expanded sufficiently to handle all subsequent production. With timing and subsidized prime-mover development in FM's favor, orders were not long in coming. Electro-Motive was booked up for months ahead, and both Alco and Baldwin had considerable backlogs when the national rush to dieselize began in 1948. Consequently, FM was able to promise delivery much earlier than its competitors, sometimes by as much as six months, and thus profited from the rush.

Unfortunately for its long-term prospects, the opposed-piston prime mover, which had performed admirably in maritime service, was not as well suited to railroad application. Problems arose quickly, involving heavy expenditure on warranted parts and taking a rapid toll on FM's reputation. Thus the O-Ps were early candidates for replacement with EMD prime movers when the owners could justify this expense, and a high percentage of FM units lost their opposed-piston power before their time on the road ended.

To its credit, FM improved the basic O-P design as rapidly as possible, introducing a potentially revolutionary unit in the 2,400-hp Trainmaster in 1953, when the competition was generally around 1,800 hp; and it even in-

Fairbanks-Morse developed an opposed-piston diesel engine that was widely used first by U.S. submarines and later for railroad locomotives. Raymond Loewy designed the locomotive's refined exterior. Minnesota Western Railway No. 10 was a 1,200-hp switcher built at the company's Beloit, Wisconsin, plant in January 1951. —Middleton Collection

In the immediate postwar period Fairbanks-Morse, followed shortly by Alco, introduced the largest single-unit diesel locomotive, operating on six-wheel trucks and equipped with a 2,000-hp, 10-cylinder opposed-piston engine. These were operated in both passenger and freight service. This three-unit Kansas City Southern set was seen at Pittsburg, Kansas, in 1950. —Louis A. Marre Collection

vested in the lightweight train fad of the mid-1950s. Ultimately, the theoretical advantage of the O-P engine evaporated under the rigorous conditions of railway service, and the dominance of Electro-Motive could not be overcome. Final domestic production came in January 1958, with a few units trickling out to established customers in Mexico as late as March 1963. All in all, FM made a valiant effort to crack the new market when full-scale conversion to diesels was getting under way. A total of 1,256 units, from 1944 to 1963, called Beloit their home.

—Louis A. Marre

A Second Generation

The first generation of dieselization ended around 1961, when the immediate postwar designs began to reach the end of their economic life span—generally 15 to 20 years, dictated by financing arrangements if not mechanical obsolescence. But there was also another strong influence on builders. Now roadbeds were better, trains were longer, and speed was a selling point for railroad traffic solicitors. The need was to make locomotives more powerful without continuing to add more units. (By the early 1960s some western roads were using as many as ten

F-M continued to exploit the high horsepower available from its proprietary opposed-piston diesel-engine design. In 1953 the builder introduced the most powerful single-unit locomotive yet offered, a C-C road switcher design powered by a single 2,400-hp, 12-cylinder engine called the Trainmaster. A demonstrator pair is seen on the Wabash at Decatur, Illinois, in 1953. —Louis A. Marre Collection

1,500-hp units on long-distance runs.) In response, builders began increasing engine horsepower.

At EMD, for example, the 1,500-hp engine in the F7 and GP7 series increased with the 9 series to 1,750 and then to 1,800 hp in the 18 series. In 1959 a turbo-supercharger was added to give 2,000 hp in the 20 models. EMD's selling point was termed "unit reduction," since three new GP20s could replace the classical lash-up of four F7s. The company urged railroads to trade in their oldest units and thus decrease the total number of locomotives requiring maintenance. The GP20 and GP18 were offered in both the traditional high-nose and the newer low-nose configurations that some roads preferred because of the better visibility for those in the cab.

Meanwhile, improvements in EMD's SD models (on C-C trucks) had kept pace. These units were often used to spread weight over more axles rather than as a power booster (except at low speed). But there were still some roads looking for even more power. So in 1958 EMD dropped a turbo-supercharged engine onto an SD9 frame, beefed up the generator, and rolled out the SD24 (2,400 hp). Now a four-unit consist had more power than half a dozen F7s.

But EMD was not alone in the race for brawnier units, nor was it the first to build a single diesel locomotive producing more than 2,000 hp. In fact, it was the last of the four early competitors to pass this power milestone. As noted earlier, General Electric had developed leadership in production of small industrial switchers, commonly known by their nominal weights (45 and 70 tons). However, in addition, GE had gradually developed a series of heavier, main-line power for the export market, where it generally outsold EMD. These models, touted as universal in design, were denoted by the letter U followed by the horsepower (in hundreds). For example, a common export switcher model was the 800-hp U8.

Building on this expertise, GE unveiled in 1954 a demonstration set of A-B-B-A cab units for the domestic market. One A-B set was powered at 1,800 hp per unit, while the other set was at 2,000 hp. To those watching the evolution of diesel power, this signaled that GE was ready to challenge Alco, Baldwin, and EMD. Indeed, only a year after EMD introduced its SD24, GE made a frontal assault on the industry as it began a nationwide demonstration tour by a pair of new, 2,500-hp road switchers riding on B-B trucks and designated U25B. This model included some new features such as a sealed carbody and a central air management system. After the two initial units completed a successful tour, GE produced another demonstration set of four units that included one low-nose unit. After its demonstrations, these were sold and GE began a steady U25B production run that lasted almost seven years (and 476 units).

Reacting to this major threat to its technical leadership, EMD unveiled in July 1961 its own new B-B unit, powered at 2,250 hp. It also featured a new type of carbody that included a largely decorative cowling over the cab that extended backward over the engine compartment to include the dynamic brake housing. With this model EMD also departed from its previous practice of identifying units by horsepower: instead of being the GP22, it was designated the GP30 to emphasize what GM called "30 improvements" over the GP20. The GP30 was also the first EMD unit for which the low nose was standard. The GP30 and its cabless counterpart sold 948 copies (including 2 for Canada) in 18 months.

General Motors pulled even with GE in the horsepower race by introducing the 35 series in 1963 and then jumped ahead slightly by unveiling the 40 series at 3,000 hp in 1965. But GE was also up to this challenge and gradually increased the power of its U25 line to U28 in 1966 and to U36 in 1967. Although Alco made similar power advances for its road switcher models between 1956 and 1966, its total sales lagged behind those of GE, which was clearly in second place by 1958. Indeed, Alco's C430 of 1966 (a 3,000-hp B-B unit) was the last locomotive produced in the historic Schenectady shops.

Diesel-Electric Derivatives

Although the diesel-electric locomotive was much more efficient than its steam-powered predecessor, this revolutionary type of motive power was not without its weaknesses. During the decade after World War II, as early diesel-electric designs from half a dozen builders were flooding onto American railways, there was a growing concern in the industry that improvements might be possible in two areas: low-speed drag service and overall fuel economy. These concerns spawned a group of experimental machines that could be described as diesel derivatives.

The earliest effort involved replacement of the thermally efficient diesel engine with an equally efficient gas turbine that operated with a much cheaper fuel, a thick, residual oil that required preheating in order to flow through the fuel supply lines (much like an oil-burning steamer). General Electric, a major producer of aircraft gas turbines (jet engines), constructed the first gas-turbine-electric locomotive (GTEL) for main-line service in 1948. It featured a double-ended carbody design, enclosing a 4,500-hp turbine (3,900 at railhead) and riding on a B+B-B+B wheel arrangement. The solid black engine was first demonstrated on the Pennsylvania and the Nickel Plate railroads but eventually found a home on the power-hungry Union Pacific, where it was painted yellow and gray and given the number 50. Two years after this engine began service, GE's competitor in the aircraft business, Westinghouse Electric, produced a cowl unit containing a pair of 2,000-hp gas turbines. With a ship's prow nose treatment and nicknamed the Blue Goose, it also rode on four B-trucks. But there was little interest, and it was scrapped after two years of demonstrations.

In 1952 Union Pacific took delivery of 10 new GTELs that were virtually identical to the demonstrator No. 50 except for the omission of one cab. There was also a small fuel tender to satisfy the turbine's thirst for fuel. To minimize use of the main turbine within the yard, these units were fitted with small auxiliary diesels for hostling moves. This design was further improved in 1954 when 15 more units were delivered with a gallery walkway cut into the side of the cowl carbody. These units also used larger fuel tenders (taken from retired 800-class 4-8-4s) and were usually used with a small B-B diesel unit as a reliability measure.

The pinnacle of American GTEL technology was embodied in 30 GE units delivered to the UP in 1958–1961. Housed in two long-cowl carbodies, the lead unit contained an 850-hp Cooper-Bessemer diesel for hostling and dynamic braking, while the 8,500-hp main turbine (7,000 on rail) rode within the second unit, with a usual fuel tender at the rear. In 1964 power at rail was increased to 8,500 hp (10,000 gross), and some units were fitted with nose M.U. connections in order to operate as a 17,000-hp power block. Other units were fitted with traction motors beneath their fuel tenders.

While the UP fleet, whose units were popularly known as Big Blows for their jetlike noise, was specialized for high-speed main-line service, the gas turbine's inability to operate economically except at full load eventually doomed this diesel derivative. All were returned to the GE plant between 1963 and 1969, where trucks and other components were used on more advanced diesel models (discussed later).

The second major attempt to improve the basic diesel-electric configuration involved shortcomings in the performance of heavily loaded DC-traction motors at low speeds. These machines, when running for an extended time in an overload condition, were prone to overheat and, if the insulation failed, to flashover and burn. With increasing use of heavy trucks for industrial and mine service, there was widespread development of hydraulic couplings between engines and drive wheels, employing liquid turbines rather than solid shafts to transmit torque. In operation the power turbine would blast a swirling liquid onto the driven turbine with great torque, causing the output of the second turbine to be virtually the same as that of the input (high efficiency).

When applied to locomotives, such heavy-duty hydraulic transmissions also assured that there would be no wheel slip or overheating in continuous low-speed service. Although Electro-Motive and its Canadian subsidiary produced some low-powered diesel-hydraulic units for industrial switching in 1951, it was German companies that moved ahead with this propulsion technology, producing a wide range of railroad applications for European lines. In the early 1960s two American lines with extensive routes in mountainous territory contracted with the Kraus-Maffei Co. of Munich to construct six main-line locomotives using Voith hydraulic transmissions. In 1961 three units were delivered to the Denver & Rio Grand Western and an equal number to Southern Pacific. These were cowl units with a turretlike cab, while the tops of the carbody sides were slanted inward to conform to Euro-

pean clearances. Riding on K-M design C-C running gear, they were powered by a pair of small Maybach diesels (1,770 hp) of V-16 configuration with a separate turbocharger for each bank of cylinders. With the diesels running at nearly 1,600 rpm, engine overheating inside tunnels became a problem, and extra louvers were added (as would later be needed for large diesel-electrics).

It took only three years for the Rio Grande to decide that these imports were not the answer to its operational problems. In 1964 it shipped its K-M units to SP, which was having more success with its hydraulics. Indeed, the road ordered 15 additional K-M units, similar in overall specifications, in 1963. These C-C units featured a hood-type road switcher carbody and rode on trucks of modified Alco design. In fact, Alco built the only American-designed hydraulics for SP in 1964 when three C-C road-switcher-type units were delivered. Carrying two 2,130-hp 12-cylinder 251-series engines driving through the Voith transmissions, they were substantially more powerful than the earlier K-Ms.

Southern Pacific's 24-unit fleet of diesel-hydraulics began to be scrapped in 1967, with the final K-M unit going in late 1968 and the big Alcos in 1973. It is clear in retrospect that these two types of diesel-electric derivatives were overtaken by continuous improvements in both engine and electrical technologies embodied within the original configuration unveiled before World War II.

—J. Parker Lamb

UP's Thirst for Power

The early race for more powerful locomotives was led by the Union Pacific Railroad, which had a long history of such quests. Beginning with its World War II successes in acquiring and operating monster steam engines such as the Challenger and Big Boy on down to its role as one of the nation's first owners of main-line diesels, UP felt a continuous need to increase average train speed across the vast West.

Among UP's thrusts for new technologies with post-steam motive power were its experiments with turbochargers for GP9s, as well as its later attempt to replace the diesel engine with a gas-turbine unit. So it was no surprise when, in the early 1960s, UP flexed its economic muscles with the three diesel builders and commissioned them to build twin-engine units that would generate at least 5,000 hp. The models constructed by GM and GE generally operated successfully, in contrast to Alco's entry, which saw only three prototypes built.

EMD's entry was the DD35B, a giant booster unit consisting of two (−35) power systems mounted on a 70-foot platform supported by D-D running gear. EMD's advertisements suggested that by attaching a GP35 lead unit, a road could easily create reliable power blocks of 7,500 hp. After purchasing 30 of the big boosters, UP ordered 15 more with cabs, denoted DD35A. In contrast, GE's first entry was the U50, containing two (−25) power assemblies and a control cab mounted on two pairs of bolster-connected B trucks, running gear commonly used in electric locomotives. A total of 26 U50s were produced.

In 1969 UP ordered a second round of twin-engine locomotives; the result was EMD's 98-foot-long DD40X, a souped-up version of the DD35A that incorporated two (−40) power systems producing 6,600 hp. Forty-seven of these mammoth engines were delivered. As the pinnacle of dual-engine diesel production, they stand as iconic counterparts of the powerful Big Boys of World War II. UP decided to call these Centennial units in honor of the 100th anniversary of the golden-spike ceremony on the UP's line at Promontory Summit, Utah.

In its second design GE reverted to C-C running gear for the U50C, using trucks from scrapped UP gas-turbine locomotives that GE had built in 1958. The two GE designs (U50 and U50C) have a similar appearance from the front, but from the side it is seen that the radiators were at either end of the unit in the original design. In contrast, the U50C cooling units were clustered in the center, a configuration similar to that used by the three EMD designs. UP bought a total of 40 U50Cs starting in 1969. Incidentally, the only other railroad to indulge in this grand experiment was the Southern Pacific, which bought three each of the first two offerings by each builder but was not interested in further developments. The major difficulties with dual-engine units were related to maintenance. With two engines on board, half the locomotive sat idle when the other half was under repair. In the long run they were doomed more by their economics than by their technology.

More Brawn for the Diesel

Sensing that pulling power was the overriding goal and determined in its competition with GE, in 1965 EMD unveiled a unique locomotive configuration with its SD45. Under its hood was a 3,600-hp diesel with 20 cylinders and a massive carbody that featured long, slanted radiator grills at the rear. Despite some early problems with its long crankshaft, this model sold 1,312 units in six years (including 52 of a passenger version that included a steam generator). However, it is significant that no builder again attempted to use a 20-cylinder diesel engine during the next 30 years.

Indeed, between the start of SD35 and U25C production (1963–1964) and the start of C30-7 production (1976), the standard main-line power for many major roads became a C-C unit powered by a V-16 engine. The total production for these three designs, and those in between, exceeded 9,000 units. EMD was the leader (6,500 to GE's 2,600), with over 80 percent of its total composed of the extremely popular SD40 series and its (−2) modification that featured modularized controls, which were more compact and easier to maintain.

Unfortunately for EMD, these production figures masked the fact that General Electric was beginning to win the technology race. Exhibit A for this conclusion occurred in 1980 when GE introduced the 30-7A line that produced 3,000 hp from a 12-cylinder FDL engine. This was followed in 1984 by the 16-cylinder, 4,000-hp 40-8 line, referred to by GE's marketing department as Dash 8-40. The pivotal year turned out to be 1983 when, after 38 years, General Motors was finally overtaken by General Electric in annual production numbers. But in that same year EMD's GP60 model, with 3,800 hp from a 16-cylinder engine, was introduced and proved to be a worthy competitor to GE's B40-8. EMD also rolled out its SD60 in 1985 to compete with the C40-8.

In the late 1980s GE solidified its position as the nation's largest locomotive builder when General Motors shut down a major part of its large La Grange plant and transferred locomotive assembly to the GM Diesel Division plant in London, Ontario. This facility was later renamed the General Motors Locomotive Group. Later increases in EMD orders caused the company to begin contracting out final assembly to independent shops located in all three nations of the NAFTA alliance.

—J. Parker Lamb

Remotely Operated Units

Helpers

In the 1960s radio communication was adopted by many railroads not only for voice messages but for the transmission of data. An early use of the latter was the control of midtrain helper locomotives from the lead unit, thus allowing closer coordination of the two sets of power than was possible when the helper was operated by a separate crew. Of course, there were savings in labor costs as well. Among the major roads that embraced this technology was Southern Railway, which routinely operated extremely long trains on its major routes leading from Atlanta (to Cincinnati, Washington, D.C., and New Orleans). The state of electronics at that time required a separate radio receiver and transmitter car to be coupled to the helper engines. Although this was partially successful, there were some problems in mountainous territory, especially around tunnels, and within a decade this type of operation was discontinued throughout the United States. Not only were locomotives much more powerful, but newer cars (and their couplers) were larger and stronger.

However, by the mid-1990s a much more sophisticated system of radio control was possible, with transmitting and receiving modules in each locomotive. Denoted as distributed power units (DPUs), this new arrangement gave the engineer independent control of every unit. Indeed, it was possible to have locomotives on one end of the train pulling while those in another location were braking. With the engineer in full control, it is also possible to operate a train backwards (through sidings and wyes). With the advent of long-distance coal trains originating in the

Powder River Basin of Wyoming and Montana, the DPU system has become standard for many other unit trains as well (including grain and other loads).

Remote Control

Remote-control operation of a locomotive from a position outside the cab first became practical in the early 1980s, when it was widely used in industrial settings where speeds were low (10 mph maximum) and train lengths short. In such operations the "train operator" may be on the ground or riding on the outside of the locomotive for better visibility. The fact that a diesel locomotive does not require constant attention has made it practical for an operator to govern its movements by a radio-based system for distances up to about half a mile. Using a control unit strapped to his body, the operator commands both power and braking while allowing the control system to determine the correct combination of engine power, drifting, and braking to maintain a given speed.

In addition to running the diesel locomotive, the control unit also operates lights, horn, and sand. It incorporates many safety features as well. There is, for example, a "tilt" feature that promptly applies the locomotive brakes if the operator stumbles. If the operator takes no control action for, say, 50 seconds (suggesting that the operator may have become distracted), a warning tone is sounded. The operator must then press a button to cancel the warning, or, again, the locomotive will stop. At the same time the unit signals other workers. The locomotive will also stop if it loses the signal from the portable unit. It is usual practice to have locomotive operators work in pairs, and either of them can override the other to stop the en-gine at any time. Another feature of the system permits one operator to pass control over to the other whenever desired.

Remote control has been widely used by Canadian roads since 1989, and the Canadian National Railways now has over 125 portable units. In the United States virtually all Class 1 railroads are experimenting with this technology, and a number are heavily committed to it for use within yard limits. Among these are Burlington Northern Santa Fe, Kansas City Southern, and CSX, all of which have 100 locomotives so equipped. Less extensive use has occurred on Union Pacific, Norfolk Southern, Florida East Coast, Montana Rail Link, Indiana Rail Road, and Wheeling & Lake Erie.

Because this technology brings into focus the long-lasting traditions of railway labor unions, it was bound to be controversial, and the final regulatory environment for its use is not yet at hand. While railroad managements emphasize that remote control is safer than traditional operation because there are two "drivers" for each unit, union leaders point out that remote-control operators are not fully trained as engineers, having only 3 weeks of preparation rather than the traditional 26. Despite these immediate uncertainties, there is little doubt that in the future, more and more locomotives will operate this way and, possibly, over longer distances.

—Dan LeMaire-Bauch

The AC Revolution

While relatively simple DC machines had many advantages, their major disadvantage became amplified with the continued increases in power produced by diesel locomo-

The newest generation of diesel locomotives incorporates AC-traction motors, radial trucks, and diesel engines that can produce as much as 6,000 hp. This is a Canadian Pacific AC4400 General Electric unit at Clearing, Illinois, which can produce 4,400 hp from the latest 16-cylinder turbocharged 7FDL16 version of the former Cooper-Bessemer engine that GE has used for more than 40 years.
—Louis A. Marre Collection

General Electric increased its single-unit horsepower to 6,000 hp with the development of a new design by Deutz MWM of Mannheim, Germany, which used 16 still larger (250 by 320 mm) cylinders than those used by the former Cooper-Bessemer engines. CSX Transportation's AC6000 No. 602 headed a train at Race Pond, Georgia, in 1997. —Louis A. Marre Collection

tives. The weakness of all machines is the need to lubricate and protect moving parts that slide over one another in direct contact. For example, performance of steam locomotives was improved immensely with the application of roller bearings to replace journal (friction) bearings that required constant lubrication. With DC motors and generators the equivalent problem was the commutator, in which solid carbon blocks (contact brushes) scraped continuously over soft-metal rotor elements. This was an essential process that produced a rotating magnetic field in the armature and thereby the torque on the motor shaft. However, as voltages and currents became larger, the prob-

ability of arcing (flashover) and burnout at the commutator became higher, and DC machines became heavier because of the need for more protection.

For electrified railroads there had been a standard practice of using AC on long transmission lines and then converting it to DC within the locomotive. Originally it was necessary to use motor-generator sets (AC motors running DC generators), but in the early 1950s there was a switch to smaller ignitron rectifiers. These were mercury arc devices inside large vacuum tubes that required triggering circuitry, as well as extra cooling. With the arrival of solid-state electronics a decade later, it was pos-

Electro-Motive's SD70MAC diesel, first produced in 1993, incorporated a 4,000-hp 16-cylinder engine, AC-traction power, and radial trucks. BNSF's No. 8941 was at Heavener, Oklahoma, in May 2000. —Louis A. Marre Collection

The latest version of Electro-Motive's high-horsepower locomotives has been its SD70ACe unit, which began to enter regular service in 2004. Its 16-cylinder, two-cycle engine produces 4,300 hp, and its emissions have been reduced to meet EPA Tier 2 regulations. It incorporates AC traction, with optional DC, and radial trucks. Demonstrator GMDX70 was on the Union Pacific at Council Bluffs, Iowa, in April 2005. —George Cockle, Louis A. Marre Collection

sible to employ silicon-diode rectifiers in industrial applications. These were even more compact and did not require any extensive cooling. Thus the initial step toward eliminating DC in locomotives occurred in 1966 when GE coupled its FDL engine to an alternator-rectifier in the U28B model. EMD followed suit with its GP38AC in 1972. Soon the DC generator could be eliminated on most new locomotives.

Although AC motors and their controls are superior to corresponding DC devices in low-speed pulling ability and in reliability, their transfer to locomotive technology required a number of years of development. Thus it was not until the 1980s that EMD began serious experimentation. In 1991 it produced two SD60MAC test engines, followed by two more in 1992. This led the way to its first production AC model, SD70MAC (4,000 hp) in 1993. GE reacted quickly to this leap forward by its competitor and, in only two years, was ready with an AC version of its 4,400-hp DC locomotive (Dash 9-44CW), designated as the AC4400CW. Many observers have concluded that these locomotives represented the beginning of American dieselization's third generation of development.

General Electric's Genesis-series locomotives have become the standard for Amtrak services. The basic design uses a 4,000-hp, 16-cylinder engine and incorporates AC traction, microprocessor control, and other advanced features. Amtrak 94 was on the *Sunset Limited* at Tallahassee, Florida, in October 2000. —Riley Kinney, Louis A. Marre Collection

Widely used for commuter rail services is Electro-Motive's 3,000-hp F59PH, originally developed for Toronto's GO Transit in 1988. A later variation provided this streamlined design, seen in Amtrak California service at Los Angeles in 1998. —Bryan Griebenow, Louis A. Marre Collection

At the heart of AC propulsion systems is the traction motor, a three-phase induction machine, also known as an asynchronous motor, that can operate at various speeds by receiving an input current of variable frequency and voltage. These motors are particularly outstanding at low speeds and heavy loads that might damage a comparable DC motor. An important feature for maintenance is that because of the lack of a commutator, AC-traction motors can be sealed to provide better protection from the environment. Feeding the traction motor are the rectified outputs from the three-phase alternator. The three phases represent identical AC wave forms that are 120 degrees out of phase. Because the raw AC from the alternator is not satisfactory to run the traction motors, the three rectified signals pass through an inverter that "chops" the DC outputs into the required AC wave forms for the motor. This is made possible by power electronic devices such as gate turn-off thyristors (GTOTs) and insulated gate bipolar transistors (IGBTs) that are controlled by digital computers (microprocessors). One of the primary differences between GM and GE locomotives is the number of inverters employed. The older GM system uses one inverter package per truck, while the GE system contains one for each traction motor, thus providing greater flexibility in operation.

Because of the extremely high power of AC motors at low speeds, a new type of truck design was required for maximum efficiency. Instead of a rigid truck frame that restricted axles to vertical movements, new designs also permitted lateral motion. The result was a steerable, or radial, truck that can provide full power while negotiating curved trackage and any other surface irregularities. This combination of power and axle flexibility provides a 5 percent increase in adhesion from the traditional value of 30 percent from traditional DC motors.

—J. Parker Lamb

Environmental Influences

During the half century after World War II the proliferation of diesel engines for transportation (primarily highway trucks, construction vehicles, barge towboats, and locomotives) produced a significant public health concern regarding their emissions. Despite its many performance advantages, the diesel, like other combustion-based devices, releases both particulates (soot) and chemical toxins into the atmosphere. As federal government oversight has increased, more stringent regulatory limits have periodically been introduced. The U.S. Environmental Protection Agency began studying diesel locomotive emissions and their contribution to air pollution in 1977. One of the first environmental aspects to be tackled by railroads was not any of those just mentioned, but exhaust noise. An EPA regulation in the late 1970s required new locomotives to include stack mufflers after 1980.

To understand the origin of diesel pollutants, one must be aware of some chemical aspects of both the fuel and the transformation processes in burning. Diesel fuel is a heavy product (low volatility) of the distillation of crude oil, a mixture of hydrocarbon liquids. It also contains trace amounts of sulfur, as well as more carbon than gasoline (a lighter product). Furthermore, almost two-thirds of the air entering the combustion chamber is composed of nitrogen, a nonparticipant in the high-temperature combustion process dominated by oxygen, which reacts with all components of the fuel and air to produce the flame and heat release needed to drive a diesel engine. Thus the products of combustion include carbon dioxide (CO_2), carbon monoxide (CO), sulfur dioxide (SO_2) from the fuel, and oxides of nitrogen (NO_x) from air. These were the principal pollutants identified in the 1977 government study.

A 1985 EPA report recommended that regulations for highway truck emissions be extended to locomotives. This result was formalized in the 1990 amendment to the Clean Air Act, which set a five-year period for development of final regulations, a deadline later extended to mid-December 1997. As is usually necessary, the physical implementation of these new standards will be gradual. The so-called Tier One set of regulations was effective for new locomotives built through 2004 and will focus on reducing NO_x emissions from about 18.1 grams per kilowatt-hour to about 8.7 grams. Tier Two levels will cover new locomotives starting in 2005 and will strive to reduce NO_x to 7.4 grams per kilowatt-hour, as well as lower particulates.

One of the first approaches to pollutant reduction was to employ electronic fuel injection in new engines. This has been a common feature of automotive engines for many years, and both GE and GM began implementing it in the early 1990s. More recent technical approaches include a four-degree retardation of fuel injection that reduces NO_x by 28 percent to 35 percent with only a 1 percent or 2 percent increase in fuel consumption. Since the normal injection point is at top dead center (when the piston reaches its topmost position), this amount of retardation means that the crankshaft will rotate four degrees past TDC and will have begun its downward motion when injection begins. Another promising approach is to cool the exhaust gas manifold in order to reduce NO_x without affecting fuel economy. With a large amount of unused cooling capacity available in recent locomotives, this technology is relatively easy to implement and, indeed, has already been tested successfully in a number of locomotives. With the probability of more stringent requirements in the future, all builders and some operators, especially those in highly affected urban areas such as Southern California, are looking toward further improvements that might be attained through the use of new fuels (low-sulfur diesel fuel and liquefied natural gas).

—J. Parker Lamb, with William D. Middleton

REFERENCES

Kirkland, John F. *Dawn of the Diesel Age*. Glendale, Calif.: Interurban, 1983.

———. *The Diesel Builders*. Vol. 1, *Fairbanks-Morse and Lima-Hamilton*. Glendale, Calif.: Interurban, 1985.

———. *The Diesel Builders*. Vol. 2, *American Locomotive Company and Montreal Locomotive Works*. Glendale, Calif.: Interurban, 1989.

———. *The Diesel Builders*. Vol. 3, *Baldwin Locomotive Works*. Glendale, Calif.: Interurban, 1994.

Marre, Louis A. *Diesel Locomotives: The First 50 Years*. Waukesha, Wis.: Kalmbach, 1995.

Marre, Louis A., and Paul K. Withers. *The Contemporary Diesel Spotters Guide*. Halifax, Pa.: Withers, 2000.

McDonnell, Greg. *Field Guide to Modern Diesel Locomotives*. Waukesha, Wis.: Kalmbach, 2002.

Pinkepank, Jerry A. *The Second Diesel Spotter's Guide*. Milwaukee, Wis.: Kalmbach, 1973.

Disasters and Railroads

Great disasters, both natural and man made, have been among the misfortunes of North America. Railroads, traveling nearly everywhere as they did, inevitably were involved in rescue and restoration after many of these. In the nineteenth and early twentieth centuries particularly, often only the railroads had the staff and resources, as well as the experience with large-scale engineering and construction, to deal with such crises. Consequently, after floods, fires, and the like, a railroad often was the first line of aid to stricken communities.

Johnstown Flood, 1889

Pennsylvania's Main Line of Public Works (begun in 1831 and closed in 1852) linked Philadelphia and Pittsburgh across the Allegheny Mountains with an ingenious combination of canals and rail portage. Though the new, all-rail Pennsylvania Railroad soon rendered it obsolete, the canal's Lake Conemaugh reservoir remained, serving as a private resort for wealthy Pittsburghers, including Andrew Carnegie and Henry Clay Frick. Its waters were held back by the original earthen dam, located 14 river miles east of Johnstown, Pennsylvania. By 1889, however, alterations and neglect over more than 30 years had made the dam unsafe. Then, on the morning of March 29, an extraordinary eastbound storm moved into Johnstown, with what was reportedly one of the heaviest downpours ever seen in the area. Rainfall was estimated at six to eight inches in 24 hours, and some places saw as much as ten inches. It rained heavily on May 30 as well. Johnstown and neighboring Conemaugh and East Conemaugh, across the Little Conemaugh River, were soon under rising water.

By 11:30 A.M. on May 31 water reached the top of the dam, and there was growing concern. At 3:10 P.M. the dam gave way, and an enormous wall of some 20 million tons of water went roaring down the river to Johnstown. Sweeping everything in its path, the water destroyed hundreds of buildings, made thousands homeless, and created terrible scenes of disaster in Johnstown and nearby communities. More than 2,200 people died.

Since it immersed the main east-west line of the Pennsylvania Railroad through Little Conemaugh, the John-

Two sections of the Pennsylvania's *Day Express* had been halted at the East Conemaugh yard just above Johnstown. In the wake of warnings that the dam had failed, some passengers ran for higher ground, while others remained with the cars. The train was heavily damaged by the flood and then caught fire. Almost miraculously, some of the passengers who stayed with the train survived. Artist Hughson Hawley recorded the aftermath for *Harper's Weekly*. —Middleton Collection

stown Flood was the railroad's most serious disaster ever. It destroyed more than 10 miles of track and bridges, much of the East Conemaugh terminal, and 34 locomotives, 24 passenger cars, and 561 freight cars. It obliterated whole stretches of roadbed.

Even before the dam burst, the Pennsylvania Railroad sounded alarms. The railroad's tower operators between the dam and the towns repeatedly telegraphed warnings, but comparatively little was done. (Similar warnings had been made about that dam for years, but nothing had ever happened.) Later the telegraph poles fell and ended these communications.

East Conemaugh had yards, a roundhouse, coal and water facilities, and shops. Because of washouts east of there, eastbound trains were being held on several parallel tracks leading into the town. They included two sections of the *Day Express* waiting abreast, a freight standing between them, and a mail train behind the first section.

A work train with locomotive 1124 and engineer John Hess had spent all day helping clear the line. When sent far east of the town, they were stopped by a flagman who advised of a washout ahead. Hess and his conductor walked forward. Then, hearing that the dam had let go,

Hess ran back to his engine. Knowing that residents of railroad centers like Johnstown and East Conemaugh understood a continuous whistle to mean danger, he tied the cord down and steamed backward toward the towns. This was the only clear warning they received. People scrambled for high ground, but many were swept away. Blocked at East Conemaugh, Hess and fireman J. C. Plummer ran, leaving their whistle blowing. It continued sounding the alarm until 1124 was engulfed.

Trainmen waiting aboard the *Day Express* at East Conemaugh heard the whistle and ran from car to car telling passengers to flee. Most did, though many of them failed to reach safety. On the other hand, a large number stayed in the train, and some of these survived.

Slaked by the water, a cargo of lime on a freight train between the two sections of the *Day Express* was set on fire. This soon spread through the freight and nearby passenger cars, including the *Day Express*. Many were completely consumed.

The roundhouse and the remainder of the terminal were wiped out by the rushing waters. Twenty-six of 33 locomotives were wrecked. Strangely, the mail train and the *Day Express*'s second section, with engine 1309, were virtually

Somehow, Consolidation 2-8-0 No. 1309 survived the flooding of the second section of the *Day Express* with little damage, even with the fire still burning in the firebox. *Harper's Weekly* artist F. D. Nichols depicted what he called "the only locomotive rescued 'alive'" after the great flood had raced through the East Conemaugh yard.
—Middleton Collection

untouched. No. 1309's fire actually remained alight for several days.

The Pennsylvania's great stone arch bridge across the Conemaugh, farther downstream at Johnstown, held. But the bridge site became a horror scene. The arches filled up with debris of every description; hundreds of people were trapped and killed by the fires that followed.

The rain had stopped by June 2, but long sections of Pennsylvania lines were demolished in both directions. A Pennsylvania Railroad train arrived from Pittsburgh, for

As the flood roared through Johnstown, wreckage of every description was trapped by the Pennsylvania Railroad's stone arch bridge. Artist W. A. Rogers drew the catastrophe for the June 15, 1889, *Harper's Weekly*. —Middleton Collection

example, but could get no closer than the little town of Sang Hollow, and by late Saturday men were carrying supplies the remaining 3 miles into Johnstown. By early Sunday the Baltimore & Ohio had come to Johnstown from Somerset in the south, via the much less damaged Stony Creek. Later in the day, through extraordinary effort, the Pennsylvania Railroad opened the line east from Sang Hollow all the way to Johnstown.

With its main east-west lines interrupted, the Pennsylvania poured all of its resources into reconstruction. (Engineer Hess's work train had been repairing the line even before the dam gave way.) In eight days a detour over the Philadelphia & Erie, also badly damaged in the flood, as well as the Allegheny Valley and the Northern Central—all Pennsylvania allies—provided passenger service; heavier freights used this route until June 17. By June 14 most Philadelphia-Pittsburgh passenger service was operating over the main line. By June 24, only slightly over three weeks after the tragedy, the track was sufficiently restored for resumption of the *New York and Chicago Limited*.

Hinckley Firestorm, 1894

Hinckley, in the great timber forests of eastern Minnesota, is located midway between St. Paul and Duluth and not far from Wisconsin. Lumbering was the town's major industry, and about a third of its 1,200 residents were employed at a big timber plant. Just south of Hinckley two railroads crossed: the St. Paul & Duluth and the Eastern Minnesota, later the Northern Pacific and the Great Northern, respectively. A rather small stream, the Grindstone River, crossed the two railroads just north of Hinckley. Aside from the little river, the only other nearby water was in a shallow gravel pit on the east.

In early September 1894 there was cause for concern. No rain had fallen since April 30, and by September 1 the sloughs and lakes carried little or no water. Forest fires sprang up periodically, but petered out. A bluish haze, however, hung over the area, and smoke from the fires was causing some discomfort that morning. By midday the smoke was thicker, and there was a disquieting warmth to the air. Gradually the smoke became more intense, darkening the sky.

By 2 P.M., when the northbound *Duluth Limited*, running two hours late from St. Paul to Duluth, made its stop at Hinckley, the smoke had grown worse and the forest fire was drawing closer. People were uneasy, but had not yet seen the flames. Only a few inhabitants were sufficiently worried to abandon everything and climb aboard the northbound trains. But in less than an hour the situation had changed drastically for the worse.

A small fire had sprung up in the western side of Hinckley. The fire department rushed in, but to no avail. More and more buildings were engulfed, and the heat and smoke became almost unendurable. Panic spread. Probably because of it, few thought of the gravel pit, the one safe place.

The Eastern Minnesota's southbound local freight out

of Duluth, with engineer Ed Barry, had arrived at Hinckley about 2:40 P.M. Despite the fire, the freight was sidetracked for southbound passenger train No. 4, with engineer Best and conductor Powers. By this time the town was overcome by the intense heat, the smoke was suffocating, and the sky was black. Barry, Best, and Powers worked quickly. A train crew was assembled, and engineer Barry ran to an engine, coupled on three empty boxcars and the caboose, and hooked this makeshift consist onto the passenger train. The train crew waited as long as possible so that the maximum number of people could board. At 4:15 the train started north and crossed the Grindstone River bridge. Again it paused, permitting some 40 more to climb on.

By now the paint on the cars was blistered and the wooden cars were becoming scorched. Finally, over burning ties and warping rails, the train moved out. The engines had to crawl because visibility was poor and they were running on a single track against a southbound freight whose position was unknown. The headlights were useless, as the locomotives were backing. They crossed many burning timber bridges; at least 19 were eventually destroyed. Two brakemen rode lookout on the rear of the leading tender, now the front of the train, to ascertain the safety of each bridge.

At Sandstone, the next town north, the train again paused. People were urged to get aboard, but most did not. The crew, however, learned that the oncoming freight had stopped some distance away, so that hazard was removed. Again the train got under way. It shortly reached the badly burned Kettle River bridge. Warned by the watchman that they had only minutes to get over, the engineers opened up and rushed across. Minutes later the bridge was gone. Now they stopped at Partridge, where both locomotives and passengers received water. Here again, most residents discounted the danger and let the train depart without them. Eventually it reached West Superior and relative safety.

Meanwhile, the smoke was evident as far as Duluth, 60 miles to the north, whence a four-car, southbound St. Paul & Duluth limited left at 2:00 P.M. en route through Hinckley. The crew, including engineer James Root, fireman Jack McGowan, and conductor Thomas Sullivan, little realized the agonies ahead. The darkened sky necessitated lighting the car lamps, and flames were frighteningly visible beside the right of way. Near Hinckley some 150 or more terrified people flagged them down and were taken aboard. Initially, the engineer hoped to run through the blaze, but as he noted the intensity of the fire and the power of the wind fanning it, he changed his mind, realizing that the only hope was to reverse his locomotive and dash for Skunk Lake, four miles behind.

Slowed by the overwhelming smoke and darkness, they were being overtaken by the wind-propelled fire. Flames penetrated the cars through clerestories, windows, and door crevices. The cars caught fire one by one, and the fear-crazed passengers crushed forward to escape. An undetermined number jumped or fell from the train and perished. Screams, wind, and crackling flames blended into one nightmare of noise. In the cab the crew's clothes were blazing and their hands were blistering. The fireman jumped into the tank to extinguish his own garments, then poured water over engineer Root to offer him some relief. Adding to Root's woes, the cab window broke, and he was gashed by the glass.

When they reached their goal, Skunk Lake, they saw that it was only a muddy hole. However, it was all they had, and they gratefully immersed themselves in it. Porter John Blair swelled the "lake's" meager resources with a fire extinguisher. Once the engine crew had recovered somewhat, they returned to their locomotive, only to find it threatened by the furiously burning coal in the tender. Hastily they uncoupled the locomotive and ran it some distance from the tank.

Still another rescue train was the southbound *Duluth Limited*, which turned out to be the last train of the day to carry passengers from Hinckley to safety. The disaster produced other railroad heroes. Tom Dunn, the Hinckley telegraph operator, knowing that without him, trains could not safely arrive or depart the town, remained to a fiery death at his post. Bull Henley, a section hand at Hinckley, stood in the street, reminding panic-stricken Hinckleyites of the shallow gravel pit, saving many lives at risk of his own. Conductor Sullivan, in the meantime, recalled that a following freight was due. Though doubting that its crew would attempt a run through the fire, he felt compelled to walk back to the station at Miller, the first telegraph office behind him. After warning the freight of his stopped consist, he collapsed.

The fire continued to burn until September 6, when welcome rain finally fell. Altogether, 2,500 acres of forest were burned out. The official death toll was 476, and the actual total was probably 500 or higher, but the trains and their heroic crews had saved many more.

Galveston Hurricane, 1900

America's deadliest hurricane struck Galveston on September 8, 1900. Galveston housed 40,000 people and, as the largest seaport in Texas, looked forward to a time of growth and prosperity. The city had survived many storms, but never one like this. The hurricane came raging straight up the Gulf of Mexico. Galveston had no defenses toward the Gulf; it presented only a low-lying island, often only a few feet above the seawater and separated from the mainland by wide Galveston Bay.

The first warning came on September 7, and the storm was into Galveston by the next day. Winds reached more than 84 mph—Beaufort No. 12, the highest strength recognized—and gusts of 120 mph or more were reported. Rising tides ultimately swamped virtually every part of the city. The damage was further aggravated by Galveston Bay. High waters flowed into the bay until the storm changed direction, and the huge body of water flowed back into Galveston. Fifteen-foot tides inundated block after block, with every house in the city destroyed, damage estimated at perhaps $30 million, and something like 8,000 deaths as a result.

In the aftermath of this unequaled disaster, the railroads provided major help to the survivors. The two-mile low rail viaduct crossing the bay was heavily damaged and unusable. Trainloads of tents and rations were shipped to

The Galveston hurricane left a locomotive and cars turned over in the ruins of track at Virginia Point. *Munsey's Magazine*, in its December 1900 issue, provided a description and illustrations of the storm. —Middleton Collection

The two-mile railroad viaduct into Galveston was heavily damaged, and miles of track were washed out and heaped with debris. Determined railroaders had the trains back into the city only 12 days after the storm. An illustration from *Munsey's* gave some idea of the damage. —Middleton Collection

Texas City and then moved by barges. Hundreds of survivors were moved out of Galveston by the same route. Within another day the existing track had been opened to the Virginia Port on the north side of the bay. After another week's effort the railroad line opened to Galveston itself, and relief trains began running into Galveston from all over the country.

Dr. William L. Crostwait, a Texan who was visiting Chicago, hastened to the *Chicago American* offices for information about the storm. William R. Hearst, the newspaper's publisher, was on hand and quickly saw an opportunity. Ever alert to publicity values in human drama, Hearst arranged for a Santa Fe train to rush Crostwait to Galveston, bearing Hearst's $50,000 check. Who paid for the train is unclear. Hearst papers reported, "Santa Fe gives trains freely" in one place and referred to "A special train, chartered by the *Chicago American*" in another.

Enterprising Hearst reporter Annie Laurie (a nom de plume) entered closely guarded Galveston in disguise, while other reporters and photographers were still denied access. Hearst wired her to have hospital facilities organized by the time the trains arrived. She did. Additional trains came from Hearst papers on both coasts: the *New York Journal* and the *San Francisco Examiner*. Of course, there were sources of aid closer to Galveston, but none that had Hearst newspapers.

The trains were prominently marked with their newspapers' names, and their news value was thoroughly exploited in print. "Succor for Stricken Galveston Organized by W. R. Hearst," blared one headline. "Hastening Relief for the Children," shouted another; beneath it was stated, "Each train will carry . . . doctors and nurses with surgical and medical supplies and emergency rations . . . a race to see which [arrives] first. It is expected to get the *Journal* train started from Jersey City [N.J.] tonight" (datelined

September 11). The expected progress of the Chicago train was published, departing at 6:00 P.M. from Chicago and arriving at Galveston just two days later.

The San Francisco train was a bit slower starting; there were apparently several sections, the last delayed until 6:30 P.M. on September 14. The first section, whenever it left, reached Galveston only on the 23rd. But it must have been worth waiting for. "Them Californians is all right," an assistant yardmaster supposedly said. "I believe they've sent the best . . . they make wine and brandy and grow . . . fruit." Mundane items—potatoes, crackers, evaporated milk, and clothing—were also carried.

Hearst's highly publicized efforts were not unique. The federal government chartered a train from the International & Great Northern Railroad, which also sent one of its own. The Missouri, Kansas & Texas and others sent trains as well.

Galveston made an amazing recovery. Essential services, banking, telegraph, long-distance telephone, streetcars, partial water and electricity, and newspapers were operating by September 17. Later efforts included a long-awaited seawall, completed by 1904. The entire city was raised as much as 17 feet by 1910, and another year saw completion of a new two-mile crossing into the city.

Imperial Valley Flood, 1904–1907

Geologic ages ago, the Bay of California extended to about the latitude of Los Angeles. Over time the Colorado River, flowing into the bay from the east, deposited a silt dike. North of that dike, the remnant of the bay became a huge dry basin (the Salton Sink), as much as 280 feet below sea level. Saturated with alkali, the hot, dry area was useless for agriculture.

By the 1870s, when the Southern Pacific decided to ex-

388   DISASTERS AND RAILROADS

tend its track from Los Angeles to the then territory of Arizona, it was an easy choice to follow the level, featureless rim of the Salton Sink, some 250 feet below sea level. Meanwhile, various promoters had noticed the rich alluvial soil that the Colorado had deposited in the Salton Sink. Arid and alkali tainted though it might be, with proper irrigation it could produce lush vegetation. And the river was near. First to take real steps were two former SP construction engineers and four associates. Forming the California Development Co. about 1900, they staked a claim to 20,000 acre-feet of Colorado River water. After obtaining federal permission for a canal right of way, they announced that they would irrigate, at nominal cost, land that anyone could buy from the government at $1.25 per acre.

They contracted with George Chaffey, who had done much to irrigate Lower California, which had become a major orange-growing area as a result. Chaffey soon fell out with them (they had gone bankrupt), took over the operation, and gave the region the euphonious name Imperial Valley. Canal work began late in 1900 and was completed by May 1901. Its principal inlet, or headstock, was at Pilot Knob, near the Mexican border. It then ran through Mexico, on land purchased for that purpose, and connected with the Alamo River. There was another control gate where that river crossed into the United States. All worked splendidly, and the valley soon began to blossom. By May 1904 the Southern Pacific had even built a new Imperial and Gulf Branch, running almost due south through this area, toward Mexico.

Within months, however, disaster struck. Arizona's Gila River drains into the Colorado near Yuma. In February 1905 heavy rains fell in Arizona. So severe was the rain that SP trains between Yuma and El Paso, Texas, were under slow orders for months. Runoff from these rains, coursing down the Gila, swelled the Colorado just north of where the irrigation canals began. By March the waters had begun to do serious damage to the irrigation works and to encroach upon the SP main line. Anticipating neither the duration of the flooding nor its potential severity, the irrigation operators laid 10,000 sandbags to control flooding, plus innumerable brush mats secured by pilings, in an attempt to stem the rising waters. By May all had been washed away.

In July a flash flood struck. Perversely, the torrent ran not into the gulf, the river's usual outlet, but into the irrigation canal. Following the Alamo and New rivers, the water inundated the Imperial Valley and the Southern Pacific roadbed (which, one must remember, was 250 feet below sea level). Now 30,000 sandbags were brought in. Still the waters rose, and trackwalkers had to precede each train to verify the condition of the line. Clearly, the track could not withstand much more, so the railroad built shooflies (detours) around the threatened sections. Each time, the water rose to meet the rails, and more shooflies were built. Eventually there were seven in all, amounting to 21 miles of diversion around an original 11-mile track section.

Naturally enough, the railroad considered that the problem was the responsibility of the California Development Co., builder of the canal system. Entreated by the railroad to take steps against the flood, the company sank more pilings and built a barrier of wire-woven brush. It hoped that reducing the velocity of the water would cause it to deposit silt and create its own levee, rerouting itself back toward the gulf. By August 1905 this too failed. Financially strained by its efforts, the development company pleaded for aid from the Southern Pacific. President E. H. Harriman agreed to a loan of $200,000, along with the expertise of SP bridge engineer F. S. Edinger. The first plan was to construct a new control gate inside a cofferdam—a fencelike waterproof enclosure. This was begun, but hopes for it waned, and they returned again to the concept of the brush dam. Nearly completed by November, this was destroyed by yet another flood out of the east.

Obviously, some more permanent barrier was called for. A concrete dam was decided upon and was under construction from November 1905 to April 1906. Just as the $200,000 loan was running out, the earthquake hit San Francisco, home of the Southern Pacific. It was a bad moment to ask for more money, but newly appointed engineer Epes Randolph did just that. Harriman granted another loan, this time of $250,000.

In the meantime, further shooflies had been built, lifting the entire line to a mere 200 feet below sea level. Thirty-six miles of the original line had now been replaced. Elsewhere, floods were a problem as well. The Inter-California Railroad, a Mexican branch of the SP, was being constructed to run from the Imperial and Gulf Branch on the west to Yuma on the east, where it would rejoin the SP main line. Much destruction occurred along both of these, followed by reconstruction and the building of shooflies.

Still the waters rose. By the end of the first year, the canal break had become half a mile wide. The SP, under Epes Randolph, stepped up its efforts. Randolph decided to build a new dam, south of the Mexican border. The first major step was to lay a spur running south from Hanlon's Junction, near Yuma. Meeting the canal at the point where the new dam was to be erected, this spur would permit bringing in the requisite huge volume of supplies and materiel, along with a large workforce. Ten work trains were assigned to the task, and at Andrade, just north of the border, a complete rail terminal was erected. It included a roundhouse and a large stock of repair components. A fleet of purpose-built side-dump cars, eventually numbering some 300, was brought in. (These had originally been constructed for work on the Lucin Cutoff across the Great Salt Lake.)

Recruiting a workforce was difficult at a time when many were involved in rebuilding San Francisco after the earthquake and fire, on flood control on the Imperial Valley Branch and the Inter-California Railroad, and on still other construction. Migratory workers had, however, heard of the effort being waged and arrived seeking jobs. In addition, six tribes of Native Americans were drawn upon. They were brought together in a camp of 2,000 family members, of whom some 400 became workers on the project. Closing the half-mile gap began with the driving of piles from one side to the other. Floating pile drivers were employed, and once the pilings were in place, a timber trestle was built upon them. The first train set out cautiously to cross it on October 11, 1906. Some timbers broke and several cars were derailed, but the cars were put back on the track, and the train made it across.

Then, without warning, an earlier wood barrier, upstream from the trestle, gave way, sending a rush of water and debris against the new structure. It began to collapse, nearly leaving one train stranded at the far end. However, that train did get back, and just in time. Once again, repairs were undertaken, and the gap was closed by November. This, too, was swept away by new flooding the following December.

The Southern Pacific decided to admit defeat. After all, it was principally interested in rail transportation. If it could reroute its line to avoid the waters, its own problems would be solved. So another shoofly (the twelfth) was laid out, this time at 100 feet below sea level. Calculations indicated that this should stay dry for up to five years, during which time a permanent line could be constructed, and the railroad's troubles would be over.

Upon hearing that, various interested groups and municipalities begged aid from Washington. President Theodore Roosevelt called upon the railroad to resume work. Harriman demurred. He telegraphed Roosevelt on December 13, 1906, to the effect that national interests, not just those of the railroad, were at stake: "In view of [this], it does not seem fair that we should be called to do more than join in to help the settlers." Ignoring Harriman's objections, Roosevelt wired back, "I assume you are planning to continue work immediately on closing break in Colorado River."

On December 19 Harriman telegraphed once more, "Our engineers advise that [the work will cost] $300,000 to $350,000. The Southern Pacific Co., having been at an expense of about $2,000,000 already, does not feel warranted in assuming this responsibility. . . . We are willing to cooperate with the Government, contributing train service, use of tracks and switches, use of rock quarries, train crews, etc. and the California Development Co. will contribute its engineers and organization, the whole work to be done under the [U.S.] Reclamation Service. Can you bring this about?"

The answer was no. While men in California were struggling up to their waists in water (and some had been swept away to their deaths), the president in faraway Washington responded thus on December 20: "Reclamation Service cannot enter upon work without authority of Congress and suitable convention with Mexico. Congress adjourns today for holidays. Impossible to secure action

at present. It is incumbent upon you to close break again. Reclamation engineers available for consultation. That is all the aid that there is in the power of the Government to render. . . . Through the Department of State, I am endeavoring to secure such action by the Mexican Government as will enable Congress in its turn to act." The telegram continued in this vein, concluding, "It is [the California Development Co.'s] duty to meet the present danger immediately, and then this government will take up with it, as it has already taken up with Mexico, the question of providing . . . against . . . recurrence of the danger."

Although Harriman promptly protested what he saw as a misunderstanding on the president's part, he also appreciated that 12,000 settlers and 1,600,000 acres of land were in jeopardy. Unwilling to be responsible for such a disaster, he telegraphed once more, "We have determined to remove the tracks onto high ground anyway. However, in view of your message, I am giving authority to Southern Pacific officers . . . to proceed at once . . . to repair the break, trusting that the Government, as soon as you can procure the necessary Congressional action, will assist us with the burden."

His good humor restored, Roosevelt jovially rejoined: "Am delighted to receive your telegram. Have at once directed the Reclamation Service to get in touch with you, so that as soon as Congress reassembles I can recommend legislation . . . for the equitable distribution of the burden." Harriman understood this to mean that the federal government would reimburse the carrier for its expenses.

Once more the Southern Pacific returned to the fray. Now, in addition to the 300 side-dump cars, 1,000 flatcars were brought in. The branch line was expanded with longer sidings. This time, it was decided to build a double trestle that, hopefully, could resist the angry waters. The first trestle was completed just before the end of 1906; a December flood demolished about a third of it. Twice later, sections were destroyed. Finally, however, fanatical efforts paid off, and on January 27, 1907, the side-dump cars and flatcars went to work dumping fill over the sides of one finished trestle. With this done, the second trestle was hurried to completion, and further dumping was carried out.

All traffic, including crack passenger trains, yielded to the work trains. Numerous quarries provided material, from gravel to 15-ton boulders. These last could only be carried on the flatcars, which, once brought to the site, had to be chained in place before the massive stones could be pushed over their sides (the side-dump cars inherently remained balanced during unloading). Train dispatching at the rail terminal was a complex task in itself, with waiting trains, incoming loads, returning empties, and the marshaling of properly laden trains to crawl out carefully onto the trestle. Dumping went on 24 hours a day for 15 days. At first, much material simply disappeared. Eventually, however, the fill reached the surface and held. Higher and higher it rose until the trestle was buried and the water was kept back. Success was achieved on February 11, 1907, and it was decided that the minus-100-foot shoofly would not be needed. That portion of the railroad would remain at 200 feet and still does. Nonetheless, for some months, work trains were stationed in readiness near the dam whenever the river rose. Now the flood repair branch from Hanlon's Junction was linked with the Inter-California Railroad, forming a complete alternate route, via Mexico, between that junction and Niland, California.

With its heroic task completed, the Southern Pacific billed Washington for $3,113,677 and, about 1929, received $1,012,655. In view of the inflation that had taken place in the interim because of World War I and other factors, this was a pittance indeed.

Florida East Coast and the Great Florida Keys Hurricane, 1935

Enchanted by Florida during an 1880 visit, Henry M. Flagler, a wealthy Standard Oil associate of John D. Rockefeller, began a Florida building program that included numerous luxury hotels, a palatial residence, a shipping line, and the Florida East Coast Railway, which reached newly named Miami in 1896. The visionary Flagler saw a deepwater port at distant Key West as a strategic jumping-off point for freight and passenger shipping, closer to the new Panama Canal than that provided by any other U.S. railroad. Convinced that it could be done, Flagler in 1905 announced that the FEC would build across the Florida Keys to Key West. To do it, the builders had to leapfrog more than 100 miles across 29 islands, building long concrete viaducts and steel bridges, including a 7-mile span across open water just below Knights Key.

Hurricanes hit the Keys in 1906, 1909, and 1910, with much loss of life and damage to equipment and the already-completed construction. But Flagler's men repaired the damage, and work continued. The job was finally complete on January 22, 1912, when Flagler arrived at Key West on a five-car ceremonial train. Regular freight and passenger service was soon operating over the Key West extension, with through passenger trains from New York connecting with steamers for Havana.

A little more than two decades later, this extraordinary "railroad that went to sea" became the setting for disaster. In 1928 work had begun on the construction of the Overseas Highway across the Keys that paralleled the railroad. Much had been done by 1935, but there were still gaps that required ferries: one connected Islamorada with the mainland. A force of World War I unemployed veterans had been put to work building a bridge there. On September 2 of that year, what still ranks as the strongest hurricane ever to hit the United States swept across the Middle Keys. As winds reached 155 mph, it became obvious that nearly 1,000 stranded residents and highway workers were in mortal danger. The only way out was by rail.

As FEC executives later contended, the federal managers of the highway project should have called for evacuation early. To succeed, they said, a train would have had to get under way by 10:00 A.M. Yet the railroad got no summons until work-camp supervisors begged for help at 2:00 P.M. Though minutes counted, the effort was plagued by delays. The first was in making up a train and finding a crew (this was the weekend before Labor Day). But trainmaster G. R. Branch, engineer J. J. Haycraft, fireman Will Walker, and conductor J. F. Gamble agreed to man the train. A car needed repair, another delay. Finally, at about 4:40 P.M., a train of six coaches, two baggage cars, and three boxcars crawled out of Miami, headed by Mountain-type locomotive No. 447. Barely rolling, it was again delayed at an open drawbridge for 10 minutes.

At Homestead, the last mainland station, Haycraft made a tactical decision. Noting the growing intensity of the storm, he felt that the locomotive should face north, at the rear of the train. They could back down to Islamorada and, having embarked their passengers, would run full steam for home. There was a 15-minute delay for the engine to run around the train. It was now almost 5:30 P.M., and they could go no more than 20 mph in the face of the storm and water-covered rails. By 7:00 P.M. they had reached only Snake Creek Bridge at Windley Key. There Haycraft stopped for a group of terrified people. When he tried to start, a heavy steel cable snagged the engine. There was another hour-long delay until they found tools to cut it.

During the final 20 miles to Islamorada, the wind reached almost 200 mph; rain painfully pelted the crew in their rear-facing cab. The train ran slower and slower; no one knew whether the rails were still in place. They finally reached Islamorada. Haycraft stopped about 1,500 feet south of the station at the island's widest point and clear of structures that might be swept away at any time. A panicky crowd rushed up. As they were struggling aboard, a tidal wave, later estimated at 18 to 20 feet high—the worst in U.S. history—struck the island. Haycraft opened his throttle, but the train promptly jerked to a stop: boxcars at the rear had been derailed by the wave, dumping the air and locking the brakes. The rest of the train was soon tossed alongside the track, and few of its passengers escaped death. No. 447 clung to the rails, however, and Haycraft, Walker, and Gamble lived to tell the tale.

Somewhere around 400 to 600 people died in that terrible storm, and the FEC's Key West extension died with them. Much of the roadbed in the 42 miles between Key Largo and Key Vaca was swept away. The line had never been a financial success, and the bankrupt Florida East Coast decided to abandon the endeavor rather than rebuild it. Remarkably, all the railroad bridges had survived the storm. They and the abandoned roadbed were incorporated into the Overseas Highway, completed all the way to Key West in 1938.

Tehachapi Earthquake, 1952

One of the worst earthquakes in California's history struck at 4:52 A.M., July 21, 1952. With its 7.5 magnitude, in just 30 seconds it brought death and widespread property loss to the city of Tehachapi and immobilized the Southern Pacific's main north-south line through the Tehachapi Mountains. For the SP and for the Santa Fe, which shared trackage rights, the quake paralyzed their principal connection between southern and northern California. Only the SP's Coast Line remained as the rail link. In town, 12 persons died and virtually every building was damaged. The railroad's water tank was wrecked, producing brief, severe flooding; highway and telephone communications were cut off.

Miraculously, SP's No. 55, a passenger local, was unscathed, though the tunnel behind it collapsed and a 125-foot-long, 15-foot-high section of fill ahead of it was jolted out of place, leaving rails and ties dangling. Equally fortuitous, Los Angeles–bound Train No. 60, the *West Coast*, running a bit ahead of schedule, got safely east of the quake area in time. On the other hand, the Caliente water tank dropped right atop a standing freight.

The line's entire centralized traffic control (CTC) system—signals, switches, rail bonds, and communications—was wiped out. In one place rails were as much as 22 feet out of line. Worst hit were six of the segment's ten tunnels. No. 3 was blocked; one wall had apparently been lifted, letting a bent rail slide beneath it, after which the wall fell on the iron. The east end of No. 4 dropped 4½ feet below the west end. No. 5 had totally collapsed. Nos. 6 and 7 escaped with relatively light wall damage, but three fallen boulders obstructed No. 8.

Within hours of the quake, SP's president and other top officials arrived by train and Jeep. Morrison-Knudsen was retained to repair the damage. Some 100 bulldozers and other earthmovers, rushed from as far away as Texas, began arriving by midnight of the first day. About 175 maintenance-of-way crews were drawn from the SP, Santa Fe, and Western Pacific. Material was brought in by the heaviest locomotives, chosen to tamp down newly placed ties and ballast.

Within 24 hours roads for earthmoving equipment were cut around tunnels 3 through 7. The crews opened up over 200 feet of tunnel No. 3's 700 feet. Tunnel No. 4 was permanently filled and the track run around it. Tunnel No. 6 was cut open and the track put back in place. Nos. 7 and 8 and the remainder of No. 3 were reinforced. Meanwhile, engineers addressed the problem of tunnel No. 5. Longest of all at 1,163 feet, it could not quickly be restored. They decided to construct a 4,358-foot temporary shoofly. This involved cuts and a deep fill that necessitated moving nearly 300,000 cubic yards of earth. Even so, the shoofly wound up with a 2.37 percent grade and curvatures as sharp as 14 degrees. But it all got done in 25 days, and trains were running by August 15. Tunnel No. 5 was eventually rebored and the shoofly abandoned.

—Dan LeMaire-Bauch

REFERENCES

Findley, Rowe. "The Bittersweet Waters of the Lower Colorado." *National Geographic* 144, no. 4 (Oct. 1973).

Herron, Edward A. "The SP's Mexican Venture." *Railway Progress* (Washington, D.C.: Federation for Railway Progress), July 1953.

Hosmer, Helen. "Triumph and Failure in the Colorado Desert." *American West*, Winter 1966.

Hubbard, Freeman H. *Railroad Avenue*. New York: McGraw-Hill, 1945.

Kennan, George. *E. H. Harriman: A Biography*. Boston: Houghton Mifflin, 1922.

Larkin, Edgar L. "A Thousand Men against a River." *World's Work* 13, no. 5 (Mar. 1907).

Lester, Paul. *The Great Galveston Disaster*. 1900. Reprint, Gretna, La.: Pelican, 2000.

McCullough, David G. *The Johnstown Flood*. New York: Simon & Schuster, 1969.

Morgan, David H. "Earthquake!" *Trains* 13, no. 1 (Nov. 1951): 14–20.

Standiford, Les. *Last Train to Paradise*. New York: Crown, 2002.

Stauss, Ed, and Mike Martin. "The Old Espee and the Sea." *Rail Classics* 4, no. 1 (Jan. 1975).

"When SP Saved the Imperial Valley." SP Bulletin (as author), *Western Railroader* (San Mateo, Calif.) 22, no. 9 (July–Aug. 1959).

Dispatchers

The train dispatcher is the controlling voice for the railroad superintendent who directs train movements over a territory that can range anywhere from 30 miles in the heavy traffic of a commuter area to as many as 1,000 miles involving lighter-traffic lines. A dispatcher can be the hero who gets a fast intermodal train over the road in only three hours or the much-maligned "train delayer" who leaves a drag freight train stuck in a siding for hours while a dozen more important trains roll by.

Dispatchers have been a part of North American railroading for over 150 years, ever since the day on September 22, 1851, when the Erie Railroad's superintendent, Charles Minot, issued a now-famous telegraphic order changing the scheduled meeting point between eastbound and westbound trains. Minot himself, according to old stories, ran the 4-4-0 of the westbound train to the next station, with his engineer and fireman cowering in the tender expecting death at every bend. Minot's use of the telegraph to control train movements began a revolution that became the standard of North American railroading—one person controlling specific territory either by train orders or, after its introduction in 1927, with centralized traffic control (CTC) or, still later, with the use of track warrants or direct train control.

The concept was slow to catch on, but during the Civil War dispatchers were used by both sides. In 1870 a reporter glorified the far-off dispatcher in the *Railroad Gazette* (forerunner of *Railway Age*). By then train dispatchers were common.

Many changes in operating rules and practices were made in the 1870s and 1880s, but by the 1890s the idea of a centralized division dispatcher was common. By then railroads were usually divided into regions under a general manager and then into divisions headed by the superintendent. On his staff was the chief dispatcher, the legendary "Chief" who, together with his assistant chiefs and the trick dispatcher, supervised the movement of trains over their territories. The chief and his assistants handled the power and crews, decided which trains to run and how big they would be, and determined their pickups and setouts.

In the nineteenth and the early twentieth centuries, when train movements were controlled only by telegraph, the dispatcher had a copy operator who recorded the notice of the time trains passed stations, or the "OSs" (which stood for "on sheet"), as they were commonly known, and kept the train sheet up-to-date. The paper train sheet was the dispatcher's main tool. On it were written the train numbers, engines, crew members, cars, and times by certain stations. In non-CTC territory it was the OS's by operators reporting trains past their stations on which the dispatcher based his decisions where to meet opposing trains or run fast trains around slow ones on double- or multiple-track territory. The train sheet was the ultimate record and a legal document that was required by the Interstate Commerce Commission (ICC), and later the Federal Railroad Administration, to be kept for a minimum of three years.

CTC did not dispense with the train sheet, though. Although some CTC systems employed graphs to record trains passing controlled points, on many railroads the dispatcher recorded those times on the sheet. Weather was usually recorded at least four times a day, and delays or unusual occurrences were recorded. In train-order and in CTC territory the dispatcher's other main tool was the train-order book. In it were recorded train orders as the dispatcher issued them. Some train-order books were rather formal affairs (the New York Central's, for example), while other roads used a simple paperbound book not unlike a child's copybook. Like the train sheet, the train-order book was a legal document and was required to be on file for at least three years.

After the passing of the telegraph (and the copy operators), the typical dispatcher's desk, well into the 1980s, had a selector for "ringing" operators and towers and, of course, a telephone for the open dispatcher's line on which everybody could talk, plus a "side phone" or "conversation phone" for more private conversations. After telephones came into use, particularly in the West and on a few eastern and southern carriers, there was also a Morse key in the event of telephone failure. This could be fairly common in the years when railroads still depended on physical pole lines. The other necessity was a clock or watch. The Illinois Central, for which this writer worked for several years, did not provide a clock, and one depended on one's own Hamilton 992B.

A train dispatcher at work in the Santa Fe's Amarillo, Texas, general office in March 1943. —Jack Delano photograph, Office of War Information, Library of Congress (Neg. LC-USW3-20163-D)

Every dispatcher's nightmare was the lap order—that is, issuing orders to opposing trains with overlapping authority. With the advent of automatic block signaling there was some element of protection, but in nonsignaled territory it could be disastrous. The busy eastern roads, with their numerous passenger trains even on branches, depended on manual block, so that even if the dispatcher "lapped" them up, the manual block rules would not permit opposing trains to be in the same block at the same time. Lap orders were costly even if no one was hurt. A dispatcher could expect a 30-day vacation—unpaid, of course.

Although the southern and western roads depended mostly on single-track timetable and train-order dispatching, the eastern roads with their multiple-track mains presented a different problem. By the 1920s interlockers were located every 10 miles or so under the control of tower operators who routed trains per the dispatcher's instructions. Their main problem was keeping the slow trains out of the way of the fast ones, and even with four tracks congestion could be a problem. A 1944 station record from OD tower on the New York Central at Ashtabula, Ohio, for example, showed 98 trains between 3 P.M. and 11 P.M.

Then came the wholesale introduction of centralized traffic control (CTC) during World War II. CTC eliminated train orders (as well as operators), and the switches and signals were under the direct control of the dispatcher, who could actually see his charges as red lights on a CTC board. It was a major change. It was claimed by its makers that CTC increased the track capacity of a single-track line to as much as 80 percent of that of a double-track line. That figure may be doubtful, but there was no doubt that it was a big improvement over train orders. CTC was expensive, but the railroads could see the savings inherent in the elimination of operators and even combining territories. The dispatchers now had to throw small levers to line switches and signals, and running the CTC board required close and careful attention. The dispatcher had to watch the moving red lights and make decisions accordingly. There was no such thing as putting out a bunch of orders during the first few hours of one's trick and letting them run.

CTC was slow to catch on in many of the Northeast's multiple-track lines, but in 1956 the New York Central's Alfred E. Perlman announced a major program to install CTC and reduced the Central's four-track main-line railroad to a double-track CTC line. Even so, well into the Conrail era manned interlockers and double track in the time-honored fashion still predominated.

In most other parts of the country timetable and train-order railroading continued well into the late 1970s. On some roads sections and schedules were eliminated and other simplifications were made, but the operation by train order remained predominant.

The supremacy of the train order was put to rest in 1984, when the Board of Adjustment ruled that clerks on the Southern Pacific did not have the exclusive right to the copying of train-movement orders. This opened the door to the complete elimination of train orders and the operators who copied them. In their place came track warrants and direct train control, as well as still more CTC. For dispatchers this was a mixed blessing. At the start, track warrants and direct train control were all manual. Putting out a "lap" was easy, and there were more than a few close calls. There were no checks and balances, but this changed with the introduction of personal computers at each dispatcher's desk based on a system designed by the Canadian National, which could prevent conflicts of authority. Indeed, this is the system still in use today. But no system is perfect. Dispatchers and train crews sometimes hear what they want to hear and not what was really said, and occasionally a fatal collision can be the result.

In today's track-warrant territory the computer contains a model of the territory with each train. When the dispatcher needs to issue a warrant, he calls up a blank form on his computer and enters the limits, then issues it to the crew. He then underlines it (using the computer) as it is repeated. If there is any conflict of authority, the computer will not let the dispatcher complete the form. This has been the saving grace of track warrants. Direct train control is similar, but the only written requirement is on the train crew, who must record the authority the dispatcher issues.

The 1980s saw another phenomenon, the consolidated dispatcher's office. CSX moved all its dispatchers into Jacksonville, the UP into Omaha, and the BNSF into Fort Worth. The day of the division DS, a standard telegraph symbol for dispatcher, was gone. Many in the industry still look at the large "dispatcheries" as a major strategic mistake. But the railroads spent billions to make it work, and there is little likelihood they will reverse themselves.

The modern dispatcher's office is almost unrecognizable to an old veteran. The dispatcher sits surrounded by up-to-date computerized CTC machines based on the cathode ray tube (CRT) that show train symbols, as well as mere lights. He also has a fax machine and a computerized train sheet. Slow orders are issued in the computer, and gone are the folding phone and the paper train sheet. Radio is in. In track-warrant territory there may not be a CTC screen, but there is the personal computer, as well as fax machines and radios.

An important part of a dispatcher's responsibility is protection for track workers. In the early days and well into the 1980s dispatchers in non-CTC territory issued what were usually called "track car lineups." This was a lineup of trains out and running with the last OS, trains that were called, and trains that were expected to be run during the time limits of the lineup (usually for no more than four hours). Generally they were issued twice a day—in the early morning around 8 and then at noon and at other times as required. This could be one of the most dangerous aspects of dispatching, for it was easy to leave a train off. Another danger was trains running ahead of their lineup time—it was up to the dispatcher to ensure that they did not, usually by putting out wait orders or having interlocking operators holding them.

Lineups were also used on some roads in CTC territory, but as a rule track workers were protected by what is usually called "track and time" or "clock time," depending on the carrier. Under this system, which applies today even with the newest CTC equipment, a track worker requests time, and the dispatcher blocks off the signals governing movements into that section. He then issues track and time authorizing the track worker to occupy the main track or siding. This used to be written in a special book, but now it is on a computer screen. This, too, could be one of the more dangerous duties of a dispatcher, as it was easy to take down the blocking and run a train into a track rider's limits. In track-warrant territory track workers use track warrants just like a train, and with the computerized conflict-avoidance system the possibility of laps is at least minimized.

One thing has not changed: dispatching is still as stressful as ever, if not more so, as the railroads reduce the number of clerks, leaving more work to be absorbed by the DS. In addition to trying to get No. 6 around a coal train, the DS may also be busy functioning as the yardmaster at Sterling.

By tradition, dispatchers moved up from the telegraphers' ranks. As telegraphers became extinct, the carriers looked at train service people. Then came the opening of training schools and hiring people off the street. BNSF, for example, hires most of its new dispatchers from Tarrant County Junior College in Fort Worth, which offers a course in railroad science. One who can pass the aptitude tests and finish the 16-week course is almost assured of a job. Another source is craft transfers, employees in other jobs who want to be dispatchers. They must complete a 10-week course and then begin breaking in on the job. The last source, which is drying up, is experienced dispatchers off other carriers. At present BNSF, for example, estimates that 50 percent of its new dispatchers come from Tarrant County Junior College, 40 percent from craft transfers, and the remaining 10 percent from other railroads.

Still more change for dispatchers appears inevitable. No doubt newer and more powerful computers will further automate many routine duties, but it is doubtful that the dispatcher can be eliminated entirely. Jobs may be combined and the remaining number much less, but even the best computer-driven systems should still need human intervention.

—W. L. Gwyer

REFERENCE

Armstrong, John H. *The Railroad, What It Is, What It Does: The Introduction to Railroading.* 4th ed. Omaha, Nebr.: Simmons-Boardman, 1998.

See also SIGNALING; TRAIN CONTROL.

Dodge, Grenville M. (1831–1916)

The architect of Union Pacific's great westward thrust was born in Danvers, Massachusetts, the son of a Yankee peddler. Grenville Mellen Dodge briefly attended Norwich University in Vermont and a small military academy before heading west to Peru, Illinois, in 1851 to survey town lots. He also did some railroad surveying. The following year Dodge became a surveyor for the Illinois Central Railroad, where he met Abraham Lincoln, who was an attorney for the railroad. Three years later Dodge moved to Council Bluffs, Iowa, which was to be his home and base of operations for the rest of his life. Here he became involved in numerous business interests, including banking, real estate, and railroads.

When the Civil War began, Dodge received an appointment as a colonel in the Fourth Iowa Volunteer Regiment and was present at a number of battles early in the war. He used his engineering skills to rebuild bridges and railway lines. His work captured the attention of Gen. U. S. Grant, who called Dodge a first-rate soldier, but even more important, a great railway engineer. Although he was injured several times and out of action for some stretches, Dodge nonetheless rose to the rank of major general.

So highly esteemed was Dodge by the end of the war that he was selected to be the chief engineer of the Union Pacific Railroad in its transcontinental push. In this role Dodge commanded a huge army, numbering in the thousands, many of them Union and Confederate war veter-

Grenville M. Dodge. —Library of Congress (Neg. LC-USZ62-35408)

ans, joined by Irish immigrants, as well as battalions of mule skinners, grog sellers, bushwhackers, and female harpies. Indians along the right of way called Dodge "Long Eye" since he was perpetually studying the route and the work crews with a long telescope. During the years of construction up to 1869, the transcontinental line became the subject of so much nationwide publicity that Dodge became a widely known name. He was not implicated in the various financial scandals that enveloped the Union Pacific in those years.

Even before the conclusion of the transcontinental project Dodge became involved in politics. He was an Iowa congressman in 1867–1868 and went on to become the best-known public figure in Iowa for the rest of his life. But he also continued his activities as a railroad builder, overseeing the building of 9,000 miles of track in the Southwest. He served as chief engineer of the Texas & Pacific Railway and became president of the road in 1880. In association with Jay Gould, Dodge was involved in the management of several other lines.

Dodge's last railroad construction was the Cuba Railroad from Santa Clara to Santiago after the Spanish-American War. In 1905 he retired to Council Bluffs, where he wrote several volumes of memoirs. He had personally known every U.S. president from the Civil War to World War I. When Dodge died in 1916, all activities came to a stop in Council Bluffs, where he was (and remains) the city's most prominent son.

—George H. Douglas

REFERENCES

Bain, David Harward. *Empire Express: Building the First Transcontinental Railroad.* New York: Viking, 1999.
Dodge, Grenville M. *How We Built the Union Pacific Railway.* New York, 1910.
Hirshson, Stanley P. *Grenville M. Dodge: Soldier, Politician, Railroad Pioneer.* Bloomington: Indiana Univ. Press, 1967.
Klein, Maury. *Union Pacific: Birth of a Railroad, 1862–1893.* Garden City, N.Y.: Doubleday, 1987.

Vanderbilt. In the 1850s he became involved in railroad stock speculation and took a special interest in the stock of the troubled Erie Railroad. He became a director of the road in 1857 and was elected treasurer. Clearly he had no interest in the welfare of the railroad beyond his own raids on its treasury and speculation in its stock. By this time Drew was known as the Great Bear of Wall Street: his strategy was to sell short and watch his enemies take their losses.

Drew was a scheming, treacherous individual, but not without a cynical sense of humor. He wore shabby clothes and affected the manner of a country bumpkin. He ate his lunch in the basement of the stock exchange with messenger boys and counter jumpers despite his wealth and his membership in the city's best clubs.

In the 1860s Drew formed an alliance with Jay Gould and Jim Fisk, and this triumvirate later was dubbed the Erie Ring. Knowing that Vanderbilt hoped to take control of the Erie as he had the New York Central, Drew and his partners used their own printing presses to turn out as many shares as Vanderbilt wanted to buy. When this deceit was discovered, warrants for their arrest were issued, but the three rogues crossed the Hudson River to Jersey City, living in a hotel protected by armed guards and thugs. They sought rival injunctions from New Jersey courts in a battle that raged for several years. Eventually Vanderbilt withdrew, but the machinations of Gould, Fisk, and Drew wrecked the Erie Railroad.

Drew's later years were unhappy. Gould and Fisk turned on him, and he lost most of his fortune in the panic of 1873. In 1876 he declared bankruptcy. When he died in 1879, his fortune was no more than $500.

—George H. Douglas

REFERENCE

Browder, Clifford. *The Money Game in Old New York: Daniel Drew and His Times.* Lexington: Univ. Press of Kentucky, 1986.

Drew, Daniel (1797–1879)

Born in rural Putnam County, New York, Drew was unschooled and remained half-literate all his life. In his early career he was a cattle drover and made a modest income bringing cattle to market in New York. Notoriously, he watered his cattle heavily just before bringing them to market, giving rise to the term "watered stock," a notion that seems to have served him well later in the stock market.

In 1829 Drew moved to New York and subsequently drifted into stock speculation, establishing his own brokerage house. In the 1830s he invested heavily in the steamboat industry, often in competition with Cornelius

Dripps, Isaac (1810–1892)

Isaac Dripps is typical of the generation of engineers who developed the earliest American railroad technology without the benefit of academic education in engineering or science. He was born in Belfast, Ireland, on April 14, 1810, and was brought to America as an infant by his parents, who settled in Philadelphia. After attending public schools he was apprenticed as a teenager to Thomas Holloway, then the major manufacturer of steam engines in the city. Holloway was a prominent supplier to the Union Line steamboat operation on the Delaware River. The Union Line was an enterprise of the John Stevens family, who became the principals in the Camden & Amboy Railroad, New Jersey's first. With the arrival from Britain in 1831 of the *John Bull*, the railroad's first steam locomotive, Dripps was hired to take charge of assembling the locomotive and putting it into operation.

In his 22-year career with the Camden & Amboy, a number of Dripps's innovations became standards in the industry. He is credited with having designed the first "cowcatcher"-style pilot and the first locomotive with eight coupled driving wheels. In 1847 he designed the unusual high-wheeled Crampton-type 6-2-0, a locomotive capable of very high speed but ultimately unsuccessful because of limited pulling power. He worked closely with Robert L. Stevens, president of the C&A, who is generally credited as having shared in the creative effort.

In 1854 Dripps left the Camden & Amboy for a business venture as a partner in the Trenton Locomotive Works, where he originated a design for the first diamond-pattern arch-bar truck for freight cars, later to become a de facto standard in the industry. This company, however, built only a few locomotives before it failed in 1858.

Dripps moved on to become superintendent of motive power for the Pittsburgh, Fort Wayne & Chicago Railroad at Fort Wayne, Indiana. Here he turned his talents toward the development of systems, machinery, and tools for the manufacture and maintenance of steam locomotives. He built the railroad's Fort Wayne facilities into a model operation that was emulated throughout the industry. As a result of this accomplishment, in 1870 Dripps was promoted by PFW&C parent Pennsylvania Railroad to become its superintendent of motive power and machinery at Altoona, Pennsylvania, where he began the expansion and development of what was to become the most extensive railroad mechanical facility in the world.

Dripps's career at the Pennsylvania was cut short by ill health, and he was forced to give up his management job in 1872. He remained with the Pennsylvania as a consultant for another six years, doing various experimental steam locomotive design work. In 1878 his health forced full retirement, and he moved in with his son's family in Philadelphia, where he died on December 28, 1892.

—Adrian Ettlinger

REFERENCES

Dictionary of American Biography.
White, John H., Jr. *A History of the American Locomotive; Its Development, 1830–1880.* New York: Dover, 1979.

Dudley, Plimmon H. (1843–1924)

Plimmon Henry Dudley was born in a farmhouse in New Freedom, Ohio, in May 1843. He entered Hiram College at age 20, studying in winter and working on the family farm in summer. He received a Ph.D. degree in engineering and metallurgy in 1868 and spent much of his life in the pursuit of improved metals. Upon graduation he became the chief engineer for the city of Akron, Ohio, and stayed there for four years before moving into railroad engineering work.

In 1872 Dudley was the chief engineer of the Valley Railroad in Ohio (later part of the Baltimore & Ohio) and became interested in the problem of measuring locomotive performance at different speeds. In 1874 he left the Valley Railroad to concentrate on his ideas for developing a car that could accurately measure these forces. Dudley demonstrated and proved many of his theories and in 1876 designed and built the first dynamometer car. This vehicle incorporated a device called the dynagraph, which used hydraulic cylinders to record the push and pull of a locomotive, also incorporating such data as work, time, coal, water, and track condition. His work drew the attention of the Eastern Railway Assn., which engaged Dudley's services in 1876, and in 1880 he was appointed as a consulting engineer on rails, locomotive tires, and structural steel for the New York Central & Hudson River Railroad.

Dudley also developed a track indicator device that could record track conditions on a continuous paper roll, showing the vertical and horizontal irregularities of each rail, as well as high joints, loose rails, and roadbed depressions. The roll also showed the percentage of tangent and curved track, the track gauge and profile, the mileage, and the exact location of track sections and stations. Still another Dudley invention was the stremmatograph. It was placed beneath a rail to record the stresses caused in the rail by each wheel crossing over it. Dudley believed that the steel rails then in use did not have sufficient rigidity to sustain the demands of increasing traffic. A stiffer rail girder would carry the weight of trains on a smooth, level surface without sag, reducing train resistance and the damaging impact on the rails.

The New York Central built a special car incorporating all three of Dudley's inventions, which operated extensively over the railroad's system. Known as the D car, it incorporated living quarters for Dudley and his wife, Lucy, also a scientist. Furnishings included a grand piano; Lucy was musically accomplished.

Thousands of miles of track studies by Dudley demonstrated that the existing rails did not have sufficient mechanical properties to distribute the wheel loads, resulting in destructive and expensive wear to rails and crossties, while high train resistance increased maintenance and operating costs. For the Central's track, Dudley designed a new heavier and higher rail section, with a broad, flat, thin head, a design that increased rail strength by 66 percent while adding only 23 percent in rail weight. The new rails helped make possible the heavier passenger locomotives designed by William Buchanan, the Central's superintendent of motive power, and the new high-speed trains of the *Empire State Express* inaugurated in 1891. Dudley continued to modify his design, with higher sections and stiffer track sections. The New York Central's standard rail in the latter part of the nineteenth century had been 4½ inches high and weighed 65 pounds per yard. By the time Dudley completed his redesign, the rail section was 7 inches high and weighed 120 pounds per yard.

Dudley also gave much thought to improving the quality of steel rails, looking for ways to find the fissures and hidden defects in rail, and improving the manufacture to greatly reduce the frequency of broken rails. With Dudley's help, the frequency of broken rails on the New York Central was reduced from 1 in 600 in 1902 to only 1 in 142,000 by 1915.

Dudley died in New York in 1924. "[He] contributed at least as much as any other man to the development of American railroads," remarked New York Central president A. H. Smith. "He was the first engineer to realize the importance of radical improvement in the track if the railroad was to be developed as it should be. Perhaps it would not be an overstatement to say that he did more than any other one man to confer upon humanity the boon of rapid, safe and economical transportation."

—William D. Middleton

REFERENCES

Hubbard, Freeman H. "Father of High-Speed Trains." *Railroad* 43, no. 2 (July 1947): 12–27.
Tuthill, John K. "The Railroad Dynamometer Car of the University of Illinois and the Illinois Central Railroad." *University of Illinois Bulletin* 45, no. 11 (Oct. 4, 1947): 1–36.

Duluth, Missabe & Iron Range Railway

The Duluth, Missabe & Iron Range Railway (DM&IR) was formed in 1937 to consolidate the Duluth & Iron Range Rail Road and the Duluth, Missabe & Northern Railway, both owned by the U.S. Steel Corp. and each operating about 300 miles of railroad.

Duluth & Iron Range Rail Road

The reports in the 1860s of gold at Vermilion Lake north of Duluth, Minnesota, proved to be false. The mineral was fool's gold, iron pyrite, but it led to something more useful than gold, the Vermilion Range iron-ore deposit. In December 1874 the Duluth & Iron Range Rail Road (D&IR) was chartered to build a line north from Duluth to Babbitt. Although the Minnesota legislature granted it land, the railroad remained simply a charter

until Charlemagne Tower, owner of the Minnesota Iron Co., acquired control and began construction. A line was built north from what is now Two Harbors, and the company constructed a dock there to transfer ore to lake boats. The first trainload of iron ore moved to the dock on July 31, 1884. Two years later the D&IR opened an extension southwest along the shore of Lake Superior to Duluth. After the discovery of further deposits of iron ore in the Mesabi Range, D&IR built a branch west to the city of Virginia and a number of spurs to mines in the area. (Mesabi is a Chippewa word meaning "giant"; it is also spelled Missabe and Mesaba.)

Tower sold Minnesota Iron to the Illinois Steel Co., which was backed by Henry H. Porter, Marshall Field, Cyrus McCormick, and John D. Rockefeller. Illinois Steel was succeeded by Federal Steel, and Federal Steel by U.S. Steel. In 1901 U.S. Steel purchased the D&IR and began to consolidate its operations with those of the Duluth, Missabe & Northern, which the steel company had also acquired.

Duluth, Missabe & Northern Railway

The hematite iron ores of the Mesabi Range were discovered in 1890. Initially neither the Duluth & Iron Range nor the Duluth & Winnipeg (later the Great Northern Railway) was disposed to build a line into the area, so the Merritt brothers of Duluth, who had acquired tracts of land in the Mesabi Range, incorporated the Duluth, Missabe & Northern Railway (DM&N).

The DM&N carried its first load of ore to Duluth in 1892, using the rails of the Duluth & Winnipeg from Brookston and D&W's ore dock in Superior, Wisconsin. Within a year the DM&N built its own line into Duluth and its own ore dock. During the financial panic of 1893 John D. Rockefeller acquired the Merritt brothers' Lake Superior Consolidated Iron Mines and their railroad.

Ore production of the Mesabi Range soon exceeded that of the Vermilion Range. The railroad built two more ore docks at Duluth. In 1901 Rockefeller sold the DM&N to U.S. Steel, which bought the nearby Duluth & Iron Range at the same time. The railroad began a program of improvements to its track and rolling stock: iron ore is a heavy cargo that moves in long trains and requires the best in track and locomotives.

For a number of years the DM&N and the D&IR operated independently, but then began to explore the benefits of joint operation. At the beginning of 1930 DM&N leased the D&IR. During the Depression years the sharing of equipment and facilities proved to be wise economic policy. Even after the elimination of duplicate rail lines, the iron-mining area around Coleraine, Hibbing, and Virginia, Minnesota, was covered with a network of tracks of the DM&IR and two other railroads, the Great Northern (later Burlington Northern) and the Duluth, Winnipeg & Pacific (a Canadian National subsidiary).

Duluth, Missabe & Iron Range Railway

In 1937 and 1938, through a series of corporate maneuvers, the two railroads were combined to form the Duluth, Missabe & Iron Range Railway, the largest carrier of iron-ore in the United States. DM&IR iron-ore tonnages climbed to record levels during World War II and the decade that followed, reaching a peak of more than 49 million long tons in 1953. During these glory years the railroad was distinguished by its continuing reliance upon steam power, headlined by a fleet of 18 enormous 2-8-8-4 Yellowstone-type locomotives that ranked among the most powerful steam locomotives ever built. Steam power continued in service on the Missabe through 1959, well after most roads had completed their conversion to diesel-electric power.

But the Mesabi Range's veins of high-grade ore were gradually mined out, and the mining companies turned their attention to taconite, a lower-grade iron ore that is processed into round pellets for shipping. The DM&IR grew accustomed to lesser tonnages as alternate ore sources were opened elsewhere in the Western Hemisphere, and the integrated North American steel industry declined.

In 1988 the DM&IR was purchased by Transtar, Inc., a holding company owned by Blackstone Capital Partners (51 percent) and USX, successor to U.S. Steel (49 percent). In 2004 Great Lakes Transportation, then owner of DM&IR and the Bessemer & Lake Erie, was acquired by Canadian National.

—George H. Drury

REFERENCE

King, Frank A. *The Missabe Road*. San Marino, Calif.: Golden West Books, 1972. 2nd ed., Minneapolis: Univ. of Minnesota Press, 2003.

Durant, Thomas Clark (1820–1885)

Above all a man who put his own best interests first, Thomas Clark Durant was also one of the visionaries who built the Union Pacific to the completion of the first transcontinental railroad at Promontory Point in 1869. Some described him as the "first dictator of the railroad world." Born in Lee, Massachusetts, to a colonial and revolutionary family, Durant completed his studies at Albany Medical College in 1840 and briefly practiced medicine. Drawn to commerce, he went into the flour and grain business in Albany and soon moved up to head the

Thomas Clark Durant. —*Trains* Magazine Collection

firm's New York branch, expanding its business and also becoming a successful stock speculator.

In 1851 Durant joined with railroad engineer Henry Farnam to build the Michigan Southern Railroad. It completed a line from Chicago to a connection with the East in 1852, and Durant and Farnam were soon looking for even bigger prospects west from Chicago. In 1853 they joined forces with the contractor for the Chicago & Rock Island, which reached the Mississippi in 1854. Then the partners looked farther west to build the Mississippi & Missouri across Iowa to a junction with the Missouri River, and beyond that toward growing interest in the Pacific railroad. Financial reverses delayed completion of the line across Iowa until 1869, but long before this Durant had moved into the great sweepstakes for the Pacific railroad.

As the 1862 Pacific Railroad Act was moving ahead, Durant and Farnam joined an effort to bring the Pacific railroad into Omaha. Even before the Union Pacific was organized, Durant began studies of the projected route west from Omaha to Salt Lake City under civil engineer Peter A. Dey. When the UP elected its first board of directors late in 1862, Durant organized the new board to suit himself. The president, Maj. Gen. John Adams Dix, was a figurehead who had held similar positions for the Chicago & Rock Island and Mississippi & Missouri railroads and had connections in Washington. Durant himself was vice president and general manager and on both the UP's executive and finance committees. He was in full control.

Because of Durant's unethical financial practices, Henry

Farnam severed his relationship with the doctor. Peter Dey, the UP's first chief engineer, left rather than work with him. As the UP inched westward out of Omaha, Durant was involved in questionable practices and frequent interference with Dey's successor as chief engineer, Gen. Grenville Mellen Dodge. One famous example was Durant's decision to abandon the already-graded 14-mile section of the UP between Omaha and the Elkhorn River for a more difficult 23-mile roundabout "oxbow" route in order to increase the UP's per mile earnings.

But Durant was also a canny businessman. Threatened with the financial failure of the Union Pacific, Durant came up with a charter for the Crédit Mobilier, which acted as the builder for the UP. The Crédit Mobilier collected far more from UP than the actual costs of the line. The stockholders got handsome profits, some of which were shared with key members of Congress, and the affair later became a scandal.

In 1867 Durant gained even greater control for the UP board and drove the railroad forward relentlessly. He was a constant irritant to chief engineer Dodge, coming up with one scheme after another to deviate from Dodge's planned route. Durant represented the Union Pacific at the May 10, 1869, last-spike celebration at Promontory Point, but scarcely two weeks later he was dropped from the UP board when the rival "Boston crowd" finally gained the ascent. Durant's subsequent ventures were unsuccessful. He died at his North Creek, New York, mansion in 1885.

—William D. Middleton

REFERENCE

Bain, David Haward. *Empire Express: Building the First Transcontinental Railroad*. New York: Viking, 1999.

Dynamometer Cars. *See*

LOCOMOTIVE TESTING

E

Eads, James Buchanan (1820–1887)

Born in 1820 at Lawrenceburg, Indiana, James B. Eads moved with his family to St. Louis in 1833. His formal schooling ended at this time (he was 13) because of family reverses. Without previous bridge engineering experience, Eads would seem an unlikely choice to design and build a crossing of the Mississippi River. Nonetheless, this self-taught American engineer built one of the great bridges of the nineteenth century.

At age 18 Eads became a steamboat clerk and began a lifelong association with the Mississippi River. Only a few years later he designed an innovative diving bell and vessel for salvage work on the river and soon became wealthy in the salvage business. During the Civil War Eads designed and built a fleet of steam-powered, ironclad gunboats—the first eight in only 100 days—that helped the Union forces gain control of the Mississippi and its tributaries.

In 1879 James Buchanan Eads developed the idea of this ship railway as an alternative to the Panama Canal. Giant locomotives would pull an entire ship on a rail-mounted cradle over a 180-mile railway across Mexico's Tehuantepec Isthmus. Eads pursued the idea for the rest of his life, but it never materialized.
—*Railway Age*

Shortly after the end of the war a bridge company was formed to build a crossing of the Mississippi at St. Louis. Congress passed an authorizing act in 1866, and Eads was appointed chief engineer for the project. The innovative engineer spanned the river with three great tubular steel arch spans, two of 502 feet and a central span of 520 feet, representing the first major use of steel in bridge construction. To form the deep foundations required for the main piers, Eads made extensive use of the pneumatic caisson method, the first such application in North America. Constructed over a seven-year period from 1867 to 1874 and opened to rail and road traffic in 1874, the historic structure, now known as the Eads Bridge in honor of its engineer, remains in service today.

After the St. Louis Bridge project Eads planned and built the system of jetties that assured access to the Mississippi from the Gulf of Mexico. The work won him an international reputation. He later completed still other harbor and channel improvement projects all over the United States and in Mexico, Canada, and England. In 1880 he began work on the ambitious Tehuantepec Ship Railroad in Mexico that would have carried ships between the Gulf of Mexico and the Pacific, believing it to be a more feasible route than that for a Panamanian canal. He died in 1887 in Nassau, Bahamas, while visiting there to recover from illness.

—William D. Middleton

REFERENCES

Dictionary of American Biography.
National Cyclopaedia of American Biography.

Eastman, Joseph B. (1882–1944)

A giant in the field of twentieth-century transportation regulation and policies, Joseph Eastman served as a member (and, intermittently, chairman) of the Interstate Commerce Commission from 1919 until his death in 1944. In the period 1933–1936 he concurrently served as President Franklin D. Roosevelt's federal coordinator of transportation, and from 1942 to his death as director of the wartime Office of Defense Transportation (ODT).

Always a liberal social thinker, Eastman gravitated to social service work in Boston after graduating from Amherst in 1904 and then was plunged into utilities and transportation issues as secretary of the Public Franchise League there. At the league he became a protégé of the famous liberal lawyer and later Supreme Court justice Louis D. Brandeis. Through Brandeis's efforts Eastman became a member of the Massachusetts Public Service

Joseph Eastman. —Library of Congress (Neg. LC-USE6-D-4220-A)

Commission in early 1915 and then, in 1919, a Woodrow Wilson appointee to the ICC.

At the time the ICC largely consisted of undistinguished political appointees. With his high intelligence and firm, incorruptible views on what constituted the "public good," Eastman quickly made himself its intellectual and rational conscience. A lifelong bachelor, he put all his prodigious energy into his work and heavily influenced the group's thinking and practices.

Despite his antipathy to the freewheeling financial practices of the 1920s and his bias (at that time) toward public ownership of the railroads, Eastman survived three successive Republican administrations. While doing so, he often frustrated railroad executives and financiers by doing his best to block what he felt were dubious financial, commercial, and corporate actions—for example, the holding-company manipulations of Cleveland's empire-building Van Sweringen brothers.

For most of his career Eastman's strong principles had found form through piecemeal case rulings and dissents, for the ICC was a quasi-judicial agency and not a policy-making body as such. But when Roosevelt came to power in 1933, Eastman finally came into his own as a major shaper of the Emergency Railroad Transportation Act, a measure designed to reform some of the financial and legal abuses of the 1920s, particularly the use of holding companies to avoid ICC jurisdiction.

Another purpose of the transportation act was to reduce waste by "coordinating" and rationalizing the then-underused railroad facilities and equipment fleets—an effort aimed at helping rescue the Depression-ravaged railroad industry while avoiding government ownership or control. (By then Eastman had changed his views on public ownership.) To that end, Roosevelt appointed Eastman federal coordinator of transportation.

Unfortunately, this turned out to be a doomed quest, and Eastman's office was allowed to die three years later with little accomplished. But thanks to the exigencies of wartime and stronger powers, Eastman made a much greater success of his job as director of the ODT. Sadly, though, overwork brought on his death in 1944 at age 61. Said his biographer, "He had been . . . denounced scathingly by both [the railroads, and the unions] at different periods. But when he was gone, all factions joined in saluting him."

—Herbert H. Harwood, Jr.

REFERENCES

Fuess, Claude Moore. *Joseph B. Eastman, Servant of the People.* New York: Columbia Univ. Press, 1952. Repr., Westport, Conn.: Greenwood Press, 1974.
Latham, Earl. *The Politics of Railroad Coordination, 1933–1936.* Cambridge, Mass.: Harvard Univ. Press, 1959.

Edison, Thomas Alva (1847–1931)

Widely regarded as the greatest of all American inventors, Thomas Alva Edison was easily the best known as well. Born to Samuel and Nancy Edison of Milan, Ohio, in 1847, Edison was almost entirely educated by his gifted mother and early on demonstrated an extraordinary resourcefulness and accomplishment. When his family moved to Port Huron, Michigan, the 12-year-old boy was already engaged in a variety of commercial activities. Working as a newsboy on a Grand Trunk train, Edison used his spare time in the baggage car to conduct experiments and publish a newspaper. While still engaged in other chemistry and electrical studies, Edison became a telegraph operator. When still only 19 he invented the automatic telegraph repeater and then duplex, quadruplex, and sextuplex telegraph machines that sent multiple telegraph messages over the same wire, saving the Western Union Co. millions in wiring costs. It was estimated that he made some 50 separate inventions and improvements in telegraphic communications.

Edison developed a lively business in telegraphic equipment at a workshop in Newark, New Jersey, then in 1876 moved to an experimental laboratory at Menlo Park, New Jersey. Edison's research interests soon encompassed an ever-wider range of activities. In 1877 he developed the phonograph and then brought out a carbon transmitter for the recently developed telephone. He became interested in the incandescent electric light, finally developing a

suitable filament (in 1879) after thousands of unsuccessful experiments. He then went on to develop the entire system needed to generate electric power and to distribute, regulate, and measure it for electrical systems. In 1880 Edison established the Edison Electric Illuminating Co. of New York (later the New York Edison Co.) and in 1882 began operating the world's first central electric power system at Pearl Street in New York. In 1886 Edison set up the new Edison General Electric Co., later merged with the General Electric Co., of Schenectady, New York, for building electrical equipment.

Other discoveries came at a feverish pace. The dictating machine was developed in 1887; the first successful motion picture camera followed in 1891. During much of the 1890s Edison was involved in an effort to separate magnetic ores. The process was largely unsuccessful, but as a by-product he came into ownership of a cement company and developed an idea for a cement house that could be completed in a single operation in only a few hours. In 1903 Edison developed the nickel-iron-alkaline storage battery that was widely used by the Edison Storage Battery Co. for electric trucks, tractors, locomotives, and submarines and for lighting railroad cars, safety signals, and other devices. Edison's Kinetoscope (1912) was a talking motion picture machine, and his telescribe (1914) combined telephone and dictating phonographs to record both sides of a conversation.

During World War I Edison was involved in developing chemicals that had been supplied from Germany and later worked on developing a substitute for natural India rubber. As a member of the U.S. naval consulting board in 1915 he was involved in a wide variety of new devices for warships.

Edison's contributions to railroads were largely the result of the development of devices for a much wider range of uses. Among the most important of these are Edison's many inventions and improvements to the telegraph; the development of electric light, power generation, and distribution; the manufacture of electrical equipment through the Edison General Electric Co.; and the Edison Storage Battery Co.

Edison also, at least briefly, developed some early ideas on railroad electrification. A year after German inventor Ernst Werner von Siemens had demonstrated the first generator-powered electric railway, Edison in 1880 began experimenting with a similar narrow-gauge electric railway at his Menlo Park laboratory. It worked well, and Henry Villard, president of the Northern Pacific Railroad, asked him to develop an electric railway that could carry wheat from the Great Plains. Villard came up with financial support, and a larger version was operated the following year. However, the Northern Pacific soon suffered financial reverses. Villard was forced out, and nothing more came of the scheme.

At the same time inventor Stephen D. Field had applied for similar patents, and by 1883 Edison had joined with

Field to form the Electric Railway Co. of the United States. A new Edison-Field locomotive, *The Judge*, was demonstrated at Chicago in 1883. Although it worked well, the company failed to prosper, and Edison himself took little interest in the new venture. Frank J. Sprague, who soon became a leader in electric railway development, had joined Edison that same year, but found Edison disinterested in electric railways and soon left to form his own company. Edison's long opposition to the use of AC power, which became increasingly important for electric power generation, transmission, and distribution, limited his possible later contributions to electric railways.

Thomas Edison's accomplishments in invention and development have probably never been equaled or exceeded. Edison submitted about 1,500 U.S. patent applications and an equal number for foreign patents, and more than 2,300 of them were approved. He received honorary degrees from universities, medals from arts and sciences organizations, a special gold medal from the U.S. Congress, an appointment as commander of the French Legion of Honor, a gold medal from Pope Pius XI, and many more honors. Visitors to the Edison National Historic Site in West Orange, New Jersey, can see the famous laboratory, where a truck from one of the 1881 Edison electric locomotives still stands.

The great inventor's feverish work schedule, finally began to slow down in his final years. He died at his West Orange, New Jersey, home at the age of 84.

—William D. Middleton

REFERENCES

Clark, Ronald W. *Edison: The Man Who Made the Future*. New York: G. P. Putnam's Sons, 1977.
National Cyclopaedia of American Biography.

Electrification

Technology

Both steam and diesel-electric locomotives represent self-contained motive power, developing their own power supply and functioning independently of the railroad's fixed plant. Electrification, however, requires a complete infrastructure, including both the fixed plant of a centralized power supply plant and distribution system and the motive power of the electric locomotives themselves.

Electrification Plant

DIRECT-CURRENT SYSTEMS

A direct current is a steady-flowing unidirectional current that is maintained at a fixed strength. The earliest railroad electrifications employed low-voltage DC electrical systems, typically at anywhere from 550 to 600 volts, similar to those developed earlier for urban street railways and rapid-transit systems. Performance characteristics of the DC series traction motors used were well suited to railway service. These systems, however, had significant disadvantages for heavy railroad service. Because of the low voltage, large current flows were required, necessitating the use of third-rail systems to provide sufficient current-carrying capacity, and electrical substations had to be provided every few miles.

These disadvantages were largely overcome by the development of high-voltage DC systems by General Electric around 1906. The higher voltage, used at anywhere from 1,200 to 3,000 volts, greatly reduced the required current flow, allowing the use of overhead distribution systems, reducing the necessary size of feeders, and permitting a much wider spacing of electrical substations.

ALTERNATING-CURRENT SYSTEMS

Alternating currents grow to a maximum value, decrease, change their direction to reach a maximum value in the new direction equal to that in the original direction, and then return to their original state. The number of times per second that the current repeats this cycle is called the frequency, formerly expressed as cycles but now as Hertz (abbreviated Hz), after German physicist Heinrich Rudolf Hertz (1857–1894). In North America power is normally generated at 60 Hz.

Alternating current is normally generated at three phases and distributed on three-wire circuits. At any time each of the three phases is at a different voltage, one-third of a cycle out of phase with that on the other two conductors. In a three-phase electrification the locomotive draws power from all three phases, with current collection from a three-wire overhead system, or sometimes a two-wire system with the running rails as the third conductor. In single-phase electrification the locomotive draws power from just one phase, with an overhead conductor at the distribution voltage and the running rails as a ground. Each of the three phases powers a different section of line. The electrical transformer, which permitted AC voltage to be stepped up or down from high voltages, made the system a superior one for power generation and distribution, permitting economies in conductors and efficiencies in transmission that were unattainable with DC systems.

Some early European electrifications, as well as the Great Northern's 1909 Cascade Tunnel electrification, employed three-phase AC systems, which provided high efficiency in power transmission, permitted the use of highly efficient induction motors, and facilitated regenerative braking. The systems, however, were extremely complex and costly.

Single-phase AC systems, requiring only a single overhead conductor, were much more adaptable to railroad requirements. Very high contact-wire voltages afforded significant economies in conductor size and transmission efficiencies. Transformers on the locomotive stepped the contact-wire voltage down for the traction motors. Their principal disadvantage was the commutator motors normally used, which were more complex, heavier, and more expensive than comparable DC series motors and required operation at a nonstandard, low-frequency power supply (25 Hz in North America).

On several electrifications the power-distribution advantages of single-phase electrification were combined with the superior performance characteristics of the DC series traction motor through the use of motor-generator sets on the locomotive that converted the AC supply to low-voltage DC. The development of rectifiers suitable for railroad service around the mid-twentieth century paved the way for a new type of single-phase electrification. The rectifier provided an efficient way to convert alternating to direct current on the locomotive, thus permitting the use of DC series traction motors. Low-frequency current was no longer required, and railroads could now draw their power supply directly from 60 Hz commercial power. New coal lines in the United States and Canada and new electrifications in Mexico and between New Haven and Boston all used commercial-frequency single-phase systems at 25 or 50 kilovolts (abbreviated kv, equals 1,000 volts), while older high-voltage DC electrifications in New Jersey and at Montreal were converted to commercial-frequency AC electrification.

Power Supply

Early electrifications were usually required to operate their own generating plants, since the public utilities lacked sufficient capacity, but later installations depended upon the utility companies for power generation. Power plants almost always used alternating current for both power generation and distribution, using transformers to step the voltage up to anywhere from 11 kv to 132 kv for greater transmission efficiency. Substations or converter stations converted the transmission voltage to the proper current and voltage for train operation.

Railroads using DC electrification used some form of rotating conversion equipment—essentially an AC motor driving a DC generator—to provide the DC power supply. Later, mercury arc rectifiers—and more recently ignitron and silicon-diode rectifiers—have been used for conversion of AC to DC.

Substations for AC electrification were much simpler, consisting of switchgear and circuit-protection equipment and transformers to step down transmission voltage for train operation. If a change in frequency from 60 Hz commercial frequency to 25 Hz for railroad operation was required, what were essentially very large motor-generator sets were installed, with a 60 Hz motor driving a 25 Hz generator. More recent installations have made the frequency conversion with solid-state equipment.

Current-Distribution and Collection Equipment

A third-rail power distribution was almost always used for low-voltage DC electrifications, with a high-conductivity steel rail mounted alongside and slightly higher than the running rail. Most were of the overrunning type, in which the top of the third rail was the contact surface, but a few were of the underrunning type, in which the contact surface was at the bottom, affording greater protection from sleeting or accidental contact. A protective cover was usually provided.

Overhead distribution systems for high-voltage DC or AC operation usually employed some type of catenary, so called because of the curve assumed by a suspended wire under uniform load. In its simplest form the catenary consisted of a single messenger wire from which a contact wire was suspended at intervals by hangers. Sometimes a more complex system with a secondary messenger wire was used, and the New Haven's initial installation at New York used a triangular catenary consisting of two messenger wires and a contact wire.

Steel, bronze, aluminum, and copper wire were all widely used in catenary construction. Catenary spans typically varied between 150 and 300 feet, usually supported from wooden or steel poles. North American electrifications typically used what was called a variable-tension, fixed-termination catenary system, with the catenary wires rigidly attached to the supporting structure. Contraction and expansion with temperature changes sometimes caused wire breaks in the winter or sagging catenary in the summer that interfered with smooth pantograph operation at high speeds. Modern electrification practice employs a fixed-tension system, in which sections of catenary—usually up to a mile in length—are tensioned by suspended weights at each end, providing equal tension in the wire and a smooth contact-wire profile under all weather conditions.

Third-rail current collection used a flat cast-iron sliding shoe or paddle, attached to a truck or a locomotive's running gear. On overrunning third-rail systems the shoe was held against the power rail by gravity and a spring, while for underrunning systems an upward spring pressure held the shoe against the underside of the power rail.

Almost all overhead electrifications used a pantograph for current collection. On earlier installations this was a diamond-shaped frame supporting a contact shoe that could adjust to variations in the height of the contact wire. The pantograph was raised against the contact wire by spring pressure and lowered by air pressure. The contact shoe was sometimes a flat steel strip, but copper, graphite, or carbon strips were often used to increase conductivity. More recently several types of lightweight, single-arm pantographs have come into general use.

Electric Motive Power

Electric Locomotive Classification

The classification system for North American electric locomotives is based upon the number of axles, with letters used to designate powered axles and numerals to designate nonpowered axles. The number of adjacent driving axles in either a truck or a rigid frame is designated by a letter, with A representing a single axle, B two axles, C three axles, and so on. Similarly, the number of adjacent nonpowered or idler axles in either a rigid frame or a truck is designated by a numeral. When both powered and nonpowered axles are included in the same rigid frame or truck, the appropriate numerals and letters in proper order are used. For example, 1B designates a truck with one idler and two driving axles.

When trucks or motive-power units are connected by an articulated connection through which tractive force is transmitted, the connection is designated by a plus sign, while the connection between swiveling trucks, or between a rigid frame and an adjacent guiding or carrying truck, is represented by a hyphen or a minus sign. When two or more motive-power units of the same wheel arrangement are normally operated in multiple as a single locomotive, the number of units is indicated by a numeral preceding the symbol of one unit within parentheses. For example, the Pennsylvania's DD1 locomotives used at New York, which were made up of two units normally operated together, each with a wheel arrangement of one two-axle nonpowered guiding truck and two powered axles in a rigid frame, were designated as 2(2-B). When two or more units of different wheel arrangement are normally operated in multiple as a single locomotive, the classifications of each unit are put in parentheses and connected by plus signs. The combination of a unit with two powered two-axle trucks and one with two powered three-axle trucks, for example, would be designated (B-B)+(C-C).

ELECTRIC LOCOMOTIVE POWER

The normal horsepower rating of an electric locomotive is the total of the continuous ratings of its traction motors. A continuous rating is the horsepower output that a motor can produce continuously without overheating. Since most electrical machinery can operate above its normal capacity for short periods, being limited only by the effects of overheating, electric locomotives are also usually given a higher hourly rating, representing the output that can be produced over a one-hour period without overheating the motors beyond safe limits. The Pennsylvania Railroad's GG1 locomotives, for example, had a continuous rating of 4,620 hp and an hourly rating of 8,500 hp.

DRIVE SYSTEMS

A geared drive system was the earliest successful type of motor mounting for electric motive power. Usually called the axle-hung or nose-suspended arrangement, it was developed by Frank J. Sprague in 1885. One side of the motor, which was geared directly to the powered axle, was suspended from the truck frame on a spring mounting, and the other was carried directly by the axle, an arrangement that minimized unsprung weight. Bearings on the axle permitted the motor to rotate slightly about the axle, maintaining alignment between the gears on the motor shaft and the axle, regardless of the axle's movement. Widely used for street and interurban railway equipment and for rapid-transit and railroad multiple-unit (M.U.) cars, it was also used for a few early electric locomotives, but the limited space available between the wheels and its low center of gravity made it unsuitable for heavy electric locomotives. The later development of more powerful compact, lightweight motors made the nose-suspended motor the preferred arrangement for diesel-electric locomotives, and it was widely adopted for electric locomotives built after World War II.

A number of early electric locomotives employed drive systems that eliminated gearing between the traction motors and the axles altogether. In some designs this was done by placing the motor armature on the axle, while the motor fields were carried on the locomotive frame. In another type of gearless drive the armature was carried on a hollow quill surrounding the axle, and power was transmitted to the wheels through flexible spring or rubber connections.

The geared quill arrangement was among the most widely used drives for heavy electric locomotives, which employed traction motors mounted on the locomotive frame above the running gear. These were geared to hollow quills that surrounded the axles and drove the wheels through flexible connections similar to those used for gearless quill drive. Placing the traction motors above the running gear raised the center of gravity and provided room for larger motors. Intermediate gearing between the traction motors and driving axles permitted higher motor speeds. Most early geared quill drives used a single traction motor for each powered axle, but later designs typically used twin motors geared to each quill.

In order to drive more than one axle from a single large traction motor, some early locomotive designs employed a side-rod drive much like that of steam locomotives. The motor was placed on a frame above the running gear where more room for a large motor was available, and the high center of gravity afforded better tracking qualities. Each end of the armature shaft was fitted with cranks, which were connected by rods to cranks on a jackshaft. Side rods connected the jackshaft to counterbalanced driving wheels similar to those of a steam locomotive. Coupling all the driving wheels together eliminated slippage, which sometimes occurred because of uneven weight distribution on locomotives with independently powered driving axles.

A variation of side-rod drive adopted by the Norfolk & Western and the Virginian for their early electric locomotives introduced intermediate gearing between single or twin traction motors and a jackshaft, which in turn powered the driving wheels through side rods. Typically, this jackshaft was connected to the side rods though flexible couplings similar to those used in quill drives.

ELECTRICAL SYSTEMS

DC-system locomotives are relatively simple. The traction motors are typically operated at the line voltage, and motor speed is controlled by resistances, field control, and grouping of motors. This grouping is generally in even numbers of motors—most often four—and they are transitioned through full series, series-parallel, and full parallel arrangements.

Single-phase AC locomotives require transformers to step down the high line voltage to the much lower traction-motor voltage. On most single-phase locomotives the traction motors are permanently connected in parallel, and the traction-motor voltage, and hence speed, is varied by connecting the motors to different taps, or leads on the transformer, each of which produces a different voltage.

There were two locomotive designs that combined the power-distribution advantages of single-phase AC with the superior performance characteristics of the DC series traction motor. The earliest of these was the motor-generator locomotive, which was equipped with a transformer to step down the high contact-wire voltage to the lower voltage required for a single-phase synchronous motor, which in turn drove a DC generator that supplied the DC traction motors. A later development was the rectifier locomotive, developed by the 1950s, which provided a highly efficient means of converting single-phase AC power to low-voltage DC for use in DC series traction motors. A transformer steps down the high-voltage AC from the contact wire to a lower-voltage AC that supplies the rectifiers, which supply DC power to the traction motors. Early designs used a mercury-arc ignitron rectifier, while more recent designs have used silicon-diode rectifiers.

TRACTION MOTORS

The DC series motor, so called because its armature and field are wired in series, has long been the most common type of traction motor for railroad service in both electric and diesel-electric locomotives because of its superior operating characteristics. As the load on the motor increases, the field strength automatically increases, and the result is an increase in torque with a decrease in speed. Conversely, the speed increases as the load decreases. Consequently, the series motor tends to adjust itself readily to the varying tractive effort required to accelerate and power a train.

Several types of motors have been used in single-phase AC electrifications. The most common is the series-commutator motor, which is nearly identical to the DC series motor and can actually be operated on DC as well as AC power. All of these AC motors required a low-frequency power supply—25 Hz in North American practice.

Modern AC propulsion, using the recent development of power electronics, including such devices as gate turn-off thyristors (GTOTs), insulated gate bipolar transistors (IGBTs), and microprocessors, has made possible the use of squirrel-cage induction motors for traction purposes, and modern practice has shifted from the tried-and-true DC series motor to these AC induction motors. A significant difference from the induction motors in earlier locomotives, which ran at a constant speed that was determined by voltage and frequency, is the ability to vary the voltage and frequency and thus the speed of the motors, something made possible by the technology now available. AC motors can be sealed, greatly reducing the maintenance problems caused by dirt and moisture that are experienced with a DC motor, and the absence of carbon brushes eliminates one of the greatest maintenance headaches of DC motors. Because they do not require the use of resistances to vary the motor speed, as a DC motor does, AC motors have a higher efficiency.

BRAKING SYSTEMS

Some electric locomotives were equipped for regenerative braking, allowing the energy of a train descending a grade to be absorbed by operating the traction motors as generators, both providing a braking effect and returning substantial amounts of power to the distribution system. Both DC series motors and AC series-commutator motors were capable of regeneration, although special control equipment was required. Another arrangement used the energy of regenerated power from a descending train to be dissipated through resistance grids in what was called dynamic braking.

Early Development

At the start of the twentieth century electric traction had emerged as a practical form of railroad motive power. Over the next several decades its proponents saw it as a superior technology that would soon supplant steam, and indeed by the end of the century it was the dominant form of motive power in much of the world. For a time it appeared that electrification would also prevail in North America; through the first half of the century U.S. electrification led the world. But then it stalled and even declined, both because of the inherent difficulties in financing the massive capital investment that would be needed under the private ownership structure of American railroads and because of the steadily improving capabilities of the diesel-electric locomotive.

English physicist Michael Faraday and Professor Joseph Henry, then an instructor at the Albany (New York) Academy, began the experimentation that led to practical electric transportation in the 1820s. Faraday discovered electromagnetic rotation in 1821 and conducted a series of experiments in 1831 demonstrating that electricity could be produced from magnetic force. Henry developed a practical electromagnet and used it to power an experimental motor that used magnetic attraction and repulsion to produce reciprocating motion. By 1835 a Vermont blacksmith and electrical experimenter, Thomas Davenport, had used an electromagnet to operate a small electric

This train, built by German electrician and inventor Ernst Werner von Siemens and exhibited at the Berlin Industrial Exhibition in 1879, was the first successful generator-powered electric railway. —Siemens A.G.

motor. Over the next quarter century crude electric locomotives, powered by batteries, were developed by Scottish electrical inventor Robert Davidson (1838), American scientist Moses G. Farmer (1847), and Charles G. Page, a physician and U.S. patent examiner (1851).

The first electrical generator, built by the Italian physicist Antonio Pacinotti in 1860, set the stage for the next step: the operation of a small generator-powered electric railway, built by the German electrician and inventor Ernst Werner

von Siemens at the Berlin Industrial Exhibition in 1879. During the next decade American inventors and electrical experimenters Stephen D. Field, Thomas A. Edison, Leo Daft, Edward M. Bentley, Walter H. Knight, Charles J. Van Depoele, John C. Henry, and Frank J. Sprague built a series of increasingly practical electric locomotives or cars. This period of experimentation came to an end during 1887–1888 with the installation of what is generally regarded as the first commercially successful electric street railway by

A key development by electrical inventor Frank J. Sprague was his nose-suspended method for mounting an electric motor, seen here in an 1886 experiment on the Manhattan Elevated Railway. —Middleton Collection

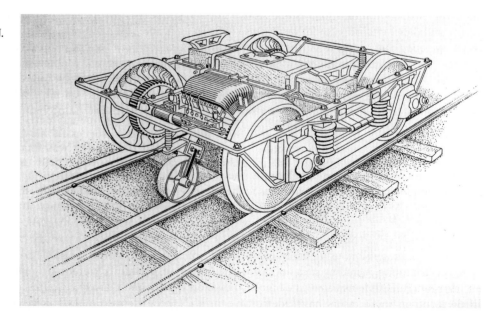

Sprague at Richmond, Virginia, setting in motion the wholesale conversion of American street railways from horse or cable power to electric operation.

Within another decade electric traction was being applied to the much heavier demands of urban rapid-transit railways. After the successful electric operation of the elevated Intramural Railway at Chicago's 1893 World's Columbian Exposition, the city's elevated railways promptly adopted electric power. Chicago's steam-operated elevated lines had all been converted to electric operation by the end of the century, and conversion of the extensive elevated system at New York City was completed by 1903.

Pioneer Railroad Electrifications

Even before electric power had reached a practical level for light street railway purposes, it was being considered for the far more demanding requirements of railroad operation. As early as 1880–1881 financier and Northern Pacific Railway president Henry Villard, with NP branch-line electrification in mind, had backed some of Thomas Edison's experiments with electric locomotives. In 1887 a 7½-ton electric locomotive built by W. M. Schlesinger began hauling 100-ton coal trains on a 3-mile line at the Lykens Valley Colliery in Pennsylvania, and similar mining and industrial electrifications soon followed. In 1892, as chairman of the NP board of directors, Villard initiated a feasibility study of a Chicago suburban electrification on the subsidiary Wisconsin Central Railroad. A year later the Baldwin Locomotive Works completed a big 60-ton,

1,000-hp electric locomotive that was intended as a prototype for the Chicago service. NP bankruptcy intervened, the project died, and the locomotive never operated.

The newly formed General Electric Co. was even more active in pursuing railroad electrification. In addition to equipping the highly successful Intramural Railway at the Columbian Exposition, GE exhibited a four-wheel, 30-ton electric locomotive at the exposition that attracted much attention. Over the next few years both GE and rival Westinghouse Electric & Manufacturing Co. equipped several experimental branch-line electrifications for the New Haven and Pennsylvania railroads. But even before its little locomotive went on exhibit at the Chicago exposition, GE in early 1892 had landed a contract to electrify some 3 miles of the Baltimore & Ohio main line through the Howard Street Tunnel then under construction as part of a new belt line at Baltimore, Maryland. The line was powered from a 600-volt DC system, initially with an overhead contact system, later a conventional third rail. Equipped with three 96-ton, 1,440-hp locomotives, the pioneer installation began regular operation in 1895. Performing well in excess of contract requirements, it established the practicality of main-line steam railroad electrification.

The New York Terminal Electrifications

For several years after the successful B&O project there was some activity in the electrification of a few branch

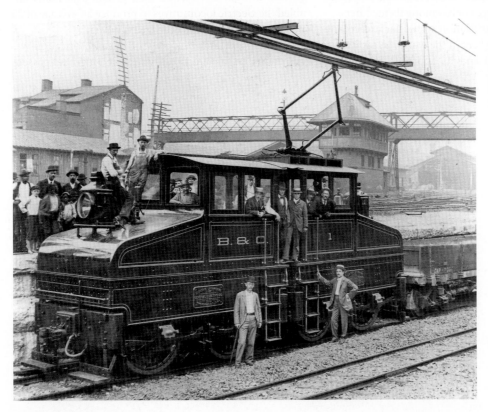

In June 1895 Baltimore & Ohio electric locomotive No. 1 paused near the north portal of the Howard Street Tunnel at Baltimore with a proud train crew and officials to celebrate the first regular freight train to be powered by electric power. —Middleton Collection

lines and switching roads, as well as a modest third-rail DC electrification of the narrow-gauge North Shore Railroad's suburban service in Marin County, California, north of San Francisco, in 1903. The next opportunity for large-scale application of electric traction was in New York City.

By the end of the nineteenth century the New York Central & Hudson River had begun to consider electrification as a solution to its major New York terminal problems. The long-distance and suburban traffic of the Central and the New Haven, which used its lines to reach Manhattan, had outgrown the railroad's Grand Central Station, and the high cost of property in midtown Manhattan made expansion of the surface terminal prohibitively expensive. The smoke, steam, and cinders of some 700 daily trains were a nuisance to the neighborhoods along the line, and low visibility in the 2-mile Park Avenue Tunnel created a severe safety problem. A collision in the smoke-filled tunnel early in 1902 that took 15 lives brought action by the New York legislature prohibiting the use of steam locomotives south of the Harlem River after July 1, 1908.

The New York Central moved ahead with plans for both a major electrification of its lines into New York and the construction of a new two-level, underground Grand Central Terminal that would solve its terminal-congestion problems, made possible by electric operation. The basic plan for this massive undertaking was the work of the railroad's vice president and chief engineer, William J. Wilgus, and its general features were worked out by a special Electric Traction Commission headed by Wilgus and with such distinguished electrical engineers as Frank J. Sprague, Bion J. Arnold, and George Gibbs among its members.

The scope of the electrification would far exceed anything yet attempted anywhere in the world. In addition to Grand Central Terminal and its approach trackage on Manhattan, the Central electrified its four-track Hudson River main line all the way to Croton, 34 miles from Grand Central, and the double-track Harlem Division as far north as White Plains, 24 miles from Grand Central. In order to meet the high power demands of the heavy-duty service, the railroad adopted a low-voltage DC third-rail system similar to that used on elevated railway systems and the B&O's pioneer installation at Baltimore.

Locomotives for the electrification were a 95-ton design built by American Locomotive and General Electric. A prototype completed late in 1904 was extensively tested against the latest New York Central Pacific-type steam locomotive on a 6-mile section of main line electrified for test purposes west of Schenectady, New York. In almost every respect the electric outperformed the steam locomotive. In one test the electric hit a maximum speed of 86 mph, and in another it accelerated an 11-car, 434-ton train to 80 mph in only two minutes.

For its suburban services the Central acquired a fleet of M.U. steel electric cars similar to those then being built for elevated railways and the New York subway. M.U. control, developed by Frank Sprague for the 1897 electrification of Chicago's South Side elevated railway, enabled a train of electric cars of any length to be controlled by the motorman in the lead car.

All operations out of Grand Central were electrified during the first half of 1907, and the full suburban electrifications were completed in 1910 and 1913. Comparative tests of the maintenance and operating costs of the new electrics conducted late in 1907 showed net savings ranging from 12 percent in transfer service to as much as 27 percent in road service, and their greater availability enabled the electric locomotives to produce an average of 25 percent more ton-miles than steam power.

The transportation capacity of this electrification was enormous. In the late 1920s, when the long-haul passen-

In 1905 the New York Central & Hudson River Railroad developed these 2-D-2 DC locomotives for its New York City electrification, the first to employ the bipolar motor design. Several of these remarkably durable locomotives remained in service for 70 years.
—General Electric

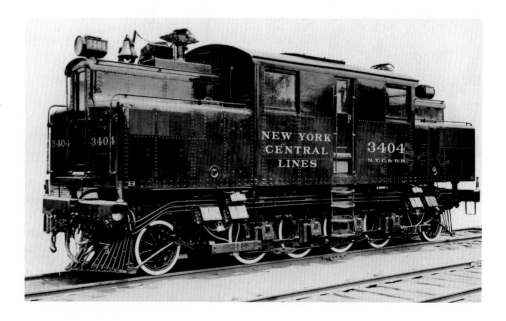

No. 01 was the 1905 Baldwin-Westinghouse prototype for the New York, New Haven & Hartford's pioneer AC electrification at New York. Forty-one of these locomotives remained in service for more than 40 years. —H. L. Broadbelt Collection

ger train was at its zenith, New York Central and New Haven traffic in and out of Grand Central averaged 500 daily trains and 134,000 passengers, and on one record day 800 trains, aggregating over 6,000 cars and carrying more than 166,000 passengers, arrived at or departed from Grand Central.

Because its trains reached New York over the New York Central, the New York, New Haven & Hartford, too, was obliged to electrify its New York terminal operations. The New Haven elected to electrify its main line all the way from its junction with the Central's Harlem Division in the Bronx to the end of suburban territory at Stamford, Connecticut, 33 miles from Grand Central.

Although the New Haven might have been expected to adopt an electrification system identical to that of the New York Central, there were clear disadvantages to the low-voltage DC system. Its high current demands required frequent substations. The New Haven, too, had experienced so many fatalities and injuries with several branch-line third-rail electrifications that they were soon discontinued. Other extensive third-rail installations—largely in the New York area—were all planned as relatively short systems.

The alternative was the newer and largely untried technology of high-voltage, single-phase AC electrification. Single-phase electrification had an important advantage of easily changing voltage as required between long-distance transmission and line voltage. Two European inventors, Lucien Gaulard of France and John D. Gibbs of England, had developed a system of alternating-current distribution in 1881–1882 that employed a transformer

that could step AC voltage up or down. Air-brake inventor George Westinghouse acquired rights to the Gaulard and Gibbs patents in 1885, and his Westinghouse Electric & Manufacturing Co. was soon engaged in developing AC generating stations, improved transformer designs, and AC electrification.

Although the Westinghouse company had a solid decade of test experience behind it at the time the New Haven began to plan its New York electrification, the only significant operating example of single-phase AC electrification was an Indiana interurban railway that had been equipped with a 3,300-volt AC system in 1905. Thus it came as a surprise to much of the railroad world when the New Haven elected to adopt an 11 kv, 25 Hz, single-phase AC system proposed by Westinghouse.

Power supply for the electrification was from an overhead catenary system. Sufficient power for the heavy railroad loads was unavailable from the public utility companies, and the New Haven constructed its own generating plant at Cos Cob, Connecticut. Initial motive power comprised 35 box-cab locomotives built by the Baldwin Locomotive Works and equipped by Westinghouse. Each was rated at 1,420 hp and was designed for a 60 mph maximum speed. The requirement that locomotives operate on both the New Haven's 11 kv AC system and the Central's 660-volt DC was met through the use of series-commutator-type motors, which could operate from either an AC or DC power supply.

Startup of the New Haven electrification in July 1907 was followed by more than a year of problems with the power plant, the overhead catenary, and the locomotives.

Gradually these were resolved, and by the end of 1908 the electric service was reported to be less subject to delays and interruptions than the steam services it had replaced. Both the efficiency and economy of electric operation proved far superior to steam power.

Over the next 20 years the New Haven's single-phase electrification was extended over two Connecticut branches, the subsidiary New York, Westchester & Boston, the railroad's six-track Harlem River branch, and the main line to New Haven. Plans to extend catenary all the way to Boston died with New Haven financial reverses, and it was almost 90 years before a full New York–Boston electrification was realized by Amtrak.

Next to initiate major New York electrifications in that extraordinary first decade of the twentieth century were the Pennsylvania Railroad and its subsidiary, the Long Island Rail Road. Electrification enabled the Pennsylvania to achieve its long-sought direct access to Manhattan across the Hudson River from its New Jersey railhead. After considering a range of bridge and other proposals over a period of nearly 20 years, the railroad in 1900 decided that it would tunnel under the Hudson to reach a new Pennsylvania Station in Manhattan, while tunnels under the East River would link the station with service facilities in Queens and permit its Long Island subsidiary to provide direct commuter service to Manhattan. Electric operation would make the tunnels feasible.

Construction of both station and tunnels began early in 1904. Electrification of the Long Island began in the same year, and an initial 38-route-mile section opened in June 1905. Reflecting the lack of significant experience with any other form of electric operation at the time, the LIRR, too, adopted a low-voltage, third-rail system that was essentially identical to rapid-transit practice. The first Long Island M.U. cars, in fact, were virtually identical to the new steel cars being built for the New York's first subway, the Interboro Rapid Transit Co., reflecting a never-realized plan for through operation of LIRR trains through the subway from Brooklyn to Manhattan. Expansion of the commuter electrification continued over the next decade. Electric service to Manhattan began with the completion of the new Pennsylvania Station in 1910, and by 1913 the LIRR was operating 89 route-miles of electrification with more than 400 electric M.U. cars.

With characteristic thoroughness the Pennsylvania set out to design an electric locomotive that could meet the exacting demands of the planned tunnel service, which included maximum grades of 1.93 percent. Two experimental third-rail DC locomotives built by the railroad's Juniata shops at Altoona, Pennsylvania, with Westinghouse electrical equipment, were acquired for an extensive test program. A third experimental locomotive was a 70-ton, 11 kv, single-phase AC unit built by Baldwin-Westinghouse, and one of the New Haven's new AC/DC units was borrowed for comparative tests that included both electric and steam power.

Extensive tests were carried out on the Pennsylvania's West Jersey & Seashore subsidiary in New Jersey, newly electrified with a third-rail DC system. The result of the tests was a design for the class DD1 electric, a 65-foot, 156-ton locomotive made up of two units, each powered by a 2,000-hp motor through a jackshaft drive. The DD1s would prove capable of a starting tractive force of almost 80,000 pounds.

Even though the Long Island had already proceeded with a third-rail DC electrification, the Pennsylvania remained undecided about its own electrification system until late 1908. A 5-mile test track for AC catenary systems was set up on an LIRR branch during the summer of 1908, and the experimental Baldwin-Westinghouse AC locomotive was employed in an extensive series of tests. Late in November the railroad, having decided that there were still too many uncertainties with the AC system, took the more prudent course and adopted the same low-voltage DC system already chosen for the LIRR.

Celebrated as "the locomotive that made Penn Station possible," the Pennsylvania's DD1 electrics proved to be exceptionally capable as the railroad began operating through the tunnels into its new Manhattan terminal in November 1910. They could handle a 1,000-ton train and were easily able to meet or exceed their 80 mph rated maximum speed. By the end of Penn Station's first full year of operation the railroad reported that nearly 10 million passengers had passed through the terminal. Almost 112,000 trains, a daily average of more than 300, operated in or out of the station in that first year. Even that level of traffic nearly doubled within less than a decade.

Competing Technologies

The difficult choices faced by the early New York electrifications in selecting a system marked only the beginning of a debate over the merits of competing systems that would last through most of the era of electrification. The low-voltage DC third-rail system adopted by the early New York Central, Long Island, and West Jersey & Seashore suburban electrifications worked well enough for these relatively short-distance installations, but had serious shortcomings for any long-distance electrification. The heavy line losses inherent in the transmission of low-voltage currents necessitated installation of costly substations at frequent intervals. The use of a third-rail power supply—required to meet the high current demand—presented obvious safety problems and potential winter-weather operational problems that were largely absent with an overhead distribution system.

Westinghouse Electric, of course, was a strong proponent of the high-voltage, single-phase AC system. Almost all such installations used the same 11 kv, 25 Hz system adopted by the New Haven's pioneer New York–New Haven installation, the only variants being a 6,600-volt, three-phase, 25 Hz system installed by the Great Northern for a 1909 electrification of the first Cascade Tunnel and a 22 kv, single-phase, 25 Hz system installed by

Henry Ford's Detroit, Toledo & Ironton in 1926. Ford talked about a DT&I all the way to the Ohio River, but the electric installation was scrapped after only four years.

General Electric, on the other hand, developed equipment and technology for a high-voltage DC electrification that obviated the disadvantages of low-voltage systems for heavy railroad loads. By employing a voltage of anywhere from two to five times that used by a typical low-voltage third-rail system, the current demand was correspondingly reduced, greatly reducing line losses and allowing the use of an overhead current-distribution system. Also important was that a DC power supply permitted the use of DC series traction motors, which offered what were usually superior performance and control characteristics to those of AC systems. Single-phase AC installations almost uniformly used an 11 kv, 25 Hz system, but there was much greater variation in high-voltage DC installations, which ranged all the way from 1,200 to 3,000 volts. Although Westinghouse and General Electric, the two principal electrical manufacturers, advocated rival systems, the two licensed the use of their patents to each other, and both were able to compete for electrification projects regardless of the system adopted.

Even apart from the variation in electrification systems, there were variations in power-distribution systems and motive power. Third-rail systems came in both over- and under-running variations, and there were dimensional differences between installations. There were similar variations in the design of overhead distribution systems. Apart from some limited standardization of apparatus, electric motive power was generally custom designed for each installation. Thus the interchangeability and the economies

of standardization were lost. As early as 1910 George Westinghouse, looking ahead to eventual merging of electrifications, had urged the adoption of a standard voltage and frequency, the establishment of uniform standards for the location of conductors, and uniformity of control equipment. His advice was unheeded, and a lack of uniformity prevailed throughout the electrification era.

Conquering Tunnels and Mountains

Such early installations as the B&O's tunnel electrification at Baltimore and the New York terminal projects clearly established electric operation as a practical alternative wherever the smoke and gases from steam locomotive operation presented problems. Among the earliest examples was an electrification of the Grand Trunk Railway's 6,032-foot St. Clair River Tunnel between Sarnia, Ontario, and Port Huron, Michigan. Opened in 1891, the tunnel was operated with specially designed locomotives that burned anthracite coal to reduce the problems of smoke and gases. Despite special operating rules developed to minimize some of the hazards of steam operation in the long tunnel, two serious asphyxiation accidents occurred over the next decade. In addition to the safety problems, increasing traffic levels were beginning to tax the capacity of the steam-operated tunnel, and by 1904 the Grand Trunk was ready to electrify.

Almost simultaneous with the New Haven's pioneer AC electrification at New York, the Grand Trunk went ahead with a similar Westinghouse single-phase AC in-

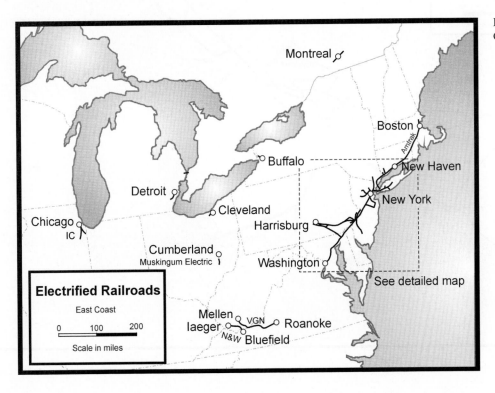

Electrified Railroads, East Coast. —Tony Howe

stallation for the tunnel. The principal difference was the adoption of a 3,300-volt power supply instead of the more common 6,600-volt or 11 kv potential because of limited clearances within the 19-foot-diameter tunnel. Opened in 1908, the electrification eliminated the safety problems and increased the capacity of the tunnel by at least a third.

Only two years later the Michigan Central Railroad opened a tunnel crossing of the Detroit River between Windsor, Ontario, and Detroit that was equipped with a 650-volt DC third-rail electrification virtually identical to the parent New York Central's New York terminal electrification. Still another electrification was installed for the Boston & Maine's 4.8-mile Hoosac Tunnel in western Massachusetts. The problem of smoke and gases from steam locomotives had steadily worsened as traffic increased through the tunnel, and delays while waiting for the tunnel to clear had become the limiting feature to the capacity of the line. By 1910, with traffic approaching 100 trains daily, the B&M decided to electrify the tunnel. By

this time the B&M had come under the control of the New Haven Railroad, and it was hardly surprising that the 11 kv, 25 Hz, single-phase electrification—designed by the New Haven's engineering department—was virtually identical to that of the New Haven. Electric operation began in 1911, and the Hoosac Tunnel's operating problems were solved.

On the other side of the continent, the Great Northern Railroad turned to electrification to overcome difficult tunnel and mountain operating problems on its crossing of the Cascade Mountains in eastern Washington. The GN had rushed its transcontinental line to completion in 1893 by crossing the Cascades with a steeply graded switchback line. Completion of the 2.63-mile Cascade Tunnel in 1900 greatly eased the crossing, but the tunnel's 1.7 percent eastbound grade and the smoke and gases from the dense traffic made steam operation through the tunnel extremely difficult and hazardous. In 1903 more than 100 passengers narrowly escaped asphyxiation when their train stalled in the tunnel and the engine crew was

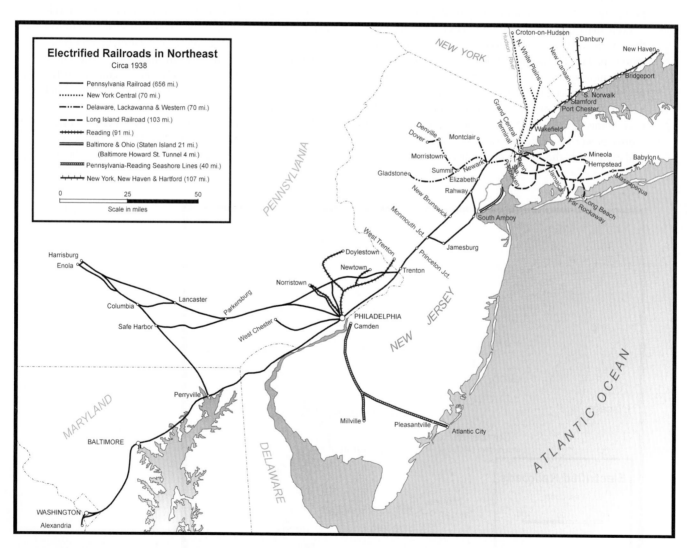

Electrified Railroads in Northeast. —Tony Howe

One of the most demanding of all U.S. electrifications was on the Norfolk & Western, where heavy Pocahontas coalfield trains encountered 1.4 percent grades on the 3,014-foot Elkhorn Tunnel on its eastbound main line. The N&W electrified a 27-mile segment of the line in 1915 with an 11,000-volt, single-phase system. Shortly after the electrification went into service, one of the 300-ton, two-unit electrics was photographed in 1915.
—Smithsonian Institution

overcome by smoke. By the end of the decade GN had electrified the tunnel with an unusual three-phase AC system supplied by General Electric, the only one of its kind ever installed in North America. The installation was also the first in North America with provision for power regeneration by locomotives operating downgrade. Soon after it was completed in 1909, studies by the railroad's superintendent of motive power indicated that the electric locomotives handled the heavy traffic through the tunnel at about twice the efficiency of the Mallet steam locomotives used previously.

Over the next decade and a half, single-phase AC electrifications were called upon to solve mountain operating problems for two Appalachian coal carriers. Despite the introduction of new compound Mallet steam locomotives, the Norfolk & Western was experiencing increasing difficulty in moving coal traffic of as much as 65,000 tons a day over the heavy grades of its Appalachian crossing in West Virginia, which was further constricted by the single-track Elkhorn Tunnel. In 1913 N&W contracted with Westinghouse Electric for an installation that represented still another variation in electrification technology. While power was distributed through an 11 kv, single-phase, 25 Hz catenary system, the locomotives were equipped with rotating-phase converters that supplied 750-volt, three-phase power to the constant-speed three-phase induction motors that were considered superior to either DC or single-phase AC traction motors for the heavy-haul demands of the N&W installation.

The results of the N&W electrification were gratifying. During the first year of operation the electric locomotives handled up to 50 percent greater tonnages eastbound over the Elkhorn grade than had ever been achieved with steam power. Fuel costs were cut by a third, and their greater availability and higher operating speed enabled just 12 electric locomotives to do the work that had previously taken 33 Mallet steam locomotives.

Within another decade the neighboring Virginian Railway was facing similar capacity constraints on its mountain lines west of Roanoke, Virginia. By the early 1920s the railroad was hauling annual coal traffic of 7 million tons, with a further increase of 100 percent forecast. Studies showed that electrification was an economical alternative to the addition of more trackage that would have been required for steam operation, and in 1923 the Virginian embarked upon a 134-mile electrification between Roanoke and Mullens, West Virginia, that employed the same split-phase technology that had proved so successful for the N&W.

Meanwhile, two western railroads had initiated heavy-haul mountain electrifications that employed the new high-voltage DC technology promoted by General Electric. The earliest of these was the Butte, Anaconda & Pacific, which in 1913 completed a 40-mile, 2,400-volt DC electrification of its copper-ore lines between Butte and Anaconda, Montana, drawing upon hydroelectric plants in the Missouri River watershed for its power supply.

Even before the BA&P installation had begun operation, the Milwaukee Road initiated a similar 3,000-volt DC electrification of the Rocky Mountain and Cascade Mountain crossings of its recently completed Pacific Extension to Puget Sound. Comprising some 647 route-miles at the time of its completion in 1920, it was the longest electrification yet undertaken anywhere in the world. The box-cab freight locomotives turned out by General Electric's Erie, Pennsylvania, plant for the Milwaukee in 1915 were proclaimed the "largest electric locomotives in the world," and in 1920 the distinctive articulated bipolar gearless locomotives—powered by a dozen traction motors mounted directly on the driving axles—built by GE for Milwaukee passenger service easily bested the railroad's big 2-6-6-2 Mallets in a highly publicized pushing contest.

Electrification quickly produced impressive gains in

Unique among electric locomotives were the Milwaukee Road's bipolar gearless passenger locomotives delivered by General Electric in 1918. Bipolar No. 10254 was photographed at Humpback Tunnel, in western Washington, on the westbound Olympian, in 1920. —Asahel Curtis Photo, Washington State Historical Society (Curtis Neg. 41124)

Electrified Railroads, Pacific Northwest. —Tony Howe

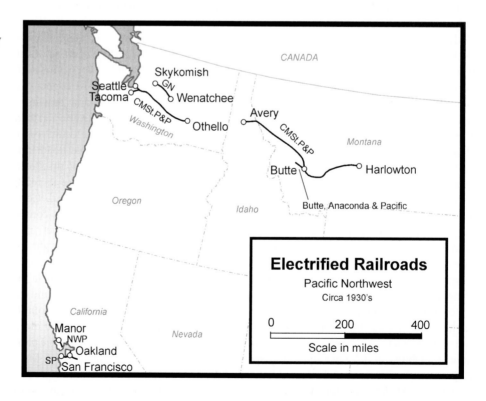

the speed and capacity of train operations over the two mountain ranges. By 1923, for example, 59 electric locomotives handled an annual freight and passenger traffic of nearly 3 million gross ton-miles that would have required an estimated 167 steam locomotives, with net savings in annual operating costs of nearly $1.2 million. To an extraordinary degree the Milwaukee electrification captured the public fancy. There was something wondrous about trains that preserved dwindling reserves of coal and oil by taking their energy from the "white coal" of rushing mountain streams ("making nature drive the wheels"), emitted no smoke or cinders, and frugally returned electricity to the wires through the magic of regenerative braking.

Commuter Electrics

The early suburban-service electrifications at New York and on the Camden–Atlantic City, New Jersey, West Jersey & Seashore quickly demonstrated the advantages of electric operation for high-density, frequent-stop suburban services. It provided much faster acceleration and afforded significant economies in operating costs. M.U. control permitted the distribution of power throughout trains of any length, providing performance characteristics that were far superior to steam power for this class of service as well. Electrification also was the answer to demands for smoke abatement in urban areas.

An early convert was the Southern Pacific, which in 1911 opened an extensive 1,200-volt DC electrification of its network of suburban services at Oakland, California. This was followed a few years later by a 2,400-volt DC terminal and suburban-service electrification of the Canadian Northern Railway's new line into downtown Montreal, which operated through the 3.2-mile Mt. Royal Tunnel.

From an early date the Pennsylvania Railroad's electrification plans extended far beyond the scope of its initial New York tunnel and terminal installation. Only a few years after the New York electrification began operation, the Pennsylvania again turned to electrification to solve increasingly severe terminal-congestion problems on its suburban lines radiating from Broad Street Station in Philadelphia. By 1913 the railroad had approved electrification of its two heaviest routes, extending to Paoli and Chestnut Hill. By this time it was considering the eventual electrification of part of its long-haul main-line system. The third-rail DC system adopted for the New York project clearly would not work well for this, and the railroad decided instead to adopt the 11 kv, single-phase, 25 Hz AC system that by this time had proven itself on the pioneer New Haven installation. The two routes began operating under electric power in 1915 and 1918, and over the next decade and a half the Pennsylvania extended its Philadelphia suburban electrification to West Chester and Norristown, Pennsylvania, and to Wilmington, Delaware, and Trenton, New Jersey.

At New York a Baltimore & Ohio subsidiary, the Staten Island Rapid Transit Railway, completed an electrification of its suburban routes in 1925. Anticipating an eventual tunnel link with the New York subway system, the line was equipped with a third-rail DC system identical to that used by the subway system.

With an unparalleled density of railroad operations, the city of Chicago was intensely interested in electrification as a means of smoke abatement. No railroad was under greater pressure on this score than the Illinois Central, which operated one of the largest U.S. suburban services at Chicago, with an annual traffic that reached 18 million passengers in 1917. Smoke from the IC's prominent lakefront location was a major source of complaint from the Chicago Loop. The railroad had considered suburban-service electrification as early as 1891, but nothing happened until the city forced the issue in 1919 with an ordinance requiring electrification of IC's suburban service by 1927. By 1921 the railroad had begun a massive electrification and terminal improvement program that would encompass both its Chicago-Richton suburban main line and branches to Blue Island and South Chicago. In addition to a 1,500-volt DC electrification, the work included extensive relocation and reconstruction of the IC's lines to create a modern electric suburban service that operated separately from the railroad's freight and long-distance passenger services. New steel and aluminum cars ordered for the service included such advanced features as fully automatic couplers, electro-pneumatic braking, and electrically operated sliding doors for high-level platform loading.

At Boston the narrow-gauge Boston, Revere Beach & Lynn completed a 600-volt DC electrification of its suburban route northeast of downtown Boston in 1928.

The last major suburban carrier in New York to electrify was the Delaware, Lackawanna & Western, which carried 60,000 daily passengers on its suburban routes radiating from Hoboken, New Jersey. Marking a new technological departure for suburban electrification, the Lackawanna adopted a 3,000-volt DC system similar to that employed on the Milwaukee Road's western electrification. Opened in stages during 1930–1931, the electric operation enabled the railroad to reduce its running times by an average of 25 percent and to increase the service frequency.

Close behind the Lackawanna was the Reading Co., which in 1929 initiated the electrification program of its five-route suburban system radiating from Reading Terminal in downtown Philadelphia. The Reading adopted the same 11 kv, single-phase, 25 Hz AC system used by the neighboring Pennsylvania, which by this time had emerged as the most popular U.S. electrification system.

Pennsylvania Railroad Electrification

The Pennsylvania had begun to think seriously about long-distance electrification as early as 1908, when studies

The incomparable GG1 electric locomotive, of which 139 were built for the Pennsylvania Railroad's eastern electrification between 1934 and 1943, operated some of the most demanding passenger and freight schedules anywhere in America. One is shown at the head of the Pennsylvania's premier train, the New York–Chicago *Broadway Limited*. —Pennsylvania Railroad, *Trains* Magazine Collection

were initiated for possible electrification of both the Low Grade Line for freight between Harrisburg and the Philadelphia area and the main line over the Alleghenies. Other studies followed, and in 1917 Pennsylvania shops turned out a huge 240-ton, 4,800-hp electric locomotive that was a prototype for a possible Alleghenies electrification.

By the mid-1920s the railroad's interest had shifted to electrification of its eastern main lines between New York and Washington, which by this time were carrying the heaviest combined passenger and freight traffic on the entire railroad. Studies promised substantial benefits from electrification; without it, for example, additional tracks would be required to accommodate projected traffic growth.

Late in 1928 the railroad announced its plans to electrify the eastern main line from New York to Wilmington, as well as the Low Grade Line west of Philadelphia to Columbia, Pennsylvania. Altogether the work would involve a total of some 325 route-miles and 1,300 track-miles, and the Pennsylvania would acquire 365 new electric freight and passenger locomotives. It was the largest single electrification program yet undertaken anywhere. Only a year later the program was expanded to include electrification all the way to Washington, D.C. A third extension to the electrification plans came in 1937, when the Pennsylvania decided to extend catenary over the main line west to Harrisburg, on the Low Grade Line from Columbia to the Enola classification yard near Harrisburg, and over the Susquehanna River line between Harrisburg and Perryville, Maryland.

Work was under way by 1929 and continued without

interruption despite the onset of the Depression. Electric operation between New York and Philadelphia began in January 1933, followed a month later by electric operation to Wilmington. Early in 1935 the entire route between New York and Washington was complete. Electric service to Harrisburg began in January 1938.

An initial fleet of heavy box-cab electric passenger locomotives proved to have significant shortcomings, and the Pennsylvania in 1933 initiated a test and development program to develop a locomotive suitable for the heavy high-speed service contemplated for the new electrification. Two years of tests produced a design for a 230-ton streamlined class GG1 2-C+C-2 locomotive that would be capable of a short-term output of 8,500 hp and a 120 mph maximum speed. Over the next decade the railroad acquired 139 of the extraordinary GG1s.

The Pennsylvania's investment quickly proved its worth. In 1938 studies showed that electrification had produced annual savings of more than $7.7 million in motive-power operating costs. Running times for both freight and passenger trains were substantially reduced. Most important of all, the electrified eastern main lines of the Pennsylvania proved capable of accommodating an unprecedented volume of freight and passenger traffic during World War II.

Modern Electrification

In 1938 the United States led the world in railroad electrification (Table 1), with 2,400 route-miles and more than 6,300 track-miles under electric power—more than

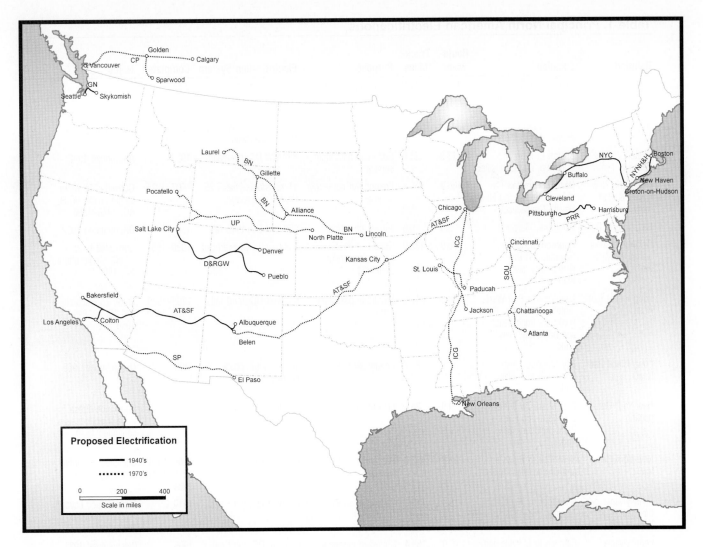

Proposed Electrification. —Tony Howe

20 percent of the world total. A 1936 study for the Federal Power Commission suggested that electrification of an additional 12,000 miles of track on 20 railroads was economically feasible. World War II only temporarily—it was thought—brought any further electrification to a halt.

The war accelerated some technological developments that would make electrification more promising than ever. Chief among these was the development of practical rectifiers for locomotives, an advance that provided an efficient means for converting AC power to DC. This would enable railroads to combine the benefits of high-voltage AC power distribution with the superior performance characteristics of the DC series traction motor, and it made it possible to distribute power at the 60 Hz commercial frequency rather than the low frequency (25 Hz) required for AC-traction motors.

With these advances, electrification proponents anticipated a major expansion of North America's electrified trackage after. Shortly after the war the General Electric

Co. identified some 1,200 route-miles of proposed new electrification, including such projects as a New York Central electrification all the way to Buffalo, an extension of PRR catenary across the Alleghenies to Pittsburgh, the New Haven's long-deferred extension of electric operation to Boston, and a Denver & Rio Grande Western electrification across the Rocky Mountains. But none of it ever materialized.

Although electrification was a proven technology for increasing performance and reducing operating costs, a major barrier to new electrification was its enormous capital cost. Perhaps an even more important contributor to the dearth of new electrification projects was the alternative provided by diesel-electric motive power, which was a proven technology by war's end. Diesel-electric power could not match the performance characteristics of electrics, but it still was a major advance in performance and efficiency over steam power, and one that could be installed at a fraction of the cost of electrification. Capital-short railroads found that it made better

Table 1. Principal North American Electrifications

Railroad	Location	Route-Miles	Track-Miles	Purpose	Electrification System	Completed	Notes
Amtrak	New Haven, Connecticut, to Boston, Massachusetts	156.0	312.0	Passenger service	25 kv, single-phase, 60 Hz AC; overhead	2000	
Boston & Maine	Hoosac Tunnel, North Adams, Massachusetts	7.9	21.4	Tunnel operation	11 kv, single-phase, 25 Hz AC; overhead	1911	Discontinued 1946
Boston, Revere Beach & Lynn	Boston to Lynn and Winthrop, Massachusetts	13.8	31.0	Suburban passenger service	600-volt DC; overhead	1928	Abandoned 1940
New York, New Haven & Hartford	New York to New Canaan, Danbury, and New Haven, Connecticut	106.9	550.7	Freight and passenger service	11 kv, single-phase, 25 Hz AC; overhead	1907–1925	Converted to 13 kv, single-phase, 60 Hz AC, 1978–1986
Baltimore & Ohio	Baltimore, Maryland	3.6	9.6	Tunnel operation	650-volt DC; third rail	1895	Discontinued 1952
Delaware, Lackawanna & Western	Hoboken to Newark, Summit, and Dover, New Jersey, and branches	70.0	133.0	Suburban passenger service and freight switching	3,000-volt DC; overhead	1930–1931	Converted to 25 kv, 60 Hz, single-phase AC, 1984
Long Island Rail Road	New York to Port Washington, Huntington, Ronkonkoma, Long Beach, and Rockaway, New York	126.5	317.5	Suburban passenger service	650-volt DC; third rail	1905–1929, 1970, 1988	Branches discontinued 1932, 1948, 1950
Long Island Rail Road	Bay Ridge to Fresh Pond Junction, New York	11.9	82.7	Freight service	11 kv, single-phase, 25 Hz AC; overhead	1927	Discontinued 1969
New York Connecting	Port Morris to Sunnyside Yard and Fresh Pond Junction, New York	9.0	25.8	Freight service	11 kv, single-phase, 25 Hz AC; overhead	1918–1927	Sunnyside–Fresh Pond Junction discontinued 1969
New York Central	New York to Brewster and Croton, New York	97.8	423.0	Passenger and freight service	600-volt DC; third rail	1906–1913, 1926, 1931, 1984	Branches discontinued 1943, 1959
Pennsylvania Railroad, New York terminal	New York to Manhattan Transfer, New Jersey	13.4	110.1	Passenger service	675-volt DC; third rail	1910	Discontinued beyond Hudson River tunnels, 1932
Pennsylvania Railroad, West Jersey & Seashore	Camden to Millville and Atlantic City, New Jersey	75.0	150.4	Suburban passenger service	650-volt DC; third rail	1906	Discontinued 1931, 1949
Pennsylvania Railroad	New York to Washington, D.C. and Harrisburg, Pennsylvania, and branches	656	2,150	Freight and passenger service	11 kv, single-phase, 25 Hz AC; overhead	1915–1938	Freight lines and Perryville, Maryland–Harrisburg, Pennsylvania, discontinued 1981
Reading	Philadelphia to Norristown, Doylestown, Warminster, West Trenton, and Fox Chase, Pennsylvania	93.2	196.0	Suburban passenger service	11 kv, single-phase, 25 Hz AC; overhead	1931–1933, 1966, 1973	
Norfolk & Western	Iaeger to Bluefield, West Virginia, and branches	55.9	208.7	Freight and passenger service	11 kv, single-phase, 25 Hz AC; overhead	1915–1924	Discontinued 1950
Virginian	Mullens, West Virginia, to Roanoke, Virginia	134.5	229.0	Freight service	11 kv, single-phase, 25 Hz AC; overhead	1925	Discontinued 1962
Cleveland Union Terminal	Cleveland, Ohio	17.0	56.0	Passenger service	3,000-volt DC; overhead	1925	Discontinued 1953
Detroit, Toledo & Ironton	Fordton to Flat Rock, Michigan	16.0	50.0	Freight service	22 kv, single-phase, 25 Hz AC; overhead	1926	Discontinued 1930
Illinois Central	Chicago to South Chicago, Blue Island, and University Park, Illinois	39.6	159.9	Suburban passenger service and freight switching	1,500-volt DC; overhead	1926, 1977	
Michigan Central (NYC System)	Detroit, Michigan–Windsor, Ontario	4.5	28.6	Tunnel operation	650-volt DC; third rail	1910	Discontinued 1953

Table 1. Principal North American Electrifications (*continued*)

Railroad	Location	Route-Miles	Track-Miles	Purpose	Electrification System	Completed	Notes
Butte, Anaconda & Pacific	Butte-Anaconda, Montana	37.4	121.8	Freight and passenger service	2,400-volt DC; overhead	1913	Discontinued 1967
Chicago, Milwaukee, St. Paul & Pacific	Harlowton, Montana–Avery, Idaho; Othello to Seattle and Tacoma, Washington	663.4	892.1	Freight and passenger service	3,000-volt DC; overhead	1915–1927	Discontinued 1972–1974
Great Northern	Cascade Tunnel, Washington	4.0	6.0	Tunnel operation	6,600-volt, three-phase, 25 Hz AC; overhead	1909	Discontinued 1927
Great Northern	Skykomish-Wenatchee, Washington	72.9	93.2	Freight and passenger service	22 kv, single-phase, 25 Hz AC; overhead	1927–1929	Discontinued 1956
Northwestern Pacific	Sausalito to San Anselmo and San Rafael, California, and branches	20.6	41.6	Suburban passenger service	600-volt DC; third rail	1903–1908	Discontinued 1941
Southern Pacific	Oakland to Alameda and Berkeley, California	49.6	118.0	Suburban passenger service	1,200-volt DC; overhead	1911	Discontinued 1941; some lines continued by Key System
Canadian Northern	Montreal to Deux-Montagnes, Quebec, and branches	27.0	46.0	Tunnel operation and suburban passenger service	2,400-volt DC; overhead	1918–1925, 1943, 1946	Branches discontinued 1969, 1988; converted to 25 kv, single-phase, 60 Hz AC, 1995
Grand Trunk	Port Huron, Michigan, to Sarnia, Ontario	4.2	12.2	Tunnel operation	3,300-volt, single-phase, 25 Hz AC; overhead	1908	Discontinued 1958
British Columbia Railway	Wakely to Quinette, British Columbia	81.0		Freight service	25 kv, single-phase, 60 Hz AC; overhead	1984	Discontinued 2000
Mexican National Railways	Mexico City to Queretaro, Guanajuato	136.0		Freight and passenger service	25 kv, single-phase, 60 Hz AC; overhead	1994	Discontinued ca. 1996
Mexican Railway	Esperanza, Puebla, to Paso del Macho, Veracruz	64.0	74.8	Freight and passenger service	3,000-volt DC; overhead	1924–1928	Discontinued 1974
Pacific Electric Railway	Puntarenas–San José, Costa Rica	79.0	93.0	Freight and passenger service	15 kv, single-phase, 20 Hz AC; overhead	1929	Operation suspended 1995
Ferrocarriles de Costa Rica	Río Frio–Puerto Limón, Costa Rica	66.0		Freight and passenger service	25 kv, single-phase, 60 Hz AC; overhead	1982	Operation suspended 1995

sense—and cost less—to dieselize the entire railroad than to electrify one or two divisions.

Indeed, instead of expanding, North American electrification began to contract in the years after the war because of the diesel-electrics. Electrifications installed for smoke abatement in long tunnels impeded the run-through efficiencies of diesel-electric power, and diesel exhausts could be managed with improved tunnel-ventilation systems. By the end of the 1950s electrification was gone from the B&M's Hoosac Tunnel, B&O's Howard Street Tunnel at Baltimore, NYC's Detroit River Tunnel, GN's Cascade Tunnel, and CN-GTW's St. Clair River Tunnel. An electrification that served Cleveland Union Terminal, originally installed for smoke-abatement purposes, was gone by 1953. Mergers shifted traffic patterns and eliminated the need for other electrifications. New coal routings after the 1959 Norfolk & Western–Virginian merger brought an end to the need for the Virginian electrification. N&W's own electrification had reverted to steam operation in 1950 after a line relocation to lower grades.

The Pennsylvania's electrification survived into the 1968 Penn Central merger, and both the PC and the subsequent Conrail considered additional electrification of the old PRR. Conrail, created in 1975, included a congressional pledge for a loan guarantee of $200 million if the railroad should electrify westward from Enola to Pittsburgh. Instead, Conrail brought changes in freight routings that took much of the freight traffic off the former PRR electrified lines, and all electric freight operation was ended in 1981. In the West declining ore traffic brought an end to Butte, Anaconda & Pacific electric operation in 1967, and the Milwaukee Road's aging electrification was shut down in 1974 in favor of run-through diesel-electric power.

Even as these older installations were fading away, there was renewed interest in new electrification, based upon a

The Great Northern Railway's electrification over Stevens Pass in Washington's Cascades combined the advantages of high-voltage single-phase AC current distribution with low-voltage DC-traction motors through the use of a built-in motor-generator system. The last ones built, two W-1-class electrics from General Electric in 1947, were billed as the most powerful single-unit electrics in the world. —Middleton Collection

new concept of high-voltage, commercial-frequency AC systems. A 1965 study by the Edison Electric Institute concluded that there were no technical obstacles to commercial-frequency electrification for high-density corridors and estimated that there were 22,000 track-miles in the United States that supported a traffic density sufficient to warrant electrification. Several new mine-to-generating-plant electrifications in 25 kv or 50 kv systems in Ohio, Texas, and Arizona were seen as prototypes for these proposed new systems. The petroleum-based energy crisis of the 1970s and early 1980s brought rising diesel fuel prices and a much more urgent consideration of electrification.

There was no shortage of potential electrification projects. Southern Pacific, Canadian Pacific, Burlington North-

The 20 Acela Express trains, built by Bombardier/GEC Alstom, are fitted with a tilting capability and are capable of 150 mph operation. Eastbound from Washington to New York, Acela Express No. 2254 raced through Trenton, New Jersey, in June 2001. —William D. Middleton

ern, Union Pacific, Santa Fe, Illinois Central, Southern, and even the bankrupt Penn Central launched studies of major new electrifications, and more than half a dozen other roads at least considered it. But electrification advocates were again doomed to disappointment.

None of the studies led to major new electrifications. There were a few more short coal-line electrifications in the west, and the British Columbia Railway electrified a new branch built for export coal traffic. The only new main-line electrification was for a new National Railways of Mexico route between Mexico City and Querétaro that never did go into full operation.

The culprit, once again, was the diesel-electric. To a degree, too, the drastic reductions of passenger trains helped lessen the importance of many lines. By the mid-1980s diesel fuel prices had begun to fall, and diesel locomotive manufacturers were producing locomotives of steadily improving performance and increasing fuel efficiency. The enormous cost of electrification and the risks and uncertainties associated with electric power cost and availability remained formidable deterrents as well.

As the twenty-first century dawned, a major new North American main-line electrification finally came on line. This was Amtrak's high-speed electrification of the Northeast Corridor between New Haven and Boston, realizing a long-deferred dream of the old New Haven and completing the conversion of the entire corridor to electric operation. Only government financing of the work, however, made it possible.

North American railroads were experiencing a steadily rising curve of annual freight ton-miles, and more and more traffic was being concentrated on key routes as the industry consolidated through mergers. It was possible to foresee a day when new electrification might be needed to meet growing capacity requirements. But would the private rail industry have access to

Eastbound on the Milwaukee Road's St. Paul Pass between Stetson and Kyle, Idaho, two big General Electric 2-D+D-2 high-voltage electrics and two diesels pulled the 70 cars of train 264 on a snowy May in 1974. —Ted Benson, *Trains* Magazine Collection

the capital that would be needed? Or would it require government support, as was necessary to extend Northeast Corridor electrification into Boston, and as has been necessary where electrification has flourished almost everywhere else in the world?

—William D. Middleton

REFERENCES

Burch, Edward P. *Electric Traction for Railway Trains.* New York: McGraw-Hill, 1911.

Friedlander, Gordon D. "Railroad Electrification: Past, Present, and Future." *IEEE Spectrum* 5, no. 7 (July 1968): 50–65; 5, no. 8 (August 1968): 56–66; 5, no. 9 (Sept. 1968): 77–90.

Manson, Arthur J. *Railroad Electrification and the Electric Locomotive.* New York: Simmons-Boardman, 1923.

Middleton, William D. *When the Steam Railroads Electrified.* 2nd ed. Bloomington: Indiana Univ. Press, 2001.

Electro-Motive Division, General Motors Corp.

First an independent company, then a subsidiary, and finally a division of General Motors, Electro-Motive became the most important U.S. diesel locomotive producer. A combination of quality products, aggressive marketing, and fortuitous timing allowed it to dominate the diesel locomotive industry for decades. Its success came at a price, however, attracting the scrutiny of Justice Department antitrust prosecutors and drawing another competitor into the industry. That rival, the General Electric Co. (GE), ultimately wrested market dominance away from Electro-Motive, and since the 1980s the two companies have periodically traded leadership roles in a highly competitive duopolistic diesel locomotive industry.

Harold L. Hamilton established the Electro-Motive Engineering Corp. on August 31, 1922, and changed the name to the Electro-Motive Co. (EMC) a year later. In a varied career Hamilton had worked as an engineer, an inventor, a railroad official (for the Florida East Coast), and a marketing executive for the White Automobile Co. At White, from 1914 until 1922, Hamilton sensed that small internal combustion vehicles, similar to highway buses, could operate reliably and economically on railroads. Hamilton spent much of his career persuading recalcitrant teamsters to accept trucks and teaching them to operate and maintain this unfamiliar technology. From this experience he developed an understanding of the importance of sales and marketing efforts to the successful introduction of a new technology.

Initially, EMC was a small organization, with no more than half a dozen employees. Aside from Hamilton himself, the most important of these was Richard Dilworth, who had worked at General Electric with noted electrical engineer Hermann Lemp. EMC employees were primarily engineers and draftsmen, since the company was a design and marketing, rather than a manufacturing, firm. Dilworth and other engineers developed designs for self-propelled railcars, which were considerably larger than lightweight rail buses. They were roughly the same size as conventional railroad passenger cars and were mechanically compatible with standard railroad equipment. EMC subcontracted the production of railcar bodies to major railway equipment producers, such as the St. Louis Car Co., the Pullman Co., the Osgood-Bradley Car Shops, the Standard Steel Car Co., and the Bethlehem Steel Co. GE provided electrical equipment for most of the railcars, and the Westinghouse Electric & Manufacturing Co. served as a secondary supplier.

EMC developed a close working relationship with the Winton Engine Co., its sole supplier of railcar engines. Between 1924 and 1927 Winton increased the horsepower of its gasoline railcar engines from 175 to 400 and later developed engines that would burn cheaper petroleum distillate. Winton was unsuccessful, however, in its efforts to develop a reliable diesel engine for railcar service.

Although the railcar bodies, electrical equipment, and engines represented the best available technology at the time, the real source of EMC's success lay in Hamilton's marketing programs. EMC bypassed railroad operating and mechanical departments, with their familiarity with and loyalty to steam locomotive technology, and targeted railcars to railroad financial officials by emphasizing their reliability and their cost savings over conventional locomotive-hauled passenger trains. Once EMC had made a sale, company representatives instructed railroad employees in proper railcar operation and maintenance. Rather than repair defective parts in their own shops, railroads returned them to EMC, and the company would send a replacement with all possible speed—employing a chartered plane in at least one instance. Although railroads could select from a variety of options when ordering a new railcar, EMC offered standard rather than custom designs. These marketing programs allowed EMC to shift the locus of railcar technology from the railroad companies and railroad mechanical officers, who controlled steam locomotive technology, to the supplier side of the industry.

EMC's marketing efforts allowed it to gain and retain market dominance throughout the 1920s. However, the onset of the Great Depression caused most railroads to curtail their equipment orders. By this time EMC had also saturated the railcar market, since many passenger and mail routes were far too heavily patronized for fixed-capacity railcars. EMC was well aware that some railroads had violated the company's advice by adding unpowered passenger and even freight cars to their railcars, in effect transforming them into internal combustion locomotives. This practice indicated a small niche market for gasoline or distillate locomotives, a market that would become far more lucrative if Winton could develop a reliable locomotive diesel engine. Despite Hamilton's enthusiasm for diesel locomotives, neither EMC nor Winton possessed the financial or technical resources necessary to launch a diesel-engine research and development program.

During the 1920s, while EMC entered the railcar industry, General Motors attempted to develop lightweight, reliable diesel engines for truck, bus, and automobile use. By the end of the decade GM had elected to purchase an established diesel-engine producer and in June 1930 acquired Winton as a wholly owned subsidiary. In December 1930 GM also bought EMC, the largest single purchaser of Winton engines. While GM initially had little interest in producing diesel locomotives, EMC's Harold Hamilton (who retained his position as EMC's president) turned the situation to his advantage. Hamilton understood that EMC's size and capital requirements, tiny by GM standards, would allow the subsidiary to avoid close scrutiny from GM executives. At the same time, EMC would have access to GM capital, facilities, and technical expertise.

Charles Francis Kettering, an extraordinarily talented GM engineer, illustrated the importance of this symbiotic relationship between EMC and GM. Kettering was intrigued by the technical challenges associated with diesel locomotives, which allowed Hamilton to lobby persuasively for R&D funds and technical support. Kettering, in turn, served as a strong advocate for EMC, and for a locomotive program, with GM president Alfred P. Sloan, Jr. As part of his research focus on automobile and truck diesel engines, Kettering worked with Winton engineers to develop lighter and more reliable fuel injectors and to transform Winton's heavy four-stroke diesel design into a much lighter two-stroke engine. Despite these improvements, the redesigned GM-Winton engine, the Model 201, was far too large for highway use, and there seemed little immediate prospect of reducing its size and weight to an appreciable degree.

Although it was ill suited to its intended application, the Model 201 was ideally sized to fit into submarines, and the U.S. Navy became an early customer for these engines. Two Model 201 engines provided power for the GM Building at the 1933 Chicago World's Fair. Although these engines malfunctioned frequently, the media and the public responded enthusiastically to this new technology. One visitor, Ralph Budd, president of the Chicago, Burlington & Quincy, was so impressed that he agreed to Hamilton's suggestion to equip a new, lightweight trainset with the Model 201 engine. Budd and Hamilton helped persuade Kettering, who in turn persuaded Sloan, that the Model 201 could operate successfully in rail service.

The Budd Co. (whose president, Edward G. Budd, was distantly related to Ralph Budd) completed the stainless-steel *Zephyr* streamliner in 1934. This four-car diesel-powered trainset was a phenomenal success, decreasing travel time, lowering operating costs, and attracting publicity and crowds. Along with the Union Pacific's distillate-powered M-10000 (with an EMC engine and a Pullman carbody), the *Zephyr* spawned a new generation of integrated trainsets. Their success was largely the result of technological convergence, since new fabrication techniques, including Budd's Shotweld process, and the increased use of aluminum and Cor-Ten steel reduced weight to a degree that would not overwhelm early GM diesel engines. These trainsets required railroads to create operating and maintenance facilities that would support long-distance diesel locomotive service and allowed EMC technicians to develop a working relationship with railroad officials. Although EMC sold fewer than two dozen trainsets, they constituted an effective point of entry into the diesel locomotive market. Electro-Motive trainsets had their limitations, however. Their articulated, fixed consist limited capacity, and they were generally not compatible with other passenger equipment. Furthermore, the Model 201 engine had not been designed for, nor was it ideally suited to, railroad service.

In 1935 GM and EMC committed to a research and development program to design a diesel engine for railroad service and to develop stand-alone diesel locomotives. EMC broke ground on a new factory at La Grange, Illinois, near Chicago. While the facility was still under construction, EMC subcontracted production of 12 box-cab test locomotives. Once La Grange opened, the company manufactured standard-design yard switching locomotives, initially employing the Model 201 engine. This was a logical first step, since switchers would rarely stray far from a maintenance facility, and since low-speed diesel switching offered the greatest economic advantage over steam switchers.

In 1937 EMC began production of its E-series passen-

Many thousands of diesels built in EMD's huge plant at La Grange, Illinois, operated all over the world. This view of the La Grange locomotive high bay dates to the time of the record-breaking F-unit diesels. —*Trains* Magazine Collection

ger locomotives, which introduced long-distance diesel locomotives to many railroads and also served as useful test beds for EMC's emerging diesel locomotive research and development program. In 1938 EMC introduced the Model 567 diesel engine (as with all Electro-Motive engines, the model number refers to cylinder capacity, in cubic inches) and also began manufacturing its own electrical equipment, based on GE designs.

In November 1939 EMC completed its prototype FT freight locomotive in an effort to tap into the largest single component of the diesel locomotive market by replacing steam locomotives on long-distance freight trains. The FT was successful from both a technical and a sales standpoint, at a time when EMC's rivals, the American Locomotive Co. (Alco) and the Baldwin Locomotive Works, were struggling to produce quality diesel freight locomotives.

World War II had a profound effect on Electro-Motive. The U.S. military flooded it with orders for diesel engines, primarily for use in landing craft and PT boats. The military used Electro-Motive engines throughout the world, exposing a generation of mechanics to that company's technology. In response to this unprecedented demand and equally unprecedented profits, GM transformed its subsidiary, the Electro-Motive Co., into the Electro-Motive Division (EMD), effective January 1, 1941. EMD accommodated wartime demand by developing standardized production techniques and organizational methods to match its earlier standardization in locomotive designs. When the War Production Board issued General Limitation Order L-97 in April 1942, it prohibited the manufacture (although not the basic research and development) of new diesel locomotive designs. Since EMD possessed the only proven diesel freight locomotive design

(the prewar FT), it enjoyed a temporary wartime monopoly in that sector of the diesel locomotive market. Although War Production Board records do not indicate any friction during the war itself, by the 1950s Baldwin and Alco alleged that L-97 had given EMD an unfair advantage just as its competitors were poised to enter the diesel freight locomotive market. It is worth noting, however, that EMD was forced to suspend locomotive production for several months during the war to accommodate more pressing military demands, and that EMD lost market share to its competitors between 1941 and 1945.

EMD enjoyed phenomenal success in the decade after 1945. Baldwin had failed to develop reliable diesel locomotives, and Alco was still struggling to compensate for a midwar decision to change the direction of its diesel-engine research program. The two new competitors who entered the diesel locomotive market, Fairbanks-Morse and Lima-Hamilton, were of little consequence. As railroads rushed to replace a generation of steam locomotives worn out by wartime service, EMD's orders soared, creating a two-year backlog. In addition to its E-series passenger and F-series freight units, EMD's GP (General Purpose) and GP9 road switcher locomotives, introduced in 1949 and 1954, respectively, ensured market dominance in the postwar years, with nearly 7,000 of those two models sold. Although La Grange had been expanded substantially during World War II, EMD opened two ancillary plants, one in Chicago, the other in Cleveland. In 1950 another GM subsidiary, GM Diesel, Ltd., opened a manufacturing facility in London, Ontario, to supply the Canadian market in conformity with that nation's domestic content laws. EMD's share of the U.S. diesel locomotive market climbed from 46 percent in 1946 to 89 percent by 1957, and in one year (1951) the division earned an impressive

An electrician at the La Grange plant completes the commutator ring for a diesel-engine traction motor. —*Trains* Magazine Collection

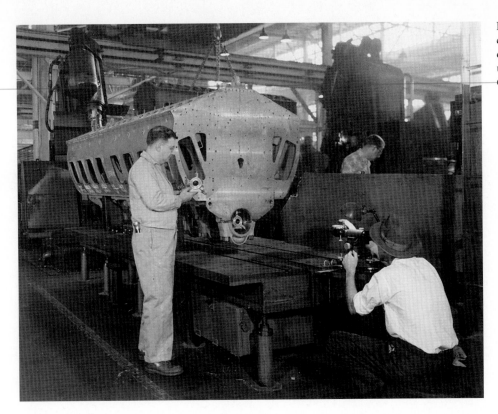

269 percent return on its investment in plant and equipment. Its overall return on investment during the entire decade of the 1950s was 144 percent.

EMD's success attracted the ire of its competitors and the scrutiny of the U.S. Department of Justice. This was, after all, at a time that predated the influence of economists like John Kenneth Galbraith and business historians like Alfred D. Chandler, Jr., who showed that underlying structural conditions, and not illegality or unfairness, could concentrate economic power in a few large corporations. In 1955 the Subcommittee on Antitrust and Monopoly of the Senate Judiciary Committee investigated GM and concluded that that company's size and financial might were crucial to EMD's success in the diesel locomotive industry. By the end of the 1950s the Justice Department had filed antitrust suits charging GM with monopolizing the bus- and highway-construction equipment industries. In a 1961 criminal suit and a 1963 civil suit the Justice Department specifically charged GM with violating both the Sherman and Clayton antitrust acts by creating a monopoly for EMD in the diesel locomotive industry. Justice Department attorneys, supported by testimony from railroad officials and executives at EMD's competitors, made three basic allegations against EMD. Some suggested that the WPB's 1942 L-97 order had crippled Alco and Baldwin just as they were poised to challenge EMD in the freight diesel market. Others argued that GM's near-simultaneous purchase of EMC and Winton in 1930 constituted acquisitions that tended to create a monopoly. Perhaps the most serious allegation involved reciprocity, suggesting that GM, as the largest single rail shipper in the United States, had promised to give preferential routing to railroads that agreed to purchase EMD locomotives. Despite these allegations, the Justice Department could not prove reciprocity or any other charge and dropped both cases in 1964.

The antitrust suits affected EMD in two significant ways. First, EMD realized that although it was possible to maintain a high market share, this course of action was politically unwise and had the added drawback of creating excess capacity in the event of a decline in locomotive orders. Second, railroad officials realized that EMD's near monopoly of the diesel locomotive industry, legal or not, tended to retard innovation and make competitive bidding on locomotive orders unrealistic. To preserve competition in the locomotive industry, railroads ordered some locomotives from Alco, EMD's last surviving competitor, even though that company produced technologically inferior products.

The evident necessity for a secondary competitor in the locomotive industry attracted the interest of GE, and that company's Transportation Systems Division, based in Erie, Pennsylvania, ultimately became EMD's rival. Since the 1930s GE had produced export diesel locomotives and small diesels for domestic industrial and shortline railway use. In 1959 GE introduced its first domestic diesel freight locomotive model, the U25B. Although these early GE U-Boats, as they were popularly called, lacked the reliability of EMD units, they were good enough to allow GE to replace Alco as the secondary producer in the diesel locomotive industry. EMD responded to the growing threat posed by GE by replacing the long-serving Model 567 diesel engine with

A crane at EMD's La Grange, Illinois, plant lowers one of 60 new SD50 diesels onto its trucks for delivery to Union Pacific System's Missouri Pacific Railroad in 1984. —*Trains* Magazine Collection

the Model 645 engine in 1965. In 1972 EMD introduced the Dash-2 series of locomotives, which incorporated improved electrical equipment and control systems. This series included the popular GP38-2 and SD40-2 locomotives, among others, and these continued EMD's success through the late 1970s.

During the 1980s EMD lost ground to GE. Railroads attempted to maximize pulling power and minimize fuel consumption through the use of increasingly sophisticated control systems, and this gave an advantage to electrical equipment producer GE. Many customers also considered GE's four-cycle diesel-engine design to be more fuel-efficient than EMD's two-cycle version. GE introduced a new Dash-8 locomotive line in 1985, using sophisticated microprocessor technology to regulate engine speed and fuel consumption. In that year EMD's market share fell to 40 percent, and the division lost market dominance for the first time since 1935.

EMD responded by spending $60 million between 1980 and 1984 to develop the Model 710 diesel engine, which the division installed in its new 60-Series locomotives. Managers at EMD also recognized that decades of success in the locomotive industry had led to complacency and the ossification of organizational routines. They tried to combat this rigidity by soliciting suggestions from customers and employees and by eliminating many traditional job classifications and work rules. EMD's new products and managerial innovations enabled the division to regain market dominance in 1984, only to lose it to GE in 1987.

New electrical equipment technology, in the form of alternating-current-traction motors, strengthened EMD's position in the locomotive industry. EMD modified European AC technology, obtained from Siemens, to suit American operating conditions. Although American freight railroads expressed interest in AC-traction motors, it was passenger carrier Amtrak that purchased EMD's first AC-motored F69PH locomotives in 1989. The success of these locomotives led to the first large order for AC-equipped EMD freight locomotives, for Burlington Northern, in March 1993. GE also introduced AC locomotive models, and, more recently, railroads have begun to return to conventional DC motor designs as the applications best suited for AC traction have been filled; both factors undermined EMD's early lead in this field.

EMD also responded to competitive pressures by allowing customers greater control over the design and manufacturing process, a flexibility that echoed traditional steam locomotive production. The division offered increasingly customized locomotive designs and in 1994 supplied locomotive components to Conrail, allowing that railroad to complete the manufacturing process at its Altoona, Pennsylvania, shops. Foreign orders have also helped EMD withstand declines in domestic orders.

In spite of these innovations, EMD experienced considerable difficulties during the final decades of the twentieth century. By 1993 GE diesels were outselling EMD units two to one, although extreme fluctuations in railroad demand make year-by-year comparisons difficult. EMD temporarily suspended production at its La Grange facility in 1983, 1987, and 1988. In 1991 GM explored the possibility of selling EMD or else transforming it into a joint venture, but was unable to interest any company in either proposal. EMD assembled its last locomotives at La Grange in 1992. In 2000 EMD demolished a large portion of the La Grange plant. EMD maintains its headquarters at La Grange and produces locomotive components (including diesel engines) at that location. Final assembly of all locomotives takes place at EMD's London, Ontario, facility. It is difficult to predict such variables as the health of the economy, the role of the railroad industry in a multinational economy, the price of oil, the impact of environmental regulation, and the maturation of locomotive technology, but EMD seems likely to remain a viable and innovative competitor in the global locomotive industry.

Early in 2005 GM sold EMD to a consortium of Greenbrier Equity Group LLC and Berkshire Partners LLC. The firm is now named Electro-Motive Diesel.

—Albert J. Churella

REFERENCES

Churella, Albert J. *From Steam to Diesel: Managerial Customs and Organizational Capabilities in the Twentieth-Century American Locomotive Industry.* Princeton, N.J.: Princeton Univ. Press, 1998.

Reck, Franklin M. *On Time: The History of Electro-Motive Division of General Motors Corporation.* Detroit, Mich.: GM-EMD, 1948.

Wilson, Jeff. *E Units: Electro-Motive's Classic Streamliners.* Milwaukee, Wis.: Kalmbach, 2002.

———. *F Units: The Diesels That Did It.* Milwaukee, Wis.: Kalmbach, 1999.

See also LOCOMOTIVE BUILDERS.

Elgin, Joliet & Eastern Railway

The Elgin, Joliet & Eastern Railway, known as the "J," describes an arc around Chicago from Gary, Indiana, to Waukegan, Illinois. It intersects with every other railroad entering Chicago and serves as a belt line; its other nickname is Chicago Outer Belt. Its primary role for many years was to serve the steel mills at Gary and their owner, U.S. Steel.

Its earliest ancestor was a railroad chartered in 1884 by a group of businessmen in Joliet, Illinois, to build west from the Indiana-Illinois state line through Joliet and Aurora to the Mississippi River opposite Dubuque. Its purpose was to give the steel mills and stone quarries of Joliet an outlet to other railroads. The Joliet, Aurora & Northern opened between Joliet and Aurora in 1886. Traffic was slow to develop, and the road's backers decided to turn the railroad into a belt line around Chicago.

J. P. Morgan was attracted by the railroad. A syndicate he directed purchased it and incorporated the Elgin, Joliet & Eastern Railway to extend the JA&N north to Elgin, Illi-

nois, and east into the northeast corner of Indiana. While the EJ&E was under construction, it backed two other railroads: the Waukegan & Southwestern, to extend the EJ&E northeast to the shore of Lake Michigan at Waukegan, and the Gardner, Coal City & Northern, which built south from Plainfield, halfway between Joliet and Aurora, into a coal-mining area. Both of those railroads became part of the EJ&E in 1891. In 1893 the EJ&E extended its line east to Porter, Indiana, where several trunk-line railroads intersected east of the south end of Lake Michigan.

In 1898 the EJ&E, Illinois Steel, and Minnesota Iron came under the ownership of Federal Steel and Elbert H. Gary. In 1901 Federal Steel and Carnegie Steel merged to form U.S. Steel. The new company built a huge steel mill in the dunes at the south end of Lake Michigan and laid out and incorporated a city nearby, named for Gary.

The EJ&E inherited trackage rights on the Chicago & Eastern Illinois south to coal mines near Danville, Illinois, for trains moving limestone and coal north. It used those trackage rights until 1947. The EJ&E had the world's first electrically operated automatic car retarders and was the first railroad to install welded rail on its main line. It completed dieselization relatively early, in 1949. In 1976 part of the Aurora Branch, the original part of the railroad, was abandoned; the rest was abandoned in 1985, as was the line between Griffith, Indiana, and Porter.

In 1988 U.S. Steel began to sell its railroads. They were acquired by Transtar Corp., of which USX, successor to U.S. Steel, owns 49 percent. The Elgin, Joliet & Eastern should get a new role as a commuter rail carrier when the Northeast Illinois Rail Corp. adds a planned Metra circumferential route between Joliet and O'Hare International Airport, part of it located on EJ&E track.

—George H. Drury

REFERENCES

Blaszak, Michael W. "Big Steel's Belt Line." *Trains* 49, no. 10 (Aug. 1989): 26–35.

———. "Crossing Bridges as They Come." *Trains* 49, no. 11 (Sept. 1989): 28–41.

Equipment Identification and Fault Detection

Since the dawn of railroading, railroads have sought to improve their ability to identify the equipment traveling over their systems. Into the mid-twentieth century equipment identification was done manually. Rail employees walked through yards doing a "yard check," writing down the numbers of the cars on hand. Operators or clerks at outlying stations used the same method, filling out forms listing the cars in their yard or siding track and passing this information on to operating crews, who in turn passed the lists to clerks, yardmasters, and other personnel.

In the 1960s technology advanced to the point where automatic equipment identification became a reality. In the spring of 1965 the Duluth, Missabe & Iron Range Railway became the first U.S. railroad to install Kartrak, Sylvania's automatic car identification system. The technology was revolutionary then: trackside scanners sent out beams of white light and received colored reflected light from colored bar codes on the sides of passing cars. The strips contained information that identified each car by number and empty weight. The system was field tested by the Missabe for more than three years before it was put into general use. It was supposed to allow railroads, car owners, and shippers to track anything that moved by rail and pass on the information about a particular car's whereabouts to a central computer.

The ACI system went into nationwide use in the late 1960s and through the 1970s. But the scanners had problems reading labels that were dirty or damaged. Since road grime is a part of railroading, railroads gradually abandoned the system, and the tags were removed from equipment. The Missabe continued to use ACI since it had an almost 100 percent captive car fleet. The railroad placed washers at various locations to keep the labels clean.

Other railroads returned to the pencil-and-paper method of checking cars. Some railroads installed cameras at key points, usually at entrances to yards. These cameras were placed in bungalows on raised platforms and had high-speed shutters to record car numbers as the train passed into or out of the yard. But this system was employed more to verify the consists of incoming or outgoing trains than to provide true electronic identification.

U.S. railroads did not seriously search for another car identification system until 1986, when Burlington Northern Railroad (BN), which had been following the efforts of various maritime shipping companies to find an automatic system to identify their containers, began testing an Automatic Equipment Identification (AEI) program using two vendors, General Railway Signal (GRS) and Union Switch & Signal (US&S). Amtech Corp. of Dallas, Texas, manufactured the US&S identification system. The technology involved applying AEI data tags to each car. These are essentially computer circuits in plastic boxes measuring roughly 3 by 10 inches. The data tags are mounted to the left of both sides of a piece of rolling stock about 48 inches above the rail. A radio transponder in each tag broadcasts a locomotive's, freight car's, trailer's, container's, or end-of-train device's information to trackside readers as a train rolls by. Each tag has information that indicates the particular piece of equipment it is attached to and includes the equipment type, owner, and road number. There is no maintenance since the tags do not use any batteries. Instead, the trackside readers use a 900 MHz radio signal to reflect off the data tag and modulate the information back to the reader.

In January 1988 BN equipped 1,500 taconite-iron-ore cars in northern Minnesota with a GRS system and an Amtech transponder. Each vendor also installed three wayside reader sites, and tags were mounted on the sides of each car. In August 1988 a presentation by BN to the Assn. of American Railroads (AAR) reported that the accuracy of both systems over a six-month period was in excess of 99.99 percent. On the basis of these results an AAR committee was formed to develop an Automatic Equipment Identification standard. Other railroads, such as Canadian National, CSX, Norfolk Southern, and Union Pacific, began their own testing and reported equal success. In August 1989 the AAR selected Amtech's identification technology as the AEI standard. The AAR mandated that two AEI tags be mounted on each railcar, one on each side, by December 31, 1994. By that date all 1.4 million railcars in North American railroad interchange service were tagged, as were over 20,000 locomotives. By the turn of the twenty-first century North American railroads had installed over 3,000 AEI readers.

The railroad's traffic or customer service department can use the AEI system to locate a customer shipment at almost any point of its trip. It also helps with billing information by eliminating entry errors normally found with manual reporting systems. The standards for the AEI system are the same as those used in the maritime and trucking industry, so intermodal equipment can be reported as well. The system is now used to identify not only railcars and locomotives, but also trucks, trailers, containers, and automobiles. New data tags have also been developed and marketed to railroads that can transmit information about a piece of equipment's well-being. These tags are called Automatic Equipment Management (AEM) data tags and can transmit information to the trackside readers such as how a locomotive is running or how much fuel a mechanical refrigerator car has left.

As railroad cars roll along the rails, they are subject to the forces of friction. Fortunately, there is very little friction between the car wheels and the rail itself, but the bearings that support the wheels are another story. For about the first 100 years of railroad operation, axle bearings on rail equipment were of the friction type. Each axle end rotated inside a journal box that was attached to a frame at each side of the truck and provided space inside the truck to house a brass bushing and a lubricant supply. The box had a cover hinged at the top for inspection and the addition of lubricants. Initially, the lubricant was fed to the bearing with packed cotton waste. Later, spring-loaded pads or wicks were used. If the lubrication failed, the bearing would heat quickly and produce what was known as a "hotbox," which could lead to the failure of the axle and possible derailment. Until technology progressed sufficiently, the only way to prevent such failures was regular inspection of the axle and the friction bearings. Once a train was out on the road, the only way to detect such faults was for an alert crew in the locomotive, caboose, or line-side station to spot the

smoking hotbox and stop the train before a catastrophic failure occurred.

Many hotboxes were prevented with the advent of roller bearings in the 1930s. Although roller bearings, were more expensive, they rapidly supplanted the friction bearing since they were sealed and required no periodic maintenance. But even roller bearings occasionally overheat and produce hotboxes. In the 1970s railroads began placing automated wayside defect detectors or "hotbox detectors" along their tracks to provide advance warning about potentially defective equipment. These detectors initially were connected to depots, towers, or dispatchers' offices and produced a paper tape readout that the operator or dispatcher examined to determine if there was a hotbox. If there was a malfunction, the operator or dispatcher called the train by radio. If no radio was available, signals or train orders were used to stop the train for inspection. Detectors were also developed that could identify dragging equipment.

The successor to the tape system was detectors with lights and/or a monitor display board. This system employed a large display board mounted on a signal bungalow or pole along the tracks. On the top or bottom of the board was a series of lights. As the train approached, one light was activated that let the train crew know that the system was working. The monitor display board indicating the condition of the train was visible from the caboose after the movement had passed the detector. Crewmembers had to look back to determine the applicable information. The board displayed large numbers that indicated the axle number of the defect or defects, and the position of the lights on the board (north or south) told the crew on which side of the train to look for the defect(s). In addition to hotboxes, some railroads checked for dragging equipment using monitor display detectors.

Another variation of the dragging-equipment detector employed a simple alarm light system. A green light mounted on a pole or bungalow indicated that the detector was working. After the train passed, the caboose crew looked back at the light; if it remained green, there were no defects. If it had turned red, the train had to stop and be inspected.

As the railroads dropped cabooses from their trains, the display board detectors were replaced by a simpler system: detectors that "talked" via radio directly to the trains. These detectors employ a computer-generated voice to send a radio signal directly to the train. The detector tells the train crew if there is a defect or not. It often also incorporates other information such as train speed, direction, and outside temperature. If there is a defect, the detector provides the crew with the axle number so the train can be stopped and inspected. These detectors are placed at regular intervals along the tracks, ranging from 10 to 30 miles apart. To minimize radio chatter on some busy main lines, the railroads have set up the detectors to talk only if there is a defect. Although these detectors are still effective for heat from a dragging brake, unless they are placed very close together, they can sometimes miss an overheated roller bearing, which can fail rapidly with a minimal amount of heat.

New acoustic detection systems employ computer technology and use microphones near the track. These detectors use "acoustic signatures" to identify bearings with defects before they fail. Under development are bearings containing an internal defect sensor, but this is an expensive option since thousands of railcars would need to be retrofitted with the new bearings.

—Steve Glischinski

REFERENCES

Car and Locomotive Cyclopedia. New York: Simmons-Boardman, 1974, 1997.
Fremont & Elkhorn Valley Railroad "Flash," no. 14 (Mar. 2003).
Interview with Bud Bulgrin, Soo Line Communications Department (retired), Nov. 17, 2003.
Thompson, Keith. "Tracking Freight Cars: AEI Data Tags and Readers." *Trains* 56, no. 1 (Jan. 1996): 86–88.

Erie Lackawanna Railroad

One of the earlier mergers in the post–World War II era of railroad consolidation involved the 2,313-mile Erie Railroad, headquartered in Cleveland, and the 940-mile Delaware, Lackawanna & Western Railroad (Lackawanna), based in New York City. They were historic competitors: both connected New York City with Buffalo, New York. The Erie had long experienced financial difficulties, including four bankruptcies, and deserved the moniker Weary Erie; the Lackawanna had enjoyed a mostly stable history and had never entered the bankruptcy court. For decades this important carrier of anthracite or "stone" coal and high-rated merchandise freight generated handsome profits, allowing its board of managers to pay extra dividends. By the 1950s, though, both companies had encountered serious money problems. Because of common interests and a closeness of officials, in the mid-1950s the Erie and Lackawanna began sharing their physical plants. After several successes, including elimination of duplicate freight facilities in Binghamton and Elmira, New York, the carriers decided that a merger might be appropriate. After considerable haggling, a corporate marriage occurred. On October 17, 1960, the 3,188-mile Erie-Lackawanna Railroad (the hyphen soon disappeared) made its debut, and its snappy diamond banner flew proudly from New York to Chicago.

After a shaky start the Erie Lackawanna showed some promise. Within several years merger savings amounted to about $21 million annually, supporting the finding reached by the company's consulting firm, Wyer, Dick. However, managerial troubles plagued the company. There existed real rivalries between former Erie and Lackawanna personnel. The new firm unfortunately inherited the corporate culture of the Erie, which was characterized by cronyism, laziness, and laxity. Some of the best administrative talent left, creating a leadership crisis that prompted EL's board of directors to respond. In 1963 the board appointed William White, former president of the Lackawanna and the New York Central, to the presidency with instructions to clean house. This he did, and EL found renewed strength. Employee morale improved, and the company stopped bleeding red ink. New equipment, including powerful locomotives, helped the road maintain its competitiveness for freight shippers. Furthermore, White closed six terminal yards to save millions of dollars annually and increase freight-train efficiency. He directed the company to reopen a heavy-car repair facility in Meadville, Pennsylvania, that, although built in the late 1950s, had never been brought into full operation. The bad-order ratio of cars in the EL freight fleet soon dropped from 15.9 percent to an acceptable 4.5 percent. White began to chip away at chronic suburban-service losses in New Jersey, ultimately leading to healthy state subsidies. Yet White and his associates were realists. Megamergers, which eventually produced Penn Central, CSX, and Norfolk Southern, were in the process of development, and smaller, poorer roads like EL needed to find corporate partners.

After White's sudden death in 1965 and deteriorating financial conditions, the course of the EL changed significantly. The Interstate Commerce Commission (ICC) pressured Norfolk & Western (N&W) to take charge. EL had wanted to be part of the 1964 merger that created an enlarged N&W from the old N&W, the New York, Chicago & St. Louis (Nickel Plate Road), and the Wabash, but the N&W did not wish to take in EL. Legal disputes followed, and on March 27, 1968, the U.S. Supreme Court upheld the ICC's position. N&W assumed control indirectly through a wholly owned subsidiary called Dereco.

The N&W did its best with Erie Lackawanna Railway, the new corporate entity. N&W president Herman Pevler sent his able senior vice president, John Fishwick, to Cleveland to head what was considered a booby prize. Fishwick labored hard, and the arrival of the N&W team boosted employee spirits throughout the railroad. EL generated a net income of $1.2 million in 1969, but it lost nearly $11 million the following year, another $2.2 million in 1971, and a whopping $16.2 million between January 1 and June 26, 1972. The N&W era came to an end shortly after Hurricane Agnes devastated large sections of the EL in New York and Pennsylvania and threw the EL into bankruptcy.

EL became a corporate basket case. Employees, shippers, investors, and politicians worried about its future. For many, EL was an ideal candidate for Conrail, the quasi-public corporation that the federal government created to absorb several bankrupt roads, including Penn Central, but EL management attempted to reorganize. Although efforts to increase traffic produced some success, the impacts of deferred maintenance, the Arab oil boycott, and rampant inflation forced EL into Conrail on April 1, 1976.

The real losers of the EL's absorption into this government-sponsored carrier were those shippers who no longer enjoyed access to the "Friendly Service Route." Particularly hard hit were freight customers along the former Erie in Ohio and Indiana. Not only did Conrail quickly end through service between New York and Chicago, but salvage dealers subsequently pulled up much of the track. Those assets not conveyed to Conrail were administered by Erie Lackawanna Inc. (EL Inc.), a Cleveland-based company that paid the remaining obligations, including back property taxes and the face value and accrued interest on secured and unsecured bonds. Before EL Inc. was dissolved in 1992, it won a protracted battle with the federal government over the value of property transferred to Conrail. The government's initial offer was approximately $60 million, but the settlement amounted to more than $350 million. This allowed the old "Erie Lack-of-money" to exit the corporate world in a blaze of glory. "We drove to the cemetery in a Cadillac," quipped a member of EL Inc.'s board of directors.

In 1974, shortly before its April 1, 1976, merger into Conrail, Erie Lackawanna operated a system of 2,928 route-miles and 6,052 track-miles, with 519 locomotives, 181 passenger cars, 21,140 freight and company service cars, and 11,664 employees. Freight traffic totaled 12.9 billion ton-miles in 1974, and food products (15 percent), transportation equipment (10 percent), chemicals (9 percent), and coal (7 percent) were its principal traffic sources. Erie Lackawanna operating revenues totaled $322.7 million in 1974, and the railroad achieved an 81.2 percent operating ratio.

—H. Roger Grant

REFERENCES

Carleton, Paul. *The Erie Lackawanna Story*. River Vale, N.J.: D. Carleton, 1974.

Grant, H. Roger. *Erie Lackawanna: Death of an American Railroad, 1938–1992*. Stanford, Calif.: Stanford Univ. Press, 1994.

Saunders, Richard, Jr. *Merging Lines: American Railroads, 1900–1970*. DeKalb: Northern Illinois Univ. Press, 2001.

Erie Railroad

In 1851 the first portion of the eventual Erie Railroad opened under the corporate banner of the New-York & Erie Railway Co. The 447-mile, 6-foot-gauge line "between the ocean and the lake" was touted as the "technological marvel of the age." Specifically, the Erie built across the rugged southern tier of New York counties from the village of Piermont, on the Hudson River about 25 miles north of New York City, to Dunkirk, a small community on Lake Erie southwest of Buffalo. It soon recognized that both Piermont and Dunkirk terminals were mistakes and subsequently built lines to the Port of New York at Jersey City, New Jersey, and to Buffalo.

In 1859, because of bad management and other factors, the New-York & Erie fell into bankruptcy. The reorganized company, the Erie Railway, never became the profitable property that its leaders had expected and led to a battle for control by speculator Daniel Drew, Cornelius Vanderbilt of the New York Central & Hudson River Railroad, and stock traders Jim Fisk and Jay Gould. The so-called Great Erie War, which erupted in 1867, created additional financial problems, but when the victorious Gould took control, he made it a much better property. "[Before Gould] its iron was worn and its roadbed in bad order," reported the *Railroad Gazette* in 1871. "There is now no better track in America. Then it was scarcely safe to run twenty miles an hour; now the road is as safe at forty-five miles as human precaution can make it." But unfortunately for both the Erie and Gould, the "scarlet woman of Wall Street" image forever haunted them.

The Erie continued to struggle. In the early 1870s the talented Gould left the Erie, and the road limped along under ineffectual leadership into its second bankruptcy. In the widespread depression triggered by the panic of 1873, the company experienced serious financial woes. By the end of the decade a better day had dawned for the Erie, reorganized in 1878 as the New York, Lake Erie & Western Railroad. Modernization of rail and rolling stock, conversion to standard gauge, and creation of an expanded, albeit patchwork, system that featured a main line nearly 1,000 miles long between Jersey City and Chicago encouraged investors, employees, and customers. But hard times returned in the wake of the catastrophic panic of 1893, and once again the Erie stumbled. A third bankruptcy followed.

In 1895 a "new" Erie emerged; the New York, Lake Erie & Western moniker gave way to simply Erie Railroad. Even though the road experienced a relatively rapid reorganization, it lacked a financial structure that would have truly enhanced its chances of avoiding future difficulties. By the early twentieth century the Erie had become a Morgan property, controlled by the giant J. P. Morgan & Co. Generally, this relationship with the House of Morgan worked to the advantage of the Erie. Its debt sold well, making possible a substantial upgrading of its physical plant. Perhaps the capstone of this rehabilitation work was an impressive line relocation in southern New York. The Erie also acquired modern steam locomotives and freight and passenger equipment. The old joke "I want to go to Chicago in the worst way . . . Take the Erie!" no longer seemed appropriate. The Morgan connection brought to the presidency Frederick Underwood, who did yeoman service for the company during his 26-year tenure.

In the 1920s the Erie underwent a major change of ownership and management. In 1923 two emerging rail titans from Cleveland, Ohio, O. P. and M. J. Van Sweringen, bachelor brothers who already controlled the Nickel Plate Road, began buying large blocks of Erie stock. The Vans particularly liked the Erie's easy-grade, double-track speedway between Ohio and Chicago. As they acquired other railroads through clever stock arrangements, the brothers attempted to receive regulatory approval to unite their properties into a great system. Twice, however, the ICC refused to let them bring the Erie under control of their Chesapeake & Ohio Railway.

The Great Depression of the 1930s sent the Vans' empire into disarray, resulting in still another receivership for the Erie. At the end of 1941 the railroad emerged from court protection and prospered from heavy wartime traffic. Reduced interest payments and robust wartime earnings prompted the Erie Railroad (its name after the reorganization remained the same) to declare a modest dividend in 1942, the first in 69 years—a proud moment for management. The press release, orchestrated by its image-conscious president Robert Woodruff, said, in part, "Wall Street tradition was shattered and Brokers were dazedly groping for reliable replacements for the immemorial dictums—When Erie Common pays a dividend, there'll be icicles in hell—and three things are certain—Death, Taxes, and no dividends for Erie Common."

Unlike the Pennsylvania and the Norfolk & Western, the Erie recognized early that substantial savings could be derived from dieselization. Even before war's end powerful General Motors road units pulled long trains over the hilly main line between Marion, Ohio, and Meadville, Pennsylvania. Full dieselization took place by the time of the Korean conflict, yet savings derived from this replacement technology could not save the Erie.

More change was in the air. By the late 1950s a variety of factors, including increased highway competition, steep property taxation, high labor costs caused by union featherbedding, and unprofitable commuter trains in the New York City metropolitan area, prompted the road to seek a merger partner. After numerous studies and negotiations, the Erie found a mate, the faltering 940-mile Delaware, Lackawanna & Western Railroad. On October 17, 1960, the new couple met the corporate world as the 3,188-mile Erie-Lackawanna Railroad (EL). By the early 1970s the EL had become the "Erie Lack-of-money" and failed. In 1976 large portions of the property entered the quasi-public Conrail, and by the early 1990s the remaining assets had been successfully liquidated.

In 1959, the last year before merger with Delaware, Lackawanna & Western, the Erie operated a system of 2,314 route-miles and 4,082 track-miles, with 484 locomotives, 538 passenger cars, 20,855 freight and company service cars, and 15,021 employees. Freight traffic totaled 7.8 billion ton-miles in 1959, and freight forwarder traffic (8 percent), vehicle parts (6 percent), iron and steel products (5 percent), and coal (5 percent) were its principal traffic sources. Erie operating revenues totaled $152.7 million in 1959, and the railroad achieved an 83.5 percent operating ratio.

—H. Roger Grant

REFERENCES

Adams, Charles F., Jr., and Henry Adams. *Chapters of Erie, and Other Essays*. Boston: J. R. Osgood, 1871.

Grant, H. Roger. *Erie Lackawanna: Death of an American Railroad, 1938–1992*. Stanford, Calif.: Stanford Univ. Press, 1994.

Harwood, Herbert H., Jr. *Invisible Giants*. Bloomington: Indiana Univ. Press, 2003.

Hungerford, Edward. *Men of Erie*. New York: Random House, 1946.

Ethnicity

The ethnicity of railroad employees reflects the populations of a particular era and area. Personnel on the pioneering railroads through 1850 tended to be of English, Welsh, Scottish, or Irish descent. Some Germans also became early employees. In the United States and Canada the ethnicities of railroaders now include Anglo, French Canadian, Mexican American, Cajun, Navajo, Cree, various other Native American, and, of late, Korean and Vietnamese. In the past it included Chinese, Japanese, Filipino, Swedish, Polish, and Italian ethnicities, among others.

Of particular note are the Navajo engineering employees whose tasks have ranged from wielding spike mauls and tamping bars to operating the giant, multifunction maintenance-of-way machines. Mexican American engineering employees, once restricted to trackmen's positions, are now also roadmasters and engineering officers. They were once mainly laborers in the mechanical departments but gradually entered the skilled shopcrafts and then became foremen and mechanical officers. In the 1950s "old heads," who hired out during the period 1900 to 1920, recalled the diligent and efficient Japanese Americans who worked in the engineering departments of the West. The Chinese American roadway laborers, performing herculean tasks, including moving mountains, who formed the core of many later Chinese communities in the West were only a historic tale of earlier generations for these "old heads."

African Americans' experience requires a particular examination, not only because they were railroaders par excellence but also because they endured hellish oppression and paved the way for the civil rights of other Americans. Slavery varies cross-societally. In the United States we can consider the "peculiar institution" as the ownership of a human as legally protected property, including the power to control the personal life of and force labor from this person.

The American South was a commercial slave subsociety, with slaves a large-scale force in an unfree labor market, in agriculture, industry, and households. Only by violence in the form of the lash and by the threat and use of armed force, including actions of troops, to prevent uprisings could society maintain it. Slave leasing had slaves working temporarily on plantations, in industry, and in mines, with rent payments going to the slaves' owners, often through intermediary contractors. In *Dred Scott v. Sandford* (1857) the U.S. Supreme Court confirmed that a slave was property legally protected by the Fifth Amendment.

Black slaves and free whites constructed and operated the railroads of the slave states. The slaves were men, women, and children. The slave trackman John Henry, who in folksong worked himself to death challenging the productivity of a steam drill, is the legendary railroad slave. He beat the steam drill, but his great exertion caused him to "die with a hammer in his hand."

Franz Anton von Gerstner, the European engineer who studied U.S. railroads during the late 1830s, noted the use and care of railroad and government slaves, while free Irish laborers died like flies in the southern swamps. In 1838 the Pontchartrain Railroad expended $5,481 for food, clothing, and medical care of its slaves, 9.2 percent of its annual budget. Gerstner mentioned the skilled construction in 1839 by 44 black slaves of complex track structure on the New Orleans & Nashville. These slaves lived in an early outfit car. The State of Louisiana owned 80 slaves as capital equipment. As part of its great profitability, the Tallahassee Railroad owned corporate slaves, and the Charleston & Hamburg had 16 corporate slaves. Most slaves on railroads were labor rented to a company. Gerstner also recorded prototypic Jim Crowism, with blacks compelled to ride in baggage cars—in the North but not always in the South.

Most railroader slaves were laborers, but some worked in the skilled shopcrafts and as locomotive firemen, brakemen, and switchmen. In both skilled and unskilled occupations their numbers grew, and by the Civil War perhaps 15,000 were working on the railroads. As the Confederate states drafted white men into the army, slaves became all the more important to run the railroads and thereby support the war effort. Kornweibel (2003) found that compared with plantation slaves, railroader slaves had greater health risks, experienced more brutality from overseers, consumed worse rations, and suffered from greater family separation.

The Thirteenth Amendment ended slavery, but black people in the South endured an exploited position in the political economy for several subsequent generations. During the postwar era a state sometimes transformed now-free blacks into felons and rented them as convict labor for railroad construction and maintenance. After the war free blacks worked not only in the railroad engineering and mechanical departments, usually as laborers, but also as firemen, brakemen, and switchmen, but not as locomotive engineers or conductors. Black operating employees became known as "unpromotable." The railroad brotherhoods that developed after the war had constitu-

tional provisos that only whites could become members. This did not prevent the southern roads from employing blacks as firemen, brakemen, and switchmen, although the related brotherhoods bitterly contested the holding of jobs by blacks. Black operating employees sometimes had their own segregated seniority rosters for a craft on a district such as a division or a point such as a yard. Accordingly, in times of depressed traffic a white conductor could not bump down into the black brakemen's ranks, as would be the case without a segregated black roster.

Black operating railroaders sometimes formed their own unions. By the 1930s the Assn. of Colored Railway Trainmen and Locomotive Firemen was the largest such union, with 60 locals in 17 states, chiefly southern, with some 3,000 reported members. The union was founded on February 17, 1912, reorganized on February 27, 1918, as the Assn. of Colored Railway Trainmen, and reorganized again in February 1936 to include locomotive firemen. This union merged with another black rail union in 1962 to form the Federated Council of the International Assn. of Railway Employees and Assn. of Railway Trainmen and Locomotive Firemen, which, in turn, merged into the United Transportation Union (UTU) in 1970.

As white-only unions developed around 1900, shopcraft jobs for blacks became rarer. Frequently southern roads pitted whites and blacks against each other in an effort to keep down labor costs. This policy led to a bitter race strike in 1909 of the Brotherhood of Locomotive Firemen & Enginemen (BLF&E) against the Georgia Railroad. The firemen's union was interested both in preventing lower wages for any fireman and in having all firemen's jobs for whites only. The Georgia employed black firemen and hostlers at lower wages. Because of pro-BLF&E violence from the white citizens, the Georgia had to cease operations and submit the dispute to arbitration. The arbitrators found for the railroad, ruling that black firemen were as competent as whites, but the road then had to pay blacks the same as whites. In 1899 the Brotherhood of Locomotive Engineers had noted that "colored" firemen were "preferred by many engineers."

Legal scholars often call *Steele v. Louisville & Nashville R.R.* (1944) a precursor to the landmark *Brown v. Board of Education* (1954). Steele, like other "unpromotable" black firemen, eventually worked his way to the top of an integrated seniority list and thereby held a highly lucrative operating job, of high-speed passenger fireman paid by the mile. (If a fireman was promoted to locomotive engineer, he would bat out cars on a night shift in a yard at a quarter to a half of his former passenger wages.) Upon pressure from the BLF&E, Steele and other blacks were reassigned to less desirable, low-paying jobs, while white firemen with less seniority took the coveted passenger runs. In *Steele* the U.S. Supreme Court unanimously found against the BLF&E: "the Railway Labor Act . . . impose[s] on the bargaining representative of a craft or class of employees the duty to exercise fairly the power conferred upon it in behalf of all those for whom it acts, without hostile discrimination against them." The Court had stopped the BLF&E in its tracks; the union legally had to represent equally its white union members and the black nonunion members. Now, black and other minority employees in any industry could seek relief from the courts.

In dining-car service blacks traditionally served as cooks, barmen, waiters, and kitchen helpers but not as stewards. The Hotel Employees & Restaurant Employees (HERE) and predecessors have represented these black employees and more recently others in such service. Today, the Amtrak Service Workers Council (ASWC) represents Amtrak's on-passenger-train, nonoperating employees providing onboard or hotel-like services. ASWC consists of three unions: HERE, the Transportation Communications International Union (TCU), and the Transport Workers Union of America (TWU).

The long struggle of Pullman porters for the right to organize a union is an epoch in American history. In the service of the Pullman Co., blacks could work as porters and maids but not as conductors in charge of sleeping and parlor cars. Although "unpromotable," porters on a train not supervised by a Pullman conductor had one of them working as a porter-in-charge, at about 58 percent of the conductor's wage. The Pullman Co. aggressively combated the forming of a porters' union, sometimes with demoralizing job threats. Some porters were Filipinos hired by Pullman allegedly to threaten the organizing efforts of the black porters. Nevertheless, working as a Pullman porter was a first step up the ladder of respectability and economic advancement for some black workers.

In 1925 the Pullman porters found a champion in A. Philip Randolph. In 1935, having fought against great odds, Randolph received, with the certification of the National Mediation Board, a victorious vote from porters and maids for their representation by the Brotherhood of Sleeping Car Porters (BSCP) as a standard railroad union. Consequently, that year the BSCP received a union charter from the American Federation of Labor (AFL). The BSCP became the earliest thriving union controlled by blacks, a model for organizing black workers, and a recognized advocate of all such workers.

Among other achievements, the BSCP helped the redcaps, who handled railroad baggage, sometimes just for tips, in their organizing of the International Brotherhood of Redcaps (IBR). The BSCP and the IBR have merged into the TCU. Many railroads directly employed black chair-car attendants for assisting coach passengers on long-distance trains. On southern railroads a complex set of issues involving discrimination against blacks concerned the now-defunct, dual position of porter-brakeman, who performed both nonoperating service and operating head-brakeman tasks. The Brotherhood of Railroad Trainmen (BRT) wanted these jobs for its brakemen members.

In 1941 the BSCP successfully campaigned to have President Roosevelt form a President's Committee on Fair Employment Practices (FEPC) to investigate discrimination in employment. After further effort by the BSCP, that June Roosevelt signed Executive Order 8802, proclaiming nondiscrimination in governmental agencies and the about-to-burgeon defense industries. Many railroads and rail unions, however, successfully thwarted both Roosevelt's order and the actions of a second FEPC that he founded as an administrative agency. Despite the progress made by the BSCP and others, it was not until after the passage of the Civil Rights Act of 1964 that the railroads began to hire African Americans, other minorities, and women in all the crafts and as supervisors and officers.

During 1918–1920 the federal government controlled the railroads through the U.S. Railroad Administration (USRA). The USRA's director general equalized, and thus pioneered for all U.S. industrial relations, national rates of pay for the same class of rail service without regard to sex or race in USRA, Interpretation No. 8, Supplement 4, General Order 2, 1918. The USRA, however, allowed a number of restrictive work rules that benefited white railroaders over blacks performing the same tasks. Generally, the brotherhoods advocated equal pay for equal work because they did not want minority or female labor to undercut their members by working for less.

Ahead of its time regarding "Employment of Women," the USRA required, in General Order 28, Article V, 1918, that "their pay, when they do the same class of work as men, shall be the same as that of men." The factors of employment of women, including discrimination, in railroading are outside the scope of this entry (*see* WOMEN IN RAILROADING). In recent decades these factors have generally resulted in segregation of women in clerical and other office, sometimes supervisory, positions.

In "The Negro in the Railroad Industry" Risher found, as have others and the courts, that the railroads and the unions did not develop their pivotal system of craft seniority on railroads to create or perpetuate discrimination in rail employment. Moreover, the system is a logical way to assure advancement in a large industry having a great range of occupations. Furthermore, "the system remains inviolate nationally regardless of the race of the workers in the lines of progression" (Risher 1971, 169).

—Frederick C. Gamst

REFERENCES

Brazeal, Brailsford R. *The Brotherhood of Sleeping Car Porters.* New York: Harper & Brothers, 1946.

Calliste, Agnes. "Sleeping Car Porters in Canada: An Ethnically Submerged Split Labour Market." *Canadian Ethnic Studies* 19 (1987): 1–20.

"Colored Firemen." *Locomotive Engineers' Journal* 33 (1899): 251–252.

Gamst, Frederick C. "The Struggle for Employment Equity by Blacks on American and Canadian Railroads." *Journal of Black Studies* 25 (1995): 297–317.

"The Georgia Railroad Strike." *Locomotive Firemen and Enginemen's Magazine* 46 (1909): 255–269.

Gerstner, Franz Anton Ritter von. *Early American Railroads.* Ed. Frederick C. Gamst. Stanford, Calif.: Stanford Univ. Press, 1997 [1842–1843].

Hammett, Hugh B. "Labor and Race: The Georgia Railroad Strike of 1909." *Labor History* 16 (1975): 470–484.

Kornweibel, Theodore, Jr. "Railroads and Slavery." *Railroad History,* no. 189 (2003): 34–59.

"The Negro Firemen Problem." *Locomotive Firemen's Magazine* 26 (1899): 539–542.

"Occupational Status of Negro Railroad Employees." *Monthly Labor Review* 56, no. 3 (1943): 484–485.

Risher, Howard W., Jr. "The Negro in the Railroad Industry." In *Negro Employment in Land and Air Transport,* ed. H. R. Northrup. Philadelphia: Univ. of Pennsylvania, 1971.

U.S. Bureau of Labor Statistics. *Handbook of American Trade-Unions.* Bulletin no. 618 (1936): 246, 272.

Wilson, Joseph F., ed. *Tearing Down the Color Bar: A Documentary History and Analysis of the Brotherhood of Sleeping Car Porters.* New York: Columbia Univ. Press, 1989.

Yancey, John L. "Red Caps' Struggle for Employee Status." *American Federationist* 46 (1939): 259–263.

Evans, Oliver (1755–1819)

Oliver Evans was born in Newport, Delaware, and his early life is obscure. By age 22, however, he already had invented a machine for making the teeth for textile cards, and he became one of the most gifted U.S. inventors of his generation. Evans's fame rests on two major innovations: the automated flour mill of 1783–1787 and an early, successful high-pressure steam engine. Evans's flour mill is the ancestor of all continuous-process manufacturing. His manual, *The Young Mill-wright and Miller's Guide,* first appeared in 1795 and remained in print for 65 years.

Evans's second great achievement lay in perfecting, independently of Richard Trevithick in England, a successful high-pressure steam engine. By 1803 Evans had a 12-hp prototype working in his shop, but the Philadelphia & Lancaster Turnpike Road Co. turned down his proposal to build a steam carriage. Instead, Evans produced a steam-powered, self-propelled dredge, the *Orukter Amphibolos,* in the summer of 1805, and in the following year he opened the Mars Works in Philadelphia for the manufacture of steam engines and other machinery. His sons-in-law, James Rush and John Muhlenberg, continued the business.

Although Evans's engines were installed in factories and in steamboats on both eastern and western rivers, and although he toyed with railroads on paper, Evans never succeeded in producing a steam wagon. Nothing in his work leads directly to the locomotive. He did, however, prophesy in 1813 that steam trains would travel on rails at speeds of 20 mph.

Lacking wealthy patrons, Evans depended upon vigorous enforcement of his patent rights, and this, combined with a truculent disposition, embroiled him in many controversies both in the courts and with contemporaries such as fellow inventor John Stevens. In 1809 Evans burned some of his papers in a fit of pique and swore off patent seeking. By then he was well established as a manufacturer and confident through the success of his inventions and textbooks that his fame would outlast that of his enemies.

—Christopher T. Baer

REFERENCES

Bathe, Greville, and Dorothy Bathe. *Oliver Evans: A Chronicle of Early American Engineering.* Philadelphia: Historical Society of Pennsylvania, 1935.

Ferguson, Eugene S. *Oliver Evans: Inventive Genius of the American Industrial Revolution.* Greenville, Del.: Eleutherian Mills-Hagley Foundation, 1980.

Evolution of Major Railroads

A number of early North American railroads never were intended to be more than local enterprises. Other promoters had grander visions. But even a local railroad ranked as a big business by the standards of the time. As late as 1850 the average U.S. manufacturing company employed only 10 workers. Individual railroads of all sizes employed more people than that era's typical corporate ventures, such as meat processors and textile mills. The larger railroads of the 1840s already ranked among the nation's leading companies in terms of revenue, capital investment, and labor force.

The U.S. rail system of 1855 counted 36 railroad companies whose individual route networks exceeded 150 miles. Largest in mileage, at 707, was the Illinois Central, which during 1856 carried more than 3,500 workers on its payroll. The New York & Erie's 464 miles reflected invested capital of $33.4 million, and in 1855 the company garnered gross revenues of $5.5 million. The New York Central, at 534 miles, led the rail industry in gross revenues that year—$6.6 million—and had invested capital of $28.5 million. Other major carriers included the Michigan Southern & Northern Indiana, 475 miles; the Baltimore & Ohio, 382 miles; and the Pennsylvania Railroad, 256 miles. The size of these corporations and the capital investment they attracted were remarkable for that era. Historian John F. Stover has written, "Few other institutions in the country did business on so vast a scale or financed themselves in such a variety of ways." As promoters gained awareness of the new mode's vast economic potential, they perceived advantages in operating or controlling even larger networks.

Civic leaders in port cities on the Atlantic Seaboard understood that rail links with the nation's interior were necessary if they were to compete with New York, which had captured an early advantage with its all-water route to the Midwest via the Hudson River, the Erie Canal, and Lake Erie. Maryland interests established the Baltimore & Ohio to gather midwestern traffic by putting down track to the banks of the Ohio River, and the company's lines reached Wheeling, Virginia, in 1853 and Parkersburg, Virginia, in 1856. After prolonged dithering and delays Philadelphia merchants resolved upon an all-rail link to the navigable interior rivers at Pittsburgh. It was completed as the Pennsylvania Railroad in 1854.

Promoters elsewhere applied similar reasoning. After the South Carolina Railroad diverted freight to Charleston from Savannah, leaders in the latter city supported the Central of Georgia Railroad, which by 1843 included 191 miles of track. Backers of the Mobile & Ohio believed that by constructing a rail line from the Alabama coast to Cairo, Illinois, they could divert to the port of Mobile traffic then moving by water down the Mississippi River to New Orleans. Commercial interests at Louisville, Kentucky, promoted the Louisville & Nashville because of concern that if a railroad was built north from Nashville to the Ohio River at some other terminal city, Louisville's stature as a regional hub for river and overland trade from the interior South would be diminished. As these and other rail ventures progressed, their sponsors discerned additional benefits resulting from operating on a larger scale.

With its fast-growing farm economy and expanding population, the Midwest was a powerful magnet for eastern railroad executives, who originally had assumed that they would interchange midwestern traffic at river or lakehead terminals on the region's eastern or southern fringes. But the farm commodities destined for export and the manufactured goods that flowed westward reached their destinations in inefficient ways—via rafts and flatboats on tributary streams or overland in wagons or herded on foot by livestock drovers. Where isolated railroads connected river ports and inland cities, the service left much to be desired, and at least two more transloadings were required for cargo hauled by steamboat or barge to reach the eastern railroads' tracks at such places as Pittsburgh and Wheeling.

Eastern rail executives calculated that this business could be tapped closer to its source, and that long-distance rail service could siphon traffic from the waterways. Midwestern promoters meanwhile were advancing their own rail projects. Eager to forge alliances that would extend their markets, eastern carriers provided encouragement and occasional financial aid to establish what would be termed "friendly connections" with these new ventures. The Lake Shore & Michigan Southern reached Chicago in 1852 and exchanged traffic with New York's railroads. In 1857 both the Marietta & Cincinnati and the Ohio & Mississippi were completed. The B&O thereby gained valuable western connections ranging all the way to St. Louis. Three railroads—the Ohio & Pennsylvania, Ohio & Indiana, and Fort Wayne & Chicago—were developed to link Pittsburgh with Chi-

cago. Their financial difficulties prompted the Pennsylvania Railroad to intervene. By 1860 these lines, which had been merged into the Pittsburgh, Fort Wayne & Chicago, were affiliated with the Pennsylvania.

Alliances, leases, and stock ownership initially were preferred because these methods were less expensive than outright extensions. Additionally, interstate ownership often required special state legislation to amend charters, which could be difficult to obtain.

Route extensions, mergers, alliances, and branch-line networks all produced financial and operating benefits. The local railroads that ultimately formed the New York Central had coordinated passenger operations from a very early date and together were able to offer superior schedules that diverted passengers from the Erie Canal. "Through" coaches and sleeping cars used by the combinations of railroads that carried passengers between the Midwest and the East Coast demonstrated that services of this type offered faster schedules, passenger convenience, and improved equipment use.

These same principles proved applicable to freight. The ability to move a shipment from origin to destination on one carrier or via a network of affiliated carriers produced operating savings and enabled managements to compete for even more business by offering lower rates. Emphasis on efficiency also accelerated the movement toward a standard track gauge, because transshipment at gauge-change points added significantly to overall transportation costs. Although an individual branch line might be only marginally profitable, each branch fed traffic to the railroad's main line, thereby increasing the economic value of the latter. Branch lines also tapped new business such as coal and other mineral deposits—important additions to a company's overall traffic base.

The quest for efficiency led to mergers, including 1853's establishment of the New York Central, which united ten small railroads serving upper New York State. The Delaware, Lackawanna & Western, originally a local line between Oswego and Ithaca, New York, by 1870 reflected the consolidation of ten railroads in New York, Pennsylvania, and New Jersey.

Rail companies also tried to win competitive advantage over their rivals. The New York & Erie had been built to a 6-foot track gauge on the theory that interchange costs would reduce traffic diversions to carriers that utilized different gauges. Other railroads soon concluded that route extensions and acquisitions would better enhance their competitive standing. The B&O's 1866 lease of the Central Ohio gave the Baltimore-based company a line running from the Ohio River at Bellaire, Ohio, to Columbus. By means of leases and new construction the B&O then completed its own track to Chicago in 1874.

Main lines supported by secondary routes and branch lines offered the potential for regional market dominance to any carrier that could unify them. Railroads acted to acquire local and regional lines. By 1868 a collection of Ohio and Indiana routes had come under control of the

Columbus, Chicago & Indiana Central, which served several important traffic centers and was an important connection to eastern carriers at Columbus. Also operating in these two states was the Cleveland, Columbus, Cincinnati & Indianapolis (a forerunner of the Big Four Railroad), controlled by the Vanderbilt interests and allied with the New York Central. Several railroads between Chicago and Quincy, Illinois, were absorbed into the Chicago, Burlington & Quincy in 1864. In four years' time the Burlington then extended its system westward to Council Bluffs, Iowa, and Kansas City.

Railroad managements also pursued expansion in order to ward off competitors and to protect existing traffic connections. At the end of the Civil War the Indianapolis–St. Louis corridor was served by only one route, the St. Louis, Alton & Terre Haute and the connecting Terre Haute & Indianapolis, each operating between the endpoint cities named in their corporate titles. Three railroads met this corridor at the Hoosier capital city. Concerned that the St. Louis–Terre Haute line could fall into unfriendly hands, interests associated with the Pennsylvania and TH&I decided to construct a second main line through Illinois, the St. Louis, Vandalia & Terre Haute, which opened in 1870. The combined TH&I/Vandalia route eventually was controlled by the Pennsylvania. The parallel route via Alton, along with a second newly built Indianapolis–Terre Haute railroad, was partially controlled by the New York Central.

Other defensive moves were made in reaction to corporate raiders. After Jay Gould attempted to expand his Erie system into the Midwest, the Pennsylvania in 1868 and 1869 was forced to lease both the Columbus, Chicago & Indiana Central and the Pittsburgh, Fort Wayne & Chicago in order to keep these properties out of Gould's hands. In 1882 Gould completed the New York, Chicago & St. Louis (commonly known as the Nickel Plate) from Buffalo to Chicago in direct competition with the New York Central's midwestern affiliates. William H. Vanderbilt then bought the Nickel Plate to protect the NYC's markets.

Within a decade after the close of the Civil War many railroad leaders and financiers had determined that the best way to manage was to merge. Unified management, coupled with the efficiencies of equipment use and single-line service, cut costs. Mergers and other forms of consolidation often provided new and better routes, reduced competition, and offered protection against rivals.

Creating larger systems had taken on special appeal by this time for other reasons as well. The United States was on a railroad-building binge. Route mileage, which had stood at 53,000 in 1870, more than tripled to 163,359 by 1890. Expansion at this frantic pace led to overcapacity in some markets and ruinous competition nearly everywhere. Efforts to preserve traffic led to savage rate cutting during the 1870s and 1880s. Economic downturns, such as the prolonged depression after the panic of 1873, weakened individual carriers to the point that they were forced into bankruptcy or were for sale at bargain prices. As the consolidation movement progressed, many smaller railroads could not afford to stand aside because, as independents, they faced the risk of isolation and eventual ruin.

In 1883 the U.S. rail system included 43 carriers whose individual systems exceeded 500 miles. The route structures of five of these exceeded 3,000 miles: Chicago, Milwaukee & St. Paul; Wabash; Chicago & Northwestern; Chicago, Burlington & Quincy; and Central Pacific. However, the Pennsylvania led the pack in gross revenues, which totaled $32 million that year from its 1,314-mile system. The New York Central collected $30.4 million from a 953-mile network. Other sizable rail companies included the Illinois Central, 1,928 route miles; Union Pacific, 1,821; Atchison, Topeka & Santa Fe, 1,821; Northern Pacific, 1,497; and Michigan Central, 1,468. Meanwhile, in Canada the Canadian Pacific was evolving into a giant enterprise that by 1890 would operate North America's first transcontinental system, from St. John, New Brunswick, to Vancouver, British Columbia.

The volume of capital flowing to rail development and operations expanded at a phenomenal rate during the second half of the nineteenth century. In 1860 rail capital investment—which included the value of all outstanding stocks, bonds, equipment trusts, and related financial instruments—stood at $1.1 billion. The amount more than doubled in a decade's time. By 1890 the industry's total capital exceeded $10.6 billion.

Between 1884 and 1888 more than 400 consolidation agreements were consummated in the United States. The panic of 1893, which temporarily stalled further expansion, created additional acquisition candidates as the brutal financial meltdown forced railroads into receivership. Within a few years of the onset of the twentieth century, ownership of a majority of U.S. route mileage had passed into the hands of a small number of railroads or financiers. Common ownership, however, did not always mean that these properties were operated as unified entities. Individual operating managements still prevailed in many instances, but business strategy, finances, and rates were dictated by those who held the leases or controlled a majority of the stock.

Although they were smaller in route mileage than several carriers elsewhere, the New York Central and Pennsylvania railroads qualified as giants within the industry because the networks they owned or controlled blanketed the nation's industrial and population heartland east of the Mississippi River and north of the Ohio River. The two companies led the industry in gross revenues, and the Pennsylvania ranked as the nation's largest industrial employer. The NYC was the crown jewel of the Vanderbilt family's holdings, which also included several midwestern railroads allied with the Central. The Vanderbilts also owned or controlled the Boston & Albany, Nickel Plate, Chicago & Northwestern, and New York, New Haven & Hartford. The Pennsylvania owned or held leases in midwestern routes extending to Chicago, St. Louis, and

Louisville and effectively controlled through stock ownership the Baltimore & Ohio, Chesapeake & Ohio, and Norfolk & Western.

Financier J. P. Morgan's rail empire included such major properties as the Southern, Erie, Mobile & Ohio, and Central of Georgia. To the west were James J. Hill's Great Northern, Northern Pacific, and Chicago, Burlington & Quincy. Edward H. Harriman controlled the Union Pacific and the Illinois Central and was the Southern Pacific's largest shareholder. George Gould had amassed dominant investment positions in the Wabash; Missouri Pacific; Texas & Pacific; Denver & Rio Grande; St. Louis Southwestern; and St. Louis, Iron Mountain & Southern. William H. Moore owned the Rock Island and the Chicago & Alton.

That era's rail magnates continued to pursue the benefits of operating on a large scale while reducing cutthroat competition by both formal and informal methods. Hill attempted in 1901 to unite the GN, NP, and Burlington into the mammoth Northern Securities Co. The Pennsylvania and New York Central collaborated on a doctrine known as the "community of interest" in which the two giants intended to divide between themselves influence over all eastern rail companies and operate them in a manner designed to deter profit-wrecking competition.

These initiatives ran afoul of public resentment against presumed abusive practices on the part of railroads, along with widespread opposition by voters and politicians to big-business combinations of all types. In 1904 the U.S. Supreme Court rejected Hill's Northern Securities merger. The PRR-NYC community of interest soon collapsed, and both carriers divested holdings in several railroads. The Interstate Commerce Commission dismembered Harriman's empire in 1913. A series of federal laws placed railroads under more intense scrutiny, regulated their rates, and created obstacles to further corporate combinations.

Subsequent developments prompted a rethinking of what was coming to be known as "the railroad problem." The industry's economic health deteriorated, and carriers operating one-sixth of U.S. route mileage were in bankruptcy by 1914. It dawned on government officials that the United States had too many railroads and too much track mileage. The railroads' difficulty in handling traffic then led to nationalization during World War I.

When the industry returned to private control in 1920, a number of interests wrestled with plans to revive its financial well-being. Rail labor advocated nationalization through the so-called Plumb Plan. Business interests, politicians, and rail executives were quick to dismiss it. The Transportation Act of 1920 instructed the ICC to devise a plan to consolidate all U.S. railroads into 25 to 30 systems of roughly equal size and earning power, while also maintaining competition. However, no railroad was compelled to accept the agency's proposal. (At the time, 118 carriers merited the agency's Class 1 designation based upon annual revenues.) The ICC engaged Harvard professor William Ripley, who fashioned a blueprint for

24 systems. Shippers and politicians feared that Ripley's approach would diminish competition. Several large railroads saw themselves as losers and worked to frustrate the process. Neither the ICC plan calling for 21 systems (finally issued in 1929) nor 1932's Prince Plan, which foresaw 7 huge systems, found acceptance.

Elsewhere in North America the railroad map had changed. A series of consolidations between 1913 and 1920 established the Canadian National Railways under government ownership. Key CN components included the Intercolonial Railway, National Transcontinental Railway, Canadian Northern, Grand Trunk, and Grand Trunk Pacific. The government-owned National Railways of Mexico was formed in 1908 and began a gradual process of bringing that nation's rail lines under governmental control.

The fortunes and prospects of many U.S. railroads, especially those in the East, deteriorated in the years after World War II. As late as 1959 *Fortune* magazine's roster of the largest U.S. transportation companies continued to be dominated by rail corporations, headed by the Pennsylvania, which posted gross revenues of $888 million that year. Southern Pacific ranked second at $788 million, and the New York Central was third with $773 million. Seventh-ranked American Airlines, the largest nonrail company on *Fortune*'s 1959 list, achieved a rate of return on investment in excess of 14 percent, while the Pennsylvania's return was less than 1 percent. None of the largest railroads earned profits sufficient to cover their cost of capital. In the face of brutal competition from trucks, airlines, and barges, railroads revived efforts to save their mode through consolidation. Finally aware of the industry's worsening condition, government officials warmed to the idea. Meanwhile, the process of pruning uneconomic lines, which had begun in the 1920s, resumed in earnest.

In 1947 approval had been gained for three mergers: Gulf, Mobile & Ohio with the Alton; Denver & Rio Grande Western with the Denver & Salt Lake; and Chesapeake & Ohio with the Pere Marquette. Ten years later the Louisville & Nashville merged with the Nashville, Chattanooga & St. Louis. Merger efforts gathered speed. In 1960 the beleaguered Erie and Delaware, Lackawanna & Western railroads united. The C&O then took over the Baltimore & Ohio. The Norfolk & Western merged with the Nickel Plate and leased the Wabash. Many observers were surprised when the East's two mightiest carriers, Pennsylvania and New York Central, announced a merger that took effect in 1968 as Penn Central. Even more astounding was Penn Central's collapse into bankruptcy two years later.

The Penn Central bankruptcy prompted second thoughts about the value of further consolidations, but 1970 also brought the merger of the Great Northern, the Northern Pacific, the Chicago, Burlington & Quincy, and the Spokane, Portland & Seattle. James J. Hill's 1901 merger plan finally had come to pass, and the new Burlington Northern system was rated a success. The federal regulatory climate improved with the passage of the Railroad Revitalization and Regulatory Reform Act of 1976 and enactment of partial economic deregulation in 1980.

By this time the B&O and C&O had combined as the Chessie System, which then merged with the so-called Family Lines, whose predecessors included the Atlantic Coast Line, Seaboard, and L&N. In 1982 the Southern Railway and Norfolk & Western combined as Norfolk Southern, and Union Pacific absorbed Missouri Pacific and Western Pacific. The Missouri-Kansas-Texas system was acquired by UP six years later. The former Penn Central properties, which together with other bankrupt eastern carriers had been restructured into the government-owned Consolidated Rail Corp. (Conrail), returned to the private sector under the same name in 1987.

At century's end the North American railroad map was dominated by six "super railroads." Norfolk Southern and CSX divided the Consolidated Rail Corp. network in 1999 and left the region east of the Mississippi River with two major carriers. Union Pacific had acquired both the Chicago & Northwestern and the Southern Pacific. Burlington Northern teamed up with Sante Fe. Canadian National absorbed the Illinois Central and the Wisconsin Central. Canadian Pacific was represented in the United States by its Soo Line subsidiary, which previously had incorporated major components of the Milwaukee Road. Still independent was the smaller Kansas City Southern, which by then had obtained a concession to operate extensive routes in Mexico in partnership with a Mexican affiliate.

These Class 1 carriers were augmented by numerous regional and shortline railroads, many of them activated after deregulation in 1980. A growing number of shortlines, however, had passed under the control of holding companies that operated these sometimes widely scattered enterprises. Many industry analysts believed that one more round of mergers was in prospect—the creation of two competing transcontinental North American systems out of the megacarriers' track. Mexico's government had decided to privatize that nation's rail system in the late 1990s, and U.S. carriers quickly entered into joint ventures with Mexican affiliates to acquire partial ownership.

—William J. Watt

REFERENCES

Chandler, Alfred D., Jr., ed. *The Railroads: The Nation's First Big Business.* New York: Harcourt, Brace & World, 1965.

Drury, George H. *The Historical Guide to North American Railroads.* Milwaukee, Wis.: Kalmbach, 1985.

Saunders, Richard, Jr. *Merging Lines: American Railroads, 1900–1970.* DeKalb: Northern Illinois Univ. Press, 2001.

Stover, John F. *The Life and Decline of the American Railroad.* New York: Oxford Univ. Press, 1970.

F

Fairbanks, Morse & Co.

Fairbanks, Morse & Co. (FM) was a railroad and marine supply manufacturer that built locomotives between 1944 and 1963. The company was noted for producing powerful locomotives with opposed-piston diesel engines, which it manufactured with great success for marine uses, particularly in submarines during World War II. The firm's locomotive-production facility was located in Beloit, Wisconsin.

Thaddeus Fairbanks of Vermont had invented the mechanical platform scale and in 1830, with his brother Erastus, began to promote the construction of railroads to serve their manufacturing business. Their company, E. & T. Fairbanks Co., expanded into a network of semi-independent branch agencies. In 1866 Charles Hosmer Morse, who had worked for the company since 1850, became a partner in the Cincinnati office, and the name Fairbanks, Morse & Co. was established. Morse headed up the firm, and the Fairbanks family dropped out. In 1885, under Morse's leadership, the company delved into markets other than the platform scale. It acquired the Eclipse Windmill Co. and the Beloit Wagon Works at Beloit, Wisconsin, and concentrated on the manufacture of steam and gasoline engines to power water pumps to replace windmills. FM entered the railroad business through the back door, building engines to power pumps to lift coal into steam locomotive coaling docks, which it also manufactured. It also purchased the Sheffield Velocipede Car Co., which put FM in the business of making railroad handcars, which later evolved into the popular gasoline-powered "speeder" cars used by railroad track-maintenance workers.

In 1922 FM began the development of diesel engines, and by the 1930s it had both two-cycle and four-cycle diesel engines available. In 1932 FM perfected the two-cycle opposed-piston engine for use in U.S. Navy submarines. The opposed-piston engine, or simply OP, has two crankshafts, one on top and another on the bottom, with open-ended cylinders lined up vertically in the engine. Each cylinder has two pistons and is connected to the crankshaft with connecting rods. The OP engine has no cylinder heads or valves; the engine is ventilated with air from a blower and runs very smoothly, producing an even,

distinctive sound. The engine is mechanically simple, with relatively few working parts. But on most railroads, diesel mechanics were used to other types of engines, primarily those of General Motors and American Locomotive. Since FMs were in the minority, mechanical forces tended to treat them as orphans, thus contributing to their downfall in railroad use. But for the railroads that properly maintained them, FM locomotives performed well.

The first railroad use of the opposed-piston engine came when FM supplied the power plants for six streamlined motor cars built by St. Louis Car Co. in 1939 for the Southern Railway. That same year St. Louis Car also built a single center-cab switcher for the Reading Co. using an FM engine. But World War II interrupted FM's entry into the railroad business, since the government limited FM diesel-engine production to submarines. However, in 1943 the War Production Board authorized FM to construct a 1,000-hp diesel-electric switch engine for railroad use. FM established a locomotive-manufacturing facility at Beloit, where the engine was unveiled in August 1944. It used frames and trucks from Baldwin and General Steel Castings Corporation and Westinghouse electrical equipment. To give the engine a touch of class, the company hired industrial designer Raymond Loewy, who had designed such classic locomotives as the Pennsylvania's GG1 electrics. The first locomotive was sold to the Milwaukee Road as its No. 1802; it remained in service until 1980. The Milwaukee Road, which served the Beloit plant, became one of FM's best customers. To enter the Canadian locomotive market, in 1950 FM licensee and subsidiary Canadian Locomotive Co. at Kingston, Ontario, began the assembly of FM designs in that country and continued to do so until the end of production in Canada in 1957.

Although FM did produce locomotives for road service, its most popular models were its switcher and road switcher locomotives. The 1,200-hp H-12-44, with 335 models sold in the United States, Canada, and Mexico, proved to be most popular. FM's 2,000-hp "Erie-built" streamlined cab units were among its most handsome designs. When FM first entered the locomotive business, it did not have different model designations for its units. From 1945 to 1949 all FM road cab units were built at the

General Electric shop in Erie, Pennsylvania, under contract. These units therefore simply became known as Erie-builts. One of their most famous assignments was on the Milwaukee Road, which in 1946–1947 received five A-B-A sets to pull the new *Olympian Hiawatha* between Chicago and Seattle/Tacoma. The A units had handsome chrome nose grills and carried the train's name below the cab. Among the other railroads that purchased Erie-builts were New York Central, Santa Fe, and Union Pacific. The Erie-builts were only produced between 1945 and 1949, with a total of 82 A units and 29 B or booster units constructed.

In 1950 FM unveiled its Consolidation line of locomotives, which became known simply as C-Liners. They were similar in appearance to the Erie-builts, but had shorter noses and larger windshields and rode on four-wheel rather than six-wheel trucks. The units came in cab and booster configurations and were available in 1,600 or 2,000-hp models. Canadian National, Canadian Pacific, Milwaukee Road, New York Central, and Pennsylvania were among the roads that bought them. Some were equipped with steam generators for passenger service. FM also offered a passenger version of the C-Liner that had a six-wheel trailing truck and came in 1,600, 2,000, and 2,400-hp versions that were purchased by the Long Island, New Haven, and New York Central.

The Consolidation never lived up to expectations, partly because railroads were moving away from streamlined cab units and toward more versatile road switchers with cab-hood designs. FM's answer was its most revolutionary design: the 2,400-hp, C-C-trucked Train Master, advertised as "the Most Useful Locomotive Ever Built." At the time the first models were produced in 1953, they were among the largest, most powerful diesels yet produced. It was a large locomotive in all respects: only FM at the time had a 2,400-hp engine with proven operating experience that enabled it to get ahead of competitors in what would soon become a single-unit horsepower race. Designated the H24-66, the 66-foot-long Train Master weighed 187½ tons, with the weight evenly distributed on all six powered axles. FM designed the engine for all-purpose duty: fast freight, local and yard switching, and passenger, mail, and suburban train service. Four Train Master demonstrators were built and toured over at least 20 railroads. The model eventually was sold to 10 North American railroads and was used in every type of service. On the Virginian Railway 19 Train Masters and 38 H16-44s helped dieselize the railroad, and with one exception, the Virginian became an all-FM-powered railroad.

While ahead of its time, the Train Master was not an unqualified success. FM was late in the market compared with its competitors, and electrical problems plagued the units at first. There was also a proxy fight for control of the company beginning in the mid-1950s that may have scared off potential buyers. The last Train Masters built were a repeat order for 7 by the Virginian in 1957. Only 127 Train Masters were ever built.

As North American railroads completed their replacement of steam engines and General Motors and American Locomotive came to dominate the market, FM's market share shrank. FM built no diesels for the U.S. market after 1958; its last deliveries were to Mexico in 1963, by which time General Electric had entered the locomotive-manufacturing business, creating an additional competitor. Between 1944 and the time locomotive production ceased in 1963, FM produced a total of 1,460 locomotives for 49 customers in Canada, Mexico, and the United States. A handful of FM switchers still operated in revenue service into the twenty-first century, working at industrial operations. Relatively few FM diesel locomotives were preserved, partly because their engines were valuable for use in nonrailroad applications, and in some instances the carbodies were preserved without the engine. Among the exceptions is the first production FM switcher, Milwaukee Road 1802, later renumbered 760, which has been preserved in operating condition at the Illinois Railway Museum in Union, Illinois. Several other FM switchers have also been saved. Only two C-Liners survive, both former Canadian Pacific units in Canada. A single Train Master, Canadian Pacific 8905, was saved and is displayed at the Canadian Railway Museum in Delson, Quebec. FM remains in business as Fairbanks Morse Engine, still based in Beloit, making diesel engines, dual-fuel engine generator sets, gas-turbine generators, and replacement parts. Its primary markets include stationary power generation and marine propulsion for the U.S. Navy.

—Steve Glischinski

REFERENCES

Boyd, Jim. *Fairbanks-Morse Locomotives in Color*. Scotch Plains, N.J.: Morning Sun Books, 1996.

Ingles, J. David. "Train Master Tribute." *Trains* 30, no. 10 (Aug. 1973): 28–43.

Pinkepank, Jerry A. "Born, at Beloit, the Cinderella of Dieseldom: Fairbanks-Morse." *Trains* 25, no. 1 (Nov. 1964): 36–49.

———. *Diesel Spotter's Guide*, 1st ed. Waukesha, Wis.: Kalmbach, 1967.

See also LOCOMOTIVE BUILDERS.

Federal Railroad Administration (FRA)

The Federal Railroad Administration (FRA) is an operating agency of the U.S. Department of Transportation (DOT), headed by an administrator, a political appointee, who reports to the secretary of transportation. FRA was established after creation of the DOT, effective April 1, 1967. It assumed some railroad policy and research activities previously conducted within the U.S. Department of

Commerce (notably the Office of High Speed Ground Transportation), took custody of the Alaska Railroad from the Department of the Interior, and became responsible for railroad safety regulatory functions previously carried out by the Interstate Commerce Commission (ICC). FRA has always been in the uncomfortable position of being both advocate for the railroad industry and judge of its safety performance. By almost all accounts, FRA's leadership in promoting regulatory reform—culminating in passage of the Staggers Rail Act of 1980—was its landmark accomplishment over the last third of the twentieth century.

The Northeast Rail Crisis (1966–1977)

A small policy agency in the early years, FRA was in no position to prevent the collapse of the northeastern railroads and then much of the midwestern rail network in the period 1966–1977. Penn Central's bankruptcy in 1970 brought down nearly all its neighbors and soon threatened cessation of essential services (including commuter trains) throughout the region. Congress acted in the Regional Rail Reorganization (3R) Act (1973) to establish a reorganization-planning process that would set up the Consolidated Rail Corp. (Conrail) to absorb key lines of bankrupt railroads in the Northeast. Importantly, Congress did not give the job to FRA, but instead created a new organization (outside the Civil Service System and presumably temporary) called the U.S. Railway Assn. (USRA).

FRA helped design the legislation that established the National Railroad Passenger Corp. (Amtrak) in 1970. Creation of Amtrak was intended to take a heavy cost burden from the private freight railroads and centralize provision of remaining improved passenger service in a new public corporation at modest cost to the taxpayer. A bright spot in the early years was FRA's small research and development (R&D) program, which launched important initiatives in the field of track-train dynamics, rail-defect analysis and prevention, and freight-car lading protection. In those years FRA owned and staffed the High Speed Ground Transportation Test Center in Pueblo, Colorado. The Pueblo campus, renamed the Transportation Technology Center, is now a world-class research and test facility managed by a subsidiary of the Assn. of American Railroads (AAR) under a care-and-custody contract with FRA.

Deregulation and Restructuring (1978–1988)

The Railroad Revitalization and Regulatory Reform (4R) Act approved USRA's plan for establishment of Conrail, but it also represented a watershed in regulatory policy. For the first time since the Act to Regulate Commerce of 1887, Congress undertook to aim transportation policy toward less rather than more regulation of railroads. The 4R Act also authorized several financial assistance programs for ailing companies and lines—loan guarantees, preference-share (quasi-equity) financing, and a federal/state continuance subsidy program for abandoned rail lines. Despite the inherent flaws and inconsistencies of these programs, and despite enormous pressure from outside interests, FRA did well in managing the financial assistance programs.

Among the studies mandated by the 4R Act, the most important requirement was that FRA survey, report, and make recommendations regarding the amount of deferred maintenance accumulated to that point. Many observers assumed that the purpose of the study was to produce an estimate of how much federal rail subsidy funding should be authorized, or even what the taxpayer bill would be when the government took over ownership and repair of rail rights of way. This was a serious possibility in 1976–1977, with midwestern railroads collapsing and with Conrail's losses reaching about a million dollars a day; indeed, there was talk of both a "Conrail-West" USRA-style planning process and even establishment of a Consolidated Facilities Corp. (ConFac) to be the vehicle for nationalization of the freight rail industry's rail infrastructure.

FRA's response to the rail crisis was to publish its report on deferred maintenance as a sweeping *Prospectus for Change in the Freight Rail Industry* (October 1978), under the mantle of the secretary of transportation. In addition to calculating the industry's capital shortfall for 1976–1985 (some $13 to $16 billion), FRA cataloged the causes of this desperate state of affairs and provided recommendations dealing with most of the problem areas it had identified. Over the ensuing months the FRA and DOT staff proposals outlined in the prospectus turned even more challenging to the status quo, essentially amounting to what would be a wholesale dismantling of the ICC regulatory regime. FRA and DOT wrote the deregulation proposals into legislative language and, with the approval of the Carter White House, carried their justification to Congress in official testimony and countless meetings with staff. After many compromises the legislation emerged as the Staggers Rail Act of 1980.

The years 1977–1982 saw FRA heavily engaged in efforts to restructure (as well as deregulate) the railroad industry. FRA believed that the bankrupt Rock Island should be dismembered and pieces sold or abandoned, and it supported the Milwaukee Road trustees' plan to exit operations west of Miles City, Montana, and reorganize as a smaller "core" railroad. Behind the scenes FRA worked tirelessly within the guidelines of its authority under Section 401 of the 4R Act to arrange joint-use agreements coupled with line rationalizations. These were aimed at combating the manifest problem of "too much track, too little traffic" (an FRA phrase). Although the yield was meager at the time, a pattern was established for successful line rationalizations a decade later.

FRA ran into a storm of opposition from other railroads by supporting Southern Pacific's eastward extension to St. Louis over the Tucumcari Route of the Rock Island. In the area of passenger service, in 1979 FRA called for sharp cutbacks in lightly used, hugely deficit-producing Amtrak trains. It was not entirely ignored—indeed, it helped bring about more rationalization of the national passenger route system than at any other point in Amtrak's history.

Conrail's management led the way in implementing new marketing efforts under the post–Staggers Act relaxation of regulation, in particular by making use of new contracting freedoms and the ability to close or discourage inefficient junctions. Also benefiting from new legislative provisions enacted in the Northeast Rail Service Act (NERSA)—especially eased labor reductions and expedited line abandonments—Conrail finally turned profitable. The carrier's newfound financial health set the stage for advocacy of privatization by the DOT secretary; after many fits and starts Conrail became a publicly traded company as the result of the largest initial public offering ever, more than $2 billion, in 1987.

Between Promise and Reality (1989–2000)

By the end of the 1980s the railroad industry was enjoying better times. As FRA had envisioned and advocated a decade earlier, Staggers Act reforms—more than any other factor the ability to enter into rate and service contracts between carriers and shippers—were yielding a better match of supply and demand. Long-term contracts facilitated the explosion of international and later domestic intermodal service using double-stack flatcars. Unit trains from the Powder River Basin in Wyoming were beginning to supply low-sulfur coal to points as remote as Georgia and Alabama under long-term rate and service contracts that often included both shipper-provided hoppers or gondolas and guaranteed annual traffic volumes. The choice of western low-sulfur coal fuel got a further boost from the Clean Air Act Amendments of 1990. Nearly all the major railroads were involved in mergers during the 1980s and 1990s, usually with FRA and DOT support.

In the last few years of the twentieth century, however, America's railroads came under attack from some of their biggest customers. Claiming that in too many cases they were "captive" to railroads that charged high rates and provided poor service, many shippers wanted to force railroads to allow "open access" to competitive operators over their own privately owned rails and rights of way. The freight railroads, on the defensive, marshaled arguments that the "forced access" proposals would lead to re-regulation— "turning back the clock" on two decades of progress.

FRA has been an observer and occasional participant in these century-ending debates, but has focused more on its safety regulatory role and (modest) promotion of higher-speed rail passenger service than on advocacy of policies promoting viability of private-sector freight railroads. At the dawn of the twenty-first century the question facing FRA and all others interested in or affected by railroad industry policy and performance is whether the renaissance begun by the Staggers Act will be sustained into the future or will slow to a trickle. Many of those observers who remember what FRA was able to accomplish in its middle period hope that it can produce a new prospectus for change that will show again how, despite significant barriers, industry initiatives and public policy can yield remarkable progress.

—Robert E. Gallamore

REFERENCE

Sampson, Roy J., et al. *Domestic Transportation: Practice, Theory, and Policy.* Chap. 21. Boston: Houghton Mifflin, 1985.

See also REGULATION.

Ferrocarril del Pacífico. *See*

PACIFIC RAILROAD (FERROCARRIL DEL PACÍFICO)

Ferry Services. *See* MARINE OPERATIONS

Fink, Albert (1827–1897)

One of the leading nineteenth-century railroad engineers to emerge from the pioneer Baltimore & Ohio Railroad, Albert Fink was also widely accomplished in railroad management. The son of an architect, he was born at Lauterbach, Germany, in 1827 and attended the Polytechnic School at Darmstadt, where he graduated in 1848 with high honors in both architecture and engineering. Fink emigrated to the United States in 1849 and secured a position in the drafting office of Benjamin H. Latrobe, Jr., the B&O's chief engineer. Well trained and capable, Fink soon became the principal assistant to Latrobe in charge of designing and erecting bridges and other structures for the expanding railroad.

REFERENCE

"Memoir of Albert Fink." *Transactions of the American Society of Civil Engineers* 40 (1898): 626–638.

Albert Fink. —American Society of Civil Engineers

While working under Latrobe, Fink designed the suspension truss that carried his name and was extensively used for long-span bridges by the B&O and other railroads. The longest of these were trusses spanning 208 feet for the Louisville & Nashville's crossing of the Green River south of Louisville. Later, Fink devised a new truss type for record-breaking main-channel spans of 370 and 400 feet for the Pennsylvania's crossing of the Ohio River at Louisville, completed during 1868–1870. These used additional intermediate members to subdivide the truss panels. A simplified variation of the design, known as the Petit, Baltimore, or Pennsylvania truss, was later widely used by the Pennsylvania Railroad.

Fink left the B&O in 1857 to take up a post as assistant engineer for the Louisville & Nashville. After the Civil War, when he was in charge of reconstruction of sections of line destroyed by Confederate troops, Fink rose rapidly through L&N management ranks, becoming general superintendent in 1865 and a vice president in 1870. At the L&N Fink devoted considerable study to the economics of railroad operation, cost accounting, and rates, and after leaving the railroad in 1875 he headed two railroad associations concerned with through traffic, rates, and tariffs. He served as president of the American Society of Civil Engineers during 1879–1880. He retired in 1889 and died in Louisville in 1897.

—William D. Middleton

Fish Cars

Livingston Stone of the U.S. Commission on Fish and Fisheries (now the U.S. Fish and Wildlife Service of the Department of the Interior) set out on a most unusual rail trip in June 1873, only four years after the transcontinental railroad had been completed. The newly established commission had set out to expand the variety of food-fishes in western states. Stone was delivering eastern fish species in a novel aquarium car modified from a Central Pacific Railroad fruit car for the long journey west. It was equipped with a tank that could carry 10,000 pounds of water, a large icebox, various equipment, and berths for the crew. The car was loaded at Charlestown, New Hampshire, with a variety of black bass, perch, bullheads, tautogs, saltwater eels, and trout, as well as a supply of breeding lobsters and a barrel of oysters. Freshwater eels, shad, and shad eggs were added during stops at Albany and Chicago. The pioneer shipment came to grief when the train was wrecked on a flooded trestle at the Elkhorn River, not far from Omaha, Nebraska. Stone and his men escaped with bruises as the car was filled with water, but the car was destroyed. Many of the fish—it was presumed—safely made their way into Elkhorn River.

Stone tried again a few weeks later with a shipment of shad fry in a baggage car, and the following year a second aquarium car completed an eight-day journey from New Hampshire to California. In both cases most of the fish arrived safely, and long-range shipment of new fish grew into a major industry for stocking the streams and waterways of the United States.

Stone and others quickly developed the techniques of moving fish safely over long distances. In one early shipment striped bass were carried from New Jersey to California with ice cooling the milk cans. Another shipment a few years later used a new aerating device: a water-filled cylinder with tiny holes in the bottom to release a fine spray of air-enriched water into the shipping cans. Colder water both absorbed more oxygen and reduced the oxygen needs of the fish. The water had to be kept free of impurities, and it was found helpful to confine the fish without food for a few days before loading. Early shipments were made in baggage cars, with government fish culturists called "messengers" along to aerate the water and to make sure the fish were in good condition.

As fish shipments grew steadily, the commission decided in 1881 to purchase its own fish car, a former Philadelphia, Wilmington & Baltimore baggage car that was specially equipped for carrying fish. A year later the Baltimore & Ohio built Fish Car No. 2, which was fitted

The Baltimore & Ohio built the second of the U.S. Fish Commission's specially equipped fish cars in 1882. It could carry 20,000 pounds of fish, water, and equipment at passenger-train speeds and provided living space and meals for its crew. Fish Car No. 2 loaded fish aboard the car. —Smithsonian Institution (Neg. 2005-10287)

with special compartments to hold fish and reinforced so that it could carry as many as 20,000 pounds of fish, water, and equipment at passenger-train speeds. Fish cans were placed in refrigerated chambers along each side at the center of the car, with portable cane-back seats above the chambers, dining space, and upper berths provided for the crew. Ice storage boxes were installed at each end, above the trucks, an office compartment was provided at one end of the car, and space at the opposite end was equipped with galley and pantry space and a pump and blower room for the refrigeration equipment. "Federally raised fish," an account of the service noted dryly, "traveled first class in railroad cars designed for their health and comfort—along with their human attendants."

Fish Car No. 3 followed in 1884. The car was equipped to hatch fish eggs in transit and got its first real-world test in 1886, when 600,000 shad eggs were sent from the Susquehanna River in Maryland to Portland, Oregon. By the time the car arrived at its destination, the eggs had hatched to become thriving fish ready for stocking in the Columbia and Willamette rivers. Fish Car No. 4 joined the roster in 1893, with cedar tanks, a pump to aerate the water, and other special equipment. By the end of the century the government had acquired two more fish cars.

Fish runs were generally operated from April through November, with some journeys lasting as long as ten days. Each car carried about 150 10-gallon cans containing some 15,000 three-inch fish. Losses en route were held to about 1 percent. The five-man crew included a fish-car "captain," several "messengers," and a cook.

Railroads welcomed the fish cars, generally charging only 20 cents a mile to haul the cars and their crews. Mes-

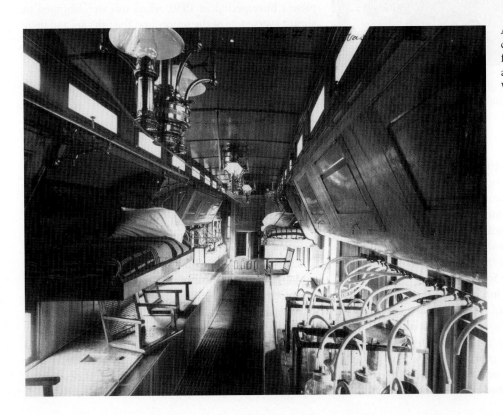

An interior view of a fish car shows accommodations for fish and their human attendants. —U.S. Fish and Wildlife Service

U.S. Fish Commission staff sit down for a formal meal atop the refrigerated chambers of Fish Car No. 2. —Smithsonian Institution (Neg. 2005-10288)

time Bureau of Fisheries man Edgar C. Fearnow. Used in place of the traditional 10-gallon milk can containers, the new pails weighed only five pounds and could carry twice as many fish as the older milk cans in only half the space. The Fearnows also had a special built-in compartment for ice to keep the water cool. Manual aeration of water in the containers began to be replaced by such methods as electric or jet aerators that used compressed air; several of the new steel cars used air from the train line.

This was a busy time for the fish cars. A 1923 report showed that over a 20-year period the fish and fisheries service had distributed more than 72 billion fish from the various hatchery activities by fish cars traveling more than 2 million miles. Most of the fish shipments were freshwater or anadromous fish, such as pike, perch, shad, whitefish, trout, carp, landlocked salmon, and others. To enrich the aquatic potential of different regions, transfers between regions were common. Regional resources such as lobsters and blue crabs, for example, were shipped from Woods Hole, Massachusetts, to San Francisco, and Dungeness crabs were shipped from San Francisco to Chesapeake Bay. Nonnative species such as brown trout, shad, and carp were introduced in many areas. Similar fish-car services for distributing hatchery stock were also operated in Canada and by at least a dozen states.

A more advanced fish car was introduced in 1929. Fish Car No. 10 was an 81-foot-long car that cost the Department of Commerce $59,000. Its insulated compartments could hold 325 cans, with room for 34,000 three-inch fish or 500,000 one-inch fish. The car even had its own generator to operate all of its equipment, including electric aerating devices. The new car helped the fisheries men complete a busy period in 1930, when fish were shipped to almost every state of the union, and the fish cars and their messengers together covered almost 506,000 miles in a year's time.

But the era of the fish car was drawing to a close. Expansion of hatcheries had reduced the need for long shipments, and trucks had proved to be a more economical way to ship fish over shorter distance. By 1937 modernized trucks equaled the mileage of the fish cars. By 1940 only three fish cars were left in service. One was wrecked in 1944; the fate of a second was unknown. The last survivor, Fish Car No. 10, was taken out of service in 1947. Most fish transport went to trucks, but shipment by air was sometimes used as well.

Another kind of fish car was built in 1929 to collect and transport fish for the new John G. Shedd Aquarium in Chicago's Grant Park, one of the largest aquaria in the world. Built by the Pullman Co., the 83-foot *Nautilus* accommodated 16 200-gallon waterproof cypress boxes and 20 30-gallon metal containers that could be rolled on and off the car, and it was fitted with tanks, pumps, air compressors, electric refrigeration coils, and steam heat to support the fish. One end of the car was outfitted with bunks, a bath, and an efficiency kitchen for a collecting crew of six.

sengers accompanying "detached" shipments rode for reduced rates or at no cost, and the empty fish cans and pails used in hauling the fish were shipped back to the commission free. The unusual fish cars became attractions themselves, appearing at such exhibitions as the New Orleans Exhibition of 1885, the World's Columbian Exhibition at Chicago in 1893, and the Pan American Exposition at Buffalo, New York, in 1901.

A new generation of fish cars began arriving in 1916, when the first all-steel car, No. 7, arrived. Larger than the wooden models, it could carry 50 percent more fish. Three more steel cars were soon delivered, with increasingly advanced equipment and greater capacity. The changing technology included a new lightweight fish container, called Fearnow pails, named after their inventor and long-

To get the new aquarium started, the Illinois Central Railroad in December 1929 completed the shipment of about a million gallons of selected seawater in 160 tank cars from Key West, Florida, to Grant Park. *Nautilus* began its maiden voyage, to Key West, Florida, in April 1930 and over the next 26 years traveled about 20,000 miles a year to destinations in Maine, Florida, and California, as well as points in the Midwest.

During its first four years *Nautilus* transported more than 21,000 fish for the aquarium, including just about anything up to a 60-pound shark. Most were tropical species, but the car could also accommodate cold saltwater fish and cold, temperate, and warm freshwater species. One marathon journey in 1933 took collectors all the way to Sydney, Australia, returning by ship with a collection of Australian fish safely on board their cypress fish boxes. Still more fish from Hawaiian reefs joined the collection at Honolulu. The steamship *Mariposa* docked in Los Angeles to be met by *Nautilus*, which reached its Shedd Aquarium destination in time for the June 1 opening of Chicago's Century of Progress. One Australian lungfish from the 1933 collection trip, known as Granddad, is still alive at the Shedd.

A 1935 collecting trip to Florida on *Nautilus* was easily the Shedd's most dramatic. Ready to depart from Key West on September 2, 1935, the car was stranded there after a record hurricane through the Florida Keys destroyed the Key West extension of the Florida East Coast Railway. Key West itself and *Nautilus* escaped damage, but the collectors spent the next two months there. The car finally came home from Key West on a car ferry after a new ferry slip was completed at Fort Lauderdale, returning the car to the tracks.

While working to keep the stranded fish alive during the enforced layover, the crew also spent some time on collecting, including among their acquisitions an Atlantic tarpon, later named Deadeye, that would remain a star attraction at the Shedd for the next 63 years. The tarpon acquired the name after a 1959 accident, when the jumpy fish leaped through several tanks and onto the gallery floor, losing half her scales and much of her vision.

The collection crew remembered the return trip home to Chicago as a pleasant outing once all the fish had been loaded, taking turns watching all the equipment and enjoying the journey. Sometimes, however, there was a little excitement. On one return from Florida a large green moray eel died on board. Wanting to get rid of it as quickly as they could, crewmembers waited until the train was in a rural wooded area in Georgia. Just as the dead moray got the heave-ho, the woods parted and a house appeared. The moray went bouncing off through the fence and landed in the house's backyard, leaving the *Nautilus* staff to wonder what the residents thought of the green snake in their backyard.

Badly deteriorated by salt water, the car could no longer be used by 1956. A replacement, *Nautilus II*, was rebuilt from a Chicago & Eastern Illinois lounge car originally

Chicago's John G. Shedd Aquarium operated special fish cars to transport its marine specimens from such locations as Florida and California. *Nautilus II*, the last U.S. fish car, is shown loading fish. —Monticello Railway Museum

used for the streamlined 1946 *Hummingbird*. For the next 14 years the car made regular trips to Florida and California to pick up specimens from the Bahamas, Hawaii, and elsewhere. By 1972 shipping live fish by airfreight had become practical, and the Shedd ended its unique fish-car operation. The *Nautilus II* is now stored at the Monticello Railway Museum at Monticello, Illinois.

—William D. Middleton

REFERENCE

Leonard, John R. *The Fish Car Era*. Washington, D.C.: U.S. Government Printing Office, 1979.

Fisk, James, Jr. (1834–1872)

One of the most flamboyant characters of nineteenth-century railroading, Jim Fisk was born in Bennington, Vermont, the son of a Yankee peddler. Following in his father's footsteps, Fisk peddled shoddy goods in his "traveling emporium," a gaudy red wagon that probably gladdened the eye of many an unsuspecting Vermont housewife. A man of supreme selling abilities, he shortly turned to more daring exploits. After working as a commission agent for a Boston wholesale firm, Fisk in 1865 opened a stock brokerage house in New York.

Fisk caught the attention of financier Daniel Drew and became an agent in some of Drew's steamboat deals. Later he became more closely allied with Jay Gould and was involved with Drew and Gould in the famous Erie Railroad wars of the late 1860s. With his blustery, extroverted personality, Fisk was a splendid foil for Gould, who was said to have the manner of a subdued undertaker. When Gould became president of the Erie in 1868, he made Fisk comptroller. In this position Fisk was largely responsible for operation of the railroad, a role for which he had no real qualification. He strode up and down the line in a resplendent colonel's uniform (having purchased the honorary title of colonel after the Civil War) and was referred to in the press as "Prince Erie." His hearty manner made him popular with employees, despite his limited skills as a railroader.

Henry Adams wrote of Jim Fisk that he was "coarse, noisy, boastful and ignorant," with "the morals of a 14-year old." But he was certainly picturesque, always thinking on a grand scale. For a while he owned the Narragansett Steamship Line and sometimes greeted passengers on the docks in an admiral's uniform. One of the nation's first playboys, he rode around New York City in a gilded carriage, usually with fancy women on his arm. For the Erie Railroad he purchased the old Pike's Opera House (renamed Grand Opera House) and converted it into "executive chambers." It was fitted out in the manner of a high-class bordello. When Gould and Fisk left the Erie in 1872, the railroad's finances were in ruins, and the company paid no dividends on common stock for 69 years.

Fisk and his antics were constantly in the pages of the cheap newspapers of the day. In 1872 he was shot and killed in a New York hotel as the result of a squabble over one of his fancy ladies, Josie Mansfield.

—George H. Douglas

REFERENCE

Swanberg, W. A. *Jim Fisk: The Career of an Improbable Rascal.* New York: Scribner, 1959.

Flagler, Henry M. (1830–1913)

Henry Morrison Flagler was a towering figure in oil, railroading, and real estate development. His most significant contribution to the railroad industry was building the Florida East Coast Railway from Jacksonville to Miami. Flagler's work on the FEC also included building the famous Key West extension, which was destroyed by a hurricane in 1935.

Flagler was born on January 2, 1830, in Hopewell, New York. He left school at age 14 and moved to Ohio, where he became successful working in the mercantile business with his half brother, Dan Harkness. After a number of years Flagler joined the oil-refining partnership of John D. Rockefeller and Samuel Andrews to form Rockefeller, Andrews & Flagler (RA&F). From 1867 through 1885 Fla-gler was a key member of the team that developed RA&F into the Standard Oil Co.

The nineteenth century was an exciting period for American business. The U.S. economy transformed local and regional markets into national ones. Railroads helped fuel this growth, and part of Flagler's work was arranging railroad transportation of his company's oil.

During the mid-1880s Flagler began to turn his attention away from Standard Oil to the young state of Florida. Flagler preferred the excitment of building businesses, and Standard Oil had matured; it no longer offered the sort of challenge he relished. Having been in American hands only since 1821, the state of Florida was a new frontier for population and development.

In December 1883, while honeymooning with his second wife, Ida Alice Shrouds (she had been the nurse of his first wife, Mary Harkness Flagler, who died in 1881), Flagler visited Jacksonville and St. Augustine and began thinking about how this region of Florida might be improved. Not only did St. Augustine need better accommodations for travelers, but the rail service between Jacksonville and St. Augustine was substandard. St. Augustine, founded in 1565, was a city focused primarily on its past. Flagler confided to a friend that he believed he could transform it into the "Newport of the South," referring to the resort town of Newport, Rhode Island. Over the next 10 years Flagler significantly changed the city into an important resort community. He built a number of private and public buildings, including the fabulous Ponce de Leon Hotel.

Flagler's first significant involvement in Florida railroading came in 1881 when the state legislature chartered the Jacksonville, St. Augustine & Halifax River Railway (JStA&HR). The road was to run from Jacksonville south to St. Augustine, then on to the Halifax River. As the railroad was built, Flagler received regular updates on its progress, and many hoped that he would become an advisor to the company. He joined the company's board of directors, but was not pleased with the quality of the construction and the overall direction of the project. On December 31, 1885, Flagler purchased the assets of the JStA&HR and over the next 11 years improved and expanded the line until it reached Miami in 1896. A year before reaching Miami, the road was renamed the Florida East Coast Railway (FEC).

Flagler continued extending the line south of Miami, and in 1905, when the federal government completed its arrangements for building the Panama Canal, he decided that he must extend his railroad to Key West, a feat that was deemed nearly impossible by everyone. His plan was to take advantage of the tremendous traffic potential of the Panama Canal by building a deepwater port close to the canal.

After years of surveys and difficult construction work the Key West extension was opened on January 22, 1912. During remarks at the opening ceremony, Flagler said, "Now I can die fulfilled." He died a little over a year later, on May 20, 1913, from complications resulting from a broken hip, at the age of 83. After the 1935 hurricane destroyed the extension, the federal government replaced it with a modern highway.

Flagler's involvement with the FEC is a great accomplishment, but his larger legacy in Florida is due in equal part to his creation of resorts and other large-scale developments. It is difficult to imagine today's Florida without Henry M. Flagler.

—David C. Lester

REFERENCES

Akin, Edward N. *Flagler: Rockefeller Partner and Florida Baron.* Kent, Ohio: Kent State Univ. Press, 1988. Paperback ed., Gainesville: Univ. Press of Florida, 1991.

Bramson, Seth H. "Henry M. Flagler." In *Railroads in the Age of Regulation, 1900–1980,* ed. Keith L. Bryant, Jr., 159–161. A volume in *Encyclopedia of American Business History and Biography,* gen. ed. William H. Becker. New York: Bruccoli Clark Layman and Facts on File, 1988.

———. *Speedway to Sunshine: The Story of the Florida East Coast Railway.* Rev. ed. Erin, Ont.: Boston Mills Press, 2003.

Standiford, Les. *Last Train to Paradise.* New York: Crown, 2002.

Florida East Coast Railway

Henry M. Flagler was one of the partners of John D. Rockefeller in the formation of the Standard Oil Co. In 1878 Flagler moved to Florida in hope that the warm climate would be beneficial for his wife (who died in 1881). Flagler saw Florida as a potential tourist destination. To open the east coast of the state to vacationers, in 1885 he acquired a narrow-gauge railroad that reached 36 miles south from Jacksonville. He renamed it the Florida East Coast Railway (FEC), converted it to standard gauge, bridged the St. Johns River to connect with other railroads at Jacksonville, and extended the line south. It reached Miami, 366 miles from Jacksonville, in 1896.

Recognizing the potential of trade with Cuba, as well as the advantage of Key West as the closest port to the Panama Canal, then under construction, Flagler pushed the railroad south from Miami and across the Florida Keys to Key West. Hurricanes in 1906, 1909, and 1910 caused setbacks in construction, but in January 1912 Flagler rode the first train to Key West. He died in May 1913.

The Florida land boom hit in 1924. The FEC double-tracked its main line, installed signals, built branch lines, and bought 90 new locomotives. The boom peaked in 1926, and competition in the form of the Seaboard Air Line Railway reached Miami in 1927. On top of that came the Great Depression. FEC went into receivership in 1931.

A hurricane in September 1935 destroyed most of the Key West extension. It had never repaid its construction cost, and FEC was unwilling to repair the line—if it could even afford to do so. The remains of the roadbed and bridges were used to extend U.S. Highway 1 to Key West, and FEC sold its excess motive power to other railroads. The FEC became essentially the Miami extension of the Atlantic Coast Line Railroad, which offered to purchase the FEC in 1944. Later the Seaboard Air Line Railway and the Southern Railway made a similar offer. Both offers were thwarted by pressure to keep control of the FEC in the state of Florida.

The company underwent reorganization in 1960 and came under the control of the St. Joe Paper Co., which was owned by the estate of Alfred I. Du Pont. In 1963 the railroad refused to go along with a pay increase that the unions had negotiated across the railroad industry. The nonoperating unions struck, and the operating unions honored their picket lines. Within two weeks freight trains were being operated by company management (through passenger trains to and from Miami detoured on the Seaboard Air Line route). The strike escalated to the point that bridges and tracks were being destroyed. Even so, in 1965 FEC was required to reinstate a daily passenger train between Jacksonville and Miami because of the provision of the company's charter, it lasted until 1968.

The strike by the nonoperating unions was settled in 1971, but the strike by the operating unions lasted until 1976. In the interim the railroad had changed completely: double track had become single, with centralized traffic control, concrete ties had replaced wood, and two-man crews operated cabooseless freight trains the length of the railroad instead of the three-to five-man crews formerly required. Revenue and earnings increased, and in 1980 FEC declared a dividend on its common stock—the first ever. In 1984 FEC changed its corporate structure and became a subsidiary of FEC Industries, a holding company that had previously been a subsidiary of the railroad. Florida East Coast operates a system of 351 route-miles and 786 track-miles, with 72 locomotives and 4,153 freight cars.

—George H. Drury

REFERENCE

Bramson, Seth H. *Speedway to Sunshine.* Rev. ed. Erin, Ont.: Boston Mills Press, 1984.

Forbes, John Murray (1813–1898)

Financier and railroad developer John Murray Forbes was raised in Milton, Massachusetts, and attended a private academy, but entered his uncle's counting house in Boston at the age of 15. Shortly afterward his uncle's firm sent him to China as a commission merchant; at age 24 he returned to Boston a fairly wealthy man. He established his own firm, J. M. Forbes, commission merchants and shipowners, and in the next decade he amassed an enormous fortune.

In 1846 James F. Joy, a Detroit lawyer, had joined with New York financier John W. Brooks to promote the development of the Michigan Central Railroad as a line through Detroit that would link to the east with the New York railroads and to the west with Chicago. Joy and Brooks, in turn, had interested Forbes with a proposal to buy and rebuild the Michigan Central and push that line on to Chicago. Forbes raised most of the needed $2 million from his fellow Boston capitalists. Later, when the Chicago connection was complete, Forbes and Joy began buying up lines already built to the west of Chicago and across the Mississippi River. Their main achievement was the creation of the Chicago, Burlington & Quincy Railroad, which took on mammoth proportions in only a few years. Forbes himself served as CB&Q president from 1878 to 1881 and groomed his cousin, Charles E. Perkins, as his successor.

During the Civil War Forbes, a vehement opponent of slavery, was a strong supporter of Lincoln. He continued his shipping interests and unsuccessfully attempted to prevent the British government from selling vessels to the Confederacy. After the war Forbes assumed a peacemaking role among the western railroads. In his earlier experiences with the China trade he had learned to be wary of lethal competition, and he hoped to form alliances between railroad companies. He arranged to eliminate cutthroat competition among rail lines between Chicago and St. Louis and set up numerous cooperative terminal agreements.

Forbes was by nature a typical New England Brahmin. He was contemptuous of the unbridled competition of the Wall Street capitalists after the Civil War and loathed railroad buccaneers like Jay Gould and Cornelius Vanderbilt. He lived the life of a cultured country gentleman in his later years; he was a good friend of Ralph Waldo Emerson and a member of the famous Saturday Club for Boston's literary elite. Emerson said of Forbes: "This is a good country that can bear such a creature as he is."

—George H. Douglas

REFERENCES

Johnson, Arthur M., and Barry E. Supple. *Boston Capitalists and Western Railroads*. Cambridge, Mass.: Harvard Univ. Press, 1967.

Larson, John Lauritz. *Bonds of Enterprise: John Murray Forbes and Western Development in America's Railway Age*. Cambridge, Mass.: Harvard Univ. Press, 1984.

Fort Dodge, Des Moines & Southern Railway

The largest of all the Iowa interurbans and one of Iowa's busiest freight railroads was the 150-mile Fort Dodge

Line, organized in 1906 using the center part of a small steam-operated coal carrier that ran between Newton and Rockwell City to create a new interurban between Fort Dodge and Des Moines. Electrification of the center part of the Newton & Northwestern and a link with a new line northward from Hope to Fort Dodge and another southward from Midvale to Des Moines created an 85-mile main line between the two cities. Electrification of the old steam line from Hope west to Rockwell City and the addition of a branch line from Fort Dodge east to Webster City completed the system. A notable feature of the line was the 156-foot-high steel High Bridge, the highest of all interurban bridges, which crossed over a ravine in the Des Moines River valley near Boone.

Electric passenger service was operated on both the main line and branches, but freight service was always the Fort Dodge Line's most important source of revenue. A busy traffic in such commodities as gypsum from the mines around Fort Dodge was interchanged with the interurban's steam railroad connections. In 1918 it was said that the Fort Dodge Line had more freight cars (2,500) than any other railroad of comparable size, and during World War I the Class 1 carrier was one of the few interurbans taken over by the U.S. Railroad Administration (USRA).

The line continued to operate until well after World War II. The last electric passenger operation came to an end in 1955, and the railroad shifted its freight service to diesel power shortly afterward. Abandonment of the branch lines followed in the early 1960s, and the railroad's main line was incorporated into the Chicago & North Western in 1971.

In 1969, shortly before it was leased by the Chicago & North Western, the Fort Dodge, Des Moines & Southern operated a system of 111 route-miles and 144 track-miles, with 9 locomotives, 219 freight and company service cars, and 72 employees. The road's operating revenues totaled $1.7 million in 1969, and the railroad achieved an 86 percent operating ratio.

—William D. Middleton

REFERENCES

Carlson, Norman, ed. *Iowa Trolleys*. Chicago: Central Electric Railfans' Assn., Bulletin 114, 1975.

Donovan, Frank P., Jr. "Interurbans in Iowa." *Palimpsest* 35, no. 5 (May 1954): 177–212.

Fort Smith & Western Railway

The Fort Smith & Western Railway (later Railroad) operated between a connection with the Kansas City Southern at Coal Creek, Oklahoma, and with the Santa Fe at Guthrie from 1903 to February 9, 1939, when it finally fell victim to the Great Depression, droughts, and floods. The principal item of traffic was coal from mines near Mc-Curtain.

In 1937 the Fort Smith & Western operated 197 route-miles and 239 track-miles, with 11 locomotives, 9 passenger cars, 282 freight cars, 33 company service cars, and 278 employees. Freight traffic totaled 60.5 million ton-miles in 1937. Operating revenues totaled $114,196 in 1937, and the railroad achieved an 86 percent operating ratio.

—George H. Drury

Freight Cars

Popular attention often emphasizes powerful locomotives or sleek passenger cars, but by far the most ubiquitous type of railroad rolling stock is the freight car. In the late 1960s there were around 2 million freight cars in North America, compared with only 30,000 locomotives and a few hundred passenger cars. Looked at from another perspective, locomotives and passenger cars have a more narrow usage than freight cars, which must exist in many configurations to handle a variety of loads. It is also important to remember that freight cars have an ancient lineage. They were at work in the eighteenth century, during the early part of the Industrial Revolution in England, at a time before rails were made of iron and locomotives had been developed.

There are several ways of understanding freight-car development. Most obvious is a direct line of progression marked by important developments along the way. This approach overlooks anomalies such as the increased use of wood for construction during both world wars (because of shortages of steel). Some innovations such as the intermodal concept and the use of aluminum in car building were introduced numerous times before they became widely accepted. Other highly touted innovations turned out to have little significance. There were also numerous regional influences. For example, car builders in Pennsylvania and other steel-producing areas were quick to increase the use of steel in their products, while car builders in timber-producing areas persisted in using wood.

The vagaries of freight cars are best viewed as a large mosaic with an ever-changing design. In order to understand the significance of each development, it is necessary to have a fairly complete record of cars produced. The trade journal *Railway Age* published annual summaries of car orders placed from 1901 to 1981. Although these data are a good starting point, there are enough omissions to warrant looking at other trade publications, railroad records, car builders' records, and field observation of freight cars. The following discussion draws heavily on largely unpublished production lists compiled from all these sources.

General Development

The earliest freight cars in North America had two wheel and axle sets attached underneath a frame with couplings at either end. Though there were many variations, the predominating design by the early 1830s consisted of longitudinal wooden beams (outside the wheels) that were bolted to the top of journal boxes on the ends of the axles. The body was mounted on the beams. It was soon discovered that a longer body could span two sets of frames, creating a double-truck freight car. The 8-wheeled freight car was generally accepted as standard on North American railroads by the mid-1840s because it operated better on less-than-perfect track than a 4-wheeled car of the same length. The ratio of load to dead weight of 8-wheeled cars does not seem to have differed much from that of 4-wheeled cars, thus favoring neither arrangement.

Early 8-wheeled cars had capacities of about 10 tons, which increased to 20 tons (40,000 pounds) by the early 1880s. Table 1 shows subsequent increases in capacity and the period during which each was built in significant numbers.

In spite of the early supremacy of the 8-wheeled car, 4-wheeled cars remained popular in coal and ore service on some railroads. They were inexpensive to build and dumped more efficiently than contemporary 8-wheeled cars. Some prices from the mid-1870s show 4-wheeled coal cars to be about a third the price of 8-wheeled coal cars. Most of the 4-wheeled cars had capacities of 5 or 6 tons, but some of the last ones built in the early 1880s could carry 22,000 pounds. According to the *Official Railway Equipment Guide*, the Lehigh Valley Railroad, Central Railroad of New Jersey, and Delaware, Lackawanna & Western Railroad alone operated 67,194 4-wheeled cars in August 1888. Approximately 10,000 more were operated by other roads, including the Philadelphia & Reading and New York Central & Hudson River railroads. The Safety Appliance Act of 1893 brought an end to the existing 4-wheeled freight cars, which could not be easily equipped with air brakes or automatic couplers. The last were retired from revenue service by August 1900.

Caboose cars were another type where 4-wheeled cars

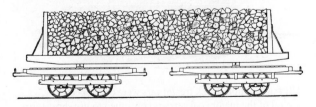

This drawing from *The American Railway* (1892) depicts an early freight car design developed by the B&O to transport firewood in 1830 for what was one of the earliest double-truck cars. —Middleton Collection

Table 1. Freight-Car Capacity

Capacity (Pounds)	Period of Construction
50,000	Late 1880s to early 1890s
60,000	Early 1890s to early 1910s
80,000	Late 1890s to early 1940s
100,000	Late 1890s to early 1960s
140,000	Mid-1910s to early 1980s
200,000	Early 1960s to present

could be found in significant numbers. Relatively short cars were found adequate by many railroads, and there was no reason to increase capacity since they did not carry freight. However, various state laws in the early twentieth century either required 8-wheeled cars or set a minimum length that made 4-wheeled cars impractical. Ten 4-wheeled caboose cars built for the Philadelphia & Reading Railroad in November and December 1921 were perhaps the last built for a major railroad.

However, that was not the end of 4-wheeled freight cars in North America. The North American Car Corp. built a 4-wheeled refrigerator car in November 1932, but it failed to become accepted. Two decades later ACF Industries developed the Adapto, a 4-wheeled flatcar for containerized freight, of which 50 were purchased by the Chicago, Rock Island & Pacific in 1956. A thousand more were ordered by the Trailer Train Co., but the order was soon reduced to 100, and none of them seem to have made it into regular service. More recently, the Front Runner, a 4-wheeled flatcar, was developed for the Trailer Train Co. in the 1980s. It was suitable for loading a single highway trailer up to 48 feet long with a 65,000 pound gross weight. At this time it was common practice to load two 45-foot highway trailers on an 89-foot car. The empty weight of the 4-wheeled car was about 26,000 pounds, a

Although double-truck freight cars were developed early, several of the major coal carriers continued to use short four-wheel cars through the end of the nineteenth century. This drawing of a Central Railroad of New Jersey four-wheel car was illustrated in *The American Railway* (1892). —Middleton Collection

value that compared favorably to an 89-foot car weighing about 69,000 pounds. Approximately 3,372 Front Runners were built by at least nine different car builders from 1983 to 1989. With the increasing use of 53-foot highway trailers, large numbers of Front Runners were taken out of service starting in 2000. Only 479 remained at the end of 2002.

The 6-wheeled freight car was much rarer. At least 81 were operated by the Baltimore & Susquehanna Railroad while James Millholland was head of its mechanical department in the 1840s. In addition, the Baltimore & Ohio Railroad had acquired 254 6-wheeled iron pot hopper cars by 1855, while Central Railroad of New Jersey began acquiring 6-wheeled freight cars in 1862, and by the end of 1875 a total of 228 6-wheeled iron, lime, and wood rack cars were in service. Further additions brought the total to 700 ore and 47 lime cars by the early 1880s. The Lehigh Valley Railroad purchased 100 6-wheeled platform cars built in 1869 and 1871 for hauling iron products. Cars on the Central of New Jersey and Lehigh Valley had capacities of 24,000 pounds and lengths of 16 feet. Some cars had cast pedestals and sprung equalizers similar in arrangement to 6-wheel passenger trucks. All were retired from interchange service by August 1900.

Even rarer was the three-truck freight car. The New York, Pennsylvania & Ohio Railroad had 40 12-wheeled side-dump ore cars (capacity of 80,000 pounds) that were built around 1890. Some were upgraded to 120,000 pounds through substitution of stronger trucks.

Small numbers of heavy-duty cars appeared in interchange service during the latter part of the nineteenth century. They were usually flat or low-side gondola cars carried on two 6-wheel trucks or two pairs of 4-wheel trucks connected by span bolsters. The earliest known example was a 16-wheeled gun car (capacity of 60,000 pounds) built for the Philadelphia & Reading Railroad in 1865. Capacities of these cars increased over the years so that, some 25 years later, special 12-wheeled flatcars were being built with capacities of 110,000 pounds. A small number of special-duty flatcars, including the Schnabel design, rode on more than 16 wheels and were built in small numbers after 1950. Each was designed for extremely large or heavy items. Various designs of heavy-duty flat and Schnabel cars are still being built.

Starting during the 1910s and 1920s, various designs of coal cars with a pair of 6-wheel trucks were used by several railroads. For many years the Norfolk & Western and Virginian railroads each operated over 2,000 cars of this type, with capacities of around 200,000 pounds. Between the mid-1960s and the early 1970s about 500 large tank cars with two 6-wheel trucks or two pairs of 4-wheel trucks connected by span bolsters were built. These cars, which held up to 60,000 gallons, were found to be difficult to handle either in the yards or in main-line service. Most existing cars remained in service, but no more were built.

Articulated cars for intermodal service were developed

in the late 1970s and early 1980s and are common today. They range from two units placed on 3 4-wheel trucks to ten units placed on 11 4-wheel trucks. They are used for highway trailers, standard intermodal containers, and garbage containers. One of the most common arrangements carries ten standard intermodal containers on five units. Some articulated flatcars with two units have racks for automobiles.

A few articulated hopper and covered hopper cars have been built for experimental purposes in both the United States and Canada since the 1960s. None have gone into regular production.

Bimodal Equipment

The idea of a freight carrier that can operate on both highway and railway is not new. Between 1853 and 1857 a special circus train did just that. The mechanical details are unknown, but apparently it inspired no imitators. Bimodal freight equipment reappeared in the late 1950s when the Chesapeake & Ohio Railway built two prototype Railvans that consisted of a highway trailer with regular tires, as well as a flanged wheel set that was lowered for operation on rails. The trailers could be coupled together with an adapter bogie under the lead trailer for connection with conventional equipment. Eighty more 29-foot trailers were built between 1959 and 1964 and operated until about 1968. Bimodal equipment again appeared in the late 1980s. The most successful proponent is Wabash National Corp., which introduced the Mark IV RoadRailer by 1987. It was similar to the Chesapeake & Ohio Railvan except that the trailers were 48 feet long. The Mark V RoadRailer was introduced by 1988 and lacked flanged wheel sets. Instead, separate rail bogies were positioned under the rear end of one trailer and the front end of the next. Trailers were 48 and 53 feet long. RoadRailers are presently operated by several companies,

An alternate approach to intermodal highway-rail freight shipment has been the use of specially designed trailers that can operate both as highway trailers and rail cars, using interchangeable rubber-tired and steel wheels. This Mark IV RoadRailer was built by Stoughton in 1988 for Triple Crown Services (TCSZ). —Eric A. Neubauer

including Norfolk Southern, whose fleet in 2000 included about 7,000 Mark V trailers. Bimodal equipment is not listed in *The Official Railway Equipment Register*, suggesting that the railroad industry does not classify vehicles of this type as freight cars.

Factors That Affect Design

To understand the evolution of freight cars, it is important to know the underlying factors that affect car design. Their significance varies by time and place, and general trends are usually driven by more than one factor. One factor has been ratio of load to dead weight. A car with more pounds of cargo per pound of empty weight will require less fuel to generate the same amount of revenue. However, if a car is too lightly constructed, repair costs increase and any savings from less fuel use are lost. Thus car design has always represented a delicate balance between strength and weight. But the bottom line is that cars have continually improved because of innovative designs, more modern construction materials, and economies of scale. The progression of hopper-bottom coal cars in similar service is a good example. In 1896 a 30-ton wooden car weighed 30,000 pounds, with a load-to-weight ratio of 2. By 1903 a 50-ton steel car weighed 37,300 pounds, with a ratio of 2.68. A 70-ton steel car of 1938 weighed 48,000 pounds, with a ratio of 2.91. By 1964 a 100-ton steel car weighed 61,700 pounds, with a ratio of 3.24, whereas in 1985 a 105-ton aluminum-bodied car weighed 50,900 pounds, with a ratio of 4.12.

It is clear that car size is limited by a railroad's infrastructure, which includes roadbed strength and clearances (both on the railroad and in customer facilities). Improvements in these areas allowed typical car capacities to increase from 20 tons in the early 1880s to 50 and 70 tons by 1920. Higher-capacity cars were envisioned, but could only be put into limited use. General clearances continued to improve, and the height of a standard boxcar grew from 14 feet 2 inches in 1918 to 14 feet 7 inches in 1937 and to 15 feet in 1942. Almost no additional increase in car size was allowed until the 1960s.

About 1963 the gross rail load was changed so that the nominal capacity of each truck journal increased by 10 percent. On March 1, 1964, a set of new clearance dimensions became effective. The new clearance diagram, known as Plate C, applied to most North American lines. Maximum height increased from 15 feet 1 inch to 15 feet 6 inches, and distance between truck centers increased from 41 feet 3 inches to 46 feet 3 inches without restricting maximum width. A number of larger cars of various types came into use during what is usually referred to as the "high-cube revolution." Clearance diagrams for even larger cars on restricted routes followed. A maximum height of 20 feet 2 inches is allowed by Plate H, which was adopted in 1991 and applies to double-stack container cars and some auto-rack cars. In 1994 the gross rail load increased from 263,000 pounds to 286,000 pounds for cars with 6-by-11-inch bearings and included the majority being built. Car designs were immediately enlarged to take advantage of this 10 percent increase in capacity.

Car design has also been affected greatly by growth of specific industrial sectors. For example, the rapid expansion and diversification of the chemical industry between 1910 and 1940 brought a whole new array of products that could not be easily shipped in existing cars. During this period cars were developed for anhydrous ammonia, carbon black, caustic soda, chlorine, dry ice, gasoline, helium, hydrogen peroxide, liquefied petroleum gas, propane, sulfur dioxide, and other chemicals. Production of plastic resins increased greatly during the 1960s and 1970s, requiring many new designs for tank and covered hopper cars.

A customer's shipping format has also affected freight-car design. Both cement and flour were originally bagged and shipped in boxcars. Around 1930 many cement manufacturers in the United States began to switch to bulk shipping using covered hoppers. With no suitable existing designs to use, builders worked quickly to develop new ones. Bulk shipping of flour in covered hopper cars began in the 1950s, but only after much effort was spent developing a functional unloading system.

Being located on a rail line has decreased in importance because of the growing highway system in North America and the use of highway trailers carried on trains. Thus it is no longer necessary for every shipper to have a railroad siding. Moreover, the rapid rise of a global economy has supported the explosive use of intermodal containers. Starting in the 1950s, railroads made a successful effort to serve off-line customers by developing cars that could efficiently handle trailers. During the 1960s the effort was expanded to include standard shipping containers. Today, intermodal business has become an important part of the railroad industry.

Construction Materials

It is obvious that car design is affected by the choice of construction materials. Throughout the nineteenth century wood was the obvious choice; it was widely available, relatively inexpensive, and easy to shape with ordinary tools. Freight-car designs usually consisted of a frame with mortise and tenon joints, held together with various iron straps, bolts, and rods. Wood flooring, sheathing, or lining was either nailed or bolted to the frame. Certain parts, including couplings, center plates for attaching the trucks, wheels, axles, journal boxes, and brake rigging, were almost always iron or steel.

Iron sheet, readily available by the 1840s, was used extensively in several isolated cases of car building. In 1844 the Philadelphia & Reading Railroad began acquiring iron hopper cars with wooden underframes. By the end of 1849 it owned 3,019 4-wheeled and 8-wheeled iron coal cars, constituting two-thirds of its coal car fleet. Most of the iron cars were retired in the 1870s and 1880s. The Bal-

timore & Ohio Railroad started building 6-wheeled iron hopper cars in 1844 and 8-wheeled iron hopper cars with wooden underframes in 1846. In 1855 a total of 254 6-wheeled and 774 8-wheeled iron coal cars were in service. The B&O cars were known as pot hoppers because the body consisted of a series of cylindrical hoppers. The original 8-wheeled pot hopper cars had a capacity of 20,000 pounds. This was increased to 26,000 pounds by 1879. Approximately 2,500 larger cars with 40,000-pound capacity were built from 1883 to 1885. By July 1888 the B&O had 4,224 8-wheeled iron coal cars in service. All were retired from interchange service by August 1900.

Tank cars, composed of a horizontal iron tank on a wooden underframe, began appearing in large numbers in the late 1860s, although iron or steel underframes were not commonly used until after 1902. The Iron Car Co. constructed about 7,000 iron-underframe cars of various types between 1887 and 1891. These were descendants of the commercially unsuccessful La Mothe designs of the 1860s and 1870s with iron underframes, predominantly composed of gas pipe. Iron Car Co.'s financial problems during 1890 brought an abrupt end to the construction of several thousand more gas-pipe cars that were in the planning stage. Gas-pipe cars were known for their great strength, but required excessive maintenance as they aged.

By the mid-1890s pressed-steel parts, advocated by steel-car promoter Charles T. Schoen, were often used for body bolsters and trucks on wooden cars. Just as wood was becoming less economical, the availability of steel and size of freight cars were increasing. The advantages of using steel were larger, lighter, and tougher cars. However, the replacement of wood by steel was not a quick or simple process. The balance began to change when Pressed Steel Car Co. began to build all-steel hopper cars in 1897. Innovative designs using pressed-steel parts resulted in cars with a much better ratio of load to dead weight and ensured rapid acceptance of all-steel cars. Although the use of pressed-steel parts was initially given the credit, it was soon found that rolled shapes had advantages of their own.

By 1901 steel's many advantages had become obvious. Although construction of all-wooden cars continued for a while, most cars built after 1909 used steel for at least the underframes. Steel supply problems during World War I caused a reversion to all-wooden cars or wooden cars with partially steel underframes for some orders in 1917 and 1918. Even in the 1920s some sizable orders were built with only partial steel underframes. By the late 1930s the use of wood had diminished to lining and flooring for the most part. There were exceptions such as Great Northern Railway's plywood-sheathed boxcars during the early 1940s, intended to promote some of the railroad's customers who manufactured plywood. Another steel shortage during World War II briefly brought wood sheathing back on most cars. Wood was eliminated from running boards along the top and sides of cars around the end of the war because any unperforated ma-

Aluminum has become increasingly competitive for freight-car construction, lowering overall car weight by about 15 percent, as well as reducing corrosion. One of the earliest unit-train hoppers, this Pullman-Standard car was delivered to the Southern Railway in 1960. —Eric A. Neubauer

terial became dangerous when covered with ice. Since the 1960s virtually no wood has been used in freight cars aside from flooring on some gondola cars and flatcars.

The types of steel used evolved along with car designs. Accelerated corrosion observed on certain steel cars during the late 1910s led to the use of corrosion-resistant copper-bearing steel alloys during the 1920s, followed by other corrosion-resistant and high-tensile steel alloys during the 1930s. Although the new alloys did not significantly affect overall design, they made lighter cars possible through reductions in plate thickness.

The use of aluminum as a structural material in freight cars occurred sporadically. Its advantages over steel are lighter weight and corrosion resistance. Its disadvantages are cost and special attention needed during construction and repair. Although some aluminum-bodied hopper cars were built during the Great Depression, the only lasting use that came out of that period was in tank-car tanks, where corrosion resistance was a factor. Some experimental aluminum-bodied boxcars and hopper cars were built after World War II, but generated little activity beyond the initial publicity. Then a burst of activity started in 1959, centered on aluminum covered hopper cars built by the Magor Car Corp. and several other builders. Although the cars were successful, with well over 5,000 manufactured in the United States and Canada by 1969, orders decreased in the 1970s and nearly disappeared in the 1980s. Most cars were used for minerals and grain, where their lighter weight allowed the carrying capacity to be maximized. Nevertheless, aluminum-bodied covered hopper cars have continued to be popular for some corrosive commodities such as sodium chlorate. Recently, partially aluminum cars have been built for grain, salt, and plastic-resin service. About 8,000 to 10,000 pounds of car weight are saved compared with all-steel cars weighing about 63,000 pounds.

In retrospect, the most important aluminum-bodied

cars were 750 coal gondola cars built for the Southern Railway by Pullman-Standard in 1960. Both their lighter weight and corrosion resistance were factors in their success. They could carry about 10 percent more coal than similar steel cars and lasted almost twice as long without body replacement. Over 95 percent were still in service in the beginning of 1998, shortly before the series was retired. Several orders for similar cars were built by other companies, including Magor, through the early 1970s. By the 1980s several builders had developed aluminum-bodied prototype coal cars and started production of similar cars. One was the Bethlehem Steel Corp., now known as Johnstown America Corp. It had always been a major producer of coal cars and, as the popularity of aluminum-bodied cars increased, built its last all-steel coal car about 1993. Today, more aluminum-bodied coal cars are built than steel-bodied coal cars. A typical aluminum coal gondola weighs about 44,000 pounds, while a steel counterpart weighs about 58,000 pounds. As on other aluminum cars, the center sill, body bolster, and trucks are steel. Aluminum has also been used for hatch covers on covered hopper cars since the 1960s.

Another unusual material used in car construction is stainless steel. Its sole advantage is corrosion resistance, and because of high expense it is normally used only for components that are in contact with lading. Perhaps 1,000 covered hopper and tank cars are sheathed or lined with stainless steel.

Several attempts have also been made to use fiber-reinforced plastics and other composites in covered hopper and refrigerator cars, but these materials are still far from being generally accepted. The use of nonmetals in refrigerator cars shows promise because of better insulating properties. A primarily wooden superstructure persisted in refrigerator cars into the mid-1930s for the same reason. Fiber-reinforced plastics have also been used for hatch covers on covered hopper cars and for removable covers on gondola and hopper cars since the 1960s.

Fabrication Techniques

Wooden cars were made with a variety of woods. Frame members were at first made of oak, but hard pine was substituted for the larger members when oak became scarce. The body bolster was sometimes reinforced with iron or made entirely from iron. Flooring was hard pine or oak. Sides of gondola and hopper cars generally consisted of oak stakes and hard pine planks. Sheathing on boxcars and refrigerator cars was usually white pine. By the late 1880s most new cars were about 34 feet long. The center of the car was supported by a series of truss rods and queen posts. The truss rods ran the entire length of the car and also served to hold the underframe together. The side and end framing of most covered cars formed a truss. Some open-top cars had a trussed side frame, but a simple post and plank construction was more common. A variety of iron parts held the car together. Weathertight roofing on boxcars was an ongoing challenge. By 1890 many boxcar roofs were galvanized iron panels in a wooden framework covered by a layer of wood sheathing.

Early steel cars were made primarily from sheet, rolled shapes, pressed-steel parts, and cast-steel parts that were assembled with rivets. Designs were complicated by myriad brackets and connecting plates. Steel framing made truss rods and queen posts unnecessary, and 40-foot cars became common by 1905.

In the late 1920s and early 1930s some experimental welded cars were built to confirm the advantages of fewer parts and quicker assembly. Reduced car weight was another potential advantage. In 1936 the Milwaukee Road began large-scale production of welded boxcars. Four years later the Reading Co. began a similar program with hopper cars. Several large car builders also constructed prototypes and made small production runs of welded cars in the 1930s. Welding was adopted for tank-car tanks by 1940, and Pullman-Standard began production of the PS-1 welded boxcar in 1947. By the mid-1950s welding was common for all car types. Some riveted construction still persisted, especially for hopper cars where sheets had to be replaced because of corrosion. Although some partially nonwelded cars are still produced, other types of proprietary fasteners are used instead of rivets.

Another important fabrication method was casting, a technique pioneered and perfected by General Steel Casting Corp. One-piece cast freight-car underframes were manufactured beginning in 1923. It was immediately obvious that cast-underframe flatcars were substantially lighter than those built in other ways. Casting was an easy way to achieve the complex shapes required for depressed-center flatcars. These underframes also had good corrosion resistance that made them ideal for gondola cars in sulfur service. By offering underframes that could easily be completed by adding trucks, couplers, brakes, and decking,

Specialized freight cars can transport extremely heavy and large oversized shipments. This depressed center flat car built for the New York Central in 1962 was over 72 feet long, with a depressed loading deck only 25 feet long, and capable of a load of over 200 tons. General Steel Industries supplied the special castings. —Eric A. Neubauer

General Steel Casting made it possible for many smaller railroads to assemble their own fleets of cars as needed. The last cast-underframe cars were built about 1973.

Standardized Designs

For many years there were proponents of standardized freight-car designs. At first, standard lumber sizes were proposed for various components to facilitate repair of cars off-line. The next step was the development of standard designs. The height of this movement lasted from 1917 until the mid-1940s. Detailed standard designs were prepared by committees of the U.S. Railroad Administration (USRA), American Railway Assn., and Assn. of American Railroads. The USRA had the most effect because of the government control of all major railroads under its administration. From late 1918 until early 1920 nearly all freight cars for U.S. railroads were built to USRA designs. Next, the ARA developed several designs during the 1920s, and a number of railroads chose to follow these closely. Additional designs were developed by the AAR in the 1930s and early 1940s. Although many cars were nominally built to these designs, the details often varied greatly. Later standards left most design details to the individual car builders. In retrospect, standardized designs were an attractive idea that was operationally impractical because of the constant changes in engineering design, manufacturing methods, and customer needs.

In contrast to freight-car design, there was an area where standardization was successfully achieved. The Safety Appliance Act of 1893 mandated automatic couplers and air brakes on cars used in interstate commerce. Final implementation of the act in 1900 caused some railroads to retire large numbers of older cars prematurely because their design did not permit upgrading. The Safety Appliance Act of 1911 spelled out very clearly where appliances should be located. At that time there was great variation even on cars owned by the same railroad. Among other things, the new standards required that steps and handholds be located at all four corners, that ladders be located on both the car side and end at the front right and back left corners, that the hand brake be located near the back left corner, and that ladder rungs have a certain spacing. Older cars were soon upgraded, and freight cars in the United States took on a more uniform appearance. Elimination of the running board on the roof of most boxcars in 1966 allowed subsequent designs to have a greater inside height and larger volume while staying within the same envelope. In general, Canadian practice closely followed U.S. practice, though some differences existed.

Development of Certain Common Components

Several components of freight-car design evolved somewhat independently of car type. They included draft components, braking systems, and trucks. Sometimes components seemed to have an existence of their own, predating or outlasting the rest of the car. The same could also be said about tank-car tanks, but they are clearly associated with a specific car type and are not discussed here. Draft components include couplings, draft gear, draft sills, and center sill, all of which are located under the center of the floor and stretch from one end of the car to the other. Their primary purpose is to transmit pulling and pushing forces from car to car throughout the train.

The center sill and draft sills are also part of the underframe of the car and are supported on the trucks at their intersections with the body bolsters. Body bolsters are cross-members that interface with the trucks and extend the width of the car. The draft sill is an extension of the center sill that supports the draft gear and couplings. Steel center sills on many cars built before the Great Depression and on most flatcars built through the present have a fish-belly shape and are also intended to support at least part of the weight of the car and its lading, as well as transmitting forces along the train. Starting during the 1920s, the ARA and AAR developed standard rolled-steel center-sill sections, which have been used on most cars built since then. An increasing number of designs do not have a continuous center sill, so that the transmitted pulling forces pass through the side sills or carbody between the body bolsters instead.

Wooden underframes were typically constructed with draft sills and body bolsters attached beneath other underframe members, including the center sill. Extensions (dead blocks) were attached to ends of the underframe in order to transmit compressive (pushing) forces to and from adjacent cars. Thus the couplings were subjected only to pulling forces. The use of steel for underframes and the use of automatic couplers and stronger draft gear allowed all underframe components to be placed in the same plane and dead blocks to be eliminated. The floors of the revised cars were thus lowered, increasing cubic capacity without increasing overall dimensions. Late wooden cars contained steel draft sills and body bolsters connected by continuous drawbars to achieve the same result.

Early couplings were mostly of the link-and-pin type. Although effective, this design was dangerous to use because it required a worker to stand between cars during coupling and guide the pin into the link while the cars were being pushed together. Another trip was necessary while they were being uncoupled. By the late 1880s the Master Car Builders (MCB) had adopted a standard automatic coupler based in part on the Janney patent of 1873. Automatic couplers could be adjusted so that they coupled automatically when cars were pushed together. They could also be uncoupled from the side of the car through a connecting linkage. Thus workers no longer had to stand between cars during coupling and uncoupling, except that the adoption of air brakes around the same time did require them to go between cars to connect air hoses, but that action was less dangerous since cars were at rest.

Early MCB couplers had slots in the knuckles, which made them compatible with existing cars with link-and-pin couplers. Many railroads quickly adopted the MCB coupler for new cars. For example, the Philadelphia & Reading Railroad had about 15,000 cars built with automatic couplers between 1890 and 1892. When delivered, they represented nearly half of the railroad's fleet. The main problem for railroads was the retrofitting of older cars because of the considerable expense and inadequate space provided by certain designs. When the Safety Appliance Act of 1893 finally took effect in 1900, all freight cars in interstate commerce had to be equipped with automatic couplers. Since 1900 the size and strength of couplers have increased gradually, but always with backward compatibility in mind. Since 1970 tank cars carrying hazardous materials are required to have special couplers that resist uncoupling during a derailment for safety reasons. They are compatible with standard couplers. Couplers with special shanks have been developed for extra-long cars and for open-top cars that are rotary dumped without uncoupling.

The draft gear connects the couplings to the draft sill. On many early freight cars the couplings were bolted directly to the draft sill without the use of draft gear. Because of the slack in the couplings, the entire car and its contents could be subjected to severe shocks when the train was started or stopped. Draft gears were developed to act as a shock absorber to reduce damage. Early types involved spring action, but later designs used sliding friction to achieve greater capacity. Couplers travel several inches inside the draft sill as shocks are absorbed by the draft gear.

The limited absorbing capacity of draft gear was not always sufficient to protect the lading. This led to the development of cushioned underframes during the 1920s. The O. C. Duryea Corp. was the leading manufacturer until the 1950s. In its design the entire center sill was free to travel 8 inches within the rest of the underframe. Longer travel allowed better cushioning, which was accomplished in a manner similar to standard draft gear. The Duryea design was widely used, but was most popular on the Baltimore & Ohio Railroad, which placed it on virtually all its new cars between 1928 and 1948. Cars with these cushion underframes were about 2,000 pounds heavier than other cars because the traveling center sill had to be partially duplicated with a fixed center sill in certain sections of the underframe. Many years later the Duryea design was found to have a design defect that led to cracking of the center sill. This led to it being banned from interchange service in the early 1970s, but by then many cars had been rebuilt as fixed-sill cars, and most were reaching retirement age.

Several other cushion underframe systems were developed in the 1950s and 1960s. Most used hydraulic cushioning, often with a travel of 20 or 30 inches. A full fixed center sill was used along with the traveling sill, avoiding the problems associated with the Duryea underframe.

The new cushioned cars were about 6,000 to 8,000 pounds heavier than ordinary cars. Although they were popular in the 1960s and 1970s, few have been built in recent times.

End-of-car cushioning was introduced during the 1960s and became even more popular during the 1970s. Essentially, the draft-gear area was enlarged to permit hydraulic cushioning with travels of 10 or 15 inches. While not quite as effective as cushioning with a traveling sill, it has the advantage of adding little weight to the car. End-of-car cushioning remains popular today and is most frequently used on boxcars and flatcars where the lading requires shock protection. Conventional draft gear is still used on cars where the lading does not require shock protection.

Illustrating the potential independence of the draft system from the remainder of the body, it was common for wooden cars to be rebuilt with steel center sills from the late 1900s to the early 1920s. It was a simple matter to jack up a car, make a few cuts to remove some of the old wooden underframe components, and install a new steel draft sill, center sill, and body bolster assembly. Numerous builders offered subassemblies for that purpose. There was a less common practice during the 1920s in which old steel cars were stripped down to the center sill and rebuilt as a different type of car. As an example, the New York Central rebuilt many of its unused coke cars into boxcars, stock and gondola cars, and flatcars.

A frequent practice is to rebuild bodies of steel coal hopper and mill gondola cars that are often in poor condition after 20 years of service. Again, old steel cars were stripped down to the center sill and rebuilt with predominantly new bodies. Recently, Conrail, CSX Transportation, and Norfolk Southern have had extensive rebody programs for both types of cars.

Each freight car in regular service today has its own braking system that can be applied manually to prevent the car from rolling. For the first 50 years of steam-operated railroads in North America, manual (or hand) brakes were also used to control trains as they descended steep hills since the locomotives weighed much less than the train and thus could not provide sufficient braking alone. A typical freight-car braking system has always included a hand wheel or lever that is connected through various guided chains, rods, and levers to brake shoes, which press on the wheel tread.

During the mid-1880s several western railroads adopted air brakes that included an air cylinder on each car connected to the existing hand-brake system. The brake cylinders were interconnected by an air line that ran the entire length of the train so that all brakes could be applied at once with pressurized air from the locomotive. The air line could be disconnected when cars were uncoupled. The use of air brakes was already established on passenger equipment and made train operation in mountainous areas safer. Trials of various kinds of air brakes conducted in the late 1880s resulted in a successful Westinghouse air brake consisting of a combined cylin-

der, reservoir, and triple (or control) valve assembly. A small pipe led from the triple valve to a retaining valve mounted on the end of the car that could release the brakes. The air reservoir was a necessary addition because it was found that the locomotive alone could not provide enough air fast enough for safe application of the brakes on longer trains. After 1892 almost all new cars were built with similar air brakes. The Westinghouse Air Brake Co. was not the only manufacturer of freight-car air brakes; the New York Air Brake Co. was also involved at least as early as 1899. By August 1900 all cars used in interstate commerce were required to have air brakes.

Several improvements were made to air brakes through 1906. A version with a detached air cylinder was introduced for easier mounting in the limited area available on hopper cars. A 10-inch-diameter cylinder was added to the product line in addition to the original 8-inch cylinder for use on heavier cars that were coming into use. The original type H triple valve was redesigned as the type K triple valve.

An improved AB air brake was tested in the early 1930s and became mandatory on new cars built after September 1, 1933. Twenty years later it was finally required on all cars in interchange service. The AB air brake had a cylinder, a two-chamber reservoir, and an AB triple valve as individual components. The AB valve was subsequently improved as the ABD and ABDW valves in 1963 and 1976.

Other special variations of air brakes exist. The most notable is the empty-load brake, which varies the braking force according to whether the car is loaded or not. In that way a greater braking force can be used on a loaded car while preventing the wheels from locking up, sliding, and becoming damaged when the car is empty. Empty-load brakes were used on large coal cars at least as early as 1922, and they are still used on some new cars today. Many other brake systems have been proposed and tested over the years, but the necessity of backward compatibility makes any radically new systems unlikely except in special situations.

Several changes have also been made to the mechanical portion of freight-car brakes. Around 1930 power hand brakes mounted on the end or side of a car started replacing the horizontal brake wheel on a vertical staff that extended above the top of the car. The advantages were twofold. Power hand brakes were easier and safer to use, and freight cars, especially boxcars, could be made taller without exceeding clearance limits.

Slack adjusters, both manual and automatic, were developed to adjust the rigging as brake shoes wear. Most freight cars built since 1960 have automatic slack adjusters. During the same period traditional cast-iron brake shoes were replaced with composition shoes, which are more efficient and require less force to operate. However, because of these differences, metal shoes cannot simply be replaced by composition shoes without either changing brake-lever lengths or modifying the brake cylinder to get the correct force.

460   FREIGHT CARS

Much effort has gone into truck design since the 1830s. A truck normally consists of two wheel-axle sets held in place by a pair of side frames including journal boxes that rest on the ends of the axles. On some early trucks the journals were located inside the wheels. The side frames are connected by a bolster that bears the weight of the car and is attached to the carbody by means of a centrally located pin, around which the truck can pivot. Lateral rocking of the carbody is limited by side bearings attached near the ends of the bolster on either side of the center pin. Some trucks have three or four wheel sets that require a more complicated assembly of side frames and bolsters. A good truck design gives the most strength with the least weight, an important consideration since trucks account for about a third of the car weight.

In its earliest forms a truck frame was rigid and unsprung. It was soon discovered that a pedestal could hold both a spring and the journal box, resulting in a sprung pedestal truck with a rigid frame. The next major advance was the diamond-arch-bar truck that became common by 1870. In this design journal boxes were bolted to the side frame, made of three iron or steel bars that formed a truss. A lower cross-member, the spring plank, connected the bottoms of the side frames. An upper cross-member, the truck bolster, was free to move vertically above the spring plank and was supported on two nests of springs. A variation of the arch-bar truck was the swing-motion truck, which allowed the body bolster some lateral as well as vertical motion. The swing-motion truck became popular with some railroads during the early part of the twentieth century and was later favored for caboose cars, though by that time the trucks had cast side frames.

The advent of pressed-steel parts in the late nineteenth century led to the introduction of the Fox truck, which was soon followed by various imitators. The Fox steel truck design reverted to the earlier sprung pedestal truck type, but was riveted together from heavy pressed-steel parts rather than bolted together from wood and iron parts. Some of the imitators' trucks were made from cast-steel or rolled-steel shapes instead of pressed steel. Steel pedestal trucks were very popular from the early 1890s to the early 1900s.

The Bettendorf Co. took a different route and began producing cast-steel trucks based on the arch-bar design in 1902. The entire side frame, including the journal boxes, was cast in one piece. Essentially the same design is commonly used today. Other manufacturers made similar trucks, though the journal boxes were not necessarily part of the casting.

Arch-bar trucks continued to be manufactured into the 1920s, even though their multiplicity of parts and the possibility of any one becoming loose made them less reliable than trucks with one-piece cast side frames. They were eventually banned from interchange service on January 1, 1938. However, the effective date was later extended to July 1, 1940.

Lighter truck designs of cast-steel trucks without spring planks were developed in the 1930s and have become standard. Other more recent changes in truck design have centered on trucks with smoother riding, better tracking, and greater stability. Special radial trucks have been developed to reduce friction and wear on curves. None of the recent, radically different designs have come into general use, though some have been in service for over 20 years.

Another factor that has improved the efficiency of freight cars is the use of roller bearings on the axle ends. They replaced journal bearings that were subject to dangerous overheating when improperly maintained. Although roller bearings were introduced on freight cars by the 1930s, it was not until the mid-1950s that they gained general acceptance. The advertised advantages were lower rolling resistance, higher speeds, less maintenance, and greater reliability. Roller bearings were required on all new freight cars built for interchange service starting on August 1, 1968, and on every car in interchange service after January 1, 1994.

Most freight-car wheels were a standard 33 inches in diameter after about 1840. During the 1960s, 36- and 38-inch-diameter wheels were adopted for cars with 100- and 125-ton capacity, while low-deck flatcars, mostly with auto racks, used 28-inch-diameter wheels. Spoked wheels were among the earliest used, but one-piece cast wheels became the norm by about 1850. Wrought- and cast-steel wheels were introduced much later. Cast-iron wheels were not permitted in interchange service after 1969 because of inherent defects. Currently, both cast- and wrought-steel wheels are in use.

It was not unusual for a freight car to receive new trucks during its lifetime, especially if the old trucks were about to become restricted from interchange service. It is also not unusual for trucks to outlast the car bodies they carried. New cars were sometimes built with lower capacities so that old trucks could be reused.

Identification

With the proliferation of freight cars, railroads eventually needed a way to identify and keep track of their cars as they roamed across North America. During the 1800s it became common practice for a railroad to assign a unique number to each of its cars. Cars owned by different railroads might have the same number, so it was necessary to record both the railroad and the number to clearly identify a particular car. Moreover, many railroads and private owners had identical or similar initials that were easily confused. A system that assigned a unique letter code for each owner emerged during the 1910s. Consisting of a combination of letters and the car number, such reporting marks are still in use.

Assignment of the correct car type for each shipper became a major concern as railroad systems became more extensive. The variety of commodities carried by North American railroads meant that no one type of car could

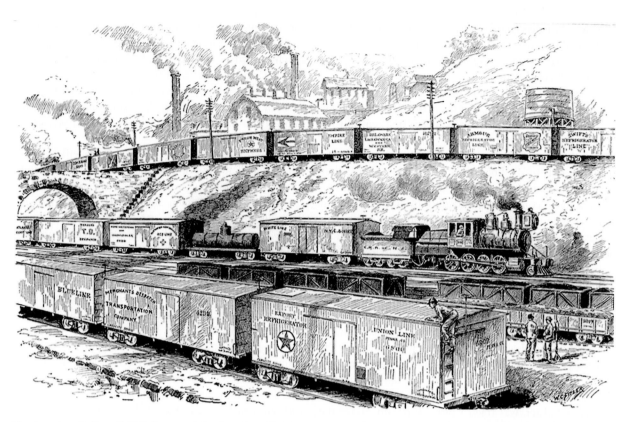

The American Railway (1892) illustrated the diversity of freight equipment. Boxcars and refrigerator cars appeared in large numbers, but such other cars as tank cars, gondolas, and hopper cars were also evident. —Middleton Collection

be suitable for all purposes. Therefore, a classification system had to be developed. By 1890 the following eight major classes of cars were recognized:

1. Boxcars were used where protection from weather or theft was necessary. Boxcars were totally enclosed and had doors in the sides. Commodities included merchandise, grain, lumber, and furniture. They were once known as house cars on some railroads.
2. Refrigerator cars had all the attributes of boxcars and were also fully insulated, though not necessarily refrigerated. They were used for commodities that required protection from heat or cold: meat, produce, provisions, and beer.
3. Gondola cars had sides and ends, but no top. The floor was generally level. Two common options were drop ends for loads longer than the car and drop doors in the floor for bulk commodities like coal and coke.
4. Hopper cars also had sides and ends, but no top. However, they had self-clearing, sloping floors with doors at the bottom for easier unloading. They could only be used for bulk commodities like coal and ore, as none of the floor was flat.
5. Flatcars lacked enclosing sides and ends. They were easy to load with long or bulky items such as lumber and rail. Some were fitted with racks for special loads such as barrels. Flatcars were some of the earliest cars

used on railroads and were sometimes known as platform cars.
6. Tank cars usually consisted of a longitudinal metal tank mounted on an underframe. They were used for many liquids, including vegetable oil, petroleum, turpentine, acid, and water.
7. Stock cars were similar to boxcars except that the sides and doors were slatted to provide ventilation and allow easier cleaning. As the name implies, they were used for livestock, but could also be used for other commodities, including produce, if necessary.
8. Caboose cars were for the accommodation of the train crew. Most had bunks, stoves, desks, and a lookout to observe the train ahead.

Because a formal, universally recognized taxonomy of freight cars was as yet undeveloped, the Baltimore & Ohio and Pennsylvania railroads each established their own classification systems before 1900. The Atchison, Topeka & Santa Fe and Harriman-controlled railroads did the same shortly after 1900. All of the railroad-developed systems had two components. The first identified the general car type. For example, boxcars were M on the B&O, X on the PRR, Bx on the AT&SF, and B on the Harriman roads. The second component identified a specific design and was applied chronologically. The AT&SF and PRR used letters for the design component, while the B&O and Harriman roads used numbers. The Harriman roads had a third component based on capacity in pounds. Two examples are Bx.E. (fifth boxcar design on AT&SF) and B-100-5 (fifth 100,000-pound-capacity boxcar design on the Harriman roads).

In 1910 the Master Car Builders Assn. (MCB) published a list of mechanical designations that identified the various types of cars. An example is XM, applied to boxcars suitable for general service. The MCB mechanical designations did not identify specific construction designs because the large number of different designs made that impractical. Although some railroads continued to have their own classification systems for internal purposes, the MCB mechanical designation was used by all railroads in *The Official Railway Equipment Register*. The original list recognized all eight major classes described earlier and added a ninth for ventilator cars with attributes of both boxcars and refrigerator cars. A tenth class for special cars was introduced in the late 1920s. The MCB mechanical designation definitions were continued by the American Railway Assn. and then by the Assn. of American Railroads. From about 1958 until 1988 the applicable designation was stenciled on every freight car in North America. Though no longer shown on cars, they are still used to classify cars today.

A parallel system of AAR car-type codes came into use in 1966 for use in data processing. They consist of a letter followed by three numerals. They are based on the mechanical designation and include additional information regarding capacity, size, and construction. Over 20 letter codes were assigned to different car types. In the example J401, the J identifies the car as an AAR type GT rotary-dump gondola car, the 4 indicates that it is a 100-ton car with capacity over 190,000 pounds, the 0 is for a flat bottom, and the 1 is for an inside length of at least 48 but under 52 feet. Information on these or the mechanical designations may be found in *The Official Railway Equipment Register*.

Specific Car Types

Boxcars date back to the 1830s. They usually had outside sheathing and a partial inside lining. Until the late 1870s most had capacities of 20,000 to 24,000 pounds and inside lengths of 30 feet or less. During the 1880s capacities of 40,000 or 50,000 pounds and inside lengths of about 34 feet became common. Some were fitted with small end doors so that long pieces of lumber could be more easily loaded. By 1901 a typical boxcar was about 36 feet long, with capacities of 60,000 or 80,000 pounds and about 2,400 cubic feet. They had sliding doors with openings about 6 feet wide. Some had auxiliary slatted doors or other provisions for ventilation so they could be used for produce. Insulated cars were used for ice. Some cars were longer and higher for transporting furniture that was bulky by nature. A few had wider side or end doors for shipping carriages. Automobile cars started appearing in larger numbers by 1907 and were essentially the same

By the early 1900s freight-car construction had largely shifted over to steel. This all-steel Southern Pacific bottom dump gondola, built in 1918, was equipped with cast-steel trucks.
—Middleton Collection

as carriage cars. They usually had double side doors with a total opening of 10 feet.

Starting around 1908, most boxcars were built with steel underframes and one of three different superstructure arrangements: outside wood sheathing on a wood frame, inside wood sheathing on a steel frame, and outside steel sheathing on a steel frame. Although all types were manufactured concurrently through the late 1920s, the trend was toward using more steel. Steel or steel-framed ends were required on new construction after about 1915, addressing a weakness that had been observed for some time. By the mid-1930s outside-sheathed steel cars with wooden linings had become the standard.

During the early twentieth century several attempts were made to design a drop- or hopper-bottom boxcar that could also be used for grain, coal, or coke. The Great Northern Railway and Chicago, Burlington & Quincy Railroad were each operating over 10,000 cars of this type by 1910. Although other railroads in the United States and Canada experimented with the idea, it mostly remained a peculiarity of those two railroads for just a few decades.

In the 1920s a dual-purpose automobile-furniture car

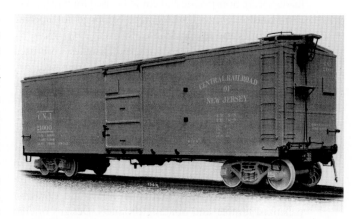

A typical early twentieth-century boxcar, this Standard Steel Car Co. design for the Central Railroad of New Jersey had a steel frame and boxcar, with wooden flooring and lining.
—D. K. Retterer Collection

Covered hopper cars were widely used for a variety of bulk materials and agricultural products. This Norfolk & Western car was smaller, suitable for such dense materials as cement. Built by American Car & Foundry Co. in 1981, it featured ACF's popular Center Flow™. Other companies developed similar cars. —Eric A. Neubauer

came into use. It was 50 feet long and had wide door openings. Automobile cars were usually only 40 feet long at this time. Two new types appeared during the late 1930s. Some automobile cars were fitted with proprietary racks in order to increase their capacity. When not in use, some racks could be folded against the ceiling so that the car could be used in general service, with some loss of headroom. Some boxcars had special linings and permanent racks for holding auto parts being shipped to assembly plants. These cars were not intended for general service.

During the late 1940s the use of forklifts and pallets by shippers made wider doors increasingly advantageous. The idea that boxcars with wide doors were only for automobile loading quickly disappeared. Several proprietary load-restraint systems were developed for boxcars in the 1950s. They used a system of adjustable cross-members or bulkheads to secure the cargo and prevent it from moving around and becoming damaged during transport. The loaders were nonspecific and could be used for any kind of merchandise. Other boxcars were equipped for specific commodities and restricted in use.

Special types of boxcars with roof hatches were used for sand, hides, and clay. Most were rebuilt from ordinary boxcars before the 1970s. A few experimental cars with roof hatches and hopper bottoms failed to revive the old dream of a multipurpose boxcar during the late 1980s.

Some boxcars of the 1940s and 1950s contained permanent tanks used to transport cryogenic gases. When new tank cars were designed especially for cryogenic gases in the 1960s, the box-tank design became obsolete.

All-door boxcars were built in the 1960s and 1970s for palletized lumber and building products. Designs offered by several builders had sides composed almost entirely of doors and heavy underframes reminiscent of those on flatcars. Their relatively heavy empty weight, about 15,000 pounds more than a typical boxcar, and the advent of

larger ordinary boxcars eventually made them obsolete. Also during the 1960s and 1970s the outside-sheathed boxcar gave way to the inside-sheathed boxcar, which eliminated the need for a lining and saved some weight.

An overproduction of boxcars during the late 1970s was followed by an economic recession during the 1980s. Many railroad observers declared that the boxcar was obsolete, citing the widespread use of covered hoppers for cement, flour, and grain and containers for general merchandise. Surprisingly, however, boxcar orders began to increase in the late 1990s. Many of the new cars are used for auto parts, paper products, or building materials and have up to 107-ton capacity, 50- to 86-foot inside length, and 10- to 20-foot-wide door openings.

Early refrigerator cars date back to the 1840s, but they did not become a commercial success until the late 1860s. Three common types of refrigerator cars were well established by 1889. One type had ice bunkers with hatches in the roof at both ends of the car. Hinged side doors at the center of the car were used for loading the cargo, usually produce. Many later cars of this type had ventilating devices associated with the roof hatches and could be operated as ventilated boxcars. The second type, used for meat and provisions, was shorter, included brine tanks instead

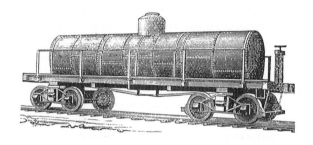

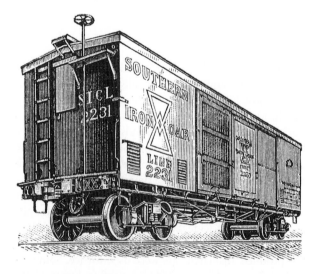

These late-nineteenth-century freight cars were framed in wood and fitted with truss rods, while the trucks employed the built-up arch-bar design. —Jim Harter, *American Railroads of the Nineteenth Century* (Lubbock: Texas Tech University Press, 1998)

of ice bunkers, and lacked ventilating devices. The third type, used for beer, was similar to the first except that it lacked ice bunkers and roof hatches. Although it was considered a refrigerator car by railroads, it was insulated but not actually refrigerated.

A fourth type, the Eastman heater car, started appearing during the 1880s. By 1892 over 2,000 were in service on railroads stretching from Maryland north to New Brunswick and west to Chicago. The cars were insulated and heated to protect produce, including potatoes, from freezing. A minority had ice bunkers as well. Eastman heater cars were considered boxcars rather than refrigerator cars.

Refrigerator cars were the last stronghold of wooden construction because the use of steel made insulation more difficult. The transition from wood to steel sheathing was made during the 1930s and 1940s. Two other innovations arose during this period. Many cars with bunkers were equipped with electric fans rather than relying on natural convective circulation to maintain a uniform temperature. Some cars were equipped with special racks suspended from the ceiling for loading meat.

During the 1920s and 1930s several other refrigeration systems were tried, but none achieved widespread use at that time. However, some designs eventually began to include a self-contained refrigeration unit that occupied about 5 feet in one end of an otherwise ordinary car because of the increased use of frozen foods in the 1950s. The refrigeration compressors were powered by gasoline or diesel engines. The 1950s also saw increased use of nonrefrigerated cars for produce and beer and a transition from hinged to rolling plug doors with larger openings. A large number of refrigerator cars both with and without mechanical refrigeration were built in the 1960s and 1970s. By this time cars with ice bunkers were no longer being built. The use of load-restraining devices became common by the 1960s.

Toward the end of the 1970s orders for new refrigerator cars began to drop rapidly, and by 1983 production had stopped entirely for lack of demand. However, a new arrangement was introduced in the late 1980s. It used a cryogen, such as liquid nitrogen, for cooling. Similar, much smaller cars of the 1930s had used dry ice. Space that had been used for refrigeration equipment became available for cargo. Hundreds of cryogenic refrigerators were built from scratch or converted from mechanically refrigerated cars. Starting about 2000, mechanical refrigerator cars were again in production, along with cryogenic refrigerator cars.

Attempts were made in the late 1960s and early 1970s to employ bulk shipping for produce and frozen foods. During this period American Car & Foundry constructed 162 insulated, mechanically refrigerated covered hopper cars for such use. Although the trials were positive, no additional cars were built, and the insulation and refrigeration were ultimately removed from the existing cars. Also during the early 1970s some refrigerator cars were fitted

An 1868 photograph of a Philadelphia & Reading car, the typical coal hopper car of the time. It was built with heavy wooden framing, wood sheathing, and sheet-iron slope sheets and hopper. —Eric A. Neubauer Collection

with interior slope sheets and conveyors for potatoes and similar commodities. These and other refrigerator cars were sometimes equipped with heaters.

Gondola cars date back to at least the early 1830s and were once occasionally referred to as boxcars, although they were not completely enclosed. The gondola is extremely versatile and thus has appeared with many options, including fixed or drop ends. The latter can be tipped inward to lie flat on the floor, and therefore these gondolas can carry items that exceed the inside length of the car. Flatcars are often used as spacers if the load is longer than the gondola. Many early gondola cars had very low sides and were useful for commodities like pig iron. Car floors may be solid or drop bottom, the latter being useful for bulk commodities. A hopper bottom increases volume and makes a larger amount of the car self-clearing during unloading. Hopper-bottom gondola cars were commonly built from the 1870s into the 1910s, but are now largely obsolete. They were popular because they could be used for both coal and lumber. Cars with drop doors have an entirely flat floor. At first, doors were hinged crosswise of the car so as to dump between the rails. Starting about 1905, several companies developed general-service cars with doors hinged lengthwise along the center sill. Some had drop doors along the entire length so that the car was largely self-clearing. All dumped outside the rails. General-service cars were popular in western North America through the 1950s. Of course, unloading facilities had to accommodate whether cars dumped between or outside the rails.

Starting around 1890, many gondola cars were equipped with racks for bulk coke shipments. Coke was relatively light, and the racks increased the volume capacity. After hopper cars designed for coke became available and some steel mills started making their coke in-house, the role of the gondola car in the coke trade diminished. However, as recently as 1982 several hundred gondola cars were built for coke service.

Gondola cars with side doors rather than drop bottoms were quite popular in New England through the early 1900s. Each side of the car was hinged at the top, allowing the bottom of the side to swing outward and upward

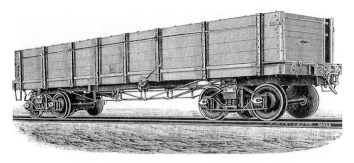

Car builder F. E. Canda designed this wood-framed gondola with a sliding bottom in 1894. —Jim Harter, *American Railroads of the Nineteenth Century* (Lubbock: Texas Tech University Press, 1998)

when unlatched. When the sides were opened, the contents could easily be pushed out of the car.

Multipurpose gondola cars were developed early in the twentieth century. The Rodger Ballast Car Co. had large numbers of Hart Convertible Ballast Cars built, which served as gondola cars with drop ends and a flat bottom, as gondolas with side doors, or as hopper cars dumping between the rails.

Gondola cars with solid bottoms and fixed ends designed for unloading only on rotary dumping machines came into common use during the 1920s. They were originally intended for coal, but their uses were later expanded to include ore and wood chips. Each use required a different car size because of the different cargo densities. Some wood-chip cars have hinged end doors and can be unloaded by upending the car rather than tipping it sideways. Starting in the 1960s, increasing numbers of rotary gondola cars have been built for unit coal trains operating between mines and electric generating stations. They are now far more popular in this service than hopper cars.

One important type of car was developed in the 1960s for shipping coils of steel. They included a shallow trough, bulkheads for securing the coils, and, often, removable covers. At first considered flatcars, they have been classed as gondola cars since the early 1970s.

Gondola cars have been fitted to carry special commodities, including auto frames, ingot mould, and non-intermodal containers for cement, coke, and minerals. In the 1970s and 1980s some gondola cars were built with extra-high ends for handling large pipes.

Since many early railroads were associated with coal mines, it is not surprising that some of the earliest cars were hopper cars. Originally, low, short 4- or 8-wheeled cars were common. As capacities increased during the 1880s, restricted overhead and side clearances at loading facilities on some railroads forced coal-car designs to grow in length when capacity was increased. The new cars were too long to have a sloping, self-clearing floor the entire length of the car, and the hopper-bottom gondola car started replacing hopper cars on some railroads. While unloading costs increased significantly because of the ne-

cessity of shoveling out part of the car, the railroads were somewhat mollified by having a car that could be used for other commodities because of the partially flat bottom. Ultimately, clearances at loading facilities were improved, and the first modern hopper cars with a shorter, higher silhouette were built in the late 1880s. Large numbers began to appear in the mid-1890s.

An important early development was the King or sawtooth hopper that replaced the usual drop door at the bottom of the hopper with a more reliable door in the side of the hopper (near the center). The sawtooth hopper was introduced about 1895 and was also used on hopper-bottom gondola cars. Although other arrangements coexisted with the sawtooth hopper into the 1920s, most hopper cars built from then on had sawtooth hoppers except for some specialized cars in ballast, coke, or ore service.

The first cars produced by the Pressed Steel Car Co. were hopper cars built in 1897. Since the complex hopper geometry was much easier to create in steel than in wood, steel hopper cars quickly became the norm. A few railroads continued to acquire wood-sheathed cars with outside steel frames because the high-sulfur coal they transported caused rapid corrosion of steel.

Some early hopper cars were equipped with coke racks that extended the height of sides and ends. Others were arranged to dump outside the rails instead of between the rails. Occasionally, hopper cars were equipped with removable roofs.

The first steel hopper cars had sheathing placed inside the side posts. Starting in the late 1910s, some cars were built with sheathing outside the side posts, resulting in increased inside width and cubic capacity. The idea gained popularity and was applied to most cars built from about 1925 to 1955. Then, in one of those peculiar reversions of technology, sheathing inside the side sheets again became standard, presumably to protect the side posts from corrosion. Later, some designs again used outside sheathing to reduce air resistance and fuel costs. Although hopper cars are still being built today, they are not as common as they once were, largely because of the increased use of rotary gondola cars in unit coal trains. Hopper cars with permanent roofs (discussed later) are a different story.

Ordinary flatcars have an unobstructed deck; loads must be secured by stakes inserted into side pockets or by blocking attached to the deck. The deck was also ideal for mounting a superstructure, as on barrel-rack cars, used by the late 1880s, or auto-rack cars, introduced around 1960.

Heavy-duty cars with plain decks used for large guns and other heavy loads were in service at least as early as 1865. Well flatcars contain a hole in the middle of the deck and are used for large loads that must extend below the deck line. Well flats existed at least as early as 1898, but few appeared on the rosters of major railroads until the 1910s. Depressed-center flatcars were developed in the 1920s for electric transformers and other large machinery that was too wide for well cars. They did not have an opening in the middle of the floor; instead, the entire center section between the trucks was about 15 to 21 inches lower than the rest of the floor. Another special design, introduced to North America from Europe in 1957, is used to move extremely heavy and large loads of up to a million pounds or more. The Schnabel car consists of two independent assemblies that are separated before loading. Each half of the car is attached to one end of the load so that it becomes an integral part of the car during shipment. All four of these car types are uncommon, yet essential to certain businesses. Virtually all ride on various special truck combinations totaling 6 to 24 axles to spread the weight of the car and load.

For many years the logging industry used casually laid rail lines to haul timber to the mills. The two most popular car configurations were normal flats with log racks and, at the other extreme, skeleton cars (a thin spine supported by two trucks) where the loaded timber became part of the car structure. The several hundred log-rack cars currently in interchange service are often used for shipping electric utility poles.

The bulkhead flatcar was introduced for gypsum board in the 1950s. Similar cars have also been used for lumber, plywood, pipe, aluminum ingots, and other commodities. These cars all have level floors and should not be confused with the somewhat similar pulpwood cars having V-shaped floors (discussed later). Starting in 1969, some bulkhead flatcars included a full-height beam (or truss) running between the bulkheads and above the center of the deck. Center-beam flatcars have become popular since the early 1980s for lumber transport. They are substantially lighter than a conventional bulkhead flatcar.

An important development after World War II was the use of flatcars for transporting loaded highway trailers. This general idea had been tried out with wagons or trailers several times since the 1800s, but it was not until the 1950s that it finally became popular. Introduction of especially long cars (for multiple loads) and the use of hitches for securing trailers helped the business grow steadily into the 1960s. Some railroads used proprietary container systems in the late 1950s, but these are largely obsolete. All-

The use of articulation and double-stacked containers for intermodal operation has produced some enormous cars. This five-unit articulated car built by Trinity Industries in 1990 for Trailer Train Co. is over 307 feet long and can accommodate 10 48-foot containers. —Eric A. Neubauer

The development of long, high-capacity bilevel and trilevel automobile cars enabled railroads to recapture a substantial share of new automobile and truck shipment. This 89-foot flatcar incorporated an enclosed bilevel rack for automobiles and small trucks. The car was built by Bethlehem Steel Corp. in 1973 for use by TTX Co. (Trailer Train). —Eric A. Neubauer

purpose cars for highway trailers and standard intermodal containers were developed in the late 1960s. Since then the designs have continued to change, but the basic business has continued to grow. There are a surprising variety of cars, considering the relative uniformity of the cargo. Some modern intermodal cars have only 4 wheels and are 50 feet long, carrying but a single trailer. At the other extreme are five-unit articulated well cars that allow two containers to be stacked on each section. These can be over 300 feet long and carry ten 48-foot containers. Recently, municipal waste and plastic resins have been transported in nonstandard containers on flatcars.

Another recent development is the multilevel auto-rack car with two or three decks. Early rack cars of the 1960s were open, but now virtually all are entirely enclosed to prevent damage from vandalism. Recently, two-unit articulated auto-rack cars have been favorably received, and about 2,000 are in service.

Cars for pulpwood used in the paper industry originated in the 1930s. There were initially several different types with gondola, flatcar, or boxcar origins. By the 1950s pulpwood cars usually had V-shaped floors and end bulkheads. Pulpwood cars are becoming uncommon because wood chips are being shipped in preference to pulpwood. The last new pulpwood cars were built about 1981. In a strict sense, pulpwood cars are not flatcars because of the V-shaped floor, but most observers would recognize them as such.

At the turn of the twentieth century only 0.1 percent of the freight-car fleet was covered hopper cars. However, by 1985 this configuration had become the most numerous type in North America. This significant change occurred gradually, as new designs were developed to haul new commodities.

Some covered hopper cars were in grain service by the late 1830s, but their use was not widespread, perhaps because the need was only seasonal. Lime cars started appearing on some eastern railroads about the 1860s, and hundreds were in service within 20 years. Most appear to have been covered hopper cars similar to coal or ore cars in design. Another example of an early application was a fleet of 70 covered hoppers built by Pressed Steel Car between 1901 and 1906. They were owned by the Central Railroad of New Jersey and carried zinc ore from nearby mines to a smelter in Pennsylvania.

The first major market niche captured by covered hopper cars was phosphate rock, a necessary component of agricultural fertilizer. Most North American phosphate mines are located in Florida and North Carolina, from which large amounts of fertilizer are shipped throughout the nation. The first covered phosphate cars were built in 1902. By 1926 over 1,500 were owned by railroads serving the southeastern United States.

The next significant development occurred in the 1920s when cement companies started to investigate bulk shipment methods. Between 1928 and 1931 Hercules Cement Corp. received 50 steel-covered hopper cars from Standard Steel Car. After this, large numbers of cement cars were built new or converted from open hopper cars to meet the increased demand. A capacity of 70 tons became standard for cement cars until the 1960s. Cars designed for cement were suitable for other commodities, including sand. Interestingly, this trend did not immediately extend outside the United States. It was not until 1948 that the first covered hopper cars suitable for cement were built in Canada.

The automobile industry was one of the first to show signs of recovery during the Great Depression. Automobiles needed tires, and tires contained carbon black. The first covered hopper car for carbon black was built by American Car & Foundry in 1933. By the end of 1942, 368 carbon-black cars were in service.

Large-size covered hoppers started appearing in both the United States and Canada during the late 1940s. At first they were used for less dense commodities such as grain or malt. After a lengthy period of development General American introduced the Airslide covered hopper car in 1953. The unloading system fluidized the contents with air and allowed more difficult materials like flour and starch to be unloaded easily. Unlike later pressure-differential cars, the interior of the car was not pressurized during unloading. The design was successful and remained in production for over 40 years.

The use of welding in covered hopper cars was introduced gradually, starting in the 1930s. Most cars built after 1953 were almost entirely welded, with much simpler details than earlier designs.

A transition in covered-hopper-car design between 1958 and 1964 led to larger units and more applications such as grain, plastic resins, clay, and other minerals. Design advances for rapid outflow occurred during this time as well. A radically different configuration was popularized by American Car & Foundry's Center Flow models starting in 1961. The new design was lighter and easier to load and unload. Numerous innovations were brought together in one package. Whereas older cars had roofs with central running boards and two rows of hatches, and hoppers divided by the center sill, new Center Flow cars featured centerline loading hatches and outlets and completely unobstructed hoppers because center sills were used only at the ends of the car. The cross section of the car was also simplified. Older cars had flat sides with outside posts and peaked roofs supported by carlines (analogous to roof beams). The new Center Flow cars had curved sides and roofs without either posts or carlines. Although all these innovations had already been applied to tank cars and some had been used previously on other covered hopper cars, the Center Flow was unique in using them all together. Weight savings were about 8,000 pounds for a car with a capacity of 140,000 pounds and 3,500 cubic feet. Designs further improved so that current cars deliver about 50 percent more capacity with only 20 percent greater car weight. Other builders gradually adopted the new arrangement, and today very few cars are being built with the old arrangement.

Several car designs using a pressure-differential unloading method were developed during the 1960s. Cars of this type were pressurized with air to help evacuate the contents and maintain sanitary conditions. Starting in the 1980s, successful pressure-differential designs were produced by several builders and are now commonly used for flour, starch, cement, clay, and other commodities. Most have provisions to fluidize the lading with air during unloading.

The development of the petroleum industry led to a rapid increase in tank-car use. Although some of the earliest successful cars were built in 1865 and consisted of two wooden vats mounted on the deck of a flatcar, they were generally supplanted by cars with horizontal metal tanks by the late 1860s. Early tank cars were relatively expensive, costing about twice as much as other freight cars. Insulated tank cars were built at least as early as 1883 by adding a wooden enclosure around the tank. Cars with internal piping for steam to heat viscous commodities like asphalt and molasses before unloading were built at least as early as 1892. Cars with copper lining for brandy were built at least as early as 1894. By 1901 the typical tank car consisted of a 6,000- or 8,000-gallon cylindrical steel tank placed on a wooden or, rarely, steel underframe. Some cars were equipped with steam coils or had special inlet and outlet fittings for acid. A few cars were lined or insulated. Acid, ammonia, lard, mineral water, molasses, petroleum, syrup, and vegetable oil were some of the commodities carried. Cars used for vinegar and pickled produce had wooden tanks or vats.

Wooden underframes were generally obsolete after 1902. Some early steel designs lacked center sills, a feature that first fell out of favor, but ultimately became standard in the 1960s. Early tank cars were prone to leak at the seams, so a double row of rivets was required for seams on cars built after 1902.

Diversification of the chemical industry after 1915 led to the development of many new designs. By 1940 variations included cars for gasoline, chlorine, sulfur dioxide,

Tank cars became much larger by the 1960s. This American Car & Foundry Co. car built in 1963 could transport 32,195 gallons of liquid petroleum gas in its large welded tank. —Eric A. Neubauer

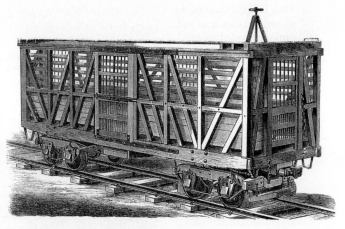

An open slatted wooden stock car of 1867 moved cattle and other animals. —Jim Harter, *American Railroads of the Nineteenth Century* (Lubbock: Texas Tech University Press, 1998)

helium, liquefied petroleum gas, propane, butane, anhydrous ammonia, and beverages. Advances included high-pressure tanks, aluminum and welded tanks, improved insulation, and new lining materials. Some chlorine and sulfur dioxide cars included up to 15 portable canisters. Helium was also transported in cars with multiple tanks.

The 1960s saw further tank-car developments. With full-length center sills no longer required, cars could become lighter and larger. During this time a double-shell vacuum-insulated tank car for cryogenic gases was introduced, thus making obsolete those boxcars with enclosed tanks. Several hundred extremely large tank cars running on 6 or 8 axles were built in the 1960s and early 1970s, but further development was not pursued because of safety concerns. A large number of tank cars are now used for kaolin clay or calcium carbonate slurry used in the paper industry. Today's most common tank cars range in size from 13,500 to 34,000 gallons, with gross rail loads of either 263,000 or 286,000 pounds.

Stock cars date back to the 1830s. Some early cars, lacking a roof, were essentially a stock pen built on a flatcar. Stock cars became more common in the latter part of the nineteenth century. Later cars had provisions for feeding and watering the livestock. Specialized cars used for poultry and horses were developed in the 1880s.

In 1901 there were four kinds of stock cars, the most common of which was the single-deck car for cattle. There were also double-deck cars for smaller animals such as pigs or sheep. Relatively rare were enclosed cars equipped with stalls for use with horses, which were also transported in special baggage cars on passenger trains. The fourth type of stock car was for poultry. The cars were arranged for crated live birds with wire-netted sides and provisions for an attendant who provided feed and water. A rare hybrid car was introduced about 1930. It accommodated live poultry in one end and refrigerated dressed poultry, eggs, and butter in the other. Most poultry cars

were owned by private companies, and their number declined greatly during the 1940s.

Since stock cars were subject to seasonal use, railroads were interested in increasing their versatility. Consequently, general-service stock cars included drop doors in the floor so they could also be used for coal or coke. Several such designs were popular in the western United States between 1904 and 1924. Later a convertible car (both single and double decks) was also developed, while the last variation was the triple-deck car that took advantage of the increased heights allowed after 1963. As large slaughterhouses were replaced by smaller facilities within trucking distance of where the stock was raised, the demand for stock cars diminished in the 1960s and 1970s. Fewer than 100 were built after the 1960s, and few remain in service at present. Some of the last stock cars built about 1970 were 85 feet long.

Many different stories have been written about the origin of the caboose. It was recognizable on some railroads in the 1850s but not on others until the 1870s. These cars were originally needed for lodging the crew, for record keeping, and for observing the train. Both 4- and 8-wheeled types were common by 1901. Steel underframes came fairly quickly to caboose cars, especially where trains were assisted by additional locomotives pushing behind the caboose car. By the 1910s laws in several states regarding number of wheels or length of caboose cars effectively outlawed 4-wheeled cars as unsafe. The last 4-wheeled cabooses for a major railroad were built in the early 1920s. More recent changes in rules have made the caboose car obsolete in all but a few cases, with air-brake-pressure-monitoring functions carried out by a small end-of-train radio device placed on the coupler of the last car. The last new caboose cars were built in 1981. Cabooses are still used today in situations where a train must back across grade crossings on a regular basis. They provide a safe riding place for the crewman who needs to observe and direct the highway traffic at the crossings.

Their long drive across the western prairies at an end, cattle are loaded aboard the cattle cars on the way to market, as illustrated in the June 1892 *Scribner's Magazine.* —Middleton Collection

Railroads usually operate a number of cars for nonrevenue purposes that are either built new or adapted from retired revenue freight and passenger equipment. They are used for construction, inspection, and maintenance of facilities, for transportation of supplies and waste products, and to handle emergencies. Some of the more common are listed here.

Coal, oil, and sand cars are used in company service for materials used by locomotives. Ballast cars, ballast unloaders, ballast spreaders (or plows), and ballast trimmers are used to distribute ballast on the roadbed. Ballast tampers, ballast cleaners, and tie extractors are used in maintaining roadbed. Side-dump cars and steam shovels are used for grading work when extending or improving the roadbed. Pile drivers are used to stabilize roadbed or build trestles. Cinder (or ash) cars and refuse cars are used at engine terminals and other facilities.

Wreck trains include wrecking derricks and cars for tools, blocks, and trucks used to put errant rolling stock back on the tracks. Snowplows, flangers (which clear the area below the top of the rail), and sweepers are used to remove snow. Scale test cars are used to calibrate track scales. Clearance cars are used to check clearances above and along tracks. Idler cars are used for switching cars in areas where locomotives are restricted, such as on car floats (ferries for freight cars). Modified passenger cars are often used for officials, paymasters, and the instruction, transportation, and boarding of employees.

Weed burners, weed sprayers, grass cutters, and brush cutters are used for clearing vegetation along the tracks. Ditching cars are used for excavating drainage ditches along the track. Rail saw, rail bender, and tracklaying cars are used to prepare and lay rails.

Small, self-propelled vehicles became common during the twentieth century as soon as the internal combustion engine became available. Recently, bimodal work equipment that can operate either on or off the rails has become popular, because it is easier to move out of the way of trains.

The line between revenue and nonrevenue equipment is not always clear. Certain convertible ballast cars were purchased for both revenue and company service and were sometimes listed as freight cars rather than company service cars. Automatic side-dump cars are considered nonrevenue cars on most railroads, but are used for revenue purposes on a few. Caboose cars are used for nonrevenue purposes, yet their close association with freight trains has led railroads to list them with freight cars more often than not.

History of Production

The demand for freight cars in Canada and Mexico did not always follow the same trends as in the United States for a number of reasons, including both political and economic factors. A significant number of cars were built in the United States for Canadian railroads from 1901 to 1920. On the other hand, quite a few cars have been built in Canada for U.S. railroads and companies since 1994. The United States exported thousands of cars to Mexico through the 1930s. Several thousand cars were built in Mexico for U.S. railroads and companies between

Table 2. Domestic Freight Car Production

Years	Total	Comments
1901–1905	671,189	
1906–1910	859,462	
1911–1915	549,219	
1916–1920	469,405	Also significant export business
1921–1925	501,775	Also significant heavy repair business
1926–1930	354,802	
1931–1935	51,309	The Great Depression
1936–1940	228,053	
1941–1945	262,199	Also significant export business
1946–1950	359,670	Also significant export business
1951–1955	328,038	
1956–1960	303,996	
1961–1965	259,936	
1966–1970	364,644	
1971–1975	300,979	
1976–1980	354,660	
1981–1985	92,365	Economic recession
1986–1990	108,948	
1991–1995	199,808	
1996–2000	314,387	

Sources: 1901–1919 figures are from the *Railway Age Gazette*; 1920–2000 figures are from the American Railway Car Institute and consistently include both contract and company shop output.

1901–1911 figures exclude company shop output, which may have been about 20,000 cars per year.

1905–1912 figures include Canadian output, which gradually increased from about 2,000 to 10,000 cars per year.

The export business peaked around the two world wars. Many orders were placed by governments for military and reconstruction purposes.

The large amount of repair business in the early 1920s was due to a build up of unserviceable cars during the USRA control of railroads.

When looking at the totals, consider that the average capacity rose from about 80,000 pounds in 1901 to about 220,000 pounds in 2000. This means that 4 cars built in 2000 carry roughly the same amount as 11 built in 1901.

1963 and 1988. Two U.S. car builders have opened plants in Mexico, which have built cars for the U.S. market since about 1998.

There were many ways businesses got into car building. Some companies were created to build cars under contract. Some existing companies added car building to use or diversify their product lines. Some railroads and equipment leasing companies got into car building to provide the cars that they used. There were also several ways to go out of the car-building business. A close look at the annual variations in orders shows great volatility that made car building a challenging business (see Table 2). The Great Depression and especially the recession of the 1980s were difficult times and resulted in numerous plant closings and mergers. At other times certain companies gradually lost market share until they disappeared. A few companies did not or could not modernize at a critical time, such as builders of wooden cars that had not added steel shops by 1910. However, one recurring theme is that having a specialty product or two could keep a company going through tough times.

—Eric A. Neubauer

REFERENCES

American Engineer & Railroad Journal, various issues.

Combes, C. L., ed. *1970 Car and Locomotive Cyclopedia*. New York: Simmons-Boardman, 1970.

Dahlinger, Fred, Jr. "Development of the Railroad Circus." *Bandwagon*, Nov.–Dec. 1983.

Dow, Andrew. *Norfolk & Western Coal Cars*. Lynchburg, Va.: TLC, 1998.

Ellsworth, Kenneth G., ed. *Car and Locomotive Cyclopedia*. New York: Simmons-Boardman, 1984.

Epstein, Ralph C. *GATX: A History of the General American Transportation Corporation, 1898–1948*. New York: North River Press, 1948.

Kaminski, Edward S. *The Magor Car Corporation*. Wilton, Calif.: Signature Press, 2000.

Kratville, William W., ed. *Car and Locomotive Cyclopedia of American Practice*. 6th ed. New York: Simmons-Boardman, 1997.

Morgan, Tom. *1991–92 Car & Locomotive Yearbook*. Chicago: Murphy-Richter, 1991.

Voss, William. *Railway Car Construction*. New York: R. M. Van Arsdale, 1892.

White, John H., Jr. *The American Railroad Freight Car*. Baltimore: Johns Hopkins Univ. Press, 1993.

———. *The American Railroad Passenger Car*. Baltimore: Johns Hopkins Univ. Press, 1978.

Freight Terminals

The line-haul operation of trains may be the most visible element of the railroad industry, but what happens in the less visible world of freight terminals is of at least equal importance. The American Railway Engineering Assn. once defined a freight terminal simply as "the arrangement of terminal facilities for the handling of freight traffic." We can take that to include facilities at which freight is delivered, stored, made available for pickup, or transferred to another rail movement or another mode of transportation, such as motor truck or waterborne vessel. This covers such diverse installations as team tracks, where railcars are spotted for loading or unloading by shippers who do not have their own rail sidings; the enormous facilities required for the transshipment of bulk materials between rail and ships; the once-common urban freight house that processed less-than-carload (LCL) shipments moving by rail; waterfront break bulk terminals; or the relatively new intermodal terminals for transshipment of truck trailers and containers between rail and motor carriers or ships.

Freight terminals can also be considered in terms of the type of freight they handle. They can be designed to handle either a variety of freight or a single commodity. For example, both the traditional freight house and the modern intermodal terminal are built to handle general freight, although in a very different manner. The coal pier, on the other hand, is designed for the single purpose of efficiently transferring coal between railcars and the holds of ships. Similarly, grain elevators are designed and built solely to store and transship grain between railcars, motor carriers, or ships. Still other examples of commodity-specific terminals include those for chemicals and automobiles.

Whatever the type of terminal, operating speed and efficiency are required for railroads to provide the best possible service to shippers. Efficient terminal operation is critical because any unnecessary time that freight spends in a terminal delays customer delivery and carries significant economic costs. Terminal delays affect not only the rail customer's business, but the business of the railroad as well. When traffic backs up at one or more terminals, the flow of freight throughout the system can be severely degraded. If not corrected quickly, terminal problems can significantly affect regional economies and even, in extreme cases, the economic health of the nation.

The importance of the freight terminal is illustrated by two examples. In 1997 operational problems centered around Houston, Texas, on the newly merged Union Pacific and Southern Pacific—many of them freight-terminal delays—brought about a massive traffic jam that soon spread over a much broader area of the system. Recovery from the terminal backlogs required months. In the meantime, chaotic service and late deliveries of freight cost shippers millions of dollars, and many moved their business to other carriers if they could.

In the fall of 2002 failed contract negotiations between longshoremen and the operators of West Coast ports resulted in a backlog of container ships, many of them transporting holiday-season merchandise. At one point more than 100 container ships sat anchored offshore at the ports of Los Angeles and Long Beach, waiting to move into port for unloading. By the time the labor dispute was resolved, the ships were unloaded, and the backlog of thousands of containers were moved to their destinations, this freight-terminal delay had exacted a significant adverse impact on the U.S. retail economy during its most important season of the year.

Since the types of rail freight terminals in use have changed over time, it is important to consider them from a historical perspective. Some terminals are no longer used because of changes in the domestic transportation industry, while new ones have been developed as the result of those same changes. The development of the motor-trucking industry, for example, had a profound effect on the evolution of rail freight terminals. The freight house, a common fixture in most small towns and urban areas during the first half of the twentieth century and before, virtually disappeared as LCL traffic rapidly shifted to the more flexible motor-trucking mode. On the other hand, the growth of intermodal services in the last half of the twentieth century, linking the pickup and delivery flexibility of motor trucking with the economies of moving containers over long distances by rail or water, required the development of an entirely new type of intermodal terminal for the fast and efficient transfer of trailers or containers between transport modes.

Other types of freight terminals function largely as they have for a century and more. Although technological advances in loading and unloading equipment have materially improved efficiency and throughput, for example, terminals for handling the bulk commodities that are well suited for rail transportation—coal, ore, and grain—have changed relatively little.

Industrial Sidings and Team Tracks

The ideal arrangement for industries that ship and receive carload quantities of freight is a private rail siding on which the railroad can deliver and pick up cars as needed by the particular business. This enables an industry to receive or ship its freight directly from the railroad with the least amount of handling. However, only plants or facilities with a substantial traffic volume can justify a private siding. The track and roadbed of the siding must be built and maintained, and special switching moves are required to deliver and pick up the freight cars. Most industries of significant size have their own sidings. Large industries, such as steel mills, often have a number of tracks to handle the number of cars needed to deliver inbound raw materials and transport outbound finished goods. Some even have their own locomotives and cars.

Although most industries that use rail freight service today have their own sidings, the team track was once extensively used by those industries that did not have the traffic volume to support a private siding. Team tracks were essentially sidings at which the railroad spotted cars for a number of shippers to load and unload their freight. Team tracks were located in areas as close to as many industries as possible and derived their name from teams of horses used to pull wagons, or drays, to the door of the freight car for manual loading or unloading. Depending on the number of shippers to be served, team-track facilities ranged from as few as one or two tracks to substantial yards in urban industrial areas. The spacing between the tracks had to allow teams to maneuver and position their wagons next to the freight car for easy loading or unloading. As early motor trucks began to replace teams and drays, consideration had to be given to the space needed for trucks to perform the same pickup and delivery. Indeed, as the motor-trucking industry grew, the need for team tracks diminished, since the line haul, as well as retail pickup and delivery of freight, could be accomplished by the trucks themselves.

Freight Houses

Until the late 1950s LCL freight was a significant source of railroad traffic. Small shipments that are handled today by motor carriers and package express companies were shipped primarily by rail. In order to effectively process this type of traffic, railroads developed freight houses for customer drop-off and pickup of their goods. Freight houses that served large urban areas were usually massive facilities, and many employed technology that was sophisticated for the time, so that shipments could be efficiently sorted and routed to their proper destinations. The railroad freight house was operated in a fashion similar to today's large motor carrier and express terminals and served essentially the same function.

Railroads that served smaller towns usually had a single freight house that handled both inbound and outbound traffic. Large cities usually required two separate houses, one for inbound and one for outbound traffic. Customers delivered goods to the outbound freight house for shipment and picked up delivered goods at the inbound freight house. Larger urban areas often also had a third type of freight house—a transfer house—in which freight would be transferred from one rail movement to another.

Depending on the volume of freight handled, freight houses typically had one or two levels, with rail sidings on one side and a driveway on the other. Some in larger cities had three or four levels, and a number had tracks inside so cars could be loaded or unloaded out of the weather. Freight houses with multiple levels often offered shippers the opportunity to store goods on one of the upper floors until it was convenient for them to take delivery. These freight houses grew to enormous facilities in major urban areas. The Chicago & North Western's Proviso Yard LCL transfer facility near Chicago, said to be the largest of its kind in the world, had some 21 acres under roof. Its 23 tracks had a capacity of 680 cars, and there was tailboard space for 113 highway trucks. The highly mechanized facility handled a daily average of 1,500 tons of freight.

The land available for locating a freight house was a major factor in determining its design, but careful consideration of its size and layout was also important. The longer or wider the house, the farther freight had to be moved within the facility while being transferred from one location to another. The number and spacing of doors in the facility were an important design element for providing maximum capacity and flexibility for spotting cars alongside the house. Elevators were necessary in multilevel freight houses, and careful consideration had to be given to the location of these and other fixed freight-handling equipment, such as scales, to facilitate the workflow.

Movement of freight within the house posed a particular challenge. Perhaps the most basic way to move freight through the house was the simple two-wheeled hand truck. Laborers unloaded freight from cars and used the hand truck to move it to the loading area and onto the outbound freight car. This was both labor and time intensive, and much more efficient four-wheel platform trucks were introduced. Freight could be unloaded onto a platform truck, moved to the section of the freight house where it was needed, and then unloaded in the outbound freight car. The platform trucks could carry much more freight than the two-wheel hand truck, and in many cases the freight never touched the freight-house floor, saving considerable time and labor expense.

The biggest LCL terminal in the world was the Chicago & North Western's facility at Proviso Yard near Chicago. It had 21 acres under roof, with 23 tracks that could accommodate 680 cars. Jack Delano photographed it in December 1942. —Library of Congress (Neg. LCV-USW 3-12457-E)

A significant further improvement was the introduction of the tractor-trailer system, which enabled one person to move larger and heavier loads of freight quickly to multiple destinations throughout the house. Three- or four-wheeled battery-powered electric tractors were used to pull anywhere from three to eight linked platform trucks.

In addition to wheeled vehicles operating on the floor of the house, railroads devised mechanical systems for moving freight through the house. Moving platforms installed in the floor were one example. These moved slowly enough that workers could safely cross them, and they could be loaded directly with freight or with loaded platform trucks.

Overhead carrier systems were also used. These consisted of an elevated runway along which a pair of electric-powered trolleys carried a frame on which loaded platform trucks were carried. The overhead carrier system also had a unit for an operator who traveled with the freight and raised or lowered the hoists as required. These systems ran throughout the freight house and were particularly useful for handling heavy freight.

Throughout most of the years during which freight houses were important elements of rail operation, customers were required to deliver and pick up their goods at the freight house before or after the rail movement. As motor trucking began to provide serious competition to the rail freight business, railroads began offering retail pickup and delivery service in their own trucks, visiting the shipper's place of business much as parcel and express companies do today.

As the motor-trucking industry grew during the 1950s, the railroads' share of LCL freight declined significantly. The freight houses were no longer needed and quickly disappeared from the landscape. Some LCL freight still moves by rail, but it is typically combined with other LCL shipments by freight forwarders to fill an entire car and therefore move at a carload rate.

Bulk-Commodity Terminals

Rail transportation is ideally suited for bulk materials that must be moved cheaply over long distances, and the terminal requirements for these materials are unique. Coal is the predominant bulk commodity carried by U.S. railroads. Indeed, coal is the single most important commodity carried by the railroads in both tonnage and revenue. In 2000 coal accounted for 44 percent of the industry's tonnage and 21 percent of its revenue, with an annual traffic of approximately 700 million tons, generating 543 billion ton-miles. The three primary destinations for U.S. coal are domestic coal-fired power plants, ports for export to international destinations, and domestic facilities that use coal to make coke, which is used in iron and steel production. Electric power generation is by far the largest domestic consumer of coal and accounted for 91 percent of all U.S. coal production in 2000.

Much of this coal moves in unit trains, which consist of equipment dedicated to continuous service in round trips from mine to power plant or port. Most coal not moving in unit trains usually moves in trainload quantities, especially when the volume of coal to be moved to a single destination requires a substantial number of cars.

Coal usually begins its journey on a conveyor system at the mine to a loading facility, usually called a tipple, which loads the coal directly into railcars on the track below. The train travels at an extremely slow speed, 1 mph or less, to avoid having to start and stop as each car is positioned under the loading chute.

When coal arrives at a power plant, it is often unloaded into a large storage area located under a trestle simply by being discharged through the bottom of the cars onto the ground below and is then moved to an adjacent storage location by ground equipment. The trestle forms a loop from the main line, enabling the train to unload its cargo without complicated switching moves, and unloading is often accomplished while the train is in motion. Once unloading is complete, the train returns to the main line for its journey back to the mine. Some power plants have rotary-dump equipment, which takes a single car and literally turns it upside down to discharge the load into a storage area or a conveyor system that takes the coal directly into the plant for consumption.

Early coal piers for transferring coal from railcars to ships were simple elevated structures. The coal cars were pushed out along the top of the pier, and their loads were discharged through chutes to the waiting ships or into pockets for later loading. Typically there were tracks for loaded cars on each side of the pier, with a center track for the removal of empty cars.

Later a variety of mechanized coal-pier designs were developed. Some of these employed giant car dumpers that could pick up loaded cars, turn them over, and dump their contents into a pan or chute that then conveyed the coal into a telescoping chute for placement in the hold of a ship. A coal pier of this type built in the early 1920s at the Reading's Port Richmond Terminal on the Delaware River at Philadelphia, for example, could handle cars weighing as much as 165 tons, car and contents, at a rate of about 40 cars an hour. Loaded cars were pushed up to the dumper on an inclined trestle by a barney car. Once emptied, cars were returned by gravity to a switchback at the end of the pier and then to a storage yard for empty cars.

The B&O built a coal pier at Curtis Bay, Maryland, near Baltimore, that operated in a very different manner. Capable of loading 12 million tons of coal a year aboard ships, the Curtis Bay pier employed two car dumpers at the land end of the pier, each capable of dumping 40 cars an hour. The contents of loaded coal cars were dumped into a huge "pan," which then deposited the coal into hoppers, from which it was transported by conveyors to storage bins at the inner end of the pier. Coal was then fed from these bins by high-speed conveyor belts to big loading towers on the pier that could each load 2,000 tons an hour into a ship.

Duluth, Missabe & Northern Dock No. 5 at Duluth, Minnesota, was the largest on the Great Lakes when it was completed in 1914. Standing 80 feet above the water and 2,304 feet long, it could store 115,200 long tons of ore. Here the Pittsburgh Steamship Co. steamer *Mataafa* was ready to load ore. —Northeast Minnesota Historical Center (Collection S3742)

Still another arrangement was devised by the Virginian Railway for its first coal pier at Sewalls Point in Norfolk, Virginia. A rotating car dumper emptied loaded cars into big electrically powered conveyor cars, which were then raised to the top of the pier either by an elevator or by hauling up an incline. The conveyor cars then operated under their own power up and down the pier to dump their coal into pockets on either side, from which it was discharged through chutes to the holds of ships.

Modern export coal piers are designed to accommodate the extremely large "super-colliers," which transport upwards of 150,000 tons of coal. When export coal shipments arrive at a modern port terminal, the cars are staged in a special yard according to the type of coal they carry and the vessel they are scheduled to load. These coal terminals use enormous piers that are equipped with some combination of rotary car dumpers, bins, chutes, conveyor belts, and moving shiploaders that deposit the coal in a ship's hold. Entire trainloads of coal can be transferred from rail to ship in just a few hours. The Norfolk Southern's Coal Pier No. 6 at Norfolk, Virginia, for example, is a 1,650-foot-long structure with two enormous 2,800-ton traveling shiploaders that receive coal from conveyer belts either directly from rotary car dumpers or storage silos. This facility is capable of dumping more than 170,000 tons of coal in a 24-hour period. Inland waterway terminals often use similar technology, although usually on a smaller scale, for rail-water transloading of coal. River and port terminals usually have facilities for blending different grades of coal to meet specific customer needs.

Iron ore is another bulk commodity well suited to rail movement. Ore transported from the Mesabi Range in northern Minnesota to the steel mills in and around Pitts-

burgh, for example, moves in a combination of rail and water movement. The initial movement is by rail, then by ship, then by rail again for delivery to the mill. Therefore, facilities are required not only for transferring the ore from rail to ship, but from ship to rail as well.

Facilities for loading ore into ships from railcars once consisted of long elevated piers with tracks on the top. Loaded ore cars were pushed out onto the dock, and their contents were emptied into ore pockets, which were then emptied through chutes into the holds of ore ships. Transferring ore from the ship back to railcars was more challenging, however. Early facilities for unloading ore boats in the lower Great Lakes typically used manual labor, but this was soon replaced by ore-unloading machines that could travel up and down a dock, employing clamshell buckets to remove the ore through hatches on the ore boat. By the beginning of the twentieth century these were being displaced by the more efficient Hulett Automatic Unloading Machine.

The ingenious Hulett unloader was a huge rail-mounted machine that could move up or down the length of a dock. A carriage or trolley that could move back and forth at right angles to the dock face carried a walking beam with a hoisting mechanism at the inner end, while the outer end supported a leg equipped with a large bucket at its lower end. This bucket leg was suspended in a vertical position, and the bucket could rotate to reach out in any direction beneath an ore-boat hatch, while it could be moved laterally across the width of the vessel. An operator in a cab inside this vertical leg rode up and down with each load and was able to see and control the operation of the bucket at all times. The bucket was lowered through a ship's hatch and filled with ore, then raised and carried back over the

Each of these giant Hulett Automatic Unloading Machines could move about ten tons of ore at a time, completing each movement in about one minute. Great Lakes Steamship Co. ore boat *J. Burton Ayers* was unloading ore at the Pennsylvania Railroad's Cleveland, Ohio, dock. —Tom Hollyman, Hagley Museum and Library

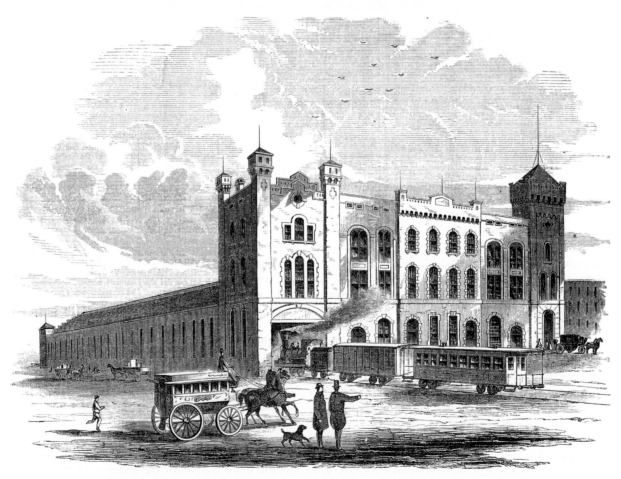

The massive Chicago & Galena Grain House at Chicago, illustrated in an 1857 issue of *Ballou's Pictorial Drawing-Room Companion.* —Middleton Collection

Enormous quantities of grain arrived from the west at the New York Central & Hudson River elevator at the foot of 61st Street on the North (Hudson) River in New York. This wood engraving appeared in the November 10, 1877, *Frank Leslie's Illustrated Newspaper.* —Library of Congress (Neg. LC-USX62-2110)

dock to be discharged into a hopper. A typical Hulett unloader had a capacity of about 10 tons of ore and could complete about one unloading cycle a minute; production rates as great as 783 tons an hour were reported for a single Hulett.

By the late twentieth century a shift to much larger ore carriers, together with the adoption of advanced bulk-material-handling systems, had transformed the way ore is loaded and unloaded at the Great Lakes iron-ore ports. Fast conveyor-belt ship-loader systems have proved a quicker and more efficient way to load the ore boats than the traditional gravity-pocket system. Ore carriers are now

Duluth, Minnesota, was one of the principal grain-shipping ports, transferring its western harvest to Great Lakes ships. A grain boat had begun to load at the Occident elevator at Duluth in August 1941.
—Library of Congress (Neg. LC-USF 34-63615-D)

In this modern view of grain shipment, taken on the Illinois Central Gulf at Savoy, Illinois, in March 1980, the grain is transferred from the elevator to a covered hopper car. —J. David Ingles, *Trains* Magazine Collection

(now Thunder Bay), Ontario, in 1924 had a capacity of 8.5 million bushels. The Great Northern Elevator on Lake Superior at Superior, Wisconsin, had a total storage capacity of more than 12 million bushels.

When boxcars were used for grain shipment, the elevators were usually equipped with car dumpers that rotated or tilted the car to unload its contents into a hopper under the dumper, but the covered grain hoppers of modern practice can simply be emptied into the hopper as they pass over it. Grain is then conveyed to an overhead "garner" and thence to scales or for drying, cleaning, or mixing before finally moving to storage bins for eventual loading into ships, trucks, or railcars.

Waterfront Terminals and Car Floats

Terminals for "break bulk" freight moving between rail and water were typically made up of waterfront rail yards, warehouses, and piers or wharves. If possible, vessels were docked at the piers for loading or unloading, and freight was sometimes handled directly between ships and railcars. This was the most economical practice, but more often freight was stored to await a particular vessel or rail movement, and much of the movement of freight to and from ships was accomplished with lighters, or covered barges. One of the largest such terminals, the Bush Terminal at Brooklyn, New York, had six enormous six-story warehouse buildings, an extensive rail yard, and seven piers.

Car-float service was developed to provide access to other rail lines or terminals that could not be reached directly by rail (*see* MARINE OPERATIONS). Railcars could be delivered to some waterfront freight terminals only by car float. The most extensive car-float operations in North America were operated in New York Harbor. Car-float operations were labor and time intensive and costly. The greater use of motor trucking and the shift of most ocean freight traffic to containers in the last half of the twentieth century brought an end to most car-float operations, as well as the massive waterfront "break bulk" freight terminals themselves.

Specialty Terminals: Chemicals and Automobiles

Railroads haul a substantial portion of the nation's chemical output because both the hazardous nature of the traffic and the need to respond quickly to changing market conditions make them ideally suited for it. Railroads that serve industries producing hazardous chemicals usually provide special yards and switching moves for these products because of the danger inherent in transporting them. In addition, the chemical industry often relies on railroads to provide storage of excess production, for which the railroads have "storage-in-transit" yards. The extensive facilities that serve the petrochemical in-

almost always equipped with their own self-unloading systems, ending the need for such big dinosaurs as the Hulett unloaders or similar systems. The old existing docks are being adapted to these new systems, and new docks are likely to be entirely different from the older facilities they replace.

The western prairies of the United States and Canada produce upwards of 400 million tons of grain every year, and much of it moves by rail toward domestic and international destinations. Grain shipments include barley, corn, oats, rye, sorghum, soybeans, and wheat, with corn being the most important grain carried by the railroads, accounting for about 50 percent of both grain tonnage and revenue. From trackside elevators on the prairies this great flood of grain flows in boxcars or specialized grain hoppers to the milling centers or to the ports of the Great Lakes, the Gulf of Mexico, or the two oceans for export. Here it is loaded into great elevator storehouses where it may be cleaned, dried, mixed, and stored until it goes to the mill or is loaded into ships for export.

These terminal elevators are often enormous structures. A Canadian National elevator built at Port Arthur

dustry in and around Houston, Texas, are good examples of the specialized service provided to the industry.

The automobile-manufacturing industry is also heavily reliant on the railroads, and special yards are provided for this industry as well. Rail service is used for movement of certain auto parts, as well as for the delivery of finished automobiles. Finished automobiles may be picked up from domestic assembly plants or at port terminals when the automobiles are manufactured overseas. Domestic assembly plants typically have a moderately sized yard for the delivery of auto parts and pickup of finished automobiles. These yards must be designed to allow room for trucks carrying automobiles to load and unload in close proximity to the railcars. Special switching moves are also required for these large facilities.

One U.S. railroad, Norfolk Southern, operates what it calls "mixing centers" to consolidate shipments of finished automobiles for one manufacturer's 21 domestic assembly plants. There are three of these centers in the United States, and each serves as a consolidation point for shipments bound for a particular region of the country. This system reduces the time that finished automobiles sit at an assembly plant awaiting a full carload before being shipped to their destination.

Intermodal Terminals

From 1980 to 2002 rail intermodal traffic tripled, from 3.1 million trailers or containers moved in 1980 to 9.3 million in 2002. In 2002 intermodal accounted for about 20 percent of revenue for major U.S. railroads. This traffic developed in the early twentieth century with the movement of highway trailers on conventional railroad flatcars. These were loaded from simple endwise "circus-style" ramps that loaded trailers on one or a string of bridge-plate-equipped flatcars, enabling a truck tractor to move between cars and load an entire cut of cars.

As the demand for this service grew, railroads developed special yards and such specialized loading equipment as top- or side-loading gantry cranes to speed the loading and unloading of trailers on or off specialized flatcars. After several years of experimentation with various lifting devices, individual railroads settled on one of several types of overhead gantry cranes that spanned the yard track and an area of pavement wide enough to enable a trailer to be spotted for lifting. Some cranes moved along special rails built into the pavement, others on large rubber tires.

After several decades of experimentation standardized freight containers had come into common use for intermodal traffic by the beginning of the 1970s. Designed to carry a variety of general freight, the container could be easily carried by and transferred between a motor carrier chassis, a railcar, and a container ship. Railroads developed specialized cars, equipment, and yards for handling containers. Usually rail-mounted or rubber-tired overhead gantry cranes and tractor-drawn yard trailers are used to transfer containers between railcars and truck chassis or to and from storage areas. In addition to rail tracks, modern container yard facilities include extensive paved areas for container storage.

The integration of rail and motor-truck movement of containers with movement on ocean vessels has created an integrated global transportation network that has brought significant economies to the international transportation of goods. The use of extremely large, specialized fast container ships has necessitated the development of comparable container terminal capacity. Enormous high-speed, rail-mounted gantry cranes are used to load and unload the ships. Those at the modern Deltaport Intermodal Terminal at Vancouver, British Columbia, for example, are 238 feet high, with an ability to reach out 155 feet over the water, and can load or unload 40 containers per hour.

—David C. Lester

REFERENCES

DeBoer, David J. *Piggyback and Containers: A History of Rail Intermodal on America's Steel Highways.* San Marino, Calif.: Golden West Books, 1992.

Droege, John A. *Freight Terminals and Trains.* 2nd ed. New York: McGraw-Hill, 1925. Repr., Chattanooga, Tenn.: National Model Railroad Assn., 1998.

Lamb, Parker J. "Texas' Chemical Coast." *Trains* 59, no. 10 (Oct. 1999): 36–49.

LesStrang, Jacques. *Cargo Carriers of the Great Lakes.* Boyne City, Mich.: Harbor House, 1985.

Middleton, William D. *Landmarks on the Iron Road.* Bloomington: Indiana Univ. Press, 1999.

White, John H., Jr. *The American Railroad Freight Car.* Baltimore: Johns Hopkins Univ. Press, 1993.

See also INTERMODAL FREIGHT.

Funeral Trains

Funeral trains carried 11 presidents at least part of the way to their final resting places, but it was the operation of those for Presidents Abraham Lincoln, Warren Harding, Franklin Roosevelt, and Dwight Eisenhower that are the most significant. Lincoln's 1865 train departed from Washington, D.C., and traveled through seven states to Springfield, Illinois, tracing a roundabout 1,662-mile, 12-day itinerary to allow as much of the nation as possible to salute its first assassinated chief executive. Only two cars traveled all the way: the *United States*, a private car built by the U.S. Military Railroads for—but never used by—Lincoln in his lifetime as the funeral coach, and a second car behind it for the honor guard. The rest of the equipment for the funeral train and pilot train was furnished by most of the 26 participating railroads, amounting to at

Franklin D. Roosevelt died suddenly at Warm Springs, Georgia, on April 12, 1945. Millions watched the funeral train that carried his body to Washington and then to his burial at Hyde Park, New York. A military honor guard and spectators waited at the Southern Railway's Warm Springs station as a hearse transported the body to Pullman sleeping car *Conneaut* to begin the long journey home. —National Archives (Neg. NA 208-PO-169-150), from Bob Withers

least 42 locomotives and more than 80 wooden passenger cars.

Harding's sudden death in San Francisco on August 2, 1923, transformed his cross-country touring train into a funeral procession that returned his body to Washington and then to Marion, Ohio, for burial. His car on that trip in both directions was the Pullman private car *Superb*, which had been fitted with a newfangled loudspeaker system. Three years later the car was temporarily repainted and renamed *Pope Pius XI* for use on the Cardinals Train for the College of Cardinals from New York to Chicago.

Roosevelt's train was resting in Atlanta when he died of a cerebral hemorrhage in Warm Springs, Georgia, on April 12, 1945. The Southern Railway quickly dispatched it southward, where it became a funeral train the next day and began a journey headed by various classes of Pacific-type steam locomotives to Washington for a White House funeral and—behind a Pennsylvania Railroad class GG1 electric locomotive and a New York Central class J-1 Hudson-type steam engine—to the family home at Hyde Park, New York, for burial. Two other trains accompanied the procession from Washington, one for members of

Congress, Supreme Court justices, and diplomats, the other for a marine escort. Since FDR's private car, the armor-plated *Ferdinand Magellan*, was equipped with a narrow, bombproof door and sealed windows, the *Conneaut*, the Secret Service's staff car, was placed on the rear of the train and the casket placed in it.

Although Robert Kennedy never became president, by many accounts he was on his way to receive the Democratic presidential nomination when an assassin's bullet brought him down in Los Angeles on June 5, 1968, as he celebrated a California primary victory. Penn Central fielded a 21-car train, pilot train, and chase train to carry Kennedy's body from the funeral at St. Patrick's Cathedral in New York to Arlington National Cemetery near Washington. The operation was plagued by a lack of planning, mismatched coaches, sticking brakes, faulty air conditioning, and an unrealistic four-hour schedule for the 226.6-mile route. The catafalque, placed in the private car *Philadelphia*, was not high enough to be seen by those at trackside, and family members lifted it up on chairs and spent the rest of the afternoon making sure that it would not tip over. Before the day ended, that car ran out of drinking and flush water, food, drinks, and ice. Even the locomotives' motors overheated. The bungled operation was compounded at Elizabeth, New Jersey, when two people were killed and six injured when they ventured too close to the track and were struck by the eastbound *Admiral*. Too late, Penn Central ordered all advance and opposing movements to halt and called in more police to control the crowds. Even then, at Trenton, New Jersey, 17 people were severely burned when an 18-year-old boy perched atop a boxcar stood up for a better view and touched an 11,000-volt overhead wire used to power electric locomotives.

In contrast, the following year's funeral train to Abilene, the last such major event, ran flawlessly. A train would never have borne Dwight Eisenhower's body to its grave had Mamie Eisenhower not hated to fly. But as it was, his 10-car special traversed four lines—Chesapeake & Ohio Railway, Baltimore & Ohio Railroad, Norfolk & Western Railway, and Union Pacific Railroad—to carry his body from Washington, where he died on March 28, 1969, to Abilene, Kansas. The movement, which took place even as U.S. rail passenger service was disintegrating each day and the Pullman Co. was preparing to get out of the passenger business altogether, was carried off in textbook fashion, taking 85 hours to go 2,805 miles in well-maintained, sparkling equipment. Indeed, the project had been in the planning stages virtually since Ike had left office in 1961.

Eisenhower, who had served as supreme allied commander during World War II, ordered that his plain gun-metal steel casket be carried in a simple baggage car just like any other soldier's. Operation of the train was a closely held military secret, but the word got out, and thousands of people, some of them retired military in full dress uniforms, stood in respect at trackside. Finally, Mrs. Eisenhower and the family began to acknowledge the condolences and allowed bunting to be placed on the baggage car at Cincinnati. When some of it fell off the speeding train, officers were ordered to stop and pick it up, lest souvenir hunters destroy the dignity of the occasion.

—Bob Withers

REFERENCES

Monroe, Herbert G. "President's Special." *Railroad Magazine* 38, no. 6 (Nov. 1945): 8–44.

Starr, John W., Jr. *Lincoln & the Railroads*. New York: Dodd, Mead, 1927.

Trostel, Scott D. *The Lincoln Funeral Train: The Final Journey and National Funeral for Abraham Lincoln*. Fletcher, Ohio: Cam-Tech, 2002.

Withers, Bob. "Ike's Trains, Part 2: Final Journey to Abilene." *Trains* 50, no. 5 (March 1990): 44–57.

———. *The President Travels by Train*. Lynchburg, Va.: TLC, 1996.

G

Gallatin, Albert (1761–1849)

Albert Gallatin served the United States well as its third secretary of the Treasury under President Thomas Jefferson. Gallatin was born in Geneva, Switzerland, on January 12, 1761. Educated in his native country, Gallatin came to North America and found a home in Pennsylvania. He entered politics in 1788 as an Anti-Federalist, that is, a person objecting to certain parts of the new U.S. Constitution. By 1790 he was widely enough known to win election to the Pennsylvania legislature.

In 1793 he was elected by the legislature to the U.S. Senate at a time when state legislatures chose Senators. The Federalists, who focused on a strong federal government, were dismayed by Gallatin's well-informed attacks on their agenda and saw to it that his election to the Senate was nullified. Undaunted, Gallatin stayed in politics and was elected to the U.S. House of Representatives from Pennsylvania in 1795. When Jefferson became president in 1801, he appointed Gallatin secretary of the Treasury, a post he held for 13 years in two administrations.

As Treasury secretary, Gallatin reduced the national debt while at the same time paying for the Louisiana Purchase. His party changed its name to the Democratic Republicans (more positive sounding than Anti-Federalists) and opposed the rechartering of the First Bank of the United States. However, Gallatin saw the bank, with both private and public investors, as a means of stabilizing the economy of the new nation without harm to the public. He was unsurpassed as a visionary, particularly in the growth of the trans-Appalachian West, and saw that it was vital to the future of the nation to support agriculture, trade, and industry. Although many Jeffersonians were opposed to big government, Gallatin felt that federal programs and financial support were necessary to assure future U.S. prosperity.

Gallatin's great contribution was his recognition of the need for a national system of transportation at least partially funded by the federal government. His landmark work of public planning, the 1808 *Report of the Secretary of the Treasury on the Subject of Public Roads and Canals*, advocated a system of highways and canals to connect the East with the rapidly developing West. Railroads as common carriers did not exist when Gallatin devised his transportation plan, but eventually his combination of public and private ventures created the very system he had envisioned. For example, his proposed Cincinnati–St. Louis road became the route of the Ohio & Mississippi Railroad and subsequently a part of the Baltimore & Ohio.

Gallatin had problems in financing the War of 1812, in part because the charter of the First Bank of the United States had not been renewed. Before the war was over, Gallatin resigned and went to Europe to serve the United States as a diplomat. After his return to the United States in 1823 he was chosen to be William Crawford's vice presidential candidate in the 1824 election, but so much controversy was mounted in opposition that Gallatin withdrew from the race. He spent his remaining years mainly as a diplomat; perhaps his greatest service in that role was preventing war between the United States and Great Britain over the Oregon Territory. After retiring, Gallatin became an ethnologist, studying the cultures of Native Americans. A great friend of fur trade magnate John Jacob Astor, he died in Astoria, New York, in 1849.

—George M. Smerk

REFERENCES

Kuppenheimer, L. B. *Albert Gallatin's Vision of Democratic Stability: An Interpretive Profile.* Westport, Conn.: Praeger, 1996.

Larson, John Lauritz. *Internal Improvement: National Public Works and the Promise of Popular Government in the Early United States.* Chap. 2. Chapel Hill: Univ. of North Carolina Press, 2001.

Meinig, D. W. *The Shaping of America.* Vol. 2, *Continental America, 1800–1867,* 311–352. New Haven, Conn.: Yale Univ. Press, 1993.

Garrett, John W. (1820–1884)

A Baltimore native, John Garrett joined his father's commission house at age 16 and by age 19 became a partner in the new family firm of Robert Garrett & Sons.

Thanks in part to John's enterprise, the firm expanded into investment banking and by the early 1850s had large holdings in the Baltimore & Ohio. After a 25-year struggle the B&O had reached the Ohio River at Wheeling (later West Virginia) in 1852 and established a connecting route to St. Louis in 1857. However, its policies were heavily influenced by political interests who preferred to use the railroad to develop Baltimore and Maryland rather than as a dividend-producing enterprise.

Backed by the powerful Baltimore banker and financier Johns Hopkins, Garrett was elected the B&O's president in 1858 with the goal of making the railroad pay dividends. He ruled the B&O for the next 26 years and presided over both its greatest expansion and worst traumas. He also held firmly to his dividend pledge, ultimately to the railroad's financial and operational detriment.

Soon after his ascension Garrett faced the challenge of his life. When the Civil War broke out, the B&O formed the only rail link between Washington and the North, and its east-west line straddled the Union and the Confederacy. Furthermore, Maryland's loyalty to the Union initially was uncertain at best. Garrett kept the B&O on the Union side and kept Washington's lifeline open, although his western main line suffered heavy damage and numerous service disruptions.

Garrett then faced the challenge of postwar rebuilding while at the same time trying to match the aggressive expansion of the Vanderbilt system and his chief rival, the Pennsylvania Railroad. He extended the B&O to Pittsburgh in 1871 and to Chicago in 1874, opened a direct route between Washington and the West in 1873, and expanded in several other directions. Garrett also helped build Baltimore into a major port, particularly for bulk materials such as coal and grain.

Partly because of Garrett's financial policies, however, the B&O was financially and competitively weaker than its large rivals and was often blamed for destabilizing the eastern railroad environment by rate cutting. During the economic depression of the mid-1870s Garrett refused to reduce dividends but instead cut wages further, precipitating the first violence that led to the national railroad strike of 1877.

In his last years Garrett was increasingly beset by a combination of physical and emotional problems. Nonetheless, he remained steadfastly in control, although he relied more heavily on his son, Robert, who eventually succeeded him. After the Pennsylvania outmaneuvered him by buying control of the Philadelphia, Wilmington & Baltimore in 1881, Garrett impulsively ordered the construction of a competing route between Baltimore and New York Harbor. It was his last major act, and he never lived to see the new line's completion to Philadelphia. On September 26, 1884, he died at his cottage in the Allegheny resort of Deer Park, Maryland.

—Herbert H. Harwood, Jr.

John W. Garrett. —Middleton Collection

REFERENCES

Harwood, Herbert H., Jr. *Royal Blue Line.* Repr., Baltimore: Johns Hopkins Univ. Press, 2002.

Hungerford, Edward. *The Story of the Baltimore and Ohio Railroad.* New York: Putnam's, 1928.

Stover, John. "John Work Garrett." *Encyclopedia of American Business History and Biography: Railroads in the Nineteenth Century.* New York: Facts on File, 1988.

General Electric Co.

Ever since its formation more than a century ago, the massive General Electric (GE) conglomerate, now ranked as the fifth-largest U.S. corporation, has been a major supplier to the railroad industry. The firms that were to become General Electric were organized in the 1880s. Thomas Edison had operated an experimental electric locomotive at his Menlo Park, New Jersey, laboratories as early as 1880 and two years later built a test installation for Northern Pacific president Henry Villard, who was considering electrification of NP branch lines. Villard believed in the future of the electrical industry and soon entered the business himself. In 1889 he consolidated the various Edison electrical enterprises with the Sprague

Electric Railway & Motor Co. to form the Edison General Electric Co. The Sprague firm, organized by electric railway pioneer Frank J. Sprague, had completed the first fully successful electric street railway at Richmond, Virginia, during 1887–1888. In 1892 Edison General Electric, in turn, was merged with the rival Thomson-Houston Co. of Lynn, Massachusetts, to form the present-day GE. Thomson-Houston's predecessors included electric railway firms established by such notable electric-traction pioneers as Charles J. Van Depoele, Walter H. Knight, and Edward M. Bentley.

Energized by Sprague's success at Richmond, electric street railways were replacing horse and cable railways all over North America, and the experience and patents that had come into the new firm from its Edison, Sprague, and Thomson-Houston predecessors made GE a leader in the fast-growing business. The success of the electric streetcar soon led to talk of a coming age of railroad electrification, and even before the 1892 merger the companies that were to form GE had begun to develop electric equipment suitable for railroad use. A 30-ton electric locomotive that rolled out of the former Thomson-Houston plant at Lynn in 1893 was exhibited at the World's Columbian Exhibition at Chicago that year and went on to serve a long and

The newly formed GE built this 35-ton, double-truck electric locomotive to do the work of a steam locomotive in 1894. Equipped with four 500-volt DC-traction motors, it was capable of a 14,000-pound drawbar pull. The sturdy engine served for the next 70 years, finally retiring into a museum collection in 1964. —Duke-Middleton Collection

useful life on a Connecticut industrial line. It was, claimed GE, "the first practically operative high speed electric locomotive in the world adapted to the requirements of the steam railroad."

Even before this pioneer locomotive appeared, and only a month after the formation of the new company in April 1892, GE had taken on an ambitious railroad electrification project. The Baltimore & Ohio was building a new belt line around Baltimore that included a mile-and-a-half-long tunnel under the city's downtown Howard Street, and it contracted with GE to supply the electrical equipment and locomotives for an installation that could handle 500-ton passenger trains at 35 mph or 1,200-ton freight trains at 15 mph up the tunnel's 0.8 percent grade. Nothing like it had ever been done. It was the world's first electrification of main-line steam railroad freight and passenger operation, and GE's successful accomplishment of the 3-mile installation was an extraordinary technical triumph.

Propelled by such early successes, GE was soon on the way toward a dominant position in the new world of electric traction. Competing vigorously with its principal rival, Westinghouse Electric & Manufacturing Co., GE produced a full range of traction motors, controls, and other equipment for the fast-growing street railway industry. The company acquired the rights to the multiple-unit control system developed by Frank Sprague in 1897 and soon gained a dominant position in the electrification of elevated railways, subways, and electric interurban railways.

Early in the new century GE landed a contract for the largest North American main-line electrification yet, the conversion of the New York Central's lines into the new Grand Central Terminal at New York. The project included all the electrical equipment required for a third-rail DC electrification of some 285 track-miles, as well as an initial fleet of 35 electric locomotives and 180 multiple-unit suburban cars.

There were still other triumphs for GE electrification. While rival Westinghouse strongly advocated the use of single-phase AC power for heavy railroad traction, GE touted the high-voltage DC system it had first installed on an Indiana interurban line in 1907. Westinghouse landed several major orders for AC installations, but GE's high-voltage DC system was selected for a Southern Pacific suburban electrification out of Oakland, California, that opened in 1911 and, several years later, for a major electrification of Montana's Butte, Anaconda & Pacific with a 2,400-volt DC system. Even before the BA&P electrification was complete, the Milwaukee Road had selected a virtually identical 3,000-volt DC GE system for an electrification of its western mountain crossings. Extending a total of 647 route-miles by the time it reached Tacoma, Washington, in 1920, the Milwaukee installation was the greatest single electrification project undertaken anywhere in the world up to that time. By the end of the decade GE high-voltage DC systems were also powering

A close-up view of one of the
GE locomotive's power trucks.
—Duke-Middleton Collection

suburban electrifications on the Illinois Central and South Shore Line at Chicago and on the Lackawanna in New Jersey.

As its electric-traction and other businesses grew early in the century, GE's plants at Lynn and Schenectady both reached capacity. Rather than expand either plant, the company selected a site at Erie, Pennsylvania, for an entirely new plant. In 1911 electric-traction manufacturing was shifted to the new Erie works, which has been the center of GE's railroad business ever since.

Until World War II the United States led the world in railroad electrification. U.S. manufacturers became world leaders in electric traction, and GE electrification projects were worldwide in their scope. In Canada GE's high-voltage DC system was selected for a Canadian Northern suburban electrification at Montreal. The company's high-voltage DC technology was triumphant in Latin America, too. In 1920 Brazil's Paulista Railway adopted the same 3,000-volt DC system used by the Milwaukee Road for an electrification that eventually reached more than 300 route-miles, and over the next two decades Brazil's Central and Sorocabana railroads followed suit. In 1922 the Ferrocarril Mexicano electrified the severe mountain grades on its Veracruz–Mexico City line with the same system.

GE's high-voltage DC technology reached Japan in 1923 with an order for DC locomotives for the Imperial Government Railways, and Europe a year later with an electrification of severe mountain grades on the Northern Railway of Spain. In 1932 the USSR adopted the 3,000-volt DC system for its first electrification, on a section of the Trans-Caucasus line, and GE's Erie works supplied an initial fleet of electric locomotives for the line.

Although GE favored high-voltage DC and Westinghouse preferred its single-phase AC system, the two manufacturers had licensed each other to manufacture under the other's patents as early as 1896, and both were ready and able to supply equipment for either system. Thus, although the New York, New Haven & Hartford had been persuaded to adopt the Westinghouse single-phase AC system for its important main-line electrification out of New York in 1905, GE subsequently became a major supplier of AC motive power to the New Haven. In 1909 GE was chosen to supply the entire electrical system and motive power for a three-phase AC electrification of the Great Northern's Cascade Tunnel. During the 1920s and 1930s GE became a major supplier of both electrical equipment and complete locomotives for the Pennsylvania's extensive single-phase AC electrification of its principal eastern lines.

As one of only two principal North American suppliers of electric motive power, General Electric enjoyed a substantial business from the very beginning of railroad electrification. Through World War II GE had built or equipped nearly 600 heavy electric locomotives for U.S., Canadian, and Mexican main-line railroads and heavy mining roads and over 100 more of its line of standard light electric locomotives for interurban railways and switching lines. Specialized electric locomotives for mining and industrial use and orders for overseas railroads added up to hundreds more. GE was also a principal supplier of the electrical equipment for the fixed plant of generating stations, transmission lines, substations, and distribution systems that powered more than 6,600 track-miles of North American electrification.

The further expansion of North American electrification that many had anticipated never materialized in the years after World War II, because railroads opted instead for diesel-electric motive power. GE continued to promote the advantages of electrification, but found its market limited largely to replacement equipment for the already-existing electrifications, while a few advanced thyristor rectifier units were supplied to several new coal-mining roads during the 1970s. In 1971 GE expanded its facilities at Erie to add complete electric multiple-unit

GE had begun to look at internal combustion engine power as early as 1904 and by 1910 was marketing a gas-electric motor car. Gas-electric car 7 was operated by the Minneapolis, St. Paul, Rochester & Dubuque Electric Traction Co., a shortline out of Minneapolis. —Duke-Middleton Collection

(M.U.) cars for commuter railroads and rapid-transit systems to its product line. Before the end of the decade, however, it quietly withdrew from the passenger-car market after manufacturing a little over 1,100 cars for New York– and Philadelphia-area commuter lines.

Even as North American railroads began their wholesale shift to diesel-electric power, GE and the American Locomotive Co. (Alco) saw promise in a third type of motive power, and in 1948 the two builders rolled out a prototype 4,500-hp gas-turbine-electric locomotive. After trials on the Pennsylvania and the Nickel Plate the unit went into extended test operation on the Union Pacific, where it proved promising enough to win an order for 10 near duplicates that were delivered in 1954. Another 15 followed in 1954, and during 1958–1961 UP took delivery of 30 massive two-unit gas-turbine locomotives rated at 8,500 hp. Although fuel costs were higher than those for diesel-electric power, the gas turbines delivered higher speeds and lower maintenance costs. No other railroad followed UP's lead, and the railroad soon turned its attention to high-horsepower diesel power. In 1963 UP began trading in its gas turbines for GE diesel-electrics, which employed the running gear from the retired units. GE's—and UP's—venture in gas-turbine power came to an end in 1969.

GE first seriously looked at the internal combustion engine in 1904, when it set out to develop and market a self-propelled railroad car. GE was far from the only manufacturer to pursue the idea of the self-propelled railcar at this time, but it was one of the most successful. By 1910 the company had developed a successful design for a lightweight gas-electric motor car powered by a V-8 gasoline engine of its own design and was soon taking orders for the car. A locomotive version of the design, produced in

1913 for a Minnesota shortline, was probably the first successful electric-drive, internal combustion locomotive operated anywhere.

The company's first involvement with diesel-electric power came in 1905, when it supplied the generator and electrical apparatus for what may have been the very first diesel-electric locomotive ever built, a little-known experimental unit designed by the International Power Co. for the Southern Pacific. In 1911 GE engineers traveled to Europe to visit the major diesel-engine manufacturers, returning to Erie with U.S. production rights for a Junkers two-cycle engine. By 1916 it had developed an improved version of the design rated at about 200 to 250 hp that was installed in three switching locomotives completed in 1917. The engine had its weaknesses, however, and there were no more orders for this early GE diesel-electric.

A difficult problem for GE's early gas-electric cars and locomotives had been that of the control system, which required simultaneous or alternate shifting of both the throttle lever of the engine and a selector for the generator field strength, a process that was inherently difficult to do well. In 1914 GE engineer Hermann Lemp developed and patented a control system that linked the generator loading to the engine capability through a mechanical system. Lemp continued to improve this system and by 1922 had developed a much-improved, entirely electrical system through which an engineer could properly control both engine output and generator field excitation from a single control handle. The principles established by this improved control system were a milestone in the development of the diesel-electric locomotive, and it set the stage for the next step in GE's involvement in diesel-electric power.

GE had left the gas-electric-car field in 1917, but by

General Electric became involved in early diesel-electric tests by 1922 and by 1930 had become an active supplier of diesel locomotives. This center-cab, 600-hp diesel-electric was built for the Lackawanna in 1934.
—General Electric

1922 it was back in the business, this time only as a supplier to the new Electro-Motive Co. of Cleveland, which was marketing a new line of gas-electric cars. GE supplied the motors, controls, and electrical equipment, the Winton Engine Co. built the gasoline engines, and any one of several car builders supplied the carbodies. The new version of Lemp's control system proved an important element in the success of Electro-Motive's gas-electric cars. By 1930, when General Motors acquired the firm and its Winton engine supplier, over 700 of the sturdy railcars had been supplied to North American railroads.

Lemp control was important, too, to a new GE venture in diesel-electric locomotives launched in 1920. Ingersoll-Rand supplied a 300-hp diesel engine for a demonstrator

"oil-electric" locomotive completed late in 1923 at the Erie works. Highly successful in demonstrations on more than a dozen railroads, the locomotive showed the reliability and economy of operation that were possible with the diesel-electric, and it led to the first significant application of diesel-electric power on U.S. railroads. GE soon took the lead in a joint venture with Ingersoll-Rand and Alco to build and market locomotives based upon the prototype design. Over a six-year period from 1925 through 1931 GE and its partners delivered a total of 50 box-cab diesel-electric locomotives to U.S. and Canadian railroads and industrial plants, among them Central Railroad of New Jersey No. 1000, generally regarded as the "world's first commercially successful diesel-electric locomotive."

The big GE plant at Erie, Pennsylvania, has been GE's railroad business center ever since it opened in 1911. The Erie plant built six streamlined, 3,600-hp electric passenger locomotives for the New Haven in 1938.
—General Electric

GE largely stood on the sidelines during the early post–World War II period of dieselization. This changed in the 1950s when the company began the development of a line of main-line diesel-electric export locomotives. This set of experimental units completed in 1954 was used as a test fleet, seen here at work on the Erie Railroad. —General Electric

Alco dropped out of the three-company venture in 1929, but GE continued to work with Ingersoll-Rand and later Cooper-Bessemer as engine suppliers for a line of switching units that ranged from 300 to 1,100 hp. By the late 1930s GE was producing a line of standard industrial diesel-electrics ranging from 25 to 80 tons and powered by such engine suppliers as Cummins and Caterpillar. This was to prove a promising market niche for GE. By 1948 it had more than 1,500 of these units at work for industrial customers all over the world.

When other builders, led by Electro-Motive, began to move into the manufacture of high-horsepower diesel-electrics for road service during the 1930s, GE stayed out of this market, acting instead as an electrical supplier to other builders. In 1935 GE's Erie plant built two 1,800-hp Winton-powered demonstrators and a single B&O unit, as well as a pair of Lackawanna switchers for Electro-Motive, and GE was the principal supplier for the electrical components of EMD diesels through 1938, when the builder switched to the manufacture of its own traction motors and electrical equipment. Similarly, GE was the principal supplier of traction motors, generators, and electrical equipment for Alco's line of diesel-electric locomotives, and from 1940 through 1953 the two firms jointly marketed a line of Alco-GE locomotives. After World War II, when diesel-engine builder Fairbanks, Morse & Co. entered the locomotive market, GE supplied its electrical components and even manufactured more than 100 road units for capacity-strapped FM at its Erie works.

But as Electro-Motive increasingly dominated the diesel-electric market, GE began to have second thoughts about its decision to limit its role in the market to that of electrical supplier. In 1954 a big four-unit GE road freight locomotive powered by Cooper-Bessemer engines began extended test operation on the Erie Railroad. A year later GE set up an engine development laboratory at the Erie plant, and in 1958 it acquired rights to design and develop the Cooper-Bessemer engine. Ostensibly, GE was developing new "universal" road units for the export trade, and indeed by the end of the decade the Erie plant had shipped nearly 400 of its new Universal-series units to overseas markets. But in 1961 GE surprised the industry with the introduction of its own line of high-horsepower road units for the North American market.

Beginning with the 2,500-hp U25, GE produced a line of increasingly powerful U-series units that set the builder on the path to a dominant position in the diesel-electric market; more than 3,100 were produced between 1960 and the end of production in 1977, as GE displaced Alco as the second-ranked builder. Still more powerful Dash-7 and Dash-8 units ranging upward to 4,400 hp followed, and by 1987 GE had overtaken Electro-Motive as the leading builder. During the 1990s GE introduced the 4,000-hp, 100 mph Genesis passenger unit that began displacing Amtrak's aging F40PH units in 1993, switched to more efficient AC traction motors for much of its production, and teamed up with Germany's Deutz MWM to develop a 6,000-hp, 16-cylinder engine for a new AC6000 CW locomotive that went into production in 1996. From the early 1960s through the end of the century GE produced almost 14,000 road units for North American railroads.

—William D. Middleton

REFERENCES

A Century of Progress: The General Electric Story. Schenectady, N.Y.: Hall of History, 1981.

Hammond, John Winthrop. *Men and Volts.* Schenectady, N.Y.: General Electric, 1941.

See also LOCOMOTIVE BUILDERS.

General Railway Signal Co. *See*

ALSTOM SIGNALING (GENERAL RAILWAY SIGNAL CO.)

Geography and Railroad Development

Geography profoundly influenced North American railroad construction, operations, and traffic. Physical geography guided route selection and imposed obstacles. Economic geography defined the markets. Political geography affected governmental rail development policies. Railroads in turn altered the continent's geography in fundamental ways.

Geography dictated early transportation strategy. After the War of 1812 the region northwest of the Ohio River emerged as a grain and livestock center. The combined population of Ohio, Indiana, and Illinois increased from 270,000 in 1810 to 2.7 million by 1840. Midwestern farm output moved by river to New Orleans, but the Erie Canal–Hudson River route then captured a portion of this trade for New York. If rival ports were to survive, transportation links that reached beyond the Appalachians were essential. Since the terrain ruled out canals, commercial interests at Baltimore and Charleston, South Carolina, endorsed railroads. Philadelphia was slower to react, settling at first for an unworkable combination of canals, inclined planes, and railroads across Pennsylvania.

Political factors took on importance. States and cities opposed standardized track gauges to protect individual ports and terminal cities that profited from the inconvenience. The 1862 decision to build a Pacific railroad was driven by the need to bind California to the Union during the Civil War. Similar logic later was applied in Canada, whose far-flung provinces could be united only by rail. Although early railroad builders aimed for specific geographic objectives—cities or navigable waterways—many post–Civil War promoters sought geographic advantage by forging territorial monopolies that included extensive branch-line networks. Since tracklaying preceded economic activity in the Great Plains and West, territorial dominance was deemed necessary if a railroad was to generate profitable volumes of traffic.

Appalachian Barriers

On all but the Erie Canal's Mohawk Valley route, rail lines that originated at midatlantic ports confronted the Appalachian ranges. This often required track rising to elevations of 2,000 feet. Surveyors followed rivers where possible, but running parallel to watercourses involved bridging tributaries at their widest points and putting down roadbeds that would not crumble with every flood. Building west along the Potomac, the Baltimore & Ohio was hemmed in by mountains, the Chesapeake & Ohio Canal, and the river itself. Although water gaps offered easier gradients, extensive blasting and fills were needed for suitable rights of way. Pennsylvania Railroad crews at Kittanning Point west of Altoona, Pennsylvania, labored to complete numerous rock cuttings, embankments, and culverts. On the approaches to Pittsburgh crews bridged Brush Creek at 14 different locations.

Acceptable grades also mandated tunneling. To complete its route between Cumberland, Maryland, and the Ohio River with grades no steeper than 2.2 percent, the B&O drilled 11 tunnels. At Allegheny Summit the Pennsylvania dug from both ends and bored three vertical shafts, two of which were 200 feet deep. Water seepage required constant pumping, and much of the 3,412-foot tunnel was supported by arches after unstable rock overhangs collapsed. Building the Fitchburg Railroad's Hoosac Tunnel in Massachusetts proved so daunting that 20 years elapsed between the initial contracts and completion of the record 4.75-mile bore in 1875.

By the mid-1850s seven railroads traversed the Appalachians. Construction costs had exceeded estimates by a wide margin. The Western Railroad of Massachusetts spent $241,311 to build 1.8 miles of its summit section near Washington, Massachusetts. The New York & Erie's 1,200-foot Starrucca Viaduct cost $320,000, a huge sum for that era. Mountain operations also called for more powerful locomotives than managers had imagined. Rock slides, washouts, and snow added to operating and maintenance outlays. Serious floods later caused widespread outages on water-level routes.

The Continent's Midsection

Ohio Valley terrain was less imposing, but builders still faced engineering challenges. Northwestern sections of Ohio and Indiana contained vast swamplands. Watersheds of the major rivers included many tributaries that had to be bridged. Hilly regions bordering the Ohio and Tennessee rivers resulted in numerous curves, which even in the 1850s were recognized as enemies of efficient operations and a source of constant track maintenance. Areas adjacent to the south shoreline of the Great Lakes were prone to heavy snowfall.

The region's great rivers posed unique problems. In order to bear the weight of railroad equipment, timber bridges required so many supports that they impeded waterway operations. The St. Lawrence's width at Montreal defied wooden bridge technology; temporary track was placed upon the ice in winter, and freight and passengers were ferried in other seasons. When the Chicago & Rock Island conquered the Mississippi in 1856 at Davenport, Iowa, the six-span structure consumed 1,000,000 board feet of timber and 150 tons of iron. Although rail connections east and west from Parkersburg (now West Virginia) existed by 1857, these routes were not joined by an Ohio River bridge until 1871.

The advent of iron, steel, and better engineering ultimately closed the gaps. In 1866 the Chicago & Northwestern spanned the Mississippi at Clinton, Iowa, as did the Chicago, Burlington & Quincy at Burlington, Iowa, two years later. The Eads Bridge at St. Louis opened in 1874. The Ohio was crossed at Cincinnati in 1870, and the Missouri River at Kansas City in 1869 and at Omaha in 1871. The lower Mississippi was not bridged at Memphis until 1892 and at New Orleans until 1935.

Delays in overcoming the major river barriers exerted long-term influences upon U.S. railroading by creating breaking points that segregated the nation's major railroads into three regions: South, Northeast, and West. These boundaries affected such issues as freight rates for more than a century.

The most formidable midcontinent obstacle existed to the north. After forming a confederation in 1867, Canadians desired to unify the dominion with a transcontinental railroad entirely within its boundaries. West of the St. Lawrence Valley was a forbidding expanse known as the Canadian Shield, a land overlaid with thick rock interspersed with forests, lakes, and streams. The Shield extended for more than 600 miles along the proposed Canadian Pacific Railway. It was believed that a railroad in such unpromising terrain would attract little local traffic, unlike the U.S. routes west of the Appalachians, which added to their traffic base with every mile of track put down. Between the Shield and Winnipeg were 400 miles of swamps and peat bogs.

Canadian Pacific contractors blasted rocky outcroppings. Dozens of workers were killed in accidents with nitroglycerine. Subzero cold and deep snow hampered progress. In 1884 an estimated 15,000 workers and 4,000 horses were engaged between Lake Nipissing and Thunder Bay. Expenditures far exceeded estimates. With construction sites unconnected to railroad lines, supplies were delivered by steamboat, flatboat, and canoe. Work already had begun on segments west of Lake Superior, where pilings were hammered nearly 100 feet before stable rock was found. Track was built through bogs on what amounted to log mattresses, and 250,000 yards of earth fill were required at Lake Maquistananah alone. The weight of locomotives and rolling stock often caused the trackbed to sink. Ongoing filling, stream diversions, and swamp drainage were necessary.

Conquering the West

The difficulties of western railroad construction were partially offset by 25 years of experience elsewhere, along with improved equipment and technology. This offered small comfort to those who labored in the Rockies, Cascades, or Sierra Nevada. Although the Union Pacific enjoyed easier grades along the Platte River and Lodgepole Creek through Nebraska, work progressed in an environment of harsh winter storms, stifling summer heat, periodic Indian raids, and severe shortages of timber for crossties, bridges, and locomotive fuel. Until the track reached the Medicine Bow Mountains, virtually all wood was hauled from Omaha. West of Cheyenne were the Laramie Mountains, which forced the Union Pacific to an altitude exceeding 8,200 feet through many cuts and fills, including the famous Dale Creek Bridge, a 700-foot span with a mile of rock cuts at both ends. West of the Medicine Bows was the Red Desert, in which water sources were fouled by alkali. The route to Salt Lake entailed intensive blasting and filling in Echo and Weber canyons.

Forging east from Sacramento, the Central Pacific confronted even more troublesome terrain. The 50 miles from Illinoistown to the Sierra Nevada summit required an ascent of nearly 4,800 feet. The Sierras were a wide system of massive granite formations cut by deep gorges. Tunnel projects consumed 500 kegs of blasting powder each day. Above the canyon of the American River's north fork the trackbed was carved from the mountainside by Chinese laborers drilling powder holes and setting charges. Progress in the summit tunnel, one of 15 such borings, was measured in inches per day during 1865 and 1866. Crews endured snowstorms, avalanches, floods, and landslides. Nearly 50 miles of snow sheds ultimately were installed.

Rail ventures in the U.S. northern tier met challenges in the Rockies and Cascades. The Northern Pacific's grades at Bozeman Pass west of Livingston, Montana, exceeded 2.2 percent, and the roadbed then ascended 1,600 feet in 20 miles to Homestake Summit, where a 3,875-foot tunnel was drilled. The Stampede Pass line over the Cascades required many switchbacks and steep grades. Supply wagons were moved by block-and-tackle rigs, or on skids through snowfields. The Stampede Pass Tunnel was completed in May 1888 after 28 months of back-breaking labor. Great Northern surveyors discovered a low route over the Rockies at Marias Pass, Montana, which was completed in 1891. A year later the GN assaulted Stevens Pass in the Cascades. A temporary summit grade exceeded 5 percent. Difficult operating conditions existed at Stevens Pass until 1929, when the 7.8-mile Cascade Tunnel reduced grades to no more than 1.6 percent and eliminated 4 miles of tunnels and 8 miles of snow sheds.

The southern transcontinentals had an easier time. Except for its crossings of Raton Pass on the Colorado–New Mexico border and the Sangre de Cristo gap south of Santa Fe, the Atchison, Topeka & Santa Fe operated through open country. The Southern Pacific's Texas-California line bypassed most of the area's isolated mountain ranges. More troublesome were Colorado's mountains. The Denver & Rio Grande's narrow-gauge line from Pueblo, Colorado, to Ogden, Utah, was forced to an altitude of 10,000 feet at Tennessee Pass. Needing 4 percent grades, the Denver & Salt Lake reached the Continental Divide at 11,678 feet. Heavy snows impeded operations until the Moffat Tunnel opened in 1928.

Western Canada was equally daunting. The Canadian Pacific Railway's line over Kicking Horse Pass in the Rockies involved a maze of tunnels, cuts, trestles, switchbacks, and 4 percent grades until the track was rerouted through spiral tunnels in 1909. Rogers Pass in the Selkirks was no less troublesome, and a full century later the CPR continued to upgrade the route with North America's longest railroad tunnel. Building east from Prince Rupert, British Columbia, in 1908 the Grand Trunk Pacific moved 12 million tons of earth in the first 100 miles.

Rough terrain also confronted Mexico's railway builders. From Veracruz to Mexico City the Ferrocarril Mexicano climbed 8,000 feet and was forced onto grades exceeding 4.7 percent as it traversed the Sierra Madre Oriental range. Routes from Texas to the Mexican interior were constructed through a rising plateau region dotted with old volcanic cones. The segment of the Kansas City, Mexico & Orient between Chihuahua and the Pacific Coast was begun in 1897, but because of the difficult crossing of the Sierra Madre Occidental (and limited traffic potential) was not completed until 1961.

Railroads Alter Geography

The staggering impact of railroads upon North America's geography—physical, political, economic, and cultural—almost defies description. At the industry's peak the United States, with 6 percent of the world's population, possessed 30 percent of its railroad route mileage.

In political geography railroads forged links that helped keep midwestern states loyal to the Union. The North's superior network was a major factor in winning the Civil War. Western transcontinental routes closed the frontier. New states were admitted to the United States after railroads delivered a flood of settlers, provided them with goods, and carried back the output of their farms, ranches, and mines.

The transition in economic geography was equally stunning. Before the railroad age interior freight traffic had flowed on a north-south axis along the Ohio and Mississippi rivers. Rail lines substituted an east-west pattern of trade and travel. The Midwest replaced the Northeast as the nation's granary and livestock center. The value of public lands in the West tripled as railroads opened routes and millions of acres were brought under cultivation. Railroads also tapped the continent's mineral resources, gathering vast tonnages of Appalachian and Ohio Valley coal, the Canadian Shield's huge copper deposits, and ore from the iron mines of the western Great Lakes, Alabama, and Colorado.

Railroads made possible the evolution of the world's leading industrial economy. A triad of industries—coal, steel, and railroads—united to transform factory production from small local enterprises to immense facilities of national market reach. Railroads were the steel industry's leading customer and delivered its coke, coal, and finished products. Thriving industrial cities were defined by two characteristics: quality rail service and access to coal for factory steam engines.

Equally important, railroads created demand by connecting producers and consumers with reliable, low-cost service. In 1820 wagon freight rates had exceeded 30 cents per ton-mile, and canal rates averaged 6 cents. By 1850 railroads carried freight for 4 cents per ton-mile and within a decade cut the cost to 2 cents. Mass factory production became possible. The consumer in turn paid lower prices and purchased more goods.

Patterns of urban geography changed radically. Existing cities on the interior rivers attained greater prominence as transfer points among the regionalized rail systems: Cincinnati, St. Louis, Memphis, New Orleans, and Kansas City. Aided by rail-delivered coal, coke, and iron ore, Pittsburgh emerged as the continent's leading iron and steel producer.

Chicago's rise was even more spectacular. Cincinnati had been the Midwest's economic hub, with ten times Chicago's population in 1840. After railroads reached Lake Erie and the Ohio River in the early 1850s, builders were attracted to Chicago as their final objective because several railroads that offered the potential for valuable connecting traffic already were under development from that city to the south and west. Chicago then prospered beyond all expectations as the nation's primary rail center. Railroads converted Denver, Seattle-Tacoma, Atlanta, Indianapolis, Minneapolis–St. Paul, Omaha, Spokane, and Nashville from cities of local influence to major regional hubs of commerce. Railroads indirectly contributed to New York's rise as a global finance center because trading in railroad securities fueled the growth of the New York Stock Exchange. Within rail-served cities large and small, the factories, warehouses, hotels, and merchants clustered around downtown tracks and depots.

Meanwhile, older towns in the East and Midwest that had been bypassed by the new lines stagnated or died. With the exception of twentieth-century suburbs, few

American cities with year 2000 populations exceeding 25,000 never had rail service. Major cultural changes occurred. The railroads' closure of the frontier all but extinguished Native Americans' traditional way of life. Trains accelerated the pace and range of communication. Regional cultural identities were diminished by mass intercity travel and by the railroads' role in delivering books, catalogs, mail, and newspapers. Mail volumes multiplied 120-fold between 1850 and 1900. However, as towns and smaller cities lost their insularity, their distinctive community identities suffered. The rise of big-city railroad suburbs spurred a population shift to the urban fringe.

Geography Alters the Railroads

Railroads created patterns of economic geography that worked in the mode's favor as long as it dominated intercity traffic. By giving industry wider options for factory siting, the immense rail network rendered individual carriers vulnerable to future changes in economic geography. Moreover, the route system was overbuilt, perhaps by as much as 30 percent, which weakened the underlying economics of rail transportation.

After 1914 the Panama Canal diverted a portion of Asian freight that had moved via the railroad "land bridge" to the East Coast. Late nineteenth-century urban street congestion produced political demands that railroads expend huge sums of money on downtown grade-separation projects. The acceleration of federal and state highway development after World War I changed the landscape in the United States and Canada, diverted passengers to the private auto and intercity bus, and eroded branch-line freight volumes. Army Corps of Engineers waterway projects made barge operations more competitive. The government-funded St. Lawrence Seaway opened in 1959. "Automobile suburbs" expanded during the post–World War II years and deeply cut into rail commuter business. The interstate highway program delivered immense benefits to the trucking industry. Before the interstates, railroads enjoyed an advantage for shipments exceeding 300 miles. In certain traffic categories trucks were now competitive in hauls up to 1,000 miles. By 1950 a government-financed airport and airway network was siphoning passenger traffic, mail, and express from the railroads.

Changes in the sources and uses of energy had an enormous impact. Primarily mined in Appalachia and the Ohio Valley, coal had provided two-thirds of U.S. energy consumption in 1919. By the mid-1950s petroleum and natural gas had replaced coal at that level of market share, in part because of government-financed wartime pipelines built from the Gulf Coast and Southern Plains to the Midwest and Northeast. Eastern railroads suffered deep erosion of a key commodity. Economics joined with environmental regulations to open low-sulfur coal mines in Wyoming and Montana, which benefited western railroads at the expense of eastern carriers.

The dispersion of industry and population escalated in the 1920s, was further augmented by the building of defense factories in the South and Pacific coastal states during World War II, and continued after 1945. This trend favored trucks in a number of traffic categories because they offered more flexible endpoint-to-endpoint haulage. The globalization of manufacturing, due in part to inexpensive transportation, also changed distribution patterns, with both favorable and unfavorable impacts upon North American railroads.

—William J. Watt

REFERENCES

Ambrose, Stephen E. *Nothing like It in the World: The Men Who Built the Transcontinental Railroad, 1863–1869.* New York: Simon & Schuster, 2000.

Berton, Pierre. *The Impossible Railway: The Building of the Canadian Pacific.* New York: Knopf, 1972.

Cronon, William. *Nature's Metropolis: Chicago and the Great West.* New York: W. W. Norton, 1991.

Meinig, D. W. *The Shaping of America.* Vol. 3, *Transcontinental America, 1850–1915.* New Haven, Conn.: Yale Univ. Press, 1998.

Vance, James E., Jr. *The North American Railroad.* Baltimore: Johns Hopkins Univ. Press, 1995.

Georgia Railroad. *See* ATLANTA & WEST POINT RAIL ROAD

Gerstner, Franz Anton Ritter von (1796–1840)

Franz Anton Ritter von Gerstner built what are often labeled the first railroads on the European continent and, later, the first Russian railroad. During 1838–1839 Gerstner, an experienced railroad engineer, extensively investigated the railroads and other internal transportation of President Martin Van Buren's America. From Gerstner's research, an encyclopedic two volumes of source material resulted. His *Die innern Communicationen der Vereinigten Staaten von Nordamerica* covered the development, finance, operations, and pioneering leaders of American railroads and canals.

Gerstner was born in Prague on April 19, 1796. His father, Franz, was an illustrious engineer and an early advocate of railroads. Young Franz attended the University of Prague and then studied engineering at the Polytechnic founded by his father in that city. In 1818, at age 22, the younger Gerstner became professor of practical geometry (surveying) at the Polytechnic Institute of Vienna. During

1822 he made the first of four trips to Great Britain to study railroad and other technology and operating practices. From 1825 through 1828 he built half of an overengineered railroad planned to link the cities of Budweis, Bohemia, and Linz, Austria. It is widely considered to be Europe's first public railroad. But the project was difficult, and the shareholders sacked him in 1828 because of cost overruns. During 1836–1837 Gerstner constructed a 17-mile line out of St. Petersburg, Russia, and next turned his attention to learning about America's expanding railroads.

Arriving in New York in 1838 with his new wife, Clara, Gerstner got an enthusiastic reception from America's growing community of railroad interests. He was given major opportunities to study railroads and other transport modes. Gerstner found that fossil-fuel-energized industrialization was beginning its inexorable transformation of American society and its agrarian culture. Alongside its stationary, external combustion brethren was the locomotive engine, a socially revolutionary machine that diminished the barriers of time and space within the vast, developing country. Gerstner saw that production distant from marketplaces was becoming cost effective, and that railroads facilitated the replacing of a natural environment with an artificial, technological one.

In analyzing America's internal systems of transportation in his two-volume book, Gerstner presented innumerable technological data found in no other published source and offered insights and commentary. He described the management and organization of railroads and canals and discussed the state boards that oversaw transportation firms. Gerstner also presented cultural snapshots of American life at that time. He died on April 12, 1840, in Philadelphia when his frail health succumbed to his punishing work schedule. An assistant later published his book, in German.

—Frederick C. Gamst

REFERENCES

Gamst, Frederick C. "Franz Anton Ritter von Gerstner, Student of America's Pioneering Railroads." *Railroad History*, no. 163 (1990): 13–27.
———. "Letters from the United States of North America on Internal Improvements, Steam Navigation, Banking, &c., Written by Francis Anthony Chevalier de Gerstner . . . in 1839." *Railroad History*, no. 163 (1990): 28–73.
Gerstner, Franz Anton Ritter von. *Early American Railroads.* Ed. Frederick C. Gamst. Stanford, Calif.: Stanford Univ. Press, 1997 [1842–1843].

Ghega, Carl Ritter von (1802–1860)

Carl Ritter von Ghega is well known in Europe for constructing the Semmering Railroad from Mürzzuschlag to Graz and the Kaiser Ferdinand North Railroad from Brno to Breclav, in the Austrian Empire. An ethnic Italian, Carlo Ghega was born in Venice, then part of the Austrian Empire. In his late teens he earned a doctorate in mathematical sciences at the University of Padua. For his engineering work, in 1844 he received the title of imperial advisor, and in 1851 he was knighted by Kaiser Franz Josef and thereby became Carl Ritter von Ghega.

Ghega's Semmering line, a harmonious blending of commercial structures and nature, is on UNESCO's list of World Heritage Sites of cultural landscapes. The line's viaducts are splendid beyond any utilitarian function. Construction of the line, when completed in 1854, included the then-highest railroad station in the world and traversed the engineering challenge of the rugged Semmering Mountains. For his Semmering crossing, Ghega walked the route to learn its topographical features and supervised the design of special locomotives for mountain service. Tourism in the Alps began with the completion of the line. The Semmering challenge sparked Ghega's study of the Baltimore & Ohio's crossing of the Alleghenies.

Ghega's engineering of railroads followed successful civil engineering work on Austrian highways and waterways. During 1836–1837 Ghega investigated the railways of Great Britain. In 1842 he visited America to research the Baltimore & Ohio, thereby following in the footsteps of Franz Anton Ritter von Gerstner and of Russian colonels Pavel P. Melnikov and Nikolai O. Kraft, who studied all U.S. railroads. From Ghega's American journey, the 273 pages and nine plates plus a map of his *Die Baltimore-Ohio Eisenbahn über das Alleghany-Gebirg* covered the engineering and operations of this pioneering long-distance line. He gave special attention to line curvature and the capacity of American locomotives with reference to different grades. The acclaimed civil and mechanical engineer died in Vienna of tuberculosis before he could complete another railroad project in mountainous Transylvania.

—Frederick C. Gamst

REFERENCES

Ghega, Carl Ritter von. *Atlas pittoresque du chemin de fer du Semmering, précédé d'un aperçu historique et statistique sur les chemins de fer en exploitation en Autriche.* Vienna: C. Gerold et fils, 1854.
———. *Die Baltimore-Ohio Eisenbahn über das Alleghany-Gebirg, mit besonderer Berücksichtigung der Steigungs- und Krümmungsverhältnisse, untersucht von Carl Ghega . . . auf seiner Reise in den Vereinigten Staaten von Nordamerika.* Vienna: Kaulfuss Witwe, Prandel, 1844.

GO Transit. *See* GREATER TORONTO TRANSIT AUTHORITY (GO TRANSIT)

Gould, Jay (1836–1892)

Jay Gould was born the son of a farmer in Roxbury, New York. He left school at an early age but taught himself surveying and mathematics as a teenager. By age 20 he was running a tannery in a town that now bears his name, Gouldsboro. It is widely believed that he fleeced his partners in this business, but shortly he moved on to other things. At the time of the panic of 1857 Gould began speculating in railroad stocks and accumulated a modest fortune.

By the time the Civil War began in 1861, Gould had his own brokerage house in New York and was speculating in stocks and in gold. In 1867 he formed an alliance with financier Daniel Drew, who brought Gould and Jim Fisk onto the board of directors of the Erie Railroad. In the following year Gould, Drew, and Fisk began a contest with Cornelius Vanderbilt for control of the Erie. In the resultant Erie wars the Gould ring issued millions of dollars in watered stock. The battle went on for several years. Even though Commodore Vanderbilt certainly had the law on his side, he eventually withdrew from the fray. But Gould's reputation on Wall Street was tarnished by his various financial schemes.

In the late 1860s and early 1870s Gould's chicanery seemed to know no bounds. Although shrewd and hard-driving, he was mild in appearance, and in contemporary portraits he looks like a benevolent country parson. But he was solitary and secretive. Historian Henry Adams described him as a man of "silent intrigue." Some of his intrigues almost defy description today. In 1869 Gould conceived a complex, even implausible, plan to corner the gold market in New York. Although this did not come off, Gould profited immensely from the plot, while many of his friends took big losses on "Black Friday," September 24, 1869. From that day forward a long shadow of villainy followed Gould the rest of his life.

Gould's later career was not altogether reprehensible. He had become president of the Erie in 1868 and made serious attempts to bring some order to that troubled railroad. He had the intelligence to see that a broken and tatterdemalion railroad had little worth to investors. Still, he did not completely succeed with Erie, and in 1872 the (mostly English) stockholders ousted him. Gould, however, was not through with the railroad business. He lay low for a short time, but in 1874 wrested control of the Union Pacific Railroad, which, like the Erie, had had a shady past. He was modestly successful in turning the Union Pacific around, but had to give up control in 1878.

The following year Gould bought a controlling interest in the Kansas Pacific Railroad, and from this time until shortly before his death he bought up railroad properties at a dizzying pace. Among his acquisitions were the Missouri Pacific, the Wabash, and a number of lines in the Southwest. He also bought heavily into some eastern railroads such as the Reading and the Central of New Jersey. His ambition led him to believe that he could one day control a complete transcontinental system. Although this never materialized, as early as 1880 Gould controlled 8,160 miles of railroad, more than anyone else in the world. In 1890 he once again took control of the Union Pacific.

Gould became one of the wealthiest Americans of his time. He had a controlling interest in the Western Union Telegraph Co., the Manhattan Elevated Railroad, and the *New York World* newspaper, which he bought to whitewash his tarnished reputation. He later sold the paper to Joseph Pulitzer. Gould was called many things in his day: Mephistopheles, the Wizard of Wall Street, the most hated man in America. Historians have invariably treated him as the archetypal robber baron, but this may not be entirely fair. Although his maneuvers in the Erie days clearly bordered on the criminal, one can find some good things to say about his later career in railroad management. Gould long suffered from tuberculosis and died in 1892, leaving almost his entire fortune to his wastrel son George Jay Gould.

—George H. Douglas

Jay Gould. —Library of Congress (Neg. LC-USZ62-067998)

REFERENCE

Klein, Maury. *The Life and Legend of Jay Gould*. Baltimore: Johns Hopkins Univ. Press, 1986.

Grade-Crossing Safety

The inherent conflict between road traffic and trains wherever highways and railroads cross at grade has existed from the beginning of the railroad era. Since the heavier train can neither deviate from its path nor be brought to a stop in sufficient time to avoid striking a road vehicle on the tracks, it was recognized from the start that a train must have the right of way. As early as 1843 warning devices such as bells and crossing signs, which soon evolved into the familiar "cross-buck" grade-crossing sign still in use today, were imposed upon early railroads. Watchmen were often employed at crossings, standing in the road when a train approached to wave a red flag in daytime and a red lantern at night to warn road users to stop.

As the railroads grew—along with opportunities for vehicle-train collisions—devices to improve highway-grade-crossing safety became a fertile field for inventors. The first improvement came about 1870, when hand-operated gates were first installed. Development of the direct-current track circuit in 1872 provided a means to automatically control warning devices upon the approach of trains. By the end of the century compressed-air or electric operation had often replaced manual operation of crossing gates. The practice of completely blocking the road at the crossing was continued into the 1920s. Some of these installations were controlled electrically upon the approach of a train. In 1924 barriers were developed that dropped down to the road from an overhead structure, completely blocking it on each side of the tracks. Damage to the lowered barrier by a vehicle, or other malfunctions, would sometimes cause the barrier to fail to rise after a train had cleared the crossing. Delays to vehicular traffic

As evidenced by this drawing, which appeared in the August 1885 *Harper's New Monthly Magazine*, railroad grade crossings were a very real danger long before the appearance of the automobile. —Middleton Collection

Grade-crossing warnings came in endless variations before the cross-buck warning sign became standard. This interesting warning signal was still in use on the Delaware & Hudson as recently as 1951. —Edward H. Weber, *Trains* Magazine Collection

became so numerous that these barrier systems were eventually removed.

In 1927 a new cable-gate system that combined extra-long gate arms with cables extending above and below the arms was first installed at some crossings. The arms were long enough to block the road, and the outer end of an arm was supported in a saddle to provide greater stability. The cabling would stop a vehicle hitting the downed gate. These systems were often installed about 25 feet in advance of the tracks, allowing room for the cable to stretch and yield toward the track.

A new warning device that came into use around the turn of the twentieth century employed a round disc with a flashing red lamp in the center that swung back and forth like a pendulum, giving rise to its "wigwag" nickname. The disc was typically mounted below or beside a cross-buck sign. Like the crossing bell, an approaching train actuated it. In one version of the wigwag, a shelter was provided for the swinging disk. When no train was approaching, the disk remained inside the shelter or housing, which was lettered "Look, Listen" on the side visible from the road. When a train approached, the disk swung free and its red light flashed.

In 1913 the L. S. Brach Co. installed a new type of flashing-light signal at a Central Railroad of New Jersey crossing in Searen, New Jersey. This employed red lamps arranged in a half circle (bowl up). On the approach of a train, the lights flashed in sequence starting from the left and going to the right. When the last right-hand red light

went off, the first left-hand lamp came on, thus simulating a man waving a red lantern to alert drivers to stop.

Early installations placed just two flashing red lamps at the right side of the road on each side of a crossing. To provide greater visibility, flashing-light signals were later installed back-to-back on each side of a crossing. Thus before a train arrived at the crossing, a driver might see flashing red lights on both sides of the road, those on the left being the lights on the back side of the lights installed on the far side of the tracks for drivers going in the opposite direction. Similarly, to provide better visibility to road users, especially on multilane highways, flashing-light signals were mounted on cantilevered structures over highway lanes at the approach to a crossing.

By the 1930s flashing-light signals were standardized at $8\frac{3}{8}$ inches in diameter. (By 1971 a more visible 12-inch roundel became available and is now widely used.) Beginning around 1928 the state of Minnesota required a rotating "Stop" sign to be mounted under the flashing-light signals. When there was no train, the vehicle operator saw only the edge of the sign. When a train approached, the sign turned, and "Stop" was visible.

In 1938 Harry C. Sampson of the Chicago & Alton patented a new standard gate design for a "Combination Crossing Gate and Signal Protective Means." This device incorporated a flashing-light signal and gate mechanism, using low-voltage DC on the flashing lights and the operation of the gate mechanism and control, and was equipped with standby power. The combination caught on rapidly, and thousands have been installed.

Modern advances in grade-crossing safety have included new technology, expanded funding for grade separations, the installation of warning devices, and educational safety campaigns to alert drivers. In the early 1950s, for example, audio-frequency overlay track circuits were developed to control highway-rail grade-crossing warning devices. This track circuit control was overlaid and separate from the block signal or cab signal track circuits. The big gain with this technology was that crossing warning-device track circuit could be used in conventional signal territory without cutting the rail for insulated joints. Later developments in the decade produced the motion sensor using AC to determine that trains are moving toward or away from a crossing.

Ever since it was adopted in June 1922 by the Signal Section, the American Railway Assn. (now the Assn. of American Railroads) has set the minimum warning time of 20 seconds before a train arrives at a highway-rail grade crossing. An important development of the 1950s was the constant warning time (CWT) device, which determined train speed and motion so that it could provide the minimum warning time with various train speeds. The CWT was based on existing track circuits and train speeds. The concept was first developed in 1956 by Arlo C. Krout, a Southern Pacific signal engineer, who worked with researchers at the Stanford Research Institute to develop the system. A key element was putting an AC into the track rails to feed toward the approaching train. The first CWT was tested on the SP in 1960 and placed in regular service within the next two years.

Today, computer controls, especially microprocessors, have become standard for highway-rail grade-crossing warning systems, while railroads are upgrading existing systems with motion sensors or constant warning time devices. Warning-device-monitoring systems that include recording equipment and communications capability to alert personnel to maintenance problems are now being used. Another recent advance is the use of toll-free telephone numbers at highway-rail grade crossings, allowing road users to call in any problems.

Improved and standardized signage has helped better alert road users about what to expect at highway-rail grade crossings. As early as the 1930s the Assn. of American Railroads worked with its railroad members to develop standards for signs, flashing-light signals, and gates. Later, *AAR Bulletins* included plans for location of devices at crossings that were accepted by the American National Standards Institute (ANSI). In 1970 these ANSI standards were incorporated into the *Manual on Uniform Traffic Control Devices* issued by the Federal Highway Administration. The Federal Railroad Administration's Regulations on Grade Crossing Signal System Safety cover reports, response to system malfunctions, and maintenance, inspection, and testing of warning devices and systems.

Flashing yellow lights above and below advance warning signs alert road users that a train is approaching the highway-rail grade crossing ahead of them. At some locations where double tracks are in service, signs are installed with the words "Look for Train on 2nd Track." At some crossings red lights above and below the sign flash when a train on the second track is approaching the crossing. Gate arms were once painted with black and white stripes, but red and white stripes make them more visible and are now standard. About 1994 light-emitting diodes (LEDs) were developed for highway traffic signals and for flashing-light signals at highway-rail grade crossings. The small light units for a 12-inch flashing-light signal provide more complete light coverage than a single incandescent lamp, with its lens system to spread the light over the entire surface.

The standard "Railroad Crossing" cross-buck sign re-

Warning gates like this one shown in *The American Railway* (1892) are still in common use, along with automatic warning lights and gates. —Middleton Collection

mains a well-recognized warning to motorists that railroad tracks are present. Some states now require that the cross-buck be treated as a "Yield" sign, requiring highway users to yield to trains. Mississippi requires road users to make a complete stop at all passive highway-rail grade crossings (crossings without active warning devices) equipped with cross-buck signs and to continue across only after determining that it is safe to do so. The Intermodal Surface Transportation Efficiency Act (ISTEA) of 1991 gave local road authorities legal rights to put up stop or yield signs at passive grade crossings if more than 2 trains per day, and at least 730 trains per year, are operated.

Still another new idea was an automated horn system that was put into a pilot trial at Mundelein, Illinois, in 2002. The required minimum locomotive horn at a rail crossing is 96 decibels, 100 feet in front of the locomotive. Nearby residents, particularly those on high-density corridors, would prefer less noise. The trial installation is a fixed horn on the crossing activated by an approaching train. Although the sound meets the federal minimum noise level at the direction to the road crossing, there is far less general sounding.

For Amtrak high-speed operation, new road-crossing gates have now been installed in New England and elsewhere, where trains operate at up to 110 mph. This system uses four-quadrant gates, completely blocking the highway used by high-speed trains, while presence detectors are buried under the roadway between the railroad tracks to warn train operators that a vehicle is on the tracks. If a vehicle is stopped on the tracks, the train operator is alerted in time for the train to be brought to a stop before it reaches the grade crossing.

The best solution to highway-rail grade-crossing conflicts, of course, is to eliminate them altogether, and efforts to do so go back well into the nineteenth century. From the 1890s through the 1920s several major cities and states passed laws requiring railroads to raise tracks to eliminate highway-rail grade crossings. Some of the major crossing elimination projects took place in Buffalo and Rochester, New York, Chicago, and Philadelphia. Costs were apportioned in many ways, usually among railroads and state and city governments. In one case the Old Colony Railroad providing commuter service into Boston increased its capitalization so it could elevate its lines. Eliminating grade crossings enabled it to operate trains at higher speeds and improve service. Another major crossing elimination program during the 1930s was that of the Pennsylvania when it electrified its line between Washington, D.C., and New York City.

Much more recently, in 2002, a major new project completed in the Los Angeles area eliminated over 200 highway-rail grade crossings used by a daily average of more than 40 freight trains. The Alameda Corridor includes a 10-mile section in which the railroad tracks were lowered by building a trench between downtown Los Angeles and the ports of Long Beach and San Pedro. Similar projects are being planned.

Table 1. Warning Devices at Highway-Rail Grade Crossings

	1939	1996	2000
Crossings	231,410	162,426	155,370
Flashing-light signals	7,792	28,614	27,100
Flashing-light signals and gates	4,005	30,813	34,296
Bells, wigwags, highway traffic signals	3,465	1,557	1,417
Total Devices	15,262	60,984	62,813
Crossings with devices	7%	38%	40%

There is nothing new about efforts to improve the safety of highway-railroad crossings, but the effort has reached a much higher level of attention with some encouraging results. Several states as far back as the 1920s began to provide funds to install active warning devices at highway-rail grade crossings. In the 1930s the federal Bureau of Public Roads was able to get the U.S. Congress to appropriate money for safety improvements at crossings. The Interstate Commerce Commission in 1966 ruled that public funds could be spent on improving safety at these crossings, since the public is the major beneficiary.

Since 1973 federal money from the Highway Trust Fund has been applied to improve safety at highway-rail grade crossings (about $2.5 billion). Estimates are that through 1994 this funding program saved 8,000 lives and prevented over 36,000 injuries. With a cost/benefit ratio of 35 percent, it saved $5.4 billion during a period when only $2.5 billion was spent in federal money (1973–1994). During this period deaths fell by 44 percent and injuries were down by 59 percent. A major portion of the spending (some $160 million per year for the states) has been for the installation of warning devices (Table 1 shows numbers of warning devices at grade crossings in 1939, 1996, and 2000).

In 1972 the Union Pacific began an educational campaign to highlight the dangers at highway-rail grade crossings, enlisting the help of local government officials, police officers, teachers, and its own employees, especially locomotive engineers. The program was successful and soon spread to other railroads and states. Called Operation Lifesaver, Inc., it now operates nationwide. Its three key elements of education, engineering, and enforcement are widely publicized. Pamphlets, radio and television spots, training seminars, classroom participation, and trooper on the train bring the crossing safety situation to millions.

Table 2. Accidents at Highway-Rail Grade Crossings

	1937	1996	2000
Accidents	4,007	3,612	3,502
Fatalities	1,607	377	425
Injuries	4,904	1,428	1,219

A tabulation of major improvements to highway-road crossing safety clearly shows the progress in reducing accidents, despite increased motor vehicle operation (Table 2).

—Robert W. McKnight

REFERENCES

Burnham, Archie C., Jr. *Roadway through the Millennium MUTCD*. Tucson, Ariz.: L&J, 2001.
Pline, James L., ed. *Traffic Control Devices Handbook*. Washington, D.C.: Institute of Transportation Engineers, 2001.

Grand Trunk Western Railway

The Grand Trunk Railway reflected early and important strategic plans to link western Europe with the heartland of North America through East Coast ports in the United States and southeastern Canada. The early eastern entrepôt was Portland, Maine, which had a harbor that was free of ice year-round. Service on the full 1,138-mile route from Portland to Chicago through Montreal, Toronto, and Sarnia began in 1880. A tunnel under the St. Clair River between Sarnia, Ontario, and Port Huron, Michigan, opened in 1890, giving the lines in Michigan a rail connection with those in Canada.

Railroad expansion continued in Canada—too much of it, as it turned out—and after 1919 huge chunks of Canadian rail property were pressed into a new Crown corporation, Canadian National Railways. The Grand Trunk became part of Canadian National Railways in 1923. Grand Trunk's lines in the United States became separate companies. The Grand Trunk Western Railway was incorporated in 1928 to consolidate Grand Trunk's lines in Michigan, Indiana, and Illinois. The Grand Trunk name continued in use to designate the line from Portland, Maine, to Island Pond, Vermont. (The Central Vermont Railway was owned by Grand Trunk and later Canadian National, but it was always a separate company. The Duluth, Winnipeg & Pacific Railway, which ran from Fort Frances, Ontario, to Duluth, Minnesota, had been a subsidiary of the Canadian Northern Railway.)

The great promise of traffic to and from Portland's year-round ice-free harbor never materialized; CN looked with greater favor on an alternative, Halifax, Nova Scotia. The American apple of CN's eye was GTW with its access to Chicago. GTW also had valuable access to Detroit and its burgeoning motor vehicle industry. Indeed, GTW's fortunes were tightly tied to names such as Dodge, Ford, and Olds. This was especially acute during World War II and after when entire trainloads of automobiles and parts rolled out of GTW's trackside plants. GTW was considered an integral part of Canadian National Railways, and its schedules were always buried deep in the Canadian National pages of *The Official Guide of the Railways*.

Grand Trunk Western's main line ran from Port Huron west to Flint, then southwest through Lansing and Battle Creek, Michigan, then through South Bend and Valparaiso, Indiana, and entered Chicago from the south. It was crossed at Durand, Michigan, by a line from Detroit through Grand Rapids to Muskegon, Michigan; a car ferry across Lake Michigan carried the Grand Trunk Western name to Milwaukee. Several branches reached such Michigan points as Jackson, Bay City, and Cassville. GTW operated commuter trains between Detroit and Pontiac; they were noteworthy for being the last regularly scheduled steam-powered passenger trains in the United States. Grand Trunk Western was a half owner (with Nickel Plate) of the Detroit & Toledo Shore Line Railroad, which ran between Detroit and Toledo.

In 1970 most of Canadian National's U.S. properties were gathered under the canopy of Grand Trunk Corp., a holding company formed under the laws of Delaware. Individual entities under Grand Trunk Corp. were to be separated from direct CN control and managed innovatively by American railroad executives. The move recognized differences in the business cultures of Canada and the United States and allowed Grand Trunk properties flexibility in meeting changing and deteriorating rail markets. From the Canadian perspective Grand Trunk Corp. was an experiment, and under the enthusiastic leadership of Robert A. Bandeen, John H. Burdakin, and Gerald L. Maas it succeeded. GTW expanded in 1980 by acquiring Detroit, Toledo & Ironton and then made a spirited run at acquiring the slimmed-down Chicago, Milwaukee, St. Paul & Pacific, which would have extended Grand Trunk's reach to Kansas City and provided a marvelous means of connecting GTW with Duluth, Winnipeg & Pacific. It was not to be. Eventually the Milwaukee Road's rail assets passed to Soo Line as part of merger mania in the industry.

That merger fever increased so that CSX and Norfolk Southern dominated in the East, Burlington Northern Santa Fe and Union Pacific in the West. The fever did not honor international boundaries. Canadian Pacific took full ownership of the Soo Line, and Canadian National shed its Crown corporation shackles to become a remarkably aggressive and well-managed player, soon acquiring Illinois Central and then Wisconsin Central. In many ways Grand Trunk Corp. had shown the way as an experimental model, buying time for Canadian National during the frightening and fluid last three decades of the twentieth century and in the end providing an invigorated Canadian National with excellent pathways to take advantage of deregulation and free trade.

—Don L. Hofsommer

REFERENCE

Hofsommer, Don L. *Grand Trunk Corporation: Canadian National Railways in the United States, 1971–1992*. East Lansing: Michigan State Univ. Press, 1995.

Granger Laws and Cases

The Granger laws were passed by four midwestern states in the early 1870s to establish more effective public control over railroad rates and related business practices. Before the Civil War several states had tried to regulate the emerging railroad industry by corporate charter provisions and by formation of state railroad commissions. Neither approach proved particularly successful. Regulation by charter was cumbersome and ill suited for a rapidly changing industry. Railroad commissions typically had only limited jurisdictions, no authority over rates, and little power to enforce their decisions.

Public concern with railroad rates and other management practices intensified soon after the Civil War. Although the development of eastern trunk-line and western transcontinental systems contributed to a gradual overall decline in rates, individual carriers frequently offset the decline by exploiting shippers and localities that lacked competitive service. Agricultural prices also began to decline in the late 1860s and dropped more sharply than the costs farmers had to meet. When the inflated post–Civil War market in railroad securities collapsed in the panic of 1873, western farmers found themselves deeply in debt, facing rock-bottom commodity prices, and convinced that much of their distress was due to the unchecked economic and political power of the railroads.

Farmers, as well as businessmen dependent on agriculture, rapidly changed from railroad boosters to champions of reform. Leadership was provided by the Patrons of Husbandry or Grange, founded in 1867 by Oliver Hudson Kelley, a Minnesota farmer turned government clerk in Washington, D.C. Kelley's initial vision of the Grange was a social organization to improve the intellectual life of farmers and reduce rural isolation. Grange membership grew rapidly, and its activities expanded to include economic cooperation, educational programs, and political action to address the economic hardships faced by American farmers.

Between 1871 and 1874 farmers organized by the Grange persuaded legislators in Illinois, Iowa, Wisconsin, and Minnesota to pass far-reaching legislation regulating railroads, grain elevators, and public warehouses. The Granger laws varied in detail, but reflected common grievances. Because freight rates were considered too high (especially relative to commodity prices), maximum rates were set by statute or by newly established railroad commissions. Farmers and businessmen also bitterly resented carriers' widespread practice of offering preferential freight rates to some ship-

Distrustful farmers in the post–Civil War period struggled to gain some regulatory control over the railroads. There is little doubt about where cartoonist Ty Wilst stood in this August 14, 1873, cartoon from a New York newspaper titled "The Farmer and the Railroad Monster. Which Will Win?" —Library of Congress (Neg. LC-USZ62-43587)

pers and localities. Discriminatory treatment of persons and places was considered fundamentally unfair and not justified by competitive forces or other market circumstances. Pro rata clauses that declared that rates for shorter hauls should not be higher than for longer hauls in the same direction and by the same line were a prominent feature of legislative efforts to prevent place discrimination.

The Granger laws also typically blocked consolidation of competing rail carriers and prohibited railroads from granting free passes to public officials. The industry practice of using free passes to court the favor of legislators, judges, and other public officials had become a widespread form of petty bribery that deterred officials from acting in the public interest in many railroad matters.

Opponents of the Granger laws, including eastern business and financial interests, launched a vigorous two-front war against the legislation. Lawsuits were promptly filed to have the laws declared unconstitutional on the grounds that they illegally confiscated property without due process of law, impaired the obligation of contracts, and infringed upon Congress's plenary power over interstate commerce. Railroad lawyers were especially confident that the federal judiciary would agree that the rate-setting provisions of the Granger laws violated the due process clause of the recently adopted Fourteenth Amendment to the U.S. Constitution because limitations on rates and charges reduced railroad earnings and thereby the value of their properties.

While litigation was under way, the railroads also sought to convince legislators and public opinion that the Granger laws should be modified or repealed because they brought more hardship than relief. Some Granger provisions were poorly drafted and inflexible, but the railroads wanted the laws to fail and took numerous steps to make the statutes as obnoxious as possible to the public. In Wisconsin the carriers undercut the detested Potter Law, by which the state had established freight and passenger rates, by deliberately providing dilapidated cars and erratic service: "Potter cars, Potter rails, and Potter time." Industry efforts to persuade the public that the Granger laws were a mistake also cited the panic of 1873 and the ensuing depression as evidence that capital was being driven away from the railroads by the "harsh and restrictive" legislation, especially legislative determination of maximum rates, pro rata provisions, and prohibitions against consolidation of competing carriers.

The public campaign to revise or repeal the Granger laws proved highly successful. Between 1875 and 1878 the legislatures of Illinois, Iowa, Wisconsin, and Minnesota replaced the original Granger legislation with considerably weaker regulatory systems. Active commissions "were replaced with advisory ones having no control over rates and little control over services and discrimination" (Robertson 1964, 290). However, the principle of railroad regulation survived and soon found additional support in other states and in Washington, D.C.

To the surprise and dismay of the railroad industry, the judicial challenges to the Granger laws proved unsuccessful. Seven cases involving railroads and one involving a grain elevator were brought to test the laws. When state courts affirmed the legality of the statutes, the Granger cases slowly made their way to the Supreme Court. On March 1, 1877, the Court announced its decisions. By a vote of 7 to 2 the Court upheld the actions of the states in all eight Granger cases.

The justices were well aware of the importance of the cases, which represented the Supreme Court's "first major statement on the constitutionality of regulating the new industrial capitalism" (Magrath 1964, 122) Chief Justice Morrison R. Waite chose the Chicago grain elevator case, *Munn v. Illinois*, as the lead case for the court's views because the constitutional issue of state authority to regulate private property was not complicated by secondary or peripheral issues. Writing for the majority, Chief Justice Waite declared that while it was well established that a person could not be deprived of property without due process of law, when businesses were substantially affected with a public interest, their regulation as public utilities was a legitimate constitutional exercise of a state's police power. Moreover, Waite said, "For protection against abuses by legislatures the people must resort to the polls, not to the courts" (Magrath 1964, 124).

The Court found the constitutional principles enunciated in *Munn v. Illinois* to be equally applicable to the railroad cases before it, that the statutes in those cases did not infringe upon Congress's exclusive power over interstate commerce, and that claims that the statutes impaired the obligation of contracts were without merit. Although the eight Granger cases clearly affirmed the constitutional power of states to regulate railroads and other enterprises affected with a public interest, the legality of specific regulatory provisions and possible state infringement of federal authority over interstate commerce remained important legal issues for future resolution.

—Richard W. Barsness

REFERENCES

Locklin, D. Philip. *Economics of Transportation*. 7th ed. Homewood, Ill.: Richard D. Irwin, 1972.

Magrath, C. Peter. "The Case of the Unscrupulous Warehouseman." In *Quarrels That Have Shaped the Constitution*, ed. John A. Garraty. New York: Harper & Row, 1964.

Robertson, Ross M. *History of the American Economy*. 2nd ed. New York: Harcourt, Brace & World, 1964.

Stover, John F. *American Railroads*. 2nd ed. Chicago: Univ. of Chicago Press, 1997.

See also REGULATION.

Granite Railway

The Granite Railway of Quincy, Massachusetts, chartered in 1826, is commonly called North America's first railroad. The statement has been repeated so widely that it has become a truism of railroad history. Since some historians have questioned it, some commentary is necessary. Research has revealed numerous earlier installations that could be described as railroads. They fall into three categories: railroads constructed only for demonstration purposes; railroads with wooden rails; and inclined planes, with haulage by rope or chain. None of these earlier installations was constructed under a charter from a state government, and although several states granted a number of charters for railroads before 1826, none ever reached the construction stage. Thus, with qualifications, the Granite Railway could justifiably be called the first "serious" railroad constructed in North America.

The Granite Railway owed its existence to the Bunker Hill monument in the Charlestown section of Boston. The contract for supplying the stone for this monument was held by Gridley Bryant, a self-educated engineer and building contractor. Bryant purchased a ledge of granite in Quincy from which to quarry the stone. His quarry was over three miles from the nearest water transportation, and he decided that the most efficient means to transport the stone to the dock would be a railroad. Bryant was aware of railways in England and is believed to have studied their development as part of his planning.

Bryant adopted a substantial track structure, including a solid roadbed excavated to a depth of two feet. Bryant, in earlier times, was credited with having invented the first track switch, the first turntable, and the first swiveling truck for eight-wheeled cars used on this continent. All of these devices had existed previously in Britain, and whether Bryant invented them independently or not, he deserves credit for being the first engineer in North America to use the technology. Bryant seems to have regarded his railroad design as merely a means to an end, and for the remainder of his career he concentrated on his contracting business.

The promotion of the charter and financing of the enterprise were the work of Col. Thomas H. Perkins, who furnished most of the $50,000 capital from his own resources. A charter was granted by the Massachusetts legislature on March 4, 1826, and the first train operated on October 7, 1826. In addition to being a talented engineer, Bryant must have been a very skilled manager. Operation was by horsepower. The quarry continued to be a prime source of stone for building construction in Boston for nearly another 40 years, and the railroad continued in operation, always by horsepower, throughout that period.

The Granite Railway has the dubious distinction of the first fatal accident to a nonemployee on a U.S. railroad. On July 25, 1832, a chain broke on an inclined plane, and a car carrying an inspection party ran away, resulting in a death.

In its early years the Granite Railway attracted much attention and was influential in fostering the development of the American railroad network in the 1830s. Officials of the pioneer Baltimore & Ohio Railroad inspected it during that enterprise's planning period.

In 1870, after several years of disuse, the Old Colony Railroad purchased the right of way, and part of it was incorporated into a new Granite Branch, opened in 1871. The Old Colony became part of the New Haven system in 1893, and the route was abandoned in 1953. Parts of the right of way and track structure are still visible, and historical markers commemorate the site.

—Adrian Ettlinger

REFERENCES

The First Railroad in America: A History of the Origin and Development of the Granite Railway at Quincy, Massachusetts. N.p.: Privately printed for the Granite Railway Co., 1926.

Gerstner, Franz Anton Ritter von. *Early American Railroads.* Ed. Frederick C. Gamst. Stanford, Calif.: Stanford Univ. Press, 1997 [1842–1843].

Harlow, Alvin F. *Steelways of New England.* New York: Creative Age Press, 1946.

Karr, Ronald Dale. *The Rail Lines of Southern New England.* Pepperell, Mass.: Branch Line Press, 1995.

Great Northern Railway

The Great Northern Railway (GN) spanned the northern-tier states from Lake Superior to Seattle. It became part of Burlington Northern in 1970. (Burlington Northern Railroad became part of the Burlington Northern & Santa Fe Railway at the end of 1996.)

Like most frontier railroads, Great Northern's predecessors had difficult beginnings. The direct antecedent of the road was the Minnesota & Pacific Railroad Co., chartered on May 22, 1857, to build a line from Stillwater on the St. Croix River to St. Paul and on to St. Anthony, the site of the falls that powered the Minneapolis flour mills. From that point the railroad was to divide into two lines: one, later dubbed the Main Line, going northwest to the Red River near Breckinridge (220 miles) and the other, subsequently known as the Branch Line, following the Mississippi River through St. Cloud to the Red River farther north (428 miles). Minnesota & Pacific's promoters anticipated building due north along the Red River to the Canadian border near present-day Pembina, North Dakota, and St. Vincent, Minnesota. Armed with an initial land grant of 2,460,000 acres by the territorial legislature, led by Vermont native and prominent frontier entrepreneur Edmund Rice (the first president and the principal moving force in the enterprise), and with its stock capitalized at $15 million, the railroad seemed to hold much promise.

For all that, the fledgling line was unable to meet the terms of its charter and defaulted in 1862. The Minnesota legislature immediately transferred the charter and all assets to a successor, the St. Paul & Pacific Railroad, again led by Rice and directors from the former company. Later that year, using the state's first locomotive, the *William Crooks*, it began operating along the 10-mile stretch between St. Anthony and St. Paul, providing the young state its first rail transportation.

Problems persisted. The railroad proved unable to complete construction and satisfy the terms of its charter. It still had not reached the Red River by 1871. It was able to claim only a small fraction of its land grant; as costs soared and construction languished, many in the state dubbed the line "two streaks of rust and a right of way."

Hoping to jump-start the operation, in 1870 the company's officers sold a controlling interest in part of the line to the Northern Pacific Railroad (NP), itself incorporated in 1864 with an enormous land grant and controlled by financier Jay Cooke of Philadelphia. However, the panic of 1873 quickly dashed hopes for the small line, as it did for the NP, when both fell into receivership.

New leadership quickly emerged and inaugurated the era of Canadian-born James J. Hill that lasted until his retirement in 1912. Railroading was a second career for Hill, who came to be called the Empire Builder. Up to 1877 he had been concerned primarily with warehousing and the steamboat trade on the Mississippi and Red rivers. As he approached middle age, however, Hill joined with other business leaders to complete the St. Paul & Pacific up the fertile Red River valley to Canada and earn its land grant.

Initially Hill was the junior member of the new leaders, or Associates, as they were known. This consortium included Donald Alexander Smith (Lord Strathcona and Mount Royal), George Stephen (Lord Mount Stephen), Norman W. Kittson, and John S. Kennedy. Smith was chief commissioner of the Hudson's Bay Co., a director of the Bank of Montreal, and a powerful Conservative figure in Canadian politics. He was deeply involved in the dominion's transcontinental railroad debates. Stephen was a cousin of Smith's and president of the Bank of Montreal. Kittson was Hill's partner in the steamboat business on the Red River and Hudson's Bay agent in Minnesota. Kennedy was a vital figure in the New York investment banking community. He played a central role in attracting capital, particularly from the Netherlands, that transformed the St. Paul & Pacific and its successors into a healthy, prosperous rail system.

After completing the line to the Canadian border and earning the railroad's land grant, Hill and his associates turned their attention west with the renamed St. Paul, Minneapolis & Manitoba (nicknamed the Manitoba). Much of their decision turned on strategic considerations. The rival Northern Pacific completed its transcontinental line to Tacoma in 1883, while not far north of the international border the Canadian Pacific completed its own line shortly thereafter. For the Manitoba, this funda-

Herald and reporting marks of a Great Northern wood-framed boxcar were photographed on the Southern Pacific at San Bernardino, Calif., in March 1943. —Jack Delano photograph, Office of War Information, Library of Congress (Neg. LC-USW3-21561-E)

mental economic reality meant either building west or eventually being taken over or driven out of business by the Northern Pacific or the Canadian Pacific.

Hill, who was president of the Manitoba, decided to compete with his more powerful rivals and build the line west. He did it in two measured phases. First he launched his crews from Devil's Lake, Dakota Territory, laying a record-breaking 634 miles of track across the northern Great Plains in 1886. Anxious to thwart a future rival, the Canadian Pacific joined with the Northern Pacific and Union Pacific lines, which had a rate-pooling agreement for controlling the booming trade of the Anaconda mining region in western Montana Territory. The fact that Montana's mines had just surpassed those of Michigan's Upper Peninsula and become the leading copper-producing properties in the nation only intensified the competition.

The confident Hill was dumbfounded when President Grover Cleveland, whom he had supported politically and financially and counted upon as a firm ally, vetoed the right-of-way bill necessary for the Manitoba to build across the Fort Berthold and Blackfeet Indian reservations. Worse, in his veto message to Congress Cleveland implicitly insulted his supporter, charging that the legislation would open Indian lands to a class of corporations carrying with them many individuals not known for any scrupulous regard for the interest or welfare of the Indians, and would likely ignite a new round of warfare on the plains.

The next round belonged to Hill and the Manitoba; he promptly regrouped and used all his political, financial, and personal allies to pressure Cleveland into a reconsideration of his veto. The president did so and, only a few months later, signed a bill that was markedly similar to the original right-of-way legislation. Further, the administration immediately commenced negotiations that resulted in land cessions that reduced the Fort Berthold and Blackfoot reservations by over 19 million acres. With vast new lands opened to white settlers and a right of way across the northern plains, the Manitoba enjoyed clear access to the fast-growing mines and lands of the north central frontier.

In its second expansionist phase the railroad completed its line through the Marias Pass in the Rocky Mountains to Seattle in 1893, possibly the worst year of the nineteenth century to begin operation of a transcontinental railroad. The panic of 1893 seared the economic and social landscape and forced all the transcontinental railroads except the Great Northern, as it had been called since 1890, into receivership. To stave off a similar fate, the GN instituted a wide range of layoffs and wage reductions throughout its system. Those measures resulted in severe labor turbulence when GN workers flocked to the new industrially organized American Railway Union of Eugene V. Debs the following spring. In a surprise strike they won an important victory over Hill, though their gains were quickly undone by the disastrous Pullman strike in the summer of 1894 in which the young union was destroyed.

Amid the turbulence of the 1890s Hill cemented an important alliance with J. P. Morgan to control most of the rail transportation in the American Northwest. Toward that end Hill, Morgan, Stephen, and Arthur Gwinner of the Deutsche Bank of Berlin (which represented the bankrupt Northern Pacific) met in London to end the two railroads' long rivalry. The so-called 1896 London Memorandum stipulated that the GN and NP would "form a permanent alliance, defensive, and in case of need offensive, with a view of avoiding competition and aggressive policy and of protecting the common interests of both Companies." Further, the railroaders and bankers determined that "all competitive business, such as [that] of the Anaconda Copper Company [the principal mining company, the single largest shipper in the Northwest, and the only shipper mentioned in the agreement], would be divided upon equitable terms between both Companies. Tariff wars and rate cutting [were to] be absolutely avoided," while neither road would in the future "ingress into the other's territory by new construction or purchase or acquiring of control of existing lines."

At the same time Hill and Morgan were purchasing the NP's outstanding stock and obtained de facto control of the railroad, which they reorganized. As part of that effort, in 1899 Hill sold over 900,000 acres of prime timberland, largely in Washington State, from the NP's land grant to Frederick Weyerhaeuser (who was a neighbor of Hill's in St. Paul) to obtain the capital to resurrect the Northern Pacific.

By 1901 the Hill-Morgan alliance effectively controlled the GN, the NP, and the highly profitable Chicago, Burlington & Quincy (Burlington) railroads, with lines stretching from the Northwest to Chicago and south to the Gulf of Mexico. However, their control was not absolute. Edward H. Harriman, whose empire included the Union Pacific and Southern Pacific, feared that the Hill Lines, as they were often called, threatened his own rail system. Consequently, he allied himself with Jacob Schiff of Kuehn, Loeb (Hill's erstwhile ally and the second-largest investment banking firm in America) and the Standard Oil Group led by William Rockefeller, Henry Rogers, and James Stillman of the National City Bank to surreptitiously purchase outstanding shares of the NP. Control of the NP, which held a significant block of Burlington stock, in turn held the promise of absolute control of the Northwest, unchallenged access to Chicago from the west, and the safeguarding of the Harriman system.

What followed was a titanic struggle that rocked Wall Street and nearly precipitated a depression. Through a series of straw men Kuehn, Loeb began purchasing NP shares on the orders of the Harriman-Rockefeller alliance while Morgan was vacationing in Europe. Hill got wind of the activity and alerted Morgan, and a full-scale bidding war ensued. Shares of the crucial Northern Pacific common stock soared to over $1,000 in the span of a few weeks as each side desperately sought control. Other stocks plummeted in the single largest trading day the markets had ever experienced, as the "shorts" scrambled to cover their losses and avert personal disaster. Ultimately, the Hill-Morgan forces triumphed after Schiff delayed too long in a final purchase.

Anxious to avert any more damage, the combatants agreed to a compromise, the Northern Securities holding company, an important part of the great merger boom then sweeping the country. Chartered in November 1901 in New Jersey, Northern Securities was the direct predecessor of the Burlington Northern, created in 1970. The holding company included controlling shares of the Great Northern, Northern Pacific, Chicago, Burlington & Quincy, and Spokane, Portland & Seattle lines. The Hill-Morgan group, with Hill as president, held a firm majority in the enterprise, although Harriman and others were represented on the board.

Northern Securities constituted a near monopoly on rail transportation from Minnesota to Washington State and immediately drew the attention of Theodore Roosevelt, who directed his attorney general to file suit to dissolve Northern Securities as a violation of the Sherman Antitrust Act. The case wound through the lower courts, and in 1904 the U.S. Supreme Court affirmed Roosevelt's position to break up the company. In a famous dissent, newly appointed Justice Oliver Wendell Holmes, Jr., opined, "Great cases like hard cases make bad law." Bad or not, the decision proved generally popular to progressives, and the individual railroads reverted to their former relationships.

In the aftermath Hill continued to lead the GN energetically. He tilted with the Harriman lines as he laid more track in Oregon and attempted to tap the northern California markets by that route. At the same time he and his railroad launched repeated efforts to attract new settlers to the northern-tier states, where Hill preached the gospel of dryland farming and agrarian reform until his formal retirement as chairman of the board in 1912.

He was succeeded first as president and later as chairman of the board by his son, Louis W. Hill. After the period of federal control under the U.S. Railroad Administration (USRA) during World War I, Ralph Budd was named president. During Budd's tenure the road faced a new economic environment, including worsening labor relations that culminated in the 1922 shopmen's strike. At the same time the GN embarked upon new policies to increase its volume of business and dramatically reduce its expenses by upgrading its grades, roadbed, and rolling stock. In January 1929 it completed a new tunnel, the longest in the Western Hemisphere, through Washington's Cascade Mountains. Other significant activities included a renewed effort to merge the GN with the Northern Pacific, while leasing the SP&S and Burlington lines. Opposition by shippers, other railroads, and a variety of other antimerger groups throughout the 1920s and the early years of the Great Depression militated against the consolidation, and the GN withdrew its application with the Interstate Commerce Commission in 1931.

The railroad survived the hard times of the 1930s, despite the generally poor economy and growing competition from trucks. Similar considerations affected passenger traffic on the line, although the GN invested heavily in the bus industry.

With the coming of World War II and the end of the Depression, freight traffic boomed to unprecedented heights, and GN entered a new era of unprecedented prosperity under the leadership of John M. Budd. Increasingly, though, Budd encountered a world in which the highly regulated rail industry faced competition from trucks, airplanes, buses, and automobiles. Budd introduced a variety of reforms, including dieselization, to make the Great Northern competitive.

But such measures by themselves were inadequate. To compete effectively in the rapidly changing marketplace, in 1956 Budd joined with the Northern Pacific in a renewed campaign to merge the GN, NP, Burlington, and SP&S lines. The plan worked slowly through the ICC and the Supreme Court, resulting in the creation of the Burlington Northern on March 2, 1970.

In 1968, just prior to the merger that created Burlington Northern, the Great Northern operated a system of 8,275 route-miles and 11,399 track-miles, with 589 locomotives, 491 passenger cars, 36,966 freight cars, 2,305 company service cars, and 15,913 employees. Freight traffic totaled 18,027 million ton-miles in 1968, and farm products (23.7 percent), lumber (19.5 percent), metallic ores (8.4 percent), and food products (7.8 percent) were its principal traffic sources. Passenger traffic totaled 349 million passenger-miles. Operating revenues totaled $266.3 million in 1968, and the railroad achieved an 81.6 percent operating ratio.

—W. Thomas White

REFERENCES

Hidy, Ralph W., Muriel E. Hidy, Roy V. Scott, and Don L. Hofsommer. *The Great Northern Railway: A History.* Boston: Harvard Business School Press, 1988.

Malone, Michael P. *James J. Hill: Empire Builder of the Northwest.* Norman: Univ. of Oklahoma Press, 1996.

Martin, Albro. *James J. Hill and the Opening of the Northwest.* New York: Oxford Univ. Press, 1976. Repr. with introduction by W. Thomas White. St. Paul: Minnesota Historical Society Press, 1991.

Veenendaal, Augustus J., Jr. *The Saint Paul & Pacific Railroad: An Empire in the Making, 1862–1879.* DeKalb: Northern Illinois Univ. Press, 1999.

Greater Toronto Transit Authority (GO Transit)

Toronto, Ontario, was long among the major North American urban areas without a significant regional or commuter rail service. In the face of growing regional traffic congestion, this changed in the mid-1960s. Originally known as Government of Ontario Transit or GO Transit, the regional commuter transit agency was established as a Crown agency of the Ontario provincial government in 1965 to operate a 60-mile commuter service over the Canadian National main line from Pickering, east of Toronto, to Hamilton, to the west. The provincial government assumed responsibility for all GO Transit capital costs and for operating costs not covered by revenues. The name change to Greater Toronto Transit Authority came after the province handed off funding responsibility to the Greater Toronto municipalities in 1997. More recently, in 2001, the Ontario government resumed funding for the service. The current Greater Toronto service area served by GO Transit covers approximately 3,000 square miles with a population of about 5 million.

GO Transit's initial Lakeshore East and West routes began operation in May 1967. They were an immediate success, and the system has been expanding ever since. Since its startup GO Transit has added routes to Georgetown (1974) and Richmond Hill (1978) over CN lines and a service to Milton (1981) over Canadian Pacific. VIA Rail services over CN to Stouffville and Bradford were turned over to GO Transit in 1982. The original Lakeshore East route was extended to Whitby in 1988 and to Oshawa in 1994. Rail and related bus ridership has grown steadily from an annual total of 2.5 million in its first year of operation to almost 35.9 million annual passengers in the 2002–2003 fiscal year. Toronto Union Station is the hub for all seven rail lines, with at least 96 percent of the system's rail passengers boarding or detraining there. The system also operates an extensive bus service that supplements and extends its rail routes.

GO Transit was the first new North American commuter rail service in more than half a century, and the system reflects many of the new operating practices that have since been adopted by other new systems. Trains operate in push-pull mode, and the system pioneered the barrier-free, proof-of-payment fare-collection system for commuter rail service. Original GO Transit equipment included single-level, lightweight aluminum coaches and a number of self-propelled cars, but the system has since standardized on the distinctive high-capacity bilevel car developed by Hawker Siddeley Canada, Ltd. (now Bombardier), which entered service in 1978. The same car is now in service on half a dozen other new commuter rail systems. General Motors Canada, working closely with GO Transit, developed the F59PH diesel-electric for the rigorous start-and-stop operation of commuter service, with the first units introduced in 1988.

GO Transit's current commuter rail system includes two routes, Lakeshore East and Lakeshore West, that provide off-peak and weekend as well as peak-period service. The five other routes, to Milton, Georgetown, Bradford, Richmond Hill, and Stouffville, operate only during weekday peak periods. In 2005 GO Transit operated a commuter rail system of 224.4 route-miles, serving 56 stations on seven routes, with a fleet of 45 locomotives and 385 bilevel commuter cars. A total of 179 weekday trains were transporting an average of 150,000 weekday passengers.

—William D. Middleton

Green Bay & Western Railroad

In many ways the Green Bay & Western Railroad, which ran straight across the middle of Wisconsin from Lake Michigan to the Mississippi River, was a microcosm of U.S. railroads: it was built by a construction contractor, it continued in operation by virtually the same people through two foreclosures, it emerged as a small, profitable trunk-line railroad in the 1920s, and it faced difficult times as a result of the deregulated railroad environment of the 1980s. The Green Bay & Lake Pepin Railway was incorporated in 1866 by business leaders of Green Bay, Wisconsin, and the upper Midwest. David Marsh Kelly joined the Green Bay & Lake Pepin company in 1870, stepped down to become its builder, and returned as vice president and general manager. Kelly obtained financial backing from Moses Taylor, a New York banker and capitalist

who owned controlling interests in the Delaware, Lackawanna & Western Railroad and the Lackawanna Coal & Iron Co., and from John I. Blair, at one time president of 16 different railroads and owner of large blocks of shares of stock in railroad and iron companies.

By the time Kelly completed the line to the Mississippi River in 1873, the company had been renamed Green Bay & Minnesota. It obtained trackage rights on the Chicago & North Western to reach Winona, Minnesota, and La Crosse, Wisconsin, both important lumber towns. Its bondholders forced the company into reorganization in 1878, and the property was turned over to the Green Bay, Winona & St. Paul in 1881. Samuel Sloan, president of the Delaware, Lackawanna & Western, was president of the GBW&StP from 1882 to 1896. As part of the Lackawanna's plan to establish a through route to Omaha, in 1891 the Mississippi River was bridged at Winona, and GBW&StP's credit was used to start construction of the Winona & Southwestern.

Also in 1891 the Kewaunee, Green Bay & Western opened from Green Bay east to Kewaunee, an all-weather port on Lake Michigan. Much of the financing for the KGB&W came from W. W. Cargill, the La Crosse grain merchant. The next year, 1892, car ferries on Lake Michigan completed the east-west connection.

The main line and La Crosse branch were sold separately in the 1896 foreclosure to the reorganization committee, a group of first-mortgage bondholders made up of members of the Winthrop and Blair investment banking firms of New York City. The railroad, renamed Green Bay & Western in 1896, was improved with funds acquired from the reorganization committee, which did not disband until 1913. The principal executive officers, elected from the Winthrop and Blair firms, made only occasional trips to Green Bay.

In the reorganization George Wickersham devised a unique financial structure under which the GB&W could not be placed in receivership or experience financial difficulties as long as it earned operating expenses. The class B debentures, a part of the reorganization, were the subject of many lawsuits through the years; the last ended in the railroad's favor in 1993.

The federal transportation law of 1920 gave greater scope and power to the Interstate Commerce Commission, which could set minimum and maximum rates. Rates were the same between cities regardless of routing, and the GB&W could compete by furnishing a route in conjunction with other railroads around congestion in Chicago. Nothing in the experience of the New York investment bankers prepared them to deal with ICC regulations and requirements. The financially strapped GB&W ran up increasingly large legal fees. Something needed to be done.

The board hired Homer E. McGee as president in 1934 and moved all executive duties to Green Bay. McGee immediately set about rebuilding the railroad for heavier locomotives and higher speeds. Suggestions, never implemented, included a *Zephyr*-like lightweight train in 1935 and a streamlined 4-4-2 steam locomotive proposed in 1936. The Lackawanna influence was still felt, as its president was named to GB&W's board in 1935.

Anticipating a decline in short-haul traffic, the GB&W made itself into a bridge route, primarily for auto parts going to the Ford assembly plant in St. Paul, Minnesota. Cars received from ferries at Kewaunee had to be in East Winona and Winona by 3 A.M. so connecting railroads could place them for unloading at St. Paul by 7 A.M.

About 1970 Ford traffic shifted to a unit train through Chicago to take advantage of volume rates permitted by the Transportation Act of 1958. The GB&W felt vulnerable and in 1971 initiated negotiations with Burlington Northern. BN offered to purchase GB&W in 1974 (BN predecessor Chicago, Burlington & Quincy had considered purchasing GB&W in 1965). A counteroffer from Soo Line, Milwaukee Road, and Chicago & North Western called for abandoning 60 percent of the GB&W's mileage and dividing the rest among the three larger roads. BN received approval from the ICC in 1978, but withdrew its plan after Brae Corp. and Itel made larger offers.

When Itel assumed control in 1978, Weldon McGee (who had succeeded his father in 1962) resigned as president but remained on the board of directors. The new board hired Joe Galassi from the Burlington Northern to replace McGee as president, and the new management embarked on an aggressive marketing campaign. A few years of prosperity ensued. GB&W used the profits of 1979, 1980, and 1981 to upgrade its right of way in hopes of attracting unit trains of western coal moving to industries and power plants in Green Bay.

But then GB&W's fortunes tumbled. In May 1981 BN hired Galassi back. In 1982, most of the Lake Michigan ferries ceased operating, bridge traffic disappeared, and GB&W suffered the first of five consecutive years of operating losses. Deregulation of the rail industry especially hurt regional carriers such as GB&W in the transcontinental market. The GB&W had come full circle. When it opened in the 1870s, its business came from communities along its line; in the 1980s it again relied on on-line communities for traffic, especially from the paper mills at Wisconsin Rapids.

To expand its presence in the Green Bay market, Itel purchased 208 miles of track in December 1988 from the Chicago & North Western and incorporated the Fox River Valley Railroad to operate it. The new railroad required heavy investment and produced no profit, so in 1990 Itel started negotiations to sell it and the GB&W. Wisconsin Central announced its plan in January 1992 for a subsidiary, Fox Valley & Western, to purchase both railroads.

While Fox Valley & Western negotiated agreements with six labor unions, Green Bay & Western trains continued to operate and business increased. Fox Valley & Western's last negotiation came to fruition on August 27, 1993. Early the next morning GB&W's final freight train, still carrying a caboose, rolled into Wisconsin Rapids, marking the end of a Wisconsin railroad tradition.

A traditional railroad right to the end, the GB&W is remembered for its dependable freight service, financial structure, and well-maintained property. It was always very much a family railroad. Of 137 hourly employees on the summer 1993 payroll, 45 had a father, son, or brother also working for the GB&W. In 1992 Green Bay & Western operated a system of 255 route-miles and 345 track-miles and had 202 employees.

—John E. Gruber and Thomas O. Kloehn

REFERENCES

Gruber, John. "A Death in the Family." *Trains* 54, no. 5 (May 1994): 56–61.

Specht, Ray, and Ellen Specht. *The Green Bay Route*. Boston: Railway & Locomotive Historical Society, Bulletin No. 115, 1966.

Guatemalan Railroads

On April 15, 1999, when Ferrovias Guatemala (FVG) hauled a trainload of cement over 37 miles of 3-foot-gauge rails to Guatemala City, the country's capital, from El Chile, it was doing something unprecedented. For the first time ever, a national rail system that had been totally shut down had been brought back to life. This revival, especially remarkable in that it was a private-sector initiative, took place under the banner of Railroad Development Corp. (RDC), a Pittsburgh-based investment and management company, working in partnership with a local investor group.

The Guatemala Central, the county's first railroad, had been completed in 1884, running 75.5 miles from Puerto San José on the Pacific Ocean to Guatemala City, perched atop a high plateau in the midst of nearly impenetrable mountains. This meter-gauge line had been begun in 1879; it was chartered in California and built under the skillful guidance of Collis P. Huntington, its president, who had earlier made his name with the Central Pacific. The climb up Palin Hill from Escuintla to the capital was a stiff 3.5 percent for 16 miles (peaking at 3.7 percent).

The Guatemala Central's success spawned another line to the Pacific, the 3-foot-gauge Champerico & Northern (chartered in 1881), reaching 27 miles from the port city of Champerico to Retalhuleu. In 1887 this railroad, now reorganized as the Guatemala Western (Ferrocarrilo Occidento de Guatemala), built 14 miles eastward to Mazatenango, where it would connect with a 59-mile branch of the Guatemala Central from Santa María. (In 1890 the GC converted to the 3-foot gauge that had become Guatemalan standard.) In the far west yet another line to the Pacific, the Ocos Railway (Ferrocarril Ocos), was organized in 1884 to build from the port city of Ocos north along the banks of the Río Suchiate to Ayutla (because Mexico was just across the river, it later became the interchange point with that country's railroads) and east to eventual connection, in 1913, with the Guatemala Western.

The 197.4-mile line to the Caribbean coast, the route reopened by RDC in 1999, was not finished until 1908, as the Guatemala Northern (Ferrocarril del Norte de Guatemala). By then Minor C. Keith, a founder in 1899 of the United Fruit Co., had begun buying railroads in hopes of establishing a Central American railroad linking North and South America. In 1904 the in-progress Guatemala Northern, Guatemala Central, Guatemala Western, and Ocos Railway were all consolidated operationally (but with corporate identities intact) as the Guatemala Railway.

The western end of the Guatemala Northern traversed spectacular terrain, which explains why the railroad was not completed until 25 years after being contracted. In the 61 miles from El Rancho to Guatemala City, the line uses 3.3 percent grades to hoist itself from 900 to 4,910 feet.

On April 19, 1912, the Guatemala Railway and the Central de El Salvador became the International Railways of Central America (Ferrocarriles Internationales de Centro América). The railroad was incorporated in New Jersey and controlled by United Fruit; Keith was president of both. In 1929 IRCA's Guatemalan and El Salvadoran operations were consolidated by the completion of a 161-mile link from El Salvador to Zacapa, on the Barrios–Guatemala City line.

Though narrow gauge, IRCA was a big, well-run railroad, supported by United Fruit money (though in most years bananas accounted for less than 10 percent of this common carrier's revenue). Listed on the New York Stock Exchange until 1965, the railroad was predominantly North American in ownership, management, and operating practices. Locomotive shops in Guatemala City were extensive and impressive. At more than 500 miles, the Guatemalan network—linking Mexico, El Salvador, and the Atlantic and Pacific oceans with Guatemala City—was the most extensive in Central America.

Steam locomotives served exclusively until 1954, with the most modern power being 32 outside-frame 2-8-2s delivered by Baldwin from 1946 through 1948. (Two of these remain operable today, available for railfan charters.) In 1947 the railroad bought a pair of former Sumpter Valley, former Uintah 2-6-6-2s to work as helpers on Palin Hill. The first diesel-electric locomotives to arrive were 6 1,000-horsepower units from General Electric. Though delivered in 1950, they did not enter service until four years later because the operating unions, fearing loss of jobs, would not run them. In 1956, 6 identical units were delivered, along with 6 400-horsepower switchers, also from GE. In 1960 came 2 more 1,000-horsepower units.

By the 1950s the railroad had begun to decline, however, and the opening of the Atlantic Highway from Guatemala City to Puerto Barrios in 1959 was a shatter-ing blow. A year earlier, as the result of an antitrust suit brought in 1954, United Fruit had divested itself of its substantial ownership interest in IRCA, which had had what would prove to be its last profitable year in 1957.

For the next decade the Guatemalan government shored up IRCA with loans. In 1968, with the railroad in default, the government foreclosed and began operating IRCA's lines in Guatemala as Ferrocarriles de Guatemala, or Fegua. In 1971, 18 new 1,050-horsepower Babcock & Wilcox/GE Spain diesels arrived on the property. Ten 2,000-horsepower units from Bombardier/MLW joined them in 1982, finally spelling the end of regular steam operations.

Fegua struggled on until March 1996 when, with its deteriorated tracks virtually impassable, the railroad shut down. Aside from the occasional railfan charter, it stayed shut down until RDC (which also has ownership interests in railroads in Argentina, Peru, Malawi, Mozambique, and Estonia, as well as the United States) entered the picture. After receiving in October 1997 a 50-year concession to restore and operate the line, RDC began to repair the 197-mile route from the capital to Puerto Barrios and Puerto Santo Thomas on the Atlantic. A major setback came in October 1998 when Hurricane Mitch swept through, delaying the project by some ten months.

In December 1999 the line was finally opened to the coast, Phase I of RDC's overall plan. On this route trains now haul coil steel, containers, and sugar. Later phases will open other IRCA Guatemala lines if business potential warrants and financing becomes available.

—Karl Zimmermann

REFERENCES

Best, Gerald M. "The Railroads of Guatemala and El Salvador." *Bulletin of the Railway and Locomotive Historical Society*, no. 104 (April 1961): 31–53.

Polinder, Douglas W. "Real Railroaders Never Quit." *Trains* 62, no. 8 (Aug. 2002): 34–41.

Gulf, Mobile & Ohio Railroad

The Gulf, Mobile & Ohio Railroad was formed by the combination of the Mobile & Ohio Rail Road and the Gulf, Mobile & Northern Railroad in 1940, creating a rail system reaching from St. Louis to New Orleans, Mobile, Montgomery, and Birmingham. In 1947 GM&O acquired the Alton Railroad, extending its reach to Chicago and Kansas City.

Mobile & Ohio

The Mobile & Ohio was intended to gather river trade at Cairo, Illinois, and funnel it to the port of Mobile, Alabama. States, counties, and cities along the route purchased M&O stock, and in 1850 Congress passed a land-grant bill aiding the railroad. In 1852, 30 miles of railroad from Mobile to Citronelle, Alabama, opened, and on April 22, 1861, the entire line was completed north to Columbus, Kentucky, a few miles south of the confluence of the Ohio and the Mississippi. Steamboats connected the new railroad with the Illinois Central at Cairo.

The completion date was just ten days after the Confederates fired on Fort Sumter. Anything the railroad could have done for the port of Mobile was lost in the Civil War. In addition, the war wore out the rolling stock and track, and the cost of rebuilding the railroad after the war combined with the Mobile & Ohio's construction debt to put the railroad in receivership in 1875.

The M&O extended its line 20 miles to Cairo in 1882. Four years later the railroad reached St. Louis by acquiring and standard-gauging the 3-foot-gauge St. Louis & Cairo. The M&O reached Montgomery, Alabama, in 1898 with a line from Artesia and Columbus, Mississippi, and a few years later reached Birmingham by trackage rights on the Illinois Central and the Southern Railway from Corinth, Mississippi.

The Southern Railway saw strategic value in M&O's route between Mobile and St. Louis and in 1901 offered an exchange of securities, which the M&O accepted. M&O's relations with the Southern grew closer, but the governor of Mississippi vetoed a merger. Southern Railway control of the M&O continued, but when M&O posted a deficit in its ledger in 1930, the Southern was unable to help. M&O entered receivership on June 3, 1932. In 1938 the Southern sold its M&O bonds to the newly created Gulf, Mobile & Ohio Railroad. GM&O bought the M&O at a foreclosure sale on August 1, 1940.

Gulf, Mobile & Northern

The Mobile, Jackson & Kansas City Railroad was aimed primarily at the pine forests of southeastern Mississippi when it was chartered in 1890. Its rails reached Hattiesburg, Mississippi, in 1902. That year the railroad was purchased by the group that had bought the Gulf & Chicago, a 62-mile narrow-gauge line from Middleton, Tennessee, to Pontotoc, Mississippi. The new owners began construction of 240 miles of railroad to connect the two ends.

Soon after the construction was finished, the railroad entered receivership. It was reorganized in 1909 as the ambitiously named New Orleans, Mobile & Chicago Railroad. In 1911 it came under the joint control of the Louisville & Nashville and the St. Louis & San Francisco. The railroad's finances fell apart again in 1913.

A reorganization as the Gulf, Mobile & Northern Railroad on January 1, 1917, was successful because of the new president, Isaac B. Tigrett, a banker in Jackson, Tennessee. One of his first actions was to construct 40 miles of track from Middleton to Jackson, where the GM&N could connect with the Illinois Central and the Nashville,

Chattanooga & St. Louis. In 1926 the GM&N began operating freight trains on NC&StL rails to Paducah, Kentucky, 145 miles north of Jackson. There the GM&N connected and made a preferential traffic agreement with the Chicago, Burlington & Quincy, which eventually acquired almost 30 percent of GM&N's stock.

The GM&N merged several small railroads: in 1928 the 49-mile Birmingham & Northwestern (Jackson to Dyersburg, Tennessee), in 1929 the Meridian & Memphis (Union to Meridian, Mississippi), and also in 1929 the Jackson & Eastern (Union to Jackson, Mississippi).

In 1935 GM&N purchased the diesel-powered Rebels, the first streamliners in the South, for New Orleans–Jackson, Tennessee, service. GM&N shifted its Jackson, Tennessee–Paducah freight trains to the Illinois Central and a route 35 miles shorter on June 1, 1933. In 1934 GM&N began to consider acquisition of the Mobile & Ohio in order to connect with numerous other railroads at St. Louis. Objection was raised by Ralph Budd, president of the Burlington and a member of GM&N's board of directors, because the Burlington would lose its favored-connection status.

In 1936 problems developed over the matter of GM&N crews operating on Illinois Central rails. GM&N made a traffic agreement with the Mobile & Ohio and discontinued its trains to Paducah. Despite the objections of the Burlington and the Illinois Central, which stated that eventually it would purchase the GM&N and the M&O, merger negotiations between GM&N and M&O continued.

New Orleans Great Northern

The New Orleans Great Northern was incorporated in 1905 and that same year purchased the East Louisiana Railway, which had a network of lines north of Lake Ponchartrain and trackage rights from Slidell, Louisiana, to New Orleans on the New Orleans & Northeastern (part of the Southern Railway system). NOGN opened its line to Jackson, Mississippi, in 1909.

NOGN's route to New Orleans was crucial to Gulf, Mobile & Northern's traffic agreement with the Burlington. GM&N acquired control of the NOGN on December 30, 1929. The NOGN entered receivership in 1932; the receiver was Isaac B. Tigrett of the GM&N. It was leased to GM&N on July 1, 1933.

Chicago & Alton Railroad and Alton Railroad

In 1847 the Alton & Sangamon Railroad was chartered to connect Alton, Illinois, on the Mississippi River 20 miles north of St. Louis, with Springfield, Illinois. The railroad opened in 1851, and by 1861 it had been extended northeast to Joliet and purchased by a new company, the Chicago & Alton Railroad. In 1864 its line reached Chicago by leasing the Joliet & Chicago Railroad, and in the 1870s it leased other railroads to create the shortest Chicago–Kansas City route until 1888, when the Santa Fe opened its Chicago–Kansas City route, 32 miles shorter.

In the 1890s the C&A caught the attention of George Gould, John D. Rockefeller, and E.H. Harriman, who formed a syndicate of financiers that purchased the railroad. Then the railroad's fortunes began to fail. Its coal traffic disappeared, and it lost the Kansas City–Chicago livestock business. The Union Pacific and the Rock Island took control of the C&A in 1904; three years later control passed to the Toledo, St. Louis & Western. The C&A began posting deficits on its ledgers in 1912 and entered receivership in 1922.

The Interstate Commerce Commission's proposal of the 1920s to reduce the number of railroad systems in the United States placed the C&A with the Baltimore & Ohio—and the B&O was pretty much the only road to take the ICC's recommendations to heart. The B&O purchased the C&A at foreclosure in 1929 and incorporated the Alton Railroad in 1931. The Alton operated as part of the B&O until 1943, when the B&O restored its independence. Gulf, Mobile & Ohio purchased the Alton from the B&O in 1945, and the merger took effect on May 31, 1947.

Gulf, Mobile & Ohio

On November 10, 1938, the Gulf, Mobile & Ohio Railroad was incorporated. It purchased the Mobile & Ohio at a foreclosure sale on August 1, 1940, and consolidated with the Gulf, Mobile & Northern on September 13, 1940.

During 1944 the GM&O began to consider acquisition of the Alton Railroad. The Alton's Kansas City route did not fit with GM&O's Chicago-to-Gulf idea, so GM&O, Burlington, and Santa Fe worked up a plan: the Burlington would buy the Kansas City line, and an exchange of trackage rights would put the Santa Fe in St. Louis and give the Burlington a short route into Kansas City. Other railroads protested the idea of the Santa Fe in St. Louis, so GM&O retained ownership of the Kansas City line and granted the Burlington trackage rights between Mexico,

Missouri, and Kansas City. The Santa Fe never did reach St. Louis.

The Alton was the principal passenger railroad between Chicago and St. Louis, and GM&O continued that service. South of St. Louis, though, the GM&O was a secondary rail passenger carrier. Its subsidiary, Gulf Transport, operated an extensive network of bus routes south of St. Louis to supplement the train service. GM&O discontinued passenger-train service to New Orleans in 1954 and its remaining passenger trains south of St. Louis in 1958.

The GM&O of the 1950s and 1960s was an efficient, well-run railroad, but one vulnerable to mergers around it. More important, the men who had put GM&O together had retired or died, and the company had little in the way of potential replacements for those men. When Isaac Tigrett created the GM&O in 1940, the Illinois Central vehemently protested the new competitor. GM&O held its own until August 10, 1972, when it was merged by Illinois Central to form the Illinois Central Gulf Railroad. In 1970, its last year before the ICG merger, Gulf, Mobile & Ohio operated 2,734 route-miles and 3,947 track-miles, with 252 locomotives, 92 passenger cars, 13,064 freight cars, 540 company service cars, and 4,947 employees. Freight traffic totaled 8,285 million ton-miles in 1970, and pulp and paper (14.7 percent), lumber and wood products (12.5 percent), chemicals (11.3 percent), and coal (7.5 percent) were its principal traffic sources. Passenger traffic totaled 44 million passenger-miles. Gulf, Mobile & Ohio operating revenues totaled $104 million in 1970, and the railroad achieved a 76.2 percent operating ratio.

—**George H. Drury**

REFERENCES

Covington, Stuart. "Rebel Route." *Railroad* 37, no. 2 (Jan. 1945): 6–33.

Glendinning, Gene V. *The Chicago & Alton Railroad: The Only Way.* DeKalb: Northern Illinois Univ. Press, 2002.

Hubbard, Freeman H. "The Expanding GM&O." *Trains* 8, no. 4 (Feb. 1948): 10–17.

H

Hamilton, Alexander (1755–1804)

Tall trees cast long shadows. Thus does Alexander Hamilton, who died decades before the advent of railroading, rate an entry in this encyclopedia. Hamilton is best remembered as a coauthor of *The Federalist Papers*, as the nation's first Treasury secretary, and as Thomas Jefferson's antagonist in competing visions of America's economic destiny. It is in that last connection that he was to play a crucial role in the development of government policy that would later have implications for railroading.

Where Jefferson saw a nation of independent farmers and small government, Hamilton envisioned a nation of industry aided by a strong central power. His economic thinking was best articulated in his *Report on American Manufactures*, issued in 1791 at the dawn of the Industrial Revolution. In it Hamilton observed that new ventures carry new risks, which hinder capital investment. "To produce the desirable changes as early as may be expedient," he wrote, "may . . . require the incitement and patronage of the government."

Those words are a lineal forebear of the Pacific Railroad Act of 1862, which provided federal loan guarantees and land grants to aid construction of the first transcontinental railroad. Similar legislation was later passed for most other transcontinental lines. True to Hamiltonian theory, the intent was not pro-business per se (or, at least, that was what was said for public consumption); rather, the idea was to accomplish socially desirable goals for the common good.

Despite Jefferson's ascension to the presidency in 1801, the Hamiltonian vision persisted and prevailed. The Whigs of the second U.S. party system carried the banner of "internal improvements" from the Jacksonian era to the Civil War, when the Republicans took up the idea. The Civil War itself can be interpreted as a clash in part between the Jeffersonian and Hamiltonian views, with the latter prevailing in resounding fashion and setting the stage for the era of western railroad expansion.

Hamilton died as the result of a famous 1804 duel. Political rival Aaron Burr, still resentful of Hamilton's role in denying him the presidency in 1800, challenged the former Treasury secretary. On the appointed day Hamilton fired into the air, while Burr shot to kill.

—Peter A. Hansen

REFERENCE

Chernow, Ron. *Alexander Hamilton*. New York: Penguin Press, 2004.

Harriman, E. H. (1848–1909)

Edward Henry Harriman is generally recognized as the greatest rail baron in American history, not only for the extent of his empire, but for the revolutionary and enduring nature of his accomplishments in operations, business practices, and safety. There was little in Harriman's family history to suggest such fabulous achievement. He came from a long line of modestly successful merchants, and his father was an Episcopal clergyman. However, business was the only career young Harriman ever wanted, so he went to work as an office boy on Wall Street at 14. At the age of 22 he purchased a seat on the New York Stock Exchange, where he gained a reputation as solid but not especially clever. His interest in railroads began with his marriage to Mary Averell, whose father was a banker and president of the Ogdensburg & Lake Champlain shortline in upstate New York. Harriman purchased another New York shortline, the Sodus Bay & Southern, in 1881. He shrewdly maneuvered the New York Central and the Pennsylvania into a bidding war for the property, pocketing a tidy profit when Pennsy emerged the winner.

Harriman's association with the two shortlines resulted in a close and useful friendship with fellow board member Stuyvesant Fish, a leading figure at Illinois Central. Fish helped his protégé to a seat on the IC board in 1883, and four years later Harriman became vice president.

Illinois Central was Harriman's first exposure to big-time railroading, and he used his tenure there to learn everything he could about finance and operations. The ex-

511

Edward H. Harriman. —Library of Congress (Neg. LC-USZ62-7874)

tions, Harriman was uniquely suited to implement that vision. He applied the same formula to other properties he controlled, most notably Southern Pacific, which he acquired in 1901. (He also had interests in Baltimore & Ohio, Chicago & Alton, and Erie.)

In a less successful chapter of his career, Harriman sought to control the Burlington in 1901. When he was outmaneuvered by the James J. Hill interests, Harriman brazenly made a play for Northern Pacific, which was controlled by Hill. A panic erupted on Wall Street as investors sought to ride the coattails of the titans. Peace was declared when Hill and Harriman agreed to joint ownership of Burlington through a holding company called Northern Securities, controlled mostly by Hill.

Harriman is often derided as the embodiment of robber baron excess, an image rooted in his pugnacious manner and in turn-of-the-century trust-busting politics. With a century's perspective his reputation has rebounded, and he is now considered on balance to have been a positive force. Changing politics and Harriman's changing reputation are perhaps best seen in two related events: the 1912 Supreme Court decision to dissolve the UP-SP combination and the 1996 merger that reunited them.

—Peter A. Hansen

REFERENCE

Klein, Maury. *The Life and Legend of E. H. Harriman*. Chapel Hill: Univ. of North Carolina Press, 2000.

perience served him well when, in 1897, he sought to buy the Union Pacific out of receivership. Although he was still an unknown compared with the Gould and Vanderbilt interests that also vied for UP, Harriman's bid was credible enough that he was offered a seat on the board of the reorganized company. Within five months Harriman had demonstrated such mastery of detail that he was elected board chairman. Even in 1898, however, few would have guessed that he was on the threshold of greatness.

Harriman's chief contribution—to UP, to other railroads he owned, and to the industry as a whole—was an operational philosophy that prevails today. He was among the first to realize that a new era had arrived in railroading. The age of speculation was over: no longer would it be possible to make money from construction contracts or by playing one road against another, as he himself had done with Sodus Bay. Instead, success would come from carrying high volumes of traffic for long hauls at lower rates.

Union Pacific was in no condition to support such traffic in 1898 (nor was most of the industry), so Harriman straightened curves, reduced grades, laid heavier rail, and installed block signaling. The result was a railroad with more, heavier, and faster trains, capable of fulfilling the new operating vision. With his combination of financial acumen, access to capital markets, and affinity for opera-

Harriman, William Averell (1891–1986)

The son of magnate E. H. Harriman, Averell Harriman made significant contributions in railroading and finance before going on to a career in diplomacy and politics. The Union Pacific was the crown jewel of the Harriman family empire, and Averell went to work there as vice president of purchasing in 1915. He served as board chairman from 1932 to 1945, where he is best remembered for two initiatives intended to boost sagging passenger revenues: streamlined trains and on-line resorts. UP's early streamliners—including the M-10000, the first streamlined train in America—were a product of Harriman's vision more than anyone else's. As a figure in international social circles in the 1920s, Harriman encountered the new European phenomenon of winter resorts, and on his initiative Union Pacific developed Sun Valley, Idaho, the first ski resort in the western United States. The railroad's engineering personnel are credited with the design of the world's first chairlift, also at Sun Valley.

Although the streamliners were a storied epoch in American railroading, they failed to revive passenger trains permanently, and such industry historians as Maury Klein have asked whether the railroads' money might have been better spent on upgrading freight service. To Harriman, obligated by regulation to keep unprofitable services and not yet able to see the full extent to which the auto and airline industries would redefine America's transportation habits, the new trains were a valiant attempt to win back business. If America should ever embrace high-speed rail, Harriman's vision will be at least a spiritual antecedent.

Besides his railroading background, Harriman also was a financier. In 1931, together with other family members and classmates from Groton and Yale, Harriman merged the family banking business with Brown Brothers, a firm whose roots dated to 1800. The resulting firm of Brown Brothers Harriman & Co. still operates as a leading private banking house.

Disillusionment with Republican economic policies and a personal relationship with Franklin D. Roosevelt led Harriman into public service, first as an official of the Depression-era National Recovery Administration. He later became a special emissary to Great Britain before U.S. entry into World War II, and ambassador to the Soviet Union (1943–1946). He served as ambassador to Great Britain (1946), U.S. secretary of commerce (1946–1948), and governor of New York (1955–1959) and was a two-time candidate for the Democratic presidential nomination. He was credited by John F. Kennedy with negotiating the 1963 nuclear test ban treaty and was appointed by Lyndon Johnson to lead the U.S. delegation to the Vietnam peace talks. He worked for every Democratic president of the twentieth century except the first and the last, Woodrow Wilson and Bill Clinton.

—Peter A. Hansen

Harvey, Fred (1835–1901)

Civilizer of the American Southwest, as he was sometimes called, Frederick H. Harvey established a system of hotels, eating houses, and dining cars along the Santa Fe Railway that earned an unparalleled reputation among North American railroads. Born in England in 1835, Harvey came to America at age 14. During his youth he worked in several restaurants in New York as a dishwasher, waiter, and finally chef. He later worked for a hotel in New Orleans and then a restaurant on a Mississippi River steamer. After several years in the postal service on the Pony Express and as a mail clerk on the Hannibal & St. Joseph Railroad, Harvey became a cattle agent for the Chicago, Burlington & Quincy and settled with his wife in Leavenworth, Kansas.

Traveling extensively for the Burlington, Harvey was all too familiar with the poor quality of restaurants and hotels that catered to rail travelers. For these eating houses,

speed, not food, was what mattered. Fred Harvey decided to change this sorry situation.

Still employed by the Burlington, Harvey made his first venture in the hotel and restaurant business in 1872, purchasing the Ellsworth Hotel in Ellsworth, Kansas. Working briefly with a partner, in 1875 he began to operate eating stations on the Kansas Pacific Railroad at Wallace, Kansas, and Hugo, Colorado. These ventures were successful, so Harvey further developed a plan for a chain of eating houses affiliated with a specific railroad.

Harvey first took his idea to his employer, the Burlington, but the railroad was not interested. Then he got a positive response from the Atchison, Topeka & Santa Fe Railway. Harvey and the railroad agreed to begin with a first-class restaurant at the Topeka, Kansas, railroad station. This first Harvey House was a huge success for the Santa Fe. Harvey next opened a restaurant and hotel in Florence, Kansas. He bought handsome new walnut furniture, silverplated flatware from England, and linens from Ireland and hired away the chef from Chicago's Palmer House. People came from miles around to enjoy a quality meal.

Harvey was soon offering similar services at other Santa Fe locations, with the railroad providing the facility and Harvey running the restaurant and hotel. Harvey finally quit his job as a Burlington agent in 1882. By 1883 he was operating 17 eating houses, and by 1893 he had a verbal agreement to control eating houses and hotels along the AT&SF all the way from Chicago to Los Angeles.

Harvey maintained high standards of quality and service, and his partnership with Santa Fe soon transformed lodging and dining in the Southwest, creating an excellent reputation for the railroad. Inspectors posing as passengers reported dirty kitchens, soiled tablecloths, or cold food. Canned foods and cold-storage eggs were not allowed; necessary supplies were brought in from distant points by refrigerator cars. During the winter out-of-season fruits and vegetables were supplied from Mexico. Tank cars brought in fresh water so Harvey customers always had consistently good coffee. Table service resembled that of Chicago's Palmer House. Each table had fresh flowers, even at desert stops.

Before a train arrived at a Harvey stop, passenger crews went through taking restaurant or lunch-counter orders. The restaurant staff was ready to serve meals as soon as the train arrived. A manager always greeted passengers as they entered. A melodious gong notified them that it was time to seat themselves either at the lunch counter or in the dining room. Men were required to wear coats in the dining room; Harvey would loan one if necessary. The Harvey House always made sure a passenger never missed his train.

The Harvey House waitresses were legendary. Harvey advertised for single women aged 18 to 30. No experience was necessary, but successful applicants were expected to be of good character and to be attractive and intelligent. Applicants were sent to Kansas City for interviews, and

taste of Harvey service in the highly fictionalized 1946 MGM musical *The Harvey Girls*, starring Judy Garland. The film introduced the popular Johnny Mercer/Harry Warren song "On the Atchison, Topeka and the Santa Fe."

By the mid-1880s Santa Fe began contracting with Harvey to operate dining-car service on first-class trains. Regular and local trains continued to stop at railroad hotels and eating houses.

In 1882 the Santa Fe and Harvey began to build a chain of resort hotels to attract train passengers to the Southwest. Facilities were patterned after the indigenous Spanish colonial and Pueblo, Hopi, and Navajo styles of architecture. This type of design became known as Santa Fe. Some of the most notable were the Alvarado at Albuquerque, the La Fonda at Santa Fe, and the Bright Angel Lodge and the El Tovar Hotel at Grand Canyon. One of the grandest of all was the Montezuma near Las Vegas, New Mexico, a 270-room resort hotel built in 1882 in Queen Anne style. Mary Elizabeth Jane Colter was hired to design the interiors of all the resort hotels. At that time Colter was the nation's foremost interior decorator and had extensively studied Southwest Indian art.

Fred Harvey died on February 9, 1901. At the time of his death the chain operated 15 hotels, 47 restaurants, 30 dining cars, and a San Francisco Bay ferry. On his deathbed Harvey is said to have whispered into the ear of one of his sons, "Don't cut the ham too thin." Harvey's two sons, Ford and Byron, assumed control of the Harvey Co.

No American railroad dining-car service ever equaled that aboard the Santa Fe's Fred Harvey dining cars. The need for faster trains and schedules began to eat away at the railroad eating house, and by World War II nearly every Santa Fe train was equipped with a diner. Yet as people moved to travel on the highway, the hotels and eating houses remained an important stop between Chicago and the Far West.

During World War II the Harvey system faced the challenge of feeding servicemen embarking for the Pacific theater. Since Harvey served the railroad, and the trains were the primary means of transportation, Harvey became a "mess hall on wheels." During 1943 the Harvey system served some 30 million meals.

At the end of the war Byron Harvey's sons took over the company. As more people began to travel by highway or by air, the dining cars, eating houses, and hotels began to fall from favor. Harvey's hotels and eating houses began to close. Seeing the handwriting on the wall, the sons sold the Harvey system to Amfac, Inc., in 1968. Santa Fe's Fred Harvey dining-car service ended when Amtrak began operating most U.S. passenger service in 1971.

—Donald Duke

The Harvey Girls, the capable young waitresses who served passengers at the Harvey Houses, helped Fred Harvey establish an unparalleled reputation for his hotels, restaurants, and dining cars on the Santa Fe Railway. —Donald Duke Collection

those selected were sent for training at Kansas City or Topeka. The Harvey Girls lived in dormitories under the stern eye of a matron, and all were expected to be in by 10 P.M. unless a late train was expected. The women dressed in black shoes and stockings, plain black skirt precisely eight inches off the floor, high-collared blouse, starched white apron, and black bow tie. Their hair was simply done, ornamented only with a neatly tied white ribbon. In some Harvey Houses the lunch-counter girls wore all-black uniforms, while those in the dining room wore all white. Sometimes it was the reverse. Women who signed up had to promise not to marry for at least one year, and it was estimated that some 5,000 Harvey Girls married Santa Fe or other railroad men. The moviegoing public got a

REFERENCES

Bryant, Keith L., Jr. *History of the Atchison, Topeka and Santa Fe Railway*. New York: Macmillan, 1974.

Duke, Donald. *Fred Harvey: Civilizer of the American Southwest.* Arcadia, Calif.: Pregel, 1995.

Marshall, James. *Santa Fe: The Railroad That Built an Empire.* New York: Random House, 1945.

Haupt, Herman (1817–1905)

One of the most versatile and accomplished engineers of his time, Herman Haupt, a key figure in the development of the Pennsylvania Railroad, was born in Philadelphia in 1817. He won an appointment to West Point at the age of 14, reportedly the youngest cadet ever to enter the academy, and graduated in 1835.

Instead of a military career, however, Haupt took up work as an assistant engineer with locomotive designer and railroad engineer Henry B. Campbell at Philadelphia. Over the next decade Haupt did railroad location work and taught for several years at Pennsylvania College in Gettysburg. In 1847 he was hired by J. Edgar Thomson to do location work for the new Pennsylvania Railroad, and only two years later he became its superintendent of transportation and, later, general superintendent. He left the PRR for other railroad location work at the end of 1851, but returned as its chief engineer in 1853 to complete the line over the Allegheny Mountains to Pittsburgh.

Haupt became interested in bridge construction early in his career and patented a bridge truss design in 1839. He began a serious study of stress analysis in 1840, building models to test his theoretical designs. Soon after Squire Whipple had published his work on bridge design in 1847, Haupt completed his own book on the subject, *General Theory of Bridge Construction*, which was published in 1851 and widely used by engineers for more than 30 years.

Haupt left the Pennsylvania in 1856 to take over construction of the Hoosac Tunnel, an effort that finally defeated him. In 1862 he was called to Washington to take on the reconstruction of the Richmond, Fredericksburg & Potomac, wrecked by Confederate forces. After viewing a bridge that Haupt's men had rebuilt in only nine days, President Lincoln commented, "That man Haupt has built a bridge across Potomac Creek, about 400 feet long and nearly 100 feet high, over which loaded trains are running every hour, and, upon my word, gentlemen, there is nothing in it but beanpoles and corn stalks." Later, as a brigadier general, Haupt headed all Union military railroads.

After the war Haupt built more railroads and designed and built the first long-distance petroleum pipeline in the United States, served as general manager of three railroads, including the Northern Pacific, and was president of the Dakota & Great Southern. From 1886 until his death at Jersey City, New Jersey, he was involved in a variety of projects, chief among them an effort to develop compressed-air power for street railway and rapid-transit operation.

—William D. Middleton

REFERENCE

Ward, James A. *That Man Haupt: A Biography of Herman Haupt.* Baton Rouge: Louisiana State Univ. Press, 1973.

Hawaiian Railroads

By 1959, when Hawaii became a state, nearly all the railroads in Hawaii had been abandoned. Earlier, though, Hawaii had a considerable railroad mileage. There were two salient features about railroading in Hawaii. Much of it was the province of plantation railroads that served sugar plantations. A century ago, "industrial transportation" meant either wagons drawn by horses, mules, or oxen or light railroads. The former were limited in speed and capacity; the latter were hardware intensive. Reliable gasoline- and diesel-powered trucks required little more infrastructure than wagons and could carry almost as much as a light railroad, and eventually trucks replaced the plantation railroads. The other notable feature of Hawaiian railroading was its lack of connectivity. With one exception, the common-carrier railroads did not connect with each other, though in large measure that was because Hawaii consisted of several widely separated islands.

Oahu Railway & Land Co.

The largest common-carrier railroad in Hawaii, the Oahu Railway & Land Co. was organized in 1888 by Benjamin F. Dillingham to build a railroad from Honolulu 20 miles west to a sugar plantation at Ewa. The 3-foot-gauge railroad reached Ewa in May 1890, then was gradually extended along the western shore of Oahu to a terminus at Kahuku at the northern tip of the island, 71 miles from Honolulu by rail and 26 miles as the crow flies. In 1906 the railroad built a steeply graded 11-mile branch into the interior of the island, north from Waipahu to a Dole pineapple plantation at Wahiawa and the U.S. Army installation at Schofield Barracks.

Business was good enough in the early years of the twentieth century that the railroad added automatic block signals to the double-track line between Honolulu and Waipahu and undertook a thorough modernization of its rolling stock. By 1927 the company had retired its bonds and was free of debt. Even during the Depression it prospered. Passenger traffic fell off, but the freight business remained good. As World War II began, traffic to army and navy bases increased. The bombing of Pearl

Harbor on December 7, 1941, completely changed the railroad. To handle the increased volume of both freight and passenger traffic, it acquired secondhand cars and locomotives from the Pacific Coast Railway, the Nevada County Narrow Gauge, and the Boston, Revere Beach & Lynn. It extended the branch from Wahiawa to a connection with the main line at Waialua as an alternate to the vulnerable line along the shore. At the end of 1945 the company operated 93 route-miles of railroad.

At war's end passenger traffic dropped by half, and plantation owners gradually turned to trucks to haul their freight. The Oahu Railway & Land Co. abandoned most of its lines at the end of 1947. Some of the company's locomotives returned to the mainland to work in El Salvador. A short stretch of track in Honolulu remained in service until 1971, and the U.S. Navy purchased a portion of the main line and used it to transport munitions between the Lualualei ammunition depot and Pearl Harbor until 1970. A short section near Ewa remains in operation as a tourist line.

Other Common-Carrier Railroads

The Koolau Railway (3-foot gauge) ran from Kahuku (where it connected with the Oahu Railway & Land Co.) along the northeast shore of Oahu to Kahana, 11 miles. It was absorbed by a plantation railway.

The Ahukini Terminal & Railway (30-inch gauge) ran about 12 miles along the east coast of the island of Kauai. It too was absorbed by a plantation railway.

The Kauai Railway (30-inch gauge) ran 19 miles along the south shore of Kauai. The abandonment date is uncertain.

The Hawaii Railway (3-foot gauge) ran 18 miles on the island of Hawaii. It was abandoned in 1945.

The Hawaii Consolidated Railway (standard gauge) had 77 miles of main line along the east coast of the island of Hawaii. It was destroyed by a tidal wave on April 1, 1946.

The Kahului Railroad (3-foot gauge) had 16 miles of main line along the north coast of the island of Maui. It was abandoned in 1966, and its rails were used in the construction of a tourist railroad, the 6-mile Lahaina, Kaanapali & Pacific Railroad.

—George H. Drury

REFERENCE

Best, Gerald M. *Railroads of Hawaii*. San Marino, Calif.: Golden West, 1978.

Heavy-Haul

American railroads largely gave up the European practice of using small four-wheel freight cars at an early date, and by about 1835 a preference for larger eight-wheel or double-truck cars had become standard. The argument for larger cars was simply that they were more efficient. Large cars could haul a given freight tonnage at lower costs than could smaller cars. In a 1900 issue of *Railroad Gazette*, cited by John H. White, Jr., in *The American Railroad Freight Car*, Leonor F. Loree commented that moving a big car cost only marginally more than hauling a standard car. The annual cost of hauling a 40-ton car, claimed Loree, was only $23.10 more than that for hauling the then-standard 30-tonner, which could be recovered in a single revenue trip. Big cars had greater payload and earning capacity and reduced yard space requirements and switching costs. Ever since the beginning of the railroad industry, then, railroaders have been building ever-larger freight cars.

Building larger freight cars was not a simple task. The capacity of the roadbed was governed by the track system and its supporting structure. Heavier and stronger foundations, ties, and rails and stronger bridges were all required before the axle loading of freight-car trucks could be increased. The freight car itself had to be built to handle the greater carrying capacity. The materials of wheels, axles, and trucks had to be improved. Couplers and drawbars had to be strengthened. The carbody itself had to become larger and stronger. All of this went on in an evolutionary process, for even as larger and stronger equipment came into service, the railroads still had to operate it together with their older equipment.

Until about 1870 freight-car size was held to about a 10-ton capacity, but then a rapid change to heavier cars began as rail traffic grew. The size of freight cars grew from less than 30 feet in length to 35 and then 40 feet. Double-truck freight cars grew to 15-ton and 20-ton capacity. By the end of the century a 30-ton-capacity car was typical, and many cars carried as much as 40 tons. The adoption of steel for freight cars beginning near the end of the nineteenth century produced some hopper cars capable of transporting as many as 50 tons in heavy coal or ore service.

The continuing effort to increase the efficiency of freight transport brought even heavier double-truck cars into service, greatly aided by the transition to steel freight equipment in the early twentieth century. By mid-twentieth century a typical modern steel boxcar had a payload capacity of 50 tons, while a coal or ore hopper could transport 70 tons. Some lines operating in extremely heavy coal or ore service used hoppers that carried as much as 90 tons. Typical axle loadings had climbed to anywhere from 20 tons per axle to more than 30 tons per axle. By the beginning of the twenty-first century freight cars had grown still larger. A typical double-truck boxcar was anywhere from 50 to 60 feet in length, 17 feet high, and 10 feet 8 inches wide. Cars with a gross weight of 263,000 pounds for a four-axle freight car—a nominal payload capacity of 100 tons—were in unrestricted interchange service well before the end of the twentieth century, bringing axle loads to almost 33 tons.

The operating benefits of higher freight-car capacity remain the same as always; "increasing the capacity and gross weight of freight cars can improve freight train productivity," wrote Semih Kalay and Carl Martland. These benefits are particularly significant for high-capacity heavy-haul requirements, and intensive research has been conducted on the technology of equipment and track structure to maximize them. "In general, heavier axle-loads will increase track and facility costs, but reduce operating and equipment costs," they continued. "As track costs are much less than operating plus equipment costs, HAL (Heavy Axleload) operations can be worthwhile even if the percentage increase in track costs is far greater than the percentage reduction in operating plus equipment costs." Successfully meeting the demands of heavy-haul rails, ties, and special track work required to support these steadily increasing axle loads has presented a number of difficult challenges for railways.

The Assn. of American Railroads (AAR) has carried out long-term studies of high-axle-load operation since 1986, using both the Facility for Accelerated Service Testing (FAST) on the AAR's Transportation Technology Center, Inc. (TTCI) at Pueblo, Colorado, and on-site locations. Between 1988 and 2004 the FAST program at TTCI operated 1.5 billion gross tons of traffic over the test line, using 100-ton, 110-ton, and 125-ton cars and studying several different combinations of cars with standard truck and track components, improved truck or track designs, and several variations of rail lubrication. The overall objective has been to determine the economic consequences of heavy-haul on equipment and track structures.

Evaluation of track components has included wheel and rail wear and fatigue studies, rail grinding, tests with different types of high-hardness rail steels, studies of concrete and plastic or composite crossties, and evaluation of track special work. Subgrade track improvements have included the widespread use of geotextiles, asphalt, and concrete beneath the ballast at diamond crossings and turnouts to improve track support. The impact of heavy axle loads on such special work as crossing diamonds and turnouts has shown particularly high maintenance costs and short service lives under high levels of traffic, and a number of premium track components are being evaluated. New premium frogs of bainitic steel composition, considerably stronger than even the manganese steel typically used, have been tested. Union Pacific and others have used movable-point frogs to eliminate the impact of high-axle-load cars on turnout frogs. TTCI has also evaluated tests made of ramped flange-bearing frog (FBF) crossing diamonds and turnouts in which the wheel tread is lifted above the running surface while the wheel flange is supported by a flange-bearing section across the flange-way gap, eliminating the high impact of each wheel as it jumps the gap in a conventional frog (Figure 1).

The HAL studies showed higher capital and maintenance costs for the track infrastructure with the heavier axle loads, but these were more than offset by reductions

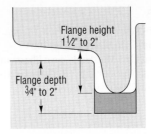

Figure 1. Ramped Flange-Bearing Frog. —Rick Johnson

in the much larger operating costs. The key result of benefits from heavy-load operation was the ability to operate trains with a higher net tonnage per train, with constraints on train length and the ratio of net-to-gross tonnage helping further increase the operating benefits. North American heavy-haul trains now typically operate with distributed motive power in 135-car coal trains.

For North American railroads, heavy-haul experience with improved track performance brought another upward step with the approval of a heavier unrestricted interchange weight for a four-axle car on July 1, 2004. With a new gross rail load standard of 286,000 pounds, nominal carrying capacity has been raised to 110 tons. Built with low-tare-weight aluminum gondolas, some of these cars are now carrying a payload capacity of as much as 122 tons. Maximum freight-car axle loadings in unrestricted interchange have now reached 35.75 tons per axle. Even heavier four-axle cars in a 315,000-pound range, with a 125-ton payload for double-stack containers and heavy-duty flatcars, are now being operated on a controlled interchange basis.

Extensive heavy-haul experience has come, too, from other countries: for example, iron ore and coal lines in Australia, South Africa, Brazil, Colombia, and elsewhere. Particularly useful experience has come from the BHP Iron Ore (formerly Mt. Newman Mining) and the Hamersley Iron Railway in Western Australia, both of which operate heavy-haul services in dedicated ore lines that rank among the heaviest axle loads and most productive railroads anywhere in the world. BHP Iron Ore, which began operation in 1969 with axle loads of 33 tons, has carefully studied the impact on rolling stock and track at high axle loading and has gradually increased its axle loads to 40.7 tons, representing a gross freight-car weight of over 325,000 pounds. Just between 1994 and 1999, for example, BHP was able to halve its operating cost per net ton-mile. Illustrating the enormous capacity of modern heavy-haul operation, BHP Iron Ore set a new world's record for the longest and heaviest freight train in June 2001 on a 171-mile run on the Mt. Newman line. Powered by eight GE AC6000CW locomotives and made up of 682 freight cars, the train carried 90,200 tons of iron ore, with a gross train weight of 110,000 tons.

—William D. Middleton

REFERENCES

Benefits of HAL Research in the Past Decade. Pueblo, Colo.: Transportation Technology Center, 2004.

Kalay, Semih, and Carl Martland. "Five Phases of HAL Research Bring Billion Dollar Savings." *Railway Gazette International* 157, no. 6 (June 2001): 407–411.

Highway Transportation

The first automobiles were developed by inventors in western Europe and North America toward the end of the nineteenth century. As was true of some other landmark inventions, motor vehicles powered by internal combustion engines initially were treated as technological novelties and playthings of the rich—intriguing, but too crude, unreliable, and expensive to have a practical future role. However, public fascination with automobiles, significant technological improvements, and declining prices led to a rapid increase in automobile production and the start of motor-truck production. U.S. passenger-car output jumped from 24,250 vehicles in 1905 to 181,000 in 1910 and 895,930 in 1915. In the same period annual commercial motor vehicle output increased from a minuscule 750 vehicles in 1905 to 6,000 in 1910 and 74,000 in 1915.

Passenger cars were initially driven around cities and towns for status and pleasure; physicians and farmers were also among early buyers. Motor trucks were used for local pickup and delivery of goods. However, the poor condition of streets and roads made intercity motor vehicle travel impractical in most states. In 1904 only 8.7 percent of the nation's 2,300,000 miles of public streets and roads had any kind of surfacing. Responsibility for early road construction and maintenance rested almost entirely with poorly funded local and county authorities.

The competitive possibilities of motor vehicle transportation began to emerge on the eve of America's entry into World War I. In 1916, the same year the nation's railroad network reached its peak of 254,000 miles, Congress passed the Federal-Aid Road Act of 1916, which provided a long-term framework for federal funding to help state and local governments expand and improve intercity highways, secondary roads, and urban connections. Automobile ownership became more affordable as a result of numerous industry improvements, especially Ford Motor Co.'s mass production of its simple, functional Model T on a revolutionary moving assembly line in Highland Park, Michigan.

Total passenger-car registrations in the United States more than trebled from 2.3 million in 1915 to 8.1 million in 1920. Meanwhile, World War I gave a significant boost to trucks, which had the advantage of being a natural by-product of the automobile. More than 130,000 trucks were used to carry supplies and serve as ambulances, and military requirements accelerated improvements in vehicle technology. The war also gave trucks an opportunity to demonstrate their transport potential in the United States. Increasing congestion and the eventual collapse of U.S. rail service in late 1917 led to the use of motor trucks to move less-than-carload (LCL) shipments to and from rail terminals and for short intercity hauls, especially in the East.

During the 1920s all aspects of the motor vehicle industry grew at a remarkable rate. Annual U.S. production of passenger cars doubled from 1.9 million in 1920 to 3.7 million in 1925 and remained surprisingly strong even after the onset of the Great Depression (2.8 million cars in 1930). Annual production of commercial vehicles increased from 321,789 in 1920 to 530,659 in 1925 and 575,364 in 1930. Output continued to grow moderately throughout the Depression.

The manufacture and use of motor vehicles became the backbone of a new consumer-goods-oriented society and economy. Among American industries automobile manufacturing ranked first in value of product, with a wholesale value in 1926 of more than $3 billion. In that same year motorists incurred over $10 billion in operating expenses to travel an estimated 141 billion miles. The motor vehicle industry was the largest consumer of petroleum products, as well as a major user of steel, glass, rubber, and other industrial products.

Because the number, use, and technology of motor vehicles consistently exceeded the quality and capacity of existing roads, all levels of government faced continuing public pressure to expand and improve the nation's network of surfaced streets and roads. Although many governmental units were reluctant to levy sufficient taxes to pay for what was needed, street and highway construction nonetheless became the second-largest category of governmental expenditures. As noted by historian James J. Flink, "In 1929, the last year of the automobility induced boom, the 26.7 million motor vehicles registered in the United States (one for every 4.5 persons) traveled an estimated 198 billion miles, and in that year alone government spent $2.237 billion on roads and collected $849 million in special motor vehicle taxes." More than three-quarters of the nation's total passenger-miles consisted of private automobile travel.

Other ramifications were equally far-reaching. Motor vehicles triggered a suburban real estate boom and a host of new business enterprises serving motor vehicle owners and operators. These included service stations, auto repair shops, and new tourist accommodations. The motorbus industry, which historian Owen D. Gutfreund has called "originally a product of entrepreneurial experimentation in the taxi industry," also developed, in a review of Margaret Walsh's book *Making Connections: The Long Distance Bus Industry in the USA*, rapidly during the 1920s. Literally thousands of small bus companies offered a receptive public convenient service over short intercity routes and to small communities.

Private automobile travel and commercial bus service had a devastating impact on steam railroad and electric

interurban passenger traffic. The number of railroad passengers dropped from 1 billion in 1916 to 700 million in 1930, a 30 percent decline in just 14 years. Some railroads, including the New York Central, Pennsylvania, and Chicago, Burlington & Quincy, responded to the new competition by launching their own bus systems or establishing partnerships with bus companies. Railroad bus operations grew to some 1,000 buses serving over 10,000 route-miles. By the end of the decade motorbus transportation "had achieved respectable popularity," generating approximately 7 billion passenger-miles annually, or 18 percent of total commercial intercity passenger traffic. The bus industry also began to consolidate into larger firms offering service over longer distances. For example, when Greyhound Corp., the future leader of the intercity bus industry, was created by the consolidation of several small firms in 1929, it triggered similar consolidation among some of its competitors.

From its wartime nucleus intercity trucking developed rapidly during the 1920s into an important factor in both the transport market and the economy as a whole. Several circumstances contributed to this growth. Motor trucks possessed an inherent competitive advantage in their ability to provide fast, direct store-door pickup and delivery of small and medium-sized shipments. Technological developments such as more powerful engines, better transmissions, and pneumatic tires led to larger, more reliable vehicles, and federally aided highway construction during the decade also facilitated increases in truck size, speed, and average length of haul.

The number of trucks in service increased from 1,006,000 in 1920 to 3,481,000 in 1930, and total intercity ton-miles carried by for-hire and private trucks jumped from 4.5 billion in 1920 to 19.7 billion in 1929. However, the structure and character of the trucking industry changed relatively little. The trucking industry consisted of thousands of small firms characterized by financial instability and a high rate of turnover. Initially, railroad industry managers did not show as much concern about trucking competition as about bus competition. Many managers were slow to recognize that truck transport was more competitive with rail service than complementary. Other railroad executives feared regulatory responses if the railroads entered the trucking business. In any event, railroad management remained relatively passive while trucking grew apace.

During the Great Depression of the 1930s motor vehicle transportation suffered less than most other sectors of the economy. For example, production of autos, buses, and trucks declined sharply during the decade, but motor vehicle usage continued to grow, largely at the expense of the railroads. Autos generated 154.3 billion intercity passenger-miles in 1929, 178.3 billion in 1935, and an impressive 292.7 billion in 1940. By 1940 the automobile was the dominant mode of both local and intercity passenger transport, with far-reaching consequences for industrial and commercial activity, land use, housing, and auto-related service industries.

Intercity passenger traffic data for bus and rail transport underscored the dominance of the private automobile. Intercity bus traffic increased from 6.7 billion passenger-miles in 1929 to 9.4 billion in 1935 and 10.2 billion in 1940. Meanwhile, intercity rail passenger-miles plummeted from 33.9 billion in 1929 to 13.3 billion in 1932 and recovered only moderately to 24.8 billion in 1940. The market share of intercity passenger traffic held by private autos increased from 77.7 percent in 1929 to 89.0 percent in 1940, while the railroad industry's share declined from 17.1 to 7.5 percent. Bus transport remained relatively unchanged at 3.1 percent, and the emerging airline industry in 1940 had a barely measurable 0.4 percent market share.

Intercity truck transportation grew even more rapidly than automobile traffic. Ton-miles generated by private and for-hire carriers trebled from 19.7 billion in 1929 to 62.0 billion in 1940. In the same time period waterway and pipeline traffic also increased, and Great Lakes traffic recovered to its pre-Depression level. Meanwhile, railroad ton-miles declined precipitously from 454.8 billion in 1929 to 237.6 billion in 1932 and did not fully recover until 1941, when national defense priorities began to drive the economy. Between 1929 and 1940 trucks increased their market share of overall intercity traffic from 3.3 to 10.0 percent. On a revenue basis trucks performed even better because they typically handled higher-value shipments.

The rapid growth of trucking during the Great Depres-sion was accompanied by increased financial instability. Entry into the industry was wide open and attracted individuals eager to earn a living as self-employed truckers. Unstable freight rates and dubious competitive practices became a serious problem for shippers, established trucking companies, and the railroad industry. To bring a measure of stability to interstate trucking, Congress passed the Motor Carrier Act of 1935.

This statute, which officially became Part II of the Interstate Commerce Act, provided the basic framework for federal regulation of trucking until 1980. The Interstate Commerce Commission typically certified the existing operations of common and contract carriers under the "grandfather clause" but made it difficult for carriers to expand their operations and for new companies to enter the industry. Competition also was muted by the ICC's power to control minimum rates. Private carriage, agricultural cooperatives, and shipments of agricultural products were exempted from federal regulation, and individual states remained free to regulate traffic within their borders. Because railroad freight rates were relatively inflexible and a matter of public information, trucking companies shaped their marketing plans and freight rates to capture as much high-value traffic from the railroads as possible. This strategy proved enormously successful in the postwar period.

U.S. entry into World War II brought abrupt changes to all forms of motor vehicle transportation. New highway construction came to a standstill except for roads to defense facilities. Production of new automobiles, buses, and commercial trucks dropped almost to zero, and automobile usage and private trucking activity declined sharply because of severe shortages of tires, gasoline, and replacement parts. Intercity buses and common-carrier trucking, both essential players in the wartime economy, struggled to maintain existing operations in the face of these same shortages. Total highway carriage (private and for-hire) dropped from 81.3 billion ton-miles in 1941 to 60 billion in 1942 and did not recover to its prewar level until 1946.

Wartime traffic growth fell principally on the railroad industry, which overcame a decade of severe financial distress to successfully handle unprecedented volumes of passenger and freight traffic. Intercity railroad passenger-miles quadrupled from 24.8 billion in 1940 to 97.7 billion in 1944. Moreover, the industry's market share kept pace, skyrocketing from 7.5 percent of total intercity passenger-miles in 1940 to 34.8 percent in 1944. Railroad freight traffic jumped a remarkable 55 percent from 481.7 billion ton-miles in 1941 to 746.9 billion in 1944. The industry's market share peaked at 71.3 percent in 1943.

Despite the railroad industry's heroic performance during World War II in moving passengers, freight, and even petroleum shipments previously carried by coastal tankers, postwar public policy and the dynamics of the transport marketplace strongly favored the railroads' competitors. Once the transition was completed from wartime production and civilian shortages to a peacetime economy, automobile and truck output resumed and reasserted the dominant role of cars and trucks in local and intercity travel. Total U.S. motor vehicle registrations, which had declined slightly during the war, trebled between 1945 and 1965 and continued to grow rapidly in subsequent decades. Automobile registrations increased from 25.8 million in 1945 to 75.3 million in 1965 and reached 132.4 million in 1999. Truck registrations more than kept pace, growing from 5.1 million in 1945 to 14.8 million in 1965, then to 83.1 million in 1999. Bus registrations nearly doubled from 162,125 to 314,284 in 1965 and reached 729,000 in 1999. More than half the buses registered were publicly owned.

The convenience and affordable cost of private automobiles, major highway improvements (especially the interstate and defense highway system), and the rapid growth of airlines as a significant competitor for long-distance passenger travel devastated the railroad passenger business (see Table 1). Between 1945 and 1965 intercity passenger-miles by private automobile almost quadrupled from 220.3 to 817.7 billion. Airline traffic soared from 4.3 billion to 58.1 billion passenger-miles. Intercity bus traffic dropped slightly from 27.4 to 23.8 billion passenger-miles. However, railroad passenger traffic dropped 81 percent from 93.5 billion passenger-miles in 1945 to 17.6 billion in 1965. In 1965 private automobiles held 89.2 percent of the market,

Table 1. Intercity Passenger Market Share by Mode (Percentage of Passenger-Miles)

	1940	1950	1960	1970	1980	1990	2000
Automobile	89.0	87.0	90.4	86.9	82.4	78.6	76.6
Bus	3.1	4.5	2.5	2.1	1.8	1.2	1.5
Rail	7.5	6.5	2.8	0.9	0.8	0.7	0.6
Air	0.4	2.0	4.4	10.0	14.9	19.4	21.3

Note: Totals may not equal 100 due to rounding.

Sources: U.S. Census Bureau, *Statistical Abstract of the United States: 2004–2005* (Washington, D.C.: U.S. Government Printing Office, 2005); *Motor Vehicle Facts & Figures, 1996* (Detroit: American Automobile Manufacturers Assn., 1996); Donald V. Harper, *Transportation in America: Users, Carriers, Government* (Englewood Cliffs, N.J.: Prentice-Hall, 1978).

Table 2. Intercity Freight Market Share by Mode (Percentage of Freight Ton-Miles)

	1940	1950	1960	1970	1980	1990	2000
Motor trucks	10.0	16.3	21.7	21.3	22.3	25.4	28.7
Railroads	61.3	56.1	44.1	39.8	37.5	37.7	40.9
Inland waterways	19.1	15.4	16.7	16.5	16.4	16.4	13.5
Pipelines	9.5	12.1	17.4	22.3	23.6	20.2	16.5
Domestic airlines		0.03	0.07	0.17	0.20	0.34	0.42

Note: Totals may not equal 100 due to rounding.

Sources: U.S. Census Bureau, *Statistical Abstract of the United States: 2004–2005* (Washington, D.C.: U.S. Government Printing Office, 2005); *Motor Vehicle Facts & Figures, 1996* (Detroit: American Automobile Manufacturers Assn., 1996); Donald V. Harper, *Transportation in America: Users, Carriers, Government* (Englewood Cliffs, N.J.: Prentice-Hall, 1978).

airlines 6.3 percent, buses 2.6 percent, and railroads only 1.9 percent. Despite some regulatory relief provided by the Transportation Act of 1958, the pre-Amtrak collapse of intercity railroad passenger service was essentially complete.

A similar story occurred in freight transportation (Table 2). The inherent service advantages of trucking, the ICC's refusal to let railroads use aggressive pricing as a competitive tool, and the new opportunities for efficient long-distance trucking provided by the interstate and defense highway system gave trucking companies an overwhelming competitive advantage over the railroads. Organized labor, particularly the International Brotherhood of Teamsters (IBT), which had a better relationship with the motor carriers than railroads had with the railroad brotherhoods, also proved more willing to accommodate technological change than railroad industry unions. Total intercity trucking (private and for-hire) more than quintupled from 1945 to 1965, from 66.9 to 370.8 billion ton-miles.

The interdependence of motor vehicle transportation and the American economy became more pronounced with each postwar decade. Motor vehicles were the most important product category in American manufacturing, and motor fuel was the largest market segment in the petroleum industry. The trend toward suburban housing, which began in the 1920s, resumed in the postwar period as residential developments sprang up ever farther from traditional city centers. Moreover, as the nation's economy gradually shifted from agriculture and heavy industry toward lighter manufacturing, distribution activities, and services, new manufacturing plants, distribution facilities, retail shopping malls, and office buildings sprang up along high-density highways (urban expressways and beltways), most of which were funded by the interstate highway program. Many manufacturing plants and distribution facilities were built without rail access, and the dispersed nature of suburban housing, jobs, and travel patterns provided little opportunity for traditional mass-transit services.

By the 1970s the economic dominance of automobile and truck transportation was fully established. In 1975 total expenditures (capital and operating expenses) for the movement of passengers in the United States were estimated to be $177.0 billion. Of this total, private automobile transportation accounted for $149.6 billion (84.5 percent), commercial and private air transportation $16.3 billion (9.2 percent), buses $1.0 billion (0.6 percent), and railroads only $340 million (0.2 percent). Total expenditures for the movement of property were estimated to be $140.6 billion. Of this total, highway carriage accounted for $109.7 billion (78.0 percent), railroads $16.6 billion (11.8 percent), water transport $8.1 billion (5.8 percent), and oil pipelines $2.2 billion (1.6 percent).

Federal deregulation of railroads and motor carriers in 1980 increased competition within each mode and increased freedom to compete between modes, but did not fundamentally change the scale or character of truck-rail competition. The inherent advantages of trucking—fast, direct, flexible, reliable service at reasonable cost—were not materially enhanced or diminished by deregulation. However, price competition within the trucking industry intensified. This resulted in better rates for shippers but numerous carrier bankruptcies and some industry consolidation.

Because railroad service could not match the flexibility and reliability of trucking, railroad executives increasingly focused on the industry's inherent advantage: low-cost transportation based on economies of scale. The severe financial distress experienced by railroads in the 1960s and 1970s resulted in widespread corporate restructuring and industry consolidation. The number of Class 1 railroads shrank from 71 in 1971 to 28 in 1984 and subsequently to 9 in 1997. Surviving carriers sought to achieve reasonable financial returns by eliminating excess capacity and raising traffic density on remaining lines. Managers also sought to improve returns by focusing on large, steady, long-distance carload shipments of commodities such as coal, chemicals, farm products, motor vehicles and equipment, food products, minerals, and lumber. Important segments of this traffic were not particularly truck competitive because of weight and distance considerations and the hazardous nature of many chemicals.

After deregulation in 1980 rail traffic increasingly moved under contract rates negotiated between railroads and large shippers. Contract rates helped provide the volume sought by rail carriers, but profit margins were typically thin and did not dramatically improve industry finances. A major case in point was intermodal traffic (trailers and containers carried on flatcars). Rail movement of trailers and containers increased rapidly during the postwar period, reaching 1.7 million units in 1965 and 8.7 million units in 1997. However, the investment required for this service, low contract rates, and competitive pressure from long-distance truckers made intermodal service only marginally profitable for most rail carriers despite the high volume of traffic.

The railroad industry's share of intercity freight ton-miles, which peaked at 71.3 percent in 1943, declined steadily to a postwar low of 36.0 percent in 1979. Deregulation enabled the railroads to slightly improve their market share to around 40 percent in the 1990s, but most of the improvement was due to greater average length of haul, not more tonnage. The railroad industry's average length of haul increased from 503 miles in 1965 to 851 miles in 1997, a striking 69 percent. However, the trucking industry did far better in terms of tonnage and revenue gains. For example, in 1999 outlays for intercity trucking ($304.6 billion) were more than eight times greater than railroad industry revenues ($35.9 billion).

—Richard W. Barsness

REFERENCES

Filgas, James F. *Yellow in Motion: A History of Yellow Freight System, Inc.* 2nd ed. Bloomington: Indiana Univ. Graduate School of Business, 1971.

Flink, James J. *The Car Culture.* Cambridge, Mass.: MIT Press, 1975.

Harper, Donald V. *Transportation in America: Users, Carriers, Government.* Englewood Cliffs, N.J.: Prentice-Hall, 1978.

Motor Vehicle Facts & Figures, 1996. Detroit, Mich.: American Automobile Manufacturers Assn., 1996.

Roberts, Merrill J. "The Motor Transportation Revolution." *Business History Review* 30, no. 1 (Mar. 1956): 57–95.

U.S. Census Bureau. *Statistical Abstract of the United States: 2001.* Washington, D.C.: U.S. Government Printing Office, 2001.

Walsh, Margaret. *Making Connections: The Long-Distance Bus Industry in the USA.* Aldershot, U.K.: Ashgate, 2000.

Hill, James J. (1838–1916)

James Jerome Hill was born in Rockwood, Eramosa Township, Ontario, on September 16, 1838, and died of peritonitis in St. Paul, Minnesota, on May 29, 1916. Through his founding and leadership of the Great Northern Railway the Empire Builder, as he came to be known, linked the Great Lakes and upper Mississippi River with the Pacific Ocean at Seattle. By 1893 Hill dominated rail transportation and played a significant role in the economic development of the American Northwest during the late nineteenth and early twentieth centuries.

Reared on a farm, James Hill was 14 when his father died, and he was forced to quit school for work in a coun-

James J. Hill, 1902. —Pach Photographer, James J. Hill Library (Neg. JH120)

try store. As a teenager, he left Canada for the United States, where he took up residence in St. Paul, Minnesota Territory. There he soon became an integral figure in the transformation of Minnesota from a raw frontier to an economically diverse region. Active in the steamboating trade on the Mississippi and Red rivers, he expanded into warehousing and the fuel business, and he later invested heavily in Minnesota's Iron Range and the mining industries of Iowa, Montana, and Washington State. During that period the Methodist Hill married Mary Theresa Mehegan, a Roman Catholic, and they had ten children, of whom nine survived to adulthood.

Approaching middle age, he entered the railroad business, joining in 1877 with Norman Kittson, John S. Kennedy, and Canadians Donald Smith and George Stephen to complete the St. Paul & Pacific from Minneapolis–St. Paul to the Canadian border via the Red River. Subsequently he built west, finally completing what became the Great Northern Railway from St. Paul to Seattle, Washington, in 1893. Alone among U.S. transcontinental lines, the Great Northern remained solvent and avoided bankruptcy in the hard times of the 1890s. Allying himself with the nation's preeminent investment banking firm, the House of Morgan, Hill obtained control of the Northern Pacific and Chicago, Burlington & Quincy railroads. He became one of the leading figures in the rise of big business in America.

After a dramatic conflict with Edward H. Harriman and William Rockefeller, Hill presided over the Northern Securities holding company (1901–1904), the largest railroad organization of its day, which included the Hill Lines that he and Morgan controlled. Although the U.S. Supreme Court ordered the dissolution of Northern Securities under provisions of the Sherman Antitrust Act, the same railroads merged again in 1970 to become the Burlington Northern (now Burlington Northern Santa Fe) system.

After 1900 Hill involved himself in a wide variety of other pursuits. He delivered countless public addresses on a wide range of topics, including international trade, agronomy, finance, and the environment. The Empire Builder also invested heavily in maritime shipping, first on the Great Lakes and, later, in commerce with Asia.

From the 1880s until his death he was active in political affairs. A low-tariff Democrat in presidential politics, Hill switched parties in 1896 when William Jennings Bryan captured that party's nomination. Supporting William McKinley, he played a pivotal role in raising funds for the Republican nominee's successful campaign.

At the same time Hill ran model experimental farms in Minnesota, particularly at his North Oaks estate north of St. Paul, to develop superior livestock and crop yields for settlers locating near his railroads. His philanthropic interests also were wide ranging and included significant support to educational, religious, and charitable organizations throughout Minnesota, the Northwest, and the nation. In his adopted hometown he constructed the St. Paul Seminary, which he dedicated to his wife, and the James J. Hill Reference Library, which houses his personal papers, to encourage individual self-improvement. When he died suddenly in 1916, James J. Hill was still at work, penning his thoughts on the wisdom of the nation's military preparedness in light of the raging World War I.

—W. Thomas White

REFERENCES

Hidy, Ralph W., Muriel E. Hidy, Roy V. Scott, and Don L. Hofsommer. *The Great Northern Railway: A History.* Boston: Harvard Business School Press, 1988.

Hill, James J. *Highways of Progress.* New York: Doubleday, Page, 1910.

Holbrook, Stewart. *James J. Hill: A Great Life in Brief.* New York: Knopf, 1955.

Malone, Michael P. *James J. Hill: Empire Builder of the Northwest.* Norman: Univ. of Oklahoma Press, 1996.

Martin, Albro. *James J. Hill and the Opening of the Northwest.* New York: Oxford Univ. Press, 1976; Repr. with introduction by W. Thomas White. St. Paul: Minnesota Historical Society Press, 1991.

Pyle, Joseph Gilpin. *The Life of James J. Hill.* 2 vols. Garden City, N.Y.: Doubleday, 1916–1917.

Strom, Claire. *Profiting from the Plains: The Great Northern Railway and Corporate Development of the American West.* Seattle: Univ. of Washington Press, 2003.

Veenendal, Augustus J., Jr. *The Saint Paul & Pacific Railroad: An Empire in the Making, 1862–1879.* DeKalb: Northern Illinois Univ. Press, 1999.

Hoboes

In the public mind hoboes are often connected with railroads because in the past these knights of the road traveled by freight train. Over more than a century the hobo is defined primarily as an itinerant worker possessed of a degree of wanderlust.

The hobo phenomenon was first noted in the depression that followed the Civil War and, most particularly, the depression and business and employment calamity of the 1870s. Many Civil War veterans, detached from a normal home life, took to riding freight trains in the hope of finding work, usually on farms. Many of these itinerants carried hoes as a tool for farming and evidence of a willingness to work; they were called, so the story goes, "hoe boys."

The railroads were not happy to have these freeloaders on board the freight trains, and they were often literally kicked off by railroad police or train crews. Some hoboes were not merely honest, unemployed men; the bad apples stole freight and attacked and robbed train crews. Legend has it that many hoboes rode on grain doors laid across the truss rods of wooden freight cars; in reality the usual place to ride was an empty boxcar or other empty equip-

In a June 1899 article for the *Century Illustrated Monthly Magazine*, artist Jay Hambige depicted the life of the railroad hobo. He is seen here (*right*) riding in the "side-door Pullman" of an empty boxcar, "collecting a fare" from a freight-car brakeman (*bottom left*), and climbing on a boxcar (*bottom right*). —Middleton Collection

Railroad men usually had a less tolerant view of hoboes. This drawing by A. B. Frost in *The American Railway* clearly presents the tramps as a danger. —Middleton Collection

ment. In riding the rods amid the dust and clamor of a speeding freight train, the odds were good of slipping off and being seriously injured or killed.

The second big explosion of the hobo tribe took place in the Great Depression of the 1930s. Again, the large majority were men of all ages looking for work in desperate times. The wandering for work in the Great Depression came to an end with the military draft and full employment of World War II. In the 1950s the mode of travel began to change because hitchhiking often became a better way to travel expeditiously across the country, especially when railroads cut back on the number of trains and branch and other lines were abandoned. Some hoboes traveled because they wanted the freedom of rootlessness, and in recent times that wish may be best fulfilled by purchase of an old car that can also serve as an abode.

Many hoboes had a talent or skill, often in the construction trades. This meant following the construction season. No hobo in his right mind would head to Montana on the Great Northern in December; winter was the time to head south, where buildings were under construction or there were crops to pick.

During the heyday of the hobo, a hobo camp or hobo jungle was an adjunct of most railroad yards of significant size. Here the hoboes would gather in a sheltered spot in a grove of trees or a gulch, build a fire to keep warm and cook food, and tell stories and get tips on where work might be found. Older hoboes instructed younger ones on how to board and deboard a train safely or where to stand by the road to hitch a ride in a car or truck.

For persons stuck in a routine existence, a certain romance about the hobo life grew up, and the writings and songs of hoboes were sought after. Screenwriter and director Preston Sturges portrayed a view of hobo life in the movie classic *Sullivan's Travels*. A hobo convention is held annually in Britt, Iowa, on the second weekend in August, and a hobo museum is located there.

Hobo graffiti chalked on railroad cars included drawings, verse, and writings. One of the most popular images is that of Bozo Texino, whose first appearance was supposedly in San Antonio in the 1930s. This one was photographed on a tank car at Carbondale, Illinois, in 1973. —*Trains* Magazine Collection

A distinction must be made between hoboes, tramps, and bums. A hobo travels and works; a tramp travels and begs; a bum drinks or takes drugs and may or may not travel. Real hoboes usually want nothing to do with tramps and bums.

The train-riding hobo era may be at an end. With the increased security concerns around railroads in the twenty-first century, boarding a train in a yard or nearby, or life in a hobo jungle adjacent to the railroad, may become virtually impossible. But, for a time, the hobo stories will persist.

—George M. Smerk

REFERENCES

Allsop, Kenneth. *Hard Travelin': The Hobo and His History.* New York: New American Library, 1967.
Britt Hobo Museum, 51 Main Avenue South, Britt, Iowa 50423, 641-843-9104. www.hobo.com
Williams, Cliff. *One More Train to Ride: The Underground World of Modern American Hoboes.* Bloomington: Indiana Univ. Press, 2003.

1891. By all accounts a modest man, Hobson declined a knighthood offered by Queen Victoria at the completion of this great work.

By 1896 Hobson had become the Grand Trunk's chief engineer, and the notable works under his charge included the replacement of John Roebling's suspension bridge over the Niagara River with a steel arch span in 1897 and the rebuilding of Robert Stephenson's Victoria Bridge at Montreal during 1897–1898. Both projects were accomplished without interruption to traffic. He retired in 1907 but remained a consulting engineer to the Grand Trunk for the rest of his life. He died at his home in Hamilton, Ontario, in 1917 at the age of 83.

—William D. Middleton

REFERENCE

Legget, Robert F. "Joseph Hobson—Another Name to Add to Our List of Engineering Greats." *Canadian Consulting Engineer* 24, no. 3 (Mar. 1982): 41–42.

Hobson, Joseph (1834–1917)

One of Canada's most accomplished railroad engineers, Joseph Hobson rose to eminence without benefit of a formal engineering education. He was born near Guelph, Ontario, in 1834 and attended school there. Before he was 18, Hobson was apprenticed to John Tully, a Toronto civil engineer and land surveyor. He passed the examination for land surveyor in 1855 and began a survey and civil engineering practice, serving most of the next ten years as a county engineer. Hobson performed a number of railroad surveys in Canada and the United States and during 1858–1860 was engaged as an assistant engineer in the construction of the Grand Trunk Railway in Ontario.

In 1869 Hobson was appointed an assistant engineer for the Great Western Railway and began a career in railroad engineering that was to last the remainder of his life. In 1870 he was appointed the Great Western's resident engineer for construction of the great International Bridge across the Niagara River at Buffalo, and by 1875 he had become the railroad's chief engineer. He became chief engineer of the Grand Trunk's Western Division when the two railroads were amalgamated in 1882.

Hobson's arrival at Grand Trunk ultimately led to the greatest achievement of his career: drilling the Grand Trunk's great tunnel under the St. Clair River between Sarnia, Ontario, and Port Huron, Michigan. Despite the lack of any previous tunneling experience, Hobson successfully employed the pneumatic shield method to complete the world's first large-scale underwater tunnel in

Hood, William (1846–1926)

Like many ambitious young men of his generation, William Hood headed west to build the first transcontinental railroad. Born in Concord, New Hampshire, in 1846, Hood served as a private with the 46th Massachusetts Volunteers during the Civil War before entering Dartmouth College. Newly graduated with a science degree in 1867, he went to California to begin a distinguished 54-year engineering career with the Central Pacific and Southern Pacific railroads.

Hood first worked as a rodman during construction of the Summit–Donner Lake section of the Central Pacific's Donner Pass crossing of the Sierra Nevada. Within only a year he was made an assistant engineer and spent the next two years in construction of the CP eastward across Nevada and Utah to its junction with the Union Pacific at Promontory Point. Over the next several decades Hood worked almost everywhere on the expanding CP and SP system. He helped build CP lines north from Sacramento toward Oregon and south into the San Joaquin Valley.

One of the greatest achievements of Hood's career came in 1875, when he located the SP's line across the Tehachapi Mountains to link the San Joaquin Valley with Mojave and Los Angeles. In an airline distance of only 16 miles the line had to climb some 2,737 feet through rugged and inhospitable terrain. Hood did it with an innovative alignment that held the ruling grade to 2.2 percent. He achieved this with sweeping curves, no less than 17 tunnels, and the celebrated Tehachapi Loop, where the line "made distance" to maintain the ruling grade by curving around a conical hill in a great 360-degree loop to cross over itself. Hood went on to help build SP's lines through the Mojave and Colorado deserts and the Sunset Route across Arizona and New Mexico to El Paso. Hood became chief engineer for the CP in 1883 and was then chief engineer for SP's Pacific system during a 15-year period that saw the SP complete its Shasta Route into Oregon.

In 1900 Hood became chief engineer for the entire Southern Pacific Co., and over the next decade he directed completion of the Coast Line between Los Angeles and San Francisco. He also led a massive improvement program under E. H. Harriman that included such notable projects as the reconstruction and double-tracking of CP's line over Donner Pass, construction of the 32-mile Lucin Cutoff across the Great Salt Lake, and the building of the San Diego & Arizona. Hood retired from SP in 1921 and died in San Francisco in 1926.

—William D. Middleton

REFERENCE

National Cyclopaedia of American Biography.

Mark Hopkins. —Library of Congress (Neg. LC-USZ62-090102)

Hopkins, Mark (1813–1878)

Mark Hopkins, one of six children, was born in 1813 in Henderson, New York. As a child he lived for about six years in St. Clair, Michigan, where his father ran a store. When his father died, he left school to run the store. Later he held a variety of other jobs and was working as a bookkeeper in New York City when word came of the Gold Rush. He quit, made the difficult journey by ship to California, and ended up in Sacramento, where he first went into the wholesale grocery business and, six years later, into partnership with Collis Huntington in his hardware store. Here he tended to the bookkeeping and accounting side of things and with his analytical mind and deliberate manner quickly made himself indispensable. Huntington once said, "[Hopkins] had general supervision of the books and the papers, contracts, etc. When he said they were right, I never cared to look at them."

Originally a Know-Nothing, Hopkins soon switched to California's burgeoning Republican Party. He, his partner, and fellow merchants Leland Stanford and Charles Crocker (along with Crocker's lawyer brother Edwin) were devout Republicans and abolitionists. It was in the Huntington, Hopkins & Co. store that the idea of building a railroad was first discussed in 1860. Engineer Theodore Judah had come to Huntington's notice in 1860 when he averred that Congress would soon pass legislation to build a transcontinental railroad (*see* Pacific Railroad). Huntington saw that such a venture could be immensely profitable to those who got in on the ground floor. Hopkins was cautious, but he too saw the possibilities. Along with Crocker, Huntington, and Stanford, he put $1,500 into the new company and assumed a place on its board. In June 1861, when the directors gathered to select their officers, the bookkeeper was, of course, named treasurer. He kept that post until his death.

A virtual vegetarian, Hopkins disliked physical labor. He was also exceedingly frugal, picking through the company's wastebaskets in hopes of rescuing still-serviceable office supplies. A cautious businessman, he was "wise enough to overcome that weakness by allying himself with speculators," as Oscar Lewis has observed.

Hopkins ran the Central Pacific's finances much as he had the store, except that the stakes were higher. He kept out of the limelight but was ever attentive to the financial ramifications of the company's shenanigans. In 1872, when the Central Pacific found itself in hot water and a congressional committee asked to see the record books, Huntington claimed that Hopkins had unfortunately burned them to save space.

Hopkins was the best liked of the Big Four. It was said that one would cross the street to shake Hopkins's hand and to avoid the other three. Although he became very wealthy, he continued to live frugally. He and his wife rented a cottage in San Francisco until she insisted that they build a larger home—a showplace on Nob Hill—which he did not live to see completed. In his later years he suffered from poor health, and in 1878 he died in his sleep in Arizona while aboard a railroad car. The oldest of the Big Four and the first to die, he left an estate estimated at $19 million.

—Roberta L. Diehl

REFERENCES

Bain, David Haward. *Empire Express: Building the First Transcontinental Railroad.* New York: Viking, 1999.

Lewis, Oscar. *The Big Four.* New York: Alfred A. Knopf, 1938.

Public Broadcasting Service, "American Experience," *The Transcontinental Railroad*, People & Events: Mark Hopkins (1813–1878), www.pbs.org/wgbh/amex/tcrr/peopleevents/p_hopkins.html

REFERENCE

Dictionary of American Biography.

Howe, William (1803–1852)

Although he had an unlikely background for a bridge engineer, William Howe developed what was by far the most successful design for a wooden truss bridge. An uncle of sewing-machine inventor Elias Howe, William Howe was born in Spencer, Massachusetts, in 1803 and was working as a farmer when in 1838 he was commissioned by the Western Railroad of Massachusetts to construct a bridge at Warren, Massachusetts. Howe designed and later patented a truss for this bridge that employed top and bottom chords and diagonal members, each extending across two panels, framed of heavy timber. The vertical-tension members were made of wrought iron. In 1840 Howe joined with his brother-in-law, railroad builder Amasa Stone, Jr., to build the Western Railroad's seven-span bridge across the Connecticut River at Springfield, using a modified form of the Howe truss. Stone and others later further modified the design into a simplified form with a single diagonal across each panel, for which stresses could be calculated mathematically. In 1842 Howe designed and built a truss-design trainshed roof for the Boston & Worcester Railroad's station at Boston; soon the Howe truss saw wide use in roof construction, as well as in bridges.

Howe and Amasa Stone worked together for a time, and Stone later acquired Howe's patent rights and formed a company to build Howe truss bridges of both timber and iron. Howe himself became wealthy selling the rights to his patent and continued to build bridges and roof trusses until his death in Springfield in 1852.

Quickly and cheaply built, Howe trusses were widely used in both North America and Europe during the nineteenth century. Among notable Howe truss spans were the Attica & Hornellsville's (later Erie) bridge across the Genesee River at Portage, New York, perhaps the greatest timber bridge ever built, and the first bridge across the Mississippi River, completed by the Rock Island in 1856, which employed modified Howe trusses, each spanning 250 feet. At the very end of the wooden bridge era, in 1886, the Philadelphia, Wilmington & Baltimore completed a great timber truss bridge across the Susquehanna River at Havre de Grace, Maryland. The huge span incorporated a dozen Howe truss main spans, each 250 feet long. Each of these heavy trusses was reinforced by a pair of arch ribs, one on each side, a variation of the basic Howe design similar to one patented by Howe in 1846.

—William D. Middleton

Hungerford, Edward (1875–1948)

Railroading's preeminent twentieth-century dramatist, Edward Hungerford was born in Dexter, New York, in 1875. After attending Syracuse University he went to work as a reporter for the *New York Sun.* But the railroad bug soon bit, and in 1905 he created for the Erie what he claimed to be the first railroad employee magazine. Afterward he seldom left railroads for long, sometimes working as a full-time employee, more often as a freelance writer and producer of public relations events.

Hungerford's early résumé included stints as a publicity representative for the Brooklyn Rapid Transit Co. and advertising manager for Wells Fargo & Co. Mostly, however, he churned out books and magazine articles, most of them about railroading: *The Modern Railroad* (1911), *Our Railroads Tomorrow* (1922), *The Story of the Rome, Watertown & Odgensburgh Railroad* (also 1922), *The Personality of American Cities,* and articles for *Collier's* and the *Saturday Evening Post*, as well as three long-forgotten novels.

But his real genius appeared when Baltimore & Ohio president Daniel Willard hired him in 1925 to plan, produce, and publicize the events celebrating the railroad's centenary in 1927. The result was the legendary Fair of the Iron Horse, built around something new in railroad showmanship—a full-scale historical pageant in which the principal actors were working locomotives of all ages. It was a spectacular success, and similar productions followed during the 1930s to help publicize the railroads and brighten Depression gloom: *Wings of a Century* at the 1933–1934 Chicago Century of Progress Exposition, *Century on Parade* at Rochester, New York, in 1934, *Parade of the Years* at Cleveland's 1936 Great Lakes Exposition, and, most memorable of all, *Railroads on Parade* at the 1939–1940 New York World's Fair.

More books appeared too, primarily company-sponsored histories that reflected Hungerford's flair for drama: the monumental two-volume *Story of the Baltimore & Ohio Railroad* (1928), *Daniel Willard Rides the Line* (1938), *Men and Iron,* a New York Central history (also 1938), *Locomotives on Parade* (1940), and *Men of Erie* (1946).

Hungerford's final effort was still another grand pageant, *Wheels-a-Rolling* for the 1948–1950 Chicago Railroad Fair. The show opened in July, but Edward Hungerford never saw it. He died on July 29, 1948, at age 72.

—Herbert H. Harwood, Jr.

REFERENCES

Kalmbach, A. C. "Edward Hungerford Dies in New York." *Trains* 8, no. 1 (Sept. 1948): 4.

Who's Who in Railroading. 1940 ed. New York: Simmons-Boardman, 1940.

Huntington, Collis Potter (1821–1900)

Collis Huntington was born in Harwinton, Connecticut, in 1821, the fifth of nine children of Elizabeth Vincent and William Huntington. His formal schooling ended at 14 when he hired himself out to a neighbor for $7 a month and board. After a brief residence in New York City he worked for six years as a peddler in the South, accumulating sufficient money to open a general store with his brother Solon in Oneonta, New York, in 1842. When the Gold Rush began, Collis made his way to Sacramento, where he soon went into business selling mining supplies. He acquired a partner, Mark Hopkins, and the business evolved into a hardware store well known as Huntington, Hopkins & Co.

In 1860 engineer Theodore Judah was drumming up support among Sacramento businessmen for a proposed route across the Sierra Nevada that would make feasible the long-discussed transcontinental railroad (*see* PACIFIC RAILROAD). Others had made similar proposals, but in addition to a viable route Judah had the beginnings of a company structure and some idea of the costs involved. Huntington attended one of Judah's presentations and, smelling myriad opportunities for profit in the scheme, recruited partner Hopkins, fellow merchant Charles Crocker, and Leland Stanford, soon to be governor of California, to help finance Judah's attempts to obtain government support for the project. Both Judah and, later, Huntington himself traveled to Washington, D.C. The Civil War had broken out, which complicated matters, but eventually Congress chartered the railroad in 1862, authorizing construction from east to west (by the Union Pacific) and from west to east (by the Sacramento group's Central Pacific). Judah barely lived to see his project started. He died in 1863 of yellow fever, which left Huntington essentially in control (although Stanford had been named president of the company because of his political connections).

One group, Huntington's Central Pacific, built eastward from Sacramento, while the Union Pacific pushed westward from Omaha, Nebraska. The two met at Promontory Point, Utah, on May 10, 1869. Most of the construction had been financed by government loans, and Huntington and his partners made huge profits by controlling the Central Pacific's construction company, which turned in inflated bills for its work. Precise figures are unknown, be-

Collis P. Huntington. —Library of Congress (Neg. LC-USZ62-063955)

cause the company's books were fortuitously destroyed (burned by Hopkins, so the story goes).

After the transcontinental route was completed, Huntington and his colleagues built tracks to southern California and on to El Paso, Texas, and New Orleans, forming what in essence was a second transcontinental railroad. Their motives were twofold: to discourage competing railroads from moving in and to take advantage of the land grants that ensued. Their various railroads were eventually merged and became the Southern Pacific Co. Frank Norris's novel *The Octopus* (1901) is a fictional representation of the unequal struggle between ordinary Californians and the railroad. The Southern Pacific and its bosses—the Big Four, as they were known—were exceedingly unpopular in California, and the cold and reclusive Huntington was the least liked of all. Huntington returned the favor, disliking both the state and its people (he felt that its mild weather bred weaklings), and spent as much time as possible in New York.

Huntington wore several hats at the Central Pacific and its successor companies. He served as financial agent, selling stocks and bonds and arranging bank loans, and also as a lobbyist in Washington, where he staved off efforts to secure aid for other railroads that were potential competitors and averted damage to the company during the Crédit Mobilier scandal. In 1890 he took over from Stanford as president of the Southern Pacific. For most of this time Huntington also controlled the Chesapeake & Ohio Railroad.

The last surviving member of the Big Four died suddenly on August 13, 1900, at his summer place in the Adirondacks. Few made any pretense of grieving. His funeral in New York City was poorly attended. The *San Francisco Examiner* noted in his obituary that Collis Huntington had been "ruthless as a crocodile." At the time of his death he controlled enough miles of railroad to connect the North and South poles, in addition to steamship lines, coal mines, timber holdings, land, and much more. He left an estate of approximately $50 million, the bulk of it to his second wife, Arabella, and his nephew Henry Edwards Huntington.

—Roberta L. Diehl

REFERENCES

Bain, David Haward. *Empire Express: Building the First Transcontinental Railroad.* New York: Viking, 1999.
Dictionary of American Biography.
Lewis, Oscar. *The Big Four.* New York: Alfred A. Knopf, 1938.
Thorpe, James. *Henry Edwards Huntington: A Biography.* Berkeley: Univ. of California Press, 1994.

Huntington, Henry Edwards (1850–1927)

Henry Edwards Huntington, usually called Edward, was born in 1850 in Oneonta, New York, to a family of modest means. He started out clerking in a hardware store, but soon went to St. Albans, West Virginia, to manage a sawmill purchased by his wealthy uncle, Collis P. Huntington, and eventually to own it, first in partnership with another young man and then outright. The mill encountered financial difficulties, and at one point Edward was forced to part with his first collection of books, valued at the not-inconsiderable sum of $1,700. Years later he still grieved at their loss. Despite Edward's efforts, the sawmill was ultimately unsuccessful, and he returned to Oneonta with his young family. There he scraped by, managing properties owned by his father and by Collis in the town.

In 1881 he moved to Kentucky when his uncle made him superintendent of construction on what was to become the Chesapeake, Ohio & South-western Railroad.

Beginning in 1884 he took a series of increasingly responsible positions at other railroads in which his uncle had an interest. His decades of loyalty and diligence on his uncle's behalf were at last rewarded when in 1892 he was summoned to San Francisco to be Collis Huntington's assistant at the Southern Pacific Railway. By 1900, when his uncle died, he had risen to first vice president. He had a shy but pleasant manner and was popular in the city. Through savings and investment Edward was a millionaire in his own right by this time, but his wealth greatly increased when he inherited about $25 million from Collis. Soon after, he sold out of SP and left San Francisco; he and his wife, who remained in the city, were later divorced.

The Los Angeles area became Edward's home, and he gradually transferred the bulk of his interests there. These consisted mainly of buying real estate on a vast scale and improving the city's inadequate and ailing public transportation system, which in 1898 consisted of only 50 miles of track with equipment in poor condition. Twelve years later, when Huntington stepped down, there were 918 miles of track, 350 in the city and 568 interurban (*see* PACIFIC ELECTRIC RAILWAY), it was considered the best urban rail system in the world, and the population of Los Angeles had grown to over 300,000. (By 1920 it was half a million.) He also purchased numerous power, water, and telephone companies. All of this aided in the development of Southern California, as well as the enrichment of H. E. Huntington.

In 1911 he sold his transportation network to the Southern Pacific. Two years later he and Collis's widow, Arabella Duvall Huntington, married. Both were in their 60s. It is often said erroneously that with this marriage Collis's money was reunited. In fact, Arabella kept her fortune separate from Edward's, and when she died most of it went to her son, Archer. Edward spent his retirement years mostly at his San Marino estate, indulging in horticultural pursuits and acquiring rare books and works of art until his death in 1927. The Huntington Library in San Marino is only one of his legacies.

—Roberta L. Diehl

REFERENCES

Dictionary of National Biography.
Thorpe, James. *Henry Edwards Huntington: A Biography.* Berkeley: Univ. of California Press, 1994.

I

Illinois Central Gulf Railroad.

See Illinois Central Railroad

Illinois Central Railroad

For two decades after World War II the Illinois Central was a traditional, conservative, well-managed railroad. It hauled coal north from the mines of southern Illinois, and it gained a reputation for the speedy movement of perishables: strawberries from Louisiana, bananas from the port of New Orleans, and meat from Iowa. It operated an exemplary electrified commuter service along Chicago's lakefront, and its glossy orange and brown streamliners were considered the best in North America. It was one of the last U.S. railroads to switch from steam to diesel power for its freight trains. But it was nontraditional in its route structure and traffic flow—it was a north-south railroad in an east-west country.

The Illinois Central Railroad received its charter in 1851. It was to build a railroad from Cairo, at the south end of Illinois, where the Ohio and Mississippi rivers meet, to Galena, in the northwest corner of Illinois. The charter included a branch from Centralia, perhaps one-third of the way up the state, to Chicago. The railroad was aided by a land-grant act of 1850 signed by President Millard Fillmore. Illinois Central's original Y-shaped system was completed in 1856.

North-South Routes

The purpose of the Illinois Central Railroad was to funnel trade to and from a connecting steamboat line that operated on the Mississippi between Cairo and New Orleans. Soon, however, the Illinois Central made a traffic agreement with the New Orleans, Jackson & Great Northern Railroad and the Mississippi Central Railway. The NOJ&GN ran from New Orleans 183 miles north to Jackson, Mississippi, and 23 miles beyond to Canton, Missis-

sippi, and opened in 1858. The Mississippi Central was completed in 1860 between Canton, Mississippi, and Jackson, Tennessee, 263 miles. (The Mississippi Central name was later used by a railroad between Natchez and Hattiesburg, Mississippi; that company was purchased by the Illinois Central in 1967, to get ahead of the story.) Illinois Central was the principal bondholder of the New Orleans, Jackson & Great Northern and the Mississippi Central and absorbed those two lines in 1874 as the New Orleans, St. Louis & Chicago Railroad. Further reorganization resulted in the Chicago, St. Louis & New Orleans Railroad, a subsidiary of the IC.

At first the Mobile & Ohio Railroad provided a connection north from Jackson, Tennessee, to Columbus, Kentucky, and steamboats on the Mississippi River shuttled between Columbus and Cairo. In 1873 Illinois Central completed its own line from Jackson, Tennessee, to a point across the river from Cairo. IC's lines north of the Ohio River were built to standard gauge (4 feet 8½ inches). The lines south of the Ohio were built to the 5-foot gauge used throughout the South. They were converted to standard gauge on July 29, 1881.

In 1882 the Yazoo & Mississippi Valley Railroad, an Illinois Central subsidiary, was incorporated to build west from Jackson, Mississippi, into the Yazoo delta area. At the same time the Louisville, New Orleans & Texas Railway built a line from Memphis to New Orleans, running down the western edge of Mississippi and passing through Vicksburg and Baton Rouge. The LNO&T was backed by Collis P. Huntington, who saw the line as a connection between his Chesapeake, Ohio & South-western at Memphis and his Southern Pacific at New Orleans. It was completed in 1884. Huntington's forces also bought the Mississippi & Tennessee Railroad, which had a line from Memphis to Grenada, Mississippi, where it connected with the Illinois Central. However, Huntington's empire was in financial trouble. Illinois Central purchased the Mississippi & Tennessee and the Louisville, New Orleans & Texas and brought them into the Yazoo & Mississippi Valley, increasing IC's presence in the South and its overall mileage by more than one-fourth. IC bridged the Ohio River at Cairo in 1889, connecting the northern and southern parts of its system by rail.

East-West Routes

IC extended its original line, the route to Galena, west a few miles to the Mississippi River. It then extended itself all the way across Iowa by leasing the Dubuque & Sioux City Railroad, whose rails reached Sioux City in 1870. In the early 1880s the Illinois Central came under the control of E. H. Harriman and launched a western expansion program. It built branches to Cedar Rapids, Iowa, Sioux Falls, South Dakota, and Omaha, Nebraska, and it incorporated the Chicago, Madison & Northern in 1886 to build a line from Chicago west to a connection with the Centralia-Galena route at Freeport, Illinois, then north to Madison and Dodgeville, Wisconsin.

IC bought another part of Huntington's empire, the Chesapeake, Ohio & South-western, in 1893, acquiring a direct route into Memphis from the north and a route east through Paducah, Kentucky, to Louisville. In 1895 IC built a line into St. Louis from the southeast. In 1906 it completed a line from Effingham, Illinois, on the Centralia-Chicago line, east and north to Indianapolis. Part of the line to Indianapolis was new construction, and part consisted of former narrow-gauge railroads. Two years later, in 1908, IC created a route from Fulton, Kentucky, southeast to Birmingham, Alabama, partly by trackage rights and partly by new construction. The reason for the new route was to connect with the Central of Georgia Railway. E. H. Harriman had acquired control of the CofG in 1907 (and sold his interest to the IC in 1909).

Further Improvements

In Chicago, a city dominated by railroads, IC's locomotives were perhaps the most conspicuous source of smoke and cinders. On its line along Chicago's lakefront IC operated one of the nation's busiest and most intense suburban services. Even before smoke abatement became the primary issue, though, IC investigated electrification. In 1891 the available technology was not up to the job. Studies in 1897 and again in 1907 recommended electrification, with no concrete result. It took a 1919 ordinance of the City of Chicago to force electrification of IC's suburban service. The project began in 1921 and was completed in 1926. It created a multiple-track railroad completely separate from IC's other lines and fully grade separated from Chicago south to Richton, 29 miles. The project included branch lines to South Chicago and Blue Island. The economies of electric operation turned a money-losing service into a profit-maker, and the speeding up of the trains touched off a real estate boom in the suburbs along the line.

The Illinois prairie was almost an ideal place to build a railroad. IC's line from Centralia to Chicago was flat and straight, essentially a racetrack. The southern part of the state of Illinois, though, is hilly. IC's line was afflicted with grades and curves, and Cairo was a bottleneck. IC reasoned that only so much could be done to improve its original line and in 1925 began building the Edgewood

Cutoff south from Edgewood, Illinois, on the Centralia-Chicago route, to Fulton, Kentucky. The line started with a 63-mile stretch of straight track south from Edgewood, and even in the hilly country the new line was as straight and level as possible. The Edgewood Cutoff included three tunnels and crossed the Ohio River on the Chicago, Burlington & Quincy's bridge at Metropolis, Illinois. It bypassed the congestion of Cairo, and it avoided state land grant taxes levied on traffic moving on its original line.

Corporate Simplification and Expansion

After World War II the Illinois Central took steps to simplify its corporate structure. The first subsidiaries purchased and dissolved were the Gulf & Ship Island and the Yazoo & Mississippi Valley in 1945 and 1946. In 1948 IC lost its holdings in the Central of Georgia when CofG reorganized upon coming out of bankruptcy. In 1951 IC purchased the Chicago, St. Louis & New Orleans, essentially everything south of Cairo that was not part of one of the other subsidiaries. In 1953 IC acquired control of two companies that had been leased by the Yazoo & Mississippi Valley, the Vicksburg, Shreveport & Pacific and the Alabama & Vicksburg.

IC acquired several connecting short lines. It teamed up with the Rock Island in 1956 to form the Waterloo Railroad to purchase the Waterloo, Cedar Falls & Northern, an interurban line in northern Iowa. IC bought several short lines on its own: the Tremont & Gulf in 1959, the Peabody Short Line in 1960 (merged with IC in 1961), the Louisiana Midland in 1967, and the west end of the Tennessee Central (Hopkinsville, Kentucky, to Nashville) in 1968.

Illinois Central had objected to the 1940 merger that created the Gulf, Mobile & Ohio from the Gulf, Mobile & Northern and the Mobile & Ohio and said that one day it would purchase the GM&N and the M&O. That came to pass, sort of, in 1972. The group of men who had put together the GM&O were no longer young, and in GM&O's ranks there was no one to replace them. GM&O saw mergers taking place around it and sought inclusion in one. In 1972 Illinois Central and Gulf, Mobile & Ohio merged to form Illinois Central Gulf.

Contraction

About the time ICG was formed, it acquired three more short lines: the Columbus & Greenville, the Bonhomie & Hattiesburg Southern, and the Fernwood, Columbia & Gulf. In the mid-1970s ICG sold the Louisiana Midland and the Columbus & Greenville and in addition spun off a number of branch lines to form shortline and regional railroads. At that point Illinois Central Gulf consisted of a main line from Chicago to New Orleans and eight east-west lines that were at best secondary through routes. They could furnish some local business, but for the most part through traffic would require a connecting railroad to short-haul itself (turn traffic over to another railroad before it had gone the maximum distance on the first road).

ICG began to sell those east-west routes. In July 1985 most of the former Gulf, Mobile & Ohio south of Tennessee became the Gulf & Mississippi Railroad. The Chicago-Omaha line became the Chicago, Central & Pacific Railroad at the end of 1985. August 1986 saw the startup of the Paducah & Louisville Railway, linking the cities of its name. MidSouth Rail Corp. acquired the Meridian, Mississippi–Shreveport, Louisiana, line that had been the Alabama & Vicksburg and the Vicksburg, Shreveport & Pacific. The north end of the GM&O (the former Alton), except from Joliet to Chicago, became the Chicago, Missouri & Western (which quickly went bankrupt; Southern Pacific acquired the St. Louis–Joliet line, and an independent company, the Gateway Western, acquired the Springfield–Kansas City line). From 9,634 route-miles in 1973, IC dropped to 2,872 route-miles at the end of 1989.

In 1988 Illinois Central Gulf changed its name back to Illinois Central. It was sold by its owner, the Whitman Corp. (formerly IC Industries) to the Prospect Group, which had previously controlled MidSouth. IC offered to purchase MidSouth, MidSouth rejected the offer, IC withdrew it, and Kansas City Southern acquired MidSouth. In 1996 Illinois Central bought the Chicago, Central & Pacific for about twice what it had received for it 11 years earlier, seeing the line as a route for grain and coal traffic. In February 1998 Canadian National Railway Co., agreed to purchase the Illinois Central, creating a rail system that reaches the three coasts of North America: Atlantic, Pacific, and Gulf of Mexico.

In 1970, its last year before the ICG merger, Illinois Central operated a system of 6,761 route-miles and 11,159 track-miles, with 767 locomotives, 462 passenger cars, 50,915 freight cars, 2,233 company service cars, and 17,075 employees. Freight traffic totaled 23,701 million ton-miles in 1970, and food products (15.7 percent), coal (14.5 percent), farm products (8.9 percent), lumber and wood products (7.2 percent), and pulp and paper (7.1 percent) were its principal traffic sources. Passenger traffic totaled 764 million passenger-miles. Illinois Central operating revenues totaled $338 million in 1970, and the railroad achieved a 78.9 percent operating ratio.

—George H. Drury

REFERENCE

Corliss, Carlton J. *Main Line of Mid-America*. New York: Creative Age Press, 1950.

Illinois Terminal Railroad

A giant among midwestern interurban railways was the Illinois Traction System, assembled by Illinois congressman and utilities entrepreneur William B. McKinley. Its earliest component was the Danville, Paxton & Northern, which began operating in 1901 over a 6-mile route between Danville and Westville, Illinois. Within seven years McKinley expanded this modest start into a traction empire that extended 167 miles north from Granite City, across the Mississippi River from St. Louis, to Peoria; 125 miles eastward from Springfield to Decatur, Champaign, and Danville, on the Indiana border; and from Decatur to Peoria via Bloomington. In 1910 McKinley completed a Mississippi River bridge that brought his trains into a new terminal in downtown St. Louis.

The system was further expanded a few years later with the acquisition of the Illinois Valley lines of the Chicago, Ottawa & Peoria, which then extended from Joliet to Princeton, with a branch to Streator. McKinley rapidly acquired other midwestern electric railway and utility properties, and by 1916 he owned some 40 railway, light, and power companies in Illinois, Kansas, Missouri, Iowa, Nebraska, and Wisconsin. Nearly 800 miles of electric railway track were under ITS management.

The system grew still larger in 1928 when ITS was merged with the Illinois Terminal Co., a prosperous and strategic steam-operated terminal line in the Alton–East St. Louis area. Two years later still more electric mileage was added to the system when the Illinois Terminal Railroad System (as it had been renamed) leased the St. Louis & Alton Railway.

Further expansion was forestalled by the lack of investment capital for key links. St. Louis–Indianapolis service was planned as early as 1906, but a 20-mile gap between ITS and the Terre Haute, Indianapolis & Eastern was never closed. Similarly, the failure to complete a link between ITS and its Chicago, Ottawa & Peoria affiliate in northern Illinois precluded the establishment of St. Louis–Peoria-Chicago interurban service.

In addition to local and short-distance passenger services typical of most interurban roads, ITS operated extensive long-distance services, notably over its St. Louis–Peoria main route, on which it had no direct steam railroad competition. Fast express trains with parlor-car and dining services were operated over this and other principal ITS routes until well after World War II. The railroad was one of the few interurbans that used sleeping cars, and it operated them longer than any other interurban (from 1906 to 1940).

Illinois Terminal was more successful than most midwestern interurbans in developing a substantial carload freight business interchanged with its steam railroad connections. The original ITS lines typically traversed the streets of cities and towns, where sharp curves or legal limitations often precluded the operation of long freight trains. As early as 1906 the company began the construction of freight belt lines around many of these communities. It was successful in establishing through rates and divisions with most of its steam road connections and was able to develop a less-than-carload-lot freight service between on-line points and Chicago that used special cars interchanged with the Chicago & Eastern Illinois and Rock Island railroads.

The IT continued to develop its passenger services long after most interurbans had given up. Air conditioning was introduced on a new high-speed St. Louis–Peoria service in 1935. An elevated structure and subway completed in 1932 linked the railroad's Mississippi River bridge with a new downtown St. Louis Central Terminal Building. New passenger stations were completed at several principal cities. Encouraged by the high volume of its World War II passenger business, the railroad spent $1 million on three deluxe streamlined trains for its principal long-distance services and eight modern, streamlined Presidents' Conference Committee (PCC) cars for its St. Louis–Granite City, Illinois, suburban service.

The investment proved ill advised as passengers returned to their automobiles. Despite the new trains, IT's interurban passenger traffic dropped precipitously. Parlor-car and dining services on the streamliners were discontinued in 1951, and by the time the railroad's interurban passenger service ended in 1956, the expensive streamliners were operating as single-car locals. The Granite City suburban service lasted only another two years before it, too, was given up.

As electric passenger operation neared an end, IT began a shift to diesel motive power for its substantial freight service. Electric freight operation ended in 1955, and the railroad was acquired in 1956 by a consortium of nine connecting steam railroads, later joined by two others. Most of IT's main-line freight operations were shifted to trackage rights on the parallel steam railroads over the next 15 years, and what was left of the railroad was acquired by Norfolk & Western in 1981. Only a few remnants of the once-great system, most of them in the St. Louis area, remain in service today.

In 1980, its last year before Norfolk & Western purchased it, Illinois Terminal operated a system of 420 route-miles and 578 track-miles, with 36 locomotives, 2,624 freight cars, 13 company service cars, and 605 employees. Operating revenues totaled $26.8 million in 1980, and the railroad achieved a 103 percent operating ratio.

—William D. Middleton

REFERENCE

Stringham, Paul H. *Illinois Terminal: The Electric Years.* Glendale, Calif.: Interurban, 1989.

Inclined-Plane Railways

Railroads like level terrain and prefer to avoid hills and mountains. But it is generally necessary to route tracks through undulating territory, so engineers typically build meandering lines that curve back and forth to gain altitude gradually. Main-line grades are thus generally held to about 1 percent. However, this makes for a long and indirect route. One alternative was the inclined plane, a system that involved a cable helper to hoist trains up a steep gradient. Grades could be overcome in a short and direct fashion, but at a price. Inclines worked by attaching a cable or rope to a train at the bottom of the hill. The cable was attached to a winding drum at the top that revolved and so pulled the train to the top of the incline. The cost of building and maintaining the incline negated much of its benefits. The attaching and unhitching of the cable slowed the operation. Long trains had to be broken into segments, for few inclines could hoist more than a few cars at a time, so the incline could slow down rather than speed up operations. Many inclines were built in this country, especially in the 1830s, but most were abandoned after only a decade or two in favor of the conventional uphill tracks that curved and meandered to overcome grades.

Several plans were devised for these hill-climbing railways. The simplest involved a hoist or winding engine at the top of the hill that pulled a car attached to a cable or rope. Cars were raised or lowered on a single track. Generally, only industrial operators used these elementary inclines. Most inclines had two parallel tracks, one for uphill and the other for downhill service. In some cases the upper and lower ends were single track with a double track at the center, so the cars could pass around each other. Self-acting inclines were favored by many early operators. Loaded cars heading downgrade pulled up empty cars. The number of empties was calculated to weigh somewhat less than the loaded cars yet had to be heavy enough to control the downward travel of the full cars. A common rope, chain, or cable connected the two sets of cars. It wrapped around a large pulley at the top of the grade and was often made in the form of a loop. A second pulley was in place at the bottom station. A manually powered brake at the top station was a safeguard against runaway trains.

Counterbalancing, a regular feature of most inclines, helped control the speed of the cars and greatly reduced power needs. Ideally the up and down loads would be equal. Because this could not always be achieved, the winding drum or wheel was powered by a steam engine, a water wheel, or an electric motor. In a few cases water tanks mounted on incline platforms or as a separate vehicle powered the incline. When full, the tank was heavy and so worked as a counterweight. It was emptied at the bottom station and its opposite member at the top of the grade was filled, and so the process was repeated to create up and down travel. The system was cheap and simple, but it required an ample water supply to be economical.

The barney or tender system worked best for the movement of conventional railroad cars on a steam railroad. The barney was a small but sturdy four-wheel car that acted as a pusher. It was attached to the hoisting cable and had adjustable-gauge axles so that it could drop into a pit placed between the incline's tracks on a separate narrow-gauge track. The standard-gauge cars were rolled into place at the bottom of the incline, just ahead of the barney's pit. The hoisting cable pulled the barney up to and behind the cars, and the pusher head of the barney came against the coupler and draft gear of the rear car. As the cable pulled, the barney and its cluster of cars went uphill. They were counterbalanced by a second group of cars descending. The barney of the down cars was at the head rather than the rear of the train and so controlled the speed of the descending cars. A common cable connected both barneys and looped around the several large sheave wheels of driving machinery. One of the chief advantages of the barney system was that it eliminated the need to attach the cars to the hoisting cable by tail ropes or hitches.

Inclines are one of the oldest forms of railways on record. The ancient Greeks used inclines to carry ships across the Isthmus of Corinth starting around 427 B.C. An incline was set up near Niagara Falls in 1762. It was actually a sledgeway rather than a proper railway, for the cars had no wheels. A wooden track was laid on the steepest portion of the portage trail. It was worked by a manual capstan and proved effective for moving ammunition, baggage, and barrels of supplies. Apparently the first incline in the United States was opened in Boston about 1805. It was a short self-acting affair, only about a quarter of a mile long, but it did good work in removing spoils from the top of Beacon Hill, which was being lowered for development. The earth was used to fill in part of the Back Bay.

Another incline appeared in the Boston area around 1830 as part of the Granite Railway at Quincy, Massachusetts. This horse-powered shortline was opened in 1826 to carry stone from quarries to a dock about three miles distant. The incline was added to service quarries at a higher level than the main track could conveniently reach. It was short (275 feet) and self-acting and used an endless chain. The Granite Railway did not carry passengers but apparently allowed sightseers to hitch a ride. Four unlucky travelers were riding on the incline in July 1832 when the chain broke. Two were killed.

A far larger railway for the carriage of coal was opened near the Pennsylvania–New York border at Honesdale, Pennsylvania, in 1829. The Delaware & Hudson Canal Co.'s railway was 16 miles long and had five steam-powered and two self-acting inclines. This short gravity line was one of the first commercial railroads in the United States and moved a huge amount of coal during its 70 years of operation. It was a two-track system, with the up and down lines crossing over each other at several points. The down track carried the loaded cars. It was extensively rebuilt and improved over the years, and additional inclines were added from time to time. Passengers and mail were carried as well after 1877, but its odd gauge of 4 feet 3 inches prevented it from becoming part of the national rail system.

Some 50 miles to the south and west of the D&H was the railway of the Lehigh Valley Coal & Navigation Co. at Mauch Chunk, Pennsylvania. This pioneering line opened in May 1827 and ran 9 miles from an open-pit coal mine at the top of the mountain to the Lehigh River, where the coal was transferred to canal boats. Loaded cars came downhill powered by gravity in groups of 14. One or two brakemen worked manual brakes on all cars through a rope that connected rods and levers on each car of the train. The four-wheel cars were small, with a capacity of 1½ tons each and a track gauge of 42 inches. The empty cars were pulled uphill by mules. The downhill trip required just 30 minutes, but the uphill journey took about 3 hours, mostly because the mule-powered cars had to stand by in sidings as the loaded trains passed. The diminutive line cost just $38,726 but was carrying 268 tons of coal a day by 1830.

By 1844 the railroad was rebuilt; it was in fact doubled in size with separate uphill and downhill lines that formed an 18-mile loop. The uphill line was westbound and carried the empties to the mine. The mules were retired and replaced by two large inclined planes. The first incline was called Mt. Pisgah after the mountain in Jordan from which Moses first saw the Promised Land. It was 2,250 feet long with a rise of 664 feet. A 90-hp engine drove two 27-foot-diameter winding drums that were geared so as to revolve in opposite directions—hence one would pull cars up the plane while its counterpart let a second set down. Flat iron bands 7½ inches wide by 3/16 inch thick were used in place of cables or ropes. Once at the top, the cars went downgrade for 6 miles to the foot of the Mt. Jefferson incline. It was somewhat smaller than Mt. Pisgah and had a length of 2,070 feet and a rise of 462 feet. It was a short run from the second plane to the mine. The loaded cars coasted eastward down the old gravity line to the river level. The inclines and the second track greatly improved the railroad's capacity; it was now carrying around 200,000 tons a year.

Clearly coal was the main reason for the Mauch Chunk railway's existence, but some passengers were carried as well. From the beginning, tourists arrived at the remote mountain station demanding a ride on the curious gravity railroad, and they were accommodated. For reasons never explained, the line became known as the Switchback, although in truth it used not one switchback. For another quarter century coal and tourists rode up and over the so-called Switchback. Then in 1870 the Lehigh Coal & Navigation Co. opened a new railroad to the mine. The antiquated gravity line appeared doomed, but the managers felt that the tourist trade would continue, and so the line was retained as a scenic railroad. Local businessmen leased the property and promoted the area as the Switzerland of America. Special trains brought day-trippers from New York City to ride the Switchback. Thousands of urban visitors came to enjoy the view and the clean air. But the automobile did much to distract from the Victorian charms of scenic railways. The lean years of the Great Depression dealt the final blow to the aging attraction. It closed in 1933 and was scrapped four years later.

A few inclines began to open on public or common-

In 1844 the Lehigh Coal & Navigation Co. replaced its mule-powered coal line at Mauch Chunk (now Jim Thorpe), Pennsylvania, with an inclined-plane system. The largest of these, at Mount Pisgah, was 2,250 feet long and climbed 664 feet. It was also popular with sightseers. —Library of Congress (Neg. LC-USZ62-51873)

carrier railroads in the early 1830s. Among the first were two inclines on the Mohawk & Hudson Rail Road built to connect Albany and Schenectady, New York. The 16-mile line opened in 1831 and was challenged by steep grades at each end. The quick and easy solution was two steam-powered inclines. The Albany incline was 3,100 feet long, and the Schenectady plane was 2,046 feet. The grade of both was a rise of one foot in eight. They cost $14,000 each but proved expensive to operate. The Schenectady plane's annual expenses, labor, fuel, and repairs, were $7,800. Wood fueled the boilers. The M&H had by this time decided that both were not only costly to run but inconvenient to operate. They slowed down the passage of trains, and because the line was built to offer a speedy passenger conduit in competition with the Erie Canal, the expeditious handling of trains was important. New routes

for conventional tracks were built, and the Schenectady plane shut down in September 1841. Its mate was eliminated exactly three years later.

The Baltimore & Ohio became disenchanted with incline operation even more quickly than its neighbor to the north. When the Baltimore line encountered the first major gradient some 40 miles to the west, its engineers concluded that inclined planes were a necessity. Locomotives could not overcome grades much greater than 0.5 percent according to conservative estimates of the time, and so four inclines were laid out in 1830. The gradients varied from 3.3 to 5 percent, and their lengths from 1,900 to 3,200 feet. The machinery was slow to come, but operations, at least limited operations, of the railroad began at Mt. Airy, over Parr's Ridge, in early 1832. Horses were used to move a few cars at a time up and down the incline.

Then locomotives were tried; in late 1834 one of the Davis Grasshoppers ran up and over the inclines with no problem. It is not certain if all four of the inclines were actually put in operation. By early 1838 work was started on a new railroad to bypass the inclines. It opened during the next year, and so ended the B&O's brief but costly romance with inclined-plane railways.

Kentucky's pioneer railroad, the Lexington & Ohio, opened the first section of its line in 1832. It aimed to connect Lexington and Louisville via the state capital of Frankfort, but poor finances and light traffic defeated this ambitious plan for many years. The line did reach Frankfort by 1834. The city was in a river valley, and an inclined plane 2,200 feet long was built to overcome this drop in elevation. The Frankfort incline tended to be more accident-prone than most. In April 1836 a broken hoisting rope caused a crash that killed three. Three years later a passenger car got away before it was attached to the cable. Some passengers jumped out during the runaway plunge to the bottom, but how many were injured or killed is unknown. The railroad was sold at foreclosure in 1842, and the new owners began plans for a cutoff to avoid the incline that included a 500-foot tunnel. When the new line opened in 1848, the incline was closed.

The Old South's first major railroad, the South Carolina Railroad, was built quickly and cheaply on wooden pilings in the early 1830s across its native state to the Georgia border. Its promoters were aiming for Augusta, Georgia, but just before reaching that terminal they encountered a large hill at Aiken, South Carolina. Once again the expedient solution was a steam-powered inclined plane. The 3,800-foot-long incline was opened in 1834, but it was not long before the road's managers were dissatisfied with their rope haulage system. It was shortened and the grade made uniform. By 1841 the stationary engine was abandoned and locomotives were used to propel trains up and down the incline in a most curious fashion. The rope and pulley system was retained. The rope was attached to cars on one track and to a locomotive on the parallel track. As the locomotive went downhill, the cars were pulled uphill. Plans were soon under way, however, for a new line to bypass the incline. When it opened in May 1852, the Aiken incline was abandoned.

The largest and best-known American incline installation was on the Allegheny Portage Railroad, which formed the mountain division of Pennsylvania's Main Line of Public Works. This transport system was composed of two railroads and two canals that stretched some 390 miles across the Keystone State. The section between Hollidaysburg and Johnstown traversed the most elevated region on the system in 37 miles. Ten inclines and 11 levels carried the railroad over an elevation of 2,570 feet, 2,007 feet of which were accomplished by the inclines. Each incline varied somewhat in length and elevation but averaged about half a mile long with a grade of around 10 percent. The general plan was praised by a Scottish engineer of the time for its "boldness of design and the difficulty of execution."

Each head house had a pair of two-cylinder steam engines. The second set was in place to take over should the first set break down. An endless rope was driven by drive sheaves 8½ feet in diameter. There were tension wheels at the top and bottom stations to keep the rope tight. The haulage rope was around 3 inches in diameter and was made from Italian or Russian hemp. The ropes cost $3,000 and lasted for only 12 to 18 months. The cars were attached by short lengths of rope tied to the cars and the haulage rope. The rope traveled at 4 mph. A hydraulic regulator with a cylinder 14 inches in diameter by 72 inches long could be engaged to regulate the speed of descent and proved effective when unbalanced loads were being handled. The safety record of the Portage was excellent during its 20 years of operation.

The Portage opened in March 1834. In its early years six to ten trips were made each hour. Four cars were taken at a time. During its first full year of operation (1835) 20,000 passengers and 50,000 tons of freight passed over the Portage. Wire rope replaced the hemp ropes by 1849, but the system was increasingly viewed as a bottleneck because it was far slower than a conventional railroad. Because each incline required a crew of four or five, labor costs were high. A new railroad was built during 1851–1854 to bypass the Portage, and so ended one of America's most novel railway operations.

By the mid-nineteenth century the incline era was ending on main-line railroads. The transit industry would pick on the idea 20 years later, but uphill pulley power was otherwise no longer in favor. As with most general rules, there are always a few exceptions. We will discuss only one of these holdouts, the three planes on the Central Railroad of New Jersey (CNJ) at Ashley, Pennsylvania, near Wilkes-Barre. They were built by the Lehigh & Susquehanna Railroad in 1842–1843 as three separate inclines all in a row. The L&S was leased to CNJ in 1871. The first incline started at the top of the hill and ran for 3,700 feet at 9.2 percent; the second ran 3,000 feet at 14.6 percent; and the last was 5,000 feet long at 5.7 percent. Hoisting engines were placed at the head of each incline. The machinery was enlarged periodically to keep up with the increase in freight-car size over the years. A back track was built around the inclines for passenger trains in 1867, so Ashley was used only for freight cars after this time. The barney pusher system was employed, and cars were whisked uphill in just 20 minutes, 6 at a time. Only 3 cars were hoisted at a time on the steeper central plane. It could handle 45 cars an hour. A 2½-inch-diameter cable was used for the hoisting service. A smaller cable was attached to the rear of the barney and passed around a pulley. A large counterweight kept tension on the tail cable that pulled back on the barney and so kept the hoisting cable taut and stretched out. This eliminated kinks and made for smoother operation. This plant, which harkened back to the earliest times of railway operations, was finally closed down on July 6, 1948. All traffic on the CNJ was diverted to the back track. The Ashley planes were dismantled in 1950.

Table 1. Principal Railroad Inclines

Name	Location	Length	Rise	Dates	Remarks
Allegheny Portage	Western Pennsylvania	About 2,600 ft each	About 200 ft	1834–1854	Ten inclines; part of the Pennsylvania Main Line of Public Works
Ashley	Eastern Pennsylvania	2.4 miles	1,000 ft	1843–1948	Three inclines; Central Railroad of New Jersey
Baltimore & Ohio Railroad	Parr's Ridge, Maryland	10,200 ft	550 ft	1831–1838	Four inclines
Belmont	Philadelphia	2,800 ft	180 ft	1834–1850	Part of the Pennsylvania Main Line of Public Works
Columbia	Columbia, Pennsylvania	1,900 ft	90 ft	1834–1840	Part of the Pennsylvania Main Line of Public Works
Delaware & Hudson Railroad	Eastern Pennsylvania		900 ft	1829–1899	Multiple inclines and levels
Gordon	Eastern Pennsylvania	12,000 ft	700 ft	1854–1896	Two inclines; Reading Railroad
Lexington & Ohio Railroad	Frankfort, Kentucky	2,200 ft		1834–1848	
Mahoning	Eastern Pennsylvania	2,400 ft	344 ft	1862–1932	Reading Co.
Mohawk & Hudson Rail Road	Albany and Schenectady, New York	5,150 ft		1831–1840s	Two inclines
South Carolina	Aiken, South Carolina	3,800 ft	180 ft	1834–1852	

Note: All dimensions are approximate.

Principal railroad inclines are shown in Table 1.

Urban and scenic inclines were once widely used. Some 50 hillside railways once carried passengers up grades too steep for conventional transit operations. Most of these lines were short and functioned much like a large-scale elevator. They should not be confused with cable railways that propelled cars through the streets of many major cities. Inclines were built in all parts of the United States, with the largest concentration in Pittsburgh, about 17, and Cincinnati, 5. The urban inclines worked as part of the city transit system and proved effective in moving large numbers of pedestrians to the top of large hills before the advent of electric traction in 1890. Many continued to function for decades after their supposed obsolescence. Several remain in operation today, and examples can be found in Pittsburgh; Johnstown, Pennsylvania; Chattanooga; Dubuque, Iowa; Los Angeles; and Canyon City, Colorado. A modern incline was built in the Los Angeles suburbs to serve the Getty Art Museum in 1996.

The city-style incline had its beginnings in 1870 when the Monongahela Incline opened in Pittsburgh. It connected downtown with the hilltop community of Mt. Washington. It was comparatively short, just 640 feet long, but it overcame a 71.5 percent grade. It proved very popular and carried well over a million passengers annually during its peak years. Other cities with hill transit problems copied Pittsburgh's premier incline. Some were made to carry wagons and horses to facilitate the carriage of goods before the introduction of motor trucks. In a few cases a separate freight incline was built next to the passenger plane. City inclines earned extra revenues in freight business and carried as many as 250 teams a day. Hun-

dreds of horses were spared the rigors of an uphill climb that could be life threatening considering the heavy loads transported in most city wagons. Both man and beast were well served by the steam-powered inclined railway.

Most inclines were built to satisfy urban transit needs, but a few were constructed for other reasons. The Cambria Incline at Johnstown, Pennsylvania, was built in reaction to the devastating flood in 1889; it was to serve as an escape route should another flood ever again threaten a population that lived in the deep river valley. It promised to whisk people to the heights well above the raging water in just seconds. Conversely, the Mount Manitou incline in Colorado was built in 1907 to carry water pipe and other needed materials uphill for a water supply system. Once the construction project was complete, the line continued as a tourist railroad. It remained in service until a large rock toppled down the mountainside and destroyed the lower end of the incline in 1990. Once closed, most inclines become only a memory, but when the Angels Flight incline closed in Los Angeles in 1969, it was disassembled and put in storage. To the surprise of many skeptics, it was restored to service in 1996. An accident in February 2001 closed it again, and because of a prolonged safety investigation it has not reopened.

Safety was an obvious consideration with inclines. The steep gradient made them look dangerous. No overall statistical records were kept, so far as we can determine. But the anecdotal record, incomplete as it may be, indicates a favorable history. There were accidents, and some persons were killed or injured. The Main Street Incline in Cincinnati (1872–1898) had a major mishap in 1889 that killed six passengers. This was the only accident on any of the five Cincinnati inclines that resulted in a passenger death. Twenty years later the operator of the Pittsburgh St. Clare Incline fainted, and as he fell to the floor of the operator's cab, he pushed the throttle fully open. The engines continued to pull after the car reached the top station, and the cables were pulled loose. The car fell to the bottom. On the way down, four passengers jumped out; two of those fleeing the runaway were killed.

Safety came through very heavy machinery, well-trained operators, careful inspections and maintenance, and various safety apparatus. Some inclines had deadman controls, large hooks to hold the car at the top station, and more than one set of brakes. Extra-large cables were used. Those of the Mt. Adams Incline in Cincinnati, for example, had a safety factor of four. They were inspected and adjusted each morning when a test run was made with no passengers on board. The Otis Elevator Co. inspected the cables on a monthly basis. The hoisting cables (1¼ inches in diameter), two for each car, were replaced every 9½ years. The larger safety or balance cable (1⅜ inches in diameter) that connected the two cars was replaced every 7 years. The Mill Mountain Incline in Roanoke, Virginia, felt that a good slogan was the best way to reassure nervous patrons. It claimed that its incline was as "Safe as the Bank of England and as strong as the Rock of Gibraltar."

Some city inclines had pleasure resorts adjacent to their top stations. Cincinnati's Hill Top Houses were famous in the 1870s and 1880s. They offered food, beer, cool breezes, and a view of the city below. Concerts, theatrical performances, and fireworks were staged at regular intervals. But inclines were also built in more rural settings to take advantage of the scenery and as an escape from the heat and noise of city life. Mention has already been made of the Mauch Chunk railway that was adapted for scenic railway operations in 1870. Some years earlier, the Summit House at Mt. Holyoke, Massachusetts, built a short incline for its guests. The hotel was perched on top of a small mountain that offered its guests a fine view of the Connecticut River valley. Neighboring Mt. Tom became home to a much larger scenic incline in 1897. A resort hotel was built at its peak. Other mountain summits could be seen as far away as Vermont and Maine. Visitors could enjoy daily opera and musical comedy performances, dancing, scenic walks, and flower gardens. There were a zoo and a merry-go-round for the children. Similar incline resorts were built at Mt. Beacon, New York, Lake George, New York, and Orange Mountain, New Jersey. The Otis Elevating Railway carried visitors up 1,600 feet to a promontory at the eastern end of the Catskill Mountains. The Otis Elevator Co. planned and built this very long (7,200 feet) incline in 1891–1892.

Scenic inclines were not limited to the northeastern states. Tennessee claims a spectacular incline that runs up the face of Lookout Mountain near Chattanooga. It opened in 1895 and remains in service. The western states were also home to a number of scenic inclines. The Mount Lowe incline, near Los Angeles, opened in 1893. It lifted passengers 1,300 feet high in the San Gabriel Mountains. This attraction included a trolley ride, the Echo Mountain House, an observatory with a 16-inch telescope, and a small zoo. A fire in 1936 and a flash flood in 1938 destroyed parts of the complex, and it was never rebuilt. By this time most other inclines in the United States were already or about to be abandoned. Today just a handful remain to remind us of another era in transport history.

—John H. White, Jr.

REFERENCES

Duke, Donald. *Incline Railways of Los Angeles and Southern California*. San Marino, Calif.: Golden West, 1998.

White, John H., Jr. *Cincinnati: City of Seven Hills and Five Inclines*. Cincinnati: Cincinnati Railroad Club, 2001.

Incorporation Laws and Charters

During the colonial period U.S. businesses organized as proprietorships, partnerships, and joint-stock associations. Since these informal arrangements were inadequate to generate capital for large-scale enterprises, state legislatures by 1820 adopted more than 300 separate acts conferring state charters upon individual corporations. Incorporation by state legislative charter predominated during the railroad industry's early years.

A typical charter enabled a business to incorporate, set its maximum capitalization, fixed the number of common shares to be subscribed before it could organize, placed limits on its debt, and shielded shareholders from liability arising from third-party claims. Because railroads were deemed to engage in a public service, additional provisions normally were added.

South Carolina's acts of 1827 and 1828, for example, empowered the Charleston & Hamburg to build canals or railroads from Charleston to Columbia, Camden, and Hamburg and to hold a monopoly between Charleston and the towns named for 36 years. The company's charges were limited to 35 cents per hundredweight for transporting freight 100 miles, and 5 cents per mile for passengers. To preserve its charter rights, it was required to begin construction within 2 years and complete its route within 6 years.

Granting monopolies ran counter to prevailing political sentiment, but was considered essential if the chartered railroad was to have a decent prospect of financing its construction and operating profitably. The Boston & Worcester's charter barred parallel lines within 5 miles of its route for 30 years. Kentucky's Green River Railroad won a provision prohibiting a parallel line within 20 miles for 25 years, and Georgia legislated a similar benefit for the Brunswick & Florida. New Jersey awarded the Camden & Amboy exclusive rights between New York and Philadelphia. Special privileges occasionally were challenged. The Boston & Lowell's 1830 charter gave it a 30-year monopoly between the cities named in its title, but a Massachusetts act of 1852 allowed competitors to circumvent this provision. The Boston & Lowell successfully defended its rights before the state's supreme court.

Another common provision granted railroads the power of eminent domain to acquire private land for their rights of way. Although legislators justified taking land for the "public purpose" railroads served, some landowners viewed eminent domain as an unreasonable infringement upon their property rights. Disputes over what constituted a fair price for land taking often resulted in lawsuits or proceedings brought before state regulatory agencies.

To facilitate investment and profitability, other inducements sometimes were added. The Richmond, Fredericksburg & Potomac was perpetually exempted from property taxes, and the Louisville, Nashville & Knoxville was granted tax exemptions until dividends exceeded the legal rate of interest. The Vermont Central received a 25-year exemption. Early Indiana charters allowed county commissioners to buy stock on the county's behalf. Kentucky permitted local officials to purchase stock in the Louisville & Nashville if voters approved in a referendum. The Baltimore & Ohio's 1827 charter reserved one-half of its authorized shares for purchase by the State of Maryland and City of Baltimore. In exchange for extensive land grants, the Illinois Central's 1851 charter required the railroad to pay 5 percent of its gross revenues to the state and to seat the Illinois governor as an ex officio board member.

A few early railroads were authorized to raise funds by conducting lotteries. A more common charter provision, especially in the South, was the right to engage in banking. Most railroad banking privileges were granted during the 1830s to give companies access to additional capital and to let them issue negotiable currency to pay employees, contractors, and suppliers.

Charter grants varied with respect to the routing of new lines. Some companies were given wide latitude. Mindful of constituents' desires not to be bypassed, lawmakers occasionally took pains to prescribe proposed routings in detail. Disputes arose when rival communities sought designation as terminal points. After civic leaders at Louisville and Maysville complained, Kentucky chartered the Cincinnati & Charleston with the stipulation that it build branch lines to those cities in addition to its intended destination of Cincinnati. Worried that Nashville would become a mere way station on the Louisville & Nashville instead of a railroad hub, Tennessee's L&N charter ordered that its tracks stop short of Nashville at the north bank of the Cumberland River. Freight was to be drayed to Nashville.

Not all early lines were created by charter. Several were launched as state-owned enterprises, often in connection with ambitious canal and turnpike schemes. Among early state-owned railroads were the Western & Atlantic (Georgia), Madison & Indianapolis, and Michigan Central. The city of Troy, New York, financed and built the Schenectady & Troy Railroad.

Critics asserted that special legislation of this type gave rise to political corruption. In the 1830s and 1840s the clamor for rail service was so intense that the need to secure legislative support with cash, stock, or other inducements would have been minimal. As rail lines proliferated, obtaining lawmakers' backing became a more competitive process that almost certainly was not always resolved on merit alone. Railroads frequently needed charter amendment laws to increase capitalization, extend routes, acquire other lines, or enter into mergers. Lobbyists from companies with competing claims descended upon state capitals. Bruising political battles often ensued, and the outcome could potentially be influenced by distributions of stock, cash, and other favors.

Defects of the charter system grew as the railroad system gained maturity. Lawmakers of the 1830s and 1840s could not have anticipated the wave of consolidation that would begin within two decades, and each merger or acquisition could require one or more amending statutes. Legislators also had assumed that railroads would be financed through the sale of stock, but bonds emerged as the primary source of investment capital. Charter holders then sought amendatory laws to raise debt limits and to allow mortgages on their assets. When attorney Samuel J. Tilden restructured the bankrupt Pittsburgh, Fort Wayne & Chicago in 1860, conforming legislation was required in four states.

The volume of laws, coupled with public disapproval of special privileges for private interests, prompted states to adopt more general railroad incorporation acts. New York did so in 1848 and 1850. Indiana adopted a general railroad act in 1852 that allowed any group of 15 or more individuals with a total capital stock of $50,000 (or $1,000 per mile of the proposed line) to incorporate. The new entities were permitted to sell bonds and mortgage property as security. Michigan's 1855 law allowed incorporation if financial requirements were met, but mandated the installation of safety devices: locomotive bells, steam whistles, and grade-crossing signs. Pennsylvania's general incorporation law of 1868 required stock subscriptions of $5,000 per mile. With his state still operating under the charter system in 1872, Massachusetts governor William Washburne commented that nearly 400 charters had been issued, noting that this amounted to "more than one charter to every five miles of railroad constructed within our limits." By 1880 general incorporation laws were nearly universal in the United States. This solution did not always eliminate the need for amendatory laws affecting railroads chartered before the enactment of general incorporation procedures. To avoid a deluge of amendments during the post–Civil War consolidation era, many legislatures passed general laws to allow railroads to lease other lines if shareholders approved.

Congress approved charters in connection with ambitious railroad projects in the American West. The Pacific Railroad Act of 1862 created the Union Pacific Railroad to build from a point near Kearney, Nebraska, to the California boundary. In addition to aid through government bonds and land grants, the act authorized the President of the United States to appoint two members of UP's board of directors. Under the law the Central Pacific Railroad, already chartered in California, was given a contract to build within that state under terms similar to those granted the UP. Congress chartered the Northern Pacific in 1864 with extensive land grants and also enacted laws enabling the Texas & Pacific and Atlantic & Pacific to build routes westward.

Given Canada's vast territory, small and scattered population, and limited sources of private capital, early railway enterprises faced formidable obstacles. Following English precedents for incorporation by charter, the legislative assembly of Lower Canada (now Quebec) chartered the Champlain & St. Lawrence Railroad in 1832 and set its capital requirement at £50,000. If dividends exceeded 12 percent, rates were to be reduced on a fixed scale. The government reserved the right to buy the line from its private owners. Upper Canada (now Ontario) issued seven charters by 1841, but none was acted upon. New Brunswick chartered the St. Andrews & Quebec in 1836.

It became clear that no major private railroad project could be undertaken without aid from the British government and British investors. Government-owned railroads of modest size were built in New Brunswick and Nova Scotia and were supervised by public boards that had the power to secure loans and issue debentures. In 1845 the St. Lawrence & Atlantic was chartered at a capitalization of £2.4 million, with rates set by law. If earnings exceeded 12 percent, the government was to receive one-half of the surplus. Progress was impossible until adoption of the Guarantee Act of 1849, which guaranteed 50 percent of the debt of any railroad over 75 miles in length.

The Railway Clauses Consolidation Act of 1851 set rules for future incorporation and permitted new companies to fix their own rates. However, certain large projects that needed public subsidy were treated under their own statutes. The Grand Trunk Railway was created in 1853 as a government-sponsored enterprise to link Toronto and Montreal. Its board included five cabinet ministers. Provinces were to guarantee construction debt in the amount of £3,000 per mile, and municipalities were authorized to borrow funds to contribute to the project. The charter qualified the railroad to receive a million-acre land grant to build an extension from Montreal to New Brunswick. A special law was adopted in 1880 to incorporate the Canadian Pacific Railway as a private company, and the measure conferred land grants along its route between Winnipeg and Jasper House. The Canadian National Railways was created as a government-supervised corporation by a 1919 statute.

Early railroads in Mexico were undertaken as the result of individual decrees by the nation's president, and these actions came to be known as "concessions." In 1837 Francisco Arrillaga was given exclusive privilege to construct a Veracruz–Mexico City line, but the concession was declared forfeit when he failed to commence work. Subsequent concessions to this and other proposed routes included provisions for governmental financial aid. U.S. and British interests eventually obtained concessions to build lines, and a number of projects qualified for government subsidies. In time, rail properties in Mexico passed to government ownership, but as part of its decision to privatize the railroads, beginning in 1997 the Mexican government granted concessions to private-sector joint ventures between U.S. railroads and companies domiciled in Mexico.

—William J. Watt

REFERENCES

Baker, George P. *The Formation of the New England Railroad Systems.* New York: Greenwood Press, 1968.

Cleveland, Frederick A., and Fred W. Powell. *Railroad Promotion and Capitalization in the United States.* New York: Longmans, Green, 1909. Repr., New York: Johnson Reprint, 1966.

Glazebrook, G. P. de T. *A History of Transportation in Canada.* Toronto: Ryerson Press, 1938.

Phillips, Ulrich B. *A History of Transportation in the Eastern Cotton Belt to 1860.* New York: Columbia Univ. Press, 1908.

Indiana Rail Road

An Illinois Central subsidiary, the Indianapolis Southern Railroad, opened a 177-mile line in 1906 from Effingham, Illinois, on the IC main line, to Indianapolis. Part of the line was new construction; part of it—the segment between Effingham, Illinois, and Bloomfield, Indiana—was the former Indiana & Illinois Southern Railroad, a narrow-gauge railroad incorporated in 1880 as the Springfield, Effingham & Southeastern and reorganized several times before it came under Illinois Central control in 1900. The line was obviously aimed at local business; the distance between Effingham and Indianapolis on the Pennsylvania Railroad's more direct line was only 140 miles.

Over the years Illinois Central moved much interchange traffic over this branch to the major eastern railroads at Indianapolis, principally the New York Central and the Pennsylvania, because it received larger revenue divisions than if traffic were interchanged at Effingham or Chicago. This was because of the way divisions broke over the Illinois-Indiana state line to allow IC to move traffic into Eastern Territory. After Conrail was formed and closed Indianapolis as a major interchange point, much through traffic dried up and traffic gradually declined. In 1977 Illinois Central Gulf, successor to the IC, petitioned to abandon about half the branch, from Linton to Indianapolis. Track conditions on much of that segment required a speed limit of only 10 mph and, in 1978, caused the Federal Railroad Administration to embargo the line between Bloomington and Indianapolis.

Thomas Hoback had negotiated with ICG in the late 1970s to purchase the line, but ICG decided to retain the line when it received state and federal funds to repair the track sufficiently to raise the speed limit to 25 mph. In 1983 ICG changed its mind and resumed negotiations with Hoback, who in conjunction with several other investors acquired the Sullivan-Indianapolis portion of the line through a holding company, the Indianapolis Terminal Corp.

The Indiana Rail Road (INRD) started operations on March 18, 1986, between Indianapolis, Indiana, and Palestine, Illinois. It subsequently acquired additional trackage from Illinois Central to extend its line to Newton, Illinois, on August 22, 1990, for a total main-line mileage of 155 miles. Its principal customers are power plants at Indianapolis and Merom, Indiana, and one at Lis, Illinois, and an oil refinery at Robinson, Illinois. The application of innovative technology and operating practice, improved service, and attention to customers' needs soon brought significant increases in traffic. Carloadings increased more than eightfold in the railroad's first fifteen years.

INRD briefly operated a 40-mile line from Indianapolis north to Tipton, Indiana, under a lease from Norfolk Southern. It also owned a former IC line from Newton southeast to Browns, Illinois, before selling the line to Indiana Hi-Rail. In 1995 CSX purchased a 40 percent interest in the Indiana Rail Road. As of 2006 it owns 85 percent.

Indiana Rail Road acquired a major expansion with the acquisition of the CPR Latta Subdivision in May 2006, which encompassed 93 miles of main line between Terre Haute and Bedford, Indiana, and linked to the INRD at Linton. Access to Chicago over CSX and over Norfolk Southern to Louisville gave the railroad a through road between Chicago and Louisville. Built by the Chicago, Terre Haute & Eastern, the line was acquired by the Milwaukee Road in 1923, and in more recent years had been part of the Soo Line and then CPR.

—George H. Drury

REFERENCES

Dolzall, Gary W., and Stephen F. Dolzall. "High Times on the Hi-Dry." *Trains* 48, no. 8 (June 1988): 24–29.

Rund, Christopher. *The Indiana Rail Road Company: America's New Regional Railroad.* Bloomington: Indiana Univ. Press, 2005.

Indiana Railroad

Although several other states had a greater interurban electric railway mileage, Indiana came closest to boasting a statewide system. With a total of some 1,825 miles, the Indiana interurban network was largely centered on the state capital of Indianapolis. From the city's great Traction Terminal, a dozen interurban routes reached out to almost every point of consequence in the state.

The Indiana interurbans had already come on hard times and had entered a period of decline when Chicago-based utilities entrepreneur Samuel Insull moved in to consolidate them into a nearly statewide system. Insull, who had extensive electric railway and power holdings in the state, first proposed a merger of these and other utility properties as early as 1925. The state's Public Utilities Commission rejected the plan, but by 1930 Insull managed to consolidate four of the principal lines into the new Indiana Railroad. Insull's Midland United Corp. first acquired the bankrupt Union Traction Co. at a receiver's sale in July 1930 and reorganized the property as the Indiana Railroad Co. The Union Traction routes north and northeast from Indianapolis linked three properties already controlled by Insull: the Interstate Public Service Co., which operated between Indianapolis and Louisville, and the Fort Wayne–based Indiana Service Corp. and the Kokomo-based Northern Indiana Public Service Co., both of which operated lines in central Indiana. Although the four companies remained separate corporations, they were placed under centralized management as the Indiana Railroad System.

The new system comprised a network of almost 700 interurban route-miles, as well as three intercity bus routes and local streetcar and bus service in 11 on-line cities. In terms of interurban route-miles, it would rank—if only briefly—as the largest interurban railway system in the world.

The new Insull management quickly initiated a major rehabilitation and modernization of the IR system. Services and schedules of the four companies were closely coordinated, and business was vigorously promoted through advertising and marketing efforts. An improved dispatch freight service was developed that enabled the IR to offer 72-hour delivery between any point on its system and connecting lines in the upper Midwest territory of the Central Freight Assn. Extensive improvements to track and power systems were begun, older heavyweight steel cars were refurbished, and a new fleet of 35 lightweight, high-speed cars was ordered. Delivered in 1931, the new cars enabled the IR to drastically reduce running times on its principal routes.

Another major property was added to the IR system in 1931 when the bankrupt Terre Haute, Indianapolis & Eastern, which operated routes east and west of Indianapolis, was acquired at another receiver's auction. The weaker THI&E lines were abandoned, leaving a single route east from Indianapolis to a junction with the Dayton & Western at Richmond, Indiana, and a line west to Terre Haute and Paris, Illinois, that were incorporated into the IR system.

Before long, however, the Indiana was feeling the combined effects of the Great Depression and the inroads of highway competition on its passenger and dispatch freight services. Despite the new equipment and improved services, traffic fell off drastically. The Indiana Railroad entered bankruptcy in 1933; only their strong electric power business kept the other three companies solvent.

One by one, the system's weaker lines were abandoned. Still, the IR struggled mightily to keep going. Traffic was heavily promoted with aggressive marketing and slashed fares. In 1935 the interurban began operating two Railway Post Office (RPO) routes. In 1936 the Indiana Railroad made one last, bold move toward expansion of its system when it leased the bankrupt Dayton & Western to preserve a connection with Ohio.

The Indiana Railroad ended 1936 with a modest net income, but it proved to be the only one in its history, and the company's operating results grew steadily worse from 1937 onward. More lines were abandoned, and the Dayton & Western connection was given up less than a year after it had been acquired. Over the next several years the system was gradually converted to bus and truck services. The IR's route between Indianapolis and Fort Wayne via Kokomo and Peru was converted in 1938, and a major segment of the Indianapolis-Louisville route was closed the following year. The Indianapolis–Terre Haute line was converted to bus and truck early in 1940, and the remaining route between Indianapolis and Fort Wayne followed a year later. The last passenger operation on the once-great system, a daily franchise run between Indianapolis and Seymour, Indiana, ended abruptly with a head-on collision near Columbus, Indiana, in September 1941.

Mounted in the face of a secular decline in the interurban electric railway industry and a growing national depression, the Insull effort to consolidate and modernize the central Indiana interurban network seemed quixotic indeed. Yet in the brief decade of their struggle for survival, the Indiana Railroad and its determined managers wrote one of the most colorful chapters in the history of the industry.

In 1938, the last year for which figures are available, the Indiana Railroad operated a rail system of 221 route-miles and 263 track-miles, with 59 passenger cars, 92 freight cars, 16 company service cars, and 947 employees. Operating revenues totaled $1.7 million in 1938.

—William D. Middleton

REFERENCE

Bradley, George K. *Indiana Railroad: The Magic Interurban.* Chicago: Central Electric Railfans' Assn., 1991.

Industrial Shop Practice

The history of railroad industrial practice—that is, of shop work—cannot be separated from the broader story of the evolution of railroad shops in general. Although on-train employees were expected to take care of minor repair work on the road, more serious repairs, as well as regular maintenance, required heavier, specialized tools. Equipment-maintenance and repair shops dated from the dawn of the railway age, and the railroads quickly became very large-scale industrial as well as transportation companies. Their industrial practice is a tale that usefully divides into four parts. The early years date to the mid-1880s. These were followed by a period of enormous expansion and modernization down to about World War I. The interwar years were marked by the quest for efficiency. Finally, after World War II diesel locomotives, decline, and deregulation reshaped railroad industrial practice.

Shops and Shop Work, 1830–1885

The shops of early railroads grew up along with private car and steam locomotive builders and machinery and machine-tool makers, and each influenced the other. It was a time of rapid development and perfection of machinery; interest in shop methods and practice came at a late date. Most of the modern wood- and metalworking tools had been developed before the 1850s, and some such as lathes were of ancient origin. Steam hammers, planers, shapers, drill presses, standard taps and dies, limit gauges, and many others were general-purpose tools that grew out of the special needs of a host of developing industries, including guns, clocks, textile machines, and railroad equipment. Technological convergence allowed machinery developed for one special purpose to be used widely on other practices. Milling machines, for example, might be developed to produce parts for guns, but then, with suitable modifications, could turn out locomotives or cars. Similarly, the heavy machine tools needed for railroad work proved useful in later marine construction.

Every early railroad had some kind of shop. On the larger carriers, because equipment was always breaking down and because locomotive runs tended to be about 100 miles, each division usually had its own roundhouse and repair yards, although there was a tendency to centralize heavy work from an early date. Most of the activity was repair, as opposed to the manufacture of new cars and locomotives. Although a number of carriers manufactured locomotives, only the Pennsylvania became a substantial producer. Car manufacture was a more important activity, for about a quarter of all freight cars came from the railroad shops, and probably a similar proportion of passenger cars as well. The Pennsylvania, the Chicago, Milwaukee, St. Paul & Pacific, the Canadian Pacific, and a few others eventually manufactured many of their own wheels, and some carriers also produced frogs and switches, bridges, and treated ties.

The earliest census data (Table 1), which combine both railroad repair shops and independent car builders, reveal a rapid increase in the size of the typical establishment

Table 1. Railroad Repair Shops and Independent Car Builders, Selected Characteristics, 1850–1900

	1900	1890	1870	1860	1850
Establishments	1,361	787	170	62	41
Capital*	$205,845	$109,942	$10,594	$2,954	$953
Officials	8,462	2,661	—	—	—
Employees	207,105	137,986	15,931	3,179	1,554
Value of products*	$305,691	$183,069	$19,790	$4,303	$2,653
Capital/worker	$958	$596	$550	$906	$365
Workers/establishment	156	177	94	51	38

Source: U.S. Bureau of the Census, Twelfth Census, *Manufacturers IV, Special Reports* (Washington, D.C., 1902), "Cars, Steam Railroad," 263–289, Table 6.

Note: Data for 1880 are unavailable.

*Capital is in thousands of 1899 dollars. Product is gross output in thousands of 1899 dollars.

Table 2. Railroad Car Repair Shops, Selected Statistics, 1890–1929

	1929	1923	1914	1900	1890
Establishments	1,851	1,801	1,362	1,292	716
Capital*	—	—	$295,077	$119,473	$69,901
Salaried officials	29,974	39,022	22,407	7,094	—
Employees	368,681	488,505	339,528	173,595	107,000
Horsepower*	1,077	735	434	99	—
Value added*	$362,267	$435,654	$225,177	$99,670	—
Capital/worker	—	—	$870	$690	$651
Horsepower/worker	3	1.5	1.3	.6	—
Value added/ worker	$983	$892	$663	$574	—

Source: U.S. Bureau of the Census, *Census of Manufacturers*, various years.

*Capital and value added are in thousands of 1899 dollars; horsepower is in thousands.

from the 1850s on. Repair shops are reported independently only from 1890 on (Table 2), and although divisional shops remained small, an average shop employed about 149 employees by that date. But by the 1880s the central shops of large carriers such as the Baltimore & Ohio, the Pennsylvania, and the Central Pacific had evolved into major industrial complexes. The Central Pacific's Sacramento shops employed 600 to 1,000 shop men by 1880, and the floor space of the Pennsylvania's Altoona shops, built about 1870, covered 19.7 acres. As on the Pennsylvania, the major shops were usually located near the carrier's traffic center to minimize unnecessary movement.

The shops were under the jurisdiction of the master mechanic (who was responsible for locomotives) and the master car builder (who ruled car building and repair), and employees were mostly highly skilled. Carpenters were the largest trade, reflecting the widespread use of wood in car construction; then came machinists. There were also blacksmiths and boilermakers, as well as helpers—who were paid by the artisan—and many other trades, as well as laborers. Labor turnover was usually high; one survey of the

Cleveland & Toledo in the 1860s showed that half the skilled mechanics had been there six months or less. Mostly the skilled men learned their trades on the job; probably every large shop employed apprentices, and by the end of the century some were formalizing training programs. Some shops paid men by the hour, but the trend seems to have been toward piecework. On the Pennsylvania the Altoona shops had been on a piecework basis since the 1870s. Pieceworkers were often called contractors; the term reflected both an older era when many artisans were independent and the nature of railroad work, in which craftsmen might do many different jobs over the course of the day, and each job had a price. By the 1880s a typical large repair complex exhibited a good deal of functional specialization. It might include a boiler house, a roundhouse or two, a sand house, an engine house, usually with a transfer table, a foundry, blacksmith, and machine shop, separate freight- and passenger-car shops, paint and upholstery shops, a planing mill, and a woodworking shop, among others. Standard construction seems to have been stone or brick, one- or two-story buildings, the largest of which might be 100 by 200 feet, often with a clerestory at the center running lengthwise with many windows for better lighting. Even so, in the days of coal power, shops were dirty and interiors were dark indeed, making precision work difficult.

Table 1 suggests a slow accretion in capital per worker during these years. An early locomotive shop of modest size had 30 lathes, 10 drills, 8 planers ranging from 6 to 16 feet long, and a handful of other large equipment. By the 1870s the Baltimore & Ohio's Piedmont shop contained an immense number of highly specialized saws, planers, lathes, hammers, boring machines, drill presses, and other equipment. The tendency was to group them by type of machines (e.g., all the lathes together) rather than by type of work (truck repair). Most early equipment was hand operated, but workers also had a few hydraulic jacks, lifts, and presses. At most shops large tools were usually driven by steam from a centrally located boiler. Companies also employed steam tractors with hoists in yard work.

A surprising amount of new equipment was homemade, a product of artisans' "learning by doing." In every shop machinists developed special-purpose tools, often made from scrap, to solve peculiar problems. These were widely reported in sections of technical journals termed "shop kinks," so they could be copied, and some were patented and marketed. An example, from the shops of the Lake Erie & Western, was a small cannon, made from a drilled-out piece of scrap axle, that when loaded with powder and ball was used to blow out rusty bolts. Its use required a light touch, however; when overcharged it once blew a hole through a locomotive cab and the roof of the shop.

Railroad shops not only repaired and produced rolling stock and other equipment, but also pioneered in quality control. Before the Civil War the Pennsylvania and some other large companies had begun to employ physical tests of the wheels and rails they purchased. With the growth of the Master Mechanics and Master Car Builders, and as their members became increasingly trained in engineering, testing spread and became more sophisticated. In 1874 the Pennsylvania also hired Yale Ph.D. Charles B. Dudley, who set up a laboratory and began to develop chemical specifications and test lubricating oils, paints, and a host of other materials to improve quality and reduce cost. Dudley represented a new kind of white-collar, highly educated employee. Similar organizations were soon founded on the Chicago, Burlington & Quincy (1876), Atchison, Topeka & Santa Fe (1883), Erie (1883), Baltimore & Ohio (1884), Milwaukee (1886), Chicago & North Western (1886), and other large carriers.

Modernization and Expansion, 1885–1914

Although the 1880s do not represent a sharp break with previous years, new trends emerged. In particular, both compressed air and electricity emerged as novel power sources at about the same time, profoundly changing the work environment. Compressed air began to be used in the mid-1880s. By the 1890s it had replaced steam in lifts and hoists; it was used for spray painting and made possible the application of power to a host of hand tools, thereby raising productivity and lightening work.

Like compressed air, electricity was far more portable than steam. Initially a large electric motor might be used to drive all the shafting in a shop. Later, as the costs of smaller motors declined, companies recognized the advantages of group and then unit drive. Such arrangements saved power, for they did away with shafts and pulleys, and unlike steam, with electricity one did not have to power the whole shop just to drive one machine. More important, they allowed greater flexibility in tool speed and location, and by getting rid of shafting they increased lighting and allowed use of overhead cranes instead of bulky transfer tables to move locomotives, thereby saving space. The spread of electricity was largely a twentieth-century event; census figures show only 241 electric motors in railroad shops in 1900, but by 1914 there were nearly 25,000.

The 1890s also saw the beginning of a major period of shop expansion and construction. By this time the railroads had simply outgrown many of their older facilities as the expansion of traffic and the increasing size of equipment required larger, more mechanized shops. Discussions at the annual meetings of the Master Mechanics and Master Car Builders during these years also reveal for the first time a self-conscious focus on shop location, layout, and organization. Books on railroad shop organization began to appear, and technical journals began to focus on the subject. In the 1890s the North Western rationalized its repair work, closing many small shops it had inherited from predecessor lines and concentrating work in its Chicago shops. These were organized with an eye to efficient work flow; materials and bad-order cars entered from one end and emerged at the other. As the *American Engineer & Railroad Journal* noted in describing the shops of the Flint & Pere Marquette, it was a "settled principle" that "there shall be no doubling back on the movement of work."

In the early decades of the twentieth century shop construction increasingly shifted to steel-frame buildings that took the load off walls, allowing much greater window space. And as companies discovered that better light improved both productivity and safety, they increased artificial lighting. In 1903 the new Collingwood shops of the Lake Shore featured electric lights attached to each machine tool. The new shops became increasingly mechanized as companies installed a host of electric motors and traveling cranes. Use of newer, very hard steel alloys ("high-speed steel") in cutting tools encouraged purchase of faster, heavier machine tools. Mechanization encouraged shop centralization; it was inefficient to have expensive tools in small shops where they would be underused. Because of the increased mechanization and the growth in car and locomotive size, the new shops were also larger than those they replaced. In 1903 the Philadelphia & Reading built what was then the largest locomotive repair shop in the country at Reading, Pennsylvania, measuring 750 by 200 feet.

On the eve of World War I such shops had come to dominate, as Table 3 reveals; although over 70 percent of establishments were small, employing fewer than 250 workers, over half of all employees labored in shops with over 500 workers. For most shop workers railroad employment would have been little different from working at any of the other large industrial concerns then emerging. Mechanization may also have diluted skill requirements; the ratio of machinists to total employment fell from 25 percent to 16 percent from 1880 to 1910.

As the carriers concentrated employment in large, capital-intensive shops, they became increasingly concerned with productivity. In 1895 Frederick Winslow Taylor's paper on "A Piece Rate System" for the American So-

Table 3. Railroad Shop Employment by Establishment Size, 1914

	Number of Establishments	Average Employment	Percentage of Workers
All	1,362	249.3	
1 to 50 employees	472	20.2	2.7
51 to 250 employees	500	94.7	17.4
251–500 employees	197	342	22.6
501–1,000 employees	131	695	30.0
Over 1,000 employees	62	1,774	27.4

Source: U.S. Bureau of the Census, *Census of Manufacturers, 1914*, vol. 2 (Washington, D.C., 1919), "Railroad Repair Shops," Table 30.

ciety of Mechanical Engineers touched off an efficiency craze that swept through railroading and much of the rest of society. In fact, Taylor's system included much more than piece rates, which seem to have been widespread in railroad shops by that time. Industrial engineers, as the Taylorites came to be called, also emphasized employee selection, tool and job design, and time and motion studies, in addition to compensation schemes. The first large-scale application of these ideas to railroads began in 1903 when the Atchison, Topeka & Santa Fe hired Harrington Emerson, a Taylor disciple, to rationalize shop work.

The Santa Fe was then experiencing much labor unrest in its shops, and the decision to hire Emerson was probably motivated in part by the hope that he could help management weather a strike, which began shortly after he arrived. Ironically, however, it was not workers but mid-level managers who opposed his efforts. At the Santa Fe Emerson found an organization with very poor cost controls. He began small, with belting used to run tools; he upgraded belt quality and improved maintenance, which reduced expensive machine downtime. He then proceeded to do the same for grinding wheels and pneumatic equipment and redesigned tools to use the new high-speed steel. By these methods Emerson claimed that he was able to reduce costs of tool maintenance greatly. He also introduced preventive locomotive maintenance, developed fuel-use records, and introduced cost accounting and standard timekeeping, which allowed comparison of repair costs with outside sources. There is little doubt that Emerson's system raised wages and improved shop efficiency, although the extent of the improvements is still debated; yet because his reforms threatened managerial prerogatives, many were undone after he left.

Despite these efforts, railroaders revealed an undercurrent of concern that shops were not as efficient as they should be, because the carriers treated them like stepchildren. Capital, horsepower, and productivity (value added per worker) were far below levels in commercial shops, and the carriers lagged in employing white-collar, salaried workers as well (Tables 2 and 4). As early as 1901 the *Railroad Gazette* complained that "railroad shop equipment as a whole is antiquated and out of date." These worries resulted in much discussion and some experimentation with contracting out repair work. Small railways especially had always contracted out heavy locomotive repairs to builders, and large companies had done so from time to time. In 1909 *Railway Age*, echoing Harrington Emerson, complained that railway accounting gave false cost estimates and suggested that more outside contracting might be in order, but little was done in the prewar years.

Taylorism and Emerson's work were widely reported and discussed in the technical press, and both played a key role in the railroads' request for a general rate increase. Railroad rate regulation had become increasingly strict with the Mann-Elkins Act of 1903; yet the general price level was rising, and the carriers, caught in a cost-price squeeze, appealed for a general rate increase in 1910. At the hearings the lawyer for business interests that opposed the increase, Louis D. Brandeis, put Emerson on the stand to condemn railroad industrial practice. The latter testified that through efficiency measures such as those he had employed on the Santa Fe, the carriers could save $300 million a year. The inference was that the carriers did not need a rate increase, and the Interstate Commerce Commission (ICC) denied their request. It was the beginning of a profit squeeze that had far-reaching consequences for the future of American railroading.

Industrial Practice, 1914–1939

World War I resulted in a federal takeover of the railroads. Under the U.S. Railroad Administration (USRA), employment expanded (Figure 1), union membership spread, piece rates were abolished, and the workday was shortened, the combined effect of which was to reduce productivity and balloon costs. When federal control ended in 1920, the carriers determined to reassert control. They increasingly began to contract out repair work, sometimes to other shops, sometimes to outside companies to run the railroads' own shops. *Railway Age* claimed that a comparison of comparable work on 50 freight cars in railroad and contract shops demonstrated the latter to be 28 percent more efficient. In early 1922 the journal *Machinery* published an article titled "What Is Wrong with Railroad Shops?" The answer, it thought, was in good part the labor inefficiencies imposed by the USRA, for which it prescribed a return to piecework. In addition, however, the author blamed unsuitable equipment that resulted from weak railroad finances. The journal compared identical operations on identical engines in different shops and discovered wide variation in the time required. Another journal, *American Machinist*, chipped in, asking the same question and adding poor methods to the indictment, which it blamed on "inbreeding" and "lack of new blood" among officials. It went on to detail the need for newer machines, interchangeable parts, production schedules, and production engineers.

Table 4. Independent Railroad Car Builders, Selected Characteristics, 1890–1929

	1929	1923	1914	1900	1890
Establishments	147	131	103	65	71
Capital*	—	—	$131,508	$88,324	$40,038
Salaried officials	6,098	8,858	4,700	1,366	—
Employees*	40,015	76,612	54,288	33,453	31,354
Horsepower*	238	240	136	35	—
Value added	$50,893	$87,709	$52,146	$28,767	$23,311
Capital/worker	—	—	$2,232	$2,666	$1,290
Horsepower/worker	6	3	2.3	1.1	—
Value added/ worker	$1,272	$1,026	$960	$860	$743

Source: U.S. Bureau of the Census, *Census of Manufacturers*, various years.

*Capital and value added are in thousands of 1899 dollars; horsepower is in thousands.

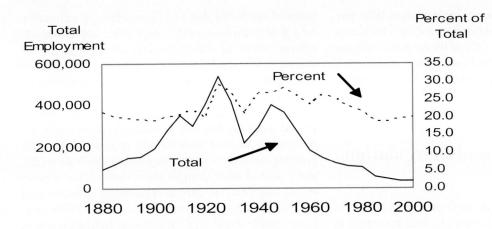

Figure 1. Railroad shop employment, 1880–2000. —U.S. Census and ICC *Statistics of Railways*, various years

Even as critics were excoriating the railroad shops' inefficiencies, the combination of contracting out and wage cuts provoked the shopmen to strike. It was a long, bitter, and bloody affair that they ultimately lost and that destroyed shop unionism for a decade. At its end the carriers promptly ended outside contracting, suggesting that its motive had been union busting as much as efficiency, but the experience helped spread new, more efficient methods of repair.

In 1923, under the guidance of Daniel Willard, the B&O introduced a "cooperative plan" in its shops that involved what was later called worker-manager "quality circles." The plan's origin lay with the company's earlier experience using safety committees and was an effort to improve both human relations and productivity. Although it seems to have been successful, the approach never spread beyond the B&O.

A more lasting change occurred when the Big Four contracted out operation of its Beech Grove Shops to the Railway Service and Supply Co. The latter promptly reinstituted piece rates and also instituted what came to be called the "progressive," "unit," or "straight-line" system of car repair that had been employed by manufacturers for some time. In a large shop this method repaired groups of similar cars, thereby allowing longer production runs of machine tools, and it worked on a semi-assembly-line basis. A car would come in and be stripped; it would then be dragged through the shed to be progressively reassembled. Even skilled workers therefore now specialized in a narrow selection of tasks. At Beech Grove productivity tripled, and the methods soon spread to most other large repair shops. By 1927 a survey by the American Railway Assn. (ARA) Mechanical Division found such methods employed on carriers owning two-thirds of all freight cars.

The return of piecework and the progressive system of car repair helped boost productivity (Tables 2 and 4), and so did a number of other changes in shop work. As locomotives became more sophisticated and expensive, downtime became more costly. Companies began to stock spare parts so that defective items might simply be replaced rather than repaired, thus speeding up the process. The progressive system encouraged new interest in shop layout, and many companies built new facilities in the early 1920s. These continued the trend toward greater size and centralization—some of them took as many as 400 acres—and they employed increasing amounts of glass for natural lighting. With better windows and lighting, and with electric power, shops were cleaner, which contributed to employee well-being. Along with other employers, the railroads had begun to introduce new systems of human relations, termed welfare capitalism, in the prewar years. These included improved safety and other working conditions and were an effort to build employee loyalty and so raise productivity and reduce the lure of labor unions. New shops were painted to improve lighting and reduce eye stress. Companies installed lockers and showers. On the Great Northern employees even built a greenhouse as part of a shop beautification campaign.

If the new welfare policies made shop work more pleasant and helped balance its increasing assembly-line quality, improving technologies in shops and rolling stock also made it less common. By the 1920s passenger traffic and some forms of freight traffic were in decline. In this context improving shop productivity reduced employment. In addition, both cars and motive power were becoming larger, more efficient, and more reliable, all of which reduced maintenance needs. Collectively these changes reshaped shop employment in predictable ways; both the number and proportion of shop-men peaked in the 1920s and then began a long decline (Figure 1).

In 1925 *American Machinist* again wondered what was wrong with railway shops. This time it blamed top management for starving the shops of new tools, and later surveys by the magazine showed that the shops were increasingly saddled with aging equipment, a result it blamed on weak profitability. The 1920s saw proliferation of increasingly sophisticated electric and air-powered machinery, and a number of carriers invested heavily. Yet the railroads were too poor to participate fully in the feast, and many writers wondered how men could perform good work with such poor equipment. In 1923 *Railway Age* reported that shop machine tools averaged 20 years old, and several years later it reported in amazement a wheel lathe purchased in 1854 that was just being retired from the Chesapeake & Ohio shops. After 1929, as the economy collapsed and many railroads slid into bankruptcy, machine-tool purchases nearly ended for a decade. In 1931 a survey indicated that 70 percent of tools were at least a decade old, and the proportion rose throughout the 1930s.

Diesels, Decline, and Deregulation, 1945–2000

World War II brought an explosion of traffic to the railroads that carried with it a brief burst of prosperity. In response, inflation-adjusted spending on maintenance of equipment doubled from 1940 through 1945 as the carriers invested in improved rolling stock and modernized shops. The pressures to cut costs and modernize were also pressing them to scrap the iron horse in favor of more efficient diesels. In combination with longer-term changes that had been reshaping railroading for decades, the new motive power revolutionized shop work.

Diesels reshaped industrial practice in several ways. They were more powerful than the steam locomotives they replaced, and so a given amount of traffic required fewer locomotives to maintain. They were more expensive than steam units, and so shop time was more costly, increasing the incentive to minimize it. And their maintenance requirements were profoundly different. Joseph Fellenz, a longtime crane operator in the Chicago & Alton shops, remembered that "they had to change the shop altogether" when diesels arrived. Gone were the water troughs, coaling stations, and ashpits. The move to diesels accelerated the shift to parts replacement rather than repair. For steam, many parts had been made in the blacksmith shop or foundry; now they were purchased. Such changes reduced labor requirements, and diesel repair also sharply changed the mix of skills among shop workers. At the Canadian Pacific Angus shops in Montreal, dieselization reduced the number of boilermakers by 84 percent from 1948 to 1961, while electricians increased 72 percent.

Diesels also reconfigured shop layout. Their longer runs continued the trend to shop centralization, and they had different shop requirements. In particular, diesels required cleanliness; companies that tried to maintain both steam and diesel in the same shop found that they needed to partition off the diesel section. Pits had to be redesigned to allow drop tables for truck removal. And although men had often worked on steam locomotives from ladders, the expense of diesels and the need to keep them on the road encouraged construction of permanent multilevel flooring to facilitate access. Similar motives impelled companies to employ spectrographic analysis of lubricating oil to look for signs of wear and Magnaflux or ultrasound investigation of wheels, axles, pistons, and other moving parts.

Yet the diesel was by no means the entire cause of changes in industrial practices after World War II, for many of the forces that had been reshaping railroading for a generation continued. Unionization had returned to railroad shops in the 1930s, and after World War II sharply rising wages encouraged companies to substitute new capital and technology for labor. In combination with larger and more reliable cars and locomotives, such forces continued the trend to centralization and therefore toward assembly-line-like production. Increasingly sophisticated machine tools and the spread of lift trucks, portable diesel cranes, vapor degreasing, synthetic paints, and a host of other changes also reduced labor requirements, and the steady erosion of passenger traffic reduced the need for equipment maintenance. In the 1950s companies finally abandoned the cast-iron freight-car wheel, thereby closing the wheel foundry at the Canadian Pacific and some other lines. Freight cars increasingly came to be made of alloy steel or aluminum, used nailable steel floors, and employed lubricating pads or roller bearings, all of which reduced maintenance needs.

Since about 1960 economic decline of eastern and midwestern roads, along with mergers and later deregulation, has continued to reshape railroad industrial practice. The devolution of many branch lines into smaller independent carriers, along with the increasing use of private cars and leasing, has encouraged the expansion of independent maintenance contractors. In 1965, when the North Western leased 600 reefers, the lessor did the maintenance. In 1972 *Railway Age* began an annual survey of outside repair contractors; in 1975 it listed 68 such firms, and by 1980 the number had risen to 131. These trends have continued, and as a result shop employment has plummeted even more sharply than total employment (Figure 1).

—Mark Aldrich

REFERENCES

American Engineer and Railroad Journal, 1890–1915.

Berg, Walter. *American Railway Shop Systems.* New York: Railroad Gazette, 1904.

Canadian Department of Labor. *Technological Changes in the Railway Industry: Employment Effects and Adjustment Process.* Ottawa: Department of Labor, 1967.

"A Century of Progress in Car and Locomotive Maintenance." *Railway Mechanical Engineer* 106 (1932): 413–424.

Davis, Colin. *Power at Odds: The 1922 National Railroad Shopmen's Strike.* Urbana: Univ. of Illinois Press, 1997.

Matejka, Michael, and Greg Koos, eds. *Bloomington's C&A Shops: Our Lives Remembered.* Urbana: Univ. of Illinois Press, 1988.

U.S. Bureau of the Census. *Report on Manufactures,* 1880–1929.

Insull, Samuel (1859–1938)

Born in London, Samuel Insull began his career at 14 as a five-shilling-a-week office boy and became a wizard

Samuel Insull. —Samuel Insull, Jr.

sull's empire fell apart in the early 1930s, and many stockholders lost their entire fortunes. Extradited from Europe, where he had gone after the collapse of his empire, Insull was tried three times on a variety of charges. Each time he was acquitted, but the once-admired Insull died in 1938 a sad, broken, and hated man. There is no indication that his financing was illegal by the standards of the day, but the Securities and Exchange Commission subsequently outlawed the template for his holding company.

In his prime, Insull was a business leader of the first cut. There is no better proof of this than his excellent oversight of the transportation companies he controlled in the Chicago area. He took over the city's elevated lines in 1914 and subsequently controlled all the streetcar lines. More important, perhaps, he acquired three important regional interurban railroads: the Chicago North Shore & Milwaukee, the Chicago South Shore & South Bend, and the Chicago Aurora & Elgin. Built and maintained to Class 1 railroad standards, they became the leading electric carriers of the era.

—George H. Douglas

REFERENCES

Insull, Samuel. *Memoirs of Samuel Insull: An Autobiography*, ed. Larry Plachno. Polo, Ill.: Transportation Trails, 1992.
McDonald, Forrest. *Insull*. Chicago: Univ. of Chicago Press, 1962.

of finance and a public utilities magnate. At the age of 21 he immigrated to the United States, where he soon obtained a position as private secretary to Thomas Alva Edison. A poor businessman himself, Edison must have perceived rare executive talent in Insull, for he sent Insull to Schenectady, New York, where he subsequently became a vice president of Edison's manufacturing unit there (later General Electric). In 1892 Insull moved to the Midwest and became president of the Chicago Edison Co., which was in time the sole electric supplier to the city of Chicago. Within a few years Insull gained control of his own utilities empire, which included not only Chicago but many other companies throughout the Midwest.

In 1912 Insull established a holding company, Middle Western Utilities, which controlled many operating companies. His system worked splendidly for many years, and Insull became one of Chicago's leading citizens, as well as a great patron of the arts (he established the Civic Opera Co. of Chicago). But his holding company involved elaborate pyramiding and eventually became his undoing. In-

Intermodal Freight

Intermodal transport is the movement of cargo or people using more than one type of vehicle. Loosely defined, its history can go back as far as biblical times, with the movement of a barrel of wine from a donkey on land to a sailing vessel. For freight, a more rigorous definition would include a door-to-door movement between modes without a transfer of cargo. This would bring one to the movement of farm wagons to market by rail on Long Island in the 1800s. Samuel Insull's Chicago North Shore & Milwaukee interurban haulage of specially built highway trailers on flatcars in 1926 would be recognizable today. All of these operations were eventually scrapped. Credit for the first, continuous operation of standard, loaded highway vehicles by a Class 1 railroad belongs to the Chicago Great Western in 1935.

This Depression-bred innovation produced decades of controversy both within and outside the railroad business. During this time intermodalists improvised and innovated until, by the end of the twentieth century, intermodal was the largest or second-largest revenue producer on virtually every North American railroad. Intermodal was also the first leg of a three-legged stool that would produce efficiencies that would lead to a true economic globalization.

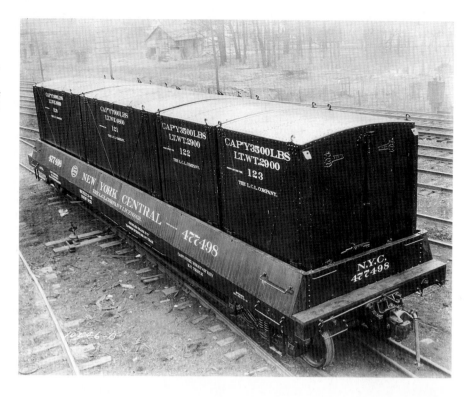

Intermodal freight was an idea that had been around for a long time, but not until after World War II did it become significant. One early attempt was an LCL container service initiated by the New York Central in 1921. Small containers were carried on a modified flatcar. —*Trains* Magazine Collection

Narrow modal interests have fought the intermodal concept in both passenger and freight for many years. Modally oriented thinkers in freight included railroaders and truckers who felt that cooperation with another mode was "selling out to the enemy." Many on the passenger side, including transit, airlines, and railroads, agreed with that view.

Regulators, including the Interstate Commerce Commission (ICC), the Civil Aeronautics Board, and the Federal Maritime Commission, were all charged by Congress with the protection of both "their" modes and the shippers. Only those working in intermodal—and the ship-

pers who used intermodal—saw the benefits and continued to push and develop the concept that, using a combination of modes, could produce a cheap, reliable, fast service that no single mode could match.

Growth in freight intermodal began in the mid-1930s but was interrupted by World War II. Serious development began in the 1950s when former General Motors executive Eugene Ryan, feeling constrained, left to develop the idea of promoting the haulage of highway trailers by rail. This was dubbed trailer on flatcar (TOFC), popularly known as "piggyback."

Early supporters of the concept included the Pennsyl-

Early intermodal service, usually called "piggyback," consisted of standard truck trailers and flatcars, modified as required. This 1954 photograph shows the Chicago & North Western's newly established service. —Chicago & North Western

Early piggyback operations used a ramp at one end of a train to load or unload truck trailers over a string of flatcars, "circus loading" style. A tractor truck at Chicago is unloading a string of inbound Illinois Central trailers just arrived from New Orleans in August 1957. —William D. Middleton

vania Railroad, the New Haven, the Chicago & Eastern Illinois, the Burlington, and the Southern Pacific. In 1953 the New Haven brought what became known as the Twenty Questions case before the ICC requesting rulings on the legality of railroads hauling truck freight. The ICC could easily have continued the "silo thinking" of the past and prohibited or severely limited piggyback. Instead, it permitted the railroads to work with truckers, shippers, and third parties (at that point, freight forwarders, brokers, and shippers' agents) to develop this new thing called intermodal.

Modern intermodal began in the 1950s with a couple of hundred thousand loads. It has continued as a growth business virtually every year since. In 2000 it became the largest single revenue producer for the U.S. Class 1 railroads, surpassing coal that year. Early intermodal customers included UPS (still the largest individual customer) and so-called third parties or logistics companies. Current major customers also include major truck lines and containership operators.

The physical loading of trailers evolved from circus trains, which loaded wagons on flatcars for movement between towns. "Circus loading" of piggyback trailers involved backing the trailer up a ramp and onto a cut of flatcars, using fold-down bridge plates to cross between cars. At the end of the car a hitch was dragged or raised in place to secure the trailer kingpin and hence the trailer to the flatcar (hitches were made in various styles). In most cases two trailers fit on each flatcar.

Equipment innovation became a watchword in intermodal from the beginning. Service in the 1950s began with 75-foot flatcars. As trailer sizes grew, so did flatcars, from 75 to 85 to 89 feet. Equipment supply for this busi-

A close-up view of a piggyback Illinois Central trailer at New Orleans in August 1957 illustrates the complicated attachment system required. —William D. Middleton

Intermodal freight operators soon abandoned the cumbersome circus-loading arrangement in favor of movable gantry units or large rubber-tired side-loading forklift machines that could handle trailers or containers anywhere in the train. This was a rubber-tired Letourneau gantry unit on CSX at Queensgate Yard in Cincinnati. —*Trains* Magazine Collection

ness was also innovative. Carload business grew almost exclusively with railroad-owned equipment. Car-pooling companies largely supplied intermodal cars. Originally two large competing companies, GATX (a private leasing company) and Trailer Train (a company originally owned by participating railroads, a freight forwarder, and Eugene Ryan, later owned exclusively by railroads and renamed TTX), supplied the flatcars. Trailer Train was originally set up and initially staffed and supported by the use of high-level PRR people. This included the initial president of Trailer Train, Jim Newell, who was simultaneously vice president of operations of the PRR. Rather surprisingly, this all occurred in a time when most operating people were decidedly antipiggyback.

Trailers also increasingly were supplied by outside sources. Initially the trailer manufacturers made simple term leases for intermodal. As the business grew, two firms were established that offered both term leases and trailer pools with daily leases and freedom of interchange. Initially XTRA Corp. offered this flexibility, to be followed by Realco, which was initially started by Railway Express Agency and later was sold to Transamerica. These equipment supply companies became critical to the growth of the intermodal business.

Equally important was the development of terminal handling equipment, which allowed for the growth in size of intermodal terminals. As intermodal growth took off, the labor-intensive circus-loading terminals quickly be-

A similar piece of equipment for handling on and off lifts for intermodal equipment were these large gantries, which could operate either on track or tire mounted, as seen here on the Pennsylvania Railroad at Kearny, New Jersey. —Don Wood, *Trains* Magazine Collection

Intermodal rolling stock quickly evolved into highly specialized cars. This was a five-platform, articulated Southern Pacific car designed to handle double-stack container loads, operated here with Sea-Land containers. —*Trains* Magazine Collection

came crowded and inefficient. Suppliers of industrial material-handling equipment attracted early to intermodal included Drott and Paceco. Paceco built ship stowage cranes for ports and placed a couple of cranes in the early 1960s. Paceco quickly lost interest in piggyback and focused on marine cranes. In 1964 Southern Pacific's Tom Fante and Jack Sherbourne worked through Scott Corbett, a dealer for Wagner Tractor, a builder of logging equipment, to develop the first side-lift machine, the Piggypacker. Their work was supported by the Milwaukee Road, and the Piggypacker became the early lift machine of choice. LeTourneau, also a builder of logging machines, became an early builder of lift equipment. Chico Clark sold LeTourneau machines but switched to Wagner machines. Drott initially acquired Travelift, a boat-lifting device, and adapted it for intermodal use. An employee, Jack Lanigan, established a close working relationship with the Santa Fe and later acquired a dealership in Chicago. In 1970 J. I. Case bought Drott. After a difficult ten years Case dropped the Drott line, and Lanigan bought the patents, redesigned the

machines, and launched Mi-Jack. In 1985 Lanigan bought the patents for Piggypackers from Raygo-Wagner. In the 1980s Taylor Machine Works, longtime builders of marine terminal handling equipment, entered the intermodal market. In this period both Clark, who also operated intermodal terminals, and Lanigan, who later established a terminal-operating company, evolved major terminal design innovations for more efficient terminals.

Many foreign and domestic manufacturers have entered the intermodal lift market, only to exit again. Mi-Jack and LeTourneau have stayed the course through the years, and Taylor, a somewhat later entry, has also proven to be a major player.

A variation of TOFC service first developed under the Chesapeake & Ohio's Robert R. Young in 1956 was the Railvan, which eliminated much of the excess weight of a TOFC by doing away with the flatcar altogether. These were specially built trailer cars designed to operate in a train of cars and equipped with retractable rail wheels that could be lowered for rail movement or raised for

Modern terminals can accommodate enormous intermodal traffic between ship, highway, and rail. Two high-speed gantry cranes load and unload containers at the Deltaport terminal in Roberts Bank near Vancouver, British Columbia. Each handles up to 40 containers an hour. Containers were being unloaded from the American President Line's container ship *President Kennedy* on September 2, 1997. —William D. Middleton

highway use. A similar concept developed in 1982 by the RoadRailer has had much more success.

On April 26, 1956, a major intermodal milestone event occurred. After unsuccessfully trying to persuade existing steamship lines to try his concept of loading containers, with cargo intact, aboard ships (in lieu of transferring cargo in loading nets, with huge labor cost and damage), Malcolm McLean loaded 58 containers on the *Ideal X* and established a company that would become Sea-Land. It would provide the second leg of the revolutionary stool— the birth of containerization.

New ideas in equipment continued as intermodal traffic grew and changed. Freight cars were developed that could readily be used for either TOFC trailers or containers. There were a number of tests of six- and ten-car designs for lightweight, center-sill articulated cars. By the early 1980s double-stack articulated cars were entering production, placing one container into a low-level well between the trucks, with a second container on the upper level. Fast double-stack container trains were being moved in trainload movements.

While it would take years to work out the kinks of "silo thinking" among the regulators, the die was cast in terms of the efficiency of haulage of cargo at sea. The container would sweep virtually all other forms of nonbulk movement from the seas. On land they could move efficiently by highway or rail.

The key to the modern container era was the development of the corner casting, a hollow steel casting about 6 by 6 by 6 inches, placed on all eight corners of the container. The top is slotted for pickup anywhere in the world, the sides are slotted for lashing tie-down, and the bottom corners are used for interbox connectors in stacking. The corner casting, together with a corner post, a hollow steel tube about 8 by 8 inches, allows containers to be stacked up to nine boxes high in ship cells or two high in railcar stacks, without the floors touching. Since the corner posts are used in 40-foot modules, the posts are not always actually at a corner for containers over 40 feet in length.

Major trade flows developed where none had existed before. Although containers were a small part of rail intermodal in the beginning (about 5 percent in the 1960s), the development of double-stack container cars, initially by SP, Sea-Land, and American Car & Foundry and later also Gunderson, American President Lines, and Thrall, provided an additional economic boost to international trade on the inland leg. So powerful was the combination that by the turn of the twenty-first century containers constituted 75 percent of rail intermodal business.

Finally, increasingly powerful computers allowed for the development of logistics—the integration of production, transportation, and storage functions. Logistics companies now have the overview data to design the most efficient movement of materials through the production process to final delivery of the product.

The combination of intermodal, containerization, and logistics constitutes a revolutionary triumvirate that has produced estimated annual savings of $1 trillion to the U.S. economy alone. It has also sparked a revolution of global production and world trade. Though largely invisible in our daily activity, the mighty triumvirate has created huge benefits for the world economy.

—David J. DeBoer

REFERENCES

Association of American Railroads Fact Books, various years.

Cass/Pro Logistics 11th Annual State of Logistics Report, 1999.

DeBoer, David J. *Piggyback and Containers: A History of Rail Intermodal on America's Steel Highways*. San Marino, Calif.: Golden West, 1992.

Intermodal Revenue, Class 1 U.S. Railroads 2000 Annual Reports.

Muller, G. *Intermodal Freight Transportation.* 2nd ed. Westport, Conn.: Eno Foundation, 1989.

White, John H., Jr. *The American Railroad Freight Car.* Baltimore: Johns Hopkins Univ. Press, 1993.

———. "The Magic Box: Genesis of the Container." *Railroad History*, no. 158 (Spring 1988): 72–93.

Internal Improvements

Before the ink was fairly dry on their brand-new constitutions, the American states took up the task of "internal improvements"—developing roads, bridges, and canals to facilitate trade and transportation. Before 1776 most residents of British North America faced east or southeast, looking to the mother country and its Caribbean colonies for connections with the outside world. Wooden ships sailed from American ports—the best were Boston, New York, Philadelphia, Baltimore, and Charleston—for all parts of the Atlantic community. A limited coastwise trade united some lesser ports around Chesapeake Bay, Narragansett Bay, the Hudson and Connecticut rivers, and Long Island Sound; still, the vast majority of commercial intercourse took place not among neighbors but across the water. Towns and cities hugged the coast and inland waterways. Notoriously bad colonial roads—unpaved tracks filled with stumps—radiated out into the urban hinterlands but seldom offered arterial connections. Travel on land rarely exceeded the pace of human perambulation; equestrians typically walked their mounts, and wagons excelled handcarts only in the magnitude of the load (and then only where roadways would accommodate the larger vehicle).

Working from traditional assumptions common to Britons living anywhere, early Americans looked to local taxpayers to build and maintain common roads in their immediate vicinity. Bridges were few; well-regulated ferries carried man and beast across the larger streams. Municipal authorities (if any) and private associations of interested merchants shared the burden of keeping up docks and wharves, although everyone seemed to think of these as public facilities. For improvements of any magnitude, Americans turned for assistance to their governments. Those governments, burdened by war debts and leery of offending their tax-averse constituents, in turn chartered private corporations to encourage men of means in the locale to invest in public infrastructure. The Charles River Bridge, for example, first chartered in 1785, offered shareholders a 40-year monopoly of tolls if they would erect a bridge in the place where Harvard College had maintained a ferry. Similar terms soon were offered to local turnpike companies in Pennsylvania, Massachusetts, Maryland, and Virginia, each promising steady profits to private parties who would undertake the "traditional" work of the sovereign.

Such efforts by local authorities and corporate enterprises sufficed for only the smallest and most local transportation improvements. Great interregional thoroughfares and expensive new technologies (canals) necessarily required the patronage of government at the state and even national levels. In the 1790s Congress assumed responsibility for "establishing" and "laying out" post roads, creating for the first time a communications "backbone" of sorts. Meanwhile, restless Americans trekked west toward the Ohio River and Great Lakes (as well as east into Maine), and these pioneers demanded improved access back to tidewater markets. Accordingly, boosters in Virginia, Pennsylvania, New York, and Massachusetts stumped for support for developing arteries deep into the continent, using (respectively) the James or Potomac, Susquehanna, Hudson, and Merrimack rivers as their routes of penetration to the heartland.

All such projects—envisioned before 1800, but still out of practical reach—promised to swallow up great sums of money, while the benefits seemed more likely to fall (like the rain) on communities more than on the investors who advanced the capital. Furthermore, rivalry among these routes for potential control of the American interior trade subverted cooperation on the federal level. Nobody doubted that these routes should be developed, and no one thought that it could be done without significant government assistance; but who would privilege any project at the expense of others? By the first decade of the new century, while local roads and bridges proceeded apace, the frustrating outlines already could be seen of an intractable problem with any national system of internal improvements.

In 1807, at the request of the Senate, Treasury Secretary Albert Gallatin gathered information on all the internal improvement projects proposed or under way in the several states. His goal was to assemble a blueprint for a national system of roads and canals, but he produced a remarkable inventory as well. Of first importance, Gallatin believed, was a series of canals cutting the four major necks of land that interrupted coastal navigation—Cape Cod, New Jersey, Delaware, and the Great Dismal Swamp that separated Chesapeake Bay from Albemarle Sound.

Massachusetts already was investigating routes for a canal at Barnstable Bay. Three corporations—the Raritan & Delaware, the Chesapeake & Delaware, and the Dismal Swamp canals—had failed for lack of capital paid in by the shareholders. With hydraulic engineering in its infancy, early canal companies fell victim to competing claims of "experts" whose overoptimistic estimates typically raised enough cash in early subscriptions to pay the consultants but not many navvies. Gallatin proposed that Congress adopt these projects as one axis of a national system.

Next, Gallatin advocated linking the coast with the "western waters." Three great rivers—the James and Potomac in Virginia and the Susquehanna in Pennsylvania—pointed the way west and nearly touched at their heads with others—Kanawha, Monongahela, and Allegheny—flowing into the Ohio. State or corporate efforts had begun to improve navigation on each of these, as well as the Roanoke, Santee, Cooper, and other Carolina rivers. Once again, technical ignorance coupled with wishful thinking fostered woefully inadequate plans for slack-water navigations, sluice dams, channel dredging, and the occasional flight of real canal locks. Once again, most of the money paid out went for surveys and exploration, much of it proving that original designs would not work. Nevertheless, the James River Co. did improve navigation above Richmond and built a canal around the falls at that city (though not down to tidewater). To the north, the Potomac Co. cut canals around the Great and Little Falls, making it possible for boats from above the Fall Line to descend 143 feet to tidewater. Additional works in the vicinity of Harpers Ferry and experimental dams and sluiceways raised the hope (never realized) of navigation in the natural riverbed all the way to Cumberland, Maryland. In Pennsylvania politics frustrated geography, because the falls that kept Susquehanna traffic from flowing smoothly into Chesapeake Bay (and thence to Baltimore) provided "natural" protection to Philadelphia as the state's entrepôt. A Maryland company had cut a canal up the lower end of the river, but Pennsylvania balked at further opening this "foreign" outlet. Instead, the Quaker State focused on interior routes along the Schuylkill and upper Susquehanna that reached into the rugged northern and central parts of the state.

New York possessed a unique natural endowment, nearly water-level routes to outlets in the North and West. At the time of Gallatin's report, companies existed for cutting canals to link the Hudson to the St. Lawrence via Lake Champlain and the Hudson to Lake Ontario via the Mohawk and Oswego rivers. A third canal around the 450-foot Niagara escarpment would place boats on Lake Erie in easy reach of the entire Great Lakes basin. Massachusetts's Middlesex Canal linked the Merrimack River with Boston Harbor at a cost of just over half a million dollars. A Virginia company, the Appomattox, was nearly finished with a short canal lowering the south branch of the James at Petersburg to tidewater. Two companies in Pennsylvania, the Schuylkill & Delaware and the Schuylkill & Susquehanna, had begun useful canals, but both were suspended for want of funds "or from other causes not fully understood." Equally fruitless enterprises had been created to cut canals at the Falls of the Ohio at Louisville and improve navigation on the Neuse, Beaufort, Deep, Haw, and Cape Fear rivers in North Carolina. Finally, the Carondelet Canal at New Orleans opened an inland communication between the Mississippi River and Lake Pontchartrain.

Turnpike roads had been much more successful than canals (technically, if not always financially) in the first decades since independence. Gallatin reported 50 charters in Connecticut alone, 39 of which were finished for a total of 770 miles. Massachusetts Yankees spent most lavishly on turnpikes, up to $12,500 per mile. Major pikes connected Boston with Newburyport, Providence, and Salem. New York spent more in aggregate (if less per mile), reporting 67 turnpike and 21 toll-bridge charters. The New Jersey turnpike from Trenton to Brunswick already was a cultural landmark.

In Pennsylvania short pikes radiated out of Philadelphia in all directions, and the 62-mile Lancaster Turnpike, the first thoroughfare of its kind in the country, gave the metropolis all-weather access to a rich agricultural hinterland and, by an extension, the banks of the Susquehanna. A new branch was just then being built to Harrisburg farther north on the river. Maryland likewise sported excellent roads in and out of Baltimore, most famously the Frederick Town Pike (which would eventually carry traffic to the start of the National Road at Cumberland). South of Washington, road building apparently lost its appeal. Gallatin attributed the "greater progress" in the North to a "more compact population" and noted as well the convenience of many good bridges of stone and wood spanning some of the "broadest and deepest rivers." The best roads to date tended to reduce grades to 5 percent or less, crown the roadway to drain off surface water, and reinforce the surface with broken stone or gravel to support the weight of carriages. As part of his final recommendation, Gallatin urged a Maine-to-Georgia post road, built to the highest specifications (anticipating I-95 by 150 years).

Gallatin's report yielded nothing but frustration for friends of a national system of internal improvement. Fed up with jealous resistance from Congress, in 1817 New York promoters, led by former New York City mayor De Witt Clinton, stirred their state to take the enormous risk of borrowing $7 million to build a "Grand Canal" linking the Hudson River with Lake Erie. Guided by the prudent experimentation of four local, self-taught engineers and enjoying good luck, as well as bold leadership, New York's Erie Canal soon poured agricultural produce from a vast interior breadbasket into the city's export markets. Rome, Utica, Syracuse, and Rochester mushroomed into cities virtually overnight. Lumber, wheat, and flour exports soared, and imports and immigrants filled the westbound canal boats; a rough-and-tumble market revolution—with all its energy and chaos—transformed life in the entire region. Revenues serviced both overhead and debt, paid for an extensive network of additional state canals (never profitable themselves), and for a while even lightened the ordinary load on New York taxpayers. Anchored by this interregional "river of gold," New York City quickly engrossed the commerce of the nation, establishing a leadership position that would dictate the terminus of the railroad networks yet to come.

The great 365-mile Erie Canal climbed 627 vertical feet in 83 locks to link the Hudson River and Lake Erie. Its completion late in 1825 helped shape the future growth of the United States. This 1873 engraving by E. A. Abbey in the December 1873 *Harper's New Monthly Magazine* shows canal boats at the Erie's Troy, New York, entrance.
—Middleton Collection

New York's rival seaports launched frantic efforts to compete for a share of this new American domestic commerce. Boston's commercial leaders turned their attention to the prospect of stealing some of New York's eastbound trade, but representatives from districts not served by a Boston-Albany connection (and wary of incurring any tax liability) blocked all efforts to build a public railroad or canal. In 1831 exasperated promoters finally secured a corporate charter for the Boston & Worcester Railroad, and when that project reached completion, they gained a public subscription to the Western Rail Road, which continued the line to New York. In Philadelphia merchants desperate to recover their colonial hegemony cobbled together a system of canals and primitive railroads across the Appalachian barrier. Spurred on by the home-market enthusiast Matthew Carey, Pennsylvania lawmakers embraced the public works model in a conscious effort to promote a state-centered thoroughfare that did not feed business down the Susquehanna toward Baltimore. In 1826 they narrowly rejected railroads for "tried-and-true" canals and launched the Main Line over, around, and through their difficult interior terrain. (Unable in the end to conquer the Allegheny summit except with an inclined railway and stationary winding engine, these intrepid canalers inadvertently contributed to the perfection of railroad technologies that soon rendered their canals unsustainable.)

Even while Philadelphia struggled to control the commercial destiny of its "own" hinterland, two Chesapeake projects cut their way up the Potomac River valley toward Pittsburgh. Resuscitated by friends in Congress, George Washington's old Potomac Canal found new life in 1826 as a national public work, the Chesapeake & Ohio Canal. In frank self-defense against this federally funded threat from Georgetown and Washington City, Baltimore merchants pooled their private capital to build the Baltimore & Ohio Railroad. Each of these initiatives directly resulted from the challenge of the Erie Canal.

Out west, Ohio, Indiana, Illinois, and Michigan each launched massive programs of public works designed to exploit natural linkages suggested by the transmontane initiatives. In each case the logic of regional and national networks competed with local ambitions for scarce funds and political favor. In 1825 Ohio set out to connect Lake Erie with the Ohio River (thus completing a waterborne circuit all the way back to New York). But before this was done, voters in the Buckeye State had demanded two major canals and several feeders, railroads, and turnpikes, all aimed at gratifying local interests. Indiana in 1836 adopted a "Mammoth System" of internal improvements centered on the federally funded Wabash & Erie Canal but also bent to the will of the landlocked capital, Indianapolis, and to additional pockets of voters in the southeastern and northwestern corners of the state. Illinois faced similar tensions when Congress offered land to aid the Illinois & Michigan Canal (linking Chicago with the Illinois River near La Salle) even though most voters lived on southern and western prairies, where railroads seemed more likely to provide satisfactory transportation improvement. Still a territory until 1837, Michigan nevertheless adopted a program of cross-state canals and railroads, hoping to lure settlers with dreams of cheap and easy transport of grain to Great Lakes steamers and, via the Erie Canal, the port of New York. In every case these state-funded programs of public works honored frontier democracy with promises of widespread spending and benefits while they hoped to take advantage of eastern "capitalists" who seemed almost irrationally willing to invest in canals and railroads in the West.

The mania came to an abrupt end in 1837 when the banking panic sparked a market contraction and wrecked the loans of the midwestern states. Ohio managed to survive without default, but Indiana, Illinois, and Michigan each stopped payment on their bonds and had to renegotiate their obligations. Construction, scattered widely to appease jealous voters, yielded no finished arteries for trade and thus no tolls that might finance continued work or pay the interest on debts. Technical difficulties further plagued canals and railroads, neither of which by 1840 (the success of the Erie notwithstanding) had quite reached the level of real technological maturity. Before the depression lifted in the middle 1840s, politicians in these midwestern states had sworn off public works and public debt, setting the stage after 1845 for the next round of private investments in railroad corporations.

South of the Mason-Dixon Line, because of slave labor and the plantation economy, internal improvements generated more complicated arguments. Tidewater planters were overrepresented in all southern legislatures, and they generally opposed public works, both to protect their sectional advantage from rising backcountry enterprise and to protect themselves from tax burdens on land and slaves. Sometimes these coastal elites marshaled support from poor men and western voters by casting their resistance in frankly antimodern, anticapitalist terms (one North Carolina farmer groused that roads only made it easy for bankers to come foreclose the mortgage). Just as often they chided Piedmont developers with the "liberal" claim that if markets warranted investment in roads and canals, private capital would fill the bill. Staple-crop exports long had been handled at private saltwater quays, which never developed into cities with a real merchant class.

All along the sandy southern coastline, keeping rivers open to shipping worried planters more than improving downstream trade from the interior. North Carolina spent money to improve the Ocracoke inlet, as well as the lower Cape Fear River. The very early Santee River improvement (begun in 1792) tried to link South Carolina's primary waterway with the South's only true port city, Charleston. Interstate projects, such as the Great Dismal Swamp Canal and the Roanoke Canal, both logical objectives from a geographic perspective, stirred up the same political rivalries that plagued improvements in the upper

By about 1850 the railroads had begun to take a significant share of traffic formerly handled by steamboats, and the great years of the steamboats began to fade after about 1870. The Vicksburg, Natchez & New Orleans fast packet *Natchez* ran on the lower Mississippi and in one of the most celebrated steamboat races raced the *Robert E. Lee* between New Orleans and St. Louis in 1870. The *Lee* won the race. —From Jim Harter, *Transportation* (New York: Dover, 1984)

Chesapeake: success would only draw money away from the people who built them.

In southern states the challenge of the Erie Canal produced a great deal of rhetoric but through the 1830s very little real investment. Virginia halfheartedly reformed the James River Co. and set up a fund for aid to internal improvements, the great majority of which turned out to be turnpike roads. North Carolina did the same but put even less real money behind it. Kentucky and Tennessee lacked the wealth to do more than local works, such as a canal around the Louisville Falls and a few turnpikes (often aided by federal money under the guise of post-road development). But the real improvement mania, such as swept the upper Midwest in the 1830s, only struck the South after 1845, by which time railroads had become the universal focus of improvers' desires. All over the South, even as the sectional crisis mounted, states launched public programs or threw public money at private railroad companies in a frantic effort to develop an infrastructure—some freely admitted, in preparation for secession.

Between 1845 and 1855 American steam railroads finally reached their first modern, effective form in terms of technical hardware, corporate organization, and internal operations. After that (outside the South), state public works of internal improvement practically vanished as private railroad corporations expanded and consolidated to form the iron network that would serve the next 100 years of industrial development. In the South, coming late to the game and distracted by slavery and the Civil War, railroads typically appeared as public works or lavishly subsidized public-private partnerships. As if the embarrassments of midwestern canal states were not enough, wholesale corruption so typified these southern railroad programs that the very idea of public investment acquired a permanent taint in American business and political culture. Regardless of their early importance in opening markets and stimulating experimentation, internal improvements by the states commonly found their places in the history books wrapped in stories of disappointment and wrongheadedness, comic-opera preludes to the heroic age of the railroad.

—John Lauritz Larson

REFERENCES

Dilts, James D. *The Great Road: The Building of the Baltimore and Ohio, the Nation's First Railroad, 1828–1853.* Stanford, Calif.: Stanford Univ. Press, 1993.

Gerstner, Franz Anton Ritter von. *Early American Railroads.* Ed. Frederick C. Gamst. Stanford, Calif.: Stanford Univ. Press, 1997 [1842–1843].

Larson, John Lauritz. *Internal Improvement: National Public Works and the Promise of Popular Government in the Early United States.* Chapel Hill: Univ. of North Carolina Press, 2001.

MacGill, Caroline, et al. *History of Transportation in the United States before 1860.* 1917. Repr., New York: Peter Smith, 1948.

Shaw, Ronald E. *Canals for a Nation: The Canal Era in the United States, 1790–1860.* Lexington: Univ. Press of Kentucky, 1990.

Sheriff, Carol. *The Artificial River: The Erie Canal and the Paradox of Progress, 1817–1862.* New York: Hill & Wang, 1996.

Stover, John F. *History of the Baltimore and Ohio Railroad.* West Lafayette, Ind.: Purdue Univ. Press, 1987.

———. *Iron Road to the West: American Railroads of the 1850s.* New York: Columbia Univ. Press, 1978.

Summers, Mark Wahlgren. *The Plundering Generation: Corruption and the Crisis of the Union, 1849–1861.* New York: Oxford Univ. Press, 1987.

———. *Railroads, Reconstruction, and the Gospel of Prosperity: Aid under the Radical Republicans, 1865–1877.* Princeton, N.J.: Princeton Univ. Press, 1984.

Interstate Commerce Commission. *See* REGULATION

Interurban Electric Railways

For much of the nineteenth century inventors and experimenters worked to harness the new science of electricity to the needs of transportation. The need was particularly acute for urban street railway systems, which were obliged to use inefficient animal or cable propulsion systems. Electric transportation finally reached a level of commercial practicality during the 1880s with the successful electrification of several street railway systems, most notably that of the Richmond (Virginia) Union Passenger Railway Co. during 1887–1888 by inventor Frank J. Sprague. Sprague's success at Richmond set in motion a wholesale electrification of street railways; by 1890 there were more than 200 electric street railway systems in the United States.

The technology was relatively simple. Direct-current power was generated and distributed at around 600 to 700 volts. Current collection from an overhead wire was accomplished by means of a trolley pole, with the return circuit to the power plant through the running rails. Two ingenious inventions made this system workable. One was the trolley pole, generally credited to inventor Charles J. Van Depoele, which employed a pivoted pole held against an overhead power supply wire by spring tension and a wheel or sliding shoe that ran along the wire to maintain a continuous contact for current collection. The other was a method of motor mounting devised by Sprague in which one side of a traction motor was supported from the car body or truck, while the other was carried by an axle, thus assuring that the motor gearing was always properly aligned with the axle gearing.

Within a few years this technology was being applied to short intercity electric railways. One of the first was a long electric line opened in 1891 to connect the Twin Cities of Minneapolis and St. Paul. What is more generally regarded as the first true interurban railway was the 15-mile East Side Railway, which began operating between Portland, Oregon, and nearby Oregon City in February 1893. Other similar lines were soon operating. A practical obstacle to the development of long intercity lines was the relatively short distance that DC could be transmitted without incurring severe voltage and energy losses. This was solved by 1896 with the introduction of high-voltage alternating-current distribution systems that could transmit power with low line losses. Substations at intervals along a rail line then stepped the AC voltage down through transformers to power motor-generator sets that drove DC generators with AC motors to produce the low-voltage DC for the trolley wire. The development by Sprague at about the same time of a system of multiple-unit control, permitting the operation of a train of electric cars under the control of a single motorman in the lead car, was another technological advance. The term "interurban" itself is credited to Charles L. Henry, an Indiana state senator who developed the state's first interurban line in 1897. He is said to have come up with the term after seeing the "intramural" electric railway at the 1893 Chicago World's Columbian Exposition.

Rise of the Interurbans

With a workable technology in place, a modest boom in interurban railway construction was under way before the end of the 1890s. Although interurbans frequently competed with steam railroads for intercity passengers, their particular strength was the ability to provide frequent, convenient service to rural America in a preautomobile era. The interurbans were bright and clean and usually charged lower fares and ran far more frequently than the steam trains, for one car made a train. Interurban service was more convenient, too; they stopped almost anywhere, and most lines entered cities and towns through the streets to carry their passengers right downtown.

Most steam railroads viewed the interurbans as competitors for their local passenger and package freight business and opposed them in any way they could. Attempts to build an at-grade steam road crossing, for example, were often met with an injunction. Unable to obtain approval, interurbans were sometimes obliged to build an expensive overpass or underpass. On several occasions attempts to build a crossing ended in violence between forces of the competing carriers. Once the electric cars were running, the steam roads sometimes tried to meet the new competition by matching the interurbans' frequent service and low fares. This usually proved to be a costly business, however, and seldom lasted long.

Construction of new interurban roads continued at a moderate pace through the end of the 1890s; at the end of 1899 little more than 1,500 miles of interurban railway were in operation in the United States. This changed rapidly as interurban railway development gathered strength. For all but one year from 1901 through 1908 more than 1,000 miles of new interurban lines began operation each year. Construction of new lines continued at a brisk pace into the World War I period. By 1917 over 18,000 miles of interurban lines and nearly 10,000 interurban cars were in operation in virtually every state in the Union. Enthusiasm for interurbans proved short lived, and after about

1918 what little new interurban mileage was built was always exceeded by that abandoned.

More than 40 percent of U.S. interurban mileage was concentrated in the five central states of Ohio, Michigan, Indiana, Illinois, and Wisconsin. Ohio and Indiana both had virtually complete statewide systems. An extensive network of intercity electric lines, most of them little more than roadside trolley lines, in the New England states was largely concentrated in Connecticut, Rhode Island, Massachusetts, and Maine. New York's extensive system provided an almost unbroken chain of east-west electric lines extending from the Hudson River to the Pennsylvania line. Pennsylvania's interurbans were largely grouped in the southeastern part of the state between Philadelphia and Harrisburg, but major lines also radiated from Scranton and Pittsburgh.

Interurban development was limited in the South and Southwest, and most of it was concentrated around such major urban areas as Washington-Baltimore, Richmond, Atlanta, Nashville, Dallas–Fort Worth, Houston, and Oklahoma City. In the mountain states major lines radiated from Denver and Salt Lake City–Ogden. On the Pacific Coast major interurban lines were grouped around Seattle-Tacoma, Portland, and the San Francisco Bay Area, while the largest system of all, the Pacific Electric Railway, served the Southern California area around Los Angeles.

Most Canadian interurban development was concentrated in southern Ontario, north of Lake Erie, and there were major lines at Montreal and Quebec. A single interurban line operated from Winnipeg. The largest of all Canadian interurbans, the British Columbia Electric Railway, operated an extensive system at Vancouver, British Columbia, as well as a single route at Victoria, British Columbia. In Latin America the only interurban system of note was the Hershey Cuban Railway, a heavy-duty freight and passenger line developed primarily to support the Hershey Chocolate Co.'s extensive Cuban sugar enterprise.

Technology

Construction standards for interurban roads reflected their planning for a predominantly passenger service, usually with provision for a light freight service, if that. Right of way and track construction followed typical steam railroad practice, but there was usually much less grading, and grades were steeper, curves sharper, and track lighter. A majority of interurbans entered towns and cities through public streets, sometimes over the tracks of the street railway companies, which often necessitated extremely short-radius curves and restrictive clearances. There were, however, many variations from this typical practice. The "roadside trolley" intercity lines common in New England and some of the other eastern states operated over track that was little different than that built for urban streetcar lines. Some lines planned for high-speed operation built rights of way and track that were comparable to main-line railroad standards. A number of midwestern and western lines were planned from the very beginning as freight and passenger shortlines integrated with the steam railroad system and were built to those standards. Most interurbans were built to 4-foot 8½-

A heavy, railroad-roofed wooden interurban car lorded it over its lesser street competitors as the Inter-Urban Railway headed out from downtown Des Moines, Iowa, to Perry in 1910.
—Library of Congress

inch standard gauge, but a few were narrow gauge. More often local streetcar systems and their connecting interurbans used a broader track gauge. These nonstandard gauges were usually imposed by local governments fearful of future freight-car operation through the streets. Most Pennsylvania interurbans were built to the 5-foot 2½-inch Pennsylvania trolley gauge used by most of the state's street railways.

The great majority of interurbans employed the same low-voltage DC power supply technology as the street railways, with trolley-pole current collection from an overhead trolley wire. Most often this was a single wire supported by brackets mounted on wooden poles, which also carried power-distribution and communication wires. On roads planned for heavy traffic or high speeds, catenary

At the beginning of the 1930s several car builders developed extremely lightweight, high-speed interurban cars. Some of the most successful were the Bullet cars built in 1931 by the J. G. Brill Co. for the Philadelphia & Western Railway. They were capable of speeds as high as 92 mph, and each logged something like 5 million high-speed miles before they were retired after almost 60 years of operation. —Library of Congress

The most successful of all interurbans were the Chicago North Shore & Milwaukee's two Electroliner streamliners. Completed by the St. Louis Car Co. in 1941, the two trains operated for more than 20 years in high-speed service between Chicago and Milwaukee. After the North Shore ended operation, they went on for another 10 years of operation on the Philadelphia & Western Railway. One of the trains was photographed at speed near Milwaukee in 1962.
—John E. Gruber

systems were sometimes used to provide a more uniform and rigid support for the contact wire, with heavier supporting structures similar to main-line railroad electrification practice. Still other roads employed the same type of third-rail power collection that was typically used by rapid-transit lines or steam railroad electrification.

A number of lines built early in the century adopted single-phase AC systems at voltages anywhere from 3,300 to 11,000 volts. These systems soon fell out of favor, largely because of high maintenance costs and other problems, and most were replaced with DC systems. More satisfactory were high-voltage DC systems, first introduced around 1907, which operated at anywhere from 1,200 to 1,500 volts. At first, most interurbans generated their own power supply, and many functioned as both transportation and public utility power supply companies. In time, the power business proved far more important than transportation.

Interurban rolling stock typically represented a combination of streetcar technology with scaled-down steam railroad equipment. Passenger cars were about 40 to 60 feet long and usually somewhat narrower than steam railroad equipment. Commensurate with higher interurban operating speeds, trucks were usually equalized, had a longer wheelbase, and were equipped with more powerful motors than street railway equipment. Although passenger cars were built in a wide variety of configurations, the most common arrangement was a combination car with a main passenger compartment, a smoking section, and a baggage and express compartment. Many interurbans used single-end cars that normally operated in only one direction, but double-end equipment was also common.

Early interurban cars were of heavy wood construction similar to that used for steam railroad cars. Soon after the turn of the century car builders began to employ an in-

The General Electric Co. built two of these 36-ton steeple-cab locomotives for the Buffalo & Lockport Railway in 1898. GE and its chief competitor, a Baldwin-Westinghouse combination, built hundreds of these light electric locomotives for interurban railways.
—Middleton Collection

creasing amount of steel, and by about 1913 the industry had largely completed a transition to all-steel construction. While they provided a high degree of safety and durability, heavy steel cars proved both expensive to operate and hard on track, and builders soon began to produce a variety of lightweight steel-car designs. As the declining industry faced the growing challenge of the private automobile in the early 1930s, several lines—most notably the Cincinnati & Lake Erie, the Indiana Railroad, and the Philadelphia & Western—worked with car builders to develop lightweight high-speed cars of aluminum construction that were capable of speeds approaching 100 mph. Interurban passenger equipment reached its peak development in the 1940s with the production of high-speed streamlined trains for the Chicago North Shore & Milwaukee and the Illinois Terminal that offered amenities rivaling those of competing steam railroad streamliners in every respect.

Many interurbans offered express and light package freight service with what were often called express or box motor cars—a sort of motorized baggage car. For the interurban roads on which the curves, grades, or clearances of the street railway tracks used in cities and towns along the way precluded the operation of standard steam railroad freight cars, special freight cars with such features as rounded ends and radial couplers were developed that could negotiate the electric lines. For lines that could accommodate standard freight equipment, both General Electric and a Baldwin-Westinghouse combination developed a range of standard small electric locomotives for interurban freight service.

Passenger Service

Although passenger travel by interurban was predominantly short-haul, local traffic, many interurban companies also began to develop long-distance services as some of the lines reached major dimensions, or as interconnecting networks were established. Long-distance services involving two or more interconnecting lines were particularly prevalent in Ohio and Indiana, where extensive interurban networks developed. Long-distance service between important destinations as much as 100 to 200 miles apart was often operated over two or more connecting roads with through cars outfitted with such amenities as parlor seats and heavy carpeting and equipped to provide light meal service. A few lines even offered overnight sleeping-car services. Some of the longest through services included Illinois Traction's Peoria–St. Louis services (172 miles), Sacramento Northern's San Francisco–Chico limiteds (185 miles), and—the longest of all—Cincinnati-Detroit limiteds that operated for a few brief years over the Cincinnati & Lake Erie and the Eastern Michigan–Toledo Railway (277 miles).

Even longer interurban trips were possible over connecting lines, and leisurely, long-distance trolley vacations were popular early in the twentieth century. In 1904, for example, one could travel between New York and Boston in just two days by "hard and steady electric travel" at a cost of only $3.28 in fares. Except for a few short gaps that had to be filled by travel on the steam roads, the hardy interurban traveler could make the 1,163-mile electric journey between New York and Chicago in only 45 to 50 hours of continuous trolley riding, or in a week's time by daylight travel. The possibilities of long-distance interurban travel were demonstrated in 1910 by the "Utica (New York) Electric Railway Tour," a two-week journey by chartered interurban that took 26 "Utica Boosters" on a 2,000-mile tour through six states to points as far west as Indianapolis and Detroit.

Excursion traffic was intensively promoted by the interurbans, and many lines operated special sightseeing cars. The Pacific Electric Railway operated popular excursions all over Southern California. Many electric railways also operated amusement parks as a way to develop extra traffic. Almost any line of consequence maintained a deluxe parlor car that was available for chartered outings. A few even operated interurban funeral cars to serve suburban cemeteries.

Freight Service

Interurban roads were built primarily for passenger traffic, and little attention was given in their design and construction to the requirements of freight traffic. Most soon found, however, that express and light freight traffic, much of it carried in the baggage compartments of their regular passenger trains, could be a profitable sideline. As the passenger business began to be eroded by the expansion of automobile ownership and operation after World War I, interurbans saw an expanded freight business as a good way to make up the lost revenues.

The light construction standards, steep grades, sharp curves, and urban street operation of most interurbans precluded the operation of standard freight cars interchanged with the steam railroads. For some, lines built to nonstandard track gauges made interchange impossible. Many such lines developed freight services using equipment that was not interchangeable with steam roads, often operated over connecting lines. In the north central states, where the most extensive interconnected interurban network was developed, more than 25 lines interchanged freight trailers and offered freight services throughout most of Michigan, Ohio, and Indiana, to Louisville, Kentucky, and to points in western New York and Pennsylvania.

Some interurbans were built with carload freight service in mind and interchanged traffic with the steam roads from the outset. Others made the improvements to their lines that were necessary to accommodate carload freight. The largest midwestern system, the 550-mile Illinois Traction System, realized at an early date that freight traffic development was essential to its success and built bypasses around major on-line cities and other improvements needed for steam road freight interchange, ultimately developing into a major freight line.

Often, attempts by interurban roads to establish connections with steam railroads and offer regular interchange freight service were met by rejection. One such case went all the way to the U.S. Supreme Court before a Michigan interurban could get the carload freight connection it wanted. Some steam railroads, however, viewed the electric lines as potentially useful feeders and developed extensive subsidiary interurban systems. The Chicago Great Western, for example, acquired control of a number of Iowa interurbans as feeders to its steam lines. The Southern Pacific acquired control of several West Coast interurbans and built one of them, Southern California's Pacific Electric system, into a major freight feeder for the parent system that ranked as California's third-largest freight originator.

Always innovative in their efforts to develop traffic, the interurbans pioneered the concept of intermodal freight transportation through the development of trailer-on-flatcar "piggyback" service, or the use of intermodal containers transferred between road vehicles and railcars. Perhaps the earliest example of this was a road-rail-steamship service for freight and express wagons established by California's Oakland, San Leandro & Hayward Electric Railway in 1895, and the Chicago North Shore & Milwaukee established the first trailer-on-flatcar service for truck trailers in 1926. Both the Chicago South Shore & South Bend and Ohio's Lake Shore Electric Railway also operated extensive trailer-on-flatcar services.

Decline of the Industry

Few major industries enjoyed so brief or ephemeral a period of prosperity as did the interurbans. Most were built with debt financing and found it exceedingly difficult, if not impossible, to earn enough to cover both operating costs and debt service. Even in 1909, one of the industry's best years, 22 electric railway properties entered receivership, and in 1910 it was estimated that nine out of ten projected electric railways were stillborn. The industry reached its peak mileage in 1917 and then began a slow decline. The problem, of course, was rapidly expanding automobile ownership and the "good roads" movement of the post–World War I period.

Through the beginning of the Great Depression there were some notable efforts to rebuild and modernize some of the major interurbans. Utilities tycoon Samuel Insull, for example, acquired control of the three major Chicago area interurbans and rebuilt them into superb properties that continued as major carriers until well after World War II.

One, the Chicago–South Bend South Shore Line, continues to operate today. During the late 1920s Thomas Conway, Jr., a professor of transportation at the University of Pennsylvania's Wharton School, assembled several run-down Ohio properties into the extensive Cincinnati & Lake Erie Railroad, operating between Cincinnati and Toledo, with a branch to Columbus, and thoroughly modernized the property. Beginning in 1930, the Insull interests did the same thing to create the nearly statewide Indiana Railroad System.

Efforts such as these, however, did little to stem the tide. For 40 major interurbans the trade journal *Electric Railway Journal* reported 1930 operating revenues that were down 46 percent from the year before. Results were even worse in 1931, when a survey of 23 interurbans revealed that operating revenues had dropped as much as 60 percent below 1930 results, and only 6 of the lines had any net income at all. By 1933 abandonments had reduced total U.S. interurban mileage to little over 10,000 miles, a decline of almost 6,000 miles in 10 years. The decline continued through the 1930s. By the end of the decade both the rebuilt Cincinnati & Lake Erie and Indiana railroads were gone. The transportation demands of World War II brought a few years' respite, but by 1960 the industry had largely vanished. Only three onetime interurbans survive today as passenger-carrying electric lines. At Chicago the South Shore Line, now operated by the Northern Indiana Commuter Transportation District, continues to operate as a major commuter carrier, while at Philadelphia the former Philadelphia & Western still operates as a high-speed suburban line of the Southeastern Pennsylvania Transportation Authority. In Cuba the former Hershey Cuban Railway soldiers on as a division of the Ferrocarriles de Cuba system. Some lines that had developed a substantial freight traffic survived as diesel-operated shortlines, most of them sooner or later absorbed by main-line railroads. A single example, the Iowa Traction Railroad at Mason City, continues to operate as an electric freight line.

—**William D. Middleton**

REFERENCES

Hilton, George W., and John F. Due. *The Electric Interurban Railways in America.* Stanford, Calif.: Stanford Univ. Press, 1960.

Middleton, William D. *The Interurban Era.* Milwaukee, Wis.: Kalmbach, 1961.

J

Jackson, William Henry (1843–1942)

William Henry Jackson, the photographer famous for views of Yellowstone Park in Montana and Mount of the Holy Cross in Colorado, made magnificent panoramas of mountain railroading in Colorado. Jackson photographed for the Union Pacific in 1869 but missed the May 10 golden-spike ceremony at Promontory, Utah. He spent eight summers in the West with the federal government's Hayden Survey before opening a studio in Denver in 1879.

Some of Jackson's Colorado narrow-gauge views are almost as famous as the locations themselves. For example, his photo of a passenger train high in the Animas Canyon on the Denver & Rio Grande's Silverton Line has been seen far and wide. His image of the Colorado Central's Georgetown Loop runs a close second. These and many others have been reproduced in a wide range of black-and-white and Photochrome color formats and have been retouched to add trains and more dramatic backgrounds.

Jackson started his railroad work in 1880 as the D&RG opened its line through the Royal Gorge. He set out from Denver in June 1881 with artist Thomas Moran, writer Ernest Ingersoll, and engraver "Apple Jack" Karst for a visit to the San Juan mining region in southwestern Colorado; the D&RG's line was open to Durango and graded to Silverton. Results of their work were evident by April 1882: Ingersoll's report on the "Silver San Juan," illustrated by Moran's drawings and Karst's engravings, appeared in *Harper's New Monthly Magazine*. The journey provided Ingersoll with the opening chapters of his popular travel book, *Crest of the Continent*, published in 1885.

Jackson continued the photographic work as the D&RG opened more routes, and he covered other narrow-gauge lines as well: Colorado Central (1884, 1885, 1889), Denver South Park & Pacific (1885, 1886), Florence & Cripple Creek (1894), and Rio Grande Southern (1892). He also found time for trips on the Baltimore & Ohio in 1885 and 1892 and on the New York Central in 1890, among others.

Jackson moved to Detroit in 1897, taking his negatives to the Detroit Publishing Co., where many were reissued in the colorized Photochrome versions. Tracing his activities in the railroad period—the years from 1897 to 1903—is sometimes difficult, since dates in *Time Exposure*, his autobiography written late in his long life in 1940, are not always dependable. For example, although the autobiography says that a Chicago & North Western trip took place in 1899, contemporary newspaper accounts, copyright notices, and his assistant's diary support an 1898 date.

For the six-state tour of the C&NW in its "official photographic car," the *Winona (Minnesota) Daily Republican* explained that the views "will represent not only the scenery along the lines, but will also show the industrial conditions." The car "has all the equipment of a photographic gallery, so that whatever work is necessary can be done easily at once," the newspaper said. Jackson continued his travels in C&NW car 104 on an extended trip on the Santa Fe Railway to California in 1899, returning home through Denver to visit his son, Clarence, who operated a studio there. Other photographic endeavors included the Delaware, Lackawanna & Western later in the year. After a trip to Georgian Bay in Canada in 1903, he took over as full-time superintendent at the Detroit plant. Jackson's professional photo career ended then. Jackson's association with the Detroit company ended in 1924. The negatives, acquired by Henry Ford, were split between the Colorado Historical Society and the Library of Congress (views east of the Mississippi River). Many of the views can be seen today on the Internet sites of the Library of Congress and the Denver Public Library.

—John E. Gruber

REFERENCES

Gruber, John. In *Railroad Heritage*, the journal of the Center for Railroad Photography and Art: "Animas Canyon, a Photographic Landmark," no. 4 (2001); "Jackson Heads West on C&NW Car," no. 8 (2003); and "Jackson's Camera Turns East," no. 9 (2003).

Hales, Peter B. *William Henry Jackson and the Transformation of the American Landscape*. Philadelphia: Temple Univ. Press, 1988.

Hughes, Jim. *The Birth of a Century: Early Color Photographs of America*. London and New York: Tauris Parke, 1994.

Jackson, William Henry. *Time Exposure: The Autobiography of William Henry Jackson*. New York: G. P. Putnam's Sons, 1940.

Janney, Eli Hamilton (1831–1912)

The search for a cheap, practical, automatic car coupler had been under way almost since the beginning of American railroads in the 1830s, but the old-fashioned and dangerous link-and-pin couplers remained in service despite the death or injury of about 10,000 trainmen each year. Many inventors were drawn to this problem, so many, in fact, that it was difficult to make a choice. Only one could be used to serve the entire industry. Patent designs continued to pile up. By 1875 there were 900 car coupler patents; a dozen years later the number had grown to over 4,000. A little man in Alexandria, Virginia, would solve the problem with a plan he patented in 1873, but he was lost in the crowd for many years.

Eli Hamilton Janney was born to a respectable, if not prosperous, farm family. His education was better than that most Americans received at the time, for he attended a seminary for two years. When the Civil War began, he joined the Confederate army and served as a field quartermaster. He rose to the rank of major. The end of the war found Janney too poor to rebuild his farm, so he became a dry goods store clerk. Just how he was drawn to the car coupler problem is not recorded, but he set to work on it in 1865, carving wooden models with a penknife to put his ideas into tangible form.

His first patent of 1868 led nowhere. But Janney soon devised the basic design for the car coupler that remains in service to this day. It worked like the crooked fingers of the left hand clasping the crooked fingers of the right hand. If you straighten either set of fingers, the grip is broken. Janney used this principle to make a device with opposite hooks or, as he called them, knuckles that would hook or engage each other. A locking pin held the coupler knuckles closed. By lifting the pin, the knuckle was opened and the car was thus uncoupled. Best of all, the unlocking could be done from the side of the car so as to keep the trainman out of harm's way between the cars.

Janney raised money from friends to have a full-size pair of couplers made for testing on a local railroad. The test went well enough, but there was no rush to adopt his patented idea of April 1873. During the next year the Pittsburgh, Fort Wayne & Chicago Railroad, a western subsidiary of the Pennsylvania Railroad, adopted Janney's invention for its passenger cars. This was an encouraging event for Janney, but it involved only 150 cars. When the PRR followed the Fort Wayne line's lead in 1876, prospects for the major's coupler greatly improved. In the following year Janney made an agreement with McConway and Torley iron foundries of Pittsburgh to manufacture and promote his creation. His new associates were able to advise him on manufacturing details to improve his design. The Pittsburgh foundries took over rights to the Janney patents about 1878. By 1888, 150 railroads were using Janney's coupler, but the actual number in service was comparatively small because most lines limited their use to passenger cars. The bulk of the car fleet was in freight service, and the railroads felt that the cost of equipping approximately 1 million cars with safety couplers was too great.

At the same time a zealous preacher/farmer named Lorenzo Coffin was lobbying anyone who would listen that the adoption of self-acting couplers was a prime necessity to protect the lives and safety of thousands of railroad workers. These working men must receive protection; the cost of the conversion was irrelevant. Coffin was the best salesman the Janney coupler ever had. His crusade won enough public support that a national law was enacted in 1893 requiring safety couplers and air brakes on freight cars. The industry was given five years to complete the conversion, but two extensions of the law were required before the job was finally done in August 1900.

One might assume that Janney became a rich man, but he apparently signed the patent rights over to McConway and Torley too cheaply. They did not enjoy a monopoly, for the railroad industry required that two basic provisions of the design be given over to the public domain so that other manufacturers could make similar couplers that would be compatible with the Janney plan. And so the inventor lived on modestly in Alexandria. When he died there in June 1912, his estate was so small that no monetary value was placed on it by the probate court.

—John H. White, Jr.

REFERENCES

Dictionary of American Biography.
White, John H., Jr. *The American Railroad Passenger Car.* Baltimore: Johns Hopkins Univ. Press, 1978.

Jenks, Downing B. (1915–1996)

Downing Bland Jenks is best known for his accomplishments at the helm of the Missouri Pacific Railroad from 1961 until 1983, when the MoPac became part of the Union Pacific Corp. Jenks joined the Missouri Pacific in 1961 as president after building a successful railroad career for the previous 25 years. When the Union Pacific acquired the Missouri Pacific in late 1982, Jenks was chairman and chief executive officer of the Missouri Pacific Corp., and joined the board of directors of the Union Pacific upon consummation of the merger. Jenks served on the Union Pacific board through 1988 and died on October 26, 1996, at the age of 81.

Jenks was born into a railroad family on August 16, 1915. His paternal grandfather was a superintendent on the Great Northern, and his father was vice president of

Downing B. Jenks. —Missouri Pacific, *Trains* Magazine Collection

operations of the same road. Jenks graduated from Yale in 1937 with a bachelor's degree in engineering. While he was at Yale, he spent summer vacations working as a chainman on the Spokane, Portland & Seattle. Upon graduation he joined the engineering department of the Pennsylvania as an assistant. After a year at the Pennsy, Jenks spent the next 10 years in positions of increasing responsibility with the Great Northern. After a year as general manager of the Chicago & Eastern Illinois, he joined the Chicago, Rock Island & Pacific in 1949, where he held a series of executive positions, culminating in his promotion to president in 1956, a position he held until 1961, when he joined the Missouri Pacific.

When Downing Jenks assumed the presidency of the Missouri Pacific, the railroad had emerged from receivership only five years before, and its physical plant, as well as its financial performance, was in serious need of revitalization. Jenks's management style was built on the belief that managers must spend considerable time on the property, seeing how the railroad runs and getting to know and understand the people who run it. Consequently, during his first three months with the MoPac he traveled over 30,000 miles for a firsthand look at the line. He was not impressed.

The first order of business was to upgrade track and roadbed, particularly on the southern end of the railroad. Jenks then ordered the destruction of many unneeded structures on the railroad, earning the railroad $35 million in revenue from the scrap. Remaining structures were cleaned and painted, work areas were organized, and directives were given that all facilities were to be maintained in top condition. This penchant for organization and cleanliness earned Jenks the nickname Mr. Clean among MoPac railroaders and set high expectations for job performance and success throughout the railroad.

Early capital improvements initiated by Jenks included an order for over 1,000 new freight cars at a cost of $12 million, as well as $9 million worth of new locomotives from the Electro-Motive Division of General Motors to begin the replacement of a hodgepodge motive-power fleet. Industrial development along MoPac lines received considerable attention and created a stronger traffic base for the railroad. Jenks also began the process of moving MoPac out of the unprofitable business of carrying passengers, and the railroad's famed fleet of *Eagle* passenger trains began to succumb to the hard-nosed business realities of 1960s railroading.

Perhaps Jenks's single most important contribution to the Missouri Pacific was initiating a program to apply computer technology to the operation of the railroad. Although this technology was still in a relatively early stage of development, Jenks saw its potential and promoted it aggressively. First employed as a means to facilitate the control of the tens of thousands of inventory items needed to run the railroad, the use of computers expanded to tracking car movements throughout the railroad and communicating their locations to terminals and shippers. Indeed, from the mid-1960s through the late 1970s MoPac implemented an automated car-tracking and control system known as the Transportation Control System (TCS). TCS was implemented in multiple phases and yielded significant benefits in customer service and productivity. The system also received accolades from the Federal Railroad Administration in the form of a $5.5 million grant to support further development for the benefit of the entire railroad industry.

In addition to being a strong railroad manager, Jenks possessed keen insight into the structure and operation of the industry as a whole. He knew that the industry would not survive, much less prosper, unless the restrictive federal regulation was eased. When and if deregulation did arrive, which it did with the passage of the Staggers Act of 1980, Jenks was confident that significant industry consolidation would occur as a result. Therefore, positioning the Missouri Pacific as a strong merger partner was a key goal during his watch. His work bore fruit when, in late 1982, the Union Pacific added to its system the railroad that Downing Jenks had spent over 20 years reshaping into a first-class property.

—David C. Lester

REFERENCES

Miner, H. Craig. "Downing Jenks." In *Railroads in the Age of Regulation, 1900–1980*, ed. Keith L. Bryant, Jr., 235–238. A volume in *Encyclopedia of American Business History and Biography*, gen. ed. William H. Becker. New York: Bruccoli Clark Layman and Facts on File, 1988.

———. *The Rebirth of the Missouri Pacific, 1956–1983*. College Station: Texas A&M Univ. Press, 1983.

Jervis, John B. (1795–1885)

One of many 19th-century engineers who rose to the top ranks of the profession without benefit of formal engineering education, John Bloomfield Jervis was a civil engineer of rare talent and significant accomplishment in the planning and construction of railroads, canals, and water supply works. The son of a carpenter, he was born at Huntington, New York, and grew up in Rome, New York. Young Jervis ended his formal schooling at the age of 15 and went to work in his father's sawmill and on the family farm.

Jervis moved into a career in civil engineering in 1817, when he went to work for Benjamin Wright as an axman on surveys for the Erie Canal. He was soon promoted to rodman and began the study of civil engineering and surveying. By 1819 he was the resident engineer for a 17-mile section of the canal and within another four years had become superintendent of a 50-mile section of the canal. After the completion of the Erie Canal in 1825, Jervis moved on to the Delaware & Hudson Canal Co., which was building a canal and inclined-plane railroad to link Pennsylvania anthracite mines near Honesdale with the Hudson River. First as principal assistant to Wright and then as chief engineer after Wright resigned in 1827, Jervis did much of the survey and location work for both the canal and the railroad. He then became chief engineer of the Mohawk & Hudson, New York's first railroad, and the Schenectady & Saratoga.

In addition to his civil engineering work for these early railroads, Jervis developed plans for some of the earliest steam locomotives to operate in North America. For the railroad section of the D&H Jervis drew up the specifications for four locomotives that were constructed by English builders, among them the *Stourbridge Lion*, the first locomotive to operate in North America. English locomotives proved ill suited to American railroads, though, and for the Mohawk & Hudson Jervis developed plans for a radically different type of locomotive. Built by the West Point Foundry in 1832, the *Experiment* employed a four-wheel swivel leading truck and two driving wheels. The first locomotive ever built with a swivel lead truck, it was a great success and established the design path for a uniquely American approach to locomotive design that was later adopted around the world.

Throughout his career Jervis moved among a diverse range of railroad, canal, and water supply projects. In 1833 he became chief engineer for the 98-mile Chenango Canal in New York, then filled similar posts for enlargement of the eastern section of the Erie Canal and the construction of the 40-mile-long Croton Aqueduct that supplied New York City with water. During 1846–1848 he served as consulting engineer for a water supply aqueduct for Boston. Jervis returned to railroad work in 1847 as the chief engineer for construction of the Hudson River Railroad between Albany and New York, which was notable as the earliest American railroad to operate at high speeds, with schedule speeds of almost 50 mph.

In 1850 Jervis moved west to become chief engineer of the Michigan Southern and Northern Indiana railroads, rebuilding and completing the two lines between Lake Erie and Chicago. Jervis became an accomplished railroad manager as well, serving as the Michigan Southern's president intermittently from 1852 through 1858. In 1852 he also took on the presidency of the Chicago & Rock Island, remaining in the post until the line was completed in 1854 between Chicago and the Mississippi River. In 1861 he took up an appointment as general superintendent of the bankrupt Pittsburgh, Fort Wayne & Chicago, restoring the line to good condition and profitability. Jervis retired to his home in Rome, New York, in 1866, but remained active into his 80s with occasional consulting assignments and writing and lecturing on railroad and industrial topics. He died in Rome in 1885 at the age of 89.

—William D. Middleton

REFERENCES

Dictionary of American Biography.

Fitzsimons, Neal, ed. *The Reminiscences of John B. Jervis, Engineer of the Old Croton.* Syracuse, N.Y.: Syracuse Univ. Press, 1971.

Larkin, F. Daniel. *John B. Jervis: An American Engineering Pioneer.* Ames: Iowa State Univ. Press, 1990.

National Cyclopaedia of American Biography.

Jones, John Luther "Casey" (1864–1900)

"Come all you rounders if you want to hear / a story about a brave engineer." These lyrics made a legend of Casey Jones, who might otherwise have been just another statistic among the 2,500 railroaders who died in the line of duty in 1900. His story was compelling, all-American stuff, so it is not hard to see why he became a legend. When he was growing up in Cayce, Kentucky (from which he derived his nickname), his greatest ambition was to drive trains. Seized by wanderlust, the tall, handsome teenager hired on with the Mobile & Ohio as a brakeman, rose to fireman, switched to the Illinois Central, and became an engineer in 1890 at the age of only 26. Jones worked freights out of Water Valley, Mississippi, for most of his IC career, then bid successfully on an assignment to the road's premier passenger train in the closing days of 1899. Liked and respected by his fellow engineers, he was known as a man with a knack for making up time.

Barely four months into the assignment Jones was asked to work a double shift on April 30, 1900, to fill in for a sick colleague. Train No. 1, the *New Orleans Special*, was 95 minutes late at Memphis when Jones took the throttle for his 188-mile run to Canton, Mississippi. It was nearly 1 A.M., he had already been on duty for 11 hours, and there were six other trains in his way on IC's single-track line, but Jones vowed to arrive in Canton on time.

He nearly succeeded. Two freight trains tried to share a passing track in Vaughan, Mississippi, however, and together they were several car lengths too long. When an air hose broke on one of the freights, its brakes went into emergency, and it was unable to move. At that moment Jones came roaring around a curve at an estimated 70 mph. Ordering his fireman, Sim Webb, to jump, Jones cut his train's speed in half before impact, and he was the only fatality on either train. The official IC accident report blamed the wreck on Jones, but some eyewitnesses considered him a hero nonetheless, since the death toll could have been much higher if he had not stayed at his post.

He might have been forgotten had it not been for Wallace Saunders, an engine wiper in the Canton roundhouse. Saunders had a talent for composing little ditties, and his song about Casey Jones was overheard by a couple of vaudevillians. With facts and music heavily altered, the song was published in 1902 and became a huge hit, both in sheet music and on the vaudeville circuit. The song had everything: a brave engineer, fast and daring, striving against all odds to put the crack express through on time, only to die in a twisted mass of wreckage, sacrificing his life so the passengers might live. It had fast machines for the men, chivalry for the women, implied gore for the kids—and heroism for everyone. Casey Jones's place as a folk legend was secure.

—Peter A. Hansen

REFERENCE

Hansen, Peter A. "The Brave Engineer." *Trains* 60, no. 4 (Apr. 2000): 34–43.

Joy, James F. (1810–1896)

Lawyer and railroad president James Frederick Joy was born in Durham, New Hampshire, and graduated from Dartmouth College in 1833 and Harvard Law School in 1836. He moved to Detroit and began a lifelong legal career. Admitted as a state in 1837, Michigan began an aggressive program of railroad building. But numerous lines were poorly routed and engineered, and by the early 1840s difficult economic times brought all construction to a halt.

At the suggestion of John W. Brooks, a New York financier, Joy came to see the possibilities for huge profits in a line across Michigan that would link Chicago with the East, connecting with New York railroads and the Erie Canal. In a series of articles written for Detroit newspapers he suggested that the so-called Michigan Central Railroad, a state-owned primitive strap-iron line, should be sold to private interests. Joy and Brooks interested a Boston financier, John Murray Forbes, in underwriting the purchase. The Michigan Central was sold to a Joy-Forbes syndicate in 1846 for $2 million.

With adequate capital at hand, upgrading of the existing track and construction of the rest of the line to Chicago began almost immediately. Joy correctly foresaw Chicago as the major railroad junction of the Midwest. Although numerous competing lines in the Chicago area raised doubts that the MC could get a foothold in the city, Joy, who for some time had been counsel to the Illinois Central, arranged for the MC to reach Chicago via IC's main line in 1852.

After bringing this project to fruition, Joy came to believe that lines going west from Chicago might be an even bigger gold mine. Joy and Forbes cobbled together a group of small lines that eventually became the Chicago, Burlington & Quincy Railroad. Joy served as president of the CB&Q from 1853 to 1857 and later from 1865 to 1871. He was also president of the Michigan Central from 1867 to 1877. Both of these lines were successful.

After 1875 Joy and Forbes had a falling out, and Joy was obliged to withdraw from Burlington management. He then got involved in the affairs of the Wabash Railroad and was instrumental in bringing that road to Detroit. He correctly perceived the need for a tunnel between Detroit and Canada under the Detroit River, but this project did not succeed in his time. Joy was president of the Wabash from 1884 to 1887.

Joy was often involved in politics. He was a Whig (later a Republican) and one of the strongest supporters of Abraham Lincoln. Over the years Joy was a director of 20 different railroads; he also continued his law practice. He died at his home in Detroit in 1896.

—George H. Douglas

REFERENCES

Cochran, Thomas C. *Railroad Leaders, 1845–1890: The Business Mind in Action*. New York: Russell & Russell, 1965.
Overton, Richard C. *Burlington Route: A History of the Burlington Lines*. New York: Knopf, 1965.

Judah, Theodore Dehone (1828–1863)

An accomplished railroad builder, Theodore Judah in 1854 moved west to California, where he soon became captivated by the vision of a transcontinental railroad. Of Judah, his wife wrote "that everything he did from the time he went to California to the day of his death was for the great continental Pacific railway. It was the burden of his thought day and night and largely of his conversation."

Judah was born in 1828 in Bridgeport, Connecticut, where his father was rector of a church. Soon afterward the family moved to a new church at Troy, New York, where Judah received most of his education, studying for a time at Rensselaer Polytechnic Institute. His family left Troy for New York City after his father's death and before his studies were completed.

Judah was convinced that his talents lay with engineering. Still only 13 years old, he joined the staff of civil engineer A. W. Hall, who was then the engineer of the Troy & Schenectady Railroad. By the time he was 18 Judah moved on to other railroad engineering work, including the New Haven, Hartford & Springfield and the Connecticut River railroads. Next he built a railroad bridge at Vergennes, Vermont, served as a resident engineer for the Erie Canal, and was the engineer for a difficult railroad down the deep Niagara Gorge.

Judah was engaged in construction of the Buffalo & New York Railroad in 1854 when he was offered the position of chief engineer for a proposed new railroad between Sacramento and Folsom, California. Judah soon moved with his wife to Sacramento to work on locating and building the Sacramento Valley Railroad. The new railroad, the first on the Pacific Coast, reached Folsom early in 1856. Even before then, however, Judah had become a tireless advocate for a great Pacific railroad that would link California with the East.

Judah spent several years exploring and surveying in search of the best route across the Sierra Nevada, and he and his engineering parties crossed the mountains more than 20 times in making the line's final location. He spent much of his time over the next several years in Washington, D.C., seeking passage of a land-grant bill that would aid railroad construction. Judah was one of the principal organizers of a railroad convention at Sacramento in 1859, attended by delegates from all over California, Oregon, and Washington. The convention adopted the central Dutch Flat route he advocated and appointed him to travel to Washington, D.C., again to advocate a Pacific railroad bill.

Unsuccessful, he returned to California to raise funds,

Theodore Judah. —Union Pacific Railroad

ultimately finding his principal support from the Big Four, Sacramento merchants Collis P. Huntington, Leland Stanford, Mark Hopkins, and Charles Crocker. Judah joined with them to form the Central Pacific and then returned again to Washington, where his efforts finally succeeded with the passage of a Pacific railroad bill in July 1862. Construction began early in 1863.

Judah returned east once again that same year, this time to attempt to raise money to avoid being forced out of the Central Pacific by his four partners. In October Judah contracted yellow fever during the passage across the Isthmus of Panama, and he died in New York early the following month. Others completed the Pacific railroad of which he had dreamed for so long. But the CP's route over the Sierra Nevada is his enduring legacy.

—**William D. Middleton**

REFERENCES

Bain, David Haward. *Empire Express: Building the First Transcontinental Railroad*. New York: Viking, 1999.

Hinckley, Helen. *Rails from the West: A Biography of Theodore D. Judah*. San Marino, Calif.: Golden West, 1969.

K

Kansas City, Mexico & Orient Railroad

The Kansas City, Mexico & Orient Railroad, colloquially known as the Orient, was steeped in political intrigue. The company had track in two nations, one of which suffered through a series of bloody revolutions, and completion of the line, ultimately by another company, took 68 years.

The idea behind the railroad was a shorter route to the Orient through the Mexican port of Topolobampo and the Gulf of California. The scheme was first taken up by Albert Kimsey Owen, a visionary promoter. Owen incorporated a company to build the line in 1881, but that was as far as he ever got. Two decades later the idea was taken up again by Arthur Stilwell, a flamboyant Kansas City insurance salesman and railroad promoter who had developed the Kansas City, Pittsburg & Gulf, the predecessor of the Kansas City Southern Railroad.

Financially overextended, Stilwell was forced out of the KCP&G presidency in 1898. He was soon back in the railroad business, announcing on February 10, 1900, his plan for a 1,600-mile railroad that would be 400 miles shorter than any existing route from Kansas City to the Pacific Ocean, with its western terminal at the port of Topolobampo. Enrique Creel, governor of the state of Chihuahua, granted Stilwell concessions and trackage rights from the Mexican city of Chihuahua southwest to Miñaca, 124 miles, on the Chihuahua Pacific Railway, which had been organized in 1897.

By May 1900 grading had begun near Milton, Kansas, southwest of Wichita. Stilwell felt that the line from Milton to Kansas City could be built later (it never was). By mid-1903 the company had track from Milton to Carmen, Oklahoma, 75 miles, plus two segments in Mexico: 34 miles east from Chihuahua and from Topolobampo inland to El Fuerte, 63 miles. By 1912 the American segment of the KCM&O reached from Wichita to Girvin, Texas, on the Pecos River, 642 miles through uninhabited, barren country. The Mexican portion consisted of two disjointed pieces, one of which was spliced by trackage rights on another railroad—and Mexico was deep in revolution. Neither portion of the KCM&O brought in much revenue.

The company entered receivership in March 1912. There followed at least two reorganization plans, operation by the U.S. Railroad Administration (USRA) during World War I, a brief spurt of oil traffic, and sale at auction. William Kemper, the purchaser and, before that, the receiver, saw that the KCM&O could not survive on its own, let alone complete the line, and arranged to sell the railroad to the Santa Fe. There is some speculation that the Santa Fe never saw the Orient as fitting into its expansion program; rather, the purchase was made to keep another railroad from acquiring the property.

The Santa Fe sold the Mexican portions of the line to B. F. Johnston and the United Sugar Co. of Los Mochis. Johnston combined the lines with those of the Mexico North-Western, which already connected with the middle section of the KCM&O. In October 1930 the Mexican portion was completed to Ojinaga on the Rio Grande, and the Santa Fe extended its line from Alpine to Presidio, opposite Ojinaga, and bridged the river in the same year.

In 1940 the Mexican portion of the railroad came under the control of the government, which announced that the railroad would be completed—with a line through some of the roughest territory in North America. In 1952 the Mexico North-Western was taken over by the government, and in 1955 it was merged with the Ferrocarril Kansas City, Mexico y Oriente to form the Ferrocarril de Chihuahua al Pacífico. The pace of construction accelerated, and on December 6, 1961, Mexican president Adolfo Mateos dedicated the last segment of track. In the mid-1980s the Santa Fe abandoned a few portions of the Orient, and by the end of the twentieth century little remained of the Orient north of San Angelo, Texas.

In 1928, the year it was purchased by the Santa Fe, the Kansas City, Mexico & Orient operated 951 route-miles, with 74 locomotives, 31 passenger cars, 1,398 freight cars, and 563 company service cars. KCM&O operating revenues totaled $3 million in 1928.

—Cary Franklin Poole

REFERENCES

Bryant, Keith L. *Arthur E. Stilwell: Promoter with a Hunch.* Nashville, Tenn.: Vanderbilt Univ. Press, 1971.

Kerr, John Leeds, and Frank P. Donovan, Jr. *Destination Topolobampo*. San Marino, Calif.: Golden West, 1968.

Kansas City Southern Railway

The Kansas City Southern had (and has) a streak of unconventionality. It was built relatively late (in the 1890s); it ran north-south in a country of east-west railroads; for years it ignored advancements in steam locomotive technology (though it eventually bought large, modern freight locomotives); and it ran first-class passenger service long after neighboring railroads had given up on sleeping and dining cars and even passenger trains themselves.

In the 1940s and 1950s KCS's map was simple: the railroad ran from Kansas City to Port Arthur, Texas. A subsidiary, the Louisiana & Arkansas Railway, ran from Shreveport, Louisiana, southeast to New Orleans and west to Dallas. Branches—short ones for the most part—reached to Fort Smith, Arkansas, Hope, Arkansas, and Lake Charles, Louisiana.

Arthur Stilwell was the promoter behind the incorporation in 1887 of the Kansas City Suburban Belt Railroad, which soon reached from Argentine, Kansas, east perhaps 15 miles to Independence, Missouri. The railroad was a success, and Stilwell proposed an extension south into coalfields near Hume, Missouri, and Pittsburg, Kansas, and to lead and zinc mines near Joplin, Missouri. The Kansas City, Nevada & Fort Smith Railroad was organized in 1889 to build the line, and it pushed the railhead south to Joplin. In 1892 Stilwell acquired the Texarkana & Fort Smith Railroad, which consisted principally of a bridge across the Red River, and combined the two companies as the Kansas City, Pittsburg & Gulf Railroad. In 1893 Stilwell bought the Kansas City, Fort Smith & Southern, which reached from Joplin south to Sulphur Springs, Arkansas, just across the Missouri-Arkansas state line.

Further extension was halted by the panic of 1893. Stilwell, however, was able to raise funds in the Netherlands. Then William Jennings Bryan ran for president in 1896 on the free-silver platform. The Dutch investors said that they would wait to see how the election turned out; if Bryan won, all bets were off. Stilwell called on several industrialists, among them George M. Pullman, and persuaded them to invest in the railroad. Receivership was averted, and construction continued southward.

Stilwell and the KCP&G had an opportunity to buy the Houston, East & West Texas Railway, which ran from Shreveport to Houston and on to Galveston. The night before the purchase was to be ratified, Stilwell had a sudden premonition of the destruction of a coastal city by a hurricane (as would happen to Galveston on September 8, 1900). KCP&G redirected its efforts straight south to Lake Sabine, a widening of the Sabine River before it flows into the Gulf of Mexico. The railroad built a port and a city named Port Arthur, 789 miles from Kansas City, a bit over half the distance from Kansas City to East Coast ports. Trains began operating between Kansas City and Port Arthur on September 11, 1897. (The Houston, East & West Texas became part of the Southern Pacific system.)

Business was good to the point that the KCP&G needed cars and locomotives. For financing, Stilwell turned again to George M. Pullman, who agreed to provide the necessary funds, but Pullman died before signing the necessary papers, stranding the KCP&G and Stilwell. The railroad entered receivership and was reorganized on April 1, 1900, as the Kansas City Southern Railway. Stilwell was forced out and turned his attention to building a railroad from Kansas City to the Pacific, the Kansas City, Mexico & Orient. (Stilwell lost the KCM&O when it entered receivership in 1912; he died on September 26, 1928, just two days after the Atchison, Topeka & Santa Fe purchased the properties of the KCM&O.)

The new Kansas City Southern was almost immediately the beneficiary of the discovery of oil in eastern Texas. Along with petroleum and petrochemicals, the KCS hauled considerable amounts of lumber. From the beginning, the KCP&G (and later the KCS) had used 15 miles of St. Louis–San Francisco track between Leeds and Grandview, Missouri. In 1929 KCS opened its own line, which had easier grades and was located above the reach of flooding creeks and rivers. In July 1939 a Kansas City Southern subsidiary, the Fort Smith & Van Buren Railway, purchased the 18-mile Coal Creek–McCurtain, Oklahoma, remnant of the Fort Smith & Western Railway (Fort Smith, Arkansas, to Oklahoma City), which had ceased operation five months earlier.

Louisiana & Arkansas Railway

In 1882 the Vicksburg, Shreveport & Texas Railway (later Vicksburg, Shreveport & Pacific, then Illinois Central), building straight west across Louisiana, bypassed the town of Minden by 5 miles. A railroad was built from Minden south to the VS&T at Sibley, and in 1897 it was extended north of Minden as the Arkansas, Louisiana & Southern Railway. North of there, over the state line in Arkansas, William Buchanan, who was in the lumber business, took a small logging railroad and incorporated it as the Louisiana & Arkansas Railroad in March 1898. Six months later the AL&S and the L&A met, the AL&S bought the line to Sibley, the L&A bought the AL&S, and the L&A had its charter changed so it could build extensions to Alexandria, Louisiana, and Natchez, Mississippi.

A new company, the Louisiana & Arkansas Railway, owned by William Buchanan, took over in 1902. The railroad opened lines north to Hope, Arkansas, in 1903, west from Minden to Shreveport in 1910, and southeast from Packton to Jonesville, Louisiana, in 1913. The branch to Jonesville was extended to Vidalia, on the west bank of the Mississippi opposite Natchez, in 1917 on Missouri Pacific rails. When Buchanan died in 1926, the L&A was purchased from his heirs, who had no interest in running a railroad, by a syndicate headed by Harvey Couch.

Louisiana Railway & Navigation Co.

William Edenborn began building the Shreveport & Red River Valley Railway southeast from Shreveport in 1896. Edenborn was originally interested only in local business, but in 1903 he organized the Louisiana Railway & Navigation Co. to take over the railroad and extend it to New Orleans, crossing the Mississippi north of its confluence with the Red River by ferry. The rails reached New Orleans in 1906, and passenger service between New Orleans and Shreveport began on April 14, 1907.

Although business was good, the railroad operated at a deficit—but the principal creditor and stockholder was Edenborn. In 1923 the company purchased a Missouri-Kansas-Texas branch from Shreveport west to McKinney, Texas, 20 miles north of Dallas, and in 1924 it opened its own station in New Orleans. In the mid-1920s Edenborn approached the Kansas City Southern with an offer to sell the LR&N. The Mississippi River crossing was considered a hindrance to the sale, so in 1925 and 1926 LR&N undertook a line relocation that included a bridge over the Atchafalaya River and a new ferry crossing of the Mississippi. Edenborn died just before the new line was finished. His widow sought a purchaser and found it in the Louisiana & Arkansas, which purchased the LR&N in 1928.

Louisiana & Arkansas Railway in the 1930s

The Louisiana & Arkansas was well maintained but had no routes of any consequence; the LR&N had the short route between Shreveport and New Orleans and passed through Baton Rouge, the state capital. The L&A set out to upgrade its properties. It established two named trains, the Shreveport-Hope *Shreveporter*, which carried a sleeping car to and from St. Louis, and the overnight Shreveport–New Orleans *Hustler*. It extended the Texas line to Dallas, first by trackage rights on Missouri-Kansas-Texas and later by rights on the Santa Fe. The L&A remained solvent through the Depression.

Kansas City Southern and Louisiana & Arkansas

The Kansas City Southern recognized that there was little future for a Kansas City–Port Arthur railroad and began to consider acquiring a route to New Orleans (the attempt to acquire the LR&N had been stopped by the death of William Edenborn). During the 1930s Harvey Couch, president of the Louisiana & Arkansas Railway, acquired an interest in the KCS. In 1939 the Interstate Commerce Commission approved control of the L&A by the KCS. Couch became president of the KCS, and the KCS acquired routes to New Orleans and Dallas. The two roads combined their operations quickly, but L&A kept a separate corporate existence until 1992. The KCS opened a new bridge over the Mississippi at Baton Rouge in 1940, inaugurated the diesel-powered, streamlined Kansas City–New Orleans *Southern Belle* that same year, and sold the Packton-Ferriday branch (the line to Natchez) to the Louisiana Midland Railway in 1945.

In the two decades after World War II the KCS was a well-managed, progressive railroad that was constantly upgrading its physical plant and rolling stock. In the late 1960s, though, it began to unravel. All the improvements of previous years seemed to wear out at the same time, and management's attention was diverted by the creation of Kansas City Southern Industries, which became the parent of the Kansas City Southern Railway.

Starting in the mid-1950s, Kansas City Southern saw neighbor railroads absorbed into larger systems. None of the larger railroads, however, showed much interest in the KCS. Through its absorption of Missouri Pacific, Union Pacific already went everywhere KCS did; Burlington Northern reached the Mississippi River and the Gulf of Mexico at several points; and so did Southern Pacific. Besides, KCS lay crosswise to the traffic flow of UP, BN, and SP.

KCS finally entered the merger game on September 21, 1992, not as a smaller railroad to be absorbed but as a larger system: it announced that it was acquiring Mid-South Rail Corp. MidSouth's main line ran east from Shreveport to Meridian, Mississippi, essentially an eastern extension of KCS's route from Shreveport west toward Dallas. Between 1992 and 1995 KCS negotiated and completed the purchase of the Santa Fe line from Farmersville, Texas, into Dallas. Kansas City Southern, long a north-south railroad, had acquired a significant east-west route.

Shortly after the North American Free Trade Agreement was signed in 1994, Kansas City Southern acquired 49 percent of the Texas Mexican Railway (Corpus Christi to Laredo, Texas), and then as part of the privatization of National Railways of Mexico, acquired a 50-year concession to the privatized Nuevo Laredo–Mexico City northeast line, the Transportacion Ferroviaria Mexicana (TFM). In 2005 KCS became a transportation holding company with its primary investments in the United States including the Kansas City Southern Railway Co. (KCSR) and Texas Mexican Railway Co., which was acquired by KCS on January 1, 2005; the former TFM, which came under KCS control on April 1, 2005, and became the Kansas City Southern de Mexico, S.A. de C.V. (KCSM); and the 50 percent–owned Panama Canal Railway Co.

In 2005 Kansas City Southern operated a system of

3,108 route-miles and a total of 4,353 track-miles on the KCSR, and 2,650 route-miles on the KCSM in the United States and Mexico. KCSR owned and leased locomotives were 576 on KCSR and 465 on KCSM, while owned and leased freight cars (in 2004) were 10,522 on KCSR and 12,997 on KCSM. Combined freight traffic in 2005 totaled 88,040 million ton-miles, and its commodity groups were coal (8 percent), chemicals and petroleum products (19 percent), agricultural and minerals (27 percent), paper and paper products (28 percent), and intermodal and automotive traffic (17 percent). In 2005 the consolidated KCSR and FCSM operating revenues totaled $1,534.2 million, with operating expenses of $1,329.8 million, representing an 87 percent operating ratio.

—George H. Drury

REFERENCE

Frailey, Fred W. "The Kansas City Southern Story." *Trains* 39, no. 10 (Aug. 1979): 22–29; 39, no. 11 (Sept. 1979): 22–32.

Knight, Jonathan (1787–1858)

One of the many largely self-taught civil engineers of early railroad construction, Jonathan Knight studied surveying under his father, Abel Knight, a weaver who sometimes worked as a surveyor and schoolteacher, and also studied algebra with a local tutor. Born in Bucks County, Pennsylvania, he moved with his family in 1801 to East Bethlehem, in Washington County in southwestern Pennsylvania. Knight began work as a teacher at the age of 21 and acquired a farm in 1815, but he also continued to do survey work. In 1816 he was appointed by the State of Pennsylvania to survey and map Washington County, following which he served as the county's commissioner for three years. Knight then became involved in national internal improvements, assisting in preliminary surveys for the Chesapeake & Ohio Canal and for the National Road between Cumberland, Maryland, and Wheeling, later West Virginia. From 1822 to 1828 Knight served in the Pennsylvania legislature, and he was appointed by the federal government in 1825 as a commissioner for the extension of the National Road from Wheeling through the states of Ohio and Indiana to Illinois.

Knight's work on the important National Road project brought him to the attention of the new Baltimore & Ohio Railroad. In April 1828 Knight joined with already-active army topographical engineers Dr. William Howard, Lt. Col. Stephen H. Long, and Capt. William Gibbs McNeill to begin surveying routes for the B&O between Baltimore and the Ohio River. With Knight came Caspar W. Wever, who had worked with Knight on the National Road. In 1828, not long after early construction has started, Knight joined with West Point engineers William Gibbs McNeill

and George W. Whistler on an extensive survey of railroad engineering practice in Great Britain, experience that would be valuable in the construction of the B&O.

For the first several years of B&O construction, Knight was one of a three-man board of engineers, but in February 1830 he was appointed the railroad's chief engineer, with sole responsibility for design and construction. He remained in that position through 1842. Knight's contributions to the new B&O were critical. Among his accomplishments were planning the strategic branch to Washington, D.C., supervising the location of the line westward to Cumberland, Maryland, and negotiating the mountainous country west of Cumberland to eventually reach Wheeling and Pittsburgh.

Knight left the B&O in 1842 to become a consulting engineer, often taking on work for the railroad. In 1844–1847 he worked for the city of Wheeling, later West Virginia, as it fought with his former employer over a suitable route into the city. He also continued to be involved in agriculture and became the first agricultural secretary of Washington County. Knight's interest in politics was renewed in 1855 when he was elected as a Whig to the 34th Congress (1855–1857), although two subsequent candidacies for reelection in 1856 and 1858 proved unsuccessful. He died soon afterward at East Bethlehem, Pennsylvania, on the 71st anniversary of his birth.

—William D. Middleton

REFERENCES

Dilts, James D. *The Great Road: The Building of the Baltimore and Ohio, the Nation's First Railroad, 1828–1853*. Stanford, Calif.: Stanford Univ. Press, 1993.

Harwood, Herbert H., Jr. *Impossible Challenge: The Baltimore and Ohio Railroad in Maryland*. Baltimore: Barnard, Roberts, 1979.

Kruttschnitt, Julius (1854–1925)

According to his obituary in the *New York Times*, Julius Kruttschnitt used to say that it "was more fun to run a railroad than to loaf or play." It was an uncharacteristic comment for the quiet, dignified Kruttschnitt, a dominant force in railroading for the first quarter of the twentieth century. Kruttschnitt had been associated with the Southern Pacific since 1885 and at the time of his death had just retired as chairman of SP's executive committee, but was still a director.

Born in New Orleans in 1854, Kruttschnitt graduated from Washington & Lee University in Virginia in 1873, then taught school for five years in Baltimore. His first railroad job came in 1878 with J. P. Morgan's Louisiana &

Texas Railroad & Steamship Co. He joined SP as assistant manager of the Atlantic System, moving up to assistant to the president in 1901, the year Edward H. Harriman gained control of the SP and linked it to Union Pacific as the Harriman Lines. Kruttschnitt was credited with the initiation in 1903 of unannounced safety inspections for operating staff, which are still widely used by North American railroads.

Kruttschnitt and his staff moved to Chicago in 1904 when Harriman named him director of maintenance for the combined system and SP vice president and general manager. When the U.S. government split the UP and SP in 1913, Kruttschnitt stayed with the latter as chairman and chief executive officer in New York City.

During Kruttschnitt's tenure the UP tried to gain control of SP's subsidiary, the old Central Pacific route from Ogden, Utah, to the San Francisco Bay Area. The federal government in 1914 sued to thwart UP, but the case was not prosecuted vigorously until after World War I. In a 1923 court decision the CP stayed with SP. Kruttschnitt spent his last two years building up the SP.

Kruttschnitt embraced new technology as a way to cut costs. For example, he expressed enthusiasm in 1904 when the International Power Co. began construction of a diesel-electric locomotive for SP (apparently unsuccessfully, since it was never heard of again). Two years before he retired, he again suggested adapting the diesel engine for locomotives.

Kruttschnitt spent a lifetime on the Southern Pacific. When he died of a heart attack in 1925 only a few weeks after his retirement as SP chairman, he had served the railroad for some 40 years. At the start of his funeral in New Orleans, SP honored him for a job well done: all trains and machines across the system stopped for one minute.

—John E. Gruber

L

Labor

Working on the railroads, which were America's first big business and pioneered a wide variety of modern management practices, railway laborers themselves were pioneers in many respects. They were among the first to work in large numbers for the new, impersonal corporate organizations that quickly emerged within the industry. As such, they were in the vanguard of the development of modern labor relations.

In general, the railroads opened up a vast array of new possibilities for young men, carving metropolitan corridors everywhere they went in an overwhelmingly rural America. The promise of travel, adventure, and new careers held enormous appeal. At the same time, the rising tide of immigrants also sought opportunities in the glamour industry of the Victorian age. Many did achieve success, developing new skills; and a smaller number advanced through the ranks to executive positions. Yet the glamour did not erase the problems created by the rise of the industry, which also took a heavy physical and financial toll upon its employees.

To address those new problems, endemic to the emerging industrial order, railroaders pioneered in union organization, through which they sought collectively to bargain with the new class of managers that dominated the industry. Most in the industry remained unorganized, however, until the 1930s. Like other wage earners, they often faced the inherited obstacle of English common law that dubbed organizational efforts as conspiracies in restraint of trade. Also, sharply divided by race, class, craft, ethnicity, and gender, the railroad workforce proved far too diverse to organize until well into the twentieth century.

For all that, those skilled workers who operated the trains, the railroad telegraphers, machinists, and others were linchpins within the industry. Using that advantage, they built important and powerful organizations called burial societies, similar to modern insurance companies, that were among the first continuous unions in the nation. The operating workers formed the so-called Big Four, consisting of independent organizations representing locomotive engineers, firemen, brakemen, and conductors, or roughly 20 percent of the industry's workforce.

Leading the way were the engineers, sometimes called the "aristocrats of labor" by their critics. In the midst of the Civil War they formed the first railroad labor union. The Brotherhood of the Footboard was formed in 1863 at Detroit by a number of engineers, angered by wage cuts and extended working hours on the Michigan Central Railroad. Within ten years it had become the Brotherhood of Locomotive Engineers (BLE), a national organization that included over 9,500 members. However, although the brotherhood maintained a staunchly independent stance and did not join the great railroad strike of 1877, the panic of 1873, coupled with several disastrous strikes, sharply eroded the organization. The BLE recovered, and by 1886 it had 20,000 members and was one of the most powerful unions in the country.

Others of the Big Four followed suit. The Order of Railway Conductors and Brakemen organized in 1868, followed by the Brotherhood of Locomotive Firemen and Enginemen (1873) and the Brotherhood of Railroad Trainmen (1883). Their national leaders all maintained an independent course, avoiding alliances with the National Labor Union, the Knights of Labor, or the American Federation of Labor (which was formed in 1886 and included some shopcraft organizations, most notably the International Assn. of Machinists). Later they actively opposed the industrially organized American Railway Union (ARU). Although many of their members joined the other rival organizations, the Big Four's national leadership refused to do so until much later in the late twentieth century.

The Great Railroad Strike of 1877

The great railroad strike of 1877 was the first national labor conflict and enlisted thousands of railway workers and their sympathizers from Maryland to San Francisco. After the principal eastern rail lines sharply reduced wages in the wake of the panic of 1873, workers in Martinsburg, West Virginia, walked off the job and blocked the tracks. Sympathy actions spread throughout the country; without organized leadership, violence and widespread destruction followed, most notably on the Pennsylvania Railroad at Pittsburgh. Federal troops and various state militias quelled the rioting, but it left a lasting legacy of industrial violence. To many it also underlined the need for union representation to agitate for improved wages and working conditions.

The great railroad strike of 1877 began with Baltimore & Ohio employees at Martinsburg, West Virginia, and quickly spread to other railroad workers, most notably in the violence and widespread destruction of Pennsylvania Railroad strikers at Pittsburgh. This drawing shows the destruction of the PRR's Union Depot and Hotel at Pittsburgh. —Jim Harter, *American Railroads of the Nineteenth Century* (Lubbock: Texas Tech University Press, 1998)

The following decade saw more conflict. Calling for the eight-hour day and other reforms, the Knights of Labor attracted large numbers of railroaders, particularly after its initial successes against the Jay Gould rail system in the Southwest during the mid-1880s. However, Gould counterattacked in 1886, and his success, coupled with public reaction after the Haymarket Square bombing, signaled the Knights' rapid decline.

In 1888, too, the BLE launched a disastrous strike against the Chicago, Burlington & Quincy. The railroad had infuriated its engineers by wage cuts and other abuses. When they called a work stoppage, the railroad had little difficulty recruiting strikebreakers and quickly defeated the BLE. The brotherhood turned inward, focusing on rebuilding the organization and reaffirming its independent course of noncooperation with other unions until the Progressive Era.

The Pullman Boycott and Strike of 1894

Many brotherhood officials, disillusioned by the defeat on the Burlington, left the brotherhoods to form a broad industrially organized union. Led by Eugene V. Debs, they established the American Railway Union at Chicago just as the panic of 1893 unleashed the worst economic depression of the nineteenth century. Determined to avoid the narrow confines of craft-based unionism, the ARU was open to all "[white] persons employed in railway service," including those who worked in the shops, maintained the lines, or manufactured railroad equipment, as well as operating workers who ran the trains.

After initial successes on the Union Pacific and in the Great Northern strike of 1894, the ARU enjoyed a boom in membership, despite the hostility of the brotherhoods, which often sided with railroad managers to combat their jurisdictional rival. At the same time the ARU enjoyed an important degree of popular support.

At its first annual convention in Chicago, delegates ignored Debs's pleas for caution and responded to a petition by Pullman Co. workers by declaring a sympathetic boycott on all trains that included Pullman Palace Cars. Led by the General Managers Assn. (GMA), an organization of all railroads with terminals in Chicago, the railroads defied the boycott. When ARU members added calls for a restoration of wages and other benefits that had been sharply cut, the GMA adamantly refused to negotiate, recruited strikebreakers, and called upon the national government for aid. The

A strike of some 400 workers of the Switchmen's Union at Buffalo, New York, in August 1892 soon turned ugly, with a series of fires and derailments, and battles between strikers and strikebreakers. The local militia and the New York National Guard were called out, and 3,000 guardsmen left for Buffalo. Artist W. P. Snyder depicted the men at work as sentries in the August 27, 1892, *Harper's Weekly*. —Middleton Collection

ensuing strike spread rapidly, paralyzing all transcontinental lines, aside from the Great Northern, in what became the greatest labor-management conflict of the century.

As the conflict escalated, the Grover Cleveland administration intervened decisively to defeat the ARU and reopen the nation's rail network. Since many state militias were sympathetic to the ARU cause—there were mutinies in California and Washington State—the national government overrode many state governments' wishes. In the largest troop movement since the Civil War, Cleveland called out the entire western garrison, and troops patrolled important rail points from Chicago to the West Coast. At the same time federal "omnibus injunctions" precluded strike activity, and most ARU officials, including Debs, were arrested. In the face of this massive show of force, the Pullman boycott and strike quickly ended,

but with lasting consequences. In the wake of the strike, managers' thorough efforts to blackball former strikers left a legacy of mistrust. Defeat in the strike made it the last serious attempt at industrial unionism on the nation's railroads. For the Big Four brotherhoods, which had allied themselves with railroad managers, it took a decade to recover their membership, since many of the rank and file had rejected their national leaders, torn up their local charters, and sided with the ARU. The violence of the strike horrified many and led to the formation of the National Civic Union to promote mediation as an alternative to massive labor confrontations.

Concerns over the common cause made by strikers and citizens along the affected lines led to the railroads' recruitment of a more diverse workforce. In the Pacific Northwest, for example, where the railroad workforce and the general populace were composed largely of native-born whites and northwest Europeans, rail managers hired thousands of Japanese and, later, southern and eastern Europeans to perform their seasonal and unskilled work. Most of the strikers were blacklisted and forced to find other work, and a good number probably joined in the populist revolt against the Cleveland administration. Among the ARU leadership, most of whom had been imprisoned, many migrated to more radical causes. Most notably, upon his release from prison Debs became a democratic socialist and campaigned regularly for the presidency through the 1920 election.

In the Progressive Era many in the shopcraft unions formed the Railway Employees Department (RED) within the AFL. Although not an experiment in pure industrial unionism, the RED represented a structural compromise through which the shopcraft unions hoped to gain the benefits of mutual, concerted action within the industry. By allowing each member organization to retain its individual jurisdiction and identity, the RED held the promise for the full realization of the goals of industrial unionists.

However, that promise proved illusory during those years. The RED was thoroughly defeated in its first test, the Harriman Lines strike of 1911–1915. At the same time its members, like the AFL in general, discriminated and lobbied hard against Asian and southern and eastern European immigration, thereby cutting itself off from potential members in the large maintenance-of-way sector of the industry. Meanwhile, the Big Four brotherhoods continued to rebuild themselves and successfully lobbied for passage of the eight-hour day for operating workers in the 1916 Adamson Act. The other 80 percent of workers in the industry often had only skeleton organizations, and many joined more radical groups, such as the Industrial Workers of the World.

America's entry into World War I significantly altered that state of affairs, however. To rationalize the chaotic railroad industry, President Woodrow Wilson established the U.S. Railroad Administration to operate the nation's rail system. As part of that effort and anxious to avoid labor turbulence, the USRA extended a wide variety of hitherto-unattainable benefits to all railroad workers, including women, who were recruited in significant numbers for the first time in the industry's history. Those benefits included the eight-hour day, increased pay, improved working conditions, and the right to union membership. Consequently, nonoperating workers were able to achieve much of what had already been accorded members of the Big Four operating brotherhoods.

After the war the independent brotherhoods allied themselves with the newly empowered nonoperating workers unions to promote continued government operation of the railroads under the Plumb Plan. To further that effort, they jointly published a Washington, D.C.–based paper, *Labor,* that enjoyed a national circulation of 400,000. Although the Plumb Plan campaign failed, *Labor* continued to publicize railroad labor's concerns throughout the 1920s and served as an important political tool supporting friendly political candidates. Jointly, the independent brotherhoods and the AFL unions continued to find common political cause and together played a significant role in fostering the Conference for Progressive Political Action, which was a springboard for the independent presidential and vice presidential ticket of Robert M. La Follette and Burton K. Wheeler in 1924. Finally, the alliance of organizations representing skilled, semiskilled, and unskilled railway workers persisted throughout the decade and survived the national shopmen's strike of 1922.

The Shopmen's Strike of 1922

The greatest labor conflict of the decade, the shopmen's strike was the first truly national railroad strike since 1894. Nonoperating workers, angered by the erosion of the gains they had made during the Great War, walked off the job and paralyzed most of the nation's rail network. After vacillating for a period, the Warren Harding administration intervened decisively to end the strike in a fashion similar to that of the Cleveland administration's actions in the Pullman strike nearly 30 years before. Defeat was followed by widespread layoffs and blacklisting of participants. At the same time railroad managers immediately instituted the period of company unionism for all employees, aside from the Big Four brotherhoods, that persisted until the 1930s. For their part, railroad labor organizations turned aggressively to the political arena, supporting friendly candidates and lobbying for reform legislation in the nation's capital.

Most notably, the brotherhoods and their AFL allies campaigned hard for the Railway Labor Act of 1926. Passage of that legislation contrasted sharply with the lack of gains made by other industrial workers of the time. Although it was riddled with loopholes, the 1926 measure set a fundamentally important precedent for union recognition within the railroad industry. It abolished the hated Railroad Labor Board, which had been created in 1920, and established the basic collective bargaining machinery for the roads that has endured, with modifications, to the present. The 1926 Labor Act guaranteed (in principle, at least) employees' rights to organize and bargain collectively. Although that guarantee was violated far more often than obeyed in the case of nonoperating workers, it was upheld by a U.S. Supreme Court ruling in 1930.

To halt widespread abuses, Congress enacted a series of amendments in 1933–1934 that plugged many of the loopholes in the 1926 law. They outlawed company unionism and the use of "yellow dog" contracts, which prohibited employees from joining unions as a condition of employment. Together, the amendments granted railroad workers the same benefits promised all industrial workers by the Wagner Act, which failed to pass in 1934 but became law the following year. Consequently, they proved an important model for the New Deal's labor policy that extended the same rights to all workers in the nonagricultural sectors of the nation's economy.

Although the general economic revival triggered by World War II benefited the rail industry in general, including those who worked in it, other broad economic trends undercut those gains. Beginning in the 1950s, dieselization increased productivity at the cost of thousands of jobs. Increased automation, the growing use of trucks and airplanes, and general corporate reorganizations within the industry also eroded railroad labor gains. To obtain the benefits of joint action, most of the operating brotherhoods merged in 1969, forming the United Transportation Union (UTU); only the Brotherhood of Locomotive Engineers opted to remain independent.

The UTU immediately became the largest transportation union affiliated with the American Federation of Labor–Congress of Industrial Organizations. Since its formation the UTU's jurisdiction has grown to include other railroaders, those working in the bus and transit systems, airline pilots, dispatchers, and others. However, within the railroad industry it continues to face persistent challenges, including the decline in the number of railroad employees, corporate consolidations among the largest carriers, rail-line abandonments, and an often-hostile political climate.

—W. Thomas White

REFERENCES

Bernstein, Irving. *The Lean Years: A History of the American Worker, 1920–1933.* Boston: Houghton Mifflin, 1960.

————. *Turbulent Years: A History of the American Worker, 1933–1941.* Boston: Houghton Mifflin, 1969.

Chandler, Alfred D., Jr., ed. *The Railroads: The Nation's First Big Business.* New York: Harcourt, Brace & World, 1965.

Cooper, Jerry. *The Army and Civil Disorder: Federal Military Intervention in Labor Disputes, 1877–1900.* Westport, Conn.: Greenwood Press, 1980.

Davis, Colin J. *Power at Odds: The 1922 National Railroad Shopmen's Strike.* Urbana: Univ. of Illinois Press, 1997.

Licht, Walter. *Working for the Railroad: The Organization of Work in the Nineteenth Century.* Princeton, N.J.: Princeton Univ. Press, 1983.

McMurry, Donald L. *The Great Burlington Strike of 1888: A Case History in Labor Relations.* Cambridge, Mass.: Harvard Univ. Press, 1956.

Montgomery, David. *The Fall of the House of Labor: The Workplace, the State, and American Labor Activism, 1865–1925.* New York: Cambridge Univ. Press, 1987.

Richardson, Reed C. *The Locomotive Engineer, 1863–1963: A Century of Railway Labor Relations and Work Rules.* Ann Arbor: Univ. of Michigan, 1963.

Salvatore, Nick. *Eugene V. Debs: Citizen and Socialist.* Urbana: Univ. of Illinois Press, 1982.

Schneirov, Richard, Shelton Stromquist, and Nick Salvatore, eds. *The Pullman Strike and the Crisis of the 1890s: Essays on Labor and Politics.* Urbana: Univ. of Illinois Press, 1999.

Stowell, David O. *Streets, Railroads, and the Great Strike of 1877.* Chicago: Univ. of Chicago Press, 1999.

Stromquist, Shelton. *A Generation of Boomers: The Pattern of Railroad Labor Conflict in Nineteenth-Century America.* Urbana: Univ. of Illinois Press, 1987.

Zieger, Robert H. *Republicans and Labor, 1919–1929.* Lexington: Univ. of Kentucky Press, 1969.

Lake Shore Electric Railway

Linking the well-populated communities along the south shore of Lake Erie between Cleveland and Toledo, the Lake Shore Electric ranked as one of the most important midwestern interurbans. The LSE was organized in 1901 from four predecessor firms by the Everett-Moore syndicate. Through service between Cleveland and Toledo began in late 1901, and in 1907 a new line between Sandusky and Fremont cut 5 miles and about 30 minutes from the 116-mile trip between the two cities.

Two major cities, the populated communities along the Lake Erie shore, and access to the resorts along the lake provided heavy passenger traffic for the LSE, and it formed a key connection between the interurban systems that radiated east, south, west, and north along the west shore of Lake Erie. The LSE joined with connecting lines to provide through passenger service between Cleveland and Lima in 1911 and between Cleveland and Detroit via Toledo in 1916. Like a majority of the interurbans in Ohio, Indiana, and Michigan, the LSE was unable to accommodate interchange equipment with the steam railroads. Instead, it operated a busy less-than-carload (LCL) and carload trolley freight service that was one of the key links in a coordinated electric railway freight service that connected interurban lines throughout Ohio and Indiana, southern Michigan, and western Pennsylvania and reached to Louisville, Kentucky.

Business was good well into the 1920s, but this changed with the Depression. In 1930 the LSE started an innovative Bonner Railwagon trailer-on-flatcar intermodal service for its freight customers, but the collapse of many of the connecting railroads came so fast that the intermodal service never materialized. In 1932 and 1933 LSE failed to cover its operating costs by $500,000 each year, and the company went into receivership in 1933. The line kept going in the hope that things would improve as the Depression eased, but they did not. A strike by the freight-service employees in 1937 led to the abandonment of freight service, although by this time most of the connecting freight services had already been abandoned. The Lake Shore Electric ended operation in May 1938, by which time it had run up operating losses of some $3 million in just eight years. In 1938 the Lake Shore Electric operated 164 miles of track with 72 passenger cars and 79 freight cars.

—William D. Middleton

REFERENCE

Harwood, Herbert H., Jr., and Robert S. Korach. *The Lake Shore Electric Railway Story.* Bloomington: Indiana Univ. Press, 2000.

Land Grants

A major question during the new American republic's early days was just how much the federal government should do to help stimulate national economic growth. The practical reach beyond the Eastern Seaboard of the original colonies and states was severely limited by the transportation available. Tidal rivers penetrated into only a limited part of the new country. Inland rivers offered the possibility of transportation, but many streams were shallow or blocked in places by rapids. Roads were few and wretched.

Much of the limited development of transportation facilities was left to the states. As an example, the Erie Canal, completed in 1825, was a project of the State of New York. The first really large investment in transportation in the United States, it was innocent of any significant participation by the national government. Ideas and plans for federal involvement were not lacking, but were almost always blocked in Congress by the southern states. The South too needed better roads and waterway improvements, but if these projects were supported by the national government, the southerners feared interference by the northern states, particularly the New England states, which were hostile to slavery.

The result was very slow development of transportation because of the limited ability of states to fund projects and often a lack of bold ideas. The Erie Canal, which was constructed at great financial risk but paid for itself in a few years, had a happy outcome. It generated toll revenue that greatly reduced taxes for citizens of New York State. This was not lost on other states; many schemes for canals were floated, and some were realized. In parts of Pennsylvania and New Jersey several canals were built with private capital by coal companies to bring their product to market.

Some canals in Pennsylvania and Ohio were public ventures to help stimulate settlement and grow the economies. Ohio had a large investment in canals, as did Indiana and Illinois. But these ventures were expensive, and maintenance was constant and costly. One severe thunderstorm could wash out portions of a canal and require large expense to put it right. As long as this situation continued, the development of the West would be limited by the relatively sparse resources of the new states, particularly in the former Northwest Territory.

The advent of privately financed and operated railroads markedly changed circumstances and national policy. Rail technology meant that entrepreneurs could risk their capital and relieve the states and the federal government of the responsibility of providing transportation. By the 1840s it was obvious that the direction of U.S. public transportation policy was to let private enterprise develop the national transportation system by means of building and operating railroads. As time proved, the private railroad firms developed improved technology, figured out ways of interlining cars without the need for transload-ing, and developed standards for equipment interchange, track gauge, and means of serving customers and communities. But there was a limit to what private enterprise could do. Enormous areas of public land had been acquired in President Thomas Jefferson's purchase of the Louisiana Territory from France. By the mid-nineteenth century much of this territory, particularly west of the Mississippi, was still uncharted and unoccupied. These public lands, some of the richest on earth for farming or the gathering of mineral wealth, were for sale by the U.S. government for an average price of $1.25 per acre. There were few takers; it was too remote and too difficult or dangerous to get to. The railroad companies were reluctant to build into it because of the limited number of customers or potential customers. A means had to be found to encourage the private companies to provide transportation by reducing the risks. The solution was the land grant. The Railroad Land Grant Act was passed in 1851.

The Illinois Central Railroad was the first to take advantage of the new law. Because of uncertainty about the legality or wisdom of the national government granting land directly to private firms, the first grant went to the State of Illinois, which then granted the land to the Illinois Central Railroad. There was an interesting wrinkle in this first grant. According to arrangements with the Illinois Central, the state of Illinois would receive 7 percent of the gross revenue from the charter line of the Illinois Central. The arrangement also stipulated that no other taxation of the railroad's charter land by local government was allowed.

There was some variation in land grants depending upon the circumstances of the particular railroad-construction project. A common factor was the grant of alternate sections of land along the proposed right of way. This land was public land valued at $1.25 an acre; by keeping alternate sections in the public domain, the increase in value that would accrue to that property after construction of the railroad would go to the national government. Usually the railroad lands would sell for at least $2.50 an acre, as would the government-retained land immediately adjacent. Ease of access makes land more valuable.

The land granted to the railroads was to serve two purposes: the railroad could be constructed upon it, and it could be sold to help finance construction. The railroad company could use it to develop town sites or to build facilities for locomotive maintenance and freight and passenger yards. In the main, the grants were to be disposed of for construction capital. In some situations the railroad could exploit the minerals or timber located on the land that was obtained from the grant.

The distance from the proposed rail right of way in which land could be granted depended upon circumstances. If the land that might otherwise be granted was already occupied, land several miles away could be granted as an alternative section or sections if the distance was great enough. It was presumed that much of the land granted to the railroads would be sold for agricultural purposes. If the land through which the rail line was to be extended was poor in quality for agriculture, the amount granted was increased to enable the railroad to realize sufficient funds to allow construction to proceed. More sections were granted at greater distance from the line if the construction was expected to be difficult and costly. The grant to the Atlantic & Pacific Railroad, later part of the Santa Fe, was expanded because of the poor quality of the land in the Southwest for farming; the expected alternate use was for cattle grazing. In the case of the Northern Pacific, construction through the mountains was expected to be difficult and expensive, so the grant was more extensive; the grant was also expanded to include coal-bearing lands to supply fuel for the locomotives in a place remote from the better-known coal sources in the East and Midwest. In the case of the Pacific railroad, land grants were combined with the award of bonds to encourage private capital to join in the important national objective of tying California and the West into the federal union. Expediting railroad construction benefited both the government and the public. Both gained because of the higher price commanded by public lands adjacent to the railroad lines.

In return for the land grant, the railroads were also expected to move government freight and passengers free of charge. The high cost of moving troops and supplies for the wars against the Indians in the late nineteenth century proved that this provision was impractical at a time when there was little additional traffic on some lines. A compromise was reached based on the assumption that although the railroad companies could not charge for the use of the land that had been granted free of charge, they had improved the land, purchased equipment, and built facilities; these improvements could be the basis for a charge of half the going rate for private goods and passengers for federal property and personnel. The U.S. mail was moved at a rate 80 percent of the rate levied on non-land-grant lines.

Over the years there was some variation in the scope of the grants. For the Illinois Central land grant, the right of way was 200 feet wide and the railroad received six sections of land for each mile of line; if any of the land was already occupied, the railroad was free to select an equal amount of land within 15 miles of the line. Later the width of the right of way was increased to 400 feet, and the sections could be increased as noted earlier. Some grants received 10 sections per mile, some 20 sections, and others 40.

There were 89 separate land grants made to the railroads; not all were used, and 17 were forfeited because of failure to construct a railroad. There were land transfers in 72 instances. A significant amount of land was involved in the railroad land-grant policy. The Illinois Central received 4,600,000 acres; the Chicago & North Western, 7,400,000; the Chicago, Burlington & Quincy, 3,200,000;

the Union Pacific, 19,000,000; and the largest grant of 41,000,000 acres went to the Northern Pacific. The total acreage of railroad land grants was 130,000,000, which is equal to the land area of Indiana, Michigan, Wisconsin, Illinois, and about half of Ohio. In some cases the railroads sold the land to raise capital; in others they held on to it so that it increased in value. Some grant land is still held by railroads; the Burlington Northern's vast holdings of low-sulfur coal are on land granted to the Northern Pacific and the Chicago, Burlington & Quincy.

There has always been speculation about whether the land grants truly benefited the U.S. government and the public. The railroads would probably have been built eventually without them, but the construction was carried out more quickly and enabled the nation to be settled faster and was a benefit to those persons who settled earlier than would have otherwise been the case. It is speculated that the land could have been sold at a higher price than $1.25 an acre after the railroads were built without the aid of the grants of land. The savings in transportation cost of the land grants was a matter of interest to the federal coordinator of transportation in the 1930s, when the number of federal agencies using transportation expanded greatly. A study carried out by the coordinator estimated that between the beginning of the land-grant policy and June 30, 1934, the savings to the federal government totaled $138,700,000; the coordinator's study estimated a savings of $7,000,000 in 1937 alone. Further estimates put the savings to the government up to June 30, 1943, including rate equalization by non-land-grant lines, at $580,000,000.

From the beginning the policy was controversial, and in 1871 Congress halted it. One reason was to stop complaints. Another was the diminishing amount of public land, thanks not only to the sales of granted land by the railroads, but also to the effects of the Homestead Act and general infilling of the public lands in the West; at least some of the public land remaining was probably unsellable. The land-grant requirement that railroads give reduced rates to the government was phased out by the Congress in 1940, except for the obligation to move military goods and personnel at reduced rates, and the land-grant rate reductions ceased on October 1, 1946.

—George M. Smerk and Lloyd J. Mercer

REFERENCES

Federal Coordinator of Transportation. *Public Aids to Transportation.* Vol. 2. Washington, D.C.: U.S. Government Printing Office, 1938.

Holbrook, Stewart H. *The Story of American Railroads.* Chap. 13. New York: Crown, 1947.

Larson, John Lauritz. *Internal Improvement.* Chapel Hill: Univ. of North Carolina Press, 2001.

Locklin, D. Philip. *Economics of Transportation.* 7th ed. Chap. 6. Homewood, Ill.: Richard D. Irwin, 1972.

Langdon, Jervis, Jr. (1905–2004)

Jervis Langdon, Jr., held key positions on several railroads, including the presidency of the Baltimore & Ohio and the presidency of the Chicago, Rock Island & Pacific Railroad. After a successful railroad career Langdon retired in 1976 after having served as trustee and president of the Penn Central. Langdon died on February 13, 2004, in Elmira, New York.

Langdon was born in Elmira on January 28, 1905, and graduated with a B.A. from Cornell University in 1927 and an LL.B. from the same institution in 1930. He worked for a year as a traffic clerk with the Lehigh Valley Railroad between graduation from Cornell and his entry into law school. Upon finishing law school, Langdon returned to the Lehigh Valley to work in the legal department, where he served in several positions before moving to the New York Central in 1934. There he spent two years with the legal department. He then moved to the Chesapeake & Ohio as an assistant general attorney. He worked his way up in the legal department, then was transferred to the C&O's traffic department in 1941 and was promoted to assistant vice president. The advent of World War II put his career on hold for four years while he served with the Army Air Forces during the war, stationed in China, Burma, and India. He left the military in 1946 with the rank of colonel.

Langdon worked as legal counsel for many of the large southern railroads that were working with the Interstate Commerce Commission (ICC) in an effort to resolve problems involving freight rates on traffic moving between the southern and northern United States. From 1953 to 1956 he was chairman of the Assn. of Southeastern Railroads.

In 1956 Langdon took the position of general counsel with the Baltimore & Ohio and was promoted to vice president and general counsel in 1958. In 1961 he became president of the B&O, where he remained until 1964. Langdon is best remembered for his work as B&O's president. He introduced a number of organizational and operational changes that took the railroad from a $31 million deficit in 1961 to a $5.5 million profit in 1964. Among these changes was ratemaking that reflected both the needs of the market and understanding of the costs incurred to provide the service. In addition, Langdon placed strong emphasis on piggyback service and dedicated coal trains—two forms of service that are very important to the railroad industry today.

In 1964 the Chesapeake & Ohio Railway gained control of the B&O, whereupon Langdon became president of the Chicago, Rock Island & Pacific. The Rock Island was in the process of trying to win approval for merger with the Union Pacific Railroad, and Langdon's role on the Rock Island was to improve the operations and financial condition as much as possible in order to make the road a stronger merger partner. The railroad was struggling at the time, but Langdon did his best to keep it running. In 1970 Langdon became a trustee of the Penn Central Railroad, which had just declared bankruptcy. Langdon was named president of the road in 1974, then retired in 1976 when Penn Central became part of the Consolidated Rail Corp. (Conrail), which was the federal government's ultimately successful effort to bring order to the chaos of northeastern railroading in the 1970s.

—David C. Lester

REFERENCES

National Cyclopaedia of American Biography. New York: James T. White, 1967.

Rasmussen, Frederick N. Obituary of Jervis Langdon, Jr. *Baltimore Sun,* February 17, 2004, www.baltimoresun.com

Las Vegas & Tonopah Railroad

Even before W. A. Clark completed the Los Angeles & Salt Lake Railroad to join those two cities, his brother, J. Ross Clark, surveyed a railroad line from Las Vegas to Tonopah, Nevada. Construction began in November 1905, and in October 1906 trains began operating between Las Vegas and Beatty, Nevada. Two months later the rails reached Rhyolite, and track crews continued working north, reaching Goldfield, 197 miles from Las Vegas, in October 1907.

In 1914, after mining in Nevada had begun to slump, the LV&T and the Bullfrog Goldfield consolidated their parallel lines between Beatty and Goldfield to form a single line. The LV&T abandoned its line between Las Vegas and Beatty on October 31, 1918. The Tonopah & Tidewater took over operation of the line between Beatty and Goldfield; it continued to operate until 1928.

In 1917 the Las Vegas & Tonopah operated 119 route-miles and 125 track-miles, with 14 locomotives, 3 passenger cars, and 5 freight and company service cars. Operating revenues that year were $16,568; the company's deficit that year was $20,315.

—David F. Myrick

REFERENCE

Myrick, David F. *Railroads of Nevada and Eastern California.* Vols. 1–2. Reno: Univ. of Nevada Press, 1962, 1990.

Latrobe, Benjamin H., Jr. (1806–1878)

Benjamin H. Latrobe, Jr., came to civil engineering over an unlikely path. The gifted son and namesake of the great

British-born architect and engineer, one of the architects of the U.S. Capitol, the younger Latrobe was born at Wilmington, Delaware. He attended Georgetown College in Washington and St. Mary's College in Baltimore before practicing law with his older brother John. The law proved not to his liking, and in 1831 Latrobe left the practice to join the pioneer Baltimore & Ohio as a civil engineer. He soon became the principal assistant to chief engineer Jonathan Knight.

A year later Latrobe was appointed to lay out the railroad's Washington branch and to design and build the viaduct at Relay, Maryland, that would carry the branch across the valley of the Patapsco River. The difficulty of the latter task was compounded by the need to build the structure on a 4.5-degree curve. Latrobe designed a stone masonry structure 704 feet long, including its approaches, with eight elliptical arches, each spanning 58 feet. It took two years to build and ranked as one of the great works of early American railroad engineering. Named the Thomas Viaduct after the B&O's first president, Philip E. Thomas, Latrobe's great structure remains in service today.

Latrobe left the B&O briefly in 1835 after completion of the viaduct to take up the post of chief engineer for the construction of the Baltimore & Port Deposit between Baltimore and Havre de Grace, Maryland. He returned to the B&O a year later to resume what was to be a long and distinguished engineering career with the railroad. After directing surveys and construction of the line west through Harpers Ferry and across the mountains to Cumberland, Maryland, he succeeded Knight as the B&O's chief engineer in 1842. He completed construction of the railroad to the Ohio River at Wheeling, Virginia, in 1852 and then built several other lines for the B&O. Still later Latrobe was a consulting engineer for the Hoosac Tunnel and the Portland & Ogdensburg. He retired from the B&O in 1875 and died at Baltimore three years later.

—William D. Middleton

REFERENCES

Dictionary of American Biography.
National Cyclopaedia of American Biography.

Lehigh & Hudson River Railway

In 1860 the Warwick Valley Railroad was built from Warwick, New York, to a connection with the New York & Erie at Greycourt, 10 miles away. The line was built to a 6-foot track gauge and was operated with New York & Erie cars and locomotives until 1880, when it was converted to standard gauge. The Warwick Valley was pushed southwest into New Jersey to serve iron mines, and an extension was built to the Delaware River by the Lehigh & Hudson River Railroad. In 1882 the two railroads consolidated to form the Lehigh & Hudson River Railway (L&HR).

The Hudson River was bridged at Poughkeepsie in 1889, and the L&HR built a 10-mile line from Greycourt to Maybrook, New York, to connect with the bridge via the Central New England & Western Railroad. At the other end of the line the L&HR bridged the Delaware River between Phillipsburg, New Jersey, and Easton, Pennsylvania. It traded trackage rights with the Pennsylvania Railroad: L&HR on the Pennsylvania between Belvidere and Phillipsburg, New Jersey, and the Pennsylvania the length of the L&HR to Maybrook.

The L&HR at first carried the products of farms and mines, but when the New Haven purchased the Central New England and the Poughkeepsie Bridge, the L&HR became a bridge railroad, connecting the west end of the New Haven at Maybrook with the Pennsylvania, Lehigh Valley, Lackawanna, and Central Railroad of New Jersey. At the request of the New Haven, these connecting railroads plus the Reading and the Lehigh Coal & Navigation Co. (owner of the parallel Lehigh & New England) purchased the Lehigh & Hudson River in 1905. About 1950 Lehigh Coal & Navigation's interest in the L&HR passed to the Pennsylvania and Lehigh Valley.

Traffic patterns shifted in the 1960s. After the Erie-Lackawanna merger of 1960, bridge traffic between the New Haven and the former Lackawanna moved to a former Erie line, which connected directly with the New Haven. After the formation of Penn Central in 1968, traffic between New England and the South that had moved via the Poughkeepsie Bridge was rerouted to a roundabout but all–Penn Central route via Selkirk Yard, near Albany, New York. The Lehigh & Hudson River entered bankruptcy on April 18, 1972. What little traffic it still carried was lost when the Poughkeepsie Bridge burned in 1974. L&HR's properties became part of Conrail on April 1, 1976.

In 1975, the year before the road became part of Conrail, the Lehigh & Hudson River operated 90 route-miles and 115 track-miles, with 6 locomotives, 2 freight cars, 9 company service cars, and 86 employees. Nearly 80 percent of its traffic was merchandise; ores constituted another 13.9 percent. L&HR operating revenues totaled $1.9 million in 1975, and the railroad achieved a 92.5 percent operating ratio.

—George H. Drury

REFERENCE

Pennisi, Bob. *The Northeast Railroad Scene.* Vol. 2, *The Lehigh & Hudson River.* Flanders, N.J.: Railroad Avenue Enterprises, 1977.

Lehigh & New England Railroad

The Lehigh & New England (L&NE) reached from the anthracite-mining area of eastern Pennsylvania across the northwest corner of New Jersey to Campbell Hall, New York. It was not a large railroad. Its main line, from Slatington, Pennsylvania, to Campbell Hall, was about 100 miles long, and at its greatest extent it operated about 100 miles more of branch lines. It was of strategic importance, though, as a connection between the trunk-line railroads of the East and the New Haven's Poughkeepsie Bridge, the only freight route across the Hudson River south of Albany, New York.

The South Mountain Railroad was chartered in 1873 to build from Harrisburg, Pennsylvania, to Boston, Massachusetts. The railroad that resulted from that activity after several corporate reorganizations was the Pennsylvania, Poughkeepsie & Boston, which ran from the Lehigh River at Slatington, Pennsylvania, to Pine Island, New York, where it connected with the Erie. Trackage rights over the Erie extended the railroad to Maybrook, New York, and a connection with the Poughkeepsie Bridge. The Philadelphia & Reading, which connected with the L&NE at Slatington, leased the railroad briefly from 1891 until 1893, when the Pennsylvania, Poughkeepsie & Boston entered receivership. It emerged in 1895 as the Lehigh & New England Railroad.

The Reading Co., successor to the Philadelphia & Reading, and the L&NE agreed to another lease in 1926, but the Interstate Commerce Commission denied it. Three years later the Baltimore & Ohio and the Chesapeake & Ohio asked for four-way control of the L&NE by those two roads and the New York Central and the Pennsylvania, and at the same time the Wabash asked to control the L&NE. The ICC's merger plan of 1929 assigned the L&NE to the New Haven. The various applications to control the L&NE were withdrawn in 1930.

As oil replaced coal as a home heating fuel after World War II, L&NE's anthracite traffic declined, followed by a decline in the road's cement traffic. The future of the railroad was obvious to L&NE's owner, the Lehigh Coal & Navigation Co. Although still solvent, the railroad petitioned for abandonment in 1960. The Central Railroad of New Jersey formed the Lehigh & New England Railway to acquire and operate two portions of the line totaling about 40 miles. The rest was abandoned in 1961.

In 1960, the year before it was abandoned, the Lehigh & New England operated a system of 177 route-miles and 302 track-miles, with 32 locomotives, 2,608 freight and company service cars, and 468 employees. Freight traffic totaled 142.9 million ton-miles in 1960, with products of mines and manufactured goods each accounting for about half of L&NE's traffic. Lehigh & New England operating revenues totaled $3.6 million, and the railroad achieved a 154.7 percent operating ratio.

—George H. Drury

REFERENCE

Crist, Ed. *The Lehigh and New England Railroad*. Newton, N.J.: Carstens, 1980.

Lehigh Valley Railroad

Among the railroads that linked New York and Buffalo, the Delaware, Lackawanna & Western was the shortest (396 miles), and the New York Central was the fastest and had the advantage of continuing west from Buffalo. At 448 miles the Lehigh Valley was the longest (except for the Pennsylvania Railroad, which was not really in the New York–Buffalo market) and the slowest. For much of its life it was owned or controlled by other railroads, and it often gave the impression of valiant poverty—the streamlined trains, for example, that appeared to have been run up by loving hands at home (which indeed they had been). It was far more a regional railroad than part of a through route, and, to its credit, it served its territory well.

In 1791, when anthracite was discovered at Mauch Chunk, Pennsylvania, the only way to transport it to market was to boat it down the Lehigh River. Because the river was often unnavigable, a canal was built. By the 1820s the Lehigh Coal & Navigation Co. dominated coal mining and transportation in the area. The Delaware, Lehigh, Schuylkill & Susquehanna Railroad was incorporated in 1846 to break the transportation monopoly with a railroad from Mauch Chunk to Easton, Pennsylvania, on the Delaware River. Construction began in 1851, and soon the company came under the management of Asa Packer. It was renamed the Lehigh Valley Railroad (LV) in 1853, and in 1855 it began operating between Mauch Chunk and Easton. Meanwhile, a competitor was built through the Lehigh River valley: Lehigh Coal & Navigation's Lehigh & Susquehanna Railroad.

The LV acquired the Lehigh & Mahanoy in 1866 and a year later reached north to Wilkes-Barre in the Wyoming Valley. Packer purchased a flood-damaged canal in 1865 and renamed it the Pennsylvania & New York Canal & Railroad. Packer used its towpath as a roadbed to build a railroad north from Wilkes-Barre to Waverly, New York, where it connected with the New York & Erie. The New York & Erie had a track gauge of 6 feet; the Pennsylvania & New York and the Lehigh Valley were standard gauge. After seven years of transferring passengers and freight at Waverly, in 1876 the LV furnished materials and financing for the New York & Erie to lay a third rail for standard-gauge trains from Waverly to Buffalo. The LV leased the Pennsylvania & New York in 1888 (to get ahead of the story).

The use of Erie rails to reach Buffalo was not an ideal situation. In 1876 LV reached Geneva, New York, by acquiring the Geneva, Ithaca & Sayre Railroad. It built a rail line west from Geneva to Buffalo (opened in 1892), constructed a line to bypass the heavy grades near Ithaca, built a station in Buffalo, and established a shipping line on the Great Lakes. In 1890 the companies involved in the extension to Buffalo were consolidated as the Lehigh Valley Railway. Other lines in western New York acquired or built at the same time were a branch to Rochester, a line north to Fair Haven, on Lake Ontario north of Geneva, a bypass around Buffalo for traffic to and from Canada, and a long, meandering branch from Elmira through Cortland to Camden, north of Oneida Lake.

At the east end of its system, LV saw its connecting railroads become competitors. The Lackawanna acquired the Morris & Essex in 1868, and the Central Railroad of New Jersey put itself into competition with the LV by leasing the Lehigh & Susquehanna in 1871. The Lehigh Valley bought another canal, the Morris Canal, for the canal company's property at Jersey City. By 1875 the LV had built a line from Easton to Perth Amboy, but LV's own rails did not reach Jersey City until 1899.

The Philadelphia & Reading Railroad (P&R), which was much involved with anthracite mining, began expanding in 1890 under the leadership of Archibald McLeod. It saw LV's line to Buffalo as an outlet to the Great Lakes for its anthracite; LV was glad of the prospect of additional traffic on its new extension to Buffalo, because traffic had not been as vigorous as LV had expected. The P&R leased the LV in 1892. J. P. Morgan and Anthony Drexel, who had been backing the P&R, suddenly became alarmed at its expansionist tendencies (the P&R had just acquired control of the Boston & Maine). They withdrew their support, the P&R fell into receivership, and in August 1893 the lease of the LV was canceled.

Morgan then undertook to rebuild the LV, but other LV stockholders protested the diversion of money from dividends into physical plant. By 1902 the Lehigh Valley was independent again. Several other railroads—New York Central, Philadelphia & Reading, Erie, Lackawanna, and Central Railroad of New Jersey—bought LV stock, and the LV was briefly part of the expanding empire of the Chicago, Rock Island & Pacific.

Until 1913 the eastern terminal of LV's passenger trains was Pennsylvania Railroad's Jersey City station. In 1913 the Pennsylvania evicted the LV, which moved its trains to the Central of New Jersey's station; in 1918, under the direction of the U.S. Railroad Administration (USRA), LV's passenger trains were moved to Pennsylvania Station in New York. That remained their terminal until the LV discontinued its passenger trains. The Lehigh Valley was adversely affected by several events during the years that led up to World War I: a munitions explosion on the Jersey City waterfront in 1916, loss of the Great Lake shipping company in 1917 (divestiture was required by the Panama Canal Act), divestiture of the anthracite-mining subsidiary (required by the Sherman Antitrust Act), and a significant drop in traffic as oil and gas replaced coal as home heating fuels.

In the 1920s the Interstate Commerce Commission (ICC) proposed that U.S. railroads merge into 19 large systems, 4 of them in the territory between New York and Chicago. In response, Leonor F. Loree, president of the Delaware & Hudson, proposed a fifth eastern system to include Delaware & Hudson, Lehigh Valley, Wabash, Wheeling & Lake Erie, and Buffalo, Rochester & Pittsburgh. Loree purchased stock in LV, but not enough to gain control. He later sold that stock to the Pennsylvania

Railroad. The Pennsylvania's ownership of LV (31 percent) was enough to keep it out of the hands of the New York Central, but the Pennsylvania exercised no influence on the operation and policies of the LV.

When the Depression began, the LV was generally in good condition and had little debt about to mature. However, between taxes in the state of New Jersey and interest on debt, LV soon owed the federal government $8 million. What little traffic there was, passenger and freight, was being eroded by the highways. LV began to prune branches and service.

The decline reversed during World War II but resumed in the late 1940s. Hurricane damage to LV's tracks in Pennsylvania in 1956 was expensive to repair. New highways and the faster, newer trains of the Lackawanna and the New York Central accelerated the drop in passenger-train ridership. LV dropped all but two of its passenger trains in 1959 and the remaining two in 1961.

Discontinuance of the passenger trains seemed to have no effect on LV's finances. Matters only got worse. In 1961 the Pennsylvania Railroad purchased the remainder of LV's stock to protect its investment. When the Penn Central was created by the merger of the Pennsylvania and the New York Central, the Lehigh Valley was offered as a potential merger partner to both the Chesapeake & Ohio (which by then controlled the Baltimore & Ohio and the Western Maryland) and the Norfolk & Western (which had recently expanded by acquiring the Nickel Plate, the Wabash, and two smaller railroads). Neither wanted it. Lehigh Valley declared bankruptcy on June 24, 1970, three days after Penn Central did the same. It continued to decline, and on April 1, 1976, LV's properties were included in Conrail. Most of LV's track in New York—west of Sayre, Pennsylvania, and Waverly, New York—was subsequently abandoned.

In 1974, two years before it became part of Conrail, the Lehigh Valley operated a system of 991 route-miles and 1,891 track-miles, with 149 locomotives, 3,965 freight cars, 161 company service cars, and 2,645 employees (1973 figure). Freight traffic totaled 3,602.7 million ton-miles in 1974, and foodstuffs (14.5 percent), pulp and paper (12.6 percent), and chemicals (9.9 percent) were its principal traffic sources. Lehigh Valley operating revenues totaled $69.5 million in 1974, and the railroad achieved an 84.3 percent operating ratio.

—George H. Drury

REFERENCE

Archer, Robert F. *Lehigh Valley Railroad*. Burbank, Calif.: Howell-North Books, 1977.

Lehigh Valley Transit Co.

Among the most successful of the traditional interurbans, Pennsylvania's Lehigh Valley Transit Co. was formed late in the 1890s by Albert L. Johnson, who consolidated streetcar and suburban electric lines in the Lehigh Valley area around Allentown. Johnson had ambitious plans for Allentown-Philadelphia and Philadelphia–New York interurban lines. These plans were greatly scaled back after his death in 1901, when a Philadelphia–New York division was canceled, and work went ahead on only the Allentown-Philadelphia line. Work was completed in 1903 on a lightly built, side-of-the-road route connecting with a Philadelphia streetcar line at Chestnut Hill, but between 1905 and 1912 it was extensively rebuilt, and an alternate connecting route was built between Lansdale and Norristown, allowing fast LVT interurban cars to operate through on the Philadelphia & Western's new high-speed line to a connection with Philadelphia's Market Street elevated at 69th Street. The original line between Lansdale and Chestnut Hill was closed in 1926.

The populous region served by the Lehigh Valley area and the fast service provided by the interurban generated a substantial traffic. In 1938, when many other interurbans had failed, LVT still saw a profitable future in passenger service and carried out an extensive modernization of its equipment with modern secondhand cars. Thirteen of the Cincinnati & Lake Erie's lightweight, high-speed cars and a single Indiana Railroad car were extensively refurbished for LVT's Allentown-Philadelphia *Liberty Bell Limited* trains, and four former Dayton & Troy curved-side lightweight cars were refurbished for Allentown-Easton service.

Interurban travel boomed during World War II, but LVT's passenger business declined rapidly after the war. In 1949 LVT ended its Allentown-Easton interurban service and discontinued through runs over the P&W connection between Norristown and 69th Street. The remaining Allentown-Norristown operation ended in 1951. LVT had never been able to establish interchange service with the freight railroads, but it continued to operate a busy interurban package freight service with multiple-unit electric cars until the end. In 1948, when it was still running between Allentown and Easton and still operating through service to 69th Street in Philadelphia, Lehigh Valley Transit operated 118 track-miles and 148 cars.

—William D. Middleton

REFERENCE

Kulp, Randolph L., ed. *History of Lehigh Valley Transit Company.* Allentown, Pa.: Lehigh Valley Chapter, National Railway Historical Society, 1966.

Lima Locomotive Works

The Lima Locomotive Works was an unlikely competitor in the railway locomotive industry. It was neither an early participant in that industry nor one that could trace its origins to traditional machine-shop practice. Its location in small-town Lima, Ohio, placed it far from a pool of skilled workers who could respond readily to upsurges in locomotive orders. The company succeeded by dominating a niche market for logging, mining, and industrial locomotives with its patented Shay technology and later entered the main-line steam locomotive market, establishing a reputation as a technologically innovative firm. Lima also embraced the difficult transition from steam to diesel locomotive production, but inadequate capitalization and poor technical knowledge doomed both the effort and the firm.

Lima began as a producer of agricultural equipment. The Lima Agricultural Works began operations in 1863 in a former sash and door factory that dated to 1859. The plant closed in 1866 after the death of its proprietor, but reopened in 1869 as Carnes, Harper & Co. The renamed Lima Machine Works manufactured the patented, portable Carnes' Oscillating Sawmill, which initially sold well in the local area and then, as the forests of northwestern Ohio disappeared, found a ready market in Michigan.

The Lima Machine Works incorporated in December 1876, at a time when most steam locomotive producers remained partnerships. By that time it had deemphasized agricultural equipment in favor of sawmills, foundry products, and Disman Metal, a low-friction metal popular in wagon and railroad journal boxes. Other products included steam tractors, which were, in effect, locomotives that did not operate on rails.

Ephraim Shay, a Michigan lumberman, helped transform Lima into an internationally recognized producer of specialty locomotives. During the 1870s Shay built a crude, wood-rail, horse-powered tramway to transport timber to his sawmill. Recognizing the limitations that poor track, steep grades, and sharp curves imposed on conventional steam locomotives, Shay developed an alternate power-transmission system. Unlike a conventional rod locomotive with horizontal cylinders and drive rods, the Shay locomotive employed vertical cylinders connected to a horizontal camshaft that in turn powered the wheels through a system of beveled gears. This system ensured that all of the locomotive's wheels were powered and, therefore, that all of the locomotive's weight contributed to tractive effort. The flexibility of the camshaft allowed the Shay to negotiate extremely sharp curves, while the small wheels and equalized trucks tolerated even the roughest track. Although the Shay had a low top speed (rarely more than 10 miles per hour), it could pull heavy loads and climb grades that were too steep for rod locomotives. Other companies, most notably Climax and Heisler, offered geared locomotives, but none could match the Shay's reputation.

In 1878 the Lima Machine Works built an unsuccessful prototype locomotive based on Shay's concepts. Two years later Lima machinist John Carnes oversaw a redesign of Shay's locomotive, incorporating many im-

Lima earned a worldwide reputation for the geared Shay locomotives that it built during some 65 years. This view of the Lima production line in 1924 shows Shays rolling off in record numbers.
—Eric Hirsimaki Collection

provements in the gears, cylinders, and other elements of the power-transmission system. The end product, Construction Number 6, is widely regarded as the first true Shay locomotive. By 1881 Ephraim Shay had patented his designs and granted the Lima Machine Works manufacturing rights. Lima made incremental improvements to the Shay design and soon offered a range of standard designs in various sizes. Although the company also produced a few conventional rod locomotives, the 2,761 Shays that Lima manufactured before production ceased in 1945 ensured that company's initial success.

In order to secure sufficient capital for a new manufacturing facility, the company reorganized as the Lima Locomotive & Machine Co. in 1892. Two years later the firm acquired the Lima Steel Casting Co., an important supplier of locomotive components. The depression of 1893 and infighting among stockholder factions for control of the company delayed the opening of the new plant until 1902. George L. Wall, who replaced Ira Carnes as mechanical engineer in 1904, made improvements to the Shay design, patenting a massive four-cylinder version. He also developed a "fireless cooker" locomotive, powered by stored steam, that could safely operate near inflammable materials. In 1909 he supervised the construction of a small gasoline-mechanical locomotive, Lima's first internal combustion product. Of more immediate concern, Wall also oversaw the completion of increasing numbers of rod locomotives in addition to the steady production of Shays.

Lima placed increasing emphasis on rod locomotive production in order to compensate for fluctuations in demand for Shays. A turning point came in 1911, when Lima supplied 23 switching locomotives to the Mobile & Ohio. These constituted the first steam locomotives produced by Lima for a major (Class 1) main-line railroad customer. One year

later increasing capital needs led to rechartering as the Lima Locomotive Corp. on June 21, 1912. In that year Lima Locomotive began a new plant geared to the construction of conventional locomotives. Also in 1912 a $1 million order from the Great Northern for 40 freight and passenger locomotives signaled Lima's presence as a major player in the main-line locomotive industry along with the two industry giants, Philadelphia-based Baldwin Locomotive Works and Schenectady-based American Locomotive Co. (Alco). As orders for Shay locomotives declined and those for conventional rod locomotives increased, 1913 marked the final year that the former category of production exceeded the latter.

In 1915 a consortium of eastern financial interests headed by Joel S. Coffin, who also controlled the Locomotive Superheater Co. and the Franklin Railway Supply Co., purchased Lima Locomotive. The sale, announced on January 28, 1916, meant that for the first time in its history local interests no longer controlled the company that Lima residents still referred to as the Loco. On April 25, 1916, the company was rechartered in Richmond, Virginia, as the Lima Locomotive Works, Inc. By that time the Lima facility employed some 1,700 workers and could complete several hundred locomotives per year. Under the new management orders increased only slightly. U.S. entry into World War I, which flooded Alco and Baldwin with orders, had little effect on Lima; that company produced less than 9 percent of the standard-design U.S. Railroad Administration (USRA) locomotives manufactured during the war. A postwar recession reduced Lima's sales to a trickle, and with only 10 conventional rod locomotives ordered during 1921 the Lima facility was virtually abandoned, and much of the workforce was laid off.

In 1922 Lima raised additional capital, which it used to

rebuild and expand its production facilities. Since demand for Shays had virtually evaporated, the modernized plant's main erecting shop was designed for the efficient production of conventional rod locomotives. Cranes moved locomotive parts and subassemblies from two side bays and an adjacent machine-shop building into the main erecting-shop area, where 11 tracks allowed for assembly of 14 locomotives at a time.

At the same time Lima revolutionized the locomotive industry by developing designs for more powerful and efficient Super-Power steam locomotives. Even though the New York Central ordered most of its locomotives from Alco, that railroad authorized Lima to construct an experimental, high-efficiency 2-8-2 freight locomotive. This prototype Class H-10 locomotive featured a larger grate area, a brick-arch firebox, an improved superheater, uniform-size flues, changes in the cylinder dimensions (larger bore and shorter stroke), lightweight alloy steel side rods, a larger smokebox, and an external dry pipe to transmit steam to the superheater. The locomotive, NYC 8000, featured horsepower gains of up to a third (unlike a diesel locomotive, steam locomotive horsepower varies

according to speed and boiler pressure), coupled with decreased fuel consumption, when it was first tested in June 1922. The New York Central ordered 75 locomotives of the same design.

By 1925 Lima had completed, at its own expense, a larger and more powerful version of the H-10. Dubbed the A-1, this 2-8-4 locomotive featured a larger firebox (made possible by the extra axle on the trailing truck and by stronger and lighter cast-steel cylinders, among other improvements). This locomotive impressed the New York Central, which ordered 25 copies for subsidiary Boston & Albany. As information regarding these locomotives spread through the small community of railroad motive-power officials, other railroads expressed considerable interest in this first true Super-Power design. The Texas & Pacific ordered 10 even larger and more powerful I-1A Texas-type 2-10-4 locomotives in July 1925. Ultimately, Lima built nearly 700 locomotives based on Super-Power innovations, ensuring the company a place as one of the big three steam locomotive producers, with about 20 percent of the overall market. Since Super-Power was more a design philosophy than a collection of patented inventions (and even that technology

Probably the best known of the nearly 900 Super-Power locomotives built by Lima were Southern Pacific's streamlined 4-8-4 Northerns. Hardly streamlined at all, they employed a "skyline" casing over the boiler, a silvered smokebox door, a bit of streamlined metal skirting, and a red, orange, and black color scheme to create a memorable train. Here GS-5 No. 4458, one of only two equipped with roller bearings, is eastbound from San Francisco to Los Angeles as train 98, the *Daylight*, in August 1950.
—William D. Middleton

could be produced by other firms under license), Alco and Baldwin each produced about 1,000 similar locomotives.

Lima enjoyed record sales (324 rod engines and 49 Shays) and profits ($2.4 million) in 1923. By the late 1920s, as railroads stagnated under restrictive rates and chronic capital shortages, they ordered far fewer Lima locomotives. The Great Depression caused locomotive orders to fall to 31 in 1931, and only 1 of these was actually completed and sent to its intended buyer. Lima had no orders at all in either 1932 or 1933. Lima lost more than $2.5 million during the Depression years, but avoided the bankruptcy that befell Baldwin in 1935. During those dark days one of Lima's brightest moments, both literally and figuratively, involved the production of 6 4-8-4 passenger locomotives for the Southern Pacific in 1935.

In addition to the sluggish Depression-era economy, Lima faced the same problem of technological obsolescence that confronted Alco and Baldwin. Although Super-Power locomotives embodied significant technological advancements, these were primarily marginal and incremental improvements that could do little to increase the thermal efficiency of steam locomotives or to reduce their high operating and maintenance costs. The only way to increase horsepower while avoiding costly doubleheading was to increase the size of steam locomotives, yet such locomotives still had to conform to weight and clearance requirements. Diesel locomotives, with their inherently higher thermal efficiency and lower operating and maintenance costs, particularly in yard switching service, offered the railroads a solution to their motive-power dilemma, but this radically different technology threatened the traditional expertise of Lima and the other steam locomotive builders. Although Alco and Baldwin had begun the manufacture of diesel locomotives by the 1930s, Lima lacked the capital and the technical expertise to rebuild its facilities and retrain its workforce for the full-scale manufacture of diesel locomotives.

Lima had experimented with internal combustion as early as 1910, when it completed two small gasoline-mechanical industrial locomotives. In 1929 Lima completed a prototype 100-hp gasoline-mechanical locomotive that employed a Hercules engine. By 1940 Lima had developed designs for 80-hp and 200-hp variants of this locomotive, in addition to the 100-hp version. Aside from the prototype locomotive, Lima built only two others to these designs (both 200 hp), and one of these served as the plant switcher. Lima applied its expertise in Shay geared locomotives to these experimental units, employing a cumbersome system of gears instead of a more efficient electrical transmission system. These small, underpowered gasoline locomotives were not suited for main-line railroad service. This was at a time when the Electro-Motive Co. was beginning full-scale diesel locomotive production, and when Alco and even Baldwin were moving aggressively into the diesel locomotive market.

During the 1930s Lima developed preliminary designs for larger diesel-electric and diesel-hydraulic locomotives of up to 3,000 hp. These designs featured Fairbanks, Morse & Co. (FM) and Cooper-Bessemer engines and, in one instance, a hydraulic transmission manufactured by the General Machinery Corp. in Hamilton, Ohio. In 1935 the Westinghouse Electric & Manufacturing Co. explored the possibility of producing diesel locomotives jointly with Lima before joining forces with Baldwin the next year.

World War II caused Lima to suspend all internal-combustion-related research and development work, and the war also led to substantial increases in steam locomotive orders. In 1942, for example, Lima received orders for 320 steam locomotives. Lima also built 1,655 M-4 Sherman tanks in 1942 and 1943. In May 1945 Lima completed its last Shay locomotive, for the Western Maryland. Although Shay orders had been in steady decline for decades, the postwar collapse of steam locomotive demand created far more serious problems. By 1955 U.S. railroads had replaced most of their steam locomotives with diesels, and Lima seemingly had little choice other than to build diesels or exit the locomotive industry entirely. Initially, however, Lima chose a third option, continuing to make incremental improvements to its steam locomotive technology in the hopes of securing postwar orders and halting, or at least slowing, the dieselization rush. In attempting to soldier on in the steam locomotive industry, Lima delayed and diverted resources away from any potential diesel locomotive research and development program. Postwar steam locomotive orders dwindled to a trickle, and the last Lima steam locomotive left the shops in 1949.

In 1947, after an unsuccessful FM effort to negotiate an agreement to manufacture diesels at the Lima facility, Lima managers merged with the General Machinery Corp. of nearby Hamilton, Ohio. At the new Lima-Hamilton Corp. the Hamilton plant supplied diesel engines and did most of the design work, while the Lima facility constructed the carbody, trucks, and underframe and assembled the units. Westinghouse Electric served as an independent supplier of electrical equipment. George A. and Walter A. Rentschler, former General Machinery executives, dominated the management of Lima-Hamilton. They fired many Lima employees and ordered engineers to stop all work on steam locomotive technology, utterly demoralizing a group of skilled workers who despite all odds tenaciously clung to their faith in steam. Since General Machinery had typically built diesel engines for marine applications, engineers in Hamilton developed a new diesel engine for locomotive use by October 1948.

In May 1949 Lima-Hamilton completed its first diesel locomotive, a 1,000-hp switcher. Higher-quality locomotives from other builders had saturated the switcher market by this time, most notably the GP-7 road switcher built by the Electro-Motive Division (EMD) of General Motors Corp. Since railroads were already beginning to standardize on designs from EMD and, to a lesser extent, Alco, they had little incentive to purchase Lima-Hamilton's designs. Ultimately, Lima-Hamilton completed only 174 diesel locomotives, all either 1,000 hp, 1,200 hp, or 2,500 hp, before locomotive production ceased in September 1951.

The 1950 merger of Lima-Hamilton with the Baldwin Locomotive Works to create the Baldwin-Lima-Hamilton Corp. (B-L-H) led to the cessation of all locomotive production at the Lima facility. The merger united two of the weakest competitors in the diesel locomotive industry and allowed Westinghouse Electric, which owned a controlling interest in Baldwin, tighter control over electrical equipment sales. B-L-H moved all locomotive production to its Eddystone, Pennsylvania, facility, and manufactured only Baldwin designs. B-L-H ended all locomotive production in 1956.

After the merger the Lima plant continued to produce shovels and cranes. In 1928 Lima had purchased the Ohio Power Shovel Co., originally a wholly owned subsidiary of the Ohio Steel Foundry Co. In 1934 it became Lima's Shovel & Crane Division and, by that time, manufactured shovels and cranes with gasoline, diesel, and electric motors. Although shovel and crane production was initially a small component of Lima's output, it allowed the company to avoid bankruptcy during the 1930s and, as locomotive production declined, became an increasingly important part of Lima's existence. In March 1951 B-L-H purchased the Austin-Western Co. and shifted production of that firm's road-construction equipment to the Lima plant. This equipment found few buyers.

In July 1965 B-L-H merged with Armour & Co., and the Greyhound Corp. acquired Armour in May 1970. Greyhound sold the Construction Equipment Division (including the Lima plant) to Clark Equipment Co. later that year. Construction of new equipment continued at Lima until December 1980. The facility manufactured replacement parts for a few more months, then was closed and sold in August 1981. Despite efforts to find other industrial tenants or even preserve the site as an industrial heritage museum, most of the factory's buildings have since been demolished.

—Albert J. Churella

REFERENCES

Hirsimaki, Eric. *Lima: The History*. Edmonds, Wash.: Hundman, 1986.

Kirkland, John F. *The Diesel Builders*. Vol. 1, *Fairbanks-Morse and Lima-Hamilton*. Glendale, Calif.: Interurban, 1985.

Koch, Michael. *The Shay Locomotive: Titan of the Timber*. Denver: World, 1971.

Weitzman, David. *Superpower: The Making of a Steam Locomotive*. Boston: David R. Godine, 1987.

See also LOCOMOTIVE BUILDERS.

Lincoln, Abraham (1809–1865)

The signature of Abraham Lincoln, 16th president of the United States, on the Pacific Railroad Act of 1862 provided the funds for construction of the first transcontinental railroad. As a man of the frontier, Lincoln had a native interest in the settlement of the West and in economic policies to further that cause. His only Washington experience before he became president was a single term in Congress (1847–1849). Elected as a Whig, the more business oriented of the two major parties at the time, Lincoln was a strong proponent of what were then called "internal improvements." Since river and rail development was largely beyond the means of private investors, Whigs supported a policy of government loan guarantees and other inducements to private capital. Lincoln favored steamboat interests early in his career, but by the 1850s he had seen the wave of the future and began to back the railroads.

Returning to Illinois after his congressional term, he built a lucrative legal practice representing the rail industry. In an 1854 case he argued successfully in the state Supreme Court that the Illinois Central should be exempt from county property taxes. He asserted that railroads were a public benefit and already paid state taxes—persuasive arguments in the railroad fever of the 1850s. The case established a precedent that facilitated railroad construction statewide.

Lincoln's railroad practice is best remembered for the case *Hurd v. Rock Island Bridge Co.* The Rock Island built the first bridge across the Mississippi River in 1856, a move that was not welcomed by steamboat interests. When the sidewheeler *Effie Afton* crashed into the bridge the following year, her owners sued, claiming that the bridge was a hazard to navigation. Thanks to Lincoln's technical understanding of the river and its currents, he proved in federal district court that the accident was caused by negligence on the captain's part, not by the bridge. The right of railroads to bridge navigable rivers was established.

If Lincoln had done nothing else for railroads, his place in the industry's history would have been secure. But his support for the Pacific railroad is regarded as his most noteworthy contribution. The need for such a railroad had been recognized for years, but during the sectional strife of the 1850s northern and southern members of Congress were unable to agree on a route. Consensus developed with the South's secession and the need to link California with the rest of the Union, and the Pacific Railroad Act was signed by President Lincoln on July 1, 1862. Empowered to establish the road's eastern terminus, Lincoln chose Council Bluffs, Iowa—possibly the result of a chance 1859 encounter with Grenville M. Dodge, who favored the Platte Valley route.

—Peter A. Hansen

REFERENCES

Bain, David Haward. *Empire Express: Building the First Transcontinental Railroad*. New York: Viking, 1999.

A painting imagined the August 1859 meeting at Council, Iowa, between Abraham Lincoln and Gen. Grenville M. Dodge to discuss the Pacific Railroad. —Union Pacific Railroad, *Trains* Magazine Collection

Ely, James W., Jr. *Railroads and American Law*. Lawrence: Univ. Press of Kansas, 2001.

Lindenthal, Gustav (1850–1935)

The Austrian-born American engineer who designed Hell Gate Bridge was the son of a cabinetmaker. Born in Brünn, Austria (now Brno, Czech Republic), in 1850, Gustav Lindenthal studied at Austrian technical schools and spent several years in engineering work on the Austrian and Swiss railways before emigrating to the United States in 1874. Upon arrival Lindenthal found work as a stonemason in the construction of the Centennial Exposition at Philadelphia, but soon advanced to design work. When exposition construction ended in 1877, he began what was to be an exceptional career as a bridge designer and builder. He first took up a position as a computer designer for the Keystone Bridge Co. at Pittsburgh and then in 1878 joined the Atlantic & Great Western Railroad, an Erie predecessor, as bridge engineer. By 1881 he had established his own engineering practice at Pittsburgh. Chief among several notable Lindenthal bridges at Pittsburgh was a lenticular steel truss span over the Monongahela River, completed in 1882, that stands today.

In 1884 Lindenthal first advanced a plan for a great road and railroad suspension bridge over the Hudson River at New York, an idea that he pursued for the next 40 years. In 1890 he moved his engineering practice to New York, and when the Hudson River project failed to materialize, he went on to other major bridge projects. Mayor Seth Low appointed him the city's bridge commissioner in 1902, and he developed designs for the Queensboro and Manhattan bridges over the East River.

In 1904 the New York Connecting Railroad, a joint Pennsylvania Railroad–New Haven venture, commissioned him as chief engineer for the Hell Gate Bridge crossing of the East

Gustav Lindenthal. —Smithsonian Institution (Neg. 90-8565)

River. Completed in 1917, the massive four-track structure incorporated a 977-foot steel arch main span over the river that still stands as the longest railroad arch ever built. It was Lindenthal's greatest work. Other major Lindenthal bridge designs completed during this period included a replacement structure for the Southern Railway's High Bridge crossing of the Kentucky River and the enormous continuous-truss bridge that carried the Chesapeake & Ohio over the Ohio River at Sciotoville, Ohio.

Lindenthal's last design for a Hudson River crossing, put forward in 1923, proposed an enormous eyebar suspension bridge at 57th Street with a clear span of 3,240 feet and a double deck 235 feet wide that would carry 12 railroad or rapid-transit tracks and 20 lanes of vehicular traffic. But when the Hudson was finally bridged at New York by the George Washington Bridge, it was designed by Othmar H. Ammann, who had worked under Lindenthal on the Hell Gate and Sciotoville bridges. Ammann appointed Lindenthal as a design consultant for the project, and the old man rode together with Ammann to the dedication in 1931. He died at his Metuchen, New Jersey, home just four years later.

—William D. Middleton

REFERENCES

Dictionary of American Biography.
"Memoir of Gustav Lindenthal." *Transactions of the American Society of Civil Engineers* 105 (1940): 1790–1794.
National Cyclopaedia of American Biography.

Literature, American

In the early years of the railroad writers in the United States and abroad began responding to this new mode of transportation. Views of the railroad were somewhat different in England than in the United States. For the most part, Victorian authors were markedly hostile to all things connected with the railroad. John Ruskin saw it as a despoiler of the landscape. The archconservative Thomas Carlyle was similarly contemptuous. Charles Dickens was apparently fascinated with railroads, but seldom put them in a sympathetic light. A dark view is found in his novel *Dombey and Son.* In other instances he introduces railroad subjects in a comical or satirical way, as in such shorter sketches as "Mugby Junction" and "The Lazy Tour of Two Idle Apprentices." Neither Thackeray nor Trollope could evince much sympathy for the railroad. Trollope had more than a little expertise on the subject since in his role as a postal inspector he spent much time riding on trains. Like most of his contemporaries, Trollope was horrified by the various railroad stock manipulations and schemes, which appeared much earlier in England than in the United States.

The American population as a whole was more welcoming to the railroad than the people of England, probably because the railroad was quickly perceived to be an essential glue that held the country together. There was no denying that the railroad allowed the nation to expand and prosper, particularly in the trans-Mississippi West, whereas the early English railroads linked long-settled communities. Still, it would be safe to say that even in America the early literary reception of railroads was guarded and skeptical.

Consider the case of Henry David Thoreau, a man who enjoyed the solitude of his cabin on Walden Pond and prized the tranquility of nature. Thoreau seemed to be ambivalent about the new Fitchburg Railroad that ran about 100 rods south of his secluded cabin. Not really a complete loner, as some have thought (he actually spent only two years at the pond), Thoreau was in many ways drawn to the railroad. He loved walking along the line and waving to the train crews, some of whom mistook him for a track worker. He was inspired by the energy and drama of the steam locomotive and the timeliness of its arrival. There was a spiritual component there: it "sets the sand a-blowing and the blackberries a-growing." Too, he saw the railroad's power of energizing people, of pulling them out of their lassitude. The railroad as a "well constructed institution regulates a whole country. Have not men improved somewhat in punctuality since the railroad was invented? Do they not think and talk faster in the depot than in the stage-office? I have been astonished by the miracle it has wrought."

On the other hand, as might be expected, Thoreau was occasionally annoyed by the noise and pollution of the railroad. "I will not have my eyes put out and my ears spoiled by its smoke and steam and hissing." There had been damage to the environment around Walden Pond.

"That devilish Iron Horse, whose ear-rending neigh is heard throughout the town, has muddied the Boiling Spring with his foot." Thoreau had little interest in where the railroad actually went. "What's the railroad to me? I never go to see where it ends." Nevertheless, here was something new, exciting, life affirming.

Ralph Waldo Emerson, Thoreau's longtime friend and mentor, was on the whole optimistic about the rise of technology, most especially the steamboat and the railroad. Like Thomas Jefferson, he believed that technology, freed of the worn-out cities of Europe and the demoralizing class systems of the Old World, could do much to fashion a new way of American life. In his essay of 1844, "The Young American," he asserted that the railroad could minimalize factionalism, overcome local peculiarities, bring the nation together, and (obviously) settle the West. "Railroad iron," he wrote, "was a magician's rod, in its power to evoke the sleeping energies of land and water."

But in the New England Renaissance there were writers who saw the railroad in much more sinister terms. Nathaniel Hawthorne found little that was reassuring in the railroad. In one of his most famous stories, "The Celestial Railroad," he asks the question that Thoreau avoids—where does the railroad go? In this story, which appears to be a dream vision and an updating of Bunyan's *Pilgrim's Progress,* Hawthorne was undoubtedly satirizing various forms of moral complacency, perhaps most obviously that of the transcendentalists, including, of course, Emerson. But he also takes a swipe at modern business, public relations types, aggressive promoters, and yes, the railroad. Its travelers have been promised a smooth voyage to the "Celestial City," but as the story's dreaming narrator wakes up, the locomotive that has been transporting him appears to have been nothing but fire and brimstone, the blazing work of the devil himself. How much the railroad itself is seen as the work of the devil is up to the reader's imagination, but Hawthorne leaves little room for doubt.

In the final years of the nineteenth century and the early years of the twentieth, the railroad was such an overwhelming presence in American life that it is hardly surprising that it appears regularly in novels, poems, and plays (*see also* THEATER). The writings of the American realists and naturalists are strong witness to this. William Dean Howells, often called the father of the realist novel in America, is not concerned primarily with making moral judgments of the railroad, but invariably shows how it fits into the warp and woof of American society. One of Howells's principal concerns was the human adjustments between the older small-town or rural America and the giant cities that were growing so rapidly. In his novel *A Hazard of New Fortunes* (1890) a well-to-do Pennsylvania German named Dryfoos moves to New York, flush with success. But urban life overwhelms his family with troubling new landscapes. At one point Howells describes the then-open yards of the New York Central north of the (old) Grand Central Station. These yards, with their smoke, constant noise and motion, and inscrutable flashing lights, seem to be a metaphor for the baffling complexity of modern life.

Howells was never a successful playwright, but his plays, either farces or melodramas in the vogue of the time, made considerable use of the railroad as an engine of social change. The very titles of some of these give an idea of the railroad's importance in his thinking: *The Albany Depot, The Parlor Car, The Sleeping Car, The Smoking Car.* The locale of *The Albany Depot,* which is the Boston & Albany station in Boston, presents us with a frivolous little social drama. A member of the Boston gentry is asked to meet a new cook in the waiting room while his wife is out shopping. Mr. Roberts picks out a plump, nice-looking lady who turns out to be the wife of a somewhat inebriated Irishman, and a farcical imbroglio results. Howells, of course, is dealing with the social leveling and the mingling of human types that the railroad was rapidly producing on the American scene.

The railroad in American literature is often seen as an agency of social and personal change, a link between the city and the country, and therefore, somehow the hand of fate and destiny. Theodore Dreiser's great novel *Sister Carrie* (1900) begins with a railroad journey that brings the book's 18-year-old heroine from her stifling Wisconsin town to a new and beguiling life in bustling and exuberant Chicago. The railroad is thus clearly an agency of deliverance, as it was to thousands of Americans in those times. Yet later in the novel a subsequent train journey under much more trying circumstances brings down another curtain on her life as she moves on with her lover Hurstwood to New York and a tragic denouement.

Social historian John R. Stilgoe speaks of the railroad as creating a "metropolitan corridor," an agency that brings about human change, social upheaval, and feelings of longing and desire. Certainly this aspect of the railroad is found over and over again in American literature between 1880 and World War II. Often the railroad depot is depicted as the place where human links are forged or broken. Especially in small villages it is the place where the city beckons to the hamstrung or stifled young. Here is the telegraph office, which brings news of the outside world. Here is where newspapers and magazines are dropped off. Here is where, often through the agency of the Sears Roebuck or Montgomery Ward catalogs, everything "new" arrives in town, from the latest ladies' frocks or summer hats to the most modern kitchen range. The depot is often the liveliest place in town, especially when a train is due. It becomes a tempter, a Lorelei, enticing especially the young away from their roots to some new and glamorous world beyond. In Sherwood Anderson's *Winesburg, Ohio* (1919), a series of sketches of the narrow horizons and deviant passions of a midwestern town, it is not hard to understand why a local preacher forbids his son to hang out at the railroad depot, for it is here that a lust for city habits and ways is engendered.

Such themes recur over and over in the American literature of this period. The heroine of Ellen Glasgow's 1925 novel *Broomsedge* feels the impact of the railroad, which provides some glamour compared with the drab environment of the church, the general store, the schoolhouse. The gleaming track, the telephone poles, offered some pulse of romanticism, even after the trains had passed. "The passing trains had been a part of the expected miracle, the something different in the future": excitement perhaps, vitality, energy, possibility.

In Sinclair Lewis's *Main Street* (1920), which takes place in the maliciously named small Minnesota town of Gopher Prairie (closely resembling the author's hometown of Sauk Center), the railroad is a constant and tantalizing presence for both the book's hero, Dr. Will Kennicott, and Carol, his new young wife. Kennicott, a kindly, well-intentioned, but unimaginative town doctor, is aware of all the trains that pass through the town, even, of course, the limited express trains that do not stop. One morning on his rounds he hears a whistle and pulls out his watch: "No. 19. Must be 'bout 10 minutes late." Everyone in town is aware of the railroad and its eternal verities; they all know the name of the president of the road. But for Kennicott, like many others, the railroad has little wider significance beyond their own world.

For Carol Kennicott, college educated and from "the big city," the railroad has a much more portentous meaning. She came up here on the dreary way train, passing town after town, none of them any more invigorating than Gopher Prairie. To her, the railroad is the link to the larger world outside, the only sign that there is a greater and more vital civilization elsewhere. The passing trains are "magic." They symbolize freedom, escape, promise.

One of the common themes in early twentieth-century American literature is the chasm that exists between the passengers in the luxurious Pullman cars and the indistinguishable bystanders watching the limited train speed by—the forgotten farmers, the small-town functionaries, the "grotesques," as Sherwood Anderson would have it—those closed off from the charms of the metropolitan corridor and the smart, sophisticated denizens of those cities to which all such trains seem to be headed. Booth Tarkington begins his first novel, *The Gentleman from Indiana* (1899), with a description of a train journey through the Midwest from inside an elegant Pullman car. To the passenger, the outside world with its isolated barns and farm dwellings occasionally provides meager visual interest, but nothing in comparison with the plush surroundings inside, which carry with them the ambiance of the sophisticated East left behind. The same feeling of alienation between railroad traveler and the endless agrarian world outside is expressed, perhaps even more brutally, by Willa Cather in her 1918 novel *My Antonia*. Passengers passing through Cather's beloved Nebraska seldom even bother to look out the large picture window—there is just too much of it. When they do, it is only for an unknowing, uncaring, momentary glance—a snapshot.

The point is made once again by F. Scott Fitzgerald at the end of *The Great Gatsby* (1925). His narrator, the son of a prosperous midwestern family (perhaps from St. Paul, Minnesota, Fitzgerald's own hometown), recalls trips back home from his eastern prep school—the "returning trains" of his youth. He remembers the dimly lit old Union Station in Chicago at Christmas, other students returning doubtless from some eastern school or college. He remembers the long green tickets clasped in his gloved hands. He recalls "the murky yellow cars of the Chicago, Milwaukee and St. Paul Railroad looking as cheerful as Christmas itself beyond the gates." Yes, it was the trains themselves—their panache, perhaps—that provided the excitement, not the small stations of Wisconsin fleeting by. "That's my Middle West—not the wheat or the prairies or the lost Swede towns, but the thrilling returning trains of my youth."

For many U.S. writers of this period travel by train, especially inside the splendid Pullman car, leads to a heightened awareness of the good life, of an almost libidinous excess. The heroes of Thomas Wolfe's novels *Of Time and the River* (1935) and *You Can't Go Home Again* (1940) are enthralled by railroad travel, especially on speeding luxury trains, which have the effect of sharpening one's senses and desires. On trains we want to wear our best clothes, we are alert to the people around us, we form relationships, however brief, but in the club car, with men of affairs; as we eat in the grandeur of a dining car, we knew that it is quite unlike anything found in our own small town. We live, even though only briefly, in an electrically charged environment. "One looks at all the pretty girls with a sharpened eye and an awakened pulse." The environment of the luxury passenger trains somehow raises us above the mundane and the humdrum, raises us, however briefly, to heroic stature.

It is probably fair to say that for these writers the railroad is always employed as an agency of social transition. Rarely is the railroad itself the central focus (*see* LITERATURE, POPULAR). One obvious exception, of course, is Frank Norris's *The Octopus* (1901), in which the railroad is the leading character—a villainous character, to be sure, but clearly the very center of the novel. Here it is the business side of railroading that comes to the fore (something that British writers had done years before) as the ill-disguised Southern Pacific Railroad uses its octopus-like tentacles to strangle the wheat farmers of California. Perhaps the only other major novel to take the railroad as its very center of focus was Emile Zola's *La bête humaine*, a work of violent passions and deep tragic import, surely the best novel ever written with the railroad at its core.

Still, any study of the American novel from, say, the 1880s until the 1930s will reveal the railroad as a constant presence in the American landscape. In addition to the writers already mentioned, the railroad can be found almost everywhere in any honor roll of the American novel in this period. It was ruminated on seriously by Henry James, Stephen Crane, O. Henry, Mark Twain, Upton Sinclair, Jack London, Owen Wister, Edith Wharton, Hamlin

A powerful novel that made the railroad the villain of the story was *The Octopus* (1901) by Frank Norris. —George H. Douglas Collection

Ogden Nash, Sara Teasdale, Christopher Morley, Arthur Crew Inman, Hart Crane, and Louis Untermeyer.

At the same time one cannot neglect to mention the many other men of letters, essayists, historians, travel writers, and others who wrote frequently on the American railroad scene. Although America has not been as addicted to the formal essay as England, its vast public prints have made room for many leisurely journalists, informal historians, and other men of letters who have devoted themselves to railroad topics, sometimes exhaustively. One thinks of Christopher Morley, long associated with the publishing industry in Philadelphia and New York, and one of the founding editors of the *Saturday Review of Literature*. Among his most loved essays were "The Paoli Local," "An Early Train," "Consider the Commuter," "The Broadway Limited," "The Owl Train," and "Going to Philadelphia." Morley was especially enchanted with the Pennsylvania and the Reading.

Another writer with strong journalistic background and connections was Lucius Beebe, who published nearly 20 volumes on railroad topics, always written in a rich magenta style. Many of his books were illustrated informal histories, a good number done with the collaboration of his photographer friend Charles Clegg. Altogether, Beebe was one of the most prominent railroad writers of the twentieth century, although he also lavished his wit on numerous other topics: café society, the rich and famous, posh hotels, lobster palaces, the West, and the Boston Brahmins. But many others can also be mentioned. One thinks of Brander Matthews, E. V. Lucas, Frank H. Spearman, Rogers E. M. Whittaker (a *New Yorker* writer and editor who wrote on railroad topics under the name E. M. Frimbo), E. B. White, August and H. L. Mencken, Herbert Hamblen, Stewart H. Holbrook, Alvin F. Harlow, Edward Hungerford, Rollo Walter Brown, Oscar Lewis, Oliver Jensen, Jacques Barzun, Freeman H. Hubbard (long editor of *Railroad Magazine* and author of the wonderfully nostalgic *Railroad Avenue*), Garrison Keillor, and Paul Theroux. Literary interest in the American railroad may well have faded somewhat since World War II, but it is still alive and well, and it would be foolish to predict its coming demise.

—**George H. Douglas**

REFERENCES

Donovan, Frank P., Jr. *The Railroad in Literature.* Boston: Railway & Locomotive Historical Society, 1940.

Stilgoe, John R. *Metropolitan Corridor: Railroads and the American Scene.* New Haven, Conn.: Yale University Press, 1983.

Garland, Ellen Glasgow, and John Dos Passos. (It will probably be remembered that Dos Passos's novel *Manhattan Transfer* was named for the once well-known station in the New Jersey industrial marsh where the Pennsylvania Railroad changed to electric engines for the trip under the Hudson River to New York's Pennsylvania Station.)

It should also not be forgotten that during these same years the railroad frequently fascinated American playwrights and made numerous appearances on the stage (*see* THEATER). Too, and perhaps more curiously, the railroad was not neglected by American poets of the day. It might be thought that only casual versifiers or newspaper poets would embrace this industrial contrivance, but not a few major poets make reference to trains and railroads, many of them with fondness and nostalgia. Some of note are Emily Dickinson, Walt Whitman, John Greenleaf Whittier, Edwin Arlington Robinson, Carl Sandburg, Ambrose Bierce, Vachel Lindsay, James Whitcomb Riley, Joyce Kilmer, Joaquin Miller, Archibald MacLeish, Edna St. Vincent Millay, Witter Bynner,

Literature, Popular

During its golden age in America, between 1880 and World War I, there grew up a sizable body of popular literature dealing with the railroad. These works involved everything from novels and stories to poetry, ballads, boys' books, children's literature, and popular magazine articles. In these same years numerous railroad workers had a legendary status in the public mind. The locomotive engineer, the brakeman, the boomer, the telegrapher, and the station agent were often perceived as heroic figures. Mass-circulation magazines were ever on the lookout for creative stories and other materials about these well-known figures. Among them were the *Saturday Evening Post, McClure's, Scribner's, Collier's,* and *Youth's Companion.*

It was not surprising, then, that a group of writers appeared who were regularly thought of as "railroad writers." They were individuals who had either worked for railroads themselves or otherwise drew on extensive personal experiences. Today, the railroad novel and the railroad short story have almost completely disappeared, but a century ago they constituted a respected and even lucrative genre.

Probably the best known of the railroad novelists was Frank H. Spearman (1859–1937). Although he was a banker by profession, Spearman developed such an overwhelming interest in the railroad that he has been called the dean of railroad writers. Certainly he was the most skilled stylist of all such writers in his day. He entered the field in 1901 with a book of stories titled *Held for Orders.* Five years later emerged probably the best-selling railroad novel in American history, *Whispering Smith.* A kind of detective mystery in a western setting, it was twice made into popular silent movies, and the "Whispering Smith" legend continued in the movies long after Spearman's death. There was a 1948 version of the story with Alan Ladd; three years later the British Hammer Studios took up the story of Whispering Smith in *Whispering Smith Hits London. Held for Orders* was made into a successful movie, *The Yellow Mail.* Other popular works of Spearman's were *The Daughter of a Magnate* (in the movies, *The Love Special*), *Flambeau Jim,* and *The Mountain Divide. The Nerve of Foley* was a fine collection of stories.

Another prolific writer was Cy Warman (1855–1914). Warman, for years an engineer on the Denver & Rio Grande Railroad, wrote two novels, *The White Mail* and *Snow on the Headlight,* but he was best known for his short stories. He also wrote poetry and ballads of the rails, many of them published in newspapers. Then there was Francis Lynde (1856–1930), who for a time held various executive positions with the Union Pacific, but in the 1890s began to support himself as a full-time writer. He was the author of 35 novels, about half of them on railroad topics. His main concerns were not so much with the rank and file, but with clashes of rival interests, the shenanigans of railroad brass, and the like. Others identified with the "railroad school of writers" were Frank L. Packard, John Alexander Hill, Alva Kerr, Samuel Merwin, Thomas Nelson Page, Henry W. Phillips, and A. W. Somerville.

Another huge literary market in these same years was the American boy. Needless to say, in the great days of

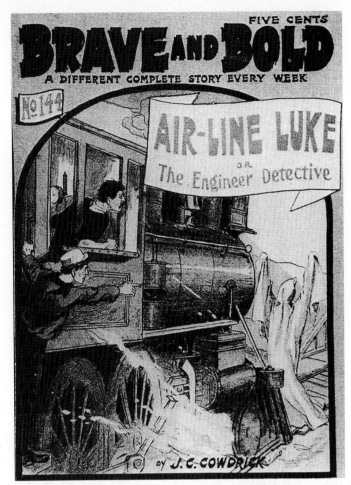

Brave and Bold, a turn-of-the-century pulp magazine, brought out an exciting new story every week. —George H. Douglas Collection

steam locomotion the railroad was a perpetual fascination to all boys, so boys' books appeared early. Leading the way as early as 1883 was Horatio Alger (1832–1899), whose novel *The Train Boy* brought a new American folk legend to the fore. In this and Alger's later railroad novel *The Erie Train Boy,* the formulaic saga of rags to riches, of pluck and luck, entered the American imagination. It infused nearly all boys' stories for several generations. One of Alger's imitators and followers, Edward Sylvester Ellis, gave the formula forceful emphasis in the title of one of his books, *From the Throttle to the President's Chair.*

Not all the juvenile authors of the day followed this formula slavishly, and by the early twentieth century there were a number of authors working assiduously in a broad field of juvenile railroad literature. Among the best known and most successful was Burton Egbert Stevenson, a librarian, who clearly grasped what young readers were looking for. Before going into library work Stevenson had been a "railroad reporter" for the *Chillicothe Daily News.* Although his books were fictional, they were solidly grounded in railroad knowledge and also somewhat didactic. They had titles such as *The Young Train*

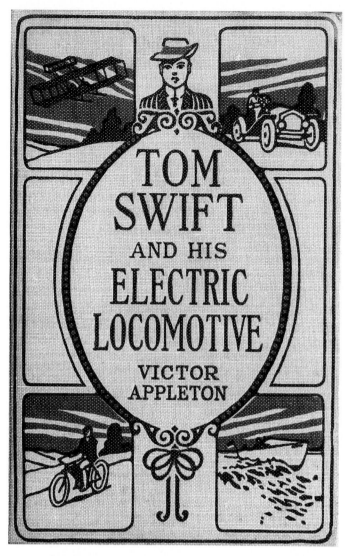

Tom Swift, the youthful genius of the Stratemeyer syndicate, sometimes turned his attention to railroads, as in *Tom Swift and His Electric Locomotive,* by Victor Appleton. —George M. Smerk Collection

Dispatcher and *The Young Trainmaster.* There was, of course, an air of the Horatio Alger pluck and luck formula about them. In the first two decades of the twentieth century a number of authors were writing railroad-centered stories for the juvenile market. Among them were Alva Kerr, Herbert Hamblin, and Francis Coombs. Allen Chapman, a pen name of the Stratemeyer syndicate, produced many railroad stories involving "Ralph": *Ralph of the Roundhouse, Ralph in the Switch Tower, Ralph on the Overland Express,* and many others. Some originators of general boys' series occasionally took a try at railroad topics. One such was Edward Stratemeyer, whose giant syndicate turned out Rover Boys, Tom Swift, Hardy Boys, and numerous others. Stratemeyer occasionally turned his attention to railroad topics. For example, his boy genius inventor Tom Swift is at the top of his form in *Tom Swift and His Electric Locomotive* (1922).

Popular railroad literature—narrative and imaginative works—had almost entirely disappeared in the last half of the twentieth century. Some might say that it had faded by the 1920s. On the other hand, the revival of the old *Railroad Man's Magazine* (later *Railroad Magazine*) in 1929 did offer the authors of stories and ballads a thriving new venue for a time. Among the most popular were E. S. Dellinger and Gilbert A. Lathrop. The latter, a Denver & Rio Grande trainman, turned out dozens of short stories and novellas for *Railroad* under his own name and several pseudonyms and published two juvenile novels, *Whispering Rails* (1936) and *Mystery Rides the Rails* (1937). Probably the most popular of all was Harry Bedwell, a boomer telegraph operator, whose stories frequently featured the exploits of Eddie Sand, a boomer telegraph operator. Bedwell tried his hand as a novelist on at least one occasion, with *The Boomer* (1942).

In the 1940s the newly established *Trains* magazine turned its back on stories, ballads, and poems in favor of articles and photography. This seemed to fit the mood and taste of the newer railroad enthusiast, so the older kinds of popular literature faded away. (It should be said that *Trains* magazine has not turned entirely away from the narrative form. It does run first-person narratives of railroad men and aficionados—many of them excellent.)

Quite remarkably, the older forms of railroad literature have not completely died. Many poems and ballads have been kept alive in folk music, country music, and sometimes popular music. One can still hear such old standbys as "The Wreck of Old 97," "The Wabash Cannon Ball," "Casey Jones," and "Big Rock Candy Mountain" (*see* MUSIC).

Adult railroad novels have disappeared, with a few exceptions from time to time, such as Hollister Noble's *One Way to Eldorado* (1954). On the other hand, there are small signs of life in the juvenile field. There continue to be books written for very young children—works like *The Little Engine That Could.* Series of such books for the very young still thrive in England. Boys' books have almost entirely vanished from the American scene, so there is little for older children except informative or historical juveniles. On the other hand, and curiously, the last half of the twentieth century has seen the arrival of several series of "Orphan Train" books. These historical narratives are intended for older children, but apparently are read almost entirely by girls.

—George H. Douglas

REFERENCE

Donovan, Frank P., Jr. *The Railroad in Literature.* Boston: Railway & Locomotive Historical Society, 1940.

Locomotive Builders

From the earliest years of railroad construction, American machine shops had the technical expertise necessary to manufacture steam locomotives, yet they could not keep pace with the demands of a rapidly expanding railroad network. As a result, many North American railroads initially purchased their steam locomotives from Britain; the first four were destined for the Delaware & Hudson Canal Co. in 1829. Perhaps the most famous of the more than 120 locomotives imported between 1829 and 1841 was the *John Bull*, of the Camden & Amboy Railroad. It soon became apparent that imported locomotives were not suited to North American railroads, which tended to have rougher track, sharper curves, and steeper grades than their more heavily engineered British counterparts.

Although British railroads typically manufactured steam locomotives in their own shops, most American railroads purchased their motive power from independent builders. There were exceptions, most notably the Altoona shops of the Pennsylvania Railroad, which began locomotive production in 1866. Early U.S.-built locomotives mimicked their British counterparts, but differences in operating conditions soon led to the development of distinctively American locomotive designs. In 1830, only a year after the first British locomotive was imported, the West Point Foundry Assn. at New York City completed the *Best Friend of Charleston*. Rapid changes in locomotive design, some of which were based on British practice, resulted in the nearly universal adoption of the horizontal boiler, lead trucks to guide the locomotive through switches and around sharp curves (1832), sprung and equalized driving axles (1837), and larger fireboxes to burn readily available wood instead of coal. The 4-4-0 wheel arrangement (a four-wheel lead truck followed by four driving wheels on two axles), introduced in 1837, marked the apogee of the early locomotive builder's art. These aptly named American locomotives could produce substantial tractive effort, yet were rugged and flexible enough to tolerate the roughest track. American builders constructed more than 13,000 locomotives with this wheel arrangement.

Although steam locomotive builders may have appreciated the advantages inherent in design and production standardization, several factors mitigated against this practice. First, the inability of early manufacturers to achieve close tolerances precluded truly interchangeable parts. Furthermore, the extraordinary variety of operating conditions on American railroads, ranging from freight to passenger to switching service and from prairies to mountains to deserts, mandated a corresponding multiplicity of designs. Moreover, railroad motive-power officials, particularly on the larger roads, were seldom willing to cede control of the design process to the builders. Frequently, railroads developed a close working relationship with a favored locomotive builder, and in exchange for regular orders, the builders built what the railroads wanted. These factors led to a wide variety of wheel arrangements and ensured that two locomotives of the same wheel arrangement and from the same builder could look quite different when designed for different railroads.

The Pennsylvania Railroad, the self-proclaimed "Standard Railroad of the World," came closest to true design and manufacturing standardization, but this was less true of independent builders. Given the diverse nature of the market, the Baldwin Locomotive Works made impressive efforts at standardization. That company maintained detailed records of each part of every locomotive that it had constructed. As Baldwin draftsmen developed new locomotive designs, they attempted to incorporate as many preexisting parts and subassemblies as possible. Designers shaped each part from wood before casting or machining it in metal. These wooden patterns, stored in a pattern vault, became the collective technological memory of the company, essential for standardization, albeit limited, and vital to the creation of replacement parts. Smaller builders, lacking Baldwin's high output, scale economies, and relative control over the locomotive market, were far less effective at enforcing standardization.

Given the size and complexity of steam locomotives, the cyclical nature of locomotive demand, and the ability of railroad customers to influence the design process, builders were rarely able to exploit high-throughput economies of scale associated with industries such as steel or oil. Instead of mass production, builders used flexible, small-batch production techniques that minimized fixed costs and allowed them to withstand business downturns by curtailing production, temporarily releasing a substantial portion of their workforce, and shifting into other product lines. Most early manufacturers built other types of machinery, including stationary and marine steam engines, in addition to locomotives. In so doing, they exploited economies of scope, making use of talented workers and general-purpose machine tools and foundry equipment. A diverse product line also enabled builders to ride out the inevitable boom-and-bust cycles inherent in one of the most volatile industries within the capital goods sector of the economy. By 1850 there were approximately 40 locomotive builders in the United States, and although that number declined precipitously after the Civil War, more than 150 companies manufactured steam locomotives at some point between 1829 and the cessation of U.S. domestic steam locomotive production in 1949.

The capital requirements of early locomotive builders tended to be modest, and this contributed to the large number of startup firms in the early years of the industry. Periodic financial panics, combined with the willingness of many builders to accept heavily discounted railroad securities in lieu of cash, quickly weeded out the marginal producers and left even the strongest firms on the verge of bankruptcy. Most firms were organized as partnerships, and this remained the case even with the largest producers until comparatively late in the steam locomotive era.

Most successful builders were located in the Middle Atlantic states, particularly in Philadelphia, Pennsylvania, and Paterson, New Jersey. These two cities allowed builders ready access to a pool of highly skilled labor, and during slack periods these workers could readily secure less remunerative work in other local manufacturing industries.

By the late nineteenth century Baldwin, based in Philadelphia, had emerged as the preeminent U.S. builder of steam locomotives. Its founder, Matthias W. Baldwin, began a career as a jeweler in 1819, produced a working model locomotive in 1831, and completed a full-sized version a year later. By 1837 his company was manufacturing more than 40 locomotives a year, an impressive number at that early date. Even after several brushes with bankruptcy and the death of its founder in 1866, Baldwin remained a partnership until 1909, by which time it had produced more than 33,500 steam locomotives. In that year the need for additional capital transformed the partnership, then known as Burnham, Williams, & Co., into the Baldwin Locomotive Works. In 1910 Baldwin employed some 19,000 workers and had a production capacity of 2,500 locomotives per year. Output soared during World War I, reaching 3,580 locomotives in 1918. In the 1920s a decline in Baldwin's orders accompanied the beginning of a long-term decline in the American railroad industry. Baldwin's move of its operations into the massive new Eddystone facility, completed in June 1928, proved to be particularly unfortunate timing. The Great Depression ensured that aside from the World War II years, Eddystone would never operate at even close to full capacity. Baldwin completed its last steam locomotive for domestic use in 1949 and continued to build a few steam locomotives for export for several years thereafter.

Aside from Baldwin, the Norris Locomotive Works dominated early steam locomotive production in Philadelphia. Established by William Norris and later controlled by his brother Richard, the company enjoyed its greatest success before the Civil War, building more than 1,000 locomotives by 1860. Production soon declined, and only 200 or so additional locomotives had been completed by the time Baldwin purchased the facility in 1873.

In Paterson the Rogers Locomotive Works was established as a machine shop in 1832. It built its first locomotive five years later and soon acquired a reputation as an innovative producer. The American Locomotive Co. purchased stock in the Rogers Locomotive Co. in 1905 and merged with that firm in 1909. Production continued in Paterson until 1913, amounting to nearly 6,200 locomotives. The Grant Locomotive Works, also located in Paterson, manufactured nearly 1,900 locomotives between 1848 and 1893. The Cooke Locomotive and Machine Works, another Paterson firm, completed some 2,750 locomotives between 1853 and its 1901 Alco merger.

In addition to the Philadelphia and Paterson firms, major producers emerged elsewhere in the United States. Two more Norris brothers from Philadelphia, Septimus and Edward, organized the Schenectady (New York) Locomotive Works in 1848. After initial difficulties, and under the leadership of John Ellis and Walter McQueen, the firm prospered. By 1901, when Schenectady became the nucleus of the newly formed American Locomotive Co. (Alco), the company had completed more than 1,200 locomotives. Based in Dunkirk, New York, the Brooks Lo-

comotive Works built more than 13,000 locomotives between 1869 and 1928, although only slightly more than 4,000 of these were completed before the company became part of Alco in 1901.

In June 1901 eight small locomotive builders, the Schenectady, Rhode Island, Cooke, Brooks, Manchester, Pittsburgh, Richmond, and Dickson Locomotive Works, joined in a defensive merger against Baldwin's market dominance. Alco, created as part of a great merger wave that swept through corporate America at the turn of the twentieth century, soon concentrated production in Schenectady. Alco's manufacturing rationalizations enabled the company to achieve rough parity with Baldwin over the next two decades, each with about 40 percent of the market. Like Baldwin, Alco suffered through the Great Depression, producing only 89 steam locomotives between 1931 and 1935. After a surge in wartime orders, Alco completed its last steam locomotive in 1948.

By the early twentieth century Lima was the only other significant U.S. producer. Lima, like many other small locomotive builders, initially exploited a niche market. Ephraim Shay, a Michigan lumberman, inventor, and entrepreneur, developed a geared (rather than rod-driven) locomotive whose low speed, high adhesion, and flexibility were ideally suited for lightly built and steeply graded logging and mining railroads. Lima acquired the patent rights and built 2,761 Shay locomotives between 1880 and 1945. Other companies, most notably Heisler and Climax, emulated Lima's production of specialized geared locomotives, but only Lima made the transition into the mainline steam locomotive market. In 1925 Lima introduced Super-Power steam locomotives, which incorporated many incremental improvements to steam locomotive technology, increasing power while lowering fuel consumption. Lima's reputation as an innovative producer allowed the company to capture most of the remaining 20 percent of steam locomotive orders in the United States until it ceased steam locomotive production in 1949.

Many smaller producers survived by manufacturing light locomotives for logging, mining, or industrial use or else by producing for regional markets. The Hinkley Locomotive Works, established as a machine shop in Boston in 1826, began locomotive production in 1840. By the time production ceased in 1889, the company had completed more than 1,800 locomotives. The Mason Machine Works (over 700 locomotives) and the Taunton Locomotive Manufacturing Co. (nearly 1,000 locomotives) were also located in Massachusetts. The Portland (Maine) Locomotive Works and the Dickson Manufacturing Co., located in Scranton, Pennsylvania, exhibited additional geographic dispersion. Cincinnati, Ohio, was a significant regional center of locomotive production, with such firms as the Cincinnati Locomotive Works. Although locomotive production was rare in the South, there were such firms as the Richmond Locomotive and Machine Works (4,500 locomotives, including many completed after Alco acquired the facility in 1901) and the much smaller Marietta, Georgia–based Glover Machine Works. On the West Coast companies that specialized in mining and logging machinery occasionally manufactured a few steam locomotives as well. The Pacific Iron Works in San Francisco was established in 1850 and remained in business for the next half century. In the same city the Union Iron Works and the Vulcan Iron Works produced small numbers of locomotives. Farther north the Willamette Iron and Steel Works, in Portland, Oregon, built more than 30 copies of Lima Shay locomotives in the 1920s.

Canadian railroads used steam locomotives well after U.S. railroads had dieselized, in part because their executives adopted a wait-and-see attitude regarding diesels, and in part because they feared that early diesels could not withstand the rigors of the Canadian climate. The Montreal Locomotive Works (MLW) and the Kingston, Ontario–based Canadian Locomotive Co. (CanLoCo) dominated steam locomotive production in Canada. In 1904 Alco purchased a controlling interest in the 21-year-old Locomotive & Machine Co. of Montreal, changing the company's name to the Montreal Locomotive Works in 1908. During the diesel locomotive era MLW initially assembled Alco diesel locomotives. After Alco ended U.S. production in 1969, Alco sold its diesel designs to MLW. Snowmobile manufacturer Bombardier acquired MLW in 1975 and continued to produce Alco-design locomotives until 1985. Bombardier is currently a major builder in the passenger-car and mass-transit market and, with European supplier Alstom, the market for high-speed electric locomotives. CanLoCo produced more than 3,000 locomotives between 1854 and 1968. In addition to building steam locomotives for Canadian railways, the company was Baldwin's diesel locomotive sales outlet in Canada and also manufactured diesels under license from Fairbanks-Morse.

Although the United States possessed some of the earliest electrified main-line trackage in the world, North American electrification was ultimately much less widespread than in Europe, and, accordingly, American locomotive producers lagged behind European firms in the manufacture of electric locomotives. Baldwin and Alco both participated in this industry, but only as producers of underframes, bodies, and running gear. General Electric (GE) and the Westinghouse Electric & Manufacturing Co. were the primary innovators and exploited economies of scope by transferring their expertise in stationary electrical equipment and in streetcar, subway, and interurban electric railways to the field of main-line electrification. Each company developed a loosely affiliated production consortium with a locomotive builder. As early as 1895 Baldwin and Westinghouse collaborated on the manufacture of an experimental electric locomotive, and the two firms continued to jointly produce electric locomotives for more than half a century. GE and Alco, both based in Schenectady, similarly produced hundreds of electric locomotives for both North American and overseas markets, although GE later began to build entire locomotives itself at its Erie, Pennsylvania, plant.

Electric locomotives had little lasting effect on the structure of the American locomotive industry. GE and Westinghouse did employ their overall expertise in electrical equipment technology to enter the diesel-electric locomotive industry, the former firm far more successfully than the latter, but the link between GE's involvement in heavy main-line electric locomotives and its success in the diesel-electric locomotive industry is tenuous at best. Since Alco and Baldwin manufactured only the relatively unsophisticated mechanical portions of electric locomotives, they did not develop an expertise in electrical equipment or control systems that might have transferred to diesel-electric locomotive production. European firms or designs have recently dominated the limited market for main-line (passenger) electric locomotives. Diesel builder Electro-Motive Division (EMD) has supplied locomotives built under license from Sweden's ASEA to Amtrak and others, and Bombardier has supplied electric locomotives either built jointly with European builder Alstom or built entirely at former Adtranz (now part of Bombardier) European plants.

The three major steam locomotive manufacturers, Alco, Baldwin, and Lima, manufactured diesel locomotives, yet ultimately none was a competitive producer. Diesel locomotives are, more precisely, diesel-electric locomotives, since most use a diesel engine to generate electricity, which in turn powers the axles. This new technology was more amenable to firms such as General Motors (GM) that understood internal combustion engines and to companies, such as General Electric, that were innovators in electric generators and related control equipment.

Although the German inventor Rudolf Diesel recognized the potential railroad applications of his engine, early versions were too heavy and unreliable for railroad service. By the 1920s advances in metallurgy had reduced engine weight, yet railroads considered diesel locomotives suitable only for niche applications, for locations with a high fire risk, or in areas where environmental regulation (in the form of local smoke ordinances) banned steam locomotives.

As with electric locomotives, early diesels were often manufactured by a consortium of companies. The first commercially successful diesel locomotives, built between 1923 and 1928, were joint efforts by Alco (body and underframe), GE (electrical equipment), and Ingersoll-Rand (diesel engine). By 1929 Baldwin and Westinghouse were collaborating on the production of diesel locomotives. These early locomotives were often custom-built one-off products with minimal standardization. Although standardization counteracted the accepted steam locomotive industry practice of allowing railroad motive-power officials influence over the design process, it was necessary in order to amortize high initial research and development costs.

Baldwin did not standardize its locomotive designs or even commit to a sustained diesel locomotive research and development program until the late 1930s. Baldwin's

1935 bankruptcy contributed to this delay, as did the disinterest of longtime Baldwin executive Samuel Vauclain in diesel locomotive technology. Alco did better, developing standard-design diesel switching locomotives as early as 1931. The company's use of a narrow hood (covering the engine and generator) allowed for superior visibility from the cab and marked a major innovation in diesel locomotive design. However, although Alco purchased the McIntosh & Seymour Engine Co. in 1929, the company still lacked adequate diesel engine technology. In 1940 Alco and GE signed a joint-production agreement in which GE agreed to manufacture only export diesel locomotives and small industrial diesel locomotives (such as the GE 44- and 70-tonners) while supplying Alco with electrical equipment for the domestic large diesel locomotive market.

During the 1930s a new producer, Electro-Motive, supplanted these early entrants. Harold Hamilton, a former marketing executive at the White Automobile Co., established the Electro-Motive Co. (EMC) at Cleveland in 1922. Initially EMC designed self-propelled gasoline-engine railcars, subcontracting manufacturing to various established railcar builders. EMC purchased electrical equipment from GE and, to a lesser extent, Westinghouse, but bought all of its engines from the Winton Engine Co., also located at Cleveland. EMC succeeded primarily because of its advanced marketing programs and its elaborate post-sale training and support programs. By the late 1920s EMC's standard-design railcars dominated the industry, but market saturation and the onset of the Great Depression threatened to forestall further growth.

In 1930 General Motors purchased Winton as part of an effort to develop automobile and truck diesel engines and, since EMC was Winton's largest customer, purchased that company as well. Although GM did not develop highway diesels until later, the company did produce an engine, the Model 201, that was suitable for submarine use, and two of these engines powered the GM Building at the 1933 Chicago World's Fair. Ralph Budd, president of the Chicago, Burlington & Quincy, saw these engines in operation and persuaded GM and EMC to use a diesel engine to power a new lightweight passenger train, the *Zephyr*. In this roundabout and largely unintentional way EMC moved into diesel locomotive production. After producing other lightweight integrated trainsets, EMC tested experimental locomotives and then began building switch engines for yard service. EMC began construction of a new manufacturing facility at La Grange, Illinois, in 1935. It introduced the Model 567 diesel engine as a replacement for the Model 201, and began the production of locomotive generators and related electrical equipment based largely on GE designs in 1938. In 1939 EMC completed a prototype FT (Freight Type) diesel locomotive that performed well in demonstration service, particularly on the Atchison, Topeka & Santa Fe.

World War II affected the locomotive industry, but did little to hinder Electro-Motive's success or alter the long-term decline of the steam locomotive builders. In April 1942 the War Production Board issued General Limitation Order L-97, which restricted diesel locomotive production to existing designs. With the only viable prewar freight locomotive (the FT), Electro-Motive had a temporary monopoly over that sector of the diesel locomotive market. Although Alco and Baldwin executives later alleged that L-97 had crippled their chances for success in the diesel locomotive industry, they made no such complaints during the war itself, and during the war Electro-Motive's share of the diesel locomotive market fell, while those of Alco and Baldwin increased. Alco, Baldwin, and Lima all benefited from a temporary increase in steam locomotive orders during the war, since diesels were difficult to obtain. L-97 allowed research and development programs to continue uninterrupted, and both Alco and Baldwin developed new designs during the war. Alco attempted to replace its prewar Model 531 diesel engine with the Model 241, but dropped this engine in favor of the Model 244, only to discard that engine in favor of the Model 251 in the early 1950s, at the height of the dieselization rush. Baldwin never did develop quality diesel engine or diesel locomotive designs.

The most important effect of the war on Electro-Motive, and on the locomotive industry as a whole, occurred as a result of a surge in military orders, primarily for marine diesel engines, that swamped La Grange and forced Electro-Motive to standardize production through the use of careful record keeping and through the application of jigs and fixtures. The profitability of diesel engines also led GM to transform its EMC subsidiary into the Electro-Motive Division (EMD) on January 1, 1941.

After 1945 U.S. railroads dieselized within little more than a decade. EMD opened two ancillary plants in the United States and established a manufacturing facility in London, Ontario. EMD's production and profitability soared as its market share increased from 46 percent in 1946 to 89 percent in 1957. This degree of market dominance led the U.S. Justice Department to initiate two antitrust suits against EMD in 1961 and 1963. Both suits were dropped, but rumors persisted that EMD had enjoyed an unfair wartime advantage, and that EMD had relied on reciprocity, allegedly promising to divert GM freight traffic to railroads that purchased EMD locomotives. More evident reasons for EMD's success lay in its dependable technology and its ability to offer railroads training programs, spare parts, and locomotive-rebuilding services. Although Alco's RS-1 had pioneered the road switcher design in 1941, U.S. railroads favored EMD units, purchasing more than 2,600 GP7 (General Purpose) and more than 3,400 similar GP9 road switchers between 1949 and 1959.

As customers standardized on EMD designs, other producers were squeezed out of the diesel locomotive industry. Fairbanks, Morse & Co. (FM), a producer of submarine diesel engines, introduced diesel locomotives in 1944, initially contracting production to General Electric's Erie, Pennsylvania, facility and later building locomotives at its own plant in Beloit, Wisconsin. FM exited the industry in 1959. Lima did not offer diesel locomotives until 1949, after a 1947 merger with the General Machinery Corp., and built only 174 diesel locomotives by the time production terminated in 1951. Baldwin since the 1930s had endured bankruptcy, oversized production facilities, mismanagement, and poor diesel locomotive designs. In 1950 Baldwin merged with Lima-Hamilton, and the new Baldwin-Lima-Hamilton Corp. struggled on until 1956, when production ceased. By 1960 Alco alone survived to challenge EMD, but it ran a very distant second in terms of product quality and market share. Railroads kept Alco afloat primarily to ensure that EMD did not monopolize the industry and thus increase prices and retard innovation.

Several small producers entered the North American locomotive market, typically producing only a few industrial locomotives before exiting the industry. For example, the Columbus, Indiana–based Cummins Engine Co. manufactured only one locomotive (in 1937) before company officials decided not to seek further railroad applications for their products. The Davenport (Iowa) Locomotive Works was more successful, manufacturing gasoline and diesel locomotives of up to 1,000 hp (although much smaller industrial units were far more common) from 1902 until 1956. H. K. Porter, established in 1866, began to build small steam locomotives a year later and completed 287 small internal combustion locomotives (mainly diesels) between 1911 and 1950. In 1914 the J. D. Fate Co. began producing internal combustion locomotives at its Plymouth, Ohio, facility. Renamed the Fate-Root-Heath Co. in 1919, it later became the Plymouth Locomotive Works. The company has manufactured nearly 10,000 small industrial locomotives, shifting production to a facility in Bucyrus, Ohio, in 1999, and is currently based in Akron, Ohio, as part of Williams Distribution. Based in Rochelle, Illinois, the George D. Whitcomb Co. began production of gasoline locomotives as early as 1906, followed by diesels in 1929. Bankruptcy in 1930 led to sale of a controlling interest in the company (by then known as the Whitcomb Locomotive Works) to Baldwin in 1931. Whitcomb became a Baldwin division in 1940, although production remained at Rochelle until it was transferred to Eddystone in 1952. As part of this reorganization process, Whitcomb locomotives were subsumed under the B-L-H nameplate. All told, Whitcomb manufactured more than 5,000 locomotives.

Although U.S. diesel locomotive manufacturers have dominated the global marketplace, foreign firms have rarely enjoyed much success in the U.S. market. Perhaps the most recognizable imports were 21 4,000-hp diesel-hydraulics manufactured by Munich, Germany–based Krauss-Maffei A.G. between 1961 and 1963. These locomotives served on the Denver & Rio Grande Western (3 units) and the Southern Pacific (18 units). Although they were powerful, they could not withstand the rigors of U.S.

rail service. In 1964 Alco built 3 similar domestic diesel-hydraulic locomotives, also for the Southern Pacific. More recently, Alstom Transport has been building diesel-electric locomotives for NJ Transit from a plant in Spain, using EMD engines.

General Electric became the last major producer to enter the diesel locomotive industry. GE had traditionally supplied electrical equipment for Alco locomotives, but GE executives worried that problems with Alco diesel locomotives would damage GE's overall reputation. Furthermore, GE marketing studies concluded that its Erie, Pennsylvania–based Transportation Systems Division could displace Alco from its secondary status in the diesel locomotive industry, although it could not overtake EMD. GE redesigned its large export locomotives for domestic service and in 1959 introduced the U25B. While EMC commenced production with a proprietary diesel engine and later expanded into the production of electrical equipment, GE combined its own electrical equipment with Cooper-Bessemer diesel engines, later setting up its own engine development laboratory and acquiring rights to design and develop the Cooper-Bessemer engine. Early GE U-series locomotives (popularly dubbed U-Boats) performed poorly, but GE's quality and market share improved rapidly, forcing Alco to suspend diesel locomotive production in 1969.

By the 1980s GE had become a formidable competitor to EMD. GE's Dash-8 locomotives contained sophisticated control systems and were more fuel-efficient than their EMD counterparts. By 1983 EMD had lost market dominance for the first time since 1935. Improved EMD designs, such as the 60-Series locomotives and the development of alternating-current-traction motors, allowed EMD to regain its lead. In recent years market share has fluctuated wildly in response to technological innovations and the feast-or-famine nature of locomotive orders. EMD assembles locomotives at its London, Ontario, facility, and has demolished a large portion of the La Grange plant. La Grange still produces parts and components, including diesel engines, and is EMD's corporate headquarters. Some companies, such as locomotive rebuilder Morrison-Knudsen, have tried to penetrate the new diesel locomotive market, but their efforts have met with little success, and it seems likely that EMD and GE will dominate the North American, and the world, market for diesel locomotives, at least in the foreseeable future.

—Albert J. Churella

REFERENCES

Brown, John K. *The Baldwin Locomotive Works, 1831–1915: A Study in American Industrial Practice.* Baltimore: Johns Hopkins Univ. Press, 1995.

Churella, Albert J. *From Steam to Diesel: Managerial Customs and Organizational Capabilities in the Twentieth-Century American Locomotive Industry.* Princeton, N.J.: Princeton Univ. Press, 1998.

Kirkland, John F. *Dawn of the Diesel Age: The History of the Diesel Locomotive in America*. Glendale, Calif.: Interurban, 1983.

Middleton, William D. *When the Steam Railroads Electrified*. 2nd ed. Bloomington: Indiana Univ. Press, 2001.

White, John H., Jr. *American Locomotives: An Engineering History, 1830–1880*. Baltimore: Johns Hopkins Univ. Press, 1997.

———. *A Short History of American Locomotive Builders in the Steam Era*. Washington, D.C.: Bass, 1982.

See also AMERICAN LOCOMOTIVE CO. (ALCO); BALDWIN LOCOMOTIVE WORKS; BOMBARDIER; ELECTRO-MOTIVE DIVISION, GENERAL MOTORS CORP.; FAIRBANKS, MORSE & CO.; GENERAL ELECTRIC CO.; LIMA LOCOMOTIVE WORKS; WESTINGHOUSE ELECTRIC & MANUFACTURING CO.

Locomotive Fueling

The steam locomotive, prodigiously powerful for its size, had an enormous appetite for fuel and water. Extremely large engines such as the Duluth, Missabe & Iron Range's 2-8-8-4 Yellowstones could easily evaporate 100 gallons of water per mile and might consume 250 gallons, along with more than 500 pounds of coal, in that distance. Clearly, this requirement mandated a massive infrastructure for fuel and water supply and, for coal-fired locomotives, ash removal.

Water was usually supplied from a trackside water tank with pull-down waterspout. There were many materials and shapes, but most common was a cylindrical wooden tank with a conical roof, supported on heavy timbers. The tank was usually made of vertical staves held by iron or steel hoops tightened with turnbuckles, spaced at gradually closer intervals from top to bottom (water pressure increases with depth). In cold climates heating equipment beneath the tank prevented freezing. Larger steel tanks were often installed at major terminals where greater quantities of water were needed. Often one large tank supplied water through a piping network (usually underground) to strategically located water columns, which were vertical supply pipes with swiveling spouts and water-control valves. A small pump, powered by steam, electricity, gasoline, or even a windmill in rural areas, kept the tank filled.

A few railroads reduced water stops by installing track pans, from which a scoop-equipped tender could lift as much as 5,000 gallons of water at 40 to 80 mph. The New York Central and the Pennsylvania had many of these, and the Baltimore & Ohio, Reading, Central of New Jersey, and Maine Central also had some. These were steel troughs, 6 to 8 inches deep, 19 or 20 inches wide, and 1,000 to 2,500 feet long, located 25 to 30 miles apart on level sections of track. The top of the pan was about an inch below the rail top. Float valves controlled the water level, and steam pipes prevented freezing in cold weather. To take water, the fireman lowered the scoop into the pan, and the motion forced the water up into the tank. Signposts at each end of the pan told firemen when to lower and when to raise the scoop. The use of auxiliary water tenders could also minimize water stops. These might look like domeless tank cars or might be more rectangular. They are still common on steam excursions because adequate locomotive water supplies are no longer available.

Condensers to recycle exhaust water (and improve locomotive efficiency through lower exhaust temperatures) have been used successfully elsewhere in the world, notably in Russia and South America. But North American railroads disliked complexity, and the amount of extra equipment (the huge tender-mounted condenser itself, the piping between locomotive and tender, blowers for both stack exhaust and condenser, and lubricating-oil separators—all high-maintenance items) was undesirable. On remote railroads that served lumber or quarry operations, a locomotive might carry its own pump and hose to draw water from a handy lake or stream. A strainer at the bottom of the hose kept out fish and other undesirable matter.

Major railroads were deeply concerned about water quality. Although 100 percent pure water is undesirable (it promotes rust), most impurities are a detriment to proper operation in a locomotive. The most troublesome chemicals are calcium, magnesium, and sodium carbon-

In an enduring image of the steam locomotive era, the Duluth & Northeastern Railroad's 2-8-0 Consolidation No. 14 took water at the railroad's Cloquet, Minnesota, water tower on a wintry day in 1958. —William D. Middleton

Several eastern roads eliminated the need for intermediate water stops by using track pans, which enabled a locomotive to take water at speed. In 1894 a New York & Long Branch Railroad locomotive scooped water at 25 mph near Long Branch, New Jersey. —F. W. Blauvelt, Library of Congress (Neg. LC-USZ62-4410)

ates, chlorides, and sulfates. Some of these form an insulating scale (coating) on firebox sheets and boiler tubes, inhibiting heat flow into the water. This invariably reduces boiler efficiency and in extreme cases can lead to overheating and a boiler explosion. Other impurities promote corrosion below water level, especially at points where the metal has been stressed during boiler construction. Finally, some impurities produce foaming or bubbling on the water surface, causing water to be carried out of the boiler along with the steam.

Water carried with the steam may cause two different problems. If the locomotive is without a superheater the water may be deposited in the cylinders where, being incompressible, it can cause piston breakage or cylinder head blowout. Or if the locomotive does have a superheater, the water will defeat its purpose, which is to add heat to dry steam. Instead, the superheater will simply serve as a supplementary boiler.

Therefore, it was common for locomotive water to be treated to alleviate these problems. Usually the harmful impurities were removed or converted into others that were not harmful and could be periodically flushed out through boiler blowdown valves. Some railroads had elaborate treatment plants; others simply added appropriate chemicals to their water tanks. (The initial quality of the local water generally determined the method.) Alternatively, specific water-treatment compounds could be added directly to the tender. Because of the cost of water treatment, railroads usually treated the water only at every second, third, or fourth water station. Engine crews generally took water at only these, avoiding the other except in emergencies.

Merely getting water to trackside could also be a prob-

This sturdy reinforced-concrete coaling tower and an adjacent waterspout fueled the Central Vermont's 4-8-2 Mountain No. 601 at White River Junction, Vermont, in October 1949. Visible on the right side is the conveyer system that lifted coal into the tower. —William D. Middleton

Some of the most advanced steam locomotive fueling and servicing facilities were these built in 1946 by the Norfolk & Western Railroad at its Williamson, West Virginia, terminal. This massive plant supplied coal and water to N&W locomotives. —Norfolk & Western, Middleton Collection

lem. Water availability was always considered in laying out a route, but sometimes supplementary sources were essential, such as the 130-mile pipeline constructed by the El Paso & Southwestern or the pipeline and tank-car trains used by the Eastern Railway of New Mexico.

Fueling the steam locomotive was another major challenge. In its earliest days the fuel was wood, easily available almost everywhere at that time. A wood fire, however, required constant attention. Its lightweight sparks were also a fire hazard, requiring huge spark-arresting

Clean, dry sand was carried in steam locomotive domes such as this one at a Santa Fe engine terminal. Its principal use was to provide better adhesion, but it was used also to clean soot from the firetube flues of the steam engine. —Santa Fe, *Trains* Magazine Collection

smokestacks that contained elaborate spark deflectors and screens.

By about 1870 most railroads had switched to coal, primarily soft (bituminous) coal, which has 25 to 30 percent volatile matter—coal tars and the like. Lignite, an extremely soft coal with more than 50 percent volatile matter, was also sometimes used. Though railroad management maintained that soft coals could be fired without smoke, not all firemen could do so, and there was a widespread and persistent smoke nuisance. As a result, toward the end of the nineteenth century a number of eastern railroads made considerable use of anthracite (hard coal, found primarily in northeastern Pennsylvania), which has less than 7.5 percent volatile matter. (The legendary Phoebe Snow, for instance, kept clean aboard the anthracite-fueled Lackawanna: "My gown stays white from morn 'til night.") However, anthracite supplies eventually were depleted, and with the installation of power stokers, even less-skilled firemen could maintain the bright, thin fire that minimizes smoke.

As early as 1900 many steam locomotives were burning oil. For them and those that followed, fueling was relatively easy, requiring only storage tanks, pumps, and sometimes heat to keep the heavy fuel oil flowing in cold weather.

Coal supplies were usually delivered in hopper cars and placed into overhead storage until needed. The coal was then loaded into tenders via chutes. Sometimes coal was unloaded at ground level and then lifted by crane or bucket conveyor to the elevated storage bin. Occasionally, hopper cars were shoved by locomotive or cable system up an incline to be unloaded into the storage bins. A coaling plant might serve one track, but at important terminals they spanned several. Timber was probably the most common construction material for these structures, but many large ones were of steel or reinforced concrete.

Fueling on a diesel locomotive was much simpler than that for steam power. This small fuel terminal at the Southern Pacific's San Luis Obispo, California, took care of its diesels with fueling hoses hooked to storage tanks and a simple overhead structure for providing sand to the locomotives. —William D. Middleton

Fueling was even easier for electric locomotives. This facility at the Pennsylvania Railroad's Sunnyside Yard at Queens, New York, only required sand and other incidental materials. —© Dan LeMaire-Bauch

All locomotives require dry sand to avoid slippage on wet rail, and this requires a sand house with dryers, an elevated storage bin, and delivery pipes to fill locomotive sandboxes. Sanding facilities were most often located near coaling stations, enabling both functions to be completed in a single spotting.

Ash disposal was a major concern for coal-fueled railroads. In fact, ashpan capacity usually determined how far a locomotive could travel between service stops. Tenders could be made larger, and water might be picked up on the fly from a track pan, but ashpan space on a locomotive was always limited. At the terminal a special ash pit was necessary. Ash could not be dropped randomly because of the danger of igniting creosoted wooden ties. In the early days the pit was just that, and the ash was periodically emptied by hand, a backbreaking task. Later ash pits were often constructed so that small ash containers, situated on rails below the locomotives, could receive the ash directly and then be raised when full and emptied in a normal hopper car. A very common arrangement was the water-filled pit, which received and extinguished the ash. A crane lifted the ash out of the pit periodically and deposited it in a railcar for removal.

The landscape of locomotive servicing changed dramatically with the arrival of the diesel, whose liquid fuel is easily pumped. Locomotive fuel tanks hold hundreds, even thousands, of gallons, enough for runs of 200 to 1,000 miles of normal service. Since the diesel uses virtually no water, other than a few hundred gallons for cooling, providing water is a simple matter. A string of diesels can be fueled simultaneously through multiple hose connections, and some terminals have traveling sand towers on gantries that can be positioned to fill each sandbox in sequence.

Diesels have one water problem that steam locomotives do not, namely, freezing. Steam engines were usually kept hot unless boiler service was planned, in which case they were drained. But with diesels came the possibility of engine shutdown between assignments. Early diesels, however, did not use antifreeze because of its cost and also because the coolant sometimes found its way into the engine oil, impairing its lubricating properties. Diesels were also difficult to restart at low temperatures, and there was the problem of severe thermal stresses during initial warmup. Consequently, on most railroads diesels idled continually in cold weather, and some lines idled at all times.

Crews were instructed to dump coolant from diesels that had shut down and could not be restarted at below-freezing temperatures. Many locomotives still have automatic valves that dump the coolant under these circumstances. Yard locomotives or road switchers sometimes had a small oil-fired heater that kept the block from freezing if the engine shut down unexpectedly. Many modern locomotives do use antifreeze, and most also have systems that monitor diesel coolant temperature, allowing the engine to start and stop as needed. Many roads are also ordering or retrofitting locomotives with such equipment

so they can be shut down between assignments whether or not they have antifreeze.

—Dan LeMaire-Bauch

REFERENCE

Howson, Elmer T., ed. *Railway Engineering and Maintenance Cyclopedia*. Chicago: Simmons-Boardman, 1942.

Locomotive Testing

Testing of locomotive performance has been around almost as long as the railroad. The earliest means of testing was the dynamometer car, a vehicle equipped for measuring and reporting mechanical force—the tractive force or pull of a locomotive at the tender drawbar—time, and distance. The product of force and distance is the work done; work done in a given time is horsepower; speed is the distance moved in a given time; and acceleration is the rate of change of speed. A dynamometer car mechanically or electrically calculates these qualities using the pull or force on the car, distance measurement, and timing from a master clock, with a large recording apparatus in which the charts are moved proportionately to time and distance to record the data. Other data recorded may include fuel and water consumption, train resistance, road gradient or curvature, track gauge and rail condition, and the like. All of these data can provide useful information about locomotive capacity and efficiency.

The idea of a dynamometer car goes back to the early years of railroad development. As early as 1836 F. M. Guyonneau de Pambour's *Locomotive Engines* described tests to determine the pull necessary to move railroad trains, and in 1839 Charles Babbage built instruments on a car for Britain's Great Western Railway that recorded tractive force and time on rolled sheets of paper. In 1856 the Great Western's Daniel Gooch built what he described as a "Measuring Van" that was used in a series of resistance trials on freight trains. All of these early devices used a simple spring balance between the tender and a train, but they gave only a poor indication of drawbar pull.

In the United States engineer and metallurgist Plimmon H. Dudley in 1862 developed several fundamental ideas regarding the efficiency of train operation at different speeds, and in 1874 he designed and built a dynamometer car generally described as the first of its type. Dudley's recorder, called the dynagraph, incorporated many of the features of later dynamometer cars. The pull of the locomotive was registered on a chart, which was driven from one axle of the car through a hydraulic cylinder attached to the underframe of the car. The cylinder was equipped with two pistons, one to measure buff, or inward force, and the other draft, or pull. Other information made on the 30-inch graphic record included speed, work, time, coal, water, and

the condition of the track. Dudley's dynamometer equipment ended up on the New York Central.

Other builders of the equipment over the next several decades included the Erie, the Pennsylvania, the Burlington, the Chicago & North Western, the Canadian Pacific, the Chicago, Milwaukee & St. Paul, the Peoria & Eastern (under lease to the Big Four), the Illinois Central, and the Chicago Great Western. The International Correspondence Schools, which then offered extensive courses in railroads, even acquired its own dynamometer car, built by American Car & Foundry, in 1903.

Both the Peoria & Eastern and the IC worked with the University of Illinois, which had an extensive program in railroad engineering and an Engineering Experiment Station. The first car was a Big Four caboose equipped by the university, which was later fitted with an unusual "floating" rack inspection device using wheels on a split axle to record variations of track gauge and rail irregularities through oil-pressure cylinders. A second University of Illinois dynamometer car was built in a large caboose-like IC car in 1900 and was twice rebuilt over more than 40 years of service. A later addition was the installation of a roof-mounted standard anemometer to record wind direction and velocity.

A third car, built by IC at its Burnside shops in 1943, was typical of more recent dynamometer cars. The for-

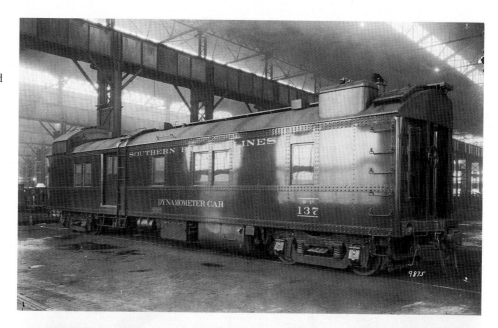

A much later version of the dynamometer car was Southern Pacific's heavy steel car 137, built by the Standard Steel Car Co. and equipped with Baldwin dynamometer equipment in 1926. The interior view shows some of the complex equipment used in locomotive testing. The car, retired in 1978, was donated to the California State Railroad Museum.
—(both) Frank C. Anderson, *Trains* Magazine Collection

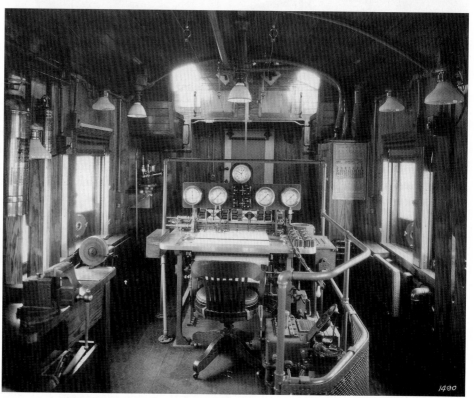

ward end of the car was outfitted with testing and recording equipment, with observation bay windows on each side. The rear end of the car was outfitted with living and dining space for a four-person operating staff. The dynamometer apparatus for measuring the pull of a locomotive was located under the frame of the car, immediately behind the drawbar yoke and in line with it. A closely fitted piston inside the dynamometer cylinder was forced by the pull on the drawbar into the oil-filled cylinder. The oil pressure on the cylinder was transmitted to a small cylinder of an indicator attached to the dynamome-

ter car's recording table. Different sizes of cylinder bushings and train weight springs made it possible to obtain a record of drawbar pull for anywhere from a single car to a train of 200 loaded coal cars.

Dynamometer cars continued as a regular testing method throughout the era of steam motive power. Some unusually extensive dynamometer tests were made in the 1948 Locomotive Interchange Trials in Great Britain, when the newly nationalized British Rail set out to develop standard steam power designs.

The accurate recording of boilers and engines, the meas-

Southern Pacific's Class GS-1 4-8-4 Northern No. 4401 had a test compartment on the pilot and dynamometer car 137 behind for a test run at Colton, California, on December 21, 1946. —Arnold Menke Collection

urement of coal and water performance, and the taking of indicator cards were all very difficult to accomplish accurately under road service conditions. Some locomotive engineers preferred to test new locomotives in stationary test plants, in which a locomotive could be operated under power in more carefully controlled conditions, although a stationary plant cannot measure total resistance of a locomotive, tender, and train or the effects of wind, speed, and curvature.

The first of these locomotive-testing plants was designed and built in 1891 by Professor W. F. M. Goss of Purdue University at West Lafayette, Indiana, where it operated in locomotive performance tests for many years. In 1894 the Chicago & North Western installed a temporary test plant at South Kaukauna, Wisconsin, followed a year later by the installation of a permanent test plant at Chicago. In 1899 Columbia University built a test plant in its mechanical engineering laboratory to operate an Atlantic-type locomotive donated by the Baldwin Locomotive Works. Other test plants were built in Europe. In 1904 the Putiloff Works at St. Petersburg, Russia, completed a test plant designed by M. V. Goloboloff and S. T. Smirnoff, and a year later G. J. Churchward of the Great Western Railway completed a similar plant at the Swindon Works in England. Other testing plants were built at Vitry, France, Rugby, England, and in Germany near Berlin.

Probably the best known and one of the largest of these in North America was the Pennsylvania Railroad's test plant at its Altoona, Pennsylvania, shops. Designed by the PRR's mechanical engineer, Axel S. Vogt, the plant was operated at the exhibits of the Louisiana Purchase Exhibition at St. Louis in 1904 and was installed at Altoona the following year. Locomotives were installed on rolling wheels, or drums, which in turn had braking equipment

so that operation of a locomotive under trains of varying length and tonnage could be simulated. New designs of steam and electric locomotives were tested at the plant for almost half a century, with increased capacity added for the Pennsylvania's increasingly large and powerful units. The plant's last tests were conducted in the 1940s, when the unorthodox T1 and Q2 duplex-drive and S2 turbine steam locomotives were introduced. The last tests were with the railroad's production class Q2 4-4-6-4 duplexes, which developed a 100,000-pound tractive effort and almost 8,000 indicated horsepower.

The University of Illinois completed an even larger test plant in 1913. The supporting bed for the locomotive was fitted with four sets of axles and wheels 52 inches in diameter that could be adjusted to the spacing of the driving axles. Brakes for the test unit were mounted at each end of each supporting axle. Each brake consisted of three cast-iron disks that operated between water-cooled copper diaphragms, which absorbed the energy of the locomotive. Varying the water pressure between the cast-iron disks and diaphragms dissipated the power generated. A dynamometer, installed at one end of the test bed to measure the tractive effort of the locomotive, was capable of a capacity of 125,000 pounds, more than half again that of the Pennsylvania Railroad's original Altoona plant. In addition to locomotive testing, the test plant could conduct other types of studies as well. In 1917, for example, the University put a Baltimore & Ohio 2-8-2 Mikado-type locomotive in service to make comparative tests of six different sizes of Illinois coal for two dozen railroads, suppliers, and coal companies.

Both the original hydraulic dynamometer cars and stationary test plants have gradually disappeared since the advent of diesel-electric locomotives. A number of old

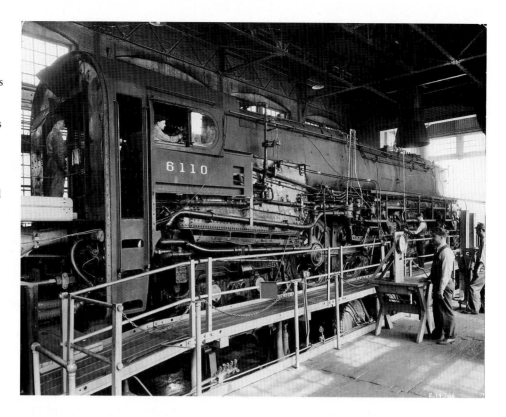

The Pennsylvania Railroad's long-lived Altoona test plant saw a wide range of steam and electric locomotives. Class T1 4-4-4-4 duplex No. 6110 was one of two experimental locomotives built by Baldwin in 1942. After 120,000 miles of road service, the engine went into test service at the Altoona plant in April 1944, where it recorded a maximum drawbar horsepower of 6,110 hp and a test-run speed equivalent to 85.5 mph. Orders for 50 T1s followed. —Pennsylvania Railroad, *Trains* Magazine Collection

dynamometer cars can be found at several major railroad museums, including the University of Illinois–Illinois Central dynamometer car 30 at the Museum of Transportation at St. Louis, Missouri, a Norfolk & Western car at the Virginia Museum of Transportation at Roanoke, Virginia, a Milwaukee Road car at the Illinois Railway Museum at Union, Illinois, a Southern Pacific car at the California State Railway Museum at Sacramento, California, and a Chesapeake & Ohio car at the B&O Museum at Baltimore, Maryland.

The dynamometer car has been replaced by what are usually called "test cars," which rely largely on electronic data transmitted from the locomotive to the test car. Almost all of this work is now done by the two principal locomotive builders, General Electric and Electro-Motive Diesel, each of which operates two test cars.

Modern diesel-electric locomotive testing requires testing and verification of each of its subsystems, as well as an integrated test of the entire locomotive. Subsystem testing can usually be accomplished on the locomotive itself, with typically 20 or more computers and software controlling a locomotive, but cabling into the adjacent test car is often required for overall integrated testing. Changes to one subsystem to meet special requirements, such as tunnel operation, high-altitude service, and the like, also require separate testing. Increasingly, however, the capabilities of the onboard locomotive systems are reducing the need for additional external installations, with data available from the locomotive by satellite and laptop computers. To record tractive-effort performance, the modern test car, instead of using the old hydraulic dynamometer, is usually equipped

with a strain gauge, or extensometer, in the drawbar, which measures minute deformations of the test instrument to record tractive- and brake-effort results.

A new locomotive-testing requirement is that new locomotives meet the standards of the U.S. Environmental Protection Agency for locomotive emissions under a variety of conditions and over an extended period. The most recent Tier 2 EPA standards became effective on January 1, 2005, and both GE and EMD have carried out extensive tests to assure that their locomotives will meet the new standards.

Dynamometer tests of steam locomotives were only a memory when the technology came back for a final performance on August 22, 1977. The occasion was one of the Southern Railway's periodic steam excursions, operated that year by former Texas & Pacific 2-10-4 610. *Trains* magazine editor David P. Morgan suggested that a test run behind the big steam engine would be interesting, and Southern president L. Stanley Crane made the necessary arrangements. An old dynamometer car was not available, but Southern produced its test car R-2, which was equipped with strain gauges in drawbars at both ends of the car that could record the tractive and brake effort from the locomotive. The car also recorded and plotted on a continuous graph paper roll speed, mileposts, pull and buff at the head end, and train resistance at the rear during a series of tests between Alexandria and Monroe, Virginia, during which the 610 reached a maximum output of more than 4,000 drawbar horsepower.

—William D. Middleton

REFERENCES

"A New Locomotive Testing Plant at the University of Illinois." *Proceedings of the Forty-Sixth Annual Convention of the American Railway Master Mechanics' Assn.*, 1913.

Ransome-Wallis, P., ed. *The Concise Encyclopaedia of World Railway Locomotives*. London: Hutchinson, 1959.

Tuthill, John K. "The Railroad Dynamometer Car of the University of Illinois and the Illinois Central Railroad." *University of Illinois Bulletin* 45, no. 11 (Oct. 4, 1947).

Westing, Frederick. "Testing the Iron Horse." *Railroad* 20, no. 3 (Aug. 1936): 91–95.

Wildhagen, Arthur R. "Dynamometer Cars of the University of Illinois." *Railroad* 13, no. 2 (July 1947): 56–62.

Withuhn, Bill. "The Great Dynamometer Test of Locomotive 610." *Trains* 38, no. 4 (Feb. 1978): 33–41.

Locomotive-Servicing, Maintenance, and Repair Facilities

Repair and maintenance facilities are essential to efficient railroad operation. As the technology of North American locomotives and cars evolved, their affiliated service and repair facilities of necessity kept pace.

The steam locomotive was based on nineteenth-century technology and had many moving parts exposed to hostile environments; it consequently required much more maintenance than did either the diesel-electric or the pure electric locomotive. The latter type of engine was in a sense the simplest of the three since it carried no power source.

Given the basic nature of railroad operations, there was a need for two types of supporting work. "Routine servicing" was the work necessary in regular locomotive operation.

"Repair work" could be classified as either "light" or "heavy." With steam power, some routine servicing was required every 100 to 150 miles, while diesels or pure electrics needed attention only at the end of their runs. Light (or "running") repairs of steam locomotives were carried out in numerous small shops located every 200 to 300 miles along a major route. On the other hand, almost every road had one shop for heavy repairs (those requiring disassembly), and large roads had several such shops, deployed at strategic points throughout their systems.

As the web of rail lines grew denser in the mid-nineteenth century, many locomotive-servicing terminals were built. The smallest of these might have only a Y-shaped track or "wye" (for turning locomotives), fuel and water facilities, and an ash pit for coal-burning engines. In some of these there was also a one- or two-track shed with service pits beneath the rails. In conjunction with large classification yards the engine facility would usually include a roundhouse and associated turntable, where heavier repairs were also possible. These included boiler washout, replacement of firebrick in the firebox, and renewal of journals and bearings. The most extensive steam repair facilities were known as back shops. These usually covered a large area and were independent of the roundhouse shops. The centerpiece of the back shop was a high-bay erecting hall.

Once diesel power became dominant, most of the earlier types of structures were unnecessary, as were many of the repair tasks. This was especially true for the turntable, although many heavy shops still retain a wye for occasional use. With diesel and electric power, most servicing and repair facilities contained parallel tracks and were long enough to house numerous locomotives at once.

Turntables

One of the most visible features of a steam locomotive roundhouse complex was the turntable (Figure 1). For

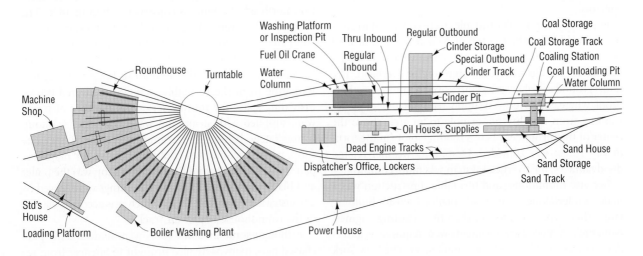

Figure 1. A typical design for a steam locomotive terminal includes space for bringing an incoming locomotive through an ash pit and washing and inspection structures, space for maintenance work and storage in the roundhouse, a turntable, coal and water for outbound locomotives, and facilities for engine crews and other maintenance workers. —Rick Johnson

optimum performance, safety, and efficiency, main-line locomotives were designed to operate primarily in one direction, so it was necessary for them to be turned at the end of each run. Though loop tracks and wyes were used in certain situations, the most common way of turning a steam locomotive was with a turntable, which was merely a bridge with a center pivot. Wheels at each of its ends rolled along a circumferential rail at the bottom of the pit in which the turntable was located.

Early turntables were of wood, with truss-rod construction (similar to that under early railcars). Later they were fabricated from metal, first cast iron and later steel. Plate-girder construction was favored, with the support structure either below the track (more common) or above. The latter configuration reduced the amount of excavation required. Originally, turntables were rotated by hand, with a man pushing an oarlike arm that projected from each end of the bridge. Such "armstrong" turntables were feasible because early locomotives were relatively light; consequently, so was the table. In addition, bridges were usually of generous length in comparison with early locomotives, so that an engineer could easily balance his engine over the center pivot. This reduced the weight at the ends of the table, thereby decreasing the force required to rotate the bridge.

However, as locomotives became longer, they eventually spanned the table, and even though the American Railway Engineering Assn. (AREA) recommended that turntables be long enough to permit balancing a locomotive with its tender empty, this was seldom the case. More important, as engine terminals became more active, there was a need to shorten turnaround time by powering the rotation of the table. Originally, air motors were favored, since pressurized air was always on tap at a terminal, and even in remote areas the locomotive's air pump and reservoir could provide it. The turntable, though it had no pump of its own, usually had an air tank for short periods of operation without a locomotive aboard. Powered tables usually had a small shanty at one end to house the controls.

Eventually, almost all turntables were converted to electric drive (though the Central of New Jersey had at least one air turntable into the 1950s). There were two supply options for the electricity: underground or overhead. The underground supply was less intrusive and more weatherproof, whereas an overhead supply required a set of cables running from a utility power pole to an arch above the center of the turntable, where a rotating joint (in the form of slip rings) was provided. Despite its weather-related disadvantages, the overhead system was more common.

Because roundhouse and turntable construction was a major undertaking, most roads planned ahead, building tables that were much longer than their existing engines. Nonetheless, special arrangements were required as latter-day locomotives became longer and longer. The New York Central, for instance, equipped its major shops with 100-foot turntables. These were ample for its 4-6-4 Hudsons, which, with tender, measured about 96 feet. Even the Central's 104-foot 4-8-2 Mohawks could squeeze on, with some overhang on each end. However, when the road decided to enlarge the tenders for its 4-8-4 Niagaras after World War II, it was necessary to construct them with a distinctive 10-foot overhang behind the rear axle so that their 115-foot length could be accommodated.

Evolution of Shops

Even before steam propulsion was developed, the Baltimore & Ohio used a multitrack car shop for its horse-drawn carriages. This building was served by some form of transfer table (possibly a turntable). Like a turntable, a transfer table is a moving bridge for aligning rail vehicles with stationary tracks or stalls. The transfer table, however, does not rotate about a pivot, but rolls sideways on rails of its own. Here, in 1830, Peter Cooper's engine *Tom Thumb* was fired up for its informal, but famous, trial run against a horse-drawn train. It is also known that the Camden & Amboy Railroad had machine shops for steam locomotives at Bordentown, New Jersey, early in the 1830s. The first manager of these shops was John Hampson, who had worked previously as a locomotive engineer on the Mohawk & Hudson Rail Road. There he operated the *Robert Fulton*, a Robert Stephenson (English) engine that was the road's second locomotive, the *De Witt Clinton* being the first.

Details concerning railroad shop development are much more sparse than comparative information on equipment. However, one major complex has been extensively documented recently and can serve as a typical example of the evolution of a heavy steam repair facility. This was Spencer Shops near Salisbury, North Carolina, named for Samuel Spencer, the first president of the Southern Railway, which Spencer assembled around 1893 from a number of lines controlled by New York financier J. P. Morgan. Because the road's primary routes stretched from Washington, D.C., to Atlanta and Chattanooga, Spencer selected a central location north of Charlotte to construct a shop in 1896. The shop complex eventually grew so large that a surrounding company town, also named after him, sprang up.

In its earliest days the shops included an armstrong turntable and a 15-stall roundhouse for minor repairs. Radiating from the turntable were 25 uncovered tracks, providing space for routine service. A number of tracks were supplied with steam and water for boiler washout. Immediately behind the roundhouse was a machine shop, where locomotives could be housed for major repair or overhaul. Beyond the machine shop was the boiler and blacksmith shop. These two buildings were served by a transfer table between them, which was accessed via one of the roundhouse's open-air tracks.

Although some machine tools were undoubtedly purchased new, many were also brought to Spencer from redundant shops scattered around the various lines acquired in the formation of the new Southern Railway. Most industrial installations of the time used a central stationary steam engine for power, but all tools in the Spencer machine shop were electrically operated, many with separate motors. Others, in accord with earlier practice, were driven by common electric motors through a system of overhead "line shafting," from which leather belts carried power to nine groups of individual tools. Electric power for machines and interior lighting was produced in an on-site generating plant, which also supplied shop heat and hot water for various purposes, including boiler washout.

Other buildings at Spencer included a blacksmith and boiler-repair shop and a wood shop for working on freight and passenger cars and on engine cabs as well. Moreover, the usual routine maintenance facilities of any steam locomotive terminal were also present, including coal, water, sand, ash removal, and lubricant supply.

Spencer Shops developed into one of Southern's most important facilities throughout the steam era. It was continually enlarged and redesigned to keep pace with the advancing technology and increasing dimensions of the road's engines. By 1905, for example, because of the growing volume of work, a new 600-foot-long back-shop building was constructed. Soon after, the boiler shop moved into the old machine-shop building. However, in 1911 a new boiler shop was constructed on the site of the 1896 boiler and blacksmith shop, and the blacksmiths moved into the old machine shop.

The original 60-foot armstrong turntable gradually became inadequate as larger and heavier locomotives were introduced. Thus in 1911–1912 the road installed a 90-foot table (still unpowered). It also served the old roundhouse, which was not replaced because of financial problems at the time. This decision proved to be a decided impediment to the required amount of shop work, especially during the demands of World War I. Other areas of modernization at Spencer included a new coaling station in 1913, capable of serving 100 or more locomotives per day. New buildings for sand and lubricating oil were constructed at the same time.

The lack of a modern roundhouse was keenly felt, and in 1924 the road razed the original one and replaced it with a much larger facility having 37 stalls, each 106 feet long. A 100-foot-long, electrically powered turntable served it. Most stalls were given pits for general locomotive repair, including 6 that contained special pits for dropping locomotive drivers and 3 equipped to drop truck and tender wheels. A specialized flue shop was completed around the same time, since work on boiler tubes and flues increased dramatically with the increases in the size of locomotives and their higher boiler pressures.

The Southern purchased its last new steam locomotives in 1928, so these changes were the final major improvements to Spencer Shops during the era of the iron horse, although a special plumbing shop for steam power was built during World War II (1942). However, with the appearance of the road's first diesel power during this time, the shops were further modified to handle their specialized needs. Of the roundhouse's 37 stalls, 12 had their rails removed and were walled off to create a diesel shop for battery maintenance, oil-filter cleaning, and repair of the steam generators required by passenger units. Nine of the remaining stalls, assigned to diesel work, were lengthened by 25 feet, necessitating removal of the rear wall of the roundhouse. Long midlevel platforms were erected for easy access to machinery mounted on diesel main frames. During this transition the flue shop became an electrical shop, and other structures were revamped in accordance with the requirements of the diesel age.

The Spencer shop complex gradually became redundant, especially upon the opening of the Southern's Chattanooga diesel shop in 1948. Spencer was closed in 1952 after the Atlanta-Washington main line was fully dieselized. Today the site, including a few of the original buildings, is home to the North Carolina Transportation Museum, which houses a number of significant pieces of rolling stock from numerous railroads of North Carolina.

Steam Locomotive Maintenance

Like its living namesake, the iron horse demanded plenty of attention. It is no coincidence that the men who handled locomotives around terminals were generally known as hostlers, an appellation derived from those who performed analogous tasks in the equine environment. Steam locomotives consumed vast quantities of fuel and water and in most cases also required disposal of coal ash. Supplies of lubricant and sand had to be checked and replenished. Boilers had to be washed out ("blown down") frequently to remove accumulated sediment left behind as the water evaporated.

Another major concern was lubrication. For most of the steam era, journal boxes on the engine and tender had to be checked and lubricated often to avoid hotboxes (journals dangerously overheated by friction). Roller bearings largely eliminated this problem, but some roads never used them on locomotives, and others did not change until the steam era was nearly over. Thus many generations of young observers gravitated to the head end of trains at stations to watch the engineer as he applied oil to various locations on the engine's rods and wheel bearings using a long-spouted pump-can. In later years this picturesque procedure was often obviated by shop workers who used heavy sticks of grease, forced by an air pump into the critical locations.

Wear of wheel treads and flanges was common to all rail vehicles. During major overhauls drivers were removed and placed in a large wheel-lathe for truing, though the rims (tires) eventually required replacement (discussed later). But removing the drivers from a steam locomotive required much more effort than removing power trucks from a diesel. In fact, present practice is to regrind diesel wheels in place.

Boiler tubes and flues were also high-maintenance components. Removing soot from their interiors was

After completion of a major overhaul, the Santa Fe's Mikado 2-8-2 No. 3261 (Baldwin, 1920) was wheeled at the railroad's Topeka, Kansas, shops in March 1943. —Jack Delano photograph, Office of War Information, Library of Congress (Neg. LC-USW3-019701-E)

The Norfolk & Western built some of the most advanced steam locomotive-servicing facilities in North America. This modern "lubritorium," built at N&W's Williamson, West Virginia, terminal in 1946, made possible a fast turnaround between runs. —Norfolk & Western, Middleton Collection comparatively easy with a sand blast. But removing scale from the exteriors (the surfaces in contact with the water) meant cutting the tubes out of the boiler and subjecting them to some form of mechanical cleaning process, such as banging them around in a "tube rattler," which knocked off the scale. New ends were then welded onto the tubes to allow for reinstallation. Not surprisingly, fireboxes had to be regularly relined with firebrick, while the multitude of staybolts had to be checked carefully for breakage, and broken ones replaced.

Many of a steam locomotive's working parts were unprotected and thus were constantly exposed to rail and brake-shoe rust particles, as well as to powdered ballast (all highly abrasive). Consequently, components such as piston rods, valve stems, packing glands, and crossheads (and their guides) fell victim to high rates of abrasive wear, far more than did the relatively closed-in pins and journals. The solution was extensive machine-shop work, which demanded high-priced labor, as well as requiring considerable time out of service for the locomotive. Indeed, it is well known that shop forces put in dozens of hours of service and repair for every hour a steam locomotive actually worked. In addition, it is estimated that during the steam era one-fourth of all railroad personnel were employed solely in maintaining and overhauling steam locomotives. Of course, it was statistics such as these that helped more easily maintained diesel power to displace steam.

Fabrication Methods in Steam Shops

Riveting was a fundamental joining process during a large part of the steam era. Boilers and many other major components were fabricated by this technique, which began by punching or drilling corresponding holes in two or more overlapping pieces of metal. The rivet (a headed pin) was inserted, often after being brought to red heat. A second head was then forged on its other end with a sledgehammer or, in the modern era, with a pneumatic hammer. After this, the gap between the two metal pieces often had to be caulked by hammering down the edges with a chisel-like tool. Riveting was largely replaced by welding in the 1930s. Welding became preferred because welded boilers were able to withstand much higher pressures, with greater reliability and less maintenance, than riveted ones. Welding was also used to replace lost metal and thus rejuvenate many worn parts on high-mileage locomotives.

Forging, by which a heat-softened raw metal was formed into a required shape, was widely employed in a locomotive shop. Many small components were formed by blows from a sledgehammer in the traditional manner of the blacksmith. However, in the modern era an automatic forging machine pressed heated metal between precision dies and thus produced large batches of items such as bolts, pins, levers, brackets, and rods. Power sawing of metal was also common to machine shops everywhere, but there was one saw especially geared to steam locomotive work: it automatically cut steel tubing into specified lengths for use as boiler tubes.

Typical Machine-Tool Inventory

The heavy machine tools of a locomotive shop were typical of any industrial installation, but were often modified or adapted specifically for locomotive work. *Lifting devices* were the first requirement because of the great weight of the components to be handled. These included a wide variety of cranes, jacks, and drop tables. In the steam period cranes had to be capable of lifting up to about 250 tons; with the advent of diesels, capacities of less than 100 tons were generally adequate.

Drop tables (track-bearing elevators) were used for removing drivers or trucks. They operated in pits between the rails and carried short segments of rail that aligned with the running track. The locomotive was positioned with the wheels to be removed on the drop table. The wheel attachments were then loosened and the drop table lowered, carrying the wheels. Jacks or a crane supported the locomotive's weight.

Lathes were used for producing components by rotating a workpiece (the item being manufactured) while a cutting tool was pressed against it, an operation called *turning*. This removed sufficient metal to bring the workpiece to the desired size and shape. If the cutting tool acted on the inside of a hollow workpiece, the operation was known as *boring*.

Railroads found many uses for standard lathes, but steam locomotives also required special types capable of handling large workpieces such as drivers and tires over six feet in diameter. A lathe could also be equipped with a variety of attachments for special operations, including the ones that allowed machinists to "quarter" drivers and turn crankpins (discussed later).

Boring mills were similar to lathes except that they generally rotated the pointed cutting tool while holding the workpiece stationary. These were often used in such operations as finishing axle holes in wheels. *Portable boring bars* were used where it was impractical to bring the work to a lathe or boring mill, as, for instance, in refinishing the interior of a cylinder or valve-chest liner. Since these were very difficult to remove, it was preferable to bore them in place on the locomotive.

Milling machines held a workpiece in place and rotated a cylindrical cutter against it, thus allowing the machine to carve a specified shape out of metal, somewhat like a hand-cranked pencil sharpener. Milling machines had many uses, including the production of side and main rods from forged blanks. Of course, railroad shop milling machines were much larger than those in most factories.

Shapers, planers, and *slotters* were similar, forcing a pointed cutting tool across a stationary workpiece to gouge a straight cut. After each such stroke the tool was shifted sidewise a small distance and made a parallel cut. After many such strokes the surface had been planed smooth or a desired slot had been cut.

Wheel-tread grinders were an alternative to the lathe for producing the proper wheel-tread contour. Many advantages are claimed for this method, one of the biggest being that the work can be done with the wheels mounted on the locomotive or truck, thus making it faster and more economical. However, it was generally not used for steam locomotive drivers.

Mechanical presses were used to force components together or apart, especially the replaceable, soft-metal bushings that were used on many surfaces. Such bushings are designed for a so-called force fit carried out by a press. Wheels were also pressed onto or off axles.

Quartering and *pin-turning machines* were specially made for a steam locomotive. They were able to carry out the following tasks: mount a pair of drive wheels on their axle with the crankpin openings of opposite wheels at precisely 90 degrees, accurately bore the crankpin openings, press the pins into place, and finally turn them to a precise shape and diameter.

Flanging machines were presses used in shaping the steel sheets that form the firebox and boiler. They trued the edges of these sheets so they would join properly with the adjacent sheets.

Locomotive spotters were used to move an engine a short distance (up to 20 feet) when reattaching a tender or rotating drivers for valve-gear adjustment. The spotter had a long rod that was coupled to the locomotive; the spotter was then clamped to the rails, and the locomotive moved via the rod as necessary. A motor within the spotter provided the power.

Tube rattlers were another specialty machine for steam engines. They consisted of a large drum into which scale-covered boiler tubes were placed. The drum was then rotated for a sufficient time to dislodge the scale. There were also other tube- and flue-cleaning machines, such as those that relied on sandblasting.

Back-Shop Layout

It was only natural that equipment for all of these specialized repair functions would be brought together in a major back shop (locomotive repair shop) for both operational efficiency and the economic advantages of a skilled labor pool in the community that usually sprang up around such facilities. Eventually most of these shop complexes became enormous, spreading over many acres. Supporting the main locomotive erecting hall would usually be a boiler shop, a blacksmith shop, a machine-tool shop, an electrical shop, a tender shop, a paint shop, a foundry, and a pipe shop (with tinsmiths). Ancillary operations usually included a powerhouse, an oil house, a tool room, and various storage areas (both indoor and outdoor). If the shop complex handled repairs for freight and/or passenger cars, there might be a wood shop and upholstery shop as well.

The usual designs for back shops followed one of three floor plans. A longitudinal shop contained long tracks that had a number of pits (between the rails) along their length, while the transverse layout contained a group of parallel tracks with pits. However, the most common plan was a combination of these, in which tracks were arranged as either an L or a cross. The choice of plans usually was a result of either the operating procedures or available land.

With the longitudinal shop, the various workstations would be set up along the track, so that a locomotive could undergo one type or group of services at each station, then move along the track for the next step. This permitted the necessary tools and supplies to be conveniently located near where they were to be used. One frequent problem with this design was that there was insufficient space between tracks, thus limiting the type of work that could be performed. The major shortcoming, however, was the difficulty in changing the sequence of locomotives under repair. An engine in the rear would have to wait for the preceding one to be finished. To solve this problem, engines were leapfrogged by means of an overhead crane.

Because of these shortcomings, the transverse design became popular since a transfer table outside the shop could position a locomotive onto the proper track, or there could simply be a single through track to bring the engine into the shop, after which a crane could place it onto the proper track. Not surprisingly, the combination shop layout was created to gain the benefits of both arrangements. Relatively minor operations, which could be performed while the locomotive was on its wheels, were taken care of in the longitudinal section, after which it was lifted over to the transverse section, where wheel removal and other major steps were carried out.

Railroads traditionally referred to shop procedures by class (or level) of the work performed. For the sake of uniformity, the federal government set up the following classes of steam locomotive repair and required railroads to report their level of activity (and date) for each engine:

Class 1: New boiler and new back end (firebox). Flues (and tubes) new or reset (rebuilt). Tires turned (reshaped to proper contour) or new tires installed.

Class 2: New firebox, or one or more boiler-shell courses, or crown sheet. Flues new or reset. Tires turned or new.

Class 3: Flues all new or reset (superheater flues might be excepted in this case). Necessary repairs to firebox and boiler. Tires turned or new. Necessary repairs to machinery and tender.

Class 4: Flues, part of a full set. Light repairs to boiler or firebox.

Class 5: Tires turned or new. Necessary repairs to boiler, machinery, and tender, including one or more pairs of driving wheel bearings refitted.

Classes 1, 2, and 3 also included "general repairs to machinery." This term included removal of driving wheels, turning or changing of tires, turning of journals if neces-

Heating expands a locomotive tire for removal or installation from the driving wheel itself. The shop crew of the Duluth & Northeastern Railroad at Cloquet, Minnesota, changed a tire on 2-8-0 Consolidation No. 27 about 1963. —John E. Gruber

sary, and overhaul of all driving boxes, with rods over-hauled and bearings refitted, and other repairs as necessary for a full term of service (four years).

Of the foregoing work, tire replacement was probably the most spectacular. Locomotive tires were made very slightly smaller than the wheel center onto which they were to be placed. To install them, a ring of gas jets was employed to heat the tire red hot, thus expanding it. It was then pushed onto the wheel center and allowed to cool, whereupon it shrank tightly into place.

Somewhat surprisingly, the schedule for Class 3 repairs in an efficient, modern shop with a combination layout took only 23 working days. The boiler jacket and lagging (heat insulation) were removed on the first day. The boiler was not removed, but miscellaneous boiler work (including descaling tubes) took 16 days; hydrostatic testing was done on the 17th day. Lagging and jacket were replaced on the 21st day. Meanwhile, drive rods, wheels, and trucks had received separate attention and were replaced on the 18th day. Valve-gear work was finished on the 19th day, and pistons, main rods, and brake rigging were finished on the 21st day. The tender was refurbished separately and finished on the 23rd day. Many additional operations were proceeding simultaneously, of course, such as the items sent to the machine shop, including cylinders, crossheads, valves, and pistons; injectors; lubricators; brake cylinders; main and side rods; and air pumps.

Obviously, many locomotives were subjected to this sequence simultaneously. In fact, this particular shop was capable of handling up to 50 locomotives and their tenders per month, typically providing new fireboxes on sev-

eral Mallets plus other engines and performing Class 3 repairs on some 40 other locomotives. Their path through the shop, which was constructed in a cross layout, was as follows:

The locomotive and tender were first separated on a track in the longitudinal section of the shop. The tender was then taken to a coal-handling facility, where it was emptied (the stoker screw was rotated by a mobile electric motor) and was then taken to wait its turn into the tender shop. The locomotive, meanwhile, was moved to an inspection track, also within the longitudinal section, where it was thoroughly checked. It was moved again, by electric winch, to a position where all pipes, gauges, and boiler fittings were removed. At successive positions within this section, the boiler jacket, lagging, rods, valve gear, air and feedwater pumps, and other accessories were removed and taken to storage areas by overhead carrier. This particular shop had a second-floor "brass room" where gauges and similar fittings were refurbished.

The locomotive was now lifted to a pit within the transverse section, which intersected the longitudinal tracks approximately at their center. The heaviest locomotives were placed on the four pits nearest the longitudinal tracks. More distant pits were employed for progressively lighter power. When repairs were completed, the engine was returned to the longitudinal section for reassembly, including connecting the pivoted front engine of articulated locomotives. As the engine moved along, its boiler lagging and jacket were reapplied, and, finally, piping was reinstalled. The partially filled tender was then coupled, both hot water and steam were injected into the boiler, and the locomotive was fired up. Safety valves were adjusted, and the refurbished engine was taken out for a test run of up to an hour, after which it was returned for any final adjustments. When these were completed, it and the other locomotives in line on the finishing track were coupled so that the newly completed engine could pull the entire string forward, each engine to its next position. It was then ready for the road.

The Diesel Shop

The arrival of diesel-electric locomotives after World War II introduced completely new requirements for the design and operation of shops. Ideally, it would have been desirable to build new facilities from the ground up. However, this would have been prohibitively expensive for most, if not all, roads. Thus older buildings were often gutted and adapted for diesel work. These were expected to last only for a few years until new facilities were constructed. Although short railroads were able to dieselize almost overnight, larger systems used a phased approach, targeting those lines with the lowest traffic levels for the first wave of full dieselization, thus allowing further savings through the closing of steam shops and roundhouses.

Not surprisingly, the diesel transition period produced some difficult times for railroad shops as they struggled through massive changes needed for their new power. A common myth of the early diesel years was that all of these new locomotives were about the same, irrespective of the builder. This misconception led some roads to make expensive mistakes. Among the worst cases was that of the Missouri-Kansas-Texas (Katy) Railroad, which inexplicably allowed its new diesel fleet to be ordered by its traffic department rather than the mechanical department. Starting in 1946, the road had acquired by 1951 a total of 170 units, composed of 14 different models from all four major builders of the period. These were entrusted to a steam-era shop force that was immediately overwhelmed by a flood of new technology and a seemingly endless shortage of spare parts. The resulting poor maintenance finally caught up with the line in 1956 when almost half its units were out of service. Its response became a common one in later years. It shipped virtually all of its older models back to one manufacturer for rebuilding in order to obtain a much greater commonality of parts and repair procedures. In later times most roads dealt with the problem of maintaining a fleet of engines from different builders by limiting the work of each shop to only one builder's products.

Not only did shop facilities change with the arrival of the diesel, but also the workers needed to staff these shops required significantly different skills. The breadth of this

A much different arrangement was required for efficient diesel locomotive servicing. This modern facility was built by the Santa Fe for its new Barstow, California, classification yard in 1975. The open-air desert servicing facilities included below-track-level pits, aboveground ramps, and overhead service arms. —William D. Middleton

change is illustrated by a comparison of the following two lists of job titles and tasks. The first, covering steam engine work, was published in the 1940s by the Assn. of American Railroads. The second is excerpted from a recent employment advertisement by CSX Transportation.

Job titles for a steam back shop included foreman, inspectors, boilermakers and boilermakers' helpers, machinists and machinists' helpers, blacksmiths and blacksmiths' helpers, lathe operators, electric-drill operators, riveters, carpenters, painters, engine cleaners, sandpipemen, crane operators, motor-truck and tractor operators, laborers, watchmen, and many other workers, skilled and unskilled. For a diesel locomotive electrician, the required tasks were listed as "maintain, rebuild, inspect and install motors and generators, switchboards, meters, controls, rheostats, static and rotary transformers, electric headlights, electric welding machines, storage batteries, axle lighting equipment, electrical clocks and electric lighting fixtures, winding armatures, fields, magnet coils, rotors, transformers and starting compensators. Inside and outside wiring at shops, buildings, yards and on structures, and all conduit work in connection therewith, including steam and diesel electric locomotives, passenger trains, and motor cars. Electrical work on tractors and trucks is also performed. Four years (min.) electrical experience (diesel locomotives preferred) and/or training is required." Interestingly, "steam . . . locomotives" were included, although this undoubtedly would involve only special, excursion-train service.

The diesel era also brought an entirely new maintenance schedule to shop work. Steam engine maintenance and repair was generally done on a calendar basis (monthly, annually, and so on), but diesel-electrics, in common with autos and trucks, were maintained on a mileage basis. Early in the diesel era GM's Electro-Motive Division recommended regular inspection of various components at intervals ranging from 2,500 miles to 1.2 million miles. Principal parts of the engine itself (such as crankcase, pistons, and cylinder heads) were to be checked every 2,500 miles, while major electrical systems, such as main and auxiliary generators and traction motors, could serve for 30,000 miles between inspections. Contemporary locomotives have such high reliability that a full-scale inspection is generally needed only four times per year.

Diesel Shop Layout

The most fundamental difference between steam and diesel shops was related to the components of each type of power. Whereas steam locomotives required frequent removal and replacement of large and heavy parts such as drivers, rods, and even boilers, the components of a diesel locomotive were much lighter, and any removal of the heaviest assemblies (entire engines or generators) was only infrequently required. Thus overhead crane capacities could be reduced, along with the support structures inside the shop buildings. Another new aspect of diesel maintenance was that because of the standardization of designs, worn parts or subassemblies could usually be removed and replaced by corresponding components obtained from outside sources. In contrast, a steam shop needed in-house capability to rework almost every part of a locomotive. Another physical difference in diesel shops was the need for three working levels. Although there were the usual below-track pits and track-level work places, diesels also needed a work platform above the trucks and main frame for easy access to most of the machinery (covered by cowls or hoods).

Southern Railway was one of the largest lines to dieselize aggressively after World War II. In 1948 the road decided to construct one of the nation's largest diesel shop complexes at Chattanooga, Tennessee, hub of its six busiest routes. This shop design was thus the prototype for many others constructed soon after. Five repair tracks were provided, four of which were stub and one through. Each was long enough for a contemporary, three-unit locomotive. Three of the stub tracks, used for running repairs, had floors depressed below rail level to facilitate work on trucks, plus elevated platforms at the level of the locomotive floor. The remaining two tracks were for major repairs. One of these had no pit, while the other, used primarily for truck repair and removal, had a short pit. A drop table for removing trucks served the four stub tracks, each of which included supports to hold the locomotive body when a truck was removed. Once removed, the truck was lifted from the drop table by a 30-ton overhead crane. Larger cranes were available for engines and generators.

The Denver & Rio Grande Western's Burnham shop complex in Denver was an example of a former steam shop that was successfully converted to diesel maintenance and further improved by later owners Southern Pacific and Union Pacific. Reopened in 1992 as an overhaul facility for EMD units, it now specializes in GE models. The redesigned shops have brought assembly-line concepts into locomotive overhaul work. Incoming locomotives move through a series of "spots" along the disassembly track. The diesel engine is lifted off the locomotive at Spot 1 and carried to an engine-stripping area to be taken apart and cleaned. Trucks are removed at Spot 3 and likewise taken to a dedicated area for disassembly and cleaning. Meanwhile, work has proceeded on refurbishing the locomotive body, including upgrading of control systems on older models. The main frame and body are then lifted by crane and remounted on the reconditioned trucks. The unit is then rolled to Spot 2 for installation of the overhauled engine. In addition to such heavy work, Burnham also performs some 90 to 100 scheduled inspections and unscheduled repairs per month on its six running repair tracks. These activities occupy more than half of the shops' 400 employees.

Diesel prime-mover overhauls at Burnham and elsewhere depend largely on whether the engine is two-stroke (GM) or four-stroke (GE). Two-stroke engines have no valves in the cylinder heads and thus are considerably simpler. In these engines the valve function is performed by inlet and exhaust ports at the bottom of the cylinder, which are uncovered by the piston at the end of its downward stroke. Four-stroke engines, however, do have valves in their cylinder heads. On these machines valve seats must be checked and either refaced (if enough metal remains) or replaced or renewed by welding and grinding. The mating valves are also checked and repaired or replaced. If valve stems are worn below limits, they may be plated to restore their diameter or turned down to fit new undersized valve guides.

Once pistons are removed, they are separated from their connecting rods, and piston rings are discarded. If the ring grooves are worn, they may be enlarged and fitted with oversized rings. Alternatively, worn grooves can be filled by welding and then new grooves machined. Pins and bushing between piston and connecting rods are inspected and usually replaced. Cylinder liners are inspected and any ridges removed by honing, which can also be used to hasten the seating of new rings. Seals are checked and replaced if necessary. Connecting rods are checked for cracks and straightness and for parallelism of both bearing openings. Oil passages are cleaned out. Crankshaft-end bearing shells are checked and repaired or replaced as required. Crankshafts, their journals and throws, and the supporting bearings are inspected for distortion, cracks, or out-of-roundness and for surface scoring. Oil holes are cleaned out. If possible, surfaces may be restored by machining or grinding, preceded by metal spraying if necessary.

The crankcase interior is cleaned and inspected for cracks. Gears are checked for looseness, tooth shape, and cracked teeth. Fuel-injection components (nozzles, pumps and drives, injectors, cams, levers, and so on) are removed and separately inspected. They are repaired or replaced as needed. Filters are cleaned or replaced. Water and oil radiators and heat exchangers are removed. These, along with associated piping, are tested for leaks and cleaned out. Regulating and relief valves are tested and reset or replaced. Similar refurbishing is carried out on numerous other components such as superchargers; fuel, lubricating-oil, and water pumps; radiator fans and their drives; governors and overspeed shutdowns; and gauges and liquid level indicators. Fuel tanks are cleaned and their interiors usually repainted.

Main generators also must be carefully inspected and repaired as necessary. Since these are attached directly to the engine, they are subjected to high temperatures, oil fumes, and smoke. Moreover, their role exposes them to high internal temperatures as well. Generator windings are checked for electrical leakage, which, if small, can be corrected by a light varnish spray. More serious cases require dipping in varnish and subsequent baking. Dipping and baking do, however, add another coating of material that may retard cooling and are therefore not used unless clearly necessary. Although many generator inspections and maintenance steps can be performed without removing this component, a major overhaul does require it. Auxiliary generators (for lights, battery charging, and so on) and exciter generators (which power the field coils of the main generator) are treated similarly. However, because they are much more lightly loaded, they require major service only infrequently. The same considerations apply to auxiliary motors that power radiator fans, cool the traction motors, pump fuel, or meet other needs.

Commutators are a key component of any rotating machine operating on direct current. They have always been the most troublesome element of otherwise reliable and durable electrical machines. Being made of copper, a soft metal, undergoing continual friction from carbon brushes, and subject to damage from electric arcing, they deteriorate rapidly in service. During overhaul the commutator can be machined, interbar insulation undercut, brushes and springs replaced, and bearings checked. A major step forward in locomotive reliability occurred around 1965 when DC main generators gave way to alternators (AC generators). The current is then rectified for the DC-traction motors, which have commutators. Thus commutators remain on all but the latest AC-drive locomotives.

During a major overhaul the power trucks are also removed and likewise taken to a dedicated area for disassembly and cleaning. Traction motors operate under much more severe conditions than do main generators. Despite the best efforts at enclosure, a traction motor is exposed to powdered rust, pulverized ballast, rain, and snow. Clean cooling air must come from within the engine compartment and is already warm by the time it reaches the motors, making their ambient temperature generally high.

In addition, traction motors are subject to severe vibration since, although the motor mounts include some spring support, much of the weight is carried directly on the axle and, thus, the rails. Consequently, the motor is subjected to the pounding produced by uneven track and rail joints.

Apart from the traction motors, engine trucks receive the same service as those of other rolling stock. Journals and journal boxes (in early days) or roller bearings must be checked and relubricated. Wheels must be inspected for cracks, and treads must be turned or ground to proper contours.

In parallel with component overhaul, the shop force also devotes attention to the locomotive body, both outside features and control-cab upgrade when needed. The latter has been a common type of upgrade in recent years, as early mechanical control elements have been replaced by successive new generations of electronic and microelectronic design.

Current Practices

Every major railroad once followed the steam tradition of operating its own shop facilities, but since the mid-

Good servicing for a locomotive included regular washing and cleaning. A yard worker cleaned the locomotive windows for the Atlantic Coast Line's fast *Havana Special,* about to continue its New York–Miami run from the Florence, South Carolina, servicing facilities in August 1957. —William D. Middleton

1980s there has been an increasing practice of consolidating railroad-owned facilities and also contracting out (outsourcing) work to independent maintenance and rebuilding companies. Because of the high mileages between major overhauls, even some large roads have insufficient overhaul work to justify maintaining a comprehensive shop system. Some of the largest roads have adopted a mixed policy, having their own employees perform the work, but contracting with a builder or independent company for overall management of each shop. Moreover, in recent years numerous roads have carried out routine servicing of small locomotives in the field, thereby eliminating the time required for them to travel to centralized facilities. This work is done by either railroad employees or private companies.

—Dan LeMaire-Bauch

REFERENCES

American Railway Engineering Assn. *Manual.* Chicago: American Railway Engineering Assn., 1915.

Brown, William H. *The History of the First Locomotives in America.* New York: D. Appleton, 1871.

Foell, Charles F., and M. E. Thompson. *Diesel-Electric Locomotives.* New York: Diesel Publications, 1946.

Galloway, Duane, and Jim Wrinn. *Southern Railway's Spencer Shops.* Lynchburg, Va.: TLC, 1996.

Howson, Elmer T., ed. *Railway Engineering and Maintenance Cyclopedia.* Chicago: Simmons-Boardman, 1942.

Ransome-Wallis, P., ed. *The Concise Encyclopedia of World Railway Locomotives.* New York: Hawthorn Books, 1959.

Textbook on Civil Engineering. Scranton, Pa.: Colliery Engineer, 1896.

Williamson, G. V. *Locomotive Rod, Wheel, and Pin Work.* Scranton, Pa.: International Textbook, 1929.

Wright, Roy V., and Robert C. Augur, eds. *Locomotive Cyclopedia.* New York: Simmons-Boardman, 1947.

Loewy, Raymond (1893–1986)

Raymond Loewy was one of the preeminent industrial designers of the mid-twentieth-century machine age. He was born in 1893 in Paris and in 1919 moved to New York, where he established himself as a commercial artist and fashion illustrator and was soon widely known in New York design circles. Loewy's interest in electrical engineering and all modes of transportation led him to establish an industrial design firm in 1929. The firm's first important commissions, modernization of the Gestetner Duplicating Co.'s duplicating-machine housing (1929) and the Coldspot refrigerator (1934), established its reputation.

Loewy's first transportation commission came from the Pennsylvania Railroad in 1932 when PRR president Martin W. Clement commissioned him to redesign waste cans at Pennsylvania Station in New York City. Loewy later recalled the meeting: "The president was intriguing, a handsome, white-haired giant of a man who sat on a high-back chair, like Mussolini behind his desk, in a huge black and brown office matching his dark clothes and black necktie." It was a fruitful partnership that spanned some 20 years.

In 1934 Loewy won the assignment to streamline the PRR's new GG1 electric locomotive. Loewy's singular innovation was to weld the prototype's riveted carbody, producing a smooth skin that the *New Yorker* magazine termed "as sleek and hard as the back of a beetle." The design so satisfied PRR management that it assigned him to the steam locomotive equivalent, the 4-4-4-4 duplex-drive class S1. Loewy's bullet-nosed monster, displayed at the 1939–1940 New York World's Fair, came to embody popular notions of the streamlined steam locomotive.

Apart from the famous steam locomotive, Loewy's designs for the PRR's first streamlined passenger trains, the Fleet of Modernism of 1938, stand out. The train's interiors featured strong Art Deco motifs, incorporating soft cove lighting, gilt ceilings, and rich finishes such as cork and mahogany. The cars' exterior paint scheme exhibited a two-tone interpretation of the carrier's hallmark Tuscan red and incorporated semicircular curves at the ends of the pier panels, reminiscent of a mockup of the designer's office displayed at New York's Metropolitan Museum of Art in 1934. Commissions from other lines followed, notably Missouri Pacific's *Eagle* streamliner, built by American Car & Foundry in 1940.

During World War II Loewy's firm anticipated the coming need to make passenger trains more cost- and labor-efficient, submitting visionary designs of double-deck coaches and diners able to fit Pennsylvania Station's confining clearances. Unfortunately, his client chose not to pursue the initiative.

Among his outstanding postwar designs were the Pennsylvania's twin-unit dining cars and recreation cars. These bore his hallmark "tumble-down" design, which set the normally 90-degree vertical interior walls at a slight angle in order to emphasize the width of the passenger car's typically elongated, narrow interior.

Other rail-related work included remodeling of the Norfolk & Western's passenger station in Roanoke, Virginia, opened in 1949 (now the O. Winston Link Museum); logo and train styling for the Monon in 1947; and carbody designs for Fairbanks, Morse & Co. diesel locomotives in 1945–1946, modified by the FM engineering staff.

Loewy's last railroad commission was Northern Pacific's *North Coast Limited* two-tone green exterior paint scheme of 1952. Among his other outstanding transportation work were the 1938 Studebaker automobile and its 1961 Avanti model, Greyhound's double-deck Scenicruiser bus of 1946, the paint scheme and interiors for Air Force One (Loewy counted President and Mrs. John F. Kennedy as friends) in 1963, and the interior of NASA's Skylab of 1972.

More than most industrial designers, Raymond Loewy became a public figure. He was featured on the cover of *Time* magazine's October 31, 1949, issue. He died at Monte Carlo, Monaco, in 1986.

—John E. Gruber and Michael E. Zega

REFERENCES

Johnson, J. Stewart. *American Modern, 1925–1940: Design for a New Age.* New York: Harry N. Abrams, 2000.

Markey, Morris. "A Reporter at Large, down the Main Line." *New Yorker*, June 20, 1936, 42–52.

Pennsylvania Railroad Technical & Historical Society magazine, *Keystone* 24, no. 1 (Spring 1991), and 26, no. 3 (Autumn 1993), contains a detailed account of Loewy and PRR.

Logging Railroads

From the earliest years of European settlement of North America, lumbering was among the dominant industries. Much of the continent was originally covered in stands of magnificent trees. As James Fenimore Cooper put it, "a birds-eye view of the whole region east of the Mississippi must have offered one vast expanse of woods." Geographer J. Russell Smith estimated that the virgin forests in the eastern United States covered almost 1,100,000 square miles; another 220,000 square miles stood in the western region. It was estimated that forested areas of about 1,700,000 square miles once covered Canada.

Early settlers wasted no time in cutting away these forests. The clearing of land for agriculture was the primary reason. But the wood was also useful for building houses, barns, and fencing and for firewood, and the demand for lumber quickly grew. By 1839 annual lumber production exceeded 1,600 million board feet, a number that more than tripled over the next decade. A few years after the end of the Civil War annual U.S. lumber production reached almost 13,000 million board feet, and soon after the turn of the twentieth century it passed 40,000 million board feet, reaching a peak annual production level of 46,000 million board feet in 1906–1907.

The development of the lumber industry closely followed the expansion of agriculture and the westward movement of the population. Maine led American lumber production in the early years, but the southeastern states also produced large quantities. By 1840 the center of the lumber industry had moved to New York; it shifted to Pennsylvania by 1859 and to Michigan by 1869. Wisconsin took the lead by 1899; then the Pacific Coast states, notably Washington and Oregon, became the leading lumber producers. In Canada, Quebec and Ontario were major timber producers, but the lead later shifted to the vast forests of British Columbia, which accounted for more than half of all Canadian timber production.

Harvesting and removing the timber were seldom easy. Crude camps were set up at the logging sites, with rough log shacks or bunkhouses for the loggers or lumberjacks and usually a separate cooking shack, and the men worked from dawn until the light faded. In the northeast and northern states during the fall and winter season the trees were felled and then hauled over snow sleds to a sawmill or a river, often pulled by huge teams of 10 to 12 oxen, or sometimes horses. In most areas logs were cut in 16-foot lengths, but 24- to 40-foot lengths were common in the Northwest. Lengths up to 65 feet later became standard. In the huge stands of the Pacific Northwest and in California's redwood groves logs could easily run to 14 feet in diameter. At the rivers a "dumpsite" was established to move the logs into the water to be floated in rafts downriver to sawmills as soon as the streams had thawed. In the South the lack of winter snows and swift-moving streams required the movement of logs over rough roads with high-wheeled carts and ox teams. In mountainous areas chutes and flumes were built to transport logs. Later, wire cables were stretched across valleys and canyons, and the logs were carried on pulleys to travel by gravity to the lower end of the cable.

Logging was seldom very far ahead of the railroads, for cheap transportation was needed to move the finished lumber to wherever it was needed. Thus the movement of logging operations from east to west followed both the demand for more timber and the growth of western railroads to transport it.

As North American lumbering expanded in the latter part of the nineteenth century, railroads took on a new role as logging railroads, transporting logs from the landing area in the woods to the log dump at a sawmill or a rafting ground for water transport. Moving the huge logs by animal had been a slow and expensive process, and the distances to cover were growing longer as close-by stands of timber were used up. Steam power provided more economical transport, and logging railroads became common well before the end of the nineteenth century.

Steam power also helped the logging companies improve the efficiency of the yarding operations in the woods, where logs were moved from the stump to be assembled and loaded for shipment. Steam-powered winches moved the newly cut loads to the landing area, where loading cranes were used to load the logs on cars. A stationary steam engine, winches, and wire ropes often used a tall spar tree that stood as much as 150 to 200 feet high to drag or carry the logs over the ground from the stump site to the landing area. Many of the large logging companies used enormous "tower skidders," weighing 300 to 400 tons, that combined yarding and loading donkeys under a single steam engine. These were often called Lidgerwoods after the company that built or licensed many of them. Instead of a spar tree, the machine used an enormous folding steel tower. Multiple trucks and a battery of geared locomotives were required to get the machine into place for logging operations.

Typically the new logging railroads were hastily built lines constructed to low standards, reflecting what was usually a relatively short period of use. Once the logging was done, the tracks were pulled up and reused elsewhere. Ties and rails were light, and roadbed and ballast were minimal. Track curvature was as sharp as 40 degrees. Grades on principal routes typically ranged from 2 to 3 percent, and spur lines were often as steep as 5 to 6 percent, or even as much as 7 to 8 percent when necessary. Switchbacks were commonly used to get trains up the steep slopes. Where even steeper grades were required, some roads used inclines to bring the loads down. One example on the Yeon & Pelton Co. at Rainier, Oregon, had a 3,200-foot incline with a maximum grade of 33 percent, with a cable line and incline machine to lower the log cars down to the dumpsite along the river. Another, on the Wisconsin Logging & Timber Co. above Oak Point, Washington, on the lower Columbia River, had a grade of 66 percent.

Instead of metal rails, some early logging lines used wooden poles, and the engines and cars ran over the pole road on double-flanged wheels. Early track was sometimes built over the skid roads built of logs for the earlier bull teams. Both standard- and narrow-gauge—often 3-foot or 3-foot 6-inch—lines were common. Track was typically laid with 60-pound or lighter rail, usually with used relay rails acquired from the main-line railroads. Track was often built in the usual manner, with a graded roadbed and ballast, but many lines found it more economical to build a line entirely on low pile trestling.

Given its ready availability, timber was widely used in railroad construction whenever possible. Cribbed log structures were used instead of earth and rock fill to carry lines across depressions or valleys, or as bridges. Timber trestles of impressive dimensions were frequently installed. Where long bridges were needed, they were sometime spanned with large logs, some of them as much as 100 feet long. Even longer bridges were spanned with timber Howe trusses. The largest logging bridge in British Columbia, and what was probably the highest wooden structure anywhere in Canada, was built to cross Bear Creek on Vancouver Island to reach new stands of timber in 1939. The 548-foot-long bridge stood 243 feet above the streambed and used timber trestling and massive tower structures to carry three 90-foot timber Pratt truss spans over the valley. In 1940 the Weyerhaeuser Timber Co. completed an enormous timber-framed structure for its Columbia & Cowlitz Railway near Longview, Washington, that was 1,130 feet long and stood 230 feet above the bottom of the canyon. Sloped frames created a timber arch over the center of the canyon.

Logs were transported over the railroad by flatcars. Some lines simply used standard main-line railroad flatcars, usually with wooden stakes along each side to increase their capacity, but far more often special cars were used. One car design, usually called disconnects, consisted simply of a pair of trucks, with logs spanning between them to form a rudimentary flatcar. A horizontal "log bunk" above each truck at the bolster was provided to firmly attach the logs to the car. One very real disadvantage of the disconnects was that they could not accommodate air braking and required hand braking as a train descended from the forest. The most popular car type was the skeleton car, which employed a center sill of wood or steel to connect the two trucks and included the air cylinders and brake rigging required for air braking. These cars were typically about 41 feet long, but some were as long as 70 feet to transport poles, piling, and other long timbers. A log bunk was provided across the bolster of each car, sometimes at an intermediate location for long cars. A Washington logging company even managed to transport a 230-foot log on two of the disconnect trucks for the "world's largest flag pole," a gift from Astoria, Washington, to San Francisco's Pan Pacific Exposition.

Many logging railroads used locomotives from main-line railroads or other sources. Most were relatively small, capable of negotiating the sharp curves and steep grades of most logging roads. Wheel arrangement ranged from little 0-4-0 locomotives to 4-4-0s, 2-6-0 Moguls, and 2-8-2 Mikados. Many lines used tank engines. One line, the Yeon & Pelton Co., operated with a whole fleet of diminutive 0-4-2T engines acquired secondhand from the Portland Street Railways. Some larger logging companies used steam power comparable with main-line railroads. A few large lines even used compound Mallet locomotives, the largest of which were two 2-8-8-2s built by Weyerhaeuser Timber Co. in 1929 and 1933. Operated over Weyerhaeuser's Co-

A train of large timbers from the Washington forests is loaded up on a train of "disconnects," which simply used the timber itself to span between independent trucks at either end of the car. —Middleton Collection

lumbia & Cowlitz, the 355,000-pound locomotives developed a tractive effort of 75,000 pounds and routinely handled trains of about 90 cars of logs. One California logging line, the Red River Lumber Co., even operated its locomotives with electric power near Chester in the Sierra Nevada. As long as steam locomotives were operated with wood fuel, some form of spark arrester on the stack was a common device to reduce the likelihood of fires.

Conventional rod locomotives worked well under reasonably good track conditions, but were ill suited to the extremely sharp curves and steep gradients of many logging lines. It was not long before several ingenious inventors came up with a specialized design to meet the needs of the logging roads. The earliest of these, and by far the most successful, was the Shay geared steam locomotive, patented in 1881. This ingenious design was developed by Ephraim Shay, a sawmill operator in Michigan's Upper Peninsula near the town of Haring. Born in Huron County, Ohio, in 1839, Shay had taught school in New Jersey, studied medicine, and served in the Union army's Corps of Engineers from 1861 to 1864. He returned to Ohio to marry and begin his medical practice, but, unable to make a proper living in medicine, he moved his family to Michigan. Lumbering was then the chief industry in upper Michigan, and in the early 1870s Shay set up a sawmill.

It was a time of unusually mild winters. The lack of adequate snowfall made it impossible to sled the timber to the mill, and the slush and deep mud of a snowless winter made moving the logs impractical. Shay thought of giving up his business, but instead developed a tramway to haul the timber to the mill, operating on maple rails with a

horse-drawn two-truck car. Shay was soon thinking of a steam locomotive to operate the road. The small steam locomotive was a big improvement over horses, but proved extremely damaging to the maple rails. During 1873–1874 the mechanically gifted Shay began to experiment with a design for a locomotive that would spread its load over two trucks and be easier on the track. Shay and his mechanic built a crude machine that was the prototype of what would be called the Shay locomotive. Work continued on the machine for the next six winters until Shay was satisfied with his locomotive. Around 1879–1880 Milton J. Bond, a neighbor and lumberman, asked Shay to build a locomotive for him. Shay declined, but suggested that Bond go to the Lima Machine Works in Lima, Ohio, which had helped Shay develop the gearing and journal boxes used in his locomotive. Lima took the assignment, beginning the company's noteworthy locomotive-building career. The new locomotive was shipped to Bond in 1880, and the following year Shay received patent papers for the design.

As initially conceived by Shay, the locomotive was a double-truck flatcar weighing around 6 tons and about 22 feet long, with a vertical boiler, fitted at one end with a water tank and at the other with a fuel supply. Attached on the right-hand side of the boiler was a pair of vertical cylinders, which powered a crankshaft that was linked by means of a longitudinal shaft with universal joints and sliding shafts to each wheel of the locomotive. Bevel spur gears were mounted on the shaft at each wheel and linked to a larger bevel gear on the outer rim of each wheel, reducing the operating speed and increasing the locomotive's torque.

The Shay design proved to be just what was needed for logging lines. It could operate equally well in either direction. With all of its fuel and water carried on the locomotive, the Shay contributed its full weight to tractive power, and the geared arrangement gave maximum pulling power on the often-steep grades. The Shays were easily capable of operating on slopes as high as 7 to 8 percent. The locomotive's short-wheelbase trucks were capable of operating easily around curves as sharp as 40 degrees.

The Shay design was a winner for the Lima works. The locomotives came in many variations. Although the earliest models had vertical boilers, almost all employed horizontal boilers. The later versions usually had three cylinders, and larger units added a short tender, carried by a third powered truck geared into the universal joints, sliding shafts, and bevel gears of the longitudinal shaft. Shays came in sizes all the way from the 6-ton originals to a record-breaking 162-ton locomotive built for the Western Maryland in 1945. Lima built about 2,770 Shays over a 65-year production period, and Shays served all over North America, South America, Asia, and Australia. Although logging operation was the Shay's principal task, the Shay and other geared locomotives also sometimes operated under similarly difficult operating conditions for coal mines, quarries, and the like.

The inventive and long-lived Ephraim Shay continued to supply new ideas to Lima. In 1888 he established a new logging railroad at Harbor Springs, Michigan, equipped—naturally—with geared Shay locomotives. Later he built an all-steel boat powered by a triple-expansion engine and designed an all-steel house. When the automobile was first introduced, Shay was among the first to own one. He died in 1916 at the age of 77.

The closest rival to the Shay was the Climax geared locomotive first produced in 1888 by the Climax Manufacturing Co. of Corry, Pennsylvania. Designed by George Gilbert, the Climax had a number of similarities to the Shay, but the early designs used two cylinders mounted on the center line of the locomotive, which powered a set of spur gears connected to a longitudinal shaft linked to the trucks by means of universal joints and sliding shafts to permit them to swing freely, while bevel gears were used to transmit power to the wheels. A lever permitted the Climax to obtain two gear ratios, based upon torque requirements. A later version, in 1891, used inclined cylinders, one on each side of the boiler, and in 1903 Climax developed a three-cylinder version. A strong competitor for Shay locomotives, the Climax company sold about 1,100 locomotives between 1888 and 1928.

Charles Heisler, a young engineering student at the Brooks Locomotive Works, developed still another significant design for geared steam locomotives. It used two cylinders centrally arranged across the engine in a 90-degree V, extending upward on either side of the boiler. The cylinders were connected to a crankshaft under the center of the boiler, which drove the two truck axles through universal joints and bevel gears. The bevel gears drove the outer axle of each truck; side rods connected the outer and inner axles. The Dunkirk Engineering Works built the first version of the Heisler in 1891, and Heisler finally began building locomotives at his own Heisler Locomotive Works at Erie, Pennsylvania, in 1894. Heisler built more than 600 locomotives between 1891 and 1941.

Logging railroads employed a wide variety of steam motive power, but the favorites were the Shays built by Ohio's Lima Locomotive Works, whose geared design could easily handle the steep grades and sharp curves of logging lines. Shay No. 3, seen on an unidentified Washington logging line, was one of Lima's larger three-cylinder, three-truck locomotives. —Middleton Collection

There were still other geared-locomotive competitors for the logging railroads. In 1911 the Baldwin Locomotive Works tried its hand at a geared-locomotive design, which had some similarity to the Climax. Only five were built, and design flaws and a slump in the logging industry soon ended the Baldwin effort. Another geared-locomotive competitor appeared in 1922 with somewhat greater success. This was a design of Willamette Iron & Steel Co. of Portland, a longtime manufacturing supplier for the logging industry. Based largely on now-expired Lima patents, the Willamette was a well-designed Shay lookalike. Willamette sold 33 of them over a seven-year period before giving up the business because of a lack of orders.

Some logging railroads survived for relatively long periods, but many more served only short periods and were taken up when the timber had all been logged out. Because of the frequently shifting nature of the logging lines, as well as their private ownership as part of timber companies, comprehensive data about them are scarce. In 1910, about the time that U.S. lumbering reached a peak, *American Lumberman* estimated the existence of some 2,000 logging railroads operating a total of over 30,000 miles of track. Most of these were small lines, but such major lumbering firms as Weyerhaeuser, Crown-Zellerbach Corp., and Rayonier also operated sizable logging roads.

Logging continued at a high level through the end of the 1920s, at an annual average of 37,000 million board feet, and then dropped by almost half during the Depression years. Many logging roads closed, only to be restored when demand returned to a high level. By the late 1950s it was estimated that about 30,000 miles of private logging railways were still in use, but the day of the logging railroad was about over. New haul roads and the development of diesel-powered tractors, heavy trucks, and other specialized logging equipment had taken over from the logging railroad, sometimes reaching places that were inaccessible even for the versatile logging locomotives. There would be still other chores for the railroad in North American lumbering, but the colorful era of the logging railroads that transported the logs from the stump face through the woods to the dump or sawmill was over.

—William D. Middleton

REFERENCES

Hidy, Ralph W., Frank Ernest Hill, and Allan Nevins. *Timber and Men: The Weyerhaeuser Story.* New York: Macmillan, 1963.

Holbrook, Stewart, with Al McCready. "Engine Smoke in the Big Woods." *Railroad* 66, no. 5 (Aug. 1955): 12–23, 50–51.

Labbe, John T., and Vernon Goe. *Railroads in the Woods.* Berkeley, Calif.: Howell-North, 1961. Repr., Arlington, Wash.: Oso, 1995.

Ranger, Ralph D., Jr. "Shay: The Folly That Was Worth a Fortune." *Trains* 27, no. 10 (Aug. 1967): 32–49.

Ryan, W. J. "The Modern Logging Railroad." *Railroad* 29, no. 6 (May 1941): 52–62.

Long, Stephen Harriman (1784–1864)

An explorer, pathfinder, and engineer, Stephen Long was one of a small corps of U.S. Army engineers who helped locate and build many of America's earliest railroads. Born at Hopkinton, New Hampshire, in 1784, Long graduated from Dartmouth College in 1809 with a classical education. After several years as a teacher, his bent for mathematics and things mechanical led him to a career as an officer in the U.S. Army's Corps of Engineers.

Long taught mathematics at West Point for a year beginning in 1815 and then won a transfer to the army's Corps of Topographical Engineers and a promotion to brevet major. Over the next several years he led a remarkable series of expeditions that explored the upper Mississippi River and its tributaries, much of the territory between the Mississippi and the Rocky Mountains, and the northern boundary of the United States from Minnesota to the Great Lakes. In 1820 he discovered the Colorado Rockies peak later named in his honor.

In 1824 the army's topographical engineers took on new responsibilities in support of the young nation's program of internal improvements, and Long was soon engaged in such work as improvements to navigation in the Ohio River and the location of new national roads. Long's railroad career began in 1827 when the army made him available to the pioneer Baltimore & Ohio, for which he surveyed potential routes from the Potomac to the Ohio.

As far back as 1825 Long had developed ideas for a system of canals and inclined planes. An opportunity to put these into practice came in 1830 when he was assigned to survey a route for the inclined planes and rail lines that carried Pennsylvania's Allegheny Portage Railroad over the Alleghenies. Over the next decade Long conducted still other railroad location surveys in New England and the South, most notably the route for Georgia's Western & Atlantic.

The versatile Long was a notable early bridge engineer as well. In 1830 he designed and built a wooden bridge that carried a turnpike over the B&O; his patented timber truss design was later used for a number of early road and railroad bridges. In 1818 he designed and built an early steamboat, the *Western Engineer*, for his Yellowstone expedition of 1819–1820, and he later built a number of steamboats for the army's work on the western rivers. He obtained several patents for locomotives and, in association with William Norris, built several early coal-burning locomotives for the Newcastle & Frenchtown and other railroads during 1832–1834. Using his B&O experience, Long in 1829 published one of the earliest manuals of railroad design, and in 1836 he published a bridge design manual that was one of the first works of its kind.

Long served out an extraordinarily long army career, much of it in river and harbor work. He was promoted to colonel and appointed chief of the Bureau of Topographical Engineers in 1861. By then 78 years old, Long was placed on the army's retired list in 1863, and he died at Alton, Illinois, the following year.

—William D. Middleton

REFERENCES

Dictionary of American Biography.
National Cyclopaedia of American Biography.
Wood, Richard G. *Stephen Harriman Long, 1784–1864: Army Engineer, Explorer, Inventor.* Glendale, Calif.: Arthur H. Clark, 1966.

Long Island Rail Road

One of the oldest railroads in America—it was chartered in 1834—the Long Island Rail Road began with some grand plans that were never realized and became North America's biggest commuter railroad, something it had never thought of in the beginning. The LIRR's original plan was to form part of an all-rail route between New York and Boston. The idea of an all-rail route across the Connecticut shore of Long Island to New York was considered infeasible. Instead, the LIRR could take a direct and level "main line" across Long Island from Brooklyn to the northeastern shore at Greenport, where a connecting ferry would link passengers to the Old Colony Railroad from Stonington, Connecticut, to Boston. The new route would halve the 16 hours required by the previous combination of Old Colony trains and Long Island Sound steamers.

The LIRR leased the 10-mile line of the Brooklyn & Jamaica Railroad & Turnpike in 1836, and by 1837 trains were running over a 30-mile route from Brooklyn to Hicksville. The full length of the 95-mile railroad to Greenport was opened in 1844, and the all-rail New York–Boston service became a prosperous reality. But it did not last long. By 1850 the line that "couldn't be built" along the Connecticut shore was a reality, and its faster service brought an end to New York–Boston trains over the Long Island. The LIRR soon went into bankruptcy.

With its prospects now confined to local traffic, the railroad began to develop its Long Island network. In 1851 it began a branch northeast from Hicksville that grew over several decades all the way to Port Jefferson, on Long Island Sound. A second line to the north shore was extended from Mineola to Locust Valley by 1869 and ultimately reached Oyster Bay in 1889. In 1870 the LIRR completed a line southeastward from a junction with the main line at Manor to Babylon, then east to Sag Harbor. It extended the line to the tip of the island at Montauk in 1895. Originally the LIRR focused on a Brooklyn terminal, but later added a second terminal at Long Island City, linked to East River ferries to Manhattan.

There was no shortage of competitors for developing Long Island's rail network. A major competitor was the South Side Railroad, which built a line across the south shore communities of Long Island from Jamaica to Babylon in 1867 and then a western extension to Williamsburg, on the East River, and an eastern extension to Patchogue, followed by a connection to the Rockaways. Another major competitor was the Flushing, North Shore & Central Railroad, and there were several dozen others as well. All of the principal competing railroads were merged into the LIRR by the early 1880s. A major branch was completed to Long Beach on the south shore in 1880, and another to Port Washington, on Long Island Sound, in 1898.

By 1877 the badly run LIRR had entered receivership. A powerful and visionary leader, Austin Corbin, came on the scene as the bankrupt railroad's receiver and then president in 1881. Over the next 15 years he extensively rebuilt the LIRR, completing new lines, rationalizing previously separate systems, and restoring the railroad to profitability.

The Long Island's second great plan originated with Corbin in the 1890s. Corbin's idea was to assure the future of the LIRR through the creation of a major transatlantic port in a deepened Fort Pond Bay at Montauk, on the far eastern end of Long Island, making the LIRR into a major trunk line. The project seemed close to approval when Corbin died in 1896, and the LIRR's great seaport on Long Island never materialized. It was back to local travel again. But by the beginning of the twentieth century the population of the New York area was expanding in all directions, and there was a rapid increase in commuter travel to the suburbs of western Long Island. The possibilities of this traffic aroused the interest of the Pennsylvania Railroad, which had been looking for nearly three decades for a way to bring its main-line terminal at Jersey City across the Hudson River into Manhattan.

Bringing Long Island commuters into Manhattan along with PRR trains would spread the terminal costs for a new Manhattan station over a much greater number of users. The Pennsylvania's president, Alexander Cassatt, acquired control of the LIRR in 1900 and set out to build an enormous project that would take tunnels under both the Hudson and the East rivers to reach the new Pennsylvania Station. Electrification was a necessity for the tunnel operation, and LIRR extended it to much of the railroad's lines on the western end of Long Island as well. The first 38 miles of LIRR electrification went into operation from Brooklyn to Belmont Park, Rockaway Park, and Valley Stream in 1905, the first major electrification in North America, and electrification continued to expand over the next 30 years. The railroad's new electric multiple-unit (M.U.) cars of 1905 were the first all-steel passenger equipment in North America, and by 1927 the railroad operated the first all-steel passenger-car fleet. The LIRR's electrification enabled operation through the East River tunnels to Pennsylvania Station in 1910, but it also made possible a capacity for a traffic density and frequency of service that would never have been possible with steam power. The combination of electrification and direct service to Manhattan created a growing flood of commuters into New York that made the Long Island the busiest passenger railroad in North America.

The addition of service into Pennsylvania Station created an unusually complex routing for Long Island trains. The railroad has three different New York terminals—Flatbush Avenue in Brooklyn, Long Island City in Queens, and Penn Station on Manhattan—and operates 11 branches, all of which except the Port Washington branch operate through the busy Jamaica station, which LIRR calls the busiest through station in North America. To interchange riders from its three terminals to 10 connecting branches, LIRR uses a remarkable "bridge train" arrangement to make multiple connections at Jamaica. Three trains, one from each of the terminals, arrive at Jamaica on three parallel tracks, each one destined for a different point. The middle track of the three has a platform on each side, and passengers changing trains can use the train on the middle track as a bridge, a shortcut, between two platforms.

By the mid-twentieth century the LIRR was in serious trouble. Money-losing commuter service, the heavy traffic of the wartime period, and accumulated deferred maintenance had left the railroad in poor condition. The parent Pennsylvania tried to help with some new equipment and other improvements in 1947, but by 1949 it had given up, and the Long Island went into bankruptcy. Two major collisions on the railroad in 1950 further aggravated the problems. In 1954 the railroad and a newly appointed public authority worked out a plan for a 12-year redevelopment program that would get the LIRR out of bankruptcy and provided a basis for financing major improvements. At the end of the redevelopment program the State of New York purchased the LIRR from the Pennsylvania, set up the new Metropolitan Transportation Authority to run it, and began a major investment program to replace almost its entire fleet of cars and thoroughly upgrade the railroad's physical plant to establish a new standard of performance. America's largest commuter railroad had become the first publicly owned commuter line.

By the early 1970s New York's MTA had supplied 620 modern M-1 M.U. electric cars, and subsequent equipment orders entirely replaced the LIRR's old M.U. cars. Major improvements upgraded the railroad's physical plant, and expansion of LIRR's electrification added M.U. car service east to Huntington in 1970 and to Ronkonkoma in 1988. In 1999 a new fleet of 23 dual-mode diesel-electric/electric locomotives and 134 bilevel cars was acquired, and LIRR has begun to receive the first deliveries of almost 500 M-7 M.U. cars to replace the first new cars built for MTA more than 30 years before.

Work is under way for a massive East Side Access project that should restructure Long Island train operations in a way unparalleled since the completion of service into Pennsylvania Station a century ago. The new access will be linked to the existing main line at Sunnyside Yard, east of the East River, to follow new tunnels to the MTA's existing East River tunnel at 63rd Street and then to a new, third-level underground terminal at Grand Central Terminal. The work should both expand passenger capacity to Manhattan and provide better distribution of LIRR commuters en route to Manhattan's East Side destinations. The $6.3 billion project should be complete by 2011.

The Long Island Rail Road operates 11 commuter rail lines over 701 miles of track and serves 124 stations. A total of 1,008 passenger railcars and 46 diesel locomotives from 733 weekday trains carry an average of almost 262,000 passengers. Annual ridership in 2005 was 80.1 million passengers.

—William D. Middleton

REFERENCES

Greenstein, Joe. "Nobody Said This Was Gonna Be EASY." *Trains* 66, no. 2 (Feb. 2006): 43–55.

Middleton, William D. "Deciding the Future of the 5:15." *Trains* 31, no. 4 (Feb. 1971): 40–46.

———. "Long Island: Back from Looneyville?" *Trains* 31, no. 3 (Jan. 1971): 20–26.

———. "The Long Island Comes Back." *Trains* 18, no. 2 (Dec. 1957): 14–32.

Ziel, Ron, and George H. Foster. *Steel Rails to the Sunrise*. New York: Duell, Sloan & Pearce, 1965.

Loree, Leonor F. (1858–1940)

Born in Fulton City, Illinois, Leonor F. Loree studied civil engineering at Rutgers and went to work at age 19 as a rodman on the Pennsylvania Railroad. After time spent on several other lines, he returned to the Pennsylvania, rising rapidly through the ranks. He became superintendent of the Cleveland and Pittsburgh Division in 1889 and in 1896, at age 38, general manager of the entire system and subsequently vice president.

In 1901 Loree was elected president of the Baltimore & Ohio, and in 1904 he accepted a similar position with the Chicago, Rock Island & Pacific. Capturing the attention of E. H. Harriman, he was brought to the smaller but prosperous Delaware & Hudson in 1907 as president and chairman of the board of managers, a position he held for 31 years. When he retired in 1938, he was one of the best-known railroad executives in the United States.

Equally proficient in financial and operating matters, Loree rapidly put the finances of the D&H in order and began a complete rebuilding of the line and acquisition of more powerful and efficient locomotives. A bearded patriarch of the old school, Loree was seen by many of his employees as a Scots tyrant. He was a firm believer in "a day's work for a day's pay" and had several periods of bad

Leonor F. Loree. —Library of Congress (Neg. LC-USZ62-135611)

relations with labor, including a nasty strike in 1922 that left much bitterness on the D&H. On the other hand, he was innovative in establishing accident insurance and pension plans, partly financed by the railroad, as well as group insurance.

At least in the first 20 years of his rule, Loree was a splendid manager, despite his imperious manner. The D&H was thoroughly modernized under his hand, symbolized by a new Flemish Gothic castle-style executive office building for the railroad in Albany. However, Loree kept his own office in New York, where he was highly successful at playing the stock market on his own behalf.

Loree should also be credited with the development of advanced steam locomotives built in the D&H's own Colonie Shops. Notable among them were four engines built between 1924 and 1933, equipped with high-pressure boilers and water-tube fireboxes. One of the engines—a triple-expansion, four-cylinder 4-8-0—was named for Loree himself.

—George H. Douglas

REFERENCE

Penrose, Charles. *L. F. Loree, 1858–1940, Patriarch of the Rails.* New York: Newcomen Society, 1955.

Louisville & Nashville Railroad

Although the Louisville & Nashville was the strong railroad of the South, its route map looked incomplete, reaching north only to the Ohio River and west and southwest to the Mississippi at only three points (St. Louis, Memphis, and New Orleans) and needing to connect with other railroads so its passengers could reach Florida and Chicago. Nonetheless, its main lines and branches pretty much covered the area south of the Ohio River, east of the Mississippi, and west of the Appalachians (except for the state of Mississippi, which the Illinois Central covered well).

From almost the beginning of the twentieth century until its inclusion in the Seaboard System, the Louisville & Nashville was under the control of the Atlantic Coast Line or its successor, the Seaboard Coast Line. L&N and ACL together owned or leased a number of smaller roads throughout the South, and the relationships among the railroads looked more like those of an extended family than those of a business-school case study.

Louisville, Kentucky, was developing into a river port and distribution center in the 1840s, but its development was hampered by seasons of low water in the Ohio River. A more dependable form of transportation was needed. Railroads were already under construction from Memphis, Nashville, and Atlanta to Chattanooga, and Nashville businessmen proposed a railroad north toward Louisville. The proposal stirred the Kentucky legislature to charter the Louisville & Nashville Railroad to build from Louisville south to Nashville (more accurately, to the state line), with branches southeast to Lebanon, Kentucky, and southwest to Memphis, Tennessee. The southern part of the line was chartered in the state of Tennessee. The charter had one restriction: the railroad could not enter Nashville but had to terminate on the north bank of the Cumberland River.

The line from Louisville to Lebanon opened in 1850. August 1859 saw the line opened between Nashville and Bowling Green, Kentucky, and two months later the route was complete between Louisville and Nashville, including a bridge over the Cumberland River at Nashville. The long line to Memphis was built by three railroads, the L&N, the Memphis & Ohio, and the Memphis, Clarksville & Louisville, and opened in 1861.

During the Civil War Kentucky was on the Union side, and Tennessee was on the Confederate side. Armies from both sides destroyed parts of the L&N. By 1863, when most war activity had moved to the Southeast, the L&N got rolling again and soon prospered.

After the war the L&N found its territory under attack by competing railroads. West of the L&N line the Evansville, Henderson & Nashville had opened from the Ohio River south to Nashville in 1872, and east of L&N's line the Cincinnati Southern Railway was under construction from Cincinnati to Chattanooga. To the south, though, there was little competition. Several railroad companies formed a route between Nashville and Decatur, Alabama; they were consolidated in 1866 to form the Nashville & Decatur Railroad. The new company proposed a lease to the L&N if the L&N would guarantee completion of the South & North Alabama Railroad, which was under construction between Montgomery and Decatur via Birmingham. The route was open from Louisville to Montgomery in 1872 (a rail line from Montgomery through Mobile to New Orleans opened in 1870). About that time L&N began pushing its Lebanon branch southeast toward Knoxville.

L&N's map in 1875 consisted of a main line from Louisville south to Montgomery, Alabama, and branches from Bowling Green, Kentucky, to Memphis and from Lebanon Junction to Livingston, Kentucky. In 1879 L&N purchased the Evansville, Henderson & Nashville at foreclosure. It also purchased the Montgomery & Mobile and the New Orleans, Mobile & Texas, completing a route under its control from Louisville to New Orleans and gaining lines into the Florida Panhandle. Alarmed by the sudden expansion of the Nashville, Chattanooga & St. Louis, it acquired control of that road and added NC&StL's St. Louis–Evansville line to the L&N system.

In 1881 L&N added the direct route between Louisville and Cincinnati, the "Short Line." Two railroad companies, the Louisville & Frankfort and the Lexington & Frankfort, had opened a route between Louisville and Lexington in 1851. There soon were proposals to continue that line north from Lexington to Cincinnati and to build a line from Louisville directly to Cincinnati, cutting off the dogleg through Lexington. The Louisville & Frankfort built the direct line in 1869, despite rivalry between the two terminal cities, arguments over track gauge (at the time, railroads in the South were of 5-foot gauge and railroads in the North were standard gauge), and a route advocated by the Louisville city council that proved to be deep under floodwater. The Louisville & Frankfort and the Lexington & Frankfort consolidated in 1869 to form the Louisville, Cincinnati & Lexington Railroad (the city of Frankfort protested that it would become simply a way station); L&N purchased the company in 1881.

L&N bought the Kentucky Central Railway in 1892 from Collis P. Huntington interests. The Kentucky Central had two lines that crossed at Paris, Kentucky: a line from Covington, Kentucky, across the Ohio River from Cincinnati, south to a junction with L&N's Lebanon Branch at Livingston, Kentucky, and another from Lexington east to the Ohio River at Maysville.

Until the turn of the century L&N was content to interchange traffic to and from Knoxville, Tennessee, with the Southern Railway at Jellico, Tennessee, just south of the Kentucky-Tennessee state line. L&N decided to build its own line to Knoxville and Atlanta. For the line beyond Knoxville, it purchased the Knoxville Southern and Marietta & North Georgia railroads, which formed a route—known as the Hook and Eye for its sharp curves and complete loop of track near Farner, Tennessee—through the

mountains from Knoxville to Marietta, 20 miles northwest of Atlanta on the Western & Atlantic. A few years later L&N built a line with easier grades and curves from Etowah, Tennessee, to Cartersville, Georgia, bypassing the Hook and Eye.

Unlike most other railroads, L&N built large numbers of its own locomotives. Between 1905 and 1923 the shops at South Louisville built more than 400 Pacifics, Consolidations, Mikados, and eight-wheel switchers.

L&N was the largest coal hauler in the South, but began to dieselize early. In the early 1940s it purchased a group of Electro-Motive diesels for passenger service and a fleet of modern 2-8-4s primarily for freight service. Steam locomotives heavy enough to handle L&N's passenger trains would have been too heavy for the line along the Gulf Coast between Mobile and New Orleans. The 2-8-4s were L&N's only large, modern steam engines, and they were assigned principally to the coalfields of eastern Kentucky. Elsewhere on the L&N system, large power—ten-coupled locomotives or articulateds—would have required that roundhouses, shops, and servicing facilities be rebuilt to accommodate them at a cost far greater than that of the locomotives themselves.

L&N's premier train was the Cincinnati–New Orleans *Pan-American*, which covered the north end of the run by day and the south end by night. Postwar modernization began not with the *Pan-American* but with two coach streamliners placed in service in 1946, the *Humming Bird* between Cincinnati and New Orleans and the *Georgian* between St. Louis and Atlanta. Both trains soon received sleeping cars and cars to and from Chicago via the Chicago & Eastern Illinois Railway—Chicago-Atlanta traffic quickly outstripped traffic on the *Georgian*'s original route.

Most of L&N's principal passenger trains were operated in conjunction with other railroads. L&N was a link in the Dixie Route, the busiest Chicago-Florida route (L&N's partners on the Dixie Route were Chicago & Eastern Illinois; Nashville, Chattanooga & St. Louis; and Atlantic Coast Line). L&N operated the Pennsylvania Railroad's Chicago-Florida trains south of Louisville. In 1949 L&N and the Seaboard Air Line Railway teamed up to inaugurate the Jacksonville–New Orleans *Gulf Wind*. The curiosity, though, was the *Crescent Limited*, the premier train of the Southern Railway, which L&N operated between Montgomery and New Orleans.

By the first decade of the twentieth century the map of the Louisville & Nashville was virtually complete. By then, though, the L&N had begun to reach out to lease and control other railroads. In 1880 it acquired control of the Nashville, Chattanooga & St. Louis. In 1898 L&N leased the Georgia Railroad and the West Point Route—the Atlanta & West Point Rail Road and the Western Railway of Alabama. Almost immediately L&N assigned a half interest in that lease to the Atlantic Coast Line.

In April 1902 John W. Gates and Edwin Hawley (whose name is usually linked with the Iowa Central and the Chicago & Alton) acquired a large amount of L&N stock, which they soon sold to J. P. Morgan & Co. Morgan in turn sold his L&N interest—51 percent—to the Atlantic Coast Line. About the same time the L&N and the Southern Railway, which were both controlled at the time by Morgan, jointly purchased the Chicago, Indianapolis & Louisville Railway (also part of the Morgan empire). In 1924 L&N and ACL jointly leased the Carolina, Clinchfield & Ohio Railway and created the Clinchfield Railroad Co., an unincorporated entity, to operate it.

On August 30, 1957, the L&N merged the Nashville, Chattanooga & St. Louis, which it had controlled for almost eight decades. Some consider that date to be the beginning of the modern railroad merger era; others set the day ten years earlier, when Denver & Salt Lake, Alton, and Pere Marquette were merged by larger railroads. It definitely marks the beginning of L&N's modern-day expansion. In 1969 L&N acquired the Woodland, Illinois–Evansville, Indiana, leg of the Chicago & Eastern Illinois and a half interest in C&EI's line from Woodland to Chicago. That same year L&N acquired 140 miles of the abandoned Tennessee Central Railway east from Nashville. In 1971 L&N merged the Monon, acquiring a second route from the Ohio River to Chicago. (L&N's previous interest in the Monon had been wiped out in the Monon's 1946 reorganization.)

The Atlantic Coast Line and the Seaboard Air Line merged in 1967 to form the Seaboard Coast Line Railroad. SCL began to refer to the "Family Lines" in its advertising, meaning the SCL, the L&N, the Clinchfield, the Georgia Railroad, and the West Point Route. Family Lines was not an official railroad name, but it foreshadowed a merger: on December 29, 1982, Seaboard Coast Line merged with L&N to form the Seaboard System Railroad.

There was also merger activity higher up on the organization chart: On November 1, 1980, Seaboard Coast Line Industries, parent of the Seaboard Coast Line Railroad, and Chessie System merged to form CSX Corp. On July 1, 1986, the Seaboard System Railroad was renamed CSX Transportation, and on August 31, 1987, it merged the Chesapeake & Ohio Railway, which four months earlier had merged the Baltimore & Ohio Railroad.

In 1982, its last year before becoming part of the Seaboard System Railroad, Louisville & Nashville operated a system of 10,396 route-miles and 14,351 track-miles, with 1,086 locomotives, 53,095 freight cars, 1,554 company service cars, and 11,829 employees. Freight traffic totaled 34,449.7 million ton-miles in 1982. Coal accounted for more than a third of L&N's traffic, and chemicals were a distant second (6.9 percent). L&N operating revenues totaled $1,103.9 million, and the railroad achieved a 95.7 percent operating ratio.

—George H. Drury

REFERENCES

Herr, Kincaid A. *The Louisville & Nashville Railroad, 1850–1963*. Louisville: Public Relations Department, Louisville & Nashville Railroad, 1964.

Klein, Maury. *History of the Louisville & Nashville Railroad*. New York: Macmillan, 1972.

M

Mail and Express

The first intercity mail and parcels usually moved by horseback, stagecoach, or watercraft. Well into the 1830s some long-distance mail was carried on foot, such as the 210-mile Chicago–Green Bay, Wisconsin, route, which entailed a 30-day round trip. Delivery times for letters and newspapers from the East Coast to the Midwest varied from two to six weeks depending upon weather and accidents. The passenger train established a nearly universal network that was far superior in schedule time and reliability. Mail and express business in turn gave railroads a profitable increment of business, often amounting to 10 to 15 percent of total revenue from passenger operations. As revenue per passenger-mile deteriorated after 1890, mail and express income sustained some passenger trains for another 60 years.

The economic and social impact of rail-based mail and express delivery was impressive. In 1853 the U.S. Post Office sold 61 million stamps and stamped envelopes. By 1886 the total surpassed 3.7 billion; by 1900, 7.4 billion; and by 1913, 18 billion. Next-day service between cities up to 300 miles apart was commonplace.

In 1832 the postmaster general established a mail route over the Camden & Amboy, and in 1838 Congress designated all railroads as "post roads," which qualified them for mail carriage. In that year mail cars in which en route sorting took place ran between Washington and Philadelphia. After an 1862 test on the Hannibal & St. Joseph of a mobile postal facility to serve Pony Express operations, other Railway Post Offices were activated two years later. The expansion of these facilities led to the 1869 creation of the Railway Mail Service.

RPO cars were functional, crammed with sorting bins and cubicles and equipped with devices that allowed the crew to snag mail bags that had been placed on trackside hooks. This allowed mail to be collected at small towns without stopping trains. Higher volume, coupled with a demand for rapid delivery, led to the scheduling of fast mail trains between major cities in the 1870s. Postal authorities in Canada and Mexico used rail service in similar ways.

Highway competition emerged in the 1930s as the U.S. Post Office deployed post offices aboard trucks and buses. After World War II long-distance mail was gradually diverted to commercial airlines. The last RPO was retired in 1977. The loss of RPOs doomed a number of U.S. passenger trains; mail had been the sole remaining profit center. Canada also discontinued rail-based mail delivery, but Mexico retained the system, including onboard sorting, for much longer.

In 1839 William F. Herndon carried small packages aboard trains and boats between New York and Boston and made delivery directly to receivers. Other express messengers copied this practice, and some paid fees to railroads for exclusive franchises on their routes. Early messengers carried shipments in valises, but as business increased, they used checked baggage service. Letters were carried in violation of postal laws, but this practice was abandoned after the U.S. Post Office cracked down on violators. Pioneer parcel ventures included Adams, Southern, American, Butterfield, and Wells Fargo. Business grew rapidly. In Indianapolis, for example, 43 express firms operated in 1883, 14 of them owned by railroads. Adams, Southern, American, and Wells Fargo dominated parcel service by 1900. Rail-based package delivery also evolved in Canada. The Canadian Pacific used Dominion Express Co. for its package deliveries, eventually purchased the firm, and in 1926 renamed it Canadian Pacific Express Co.

The advent of the U.S. Post Office's parcel post service in 1913 troubled railroad managers because they now would carry competing mail parcels at government rates that were lower than their normal charges for private parcels. During the U.S. Railroad Administration's World War I control of railroads, most parcel operations of the major private companies were consolidated into the American Railway Express Co. When that firm's contracts expired in 1929, its assets and operations were conveyed to the Railway Express Agency, an entity owned by 86 railroads, whose participation was based upon their respective shares of package express service.

Although trucks and intercity buses began attracting railroads' express business in the 1920s, these operations remained profitable for nearly a decade after World War II, despite a sharp postwar decline in volume. The discontinuance of passenger trains during the 1950s and 1960s

Mail service by railroad began in the early 1830s and soon grew into a nationwide service, with specially equipped Railway Post Office (RPO) cars. On September 16, 1875, *The Fast Mail* train was inaugurated between New York and Chicago, making the run in only 26 hours. Mail was sorted en route and was received or delivered from more than a hundred post offices along the route without stopping. Illustrations in *Harper's Weekly* for October 9, 1875, showed the new train, painted white and emblazoned with the name *The Fast Mail* and the national coats of arms in gilt, ready to depart Grand Central Depot (*top*), mail being sorted en route (*bottom left*), and the equipment for picking up or dropped mail (*bottom center*). George S. Bangs (*bottom right*) was general superintendent of the Railway Mail Service. —(all) Middleton Collection

further cut into the potential rail market, which by then was under intense pressure from trucks, buses, and airlines. In 1969 Railway Express Agency was sold to its management. By then railroad express traffic had dwindled to insignificant levels. REA ceased business in 1975.

—William J. Watt

REFERENCES

Holbrook, Stewart H. *The Story of American Railroads.* New York: Crown, 1947.

Long, Bryant A., with William J. Dennis. *Mail by Rail: The Story of the Postal Transportation Service.* New York: Simmons-Boardman, 1951.

Martin, Albro. *Railroads Triumphant.* New York: Oxford Univ. Press, 1992.

Viekman, William K. "RPO: Past, Present and No Future." *Trains* 31, no. 4 (Feb. 1971): 26–36.

See also MAIL ORDER.

The RPO car provided "at-speed" delivery and pickup of mail en route. Here, in successive photos at Bruno and then Bethel, Minneapolis, the Duluth & St. Paul RPO car, operating over the Great Northern's Duluth–Twin Cities train 23, the *Badger,* "makes the catch" of a mail pouch in October 1967. —(both) Don L. Hofsommer

Inside the Chicago & Minneapolis RPO busy clerks sort the mail on Milwaukee Road train 56, *The Fast Mail,* in June 1970 (*left*). Clerk-in-charge P. C. Lundberg cancels letters on board the St. Paul & Noyes RPO, operating between St. Paul and the Canadian border at Noyes, Minnesota, on the Great Northern's *Winnipeg Limited* (*right*). —(both) Don L. Hofsommer

Mail Order

The growth of the railroad network in the United States created a national economy and a national market for goods. By the last quarter of the nineteenth century the mail service offered the possibility of expanding retailing through mass merchandising by mail. To make the possibility a reality, certain factors had to be in place. A reliable national mail service was key. Delivery of mail-ordered goods had to be convenient and inexpensive. There must be a demand on the part of the public for goods that could not be purchased locally. Encouragement to purchase by mail had to be provided either through catalogs or advertisements in newspapers and magazines. Last, mail-order merchants had to be perceived by the public as honest and reliable.

Railroad service greatly abetted the development and success of mail order. Railroads had transported the U.S. mail almost from the very start of rail development. The mail by rail was originally hauled in sealed mail sacks and was sorted when it arrived in post offices. Speeding up and improving mail service by sorting on board the trains was an idea of a St. Joseph, Missouri, postal clerk named W. A. Davis. Davis was encouraged by George B. Armstrong, the assistant postmaster in Chicago. Further encouragement by Postmaster General Montgomery Blair led to the trial of the Railway Post Office (RPO) scheme. The Chicago & North Western Railway outfitted several cars as rolling post offices, and on August 28, 1864, the first RPO operated between Chicago and Clinton, Iowa. RPOs greatly improved the speed and reliability of national mail service and were a major factor in mail movement for a century.

Delivery by mail was not always convenient in the nineteenth century. In rural areas residents had to come into town to pick up their mail. City dwellers had enjoyed home delivery of mail beginning in 1861, although complete home delivery was not always provided. However, the postal service did not handle packages; package delivery had to be entrusted to half a dozen large express companies, and these firms were often accused of price gouging. Rural free delivery and parcel post were needed to improve convenience and make mail-order retailing a reality.

Postmaster General John Wanamaker pressed for these improvements during his term of service from 1889 to 1893. Wanamaker felt that the government should play a role in putting the widest possible range of goods in reach of the public at low cost. Wanamaker, of course, owned large and successful department stores in Philadelphia and New York. With Wanamaker's support, rural free delivery began on a small scale in 1892 and grew slowly at first; five years later there were only 82 rural routes, but by 1905 the number had grown to 32,000. With pressure from large merchants and mail-order companies, parcel post was instituted by the Post Office in 1912. The express companies and small-town merchants fought parcel post, but to no avail.

Demand from the public for goods not available locally was greatly stimulated by newspapers and magazines. The railroads, in conjunction with the U.S. mail, helped distribute this information across the nation. Those who lived in small cities and rural areas were no longer ignorant of the latest blandishments of life. General prosperity over the years after the Civil War and before World War I allowed citizens to back up their wishes with cash. Potential customers also had their appetite for goods whetted by the illustrated catalogs from the mail-order houses and the large merchants that cultivated sales by mail.

The perception of mail-order merchants as honest and reliable was a development of the late nineteenth century. Some dry goods houses had attempted to sell by mail in the 1860s, but little came of it. Aaron Montgomery Ward saw an economic opportunity and played a large role in pioneering the mail-order business. As a young man, Ward had worked in a general store in Michigan and then in a Chicago department store. For a time he was a traveling salesman for a St. Louis dry goods establishment. As the *The Music Man* proclaims in its opening chorus of traveling salesmen, "You gotta know the territory." In riding the trains to make calls in small towns in the rural Mississippi Valley, Ward came to know his territory well. He learned that rural people wanted a wide variety of goods, delivered directly to avoid middlemen, with low prices possible because of high volume.

Ward and his brother-in-law, George R. Thorne, launched the first general mail-order house in 1872. The first Montgomery Ward catalog was a price list of 163 items. By 1900 the catalog reached 1,200 pages, with 17,000 illustrations, and showed 70,000 items, and the orders of 2 million customers in that year were handled by an army of 2,000 clerks at the center of Montgomery Ward activity in Chicago. Chicago is also the site of Sears, Roebuck & Co., which eventually outdistanced Montgomery Ward.

Sears originated in 1886 when Richard Warren Sears was a station agent of the Minneapolis & St. Louis Railroad in North Redwood, Minnesota. His railroad duties were light, and Sears took up part-time business activities. A local jewelry store refused to accept a carton of watches; the manufacturer offered Sears the opportunity to sell them and keep for himself anything over $12 apiece. He wrote letters to other station agents offering the watches at $14. The watches were soon sold, and Sears bought more to sell at a profit. Giving up the railroad job, he moved to Minneapolis and then to Chicago and broadened his line of goods to include silverware and jewelry. Repair was a part of the watch business, and Sears hired Alvah C. Roebuck, who was skilled at repair, as well as assembling timepieces from parts, to handle that part of the business.

Sears began to advertise widely and to issue catalogs promoting its goods. Sears, Roebuck & Co. was a thriving mail-order business by the 1890s and was fortunate for the next 50 years to enjoy excellent leadership, after both Sears and Roebuck departed, in the person of Julius Rosenwald and, later, Gen. Robert E. Wood. Under their management Sears became the largest retailer in the world and remained so for many years. General Wood broadened Sears's outreach by constructing many department stores, each with a mail-order department. By the 1920s Sears sold an enormous variety of goods, including complete houses; the pre-cut homes were delivered by rail in kit form, along with detailed blueprints. Seeking more outreach, Wood led Sears to join with Simpsons Ltd. of Canada to form Simpson-Sears Ltd. Simpsons' already-large mail-order business was expanded greatly by the combination.

Much has changed over the years, but mail order remains a favorite means of purchase in the United States. The Railway Post Office cars are no longer in operation, and the railroads carry only storage or pouch mail. Information about goods still arrives in catalogs and newspaper and magazine ads, but radio, television, and the Internet have added to the flow of information available to the public. Sears, Roebuck & Co., at one time the largest retailer and the largest mail order house, has drifted away from catalog sales to serve the public through hundreds of local department stores. Montgomery Ward is now only a memory. The U.S. mail still delivers a huge proportion of parcels, but it faces severe competition from United Parcel Service and Federal Express. The railroads continue to play a role in the mail-order business.

—George M. Smerk

REFERENCES

Leach, William. *Land of Desire: Merchants, Power, and the Rise of a New American Culture.* New York: Pantheon, 1993.

Stevenson, Katherine Cole, and H. Ward Jandl. *Houses by Mail: A Guide to Houses from Sears, Roebuck and Company.* Washington, D.C.: Preservation Press, 1986.

Worthy, James C. *Shaping an American Institution: Robert E. Wood and Sears, Roebuck.* Urbana: Univ. of Illinois Press, 1984.

See also MAIL AND EXPRESS.

Maine Central Railroad

Much railroad development in the state of Maine was driven by the desire to link Canada with an Atlantic seaport that would remain free of ice, unlike the St. Lawrence River. Many of the railroads chartered in Maine had Montreal or Quebec as their goal. The first Portland-to-Canada railroad was the Atlantic & St. Lawrence (A&StL), opened between Portland and Montreal in 1853 and immediately leased by the Grand Trunk Railway.

The A&StL provided the starting point for two Maine Central predecessors, which were not concerned with building to Canada, but rather with replacing coastal and river navigation with railroads. The Kennebec & Portland was chartered in 1836 to build from Yarmouth, 12 miles from Portland on the A&StL, east to Brunswick and then up the Kennebec River to the state capital, Augusta. The Androscoggin & Kennebec was chartered in 1845 to build from Danville, 27 miles north of Portland on the A&StL, northeast through Lewiston to the Kennebec River somewhere between Hallowell and Waterville. The Kennebec & Portland was to be standard gauge; the Androscoggin & Kennebec would have a track gauge of 5 feet 6 inches, like the A&StL.

Chartered at the same time as the Androscoggin & Kennebec was the Penobscot & Kennebec, which would continue the Androscoggin & Kennebec's line east to Bangor. The Somerset & Kennebec was chartered in 1848 to extend the Kennebec & Portland's standard-gauge line north to Waterville and Skowhegan. In 1850 the Kennebec & Portland built a line of its own west into Portland from Yarmouth. The Kennebec & Portland was reorganized as the Portland & Kennebec in 1862.

In central Maine, then, in the 1850s were two broad-gauge and two standard-gauge railroads, all named [Something] & Kennebec. Added to those was the Androscoggin Railroad, which opened a broad-gauge line from Leeds Junction, northeast of Lewiston on the Androscoggin & Kennebec, north to Farmington. The Androscoggin had hoped that the Androscoggin & Kennebec would take it over; when that did not happen, it built a standard-gauge line south to a connection with the Kennebec & Portland at Brunswick and then standard-gauged the original portion of its line.

In 1862 the Maine Central Railroad (MEC) was incorporated to consolidate the Androscoggin & Kennebec and Penobscot & Kennebec railroads. The MEC leased the Portland & Kennebec (the reorganized Kennebec & Portland, which by then included the Somerset & Kennebec) in 1870 and the Androscoggin in 1871, clearing up much of the confusion over the various Kennebec names. It standard-gauged its Danville-Waterville-Bangor line in 1871 and built an extension from Danville south to Portland. Soon afterward it absorbed the leased lines and came under the control of the Eastern Railroad (Boston to Portland). Boston & Maine, which also had a line from Boston to Portland, acquired control of the Maine Central when it leased the Eastern in 1884.

Soon after it established a monopoly on railroading in the territory between Portland and Bangor, the Maine Central began to expand. It leased the European & North American Railway (E&NA) in 1882. The E&NA intended to build to Cape Canso in Nova Scotia, from where transatlantic steamers would make a short, quick crossing of the Atlantic; the road also saw itself as a link in the rail line between Montreal and the Maritime Provinces. The E&NA opened from Bangor to the Canadian border at Vanceboro, Maine, in 1871, consolidated with the Canadian portion of the line (Vanceboro to St. John, New Brunswick), and leased two nearby short lines. In 1875 the E&NA entered receivership and lost most of the railroads it had acquired.

In 1888 the MEC leased the Portland & Ogdensburg, the Maine and New Hampshire part of a railroad that was intended to connect Portland with Great Lakes shipping at Ogdensburg, New York. The railroad had been built by three companies, which fell into financial difficulties and came under the control of other railroads that had other goals in mind than a Portland–Great Lakes route (the middle portion of the Portland & Ogdensburg became the St. Johnsbury & Lake Champlain; the western portion became the Rutland's long line that reached across upstate New York). Lease of the Portland & Ogdensburg gave MEC a route for traffic to and from Montreal via St. Johnsbury, Vermont. In 1890 MEC leased the Upper Coos Railway and the Hereford Railway, which connected with the Quebec Central Railway. Between 1891 and 1907 MEC leased or obtained control of the Knox & Lincoln Railway (from Woolwich along the coast to Rockland), the Washington County Railroad (Ellsworth east to Calais), the Somerset Railroad (Oakland north to Moosehead Lake), and the Portland & Rumford Falls Railway (Auburn through Rumford to Kennebago).

The Portland Terminal Co. was created in 1911 as a Maine Central subsidiary to acquire and operate the MEC and Boston & Maine properties around Portland. At that same time the most prosperous of Maine's 2-foot-gauge lines, the Sandy River & Rangeley Lakes and the Bridgton & Saco River, came under Maine Central control (the 2-footers, considerably less prosperous, regained independence in 1923 and 1927, respectively).

In 1925 the lease of the Hereford Railway expired, and MEC pulled back south across the international border. Some of the Hereford Railway was abandoned; some of it was sold to Canadian Pacific. In 1927 the Belfast & Moosehead Lake, which MEC had operated from its opening, assumed independent operation under the ownership of the City of Belfast. In the 1930s MEC abandoned the long north-reaching lines that had been the Somerset Railroad and the Portland & Rumford Falls.

Boston & Maine control of the Maine Central had ended in 1914, but in 1933 MEC made an agreement with B&M for joint employment of some officers, a cooperative arrangement that provided most of the benefits of a merger. In 1952 MEC began to resume its independence and by the end of 1955 had become totally independent of the Boston & Maine.

Maine Central ceased carrying passengers in 1960, though the trains themselves continued to run carrying mail and express for a short period. About the same time Boston & Maine, MEC's principal connection, decided to discontinue its mail and express business and operate passenger-only trains.

Canadian Pacific's Montreal–St. John trains ran on Maine Central rails between Mattawamkeag and Vanceboro. In 1974 MEC sold that stretch of the former E&NA to Canadian Pacific, retaining trackage rights for itself. In 1976 MEC sold the North Stratford, New Hampshire–Beecher Falls, Vermont, line, the former Upper Coos Railroad, to the State of New Hampshire. During the 1970s MEC upgraded the track on the former Portland & Og-

densburg. The line had little local business, but traffic interchanged with Canadian Pacific at St. Johnsbury, Vermont, remained vigorous.

U.S. Filter Corp. purchased the Maine Central in December 1980. Ashland Oil took over U.S. Filter about the same time and sold the railroad in June 1981 to Guilford Transportation Industries. Two years later Guilford bought the Boston & Maine and in 1984 added the Delaware & Hudson. Guilford's revenues would increase if traffic to and from the West were routed over the Boston & Maine and Delaware & Hudson. The Mountain Division, the former Portland & Ogdensburg, no longer had a job and was abandoned. About the same time MEC abandoned the branches to Rockland and Calais and most of the Portland-Augusta-Waterville line, essentially pruning the Maine Central to a single main line between Portland and Mattawamkeag via Lewiston, Waterville, and Bangor, a branch to Rumford made up of parts of the former Androscoggin Railroad and a short segment of the former Portland & Rumford Falls, and a few short branches. In the mid-1980s Guilford leased portions of the Maine Central to Boston & Maine subsidiary Springfield Terminal to take advantage of the lower wage scale and more flexible work rules of shortlines. The Maine Central appeared destined to disappear not with a bang but a whimper.

In 1981, the year it was sold to Guilford Transportation Industries, Maine Central operated a system of 818 route-miles and 1,062 track-miles, with 73 locomotives, 4,523 freight cars, 215 company service cars, and 1,265 employees. Freight traffic totaled 898.3 million ton-miles in 1981, with pulp and paper (53.2 percent), lumber and wood products (10.9 percent), and chemicals (9.0 percent) representing its principal traffic sources. Maine Central operating revenues totaled $65.4 million in 1981, and the railroad achieved a 94.1 percent operating ratio.

—George H. Drury

REFERENCES

Baker, George Pierce. *The Formation of the New England Railroad Systems.* Cambridge, Mass.: Harvard Univ. Press, 1937.

Harlow, Alvin F. *Steelways of New England.* New York: Creative Age Press, 1946.

Maintenance-of-Way

The fundamental aspects of railway track—a system that supports and guides vehicles traveling upon it—can be traced to Babylonian times. As early as 2245 B.C. Babylonians, Greeks, and Romans used a system of stone blocks with grooves down the centers to guide their wagons. Remnants of these wagon ways, with the distance between the running grooves ranging from 5 feet to 5 feet 4 inches, can still be found.

Track Gauge

Wagon ways evolved over time from carved grooves to raised rails, and "rail roads" were born. First, horse-drawn carts operated on wooden rails; later, mechanical engines on iron rails. Inventing all the way, these first railroads built track to various dimensions and gauges—the distance between the rails, measured from the inside head of one rail to the inside head of the opposing rail. What we consider standard gauge today was first used by George Stephenson, based upon the selection of the 4-foot 8-inch gauge already used by colliers, with ½ inch added for side play of the engines, but decades passed before it became the standard.

In North America the earliest railroads adopted a wide variety of track gauges. Some used the 4-foot 8½-inch gauge that by then was widely used in England. The Erie built at 5 feet 6 inches, and many southern lines were built at 5 feet. Coal roads in Pennsylvania used a 4-foot 3-inch gauge, and the Pennsylvania Railroad originally adopted a 4-foot 9-inch gauge. But Stephenson's standard became the de facto North American standard when President Abraham Lincoln declared in 1863 that the transcontinental railway would be built to 4-foot 8½-inch gauge. By 1887 nearly every major U.S. railroad had adopted standard gauge. There were exceptions, of course. Mining roads in Colorado and other locations were built and operated at "narrow," 3-foot gauge. But while exceptions remain, they are few and far between. Adoption of the standard gauge was necessary for railroads to interchange railcars with other railroads so that railcars could move virtually anywhere in the country as the rail network grew.

Slight variations in gauge are also used in a few other specific situations. For example, ¼-inch-wide gauge is sometimes introduced in tight-radius curves to improve vehicle-curving characteristics. In other instances gauge is set ¼-inch tight to extend the period in which the gauge will eventually spread under lateral vehicle loads. Track typically is regauged when it reaches ½-inch-wide gauge.

Track Grading and Construction

Like track gauge, the North American railway track structure has been a work in progress. Although the basic structure—rail or steel rails fastened to wooden crossties laid on a ballasted roadway—looks much the same today as when it was first established nearly 200 years ago, track materials and components have evolved, and track design has been refined over time. Not surprisingly, the level of engineering and the number of improvements to track components increase as they work their way up from the below grade, or substratum, of the roadbed (which is generally considered to extend 6 feet beneath the ballast section) to the top of the rail.

In most cases the roadway is selected not for its native structural qualities, but for its alignment: the straighter and flatter, the better. In early years the roadway was cut, cleared, and graded by horse- or oxen-drawn blades, blasting powder, and backbreaking pick and shovel work. As chronicled in Stephen Ambrose's *Nothing like It in the World*, the building of the transcontinental railroad through the mountains of the West in the 1860s was a feat unto itself: "Grading work," as Lynn Farrar, a Southern Pacific historian described it, "uses pick-and-shovel work most efficiently when low cuts or fills—one and a half to two feet—are required. Fills are made by what is called 'casting'—i.e., shoveling. If there are over three feet of material, it can be double-casted—that is, it requires two 'throws' to get the material into place for the grade. In most cases earth was plowed by heavy steel plows drawn by up to twelve oxen. . . . For distances greater than 500 feet it was economical to 'waste and borrow'—that is, dispose of cut material by wasting it then 'borrow' material for an adjacent fill. The location surveyors always tried to find a line that would 'balance' the grading cuts and fills so that there would be a minimal amount of moving of material."

The alignment through the Sierra Nevada required the grade to climb to a maximum of 2.2 percent, as much as 116 feet per mile, the steepest grade allowed by Congress. Blasting powder was used to loosen the naturally cemented gravel in some of the cuts. One cut that was 63 feet deep and 800 feet long required as much as 500 kegs of blasting powder per day, which, Ambrose points out, was more than was used in most of the major battles of the Civil War.

Today, new construction is done with diesel-powered shovels, excavators, and graders that cut and fill and build the roadway to grade with laser precision. These roadbed-preparation techniques are nearly identical to those used in highway construction.

Track Bed

Strange though it may seem, the least engineered aspect of the track structure is the primary roadway, the ground upon which the track is laid. The subgrade is typically made up of native material found on the alignment. Generally speaking, the subgrade on a given right of way is what it is, and track engineers learn to live with it. Depending upon which part of the country a track is located, the subgrade can range from the hard, well-compacted soils found in the high desert of the West to the soft, clayey, moisture-retaining soils of the South. The hard-packed soils tend to promote drainage and provide a stiff track modulus. The soft, clayey soils tend to hold moisture and produce a soft, more maintenance-intensive track modulus. Fortunately, the subgrade on most railroads falls somewhere in between.

In order to quantify the effects of soft subgrade on track maintenance, particularly under today's 100- to 125-ton cars, tests were conducted in 1990 at the Assn. of American Railroads' (AAR) Transportation Technology Center, Inc. (TTCI) test facility in Pueblo, Colorado. A 700-foot-long, 12-foot-wide, 5-foot-deep trough was excavated and backfilled with what is called buckshot soil, a kind of clay that dries into pellets that resemble coarse lead shot. The moisture content was maintained at about 33 percent. It was shown that under the heavy, repeated loadings and the dynamic action caused by train traffic, saturated subgrade soils can be pumped or otherwise forced into the voids between the crushed rock in the ballast layer, reducing the ballast's drainage properties and the overall strength of the track. Test researchers concluded that track stiffness, called track modulus, of 2,000 psi (pounds per square inch) or less (represented by a conventional 18-inch granular layer over a soft, clayey subgrade) leads to degradation of the track geometry and requires frequent surfacing maintenance under 125-ton cars (39-ton axle loads).

In real-world applications in which subgrade conditions are good, ballast is often laid directly on the graded subgrade. Where conditions are poor, a subballast layer, usually about 6 inches thick, is placed between the subgrade and the ballast to help spread the loads and promote drainage. Subballast may consist of slag or other material that will promote drainage. Or, as is more common, it may consist of old ballast that has been built upon over time. In areas with clayey or otherwise unstable native soil conditions, a lime slurry or fly ash can be injected into the subballast to stabilize it without removing or disturbing it. Geosynthetic fabric filters are also sometimes laid beneath the ballast section in areas known to be unstable or to have poor drainage characteristics. These materials must be fine enough to hold the soil in place, but permeable enough to allow moisture to pass through the ballast and flow out through the subballast and subgrade. Geosynthetic materials are often used in confined areas such as inverts, or beneath highway-rail grade crossings, which tend to trap moisture. Hot-mix asphalt underlayment has also been used in troublesome spots, such as crossing diamonds and highway-rail grade crossings. In these installations a 4- to 8-inch-thick layer of asphalt is laid on the subballast and covered with 8 to 12 inches of ballast. This method has been shown to promote drainage, increase the overall stiffness of the track even in moist, clayey soils, and reduce maintenance. Regardless of the substructure, no track is perfectly rigid. Defection of up to 1/10 inch is common on stiff track structures and up to 1/2 inch on soft track structures.

Ballast

The top layer of the graded roadbed is called the ballast. Its primary functions are to promote drainage, hold the ties in place, and disperse the wheel loads to the subgrade below. In the early days of railroading, ballast consisted of whatever material—rock, gravel, slag—was readily available. The term "ballast" as used in connection with railway track material originated in England. Ships carrying coal from Newcastle returned "in ballast," that is, laden with gravel and other material to maintain stability. The ballast was dumped by the docks and was used to provide a solid roadbed for the coal-hauling tramways. The word "ballast" became a standard railway term.

The most commonly used ballasts on today's railroads are granites, trap rocks, quartzites, limestone, dolomites, and slags. Which is used depends in part on what is locally available and the type of traffic that the railroad handles. Slags, a by-product of the steelmaking process, were used extensively at one time. Limestones are used on lighter-density lines, but on heavy-tonnage main lines granites and trap rock are the preferred ballast materials. These rocks are hard and dense, and their angular particle structure provides good interlocking qualities without undesirable cementing characteristics.

On today's railroads ballast material is graded by size, and typical size gradations range from 2½ inches down to ¾ inch, 2 inches to 1 inch, and 1½ to ¾ inches. Material that is less than ¾-inch gradation is typically removed during ballast-cleaning operations. The move toward heavier cars has caused most railroads to choose hard crushed rock, such as granite, on core lines. Demanding applications, such as concrete tie installations, typically require granite or trap rock (quartzite, if available) in larger sizes. But since ballast is not manufactured—availability is limited by the local geology—railroads cannot be too choosy. Transportation is expensive. And since ballast constitutes more than 80 percent of the weight of the track structure above the subgrade, availability within reasonable hauling distances is a primary consideration.

Ballast depth, or thickness, is typically 12 inches, on top of a 6-inch subballast layer. The cribs, the spaces between the crossties, are filled and broomed during ballasting operations to the top of the ties. Embedding the ties within the ballast provides the overall lateral and longitudinal track strength. Although the width of the ballast shoulder, the width of graded ballast that extends beyond the ends of the ties, varies from railroad to railroad, they typically extend 6 to 18 inches. In most cases the broader the shoulder, the greater the overall track stability. Tests indicate that the lateral strength of the track is increased by up to 40 percent by increasing shoulder width from 6 inches to 12 inches. The typical slope of the ballast shoulder is 2:1.

Ties

Although the earliest railways used stone blocks to support the rail, North American railroads early on adopted the contemporary track structure—iron or, later, steel rails spiked to timber logs laid crosswise with stone and gravel between them. The system has been refined over the years, but some aspects remain constant. The use of timber ties, for example, remains the standard; timber accounts for more than 95 percent of the more than a half billion ties in track on U.S. railroads. Of the 12 million new ties installed on major railroads in 2001, approximately 93 percent were timber, and the bulk of these were creosote-treated hardwoods (treated softwoods are used in less demanding territories). There are good reasons for this use of wooden ties.

In many ways, timber is ideally suited to its role in track. The standard North American hardwood tie is strong in tension, enabling it to hold the rails at the proper gauge; strong in compression, enabling it to support the wheel loads; and strong in bending, enabling it to distribute loads to the ballast in a uniform fashion. And since it is nailable, rails can be easily fastened to it.

Rails at one time were nailed directly to the ties, but steel tie plates have been adopted to help spread wheel loads over a greater portion of the tie. Cast- or rolled-steel tie plates, which range from 12 to 18 inches wide, have reduced the tendency for the rail to cut into the ties and have extended the overall life of the tie. Plates are generally hot punched with two holes along each side of the rail seat and staggered outer holes that allow for various spiking patterns. Although their primary purpose is to reduce the mechanical wear at the base of the rail and distribute the load over a greater area, tie plates also provide inward rail cant that better positions the wheel bearing over the rail. After years of experimenting with tie-plate configurations ranging from 8 to 18 inches wide and with various degrees of cant, North American railroads standardized on double-shoulder plates with 1:40 cant in the rail-seat area between the two shoulders. A 1:40 cant inclines the rail toward the track centers and matches the standard 1:20 wheel-tread taper. (A steeper 1:30 cant has been used in recent years in areas in which heavy-haul traffic has led to rapid gauge widening.)

As railway engineering became more sophisticated, trackmen began to establish standards for ties. Photographs of the transcontinental line under construction show a roadbed consisting of split logs of varying lengths and thicknesses laid on the grade. Although this approach was adequate to get the railroad up and running, it did not meet the longer-term structural needs. With experience, standard tie dimensions were reduced to three lengths and five thicknesses by the turn of the twentieth century. In 1921 the American Railway Engineering Assn. (AREA) adopted six grades of crossties. A number 1 grade tie was 6 by 6 inches in section, for example, and a number 6 tie was 7 by 10 inches in section. In 1984 the size classifications were reduced to two, 7 by 9 inches and 6 by 8 inches, with each available in 8-, 8½-, and 9-foot lengths. With further experience, the use of 8-foot lengths, which conformed to the length of cordwood and commercial lumber lengths sold at the time, was discontinued, and railroads adopted the 8-foot 6-inch length, which is the standard length today. Ties are spaced between 18 and 24 inches, center-to-center, but typically at 19½ inches.

Although timber has proved to be an excellent crosstie material, untreated timber can break down fairly quickly from mechanical wear and decay. Consequently, virtually all timber ties today are creosote treated. This process has extended tie service life from 10 years or less, for untreated ties, to 25 to 30 years or more, depending on the traffic levels.

During the building of the transcontinental railroad, ties were made from the plentiful cottonwood trees found along the right of way. These rough-hewn logs, which were soft and perishable, were treated by Burnettizing, a process in which the water in the timber was extracted and a zinc solution was infused in its place. This process served its purpose, but coal tar creosote and mixtures of creosote with heavy petroleum are the most common preservatives used for ties today. In this process hardwood ties (which weigh an average of 200 pounds) are air dried for several seasons (until their moisture content is reduced by half or less), then treated with up to 25 pounds of creosote to prevent decay. Although timber-tie industries continue to look at alternatives, such as the use of borates, sulfur compounds, and copper naphthenate, creosote remains the most popular.

Timber ties remain the most common standard, but there is growing acceptance of alternative materials such as concrete, steel, composite, and, most recently, plastic. Next to timber, reinforced concrete is the most widely accepted crosstie material. Concrete ties were first used in North America by the Philadelphia & Reading Railroad in 1830. From that time until the 1930s more than 150 types of reinforced-concrete ties were designed and patented in the United States. Because of inadequate rail-fastening systems and the ready supply of timber ties, however, concrete-tie designs did not find their way into the mainstream. Development continued in other parts of the world, however, where timber supplies were inadequate or where timber could not stand up to environmental conditions. Improvements in concrete-tie and fastening-system designs generated renewed interest by North American railroads in the late 1950s. Interest spiked again in the 1980s as increased axle loadings showed that standard, or nonpremium, track components degraded more rapidly and that maintenance requirements increased by 20 to 30 percent. As the need for longer-lasting materials requiring less maintenance grew, the interest in concrete ties and other premium track components increased. Although concrete ties constitute no more than 6 percent of the annual North American tie market, they are the material of choice in new construction in both freight and passenger applications.

Early concrete-tie designs relied on unstressed reinforcing steel, but the new-generation designs incorporated prestressed reinforcing steel. Two primary types of concrete ties were developed—monolithic and dual-block. Of the two, monolithic concrete ties are the North American standard. Among the benefits of concrete ties is that the rail seat and steel shoulders are cast directly into the tie, fixing cant and gauge. Their ability to hold gauge has led to the use of concrete ties in the most difficult stretches of track—areas with frequent or sharp curves in which vehicles generate high lateral, gauge-widening forces. In these types of applications concrete ties with their fixed gauge held by steel shoulders embedded into the concrete have been shown to hold up better than timber ties, which are prone to plate cutting and gauge widening resulting from elongated, or spike-killed, holes. As a result, concrete ties have become standard issue on high-speed and heavy-tonnage main lines, particularly in severe operating environments, such as mountainous territory.

One of the limiting factors in the use of concrete ties has been their weight (an average 700 pounds each versus 225 pounds for the average treated 8-foot 6-inch timber tie) and their inability to be handled by standard timber-tie-handling equipment. Consequently, standard main-line concrete ties are installed by what is called out-of-face, when an entire section of track is replaced, and are rarely, if ever, interspersed with other tie types. Burlington Northern Santa Fe, however, recently installed concrete ties made by Rocla Concrete Tie that are roughly the same dimensions as timber ties, enabling them to be handled by typical tie-handling equipment and interspersed with timber ties.

Concrete ties used in heavy-tonnage and high-speed main lines are typically spaced at 24 inches center-to-center. Since concrete-tie track can be twice as stiff as timber-tie track, a higher grade of ballast is generally used in conjunction with concrete ties. Unlike timber ties, concrete ties require a cushioning pad between the rail and the tie. Elastic fasteners mate with cast-in-place steel shoulders to fix the rail in place. In recent years a steel wear plate has been introduced in the rail-seat area to prevent rail-seat abrasion, which has occurred in moist climates.

Steel ties have also found a place on North American railroads, albeit a much smaller place than that of concrete. Steel ties are stamped from flat steel, 8 to 10 millimeters thick. The shape of the tie, an inverted trough, is designed to trap ballast; the tie ends are shaped like spades that dig into the ballast and provide resistance to lateral displacement. Like concrete ties, a rail seat is built into the tie, so tie plates are not required. Welded or hook-in shoulders are used to hold gauge and accommodate an elastic fastening system. Steel ties are frequently used interspersed with timber ties (as gauge rods) in non-main-line track, in yard turnouts, and in special applications, such as refueling facilities, in which timber ties rapidly deteriorate.

Composite-plastic ties are the most recent entry into the market. Although several types have been available and under test for some years, serious interest in using these ties as alternatives to standard creosote-treated timber ties was spurred by an announcement by Kerr McGee, one of the largest suppliers of treated timber ties, that it would exit the tie business in 2005. This announcement sent the major railroads' tie buyers scurrying to secure enough ties for planned tie programs. It also generated significant interest in alternate tie materials, such as plastics, that can be used in main-line applications in place of timber.

Although alternative timber ties, such as very dense Azobe hardwoods and parallel-strand laminated cross-section timbers that are cut to the appropriate dimen-sions, exist, plastic or composite-plastic ties, which are made from recycled plastic, appear to show the most promise. They are considerably more expensive than timber ties, but they have performed well in tests thus far. At 260 pounds, plastic ties weigh about as much as creosote-treated timber ties. They are strong but not stiff, so they incorporate a composite of either polymer and a glass fiber or a polymer/polymer composite to increase stiffness. Tests at the TTCI have shown no major difference in track stiffness between plastic- and timber-tie track, and no tie failures after more than 550 million gross tons (MGT) of traffic. Tests also have shown that smooth plastic ties offered less lateral resistance than timber or concrete ties, but that plastic ties with a textured surface showed greater lateral resistance than either timber or concrete. Unlike timber, plastic ties are not susceptible to deterioration from moisture or insect infestation, and they are recyclable.

The 7-by-9-inch cross section of extruded plastic ties matches the dimensions and profile of timber ties, enabling them to be used interchangeably with timber ties. They also can accommodate spikes or threaded fasteners, which can be installed with traditional timber-tie hardware, including tie plates, screws, and fasteners. This means that they can be installed out-of-face or interspersed with timber, using standard tie-handling equipment. What remains to be seen is how they perform in less-than-favorable ballast conditions and, more generally, how they perform over the long term.

Rail

Of all track components, rail is the most fundamental and most highly engineered, and it is the most expensive item of the annual maintenance-of-way budget. Each year U.S. railroads install about 3,000 miles of new rail in "first position," at an average installed cost of about $100,000 per mile, or a total annual expenditure of $300 million. In 2003 the seven principal railroads ordered an estimated 512,599 tons of new rail.

Some form of rail was used in some kind of guideway for carts long before locomotive-hauled machines were developed. The earliest was oak laid upon ties, usually called stringer-tracks. The rails wore rapidly, and separate birch tiles that could easily be replaced were laid over the oak stringers. Fish-bellied cast-iron rails that acted as a bridge between stone blocks or sleepers or ties, the ancestors of modern rails, were designed in 1792 and first used in North America in 1828. Another early arrangement was the use of long plates of cast-iron strap rail laid over wooden rails. The design was cheap and popular with early U.S. rail lines.

The familiar pattern of modern T-rail began to take its present form as early as 1830, with the design for Robert Stevens, chief engineer of the Camden & Amboy. Made in wrought iron, these were rolled with a wider base resting on supporting stones, or later ties, with a vertical supporting web and a wider head on the top flange. A similar design developed at about the same time was the pear-shaped rail, similar in appearance to the T-rail, but with the section above the base plate shaped more in a pear shape than a web and upper section. This design was in widespread use into the Civil War period before being replaced by the T-rail. By 1856 the Bessemer steel blast furnaces made inexpensive and stronger steel rails readily available.

In cross section, today's T-rails resemble their ancestors of 175 years ago. The weight of rail has changed dramatically, however, from as light as 36 pounds per yard to the 155-pound rail section adopted by the Pennsylvania Railroad in 1931. There is no formula to determine which rail section to use on a given line, but track engineers are apt to consider the speed of traffic and the average annual tonnage, as well as environmental factors such as grade and curvature of the line. As gross vehicle weights have steadily increased to as much as 125 tons in unit coal and double-stack intermodal service, engineers have tended toward the use of heavier rail sections.

Although a fairly wide range of rail weights remains in track, new installations typically range from 115-pound rail on light-density lines to 132- to 136-pound rail on core, heavy-tonnage main lines. The engineering standards committees of the major railroads recently adopted a 141-pound section for use in curves and very high-tonnage track. The weight of rail in track on Class 1 railways increased from an average of about 83 pounds per yard in 1921 to 126 pounds per yard in 2001. Typical rail sections range from 6 to 8 inches in height. Rail lengths, too, have varied over the years, from 15-foot lengths during the early years of railroading to the ¼-mile strings of welded rails that are installed today. Over the past 50 years the standard rail length has been 39 feet, adopted for ease of shipment in standard 40-foot cars. The 39-foot rail lengths are laid with bolted joints that match the contour of the rail web, head, and base and are staggered at least 12 inches apart, so that joints are never opposite each other. The distance between the rail ends is set so that the gaps will close as the rail expands with high temperatures, and open an acceptable amount as the rails contract in the cold. Wheels hitting these gaps at the rail joints—135 beats per rail, per mile—create the familiar rhythmic "clickety-clack." Although this method of constructing track has been effective, it is not without its share of problems—most notably that the rail ends, which are less rigid than the body of the rail, tend to flex under traffic, causing rail wheels to batter the joint ends over time. This continual battering also leads to a breakdown of the ballast under the rail ends, creating low joints and soft spots in the track. These soft spots in turn induce harmonic "rock-and-roll," a side-to-side motion in freight cars that typically occurs between 14 and 22 mph, which further aggravates the problem. Thousands of miles of track have been laid in this manner. Though longer 78- to 82-foot rail lengths are now available, 39-foot lengths are still prevalent in North America.

Perhaps one of the most significant changes made to the track structure was the advent of continuous welded rail (CWR), a process in which lengths of rail are welded into ¼-mile strings. CWR was developed in the 1920s, and railroads adopted it in earnest beginning in the 1950s, as acceptable welding techniques were established and methods for handling and transporting long strings of rail were developed. Rail is welded at the rail mill or specialized welding plants, using an electric flash butt welding process. Unlike thermite welds, which are produced by a chemical reaction of aluminum with a metal oxide, electric flash butt welds are produced when the parent metal of the individual rails is heated and the rail ends are fused without the addition of other materials. This ensures that there are no weak or soft spots in the welded sections of the rail. After the rails are welded into 1,500-foot strings, they are loaded into specially designed, permanently coupled railcars that allow the rail strings to bend around curves. Rail strings are laid along the roadbed where they are to be installed, in most cases, by specialized track equipment. These machines are capable of removing the existing rails from track, transferring them to the track shoulders, and picking up the new rails and threading them into the rail seats of new or existing ties.

The key factor in CWR applications is installing and fastening the rail in place at its neutral, or stress-free, temperature. Unlike jointed rail, CWR does not have consistent gaps that allow the rail to expand and contract with temperature variations. Instead, CWR relies on an elastic fastening system that generates a continuous vertical clamping force at the base of the rail to hold the rail firmly in place.

Left unrestrained, a 1,500-foot CWR string will be nearly a foot shorter at 0°F than at 100°F. But if the rail is properly restrained, the length will remain the same; the shrinkage will occur in the cross section. Since rail can withstand at least 75,000 psi without permanent deformation, normal temperature variations can be accommodated within its elastic range. If CWR is allowed to expand beyond a certain temperature range, however, the track is likely to buckle. Track buckles, also known as sun kinks, occur suddenly, frequently under trains, often resulting in derailments. Conversely, if CWR contracts with too great a tensile force, the rail may break at weak points in the track, such as defective welds or existing bolt holes, or pull apart at the nearest joint. Railroads go to considerable effort, which typically includes heating the rail, in order to lay and maintain CWR at the proper neutral temperature. On Burlington Northern Santa Fe, for example, the typical neutral temperature for CWR is 95 degrees.

Rail is typically replaced because of wear—head wear in tangent track, gauge-face wear in curves—fatigue, and plastic deformation. The greater use of heavier rail sections, such as the recently adopted 141-pound section, that concentrate more mass in the head of the rail has helped delay the inevitable. But size alone is not enough. As important as rail's size and weight is its metallurgical composition. Research has shown that wear, deformation, and the fatigue resistance of rail steels are strongly influenced by the hardness and metallurgical microstructure of the steels. Consequently, researchers and manufacturers have worked to come up with cleaner, harder, more wear-resistant rail steels.

Rail is rolled from high-quality steel containing iron, carbon, manganese, and silicon. Impurities such as phosphorus and sulfur must be minimized or eliminated to prevent cracking, or making the rail brittle during the cooling process, thereby reducing the rail's impact resistance. Metallurgical cleanliness is determined by the content of nonmetallic inclusions, such as aluminum-silicon oxides, which can lead to rail surface defects, such as what is called "shelling," a failure along the rail head. Research conducted by the AAR has shown that the use of clean steels can increase the life of rail by a factor of five or more.

Rail hardness has also played a significant role in increasing the life of rail. Manufacturers introduced "head-hardened," heat-treated rails in the early 1950s. This process, which involves heating, quenching, and controlled cooling of the top and sides of the railhead, results in a fine pearlitic microstructure that produces significantly higher tensile strengths and hardnesses than standard carbon rail. Rails that are head-hardened and deep head-hardened (to 20 millimeters) typically contain alloys such as chromium and vanadium or columbium as hardness enhancers.

Rail hardness is measured by Brinell hardness (Bhn), the sample's resistance to indention with a standard load of a steel ball under hydraulic pressure. Brinell measurements have gradually increased over the past 50 years from approximately 260 Bhn for standard carbon rail to more than 400 Bhn for some premium rails. Railroads today typically use rails in the 300 to 320 Bhn range for tangent track and less demanding applications and premium rails, which the American Railway Engineering and Maintenance-of-Way Assn. (AREMA) characterizes as 341 Bhn or greater, in curves or other demanding applications. Fully head-hardened premium rails in the 380 to 405 Bhn range are currently available from Europe and Japan, and very high-hardness rails in the 420 to 430 Bhn range are in the offing.

Most metallurgists agree, however, that the existing pearlitic rail structure, a mixture of soft, near-zero carbon iron platelets and hard, brittle iron carbide platelets, has been pushed to its limits. Other materials, such as 415 Bhn bainitic rail steels, which usually have a single-phase tetragonal structure with iron carbide particles interspersed throughout, have been shown to wear better than pearlitic rails, with higher resistance to shelling, which is characterized as subsurface-initiated defects caused by cyclic rolling compression loads, spalling, characterized as surface-initiated defects, and fatigue. These tough, high-hardness steels may prove very beneficial in special trackwork, such as switches, turnouts, frogs, and crossing diamonds.

Switches

Switches are that part of the track structure that uses a set of movable rails to switch rolling stock from one track to another. Single-slip switches provide access to one track; double-slip switches provide access to two. In areas of multiple tracks with intersecting leads, such as rail yards, a series of single-slip switches is used to create a switch ladder to provide access to many tracks from a single lead.

Switch stands typically have "targets" or markings on them to indicate the position of the switch points and allow train crews to ascertain the alignment. Targets, which are mounted on the switch stands and rotate 90 degrees when the switch is thrown, use shape or colors—green for straight, red for a diverging movement—to identify the alignment of the switch when the position of the points cannot clearly be seen. In bygone years oil-burning lamps with shaded red and green windows were used to indicate alignment. Whatever the type, these devices enable train crews to look down a lead and determine the alignment at a glance. Although reflective targets are still used in yards and on branch lines, they have been replaced on main-lines in large measure by electric overhead or wayside "dwarf" signals controlled by a dispatcher.

Main-line switches are typically referred to as turnouts, arrangements of a switch and frog with closure rails that are used to divert rolling stock from one track to another. Turnouts are made up of many parts, including rods and plates to hold the switch points in the correct position, bracing to hold the stock rails in place, heel blocks to provide a rigid joint at the heel of the switch, and frogs. Frogs, so named because their shape resembles that of a frog, are castings located at the point at which wheels cross from one track to another.

Since they represent a discontinuity in the track, turnout components are notoriously high maintenance. Heat-treated rails and manganese steel tips are often used on switch rails where wear is severe. High-strength manganese steel castings, which are frequently explosion hardened before installation in track, are often used to extend the wear life of frogs in track.

Standard AREMA-recommended turnouts are built in varying lengths, with switch points ranging from 11 to 39 feet, depending on the desired crossover speeds. Turnouts are designated by number, which corresponds to frog angle and length of switch points. These aspects determine the maximum crossover speed allowed through the turnout. A typical No. 10 turnout, for example, has a recommended maximum speed of 20 mph. A No. 20 main-line turnout with curved 39-foot switch points has a recommended maximum speed of 50 mph.

Newer tangential-geometry turnouts, which feature longer switch points that provide a lower angle of entry to the switch, and movable-point frogs, which remove the wheel flange gaps to create a continuous wheel path at the frog, are currently used in both heavy-freight and high-speed applications. These premium designs require less maintenance and allow higher operating speeds. An 800-foot-long tangential-geometry turnout installed on Amtrak's Northeast Corridor, for example, allows crossover speeds of 80 mph.

Crossing diamonds—points at which tracks cross at severe 90-degree or other angles—are particularly maintenance intensive. Tests at the TTCI have shown that typical frogs and crossing diamonds generate the highest vertical forces in track. These forces, generated by wheel/flangeway impacts, also stress vehicle components and contribute to axle fatigue. Improved materials, such as high-hardness bainitic rail steels, and new crossing designs dramatically extend the life of these components.

Perhaps the most radical of the new crossing-diamond designs is the flange-bearing crossing frog. In this design the crossing frog incorporates shallow, tapered flangeways that make contact with the bottom running surface of the wheel flanges instead of the wheel tread surface, eliminating impacts with the intersecting flangeways through the crossing. Tests at the TTCI have shown that the flange-bearing crossing diamonds have minimal effect on vehicles, but dramatically reduce the impact loadings typically associated with crossing diamonds. Tests in revenue service, which required the AAR on behalf of its member railroads to obtain a waiver of the Federal Railroad Administration (FRA) Track Safety Standards relating to allowable frog flangeway depths, are ongoing. TTCI also has tested a ramped diamond crossing in which the tread-bearing approaches on either side of the crossing frog are ramped to enable the wheels to "jump" across the intersecting open flangeways at the crossing. The ramped diamond under test is made from modern, thick-web bainitic rail steel. This design incorporates ramps on either side of the open flangeways at the rail crossing. The wheel-tread surfaces ride up the ramp on one side of the flangeway, over the flangeway, then down the ramp on the other side of the flangeway. Early indications are that this design, which can accommodate 40 mph traffic, reduces vertical loads and the rail-end batter typically associated with diamond crossings.

Track Hardware

Once the rails and special trackwork components are assembled in track, they must be fastened to the ties. The simplest, most frequently used fastening system is the cut spike. The railway cut spike, or "dog" spike, dates back to 1830, and the first patent for a machine to produce the spikes dates to 1840. (The fishplate used to join rail ends was also designed around this time.) Although various fastening systems have been developed over the years, the cut spike remains the primary means of fixing rail to the ties, and despite modifications from time to time, it remains similar in shape and function to its ancestors. Current designs are typically 5½ to 6 inches long from the spike point to the underside of the spike head and 9/16 or 5/8 inches square in section. The body of a full-size finished spike is designed to withstand being bent cold through 120 degrees around a pin without cracking the outside of the bent portion.

Except for a period immediately after they are installed, cut spikes do not offer any real hold-down force on the rail. The rail remains upright because of its design and because the forces delivered by the vehicles are primarily downward forces. Rather, spikes serve to hold gauge and prevent lateral displacement of the rail. Elastic or resilient fasteners, on the other hand, exert a constant downward force on the base of the rail, holding it firmly in place. This positive downward force, or toe load, is beneficial in reducing mechanical wear in the tie/rail interface.

Since cut spikes provide no real hold-down force, they provide little if any vertical restraint once the track deflects under traffic. Cut spikes also provide little restraint against longitudinal rail movement, which can be caused by temperature changes and by rail creep, a result of the rolling wave action of the rail under traffic loads. Because of this rolling wave action, rail tends to move or creep in the predominant direction of traffic. The degree to which the rail creeps is also affected by accelerating or braking forces, locomotive tractive effort, and the rolling wave action caused by trains descending long grades.

Rail anchors combat longitudinal rail creep and are considered standard materials in cut-spike track. They are driven onto the base of the rail from one side of the rail, locked in place, and snugged up against the sides of the ties to resist longitudinal movement. Creep forces tend to cinch them tight against the ties, increasing their holding power over time. In CWR territory with cut spikes, AREMA recommendations are to box-anchor (one anchor on each side of the tie on both rails) alternating ties to prevent creepage and to restrain the rail in the event of a break.

Although cut spikes with rail anchors continue to be the primary fastening system in use on North American railroads, elastic fasteners, which hold the rails to the ties via a positive vertical hold-down force, have seen increasing usage. Unlike cut spikes, elastic fasteners provide a positive rail hold-down force that resists vertical, lateral, and longitudinal rail movement. The Pandrol e clip is the most widely used elastic rail fastener. Shaped like its namesake e, and made from high-quality spring-steel alloy with a 20-millimeter bar thickness, the e clip provides a nominal toe load of 2,750 pounds per clip and a nominal rail-seat clamping force of 5,500 pounds. This load is adequate to prevent longitudinal rail creep and eliminates the need for anchors in most applications. And since elastic fasteners hold the base of the rail more rigidly to the tie, they reduce gauge-widening lateral rail displacement. For this reason, elastic fasteners are frequently used to reduce gauge widening in curves. The clamping force provided by elastic fasteners also has been shown to resist rail rollover and the derailments that rail rollover can cause.

Elastic fasteners are standard on concrete- and steel-tie applications in which the fasteners clip into prefabricated or cast-in-place steel shoulders. In these types of installations nylon or thermoplastic insulators are placed between the toe of the clip and the base of the rail to provide electrical insulation and additional resistance to gauge widening. But elastic fasteners are also used on timber ties, typically with rolled or cast plates that are affixed to the ties with screw spikes to hold them firmly in place. With their greater resistance to horizontal, lateral, and vertical forces, elastic fasteners have been shown to increase gauge restraint and reduce the types of mechanical wear, such as plate cutting, that occur in the rail-seat area on timber-tie track.

Other fastening systems, such as the Pandrol Fastclip and the Safelock III, represent the most recent elastic fastener designs. These systems feature a captive fastening system in which all the necessary components—clips, shoulders, pads, and insulators—are preassembled on concrete ties before they are delivered to the field. These designs provide the same toe load and rail-seat clamping force as the noncaptive fastening systems in which the individual components are assembled in the field, but they simplify handling and track-construction or maintenance procedures.

One of the integral components of the fastening systems shipped with concrete ties is a rail-seat wear pad. Several years ago it was discovered that concrete ties that had been in track for only a few years exhibited various degrees of rail-seat abrasion, a condition in which the concrete under the base of the rail was being abraded by a combination of moisture and sand under the pumping action of repeated wheel loads. The problem was serious enough that hundreds of ties had to be repaired with an epoxy resin in the field. On the heels of this experience, fastener manufacturers developed a metal wear plate that is used between the rail and the rail-seat pad to alleviate the problem. In most freight applications wear plates are now standard issue.

Rail pads, which range in thickness from 5 to 10 millimeters, are made from polyurethane, ethylene vinyl acetate copolymer (EVA), rubber, or synthetic rubber, depending upon the application. They are installed in the rail seats to provide electrical insulation and to mitigate wear and reduce the impacts transferred from the rail to the concrete. A three-part system, which consists of a polyurethane pad, a steel antiabrasion plate, and a foam gasket, is designed to eliminate the potential for rail-seat abrasion on new concrete ties by sealing out dirt and water. This type of system is generally used in heavy-haul freight service in curves.

Grade Crossings

Another area in which designs and materials have evolved is at highway-rail grade crossings. Railroads have always had to contend with these intersections, but ever more so as vehicular traffic has increased. The establishment of the Highway Trust Fund in 1956 fueled the great highway boom, and along with more roads came more grade crossings and an emphasis on creating a smooth and safe means of crossing the tracks. To assist in this endeavor, the Federal Highway Act of 1976 authorized the financing of crossings on public streets. According to the U.S. Department of Transportation's Highway Safety Division, there are more than 250,000 active public and private grade crossings in the United States today.

This road/rail interface is one of the few areas that must accommodate both trains and vehicular traffic. As such, it must be designed to accommodate very different requirements. The track structure must be equivalent to open track in its ability to handle rail traffic, and it must provide a firm foundation for the crossing surface materials that allow vehicles to cross the tracks. In order to meet the demands of both highway and rail traffic, special attention is paid to the preparation of the track structure at these locations. Toward that end, AREMA has established guidelines for preparation of the ties, ballast, and rail at crossings and, more significantly, the roadbed and drainage conditions.

Providing good drainage conditions is paramount at crossings, because moisture tends to collect in the zone between the crossing surface material and the track structure. Consequently, railroads pay special attention to ensuring that crossings are well drained, frequently installing geosynthetic fabric beneath the ballast within the limits of the crossing and perforated drainpipe along the track shoulders.

Still, crossings are problematic. They tend to create transition zones—changes in track modulus—in track. They may be stiffer than open track when installed, and softer as traffic and tonnage take their toll. Compounding the difficulties inherent at crossings is that except on core main lines, crossings tend to see less track maintenance than the adjacent open track. Since the track and ballast section is not readily accessible at crossings, track-surfacing gangs, for example, tend to periodically skip over crossings during routine maintenance cycles. In some cases, where maintenance has been problematic and ensuring good ride quality through the crossing is essential for both rail and road, asphalt underlayment has been used to stiffen the crossing zone and provide a longer-lasting surface.

There have been many approaches to providing an acceptable driving surface that allows vehicles to cross the tracks. These have ranged from gravel to high-strength reinforced-concrete panels. Bituminous, hot-mix asphalt is the most commonly used crossing surface in use today. But in heavily used crossings asphalt is typically used in conjunction with steel (rail), timber (ties), or rubber headers that are spiked or otherwise fastened longitudinal to the rail to create and maintain an open flangeway. Header materials initially consisted of old rail sections and ties. These have been replaced in large measure by engineered rubber flangeways, or railseals, that match the contour of the rail web and maintain the proper flangeway widths through the crossing. Used in conjunction with asphalt, these designs provide an acceptable driving surface for vehicular traffic.

Patents for specialized grade-crossing surface designs date from the 1920s. Since that time premium surface materials have included steel, treated timber, virgin and recycled rubber, high-density polyethylene, and steel-reinforced concrete. Premium crossing materials consist of three primary pieces: gauge panels, which fit between the rails and create a flangeway, and two field panels, units that extend to the ends of the ties on the outside, or field side, of the rail. Preferences for material types have varied over the years, but the trend in recent years has been toward the use of steel-reinforced concrete. The move toward concrete has been led by the western railroads and driven by the need to be able to install (and remove and reinstall) crossing materials quickly on busy main lines. Concrete panels, which typically range in length from 8 to 12 feet, can be installed quickly. They can be lagged to the ties, or they can be left unfastened, held in place by their own weight of approximately 3,500 pounds for an 8-foot-long gauge panel. As in other areas of railway engineering, there is a move among the major railroads to standardize material and component designs and to establish common standards wherever possible.

This effort, which has been driven in part by consolidation within the industry, is expected to increase the availability and reduce the costs of common track components.

Track Inspection

To the untrained eye, railway track looks fixed, laid, and forgotten about, as permanent as the "permanent way" it is known as in other parts of the world. But those at all familiar with railways understand that the permanence of the permanent way is a direct result of maintenance-of-way—the cyclical inspection, maintenance, and renewal programs designed to combat wear and fatigue and maintain track to acceptable operating standards. Maintaining the nearly 200,000 miles of main line, yard tracks, and sidings on Class 1 railroads alone is a big, capital-intensive job. Class 1 capital expenditures for roadway and structures in 2001, for example, were nearly $4.5 billion.

Track maintenance begins with inspection. Like many of the advances that have taken place within the industry, inspection has evolved from visual inspection to quantitative, high-speed automated inspection of everything from surface and line to the internal condition of the rail. Although track inspectors still walk and visually inspect main-line track, they are armed with information gleaned from sophisticated inspection vehicles that regularly operate on primary lines.

One of the most common tools on main-line railroads is the track-geometry car. These cars are of two basic types: in-train and self-propelled (although units that can

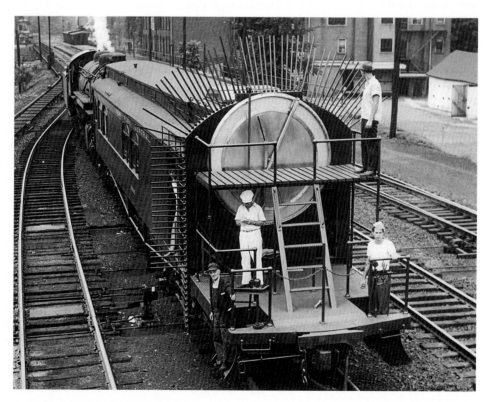

A specialized car for track maintenance was this New York Central car for verifying the clearance dimensions around the rail line to assure that equipment would clear.
—*Trains* Magazine Collection

Modern track inspection employs sophisticated equipment that continually records such data as track profile, gauge, cross-level, alignment, and surface, as well as the location of all defects for corrective maintenance. The Norfolk & Western's EM 80c track geometry car was at work testing the railroad's Shenandoah Division at Stuarts Draft, Virginia, in March 1981. —William D. Middleton

be towed by hi-rail vehicles also exist). Most geometry cars measure track surface and alignment, elevation, and gauge. Exceptions (parameters outside of acceptable track conditions) are marked with paint; a strip chart or list of exceptions identified by milepost is delivered to the local roadmaster or track engineer responsible for mainte- nance. In many cases the data can be stored and com- pared from one run to the next to measure the rate of track degradation. Using this information, track engi- neers can "predict" degradation rates and plan mainte- nance programs accordingly.

Although smaller, lighter hi-rail or self-propelled rail-

More than 10 feet wide, these whirling blades of a rotary snowplow took on the heaviest railroad snowfalls. This one, on the Denver & Rio Grande, worked in the Rockies west of Denver, with a separate steam engine to power the blades, while two steam locomotives propelled the plow through the drifts. —*Trains* Magazine Collection

bound track-inspection vehicles are more flexible in how they can be used, their ability to measure track under dynamic, or loaded, conditions is limited. The big 200,000-pound railbound track-geometry/inspection vehicles used on freight railways tend to generate a better picture of what the track actually looks like under traffic. The AAR in the late 1980s developed the Track Loading Vehicle (TLV) to better measure track strength. The TLV, a railbound vehicle that is coupled to a locomotive, incorporates a special split axle that can apply a lateral load to the rail at low speeds to measure the track's resistance to gauge-spreading forces. A similar design, known as the Gauge Restrain Measurement System (GRMS), has been adopted for use on the FRA's self-propelled track-geometry car, which is used to test track on lines with passenger service. Split-axle systems are also used on track-geometry cars in regular service on the major freight railroads.

More sophisticated geometry cars also can measure the shape and rotation of the railhead. Using laser or video technology, these can identify the size and weight of the rail and are used to measure rail-head and gauge-face wear and monitor the overall shape of the railhead as it wears. As with track-geometry data, this information can be stored and compared from run to run to determine the need for maintenance, such as rail grinding, or replacement.

With passage of the federal Railroad Safety Act of 1970, the FRA was given jurisdiction over track quality. This led to the establishment of minimum safety standards based upon inspections for roadbed and track structure and track geometry, with corresponding speed limits. State and federal inspectors can suspend operation over substandard track and impose monetary penalties for failure to correct reported track deficiencies. FRA speed limits have been established for nine classes of track, as shown in Table 1.

Among the most sophisticated of all is Amtrak's 10002 Track Geometry Car (TGC), which records track-geometry, ride-quality, and rail-profile measurements, among other information, while moving at speeds up to 125 mph on Amtrak's high-speed Northeast Corridor. The next-generation TGC 10003 is recording these and additional parameters at speeds up to 150 mph. On its Class 8–9 track (allowing speeds up to 200 mph for passenger trains), Amtrak tests at a frequency of twice every 60 days. Amtrak also operates the GRMS at speeds up to 50 mph at least once per year on its Class 8–9 track.

Another type of inspection that is critical to track maintenance is rail-flaw detection. Rail flaws, such as transverse defects, detail fractures, and horizontal and vertical split heads, come in many shapes and sizes. Internal defects typically propagate. Left undetected, defects tend to break out in dramatic fashion, often resulting in derailments. Although rail is ultrasonically inspected for defects before it is shipped from the mill, there is no assurance that it will remain defect free under traffic. Internal defects that are hidden ¼ inch or more within the railhead cannot be seen until wear exposes them. In other

Table 1. Federal Railroad Administration (FRA) Track Standards

Track Classification	Maximum Speed Limits	
	Freight	Passenger
Class 1: Yard, branch line, short line, and industrial spurs	10 mph	15 mph
Class 2: Branch lines, secondary main lines, and many regional railroads	25 mph	30 mph
Class 3: Commonly used for Class 1 secondary main lines and regional railroads	40 mph	60 mph
Class 4: Dominant class used in main-line and long-haul freight	60 mph	80 mph
Class 5: Standard for most high-speed track	80 mph	90 mph
Class 6: Used exclusively on Amtrak Northeast Corridor	110 mph	110 mph
Class 7: Amtrak Northeast Corridor passenger		125 mph
Class 8: Specific sections of Northeast Corridor passenger		160 mph
Class 9: Passenger (future)		200 mph

cases fatigue-related defects are initiated by impacts caused by flat wheels or wheel burns in the rail. Shelling, a disintegration of the rail surface that typically occurs at the gauge corner of the high rail in curves, and plastic deformation of the rail head, a result of repeated, heavy loadings, are typical of the fatigue-related defects commonly found in track today.

The means to detect internal defects before rails failed in service was developed by Elmer A. Sperry, and the first detector car was placed into service in 1928. This car relied on an induction process in which a current was passed through the rail. When a flaw was encountered, the current's flux pattern was distorted, indicating a defect. Ultrasonic rail-flaw-detection equipment, developed in the 1950s and currently available from several manufacturers, is most commonly used today. These systems use a series of transducers that scan the rail through a beam of electro-acoustic energy. Discontinuities in the beam indicate potential defects. The accuracy of these systems depends in part on the size of the defect and the percentage of the railhead that it encompasses. Accuracy also depends on the surface cleanliness of the rail, because defects are difficult to detect under greasy, surface-damaged, or extremely worn rail.

Although the primary purpose of rail-flaw detection is to find defects before they "blow up" in track, the data also can be a preventive-maintenance tool. If the number of defects detected per mile reaches an unacceptable threshold, for example, maintenance planners may elect to replace the rail. This information, used in conjunction with rail-profile data from geometry or specialized rail-inspection cars, enables track engineers to plan rail-profile grinding or other rail-maintenance programs.

Rail maintenance once consisted of ensuring that rail

joints were adequately spaced and joint bars securely fastened. Defect detection was always important, as was monitoring the rail surface for wear to plan rail renewals, particularly in curves. Until fairly recently it was a common practice to transpose the rails in curves, which entailed moving the superelevated high rail to the low position, and the low rail to the high position, at an optimal time in their wear cycle. Depending on the wear pattern, curve rails might be transposed because of gauge-face wear on the high rail or railhead flow on the low rail. Although this technique effectively extended the useful life of jointed or welded rail in curves, the procedure essentially has been discontinued because better rail steels and improved maintenance techniques, such as rail-profile grinding, have enabled railroads to use the available life of the rail while it is in its first position.

Rail grinding has been a staple of maintenance programs for many years. Early grinders were designed to remove surface corrugations and rail-end batter associated with softer rail steels. Modern rail steels and more effective lubrication programs have solved much of that problem, but corrugation still occurs, primarily in the head of low rails in curves. Current grinding techniques effectively control corrugation, as well as shelling and fatigue, gauge-face wear, and metal flow on the low rails of curves. Profile grinding is also used to remove fatigue cracks that develop at the surface and subsurface of the rail. Since normal wear rates are not sufficient in most cases to remove these cracks, artificial wear in the form of rail grinding must be introduced.

Rail-profile grinding programs are designed to remove only as much metal as necessary to maintain a "healthy" rail surface condition. This condition is achieved by obtaining what is known as the "magic wear rate," a state of balance between sufficient and insufficient wear. Too much wear results in reduced rail life; too little wear allows surface fatigue cracks to propagate and cause fatigue failures.

Contemporary rail grinders incorporate a multitude of grinding stones with variable motors that contact the rail at various angles to remove the appropriate amount of metal—usually between 0.002 and 0.008 inches—and to produce the desired shape. Loram's RG 48, for example, uses 48 grinding modules generating 30 hp each to grind and shape the rail at speeds up to 15 mph. Grinding frequency depends on the depth of the cracks and the overall condition of the rail surface and is typically based on the number of million gross tons (MGT) that the track sees. Railroads such as Burlington Northern Santa Fe, which employs an aggressive preventive-maintenance grinding program, may schedule grinding as frequently as every 10 to 20 MGT.

Another aspect of rail maintenance in which inspection and high-quality materials and methods are essential is rail welding. As a whole, Class 1 railroads installed nearly 625,000 tons of new rail and 235,000 tons of secondhand rail, typically used on secondary lines or yard tracks, in 2001. The bulk of the rail installed is CWR, which includes many plant and field welds. Plant welds are uniformly the electric flash butt type in which the rail ends are heated and fused. Since no foreign materials are introduced, these welds produce strong, maintenance-free bonds. Mobile flash butt welders are also used in the field, particularly in conjunction with rail renewal projects.

Like stationary plant welders, mobile flash butt welders must accurately match the rail ends to preserve the symmetry of the rail throughout the length of the strings. If the rail ends are not perfectly aligned, the entire rail profile must be ground. Proper alignment and weld integrity are ensured by precise techniques and computer monitoring of the welding process on these mobile machines.

In Plasser & Theurer's APT 600 mobile flash butt welder, for example, the welding head is positioned between the bogies of the four-axle, railbound machine. The rail ends are gripped and aligned by a pulling device, and the welding head, which is mounted on a telescopic jib crane, is moved into place. The rail is pulled as necessary to account for the steel that is upset, or consumed, during the welding process. An integrated hydraulic rail-tensioning device that pulls the rail can also be used to produce closure welds and maintain the rail's neutral temperature. Upset metal is sheared in one cutting action to leave all surfaces of the rail free of seams. An onboard computer analyzes and records data relating to all parameters of the process, ensuring the quality of the welds.

Although most of the major railroads own or contract the use of mobile flash butt welders, the vast majority of their maintenance work requires the use of aluminothermic, or thermite, welds. Unlike electric flash butt welds, which use no additives to fuse rail ends, thermite welds are produced by a chemical reaction of aluminum with a metal oxide. Developed at the turn of the twentieth century, the thermite weld is the standard maintenance weld in the industry. Its popularity stems from the fact that it can be made with a standard kit, which includes a crucible that clamps to the rail and straddles the gap (typically 1 inch) between the rails that are being welded and the fully consumable welding material. Thermite welds are typically used to repair the track when breaks occur, or whenever defects are cut out of the rail. In many cases repair requires the installation of a plug rail, which requires two welds to install in track. Consequently, the number of field welds in track proliferates over time.

Since thermite welds introduce foreign materials that are typically softer than the parent rail steel, they are commonly regarded as weak links in the track. A rash of failures that occurred with the onset of heavy-axle-load testing at the TTCI in the late 1980s generated a wave of concern

A long string of mechanized maintenance machinery carries out the replacement of old jointed rail by welded rail on the Louisville & Nashville Railroad south of Lafayette, Indiana, in September 1980. A Burro crane threads new 115-pound rail onto the track (*above*). A rail displacer sets out the string of the old bolted rail (*below*). —William D. Middleton (both)

A gauger-spiking machine follows the new string of rail to set it in place (*top*). A rail heater, which heats rail between 93 and 94°F to control expansion and contraction, follows the large spiker (*center*). An anchor machine follows the rail heater to set new anchors at every fourth tie (*bottom*). —William D. Middleton

throughout the industry. Welding procedures and materials have improved since then, but in the heavy-tonnage, high-density operations that prevail on the major railroads, track-maintenance personnel are eager for further improvements. Thermite weld hardness, for example, now approaches 341 Bhn, the low end of the hardness range of premium rail steels, but is well below the 400 Bhn range of some of the harder premium rails in use. When used to join harder rails, the welds create soft spots that are prone to metal flow and fatigue under traffic, particularly under heavy axle loads. Improved materials with head-hardened thermite portions are being tested.

Modern Tie Maintenance

As with rail maintenance, increasingly sophisticated inspection tools have enabled track engineers to better plan tie- and ballast-maintenance and renewal programs. With more than half a billion crossties in track and nearly 12 million or more annually laid in replacement on Class 1 railroads alone, tie maintenance and renewal are high-priority programs. Railroads determine their annual tie programs based on a number of factors, including geometry-car data, tie inspectors' defective-tie counts, and the number of slow orders on a given section of track.

Tie renewals are typically scheduled well in advance of the work, because ties and other track material (OTM) must be distributed in the field, and work gangs and equipment must be scheduled. In most cases the ties in a given section do not wear out at the same time. The number of defective ties per mile determines whether a portion of the tie population is replaced or all the ties in a given segment are replaced out-of-face. These decisions are based upon minimum requirements dictated by the FRA's Track Safety Standards and by the level of service required by the railroad. Differing levels of equipment and manpower are required, depending on the replacement approach.

One of the keys to successful maintenance programs is providing adequate work windows—track time. In instances in which track time is at a premium, railroads sometimes use small, lightweight off-trackable maintenance-of-way equipment that can be quickly lifted on or off the track to clear for trains. High-production gangs that can insert more than 1,000 ties per day, on the other hand, typically require undisturbed work windows of several hours or more for efficiency. In some cases railroads have opted to perform a maintenance blitz in which trains are rerouted and the track shut down for days on end for round-the-clock maintenance work.

Before mechanization, tie renewal was performed by teams of laborers with claw bars, spike mauls, and rail tongs. For many years system track gangs were housed in camp cars set in sidings close to the work site. Although these cars served their purpose, they have been all but abandoned, and railroads have opted instead to house track crews at motels near the tie-up locations. And although laborers using some of these same hand tools are still in evidence today, tie-renewal programs now depend on a fleet of automated equipment, such as spike and anchor applicators/removers, tie and tie-plate handlers, scarifiers, and other specialized equipment. Tie unloading alone has progressed from laborers dropping ties one at a time over the sides of gondolas to mechanized equipment such as Herzog Contracting Corp.'s Cartopper. This

Until well after World War II, maintenance-of-way was labor intensive. Working in unison, an Indian section gang lifted a heavy rail into place at Cajon, California, on the Santa Fe in March 1943.
—Library of Congress, Jack Delano photograph (Neg. LC-USW3-22234-D)

At Needles, California, a Santa Fe Indian maintenance crew joined forces to shift steel rails in March 1943. —Library of Congress, Jack Delano photograph (Neg. LC-USW3-21392-E)

High-capacity mechanical equipment has transformed modern maintenance-of-way work. This ballast regulator moves crushed rock ballast into position. —Bill Gale Photography, Inc., *Trains* Magazine Collection

system uses a tie-handler crane that rides along the tops of gondolas, moving from car to car to unload ties onto the right of way as the work train moves along the track. The crane, which is equipped with an electromagnet coupling, can also unload plates, spikes, and anchors by the bundle.

During tie-renewal operations spent ties are removed whole when possible; more frequently, however, they are removed in pieces. Cuts are made at the inside edges of the tie plates so that the center section can be lifted out and the end sections pushed clear of the track. Before insertion of a new tie, loose ballast is removed from the tie cavity, and hard-packed ballast that has formed under plate-cut ties is scarified, or broken up.

Tie-installation procedures and equipment vary from railroad to railroad, depending on the scope of the project. Most railroads plan and execute tie renewals with their own work gangs and equipment, but others, such as BNSF, have adopted another approach in which an equipment supplier (Harsco Track Technologies, in this case) owns and maintains all the equipment used in the gangs, while the railroad supplies the labor. This concept, dubbed Tie Masters, was patterned after BNSF's power-by-the-mile agreements with locomotive manufacturers and gives the equipment supplier management responsibility for tie-renewal and related surfacing work. Interest in this approach is growing.

Concrete-tie programs differ from timber-tie renewals in that they typically are handled like new construction, which requires more specialized equipment, such as Harsco's P811 or New Track Construction (NTC) machines. (The P811 operates on the existing rails, while the NTC incorporates a crawler that operates on a prepared roadbed.) In these systems concrete ties are delivered from specially designed cars via a conveyor system and dropped into place on the roadbed. Rail pads are placed in the rail seats between the steel shoulders, and the rail (which typically is new) is threaded into the rail seats. The rail is heated to obtain the proper neutral temperature and then is mechanically clipped into place by automated applicators. Tamping, surfacing, and track-stabilizing equipment typically follows.

Modern Ballast Maintenance

Done on its own or in conjunction with tie- or rail-renewal programs, ballast maintenance is key to keeping the track structure in proper trim. No matter how effective the track structure may be, however, tonnage and environmental factors cause track geometry to deteriorate over time. The frequency of ballasting and surfacing operations—the process of restoring track to the desired profile by lifting and tamping—was once based on fixed cycles or on inspectors' observations of the ride quality and geometry of the track. The observations were informed, but subjective. The Railroad Safety Act of 1970 changed all that. With the act came the FRA Track Safety Standards, which established minimum inspection and maintenance requirements that railroads must meet, depending on the class of track, which is determined by the maximum allowable speeds for freight and passenger service. Although compliance with the Track Safety Standards is mandatory (with fines levied for infractions), most railroads plan their surfacing and other ballast-maintenance programs to meet their operating needs. And although the inspector's eye remains valuable, it has been supplanted by the detailed geometry-car data that are used to plan maintenance programs today.

Evidence of past ballast maintenance is readily apparent in some areas, seen as successive layers of ballast set to grade high above the roadbed. With lifts typically ranging from 1 to 6 inches, surfacing requires new ballast—and lots of it. According to an annual survey of capital programs conducted by *Railway Track and Structures*, seven major railroads planned to surface nearly 35,000 miles of track in 2003. Norfolk Southern alone planned to surface nearly 5,000 miles of track. Although ballast has not changed much since the earliest days of railroading, the equipment used to deliver and distribute it is light years from the horse-drawn wagons that were used to haul and dump ballast during the construction of the transcontinental railroad.

Distributing the right amount of ballast in the right place is an important part of ballast-maintenance operations. The horse-drawn wagon has given way to hoppers or specialized ballast cars with bottom-mounted doors that can direct the flow of ballast between the rails or toward the shoulders for distribution. Ballast doors were operated manually by laborers with pry bars at first. Electrically controlled, pneumatically powered gates have reduced the amount of labor required. More significantly, these types of powered gates can be opened remotely, reducing workers' exposure to silica dust. Further enhancements have enabled railroads to accurately distribute ballast based on preprogrammed Global Positioning System (GPS) data. This approach allows for accurate stone placement and eliminates the tendency to spill ballast in locations where it is not needed, such as grade crossings and bridge approaches. Herzog's Programmable Linear Unloading System (PLUS) train, for example, represents the state of the art in ballast-unloading systems. Using preprogrammed GPS-based surveys, the PLUS train is able to unload ballast at speeds up to 20 mph with one operator in the cab and no personnel on the ground.

Once ballast has been unloaded, it is plowed and trimmed to a uniform depth—depending on the anticipated lift—before the ties are tamped and the track raised to the desired height. (In areas in which overhead clearances are fixed, such as tunnels and track with overhead catenary, tie-renewal, tamping, and surfacing operations must be completed without lifting the track or altering the top-of-rail elevation.)

Tamping, the process of compacting the ballast beneath the ties to provide an adequate load-bearing area, is performed on a spot and out-of-face basis. Spot tamping is done to shore up low or other types of weak spots in track, such as switches, crossing diamonds, and battered rail joints, between surfacing cycles. Out-of-face tamping is done in conjunction with large-scale tie-renewal and surfacing operations that cover miles of track. The earliest tampers were the trains themselves. Enough ballast was shoveled and packed into the tie beds to allow for the settlement generated by "train tamping," the process of running trains over the track at slow speeds until the track is consolidated. The ability to anticipate how much lift was needed to account for track settlement was gained only through experience. Train tamping is still used to some degree to consolidate the ballast after large-scale maintenance operations in which the ballast has been disturbed, particularly on smaller railroads that do not have access to modern ballast-consolidating equipment.

Combination Tamping and Ties

Because much of a railroad's ability to consistently operate trains at acceptable speeds depends on its ability to maintain track geometry, there has been a great emphasis on the use of machinery that can accomplish a lot with the least amount of track time. Toward that end, maintenance-of-way equipment suppliers have developed very efficient and very sophisticated tamping and combination tamping/track-stabilizing machines. These range from machines that tamp one tie at a time to continuous-action tampers that tamp several ties simultaneously.

The typical workhorse single-tie production and switch tampers in use today (best characterized by Harsco's Mark IV and Mark VI tampers) incorporate 16 tamping tools that are hydraulically driven by four or eight motors that vibrate the tools at 3,000 to 4,500 vibrations per minute. The tamping tines are inserted into the ballast at the tie on either side of each rail from a point 12 inches inside each rail to the ends of the ties on both sides of the track. Tamping one tie at a time, these machines can tamp up to 2,600 feet per hour. (They can also tamp through switches.) These machines also incorporate automated track-lifting devices that grip the base or ball of the rail and produce enough jacking power to accommodate up to 6 inches of lining offset or superelevation. Guided by laser-lining devices, these machines lift the track to a predetermined height and then squeeze the ballast up and under the ties to hold the track in its raised position.

At one time track was lined by hand and eye. One member of the lining crew would sight down the track several rail lengths beyond the point at which the lining operation began, identifying the last rail in a lie that was straight and true. The rest of the crew would nudge the next rail with lining bars into proper location. As rails were laid and lined, they became guides for the next rails. Later, more precise lining machines that incorporated a wire or beam of light with a target to sight the proper line were used. The advent of CWR used in place of jointed, 39-foot rails has simplified the lining process. Use of the computerized, laser-lining function that has been incorporated into most modern tampers has further improved the process.

Faster, more powerful continuous-action tampers are used by most of the major railroads as part of their major rail- and tie-renewal and surfacing gangs. The lifting and tamping units on these machines are mounted on a satellite frame that moves independently of the main frame, indexing from tie to tie while the main frame moves at a constant pace down the track. With the ability to tamp three ties at a time, continuous-action tampers can tamp up to 29 ties per minute. The most recent of these machines, Plasser's 09-16 DYNA C.A.T., for example, also incorporate a dynamic track stabilizer, further reducing the number of machines and operators required for high-production tie and surfacing operations.

Although tamping is performed to solidify the ballast under the ties, the process actually disrupts and loosens the compaction of the rock around the ties. As a result, the ballast section must be reconsolidated after tamping. This is done in some cases through train tamping, a process in which a fixed number of trains or amount of tonnage is operated at incrementally increasing speeds until the track is fully consolidated and the speed restrictions are removed. In other cases ballast consolidation is achieved more quickly through the use of a ballast compactor or dynamic track stabilizer.

The dynamic track stabilizer essentially grasps the outside surface of the rail with a number of flanged rollers that vibrate the track at up to 45 Hz. The combination of horizontal vibration and vertical loading provided by the stabilizer simulates the action created by train traffic and reconsolidates the ballast in a fraction of the time required by train tamping. In some instances the track can be returned to design speeds after the passage of only a few trains.

Ballast Cleaning

No matter how much attention it receives, ballast breaks down over time. Breakdown is caused by a number of factors, including mechanical wear from traffic loadings, freeze/thaw cycles, and particle damage caused by repeated tamping cycles. These, combined with wind-blown dirt and sand, coal or other materials falling from cars, or fines that migrate upward from the subgrade or subballast, all contribute to ballast fouling. Once ballast becomes fouled, it can no longer drain water from the track structure, and no amount of tamping or surfacing will enable it to hold surface and line. When this occurs, more drastic measures are in order, such as shoulder ballast cleaning, undercutting, or "sledding," a process in which the track is lifted clear and the ballast is scraped from the roadbed, cleaned, and returned with new ballast to which the track is tamped.

Shoulder ballast cleaning is the least invasive ballast-cleaning measure. This approach is used on a spot basis to break open mud pockets, release trapped water, and restore drainage. Equipment such as Loram's self-propelled High Performance Shoulder Ballast Cleaner uses twin 30-inch-wide buckets to dig fouled ballast up to 16 inches below the top of a tie, from the tie ends to the edge of the ballast section. A conveyor transfers up to 2,000 pounds of excavated ballast per hour to a series of shaker screens that clean the ballast and dispose of the fines. Cleaned ballast is returned, and the shoulders are reprofiled.

When ballast is fouled to the degree that shoulder cleaning is not enough, ballast-undercutting/cleaning operations are often performed. Undercutter/cleaners excavate ballast from the shoulders and from beneath the track. In this process a cutting bar with hardened steel teeth is inserted beneath the track. With cutting depths that range from 6½ inches to more than 12 inches beneath the bottoms of the ties, these machines are capable of undercutting up to 600 feet per hour. The fouled ballast is carried via conveyor belt to shaker/cleaner screens. Cleaned ballast, along with new ballast, is returned to the track; spoils are discharged along the right of way or dumped into cars for unloading. Various systems have been designed to handle spoils and to add new ballast to the track after undercutting. Track gangs follow undercutting operations to dress the track and establish the proper geometry.

In CWR territory the appropriate neutral rail temperature must be reestablished whenever ballast is disturbed. Research has shown the importance of reestablishing the lateral track strength associated with tie/ballast interaction as soon as possible. Single-tie push tests indicate that the lateral strength of track that has just been tamped is about 1,000 pounds per tie—one-third to one-half that of strong, undisturbed track.

Vegetation Control

Another factor that affects ballast and overall track conditions is vegetation—the weeds that grow in and along the right of way of every railroad. Track, with its dependence on effectively draining ballast and subgrade sections, can be compromised by the unmanaged growth of plants in drainage paths. Vegetation control also minimizes fire hazards and maintains good visibility along the right of way. Most railroads employ a combination of mechanical brush-cutting methods to control growth and application of preemergent herbicides to stop vegetation growth before it becomes a problem.

Vegetation control is performed for the most part on a contract basis. Track-mounted machines generally cut back brush to a clearance envelope of 22 to 30 feet from the centerline of track. In sensitive areas, such as the approaches to highway-rail grade crossings, brush is cut more aggressively to provide unobscured sight lines for train crews and motorists. Since the effectiveness of preemergent herbicides is dependent upon rainfall for application (not to mention local regulations), weed-spraying programs require more planning. And since the major railroads operate in several geographic regions, they tend to work with regional contractors.

The use of contract services has increased in other areas of maintenance-of-way as well. Although railroads once performed virtually all their own engineering and maintenance—each with their own standards and practices—they have begun to do more out-of-house on a contract basis. This trend extends even to the most essential aspects of maintenance, such as major tie and surfacing programs, in some cases. In all cases, however, the effects of concentrating more traffic on fewer core lines (up to 180 million gross tons per year—a lifetime of tonnage in an earlier era) have forced engineering and maintenance-of-way departments to become more efficient builders and maintainers of track. This, in turn, has pushed railway suppliers to build longer-lasting components and faster, more efficient, less labor-intensive machines. Where these trends will take railway maintenance remains to be seen. Regardless of the direction, however, the practices of railway trackmen will remain inextricably linked to those that preceded them.

—Robert E. Tuzik

REFERENCES

Ambrose, Stephen. *Nothing like It in the World.* New York: Simon & Schuster, 2000.

American Railway Engineering and Maintenance of Way Assn. *Manual for Railway Engineering.* Washington, D.C.: American Railway Engineering and Maintenance of Way Assn., 2003.

American Railway Engineering Assn. *Manual for Railway Engineering.* Washington, D.C.: American Railway Engineering Assn., 1988.

Armstrong, John. *The Railroad, What It Is, What It Does.* 4th ed. Omaha, Nebr.: Simmons-Boardman, 1998.

Assn. of American Railroads Policy and Communications Department—Track. *Progressive Railroading Track Yearbook, 2002–2003.*

Goddard, Stephen. *Getting There.* New York: HarperCollins, 1994.

Schulte, Christopher. *Dictionary of Railway Track Terms.* Omaha, Nebr.: Simmons-Boardman, 1990.

The Track Cyclopedia. Omaha, Nebr.: Simmons-Boardman, 1985.

Maintenance-of-Way Machinery

Traditionally, track walkers did track inspection, and maintenance was performed by section gangs. Tools of the trade included shovels, crowbars, mallets, pickaxes, tie tongs, and jacks. With these tools, tracks were built, adjusted, and repaired. Well beyond the mid-twentieth century this was still the case, and large section gangs engaged in the routine maintenance-of-way. In a 1926 railway track and maintenance handbook, for example, typical section gangs covered anywhere from 4 to 12 miles of track, and the workforce ranged anywhere from 3 to 12 men in each gang during the heavy spring maintenance season.

The growing cost of labor, however, combined with advances in technology, resulted in the gradual mechanization of railway maintenance. Today a handful of men operating specialized machines can accomplish the same tasks that once required dozens working on a section gang. Track-maintenance tools now include a wide range of sophisticated and highly productive self-propelled spike

pullers and spike inserters, tie cranes, tie extractors and inserters, ballast regulators, tampers, and ballast cleaners, and a variety of railway inspection vehicles.

Ballast Regulators

A ballast regulator is designed for the localized distribution and sculpting of ballast. Many railroads once used large Jordan Spreaders for this task. Oswald F. Jordan developed the Jordan Spreader in the early twentieth century, and it was a universal tool in railroad maintenance. The Jordan Spreader consisted of an adjustable front plow and large adjustable blades on extendable wings. The early Jordans used pneumatic cylinders to control the blades and wings, but later machines used hydraulic controls. A variety of specialty attachments could be connected to the wings. In addition to ballast spreading, Jordans found work as ditch-digging machines and snowplows. They were not self-propelled and required one or more locomotives for propulsion.

Most of the Jordan machines were manufactured in East Chicago, Illinois, until Jackson Vibrators bought the Jordan company in 1964. Jordan-Jackson later became Pandrol-Jackson, one of several companies merged to form Harsco Track Technologies, based in Cayce–West Columbia, South Carolina, which is now one of the largest producers of railway-maintenance equipment in the United States.

Contemporary ballast regulators are self-propelled machines generally in the control of a single operator. A typical machine has three types of tools: an angled front-end plow used for moving and spreading ballast, side-mounted ballast boxes used for sculpting, and a rotary broom used to sweep away excess ballast. Among the companies that have built modern ballast regulators are Harsco Track Technologies and its predecessor companies, Plasser American Corp. of Chesapeake, Virginia (since 1961 the American subsidiary of the Austrian-based Plasser & Theurer), Knox Kershaw of Montgomery, Alabama, and Nordco of Milwaukee, Wisconsin. One feature of modern ballast regulators and some other types of unidirectional self-propelled track equipment is a built-in turntable that allows for the rotation of equipment.

Tampers

Track tamping is the process of squeezing ballast under the ties to improve stability. It is typically combined with the straightening of tracks. Section gangs used jacks and rods to tamp track by hand. A modern mechanized tamper uses automatically controlled, hydraulically powered tamping tools, four pairs of them for each rail. These tools oscillate very rapidly in order to liquefy ballast when they are thrust into the ground on either side of a tie around the rail. Once the tools reach the proper depth, they automatically squeeze together in a scrunching motion, pushing ballast up under the tie below the rail to provide support. More elaborate tampers are designed for surfacing work and are

An example of modern maintenance machinery is this productive Harsco Mark IV track tamper, photographed at Hawkins, Wisconsin, in 2000. —Brian Solomon

Also at work at Hawkins was this mechanized ballast regulator. —Brian Solomon

equipped with jacks to lift and line track vertically and horizontally. These machines use a trusslike frame for support during lifting actions. To straighten track, tampers use triangulation principles and project an infrared beam ahead of the machine. Harsco Track Technologies manufactures a line of tampers that were originated by the old Tamper company (later Fairmont-Tamper). Plasser American Corp. began selling tampers to the American market in 1957. The earliest of these were imported from Europe. Today Plasser produces a variety of tampers, including massive production tampers used for rapid working on lines where only short work windows are available for maintenance. This type is more common in Europe than in the United States, but they are used by Amtrak on the Northeast Corridor, which has maintenance requirements similar to those of European high-speed, high-capacity lines.

Spike Pullers

A variety of machines are used in tandem with each other and other machines on steel gangs that realign, re-

place, or renew track. A spike puller is a relatively simple self-propelled machine, typically with an open-air cab designed for a single operator. The operator directs hydraulically operated spike-removal carriages that use a steel jaw to reach down, grip, and remove a spike from the tie. The most modern and advanced spike pullers use computers to aid the operator. A spike puller should work as quickly as possible in order to be effective. Many machines are set up to work on one side of the track and may work in pairs, with one machine working each rail. Some machines are designed for two operators, and these can remove spikes from both rails simultaneously. Nordco and Harsco are the primary suppliers of spike pullers.

Tie Machines

Once spikes have been removed, ties can be replaced. Ties are removed by tie extractors and replaced by tie inserters. Tie cranes are used to place ties in strategic locations along the right of way and remove old ties from the line once they have been extracted. Before mechanization, replacing a tie could take 30 minutes or more; now it can be done in seconds. A small tie extractor is a self-propelled single-operator machine. To remove a tie, the operator attaches clamps to the rails, lifts the track using jacks, and directs a telescoping boom to grip a tie from the end and pluck it from the track structure. Ties are replaced with similar equipment that works in reverse order. The most complex and elaborate tie extractors/tie inserters are massive track-relaying machines that are designed to lift old ties and rail while simultaneously laying new concrete ties with welded rail in one continuous operation.

Spike Inserters

Spike inserters may require up to three operators, one to drive the machine and insert spikes on one side of the track, one to insert spikes on the opposite side, and a third to attend to new spikes being fed into the chutes that deliver them to the driving equipment. The machine uses clamps to grip the track, and gauging equipment ensures that rails are separated precisely at the correct width. Ties are held in place and tight to the rails with claws. The operators direct the location of the spikes, which are then pounded into place with automatic rams.

Another machine, known as an anchor-boxer, automatically clips rail anchors in place. Rail anchors are used to keep rail from lengthwise sliding. They are especially important with welded rail and help keep it in place during heat-related expansion and contraction. Welded rail must be heated to a specific temperature when it is installed so that it will not buckle when temperatures rise. Rail-warming machines using banks of propane heaters are used to heat rail after it has been gauged and spiked, but before an anchor-boxer anchors it in place. Failure to do this properly can result in heat kinks, which can easily derail a train (*See* MAINTENANCE-OF-WAY, "Rail").

Ballast Cleaners and Undercutters

Ballast is designed to give track proper drainage. Over time ballast becomes soiled with debris, which clogs it and prevents it from functioning properly. If this situation is left unchecked, track can became waterlogged, undermining track structure and causing further deterioration. Ballast cleaners are machines that dig up ballast and sift away particulates and other soiling material. One type of ballast-cleaning machine is the shoulder cleaner. These dig up and clean ballast on the edge of tracks. Although only a third of the ballast is cleaned directly, this will unblock the ballast structure and improve drainage, allowing it to function as intended. Once drainage has been restored, the ballast between ties will naturally flush away remaining debris. A shoulder cleaner is an excavating machine that moves at slow speeds while it digs up ballast on both sides of the track. Soiled ballast is dumped into bins with vibrating screens, which sift away dirt. The cleaned ballast is then redeposited along the tracks, and dirt is put into hoppers or thrown from the track area by way of conveyors. Usually an area of ballast about two feet wide and six inches deep is excavated from the sides of the track.

When ballast needs to be removed either because it has become so fouled that it is no longer effective and has begun to break down, or the track structure needs to be lowered, undercutting machines are used to remove ballast from below the ties, as well as alongside. There are several basic types of undercutters. One common type uses a continuous chain placed below tracks that scoops away ballast. Some ballast cleaners combine shoulder-cleaning and undercutting work.

Loram Maintenance of Way Inc. of Hamel, Minnesota, has been contracting ballast-cleaning work since the steam era. Another traditional ballast-cleaning company was Speno Rail Services of East Syracuse, New York, which was taken over in the 1990s by Pandrol-Jackson, now a component of Harsco Technologies.

Another type of earthmoving machine is the ditch digger, which is used for constructing line-side ditches that direct water away from tracks. In earlier times men dug ditches with shovels or a specially equipped Jordan Spreader. Today, companies such as Loram build specialized rail-based ditching machines. Loram's Badger Ditch Digger is named for the furry and rapidly burrowing animal. This self-propelled machine uses two adjustable arms, one of which is equipped with a high-speed digging wheel, the other with a conveyor to remove earth, debris, and water from the site of the ditch. This machine can reach up to 18 feet from the track center and dig a drainage ditch up to 4 feet deep.

Rail Grinders

The force of steel wheels on steel rails results in friction that is damaging to both. The greater the speed, weight, and frequency of trains over a set of tracks, the more rapidly rail wears out. Hunting motion (lateral travel) causes wear on tangent track. Curved track suffers from uneven wearing as wheels gouge the outside rail. As rail is damaged, it alters the ideal contact surface between rail and wheel, which further exacerbates the problem. One solution to the problem is to replace rail. However, to extend rail life, an alternative is corrective rail grinding, which is done to reprofile the rail to the ideal shape. Modern rail-grinding techniques have taken this a step further and introduced preventive rail grinding, which is done on a scheduled basis to prevent defects before they occur and improve locomotive traction. Rail grinding has become a specialized art that is especially important to contemporary freight-hauling lines that use sophisticated wheel-slip control to achieve extremely high adhesion. This technology can take its toll on rail surfaces.

Rail grinding has long been an area of railroad maintenance handled by contract providers. Speno and Loram, also known for their ballast cleaners, were names closely associated with rail grinding. Locomotives powered Speno's production rail grinders. The biggest of these trains, known by the letters RMS (Rail Maintenance System), was self-contained and carried its own crew, who lived on the train. It used 120 rail-grinding heads to profile the rail. In addition, it carried more than 40,000 gallons of water used for fire prevention. Water is necessary because the grinding process produces a continual stream of hot sparks, which, if they escape from the machine, can ignite wildfires. Harsco Track Technologies now produces a variety of rail grinders commercially. Harsco's modern machines, such as the PGM-48, are a vast improvement over the dirty machines used in years past and provide crews with climate-controlled pressurized operators' stations. These machines, while designed for track grinding production, have fewer heads than the massive machines used for contract work. Loram has also introduced modern rail grinders, which use computer technology for profiling and rail-surface analysis. Modern grinders may measure rail shaving down to $1/1000$ of an inch.

—Brian Solomon

REFERENCE

Solomon, Brian. *Railway Maintenance Equipment.* Osceola, Wis.: MBI Publishing Company, 2001.

Mallet, Anatole (1837–1919)

Jules T. Anatole Mallet was born near Geneva, Switzerland, on May 23, 1837. Early in his life his family moved to France, where Mallet did most of his work. He attended the École Centrale des Arts et Manufactures in Paris and later taught there. He died in Paris on October 10, 1919, at age 82. Although Mallet's name is closely connected with railroads, he worked with Lesseps on the Suez Canal around 1867.

Mallet was best known for his dedication to compounding. His first essay in this area was a two-cylinder 0-4-2T, #2, named *Anglet* and built by Schneider at Le Creusot for the Bayonne-Biarritz Railway. It was not the first compound locomotive, but it was the first of "continuous history."

Mallet's idea of two-cylinder compounds was copied or exported to Russia and Germany. He was granted a patent for the articulated compound in 1884; the first example appeared in 1887, built in Belgium for Decauville of light-railway fame. The idea was seen at first as a way of packing punch into relatively small machines on lighter railways, but the idea moved to main lines, and Mallets grew to enormous size. Mallet was a strong advocate of compound locomotives and was opposed to the noncompound "Mallets" ("articulated" is a better term) that proliferated in the United States. Mallet continued to take a theoretical interest in locomotive design for many years and wrote learned papers until a year or so before his death, mainly in the *Mémoires* of the (French) Society of Civil Engineers.

—George H. Drury

REFERENCE

Van Riemsdijk, J. *Compound Locomotives.* Penryn, Cornwall, U.K.: Atlantic Transport, 1994.

Management Structure and Practice

Within two decades after the first tracklaying, railroads functioned on a scale that dwarfed other North American enterprises. The scope of their operations called for innovation; many railroad management procedures were devised by the industry's first- and second-generation leaders, and these techniques then were adopted by other businesses. Railroads therefore were important contributors to the theory and practices of modern American corporations of all types.

The primary challenges centered on size, geographic dispersion, and complexity. The largest New England 1850s textile manufacturers counted fewer than 1,000 employees, but the New York & Erie's workforce already numbered 4,000. Within an hour's time a typical factory manager could inspect the operations and personnel under his control. More than 30 railroads exceeded 150 route-miles by 1855, and direct supervision by one person was becoming impractical. Rail companies were unique among transportation enterprises in that they owned and maintained their infrastructure and also provided the service. Demand for this service varied widely by type, location, and timing.

Accurate forecasting of freight demand required a thorough understanding of customers and their transportation needs. Railroad leaders soon found that they had to know about such diverse topics as farm production, European import demand, weather, industrial development, and prices of precious metals, all of which could influence traffic and revenue. No other enterprises had to devote so much effort to the intricate process of devising appropriate rates.

In stark contrast to the present time, in which bookstore shelves are weighed down by scores of tomes dispensing management advice, few experts wrote books or pamphlets on the subject during the nineteenth century. That era's corporate executives were wary of these tracts unless the authors could demonstrate practical and beneficial results. Early railroad leaders could look to only one institution whose experience seemed to offer useful models: the U.S. Army. Beginning in the 1830s, the army had divided the nation into geographic regions for purposes of military administration. Troop units were led by line officers who answered to higher headquarters through a well-defined chain of command. Line officers rotated among command positions and staff duties at higher administrative levels. The army also used specialists to manage its support functions: quartermasters, paymasters, engineers, and the like. Given the nation's limited industrial base, the army maintained its own facilities to produce weapons, munitions, and uniforms. Every officer and soldier was governed by comprehensive sets of standard regulations. All of these principles, in one form or another, were adopted by the railroads.

Early railroads employed a simple management style. The president handled finances, raised capital, and made decisions on expansion and acquisitions. A superintendent served as chief operating officer and personally supervised train operations, maintenance of locomotives and rolling stock, track improvements, and construction. This arrangement was feasible only if the property was small enough to allow the superintendent to inspect the entire line and its scattered workforce on a frequent basis. As the routes were extended, more sophisticated organizational structures became necessary.

One approach centered on creating two or more operating divisions, each under the control of a division superintendent, who was assisted by personnel in three functions: transportation (train operations), mechanical (equipment maintenance and repair; supervision of shop facilities), and engineering (construction and maintenance of track, bridges, and support facilities). Each division superintendent reported to the railroad's chief operating officer, who might carry the title of vice president, general manager, or general superintendent. Early users of the divisional concept were the New York & Erie, Baltimore & Ohio, and Pennsylvania railroads.

Under an alternative departmental structure, the division continued to exist as the basic operating unit, but its superintendent shared responsibilities in the key areas of transportation, mechanical, and engineering. Subordinates ultimately answered to officials in charge of those functions at corporate headquarters. Under the departmental plan, the division superintendent was a coordinator, rather than a commander, of the people and assets within his territory.

The divisional structure predominated, but in practice nearly all large railroads combined the two concepts, especially as rail operations took on greater complexity. The Baltimore & Ohio pioneered the separation of finance and accounting from transportation operations because the volume of financial transactions and the number of people involved in them far exceeded the norm for American business. J. Edgar Thomson of the Pennsylvania Railroad created a centralized traffic department that solicited and processed freight and passenger business, but had no role in the actual transportation of people or goods. Other railroads copied these innovations.

Assisting the chief executive officer at headquarters were teams of specialists. The treasurer managed payments to employees and vendors and supervised the issuance and redemption of securities. Law departments expanded along with the number of damage claims, property-ownership disputes, tax issues, and other legal matters. A department of purchasing and stores managed procurement and inventories. Ratemaking functioned either within the traffic department or in a separate entity.

One of the industry's leading nineteenth-century management innovators was Daniel C. McCallum of the New York & Erie, who advocated a series of basic principles. Responsibilities should be divided, and sufficient authority should be delegated to allow executives to execute them. Management controls were essential to evaluate whether or not responsibilities were being carried out, to promptly report shortcomings, and to provide daily reports on train operations, delays, car use, and locomotive availability. Chief operating officers needed a procedure that would enable them to detect errors immediately, but also to "point out the delinquent." McCallum was a believer in the principle of economies of scale—a longer railroad should function with greater efficiency than a short one.

The ideas espoused by McCallum and others led to the acceptance of "managing through statistics," which eventually spread to American business generally. These rail executives also emphasized tight control over operations and expenses and insisted upon a high level of accountability from subordinates. They favored adherence to the "chain of command" as proposals and decisions flowed up and down the organization's structure.

Although the basic elements of these management and structural arrangements have prevailed ever since, by the 1890s rail managers detected serious flaws at the same time they were confronting fresh challenges. Route expansion, coupled with the trend toward consolidation of ownership, resulted in companies far larger than anyone originally had foreseen. Size offered economies of scale,

but only if it could be managed effectively. Yet some large railroads were better described as collections of individual companies rather than systems. The New York Central's leased lines, for example, essentially were independent units under the vice presidents in charge of each one.

Several railroads concluded that they had outgrown their organizational blueprints or decided that streamlining was called for. In 1899 the Pennsylvania Railroad owned or otherwise controlled 126 companies, but in five years' time it succeeded in doing away with 29 of these entities. Combining or eliminating subsidiaries could be difficult if lease provisions or bond covenants stood in the way. An early adopter of the divisional structure for its home-state routes, since 1870 the Pennsylvania had managed its affiliated lines west of Pittsburgh through its Pennsylvania Co. subsidiary. Quasi-independent managements had continued to run the affiliates, and this procedure had proved less than satisfactory, especially as the parent company attempted to improve the efficiency of long-distance traffic movements. In 1920 the railroad divided its entire system into four administrative regions, each under the direction of a vice president with considerable autonomy. Within each region a general superintendent supervised the divisions, as well as the key functions of transportation, motive power, maintenance-of-way, engineering, and traffic. This decision transferred most corporate-level supervision from headquarters to the four regions. Other large railroads eventually accepted variations of this approach.

Meanwhile, new responsibilities added boxes and lines to organizational charts. The advent of signalized traffic control systems required a management entity (usually within the operating department). Western railroads had activated staffs to manage their government land grants, and their immigration bureaus promoted settlement along the rights of way. Railroads created entities for tourism promotion, advertising, and public relations. Ever-increasing governmental regulation brought the hiring of governmental relations professionals. Traffic departments added personnel who focused upon key freight commodities: coal, grain, livestock, perishables, petroleum, lumber products, ore, and international freight. The rise of unions resulted in labor relations offices. Safety divisions were established within operating departments.

The size and scope of these activities led to the bureaucratization of railroad management. Some executives concluded that bureaucracy could be tamed only by a rigid, top-down management style. The extent to which this approach (hardly unique to the rail industry) stifled individual initiative has been debated in business graduate schools for a generation. Modern management analysts have observed that although railroads had been innovators in management, services, and marketing, the companies were slow to adopt new technology, even when issues such as the industry's woeful nineteenth-century safety record argued in favor of it.

Rigid hierarchies tend to resist change, which could explain the slow pace at which the industry accepted technology-based improvements. However, other factors also were involved. Capital improvement projects often were intended to create physical assets with lengthy useful lives. Executives would be predictably wary of replacing them prematurely without compelling reasons to do so. In addition, the long-term decline in rail rates restricted the availability of capital funding, a problem that worsened during the years from 1930 to 1980 when railroads frequently failed to earn rates of return sufficient to cover their cost of capital. Railroads also were bedeviled by paperwork arising from a torrent of business transactions, a byzantine array of rates and tariffs, the intricacies of billing procedures, and the demands of government regulators. Nearly one-fourth of railroad employees did clerical work.

Increasingly perplexed by these and other matters, senior managers continued their quest for more workable solutions. At times they seemed to tread water in the face of tradition-bound habits. Modest structural changes occurred, and then accelerated after World War II, but the basic framework remained intact.

Marketplace trends dictated adjustments. The rise of trailer-on-flatcar/container-on-flatcar service in the 1950s added intermodal functions to both the traffic and operating departments. In the 1960s traffic departments began evolving into marketing departments that directed their efforts toward a company's major customers. The new marketing entities often were placed in charge of corporate planning, as well as industrial development agencies.

Advances in telecommunications and computers enabled railroads to streamline customer service functions. As late as 1969 the Illinois Central, for example, had maintained 80 district freight- and passenger-service agencies throughout the United States. By the 1980s railroads had drawn these scattered offices into a handful of central locations. High-tech hubs controlled train movements, crew calling, and related functions over a company's entire system. The transfer of passenger service to Amtrak permitted railroads to abolish a huge management and employee infrastructure that had supported travel promotion, reservations, ticketing, and operations.

Operating departments continued to perform the basic duties of transportation, engineering, maintenance-of-way, communications and signaling, and safety. However, the advent of centralized dispatching transferred many routine decisions from the field to a central headquarters. In a gradual process after 1950 railroads established new administration departments, which consolidated under one executive the functions of personnel recruitment and management, labor relations, procurement, information management, and public relations. In addition to their traditional role, law departments often included the accounting and controller functions, as well as governmental relations.

Another structural change resulted from the evolution of the holding company. The Pennsylvania Co. of 1870 represented a prototype and was organized to exert a measure of control over quasi-independent subsidiaries of the Pennsylvania Railroad. In 1901 James J. Hill formed the Northern Securities Co. as a vehicle to merge the Great Northern, Northern Pacific, and Burlington lines. Although the U.S. Supreme Court rejected this merger, other holding companies were used in the century's early years to control an investor group's rail holdings. The Van Sweringen brothers' rail properties initially were controlled by the Vaness Co. and later by the Alleghany Corp., for example. The holding company typically controlled the securities, managed relations with Wall Street, appointed corporate officers to its subsidiaries, and dictated overall strategy. It had a minimal role in guiding operations or administration.

This approach took on broader appeal because of two developments. In 1906 the Hepburn Act severely restricted railroad ownership of nontransportation companies. This had the effect of making it difficult for western railroads to capture profits from the natural resources they owned as a consequence of federal land grants. In time they adopted the holding-company format to maintain subsidiaries in coal, forest products, and petroleum extraction. The holding company gained wider use in the 1950s and 1960s as railroads sought to duplicate corporate America's trend toward diversification and conglomeratization. A number of carriers became active in real estate, natural resources development, and joint ventures. The Pennsylvania's portfolio included a pipeline company and an operator of amusement parks. CSX ultimately acquired barge and ocean-carrier subsidiaries.

Throughout the industry's history a railroad's senior executive normally has held the title of president, but at times board chairmen have fulfilled the CEO role, while presidents were chief operating officers. During much of the nineteenth century entrepreneurs, financiers, and speculators dominated the CEO positions. Many of them had been merchants, traders, investment bankers, or industrialists who later branched out into real estate development, steamboats, or international trade. Occasionally, army-trained engineers who supervised the construction of railroads emerged as the presidents who ran them. Some CEOs were part-timers who simultaneously occupied CEO posts in several enterprises, including other railroads.

The industry's insatiable demand for capital placed a premium upon financial acumen, and such leaders as Edward H. Harriman, Cornelius Vanderbilt, John Murray Forbes, and Jay Gould were skilled in the tactics of high finance. Some chief executives simply were agents of Wall Street, placed in their positions to look after the interests of major investors. Although few CEOs could ignore finance and strategic planning, they varied in their other skills and priorities. Harriman had a phenomenal memory, a deft sense of timing in scheduling capital projects, and a genius for detail. Vanderbilt emphasized upgrading the quality of the rail infrastructure because he believed that this approach would enhance the value of a company's securities. Other CEOs might base their leadership upon an exhaustive knowledge of their company's route system, connections, and customers. Still others, like Forbes, seldom traveled the routes they controlled, instead managing at arm's length. In addition to dogged pursuit of industrial development, Gould routinely visited with customers and local civic leaders to gather information on economic trends and opportunities. James J. Hill believed that his Great Northern could succeed only if it gathered steamship traffic originating in Asia, and he is credited with stimulating U.S.-Asia trade, as well as bringing business to his railroad.

A president's principal subordinates were essential to his success. Julius Kruttschnitt of the Southern Pacific believed that his most important duty was to select outstanding senior managers, a priority echoed by Harriman, Forbes, and Gould. Forbes noted, "While there are a hundred good projects, you will find it hard to choose ten men to manage them." In hiring senior operating personnel, nineteenth-century CEOs sought the traits of energy, efficiency, and the ability to deliver results while keeping costs under control.

The post–Civil War consolidation movement created a pool of experienced senior managers who had been displaced by mergers. Professionalism among the top management ranks took hold, as did two other trends—leaders chosen from the ranks of their own company and senior executives who frequently moved from one railroad to another. When the era of the entrepreneurs/financiers passed early in the twentieth century, professional managers who had spent most of their working lives in railroading usually occupied the top positions.

The nature of executive promotion, coupled with highly echeloned structures, resulted in leaders who were competent conventional managers, but who in many cases had difficulty adjusting to changed circumstances. Business historian Robert Sobel has characterized these executives of the 1900–1950 era as "solid plodders." The difficulty of keeping huge bureaucracies under control often led to an authoritarian and arbitrary leadership style. Railroads' aversion to external talent also deprived the industry of the benefits of improved management techniques that had been tried and proved elsewhere. By the time CEOs concluded that outsiders were necessary, the industry's diminished stature and questionable economic prospects hampered recruitment.

A number of CEOs embraced change in the 1950s. Alfred Perlman of the Denver & Rio Grande Western applied technology to replace track-maintenance workers. Later, at the New York Central, Perlman deemed it essential to increase the speed at which freight trains operated if the NYC was to prosper. D. W. Brosnan of the Southern Railway also employed technology to improve labor productivity and advocated the use of high-capacity freight cars to improve efficiency. W. Graham Claytor, Jr., of the Southern perceived his role as that of team leader. Before his tenure more than 20 officers had reported directly to the Southern's president. Claytor created four executive vice presidents who became the senior members of his team.

Increasingly during the 1960s junior executives were drawn from among business-school graduates, instead of from the ranks of railroad personnel. Outsiders were brought into senior management posts from financial institutions and manufacturing companies, especially to positions in finance, marketing, administration, and corporate planning. Several railroads secured CEOs with little or no prior railroad experience, including Burlington Northern's Richard Bressler, a former executive vice president of Atlantic Richfield. The impact of the federal government's role in the industry's fortunes led to the hiring of CEOs with extensive federal backgrounds: Gerald Grinstein of Burlington Northern, James Hagen of Conrail, and John Snow of CSX.

—William J. Watt

REFERENCES

Chandler, Alfred D., Jr., ed. *The Railroads: The Nation's First Big Business.* New York: Harcourt, Brace & World, 1965.

Cochran, Thomas C. *Railroad Leaders, 1845–1890.* Cambridge, Mass.: Harvard Univ. Press, 1953.

Drury, George H. *The Historical Guide to North American Railroads.* Milwaukee, Wis.: Kalmbach, 1985.

Saunders, Richard, Jr. *Merging Lines: American Railroads, 1900–1970.* DeKalb: Northern Illinois Univ. Press, 2001.

Stover, John F. *The Life and Decline of the American Railroad.* New York: Oxford Univ. Press, 1970.

Mann, William D. (1839–1920)

William D'Alton Mann was a sleeping-car operator who championed room- or compartment-style accommodations that were superior to traditional Pullman open-section berth cars. He was born in Sandusky, Ohio, on September 27, 1839, to a family of modest means. Mann was a promoter who frequently changed careers and locations. His claim to be a civil engineer cannot be verified, but he apparently possessed some inventive talent. During the Civil War he patented a sling for rifles that proved successful. After the war he took on the title of Colonel Mann and plunged into Pennsylvania's Titusville oil boom, but after a brush with the law he moved south to see what profit he could find as a carpetbagger. He settled in Mobile, Alabama, as an Internal Revenue agent. Next he opened a newspaper, but this only inflamed local antagonism, and Mann was burned in effigy by an anticarpetbagger mob. Efforts to promote a railroad out of Mobile proved unsuccessful as well. Somehow during these turbulent years Mann found time to patent an improvement to sleeping cars.

Mann felt that Pullman's open-berth sleeper with its makeshift folding seats, pull-down berth, and curtains should be replaced with small rooms or compartments where passengers might enjoy true privacy and improved security behind a locked door and wooden partitions. The idea was hardly novel, but it appealed to many travelers.

Pullman's opposition to compartment cars and its growing monopoly of the sleeping-car trade undoubtedly prompted Mann to peddle his ideas in Europe. He found a partner in Georges Nagelmackers, the son of a Belgian banker, in 1873. This sleeping-car venture, later called Wagons-Lits, came to dominate the European deluxe train trade. However, Mann sold out in 1875 or 1876. He eventually returned to the United States and in 1883 formed the Mann Boudoir Car Co. The sleeping-car field was already crowded, with Pullman as the dominant operative. But Mann felt that his all-bedroom cars were so superior that he would succeed in claiming at least part of the trade. A few railroads signed on, but in general, the Colonel was only marginally successful. His 43 cars hardly compare to Pullman's fleet of 2,000. The Boudoir operation was sold to Union Palace Car Co. in 1888 and taken over by Pullman soon thereafter.

The Colonel, just 50 at this time, was far too vigorous and ambitious to retire. He reentered the publishing business, this time with a magazine in New York. His *Town Topics* was a society journal devoted to stories about the rich and famous. On the surface, Mann was a jovial fellow, cherubic in appearance and fond of offering sugar cubes to passing horses. Behind the white whiskers, though, lurked a more sinister personality. Silver dollars were passed out to butlers, bellhops, and chambermaids for scandalous tidbits about New York's leading citizens. Staff reporters sought out tales sure to embarrass Manhattan's first families.

The Colonel offered such intelligence in a weekly gossip column signed innocently "The Saunterer." The identity of the transgressors was thinly disguised; real names were never mentioned, but almost everyone could deduce who was being featured. The story would never appear in print if the intended victim or his family paid up. Many were willing to pay thousands of dollars to protect their reputation. At last, one of the subjects exposed Mann's blackmail operation. A series of lawsuits followed, and late in 1906 Mann was absolved of perjury. But few believed his innocence, and suddenly his reputation was subject to scorn. The Colonel maintained his innocence and continued his editorial duties as if nothing were amiss until his death in May 1920.

—John H. White, Jr.

REFERENCES

Logan, Andy. *The Man Who Robbed the Robber Barons*. New York: W. W. Norton, 1965.

White, John H., Jr. *The American Railroad Passenger Car*. Baltimore: Johns Hopkins Univ. Press, 1978.

Marine Operations

Car Ferries

Confronted with a water barrier, a railroad's usual options included going over, under, or around. Bridges and tunnels were costly and sometimes infeasible. The best and sometimes only choice was to ferry cars across the water.

Principal areas of car-ferry operations in North America included the Great Lakes, the San Francisco Bay Area, New York Harbor, the Mississippi and Ohio rivers and other inland rivers and lakes, and oceangoing services to distant points, including Cuba and Alaska. An earlier generation of these car ferries often carried complete freight or passenger trains, sometimes even including locomotives, but the operations that continue today are confined to freight cars.

Conditions that confronted car ferries varied from the brief crossing of a placid river to long, storm-tossed, ice-impeded journeys over the Great Lakes or even to hundreds of miles of open ocean. The vessels themselves necessarily varied as well, in size, power, and seagoing ability. Car-ferry vessels ranged from nonpowered barges, sometimes called "car floats," propelled by tugs or towboats, to self-propelled car-ferry boats, either of which might be designed for operation across the open ocean. In addition to the vessels, the car-ferry system also included the shore facilities required to move railcars between the ferry boat and the shore.

Early History

The first railcar ferry in North America was the sternwheeler *Susquehanna*, which began carrying cars of the Philadelphia, Wilmington & Baltimore Railroad across the mile-wide crossing of the Susquehanna River between Perryville and Havre de Grace, Maryland, in 1837 or 1838. A similar service began operation in 1852 across the Connecticut River between Saybrook and Lyme, Connecticut, with the steam ferry *Shaumpishuh* transporting cars of the New Haven & New London Railroad.

Car-float operations had begun serving some of the numerous railroads terminating at New York City by 1878. In the West the Southern Pacific began ferrying trains across the Carquinez Strait, north of San Francisco, in 1879. By 1881 Boston-Philadelphia trains were being ferried across the Hudson River between what are now Beacon and Newburgh, New York. By 1885 a Pennsylvania Railroad predecessor had established a car-ferry service across the mouth of Chesapeake Bay between Cape Charles and Port Norfolk, Virginia. A car ferry across the Straits of Mackinac, which divide Lakes Michigan and Huron, began running in 1888, following a less successful tug-barge operation.

The first of the many car ferries on Lake Michigan was

initiated in 1890, operating over a north-south route linking Chicago and Peshtigo, Wisconsin. The first cross-lake service, by the Ann Arbor Railroad, began in 1892. Ultimately, car-ferry services on Lake Michigan became the busiest and most complex in the world, with the greatest traffic and—on average—the longest voyages. At its peak in the 1940s, the Lake Michigan system involved nine water routes, ten ports, as many as 20 vessels, and numerous railroads, including the Michigan Central, Pennsylvania, Ann Arbor, Grand Trunk Western, and Pere Marquette.

The Great Lakes

Great Lakes car-ferry operations faced lengthy voyages and weather conditions comparable with those of the open ocean. Although there are no tides on the Great Lakes, there are both seasonal and wind-induced water-level variations of as much as 8 feet. Most Great Lakes boats operated year-round despite the high seas and heavy ice of winter. Almost all the Great Lakes services employed sturdy, self-propelled ferryboats. Car floats powered by tugs had been tried by a subsidiary of the Wisconsin & Michigan Railroad, but this operation was discontinued after a number of sinkings.

As has been noted, much of the Great Lakes car-ferry service operated on Lake Michigan. Ludington, Michigan, was a major terminal on that lake, beginning with the 1897 establishment of the first route, between Ludington and Manitowoc, by the Pere Marquette. The Pere Marquette later acquired the Chicago & West Michigan, already operating a ferry between Muskegon and Milwaukee. This later became a Ludington-Milwaukee service. Eventually the Pere Marquette added service to Kewaunee. By the 1920s as many as nine boats traveled from Ludington to the Wisconsin cities of Milwaukee, Manitowoc, and Kewaunee.

The Pere Marquette's Ludington-based fleet was continually updated and augmented; two innovative turbo-electric boats, for example, were put into service in 1930. The final additions to the fleet, the *Spartan* and the *Badger*, were built in 1952 for the Chesapeake & Ohio, which had merged with the Pere Marquette in 1947. These two, plus another Ludington-based vessel, the *City of Midland 41*, were sold in 1983 to a firm that continued car-ferry service only to Kewaunee; in 1990 this, too, ended. The *Badger* still sails, carrying automobiles and passengers, but no railcars.

Similar Lake Michigan services were operated by the Ann Arbor Railroad out of Frankfort, Michigan, connecting with Manitowoc and Kewaunee, Wisconsin, and Menominee and Manistique, Michigan. The two routes to Michigan closed in 1968 and 1970, but the two Wisconsin lines continued to operate until 1982 under Conrail after closure of the Ann Arbor in 1976. The Grand Trunk Western also operated a line between Muskegon, Michigan, and Milwaukee.

An older Great Lakes car-ferry style was the *Chief Wawatam*, built at Toledo, Ohio, in 1911, which employed a V-shaped bow section that was hinged up to allow railcars to roll on or off. The car ferry is seen here in October 1974. —Brian J. Cudahy

The newest Great Lakes car ferries were the Chesapeake & Ohio sister ships *Spartan* and *Badger,* built at Sturgeon Bay, Wisconsin, in 1952. The *Spartan* departed from Manitowoc, Wisconsin, in the summer of 1977 on a trip across Lake Michigan to Muskegon, Michigan. These ships used a rear loading arrangement. The C&O car-ferry operation continued until 1990, and the *Badger* continues to operate, but only for automobiles and passengers. —Brian J. Cudahy

A number of car ferries operated on Lakes Erie and Ontario, using boats and shore facilities much like those on Lake Michigan. One Lake Erie car ferry connected Ashtabula, Ohio, and Port Burwell, Ontario; it was operated jointly by the Pennsylvania and the Canadian Pacific and employed the steamer *Ashtabula*, built in 1906 and in operation until 1958. Another ferry, running the steamer *Marquette and Bessemer No. 2*, connected Conneaut, Ohio, and Port Stanley, Ontario. This operation was controlled by the Bessemer & Lake Erie and the Pere Marquette; it ended in 1932. The latter railroad also ran a ferry between Conneaut

Most Great Lakes car ferries employed a stern loading arrangement. This was the Chesapeake & Ohio's *City of Midland 41,* built in 1941, which used a rear loading arrangement shown here at Milwaukee in 1976. —Brian J. Cudahy

and Rondeau, Ontario. On Lake Ontario the Canadian National and the Baltimore & Ohio operated a car-ferry service between Charlotte, New York, and Cobourg, Ontario, using the boats *Ontario No. 1* and *Ontario No. 2,* until service ended in 1950.

The strait connecting Lake Erie to Lake Huron is known as the St. Clair River at its northern end and as the Detroit River at the southern. Before the St. Clair River Tunnel was completed in 1891, the Grand Trunk Railway operated a car ferry linking Sarnia, Ontario, and Port Huron, Michigan. At a much later date the service was resumed by both the Canadian National and CSX (the Pere Marquette's suc-

cessor) to transport cars too large for the tunnel, using towboats and formerly powered car ferries that had been converted to barges. The service was again discontinued when a larger St. Clair River tunnel was completed in 1995, thus ending the last car-ferry service on the Great Lakes.

The Great Western Railway, a CN predecessor, initiated car-ferry service across the Detroit River between Detroit and Windsor, Ontario, in 1867. The Canadian Pacific, Pere Marquette, and Wabash soon established similar car ferries, as did the Michigan Central until it completed a Detroit River tunnel in 1910. All of these railroads later acquired trackage rights through the Detroit River Tunnel, but car-ferry operation continued for cars too large for the tunnel. It used tugs and the ferry *Manitowoc,* cut down to a barge. The service continued until 1994, when enlargement of the tunnel ended the need.

New York Harbor

New York City has always been difficult of access, since it is all but surrounded by major water obstacles: the Hudson and East rivers, New York Harbor, the Arthur Kill, and Newark Bay. Until completion of the Pennsylvania Railroad's Hudson and East River tunnels and of the New York Connecting Railroad's Hell Gate Bridge early in the twentieth century, all rail entry to the city, other than New York Central and New Haven services into Manhattan across the Harlem River from the north, was by water. With the Pennsylvania (now Amtrak) tunnels confined to passenger traffic, rail freight into the city remains dependent upon water transport or long, roundabout routings.

In 1876 the New York & New England, a New Haven predecessor, established a car-ferry service to carry through passenger trains operating between New England and

Seen from New York's Hell Gate Bridge, a New Haven Railroad tug towed two car floats up the East River on the way from the Greenville Yards in New Jersey to New Haven's Oak Point Yard in the Bronx in April 1957. —© Dan LeMaire-Bauch

Philadelphia or Washington across the water barriers at New York. The side-wheel steamer *Maryland II*, later joined by the twin-screw steamer *Express*, operated from a terminal on the Harlem River at the south end of the Bronx around Manhattan by way of the East River and across the North River (as the lower Hudson was once commonly known in maritime circles) to the Pennsylvania railhead in Jersey City. The service ended in 1912, several years before completion of the Hell Gate Bridge created an all-rail route.

Conveying freight cars between the terminals of various railroads in New Jersey or the terminals of the New York Central and New Haven on the Harlem and East rivers to points in Manhattan, Brooklyn, and Queens was always the main work of the New York Harbor "railroad navies." Virtually every railroad operated its own fleet of car floats and tugs. Although not subject to storms such as those faced by, for example, the Great Lakes car-ferry services, New York–area float movements confronted hazards of their own, being largely cross-river operations in conflict with what was once an extensive up- and downriver traffic.

In their heyday, at the time of World War II, the railroads' New York Harbor services employed some 324 car floats, as well as a large fleet of railroad-owned tugboats and other cargo barges and vessels. Railroads involved included the Pennsylvania, Baltimore & Ohio, Central of New Jersey, New York Central, Erie, New Haven, Lehigh Valley, Long Island, Lackawanna, and several Brooklyn waterfront terminal railroads.

Today, with much better access via numerous bridges and tunnels, motor trucks transport almost all of New York City's freight, and a much-reduced number of freight cars still cross New York Harbor on tug-powered car floats. These remaining waterborne operations are conducted by the New York Cross Harbor Railroad, which operates between car-float terminals in the Greenville section of Jersey City, New Jersey, and the Bush Terminal in Brooklyn.

San Francisco Bay

Located on the west side of the broad San Francisco Bay, San Francisco was extremely hard to reach by rail except from the south. Near Vallejo, at the northeast corner of the bay, the original transcontinental railway encountered the formidable barrier of the Carquinez Strait, and its terminals at Oakland were separated from San Francisco by more than 3 miles of water. Until the completion of the Martinez Bridge in 1930, the Central Pacific and the successor Southern Pacific operated double-ended side-wheelers, as well as car floats and tugs, to move their heavy main-line traffic across the Carquinez Strait.

San Francisco Bay freight-car ferry services were also operated by three other major railroads. The North Shore Railroad, which became the Northwestern Pacific in 1907, operated freight-car and passenger ferryboats to San Francisco from a terminal at Sausalito, north of the Golden Gate on San Francisco Bay. NWP car ferryboats included two double-ended side-wheelers, a stern-wheeler, and a

side-wheel tug. Passenger operation ended with the opening of the Golden Gate Bridge in 1941. The Western Pacific moved freight cars between Oakland and San Francisco with tugs and car floats until 1957, when the modern diesel car ferryboat *Las Plumas* was placed in service. The Santa Fe used tugs and car floats for a similar transbay service until the service was ended in 1980.

Rivers and Other Lakes

Both the Mississippi and Ohio rivers and their tributaries present major barriers to rail traffic, and there were at one time many car ferries crossing them. Among the more important crossings were Trotter's Point, Mississippi, to Helena, Arkansas; Vicksburg, Mississippi, to Delta Point, Louisiana; Brookport, Illinois, to Paducah, Kentucky; and Cairo, Illinois, to East Cairo, Kentucky, all operated by the Illinois Central. The St. Louis Southwestern operated Cairo, Illinois, to Bird's Point, Missouri, and the Southern Pacific ran a ferry between Harahan, Louisiana, and New Orleans until the Huey P. Long Bridge was completed in 1935. Before the opening of the New Orleans bridge, the Texas & New Orleans Lines of the Southern Pacific ferried complete passenger trains across the Mississippi between New Orleans and the west-bank Louisiana cities of Avondale and Algiers.

Most car ferrying on the Mississippi and neighboring rivers was by powered boat. One exception was the Texas & New Orleans car ferry. This operation employed a tug and a 441-foot-long, three-track car float, or barge, as they were usually called on these rivers. It held engine, tender, and four 80-foot passenger cars on one track and five cars on each of the other two tracks.

Another ferry system, of the Nashville, Chattanooga & St. Louis, used nonpowered barges over a 21-mile route between Hobb's Island and Gunter's Landing, Alabama, on the Tennessee River. These barges were relatively small, just 240 feet long, with only two tracks, giving them a capacity of 10 freight cars. Propulsion was by stern-wheel steam towboats. These were replaced by diesel towboats in the final years of this service.

At least two electric interurban railways operated passenger-train car ferries. From 1912 to 1928 the Evansville Railways side-wheeler *Henderson* operated across the Ohio River between Evansville, Indiana, and Henderson, Kentucky. Perhaps the smallest of side-wheelers, the 130-foot-long, single-track vessel could accommodate only two 50-foot cars. The vessel's two paddle wheels were powered independently, each with its own six-cylinder gasoline engine. Unusual features of the vessel included overhead trolley and telephone wires that were connected upon docking, and an electric headlight for night operation. In California, after the operation of the short-lived wooden-hulled *Bridget* from 1913 to 1915, the steel-hulled car ferryboat *Ramon* transported Sacramento Northern passenger and freight trains across Suisun Bay, California, until the service was given up in 1954. The Northern Pacific Railway

Illinois Central smoked up the area at Trotters Point, Mississippi, around 1950 as 2-8-0 No. 726 pulled cars off the car ferry *Pelican*. The ferry crossing of the Mississippi River gave the IC its only link with Arkansas, serving the town of Helena. The *Pelican* was built at Dubuque, Iowa, in 1902. —J. M. Gray, *Trains* Magazine Collection

operated a double-ended side-wheeler, the *Tacoma*, across the Columbia River at Kalama, Washington.

Two car-ferry routes moved traffic across the St. Lawrence River. The Canadian Pacific operated one between Prescott, Ontario, and Ogdensburg, New York, consisting of a single car float lashed to a diesel tug. The National Transcontinental Railway and the Grand Trunk operated the other across the St. Lawrence between Quebec City and Levis until the opening of the Quebec Bridge in 1917.

Still another Canadian car-ferry service was conducted in the Selkirk Mountains on several lakes of southern British Columbia, providing connections to isolated lines. The first line began operation in late 1880 and ran at various times to Upper and Lower Arrow, Okanagan, Kootenay, and Slocam lakes. It used steam boats or, later, floats and tugs. The last to close was the Slocam Lake line, which ended operation at the end of 1988.

Oceangoing Car Ferries

In 1914 the Florida East Coast Railway began operating an international car-ferry service between Florida and Havana, Cuba, with three stern-loading ships very much like those used on Lake Michigan: the *Henry M. Flagler*, the *Estrada Palma*, and the *Joseph R. Parrott*. Originally the service ran from Key West, Florida, only 90 miles from Havana. After destruction of the rail connection to Key West by a hurricane in 1935, the boats sailed from Port Everglades, 180 miles farther north, making the trip 270 miles each way.

The service was interrupted by World War II, but was resumed after the war by the West India Fruit & Steamship Co. (WIF&SCo), employing the former FEC ferries *Flagler* and *Parrott*, as well as a former Grand Trunk Great Lakes car ferryboat, *Grand Haven*. The new company operated out of Port Everglades for a time and then shifted its Florida terminal to Palm Beach. Two much larger modern car ships were added to the WIF&SCo fleet, the *New Grand Haven* in 1951 and the *City of New Orleans* in 1959. In 1954 the company acquired the *Seatrain New Orleans* from Seatrain Lines and took over that line's Belle Chasse, Louisiana–Havana route. Service to Cuba ended in early 1960 after the country's socialist revolution.

The Canadian National operated two car-ferry systems in northeastern Canada. One joined Cape Tormentine, New Brunswick, to Port Borden on Prince Edward Island, a distance of some 9 miles. The 300-foot *Prince Edward Island* carried both freight and passenger cars, while the larger, 324-foot *Charlottetown*, built in 1931, handled automobiles, as well as railcars. Both ships were considered powerful icebreakers. The second CN operation in this area joined Mulgrave, Nova Scotia, to Port Tupper, Cape Breton Island, a much shorter distance. Two boats, the *Scotia* and *Scotia II*, provided the service.

An early oceangoing car-ferry service was initiated in 1885 by a Pennsylvania Railroad predecessor, the New York, Philadelphia & Norfolk, which began operating the bow-loading side-wheel steamer *Cape Charles* to ferry passenger cars over a 36-mile route across the entrance to Chesapeake Bay between Cape Charles and Port Norfolk (now Portsmouth), Virginia. Schedule-coordination problems with southern railroads brought an end to passenger-car ferrying only two years later, but freight-car ferry service with tugs and barges continued. Reflecting the open-water nature of the route, these bay barges were large, sturdy vessels of wood or steel. One, the *Nandua*, still operates in a reduced-scale service across the mouth of the bay between Cape Charles and Little Creek, Virginia.

An important oceangoing car-ferry system was operated by the Seatrain Lines over a triangular route linking New Orleans, New York City, and Havana, Cuba, the longest run of any car ferry. Ships traversed this route weekly in opposite directions. Two ships provided similar Seatrain service between New York and Texas City, Texas. Seatrain's ships were distinctive in that cars did not roll on and off the ship, but were lifted on and off by shore-mounted cranes. The innovative Seatrain service was eventually supplanted by the almost universal use of standard intermodal containers. Indeed, Seatrain was itself a containerization pioneer but dropped out of the field in the 1970s.

A more recent oceangoing car-ferry operation in the Gulf of Mexico was inspired by the substantial growth in U.S.-Mexico trade resulting from the North American Free Trade Agreement (NAFTA). In 1992 Burlington Northern began operating a high-speed railcar barge service between Galveston, Texas, and the Yucatán Peninsula. The service was terminated in 1994, but in 2001 a similar service began operating between Mobile and the Yucatán employing self-propelled vessels.

Both tug-barge and self-propelled car-ferry services operated on the waters of the Pacific Northwest. The Milwaukee Road served outlying landings from Tacoma and Seattle. The Canadian National (originally Canadian Northern) and the Canadian Pacific operate self-propelled (originally steam and now diesel) car ferries between Vancouver and Vancouver Island, transporting both freight cars and highway trucks. Numerous pulp mills along the British Columbia coast were served over the years by car-ferry barges, which delivered carloads of chemicals and brought the pulp out. The Alaska Railroad railhead at Whittier, Alaska, is served from Prince Rupert, British Columbia, by huge oceangoing rail barges.

Vessels

To withstand the fierce Great Lakes storms and severe ice conditions, car ferryboats built for this service had to be rugged and powerful, with effective icebreaking capabilities. High sides or freeboards and an enclosed train deck were standard. The bow was heavily braced and sloped back underneath so that if the boat could not push the ice aside, it could ride up onto the ice and break it by sheer weight.

To improve control when steering up to the slip, these vessels typically had two independently operated propellers at the stern. Some also had a third propeller in the bow. Its purpose was to help in icebreaking by drawing water out from under the ice as the boat rode onto it, thus weakening its support and making the ice easier to crush.

Most Great Lakes boats had four tracks and handled six to eight cars per track. A small number of automobiles were generally carried on the train deck, and passengers were accommodated as well, with a comfortable main saloon and sleeping quarters for perhaps 40 to 50. Railcars were chained to the deck, and chocks were provided to prevent them from rolling fore or aft along the track. In addition, jacks were employed to lift the cars' weight off their springs and prevent rocking in rough seas.

To make the boats seaworthy, the freeboard extended well above the track level, necessitating some form of door for loading. This could be either at the bow or stern, depending on how the boat was designed to approach its slip. The vast majority of Great Lakes boats were stern loading; their high, well-enclosed, and strongly braced prows gave them the ability to contend with rough seas and ice. A disadvantage of this arrangement was the need to back into the slip, a time-consuming operation. Some ships had a rear pilothouse for use when maneuvering into the slip.

Bow-loading ships were easier to steer into the slip but, because they needed some kind of door at the bow, were less able to withstand high seas and heavy ice. Eventually, use of bow-loading boats was limited to the comparatively smooth Straits of Mackinac between Lake Michigan and Lake Huron. One example, the Mackinac Transportation Co.'s *Chief Wawatam*, had a V-shaped bow section that hinged up to allow railcars to roll on or off.

The relatively calm waters of the Detroit River permitted the use of open-decked car ferryboats for the several Detroit-Windsor services. Originally, most were double-ended side-wheelers, but the majority were eventually operated as single-enders. All were later replaced by double-enders that had four independent propellers, two at each end. The largest and most modern of these was the 400-foot *Pere Marquette 12*, with three tracks and space for 27 freight cars.

The earliest car ferryboats operated by the Southern Pacific for its Carquinez Strait crossing were double-ended side-wheelers; each wheel had its own walking-beam engine for increased maneuverability. The first of these was the *Solano* of 1879, at that time the largest such vessel in the world. The similar and even larger *Contra Costa* was built in 1914. Constructed largely of wood and well over 400 feet long, this boat had four tracks that could accommodate two locomotives and 24 passenger cars or 36 freight cars.

The Missouri Pacific's 308-foot *Willard V. King*, built in 1910, which operated between Anchorage and Baton Rouge, Louisiana, and later between Natchez and Vidalia, Louisiana, was fairly typical of Mississippi car ferryboats, or transfer boats, as they were usually called on the Ohio and Mississippi. The *King* was a side-wheeler with two tracks, each holding up to 16 freight cars. A somewhat unusual side-wheel car ferryboat was the *George H. Walker* of the Gulf Coast Lines, which operated at Baton Rouge, Louisiana. Each paddle wheel was driven via reduction gearing by a steam engine that had two opposed, inclined cylinders. This vessel had three tracks and could handle up to 12 passenger cars or 24 freight cars.

Unique among car ferryboats was the Texas & Pacific's *Gouldsboro*, operating between its namesake city and New Orleans. This vessel's wrought-iron hull was originally built in 1863 as the two-turret Confederate monitor *Chickasaw*. It served in the battle of Mobile Bay and, in 1884, was acquired by the railroad and converted for carrying railcars.

The usual arrangement for loading and unloading car-ferry vessels called for the shore tracks to be raised or lowered to adjust to the level of the boat, which varied with the tides and loading. Several vessels that operated across the St. Lawrence at Quebec, however, did it the other way. The National Transcontinental Railway's railroad ferryboat *Leonard* had a rail deck supported by 20 engine-driven screw jacks with an overall height range of 20 feet. During crossings the deck was kept at its lowest position. After the boat docked, the deck was raised to meet the shore. At Quebec the Grand Trunk operated two ferryboats, the *John S. Thom* and the *James B. Langdon*, that had lifts that could raise or lower cars to compensate for the 20-foot tidal range.

Most oceangoing car ferryboats were similar to those used on the Great Lakes. Seatrain's ships, however, were quite different, since cars were not rolled on and off the ship, but were lifted on and off by cranes. Onshore cranes lifted cars on tracked platforms and then lowered the platforms through hatches to the desired deck of the vessel, where cables hauled the cars along shipboard rails into position for sailing. The original Seatrain ship, the 427-foot *Seatrain* delivered in 1929, had four car decks, with space for 92 freight cars. Two later ships built in 1932, the *Seatrain New York* and *Seatrain Havana*, were each 478 feet long, with four decks of four tracks each. Each of these carried about 100 cars.

By far the most extensive car-float operation in North America was located at New York Harbor. The equipment generally resembled that used elsewhere. A typical New York Harbor transfer car float was built of wood (later steel), ranged from 257 to 360 feet in length, and carried up to 25 cars on three tracks.

A station or platform float, a sort of floating freight station, was similar to other car floats. It usually had only two tracks flanking a covered floor-level freight platform. Station floats typically carried boxcars with less-than-carload lot (LCL) freight and sometimes refrigerator cars, ferrying them to piers where there were no track connections. Longshoremen unloaded the cars and transferred the goods by hand trucks to the destination pier. The freight cars never left the float but made the return trip with it.

Lighters were barges that carried no railcars. Owned by New York–area railroads in sizable numbers, they were typically used to transfer freight from waterfront terminals to ships at anchor. Covered lighters were large floating sheds with doorways through which goods could be loaded and unloaded. Tugboats transported them as they did car floats.

Other barges called "stick" or "derrick" lighters were barges with onboard cranes that could transfer freight from the lighter to a ship.

The Canadian Pacific employed a car float of unusual configuration in its service across the St. Lawrence between Prescott, Ontario, and Ogdensburg, New York. To provide increased visibility for the captain, a pilothouse was mounted high aboard the float, and the tug alongside was operated by electric remote control.

Car floats or barges used in oceangoing car-ferry services were generally similar to, but often larger than, those used in more protected waters. Most of the barges used in the Pennsylvania Railroad's Chesapeake Bay crossing, for example, were about 400 feet long and 50 feet wide, with a capacity of 26 cars. The last and largest, which entered service in 1949, was the *Captain Edward Richardson*, a 418-foot-long, 51-foot-wide vessel capable of carrying 32 40-foot freight cars. It still operates in 2006 as the *Nandua*.

Shore Facilities

Transfer Bridges

One of the most critical elements of any car-ferry operation was the installation provided for moving railcars on and off the vessels. This was an inherently difficult operation. Shore tracks had to be aligned in some manner with the elevation of the railcar deck. Large and heavy railcars had to be moved to or from a vessel that rose or fell with the tide or the weight of its lading and listed to one side or the other with shifts in the loading as cars were removed or added. The most common way to accomplish this was with a hinged section of track, usually called a float bridge or transfer bridge, that linked the shore track and the rail deck. These structures came in a wide variety of types, with almost infinite variations in their mechanical details, but all performed essentially the same function.

A vessel using a transfer-bridge facility was typically brought up to and aligned with the shore tracks by means of a guiding or funneling slip. Such a slip usually consisted of two rows of piles, one on each side, which converged toward the shore. One of these rows was shorter than the other, and a vessel entering the slip would graze the longer row, which absorbed some of its energy, slowed it, and helped guide it into the slip.

The transfer or float bridge was then used to align the elevation of the shore tracks with that of the vessel's deck. Generally, the required height adjustment could be accomplished with one bridge span of 50 to 100 feet. Where the height range was greater, two to as many as six spans were used, accommodating height variations up to about 12 feet. Early transfer bridges were typically built of wood, but more recent bridges have been built of steel.

The suspension of the float bridge and the arrangements for raising or lowering it depended upon such factors as the desired speed of railcar transfer, the extremes of distance the bridge had to be raised or lowered, the size

An Alco diesel switcher pulled a string of freight cars from the Long Island Rail Road's Long Island City car float on New York's East River in August 1956.
—William D. Middleton

The Hampton Roads and Chesapeake Bay waterways generated a substantial car-float operation for the railroads serving the port at Norfolk, Virginia. A U.S. Navy diesel switches cars off a Chesapeake & Ohio tug and car float at the Norfolk Naval Base in 1963.
—William D. Middleton

of the vessels used, and construction costs. Once adjusted, the bridge either rested on the vessel or was locked to it with steel bars and was subject to twisting forces as the vessel listed one way or the other. It thus had to be either strong enough to resist these forces or flexible enough to yield to them without damage.

There were several mechanisms for raising or lowering the outer end of the bridge. The fastest was to suspend it from an overhead structure, sometimes called a gallows frame, by motor-driven cables; these could align the heights in about two minutes. A similar earlier approach was manual, employing helmlike wheels to reel or unreel the cables as required. In most cases cable-suspended counterweights were used as well.

A similar but slightly different system was in use at Ludington, Michigan, and elsewhere. In these a counterweighted overhead rocking beam or lever supported the offshore end of the bridge by rigid hangers. A power winch reeled or unreeled cables at the inshore end of the beam, which was thus tilted to adjust bridge height. Alike in principle, but different in construction, was the beam arrangement of the Wabash Railway landing on the Detroit River. Here the beams were alongside, not above, the transfer bridge.

Yet another approach was to use no lifting machinery at all, but to rely entirely on pontoons that supported the outer end of the float bridge. One way of adjusting the latter type was to push a special heavily weighted car slowly out on the bridge until it applied enough leverage to lower the bridge to deck height. Or water could be pumped into or out of the pontoons to adjust their buoyancy as required. Raising the float bridge without pumping required the use of hydraulic jacks on the face of the bridge that bore down on the deck of the car float. These methods allowed less expensive bridge construction, but were much slower, taking perhaps 10 minutes of adjustment for each incoming vessel.

A still different system, used by the New York Central and the New Haven in the New York City area, was to adjust bridge height by means of huge vertical screws. These passed through power-rotated nuts. Both railroads employed shorter "aprons," outboard of the main bridge sections, to accommodate the listing of the car float.

This system of adjusting screws was carried to its ultimate by the Texas & New Orleans and the Texas & Pacific, which had long bridges consisting of six 45- or 50-foot spans at New Orleans that were designed to adjust for the extreme variations in elevation encountered on the Mississippi. There was a screw lift at each junction between spans, and the thread pitch of the screws was so calculated that the entire system rose in one plane (screw pitch was increased in proportion to the distance from the shore pivot). In each installation lengthy shafts allowed a single motor to turn all of the nuts, which jacked the screws.

INCLINES

The screw-and-nut arrangements of the T&NO and the T&P just noted were an exception to normal practice on the Mississippi and other inland rivers. Because of the generally very wide and gentle slope of the riverbanks, coupled with great variations in water level, a boat or float could not simply "pull up" to its slip. The majority of these river landings used what were called inclines.

Inclines were arranged with a track—the "incline"—laid down the sloping riverbank. On this incline ran a track-bearing "cradle," 200 to 250 feet long, that sloped upwards toward the river. Its rails at the shoreward end rested on the incline. Thus a car could run down the incline track and then roll up onto the cradle track. The cradle itself could roll up or down the incline on flanged wheels, thereby being adjusted to the boat's deck level. Cables, pulled by locomotives or winches, were generally used to move the cradles, although at one location the cradle was moved downgrade (toward the water) by the momentum of a braking locomotive and was shoved in the upward direction by the ferryboat.

In some other applications of the cradle system, as at Vicksburg, Mississippi, there was a moored "wharf boat" or floating freight shed at the end of a 117-foot cradle. On this shed goods were transferred between freight cars and river steamers; the cars were not taken aboard.

—Dan LeMaire-Bauch

Ferry Services

Many of America's early cities were seaports; railroad companies frequently established their terminals across a body of water from such cities and used ferryboats for the final (or initial) leg of an overland journey. Important examples of such arrangements were found on both the East and the West Coast. In New York the mile-wide expanse of the Hudson River saw many railroads terminate their trains on the New Jersey side and deploy fleets of ferryboats so passengers could reach Manhattan. In San Francisco the Central Pacific Railroad's link in the nation's first transcontinental railroad terminated its trains on the east side of San Francisco Bay, and a ferry ride was required to reach San Francisco.

The first successful steam-powered ferryboat to cross the Hudson River, the *Jersey*, was built under the direction of Robert Fulton and began operating between the foot of Cortlandt Street in Manhattan and the Paulus Hook section of Jersey City in 1812. When a rail line that was subsequently built inland from Paulus Hook later became part of the Pennsylvania Railroad, the successor of Fulton's trans-Hudson ferry service evolved into a maritime subsidiary of the Pennsy. The Central Railroad of New Jersey, the Erie, the Delaware, Lackawanna & Western, the New York, Ontario & Western, and the West Shore service of the New York Central also operated trans-Hudson ferryboat services, and the Long Island Rail Road ran similar service across the East River between Manhattan and its western terminal in Long Island City.

A distinctive style of vessel evolved for such river crossings and quickly became standard for harbor ferryboats the world over. Following the design Fulton himself used in 1812, the boats could operate in either direction, carried both foot passengers and horse-drawn carriages, and catered to short-haul cross-river traffic, as well as long-distance rail passengers. Fulton's *Jersey* was a twin-hulled vessel with a revolving paddle wheel located between the hulls. Later boats featured more conventional hulls with twin paddle wheels, one on each side of the vessel, powered by a large, single-cylinder steam engine located amidships. These vertical-beam engines, as they were called, posed an operational danger in short-haul ferry work. Should the piston in such an engine's single cylinder stall at either the very top or the very bottom of the cylinder, the engine was effectively disabled and could not be restarted without extraordinary intervention. As a ferryboat was entering a slip, though, a prompt response to a "reverse engine" command was essential to avert disaster.

Consequently, in 1888 the Hoboken Ferry Co., soon to become a maritime subsidiary of the DL&W, designed the first successful double-ended ferryboat that was powered by screw propellers. Christened *Bergen*, the boat featured propellers on each end that turned on a common shaft, with power supplied by a three-cylinder, triple-expansion steam engine, a style of propulsion that was far more responsive to the kind of rapid engine commands routine ferry service demanded. Similar vessels were quickly ordered by other railroads for trans-Hudson service, and fleets of such vessels that were built in the early years of the twentieth century remained active until the

Passengers on New Jersey's ferries across the Hudson River got incomparable views of the lower Manhattan skyline. This was the Erie Railroad's ferry *Youngstown* in 1956. —Brian J. Cudahy

demise of railroad-operated ferryboats in New York Harbor in the late 1960s. (More a matter of trivia than serious history: the final regularly scheduled steam-powered service provided by many eastern railroads was not a run along their tracks behind a steam locomotive, but a crossing of the Hudson River by ferryboat.)

There were many instances where railroads used ferryboats to connect riverside terminals with major cities. Both the Pennsylvania and the Reading Co. operated fleets of double-ended boats across the Delaware River between Philadelphia and Camden, for example, and a

The merged Erie Lackawanna Railroad's ferry *Elmira* had just departed from its Barclay Street slip at Manhattan on the way to Hoboken in September 1967. The 1,400-hp steam ferry was built in 1905. —Gerald Newman

Ready to board a crowd of passengers, the Jersey Central car ferry *Elizabeth* was ready for another trip from Manhattan to the waiting commuter trains in Hoboken in 1956. —Brian J. Cudahy

short-haul narrow-gauge railroad that linked Boston with communities to the north, the Boston, Revere Beach & Lynn, relied on a fleet of ferryboats to connect its terminal in East Boston with the city proper on the opposite side of Boston Harbor. Nor were the Central Pacific and

its successor, the Southern Pacific, the only railroads in the Bay Area to require ferryboat connections to San Francisco. Transcontinental trains operated by the Atchison, Topeka & Santa Fe, as well as local and largely suburban services provided by such companies as Northwestern Pacific and Key System, used ferryboats on San Francisco Bay until the advent of the Bay Bridge and the Golden Gate Bridge in the 1930s rendered the ferries obsolete.

In addition to short-haul waterborne services where a double-ended ferryboat was the typical vessel of choice, many railroads deployed conventional steamboats on somewhat longer ferry-style routes. There were several such services in tidewater Virginia. The Chesapeake & Ohio terminated its trains in Newport News and provided connections to Norfolk, on the opposite side of Hampton Roads, with a variety of steamboats over the years, and the most direct rail route between New York and Norfolk was a Pennsylvania Railroad service that left the New York–Washington main stem at Wilmington and proceeded down the Delmarva Peninsula to Cape Charles, Virginia, where steamboat connections were available across the mouth of Chesapeake Bay to Norfolk. In New York Harbor the Central Railroad of New Jersey supplemented its trans-Hudson ferryboat operations between Manhattan and Jersey City with railroad-operated steam-

Passengers are ready to disembark as the Central Railroad of New Jersey ferry *Elizabeth* approaches its Manhattan slip in August 1953. The ferry *Cranford* is loading for the return trip. —Wallace W. Abbey, *Trains* Magazine Collection

boats that carried passengers from Manhattan to connections with its North Jersey Coast trains down the bay in Monmouth County, New Jersey. From its opening in 1851 until its right of way reached Jersey City in 1861, the easternmost railhead of the Erie Railroad was 25 miles up the Hudson River from New York City at Piermont, New York, and a fleet of side-wheel steamboats was used for connections.

Many North American railroads also featured waterborne operations that supplemented and complemented their basic main-line operations. Chief among these was the New York, New Haven & Hartford. When J. P. Morgan gained control of the railroad in 1892, the New Haven began to acquire Long Island Sound steamboat companies, not because they provided needed connecting services with the company's rail lines—although in many instances they did; New Bedford and Woods Hole to Martha's Vineyard and Nantucket is one example—but rather because inland steamboat services on Long Island Sound and its tributaries were seen as a competitive threat to the railroad. The Long Island Rail Road operated supplementary overnight steamboats between New York and Greenport on the eastern end of Long Island, a journey the company's passenger trains could easily accomplish in a few hours, and the Pennsylvania was active in acquiring various steamboat lines on Chesapeake Bay.

A variety of factors served to minimize the importance of railroad-operated ferryboat services throughout the twentieth century and eventually led to their demise. Construction of bridges and tunnels allowed either railroad trains themselves or more economical connecting motor-coach services to substitute for costly ferry operations; the various services were cut back, curtailed, and eventually eliminated.

Although ferry services are no longer directly operated by railroads, there are still a few places where one can step off a passenger train and continue the trip aboard a passenger vessel of some kind. In New London, Connecticut, for example, the Amtrak station is just a few paces from terminals where ferries depart for various points in Long Island Sound, and in what may well be the most interesting example of the twenty-first century rediscovering aspects of nineteenth-century technology, passengers arriving at the Hoboken Terminal aboard New Jersey Transit commuter trains can now reach their Manhattan destinations aboard a fleet of new, fast-moving contemporary ferries operated by New York Waterways.

Finally, what is surely the best-known ferryboat service of all time, the famous Staten Island Ferry that links the southern end of Manhattan Island with St. George, continues to provide connections for passengers traveling aboard a Staten Island electric railway that is today operated by the same public agency, the Metropolitan Transportation Authority, that is the parent of both the New York subway and the Long Island Rail Road. The ferry service has been municipally operated since 1905. In the final decades of the nineteenth century, though, it was a

maritime subsidiary of the Staten Island Rapid Transit Co., a railway that was acquired by the Baltimore & Ohio Railroad in 1888. With a number of reservations and qualifications, then, one could say that today's Staten Island Ferry is the sole remaining North American example of a traditional ferryboat operation that provides connecting service between a central city and a rail passenger terminal across the water, and it has done so during three separate centuries.

—Brian J. Cudahy

Oceangoing Steamship Services

The development of large industrial and transportation enterprises on the North American economic scene occurred after the Civil War and the 1867 creation of the Dominion of Canada. The advent of the North American industrial revolution stimulated expansionist philosophies in transportation enterprises everywhere on the continent. In financial terms, the growth of the North American railroad industry provided the financial resources for investment in complementary services of every nature, including steamships. The dynamic transcontinental railroads pushed westward. The even more powerful eastern railroads strove to expand their interests and consolidate their control over the transportation market by developing through lines with services coordinated over vast distances.

An integral part of this stage of North American railroad development involved transatlantic expansion as American and Canadian economic ties began to stretch around the globe. This era brought a transformation in the character of the deep-sea North American merchant marines as sailing vessels increasingly gave way to steam.

Among the railroads that sought to establish transatlantic or transpacific steamship lines were the Baltimore & Ohio, Canadian Pacific, Pennsylvania, Union Pacific, Central Pacific, Northern Pacific, and Great Northern. Many railroads created business relationships with both foreign and domestic steamship lines in order to provide through services for freight and passengers, but they are not pertinent here; a direct and specific financial tie with a railroad must exist for inclusion.

Possibly the first endeavor of this nature occurred on July 12, 1865, when the Baltimore & Ohio purchased four ships of the defunct Neptune Line and established the Baltimore & Liverpool Steamship Co. to run between Baltimore and Liverpool. Appropriately the ships were renamed *Allegheny*, *Carroll*, *Somerset*, and *Worcester* (1863, 1,244 tons, 9 knots). The ships had been constructed with wooden hulls by J. B. and J. D. Van Dusen of New York and were driven by a single screw. As such, they were the only wooden-hulled, screw steamers ever to maintain a regular service on the North Atlantic. The B&O operated the steamship line from September 30, 1865, through November 1, 1868, when sailings ceased. The ships were subsequently sold in 1873 for coastal service. In its place a new service had been agreed to on January 21, 1867, by John W. Garrett, president of the B&O, as the result of negotiations encouraged by Consul Albert Schumacher with the North German Lloyd Line, allowing immigrants to purchase a single ticket from Bremen to Baltimore and westward on the B&O to the U.S. hinterland. This involved the establishment by the B&O of a new joint service with the NGL Line. The ships of the Baltimore service were financed by a special issue of Litera B shares valued at $525,000 and divided between the B&O and North German Lloyd. The first of the new ships for that operation, *Baltimore* (1868, 2,321 tons, 10 knots), received a triumphal welcome at Baltimore involving a brass band, parade, and public reception on March 28, 1868. Immigrants and manufactured goods came to Baltimore, and Maryland tobacco and lumber went to Bremen. The business partnership was sustained through January 1, 1879, when, in the midst of the economic depression, the B&O withdrew and NGL assumed full ownership of the six ships in the fleet. The Baltimore market also attracted the attention of the Hamburg-American and Baltimore Mail Line. North German Lloyd maintained its service to Baltimore and cooperated with the B&O until the outbreak of World War I.

The classic example of railroad involvement is that of the Pennsylvania Railroad, which by 1865 had become the most powerful and influential business enterprise in the United States. Among its great rivals was the New York Central, which was admirably positioned to greet the constant stream of immigrants arriving in New York and to assist those passengers on their way to the hinterland. After the conclusion of the Civil War the New York challenge could not go unanswered by the Pennsylvania. As early as November 1865 the railroad's board of directors passed a motion offering to invest $500,000 in the stock of any steamship company willing to establish a line between Philadelphia and Liverpool. Whatever the Pennsylvania Railroad wanted, ultimately, it usually got.

As with all other eastern U.S. trunk-line railroads, the Pennsylvania wanted to expand its operations in order to ensure a through service for immigrants and trade from Europe to the U.S. hinterland. Its leadership expected transatlantic trade to expand for the rest of the century. That expectation combined with the desire to offer customers a single freight bill or passenger ticket to any U.S. destination. In the East continental rivalry fostered transatlantic competition in an effort to develop global control of the transportation of passengers and freight from European points of origin, across the North Atlantic, to destinations throughout North America. This prompted the PRR to encourage international trade either through the establishment of American-flag steamship lines or through the acquisition of a foreign-flag concern. The steamship schedules and services could be dovetailed with those of the railroad to provide a universal transportation network. The PRR financed the creation in 1873 of the American-flag American Steamship Co. and the Belgian-flag International Navigation Co. (Red Star Line, Société Anonyme de Navigation Belge-Américaine), which was controlled by the Philadelphia shipping magnate Clement Acton Griscom.

When the PRR decided to end direct involvement in 1884, the railroad insisted that the INC purchase the four ships (*Pennsylvania, Ohio, Indiana,* and *Illinois*) of the American line and provided the necessary financing. Subsequently the PRR also provided Griscom with the funds necessary to buy one of the most famous shipping lines in the world, the British-flag Inman Line (1850–1886). The result was the creation of the Inman & International Steamship Co., which in 1888–1889 ordered, with PRR funds, the two largest and fastest passenger liners in the world, *City of New York* (1888) and *City of Paris* (1889, 10,800 tons, 21 knots), from the Scottish firm of J. G. Thompson. The British government canceled the mail contract of the I&I, and in 1892 the company sought American registration for its two speed queens. Congress granted this on condition that two even larger ships be built in American yards, leading to the creation of the new American Line in 1892. The result was two ships constructed by the Cramp Shipyard of Philadelphia, the *St. Louis* and *St. Paul* (1894–1895, 11,600 tons, 21 knots).

Ultimately, with the moral support of the PRR and the financial genius of J. P. Morgan, Griscom attempted to gain control of every major steamship line on the North Atlantic through the creation of the International Mercantile Marine in 1902, a gigantic American-backed shipping trust. The American owners of the IMM paid too much for their acquisitions, which included the White Star Line, and the shipping trust had a difficult financial history, but by then its operation was independent of the Pennsylvania Railroad.

Similar railroad support for the creation of worldwide transportation networks also occurred in the Dominion of Canada. Sir Hugh Allan, founder of the Allan Steamship Co., became president of the Canadian Pacific Railway (CPR) in 1873. The enormous achievement of spanning North America from the St. Lawrence to the Pacific Ocean finally was completed in 1885.

As an experiment, in 1886 CPR chartered the 800-ton *W. B. Flint* to undertake a highly successful voyage from Yokohama to Vancouver that squelched any naysayers. With this strong testimonial to transpacific trade, in 1887 CPR chartered three steamships to start a regular service between Vancouver, Yokohama, Shanghai, and Hong Kong. The trade proved so strong that three more ships were added in 1888. The Canadian government in 1889 awarded CPR a mail contract worth $300,000 for a monthly service across the Pacific Ocean with ships capable of a speed of not less than 18 knots. The new ships were the 6,000-ton *Empress of India, Empress of Japan,* and *Empress of China,* which entered service in 1891, earned the subsidy, and dominated the trade.

Some time elapsed because of political dissension before

an effort could be made to establish a Canadian Pacific presence on the North Atlantic. This finally occurred in 1902 when the Canadian government indicated its willingness to subsidize a North Atlantic service providing CPR built at least four steamers capable of sustaining 20-knot crossings between Liverpool and Quebec in the summer and Liverpool and Halifax during the winter, when the St. Lawrence was frozen. With this encouragement CPR purchased for some $7 million the Canadian interests of Elder Dempster & Co., Ltd., including some 14 ships. The freighters of this line were operated by the Beaver Line, which was long a famous freight subsidiary of the CPR. The first of the CPR liners was the *Empress of Britain* (1906, 14,000 tons, 20 knots), soon joined by the *Empress of Ireland* (1907). The *Empress of Ireland* collided with the Norwegian coaler *Storstad* in the St. Lawrence River on May 28, 1914, and sank with the loss of 1,024 lives—the third-largest death toll of any maritime disaster on the North Atlantic.

The CPR achievement was to control the "All Red Route" from Britain across the Atlantic Ocean, North America, and the Pacific Ocean to Japan, China, and Australia. In the future the Canadian Pacific could boast that it was "the world's greatest transportation system" and that its services "bridged two oceans and linked four continents." Rumors of the combination of the steamship operations of CPR and its great rival, the Allan Line, were frequent. Certain supply services were combined in Liverpool as early as 1913. In 1915 the management of CPR's marine services was reorganized with the creation of Canadian Pacific Ocean Services Ltd. to handle the combined fleets. In July 1917 CPR finally purchased the ships and goodwill of the Allan Line and immensely increased its control of the Canadian North Atlantic service. After World War I Canadian Pacific Steamships Ltd. was created in 1921 and operated passenger liners on the North Atlantic until 1971, when the oceangoing passenger trade ended, and along the Pacific Coast until 1975.

On the West Coast the Union Pacific and Central Pacific railroads joined forces in 1874 to create the Occidental and Oriental (O&O) Steamship Co. as a means of fighting the disastrous rate wars begun by the Pacific Mail Steamship Co. Pacific Mail had founded a transpacific service from San Francisco to the Orient in 1867 and patronized the American transcontinental railroads until 1873, when it began to offer greatly discounted rates for cargo shipped to the East Coast via its steamers to Panama, across the Isthmus of Panama by train, and on to East Coast ports by steamer. The Union Pacific and Central Pacific united to create the Occidental & Oriental Co., and the ensuing rate war resulted in a division of the Asiatic trade between the steamship lines, with inbound cargo from the O&O's transpacific ships traveling east over the Central Pacific. Ultimately Collis P. Huntington bought Pacific Mail in 1893. Among the most famous and valuable cargos was silk, both in cocoons and raw. Southern Pacific trains assigned to carry the precious freight met the ships at the wharves, where the cargo was transferred under armed guard and then sent east. These fabled "silk trains" took priority even over express passenger trains,

Canadian Pacific once boasted "the world's greatest transportation system," including ships that spanned both the Atlantic and Pacific Oceans. The largest ship of all, and the CPR's flagship of the 1930s, was its second *Empress of Britain*. The 42,000-ton ship is seen here in 1931. —Canadian Pacific Railway Archives (Neg. NS.22046)

and on one occasion a Southern Pacific silk train made the run from San Francisco to Chicago in an unbelievable 49 hours. When Huntington died in 1900, the steamship line was incorporated into the holdings of the Southern Pacific, which then boasted a fleet of over 30 vessels that was maintained until 1915, when the ships were sold at war-inflated prices.

Under the leadership of James Hill, the Great Northern Railroad was completed from St. Paul to Seattle in 1893. Hill also gained control of the Northern Pacific Railroad in the same year and soon laid the foundation for extending service across the Pacific to Japan. Initially, Hill contracted with the Nippon Yusen Kaisha (NYK) Line in 1896 to have its transpacific steamers meet his trains in Seattle. In 1904 Hill ordered the huge cargo-passenger liners *Dakota* and *Minnesota* (1904, 20,178 tons, 14.5 knots) for the transpacific service; they were the largest ships built in the United States when delivered. In 1906 Hill founded the Great Northern Steamship Co. to consolidate the Northern Pacific service to Yokohama, Manila, and Hong Kong, and in 1914 the name was changed to Great Northern Pacific Steamship Co. when all the steamship operations were combined. The operation lasted until the early 1920s.

The challenge of creating international commercial ties in the second half of the nineteenth century often involved establishing a unique steamship service running directly to the principal port of the railroad. As transportation networks increased in sophistication by 1890, the multiplicity of available steamship lines made it possible for many alternative business arrangements to occur. Of all the railroads, the Canadian Pacific succeeded in maintaining a first-class steamship service for the longest period of time.

—William Henry Flayhart III

REFERENCES

Bonsor, N. R. P. *North Atlantic Seaway.* 5 vols. Jersey, Channel Islands, U.K.: Brookside, 1975–1980.

Cudahy, Brian J. *Over and Back: The History of Ferryboats in New York Harbor.* New York: Fordham Univ. Press, 1990.

Esslinger, Dean R. "Immigration through the Port of Baltimore." In *Forgotten Doors,* ed. M. Mark Stolarik, 61–74. Philadelphia: Balch Institute, 1988.

Flayhart, William Henry, III. *The American Line, 1871–1902.* New York: W. W. Norton, 2000.

———. *Perils of the Atlantic: Steamship Disasters, 1850 to the Present.* New York: W. W. Norton, 2003.

Harlan, George H. *San Francisco Bay Ferryboats.* Berkeley, Calif.: Howell-North, 1967.

Krieger, Michael. *Where Rails Meet the Sea: America's Connections between Ships & Trains.* New York: MetroBooks, 1998.

Musk, George. *Canadian Pacific: The Story of the Famous Shipping Line.* Newton Abbot, U.K.: David & Charles, 1981.

Transfer (periodical of the RMIG). Ellicott City, Md.: Rail-Marine Information Group, 1993–present.

Tratman, E. E. R. "Railway Car Ferries, American and Foreign." *Proceedings of the Forty-First Annual A.R.E.A. Convention,* 965–1031. Chicago: American Railway Engineering Assn., 1940.

Tyler, David Budlong. *Steam Conquers the Atlantic.* New York: D. Appleton-Century, 1939.

Marketing and Promotion

Marketing can be defined as "the act of selling." In the American marketplace companies and their products compete on the basis of product (function, quality, or performance), price, promotion (such as advertising and purchase incentives), and distribution. In the past, railroad practice and parlance placed responsibility for the sales function with the traffic department. More recently, the function is found in a marketing department.

Two carriers in particular excelled at the practice of marketing and advertising. Both ranked among the first business organizations to develop marketing campaigns with the objective of differentiating their product or brand from that of their competitors. Both had campaigns that exhibited the characteristics of effective advertising, largely an anomalous condition among railroads. Both emphasized the unique qualities of their line and service region. Both advertised consistently about schedule frequency and strategic message. The Atchison, Topeka & Santa Fe sold an intangible: creating a distinctive corporate imagery that equated its service with a romanticized Southwest. The New York Central seized upon the very tangible benefits of speed and comfort provided by the natural advantage of its unique water-level crossing of the Appalachian Mountains barrier.

Railroad marketing's conventions were set during the period of the industry's apex (1880–1900), characterized by intense innovation and individual experimentation. The traffic man's prime tenet—that promoting passenger service was the most efficient means of growing more profitable freight traffic—won popular acceptance during this time. In an era largely defined by intense westward migration and growth, that understanding stood as an eminently logical equation: the growing populations that settled along new rail lines demanded and produced goods and services at record rates, and shipment by rail typically offered the only efficient option. Meanwhile, in the more established eastern markets, operational efficiency, most often equated with speed and ease of travel, was thought to demonstrate a carrier's capacity to handle freight traffic.

For the railroads more than most industries, physical structure (where the individual carrier's lines went) determined marketing practice. The early generations of rail service (1830–1860) established a pattern of interconnectivity between regional carriers. The determining event in railroad marketing and competition produced a sea change in that model. The 1870s and 1880s witnessed a boom in railroad construction that introduced the widespread phenomenon of multiple, parallel carriers serving important markets. The resulting competition defined the structure of competition and marketing in the rail mode. To a great extent those patterns and decisions continue to affect the industry today.

This proliferation of parallel lines brought a marketplace governed by unregulated or open competitive forces, dubbed "unfettered competition" by the railroaders. In response, they developed a system of pooling arrangements with the objective of managing the undercutting of rates, or "rebating." Most intense were the Iowa Pool battles over Granger traffic in 1873 (*see* GRANGER LAWS AND CASES).

Overwhelmingly in competitive markets negotiated pool agreements governed price, product, and the distribution of service: three of four potential competitive strategies. This situation effectively made promotion, or in rail terms "service," the only variable. Vaguely alluded to as "gentlemen's agreements" by the press, the trunk lines' model—which governed service between the nation's two largest markets, the East Coast and Chicago, and involved as many as ten carriers—proved most important. These dictated a continuum of passenger-train running times and corresponding fares and frequently even the provision of amenities such as observation cars. Similar pooling agreements governed freight traffic during the period that preceded the imposition of effective regulation (1906–1912). Even afterwards competition for freight traffic remained a much-hindered affair. Competition on the basis of product—service or transit time and, very importantly, car supply—became serious factors in influencing shipper decisions. Equally important was the maintenance of fluid, efficient connections, in industry parlance "friendly," between individuals and/or groups of carriers necessary to connect shippers to suppliers and/or markets.

Fierce competition and growth also attracted adventuresome and innovative personalities (managers). Railroaders were among the pioneers in developing the concept of branding, or consistent product and corporate identification. The introduction of railroad logos in 1880 (claimed as a first by both the Chicago, Burlington & Quincy and the Chicago & North Western) was an important by-product of Granger line competition. Likewise, the display of logos on boxcars, timecards, and letterhead inspired George J. Charlton, general passenger agent (GPA) of the Chicago & Alton, to introduce the railroad calendar in 1883 as another tool for building and maintaining consumer recognition.

Railroaders also pioneered in the business of advertising. However, their method of payment for ad space proved controversial. Understandably wary of the advertising men's unproven claims about the efficacy of their product, railroaders, like most businessmen, paid for advertising by barter, exchanging transportation for ad space. The practice produced an immediate backlash: public opinion equated the flood of "free passes" that ensued with the industry's scourge, the rebating of freight rates. By 1890 passes were so prevalent that one forced to pay full fare "looked upon himself as something of a victim, if not a fool."

The vagaries of railroad advertising expenditures were also unique. Typically, railroads budgeted 1 to 2 percent of gross system passenger revenue for advertising. By comparison, mercantile houses averaged 5 percent or more. The purchase of space in mass-circulation media—newspapers and magazines—accounted for the bulk of it (e.g., industry leaders AT&SF and Southern Pacific averaged 50 percent, as reported in Interstate Commerce Commission "advertising expenditure"). Timetables and advertising-related salaries claimed most of the remainder, averaging between a third and a half of the total budget.

The industry's plan of organization further affected media choices. The station agent functioned as the public face of marketing—the point of purchase—and advertising initiatives. The agent network's pervasive and thorough geographic coverage was ideally suited to the task of distributing illustrated booklets, the third major type of media most often used by the railroaders.

In contrast to Europe, poster advertising played a relatively minor role in U.S. railroad marketing, primarily because of contrasting competitive models. European railways each generally served a defined region with minimal overlap, whereas in the United States competition between multiple carriers set the norm. The European system lent itself to the promotion of each region's distinctive features (and carrier); the American tended to emphasize "service" features in order to draw a competitive distinction.

Rail promoters sold a golden age of innovation (1870–1900) as the young mode's technology improved. Equipment improvements such as the introduction of dining cars (1882), vestibules (1887), and electric lighting (1898) all provided leverage and were aggressively marketed. The 1880s also marked the introduction of resort hotels (SP in 1880) and national park hotels (Northern Pacific in 1883) as engines of tourism and development. The limited train (Pennsylvania Railroad, 1880) and tourist-class sleeping cars (1886–1887) were two other significant marketing-driven innovations of the decade.

Throughout the 1890s railroads ranked among the top ten nationally advertised product categories. Lines such as the Alton, NYC, Rock Island, and AT&SF in particular created corporate identities and became household names. New York Central & Hudson River's GPA George H. Daniels exemplified this trend by applying the idea of branding to the naming of passenger trains: witness the *Empire State Express* of 1891.

Ticketing facilities were likewise important to marketing efforts. The 1890s saw the advent of city ticket offices, both shared and independent. The leader in this arena was NYC passenger agent Daniels, who advertised 77 "information bureaus" by 1903. Timetable racks provided ample display space for both local and connecting schedules and booklets. However, as transportation-marketing

For the Union Pacific and Southern Pacific of the time, there was nothing finer than *The Overland Limited* to San Francisco. This 1906 advertisement pointed out such special features as electric lights in each berth and the fact that it operated daily, not weekly or semiweekly like some other trains. —Michael E. Zega Collection

pioneer Frank Presbrey pointed out (*Profitable Advertising*, 1899), by the late 1890s the major carriers had reached a state of competitive parity on this front. The first years of the twentieth century saw the search for a new sort of competitive advantage. Presbrey proposed selling scenery or other aspects unique to each individual carrier as the solution.

The two campaigns that were to dominate passenger-train marketing in the twentieth century were created in response to Presbrey's formulation. Here the key objective was to create a tangible advantage out of thin air. NYC's "The Water Level Route—You Can Sleep" and "Graceful Curves and Easy Grades" in 1899 and AT&SF's "Fred Harvey Service" and Native American–themed imagery that depicted a mythic "Great Southwest," introduced in 1898, proved the most effective examples. And, as a matter of some significance, both campaigns survived and prospered throughout the era of railroad regulation.

The Hepburn Act granted the ICC the power to review ratemaking. Increased regulation (1906–1912) greatly changed rail marketing's dynamics by effectively ending competition on the basis of price. The end of price competition dictated that the carriers' vast network of agents emphasize service: transit time, maintenance of "friendly" (or efficient) connections, and adequate car supply. Personal relationships now supplemented and often supplanted business dealings in dinners at big-city traffic clubs, on the golf course, and at other entertainment venues. On the passenger side regulation eliminated the free passes that the rails had provided for politicians and editors; now, literally from the president of the United States to the small-town editor, everyone had to pay his or her way.

Yet even with the imposition of stringent regulation, the decade saw its share of innovative accomplishments. Most important was the completion of a wave of monumental product improvements by the carriers—new stations such as New York's Pennsylvania Station (1910) and Grand Central Terminal (1913) and Kansas City Union Station (1914). Less noticed was a bold but short-lived initiative advertising freight service by the Burlington Route and Santa Fe during 1910. Both carriers broke tradition by selling quality and prompt delivery ("Advertising Railroad Freight Service," *Judicious Advertising*, October 1910, 71–73).

During the 1910s and early 1920s a new type of advertising—corporate, or institutional, advertising—came into vogue. A few lines, led by the New York Central (under the rubric "For the Public Service"), presented the aforementioned and other improvements as proof of a newly enlightened outlook that emphasized their corporate contribution to the commonweal. Their objective was to influence public opinion about issues important to the railroad industry rather than to sell actual rail service. Notably, PRR, SR, Louisville & Nashville, and Philadelphia & Reading Railway announcements emphasized freight as well as passenger service.

During the 1920s marketers faced unexpected challenges. Rail traffic, both freight and passenger, for the first time experienced inroads from competing modes. Their response was framed during a period of intense regulatory debate over valuation and forced merger into balanced regional systems. Furthermore, two critical factors effectively dimmed the industry's competitive prospects: the advent of substantial competition from other modes and the ascendancy of a new generation of railroad managers, more comfortable with the status quo. As the decade progressed, a boom in consumer advertising made the effect of the railroads' conservative outlook painfully evident. The rails whose nineteenth-century expenditures remained unchanged now found their message virtually lost in a sea of automotive and consumer advertising.

Forward-looking rail managers such as PRR president William Wallace Atterbury reacted to the new competitive environment by proposing and beginning multimodal or intermodal transportation systems. During the late 1920s PRR introduced combined air-rail passenger transport, augmented long-distance service with bus connections, and introduced multimodal freight containers. However, pressures from regulatory bodies and competing business coalitions effectively undercut the initiatives' intended benefits.

To a large extent, the railroads' competitive response was one of inaction and indecision. From the mid-1920s through the late 1930s passenger traffic officials battled

The New York Central had much to boast of—and did—in this full-page ad in *Scientific American* on December 7, 1912. Its splendid new Grand Central Terminal was simply "the most wonderful terminal in the world," and its ranking train, the *20th Century Limited,* "the most famous." The *Century's* permanence was implied by images of the Pyramids.
—Middleton Collection

over the details of mounting a united or "cooperative" response to the automobile. Their initiative, summed up in the slogan "Travel by Train," remained stillborn as even the nation's florists rallied together under the banner "Say It with Flowers."

The Depression and streamlining brought tangible improvements for passengers; air conditioning afforded clean travel, diesel locomotives provided faster schedules, and industrial designers developed private accommodations that passengers had long desired. Still, on the advertising front, longtime advertising revenue and media allocations remained virtually unchanged, as indeed they would to the end. One bright spot was the growing use of radio, which proved highly effective in gaining attention for high-speed runs, but found little other use. (By the time television arrived, the rail passenger business had so seriously declined that it never became a significant factor.)

New products, especially all-coach trains, registered competitive headway against the automotive mode. However, in transportation, as in any service business, consistency is key. The majority of railroad service, both freight and passenger, remained unimproved and therefore had difficulty in matching inroads from competing modes.

The postwar years witnessed a resurgence of innovation for both passenger and freight marketing in response to advances by other modes. A range of new products increased rail's flexibility and efficiency: trailer-on-flatcar or "piggyback," Southern's Big John hopper car, unit trains, computer control of classification yards, and centralized traffic control. Passenger innovation centered upon the Vista-Dome car, which capitalized on the market shift from business to leisure travel brought by the advent of efficient air competition. However, these improvements remained insufficient to counter automotive advances.

The railroads' media preferences remained constant through the mid-1950s, when Union Pacific and Santa Fe introduced television advertisements for their premier trains. The passenger train's broad decline effectively ended railroad advertising by the early 1960s. Yet even then a few bright spots remained: Seaboard Coast Line promoted its Florida trains as a safe alternative to the rash of airline hijackings, and Penn Central dubbed its new high-speed Metroliner service "The Ground Shuttle" (1969–1970). Amtrak continued the creative tradition with cartoonist Edward Saxon's sketches reintroducing the flagship *Broadway Limited* (1972). As of this writing, the freight railroads continue to favor a traditional network of personalized relationships in marketing their services, primarily focusing on corporate transportation managers.

—Michael E. Zega

REFERENCES

Grodinsky, Julius. *Transcontinental Railway Strategy, 1869–1893: A Study of Businessmen.* Philadelphia: Univ. of Pennsylvania Press, 1962.

Pomeroy, Earl S. *In Search of the Golden West: The Tourist in Western America.* New York: Knopf, 1957.

Presbrey, Frank. *History and Development of Advertising.* Garden City, N.Y.: Doubleday, Doran, 1929.

———. "Transportation Advertising." *Profitable Advertising,* June 15, 1899, 37–38.

Zega, Michael E., and John E. Gruber. "Advertising the Southwest." *Journal of the Southwest* 43, no. 3 (Autumn 2001): 281–315.

———. *Travel by Train: The American Railroad Poster, 1870–1950.* Bloomington: Indiana Univ. Press, 2002.

Maryland & Pennsylvania Railroad

Two former narrow-gauge railroads, one aimed northeast from Baltimore and the other southeast from York, Pennsylvania, merged in 1901 to form the Maryland & Pennsylvania Railroad, the "Ma & Pa." Its route measured 77 miles; its terminals were about 50 miles apart as the crow flies (56 miles for the Pennsylvania Railroad's former Northern Central route).

After more than a half century of existence as a purely local railroad—the archetypal shortline carrying passengers and freight—the Ma & Pa began to cut back its line at the south end. It was purchased by Emons Industries in 1971 as the basis of a freight-car-leasing operation. It acquired two former Pennsylvania Railroad lines and in 1983 abandoned the last of its original route.

—George H. Drury

REFERENCE

Hilton, George W. *The Ma & Pa.* La Jolla, Calif.: Howell-North, 1980.

Massachusetts Bay Transportation Authority (MBTA)

The Metropolitan Transit Authority of Massachusetts was formed in 1947 to take over the privately owned Boston Elevated Railway, which provided urban rail and bus transit services to Boston and 13 surrounding communities. The MTA was succeeded in 1964 by the Massachusetts Bay Transportation Authority (MBTA), with an enlarged service territory encompassing Boston and 77 other municipalities in eastern Massachusetts.

One of the principal reasons for the expanded MBTA was to provide a basis for public support of the region's failing commuter rail services. The Boston area had a long history of commuter service. As early as 1838 the Boston & Worcester Railroad began offering what were probably the first "commuted" fares for daily travel between suburban areas and city terminals, giving rise to the term "commuter." All three of the Boston area's principal railroads—Boston & Maine, Boston & Albany, and New Haven—developed extensive commuter services. By 1920, the peak year for Boston commuter service, the three railroads were transporting nearly a quarter of a million commuters every day. By the early 1960s, however, these services were in a state of rapid decline.

The initial MBTA involvement in commuter service came in the form of assistance payments to the railroads operating the services. In 1972 the authority acquired from Penn Central the former New Haven and Boston & Albany commuter properties south and west of Boston, followed by the purchase of the Boston & Maine's extensive commuter system north of Boston in 1976. Penn

Central and Boston & Maine continued to operate the trains under contract. Amtrak was the contract operator from 1987 through 2003, when a new firm, Massachusetts Bay Commuter Railroad Co., took over.

With the full Boston commuter service under its control, MBTA launched a long-term effort to rehabilitate the commuter physical plant, replace equipment, and expand and extend services. Chief among MBTA's physical plant projects were the redevelopment of the two downtown Boston terminals at South Station and North Station into modern transportation centers and the construction of a new Southwest Corridor entry into Boston that is shared with Amtrak Northeast Corridor services and MBTA's Orange Line metro. Commuter rail train operation was shifted to push-pull mode, new or remanufactured diesel locomotives were acquired, and almost 300 new single- or bilevel commuter cars replaced older rolling stock and provided additional capacity.

In addition to rebuilding the existing plant, MBTA has extended several lines and added new routes to the system. Existing Northside lines were extended from Reading to Haverhill and from South Acton to Fitchburg. On the lines south and west of Boston service has been extended from Attleboro to Providence, from Franklin to Forge Park, and from Framingham to Worcester, and an entirely new Fairmount route was established. In 1997 MBTA completed major construction projects to restore service from South Station to Middleborough/Lakeville and Plymouth/Kingston over the former New Haven's Old Colony lines southeast of Boston. A third Old Colony line to Greenbush will open in 2007, while an extension from Providence to North Kingston, Rhode Island, over the Northeast Corridor should open in 2008. Still other planned extensions include a line from Stoughton to New Bedford and Fall River.

MBTA's current commuter rail system includes eight Southside lines operating from South Station to Framingham/Worcester, Needham, Franklin, Attleboro/Providence, Stoughton, Fairmount, Middleborough/Lakeville, and Plymouth/Kingston. Another five Northside lines operating from North Station serve Fitchburg, Lowell, Haverhill, Newburyport, and Rockport. By mid-2003 MBTA was operating a commuter rail system of 377 route-miles, serving 119 stations on 13 routes, with a fleet of 83 locomotives and 377 commuter cars. A total of 462 weekday trains were transporting a weekday average of almost 134,700 passengers.

—William D. Middleton

REFERENCES

Humphrey, Thomas J., and Norton D. Clark. *Boston's Commuter Rail: Second Section*. Cambridge, Mass.: Boston Street Railway Assn., Bulletin No. 20, 1986.

———. *Boston's Commuter Rail: The First 150 Years*. Cambridge, Mass.: Boston Street Railway Assn., Bulletin No. 19, 1985.

Mass-Transit Legislation and Programs

Federal urban mass-transportation programs of the late twentieth century have played a major role in preserving and expanding urban public transportation and commuter rail service at a time when these services were seriously threatened with extinction. Federal programs and subsequent action by state and local governments have helped maintain, strengthen, and expand urban rail transportation in the United States.

Both bus and rail urban mass-transportation services fell on hard times in the post–World War II era as customers deserted transit in favor of private automobiles. The change to a five-day workweek caused a major loss in transit and commuter rail patronage. Privately owned transit properties made major cutbacks in service, raised fares, and lost riders in wholesale quantities. The federal programs that began in the 1960s provided money for transit purposes, but the federal leadership role, together with requirements for comprehensive planning on the local level, was in all likelihood much more important than the dollars involved, especially in the first 20 years. This guidance and financial aid laid the groundwork for a revival of transit for a time until state and local officials enacted the needed enabling legislation and appropriated the money to make major improvements possible in what had become a sadly neglected part of the U.S. transportation industry. Rail transit has been a major beneficiary of the renaissance of mass-transit and commuter rail services.

The postwar era began with the all-time U.S. record of public transportation use, with over 26 billion transit rides taken in 1946. By 1950 patronage had fallen to about 17 billion rides as the public began to move to the suburbs, work only five days a week, and buy and use automobiles in larger numbers than ever before. The fall-offs in transit patronage brought about a major cutback of public transportation service as privately owned transit properties became less profitable. The first contractions involved loss of public transportation service for hundreds of small cities and towns during the 1950s. Streetcar service that had managed to survive during wartime shortages of tires and gasoline was eventually replaced by buses in most cities. What remained of urban rail service was often delivered with obsolete equipment and facilities. Many commuter rail services were especially decrepit.

The move to the suburbs was not new; it began in the 1840s and continued slowly and steadily with few interruptions. Earlier suburbanization took place along the arteries of public transportation, usually rail corridors served by streetcars, interurban electric lines, or commuter railroads. In the postwar period the suburbs grew at places remote from rail lines or any other public transportation service; they were designed to be served almost exclusively by the private automobile. By the 1950s traffic congestion, a problem in cities beginning in the 1920s, spread to the auto-oriented suburbs. Massive highway projects appeared to do little to relieve it. By the late 1950s it was obvious that merely building highways was no answer to urban congestion problems that had been spurred by the federal policy of supporting only highways in urban areas. It became apparent that moving people was more important than moving vehicles.

Changes in federal policy in the late 1950s inadvertently led to the development of a federal transit policy. The Transportation Act of 1958 was aimed mainly at helping the U.S. railroads, which had failed to participate in the general economic prosperity of the 1950s, in part because of federal aid to competing forms of transportation. In addition to abetting the surge of population to the suburbs, the major highway construction programs fostered by the federal interstate highway program and by state and local programs of highway construction and improvement spurred gains in the trucking industry. The railroads lost high-revenue traffic to the motor carriers, the rails lost passengers to the airlines, and federally improved waterways allowed barge lines to siphon off low-revenue bulk traffic in some markets. The Transportation Act of 1958 sought to relieve railroads of some burdens and guaranteed loans to railroads for capital purposes. It also helped U.S. railroads rid themselves of many money-losing passenger services.

It was the relative ease of abandoning passenger service under the terms of the 1958 act that alarmed the mayors of Boston, New York, Philadelphia, Chicago, and other cities. There was just cause for concern. The first railroad to use the passenger provisions of the 1958 act was the New York Central. Immediately after passage of the law (it was signed by President Eisenhower on August 12, 1958), the New York Central dropped its ferry service that connected its commuter rail service on the west side of the Hudson River with Manhattan. The Interstate Commerce Commission did not stop the end of the ferry service, and patronage on the commuter rail service plunged with removal of the ferry link. The railroad had a case justifying the end of the west-side commuter rail service.

Big-city mayors feared that the commuter railroads serving their cities, all of which lost considerable sums of money, would eliminate the commuter trains, with the result that even more automobiles would flood the city streets. In December 1958 the Lehigh Valley Railroad and the Delaware, Lackawanna & Western made public their plans to drop all commuter service in the metropolitan New York City area. The Pennsylvania Railroad stated that it would drop all off-peak commuter service to Manhattan. Other railroads in other cities made similar threats. Mayors Dilworth of Philadelphia, Wagner of New York, and Daley of Chicago, in the absence of a federal department of transportation, approached the U.S. Department of Commerce, hoping that it would provide capital funds to help replace aged commuter equipment, facili-

ties, and motive power. Nothing came of that effort; the Eisenhower administration did not seek new commitments, especially in urban areas.

This rebuff came in the face of concern from some federal officials who felt that a more varied approach to urban transportation problems was justified by federal policies that had helped create the problems. In 1960 Senator Harrison Williams of New Jersey, seeking an issue that would be popular with his constituents and important to the United States, proposed an urban mass-transportation act that would provide capital and other aid. The legislation proposal failed at first. However, as part of the Housing Act of 1961, during the Kennedy administration, there were provisions for federal capital loans for mass transit, demonstration grants in mass transit, and planning aid for mass transportation. In preparing the legislation, Senator Williams broadened the proposed program to include all mass transportation, not just commuter railroads.

Expanding the scope of federal aid to mass transportation was a wise move. At the time, only New York, Boston, Philadelphia, and Chicago had extensive commuter rail services. San Francisco had a single service remaining that linked San Francisco with San Jose. Modest commuter services served the Washington-Baltimore area, Pittsburgh, Cleveland, and St. Louis. To succeed in gathering support in Congress, a program must have broad benefits, and aid focused on commuter rail services was too narrow in its aim to garner the necessary support.

The demonstration grants under the Housing Act of 1961 were the first federal transit actions to gain attention nationwide; even though only a small sum of money was spent, the projects were often arresting and attention getting. Support in Congress increased. The Highway Act of 1962 required comprehensive urban transportation planning; this meant that all modes of transportation had to be considered, not just highways. In 1964 President Lyndon Johnson supported a small program of capital aid for urban public transportation, along with continuation of the planning and demonstration research programs. The Urban Mass Transportation Act of 1964, as amended over time, provided the vehicle for the mass-transit legislation that followed. By 1970 the federal transit programs included capital aid, operating aid, money for planning, aid for management training for public transit managers, and research, demonstration, and development programs.

The federal aid rose to a billion dollars for the first time in 1970. During the 1970s the federal programs provided increasing sums of money for mass transit. There was a falling off during the Reagan administration in the 1980s, but the point of the importance of transit and commuter rail service in urban transportation had already been made.

The transit industry worked through the well-organized and effective lobbying efforts of the American Public Transit Assn. (since 1999 the American Public Transportation Assn.). State transportation associations pursued state and local financial support with increasing vigor. Congress has generally been supportive, and helping mass transit became a popular nonpartisan issue. In 1991 the Intermodal Surface Transportation Efficiency Act (popularly known by the acronym ISTEA) combined highway and transit aid and provided an authorization of over $4 billion annually for transit over a six-year period. Subsequent reauthorization for a second six-year period as the Transportation Equity Act for the 21st Century (TEA 21) in 1997 authorized transit aid that rose to over $6 billion annually.

State and local government officials also realized by the 1970s that it was not possible to solve all the transportation problems in urban areas simply by building or improving roads. State governments began to supply funds, as well as pass enabling legislation so that, in turn, local governments could begin to provide money to support public transportation capital programs and cover a portion of operating costs. Encouraging state and local governments to lend support was the requirement of a state and/or local financial match of federal grants. Federal comprehensive planning was required to receive federal highway and transit funds. The federal aid permitted state and local dollars to be leveraged sufficiently to make major transit improvements.

Starting in the 1970s and continuing to the present, there has been a major expansion of transit service in cities of all sizes. Large cities such as Boston, New York, and Chicago have received large sums of money, federal, state, and local, that has been used to support significant improvements of public transportation. These betterments range from completely new bus services to expanding rail lines to purchase of thousands of new railcars and buses. A number of cities that did not have urban rail service built new rail transit lines, including Atlanta, Miami, Los Angeles, St. Louis, Baltimore, Sacramento, San Jose, and Portland, Oregon.

The federal programs also involved aid for small cities and rural areas. Although often overlooked, these programs made sure that every state had a strongly valued and widespread program of rural and small-city transportation. Every U.S. senator and most U.S. representatives had constituents in nonurbanized areas who benefited from these programs. This further encouraged state aid to public transportation. Widespread benefits meant widespread political support, a fact not lost on transit's proponents.

Beginning in the 1960s and 1970s, the federal programs, allied with state and local programs, helped public agencies take over money-losing rail commuter services, as well as virtually all other local transit providers. Before 1970 the great majority of all U.S. mass-transit and commuter rail service was supplied by private-sector companies as a for-profit enterprise. The federal programs began the profound change of the transit industry. By the 1970s virtually all U.S. urban mass-transportation services were provided by public agencies. In the case of commuter railroads, the service was subsidized by the public

agencies, and in many cases the commuter lines were eventually acquired by the public transportation authorities.

In the decades after 1980 there was significant expansion of existing rail commuter services. Major improvements of service between Washington and Baltimore were carried out, and a large-scale upgrading of service in Boston, New York, and Philadelphia took place. A new commuter rail service was initiated between Miami and West Palm Beach. New commuter rail services began in Los Angeles and San Diego and in the Virginia suburbs of Washington, D.C. Nashville, Tennessee, and Albuquerque started new services in 2006, and plans were under way for a rail service between San Antonio and Austin. A highly successful rail service between Dallas and Fort Worth was initiated at the beginning of the twenty-first century. Completely new rapid-transit services were begun to serve the citizens of Atlanta, Baltimore, Miami, and San Francisco. New light-rail operations supplied service in Baltimore, St. Louis, Denver, Dallas, Salt Lake City, Sacramento, San Jose, Portland, Oregon, Salt Lake City, Los Angeles, San Diego, and Houston. At the beginning of the twenty-first century ground was broken for new light-rail services in Houston, Phoenix, Charlotte, and Seattle, Austin, and San Antonio were involved in building local support for light-rail lines.

Independent of U.S. efforts but nevertheless gaining encouragement from them were improvements in public rail transit in Calgary, Edmonton, Toronto, Vancouver, and Montreal, Canada. Mexico City, Guadalajara, and Monterrey built new rapid-transit services in Mexico.

Rail transit again appears to be attracting public interest. Moreover, urban rail transportation has succeeded in attracting very large numbers of passengers. Some facilities may have approached their practical capacity in their current form. The Washington Metrorail system is contemplating new subways parallel to the present lines, and New York appears ready to build a long-promised subway under Second Avenue, as well as extending the subway under 42nd Street to the Javits Convention Center. Some light-rail service in San Francisco is overwhelmed with passengers; Penn Station in New York and Union Station and Randolph Street Station in Chicago are apparently close to capacity. Federal funds are being sought to expand facilities.

Some observers have asked whether some of the rapid-transit and light-rail lines built since 1970 were really recent manifestations of the old interurban electric railways. Indeed, the difference between an interurban railway, light-rail transit, heavy-rail transit, and commuter rail is blurred. The far-flung operations of the Washington Metropolitan Area Transit Authority's Metrorail rapid-transit service, with lines reaching well out into the suburbs, may be seen as either an interurban or a commuter rail service. The same is true of the lines of the Bay Area Rapid Transit District in the San Francisco region. Whatever the definition, the period since 1960 has seen a major increase in the provision of rail services oriented to serve cities in North

America. Behind this phenomenon is the federal aid program in support of urban mass transportation.

—George M. Smerk

REFERENCES

Altshuler, Alan, with James P. Womack and John R. Pucher. *The Urban Transportation System: Politics and Policy Innovation.* Cambridge, Mass.: MIT Press, 1979.

Attoe, Wayne, ed. *Transit, Land Use & Urban Form.* Austin: Univ. of Texas at Austin, Center for the Study of American Architecture, 1988.

Barrett, Paul. *The Automobile and Urban Transit: The Formation of Public Policy in Chicago, 1900–1930.* Philadelphia: Temple Univ. Press, 1983.

Jackson, Kenneth T. *Crabgrass Frontier: The Suburbanization of the United States.* New York: Oxford Univ. Press, 1985.

Jones, David. *Urban Transit Policy: An Economic and Political History.* Englewood Cliffs, N.J.: Prentice-Hall, 1985.

Lyle C. Fitch and Associates. *Urban Transportation and Public Policy.* San Francisco: Chandler, 1964.

Smerk, George M. *The Federal Role in Urban Mass Transportation.* Bloomington: Indiana Univ. Press, 1991.

Vuchic, Vukan R. *Urban Public Transportation: Systems and Technology.* Englewood Cliffs, N.J.: Prentice-Hall, 1981.

Yago, Glenn. *The Decline of Transit: Urban Transportation in Germany and U.S. Cities, 1900–1970.* New York: Cambridge Univ. Press, 1984.

William Gibbs McAdoo. —Library of Congress (Neg. LC-USZ62-33041)

McAdoo, William Gibbs (1863–1941)

Few figures of twentieth-century railroading mixed business and politics as effectively as William Gibbs McAdoo. The future railroad president, Treasury secretary, and senator was born in Georgia on October 31, 1863. Educated at the University of Tennessee at Knoxville, McAdoo joined the Tennessee bar in 1885 and practiced law in Chattanooga. He moved to New York City in 1892. The prospects for commuter rail service into the city interested him, and he learned that construction of a tunnel under the Hudson River had been abandoned. While practicing law, he became president of the New York & New Jersey Railroad, and when it combined with other companies to become the Hudson & Manhattan Railroad (H&M) in 1902, he became its president. Construction of the tunnels, the first ones under the Hudson, began again in 1902, and they were opened with much fanfare on February 25, 1908.

McAdoo demanded that H&M employees treat the public with courtesy. As president, he implemented innovations such as dual platforms, so that passengers boarding and exiting trains would not collide, and portable ticket booths that could be moved to heavy traffic areas.

McAdoo became involved in Democratic politics. He served as vice chairman of the Democratic National Committee in 1912 and helped Woodrow Wilson win the party's nomination. A victorious Wilson rewarded McAdoo by appointing him Treasury secretary. McAdoo helped maneuver the Federal Reserve Act through Congress in 1913 and was made chairman of the Federal Reserve Board. McAdoo's first wife died in 1912, and two years later he married the president's daughter, Eleanor. When the United States entered World War I, McAdoo played a vital role helping finance the war, and in 1917 he became director general of the U.S. Railroad Administration. He held both posts until he resigned from the cabinet in 1918.

He returned to New York City and in 1922 moved to Los Angeles, where he resumed his law practice. Enthusiastically endorsed by the railroad unions during the 1924 election, he ran for the Democratic presidential nomination. The convention divided between McAdoo and New Yorker Alfred Smith and finally chose John Davis.

McAdoo returned to Los Angeles and in 1932 won a seat in the U.S. Senate, where he served until 1938. As a senator, he helped write the Federal Reserve Act of 1933 and served as chairman of the Patents Committee. He resigned after he failed to win renomination but served on the Democratic National Committee from 1932 to 1940. McAdoo died on February 1, 1941, and is buried in Arlington National Cemetery.

—Jon R. Huibregtse

REFERENCES

Fitzherbert, Anthony. "The Public Be Pleased: William G. McAdoo and the Hudson Tubes." Electric Railroaders' Assn., Supplement to *Headlights* 26, no. 6 (June 1964): 1–8.

McAdoo, William G. *Crowded Years: The Reminiscences of William G. McAdoo.* Boston: Houghton Mifflin, 1931.

McClellan, George B. (1826–1885)

George Brinton McClellan was born in Philadelphia, Pennsylvania, on December 3, 1826. His father was a physician specializing in ophthalmology; his mother came from a distinguished Philadelphia family. Young George received an excellent education in Philadelphia, including private tutoring. When he decided to seek a military career, his father secured an appointment for him at West Point, which he entered in the summer of 1842.

At that time West Point was probably the best engineering school in the United States, and McClellan took readily to the studies of math and engineering, where his excellent early education made him a proficient scholar. He chose the Army Corps of Engineers as his military specialty. He graduated second in the class of 1846 and was soon dispatched to Mexico to serve in the Mexican War. He returned to West Point and spent some time as an instructor in practical engineering and mathematics. He also continued his study of classic works on military strategy, tactics, and history.

McClellan's study of the art and science of war soon established for him a reputation as a highly knowledgeable young officer. He gained practical engineering field experience as a member of an expedition to trace the origin of the Red River of the South and in another assignment surveying the rivers and harbors of Texas. Successful in both these ventures, he was ordered to be a member of the engineering team conducting the Pacific railroad survey for the Department of the Army. He was involved in the survey of a rail route from St. Paul, Minnesota, to Puget Sound. McClellan's work on these projects brought him to the attention of Secretary of War Jefferson Davis. Davis ordered the young officer to investigate the established railroads of the United States and to study and report on the construction methods employed and costs.

Progress for career officers in the peacetime army was very slow, and McClellan resigned his commission and on January 15, 1857, took the position of chief engineer of the Illinois Central Railroad. The president of the railroad was mainly occupied with fund-raising in New York and abroad, and soon McClellan was named vice president of the Illinois Central; as operations manager of the railroad, he was in effect the presiding official. Hard economic times proved that he was a capable manager who ran the railroad with great economy while not discouraging business. His reputation was bolstered by his contracting with steamboat operators to provide an integrated service from the southern terminal of the IC at Cairo, Illinois, to Memphis, Vicksburg, and New Orleans, and he planted the idea with the board of directors that the IC should be extended all the way to New Orleans.

In 1860 he married and took the post of superintendent of the Ohio & Mississippi Railroad, which linked Cincinnati with the Mississippi River at St. Louis. Moving to Cincinnati, McClellan attracted the attention of the governor of Ohio. When the Civil War started, the Ohio governor had McClellan named a major general of the Ohio Volunteers, which he accepted on April 23, 1861. On May 3, 1861, he was named commander of the Department of the Ohio, and on May 14 he was appointed a major general in the federal army. McClellan was successful in efforts to protect the Ohio & Mississippi and the Baltimore & Ohio from the Confederate army, and also in keeping the western part of Virginia loyal to the Union.

Before long, impressed by McClellan's reputation, President Abraham Lincoln named him commander of the Army of the Potomac and soon after the commander of all Union forces. McClellan proved a reluctant warrior, refusing to believe that he had the advantage over the Confederates. His failure to take advantage of his superior forces and supplies led to his dismissal as commander of the Army of the Potomac. His army career over by any realistic measure, McClellan turned to politics, running unsuccessfully against Lincoln in 1864. Later he was elected governor of New Jersey. Mainly he pursued a business career and formed an engineering consulting firm. He was for a time in 1872 the president of the Atlantic & Great Western Railroad.

McClellan was a failure as a military man; his greatest success came as a railroad official with the Illinois Central and the Ohio & Mississippi. He embarked on writing a series of magazine articles on battles of the Civil War for *Century* magazine. He died of a heart attack on October 29, 1885, at the age of 58.

—George M. Smerk

REFERENCES

Corliss, Carlton J. *Main Line of Mid-America: The Story of the Illinois Central.* New York: Creative Age Press, 1950.

Sears, Stephen W. *George B. McClellan, the Young Napoleon.* New York: Ticknor & Fields, 1988.

McGinnis, Patrick B. (1904–1973)

In Northeast railroading the name McGinnis is associated with one of the industry's great graphic images: a big

Patrick B. McGinnis. —Philip R. Hastings, *Trains* Magazine Collection

N-over-H logo, on red orange, white, and black rolling stock, introduced on the New York, New Haven & Hartford Railroad in 1955. The image survives today on locomotives owned by the Connecticut Department of Transportation. It is a lasting legacy of Patrick B. McGinnis, president of the New Haven during a stormy tenure in the mid-1950s.

McGinnis was born in Palmyra, New York, in 1904, the son of Irish immigrants. Patrick McGinnis, Sr., worked in New York Central's track department, and young Patrick had much early exposure to rail operations. After college McGinnis worked for New York City brokerage and investment firms and soon became an industry authority in railroad bonds. During the Great Depression, when dozens of railroads were bankrupt, McGinnis also became an expert in rail reorganization. As many unhealthy railroads recovered when the nation moved into World War II, millions of dollars flowed to McGinnis, his employers, and those who followed his guidance.

McGinnis had identified several railroads that he believed could be particularly profitable under new leadership. He partnered with a group of investors to acquire control of the old Norfolk Southern Railway, and McGinnis was named chairman of its board of directors in 1947. Although McGinnis and his colleagues came under Inter-

state Commerce Commission scrutiny amid questions over their salaries and other benefits, the NS became profitable. Despite these difficulties, McGinnis supporters on the Central of Georgia board of directors elected him to that railroad's board in 1952. On the same day in 1953 that he resigned from NS, McGinnis became chairman of CofG, where he lasted only a month.

McGinnis next led a harsh proxy fight with several major New Haven stockholders who were dissatisfied with NYNH&H management's dividend policies. McGinnis's group emerged in 1954 with a small board majority after a long and emotional annual meeting, and the new board elected McGinnis president. Although his term as head of the NYNH&H was short, McGinnis left major marks on the 1,700-mile railroad. Most enduring, perhaps, was the new image created by graphic designer Herbert Matter of the firm Knoll Associates. (McGinnis's wife, Lucille, is often incorrectly credited for the NYNH&H's image, although she apparently influenced the final design choices.)

McGinnis was a flamboyant leader, always in the public eye. He championed new lightweight high-speed passenger trains such as the Talgo, but stayed only long enough to buy three experimental (and largely unsuccessful) trains. He cut costs all over the railroad, reduced passenger services, pushed for local government funding of passenger operations, and recommended elimination of NYNH&H's electrified operations. McGinnis advocated the purchase of dual-mode FL9 locomotives, which did allow the railroad to reduce electric operations and eliminate the diesel-to-electric engine change at New Haven, Connecticut. Amazingly, some of these FL9s continue to work in 2006—still in the McGinnis paint scheme.

While he was heading the NYNH&H, McGinnis associates won a proxy fight for control of the Boston & Maine and asked him to serve as president of that railroad as well. Protracted hearings delayed a decision. Back in New Haven, McGinnis was facing mounting criticism from NYNH&H passengers and regional newspapers over service issues. Even his supporters on the board questioned some of his decisions. McGinnis resigned his New Haven post on January 20, 1956. Later that same day B&M's board named him president.

During his six years at the B&M McGinnis maintained a much lower profile than he had on the NYNH&H. He did hire Matter to design the familiar B-over-M logo and new color schemes and bought a high-speed Talgo train identical to New Haven's. He began to eliminate most of the road's long-distance passenger service.

McGinnis stepped down as B&M president in 1962, although he was named to the unpaid position of chairman of the board. McGinnis later was sentenced to a federal prison term for involvement in a kickback scheme over the sale of B&M passenger cars. He died in 1973.

—Scott A. Hartley

Medicine

The appearance of the iron horse during the second quarter of the nineteenth century quickly led to a close and continuing relationship between the railroad enterprise and the medical community in both North America and Europe. It became obvious to managers of the first railroads that the inherent dangers involved in travel necessitated some association with physicians, no matter how poorly trained. As early as 1834 the infant Baltimore & Ohio Railroad employed a doctor, an action that may have been inspired by the common naval practice of carrying a ship's surgeon. Just as sailing vessels journeyed far from medical assistance, at times rail carriers served areas that were nearly as remote. In the mid-1840s the Rhine Railway in Holland hired physicians to attend to the medical needs of its employees and their families. By the 1860s most railroads, both domestically and abroad, had or would start some sort of regularized medical system. After all, the number of accidents increased as mileage soared, freight and passenger traffic burgeoned, and train speeds increased. Undeniably, American carriers had become extraordinarily dangerous. Moreover, railroad officials realized that providing medical assistance was humane, lessened the likelihood of expensive and troublesome lawsuits, and engendered goodwill among workers and patrons. Although common law gave little incentive for railroads to decrease the numbers of injured, most of all in the case of trespassers, who were usually vagrants, railroads customarily provided medical aid to any accident victim.

Railway medicine took several paths. The most widespread activity involved examinations and emergency care of employees. Companies wanted their workers, especially those involved in train service, to be physically capable of performing their duties. They began to have medical doctors screen applicants to make certain that these individuals had good vision and no chronic diseases or disabilities and possessed "good moral character." Regularly scheduled reexaminations took place, usually on an annual basis. If employees suffered on-the-job accidents, physicians would attend to their needs. Before the advent of Janney or knuckle couplers and other technological betterments, often inspired by the Federal Safety Appliance Act of 1893, hand and arm injuries were ubiquitous. Moreover, in the days of steam, eye injuries, usually caused by flying cinders, were numerous.

The selection process for railroad physicians evolved during the nineteenth century. Until the 1870s or so it was typical for a railroad to rely on local practitioners to examine and treat workers and to care for passengers who sustained injuries, paying them on a case-by-case basis. Then carriers started to offer retainers to a select group of reputable on-line physicians and surgeons who could meet their medical requirements. This policy change reduced the possibilities of mistakes and of physicians bilking the company. It also resulted in better quality control in a time of poorly trained physicians and widespread quackery. There was an added benefit: health care fostered employee loyalty and helped reduce worker turnover.

By the twentieth century railroads had largely formalized their relationships with physicians and surgeons. Although most of these healers received retainers and continued their own private medical practices, it became customary for railroads to hire "chief surgeons" or "chief medical officers" on a full-time basis. These physicians oversaw health programs, including the hiring and assessment of local part-time doctors. Many railroads also had a list of specialists, particularly oculists, who were more commonly engaged through a retainer arrangement. Even small carriers, including many shortlines, embraced the same practice. To make certain that the injured were treated by the proper doctors, carriers typically listed on their employee or operating timetables by city and town those individuals who had been officially sanctioned.

Physicians who became involved in railroad work frequently gathered to discuss their activities. An illustration involves professional medical groups. In the early 1880s the Wabash, St. Louis & Pacific (soon the Wabash) claimed to have the first systemwide association of railway surgeons. This organization, emulated by other carriers, held annual meetings in which members read papers covering such practical topics as "The Induction of Rapid Anesthesia in Railway Injuries" and "First-Aid Paraphernalia for the Caboose." The association, underwritten by the sponsoring railroad, published these findings. They were distributed to other physicians retained by the road and were made available to colleagues on other carriers.

In time, these professional groups disappeared. The case of the Wabash is typical. At the beginning of World War II the surgical association suspended its annual meetings for the "duration of the emergency" and never resumed them, a casualty of competing specialized professional organizations and expanded access to medical information.

After the Civil War railroads began slowly to establish "brick and mortar" facilities. The best known were the railroad hospitals. As early as 1867 the Central Pacific Railroad opened a temporary hospital in Sacramento, California, and a year later it constructed a much larger replacement structure with beds for 125 patients, making this facility one of the largest, most up-to-date hospitals in the American West. Not long thereafter the "Gould Roads," several carriers controlled by financier Jay Gould that included the Iron Mountain, Missouri Pacific, Texas & Pacific, and Wabash railroads, embarked on establishing a network of company hospitals. By the 1880s the Wabash, for one, sported such facilities in Danville, Illinois, Kansas City, Missouri, Peru, Indiana, and Springfield, Illinois.

Most of these specially created "hospital departments," whether part of the Gould Roads or not, opted for what

Some railroads operated fully equipped hospital cars. An early example was the Southern Pacific's Hospital Car No. 119, rebuilt from a business car in 1905. Located at the railroad's West Oakland, California, hospital, the car was equipped with operating and dressing rooms, space for 12 patient berths, staterooms for doctors and nurses, and kitchen and staff spaces. —Don Munger Collection

One of the leaders in establishing medical care for railroad employees was the Wabash Railway. The railroad began operating its own hospitals in the late 1800s, and three Wabash hospitals continued to operate well after World War II; the last company hospital closed in 1972 at Decatur, Illinois. This was the Peru, Indiana, Wabash hospital, which played a major role in treating injuries after the railroad's worst-ever accident in 1901. —H. Roger Grant Collection

might best be described as mutual benefit associations. A number of nonrailroad businesses, including farm machinery, hardware, and stove manufacturers, also settled on this approach. Although railroads usually covered expenditures for hospital buildings and some related expenses, employees paid much of the costs for their medical care. Those who joined—the programs were usually voluntary—were assessed a reasonable monthly fee, based on income, with a track laborer contributing somewhat less than half of what a locomotive engineer paid. If an injury occurred, all hospitalization and medical expenses would be fully covered. Unlike most medical services in Europe, American railroad hospitals treated only employees and not members of their immediate families. There was also a firm policy of not attending to certain medical conditions. "Under no circumstance will treatment be given alcoholic or venereal diseases or their afteraffects, chronic diseases arising before entering the Company's services, injuries received in fights, brawls or any other disability arising from vicious acts." In the late nineteenth and early twentieth centuries some railroads, usually the largest, maintained a network of medical dispensaries that provided first-aid services and prescription medicines.

By the latter part of the twentieth century railroads continued to provide some degree of medical coverage for employees. Private health insurance plans, backed by the representative railroads, became nearly universal. Yet free-standing "railroad hospitals" and dispensaries closed, although at times a few HMO-type railway associations grew out of the long-established railroad hospital traditions. When the federal government entered the health insurance world in a major way with passage of the Medicare Act in 1965, the role of public involvement expanded. One important constant, however, has been the use of railroad-sanctioned physicians for both examinations and emergency care and the overall commitment of the railroad industry to the good health of its employees.

—H. Roger Grant

Mellen, Charles S. (1851–1927)

Charles Sanger Mellen was an important figure in nineteenth-century railroad management and played a particularly strong role in New England. Born on August 16, 1851, in Lowell, Massachusetts, he was the son of George K. and Hannah M. (Sanger) Mellen. He graduated from high school in 1867 (a rare occurrence in mid-nineteenth-century America) after a primary education in the public schools of Concord, New Hampshire. He began his railroad career in 1869 in the office of the cashier of the Northern New Hampshire Railroad. His ability was recognized early on, and Mellen rose steadily in railroad management: Central Vermont (1872–1873), Northern New Hampshire (1873–1880), and Boston & Lowell (1880–1888).

In 1888, in a major move, Mellen became general purchasing agent for the Union Pacific and subsequently became general traffic manager of that railroad. Mellen attracted the favorable attention of financier J. P. Morgan. Thanks to Morgan's influence, in 1892 Mellen became general manager of the New York & New England Railroad and soon after was appointed second vice president of the New York, New Haven & Hartford. Again because of Morgan's influence, Mellen was awarded the presidency of the Northern Pacific in 1897. It was an important time in the history of the financially troubled Northern Pacific. Mellen had little to do with the financial side of things, concentrating instead on the acquisition of feeder railroads and making capital investments in the railroad to improve its efficiency and produce a favorable operating ratio.

The growing influence of James J. Hill in the fortunes of the Northern Pacific made life difficult for Mellen, and Morgan decided to bring him back east, where Mellen became president of the New York, New Haven & Hartford in 1903. By that time he had a national reputation in railroad circles. President Theodore Roosevelt consulted with Mellen on railroad matters and quoted Mellen extensively in his annual messages to Congress, which often dealt with railroad issues.

At the New Haven Mellen let the financial matters repose in the hands of the directors and bankers; he concentrated on making physical improvements to the railroad, including double- and triple-tracking busy parts of the property, electrification of the entry into New York City, and joining with the Pennsylvania Railroad in developing the Hell Gate route from New York City into New England. Mellen worked industriously to monopolize all transportation in New England, buying up railroads, steamship lines, and electric interurban and local streetcar lines and reputedly often paying too much for a property in order to pull together another piece of monopoly. In addition to his presidency of the New Haven, he also presided over the Maine Central and the Boston & Maine.

Mellen was not a lovable or affable person; he fawned over superiors and was dictatorial and harsh to subordinates. Whatever his talents and faults, he soon became embroiled in difficulty over the virtual monopoly of New England transportation. Resentment over his management was touched off and grew after a series of serious railway accidents. His personal life was troubled with marital difficulties in 1912 and 1913. Adding to his problems, the Interstate Commerce Commission investigated Mellen and his activities and called his management of the New England properties "one of the most glaring instances of misadministration revealed in all the history of American railroading." Mellen's faults were paraded before the public; even though some of the financial problems were not of his doing, because he was president of the railroads, the financial difficulties were his responsibility. He was also responsible for the lack of proper maintenance of equipment uncovered in the investigations. His burden of very conservative board members was not helpful in making needed improvements in the railroad properties under his control. Several investigations and a public outcry forced his resignation from leadership roles in 1913. He largely retired from all business affairs after this, moving to Concord, New Hampshire, where he died on November 17, 1927.

—George M. Smerk

REFERENCES

Batson, G. W. "Charles S. Mellen: Railroad Organizer." *Review of Reviews*, Aug. 1907.
Dictionary of American Biography.
Garrett, Garet. "Things That Were Mellen's and Things That Were Caesar's." *Everybody's Magazine*, July 1914.
Lyle, E. F., Jr. "C. S. Mellen, Master of Traffic." *World's Work*, May 1905.

Menk, Louis Wilson (1918–1999)

Louis Menk, widely credited with making the gigantic Burlington Northern merger a success, was born in Englewood, Colorado, in 1918, the son of a trainman. During the Great Depression he delivered newspapers, cut lawns, pumped gasoline, and became a champion golfer at Denver High School. He studied at Denver University for two years, at the same time learning Morse code as a messenger for the Union Pacific, after which he worked as a telegrapher for the St. Louis–San Francisco (Frisco) Railway.

At the Frisco Menk worked his way up the corporate ladder to assistant trainmaster and later division superintendent. In 1953 he graduated from an advanced management program offered by Harvard University. In 1962 he was named president of the Frisco, at age 44 the youngest company president in U.S. railroading at the time. Two years later he was named Frisco's chairman.

In 1965 Harry C. Murphy retired as president of the Chicago, Burlington & Quincy Railroad (Burlington Route). A beloved figure in the railfan community, Murphy favored passenger-train service and had a soft spot for steam locomotives, retaining a CB&Q 2-8-2 and a 4-8-4 for excursions. But when Burlington's earnings sagged, Menk moved over from the Frisco to improve CB&Q's balance sheet after Murphy's retirement. A businessman first and foremost, Menk ended the popular steam excursion program in 1966 and began the process of eliminating money-losing passenger trains. He later said that the Burlington had not been doing well at the time, that he was trying to contain costs, and that steam was not paying its way, despite the public relations value. Menk said that he never regretted the decision, although it earned him the enmity of railroad enthusiasts, some of whom wore "Menk the Fink" buttons.

With the Burlington Northern merger on the horizon, Menk moved to the presidency of the Northern Pacific in 1966 since it, along with Great Northern, would be one of the major merger players. Of lesser standing would be CB&Q and Spokane, Portland & Seattle. Menk fought antitrust laws for several years, finally achieving victory with consummation of the BN merger on March 2, 1970. Menk was named its first president and became chairman and CEO of BN in 1971.

Under Menk's leadership, BN was able to avoid many of the internal divisions that derailed the roughly concurrent Penn Central merger. The new railroad also was able to remake itself to handle the influx of coal trains from Wyoming's Powder River Basin. Low-sulfur Wyoming coal was in demand because of antipollution requirements contained in the Clean Air Act of 1970. Much of the BN route system had to be rebuilt to accommodate the heavy trains, and a new line was built in Wyoming to reach several mines.

In 1980 Menk succeeded in bringing his old railroad, the Frisco, into the BN fold. He retired as chairman of BN the following year. When Burlington Northern built a new corporate headquarters in Fort Worth, Texas, the company named the main street through the campus Lou Menk Drive. BN later merged with the Atchison, Topeka & Santa Fe Railway to form Burlington Northern & Santa Fe Railway.

In 1982 International Harvester, a maker of trucks and farm equipment, was on the brink of bankruptcy. The company asked Menk to come out of retirement to save the company. In 20 months he reorganized Harvester, administering cutbacks and installing a new management team. He served as chairman and chief executive of the company until 1983 and then retired a second time. Menk died of cancer at age 81 in Carefree, Arizona, a suburb of Phoenix, on November 23, 1999.

—Steve Glischinski

Metra. *See* Northeast Illinois Regional Commuter Railroad Corp. (Metra)

Metrolink. *See* Southern California Regional Rail Authority (Metrolink)

Metropolitan Transportation Agency (Agence métropolitaine de transport, AMT)

Created by the Quebec provincial legislature in 1995, the Metropolitan Transportation Agency (Agence métropolitaine de transport, AMT) is a regional transit agency with a charter that includes overall regional planning, coordination, integration, and promotion for public transit for the Greater Montreal metropolitan region, as well as direct management and development of its regional/commuter rail system through purchase of service agreements with Canadian Pacific Railway and Canadian National. At its formation AMT assumed responsibility for Montreal's two long-established commuter lines: the 41.3-mile, diesel-powered CPR route from Windsor Station to Dorion-Rigaud, which began hauling commuters as early as 1889, and the 19.9-mile, electrified route from Central Station through the Mount Royal Tunnel to Deux-Montagnes, which was completed as part of a new central terminal project by the Canadian Northern Railway in 1918. Both lines had begun receiving financial support from the provincial and regional governments in 1982, when the Montreal Urban Community Transportation Commission (Société de transport de la Communauté de Montréal, STCUM) took over management and funding of the service.

The former CPR service received 24 new Bombardier coaches, rebuilt locomotives, station improvements, and a new intermodal station linked to the Montreal Métro at Vendôme. Push-pull operation was established.

The CN route was severely obsolescent and operated several electric locomotives dating from 1914, the oldest main-line locomotives in regular service in North America. That route was completely rebuilt between 1992 and 1995 with a new 25 kv AC electrification and new signaling. The track was reconstructed, stations were replaced or rebuilt, and a fleet of 58 modern multiple-unit cars built by Bombardier was placed in service.

AMT took responsibility for the two lines from STCUM soon after its formation and began the development of additional Montreal commuter routes based largely upon a plan for expanded service that had been proposed jointly by CPR and CN in 1993. The first of these to begin operation was a 28-mile route operating north from Montreal over CPR tracks from Windsor Station to Blainville. Initially operated as a temporary service, the line rapidly developed a substantial traffic and was made permanent in 2000.

In June 2000 AMT established a second new service, restoring a commuter rail service over the Victoria Bridge to the CN main line south of the St. Lawrence that had been discontinued in 1988. Initially operated between Central Station and McMasterville, the service was extended to Saint-Hilaire in August 2002. A third line, operating over CPR between Windsor Station and Delson, south of the St. Lawrence, opened in September 2001. Equipment to operate these expanded services has included 80 former GO Transit single-level aluminum cars and 11 new Electro-Motive F59 units acquired during 2000–2001. Probable further expansion of the AMT commuter rail system includes extension of the Delson route to Iberville; routes on CPR rails to Mascouche, north of Montreal, on CN to Repentigny, northwest of Montreal on the north bank of the St. Lawrence, and also on CN to Varennes, northeast of Montreal on the south bank; and a new line from either the Dorion-Rigaud or Deux-Montagnes line to Montreal's Dorval International Airport.

—William D. Middleton

REFERENCE

North American Commuter Rail, 1994. Pasadena, Calif.: Passenger Train Journal, 1994.

Mexican Railroads, General History

The half century after Mexico's independence in 1821 was not kind to the former Spanish colony. Internal strife, foreign intervention, and major territorial losses to its stronger northern neighbor fostered a desire for isolation. Railroad promoters were plentiful, but with frequently changing governments, concessions were subject to abrupt cancellation, and capital was understandably difficult to secure.

"Poor Mexico," remarked strongman President Porfirio Díaz. "So far from God, and so close to the United States." These plaintive words from the man largely responsible for Mexico's greatest period of railroad growth coincided with a basic change in the internal politics of the Mexican Republic. Before the Porfiriato, as the 1877–1910 period came to be called, limited railroad building had been intentionally focused on a few internal links, with the hope of connecting Mexico City to ports on the Gulf of Mexico and the Pacific Coast. Many Mexican citizens viewed their nation's underdevelopment as a reflection of its cautious isolation; railroad links to the technologically advanced United States thus came to be seen as necessary and unavoidable steps toward the modernization of Mexico.

Ferrocarril de Veracruz al Río de San Juan

Mexico's first railway concession dated from August 22, 1837, when a line was proposed linking Veracruz, on the Gulf Coast, with Mexico City. From the government standpoint, the authorization was quite optimistic: it provided no subsidy, lasted for only 30 years, and called for large annual payments to the state after 10 years of operation. The proposal never went beyond the paper stage.

The issue of who operated the first railroad in Mexico is still subject to clarification, but most accounts give that honor to the much-delayed Veracruz to the San Juan River line (Ferrocarril de Veracruz al Río de San Juan), a project conceived in 1842 but not operated until 1850. President José Joaquín de Herrera was present on September 16, 1850, when the line's tiny Belgian-built Couillet 4-2-0 inaugurated the first 13 kilometers (8.1 miles) between the port at Veracruz and a point called El Molino.

In 1855 a concession was issued to the Mosso brothers for a continuation beyond San Juan. Passing by way of Mexico City, the proposal authorized rails all the way to Acapulco, on the Pacific Coast. On July 4, 1857, a 5 km (3.1-mile) section of track between Mexico City and Guadalupe was inaugurated. Shortly thereafter the concession changed hands, passing to the Escandón brothers, who renegotiated the original agreement, acquiring the original Veracruz link from the government, as well as a commitment for a subsidy.

Ferrocarril Mexicano

In 1864 the Escandóns transferred their rights to the Imperial Mexican Railway Co., Ltd., and that English-backed firm took the project forward, completing 216 km (134 miles) before the fall of Emperor Maximilian and the end of the French intervention. Rejecting the Jalapa route backed by some experts, American engineer An-

This colorful 1896 timetable was for the Mexican Railway Co., which operated over the difficult mountains of the Sierra Madre Oriental between Veracruz and the City of Mexico. The Mexican Railway folder featured its original English-built double-end Fairlie steam locomotives. —John A. Kirchner Collection

drew H. Talcott built via the more difficult Orizaba-Maltrata alignment. Further revisions to the concession after restoration of Mexican sovereignty led to creation of the Ferrocarril Mexicano (FCM), and service over the spectacular 423 km (263-mile) route between the capital and the coast came to fruition on January 1, 1873.

Called the "Rail Trip of a Thousand Wonders," the standard-gauge line through the Sierra Madre Oriental had 10 viaducts, 148 bridges, and 15 tunnels and for many years tackled its 4.7 percent grades with double-boilered English Fairlie locomotives. The largest of these could handle 300 tons on the climb. In 1922 work began on electrifying the steepest part of the line, using 3,000 volts DC and 2,520-hp General Electric B-B-B motors. With multiple-unit (M.U.) operation, a single crew could handle two of the electrics and more than double the prior tonnage maximum. The well-managed FCM, which also operated several narrow-gauge branches, remained an independent carrier until 1946, when control passed to the government.

Ferrocarril de Sonora

The first direct rail link between the United States and Mexico was an isolated line completed in 1882, providing the southwestern United States with a shortcut to the Pacific Coast. Connecting Nogales, on the Arizona border, with Guaymas on the Sea of Cortéz, the 419 km (260-mile) AT&SF-backed Sonora Railway (FdeS) later passed to control of the Southern Pacific of Mexico (SPdeM), but many years passed before the "West Coast Route" was tied into the rest of the Mexican rail network.

Ferrocarril Central Mexicano

Like the Sonora Railway, the Mexican Central (CM) had ties to the Santa Fe. The second link to the northern border, this standard-gauge line connected Paso del Norte (Ciudad Juárez) with Mexico City, passing by way of Chihuahua, Torreón, León, Zacatecas, Aguascalientes, Irapuato, and Querétaro. Authorized under a concession of September 8, 1880, it placed its full 1,978 km (1,226-mile) north-south line in service in 1884, well ahead of the rival Mexican National (NM). Several major branches were also built, including lines to Guadalajara, Manzanillo, and Tampico.

Ferrocarril Nacional Mexicano

One of two railroads to link Texas points with Mexico City, the Nacional Mexicano (NM) was headed by Gen. William Jackson Palmer and followed Denver & Rio Grande practice by building to the 3-foot gauge (914 mm). Under a concession dated September 13, 1880, the 1,350 km (837-mile) main line from Mexico City to Nuevo Laredo was completed in 1888. Passing by way of Monterrey, Saltillo, and San Luis Potosí, the narrow gauge, known as *via angosta* in Mexico, reached the capital via Acambaro and Toluca through a mountainous region at the southern end. It also owned the narrow-gauge Texas-Mexican Railroad, a U.S. line that connected Laredo with Corpus Christi.

The NM was troubled financially from the start. Despite its shorter route and faster passenger-train times, the border gauge change played havoc with freight. Between 1901 and 1903 it converted most of its main line to standard gauge, or *vía ancha,* and built a new, more gradient-friendly link to Mexico City. The original Toluca line became a branch, but remained narrow gauge until 1949.

Ferrocarril Internacional Mexicano

The Ferrocarril Internacional Mexicano was Mexico's first major railroad built without a federal subsidy. Its concession was issued on February 7, 1881, and called for, among other things, a line from Ciudad Porfirio Díaz (Piedras Negras) to Mazatlán by way of Torreón and Durango. The project's ties to the SP were evident, with Collis P. Huntington as a major investor and Charles Crocker's International Construction Co. as the builder. It took a decade to reach Durango, some 869 km (540 miles), but Huntington's death and the barrier of the Sierra Madre Occidental precluded reaching its original goal, and in 1901 the NM took control of the truncated system.

Other Major Narrow-Gauge Lines

After the NM conversion, Mexico's largest narrow-gauge operation was the 914 mm (3-foot) Interoceanic Railway (FCI), which, like its competitor, the FCM, connected Veracruz and Mexico City and had hopes of reaching the Pacific. The product of many different concessions, the Interoceanico was surveyed by noted railroad author and engineer A. M. Wellington and was built largely by Mexican engineers. Its main 546 km (339-mile) component opened in 1892, passing by way of Jalapa and Puebla, but its advantage of lesser gradients was compromised by its narrower track. Conversion of the main line to standard gauge, however, did not take place until 1948, and several branches remained *vía angosta.*

Several independent railroads became part of the FCI, including the 112 km (69-mile) tramway connecting Veracruz with Jalapa. Another noteworthy component, the Mexicano del Sur or Mexican Southern (MdelS), connected Puebla with Oaxaca, but maintained its separate identity after the FCI took control in 1909. Ulysses S. Grant failed in the original MdelS promotion of 1880, but the project passed to Read, Campbell & Co. of London, which completed the 367 km (228-mile) line in 1893. The Oaxaca line became standard gauge in 1952.

Among other narrow-gauge common carriers, perhaps the best known were the Hidalgo & Northeastern, the Oriental Mexicano or Mexican Eastern (OM), the Coahuila y Zacatecas (CyZ), and the various locally built lines of the Yucatán Peninsula. The latter, which also included segments of standard gauge, dated from 1880 and were unified under the Unidos de Yucatán or United Railways of Yucatán (UdeY) banner, but remained isolated from the rest of the Mexican railway network until 1950.

Other Major Standard-Gauge Lines

The SPdeM, as it was known, was Mexico's major rail link along the West Coast. Its original component, the Sonora Railway, was acquired by C. P. Harriman in 1898 in a deal that gave the AT&SF control of the SP's Mojave-Needles line in California. Under E. H. Harriman, the effort to push the SPdeM south did not come easily. Mazatlán was reached in 1909 and Tepic in 1912, the latter amid the rumblings of the Mexican Revolution. Construction was also initiated working north from near Guadalajara, but the two sections were not united until 1927. Political instability aside, a great impediment was the rugged barrancas south of Tepic, where the final 165 km (102 miles) of railroad required 33 tunnels and 29 viaducts, including the famed Salsipuedes span, 73 meters (239 feet) high and 262 meters (859 feet) in length.

For all the promise that SP interests saw in the West Coast Route, the line was rarely profitable, and in late 1951 the SP sold its 1,976 km (1,225-mile) subsidiary to the Mexican government, which created the Ferrocarril del Pacífico or Pacific Railroad (FCP). It continued to operate independently and was not tied administratively to the national system until 1986.

The dream to link the oceans by rail across Mexico's narrow southern isthmus made the 310 km (192-mile) route from Coatzacoalcos, on the Gulf of Mexico, to Salina Cruz, on the Pacific, an early candidate, with the first of many unfulfilled concessions in 1842. Influenced by the successful 1855 opening of the Panama Railroad, efforts continued. Among the failed backers were Simon Stevens and Edward Learned of New York, who by mid-1881 had laid the first 35 km (22 miles) of track. A year later the government suspended the project, paying off the backers through arbitration. A new concession went to interests headed by Chandros S. Stanhope, who completed the road in 1894, but controversy over contractor billings marked the event. Regardless of who was at fault, the line was in poor condition, and the British firm of S. Pierson & Son, Ltd., had to be brought in to rebuild and operate it. The railroad's ultimate success was limited; the major negative force was competition from the Panama Canal. It was merged into the National Railways of Mexico (NdeM) in 1925.

The Isthmian route was eventually connected to several other railroads, the Veracruz al Pacífico (later the Veracruz al Istmo), which joined Córdoba and Veracruz with the NdeT, and the Ferrocarril Panamericano, which headed south along the west coast of Chiapas to a border river gap and later direct link with Guatemala's 3-foot-gauge International Railways of Central America (IRCA).

Years later, in 1950, a rail link from Coatzacoalcos to Yucatán was established.

The list of *vía ancha* lines includes a number of formerly independent carriers. Among them were the México, Cuernavaca y Pacífico, which tried but failed to reach Acapulco, the desert-running Coahuila y Pacífico, the Ferrocarril Mexicano del Norte (Mexican Northern), the Monterrey al Golfo, the Nacozari, the Inter-California, and the border-running Tijuana y Tecate, the latter better known as part of the San Diego & Arizona. Finally, there were two other routes of significance, the Kansas City, Mexico & Orient and the Sierra Madre, Río Grande y Pacífico, later known as the Nor-Oeste de México (NodeM) or Mexican Northwestern. Both became part of a notable government project to be discussed later.

Consolidation

Because of the government's major role in financing construction during the Porfiriato, it was no surprise that the carriers' frequent financial difficulties led to state intervention. José Ives Limantour, finance minister under Díaz, in 1898 laid out a policy to control subsidies and limit building of parallel railroads. In 1903 Limantour had the government begin buying stock and, in a successful battle with rival contender Mexican National, took control of the Interoceanico. Soon after, the government surrendered its shares of the FCI to the NM and in so doing received sufficient stock to control the larger carrier. In 1906 Mexico gained control of the Mexican Central, and in 1908 a final agreement was reached placing the combined carriers, known as the National Railways of Mexico (NdeM), under government stock control.

Revolution

Mexico's "modernization" during the Porfiriato came at a high price. With political stability enforced at gunpoint and social injustices exacerbated by ruling elites, Mexico was ripe for rebellion. Indeed, some scholars, such as John Coatsworth, saw the railroads as helping foment the crisis in the first place.

In the chaos that followed the initial events of 1910–1911, the railroads played a major role. The story is a complex one, with frequently changing alliances and loyalties. Most of the famous names of the revolutionary period, Venustiano Carranza, Victoriano Huerta, Francisco Madero, Alvaro Obregón, Francisco Villa, Emiliano Zapata, and others, were part-time railroaders one moment and railroad-wreckers the next. There was hardly a part of the railway network that did not suffer. By 1915, three-quarters of all the standard-gauge boxcars in Mexico had been destroyed, with a similar fate for a third of the locomotives.

General Francisco "Pancho" Villa was active along the various rail lines in northern Mexico, and his capture of Ciudad Juárez on November 15, 1913, was a typical lesson in bravado. Bogus telegraph messages indicated that a southbound Mexican Central coal train was stranded because of track damage, and it was given permission by the federales to return north to the border town, but when it arrived under the cover of darkness its load had been replaced with 2,000 of Villa's troops.

Operation of the railroads passed back and forth between private and government hands, and for a time during the 1914–1915 period there existed an entity called the Ferrocarriles Constitucionalistas that ostensibly controlled all lines, but whose writ held sway only over areas in the south controlled by General Carranza. Coincidentally, in 1920, Carranza fled a coup attempt in Mexico City, only to meet death at the hands of one of his own men after a wild ride over the FCM's Veracruz main line.

General Alvaro Obregón, whose military exploits made considerable use of the SPdeM, became the nation's leader. During his presidency in the 1920s Mexico returned to a semblance of order. Labor, however, found new power during the period, leading to strikes that financially crippled the NdeM and slowed its rehabilitation.

Mexicanization

The 1930s were marked by socialist rhetoric, and in 1937 populist President Lázaro Cárdenas expropriated the technically still private NdeM, turning direct control over to labor. The "Workers' Administration" was a disaster and came to an end in 1940, but the public image of a disorganized railroad endured long after. Juan José Arreola's short story *El Guardajujas* (*The Switchman*) poked fun at NdeM "improvements," noting that some trains carried a funeral car so that long-delayed passengers who expired en route would eventually reach their destination, properly prepared for burial.

Mexicanization did have its impact in another area, for under the Plan Sexenal (1935–1940) Mexico began building railways to close some of the major remaining gaps in its national system. The goal was "national integration," not profit, and in 1948 and 1950 two major lines, built and operated by the Secretary of Communications and Public Works (SCOP) were completed: the 537 km (333-mile) Ferrocarril Sonora–Baja California (SBC) linking its namesake states and the 732 km (454-mile) Ferrocarril del Sureste (SE) connecting the Isthmus of Tehuantepec with Campeche and the railways of Yucatán.

The period after World War II also saw the remaining private railroads come under government control, the FCM in 1946, the SPdeM in 1951, and the Nor-Oeste in 1952. The latter, with its Ciudad Juárez–La Junta, Chihuahua, link to the old KCM&O, became part of the SCOP's Chihuahua project.

In 1961 the spectacular Ferrocarril Chihuahua al Pacífico (ChP) was completed, linking Ojinaga, opposite Presidio on the Texas border, with Topolobampo on the Gulf of California, some 941 km (583 miles). A dream come true, the work closed the final 243 km (151-mile) gap in what was once A. E. Stillwell's Kansas City, Mexico & Orient Railway, the so-called Orient line whose segments of trackage in Mexico had been acquired by the state in 1940. The new section included 73 tunnels, 38 bridges, and 3 viaducts; most dramatic were the El Fuerte span, at 45.14 meters (148 feet) in height and 481 meters (1,578 feet) in length, and the Chinipas viaduct, at 89.97 meters (295 feet) in height and 310.45 meters (1,018 feet) in length. The ChP, however, was not the last new line to the Pacific, for in 1979 the NdeM opened a 200 km (124-mile) railroad connecting the Apatzingán branch in Michoacán with the new steel mill and port complex at Lázaro Cárdenas, near the mouth of the Balsas River.

Motive Power

Operating practices and equipment on Mexico's railways followed U.S. traditions. Most locomotives came from U.S. builders, with Baldwin and Alco the major suppliers of steam power. Secondhand locomotives were also common; after the Revolution many 4-6-0s and 2-8-0s arrived from the Illinois Central, and during World War II Chicago & North Western and Rock Island 2-8-0s, Nickel Plate (NKP) U.S. Railroad Administration (USRA) 2-8-2s, and Florida East Coast USRA 4-8-2s made the trek south of the border, accompanied by a mix of other locomotives, including a pair of former D&RGW 3-foot-gauge (914 mm) Mikados later converted to standard gauge.

Because of light axle loadings and bridge restrictions, Mexican standard-gauge power was not large, and double-heading, particularly on NdeM, was uncommon. Helper engines, when used, were typically spaced a number of cars behind the lead engine.

Ten Wheelers and Consolidations dominated the roster. There were, however, some impressive locomotives. Both the NdeM and the FCM acquired three-cylinder Pacifics during the 1920s and 1930s; on the latter road they were

the mainstay of varnish on the nonelectrified trackage to Mexico City.

On NdeM 20 compound HR-3 2-6-6-2s had been acquired in 1911, and in the 1930s the railroad returned to articulated power with eight HR-4 simple 2-6-6-2s, complete with "flying" air pumps on the smokebox front. Small numbers of NR-1 4-6-4s and PR-8 4-8-0s were added at the same time.

Mexico's last new steam locomotives were ten U.S. Army–style Consolidations built by Baldwin in 1946 for the FCM. The NdeM's last new steam was also purchased in 1946, when it took delivery of 32 Alco and Baldwin QR-1 4-8-4s. Intended for passenger service and light by U.S. standards, the handsome Niágaras worked most of their lives in freight service on the main line north of Mexico City. Many were preserved and today are the largest single class of surviving steam locomotives in North America.

The NdeM narrow gauge relied primarily on modest 2-8-0s, but the largest locomotives were ten simple Alco 2-6-6-2s, delivered in 1928, 1934, and 1938. These impressive HR-01s, with flying pumps, four domes, and a maze of external handrails and pipes, worked the old FCI line to Veracruz and saw service on other mountainous routes. The post–World War II gauge changes rendered them surplus, and all were retired by the end of 1954.

Mexico's first common-carrier diesel-electrics were 65-ton GEs delivered in 1939 to the SCOP's Sonora–Baja California project. On the NdeM the original diesels were Alco switchers acquired during World War II. In the early 1950s Alco supplied 68 1,600-hp F-series cab units and followed up with numerous first-generation road switchers, including RS1s (64 units), RS11s (94 units), and RSD12s (73 units). The hood units were favorites with the Mexican road.

In 1946 NdeM bought the first locomotives ever exported by EMD, 14 1,325-hp F2 A-B sets, and eventually

The largest of all Mexican steam power were the class HR-4 2-6-6-2 articulated locomotives (eight in all) delivered by Alco in 1937. No. 2033 pulled a long train of tank cars. —John A. Kirchner Collection

Two Electro-Motive 2,000-hp GP38-2 units headed NdeM's Mexico City–Ciudad Juárez passenger train No. 7 at Aguascalientes in August 1976. —William D. Middleton

operated an additional 100 EMD covered wagons of various types. La Grange also provided 114 G12 and G16 lightweight export units for branch-line service. In addition, the Mexican road acquired Baldwin cab and hood units, including 14 of the unusual 3,000-hp 2-D+D-2 Centipedes. Second-generation hood units arrived in large numbers in the 1960s, 1970s, and 1980s, and GE gradually became Mexico's major supplier.

In the 1950s Constructora Nacional de Carros de Ferrocarril (CNCF), the government-backed car builder located at Ciudad Sahagún, Hidalgo, began supplying boxcars and other rolling stock and within a few years dominated freight-car sales in Mexico. It was also successful in exporting cars to the United States, with the AT&SF and Missouri Pacific among its customers.

Steam on the NdeM was phased out by the end of the 1960s. It, however, was not the first railroad in Mexico to be dieselized. That honor went to the SBC, whose small roster was all diesel by the time of its completion in 1948. The FCP was also an early convert, using five Alco FPA2s, 35 RSD5s, and 25 S6s to retire the last of its SP-lineage steam in 1957.

Freight and Passenger Service

Freight traffic in Mexico was and is a mix of general cargo and bulk commodities, the latter made up of cement, coal, iron ore, and other minerals, as well as chemicals, petroleum, and agricultural products, particularly maize and wheat. Produce traffic in reefers or piggyback trailers was once common, particularly on the West Coast, but that business was lost to road transport. SPdeM and NdeM once moved substantial quantities of sugarcane for milling, hauling the raw material in gondolas.

Intermodal service was slow in coming, with limited piggyback service, and when container traffic did develop, the Mexican roads lacked proper flatcars and were often forced to use gondolas. In more recent years auto parts and finished automobiles have become a growing source of business.

Passenger trains in the 1960s and 1970s continued to provide service to nearly every part of the national network, including mixed trains, or *mixtos*, on many secondary or branch lines. Long-distance trains, with sleepers, diners, and lounges, were still common, and these special car services were provided by Servicio de Carros Dormitorios (SCD), successor to the Pullman Co. of Mexico. NdeM had the distinction of operating the last all-sleeper trains in North America: *El Regiomontono (The Mountain Region)* between Mexico City and Monterrey and *El Tapatio* between the national capital and Guadalajara.

Passenger stock, both lightweight and heavyweight, came largely from U.S. and Canadian sources, much of it secondhand. Some new cars were imported from Europe during the 1950s, the best known from Swiss builder Schindler to equip the *Aguila Azteca* (*Aztec Eagle*), the premier Mexico City–Nuevo Laredo train that for many years offered through service via the Missouri Pacific to San Antonio and St. Louis.

With the rapid decline of passenger service in the United States, particularly during the 1960s and early 1970s, Mexico picked up hundreds of modern lightweight cars, including diners, lounges, and sleepers. The cars were renamed, but astute travelers could still recognize lineages from the *20th Century Limited*, the *California Zephyr*, and a host of other famous trains.

The last generation of Mexican car purchases consisted

of new coaches of Canadian and Japanese origin, many of the latter assembled by CNCF. With privatization and the 1990s discontinuance of most remaining Mexican passenger service, many of these modern coaches have gone on to a new career in Cuba.

In one of the stranger tales of modern Mexico, a costly 245 km (152-mile) double-tracked 25,000-volt AC "high-speed" line from Mexico City to Querétaro was built during the 1980s. The 6,000-hp GE E60C electrics sat unused for many years and then saw only limited service. Most wires have since been removed and the majority of the 39 locomotives sold. Privatized diesel freights rule the line today, though a section of catenary remains intact just north of Mexico City and may soon become part of Mexico's first commuter rail project.

Privatization

Freight and passenger rates in Mexico continued to be heavily subsidized, yet despite this seeming advantage to shippers and travelers, and major industrial expansion, market share continued to erode. Operating ratios soared as the labor-heavy, inefficient railroads lost the marketing game to trucks and buses and to air. At a time when U.S. railroads, with huge increases in intermodal and bulk traffic, were regaining market share, Mexico's carriers continued to decline to only 10 percent of the nation's ton-miles, or less than a third of the market share held by U.S. railroads.

By the 1990s, as economic neoliberalism spread its wings and the North American Free Trade Agreement (NAFTA) became a reality, Mexico began to seriously pursue the idea of reinventing private railroads, dividing the national network into different segments. A bidding process was established that allowed limited foreign participation, but reserved majority control (51 percent) for Mexican interests.

In 1997 the first regional segment to be offered, the prime Northeast corridor to Nuevo Laredo, surprised onlookers by going for $1.4 billion to Transportación Ferroviaria Mexicana (TFM), a consortium of Mexico's largest ocean shipping company, Transportación Marítima Mexicana (TMM) and Kansas City Southern Industries (KCS). The TFM line constituted only 19 percent of Mexico's route miles, but accounted for 40 percent of its traffic. The Laredo gateway is the biggest on the border and accounts for over half of U.S.-Mexico trade, but TFM also serves the ocean ports of Lázaro Cárdenas, Tampico, and Veracruz.

The immediate success of 2,661 km (1,650-mile) TFM is evident, for with new motive power and rolling stock, improved service, and proper marketing, traffic by 2000 had more than doubled over the volume moved by its predecessor in 1996. Train times were cut dramatically, from 60 to 34 hours for intermodal and automobile trains and to 41.5 hours for general cargo. It is also the first Mexican road to offer "Road-Railer" service. TFM now claims to have the youngest locomotive fleet of any major railroad in North America, and makes regular use

of distributed power with remote-controlled helpers on its mountainous main lines. On April 21, 2003, word was released that the KCS, TFM, and Texas-Mexican railways would be combined under a single Kansas City–based holding company to be known as NAFTA Rail. Two years later, on April 1, 2005, KCS completed purchase of a controlling interest in TFM from the financially strapped Mexican ocean carrier TMM, and in December of the same year, the name TFM was changed to Kansas City Southern de Mexico (KCSM).

The second concession, the Northwest, went in late 1997 to the new Ferrocarril Mexicano, or Ferromex, which also acquired several lesser concessions, including the Chihuahua al Pacífico and Nacozari. Ferromex is held primarily by Grupo Mexico, a leading mining enterprise, with the Union Pacific holding a modest minority stake. The largest network, with over 8,500 km (5,270 miles), includes much of the old SPdeM, Mexican Central, and Mexican International routes and serves five border crossings, Mexicali-Calexico (UP), Nogales (UP), Ciudad Juárez–El Paso (BNSF-UP), Ojinaga-Presidio (Transpacific), and Piedras Negras–Eagle Pass (BNSF-UP). Ferromex also operates Mexico's last important passenger service, the tourist-oriented *El Chepe* on the Copper Canyon route over the former ChP between Chihuahua and Los Mochis.

Another concession, the Southeast, was also offered in 1998 and went to Ferrosur, a consortium of Mexican banking and business interests. Its main line links Mexico City, Veracruz, and the Isthmus, but it uses a modern, preprivatization bypass line to avoid the steepest part of the old FCM. Ferromex has acquired the Ferrosur operation for $245 million in stock, but KCSM has filed a Mexican antitrust action to try to block the sale.

The final concessions went to shortline operators. One, the Coahuila Durango, was taken by northern mining interests, but has been operated under contract by the Genesee & Wyoming. The G&W also took direct control of the Chiapas-Mayab, which operates the lines to Yucatán and to Ciudad Tecun Uman in Guatemala, a total of 1,805 km (1,000 miles). It also has trackage rights over the old NdeT, which remains in federal hands. Finally, a joint terminal railroad for Mexico City was set up, with control of the Terminal Ferroviaria del Valle de México (TFVM) proportioned between TFM, Ferromex, Ferrosur, and the government.

Mexico's railway history has been witness to many major changes in policy and practice. The initial years, hampered by political instability and a lack of capital, saw railroads play a role in central Mexico, but only with the Porfiriato did major expansion to the northern and southern borders take place. The 1910 Revolution took a terrible toll on the nation and its railroads, and the system that eventually emerged reflected the politics of a neosocialist era with national integration and "Mexicanization" as its hallmarks. The government continued new construction and modernization after World War II, but by

Mexico's Nonexistent Railroad

Hollywood has created many fictitious railroads, but have you heard of the Mexican railroad that ran trains in the United States for many years, but never existed? The small locomotive in the photograph, seen in El Paso, Texas, in December 1946, was on a cross-border transfer run between the NdeM station in Ciudad Juárez and Union Station in El Paso. Lettered GFM, or Gobierno Federal Mexicano, the switcher is actually an NdeM B-12 class 0-6-0 (Baldwin, 1907) in disguise. The heavyweight cars also carried false identities.

In the chaotic years during and immediately after the Mexican Revolution, U.S. citizens filed claims against the NdeM for nonpayment of money owed for delivery of locomotives and other rolling stock. With vigilant sheriffs on the U.S. side of the border ready to seize NdeM property in compensation, the Mexican carrier used an alias and maintained its international connections. The engines that worked the Juárez–El Paso link were also seen at times lettered for FCM, the onetime British-owned Veracruz–Mexico City line, but it is doubtful whether that carrier ever knew that it provided direct service to the United States.

economic growth continuing, Mexico's recently privatized freight railroads appear to be in a strong growth mode, with a viable future. Mexico's psyche, however, has changed many times, and the railroads legacy remains clothed in the rhetoric of a complicated past.

—John A. Kirchner

REFERENCES

Best, Gerald M. *Central American Holiday*. Redwood City, Calif.: Pacific Coast Chapter, Railway & Locomotive Historical Society, 1960.

———. *Narrow Gauge*. Berkeley, Calif.: Howell-North, 1968.

Cloverdale & Colpitts. *National Railways of Mexico: Report to the International Committee of Bankers on Mexico*. New York: Cloverdale & Colpitts, 1929.

Coatsworth, John H. *Growth against Development: The Economic Impact of Railroads in Porfirian Mexico*. DeKalb: Northern Illinois Univ. Press, 1981.

Garma Franco, Francisco. *Railroads in Mexico: An Illustrated History*. Vols. 1–2. Denver, Colo.: Sundance, 1985, 1988.

Gurría Lacroix, Jorge. *Bibliografía mexicana de ferrocarriles*. Biblioteca técnica ferrocarrilera, no. 50. Ferrocarriles Nacionales de México. México, D.F.: Talleres Gráficos de la Nación, 1956.

Kerr, John Leeds, and Frank P. Donovan, Jr. *Destination Topolobampo*. San Marino, Calif.: Golden West, 1968.

Kirchner, John A. *Baja California Railroads*. San Marino, Calif.: Golden West, 1988.

Long, William Rodney. *The Railways of Mexico*. U.S. Department of Commerce, Trade Promotion Series No. 16. Washington, D.C.: U.S. Government Printing Office, 1925.

the 1980s Mexico's state-run system was clearly in deep trouble, with high operating ratios compounded by significant loss of market share to competitive modes, particularly trucks and buses.

With NAFTA, a conservative government, and general

To avoid the seizing of NdeM equipment on the U.S. side of the border, any NdeM locomotives and cars moving over the border were identified with a fictitious railroad. The nonexistent Gobierno Federal Mexicano, seen here at El Paso in 1946, was in reality an NdeM switcher. —Al Phelps, John A. Kirchner Collection

McNeely, John H. "The Railways of Mexico: A Study in Nationalization." *Southwestern Studies* 2, no. 1 (Spring 1964): 3–56.

Secretaría de Comunicaciones y Obras Públicas. *Ferrocarril del Sureste.* México, D.F.: Talleres Gráficos de la Nación, 1950.

———. *Ferrocarril Sonora Baja California.* 2nd ed. México, D.F.: Talleres Gráficos de la Nación, 1950.

Secretaría de Obras Públicas. *Memoria de la construcción del Ferrocarril Chihuahua al Pacífico.* México, D.F.: Editorial Rabasa, 1963.

Signor, John R., and John A. Kirchner. *The Southern Pacific of Mexico and the West Coast Route.* San Marino, Calif.: Golden West, 1987.

Mexican Railroads, Nationalization (1880–1990)

In recent years the railroads in Mexico have been privatized, but they were previously owned by the Mexican government. Until 1987 the railroad system included one large railroad, the National Railways of Mexico (Ferrocarriles Nacionales de México, NdeM), which was gradually gathered from railroads built at different times by different companies, and several regional railroads, which were owned by the government but operated separately (discussed at the end of this entry).

The two largest components of the NdeM, the Mexican Central Railway and the Mexican National Railroad, were both constructed in the 1880s from the U.S. border to Mexico City. The Mexican Central was built south from El Paso, Texas, by Atchison, Topeka & Santa Fe interests. The standard-gauge line passed through the cities of Chihuahua, Torreón, Aguascalientes, and Querétaro. The 1,226-mile line was completed in 1884.

The Mexican National was a 3-foot-gauge railroad from Nuevo Laredo, across the Rio Grande from Laredo, Texas, to Mexico City via Monterrey, Saltillo, San Luis Potosí, Acámbaro, and Toluca, 840 miles. It was begun in 1881 by Gen. William Jackson Palmer, earlier the builder of the 3-foot-gauge Denver & Rio Grande. The Mexican National had branches from Monterrey east to Matamoros, across the Rio Grande from Brownsville, Texas, and from Acámbaro southwest to Uruapan. The railroad was converted to standard gauge from Nuevo Laredo to Escobedo in 1903. A new standard-gauge line was built from Escobedo to Mexico City parallel to the Mexican Central line. The new route cut about 35 miles off the distance between Escobedo and Mexico City and was much easier to operate. In later years that line was known as the B Line between Querétaro and Mexico City (the former Mexican Central was the A Line). The old route from Escobedo to Mexico City via Toluca was converted to standard gauge in 1949. A third route from the U.S. border to Mexico City was formed by the Southern Pacific of Mexico (after 1951 the Pacific Railroad, or Ferrocarril del Pacífico) from Nogales, Arizona, to Guadalajara and the National Railways of Mexico from Guadalajara to a junction with the former Mexican Central at Irapuato.

The NdeM had two routes from Mexico City east to the port city of Veracruz. The route via Jalapa was the former 3-foot-gauge Interoceanic Railway. It was widened to standard gauge in 1948. The Mexico City–Veracruz route via Orizaba was built as the Mexican Railway (Ferrocarril Mexicano). A line from Coatzacoalcos, on the Gulf of Mexico, south across the Isthmus of Tehuantepec to Salina Cruz, 189 miles, was built as the Tehuantepec National Railway. Its promoters had the idea of creating a land bridge between the Atlantic and the Pacific; the Panama Canal took most of the traffic it might have carried.

Late Twentieth-Century Changes

In the 1960s and 1970s NdeM undertook a number of line relocations and improvements: a cutoff northeast of Querétaro (bypassing Escobedo and San Miguel Allende) for traffic moving between Mexico City and Monterrey, extensive reconstruction and relocation of the former Mexican National line between the north end of that cutoff and Saltillo, a new line from a point near Uruapan to the Pacific port of Lázaro Cárdenas, and a line that bypasses the steepest part of the Maltrata Incline on the former Mexican Railway. NdeM built a double-track electrified line from Mexico City to Querétaro to replace the A and B lines. The electric locomotives were delivered but ran only briefly, if at all. The extensive network of narrow-gauge lines was converted to standard gauge.

At the same time NdeM purchased hundreds of used passenger cars from railroads north of the border. Many of these were sleeping and dining cars, and for a number of years NdeM operated a nationwide system of first-class passenger trains. In the 1980s and 1990s NdeM removed first the dining cars, then the sleeping cars, then the trains themselves. Privatization of Mexico's railways accelerated the demise of the passenger trains. By 2000 only a few trains were listed in the *Thomas Cook Overseas Timetable,* and nearly all noted "service temporarily suspended."

Mexico's regional railroads were owned and in some cases built by the government. Most of them came under the banner of the National Railways of Mexico in 1987.

Chihuahua-Pacific Railway (Ferrocarril de Chihuahua al Pacífico)

See Kansas City, Mexico & Orient Railroad

Mexican Railway (Ferrocarril Mexicano)

The Ferrocarril Mexicano was intended to be a transcontinental route from Veracruz on the Gulf of Mexico to Acapulco on the Pacific. The company was chartered in 1855, and in the next few years it built a few miles of track at Veracruz and a few miles at Mexico City. There followed a decade of governmental instability, when Mexico defaulted on its European debts and the emperor Napoleon III of France established a monarchy in Mexico. When the situation stabilized, the Mexican Railway was able to attract British capital and complete a 264-mile line from Veracruz to Mexico City (it never built beyond Mexico City). The railroad was noteworthy for its steep climb from the coastal lowlands to the central plateau: the Maltrata Incline, with a ruling grade of 4.7 percent and curves as sharp as 16.5 degrees. The incline was operated with electric locomotives from 1923 through the 1960s. The Mexican government bought the Mexican Railway in 1946 and merged its operations with the NdeM in 1959.

Pacific Railroad

See PACIFIC RAILROAD (FERROCARRIL DEL PACÍFICO)

Sonora–Baja California Railway (Ferrocarril Sonora–Baja California)

In 1923 Mexico's Ministry of Communications and Public Works began building a railroad southeast from Mexicali, Baja California. Construction halted after 43 miles of railroad had been completed. Construction resumed in 1936. In 1940 the railhead reached Puerto Peñasco, on the Gulf of California, and it remained there during World War II. Construction resumed again in 1946, and in 1948 the railroad made a connection with the Southern Pacific of Mexico (later the Pacific Railroad, Ferrocarril del Pacífico) at Benjamin Hill, Sonora, 323 miles from Mexicali. The railroad became the Baja California Division of the National Railways of Mexico in 1987.

Southeastern Railway (Ferrocarril del Sureste)

The Southeastern Railway was built by the Ministry of Communications and Public Works to extend Mexico's railroad network along the Yucatán Peninsula. It was completed in 1950 from Allende, Veracruz, on the Río Coatzacoalcos, to a connection with the United Railways of Yucatán at Campeche, 457 miles. The railroad bridged the Río Coatzacoalcos in 1962, creating an all-rail route between Yucatán and the rest of Mexico. The Southeastern Railway and the United Railways of Yucatán were merged to form the United Southeastern Railways in 1969.

United Railways of Yucatán (Ferrocarriles Unidos de Yucatán)

The United Railways of Yucatán operated a network of standard- and narrow-gauge lines radiating from Mérida,

the capital of the Mexican state of Yucatán. One line reached 108 miles southwest to the city of Campeche in the neighboring state of the same name. The railroad was isolated until 1950, when the Southeastern Railway was completed. The line between Mérida and Campeche was converted to standard gauge between 1953 and 1967. The United Railways of Yucatan and the Southeastern Railway were merged to form the United Southeastern Railways in 1969.

United Southeastern Railways (Ferrocarriles Unidos del Sureste)

United Southeastern Railways was created in 1969 by the merger of the United Railways of Yucatán and the Southeastern Railway. It became part of the National Railways of Mexico in 1987.

—George H. Drury

Mexican Railroads, Privatization (1990–)

In the early 1990s the Mexican government began a complicated process by which the country's nationally controlled telecommunications, utilities, ports, and railroads would be privatized. The privatization of Ferrocarriles Nacionales de México (FNM), a process essentially completed by 1999, ranks as one of the more significant developments in the North American railroad industry. Prompted by enactment of the North American Free Trade Agreement (NAFTA), the privatization brought Mexico's rail system up the level of technical, operational, and service efficiency of the Class 1 railroads in the United States and Canada, creating a unified North American network in which physical and logistical borders were greatly diminished.

Although U.S. railroads, particularly the western carriers, had a beneficial relationship with their Mexican counterpart for many years, privatization opened the doors to business-growth opportunities virtually unfettered by government control and its inherent inefficiencies. These opportunities extended to railway suppliers, which reaped the rewards of over $2 billion in capital that was invested during the first few years of private operations, creating a safe, modern, and efficient railway network. Among the improvements were 136-pound continuous welded rail, concrete ties, centralized traffic control, 10,000-foot sidings, modern yards and switching facilities, new intermodal terminals, new EMD and General Electric AC-traction locomotives, new or rebuilt freight car fleets, centralized dispatching and customer service centers, and Automatic Equipment Identification (AEI).

The privatization process began in 1994, when the Mexican government split FNM operations into four main parts—the Northeast, Pacific-North, Southeast, and Mexico City Terminal railways—plus several short lines. The Northeast Railway, whose Nuevo Laredo–Mexico City main line handled 60 percent of Mexico's total rail volume, including much of the international traffic, was considered the crown jewel of the system. In addition to the Laredo (Texas)/Nuevo Laredo border crossing, the Northeast Railway connected with the United States at Matamoros/Brownsville and served the ports of Veracruz and Tampico.

The Pacific-North, which included the scenic Chihuahua al Pacífico railway winding alongside Mexico's Copper Canyon, had the majority of U.S. border connections (at Mexicali/Calexico, Nogales, Cuidad Juárez/El Paso, Ojinaga, and Piedras Negras/Eagle Pass). It also served the ports of Empalme, Topolobampo, Mazatlán, Manzanillo, and Lázaro Cárdenas. Its western spine, stretching from Nogales to Guadalajara, was originally built by the Southern Pacific and sold to the Mexican government in 1951.

The Southeast Railway also served Veracruz, as well as the port of Coatzacoalcos. All three main-line carriers reached Mexico City, with its large switching district.

Before the railroad network was privatized, the Mexican government took several preparatory steps. The employee ranks were reduced, and FNM's principal locomotive shops at Monterrey and San Luis Potosí were privatized. GEC Alsthom and MotivePower Industries (predecessor companies of Alstom Transport and the MotivePower Division of Wabtec Corp.) assumed operation of the Monterrey and San Luis Potosí shops, respectively, modernizing them and greatly improving productivity. These successful privatizations set the stage for what followed. The Mexican government initially allowed a maximum of 49 percent foreign investment.

The Mexican railroad system now consists of Kansas City Southern de Mexico, S.A. de C.V., previously Transportación Ferroviaria Mexicana S.A. de C.V. (TFM), the former Northeast Railway; Ferrocarril Mexicano S.A. de C.V. (Ferromex), the former Pacific-North Railway; Ferrocarriles del Sureste S.A. de C.V. (Ferrosur), the former Southeast Railway; a Mexico City switching district, Terminal Ferroviaria del Valle de México (TFVM), whose assets are jointly owned by the three trunk lines; and two principal shortlines—Compañía Ferrocarriles Chiapas-Mayab S.A. de C.V. (FCCM), which serves Mexico's southeastern peninsula, and Línea Coahuila Durango S.A. de C.V., located in central Mexico, west of Monterrey.

The 2,600-mile Northeast Railway was the first private concession awarded. In 1996 TFM, a consortium of Kansas City Southern and Mexican shipping conglomerate Grupo TMM S.A. (Transportación Marítima Mexicana), successfully bid $1.4 billion for the railway. Upon startup the following year, a major upgrade program got under way on the main line that reduced transit times to Mexico City by as much as one-third. Among other improvements, TFM acquired 150 new AC-traction locomotives—75 GE AC4400CWs and 75 EMD SD70MACs. New yards were constructed on both sides of the border to expedite customs clearance and allow for pre-blocking of trains, alleviating congestion on the rail bridge spanning the Rio Grande at Laredo (the bridge is also used by Union Pacific). TFM came under KCS control in 2005 and became Kansas City Southern de Mexico (KCSM). TFM transports motor vehicle parts to General Motors, Daimler-Chrysler, and Ford plants in Mexico and finished vehicles north to the United States.

The 4,900-mile Pacific-North concession was awarded in late 1997 to Ferromex, a consortium of Union Pacific and mining company Grupo Mexico, in a $527 million transaction. UP at 13 percent was the minority owner, but soon afterward increased its share to 26 percent. Unlike KCSM, whose traffic base consists primarily of import/export movements, 70 percent of Ferromex's traffic base is domestic—agricultural products, minerals, cement, and industrial products. Intermodal traffic is growing. Also unlike KCSM, Ferromex continues to operate a small number of passenger trains, among them the Tequila Express tourist service out of Guadalajara. (After privatization the Mexican government discontinued all of FNM's intercity passenger trains but is considering instituting commuter trains serving Mexico City that would be operated by a private contractor.)

The 900-mile Southeast Railway was in early 1998 the last main-line concession awarded. Ferrosur, a consortium of Mexican construction firm Grupo Tribasa and financial services company Banco Imbursa, paid $311 million. Ferrosur's principal traffic consists of grain, cement, industrial products, petrochemicals, intermodal, and finished motor vehicles.

TFM and Ferromex are members of the Assn. of American Railroads and are governed by AAR interchange rules and regulations. Both participate in the Interline Settlement System (ISS).

FCCM is 100 percent owned by Genesee & Wyoming Inc.; its network consists of the Chiapas and Mayab rail lines. The Chiapas line is situated in the states of Oaxaca and Chiapas. The Mayab line is situated in the states of Campeche, Yucatán, Veracruz, and Tabasco.

The Coahuila Durango operates in the states of Chihuahua, Coahuila, Durango, and Zacatecas. Owned by Mexican industrial firms Grupo Acerero del Norte S.A. de C.V. and Industrias Peñoles S.A. de C.V., it is operated by Genesee & Wyoming.

—William C. Vantuono

REFERENCES

Middleton, William D. "The Railroads of Mexico, the U.S., and Canada: Investing for Trans-border Growth." *Railway Age* 195, no. 10 (Oct. 1994): M3–4, M6–14, M18–20, M22.

Vantuono, William C. "Cross-border Bonanza." *Railway Age* 201, no. 10 (Oct. 2000): 31–32, 33, 36.

———. "In Mexico, a Railroad Revolution." *Railway Age* 198, no. 10 (Oct. 1997): 35–38, 40, 42–43, 45, 48, 50–51.

———. "Mexico's Railroads Prepare to Go Private," *Railway Age* 196, no. 11 (Nov. 1965): 37–42, 44, 46, 48, 50–56.

———. "A Railroad Renaissance South of the Border." *Railway Age* 199, no. 4 (Oct. 1998): 31–34, 36–37, 40–44, 46–49.

Welty, Gus. "U.S. Railroads Are Forging Stronger Connections." *Railway Age* 195, no. 10 (Oct. 1994): M23–28.

Milwaukee Road. *See* CHICAGO, MILWAUKEE, ST. PAUL & PACIFIC RAILROAD

Minneapolis & St. Louis Railway

The Minneapolis & St. Louis Railway was sired by Minneapolis manufacturing and commercial interests in response to their perception of rapacious conduct by railroad companies in Milwaukee and Chicago. Indeed, those two aspiring Lake Michigan cities enthusiastically and successfully embraced railroads as effective tools to wage urban economic imperialism that did in fact take wheat away from and deliver lumber and finished goods to what Minneapolis considered its "natural territory." A rail route from Minneapolis to St. Louis, Minneapolis leaders finally decided, would circumvent the power and influence of Milwaukee and Chicago by tapping trunk roads to the east via St. Louis and by connecting with Mississippi River shipping at St. Louis. Such a route also would tap wheat-producing regions, supply an outlet for locally milled lumber and flour, and bring coal to the fuel-starved Northwest. The great dream of linking Minneapolis with St. Louis by an independent rail line never happened, however, and good fortune mostly eluded the M&StL.

Minneapolis interests frankly were late to the party; they reacted slowly instead of acting early and affirmatively on their own behalf. By 1870 Minneapolis was well served by the St. Paul & Pacific, but that road's attention was focused on the West and Northwest, and a Milwaukee Road predecessor honored the city with an appendage off its pioneer line connecting St. Paul with Milwaukee. For Minneapolis—a mere way station on the StP&P and at the end of a plug branch on the Milwaukee & St. Paul—it was as much a matter of urgency as of ego. The eventual response of local leaders was to dust off an old charter, have the state legislature amend it, and trot out the M&StL. Money was scarce but adequate for two very short lines, one northeast to hit the already-completed Lake Superior & Mississippi at White Bear Lake, and the other southwest to tap the St. Paul & Sioux City at Merriam. The former would, by interchange, provide Min-

neapolis business a seasonal chute to Duluth and the Great Lakes, and the latter would gain access to a burgeoning market for lumber and an area sure to generate prodigious supplies of wheat for the hungry mills of Minneapolis. The local enterprise then fell to the colossal Jay Cooke empire, which took lease of the M&StL and the Lake Superior & Mississippi as well. The Cooke empire quickly unraveled, however, in the panic of 1873, and M&StL rail did not reach the Iowa border until 1877. That bit of construction did match up, though, with that of the Burlington, Cedar Rapids & Northern, and in connection with the Chicago, Burlington & Quincy, it provided a Minneapolis–St. Louis thoroughfare.

BCR&N and M&StL came under the control of the Chicago, Rock Island & Pacific, which saw in the two smaller roads a platform to make concrete the "Pacific" in its corporate name by a northwest passage. Matters did not congeal in that way, but the M&StL did press a line westward from Minneapolis to Watertown, Dakota Territory, before the Rock Island lost interest.

M&StL bounced about uncertainly, fell into receivership, and passed to control of New York interests whose purposes seemed only speculative. Edwin Hawley was one of those New Yorkers; M&StL became the first of the "Hawley roads." Another was the Iowa Central, which Hawley joined to the M&StL, now expanded to a 1,600-mile system with a 488-mile main line from Minneapolis to Peoria. Hawley dreamed of further construction north and south, which, with his Missouri, Kansas & Texas, would have forged an impressive vertical-axis transcontinental route, but he died unexpectedly in 1912, and with him passed that dream. M&StL bobbed about again and in 1923 again ended up in receivership.

The general prosperity of the 1920s failed to revive M&StL; its circumstances only deteriorated with the Great Depression of the 1930s. Dismemberment was prescribed by some, who argued that M&StL's four-state service area of Minnesota, Iowa, Illinois, and South Dakota was already cluttered with redundant rail lines. Tearing out rail in rural areas not yet served by paved roads and throwing 2,500 persons onto the breadlines during hard times proved unpalatable, however, and receiver Lucian C. Sprague argued that he could revive M&StL.

Sprague got it right. M&StL slimmed down, improved its property, and was ready to shoulder prodigious tonnage offered during World War II and after. M&StL no longer stood for "Misery & Short Life," Sprague boasted, but rather "Modern & Streamlined." The road paid dividends and bragged that it was without bonded indebtedness. Shippers praised M&StL's service, especially diesel-powered time freights 19 and 20 between Minneapolis and Peoria on schedules that cost M&StL only one day's per diem and avoided the awful congestion of Chicago. Passengers smiled at the brand-new stainless-steel coaches that trailed incongruously behind venerable gas-electric cars on the road's few remaining passenger runs.

M&StL's star shone brightly—too brightly as it turned

out, attracting unwanted suitors in the form of Ben W. Heineman and associates, who successfully wrested control through a bitter proxy fight in 1954. Heineman moved on to the Chicago & North Western two years later. At M&StL young managers embraced lively innovation that often led the industry, but going it alone in the late 1950s proved difficult. Merger was the nostrum of choice. M&StL passed into the clutches of Chicago & North Western at 12:01 A.M. on November 1, 1960. C&NW subsequently abandoned most of M&StL's routes.

In 1959, the year before the Chicago & North Western purchased it, Minneapolis & St. Louis operated a system of 1,391 route-miles and 1,735 track-miles, with 74 locomotives, 10 passenger cars, 4,178 freight cars, 116 company service cars, and 1,775 employees. Freight traffic totaled 1,388.2 million ton-miles in 1959, and manufactured goods (35.3 percent), products of mines (26.7 percent), and products of agriculture (23.7 percent) were its principal traffic sources. Passenger traffic totaled 350,617 passenger-miles. Minneapolis & St. Louis operating revenues totaled $21 million in 1959, and the railroad achieved an 84.9 percent operating ratio.

—Don L. Hofsommer

REFERENCES

Donovan, Frank P., Jr. *Mileposts on the Prairie: The Story of the Minneapolis & St. Louis Railway*. New York: Simmons-Boardman, 1950.

Hofsommer, Don L. *"The Tootin' Louie": A History of the Minneapolis & St. Louis Railway*. Minneapolis: Univ. of Minnesota Press, 2005.

Missouri Pacific Railroad

The Missouri Pacific Railroad ran west and southwest from its headquarters city of St. Louis through Arkansas, Texas, Oklahoma, Kansas, Nebraska, and Colorado. Often called the MoPac, the road spent much of its life in bankruptcy and receivership, yet saw its most prosperous years in the decade before its merger with the Union Pacific Railroad in 1982.

The Missouri Pacific originated with the charter of the Pacific Railroad in 1849, which was to build west from St. Louis to the Pacific. Construction began in 1851, and rails reached Sedalia, Missouri, 185 miles west of St. Louis, in 1860. In 1856 the additional 94 miles to Kansas City were completed. An interesting aspect of the Pacific Railroad was its nonstandard track gauge of 5 feet 6 inches. The conventional wisdom at the time was that bridging the Mississippi was impossible, so there was no concern about interchanging cars with railroads on the east side of the river. After the Rock Island bridged the Mississippi in 1856, however, and other railroads west of the Mississippi

began using standard gauge, the Pacific Railroad adopted standard-gauge track in 1869. The following year the Pacific Railroad was renamed the Missouri Pacific Railroad. In 1876 the road was reorganized as the Missouri Pacific Railway.

During the mid-1800s two railroads were being built south and southwest of St. Louis that would become components of the Missouri Pacific. The St. Louis & Iron Mountain and the Cairo & Fulton, both chartered in the early 1850s, were merged to form the St. Louis, Iron Mountain & Southern Railway in 1874. It ran southeast from St. Louis to Cairo, Illinois (reached by a ferry across the Mississippi), and southwest from St. Louis through Arkansas to the Texas border.

Another group of lines, chartered in the late 1800s and early 1900s in Texas and Louisiana, would also become key parts of the Missouri Pacific. The most significant of this group were the International & Great Northern Railroad and the Gulf Coast Lines. The International & Great Northern (I&GN) was formed in 1873 by the merger of the Houston & Great Northern Railroad and the International Railroad. The lines of the I&GN served several locations in the southeast quadrant of Texas. The International–Great Northern (I-GN) was incorporated in 1922 as the successor to the I&GN, which had entered receivership in 1914. The Gulf Coast Lines (GCL) consisted of several railroads between New Orleans and Brownsville, Texas. The two most significant of these were the GCL parent, the New Orleans, Texas & Mexico (NOT&M), and a subsidiary, the St. Louis, Brownsville & Mexico. The NOT&M purchased the I-GN in 1924.

In 1917 the Missouri Pacific Railway acquired the St. Louis, Iron Mountain & Southern, and the new entity was named the Missouri Pacific Railroad. In 1924 the Missouri Pacific purchased the NOT&M. In 1929 the Missouri Pacific gained control of the Missouri-Illinois Railroad, which was formed when the Mississippi River & Bonne Terre Railway and the Illinois Southern (both of which connected with the St. Louis, Iron Mountain & Southern) merged in 1921. By the mid-1950s the Missouri Pacific also owned all the preferred stock and over half of the common stock of the Texas & Pacific Railway, which ran from New Orleans to El Paso. During the mid-1960s the Missouri Pacific gained access to Chicago through the acquisition of the Chicago & Eastern Illinois Railroad (C&EI). In 1976 the Texas & Pacific and the C&EI were formally merged into the Missouri Pacific, and in 1978 the Missouri-Illinois was as well.

Ownership and Control of the MoPac

As the Missouri Pacific grew in the late nineteenth century, its strategic importance to the national rail network was not lost on rail magnate Jay Gould. Gould purchased control of the railroad in 1879 and was responsible for extending the system to Pueblo, Colorado, and Omaha, Nebraska. Even though the Gould empire disintegrated in 1892, the Missouri Pacific benefited from Gould's ownership from a financial and managerial perspective. For the next 20 years the railroad remained relatively stable and even grew a bit.

The Van Sweringen brothers of Cleveland, Ohio, through their Alleghany Corp., added the Missouri Pacific to their railroad empire in 1930. Their involvement with the railroad was short lived, however, as the MoPac declared bankruptcy in 1933, and the Alleghany Corp. itself was purchased in 1937 by a group of investors led by Robert Young, a financier who later became president of both the Chesapeake & Ohio and the New York Central. For the next 23 years the Missouri Pacific remained in the hands of receivers and was finally reorganized in 1956.

The terms of the 1956 reorganization were heavily influenced by the Alleghany Corp. in an effort to maintain hope that the investment in the railroad made by the Van Sweringens in 1930 would finally yield a profit. This effort by Alleghany resulted in two categories of Missouri Pacific common stock, A and B. The A stock controlled the management of the railroad, but could receive a dividend of no more than $5 per share. The B stock, the majority of which represented the common stock held by the Alleghany Corp., would presumably control the equity of the railroad and would grow in value as the railroad's value grew. This arrangement created a challenge for MoPac management as it tried to position the railroad as a merger partner for other systems through the 1960s because the holders of the B stock (i.e., Alleghany) would have to approve any merger and would only do so if they felt that the terms of the merger would be financially beneficial. This stock structure was eliminated in 1974 when the railroad and its parent company, the Mississippi River Fuel Corp., purchased the Alleghany Corp.'s interests in the MoPac.

The Reorganized MoPac

When the Missouri Pacific emerged from reorganization in 1956, it began a 26-year period of revitalization of its physical plant and financial performance. This was due largely to the ascension of William Marbury, as chairman, and Downing Jenks, as president, of the Missouri Pacific in the early 1960s. Marbury was a St. Louis attorney and chairman of the Mississippi River Fuel Corp. (MRFC), which operated a 1,500-mile gas pipeline serving St. Louis. Marbury became chairman of the Missouri Pacific when the MRFC gained control of the railroad's A stock. Marbury's knowledge of legal and financial matters provided a perfect complement to Jenks, who had been building his railroad career for the past 25 years in the operating departments of several roads and had most recently served as president of the Chicago, Rock Island & Pacific before joining the MoPac.

With Marbury supplying significant capital and mana-

gerial freedom, Jenks set about the task of improving the operations of the Missouri Pacific. Track and roadbed throughout the system were upgraded, particularly on the southern end of the railroad. Freight-car maintenance was improved, and the diesel locomotive fleet was upgraded. Industrial development efforts were revitalized, and the traffic base was strengthened. The railroad began its exit from the unprofitable passenger business. Significant amounts of computer technology were implemented, which helped the railroad improve financial accounting, traffic analysis, and other management reporting.

Jenks had a profound impact on the daily operation of the railroad through his insistence on a clean and organized work environment. Nicknamed Mr. Clean, Jenks spent much of his early presidency inspecting the railroad and its facilities, noting the need for improvements and directing that they be completed. His eye for the smallest detail and quick decision-making ability generated a culture of discipline that permeated the entire railroad. Jenks also required the officers of the railroad to spend more time out on the line instead of managing from the general office building.

Leading the early adoption of information technology on the Missouri Pacific was a key contribution of Downing Jenks. First implemented to improve the management and control of the tens of thousands of inventory items needed to run the railroad, computer technology was then applied to the management of freight cars and the communication of their whereabouts among terminals and to shippers. Working with others in the railroad and computer industries, Jenks assembled a strong team of analysts and railroaders to implement what became known as the Transportation Control System (TCS). The implementation of this system over the entire railroad required several years and yielded tremendous benefits in productivity, efficiency, and customer service. Furthermore, this effective use of information technology served as an example to the entire railroad industry of how to improve operations in a challenging business and regulatory environment.

Eagles *on the MoPac*

Although the company was bankrupt and the nation was still emerging from the Great Depression, the Missouri Pacific began to field a distinctive set of passenger trains known as the *Eagles* just before America's entry into World War II. Beginning with the *Eagle* in March 1940 (renamed the *Missouri River Eagle* the following year as more *Eagles* were introduced), the railroad launched seven streamlined trains through the end of 1948, providing comfortable and reliable service in much of its territory until the mid-1960s.

The *Eagles* covered much of the Missouri Pacific system. The *Missouri River Eagle* provided service from St. Louis to Omaha via Kansas City. The *Delta Eagle* ran from Memphis to Tallulah, Louisiana, and the *Colorado*

Eagle ran from St. Louis to Denver. Two *Texas Eagles* provided service to the Lone Star State from St. Louis: the *West Texas Eagle* ran to Fort Worth and then on to El Paso, while the *South Texas Eagle* provided service to San Antonio. The *Valley Eagle* was an all-coach train running between Houston and Brownsville, and the *Louisiana Eagle* provided service between New Orleans and Fort Worth over the Texas & Pacific. The *Aztec Eagle* was essentially a supplement to the *Texas Eagle* trains, providing service from San Antonio to Mexico City in cooperation with the National Railways of Mexico. Although Jenks was not a fan of the passenger train, he was willing to maintain basic but good service as long as the passenger traffic on a given route was sufficient to affect the public image of the railroad, and there was sufficient revenue from Postal Service contracts to minimize out-of-pocket losses.

The 1970s and Merger

Although price inflation and economic stagnation challenged many industries during the 1970s, these years were the most prosperous in the history of the Missouri Pacific. Except in 1975 the railroad's revenue and net income increased steadily each year. The significant capital investments in the railroad's physical plant and in information technology made by Jenks and Marbury after the 1956 reorganization began to pay significant dividends. In addition, the railroad no longer shouldered the burden of unprofitable passenger service after the birth of Amtrak in 1971. The relocation of significant economic activity in the late 1960s and 1970s to the Sunbelt, which encompassed much of MoPac's territory, further strengthened the railroad's financial performance. The railroad continued to benefit from the high quality of Jenks's leadership, which was widely recognized and reported on both in the railroad industry and in the business community generally.

Although the Missouri Pacific and a select few other carriers were relatively prosperous during the 1970s, the industry as a whole was in critical condition. This situation was the driving force behind the passage of the Staggers Act of 1980, which provided unprecedented deregulation of the railroad industry and set off a wave of significant railroad mergers. On December 22, 1982, the Missouri Pacific merged with the Union Pacific Railroad. The Union Pacific also acquired the Western Pacific Railroad. Despite an initial announcement that the Missouri Pacific would be a "sister" railroad to the Union Pacific and would maintain its own identity, the Missouri Pacific name all but disappeared from the scene within a few years.

In 1982, which ended with the merger with Union Pacific, Missouri Pacific operated a system of 11,167 route-miles and 17,245 track-miles, with 1,602 locomotives, 47,825 freight cars, 3,035 company service cars, and 20,830 employees. Freight traffic totaled 58,298.6 million ton-miles in 1982, and chemicals (19.8 percent), coal (13.2 percent), transportation equipment (11.2 percent), and foodstuffs (8.3 percent) were its principal traffic sources. Missouri Pacific operating revenues totaled $1,678.8 million, and the railroad achieved an 89.9 percent operating ratio.

—David C. Lester

REFERENCES

Miner, H. Craig. *The Rebirth of the Missouri Pacific, 1956–1983.* College Station: Texas A&M Univ. Press, 1983.
Stout, Greg. *Route of the Eagles: Missouri Pacific in the Streamlined Era.* Kansas City, Mo.: White River, 1995.

Missouri-Kansas-Texas Railroad

The railroad known popularly as the Katy received a Kansas charter in 1865 as the Union Pacific Railway, Southern Branch. Although physically connected with a predecessor of the Union Pacific at Junction City, Kansas, the branch had no corporate relationship with its namesake. In less than two years the UPSB came under control of New York investors, led by Judge Levi Parsons as president. By 1870 the visionary judge presented a grandiose plan, proposing that the railroad connect Kansas City with ports on the Gulf of Mexico. He soon changed its name to Missouri, Kansas & Texas Railway. It was identified on stock exchanges by the initials "KT," from which its popular nickname sprang.

Promised a federal land grant for constructing a line through Indian Territory (later Oklahoma), the MK&T battled nature, hostile natives, and competing railroads for nearly two years before reaching Texas in December 1872, ending at a company town named for the road's vice president, George Denison. Construction crews then moved north and by August 1873 had completed an extension to Hannibal, Missouri. Soon thereafter Parsons and his partners liquidated their Katy holdings, only a few weeks before the panic of 1873 wiped out much of the nation's corporate structure.

The leaderless MK&T represented a ripe opportunity for manipulator Jay Gould, who at the time controlled the Missouri Pacific and the Texas & Pacific. He gained control of the Katy for use as a collection of feeder lines. Not surprisingly, MoPac control involved a massive transfer of Katy assets to other Gould railroads, along with numerous route acquisitions in northern Texas that enlarged the MK&T so it could function better to support the MoPac-T&P system. Gould's financial recklessness led to legal action by the State of Texas that eventually cost him control of Katy, which entered bankruptcy in 1888.

Emerging from bankruptcy in 1891, the road began a 20-year rebuilding process that gave it access to Austin,

San Antonio, and Houston, Texas, and St. Louis, Missouri, along with new rolling stock and improved roadbed. However, mounting debt from earlier bond issues and increasing costs due to growing traffic because of the war in Europe pulled the road back into insolvency in September 1915. When U.S. Railroad Administration (USRA) control ended in 1920, the Katy was again ailing both financially and physically.

A financial reorganization in April 1923 brought the road its final name, Missouri-Kansas-Texas Railroad, and the shedding of nearly 500 miles of unproductive routes (from a total of 3,860). However, this rehabilitation effort ended abruptly with the stock market crash of October 1929. By 1934 operating revenues were little more than half their 1930 total.

Katy's next leader was Matthew Sloan, who came from the electric utility industry. Securing rehabilitation funds from the federal government, as well as private banks, he also sought to promote a bright public image by painting every rebuilt freight car and every company building bright yellow with black trim.

Another of his major accomplishments was the refurbishment of Katy's ancient steam locomotive fleet. Modernized locomotives were given white striping; tenders carried large, embossed red heralds featuring the road's initials. Eschewing a business car, he roamed the system in a yellow Chrysler sedan fitted with pilots and flanged wheels. He inaugurated named freights (the *Katy Komet* and *Klipper*) and improved service on the road's four major passenger trains, the *Texas Special*, *Bluebonnet*, *Katy Flyer*, and *Katy Limited*. These served both of Katy's Missouri gateways, Kansas City and St. Louis, as well as its Texas terminals, operating in separate sections north of Parsons, Kansas, and south of Denison, Texas.

Sloan died suddenly in 1945. The Katy prospered with Korean War traffic through the early 1950s, but then traffic fell rapidly. Moreover, a regional drought that lasted eight years decimated Katy's agricultural business. Major operating problems began to mount, aggravated by the premature aging of 3 million World War II crossties due to faulty creosoting. In a twist of fate, the federal government in 1946 after years of litigation rescinded the Oklahoma land grant that Levi Parsons had fought to achieve in the late nineteenth century. Had this decision been in Katy's favor, the road would have had a much brighter future.

Searching for a "tough" operating man in the late 1950s, Katy brought in William Deramus III, who had earlier rescued the Chicago Great Western. Despite a blunt approach that created public relations problems both on and off the railroad, he was able to get Katy moving forward again. Yards were modernized, and freight classification procedures were streamlined, allowing more competitive schedules between major terminals. On the downside, he presided over the reduction of Katy's passenger service. But even these measures did not bring profitability. A major shakeup of investor groups in 1961 led to another management team whose results over the following three years were not significantly better.

In March 1965 Katy's final rehabilitation effort was led by John W. Barriger III, recently retired as president of the prosperous Pittsburgh & Lake Erie Railroad. A Dallas native, Barriger chose not to leave railroading when he reached P&LE's mandatory retirement age but to return to his roots and rescue the Katy, a road he was thoroughly familiar with (he had reviewed its government loan applications during the Great Depression). Following the recipe used by Sloan 30 years earlier, he began by cleaning, repairing, and repainting equipment and structures, by starting a massive track and roadway rehabilitation program, and by becoming a tireless Katy promoter with a business card that read, in part, "Traveling Freight Agent." Unable to cover the down payment on equipment trusts, he signed 15-year leases on nearly 4,000 cars and combined trade-ins and wreck insurance claims to purchase a dozen GP40s, the road's first second-generation power.

Barriger liked bright colors and opted to paint all equipment solid red with the classic Katy herald prominently displayed. Barriger was not able to justify operating the road's last passenger train, the Kansas City–Dallas remnant of the *Texas Special*. It was discontinued on June 30, 1965.

After Barriger's second retirement in 1970, Reginald Whitman became president and built the Katy toward its pinnacle. Whitman, too, brought new colors to the Katy: green with yellow highlights. Using government-guaranteed loans, Katy rebuilt its Kansas City–Fort Worth–Houston main line to Class 4 (60 mph) condition in the early 1980s. Although its Granger legacy was a distant memory, the government's entry into the international grain business provided abundant export traffic for the new Katy, which now included the Oklahoma, Kansas & Texas (former Rock Island trackage north of Fort Worth). The most significant event in Katy's rebound was a government mandate in the 1970s that electric generating plants situated along MKT routes burn low-sulfur western coal. Unlike seasonal agricultural movements, this new traffic served a year-round demand covered by long-term contracts.

While Katy was increasing its traffic base in the 1970s, the nation's merger movement was producing larger competing railroads even faster. In the 1980s Katy found itself surrounded by the likes of Burlington Northern (which by then included the Frisco) and Union Pacific (which included the Missouri Pacific). Katy's independence was clearly in jeopardy, and eventually the resilient Katy vanished into the UP in May 1988. (Actually the Katy was merged into the MoPac, which was controlled by the UP Corp.) It is remarkable that virtually all of Katy's main lines are still in use.

The motive-power history of Katy is nearly as colorful as its corporate saga. A Granger road built with light rail over mostly prairie country with few heavy grades, it needed only modest-sized steam locomotives. Unlike neighboring railroads, Katy never had anything larger than 2-8-2s and 4-6-2s—Mikados and Pacifics. The road went through World War II with a roster of 450 engines, only one-fourth of which had been built after World War I. Main-line power consisted of 154 Mikados and 62 Pacifics, with yard work entrusted to 66 switchers and branch lines to 120 Moguls, 40 Consolidations, and 10 Americans (among the last 4-4-0s in the nation).

When it came time to dieselize, the road pursued a naive strategy, empowering the traffic department rather than the mechanical department to order new locomotives. Undoubtedly influenced by persuasive sales pitches from aggressive builders, by the end of 1951 Katy owned 14 different models from four builders of the period (American Locomotive Co., Electro-Motive, Fairbanks-Morse, and General Electric). The 14 different models included 4 switchers, 4 road switchers, 2 freight cab types, and 4 passenger cab models. By 1956 Katy had acquired 50 more units in 7 additional models. Because of the massive maintenance demands of this fleet, many were worn out by 1956 and were either repowered or scrapped. By 1963 the road's locomotive roster was virtually all built by Electro-Motive or rebuilt and repowered with Electro-Motive diesel engines. In its last years the road's 327-unit roster included many secondhand locomotives, as well as a fleet of SD40-2s for coal trains and a group of 20 GP39-2s purchased in 1984 (Katy's last locomotive purchase before merger).

In 1982, the last year for which figures were available, Missouri-Kansas-Texas operated a system of 2,211 route-miles and 3,239 track-miles, with 237 locomotives, 3,566 freight cars, 76 company service cars, and 2,499 employees. Freight traffic totaled 6,693.4 million ton-miles in 1982, and coal and farm products predominated. Katy operating revenues totaled $230 million in 1982, and the railroad achieved a 73.7 percent operating ratio.

—J. Parker Lamb

REFERENCES

Anderson, Willard V. "Katy Serves the Southwest." *Trains* 9, no. 6 (Apr. 1949): 16–25.

Hofsommer, Donovan L. *Katy Northwest: The Story of a Branch Line Railroad.* Boulder, Colo.: Pruett, 1976.

Masterson, V. V. *The Katy Railroad and the Last Frontier.* Norman: Univ. of Oklahoma Press, 1952.

Morgan, David P. "Is There a Cure for What Ails Katy?" *Trains* 20, no. 10 (Aug. 1960): 16–25.

Modjeski, Ralph (1861–1940)

Trained at an early age as a pianist, Ralph Modjeski turned away from a concert career to take up the study of civil engineering. Born Rudolphe Modrzejewski in Bochnia, Poland, in 1861, Modjeski emigrated to the United States with his actress mother, Helena Modjeska,

in 1876; the two adopted the shortened surname to ease his mother's U.S. stage debut. After touring in the United States and England for several years as stage manager of his mother's troupe, Modjeski entered the École des Ponts et Chausées at Paris in 1881. He graduated at the top of his class in civil engineering in 1885 and returned to the United States to begin a long and brilliant career during which he designed or acted as consultant for more than 50 major bridges.

After two years as an inspector in the shops of the Union Bridge Co. at Athens, Pennsylvania, Modjeski joined the noted bridge engineer George S. Morison to work on the erection of a crossing of the Missouri River at Omaha, completed for the Union Pacific in 1887. He then worked with Morison and Alfred Noble on a crossing of the Mississippi at Memphis for the Kansas City, Fort Scott & Memphis. Completed in 1892, this cantilever truss bridge was the first crossing of the lower Mississippi and marked the beginning of Modjeski's experience with major, long-span bridges.

After establishing his own consulting engineering practice in 1893 Modjeski was involved in the design and construction of still other major bridges on the Mississippi, including the reconstruction of the Rock Island's bridge at Rock Island, Illinois, in 1895, Illinois Traction's McKinley Bridge at St. Louis in 1910, and, together with Alfred Noble, an enormous double-track, 2,800-foot, five-span cantilever crossing at Thebes, Illinois, completed in 1904 for the Southern Illinois & Missouri Bridge Co. During the same period he also was engaged in major bridge projects in almost every part of the United States, including the design of two bridges for the Spokane, Portland & Seattle and work as chief engineer for all bridges built for the Oregon Trunk Railway and as a consulting engineer to New York City for the Manhattan Bridge.

Ralph Modjeski had become one of North America's preeminent long-span bridge engineers when he was appointed by the Canadian government in 1908 to the board of engineers for the reconstruction of the Quebec Bridge. He remained a member throughout the decade-long period of design and construction of what still ranks as the world's longest cantilever bridge. Modjeski went on from that successful effort to design dozens of other notable railroad and highway bridges, including the Benjamin Franklin Bridge at Philadelphia and the Ambassador Bridge at Detroit. Together with Charles H. Cartlidge he designed the Burlington's crossing of the Ohio River at Metropolis, Illinois, completed in 1917 with a 720-foot main span that still ranks as the world's longest simple truss span. His firm designed the Huey P. Long cantilever bridge across the Mississippi River at New Orleans, completed in 1935. Ralph Modjeski's last and greatest work was his design for the great double-suspension and cantilever truss San Francisco–Oakland Bay Bridge, which opened in 1937, just three years before his death at Los Angeles in 1940.

—William D. Middleton

REFERENCES

Dictionary of American Biography.
"Memoir of Ralph Modjeski." *Transactions of the American Society of Civil Engineers* 106 (1941): 1624–1628.
National Cyclopaedia of American Biography.

Mohawk & Hudson Rail Road

The Erie Canal, opened in 1825, connected the Hudson River just north of Albany, New York, with Lake Erie. Between Albany and Schenectady the canal followed a circuitous 40-mile route through a number of locks. Boats took an entire day to travel between the two cities, which were only 16 miles apart by land. The need for faster transportation was recognized, and George William Featherstonhaugh (pronounced Fanshaw) took the lead in promoting a railroad. After much controversy in the state legislature, the Mohawk & Hudson Rail Road was chartered on April 17, 1826. The original bill imposed such stringent terms on the investors that money proved very difficult to raise, and not until after charter revisions were obtained early in 1828 did financing become possible. Featherstonhaugh had a falling out with the other directors and severed his connection with the company in August 1829.

The engineer chosen to carry out the work was John B. Jervis, who had worked on the Erie and Delaware & Hudson canals. Construction started in Schenectady in the summer of 1830. The route required the use of inclined planes at each end of the line. Operation by steam power was contemplated from the start, and a locomotive, the *De Witt Clinton*, was ordered from the West Point Foundry in New York.

An excursion train was operated with the locomotive on August 9, 1831, and regular operation began the following day with horsepower. The *De Witt Clinton* required extensive reworking by its builder to correct numerous problems. It never performed satisfactorily and was scrapped in 1835.

In 1832 Jervis designed a locomotive with a swiveling front truck. The locomotive, named *Experiment*, was quite successful, and the swiveling truck, Jervis's sole contribution to locomotive design, was a genuine breakthrough in American locomotive technology.

By the early 1840s it was recognized that the inclined planes at both ends of the line were an inconvenience, and in 1844 new routes were opened at both ends to bypass and eliminate the planes. Part of the motivation for this improvement was that the Schenectady & Troy Railroad opened in 1842 and could be expected to divert traffic from the Mohawk & Hudson. The elimination of the Albany plane was financed with assistance from the City of Albany. Despite this help, the Mohawk & Hudson was not a profitable enterprise for many years and paid no dividends between 1840 and 1847. In 1847 the name of the company was changed to the Albany & Schenectady.

A chain of short connecting railroads had been constructed in stages between Albany and Buffalo. As early as 1847 consolidation of these companies was discussed. In a long and complicated agreement ratified on June 29, 1853, the ten companies, including the Mohawk & Hudson/Albany & Schenectady, were merged to form the first New York Central Railroad. Of the original 16-mile route of the Mohawk & Hudson, about half of the central section became the main line of the New York Central Railroad. It is now operated for freight service by CSX and for passenger service by Amtrak.

—Adrian Ettlinger

REFERENCES

Gerstner, Franz Anton Ritter von. *Early American Railroads.* Ed. Frederick C. Gamst. Stanford, Calif.: Stanford Univ. Press, 1997 [1842–1843].
Harlow, Alvin F. *The Road of the Century.* New York: Creative Age Press, 1947.
Shaughnessy, Jim. *Delaware & Hudson.* Berkeley, Calif.: Howell-North, 1967. Repr., Syracuse, N.Y.: Syracuse Univ. Press, 1997.
Stevens, Frank Walker. *The Beginnings of the New York Central Railroad.* New York: G. P. Putnam's Sons, 1926.
White, John H., Jr. *American Locomotives: An Engineering History, 1830–1880.* Baltimore: Johns Hopkins Univ. Press, 1997.

Monon. *See* Chicago, Indianapolis & Louisville Railway (Monon Railroad)

Monuments

Although bronze statues and granite monuments seem now to have fallen out of favor, railroad men of an earlier time came in for a goodly number of memorials. Most commemorated railroad builders and corporate leaders, but there were some that recognized the achievements of ordinary railroad workingmen or even, in one instance, the men who stole a train. This entry presents a sampling.

B&O's Relay Viaduct Monument

Probably the oldest railroad monument commemorates completion by the Baltimore & Ohio of one of North America's greatest works of early railroad construction. Built to span the Patapsco River at Relay, Maryland, for the Washington extension of the B&O, the 704-foot structure of sturdy Patapsco granite comprised eight 58-foot ellipti-

Near the dawn of the railroad era Benjamin H. Latrobe, Jr., designed this simple obelisk to honor B&O president Philip E. Thomas. Dedicated on August 25, 1835, it still overlooks the great Thomas Viaduct. —William D. Middleton

In 1883 the Union Pacific Railroad erected this 60-foot-high monument to builders Oliver and Oakes Ames. Designed by Henry Hobson Richardson, it still stands near Sherman, Wyoming, at the Continental Divide. —*Trains* Magazine Collection

cal arches on a 4.5-degree curve. To celebrate its completion, bridge engineer Benjamin H. Latrobe, Jr., planned an impressive obelisk of light-colored granite that would stand above the viaduct on the north side of the structure. The bridge was named the Thomas Viaduct in honor of railroad president Philip E. Thomas, and the monument listed the principals involved, dates of construction, and B&O directors. The bridge and obelisk were formally dedicated at the official opening of the Washington branch in August 25, 1835, and both have been there ever since.

Ames Monument

Probably the largest railroad monument was completed in 1883 by the board of the Union Pacific. It honors brothers Oliver and Oakes Ames, businessmen, financiers, and (Oliver) president of the UP during its construction. Located near Sherman station on the Wyoming prairie, the monument stands at the Continental Divide, 8,300 feet above sea level. Erected at a cost of $75,000 and designed by architect Henry Hobson Richardson, it was a rough-hewn Wyoming granite pyramid, 60 feet square at the base and 60 feet high. Huge bas-reliefs of the two brothers designed by sculptor Augustus Saint-Gaudens were carved in the sandstone of their native Massachusetts, one facing east and one west.

Some time after the monument was completed, the Union Pacific found itself in an embarrassing situation. The land-grant railroad on either side of the line was laid out with alternate odd-numbered sections owned by the railroad, while the government held even-numbered sections. The monument was supposed to have been located on a UP-owned odd-numbered section, but an enterprising local entrepreneur discovered that it was in an even-numbered section, filed a claim, and took possession of the property. The owner of the new monument was going to sell advertising or sell it to the UP at a handsome price. In the end the UP was able to get the land back at only a small cost. Union Pacific donated the monument to the State of Wyoming in 1983, where it still stands firmly astride the Continental Divide.

Commodore Vanderbilt

Probably the most expensive monument was that honoring shipping and railroad financier Cornelius Vanderbilt. Few could exceed the New York Central's Vanderbilt in his vanity. He once proposed to erect a memorial in Central Park, larger even than the Washington Monument, that would jointly commemorate George Washington and himself, and he had even hired an architect to prepare the plans before he could be dissuaded from the scheme. In 1869 Vanderbilt actually did go ahead with a huge series of bronzes to himself to be located atop the

Cornelius Vanderbilt, the "Commodore," was not wanting in self-esteem. The massive bronze memorial to himself erected at the New York Central's freight station in 1869 weighed 50 tons. Most of the memorial came down in 1929, but the figure of the Commodore was moved to a Grand Central Terminal vantage point on 42nd Street and Park Avenue, where it stands today.
—William D. Middleton

New York Central's new freight station at St. John's Park in New York. It was built at a cost of $500,000, measured 3,125 square feet, and weighed 50 tons. In the center of the piece sculptor Ernest Plassman set up a giant statue of Vanderbilt, wearing an overcoat, upholding Neptune on the right and Liberty on the left, and honoring an ocean liner and a train of cars.

Vanderbilt unveiled the new monument with some 2,000 in attendance, with bands, a bishop, and New York mayor A. Oakley Hall in attendance. "Stand there, familiar image of an honored man! Stand there to breast the storms or glitter in the sunshine of coming centuries!" proclaimed Mayor Hall. The Commodore stood there until 1929, when the statue was relocated to Grand Central Terminal atop a large pedestal on an elevated road around the station at 42nd Street and Park Avenue.

Camden & Amboy Monument

Marking the early beginnings of the Camden & Amboy Railroad, the Bordentown Monument was dedicated on November 12, 1891, to commemorate the 60th anniversary of the C&A's first train in 1831. Installed at Bordentown, New Jersey, it is a granite shaft five feet square, surrounded by a circle of square stone-block sleepers, all set in a ring around the monument, while a bronze plaque depicts the locomotive *John Bull* and cars. The monument has recently been restored and is now located at Farnsworth Avenue and Church Street, immediately above the old C&A main line. The famous locomotive itself with one of the cars is on exhibit at the National Museum of American History at the Smithsonian Institution at Washington.

The Last Spike

The ceremonial driving of the last spike has been traditional for the completion of a new railroad, with none better known than that for the Pacific Railroad on May 10, 1869. Sixteen years later came another last spike, for the completion of the transcontinental Canadian Pacific Railway, an event of at least equal importance to Canadians. Director Donald A. Smith drove the plain iron spike at Eagle Pass at Craigellachie, British Columbia, on November 7, 1885. There were no bands or politicians. Echoing the simplicity of the ceremony, the CPR's completion is marked with a stone obelisk bearing a bronze plaque with the words "Here Was Driven the Last Spike, Completing Canadian Pacific Railway from Ocean to Ocean, November 7, 1885."

Pennsylvania Station Statues

The construction of Pennsylvania Station, including the entire complex of Hudson and East River tunnels, electrification, and the opening of the Hell Gate Bridge, was one of the greatest undertakings by a railroad company, and the Pennsylvania honored two of its chief builders. Pennsylvania president Alexander Cassatt had begun this remarkable achievement. Cassatt died in 1906 while the work was still in progress and was honored at the station's completion in 1910. The bronze larger-than-life-size sculpture by Adolph A. Weinman was set in a travertine niche at the right side of the grand staircase of the main waiting room. PRR president James McCrea and Samuel Rea, Cassatt's chief lieutenant for the station project, were present at the gathering of 80 people for the monument's unveiling on August 1, 1910. The inscription on the statue told "whose foresight, courage, and ability achieved the extension of the Pennsylvania Railroad System into New York City," and the station was declared open.

Rea later became president of the PRR, and in 1930, the year after his death, a second bronze statue, also by Weinman, was installed in a similar niche on the left side of the grand staircase. The statues remained there until the demolition of Pennsylvania Station in the 1960s, after which the Rea statue was reinstalled at the Seventh Avenue entrance of the new Two Penn Plaza building. The Cassatt statue has been moved to the Railroad Museum of Pennsylvania at Strasburg, Pennsylvania, where it is on display.

Central Pacific Pathfinder

Long after his death, a monument for Theodore Dehone Judah, who pioneered the Central Pacific's path across the forbidding Sierra Nevada range, was erected in a park facing the Southern Pacific station at Sacramento, California, in February 1931. Boulders formed the monument, surmounting a large stone with Judah's portrait, surrounded by laurel leaves, and a depiction of the great CP crossing of the Sierra Nevada. Judah's great-grandniece, Janice Judah, and two still-surviving members of Judah's surveying party attended the unveiling. The monument is no longer at the Sacramento station, but it survives, although stored in a warehouse at the California State Railroad Museum.

A Monument to Casey Jones

On April 30, 1900, engineer John Luther "Casey" Jones headed south with Illinois Central Train No. 1, the *New Orleans Special*. Running fast to make up time, it overran train No. 83, which had not yet cleared the main line, at Vaughan, Mississippi. Jones rode the locomotive into the collision and lost his life. Railroad accidents were common at that time, and Casey Jones would not have been long remembered except for engine wiper Wallace Saunders's famous ballad. In several forms the story of "Casey Jones, the Brave Engineer" became popular, and Jones became a railroad legend. Almost a half century after his death he got his own monument, a handsome stone marker installed at Jackson, Mississippi: "For I'm going to run her till she leaves the rail—or make it on time with the southbound mail." Among those on hand for the 1947 dedication were the brave engineer's widow; Simeon Webb, Casey's fireman in the 1900 collision; and railroad writers and photographers Lucius Beebe and Charles Clegg, who put up the monument. Three years later, on the 50th anniversary of Casey Jones's death, the Post Office Department issued a commemorative three-cent stamp as well.

Honoring a Stolen Train

One of the great adventures of the Civil War was the bold attempt of a band of 21 Union men, headed by James

J. Andrews, to go behind Confederate lines to capture and wreck the Western & Atlantic Railroad between Big Shanty, Georgia, and Chattanooga, Tennessee, isolating the Confederacy at Chattanooga. On April 12, 1862, Andrew's men seized the locomotive *General* and three cars at Big Shanty and headed north, with the Confederates in hot pursuit. The chase went on for over eight hours, until the *General* ran out of fuel and water just south of the Tennessee line. The raiders ran for cover, but all were captured by the Confederates. Andrews and seven of his men were hanged, while the remainder went to a Confederate prison. In 1891 the eight men were reburied at the Chattanooga National Cemetery behind a large stone memorial given by the State of Ohio and topped by a likeness of the *General*. It still stands.

Railroad Workers

Many monuments honor railroad employees who served their country in times of war, perhaps few better than the Canadian Pacific's Winged Victory statue at Montreal's Windsor Station. Sculpted by Coeur de Lion MacCarthy in 1922, the heroic bronze, which towers over the station concourse, depicts a winged angel and a fallen soldier. Since installation, it has been rededicated to honor the 33,127 CPR employees, 1,774 of whom gave their lives, in both world wars. Similar CPR statues were installed in Winnipeg and Vancouver, and the railroad also commissioned 22 bronze tablets in 1922 that were erected at overseas locations in London, Liverpool, New York, and Hong Kong, as well as stations all across Canada.

The Pennsylvania Railroad remembered more than 1,300 PRR employees who died in World War II with this 36-foot bronze sculpture by Walker Kirtland Hancock. Gen. Omar Bradley presided over its dedication at Philadelphia's 30th Street Station on August 10, 1952. —Saul Zalkind, *Trains* Magazine Collection

An equally impressive memorial at the Pennsylvania Railroad 30th Street Station in Philadelphia, the Angel of Resurrection, honors 1,307 PRR employees killed in World War II. The enormous 36-foot 7-inch winged bronze statue, designed by sculptor Walker Kirtland Hancock, towers over the station's main hall. Gen. Omar Bradley presided over the dedication on August 10, 1952.

Railroad Passengers

On a busy evening on August 26, 1893, an inbound train from the Long Island Rail Road's Manhattan Beach Division, delayed by traffic ahead, was overtaken by a following Rockaway train. The last two cars were badly damaged by the collision, and the casualties included 15 fatalities and 17 severely injured passengers. Among the dead were a young couple, Oscar and Maggie Dietzel, returning from a day's outing at Manhattan Beach. The family of the tragic couple installed an impressive granite memorial in Brooklyn's Greenwood Cemetery consisting of a large stone marker surmounted by an ornate open structure and topped by a large stone angel. Within the open structure was installed a granite locomotive and the wrecked cars from the fatal train wreck. It still stands at the cemetery.

Other Financiers, Engineers, and Operating Men

People sometimes talked of empire builder James J. Hill being memorialized by the 8,200-mile Great Northern itself, but he has at least four traditional monuments as well. Bronze busts of Hill are at Superior, Wisconsin, in the Burlington Northern & Santa Fe yard office at West Superior; on the University of Washington campus at Seattle; and, appropriately, in the James J. Hill Library at St. Paul. A statue of Hill stands at Havre, Montana, in front of the depot.

Denver & Rio Grande builder William J. Palmer was best known for his Colorado railroads, but it is his service as president of the Mexican National from 1881 to 1887 that is commemorated in a bronze bas-relief at Mexico City.

In 1894, when J. P. Morgan put together several failed southern railroads to form the Southern Railway, engineer and former B&O president Samuel Spencer was brought in as the Southern's president. Spencer built the company into a strong railroad, and after his death in a railroad collision he was memorialized with a statue. This could be viewed at the Atlanta Terminal Station until demolition of that depot. The statue was moved to Atlanta's Peachtree Street Station, then again to its present location at Hardy Ivy Park in downtown Atlanta.

Henry M. Flagler, former oilman, Florida developer, and builder of the Florida East Coast Railway, was memo-

A handsome bronze statue of Samuel Spencer, first president of the Southern Railway, by Daniel Chester French, was erected at the Atlanta Terminal Station in 1910. The Spencer statue was relocated several times, most recently to Atlanta's Hardy Ivy Park. —David C. Lester

rialized in an Italian-built bronze statue. Flagler did not like it, and it remained in a freight station until after his death; it was then placed on the campus of Flagler College in St. Augustine, where it still stands.

Railroad builders have occasionally been memorialized, too. Maj. Gen. Grenville M. Dodge ended up with at least two cameo portraits. One is located at the Sherman Memorial at Washington, D.C., while the other, at Des Moines, Iowa, is part of Iowa's big Civil War Memorial adjacent to the State Capitol. Attired in suitable winter clothing, a heroic bronze statue of John Frank Stevens, who discovered the Great Northern's Marias Pass through the Rockies in a snowstorm in 1889, still stands at the summit of the Continental Divide at Marias Pass in Summit, Montana. An 8-foot bronze statue of longtime Baldwin Locomotive Works president William Matthias Baldwin, designed by Herbert Adams, was erected in 1905 and now stands in a prominent location on the north side of Philadelphia City Hall.

Charles Minot was an early general superintendent for the New York & Erie who made an important and widely adopted change in railroad operations. In 1851 railroads operated under a timetable system, under which trains moving in opposite directions on a single-track line were scheduled to meet at a scheduled meeting place. If a train was delayed, a railroad could be tied up for hours until the late train arrived. Minot conceived the idea of using the railroad's new telegraph to issue a train order to revise meeting points. Minot's first telegraphed train order was sent on September 22, 1851, and the timetable and train-order system was soon widely adopted. The occasion was marked in May 1912 by railway telegraph superintendents, who erected a bronze tablet backed by a granite stone, designed by Charles Keck, and fittingly installed on the Erie main line at Harriman, New York. Sadly, the memorial is no longer there.

—William D. Middleton

REFERENCES

Carter, Charles F. "Railroaders in Bronze." *Railroad* 22, no. 6 (Nov. 1937): 40–49.

Hansen, Peter A. "The Brave Engineer." *Trains* 60, no. 4 (Apr. 2000): 34–43.

Harlow, Alvin F. "A Monument for Rent." *Trains* 8, no. 12 (Oct. 1948): 52–53.

Heineman, E. B. "Sculptured on a Tombstone." *Railroad* 20, no. 4 (Sept. 1936): 34–39.

Jensen, Oliver. "The Great Locomotive Chase." In *The American Heritage History of Railroads in America.* New York: American Heritage, 1975.

Moody, John (1868–1958)

John Moody, born on May 2, 1868, was an early business analyst and writer at a time when corporate America was in its infancy. Moody was always interested in becoming a writer, and when he was only 14, he sold a story to a boys' magazine. But his family's savings were lost in the stock market, and Moody, then 15, had to go to work. He found employment with a New York wholesaler and then, with the help of George Foster Peabody, who was a cousin of Moody's mother, in 1890 obtained a job with Spencer, Trask & Co., a Wall Street securities firm.

While serving primarily in an administrative role with Spencer, Trask, Moody developed a serious interest in the securities industry. To this point the securities industry had been dominated by the railroads, because they were generally the only firms large enough to issue stock and have their performance tracked by investors. As the number and size of U.S. business firms continued to grow, the securities industry grew along with it. Sources of information on companies, however, were limited. The primary exception was, again, the railroad industry, about which information was available through the highly successful *Manual of Railroads,* begun by Henry Varnum Poor in 1868.

Appreciating the dearth of information on companies other than railroads, Moody seized the opportunity to do something about it. Acting on a suggestion by Thomas F. Woodcock, then editor of the *Wall Street Journal,* Moody set out to develop a reference of industrial companies that would complement Poor's railroad series. With American business growing continuously, along with the financial industry that supported it, John Moody's *Manual of Industrial and Miscellaneous Securities,* published beginning in November 1900, was a tremendous success. When Henry Varnum Poor died in 1905, Moody added railroad coverage to his *Manual.*

In 1910 Poor's began publishing information on non-rail industrial securities, and the efforts of Moody's and Poor's to publish securities manuals were eventually combined. Moody expanded the services of his firm to include investment advice, ratings of securities, and additional publications for the investor. He also wrote several important books addressing issues in the railroad industry, as well as on general business and investment.

Deeply religious, Moody was active in the Roman Catholic Church for much of his life. He believed that the teachings of Christianity should be used as a basis for business dealings. In the first volume of his two-volume autobiography, *The Long Road Home,* Moody devotes considerable space to discussing his religion and its impact on his life. He died on February 16, 1958, shortly after moving to La Jolla, California.

—David C. Lester

REFERENCES

Martin, Albro. "John Moody." In *Dictionary of American Biography, Supplement Six, 1956–1960,* 457–458. New York: Charles Scribner's Sons, 1980.

Moody, John. *The Long Road Home.* New York: Macmillan, 1933. Repr. New York: Arno Press, 1975.

Obituary of John Moody. *New York Times,* Feb. 17, 1958.

Morgan, J. P. (1837–1913)

The son of a prosperous banker, J. Pierpont Morgan was born with a silver spoon in his mouth and, as the world knows, soon turned it into gold. He himself entered the banking business in 1856 at age 19, at first working with his father, but four years later he had his own firm.

Much of Morgan's legendary power and influence came from his involvement with railroads, in his time the country's dominant industry. As a banker, he neither built nor managed "his" railroads, but by controlling much of the investment money that went into them, he came to choose their managers, dictate their policies, and shape them to his principles. His primary principle was to preserve and enhance investment values by stabilizing those businesses where large investments were at stake. His methods included reducing wasteful competition, consolidating competing companies, and reorganizing shaky operations—usually with Morgan, his banking allies, and his own handpicked managers guiding the newly "Morganized" entities. The late nineteenth-century railroad industry was one of those in greatest need of his ministrations. Not only was it the country's largest consumer of capital funds, but by the 1880s it was becoming increasingly financially unstable through overbuilding and overcompetition, and was also often victimized by speculators and empire builders.

Morgan's first foray into railroad warfare came in 1869 when he helped thwart Jay Gould's attempted takeover of the Albany & Susquehanna Railroad. A far greater opportunity to exert power appeared ten years later when, in 1879 and 1880, he helped the New York Central's William H. Vanderbilt dispose of half of his huge Central stock holdings. The sale demanded a careful strategy to avoid breaking the market with such a large bloc, and Morgan handled it adeptly. Subsequently Vanderbilt made him the railroad's principal banker. This was followed in 1880 by Morgan's infusion of new capital into the faltering, unfinished Northern Pacific, allowing it to complete its route to the Pacific Coast. Shortly afterward he changed its management and stabilized its finances, making it the first true "Morgan road."

He next resolved a ruinous power struggle between the Pennsylvania Railroad and the New York Central, then the East's two dominant rail systems. The conflict revolved around Vanderbilt's attempted invasion of the Pennsylvania's prime eastern territory through two new railroad-construction projects in the PRR's home state of Pennsylvania—the South Pennsylvania and the Beech Creek—and a suspected (but never proven) effort by the Pennsylvania to control the New York, West Shore & Buffalo, a newly built line that directly paralleled the Central between New York and Buffalo. Morgan stepped into this complex, confused, and costly situation in 1885 and brokered a peace agreement whereby the Central would take over the West Shore, while the Pennsylvania would get Vanderbilt's two Pennsylvania lines. Although legal problems frustrated some elements of the plan, Vanderbilt's South Pennsylvania project was stopped, and the broad goals were accomplished.

Numerous other Morgan reorganizations came in the late 1880s and 1890s. One example, the Philadelphia & Reading, had to be done twice—once in 1886 and again in 1895 after the company backslid under a new empire-

J. P. Morgan. —Library of Congress (Neg. LC-USZ62-8681)

building president. The second effort produced a railroad that remained solid and prosperous through the first half of the twentieth century. Some others were not as successful, notably his failed attempt with the Union Pacific (giving E. H. Harriman his opportunity) and a rebuff by the Baltimore & Ohio that eventually led to that railroad's 1896 receivership. An 1893–1895 reorganization of the perennially wayward Erie Railroad helped it somewhat, but not even Morgan could solve its basic ills.

But probably Morgan's most notable single accomplishment in the railroad business was his 1894 creation of the Southern Railway system out of a conglomeration of marginal southeastern railroads, most of which had been victimized through a holding company composed of New York speculators. Under its Morgan-appointed president, Samuel Spencer, the Southern was built up into the South's most powerful rail system.

In other cases Morgan's hand was less visible, although no less firm. By the early twentieth century the boards of many railroads were dominated by Morgan and his allies, creating a banker-controlled community of interest that stabilized competition and channeled funds into rebuilding and upgrading the stronger properties rather than building new lines. And indirectly, through his newly created United States Steel Corp., Morgan helped stop the transcontinental ambitions of Jay Gould's son George.

There were, of course, some equally spectacular failures. Unquestionably the most famous was the Northern Securities Co., a holding company created by Morgan in 1901 to resolve a power struggle involving himself, Edward H. Harriman, and James J. Hill over control of the Northern Pacific, the Great Northern, and their Chicago connection, the Chicago, Burlington & Quincy. All three lines were to come under Northern Securities' wing, thus putting all the principal routes between Chicago and the Pacific Northwest under a single control. Unfortunately for Morgan, though, President Theodore Roosevelt viewed it as the archsymbol of the evils of monopoly and made it the landmark case in his trust-busting crusade. Northern Securities was finally dissolved by a 1904 Supreme Court order.

Closer to home was the New York, New Haven & Hartford debacle. With Morgan's backing, Charles S. Mellen, his handpicked president, went on a headlong and heedless monopolistic buying spree after 1903 that soon resulted in the New Haven's control of virtually every major railroad, street railway, and steamship line in its New England territory. Some were acquired by legally and ethically dubious methods, and many were bought at premium prices that could never be recouped in earnings. In a short time Morgan's beloved but hapless New Haven was heading toward collapse and was the target of an extensive investigation and scathing indictment of its management by the Interstate Commerce Commission. Morgan himself died before the affair was over, and his New Haven never fully recovered. But if Morgan was not quite the omnipotent giant of legend, he was unquestionably the single most powerful force in rescuing the nineteenth-century railroad industry from itself, stabilizing and strengthening it, and equipping it to handle the demands of the twentieth century.

—Herbert H. Harwood, Jr.

REFERENCES

Carosso, Vincent P. *The Morgans: Private International Bankers, 1854–1913*. Cambridge, Mass.: Harvard Univ. Press, 1987.

Chernow, Ron. *The House of Morgan: An American Banking Dynasty and the Rise of Modern Finance*. New York: Atlantic Monthly Press, 1990.

Strouse, Jean. *Morgan: American Financier*. New York: Random House, 1999.

Morse, Samuel F. B. (1791–1872)

Samuel Finley Breese Morse is celebrated in the United States as the inventor of the telegraph. This is at once an exaggeration and an understatement. Long before the electric telegraph was conceived, the word "telegraph" had been in use to describe a system to relay messages over multiple steps of line-of-sight distances by manual signaling, and an electric telegraph system was used commercially with limited success in England several years before Morse's first real success in 1844. Nevertheless, the system developed by Morse proved to be by far the most practicable and was the one eventually universally adopted.

The title of Carleton Mabee's Pulitzer Prize–winning biography of Morse, *The American Leonardo*, aptly indicates the breadth of his interest and talents. He was born on April 27, 1791, in Charlestown, Massachusetts, near Bunker Hill. His father, Jedidiah, was a Congregational minister and a man of accomplishment who had authored the first geography published in North America. Morse thus had a privileged education available to him, but a restless and rebellious temperament steered him away from conventional pursuits. He attended Phillips Academy and Yale without academic distinction. With a natural talent for drawing, he determined to become a painter; in that day the technique could be learned only in Europe, and his parents agreed to support him in England for study. He spent four years (1811–1815) in England, able to pursue his artistic education despite the fact that the two countries were at war for most of the period. By fits and starts, over the next 17 years, Morse established himself as the preeminent portrait painter in the United States and was the driving force in establishing the National Academy of the Arts of Design, of which he was repeatedly elected president.

Morse's career in telegraphy began abruptly with a casual shipboard conversation late in 1832 in which the newly discovered electromagnet was mentioned. His fertile imagination immediately grasped the consequences: instantaneous communication by electricity should be feasible. At that time he thought that the concept was original with him, unaware as he was of some European scientists who had been suggesting the possibility for some time. For at least five years he dabbled in experimentation as an avocation and then started to fully devote himself to it. It took until 1844 before the first fully practical and commercially useful telegraph system was installed between Baltimore and Washington. Most of the true "invention" of the devices needed to perfect the system really sprang from others, even including the code that bears his name. But Morse was the driving force behind the effort, and his business and political skills were essential to its successful completion.

Ironically, Morse spent much time developing a means to record a coded message in permanent form on a strip of paper. He failed to realize that it would be possible for the human ear and brain to "copy" a message audibly from a sounder. Within two years of operation the sounder had become popular and largely supplanted the use of the recording system.

The telegraph made Morse a very wealthy man, despite a seemingly endless stream of lawsuits and business disputes. He maintained an active interest in politics, and many of his views today would be regarded as the epitome of political incorrectness. From the start of the abolitionist movement, Morse considered abolitionism to be a greater danger to the nation than the institution of slavery, and he became an apologist for the Southern cause. Morse lived through the Civil War, which he saw as a fulfillment of his prophecies. He died on April 2, 1872.

—Adrian Ettlinger

REFERENCES

Mabee, Carleton. *The American Leonardo: A Life of Samuel F. B. Morse.* New York: Alfred A. Knopf, 1943. Rpt. Fleischmanns, N.Y.: Purple Mountain Press, 2000.

Silverman, Kenneth. *Lightning Man: The Accursed Life of Samuel F. B. Morse.* New York: Alfred A. Knopf, 2003.

MTA Metro-North Railroad

"We have a gem of a little railroad—and we would hate to move backward from that." This unsolicited compliment from an MTA Metro-North Railroad commuter was published in the *New York Times* several years ago in connection with the Metropolitan Transportation Authority's announcement that Metro-North would be merged with the Long Island into a combined MTA Rail Road. Although some functional merger may eventually happen, the separate Metro-North and LIRR names will remain.

Things were not always this rosy on Metro-North. The railroad was formed in 1983 from Conrail's Metropolitan Region, which was created in the 1968–1976 Penn Central era to isolate the costs of the New York City commuter operations of the former New Haven and New York Central railroads. Some new equipment had been funded by the states of New York and Connecticut, but the Metro-North of 1983 nonetheless confronted decades of deferred maintenance, both in physical plant and in equipment. A ragtag fleet of former New Haven FL9 dual-mode diesel-electric and straight electric locomotives had to be retained because no other available units could operate into Grand Central Terminal's third-rail territory, and in desperation some E8s were leased from Amtrak and New Jersey Transit to help out. Even freight locomotives were used, and this motley assemblage of power hauled a similarly ragtag fleet of steam-heated former long-distance coaches. Multiple-unit electric cars provided the bulk of the service, but the majority of these were also hand-me-downs in poor condition. The main shop was a sprawling dingy relic at Harmon, with a smaller but equally ancient facility at North White Plains and a new two-track shop at New Haven. Employee morale was understandably low, and hapless passengers endured standee conditions and low 80.5 percent on-time performance.

New York and Connecticut fortunately realized that Grand Central commuter service was essential, both to the suburbs and to the city itself, and the states had already funded some improvements before 1983. New York's Metropolitan Transportation Authority (MTA) acquired the former New York Central Harlem and Hudson lines by long-term lease in 1972, as well as purchasing New Haven Line trackage within New York State. In 1971 the Connecticut Department of Transportation (CDOT) bought the New Haven Line within Connecticut as far as New Haven, as well as New Haven branches to New Canaan, Danbury, and Waterbury. This was just a step ahead of Amtrak, which was formed in 1971 and which acquired all of the Northeast Corridor between Boston and Washington except for Metro-North's New Haven Line segment between New Rochelle and New Haven. Thus Amtrak trains traverse this territory under Metro-North trackage rights and are dispatched by Metro-North rail traffic controllers.

Metro-North trackage west of the Hudson River is comprised of the New York State portions of New Jersey Transit lines. Trains on those lines are crewed and dispatched by NJ Transit.

The states also tackled the equipment problem, which requires three totally different fleets: 650-volt DC multiple-unit cars for former New York Central territory, bicurrent M.U. cars for the New Haven Line (they operate on 13,500-volt AC drawn from overhead wires or 650-volt DC from a third rail), and locomotive-hauled coaches for the nonelectrified parts of the railroad. Some M.U. cars were overhauled, but most were replaced, and all steam-heated coaches were replaced as well. The FL9s were initially overhauled, but have now been largely replaced by new General Electric Genesis dual-power locomotives. Metro-North also uses 11 GP40 and F40 variants for West of Hudson service.

Metro-North may still be a gem, but it is not little. At 250,000 weekday trips, its ridership is second only to that of the Long Island Rail Road in North American commuter operations, and its fleet of electric M.U. cars totals 825. These include 80 M-1 and 140 M-3 cars, 238 M-7 cars still being delivered, and 241 M-2 cars, 54 M-4s, and 48 M-6s for dual-voltage New Haven Line service. All these cars have subway-style quarter-point automatic doors and no passenger steps and thus require high platforms.

Locomotive-hauled equipment consists of 211 Bombardier push-pull coaches, which have end-of-car vestibules and doors, but door operation is automatically controlled (some cars have center doors as well). These cars have vestibule traps and steps for use at the few remaining low-level platforms on branch lines. A fleet of 31 GE Genesis P32DCM dual-power locomotives (plus six leased Amtrak Genesis P40s) is the primary road power, and 6 rebuilt GP35Ms handle most work train duties.

Despite the massive equipment replacement program funded by the states, a few pieces of equipment from an earlier era are still earning their keep on Metro-North.

Seven former New Haven FL9s survive. Six of these are CDOT owned and were heavily rebuilt by Morrison-Knudsen in the 1990s, and all are painted in the New Haven's red, white, and black McGinnis colors (as are the four CDOT-owned P32DCMs). The FL9s were built in 1957–1960, but are youthful compared with three F10 units purchased from Boston's MBTA; these started life in 1946 and 1947 as freight haulers on the Gulf, Mobile & Ohio, and the senior one (Metro-North 413) is reportedly the oldest diesel in regular passenger service in the nation. A pair of early GP units supplement the GP35Ms in work-train service, but the three former Niagara Junction steeple-cab electric switchers are off the roster—they were the last straight electric locomotives to work in Grand Central Terminal.

Metro-North is not resting on its laurels. Much of its infrastructure has been rebuilt, but this continues with the replacement of New Haven Line catenary, signal system improvements, and additional three-tracking on the Harlem Line. Further new equipment will be ordered for the New Haven Line, because traffic continues to grow. And so does the railroad: service has already been extended six miles north to Wassaic, New York, and an unused 50-mile former New Haven freight line on portions of the old Maybrook line and branches has been purchased and rail-banked for possible future expansion. Adjacent highways are already congested, with no room for expansion, so Metro-North's future looks bright indeed.

In 2005 Metro-North operated a system of 385 route-miles and 775 track-miles (including West of Hudson lines), with 62 locomotives, 1,036 passenger cars, and 6,000 employees. Passenger traffic totaled 2.05 billion passenger miles. Metro-North transported a total of 74.5 million passengers in 2005, a 56 percent increase since 1984. On-time performance was 97.5 percent, with 735 trains operated daily.

—J. W. Swanberg

REFERENCE

Swanberg, J. W. "Metro-North: From Faltering to First Rate." *North American Commuter Rail, 1994*, 8–15. Pasadena, Calif.: Passenger Train Journal, 1994.

Music

By its nature (at least during the nineteenth century), elite (i.e., classical) music tends toward the abstract and general; consequently, the genres that have most often used railroad themes and imagery are the vernacular ones: mass popular music and the more regional musics of particular communities, occupational groups, and ethnic enclaves. This survey will concentrate mainly on these categories. Some of the works discussed are by well-known authors and musicians; others are the creations of long-anonymous folk poets and musicians.

In a sense, the Industrial Revolution that made possible the spread of the railroads also provided the means for memorializing steel rails and their users in America's newly developing mass media. Railroads and rail travel on the continent began in 1828 and the years immediately following; the earliest railroad songs and tunes came very soon after.

On July 4, 1828, groundbreaking ceremonies were held at Baltimore for the construction of America's first public railway carrier to be put in regular service, the Baltimore & Ohio Railroad Co. A song, "The Carrollton March," was especially written for the occasion:

> And when the road is made, with the pick and the spade,
> In the locomotive engine, they will put a little fire,
> And while the kettle boils, we may ride 300 miles,
> Or go to bed in Baltimore and breakfast in Ohio.

While unremembered today, this may be America's first railroad song (that is, a song in which the subject of railroads or trains is more than merely incidental).

In the 1830s and 1840s songs reflected the mixture of exhilaration and fear that characterized then-current attitudes toward the railroads. To early nonpassengers, railroads were often a source of terror, panicking horses, frightening children, covering bystanders with soot and cinders, and sometimes setting fields ablaze from wayward sparks. A graphic example was "The Song of the Locomotive," published first in the 1840s and circulated on many broadsides in the following decades:

> Avaunt! avaunt! for I heed you not,
> Nor pause for the cry of pain;
> I rejoice o'er the slaughter my wheels have wrought,
> And I laugh at the mangled slain.

In the 1840s the railroad came to be used allegorically, with symbolic trains representing journeys to heaven or hell. In the spirit of Nathaniel Hawthorne's short story "The Celestial Railroad" (1838–1843), whose narrator dreams about a train that supposedly is taking pilgrims to heaven but actually is run by the devil taking them to hell, several broadsides from the 1840s depicted a railroad journey to heaven or hell. Two early ones were "Railway to Heaven" and "Railway to Hell," both from the 1840s. More widely reprinted was "The Spiritual Railway," also from the late 1840s. This was still sung in the 1920s, if not later:

> The line to Heaven by Christ is made,
> With Heavenly truth the rails are laid. . . .
> . . .
> There is a railway downward laid,
> Which God the Father never made.

The best known of these allegorical railroads is "Life's Railroad to Heaven" (M. E. Abbey and Charles D. Tillman, 1890), a good example of a popular style of homiletic poetry in which a railroad journey was used to represent life itself. The song became instantly popular among railroad men and appeared frequently in journals for railroaders. It has retained its popularity now for over a century and is still sung by bluegrass and gospel bands.

In the 1860s, as railroad travel became commonplace, the subject of train songs became the travelers and their experiences. One favorite, of which several variants were printed, was "The Charming Young Widow I Met in the Train." In one of these, a young man on a train meets a young "widow" with a babe in arms; she asks him to hold her infant while she detrains momentarily to greet her late husband's brother on the platform. But she never returns; the swaddling clothes cover no baby, only a dummy—and furthermore, he discovers that his pockets have been relieved of purse, ticket, watch, and gold pencil-case.

By century's end railroad lines were so extensive that an indigent traveler could venture anywhere he wanted, provided he was careful to avoid the fierce company guards known as railroad bulls. Nonpaying passengers (tramps, hoboes, and bums) became the subjects of a class of songs that tended to treat their downtrodden social position with considerable sympathy. One of the best known is "The Wabash Cannonball," popularized in the 1930s by Roy Acuff and his Smoky Mountain Boys, but derived from an earlier sheet-music composition, "The Great Rock Island Route!" (J. A. Roff, 1882), that served as a musical advertisement for the latter railroad line. (This piece is not to be confused with "Rock Island Line," mentioned later.) Other once-popular songs about tramps include "The Poor Tramp Has to Live," "The Dying Hobo," and "Because He Was Only a Tramp," all from the late nineteenth century and anonymous.

Trains and railroads have taken on many symbolic meanings over the years, most of which have found expression in folksongs at one time or another. On the one hand, they can represent luxury, comfort, freedom, and power; on the other, they can conjure up images of smoke and soot, disaster, excess profits, and corporate greed. Many blues songs of the 1920s either lamented the train that took a singer's loved one away or extolled the train as a means to freedom. Numerous folk blues of the early twentieth century gave voice to the singer's despair over a departed lover (e.g., "Train That Carried My Girl from Town," "2:19 Took My Baby," and "Railroad Blues"). In some the singer cursed the train itself, as well as the engineer and fireman, as if they were personally responsible for his gal's departure.

Until the middle of the twentieth century a high-speed train was the fastest means of travel and became a symbol of escape or flight from an intolerable situation. "The Midnight Special" is a folksong about the *Golden Gate Limited*, from Houston's Southern Pacific depot to San Antonio and El Paso. Thirty miles out from Houston its headlamp shone through the barred windows at the Texas prison farm at Sugarland, teasing inmates with the reminder of the light and freedom on the other side of the prison walls.

In the United States the first train fatality occurred in 1831, scarcely five years after the opening of the B&O. As train wrecks became more frequent, inevitably songs and poems were written about them, many of which were published in the journals of the railroad brotherhoods. "The Bridge Was Burned at Chatsworth" (Thomas P. Westendorf, 1887) recounted one of the worst train wrecks in American history. This and earlier songs focused on the passenger victims; later, attention shifted to the heroism of engineers and brakemen. One of the most enduring wreck ballads is "Wreck of the Old 97." The disaster occurred on September 27, 1903, on the Southern Railway in Virginia, the result of engineer Steve Broady's determination to make up lost time in spite of his unfamiliarity with a difficult road.

A similar situation caused the train wreck song of greatest commercial success, "Casey Jones." Outside Vaughan, Mississippi, on the night of April 30, 1900, engineer Jones was running the Illinois Central's southbound Cannonball Express late when it collided with a caboose and three freight cars that were standing on the main track, the rest of the train being on a sidetrack. Soon after the wreck African American engine wipers around the railroad yards at Canton, Mississippi, particularly Wallace Saunders, made up a ditty about Jones based on older folksongs. Two vaudevillians, Eddie Newton and Lawrence Seibert, heard one of those songs and completely rewrote it in 1909 for the stage.

Not all songs about trainmen ended in disaster, but tragedy was always a favorite ballad topic. In the 1870s and later at least three different songs were written with the title "Asleep at the Switch." In the best known of these (by Charles Shackford, 1897), switchman Tom, crazed by the thought of his son dying at home, collapses at his post. His daughter Nell runs up to tell him that the boy is better and sees his lifeless body. She picks up a lantern and waves it frantically to sidetrack the westbound freight, thus narrowly averting a disaster. Tom has died at his post, but because the wife and child of the railroad's president were on that train, Nell is handsomely rewarded.

During the decades of westward expansion songs about railroad construction flourished. "John Henry" has probably been the most oft-recorded American folksong, with over 500 versions since it was first commercially recorded in 1924. In bygone days human steel-drivers drilled holes in solid granite for implanting explosives to blast out rock. When a new, steam-driven invention was brought forward, a contest was arranged between the machine and the best of the steel drivers, an African American named John Henry. Upon its outcome would depend the livelihoods of numberless manual laborers. John Henry bested the machine, but the superhuman exertion proved fatal, and he died shortly afterward. Although it was long believed that the ballad, if true, dealt with the construction of the Chesapeake & Ohio's Great Bend Tunnel in West Virginia in 1870–1872, recently a strong case has been made for the historicity of the story but on the Columbus & Western Railroad at Dunnavant, Alabama in 1887–1988. In any case, John Henry remains an iconic testament to the dignity of labor and the ever-present threat of occupational displacement by the wheels of progress.

In the last decades of the nineteenth century Irish laborers were the subjects (and perhaps also the authors) of several ballads about rail construction, including "Jerry Go 'ile that Car" (ca. 1881), "Paddy Works on the Railway" (ca. 1850s), and "Drill Ye Tarriers Drill" (1888?). Songs were sung by the Chinese construction workers on the transcontinental building of the Central Pacific in the 1860s, but by the time folksong collectors went into the field in this country, there were few if any traces of them to be found.

Narrative ballads and songs should not wholly divert our attention from two other important categories of rail-road music: work songs and instrumentals. The former are the musical chants sung to accompany the rhythms of manual labor and serve at the least to coordinate the motions of the laborers, and sometimes additionally to give vent to their feelings and frustrations. Primarily the progeny of African American singers, they were most often heard during the post–Civil War decades when convict labor was exploited for railroad construction and maintenance. "Rock Island Line" was such a work song, first collected in an Arkansas state prison in 1934, but catapulted into a national hit by folksinger Huddie Ledbetter ("Leadbelly"), who transformed it into a story-song about an engineer hauling pig iron and not wanting to stop his train for inspection. Folksong collectors recorded some stunning examples of other work songs in the Deep South in

Not long after the Milwaukee Road inaugurated its Chicago-Seattle *Olympian,* the occasion was celebrated by songwriter and railroad editor of the *Seattle Post-Intelligencer* Charles E. Hunt with the stirring march "The New Steel Trail."

> There's a long yellow train that is built of steel, and it runs with the speed of the gale.
> 'Tis the Milwaukee's pride, an ideal ride; many patrons now sound its wide praises. . . .
> Ev'ry mile a delight as the train takes its flight, o'er the glori'us New Steel Trail

A player-piano roll of the song was also available.
—Father David Brant Collection

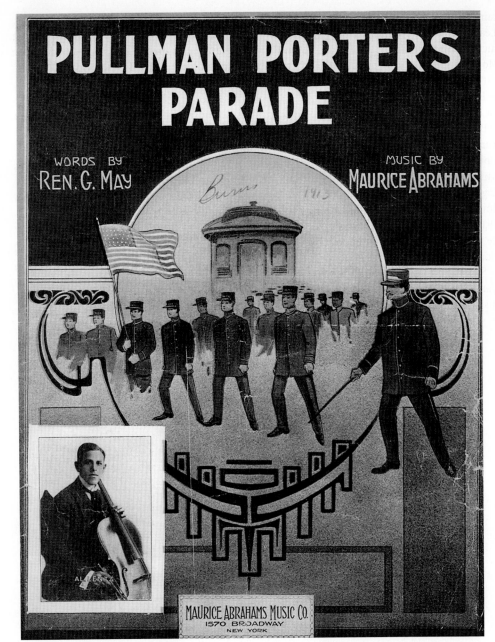

PULLMAN PORTERS PARADE

WORDS BY
REN. G. MAY

MUSIC BY
MAURICE ABRAHAMS

MAURICE ABRAHAMS MUSIC CO.
1570 BROADWAY
NEW YORK

Despite the prominence of lyricist Irving Berlin, who wrote this under the pen name Ren G. May (an anagram for Germany), the "Pullman Porters Parade" (1913) was not well known.

It's worth a thousand
dollars,
To see those tip collectors,
Those upper berth
inspectors,
Those Pullman porters on
parade.

—Father David Brant
Collection

the 1940s and 1950s, but the genre seemed to be on the wane by then.

Makers of instrumental music in several genres have turned to the sounds of railroad wheels, whistles, and engines for inspiration. Country fiddlers and harmonica blowers of all ethnicities have fashioned an impressive array of imitative compositions, including "Orange Blossom Special" (Ervin Rouse and Chubby Wise, 1938) and "Southern No. 111" (Roane County Ramblers) on fiddle; "Train Imitations and the Fox Chase" (Charlie McCoy) and "McAbee's Railroad Piece" (Palmer McAbee, 1928) on harmonica; and "Honky Tonk Train Blues" (Meade Lux Lewis, 1927) and "The Celestial Railroad" (Charles Ives, 1921–1923) on keyboards. Fully orchestrated pieces (Arthur Honegger, "Pacific 231," 1923; Duke Ellington,

"Daybreak Express," 1933) have also enjoyed great popularity. One of the most imaginative uses of train sounds is minimalist composer Steve Reich's "Different Trains" (1988), a musical montage of journeys across the American continent and across Europe to World War II Nazi concentration camps, including music, train sounds, and snippets of tape-recorded narratives of a Pullman porter and others.

In the last decades of the nineteenth century popular music favored narrative ballads of a style that would be regarded as cloyingly sentimental today. One favorite was "In the Baggage Coach Ahead" (Gussie L. Davis, 1896). A young man holds a baby whose incessant crying disturbs the other Pullman passengers. When they complain, he explains that his beloved bride now rides lifeless in the baggage coach of the train. Other sentimental songs include "Does This Train Lead to Heaven?" (Lucy A. Schlief, 1902), "Please Mr. Conductor, Don't Put Me off the Train" (J. Fred Helf and E. P. Moran, 1898; also known as "The Lightning Express"), "Just Set a Light" (Gussie L. Davis, 1896; also known as "The Engineer's [Dying] Child"), and the much later "There's a Little Box of Pine on the 7:29" (Joseph Ettlinger, George Brown, and De Dette Lee, 1931).

Popular songs of the early twentieth century still found the railroad a popular subject, but the songs moved from the sentimental to the whimsical, comical, and novel, including "That Railroad Rag" (Nat Vincent and Ed Bimbert, 1911), "When That Midnight Choo Choo Leaves for Alabam" (Irving Berlin, 1912), "Pullman Porters' Parade" (Ren G. May and Maurice Abrahams, 1913), "Chattanooga Choo Choo" (Mack Gordon and Harry Warren, 1940), and "Atchison, Topeka and the Santa Fe" (Johnny Mercer, Harry Warren, Steve Goodman, and Bruce Phillips, 1943).

As trains have been displaced by trucks, automobiles, and airplanes as the prime movers of people and freight, they have moved off center stage, musically speaking. But even the disappearance of the train has occasioned some memorable songs, notably "City of New Orleans" (Goodman, 1971) and "Daddy, What's a Train?" (Phillips, 1973).

—Norm Cohen

REFERENCES

Cohen, Norm. *Long Steel Rail: The Railroad in American Folksong.* 2nd ed. Urbana: Univ. of Illinois Press, 2000.

Lyle, Katie Letcher. *Scalded to Death by the Steam.* Chapel Hill, N.C.: Algonquin, 1983.

Mystery Train: Classic Railroad Songs, Volume 2. Cambridge, Mass.: Rounder Records, CD 1129, 1997.

Railroad Songs and Ballads [from the] *Library of Congress Archive of Folk Culture.* Cambridge, Mass.: Rounder Records, CD 1508, 1997.

Train 45: Railroad Songs of the Early 1900s. Cambridge, Mass.: Rounder Records, CD 1143, 1998.

N

Narrow Gauge

Narrowness of track gauge is a relative concept. There must be a comparative standard of gauge, or at least a wider gauge in use than the "narrow" gauge in question. When steam railroading made its appearance in the United States beginning in 1830, railroad entrepreneurs tended to lay their track to whatever gauge seemed appropriate for their largely local purposes, because as the concept of interchanging traffic between connecting railroads was not yet envisioned. For the next 40 years, as the rail network expanded, the emphasis gradually became one of readjusting the variety of gauges in existence to one standard gauge to facilitate the routing of freight between different rail lines without the expense and loss of time required for "breaking bulk"—transferring the load from one car to another (or, later, shifting the carbody to different-gauge trucks).

The present standard gauge of 4 feet 8½ inches was generally adopted by the new railroads of New England, New York, Pennsylvania, Virginia, and North Carolina. It would appear that this decision reflected emerging English practice, since the pioneering English locomotive manufacturer George Stephenson had already established that gauge as the emerging standard for England, and U.S. railroads then were designed to be operated with Stephenson's locomotives.

But in many other parts of the United States gauges varied. New Jersey opted for 4 feet 10 inches, as did early railroads in Ohio, such as the Mad River & Lake Erie and Little Miami. Michigan had a bit of both standard and 4 feet 10. The Deep South almost uniformly embraced 5-foot gauge (with the exception of a couple, such as the Arkansas Central, that attempted to compete with 3-foot 6-inch gauge).

The most conspicuous maverick was the New York & Erie, which chose 6-foot gauge. Eventually the Erie, its Ohio subsidiary the Atlantic & Great Western, and the 6-foot-gauge Ohio & Mississippi formed the first through passenger route from the Atlantic to the Mississippi. This required the laying of four-rail track over the Ohio-gauge Cincinnati, Hamilton & Dayton for 59 miles to accommodate the broad-gauge equipment; in fact, in 1867 Ohio had 152 miles of double-gauge track. But the Erie later abandoned wide gauge; the O&M was converted to 4-foot 9-inch gauge in 1871, the A&GW in 1880, and the Erie itself began three-rail conversion in 1878 and completed conversion in 1885.

The South remained isolated in 5-foot gauge until 1885–1886, when all major roads converted to 4 feet 9 inches in one great upheaval. The entire 13,000-mile Louisville & Nashville system was converted on one Sunday, May 30, 1886. Conversion of track and car trucks clearly was a major task. Old wheel sets could be reset up to three inches successfully (hence the choice of 4 feet 9 inches); locomotives were another matter. However, the planning had been many years in the process, and newer locomotives were designed for relatively easy conversion with new driver tires and pony wheels. Initially, the half-inch difference in gauges then in use seemed to be acceptable, but before long another half-inch reduction on the part of the now-minority holdouts brought the main network of railroads in the United States to the 4-foot 8½-inch standard.

About 1870 this emerging serenity of gauges was disturbed by a new idea (also imported from England) of building cheaper railroads to narrower-gauge track, using smaller, lighter equipment and lighter track constructed with less costly grading fitted more closely to the contours of the land. Even before the emergence of steam railroads in Britain, a number of short, horse-powered trams had been constructed to haul mine products—coal or slate. As the use of steam locomotives became more common, some narrow-gauge trams began to consider small steam locomotives for their use. One of the most celebrated of these "expanded trams" is the Festiniog Railway in Wales, which had been lengthened to over 13 miles of 60-centimeter track (about 2-foot gauge). The Festiniog acquired a small four-wheel locomotive in 1863 and quickly became a success story for those who promoted cheap railroads of narrower gauge. One of these promoters was Robert F. Fairlie, an engineer by training and a designer of locomotives. The concept of lighter, efficient railroads built to narrow gauge appealed to him, and he put his considerable energy and technical knowledge to aggressively promoting them. Articles and pamphlets produced by Fairlie and others of similar persuasion soon gained wide circulation.

By 1870 the essential network of U.S. railroads had been pretty well established east of the Mississippi and was taking shape in the West. But already many towns anxious for development discovered that they were not about to be included in a major rail system, and many regional opportunities for rail service were being ignored, because potential traffic flow would not support the expense of a standard-gauge railroad. The siren song of obtaining narrow-gauge railroad service at a "fraction" of the cost immediately attracted attention.

The first visionary to embrace the narrow-gauge concept with action was Gen. William Jackson Palmer. A pioneer Colorado entrepreneur, Palmer had aspirations for the future of the new state. Colorado had all the promise of a major mining frontier, and by 1870 Denver was connected to the transcontinental railroad. Palmer's next step was to ensure the future importance of Denver by building a rail line south to capture the vast trade that was sure to develop out of the Southwest. Only the promise of cheap construction and operation held out by the narrow-gauge arguments would make this possible. So in 1870 Palmer and associates chartered the Denver & Rio Grande Railway, projected as a 3-foot-gauge railroad, to go from Denver to Mexico City, with a suitable number of extensions into the mining areas. Construction was begun in 1871, and by 1872 the road was through Pueblo and was 117 miles in length.

Construction practice followed narrow-gauge theory closely. Rail was 30 pound, rather than the 56 pound deemed necessary for standard gauge. The grade could follow the dictates of the terrain, thanks to the sharper curves, narrower cuts and fills, and lighter bridges. Passenger locomotives initially weighed 12½ tons, freight locomotives 18½. Narrow-gauge coaches carrying 36 passengers weighed 15,000 pounds versus 36,000 pounds for a standard-gauge car carrying only 56 passengers—a clear saving in tare weight. The first freight cars ordered by the D&RG were four-wheeled affairs, offering great savings in tare weight, but they were soon deemed impractical in use and were quickly superseded by also light but larger eight-wheel cars (with the usual arch-bar freight trucks).

Early costs did bear out the claims of proponents. The first 117 miles of the Rio Grande's line through hilly Colorado terrain cost $13,500 per mile, considerably less than standard-gauge construction. A more striking example was soon provided by the nearby Colorado Central Railroad, a project of H. A. W. Loveland and Henry Teller of Golden, Denver's competitor 12 miles west. Loveland had entertained hopes that the Union Pacific transcontinental could be routed through Golden and up Clear Creek to a crossing over a pass discovered by Capt. Edward Berthoud, but the UP went through Wyoming instead. Now faced with a challenge to reach the mining areas up Clear Creek, Loveland chose 3-foot gauge and began construction in 1871. The first 25 miles were threaded through the twisting confines of Clear Creek Canyon to Black Hawk at a total cost of $20,000 per mile, in contrast to the earlier estimate for standard-gauge construction of $90,000 a mile. The Colorado Central locomotives were a bit smaller and much older than the Rio Grande's: the first three were second-hand 0-4-0 locomotives built in the 1860s by John Souther's Globe Locomotive Works for contracting use.

The Denver & Rio Grande "baby railroad" captured everyone's imagination and seemed to ignite the narrow-gauge explosion. A National Narrow-Gauge Convention (the first of a series of such events) was held in St. Louis in 1872, offering an opportunity for narrow-gauge proponents to expound their views and present their arguments to the many would-be railroad entrepreneurs searching for an affordable way to accomplish their dreams. There already were a dozen other 3-foot-gauge roads under actual construction in 1872, including the ambitious Cairo & St. Louis (to reach 165 miles by 1875), the beginnings of the Utah Northern that eventually reached Montana, and the short-lived Iowa Eastern and American Fork. Some other very ambitious undertakings of the early 1870s failed entirely: the projected 300-mile Farmer's Union in Iowa, the 450-mile Nashville & Vicksburg, the 450-mile Portsmouth & Pound Gap, and the champion scheme of all, the 793-mile Washington, St. Louis & Cincinnati. The financial panic of 1873 wiped out many ambitious plans; even the Denver & Rio Grande became stalled at Pueblo until 1876.

Nevertheless, within a decade—from the time of the Philadelphia Centennial Exposition, where visitors were

The first locomotive for Colorado's new Denver & Rio Grande narrow-gauge railway was the handsome 2-4-0 *Montezuma*, built by Baldwin Locomotive Works in 1871. It weighed only 12.5 tons. —H. L. Broadbelt Collection, from Cornelius W. Hauck

Heavier locomotives were soon found to be necessary for the narrow-gauge lines. By 1880 Baldwin was delivering 28- to 30-ton 2-8-0 Consolidation-type locomotives like Rio Grande No. 61. —Colorado Railroad Museum Collection, from Cornelius W. Hauck

A comparison of Denver & Rio Grande Western locomotives at Montrose, Colo. The narrow-gauge 2-8-0 Consolidation No. 318 was a 36-ton Baldwin of 1896; the standard-gauge 2-8-2 Mikado No. 1202 was a 138-ton Baldwin built in 1913. —R. W. Richardson, from Cornelius W. Hauck

A narrow gauge railroad in the Midwest: Cincinnati, Lebanon & Northern Railroad's 2-6-0 Mogul No. 6 made a passenger local stop at South Norwood, near Cincinnati, in 1887. —Cornelius W. Hauck Collection

Cheaply built narrow-gauge railroads were often popular for mining and lumbering lines. This small 1879 Porter locomotive was well suited for the needs of the Tawas & Bay County, an early Michigan lumbering line. —Cornelius W. Hauck Collection

carried about over a 3-foot-gauge railroad line, to 1886— 11,699 miles of narrow-gauge railroad had been constructed. There were narrow gauges in every state except Rhode Island, Connecticut, and Delaware in the East and the territories of Oklahoma, North Dakota, and Wyoming in the West. Largest by far was the Rio Grande, with 2,086 miles; it connected at Ogden with the 454-mile Utah & Northern, permitting a traveler to ride in Pullman luxury 1,200 miles over uninterrupted narrow gauge. Two midwestern roads vied for an even longer routing, in theory— the Toledo, Cincinnati & St. Louis and the Texas & St. Louis (plus the St. Louis & Cairo) would have taken one all the way from Toledo to Waco, Texas. But the TC&StL was already imploding—all 776 miles of it—and the T&StL was

in receivership and would shortly be standard-gauged, ending the vision of a Great Narrow-Gauge Trunk.

By 1886 more miles of narrow-gauge track were being converted to standard gauge than were being built new, and in 1909 for the first time more narrow-gauge trackage was abandoned than built new. Total narrow-gauge mileage shrank from 11,699 in 1885 to 6,733 in 1900 and 3,966 in 1920. At the end of World War II there were still over 1,000 miles of narrow gauge in operation, mostly Denver & Rio Grande Western and Rio Grande Southern. Today, only the 45 miles of the Durango & Silverton (former Rio Grande) Narrow Gauge can qualify as an operating narrow-gauge railroad; the nearby Cumbres & Toltec, the White Pass & Yukon, and the East Broad Top are

This narrow-gauge line in Alaska was the most northerly railroad in North America. Powered by an enclosed Climax geared locomotive, the Nome Arctic Railroad made a stop at Banner Station, Anvil Creek, in 1904. —Cornelius W. Hauck Collection

The lightweight construction of narrow-gauge railroads sometimes produced unfortunate results, such as this spectacular collapse of a high trestle over Nine Mile Creek, Ohio, on the New Richmond branch of the Cincinnati & Eastern. Three passengers were killed and nine injured. —Cornelius W. Hauck Collection

In its declining years the Rio Grande Southern Railroad assembled this versatile motor locomotive from an old passenger automobile. It could accommodate the U.S. mail, freight, and passengers and plow snow when necessary. It was photographed at Durango, Colorado, in September 1940. —Russell Lee photograph, Farm Security Administration, Library of Congress (Neg. LC-USF34-37777-D)

Narrow- and standard-gauge trains often shared lines in Colorado's extensive narrow-gauge system. This view of the mixed-gauge Denver & Rio Grande Western lines at Salida, Colorado, indicates the complexity required for turnouts. —Van Wilkins, *Trains* Magazine Collection

tourist-only lines. New is a reconstituted remnant of the Wiscasset, Waterville & Farmington, the last vestige of Maine's famous 2-foot-gauge lines.

What killed the narrow-gauge dream? Primarily, economics: the advantages claimed for narrow-gauge cost effi-

ciency proved untrue. The toylike "baby railroad" concept died quickly; before the Rio Grande could progress beyond Pueblo, it became necessary to abandon 30-pound rail for 45- or 50-pound, 12½-ton locomotives for 30-ton, and flimsy little freight cars for cars that would stand up in ser-

The Colorado narrow-gauge railways remain popular as tourist lines, if not as freight carriers. Then still part of the Denver & Rio Grande Western, K-28 class 2-8-2 No. 476, built by Alco in 1923, waited at Durango for the morning trip to Silverton on August 15, 1979. —William D. Middleton

vice. Hastily constructed track over wandering rights of way proved expensive to operate; light bridges of untreated wood and narrow fills had to be replaced. And, unless the line did a purely local traffic, transshipment of cargo to and from standard gauge was an added cost, even with cheap labor.

Those roads that remained narrow gauge and lasted into the twentieth century generally did so because (1) they served a local or regional traffic base sufficient to keep them viable and (2) circumstances were such that it was not practical to convert them. Farm-to-market roads such as the Newport & Sherman Valley, Ohio River & Western, and Bellevue & Cascade died when the automobile era caught up to them. Forest-product roads such as the AuSable & Northwestern and Sumpter Valley quit when the timber ran out. Mining-country roads such as the Black Hills & Fort Pierre and Eureka-Nevada faded and disappeared with local mining ventures.

During the first half of the last century design and appearance of equipment and operating routines changed very little. In many cases declining traffic put so little stress on equipment that it could be patched up indefinitely. When "new" had to be purchased, there was often little reason to deviate from old designs. In the 1930s, when the Colorado & Southern considered buying new articulated locomotives for its South Park narrow-gauge lines, it determined that there would be little advantage, and that its smaller turn-of-the-century locomotives were as efficient as newer designs anyway. But all the seeming vestiges of antiquity of the narrow gauges were an attraction to many enthusiasts, who still think of them with nostalgia and a feeling of loss.

—Cornelius W. Hauck

REFERENCES

Beebe, Lucius, and Charles Clegg. *Narrow Gauge in the Rockies*. Berkeley, Calif.: Howell-North, 1958.

Fleming, Howard. *Narrow Gauge Railways in America*. 2nd ed. 1875. Oakland, Calif.: Grahame H. Hardy, 1949.

Hauck, Cornelius W. "Early Narrow Gauge Locomotives in the West." *Railroad History*, no. 149 (Autumn 1983): 51–69.

Hilton, George W. *American Narrow Gauge Railroads*. Stanford, Calif.: Stanford Univ. Press, 1990.

See also STANDARD GAUGE.

Nashville, Chattanooga & St. Louis Railway

On a map, the Nashville, Chattanooga & St. Louis appeared to be two railroads that met at Nashville, Tennessee. The main line ran from Nashville southeast through Chattanooga to Atlanta, Georgia, and was a link in the Dixie Route passenger trains (*Dixie Flagler, Dixie Flyer, Dixie Limited,* and *Dixieland*) between Chicago and Florida that were operated by the Chicago & Eastern Illinois and Louisville & Nashville north of Nashville and the Atlantic Coast Line, Atlanta, Birmingham & Coast, Central of Georgia, and Florida East Coast south of Atlanta. The other half of the NC&StL was a line west from Nashville to Bruceton, Tennessee, where it split to go southwest to Memphis, northwest to Hickman, Kentucky, on the Mississippi River, and north to Paducah, Kentucky, on the Ohio River.

The Nashville & Chattanooga Railroad was incorporated relatively early, in 1845. Construction began at Nashville, and by 1853 the line had crossed Cumberland Mountain (even today a source of anxiety for drivers on Interstate 24) and reached the Tennessee River at Bridgeport, Alabama. A year later the line reached Chattanooga and a connection to Atlanta—the Western & Atlantic, which was owned by the State of Georgia.

In 1862 floods destroyed much of the N&C's line before retreating Confederate and advancing Union forces could, but each army destroyed one of the road's two bridges over the Tennessee River. The N&C was soon rebuilt and just as soon destroyed again. The U.S. Military Railroad rebuilt it again before returning it to its owners after the war.

The railroad began to expand in 1870 by leasing and then purchasing the Nashville & Northwestern Railroad, which ran from Nashville to Hickman, Kentucky, on the Mississippi River. The N&C added "St. Louis" to its name in 1873, reflecting the destination of the railroads across the Mississippi at Hickman.

In 1879 the president of the NC&StL, Edwin Cole, decided to reshape the railroad into a St. Louis–Atlanta route. He acquired control of the Owensboro & Nashville, which was building south toward Nashville from the Ohio River, and purchased the financially troubled St. Louis & Southeastern for its line from St. Louis to Evansville, Indiana. Cole began negotiations to lease the Western & Atlantic and the Central of Georgia, both of which connected with the NC&StL at Chattanooga.

The neighboring Louisville & Nashville Railroad decided to quash Cole's expansionism. L&N bought 55 percent of NC&StL's stock and transferred the St. Louis–Evansville line to its own system. Several years later, in 1896, it acquired and leased to NC&StL two railroads, the Paducah, Tennessee & Alabama Railroad and the Tennessee Midland Railway, which met end-to-end at Lexington, Tennessee, to form a Paducah-Memphis route that crossed the Nashville-Hickman line at Bruceton, Tennessee. The acquisition and lease gave the NC&StL an Ohio River gateway—Paducah—and a Nashville-Memphis route. At Paducah the NC&StL and the Burlington jointly built a connecting railroad and a bridge, opened in 1917. In 1924 the two roads sold a one-third interest in the Paducah & Illinois Railroad to the Illinois Central to use as part of a line it was building (the Edgewood Cutoff) to bypass the congestion of Cairo, Illinois. The Nashville, Chattanooga &

St. Louis had come under the control of the Louisville & Nashville about 1880. In 1957 L&N carried its control a step further and merged the NC&StL.

In 1956, the last year before merger by the Louisville & Nashville, the Nashville, Chattanooga & St. Louis operated a system of 1,043 route-miles and 1,785 track-miles, with 132 locomotives, 106 passenger cars, 6,761 freight cars, 517 company service cars, and 4,289 employees. Freight traffic totaled 2,072.8 million ton-miles in 1956, and products of mines and manufactured goods predominated in its traffic mix. Passenger traffic totaled 52 million passenger-miles. NC&StL operating revenues totaled $35.6 million, and the railroad achieved a 77.9 percent operating ratio.

—George H. Drury

REFERENCE

Prince, Richard E. *The Nashville, Chattanooga and St. Louis Railway: History and Steam Locomotives.* Green River, Wyo.: Richard E. Prince, 1967. Repr., Bloomington: Indiana Univ. Press, 2001.

National Parks

By the 1890s every principal western railroad was heavily engaged in the promotion of national parks. In 1883 the Northern Pacific Railroad (NP) arrived at Yellowstone, completing the support of Jay Cooke & Co. for the park's establishment in 1872. In 1890 the establishment of Yosemite, Sequoia, and General Grant national parks owed much to the Southern Pacific Railroad (SP). All in the High Sierra of California, the parks invited the possibility of developing a tourist trade based on Los Angeles and San Francisco. Afterward the Sierra Club (1892) heard from John Muir a startling admission: "Even the soulless Southern Pacific R.R. Co., never counted on for anything good, helped nobly in pushing the bill for [Yosemite National Park] through Congress." Of course, the SP had wanted all three parks and as many more as might swell passenger revenues.

Beyond altruism, the railroads hoped that eastern tourists might join farmers in settling the American West. Its cities needed people, too. There was further the advantage of corporate prestige: today's wealthy traveler might be tomorrow's corporate customer, thinking of the railroad for moving freight. If a memorable trip to Yellowstone helped recall the railroad's name, so much the better for courting business.

Railroads that hoped to sell their land grants realized, too, the advantage of having the federal government maintain the watersheds. National parks and national forests protected new farms below. Occasionally a railroad land grant included mountains covered with ice and snow. These sections the railroad would want exchanged. In that regard

the NP scored mightily in 1899, virtually writing the bill that allowed trading Mount Rainier, Washington, for timber elsewhere on the public domain. Now the fifth national park, Mount Rainier benefited SP and NP, along with the Tacoma Eastern Railroad, a subsidiary of the Chicago, Milwaukee & Puget Sound.

Still, Yellowstone National Park was the attraction, and the NP was its shrewd monopolist. Its advertisements flooded prominent magazines, extolling Yellowstone as a "wonderland" not to be missed. A guidebook of the same name, *Wonderland*, appeared in a new edition every year. Great names of western art and photography contributed to the guidebooks and the ads. Throughout the park NP hotels and camps provided for visitors as if they had never left the luxury of the train.

Both in the United States and in Canada a similar, seamless monopoly was the goal of every railroad. Mexican railroads languished, obviously lacking political stability and the flow of wealth. Mexico's national parks came later, too. Today's famous Copper River Canyon—reached by the Chihuahua-Pacífico Railroad—was not fully opened until 1961.

Canada emulated the United States, in 1885 establish-

Yellowstone, established in 1872, was the first of the great national parks. In this 1911 promotion boys are shown photographing the (tame) bears, with the Yellowstone Lake Hotel in the background. —Michael E. Zega Collection

ing a national park at Banff, Alberta. Within three years the Canadian Pacific Railway (CPR) had built and opened the first Banff Springs Hotel. After the turn of the century a second transcontinental (consolidated into the Canadian National) opened Jasper to the north, while CPR rebuilt the Banff Springs Hotel (1928) and reconstructed its hotel on Lake Louise (1925).

Simply, after providing transportation, the object of each railroad was to sell a tour. By controlling the park hotels, the railroads owned their passengers all the way. At Yellowstone NP grandly displayed its monopoly with the opening in 1904 of Old Faithful Inn. Designed by Seattle architect Robert C. Reamer, Old Faithful Inn set the standard for rustic accommodations—"parkitecture"—that thrill visitors to this day.

For the next quarter century the growing competition among the western railroads led to new parks, large and small. At times the advertising could be blunt. "See America First," proclaimed the Great Northern Railway (GN), implying that travelers should stay home. Canada and Europe drained tourist dollars but had no better scenery. Obviously, if the GN's point were to be proved, more parks needed to be established.

Pressure on Congress was the inevitable result, so the railroads tried to wrest business from each other. Yellowstone's popularity tempted several—might NP's monopoly be eclipsed? In 1908 the Union Pacific (UP) was first to answer, arriving from the west. Next the Chicago, Burlington & Quincy developed the eastern entrance, transferring passengers to buses at Cody, Wyoming. From the northwest, the Gallatin River canyon similarly enticed the Milwaukee Road, which in 1928 completed the fabulous Gallatin Gateway Inn.

In Arizona the Grand Canyon offered the Atchison, Topeka & Santa Fe (AT&SF) the traditional monopoly, with no other railroad then even in sight. On September 17, 1901, the AT&SF brought the first passenger train to the south rim. Unfortunately, Grand Canyon was not yet a national park and so lacked the magical name. While the railroad spur from Williams did double duty hauling logs and freight, AT&SF pushed Congress for the name—Grand Canyon National Park. Accommodations comparable to Yellowstone's had already been promised. Opened in January 1905, El Tovar Hotel was indeed as rustic and charming as Old Faithful Inn.

More cautiously, but no less effectively, GN campaigned for Glacier National Park, Montana, established in May 1910. Antimonopoly sentiment sweeping the state dictated that the railroad be a silent partner. That aside, no sooner was Glacier secured than GN revealed its aims—another monopoly in the proven tradition of railroad-owned camps and hotels.

A final advantage was Glacier's southern boundary, virtually hugging GN's main line along the park's southern end. Even tourists who were not stopping might look into the park. For overnight guests, the railroad built at East Glacier Park Station a major hotel, which opened to

James J. Hill, his son Louis Hill, and the Great Northern Railway were strong supporters of the formation of Glacier National Park in 1910. This 1915 promotion touts its magnificent new hotel and its chain of Swiss chalets throughout the park. —Michael E. Zega Collection

tourists in 1913. Gradually, camps deep within the park were replaced, either by chalets or hotels. In 1915 the sprawling Many Glacier Hotel opened on Lake McDermott (now Swiftcurrent Lake). As at Yellowstone and Grand Canyon, parkitecture guided all construction, replicating throughout Glacier an imaginative tie with Switzerland.

Finally, direct service to Yosemite National Park had also been realized with the completion of the Yosemite Valley Railroad—a misnomer, even in 1907, in that the railroad stopped 12 miles short. Its salient purpose, after all, was to open the sugar-pine forests west of the park. Of course, the YVRR also envisioned a profitable tourist trade. At the end of the track, the town of El Portal, it constructed a large hotel, then a road up the Merced River Canyon to connect with an existing road. Now on motor coaches, railroad visitors might enter the valley proper, continuing with side trips to Glacier Point and the Mariposa Grove of giant sequoias.

Minor parks, like major parks, similarly benefited from the aims of a nearby railroad. Generally, "minor" parks were simply those more difficult to reach. Certainly there was nothing minor about Crater Lake, Oregon; it was just that the SP main line was 40 miles away. Established in 1902, the park was also too rugged for a branch. Regardless, SP promoted the transfer, which brought in tourists by motor coach from Klamath Falls.

A prominent difference between Europe and the United States now manifested itself across the West. In Europe a final connectivity between the city and spectacular scenery was being established by nonconventional railroads. In many areas passengers transferred to cog-assisted branch lines, funiculars, and cable cars. In the United States all transferred to buses, which required roads inside the parks. Having centuries ago dispensed with wilderness Europe found no inconsistency using railroads in any landscape. America wanted the pretext of wilderness and so kept railroads of any kind outside the parks. Except for the AT&SF branch into Grand Canyon (which preceded the national park), no major railroad penetrated a park again.

The irony was that roads did penetrate, and beginning in 1913 the automobile was admitted to all the parks. Why was not the automobile considered a corporation and like the railroads entirely banned? Because the driver was an individual, allowing the pretext of pioneering. The car was a covered wagon and the driver Daniel Boone. A road was just a trail with asphalt, which is why the automobile gained everything denied the railroads, even though railroads better preserved fragile landscapes.

Ironically, the agency that favored the automobile, the National Park Service, had received its critical boost from the railroads. Annually the railroads had chafed at the lack of consistency, in management most of all. Every time the railroads needed something from the federal government, another official seemed to be in charge, or the Department of the Interior, as custodian of the parks, seemed always to be out of funds. Getting a permit to build anything was an arduous process, even when a railroad wanted to help build a road. Such was Louis W. Hill's constant complaint at Glacier; even as president of the GN, he had to beg.

Preservationists were no less frustrated by the lack of concern that without visitors there would not be parks. Why should Congress fund what the public could not see? Preservationists agreed with the railroads: The parks needed a bureau of their own. Finally, in 1916, after five years of intensive lobbying, both interest groups got their wish. On August 25, 1916, the National Park Service was enacted into law. Stephen T. Mather, as its first director, proved immediately his affection for the railroads. After all, they had been developing the national parks for half a century. Mather, himself a millionaire, spoke the railroads' language. Practically, they were the place to begin his program for more parks and accommodations. The newest model for the American wilderness, Glacier, was indeed what Mather had in mind. As a railroad park, it had a powerful sponsor capable of building new infrastructure and visitation.

Thus Mather began where the railroads had left off, pushing for parks that engaged their interest. He agreed that Grand Canyon should be a national park, along with Zion and Bryce Canyon. Accordingly, he asked Carl Gray, as president of the UP, to promote the North Rim of Grand Canyon, as had AT&SF the South. Better yet, would UP agree to help open Zion and Bryce, along with Cedar Breaks National Monument? Actually, the proposal for parks in Utah was nothing new. It was just that the lodges Mather wanted would be open only three months out of the year. Finally, Mather stressed the good publicity, and the railroad itself agreed. After all, even if UP did not make a profit, pleasing the federal government would serve it well.

Still, the automobile, Mather now believed, was as important as the railroads. Limiting park access to the wealthy was a policy the Park Service no longer could afford. Increasingly, Congress demanded an explanation why the general public could not be served. By the 1930s the Great Depression had strengthened every argument that railroads were too costly for family travel. There should continue to be railroads, yes, but there should also be more roads. Road construction, as an added benefit, would allow the Park Service to provide more jobs.

Inevitably, the consequence was a dramatic fall-off among the railroads even as travel by car continued to soar. In 1945 the Yosemite Valley Railroad was abandoned, a first (and telling) victim of the trend. Railroad interest elsewhere was sustained in the hope that new trains would recapture business. Finally, with World War II behind them, the railroads were free to experiment. The introduction of the Vista-Dome in 1945 reawakened America's interest in modern trains and western scenery. Over the next decade a constant parade of advertising told the story of an earlier age. Not only were they the finest trains in the West, but they traversed the grandest scenery.

Although the railroads had lost their edge to the automobile, the number of western travelers had dramatically grown. Even at 2 percent of national park visitors, the railroads were carrying close to their historical norms. In 1915 the railroads had carried 44,477 visitors to Yellowstone; by 1959 Yellowstone, with nearly 2 million visitors, still allowed the railroads to claim their share. In the West, at least, the railroads were satisfied that losing a majority of park visitors need not translate into losing trains.

Few railroads in the East were as confident, and by the 1960s they had begun to convince the western lines that the passenger train had become an albatross. The future of the railroads was in bulk commodities, but the passenger train demanded speed. Increasingly, the passenger train would be in the way, demanding levels of service and maintenance bulk carriers could not afford. Eastern railroads needed to reduce capacity, moving from double to single track. For the western lines emanating from Chicago, it all spelled the end of reasonable connections with the East.

One by one, branch lines with the national parks were abandoned, and in the 1970s most of the tracks themselves were torn up. The last scheduled passenger train left Yellowstone in 1960, Grand Canyon in 1968. The creation of Amtrak in 1971 restored neither connection, nor did Amtrak seem interested in the national parks. Only Glacier National Park suffered no disruptions, but only because it was on a main line east and west. Amtrak's focus remained Seattle and Chicago, not what lay between.

The first revival came in Alaska, thanks to renewed interest among the cruise lines. Market research determined that wealthy travelers overwhelmingly preferred taking the train to Denali (Mount McKinley) National Park. Using the Alaska Railroad, the cruise lines determined, they might profitably extend their reach. By 1990 Holland America and Princess Tours had revived the Vista-Dome, both new and refurbished cars. The Alaska Railroad had followed suit. Obviously, many Americans still wanted the experience of visiting the national parks by rail, as was proved by the next revival, now at Grand Canyon in Arizona. Unlike the other western railroads, the AT&SF had not torn up its branch. Although badly deteriorated, it still survived. In 1989 two Phoenix developers, Max and Thelma Biegert, reopened the entire line, which by 2003 carried more than 175,000 patrons annually.

Might Grand Canyon then be fully restored by removing all automobiles from the park? So the Grand Canyon Railway further posed the question, offering light rail laid over existing roads. Park Service resistance to the railway's proposal proved the durability of the highway lobby. Regardless, as the twenty-first century opened, at least some politicians and environmentalists were finally discussing the desirability of using railroads inside the parks.

For most Americans, the irony of allowing the automobile in while keeping railroads out remained difficult to grasp. Preservation, demanding community, asked that individual wants and desires be curtailed. That was not the American way. Whether inside the parks or outside, Americans preferred their cars.

For landscape, the question is simple: what both protects and allows access. Granted, a railroad is restrictive, allowing no one to pull off the road. It is also protective, something a park desperately needs. Every mile of highway leading to the parks is vulnerable to development and commercial aims. Historically, the railroads sold expectation, refusing to destroy the scenery along the way. Without the anticipation built by that scenery, the destination was hardly worth anyone's time.

By breaking the railroads' monopoly over the national parks, the automobile broke their pact with conventional landscapes. Suddenly, the meaning of travel was all in the destination, and Americans had tired of making time for trains.

A final conviction that the future of the passenger train was in city corridors worked against using railroads to save any landscape. In its more than 30 years of service Amtrak had lost touch with the connection, too. Finally,

with the revival of the Grand Canyon Railway, there was renewed hope for the best of the past and present. Travel need not be modernized at the expense of meaning, and every "common" landscape could mean as much as the national parks. All America need do was rediscover the railroad, learning again how best to move, and what not to miss.

—Alfred Runte

REFERENCES

Johnston, Hank. *Short Line to Paradise: The Story of the Yosemite Valley Railroad*. Corona del Mar, Calif.: Trans-Anglo, 1962.

Richmond, Al. *Cowboys, Miners, Presidents & Kings: The Story of the Grand Canyon Railway*. 5th ed. Flagstaff, Ariz.: Grand Canyon Railway, 2002.

Runte, Alfred. *Trains of Discovery: Western Railroads and the National Parks*. 4th ed. Boulder, Colo.: Roberts Rinehart, 1998.

Waite, Thornton. *Yellowstone Branch of the Union Pacific: Route of the Yellowstone Special*. Idaho Falls, Idaho: Thornton Waite, 1997.

National Railroad Passenger Corp. (Amtrak)

After World War II the railroads invested heavily in passenger operations to replace worn-out equipment. By 1949 many new passenger trains and even fleets of trains—such as Burlington's *Zephyr*s, Union Pacific's *City* streamliners, and the Milwaukee Road's *Hiawathas*—were in operation. Load factors and patronage remained good into the early 1950s, but the effects of aggressive automobile sales and advertising soon began to eat into ridership. Three events in the late 1950s caused sharp drops in passenger-train ridership.

First, in 1956 President Eisenhower signed a bill creating the National System of Interstate and Defense Highways, a nationwide system of superhighways and freeways. These highways would not only affect rail passenger travel (San Francisco to Reno would be a 4-hour trip by car versus 6 hours by train) but also would cut into freight business because trucks could move faster and compete for time-sensitive traffic such as perishables.

Second, passenger jets became reality as Boeing introduced the 707 in commercial air service in 1958, followed a year later by the Douglas DC-8. A flight from Chicago to Los Angeles on a piston-powered plane took around 6 hours; the new jets took less than 4 and were smoother, quieter, and more efficient. Santa Fe's *Super Chief* took 39¼ hours.

Third, in 1958 the Interstate Commerce Act was revised to make it easier for a railroad to discontinue a money-losing interstate passenger train. To discontinue a Los Angeles–El Paso train, for example, Southern Pacific needed to go only to the Interstate Commerce Commission instead of the public utilities commissions of California, Arizona, New Mexico, and Texas.

Train ridership continued to decline in the early 1960s. Mail and express traffic, which had been a steady source of revenue, began to dwindle. In 1967 the U.S. Postal Service ceased operating all Railway Post Office cars except in the Northeast Corridor and began sending all first-class mail by air. The Railway Express Agency closed its doors in 1968.

By 1969 there were fewer than 600 intercity passenger trains running in the United States, and discontinuance petitions had been submitted to the ICC and the state commissions (for intrastate trains) for more than half of them. While Europe and Japan were embarking on high-speed rail projects, the United States was rapidly moving toward dependence on highways and airways for passenger transportation.

In 1968 Anthony Haswell, who had been an attorney for the Illinois Central Railroad, formed the National Assn. of Railroad Passengers (NARP), which began to lobby for a system of passenger trains operating nationwide and owned by the U.S. government. The effort was successful. Congress passed the National Railroad Passenger Act in 1970. The act created a new company, the National Railroad Passenger Corp., with all its common stock owned by U.S. taxpayers and its preferred stock owned by the participating railroads. The U.S. Department of Transportation (DOT) was ordered to establish a route system that would serve all the major metropolitan areas of the country, though with train frequencies about half the existing level. The company would take over passenger-train operation on May 1, 1971.

The preliminary system was announced in November 1970. There was a great outcry from the West, which had been pretty much left off the map, thanks to intensive lobbying by the western railroads, which had essentially said that passenger trains were great as long as they stayed east of Chicago. The DOT's map showed thrice-weekly trains from Chicago to Seattle and from Chicago to San Francisco (the latter operating daily as far west as Denver) and a daily train from Chicago to Los Angeles, but no north-south service along the West Coast and nothing across the southern tier of the United States.

In January 1971 the DOT announced a revised route structure that included routes from New Orleans to Los Angeles and from San Diego to Seattle, both with tri-weekly service, except that San Diego to Los Angeles was twice daily in addition to the triweekly San Diego–Seattle train, and Los Angeles to Oakland was daily. Also added to the map were Newport News–Cincinnati and New York–Kansas City routes and extensions of the New York–Miami trains to Tampa and St. Petersburg.

In the days immediately after May 1, 1971, the only evidence of Amtrak's existence was the presence of the corporation's pointless-arrow emblem at stations. Indeed, the Amtrak name was a last-minute change from the expected nickname, Railpax.

The new company had only five employees—president Roger Lewis, who came from Pan American World Airways, and four staff members. A marketing department headed by Harold Graham, also from Pan Am, established sales offices in major cities. Advertising was contracted to Ted Bates & Co., and travel agents were wooed for bookings (at least two railroads, Southern Pacific and New York Central, had discontinued commissions to travel agents in 1965). Despite a prevailing belief that Amtrak's purpose was to get rid of all intercity passenger-train service except in the Northeast Corridor, passengers returned to trains, and ridership grew by 23 percent in the first year.

Amtrak purchased a fleet of aged locomotives and cars from the railroads, overhauled them, and gave them red, white, and blue stripes. Soon Amtrak purchased new locomotives and cars, starting with Amfleet coaches, based on Penn Central's Metroliners, for Northeast Corridor service.

Three railroads that operated passenger service did not join Amtrak in 1971: Southern Railway, Rock Island, and Denver & Rio Grande Western. Southern joined in 1974, and its New York–Washington-Atlanta–New Orleans *Crescent* was added to Amtrak's fleet of trains. The Rio Grande joined in 1983, and the Chicago–San Francisco train was rerouted over the D&RGW from Denver to Salt Lake City, as had been planned in 1971. The Rock Island's Chicago-Peoria and Chicago–Rock Island trains ceased operation at the beginning of 1979.

Amtrak gradually took over the train and engine crews that operated its trains. Dining- and lounge-car staffs and car attendants were assimilated soon after 1972. By 1983 all the operating crews received paychecks from Amtrak rather than the freight railroads.

In 1976 Congress appropriated $120 million for Amtrak's purchase of the Northeast Corridor line from the bankrupt Penn Central, and the passenger road now owns the real estate and rail properties from Boston to Washington (except for that owned by Metro-North from New Haven to New Rochelle and by Massachusetts Bay Transportation Authority from Boston to the Rhode Island state line; Amtrak has permanent operating rights over these sections). The acquisition also included Penn Central's Philadelphia-Harrisburg and New Haven–Springfield lines, as well as a line between Kalamazoo, Michigan, and Michigan City, Indiana, and a segment near Albany, New York.

A $2.5 billion Northeast Corridor Improvement Project authorized by Congress after its acquisition financed extensive rehabilitation and modernization of the corridor, while another $1.7 billion was spent for further improvements, including New Haven–Boston electrification, under a Northeast High-Speed Rail Improvement Program authorized in 1990. Although still more work will be required to fully attain Amtrak's high-speed goals for the corridor, the improved infrastructure and a fleet of high-speed AEM7 electric locomotives derived from

European practice, followed by the Acela Express high-speed train program of the late 1990s, made Amtrak the dominant passenger carrier in the corridor.

In 1978 Amtrak received the first of the double-deck Superliner cars, inspired by Santa Fe's Hi-Level fleet of 1956, to reequip trains west of Chicago. More Superliners were built in the early 1990s for trains east of Chicago that did not operate through the tight-clearance tunnels to New York City. Single-level Viewliner cars gradually replaced older cars, dubbed Heritage Fleet, on trains serving New York; the last Heritage Fleet sleeper was replaced in October 2001.

Funding for Amtrak has perpetually been barely enough to keep the basic system in operation, with little available for expansion. In 1998 Congress revised the National Railroad Passenger Act, requiring Amtrak to break even on its operations by 2003. Amtrak management tried gamely to attain this unrealistic goal in a world of heavy subsidies for the railroads' highway and air competitors, but was unable to meet the break-even target.

Although Amtrak carried a record of almost 25.4 million passengers in 2005, an unsympathetic national administration proposed to eliminate operating-cost subsidies altogether in 2005. Thus far, at least, the U.S. Congress has continued to authorize at least some annual support for both the operating and capital costs for Amtrak. Thus it is likely that Amtrak will continue to pursue an uncertain financial future, with enough money to continue operation but not enough to develop a long-range program of development and growth.

—Arthur L. Lloyd

REFERENCE

Wilner, Frank N. *The Amtrak Story*. Omaha, Nebr.: Simmons-Boardman, 1994.

New Jersey Transit

New Jersey Transit, the largest statewide public transportation agency in the United States, operates the nation's third-largest commuter rail system, as well as three connecting light-rail services, one of which is with diesel-powered light rail equipment.

NJ Transit's commuter rail system, operated by subsidiary NJ Transit Rail Operations, is a combination of diesel and electrified services that traces its roots to six railroads that once served New Jersey and the greater New York Metropolitan Area: Pennsylvania Railroad; Central Railroad of New Jersey; Erie; Delaware, Lackawanna & Western; Lehigh Valley; and Pennsylvania-Reading Seashore Lines. Mergers of several, notably, formation of the Erie Lackawanna in 1960, Penn Central in 1968, and finally, Conrail—which incorporated all of these—in 1976

led to the state's formation of NJ Transit and assumption of passenger services from Conrail in 1983. By that time the system had fallen into disrepair, with ancient, broken-down equipment and deteriorating infrastructure contributing to chronically late trains and angry passengers. Since 1983 NJ Transit has invested billions of dollars in new rolling stock and massive infrastructure renewal and expansion programs. Among these are several key links among previously unconnected lines that have produced what is widely recognized as a seamless statewide network.

NJ Transit's history can be traced back to 1959, when the New Jersey legislature created the Division of Rail Transportation within the State Highway Department. The division provided subsidies to private railroads to help pay for money-losing yet essential commuter rail services. In 1965 Governor Richard Hughes suggested that a state agency be formed to finance, and potentially operate, passenger rail service. The New Jersey Department of Transportation was formed in 1966, making the state the first to establish a governmental department in charge of public transportation and highways. At the same time the Commuter Operating Authority (COA) was formed to handle passenger service contracts with railroads and fund capital improvements. NJ Transit was formed in July 1979 under the New Jersey Public Transportation Act. At the same time the COA was dissolved. The new agency became the first in the nation devoted solely to public transportation.

The Northeast Rail Service Act of 1981 required Conrail to divest itself of passenger rail services by the end of 1982. That year, after an extensive study of potential options (among them, contracting with Amtrak for commuter rail services), it was determined that NJ Transit should assume operation of all the state's commuter trains. The first NJ Transit commuter train departed Hoboken Terminal at 12:30 A.M., January 1, 1983, bound for Dover, New Jersey, on what are today the Morris & Essex Lines.

NJ Transit's 11 commuter rail lines, which are divided among three operating divisions, serve major destinations in New Jersey and New York. The Hoboken Division includes Midtown Direct service to Penn Station New York on the electrified Morris & Essex and Montclair-Boonton lines (which connect to the electrified Northeast Corridor at Kearny, New Jersey) and service to Hoboken Terminal on the Morris & Essex, Montclair-Boonton, and nonelectrified Main/Bergen and Pascack Valley lines. The Newark Division includes the Northeast Corridor and partially electrified North Jersey Coast and nonelectrified Raritan Valley lines operating to Newark Penn Station, Hoboken Terminal, and Penn Station New York. The nonelectrified Atlantic City Rail Line operates between New Jersey's seaside resort city and Philadelphia. The agency also operates service to points in New York State on the nonelectrified Pascack Valley and Port Jervis lines for Metro-North under contract with the New York Metropolitan Transportation Authority. NJ Transit's electrified trains draw alternating current from overhead wires, with voltage ranging from 12,000 to 25,000 volts AC. Passengers can make direct transfers between all but two lines (the Atlantic City Rail Line and the Raritan Valley Line, where an additional transfer is required at Newark Penn Station) at Secaucus Junction, which provides transfers between NJ Transit trains operating on the Northeast Corridor to Penn Station New York and those on the Main/Bergen, Pascack Valley, and Port Jervis lines to Hoboken Terminal.

The NJ Transit network provides numerous links to the region's other transit systems. Transfers to the state's extensive bus system are possible at many rail stations. At Penn Station New York connections are available to Amtrak, the Long Island Rail Road, and the New York City subway system. At Trenton riders can connect to Southeastern Pennsylvania Transportation Authority (SEPTA), Amtrak, and the new River LINE, NJ Transit's diesel light rail, which follows the Delaware River to Camden, New Jersey. At Hoboken Terminal transfers can be made to Port Authority Trans-Hudson (PATH) rapid-transit trains between Hoboken, Jersey City, Newark, and midtown Manhattan; to Manhattan-bound ferry services; and to NJ Transit's Hudson-Bergen Light Rail System. At Newark Penn Station connections to Amtrak, PATH, and NJ Transit's Newark City Subway are available. On the Atlantic City Rail Line connections can be made to Amtrak and SEPTA at Philadelphia's 30th Street Station, and to Philadelphia's Port Authority Transit Corp. (PATCO) rapid-transit system at Lindenwold, New Jersey. Newark Liberty International Airport Station on the Northeast Corridor connects with the Port Authority of New York & New Jersey Airtrain monorail. Automated ticket vending machines are in use at many stations systemwide.

NJ Transit pays Amtrak trackage rights fees to operate on the Northeast Corridor and also contributes capital to fund expansion and renewal programs through the Joint Benefits and New Initiatives programs. In 2005 the agency replaced operation of Amtrak and Philadelphia–New York Clocker trains with Trenton–New York Northeast Corridor Service.

NJ Transit's commuter rail rolling stock is a mix of push-pull coaches and cab-control cars, electric and diesel-electric locomotives, and electric multiple-unit (M.U.) cars from a variety of builders. Since 1987 all equipment, with the exception of three EMD SW1500 switchers, has been acquired new or has been remanufactured.

The locomotive fleet includes 83 diesel-electric and 61 electric locomotives. The 4,400-hp ALP-44 locomotives, 32 of which were purchased from ABB Traction (now Bombardier Transportation) between 1989 and 1996, were NJ Transit's first new electric locomotives. Similar to Amtrak's AEM-7, they replaced aging E60s acquired secondhand from Amtrak in the early 1980s. (The E60s had replaced GG1 electrics originally built for the Pennsylvania Railroad in the late 1930s.) The newest electric locomotives are 29 7,000-hp ALP-46 units supplied by Bombardier. They are based on a European design, the Class

130, which is widely used in Germany and other European countries.

Thirty-three Alstom Transport 4,200-hp PL42AC diesel-electric locomotives were delivered in 2005. These units, which replaced many of the older F40PH-2C, GP40PH-2, and GP40FH-2 diesels, are powered by a 16-cylinder EMD 710 prime mover and are equipped with AC-traction motors.

NJ Transit operates 428 Arrow III M.U. cars that were remanufactured in 1992 and 1993 by ABB Traction. Originally built by General Electric, they are the only M.U.s in the fleet. All new equipment going forward will be locomotive-hauled push-pull cars, the newest of which are 277 bilevels (NJ Transit's first) from Bombardier, scheduled for delivery beginning in 2006.

The push-pull fleet numbers 743 cars (34 of which are owned by Metro-North but operated by NJ Transit): 163 cab-control cars and 580 trailer coaches. Model designations are Comet I (rebuilt from GE Arrow I M.U.s), Comet II (Bombardier, rebuilt by Alstom, 2002–2003), Comet III and Comet IV (Bombardier), and Comet V (Alstom). The design of the aluminum-carbodied Comet II–IV series can be traced back to a Pullman-Standard design also known as the Comet. This type of car was first produced in the early 1960s for Erie-Lackawanna commuter services. In the mid-1980s, after Bombardier had purchased the manufacturing rights from Pullman-Standard, the Comet car went through a redesign resulting in the Comet II, which Bombardier supplied to SEPTA, Massachusetts Bay Transportation Authority, and NJ Transit, as well as to Amtrak (as the Horizon fleet). The Comet II does not have center doors; the Comet III and Comet IV cars are equipped with sliding pocket center doors. The Alstom Comet V carbody, a departure from the Bombardier design, is of smooth-sided (non-fluted) stainless-steel construction. The Bombardier bilevel also features a smooth-sided, stainless-steel carbody and uses a 2-2 seating configuration rather than the 3-2 configuration used in all single-level coaches.

One oddity in the NJ Transit car fleet is Comet II No. 5459. The Jersey Shore Commuters Club Inc., a private organization founded on the Pennsylvania Railroad in 1933, leases half of this car. The club's space, which is separated from the regular passenger area by a bulkhead and door, is equipped with Amtrak Metroliner reclining seats and tables. The club is one of two remaining organizations of its type in the United States and the only one on NJ Transit. The car operates on the North Jersey Coast Line.

All NJ Transit rolling stock is maintained at the Meadows Maintenance Complex, a sprawling, 500,000-plus-square-foot facility in Kearny. The Meadows Complex also houses the Rail Operations Center, which contains Train Control and Power Control theaters for centralized dispatching and control of catenary in electrified territory, respectively. NJ Transit and Amtrak jointly operate the Terminal Operations Center at Penn Station New York, the nation's busiest passenger rail facility, which handles more than 1,200 NJ Transit, Long Island Rail Road, and Amtrak trains on an average weekday.

In 2005 New Jersey Transit operated 722 weekday trains on 11 rail lines totaling 951 miles and serving 162 stations. Annual passengers were 64.9 million, with a weekday average of almost 237,000 passengers.

—William C. Vantuono

REFERENCE

Rosenbaum, Joel, and Tom Gallo. *NJ Transit Rail Operations*. Piscataway, N.J.: Railpace, 1996.

New York, Chicago & St. Louis Railroad (Nickel Plate Road)

The New York, Chicago & St. Louis Railroad (NYC&StL), better known as the Nickel Plate, was chartered on February 3, 1881, to build a standard-gauge railroad between Buffalo, New York, and Chicago, with a branch from Fort Wayne, Indiana, to St. Louis. The new railroad would pass through a few large cities such as Erie, Pennsylvania, Cleveland, and Fort Wayne, but generally it would traverse rural countryside and pass through small hamlets. The main purpose of the railroad was to forward traffic obtained from the Lake Erie & Western Railway (LE&W) to eastern connections at Buffalo. Indeed, the project began as an extension of the LE&W's lines.

The Seney Syndicate, backers of the venture, owned the LE&W, which ran from Sandusky, Ohio, to Peoria, Illinois. The new Nickel Plate would lessen LE&W's dependence on traffic interchanged with the large trunk railroads of the time: the New York Central, Erie, Wabash, and Pennsylvania. It would not only provide the LE&W with access to new gateways, but would enable it to survive in an era of robber barons.

It was decided to build the Chicago-Buffalo line first and the St. Louis extension later. Construction of the 524-mile main line was quickly completed during 1881 and 1882. East of Cleveland it was in many places only a few hundred feet south of the NYC's Lake Shore & Michigan Southern subsidiary; west of Cleveland it crossed Ohio's Great Black Swamp and the Indiana prairie. Construction and equipment standards for the new railroad were high; one newspaper called it "the great New York and St. Louis double-track nickel-plated railroad." Thus the nickname Nickel Plate Road was born.

The railroad opened for business on October 23, 1882, but the company immediately passed into bankruptcy and was sold to the NYC, which wanted to remove this competitive threat and keep it out of hostile hands. As a result, for the next 34 years the Nickel Plate was a nonentity. Traffic levels were kept low, and little was done to improve the railroad.

The Nickel Plate's destiny was forever changed in 1916 by an unusual set of circumstances. M. J. Van Sweringen and O. P. Van Sweringen were developing a new residential subdivision, Shaker Heights, southeast of Cleveland. They wanted to connect it with downtown Cleveland by a rapid-transit line that needed to use a portion of the Nickel Plate's right of way. When the brothers approached the railroad for the necessary easement, they were offered an opportunity to buy the entire property. The NYC, under federal pressure to divest itself of controlling interests in competing lines, felt that the Van Sweringen brothers offered a safe, innocuous way to sell out without hurting itself. However, to help the Van Sweringens run their railroad, the NYC offered the services of John J. Bernet, one of its vice presidents. This would prove to be a fateful choice.

The Vans acquired the Nickel Plate early in 1916 and installed Bernet as president. He immediately began upgrading the physical plant and buying new, modern motive power based on NYC designs to enable it to compete for fast freight business. Almost overnight the Nickel Plate was transformed into a modern railroad that quickly lived up to its potential. To show that a new era had dawned, the tenders behind its locomotives were emblazoned with a new herald: "Nickel Plate Road." At Buffalo the Nickel Plate turned over most of its traffic to the Delaware, Lackawanna & Western, which forwarded it to the East Coast.

More significant changes took place in 1921 when the Van Sweringens expanded their railroad by purchasing the Toledo, St. Louis & Western Railroad (Clover Leaf) and the LE&W, which had been purchased by the Lake Shore & Michigan Southern in 1899. The Clover Leaf had a main line running from Toledo, Ohio, through sparsely settled portions of Ohio, Indiana, and Illinois to St. Louis. It had begun life as a narrow-gauge railroad and was later converted to standard gauge, though it never enjoyed much success. Traffic levels were low, the railroad was in continual financial trouble, its physical plant was in poor condition, and its locomotives were obsolete.

The LE&W's Sandusky-Peoria main line was complemented in Indiana by branches to Michigan City, Fort Wayne, New Castle, and Indianapolis. Like the Clover Leaf, it was in poor condition. Its main value was access to the Peoria gateway. Fortuitously, the LE&W and Clover Leaf main lines crossed in Frankfort, Indiana, the site of the latter's main repair shops.

Shortly after acquiring the LE&W and Clover Leaf, the Van Sweringens gained control of the Chesapeake & Ohio, Pere Marquette, and Erie railroads with the goal of merging them and the Nickel Plate to create one huge railroad. This effort was unsuccessful, and the railroads remained independent, though they joined together to form the Advisory Mechanical Committee, which set engineering and purchasing standards for all four railroads.

During the Depression the Nickel Plate's ability to move traffic across the railroad was enhanced by new union agreements that improved train operations. Most Clover Leaf District traffic was diverted onto the former LE&W east of Frankfort, Indiana. Frankfort became an LE&W District division point, and LE&W District crews were allowed to operate into Bellevue, Ohio, over the Nickel Plate District rather than interchanging traffic at nearby Fostoria. This allowed the Nickel Plate to concentrate traffic on its best lines, expedited the movement of freight, and yielded significant operating savings.

The start of World War II caught the Nickel Plate unprepared for the enormous growth in freight traffic that descended upon it. It was soon stressed to the breaking point. Nickel Plate bought 55 700-series 2-8-4 locomotives between 1942 and 1943 to move this freight, though this required that many bridges be strengthened and terminal facilities improved to allow their operation over virtually the entire system.

It was during the presidency of John W. Davin, from December 1942 to January 1949, that the Nickel Plate entered its golden age. Under his stewardship the railroad was transformed into a first-class, modern operation. New locomotives and rolling stock were acquired, and modern terminal facilities were built across the system. By 1950 the Nickel Plate was one of the most profitable railroads in America and had gained the reputation of being able to move freight fast; it had to if it was to survive.

Nickel Plate's last major acquisition came in December 1949 with the lease of the Wheeling & Lake Erie Railway. The new Wheeling District operated a main line extending from Toledo southeast into the Ohio coalfields that were an abundant source of traffic. The Wheeling was part of the so-called Alphabet Route for traffic heading to the East Coast. Other roads in the consortium were the Nickel Plate, Pittsburgh & West Virginia, and Western Maryland.

The Nickel Plate achieved fame in the late 1950s by operating steam locomotives in high-speed Chicago-Buffalo freight service long after most competing lines had dieselized. Rising labor and material costs finally forced the railroad to dieselize by the end of 1959, causing dramatic changes in operations and employment and in the image of the railroad. During the steam age the Nickel Plate operated locomotive repair shops at Frankfort, Indiana, and Lima, Conneaut, and Brewster, Ohio. After the diesels arrived, only the former Wheeling shop in Brewster remained.

Despite the economies of dieselization, the Nickel Plate began experiencing reduced traffic levels and declining profits. This forced the railroad to consider its future. The industry was changing, and the Nickel Plate was not in a good competitive position. The 1960 merger of former partner Delaware, Lackawanna & Western with rival Erie was a particularly serious blow. The new Erie Lackawanna could haul freight between the East Coast and Chicago without interchanging with the Nickel Plate in Buffalo. It was apparent that the Nickel Plate either had to find a merger partner or be acquired by a larger railroad.

Somewhat surprisingly, the best candidate proved to be the Norfolk & Western Railway, which offered a sizable traffic base consisting of on-line coal, which would lessen the Nickel Plate's dependence on overhead traffic. More important, unlike most eastern railroads, the N&W was financially strong. Although there was no physical connection between the two railroads, arrangements were made to buy the Pennsylvania Railroad's Columbus-Sandusky, Ohio, line, which crossed the Nickel Plate at Bellevue. The Wabash, the Akron, Canton & Youngstown, and the Pittsburgh & West Virginia railroads subsequently became part of the new Norfolk & Western system. The merger was effected on October 16, 1964, and the Nickel Plate passed from existence. In the decades that followed, much of the former Clover Leaf, LE&W, and W&LE was abandoned or sold to shortlines; only the original Chicago-Buffalo main line remains as part of the current Norfolk Southern system in its original form.

In 1963, its last year before becoming part of Norfolk & Western, the Nickel Plate Road operated a system of 2,170 route-miles and 3,992 track-miles, with 408 locomotives, 60 passenger cars, 22,305 freight cars, 700 company service cars, and 9,958 employees. Freight traffic totaled 9,052.4 million ton-miles in 1963, and manufactured goods (43.4 percent) and products of mines (39.7 percent) made up the bulk of its freight traffic. Passenger traffic totaled 13.8 million passenger-miles. Nickel Plate operating revenues totaled $132.6 million in 1963, and the railroad achieved a 74.3 percent operating ratio.

—Eric Hirsimaki

REFERENCE

Rehor, John A. *The Nickel Plate Story*. Milwaukee, Wis.: Kalmbach, 1965.

New York, New Haven & Hartford Railroad (New Haven)

The New Haven, as it was generally known, was the dominant railroad in southern New England, eventually controlling virtually all the railroads in Connecticut, Rhode Island, and much of Massachusetts. The NYNH&H main line extended from New York to Boston through New Haven, Connecticut, and Providence, Rhode Island, with principal secondary routes from New Haven north through Hartford to Springfield, Massachusetts, and from Devon, Connecticut, between Bridgeport and New Haven, west across the Hudson River to Maybrook, New York. Branches covered Connecticut, Rhode Island, and southeastern Massachusetts, and several lines extended north almost to the northern border of Massachusetts.

The New York, New Haven & Hartford was formed

through the 1872 consolidation of the New York & New Haven and the Hartford & New Haven railroads. Opened in 1839, the Hartford & New Haven had reached Springfield, Massachusetts, in 1847. The New York & New Haven opened in 1848 and had reached New London, Connecticut, in 1870 through lease of the Shore Line Railway. Lease of the New York, Providence & Boston in 1892 gave the New Haven lines in eastern Connecticut and Rhode Island that extended its reach north to Worcester, Massachusetts, and Providence. A year later lease of the Old Colony Railroad, which operated an extensive system in southeastern Massachusetts, including the former Boston & Providence, completed a New Haven rail route between New York and Boston. Acquisition or lease of still other lines gave the New Haven a dense network of lines in Connecticut. It reached its fullest extent by gaining control of two major rivals, the New York & New England and the Central New England, in 1895 and 1904, respectively. Control of the CNE gave the New Haven an important link with the anthracite coalfields of northeastern Pennsylvania via the Poughkeepsie Bridge over the Hudson River.

This final consolidation of the New Haven had been carried out after the railroad came under the financial control of financier J. P. Morgan. In 1903 Morgan installed his own man, Charles S. Mellen, as president of the New Haven, and Mellen began an extraordinary effort to bring a large part of New England's transportation system under the railroad's control. The New Haven gained control of the Boston & Maine and the Maine Central. It reached outside New England to gain control of the New York, Ontario & Western in 1904, then traded the New York Central a half interest in the NYO&W for a half interest in the Rutland. The New Haven also acquired Long Island Sound steamship companies and urban and interurban trolley lines in Connecticut, Rhode Island, Massachusetts, and New York's Westchester County. By 1913 the New Haven controlled an estimated 1,600 miles of electric railways.

By the end of the first decade of the twentieth century the New Haven controlled approximately 10,000 miles of railroads, steamboat lines, and electric railways in New England and New York State, as well as electric, water, and gas utilities companies. It was estimated that the New Haven and its associated companies employed 125,000 people.

The New Haven pioneered the new technology of railroad electrification and between 1905 and 1914 installed the first major single-phase AC electrification on its heavily used four-track main line between New York and New Haven. During 1912–1917 the New York Connecting Railroad, a joint venture of the New Haven and the Pennsylvania Railroad, completed the Hell Gate Bridge over the East River at New York, giving the two railroads a direct link at Penn Station in Manhattan. A heavy-duty electric suburban subsidiary, the New York, Westchester & Boston, was constructed in Westchester County, north of New York City.

Morgan and Mellen had paid dearly for their era of expansion and acquisition, and by 1913 the New Haven's financial house of cards began to come tumbling down. The Justice Department brought antitrust action under the Sherman Act. Mellen and 21 New Haven directors were indicted on various antitrust charges, and the New Haven was forced to give up its control of electric railway properties. Unfavorable business conditions reduced earnings, and the railroad experienced a string of serious passenger-train wrecks. The New Haven's debt load had increased fourfold in scarcely a decade, while the value of its stock had fallen by 75 percent. For the first time in 40 years the New Haven passed a dividend. Morgan died in 1913, and Mellen was soon forced out of the New Haven presidency. The once-powerful New Haven avoided probable bankruptcy only by the federal takeover of the railroads during World War I.

The railroad emerged from federal control in 1920 in poor physical and financial condition, but had returned to prosperity by the end of the decade under the favorable business conditions of the late 1920s. This all came to an end with the stock market crash of 1929 and the Depression that followed. Still loaded with debt from the Morgan-Mellen years, while operating revenues had dropped by more than half by 1934, the New Haven entered bankruptcy on October 23, 1935. Under the shelter of bankruptcy, Howard Palmer, the principal trustee, was able to divest the railroad of many of its cumbersome leases and agreements, reduce the number of unprofitable branch lines, modernize the railroad's passenger fleet, and purchase new steam and electric locomotives. Innovations of the Palmer trusteeship included the lightweight Goodyear Zeppelin *Comet* of 1935, the novel Besler steam railcar of 1936, and, more important, the establishment of one of the first trailer-on-flatcar "piggyback" services in 1938. By the time the country entered World War II, the New Haven was prepared for the challenging demands of wartime traffic.

The postwar optimism that followed the emergence of the New Haven from bankruptcy in 1947 and the election of Howard Palmer as president quickly evaporated in a series of struggles for control of the railroad and their damaging aftermath. Within a year of Palmer's election, at the first stockholders' meeting to be held in 12 years, Frederic C. Dumaine, Sr., an autocratic 82-year-old financier, and a group of Canadian corporate interests that were dissatisfied with the dividends managed to elect a two-thirds majority to the board of directors. Promising greater profits to stockholders, Dumaine wrested control away from the Palmer interests with the assistance of a rising Wall Street broker, Patrick B. McGinnis, and became the railroad's new chairman. Laurence F. Whittemore was elected president.

Dumaine had been on the railroad's board since 1923 and had a reputation for being dictatorial, inflexible, and miserly. One of his most notorious decisions was to fire all staff members who earned more than $10,000 a year.

A little more than a year after becoming the railroad's president, Whittemore resigned in protest, allowing Dumaine to assume both the presidency and the chairmanship.

Dumaine imposed draconian measures, producing profits for stockholders, but at the expense of maintenance and labor relations. Upon his death in 1951, his son, Frederic C. Dumaine, Jr., took over and set out to restore the railroad and improve employee morale and public relations. In contrast to his father, he put money back into the physical plant and reinvigorated the road's important passenger services.

This second Dumaine administration was short lived. In 1954 McGinnis won a bitter and well-publicized proxy battle, claiming that Dumaine was putting too much of the company's earnings into the railroad, earnings that should have been going instead to the stockholders. McGinnis promised greater profits and dividends if only the New Haven were controlled by a McGinnis administration. For the New Haven's customers, McGinnis promised new high-speed passenger trains and improved freight service.

Eager to make good on his promises, McGinnis strove for short-term profits by speculation in securities, cutting maintenance to inflate the railroad's earnings, taking out short-term loans, and projecting himself as a reformer. He cut the New Haven's maintenance budget by $9.5 million in 1954 and by another $2.2 million in 1955. Not surprisingly, the company's earnings for 1954 improved by $3 million. A flashy new color scheme for the railroad's locomotives and passenger equipment helped give the New Haven a progressive image. Despite the new look, McGinnis's abrasive style turned many against him. That, coupled with considerable damage from two hurricanes that struck southern New England, led to McGinnis's departure early in 1956.

Next up as president was board member George Alpert, who took over because no one else wanted the job; not long thereafter the railroad took delivery of the new lightweight trains. On an early 1957 demonstration run one of the trains caught fire, and their startup in regular service was delayed. When they did begin running, passengers disliked the trains, which were soon stored. Alpert then compounded the lightweight-train debacle with a major blunder of his own, a decision to move toward elimination of the New Haven's electrification between Stamford and New Haven and on the Bay Ridge freight line, despite the fact that the previous management had just acquired new electric locomotives and a large fleet of multiple-unit commuter cars. This was to be done with a fleet of dual-power locomotives that could operate from third-rail power into New York's Grand Central Terminal and as diesel-electrics elsewhere. These 60 new Electro-Motive FL9 diesels were troublesome initially but settled down to long working lives; there were not enough of them, however, to permit elimination of the electrification, and the supposed savings from a conversion to dual-power locomotives proved illusory.

Passengers accounted for two-thirds of the New Haven's train-miles and half its revenue. The New Haven operated frequent passenger trains connecting the population centers of Connecticut, Rhode Island, and Massachusetts with New York City: 82 percent of its passengers were traveling to or from New York. It participated in operating trains to Washington, Montreal, and Portland, Maine. Even so, most of the New Haven's passengers rode only short distances—cities and towns are close together in southern New England, and the New Haven had intense commuter operations at New York and Boston—and this was proving to be an increasingly unprofitable business. Meanwhile, the longer-haul traffic was declining rapidly as new air shuttle services, turnpikes, and interstate highways paralleled the New Haven's principal passenger routes. The New Haven's freight business declined early. New England's labor-intensive textile business moved to the South in the early 1920s; other manufacturing plants moved to the Midwest to better serve the expanding markets of the South and the West. The way to make money in the railroad freight business is to originate freight and move it a long distance. The New Haven did little of either. As manufacturing declined in southern New England, the New Haven became essentially a carrier of terminating freight, and its longest haul was 258 miles, from Maybrook to Boston. Indeed, the New Haven was described as "one vast switching yard."

By the late 1950s the New Haven was posting substantial deficits, maintenance expenditures were further reduced, and service quality and reliability had plummeted. Federal loan guarantees helped patch things together for a few more years, until the New Haven entered its second bankruptcy in July 1961. Maintenance was cut again, employees were laid off, and service was reduced. The trustees appointed by the court saw little future for the New Haven as an independent company. The apparent solution to the railroad's troubles seemed to be inclusion in the long-awaited merger of the New York Central and the Pennsylvania railroads. Although neither of them wanted the New Haven, the federal court and the government stipulated that if the Penn Central merger were to become a reality, the New Haven would have to be a part of it. The Penn Central absorbed the New Haven on January 1, 1969.

In 1967, a year before its inclusion in the Penn Central, the New Haven operated a system of 1,547 route-miles and 3,344 track-miles, with 332 locomotives, 855 passenger cars, 4,200 freight and company service cars, and 10,162 employees. Freight traffic totaled 2,928.5 million ton-miles in 1967, and foodstuffs (15.8 percent), pulp and paper (13.9 percent), and metal products (10.7 percent) were its principal traffic sources. Passenger traffic totaled 953.6 million passenger-miles. The New Haven's operating revenues totaled $120.1 million in 1967, and the railroad achieved a 96.3 percent operating ratio.

—Geoffrey H. Doughty

REFERENCE

Weller, John L. *The New Haven Railroad: Its Rise and Fall*. New York: Hastings House, 1969.

New York, Ontario & Western Railway

The New York, Ontario & Western was a hapless railroad operating between Cornwall, New York, on the west bank of the Hudson River about 55 miles north of New York City, and Oswego, New York, on the shore of Lake Ontario. Its strengths were passenger traffic to the Catskills and, in the 1940s, bridge traffic between Scranton, Pennsylvania, and the west end of the New Haven at Maybrook, New York. Its abandonment in 1957 was one of the earliest of a large railroad (541 miles) in its entirety.

The New York & Oswego Midland Railroad (NY&OM) was incorporated in 1866 to go from Oswego, New York, to New York—more precisely to a point on the New Jersey state line to connect with a railroad that could take its trains to a terminal a ferry ride away from Manhattan. The promoters of the railroad envisioned a trunk line that would be extended across Lake Ontario by ferry and connect with railroads to the West.

The railroad's first problem was with cities and towns along its proposed route: if they refused to issue bonds to finance the railroad, the railroad shifted its route to avoid them. The result was that the NY&OM went through few places of any consequence. Such financing was not allowed in the state of New Jersey, so the new railroad initially arranged with two short railroads in New Jersey for through service.

In 1869 the line opened from Oswego to Norwich, and three years later the company leased lines that formed branches to Rome and Utica. The entire route from Oswego to Jersey City opened in July 1873. The cost of construction was more than twice the estimated amount, largely because of the tunnels and bridges required—the NY&OM ran crosswise to the lay of the land. A few weeks after the entire line was opened, the company entered bankruptcy.

During bankruptcy the railroad lost its connection down through New Jersey and had to extend its line east to a connection with the West Shore at Cornwall. It was reorganized in 1879 as the New York, Ontario & Western Railway (NYO&W). Implied was its hope that it could turn Oswego into a port city. However, car-ferry connections across Lake Ontario never materialized, and Great Lakes shipping preferred Buffalo as a port—continuing to Lake Ontario meant a trip through the Welland Canal to bypass Niagara Falls.

When the West Shore came under the control of the New York Central in 1885, the New York, Ontario & Western found itself in the position of a local railroad, not a trunk line, that ran from one place on the New York Central to another place on the New York Central—from Cornwall to Oneida. The distance was 10 miles greater on the NYO&W than it was on the New York Central.

In 1890 NYO&W opened a branch from Cadosia, New York, to Scranton, Pennsylvania, to reach an anthracite-mining area. Because of that access to anthracite mines, the New Haven purchased control of the NYO&W in 1904, the same year it purchased the Central New England Railway for its bridge over the Hudson at Poughkeepsie and its connections at Maybrook and Campbell Hall, New York. A few years later, in 1912, the New Haven and the New York Central discussed trading part of their interests in the NYO&W and the Rutland, respectively. The New Haven acquired part of New York Central's Rutland stock but retained its control of the NYO&W.

The growth of the Catskill Mountains as a resort area in the 1920s brought a passenger travel boom to the NYO&W. During the Great Depression much of that business disappeared, and the Scranton Branch assumed greater importance in the road's affairs. The anthracite traffic peaked in 1932 and then declined sharply to 1937, when the anthracite mines near Scranton failed. The anthracite business had barely kept the NYO&W alive; without it, all the railroad could do was file for reorganization.

Frederic Lyford, the trustee of the NYO&W, saw that NYO&W should build its future on general merchandise traffic and develop into a bridge railroad connecting the New Haven at Maybrook with the Lehigh Valley and the Delaware, Lackawanna & Western at Scranton. Lyford also tried to recover the Catskill passenger business, primarily with a low-budget restyling of its principal passenger train for the 1937 season. Both efforts were moderately successful, to the point that NYO&W could begin dieselization, a move driven, as it was on most railroads, by a desire for economy rather than for a modern image.

Despite the surge of traffic during World War II and a brief spurt of business after the war, the bridge traffic was not enough to support the whole NYO&W. In the railroad freight business the railroad on which the cargo begins its journey usually makes the most money; making money as a bridge railroad requires a long haul, and the 145 miles from Scranton to Campbell Hall was not nearly long enough.

Various things were tried in an attempt to save the NYO&W, including a booster organization and a proposal for state aid, claiming that the NYO&W was essential for civil defense (the Cold War was going strong in the early 1950s). In 1955 the railroad posted an operating ratio of 107 percent—it was spending $1.07 for each dollar it took in from operations. The New York, Ontario & Western ceased operations on March 29, 1957.

In 1956, its last year before abandonment, the New York, Ontario & Western operated 541 route-miles and 792 track-miles, with 46 locomotives, 152 freight cars, 71 company service cars, and 1,122 employees. Freight traffic totaled 353 million ton-miles in 1956, and manufactured goods (55.2 percent) and products of mines (24.4 percent) were its principal traffic sources. NYO&W operating revenues totaled $5.6 million in 1956, and the railroad achieved a 111.5 percent operating ratio.

—George H. Drury

REFERENCE

Helmer, William F. *O. & W.* Burbank, Calif.: Howell-North, 1959.

New York Central System

Preeminent among North American railroads, the New York Central System was assembled in the last third of the nineteenth century by empire builder Cornelius Vanderbilt and his heirs. At its height, New York Central encompassed a network of more than 11,000 miles of railroad serving principal points in New York, Ohio, southern Ontario, Indiana, Michigan, and Illinois, with main lines extending east to Boston and west to Chicago and St. Louis and secondary lines that dropped down into Pennsylvania and West Virginia. Serving these heavily populated regions of the Northeast, the NYC was one of the principal American passenger carriers, and its freight trains served the heart of industrial America.

The NYC had its origin in the Mohawk & Hudson Railroad, incorporated in 1826 to replace the stagecoaches that ran the 17 miles between Albany and Schenectady, shortcutting a 40-mile dogleg in the newly opened Erie Canal. The success of the Mohawk & Hudson upon its opening in 1831 spawned a proposal to extend a railroad all the way to Buffalo in competition with the canal.

Soon a string of railroads reached across upstate New York: the Schenectady & Troy, Utica & Schenectady, Syracuse & Utica Direct, Mohawk Valley, Auburn & Syracuse, Auburn & Rochester, Rochester & Syracuse, Buffalo & Rochester, Attica & Buffalo, Tonawanda Railroad, Buffalo & Lockport, and Rochester, Lockport & Niagara Falls. From their beginnings these railroads acted in concert to provide service between Albany and Buffalo, and in 1853 they were consolidated to form the first New York Central Railroad.

Meanwhile, at New York the New York & Harlem Railroad was chartered in 1831 to build a line northward from New York City, at first only to Harlem, then to White Plains, and finally to a connection with the Western Railroad at Chatham, New York, in 1852, creating a New York–Albany rail route. In 1847 the rival Hudson River Railroad was chartered to build a railroad up the east bank of its namesake river between New York and East Albany. It opened in 1851.

Cornelius Vanderbilt, who had built a small ferry service between Manhattan and Staten Island into a shipping empire that made him a fortune, saw a bountiful future in the railroad industry. Then 63 years old, the Commodore, as he was known for his shipping activities, acquired control of the New York & Harlem in 1857, followed by control of the Hudson River Railroad in 1863 and a substantial interest in the New York Central a year after that. In 1869 he consolidated the Hudson River Railroad with the New York Central to form the New York Central & Hudson River Railroad. In 1873 the New York & Harlem was consolidated into the NYC&HR.

By this time Vanderbilt had his sights set on Chicago, and that same year he acquired control of the Lake Shore & Michigan Southern Railway, which extended from Buffalo west along the south shore of Lake Erie through Cleveland and Toledo and on across northern Indiana to Chicago. At about the same time Vanderbilt began purchasing stock of the Michigan Central Railroad (Detroit to Chicago) and then acquired the Canada Southern Railway (Buffalo to Detroit) in 1876.

The Michigan Central's origins can be traced to the Detroit & St. Joseph Railroad of 1832. The road's main line ran from Detroit west toward Michigan City, Indiana, and thence to Chicago via a connection with the Illinois Central; a long secondary route extended north from Detroit through Bay City to Mackinaw City, at the very northern tip of lower Michigan. Even though its operations were wholly integrated into the New York Central System, the Michigan Central retained its identity for years in order to avoid the legal complexities of merger. After decades of controlling the Michigan Central, NYC finally leased it in 1930.

New York Central's other major subsidiary was the Cleveland, Cincinnati, Chicago & St. Louis Railway (the Big Four). It was formed in 1889 by the consolidation of the Cincinnati, Indianapolis, St. Louis & Chicago (part of the Vanderbilt empire) and the Cleveland, Columbus, Cincinnati & Indianapolis railroads, with principal routes from Cleveland through Columbus to Cincinnati, from Cleveland through Indianapolis to St. Louis, and from Cincinnati to Chicago. Like the Michigan Central, the Big Four retained its identity for years. NYC finally leased it in 1930.

As with all empire building, there were a variety of sideshows. The biggest in the Vanderbilt empire was the matter of the New York, West Shore & Buffalo Railroad, built from Jersey City to Albany and Buffalo, practically parallel to the New York Central and often within sight of it. The Pennsylvania Railroad, the Central's archrival, was behind this scheme. The West Shore was completed in 1884 and began to wage a rate war, which ultimately was settled by J. P. Morgan: the NYC would lease the West Shore, and the Pennsylvania would gain the right of way of NYC's retaliatory move, the still-incomplete South Pennsylvania Railroad. NYC merged the West Shore in 1952. Most of the West Shore right of way west of Albany has returned to shrubs, tall grass, and forest growth; the route along the west bank of the Hudson from Albany to northern New Jersey remains a major freight route for CSX Transportation.

In 1914 the New York Central & Hudson River and the Lake Shore & Michigan Southern were combined to form a new (second) New York Central Railroad. The Vanderbilt empire, the New York Central Railroad plus a large collection of semi-independent rail lines, became known as the New York Central Lines. Among the more important subsidiaries were the Boston & Albany Railroad, leased in 1900 and finally merged in 1961; the Peoria & Eastern Railway, formed in 1890; Ohio Central Lines (the Toledo & Ohio Central Railway, which ran from Toledo through Columbus to Charleston, West Virginia, plus three leased lines, the Zanesville & Western Railway, the Kanawha & Michigan, and the Kanawha & West Virginia Railroad), acquired in 1910, leased in 1922, and merged in 1952; the Pittsburgh & Lake Erie Railroad (NYC gained control in 1889); and the Indiana Harbor Belt Railroad (originally owned jointly by Michigan Central and Lake Shore & Michigan Southern), plus the Michigan Central and the Big Four. Over the next 50 years the subsidiaries were consolidated through lease, purchase, or merger. Leasing held tax advantages over outright merger, and when it was in its best interest to lease, the Central did so.

In 1902 the railroad's flamboyant passenger agent, George H. Daniels, conceived of a luxury train traveling in record time between New York and Chicago. Called the *20th Century Limited*, it became one of the best-known passenger trains in the world. The *20th Century* was scheduled to make the 960-mile run in 20 hours, an amazing feat for the day. Critics said that the railroad and its rolling stock would never be able to maintain such a schedule; by 1905 the Central had cut the schedule to 18 hours, and by 1938 the trip was down to 16 hours.

At New York the Central's great passenger-train fleet operated out of what was—and still is today—indisputably North America's greatest passenger terminal. Commodore Vanderbilt had started it with the construction of the splendid Grand Central Depot on 42nd Street in midtown Manhattan during 1869–1871. In 1900 it became known as Grand Central Station after extensive expansion and rebuilding. Only three years later work began for a third new terminal that would be known as Grand Central Terminal. Conceived by the railroad's chief engineer, William J. Wilgus, this New York terminal scheme involved far more than just a new terminal structure. The railroad was already under a mandate from the New York legislature to end steam operation into New York by 1908, and the Central completed an extensive DC third-rail electrification—the largest electrification yet carried out anywhere in the world—of its lines into New York. Electric operation, which began at the end of 1906, permitted the design of the terminal itself with two below-ground track levels. The magnificent Beaux Arts structure designed by architects Charles Reed and Whitney Warren remains a landmark to this day. Between 1910 and the onset of the Great Depression NYC flaunted its strength with the construction of other monumental stations at such major points as Worcester (Massachusetts), Detroit, Rochester, Utica, and Buffalo.

By 1935 the New York Central and its affiliated lines formed an enormous system of more than 11,000 route-miles of railroad, operating nearly 5,000 locomotives and more than 200,000 passenger and freight cars, and the railroad had established an enviable reputation for operating a first-rate passenger service and efficient freight transport. Beginning in the 1920s, the New York Central was in the vanguard of railroads that adopted advanced steam locomotives, with such notable designs as the 4-6-4 Hudson and the 2-8-4 Berkshire. The *20th Century Limited*—streamlined in 1938—remained the premier train among a "great steel fleet" of east-west passenger trains that provided unrivalled service to principal destinations. Serving a heavily industrialized region that accounted for nearly two-thirds of American manufacturing and more than half its population, the Central gave yeoman service in successfully transporting the unprecedented traffic of the World War II years.

At war's end the railroad invested millions in rehabilitating and upgrading its plant and equipment. Early in 1946 it announced a $56 million order for 720 new passenger cars. Hundreds of new diesel-electric locomotives were placed on order, and the Central would end the operation of steam power in 1957. A new passenger station—one of the last major stations anywhere—was built at Toledo. Through sleeping-car services were inaugurated to such distant points as Los Angeles and Mexico City.

As for almost all North American railroads, however, the postwar years proved to be difficult for the Central. Despite an enormous investment in passenger equipment and facilities, the railroad's passenger traffic dropped sharply in the face of competition from improved highways and the fast-growing airline industry. From a postwar peak level of 5.5 billion passenger-miles in 1948, NYC's passenger traffic dropped to less than 2 billion in 1959; by 1967 it was down to only 939 million passenger-miles. By 1959 the Central's annual passenger deficit had reached $53 million. The Central's freight traffic fared little better as new turnpikes and—later—interstate highways paralleled its principal routes, siphoning away much of the most profitable high-value traffic.

Major changes were clearly needed as the railroad's earnings fell. Someone who thought that he knew what the railroad industry needed was Robert R. Young, then chairman of the Chesapeake & Ohio Railway and something of a maverick. Young saw the New York Central as a good place to launch his movement to transform the railroad industry and set out to gain control.

Sensing the battle ahead, NYC hired an experienced, practical "railroad man," William White, to see the company through the coming battle in 1952. A traditionalist, White poured resources into the railroad's physical plant and reestablished the *20th Century*'s famous 16-hour schedule between Chicago and New York, which had been

The New York Central periodically reequipped the celebrated *20th Century Limited* with the latest and finest rolling stock, but never was it more handsome than in its 1938 streamlining, headed by this Henry Dreyfuss–styled 4-6-4 Hudson. The train was eastbound, heading down the Hudson River to its New York terminal at Grand Central. —*Trains* Magazine Collection

allowed to slacken because of speed restrictions brought about by cuts in track maintenance.

In 1954 Young, claiming that more of the company's earnings should be going to the stockholders, won control of the railroad in a bitter proxy fight with the established NYC board and set out to change the railroad. As the railroad's new chairman, Young brought in Alfred E. Perlman from the Rio Grande to reform the company over time. Perlman began to rationalize the railroad's plant, cutting back the Central's main lines from four tracks to two and installing centralized traffic control (CTC) to create a modern high-speed freight railroad. He accelerated NYC's manifest schedules and developed an aggressive freight marketing department. Young had long championed innovative new equipment as a way to revive the passenger business, and the Central soon acquired a lightweight train, the Xplorer, that was seen as a way to restore profits to its money-losing passenger operations. The train was unsuccessful and soon taken out of service, and the decline in the Central's passenger business continued.

By the end of 1956 the New York Central's passenger and freight traffic levels dropped as the country entered a recession. Losses from passenger operations now exceeded the earnings from all other operations. Half of NYC's daily train-miles were run by passenger trains, which produced per train-mile revenues averaging only 25 percent of those for its freight trains. A nationwide coal strike and a looming economic slowdown promised more difficulties for the railroad.

In a changing market there was simply too little freight traffic for too many railroads. Young began to see consolidation as a solution to the Central's problems, and merger talks were begun with the rival Pennsylvania Railroad. Young's suicide early in 1958 brought Perlman to the fore as the Central's president and chief executive officer, with authority to reshape the railroad as he saw fit. Perlman's vision for the future was a single-track New York Central, shorn of money-losing branch lines and passenger trains, able to carry high-speed freight trains and trains carrying a single commodity, and transporting only traffic that the railroad could carry at a profit. He foresaw a railroad devoid of yards, operating trains that did not require five-man crews, trains with an engineer and a conductor, trains dispatched from one central location.

Perlman pursued that vision vigorously. As merger talks with the Pennsylvania sputtered along, he continued the rationalization of the railroad's physical plant. The Central adopted an innovative Flexi-Van container system that moved the railroad into the intermodal business in a big way. Within less than a decade the railroad was operating nearly 50 daily high-speed freights with Flexi-Van equipment. Costly long-distance and commuter passenger service operations were reduced wherever possible. Low-revenue mail transport service, that is, the carrying of second- and third-class mail, was eliminated. Costly yard operations were consolidated or eliminated. Older motive power was retired. Perlman went after changes in restrictive work rules. The New York Central of the first half of the century was history; the new New York Central was on the Road to the Future.

Merger talks with the Pennsylvania continued sporadically through the late 1950s and into the 1960s. A merger plan was finally hammered out, was approved by the Interstate Commerce Commission, and took effect with the formation of the ill-starred Penn Central on February 1, 1968. It would take two more decades and the greatest railroad bankruptcy in history before the railroad of the future envisioned by Al Perlman would begin to take shape.

In 1967, its last year before the Penn Central merger, New York Central operated a system of 9,696 route-miles and 18,454 track-miles, with 1,917 locomotives, 2,085 passenger cars, 78,172 freight cars, 2,650 company service cars, and 42,218 employees. Freight traffic totaled 38,900.6 million ton-miles, and coal (15.8 percent), transportation equipment (12.4 percent), metal products (11.1 percent), and foodstuffs (10.2 percent) were its principal traffic sources. Passenger traffic totaled 939.4 million passenger-miles. New York Central operating revenues totaled $636 million in 1967, and the railroad achieved an 83.4 percent operating ratio.

—Geoffrey H. Doughty

REFERENCES

Harlow, Alvin F. *The Road of the Century.* New York: Creative Age Press, 1947.

Hungerford, Edward. *Men and Iron.* New York: Crowell, 1938.

Nickel Plate Road. *See* New York,

Chicago & St. Louis Railroad

(Nickel Plate Road)

Norfolk & Western Railway

The Norfolk & Western's history divides at 1964. Before then the N&W was a Pocahontas Region coal carrier. It ran from Norfolk, Virginia, through Roanoke to Cincinnati and Columbus, Ohio. Its principal business was carrying coal from the mines of Virginia and West Virginia east to tidewater at Norfolk and west toward the Great Lakes. N&W was efficient and profitable, and it used steam locomotives later than almost any other railroad in North America. The Pennsylvania owned about one-third of N&W's stock.

The announcement of the impending merger of the Pennsylvania and the New York Central started a mating dance among the other eastern railroads. Traditional alliances were forgotten. In 1964 Norfolk & Western became a major U.S. railroad by merging the Nickel Plate (which ran from Buffalo to Chicago and St. Louis), leasing the Wabash (another member of the Pennsylvania Railroad family; its lines ran from Buffalo through Detroit to Chicago, St. Louis, Kansas City, and Omaha) and the Pittsburgh & West Virginia (which connected the Nickel Plate with the Western Maryland southeast of Pittsburgh), and purchasing the Akron, Canton & Youngstown (which ran west from Akron across most of Ohio) and a Pennsylvania Railroad line that connected the "old" N&W with its acquisitions. N&W suddenly blanketed the Midwest and reached west to the Missouri River.

Along the way to its 1964 expansion, N&W had merged the Virginian Railway (Norfolk through Roanoke to the coalfields of West Virginia) and purchased the bankrupt Atlantic & Danville (Portsmouth to Danville, Virginia). In the 1970s an N&W subsidiary acquired the Erie Lackawanna (New York to Chicago) and Delaware & Hudson (Scranton through Albany to Montreal), and in 1981 it purchased the Illinois Terminal (the remnant of an interurban system that connected central Illinois with St. Louis).

The Norfolk & Western grew from a 9-mile line between Petersburg and City Point, Virginia, opened in 1838. Twenty years later the Norfolk & Petersburg Railroad reached Petersburg. The head of the N&P was William Mahone, a Virginia Military Institute engineering graduate. He created a route through the Great Dismal Swamp west of Suffolk, Virginia, by laying a mat of logs and trees; the roadbed is still used today.

After the Civil War Mahone was the driving force in linking the N&P, Southside, and Virginia & Tennessee railroads to form the Atlantic, Mississippi & Ohio Railroad in 1870 (the Southside had begun service from Petersburg to Lynchburg in 1854; the Virginia & Tennessee had been opened in 1856 from Lynchburg to Bristol, on the Virginia-Tennessee state line). When the AM&O went bankrupt, Mahone's role as a railroad builder ended. In 1881 E. W. Clark & Co., bankers of Philadelphia, bought it and renamed its new property the Norfolk & Western Railroad.

Frederick J. Kimball, a partner in the Clark firm, headed the new company and merged it with another Clark railroad, the Shenandoah Valley Railroad, just completed from Hagerstown, Maryland, to a small Virginia village named Big Lick (it was soon renamed Roanoke). Kimball's interest in geology and natural resources was responsible for N&W opening the Pocahontas Coalfields in southern West Virginia and western Virginia in 1880. Between 1890 and 1892 he pushed the N&W northwest to and across the Ohio River to a connection with the Scioto & New England Railroad north to Columbus. In 1901 N&W purchased the Cincinnati, Portsmouth & Virginia Railroad for access to Cincinnati. About the same time N&W built branch lines south from Lynchburg to Durham, North Carolina, and from Roanoke to Winston-Salem.

Pocahontas coal made the N&W prosperous. It literally fueled half the world's navies, and today it stokes steel mills and power plants all over the globe. For years N&W's 100-main-line-mile Pocahontas Division from Bluefield to Williamson, West Virginia, provided 50 percent of the railway's gross revenues. Coal was also responsible for the extensive facilities (yards, car dumpers, coal-handling equipment, and piers) that Norfolk & Western maintained in and around Norfolk, facilities aimed at transferring coal from hopper cars to ships.

The Pocahontas Division also had an operating problem: the climb from Welch to the summit of the Appalachians at Bluefield, West Virginia. For much of the way the grade was 2 percent, and the curves were sharp. Near the top of the grade the single-track Elkhorn Tunnel was a bottleneck. It was too much for N&W's best, most powerful steam locomotives. In 1914 N&W electrified the Elkhorn grade, and eventually 56 miles of its main line between Iager and Bluefield, West Virginia, were under wire. The project combined the 11,000-volt, single-phase AC system pioneered by the New Haven with phase-splitting devices that permitted the locomotives to be operated with three-phase induction motors. A line relocation and a new 7,000-foot Elkhorn Tunnel that opened in 1950 made it possible for steam locomotives to handle trains. N&W shut down its electrification and reverted to steam power, perhaps the only example of a conversion from electric to steam.

West of Williamson, West Virginia, N&W had made a serious mistake in 1892 during the construction of its route to the Ohio River: the line up Pigeon Creek from Naugatuck to the mile-long Dingess Tunnel, then down Twelve Pole Creek to Kenova. The route was expensive to operate, but Kimball thought that the coal and timber along the way would compensate. However, neither was worth the effort, and the N&W soon started building the route it should have built in the first place, along Tug Fork and the Big Sandy River. The expense and lack of return on the Twelve Pole Line—which still exists in shortened form as a major coal branch—apparently had much to do with the N&W's financial position and 1896 bankruptcy.

Kimball survived the financial crisis and served as the new company's receiver until his death in 1902.

N&W operated profitably through both world wars and paid regular dividends through the Depression. Because of its fleet of modern coal-burning steam locomotives (which it built at its shops in Roanoke), N&W remained with steam longer than any other major U.S. railroad, making its last two steam-powered runs on May 6, 1960. Indeed, N&W was something of a renegade in the matter of steam locomotion. It developed efficient steam locomotives—conventional machines except for one steam-turbine-electric, which suffered the dual handicaps of complexity and uniqueness—and, just as important, modern servicing facilities, including innovative "lubritoriums" that accelerated inspection and servicing of a locomotive between runs. Most other railroads that developed modern steam locomotives never modernized the facilities for their maintenance.

Norfolk & Western was not a major operator of passenger trains. The two principal passenger routes of the "old" N&W ran from Norfolk to Cincinnati and from Lynchburg, Virginia, to Bristol, on the Virginia-Tennessee state line. The two routes coincided for the 85 miles between Lynchburg and Christiansburg, Virginia. The Norfolk-Cincinnati line carried the streamlined daytime *Powhatan Arrow* and the overnight *Pocahontas*. The Lynchburg-Bristol route was the middle part of Southern Railway's Washington-Chattanooga route.

N&W's late operation of steam attracted the singular attention of O. Winston Link, a New York City industrial photographer, who spent every spare moment from 1955 into early 1960 photographing (mainly at night) and recording the N&W's steam locomotives. Link's talent and perseverance had the blessing of N&W president R. H. Smith and all his employees. A museum of Link's work opened on January 10, 2004, in the former Roanoke passenger station.

In the late 1950s the export market for coal was growing, which meant that N&W was hauling considerably more coal east from Roanoke than it had previously. The N&W's line east of Roanoke climbed over three summits; the Virginian Railway's line had a water-level grade along the Roanoke River. For years N&W had envied and even coveted, the Virginian's route, and in 1925 the two roads agreed that N&W could lease the Virginian, but the Interstate Commerce Commission withheld its approval. More than 30 years later the situation had changed. On December 1, 1959, Norfolk & Western merged the neighboring Virginian Railway. N&W established one-way traffic on which the N&W line was westbound and the old Virginian eastbound on parallel lines west of Roanoke. An early casualty of one-way operation was Virginian's extensive electrification.

On October 31, 1962, N&W purchased the bankrupt Atlantic & Danville Railway, a secondary line between Danville and Portsmouth, Virginia, which had served as a route to Portsmouth for the Southern Railway (Southern turned to trackage rights on Atlantic Coast Line). N&W formed a subsidiary, the Norfolk, Franklin & Danville Railway, to operate the line.

The creation of Erie Lackawanna and the announcement of the creation of Penn Central kicked off an extensive realignment of the other railroads in the Northeast. One of the conditions of the Penn Central merger was that the Pennsylvania divest itself of its interests in the Norfolk & Western and the Wabash. The Nickel Plate lost the traffic it interchanged at Buffalo with the Lackawanna and looked around for a merger partner.

The Erie Lackawanna and the Delaware & Hudson petitioned for inclusion in the enlarged N&W; N&W formed a subsidiary holding company, Dereco, to acquire them and essentially hold them at arm's length for a while. At the beginning of 1984 Guilford Transportation Industries bought the Delaware & Hudson. GTI placed it in bankruptcy in 1988 and a few years later sold it to Canadian Pacific. The Erie Lackawanna declared bankruptcy on June 26, 1972, and eventually became part of Conrail. In 1983 N&W donated its 1,000 shares of Erie Lackawanna stock and EL's corporate records to the University of Virginia.

The merger made N&W into a midwestern railroad, quite able to hold its own in competition with Penn Central and the combination of Baltimore & Ohio and Chesapeake & Ohio—indeed, with an advantage in the form of its former Wabash routes to Kansas City and Omaha. Railroads continued to merge during the 1970s and 1980s. In the eastern United States there were five major railroad systems: Conrail, Chessie System (Baltimore & Ohio and Chesapeake & Ohio), Seaboard System (Atlantic Coast Line, Seaboard Air Line, and Louisville & Nashville, plus all the roads they controlled, owned, or leased), Southern Railway, and Norfolk & Western. Chessie System and Seaboard System merged as CSX. At the end of 1990 the N&W became a subsidiary of the Southern Railway, and the Southern Railway changed its name to Norfolk Southern, reusing the name of a regional railroad the Southern had purchased a few years earlier.

In 1981 the Norfolk & Western operated a system of 7,803 route-miles and 14,931 track-miles, with 1,372 locomotives, 87,903 freight cars, 2,978 company service cars, and 21,208 employees. Freight traffic totaled 48,698.2 million ton-miles in 1981, and coal (50.1 percent) and transportation equipment (10.5 percent) were its principal traffic sources. Norfolk & Western operating revenues totaled $1,785.9 million in 1981, and the railroad achieved a 75.1 percent operating ratio.

—Lloyd D. Lewis and George H. Drury

REFERENCE

Striplin, E. F. "Pat." *The Norfolk & Western: A History*. Roanoke, Va.: Norfolk & Western Railway, 1981.

Norfolk Southern Railway (1942)

This Norfolk Southern Railway is not today's Norfolk Southern, but a regional railroad that ran south from Norfolk, Virginia, crossed Albemarle Sound, and then ran west through Raleigh, North Carolina, to Charlotte, a railroad that had narrow-gauge and trolley predecessors and operated American Car & Foundry railbuses and five light 2-8-4 locomotives built by Baldwin in 1940. Further confusing matters is the Southern Railway's purchase of this Norfolk Southern in 1974, changing its name to Carolina & Northwestern, and its reuse of the Norfolk Southern name for a holding company and later for the railroad that resulted from merging the Norfolk & Western Railway and the Southern Railway.

In 1870 the Elizabeth City & Norfolk Railroad was chartered. Construction began in 1880, and by December 1881 its line reached from Berkley, Virginia, now part of Norfolk, south through Elizabeth City, North Carolina, to a boat connection at Edenton, on Albemarle Sound. The railroad got a new name in 1883: Norfolk Southern Railroad. It entered receivership in 1889. In 1891 it was reorganized as the Norfolk & Southern Railroad. In 1900 the N&S absorbed the Norfolk, Virginia Beach & Southern Railroad, a former 3-foot-gauge railroad with lines to Virginia Beach, Cape Henry, and Munden. In 1902 N&S acquired the 3-foot-gauge Washington & Plymouth, which ran between the North Carolina towns of its title, standard-gauged it, extended it northeast to the south shore of Albemarle Sound, and started ferry service across Albemarle Sound to Edenton.

Several railroads in coastal North Carolina were consolidated with the Norfolk & Southern Railroad in 1906 to form the Norfolk & Southern Railway. The new company leased the Atlantic & North Carolina Railroad, a state-owned line from Goldsboro through New Bern to Morehead City. The Norfolk & Southern entered receivership in 1908 and was reorganized in 1910 as a new Norfolk Southern Railroad. The NS built a long trestle across Albemarle Sound to replace the ferry and resumed an expansion program: through purchase and construction it extended its main line west to Charlotte, with branches to Fayetteville, Aberdeen, Asheboro, and (in 1920) Durham.

NS again entered receivership in 1932, largely because of the Depression. The Atlantic & North Carolina withdrew its lease for nonpayment, and the electrically operated services to Virginia Beach and Cape Henry were replaced by gasoline cars. In the late 1930s NS abandoned some of its lines, and it was sold at foreclosure in 1941.

In 1942 the property was taken over by the Norfolk Southern Railway, and in 1947 Patrick B. McGinnis led a takeover by a group of investors. The NS leased luxurious apartments in Miami, Washington, and New York, acquired two office cars, entertained its shippers lavishly, and was the focus of an investigation by the Interstate Commerce Commission. McGinnis moved on, eventually to the New Haven and the Boston & Maine, and new management took over in 1953.

The Southern Railway bought the Norfolk Southern in 1974 and merged it with the Carolina & Northwestern, continuing to use the NS name. In 1981 the name of the NS was changed to Carolina & Northwestern, and the Norfolk Southern name was applied to a new holding company created to facilitate the merger of the Southern Railway and the Norfolk & Western Railway.

In 1973, the year before it was purchased by the Southern Railway, Norfolk Southern operated a system of 622 route-miles and 794 track-miles, with 37 locomotives, 2,245 freight cars, 50 company service cars, and 612 employees. Freight traffic totaled 73.1 million ton-miles in 1973, and stone, clay, sand, and gravel (23.8 percent), chemicals (23.8 percent), lumber and wood products (12.5 percent), and pulp and paper (11.9 percent) were its principal traffic sources. Norfolk Southern operating revenues totaled $16.2 million in 1973, and the railroad achieved an 86.5 percent operating ratio.

—George H. Drury

REFERENCE

Prince, Richard E. *Norfolk Southern*. N.p.: Richard E. Prince, 1972.

Norfolk Southern Railway (1990)

Until the mid-1970s the Norfolk Southern was a regional railroad that ran south from Norfolk, Virginia, then west to Charlotte, North Carolina. The Southern Railway bought the Norfolk Southern in 1974 and merged with it another Southern subsidiary, the Carolina & Northwestern, continuing to use the Norfolk Southern name for the regional railroad until 1981, when the Norfolk Southern was renamed Carolina & Northwestern—the Southern had a new job for the Norfolk Southern name.

On March 25, 1982, the Interstate Commerce Commission gave its blessing to the acquisition of the Southern Railway and the Norfolk & Western Railway by a new holding company, the Norfolk Southern Corp. The two railroads kept their identities and images for a while, but gradually the image of the Norfolk Southern replaced them. In late 1990 the Norfolk & Western ceased being a subsidiary of the Norfolk Southern Corp. and became a subsidiary of the Southern Railway, which changed its name to Norfolk Southern Railway.

By virtue of the Conrail acquisition described later, Norfolk Southern reaches from northern New Jersey southwest through Washington, Charlotte, and Atlanta and also through Harrisburg, Roanoke, and Chattanooga to Birmingham and New Orleans, with branches reaching to the Atlantic Coast at numerous points from northern New Jersey to Jacksonville; from Philadelphia west through Pittsburgh and Cleveland to Chicago; and from Buffalo and from Detroit southwest to St. Louis and Kansas City. Secondary lines connect the main trunk routes, and branches cover much of the territory along the trunk routes. Trackage and haulage rights extend NS to such diverse points as Dallas, Des Moines, Rouses Point, New York, and Waterville, Maine. NS's line to Kansas City, a former Wabash route, is unique in crossing the railroad world's division between East and West: an imaginary line from Chicago to St. Louis, then south along the Mississippi River to New Orleans.

After Conrail became profitable in the early 1980s, the U.S. Department of Transportation began to urge that the federal government sell it. In 1985 Norfolk Southern made an offer to purchase Conrail. Conrail management, however, held out for independence for the railroad. The public sale of Conrail stock in 1987 netted the federal government roughly one-third of the amount it had spent on Conrail in the preceding decade. Conrail resumed merger negotiations with Norfolk Southern in 1994 (they were inconclusive), offered to buy St. Louis Southwestern from Southern Pacific in 1995, and began merger negotiations with CSX in 1996. Norfolk Southern made a counteroffer. In 1997 Norfolk Southern and CSX agreed to split Conrail between them. The Surface Transportation Board authorized the deal. In May 1999 Norfolk Southern received the former New York Central line between Cleveland and Chicago, the former Pennsylvania Railroad main lines east of Cleveland and Pittsburgh, and former Erie Lackawanna, Reading, Central of New Jersey, and Lehigh Valley routes. NS and CSX jointly own lines in New Jersey and eastern Pennsylvania under the Conrail Joint Assets name.

At the beginning of the twenty-first century the railroad industry seemed to be waiting. West of Chicago and the Mississippi River two railroads, Union Pacific and Burlington Northern Santa Fe, dominated the railroad industry. East of Chicago and the Mississippi two other railroads did most of the railroading: CSX and Norfolk Southern. It was uncertain what the railroads were waiting for; however, it was certain that if one eastern railroad and one western railroad formed an alliance of almost any kind, the other two railroads would do the same.

In 2005 NS operated a system of 21,184 route-miles and 38,041 track-miles, with 3,791 locomotives, 99,454 freight cars, 5,425 work cars, and 30,433 employees. Freight traffic totaled 203 billion revenue ton-miles in 2005, and its principal traffic was coal (24 percent), general merchandise (54 percent), and intermodal traffic (21 percent). NS operating revenues totaled $8,527 million in 2005, with $6,410 million in operating expenses, and the railroad achieved a 75.2 percent operating ratio.

—George H. Drury

North Shore Line. *See* Chicago

North Shore & Milwaukee Railroad

Northeast Illinois Regional Commuter Railroad Corp. (Metra)

In 1973 the Regional Transportation Authority (RTA) was formed to coordinate and assist public transportation in the six-county Chicago metropolitan region, with an emphasis on the declining commuter rail system. By the end of 1976 the RTA had entered into purchase-of-service contracts with the city's commuter railroads and had begun to acquire new equipment and improve the facilities used for the commuter systems.

The RTA moved into direct operation of commuter lines after the bankruptcy of the Rock Island in 1975 and its liquidation five years later. The Chicago & North Western had established an operating contract for the former Rock Island line between Chicago and Joliet, but withdrew from the operating contract in 1981. With no one else interested in operating the former Rock Island services, RTA took over the railroad in 1982 and formed the Northeast Illinois Railroad Corp. to operate the line itself. In much the same manner, the NIRC began operating the two lines of the bankrupt Milwaukee Road in 1982, and the RTA took ownership in 1987.

In 1983 the RTA restructured the NIRC to provide for direct operation and oversight of contracted services and for long-range planning and marketing of regional rail services. Popularly known as Metra (*Me*tropolitan *Ra*il), the new system established its own Metra service mark and logo to give a unifying identity to the entire commuter rail system. Metra's directly operated system was further expanded in 1987 when Metra took over ownership of the Illinois Central Gulf's electrified suburban main line and branches south from downtown Chicago. All told, Metra in 1987 was operating a system of nearly 500 miles, made up of four directly owned and operated lines and another seven operated under lease, trackage rights, or purchase-of-service contracts.

Since 1984 Metra has spent some $2 billion to rebuild and modernize the system. Track and structures have been rebuilt, signaling and communications have been upgraded, and support and yard facilities have been rebuilt or replaced. Equipment modernization, however, has constituted the largest share of Metra's capital renewal spending, for both equipment overhaul and the purchase of new locomotive and bilevel car replacements. When current orders are complete, Metra will have built 477 bilevel coaches and 25 bilevel electric cars. Virtually the entire fleet is operated in a "Chicago standard" of service, with bilevel gallery cars operated in push-pull operation for nonelectrified lines and bilevel cars for electric lines.

Although rebuilding the old system has taken the largest share of Metra's spending, the rail system has also seen significant expansions. The largest of these was the 1996 opening of an additional northwest route extending 41 miles over the Canadian National (formerly Wisconsin Central) to Antioch in northern Lake County, just south of the Wisconsin state line, which provides Metra with a direct connection to O'Hare International Airport. Other new construction has included both capacity improvements on existing lines and line extensions. Two major extensions now high on Metra's priority list include a 55-mile circumferential line, partly on existing Elgin, Joliet & Eastern track, that will link Joliet with O'Hare International Airport, while the planned SouthEast Service line will add 32 miles to link Crete, south of Chicago, with Metra's existing Rock Island line to LaSalle Street Station.

Metra's current commuter rail system comprises 546 route-miles on 12 main lines and 4 branches. From Chicago's downtown Randolph Street Station Metra Electric operates south to University Park, with branches to Blue Island and South Chicago, and the South Shore line runs into northwestern Indiana. The Rock Island District operates trains southwest to Joliet from LaSalle Street Station. The busiest Metra terminal is Chicago's Union Station, from which operate Metra's Norfolk Southern line (the former Wabash) and the Metra/Heritage Corridor (over the former Gulf, Mobile & Ohio) to Joliet, the Burlington Northern & Santa Fe's western corridor to Aurora, the northwest corridor over Canadian National to Antioch, and Milwaukee District lines northwest to Elgin and to Fox Lake and Big Timber. Three Union Pacific lines operate from Chicago's Metra Passenger Terminal (the former Chicago & North Western Station): the West Line to Geneva, the Northwest Line to Harvard, and the North Line to Kenosha, Wisconsin.

In 2006 Metra served 230 stations, with a fleet of 140 diesel locomotives, 762 diesel-hauled bilevel cars, and 243 bilevel electric multiple-unit (M.U.) cars. A total of 705 trains transported an average of 283,000 passengers every weekday.

—William D. Middleton

REFERENCE

Middleton, William D. "Second City Commuter Trains Are Second to None." *Railway Age* 195, no. 3 (Mar. 1994): 57–62, 64–66.

Northeast Rail Services Act. *See*

REGULATION

Northern Alberta Railways

The province of Alberta was in the railroad business in the late 1920s with the ownership of four railways. The longest was the Edmonton, Dunvegan & British Columbia Railway. Construction began in 1912; by 1930 the line reached Dawson Creek, British Columbia (495 miles from Edmonton) via Smith, McLennan, and Grande Prairie, Alberta. Connecting with the ED&BC at McLennan was the Central Canada Railway. Its track reached Peace River in 1916 and was later extended west to Hines Creek (382 miles from Edmonton). Both the ED&BC and the Central Canada had been built by the J. D. McArthur Co. of Winnipeg. The construction company operated the two railroads until World War I created financial difficulties. Alberta leased the two railways in 1920 and arranged with Canadian Pacific Railway to operate them.

The timetable of the Edmonton, Dunvegan & British Columbia in the June 1916 *Official Guide of the Railways* is noteworthy for the use of 24-hour notation, which was also used by Canadian Pacific, but only west of Fort William, Ontario.

The Alberta & Great Waterways Railway had a similar history. It was chartered in 1909 and built by the McArthur Co. between 1914 and 1925 from Carbondale, 14 miles north of Edmonton on the ED&BC, to Lac La Biche and Waterways (305 miles from Edmonton). During its first years it was operated by the construction company as part of the ED&BC. The provincial government purchased the railway from the construction company and operated it through its Department of Railways and Telephones but later arranged for Canadian Pacific to operate it.

The fourth provincial railway was the 26-mile Pembina Valley Railway, which reached northwest to Barrhead from Busby, on the ED&BC 40 miles north of Edmonton. The Pembina Valley was chartered and built by the province; it opened in 1927. In the early 1920s the province endeavored to sell its railways to either the CPR or the newly created Canadian National Railways. In 1926 the province assumed their operation while negotiations continued. Canadian Pacific in 1928 said that it would be willing to purchase the railroads jointly with Canadian National. The arrangement was agreeable to the provincial government. The jointly owned Northern Alberta Railways was incorporated on June 14, 1929, and on July 1 of that year purchased the four railways from the government.

During World War II NAR's traffic increased greatly because of the construction of the Alaska Highway north from Dawson Creek. In 1955 the opening of a provincial highway cut 130 miles off the route from Edmonton to Dawson Creek; the new road took considerable business from NAR. In 1958 the Pacific Great Eastern Railway (later BC Rail) reached Dawson Creek from North Vancouver and Prince George; it too took traffic from NAR.

The opening in 1964 of the Great Slave Lake Railway, built by the Canadian government and operated by CN, provided interchange traffic for NAR—lead and zinc ores

(NAR's principal commodity was grain). The new railway connected with NAR at Roma Junction, west of Peace River. In 1969 the Alberta Resources Railway, owned by the province and operated by CN, reached Grande Prairie from the south. Canadian Pacific sold its half of Northern Alberta Railways to Canadian National in 1980, and CN absorbed its operations at the beginning of 1981.

In 1980, the year before it was purchased by Canadian National Railways, Northern Alberta operated 923 route-miles, with 21 locomotives, 9 passenger cars, and 100 freight cars. Northern Alberta's operating revenues for 1972, the last year for which figures are available, totaled C$12.8 million.

—George H. Drury

Northern Pacific Railway

The construction of the Northern Pacific Railway (NP) was the single greatest corporate undertaking in the history of the United States up to that time. It constructed a rail line that traversed the nation's northwestern quadrant, connecting the Great Lakes at Duluth and the Mississippi River at St. Paul, Minnesota, with Puget Sound at Tacoma, Washington. By linking the upper Midwest with the Northwest's Pacific ports, it opened the area to settlement and rapid economic development that in turn fostered the national marketplace and further encouraged international trade among Pacific Rim nations.

The Northern Pacific was the nation's second transcontinental rail line. As with the first line, the Union Pacific/Central Pacific (UP/CP), approval of its charter had been delayed by the growing sectional tensions between the North and the South. Spanning the northern-tier states from Duluth, Minnesota, to Portland, Oregon, and Tacoma, Washington, the NP in large measure followed the route established by the 1804–1806 Lewis and Clark Expedition. New York merchant and entrepreneur Asa Whitney lobbied hard for a northern railroad throughout the 1840s, and in 1853–1854 Isaac I. Stevens, governor of Washington Territory, led a notable Pacific railroad survey that further refined the northern route as a feasible line from the Great Lakes to the Pacific Ocean.

With the departure of southern senators during the Civil War, the way was cleared for the issuance of the NP's charter. In 1864 President Abraham Lincoln signed the legislation to construct the northern transcontinental. The Northern Pacific, unlike the UP/CP, received no direct monetary support from the national government, although its charter provided the largest land grant in the history of the Republic to offset construction expenses: rights to alternating sections of land along its line that totaled almost 60 million acres.

However, the lack of cash severely hampered the actual

building of the line. In 1869 the Philadelphia banking firm of Jay Cooke & Co. assumed financial control of the project, issued bonds, and finally commenced construction. At the same time the NP launched an extensive advertising campaign to attract settlers. Toward that end, Cooke advised the road to open land offices in Germany, Scandinavia, and the Netherlands, as well as in the United States. By 1873 the main line reached Bismarck, Dakota Territory, but construction stopped immediately with the panic of 1873 and the financial collapse of the NP and Jay Cooke & Co., which signaled the onset of the economic debacle.

Matters languished until the late 1870s, when Frederick Billings of Vermont led a team of eastern investors, the Pennsylvania Group, to reorganize the NP. By 1878 construction resumed as crews built west from Bismarck and, at the other end of the line, east from Wallula Junction, Washington Territory. Dealing with enormous problems that included the railroad's voracious need for capital, the sparse population along most of the line, growing anti-railroad sentiment in Congress in the wake of the Crédit Mobilier scandal, and other issues, Billings made significant headway in an effort to complete the transcontinental line. However, a threat to his leadership had emerged in the person of Henry Villard, a German-born journalist turned financier. A latecomer to railroad affairs, Villard created a transportation empire that included rail and steamship operations emanating from Portland, Oregon, in the 1870s. To protect and expand access to that city, he worked hard to persuade the Northern Pacific to use his Oregon Railway & Navigation line along the south bank of the Columbia River to Portland. When Billings remained unreceptive to his overtures, Villard took a dramatically different tack. In 1881 he organized the famous "blind pool" to raise the capital to capture control of the NP and mesh it with his other interests in the Pacific Northwest. That curious arrangement, so named because the participants knew Villard but did not know what project or projects their investments would be used to finance, was one of the first hostile takeovers in Wall Street history.

As soon as he installed a new board of directors and became president of the NP that September, Villard plunged into a frenetic round of activity. He escalated road construction by his branch lines in Washington and Oregon. However, his principal concern was completion of the Northern Pacific's transcontinental line. Toward that end, he launched an explosive round of tracklaying at both ends of the railroad's main line, while he simultaneously built a terminal and hotel in Portland and numerous other structures along the road. Heedless of cautionary advice, Villard simply poured money into the grand scheme that would spread a transportation network throughout the Pacific Northwest and eastward to the Great Lakes.

Finally, in the summer of 1883 the Northern Pacific line was completed. Villard staged an extravagant celebration, lavish even by Gilded Age standards. He spent nearly a quarter of a million dollars for four special trains and invited over 200 American VIPs, as well as a bevy of foreign diplomats and financial figures, primarily from Great Britain and Germany, who had made substantial investments in the line. The grand excursion began in the Twin Cities of St. Paul and Minneapolis, which held twin parades that ran some 15 to 20 miles each and were attended collectively by over 120,000 onlookers. Riding west, the special trains arrived at Gold Creek, Montana Territory, near present-day Helena, for the golden-spike ceremony on September 8, which was broadcast by telegraph throughout the nation.

The enormous expenditure of treasure and energy had exhausted the company and its leader. Four months later, when the financially overextended NP simply could not meet its obligations, Villard was forced to resign as president and suffered a nervous breakdown, although he later returned as a director of the company. The troubled railroad struggled through the remainder of the 1880s and managed to complete an important line from Pasco to Tacoma via Stampede Pass through the Cascade Mountains. That feat made Tacoma the most prominent port on Puget Sound until the rival Great Northern Railway arrived at Seattle ten years later.

Despite an enormous campaign to attract settlers and market its lands from federal grants and despite its efforts to improve operational expenses, the NP proved unable to weather the panic of 1893. Like all other transcontinental railroads except the Great Northern, the company fell into receivership as hard times swept the nation. The Pullman strike of 1894 added intense labor turbulence to the already-burdened railroad.

Shortly thereafter the NP entered into an agreement with its longtime nemesis James J. Hill of the Great Northern, who in alliance with the House of Morgan took de facto control of the line. The first step in the process was the so-called London Memorandum of 1896, in which Hill, Morgan, George Stephen, and, representing the Northern Pacific, Arthur Gwinner of the Deutsche Bank of Berlin cemented a momentous agreement. The signatories specifically stipulated that the GN and NP would "form a permanent alliance, defensive, and in case of need offensive, with a view of avoiding competition and aggressive policy and of protecting the common interests of both Companies." Further, the railroaders and bankers determined that "all competitive business, such as [that] of the Anaconda Copper Company [the principal mining company, the single largest shipper in the Northwest, and the only shipper mentioned in the agreement], would be divided upon equitable terms between both Companies. Tariff wars and rate cutting [were to] be absolutely avoided," while neither road would in the future "ingress into the other's territory by new construction or purchase or acquiring of control of existing lines."

Within three years the Hill-Morgan alliance controlled the Northern Pacific. To make the line viable, it sold over 900,000 acres of prime lumber from the NP's land grant to Frederick Weyerhaeuser, Hill's neighbor in Saint Paul, who subsequently moved his headquarters from the Midwest to Federal Way, Washington. That transaction allowed the NP to obtain the necessary infusion of capital to recover from the debacle of the 1890s.

The alliance's control was not absolute, however, and Northern Pacific quickly became the target of an attempted takeover that rocked the nation's financial community. Embittered rival Edward H. Harriman of the Southern Pacific system desperately wanted to limit the influence of the Hill Lines and preserve his own rail empire. To that end, he allied with Jacob Schiff of Kuehn Loeb and the Standard Oil Group, led by William Rockefeller. Pooling their resources, they began surreptitiously buying NP stock. The NP was central to their plans, since control of that line would give the Harriman group nearly absolute control of the Pacific Northwest and control of the Chicago, Burlington & Quincy with unchallenged access to Chicago from the West, and would safeguard the Harriman system.

The ensuing struggle rocked Wall Street and nearly precipitated a depression. As soon as he realized what was going on, Hill wired Morgan, then vacationing in France, and an unrestrained bidding war erupted. As each group vied for control, the price of NP stock roared from a little over $35 to over $1,000 per share in only a few weeks. Ultimately, the Hill-Morgan alliance triumphed when Schiff neglected to purchase the crucial final block of stock necessary for control of the NP.

Anxious to avert any more damage, the combatants agreed to a compromise, the Northern Securities holding company, an important part of the great merger boom then sweeping the country. Chartered in November 1901 in New Jersey, Northern Securities was the direct predecessor of the Burlington Northern, created in 1970. The holding company included controlling shares of the Great Northern, Northern Pacific, Chicago, Burlington & Quincy, and the new Spokane, Portland & Seattle lines. The Hill-Morgan group, with Hill as president, held a firm majority in the enterprise, although Harriman and others were represented on the board.

Northern Securities constituted a near monopoly on rail transportation from Minnesota to Washington State and immediately drew the attention of Theodore Roosevelt, who had just acceded to the presidency upon William McKinley's assassination. Roosevelt quickly directed his attorney general to file suit to dissolve Northern Securities as a violation of the Sherman Antitrust Act. The case wound through the lower courts, and in 1904 the U.S. Supreme Court affirmed Roosevelt's position to break up the company. In a famous dissent, newly appointed Justice Oliver Wendell Holmes, Jr., opined, "Great cases like hard cases make bad law." Bad or not, the decision proved generally popular with progressives, and the individual railroads reverted to their former relationships.

During and immediately after the Hill-Morgan domination of the Northern Pacific, the line prospered. It benefited substantially from the arrival of new settlers on the northern Great Plains, where agricultural reformers, pundits, and the railroads themselves decreed vast new potential through "scientific" dryland farming practices. Responding to those pronouncements, tens of thousands of new settlers established homesteads on the plains, many on purchased NP lands. Similarly, higher yields of wheat and lumber significantly increased freight traffic on the railroad. Transportation generally benefited from the "golden age" of American agriculture in the first two decades of the twentieth century.

To expand its service area, the Northern Pacific cooperated with the Great Northern to build new lines. Barred by its charter from building branch lines, the NP continued its practice of establishing a number of separately incorporated companies, which it controlled, to access new areas. In 1908, with the GN it completed the Spokane, Portland & Seattle Railway along the north bank of the Columbia River, linking Pasco, Washington, with Portland, Oregon. By the close of the Progressive Era the NP had increased its total trackage to more than 6,000 miles and had warded off the threat posed by the completion of the Chicago, Milwaukee & St. Paul Railway (Milwaukee Road) extension to the Pacific in 1909.

After World War I the Northern Pacific faced a more difficult economic environment. The collapse of the international market for foodstuffs, combined with an end to the "wet" rain cycle on the Great Plains and a consequent large depopulation of that area, hurt its freight traffic. At the same time it faced serious new competitors from oceanic shipping for the vital lumber traffic. In the 1922 shopmen's strike the road, like its counterparts throughout the nation, again faced significant unrest by its employees. Finally, a renewed attempt to merge with the Great Northern failed in 1927 when the Interstate Commerce Commission decreed that the two railroads must give up control of the Chicago, Burlington & Quincy as a condition for allowing the proposed merger. Matters only worsened when the Great Depression struck the nation.

The Northern Pacific did survive the interwar period, unlike the parallel Milwaukee Road, which filed for bankruptcy in 1925 and was the largest business failure in the nation at the time. With the economic revival sparked by World War II and the end of the Depression, the NP's fortunes also improved. By 1941 it was able to purchase outright the Minnesota & International Railway, connecting Brainerd with International Falls, Minnesota, which it had controlled informally for several years. After the war population growth and a burst of construction in the area it served allowed the railroad to continue to improve.

Beginning in 1956, the Northern Pacific again joined with the Great Northern in a campaign to merge along with the Chicago, Burlington & Quincy and the Spokane, Portland & Seattle. The campaign proved quite long as the plan worked its way through the ICC and finally went to the U.S. Supreme Court. The result was the Burlington Northern, created officially on M-Day (March 2, 1970). Upon its creation the new BN immediately became the world's longest privately owned railroad system and, since it included the same lines as those of the Northern Securities Co., the fulfillment of James J. Hill's original dream.

In 1969, its last year before the Burlington Northern merger, Northern Pacific operated 6,771 route-miles and 10,457 track-miles, with 604 locomotives, 192 passenger cars, 34,961 freight cars, 3,970 company service cars, and 13,236 employees. Freight traffic totaled 14,519.6 million ton-miles in 1969, and lumber and wood products (25.3 percent), farm products (18.2 percent), and foodstuffs (10.8 percent) were its principal traffic sources. Passenger traffic totaled 207.4 million passenger-miles. Northern Pacific operating revenues totaled $214.1 million in 1969, and the railroad achieved an 87.8 percent operating ratio.

—W. Thomas White

REFERENCES

Frey, Robert L., and Lorenz P. Schrenk. *Northern Pacific Super-steam Era, 1925–1945*. San Marino, Calif.: Golden West, 1985.

Mickelson, Sig. *The Northern Pacific Railroad and the Selling of the West*. Sioux Falls, S. Dak.: Center for Western Studies, Augustana College, 1993.

Renz, Louis Tuck. *The History of the Northern Pacific Railroad*. Fairfield, Wash.: Galleon Press, 1980.

Schwantes, Carlos A. *Railroad Signatures across the Pacific Northwest*. Seattle: Univ. of Washington Press, 1993.

Northwestern Pacific Railroad

The Northwestern Pacific served the large area of California north of San Francisco. For the most part its lines lay one mountain range east of the Pacific Coast. No other railroad its size had as wide a variety of operations: standard-gauge trains, narrow-gauge trains (until 1930), a dense electrified suburban service in Marin County (until 1941), and ferries on San Francisco Bay. NWP's main line from Sausalito north to Eureka measured 278 miles; the road's total mileage peaked at 534 miles in 1920.

Thirty-four railroad companies preceded the Northwestern Pacific. The earliest, the Petaluma & Haystack Railroad, was opened in 1864 by Charles Minturn to connect with a steamer line from Haystack to San Francisco. Six years later another railroad opened to link San Rafael with the port of San Quentin for a shorter ferry ride to San Francisco (that line was built to standard gauge, then was narrowed to 3-foot gauge, then was standard-gauged again before it was abandoned).

The North Pacific Coast Railroad commenced building a narrow-gauge line at Sausalito in 1872. After boring several tunnels and laying rails along the shore of Tomales

Bay, it reached the town of that name in January 1875 and the Russian River at Monte Rio the next year. Construction ended at Cazadero in 1886. The little railroad hauled timber during the week and picnickers on Sundays.

The standard-gauge San Francisco & North Pacific Rail Road was formed in 1869. After an interlude of ownership by Central Pacific, it came into the hands of Peter Donahue. He built a line to Cloverdale, 46 miles north of Petaluma, and extended the existing railroad, the Petaluma & Haystack, south to San Rafael. Scheduled service began in 1879. To create a faster route to San Francisco, Donahue formed the San Francisco & San Rafael Rail Road in 1882. In May 1884 it began service between San Rafael and Tiburon, where passengers boarded ferries for San Francisco.

John Martin, who was in the electric power trade, purchased the North Pacific Coast in 1902 and transferred ownership to his new North Shore Railroad. Martin electrified the North Shore with a third-rail system from Sausalito through San Anselmo to San Rafael and west from San Anselmo to Manor.

Meanwhile, about 300 miles north of San Francisco, lumbermen used nine little railroads located between Shively and Trinidad to bring redwood lumber to coastal ships in Humboldt Bay at Eureka. The Eel River & Eureka Railroad began transporting lumber from Burnell's (near Alton) to South Bay in 1884.

In 1903 Southern Pacific obtained control of most of the railroads reaching north from Sausalito and Tiburon and extended the main line of the San Francisco & North Pacific north over a 3 percent grade to reach Willits in 1902. The Atchison, Topeka & Santa Fe owned four lumber railroads around Eureka and the isolated line from Albion. The two railroads recognized that no more than a single railroad north to Eureka could be justified economically, and they jointly formed the Northwestern Pacific Railroad Co. on January 8, 1907 (the deal included the transfer of some track in southern Arizona).

New surveys of a line to close the 106-mile gap between Willits and Shively were necessary because the previous work had been lost in the 1906 San Francisco fire. Construction began at both ends in November 1909, and W. S. Palmer, president of the NWP, drove the last spike on October 23, 1914, at Cain Rock, 12 miles south of Fort Seward. Through operations began on July 1, 1915.

Southern Pacific became sole owner of the Northwestern Pacific on January 17, 1929. Four years later NWP acquired the Petaluma & Santa Rosa Railroad, an interurban that linked the towns of its title. During the 1930s various branches became superfluous because of the growth of highway competition. The opening of the Golden Gate Bridge brought an end to suburban train service in Marin County on February 28, 1941. Freight kept the railroad busy during World War II; the postwar building boom kept traffic high, but that was not to last.

The Eel and Russian rivers were prone to flood; wood-lined tunnels burned readily; and much of the NWP was built on unstable soil. Storms in December 1964 devastated 100 miles of NWP track at 25 places in the Eel River canyon. Restoration of the line under the direction of Charles E. Neal, general manager of the NWP, was celebrated on June 16, 1965, with a redriving of the 1914 golden spike.

The end of the Northwestern Pacific began on September 1, 1983, when the company applied to abandon all track north of Outlet, 4 miles north of Willits. No action ensued immediately, but on November 1, 1984, Brian Whipple, a former SP staff member, negotiated purchase of the railroad north of Outlet and formed the Eureka Southern Railroad.

In 1985 and in some succeeding years another group operated a passenger train, the *North Coast Daylight*, through the scenic Eel River canyon. The river allowed the railroad one trouble-free season, but flooding in February 1986 caused the suspension of Eureka Southern trains for months. Costly repairs and insufficient business forced the Eureka Southern into bankruptcy in December 1986, but operations continued until April 1, 1992, when the North Coast Railroad (authority) bought the property.

Ownership of the NWP south of Ignacio passed to the Golden Gate Bridge, Highway & Transportation District, while another public agency, the Northwestern Pacific Railroad Authority, acquired the remainder of the railroad. The California Northern Railroad began running trains over the NWP from Schellville to Willits in September 1993 but terminated its operating agreement in 1996 after two seasons of floods.

Marginal operations struggled while state or federal aid was anticipated to restore the physical plant and assist with expenses, but bureaucratic confusion prevented any success. The Federal Railroad Administration ordered the authority to install highway crossing signals and other safety improvements. The railroad had no money to do the work, and the FRA ordered the railroad shut down on November 25, 1998. Although politicians frequently expound on the necessity of restoring the line to Eureka, the former Northwestern Pacific Railroad remained dormant in 2006.

By 1959 the Northwestern Pacific was essentially a division of Southern Pacific and had no rolling stock of its own. It operated 328 route-miles and 467 track-miles; its primary item of freight traffic was outbound lumber and wood products. A diesel car operated triweekly (later twice a week) until 1971 carrying passengers between Willits and Eureka. NWP operating revenues totaled $13.9 million in 1959.

—David F. Myrick

REFERENCES

Dunscomb, Guy L., and Fred A. Stindt. *The Northwestern Pacific Railroad*. Kelseyville, Calif.: Fred A. Stindt, 1964.

Kneiss, Gilbert H. *Redwood Railways*. Berkeley, Calif.: Howell-North, 1956.

O

Occupations

Railroaders have many occupations, grouped in various ways. An informal distinction sometimes made is between *railroaders* and *civilians*, those not working on a railroad. A formal distinction is between *operating employees* (also called *ops*), who operate trains and engines and handle cars, and *nonoperating employees* (*nonops*), who provide support of all kinds to the former. Among the operating employees, the railroads often distinguish among those in *engine service* (locomotive engineers, locomotive firemen, hostlers, assistant engineers, and student engineers), *train service* (conductors and brakemen), and *yard service* (switchmen and switchtenders).

The largest organizational part of a railroad is the *operating department*, with about 80 percent of all employees. This superdepartment is sometimes divided into three functional units, the *transportation department*, which operates the trains and engines and handles the cars, the *mechanical department*, which inspects, services, repairs, and constructs locomotives and cars, and the *engineering department*, which inspects, maintains, repairs, and constructs track and structures. On some roads, the mechanical and (civil) engineering departments are within an overall engineering department. The civil engineering department usually has three large subunits, *maintenance-of-way* (MOW), *bridge and building* (B&B), and *communications and signals* (C&S). The mechanical department crafts are grouped as *shopcrafts*. A now-small engineering unit is *water service* (sometimes now included in an electrical and water *utilities department*). Confusing to "civilians," the employees of the mechanical and engineering departments are in the operating department but are called nonops by railroaders. This insider usage equates ops with most transportation employees. Such employees also call themselves *rails*.

Departments outside the giant operating department include *executive* (or *administration*), *law*, *traffic* (with subdepartments *marketing* and *sales*), *finance and accounting*, *personnel* and *labor relations* (often grouped as *human resources*), *management information services* (MIS), and an independent *special agent* unit. Depart-

The train crew of Chicago & North Western train 501, the Chicago-Minneapolis *Viking,* is ready for departure from Madison, Wisconsin, in May 1955. —William D. Middleton

ments or subdepartments are *planning and development*, *real estate*, *insurance*, *purchasing*, *materials management*, and *comptroller*. Most of the positions in the departments outside the operating department have tasks similar to those in other industries, with exceptions noted later. Law and labor relations personnel deal with the Railway Labor Act, unique to the railroad and airline industries. *Agreement employees* are subject to the terms of a labor agreement between a railroad and a union. *Exempt employees* are not covered by a labor agreement.

Operating Employees

Brakeman: Also called trainman (which see). At times inspects train before departure; attends to any setouts and pickups of cars en route; couples and uncouples cars; aligns track switches and derails; flag-protects train when necessary; inspects other trains en route for defects; today, sometimes sets and releases retainers; sets and releases hand brakes on cars; gives and receives hand and voice-radio signals; bleeds air from brake system; couples air-brake hoses and makes air-brake tests; and monitors operations by the operating rules and authority to occupy the main track. Brakemen in passenger service today are often designated as *assistant conductors*. In passenger service brakemen have the same duties as in freight service, although setouts and pickups of cars are rare, and they attend to tickets and other matters for passengers. Today, except for local freights doing heavy switching of cars, few brakemen remain in freight service. The brakeman on the freight engine or front passenger cars was the *head* (i.e., front) *brakeman*, the one on the caboose or the rearmost passenger car was the *rear brakeman/flagman*, and any other brakemen on a train were the *swing brakemen*. In the nineteenth century brakemen hand-braked trains to control speed or stop in response to the engineer's whistle signals. As late as the 1950s swing brakemen were still required continuously to "decorate the tops" of freight cars in certain territories, for example, on the descending grade of the Santa Fe's Cajon Pass. I observed this practice in Mexico in the 1970s.

Conductor: On most railroads, since at least the late 1830s, the conductor is the employee in charge of a train or yard engine and all employees on it and is responsible for prompt and timely operations. On yard engines the conductor is usually called an *engine foreman* (see *switchman*). In freight service, at times inspects train before departure; attends to any setouts and pickups of cars en route; monitors, makes, and communicates records for train movement and for cars handled; couples and uncouples cars; aligns track switches and derails; receives traffic control directives from the train dispatcher; monitors the train movement directly controlled by the engineer regarding rail traffic control, observing signals, compliance with rules, and speed limits; flag-protects train when necessary; bleeds air from

The brakeman's job was particularly demanding and dangerous in the days before air braking. This drawing by A. B. Frost appeared in *The American Railway* (1892). —Middleton Collection

A nineteenth-century conductor. This drawing appeared in the August 1874 *Harper's New Monthly Magazine.* —Middleton Collection

Conductor Don Downer looks over his paperwork on the way into Stockton, California, on board the *California Zephyr* in March 1970. —Ted Benson, *Trains* Magazine Collection

brake system; inspects other trains en route for defects; gives and receives hand and voice-radio signals; today, sometimes sets and releases retainers; sets and releases hand brakes on cars; and couples air-brake hoses and makes air-brake tests. In passenger service conductors have the same duties as in freight service, although setouts and pickups of cars are rare, and they attend to tickets and other matters for passengers.

Engineman: Originally and still a synonym for locomotive engineer but expanded on some roads to include all engine service employees.

Groundman: A generic term designating switchmen, brakemen, conductors, switchtenders, and herders.

Herder: Transportation department employee, usually from the ranks of switchmen, (1) who assists a hostler in moving locomotives to and from trains or who couples and uncouples locomotives from departing and arriving trains; (2) who has duties similar to those of a switchtender (which see).

Hostler: Originally a transportation department locomotive engineer or fireman or a "permanent fixture" (i.e., one permanently assigned to a position) who operates locomotives without cars in roundhouse and shop areas (*inside hostler*) and who delivers locomotives to trains, sometimes at distant points in a terminal (*outside hostler*). Now also a mechanical department employee such as a machinist certified to move locomotives.

Hostler helper: A mechanical department employee who works with a hostler to service locomotives. This includes fuel, sand, and water servicing.

Locomotive engineer: The employee in immediate control of and with direct responsibility for the movement of a train or engine. On intricate levels, the locomotive engineer is an information processor and controller of a human-machine system that is often demanding to monitor. For safe, efficient operations, an engineer, among other things, must learn the train-handling constraints of every upgrade, downgrade, curve, turnout, crossover, auxiliary track such as passing siding, fixed signal location, crossing at grade, and speed restriction. He or she observes signals of all kinds, watches for obstructions and potential hazards along the right of way, and visually inspects his or her own and other trains. The engineer has little advance information on a particular train's handling characteristics. These comprise numerous dynamic, variably simultaneous and sequential events to be monitored continuously by the engineer for constantly changing inputs. In short, the engineer is the operator of an electromechanical system that is long (often a mile or more), heavy (usually many thousands of tons), fragile (it is easy to derail or "break in two" a train), mobile (at speeds from 1 to more than 100 mph and requiring great braking distances, proportionate to speed and weight), and highly dynamic (having up to a foot of drawbar slack for each entrained freight car and with individual car air brakes of varying power).

With hands on the responsive controls and eyes and ears on the informing indicators, the engineer handles and dynamically monitors a machine system with complex

The locomotive engineer and fireman pass through Tulsa, Oklahoma, on a freight train in October 1942. —John Vachon photograph, Office of War Information, Library of Congress (Neg. LC-USW3-9577-D)

subsystems, each having ever-varying critical statuses, while transiting a continuously changing environment that itself could have altered from trip to trip. He or she manipulates and monitors dynamic variables such as velocity, drawbar pull and compression on draft equipment, amperage in traction motors, train brake-pipe pressure and related brake-cylinder pressure on cars, brake-pipe leakage, independent locomotive brake-cylinder pressure, statuses reported by the end-of-train device, statuses reported by any "rear" and "swing" helper units back in the train consist remotely controlled by the engineer through radio signals, profile of train by car weight and type and by weight of blocks of cars, and power of dynamic electrical brakes. On steep grades any failure of the dynamic brake necessitating a short cycling of the automatic air brakes, perhaps with use of retainers and car wheel-cooling stops, must be anticipated. Too many operative dynamic brakes can cause a light car to compress in its draft gear, with buff forces causing its wheel flanges to ride up over the head of a rail to a derailment.

Locomotive engineer, assistant: Someone who assists the locomotive engineer with his or her tasks and monitors

Traveling at 80 mph, locomotive engineer Martin Lee was all business at the controls of his steam locomotive. —*Trains* Magazine Collection

operations by the operating rules and authority to occupy the main track.

Locomotive engineer, student: Someone in a training program to become a locomotive engineer. Training includes classroom, locomotive simulator, and hands-on instruction on trains under the tutelage of a locomotive engineer.

Locomotive fireman: Rarely found today on locomotives other than steam. Student and assistant locomotive engineers perform training and assisting tasks formerly done by firemen. On steam locomotives, fires a coal- or oil-fueled boiler via the firebox and keeps water (by an injector and water pump and water-level sight glass) and steam pressure at proper levels. Assists the engineer by servicing and maintaining the locomotive above the running board, including taking on fuel and water, and displaying the required train signals on the head end. On steam locomotives, "took on water" at water service facilities in locations including "jerkwater towns" or "tank towns." On locomotives other than steam, assists the engineer by inspecting and monitoring locomotive statuses and trouble-shooting to correct failures of locomotive equipment. On both kinds of locomotives, the fireman observes signals of all kinds, watches for obstructions and potential hazards along the right of way, visually inspects his or her own and

In a different era locomotive engineer Don Schlegel runs an Illinois Central GP7 diesel. The train was Omaha-Chicago freight train 2nd 76 eastbound across Illinois. —William D. Middleton

The work of the locomotive fireman was never easy in the steam era. This view is from the August 1874 *Harper's New Monthly Magazine.* —Middleton Collection

other trains, and monitors operations by the operating rules and authority to occupy the main track.

Messenger: A locomotive fireman who travels with and fires a live steam locomotive being moved in the consist of a train.

Pilot: An employee, ordinarily one promoted to engineer or conductor, on a train assisting an engineer or conductor who is unfamiliar with the rules for or the physical characteristics of the railroad on which he or she will operate.

Porter-brakeman: Formerly, on certain southeastern railroads, in passenger service, a black employee performing some head brakeman plus chair-car attendant or porter tasks.

Remote-control operator (RCO): A position not to be confused with *control operator* (see *operator, control* under "Nonoperating Employees, Not on Trains"). From the ranks of switchmen, conductors, brakemen, and locomotive engineers, an employee operating a remote-control locomotive (RCL) via digital, coded radio signals by manipulation and observation of a body-mounted console ("the box"). The *primary RCO* is the person who controls an RCL. When part of an RCL crew, the *secondary RCO* does not control the RCL, other than to stop it if necessary, but sole control can be transferred to him or her by the primary RCO.

Student: Any operating employee while training and, by extension, any operating employee in the first year or two of service, while still learning to be safe and effective.

Switchman: At times checks the cut of cars handled before departure; attends to setouts and pickups of cars at industrial and other sites; couples and uncouples cars; aligns track switches and derails; flag-protects movement when necessary; gives and receives hand and voice-radio signals; sets and releases hand brakes on cars; bleeds air from brake system; and couples air-brake hoses and makes air-brake tests. The head switchman is called an *engine foreman* (sometimes, *yard conductor*) and has the authority of a conductor for a yard locomotive and its crew. Within yard limits and other designated limits, the engine foreman and his or her crew conduct operations on main tracks, in yards, and in industrial areas. The one or more subordinate switchmen on a crew are collectively called *helpers*. If there are two or more helpers, the one "who follows the engine" is the *pin puller* and the other one (or two), working further afield, is a *field man*.

Switchtender: A switchman specifically assigned to tasks of the aligning of switches and giving of hand and voice-radio signals for entrance to and exit from a yard or an important route.

Trainman: Originally a synonym for brakeman but now a generic term meaning either conductors and brakemen or, instead, these two plus switchmen and switchtenders.

Yardman: A generic term meaning switchmen and switchtenders.

Nonoperating Employees, on Trains

Except for the express messenger, maintainer, and railway mail service employee, the following occupations have "hotel" tasks. By hotel tasks are meant those typically found in a large hotel concerning provision of beds, seating, meals and beverages, restrooms, baggage handling, entertainment (at times), and other services for paying people.

Attendant, chair car/coach: A railroad employee who

A switchman on the Indiana Harbor Belt Railroad gave a "go-ahead" to a cut of cars in the yard in January 1943. —Jack Delano photograph, Office of War Information, Library of Congress (Neg. LC-USW3-14190-D)

A baggage man wrestled cream cans into the combine car of Northern Pacific mixed train 154 at Glover, North Dakota, in April 1959. —William D. Middleton

attends to the needs of passengers in a chair car/coach (non-first-class car).

Baggageman: Traditionally, this position was taken from the ranks of brakemen. In baggage cars of passenger and mail and express trains, he or she loads, stores, and unloads luggage, mail, and railroad material and maintains related records. Tasks formerly were also done in combine cars and included handling milk cans, sometimes on a "good job" called a milk run. A *milk run* is a job with regular hours, making many stops, and having no great pressure on it.

Conductor, Pullman: A white employee of the Pullman Co., with a distinctive gold badge on his cap displaying "Pullman Conductor." He supervised black (and more rarely Filipino) Pullman porters and maids on Pullman sleeping cars and parlor cars and attended to the needs of the passengers (all first class) on these cars. The Pullman Co. built, owned, and operated its own cars and came to be designated a carrier by railroad under U.S. laws.

Cook, dining car: These employees, formerly often in a dining-car and hotel department, supervise galley helpers and prepare food and beverages for dining-car patrons.

Express messenger: An express-company employee who rode certain express cars in passenger and mail and express trains to handle and keep records of packages loaded and unloaded en route.

Maid, sleeping car: A Pullman Co. employee, rare after the 1930s, who attended to the needs of female passengers traveling in Pullman cars.

Maintainer: A mechanical department electrician who rode the diesel-electric locomotives on certain named passenger trains, such as the Union Pacific's *City of Los Angeles.* His responsibility was to keep the diesel-electric power plants in each unit at full performance. Thus, besides the engineer and fireman, he was, de facto, a third engine crew member.

News butcher/butch: A person, usually not a railroad employee, who sold newspapers, magazines, souvenirs, snacks, and sometimes sandwiches while walking and hawking in the aisles of passenger trains.

Porter, sleeping car: A Pullman Co. employee who attended to the needs of passengers traveling in Pullman cars, including making beds and shining shoes.

Railway mail service employee: One of a crew of post office employees who received, sorted for destination, and discharged mail on a railway post office car. Often mail sacks were caught "on the fly" from a wayside frame by using a special long, pivoted hook mounted in the doorframe of the post office car. Delivered mail sacks were tossed to a depot platform.

Steward, dining car: The employee, formerly always white, in charge of a dining car and its crew. He attended to the dining needs of passengers and made records of food inventories and money collected.

Waiter, dining car: The employee, formerly always black, who waited on tables in a dining car, taking orders and bringing food and beverages.

Nonoperating Employees, Not on Trains

Agent: A transportation department employee, usually from the ranks of clerks, who supervises a railroad's commercial interests at a large station, in a terminal, or across a district. An agent's *agency* is such a location for railroad business and is identified by accounting and station numbers.

Blacksmith: Tasks include repairing, welding, and fabricating items of heavy metal. Metal is often heated and softened in a forge and then joined to other such pieces, frequently with a power hammer. The metal is finally hardened and tempered.

Blacksmith-welder (B&B): Tasks include inspecting, modifying, repairing, and installing large steel components, such as on bridges.

Boilermaker: Tasks include working on boilers and related equipment such as tanks, drums, retorts, and large metal structures such as pilot snowplows. Inspects, repairs, and rebuilds boilers and other heavy sheet-metal assemblies. Tasks include laying out, cutting and grinding, fabricating, fitting, and then welding, riveting, and bolting components together. Components worked on include locomotive fronts, doors, running boards, and truck frames and roadway-machine derricks and booms.

Bridge tender: A transportation department employee who operates a movable bridge, usually over water.

Business representative (title varies): Tasks include working as the customer contact for small to medium accounts, handling development and coordination of the ongoing transactions for a particular line of business, and negotiating and developing prices. The representative determines customers' transportation needs, coordinates service from all departments, and achieves assigned revenue targets.

Caboose cleaner: Cleans and supplies cabooses on a caboose track. Few cabooses are still in service.

Carman: Today also called *freight car repairer.* Inspects, services, repairs, rebuilds, and constructs freight and pas-

Boilermaker's helper Homer Brandon crawled out of the firebox of a Santa Fe locomotive in the shops at Topeka, Kansas, in March 1943. —Jack Delano photograph, Library of Congress (Neg. LC-USW3-19446-D)

New York Central car inspectors Van Slyke and Whalen, better known as "car knockers," checked the wheels of a passenger train at Utica, New York, in 1950. —Tranquille, *Trains* Magazine Collection

senger cars. The craft uses hand tools, power tools, hoists, cutting torches, and welding equipment. Today carmen often inspect trains from a moving vehicle.

Carpenter (B&B): Work includes carpentry and other tasks related to the repair, maintenance, rebuilding, and construction of steel and timber bridges, tunnels, culverts, abutments, and buildings. Specific duties include painting, framing, installing timbers, pile driving, repairing masonry, pouring concrete, and other tasks. Some B&B positions specifically include *painter* and *mason*.

Claim agent: Tasks include managing and executing in the field claim processes regarding employee injuries and other personal injuries or allegations of injuries affecting the railroad. A claim agent investigates and records facts and arranges medical, rehabilitation, and vocational services for an injured employee's return to work. Also handles claims for damage to a freight shipment. Evaluates and resolves claims on behalf of a railroad and has a duty to minimize payout of claims. At times works with railroad or contract attorneys in a railroad's legal defense.

Clerk: An employee who does clerical work (preparing, maintaining, manipulating, distributing, and filing paper and electronic documents) in the various departments and the general office.

Clerk, bill: A transportation department employee who prepares waybills and other information regarding loaded freight cars. Other information includes freight shipping documents that includes routing, such as bills of lading, freight bills, arrival notices, delivery receipts, and copies, as necessary, for stations of origin and destination and accounting department(s) of carrier(s) involved. A *waybill* is an electronic or paper document prepared for a freight shipment on a common carrier containing origination point, destination, route, consignor, consignee, kind of freight, and transport charge.

Clerk, crew dispatching: A transportation department employee who calls on duty and assigns to jobs engine, train, and yard crews in accordance with their bids, bumps, seniority ranking, and contract provisions. He or she also maintains lists of assigned personnel and their jobs and those furloughed, on vacation, and on leave of absence. Today most calls are by telephone. Years ago, *call boys* of the crew dispatcher's office would also call in person those living or rooming in a stipulated proximity to the on-duty point. At some away-from-home terminals, those rooming in company-designated facilities still receive in-person calls from a *crew caller.*

Briefly, a *bid* occurs when an employee applies in writing (today, by computer) for a vacant or newly created job for which that employee qualified in his or her craft and

Clerks in the Milwaukee Road's Car-Scope car-tracing office in Chicago work to provide information on car location throughout the railroad's 10,600-mile system. —Milwaukee Road, *Trains* Magazine Collection

on his or her seniority district. The job is filled by seniority rank order on the governing "seni list." A *bump* occurs when an employee's job is either abolished or "readvertised" by the company because of a change in job characteristics. Then the employee has a bump and can thereby take the job, for which he or she is qualified, of any person

on his or her district, in his or her craft, and ranked lower on the "seni list." This process continues on down the line until the "low man" on the list is "furloughed," that is, "out on the street."

Clerk, intermodal: Tasks include receiving and dispatching intermodal containers and trailers, including re-

Clerks at Canadian Pacific's motive-power operations center at Montreal, Quebec, monitor the location of trains throughout the system in January 1975. —Kenneth A. W. Gansel, *Trains* Magazine Collection

lated preparing, maintaining, manipulating, distributing, and filing of paper and electronic documents.

Clerk, rate: This employee, among other things, must understand and use the rules of rail freight classification and contracts regarding the obligations and rights of shippers, consignees, and carriers; special freight services; and, in the past, matters of less-than-carload shipments and livestock contracts. Tasks include the divisions of rate agreements between involved carriers, which beyond the railroad can include waterway, trucking, and airline carriers. Rate work is computerized nowadays.

Clerk, tie down: Tasks include helping load and unload containers and trailers on long cuts of stationary cars, which must be mounted and dismounted.

Clerk, typist: Using a personal computer, this employee performs various clerical duties, including typing and filing correspondence and documents, helping prepare instructional materials and arrange for instructional space and conferences, ordering and maintaining levels of office supplies, preparing payments for invoices, serving as a receptionist, including answering telephones and taking messages, receiving and distributing mail, and making reservations.

Clerk, Utility: Tasks include driving operating employees to and from assignments, ordering and maintaining levels of supplies, distributing supplies to train and engine crews, supplying and servicing office machines, assisting in service to automotive vehicles, and doing janitorial tasks.

Clerk, yard: Assists a yardmaster by performing tasks that include checking cars into and out of a yard, preparing yard and industrial switch lists, and working on waybills. Today, computerization has reduced or replaced many of these tasks.

Coach cleaner: Cleans and supplies passenger cars.

Draftsman: In various departments, draws plans and diagrams of structures and machinery.

Drover: A nonrailroad employee formerly mentioned in the rules of many railroads as permitted to ride in the caboose. Drovers attended livestock under their care shipped in livestock trains, which no longer exist.

Electrician: Inspects, diagnoses, repairs, rebuilds, constructs, and installs electrical equipment. Tasks include work on electrical motors, generators, alternators, switching equipment found in electrical control cabinets, and electrical circuits for locomotives, cars, and buildings. Electricians use power and hand tools and hoists and cranes and have bench assembly tasks.

Electrician, catenary: Tasks center on installing, maintaining, and inspecting the catenary wiring and its supports. Catenary is a system of wires and insulators suspended from poles and overtrack bridges, supporting overhead *contact* (also *trolley*) wires having high voltages to energize, through a sliding contact shoe on its roof-mounted pantograph, an electric locomotive or self-propelled railcar. The contact wire is suspended from a supporting *messenger* wire by *auxiliary* wires.

Electrician, diesel-electric: Tasks specialize on diesel-electric locomotives and cranes.

Electronics technician: Builds, repairs, and maintains pole lines and supports; strings, connects, and maintains overhead and underground line wires, service wires, and cables, includ-

An electrician works to position preformed coils in the slots of the armature for a diesel-electric traction motor in 1956. —Robert Hale, *Trains* Magazine Collection

ing their supports; lays conduits for such wires and cables; does tasks for microwave and radio towers; and performs similar tasks in connection with telecommunications equipment.

Financial analyst: Leads, manages, and does qualitative and quantitative analyses regarding various business issues to develop reports for management. The analyst must coordinate activities with other departments and outside parties. Also develops account controls, performs analyses to monitor compliance with railroad policies and procedures, reconciles account balances, and advises on using computers and software applications.

Flagman: Any employee or contract worker providing flag protection, that is, giving hand, voice-radio, or other signals to a movement and for other purposes, in accordance with the rules.

Floating-equipment (marine) employee: A transportation department employee who crews tugboats, railcar floats, and ships carrying railroad equipment and/or passengers.

Foreman: This position, which includes those of the following five foremen, is that of a first-line supervisor that can be unionized under the provisions of the Railway Labor Act of 1926 as amended. Train dispatchers and yardmasters have the same variable status. Depending upon the desires of the holders of such a position on a particular railroad, the occupation may or may not be unionized. Foremen supervise the workers under their charge, including assurance of safe and efficient use of labor and materials. They see to the safe condition of track, structures, and rolling equipment in their care and prepare and maintain records of labor, materials, and work done.

Foreman, bridge and building: Bridge and building foremen additionally inspect bridges and culverts after a heavy rain or water flow and repair or protect them as necessary.

Foreman, car: Car foremen additionally see that freight and passenger cars remain in service only when in a safe condition and, if they are not, take them out of service for repair.

Foreman, roundhouse: Roundhouse foremen additionally see that locomotives and self-propelled railcars remain in service only when in a safe condition and, if they are not, take them out of service for repair.

Foreman, signal: Signal foremen additionally inspect wayside signals and highway grade-crossing equipment to see that they are in operable condition and repair or protect them as necessary.

Foreman, track: Track foremen additionally inspect track and the right of way, including after a heavy rain or water flow, and repair or protect them as necessary.

Freight handler: In the past, railroads handled less-than-carload (LCL) freight at their freight houses, which employed this occupation to load and unload railcars and highway trucks.

Gateman/watchman, grade crossing: These employees of the transportation department manually operate gates at a highway grade crossing or bodily flag these crossings on foot. These employees are rare today. Formerly their ranks were filled from employees who were severely injured on the job, usually with loss of limb(s).

Ice dock man: When manually iced refrigerator cars still plied the rails carrying fruit, vegetables, meat, and beer, these employees moved, with hooked poles, blocks of ice into the roof hatches of long cuts of "reefers" spotted alongside a long, car-high ice dock (icing facility). In the early 1950s the Watsonville-Salinas, California, area of the Southern Pacific's Coast Line generated as many as 600 dripping, iced loads daily in season. Today, only mechanical or specially insulated nonmechanical "reefers" and refrigerated containers on flatcars ply the rails. Most produce traffic was lost to trucks.

Instrumentman and *rodman:* Engineering department employees who perform tasks concerning surveying, in determining the location, form, and boundaries of a piece of land, by measuring lines and angles through principles of geometry and trigonometry.

Iron worker/welder (B&B): Iron workers inspect, repair, maintain, and construct bridges.

Laborer, automotive and MOW equipment: Work includes various tasks in shops for maintaining highway trucks and MOW equipment and on-track MOW equipment.

Laborer, engineering: A track laborer's job, using hand tools, consists of repairing, maintaining, rebuilding, and constructing railroad track. Duties include removing and replacing ties, pulling and driving spikes, shoveling rock ballast, loading and unloading equipment and material, and other tasks.

Laborer, mechanical: Mechanical laborers assist in the movement of locomotives in the shop area, perform servicing and cleanup of locomotives and work areas, and assist in fueling. See also *wiper* and *hostler helper.*

Machine operator (MOW): Operates various roadway machines for track work, both flanged wheeled on rails and rubber tired. Some on-rail machines are self-propelled and can pull up to 40 loaded freight cars.

Machinist: Inspects, repairs, maintains, rebuilds, and constructs machinery with hand and power tools and hoists. Some tasks include bench disassembly and assembly of components.

Machinist, diesel-electric mechanic: At large terminals, some machinists work as mechanics on locomotive diesel engines, air compressors, blowers, fuel pumps, and other components.

Mechanic, work equipment: In the engineering department, maintains and repairs the flanged-wheeled and rubber-tired machines used by machine operators for track work. Work is often done at the sites of track gangs.

Operator (telegrapher): Operators on railroads were originally all telegraphers capable of rapidly transmitting and receiving messages via electric dot-and-dash impulses sent over a wire. By the 1950s telephonic, teletype, and radio apparatuses largely replaced any requirement for an operator to "sling Morse." From railroad telegraphers' practice and terminology come several survivals

A Gulf, Mobile & Ohio car washer at Glenn Yard in Chicago cleans a car for the Chicago-Joliet commuter run in May 1974. —William A. Raia, *Trains* Magazine Collection

found in other industries. Radio and television are broadcast from *stations*, each of which has unique *call letters*. Some radio operators are called *hams*, and the telephone industry employs *operators*. All of these are transfers from railroading, as when a *ham* who was employed by, say, the Southern Pacific as an *operator* at San Luis Obispo would respond to the train dispatcher who sent him the *station call letters* for San Luis O*bispo—BI*. Railroad telegraphers would listen in on the *grapevine* (telegraphic network) for messages destined for other stations, to hear the latest news. Journalistic transmissions still sometimes end with the telegraphic code number *30*, railroadese for "end of transmission." Code *31* meant "do you understand [a train order]?" Originally, 31-orders from the *DS*, code for train dispatcher, had to be signed by the *C&E*, code for conductor and engineer.

Operator, block: Employee at a designated station at which the movement of trains is controlled by block signals manipulated by him or her.

Operator, control: Employee operating a centralized traffic control (CTC) or interlocking control machine or issuing track permits.

Operator, towerman: Employee using an operating con-

Northern Pacific operator Dan McDonald at Central Avenue Station, South Superior, Wisconsin, alongside the operator's traditional telegraph key and telephone in June 1966. —William D. Middleton

Operator L. S. Guyton controls the Atlantic Coast Line's busy RA Tower at Florence, South Carolina, in August 1957. —William D. Middleton

The work of an operator, towerman, was arduous in the manually operated interlocking switches of a large switch tower like this early one, illustrated in *The American Railway* (1892). —Middleton Collection

A more recent pneumatically operated interlocking tower like this one at Union Station, Chicago, in February 1943 made the work of the operator, towerman, a little less taxing. —Jack Delano photograph, Office of War Information, Library of Congress (Neg. LC-USW3-015830-D)

sole or older, long "armstrong" levers to change aspects of wayside signals and positions of appliances such as track switches and derails in an interlocking plant. The plant's signals and appliances are interconnected so that their aspects and movements must succeed each other in a predetermined sequence. The signals cannot be made to display conflicting routes. British towers are called signal boxes because all towers/boxes developed, in the 1830s and 1840s, from standard one-man sentry boxes, from which the first wayside signalers to trains plied their tasks.

Paymaster: A now-defunct railroad position. He and subordinates once traveled the railroad in a pay car to pay employees in cash.

Rail detector car operator: Employee or contract worker operating a self-propelled rail detector car for inspection of rails in the track. Uses automated and semiautomated ultrasonic test systems.

Ramp loader: Tasks comprise assisting in loading and unloading containers and trailers from flatcars, including mounting and dismounting such equipment in long cuts of cars.

Roadway worker: Any engineering department employee or contract worker doing engineering work, including MOW, B&B, and C&S, on or along the right of way.

Sheet-metal worker: Using hand and power tools, cutting torches, welding equipment, and hoists, inspects, maintains, and repairs pneumatic, fuel, water, sand, and hydraulic systems on locomotives. Also performs daily locomotive inspections for visible or audible defects in air, fuel, and water systems; disconnects or connects any piping coupling or piping necessary; and diagnoses malfunctions in diesel engines, air equipment, trucks, and other components.

Signal inspector (C&S): A *signal maintainer* (which see) who inspects wayside signals and grade-crossing protection equipment.

Signal maintainer (C&S): Installs, repairs, tests, and maintains railroad wayside signals and grade-crossing protection equipment. Tasks include loading and unloading supplies and heavy equipment on and from trucks, digging holes and trenches for cable, painting equipment, climbing and working on poles and signal masts and bridges, stringing cable and wire, and making electrical connections.

Special agent: An employee independent of any other department who serves as a railroad police officer, including detective. Provides safety and security to railroad employees and rail passengers and for rail freight and railroad property. The agents respond to hazardous-material incidents, property damage, and environmental degradations; investigate grade-crossing accidents and injuries and fatalities to outsiders involving the railroad; investigate criminal activities resulting in a loss to or on the railroad; assist claims personnel with investigating personal injuries to employees or outsiders; inspect shipments and their vehicles; and coordinate activities with outside police, fire, emergency, and other personnel.

Station master: A transportation department employee at a *station* (a place on the timetable designated by name) with a passenger depot. Such employees and *assistant station masters* attend to the comfort and convenience of passengers. They make informational announcements for passengers, handle mail, express, and baggage, and prepare and maintain reports.

Stationary engineer: A mechanical department employee who operates and maintains a stationary boiler, any

A signal maintainer worked on semaphore signals on an eastern line in the 1940s. —Ernest Black photograph, *Reading–Jersey Central Magazine*, *Trains* Magazine Collection

attached steam engine, and related equipment, mainly to provide steam and heat to railroad facilities.

Steel erector (B&B): He or she joins steel members in structures such as bridges.

Surgeon, company: A position much more common before the 1920s, when rail accidents to persons were common and railroad company hospitals existed, but now a rare medical and health administrative position, for policy rather than practice. In official railroad terminology *surgeon* includes *physician*.

Surgeon, local: Common before the 1960s, such contractors usually had their own local practice, were listed in the employees' timetable by station locale, and were on call as needed.

Timekeeper: An employee who reviews and approves the trip claims for the pay of operating employees.

Trackman: An MOW track laborer. See *Laborer, engineering*.

Train dispatcher: A transportation department employee who controls and supervises the safe and efficient movement of trains and their crews and authorizes the occu-

pancy of main tracks and sidings for train and roadway worker operations. Is a rail traffic controller who authorizes track occupancy by absolute signal indication or issuing written track permits, track bulletins, track warrants, direct-traffic-control directives, Form D permits, and, rarely today, clearances and train orders. Communicates such authorities to train crews, MOW and B&B gangs, track-car and hi-rail vehicle operators, and others. The train dispatcher maintains electronic and paper records of all operations for which he or she is responsible, ensures compliance with the operating rules and federal hours-of-service law and related tie-up requirements, and coordinates responses to train accidents and hazardous-material spills. Some dispatchers monitor and adjust a computer-aided dispatching (CAD) auto-routing system, and some either monitor and adjust or make decisions for and manipulate, from a console or keyboard, a centralized traffic control (CTC) system integrated with or independent of a CAD system.

Train dispatcher, chief: A transportation department employee who supervises train dispatchers. Also balances train crews, locomotives, and, formerly, cabooses so that these do not inefficiently accumulate or become in short supply on one or the other end of a dispatching district. A "chief" collects data and maintains databases for the efficient conducting of transportation.

A Santa Fe train dispatcher issued train orders in the telegraph room at Argentine, Kansas, in March 1943. —Jack Delano photograph, Office of War Information, Library of Congress (Neg. LC-USW3-19145-D)

A yardmaster at an Illinois Central hump yard at Chicago, Illinois, operates the retarders on the south hump in November 1942. —Jack Delano photograph, Office of War Information, Library of Congress (Neg. LC-USW3-10562-E)

REFERENCES

Christie, Hugh K., and James McKinney. *The Railway Foreman and His Job*. Chicago: American Technological Society, 1947.

Cottrell, W. Fred. *The Railroader*. Stanford, Calif.: Stanford Univ. Press, 1940 [most crafts].

Early, A. W. *The Train Dispatcher: A Manual of Railway Telegraphy*. Chicago: Henneberry, 1903 [telegrapher/operator, train dispatcher, chief train dispatcher].

French, Chauncey Dell. *Railroadman*. New York: Macmillan, 1938 [call boy, telegrapher, switchman, brakeman, baggageman, conductor, locomotive fireman, agent, yardmaster, 1873–1930].

Gamst, Frederick C. *Highballing with Flimsies: Working under Train Orders on the Espee's Coast Line*. Railway History Monograph: Research Journal of American Railways 19, nos. 1–2 (1990): whole issue [locomotive engineer, locomotive fireman, conductor, brakeman, operator, train dispatcher, yardmaster].

———. *The Hoghead: An Industrial Ethnology of the Locomotive Engineer*. New York: Holt, Rinehart & Winston, 1980.

Katz, Daniel, Nathan Macoby, Gerald Gurin, and Lucretia G. Floor. *Production, Supervision, and Morale among Railroad Workers*. Ann Arbor: Univ. of Michigan, 1951 [MOW employees].

Santino, Jack. *Miles of Smiles, Years of Struggle: Stories of Black Pullman Porters*. Illini Books ed. Urbana: Univ. of Illinois Press, 1991.

Spier, John S. "The Railroad Switchman: A Study in the Meaning of Work." Master's thesis, Univ. of California, Berkeley, 1963.

Winkler, Fred A. *Railroad Conductor*. Spokane, Wash.: Pacific Book, 1948.

Wyckoff, D. Daryl. *Railroad Management*. Lexington, Mass.: Lexington Books, 1976 [most departments].

Watchman, engine: Perhaps nonextant today. Formerly an employee who watched a steam locomotive left unattended at a remote location. For example, on the Glendale Branch of the Los Angeles & Salt Lake Railroad, an engine watchman attended the steam locomotive left behind by the crew of a local freight train who had to use an electric locomotive over city streets.

Water service employee: An engineering department employee who performs tasks for maintaining, repairing, installing, constructing, and sometimes operating machinery, piping, and storage tanks for water supply. Specific positions included *water service mechanic* and *water service pipe fitter*. Such employees became rare after the age of steam ended.

Wiper: A mechanical department employee who cleans engines with long-handled brushes, power hoses, and washrack facilities, especially in the time of steam locomotives. See also *Laborer, mechanical department*.

Yardmaster: A transportation department employee, usually from the ranks of switchmen, who controls train and yard engine movements within a yard or group of yards and, with the train dispatcher, on adjacent main tracks within yard limits (an operating designation). Also plans and directs the handling and timely distribution of empty and loaded cars in the yard(s) and adjacent industrial tracks and makes up departing and classifies (switches out) arriving trains in accordance with schedules. Other tasks include interchanging cars with other railroads, ensuring that cars are inspected, and spotting cars to be repaired at repair sites.

—**Frederick C. Gamst**

Official Guide of the Railways

As North American railroads developed into a regional system of connecting lines, growing numbers of passengers used them for extended journeys. Traveling for any distance among these individual railroads could be a daunting task. One was obliged to learn about connecting schedules, transfers between stations, fare information, and the like to successfully travel among the many separate companies. For Great Britain's growing railway network, and soon afterward in separate guides for the entire continent, this information was admirably provided by such national timetables as *Bradshaw's Guide* (published from 1838 until 1961) or the more recent *Cook's Continental Timetable* (published since 1873), and there was soon a host of similar timetables available for North American travelers.

Probably the first North American timetable guide was Disturnell's *Railroad, Steamboat and Telegraph Guide,* established in 1846. Another early guide, and one of the longest lived, was Appleton's *Railroad and Steam Navigation Guide*, established in 1848. Still other early publishers included Doggett's *Railroad Guide and Gazetteer*, also founded in 1848; Dinsmore's (later Batterman's) *Ameri-*

can Railway Guide, which began publication in 1850; and Lloyd's American Guide, established in 1857. The latter guide was particularly proud of its timetables, "new arranged time-tables, so easy that a child can understand them; it being universally acknowledged that all other guide books are so complicated that not one in a hundred can understand them."

Establishment of what would be called the Official Guide in 1868 emerged from apparent widespread dissatisfaction by railroad ticket and passenger agents with the accuracy of the Appleton or other guides or their financial arrangement with the railroads. The idea of the new official guide had been discussed over several years in meetings of the National Assn. of General Passenger and Ticket Agents of the railroads, which proposed that the guide would be the only one with the authority of, or recognized by, the passenger and ticket agents' association. For many years the front cover of the guide informed the National General Ticket Agents' Assn. of this resolution: "That The Official Railway Guide be considered the recognized organ of this Association." The editor for the new guide would be Edward Vernon, a former ticket agent for the St. Louis, Alton & Terre Haute Railroad. More than 30 passenger or ticket agents, representing some 12,000 miles of line, joined the new arrangement.

The first Travelers Official Railway Guide of the United States and Canada, to give it its full title, was published on June 1868, and the 280-page publication was impressive from the first. Railroad travel was the primary purpose of the guide, of course, and it included more than 200 pages of timetables, maps, and the names of principal officers of each railroad. There were some 360 railroads that extended all the way from New England and eastern Canada to the western reaches of the new Pacific Railroad, showing the schedules thus far complete and open from Omaha to Cheyenne on the Union Pacific and from Sacramento to Cisco, California, on the Central Pacific.

Sleeping-car services were noted on the timetables. Dining was typically confined to stopping points along the railways. The Bellefontaine Railway, in Ohio and Indiana, helpfully listed the locations at which its principal trains would stop for meals. The Union Pacific simply advised, "good eating houses at convenient points on the lines."

Until a national time standard was established in 1883, determining the correct time was one of the traveler's most vexing problems (see STANDARD TIME). The Official Guide tried to help with its "Comparative Time-Table," which compared the local time at principal cities with noon at Washington. The traveler between New York and Chicago, for example, could add the 12 minutes that New York was ahead of Washington to the 42 minutes that Chicago was behind Washington to get the 54-minute difference. Every railroad operated on its own timetable. The Grand Trunk Railway of Canada, for example, ran its trains on Montreal time, which meant that train schedule times would run 10 minutes slower than the local Quebec

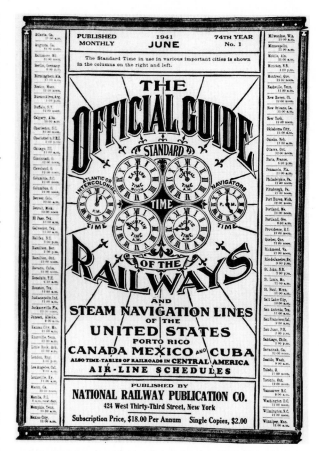

Official Guide of the Railways. —Trains Magazine Collection

time and 15 minutes slower than the local Portland time, while Buffalo train schedules would run 20 minutes faster than local Buffalo time and 21 minutes faster than local Toronto time. The Chicago, Alton & St. Louis Railway helpfully advised that it would operate on a standard time based upon the freight depot at Bloomington, Illinois.

The guide included a variety of what Vernon called "all such miscellaneous information relative to railway improvements and progress as may be useful to the traveling public." An appendix listed more than 5,000 railroad stations, together with the railroads served by each of them. The routes of principal express companies were included. There were a few miscellaneous advertisers. The Illinois Central was selling farmland along its railroad. The editorial section covered such diverse topics as annual reports from a number of railroads, noteworthy appointments and resignations, railway statistics from the State of Ohio, data on emigration to the United States in 1867, and various railroad developments. There was an account of coal-mining practice in Pennsylvania, a long paper on the various uses of India rubber, and a treatise on "What shall we do with our Young Ladies?" advocating a broader range of suitable female occupations.

The Official Guide grew with the railroads as new railroads expanded all over North America. There were other guides as well. Gilbert S. Baldwin's Free Railroad Guide was active in 1868 and in 1871 became Rand McNally & Co.'s *Western Railway Guide*, soon changed to the *Railway Guide*. Except for a suspension after the great Chicago fire in 1872, the *Railway Guide* continued as a separate publication until 1919, although it was taken over by the National Railway Publication Co., also the publisher of the *Official Guide*, in 1877. But National Railway Publication acquired the rival Appleton's *Railroad and Steam Navigation Guide* and set up the new *Knickerbocker Ready Reference Guide*, a specialized guide for the New York area. The Knickerbocker Guide Co. began publication of the *Travelers' Ready Reference Guide*, which incorporated such useful additions as the "Ready Reference Index to Routes between Principal Cities" and the extensive "Tourist Guide to the Principal Watering Places, Springs and Places of Fashionable Resort in the United States and Canada." This publication went through several title changes before becoming eastern and western guides titled *Pocket Edition of the Official Railway Guide*. Both were discontinued in 1919.

The main *Official Guide* became enormous. In its 50th edition the *Guide* proclaimed that it was "undoubtedly the largest monthly publication in the world." Virtually every North American railroad, both passenger and freight, was listed. In addition to timetable information, passenger schedules provided full information about train names, accommodations, and connecting services. The publication's original scope was ultimately expanded to include Mexico, Central America, Puerto Rico, and Cuba. In addition to showing connecting steamship and barge lines in North America, the *Guide* advertised for both passenger and freight ships operating as far afield as the Far East or the Mediterranean. In later years many airline companies advertised in the guide, and there was a separate guide to air passenger lines throughout the world. Many railroads also advertised the schedules of their premier scheduled freight trains. Interstate and over-the-road bus schedules were once included. Hotel advertising became an important addition to the guide. Every issue provided extensive editorial comments about new equipment and services, official changes and appointments in the railroad industry, and the like. The guide listed all U.S. military installations, complete with connecting railroad stations, and U.S. government hospitals. U.S. and Canadian national parks were listed, together with their connecting railroad stations.

Any required changes to timetables were submitted to the guide from the railroads on a monthly basis, to be incorporated into the next edition. At the time of its 100th anniversary, the publisher advised that it could make a train time change and put it on press within 20 minutes of receipt. From its very first issue, Edward Vernon had made the correctness and reliability of the guide his watchwords. Its reputation for accuracy was said to have been such that once, when someone brought an erroneous scheduled stop in the guide to the railroad's passenger traffic manager, the manager replied: "Well, if the *Official Guide* says the train stops there, then, dammit, have it stop there!"

The guide was also widely used for the routing of freight traffic, providing an index of stations and railroad routes at thousands of locations. In 1968, for example, less than 20 percent of the railroads listed in the guide even carried passengers.

The *Official Guide* reached its zenith in its issue of January 1930, when it published an issue of 1,796 pages, its largest ever. Official maps, timetables, and other information were supplied for 992 railroads, 176 marine and barge lines, 5 airlines, and 10 other shipping lines. Its railroad station index alone took 263 pages to list some 76,000 points. With the transportation decline of the Great Depression, and with the growth of competing transport modes, the guide gradually retrenched, but remained a significant transportation source for several decades after World War II. During World War II and immediately after, the railroads transported an unprecedented passenger volume, and the *Official Guide*s of that period typically carried 1,500 pages or more. For more than a century the monthly issues of the guide provided an extraordinary insight on railroad travel in North America. "The files of *The Official Guide*," remarked the publishers on its 50th year, "contain almost the only record of many phases of transportation development, particularly in the combination of through routes, the accelerated time of trains, the improvement in the comfort of equipment, and many other features which distinguish American travel."

By the date of the guide's centennial in June 1968, the number of railroad timetables required for North American schedules had shrunk to less than half the number carried in the record issue of January 1930. By the time the substantial reductions and consolidation of trains had been made by Amtrak in 1971, the guide had declined still more, to less than a quarter of the pages that it had had only a few years before. Nevertheless, for over two decades more the guide kept coming out every month, or later every two months, with current timetables and equipment schedules, an index of all railroad stations, tour operators and tourist lines, editorial material, and the like. The *Official Railway Guide* published its final edition of North American railroad passenger service in 1995. The current publisher, Commonwealth Business Media, continues to publish the *Official Railway Guide*, covering North American freight service, every other month, a quarterly *Pocket List of Railroad Officials*, and other railroad freight directories. North American passenger rail, selected motorcoach, and shipping service schedules are still published every two months by Great Britain's *Thomas Cook Overseas Timetable*.

—William D. Middleton

REFERENCES

Official Guide of the Railways, 101st Year, no. 1, June 1968.
Travelers' Official Railway Guide of the United States and Canada, June 1868. Facsimile. New York: National Railway Publication Co., 1968.

Ontario Northland Railway

In 1884 the boundary between the Canadian provinces of Ontario and Quebec was determined. The lower part of the boundary was formed by the Ottawa River, from a point near its mouth to Lake Temiskaming. Soon afterward settlers living in Ontario near Lake Temiskaming asked for a railway, both to help with colonization and to tie their area to Toronto, about 350 miles south. In 1902 Ontario's legislative assembly created a commission to build and operate the Temiskaming & Northern Ontario Railway (T&NO). The commission opted to create a government railway rather than authorize a new privately financed one through the sparsely settled area or build a railway to be operated by one of the existing railroads, such as Grand Trunk or Canadian Pacific.

Construction of the T&NO began at North Bay, located on Canadian Pacific's Montreal-Sudbury line and at the end of a Grand Trunk line from Toronto. The railhead reached Englehart, well past Lake Temiskaming, in 1906, and by 1909 the T&NO had reached Cochrane, where it connected with the National Transcontinental Railway (NTR), still under construction. Early on, the T&NO was a supply line for the NTR, and later it formed part of a through route to the West, in conjunction with the Grand Trunk south of North Bay and the NTR west of Cochrane.

The discoveries of silver at Cobalt in 1903 and of gold near Timmins in 1909 were a major boost to the railway's ledgers. In addition, the railway helped develop the Clay Belt agricultural area and the forest through which it ran. A subsidiary, the Nipissing Central Railway, built east from Swastika across the provincial border to the gold-mining center of Noranda, Quebec. In 1931 the T&NO opened a line from Cochrane north to the shore of James Bay at Moosonee.

Shortly after World War II, in 1946, the name of the railway was changed to Ontario Northland (ON) to avoid confusion with Southern Pacific's Texas subsidiary, the Texas & New Orleans Railroad, and also to more accurately describe its territory. Still owned by the province of Ontario, the ON earned most of its revenue carrying the products of Ontario's mines and forests. Passenger services included a daily Toronto-Cochrane round trip, the *Northlander*; a year-round triweekly Cochrane-Moosonee mixed train, the *Little Bear*; and a summertime daily Cochrane-Moosonee *Polar Bear Express* round trip aimed at tourists. Ontario Northland Transportation Commission (ONTC), parent company of the railway, also operated buses, trucks, boats, airplanes, and communications services in northern Ontario.

—George H. Drury

REFERENCE

Tucker, Albert. *Steam into Wilderness*. Don Mills, Ont.: Fitzhenry & Whiteside, 1978.

Opera and the Railroads

Early in the nineteenth century small opera companies began traveling wherever transportation was available. Needless to say, not all of what went under the name of opera was what we would call opera today. Some were musical shows, western "horse operas," or minstrel shows. On the other hand, the word *opera* had a magic to it, and many small towns, some with nothing more than a few barns, corn cribs, a saloon, and a jail, built "opera houses," hoping that eventually opera companies would come. Most of these houses never saw an opera company, although many were eventually able to draw in poor-quality theatrical companies or stock companies (*see* THEATRICAL TOURING COMPANIES). Some of those lasted over the years to become movie houses or "little theaters" in modern generations.

The United States was, however, to witness the largest movement of grand opera companies in human history, but this had to wait until after the Civil War, when the railroad network, at least in the East, was essentially complete. For well over a century opera companies have toured, and for most of the time this touring was accomplished on the railroad. The movement of entire casts, scenery, costumes, support personnel, and everything needed to put on professional productions often required two or more long trains of Pullmans and baggage or freight cars. Touring by rail became commonplace for opera performers in America and remained so until the 1960s.

Consider the case of the Metropolitan Opera Co. of New York, which surely holds the record for the number and quality of tours over the years, most of them by rail. The Metropolitan began tours as soon as the company took its present name in 1883 and, with a few interruptions, toured until the 1980s, managing to visit nearly all the major cities of the eastern United States. Occasionally it ventured west of the Rockies. And it invariably played to sold-out houses. Until the advent of the movies, opera was a popular art form, not thought of exclusively as "highbrow." The names of opera stars were known far and wide, and their coming was often greeted with wild enthusiasm.

So great was opera's popularity that in the late nineteenth century numerous companies began to compete with the Metropolitan's juggernaut and with one another. The German-born conductor Walter Damrosch established a company devoted exclusively to touring in 1894. Early in the twentieth century the touring company of the Met was aggressively challenged by the very resourceful Oscar Hammerstein (grandfather of Oscar Hammerstein II, the famous lyricist) with his Manhattan Opera Co. For a number of years Boston had its own company, which also gave the Met a run for the money. Some other cities, such as Chicago and San Francisco, had opera companies, and beginning in the 1920s these companies entered the big time, with first-rate stars. They too took to the rails to show off their wares.

The touring of the large opera companies was by no

The Chicago Opera Assn., headed by General Director Mary Garden, made a stop for publicity photos at tiny Drexel, Montana, on its Milwaukee Road special tour to the Pacific Northwest in March 1922. —Asahel Curtis Photo, Washington State Historical Society (Curtis Neg. 42761)

means a minor operation. In 1940, for example, the Metropolitan Opera Co. visited 13 cities. In Cleveland, one of its regular venues, it put on eight different operas between April 8 and April 18: *Aida, Tannhäuser, La Bohème, Carmen, Madama Butterfly, Tristan und Isolde, La Traviata,* and *La Gioconda*. All had their own stars, costumes, and scenery, which had to be moved by railroad transportation.

The rule at the Met was "everything but the opera house itself must go." Accordingly, huge trunks and crates of scenery had to be loaded. In addition to the stars and members of the orchestra and chorus, there were stagehands, makeup artists, wardrobe people, paymasters, secretaries, and roustabouts—all had to go so that no temporary hiring on location would be needed. Around the time of the Cleveland productions just mentioned, the Met used two special trains consisting of 18 sleeping cars and about 22 baggage cars. All scenery had to be capable of being reduced to dimensions not exceeding six feet so the pieces could fit through a baggage-car door.

The usual procedure for the famous annual spring tour was for preparations to be made the moment the last show in New York was staged. The scenery was taken apart, costumes were put in huge wardrobe trunks, and an army of trucks (in earlier times drays or wagons) were dispatched to the Mott Haven Yards of the New York Central Railroad. (Naturally, if the company was going south, to Philadelphia, Baltimore, or Atlanta, which it did almost every year, the properties might be sent to the Pennsylvania's station in Jersey City.) Most of this activity took place at night, carried out by local hauling companies at considerable expense. Early in the morning the trains would back into Grand Central or Penn Station and pick up the personnel. And off they went.

Members of the company had their own Pullman sleeping rooms, although there were dining and lounge cars for camaraderie. When the trains reached their destinations, the cast invariably stayed in comfortable commercial hotels. In earlier times the great stars had their own private cars, sometimes owned by them personally. Invariably such cars were attached to the end of the train. Divas Adelina Patti and Lillian Nordica, who dominated the opera world a century ago, traveled like royalty. Dame Patti had a palatial car with her name in gilt lettering on the side. She toured with her own retinue of servants, including her personal chef. Such extravagances were long gone by the middle of the twentieth century, but later companies traveled in very comfortable circumstances.

In the great days of railroad travel a performance was seldom missed because of failure of the special opera trains to arrive. Usually when there were mishaps, they were at the local destination, not en route. In 1948 Atlanta was to have a performance of *Carmen,* but a coal strike called by mine workers' chief John L. Lewis caused the opera specials to be hitched to the *Peach Queen* and the *Piedmont*. The costumes failed to arrive on time, and Risë Stevens and Kurt Baum improvised costumes with scarves; Licia Albanese performed in a black street dress.

The Metropolitan generally limited itself to the eastern United States, but in April 1906 the company reached San Francisco and gave two performances before the San Francisco earthquake and fire. The world's most famous tenor, Enrico Caruso, was tossed out of his bed in the St. Francis Hotel and appeared in the lobby wearing pajamas and a scarf. "'ell of a place, 'ell of a place," he swore. "I never come here again." And he did not. No one from the company was killed, but thousands of dollars worth of costumes were lost, as well as personal possessions and mementos. Members of the company, all with horror tales to tell, returned to their train at the Southern Pacific's Oakland Mole in shattered and battered condition for the trip back to Chicago.

Since San Francisco established a major opera company of its own in 1923 and was able to adequately serve West Coast cities, the Met seldom had to venture to the West. When it finally decided to visit Los Angeles in 1948, bad luck struck again. In a tour that also included Denver, the special train struck a car stalled on the tracks at a crossing in El Paso, and several people were killed. There was a long delay, but somehow the company was able to open on time at the Shrine Auditorium in Los Angeles with *Carmen*. Fortunately, serious mishaps were few, and never did they have the effect of completely canceling any engagement.

The Met continued touring until the 1980s, but after the 1960s the casts went by air and the properties by truck. Many old-timers lamented the loss of the special trains. Soprano Roberta Peters, who came to the Met in 1950 and stayed for 35 seasons, remembers rail touring with great fondness. In the early days she traveled with her mother, later with her husband, in her own private drawing room. She recalled endless card games in the lounge cars, plenty of gossip, and adequate opportunity for reading, relaxing, and fraternization. This experience created a bond that could be formed in no other way. She might perhaps have added that rail travel in those days was just plain fun. It certainly beat being shipped like eggs in a crate, however speedily.

—George H. Douglas

REFERENCES

Eaton, Quaintance. *Opera Caravan: Adventures of the Metropolitan on Tour.* New York: Da Capo, 1978.

Hamilton, David, ed. *Metropolitan Opera Encyclopedia: A Comprehensive Guide to the World of Opera.* New York: Simon & Schuster, 1987.

Operating Rules and Enforcement

The nature of railroading, with trains operating day and night in every weather condition and a workforce typically operating remote from supervisory management, has made individual accountability for rules compliance of para-

mount importance. Steady growth of rail traffic, heavier locomotives and cars, higher operating speeds, and the impact of new technologies have all required continuous effort to develop improved operating procedures. Railroad rulebooks require frequent revision. Operating staff training and testing have been established to assure that the rulebook is understood and followed, and North American railroads have historically imposed severe penalties for failures.

The Rulebook

In the industry's earliest days train movements were governed strictly by timetables for the operating staff, which contained not only the schedules but also rules and special instructions. The timetable was the sole authority for the movement of a train. Trains were assigned numbers, and meets were positive, which could lead to some lengthy delays when one train ran into difficulty. Some trains, usually running as an extra section of a scheduled train, were operated without timetable authority and were required to clear all scheduled trains. The role of the dispatcher, who planned the day's train movements, evolved from timetable operation. In addition to train schedules, the timetables contained such essential train-operating rules as whistle signals, use of the bell, hand signals, when and how to clear superior trains, the duties of engineers and conductors, and other matters that in the aggregate were essential to getting a train over the road.

By the 1840s the system had become a little more sophisticated with the introduction of directional authority, under which trains in one direction had priority. Train operation took a giant step forward with the development by Erie Railway superintendent Charles Minot in 1854 of a system of telegraphic orders, which could supersede the timetable when necessary and move inferior trains against superior trains. By the 1880s second- and even third- and fourth-class trains were established, and train orders permitted the operation of extra trains not in the timetable.

There were further requirements for clearing opposing trains, whistle signals, hand signals, and the like. Markers denoting the end of a train were introduced, and there was some standardization in the methods of transmitting and receiving train orders. Form 19 train orders did not require a signature and could be delivered to a train without stopping by "hooping" them up from an operator, while Form 31 orders required signatures by the train crew. The use of classification signals with flags or lights became common: white for extra trains and green to indicate a following section. Trains were dispatched through wayside telegraphers, and the passage of trains was recorded in the dispatcher's train sheet for the territory. In this era of classic timetable and train-order operation every dispatcher's nightmare was to put out a train-order lap that would have permitted two trains to occupy the same section of track at the same time. The lapped train order and impending disaster are a recurrent theme in railroad fiction.

The Erie published a separate rulebook as early as 1857, and evidence indicates that the U.S. Military Railroads issued one during the Civil War. But even with the added complication of telegraphic train orders and manual block, separate rulebooks did not become common until the late 1880s. After the adoption of Standard Time in 1883, the General Time Convention (a predecessor of the present-day Assn. of American Railroads) under its secretary, W. F. Allen, adopted the Uniform Train Rules and Rules for the Movement of Trains by Telegraphic Order in 1889. There was still wide variation, however, in how individual railroads adopted the standard code. There were differences in train-order signals, the exact language of train orders, when a train had to be in the clear for a superior train, the placement of class lights on a locomotive, the color of markers, and even hand signals. A greater uniformity was achieved with a new Code of Standard Train Rules adopted in 1899, but frequent updates were required because of new technology and increasingly heavy traffic.

Mechanical interlockers had been around since the 1870s, and now automatic block signaling (ABS) and electric interlocking were introduced. In another two decades automatic train stop and cab signals were adopted. An entire new section was added to the rulebook concerning signal indications and a variety of automatic block rules. Telephone dispatching was being introduced, and as early as the 1920s the Pennsylvania Railroad eliminated the use of the telegraph.

Railroad rules were becoming increasingly complex, and there was soon a body of literature available to help explain them. The best of these, long consulted by railroad operators, was *Rights of Trains*, first published in 1904 by the Western Pacific's Harry W. Forman and carried on in many editions by Peter Josserand for more than half a century. Every train dispatcher worth his salt had one in his desk drawer. Though now long obsolete, *Rights of Trains* is still in print from Simmons-Boardman.

Still more new technology was introduced in the 1920s—automatic train stop, cab signaling, and the most important of all, the first installation of centralized traffic control (CTC) (*see* SIGNALING) in 1927 on the New York Central's Ridgeway Tower in Ohio.

There were more changes in operating rules as many of the major eastern roads became multiple track, and trains were automatic block dispatched through manned interlockers. Trains moving in the current of traffic were permitted to run on signal indication alone. Train orders were necessary only to move against the current of traffic or for "slow orders."

With CTC came another major advance, with operating rules that permitted the movement of trains in both directions by signal indication only. Timetable and train-order rules continued to prevail on non-CTC-equipped single-track main lines or branch lines, but the rules were simplified. Some branch lines were turned over to some form of staff system, which required physical possession of a staff by a train crew to operate over the territory, or

Issuance of Form 19 orders "on the fly" was a familiar ritual of train operation. In June 1966 the engineer of the Great Northern's train 23, the *Badger*, picked up his copy of a Form 19 order (*top*) at South Superior, Wisconsin. The conductor's copy of a Form 19 order (*bottom*) was picked up by conductor C. W. Tevis from the caboose at the rear of an eastbound freight train at Dalies, New Mexico, in March 1943. —(top) William D. Middleton; (bottom) photographer Jack Delano, Office of War Information, Library of Congress (Neg. LC-USW3-21136-E)

train-register operation, which required that a crew sign a register book before they entered the territory that gave them exclusive right to occupy that branch. Manual block signals were often eliminated when passenger trains were discontinued. The rule for flagging behind a stopped train that could be overtaken by a following train was dropped in signaled territory in ABS and CTC territory, and some carriers allowed a train to pass a stop and proceed indication at restricted speed. Radio came on the scene with an entire new body of rules, and more than one accident was caused by poor radio procedure.

Along with simplified operating procedures, some efforts toward greater uniformity came in the 1930s. The Great Northern and the Northern Pacific agreed on the Consolidated Code, and the Rock Island, Missouri Pacific, and Cotton Belt came together on the Uniform Code. Regardless, in 1950 there were still 110 Class 1 railroads and 105 different rulebooks.

In 1955 the Bessemer & Lake Erie completed a CTC installation and a new, simplified rulebook. The traditional written Form 19 and Form 31 train orders issued by the operator were replaced by simple preprinted "train-order" Form X and Form Y, which were copied directly by the train crews without the complications of train orders. These were the prototypes of what were later called "track warrants," a temporary oral order to a train crew or track equipment operator that, after being copied in writing on a prescribed form and repeated back to the control station for verification, permits entrance and occupation of the specified main-line track. The Pennsylvania, too, was eliminating train orders and operators with its block limit stations and verbal authority on "secondary track." The Rock Island even experimented with radio dispatching. There were still more moves toward simplification. On most carriers schedules were eliminated and all trains ran extra, thus eliminating or reducing the complications of sections, rights over, waits, and the like for both train service employees and train dispatchers.

But the changes in operating rules that could be made were inhibited by the labor unions. This all changed in 1984, when the Railway Adjustment Board ruled that the clerks' union did not have exclusive rights to the copying of train-movement orders. In an instant the practice of well over a century in train operation and an entire class of employees were rendered obsolete.

The railroads lost little time in implementing the new decision. Some, such as the Southern Pacific, went to what they called direct train control (DTC), a system in which the dispatcher verbally authorized train movements by radio from block to block directly to the train instead of through written instructions to a wayside tower operator for hand delivery to a train. Most other roads opted for track-warrant control (TWC), using a preprinted form similar to the Bessemer & Lake Erie's X and Y forms, but standardized to cover a variety of potential instructions. A standard form recommended by the General Code of Operation rules, for example, lists 17 standard instructions. The dispatcher selects the appropriate lines of the warrant form and issues the form directly to the train crews by radio. Both systems were enhanced by the addition of personal computers located at the dispatcher's desk designed to avoid overlapping authority.

Over the next few years the wholesale merger of the major railroads brought new rulebooks. The western carriers joined together and developed the General Code, and, realizing that the language of the old rulebooks was out-of-date, they hired a consulting firm in 1993 to rewrite the rules from page 1 in simple, straightforward language. The result would be scarcely recognizable to an old veteran. Others soon followed, and the new Standard Code adopted in 1996 was written in the same style.

Today only five rulebooks are in use in the United States. The western roads use the General Code, CSX and Norfolk Southern each have their own, and the northeastern lines such as Amtrak use the Northeastern Operating Rules Advisory Committee (NORAC) rulebook, except for Metro-North, which has its own separate rulebook. Although all are similar, there are still differences. CSX uses direct train control, while the western lines and NS use track warrants. Supplementing the operating rules is the railroad employee operating timetable, not to be confused with a public timetable, which advertises arrivals and departures of passenger trains. Railroads issue employee timetables for each operating division as often as circumstances dictate, in some instances as often as two or three times annually. They contain localized "special instructions," noting exceptions to and changes in the operating rules; a schedule, which lists stations and the times at which numbered trains are due to pass, arrive at, and depart them; and the designation of tracks, maximum permissible speeds, and the prescribed method of operation. Day-to-day conditions that affect the movement of trains, such as temporary speed restrictions and areas where track maintenance is being performed, are delivered to individual operating crews before their departure or en route in the form of orders or daily bulletins issued by train dispatchers.

In addition to the individual system's own rules, railroads and their employees are regulated by the Federal Railroad Administration (FRA), which, among other things, limits the length of time workers directly involved in the movement of trains may remain on duty and establishes minimum periods of release before they may again perform service. The FRA, however, does not have authority over operating rules except in four cases: the flagging rule, radio procedure, yard limits, and protection of men working around movable equipment. The latter is the blue-flag rule, with a blue flag or light displayed on a locomotive or other equipment to indicate that men are working on the equipment. While the flag is displayed, the equipment may not be moved. Employee and employer are both subject to penalties and fines for violations, and this provision encompasses dispatchers, operators, signal maintainers, and some mechanical personnel, as well as the actual operating crews.

Under the original Federal Hours of Service Act, passed in 1907, engineers and conductors could work no more than 16 hours in any 24-hour period and were required to be off duty for at least 8 hours before resuming service. Amendments in the early 1970s reduced the number of permissible hours to 14 and then 12. The Hours of Service Act was similarly extended to train dispatchers and operators in 1909, and signal maintainers were later added. Still further changes are likely. Citing safety concerns arising from the operation of longer trains by fewer employees and evidence pointing to irregular work patterns and sleep deprivation as contributing to accidents caused by human error, the railroad unions have been pushing for further limits to both allowable numbers of days and hours of service, as well as mandating predictability of an employee's tour of duty.

Further changes and evolution of railroad operating rules seem almost inevitable. The present system of track warrants has proved to have weaknesses, because missed verbal repeats have sometimes resulted in major accidents. Verbal authorization of track movements in warrants is likely to be replaced by track warrants and similar authorizations printed out directly in the cab of the engine or hi-rail vehicle. Also likely in the next decade will be the implementation of some form of positive train control system based upon geographic position survey (GPS) data that will eliminate wayside signaling. Automation of much of the dispatching function is likely, and one-man crews are already on the way on some shortlines and in Canada.

Operations Testing

Operations testing—the testing of employees for rules compliance—has long been a part of the railroad industry. Originally instituted by Southern Pacific's Julius Kruttschnitt in 1909, typically it was done as surprise field rules testing by supervisory employees to observe train crews' compliance with signal indications, speed restrictions, and the like. This did not become a federal requirement until 1974, when the FRA adopted a rule requiring railroads to submit an operational testing plan and to keep adequate records of the testing. The law does not specify who is to be tested, nor does it specify how often.

Today all railroads have some sort of testing program, although there is wide variance among the different carriers. Generally the testing applies to all operating employees, including train dispatchers, operators, train service personnel, and maintenance-of-way workers. Some carriers require that an employee be tested every 180 days, while others require tests as frequently as every 60 days.

As expected, the tests are craft specific. Dispatchers are checked for proper issuance of track warrants, track and time, and the like; train service employees for compliance with such requirements as speed restrictions, signal indi-

cations, or getting on and off equipment; maintenance people for copying authorities to occupy the main track, protecting men and equipment, and the like. On some roads a failure on certain tests is regarded as mortal sin and could lead to further action. In the case of engineers such failure can lead to decertification, withdrawal of the engineer's locomotive license.

Usually testing is the responsibility of local supervisors, such as trainmasters, road foremen of engines, roadmasters, chief dispatchers, and rules staff. But at times, especially after major accidents, "flying columns" are organized whose duty is to conduct operational testing over the entire railroad.

Technology is also coming into play. It is possible for testing staff to conduct some checks from a central location using audiotapes, traffic control system playbacks, and locomotive event recorders (remotely downloaded). No doubt in the future much of this will be automated, and reports will be generated that will indicate areas in need of special attention.

Operations testing is unpopular with employees and supervision alike, but, in view of some of the spectacular accidents that have occurred in recent years, it remains a clear necessity. The old stories about a trainmaster and road foreman hiding in the weeds to conduct surprise tests are as valid today as they were 50 or 100 years ago.

Railroad Discipline

Given the potential impact of human and material damages from accidents, railroads have always had to resort to strict, well-defined, uniform operating practices in order to keep a tight rein on their vast holdings and widespread workforces. Individual accountability for rule compliance becomes of paramount importance, and North American railroads have historically tended to rely on harsh punishment of employees who fail to abide by them. Substantial strides have been made in recent years away from an exclusively punitive approach in favor of rewarding employees for positive work records, meanwhile counseling and retraining those with less exemplary ones, but joint labor/management initiatives to bridge the old history of distrust and animosity between employee and employer still have a long way to go.

Discipline in the railroad industry has always been a contentious issue because it has from the beginning been based upon suspension from duty with loss of pay for a period that could range anywhere from a few days to as many as 90 days, or even to outright dismissal from the service for some capital offenses. The only alternative method of discipline was a demerit system developed by George R. Brown, general superintendent of the Fall Brook Railroad, in the 1880s and known as the "Brown system of discipline without suspension." Instead of actual suspension, an employee would receive a record suspension of a certain number of days, or demerit counts, while continuing to work and receive compensation. When an employee's record days, or demerit count, reached a certain number—usually 100—he was dismissed. As with the system of suspension without pay, certain capital offenses could lead to immediate dismissal. An important element of the Brown demerit system was an accompanying credit or merit feature for acts of special merit, through which an employee could offset his demerit count.

The Brown demerit system was widely used, and many managers believed that it worked much better to retain, develop, benefit, and encourage good men than did the more punitive system of suspension with loss of pay. Not everyone agreed; one old-line railroad president commented, "You may catch flies with molasses, but our lives, our fortunes, our civilization we owe to our jails, penitentiaries and gallows."

Brown's demerit system vanished from use after World War II, and at the start of the twenty-first century things are much as they were before Brown came along. As an example, a yard crew that runs through a switch may serve 5 days off without pay, an engineer who passes an red absolute could receive 30 days or more and even lose his certification, a track rider who finds himself outside the limits of his authority may face a 15-day suspension, and a machinist found to have violated the blue-flag rule could face the same, although some welcome new disciplinary practices are now being tried.

Discipline for train service and maintenance-of-way employees is usually a division issue and begins with a trainmaster, road foreman, or roadmaster. In the large dispatching centers it begins with a corridor manager and in the shops with a general foreman, but the fundamental process is the same for all.

The framework by which railroads and their unions have agreed to handle employee discipline reflects the tenets of the American judicial system. A railroader accused of violating a rule is presumed innocent until proven guilty. Unless the continued presence of the accused compromises workplace safety, or unless there is definitive evidence of theft, dishonesty, disruptive behavior, or an unlawful act, the employee is allowed to continue working until after a board of inquiry has met and its findings result in acquittal or guilt where discipline is assessed. Penalties range from a formal reprimand or demerits to suspension without pay, being barred from working in a specific class of service, or even dismissal. It should be noted here that since the more recent imposition of uniform federal standards for the licensing of locomotive engineers, as well as laws governing the conduct of railroad employees with respect to the presence of alcohol or drugs, immediate removal from service is mandated, and civil and/or criminal penalties may also be levied in addition to whatever action the railroad itself may take.

The first step, once the carrier becomes aware of a rules violation, is an investigation (sometimes called a trial or hearing), the purpose of which is to develop the facts surrounding the incident. It is conducted by a carrier officer. The employee is represented by his union, whose representative speaks for the employee as an intermediary, negotiator, and protector to assure fair treatment. Both sides can bring in witnesses to bolster their case. Cross-examination is permitted, and a careful transcript is made, because this is the basis for the appeals procedure. In a minor incident the entire affair may last less than an hour, but in serious situations involving death and injury it could well take two or three days. Once the investigation is over, the transcript is forwarded to the appropriate officer, such as the superintendent, who, usually after consulting labor relations, decides the amount and type of discipline to be assessed.

There is an alternative to the formal investigation process, and that is to accept the discipline the carrier proffers before the investigation begins. If the employee accepts, he signs a waiver, serves the discipline imposed, and the issue is closed. In many cases this is a more practical solution, particularly if the facts are so obvious that to pursue the investigation route could lead to greater discipline than what the carrier has offered.

In all cases the employee and union have the right to appeal. This process may vary from carrier to carrier, but it generally starts with the superintendent. If that fails, the next step is the carrier's designated appeals officer, who is usually a director or an assistant vice president of labor relations. If that comes to no satisfactory end, then the union can ask for a joint conference, and if that still does not resolve the issue, the case goes to a "public law board" or "expedited adjustment board," both of which are authorized by the Railway Labor Act.

These boards are composed of a carrier representative, a union representative, and a referee agreed upon by mutual consent or appointed by the National Mediation Board. Both the carrier and union members are paid by the parties they represent, while the mediator is paid by the board. The case is reviewed on the basis of the transcript, and both sides present their arguments. Then a vote is taken, and a simple majority rules, with the referee casting the deciding vote. The outcome is binding on both parties. In some cases the discipline is overturned and the employee is returned to service, while in others the carrier's position is sustained. This can be a slow process, and it may take several years or more before a decision is returned.

There have been some innovations in railroad discipline in recent years. In the mid-1980s the Burlington Northern and the American Train Dispatchers Assn. signed the "alternative discipline" agreement, which allows a dispatcher who commits a rules infraction that did not result in a serious accident the option to accept some form of alternative to time off. This may be a rules refresher course, a road trip, or something similar. The advantage here is that the dispatcher remains on the payroll at 80 percent of his salary for the duration. Another change has been the introduction of "suspensions of record" (the ghost of Charles Brown, perhaps), in which the offender never serves time off, but the suspension is a part of his record. The presumption is that the employee who incurs too many suspensions may face further action that could lead to dismissal. Indeed, this is a far cry from the days when the hapless dispatcher who issued a paper lap (a train order that, if executed, would have left two trains occupying the same track at the same time) or left a train off a track-car lineup for maintenance-of-way work could look forward to 30 days of unpaid vacation.

In addition to the enforcement of operating rules established by the railroad companies, there has been a growing involvement at the federal level in the establishment of standards and enforcement for critical areas of railroad safety. After a major accident at Chase, Maryland, in 1987, attributed to an engineer operating under the influence of drugs, the Federal Railroad Administration set standards for the eligibility, training, and licensing of locomotive engineers. To identify and purge the railroads of those guilty of alcohol or substance abuse, not only were periodic, random, and preemployment substance abuse tests made law, but specific criminal and/or civil penalties for workplace violations were prescribed.

Although they are implemented, monitored, and enforced by each individual railroad, FRA standards mandate that locomotive engineers be licensed for a period of no more than three years and undergo retraining before recertification. They are tested on equipment knowledge, train-handling skills, territorial familiarity, and rule compliance. Any alcohol- or drug-related convictions appearing on their personal automotive driving record are taken into consideration when making initial or subsequent license application, and any violations occurring after certification is granted must be promptly reported to the railroad. Annual physical examinations to determine general health, as well as visual and hearing acuity, are also required. Once certified, engineers must be observed and evaluated at least once every six months, as well as being tested for adherence to operating rules during actual on-the-job situations at frequent intervals.

Under the federal legislation, entering a segment of track without authority, passing a signal requiring a train to halt short of it, or exceeding any speed limit by more than the lesser of 10 mph or 10 percent constitutes a de-certifiable licensing violation for an engineer. A single violation merits a 30-day penalty; a second within two years results in a six-month license suspension; three times in three years calls for license forfeiture for a year; and more than three incidents will cost an engineer three years without being able to legally operate a locomotive.

An employee in any covered craft testing positive for drugs or alcohol is permitted to return to work after successful treatment for a first offense, but is barred from railroad service for a second offense for two years, five years should there be a third occurrence. Nothing precludes individual railroads from imposing their own penalties, and many demand zero tolerance, as stated in their operating rules. Noting that three out of ten recent candidates for employment on a Class 1 carrier failed the preemployment drug test, the official conducting the in-terviews just shook his head and sighed. "If a person can't abide by society's laws, it's a virtual certainty that they're not going to make a good employee for us, because, after all, a railroad still runs by a reliable watch, a timetable, and the book of rules, and it always will."

This, then, is the general state of the discipline process in the industry today. Although many railroads have been combined through the major mergers of recent years, the labor agreements of the prior carriers still prevail, and the exact method of resolving discipline issues may vary from property to property. But for all of them, railroading is a potentially dangerous endeavor and demands rigid rules compliance from everyone involved. Strict disciplinary practices are likely to prevail as long as railroads operate.

—W. L. Gwyer, with additional material by Doug Riddell

REFERENCES

Armstrong, John H. *The Railroad, What It Is, What It Does.* 4th ed. Omaha, Nebr.: Simmons-Boardman, 1998.
Josserand, Peter. *Rights of Trains.* 5th ed. New York: Simmons-Boardman, 1957.

Operations Planning and Analysis

Railroads involve an enormous investment of plant and staff, and their productive assets require the complex management activities of planning and analyzing the railroad operation and some of the tools employed. The primary resources required to operate a railroad are the infrastructure (consisting of line-of-road and terminal tracks and facilities), locomotives, freight cars, and workforce. Table 1 summarizes the significance of these resources to the operation.

This table suggests several economic realities. First, railroads are very capital intensive. Infrastructure, which in the United States is owned and maintained by the railroad companies themselves, constitutes a huge portion of total industry value and annual capital investment. In the year 2000 railroad capital expenditures as a percent of revenues were 17.8 percent, compared with 3.7 percent across all U.S. manufacturing industries. As shown in Table 1, roughly three-fourths of rail investment is in infrastructure.

A second economic reality is the need for efficiency. Because infrastructure costs are so high, railroads have a tremendous incentive to minimize their facilities and to push as much volume and revenue through them as possible. Concerning the 20,000 locomotives, the drive for efficiency is to keep them on the road pulling freight and to maximize turns, miles, and tonnages handled. Similarly, the goals for the nearly 1.4 million freight cars are to max-

Table 1. Railroad Operating Resources

Resource	U.S. Industry Totals	Total Asset Value (%)	Annual Capital Investment (%)	Annual Operating Expense (%)	Workforce (%)
Infrastructure	67,275 track-miles	73	75	17	21
Equipment		25		25	20
Locomotives	20,028 units		12		
Freight cars	1,380,796 cars		10		
Workforce	168,360 people				
Train and yard operations				40	42
Resources as percentage of total value		98	97	82	83

Sources: Association of American Railroads, *Analysis of Class I Railroads, Year 2000*; Association of American Railroads, *Railroad Facts*, 2002 ed.

imize time moving under load, minimize time in terminals, and minimize empty repositioning for the next load. Regarding the mostly unionized workforce, whose wages and benefits total 40 percent of railroad operating expenses, the goal is to minimize labor required in the operation. As shown in the table, 83 percent of the workforce is engaged in running the trains and maintaining the equipment and track. Railroads continue to seek work-rule improvements and to invest heavily in technology to reduce labor requirements.

A third economic reality is the presence of trade-offs. The rail operation can be achieved through different blends of the resources, each of which has its own cost and service implications. A classic example concerns the decision of train size. Eager to minimize its labor costs, a railroad may choose to operate very large trains. For a given level of traffic, the result is operation of fewer trains and lower workforce costs, since crews are paid by the trip. However, the railroad must wait for a longer period of time to collect more cars before operating larger trains. This results in longer dwell times on the equipment, fewer trips per month, and greater overall equipment and terminal infrastructure requirements. The large-train strategy can also negatively impact the quality of service by delaying delivery of customers' freight. Numerous such trade-offs exist in blending the key operating resources.

Resource decisions are further complicated by the somewhat divergent needs of three different service networks de-signed around the three basic railroad products: premium, bulk, and manifest. The premium network generally includes intermodal and auto traffic, often operated in dedicated unit trains at higher speeds and schedule standards than those of the other networks. Bulk generally refers to coal, grain, and ore traffic, which also is often operated in dedicated unit trains from origin to destination (e.g., from mine to utility or transload facility). Manifest traffic is the traditional carload business that is collected into terminals, assembled into trains, sorted at other terminals, and then distributed to customers' plants and sidings. Each of these three basic service networks tends to have unique terminal facilities and unique freight cars, and each may use different locomotives. However, the three typically share the route infrastructure resource and the crew resource.

How do railroads drive the efficiency of their critical resources across three service networks and ensure that the right blend of resources comes together at the right place and time to move the freight? The challenge is usually structured and addressed across three time frames, strategic, tactical, and real-time, as shown in Table 2.

Portions of the organization engage in strategic planning and analysis activities well in advance of running the trains—more than 90 days and often 12 to 24 months in advance. This work is typically conducted at a railroad's headquarters to ensure integrity with the overall business plan and that proper economic trade-offs are made. The operating team takes action. Within the tactical time frame

Table 2. Planning and Analysis Activities

Time Frame	Activities	Objectives
Strategic (> 90 days)	Forecast Determine service requirements Design train plan Analyze resource trade-offs Determine resource requirements Justify and acquire resources Analyze results	Ensure capability to deliver service products Minimize total cost given traffic forecast and service requirements Define service plan Identify opportunities for improvement
Tactical (1–7 days)	Define execution plan Position resources	Maximize efficiency within the service plan
Real-Time (0–1 day)	Execute resource plan Execute train plan Achieve schedules	Move trains and cars on time Improve Efficiency

the operating team makes specific plans to distribute freight cars and locomotives, assemble trains, assign crews, and allocate infrastructure capacity. These tactical tasks are also usually performed for the network as a whole from a central location to ensure full visibility of trade-off options and good resource utilization. Finally, trains are operated real-time. The equipment comes together and is verified to be in good working order, a crew is placed aboard, printed instructions are provided, switches and signals are aligned, the engineer cracks the throttle, and the wheels turn. Most of the railroad organization is engaged real-time in running the trains, switching the cars, and maintaining the track and equipment, but it does so according to a plan devised and with resources acquired and distributed well in advance of the actual train operation.

Operations planning and analysis activities occur primarily in the strategic and tactical time frames. The infrastructure resource is analyzed for its capacity. A rail line can efficiently handle only so many trains each day before it becomes congested. Too much traffic can have the same effect on a rail line as rush hour can have on a highway. Various methods exist to quantify rail-line capacity. Traditionally it has been accomplished by calculating the amount of time it takes to operate one train in each direction over the longest single-track segment between sidings in a given territory. This time constitutes one full east-west or north-south cycle. The cycle time is then divided into 24 hours to calculate maximum theoretical trains per day that the line can handle. The resulting number is adjusted downward to allow for traffic peaking (several trains operating closely together), track maintenance, weather problems, and various failures. On a double-track line capacity is a function of train speeds and following distances (the space required between trains for safety), adjusted for the same issues just noted.

Recent expansions in computing power have allowed simulation of rail-line operation, including calculations of speed and capacity based on the profile of the track, speed limits, train sizes, and locomotive horsepower. Simulation can verify the locations of capacity bottlenecks, but its greatest value is in testing alternatives to find the most efficient solution for improving operating performance.

Simulation is applied to determine capacity improvements needed to support commuter rail operations on the freight railroads. This is a growing issue as public agencies in major urban areas wrestle with highway traffic congestion and find it increasingly infeasible to expand the road network. Commuter rail can offer a cost-effective alternative. The freight railroads have generally shown a spirit of cooperation with the public agencies so long as the agencies are willing to pay for the added rail infrastructure needed to handle the passenger trains and still keep the railroads' freight traffic moving fluidly. The most successful solutions have been win-win: the agencies gain an efficient transportation solution, and the railroads gain enhanced capabilities. The starting point in such partnerships is rail-line capacity simulation, which offers unbiased analysis of the impact of adding commuter trains to a rail corridor.

Infrastructure capacity analysis has become more critical to railroads as they have grown traffic on their networks in the modern (post–Staggers Act) era. As explained earlier, railroads seek to fill their expensive infrastructure and minimize additions to it. By understanding capacity bottlenecks, railroads can look across an entire corridor, pinpoint precise areas to be improved, and gain maximum leverage from capital spending. The right investments at the right locations can improve capacity use across dozens or hundreds of miles. Sometimes the analysis leads to other solutions that improve capacity, such as raising speed limits, changing train schedules to space traffic more evenly, or changing dispatching techniques.

Terminal capacity is analyzed in a similar fashion. Dwell time affects terminal capacity as speed affects line capacity. The longer trains or cars dwell in terminals, the more trackage is needed to hold them. Theoretical terminal capacity is thus a function of dwell time and track footage. Terminal capacity is easily calculated and then adjusted to allow for spacing between trains or freight cars, traffic peaks, maintenance, and weather interruptions. Typically this analysis is performed at a high level to design the operating plan so it will fit within each terminal's capabilities. As demand and congestion increase, several additional actions are supported with analysis. One is to modify train schedules so the cars connect from one train to another with shorter dwell times. This may suboptimize another operation up- or downstream, but be well worth while to relieve congestion at a critical terminal. Another step is to conduct further analysis within the terminal and identify precise bottlenecks in switching operations that can be eased by applying greater resources or better operating processes. The last resort is to add physical facilities (e.g., more track), but sometimes this must be a part of the solution.

In the tactical time frame the infrastructure cannot be altered. The hand is dealt, but the same analytical concepts can be applied in playing the cards to manage use of the infrastructure and to achieve good service performance. The key is to maximize throughput in the bottlenecks, whether they be line segments or terminals. The analysis previously described quantifies those capacities. Tactical management is aimed at filling but not exceeding them. This can be accomplished by spacing trains or delaying their launching so demand is smoothed and not excessive. Another tactic is to ensure that the other resources (crews and locomotives) are in plentiful supply at the bottleneck to isolate the issue of capacity. These actions may add to costs and cause minor delays to traffic, but they can avoid massive delays that occur when a critical line or terminal becomes overwhelmed and badly congested.

Locomotive and freight-car needs are highly dependent upon traffic forecasts, which ideally include the timing of demand, the type of traffic to be handled, and its origin and destination locations. Such information is often gathered from the railroad's sales and marketing forces and tempered by purchased forecasts for key sectors of the economy.

A good approach to planning locomotive requirements begins by using the forecast to estimate tonnages and the miles to be hauled by traffic type. Efficiency assumptions are made concerning the train operation, including speeds and horsepower assignments. By adjusting further for terminal and maintenance time, final horsepower demand is deduced. The focus then shifts to filling that demand by using existing locomotives, purchasing or leasing additional locomotives, and modifying maintenance and retirement plans.

In the tactical time frame specific locomotives are assigned to specific trains. At this point the objectives are to maximize efficiency and service performance. The railroad wants to assign just enough horsepower to a train to make its schedule. It wants locomotives with distinct mechanical capabilities, such as AC traction, to operate in specific services or territories that fully leverage those capabilities. It wants to distribute locomotives to the terminals throughout its network so that no trains are delayed waiting for locomotives, but without excessive idle time on the locomotives waiting for trains to be assembled.

With hundreds or thousands of locomotives, dozens or hundreds of terminals, and uneven traffic demand, tactically optimizing the locomotive resource across a rail network is a difficult challenge. Some railroads follow the scheduled-cycle approach—operate the same horsepower between the same points every day. This is predictable, but it wastes locomotives on the days and in the directions that train sizes are small. Another approach is to assign only the horsepower needed to make schedule on each train and to then reposition locomotives into deficit areas. Some railroads have developed computerized models that apply optimization logic to this task.

Compared with locomotives, freight-car planning and tactical assignment activities are even more complex. There are 12 to 20 basic car types, as many as 50 variations within those, and 1.4 million total cars in the U.S. fleet. The concepts and approaches to management are very similar to those of locomotives. In the strategic time frame the game is to meet demand calculated from forecast volumes, locations, and cycle times and to accomplish this by car type. In the tactical time frame cars are assigned and distributed to balance the objectives of being available for loading when needed without sitting idle any longer than absolutely necessary. Computerized decision support tools are usually employed to improve freight-car distribution and assignment efficiency.

The workforce resource, discussion of which is limited here to train crews, has unique attributes and challenges. The crew resource is location specific. That is, a person who works on board a train can generally operate over his or her specific territory only. This means that good sup-

ply/demand planning in the strategic time frame must be done for each crew district, which is typically a segment of 100 to 300 miles, or a specific terminal. Also, the lead time is long; it takes several months to hire and train a crew person. These challenges reinforce the need for a good geographic traffic forecast.

Another unique attribute of the workforce resource is that its behavior follows human nature and so is less predictable than track, terminals, locomotives, or cars. The crews are unionized and are generally paid by a combination of the number of miles traveled and hours worked in a given period of time. Crewmembers can take time off ("mark off") at their own discretion. Hence the capacity of the crew resource varies considerably, depending on how hard the people want to work, and it is limited only by federal laws that prescribe maximum consecutive hours on duty (12) and minimum consecutive rest hours (8) between tours of duty. If traffic increases, the demand on locomotives and freight cars is felt immediately, but crews may simply make more trips and earn more money, so crew capacity easily expands. However, if the crew resource is pushed too hard, it gets tired and rich, and then it marks off, and capacity can actually decrease to a point below where it started. Another challenging phenomenon of the crew resource is that its capacity tends to diminish around the time of critical football games and hunting seasons, largely independent of the needs of the railroad.

In the strategic time frame a good crew plan is derived by crew district on the basis of the traffic forecast, a reasonable assumption of miles and earnings, and expected attrition. Day to day, road crews generally operate back and forth across their district on any type of train on a first-in, first-out basis. Tactical decisions are made to reposition crews to compensate for imbalances in traffic flow. This activity can be complex and costly, because crews are paid even if they are taxied ("deadheaded") to the other end of their territory, but they are also paid if they are detained beyond a certain amount of time at the end point away from their home terminal. This presents yet another balancing game that receives a great deal of management attention. Railroads do not want their equipment and customers' goods to sit idle waiting for crews, but at the same time they want to minimize their high labor costs.

The operation of a modern freight train is the result of considerable thought and effort by the railroad organization. Resources have been acquired. Service plans have been sold to customers. Freight cars have been provided for loading. Sufficient locomotives have been positioned to move the train at speeds that will achieve the schedule. Crews have been assigned. The train consumes a predetermined portion of infrastructure capacity.

The goal of operations planning and analysis is to bring the railroad's key operating resources together at the right place at the right time and with minimal waste to deliver the railroad's three basic service products: premium, bulk, and manifest. In the longer or strategic time frame the tasks include setting the service plan and acquiring an efficient blend of resources to achieve it. Tactically, the resources are distributed and assigned. Finally, in real time, freight trains are operated.

—Thomas Haley

REFERENCE

American Assn. of State Highway and Transportation Officials (AASHTO). *Freight-Rail Bottom Line Report*, 2002, 41.

Orphan Trains

What we now know as slums hardly existed in the colonial period. Cities were small, and few citizens were far from rural roots. As eastern U.S. cities became more populous in the nineteenth century, increasing numbers of orphans and homeless children were living in dangerous and threatening squalor of Dickensian proportions, according to contemporary observers. Those without adequate wages or support, both young and old, often turned to crime. The homeless and orphans were categorized as members of a dangerous class and perceived as a danger to those in more comfortable circumstances. The society of the time in New York, especially in Manhattan, put young potential criminals in jail, mixed in with older hardened and proficient malfeasants. There were also grim orphanages.

It was clear to reformers that the situation was intolerable. Reformers who sought to help disadvantaged children strongly believed that they should be removed from their families and placed in a better environment. Cities were considered evil places, while the mythic purity of rural small towns and the healthy life of farming were seen as attractive antidotes to the problem of poor, homeless, or unwanted children.

Charles Loring Brace, a young New Yorker with a strong religious bent, felt great sympathy for homeless children and orphans. Resolving to help, he and others formed the Children's Aid Society. Brace originally tried to place children individually with families in New York or close by. This proved to be time consuming and difficult. The idea emerged to send groups of orphans west by train to be placed with persons or families who would take the children into their homes, feed and clothe them, send them to school in the winter months, and help them learn a skill or trade. At age 18 the children were to be released to make do for themselves. By working with groups, and without the problems of dealing with accepting families or individuals, the work of the Children's Aid Society was made simple and manageable. The idea chosen was, in effect, a reinvention of the system of indenture that had permitted many immigrants to come to America in the seventeenth and eighteenth centuries.

The CAS arranged with a religious minister or pastor in a western city or town to be the agent who would receive the children at the railroad station and then place them before interested parties for selection. A group rate was arranged with one or more railroads. The children were scrubbed up, given new clothes, and packed aboard a train to the western part of the United States, with a CAS staffer to accompany them. When not all the children were selected at the first point, those unwanted were moved further west. Children not selected were returned to New York.

The first orphan train left New York for Dowagiac, Michigan, on September 28, 1854. There were 37 boys and girls in the group, ranging in age from 6 to 15. It is not clear why Dowagiac was selected; it was a new town that had been developed by the Michigan Central Railroad a few years earlier.

Other similar organizations in New York City and in other eastern cities adopted the orphan-train scheme. Between 1854 and 1929 a quarter of a million children were sent out on the orphan trains, a little over 100,000 by the Children's Aid Society. Not all of them went west; in later years the majority of placements were in New York City, New York State, New Jersey, and Connecticut.

In a successful placement the youngster became a part of the family, and many were legally adopted; ideally, they became solid citizens. When placements were unsuccessful, the unfortunate children were put in the hands of a cruel or indifferent family or were taken on merely to work cheaply. Some youngsters from large cities simply did not fit into rural settings or small towns. Some found themselves in trouble with the law. The dearth of records and follow-up makes it impossible to determine the actual success of the program.

There were a number of problems. One was the difficulty of taking children away from their biological parents, a factor that is anathema to current thinking by social work professionals. Inadequate funding for the work of the CAS and similar agencies was a source of other problems, probably the worst of which was a lack of trained and capable staff.

As the nineteenth century progressed, there was a change in outlook, attitude, and laws. Some states prohibited the putting out of children without preselection and at least some foster home or adoption control. By the turn of the twentieth century the orphan trains continued to roll, but much of the placement was close to the city of origin. The size of the groups changed; instead of 30 to 100 children, a group would rarely be larger than 15 and sometimes only 1 or 2. The last orphan train ran from New York to Sulphur Springs, Texas, on May 31, 1929.

—George M. Smerk

REFERENCE

O'Connor, Stephen. *Orphan Trains: The Story of Charles Loring Brace and the Children He Saved and Failed.* Chicago: Univ. of Chicago Press, 2004.

P

Pacific Electric Railway

The Pacific Electric called itself the "world's greatest interurban railway," and few would argue. Radiating in every direction from Los Angeles, PE operated nearly 1,200 miles of electric railroad reaching over 125 cities and communities in a four-county area of Southern California. PE played a key role in the urbanization and development of the great megalopolis that grew up in and around Los Angeles in the early twentieth century. It was estimated that the PE accounted for nearly 10 percent of the U.S. interurban investment.

The Los Angeles & Pasadena, the first interurban line that was to become part of PE, was created in 1895 when Los Angeles traction pioneers Moses H. Sherman and Eli P. Clark linked local lines in Los Angeles and Pasadena with a new bridge across the Arroyo Seco. Pacific Electric itself was incorporated in 1901 by Henry E. Huntington, a nephew and heir of Southern Pacific's Collis P. Huntington. Huntington acquired control of the Los Angeles & Pasadena and Pasadena & Mount Lowe railways, folded them into PE, and began constructing lines to link Los Angeles with San Pedro, Long Beach, Newport Beach, Santa Ana, Glendora, and Glendale. Henry Huntington was also active in property development, and the advance of the electric cars into new territory was carefully coordinated with his real estate interests.

Huntington withdrew from active management of PE in 1910, and the company was sold to Southern Pacific early in 1911. SP then merged the original PE with the Los Angeles Pacific, the Los Angeles Inter-Urban, the Los Angeles & Redondo, and other Southern California traction properties. PE expansion continued with the construction of new lines to the San Fernando Valley, Pomona, San Bernardino, and Riverside. By 1914, one of the peak years for Pacific Electric passenger operations, a total of 1,626 trains entered or left Los Angeles daily, and the company's annual passenger traffic totaled almost 70.7 million passengers.

East and south from Los Angeles four-track rights-of-way carried intensive levels of traffic. The four-track Southern Division main line south from downtown Los Angeles to Watts accommodated both passenger services to Santa Ana, San Pedro, Long Beach, and the beach communities south to Newport and Balboa and heavy freight traffic. It was probably the most intensively used interurban route in North America.

In addition to its dense passenger traffic, Pacific Electric operated an extensive mail and express service throughout Southern California and developed a substantial freight business serving the growing industry of Southern California, becoming at one time the third-ranked freight railroad in California. The 58-mile, 1,200-volt San Bernardino line that was PE's longest and fastest route boasted its own Railway Post Office service.

Together with the growing Los Angeles area, PE thrived through the 1920s, reaching a peak traffic of just over 100 million rail passengers in 1923. Even then, however, Southern California was beginning the shift toward road transport that would make it the world's most automobile-oriented urban area, and PE began a parallel shift to motor-coach operation for many of its local and light-density routes. By 1930, when PE acquired the competing Motor Transit Lines, buses accounted for more than 15 million annual passengers, while its rail passenger business began a long decline.

The extraordinary World War II development of Southern California's aircraft, shipbuilding, and other defense industries and the population growth that accompanied it brought a resurgence in PE's rail passenger traffic, which climbed to an all-time peak of more than 100 million passengers in 1945. Aging wooden interurban cars were literally pulled off the scrap line and rehabilitated for wartime service, and surplus cars were transferred to PE from defunct Southern Pacific electric operations in northern California to help carry the loads.

At war's end, however, development of Southern California's unequaled freeway system accelerated the region's shift to motor transportation. PE's losses from rail passenger operations reached nearly $3.3 million by 1950, and it set out to complete the shift of its passenger services to buses. By 1953, when PE's rail passenger routes had declined to less than 200 miles and annual rail passenger count had fallen below 14 million, the company's entire passenger business was sold to Metropolitan Coach Lines, which continued the shift to bus operation at an accelerated pace. The last former PE rail passenger route, between Los Angeles and Long Beach, ceased operation early in 1961.

While its passenger traffic declined, Pacific Electric's freight business prospered, reaching a level of more than 5.6 million tons in 1952. Freight operations were shifted from electric to diesel motive power as rail passenger operations were discontinued, and in 1965 what was left of the PE rail system—by this time 446 track-miles—was merged into Southern Pacific.

In 1965, the year its operations were absorbed by Southern Pacific, Pacific Electric operated 316 route-miles, with 42 locomotives, 29 freight cars, and 29 company service cars. Operating revenues totaled $3.6 million in 1963, the last year for which figures are available.

A footnote to the history of Pacific Electric is the congruence of lines of the rail transit system under development by the Los Angeles County Metropolitan Transportation Authority with the PE system. MTA's Los Angeles–Long Beach light-rail route follows the alignment of the PE Long Beach line almost foot by foot, the Red Line subway between downtown Los Angeles and the San Fernando Valley serves the corridor that was developed by the PE's line to the Valley, and the Los Angeles–Pasadena light-rail Gold Line route opened in 2003 and restored rail service to what was Southern California's very first interurban route in 1895.

—William D. Middleton

REFERENCES

Crump, Spencer. *Ride the Big Red Cars: How Trolleys Helped Build Southern California.* Los Angeles: Crest, 1962.

Swett, Ira L. *Lines of Pacific Electric.* 5 vols. Los Angeles: Interurban Press, 1953–62.

Pacific Great Eastern Railway.

See BC RAIL

Pacific Railroad

Columbus and other explorers hoped to find an easy way to the Far East by sailing west. Unfortunately, a continent intruded. Nevertheless, the dream of a Northwest Passage persisted for many years. The hope was that the waterway would help join the colonies anchored to the Atlantic Coast with the Pacific Ocean. In the mid- and late eighteenth century interest in the western and northwestern portions of the North American continent was strong. French trappers and missionaries had penetrated to the Great Lakes and the Mississippi and generated tales of great rivers and rugged mountains in the West, but there was no firm evidence of a passage by water. A safe and usable land route was needed in the absence of such a waterway.

The French had explored as far to the west as Lake Superior. To journey all the way to the Pacific was the aim of Capt. Jonathan Curtis, a Connecticut native and officer in the British provincial army who had fought in the French and Indian Wars. Curtis spent two years and five months in exploration. In 1767 he reached Prairie du Chien, Wisconsin, and spent a winter with local Indian tribes in Minnesota. He did not reach his goal of the Pacific. Later, trappers operating out of St. Louis traced much of the course of the Missouri River and knew that the upper reaches of the river were in the Northwest.

The Lewis and Clark expedition, inspired by President Thomas Jefferson, discovered more about the huge area Jefferson had obtained in the Louisiana Purchase of 1803. The notion of a quick and easy portage between the upper reaches of the Missouri River and a western river reaching the Pacific was put to rest by Lewis and Clark. The courageous explorers and their team found no water route to the Pacific, but did learn much about the region, its peoples, and its resources. More information about the American West flowed back to the East through the tales of the mountain men and trappers and later the explorations of Zebulon Pike and John C. Frémont.

The Pacific Railroad Idea

The reliance upon water for improved transportation was superseded in the early nineteenth century when development of a reliable and powerful steam locomotive by George Stephenson and his son Robert stirred interest in the railroad as a way of conquering distance, even the distance across the continent. In 1819 a South Carolina engineer, Robert Mills, proposed a line of steam-powered cars to run from the Mississippi River valley to the valley of the Columbia River and to the Pacific. Despite Mills's friendship with Thomas Jefferson and Benjamin Latrobe, no immediate action was taken.

The beginning of railroad construction in the United States with the advent of the Baltimore & Ohio in 1827 made the notion of a lengthy steam-powered railroad to the West appear practical. In 1830 William C. Redfield published a pamphlet promoting the idea of a railway line from the Eastern Seaboard to the Mississippi River and then on to the Pacific. A meeting of local businessmen and community leaders was held at the Dunkirk Hotel in Dunkirk, New York, on January 10, 1832, and the end result was passage of a resolution that a railroad should be built along the southern-tier counties of New York State from the Hudson River to the Mississippi as a major link in a railroad to the Pacific. On February 6, 1832, Samuel Dexter, editor of the *Western Migrant* of Ann Arbor, Michigan published a lengthy article in his paper on the subject of a railroad to the Pacific. The idea was a bold one, given the available information about a Great American Desert that lay between the early settlements on the western shore of the Mississippi and the formidable mountains that were known to block the way to the Pacific.

Other visionaries or dreamers joined in to help plant the notion of a railroad across the continent in the minds of Americans. In 1833 Dr. Samuel Barlow espoused the cause in the *Intelligencer*. In the summer 1836 issue of the *Knickerbocker Magazine*, editor Lewis Gaylord Clark supported the dream of a transcontinental railway line. Clark later claimed that the idea was his originally.

Added to the ranks of Pacific railway promoters was Welshman John Plumbe. Plumbe had come to America as a boy and for a time worked as a member of a railway survey party in the Allegheny Mountains of Pennsylvania. Plumbe moved to Iowa, read law, and established himself as a prosecuting attorney in Dubuque, Iowa, in 1836. He contributed articles to the journals of the day on the subject of the railroad to the Pacific. One of these in the *Iowa News* of March 24, 1838, spoke of a rail connection between Lake Michigan and Dubuque as an important first step in a transcontinental railway. Plumbe called a public meeting in Dubuque to discuss the subject. In 1838 Plumbe and his fellow Iowans directed a petition to Congress promoting the idea of a Pacific railway; it was ridiculed. In the early 1840s Plumbe learned the art of the daguerreotype and established a string of studios in cities from Boston to Washington. He invented a process for copying daguerreotypes that he called plumbetypes, but neglected to patent his invention. Still interested in the Pacific railway scheme, he was caught up in the railroad fever that was then stirring in Washington, neglected his business, and went bankrupt. Plumbe journeyed to the gold fields of California to rebuild his lost fortune. In the gold camps and elsewhere he promoted the idea of Californians building a railroad to the East. His fortune unrebuilt, Plumbe returned to Iowa in 1857, found that others had adopted his idea and were in the process of realizing his dream, and committed suicide.

One of the foremost dreamers of a Pacific railroad was Connecticut merchant Asa Whitney, who had made a fortune in the China trade. It was on his return from China in 1844 that Whitney developed his idea. Goods bound for Asia had to make the journey around Cape Horn or around Africa and the Cape of Good Hope. A shorter route via the Isthmus of Panama required transfer of shipments to wagons or later a railroad to cross the 40 miles separating the Pacific from the Atlantic. To Asa Whitney, a railway across the United States would provide an easy approach to the trade with the Far East.

Whitney had been impressed by the railroad's possibilities in 1830 when, on a buying trip to Great Britain, he saw the Liverpool & Manchester Railway in action and rode the train as it sped along at 48 miles per hour. As he meditated on the long journey home from Canton, he envisioned the Pacific railway as not only a benefit to commerce, but also a boon to the people of the United States and the whole world because it would open up the vast reaches of the American continent to settlement. He set to work on a series of memoranda to Congress, innumerable letters to the editors of newspapers, and speeches and meetings to promote the idea with an almost religious fervor.

What Whitney proposed was that the federal government set aside for his railroad a swath of public land 60 miles wide from Lake Michigan—which he rightly surmised would soon be joined by rail with the East Coast—to the Pacific. He estimated the cost to be $50 million and maintenance expense until completion to be $15 million. Since the railway was to be built in phases, the public lands would be sold to pay for the construction. As it stretched westward, over time the railway could be built without the need to issue stock or to use taxpayers' money. Whitney's financial reward would come after the completion of the railroad; in his plan, Congress would allow him to retain any unsold lands along the railway, which he could then offer to buyers. He proposed that the rates charged would be sufficient to pay operating costs and to maintain the railway. He also requested that Congress establish a survey to plot the precise location of the railroad.

Whitney gave his petition to Congressman Zadock Pratt of Prattsville, New York, who took it to Washington for the second session of the 28th Congress. On March 3, 1845, the Whitney proposal was tabled by the House Committee on Roads and Canals. The committee chairman, Robert Dale Owen of New York, thought that the issue was too important for quick decision and should be carefully deliberated upon; Owen also questioned the lack of a completion date and the probable need for military escorts to protect the survey crew and the teams of construction workers from Indian attacks.

To promote the Pacific railroad, Whitney set out on a speaking tour to build public support. He also sponsored and joined an expedition to explore part of the area. The group set out in the summer of 1845 and explored an area from Milwaukee to the great bend of the Missouri. As the group moved westward, Whitney sent back detailed reports for the newspapers, which were always anxious to print stories about the western frontier. Whitney admitted to problems in his plan: much of the land to be used was occupied by Indian tribes, and their titles had not been extinguished by Congress. He held the view that the coming of the railroad and new settlers would drive the tribes out of the way to the north.

Thanks to the work of Whitney and Plumbe and to the conferences and mass meetings held to promote the transcontinental and Pacific railroad, the idea was becoming increasingly accepted. Helping to underscore that inevitability were the Treaty of Guadalupe Hidalgo, which brought much of the southwestern region into the United States, the California Gold Rush, and the admission of California into the Union in 1850. The acceptance of the Pacific railway idea concerned politicians seeking to gain advantage for their part of the nation. Whitney's general proposal was that the railway would start at Milwaukee and then head west. Stephen Douglas of Chicago wanted the railway to commence at Chicago; in a like vein, Senator Thomas Hart Benton of Missouri saw St. Louis as the ideal eastern terminus. Sam Houston of Texas wanted the Pacific railroad to pass through his state, while John C. Calhoun envisioned the Charleston & Memphis Railroad extending west across the Mississippi to the Pacific.

Pacific railway bills were introduced in Congress, but to Whitney's dismay all failed. He sought funding for the project in England in 1851, but found the bankers uninterested. After seven years of effort, with his fortune largely expended, Whitney retired to his dairy farm at Locust Hill, near the District of Columbia; he spent the remainder of his life selling dairy products in the nation's capital. Although he no longer played any role in the development of the railway to the West, he lived long enough to see his dream fulfilled.

The Idea Takes Hold

By the early 1850s it was obvious that the transcontinental railroad was an idea whose time had almost arrived, but there was to be controversy and delay over the specific route. As John C. Calhoun had already recognized, the United States was becoming two nations, with the issue of slavery as the wedge between them. If the Pacific railroad had an eastern terminus in the South, it was felt that the territories along the area that would become states would enter the union as slave states; if the eastern terminus was in the North, slavery would be absent from the new territory. Where to build was the question, and facts were necessary to select the route. In his proposal Whitney had requested that Congress fund a survey of the area between the 43rd and 45th parallels, which would mean a more northern route and thus antipathy from southern members of Congress.

Progress of a sort began on March 1, 1853, when Congress authorized the secretary of war to use the services of the Corps of Topographical Engineers to find the most practical route for the railroad from the Mississippi to the Pacific Ocean. The secretary of war was Jefferson Davis, later president of the Confederacy, who personally favored a southern route along the 32nd to 35th parallel. To show his objectivity, Davis ordered the engineers to conduct the survey from Mexico to the Canadian border. Distrusting the army engineers, Senator Benton of Missouri supported his own survey with the route planted at St. Louis. The Pacific railroad survey, as it turned out, did not form the basis of the route of the eventual transcontinental railroad; it did, however, publish in thirteen large volumes, at a cost of $1 million, an impressive compendium of information about the American West before the railroads and the settlers changed it forever.

In August 1853 President Franklin Pierce dispatched George W. Manypenny, the commissioner of Indian affairs, to go west and meet with the various tribes between the 40th and 45th parallels where the Pacific railway would eventually be built. In his dealings Manypenny made treaties ceding vast amounts of Indian lands to the federal government. By these agreements the Indians gave up 18 million of their 19,342,000 acres. The process of pushing the Indians off the lands promised them had taken another step. The treaties did not assure peace.

Judah Advances the Idea

One of those who dreamed of building a railroad from California to the East was Theodore Dehone Judah. Judah was born on March 4, 1828, in Bridgeport, Connecticut, the son of an Episcopal minister. In 1833 the Reverend Judah was called to a church in Troy, New York, the home of the Troy School of Technology (later the Rensselaer Institute of Technology). It was one of the first schools to offer education in civil engineering, including the specialized study of railroad engineering. Theodore Judah spent several years at the school. Nearby were the yards and other facilities of the Troy & Schenectady Railroad Co. Upon the death of his father Judah worked on the survey crew of the S&T and at 18 joined the surveying crew of the New Haven, Hartford & Springfield Railway. He was hardworking and precocious, was soon promoted to location engineer for the Hartford district, and before long was made assistant to the chief engineer.

Theodore Judah was at the right place at the right time; many new railroad companies were springing up, and the supply of civil engineers was small. Within a short time he was employed by the Niagara Falls & Lake Ontario Railway and ran the line down along the Niagara Gorge. For a time he was resident engineer for the western end of the Erie Canal and later served as chief engineer for the Buffalo & New York Railroad.

Judah's future arrived in New York City in the person of Col. Charles Lincoln Wilson. Wilson had gone to California to make his fortune by providing supplies to the gold miners working in the Sierra Nevada east of Sacramento. Wilson operated a supply steamer on the Sacramento River. In 1852, sensing new opportunity, Wilson and banker and retired army officer William Tecumseh Sherman incorporated the first railroad west of the Missouri River, the Sacramento Valley Railroad. Wilson was looking for an engineer to lay out the line. On the advice of New York governor Horatio Seymour, Wilson hired Theodore Judah for the job. Judah and his wife, Anna, arrived in Sacramento in 1854, and he began surveying the line to Marysville. In his work he saw other possibilities; in his first report to the directors Judah commented on the possibility of extending the line up the American River to Coloma and Shasta and eventually along the Sacramento Valley to Stockton and San Francisco. In the report Judah noted the possibility of building over the Sierra to the east and to Nevada. In February 1855 the grading on the railroad began in downtown Sacramento.

The transcontinental railroad soon became an obsession to Judah. Employed to do the preliminary survey of a railway from San Francisco to Sacramento, in his report to the directors of the proposed railway on February 7, 1856, he pressed the idea of the San Francisco & Sacramento as a key link in a transcontinental railway. Judah's report noted that the SF&S might be eligible for federal land grants that were being used to build the Illinois Central Railroad. Practical despite his enthusiasm, Judah journeyed to Washington in April 1856 to learn the process of the politics and lobbying needed to achieve his dream.

Washington was in chaos in the mid- and late 1850s as the unrest that would lead to war was playing itself out. The Republican Party was entering onto the national stage, and its presidential candidate, explorer and self-publicist John Charles Frémont, was against slavery and for a Pacific railroad. Fremont was best known as an explorer and one knowledgeable about the West; he had also been briefly the self-appointed president of California and had been appointed U.S. senator by the California legislature for half a year. Youth was not served in the election, and old, sickly James Buchanan of Pennsylvania was elected chief executive. There were others in Washington interested in pushing railroad legislation. Stephen A. Douglas of Illinois, just before his debates with Abraham Lincoln, was vigorously promoting the idea of a railroad from Chicago west across Nebraska to the Pacific.

Assessing what he needed to do, Judah issued a self-published pamphlet titled *A Practical Plan for Building the Pacific Railroad*; it was distributed to all members of Congress and to pertinent bureaus and departments. In the pamphlet he envisioned a transcontinental railroad route through the Platte Valley to the valley of the Sacramento and the Pacific.

Judah came to believe that strong local support from the West was necessary. He returned to Sacramento to carry out more survey work for Colonel Wilson and struck up a friendship with Lauren Upson, editor of the *Sacramento Union*. The newspaper would be an important source of support for Judah's plan. Judah and his small band of supporters called for an official Railroad Convention to be held in San Francisco on September 20, 1859. There were sharp differences among the delegates drawn from all parts of California, as well as from Washington, Oregon, and the Arizona Territory. With determination and eloquence, the delegates finally chose a common path. With a small delegation in tow, Judah returned to Washington, and the group visited with President Buchanan on December 6, 1859, to make the case for the transcontinental line and the need for federal aid.

Judah then went on a quick tour of major eastern cities to give talks and seek support for the Pacific railway. Back in Washington by January 14, 1860, he found support growing. Thanks to Congressmen Beech of California and Logan of Illinois, Theodore Judah was given a room in the Capitol building. It was the former office set aside for use by the vice presidents. Judah filled it with information on his favorite subject, and the room was soon known to members of Congress as the Pacific Railway Museum. Here Judah expressed his ideas, revealed facts and figures, spoke with interviewers, and answered questions.

On a positive note, Congressman Samuel Curtis of Iowa was named chairman of the House Select Committee on the Pacific Railroad, to which Judah's memorial was directed on March 5, 1860. Curtis introduced a Pacific railroad bill into the House, but it failed, a victim of what were called the Southern Obstructionists. Judah needed maps, profiles, and cost estimates to help build the case for the Pacific railroad, and he returned to Sacramento to gather more information.

The Central Pacific Associates

One constant question concerned the rugged Sierra Nevada. Was it really possible to build a railroad line across the harsh escarpment? A letter to Judah from Daniel W. Strong, a druggist in Dutch Flat, California, claimed to have knowledge of a reasonable pass. Journeying quickly to Dutch Flat, Judah met with "Doc" Strong, who took him up into the mountains above Donner Lake; there he saw a promising pathway for a railroad. Beyond Donner Lake lay the valley of the Truckee River and the way to the East. The two men immediately set out terms of agreement and sought to sell stock in the envisioned railroad, for which Judah believed he had discovered a practical route. The case needed to be convincing: Donner Summit was 7,032 feet high and 105 miles from Sacramento. To sell the idea and shares of stock, Strong and Judah called a meeting at the St. Charles Hotel in Sacramento late in November 1860. There Judah would reveal his newly discovered route across the Sierra Nevada. About 30 men attended. There was not the burst of enthusiasm Judah had hoped for, but as his audience rose to leave, one of them stopped to talk to Judah and to invite him to meet in his office in the near future. The man was Collis Potter Huntington, a successful Sacramento hardware merchant. Judah soon met with him. Huntington became interested in the moneymaking opportunities presented by a railroad to the East. He felt that the practical way to proceed was to incorporate. More to the point of progress, Huntington brought others into the group of associates that would form the core of support for the Central Pacific Railroad.

There were four Central Pacific associates, along with the lawyer brother of one of them. Huntington turned out to be the leader. A native of Harviston, Connecticut, he had been born poor, but he had a talent for working hard and making money. At one point he had been an itinerant peddler, but he had enjoyed some business success; he moved to California to seek more success in the aftermath of the 1849 gold strike. Huntington was not interested in panning or digging for gold; over the years he had become a person of some wealth and stature by selling supplies to the miners and was a partner in the largest hardware business in California. His partner was dour Mark Hopkins, born in Henderson, New York, in 1813, who, after several careers, had come west to make his fortune. Hopkins had a keen analytical mind and kept the accounts of the hardware business, as he later would for the railroad. It was reputed that no detail escaped his eye.

Another man brought into the group was Leland Stanford, born in 1824 near Albany, New York; after a variety of careers he had come to Sacramento in 1852 and operated a successful grocery store. Stanford had political ambitions and was soon to be elected governor of California. The fourth member was Charles Crocker. Born in Troy, New York, in 1822, Crocker was a large, commanding man with a talent for leadership and an interest in politics. His lawyer brother, Edwin Bryant Crocker, usually addressed as "Judge," provided legal advice.

Judah had the dream of the Pacific railroad and the technical skill of an engineer. The others were hardheaded businessmen who saw Judah's dream as a way of making money. As Judah came to see, the four could be ruthless in their pursuit of gain.

Judah was back in Washington by December 18, 1860, to assess what was happening. The House had passed a railway bill, but nothing came of it in the Senate. Abraham Lincoln had been elected president the month before, and already there was turmoil as the southern politicians tried to determine a course that would preserve slavery, an institution that the president and his fellow Republicans in Congress were sworn to eventually abolish. Sensing that more facts were needed to persuade Congress and others, Judah returned to California, and April 1861 found him high in the Sierra Nevada conducting more surveys with which to provide detailed information on location, land profiles, and cost estimates. The route he found followed in general the old emigrant trail, and he surveyed and staked the route over the summit and east to the big bend of the Truckee River.

With help from Judge Crocker, the corporate papers for the Central Pacific Railroad Corp. were filed on June 27, 1861. Each of the four major participants invested $1,500, and a like sum in stock was given to Judah, who was to be the chief engineer of the new company. From his work in the spring, Judah developed the necessary figures, profiles, and maps. Indeed, he produced a 90-foot-long map that showed the route of the railway in significant detail. The Central Pacific he had surveyed would be 140 miles long and would cost more than $12 million. He saw the need for 18 tunnels, several of which would be over 1,000 feet long. Bridges would be necessary, but he did not perceive the need for extraordinarily long structures. Snow is a major factor in the Sierra Nevada; by inspecting the growth patterns of pine trees, Judah estimated that the snow depth in winter was approximately 15 feet.

With his information in hand, Judah went to Washington on October 11, 1861. The backers of the Central Pacific hoped for another Pacific railway bill, and to help the process along Judah carried with him shares of stock in the railroad with a par value of $100,000 that were to be used to help pay his expenses and to enlist aid in the undertaking. Judah prepared a *Memorial of the Central Pacific Railroad Company of California* that presented the case of the Central Pacific, and he reopened the Pacific Railway Museum in the Capitol to argue for the Central Pacific and answer questions. Collis Huntington soon joined Judah in the lobbying effort.

Lincoln and the Pacific Railroad

The Civil War had begun in April 1861, and as the southern states seceded, pressure for a southern orientation to the transcontinental railway disappeared. At the same time the need for the railway became more obvious. From the political point of view, to preserve the Union, it was important that Californians not feel left out. There was a worry that the state might set itself up as an independent nation once again. To keep California in the Union, it was necessary to link it to the rest of the United States by rail.

President Lincoln knew railways; as probably the outstanding attorney in Illinois, he had represented the Chicago & Rock Island Railroad in the important case deciding whether or not railroads had the right to bridge navigable rivers. He had also won the case of the Illinois Central Railroad concerning double taxation of its land grant or Charter Lines.

More to the point of interest in the Pacific railway, in August 1859 Lincoln had been in Council Bluffs, Iowa, to check into some real estate holdings that secured a debt. He was also checking on a homestead allotment due him for his service in the Blackhawk War. While sitting on the veranda of his hotel, by chance he met Grenville Dodge, a young engineer who had been carrying out preliminary surveys along the Platte River valley for his employer, Henry Farnam of the Chicago & Rock Island and the Mississippi & Missouri railroads. Lincoln drew out of Dodge much of the information the engineer had gleaned in his survey work in the Platte Valley along the 42nd parallel. Dodge later recounted that he had made a point to Lincoln about the wisdom of the eastern terminus of a Pacific railway being located in the Omaha–Council Bluffs area. The meeting was of great importance to the future of the Pacific railroad.

Legislation

The 1862 Pacific railway bill was introduced by Congressman James Rollins of Missouri. It differed from earlier bills. Instead of one company to carry out the task, there were to be several. In the West the Central Pacific and the Nevada Central would be the carriers. At the eastern end the Leavenworth, Pawnee & Western (later the Kansas Pacific) and the Hannibal & St. Joseph would carry out the work. In the middle a new railroad company called the Union Pacific would do the job; it was initially envisioned that the Union Pacific would construct a railroad from the eastern boundary of Nevada to the western boundary of Kansas. Later this was changed: the Union Pacific would build west from the 100th meridian in Nebraska, with other roads from the East to connect at that point on the prairie.

Unlike the other railroads, the Union Pacific had been chartered by the U.S. Congress, not by state governments. That meant that the Union Pacific had to be constantly on the alert for lobbying efforts of parties seeking some harm to the company or some advantage in dealing with the federal government. The whole package differed from other federal efforts. The Pacific railway was to be a government project, but it was to be built by private companies supported by government aid.

Under the act the railroads, once completed, were to put into escrow 5 percent of their annual net earnings to go toward interest charges and retiring of the loans from the government. There were to be federal subsidies in the form of a land grant; the grant would involve 6,400 acres for each mile constructed, with sections of land alternating on either side of a 400-foot right of way. Mineral lands were excepted from the land grant, but the railways would have access to any timber and stone encompassed by the grant. First-mortgage bonds at 6 percent payable in 30 years would be issued. The number of bonds issued would depend upon the difficulty of construction. There would be $16,000 worth of bonds issued for each mile of easy construction, such as would be experienced by the Central Pacific in the Sacramento Valley and by the Union Pacific across the Nebraska prairies. Each mile in the mountains would yield $48,000 in bonds per mile. The mountain areas were to be measured from the western base of the Sierra Nevada and the eastern base of the Rockies. Bonds of $32,000 per mile would be issued for the construction in the High Plains between the mountains, with 15 percent of the mountain funds and 25 percent of the bonds for the easier stretches withheld until the whole line was in working order. Nothing could be drawn from the U.S. Treasury until the railroad companies had each raised $1 million from private investors and had built 40 miles of track. Two years were allowed for building the first 50 miles of track, and 50 miles were to be constructed each year thereafter.

Under the terms of the 1862 act, if the Central Pacific reached Nevada before the eastern railroad, the Central Pacific could continue construction until it met the eastern railroad. If the Leavenworth, Pawnee & Western reached the 100th meridian before the Union Pacific, the Leavenworth line was free to proceed to build to California. If the Pacific railroad was not completed between the Missouri and Sacramento rivers by January 1, 1871, all companies would forfeit to the federal government what they had built and gained. The latter condition was to assure completion.

With the Pacific railway bill passed as legislation,

Theodore Judah hastened to New York to buy supplies. Bonds were used to pay for 5,000 tons of iron rail, 8 locomotives, 8 passenger cars, 4 baggage cars, and 60 freight cars. Still undecided, and to be the choice of President Lincoln, was the gauge of the railways, exactly where the mountain sections commenced, and where on the Missouri River the eastern line would begin.

The Construction Challenge

The task was a formidable one and extraordinarily risky. No one had ever undertaken a railroad project of such scale. No one really had an idea of the magnitude of the cost. Not until the location engineers and the surveyors looked over the land very carefully would anything resembling an honest guess at cost be available. Cost aside, there was the question of whether or not it could actually be built. The rugged Sierra Nevada was a formidable hurdle for the Central Pacific, and the Rockies stood athwart the line of the Union Pacific.

Worst of all, the major revenues from the railroad would not arrive until after the railroad had been built. Moreover, the railroad would be built through an unpopulated area in which there was very little economic activity. A prospective investor would honestly wonder just what the freight and passenger traffic would consist of for years to come; no grand thoughts could hide the fact that the Pacific railway would be built through an economic desert. The land-grant land could be sold to farmers who would eventually be customers, but it would not happen quickly. To the keen observer, it was worrisome that the government had decided not to build the railroad itself.

The whole business of construction was complicated by the reality that neither the Union Pacific nor the Central Pacific had easy access to supplies and equipment. For the Central Pacific, all major supplies had to be shipped from the East Coast around Cape Horn to the West Coast, a long, dangerous, and expensive voyage. As for the Union Pacific, Council Bluffs and Omaha were not reached by rail from the East for several years after construction commenced. All manufactured goods had to be brought up the Missouri River by steamboat. When the building of the eastern portion of the line eventually started, there was likely to be a labor shortage because of the Civil War. Problems were easy to perceive, and it was not surprising that sales of stock in the venture went slowly.

Leadership and Organization

Leadership and a means of providing more than a remote hope of profit in the near future were sorely needed. For the Central Pacific, the leadership was established. Leland Stanford was president. His associates thought that it would be advantageous to have the governor of California in a key position. The real leader and driving force for the funding and completion of the railroad was Collis Huntington. Once the Central Pacific got under way, he spent most of his time in New York raising money and in Washington lobbying. Theodore Judah as chief engineer brought knowledge and facts to bear in a convincing manner that was often key to moving the project along among potential investors or in Congress. Mark Hopkins was the inside man, the one who kept the books and knew and understood the internal finances of the Central Pacific. Charles Crocker, who could get men to do what he wanted, was to be in charge of construction once the building got under way. The other associates needed Crocker's ability to push the construction crews to carry out very difficult tasks and to bring ingenuity to the process. Judge Crocker kept an eye on legal matters and played a strong role in pushing the project ahead on the West Coast, as did Huntington in the East.

Several of the Central Pacific leaders risked health and life. Collis Huntington was badly overworked and stressed at times. Judge Crocker agonized over the problems and suffered a stroke. Theodore Judah made regular trips east to find the finances and supplies to build the railroad. He usually traveled via the Isthmus of Panama and on one trip was bitten by a mosquito; he died on November 2, 1863, of yellow fever.

The leadership of the Union Pacific was more divided and chaotic. Thomas Clark Durant, for most of its early history, was vice president and general manager. A native of New York State, Durant had attended the Albany Medical College and was an accredited physician, specializing in ophthalmology. He soon turned away from medicine and toward business but still liked to use the title Doctor. Energetic and unpredictable, bright and ruthless, he wanted always to be in the center of things, especially big projects such as the Pacific railway. He did not always inform his associates of what he was up to; he regularly countermanded the orders of others and his own; under his quirky direction, the management of the construction was often confused by Durant's orders to build along different routes than those set out by the engineers. The changes demanded by the Doctor were often for the purpose of lengthening the railroad and increasing the government subsidies. Durant was no dreamer. He wanted to make money, and he was slippery and ruthless enough to be able to do so.

Before the advent of the Union Pacific, Durant had been associated with the highly respected engineer and railroad developer Henry Farnam in the construction of the Michigan Southern Railroad, the Chicago & Rock Island Railroad, and eventually the Mississippi & Missouri Railroad. Some shady dealings on Durant's part led Farnam to disassociate himself from the Doctor. Regardless, Durant was involved at the very beginning of the process of chartering the Union Pacific company and had a role in selecting the leadership of the railroad. Durant named his toady, Silas Seymour, consulting engineer to the railroad. Seymour's main function appeared to be to impede progress by issuing conflicting orders and undermining Dodge.

Durant was also instrumental in bringing the New England–based Ames brothers into the Union Pacific family.

The brothers had made a fortune manufacturing shovels, some of which assisted forty-niners in the Gold Rush and some of which helped build the transcontinental railroad. Both of the brothers invested in the Union Pacific. Oliver Ames in time became president of the railroad, and Oakes Ames, a member of the House of Representatives, played a key role in freeing up federal funds for the Union Pacific.

Construction Companies

Another player was the eccentric George Francis Train. Among other ventures, Train attempted to introduce street railways into Great Britain and designed a type of rail that would enable carriages and wagons to pass over it without harm. Given the risks associated with the Pacific railroad project, there had to be a means of assuring profit to the principals in the company, and it was Train who gave the idea of a construction company to Durant. Train, while in France, had learned about the Crédit Mobilier de France. This French company had been created in 1852 and had been involved in developing the Paris Omnibus Co., the building of the Paris Gas Works, the Grand Hotel du Louvre, and large-scale railway operations.

What was to become the Union Pacific's construction company was an obscure corporation chartered in 1859 by the State of Pennsylvania. Called the Pennsylvania Fiscal Agency, it was endowed with broad powers to buy and sell railroad bonds and other rail securities and to advance money and credit to railroad companies. In March 1864 Durant and Train bought the Pennsylvania Fiscal Agency and changed its name to Crédit Mobilier of America. Insiders on the board of the Union Pacific would own the Crédit Mobilier and let construction contracts to the Crédit Mobilier. The money to be made arose from the reality that as key members of the management of the Union Pacific, they would approve the contracts with the construction company, even if the contracts were wildly inflated in cost. As an example, engineer Peter Dey estimated that the cost of building the first stretch of track to the west of Omaha would be $30,000 per mile. Durant advised Dey to increase the amount of the estimate, and $50,000 was the new figure. The Crédit Mobilier would spend $30,000 to build a mile of line, but collect $50,000. On the face of it, the expenses could be greater than actual construction costs because costs of lobbying and other incidentals could properly be added. The holders of Crédit Mobilier stock could profit handsomely. While some dreamers saw the Pacific railroad as a work of great economic and social benefit for the nation and the world, Durant and his colleagues were interested only in making money from the certainty of the construction process and, to a lesser extent, what profit might be derived from actually operating a functioning railroad.

The Central Pacific's version of the construction company was the Contract and Finance Co., which was owned and controlled by the principal partners in the railroad corporation. The Contract and Finance Co. was empowered to build, operate, and maintain railroads, support the provision of supplies, borrow and lend money, provide transportation services on land and water, and build telegraph lines. A main purpose of the scheme was to hide the profits the insiders were making from overcharging on the construction of the Central Pacific. Both Leland Stanford and Collis Huntington took credit for the creation of the Contract and Finance Co.

Building the Central Pacific

The building of the Central Pacific got under way in Sacramento on January 8, 1863, a wet and cheerless day. The ceremonial first shovels of dirt were taken from two wagons of dry soil hauled before the platform erected for the speechifying that was an expected part of such occasions. The first miles of the Central Pacific were easily constructed in the valley of the Sacramento River. As the Sierra Nevada was approached, the work became increasingly difficult. Part of the arduous nature of the project was the primitive construction methods that were then commonly employed. Grading was done with horse-pulled scrapers and with picks and shovels. Weather was a major problem in the mountains. Judah had expected 15 feet of snow in the area toward the summit; it was all of that and more. Enormous amounts of work were done by hand to keep the line level by digging cuts, some very deep. In winter the snow would fill the cuts and then freeze, so moving supply trains up to the site of construction was seriously delayed. Constructing fills was carried out by wheelbarrows, handcarts, and horse-drawn wagons.

Titled "Taking a Level," this illustration from the August 1874 *Harper's New Monthly Magazine* shows the difficulty of locating the Central Pacific through California's Sierra Nevada. —Middleton Collection

Large numbers of hardworking Chinese laborers—some 20,000 of them were hired for the Central Pacific—made the timely completion of the railroad possible. This view by artist A. R. Waud in the May 29, 1869, *Harper's Weekly* showed Chinese and European workers late in the project. —Library of Congress (Neg. LC-USZ62-35452)

Labor was in short supply on the Pacific Coast, and Charles Crocker was hard pressed. There were many Chinese in the San Francisco area who had come to the United States to improve their fortunes and send money back home. Someone suggested hiring these as workers. At first Crocker refused, feeling that the Chinese were not large or strong enough to carry out the heavy construction work, but he was reminded that it was the Chinese who had built the Great Wall. Eventually he tried a small group of Chinese workers and was delighted to find that they were strong and diligent, complained little, stayed sober, and were reliable. The Central Pacific came to employ many thousands of Chinese workers, some recruited in China, on its construction team.

With the primitive equipment of the time, digging the tunnels was dangerous, difficult, and time consuming. Hand drills were used to punch holes in which to put black powder. It was slow work, and thousands of kegs of powder were used. This project was one of the earliest to use nitroglycerine. The danger in transporting the explo-sive was such that a laboratory was set up near each tunnel's construction site for its manufacture.

The Summit Tunnel took several years and was driven through very hard rock; often progress was only inches a day. Fortunately, work could be carried on in the tunnel when the deep snows of winter came. For a time there was a seven-mile gap in the railroad because the Summit Tunnel was still uncompleted.

To speed up construction in order to collect the bonds and other subsidies from the government, rails and other supplies were hauled by wagon over the summit of the Sierra Nevada, and construction was carried out on the easier downslope toward the Truckee River and Nevada. The gap was not disclosed by Huntington in his forays to Washington to get more funds, and subsidies were paid in the belief that the railroad had been completed through the tunnel and over the summit. Eventually the gap was closed, and new challenges presented themselves.

The land in Nevada was relatively flat, which made the work of moving earth easier. But construction continued

Men, mules, and wagons completed the enormous cuts and fills required for the Central Pacific's line through the Sierras. This view, made at Sailor's Spur in the summer of 1866, shows how material from the cut in the background was used to fill the area in the foreground. —*Trains* Magazine Collection

across an alkali desert, with the alkali dust knee deep in some places, harmful to construction workers and their animal teams. Potable water had to be hauled across the summit for use by the construction crews and the locomotives.

Snow in the Sierra Nevada was a constant problem in the long winters at the high altitudes. The track was often blocked, and locomotives were equipped with snowplows. Special snowplows were built and pushed by multiple locomotives into the drifts. The cuts were so deeply filled with snow that they often had to be dug out by hand. Eventually the Central Pacific turned to the extensive use of snow sheds, especially where avalanches were prevalent.

Crocker kept pushing the workers, and they responded

handsomely, steadily advancing the tracks toward the junction with the Union Pacific. Exactly where that point would be was left unsettled for years. Huntington and his colleagues wanted to build as far as Ogden, Utah, and into Salt Lake City. But at first it was uncertain if the railroad would approach these targets from the north, around the top of the Great Salt Lake, or from the south. In time it was decided that the northern route was preferred, and the survey stakes were pushed forward toward the Promontory Mountains. To help in the construction, Leland Stanford journeyed to Salt Lake City and approached Mormon leader Brigham Young to arrange a contract to employ Mormons in building the railroad in Utah.

To hasten construction, temporary, rickety wooden bridges were built; later, earth was dumped in from the

Perhaps the most difficult section of the Central Pacific line through the Sierra Nevada was the precipitous route at Cape Horn. Here, with perhaps a little exaggeration from the artist for the May 1872 *Harper's New Monthly Magazine,* a train is shown passing one of the Cape Horn curves. —Middleton Collection

The Central Pacific's early experience with the heavy snowfalls of the Sierra Nevada convinced the railroad that extensive snow-shed construction was needed for reliable winter operation. This drawing, from the February 10, 1872, *Harper's Weekly*, shows the terrible snowfalls encountered in that year. —Middleton Collection

bridges to create large fills, or stronger, better-designed structures were built. This work was carried on for some time after the two railroads were supposedly completed. The Union Pacific adopted the same strategy to save time and get miles of railroad built. As Crocker's construction crews gained experience, the project moved on in an assembly-line process, advancing steadily across Nevada and into and across Utah.

As the meeting place was approached, Crocker's crew built ten miles of railroad in one day; this record was set after careful preparation and a bounty paid to the grading and tracklaying staff. Despite the construction difficulties in the Sierra Nevada, the Central Pacific was fortunate in a virtual absence of trouble from Indian tribes. The associates decided to give passes to the tribal chiefs, and the train crews were instructed to allow Indians to ride freight trains without question. This practice assured relatively peaceful relations.

This drawing, from the May 1872 *Harper's New Monthly Magazine*, shows the typical interior of a timber shed. —Middleton Collection

As mentioned, a significant problem for the Central Pacific was the need for all construction supplies from the East to be moved via a long voyage around Cape Horn to the Pacific shore and then eastward to supply the construction crews. Orders could take many months to fill. The supplies included timber for bridges and crossties; this was a particularly important requirement in the deserts of Nevada and Utah, where there was no local timber. Fortunately, timber and potable water supplies were available in California, but still had to be moved long distances.

Building the Union Pacific

Construction work for the Union Pacific began later than that of the Central Pacific. On December 2, 1863, a groundbreaking ceremony was held at a point in Omaha two miles south of the ferry landing at Council Bluffs. George Francis Train delivered an impassioned address; he was joined by the governor of Nebraska and two companies of artillery. Engineer Peter Dey read messages from President Lincoln and Dr. Thomas Durant citing the commencement of a great undertaking.

At that time no railroad had yet reached Council Bluffs from the East. Not until four years later, in December 1867, did the Chicago & North Western reach Council Bluffs from Chicago and points east. Soon afterward it was joined by the Chicago, Burlington & Quincy and the Chicago, Rock Island & Pacific. There was still no direct rail connection from the East to Omaha. Supplies and people had to be ferried across the Missouri River. A bridge between Council Bluffs and Omaha was finally built in 1872.

The path the Union Pacific was to follow was laid out by Grenville Dodge. In addition to his work as an engineer, Dodge served in the Civil War, and his skillful and excellent work in difficult situations got him promoted to general. Dodge made important friendships in the Union army, including Generals Grant and Sherman. In surveying and selecting the route of the Union Pacific, Dodge's knowledge of the region and his key friendships and vision made him indispensable. The shady Dr. Durant was not an appealing figure to important constituencies, especially within the federal government; Dodge could bring stability and federal subsidies to the situation because of his reputation and integrity as an engineer. He

Hand labor, horses, and mules provided the hard labor for early railroad building. Here Union Pacific workers are armed with the famous Ames shovels. —Library of Congress (Neg. LC-USZ62-35458)

to Cheyenne and then on to Laramie; from there it followed the Green River and then on to the Wasatch Mountains, Weber Canyon, and Utah. Dodge's choice of the South Pass was significant because this crossing of the Rockies is at an altitude of 8,000 feet, much lower than alternate passes in the surrounding mountains.

One shortcoming with the route was that it took the railroad across the land of Indians who proved to be hostile. Some of the tribes had already been moved and their culture and way of life disturbed. The coming of the iron horse was the overture to complete upheaval. The tribes, so often lied to by the white man, understandably fought back. The initial surveying parties were attacked, and the construction parties were under constant threat. Soldiers under the command of General Sherman, who was in charge of the U.S. military in the western United States after the Civil War, were assigned to protect the railroad builders. The carnage continued all during construction and even after the railroad across the continent was complete.

The actual construction work of the Union Pacific was in the able hands of the Casement brothers, Jack and Dan. The former, known as General Jack, had practical experience in railroad building in Ohio and later served with great distinction in the Civil War. The contract to build the railroad was won because of Jack Casement's experience in leading men in war. When construction started, the war was still in progress, and it was difficult to find able-bodied men. After the war thousands of veterans of both armies were searching for work, and many found it in building the Union Pacific Railroad. Among the problems was the reality of friction between Union and Confederate veterans. Added to this was an influx of sometimes-temperamental Irish immigrants. Whiskey was often the fuel that ignited

also served as a member of the U.S. House of Representatives from Iowa, which increased his influence on the political side of the Union Pacific.

As a pathfinder, it was Dodge who found the best course of the railroad west from Omaha and up the Platte River valley. From the Platte the route followed Lodgepole Creek

The grading complete and the crossties in place, teams of UP track workers carried the rails into position somewhere on the prairies. From the June 1867 *Harper's New Monthly Magazine*. —Middleton Collection

The Union Pacific's "General Jack" Casement was a man of extraordinary skills and leadership. Casement's rolling train that housed workmen and equipment just behind the completion of track helped the UP maintain a fast pace of construction. In the foreground are a few Indians and a party of westbound settlers. —*Trains* Magazine Collection

fights and violence. The Casement brothers and their foremen had to bear down hard to keep peace and get the railroad built.

Like the Central Pacific, the Union Pacific employed primitive construction tools. Near the very end of building the railway, small numbers of steam shovels were used, but pick and shovel and horse-drawn scrapers were the principal means of construction.

The Casement brothers developed a new technique in building and supplying the construction crews, the construction train. It consisted of a string of oversized boxcar-like vehicles that could be moved along to keep pace with the railroad's progress. Many of the cars were dormitories that could house the workers in greater comfort than would a tent village. There was a blacksmith car to produce metal items needed as the work progressed, and a car for farriers to keep the horses well shod. A butcher's car provided fresh meat. There were kitchen cars and cars for feeding the construction crews. Hunters such as Buffalo Bill Cody supplied the butchers and cooks with fresh game, as well as buffalo meat. There were also equipment cars, and strings of flatcars arrived regularly with rails, spikes, joining bars, crossties, and bridge timbers.

Following the railroad builders was a movable city that was dubbed Hell on Wheels. It consisted of portable modular buildings of wood and supplies of canvas to create large tents and roofs for the buildings. The city was peopled by whiskey purveyors, gamblers, prostitutes, and other hangers-on. Hell on Wheels would move to a point near the end of the track, and the temporary buildings would be erected into saloons, dance halls, and other means of separating the construction gangs from their money. Gunfire was the leitmotif of these meandering cities, and drunkenness and murder were common.

After the locating engineers and surveyors set out the stakes for the pathway the railroad was to follow, the grading work would commence. To speed up the process, much of the new track work was not ballasted at first. Later the ballast train arrived, and the track structure was eventually put in good order. As first built, the track was often rickety, and derailments of the construction trains were commonplace. The grading work often moved far in advance of the actual laying of track, in part because of delays in obtaining supplies and in part in order to claim more progress so as to keep the government money flowing.

In some instances the more difficult and time-consuming work was temporarily avoided by grading and laying track around an obstacle, helping keep the gradient within practical limits but increasing distance. This expedient strategy was followed by both the Central Pacific and the Union Pacific in order to get the job done. Well into the twentieth century both the Central Pacific's successor, the Southern Pacific, and the Union Pacific were involved in a regular process of reducing curvature and diminishing gradient in order to make the railways more efficient. Old tunnels were daylighted into long cuts, and light wooden and iron bridges were replaced with stronger steel structures. In a very real sense the Pacific railway has never been completed.

Completing the Pacific Railroad

For a lengthy period the federal government did not identify the place at which the two railroads would meet. The provisions of the Pacific Railroad Act encouraged each of the railroads to build as much line as they could. Collis Huntington and General Dodge wanted to settle on a meeting place before Congress or some other party made the decision. They met on Sunday, April 8, 1869, in Washington, D.C., at the home of Congressman Samuel Hooper of Massachusetts. This was appropriate because the congressman owned shares in Crédit Mobilier, Union Pacific, and Central Pacific. Toward the end of the building process the two railroads were grading their lines parallel and virtually next to one another. When the meeting point was finally set at Promontory Point, Utah, north of the Great Salt Lake, there was a duplication of railroad; eventually the Central Pacific purchased a part of the line built by the Union Pacific to gain entrance into Ogden.

With the exception of the death of Theodore Judah, the leadership of the Central Pacific stayed much the same, with Judge Crocker playing an increasing role; indeed, he worked so hard on the project that his health was impaired. Also under great stress was Collis Huntington, who worked diligently in New York and Washington to secure the legislation and the funds needed to build the Central Pacific. Money and securities were liberally distributed to members of the House and Senate to gain favor. It could be called bribery, but it was not an uncommon practice in the nineteenth century or in the years that followed. The ownership and the profits of the Contract and Finance Co. continued to be held closely by the four Central Pacific associates.

In the case of the Union Pacific, there were similarities but also differences. Unlike the Contract and Finance Co., the shares in Crédit Mobilier were widely held and the profits distributed with a liberal hand to shareholders. Durant sought to place persons of good reputation on the board of directors to gain respectability and to help attract investment. The aforementioned Ames brothers were an example. Successful businessmen, they helped raise money and support in New England, which at the time was a major source of finance. Oliver Ames was eventually named president of the Union Pacific. Oakes Ames, as a member of the U.S. House, played a large role in distributing Union Pacific and Crédit Mobilier stock to congressmen and others who could be helpful. Thanks to his diligence, many eminent businessmen became shareholders or directors.

The date for the completion of the Pacific railroad was set for May 8, 1869, at Promontory Point, Utah. The wedding of the rails had to be put back two days because Dr. Durant's train of Union Pacific dignitaries was delayed by weather and a strike of construction workers demanding back pay. Finally, on May 10, 1869, with the nation waiting breathlessly for news by telegraph of the completion of the great work, the Central Pacific locomotive *Jupiter* ap-

One of the great moments of American history was the joining of the Central Pacific and Union Pacific railroads at Promontory, Utah, to complete the Pacific Railroad on May 10, 1869. UP locomotive No. 119, photographed from its cab, would move west to meet the CP locomotive *Jupiter* to complete the formal joining. —*Trains* Magazine Collection

proached the site from the west, and Union Pacific No. 119 from the east. The last ties were put down and the last rails placed and all but the final spikes hammered in. Leland Stanford was responsible for seating the golden spike, while Thomas Durant drove in the silver spike. The *Jupiter* and No. 119 were detached from their trains. They moved ahead until the pilots touched. The famous photograph of the most important economic event of the nineteenth century was snapped. The telegraph signaled that the project was completed. Both locomotives backed to recouple to their trains; then No. 119 moved forward to cross the point where the rails had been joined and then backed away. *Jupiter* repeated the symbolic process. The dream of the Pacific railway had been fulfilled. The ceremony led San Francisco's unofficial poet laureate, Bret Harte, to compose a poem, the opening lines of which read:

> What was it the Engines said,
> Pilots touching—head to head
> Facing on the single track,
> Half a world behind each back?

At the ceremony General Dodge gave a short speech that harkened back to the days when the Pacific railway was just a dream of men such as Theodore Judah and Asa Whitney and Thomas Hart Benton. In it he said, "The great Benton prophesied that some day a granite statue of Columbus would be erected on the highest peak of the Rocky Mounts, pointing westward, denoting the great route across the continent. You have made the prophecy today a fact. This is the way to India." The heroic statue was never erected.

The telegraph signal of completion of the Pacific railway touched off a huge celebration in New York, Washington, and other eastern cities. In Chicago the largest parade in the history of the city took place. All over the United States there were fireworks displays befitting the Fourth of July.

Grenville Dodge is the person most responsible for the actual creation of the Union Pacific. Despite interference from Durant and his sycophant Seymour, the railroad was built to his direction. It was built quickly, and in a few years much would be rebuilt. Collis Huntington provided the greatest leadership for the completion of the Central Pacific. Except for Stanford, Dodge, and Durant, none of the principal players in the great railroad drama were present at Promontory Point.

The two companies had completed a formidable task, fighting weather, mountains, and hostile Indians. The Union Pacific had built more than 900 miles of line and the Central Pacific more than 1,100 miles. Both companies were dogged by the fear of running out of money and bankruptcy. Both companies had bribed their way to success, and the profit to the insiders was in the millions of dollars. Despite the negatives, the Pacific railroad was complete.

In 1873 the *New York Sun* began a series of articles giving the behind-the-scenes story of the transcontinental railroad; the news precipitated the Crédit Mobilier scandal. Several congressional investigatory panels were established, and much of the seamy mess was made public. The bribery was only part of the story. The overcharging for the construction by insiders became a subject of gossip when it became known that Durant and Seymour had contracted at high prices to sell supplies to the Union Pacific. Oliver Ames and particularly Oakes Ames were vilified as masters of bribery and unethical conduct. Durant was likewise tarred with opprobrium. The Grant administration, already deep in dirty linen, was further burdened by the Crédit Mobilier disgrace that played out over a long period. The Central Pacific associates escaped general public disdain, in part because the books of the Contract and Finance Co. had been burned (whether by accident or on purpose remains an unsolved mystery).

The story of what was done by those who sought maximum profit to build the Pacific railway is not a pretty one. What should not be dismissed is that an extraordinarily difficult and highly risky undertaking was completed in a relatively brief period of time, once under way. The Pacific railroad tied the nation together as Lincoln hoped. It and subsequent railways to the Pacific joined with the eastern railroads to form a single economy and society. The Pacific railroad helped change the United States forever by making it into a truly continental nation.

—George M. Smerk

REFERENCES

Ambrose, Stephen E. *Nothing like It in the World: The Men Who Built the Transcontinental Railroad, 1863–1869.* New York: Simon & Schuster, 2000.

Bain, David Haward. *Empire Express: Building the First Transcontinental Railroad.* New York: Viking, 1999.

Brown, Dee. *Hear That Lonesome Whistle Blow: Railroads in the West.* New York: Holt, Rinehart & Winston, 1977.

Daggett, Stuart. *Chapters on the History of the Southern Pacific.* 1922. Repr., New York: Augustus M. Kelley, 1966.

Haney, Lewis H. *A Congressional History of Railways in the United States.* 2 vols. 1908 and 1910. Repr., New York: Augustus M. Kelley, 1968.

Holbrook, Stewart H. *The Story of American Railroads.* Chap. 30. New York: Crown, 1947.

Klein, Maury. *Union Pacific: Birth of a Railroad, 1862–1893.* Garden City, N.Y.: Doubleday, 1987.

Train, George Francis. *My Life in Many States and in Foreign Lands.* Chap. 23. New York: D. Appleton, 1902. Repr. Buckingham, U.K.: Adam Gordon, Priory Cottage, Chetwode, 1991.

White, Henry Kirke. *History of the Union Pacific Railway.* Chicago: Univ. of Chicago Press, 1895. Repr., New York: Augustus M. Kelley, 1973.

Pacific Railroad (Ferrocarril del Pacífico)

The Pacific Railroad extended from Nogales, a city straddling the border between Arizona and the Mexican state of Sonora, south to the port of Guaymas, then southeast to Guadalajara, 1,095 miles from Nogales. It was built by two American railroads, the northern part by the Santa Fe and the southern part by the Southern Pacific, and came under ownership of the Mexican government in 1951.

Sonora Railway

North America's second transcontinental rail route was created in 1881 when the Atchison, Topeka & Santa Fe, building south from Albuquerque, met the Southern Pacific, which was building eastward from Los Angeles, at Deming, New Mexico. The Santa Fe's goal in meeting the SP at Deming was the Pacific, but not in California. It arranged for trackage rights on SP west to Benson, Arizona, and from there it built a line southwest to Nogales, where it connected with the Sonora Railway, which the Santa Fe had built north from Guaymas, on the Gulf of California.

The Santa Fe also built west from Albuquerque to Needles, California, where it met a line the Southern Pacific had built across the desert from Mojave to Needles. SP's line was to have been part of its route to New Orleans until SP was persuaded to make a detour to serve the young city of Los Angeles. The line to Mojave was simply a branch to nowhere on SP's map, but it would extend the Santa Fe system much of the way to Los Angeles. SP wanted a line into Mexico, and in 1897 the two railroads worked out a swap: Santa Fe got the Needles-Mojave line, and Southern Pacific got the Sonora Railway, first leasing it in 1898, then purchasing it in 1911.

Southern Pacific of Mexico

In 1909 SP incorporated the Southern Pacific of Mexico (Sud Pacifico de Mexico, SPdeM) and in 1912 consolidated it with the Sonora Railway. The railroad began to push southeastward, though hindered by the Mexican Revolution, native uprisings, and rough country where it turned inland at Tepic. It finally connected with the National Railways of Mexico near Guadalajara in 1927.

The SPdeM was not the moneymaker its parent had hoped it would be. Southern Pacific withdrew financial support in 1940 and required the railroad to live on its income. Labor laws constrained productivity, and tariffs on produce imported from Mexico kept the traffic level low. The status of U.S.-owned holdings in Mexico became doubtful, and Southern Pacific decided to sell its subsidiary before it was expropriated. The Mexican government purchased the railroad in December 1951, and it was renamed the Ferrocarril del Pacífico (FCP), or Pacific Railroad.

Ferrocarril del Pacífico

FCP's condition gradually improved. Produce moving northward proved to be its major freight commodity, and by the 1980s that traffic was moving in fast piggyback trains. It teamed up with the National Railways of Mexico to offer first-class passenger service between the U.S. border and Mexico City.

The Mexican government set out in the mid-1980s to unify its railroads. On June 22, 1987, the FCP became the Pacific Region of the National Railways of Mexico (FNM). As Mexico privatized its rail system a decade later, the former FCP returned to private operation in February 1998 as part of a 4,000-mile FNM segment turned over to Ferrocarril Mexicano S.A. de C.V. (Ferromex) concessionaire that included Union Pacific.

—George H. Drury

REFERENCE

Signor, John R., and John A. Kirchner. *The Southern Pacific of Mexico and the West Coast Route*. San Marino, Calif.: Golden West, 1987.

See also MEXICAN RAILROADS, GENERAL HISTORY; MEXICAN RAILROADS, NATIONALIZATION (1880–1990); MEXICAN RAILROADS, PRIVATIZATION (1990–)

Pacific Railroad Survey

For more than three decades before the Pacific railroad finally became a reality in 1869 it was the object of intensive debate and a range of competing proposals. There were proposals for an Atlantic-to-Pacific road as early as 1832. For these early proposals the facilitating of commerce to the riches of the Orient often seemed to be the primary consideration. But the building of a railroad to forestall England's designs on the Oregon country, tying together the emerging West that would link the United States firmly into a great coast-to-coast union, and the growing numbers of westbound Americans were all increasingly important considerations.

The first well-developed proposal for the Pacific railroad was advanced in 1844 by an unlikely man for such a project: a 47-year-old visionary named Asa Whitney. Whitney, who had buried two wives and lost his once-prosperous French import business to foreclosure at New York, had sailed by the Cape of Good Hope for China to start anew. Conceiving the idea of a railroad as a new and faster route to the West, Whitney developed it into a detailed plan for a line from Lake Michigan to Oregon and presented it to Congress in 1844. It was under discussion for almost another decade, and there was no shortage of alternate plans. Competing proposals, compounded by sectional rivalries, slavery questions, and opposition to any public involvement in a railroad, seemed by the early 1850s to have made any consensus impossible to achieve.

A major problem was the lack of detailed information

about the nature, character, and aspect of much of the land west of the Mississippi. Despite intensive discussion in Congress in 1852–1853, no plan could be agreed upon. Instead, near the end of the session, Congress finally passed a bill that would appropriate funds for the secretary of war to conduct surveys to ascertain the most practical and economic route for a railroad between the Mississippi and the Pacific Ocean.

After careful consideration of routes already advocated and the information then available, Secretary of War Jefferson Davis planned surveys for four general transcontinental routes, including the northern or Whitney route linking St. Paul and the Oregon country (although Asa Whitney's proposal followed an alignment much farther south from Lake Michigan to Oregon), the central route proposed by Senator Thomas Hart Benton of Missouri for his National Central Highway linking Missouri and northern California, a southern route extending from Fort Smith, Arkansas, to Los Angeles, and the southernmost alignment on the Gila route, extending from Texas to San Diego. The expeditions required detailed information on the surveys, with particular attention to the mountain passes, and would provide a vast mine of new information for the study of the history, ethnology, zoology, paleontology, botany, and geology of the West. The survey parties, led by the army's Corps of Topographic Engineers and equipped with such equipment as transits, magnetometers, and barometers, began their work in the spring of 1853.

The Northern Route from the 47th to the 49th Parallel

The first survey party to get under way was the northern route, which headed west out of St. Paul early in April 1853, headed by Isaac I. Stevens, a West Point graduate and an experienced army engineer who had recently been appointed the first governor of Washington Territory. The expedition was organized into two main divisions. Governor Stevens himself headed the eastern division, which began at St. Paul, while a western division began work from Puget Sound and through the Cascades. Stevens's chief assistant, who led the western group, was Capt. George B. McClellan, who would go on to service as the commander in chief of the Army of the Potomac during the Civil War and later be the 1864 Democratic candidate for president.

The Stevens group traveled west from the Mississippi River valley and the great bend of the Missouri, typically organizing smaller groups to explore the terrain as they went. By the beginning of August the main party had reached Fort Union, at the junction with the Missouri and Yellowstone rivers in the Nebraska Territory (now northeast Montana). The group then headed west to Fort Benton and then into the eastern slopes of the Rocky Mountains, reaching there in early September, from which Stevens and his men sent out small pack-train parties to explore the passes of the Rockies.

Meanwhile, McClellan's western division moved east, leaving in July from Fort Vancouver, in Washington Territory. They moved northerly to explore the Cascades, while several reconnaissance teams explored other possible routes. By the next month McClellan's party was exploring the mountains between the Yakima and Columbia rivers. Unable to find any other acceptable pass, McClellan had chosen a crossing through the Yakima River as the best route. McClellan moved east from the Cascades, connecting with a small party led by Governor Stevens at St. Mary's village in western Nebraska Territory on October 19.

Work continued through 1854, and Stevens's report—the first one completed—was delivered at the end of June 1854. Stevens's study established feasible railroads to the Rocky Mountains through either the Missouri or Yellowstone, identified five possible routes through the Rockies between the passes to the east and the Bitterroot River, several practical passes through the Cascades, and a favorable route to Fort Vancouver and Olympia.

The Central Route from the 38th to the 39th Parallel

Capt. John W. Gunnison of the Topographic Engineers headed the central route. His work began with general reconnaissance of the features and practicality of the Missouri River, with the route later following the Arkansas River into Kansas Territory. The survey party followed the route of the Huerfano River and progressed up into the San Luis Mountains and then northward through the best pass to the Grand River valley. The route extended across Utah Territory (now Colorado) and then near Sevier River crossed the Wasatch Mountains and turned northward to Salt Lake City.

Gunnison arrived in St. Louis early in June 1853 and had reached Westport near Fort Leavenworth by the end of the month. West of this point he divided his party into two groups, with the second headed by Lt. Edward G. Beckwith, one of Gunnison's assistants, following a more southerly line along the Santa Fe Trail until the two groups rejoined at Fort Zarah in Kansas Territory. The group continued along the Santa Fe Trail, making good time over the well-defined trail along the Arkansas and reaching Bent's Fort at the end of July. Gunnison continued along the Arkansas and then followed the Raton Pass.

Separating, Beckwith headed to the northwest, to the Greenhorn River and into the mountains of the San Luis Valley, while Gunnison took a route along the Arkansas and Huerfano rivers and then followed the dividing ridges of Sangre de Cristo Pass, finally descending into the San Luis Valley almost to Fort Massachusetts. Late in August the party moved toward the north and west, following the San Luis Valley to the summit of the divide that separated the headwaters of the Arkansas and the Rio Grande and then following the Gunnison River across Cochetopa Pass and taking the route of the Spanish Trail. Following a depression through the Wasatch Mountains, Gunnison had learned of an uprising between settlers and the Utah Indians, but continued to travel west to explore Sevier Lake.

On the morning of October 26 Gunnison's small party was surprised by a band of young Paiutes. Eight of the party were found dead, including Gunnison, who was pierced by 15 arrows. There were some who attributed the disaster to the Mormons, while others blamed it entirely on the Indian group. A Mormon jury later indicted 26 Indians, but all were found not guilty. Beckwith now took charge of the party, recovering almost all the notes and instruments from the Gunnison party, and then continued north to Salt Lake City, where they wintered.

The following year, in April 1854 Beckwith set out to the north and east to explore the Weber and Green rivers of northeast Utah Territory, returning to Salt Lake City late in April. Beckwith then began the trip to the west, exploring possible passes through the region of the Humboldt River, and made a number of surveys of the Sierra Nevada, including Madeline Pass and Pitt River. Having explored all available passes from the east, Beckwith was convinced that the Feather River lay farther south. After reaching Sacramento, Beckwith made surveys from the west of Madeline Pass.

Beckwith disbanded his party and reported to Washington in September 1854. The entire length of the route along the Missouri River was estimated at 1,888 miles. The line offered many advantages for railroad construction, with ample supplies of wood and water, and with a soil capable of cultivation for the greater part of the route. Disadvantages were the heavy snowfalls and difficult grades of both the Wasatch Mountains and the Sierra Nevada.

The Southern Route along the 35th Parallel

Lt. Amiel W. Whipple came to his new assignment for the 35th parallel with an extensive experience in western exploration, having spent three years on the Boundary Survey Commission in western territory from 1850 to 1852. Issued in May 1853, the army's instructions for the survey called for a relatively straight path across the Unorganized Territory (now Oklahoma), Texas, the New Mexico Territory, and California to a western terminal at Los Angeles. The party left Washington at the end of May 1853 and was ready to begin its work from Fort Smith, Arkansas, by mid-July.

The party moved into the Choctaws, on the territorial lands that had been ceded to them (now Oklahoma), generally following the line of the Washita and then the Canadian River west through Indian Territory and the north Panhandle of Texas, with extensive side trips to explore the land. From Tucumcari Creek, in New Mexico Territory, the party was divided into two groups. One would proceed directly to Albuquerque, while the other would travel

to the northwest before following the Rio Grande south into Albuquerque.

By early November Whipple had organized his party into the two groups. Lt. J. C. Ives, Whipple's chief military assistant, took a group south and then crossed the Rio Grande at Isleta and went west, while Whipple crossed the Rio Grande at Atrisco to explore the western route to Zuñi, with the two parties rejoining at San Jose River. They continued west, dividing again at San Jose Valley, with Ives traveling directly to Zuñi while Whipple began ascending the Sierra Madre, reaching the summit of the Continental Divide at Agua Fria, 7,760 feet above sea level. On the western slope Whipple's party found Spanish inscriptions in a rock dating to as early as 1620. By late November the two parties had rejoined on the Zuñi at Fort Defiance.

Whipple's party then continued west across the Rio Puerco and the San Francisco Mountains, identifying several feasible passes through the mountain ranges and reaching the dividing ridge between the Colorado and Gila rivers in mid-December. The party continued its reconnaissance to the west, finally joining the Colorado River at its junction with the Rio Santa Maria at the junction of Bill Williams' Fork in late February. Whipple then traveled to the west across the Mojave Valley, accompanied by the Paiute tribes, who wanted to come under protection of the United States. By mid-March Whipple had reached the road to Cajon Pass to begin his descent into Los Angeles, the end of the journey.

The 35th parallel route as surveyed by Whipple was 1,952 miles in length and had many advantages. The route between the Rio Grande and the Colorado was intersected by several mountain ranges, but he had found passes that were practical, if not easy.

The Southern Route along the 32nd Parallel

The southernmost route was the last to get started and was the only one broken up into two separate survey parties. Capt. John Pope was instructed to study the 32nd parallel across Texas at El Paso eastward to the Red River, while a western segment of the survey headed by Lt. John G. Parke would conduct surveys extending east from Fort Yuma on the Colorado River, on the border of California and New Mexico Territory, to the Rio Grande at El Paso.

Pope got started first. His party was organized at Albuquerque and then set out for a starting point at Doña Ana, north of El Paso on the Rio Grande, arriving there by mid-January. Pope ran a survey to El Paso, while the main party then set out through an unexplored area east of the Rio Grande. Upon reaching the east side of Guadalupe Mountains and then eastward into the Pecos River, they encountered what was regarded as the most dangerous portion of the route, the Llano Estacado, the dreadful "terra incognita" of the western Texas desert. One party was sent east to examine the Llano Estacado from the direction of the Colorado and Brazos rivers, while another was searching for a better pass through the Guadalupe Mountains to El Paso. Camping on Delaware Creek, Pope and his party were attacked by Apaches, who set fire to the prairies, and only rapid backfiring and a retreat across the Pecos saved the expedition.

Dividing into several parties, Pope's men launched reconnoitering expeditions in the area. Pope himself had decided that it was impossible to cross the Llano Estacado with wagons and headed south along the Pecos following the emigrant train. Upon reaching Big Springs of the Colorado, Pope then headed northwest along his own trail to rejoin Captain Taplin, one of Pope's officers, at the Sulphur Springs. Meanwhile, Taplin made several forays into the Llano Estacado to secure a thorough and practical knowledge of the area. The party then traveled east from the Colorado River to the Brazos and then moved northeast along the military road that linked Forts Chadbourne and Belknap, pausing at the town of San Antonio, where the party saw its first house since leaving Doña Ana. Not quite three months since it had left Doña Ana, Pope brought the party into its eastern end at Preston, along the Red River.

Lieutenant Parke, who had been exploring the Sierra Nevada, received his instructions at San Diego from the secretary of war late in 1853. Parke's party set out at Fort Yuma. Because the section from San Diego to the Colorado and the Pima and Maricopa villages had already been explored by Lt. Col. William H. Emory during 1846–1847, Parke and his party traveled rapidly through the Gila River and Pima villages and then headed south to Tucson. The Mexican government had recently granted permission for Parke to proceed through the northern part of Mexico, and his instructions were to proceed from Tucson by Nugent's wagon train to its San Pedro crossing and then as far east as Cooke's wagon road and thence the shortest and best route to the Rio Grande somewhere between Doña Ana and Frontera.

Tucson was still part of Mexico, and Parke received his passport from the *commandante* of the presidio (the area would change to U.S. jurisdiction through the Gadsden Purchase in mid-1854) and continued his surveys to the east. Parke traveled to the southeast into the San Pedro Valley and then across the Apache Pass crossing of the Chiricahui Mountains. Crossing the valley of the Ciénega de Sauz, Parke reached the Pyramid Range and then headed east to Mesilla on the Rio Grande. Although the route across the Mesilla Valley had proved entirely suitable for a railroad, Parke also went back to the east and surveyed a more southerly line to El Paso. Parke disbanded his party and returned to Washington, although the following year, in 1855, he returned to the same alignment for further surveys of the route.

The combined Pope and Parke studies totaled 1,012 miles. Both Pope's eastern end and Parke's study in the west were shown to be favorable for railroad construction, with shortest distance and but slight opposition from the mountains. The biggest problem was water, of which only nine sources were found over the entire route.

California and Oregon Studies

In addition to the four east-west surveys, the War Department also set up survey teams to explore the most feasible lines along the Pacific ranges. Under a set of instructions from the War Department received early in May 1853, Lt. R. S. Williamson was to study the practicality of passes from the lower Colorado River west into California. Explorers familiar with the Sierra Nevada were unanimous that there was no feasible pass through the mountains in either Sacramento or the Sacramento Valley, and it was deemed unnecessary to explore any routes north of the Kern River.

Beginning from Benicia, near San Francisco, Williamson explored five different Sierra Nevada passes, but found only two that were practical. He continued south with surveys of the junctions between the Sierra Nevada and Coast ranges and of the Mojave area to the east of Los Angeles and located feasible routes east from Los Angeles through Cajon Pass and San Gorgonio Pass and to the west through Santa Susana pass. John Parke, who had worked under Williamson when he surveyed the western segment of the 32nd parallel, also made surveys in late 1853 over the Colorado Desert to Fort Yuma and the passes leading to San Diego. Lieutenant Parke, after the end of his surveys for the 32nd parallel, was appointed to head another survey at the beginning of October 1854 to study the practicality of a railroad route from San Francisco to Los Angeles west of the Coast Range, as well as further studies of the Mojave River valley to the Colorado.

Finally, a third exploration of surveys of Upper California and Oregon was set up in the spring of 1855. Headed again by Lieutenant Williamson and aided by chief assistant Lt. H. L. Abbot, the party began its work from Benicia. Traveling with pack trains instead of wagons, it surveyed the Sacramento River valley to Fort Reading, then headed east and again north to follow the western chain of the Sierra Nevada. The party reached Lower Klamath Lake and then followed the Deschutes River into Oregon to Fort Dalles and to Fort Vancouver. While Williamson continued studies in the Cascades, Abbot headed a party south through the Willamette River valley from Vancouver and finally to Fort Reading.

Survey Results

Information from these surveys gave the War Department an unequaled opportunity to study the several routes and make a well-informed choice for the Pacific railroad. Thirteen large volumes were filed with the *Congressional Record* in 1855. After studying the alternatives, Secretary of War Jefferson Davis recommended to Congress in February 1855 that the southernmost 32nd parallel route was the most practical and economical. As a southerner, Davis's recommendations were discounted,

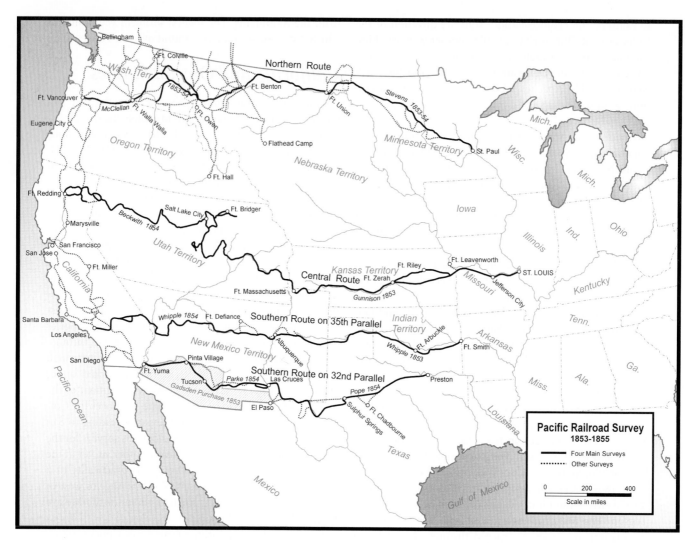

Pacific Railroad Survey, 1853–1855. —Tony Howe

but there seems little doubt that he was right. Except for the northernmost line, the 32nd parallel route had the lowest grades, the most economical construction costs, and the most favorable geography and weather.

But with slavery issues and intense political rivalries, no one was about to approve a southern route or, for that matter, anything else, and the issue went unresolved until the Civil War, when, with the southern factions gone, it became possible to proceed. Ironically, none of the four parallel studies was adopted; the route selected instead would prove much more difficult. Built by the Union Pacific and Central Pacific railroads, the line had not one but three passes at anywhere from 7,000 to 8,000 feet, higher than any other save for the central line across Utah, and some of the most difficult operating conditions. But in the end, all four Pacific railway survey routes were used by later railroads. The southernmost line closely followed Southern Pacific and Texas & Pacific. The Santa Fe and the Rock Island were built along the 35th parallel. The Missouri Pacific, Rio Grande, and Western

Pacific closely followed the 38th and 39th lines along the proposed National Central route, except for the Feather River through the Sierra Nevadas, which Beckwith had not found. Both Northern Pacific and the Milwaukee Road followed the western alignment of the northern route to the Rocky Mountain passes identified by Stevens, while the Great Northern followed the eastern end until it found the much more advantageous pass through Marias Pass, which Stevens had looked for but could not find.

—William D. Middleton

REFERENCES

Albright, George Leslie. *Official Explorations for Pacific Railroads.* Berkeley: Univ. of California Press, 1921.

Bain, David Haward. *Empire Express: Building the First Transcontinental Railroad.* New York: Viking, 1999.

Haney, Lewis Henry. *A Congressional History of Railways in the United States, 1850–1887.* Madison: Bulletin, Univ. of Wisconsin, 1910.

Packer, Asa (1805–1879)

Canal and railroad builder Asa Packer was born in Groton, Connecticut, in 1805. He received only a sketchy formal education and spent much of his youth as a tanner's apprentice, a farmer, and a carpenter's apprentice. As a carpenter, he worked for a relative, Edward Packer. Asa Packer also seems to have brought with him a gift of Yankee sagacity and foresight, which would pay large dividends in the years ahead.

In 1833, aware of the rapidly growing canal business in the Lehigh Valley, Packer moved to Mauch Chunk (now Jim Thorpe), Pennsylvania, where he used his carpenter's skills to build his own canal boat. This he used to haul coal from Mauch Chunk to Philadelphia. The endeavor was successful; he shortly bought other boats and became a major player in the canal business in eastern Pennsylvania. He also became involved in canal construction, building locks and boatyards. With the opening of the Morris Canal across New Jersey, Packer's boats found their way to New York. As a coal hauler, he also became interested in mining and bought into several mining companies, all of them successful. Already a wealthy and respected man by the 1840s, Packer served two terms in the Pennsylvania state legislature.

By the late 1840s Packer perceived that canals were not the wave of the future for coal haulers and bought into the Delaware, Lehigh, Schuylkill & Susquehanna Railroad. Finding it a poorly constructed and managed line, Packer acquired control of the majority of stock in 1851. Two years later he changed the name to the Lehigh Valley Railroad and hired a skilled civil engineer, Robert Sayre, to lay out the line. By 1855 the Lehigh Valley (LV) was completed from Mauch Chunk to Easton on the Delaware River. It quickly became one of the nation's premier coal-hauling railroads.

But there was more in store for the Lehigh Valley and Packer. In the following decade the LV built 160 miles of track in the rich coal areas of Pennsylvania, and Packer was widely believed to be the richest man in Pennsylvania. But more construction was required. Like other Pennsylvania coal railroads, the Lehigh Valley depended on the Jersey Central Railroad to haul cars to tidewater and the rich New York market. Packer was content with the Jersey Central alliance for a time, but in 1868 one of the LV's chief competitors, the Delaware, Lackawanna & Western Railroad, purchased the Morris & Essex Railroad to reach the Hudson River and New York City. This led Packer to conclude that he needed a railroad of his own across New Jersey. Opting at first for an interim solution, the Lehigh Valley leased the Morris Canal from the State of New Jersey, a lease it was unfortunately stuck with until the 1920s. The canal was already superannuated by the time the Lehigh Valley leased it, so the need for an all-rail route became apparent. Accordingly, Packer and his managers pushed through the Easton & Amboy Railroad

Asa Packer. —Library of Congress (Neg. LC-USZ62-135610)

(later LV's New Jersey division). This line was completed in 1875, offering access to tidewater and the port of New York.

Long before the first Lehigh Valley coal reached tidewater, Asa Packer had moved his base of operations from Mauch Chunk to Bethlehem, Pennsylvania. From there he continued to govern his numerous business activities, nearly every one of which was an overwhelming success. In 1865, ever conscious of his own lack of formal education, Packer bought 56 acres of land in Bethlehem on which to establish a university to train young men, especially in the areas of mining and engineering. This institution, Lehigh University, was one of his proudest achievements. In the remaining years of his life he looked after the growing university and bequeathed to it $1.5 million. As for the Lehigh Valley Railroad, by the time Packer died in 1879, it had 658 miles of track and was one of the most prosperous railroads in the United States.

—George H. Douglas

REFERENCES

Stuart, Milton C. *Asa Packer, 1805–1879: Captain of Industry, Educator, Citizen.* Princeton, N.J.: Princeton Univ. Press, 1938.

Yates, W. Ross. *Asa Packer: A Perspective.* Bethlehem, Pa.: Asa Packer Society, 1983.

Palmer, William Jackson
(1836–1909)

William Jackson Palmer was born on September 17, 1836, in Kinsale, Delaware, and enjoyed an illustrious career in business and railroading, interrupted only by service in the Union army during the Civil War, where he rose to the rank of brigadier general by war's end. His work after the war in the founding and development of the Denver & Rio Grande and the Rio Grande Western railroads helped shape the development of Colorado. He also founded the Mexican National Railway, as well as the Colorado Coal & Iron Co.

Palmer grew up in Philadelphia, and after high school he joined the Hempfield Railroad, which was building a line in Pennsylvania through the Allegheny Mountains. After two years with that railroad, Palmer had developed a strong interest in railroading and mining and traveled to England to learn about their operations there. He chronicled his experiences for an American mining publication, *Miner's Journal*. His articles drew the attention of a number of Americans associated with the railroad and mining industries, including the president of the Pennsyl-

vania Railroad, J. Edgar Thomson. Within a year of returning to the United States in May 1856, Palmer joined the Pennsy as Thomson's secretary, a position he held for about four years.

Palmer enlisted early in the war and quickly distinguished himself for his ability to organize and command his troops while earning their unwavering respect. He won a number of battles and managed to gain his return to the Union army after his capture behind Confederate lines. Palmer won the Congressional Medal of Honor for his bravery in a battle near Red Hill, Alabama, in 1865.

After the war Palmer returned to the railroad industry, joining the Eastern Division of the Union Pacific as treasurer. He began work on proposed lines from Texas and New Mexico to the West and led surveying expeditions in the southern portion of the Rocky Mountains. Battling Indians, weather, and other dangers of this rugged terrain, Palmer and his surveying parties finally arrived in San Francisco in early 1868. The published results of his surveys showed nearly 4,500 miles of proposed route.

In 1869 the name of the Union Pacific, Eastern Division, was changed to the Kansas Pacific Railway. Palmer was made a director, charged with managing construction of the line to Denver, Colorado. The railroad had already reached Sheridan, Kansas, from Kansas City, so construction west began toward Denver, while construction east from Denver was progressing as well. The Kansas Pacific was completed in August 1870. Palmer again distinguished himself during its construction, dealing with material and labor shortages, Indian attacks, and other challenges of the undeveloped region.

During the time Palmer had prepared his route surveys in the southern Rockies, he had become interested in this territory and wanted to develop a railroad there. Upon resigning from the Kansas Pacific upon its completion in 1870, he incorporated the Denver & Rio Grande Railway to build a line from Denver south to El Paso, Texas. In 1869 Palmer met attorney William Proctor Mellen, who would help Palmer obtain financing for his new railroad. Mellen also become his father-in-law upon Palmer's marriage to Mellen's daughter, Mary, in 1870.

Soon after, Palmer began work on the construction of the Denver & Rio Grande. Because of the mountainous territory the railroad would cross, Palmer decided to use 3-foot track gauge instead of the standard 4-foot 8½-inch gauge used by most American railroads, believing that the narrow gauge would make construction easier and less expensive. Before actual construction began on the railroad, however, Palmer organized several towns in anticipation of the railroad's arrival. The first to be founded was Colorado Springs.

Construction on the D&RG began in July 1871, and by October the line had extended from Denver to Colorado Springs, 76 miles to the south. During this time the Atchison, Topeka & Santa Fe was building in the same territory and crossed paths with the D&RG on two occasions—once at Raton Pass near Trinidad, Colorado, in

William Jackson Palmer. —Colorado Historical Society, *Trains* Magazine Collection

1878 and again at the Royal Gorge of the Arkansas River, west of Pueblo, Colorado, in the same year. The Sante Fe prevailed in the first contest, while the D&RG won in the second.

In the Raton Pass encounter Santa Fe's chief engineer arrived at Raton Pass with his work crew less than an hour before the arrival of the Rio Grande's chief engineer and crew. After a few tense moments, the Rio Grande crew moved to an inferior location to begin their work on the crossing. Shortly thereafter, deciding that he could not compete with the Sante Fe with a line through Raton Pass, Palmer terminated construction of the line. This incident prevented the D&RG from becoming a north-south line, prompting the railroad to expand to the west. When the two railroads met again at Royal Gorge, the claim to this route was also disputed, and no one could determine with certainty which road had arrived first. The U.S. Supreme Court eventually ruled in favor of the Denver & Rio Grande.

After the Royal Gorge matter had been resolved, Palmer continued to extend the lines of the D&RG and, in 1881, incorporated the Denver & Rio Grande Western Railway in Salt Lake City, Utah. This road enabled him to build outside of Colorado and expand farther west. By 1883 Palmer's railroads connected Denver and Ogden, Utah, with nearly 800 miles of narrow-gauge track. During this time Palmer's relationship with the D&RG board of directors had deteriorated. He resigned the presidency in 1883 and his directorship the following year.

Concurrent with his work on the Denver & Rio Grande Western, Palmer had embarked on two other corporate ventures. First, he incorporated the Colorado Coal & Iron Co. in 1880 from several Denver & Rio Grande companies. The mission of this company was to build a steel and iron works, which was completed in 1882. The business faced economic and legal problems, however, that resulted in the resignation of Palmer as president. Second, he incorporated the Mexican National Railway in 1880 in a plan to build a line from Mexico City to Texas, which he hoped could connect with the Denver & Rio Grande. Although nearly 500 miles of line had been completed by 1884, the line faced financial difficulties, requiring Palmer's resignation of the presidency of that company as well.

With these corporate misfortunes behind him, Palmer focused exclusively on the Denver & Rio Grande Western. Toward the end of the nineteenth century it became apparent that the line could no longer sustain itself as a narrow-gauge railroad, and Palmer embarked on a project to widen the track to standard gauge. Reorganizing the railroad as the Rio Grande Western Railway in 1889, Palmer also led an effort to improve the physical plant. During this time Palmer strengthened the line's relationship with the Denver & Rio Grande railroad, which, under the leadership of David Moffat, was also making improvements, including standard-gauging its track.

As the twentieth century began, George Gould purchased Palmer's two roads, the Denver & Rio Grande and the Rio Grande Western. Upon the sale of the Rio Grande Western, Palmer retired from railroading and devoted the remainder of his life to philanthropic pursuits in Colorado Springs. In 1906 he was seriously injured in a riding accident, which left him paralyzed below the waist. Despite this injury, he continued to live a relatively active life until his death on March 13, 1909.

—David C. Lester

REFERENCES

Athearn, Robert G. *The Denver and Rio Grande Western Railroad.* Lincoln: Univ. of Nebraska Press, 1977. Originally published as *Rebel of the Rockies: A History of the Denver and Rio Grande Western Railroad.* New Haven, Conn.: Yale Univ. Press, 1962.

Danneman, Mike. *Rio Grande through the Rockies.* Waukesha, Wis.: Kalmbach, 2002.

Frey, Robert L., ed. *Encyclopedia of American Business History and Biography: Railroads in the Nineteenth Century.* New York: Facts on File, 1988.

The Historical Guide to North American Railroads. 2nd ed. Waukesha, Wis.: Kalmbach, 2000.

Panama Railroad

The Atlantic and Pacific oceans were first linked by rail on January 27, 1855, in the middle of a thick jungle, more than 14 years before the Central Pacific and the Union Pacific joined with much fanfare at windswept Promontory Point in Utah. Congress had investigated construction of a railroad across the Isthmus of Panama in the early 1830s, shortly after the Baltimore & Ohio Railroad began operation. Then the California Gold Rush prompted a group of New York investors in 1849 to negotiate a 49-year concession with the government of Colombia, which controlled the area at the time, for rights to build a railroad, highway, or canal.

For quick return on investment, a railroad creating a 47-mile land bridge that would eliminate a 7,000-mile ocean voyage made the most sense. Building the line was a struggle. Five-foot-deep swamps, a tropical climate, wood-eating insects, alligators, and a June-to-December rainy season that bred malaria all had to be conquered before a roadbed was carved out. Then the rails would sink and wood would rot before the next section was completed, but the construction gangs finally prevailed.

French interests bought the Panama Railroad in 1879, intending to use it to help build the long-dreamed-of canal. Business boomed, with almost 800,000 passengers and over 300,000 tons of freight carried over the single-track, 5-foot-gauge line in 1886.

Financing difficulties and political upheaval that created a separate Republic of Panama and Canal Zone in

Opened 14 years before the Pacific Railroad was completed, the Panama's timesaving crossing of the isthmus between the Atlantic and Pacific oceans was a success. This drawing from the May 30, 1868, *Harper's Weekly* showed a busy Panama Railroad train boarding at Aspinwall on the Atlantic side, now Colón. —Middleton Collection

1903 facilitated a U.S. takeover of the railroad and canal project. During the next decade of canal construction the Panama Railroad main line was relocated to its present alignment over the Continental Divide at Summit; the original route was used to help move materials, earth, and construction crews and then was abandoned.

Freight traffic declined sharply after the opening of the canal in 1914, but the railroad continued to be a key transportation link across the isthmus. Though the 5-foot gauge was retained, later on secondhand passenger cars and new mechanical refrigerated cars were purchased, 100-pound rail was laid, and diesel-electric locomotives were obtained. The final major upgrading under U.S. government control occurred in the late 1950s.

By the mid-1970s the Panama Railroad ran seven passenger round trips a day between Colón in the north (on the Atlantic side of the isthmus) and downtown Panama City on the south (the Pacific side), along with two daily freights. The trains operated over jointed rail spiked to wooden ties and protected by automatic block signals. Passenger trains made eight stops and took an hour and a half to make the 47.6-mile journey through the jungle.

All that began to change in 1979, the year title to the railroad passed to the Panamanian government. By 1986, as President Manuel Noriega's oppressive regime tightened its grip, the Panama Railroad's payroll had ballooned from 110 railroaders to 430 employees who took paychecks but did little work. Frayed bond wires spelled the end of the block signal system, and passenger service was dropped after a lack of track maintenance took its toll on a shifting roadbed that needed constant vigilance.

In 1998, with the cross-isthmus rail link in shambles and

Panama's post-Noriega government seeking investors who might be interested in rejuvenating the property in exchange for a 25-year operating concession, container-terminal operator Mi-Jack Products and the Kansas City Southern Railway jointly came up with a business plan that used the well-tamped old roadbed to support an entirely new standard-gauge railroad with continuous 136-pound welded rail resting on mostly concrete ties laid over a 6- to 22-foot subbase and 9 inches of crushed ballast. Construction on the newly christened, $80 million Panama Canal Railway Co. (PCRC) began in 1999. In the meantime, PCRC struck a deal with the world's leading shipping company, Maersk Sealand, to transport containers between Balboa and Colón that had previously been trucked across the isthmus from large vessels on one side to smaller "feeder route" ships on the other. Maersk would gain operating flexibility by moving part of a heavily laden ship's volume by rail to avoid the typical 36-hour wait to get through the canal.

KCS chairman Michael Haverty and PCRC president David Starling saved money by rehabilitating castoff equipment from the United States. The company leased surplus Amtrak F40 diesel locomotives to bookend twin-stack, international-standard 40-foot bulkhead well cars, which were becoming obsolete for stateside traffic as domestic container lengths grew. The 480-volt head-end power from the F40s came in handy for supplying electricity to refrigerated containers of perishables.

Passenger trains were not in the original business plan, but queries from Panama City–Colón commuters and cruise-line marketing people persuaded Starling to develop another revenue stream. He leased nine Amtrak stainless-steel coaches and purchased a former Southern Pacific Daylight dome lounge that had been spending its retirement as an ice-cream parlor in Jacksonville, Florida. The passenger cars were beautified with cherry and mahogany paneling at a leased KCS shop in New Orleans.

One daily commuter train round trip began in mid-2001, and freight and cruise-ship excursion service started later that fall. Transporting an average of 600 containers a week the first two years, the PCRC has been constrained in gaining more freight traffic by the lack of dock space at Balboa near Panama City. Meanwhile, the daily commuter train continues to carry about 80 passengers each weekday, and the cruise crowd has made the excursion service a sold-out hit, with full-train, 300-passenger bookings tripling from 35 to over 100 annually.

—Bob Johnston

REFERENCES

Hull, Gene. "Panama's Transcontinental Railroad." *National Railway Bulletin* 64, no. 5 (1999): 4–35.

Johnston, Bob. "Our Railroad in Panama." *Trains* 62, no. 9 (Sept. 2002): 43–49.

Otis, F. N. Foreword by Donald Duke. *Illustrated History of the Panama Railroad.* 1861. Repr., Pasadena, Calif.: Socio-Technical Books, 1971.

Pangborn, Joseph (1844–1914)

Joseph Gladding Pangborn was a public relations man with an interest in history. His exhibits and publications did much to promote interest in railroad history at a time when rail travel was a modern form of transportation. He was born in Albany, New York, on April 9, 1844, of Dutch and English parentage and joined the Union army as a drummer boy during the Civil War. He became a cub reporter at the end of the war and worked on newspapers in New York City and Kansas City for the next several years. In 1876 Pangborn joined the Santa Fe Railroad as an advertising agent and later became clerk to the railroad's general manager.

In May 1880 Pangborn returned to the East as the general advertising agent for the Baltimore & Ohio. A few years later he was named assistant general passenger agent, with responsibility for selling tickets and promoting travel on the B&O.

Selling service over the B&O had its challenges. It was not the fastest or most direct route west. Its mountainous crossing of western Maryland and West Virginia dictated slow schedules. The Pennsylvania Railroad main line was shorter, and the New York Central had its Water Level Route. Pangborn began to push "historic" as a reason to travel over the B&O. Much was made of the nation's capital and the historic town of Harpers Ferry, West Virginia.

He presented the B&O as the nation's oldest main line, which was more or less true—true enough to be a talking point, at least. In 1883 Pangborn produced a sizable book, *The Picturesque B&O,* which was part travel guide and part history. About this time he picked up the unofficial title of "Major" even though he never earned the rank during his military service.

As 1892 approached, plans were announced for a World's Fair in Chicago to celebrate the 400th anniversary of Columbus's landing in the New World. American businesses were urged to create exhibits. The railroad industry viewed the fair as a giant traffic generator that promised to fill passenger trains for the duration of the exposition.

Pangborn was assigned to mount a large exhibit on the history of railways that would feature the achievements of the B&O. It was, at 36,000 square feet, the largest history display at the World's Columbian Exposition. Its creator had assembled so much material that the display overflowed into an annex. He had original locomotives and cars, 40 or so full-size wooden and canvas models, numerous smaller relics, and 14,000 square feet of wall space for prints, photographs, and wash drawings. The display concentrated on the history of the locomotive and traced its development in considerable detail, including its British origins.

Pangborn was not a scrupulous historian. He wanted most of all to tell a good story and entertain the public. Hence dates, names, and identities were altered to suit the story line. Four ancient Grasshopper engines, all dating from the 1830s, were rebuilt and renamed to suit the needs of the exhibit. An old freight engine, the *Memnon,* was rechristened the *Dragon* because the name was catchier. A ten-wheel Camel locomotive built in 1869 was backdated to 1853 to represent an earlier design, and its number was changed because the Major liked "firsts" and so the new number represented the first engine of that class. The public was unaware of these muddled identities, and historians to this day are confused by Pangborn's falsifications. The fair's opening was delayed until 1893, but it proved successful, and thousands visited the large, if not always accurate, display.

In the following year Pangborn published an elegant book, *World's Railways,* which repeated much of the story presented in the exhibit. Although it contains many errors, it does record much information that might otherwise have been lost.

Pangborn began a worldwide tour, sponsored by Chicago department store scion Marshall Field, to collect railway relics and illustrations for an expanded display at the Field Museum. By 1904 the museum decided that it would concentrate on natural history, and so Pangborn removed the exhibits and remounted them in St. Louis for the Louisiana Purchase Exposition. At the end of the fair the sizable collection was taken back to Baltimore for storage. Much of it was shown in 1927 at the B&O Centennial Exhibit. Today the core of Pangborn's collection resides at the B&O Museum in Baltimore. J. G. Pangborn died in Baltimore on August 15, 1914.

—John H. White, Jr.

REFERENCES

"Baltimore and Ohio Transportation Museum." *Technology and Culture* 11, no. 1 (Jan. 1970): 70–84.
National Cyclopaedia of American Biography.

Parmelee Transfer Service

As the nineteenth century passed its midway point, the rapidly growing city of Chicago was becoming a major railroad center. Railroads from east and west, north and south entered the city via a number of separate passenger stations. Frank Parmelee came to Chicago in 1853 from Genesee County, New York, and created Frank Parmelee & Co. to provide transfer service between the depots,

Frank Parmelee began surface transportation between Chicago's many railroad stations in 1853 and headed his unique transfer service until he retired at age 85 in 1901. —Illinois Historical Survey

using six omnibuses and wagons and a stable of horses. Initial success led him to diversify in 1858 by obtaining a franchise to operate a horse-powered street railway; a year later, joined by Henry Fuller, he incorporated the Chicago City Railway Co. In 1864 Parmelee rid himself of the street railway business and concentrated on the inter-station transfer operations.

The great Chicago fire of 1871 destroyed the company's new headquarters and stable at Franklin and Jackson streets; in 1872 the great epizootic, a strain of equine influenza, destroyed many of the Parmelee horses and other horses in the city. Oxen had to be employed to move Parmelee's omnibuses and wagons. The company prospered as the railroad business grew, and by 1881 Parmelee employed 130 men, 250 horses, 75 wagons, and 75 omnibuses. At age 85 in 1901, Parmelee sold the company to a syndicate of prominent Chicago businessmen led by John C. Shedd, the president of Marshall Field & Co., and retired. Parmelee died in October 1904.

The business changed again in 1919 when the Shedd syndicate sold out to Charles A. McCulloch, president of Yellow Cab Co. of Chicago. Once at the helm, McCulloch ended the use of horse-drawn vehicles; Parmelee's fleet consisted solely of motor vehicles. Another change occurred in 1929 when Morris Markin acquired the transfer business and created a holding company called the Parmelee Transportation Co.

Chicago Railroad Stations

Central Station
    Illinois Central
    New York Central (Big Four)
Dearborn Station
    Erie
    Grand Trunk Western
    Monon
    Santa Fe
Grand Central Station
    Baltimore & Ohio
    Chesapeake & Ohio
    Chicago Great Western
    Soo Line
LaSalle Street Station
    New York Central (Michigan Central)
    Nickel Plate
    Rock Island
Northwestern Station
    Chicago & North Western
Randolph Street Station
    Chicago South Shore & South Bend
    Illinois Central (suburban trains)
Union Station
    Burlington
    Gulf, Mobile & Ohio
    Milwaukee Road
    Pennsylvania

With a uniformed driver in charge of a Parmelee coach, a group of immigrants were ready to move between their connecting stations at Chicago. —Illinois Historical Survey

By the end of the 1920s there was much transfer business to do. Chicago was served by Northwestern Station, Union Station, Grand Central Station, Dearborn Station, LaSalle Street Station, Central Station, and Randolph Street Station, as well as the Chicago North Shore & Milwaukee station on the Chicago elevated structure at Wabash and Adams streets. In a stock transfer in 1930, the Checker Cab Manufacturing Co. of Kalamazoo, Michigan, acquired a large block of Parmelee stock. The action was to help Checker diversify. Not surprisingly, green- and cream-colored Checker cabs became the standard Parmelee passenger vehicle. Checker also started the Parmelee Motor Fuel Co. to supply its vehicles and those of other fleet operators.

After World War II it was clear that air travel would be a major competitor to the railroads. Parmelee formed the Continental Air Transport Co. to link the Chicago central business district with Midway Airport. Service was expanded to O'Hare Field when it opened. Continental purchased large over-the-road Flxible airport buses. In downtown Chicago the Continental buses picked up and dropped off passengers at the major hotels.

As the environment and the market changed, the company founded by Frank Parmelee also changed. In 1983 a new group of Chicago businessmen purchased it. The concentration of businesses and hotels in the central business district was changing. New, smaller hotels were being built in spread-out fashion, and the Loop business district was steadily expanding. Large buses were no longer appropriate, and the big green Flxibles were replaced with red,

white, and blue vans; the company name was changed to Airport Express. The vans linked Midway and O'Hare airports with north-, west-, and south-side neighborhoods, as well as the downtown Loop district and other business centers. Because of the vans' modest size, it was possible to provide door-to-door service. In 2001 an online reservation system was introduced, allowing reservations to be made from anywhere in the world.

In the great days of railroad passenger travel from 1900 to the 1950s, the Parmelee Transfer was included in through railroad ticketing. As an example, in the long multicoupon ticket of a journey from Philadelphia to Peoria, Illinois, there would be a coupon for service on the Pennsylvania Railroad from North Philadelphia Station to Union Station in Chicago, a coupon for the Parmelee Transfer to LaSalle Street Station, and a coupon on the Rock Island Railroad to Peoria. The transferring passenger merely gave the coupon to the Parmelee driver, and the transfer was taken care of.

—George M. Smerk

REFERENCES

"Historian Driven to Record Parmelee Transfer Co.'s Tale." *Parmelee Family Magazine* 3, no. 4 (Nov.–Dec. 1999): 269–288.

Jolly, Maria. "Well-Grounded in the Windy City." *Bus Ride* 40, no. 2 (Feb. 2004): 28.

Parmelee, Robert D. *Chicago's Railroads and Parmelee's Transfer Company: A Century of Travel.* New York: Golden Hill Press, 2003.

Parry, Charles (1821–1887)

Charles Thomas Parry was an important contributor in the early days of locomotive manufacturing, starting as an apprentice and working himself to the top of the organization of the Baldwin Locomotive Works. Parry was born in Philadelphia on September 15, 1821, the son of Samuel and Mary (Hoffline) Parry. As was typical at the time, he was put to work early and at age 15 became an apprentice in the Baldwin pattern shop. Later he worked in the drawing room preparing plans for steam locomotives. It was an excellent place to learn about locomotive design because Baldwin prided itself on being able to design engines tailored to meet particular wishes of a railroad, as well as produce a standard line of motive power.

Parry worked in all types of mechanical labor and design until 1855, when he was named general superintendent of locomotive construction. Upon the death of Matthias Baldwin, Parry became a partner in M. Baird & Co., which took over ownership and operation of the company. When Matthew Baird retired from the locomotive works in 1873, Parry became a partner in Burnham, Parry, Williams & Co., the partnership that operated the Baldwin Works until Parry's death.

Parry virtually grew up with the locomotive business. When he started his apprenticeship, Baldwin had produced only about 50 locomotives. Parry's rapid promotion was due to his ability and capacity to learn, and he became Baldwin's chief executive only 19 years after his apprenticeship began. As head of production, he developed a scientific management approach far different from the rule-of-thumb methods used in locomotive production up to that time. Among his innovations were preparation of complete drawings of locomotives in advance of construction, standardization of parts, and the introduction of more efficient shop practices.

Parry also was skilled at dealing with labor and in solving workplace problems. He installed a piecework system that brought good wages and many years of labor peace to Baldwin. He visited Europe frequently to keep informed about locomotive construction overseas. Beginning in the late 1870s, Parry was engaged by the Russian government to supervise that country's locomotive construction; Baldwin ultimately built 40 locomotives for Russia.

Under Parry's leadership, Baldwin became the largest locomotive builder in the world. Parry became active in local affairs and offered his skills to Philadelphia's Franklin Institute, where for a year he was a member of the institute's board of managers. He was also a director of the National Bank of the Republic. Parry was a lifetime subscriber to the publication fund of the Pennsylvania Historical Society. He died on July 18, 1887.

—George M. Smerk

REFERENCES

Brown, John K. *The Baldwin Locomotive Works, 1831–1915.* Baltimore: Johns Hopkins Univ. Press, 1995.
Dictionary of American Biography.

Passenger Cars

The American railroad passenger car changed remarkably in size, strength, safety, materials, and amenities during its first century. This evolution took place in measured stages that transformed the vehicle from a small wooden box into a long steel tube.

There were no car builders or designers in the United States when the railroad era opened in 1830. Just what plan was suitable for such service was unknown, and so the first cars were copies of highway vehicles. The pioneering Mauch Chunk Railway in eastern Pennsylvania used Dearborn-style carriage bodies (a early four-wheel car with two bench seats, looking something like an Amish buggy) for passenger cars in the late 1820s. Other early lines copied stagecoaches. The melon-shaped bodies, complete with leather straps called thoroughbraces in place of springs, were mounted on four-wheel undercarriages. These makeshift cars had no window glass. The openings were covered by roll-down leather curtains. They had no lights, heating, or toilet facilities. They seated about 20 inside and another 10 or so if roof seating was provided. They weighed a little less than two tons, and much of the weight was in the wheels and axles. They cost about $800 each. The boxy and oblong city omnibus provided another model for pioneer car builders to copy. These were generally built with three compartments and doors on either side for each compartment. They had glass windows and steel springs but were otherwise as devoid of passenger comforts as their melon-shaped counterparts. The worst shortcoming of the four-wheel passenger cars was their bouncy and galloping ride, even on comparatively good track.

Mounting a car on eight wheels, with two wheel sets attached to a subframe (called trucks) placed at each end of the body main frame, smoothed out the ride. The trucks could swivel or turn so that rounding curves was not a problem. The double-truck car had many other attributes. It allowed a long body that was easily double or triple the length of the four-wheelers. This increased capacity and gave passengers room to move around. It eliminated the weight and cost of duplicate end partitions, couplers, and draft gears because one double-truck car could carry the same passenger load as two or three of the older design. A center aisle with seats on either side created a central passageway. End doors and platforms allowed train crews to quickly and safely pass through the train. Passengers were prohibited from making a similar journey while the train was in motion, but not everyone obeyed this rule. This basic center-aisle, double-truck plan has remained standard in the United States to the present day. European lines remained loyal to side-door cars for many years but later adopted a compartment-style plan with an aisle on one side.

The double-truck passenger car was introduced on the Baltimore & Ohio Railroad in the summer of 1831. Ross Winans is traditionally credited with the design, but there is evidence that many others were involved. The design was

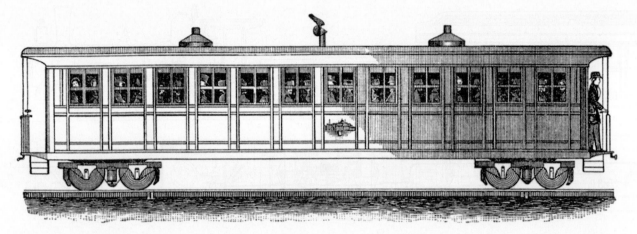

By 1834 the passenger car illustrated in *The American Railway* had evolved into this familiar format, with a long car supported by two trucks and with entrance and exit from platforms at each end. Materials, size, and technology have changed enormously over more than 150 years, but the basic configuration remains the same. —Middleton Collection

refined over the next few years. It was nearly universally accepted by all American railroads by 1840. These earliest eight-wheelers were small and cramped by modern standards. They were also lightly built, often with no center sills, in order to hold down weight. The body size was generally only 30 feet long and 8 feet 6 inches wide. The center aisle was a scant 18 inches and the ceiling height 6 feet 4 inches. Yet they seated 48 passengers. Keeping everything as small as possible achieved the goal of low weight, just 7 tons. The size was grudgingly increased during the 1840s and 1850s so that there was more legroom and ceiling height.

Space was also preserved for a simple dry-closet toilet and a stove for winter heating. Lighting was very stingy at first—just small candle lamps at each end of the car so that passengers might see their way in and out. Eventually small side lamps were introduced so that passengers might read. Still later, around 1865, center ceiling lamps were installed that improved the general level of lighting. The passenger coach in general had grown considerably in size by 1855. Bodies were 50 and even 60 feet long, and ceilings were 7 feet high inside. The toilet remained without running water, but it was roomier. Some cars had a water cooler so travelers could refresh themselves during the hot, dusty ride. This increase in size drove car weights up to 10 tons and more.

The appearance of passenger cars was greatly changed starting in about 1860 with the clerestory roof to provide both better lighting and air circulation. The center of the roof was raised high enough for a row of small windows that brightened the interior. In some cases these windows could be partially opened to let in air—a mixed blessing because smoke and cinders were also brought inside. The interior space was more elevated, providing more openness and also space for ceiling lamps. The improved ventilation and lighting of the clerestory roof remained a fixed part of American car architecture until the streamlining craze of the 1930s.

Throughout the nineteenth century American railroad cars were essentially wooden structures. The underframes, body frames, inside and outside paneling, floors, seat frames, interior partitions, window frames, and doors were all wooden. Frames were constructed of white oak or yellow pine. Only the very best grade of lumber was used for both appearance and strength. Before about 1860 interiors were painted and striped and decorated with elegant cameo paintings or scrolls. The paneling was poplar or white pine. The cars' exteriors were also decorative, with fine stripes, graceful scrolls, and lettering. Pale yellow or cream was a popular color. After 1860 fine cabinet woods such as cherry, walnut, and mahogany came into favor. Cheaper cars had varnished oak interiors. Hardware was bronze or brass. Exteriors were painted in somber shades of brown, olive, and blue. Gold-leaf strips, ornaments, and lettering were employed to lighten and highlight. Gloss varnish protected the painted surfaces from the weather. This had to be reapplied on a regular schedule. In the better cars fine upholstery covered the seats, and the best textiles were used for window coverings. Long-wearing mohair was used to cover seats in the coaches, and wooden shutters that could be raised or lowered generally replaced window blinds.

Operating improvements emerged to enhance safety and to accommodate the larger and faster cars. Cast-iron wheels had become standard by the mid-nineteenth century, and cast-steel wheels were coming into use at the beginning of the twentieth century. Wooden car trucks had begun to shift to all-metal designs by late in the nineteenth century, and the cast-steel truck frame began to be adopted in the early 1900s. Braking systems, originally some kind of mechanical lever system operated by brakemen, began to shift to various types of air and vacuum systems; the George Westinghouse air-brake system became the North American standard for passenger equipment by about 1870. By the late 1880s enclosed vestibules

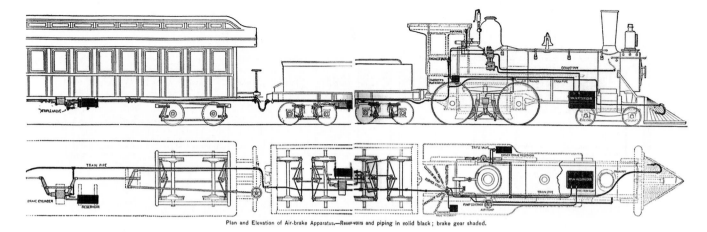

Plan and Elevation of Air-brake Apparatus.—Reservoirs and piping in solid black; brake gear shaded.

Even more important to railroad development than the automatic coupler was the automatic air-brake system. This drawing from *The American Railway* (1892) shows the application of the system on a locomotive and an attached car. —Middleton Collection

Well-to-do nineteenth-century travelers enjoyed the amenities of the railroads' first-class parlor, dining, and sleeping cars. This drawing from a May 1872 *Harper's New Monthly Magazine* article on travel to California shows a transcontinental sleeping car. —Middleton Collection

replaced the open platforms at each end of a car, with a flexible, bellowslike diaphragm to enclose the entire space between cars, affording greater safety and comfort for passengers moving between cars. These were initially narrow vestibules at the center of the platform; soon full-width vestibules covered the entire platform area, with hinged trap doors concealing the step wells.

As railroad travel became more competitive, railroads offered not only highly decorated passenger cars but also sleeping, lounge, observation, and dining cars. They also adopted such amenities as better lighting and heating systems and safety devices such as the air brake, which was widely adopted after about 1870. The basic day coach was fine for the short journeys typical of the early decades, but as longer journeys became possible by around 1855, affluent travelers expected more specialized rail vehicles for overnight trips. Even so, the bulk of the passenger-car fleet remained the common day coach. Sleepers and parlor and dining cars generally constituted only about 12 percent of the total.

At first, long-distance rail trips were broken into segments, and travelers spent the night in a trackside hotel. Businessmen objected; they needed to be at their destinations quickly and had no time or patience to lie around in a station hotel, no matter how elegant. Thus the sleeping car was born. Actually, a few eastern lines used such cars

Most travelers went by day coach. This one for the Brunswick & Birmingham Railroad (*top*) was built in the late 1800s by the Boston & Albany's Alston shops near Boston. The car employed the usual clerestory-type roof and ventilators for air circulation. The interior of a similar car (*bottom*) shows the typical unadorned walkover coach seats; the light fixtures and the ceiling headlining were the only adornments. —(both) Middleton Collection

as early as the 1830s, but the notion did not catch on for another 20 years.

Theodore T. Woodruff was the first to devise a practical sleeping car that received wide acceptance. His operation began in 1857, and within one year he had 21 sleepers in use. Some of his elegant cars cost $8,000, almost as much as a locomotive. These cars were designed to function as a first-class coach in the daylight hours but had seating that was converted into a bed after sundown. There was no shortage of sleeping-car companies that were soon in operation. The Wagner Palace Car Co. and the Case Sleeping Car Co., both established in 1858, were among the earliest. By 1870, however, George M. Pullman dominated the business, and his competitors, such as Woodruff, Wagner, and others, left the field one by one.

The Pullman Palace Car Co. operated as a concession. The revenue was shared with the railroads, and the sleepers were carried as part of regular trains. The success of the sleeping cars led to the creation of parlor cars for deluxe daytime travel. Parlor cars featured single seating on both sides of the car. An attendant was usually provided, and a premium fare was charged, so parlor-car travel was limited to affluent travelers. Dining cars came on more gradually because they generally lost money, but by 1885 the demand was great enough that most major railroads operated them, despite the losses sustained, because they were seen as a necessity by first-class travelers. Excellent meals were prepared in very small kitchens by skilled cooks. Waiters served food to diners seated at tables on both sides of the center aisle.

Amenities

A general improvement in rail passenger travel is apparent in advances made in various auxiliaries such as heating, lighting, and ventilation systems. As noted, the earliest cars were bereft of heating apparatus. Our forefathers were generally accustomed to an absence of central heating. Few homes had more than a fireplace; being cold was accepted as part of winter living. Coal stoves began to appear on some northern railway cars as early as 1835. Other lines adopted wood stoves, so that almost from the beginning of railway travel in North America some effort was being made to warm passengers. Even so, a common complaint about railway travel centered on the defects of heating by stoves. Passengers were either too hot or too cold—this was often dependent on how close they were to the source of heat. Placing a stove at both ends of the car helped somewhat. Overly zealous or negligent trainmen who tended the stoves could greatly affect the amount of heat produced. A partial solution was the introduction in the mid-1860s of hot-water heating, which provided better distribution. Yet the presence of a stove inside a wooden coach was viewed as a danger, and a number of fairly minor train wrecks were made considerably worse because of this source of open flames to the wooden cars.

Steam heating, which used low-pressure steam piped in from the locomotive, removed this danger, but it was expensive and not much used until after 1900. Ventilation was associated with heating and seemed to divide passengers equally on what was too much or too little. Opening and closing the windows was the basic method of regulating the flow of air. Unfortunately, an open window also sucked in unwanted smoke and cinders from the locomotive and a degree of dust from the track. In the 1850s several patented forced-air systems were tried with varying degrees of success. Almost all attempted to clean the air before introducing it into the car. The cost of the apparatus and its upkeep discouraged any large-scale use of these systems. Car ventilation remained a problem until the advent of air conditioning in the 1930s.

Car lighting followed the fashions and ebb and flow of illumination technology as it progressed from candles to incandescent lamps. Artificial illumination was necessary for more than reading as the train rolled through the night. Passengers and crew needed to move through the train,

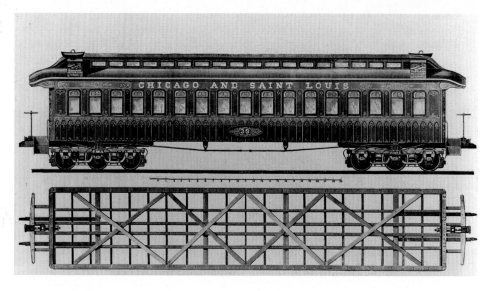

In drawings for the June 10, 1871, *Railroad Gazette,* the Chicago & Alton provided a side view of a new coach built at the company's Bloomington (Illinois) shops. The car was larger—58 feet long overall—and more luxurious than most day coaches and employed a patented ventilating system that drew air across an open water tank to cool it and remove dust. —Library of Congress (Neg. LC-USZ62-054115)

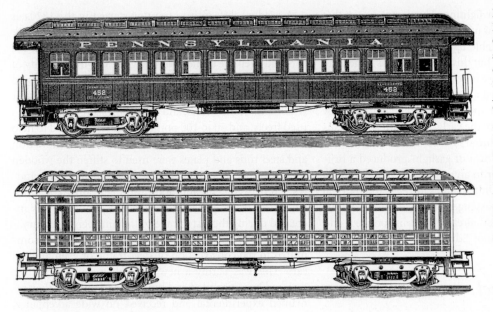

In 1878 the Pennsylvania Railroad adopted this Class PD standard coach, shown in elevation and a cutaway view of the framing published in *The American Railway* (1892). The 53-foot 6-inch car seated 52 passengers. Interiors were finished in quarter-sawn oak and ash panels, head linings were muslin painted, and windows were of polished plate glass imported from France. —Middleton Collection

which could not be done in the dark. Candles and oil lamps were the state of the art at the beginning of the railroad era. Minimal lighting was about all travelers could hope to find at first. Trainmen carried their own lamps wherever they went, but passengers were dependent on what parsimonious railroad managers were willing to provide. Candles were considered the safest form of open-flame interior lighting, because any type of oil lamp was a ready-made fire should it be broken or upset—a distinct possibility on vehicles moving along over a less-than-perfect track. The introduction of cheap lamp fuel came in the 1860s with the large-scale production of kerosene. It was too great a bargain for most consumers to resist, and this included the nation's railroads. Kerosene oil lamps were very soon nearly

Vestibules at end platforms, shown here in drawings from *The American Railway* (1892), were developed for first-class passengers about 1890. They provided an enclosed passage between cars, protecting them against the elements and providing much greater safety. This design was soon replaced by fully enclosed end platforms. —Middleton Collection

the standard form of car lighting. This is not to say that other systems were not in use—nor was kerosene lighting perfect. It gave a reasonable light if the lamps were well maintained and cleaned, but this was not always done. And even the best oil lamp gave off disagreeable odors.

Some railroads wanted a better system, and the obvious alternative was gas. Experiments had been under way with gas car lighting since the early 1850s, but a vastly superior system was introduced in 1869 by a German inventor, Julius Pinsch. This form of gaslight produced a brilliant light vastly superior to any alternative. Pinsch lights were introduced in the United States in 1882, and by 1908 over 32,000 domestic passenger cars had lamps of this type. Electric lighting had already been introduced, and gradually the handiwork of Edison displaced that of the inventive German.

The Shift to Steel

As these changes were under way, the American passenger car was growing in weight and size. By 1900 the typical passenger car was twice as long and four times as heavy as its predecessor of 50 years earlier. Cars that were 70 feet long were common, and another 10 feet would soon be added. Yet despite all the progress and ingenuity of late nineteenth-century car design, the age of the wooden car was nearing its end. The car-building industry and the majority of designers were perfectly content with wooden car construction. But other forces, some outside the railroad industry, were at work. Concerns over safety grew stronger. Well-made wooden cars were sturdy enough. They could withstand hard use and most minor collisions, but even so they had many flaws. If the car broke up in a wreck, the wood splinters became a danger to the passengers. And there was the fire hazard. It was inescapable; a wooden vehicle was very prone to burn, especially with coal stoves and open-flame lamps present. In addition, the cost of prime lumber was growing. The nation had yet to face a timber shortage; however, most of the virgin forest had been harvested, and so ended the supply of cheap, choice lumber.

A gradual shift to iron framing started in the 1870s as metal body bolsters became more common. Truss rods, running the length of the frames, did much to stiffen the cars and keep the bodies from sagging. But the majority of the material used in passenger-car fabrication remained wood until about 1890. The parts were fastened together with nails, wood screws, and bolts. Furniture glue was also used freely, and 50 to 100 pounds of glue were used to help hold a typical car together. After 1890 more and more iron and steel rods and plates were used to stiffen the wooden frames and bodies. Metal plates ½ by 8 inches were sandwiched between end and floor framing beams. The number of the rods, generally ¾ inch in diameter, was increased during the last decade of the nineteenth century.

By 1900 the more progressive car designers were committed to the construction of steel-frame or even all-steel cars. This was hardly a new concept; metallic passenger cars had been patented and built in the 1850s. Yet they remained experimental and received no wide acceptance, being both heavier and more costly than wood cars. Even so, these pioneering efforts led the way to improved designs and encouraged the railroad industry to adopt stronger, fireproof rolling stock.

By the early 1900s the New York subway was under construction. It was decided after considerable discussion that wooden cars in an underground tunnel were unacceptable; only steel cars would satisfy the safety needs of the public. A prototype was finished in late 1903. The design was refined for 300 production models built during the following year. The success of these cars encouraged the Pennsylvania Railroad to develop a larger version for main-line use. The long tunnels under way for Pennsylvania Station in downtown New York prompted the use of fireproof passenger cars. In 1907 the production of such cars began. By 1910 the Pennsylvania Railroad had over 300 of them in service. Other major U.S. railroads began to purchase steel passenger cars at this time. Yet for all the publicity, the retirement of the old wooden fleet proceeded at a leisurely pace. In 1915, 77 percent of the U.S. passenger car fleet remained wooden. It was well into the 1920s before steel cars outnumbered their wooden ancestors. A few main-line rail-

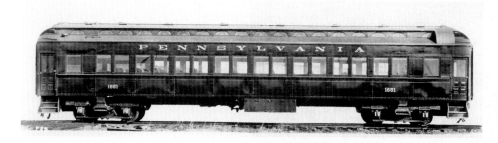

The Pennsylvania Railroad's first all-steel car for main-line service was No. 1651, built in 1906. A much-improved steel-car design, the P-70, was produced the following year, and the car was in production for more than 20 years. By the time the Pennsylvania had banished wooden cars from regular service in 1928, its all-steel cars numbered 5,501. —*Trains Magazine Collection*

roads continued to operate wooden cars in commuter service into the early 1950s.

The steel cars had many advantages, but they were not completely fire- or collision-proof. The interiors had upholstery, window blinds, and, in some cases, wooden trim. They were more accurately described as fire resistant. And for all the heavy steel plate, they could be crumpled and telescoped in a high-speed accident. Passengers were definitely safer in a steel car than in a wooden one, but it was a matter of degree. The metallic passenger-carrying railcars were also very heavy. An 80-foot-long steel coach weighed 60 tons, almost twice the weight of a wooden car. This added to the cost of operating trains. A wood coach might cost $6,000 to $7,000, while a steel one cost twice as much. These were reasons that smaller and less affluent railroads moved more slowly in converting from wood to steel.

The typical steel car was made from the most common grade of steel. The side plates were generally ⅛ inch thick, and the frame members were ⁵⁄₁₆-inch plate. Large round-headed rivets held everything together. Insulation was used between the inner and outer walls to keep the heat in during winter and out in summer. The floors were made from concrete poured over corrugated sheet metal. Steam heat and electric lighting were nearly standard by 1910. Seating was closely spaced, and many coaches carried 80 passengers.

The decor of passenger-car interiors changed dramatically about the time steel cars were introduced. This was unrelated to the new technology. Society in general was rejecting Victorian excesses. Plain, unadorned surfaces and muted colors were now in fashion. The Mission style came into favor as part of the Arts and Crafts movement of about 1900 and was adopted to give car interiors a spartan, clean appearance. Some contended that the plainer interiors were more hygienic because germs had fewer places to hide. The plain surfaces were surely easier to clean, even if they were not necessarily more sanitary. By the 1920s some railroads adopted a colonial look that was less austere than the utilitarian mode so long in fashion.

—John H. White, Jr.

The Rise of Long-Distance Travel

Although he was not the first operator of the sleeping-car business, George M. Pullman's concession approach soon made the firm the dominant company of what would become a vast network of sleeping-car services in the United States, Canada, Mexico, and Cuba. The first two Pullman sleeping cars were rebuilt from Chicago & Alton Railroad coaches at Bloomington, Illinois, in 1859. The first car completed, christened simply *No. 9*, had convertible interiors with fixed daytime seating and upper and lower berths for overnight use, and anywhere from 8 to 12 sections, depending upon later recollections. Each end of the car held a toilet and wood-burning stove, and the ever-present risk of fire was compounded by the candles used for illumination at night.

Six years after *No. 9*'s introduction Pullman built a new car that would set a new standard for overnight passengers and help him create his sleeping-car empire. Completed in 1865, the *Pioneer* was a 54-foot-long wooden car combining private room accommodation (one at each end of the car) with open sections in the center that converted from daytime seating to beds. In a configuration that would remain in use for over a century (and persists even today aboard some Canadian trains), a pair of facing settees made up each section. The seat backs and bases folded into a lower berth, with another berth folding down from the upper wall. All sleeping-car passengers thus had their own dedicated seat during the day and a corresponding bed at night. When the car was "made down" for evening use, heavy curtains concealed the berths and their occupants. The success of sleeping cars was followed by the creation of parlor cars and dining-car service.

Railroad passengers desiring to purchase and consume a meal while traveling had to wait until 1862, when Pennsylvania Railroad predecessor Philadelphia, Wilmington & Baltimore (PW&B) introduced the first dedicated food-service cars in America. Railroads that operated passenger trains during traditional meal times had long skirted the issue of passenger meals; travelers were encouraged to bring their own food. Along the line local entrepreneurs frequented station platforms and hawked all manner of food and drink to passengers through their car windows. The earliest formal efforts on the part of the railroads merely ensured that schedules allowed brief meal stops—often corresponding to locomotive service stops—during which passengers detrained to eat, en masse, in station or hotel dining rooms before their train continued its journey. The two coaches rebuilt by the PW&B in 1862 provided a stand-up counter at which precooked meals could be purchased and eaten. With the exception of a steam oven to reheat the catered fare, no cooking facilities were provided.

George Pullman also introduced the first cars aboard which meals could be cooked to order and served to seated passengers. Pullman's first such "hotel cars," the *President* and *Western World* of 1867, were otherwise standard sleeping cars to which a small galley had been added. Cooks prepared meals ordered by passengers who occupied berths in the hotel cars, and waiters served the food on temporary tables at the travelers' seats. The 1868 appearance of Pullman's *Delmonico*, named for the noted Manhattan restaurant, ushered in the era of the dining car, a vehicle dedicated solely to the preparation and serving of meals to passengers, regardless of their onboard accommodation. Many railroads initially resisted the introduction of dining cars because of their high staffing and stocking costs and the operational penalties imposed by their great weight and limited hours of operation. By the late 1880s, however, dining cars were carried by a growing number of railroads.

As famous as North America's railroads later became for their regional fare and distinctive house menu specialties, dining cars themselves exhibited a remarkably standardized layout. Kitchen and pantry—comprising ranges, ovens, freezers, refrigerated lockers, sinks, storage, and preparation areas—typically occupied the forward portion of the car, disrupted only by a narrow corridor for passenger access. Narrow doors were provided on each side of the kitchen end to permit en route restocking and refuse disposal. The remainder of a typical dining car provided table seating for as many as 48 passengers.

Variations on the standard dining car ranged from budget-oriented, limited-selection café and buffet cars—often partitioned within coaches and thus reminiscent of the PW&B's pioneers of 1862—to high-capacity twin-unit diners. The latter enjoyed limited popularity in the mid-twentieth century and comprised two adjacent 85-foot cars, one containing only table seating and the other an expanded kitchen along with still more tables and, often, a small lounge.

Most food-service-car variations reflected the railroads' desire to contain the cars' inherent high costs. The self-serve Automat cars introduced by Southern Pacific in the 1950s, with prepared food items dispensed from vending machines, epitomized this movement.

Twentieth-Century Rail Travel

Passenger cars continued to increase in size as the nineteenth century came to an end. They soon reached a length of as much as 85 feet. A standard configuration had emerged in sleeping-car construction, with the 12-1—12 sections and an enclosed drawing room—forming the core of the Pullman fleet. Over 4,000 12-1s were built for Pullman service, with only slight variations in floor plan, and they accounted for approximately 40 percent of all Pullman cars in service in the early 1930s.

The shift to all-steel construction began early in the twentieth century. Steel center sills and underframes introduced in the late nineteenth century helped, but wooden cars still presented substantial risk from collisions, derailments, or the always-present dangers from fire. All-steel passenger cars were an obvious evolutionary step, but their debut in 1907 and widespread use after 1910 were met with resistance from passengers wary of electrocution. Some feared that electricity from lightning or overhead catenary wires would contact the steel bodies. In a few instances car builders sought to quell the public's fears by giving the new steel cars and exterior sheathing a wood-grained appearance, but the unfounded anxiety soon passed. Electricity, in fact, was already present on passenger cars, with belt-driven, axle-powered generators providing current to lighting before the end of the nineteenth century. Banks of batteries, slung in boxes under the floor, were charged while the cars traveled and provided standby power during stops. All-steel passenger cars were built upon a fabricated steel, fish-belly-shaped center sill and underframe cross-members, obviating the truss-rod arrangement required by wood-underframe cars. Sides, ends, and roofs of the all-steel cars were framed with small-section structural mem-

bers, insulated, and sheathed with riveted steel plate of varying thickness.

As World War I concluded, North American passenger cars exhibited a high level of uniformity, influenced in large measure by the standardized size and geographic scope of the Pullman Co.'s operation. Modern steel cars were typically 75 to 80 feet in length, with typical end-platform and step arrangements and incorporating standard Master Car Builders practices. With notable exceptions such as the Pennsylvania and the Canadian Pacific, which favored maroons, and a handful of brightly painted seasonal or special-service consists, the exterior color of choice for North American passenger trains was dark green—in most instances, the same deep shade adopted by the Pullman Co. and known, not surprisingly, as Pullman Green. Arched roofs, referred to in some quarters as turtlebacks, stood out against the clerestory-roofed majority. Regardless of their style, virtually all roofs were coated in black to conceal the accumulation of steam locomotive and dining-car kitchen exhaust. Six-wheel trucks spread the weight of heavy steel cars and provided passengers with a smooth ride, while four-wheel trucks were less expensive and were applied most often to head-end cars and coaches.

Relying as it did on the ubiquitous 12-1 configuration to accommodate the majority of overnight passengers, it was not until 1927 that the Pullman Co. introduced private-room floor plans aimed at more affluent travelers aboard premier trains. The trouble with private sleeping-car rooms was that relatively few paying passengers could fit into a standard-sized carbody. Whereas an 85-foot-long intercity coach could accommodate as many as 70 or 80 travelers in somewhat cramped comfort, this first all-room Pullman could offer private space for only 14 individuals. Their quarters, however, were rather opulent, with private toilet and lavatory facilities and a crosswise, permanent box-spring bed in each room. No mere fold-away beds, these sleeping arrangements evoked the furnishings aboard the private cars of the era. Only 45 of these "single-room" Pullman cars were built, and most served on prestigious trains in the Midwest and East, with a few assigned to California routes.

The notion of traveling overnight with more than just a heavy curtain to protect one's modesty had a broad appeal, however, and the Pullman Co. and its car-building arm responded in the late 1920s and early 1930s with more and varied sleeping-car floor plans offering private rooms. Many older cars were rebuilt with the newer interior configurations, often retaining some original open sections with an assortment of new partitioned quarters. One popular and long-lasting room type to emerge from this process was the double bedroom; multiple occupancy of private rooms boosted a given floor plan's revenue potential. Pullman still sought ways to fit more individual travelers into its sleeping cars, though, and rebuilt a pair of club cars in 1932 to create *Nocturne* and *Eventide*. Each offered 16 single rooms in a staggered, up-and-

New York Central's *20th Century Limited* always had a car with sleeper compartments, a lounge car, and a brass-railed observation platform, complete with the train's drumhead. Photographers showed up for public relations events or celebrities. Models wearing the latest fashions were on board for an April 1931 departure from Grand Central Terminal.
—Ed Nowak, from Penn Central Co.

down duplex arrangement. That was two more than the pioneering single-room floor plan of 1927, but there was still room for improvement. However, this configuration, a means of squeezing revenue-generating rooms into the height and length constraints of a standard-sized sleeping car, saw limited use, predominantly after World War II.

As comfortable and well appointed as passenger trains were becoming, travel aboard dining cars and sleepers in particular could still be hot and stuffy. Air conditioning appeared on North American passenger trains with much fanfare in 1929 when Pullman 12-1 sleeper *McNair* was equipped with an experimental cooling system. Refined and improved, air conditioning spread through the Pullman fleet, and roads such as Baltimore & Ohio and Chesa-

The *Georgian Bay,* built by Canadian Car & Foundry in 1930, included sleeping compartments, a lounge equipped with a soda fountain–buffet, and a Vitaglass-equipped, fully enclosed solarium-observation area. Two similar cars were operated in Canadian National's Montreal-Chicago *International Limited.*
—Kevin J. Holland Collection

peake & Ohio also became early proponents. Air was cooled by ice or mechanical means and circulated through the car by fans, often via rooftop ductwork occupying the lower ends of a traditional clerestory roof. The widespread adoption of air conditioning marked the beginning of the end of opening windows. Sealed windows kept the cool air in and kept cinders, smoke, and right-of-way dust out.

Even with the comforts afforded by sleeping cars, lounges, and dining cars, it was left to the forward portion of the typical passenger train—the day coaches and head-end express and mail cars—to provide the lion's share of revenues. Coaches were, and remain, the most mundane of passenger-carrying cars, with only utilitarian seating and washroom facilities occupying the car's interior. The arrangement of paired seats flanking a center aisle has changed little since the mid-nineteenth century. Variations over the decades and among railroads have encompassed the type and total number of seats, the number and size of washrooms, and the provision of luggage storage, often in the form of an open, overhead rack running the length of the car interior above the windows.

Parlor cars offered passengers the option—for a higher fare—of more sumptuous and less crowded daytime seating. Single overstuffed chairs flanked a wide center aisle. Parlor chairs often were mounted on rotating bases, enabling passengers to position the chair for the view most to their liking.

Head-end cars, so called by virtue of their typical position at the front of a passenger train, employed the space within a standard car shell for baggage, the storage or en route sorting of mail, and the movement of express shipments by companies such as the Railway Express Agency. In addition to such adaptations of standard passenger-car shells, passenger-train head-end business also incorporated goods carried aboard boxcars and refrigerator cars more typically seen in freight trains. Boxcars and refrigerator cars used in passenger-train service, however, were required to be equipped with pass-through steam and signal lines and passenger-car safety appliances and typically rode on high-speed trucks.

Streamlining Arrives

Even more radical changes in passenger-car architecture came in the mid-1930s as practitioners in the emerging field of industrial design turned their sights on the railroads. The streamlined future of the North American passenger train had been suggested by Pullman's centerpiece exhibit at the 1933 Century of Progress Exposition in Chicago. Named to honor the company's founder, the *George M. Pullman* was, functionally, a traditional sleeper-lounge-observation car. In years past it would have taken the form of a standard heavyweight steel car with a brass-railed observation platform or a squared-off solarium observation room boasting a generous expanse of larger-than-normal windows. In its new *George M. Pullman*, however, the company dispensed with almost every car-building convention to create a gleaming, aluminum-bodied

car with a smoothly rounded roof and a sleek boat-tailed observation end—the first of its type. This car was, in many respects, the progenitor of the so-called lightweight era of passenger-car construction. By using aluminum, itself an embodiment of the future in 1933, Pullman's new showpiece weighed only about half as much as one of its all-steel contemporaries. Although some design elements of the waning era were present—square-cornered, paired windows, a riveted belt rail, and exposed step wells, for example—the gleaming new car was the shape of things to come.

By the mid-1930s industrial designers such as Otto Kuhler, Raymond Loewy, Henry Dreyfuss, Walter Dorwin Teague, and Norman Bel Geddes were literally reshaping America and defining its aesthetic tastes. Streamlined forms were everywhere, and a Depression-weary public embraced the myriad manifestations of Art Deco and Moderne design. Some were streamlined for inherently practical reasons, as in the sleek Douglas DC-1 airliner and its larger offspring, but household appliances and other more mundane items were given streamlined facelifts solely for the sake of style and marketing opportunism. Railroad passenger trains were caught up in the frenzy. Although the aerodynamic benefits of streamlining a passenger train were marginal, at best, its aesthetic—and economic—benefits were clear.

New-generation trains like the Budd-built *Zephyr*s and *Flying Yankee*, the Goodyear Zeppelin *Comet,* and the Union Pacific streamliners, all introduced between 1934 and 1936, made headlines across the continent. These early fixed-consist streamliners were so successful, in fact, that they could not accommodate the passenger loads generated by their own publicity. Moreover, the articulated, semipermanently coupled nature of these designs meant that extra cars could not be readily added to meet traffic peaks. First-generation streamliners like the Milwaukee Road's *Hiawatha*s of 1934 were more versatile, since they were composed of independent cars, and their consists could therefore be lengthened or shortened as patronage dictated.

The first large fleets of streamlined, nonarticulated passenger cars were those styled by Walter Dorwin Teague for the New York, New Haven & Hartford and the Boston & Maine railroads. Their design featured a turtleback curved roof and riveted steel sheathing that extended below the cars' floor line, covering the trucks and mechanical appurtenances. This design also formed part of the cars' strength and integrity, meeting existing Assn. of American Railroads (AAR) safety specifications for passenger equipment. The first of these cars entered service on the New Haven in 1934, and they were soon rendered in model form by toy maker A. C. Gilbert as part of the manufacturer's American Flyer line of miniature trains. The full-size versions, which eventually were also built for the Lehigh Valley, Bangor & Aroostook, Seaboard Air Line, and St. Louis Southwestern railroads, were nicknamed American Flyer cars in short order. As lightweight passenger-car designs evolved through the mid-1930s, riveted body assembly gave way to welding for the ulti-

mate in smooth-sided streamlining. The Milwaukee Road's *Hiawatha*s and groups of curved-sided cars built by the Canadian Pacific Railway employed welded sides to particularly good effect.

In Philadelphia the Budd Co. had developed its Shotweld process, a proprietary technique of welding stainless steel. Budd, a fabricator of automotive parts, became involved in the construction of railroad passenger equipment through an ultimately unsuccessful early 1930s joint venture with the French firm Michelin for railcars used both in France and in the United States. Budd had provided stainless-steel superstructures for rubber-tired railcars and subsequently leapt to the vanguard of passenger-car construction with the 1934 debut of the Chicago, Burlington & Quincy's articulated *Zephyr*. Followed less than a year later by the *Flying Yankee*, a near twin delivered to the Boston & Maine/Maine Central, the original *Zephyr* and its eventual fleet mates combined strong box-girder body construction with unpainted exteriors clad in ornamental stainless-steel fluting. This combination of corrosion-resistant construction and fluted styling, the work of architect Paul Cret, endured for decades, emulated with only limited success by other builders.

For its part, Pullman continued to innovate, introducing the first lightweight, articulated sleeping cars in 1934. *Abraham Lincoln, Oregon Trail,* and *Overland Trail* were assigned to Union Pacific's M-10001 streamliner consist, the *City of Portland*. As articulation fell from favor with railroad operating departments, however, Pullman moved away from this restrictive design approach first with the 16-section duplex-room sleeper *Advance* and sleeper-lounge-observation *Progress* in 1935 and then with *Forward* in 1936. *Forward*'s truss-supported steel superstructure was sheathed in cosmetic stainless-steel fluting, a treatment that would be the exception rather than the rule for Pullman-Standard's subsequent production.

Although articulation was avoided, for the most part, after the mid-1930s, the versatility of bidirectional consists appealed to several eastern railroads burdened with congested terminals. A train, either self-propelled or locomotive hauled, that did not need to be physically turned at an end-point station would offer increased availability and generate savings in time, manpower, and money. The New Haven was just such a property, with Boston and New York City as its principal passenger-train endpoints, and the road embraced bidirectional passenger trains with zeal. The aforementioned Goodyear Zeppelin *Comet* (1935) and the Besler steam train (1936), both vest-pocket trainsets, were the first bidirectional streamlined trains employed by the New Haven. Budd, for its part, had proposed a double-ended version of its shovel-nosed *Zephyr* to the New Haven, but was turned down. The Philadelphia builder had to wait until 1937 to create its first bidirectional train, the Reading's steam-locomotive-powered *Crusader*. This five-car stainless-steel train featured a pug-ended observation car at each end and simply reversed direction at its Philadelphia and Jersey City endpoints. Turnaround labor was limited to reversing coach seats and turning the locomotive, and even this latter task was eliminated after the train was dieselized.

Although Pullman-Standard dabbled with stainless-steel cosmetic sheathing on some cars well into the 1950s, the vast majority of lightweight P-S production followed the appearance of the *20th Century* and *Broadway* consists, with their smooth, welded sides, four-wheeled trucks, and skirted underbodies. Unfortunately, the fluted stainless-steel strips applied by P-S proved to be an Achilles' heel for many of the cars so equipped. Unlike Budd, able to employ its Shotweld process and fabricate entire carbodies of corrosion-resistant stainless steel, P-S decided to settle for the application of stainless sheathing over structural Cor-Ten steel, even though Budd offered to share the process with Pullman. The two metals proved to be incompatible, and electrolytic corrosion ate away the underlying Cor-Ten over time, while the cosmetic fluting concealed much of the ongoing deterioration.

Pullman's efforts to accommodate individual overnight travelers culminated in 1937 with the introduction of the roomette, a marvelously efficient single-room design with self-contained toilet and lavatory and a lengthwise bed that hinged down from the wall. During the day roomette occupants enjoyed an upholstered settee. Eighteen-roomette demonstrator cars *Roomette I* and *Roomette II* gave travelers and railroads alike a taste of the new rooms. With the debut of the streamlined, lightweight *20th Century Limited* and *Broadway Limited* in June 1938, the roomette emerged, along with the modernized double bedroom, as the new standard in Pullman accommodations. Early floor plans contained either 17 or 18 roomettes, or 10 roomettes in combination with 5 (6 after World War II) double bed-

rooms. The so-called 10-6 sleeper in effect became the lightweight-era version of the ubiquitous 12-1.

So prevalent was streamlining during the 1930s that a handful of railroads, economically unable to reequip all or even some of their schedules with new lightweight cars, turned to their own shops to rebuild old or obsolete rolling stock with an up-to-date, stream-styled appearance. Designer Henry Dreyfuss created the *Mercury* for New York Central in 1936, directing the road's Beech Grove (Indianapolis) shops in the conversion of old commuter coaches into a streamlined day train. Otto Kuhler oversaw a similar project for the Baltimore & Ohio, which rebuilt heavyweight cars into the semistreamlined *National Limited* and *Capitol Limited* of 1938. Other railroads took a piecemeal approach both before and after World War II, upgrading individual groups of heavyweight cars in the streamlined mold rather than creating entire stream-styled trainsets. Lehigh Valley, Erie, Nickel Plate Road, Illinois Central, Gulf, Mobile & Ohio, Missouri Pacific, Great Northern, Southern, and Atlantic Coast Line were among the roads in this frugal category.

World War II and Beyond

The newly dawned lightweight era was preempted by the materials shortages and exigencies of World War II, and no new passenger cars were delivered between 1942 and 1946. After the war a dramatic shift in travel habits occurred that brought back memories of the decline in passenger-train ridership on the threshold of the Great Depression. Although the world had changed, the manner in which railroads marketed their passenger services had not. Changing public attitudes had not made an impression on passenger department planners who, during the war, laid plans for the postwar period, which they foresaw as a rebirth of modern rail passenger travel. By 1944 several railroads had initiated passenger surveys aimed at assisting in the development of their postwar fleets. Santa Fe, New Haven, and New York Central were among the roads to solicit passenger opinions on topics ranging from seating, sleeping accommodation, food service, and lavatory facilities to window configuration and exterior finish.

By virtue of its in-house research department, the Chesapeake & Ohio (along with corporate affiliates Nickel Plate Road and Pere Marquette) emerged as an aggressive innovator in postwar passenger-car design. Among the hallmarks of C&O influence were center bulkheads in coaches (to break the bowling-alley effect of the hitherto-open interiors), air-operated sliding car-end doors, placement of higher-priced bedroom accommodation in the smoother-riding center of the car, foot-pedal controls for lavatory faucets (a nod to hygiene-minded C&O chairman Robert R. Young), and cutaway roomette beds.

Many of the C&O-inspired sleeping-car improvements were adopted by Pullman-Standard when that builder unveiled the S-Type roomette in 1954, and the refinements also appeared in Budd-built sleepers before long. Cutaway beds permitted roomette occupants to raise and lower the bed while inside their room with the sliding door closed—previous roomette designs had required the passenger to back into the corridor, with only a zippered curtain for privacy. The cutaway design also facilitated a fixed corner sink, replacing the awkward and sometimes-unreliable folding models in earlier roomette plans. Postwar coach passengers benefited from improved lighting and seating, all the while within the now-standard lightweight, streamlined carbody configuration. Seating manufacturer Heywood-Wakefield introduced its Sleepy Hollow line, with ergonomics derived from sample passenger measurements gathered by Harvard anthropologist Dr. Earnest Hooton. Seating options ran the gamut from fixed-back and walkover designs to fully reclining styles equipped with retractable leg rests.

Postwar Signature Cars

In addition to these functional improvements, railroads and car builders perceived the importance of feature cars in attracting postwar travelers out of automobiles and airliners. The premier lightweight streamliners offered observation cars, many of which emulated the boat-tail styling of 1933's *George M. Pullman*. Some of the observation cars built by Budd before the war had a blunter, but still rounded, end, while some postwar versions from Budd, P-S, and American Car & Foundry (AC&F) (both new and rebuilt) had squared-off ends in deference to occasional midtrain use.

The highlight of postwar feature-car design, however, was the dome car, with a glassed-in seating area rising above the conventional roofline to afford passengers a 360-degree view. Freight-train crews had long enjoyed such vistas from their caboose cupolas, and the Canadian Pacific Railway had even operated twin-cupola-equipped passenger cars in the Rockies at the end of the nineteenth century. In its postwar incarnation, though, the dome car was the brainchild of General Motors executive C. R. Os-

Typical of post–World War II equipment were these streamlined coaches built for the New York, New Haven & Hartford by the Pullman-Standard Worcester (Massachusetts) plant during 1947–1948. Although built largely of lightweight steel, the cars used a corrugated stainless-steel exterior material. —Kevin J. Holland Collection

born, whose memorable ride through the Colorado Rockies aboard one of his company's new diesel locomotives led him to the conclusion that passengers deserved to enjoy the same visual experience.

The Chicago, Burlington & Quincy rebuilt a Budd "flattop" coach at its Aurora, Illinois, shops in 1945, and then another, to create the first modern dome cars. General Motors and Pullman-Standard teamed up to promote the dome with their four-car, all-dome *Train of Tomorrow* in 1947. Any doubters of the dome's popularity were quickly silenced with the 1949 debut of the *California Zephyr*, a Chicago-Oakland schedule launched as the first daily cruise train. Each *California Zephyr* consist boasted multiple dome cars, and the train's schedule was arranged to pass through the best western scenery in daylight. Other domeliners followed, mostly on western railroads with their more generous lineside clearances.

Domes grew from the short variety pioneered by GM, CB&Q, and Budd into the full-length Super Domes built by P-S for the Milwaukee Road beginning in 1952. Budd built similar full-length dome cars for Santa Fe and Great Northern, and Southern Pacific rebuilt a group of three-quarter-length domes from prewar flattops, using dome

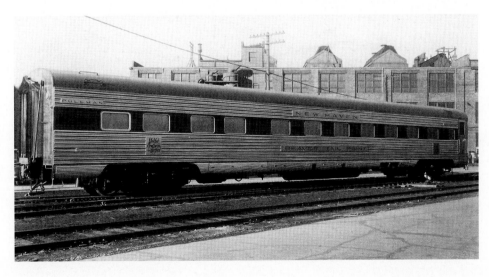

The Pullman sleeping car *Beaver Tail Point* is a good example of post–World War II standards. This 14-roomette, 4-bedroom car was built by Pullman-Standard in Chicago in 1949 and operated on overnight services into Maine, the Washington-Montreal overnight train, and others. —Kevin J. Holland Collection

For its postwar reequipping of the streamlined *20th Century Limited* in 1948, Pullman-Standard delivered the elegant observation-lounge car *Hickory Creek*. The car included five double bedrooms, a bar, and the raised Lookout Lounge, which provided splendid views of the Hudson River from its extra-high windows. —Geoffrey H. Doughty Collection

components purchased from Budd. Despite their impressive expanses of glass, though, sight lines from the longer domes, particularly to the front and rear, fell short of those afforded by their smaller kin.

The observation car, meanwhile, had reached its zenith with the Milwaukee Road Skytop cars designed by Brooks Stevens for *Hiawatha* service. These distinctive cars merged the faceted glazing of the dome car with an observation car's rounded end. Two styles of Skytop were built in the late 1940s—a group of parlor-observation cars in the railroad's own Milwaukee shops and six sleeper versions delivered by Pullman-Standard for the Chicago-Tacoma *Olympian Hiawatha*. Pullman-Standard took a similar but less spectacular approach with a trio of sleeper-lounge cars delivered to the Seaboard Air Line in 1954. Befitting their role in the New York–Washington-Florida trade, these three SAL Sun Lounge cars were fitted with skylight windows in their lounge roofs, a concession to the low clearances in the Northeast.

Larger end windows appeared on a handful of Budd, AC&F, and P-S observation cars, and the raised-floor spaces they enclosed were termed Lookout Lounges. By the mid-1950s, however, use of the observation car had begun to decline. Popular with passengers and publicists, they were expensive to build and incurred additional switching at terminals and on-line points when cars had to be added to or removed from a consist en route. Some observation cars were converted or built with flat ends for midtrain operation, but many were simply victims of rising costs and declining ridership.

—Kevin J. Holland

Experimental Ultralightweights

The passenger-train optimism of the early postwar years did not last long, and soon a few industry leaders began to look at ways of redesigning the conventional passenger car. The C&O's Robert R. Young was in the forefront of this campaign. Young saw the conventional design as outdated, based, as he claimed, on designs created in the mid-1800s for conditions that existed in those times. He believed that what made passenger service so expensive to operate and, therefore, so difficult to earn a profit was the initial cost of a modern car's construction. The material and labor costs to build each car inflated the cost of the

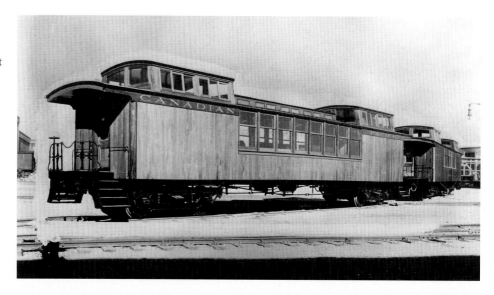

This 1904 version of a Canadian Pacific sightseeing car with two elevated domes proves that there is seldom anything completely new. The idea was revived again with the raised domes of the modern Vista-Dome in 1945. —*Trains* Magazine Collection

cars, resulting in an initial investment that took years to recoup. The typical 60-seat coach in 1950 weighed approximately 60 tons, or about 1 ton per seat. When the locomotive weight, about 300 tons, was factored in, the average weight per seat rose to roughly 1.5 tons. Because the average passenger coach cost about $135,000, or approximately $2,300 per seat, with the locomotive's portion added in, the cost rose above $2,600. Of course, diners and sleepers, with their complex interior arrangements and fixtures, cost even more.

Young argued that the railroad had to lower its investment and operating cost per seat in order to remain competitive. In effect, trains had to become lighter and faster, consume less fuel, and be less costly to operate and maintain. The rail passenger cars then under construction, Young stated, were top-heavy, and he pointed to GM's 1947 *Train of Tomorrow,* then on its promotional tour around the country, as an example. More important, he felt that the cost of the railroad passenger car was too high relative to its earning capacity. A high-capacity coach earned more in revenue than a sleeper that could carry, at most, 24 persons. This made each coach, dining car, or sleeper a poor investment. As passengers switched to other modes of travel, the opportunities for railroads to earn enough on their initial investment were made even more difficult. Young believed that travelers might be lured away from air and highway travel with the development of a real Train of Tomorrow. With the profile of the average traveler in transition, railroads had to alter their way of doing business—or else. As a case in point, by the end of 1948, approximately 1,840 passenger cars were on order—some orders had been placed as early as 1944, but had not yet been delivered. By mid-1948 railroads had ordered 184 additional passenger cars, but in the last three months of that year only 14 additional cars had been ordered.

Young's vision of new design was a lightweight, low-center-of-gravity, high-speed train that could operate over existing American roadbeds. He called it Train X. Its origins dated back to the 1930s and the New York, New Haven & Hartford Railroad's *Comet.* Young's Train X was based on a Spanish development called Talgo, the result of a privately funded project inspired by a Spanish army engineer. Alejandro Giocoechea had been approached by Spanish philanthropist Lucas de Oriol, who commissioned the design of a new lightweight train for use on the Spanish National Railways. The train drew its name from the Spanish terms *tren* (train), *articulado* (joined), *ligero* (light), Giocoechea (its inventor), and Oriol (the philanthropist).

The Talgo concept attempted to lower the overall costs of passenger-hauling systems (construction, maintenance, and operation) while increasing speed on the main line. One major issue that had to be addressed was pure physics—the centrifugal forces that combine to offset the train's equilibrium on curved track. Traditionally, railroad engineers compensated with superelevation—tilting one side of a curve, with a slight speed restriction, causing the train to tilt at the same angle as the track. The benefits

of these tactics, however, were offset by passenger comfort considerations.

During World War II a five-car test train was constructed and tested in Spain. At the end of 1944 AC&F won the contracts to build two trainsets. The specifications called for a low-slung articulated and lightweight (aluminum) train powered by a single locomotive containing an 1,150-hp Hercules diesel engine. The all-coach train carried 176 passengers, but did not offer specialty cars such as a diner or lounge. Each coach unit was 20 feet 2 inches long, coupler to coupler, and carried 16 passengers. A rubber gasket or diaphragm encircled the ends of the cars, making the interior appear to be one long tube and eliminating the use of vestibules between the cars.

A single set of wheels was located beneath the couplings between cars, and the wheels rotated on their own bearings, not on an axle. Retractable 5-inch dolly wheels were located at one end of each car to be used when the cars were detached or switched out or in. The two Talgo trainsets were exported to Spain and went into service on July 14, 1950. A third set, consisting of six cars and a locomotive, was built for AC&F's own demonstration tour around the United States.

Meanwhile, design work for Train X began during the period when Robert Young was at the helm of the C&O. He created a research and development department under the direction of Kenneth Browne, who charged a creative engineer, Alan Cripe, with the task of designing a prototype Train X car. The C&O partnered with Pullman-Standard to build a test car, which debuted on February 21, 1951.

But then the project stalled. Young became consumed by his efforts to take over the New York Central Railroad, and when that battle was won, he picked up the gauntlet and waved it in front of the railroad industry—and got its attention. He began his campaign as if it were a holy crusade. Within a short time designs for new trains were flying off the drafting tables of Pullman-Standard, Budd, and AC&F, most of them based on the Train X concept.

One of the first was the Aerotrain, developed by General Motors. Because GM was building fleets of locomotives, it felt that it should be in the forefront of developing a new train, hence its participation in the 1947 *Train of Tomorrow* project. Naturally, the company's primary interest was in developing a locomotive for Train X, and having the capacity to build the carbodies, GM decided to offer a trainset of its own design using many of the standard components then in use by its bus division. The design for the independent cars was GM's standard 40-passenger intercity aluminum bus body, widened by 18 inches and riding on a steel underframe supported by two single-axle trucks. The cars were modified to use the driver's space for an entrance and the bus engine area for a lavatory and a food-service pantry. The doors and steps of the vestibule at the front of each coach were arranged so the entrances would serve either high or low station platforms. Electropneumatic sliding doors were set in the vestibule bulkheads, and inner and outer diaphragms were applied to each end of the car.

As in the bus, luggage was carried in compartments located under the floor section, accessible from outside the car. Each 40-seat coach unit stood 10 feet 9 inches high, was 9 feet 6 inches wide, and weighed 27 tons. The center of gravity was 45 inches above the rail, close to that of other lightweight trains. The undercarriage suspension was similar to that of a standard GM bus—air-filled bellows inflated by the train's compressed-air line. The total weight of an empty coach was approximately 30,000 pounds, considerably less than that of a conventional coach.

Aerotrain's electrical system replaced the standard steam-heat systems then being used. An auxiliary oil-fired hot-water heater could be used as supplemental heat during extreme cold, and another auxiliary power source in the locomotive supplied current for train lighting and individual heating and air-conditioning units in each car. Thus steam lines were eliminated, saving weight and making possible the use of automatic couplers that completed the necessary electrical and air connections. Because cars would not be interchanged, an entirely different air-brake system with substantial reductions in cost and weight was designed, although allowance was made for a standard locomotive to haul the Aerotrain in an emergency.

Two ten-car Aerotrains were built for demonstration purposes. One was delivered to the Pennsylvania Railroad, while the other went to the NYC. The futuristic locomotives and observation cars were based on GM stylist Harley Earl's automotive designs of the period. Initial test results of the Aerotrain were mixed, with many passenger complaints of rough riding quality. Although the cars were designed to operate at 100 mph, their ride was so jostling that the Aerotrain was restricted to normal track speeds. Despite these results, the Aerotrain did fulfill most of the criteria of Young's Train X.

The Train X concept also addressed an important operational philosophy. New York Central's passenger research department found that the future of rail passenger travel lay with coach trains operating in corridors of 200 to 500 miles in length. NYC concluded that there was a better and more economical way to operate passenger trains, namely, a single locomotive pulling several coaches, strategically scheduled. Thus Baldwin-Lima-Hamilton (B-L-H) received an order to begin production of the Train X diesel-hydraulic locomotive, delivered to NYC in May 1956. Pullman-Standard, meanwhile, received orders for nine coaches. NYC's Train X was then given a new name, *Xplorer* (the neighboring New Haven purchased a similar train, the *Dan'l Webster*).

Since Pullman had done much of the preliminary design work in 1950 for the original Train X test car, it was able to quickly begin construction of the coaches, although there would be little resemblance between the test coach and those of *Xplorer*. The coaches were aluminum and consisted of a center car on each end of which were four articulated single-axle units of two cars each. The center car would be 50 feet 6 inches long and would seat 40 passengers. The other cars would be 48 feet long and seat 48 passengers. The floors of the cars were only 23 inches above the top of the rail.

Perhaps the train's biggest attribute was its ability to lean into curves at high speeds, identified early in the Talgo design. This greatly improved the riding characteristics of the cars by allowing the passenger to remain at the same angle as when the train went along on straight track. The design was Pioneered by a trio of experimental Pendulum coaches built for Santa Fe, Great Northern, and Burlington Route in the late 1930s. American interest in such carbody tilting would see a resurgence in next-generation equipment designs of the 1990s.

Each *Xplorer* car contained its own air-conditioning system, with power drawn from an auxiliary power unit in the locomotive. Forced-hot-air and electric convection units in each car provided heat in winter. The cars' electrical appliances were also fed power from a generator located in the locomotive, differing from the conventional arrangement with axle-driven generators on each car powering a battery system for each car's electrical system. The *Xplorer* consisted of nine units, each 45 feet 6 inches long. The entire body structure of each unit weighed less than 7,000 pounds, only about 40 percent of the weight of a conventional carbody. Interior trim and equipment brought the weight to 13,000 pounds for the 48-passenger compartment. The entire nine-section train weighed less than 135 tons empty (excluding the locomotive) and about 165 tons loaded. Specialty cars, such as dining cars and lounges, were not included. Instead, the train used an innovation from airline operations and the Talgo, with tray meals delivered to patrons at their seat.

On a May 1956 New York Central press run between Cleveland and Cincinnati, *Xplorer* used about $20 worth of fuel, or about one-quarter the amount of a regular train on the same run. The ride did not fare much better than the Aerotrain's, and repeated failures in service, perhaps due to inadequate testing periods, did not help the railroad's (and Young's) cause. Interior design received high marks, however, and most riders gave the train favorable ratings in regard to seat comfort. One of the major reasons for the riding characteristics that differed from a smoother ride in the C&O prototype was that when the Train X design plans arrived in NYC's mechanical engineering office, details of the designs for the cars' suspension were altered with the intention of making improvements. The Train X overhead suspension—as originally designed by Alan Cripe and placed in the C&O prototype car—was changed to a more traditional supportive system for ease of maintenance.

Although these two American experiments introduced many new design features that would later find further use, their failure was due to characteristics that counted most for the riders, namely, poor riding qualities and slow transit times. Two Aerotrains and a Talgo served out their short-lived years on the Rock Island's Chicago commuter trains.

—Geoffrey H. Doughty

The Budd Co. was the leading builder of the postwar Vista-Dome cars, which usually provided a raised center dome with all-around visibility seating about 24 passengers. The *Silver Garden* was a Budd buffet-coach car built in 1952 for the Burlington's *American Royal Zephyr* and *Kansas City Zephyr*. —Kevin J. Holland Collection

Other Initiatives in Car Design

While Pullman-Standard and AC&F were building experimental lightweight trains in 1956, Budd was building experimental trains and cars of its own. Three of Budd's designs that were intended to meet most of the criteria of the lightweight aspirations were the Keystone cars (also known as a "tubular" design) built for the Pennsylvania Railroad, the *Pioneer III* prototype car, and a modified Rail Diesel Car (RDC) design (discussed later) that was sold to the New Haven. The Keystone cars were a lightweight (stainless-steel) and simplified variation of conventional

Perhaps the ultimate in passenger-train amenities were the Budd Co. cars with both a Vista-Dome and a rear observation compartment, built for several Burlington *Zephyr*s and the *Canadian*. The *California Zephyr* car shown here incorporated three double bedrooms and a drawing room, a 24-seat dome, a buffet-lounge under the dome, and an observation lounge.
—Kevin J. Holland Collection

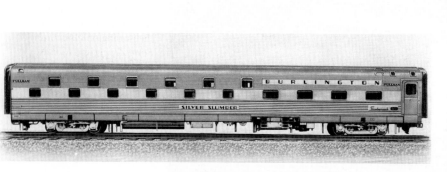

Among the major innovations of the Budd Co. was the development of the economy sleeping car. It managed to fit 40 passengers—24 single and 16 double—into the all-room Slumbercoach, which was available for only a small charge over coach fare. The *Silver Slumber* was built in 1956 for Burlington operation on the *Denver Zephyr* (*left*). The interior of a single roomette car (*right*) was obviously staged for the photographer. —(both) Kevin J. Holland Collection

stainless-steel coaches, but were intended to be pulled by a conventional or newly designed locomotive. As with the new trains from Pullman-Standard and AC&F, the cars were designed without steam heat, which was replaced with electrical power provided from a diesel-driven generator located in the first car.

Car interiors were made of plastics and stainless steel for easy cleaning and maintenance. The cars were semi-duplex, consisting of a coach section, located in the drop center of the car's main body, and a smoking lounge on a slightly raised platform over the trucks at each end of the car. Cars were heated by electric convection, and air conditioning was provided through a self-contained system in each car. The Pennsylvania Railroad was the only road to purchase the Keystone lightweight experiment (which derived its name from the PRR's keystone logo), and since it proved to be unstable in service, it was retired after a brief period of operation between New York City and Washington, D.C.

The Pioneer III was another design that was a refinement of Budd's earlier stainless-steel coaches. This car was 85 feet in length, stood 11 feet 9 inches high, and had an empty weight of 83,000 pounds. Its center of gravity was 43 inches, compared with conventional cars that had a center of gravity of 52 inches. It seated 88 persons in interiors made of low-cost plastics, simplified to reduce construction and maintenance. A head-end power source provided heat and air conditioning for the cars. Its exterior design was rounded, like the tubular design of the Keystone, and would eventually served as a starting point for Budd's later attempts at newer and improved passenger equipment (Metroliner, commuter coaches, Amfleet equipment, and others).

Self-Propelled Cars

Even before the internal combustion engine made them common, self-propelled passenger cars afforded railroads a means of providing cost-effective service on marginal routes. Although steam-powered self-propelled cars found limited application, the development of reliable distillate (gasoline) engines ushered in the age of the gas-electric "doodlebug" in the early years of the twentieth century. Outwardly resembling an arch-roofed steel combination baggage-coach car, the typical gas-electric incorporated a power plant in its blunt-faced forward end, behind which were a small baggage compartment and a coach section. Some also incorporated a small Railway Post Office apartment; still others contained no passenger space at all. The engineer was provided an operating station in the forward corner of the engine room, beside the bulky radiator housing. Individual gas-electrics often were sufficiently overpowered that they could, and frequently did, pull an unpowered trailer car.

Standouts among pre–World War I gas-electrics were the knife-prowed McKeen cars, built between 1905 and 1914. With an early streamlined design and porthole-shaped windows, these chain-driven cars hinted at a streamlined era still three decades in the future. The car was designed by Union Pacific's superintendent of motive power, William R. McKeen, who set up his own plant. Nearly 150 McKeen cars were built and eventually saw service on over four dozen railroads. Gas-electric production faltered with General Electric's departure from the market after World War I, but was rekindled in 1925 when the Electro-Motive Corp. (EMC), in conjunction with the St. Louis Car Co., built the first of more than 400 cars. EMC quit the gas-electric market in 1932, choosing instead to focus on diesel-electric locomotive development and production. Development in the field of self-propelled passenger cars remained nearly dormant for over 15 years before the next-generation doodlebug appeared.

Budd's Rail Diesel Car (RDC) was introduced in 1949 as a means for railroads to restore the profitable operation of secondary and branch-line passenger services by replacing conventional locomotive-hauled consists with one or more self-propelled, bidirectional stainless-steel railcars. Budd eventually offered the RDC in five variants: the full-coach RDC-1, the coach-baggage RDC-2, the coach-baggage-mail RDC-3, the short-bodied mail-express RDC-4, and the RDC-9, purchased only by the Boston & Maine and essentially an RDC-1 lacking engineer's control stations and end windows. Customers employed their RDCs in every role from commuter service to intercity limited-stop express. B&M eventually owned over 100 RDCs, more than any other railroad. At the other end of the scale, roads like Duluth, South Shore & Atlantic and Duluth, Missabe & Iron Range employed solitary RDCs in short-lived, stopgap runs. The RDC shared carbody attributes with Budd's conventional offerings, but stood apart at a glance by virtue of a rooftop hump that housed radiators and exhaust stacks. Twin diesel power plants were placed in under-the-floor mounts, connected to driven axles by a hydraulic transmission.

Perhaps Budd's most significant contribution to the new era, at least from a performance standpoint, was the modified RDC design sold to the New Haven and named the *Roger Williams*. Originally a six-car train, these cars were given flat stainless-steel sides, and although each car was powered and looked much like a regular RDC, the two control cars on either end were modified with a locomotive-cab lookalike. Unlike the other trains that were being developed in the Train X mold, the *Roger Williams* was not much more than a train of conventional design, although the middle cars contained vestibules at one end only. Its center of gravity was that of an RDC, its shape was that of an RDC, and although it was intended for Boston–New York service, its eventual inability to operate in New York Central's third-rail territory bumped it from that service.

In service the lack of dining-lounge facilities made the *Roger Williams* less attractive, although one coach was modified to provide food service of the grill variety. Damage to one car and the elimination of the food-service car eventually reduced the train to four cars. It lasted in service longer than any of the other lightweight experiments because of the proven RDC design. In time, another car was wrecked, and the one remaining coach and the two control cars were operated in other trains, but not as a unit.

High-Level Cars

Even with the frenzy of ultralightweight activity through the mid-1950s, conventional passenger-car design did not stagnate. Bilevel designs were seen as a means of reducing passenger-car weight per seat, as well as the number of cars needed to accommodate a given passenger load. The double-deck passenger-car concept dated back to the 1920s, with Pullman's duplex sleepers and 63 PRR/Long Island Rail Road commuter coaches among the earliest practical examples. Three prototypes were developed by Altoona in the 1930s, and 60 production units followed in 1947–1948. Neither of these designs was a true bilevel, however, because their upper and lower accommodations were reached from a single floor level and aisle. True bilevel designs, with two floor levels in a single car, began to appear on drawing boards in the mid-1940s. The Chesapeake & Ohio was among the first railroads to seriously examine the potential of bilevel equipment, even going so far as to propose a bilevel self-propelled car before the debut of Budd's RDC.

However, C&O's interest remained on paper, and the first double-height North American passenger cars debuted in CB&Q's Chicago commuter service in 1950. Cars of this configuration were ideal commuter carriers,

The Budd Co.'s successful Rail Diesel Car was an updated version of the branch-line and local gas-electric cars developed earlier. Between 1949 and 1962 nearly 400 of the stainless-steel RDCs were put into service. Some are still in operation. This Canadian Pacific car was the basic all-coach RDC-1. CPR operated some 55 RDCs all over Canada.
—Kevin J. Holland Collection

with their low cost per seat, but were not true bilevels. Rather than having a full-width second floor, these gallery cars placed upper-level seats on what amounted to a pair of shelves—the gallery—running the length of the car interior. A solitary crew member therefore needed only one pass through the car to collect tickets from both seating levels. The gallery cars' additional capacity, when compared with conventional single-level cars, permitted more passengers to be conveyed to and from terminal platforms by trains with an identical number of cars. Bilevel-car designs of American, Canadian, and Japanese origin remain the mainstay of urban commuter operations throughout North America.

The first true bilevel cars—containing two full-width floor levels, as opposed to a gallery configuration—were built by Budd for the Santa Fe's Hi-Level *El Capitan*. Testing of two experimental cars in 1954 led to delivery of stainless-steel bilevel equipment for the all-coach train in 1956. The cars' upper levels were devoted exclusively to passenger accommodation, with baggage, loading, and mechanical necessities located on the lower level. Only two other railroads employed intercity bilevel cars in the pre-Amtrak era. Chicago & North Western equipped some of its *400* schedules with smooth-sided P-S coaches, parlors, and lounge cars and even installed false high roofs on some conventional diners and head-end cars to match. A small group of CB&Q gallery coaches was fitted with washrooms and long-distance seating for assignment to tour groups and, on occasion, even the *Morning* and *Afternoon Zephyr*s.

New Car Designs

A new generation of passenger car emerged in the early 1960s, building on late 1950s efforts such as Budd's Pioneer III and funded by $90 million of federal funds under the auspices of the High Speed Ground Transportation Act of 1965. The Pennsylvania Railroad augmented this with $45 million of its own and, in concert with the Budd Co., developed the tubular, stainless-steel car design first employed on the electrified Metroliners and, in 1975, on Amtrak's Amfleet. Budd even offered the curved-sided, slit-window design in the mid-1970s as a next-generation self-propelled car, dubbed the SPV-2000.

Among the myriad passenger-car designs acquired by the fledgling Amtrak from its signatory railroads were the Metroliners, by way of PRR successor Penn Central. Santa Fe's Hi-Level *El Capitan* cars also made it onto the Amtrak roster, and their design clearly influenced the new government agency when it came time to reequip its long-distance western trains. Bilevel architecture was adopted for Amtrak's new Superliners, the first of which were delivered by Pullman-Standard in 1978. Completion of the initial Superliner order was marked by Pullman-Standard's withdrawal from the car-building business, a move already taken by minority builders St. Louis Car and AC&F. Even Budd left the market after it had given form to the single-level Viewliner design intended as a replacement for the 1940s- and 1950s-vintage cars operating as Amtrak's Heritage Fleet on long-distance eastern trains in the 1980s and 1990s. Canada's Bombardier acquired the rights to Budd and P-S designs and those of Canadian builder Urban Transit Development Corp. Bombardier's distinctive lozenge-shaped, two-level commuter coaches, originally developed by Hawker Siddeley at Thunder Bay, Ontario, were originally developed for Toronto's GO Transit and became a mainstay of other North American transit agencies by the early 1990s.

The Heritage Fleet program took the best of Amtrak's inherited rolling stock—mostly Budd-built and hence with a minimum of structural decay—and upgraded key systems (wiring, plumbing, and so on) in order to extend the cars' service lives by ten or more years. The biggest change involved conversion of the selected cars from steam heat to head-end power (HEP), whereby all on-board heat, light, and air conditioning were powered by electrical current provided via direct connections from the motive power. HEP had seen limited prior use, notably on the PRR Keystone and GM Aerotrain of 1956, Canadian National's 25-car Tempo fleet (built by Hawker Siddeley in 1967), and a few urban commuter operations. The continued use of steam for train heating, by way of a boiler within a locomotive's carbody and heavy piping and car-to-car connections, was a cumbersome, costly, and labor-intensive proposition. HEP had therefore been embraced by Amtrak as a fundamental component of both its Amfleet and Superliner programs.

Turbine-Powered Trains

Another of Amtrak's inherited orphans was the Turbo-Train, part of the same federally funded Northeast Corridor efforts that yielded the Metroliners. Developed by United Aircraft through its Sikorsky and Pratt & Whitney subsidiaries, the TurboTrains were in essence an application of aircraft technology to ground transportation that traced their roots back to Alan Cripe, the C&O, and Robert Young's ill-fated Train X.

The TurboTrain's smooth aluminum skin, tubular cross section, turreted cab, and bulbous, clamshell nose configuration reflected Cripe's early design renderings, as well as elements of Sikorsky's helicopter architecture. With two power cars bracketing each trainset, TurboTrain was well suited to operation into and out of congested urban terminals. The power-car design placed the engineer above the gas-turbine power plant, which was accessed through hinged panels on the exterior of each power car. The raised cab area was extended rearward to provide domed passenger seating, although the interior of this space was impinged by the turbine's paired exhaust ducts, which vented through the dome roof. One four-wheeled truck under the forward end of each power car propelled the train, and a single, guided axle supported each articulated coach unit.

The aluminum United Aircraft TurboTrain was equipped with articulated single-axle trucks, tilting capability, and gas-turbine power plants. One of the trains reached a still-standing record speed of 170.8 mph on the Northeast Corridor on December 20, 1967. Several were operated in service between New York and Boston and between Toronto and Montreal for extended periods, but maintenance problems ultimately sidetracked them. This was Boston–New York TurboTrain No. 3001 passing the Rhode Island Capitol at Providence. —William D. Middleton

TurboTrain's articulated, semipermanently coupled design actually harked back much farther than Train X, to the pioneering *Zephyr*s and *Comet* of the early 1930s. The lessons of fixed consists had seemingly not been learned even after more than three decades. TurboTrain's Pratt & Whitney gas-turbine power plants—designed for jet aircraft and unsuited to the rigors of railroad service—and its temperamental suspension, combined with its limited consist flexibility, led to a checkered career in Amtrak and Canadian National service. Although Amtrak favored TurboTrain configurations of five cars or less (including power cars), CN (and, later, VIA) regularly ran TurboTrains of up to nine cars on its high-speed, 335-mile Toronto-Montreal route.

Amtrak sampled turbine-powered passenger trains again in the mid-1970s, first with bidirectional ram-turbine-gas

Influenced by the successful bilevel cars developed by the Santa Fe in 1954, Amtrak used a similar design for many of its trains. Almost 500 of these Superliner cars, which include coaches, sleepers, dining cars, and lounges, were built by Pullman-Standard beginning in 1979, with a second group, shown here, following from Bombardier in 1993. —Bombardier, Inc.

(RTG) trainsets imported from France and then with modified French versions developed with the Rohr Corp. These Turboliners were employed in the Midwest and Northeast, and both types were rebuilt beginning in the late 1990s to serve New York State markets as part of Amtrak's Acela brand. Reflecting the trains' short-haul corridor assignments, passenger accommodations aboard the large-windowed cars were limited to coach and club (parlor) seating, along with limited food service.

Foreign Influences

Another next-generation passenger-train concept was Canada's LRC design (Light, Rapid, Comfortable), tested in the mid-1970s and employed with inconsistent results by VIA Rail Canada beginning in the early 1980s. Low-profile, curved-sided LRC coaches offered passengers huge windows, but the hallmark inertial banking system proved troublesome. Designed to be pulled by matching LRC diesel-electric locomotives, built by the Montreal Locomotive Works (later part of Bombardier), the LRC nonetheless avoided the Turbo's pitfalls of semipermanent consists and exotic power plants, and LRC rolling stock (excluding locomotives) remains in VIA service.

The most recent developments in North American passenger-car technology—those introduced during the last decade of the twentieth century—were mostly of European origin. After an absence of decades, Spain's Talgo reemerged as a new-generation option for Amtrak planners and was placed in operation in the Pacific Northwest. The influence of France's Train à Grande Vitesse and Germany's Inter City Express electrified trainsets, among others, can be seen in the high-speed, tilt-body Acela trainsets built by Bombardier for Amtrak service between Boston and Washington, D.C. Canada's newest passenger cars, dubbed Renaissance by VIA, were imported from Great Britain after the overnight Channel Tunnel service for which they were built never materialized. Along with Amtrak's Acela Express, VIA's Renaissance cars have maintained the European influence introduced to North America's passenger trains with the Talgo demonstrator of 1949 and reinforced in the early 1970s with Amtrak's imported French Turboliners and Ontario Northland's erstwhile Trans-Europ Express trainsets.

—Kevin J. Holland and Geoffrey H. Doughty

Running Gear

Couplers

For well over half a century both passenger and freight trains employed link-and-pin coupling. Coupling and uncoupling of cars was a dangerous task, and many attempts were made to devise safer and more efficient automatic couplers.

The first of these to be widely used for passenger cars was developed by Col. Ezra Miller in the mid-1860s. It used a combination trussed end platform, draft gear, and coupler that both eliminated the use of the link-and-pin coupler and greatly reduced the likelihood of telescoping of trains in accidents. The coupling used a hook arrangement, with drawbars with spear-shaped ends on each car. These were sprung at their ends so that when they passed by each other, they would be snapped together and held fast. A lever on the end platform was used to pull them apart for uncoupling, and a single buffer above the hook maintained tension so that cars would not separate. Miller's end-platform design replaced the dropped-end platform then used with one that put the main frame and platform in a line. This arrangement, together with the cars drawn tightly together, greatly reduced the likelihood of one car riding over another in the event of an accident. The Erie adopted Miller's design in 1866 for its passenger cars, and within less than a decade some 85 percent of all U.S. and Canadian railroads were using the Miller design. (The Pennsylvania was the only major passenger carrier that did not.)

Because so few cars were involved, passenger cars adopted semiautomatic couplers well in advance of freight cars. Freight-car conversion went much more slowly and required federal law to force adoption.

In 1873 inventor Eli H. Janney patented an open-jaw or knuckle coupler that formed a hook when closed, and opened when the grasp was broken. Because the connection was on edge, the coupler was called a vertical-plane coupler. The Janney coupler was tried on Pennsylvania passenger cars as early as 1874, and a heavier design for freight cars was developed. By 1888 the Master Car Builders (MCB) had adopted an automatic Janney coupler for freight cars that was incompatible with the Miller coupler. The Pennsylvania, of course, had gone directly from link-and-pin couplers to the Janney coupler for its passenger equipment, and by 1890 the Burlington had switched from Miller to Janney couplers for its passenger fleet. The entire rail system soon followed.

Although all couplers were interchangeable, there were a variety of designs and periodic improvements, always with compatibility for older designs in mind. In 1916 the MCB adopted a stronger-standard Type D coupler, which was used for both freight and passenger equipment, and the still heavier Type E coupler was adopted in 1930. This was followed by a new Type H Tightlock coupler for passenger cars that incorporated interlocking aligning wings at the sides of the coupler head and machined surfaces on the coupler body, knuckle, and lock that virtually eliminated coupler slack. This greatly improved passenger comfort, as well as preventing overturning or telescoping of cars during a derailment or collision. The Type H design was adopted as an alternate standard in 1937 and became mandatory for all new passenger cars in 1956. Railroads never adopted a fully automatic coupling system incorporating steam, air, electrical, or control circuits, but equipment of this type is often used for rapid-transit or multiple-unit equipment or non-

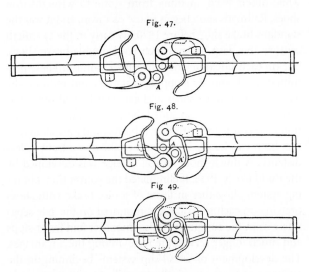

Fig. 47.

Fig. 48.

Fig 49.

The automatic Janney coupler replaced the hazardous link-and-pin system. Shown here, all from *The American Railway* (1892), are the old link-and-pin system (*top*) and the Janney automatic system (*middle*). The functioning of the Janney system is shown here (*bottom*). —(all) Middleton Collection

standard passenger equipment for which general coupler interchange is not required.

Draft Gear

The earliest railroad cars attached drawbars directly to the car frame. This was unsatisfactory, and some type of shock absorber between the coupler and the car frame was soon adopted. The apparatus attached to the rear of the coupler's shank—the draft gear—includes a spring or friction mechanism to act as a shock absorber. One early draft-gear design, patented by Charles Davenport in 1835, involved the use of a full-leaf spring at each end of the coupler shank, while another device that used coil springs was developed soon afterward. During the 1840s a rubber draft-gear design was popular. By the latter part of the nineteenth century, however, coil-spring draft gear, often with a double spring, was the most common type. In 1927 Otho Duryea developed a new type of draft gear, that used a cushion underframe that ran the full length of a car, with a large bank of coil springs to absorb the impacts. Although intended for freight cars, it was used for some passenger cars as well. Still more recently, in 1955, hydraulically cushioned draft gears were developed. Equipment using springs and friction clutches, a combination of steel springs and rubber, or hydraulic cushioning are all in use for modern passenger-car draft gear.

Brakes

For nearly half a century railroad brakes were confined to manual systems. A lever or hand wheel at the end of the car platform, operated by a brakeman, was connected by a linkage of chains, rods, and levers to force a block or shoe against the wheel treads. Originally, each hand-braking wheel or lever controlled brakes on just the nearest truck, but by about 1850 the efficiency of manual braking was doubled by the use of interconnecting that permitted a brakeman to operate brakes on all eight wheels of a car, using both trucks.

An early effort to improve railroad brakes was an attempt to develop a system of continuous braking, which connected all the brakes in a train so that they could all be operated together. A number of manual systems for achieving this were tried, but none enjoyed widespread adoption until continuous braking was linked with power breaking. There were attempts to employ a chain brake that linked all the cars of a train together. Another, intended to be used only for emergency stops, was the spring brake developed by William G. Creamer in 1853, which enjoyed a fairly wide use for passenger trains. A large clockwork spring could be activated by a locomotive engineer or trainman to set the brakes.

Braking, particularly for passenger trains, became an urgent consideration as their growing weight and speed made manual braking increasingly inadequate. A variety of proposed power-braking systems had been tried, using steam, electric, vacuum, and compressed-air power supply, but none were widely accepted until the 1870s. The two in serious contention were the Westinghouse compressed-air system and the atmospheric vacuum brake. The vacuum brake used a train line on which a vacuum could be created by a steam ejector on the locomotive. The pressure of the atmosphere would then push a piston or cause a diaphragm to collapse, with the motion transmitted through a system of rods and levers to the brake shoes. It was a simple system, requiring no compressor or storage tank, although early designs had the disadvantage of not having any kind of automatic safety feature if the vacuum system failed. This problem was later solved, but the vacuum brake also was limited in the power it could apply, and this became increasingly critical as train weights and speeds continued to advance.

The vacuum brake was adopted over air braking in Great Britain and several other countries; air braking was eventually preferred in the United States. The earliest vacuum brake was patented in England in 1844, but it was nearly 30 years before the system was being tested in the United States. The John Y. Smith vacuum system was adopted by several U.S. railroads in 1871 and was extremely successful in Great Britain. Frederick W. Eames became another vacuum-brake proponent and patented a design in 1874 that soon enjoyed wide acceptance in the United States.

At the same time the idea of a compressed-air braking system was also being advanced. George Westinghouse got into the field in 1868 and in April 1869 patented a pneumatic braking system that used a reciprocating steam pump to supply compressed air to the system. Improvements were made, and by 1870 the Westinghouse brake was enjoying wide acceptance. Eight railroads were already using Westinghouse air brakes on some 355 cars. In less than two years 85 railroads were using the brakes on 4,000 cars. By the time of the 1876 centennial nearly three-quarters of U.S. railroad passenger cars were equipped with Westinghouse brakes, and the vacuum-braking system quickly fell out of favor.

Even as Westinghouse's air brake was winning acceptance, he was at work on the idea of a fully automatic system. This involved an independent air system, auxiliary tank, and control valve under each car. Instead of using air pressure to set the brakes, they would be activated by discharging the air. The control device, called the triple valve, helped achieve more uniform braking. The operation was fail-safe because any major reduction of pressure of the train line (a broken pipe or hose, for example) would cause the triple valve to open to full emergency. By the early 1880s the Westinghouse automatic braking system had become universal on passenger equipment. It was adopted on freight cars a little later.

Passenger and freight braking systems operate under the same train-line signals for service and emergency braking, but there were many differences in the way they operated. Because passenger trains were relatively short, it was possible to regulate or graduate the level of brake release in response to a corresponding level of reduced brake command. Graduated release was not practical for the much longer freight trains; brakes on freight cars were released completely and then had to be recharged before the brakes could be applied again.

Passenger air-braking systems underwent frequent changes and improvements as speed increased and cars grew heavier. In 1894 Westinghouse introduced the high-speed brake, which raised train-line pressure from 70 to 110 psi to provide additional stopping power. Improvements over the next few decades provided greater power and smoother stops. The advent of steel passenger cars in the first decade of the twentieth century required still greater stopping power. The PC brake introduced by Westinghouse in 1910 operated with two brake cylinders instead of one, reducing stopping distance by almost 40 percent from the earlier equipment. In 1914 Westinghouse developed the even more successful UC brake.

Another major advance in air-braking equipment was the HSC brake, introduced in 1932 in time for the fast, lightweight streamlined trains that were just beginning to come into operation. This used electrical control to provide a much more rapid response and superior power and extra-smooth stopping ability over those for a purely pneumatic system. An improved version of the HSC design developed in 1935 mounted the brake cylinders on the trucks instead of under the carbody. Still another improvement in railroad braking was the introduction of the pneumatic-hydraulic brake valve in 1969 that used a high-pressure hydraulic system (at 800 psi) that was controlled by, and interchangeable with, a conventional air-braking system.

Brake shoes must dissipate the heat energy generated in braking a train. Early trains usually used wooden shoes, while others tried anything from stone to wrought-iron shoes. Railroads soon began to use cast iron, and it was the standard brake shoe before 1870. By early in the twentieth century the clasp brake, which used double brake shoes, one on each side of a wheel, became common. These permitted much shorter stopping distances and reduced the wear on both brake shoes and car wheels. Still other advances in brake shoes included the adoption of a composition shoe consisting of rubber, asbestos, and powdered iron that both was longer lasting and could stop a train in less distance. A much more radical change was developed by the Budd Co. in 1938. It eliminated the conventional braking system altogether in favor of a disc brake with shoes pressing on each side of a disc mounted on the axle separately from the running wheels. Smoother and faster stops and much longer service life were among the advantages. The development of wheel-slip systems beginning in the 1970s provides electronically controlled braking to monitor brake pressures to avoid slipping. Electrically operated multiple-unit equipment is sometimes also equipped with a dynamic braking capability.

Trucks

After trying a few early passenger cars largely patterned after stagecoach practice, with four wheels directly attached to the car, North American railroads soon adopted the double-truck car; with two separate four-wheel trucks swiveling on a long car. Early trucks were simple structures built of wood and iron. The earliest ones had only leaf springs over the journals to absorb vertical shocks. Lateral movement was directly transmitted to the truck, but by the 1840s car builders had begun to use the swing bolster, which added a flexible spring mounting that absorbed lateral forces as well. At about the same time passenger-car builders had begun to use equalization, which connected two parallel axles with a lever or equalizer so that a bump or shock from one axle was partially transmitted to the other.

These early additions established the basic form of the passenger-car truck. Subsequent evolution was largely confined to increase in truck capacity and the adoption of new materials. Early trucks were built with a wheelbase of less than 4 feet, compared with as much as 9 feet in modern high-speed cars. As passenger-car weight continued to grow, trucks were manufactured in composite designs, with iron plates and rods added to strengthen the truck assemblies. These were soon replaced by the all-metal truck and the wooden truck frame with fabricated steel assemblies. Soon after the beginning of the twentieth century railroads began using cast-steel truck frames, which created an integral, one-piece truck frame.

An important variation from this standard four-wheel arrangement was the use of a six-wheel truck. A few cars used them as early as 1845, but the design did not become common until the late 1860s, when they were sometimes used for dining, parlor, and sleeping cars to carry their greater weight on additional axles and wheels. After the development of heavyweight steel cars early in the twentieth century, six-wheel trucks became the standard for the heavy first-class passenger cars. Most passenger cars, however, reverted to the four-wheel truck with the advent of lightweight, high-speed trains in the 1930s.

From about 1960 onward an increasingly common and much lighter truck design used built-up, welded construction with an inboard location of bearings. Many of these designs have utilized air-bag suspension in place of the more conventional coil springs, or sometimes both types have been used.

A key component of every truck was the journal bearing and lubrication system, where a failure could lead to disastrous accidents. The basic form of this bearing was a simple one: the bearing at each end of an axle extended into a journal box, where a half bearing rested on the journals on the axle. Lubrication was provided by oil in the journal box, and cotton waste was used to bring oil to the bearings. Numerous improvements were made in the design or the materials, but the basic idea remained standard until the roller bearing came into common use for railroad equipment. These typically used two races of roller bearings operating in a sealed oiled housing. Several railroads were using roller bearings in tests before the end of the nineteenth century, but it was not until well into the twentieth century that they came into common use. The Swedish-based firm SKF equipped six Pennsylvania Railroad cars in 1921. Other railroads soon followed, and by 1930 there were more than 1,000 roller-bearing-equipped passenger cars in service. The Milwaukee Road, for example, found that its early roller bearings reduced bearing resistance to about 15 percent of that for conventional bearings, and that they could operate trouble free with only an annual greasing.

Both axles and wheels were components of passenger cars subject to severe stresses, and their failure could result in serious accidents. Early axles were typically made of iron, rarely much more than 4 inches in diameter. With the demands of heavier equipment and faster operating speeds, this was steadily increased. By the turn of the century passenger-car axles were increased to $5\frac{3}{8}$ inches at the center and $6\frac{3}{8}$ inches at the hub. Iron was replaced by wrought iron, and better grades of metal were used. Steel was used for axles as early as the 1850s, but it was not until the twentieth century that it was brought into common use.

Axles were rigidly attached to the wheels, which caused slippage in curved track, because one wheel covered a greater distance than the other. This was usually resolved by using a slightly coned wheel tread to accommodate the difference. The earliest railroads followed typical wooden-spoked wagon-wheel practice, with a flanged tire fastened over the wooden wheel. This arrangement was replaced about 1840 by one-piece cast-iron wheels. Some roads used a spoked wheel design, while others used a solid plate arrangement. Some wheel designers used a single-plate design, but a double-plate design was found to be superior and was almost always used for passenger cars. Good-quality cast iron produced reliable wheels, and it remained a standard for most of the nineteenth century. It was not until 1968 that the use of cast-iron wheels was finally banned in interchange service.

There was some use as early as 1850 of a wheel that had a cast-iron center and wooden wedges between the wheel and a wrought-iron tire. In 1869 inventor Richard N. Allen came up with the unlikely sounding paper wheel. This used a highly compressed strawboard center core made under intense hydraulic pressure and held in place with bolted front and rear plates, with metal centers and tires. It worked well, and the design helped reduce the noise transmission from car wheels. The Pullman Co. adopted the paper wheel, and by the 1880s there were some 115,000 of them in service. A wide variety of imitators followed. Some had a kind of cushioned wheel, while others just used a built-up steel-tired wheel. The fabricated wheels, however, proved unsuitable to handling the heavier weights and braking strains of heavier steel cars and faster trains, and by 1915 they were declared unsafe by the Interstate Commerce Commission.

A new wheel design came into use early in the twentieth century with the development of the much stronger rolled- or wrought-steel wheel for passenger cars. By 1924 an estimated 80 percent of passenger cars were equipped with them. For freight cars, however, the cast-iron wheel continued to run until 1968, when it was finally banned from interchange service. The steel wheel was further improved in 1930, when heat-treated steel came into use. This permitted the tread and flange to be hardened for improved mileage, while the body of the wheel remained a low-carbon steel that was not prone to thermal cracking.

—William D. Middleton

REFERENCES

Doughty, Geoffrey H. *Burlington Route—The Early Zephyrs.* Lynchburg, Va.: TLC, 2002.
———. *The New Haven Railroad's Streamline Passenger Fleet.* Lynchburg, Va.: TLC, 2000.
———. *New York Central and the Trains of the Future.* Lynchburg, Va.: TLC, 1997.
———. *New York Central's Lightweight Passenger Cars, Trains and Travel.* Lynchburg, Va.: TLC, 1997.
Dubin, Arthur D. *More Classic Trains.* Milwaukee, Wis.: Kalmbach, 1974.
———. *Some Classic Trains.* Milwaukee, Wis.: Kalmbach, 1964.
Duke, Donald, and Edmund Keilty. *RDC: The Budd Rail Diesel Car.* San Marino, Calif.: Golden West, 1990.
Keilty, Edmund. *Interurbans without Wires: The Rail Motorcar in the United States.* Glendale, Calif.: Interurban, 1979.
Kratville, William W. *Steam, Steel & Limiteds.* Omaha, Nebr.: Kratville, 1967.
———, ed. *Car and Locomotive Cyclopedia of American Practice.* 6th ed. Omaha, Nebr.: Simmons-Boardman, 1997.
"Lincoln Pin." *Railroad* 29, no. 6 (May 1941): 6–23.
Randall, David W. *The Official Pullman-Standard Library.* Vols. 1–10. Godfrey, Ill.: Railway Production Classics, 1987–1991.
———. *The Passenger Car Library.* Alton, Ill.: RPC, 2001.
Schafer, Mike, with Kevin J. Holland and Joe Welsh. *The American Passenger Train.* Osceola, Wis.: MBI, 2001.
Scribbins, Jim. *The Hiawatha Story.* Milwaukee, Wis.: Kalmbach, 1970.
White, John H., Jr. *The American Railroad Passenger Car.* Baltimore: Johns Hopkins Univ. Press, 1978.

Passenger Service

Despite crude equipment and defect-ridden operating conditions, early passenger trains dramatically improved mobility, offering faster travel and greater all-weather reliability. People flocked to the new mode, which revolutionized passenger transportation in North America. After experimenting with horses as motive power, industry pioneers adopted steam locomotives. In 1830 the Baltimore & Ohio's *Tom Thumb* hauled 24 passengers on a test run between Baltimore and Ellicott's Mills, Maryland, averaging 6 mph on the 13-mile trip. The South Carolina Railroad's *Best Friend of Charleston* pulled four cars at 30 mph in 1831.

The Early Years

Early passenger cars resembled stagecoaches; one historian described them as "open, wagon-like structures of cumbrous weight and uncouth appearance." Some vehicles boasted upper decks that allowed passengers and baggage to ride on top. Travelers within coaches could lower protective curtains during inclement weather. A few cars had sofalike seating along the walls. Other coaches were little more than flatcars to which benches had been added. Passengers were jolted as trains tottered over uneven track; they were showered by cinders; and those occupying seats in the open often carried umbrellas to protect themselves and their clothing from sparks and burns.

These shortcomings, coupled with rising claims for damaged clothing and baggage, prompted managements to adopt the elongated coach, which predominated by 1840. Typically 30 to 40 feet in length, the corridor coach featured a central aisle and bench seating on each side. Windows normally were uncovered openings that exposed travelers to soot, cinders, and dust. Glass windows then reduced these discomforts, but created ventilation problems that were only partially solved by ceiling vents. Candles furnished interior illumination until oil lamps replaced them. Heat emanated from a stove positioned at one end of the car. Passengers nearest the stove endured stifling heat, while those in remote seats shivered.

Other refinements evolved. In 1840 the Camden & Amboy equipped two coaches with rocking chairs. Railroads began to offer differentiated classes of service. For an extra fare travelers could ride on upholstered and adjustable seats in cars with more elegantly decorated interiors. Premium versions included seat springs and venetian blinds. Special coaches were set aside for women, and smokers were restricted to a single car. Spartan accommodations survived well into the 1850s. Confronting an equipment shortage, the Madison & Indianapolis in 1850 swept straw and manure from hog-hauling freight cars and installed wooden plank benches for passengers. When trains on Canada's Northern Railway between Toronto and Collingwood, Ontario, ran short of fuel, passengers helped the crew cut wood from trackside forests.

Ever-lengthening routes—such as the Western Railroad's 200-mile Boston-Albany run in 1842—made food service necessary. Vendors of snacks and water from communal metal cups rushed through coach aisles at station stops, along with newspaper salesmen known as butchers. Railroads then provided meal stops, and passengers raced to depot restaurants where the food ranged in quality from indifferent to barely edible. Catered meals were served on excursion trains during the 1850s, using coaches that had been reequipped with tables and benches. It is believed that dining cars first were used on scheduled trains as early as 1862 on the Philadelphia, Wilmington & Baltimore Railroad, but the food was prepared elsewhere. Despite the problems, rail service was better than any alternative.

At first, the effects of accidents were moderate because speeds were slow. Faster and more frequent trains posed a greater risk of catastrophe. Strap rail (iron strap attached to wooden planks) often failed, and errant straps ripped into coaches and riders. Equipment breakdowns and defective connecting chains added to the risk. Oil lamps and stoves ignited the wreckage of wooden car frames and furnishings after derailments. By the 1850s the frequency and severity of railroad accidents spurred lurid newspaper accounts that undermined the industry's reputation.

Fare levels varied widely in the first decade of operations. The B&O in 1831 charged 75 cents for the 26-mile round trip on its fledgling Maryland line. Fares on the combined canal/railroad operations of Pennsylvania's state-owned system averaged 1 cent per mile. Travelers on other routes might encounter rates as high as 10 cents per mile, but competition and other factors gradually depressed fares to a 2.5-cent to 3.5-cent level in the Northeast and between 4 and 5 cents elsewhere.

Early railroads adopted the booking system common to stagecoach and steamboat travel. Passengers made advance reservations, and their names were entered in ledgers. Tickets proved more efficient, and many early examples were reusable tokens of cardboard, metal, or leather. Reusability invited thievery. Paper tickets good for onetime use then appeared. Consecutively numbered tickets were adopted in the mid-1850s. Since most stations had open platforms, conductors took tickets on board. Although early travelers frequently changed railroads or modes en route, through ticketing was slow to evolve. To curry favor with influential travelers, railroads issued free passes. In time these privileges were granted to public officials, journalists, favored freight shippers, clergy, and delegates to political conventions. One writer complained that "every officeholder in Pennsylvania, from constable to governor, held an annual pass on the 'state railroad.'"

Uniformity also was lacking in baggage transport. Free allowances ranged from 50 to 100 pounds, and some carriers permitted higher weights. Several railroads tried to impose a uniform 80-pound limit, but the notion failed to take hold. Checked baggage was an early innovation, using numbered metal or leather tags. Handlers loaded and unloaded the parcels from baggage cars.

Published schedules informed travelers of train frequencies, fares, and arrival and departure times. These often took the form of classified advertisements placed prominently in newspapers. So-called broadsides printed on sheets of white cardboard duplicated this information and were displayed at depots and hotels. The value of arrival and departure information was marginal at best. Departures often were tardy, and delays en route were common. At cities where passengers interchanged between steamboats and railroads, late arrivals on one mode delayed departures on the other.

Running times improved as deficiencies were corrected. Trains of the early 1830s had been hard pressed to average 10 mph. Timetables for 1852 reflected average speeds (including intermediate stops) of 22 mph, although trains operating on the best routes averaged 35 mph.

Poor connections frustrated long-distance travelers. Although two or more railroads might serve the same city, their depots could be miles apart. Differences in track gauges meant that equipment could not be interchanged even if terminals were adjacent. Making a connection could involve a mad dash by foot or horse-drawn vehicle. Passengers idled in depots of uneven quality. By the 1850s adequate stations existed in larger cities. Elsewhere, riders loitered in hotel lobbies, restaurants, or taverns until it was time to board.

In 1850 through rail service opened between New York and Buffalo. By 1853 one could travel by rail from the Atlantic Coast to Chicago. Through service, however, did not mean uninterrupted service. Track gauges were not standardized until the 1870s and 1880s. Some schedules required overnight hotel stays at connecting cities. The lack of bridges over major waterways forced time-consuming transfers via ferryboat. Until the Allegheny River was bridged in 1858, riders transferring between the Pennsylvania Railroad and its western connections were hauled by omnibus over a highway bridge. The Mississippi River was bridged at Rock Island in 1856, but further spans over the Mississippi or Ohio rivers were not in place until after the Civil War.

Passenger Service Triumphs, 1865–1920

Passenger service was a key element of the railroad revolution that transformed North America after 1865. The burgeoning network brought service to remote towns and competing route choices between major cities. Faster trains increased the pace of life. Old concepts of time and distance were swept aside. "Do they not talk and think faster in the depot than they did in the stage office?" remarked Henry David Thoreau. Business travel gave rise to new commercial relationships and altered the retailing of consumer goods. The passenger train and its mail and express cars created a boom in the sale of newspapers, books, magazines, and catalogs.

The sleeping car enhanced the comfort of long-distance travel and created an important new category of revenue. Dating from the 1830s, sleeper service typically involved refitting coaches with seats that could be flattened and joined with boards, along with tiers of upper berths consisting of boards placed into shelves and covered with cushions. The accommodations were cramped, crude, and uncomfortable. Occupants complained of vermin infestations. One traveler griped that riding at night was "like

First-class travelers on the new Pacific railway enjoyed the elegant dining room of the Union Pacific. The coal-fired cooking range (*right*) served up oysters, turtle, mutton, beef, pheasant, and lobster; a dozen vegetables; desserts; and a wide variety of wines and liquors. The illustrations are from an article by Charles Nordhoff about travel to California in the May 1872 *Harper's New Monthly Magazine*. —(both) Middleton Collection

sleeping on a runaway horse." The first Grand Trunk sleepers consisted of benches and boards along the length of the car. No provision was made for curtains or dividers.

Over time, quality improved, and several carriers fabricated their own designs or acquired them from specialty builders, including Wagner, Knight, and Woodruff. A Canadian-built car for the Great Western included three tiers of berths, beds with springs and hair mattresses, and draperies that allowed passengers traveling in groups to partition their sections of the car. In 1869 the Pittsburgh, Fort Wayne & Chicago constructed two ornate sleeping cars whose interiors featured oiled black walnut woodwork trimmed with gold, along with ornamentation and lamp fixtures of silver. Adjustable tables could be used for writing and card playing.

George M. Pullman redefined long-distance travel with equipment and services that were adopted widely in the United States and Mexico. Founded in 1867, his Pullman Palace Car Co. built and operated sleeping cars for client railroads. The railroad transported the equipment and

collected the equivalent of a coach fare for each passenger. The Pullman Co. garnered a surcharge of $2 to $3 per night. Pullman insisted upon a high standard of customer service. His initial 48-car fleet expanded so rapidly that by the 1890s the company held a near monopoly in the United States. (Most Canadian railroads operated their own sleeping-car services.) There were many Pullman configurations, but most common was a car divided into 12 open sections of upper and lower berths and two washrooms. Some included one or more private rooms. "Hotel cars" included kitchens, and the company then deployed separate dining cars, although railroads eventually supplanted them with diners operated under their own management. Day travelers could ride in Pullman-owned parlor cars with ornate chandeliers and swiveling easy chairs.

Luxurious rail travel became the rage for those who could afford it. On lengthy trips sleeping-car service was more than an amenity; journeys from the Midwest to the Pacific Coast could be five-day adventures. By the 1880s many railroads offered daily all-Pullman trains on their major routes.

Seasonal trains intended for peak-period tourism demand appeared in the late nineteenth century. Florida's tourism boom prompted the Atlantic Coast Line in 1888 to launch the winter-only, all-Pullman *New York Florida Special* in partnership with the Florida East Coast. The *Seaboard Florida Limited* began operations in 1903 over the tracks of the Pennsylvania, the Richmond, Fredericksburg & Potomac, and the FEC. The Santa Fe aimed for a premium market with its *de Luxe*, a winter-only weekly run between Chicago and Los Angeles from 1911 to 1917. This service was limited to 60 passengers per train and was advertised by Santa Fe as "extra fast, extra fine, extra fare."

Service quality improved markedly between 1870 and 1920. Dining cars eliminated the need for meal stops and lopped hours from intercity schedules. The New Haven Railroad's *Merchants Limited* carried two diners, one of which offered seven-course meals. By 1906 the Chicago & North Western's *North-Western Limited* menu listed 28 different wines. First-class passengers could ride in club and observation cars. Premier trains offered barbershops, bath facilities, and telegraph service. Coach travelers also benefited. Oak ceilings replaced canvas linings. Oil lamps yielded to gaslights and electric lamps. Comfortable seats and flush toilets were installed. Pennsylvania Railroad coaches contained a small "retiring room" with sofa and washstand. The 1880s brought vestibule cars in which fabric-covered flexible canopies connected the open platforms at car ends, enabling travelers to move safely throughout the train.

The affluent passenger traveled by Pullman Palace Car. This shows the comfortable arrangements for Sunday church services conducted on the car. The wood engraving by Lumley after W. Hollidge was in the April 30, 1876, *La ilustración española y americana*. —Middleton Collection

This drawing from *The American Railway* (1892) shows the much less luxurious coach class experienced by the great majority of railroad travelers. —Middleton Collection

Impressive depots were erected, and attempts to improve connections led to union stations in which several railroads used a common terminal. The union station concept failed to take hold in the largest cities. Six depots handled intercity passengers in Chicago. Railroads also strove to enhance the image and performance of onboard employees. Managers of Canada's Intercolonial Railway had noted in the 1870s that employees resisted wearing uniforms, and the company frequently imposed fines for "uncouthness," rudeness to women passengers, cursing, and spitting in the aisles. Most railroads adopted detailed rulebooks for employees and passengers. The latter were forbidden from jumping on or off moving trains, traveling as standees, using vulgar language, or riding in baggage or mail cars.

Accident and fatality rates continued to be worrisome as the volume of passenger and freight trains soared. Air brakes, automatic couplers, block signaling, heavier rail, multiple tracks, and better roadbeds all improved safety, as did the advent of the more durable steel passenger car in the twentieth century's first decade. The passenger death rate dropped from 24 to 4.8 per billion passenger-miles between 1890 and 1920.

The 1870–1920 era marked the emergence of "name trains"—often known as "limited" or "express" runs

This 1870s example of the railroad smoking car shows a card game in progress. Players are enveloped in a cloud of pipe and cigar smoke. —Library of Congress (Neg. LC-USZ62-54183)

SCENE IN BUFFET - SMOKING LIBRARY COACH

ON THE FAMOUS "NORTH-WESTERN LIMITED."

BETWEEN MINNEAPOLIS, ST PAUL & CHICAGO.

HAYNES, PHOTO. — MN'PLS.

NO EXTRA FARES ON THIS TRAIN.

This photograph of the Chicago & North Western's Chicago, St. Paul & Minneapolis *North-Western Limited* shows an elegant version of the railroad's buffet, smoking, and library coach, with a uniformed waiter uncorking a bottle of wine. —State Historical Society Wisconsin (Neg. Whi (X3) 14820)

because they stopped only at larger cities and maintained average speeds (stops included) in the 40 mph range. The Pennsylvania Railroad's *New York–Chicago Limited* of 1881 cut 7 hours from the previous schedule between those cities. Southern Pacific's *Sunset Express* opened between Texas and California in 1884. Among the era's memorable trains were the Union Pacific's *Overland Limited* (1887), Atlantic Coast Line's *Florida Special* (1888), New York Central's *Empire State Express* (1890), and Canadian Pacific's Montreal-Vancouver *Imperial Limited* (1899). The new century brought the Northern Pacific's *North Coast Limited*, which operated between St. Paul and Puget Sound in 62½ hours. On each run an onboard electrician maintained the power plant and more than 300 electric lamps. Eight trainsets were required to provide daily service by the Great Northern's *Oriental Limited*, which first ran between Chicago and Tacoma in 1905. Perhaps most celebrated was the *20th Century Limited*, launched by the New York Central between New York and Chicago in 1902. The Pennsylvania countered with the *Broadway Limited*, and by 1905 running

times between those cities were cut to 18 hours. Three routes served Mexico City from the United States, and another opened between Mexico City and Veracruz. The equipment was on a par with that used on the better U.S. operations.

Luxurious rail travel was not universal. On some branch lines and secondary routes riders were transported in coaches scarcely altered since the Civil War. The lowest fares were available to immigrants seeking new homes and jobs, and their accommodations reflected this. Racial segregation in coaches and station waiting rooms became common in the South.

Fares averaged 2.4 cents per mile in 1881, but dropped to 2 cents by 1890 and remained in that range until World War I. Higher fares survived on some routes. The Union Pacific's charges amounted to about 3.3 cents per mile for service between the Midwest and California. Railroads offered group rates and discounts for travelers to conventions, state fairs, veterans' reunions, and expositions.

Although coupon tickets became standard for travelers

For first-class passengers only: "On the way to Chicago—the Observation Car," drawn by Childe Hassam for the July 22, 1893, *Harper's Weekly*. —Middleton Collection

using more than one carrier, the railroads failed to achieve uniformity in ticketing. They attempted to end cash payments because conductors pocketed much revenue. Meanwhile, commission agents made a joke of published rates. These agents besieged passengers at train stations with offers of steep discounts. By waiting until the last minute to buy a ticket, a passenger might travel for half the published price. Some agents, known as scalpers, resold unused portions of tickets or dealt in stolen ones. Rail managements moved to abolish these practices in the 1880s.

The frequency of trains and route choices boosted demand for printed timetables, which also proved to be effective promotional forums. Publishers offered compendiums of timetables and guides that provided information about routes, services, and hotel accommodations. Western railroads aggressively promoted tourist travel and distributed posters and calendars emblazoned with impressive scenery. Land cruises and group tours were offered, and railroad-sponsored hotels were built at popular tourist sites. The Canadian Pacific established elegant hotels at its major terminal cities and tourism destinations. Railroads were partly responsible for opening national parks in the West, as well as Florida's tourism boom of the 1890s. In 1898 the Southern Pacific launched *Sunset Magazine*, which promoted scenic wonders, cities, and job opportunities in its service territory. The Grand Rapids & Indiana advertised itself as "the fishing line" in a bid to win the patronage of sports enthusiasts.

Fading Glory, 1920–1970

When railroads returned to private control after World War I, the companies acted to restore name trains curtailed during wartime and to place orders for more all-steel equipment. From 1920 to 1940 they emphasized service, speed, and streamlining in the face of massive traveler defections to the automobile and intercity bus. The Great Depression also delivered a punishing blow to passenger volumes and revenue. Passenger service ended on many branch lines or was replaced by gasoline-powered motor cars and mixed passenger-freight trains. To cut operating losses, several railroads activated bus lines to serve light-density markets. Trains were consolidated into fewer frequencies on secondary routes, and all-coach long-distance trains were scheduled. Railroads meanwhile invested heavily in new and improved rolling stock to hold on to their main-line passenger business.

The fastest passenger trains posted average speeds exceeding 50 mph, including stops. Several hours were slashed from intercity schedules. Although 12-section Pullman sleeping cars with lower and upper berths survived, they increasingly were replaced by more private accommodations. By 1940 the Pennsylvania Railroad, for example, offered six different configurations: roomettes, duplexes, double bedrooms, compartments, drawing rooms, and master rooms (which included private showers). Long-distance trains copied the airline practice of placing nurses or stewardesses aboard. Radio receivers were installed. Air conditioning was added in the mid-1930s. Some trains offered telephones and typewriters. Long-distance runs carried dedicated equipment that rolled over the tracks of more than one carrier, especially in service between the Midwest and the Pacific Coast. When the Southern Railway activated the *Crescent Limited* in 1925, the train used the track of four different railroads—Louisville & Nashville, West Point Route, Southern, and Pennsylvania—on its New Orleans–New York run.

More name trains entered service, including Canadian National's *Continental Limited*, Southern Pacific's *Daylight*s, Seaboard's *Orange Blossom Special*, Santa Fe's *Chief* and *Super Chief*, and B&O's *Capitol Limited*. Luxury trains in Mexico included the all-Pullman *City of Mexico*. Particularly striking in design and appeal was the Chicago, Burlington & Quincy's streamlined *Zephyr*, which averaged 77 mph in a spectacular nonstop Chicago-Denver run in 1934. Powered by diesel-electric locomotives, *Zephyr*s were added to other Burlington routes. Diesel-powered streamliners soon were adopted by other carriers.

New seasonal trains designed for major tourist destinations augmented the existing East Coast winter runs to and from Florida. The Grand Rapids & Indiana offered summer-only service to Michigan resort destinations. The New York–Montreal *Laurentian,* operated jointly by the New York Central and the Delaware & Hudson, added extra sections to principal vacation destinations in the Adirondacks during the summer. The Colorado & Southern's summer season *Buffalo Bill* carried travelers between Denver and Yellowstone National Park. The Pennsylvania's all-Pullman *Bar Harbor Express* used tracks of the PRR, the New Haven, and the Boston & Maine in its summer-only schedule between Washington and Ellsworth, Maine.

A waitress served beverages in the ladies' sitting room on the Milwaukee Road's elegant Chicago-Seattle *Olympian* in October 1929. —Asahel Curtis photograph, Washington State Historical Society (Neg. 56077)

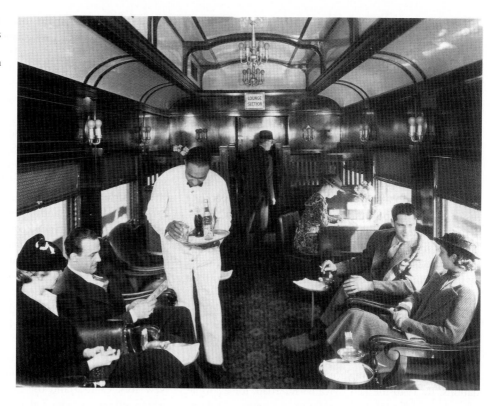

A white-uniformed waiter served drinks in the train's parlor-lounge section.
—*Trains* Magazine Collection

In 1941 the Illinois Central's winter-season *Floridian* was inaugurated and also used the routes of the Central of Georgia, Atlantic Coast Line, and Florida East Coast. Nearly all of these and other seasonal trains disappeared when World War II travel restrictions were imposed, but a few survived through the 1950s.

The Pennsylvania also tried to tap a potential market created by public concern about night air travel by fashioning a rail-air service in 1929 that offered a 48-hour schedule between Philadelphia and Los Angeles. Passengers traveled by train from Philadelphia to Columbus, Ohio, and then were airborne on TAT Ford trimotors to

The unusual Beaver Tail observation lounge provided passengers a splendid view from the Milwaukee Road's 1939 Chicago-Minneapolis *Hiawatha*, which sometimes attained speeds in excess of 100 mph.
—Milwaukee Road, *Trains* Magazine Collection

Passengers of the Burlington enjoyed elegant dining-car surroundings in a Budd-built streamliner. —Kevin J. Holland Collection

The chef on a Baltimore & Ohio dining car was quite proud of the roast turkey he was serving up for his passengers. —*Trains* Magazine Collection

Pullman porter Alfred MacMillan made up an upper berth for a passenger in the Baltimore & Ohio's *Capitol Limited* westbound from New York via Baltimore and Washington to Chicago in March 1942. —Jack Delano photograph, Office of War Information, Library of Congress (Neg. LC-USW3-50-D)

Waynoka, Oklahoma, where they were handed off to the Santa Fe for rail travel to Clovis, New Mexico. TAT provided air service on the Clovis–Los Angeles trip segment. The rail-air tickets were expensive, with one-way travel priced at $350. Typically, no more than 10 to 15 passengers used this arrangement on a daily basis, and in 1930 TAT launched a 36-hour, all-air coast-to-coast service, which included an overnight stop in Kansas City. In the face of improved air service and the effects of the Great Depression, the rail-air concept soon expired.

Railroads continued to promote tours and special trains to expositions and football games. In 1921 alone the Southern Pacific distributed more than 6.2 million promotional materials: timetables, pamphlets, posters, and calendars.

After their impressive passenger-hauling feats during World War II, railroads moved quickly to replace equipment exhausted by wartime overuse. Since rail passenger service was now a mature industry, the nearly 5,000 cars ordered between 1946 and 1950 represented incremental improvements to previous designs. Private-room sleeping cars continued to supplant open berths; exteriors and inte-

riors were more stylish; amenities such as recorded music, telephones, lounges, and children's play areas were added; and several carriers acquired Slumbercoach economy sleeping cars, which appealed to budget-conscious travelers. In 1949 the Burlington and its Denver & Rio Grande Western and Western Pacific connections launched the *California Zephyr*, which included raised Vista-Dome sections atop coaches and sleeping cars for viewing the spectacular scenery along the route. Other railroads rushed to acquire similar equipment, and the Santa Fe purchased high-level cars for its Chicago-California runs in 1956. These postwar alterations increased the costs of equipment and operations while often failing to deliver corresponding gains in ridership and revenue. The coach passenger who wandered into the lounge and Vista-Dome was getting several seats for the price of one.

The opening of multilane highways and better air service soon delivered cruel blows. In 1947 an antitrust decision required that the Pullman Co.'s car-building plant be separated from its train operations entity. Pullman kept the former; the latter was acquired by a consortium of 57 railroads. With demand for long-distance rail travel declining, all-Pullman trains no longer could be justified. When the New York Central added coaches to its fabled *20th Century Limited* in 1957, it symbolized the passing of an era. To stem financial losses from dining cars, railroads substituted dinettes and combination coach/snack-bar equipment. Through service to Mexico vanished, although the Mexican rail system improved its passenger fleet by purchasing surplus equipment from U.S. railroads. Railroads in Canada and the United States tried to lure travelers with bargain excursion fares and group rates. These were essentially futile exercises.

In 1971 most U.S. intercity service was placed in the hands of the government-sponsored National Railroad Passenger Corp. (Amtrak). Canada's intercity services were taken over by a Crown corporation, VIA Rail, in 1977. Ironically, two innovations were arriving just as private intercity service was dying. The New York–Washington Northeast Corridor was in the process of becoming a true high-speed route, and Auto-Train Corp. began hauling tourists and their automobiles between Virginia and Florida. The Amtrak-era shrinkage of long-distance rail passenger service rekindled interest in the cruise train, intended primarily to provide a travel experience on its own, rather than a means of conveying travelers from origin to destination. A limited number of cruise trains had been operated years earlier by the private railroads. The Pennsylvania, for example, in 1891 activated a series of land cruises in special trains using top-of-the-line equipment. Representatives of the railroad's tourist bureau accompanied the passengers on cruises to California, Florida, Mexico, and other locations. This service was discontinued about the time of World War I.

Post-1970 cruise trains were concentrated in the western United States and Canada. Since 1996 American Orient Express has operated land cruises from major cities in the western states with stopovers in the region's national

On the eve of World War II the Burlington's Chicago-Minneapolis *Twin Zephyr* drew an expectant crowd of passengers at East Dubuque, Illinois, before beginning its race up the bank of the Mississippi River in April 1940. —John Vachon photograph, Farm Security Administration, Library of Congress (Neg. LC-USF33-1708-M1)

parks, as well as Montreal-Vancouver service, and more recently in Mexico's Copper Canyon. Ocean cruise lines have teamed up with the Alaska Railroad to include rail visits to Denali National Park as part of their itineraries. Montana Rockies offers weekly round trips over Montana Rail Link's route in that state. Great Canadian Railtour Co. runs special trains in Alaska and between Vancouver and the national parks of Alberta and British Columbia. Land cruises in western Canada are operated by Canadian Pacific.

—William J. Watt

During World War II a crowd of soldiers and civilians boarded the Rock Island *Rocket* at Amarillo, Texas, in November 1942. —John Vachon photograph, Office of War Information, Library of Congress (Neg. LC-USW3-11463-D)

REFERENCES

Douglas, George H. *All Aboard: The Railroad in American Life.* New York: Paragon House, 1992.

Dunbar, Seymour. *A History of Travel in America.* Vol. 3. Indianapolis: Bobbs-Merrill, 1915.

Gordon, Sarah H. *Passage to Union: How the Railroads Transformed American Life, 1829–1929.* Chicago: Ivan Dee, 1996.

Martin, Albro. *Railroads Triumphant.* New York: Oxford Univ. Press, 1992.

Passenger Traffic Categories and Trends

Passenger trains quickly gained advantage over stagecoaches and steamboats by reducing travel time. Route expansion—along with improved service quality, higher frequency, and greater capacity—then led to a virtual railroad monopoly of intercity traffic that prevailed until about 1920. Of equal importance was railroads' ability to generate new categories of demand. This trend also continued until about 1920, when other modes began cutting into rail's supremacy and captured much of the added intercity travel that accompanied robust population growth and Americans' desire for greater personal mobility.

Services and Markets: 1830–1870

Traffic was local in passenger railroading's first decade. Isolated routes served nearby city pairs or connected cities with navigable waterways. Business flourished anyway. In 1833 the Camden & Amboy averaged nearly 10,000 passengers a month on its segment of the rail/steamboat link between Philadelphia and New York. With 70 miles of route completed west from Baltimore in 1835, the Baltimore & Ohio carried 8,000 passengers a month. That railroads achieved more than a mere diversion of stagecoach and watercraft travel is evidenced by the Charleston & Hamburg, which in 1835 hauled more than 2,500 passengers monthly between those cities. Prior to the line's completion a single stagecoach had rumbled between Charleston and Hamburg, making three round trips per week. People who had been reluctant to travel rushed to embrace the new mode—some of them for the sheer novelty.

From the outset passengers were important to rail carriers. Historian John F. Stover has estimated that a typical 1850s railroad received one-fourth to one-third of its total revenue from this source. The share was higher on certain railroads. With 600 miles of road in service in 1855, the Illinois Central's (IC) passenger revenue exceeded its freight revenue. A decade later, however, the IC's revenue ratio had changed to 2:1 in favor of freight.

Passenger traffic expanded rapidly as system mileage increased. For example, in 1855 the Pennsylvania Railroad operated 69 coaches and 24 baggage/mail cars. Two years later the coach fleet counted 119 cars, and by 1880 the Pennsylvania's passenger fleet exceeded 840 units. In 1857 the company noted that a majority of its passengers' trips were 40 miles or less. True long-distance travel then took hold as track extended to the Midwest. In 1860 the Pennsylvania reported that 34,848 passengers originating or terminating at Philadelphia had started or ended their journeys on its connecting lines west of Pittsburgh—an average of nearly 100 per day. By this time mail and express carried on passenger trains contributed a modest increment of additional income. Sleeping accommodations still represented a niche traffic category, as only a handful of cars were deployed by the carriers that offered this premium service.

At an early date the passenger train began reshaping urban America. Cities were compact, crowded, noisy, dirty, and polluted. Workers usually lived within walking distance of their jobs. Railroads then enabled those who could afford daily commuter tickets to relocate to the outskirts. During the 1830s three railroads served Boston-area commuters, and by 1858 the Boston & Worcester transported more than 1,000 commuters daily between Boston and Auburndale. Extensive commuter service also existed in New York and Philadelphia. The Illinois Central opened its commuter runs between downtown Chicago and the southside community of Hyde Park in 1856.

The completion of rail links among the major cities of the East, Midwest, and South doomed long-distance steamboat passenger service. Railroads offered greater geographic reach, faster trip times, and shorter routes. Water travel between Cincinnati and New Orleans involved a journey of 1,484 miles. A network of connecting railroads cut the distance to 922 miles. Steamboats retained a role in transporting local traffic, often in conjunction with railroads, by ferrying riders across waterways that had yet to be bridged or tunneled.

Unparalleled Dominance: 1870–1920

Aggressive tracklaying in the post–Civil War era delivered rail service to nearly all U.S. and Canadian population centers. The U.S. rail system peaked in 1916 at more than 254,000 route-miles. The scope of rail passenger operations eclipsed all prior experience. U.S. passenger-miles surpassed 7 billion in 1865, 12 billion in 1890, 16 billion in 1900, and 34 billion in 1916. Railroads carried 98 percent of U.S. intercity commercial ridership in 1916, and the average citizen boarded a passenger train 10 times that year. Passengers carried by the Canadian Pacific totaled fewer than 400,000 in 1882, but in a decade's time passenger trips exceeded 3 million, and then boomed to 15.5 million by 1913.

The sheer size of the rail system did not account fully

for the passenger traffic it attracted. Several trains ran daily in each direction on major corridors, affording greater convenience—especially for business travelers. Competition among carriers expanded choices, constrained fare levels, and prompted railroads to deliver better service and faster trains. Railroads created a market for tourism and land cruises. The business traveler was pampered. Low-cost trips were offered in emigrant cars, and entire trainloads of emigrant coaches transported settlers and seasonal farm workers. Between 1890 and 1920 the number of U.S. railroad-owned passenger cars in service increased from 26,820 to 56,102. Although industry-wide statistics by traffic category are not available for most of this period, in 1916 travel in Pullman Company sleeping and parlor cars accounted for 9.2 billion passenger-miles, or 27 percent of the total.

These staggering achievements placed heavy demands upon the railroads: an army of line managers, a huge workforce allocated to passenger operations, and daunting levels of capital investment. Growing passenger (and freight) traffic masked underlying problems. The 1900–1920 years were marked by high inflation, which coincided with the conversion from wooden rolling stock to steel equipment. Baggage cars, diners, and other specialty equipment produced little net income, but they had to be hauled because the public now expected these amenities. Heavier steel rolling stock required more powerful locomotives. Multiple-tracking and passing sidings were built to keep everything flowing on schedule. Impressive urban stations constructed between 1880 and 1920 carried a hefty price tag.

Rail managements reacted to cost pressures by improving productivity. The Chicago, Burlington & Quincy, for example, doubled the passenger-miles on its system between 1901 and 1915, and did so by increasing passenger train-miles by only 27 percent. The underlying economics of passenger service, however, were deteriorating. Revenue per passenger-mile, which had stood at 2.4 cents in 1881, declined to 2 cents within a decade and remained at those levels until World War I. More troublesome was the downward trend in operating profit. In 1879 the Pennsylvania Railroad had retained about half a cent of revenue per passenger-mile as operating profit. The yield declined to .38 cents by 1896 and dropped below one-tenth of a cent in 1914.

The severity of these trends largely went unappreciated by government regulatory agencies because overall revenues were rising at a brisk pace. In 1903 U.S. railroads gathered $421.7 million in passenger revenues. By 1916 the total had risen to $722 million, but the inflation rate, coupled with the railroads' capital investments and labor costs, more than offset the gain in gross revenues. Meanwhile, freight revenue per ton-mile also was declining, railroad tax liabilities doubled, and revenue from mail and express parcels carried on passenger trains was diminished by the Post Office's decision to offer parcel post service in 1913. The carriers obtained little relief from the Interstate Commerce Commission or from state agencies that set commuter rates. Politicians cared only about maintaining cheap fares.

Railroads also confronted competition. By 1917 motor vehicle registrations surpassed 5 million. A network of electric intercity trolleys, known as interurbans, was developed in the early years of the twentieth century, and its mileage expanded to 15,580 by 1916. Concentrated in the Great Lakes states, interurbans competed for both commuter and short-trip intercity rail travel. Some railroad executives initially believed that automobiles and trucks would benefit freight and passenger service by delivering more people and goods to trainside. The more far-seeing among them recognized a serious threat.

Rail commuter operations still enjoyed solid growth during this era. Most large urban areas included "railroad suburbs," and impressive commuter operations existed in New York, Philadelphia, Boston, and Chicago, with the Long Island Railroad emerging as the nation's leading commuter carrier. The Illinois Central's Chicago service had transported 200,000 passengers in 1870. By 1880 ridership had increased to 1.5 million, and by 1890 to 4 million. Electrification and steel coaches spread to commuter routes.

The Golden Age Tarnished: 1920–1945

Although 1920s total of 47.3 billion passenger-miles was a record for that time, railroads' share of the intercity and commuter markets already had begun to ebb. After the end of World War I federal control, managements moved aggressively to defend their passenger business. Even as traffic slipped during the 1920s, the carriers' equipment deliveries between 1921 and 1930 slightly exceeded the prior decade's levels as the conversion to steel equipment was completed and equipment of greater carrying capacity was placed into service. Yet the new equipment was expensive—with the Illinois Central reporting that the acquisition cost of a trainset (including locomotive) had doubled since 1900.

Nevertheless, the downturn in fortunes was abrupt. Combined U.S. commuter and intercity passenger-miles slumped to 38.3 billion by 1923, a 20 percent drop in only three years. By 1929 the volume had eroded to 31.1 billion. In nine years the railroads lost 35 percent of their traffic (measured in passenger-miles). Statistics from Canada were only marginally less dreary, with the number of passengers carried declining to 39 million in 1929 from a 1920 peak of 51 million.

Although the heyday of interurban trolleys had passed, automobile and bus competition was proving to be brutal. In 1930 U.S. bus industry passenger-miles exceeded 11 billion, and it is estimated that automobile mileage was six times greater than railroad passenger-miles. Railroads acted to substitute gasoline-electric motor cars on light-density routes, and by the late 1920s several railroads operated intercity bus subsidiaries. By 1930 the Pennsylvania Railroad's bus system carried more than 4 million riders and produced an annual operating cost savings of $500,000. The Chicago, Burlington & Quincy's diversion of passengers to its motor car fleet saved $300,000 yearly. A number of long-distance trains running on secondary routes were consolidated.

Managements also worried about the future of sleeping cars. Revenue passenger-miles in Pullman-owned equipment had increased from 8.9 billion in 1915 to 14 billion in 1925, but the service carried a high overhead in crew wages and other operating costs. Sleeping cars gradually were pulled from light-density routes in the latter 1920s.

The Great Depression then struck a stunning blow. U.S. passenger-miles plummeted to a low of 16.4 billion in 1933 before beginning a gradual recovery to 26.9 billion in 1940. The number of riders carried on Canadian railroads was cut in half between 1928 and 1933—to 19.2 million. U.S. revenue passenger-miles in Pullman equipment also were decimated, to 7.1 billion by 1935. Although commuter trends had been modestly favorable through the 1920s, rising from 6.1 to 6.7 billion passenger-miles between 1922 and 1930, the trend quickly reversed, and by 1940 this category had been slashed to 4 billion.

The financial impact was equally devastating. Fare increases granted during World War I, coupled with railroads' productivity initiatives, had boosted revenue per passenger-mile to 3 cents through the late 1920s, but that income level could not be sustained during an unprecedented economic downturn. In 1935 per-mile fare averages dropped below 2 cents. Total U.S. passenger operating revenue, which had exceeded $1 billion in 1926, plunged to $358.5 million in 1935 before recovering slightly to $418 million in 1940.

Despite aggressive employee layoffs and other measures, given the industry's high fixed costs it was impossible to cut expenses sufficiently to preserve profits. Total deliveries of new passenger cars between 1931 and 1940 dropped to 2,678. Since the worst damage had been inflicted upon short-distance intercity and commuter ridership, managements focused on preserving the quality of their long-distance "name" trains. Buses, meanwhile, had nearly doubled their ridership volume during the Depression decade, and by 1940 had captured one-fourth of the intercity commercial travel market.

Postwar Collapse: 1945–1970

While their superb passenger-carrying performance during World War II was not sustainable in peacetime, rail industry executives believed that long-distance trains could occupy a profitable and meaningful role in the years ahead. Two factors seemed to support this opinion. U.S. population had increased by 30 million since 1929. Many Americans had not traveled for pleasure since that time, owing to the Great Depression's financial strictures and followed by wartime bans on nonessential trips. Premier trains were reequipped, and car deliveries between 1946 and 1950 totaled 4,986. The carriers meanwhile petitioned state regulatory commissions to discontinue trains on branch lines and secondary routes because this ridership already had abandoned the railroads in favor of the automobile and bus.

Although the 1946 U.S. intercity passenger-mile volume of 58.9 billion was double the 1941 prewar total, traffic then went into a rapid slump, declining to 26.8 billion by 1950, the year in which railroads ceased to carry a majority of intercity commercial traffic. Passenger revenue was halved during that period, and runaway postwar inflation cut deeply into its actual value. Labor and equipment costs had risen sharply. By 1953 the industry's passenger operating ratio (operating expenses expressed as a percentage of passenger income) stood at an alarming 138 percent. Pullman travel, which had increased from 7.3 to 9.3 billion passenger-miles between 1946 and 1950, then went into a tailspin as business travelers deserted the rails in favor of airline travel. By 1960 the Pullman total plummeted to 3.6 billion passenger-miles.

In the late 1950s passenger deficits threatened the industry's meager freight profits. Train discontinuance petitions accelerated. State regulatory commissions' opposition to cutbacks often forced railroads to appeal to the courts, but the Interstate Commerce Commission took control of these proceedings in 1958. Significant reductions ensued, but they didn't alter the economics. Intercity non-Pullman passenger-miles dropped to 17.1 billion in 1960. Seven years later Southern Pacific CEO Donald J. Russell told shareholders that the "long-haul passenger train has outlived its usefulness." In 1967 the New York Central petitioned to end all intercity passenger service on its tracks. Railroad timetables of 1950 had listed 9,000 passenger trains. Twenty years later only 450 trains were running—and 100 of them were in the process of discontinuance. Intercity passenger-miles in 1970 stood at 6.2 billion, and the total for sleeping cars had dropped to a meager 765 million. (For post-1970 intercity trends see NATIONAL RAILROAD PASSENGER CORP. [AMTRAK].)

Commuter ridership declined from its postwar high of 5.8 billion passenger-miles in 1946, but the falloff was less severe than the intercity trend. After slipping to 5 billion in 1950 and bottoming out at 4.1 billion in 1963, modest ridership gains then were posted. Commuter fleets were reequipped, and the 1950s brought streamlined double-decked coaches called "gallery cars" to several systems in Chicago, California, and Canada. Ridership was concentrated heavily in three Chicago railroads (Burlington, Chicago & Northwestern, and Illinois Central) and five serving East Coast urban regions (New York Central, Pennsylvania, New Haven, Long Island, and Erie-Lackawanna). By 1968 these railroads sold more than 80 percent of U.S. commuter rail tickets.

Operating deficits rose, but regulators resisted fare increases. The Illinois Central's Chicago service began losing money in the early 1950s. Southern Pacific's San Francisco–San Jose runs lost $1 million annually in the late 1960s. With new equipment and aggressive marketing the Chicago & Northwestern managed to restore profitability.

These deficits, along with the railroads' inability to finance commuter equipment purchases, then brought local and state governments into a leadership role, often using federal funds. Some local transit agencies covered the deficits while private railroads continued to run the trains. In others, transit agencies took over the entire operation. Ontario's government activated GO Transit in 1967, operating a 60-mile system on tracks of the Canadian Pacific and Canadian National. In 1982 Montreal assumed responsibility for 57 miles of routes. As federal and state funding increased in the United States, commuter rail systems were modernized and service improved.

Worsening highway congestion and urban air pollution then prompted consideration of an expanded role for commuter rail—although some urban planners favored "heavy-rail" or "light-rail" operations that utilized dedicated guideways. Traditional rail commuter lines recorded significant growth, rising from 7 billion passenger-miles in 1990 to a 9.4 billion in 2000. Roughly 20 percent of public transit riders in the urban United States were carried in 2000 by these trains. New commuter rail services began running at Miami, Nashville, Albuquerque, San Diego, Los Angeles, Seattle-Tacoma, and Vancouver, and still others were planned.

—William J. Watt

REFERENCES

Stover, John F. *The Life and Decline of the American Railroad.* New York: Oxford University Press, 1970.
Wattenberg, Ben J. *The Statistical History of the United States.* New York: Basic Books, 1976.

Peninsula Corridor Joint Powers Board (Caltrain)

The San Francisco & San Jose Railroad, California's second railroad, was completed as far as Mayfield (now the California Avenue station in Palo Alto) in October 1863. Train service began on October 18, 1863, and was extended to San Jose on January 16, 1864. The fare from San Francisco to San Jose was $2.50; the former stagecoach tariff was $32 (the fare in 2001 was $4.75).

The original route of the SF&SJ ran southwest from San Francisco through Daly City and over the San Bruno Mountains to avoid the tunneling that a route along the shore of San Francisco Bay would require. In 1906 Southern Pacific, successor to the SF&SJ, completed the Bayshore Cutoff. The new line had five tunnels and cut 3 miles off the distance to San Jose. It joined the original route at San Bruno.

In 1956 Tunnel 5 was eliminated as part of the construction of the Bayshore Freeway, U.S. Highway 101. The new highway began to take ridership away from the trains. Southern Pacific improved the westbound track (San Jose to San Francisco) in anticipation of discontinuing its commuter trains and single-tracking the line. In 1975 Southern Pacific applied to discontinue all service, and it was apparent that the Interstate Commerce Commission would grant the application, based on the financial losses SP said it was experiencing.

The State of California Department of Transportation (Caltrans) took over the operation of Southern Pacific's commuter trains between San Francisco and San Jose in 1980. Ridership then was at its low point, 14,000 daily passengers. SP continued operating the trains with its crews, coaches, and locomotives; Caltrans reimbursed SP's losses. In an effort to increase ridership, San Mateo and Santa Clara counties provided 30 percent discounts to monthly, weekly, and 20-ride ticket purchases. More trains were added. Hourly service with a "memory schedule" was instituted on weekdays, with two-hour headways on weekends and holidays. In 1985 Caltrans purchased 20 F40 locomotives and 73 gallery cars (20 of them cab cars for push-pull operation). Ridership increased slowly, reaching 22,000 in 1992.

The Peninsula Corridor Joint Powers Board (Caltrain) took over the 77-mile corridor from San Francisco through San Jose to Gilroy in 1992. The three counties involved, San Francisco, San Mateo, and Santa Clara, purchased the 47 miles of line between San Francisco and San Jose from Southern Pacific for $222 million and secured trackage rights to Gilroy from Union Pacific, successor to Southern Pacific. The San Mateo County Transit District (SamTrans) assumed oversight of the JPB by providing Caltrain with staff and such functions as accounting, human resources, and planning. A nine-member board of directors, three from each county, directs policy.

In a little over a decade after 1992, weekday trains increased to 96, with half-hour headways midday and hourly service on Saturday. Ridership rose to 32,000 on weekdays. Equipment purchases included 20 more coaches and 3 more locomotives for regular service. Service to San Francisco Giants baseball games at Pacific Bell Stadium, a block from the San Francisco station, generates up to 6,000 riders per game.

Extensive line improvements included track upgrades with welded rail, construction of seven grade separations, and a new Millbrae station that provides across-the-platform transfers with Bay Area Rapid Transit (BART) trains at the San Francisco International Airport. A major Caltrain Express project completed in 2004 finished the rebuilding of the tracks, provided two sections of four-track lines, each 2 miles in length, and completed a new centralized traffic control (CTC) installation. The new four-track segments enabled Caltrain to install a system made up of Baby Bullet express, limited-stop, and local trains. Five additional MotivePower locomotives and 17 Bombardier bilevel cars were added to the Caltrain fleet. Planned track improvements to the Union Pacific line between San Jose and Gilroy will permit the operation of additional trains. Still other major improvements include a planned extension from the present 4th and Townsend terminal in San Francisco to a more central site and the electrification of the railroad.

Extensions of the service to Salinas and Monterey have been proposed by Monterey County and to Hollister by San Benito County. Both counties are negotiating to purchase branch lines from Union Pacific. Caltrain is also considering operating train service across the Dumbarton Bridge from Palo Alto to a connection with BART at Union City. The trains would be supported by San Mateo, Santa Clara, and Alameda counties. Caltrain is operated under contract by Amtrak, which furnishes engine and train crews, supervision, security, and maintenance of rolling stock and right of way.

—Arthur L. Lloyd

REFERENCE

Johnston, Bob. "Caltrain's Commuter Choreography." *Trains* 65, no. 2 (Feb. 2005): 52–59.

Penn Central Co.

Penn Central was initially incorporated in 1846 as the Pennsylvania Railroad, changed its name to Pennsylvania New York Central Transportation Co. on February 1, 1968, when it merged the New York Central Railroad, and changed it again on May 8, 1968, to Penn Central Co. On October 1, 1969, it was renamed again: Penn Central Transportation Co., a wholly owned subsidiary of a holding company, a new Penn Central Co.

For decades the Pennsylvania Railroad and the New York Central Railroad were rivals. They surprised the industry in November 1957 by announcing their plan to merge. The stockholders of the two companies approved the merger on May 8, 1962, and the Interstate Commerce Commission approved it nearly four years later with three conditions:

- The new company had to take over the freight and passenger operations of the New Haven Railroad, which was in reorganization and squeezed by new superhighways and declining industry in its territory.
- It had to absorb the New York, Susquehanna & Western, a shortline in northern New Jersey (this did not happen).

- It had to make the Lehigh Valley, which was owned by the Pennsylvania, available to either the Norfolk & Western or the Chesapeake & Ohio—and if neither of them wanted it (which was the case), merge it into Penn Central (this did not happen).

Despite the ten years between the initial announcement and the formation of Penn Central, little was done to unify the railroads. New York Central had pruned its physical plant and had a young and eager management team. The Pennsylvania had far more track than it needed, and its management was extremely conservative and traditional. The Pennsylvania's ways dominated the new company. Moreover, the area served by both railroads was losing its industry, and the Pennsylvania and New York Central had duplicate facilities nearly everywhere.

Both railroads were profitable when they entered the merger. Penn Central's first year of operation resulted in a deficit of $2.8 million. The next year the deficit was $83 million. For 1970 it was $326 million. By then the nation's sixth-largest corporation had become the nation's largest bankruptcy—PC declared bankruptcy on June 21, 1970.

Something had to be done. PC was by far Amtrak's largest passenger-train operator, with commuter services around Boston, New York, Philadelphia, Washington, and Chicago, and it was the predominant freight railroad in the northeast United States. In May 1974 the reorganization court decided that PC could not be reorganized on the basis of income. The U.S. Railway Assn. (USRA, which is the same set of initials used by the U.S. Railroad Administration during World War I), a federal government corporation, was established under the provisions of the Rail Reorganization Act of 1973. Consolidated Rail Corp. (Conrail), owned by the U.S. government, was created to take over the properties and operations of Penn Central and six other railroads, all but one of which were bankrupt: Central of New Jersey, Erie Lackawanna, Lehigh Valley, Reading, Lehigh & Hudson River, and Pennsylvania-Reading Seashore Lines (PRSL was not bankrupt, but it was on the verge of financial and physical collapse).

Penn Central cooperated with the U.S. Department of Transportation in two experimental passenger-train operations that were a first try at improving rail passenger service in the Northeast Corridor. The first was the Metroliner, which PC inherited from the Pennsylvania Railroad. Although the start of the high-speed electric train service was postponed several times and the schedules of the handful of Metroliners did not appear in *The Official Guide*, the service reversed a long decline in passenger-train ridership between New York and Washington. The second was the operation of a United Aircraft TurboTrain between Boston and New York in an attempt to beat the 3-hour 55-minute timing of the New Haven's best express trains of the early 1950s. TurboTrain service was not as frequent or as well publicized as Metroliner service. The combination of untested equipment and deteriorated track and the problems of meshing space-age technology with traditional railroad thinking made both experiments the object of a great deal of satire and humor.

Penn Central and its problems were the subject of countless books and articles. Despite the prophecies of doom or worse, Penn Central's successors have done well. Amtrak took over PC's long-distance passenger service on May 1, 1971; Conrail took over the commuter service, then turned it over to state and regional authorities. Amtrak's greatest success has been in the Northeast Corridor, where the Metroliner and the TurboTrain first ran; former Penn Central commuter services have flourished; and Conrail became profitable.

In 1975, the year before it became part of Conrail, Penn Central operated a system of 19,300 route-miles and 39,059 track-miles, with 4,033 locomotives, 1,173 passenger cars, 137,546 freight cars, 4,354 company service cars, and 79,503 employees. Freight traffic totaled 78.1 billion ton-miles in 1975, and coal (14.4 percent), transportation equipment (12.8 percent), and foodstuffs (11.2 percent) were its principal traffic sources. Passenger traffic totaled 1,544.5 million passenger-miles. Penn Central operating revenues totaled $2,173.4 million in 1975, and the railroad achieved an 88.2 percent operating ratio.

—George H. Drury

REFERENCES

Daughen, Joseph R., and Peter Binzen. *The Wreck of the Penn Central*. Boston: Little, Brown, 1971.

Salsbury, Stephen. *No Way to Run a Railroad*. New York: McGraw-Hill, 1982.

Saunders, Richard, Jr. *Main Lines: Rebirth of the North American Railroad, 1970–2002*. DeKalb: Northern Illinois Univ. Press, 2003.

Pennsylvania Railroad

The heart of the Pennsylvania Railroad was the line from Philadelphia to Pittsburgh. Long routes extended from Pittsburgh to Chicago and St. Louis. Secondary lines reached the shores of Lake Ontario and Lake Erie at eight points from Sodus Point, New York, to Toledo, Ohio; several lines touched the Ohio River in Ohio and Indiana. A long tentacle ran all the way to the top of Michigan's Lower Peninsula at Mackinaw City. Networks of branches covered the Delmarva Peninsula, central and western Pennsylvania, Ohio, and Indiana. The line from New York through Philadelphia to Washington and across the Potomac to Alexandria was the Pennsylvania Railroad's best-known and most traveled route; it came later in the railroad's history.

The Pennsylvania declared itself to be the standard railroad of the world, but much of its standardization was internal and at variance with customary American practice: steam locomotives with square-topped Bellaire fireboxes instead of the usual radial-stay fireboxes, passenger cars painted red instead of olive green, and signals that used rows of amber lights instead of the usual red and green lights. Two classes of Pennsylvania Railroad freight locomotives numbered nearly 600 each, and the Pennsylvania's passenger trains were pulled by a fleet of 475 class K4s Pacific-type locomotives.

The Main Line of Public Works

The Erie Canal carried commerce to New York, and the National Road and the Baltimore & Ohio Railroad carried commerce to Baltimore—commerce that might well have gone to Philadelphia, had the people of that city been alert. A canal was proposed to run east and west across Pennsylvania along the Susquehanna, Juniata, Conemaugh, and Allegheny rivers. The idea, which included a four-mile tunnel under the summit of the Alleghenies, was declared impractical. Instead, the Main Line of Public Works was chartered in 1828 to connect Philadelphia with Pittsburgh by a combination of railroads and canals.

Canals were open from Columbia to Hollidaysburg and from Johnstown to Pittsburgh by 1832. A railroad began operation between Philadelphia and Columbia in 1834. That same year the Allegheny Portage Railroad was opened over the mountains between Hollidaysburg and Johnstown. The portage railroad was a series of inclined planes; the canal boats were designed to be taken apart and the sections pulled over the mountains.

A request from the Baltimore & Ohio for a charter to build a line to Pittsburgh spurred the Commonwealth of Pennsylvania to action. It chartered the Pennsylvania Railroad on April 13, 1846, to construct a line from Harrisburg to Pittsburgh, with a branch to Erie. The B&O's charter would be valid only if the Pennsylvania Railroad did not build its line.

The Pennsylvania Railroad's route was surveyed by J. Edgar Thomson, who had laid out the Georgia Railroad. Rather than a route with a steady climb all the way, Thomson laid out a line that was almost level from Harrisburg to Altoona. At Altoona the line became steeper (but not as steep as the Baltimore & Ohio) for the short climb to the summit (using the celebrated Horseshoe Curve) of the Alleghenies. Thomson's arrangement concentrated the operating difficulties of mountain railroading in a small area.

Construction of the Pennsylvania Railroad (PRR) began in 1847. In 1849 the PRR made an operating contract with the Harrisburg & Lancaster (in full, the Harrisburg, Portsmouth, Mountjoy & Lancaster). By 1852 rails reached from Philadelphia to Pittsburgh by way of the Allegheny Portage Railroad. PRR's tunnel at the summit of the Alleghenies was opened in 1854, bypassing the inclined planes of the portage railroad.

PRR bought the Main Line of Public Works in 1857

and leased the Harrisburg & Lancaster in 1861, creating a route under a single management between Philadelphia and Pittsburgh. (By then the B&O had long since reached the Ohio River; predecessors of the New York Central had created a rail route between New York and Chicago; and the Rock Island had bridged the Mississippi River.)

PRR's charter included a tax on the freight it carried to protect the canals, which were part of the PRR after 1857. The charter was eventually amended, but only to the point that the funds were used to aid shortline railroads that connected with the PRR. (The State of New York had released the railroads from the need to pay Erie Canal tolls in 1851.)

Early on, the PRR acquired interests in two other railroads, the Cumberland Valley and the Northern Central. The Cumberland Valley reached from Harrisburg southwest to Hagerstown, Maryland. The Northern Central was incorporated in 1828 as the Baltimore & Susquehanna. It built north from Baltimore and reached Harrisburg in 1851 and Sunbury in 1858. By then its component companies had been consolidated as the Northern Central Railroad. A block of its stock was held by John W. Garrett, president of the Baltimore & Ohio. J. Edgar Thomson bought the stock about 1860 and transferred it to the PRR. PRR gained majority ownership of the Northern Central about the turn of the twentieth century.

In 1862 PRR acquired an interest in the Philadelphia & Erie Railroad and helped it complete a line from Sunbury to Erie. The line to Erie was never outstandingly prosperous, but from Sunbury to Driftwood the Philadelphia & Erie became part of a freight route with easy grades. The line between Driftwood and Pittsburgh was built as the Allegheny Valley Railroad. It was intended to be a feeder from Pittsburgh to the New York Central and Erie railroads, but the PRR obtained control in 1868 and leased it in 1900.

Pittsburgh, Fort Wayne & Chicago

Even before the PRR had been completed to Pittsburgh, its directors were looking westward. In 1851 they discussed financial assistance to the Ohio & Pennsylvania Railroad, which was already in service between Salem, Ohio, and Allegheny, Pennsylvania (across the Allegheny River from downtown Pittsburgh and now a part of the city of Pittsburgh). The O&P was projected west to Crestline, Ohio, and beyond Crestline the Ohio & Indiana was constructing a line west to Fort Wayne, Indiana, and Burlington, Iowa—and to Chicago, almost as an afterthought.

The Ohio & Pennsylvania, Ohio & Indiana, and Fort Wayne & Chicago were consolidated in 1856 to form the Pittsburgh, Fort Wayne & Chicago Rail Road (the Fort Wayne), a company in which the Pennsylvania Railroad held an interest. Two years later the Fort Wayne effected a junction with the PRR at Pittsburgh; by the end of 1858 its rails had reached Chicago. In 1860 the Fort Wayne cre-

ated a branch to Cleveland by leasing the Cleveland & Pittsburgh, which had a line from a connection with the Fort Wayne at Rochester, Pennsylvania, southwest along the Ohio River to Wellsville, then northwest through Alliance (where it crossed the Fort Wayne) to Cleveland. Jay Gould tried unsuccessfully to get control of the Fort Wayne in 1869 to serve as a Chicago extension of the Erie. The PRR leased the Fort Wayne and the Grand Rapids & Indiana, a line from Grand Rapids, Michigan, south through Fort Wayne to Richmond, Indiana. In 1873 the PRR built and acquired a route from Mansfield, Ohio, to Toledo; in the 1920s PRR extended it to Detroit, mostly by trackage rights on other railroads.

Pittsburgh, Cincinnati, Chicago & St. Louis

A string of railroads reached from Pittsburgh through Columbus, Ohio, to Cincinnati: Pittsburgh & Steubenville, Steubenville & Indiana, Central Ohio, Columbus & Xenia, and Little Miami. The first named, the Pittsburgh & Steubenville, was the last to be completed because the Commonwealth of Virginia, which owned a large block of Baltimore & Ohio stock, refused to permit the railroad to be built across what is now the Panhandle of West Virginia.

The Pittsburgh & Steubenville was sold at foreclosure to a new company, the Panhandle Railway, which began operation in January 1868. The Panhandle was soon consolidated with the Steubenville & Indiana as the Pittsburg, Cincinnati & St. Louis Railway, a PRR subsidiary (for a period the city of Pittsburgh spelled itself "Pittsburg"). The Panhandle nickname stuck with the new railroad and its successors.

In 1869 Jay Gould also tried to acquire the Columbus, Chicago & Indiana Central Railway, which had lines from Columbus to Indianapolis and from Columbus through Logansport, Indiana, to Chicago. The PRR leased the CC&IC as it did the Fort Wayne.

West of Indianapolis was the Terre Haute & Indianapolis, and beyond that was the St. Louis, Alton & Terre Haute. Disagreements among several railroads about the division of traffic led to the construction of the St. Louis, Vandalia & Terre Haute between 1868 and 1870. The Terre Haute & Indianapolis leased it and made traffic agreements with the Panhandle and the CC&IC. The St. Louis, Alton & Terre Haute was left on its own; it became part of the New York Central System in 1882.

PRR's line to Cincinnati was built as the Little Miami Railroad. It was incorporated in 1836, and within ten years it reached from Cincinnati through Xenia to Springfield, Ohio. It soon had lines that reached to Columbus and Dayton. The Pennsylvania Railroad wanted the Little Miami and forced the issue of a lease by getting control of the Zanesville & Cincinnati, a secondary railroad, which gave PRR access to Cincinnati. The Little Miami was leased by the Panhandle in 1869.

An 1890 consolidation created the Pittsburgh, Cincinnati, Chicago & St. Louis Railroad from the PC&StL and several other railroads. The Vandalia Railroad was created in 1905 to consolidate the lines west of Indianapolis. In 1916 the PCC&StL, the Vandalia, and several other railroads were consolidated as the Pittsburgh, Cincinnati, Chicago & St. Louis Railway; the Pennsylvania Railroad leased it in 1921.

Pennsylvania Co.

In 1869 the Pennsylvania Railroad found itself running about 3,000 miles of railroad west of Pittsburgh from its offices in Philadelphia. It formed the Pennsylvania Co. to hold and manage the lines west of Pittsburgh. The division of the PRR was not entirely successful, primarily because everything came together at Pittsburgh, where the terminals and yards were under three managements. In 1918 the Pennsylvania Co. ceased to be an operating company (it continued to exist as a holding company) and transferred its leases to the Pennsylvania Railroad.

East of Philadelphia

Even though the Pennsylvania Railroad was headquartered in Philadelphia, it recognized that considerable traffic moved to and from New York. In early years it had to turn that traffic over to a predecessor of the Reading at Harrisburg because there was no rail route between Philadelphia and New York. In 1863 the PRR made traffic arrangements with the Philadelphia & Trenton, the Camden & Amboy, and the Delaware & Raritan Canal Co. In 1871 PRR leased those companies plus the United Canal & Railroad Companies of New Jersey, gaining a Philadelphia–Jersey City route and lines south to Cape May and north to Belvidere, on the east bank of the Delaware River. A decade or so later PRR acquired lines from Camden, New Jersey, east to Atlantic City and constructed a line up the Schuylkill valley from Philadelphia to Reading.

The PRR looked enviously at New York Central's terminal on Manhattan Island. It was determined to have one of its own, rather than use ferries across the Hudson, as did the other railroads that approached New York from the west. PRR acquired the Long Island Rail Road in 1900, attracted by its intense commuter traffic and seeking to spread the cost of PRR's New York terminal over as many trains as possible. Construction began in 1904 on a station between Seventh and Eighth avenues and 31st and 33rd streets—Pennsylvania Station—plus tunnels under the Hudson and East rivers. The new station opened in 1910. In 1917 the New York Connecting Railroad, a joint project of the PRR and the New Haven, opened, creating a route from Penn Station to New Haven, Providence, and Boston and, as some people put it, making New York a way station on the line between Boston and Washington.

South of Philadelphia

The Baltimore & Ohio's charter protected its monopoly on traffic to and from Washington, and B&O refused to make arrangements for through traffic, whether passenger or freight, with the Northern Central and the Philadelphia, Wilmington & Baltimore. PRR bought the charter of the dormant Baltimore & Potomac, which was to have run from Baltimore south-southwest to the Potomac River at Popes Creek, Maryland. B&P's charter allowed it to build branches no more than 20 miles long, and the distance from Bowie, Maryland. to Washington was slightly less than that. PRR's Baltimore-Washington route opened in 1872. It was only 2 miles longer than the B&O route, which it quickly relegated to secondary status.

Through service between Jersey City and Washington was established in 1873 via the Philadelphia, Wilmington & Baltimore and the Baltimore & Potomac (the PRR had quickly connected the two in Baltimore). In March 1881 the Pennsylvania purchased the majority of the PW&B's stock. Ten years later PRR leased its Baltimore & Potomac subsidiary to the PW&B, and in 1902 the PW&B merged with the Baltimore & Potomac to form the Philadelphia, Baltimore & Washington Railroad. (The Baltimore & Ohio also wanted the PW&B. Its reaction was to build its own line to Philadelphia and a connection with the Reading-Central Railroad of New Jersey route to Jersey City.)

Late Nineteenth and Early Twentieth Centuries

In 1882 the Grand Rapids & Indiana was extended north to Mackinaw City, Michigan. In 1892 PRR opened the Trenton Cutoff, a freight line that bypassed Philadelphia. A year later it purchased stock in the Toledo, Peoria & Western (PRR later sold it and even later reacquired an interest in it). About that same time PRR acquired the Western New York & Pennsylvania Railroad, reaching deep into New York Central territory at Buffalo and Rochester.

About 1900 PRR purchased stock interests in the Norfolk & Western, Chesapeake & Ohio, Baltimore & Ohio, and (through B&O) Reading. It sold the B&O and C&O interests in 1906. The Pennroad Corp., a holding company, was formed in 1929. It bought interests in the Detroit, Toledo & Ironton, Pittsburgh & West Virginia, New Haven, and Boston & Maine. Had PRR bought railroad stock directly, it would have required approval by the Interstate Commerce Commission; the holding company did not need ICC approval for its actions.

In the 1920s and 1930s PRR electrified its New York–Washington and Philadelphia-Harrisburg routes. At the same time it changed the New York terminal electrification from low-voltage DC to high-voltage AC to match its long-distance electrification. PRR wanted to extend its electrification west from Harrisburg to Pittsburgh, but could never afford to. The electrification allowed PRR to handle record traffic levels during World War II and also to put off the need to develop modern steam locomotives. In the 1940s it rushed into production the modern steam locomotives it lacked; some were quite good and some were terrible.

The Pennsylvania Railroad put off dieselization as long as it could, then dieselized quickly with an array of locomotives from all the major builders. It was slow to react to declining traffic in the 1950s and had far more capacity than it needed.

The Pennsylvania Railroad operated an extensive passenger service. In addition to its east-west passenger trains, between New York and Philadelphia on one hand and Pittsburgh, Chicago, St. Louis, and Cincinnati on the other, the PRR also ran trains between New York and Washington in what would eventually be called the Northeast Corridor and operated commuter service at New York, Philadelphia, Baltimore, Washington, and Pittsburgh plus minimal commuter service east from Chicago.

After World War II, the Pennsylvania assigned most of its new equipment and management attention to the east-west trains; modern, streamlined cars were notably absent from the New York–Washington line except for a token streamlining of the *Congressional* in 1952—and the streamlined cars running through from connecting railroads such as the New Haven, the Atlantic Coast Line, the Seaboard Air Line, and the Southern. Even in the late 1960s, heavyweight P70 coaches were the mainstay of the New York–Washington trains. However, even the east-west trains seemed to lack polish. It could have been the PRR's tendency to use boxcars to carry mail and express on passenger trains; it could have been simply that the revered Tuscan red paint didn't hold up well. Ultimately, passengers disappeared from the east-west trains but traffic remained strong in the Northeast Corridor, both within the corridor and on trains to and from the South.

The Pennsylvania Railroad was very much traditionalist in the matter of freight service.

In November 1957 PRR and New York Central announced plans to merge after decades of intense rivalry. It took a decade to plan the merger: Penn Central was created on February 1, 1968, and fell into bankruptcy in little more than two years.

In 1967, its last year before the Penn Central merger, the Pennsylvania Railroad operated a system of 9,538 route-miles and 21,868 track-miles, with 2,211 locomotives, 2,632 passenger cars, 112,431 freight cars, 2,489 company service cars, and 56,318 employees. Freight traffic totaled 50.7 billion ton-miles in 1967, and coal (16.3 percent), metal products (11.9 percent), and foodstuffs (10.1 percent) were its principal traffic sources. Passenger traffic totaled 1,757.2 million passenger-miles. Pennsylvania Railroad operating revenues totaled $873.8 million in 1967, and the railroad achieved an 80.4 percent operating ratio.

—**George H. Drury**

REFERENCES

Alexander, Edwin P. *On the Main Line: The Pennsylvania Railroad in the 19th Century.* New York: Clarkson N. Potter, 1971.
———. *The Pennsylvania Railroad: A Pictorial History.* New York: Bonanza Books, 1967.
Bezilla, Michael. *Electric Traction on the Pennsylvania Railroad, 1895–1968.* University Park: Pennsylvania State Univ. Press, 1980.
Burgess, George H., and Miles C. Kennedy. *Centennial History of the Pennsylvania Railroad Company, 1846–1946.* Philadelphia: Pennsylvania Railroad, 1949.
Cupper, Dan, ed. *The Pennsylvania Railroad: Its Place in History, 1846–1996.* Wayne, Pa.: Pennsylvania Railroad Technical & Historical Society, 1996.

Pere Marquette Railway

The Pere Marquette was one of the first railroads to be merged after World War II—by the Chesapeake & Ohio on June 6, 1947. For several years it continued to exist as it had been as C&O's Pere Marquette District, but then it was redesignated C&O's Northern Region, and its identity gradually disappeared.

Pere Marquette's main routes ran from Detroit northwest to Grand Rapids, Michigan, and from Chicago around the south end of Lake Michigan through Grand Rapids to Traverse City and Petoskey. Branches covered central parts and the thumb of Michigan's Lower Peninsula. Lines from Sarnia and Walkerville, Ontario, met at Blenheim, Ontario, and a single line continued east to St. Thomas; from there to Buffalo and Niagara Falls, PM operated on Michigan Central (New York Central System) rails. Ferries reached across Lake Michigan from Ludington to Kewaunee, Manitowoc, and Milwaukee, Wisconsin.

On January 1, 1900, the Pere Marquette Railroad was created as a consolidation of the Chicago & West Michigan Railway, the Detroit, Grand Rapids & Western Railroad, and the Flint & Pere Marquette Railroad. PM's predecessors had been built to serve the lumber industry in Michigan, and at the turn of the century all three were feeling the effects of the disappearance (through logging) of the forests of lower Michigan.

The Chicago & West Michigan had lines from La Crosse, Indiana, north along the east shore of Lake Michigan to Pentwater, Michigan, and from Holland, Michigan, east to Grand Rapids, then north through Traverse City and Petoskey. The Flint & Pere Marquette completed a line in 1874 from Monroe, Michigan, south of Detroit, north and then northwest through Flint and Saginaw to a ferry dock at Ludington (originally called Pere Marquette) on the shore of Lake Michigan. The Flint & Pere Marquette included the former Port Huron & Northwestern, a narrow-gauge line built from Port Huron to Saginaw between 1879 and 1882. The Detroit, Grand Rapids & Western ran from Detroit to Grand Rapids and had a network of branches northeast of Grand Rapids.

The predecessor companies carried a considerable amount of debt, which the new Pere Marquette acquired along with the rail, ties, locomotives, and cars. To make matters worse, PM's management concentrated on absorbing shortlines rather than building a line to Chicago. However, new management in 1903 acquired the Canadian lines and trackage rights and launched construction of a line from New Buffalo, Michigan, to Porter, Indiana, from where PM reached Chicago by trackage rights on the Lake Shore & Michigan Southern (part of the New York Central System) and the Chicago Terminal Transfer Railroad (a forerunner of the Baltimore & Ohio Chicago Terminal).

From 1904 to 1907 the PM was acquired or leased by several railroads in succession: the Cincinnati, Hamilton & Dayton, the Baltimore & Ohio (through the CH&D), and the Erie. PM emerged from one receivership in 1907 and entered another in 1912.

The Pere Marquette Railway was incorporated in 1917 to acquire the property of the Pere Marquette Railroad. The Van Sweringen brothers of Cleveland acquired control of the PM in 1924, seeing that it could furnish a market for coal moving from the Chesapeake & Ohio. PM's interchange with the Hocking Valley (controlled by the Chesapeake & Ohio) at Toledo soon became PM's largest source of freight traffic. In 1928 the Interstate Commerce Commission approved control of the PM by the C&O.

In addition to serving Detroit's growing automobile industry well, the PM carried a significant amount of bridge traffic from Buffalo, New York, to the west shore of Lake Michigan. The advantage of bypassing the terminal congestion of Chicago more than made up for the ferry crossings of the Detroit River and Lake Michigan.

The first complete streamlined trains to enter service after World War II were PM's diesel-powered *Pere Marquettes*, which entered service between Detroit, Lansing, and Grand Rapids in 1946. The *Pere Marquette* name was also later applied to Chicago–Grand Rapids trains, and Amtrak used it when it established Chicago–Grand Rapids service in 1984. The Chesapeake & Ohio merged the Pere Marquette Railway on June 6, 1947, but the PM continued a nearly autonomous existence for several years before the Chesapeake & Ohio name and image replaced those of the Pere Marquette.

In 1945, shortly before merger by the Chesapeake & Ohio, the Pere Marquette operated a system of 1,949 route-miles and 3,390 track-miles, with 283 locomotives, 113 passenger cars, 14,335 freight cars, 541 company service cars, and 7,817 employees. Freight traffic totaled 5,229.4 million ton-miles in 1945, and manufactured goods (23.5 percent) and coal (14.5 percent) were its principal traffic sources. Passenger traffic totaled 161 million passenger-miles. Pere Marquette operating revenues totaled $51.5 million in 1945, and the railroad achieved an 88.5 percent operating ratio.

—George H. Drury

REFERENCE

Dixon, Thomas W., and Art Million. *Pere Marquette Power*. Alderson, W. Va.: Chesapeake & Ohio Historical Society, 1984.

Performing Arts and the Railroads. *See* CINEMA AND RAILROADS; MUSIC; OPERA AND THE RAILROADS; RADIO AND TELEVISION; THEATER; THEATRICAL TOURING COMPANIES

Perkins, Charles E. (1840–1907)

Charles Elliott Perkins played a major role in the formation and development of the Chicago, Burlington & Quincy Railroad, helping make it one of the largest and best-managed U.S. railways in the nineteenth century. He was born in Cincinnati, Ohio, the son of James Handasyd Perkins and Sarah Hart (Elliott) Perkins, on November 24, 1840, and was educated in the public schools of Cincinnati and Milton, Massachusetts. For a time he clerked in a store; then, on the advice of his cousin, John Murray Forbes of Boston, who had a financial interest in railroad development in the Mississippi Valley, Perkins went into railroading. In 1859 he moved to Burlington, Iowa, and became a $30-a-month clerk in the offices of the Burlington & Missouri River Railroad. The B&MR had received a federal land grant in 1856 and had begun to build west across Iowa. After the financial panic of 1857 the line had been purchased by the Chicago, Burlington & Quincy, of which Detroit's James F. Joy was president.

The affable and able Perkins's abilities were recognized; he was soon made cashier of the combined railroads and shortly thereafter promoted to assistant treasurer and secretary. In 1865 he was promoted to acting superintendent and later became general superintendent of the CB&Q. The railroad was completed to Omaha in 1869, and a separate corporation, the Burlington & Missouri River Railroad in Nebraska, received a charter to build west from Omaha. It reached Fort Kearny and a connection with the Union Pacific in 1873. Perkins played an active role in the construction of the extension, and he was an incorporator and director of the Nebraska railway from the beginning. He was soon elected vice president of the railway line in Iowa; this was consolidated with the Chicago, Burlington

& Quincy in 1873. Perkins was employed as the vice president and general manager of the lines west of the Missouri River. In 1875 he was made a director and in 1876 a vice president of the Chicago, Burlington & Quincy.

In 1880 the Burlington & Missouri River Railroad in Nebraska was consolidated with the Chicago, Burlington & Quincy; in 1881 Perkins was named president of the whole system, replacing his cousin John Murray Forbes. He had worked closely with Forbes and because of his substantial knowledge of western railroads was well placed to take the lead of a major U.S. railroad. Perkins was trusted by the eastern investors and financial markets and was able to reorganize the railroad and to expand and take advantage of opportunities to serve new markets and production points. Railway lines that did not meet the longer-range needs of the CB&Q were disposed of during his administration, and new acquisitions were made to expand the railroad advantageously to the west. By 1882 the Burlington reached Denver; the railroad built into St. Paul in 1886 and into Billings, Montana, in 1894.

By the time Perkins resigned the presidency of the CB&Q on February 21, 1901, the railroad was 7,661 miles long and was stable and financially successful. Until his death on November 8, 1907, in Westwood, Massachusetts, Perkins remained a director of the CB&Q.

—George M. Smerk

REFERENCES

Delano, F. A. "Perkins of the Burlington." *Appleton's Magazine*, March 1908.

Dictionary of American Biography, Base Set, "Charles Elliott Perkins." N.P.: American Council of Learned Societies, 1926–1936.

Perlman, Alfred E. (1902–1983)

His name will always be associated with the merger that created the unfortunate Penn Central, but Alfred E. Perlman's accomplishments as a superlative railroad executive transcend the industry's most famous bankruptcy. His success at transforming troubled railroads—most notably the New York Central—led John W. Barriger III to describe Perlman's life as "a chronicle of brilliant achievement."

Perlman was born in St. Paul, Minnesota, on November 22, 1902. His father, a civil engineer, was a profound influence; Perlman also became a civil engineer, graduating from MIT in 1923. He had already demonstrated a strong interest in railroads, having worked as a car cleaner in St. Paul at age 16 and over subsequent summers.

After MIT Perlman went to work for the Northern Pacific as a track laborer and a draftsman until 1930, when the railroad sent him to the Harvard University Graduate School of Business Administration to study railroad management. He returned to NP in 1931. His success there attracted the attention of the Roosevelt administration, and in 1934 NP "loaned" him to the new Reconstruction Finance Corp. (RFC) to assist with the rehabilitation of ailing railroads.

Fate soon conspired to help Perlman crystallize his reputation. On May 31, 1935, torrential rains in southern Nebraska caused an epic flood along the Republican River, killing 100 people and taking out 41 miles of Chicago, Burlington & Quincy main line. NP dispatched Perlman to help its Hill Lines partner, and within 23 days Perlman and his crews reopened the railroad, 2 days earlier than anyone thought possible. In battling the floods, Perlman pioneered the use of off-track equipment instead of work trains, a technique that gradually became the industry standard.

Perlman's work with the RFC and troubled railroads led him to the Denver & Rio Grande Western. He joined the Rio Grande in 1936 as maintenance-of-way engineer, then rose through the ranks to the positions of chief engineer, general manager, and executive vice president. He was a prime mover in a reorganization plan that helped lift D&RGW out of bankruptcy and bring dividends in 1947, the first time such payments had been made in 76 years.

Alfred E. Perlman. —Western Pacific Railroad, *Trains* Magazine Collection

Perlman's success at D&RGW attracted the attention of Robert R. Young, the anarchical financier who had won control of the New York Central after a high-profile proxy fight with old-line NYC management led by William H. White. Young hired Perlman to lead the Central, and the new president embarked on one of the most dramatic turnarounds in railroad corporate history. Wielding a razor-sharp financial ax, Perlman boldly cut costs on the elephantine NYC, reducing its famous four-track main line to two tracks, closing numerous yards and servicing facilities, installing centralized traffic control signaling on a large scale, and dramatically downsizing NYC's famous fleet of passenger trains. The last run of the famed *20th Century Limited* on December 3, 1967, symbolized the stark changes Perlman brought to the Central.

Perlman's efforts improved NYC's bottom line and made the company the talk of railroading, but long-term prospects for an independent Central were discouraging. Perlman led his company in search of a merger partner and for much of the early 1960s focused on Chesapeake & Ohio and Baltimore & Ohio. Thwarted by the Interstate Commerce Commission, NYC instead was pushed toward a union with archrival Pennsylvania, and in 1968 the two combined to form Penn Central Transportation Corp. Perlman became PC president, while Pennsy chief Stuart Saunders was the new company's chairman. Despite his best efforts, Perlman and his team could never resolve the profound problems that beset PC, and in 1970 the railroad declared bankruptcy, at the time the largest corporate failure in U.S. history.

Although many PC executives were embroiled in legal problems after the bankruptcy, Perlman survived with his reputation mostly intact, and within months of PC's failure he became president and then chairman of Western Pacific. Through dedication to service and his usual hard-nosed attention to costs, WP soon regained profitability. He retired from WP in 1976 and continued to serve on various conferences and boards until his death in 1983 at age 80.

—Kevin P. Keefe

REFERENCES

Morgan, David P. "A Conversation with A. E. Perlman," *Trains* 34, no. 10 (Aug. 1974): 42–45.

———. Perlman obituary. *Trains* 43, no. 9 (July 1983): 4.

Perlman obituary. *New York Times*, May 2, 1983.

Philadelphia, Wilmington & Baltimore Railroad

Early transportation between Philadelphia and Baltimore was largely by water, using the Delaware River and Chesapeake Bay. To facilitate the trip across the narrow isthmus between the two bodies of water, a turnpike company was chartered in 1809. The company was reconstituted in 1829 as the New Castle & Frenchtown Turnpike and Rail Road. The 16-mile railroad operated with steam power from its opening in October 1832. It remained an important transportation link only until 1838, when the Philadelphia, Wilmington & Baltimore Railroad was completed between Philadelphia and Baltimore. It then became a branch of the PW&B and was abandoned in the 1850s.

The PW&B had been chartered on April 2, 1831, as the Philadelphia & Delaware County Rail-Road, to build from Philadelphia to Wilmington. The name was changed to Philadelphia, Wilmington & Baltimore on March 14, 1836, before construction started. In Philadelphia a short street line, the Southwark Rail Road, reached the center of the city from Gray's Ferry Bridge over the Schuylkill River. The Philadelphia-Wilmington route was completed in 1838.

Three separate companies built the route between Wilmington and Baltimore. From Wilmington to the Susquehanna River, the states of Delaware and Maryland in 1832 chartered, respectively, the Wilmington & Susquehanna Rail Road and the Delaware & Maryland Rail Road. The two companies merged under the name of the former on April 18, 1836, and completed their railroad in 1837. The Baltimore & Port Deposit Rail Road was chartered, likewise in 1832, to build between the Susquehanna and Baltimore. It began operation in 1837. The companies of the Philadelphia-Baltimore route were consolidated under the Philadelphia, Wilmington & Baltimore name on February 5, 1838.

The wide Susquehanna River, crossed by ferry, was a major obstacle and inconvenience. Baggage cars were transferred by ferries, but passenger cars were not. Passengers were required to detrain, walk on and off the boat, and board the waiting train on the other side. A large ferry, the *Maryland*, which had two tracks of sufficient length to take an entire passenger train, was put into service in 1854. The Susquehanna was finally bridged in 1866, and the *Maryland* later saw service in New York Harbor transferring trains between the New Haven and Pennsylvania railroads. The three major on-line cities also proved to be obstacles: the railroad was required to haul its cars with horses in Philadelphia and Wilmington into the 1850s and in Baltimore until after the Civil War.

The PW&B grew into a substantial system by the acquisition of additional routes, primarily on the Delmarva Peninsula. It took control of the Delaware Railroad in 1853 and leased it in 1855. Its route was completed to Delmar, at the southern edge of the state of Delaware, in 1859. After the Civil War it extended numerous branches, all operated as part of the PW&B, to the eastern shore of Chesapeake Bay. In 1880, shortly before the end of its independent life, the PW&B acquired two other short railroads: the West Chester & Philadelphia and the Philadelphia &

Baltimore Central, which extended from a junction with the WC&P to the Susquehanna River upriver from Port Deposit. From the outset the PW&B was a passenger railroad. While most railroads developed two-thirds or more of their revenue from freight, on the PW&B the revenue mix was about equally divided between passengers and freight.

By the 1870s a spirited rivalry had grown up between the Baltimore & Ohio and the Pennsylvania Railroad. Both were using the Philadelphia, Wilmington & Baltimore to route traffic to New York. The two railroads came into conflict over connection arrangements in Philadelphia, and they vied to gain control of the PW&B. In March 1881 the Pennsylvania purchased a majority of the PW&B's stock. The railroad continued to operate under its own name, but in 1891 the Pennsylvania leased its Baltimore & Potomac subsidiary to the PW&B and in 1902 consolidated the railroads of the Philadelphia-Washington route into one company by merging the PW&B with the Baltimore & Potomac to form the Philadelphia, Baltimore & Washington Railroad.

The subsequent history of this route is part of the history of the Pennsylvania Railroad. Today, the main line forms part of the Amtrak Northeast Corridor, the busiest intercity passenger railroad route in the United States. Norfolk Southern now operates the former Delaware Railroad route from Wilmington south, while the former West Chester & Philadelphia is now an electrified South Eastern Pennsylvania Transit Authority (SEPTA) commuter line. Of the various branch lines, about half the mileage has been abandoned, while the other half is still operated by shortline companies.

—Adrian Ettlinger

REFERENCES

Burgess, George H., and Miles C. Kennedy. *Centennial History of the Pennsylvania Railroad Company*, 1846–1946. Philadelphia: Pennsylvania Railroad, 1949.

Gerstner, Franz Anton Ritter von. *Early American Railroads.* Ed. Frederick C. Gamst. Stanford, Calif.: Stanford Univ. Press, 1997 [1842–1843].

Poor, H. V., and H. W. Poor. *Poor's Manual of Railroads, 35th Annual Number.* New York: H. V. and H. W. Poor, 1902.

Taber, Thomas T., III. *Railroads of Pennsylvania Encyclopedia and Atlas.* Muncy, Pa.: self-published, 1987.

White, John H., Jr. *American Locomotives: An Engineering History, 1830–1880.* Baltimore: Johns Hopkins Univ. Press, 1997.

Piedmont & Northern Railway

The Piedmont & Northern began its existence as a more or less typical interurban electric railway, with two separate divisions, one in North Carolina and the other in South Carolina. From the very beginning, however, it carried a heavy freight traffic and soon evolved into what was more like an electrically operated conventional (or steam) railroad. Financially, it was one of the most successful of all intercity electric railways.

James Buchanan Duke, head of both the American Tobacco Trust and the Duke Power Co., had a vested interest in the development of the Piedmont area of North and South Carolina. In 1909 Duke agreed to support a plan proposed by William States Lee, vice president of Southern Power & Utilities, that called for the construction of an electrically powered interurban railway system that would serve the major communities of the Piedmont area.

Two companies were organized, one for each state. The North Carolina company was organized on January 8, 1910, as the Piedmont Traction Co., with Duke as president and Lee as vice president. The South Carolina legislature chartered the Greenville, Spartanburg & Anderson Railway Co. on March 10, 1910, for operations in South Carolina. The entire project would be capitalized at $5,000,000, and as soon as the two divisions were constructed, the Piedmont & Northern Railway Co. would assume control over the two companies.

Construction began early in the spring of 1910 on a 21-mile section from Gastonia to Charlotte, North Carolina, and a 98-mile line from Greenwood to Spartanburg, South Carolina. The railroad was built to unusually high standards for an interurban road and was one of the first to employ a high-voltage (1,500-volt) DC power system. By that summer the railroad had placed its initial rolling stock orders for 23 passenger cars, 8 express motors, and 6 freight motors. Trains began running over a portion of the South Carolina section in September 1911, and service began over a portion of the Charlotte-Gastonia line in April 1912. The completed system comprised a total of 127 route-miles in the two states.

An unusual double signaling system was used by the P&N. Lower-quadrant signals were tripped to a stop position by the dispatcher when he had modified orders for an engineer, who would use a trackside-mounted call box to issue the modifications. The train crew could answer the signal, telephone the dispatcher, record the order in an order book at the signal box, and, upon the dispatcher's instructions, proceed.

Shortly after America's entrance into World War I, two army training camps were established in the railroad's area. With increased traffic, the P&N was forced to run as many as 80 passenger trains a day. Additional passenger cars were acquired, and the railroad began to build its own electric freight motors. With other railroads, the P&N was placed under the control of the U.S. Railroad Administration (USRA) on December 28, 1917.

By the time USRA control ended in 1920, the Piedmont & Northern was in a badly deteriorated condition. The company spent two years and $300,000 rebuilding its track and locomotives and luring shippers back to using the line once again. Freight traffic development was emphasized, and by the mid-1920s the railroad could boast

135 cotton mills, with a total of 3 million spindles in operation, located along its line. The P&N also carried large amounts of coal traffic for the parent Duke Power Co.

In March 1927 the P&N applied to the Interstate Commerce Commission (ICC) for permission to commence construction of a 51-mile link between the two separate sections of the railroad. The company felt that the filing was a courtesy, as the ICC had no formal jurisdiction over an interurban. The Southern Railway, controlled by J. P. Morgan interests, filed a brief in protest with the ICC. The case ground on for many years and ended up in the U.S. Supreme Court. The courts determined that the P&N had ceased to be an interurban railroad and had developed into an electrified railroad (essentially a "steam railroad"), which placed it under ICC jurisdiction. The case was finally affirmed on May 16, 1932, when the Supreme Court upheld an injunction against further construction. The case made legal precedent and was later used in cases against the Pacific Electric Railway and other electrified lines. A P&N plan to build northward from Charlotte to Winston-Salem, North Carolina, fared no better.

Electric operation continued until well after World War II. In 1950 P&N president W. I. Rankin, in a statement to stockholders, forecast the end of passenger service and electric operation. In the same year the P&N ordered its first diesels. On February 28, 1951, passenger service ceased on the North Carolina Division; it lasted only eight months longer on the South Carolina Division. Freight operation was fully dieselized by 1954.

In November 1965 the Duke Power Co. announced its intention to divest its portfolio of the railroad. By December 1967 the Seaboard Coast Line and the P&N had reached a tentative agreement, only to be opposed by the Southern Railway. After a bitter legal battle the ICC ruled on September 12, 1968, giving SCL and P&N permission to merge. The merger became effective and the P&N ceased to exist on July 1, 1969.

In 1968, the last year before merger by Seaboard Coast Line, Piedmont & Northern operated a system of 150 route-miles and 237 track-miles, with 18 locomotives, 23 freight and company service cars, and 344 employees. Coal made up almost half the carloadings; foodstuffs were the next most important commodity. Piedmont & Northern operating revenues totaled $6.7 million in 1968, and the railroad achieved a 55.3 percent operating ratio.

—Cary Franklin Poole

REFERENCE

Fetters, Thomas T., and Peter W. Swanson. *Piedmont and Northern: The Great Electric System of the South*. San Marino, Calif.: Golden West, 1974.

Piggyback. *See* INTERMODAL FREIGHT

Pipelines

The successful completion of Col. Edwin L. Drake's well near Titusville, Pennsylvania, on August 28, 1859, marked the beginning of the modern petroleum industry. Early production was transported from the field to marine and railroad terminals by drays, and 2,000 wagons and teams were used daily to move the oil. Initial attempts to replace the unreliable and expensive drayage with pipelines were unsuccessful because the cast-iron pipe leaked badly, and teamsters also destroyed the pipeline facilities.

Samuel Van Syckel solved the leakage problem by using wrought-iron pipe. He organized the Oil Transportation Assn., which completed the first successful pipeline on October 7, 1865. The 2-inch-diameter 5-mile line moved 81 barrels of crude oil per hour from the Pit Hole Creek Field to the railroad at Miller Farm, Pennsylvania. Van Syckel initially charged $1.00 per barrel, significantly lower than the average teamster charge of $2.50. Despite the cost of armed guards to protect the line and the addition of a telegraph line to keep track of oil movements, Van Syckel recovered his investment in a few months. Over the next 16 years pipelines expanded to connect the Appalachian fields in northwest Pennsylvania with refining centers in Pittsburgh, Cleveland, and the Eastern Seaboard.

John D. Rockefeller and his associates at Standard Oil were quick to see the importance of transportation to the success of the firm. The railroads were reluctant to build specialized cars, such as tank cars, so Standard designed and built its own cars. Standard, recognizing the economy of pipeline operation, soon went into the pipeline business. Standard's near monopoly in the oil business was due to its control of petroleum transportation.

By 1900 there were 6,800 miles of crude-oil pipelines concentrated east of Chicago. This changed with the coming of the twentieth century. The Lucas gusher at Spindletop, near Beaumont, Texas, in early 1901 was the first of several major discoveries in the area. Further inland, the Mid-Continent Field was gradually extended from Kansas into Indian Territory (now the state of Oklahoma), culminating with the prolific Glenn Pool discovery of 1905. Prairie Oil & Gas built a 460-mile, 8-inch pipeline from the field to Griffith, Indiana, just south of Whiting, in 1905. Two years later both the Texas Co. and Gulf Oil built 8-inch lines from Glenn Pool to southeast Texas, and in 1909 Standard of Louisiana completed another 8-inch system to Baton Rouge, Louisiana. Between 1900 and 1910 pipeline mileage more than doubled. As the petroleum industry expanded into more areas, pipeline construction kept pace. Mileage again more than doubled between 1910 and 1920 and doubled again between 1920 and 1930. By 1940 there were more than 63,000 miles of trunk crude-oil pipelines.

Although there was initial hostility between the railroads and the expanding pipeline network, the railroads soon conceded the transportation of most crude to the pipeline industry. Several railroads invested in pipeline companies and others made their right-of-ways available for pipeline construction. While the railroads lost the crude market, they continued to handle the distribution of the refined products. This transportation pattern established by the early 1870s remained virtually intact for nearly 60 years. In 1930, however, Standard Oil Co. of New Jersey's Tuscarora subsidiary, no longer required for crude service, reversed the flow of its pipeline and in October began moving gasoline from SONJ's New Jersey refineries to Pittsburgh. Sun and Atlantic quickly built their own product lines across Pennsylvania in order to stay competitive. In 1931 Phillips Pipe Line Co. completed a 681-mile, 8-inch gasoline pipeline from Borger, Texas, to East St. Louis, Illinois. At the same time a group of Mid-Continent refiners organized the Great Lakes Pipe Line Co. as a joint venture and by July 1931 had completed a line from the Tulsa area to Chicago, Omaha, and Minneapolis–St. Paul. By the end of 1940 there were nearly 8,300 miles of product pipelines in operation, which grew to over 23,300 miles by 1950.

When the United States entered World War II, tankers were still moving nearly 1 million barrels of oil per day from the Gulf Coast to the Eastern Seaboard. The need for tankers to move military cargos, as well as the loss from U-boat attacks, required that this traffic be diverted to other modes. For a time the railroads provided pipelines on wheels in the form of solid trains of tank cars moving crude from the oil fields to East Coast refineries. The pipeline industry responded by building new pipelines, temporarily extending others, and adding interconnections for increased system flexibility. However, the largest project was the government-financed War Emergency Pipeline, consisting of a 24-inch, 1,245-mile crude line from Longview, Texas, to Linden, New Jersey, and a 20-inch, 1,475-mile product line from Beaumont, Texas, to Linden. These were commonly called the Big Inch and the Little Big Inch. Construction began on the Big Inch on August 3, 1942, and the line was fully opened to Linden in October 1943. The Little Big Inch was completed in December. In 1947 the lines were sold to the Texas Eastern Transmission Co., and both were initially converted to natural-gas-transmission lines.

Van Syckel's original line used 15-foot lengths of lap-welded wrought-iron pipe and screw-threaded connectors. Steel line pipe became available in 1895, and the first use of welded joints using the oxyacetylene process occurred in 1911. In 1928 the electric arc-welding process and 40-foot lengths of seamless line pipe became available. These technological advances, along with automatic controls, made possible the construction of product pipelines, beginning during the 1930s, and the War Emergency Pipeline lines of World War II. By the early 1960s pipe of up to 40 inches in diameter and in joint lengths of 60 to 80 feet was available, and 48-inch-diameter line pipe was used on the 800-mile Trans-Alaska Pipeline System (TAPS) completed in 1977.

Early pumping stations used steam-powered displacement pumps, which began to be replaced by diesel prime movers in 1914. Electric motors and centrifugal pumps made their appearance in the 1920s, and control of the oil movements has advanced from telegraph to microwave. Centralized operation centers now control the flow through the lines, and staffed pipeline pumping stations are virtually a thing of the past.

With a sufficient volume of throughput, pipelines are the most efficient method of moving crude and refined products overland and have significant economies of scale. The 8-inch-diameter lines standard before World War II could nominally move 20,000 barrels per day, the 24-inch-diameter Big Inch 300,000 barrels per day, while the 48-inch-diameter TAPS has had throughput in excess of 2.1 million barrels per day. On a per barrel basis, the operating cost of a 36-inch line is about one-third the cost of a 12-inch line, while the capacity of a 36-inch line is equivalent to 17 12-inch lines. Because of capacity constraints, early pipelines attempted to limit their throughput to liquids owned by the pipeline's owners and frequently set tariff rates equal to rail rates and required large tenders of 100,000 barrels in order to discourage outside business. The War Emergency Pipeline proved the practicality of large-diameter lines, which subsequently became standard for major projects. This has resulted in an increase in joint-venture projects in order to spread the pipeline capital costs and risks as widely as possible, as well as obtain a sufficient traffic base. These lines and newer proprietary lines also seek throughput from nonowners.

The Hepburn Act of 1906 extended the 1887 Interstate Commerce Act to include interstate oil pipelines, and the Elkins Act of 1903 became applicable to common-carrier oil pipelines. Although the pipeline industry filed suit, in 1914 the U.S. Supreme Court ruled in the *Pipe Line Cases* that the language of the Hepburn Act made all pipelines engaged in interstate commerce a common carrier and subject to Interstate Commerce Commission jurisdiction. In 1934 the ICC began its valuation work for ratemaking purposes on individual pipelines, and in 1940 it ruled that tariff rates should be adjusted to allow crude-oil pipelines to earn a maximum of 8 percent of the property valuation. The following year the maximum return on product pipelines was set at 10 percent. Probably the most significant action regarding pipelines was the 1941 *Atlantic Refining* consent decree whereby, effective January 1, 1942, any defendant pipeline was prohibited from paying out more than 7 percent of its valuation to its shipper-owner in any year. As interpreted by the Justice Department, the limitation included repayment of debt from the pipeline to its owner. As a result of these restrictions, pipeline tariffs were reduced to levels that could not be matched by other land-based transportation modes.

Another consequence of the decree has been the increase in the debt-equity ratio of pipelines from about 20 percent in 1940 to 90 percent for recent large joint-venture projects. Inasmuch as the financial community considers pipelines to be high-risk investments, it is necessary for the owner-shippers to guarantee sufficient throughput to make the project attractive to lenders. On October 1, 1977, the responsibility for the regulation of pipelines was transferred to the Federal Energy Regulatory Commission. Many of the states also regulate intrastate pipelines within their borders and have aided pipeline construction by granting the right of eminent domain, which was pioneered by Pennsylvania and Ohio in 1872.

Throughout its history the pipeline sector has mirrored the trends in the overall petroleum industry. With the decline in domestic production has come a reduction in the mileage of crude pipelines from a peak of 82,000 miles in 1957 to 50,555 in 1999. Product pipelines, however, continue to expand and total nearly 84,000 miles. The increase in throughput of product pipelines has offset the decline in crude lines, and in 1999 pipelines accounted for 67.1 percent of petroleum ton-miles, compared with 28 percent for water, 3.1 percent for trucks, and 1.8 percent, primarily lubricants and specialty products, for rail.

—George C. Werner

REFERENCES

Johnson, Arthur M. *Petroleum Pipelines and Public Policy, 1906–1959.* Cambridge, Mass.: Harvard Univ. Press, 1967.

Petroleum Extension Service. *Introduction to the Oil Pipeline Industry.* Austin: Univ. of Texas, 1978; 2nd ed., 1980.

Wolbert, George S., Jr. *U.S. Oil Pipe Lines: An Examination of How Oil Pipe Lines Operate and the Current Public Policy Issues Concerning Their Ownership.* Washington, D.C.: American Petroleum Institute, 1979.

Poor, Henry Varnum (1812–1905)

A leading nineteenth-century economist and writer who specialized in the railroad industry, Henry Varnum Poor was born in Andover, Maine, on December 8, 1812, and after an intellectually active childhood entered Bowdoin College in 1831, from which he graduated in 1835. After graduation he decided to pursue a legal career and entered practice with his uncle's law firm in Bangor, Maine.

Writing and analysis were two things that Poor enjoyed most in his professional life, and after practicing law for 14 years, he purchased the *American Railroad Journal.* He served as its editor for the next 14 years. During this time Poor was champion, critic, and key spokesperson for the railroad industry. In his writings for the *Journal* Poor tackled many financial and legislative issues, arguing for or against them as necessary in order to promote the best interests of the rail industry. Poor was a true pioneer in the field of business reporting in that he focused on interpretation and analysis of railroad issues, rather than simply documenting and publishing information.

In 1861 the onset of the Civil War initiated a change in direction in Poor's career, and he spent his time working on business interests in Washington, D.C., and New York. While the time he spent on writing diminished somewhat, he joined the editorial staff of the *New York Times,* to which he contributed for several years. Much of Poor's writing focused on the financial issues associated with the war, as well as general issues in business and economics. At this point Poor decided to sell the *American Railroad Journal.* In 1862 he accepted the editorship of *Samuel Hallett's North American Financial Circular,* which was devoted to informing those outside the United States about American financial markets.

In 1867 Poor and his son, Henry William Poor, joined in developing a firm that specialized in railroad insurance, along with the publication of information about the industry. As the business became established, Henry Varnum Poor, deciding once again to turn his attention to serious writing, founded the *Manual of the Railroads of the United States* in 1868. Poor's personal involvement with the *Manual* varied over the years, but it was very successful and served as the leading resource for investors in railroad securities during the late 1800s and through and beyond the turn of the century, as well as an important reference for railroad historians. Eventually, Poor turned responsibility for the *Manual* over to others, but continued to write the annual introduction for several more years and was periodically consulted on its business affairs.

In 1886 Poor retired from the firm he and his son had founded in 1867, but continued his writing on business and economic analysis for both the financial community and the political arena. Although Poor wrote several useful books and articles on general business and economics, his work on the *American Railroad Journal* and the *Manual of the Railroads of the United States* was his greatest contribution to railroad history and journalism. After a comfortable and busy retirement Henry Varnum Poor died on January 4, 1905.

—David C. Lester

REFERENCES

Chandler, Alfred D., Jr. *Henry Varnum Poor: Business Editor, Analyst, and Reformer.* Cambridge, Mass.: Harvard Univ. Press, 1956. Repr., New York: Arno Press, 1981.

Redinger, Matthew A. "Henry Varnum Poor." In *Railroads in the Nineteenth Century,* ed. Robert L. Frey, 330–332. A volume in *Encyclopedia of American Business History and Biography,* gen. ed. William H. Becker. New York: Bruccoli Clark Layman and Facts on File, 1988.

Portland & Ogdensburg Railroad

The Portland & Ogdensburg Railroad was incorporated in 1867 to build a railroad northwest from Portland, Maine, to the Connecticut River east of St. Johnsbury, Vermont. Its purpose was to form the eastern portion of a link between the year-round port of Portland and navigation on the Great Lakes.

Geographic obstacles included the White Mountains of New Hampshire and Lake Champlain. Organizational and financial obstacles were worse. The middle portion of the route, the Portland & Ogdensburg (Vermont Division) went bankrupt in 1877, the year it opened. It was reorganized in 1880 as the St. Johnsbury & Lake Champlain Railroad (StJ&LC), controlled by the Boston & Lowell, which was eager to carry traffic to the port of Boston. The western part of the route, the Ogdensburg & Lake Champlain, was controlled by the Vermont Central Railroad, which had its own seaport at New London, Connecticut. When the StJ&LC built an extension west to connect with the O&LC, the Vermont Central refused to interchange traffic.

The Maine Central leased the Portland & Ogdensburg in 1888, giving the Maine Central a westerly connection with the Canadian Pacific, in earlier years north of the border in Quebec, later at St. Johnsbury, Vermont. The StJ&LC's line across northern Vermont was sold and resold, becoming successively the St. Johnsbury & Lamoille County, the Lamoille County, the Vermont Northern, and the Lamoille Valley. The Ogdensburg & Lake Champlain became part of the Rutland and was abandoned after the demise of that railroad in 1961. Only a few short pieces of each segment remain in service.

—George H. Drury

REFERENCE

Baker, George Pierce. *The Formation of the New England Railroad Systems*. Cambridge, Mass.: Harvard Univ. Press, 1937.

Preservation

Preservation efforts reach back to the beginnings of railroading in Great Britain in the 1830s, but in the United States the effort largely followed the Civil War. Through the years railway preservation activities have shifted from the railroads themselves to enthusiast and civic groups as the companies' resources and priorities have changed. The Chessie Steam Specials of 1977–1978, the Chessie Safety Express of 1980 and 1981, and the Norfolk Southern steam train excursions ending in 1994 were the last large industry-sponsored extravaganzas.

Many early promotions (and some myths) are credited to the Baltimore & Ohio, the first successful commercial line. William Prescott Smith, its master of transportation, wrote a formal railroad history book in 1854. About the same time the Pennsylvania Railroad saved the locomotive *John Bull*, imported in 1831, from being scrapped, leading to a decision to donate it to the Smithsonian Institution in 1885.

The 1876 U.S. Centennial Exposition in Philadelphia, the 1880 Chicago Railway Appliance Exposition, and other expositions featured preserved equipment, but by far the most influential nineteenth-century event was the World's Columbian Exposition in 1893 at Chicago. Joseph G. Pangborn, the B&O's master publicist, assembled an impressive collection of relics and replicas. The B&O's 12-acre exhibit, titled The World's Rail Way, showed the entire history of land transportation, with the railroad as the centerpiece. Reconstituted as part of the Field Columbian Museum, that exhibit constituted the first real railroad museum, but it was replaced in 1904 when Marshall Field decided to emphasize natural history instead.

Before going into storage, a recycled B&O exhibit and many by-then-familiar railroad artifacts traveled to the 1904 Louisiana Purchase Exposition in St. Louis. The Panama-Pacific Exposition in San Francisco opened in 1915 with a railroad exposition. It marked a reorientation of the nation westward across the Pacific, with exhibits highlighting Asian culture, trade, and the emerging industries of the twentieth century.

The B&O's Fair of the Iron Horse in 1927, celebrating that railroad's centennial, featured the same Pangborn exhibits assembled for the Columbian Exposition. That was the most elaborate of a season of railroad centennial celebrations extending from 1925 through 1929. Quickly following were the "Wings of a Century" pageant at the 1933 Century of Progress, celebrating the founding of Chicago; the "Railroads on Parade" exhibit and pageant at the 1939–1940 New York World's Fair; and the 1948 and 1949 "Wheels a-Rolling" pageant at the Chicago Railroad Fair, celebrating the first railroad in Chicago. The B&O Transportation Museum, founded in 1953, re-created as much as possible the 1927 Fair of the Iron Horse and had many of the earlier Pangborn exhibits on display.

One late example of old-fashioned celebratory railroad history presentation came in 1969 when the Union Pacific mounted a Gold Spike Centennial Celebration, which belied the sorry state of the industry in general at that time. The Expo 86 world's fair at Vancouver, British Columbia, in 1986 adopted transportation as its theme and delivered a Steam Expo railroad extravaganza.

Purdue University engineering preserved, beginning in 1901, three locomotives and an interurban car for use in education. In 1951 these became an important part of the collection at the Museum of Transportation in St. Louis.

Henry Ford began collecting steam locomotives in 1925 for the Edison Institute. These locomotives are displayed today in the Henry Ford Museum and Greenfield Village in Michigan. The Franklin Institute science museum in Philadelphia opened a few years later in 1933 with Baldwin three-cylinder demonstrator No. 60000 (4-10-2) and 1838 *Rocket* 0-4-0 and an 1842 Reading 4-4-0.

When vintage equipment and lines were no longer needed for everyday services, enthusiast groups stepped in to preserve a part of the past. The electric streetcar and interurban lines were the first to be shut down, resulting in formation of the Seashore Trolley Museum, Kennebunkport, Maine, in 1939 and the Branford Electric Railway Assn., East Haven, Connecticut, and Connecticut Electric Railway Assn. at Warehouse Point, Connecticut, in 1940. Groups such as the Pennsylvania Trolley Museum in the East and the Orange Empire and Western Railroad Museum in California came later.

The impending end of main-line steam (which happened in 1960) brought an array of steam-powered tourist lines, including Illinois Railway Museum, Union, Illinois; Minnesota Transportation Museum, Minneapolis–St. Paul; National Railway Museum, Green Bay, Wisconsin; Mid-Continent Railway Historical Society, North Freedom, Wisconsin; Museum of Transportation, St. Louis (1946), as the National Museum of Transport; Los Angeles' travel town at Griffith Park (1954); and Midwest Central, Mt. Pleasant, Iowa. The Strasburg Rail Road in Pennsylvania, a shortline founded in 1832, turned into a tourist line in 1958.

Some main-line railroads returned steam to the rails as public relations ventures. Union Pacific has retained two steam locomotives and four historic diesel-electric locomotives for special operations. No. 844, the last locomotive built for UP, in 1944, continues to run in special public relations service. Volunteer Union Pacific employees restored a second locomotive, Challenger No. 3985, which had been on display in Cheyenne, Wyoming, to operating condition in 1981. It too has been used in excursion service since then. UP maintains a history museum at Council Bluffs, Iowa.

The Burlington operated main-line steam excursions through 1966. Reading's Iron Horse Rambles from 1959 to 1963 were popular. Southern Railway, later Norfolk Southern, virtually institutionalized its steam program from 1966 to 1994. From 1977 through 1981, Chessie System invested millions of dollars in renovations at the B&O Railroad Museum and operated main-line excursions. And the Chicago & North Western put a small Ten Wheeler into service for a few years. Canadian Pacific locomotive 2816 (Montreal, 1930) reentered service in 2001; as a component of the CPR's Community Connect program, it has toured Canada and the United States. Main-line steam continues through the efforts of such organizations at the Friends of the 261, which teamed up with Amtrak and railroad companies to run the former Milwaukee Road Northern 4-8-4 as part of the 2004 Grand Excursion activities along the Mississippi River. Southern Pacific locomotive 4449, restored to operating condition to pull the 1976 Bicentennial American Freedom Train, is maintained and operated on special excursions by the Friends of 4449, a volunteer group.

Federal policy with the passage of the National Historic Preservation Act of 1966 brought recognition of places of state and local significance (previously, only landmarks of national importance, such as Mount Vernon, had been recognized). Thousands of stations, locomotives, and passenger and freight cars are listed in the National Register of Historic Places, an indication of the high regard accorded preservation.

Among the most significant historic operating museums, all listed on the National Register, are East Broad Top Railroad, Rock Hill Furnace, Pennsylvania, which was sold for scrap in 1956, started tourist operations in 1960, and was placed on the National Trust for Historic Preservation's "endangered" list in 1996; Cumbres & Toltec Scenic, Chama, New Mexico; and Nevada Northern, Ely, Nevada. But the honors for the busiest (most riders) go to White Pass & Yukon in Alaska; Durango & Silverton in Colorado; Great Smoky Mountain at Dillsboro, North Carolina; Grand Canyon at Williams, Arizona; Strasburg Railroad at Strasburg, Pennsylvania; Huckleberry Railroad at Flint, Michigan; and Lahaina Kaanapali & Pacific Railroad in Hawaii.

State and city efforts also have been influential. Demolition of New York City's Pennsylvania Station in 1963 led to a landmark law that was responsible for preservation of Grand Central Terminal. The U.S. Supreme Court upheld the law in 1978.

In 1991 the U.S. Congress created a special fund that encouraged states to dedicate transportation money to projects that enhance the travel experience and community quality of life. Since then, states have dedicated federal highway funds to enhancements; many of these projects have involved historic preservation.

Publicly funded or nonprofit museums include B&O, Baltimore (1953); California State Railroad Museum, Sacramento (1981); Railroad Museum of Pennsylvania, Strasburg (1975); and North Carolina, Spencer (1977). The California museum repeated its opening Railfairs in 1991 and 1999.

Steamtown started in 1959 when Nelson Blount begin collecting standard-gauge locomotives, with operations on the Claremont & Concord in Vermont in 1961. The collection moved to Scranton, Pennsylvania, in 1985 and became the National Park Service's Steamtown National Historic Site, opened in 1995.

Enthusiast organizations and publications proliferated. To the Railway & Locomotive Historical Society (1921) and National Railway Historical Society (1935) were added groups for almost every railroad, each with magazines and archives. Books are turned out by the thousands. The field had its own magazine, *Locomotive & Railway Preservation*, from 1986 to 1997 (issue 25, March–April 1990, had a review of preservation). The *Steam Passenger Service Directory*, first published by the Empire

State Railway Museum in 1966, has evolved into Kalmbach's *Guide to Tourist Railroads and Museums.*

Gradually, throughout the last 10 or 20 years, the ways we think about railroad history and present it to the public have begun to change. The Smithsonian Institution, forced to rethink its exhibit philosophy, replaced a railroad hall with America on the Move in 2003. The 92-foot Southern Railway locomotive, No. 1401, was retained, but is surrounded by a 1920s scene of the Salisbury, North Carolina, station. The B&O Railroad Museum moved to nonprofit status in 1989. After its roof collapsed in a heavy snowfall, it reopened in 2004 with a stronger roof covering new interpretive displays. The railway preservation movement is maturing. It is telling the stories of railroad labor, of the millions of men and women who worked for the railroad. It is making the link between Asa Philip Randolph, who led the Brotherhood of Sleeping Car Porters in its struggle against the Pullman Co., and modern civil rights ideals. And photography has a growing role in documentation and interpretation.

Railway preservation in general is moving away from an emphasis on equipment to a more sophisticated and inclusive approach to the heritage of railroading. The Center for Railroad Photography and Art is one example. It treats the use of images of railroading and advocates the reinterpretation of railroading's visual culture. The fact that railroad heritage is recognized so emphatically by the National Park Service, the Save America's Treasures program, the American Society of Civil Engineers, the American Society of Mechanical Engineers, and other nonrailroad cultural heritage organizations is further evidence of the field's maturity and significance. As the celebrations of the last 100 years are being replaced by commemoration, it marks the beginning of a new era for museums and operating lines and the final step away from the traditional railroad-company way of marking history.

—John E. Gruber, Richard Gruber, and John Hankey

REFERENCES

Hankey, John P. "Railroads on Parade." *Vintage Rails*, no. 18 (May–June 1999): 32–40.
"Kaleidoscope." *Locomotive & Railway Preservation*, no. 25 (Mar.–Apr. 1990).

Presidential Campaigns and Travel

North American heads of state were slow to warm up to the idea that they could see and be seen by riding trains. The idea caught on gradually at first. Abraham Lincoln and successive chief executives used trains to some advantage, but it was William Jennings Bryan and Theodore Roosevelt who began to employ special cars, then dedicated trains, about the turn of the twentieth century. Presidential rail travel reached its zenith during Franklin Roosevelt's administration, continued unabated under Harry Truman, and started to decline during Dwight Eisenhower's first term.

Trains operated for these three men reached enormous—and complicated—proportions. They usually included a baggage car that carried automobiles for the principal transportation during stops, a communications car that kept the president in touch with the White House and most capitals of the world, three or four sleepers for the traveling press, a press car equipped with long benches at typing height, a diner or two, a lounge car for the press and White House staff, two or three sleepers for White House staff, a sleeper/lounge for the Secret Service and railroad special agents, and, finally, the president's private car.

Campaign trains could cover 10,000 miles in 30 days, with the president giving 35 or 40 major off-train speeches and 60 to 90 rear-platform talks. Often the specials were shunted off on lonely spurs or spotted in a yard in some great city overnight, and everyone used the train as a hotel. Telephone connections were plugged in, typists worked far into the night, and there was all the hustle and bustle of any political headquarters. Sometimes the train continued moving through the night, especially in the West, where great unpopulated distances had to be covered. But the normal procedure was to call a halt so the president could start his day of speechmaking at the next town on the route.

Long campaign tours had a downside—the lack of laundry facilities and access to showers. Reporters and politicians often had to go several days between showers and clean clothes. Atmospheric conditions aboard the cars became so unbearable that porters burned incense.

Presidential trips were planned months in advance, and long sheets of detailed instructions were issued to scores of officers on every participating railroad. Track foremen inspected the trains' entire routes inch by inch, facing-point switches were spiked shut, and watchmen patrolled long tunnels, bridges, and canyons. Plainclothesmen scrutinized every station, coaling tower, and water tank for suspicious characters and kept crowds from getting in the way.

A pilot train always preceded a presidential special, and sometimes a chase train followed. Spare locomotives with steam up were spotted at strategic points, ready to take over in case of a breakdown. Most roads brought other trains in either direction to a stop 30 minutes in advance of the special, although a few permitted them to continue slowly. Engineers working near the special were ordered to silence their bells and whistles or horns.

Car inspectors accompanied the special with all manner of spare parts; linemen also were aboard with portable telegraph and telephone sets and blueprints showing the location of the wires along the right of way. Sometimes an

Presidential campaigners —and many other lesser candidates—long made the railroad "whistle stop" an important campaign tool in the American heartland. Republican presidential candidate Dwight Eisenhower is shown on September 24, 1952.
—Weirton Steel/Eisenhower Library, from Bob Withers

extra crew rode along in case illness struck any of the regulars. Secret Service agents screened everyone who boarded.

The classic example of presidential campaigning has to be Democrat Harry Truman's 1948 upset of Republican Thomas E. Dewey. No one—except maybe Truman—expected him to win against the dapper New York governor, but how he did it has been cited many times since as the way to win an election.

Truman's first big coup came in June when he was invited to deliver the commencement address and receive an honorary degree at the University of California at Berkeley. His aides saw this as an opportunity to cross the nation by rail and campaign in a grand fashion, with taxpayers picking up the tab instead of the financially strapped Democratic Party. The trip turned into a 15-day, 18-state, 9,504-mile journey that called for 5 major speeches and 68 other talks.

The trip amounted to a shakedown cruise that exposed procedural weaknesses and gave Truman's handlers a chance to hone his political skills. This helped turn the tide for the underdog incumbent beginning in September. Truman had trained himself to talk extemporaneously from outlines instead of written-out speeches—which, with his poor eyesight, he read rather stiffly. He also had put together a research team to collect background data on all the issues and add sparkle to the stops by compiling local color about each town he would visit. With all the preplanning, research, and development of a down-home speaking style, the candidate knew that he would triumph by meeting America face-to-face.

In fact, the very term "whistle-stop campaign" resulted from a Republican gaffe in June. Truman had continually assailed the "do-nothing 80th Congress" in general, and Senator Robert Taft (R-Ohio) in particular, who, speaking in support of the Republican line, had called on Americans to fight inflation by eating less. "I guess he would let you starve, I don't know," Truman remarked. Three days later Taft responded on nationwide radio, digging himself in deeper and inspiring the addition of a new term to the American political dictionary. Speaking before the Union League Club in Philadelphia, Taft berated Truman for "blackguarding Congress at every whistle station in the West." Truman and his staff loved it. A few days later, in Los Angeles, he nailed Congress again and joked that the city was the biggest "whistle-stop" he had visited, editing slightly Taft's "whistle station" and permanently planting in the public's mind an apropos description of his style of campaigning.

Truman won in 1948, and he and most of his staff credited that victory to the fact that he had crisscrossed America on a train. "You get a real feeling of this country and the people in it when you're . . . speaking from the back of a train," he said. "And the further you get away from that, the worse off you are, the worse off the country is. The easier it gets for the stuffed shirts and the counterfeits and the fellas from Madison Avenue to put it over on the people."

Several North American rail trips involved a U.S. president and other heads of state. On a 1943 outing Franklin Roosevelt planned a detour from his secret inspections of military installations and defense plants long enough to visit Mexican president Manuel Avila Camacho. When Roosevelt's train arrived in Monterrey, Avila Camacho's train was already there, headed north. FDR's special backed into the same siding so that the two presidents' private cars were end-to-end, with only a street over which the auto caravan into town would pass separating the two. They went into town to visit the governor's palace, review troops, witness a demonstration by schoolchildren, attend a seven-course dinner, and address the Mexican people by radio.

Avila Camacho paid a return visit to the United States instantly. When the party returned to the trains, Avila Camacho's private car and one other were cut in ahead of the rear two cars on Roosevelt's train for the trip back to Corpus Christi, Texas, to give the presidents more time together and provide tighter security. Avila Camacho's train followed Roosevelt's.

On March 25–28, 1956, Palm Sunday weekend, President Eisenhower rode a 14-car President of the United States (referred to by railroad men as POTUS) train from Washington to White Sulphur Springs, West Virginia, for a three-way summit with Canadian prime minister Louis St. Laurent and Mexican president Adolfo Ruiz Cortines. The trip was nearly derailed before it started. Ike's private car, *Chessie 29*, departed Cleveland, Ohio, fully stocked several days before the journey and stopped over in Huntington, West Virginia, for a mechanical check. It was to proceed to Washington on March 22 to join the special. But early that evening a mechanical officer allowed nine members of his family to visit the car. A well-meaning chef gave them all cocktails. Some detected a cloudy look or a bad taste and set the drinks aside. Three drank their glasses dry and became ill. The incident resulted in a big flap, with charges that someone was trying to poison the president. Tests were conducted on the leftover beverage, and section gangs combed the entire route to Washington looking for empty bottles that might have been tossed off the car after it left Huntington. The problem was traced to cleaning fluid, often stored on board in club soda or ginger ale bottles. Apparently the party was served from a bottle containing the cleaner.

—Bob Withers

REFERENCE

Withers, Bob. *The President Travels by Train*. Lynchburg, Va.: TLC, 1996.

Public Relations

Public relations, public affairs, media relations, press office, corporate communications—all these titles apply to both the concept and the institution of influencing public opinion about corporations, associations, political movements, and public policy issues. Variously referred to as press agents, spokespersons, or—more pejoratively and sometimes unfairly—"flaks," "damage control officers," and more recently "spin doctors," public relations practitioners are important players in American business.

Railroad public relations evolved as a professional discipline and universally accepted component of the corporate hierarchy at roughly the same time and pace as for other industries. However, to a considerable degree, the railroad industry itself was the incubator for the growth and development of public relations precepts and practices as we know them.

Modern public relations is generally held to be a creation of the twentieth century, and many observers point to long-lived (1891–1995) Austrian-born Edward L. Bernays as the chief architect of contemporary public relations. Bernays was a visionary, a philosopher who combined psychology and salesmanship to influence public thinking. He theorized that linking events, products, or beliefs with prevailing social consciousness had the ability to spark public interest. Bernays's critics might dismiss him as a mere propagandist, but others praise him for discovering ways to influence public thought with the precision of an engineer.

Perhaps the best-known railroad public relations pioneer was Ivy Lee (1877–1934). Lee was dedicated to disseminating the truth to the news media so that the public could judge for itself the merits of all sides of an issue. When Lee came to the powerful Pennsylvania Railroad in 1906, he saw as his mission reconciliation between railroad management and the media, two formidable institutions that deeply mistrusted one another after several decades of perceived railroad management misbehavior in tumultuous conflict with muckraking journalism.

In the early years of the twentieth century railroad accidents occurred with deadly frequency, and the news media—and thus the public—resented railroad management's secrecy and inaccessibility. Ivy Lee convinced the Pennsylvania Railroad's top management that the news media could be used to get the company's message to the public if reporters were allowed access to railroad property and officials. Lee's "Declaration of Principles" outlined his public relations theory, which emphasized placing accurate facts in front of news editors for their information and use. In addition to his best-known work, for the Pennsylvania Railroad, Lee and his associates worked for many other railroad and transit interests, including New York City's Interborough Rapid Transit Authority, the Assn. of Railroad Executives, the American Locomotive Co., the American Railways Assn., and the Electric Railroads of New York State.

Over time, Ivy Lee's principles were adopted by other railroads, and public relations became an integral part of the industry. In 1952 the Assn. of American Railroads formed the Railroad Public Relations Assn. (RPRA). This professional organization, composed of top railroad public relations executives, held annual meetings at which members and guests gave presentations on the changing world of public relations and media relations. Because of mergers and a dwindling number of railroads, RPRA was dissolved in 1997.

As railroads consolidated during the latter half of the twentieth century, their public relations departments combined, too, often producing offices in several regions of the increasingly vast railroad companies' territory. Far from being merely propaganda producers, modern railroad public relations departments are an integral part of the decision-making process of most major North American railroads. To the public—and therefore its decision makers—perception is reality, and that reality in many ways drives the direction of the regulatory arms of government and the business climate in which railroads work. Railroad public relations guide the way in which the industry is perceived.

—R. Clifford Black IV

Puerto Rican Railroads

Railroads virtually encircled the prosperous coastal plains of the almost 3,500-square-mile mountainous island of Puerto Rico. Construction began under the Minister of Colonies of Spain in 1888. The meter-gauge Compañía de los Ferrocarriles de Porto Rico began operation in 1891, and by the next year the company had a total of 100 miles of track operating in three isolated segments of the planned around-the-island railway.

The island became part of the United States in 1898, after the end of the Spanish-American War. Puerto Rico saw new American investment in the island, much as it had with the new independence of Cuba from Spanish control. In 1902 the New York–controlled American Railroad Co. of Porto Rico took over the Spanish railway and by the end of World War I had closed the remaining gaps in the line, completing a route from San Juan across the northern and western shores of the island and around the south shore to the city of Ponce. The line prospered as sugarcane production was developed along the coast. The railroad by 1925 operated a total of 52 oil-burning locomotives built by Baldwin and Alco, notable among them three 0-6-6-0 Mallet compound articulated locomotives built by Baldwin in 1904, the first of their kind built by the Philadelphia builder. The American Railroad operated over 1,000 freight and sugarcane cars and more than 40 passenger cars. Running time between San Juan and Ponce was leisurely in the extreme, requiring upwards of 9 hours for the 172-mile journey and including an overnight service between the two cities.

Ponce was as far east as the American Railroad would ever get along the south shore of the island. Linked with the American Railroad was the Ponce & Guayama Railroad, also meter gauge, which completed a 30-mile line between the fertile cane fields of the two cities. Plans were made in 1921 to complete the line around the southern and eastern portions of the island, much of it using already-existing private sugarcane lines, but they never materialized.

Other railways included a shortline between San Juan and Humacao, on the eastern shore of the island, and the 8-mile Northern Porto Rico Railroad, which operated on the north coast of the island. Puerto Rico even got a short electric interurban, the Canadian-financed Porto Rico Railway, Light & Power Co., which operated an 18-mile steam line between Río Piedras and Caguas, and an 18-mile, 600-volt electric line between San Juan, Santurce, and Río Piedras. Unlike other Puerto Rico railroads, the line was built to standard gauge.

By 1925 Puerto Rico's public service railways totaled almost 350 miles, and over 600 miles of private sugar and industrial railways were operated. Almost all were built to meter gauge, allowing sugarcane shipments to be shipped over the American Railroad to be interchanged.

The development of improved highways brought an early end to railroad passenger service, and freight service was not far behind. By 1947 the American Railroad had gone into bankruptcy, and the company was reorganized as the Puerto Rico Railroad & Transportation Co. Passenger service was quickly ended, and the company continued to operate as a sugarcane carrier until all operation ended in 1957. The last segment of Puerto Rico's railroad system, the Ponce & Guaymas Railway, continued to operate as a sugar line until it was closed in the 1990s.

—William D. Middleton

REFERENCE

Rollinson, David C. *Railways of the Caribbean.* London: Macmillan Education, 2001.

Pullman, George M. (1831–1897)

Most popular American texts claim that George Mortimer Pullman invented the sleeping car and that he introduced luxury to railroad travel. These claims are at best half-truths. A large number of persons contributed to the introduction of sleeping cars and deluxe accommodations, many years before Pullman entered the trade. Pullman did, however, come to dominate the sleeping-car business, and many of his cars were indeed palatial. He was a great capitalist and business manager. He was daring, energetic, and shrewd in an age in which only the strong survived in the business world. His rise to fame and fortune was a classic American success story.

He was born in Brockton, New York, on March 3, 1831.

Railroads were a new idea at the time. Pullman started life modestly enough; he was one of ten children, and his school days ended at age 14. He became a store clerk and then joined an older brother in the cabinet-making trade. In 1853 he became a contractor in the house-moving trade. His ambition drove him to relocate to Chicago several years later. He continued moving buildings and was also active in elevating streets, for his new hometown struggled to raise itself above the swamps on the edge of Lake Michigan. He made good money over the next few years but yearned to get into something bigger.

Pullman tinkered with sleeping cars briefly in 1859 and then headed to the Colorado gold fields. About 1864 he was ready to settle on sleeping cars as his main business and formed the Pullman Palace Car Co. in 1867. He faced several established competitors, notably the Central Transportation Co., which operated a fleet of sleepers on many eastern lines. But Pullman felt that he could succeed. He put cars on some midwestern lines and in 1870 contracted with the Union Pacific Railroad to run cars as far west as Ogden, Utah.

At the same time he leased the Central Transportation Co. Pullman now had a national operation. By 1876 he had 600 cars and 2,000 employees. The business grew and prospered. By 1880 the Pullman Palace Car Co.'s stock was worth $6 million, and the earnings on investment were an astonishing 18 percent.

In the next year he opened a giant car plant south of Chicago. The largest such facility in the world, it was more than just a collection of industrial buildings. It was a complete town with a shopping center, a hotel, and homes for the workers. This model town became known as Pullman and was home to 12,000 residents. The car works cranked out about 12,000 freight and 1,000 passenger cars each year. Pullman was proud of this scientifically designed town and enjoyed showing it to visiting VIPs. But many of the residents were less enthusiastic. They found life in Pullman limited, undemocratic, and puritanical. The town's founder was not bothered by these negative feelings, however, if he even knew about them.

But his world was about to fall apart. His business slowed significantly in 1893. Orders for new cars diminished. Pullman decided to cut wages at the car plant by 25 percent. The workers protested and walked out. Pullman refused to negotiate, and the strike went on for months with no movement on either side. The American Railway Union refused to handle Pullman cars in support of the striking car builders. The sympathy strike turned violent, and federal troops were brought in to restore order. A month later the Pullman car shops reopened, but with ill feelings between management and labor.

Bewildered by the criticism in the public press of how he had handled the strike, Pullman grew bitter and resentful. His success and wealth were of little comfort, for he felt that his reputation had been sullied. The stress affected his health, and he began to decline. On October 19, 1897, Pullman suffered a fatal heart attack at his luxurious Prairie Avenue home in Chicago.

—John H. White, Jr.

REFERENCE

Leyendecker, Liston E. *Palace Car Prince: A Biography of George Mortimer Pullman.* Niwot: University Press of Colorado, 1992.

Pullman Co.

George M. Pullman first came into the sleeping-car business in a partnership with Benjamin C. Field in 1859, rebuilding two day coaches from the Chicago & Alton Railroad. The 44-foot cars, each accommodating 10 sleeping-car sections, a linen cupboard, and two washrooms, operated between Chicago and Bloomington, Illinois. After a brief divergence into the Colorado gold fields, Pullman returned to Chicago in 1863 to make the sleeping car his life's work.

He was far from the first in the business. The earliest North American sleeping car had begun operation a good two decades previously, and by the time he entered the field there were close to a dozen other companies, several of them well established. But Pullman noticed a growing demand for luxury travel accommodations and possessed the ambitious and aggressive nature and the shrewd business sense to build the Pullman Co. into a near-national cartel of the U.S. sleeping-car business and make his name synonymous with quality transportation service.

In July 1863 Field and Pullman ordered a splendid new 16-wheel palace car from the Wason Car Co. in Springfield, Massachusetts, that would rival anything offered by their competitors. Named the *Springfield*, the 58-foot car could accommodate a total of 56 passengers in 14 lower and upper sections. Interiors were finished in polished black walnut; costly damask curtains surrounded the berths. Bed linens were changed daily. The *Springfield* was provided with every convenience found in first-class hotels.

An even more luxurious car was designed and built in a rented shop at Chicago and completed in the spring of 1865. The 54-foot car had 12 open sections and was said to have been 1 foot wider and 2½ feet higher than any previous car. Originally known simply as the A, it was later named the *Pioneer*. Its elaborate interior furnishings helped drive the car's cost up to $20,000. At least according to later Pullman accounts, the luxurious *Pioneer* was in-

cluded in the President Lincoln funeral party between Chicago and Springfield in April 1865. This legend was carefully polished by Pullman men for years afterward. The new car did attract considerable press attention on trial runs over the Chicago & Alton in May 1865. Similar cars were soon added, and by the end of 1866 the Chicago & Alton had joined other roads, with more than 40 cars operating over seven Chicago lines. The luxurious cars were outfitted with veneer panels, polished glass and brass, and ornate carpets and curtains. Trained attendants made up the beds and saw to the comfort of their passengers.

In 1867 Pullman decided that it was time to attract more capital and expand the company beyond its Chicago base. Field had already decided to retire, and Pullman incorporated the company as the Pullman Palace Car Co. early in 1867, with a capital of $1 million. Andrew Carnegie and Chicago moneymen John Crerar and Marshall Field were among Pullman supporters, and he soon began to build a national sleeping-car company. This was accomplished both by expanding his operations and acquiring competing companies. Pullman began running cars over the Central Pacific and Union Pacific in 1868, and in 1870 he leased the Central Transportation Co., a major competitor. Other small operators were similarly absorbed, and Pullman's last big rival, the Wagner Palace Car Co., which ran over the New York Central and other Vanderbilt-controlled lines, finally sold out in 1899. Except for several railroads that operated their own sleeping cars, the Milwaukee, New Haven, and Great Northern chief among them, Pullman now had a virtual monopoly of the U.S. sleeping-car business, with significant extensions into Mexico and Canada as well.

Early railroad dining consisted of a brief stop at a station restaurant, where the traveler was obliged to gulp down what was rarely good food. In 1867 Pullman came up with the idea of the hotel car, which provided both overnight sleeping facilities and high-quality meals. More practical separate dining cars soon followed, but once again Pullman had helped pioneer more comfortable travel. The first separate dining car was the elegant *Delmonico*, named for the legendary New York restaurant, which went into regular service on the Chicago & Alton. Another early Pullman idea was the operation of long sleeping-car runs over different roads, which became increasingly possible as American railroads moved toward the 4-foot 8½-inch standard gauge. In 1870 a charter trip for the Boston Board of Trade became the first through car with Pullman equipment to run from the Atlantic to the Pacific. About the same time Pullman first employed an African American as a porter, which became a standard arrangement for Pullman cars.

As Pullman's business continued to grow, the company decided that it was time to establish its own facilities for construction and repair of its sleeping cars. The Detroit Car & Manufacturing Co. at Detroit, Michigan, was the first to be acquired, in 1870. Another was added by purchase of the Erie & Atlantic Sleeping Coach Co. at Elmira,

New York, in 1873, and a third was built at St. Louis, Missouri, in 1880. But even these became inadequate, and in 1879 Pullman was ready to build an enormous new plant for railroad-car construction that would represent the most modern car-construction practice. Chicago was already becoming a national rail center, and Pullman bought a 3,600-acre site at Lake Calumet, 14 miles south of Chicago, that would be the home of both the new plant and many of its employees and their families. The planned industrial community of Pullman grew into a city of some 12,000 and attracted both praise and criticism for its innovative social experiment arrangement.

As both the magnitude of rail passenger travel and Pullman's share of the sleeping-car business increased, the company grew rapidly. The number of Pullman cars grew from an estimated 300 in 1870 to twice that number by 1875, doubled to 1,195 by 1885, and doubled again to 2,556 cars by 1895. The route-miles operated by Pullman more than doubled from an estimated 30,000 in 1875 to 71,400 in 1885 and nearly doubled again to 126,600 miles by 1895. Pullman's gross income in 1870 was $750,000; by 1880 it was over $2.6 million, and by 1890 it was almost $8.9 million.

Pullman continued to improve the quality and comforts of its equipment. Although a number of car arrangements were tried, the long-standing Pullman favorite was the open-berth car, with 12 open sections (24 berths), a single drawing room, and ladies' and gentlemen's toilet facilities at opposite ends. Interior accommodations featured fine woods, paneling and molding, ornate decoration, and up-to-date equipment. Older cars were regularly upgraded. Air brakes and coupling systems were installed. Heating systems were improved. Kerosene lanterns were replaced by Pintsch gas and later by electric lighting.

Much more elaborate interior arrangements were developed for the equipment used in the luxury trade. In 1887 Pullman adopted the idea of the vestibule car, which provided an enclosed passageway at the center of the end platforms, protecting passengers from the elements and smoke from the locomotive. The vestibule car was soon adopted by railroads for their extra-fare trains, and by 1893 Pullman had developed a new design that enclosed the full width of the vestibule, using trap doors to enclose the stairwells at each side.

Pullman and other companies led the world in developing comfortable first-class equipment, and representatives of European railroads were soon looking at the American experience. The first was Belgian engineer Georges Nagelmackers, who returned from a U.S. visit in 1870 determined to introduce international sleeping cars in Europe. His company, originally named Mann's Railway Sleeping Car Co., Ltd., used the boudoir sleeping-car design developed by U.S. sleeping-car operator Colonel William D'Alton Mann. It soon became known as the International Sleeping Car & European Express Trains Co., or Wagons-Lits, and eventually operated throughout Europe and into Asia and North Africa.

Next came Sir James Allport, general manager of Great Britain's Midland Railway, who visited with George Pullman in 1872 and soon invited him to a shareholders' meeting of the Midland Railway, which signed a 15-year contract to operate sleeping-, parlor-, and dining-car services. The first six Pullman sleeping and parlor cars for the Midland were built in the Pullman plant at Detroit, Michigan, and began operation in 1874. By 1876, 36 Pullman cars were in operation on the Midland. In 1882 Pullman organized the subsidiary British Pullman Palace Car Co., and Pullman services were operated over half a dozen other British railways. Pullman ownership of the British venture continued until 1907, when it was taken over by a British firm, but the company carried the Pullman name for another 60 years, until it was finally incorporated into the nationalized British Rail.

A less successful European venture was the 1875 establishment of a Pullman plant in Italy, which was soon taken over by the Wagons-Lits company. The Pullman name later returned to continental Europe in 1925, when deluxe first-class Pullman parlor cars were widely operated by Wagons-Lits all over Europe and even into Egypt. Although they were never part of the Pullman company, more than 200 of these Wagons-Lits cars, proudly lettered "Voiture-Salon-Pullman" and painted in a distinctive Wagons-Lits blue and ivory, were operated in such premier daytime services as the Calais-Paris leg of the London-Paris *Golden Arrow*, the Paris-Brussels-Amsterdam *North Star*, and the Paris-Menton *Côte d'Azur* until the late 1960s.

By the beginning of the twentieth century Pullman had become an enormous corporation. The name had been changed simply to the Pullman Co. at the time of the Wagner acquisition in 1899, and by 1900 the company owned 3,258 cars and operated its services over 158,500 miles of line. It transported over 7.75 million passengers, and its annual gross was over $6.6 million. Its car-building and repair shops were again expanded. The Dure Manufacturing Co. at Wilmington, Delaware, was acquired in 1886 to add another repair plant; another at Buffalo, New York, was added by the 1899 acquisition of the Wagner Palace Car Co.; and two others followed at Richmond, California, in 1901 and Atlanta, Georgia, in 1909.

Soon after the new century Pullman faced the need for a complete replacement of its sleeping-car fleet. Fearful of the effect of fire in such tunnels as New York's new Interborough Rapid Transit subway and the Pennsylvania Railroad's Hudson River Tunnel, car builders were anxious to develop all-steel passenger cars. Pullman was not the first to make the transition; the American Car & Foundry Co. began to build the first all-steel cars in 1904. But Pullman soon began an enormous conversion program. Over the next several years Pullman built several prototypes to develop the lightest possible design, and a new steel-car works was completed at Chicago in 1909. A new prototype car, the *Carnegie*, was completed early in 1910. Within another month 500 new steel cars were on order, and Pullman had produced its last wooden sleeping car. By 1913, 2,100 all-steel sleeping cars were in service. In 1926, three-quarters of the Pullman fleet were all-steel, and by the mid-1930s the last wooden sleeping car had been retired. In just a quarter century of construction, from 1910 to 1935, Pullman had produced 8,000 heavyweight, all-steel cars.

Pullman reached its peak in the late 1920s. Every night almost 100,000 people traveled by Pullman, each carried on board a comfortable car attended by a well-trained, white-jacketed porter. Pullman operated 130,000 miles of line, transported around 14 billion passenger-miles a year, and employed up to 29,000 persons, as many as 9,000 of them as Pullman porters alone. In 1930 Pullman owned 9,860 cars and was capitalized at $129 million.

Under the most common arrangement between Pullman and the individual railroads, the sleeping car was owned and maintained by Pullman. The Pullman equipment was transported by the railroad company, which received the coach-fare portion of the ticket, while Pullman received the additional first-class fare. Another common arrangement was what was called an association contract, under which the sleeping cars were jointly owned by the two companies with an appropriate division of revenues. Gradually, however, most of these association arrangements were shifted to the more usual Pullman ownership. A major benefit of the nationwide operation by Pullman was the advantage of through operation over connecting railroads, while Pullman's large national pool of sleeping cars made it easy to meet the needs of seasonal services or special movements. These extra cars could accommodate summer vacation traffic to the West or winter travel to Florida or be used for extra holiday service. Franklin D. Roosevelt's first inauguration in 1933 required a special move of 845 extra cars, but the largest special move of all was for the 1926 Eucharistic Congress at Chicago, which took 1,199 cars to handle the delegates (see SPECIAL TRAINS).

Pullman and other early sleeping-car operators quickly learned that any kind of a numbering system for their equipment was likely to create confusion with railroad-owned cars and soon shifted to car names established by a committee. Geographic names were an early favorite, parlor and drawing-room cars were named for flowers or women, and dining cars were named for famous hotels. In the 1920s Pullman adopted a system of names with common prefixes or suffixes for the principal car types. *Saint* cars were 12-section, 1-drawing-room cars, *Camp* cars were 10-section, 1-drawing-room, and 2-compartment cars, and so forth. As special sets of cars were built for custom-designed luxury trains, special names were developed that reflected the people and territories they served.

In the 1920s Pullman began to make the first significant changes from the organization established with the formation of the first Pullman incorporation in 1867. In addition to building its own equipment, Pullman had long built both passenger and freight equipment for other companies and had developed a major business in the manufacture of street railway, rapid-transit, and interurban cars. Pullman substantially increased its freight capacity in 1922 with the acquisition of the Haskell & Barker Car Co. at Michigan City, Indiana. In 1924 the separate Pullman Car & Manufacturing Corp. was established, and in 1927 a new holding company, Pullman Inc., was established under the laws of the State of Delaware. It owned both the manufacturing company and the Pullman Co. that operated Pullman's sleeping-car services. Still more manufacturing assets joined Pullman in 1930 with the acquisition of the Standard Steel Car Co. at Pittsburgh, Pennsylvania, and the Osgood Bradley Car Co. at Worcester, Massachusetts. All of these were rolled up in 1934 as the Pullman-Standard Car Manufacturing Co.

The early 1930s proved to be a poor time for expansion. New car orders had all but vanished, and by 1933 sleeping-car travel had fallen to only 6,142 million passenger-miles, less than half its 1930 traffic. Sleeping-car fares were drastically reduced, shops were closed, and men were laid off. Pullman incurred its first loss ever in 1932, but the company had enough resources to weather the storm until business began to improve in the latter part of the decade.

With conversion to all-steel cars largely complete by the end of the 1920s, Pullman had soon taken on other major changes to its equipment fleet. During 1927–1929 Pullman began testing of mechanical air conditioning in Pullman sleepers, and by 1935 it had equipped some 6,000 of its cars with air conditioning at a cost of more than $30 million.

Pullman was a leader in the development of new lightweight passenger cars with the construction of the all-aluminum observation-lounge-sleeper *George M. Pullman*, exhibited at the 1933 Chicago World's Fair. The next year the Pullman-Standard Car Manufacturing Co. built the country's first streamlined, lightweight, air-conditioned train, the three-car Union Pacific M-10000. Together with the Budd Co.'s streamlined *Zephyr*, it was in the vanguard of the streamliner era that brought new life to North America's passenger trains. Pullman's first lightweight, streamlined sleeping cars were completed in 1934, and by the time World War II interrupted their development, Pullman had produced more than 600 of them for the new trains.

Like the railroad industry as a whole, the Pullman Co. met the extraordinary transportation demands of World War II superbly. Operating every sleeping car it had and augmented by 1,200 wartime troop sleepers and 400 kitchen cars for troop-train service, Pullman saw traffic on its fleet of 8,590 sleeping cars (in 1945) grow by almost four times, from 8,214 million passenger-miles in 1940 to a record 28,267 million passenger-miles in 1944, by far the largest traffic ever carried by the Pullman Co.

Pullman's long-held cartel of North American sleeping-car construction and operation moved to an end soon after World War II. In 1940 the federal government initiated an antitrust suit against the group of Pullman companies, alleging that the purchase of new sleeping cars by builders other than Pullman-Standard had been suppressed. The Budd Co., which had lost out on orders for all except a few new sleeping cars, was undoubtedly behind the suit. It took seven years to complete the action, but in the end Pullman lost. In 1944 Pullman was required to separate its car-construction and sleeping-car-operation businesses. The company decided to stay with car manufacturing, but it was not until June 30, 1947, that the sleeping-car operation was sold off to a consortium of 57 (later 59) railroad companies with the transfer of 731,350 shares of stock at a cost of just over $40.2 million.

For a few years after the end of World War II there was considerable optimism about the future of the railroad passenger business and the Pullman Co. The new streamlined trains of the late 1930s had proved enormously successful, and the railroads had transported the greatest passenger traffic in history during the war. There was, many railroad men believed, a substantial market for modern, comfortable new trains. During the next decade more than 2,000 new lightweight, streamlined cars were added to the Pullman rolls, some of them this time built by rivals Budd Co. and American Car & Foundry.

But well before the last of the new cars rolled off the assembly line, it had become apparent that there was not much of a future for the passenger train or Pullman cars after all. The number of Pullman passengers fell by more than half between 1945 and 1950, to just over 16.6 million, and then decreased again to reach a 1960 level of fewer than 4.5 million. Pullman drastically cut back its staff, equipment, and shops. The Pennsylvania Railroad took over its own parlor-car services in 1957, and the New York Central withdrew all of its Pullman services in 1958. By the mid-1960s Pullman had sustained heavy losses, and in 1968 the company's railroad owners decided to end operations at the end of the year. In that final year Pullman operated fewer than 800 sleeping cars and transported just over 1 million passengers. What was left of the sleeping-car business was taken over by the individual railroads.

Pullman-Standard continued its car-building business for both passenger and freight cars. Most passenger car orders were for commuter equipment, although what turned out to be the company's last passenger-car order was for 284 Superliners delivered for Amtrak during 1978–1981. The last car off the line and the last one built at the old Pullman plant was fittingly named for George M. Pullman. On hand for the May 22, 1981, occasion was Pullman's granddaughter, Mrs. Philip Miller. Plagued by losses, Pullman-Standard had said that the Superliners would be its last passenger-car order. Late in 1983, with empty freight-car order books in hand, Pullman Transportation Co., as it was now called, announced that it would leave the freight-car business as well, selling its Butler, Pennsylvania, Bessemer, Alabama, and Asheville, North Carolina, plants and the designs and rights for its freight cars to Trinity Industries. Bombardier Transportation acquired the designs and rights to Pullman passenger cars.

—William D. Middleton

REFERENCES

Dubin, Arthur D. *More Classic Trains*. Milwaukee, Wis.: Kalmbach, 1974.

———. *Some Classic Trains*. Milwaukee, Wis.: Kalmbach, 1964.

Husband, Joseph. *History of the Pullman Car*. Chicago, A. C. McClurg, 1917. Repr., Grand Rapids, Mich.: Black Letter Press, 1974.

Morel, Julian. *The Pullman Car Company: Its Services, Cars, and Traditions*. North Pomfret, Vt.: David & Charles, 1983.

Welch, Joe, and Bill Howes. *Travel by Pullman: A Century of Service*. St. Paul, Minn.: MBI Publishing Co., 2004.

White, John H., Jr. *The American Railroad Passenger Car*. Baltimore: Johns Hopkins Univ. Press, 1978.

Pullman Works

The Pullman Palace Car Co.'s (PPCC) Chicago works was planned to be both the largest and most modern railcar-manufacturing facility in the world and a model of the planned, industrial community. Although the company and its founder, George M. Pullman, were widely heralded for both of these endeavors at the outset, both were in a sense failures (although the former not nearly so spectacularly as the latter; the PPCC did, after all, go on to dominate the railcar industry for the next four decades).

Within 17 years of its establishment, Pullman's planned community experiment had failed, a victim of the 1894 Pullman strike. The Pullman Palace Car Co. was ordered by the Illinois State Supreme Court in 1898 to divest itself of its nonindustrial holdings. The original factory, for its part, which had been designed with as much care as the community, proved inadequate for the demands that the PPCC's growing business placed on it, as well as for the technological changes that overtook the railcar industry (particularly the transition from the production of wooden to steel cars). After a history of structural and functional modifications, what was left of Pullman's original factory building ended its working life as a warehouse for a local steel company.

By the time Pullman began construction of his industrial complex and model community in the spring of 1880, he was already a successful railcar manufacturer with factories in Atlanta and Detroit. He chose his location, some 14 miles south of Chicago's downtown, with care. Like many of his class at this time, he was concerned with the growing specter of labor unrest. He reasoned that if his workers were provided with attractive, orderly, and healthy living conditions in a community with all the amenities of urban life (schools, churches, markets, library, theater, and recreational facilities), they would be protected from "baneful elements," particularly saloons, and be happier and more productive. The distance from Chicago was seen as a distinct advantage. There was a darker side to this paternalism, of course. The workers were paid on a piece-rate basis, their rents were deducted from their pay, and labor organizers were excluded from the community. Like the factory, the community was a business venture intended to make a profit. These factors contributed to its ultimate failure.

The factory too was planned to reflect the aesthetic of the community. No sign of industrial activity was to be visible from outside the grounds, the facades of the factory buildings shared the same Romanesque architecture as the buildings in the community, and the grounds were carefully landscaped (the condensing pond for the Corliss steam engine, discussed later, was crafted as a small lake [Lake Vista] in front of the administrative building). Pullman also wanted to build for the ages; the buildings were constructed of locally made brick atop massive limestone foundations. The durability of construction, however, hampered efforts to adapt the facility to changing demands and technologies.

In addition to the facilities directly related to the construction of railcars, Pullman also included facilities for the production of virtually everything needed for the production of railcars apart from the raw materials: the only components that were not made on-site were carpets and iron piping. Even the majority of the bricks used in the construction of the factory were made on-site from Lake Calumet clay, and the sewage produced by both factory and community was piped to Pullman's farm to fertilize the crops.

The factory and community were both designed by the team of architect Solon Spencer Beman and landscape architect Nathan F. Barrett. It is said that Beman, not taking Pullman's initial request for a design seriously, had not prepared his initial drawings until Pullman asked to see them, and he had to complete them overnight. This kind of extemporaneous adaptation seems to have been characteristic of the early enterprise; the first publicly released plan of the complex differs in several respects from the finished project, and the administrative pavilion, still extant today, is slightly asymmetrical.

As originally laid out, the factory complex consisted of the administrative pavilion and clock tower, located on the west side of the property facing the Illinois Central tracks (and today, Cottage Grove Road) and flanked north and south by the front erecting works, each having ten construction bays, terminating in smaller pavilions (altogether measuring nearly 1,000 feet in length). Behind (to the east of) the front erecting works was a transfer table (more about this feature later) and another rank of buildings; the southern half consisted of two parallel erecting shops, and the northern half was a single large building housing wood shop, iron machine shop, blacksmith shop, and other ancillaries. Further to the east was yet another transfer table and a final erecting shop. Additionally, there were buildings that housed the Corliss steam engine, foundry, hammer shop, drying kiln, and coalhouse, as well as the water tower and lumberyards.

The design of the factory included a number of specialized features. Much of the machinery was powered by the Corliss steam engine (originally built for the Centennial Exhibition of 1876 by George Corliss and at the time the largest and most powerful steam engine in the world). Power from the engine was mechanically distributed to the erecting shops through shafts measuring five to eight inches in diameter, housed in underground conduits. Individual machines, as well as elevators in the taller buildings, were powered by leather belts connected to the shafts, which ran along the inside edge of each building. In addition to the Corliss engine, there were several other steam engines used to power other parts of the factory (19 others were in use by 1893). Steam from the Corliss also was used to heat the factories and residences in the community. The Corliss engine was in use at the factory until 1910, when it was finally retired and sold for scrap.

Another feature of the factory, unique at the time, was the construction of the cars themselves. Pullman developed an early form of the assembly line in which the cars were moved from one specialized shop to the next through the various stages of construction. The process began by placing the trucks for the car on the tracks in the construction bay (which were oriented perpendicular to the long axis of the erecting shop), and the bottom frame of the car was built atop them. The car was then moved along the tracks, out of the erecting shop, and onto the transfer table (by means of a winch that was attached to a movable eyebolt in the floor of the erecting shop). The transfer table consisted of a pair of tracks oriented perpendicular to the erecting shop, mounted on trucks that were themselves set on a set of six tracks that ran parallel to the erecting shop. A dummy engine (a small, boxy, steam locomotive) then pushed the table to the bay in which the next phase of construction would take place, and the car was winched in.

Altogether, there were several stages in the process of constructing a passenger car (which might vary, depending on the complexity of the order): constructing the bottom frame of the car, building the body, putting on the roof boards and moldings, applying the tin roof cover, external painting and interior finishing (both done at the same time), installing the heating and lighting fixtures, finishing the interior woodwork, and final trimming and installation of seats and drapery. At each stage of construction prefabricated components, constructed at the various specialized shops within the complex were used in the assembly of the cars. With the exception of refrigerated cars, the construction of freight cars was less complex and followed a linear assembly-line process in a separate facility (beginning in 1883, as discussed later).

Actual construction of the Pullman complex began in May 1880 and continued into the winter of 1880–1881. In addition to building the factory and community, it was necessary to drain and fill the building site, which was prone to flooding during the spring months. Pullman began hiring in February 1881 and officially inaugurated the facility on April 2, 1881 (Figure 1).

Almost from the beginning, the productive capacity of the original factory was outpaced by demand. According to the original plan, both passenger and freight-cars were to be produced in the front and rear erecting works. The

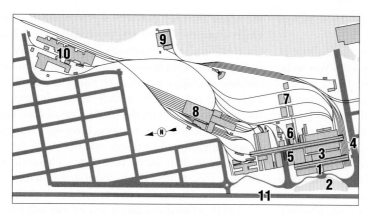

Figure 1. Pullman Works, 1886. —Rick Johnson

1-Pavilion
2-Lake Vista
3-Erecting Shops
4-Transfer Tables
5-Corliss Engine
6-Wood Shops
7-Lumber
8-Freight Shop
9-Iron and Steel Works
10-Foundry and Wheel Works
11-Illinois Central Tracks

demand for new passenger cars, however, relegated freight-car construction to just a few bays in the original facility. By 1883 it was necessary to construct a separate facility for the production of freight cars, which was built to the northeast of the original factory buildings.

Pullman's planned community also ran into trouble, in this case terminal, fairly early on. Pullman was forced to reduce wages in response to the depression of the early 1890s. However, insisting that the community generate a profit, like all his other ventures, he did not reduce rents. Because rents were deducted from the workers' pay, many were left with insufficient cash to support their families. This led directly to the Pullman strike. Before it ended (after less than four months and in Pullman's favor), it had drawn in the entire railroad industry and federal troops, and had cost the lives of 13 strikers. Although Pullman won the strike, the company was ordered to divest itself of its residential properties in 1898. Pullman had died by this time, and it is thought that the strike was a contributing factor.

During the 1880s and 1890s the factory complex continued to grow, adding new repair shops, a laundry, and a knitting mill. Streetcars were added to the Pullman lineup in the late 1880s. A fire in 1890 destroyed the hammer shop, which had to be rebuilt. By the turn of the century the workforce at the factory complex was over 7,000, and the company had a virtual monopoly on the production of sleeping cars in the United States.

The next major change at the Pullman factory was initiated in 1907 when the company began the production of steel cars. Their greater length made the existing facilities obsolete, and the lack of appropriate facilities appears to have cost at least one contract (Pennsylvania Railroad). By 1910 much of the original facility had been rebuilt to accommodate the new cars. The southern arm of the front erecting works was largely demolished, and a larger building (the front steel erecting shop) was erected in its place, as well as covering part of Lake Vista (which was filled) and the southern extent of the westernmost transfer table. The parallel pair of rear erecting shops was modified to form a single building. Other new facilities,

particularly a steel freight-car shop, were constructed elsewhere on the site. The transition to electrical power also was made at this time, and the Corliss steam engine was finally retired. By 1920 the conversion to all-steel construction was essentially complete.

The succeeding years saw further new technology, such as the introduction of welding as opposed to riveting, new steel alloys, and aluminum siding, as well as new car models. However, beginning with the Depression, orders for passenger cars declined, and although there were periodic upswings in orders, the impact of air travel and automobiles on passenger rail was inevitable. Sagging rail-car orders were supplemented by the production of aircraft wings, landing craft, and munitions. By the mid-1950s the original factory had outlived its usefulness, and operations were shifted to other facilities that the Pullman Co. had acquired over the years.

In 1957 most of the original buildings were demolished, leaving only the north wing of the front erecting works, the administrative pavilion, and the two steel erecting shops on the original property. Portions of the property were sold off to a variety of companies. The few remaining original buildings, on a 12.6-acre parcel bounded by Cottage Grove Road and 111th Street, were sold to the Kasel Steel Co. in 1965. The foundations of the demolished buildings were covered with cinders and other debris, and rail sidings were run into the area bounded by the remaining buildings, which were used as warehouses.

As the Pullman Co. wound down its Chicago operations, there were thoughts of developing the former industrial site and the community as an industrial park. The residents of the former community (now individual property owners) resisted the plan and pressed for landmark status. Pullman became a state landmark in 1969, a national landmark district in 1971, and a City of Chicago landmark in 1972.

The factory site was purchased by the State of Illinois in 1991, along with the Hotel Florence (part of the Pullman community). In 1998 the remaining architecture at the factory was badly damaged in an arson fire. The two steel erecting shops and the administrative pavilion and clock tower were nearly destroyed. A collapsed section of roof saved the north wing of the front erecting shop, which is still in good condition. Damage to the front steel erecting shop was so severe that it had to be leveled. All that remains of it today is its foundation pad. The rear steel erecting shop lost its roof and about half of its remaining external walls. The State of Illinois has undertaken stabilization work on the remaining architecture, but limited funding restricts it to only what is absolutely necessary to prevent further collapse of the remaining structures.

During the summer of 2004 DePaul University, Chicago, in conjunction with the Illinois State Historical Society, began archaeological work as part of its Summer Field School in Archaeology Program under the direction of William Middleton of DePaul University and Scott Demel of the Chicago Field Museum of Natural History. The project documented the extent of remaining building foundations, including the foundations of the building that had housed the Corliss steam engine, located several of the underground conduits that had originally housed the power shafts from the Corliss steam engine, cleared part of the work floor of the original wood shop building, and excavated a portion of one of the transfer tables. Archaeological work at Pullman will continue for the next several years.

—William D. Middleton III

REFERENCES

Buder, Stanley. *Pullman: An Experiment in Industrial Order and Community Planning, 1880–1930.* New York: Oxford Univ. Press, 1967.

Doty, Mrs. Duane. *The Town of Pullman: Its Growth with Brief Accounts of Its Industries.* Chicago: Pullman Civic Organization, 1893.

Historic American Building Survey. *Pullman Company Administrative Building and Shops.* HABS ILL, 16-Chig, 90–.

Historic American Engineering Record. *Pullman Industrial Complex*, HAER ILL, 16-Chig, 102–.

Purchasing and Stores

Railroads consume an enormous amount of supplies and capital goods. The act of buying what is needed is an important function because it involves the expenditure of large sums of money. Storing and keeping track of the purchases is also a large-scale function.

As railroads grew in size toward the end of the nineteenth century, it was obvious that it was inefficient, as well as awkward, to have each department or each functional site purchase goods and supplies separately. A purchasing agent was employed, and all orders were directed to the purchasing department, which typically reported to a vice president or the general manager of the carrier. The task of the purchasing department is to acquire what is needed and make sure that it is of the desired quality and is purchased on the most favorable terms.

Railroads share with other businesses many of the tasks and methods of conducting the job of purchasing. At the same time there is a difference because the carrier itself may be involved in the transportation of its goods, as well as the goods of other carriers. The purchases of a railroad are usually dubbed company materials; these materials range from ballpoint pens and paper towels to diesel locomotives and thousands of tons of steel rails.

There is a definite trend in the railroad industry to substitute capital equipment for labor. There are examples in a variety of areas, but perhaps the most obvious is the mechanization of much of the maintenance work on track and track structure. Train control and signaling have also shifted away from use of labor toward communication equipment.

As with most other enterprises, about 70 percent of the items purchased account for only about 10 percent of the expenses, about 20 percent reflect 20 percent of the expenditures, and 10 percent of the items are probably responsible for about 70 percent of the money spent. The values involved are indicative of the care in managing the purchases and the inventory. Great care must be taken with the items that involve the greatest sums of money. New locomotives range in cost from $2.5 million to $4 million; freight cars range from $8,000 to $30,000 or more, depending on the complexity of the equipment and the size of the order.

The orders for purchases are gathered in the purchasing department, and, where possible, the often-numerous requests for similar items are combined to take advantage of economies of scale in buying. The purchasing department maintains a regular relationship with vendors who sell what the railroad wishes to buy. The purchasing agents note the quality of products, the location of vendors, the delivery time, and the ability of a vendor to satisfy the particular specifications of the purchase. A carrier with multiple facilities and sites may need diesel fuel, paper forms, computers, paper clips, and staple guns at a variety of places. The advantages in purchasing in large quantities from a vendor must be balanced against the opportunity costs of the money tied up in inventory that cannot be used for other purposes. Fifty million dollars spent on an inventory of steel rails is money that cannot be placed in interest-bearing securities or used to pay for bridge replacement.

In placing an order, the purchasing staff works closely with the freight traffic or marketing departments to find the cost of transporting the goods to the purchaser. Another piece of important information is how much of a vendor's products were shipped by the purchasing railroad. As an example, in the purchase of steel for structural purposes, the purchasing department may find that in reviewing the movement of steel by several steel firms, firm A moved 40 percent of its traffic via the purchasing carrier, and steel firms B and C each moved 30 percent of their rail freight movement by the purchasing carrier. Assuming that each steel firm can meet the price, specifications, and delivery time, the purchase would be split, with 40 percent going to firm A and 30 percent each going to firms B and C. This is a simple process of rewarding vendors who have been customers.

In a similar vein, railroads pay close attention to other railroads and carriers who have used their services in the movement of company materials. For example, the purchase of freight cars usually entails the movement of component parts to the car builder. These components include steel shapes, truck frames, brake systems, and couplers. Railroad A would remind railroads B and C, both of whom are ordering new cars, that railroad A routes so many carloads of its company materials via railroads B and C. Railroad A, in finding that motor carrier Z was purchasing 100 new trailers, would remind Z that railroad A routes a certain tonnage of company freight by Z. Reciprocity is the cherished business dictum of "You scratch my back and I'll scratch yours."

Another railroad purchasing practice has been to take possession of costly items in a way to avoid sales tax, depending, of course, on the tax policies of given states. As an example, for many years the Illinois Central Railroad purchased diesel locomotives manufactured in Illinois, but took possession of the locomotives in Paducah, Kentucky. For several years thereafter, the new locomotives would not be used in Illinois; as a result, the railroad avoided paying the Illinois sales tax, and the newest motive power was employed on the IC lines south of the Ohio River.

Purchases are divided into several categories. One of these includes those expendables used on a fairly consistent basis, such as office supplies, locomotives and diesel fuel, freight-car wheels, and brake shoes. Tracking use and purchase over time allows such expendables to be ordered on a routine basis. Knowledge of the location of routine needs permits large-scale purchases, with delivery to a number of specific sites.

Another category is those items associated with heavy repairs to locomotives and rolling stock. This work, carried out at a main shop area, requires the service of a major storehouse that contains all the items needed to put locomotives and freight cars in good condition. Some of this work must be continuous in order to keep a car or locomotive fleet functioning. In other instances a rebuilding and upgrading program stretching over a period of years has different requirements. Still another class of work is maintenance of the right of way; this entails the purchase of rail, crossties, and ballast and specialty items such as switch stands, frogs, and other truck components and hardware.

Purchasing is usually centralized, and many items are kept in one great storehouse, usually at the main car and locomotive shops. In the past, some storehouses were several blocks long and a block or more wide. In them was every item needed. Better communication and delivery methods have changed some of the centralization of storage that was common in the past. For example, all paper supplies and other office needs may be centrally purchased but delivered directly to the individual offices by the manufacturer. Likewise, rail and ballast and crossties are centrally purchased but are usually delivered to a place near where they will be used.

The central storehouse will have a different variety of goods if the railroad rebuilds its own locomotives than if it sends them off for the heavy maintenance. A supply of spare diesel engines, generators, and traction motors will be necessary to keep a rebuilding program on schedule.

Heavy repairs on cars are usually handled at main car shops. Minor repairs, such as replacing brake shoes, new hopper doors for covered hopper cars, or new wheels, are carried out at repair tracks around a system, and the parts have to be delivered on a timely basis. Good records collected over time enable the supply process to be planned carefully.

The contents of the central storehouse were greatly simplified and reduced in size when Amtrak took over railroad passenger service. An inventory of seat cushions, seat frames, lavatory equipment, dining-car tables and kitchen equipment, and myriad items associated with passenger service could all be eliminated. Dropping the use of cabooses likewise reduced inventories of materials peculiar to cabooses.

The size and importance of railroads caused them to pioneer some technology. Because of the size and complication of a railroad's purchases, the purchasing and stores area was one of the first to use punch-card accounting shortly after the turn of the twentieth century. This attention to better control of inventory has continued, and electronic computers have been employed to manage purchases and stores since they became available.

—George M. Smerk

REFERENCE

Monczka, Robert, Robert Trent, and Robert Handfield. *Purchasing and Supply Chain Management*. Cincinnati, Ohio: South-Western, 1998.

Q

Quebec North Shore & Labrador Railway

One of the largest deposits of iron ore in the world was found in Labrador along the Quebec-Newfoundland border. Exploration in the 1930s and 1940s determined the economic feasibility of mining and transporting the ore. The Iron Ore Co. of Canada (IOC) was formed in 1949 with the backing of several U.S. steelmakers. Bringing the ore out required a railroad—trucks would not be able to handle the volume—so among IOC's initial projects was a 356-mile railroad north into the wilderness from Sept-Îles, Quebec, on the north bank of the St. Lawrence River, about 400 miles northeast of Quebec City. Because of the remote location, most of the railroad was surveyed from helicopters, and materials and construction machinery came in by air.

Construction of the railroad began in 1951 and took three years. The line crosses the Quebec-Newfoundland border about halfway along its length, then returns to Quebec a few miles before it reaches its northern terminal at Schefferville. Iron ore moves south to Sept-Îles, where it is transferred to ships to continue its journey to ports along the St. Lawrence River and the Great Lakes. The Quebec North Shore & Labrador is connected to the rest of the North American rail network only by a car ferry operating between Sept-Îles and Matane, Quebec, on the south bank of the St. Lawrence.

In 1960 a branch, jointly owned by IOC and the Wabush Lake Railway, was constructed west from Ross Bay Junction (224 miles from Sept-Îles) to the mining area at Labrador City and Wabush Lake. Trains from the branch move south along the QNS&L to Arnaud Junction, 8 miles north of Sept-Îles, then follow the Arnaud Railway to ore docks at Pointe-Noire.

The QNS&L embodied the best of modern technology when it was built—welded rail, centralized traffic control, and roller bearings—and since then it has adopted such concepts as radio control of midtrain helper locomotives. Its trains are among the longest and heaviest in the world, usually 230 cars stretching 1.6 miles and carrying a total of 28,000 tons of ore. It carries raw ore only during the summer and fall but carries processed ore in pellet form all year long. The QNS&L is a common carrier and operates biweekly passenger trains; there are no highways into the wilderness from Sept-Îles.

—George H. Drury

R

Radio and Television

During radio's so-called golden age, between 1930 and 1950, railroads continued to be important in American life. Scenes with trains were common on radio programs, although there were no network programs devoted solely to railroad situations. Several programs, however, were developed around railroad themes and places. One of the most popular was *Grand Central Station,* heard on CBS from 1937 to 1953. Each broadcast was a self-contained new drama, built around people arriving at the train station. Many listeners recall the dramatic opening sequences in which the announcer described trains rushing down the Hudson River, past tenement houses in upper Manhattan, and then with a roar into the tunnel leading to Grand Central Station, "crossroads of a million private lives." After the characters arrived in New York, they went their own ways, and neither train nor station was thereafter a part of the drama. The sound effects—steam locomotives, trains squealing to a stop—were superb, but not realistic since steam trains did not operate into Grand Central. The approaches were all electrified when the new station opened in 1913.

Among the charms of old-time radio were the sound effects. Radio sound-effects men developed railroad sounds to a high and dramatic art. So whenever trains did appear, their presence was both dramatic and carefully researched (sometimes recordings were used). Needless to say, radio sound-effects men were much less drawn to the diesel when it arrived and could do almost nothing meaningful with electric traction. Steam trains could still be heard on radio dramas long after they had disappeared from the American scene.

A radio program actually sponsored by the Assn. of American Railroads and heard in the late 1940s and early 1950s was *The Railroad Hour.* The program was devoted to musical comedies, operettas, and Broadway plays, with Gordon McRae nearly always the lead singer. Announcer Marvin Miller began the program with "Ladies and Gentlemen, *The Railroad Hour.* And here comes the star-studded show train." This was accompanied by the sound of escaping steam and other train noises. But the railroad invariably had nothing to do with the musical plays that followed.

A program of an entirely different nature was *Bob Elson aboard the Century,* a 15-minute interview program heard on the Mutual network from 1946 to 1951. Bob Elson was a popular Chicago sportscaster who worked with a microphone at Chicago's LaSalle Street Station, where he attempted to interview the many celebrities who rode the *Twentieth Century Limited* to New York in those days. There were plenty of steam train noises recorded for the program, although the *Century* was already dieselized by this time. Elson was never actually on board the train as the title suggests.

With the arrival of the television era the railroad fared somewhat better since trains provide both dramatic audio and visual action. When old movies began to appear on television, the networks had a rich source of material to mine (*see* CINEMA AND RAILROADS). Naturally trains appeared sporadically on television programs when required by plot lines and other situations. In addition, a few serial programs were built around railroad themes and settings over the years. Among them were *Petticoat Junction, Iron Horse, Casey Jones, The Wild Wild West, Union Pacific,* and *Supertrain.*

One of the principal ways the American public has kept in touch with the railroads is by means of television documentaries. There have been many of these, and many more with the growth of cable television in recent decades. The History Channel, Arts and Entertainment, the Learning Channel, Public Broadcasting, and Discovery have offered a great deal of historical material relating to the railroad in documentaries that blend old still photographs, available moving shots, interviews with experts, and miscellaneous file material. Among the better ones were the History Channel's *Trains Unlimited* and *Great Railway Journeys* and *Tracks Ahead* on Public Broadcasting. Using the best of modern resources, in 2003 the Public Broadcasting System created a very successful two-hour historical profile of the building of the transcontinental railway.

But for the home television viewer, living-room sets also offer much more specialized and well-focused material directed to the railroad aficionado. In recent decades an enormous industry has grown up providing railroad videotapes. Such tapes, some highly professional, others crude and amateurish, nonetheless provide a rich lode of material to those with a specialized interest in railroads. There is, of course, much film made by recent video photographers, but there has also been a good deal of borrowing of older historical material, some of it converted from 16 mm or even 8 mm movies. During the 1930s and 1940s the public relations departments of major railroads made films for educational and promotional purposes, many of them lost treasures that were fortunately preserved or uncovered in archives or vaults, then converted to videotapes for large and grateful railfan audiences.

—George H. Douglas

REFERENCE

Dunning, John. *On the Air: The Encyclopedia of Old-Time Radio.* New York: Oxford Univ. Press, 1998.

Rail Defects, Detection of

Rails are the most crucial components of track structure, providing both support and guidance for trains. In the course of day-to-day operations minor ballast problems, broken ties, missing spikes, and other track defects can be tolerated, but rail fracture can be catastrophic. As the size and speed of trains increased, the likelihood and threat of fractured rails became more serious. By the turn of the twentieth century the development of powerful steam locomotives, air brakes, and automatic signaling systems permitted passenger trains to operate at speeds of 80 mph and more. Not only did heavier trains and faster speed place much greater stress on rails, but the consequences of a rail fracture at high speed could be disastrous.

Rail fractures can be caused by a variety of structural flaws. They can be introduced during the manufacture of the rail or be caused by circumstances of operation, or by some combination. Daily operation over a minor structural imperfection in a rail can gradually lead to a critical flaw that suddenly, without warning, results in a fracture. Traditional visual inspection of tracks and rails cannot detect several varieties of critical rail flaws. Invisible defects such as tiny cracks inside the body of the rail or in the railhead can easily go unnoticed. One of the most serious internal defects is the transverse fissure—a crack that bisects the width of the rail. This is largely undetectable by traditional inspection, yet can shatter under the weight of a train and result in a serious derailment.

Such a disaster befell the Lehigh Valley Railroad in 1911 when a passenger train derailed near Manchester, New York, killing 29 people and seriously injuring another 60. Investigation revealed that the rail had failed as the result of an internal transverse fissure. In response to the public outcry, the U.S. Bureau of Standards began researching ways to detect internal rail defects that could prevent similar accidents.

Elmer Sperry (1860–1930)

The railroads' problem with rail defects was an opportunity for Elmer Ambrose Sperry, a prolific scientific inventor-entrepreneur who developed more than 350 patents during a 50-year career. Born at Cortland, New York, in October 1860, Sperry completed a little over two years of a three-year program at the Cortland Normal School between 1877 and 1880, concentrating his studies in science and technology. Sperry quickly developed his extraordinary range of technical interests and new technologies. His diverse inventions included electric light and power, mining machinery, electric traction, automobiles, batteries, industrial chemistry, internal combustion engines, ship stabilization, the gyrocompass, aviation instruments, marine and aerial equipment, searchlights, marine gyropilots, antisubmarine equipment, and rail flaw detection and testing. He was only 23 years old when he formed his first company, the Sperry Electric Light, Motor & Car Brake Co., to develop improved electric dynamos and arc lights, followed by a number of other companies. His numerous inventions in electric traction were eventually sold to the General Electric Co. Sperry is best known, however, for his work with gyroscopes. The development of steel-hulled ships had made the use of traditional magnetic compasses problematic. Sperry developed his first gyrocompass during 1908–1909. The U.S. Navy made good use of the device during World War I. Sperry developed a gyroscopic aircraft autopilot in 1909, followed in 1915 by a two-frame gyroscopic device to improve ship stability.

As early as 1912 Henry W. Thornton, then president of the Long Island Rail Road and later of the Canadian National Railways, had asked Sperry to consider the use of gyroscopes as a means for determining the alignment and level of tracks. Little was accomplished until after World War I, when the Santa Fe in 1923 asked Sperry to develop a gyro-equipped track recorder car. Fitted with two gyros, the Santa Fe car proved highly succesful in providing a much more accurate assessment of track conditions.

Today, Sperry is best known in the railway field for his work in rail-flaw-detection systems. Sperry began to look at the problem by studying earlier detector cars that had proved inadequate. By 1927 he developed an initial detector-car design that worked well in the laboratory but failed in actual service. The American Railway Assn., which had funded this first test, discontinued further support, but Sperry continued his work. By 1928 he had developed an induction system capable of detecting internal rail defects, including the dreaded transverse fissure. Sperry hoped to build and sell defect-detection cars directly to the railroads, but found them hesitant to make such highly specific purchases. Ultimately he found it more practical to start a company that would contract detection service to individual railroads, and he founded the

Ever since the prolific scientist and entrepreneur Elmer Sperry developed the first successful rail-defect-detection car in 1928, the self-propelled Sperry Rail Service cars have been periodic visitors to North American railroads. Sperry car No. 130 was seen on Conrail track at Middlefield, Massachusetts, in 1997.
—Brian Solomon

Sperry Rail Service. Sperry himself died at a Brooklyn, New York, hospital in 1930, but the Sperry Rail Service went on to a long and still-continuing success in rail-defect detection.

In the early years Sperry Rail Service defect-detection cars, colloquially known as Sperry cars, used commercially manufactured self-propelled gasoline-electric railcars as the basic platform to house the specialized induction testing equipment. Self-propelled gas-electrics had become a popular cost-cutting tool for branch-line passenger operations and enjoyed robust sales in the 1920s. For its earliest defect cars, Sperry bought new gas-electrics from the J. G. Brill Co. and outfitted them with crew quarters and his patented induction detection equipment. By the time Sperry died in 1930, Sperry Rail Service had a fleet of ten gas-electric defect-detection cars in operation, known by the Sperry Rail Service as the "large cars," as well as smaller rail-defect-detection equipment.

During the 1930s and 1940s, when branch-line passenger services suffered a serious decline, many railroads dumped lightly patronized and unprofitable passenger services, which allowed Sperry to acquire additional gas-electric cars relatively cheaply secondhand. Gradually Sperry amassed a fleet of more than 25 self-propelled cars from Baltimore & Ohio, Chicago & North Western, Lehigh Valley, New York Central, and Seaboard Air Line and converted them for its specialized use. The old railcars required substantial rebuilding. The interior was entirely reconfigured, most windows were blanked up, and specialized rail-testing equipment was installed. When the supply of used railcars dried up, Sperry built its own detection cars, and gas-electric propulsion was later replaced with diesel-electric power.

When working, a Sperry crew lives on its car for months at a stretch. Typically after a day of testing the car will tie up overnight on a siding or railroad yard. The crew is provided comfortable living space, and most cars

are set up to accommodate three or four employees. The front of the car contains a motor compartment. Beyond is a meal galley, followed by a dining and lounge area. At the center are upper and lower berths and toilet and shower facilities. Toward the rear is a generator and storage facilities, followed by the car's most important equipment, that used for detection, recording apparatus, and analysis, and crew work space.

How Induction Testing Works

Sperry cars roll along at just 6.5 to 13 mph when searching for defects. The induction system produces a powerful magnetic field in the rail using low-voltage current at about 2,000 amps. Electrical brushes are put in contact with the rail to set up the magnetic field, and a sensing coil is used to detect deflections or changes in the field that indicate the presence of a rail fracture or other flaws. Field changes are automatically logged and tracked on a paper-strip chart with ink pens. The traditional method required just one pen for changes in the field for each of the two rails. As the car moves along, a skilled operator monitors the strip chart, interpreting incoming data. Interpretation is key to making use of the car's equipment.

Magnetic induction detects transverse fissures, but it also senses other imperfections in the rail such as seams and corrosion. Also, rail joints are revealed by induction testing. The operator must distinguish normal occurrences from abnormal and separate serious flaws from more minor problems. Potential defects are marked on the track. Traditionally, a crew member would inspect the problem area and mark it for repair if necessary, using yellow paint for minor problems, red for more serious flaws. In addition to the Sperry crew, typically a railroad official rides along in the car, while a repair gang follows the car to repair rails. In their first two decades Sperry cars only used induction testing to look for defects.

Ultrasonic Testing

In the early 1950s Sperry began augmenting the traditional induction tests with ultrasonic signals. Ultrasonic tests can be used to locate different types of invisible rail flaws not revealed by induction testing. In its earliest application ultrasonic testing was performed manually with handheld units. Sperry's first ultrasonic railcar was built for subway use on the New York City Transit Authority, using an old New Haven Railroad Mack railbus. Since its introduction Sperry has advanced ultrasonic testing, making it much more useful for finding rail flaws and more practical to perform at higher speeds. Early ultrasonic systems were adversely affected by grease on the rail surface. The use of automated compensation systems overcame this problem.

Sperry now uses ultrasonic inspection to complement its traditional testing; it maintains that by using both systems it can provide more thorough rail inspections than was possible by either system operating independently. Using the two systems in tandem enables Sperry to locate greater numbers of rail defects, and with greater accuracy. The two systems combined can identify more than 20 types of hidden flaws. By the mid-1960s all the big Sperry railcars were equipped to do both induction and ultrasonic testing. Today, information-processing methods blend the systems. When a potential defect is found with one system, positive confirmation is possible with the other, a valuable feature when dealing with defects invisible to the eye. Induction tests are most effective for analysis of the railhead. Ultrasonic tests are better for finding flaws in the body of the rail and in locating defects such as fatigue cracks that may be disguised by other types of imperfections. Ultrasonic testing is especially useful for identifying bolt-head cracks at the end of rails.

To project high-frequency sound impulses into the rails and rail joints, Sperry employs transducers, devices that transmit power. In a typical system transducers are coupled to the rail using a roller search unit (RSU), essentially a tire filled with fluid that rolls along below the car. Each RSU contains three transducer heads used to project high-frequency sound at three distinct angles. The different projection angles are designed to make the best use of the information received from the reflection. This is analogous to having three video cameras at different angles aimed at the same scene. Sound reflection is recorded, and the signals from the different heads are amplified, processed, and combined electronically to create the most accurate rail profile. This provides operators with a distinct image of internal and external rail conditions.

Different rail areas have various inspection requirements. Ends of the rails at the joints are critically important because of the unusually high stress placed on them. As a result, joints are more prone to specific types of flaws than the rest of the rail. The three-angle ultrasonic picture helps minimize detection errors, such as when routine imperfections, as with normal bolt holes, are highlighted as actual defects. However, bolt holes cannot be categorically ignored, since these areas are subject to stress-related fractures. Traditionally, ultrasonic output was monitored in the same way as the induction system, using ink pens and paper-strip charts.

Hi-rail Detection Trucks

In addition to its traditional railcars, Sperry has developed detection equipment for use on hi-rail trucks. Until a few years ago, it was impractical for trucks to carry induction equipment, and as a result they were limited to ultrasonic testing. By 2000 Sperry had developed an improved induction system capable of application on hi-rail trucks, and now trucks can do both types of testing. Sperry plans to retire many of its older railcars, some of which are more than 60 years old, and replace them with dual-inspection hi-rail trucks. This follows the trend in North American railway maintenance, which has moved away from traditional rail-based equipment in favor of hi-rail-type maintenance machinery. Hi-rail vehicles are easy to get on and off the tracks, giving a railroad greater flexibility when testing a section of line. A truck can be taken off at virtually any highway grade crossing and so does not tie up valuable track space, as do the traditional Sperry railcars. Sperry will not replace all of its old cars, because in some situations they are still preferred, such as remote lines where there are very few grade crossings and no local accommodation, as well as heavily traveled passenger routes.

Sperry's fleet of testing equipment reflects systematic and modal shifts. In 1978 Sperry had 26 traditional railcars equipped for both induction and ultrasonic testing and just 2 all-ultrasonic testing cars. By 1990 it had boosted its fleet to 5 all-ultrasonic cars, in addition to the 26 traditional cars. By 1997 it had just 19 of the traditional cars left and 10 all-ultrasonic cars operating in North America. In 2002 Sperry was operating a total of 62 testing vehicles worldwide.

In Sperry's first few decades its rail-analysis business grew rapidly. By 1930, after less than two full years in business, it had tested 36,000 miles of track. By 1950 it had tested more than 2 million miles of track on 124 different railroads. After 50 years it had tested more than 6.4 million miles and found more than 3.5 million rail defects. In 2004 it claimed to have tested 10 million track-miles and to have located 5.5 million rail defects. Every defect found prevents a potential wreck. Today, Sperry Rail Service is a division of Rockwood, one of the world's fastest-growing materials engineering and inspection companies.

Although Sperry is the most prominent rail-defect-detection service, several other companies also offer rail-defect-detection service, among them Harsco Track Technologies, Herzog Services, and Speno International. Sperry, however, is the only company that continues to offer the combination of induction and ultrasonic testing.

Speno has marketed its VUR-505 rail-inspection car, which performs ultrasonic rail testing, on the world market. Its system uses a probe carrier to hold eight different ultrasonic projectors to scan for various types of defects. One probe scans for horizontal fissures; a bank of four probes, each set at 70-degree range, searches for transverse fissures throughout the entire rail profile; another probe set at 55 degrees looks for longitudinal defects; and a pair of 35-degree probes is reserved to examine bolt holes for stress cracks. Instead of a liquid-filled roller search unit (RSU), Speno sprays a continuous film of water bridging the gap between the probe heads and the rail surface to allow for optimum sonic wave transmission. As a result, these detection cars must carry a large water tank, which is designed to carry enough water for about 95 miles of uninterrupted testing. The sound-reflection data are processed and interpreted using a specialized computer. An audio warning indicates when a serious rail defect has been located, and an onboard spray gun automatically marks the location of defects. For later reference the onboard computer prints a hard copy of the rail profile. The VUR-505 is designed to operate at about 25 mph and requires a four-person crew.

The frequency of rail inspection varies greatly depending on the type and density of traffic over a line. American Class 1 carriers may employ Sperry once or twice a year as part of a routine maintenance program. One of the most intensive ultrasonic rail-inspection regimens is on Australia's BHP Iron Ore line, where trains have an abnormally high axle loading of more than 40 tons (based on the 2,000-pound U.S. ton) and operate up to 240 cars on a single train. Here ultrasonic testing is performed about every 10 days. This strict maintenance regime keeps rail failures at a minimum on a line that carries some of the world's heaviest trains in regular operation.

—Brian Solomon

REFERENCES

Hughes, Thomas Parke. *Elmer Sperry: Inventor and Engineer.* Baltimore: Johns Hopkins Univ. Press, 1971.

Solomon, Brian. *Railway Maintenance Equipment.* Osceola, Wis.: MBI, 2001.

Rail Revitalization and Regulatory Reform Act (4R Act). *See* REGULATION

Railroad Costs: Their Nature, Uses, and Effects

Knowledge of costs and the methods for measuring them are indispensable for effective and efficient management of railroads. Decisions requiring cost data span all sectors of a rail carrier's business. They involve choices concerning operation and marketing of the carrier's service and the sizing of its capital asset base.

Operations and marketing-related choices include service frequency (number of trains to be run within a specific period of time); pricing of services (setting of freight rates and passenger fares and ancillary charges to customers); personnel available to handle customer inquiries; maintenance of motive power and rolling stock, and of track, bridges, communication and signal equipment,

buildings, and other infrastructure (fixed-plant) components; and the scope and intensity of marketing and sales initiatives. Capital asset choices encompass acquisition and retirement of all types of physical durables (i.e., items with a life cycle of more than one year) such as track, bridges, locomotives and cars, maintenance-of-way machinery, buildings, signal, and communication systems.

The need for cost knowledge extends beyond railroad managerial personnel. Such knowledge is also vital for the guidance of actions by investors, creditors, government regulators and taxing agencies, freight shippers, and other outside parties concerned with rail systems' economic and financial performance and condition.

Railroad operating costs are multifaceted. They can be viewed from many different vantage points, and can be classified in different ways. One way of looking at railroad costs is by type of expense category, and by the proportion that each category represents in relation to total costs, as depicted in Table 1 for U.S. Class I freight railroads in 2002.

These expenses depict costs of railway operation as calculated on the basis of generally accepted principles of financial accounting. Financial accounting endeavors to measure the performance and condition of a business firm from a historical vantage point and within a specific period of time, such as a fiscal year. (In contrast to financial accounting, managerial accounting provides data for economic decision making within a current and forward-looking perspective.) Under this approach, only those expenses judged to have been incurred for the generation of revenue from railway operations in that period are recognized as expenses. Hence, the $3.19 billion of depreciation reported for Class I freight railroads in Table 1 represents an apportionment of capital expenditures made in past years for assets with useful service lives expected to extend over periods longer than the years in which they were acquired. This means that the capital expenditures that a railroad makes in any particular year are not

Table 1. Railroad Costs by Expense Categories, 2002

Expense Category	Amount (millions of dollars)	Percent of Total
Labor costs, including wages, benefits, and payroll taxes	$11,476	37.67
Locomotive fuel	3,191	10.48
Loss and damage, injuries and insurance	976	3.20
Depreciation	3,192	10.48
Income taxes on ordinary income	538	1.76
Provision for deferred taxes	1,076	3.53
All other expenses	10,016	32.88
Total	$30,465	100.00

counted as operating costs in that year. Instead, they are entered on the railroad's balance sheet as assets. Then, over the years of their estimated service lives, they are moved "bit-by-bit" from the balance sheet to the railroad's income statement, where they appear as depreciation expense (a charge against income).

Thus, for example, if a railroad acquired a locomotive on December 31, 2000, for $1.5 million, the $1.5 million would be included in the asset values listed on the railroad's balance sheet for the year 2000. Assuming that the locomotive is judged to have an estimated service life of 15 years, and that the railroad's accountants calculate depreciation on a straight-line basis, $100,000 of depreciation expense ($1,500,000 ÷ 15) would be deducted from the locomotive's balance sheet value and entered as an expense item in the railroad's income statements for each of the next 15 years. After the end of the 15-year depreciation period for the locomotive, no amount of value for it would appear on the railroad's balance sheet (even if the railroad continued to own the locomotive).

Another way of viewing railroad operating costs is by the several basic functional and physical elements required for the conduct of railroad operation. They are transportation, which encompasses train and engine crew wages and benefits, fuel, and other costs of train operation; equipment, such as locomotives and freight cars; way and structures, including track, bridges, buildings, and other site-fixed facilities; and general and administrative expenses. Table 2 shows their magnitude and composition for U.S. Class I railroads in 2001.

It is important in a discussion of railroad costs to distinguish between accounting costs and economic costs. Accounting costs are costs that are represented by past or completed financial transactions for the purchase of all types of material items and human resource services required for the conduct of all aspects of a railroad's business. Economic costs are the *future* costs of choosing one alternative over another. In the locomotive acquisition example presented above, suppose that the railroad's need for the locomotive ended unexpectedly after seven years of use. Since at that point in time $800,000 of the locomotive's original purchase price would remain in the company's capital asset account and on its balance sheet, the railroad's financial accountant would view the locomotive's value as $800,000. If, however, the railroad's *only* alternative would be to sell the locomotive for $250,000, the economic cost of keeping it would be $250,000, that is, the value forgone or the opportunity cost incurred by not selling it. In this situation, the undepreciated $800,000 balance of the locomotive's original cost has become irrelevant in an economic sense.

The concept of opportunity cost bears on virtually every decision made in managing every sector of a railroad's activity. One example involves determination of priority for use of track capacity: some types of freight traffic are seen as more profitable, and their customers more sensitive to timeliness of delivery, than others. If trains carrying such traffic were ordered to take siding (or delay departure from initial terminals) in preference to others carrying less remunerative and less time-sensitive commodities, the railroad might well incur an opportunity cost through loss of the higher-profit traffic and its revenue to a competing carrier.

A distinction of critical importance to the analysis of railroad costs is the difference between fixed or constant and variable costs. Fixed costs (often called overhead costs, indirect expenses, fixed expenses, or burden) are costs that do not vary in relation to changes in the quantity and/or quality of service that a railroad produces within a specific period of time. In contrast, variable costs (sometimes called direct expenses or prime costs) are costs that vary with changes in the volume of a railroad's business activity. Measures of such activity include number of trains operated, carload shipments moved, tons of freight carried, number of passengers carried, freight ton-miles (ton-kilometers) produced, and passenger-miles (passenger-kilometers) produced.

Determination of a railroad's total cost of doing business within a specific period of time, such as a 12-month fiscal year or some multiple thereof, is relatively straightforward. However, the task of costing or cost-finding in a rail firm, that is, assigning, tracing, or allocating specific elements or portions of a railroad's total costs to specific categories of its business activity, is difficult. This difficulty stems from the fact that relatively large portions of a railroad's total costs are indivisible. That is, they cannot be identified or linked with specific individual rail production (output) and sales units (e.g., individual trainloads and carloads) on the basis of clearly observable and unambiguously measurable cause-and-effect relationships.

These indivisible or non–casually traceable costs arise from the conditions of commonality and jointness under which most individual units of railroad service are produced. To illustrate, mainline track typically is used for the movement of three basic types of freight trains: mixed freights, or general-service freight trains; unit trains; and intermodal trains. Some sections of mainline track also host the movement of intercity and/or commuter (suburban) passenger trains. The costs of maintaining the track and related signal and communications facilities are "common" to all trains of all types that use the track. Other common costs include administrative overhead,

Table 2. Railroad Costs by Functional and Physical Elements, 2001

	Amount (thousands of dollars)	Percent of Total
Transportation	$13,309,186	45.64
Equipment	7,180,965	24.62
Way and structures	5,127,429	17.58
General and administrative	3,546,287	12.16
Total	$29,163,867	100.00

ranging from transportation department costs such as the wages and salaries of train dispatchers, trainmasters, and superintendents who manage train movements to the salaries of senior executives charged with leading the overall rail enterprise. Some common costs are fixed in relation to changes in rail traffic volume, some are partially fixed or semivariable, and some are variable.

Categories of cost that at face appear to be common and thus indivisible can sometimes be traced or assigned on the basis of causal evidence to particular types of trains. In the case of track carrying both freight and passenger trains, accommodation of the latter might require a different and higher-cost signal system than if only freight trains were operated. The difference in cost between the type of signal system required for freight-only operation and that required for passenger train movements can be assigned to the passenger service on a causal basis. However, within the passenger service category, this amount becomes a cost common to all of the passenger trains operated. It cannot be assigned on a causal basis to each individual passenger train (but could be allocated to each train by means of gross averaging). In the case of different types of freight trains, engineering-based studies can be conducted in an attempt to identify differences in impact on track structure (rail, ties, and ballast), and on bridges for the purpose of attempting to obtain causal evidence of the cost impacts of each type of train (e.g., heavily loaded unit coal trains versus less heavily loaded intermodal trains). As with the passenger example, however, any differential costs that might be causally identified with a particular type or category of freight train are common to all trains *within* that category and hence indivisible and assignable to each train only by gross averaging.

Cost indivisibility is greatest in the operation of mixed or general-service freight trains. Mixed freight trains can and do carry many different types of commodities in different types of freight cars that have different ownership and maintenance costs. Such trains can be either through freight trains, running nonstop or almost so between major classification yards, or they can be local freight trains that pick up and set out loaded and empty cars at shippers' private sidings and, in some instances, at interchanges with other railroads. The costs of mainline track are incurred in common for each individual carload or multiple carload freight consignment moved over that track. In addition to mainline track, both through freight and local freight train operations require relatively extensive yard and related terminal facilities, and operation of switching locomotives within yards to make up or build outbound trains and break apart and sort the cars of inbound trains. Many if not most of the capital, maintenance, and operating costs of yard and terminal facilities are *incurred in common* for all individual train and freight car movements handled through those facilities.

Among working railroaders, the term *joint costs* is often used in reference to costs that have been characterized in the preceding paragraphs as common costs. Thus, costs of providing track used by both passenger and freight trains are said to be joint between passenger and freight service. Another application of the term is to denote costs incurred in the provision of joint facilities, that is, trackage and related infrastructure shared by two or more rail carriers. Still another use of the term (more often by economists than by rail employees) is in reference to costs incurred in joint-product situations.

A true joint-product situation, as seen by economists, is that in which the production of one item or service necessarily or unavoidably also results in the production of another. Under this definition, the only true joint-product in a railroad is the backhaul, which occurs because of (and as an inescapable by-product of) the production or operation of a front-haul movement. The cost of the empty-return movement thus is viewed as being joint (and hence also indivisible) with the cost of the front-haul movement. In contrast to joint costs, common costs are seen by economists as costs incurred for the production of two or more units of a good or service, with production of any one particular unit (such as one among many individual carload consignments moved within a mixed or general-service freight train) neither causing, nor resulting from, the production of another.

The presence of relatively large proportions of indivisible costs vis-à-vis causally identifiable (divisible or traceable) costs within the overall cost structures of most rail firms has exerted heavy influence on rail pricing practices ever since the inception of the railroad industry. That is, given that indivisible costs comprise the dominant portion of a railroad's total costs, the causally identifiable or divisible costs (also termed variously as marginal, incremental, direct, prime, and out-of-pocket costs) of handling each of the individual carload and trainload units of traffic within the railroad's total traffic base will, when added together, be substantially smaller than the carrier's total costs. Thus, if the railroad were to set its freight rates and/or passenger fares (prices) on all or a significant portion of its total traffic at levels equal to or slightly above the causally identifiable costs of handling individual units of traffic, the railroad would fail to generate total revenues in an amount sufficient to cover total costs and hence incur a deficit (i.e., total indivisible costs + total divisible or causally identifiable costs = total costs = revenue required to break even). To counteract the risk of insufficient revenue posed by its inability to causally trace a significant proportion of total costs to individual traffic sales units, the railroad will be compelled to try to extract as much revenue as it can from each category or type of traffic that it carries. Rates charged for freight service will therefore vary with the differences (as perceived by rail pricing officers) between individual freight transportation customers or customer groups' ability and willingness to pay for the railroad's service.

This form of pricing has traditionally been referred to as either "value-of-service pricing" or "charging what the traffic will bear." More recently, it has come to be called "differential pricing," "demand-based pricing," and "value pricing" by persons involved with its practice. Economists term it "price discrimination," "discriminatory pricing," "differential pricing," or "Ramsey pricing." They define it technically as occurring under two circumstances. The first is when a railroad (or any other form of business) charges different prices to different buyers or buyer groups in situations where the railroad's unit costs of serving each buyer or buyer group are identical or almost so. The second is when a railroad charges identical prices to each buyer or buyer group when the railroad's costs of serving them differ.

Differentiation in rail freight pricing can and does occur between (1) types of commodities transported, (2) locations served, (3) times at which service is provided, (4) direction of movement, and (5) persons or entities served. Railroads traditionally have tried to charge higher rates for moving commodities with relatively high market values than for lower value commodities (e.g., new automobiles versus steel scrap). This approach works relatively well when a railroad faces little or no competition from another railroad and/or carriers in other modes of transport. It must be emphasized, however, that not all commodity-based differences in rail freight rates are demand or market-power driven. Higher-value commodities can require higher-cost levels of service in the form of greater speed and specialized rolling stock (e.g., freight cars equipped with special load-restraining devices and cushioning mechanisms to protect lading against damage from the shock of coupling of cars in switching and slack action in line-haul freight train operation). Movements of higher-value commodities as well as fragile products and perishables such as fresh fruits and vegetables also impose higher costs on a railroad by exposing it to greater risk of having to compensate shippers for loss-and-damage stemming from theft, rough handling, accidents, and product spoilage. Similarly, a railroad's risk costs are higher for the transport of hazardous commodities due to the injury to persons and damage to property and the environment that can result from fire, explosion, and release of toxins.

Differentiation between locations served by a carrier (place or spatial discrimination) occurs when the carrier charges different rates for moving the same commodity over different segments of its network (and where the differences in rates cannot be explained by differences in segment operating and capital costs). An historic example of demand-driven rate differentiation based on time-of-service provision occurred in 1959, when the opening of the St. Lawrence Seaway threatened diversion of export and import freight traffic from joint rail-water movements via East Coast ports to all-water movements via Great Lakes ports. Upon the opening of the seaway, the former New York Central Railroad (NYC), which linked Chicago with the ports of New York and Boston, reduced its rates on export-import freight traffic during the seaway navigation season. During winter closure of the seaway, the NYC's export-import freight rates reverted to higher levels. A classic example of differential pricing by direction of movement is the charging of relatively low rates designed to attract so-called backhaul traffic and revenue and reduce or eliminate empty-return movements of rolling stock.

Differentiation by persons or entities (personal discrimination) occurs when a carrier charges different rates to different shippers of the same commodity in instances where the carrier's costs of serving each shipper are the same or substantially so. Personal discrimination by railroads became illegal per se in 1887, when the railway industry was made subject to federal economic regulation. However, legalization of contract rail rates with the post-1975 reductions in economic regulation of the rail industry made it possible for railroads to once again engage legally in personal discrimination. The terms of contract rail rates apply to particular movements of traffic for particular shippers, and are secret between the railroad and the shipper to which they apply. A railroad is free within the limits of its bargaining power (and modest residual federal regulatory power, if exercised) to charge whatever contract rates it can obtain from each shipper with which it deals, regardless of the type of commodity carried or the points served.

Cost indivisibility does not stand alone as a key driver of pricing and other dimensions of railroad marketing and related operating policies and practices. Its influence is exerted in tandem with three other conditions: economies of scale, economies of density, and economies of scope.

Economies of scale exist when a larger-sized production unit, such as a locomotive, a train, a freight yard, or a passenger terminal, can produce rail service at a lower cost per unit than two or more smaller production units. Economies of density occur when an increase in the utilization of a production unit that is fixed in size or capacity results in lower cost per unit than two or more smaller production units. Economies of scope ensue when an increase in the range of a railroad's service offerings or markets served results in a decrease in the railroad's unit costs.

Thus, as illustration, economies of scale are manifested in the situation where one 4,000-horsepower-capacity locomotive working at an optimum or desired level of performance (as measured by some combination of speed and tonnage moved) can produce freight or passenger service at less cost per ton-mile/ton-kilometer than two 2,000-horsepower locomotives running in multiple (and working at a level of performance deemed optimal for locomotives of their size). In contrast, economies of density result when the cost per unit of service produced decreases as utilization of the locomotive's horsepower capacity increases. This decline in unit cost results from a spreading of the locomotive's capital, operation, and maintenance costs over an increasing number of units of freight or passenger service produced by operation of the locomotive. Economies of scope prevail when a railroad's average cost of producing service decreases as it expands its service territory and/or increases the variety of types of traffic carried within its system.

The existence of economies of scale and economies of

density at the locomotive, freight and passenger car, and train operating unit levels underpins the growth trend in locomotive, car, and train size that has prevailed since the beginning of the railway industry. Realization of these economies through the increases in productivity underlying them has provided the incentive for many generations of rail managers to prefer operation of longer and heavier rather than shorter and lighter freight trains. This quest for minimization of unit costs at the train operating unit level can contribute, and has contributed, to the freight railroad industry's continued viability in the face of severe competition from other modes of transport, and in offsetting the burden of increasing costs of doing business in areas such as wages, salaries, employee benefits, and locomotive fuel. However, focus on cost minimization at the train operating unit level, to the exclusion of its impacts on attraction and retention of revenues from rail customers, can exert a negative impact on rail operating profit and even threaten a rail carrier's existence. That is, if operation of freight trains of lengths and weights sufficient to achieve minimum direct total and unit costs requires the holding of shipments in yards until trains of sufficient size can be made up, shippers will receive lower-quality service in the form of slower transit time and less consistent delivery time, as well as increased loss and damage to lading stemming from the more severe slack action–induced shock associated with operations of very long trains. This raises the probability of loss of rail traffic and revenue to competitors. Also, less frequent and irregular train operation can increase other categories of costs by reducing the productivity of rolling stock and motive power through higher levels of idle time.

Near the close of the 1990s, some railroads began to scrutinize the full array of costs resulting from unscheduled maximum-tonnage freight-train operation. They concluded that a shift toward scheduled operation would yield lower total costs and improve opportunities for maintaining and growing revenue and net profitability by raising service quality to levels more competitive with trucking. Other railroads have since reached and acted on the same conclusions.

Despite these changes, however, other policies and practices exist that raise questions about rail managers' use of unit cost data. They involve the setting of high minimum quantities for individual rail shipments of bulk commodities, including coal.

Coal, when transported from mines to electric power stations, steel mills, and ocean ports (for export), has come to be moved almost exclusively in trainload lot–sized shipments totaling 10,000 tons or more. Order quantities of such size fit the consumption requirements of coal buyers in these markets. However, they are too large for many buyers of industrial coal, that is, coal used in manufacturing plants, steam-heat and smaller-sized electric generating plants operated by universities, prisons, and other institutions, and in various miscellaneous applications such as kilns for lime processing and cement production.

Rail deliveries of coal to these smaller buyers were common in the days before unit trains came to dominate rail coal movements. More recently, they have become difficult or impossible to make, regardless of what a shipper might be willing and able to pay for rail service, because of the establishment of minimum shipment sizes (e.g., 25 or more cars, moved in one block) by some Class I railroads that exceed the economic order quantity limits of smaller buyers.

These Class I carriers reportedly have declined to participate in interline industrial coal movements in shipment sizes of from one to about 15 cars that have been proposed by other railroads with which they connect. Personnel on the connecting railroads contend that the small movements would be profitable for all participants and that personnel on the Class I carriers have rejected them out of hand because they have become mesmerized by the economies of scale of large unit trains.

The immediate lesson from this in an entry on railroad costs is not who is right and who is wrong. Rather, it is that careful evaluation of the economic desirability of particular movements of rail traffic between particular pairs of points requires the application of methods that will reveal the causally identifiable costs specific to those movements (and relate them to the revenue that the movements will generate). Decision making based on systemwide or regional average costs, or on the belief that rail traffic is economically worthwhile only if moved under cost conditions distinctive to unit-train operation, might well result in the rejection of profitable traffic and missed opportunities for capturing new traffic that will contribute to long-term growth of rail business.

—John C. Spychalski

REFERENCES

Achworth, Sir William M. *The Elements of Railway Economics.* Rev. ed. Oxford: Oxford University Press, 1924.

Keeler, Theodore E. *Railroads, Freight, and Public Policy.* Washington, D.C.: The Brookings Institution, 1988.

Milne, A. M., and J. C. Laight. *The Economics of Inland Transport.* 2nd ed. London: Sir Isaac Pitman & Sons, 1963.

Talley, Wayne K. "Costing Theory and Processes." In *Handbook of Logistics and Supply Chain Management*, ed. A. M. Brewer, K. J. Button, and D. A. Hensher, 313–323. Oxford: Pergamon/Elsevier Science, 2001.

Wilson, George W. *Essays on Some Unsettled Questions in the Economics of Transportation.* Bloomington: Foundation for Business Studies, Indiana University, 1962.

Railroad Engineering

Civil Engineering

Railroad engineering began in England, but it was soon adopted by railroad builders on the other side of the Atlantic and developed in uniquely American ways, suitable to the formidable tasks of building a railroad system across the vast North American continent. The technical challenges were demanding enough, but engineers also had to learn to build their lines cheaply because of the shortage of capital. For, unlike Britain, where railroads were built to serve an already-developed population base and industry, American railroads were built largely to bring civilization to the vast open spaces of the North American interior and the West. Until that process occurred, there would be too little traffic to finance the debt service that would be required for railway lines built to the advanced English standards. Consequently, American railway lines, though much longer than those in England, did not achieve the same level of performance until after the U.S. Civil War.

To a remarkable degree, the building of the railroads and the internal improvements—roads and canals—that preceded them nurtured the new profession of civil engineering in the nineteenth century. Most of the earliest trained engineers came from the U.S. Military Academy at West Point, the first American educational institution to offer a technical education. The U.S. Army made its engineers available to early road, canal, and railroad projects. The engineering corps that built the pioneer Baltimore & Ohio, for example, included West Pointers George W. Whistler and William Gibbs McNeill, both of whom went on to other notable achievements in early railroad building. The U.S. Army's Topographical Corps mapped and planned many of the routes that would be followed by the growing railroad system, including the Pacific railroad survey of 1853–1855, which studied alternate transcontinental routes.

Soon other schools took up the teaching of engineering. Rensselaer Polytechnic Institute at Troy, New York, established in 1824, was the first nonmilitary engineering school in the United States. Theodore Judah, who would find a route for the Central Pacific across California's Sierra Nevada, studied there. Other trained engineers came from the technical schools of Europe. Such noted early bridge engineers as Albert Fink and John A. Roebling were trained in German technical schools. Many more of these early American engineers were self-taught, with little or no formal technical education at all. Bridge builders William Howe, a farmer, and Wendell Bollman, a carpenter, were among their number.

These early engineers quickly acquired the skills and experience needed for the location and construction of railroads that could be quickly and economically built. They transformed bridge engineering from a trial-and-error art to an analytical science, fathered modern structural engineering practice, and advanced the development of structural materials. They developed the methods and machines that changed tunneling from a hand-drilling and black-powder-blasting art to a modern technology of shields and tunnel-boring machines. As the North American railroad network was substantially completed during the late nine-

teenth and early twentieth centuries, the responsibilities of railroad civil engineers gradually shifted from a primary emphasis on construction to maintenance-of-way—the inspection and maintenance of bridges, tunnels, and other structures and the improvement, maintenance, and renewal of track.

American civil engineers formed the first national engineering society on November 5, 1852, when 12 engineers gathered in New York to organize the American Society of Civil Engineers and Architects, later the American Society of Civil Engineers (ASCE). Appropriately, the society's first president was the prominent railroad engineer James Laurie.

—William D. Middleton

Mechanical Engineering

Military engineering and its civilian counterpart, civil engineering, served as the progenitors of the engineering profession. One of the first offspring was a specialty field related to the design and construction of machines. In parallel with civil engineering, the first practitioners of machine design used intuition and experimentation to develop a body of knowledge in mechanical art. Although they had already developed the cars for passengers and freight that were pulled by animals and even by humans, these early mechanical engineers gained everlasting recognition as developers of the first successful machine for producing power, the stationary steam engine spawned by the Industrial Revolution during the early part of the eighteenth century. The first steam engine to be used commercially was developed by Thomas Newcomen in 1724. At the time of his death in 1729 there were hundreds of these primitive engines at work in England and Europe.

James Watt of Scotland was an early inventor and steam-engine innovator. His first successful engine was built in 1781, and he soon became part owner of Boulton & Watt, the largest engine manufacturer in England. By 1800 they had constructed over 500 engines. Richard Trevithick, Jr., developed an early steam locomotive in 1804. George Stephenson, a practical man with no formal education, but with great instincts as a mechanical designer, perfected current locomotive designs and became the first to build a commercially successful steam locomotive in 1814. With his son Robert he founded the world's first locomotive works in 1825.

English-built locomotives first came to America in 1829 in the form of the seven-ton *Stourbridge Lion*, which proved to be too heavy for the primitive rails on the Delaware & Hudson Canal and Railway and was immediately rebuilt as a stationary boiler. Although over 120 English steam locomotives crossed the Atlantic during the 1830s, American designers and machinists immediately grasped the importance of railway travel and began producing their own designs. Early builders were led by Matthias Baldwin of Philadelphia and also included another Philadelphian, William Norris, along with Thomas Rogers of Patterson, New Jersey.

By the 1850s over 150 American locomotive builders were at work throughout the nation. There were also as many builders of railway cars, with each builder specializing in only one or two types of freight cars. Nor did many companies try to build both passenger and freight cars. Most early companies were wiped out by the national financial panic of 1857, and by 1930 the number of locomotive builders had diminished to three major companies (Alco, Baldwin, and Lima), which constructed the majority of American steam locomotives after 1900. Although many railroad shops made small numbers of engines for their own use, the Pennsylvania Railroad's shops at Altoona became the largest proprietary builder. The number of car builders stabilized at a higher level (approximately a dozen) than engine builders because of their specialization.

By the twentieth century growing numbers of formally trained mechanical engineers began to develop a greater knowledge of combustion and thermodynamics, as well as stresses in boilers and running gear, mechanical properties, and the like. By the mid-twentieth century American-built locomotives were the largest and most technically advanced anywhere. They were exported to developing countries around the world and powered America's railways through World War II.

The mechanical engineering profession gained national recognition in November 1880 when the American Society of Mechanical Engineers (ASME) was organized in New York City by 50 leading practitioners. English mechanical engineers had organized their society in 1847.

—J. Parker Lamb

Electrical Engineering

A third major engineering discipline emerged in the last half of the nineteenth century as electrical experimenters in both North America and Europe began to develop useful applications of the science of electricity to communications, lighting, machinery, and transportation. Railroads were among the early users of the new electrical technology. Samuel F. B. Morse's telegraph was first used for train dispatching in 1851 on the Erie Railroad. Signaling and train lighting were other applications that were later taken up. Early experiments with the use of electricity for motive power included a battery-operated locomotive developed by Dr. Charles Grafton Page that made a trial trip over the Baltimore & Ohio's Washington branch in 1854, a generator-powered electric railway constructed by Dr. Ernst Werner von Siemens at the 1879 Berlin Industrial Exhibition, and several experimental electric locomotives developed by Stephen D. Field and Thomas Edison around 1880 to 1882. During the 1880s the work of Leo Daft, Charles J. Van Depoele, Frank J. Sprague, and others brought the electric operation of

street railways to a commercially practical level, and over the next decade the technology was being applied to railroad motive power as well, beginning with the successful electrification of the Baltimore & Ohio's Howard Street Tunnel at Baltimore in 1895. The requirements of these heavy-duty installations brought significant developments in the technology of power generation, transmission, and conversion. During the last half of the twentieth century the responsibilities of railroad electrical and electronics engineers were greatly expanded with the application of computers to a wide range of administrative, analysis, and control tasks; electronic data transmission; electronically controlled braking systems; locomotive diagnostic systems; and sophisticated new signaling systems.

As the electrical industry began its rapid growth in the last quarter of the nineteenth century, 25 prominent electrical engineers, among them Thomas Edison and Elihu Thomson, proposed the formation of a professional society to promote their growing discipline, leading to the formation of the American Institute of Electrical Engineers (AIEE) at New York on May 13, 1884. The AIEE merged with the Institute of Radio Engineers in 1963 to create the present-day Institute of Electrical and Electronics Engineers (IEEE).

—**William D. Middleton**

Railroad Hotels and Resorts

In order to make long-distance travel practical before the advent of a national sleeping car network, the railroads built hotels at division points. By the 1930s most of these were rendered uneconomical and functionally obsolete by the Depression, shortened train schedules, and increased automotive use.

Railroad hotels and eating houses date from the industry's first generation of expansion, 1840 to 1860. The establishments were intended to accommodate the need for food and lodging as travel distances increased. Although they were an indispensable adjunct to rail terminals, there was no pattern to their management. As many as not were company operated and often also served as resorts.

The trunk-line railroads, which linked East Coast cities with the Midwest, developed the most extensive operations. Their example soon set the model for the nation. The Erie, Baltimore & Ohio, and Pennsylvania located their establishments at intervals of some 150 miles. PRR, for example, operated hotels at Bryn Mawr (Bryn Mawr Hotel, 1872), Mifflin (Patterson House, 1852), Altoona (Logan House, 1854), Cresson (Mountain House, 1881), Latrobe (Gilchrest House, ca. 1853), and Pittsburgh (Union Depot Hotel, destroyed 1877). However, the fourth major trunk line, the New York Central, operated few hotels because its line followed a commercial corridor already well established by the Erie Canal (1825).

Although European railroad terminals often incorporated hotels (e.g., London, St. Pancras, 1868), comparatively few in the United States followed suit. The singular noteworthy example was St. Louis Union Station (1893).

West of Chicago, Fred Harvey began his famous alliance with the Atchison, Topeka & Santa Fe (AT&SF) at Topeka, Kansas, in 1876. Still, it was Southern Pacific's Hotel Del Monte at Monterey, California, opened in June 1880, that set the prototype for the industry's most enduring (and remunerative) venture into the lodging business. Del Monte's purposeful mix of spectacular natural setting and premium service catered to prosperous tourists. Its business objective was to spur development, and thereby rail traffic, in and to California. Ironically, by contrast, Harvey's first tourist hotel, the Montezuma at Las Vegas, New Mexico, proved a business failure and was sold in 1901.

Various railroad and business alliances built upon SP's model. Noteworthy were the Raymond at Pasadena, Cali-

Mindful of the great scenic potential of the Canadian Pacific's crossing of British Columbia, CPR president William Van Horne made provisions for it from the beginning. Just west of the CPR's crossing of Rogers Pass in the Selkirks, the railroad built the Glacier Hotel overlooking the great Illecillewaet Glacier in 1886. The hotel was closed in 1930, but Canada's Glacier National Park remains. The drawing was made from a photograph by William Notman of Montreal for the August 3, 1889, issue of *Harper's Weekly*. —Middleton Collection

fornia, opened in 1886, Hotel Del Coronado at San Diego (1888), and C&O's Greenbrier, West Virginia (1910). Likewise, Henry M. Flagler developed Florida by building hotels along the Atlantic Coast, beginning with the Hotel Ponce de Leon at St. Augustine, Florida (1888), and the Royal Poinciana at Palm Beach (1893).

A natural extension of SP's initiative was the railroads' role in the development of the national parks system. Here Northern Pacific & Yellowstone Park Improvement Co. pioneered, opening the National Hotel at Mammoth Hot Springs, Yellowstone, in 1883. The initiative matured some 20 years later with NP's Old Faithful Inn at Yellowstone and AT&SF–Fred Harvey's Hotel El Tovar on the Grand Canyon's south rim (both 1904–1905).

Many railroad establishments retained a substantial business long after their utility had been supplanted by the adoption of dining-car (1882, PRR) and sleeping-car service during the 1880s. Noteworthy were Erie's Starrucca House at Susquehanna, Pennsylvania, some 8 miles west of its namesake viaduct, SP's iconic station and springhouse at Shasta Springs, California, and PRR's Logan House, which operated through World War II.

As of this writing, the B&O hotel at Grafton, West Virginia, sits vacant awaiting disposition. Hotel Del Coronado continues to operate its original wood-framed structure, now a designated national historic landmark. And a new sort of railroad hotel has recently emerged: that catering to rail enthusiasts, modeled on the Station Inn, which adjoins the historic Norfolk Southern (PRR) main line at Cresson, Pennsylvania.

Some Notable Hotels and Resorts

The complementary and synergistic relationship of railroad and hotel dates practically from the introduction of travel by the new mode.

Niagara

The first resort to be served by rail was Niagara Falls in the 1830s. Through service began with the 1853 formation of the New York Central Railroad. Even before the advent of the rail mode, Niagara's popularity demonstrated the attraction of the New World's wonders. Witness Horatio Parsons's guide (1835): "The fashionable, the opulent and the learned congregate here from the principal cities of the country." J. W. Orr's *Pictorial Guide to Niagara* of 1842 concurred: "The wonderful cataract of Niagara, the most grand and sumptuous natural curiosity in the world, is annually visited by so many thousands of people from the different countries of Europe and America." By 1842 a railroad connected Buffalo and the falls, a distance of 22 miles, "propelled by steam and making two trips daily."

Advertised as "the Queen of Wonders," Niagara furnished overnight accommodations for about 4,000 as late as 1938. Michigan Central, whose first ads featured the suspension bridge, still paused its trains at the Falls View station on the Canadian side, while the New York Central ran the famous "layover" sleeping car en route from New York to Chicago.

Saratoga Springs

The popular watering place or spa at Saratoga, New York, followed Niagara within a decade. Saratoga's first hotel dates from 1802. Through rail service from New York City was established in the summer of 1836, taking 16 to 18 hours. By 1893 Saratoga had been famed as a resort for over half a century and boasted the largest and finest summer hotels in the world. Its summertime population swelled to 100,000, and it counted upwards of half a million seasonal visitors. The most renowned of Saratoga's 50-odd hotels, the Grand Union and the United States, slept thousands and offered acres of ballrooms, verandas, and lawns. Activity peaked at the racing season, which opened in mid-July. Accordingly, it enjoyed a more developed railroad service than any similar resort.

Among the resort's most prominent promoters was New York Central's general passenger agent, George H. Daniels, who dubbed it "the World's Greatest Watering Place, Queen of Spas." Popular demand prompted Daniels to introduce the *Saratoga Limited* in 1896. One of the finest and fastest trains in the nation, it reached New York City in 4 hours, a carding second only to the *Empire State Express*.

California

Out west the first railroad-owned resort was SP's Hotel Del Monte at Monterey, California, opened in June 1880. Modeled after European spas, its two-story Swiss-Gothic structure accommodated 500 guests. Designed with the objective of inducing its wealthy guests to settle and develop California, it scored an immediate success. In no time Del Monte spawned a flood of imitators, many planned and operated in close association with the two major California railroads. A deteriorating Del Monte served as a naval hospital in World War II, only to be demolished soon thereafter. Today the famous Pebble Beach golf club occupies its grounds.

The Raymond and the Green at Pasadena set the foremost example of rail/hotel synergy. The Raymond, the first great hotel to be built in Pasadena, opened on November 17, 1886. Set on a site chosen for its view and proximity to the tracks, it became a mecca for winter tourists. Its namesake and proprietor, Walter Raymond (1851–1934), was the son of Emmons Raymond, who with I. A. Whitcomb organized the well-known Boston excursion agency in 1879. The firm's first California excursion dates from 1882. The hotel closed in 1933. The Green, which directly adjoined the AT&SF depot, was also named for its proprietor, Colonel G. G. Green. Green acquired and expanded the property in 1891 from Edward C. Webster, who had built a depot for the railroad on the condition that it move its offices to the hotel; both opened in 1887.

"Golf in California, under summer skies in midwinter," advertised the Santa Fe in this 1900 scene in the foreground of the company's Hotel Del Coronado at San Diego, drawn by Hardesty G. Maratta. —Michael E. Zega Collection

February 19, 1888, marked the opening of the Hotel Del Coronado, at San Diego, whose original wooden structure operates to this day, a rare testament to vigilant management. It was built by Elisha S. Babcock, Jr., a retired railroad executive, and his partner H. L. Story, who began construction in January 1887. Babcock had purchased land on Coronado Island, a storm-swept wilderness, a few months before the railroad's arrival. Popularly termed "Babcock's folly" while under construction, the hotel was an immediate success. Demand for accommodation of guests of more moderate means prompted the construction of Coronado Tent City in 1902.

AT&SF and Fred Harvey Co.

Perhaps the most influential and best-known railroad restaurants and hotels were those operated by the Fred Harvey Co. in association with the AT&SF. In an era when railroad meals at best were a haphazard affair, London-born Fred Harvey opened his first eating house in 1876 at Topeka, Kansas. He embraced the novel business model of tempting travel rather than discouraging it. His method was straightforward—unwavering maintenance of standards; it caught on immediately.

In 1882 Harvey opened his first hotel, the Montezuma at Las Vegas Hot Springs, New Mexico, after SP's Del Monte the second western resort of note. Harvey died at age 65 in 1901, but his progeny maintained his tradition. By 1915 the firm operated some 65 hotels and restaurants, expanding to a high point of 38 hotels in 1930. Longtime AT&SF advertising manager William H. Simpson attested to his genius, noting, "On almost every piece of AT&SF ad copy is this line: 'Meals by Fred Harvey.'" Hotel El Tovar at the south rim of the Grand Canyon and La Fonda at Santa Fe continue very much in the Harvey Co. tradition today.

Yellowstone National Park

The early years of the twentieth century saw the popularization of active vacations as advocated and personified by President Theodore Roosevelt himself. The trend fostered a new building model: the rustic Old Faithful Inn of 1904 in the log or chalet style popularized by Adirondack camps. AT&SF/Harvey Co.'s El Tovar, at the Grand Canyon (also 1904), Great Northern's Glacier Lodge (1913), and Union Pacific's Bryce and Zion lodges emulated the design.

Northern Pacific and the Yellowstone Park Improvement Co. (characterized by historian Edward Nolan as not quite a subsidiary, but "a private company largely under NP control") opened Yellowstone's first hotel, the National Hotel at Mammoth Hot Springs, in 1883. The famous Old Faithful Inn followed two decades later. Ad copy of 1905 pointed to its innovative design: "It is a structure of boulders and logs, peaks, angles, dormers, French windows, etc., artistically combined. . . . a marvel of ingenuity and comfort," and forecast that it "will become one of the most popular hotels in the country."

Glacier National Park

Great Northern Railway's Glacier Park Lodge opened in May 1913. "Built entirely out of huge logs, four feet in diameter and forty feet long," according to mystery and travel writer Mary Roberts Rinehart, it was personally planned by the line's president Louis W. Hill. By 1915 GN operated two hotels and eight smaller chalets for 50 to 100 guests. One can still visit many of them as of this writing.

Florida

Henry Morrison Flagler's Florida East Coast Railway opened the first resort hotel in Florida, the Hotel Ponce de Leon at St. Augustine, in 1888. It marked "a new era in the building of public inns. . . . the idea of constructing, almost in the heart of the ancient city of St. Augustine, a mammoth hotel reproducing the architecture of the

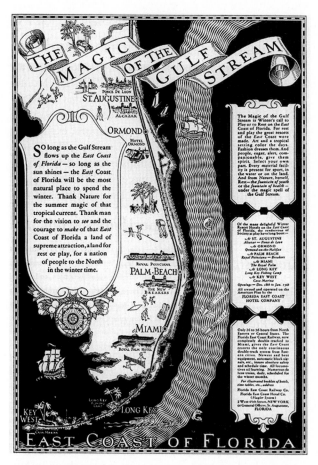

In its 1926 promotion, "The Magic of the Gulf Stream," the Florida East Coast advised of the advantages of the Gulf Stream and the superior winter attractions of the company's resort hotels along the East Coast. —Michael E. Zega Collection

sixteenth century . . . was in itself a bold one; but the successful embodying in it of every detail of that time is something marvelous," said Jacksonville's *Daily News Herald* on January 1, 1888.

Early in January 1888 Flagler inaugurated the *Florida Special* to provide its equivalent in transportation. Together the pair begat a chain of resorts that stretched the length of Florida's Atlantic Coast. Most renowned was 1893's Royal Poinciana at Palm Beach, which boasted its own trestle and private car siding. The title of an 1898 FEC booklet best summed up Flagler's marketing strategy: *The East Coast of Florida Is Paradise Regained.* Constructed primarily of concrete, the Ponce de Leon still stands on the campus of Flagler College.

Virginia

The Virginias counted two early resorts: Virginia Hot Springs at White Sulfur Springs, West Virginia, settled around 1750 and known for its mineral springs, and Old Point Comfort, "a popular bathing and fishing resort" on Chesapeake Bay at the entrance to Hampton Roads. White Sulphur Springs, advertised as "the Saratoga of the South," was served by Chesapeake & Ohio's *F. F. V. Limited* (for

Fast Flying Virginian), one of the first vestibuled trains. The line's famed Greenbrier Hotel opened there in 1910. Although under railroad management only through 1922, it retains a uniquely close association with C&O's corporate heritage.

Canada

Canadian Pacific's Banff Springs Hotel, Alberta, opened in 1888, and Chateau Frontenac, Quebec City (1893), introduced the Canadian Chateau style of architecture that came to symbolize the company.

Other Notable Resorts

Ultraexclusive Bar Harbor on Mt. Desert Island, Maine, termed "a summer center of wealth and fashion" by a 1905 Boston & Maine booklet, remains "one of the most beautiful localities in North America." Its august clientele warranted the introduction of the second train in the nation to feature George Pullman's new vestibule car: the *Mt. Desert Limited* of July 4, 1887. Dubbed the Cyclone for its speed, it operated for only three seasons. Its successor of 1902 proved more durable: the *Bar Harbor Express* continued through 1960.

Both Seaboard Air Line and Southern Railway served Pinehurst, North Carolina, "a natural sanitarium," best known for autumn golfing. SR's booklet *The Land of the Sky* (1901) dates its founding at 1895. The northern New Jersey Atlantic Coast resort towns of Asbury Park, Ocean Grove, and Long Branch, served by the New York & Long Branch, were home to five U.S. presidents, most famously U. S. Grant. Colorado claimed the Antlers at Colorado Springs, operated by the Rio Grande, and the Broadmoor at Manitou, at the foot of Pike's Peak, dubbed by Chicago Rock Island & Pacific "the Saratoga of the West."

—**Michael E. Zega**

REFERENCES

Alexander, Edwin P. *On the Main Line: The Pennsylvania Railroad in the 19th Century*. New York: Clarkson N. Potter, 1971.

Ellis, Hamilton. *The Pictorial Encyclopedia of Railways*. Feltham, Middlesex, U.K.: Hamlyn House, 1968.

Grant, H. Roger, Don L. Hofsommer, and Osmund Overby. *St. Louis Union Station: A Place for People, a Place for Trains*. St. Louis: St. Louis Mercantile Library, 1994.

Joki, Robert. *Saratoga Lost*. Hensonville, N.Y.: Black Dome Press, 1998.

Nolan, Edward W. *Northern Pacific Views: The Railroad Photography of F. Jay Haynes, 1876–1905*. Helena: Montana Historical Society, 1983.

Pangborn, J. G. *Picturesque B. and O.* Chicago: Knight & Leonard, 1883.

Pomeroy, Earl. *In Search of the Golden West*. New York: Alfred A. Knopf, 1957.

Pullman Co. scrapbooks. Newberry Library, Chicago.

Runte, Alfred. *Trains of Discovery*. Niwot, Colo.: Roberts Rinehart, 1990.

Simpson, William Haskell. "Article for Fred Harvey for Printer's [sic] Ink." ca. 1915. Not published. Fred Harvey Co., Papers. Heard Museum, Phoenix, Ariz.

Travelers' Official Railway Guide. New York, June 1870, June 1893, Oct. 1911.

United States Official Hotel Directory. New York, 1886, 1890, 1893.

Wood, J. W. *Pasadena, California, Historical and Personal.* Pasadena, Calif.: Self-published, 1917.

Young, William S. *Starrucca: Bridge of Stone.* N.p.: Privately published, 2002.

Railroad Retirement Acts (1934–1935)

The Railroad Retirement Acts (RRAs) of 1934 and 1935 were important forerunners to the Social Security Act. Enactment of the RRA of 1935 helped lay to rest troubling constitutional issues, the most important of which involved the legality of Congress establishing a mandatory pension system, and it demonstrates the growing willingness of the federal government to assert its power to help stabilize the economy. Enactment of the two bills brought order to an area formerly distinguished by chaos: disjointed and uncoordinated efforts of the private sector, some government agencies, and a few unions to deal with the growing number of elderly Americans. Labor leaders who helped write the railroad legislation also played important roles in helping shape Social Security legislation.

The idea of old-age pensions first gained popularity among reformers during the Progressive Era as demographic and technical changes altered the nation. In response to these changes numerous pension schemes were introduced into Congress, 47 of them before 1929. The power of Congress to administer pensions was a murky issue. Consequently, before the Great Depression none of the pension bills was seriously considered. Pension advocates in the 1930s readily found support for their program, in part because of the diligent work throughout the 1920s to enact pension laws in many states. The most important ally of labor was Senator Robert Wagner (D-N.Y.), who wanted railroad retirement legislation enacted because of its wider implications. Establishing a pension system for railroad workers, who he believed clearly fell under the authority of the federal government, would provide a "laboratory for experiment" and "blaze the way for full treatment of the problem."

Railroad companies had a long history of offering pensions to their employees, and firms in other sectors followed suit. The Baltimore & Ohio Railroad initiated the first pension program in 1884. By the time the federal government took over operation of the nation's rail system late in 1917, 39 carriers operated pension programs. By 1932, 51 Class 1 carriers offered their employees some form of pension plan. However, many operatives, especially those who worked on small carriers not involved in interstate commerce, were not covered. Nationwide, by 1929 the number of firms offering pensions increased to approximately 400, and the number of workers covered rose correspondingly to about 4 million. Between 1929 and Franklin Roosevelt's inauguration many pensioners saw their benefits reduced or their pension system go bankrupt. By 1933 pensions covered less than 15 percent of the American workforce. Many industrial pensions were little more than discretionary awards requiring a working retirement. For instance, pensioners might be called back to work if their former employer was experiencing labor problems. If they refused, their pensions would be cut off.

Unions also had a long history of offering various pension plans. By 1930 approximately 28 percent of the trade unions in the United States and Canada offered pensions, but only 21 percent of members took advantage of the programs. The strict rules of eligibility imposed by unions prevented some interested workers from participating. Of the ten international unions with retirement pensions, four required recipients to be members for 20 years, two required 25 years, and another required 30 years. The plans typically prohibited men from entering the pension department after they had reached a certain age, usually 45 or 50. Like other pension schemes of the day, most union plans were hurriedly drawn up to meet growing demands, and little foresight went into their creation. In other words, they were built on a weak financial foundation.

The Railroad Labor Executives Assn. (RLEA) first addressed the pension question in the spring of 1929, and in the autumn the American Federation of Labor (AFL) went on record as endorsing government-sponsored pensions. As the Great Depression deepened, the idea of national old-age pensions began to gain momentum within the labor movement and the general public. Actions of the RLEA were at first slow and confused, prompted mostly by pressure from the Railroad Employees National Pension Assn. (RENPA), an independent group that was critical of the RLEA for moving slowly on the pension issue, rather than by any firm conviction that pensions were needed.

The Depression forced many operatives to seek employment, often for short periods of time, on other carriers, which made it impossible to qualify for a company pension. This situation also made it difficult to earn a union pension because men were willing to take any available position, including jobs that were not affiliated with their union or were simply nonunion. The RLEA hoped that establishing a national retirement system would allow for continual coverage.

Two railroad retirement bills were introduced in 1932, one sponsored by the RLEA and one by RENPA, but neither had a fighting chance of being enacted. The bills advanced a new idea into American industrial life—that the government mandate that all employees and all companies in a particular field contribute to a fund from which annuities for retired employees would be paid. The preamble of the RLEA-sponsored bill stated that its purpose was "to increase safety and efficiency in interstate transportation service." Questions arose because it was not clear that the legislation fell within the purview of the commerce clause of the Constitution. Closely related to the issue of constitutionality was another important question: Should the federal government pass legislation that so dramatically altered its responsibilities to so many Americans? The following year, with Roosevelt in the White House, the scales tipped slightly in favor of the railroad retirement bill. FDR was not an enthusiastic supporter of railroad pensions, but he did favor federal old-age insurance and as governor of New York had worked to enact state old-age pensions.

In 1934 the Senate sponsors of the two original bills, Wagner and Henry Hatfield (R–W. Va.) reconciled their differences, and this bill became the basis for the Railroad Retirement Act of 1934. The new bill's preamble stated that its purpose was to relieve unemployment in the industry. Hatfield claimed that its passage would allow the retirement of 100,000 aged workers and the immediate hiring of an equal number. By the spring of 1934 many congressmen supported the bill, and the president had given his lukewarm approval. As the congressional debate unfolded, it became apparent that many members, like Wagner, viewed the bill as a precursor to more far-reaching federal retirement legislation. On the Senate floor James J. Davis (R-Pa.) stated, "I think it is reasonable to pioneer in this field in connection with the railroad industry because so many excellent improvements in our social and industrial life have been made possible through it."

The Senate Interstate and Foreign Commerce Committee reported the bill favorably. On June 14, 1934, it passed the Senate 66–0. The most significant features of the bill included compulsory retirement at 65, provided the operative had worked 5 years, or after 30 years of service; each operative would pay 2 percent of his monthly compensation into the annuity fund, an amount that his employer would double; his retirement compensation was to be computed by multiplying 2 percent of his average monthly income by the number of years of service. A three-man board would administer the program. The Railroad Retirement Act passed in the House in only slightly different form, and the Joint Conference Committee quickly resolved the differences. Roosevelt signed the bill into law on June 28.

Opponents immediately challenged the act; 134 Class 1 carriers or their receivers or trustees in bankruptcy, the Pullman Co., the Railway Express Agency, and the Southeastern Express Co. filed suit for the carriers, naming the members of the Railroad Retirement Board as defendants. Chief Justice A. A. Wheat of the Supreme Court of the District of Columbia ruled late in October in favor of the companies, arguing that Congress could pass pension legislation that covered employees engaged in interstate commerce; however, the act went beyond that by covering workers who were employed in intrastate commerce. He also faulted the law because any person who left a carrier within one year before its passage was eligible for an annuity.

The U.S. Supreme Court upheld Wheat, 5-4. The majority argued that the bill was an attempt to create social legislation and therefore fell outside congressional authority as defined by the commerce clause of the Constitution. Further, the majority struck down the taxing mechanism, which it ruled took the carriers' property (money) without due process, and confirmed the lower court's ruling that the law covered workers not engaged in interstate commerce.

Within two weeks Robert Crosser (D-Ohio), one of the original sponsors back in 1932, and Wagner introduced new pension legislation. The mechanics of the pension system remained largely unchanged. The underlying philosophy had been subtly altered, however. Framers based the new legislation upon congressional power to tax, not on its power to regulate interstate commerce. The second Railroad Retirement Act inferred that all employees could be covered because they all were subject to federally imposed taxes. Actually two bills were submitted. One established the machinery of the railroad retirement system, and the second bill, in theory unrelated, created a tax on the pay of railroad operatives and the payrolls of the carriers, to be paid into the U.S. Treasury. The formula used to compute the taxes was essentially unchanged from the overturned retirement law. Roosevelt signed the measure into law on August 29, 1935.

Retirement insurance proponents learned valuable lessons from the failed retirement legislation. The U.S. Supreme Court did not believe that the commerce clause gave Congress the authority to establish pensions, which compelled pension advocates to base the bill on congressional authority to tax. The debate and controversy that surrounded the Railroad Retirement Act was well covered in both the labor press and the regular press and helped educate the public. The court challenge illuminated further faults in the law and helped framers of the Social Security Act avoid similar mistakes. The experience gained from the controversy surrounding the Railroad Retirement Act ensured that the Social Security Act would have an excellent chance of withstanding the inevitable legal challenge.

—Jon R. Huibregtse

REFERENCES

Lubove, Roy. *The Struggle for Social Security*. Cambridge, Mass.: Harvard Univ. Press, 1968.

McCoury, Phillip D. "A Legislative History of the Railroad Retirement Act." Master's thesis, Duke Univ., 1950, 18–23.

Witte, Edwin E. *The Development of the Social Security Act*. Madison: Univ. of Wisconsin Press, 1962.

Railway Assn. of Canada (RAC)

The Railway Assn. of Canada (RAC) is an association of Canadian railroads, including some 60 Class 1 freight line, intercity passenger, tourist, commuter, and shortline and regional railroads with a main-line trackage of about 38,000 miles. Its activities include safety and operations management for Canadian railroads, the conduct of research, policy development, and advocacy to promote to the Canadian government an understanding of railroad advantages and fair treatment among competing modes, and the development of an effective national transportation policy. The RAC's role in the fields of policy and advocacy on behalf of its member railroads was added to the RAC mandate in 2000, which led to its relocation from its previous headquarters at Montreal, Quebec, to the national capital in Ottawa, Ontario.

At the suggestion of the Canadian government, a group of railway executives met on October 23, 1917, as the Canadian Railway War Board to coordinate railway activities during World War I, ensuring efficient movement of troops, war supplies, and services. Having proved its effectiveness, the Railway Assn. of Canada (RAC) was officially established in 1919 and incorporated in 1953. Until its expanded role was established in 2000, the RAC was primarily concerned with member services and safety and operations activities at the national level, and with coordination of standards with the Assn. of American Railroads (AAR) on an international level. The expansion of RAC's role in policy and advocacy in 2000, as well as the impact of such changes as the establishment of the North American Free Trade Agreement in 1994, the privatization of the Canadian National in 1995, and the deregulatory changes imposed by the National Transportation Act of 1987 and the Canada Transportation Act of 1996, have all brought major changes to the association.

The public affairs and governmental relations group is the RAC's advocacy arm. It lobbies for improvements to public policy and regulatory frameworks. Such publications as RAC's *Policy Directions 2001* inform the government, transportation officials, industries, and others of the public policy changes that will be needed to create a highly effective, privately funded railroad network. RAC is promoting eight distinct components toward a new comprehensive Canadian Surface Transportation Policy to create an efficient and competitive intermodal transportation environment. Public investment in infrastructure and Canada's heavy taxation burden are among other important issues. The operations and regulatory affairs group of RAC includes dangerous-goods standards and training, mechanical services standards, radio-spectrum management, a variety of training initiatives, developing work regulations and standards, and active participation in Operation Life Saver.

Deregulation made possible by passage of the National Transportation Act of 1987 has led to large-scale shifts of low-density or branch lines from Class 1 railroads to new shortline or regional railways, some 40 of which have been established since 1987, with almost 10,000 miles of track, greatly increasing their importance in the national transportation network. RAC Class 1 and shortline railroads have worked jointly on improved communications between the two, as well as a joint federal-railroad funding arrangement to upgrade shortline bridges to meet the North American 286,000-pound heavy-car standard.

—William D. Middleton

Railway Enthusiasts

Railway enthusiasts number in the many thousands and range from casually interested to ardent. Their leading journals, *Trains, Railfan & Railroad,* and *Classic Trains,* sell 108,000, 50,000, and 60,000 monthly copies, respectively. *Trains* has estimated that combined annual expenditures for books, videos, and journals, collections of materials of every description special excursion trains, and the like come to somewhere around $135 million. Interest in model railroading is even stronger. *Model Railroader* sells 175,000 copies, while *Railroad Model Craftsman* circulates about 80,000 monthly copies. The Model Railroad Industry Assn., a trade group of manufacturers, has estimated that model railroaders spend $500 million annually.

Diverse Railway Interests

The wide scope of these interests has left few areas of the railroad unexplored. Organizations number into the many dozens. The oldest of these is the Railway & Locomotive Historical Society, founded in 1921, which is particularly interested in railroad history. The R&LHS has close to 4,500 members and eight local chapters and publishes a well-researched, twice-yearly journal, *Railroad History*. In contrast, the National Railway Historical Society, formed in 1935, is more oriented to current activities in railroad museums and trips and has more than 170 regional chapters and a membership in excess of 19,000. Its annual meeting typically brings together an extensive series of special rail trips. It publishes the bimonthly *National Railway Bulletin*. Established in 1932, the 900-member Canadian Railroad Historical Assn. is oriented to the history of Canadian railroads and publishes the bimonthly *Canadian Rail*. Two more specialized groups focus on electric railways. The Electric Railroaders' Assn., founded in 1934, embraces everything from street railways to main-line electrification all over North America, with some 1,600 members, and publishes a twice-yearly magazine, *Headlights*. The similar Central Electric Railfans' Assn., established in Chicago in 1938, also has about

Some 54 men and women of the National Assn. of Railroad Enthusiasts gathered for a special excursion over the Hoosac Tunnel & Wilmington in western Massachusetts. The outing, on August 24, 1934, was generally believed to be the first organized railfan trip in the United States. Thousands of similar outings have followed.
—H. W. Pontin, *Trains* Magazine Collection

1,600 members and publishes periodic bulletins, each a major history of electric railroads. Many other organizations are more specialized or serve on a regional basis. Often these are devoted to the history of an individual railroad, or sometimes a group of related railroads. Most have some kind of periodic publication, and there are now well over 100 of these. One of the oldest and largest, for example, the Pennsylvania Railroad Technical and Historical Society, now numbers almost 3,200 members and publishes a quarterly magazine.

There are more than 350 railroad museums and tourist railroads in the United States and Canada. Many feature some kind of equipment operation. The Seashore Trolley Museum at Kennebunkport, Maine, has probably the largest equipment ownership, with more than 200 pieces of rolling stock. The longest line operated by a tourist train is the Cumbres & Toltec Scenic Railroad, which climbs above a 10,000-foot summit on a 64-mile line in Colorado and New Mexico. The Illinois Railway Museum, near Union, Illinois, occasionally operates the entire *Nebraska Zephyr* or the North Shore Line *Electroliner* streamliners. Cog railways climb New Hampshire's Mount Washington and Colorado's Pikes Peak.

Dinner trains make for a popular outing. One of the most elegant is the Napa Valley Wine Train, offering brunch, lunch, and dinner service year-round over a leisurely 19-mile trip through the vineyards of northern California's Napa Valley. Some tourist trains are operated in addition to regular freight services. The Alaska Railroad, for example, operates what are primarily tourist services over the 470-mile run between Seward and Fairbanks. In addition to its freight business, Canada's Algoma Central Railway operates regular tourist trains over Ontario's spectacular Agawa Canyon north of Sault Ste.

Marie, and the Ontario Northland runs summertime Polar Bear Express trips to Moosonee on Hudson Bay. In Mexico regular tourist trains are operated over the Chihuahua Pacific line over the Copper Canyon of the Sierra Madre. Also popular are special excursions of steam locomotives or vintage diesels operated over the regular freight rail system. Union Pacific and Canadian Pacific operate restored steam locomotives and, at Canadian Pacific, restored older diesels. Other locomotives are owned by enthusiast organizations or private owners.

Then there is the cruise train, which operates over scenic settings as much for those who simply enjoy the scenery and pleasure of rail travel as for railway enthusiasts. Rocky Mountaineer Railtours, for example, operates summer trips from Vancouver, British Columbia, to Banff, Calgary, and Jasper, designed for enjoyment of the scenery. Trains Unlimited Tours schedules a number of special trips in Canada, Mexico, Alaska, and other U.S. locations, as well as a few overseas trips. There are travel agents who specialize in planning rail trips. A number of inns and hotels situated at good trackside locations advertise to the railway enthusiast market.

Hardly anything connected with railroading is not collected. Lamps, railroad signs, railroad heralds, items of clothing, dinnerware, flatware, and dining-car menus are sought after. Photographs, slides, and such ephemera as maps, tickets and passes, broadsides, and calendars are all collected. Old passenger-train timetables are of interest to many; there is even a National Assn. of Timetable Collectors, and reprints of old copies of *The Official Guide of the Railways* are available. Railroad hobby shows are featured regularly.

Videotapes have become enormously popular, usually made by railway enthusiasts themselves. A number of professional programs such as the *Trains Unlimited* series for the History Channel and the *Tracks Ahead* series for Public Broadcasting Service have been widely shown.

Books are available on virtually any topic. Among the principal publishers are Barnard, Roberts & Co., Golden West Books, Indiana University Press, Johns Hopkins University Press, Kalmbach Books, MBI Publishing, Morning Sun Books, Northern Illinois University Press, Signature Press, Stanford University Press, TLC Publishing, University of Illinois Press, and University Press of Kentucky. Used railroad books always sell well.

—William D. Middleton

Model Railroading

Model railroading can be as simple as collecting models or as involved as constructing a miniature empire featuring highly detailed trains operating through elaborate scenery. A variety of skills are used to build a layout, which can make it a great family activity and teaching tool. It offers a chance to learn carpentry, acquire a basic knowledge of electricity, develop artistic talents, and gain mechanical aptitude.

The roots of model railroading stretch back to the mid-nineteenth century, when the nation's first railroads were under construction. Enthralled by locomotives that did work no beast could handle, children dreamed of becoming engineers and riding trains to distant places. It was not long before toy makers cashed in on those dreams by offering wood and tin replicas that could be pulled across the floor. By the time America's first transcontinental railroad was completed in 1869, toy trains were readily available. The wooden trains were decorated with pasted-on lithographed paper sides, while the tin ones were often brightly painted and adorned with stenciling.

As early as the 1840s toy makers in Europe were marketing locomotives that were propelled in the same manner as real locomotives—using steam. These featured a metal boiler and a small fuel reservoir that held either alcohol or kerosene that, when burned, heated the water to produce steam. Along with the excitement of a working steam engine came occasional burned hands or fingers, scalded floor boards, and charred spots in the carpet. An example of a very early trainset in the early 1870s was produced by Eugene Beggs with an American-built live-steam locomotive and a circle of track made of steel strips pressed into slots of precut wood. Other manufacturers soon followed. In 1888 the Weeden Manufacturing Co. introduced the successful Weeden Dart, a small, live-steam engine that was also available with a circle of track for $2.50. During this same time cast iron became a popular material for making toy trains, and clockwork and windup trains were introduced.

The first electric toy trains came along in the 1890s. Carlisle & Finch, of Cincinnati, Ohio, produced a simple, four-wheel trolley that proved popular and led to an expanded line that included an 0-4-0 steam locomotive, an interurban car, and an electric mine train. With few homes wired for electricity, these early electric toys were powered by either chromite or sulfuric acid wet-cell batteries, which the operator had to make up. Like the live-steam engines, these toys were not designed for the careless or fainthearted.

Joshua Lionel Cowen, a man whose middle name became synonymous with toy trains, produced his first electric toy train in 1900. It, too, ran on battery power, but in 1906 Lionel introduced a transformer that reduced 110-volt household current to a range that could safely operate its trains. The same year that Lionel brought out its first transformer, it also began producing all-metal, three-rail, sectional tubular track with a gauge of 2⅛ inches. Known as standard gauge, it became the most popular size for early electric trains, and its powered, center third rail caught on with the toy train industry.

In 1910 the Ives Co. became the first American toy maker to offer a line of smaller electric toy trains. These, too, ran on three-rail track, but with a more compact gauge of just 1¼ inch. Known as O gauge, it proved to be the beginning of a trend toward smaller model trains (also referred to as "tinplate" trains because they were originally made from sheet iron or steel plated with a thin layer of tin). Other American toy train manufacturers, including Lionel, American Flyer, and Dorfan, followed Ives's lead.

Along with this trend came an increased level of detail and greater scale fidelity. Toy trains may have originally been marketed for children, but there was no denying that they had a broader appeal. By the 1930s a new phase of the hobby, scale-model railroading, was emerging. Over time the hobby evolved into two main segments, one centered on collecting and operating toy trains and the other focusing on building and operating scale-model railroads.

Scale (Figure 1) refers to the relationship in size between the model and the actual object being modeled. For example, O-scale models are built to a scale of 1:48, which means that the model is 1¹⁄₄₈ the size of its prototype, and, therefore, ¼ inch equals 1 foot 0 inches. (It must be noted, however, that there is a difference between ¼-inch O-scale models and O-gauge tinplate trains. Although both use a track gauge of 1¼ inches, O-scale trains run on two-rail track and are built to scale. O-gauge tinplate trains, on the other hand, run on oversized three-rail track, have wheels with extra large flanges and big couplers. Most O-gauge tinplate trains are also designed smaller than ¼-inch scale so that they can operate on the tight-radius curves and take up less space.) O scale accounts for only a small percentage of today's scale-model railroads. Its large size allows those who specialize in model building to showcase their work, but it is an impediment when designing a layout in a limited space. Among toy train operators, however, O gauge still retains its popularity.

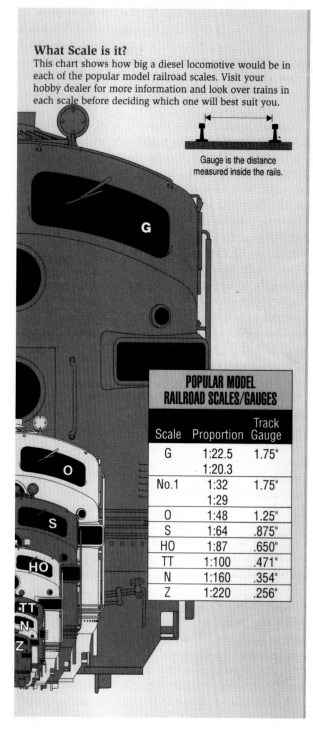

POPULAR MODEL RAILROAD SCALES/GAUGES

Scale	Proportion	Track Gauge
G	1:22.5	1.75"
	1:20.3	
No.1	1:32	1.75"
	1:29	
O	1:48	1.25"
S	1:64	.875"
HO	1:87	.650"
TT	1:100	.471"
N	1:160	.354"
Z	1:220	.256"

Figure 1. Model Railroad Scale and Gauges. —Model Railroad Industry Assn.

HO models are built to a scale of 1:87.1 (3.5 mm equals 1 foot 0 inches). At 55 percent the size of O scale, HO allows almost twice as much railroading in the same space. Today, approximately 75 percent of American modelers work in HO scale. Along with HO's enormous popularity comes a wealth of products, by far the most available in any scale. There are hundreds of locomotives and cars that can be purchased either ready-to-run or as kits.

The second most popular scale is N, which was devel-

oped in the 1960s. Built to a scale of 1:160, N-scale models are often favored by modelers with limited space and those who prefer to model large scenes that can dwarf their trains.

Rounding out the scales in general use today are S and Z. S-scale models are built to a scale of 1:64 (³⁄₁₆ inch equals 1 foot 0 inches) and fall midway in size between O and HO scales. S scale's popularity is due in large part to the introduction of American Flyer's line of ³⁄₁₆-inch-scale, two-rail tinplate trains in the post–World War II years. Z, with a scale of 1:220, is the newest. While its small size does not lend itself to a high level of detailing, it does offer the possibility of building a layout in a very small space.

The exception to the downsizing trend has been the growing popularity of G scale (1:22.5), introduced by the German firm LGB in 1968. Slightly smaller than the old standard-gauge trains, these large-scale models not only are popular as children's toys, but are also favored by many adults who use them for outdoor garden railways.

It is estimated that there are approximately 250,000 scale-model railroaders in America. They range from those with a casual interest to those who have spent countless hours building and operating model trains. Some modelers choose to concentrate on modeling narrow-gauge railroads (those with a track gauge less than the standard 4 feet 8½ inches). Although such railroads made up only a small percentage of the nation's overall rail system, they are popular modeling subjects. These layouts are often based on Colorado's legendary 3-foot-gauge railroads or Maine's unique 2-foot lines. Modeling electric interurban and trolley lines is another specialty, as is modeling pre-1900 railroads. Most modelers, however, concentrate on standard-gauge steam and diesel operations in the years between World War II and the present. Even here, though, they follow different paths. Some choose to model portions of Class 1 railroads, such as the Pennsylvania or the Union Pacific, while others choose much smaller railroads, known as shortlines. Finally, there are modelers who create their own railroad. They take various aspects of different railroads that appeal to them and design their own line. This is known as freelancing.

There are also modelers who build their layouts outdoors. Garden railroads are usually constructed with G-scale trains and feature a creative mix of garden landscaping and modeling. Most garden railways are powered by electricity, but some use live-steam models. Building and operating large, highly detailed, live-steam models is the focus of some clubs, and many of them have track in a variety of gauges. Some of these trains are large enough to ride on.

Whatever the scale, modelers today have more products available than at any other time. From expensive, handmade brass locomotives to mass-produced plastic rolling stock, the selection and attention to detail have never been better. And although live-steam models are still produced, model railroading has entered the digital age. Using Digital Command Control (DCC), modelers can install decoders in their locomotives and program them to operate independently of each other, even on the same track. Decoders can also be programmed to control light and sound functions.

There are a variety of organizations that support the hobby. As scale-model railroading came into its own, so did the need for standards among the different manufacturers. The National Model Railroad Assn. (NMRA), founded in 1935, is the largest organization devoted to scale-model railroading. For those interested in toy trains, there are the Train Collectors Assn. (TCA) and the Toy Train Operating Society (TTOS). Model railroad manufacturers have their own organization, too, the Model Railroad Industry Assn. (MRIA).

Leading publications for modelers include *Model Railroader*, published by Kalmbach, and *Railroad Model Craftsman*, published by Carstens. Both companies also publish books about the hobby. There are also specialty magazines. Small niche publications, such as *LGB Telegram*, *O Gauge Railroading*, *S Gaugian*, and *N-Scale*, cater to modelers in their respective scales. *Narrow Gauge and Short Line Gazette*, published by Benchmark, concentrates on modeling narrow-gauge railroads, shortlines, and small industrial railroads, while *Classic Toy Trains*, published by Kalmbach, focuses on collecting and operating toy trains.

Excellent scale-model railroads can be found throughout the country. Two of the nation's best known are the HO-scale New England, Berkshire & Western layout operated by the Rensselaer Model Railroad Society at the Rensselaer Polytechnic Institute in Troy, New York, and the stunning HO-scale re-creation of Tehachapi Pass built by the La Mesa Model Railroad Club at its home in the San Diego Model Railroad Museum in San Diego, California. One of the best places to view toy trains of all types is the Train Collectors Assn.'s Toy Train Museum in Strasburg, Pennsylvania.

—Christopher P. D'Amato

REFERENCES

Hayden, Bob, ed. *6 HO Railroads You Can Build*. Waukesha, Wis.: Kalmbach, 2001.

Johnson, Kent, ed. *Garden Railroading: Getting Started in the Hobby*. Waukesha, Wis.: Kalmbach, 2001.

———. *Project Railroads You Can Build from Benchwork to Finished Scenery*. Waukesha, Wis.: Kalmbach, 2001.

Posey, Sam. *Playing with Trains*. New York: Random House, 2004.

Souter, Gerry, and Janet Souter. *The American Toy Train*. Osceola, Wis.: MBI, 1999.

Railway Express Agency

The most familiar railroad-oriented express company in the mid-twentieth century was Railway Express with its forest green trucks adorned with the red diamond. At its peak it had more than 23,000 offices in the United States and 1,500 offices in Canada. At the end of World War II it had almost 86,000 employees. Railway Express was known for taking any kind of freight—elephants or eggs, cash or cornets—and moving it wherever the shipper desired.

Express service began in 1834 when William F. Harnden offered to carry goods for a charge while traveling as a passenger on trains and boats between Boston and New York City. The service proved to be attractive to the shipping public, and during the latter part of the nineteenth century many express companies were formed. Gradually these merged so that only a few survived. By the early twentieth century four major express companies remained: Adams Express, American Express, United States Express, and Wells Fargo.

Almost every passenger train included an express car or an express section of a baggage or mail car. Many trains moved more than one express car, and at times there were solid trains of such cars moving between important centers. Each express car was staffed by an armed express messenger who had responsibility for the contents. A safe was bolted to the floor to hold valuables such as securities and shipments of cash.

During World War I the U.S. Railroad Administration took over the railroads and the express companies in order to operate them for the benefit of the war effort. USRA director general William Gibbs McAdoo believed that it would be most efficient if the three major express companies—Adams, American Express, and Wells Fargo—were merged into one firm. The American Railway Express Co. was formed on June 30, 1918. When the war ended and the Transportation Act of 1920 returned the railroads to private ownership, American Railway Express became a private firm under the jurisdiction of the Interstate Commerce Commission (ICC). In 1921 the soon-to-be-familiar green and red colors were adopted.

During the 1920s the railroads came to believe that it would be in their best interest to own the express business themselves. On December 7, 1928, the Railway Express Agency was granted a corporate charter, and on February 28, 1929, the railroads' contracts with American Railway Express expired. On March 1, 1929, the 86 Class 1 railroads chose not to renew contracts with American Railway Express, and the Railway Express Agency took over the majority of U.S. express business.

The decision to own the express business was based on the railroads' dissatisfaction with the compensation received from American Railway Express. Before World War I the railroads had individual contracts with the express companies that operated over their lines, which typically meant that the railroads received about half of the revenue for the express traffic. In dealing with American Railway Express, the division of revenue was in the main about 48 percent and in some cases as low as 38 percent. The railroads bought out American Railway Express for $30 million and acquired all the assets of that company.

The two major holders of Railway Express Agency stock were the New York Central Railroad, with 144 shares, and the Pennsylvania Railroad, with 126. Holding 45 or fewer shares were the Atchison, Topeka & Santa Fe Railway, the Southern Pacific, the New York, New Haven & Hartford, the Baltimore & Ohio, the Chicago & North Western Railway, the Illinois Central, the Chicago, Burlington & Quincy, the Chicago, Milwaukee, St. Paul & Pacific Railroad, the Erie, and the Union Pacific. The Railway Express Agency was guided by a board of 15 directors; six were named by the eastern railroads, southern railroads named 3, 5 were named by the western railroads, and 1 director was chosen at large. Revenues collected from shippers were used to pay wages, salaries, and other operating expenses. Any residue was to go to the owning railroads on a pro rata basis. From the start the railroads were never sufficiently reimbursed to cover their costs.

The Great Depression was a terrible burden on all businesses, and the railroads and the Railway Express Agency were not immune from the sharp downturn in the economy. Nonetheless, the Railway Express did not stand still. It purchased the small Southeastern Express for $1 million in 1938 and thus achieved a complete monopoly of the express business in the United States.

Air Express had its roots in American Railway Express, with service initiated on November 14, 1919. It was attractive to some shippers who required very fast deliveries, but the service grew slowly, as did the entire air transportation industry in the 1920s. On September 1, 1927, the American Railway Express began a regular daily Air Express service for 80 cities. By 1930, 100 airports were involved in Air Express service. The higher rates charged by Air Express were difficult to sell during the 1930s; even so, the business began to grow steadily. Railway Express expanded Air Express to international scope with the cooperation of Pan American Airways in 1934, as International Air Express. The idea caught on, and on February 1, 1936, 18 airlines joined with Railway Express in the Air Express business. As the decade moved on, Railway Express also became involved in water transportation and had contracts with 12 steamship lines.

The Railway Express Agency boomed during World War II. Its eventual decline was caused by several factors. After World War II the flurry of highway construction and the widespread purchase of automobiles, along with the sharp increase in air travel, offered competition in passenger travel that the railroads were hard pressed to meet. By the mid-1950s the railroads began sharp reductions in the number of passenger trains and a resultant cutback in the reach of Railway Express. Other competition arose from the rapid growth in the motor carrier industry. Nevertheless, as late as 1967 the Railway Express Agency had 17,000 trucks, moved over 300,000 shipments daily, and had gross revenues of more than $450 million.

Despite rate increases after the war, revenues fell, and the owning railroads grew weary of making up the losses. By the end of 1950 the railroads were making up an annual Railway Express loss of $97 million. They were losing money not only on passenger service, but also from the express service. Although the railroads signed the contracts in 1954 to extend the life of Railway Express, they saw it as a losing proposition. In 1960 the largest shareholder, the New York Central, dropped its ownership stake. Other railroads began to call for doing away with Railway Express.

In September 1960 Railway Express took on the trade name REA Express. It was felt that dropping the word "Railway" from the name would betoken a new and more modern approach to small shipments. There were offers to purchase Railway Express by the investment banking firm of Lehman Brothers and by the U.S. Freight Co., but both bids were rejected. Negotiations began with the Greyhound Corp. in 1965, in which Greyhound would acquire $10 million in REA stock, but the ICC would not go along with the arrangement. An attempt by Data Processing Financial & General Corp. to buy Railway Express also fell through.

In 1968 Spencer D. Moseley, who had been with freight-oriented General American Transportation, organized a group of management people and purchased Railway Express from the railroads for $2.5 million. By this time competition was growing as United Parcel Service and Federal Express began to offer service on a national and international basis. The airlines and motor carriers that had once cooperated with Railway Express became indifferent and then hostile.

Payroll was cut sharply; offices closed; morale failed. The integrity of Railway Express was tarnished when several employees were found to have been pilfering from the company. In 1974 the Civil Aeronautics Board ordered the airlines to end their contracts with REA. In early 1974 REA entered Chapter 11 bankruptcy proceedings, and in 1975 a federal judge in New York ordered the liquidation of REA. In 1976 another judge ordered that all assets of REA be auctioned. Worse was to come: Several REA officials were convicted of embezzlement and bribery. The end of Railway Express came with a whimper and not a bang at a court-ordered auction in 1979.

—George M. Smerk

REFERENCES

Garrett, Klink, and Toby Smith. *Ten Turtles to Tucumcari: A Personal History of the Railway Express Agency*. Albuquerque: Univ. of New Mexico Press, 2003.

Roseman, V. S. *Railway Express: An Overview*. Denver: Rocky Mountain, 1992.

Yoder, Wallace Omer. "An Evaluation of the Express Business in the United States as Conducted by the Railway Express Agency, Incorporated." Ph.D. diss., Indiana University, 1953.

Randolph, A. Philip (1889–1979)

When he died in New York on May 16, 1979, at age 90, Asa Philip Randolph was mourned by President Jimmy Carter as an American giant. Leaders of organized labor and the civil rights movement also mourned. Millions more owed him a debt as a key figure in the history of unions, particularly for African Americans.

Born on April 15, 1889, in Crescent City, Florida, Randolph was the son of a Methodist minister. Although he was class valedictorian, the customs of the South conspired to condemn him to menial work. Randolph moved to Harlem in 1911, where he attended City College and New York University at night. In 1917 he and progressive fellow student Chandler Owen launched the publication the *Messenger* (later *Black Worker*). A hallmark of this radical magazine was an advocacy of civil rights for all through the labor movement, always Randolph's basic philosophy. Trade unionism was Randolph's secular gospel. "The Negro question" was part of a larger issue concerning all workers.

During World War I Randolph and Owen advocated more jobs in the defense industries and better military positions for blacks, although they strongly opposed the Great War. They vigorously fought the American tradition of terrorism enacted in mutilations and lynchings. They opposed other national core values of discrimination, just as they later confronted unions for refusing to admit blacks. After the war Randolph ran unsuccessfully as a Socialist for a number of political offices.

Randolph's advocacy ideas in the *Messenger*—"No intelligent Negro is willing to lay down his life for the United States as it now exists"—began to attract the attention of Pullman sleeping-car porters. The company built, maintained, and operated sleeping and parlor cars, staffed with porters and maids, mainly black but also Filipino, and supervised by white Pullman conductors. By the end of World War I almost all railroad crafts were organized, except for traditionally black crafts such as porters and redcaps.

The powerful, antiunion Pullman Co. attacked porters who tried to organize an independent union and threatened them with firings in an era when few jobs except the most menial were open to blacks. The porters needed an effective outside leader with a message. In 1925 *Messenger* editor Randolph accepted an invitation to organize Pullman's porters and maids as the president of the Brotherhood of Sleeping Car Porters (BSCP). For 12 years Randolph persisted in his efforts. He brought his union into the American Federation of Labor at a time when about half of the umbrella organization's unions prevented blacks from joining, at least in practice or as full members.

After resisting charges of communism, fighting Pullman's sham company union, and lobbying the U.S. government for changes in the Railway Labor Act, the BSCP in 1935 won recognition by Pullman after the National Mediation Board certified the union. In 1937 Randolph finally negotiated the first BSCP labor agreement with Pullman. The BSCP, a standard railroad union, now had a standard labor agreement under the Railway Labor Act, centered on the principle of craft seniority.

The BSCP president, however, did not rest on his hard-won laurels. According to Randolph, life for all Americans centered on decent jobs. After Randolph's threat of a 100,000-person March on Washington, President Roosevelt in 1941 signed Executive Order 8802 banning discrimination in government agencies and the defense industries. With the enactment of the Selective Service Act of 1947, Randolph pushed for integration of the armed forces and an end to its "Jim Crow conscription." Needing the black vote in the tight race of 1948, President Truman a few months before the election ordered the end of military discrimination. In 1955 Randolph was elected a vice president of the newly formed AFL-CIO. From this position he strove for civil rights both within and outside the labor movement.

Randolph's long, eventually successful practice of organizing peaceful marches and civil disobedience culminated when he conceived and chaired the March on Washington for Jobs and Freedom of 1963, at which Martin Luther King, Jr., delivered his famous "I have a dream" speech. In 1964 President Lyndon B. Johnson signed the Civil Rights Act and honored Randolph with the Presidential Medal of Freedom.

Randolph retired as president of the BSCP in 1968 but continued to be active in the labor movement, including the AFL-CIO Executive Council, through 1974. The A. Philip Randolph Pullman Porter Museum, in Chicago, honors this American leader and the Pullman porters and maids.

—Frederick C. Gamst

REFERENCES

Anderson, Jervis. *A. Philip Randolph: A Biographical Portrait.* Berkeley: Univ. of California Press, 1986.

Hanley, Sally. *A. Philip Randolph.* New York: Chelsea House, 1989.

Minton, Bruce, and John Stuart. "A. Philip Randolph: Negro Labor's Champion." In *Men Who Lead Labor.* New York: Modern Age Books, 1937.

Neyland, James. *A. Philip Randolph.* Los Angeles: Melrose Square, 1994.

Reef, Catherine. *A. Philip Randolph: Union Leader and Civil Rights Crusader.* Berkeley Heights, N.J.: Enslow, 2001.

Wright, Sarah E. *A. Philip Randolph: Integration in the Workplace.* Englewood Cliffs, N.J.: Silver Burdett, 1990.

Rates and Rate Associations

From the outset, railroads' successful operation as businesses required techniques different from those employed for waterways and highways. Turnpike companies built and maintained an improved roadway and then let anyone use it who was willing to pay the toll; they did not operate the vehicles using the roadway. Likewise, when canals were built, the waterway was open to any party willing to pay the toll; the canal company was not an operating company. But early on, it proved ineffective and inefficient to let a railway line be used by any party other than the rail-line owner.

The problem was the mixing, or potential mixing, of rapidly moving steam-powered trains and slow-moving wagons or cars pulled by horses, mules, or oxen. To maximize efficiency of the costly rail line and its capability to move freight and passengers, it was necessary to operate steam locomotives exclusively, and it was best if movement on the railroad was controlled by one management team. The railroads needed an operating monopoly. Moreover, because of the expense of railway construction, it was obvious that railways could not be ubiquitous. It was inefficient to build more than one railway line to a place that could be well served by just one. The necessary operating monopoly meant that in many, if not most, places railways would have a market monopoly as well.

Competition, the usual guarantor of quality products and services provided at reasonable prices, would not work well in the case of railroads. Some points would generate enough traffic to warrant being served by more than one railroad, but less busy points would only be served by one railroad under conditions of monopoly. Where there is competition, rates tend to fall toward cost. A problem with railroads is that large portions of the costs are fixed—they do not vary with output—and are therefore difficult, if not impossible, to allocate objectively to given units of traffic. Indeed, railroads may not have a clear idea of the costs associated with a given freight movement. In vigorous competition it is easy for rates to fall below cost. There was strong pressure to increase traffic on the expensive facilities required of a railroad, and reducing rates was a way to attract more business.

In the short run rates need only cover out-of-pocket costs, but in the long run rates must cover not only all fixed and variable costs but also fully allocated costs, which include a reasonable profit. If rates cover only fixed and variable costs and there is no profit, there is no reason for the carrier to stay in business.

In conditions of ignorance of costs and zealous pursuit of traffic, railroad competition can easily become ruinous or cutthroat competition, in which rates may fall well below the cost of providing the service. In the 1870s and 1880s many railroads suffered from cutthroat competition. In order to continue in business, railroads had to develop means of staying alive economically. Unfettered competition could cause railroad revenues to suffer, and vigorous attempts to gain traffic might lead to rapid changes in rates, both up and down. Under such conditions freight rates might become highly unstable and unattractive to shippers.

Rate Discrimination

The pressure on railroads to stay economically viable led to rate discrimination. Discrimination takes place when two services cost the same to produce, but different rates are charged, or when costs are different, but the same rate is charged. At points served by several railroads, rates were likely to be low and perhaps unremunerative. To make up for losses or lower profit margins at competitive points, high rates would be charged at noncompetitive points in rural areas.

Recognizing the destructive possibilities of unabated competition, railroads devised means of self-preservation. One method was to divide up territory to avoid competition; the rail carriers reached agreements not to invade one another's territory. A variation was to agree not to solicit traffic in the territory of another railroad. Territorial agreements were sometimes effective in preventing the construction of a new rail line into another railroad's territory, but were less successful where competitive lines already existed. Rate agreements were used in such circumstances, in which the competing railroad lines agreed to maintain specific rates to avoid rate competition. These agreements became commonplace in the post–Civil War period as more railroad lines were constructed. Rate agreements were difficult to maintain because of the temptation to break them in the face of an economic opportunity. Worse, there was no legal basis for territorial agreements under common law. Rate agreements to avoid competition were assumed to be conspiracies in restraint of trade and a clear violation of the precedents of common law.

Because rate agreements were of questionable value, traffic pools and money pools were created. In a traffic pool the competitive rail lines agreed to divide the traffic up among themselves. In a money pool the traffic moved according to the wishes of shippers on their lines of choice, but the revenues from the traffic were divided according to agreements between the carriers. The legal status of pools under common law was questionable; nevertheless, some pools appeared to have been successful in limiting destructive competition. The Act to Regulate Commerce of 1887 (more often known as the Interstate Commerce Act) changed the situation because it specifically prohibited pooling, despite its apparent value in reducing destructive competition.

Traffic Associations

In reaction to passage of the Interstate Commerce Act, various traffic organizations that had administered the pools were reformulated, and the stability of rates was once again sought by rate agreements between railroads. When this practice was deemed questionable under the Sherman Antitrust Act, another method evolved. Traffic associations had existed for years to administer matters associated with interchange of traffic between railroads, standardization of the rules of bills of lading, the collection of freight bills, and the need to standardize equipment handling. All this was necessary because much traffic moved over more than one railroad and in and through different parts of the nation. Rate bureaus or traffic associations evolved as the means to process rate adjustments and thereby prevent ruinous competition.

What the rate bureaus did was twofold: they published tariffs and fixed prices. In fixing prices the rate associations acted as a cartel, that is, a combination of independent commercial enterprises designed to limit competition.

To carry out the work of the rate bureaus, the nation was divided into a number of rate territories. Originally there were three: Official Territory, which was the area east of the Mississippi and north of the Ohio and Potomac rivers; Southern Territory, which was the area east of the Mississippi and south of the Ohio and Potomac rivers; and Western Territory, which was all the area west of the Mississippi. These large territories were further subdivided over time. Western Territory, for example, was divided into the Trans-Continental Freight Bureau, the Western Trunk Line Assn., and the Southwestern Freight Bureau. There was further division in some of the larger territories. The territories were based on the operating and traffic conditions in the various geographic areas and the competitive situation existing between the carriers.

The rate bureaus followed procedures that permitted all parties to consider, advise, and share information and have input on rate changes. Each of the railroad rate bureaus was supported by dues levied on the carriers within the given territory and prorated upon the rail mileage of a carrier within the territory. Each carrier contributed personnel to what was called the standing rate committee. The task of this committee was to study rate proposals carefully to make sure that the proposed changes would not have a negative impact on the carriers as a whole or on specific carriers for whom the standing rate committee members worked. The rate bureaus considered and published rates for movement within their territory and from that rate territory to the other territories. Railroads could also publish their own freight tariffs.

Rate Types

There are two basic types of rates. In the class rate system, all commodities are divided into a relatively small number of classes; the classes represent a cost factor called a rating. Some observers hold that the class rating represents the value of the service, or what the traffic would bear. In other words, it is the highest rate that would still attract a reasonable volume of traffic. In effect, the class rating assigned to each commodity was a crude reflection of cost. Another element is the rate basis, which is a distance factor, typically the shortest rail distance between origin and destination points. The cost and distance factors interacted to produce a class rate. Class rates

were high enough to cover costs and were generally considered to cover fully allocated costs. The class rate system provided a means by which anyone could move any commodity between any two points in the United States or Canada.

Commodity rates are the other principal type of rates. These rates are tailored to given demand and volume situations. Class rates, by their very nature, were generally insensitive to demand for the service. Class rates are a standby to be used for infrequent movement, but they are useful because there is no need to spend time or money in negotiating them. In contrast, commodity rates are negotiated and thus take effort and expense, as well as time, to reach fruition. It was for the purpose of arriving at commodity rates that rate bureaus came into their own. Commodity rates are always lower than class rates and are therefore most attractive to shippers, but unless an existing commodity rate can be used, a new commodity rate must be negotiated, which costs time and money. Commodity rates, like class rates, are made between places and not between shippers and consignees, so a commodity rate, once negotiated, is available to all shippers and by means of all carriers that are parties to the agreement.

Ratemaking Procedures

Over time a procedure evolved. Rate-change proposals were usually initiated by shippers working through a rail carrier to establish a new commodity rate or adjust an existing rate. Reasons for rate changes were varied: a shipper might find a new market for its products and seek to establish a rate from its production point to its new markets that was lower than the class rates. By the 1950s and beyond, many, if not most, rate adjustments were made because of competition from motor carriers. In some cases water carrier competition was the instigating factor. Regardless of the impetus, the proposed rate change had to be approved by all the territories through which the shipment passed, and that meant that all the railroads that could potentially handle the shipment had to agree to the rate or request that they be left out of the movement and not be party to the rate.

The rate change or adjustment was usually introduced first in the rate bureau of the railroad that would initiate the shipment; subsequently it would be introduced in the other territories to be affected. The idea of precedence was that if one territory agreed to the change, it would be easier to win the approval of subsequent territories. Suppose that a shipper in Des Moines, Iowa, wished to obtain an attractive rate on goods to be sold in Atlanta, Georgia. The rate proposal would first be introduced in the Western Trunk Line Assn. If successful, the proposal would then follow the routing of the shipment and the rail carriers involved and move to the Illinois Freight Assn. and, if successful there, would finally be introduced in the Southern Freight Assn.

The proposal to the Western Trunk Line Assn. would be

prepared showing the arguments in favor of the change, noting the carriers that would or could participate in the movement, and indicating how the revenue from the rate would be divided among the participating carriers. The proposal would be distributed by mail to the members of the Western Trunk Line and would also be published in the *Daily Traffic Bulletin*. Members were asked to vote upon the proposal by mail within a given time frame. If the proposal was defeated by the mail vote, it usually died or might be modified for later introduction.

Often, however, the proposal would be docketed for more consideration at a monthly meeting of freight traffic officers of each of the carriers participating in the rate bureau. Each rail carrier in its general freight office had analysts familiar with commodity and competitive conditions within or between territories. They would also be familiar with the nature of the competitive conditions for the particular commodity in question. The rate analysts would study the proposal and prepare documentation on the rate proposal and create a file containing the information and supporting or negative arguments to be given to the officer to represent the particular railroad at the monthly meeting.

The railroad representative, usually an assistant general freight agent, would attend the meeting and support his employer's position regarding the rate. All the representatives would literally sit around a table and come to an agreement, or they would agree to negotiate further or drop the matter. Perhaps they would send the proposal to the standing rate committee of the association for further analysis. The standing rate committee would then develop a final version of the proposal and distribute it for a final vote by mail. When the proposal was finally approved, a rate advice would be issued by the association. In the example here, the approval of the Western Trunk Line would be passed on to the Illinois Freight Assn. and, if approved, then on to the Southern Freight Assn. The final rate advice would indicate the conditions surrounding the change, which tariff would contain the new rate, and the basis upon which the revenue would be divided.

This procedure gave all parties an opportunity to voice their feelings and concerns, including the concerns of other shippers working through the railroads that served them. The process was time consuming; a rate proposal affecting only one rate association would take about four months if there were no substantive questions raised. A shipper anxious to move more quickly where several rate bureaus were concerned might work with several railroads to introduce the proposal in all the rate bureaus involved at the same time in order to speed the matter.

The work of the participants in the monthly rate meetings was often difficult because of the need to balance all the conflicting interests of all the carrier members. A railroad that felt a threat could delay the final rate decision interminably. In many cases the motor carriers would win the business. Many railroads blamed regulation and unfair competition for loss of traffic when it was the slowness or inaction of the rate bureaus that caused the traffic to go to competing modes of transportation.

There were several reasons for turning down a proposal. One was the divisions of the interline revenue from a joint rate. (A joint rate involves two or more carriers; the rate to be charged is always lower than the aggregate of the existing rates. Joint rates are obviously attractive to shippers seeking to save money.) A carrier that felt that a division was unremunerative could block the proposal unless the divisions were renegotiated. Or a carrier might simply require that it be left out of the routing. Another reason for turning down a proposal was the belief that it would set a bad precedent and might affect other rates and the competitive situation.

When an agreement was finally negotiated within the rate bureau, all the carriers would charge the same rate on the same commodity moving between similar points; there was no price competition. Individual railroads could charge different rates if they chose by exercising independent action. For example, a railroad with a lengthy route between two points in comparison with its railroad competition might charge a lower rate because the service was slower and thus less attractive.

The practice of collective rate agreements was begun shortly after passage of the Interstate Commerce Act. For decades the Justice Department feared that the collective ratemaking of the rate bureaus was in violation of the Sherman Act. There was no major outcry against the rate bureaus because they solved a problem. It was conceded by government and the business world that they performed a useful function in avoiding rate chaos and destructive competition. In fact, collective ratemaking was explicitly legalized by the Reed-Bulwinkle Act of 1948. Under Reed-Bulwinkle the rate bureaus were legal if their procedures, rules, and regulations met the approval of the Interstate Commerce Commission. The rate bureaus had to make their records, accounts, and files available to the commission.

The other modes of transportation also adopted collective ratemaking as they grew to compete with the railroads. The general procedures used by the railroads were echoed by the other modes. The rate bureaus successfully reduced cutthroat competition in transportation. One major negative of the process of collective ratemaking is that a high-cost carrier may work to hold all rates higher than they would otherwise be.

Under regulation the railroads were required to publish their rates. The rail customers and, in time, the customers of other regulated carriers had a right to examine the tariffs. Because publication and purchase of tariffs were often expensive, the carriers were required to keep a public tariff library or public tariff file at their principal place of business or at other major offices. Not only did shippers make use of these tariff files, but the competitors also visited the public tariff files in order to save themselves the cost of buying tariffs. Motor carriers often used railroad tariff facilities for information used to engage in rate adjustments that took business from the railroads. The water carriers, many of which were and are small firms, used rail tariff files to their advantage. Often, after checking out a rail rate along a waterway, the barge operator would quote a rate a given percentage lower. This was justified on the assertion that water transportation was cheaper than rail, slower, and thus less attractive to shippers. The railroads were thus put in the position of doing the costly work of rate analysis, and competitive modes could take advantage of the public nature of tariffs.

With the changes in railroad regulation in the Staggers Act of 1980, collective price fixing was for all practical purposes eliminated. Carriers were forced to rely more on market conditions, and the role and power of the rate bureaus greatly diminished. In addition, railroad mergers and combinations have greatly reduced the number of railroads and changed the conditions of competition. Railroad and motor carrier rate bureaus may still play a role, but only those carriers that may actually participate in a traffic movement may join in the collective ratemaking procedures; this is to prevent high-cost carriers from keeping rates higher than necessary.

—George M. Smerk

REFERENCES

Coyle, John J., Edward J. Bardi, and Joseph L. Cavinato. *Transportation*. 3rd ed. Chap. 14. St. Paul, Minn.: West, 1990.

Kolko, Gabriel. *Railroads and Regulation, 1877–1916*. Chaps. 5–9. Princeton, N.J.: Princeton Univ. Press, 1965.

Locklin, D. Philip. *Economics of Transportation*. 7th ed. Chap. 4. Homewood, Ill.: Richard D. Irwin, 1972.

Martin, Albro. *Enterprise Denied*. Chaps. 2, 5–8. New York: Columbia Univ. Press, 1971.

Shinn, Glenn L. *Freight Rate Application*. New York: Simmons-Boardman, 1948.

Rea, Samuel (1855–1929)

"His studious, deeply penetrating mind and his firm decision were more largely responsible than any other factor for the successful completion of the Pennsylvania Railroad's prodigious tunnel and terminal system at New York and its connection with the New England track network," wrote the *Engineering News-Record* at the time of Samuel Rea's death in 1929. Born in Hollidaysburg, Pennsylvania, in 1855, Rea, like many other nineteenth-century engineers, learned his practice as an apprentice rather than through formal training. Thrown on his own resources at the death of his father, the 16-year-old Rea went to work as a chainman and rodman for the Pennsylvania Railroad. Temporarily idled by the Pennsylvania in the panic of 1873, Rea returned to the railroad in 1875 and—except for a period of locating surveys for the Pittsburgh & Lake Erie—developed his experience in a succession of construction posts, becoming the principal engi-

neer assistant to Vice President J. N. DuBarry in 1883. Rea left the Pennsylvania in 1889 to become vice president of the Maryland Central and chief engineer of the Baltimore & Ohio's Baltimore belt-line and tunnel project, returning again to PRR in 1892 as an assistant to President George B. Roberts.

In 1884 bridge engineer Gustav Lindenthal developed a plan for a great suspension bridge across the Hudson River at New York. For a long time the Pennsylvania had as an urgent goal a crossing that could carry the railroad from the New Jersey shore of the river into Manhattan. Rea took up the bridge proposal, at one point becoming an incorporator of Lindenthal's North River Bridge Co. Upon his return to the PRR in 1892 Rea visited and reported on underground electric railways in London, an assignment that gave him an appreciation for the potential of electric traction. Later in 1892 Rea developed a report for Roberts on all the alternatives for a New York entrance, leading to a decision to pursue a high-level bridge.

Appointed fourth vice president after A. J. Cassatt's election as president in 1899, Rea soon was placed in overall charge of the New York extension work. When the plan for the high-level bridge failed because of the unwillingness of other railroads to join in the costly project, Rea urged Cassatt to consider electric traction and tunnels under the Hudson and East rivers, and the great work was soon under way.

After successfully completing the New York tunnel projects and Pennsylvania Station, Rea continued to move up through the Pennsylvania's vice presidential ranks and was elected president in 1913. He served a distinguished 13-year term that saw major expansions of PRR capacity. Completion of the New York Connecting Railroad and Hell Gate Bridge in 1917, linking the Pennsylvania with New England, concluded the railroad's great New York terminal project.

Under Rea's presidency the Pennsylvania began an extensive program of suburban electrification at Philadelphia, which later grew into the great main-line electrification program of the 1930s. Rea retired in 1925 and died four years later. In recognition of his achievements, a larger-than-life-size bronze statue of Rea by sculptor Adolph A. Weinman was erected in the main waiting room at Pennsylvania Station (*see* MONUMENTS).

—William D. Middleton

REFERENCE

"Samuel Rea, Former President of Pennsylvania R.R., Dies." *Engineering News-Record* 102, no. 13 (Mar. 28, 1929): 487, 520.

Reading Co.

The Philadelphia & Reading Railroad Co. was incorporated in 1833. It opened from Philadelphia to Reading in

1839 and was extended to Pottsville in the center of the Schuylkill anthracite coalfield in 1842. At Philadelphia a branch passed north of the city to Port Richmond on the Delaware River, the nation's first large rail-to-water coal terminal. The Reading was built directly alongside the profitable Schuylkill Canal, whose traffic levels and earning power rivaled those of the Erie Canal. In the struggle that followed, the canal was forced to rebuild wider and deeper but became so burdened with debt that it forever lost its blue-chip status. The Reading had exploded the conventional wisdom that a railroad could not compete with a waterway for heavy freight.

The Reading had been promoted by Nicholas Biddle of the Bank of the United States, and after the bank's failure it was controlled by British capitalists and their handpicked American managers down to the 1880s. For its first 30 years it focused almost exclusively on the coal trade, in which it became the dominant carrier. Completion of the Lebanon Valley Branch from Reading to Harrisburg in 1858 made the Reading a direct competitor of the Pennsylvania Railroad. The PRR quickly contained the threat by securing most of the viable routes west of the Susquehanna River. President Charles E. Smith (1861–1869) perfected the Reading's control of the Schuylkill trade by buying or leasing all the lateral mine railroads, most of which had been feeders of the canal since the late 1820s.

In 1869 Smith was succeeded by the company's counsel, Franklin B. Gowen, who, with brief periods of exile, dominated the company through 1886. A mesmerizing courtroom orator, Gowen beguiled investors, and ultimately himself, with visions of empire. Through the Philadelphia & Reading Coal & Iron Co. (1871) he bought over 100,000 acres of coal lands at inflated prices and without regard to quality. He organized the anthracite roads into a cartel and ruthlessly crushed the miners' union when it stood in his way. He leased the canal (1870) and branch lines, notably the East Pennsylvania (1869) and the Philadelphia, Germantown & Norristown (1870).

Most important, Gowen sought to break out of the box in which the PRR had contained the Reading and achieve trunk-line status. The PRR became Moby Dick to Gowen's Ahab, with the important exception that it was the leviathan that had the last word. Gowen found allies in the Baltimore & Ohio and the Vanderbilts, and the Reading remained their link to Philadelphia and New York for a century. Lease of the Catawissa Railroad (1872) brought the Reading to the Williamsport gateway and eventual connections with the Vanderbilt lines. The North Pennsylvania (1879) gave the Reading control of a rival line between New York and Philadelphia.

In 1880 Gowen spent and borrowed his way into bankruptcy. The English shareholders voted him out in 1881; William H. Vanderbilt voted him back in 1882. The receivership was lifted, and the war entered its final phase. Gowen leased the Central Railroad of New Jersey (CNJ) in 1883, cementing his access to New York. With control of the Philadelphia & Atlantic City, Gowen struck at the PRR's New Jersey resort traffic. High-speed Reading and PRR passenger trains dueled on the New York and Atlantic City runs into the next century. Gowen joined Vanderbilt in starting the construction of the ill-starred South Pennsylvania Railroad to Pittsburgh, and the PRR paralleled the Reading's main line to Pottsville. The Reading failed again in 1884, and Gowen was finally deposed in 1886 by a bankers' syndicate headed by J. P. Morgan, who had already brokered a truce between the PRR and the Vanderbilts.

Archibald Angus McLeod, who became president in 1890, decided to go Gowen one better. Over PRR opposition McLeod built the grand Reading Terminal in Philadelphia. A new line from Harrisburg to Shippensburg (1891) created a connection with the B&O at Cherry Run, West Virginia (1892) and brought the Reading substantial western traffic bound to and from New York and New England. Then, in a wild spree during 1892 and 1893, McLeod leased the CNJ and the Lehigh Valley, built his own line to a New York coal terminal at Port Reading, and, with the goal of controlling the distribution of anthracite to New England, acquired the Poughkeepsie Bridge Route, the New York & New England, and the Boston & Maine. His move on the Old Colony Railroad failed when the whole house of cards collapsed. Again, Morgan stepped in to pick up the pieces.

Because the old Philadelphia & Reading was so encumbered with debt, it was necessary to clear the books with a foreclosure sale. However, Pennsylvania had since prohibited railroads from owning coal companies. Morgan's local lawyer, George F. Baer, found the solution. Forgotten among the North Pennsylvania's assets was an 1871 charter for a holding company with almost unlimited powers. Rechristened the Reading Co. in 1896, it became the common owner of the old Coal & Iron Co. and the new Philadelphia & Reading Railway Co.

By this time the Reading system was nearly complete. The Wilmington & Northern was purchased from the du Ponts in 1898, and the Reading secured stock control of the CNJ in 1901. Under the community of interest negotiated by the PRR and the Morgan roads, the B&O and New York Central each acquired 40 percent of the Reading in 1902. George F. Baer's handiwork withstood two decades of antitrust prosecution, but in 1920 the Supreme Court finally ordered the divorce of the Coal & Iron Co. and the railroad and of the Reading and CNJ. In 1923 the Reading Co. sold the Coal & Iron Co., absorbed the Philadelphia & Reading Railway and other rail subsidiaries, and became an operating company. The CNJ stock was placed in the hands of trustees but was returned to the Reading in 1933.

In the same year the web of parallel lines in southern New Jersey was consolidated as the jointly owned Pennsylvania-Reading Seashore Lines, and the Reading completed the electrification of its Philadelphia suburban lines. Through the Reading Transportation Co. (1928) it had begun to operate a network of trucks and buses for local traffic. The 1937 Budd streamliner *Crusader* added a touch of class to the New York–Philadelphia run, as did, until 1958, the B&O's Washington–New York Royal Blue Line trains. During the 1960s the Reading was one of the last regular operators of steam in the Northeast with its popular Iron Horse Rambles.

Although bankrupt again in 1971, the Reading was anything but demoralized and fought in vain to stay out of Conrail. Its strength is reflected in the fact that its Allentown-Shippensburg and Reading-Philadelphia routes became Conrail main lines. Many of the coal-country branches are owned by the Reading, Blue Mountain & Northern, which continues some Reading traditions. The Southeastern Pennsylvania Transportation Authority (SEPTA) assumed the passenger operations, dropped the last Philadelphia-Reading runs in 1981, and continues to run the electrified lines around Philadelphia. The Reading Co. now does business in Los Angeles as Reading Entertainment, Inc., the owner of theater chains in Australia and New Zealand.

In 1975, the last year before its properties were absorbed by Conrail, the Reading Co. operated a system of 1,149 route-miles and 2,591 track-miles, with 225 locomotives, 176 passenger cars, 12,213 freight cars, 168 company service cars, and 5,756 employees. Freight traffic totaled 3,136.2 million ton-miles in 1975, and coal (29 percent), pulp and paper (7.7 percent), foodstuffs (6.3 percent), and chemicals (5.8 percent) were its principal traffic sources. Passenger traffic totaled 189.7 million passenger-miles. Reading operating revenues totaled $136.9 million in 1975, and the railroad achieved a 92.4 percent operating ratio.

—Christopher T. Baer

REFERENCES

Hare, Jay V. *History of the Reading: The Collected Articles by Jay V. Hare*. Philadelphia: John Henry Strock, 1966.

Holton, James L. *The Reading Railroad: History of a Coal Age Empire*. 2 vols. Laury's Station, Pa.: Garrigues House, 1989–1992.

Schlegel, Marvin W. *Ruler of the Reading: The Life of Franklin B. Gowen, 1836–1889*. Harrisburg: Archives Publishing of Pennsylvania, 1947.

Regional Rail Reorganization Act (3R Act). *See* REGULATION

Regulation

The first action of the federal government that created statutory economic regulation and oversight of private enterprise dealt with the railroads. Economic regulation involves three elements: entry into the field of transportation or other enterprise, the rates that may be charged, and quality and quantity of service.

Economic regulation of entry, rates, and service can be achieved in several ways. The best and strongest is competition. New entrants will be wary of entering a field already well occupied. The rates charged will also be affected by the number of competitors, their costs, and the prices they charge. Many competitors in a free market will usually keep prices down and encourage efficient operation. The quantity and quality of service will also be a factor; in a market structure the competition that cannot match the quality standard of the other participants or offer sufficient quantities and qualities of goods or services will eventually be forced out.

Public investment, or the power of the public purse, is another source of nonstatutory economic regulatory control. An example is the construction of the interstate highway system by the federal government. The possibility of moving motor freight quickly and easily made entry attractive for those who wished to go into the trucking business. At the same time other modes of transportation, particularly the railroads, would tend to be very cautious about entering a market because the highway investment was perceived as giving motor carriers a distinct advantage. Federally improved waterways with facilities for barge service are another example, as are government-supported air transport facilities and operations. To prudent rail managers, the competition from carriers that used the publicly provided right of way might be assumed to be too great. The rates charged by all participants would be affected by the competition offered by carriers that used publicly provided facilities. The quality of the service would also be affected by the types of service offered by highway and other carriers.

Third-party pressure can also affect entry, rates, and service. A major shipper may demand that certain carriers enter a field, may demand and vigorously negotiate attractive rates, and may demand certain qualities and quantities of service. In return, the customer ships large quantities of freight or routes many passengers via the carrier that meets its requirements.

In all these examples the play of market forces and the circumstance of competition, public investment in facilities, or third-party pressure determined whether or not a carrier entered a market, the prices it charged, and the amount and quality of service it offered; no regulatory statutes were passed to achieve sufficient participants, reasonable rates, and acceptable service. In the earliest days of U.S. railways it appeared that there would be no need of any regulation to protect the public and the railroads other than usual market forces. Eventually, however, it seemed necessary for government to play a role in economic regulation, and, of course, there was the matter of the role of government and its rules in starting a railroad.

When railway development began in the 1820s and

1830s, corporate charters from the states were the first sort of government control or regulation to be faced. Charters were general in some cases, too specific in others. The points to be served were usually laid out in the charter, as was the deadline for completion. The reason for the specificity is that the charter granted a franchise of value to the public, as well as to the railroad corporation. If service did not commence by a certain time, the states wanted to give other entrants an opportunity to participate and serve the public. The type of locomotion to be used was set forth in some charters, and in some cases the maximum rates to be charged for passengers and freight were stipulated as well. Upon examination, many early charters appear to be very naive; the railroad business was not well understood.

Shortly after their advent it was clear that railroads were very different from the turnpikes and canals that had preceded them as transportation improvements. The turnpike or canal companies created by private capital or in some cases—particularly in later years—by public bodies built and maintained their facilities and allowed others to use them upon payment of a toll; turnpike and canal companies were not necessarily operators of the facility they owned and maintained. As first chartered, some of the early railways were expected to be simply another kind of turnpike company; the railroad would own the right-of-way facility, but many different individuals or firms would operate on its lines upon payment of a toll.

But the speed of the steam locomotive made it impractical, ineffective, and inefficient to share the right of way. The railroad had to be an operating monopoly, as well as a market monopoly. In the latter case, except in very large and busy towns, railways would not be built anywhere and everywhere in a fine-grained fashion, but would confer this transportation advantage only to a limited area.

Absent effective competition from other modes of transportation, the railroads could with impunity establish the service standards and rates they charged. The expense of railway construction, rolling stock, locomotives, and fixed facilities was so great as to practically limit where railroads would be built; areas with small populations and limited resources would not enjoy the presence of a railroad except for a line built to serve some other place or places and merely passing through.

At points served by more than one railroad, the level of rates and quality and quantity of service were usually attractive because of the force of competition. But passengers and shippers soon found reason to demand lower rates and better service if they were served by a single rail carrier. Public cries for economic regulation came on the heels of the Civil War. Farmers and others at noncompetitive points saw themselves as hapless captives of greedy railroads. In fact, the railroad companies sought to make up losses or less-than-adequate revenues gleaned from competitive points by charging higher rates at points where they had a true monopoly position.

One trigger of public discontent was the federal government's attempt to pull back into the U.S. Treasury the greenbacks or paper money that had been printed to help pay for the Civil War. Greenbacks made money readily available around the nation, particularly in rural areas in the West and South where hard money based on the gold standard rarely found its way. Upset, the farmers and businesspeople in small cities and towns reacted against the economic problems fostered by the end of the greenback.

A particularly sore point in these locations was the high freight rates charged by the railroads. Farmers were especially angered by what they perceived as the high rates they paid to bring in supplies and equipment or to ship out the products of their fields. Although notoriously difficult to organize because of their scattered locations, outraged farmers eventually joined together in an alliance. There were other grievances, but the rural organizations called for government regulation to help control high railroad rates at noncompetitive points. Usually called the Granger movement because of the nickname of one of the largest of such groups, the Patrons of Husbandry or Grange (*see* GRANGER LAWS AND CASES), the alliance gathered strength. Under strong pressure from the angry farmers, the states of Wisconsin, Minnesota, Iowa, and Illinois passed the so-called Granger laws in 1870 and 1871. These laws were aimed at railroads and other important enterprises delivering vital public services, such as grain elevators or ferry service.

Although many of these laws were unworkable and impractical (some specified maximum freight rates despite no knowledge by legislators of railroad costs), the concept of state regulation of railroads and other public businesses withstood the test in the U.S. Supreme Court. In the case *Munn v. Illinois* the Supreme Court found in 1877 that enterprises that were clothed with the public interest could indeed be regulated by the state. In the decision the Court looked back to the rulings of Lord Chief Justice Hale in seventeenth-century England. In short, regulation of vital private enterprise by the state was legal in the eyes of the Court.

Abetting the move toward statutory regulation was the failure of common law to provide protection. Under common law, a plaintiff must be injured before redress could be sought. That is, a farmer who believed that the rates on shipping his corn were too high could not complain to the court until the grain had been shipped and the too-high price actually charged. In short, common law was and is remedial, not preventive.

Another problem with common law is that the concept, which dated back to medieval times, assumed that the parties to a dispute were equal in their ability and economic power. In the real world of the post–Civil War United States, the railroad companies were formidable adversaries to the ordinary citizen seeking redress of grievance. Most railroads had large and talented legal staffs, and it was also their practice to put the outstanding lawyers in the territory along the line on retainer. (Abraham Lincoln, considered the top lawyer in Illinois, was on retainer to both the Chicago, Rock Island & Pacific Railroad and the Illinois Central Railroad. The future president won major cases for these carriers.) Ordinary citizens could not afford to hire the legal talent to win a case against a railroad.

In 1874 the Windom Committee was established by the U.S. Senate to investigate the outcries from around the United States. In its report it agreed that high railroad rates were damaging to noncompetitive points and recommended that the federal government build a railroad from St. Louis to the Atlantic Seaboard that would charge prices that were fair and honest. It was expected that competition from the federal railroad would bring down the rates charged by the other, privately owned railroads. Considered impractical, as well as highly expensive, and flying in the face of the national mood of laissez-faire, the recommendations were not carried out.

A huge expansion of railroad construction began in the late 1870s and continued through the 1880s as the nation virtually doubled its rail mileage. There were mergers and consolidations on a large scale, and railroad networks and systems were formed. Some railroads became huge enterprises. Again there were many complaints from shippers, especially small businesses and farmers, at noncompetitive points. This time they were not so much about excessively high rates as about the vast discrimination practiced by the rail companies. For example, major shippers were given rebates that refunded part of the freight charges. In some cases drawbacks were given, in which a major shipper would be refunded part of the freight charges levied against its competitors. Revelations of the favorable rates and drawbacks given to John D. Rockefeller's Standard Oil Co. outraged small shippers. This information was revealed by the Cullom Committee of the U.S. Senate, which reported upon its investigation in 1886 and called on the federal government to regulate interstate commerce by rail.

At virtually the same time a landmark Supreme Court decision made federal regulation inevitable. In *Wabash, St. Louis & Pacific Railway Co. v. Illinois* (1886) the Supreme Court found that the State of Illinois could indeed regulate the railroads within its borders, as it had done since the early 1870s, but on shipments of corn from Illinois to New York, Illinois had no jurisdiction over the interstate portions of the trip. The Court ruled that only Congress could regulate interstate commerce. With a decision in the *Wabash* case and the report of the Cullom Committee, the stage was set for the federal government to provide statutory economic regulation of the railroads.

—George M. Smerk

Act to Regulate Commerce

The Act to Regulate Commerce of 1887, popularly known as the Interstate Commerce Act, was the first major step by Congress under its commerce power to regulate economic activity. It sought to remedy perceived abuses in America's first big business, the railroad industry.

Although the states had experimented with regulatory schemes, they found it difficult to effectively govern the growing network of interstate rail lines. Their power, after all, only reached to their borders. At the same time railroads were frustrated by inconsistent and piecemeal state legislation. State regulations made the rate structure even more confused. There was mounting pressure for Congress to address the problems of the rail industry and impose a uniform law throughout the United States. In 1883 President Chester A. Arthur called for congressional action to regulate the carriers. But Congress moved cautiously, in part because there was little agreement on either the nature of the problem or the desired legislative remedy. As a result, the House of Representatives and the Senate passed quite different bills. It was clear, however, that some type of federal legislation was likely. At this point the Supreme Court concluded in *Wabash, St. Louis & Pacific Railway Co. v. Illinois* (1886) that state regulation of interstate railroad charges invaded federal authority under the commerce clause. The Court in effect ruled that interstate transportation charges could only be controlled by Congress. The *Wabash* decision helped break the legislative impasse and bring about passage of the Act to Regulate Commerce in 1887.

The act was an untidy compromise between the House and Senate bills. It created a five-member Interstate Commerce Commission (ICC) whose members were appointed by the president for six-year terms. The ICC was authorized to conduct hearings and issue orders to halt practices found to be in violation of the statute. If a carrier failed to heed an order, the ICC could petition the federal courts to compel compliance. The act provided that charges for interstate rail transportation should be "reasonable and just," but did not define this standard or confer ratemaking authority on the ICC. It also banned rebates or preferential treatment for any shipper. The pooling of traffic or earnings among carriers was outlawed. The prohibition of long-haul/short-haul rate differences, however, was softened by inserting the imprecise phrase "under similar circumstances and conditions." This wording seemingly allowed the railroads to keep long-haul/short-haul rate differences when they were warranted by special circumstances. Finally, the act obligated carriers to file public rate schedules and to furnish information on financial matters and operations to the ICC. Having satisfied the public desire to curb perceived railroad excesses, Congress left unresolved policy matters and interpretive issues to the ICC and the courts.

Implementation of the measure was beset with difficulties. Many of these can be traced to the act itself. Fundamental policy questions, such as the role of competition, were not clearly addressed. Was the act intended to encourage competition among railroads, or to stabilize the industry by cartelization? Moreover, the ICC had to rely on the federal courts to enforce its orders. Yet the federal courts, skeptical about the regulatory process, insisted that the factual basis for ICC findings be reexamined de novo. This undercut the ICC's authority and delayed the enforcement of its orders.

During the 1890s the Supreme Court in a line of cases narrowly construed ICC authority under the act. The commission assumed that its authority to review the reasonableness of existing rates encompassed the implied power to set charges. In *ICC v. Cincinnati, New Orleans & Texas Pacific Railway Co.* (1897), however, the justices held that the act did not by implication empower the commission to fix railroad rates. Further, in *ICC v. Alabama Midland Railway Co.* (1897) the Court greatly limited the scope of the long-haul/short-haul clause. It determined that the existence of railroad competition must be considered in applying the proviso "under substantially similar circumstances and conditions." As a practical matter this decision rendered the long-haul/short-haul clause of the act null. It was usually possible to demonstrate that competition at one point created dissimilarities.

By the turn of the twentieth century the ICC was largely toothless and devoted much of its energy to collecting statistics. Its supervision of the railroads was almost entirely nominal. Some historians have accused the Supreme Court of emasculating the act, but this charge is wide of the mark. The Court's restrictive interpretation of the act undoubtedly reflected judicial preference for private market ordering. Congress, however, was responsible for the underlying problems. The measure was a patchwork of shadowy provisions. The Supreme Court did not frustrate any clear intent of Congress concerning the rail industry. In fact, neither Congress nor the presidents seemed bothered by the Supreme Court's rulings. Not until the emergence of the Progressive movement in the early twentieth century did Congress take steps to strengthen railroad regulation. The Elkins Act of 1903 and the Hepburn Act of 1906 amended the 1887 Act to Regulate Commerce to enhance the powers of the ICC. Since then the 1887 act has been repeatedly amended to reflect changed thinking about regulatory policy.

Despite many shortcomings, the Act to Regulate Commerce constituted a watershed in American economic and legal history. It was the initial hesitant move by Congress toward administrative regulation of economic activity. The ICC, moreover, became the model for other independent regulatory commissions that characterized the administrative state of the twentieth century.

—James W. Ely, Jr.

Interstate Commerce Commission

The Act to Regulate Commerce of 1887, commonly called the Interstate Commerce Act, created the Interstate Commerce Commission (ICC) as the first federal independent regulatory commission. These commissions became an important part of the federal government structure in the twentieth century. As an independent body, the ICC was a product of agrarian and labor protest that played an important part in American life in the period between the end of the Civil War and World War I. Various reform groups saw that there was much wrong in American life and government and sought to improve the situation through problem-solving legislation and programs.

Many reformers believed that politics was essentially evil. By the 1870s the wretched excesses of political bosses like William Marcy Tweed in New York, the Crédit Mobilier scandal of the Grant administration, and the flowering of corruption at all levels of government offered good cause for this distrust. To the reformers, the regulation of a business as big and vital as the railroads demanded that nonpolitical bodies be created to carry out state and federal regulation.

The geographic and legislative scope of the Interstate Commerce Act also underscored the need for an expert body to interpret its provisions. This was a realistic appraisal of the legislative process because laws cannot possibly be specific enough to deal with all situations. For example, the first section of the act required that all rates be just and reasonable and stated that any unjust or unreasonable rate was unlawful. This was, of course, no more than the tenets of common law written into statutory law. The law states a general principle, but an expert body would sift the facts and make a judgment of what was just and reasonable in a given case. The same was true of Section 3, which prohibited undue preference or prejudice in rates. The key word was "undue"; the act did not attempt to outlaw all preference and prejudice, only that which was undue. Some expert body was needed to decide what constituted undue preference and prejudice.

The Interstate Commerce Act created the ICC as an independent body that was to have legislative, executive, and judicial functions, but was not to fall within those branches of the federal government. As originally established, the ICC consisted of 5 commissioners appointed by the president with the advice and consent of the U.S. Senate. The commissioners would annually choose the chair on a rotating basis. This was finally changed by legislation passed in 1969. Since January 1, 1970, the president has selected the ICC chairman.

The first chairman of the ICC was Judge Thomas M. Cooley. As a lawyer, he was largely responsible for the commission's legalistic, case-by-case approach to regulatory matters. Cooley was instrumental in setting the tone for the ICC, which regarded itself as a body to adjudicate disputes between private parties rather than a promoter of the public interest.

A major duty of the ICC was to hear complaints concerning alleged violations of the act. For example, carriers under the jurisdiction of the ICC were obliged to file rates with the commission; this did not mean that the commission reviewed or investigated each rate. Instead, the ICC looked into rate matters only upon complaint or when the proposed rate was extraordinary.

The ICC had investigative powers and was to look into alleged violations and to order violators to cease and desist from unlawful practices. The commission also was empowered to assess the damages suffered by a party harmed by violations of the act. In carrying out its work, the commission possessed the authority to inquire into the business of common carriers and could require testimony of witnesses and demand a review of documents and records relevant to matters being investigated. The commission was given power to require annual reports from the carriers and to prescribe a uniform system of accounts. The ICC was to report annually to Congress in order to offer information pertinent to the regulation of commerce and to make suggestions for modifications of existing legislation or proposals for new legislation.

As new regulatory statutes were enacted, the work of the ICC expanded beyond its original jurisdiction of railroads and some joint rail-water movements to embrace all modes of transportation. Even air transport for a time was partially under its jurisdiction. Over the years, as the workload increased, the size of the commission grew to 11 members, and terms were increased to seven years. The ICC staff also expanded to approximately 2,500. To hasten matters and carry out more work, the Commission Division Act of 1917 authorized the ICC to organize itself into divisions of not less than 3 commissioners each. This precluded the need for all the commissioners to hear all the cases. In difficult cases the matter could be reheard by the whole commission.

During the 1890s court decisions placed much of the Interstate Commerce Act in doubt. Under the original act of 1887, ICC orders had to be enforced by the federal courts, and many jurists were skeptical or hostile to commission decisions. It was not until passage of the Hepburn Act in 1906 that the ICC was given power to make legally binding orders. This power placed the commission in a position to provide leadership and vision in the formulation of an effective transportation policy for the United States, but relatively little came of it. Transportation legislation continued to be mainly a reaction to the perceived problems and political pressures of a given time rather than a comprehensive approach to changing transportation needs and circumstances.

In the first decade of the twentieth century the ICC did attempt to keep up with changes in competition and improve its understanding of the economics of the railroad industry, including the impact of inflation on rates once thought to be fixed permanently. However, from the perspective of both the railroad industry and knowledgeable observers, the commission was seen as having a largely negative influence. The industry and the national economy were not strengthened.

After the federal government's takeover of rail operations during World War I, the Transportation Act of 1920 returned the industry to private control and placed the ICC in a position to help shape a rationalized national rail system. The commission and some members of Congress also recognized the transportation potential of motor carriers as the federal and state governments moved to provide a network of paved highways and the automobile industry turned out increasingly reliable and powerful trucks. The commission and Congress encouraged the railroads to go into the trucking business. It was seen as a way for a well-established industry to help a budding but chaotic transportation industry that could also act as a complement to railroad service. Despite the encouragement, only a few rail carriers chose to go into the motor carrier business on a large scale; however, they did enter the intercity motor bus industry on a fairly aggressive basis. The act of 1920 also encouraged the consolidation of railroads into rational systems in an effort to overcome the difficulty of dealing with railroads of varying levels of financial success. Because of railroads' reluctance to join wholeheartedly into the consolidation idea, little came of it.

The Great Depression plunged the railroads into numerous bankruptcies, and the skilled ICC staff and knowledgeable commissioners helped guide Congress in the passage of legislation that was hoped to be effective in preserving a healthy system of carriers. With competition from water carriers, motor carriers, and pipelines, and a fledgling airline industry forming, it would have made economic sense to reduce regulation and allow market forces to work. Such action was politically unfeasible.

The regulation of interstate motor carriers in 1935 placed a huge burden on the ICC. The motor carrier law permitted carriers that could prove bona fide existing interstate operations to be grandfathered into receiving operating authority. Because of the proliferation of motor carriers, the grandfather case burden was enormous, and ICC staff and commissioners were swamped. The commission's legalistic, case-by-case approach to its work made the process a slow one, and the cases took 20 years to be completed.

The work burden of the commission was increased again when water carriers were regulated in 1940 and freight forwarders in 1942. The task of working with rate adjustments and operating authority, as well as overseeing stock issues and financial matters of the carriers under its jurisdiction, also slowed the work of the commission. Commission oversight of controversial carrier mergers led to proceedings that dragged on for years. The proposed merger of the Chicago, Rock Island & Pacific into the Union Pacific took 12 years, and when the decision was finally rendered, the Rock Island was hopelessly bankrupt and the merger did not take place.

The slowness of action proved to be a burden on the transportation industries under the jurisdiction of the ICC. It was clear that the regulated transportation industries were not enjoying the same success as the unregulated businesses in the 1950s, 1960s, and 1970s. Regulation came to be held in low regard, especially given the sad financial and physical state of the railroads in the 1960s and 1970s. Deregulation and more reliance on market forces, originally a position mainly taken by academics in the 1950s, came to be recognized by some members of the commission, the carriers, Congress, and the public by the late 1970s as a sensible public policy for the transportation industries.

The initial move toward deregulation came with the Railroad Revitalization and Regulatory Reform Act of 1976, which provided more rate freedom for railroads and made rail abandonment and mergers easier. A major aim was to help prevent the economic disaster of the Penn Central merger and subsequent bankruptcy from repeating itself. The pace of deregulation picked up. Air cargo movements were deregulated in 1977. The Airline Deregulation Act of 1978 did away with economic regulation of airline passenger service and led to the sunsetting of the Civil Aeronautics Board. In 1980 the Motor Carrier Act eased entry restrictions and permitted rate negotiations based on market forces for the trucking industry. It was followed quickly by the Staggers Act of 1980, which greatly eased rail regulation and gave railroads the authority to negotiate contracts; the act allowed rate flexibility and defined rail maximum rates. In short, by the end of 1980 railroads were largely deregulated, and the ICC had less to do with rail transport. The 1994 Trucking Industry Regulatory Reform Act did away with the need for motor carriers to file individual tariffs with the ICC, and the commission was given the power to deregulate categories of truck traffic. With less and less to do, the ICC was abolished in the ICC Termination Act of 1995. It closed up shop on December 31, 1995. The Termination Act created the Surface Transportation Board to continue the tasks of the ICC that needed to be carried out.

Over its long history the ICC took on the difficult task of putting acts of Congress into practical regulatory form. It provided expertise for Congress and the courts in shaping legislation and judicial decisions. The ICC developed a uniform system of accounts that not only served the needs of the commission but also provided a stable means of comparison for the companies under its jurisdiction.

What the commission was unable to do was adjust quickly to change. It began its existence regulating the railroad industry's virtual monopoly of U.S. transportation and eventually took on the job of regulating competition, which is an oxymoron. It successfully adjusted to much of the legislation it had to interpret and implement, but reacted slowly and did not keep pace with fundamental changes in the market for transportation service. The ICC was overwhelmed with a huge burden of work, which included safety regulation, as well as economic regulation. Although the staff was large, it was not really adequate to handle all the work quickly. The ICC was a great training ground for economists and lawyers; there was a problem of retaining the services of these skilled staff, many of whom went to work for the carriers regulated by the ICC, which could pay higher salaries.

In retrospect, as workable competition in transportation became truly possible in the 1930s, strict economic regulation should probably have been phased out to let market forces play a larger role. But deregulation would have been unthinkable during the Depression, which was popularly blamed on big corporations. The commission was already gaining a reputation for being old fashioned and slow; this is a reason Congress saw to it that airlines were regulated by a separate body, the CAB. The ICC was generally seen as an agency of government that had maintained its integrity despite its task of handling obsolete and inconsistent policies developed by Congress.

—George M. Smerk

The Elkins Act, the Hepburn Act, and the Mann-Elkins Act

The passage of the Act to Regulate Commerce (usually called the Interstate Commerce Act) into law in 1887 did not end the problems related to the economic regulation of the railroads. At first, the railroads generally accepted the provisions of the act and complied with ICC orders. There were weaknesses in the Interstate Commerce Act— the orders of the ICC could only be given force by a federal court—and when court decisions of 1896 and 1897 essentially emasculated the law, there was public concern over the viability of the regulatory system.

As the weaknesses were perceived, newspapers and periodicals painted vivid pictures of malevolent practices of big business. Unfortunately, at that time the railroads were the biggest businesses of all. Muckraking journalists had much to feed on with the business and financial scandals of the 1890s and early 1900s. Even when the muckrakers did not focus on the railroads in particular, the carriers were a very visible symbol of big business. Railroad officials also felt the need for more effective regulation that would protect them from the plague of rebates and concessions that siphoned off what one observer estimated was 10 percent of the rail carriers' revenues. The railroads wanted protection against the pressure of large shippers that forced rebates.*

Early on there had been modifications to help strengthen the Act to Regulate Commerce. The act was first amended in 1889. One provision required three days' advance notice of rate reductions. Ten-day notices were required in the original act for rate increases, but none for reducing rates. Another modification involved penalties to be imposed upon shippers seeking advantages, which brought pressure upon the rail carriers to discriminate. In the original act

---

*A rebate is a return of a portion of the published rate to the shipper. For example, if a published rate was 100 cents per hundredweight, the carrier might rebate 20 cents to the shipper in order to gain the business. A concession often took the form of a carrier performing work without payment. As an instance, a railroad might perform intensive switching and placement of cars at a factory without receiving reimbursement.

there was no provision to enforce the orders of the ICC; the 1889 amendments gave injured shippers the right to take court action to compel the payment of damages awarded by the commission.

The act of 1887 gave the ICC the power to compel witnesses to testify, but the Fifth Amendment to the Constitution prevents persons from being compelled to testify against themselves. The Compulsory Testimony Act of 1893 held that persons could be compelled to testify in proceedings of the ICC, but that the witnesses could not be prosecuted or subjected to any penalty on account of the testimony.

Pressure for stronger regulation came from both the industry and the public. The railroads wished for statutes to help them with problems that could not be solved by common law. The excesses by railroads in some cases and the general unhappiness with big business and predatory practices by corporations were highlighted by the writings of such authors as Ida M. Tarbell, Ray Stannard Baker, and Lincoln Steffens. As for greater regulation of the railroads, President McKinley was uninterested, but this was not the case with his vice president, Theodore Roosevelt. Upon McKinley's assassination, President Roosevelt pressed for new legislation.

The first action to move ICC cases through the federal court system with greater speed was the Expediting Act of 1903. The ICC had no power to enforce its orders; the commission had to rely on the action of the federal courts, which averaged about four years for the prosecution of ICC cases. The delay meant that commission orders were often unobserved, and condemned practices continued for a considerable period. Under the Expediting Act, cases brought under the Sherman Antitrust Act or the Interstate Commerce Act were to be given expedited treatment upon certification by the attorney general of the importance of the case. The federal court was to push such cases forward at the earliest opportunity. Any appeal to a decision by a circuit court was to be appealed directly to the U.S. Supreme Court.

The departure from published rates by some railroads was a matter of concern both to the railroads and to the public. The railroads pushed for legislation because they were losing money as a result of departure from published rates. The Elkins Act of 1903 addressed solely the issue of personal discrimination. One of its provisions held the railway corporation itself, rather than individuals employed by the carrier, liable for prosecution for unlawful discrimination or concessions. A second provision of the Elkins Act made the receiver of a rebate or concession guilty of violating the law whether the rebate had been offered voluntarily by the rail carrier or given under pressure by the shipper.

The Act to Regulate Commerce made it illegal for carriers to charge rates above or below those published in tariffs. The Elkins Act made any departure from the published rate a misdemeanor; it was not necessary to prove that discrimination had taken place. Another provision of the Elkins Act was to authorize the courts to enjoin carriers from continuing unlawful discrimination or departure from the published rate.

Between the Interstate Commerce Act of 1887 and the Transportation Act of 1920, the most important piece of railroad regulatory legislation was the Hepburn Act of 1906, named after Congressman William Hepburn of Iowa, then chairman of the House Commerce Committee. The law closely reflected the views of President Theodore Roosevelt and his Department of Justice; indeed, an earlier and more stringent version of the legislation had been drafted by the Justice Department.

The Hepburn Act greatly increased the power of the ICC and put teeth back into the Interstate Commerce Act. That act had been weakened by decisions that mirrored the attitude of a conservative federal judiciary uncomfortable with the regulatory role of government. Although the legislation was enthusiastically supported by President Theodore Roosevelt, it was bitterly opposed by the railroads and by J. P. Morgan, the National Assn. of Manufacturers, and financial interests. Opponents saw the legislation as weakening the railroads' ability to prosper and thus making it difficult for carriers to attract the funds needed to make necessary capital investments. Some railroad executives favored the legislation as the best they could expect at a time when the public was often hostile to big business and particularly disaffected with the railroads.

Leading up to passage of the act was an effort by the railroads to increase their rates, a fact not appreciated or fully understood by the Congress or the ICC. Earlier than most businesses, as well as the American public and the federal government, American railroads began to grasp the influence of inflation and to realize that costs were going up.

When the Interstate Commerce Act was passed in 1887, Congress believed that the freight rates that would eventually be published under the act would stay the same. This was understandable; by 1887 the United States had experienced a period of very stable or even declining costs and prices for 20 to 25 years. By early in the twentieth century it was clear to the railroads that a dollar in 1904 or 1905 would not buy as much as a dollar in 1887. The falling value of a revenue dollar was a great problem because steadily increasing freight and passenger traffic strained available resources. Major bottlenecks developed, and failure of the railroads to provide a high level of service could have a detrimental effect on the economy.

Several components of the federal government misunderstood the economic pressures and needs of the rail carriers. The railroads needed to make capital improvements in track and structure and purchase more and better rolling stock and newer, more powerful locomotives to handle the burgeoning traffic. Newer, larger freight and passenger terminals and facilities were needed, along with double- and triple-tracking of busy lines and the installation of modern signal systems to increase capacity and improve safety. The efforts of the railroads in the first five years of the twentieth century to raise rates created a reaction from Congress and the White House to curb what was perceived as rapacity on the part of greedy railroads and the bankers who financed them. The act of 1906 was aimed at greater control of the railroads, as well as the pipelines that had been key to the formation of the Standard Oil monopoly.

The Hepburn Act expanded the reach of ICC regulation of the railroad industry. It now included express companies, sleeping-car companies, and pipelines. In the matter of petroleum pipelines, President Roosevelt and his administration were frustrated by their inability to bring the Standard Oil Co. to heel under the terms of the Sherman Act. By declaring pipelines to be common carriers and thus under the jurisdiction of the ICC, the Roosevelt administration believed that the monopoly power of Standard Oil would be mitigated, and to a large extent that was true.

The Hepburn Act also gave the ICC jurisdiction over various accessorial services that railroads provided, such as storage, refrigeration, heating, and ventilation. The lawmakers felt that discrimination was possible unless the ICC had regulatory oversight of these services. The rail carriers usually levied extra charges for accessorial services, and without regulation certain shippers could be fa-

vored at the expense of others. An aim of the act was to assure that all shippers would be treated without discrimination.

Strength was reinstated in the Interstate Commerce Act under the Hepburn Act by empowering the commission to prescribe maximum reasonable rates. This power was to be employed only upon complaint, but it was the greatest example of governmental power vis-à-vis the railroads up to that time. In the absence of the power to prescribe maximum reasonable rates, the public and shippers were given inadequate protection from unreasonable charges by carriers. It should be noted that this power could only be used if existing rates were found to be unreasonable or otherwise unlawful. Under the Hepburn Act, a specific rate could not be set, but the maximum rates could be prescribed. Even under the act, the ICC was not empowered to prescribe minimum rates to help prevent the carriers from levying unremunerative rates.

Under the Hepburn Act, the commission also was given the power to establish through routes for freight movement when carriers refused to do so. The commission also prescribed maximum joint rates and, under certain conditions, could prescribe the division of revenues among the participating carriers in joint-rate interactions.

Under the new law, 30 days' notice had to be given for all changes in rates, whether increases or decreases. Under

Theodore Roosevelt was hardly a friend of the railroads, but there were some railroad executives who thought that some of the control measures being proposed in the Congress could help the railroads. Chief among them was Pennsylvania president Alexander Cassatt, who often advised Roosevelt. When the Hepburn Act was finally passed in 1906, it included a number of provisions that were helpful, among them prohibition of the free passes and rebates and concessions practices that had become costly for railroads. New York *Herald* cartoonist W. A. Rogers, at least, felt that Roosevelt had done some good work for the railroads. —Library of Congress (Neg. LC-USZ62-10327)

emergency conditions, such as a misprinting of the rates in a tariff, the commission could authorize rate changes on briefer notice.

The issue of discrimination, a sore point with shippers and the American public, was covered in the legislation. Free passes had long been used by the railroads as a marketing device. Under the act, these were prohibited, except for railroad employees.

The Hepburn Act also included what came to be called the commodities clause. It prohibited railroads that owned coal mines or engaged in producing other commodities from doing so. For example, a railroad that owned coal mines could charge very high prices for shipping the coal and merely take the money from one pocket and put it in the other when the coal was transported by the railroad controlling the mines. Coal-mining competitors would be forced to pay the high rates to move their coal and would be at a disadvantage in the marketplace. In short, the Hepburn Act prohibited railroads from transporting materials in interstate commerce that the carrier had produced or in which it had some interest. There was an exception for lumber. Also, the commodities clause did not prevent railroads from producing materials for their own use, such as owning coal mines to supply locomotive fuel.

In a very important legislative action, in order to enforce the provisions of the Interstate Commerce Act, as amended, the Hepburn Act gave the force of law to the orders of the ICC. Heretofore, commission orders had not been binding on the railroads unless there was a court order that compelled carriers to respond.

To help in its regulatory work, the Hepburn Act authorized the ICC to employ a staff of examiners and agents to review railroad accounts. It also made reporting key information to the ICC annually a requirement and set penalties for railroads that failed to comply. Finally, the ICC was increased in size from five to seven members. The term of office of an ICC commissioner was raised from six to seven years.

All in all, the Hepburn Act created comprehensive control over the actions of the railroad industry. Many railroad managers and observers of the railroad scene viewed the act as detrimental to the rail carriers because it prevented them from working freely in the market to sell their services. This control and lack of rate freedom had a negative impact on the railroads when other modes of transportation were developed and entered the transportation marketplace in the 1920s.

The Hepburn Act did much to strengthen railroad regulation, but there were still weaknesses perceived. Indeed, when William Howard Taft ran for the presidency in 1908, an important part of his platform was further economic regulation of the railroads. Insurgents in the Congress made many changes, and the Mann-Elkins Act that eventually made its way into law in 1910 was unlike the legislation originally proposed by President Taft.

An important feature of the Mann-Elkins Act was amendment of the long-and-short-haul clause of the Interstate Commerce Act. In the original act there was a provision that railroads could not "under substantially similar circumstances and conditions" charge a higher rate for a shorter than a longer haul over the same line in the same direction. In the Alabama Midland case (*ICC v. Alabama Midland Railway Co.*, 168 U.S. 144, 1897), it was held that railroads themselves might decide whether or not conditions were similar and that competition at both intermediate and through points might create a difference in circumstances so that the prohibitions in the law did not apply. The upshot was wholesale disregard of the fourth section of the Interstate Commerce Act.

In the Mann-Elkins Act the phrase "under substantially similar circumstances and conditions" was removed. Charging more for a short haul than a long haul was prohibited unless an exception was granted by the ICC. A railroad that wished to avoid the prohibition had to pray for relief from Section 4 of the act and explain to the ICC why it wished to do so. Usually the argument used cited cost as the reason for the exception.

Another element of the new law involved rate changes. The Hepburn Act empowered the commission to change only rates already in place; the ICC was not empowered to assay the reasonableness of proposed rates. Until the Mann-Elkins Act, the only means of determining the reasonableness of a proposed rate was to let the rate go into effect; upon complaint, if the ICC found the rate to be unreasonable, it could order that the rate be changed and that the parties that paid the unreasonable rate could receive reparations. Because delays could be harmful to the public, as well as to carriers, the Mann-Elkins Act permitted the commission to suspend a proposed rate change for up to 120 days while the reasonableness was investigated. Additional suspension time was authorized if the investigation needed more time.

The rate-suspension provisions of the act affected the burden of proof. The theory was that the party proposing a rate change had the burden of proof, so it was up to the railroad to show that a rate increase was reasonable.

—George M. Smerk

Transportation Act of 1920

As the nation's first big business, railways acted profoundly in moving the American economy and society from one mostly rural and agrarian to one primarily urban and industrial, in the process challenging tightly held devotion to laissez-faire principles. State regulation of rails came first, and regulation at the federal level began with the Interstate Commerce Act of 1887. The ICC was greatly strengthened during the Progressive Era with the Hepburn Act (1906) and the Mann-Elkins Act (1910), which collectively put a chill on investors and drove the spirit of entrepreneurship from the industry. By 1912 newspapers were printing stories headlined "Pitiful

Plight of the American Railroads" and "Our Starving Railroads." By 1915, one-sixth of U.S. rail mileage was in the hands of receivers; fewer miles of railroad were built in 1915 than in any year since 1864. Nevertheless, in 1916, four operating-craft brotherhoods demanded federal legislation mandating an eight-hour day without reduction in wages, and to avoid a threatened nationwide strike, Congress passed and President Woodrow Wilson signed into law the Adamson Act giving labor what it wanted. In the end, railroad managers were prevented from deciding what they would pay for labor and what they would charge for service.

Then came the Great War. Europe in flames craved American production; industrial and agricultural tonnage swelled traffic on the rails. That swell only increased when the United States itself entered combat early in April 1917. But problems were great. War traffic tended to move only in one direction—east—and when Atlantic ports and oceanic transport proved inadequate, railcars simply piled up as unintended warehouses. Gridlock was at hand. President Wilson, to complete mobilization of the country's resources required for war, took possession of the railroads by proclamation issued on December 26. Control passed to the U.S. Railroad Administration (USRA) and to William G. McAdoo, director general, effective at noon on December 28, but for accounting purposes on January 1, 1918. Congress subsequently passed and Wilson signed into law the Railway Control Act, which provided that the federal government would make annual compensation to the carriers on the basis of net operating income for the three years preceding and ending June 30, 1917. It also promised adequate maintenance of property during the time of government operation. Regional federal directors were appointed to oversee general operation, and local federal managers were assigned to on-the-job responsibilities, but with final authority resting in Washington.

Railroad owners and managers were understandably perplexed by this turn of events. There was nothing in the history of American railroading parallel to the new federal control. The ICC and antitrust law were summarily put on the shelf, and USRA's sweeping authority superseded them. ICC and antitrust had obliged railroads to compete with one another; USRA now obliged them to cooperate. Then, on November 11, 1918, the awful international conflict came to an end. The Railway Control Act required return of the railroads to their owners within two years of the end of hostilities.

It was in this milieu that a strenuous debate occurred regarding the disposition of the railroads. President Wilson earlier had promised that they would be returned to their owners as soon as the "emergency" passed, but one month after the armistice, McAdoo proposed continuing government operation for another five years. Glenn E. Plumbe, representing labor, vigorously advocated purchase of railroad properties by the federal government, the creation of a national operating corporation, and the lease of these lines to it. Others joined the fray. The ICC (frozen out of power by the USRA) and others opposed nationalization but wanted additional regulation of one sort or another.

Senator Albert E. Cummins, chairman of the Interstate Commerce Committee, was at the vortex of these debates and would have a strong hand in any forthcoming legislation. His task was to frame a plan of solid economics but capable of political passage. A Republican, Cummins had the advantage of dealing with a Congress controlled by that party, but Woodrow Wilson would hold the presidency until March 1921. And railroad managers and owners were not of one mind. Cummins would have his hands full trying to satisfy diverse constituencies.

One part of the legislative effort was to resolve the problem of inadequate earnings. The rule of ratemaking was changed to follow the model of *Smyth v. Ames* in which the regulated entity was to earn a fair return on a fair valuation of the property. To address the weak-railroad problem, the recapture clause was added to the law. Those carriers earning more than a fair return would have the excess earnings taken by the ICC: Half of this money would be returned to the donor to be invested in capital improvements that could not be added to the value base; the remainder of the money would be made available to weak railroads for productive investment at very low rates of interest. The revised rule of ratemaking proved unworkable. Assuming that a fair value could be estimated with a high degree of accuracy, should rates be raised or lowered to achieve a fair rate of return? What to do depended upon the price sensitivity of various commodities; this is very difficult to ascertain and may vary substantially over time. The revised rule was eventually dropped, along with the recapture clause, in later legislation.

Senator Cummins proved a skillful legislator, fully engaging himself in the art of the possible. Recognizing that there was unequal earning capacity in the family of railroads, he counseled "a series of consolidations which will merge weak roads with strong ones, to the end that the resulting systems, and they will be comparatively few in number, may do business on substantially even terms." Railroad consolidation would be a hallmark and the most publicly visible element of what became the Esch-Cummins bill. Pulling and hauling added other important elements, including, not unimportantly, return of railroads to their owners, a labor board with authority to arbitrate labor disputes, establishing 5.5 percent as a fair return on the aggregate value of property, allowing the pooling of traffic if it was found to be in the public interest, and variously strengthening the ICC. Esch-Cummins reflected shipper interests more than railroad interests, but given the political landscape of the time, it was about all that railroaders and investors could hope for. President Wilson signed Esch-Cummins, or the Transportation Act of 1920, into law on February 28, 1920. Owners took possession of their property the next day.

Yet the extinct USRA continued to cast a long shadow,

and the Transportation Act of 1920 in some ways added to industry woes. Even as Esch-Cummins returned railroads to owners, it also reaffirmed the authority of the ICC, and in its wake the USRA had saddled the industry with a 16 percent larger labor force and a payroll expanded by a startling 86 percent. Indeed, no industry issue loomed larger than labor conditions—the size of the workforce, wages, and work rules. Matters worsened. In 1920 the Labor Board, established as part of the Transportation Act of 1920, granted a substantial increase to nearly all rail employees. The ICC tried to offset this additional expense and to secure a 5.5 percent return on the property of carriers by authorizing rate increases, but depressed business conditions left the railroads with high rates and little traffic. To this the ICC responded by lowering rates, but for railroads that had the effect of decreasing gross revenues. Managers shook their heads. The only solution was to bring down costs, and since the most significant operating expense was wages (60 percent of the total in 1920), managers turned to that area. The result was the shop strike of 1922, an ugly matter not settled until February 1923, and without any winners.

A major component of the Transportation Act of 1920 gave the ICC authority over railroad combinations and even obliged the commission to provide a comprehensive plan for amalgamation of the nation's rail carriers. This reflected the view of Senator Cummins, who had argued that private ownership under public control could not endure unless railways were able to earn the cost of their maintenance. Weak railroads, in Cummins's view, should be sheltered by strong roads through combination—a process of public policy that would provide the greatest good for the greatest number. In formulating this grand plan, the ICC was required to preserve competition and to maintain existing routes and channels of trade while arranging systems that would earn essentially the same rates of return under a system of uniform rates.

The regulatory agency had no enthusiasm for this task, but it had no choice in the matter, and during the 1920s it spewed forth three plans. The first, by Harvard University's William Z. Ripley, proposed 24 systems, usually clustered around one or two principal roads. Ripley's report was done on behalf of the ICC, but the commission's own "tentative plan" in 1921 differed in detail, seeking especially to minimize dismemberment of existing lines of systems. The ICC invited comment before rendering a final plan of 21 systems; it was not long in coming. But concrete action, as opposed to blather and complaint, by carriers and bureaucrats alike, was absent. In 1929 the ICC rendered its "final plan" for consolidation of the nation's railroads into limited systems. By that time, however, the blight of depression was abroad in the land, and any proposal to reduce service or employment was not politically palatable.

Consolidation efforts under the Transportation Act of 1920 proved a monumental bust, showering distinction neither on railroad owners and managers nor on politicians or bureaucrats. Esch-Cummins of 1920 was a modest public policy admission that the age of railways had passed, and it served as an oblique prelude to additional federal legislation in 1940 and 1958 and finally to partial deregulation under the Staggers Act of 1980.

—Don L. Hofsommer

Public Policy in the Great Depression

The stock market crash of October 1929 was not followed immediately by a precipitous decline in the economy. However, by the summer of 1930 there had been a perceptible softening, and by mid-1931 the bottom had indeed fallen out of the U.S. business world. Once the Great Depression began, it affected the railroads severely. In 1930 weekly carloadings varied from about 800,000 to 1,000,000; in 1932 weekly carloadings were only about 550,000. In the same year railroads constituting 72 percent of U.S. mileage did not earn enough to fully cover interest charges or other fixed obligations.

It was clear by late 1932 that extraordinary national economic conditions prevailed as millions had been thrown out of work and business and personal bankruptcies were commonplace. It was also apparent that something extraordinary had to be done on the national level to handle the rash of railroad bankruptcies. The usual way of handling the failure of railroads to cover their fixed obligations was for the bankruptcy court to place the carrier into the hands of a receiver. The receiver would manage the railroad while the court worked to revise the capital structure. This was often a lengthy process because it required the holders of debt and equity in the railroad corporation to come to an agreement. The holders of debt were usually reluctant to agree to a reorganization plan in which there would be a judicial sale of the rail property to a new corporation in which the security holders would participate. Usually this meant that most holders of common stock lost their equity and the bondholders became common stockholders. Creditors often held off settlement for years, trying to get the best deal.

The railroad industry's financial distress was so great in the early 1930s that traditional bankruptcy proceedings would not work. Congress responded to the emergency by adding Section 77 to the Bankruptcy Act of 1898. Under the provisions of Section 77, the railroad corporation or holders of debt aggregating 5 percent or more of the total indebtedness could file a petition with an appropriate court by declaring that the carrier was insolvent and incapable of paying its debts and thereby seeking a financial reorganization of the corporation. Upon acceptance of the petition, the court was obligated to appoint one or more trustees to take charge of the railroad's property.

Under Section 77, after approval of the petition by the

court, the bankrupt railroad was required to submit a plan of reorganization to the court and the ICC. Additional reorganization plans could be submitted by the trustees, creditors, stockholders, and other interested parties. A public hearing was also mandated to consider the various reorganization plans. Finally, the ICC was required to issue a reorganization plan that could be different from any of the other plans submitted.

Before approving any plan from whatever source, the commission had to see that certain requirements were met: the plan had to be compatible with the public interest; the fixed charges resulting from the plan had to fit within the earning capacity of the railroad; the plan was also required to be fair and equitable, recognizing the right of each class of creditors and stockholders; and last, the plan also had to meet the requirements of existing laws regarding the participation of each class of stockholders and creditors. When the ICC approved a plan, it was submitted to the court for judicial approval.

The plan had to be submitted by the court to the relevant classes of creditors and shareholders for their approval. When it was approved by creditors or stockholders representing two-thirds of the amount of such claims or stock, the bankruptcy judge had to approve the plan. Once confirmed by the bankruptcy judge, the plan was binding upon all the parties involved. The role of the commission was to ensure that the reorganized railroad possessed a sound financial structure.

Another provision of Section 77 was that the court or the ICC was not obliged to accept a reorganization plan of stockholders if the court determined that the stock of the corporation had no value. Under this condition, the court and the commission might hold that the stockholders could not play a role in the reorganization; in other words, the stockholders would be wiped out. Another provision enabled the court to accept a plan that had been rejected by a class of creditors or stockholders. The court had to show that it was satisfied that the adopted plan provided for fair and equitable treatment of the objecting parties and that the rejection was unreasonable. This was necessary to prevent certain classes of creditors from holding up proceedings in order to gain more favorable treatment.

The bleak economic situation of the early 1930s also caused the passage of the Emergency Transportation Act of 1933. Under Title I of the act, there were measures of a temporary nature aimed at alleviating the Depression conditions of declining traffic, reduced earnings, and financial distress. Title II contained amendments to the Interstate Commerce Act.

Under the Title I emergency provisions, the act created the position of federal coordinator of transportation. The coordinator was to be selected by the president of the United States from the members of the ICC. The person chosen in 1933 was Commissioner Joseph B. Eastman, who held the position until it was phased out in 1936. The coordinator was to seek means to improve the efficiency of the railroads. Cooperative efforts were to be encouraged, including sharing of equipment and joint use of trackage and terminal and other facilities. Working out the cooperative plans was the job of regional coordinating committees. The committees, of which three were established, were to consist of seven railroad representatives. If the committees could not carry out a plan voluntarily for legal or other reasons, the committee could request the coordinator to require that the plan be carried out. The order of the coordinator could override the antitrust laws if necessary.

The coordinator was also to study and investigate other means of improving U.S. transportation. His recommendations were to be submitted to the ICC. The commission would then, with its own comments included, submit the recommendations to the president and Congress.

In retrospect, the emergency provisions seeking greater coordination and improved efficiency were unsuccessful. Railroad management had developed in a competitive environment, and managers were haunted by the possibility of another carrier obtaining an advantage; no plan for cooperative or coordinated action was ever adopted. Moreover, there were labor-protection provisions within the Emergency Act that were unacceptable to the railroad industry as a whole. For example, the number of railroad employees in service could not be reduced below the number serving in May 1933.

Coordinator Eastman studied the situation carefully and issued many reports for improving railroad efficiency through cooperation. None of these was acceptable to the railroads. Indeed, some of the proposals would have been in conflict with the labor-protection provisions of the Emergency Act. Eastman was more successful in his studies of other ways of improving the transportation situation in the Great Depression. The eventual regulation of the motor carriers, airlines, and water carriers was based on recommendations from Eastman.

The Emergency Act did have an impact on the Interstate Commerce Act itself, as in the case of railroad consolidations and acquisitions of control. Combinations that were enabled by holding companies were brought within the Interstate Commerce Act. This overcame the difficulty of encouraging mergers and combinations promoted by the Transportation Act of 1920, but made impossible by other provisions of the 1920 law. The rule of ratemaking was also affected by the Emergency Act. The provision for fair return on fair value of Section 15a of the 1920 act was repealed. The revised Section 15a also held that in prescribing rates the ICC had to consider the need for the carriers under its jurisdiction to earn sufficient revenue to enable them to offer adequate and efficient service. The commission was also to consider the level of rates on the movement of traffic. The public's need for adequate service at low cost was also to be carefully considered.

The repeal of the recapture clause of the 1920 act was recognition of reality. Excess earnings under the 1920 act that had been paid to the commission were to be returned to the carriers. In the Depression those carriers that had generated excess earnings were in need of all the revenue they had previously generated and were generating.

The Great Depression was an extraordinary event. Marked ups and downs in the U.S. economy were not unusual, but the extent, severity, and duration of the economic troubles of the 1930s were unusual. The Emergency Act tried to recognize reality. The studies by the ICC and the co-ordinator were instructive of a great change in the U.S. transportation picture. The virtual monopoly of interstate and long-distance transportation once held by the railroads had significantly eroded by the 1930s. The motor carrier industry was proving to be a strong competitor for the higher-rated and more profitable freight traffic. Low-value commodities were being moved in larger amounts by the revitalized water carrier industry, and the pipelines made huge inroads on the movement of petroleum and petroleum products. The airlines eventually threatened first-class, long-distance passenger business. Clearly there was effective competition in transportation. Some observers, looking back, lament the movement toward more regulation in the 1930s when there was finally effective competition in place. But given the Depression and the low esteem for business in the United States during this period, substantial lessening of regulation of the railroads would have been unthinkable.

—George M. Smerk

Transportation Act of 1958

The Transportation Act of 1958 was a reaction to the problems faced by U.S. railroads after World War II. In many ways the U.S. economy was at its best in the 1950s. However, there was an anomaly to be found in transportation. The motor carrier industry expanded rapidly, air travel became commonplace by the late 1950s, new crude-oil and petroleum-product pipelines were built, and new gas pipelines brought low-cost natural gas to new homes. The U.S. Army Corps of Engineers improved additional miles of inland waterways, and the interstate highway system was built to the delight and benefit of motorists, truckers, and intercity bus operators. Left out of the boom were U.S. railroads.

They had entered the postwar era with a degree of optimism. The wartime years had been profitable, and the railroads basked in the accolades earned by carrying the bulk of the wartime freight and passenger traffic. Steam locomotives were being replaced by new diesels, worn track and roadbed were replaced, and modern signal systems were installed. Fleets of fine passenger equipment were ordered and introduced to the public, and new freight cars with large carrying capacity were ordered and delivered. But the proportion of freight moved by rail diminished markedly in the 1950s, as did patronage of passenger trains. Between the end of the war and 1960 the railroads lost substantial market share, and the passenger train deficit grew steadily.

Despite the erosion of freight and passenger traffic, the railroads continued to be regulated by government as if their old monopoly power of the late nineteenth century continued. Worse yet, state, local, and federal governments were busy building new highways and improving existing roads; it was no secret that highway users, including truckers, did not pay their full cost. Air transportation benefited from the construction of publicly owned airports and the federal air traffic control system. The waterways improved by the U.S. government were free to their commercial users. Motor bus companies took advantage of highway improvements to provide relatively inexpensive transportation in many parts of the country, particularly small cities and rural areas that were not well served by rail or air transportation. Prosperous times had also permitted millions of individuals and families to buy an automobile, bypassing the use of commercial carriers altogether.

The decline in the railroads' share of the booming freight business was alarming, but in the main there were no immediate deficits from freight operations in the postwar era. Passenger service was a different story. Except for the four wartime years, it had operated at a loss since the beginning of the Great Depression. In 1948 the passenger deficit was estimated at half a billion dollars. By 1957 the passenger deficit was estimated at $723 million. Much of this loss was from commuter rail services around large cities where railroads were forced to continue service by regulators and, at the same time, prevented from raising fares.

The plight of the railroads and the idea of railroad nationalization finally attracted the attention of Congress. A strong lobbying effort by the railroads helped produce the Transportation Act of 1958, which was plainly put into law to help the rail carriers survive as private enterprises. It addressed several of the most serious problems.

The issue of discontinuing money-losing trains in rail passenger service, whether intrastate or interstate, had not been under the jurisdiction of the ICC, but had been left in the hands of state regulatory agencies. It was usually difficult and time consuming for a railroad to gain permission to rid itself of a passenger service. Under the new law, to discontinue an interstate passenger service, the railroad need only give 30 days notice to the public, the ICC, and the governors of the states affected. Unless there was a complaint to the ICC, the train in question could be dropped. Upon petition, the ICC could cause the train service to be continued for one year in order to see if the money-losing situation could be mitigated; if not, the service could be terminated. In the case of an intrastate passenger train, the rail carrier rebuffed by state regulatory agencies for more than 120 days could petition the ICC to discontinue service. The railroad had to show that public convenience and necessity did not require the continuation of service and that maintenance of service would be a burden on interstate commerce.

The inability of the railroads to raise capital at attractive rates of interest to carry out needed maintenance was another target. Loan guarantees for over $200 million were provided for purposes of maintenance. The timeline was extended twice, and the loan guarantees were phased out as of June 30, 1965. By that time nearly $240 million in loans were guaranteed. In the opinion of the ICC, some eastern railroads survived only because of the loan guarantees. The carriers had to show the need for the money and the need for a guarantee in order to obtain the funds at a reasonable rate of interest.

The 1958 law offered railroads relief from unduly low intrastate rates and fares. The rationale for the legislation was that unduly low rates and fares could be a burden on interstate commerce. It was not necessary for the railroads to show that the charges in question were higher than other intrastate rates or that intrastate costs were higher than costs for the movement of interstate traffic. The new law also speeded up the processing of carrier complaints.

A major complaint of the railroads was that they were often obliged by the ICC to hold their rates above those of other modes of transportation to help those modes survive. What may have been a decent argument for survival in the 1920s or 1930s had lost relevance in the highly competitive 1950s. The ICC policy of preventing railroads from lowering rates to meet the competition was dismissed, and railroads were encouraged to experiment with a variety of ratemaking ideas.

One unexpected result of the Transportation Act of 1958 was the development of federal aid policy toward urban mass transportation. Commuter trains were big money losers in the 1950s, and the threat of losing this service because of the train-off provision of the 1958 act persuaded local government officials to work with Congress to develop a program to provide federal support to commuter rail and other urban transportation programs.

—George M. Smerk

Regulatory Reform

In the late 1950s, after 70 years of regulation, U.S. railroads had entered a new era. The traffic surge of World War II and the Korean War and the prosperity of the postwar period began to give way to the rapid growth of competition for freight traffic from trucks and waterways and to a massive diversion of passenger traffic to the automobile and the airlines. Government-sponsored public works programs, such as the interstate highway system, inland waterway improvements (including the St. Lawrence Seaway), and the air traffic control system and the construction of airports throughout the country, stimulated the growth of competition for the railroads on all fronts. Stringent government regulations made it all but impossible for the railroads to react effectively to that new competition. In addition, 70 years of regulation had

driven competitive instincts out of the management of railroads. The precipitous fall of railroad revenues was in part offset by significant economies derived from the replacement of steam locomotives with more efficient diesel-electrics, the mechanization of track maintenance, and the automation of data processing, all of which made it possible for the railroads to sharply reduce employment, which accounted for about half of their costs. In addition, of course, the railroads cut back on services, which tended to compound the loss of revenues.

As more of the interstate highway system came on line in the 1960s, the truckers' service capabilities improved sharply and their costs decreased, resulting in the diversion of more and more freight to trucks. The nation's love affair with the automobile, along with the much shorter trip time for medium-distance journeys, and the introduction and growth of jet services by the airlines virtually killed the passenger train for longer trips. The shift of U.S. mail contracts from the railroads to trucks and air caused the railroads to petition the ICC to discontinue many of their remaining passenger services, which were generating substantial losses. The Rail Passenger Service Act of 1970 provided for the creation of Amtrak, which relieved the freight railroads of their intercity passenger services in 1971.

Beginning in 1967 with the bankruptcy filing of the Central of New Jersey, one by one the nation's eastern railroads entered reorganization under Section 77 of the Bankruptcy Act, the Boston & Maine in March 1970, the Penn Central, the nation's largest railroad, in June 1970, followed shortly thereafter by the Reading, the Lehigh Valley, the Lehigh & Hudson River, the Ann Arbor, and the Erie Lackawanna. In the late 1970s these were joined by two primarily midwestern railroads, the Rock Island and the Milwaukee.

In the railroad bankruptcies of the 1930s the fundamental problem was that the net operating income of the railroads was not sufficient to service their existing capital structures. This could largely be addressed by paring down the capital structures in a financial reorganization in bankruptcy. The railroad bankruptcies of the 1970s were different. Now the railroads were not generating sufficient operating revenues to cover their operating expenses, exclusive of debt service. Every day of operation in bankruptcy reduced the stock of assets available to pay creditors. The issue came to a head on March 6, 1973, when Judge John P. Fullam, supervising the bankruptcy of the Penn Central, after reviewing January 1 and February 1, 1973, reports of the trustees, issued Memorandum and Order No. 1137 stating (*In the Matter of Penn Central Transportation Company, Debtor*, 355 F. Supp. 1343 [E.D. Pa. 1973]): "[T]his Court cannot ignore the realities of the Debtor's situation. On the basis of the record to date, it appears highly doubtful that the Debtor could properly be permitted to continue to operate on its present basis beyond October 1, 1973."

Regional Rail Reorganization Act of 1973

Judge Fullam's opinion and accompanying order directing the Penn Central trustees to file by July 2, 1973, either a feasible plan for reorganization or their proposals for liquidation or other disposition of the enterprise provided a powerful stimulant to congressional action, which culminated in enactment of the Regional Rail Reorganization Act of 1973 (the 3R Act). The 3R Act established a process and institutions that would lead to the physical reorganization and restructuring of the railroad system in the northeastern United States.

In the 3R Act Congress established two principal institutions, the U.S. Railway Assn. (USRA), a nonprofit corporation on whose board of directors were representatives of the federal government, the states, municipalities, labor, shippers, financial institutions, and the private railroad industry, and the Special Court, a three-judge U.S. district court to which Congress gave exclusive jurisdiction over most legal issues arising under the 3R Act. The USRA's principal task was to prepare a plan (the Final System Plan) to physically restructure the railroads in the Northeast into a viable system, to deliver that Final System Plan to Congress, and if neither house of Congress disapproved it, to certify it to the Special Court. The USRA was to finance the continuing bankrupt railroad operations during this period. The Special Court was required to order the conveyance of the property of the bankrupt railroads as outlined in the Final System Plan and had jurisdiction subsequently to determine the value of the conveyed properties for compensation purposes.

The 3R Act process was in principle straightforward. The individual reorganization courts would determine whether the railroads subject to their jurisdiction could be reorganized on an income basis. If not, they would be subject to the 3R Act process. The USRA would then devise the Final System Plan to restructure the lines of the railroads subject to the 3R Act, Congress would have an opportunity to disapprove the Final System Plan, and if it did not disapprove, the Special Court would order the necessary conveyances of property by the bankrupts.

In practice it was not that straightforward. Its constitutionality was challenged by creditors of the bankrupt railroads and ultimately upheld by the Supreme Court after finding that the bankrupts would have a claim for damages against the United States under the Tucker Act in the event the 3R Act took their property without providing the just compensation required by the Fifth Amendment. The principal profitable railroads in the Northeast, Norfolk & Western, Southern, and Chessie, refused to take any substantial properties of the bankrupts they were offered, so ultimately the Final System Plan reorganized most of the lines of the bankrupts into Conrail, conveyed competitive access to a limited number of lines to the

Delaware & Hudson and others, conveyed the Northeast Corridor to Amtrak, and permitted the abandonment of most of the remainder. The Final System Plan was implemented pursuant to an order of the Special Court on April 1, 1976.

Rail Revitalization and Regulatory Reform Act of 1976

The Rail Revitalization and Regulatory Reform Act of 1976 (the 4R Act) was a critical piece in the restoration of U.S. railroads. The act was extensive and dealt with many issues in addition to those discussed here. The issues selected for discussion are those that, in the long run, contributed significantly to the restoration of the health of the country's freight railroads. The most immediate significance of the 4R Act was to fine-tune the 3R Act process. The 4R Act permitted and approved additional designations of property under the 3R Act and made provision for supplemental transactions permitting reconveyance of lines conveyed to Conrail. It provided over $2 billion for funding Conrail and additional sums for funding certain preconveyance obligations of the bankrupts whose nonpayment would have been disruptive to Conrail's operations. Finally, it provided for the USRA to issue to the bankrupts "certificates of value," securities guaranteed by the United States, which would ensure that the compensation received by the bankrupts for their properties would be equal to their constitutional due, thus greatly reducing the possibility of Tucker Act suits against the United States.

The long-term objective of the 4R Act was to begin a basic reform of the Interstate Commerce Act's regulation of railroads. The reforms focused on rate regulation, the establishment of standards for revenue adequacy of railroads, and the provision of an exemption process whereby persons or transactions could be exempted from regulation.

Rate regulation: The 4R Act limited the ICC's jurisdiction over minimum rates, specifying that rail rates that covered costs that varied directly with the level of service could not be held to be unreasonably low. In the past, a large number of rate cases against railroads had been based on complaints by competitors that the rail rate was unreasonably low. These cases had had the effect of forestalling railroad competitive and productivity initiatives. The 4R Act also limited the ICC's jurisdiction over maximum rates, providing that rates could not be found to be unreasonably high unless the commission first found that the railroad had "market dominance" over the service in question. Finally, the act imposed some limits on the ICC's power to suspend a rate change pending an investigation of the change.

Revenue adequacy: The 4R Act began the process for establishing revenue adequacy levels that satisfied basic economic requirements for a viable railroad system. Specifically, Congress directed the ICC to establish a process to develop "reasonable standards and procedures for the establishment of revenue levels adequate under honest, economical, and efficient management to cover total operating expenses, including depreciation and obsolescence, plus a fair, reasonable, and economic profit or return (or both) on capital employed in the business" (4R Act, Section 205). Equally important was Congress's injunction that the ICC "shall make an adequate and continuing effort to assist such carriers in attaining such revenue levels." For the first time Congress unambiguously directed the ICC to use economically rational criteria to determine adequate revenue levels and unambiguously directed the ICC to help the railroads attain those revenue levels.

Exemptions: The 4R Act began the process whereby the ICC could grant exemptions from most economic regulation. The 4R Act step in this direction was limited, permitting the ICC to exempt persons, classes of persons, transactions, and services relating to a rail carrier from regulation when certain restrictive criteria were met. The significance of this exemption authority flows from its subsequent broad development and exercise after enactment of the Staggers Act in 1980.

In addition to dealing with 3R Act and Interstate Commerce Act problems, the 4R Act addressed two related issues: discriminatory state taxation of railroads that imposed a greater tax burden on them than on other industrial property, and the difficulty the railroads were having, in light of their financial straits, maintaining their plant and equipment. Discriminatory state taxation of railroads was prohibited, and states were required to deal with railroads on the same basis as they dealt with other commercial and industrial property. To address maintenance programs for plant and equipment, Congress established two funding mechanisms, one under which the secretary of transportation could purchase railroad preferred stock on terms generous to the railroad, and another under which the secretary could guarantee loans to railroads that ensured that the railroads would obtain financing terms approximating those obtained by the United States itself.

The Staggers Act

The regulatory reforms of the 4R Act did not appear to produce significant improvement in the railroads' financial condition. In particular, they did not seem to produce significant improvements in Conrail's financial performance. To some degree Congress viewed this as a result of a timid implementation of the 4R Act reforms by the ICC, though the 4R Act had failed to address critical issues that were coming to the fore at the end of the 1970s, particularly the need for railroads to enter into confidential long-term contracts with their customers. Congress's response was the Staggers Rail Act of 1980, which focused

primarily on reform of the ICC's economic regulation of railroads.

Rate regulation: Congress addressed railroad rate regulation comprehensively. The Staggers Act deprived the ICC of jurisdiction over maximum rates unless the complaining shipper could show that the railroad had market dominance over the transportation and that the rate was above 180 percent of variable cost (a threshold that was phased in). The 4R Act restrictions on the ICC's ability to suspend proposed rate changes were further tightened.

Revenue adequacy: Congress sent the ICC back to take another look at its revenue adequacy standards, required an annual determination of which railroads were meeting them, and again enjoined the commission to assist the railroads in attaining adequate revenues.

Contract rates: Congress permitted the railroads to enter into rail transportation contracts subject to narrow exceptions. Once a rail transportation contract became effective, the ICC lost jurisdiction over it, and any disputes were resolved in court. Moreover, the ICC interpreted the statutorily required disclosures narrowly and did not include publicly disclosing the rate or rates in the contract. The contract rate provision of the Staggers Act thus permitted the railroads to enter into confidential contracts with their shippers, contracts that were expressly exempted from the antidiscrimination provisions of the Interstate Commerce Act.

Exemptions: Congress broadened the ICC's exemption power and made clear in the legislative history that it wanted the ICC to exercise its exemption power vigorously.

Intrastate regulation: State regulation of railroads with respect to rates, classifications, rules, and practices was subjected to and, where exercised by the state, required to conform to the federal structure. State regulatory standards were subject to prior approval by the ICC, and decisions of state regulatory agencies could be appealed to the ICC. State economic regulation of the railroads was preempted by the federal government in substance if not in name.

Conrail: Congress addressed the continuing need of Conrail for government funding. Specifically, it provided additional authority for the USRA to purchase Conrail securities and required Conrail, the USRA, and the secretary of transportation to submit reports to Congress by April 1, 1981, containing proposals for Conrail's future structure. These reports laid the foundation for the Northeast Rail Services Act of 1981, which put Conrail on the road to reform and economic viability or liquidation.

Whereas the ICC was somewhat timid in its use of deregulatory powers granted under the 4R Act, a majority of the newly appointed members of the ICC interpreted the act (and the mood of the country) to aggressively implement the Staggers Act. The railroads also became aggressive in their use of the provisions of the act.

Northeast Rail Services Act

The Staggers Act had called for a number of reports on the future of Conrail to be submitted early in 1981. These reports formed the background for the Northeast Rail Services Act, which dealt with issues the 3R Act and the 4R Act had avoided. Conrail was freed entirely of the obligation to provide commuter service to commuter authorities; Conrail's labor costs were directly addressed through actual wage reductions and elimination of redundant positions; and a number of profitability benchmarks were established that Conrail had to meet or face liquidation.

Recent Legislation

Although it is difficult to precisely measure the impact of changes in regulation of the U.S. railroads because the bases of calculating return on freight investment have changed, it is clear that the railroads as a whole have become much more competitive and profitable since the Staggers Act. Conrail became profitable in the early 1980s, was privatized in 1987, and was split between CSX and NS to enhance rail-to-rail competition in the northeastern United States in 1999.

—John H. Broadley and Charles W. Hoppe

REFERENCES

The American Railroad Industry: A Prospectus. Washington, D.C.: America's Sound Transportation Review Organization, 1970.

Bernstein, Marver H. *Regulating Business by Independent Commissions.* Princeton, N.J.: Princeton Univ. Press, 1955.

Coyle, John J., Edward J. Bardi, and Robert A. Novack. *Transportation.* 5th ed. Chap 2. Cincinnati: South-Western, 1999.

Ely, James W., Jr. *Railroads and American Law.* Lawrence: Univ. Press of Kansas, 2001.

Fair, Marvin L., and John Guandolo. *Transportation Regulation.* 9th ed. Esp. Chap 2. Dubuque, Iowa: William C. Brown, 1983.

Friedlaender, Ann Fetter. *Freight Transport Regulation: Equity, Efficiency, and Competition in the Rail and Trucking Industries.* Cambridge, Mass.: MIT Press, 1981.

Friedlaender, Ann Fetter, and Brookings Institution. *The Dilemma of Freight Transport Regulation: Studies in the Regulation of Economic Activity.* Washington, D.C.: Brookings Institution, 1969.

Hines, Walker D. *War History of American Railroads.* New Haven, Conn.: Yale Univ. Press, 1928.

Hoogenboom, Ari, and Olive Hoogenboom. *A History of the ICC: From Panacea to Palliative.* New York: W. W. Norton, 1976.

Keeler, Theodore E. *Railroads, Freight, and Public Policy: Studies in the Regulation of Economic Activity.* Washington, D.C.: Brookings Institution, 1983.

Kerr, K. Austin. "Decision for Federal Control: Wilson, McAdoo, and the Railroads, 1917." *Journal of American History* 3 (Dec. 1967): 550–560.

Kolko, Gabriel. *Railroads and Regulation, 1877–1916.* Princeton, N.J.: Princeton Univ. Press, 1965.

Leonard, William Norris. *Railroad Consolidation under the Transportation Act of 1920.* New York: Columbia Univ. Press, 1946.

Locklin, D. Philip. *Economics of Transportation.* 7th ed. Chap. 12. Homewood, Ill.: Richard D. Irwin, 1972.

MacAvoy, Paul W., and John W. Snow, eds. *Railroad Revitalization and Regulatory Reform.* Ford Administration Papers on Regulatory Reform. AEI Studies, 173. Washington, D.C.: American Enterprise Institute, 1977.

Martin, Albro. *Enterprise Denied: Origins of the Decline of American Railroads, 1897–1917.* New York: Columbia Univ. Press, 1971.

Options for ConRail: ConRail's Response to Section 703 (C) of the Staggers Rail Act of 1980: Executive Summary. Philadelphia, Pa.: Consolidated Rail Corp., 1981.

Phillips, Charles F., Jr. *Economics of Regulation.* Homewood, Ill.: Richard D. Irwin, 1965.

Stover, John F. *American Railroads.* 2nd ed. Chap. 8. Chicago: Univ. of Chicago Press, 1997.

————. *The Life and Decline of the American Railroad.* New York: Oxford Univ. Press, 1970.

United States Railway Assn., ed. *Conrail at the Crossroads: The Future of Rail Service in the Northeast.* Washington, D.C.: USRA, 1981.

White, W. Thomas. "Railroad Labor Relations in the Great War and After, 1917–1920." *Journal of the West* 25 (April 1966): 36–43.

Court and Agency Decisions

Blanchette v. Connecticut General Insurance Co., 419 U.S. 102 (1974).

Coal Rate Guidelines, Nationwide, 1 I.C.C.2d 520 (1985).

In re PennCentral Transportation Company, 384 F. Supp. (Sp. Ct. RRRA 1974).

Market Dominance Determinations and Consideration of Product Competition, 365 I.C.C. 118 (1981).

Matter of Valuation Proceedings under Sections 303(c) and 306 of the RRRA, 439 F. Supp. 1351 (Sp. Ct. RRRA 1977).

Matter of Valuation Proceedings under Sections 303(c) and 306 of the RRRA, 445 F. Supp. 994 (Sp. Ct. RRRA 1977).

Standards for Railroad Revenue Adequacy, 364 I.C.C. 803 (1981).

Reorganization and Receivership

"Reorganization" of a railroad (or any other business enterprise) is a euphemism for a legal procedure for reducing its debt burden. The process was developed by courts of equity in nineteenth-century railroad mortgage foreclosure actions to forestall piecemeal liquidation of the railroad and force compromise of the bondholders' claims while operation of the railroad continued without interruption. The equity reorganization process evolved in the twentieth century into Chapter 11 bankruptcy reorganization, available to all businesses and all forms of debt.

Railroad reorganization worked its greatest effects in the nineteenth century when its greatest public impact was no impact. That is, the railroads, whose prosperity and financial viability tended to fluctuate with the national economy, continued to operate trains through boom and bust with unparalleled reliability, albeit at the expense of creditors and investors. Estimates have placed the percentages of railroad corporations in reorganization during the panics of 1859, 1873, the 1880s, and 1893 at 20 to 40 percent. Near the end of the nineteenth cen-

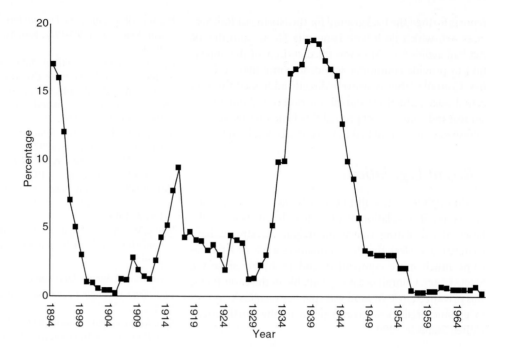

Figure 1. Railroad Receiverships

tury the U.S. Census Bureau began recording the year-end numbers of miles of track in use and the numbers operated by receivers or trustees, allowing the role of reorganization—and of the general economy—in the railroad industry to be arithmetically demonstrated. Between 1894 and 1968 the percentage of miles operated by receivers or trustees varied, with large percentages during bad economic times and small percentages during more favorable times, never rising to 20 percent and often below 1 percent (Figure 1).

Beginning as American versions of the English Court of Chancery, the equity courts were separate from the courts of law; each had its own body of laws, procedures, and remedies. Over a century and a half law and equity merged into a single judicial system, culminating in the 1938 Federal Rules of Civil Procedure. Although state courts presided over some railroad reorganizations, the spread of railroads across state lines made the federal courts with their nationwide jurisdiction the courts of choice for most railroad reorganizations.

The seeds of railroad equity reorganizations were planted by the financing of the original construction. Equity financing was desired because stockholders have no rights in any corporate assets until after dissolution of the corporation, when assets remaining after payment of all debts, that is, the equity, can be distributed among them pro rata, and no rights to income until the board of directors declares a dividend, which it may not do unless there are profits from which to pay the dividend. But the usual occasion for dissolution of railroad corporations was insolvency, leaving the stockholders only the comfort of knowing that their losses were limited to their investment. Since the price a stock can command depends on the security of the holder's investment, coupled with the anticipated size and imminence of dividends, the failure

of stock issues to generate sufficient capital to build a railroad is no surprise. So promoters turned to debt financing. Fortunately, hope sprang eternal in the nineteenth-century breast so long as bonds were issued that bore engravings of the latest locomotives speeding out of the picture ahead of long strings of cars and sold at substantially discounted prices.

Although the terms of railroad bonds were limited only by the imaginations of promoters and their investment bankers and lawyers, typically a railroad bond was an IOU payable to bearer, promising to pay a fixed interest on specified dates and a stated principal on a certain distant future date, secured by a mortgage, and transferable by delivery. The bonds often came with sheets of coupons, one for each promised interest payment, to be presented to the corporation when payment was due. Alternatively, the bonds had spaces on the backs for the corporate treasurer to record and sign each interest payment made.

Since mortgages could not be granted to each of the thousands of bondholders, the bond issue was accompanied by a document called an indenture that conveyed the mortgage to a trustee for all bondholders. The indenture authorized the trustee, in the event of a default in interest payments, to make formal demand on the railroad corporation for payment, and if it refused, upon request of a percentage of the bonds—typically holders of at least 25 percent of the outstanding bonds—to proceed in court for foreclosure of the mortgage. The railroad corporation also contracted to turn over to the trustee, upon demand after default, full possession and control of all the corporation's railroad and property.

A voluntary reorganization might be negotiated between the railroad and its securities holders before a foreclosure suit was started, but this solution was often only

REORGANIZATION AND RECEIVERSHIP

"funding" the defaulted interest payments, which meant issuing another series of bonds on the same mortgage for the amount of the defaulted interest. Although funding the interest exacerbated the financial problem that caused the default in the first place, it postponed more heroic measures to a later default. Then, if enough bondholders agreed that more than optimism was needed, the trustee could proceed with the foreclosure suit.

After the railroad refused the formal demand for payment, the trustee appointed a receiver acceptable to the trustee and the bondholders and demanded possession and control of the railroad and property under the trustee's contract with the railroad, placing the designated receiver in charge of the railroad. Meanwhile, the trustee filed a petition in a court of equity starting the suit for foreclosure and, to avoid the expense, risk, and delay of a trial, requested the court to stay foreclosure and confirm the appointed receiver, who thus became an officer of the court backed by the court's authority.

Receivers had a long history as officers of equity courts, where they performed two functions, generally (1) holding property in dispute while the court decided which of the parties before it was entitled to it and then delivering the property as ordered by the court and (2) holding property to be liquidated for payment of a debt until the sheriff or a master (another officer of an equity court) consummated the sale and then receiving and distributing the proceeds as ordered by the court. But in railroad reorganizations the receiver was more than a brief and passive custodian of the railroad and property. He supervised the operation of the railroad for the court until the foreclosing bondholders' negotiations reached a reorganization agreement, and that could consume months or even years.

The person appointed receiver might be a respected railroad manager, or the receiver might be the same management that had operated the railroad for the corporation. In either case control of the railroad and property was taken from the stockholder-controlled corporate board of directors and turned over to the bondholders' trustee-appointed receiver. During the receivership the receiver would file monthly reports and income statements with the court and, if capital were needed for improvements, prove the need to the court and obtain authority to borrow the needed funds with a first-priority security interest in the property. The receiver would also respond to all claims against the railroad with payment or a defense, as appropriate.

Predictably, creditors, investors, other courts, states, and competitors did not experience railroad receiverships with the same equanimity as the general public. British bondholders, who supplied much of the capital for American railroads, cried foul. Accustomed to British mortgage law, which gave the mortgagee title to the property subject to the mortgagor's redemption by timely payment of the debt, they expected that when the railroad defaulted, its property would immediately vest in their mortgage trustee for liquidation to pay them the defaulted interest and principal. But the American mortgage gave the mortgage trustee only a lien on the property and the burden of trying to obtain foreclosure. This could be done only after a long, hard-fought, expensive, and risky trial involving all claimants to the corporation's assets before a court attuned to the public's need for the operating railroad and armed with the doctrine that property in a railroad was property affected with a public interest.

Competitors saw unfair advantage. The receivership relieved the insolvent railroad of all interest and principal obligations until the reorganization was completed, significantly reducing its cost of operation for months or even years. Commonly the debtor railroad had struggled long to avoid default, deferring maintenance all the while, but under the court's protection it could get credit to replace worn iron rails on broken ties with new steel rails on new ties and ballast for new rolling stock.

Others saw obstruction. All claims against the railroad—for example, personal injury, property damage, lost or damaged shipments, late deliveries, or breach of contract—had to be brought in the court whose receiver was operating it, putting the claimant in the delicate role of suing the judge who would decide his case. State tax collectors were sometimes thwarted by unsympathetic reorganizing courts. Other courts also found their authority conflicted by the orders of the reorganizing court. Resulting controversies crowded the U.S. Supreme Court's docket along with all the other railroad cases.

Meanwhile, the bondholders and others looking to the railroad property for payment, grouped according to their claims' priorities, elected small committees to represent them, and the committees began negotiating a reorganization agreement. Because the corporation's default had proved that the railroad and property could not support the debt burden of the original securities, the committees negotiated how much each of the securities holders and other creditors needed to relinquish in order to reduce the burden to a sustainable level. No one gave up easily, and the negotiations tended to inspire inflated estimates of the railroad's future earnings. Committees unable to reach agreement on a realistic plan settled for lesser reductions and wishful hoping that soon produced a second default and reorganization to force further reduction of the debt burden, and maybe a third round after that.

When the committees settled upon a reorganization plan, they presented it to their securities holders, who could sign their consent and tender their securities to their elected committees, conditioned on adoption of the reorganization agreement by all securities holders. A reorganization agreement usually provided reduction of principal or interest, or both, owed by the railroad on each security.

The reductions were achieved by issuance of new securities in exchange for the original, conditionally tendered securities. First-mortgage bondholders might accept new bonds promising less principal or interest, or both, perhaps sweetened by the addition of stock. Interest-bearing second-mortgage bonds might be exchanged for income bonds that promised payments only as corporate profits warranted. Debentures, which are bonds secured only by the debtor's general credit, could be issued for second-mortgage bonds. Debt holders and stockholders certain to be wiped out by a liquidation of the railroad and property were usually content to get preferred or common stock.

If all the original securities were tendered according to the reorganization plan, reorganization was achieved voluntarily, and the foreclosure proceeding was dismissed. If a small minority of securities holders held out, the mortgage trustee would ask the court to proceed with the foreclosure implementing the terms of the reorganization agreement. Absent persuasive opposition to the reorganization plan, the court would issue an order for the sale of the railroad and property as a unit at public auction following proper notice and allow an elected reorganization committee to bid at the sale and, if its bid won, to pay the bid price with all the tendered securities. The order would condition eligibility to bid on a cash payment to pay the costs of the foreclosure. The order would also provide that the total face value of tendered securities paid by the reorganization committee be divided by the amount of its winning bid to arrive at a liquidated value for each security, and that the dissenting security holders be paid that liquidated value for their securities. Finally, the order would bar forever all other claims, if any, against the railroad and property.

The reorganization committee, which now owned the railroad and property, would form a new corporation capitalized according to the reorganization plan and convey the railroad and property to it in exchange for all its securities. The reorganization committee would distribute those securities according to the terms of the reorganization agreement. The old corporation could then be dissolved.

In March 1884 a singular departure from established reorganization procedure occurred when the Wabash Railroad, facing an interest payment date for which it had no funds, under the leadership of its chief officers, Jay Gould and Russell Sage, persuaded a Missouri court to place it under the protection of a receiver of its nomination. The receiver's first act was to obtain court authority to borrow funds on a first-priority security to pay off several million dollars in notes also becoming due. Those notes had been cosigned by Gould and Sage, who therefore would have been called upon to pay the notes if the railroad failed to do so. When that novelty reached the U.S. Supreme Court, the justices had unkind words for the manipulation of equity foreclosure and implicitly, if not expressly, the manipulators. But the precedent was set, making reorganization available to debtors as well as creditors and cutting its umbilical cord to mortgage foreclosures. The way was thus pointed toward Chapter 11 of the Bankruptcy Act, offering reorganization to all creditors and distressed debtors.

In 1933 Congress added Chapter 77 to the Bankruptcy Act, which made reorganization in the bankruptcy courts an alternative to equity reorganization, and railroad reorganizations proceeded in both venues until 1935, when Congress enacted Section 205, which gave exclusive jurisdiction over all railroad liquidations and reorganizations with all of the powers of equity receivers to the bankruptcy court. The bankruptcy court replaced the receiver with its trustee. The provisions for railroad reorganization can now be found in Sections 1161–1174 of the Bankruptcy Act, Title 11 of the U.S. Code.

—Thomas O. Kloehn

REFERENCES

Chandler, Alfred D., Jr. *The Visible Hand: The Managerial Revolution in American Business.* Cambridge, Mass.: Belknap Press of Harvard Univ. Press, 1977.

Daggett, Stuart. *Railroad Reorganization.* Boston: Houghton, Mifflin, 1908.

Ely, James W., Jr. *Railroads and American Law.* Lawrence: Univ. Press of Kansas, 2001.

Klein, Maury. *The Life and Legend of Jay Gould.* Baltimore: Johns Hopkins Univ. Press, 1986.

Martin, Albro. *Railroads Triumphant: The Growth, Rejection, and Rebirth of a Vital American Force.* New York: Oxford Univ. Press, 1992.

U.S. Bureau of the Census. *Historical Statistics of the United States, Colonial Times to 1970.* Bicentennial ed., U.S. Dept of Commerce. Washington, D.C., U.S. Government Printing Office, 1975.

Richmond, Fredericksburg & Potomac Railroad

The Richmond, Fredericksburg & Potomac Railroad (RF&P) was chartered in 1834 to construct a rail line north from Richmond, Virginia, through Fredericksburg to some port on the Potomac River. The goal was not to create a rail route between Richmond and Washington, D.C., but instead to connect Richmond with the steamships plying the Potomac. The railroad was envisioned as a competitive improvement on the combination of steamships and stagecoaches that were then ferrying passengers up and down the Eastern Seaboard. The line's supporters hoped that the RF&P would, in combination with other proposed rail lines south of Richmond, offer a more advantageous overland route.

Construction commenced in 1835, and the first 20 miles of road opened for business in 1836. The line was built using the strap-rail method of construction. Thin iron straps were nailed to the inside edges of longitudinal wooden stringers that were placed atop wooden crossties.

Grading was minimal and ballast nonexistent. Bridges over the numerous creeks and rivers were built of wood. Fredericksburg was reached by January 1837. An extension north to Aquia Harbor on the Potomac River was opened by November 1842.

All of the RF&P's earliest locomotives were built by English manufacturers. Within a few years the company began to manufacture locomotives in its own shops, as well as to purchase them from American builders. The company built most of its own freight and passenger cars. The company was immediately profitable, securing a substantial amount of north-south traffic, including contracts for carrying the mail.

Located where it was, the RF&P found itself surrounded by combatants during the Civil War. Many times either retreating Confederates or attacking Union soldiers destroyed sections of the line. By the war's end in 1865 nearly the entire road lay in ruins. In the spring of 1862 Union forces landed at Aquia. Retreating Confederates destroyed the section between Aquia and Fredericksburg, carting off rails and burning bridges. To repair the line, the U.S. Military Railroads brought in engineer Herman Haupt. Under Haupt's supervision the line from Aquia to Fredericksburg was reopened within 21 days. This included the reconstruction of several major bridges, chief among which was the bridge over Potomac Creek, which required a span some 400 feet long and over 80 feet high; it was constructed in 9 days from over 2 million board feet of raw lumber cut from area forests. After he had viewed Haupt's creation, President Lincoln supposedly remarked that Haupt had built the bridge out of nothing but "beanpoles and corn stalks."

The RF&P recovered slowly after the war. In 1867 a direct connection between the RF&P and the railroads running south of Richmond was established. A direct rail connection between Richmond and Washington was finally realized in 1872 after the RF&P joined tracks in Quantico with the Alexandria & Fredericksburg Railway. The A&F was a subsidiary of the Pennsylvania Railroad, which had that same year taken control of the Alexandria & Washington Railroad, thus providing a link to Washington. In 1890 the PRR consolidated its two subsidiaries into the Washington Southern Railway. The RF&P ran trains from Richmond to Quantico; the Washington Southern ran from Quantico to Washington.

In 1901 the six railroads that connected with or had trackage rights over the RF&P agreed to the formation of a new company to control the RF&P, the Richmond-Washington Co., in which each would have an equal interest. (The six railroads were the Pennsylvania, the Baltimore & Ohio, the Southern, the Chesapeake & Ohio, the Atlantic Coast Line, and the Seaboard Air Line.) The RF&P-WS Railway would now operate trains directly between Richmond and Washington. In 1920 the RF&P absorbed the Washington Southern.

In response to increased traffic, the entire 110-mile-long RF&P was double-tracked between 1903 and 1907. In 1905 the RF&P opened Potomac Yard in Alexandria. It was one of the largest and most important freight classification yards in the country, breaking down and reorganizing shipments for the many railroads that connected with the RF&P. In 1919 the company opened Broad Street Station in Richmond, a magnificent Neoclassical structure designed by John Russell Pope.

Traffic increases throughout the first half of the twentieth century required the RF&P to purchase increasingly more powerful locomotives. Of special note were the 27 4-8-4 locomotives it purchased from Baldwin Locomotive Works beginning in 1937. Named after famous Virginia generals, governors, and statesmen, these locomotives were designed for high-speed passenger and freight service.

Traffic demands during World War II placed a tremendous burden upon the RF&P. At the peak of demand during 1943, the RF&P was running an average of 103 trains per day, the equivalent of a train every 14 minutes. To help meet the demand, the RF&P placed into service its first diesel locomotives, two Alco S-2 switchers. Orders for diesels increased after the success of the initial units, the first road diesels being received in 1949. By 1954 the RF&P was completely dieselized. The RF&P had the rare habit of operating directional diesels. Even-numbered units pointed north; odd-numbered units pointed south.

Like most railroads, the RF&P experienced declines in its passenger and freight business after World War II. The company handed over passenger operations to Amtrak in 1971. As the number of rail mergers increased in the last third of the twentieth century, the independent survival of the RF&P became doubtful. After a protracted legal battle with the State of Virginia, which owned about one-fifth of the company, CSX Transportation acquired control of the RF&P in October 1991. The line remains an integral part of the nation's rail infrastructure, serving not only CSXT freight trains, but also Amtrak and commuter operator Virginia Railway Express.

In 1990, the last year before CSX absorbed its operations, the Richmond, Fredericksburg & Potomac operated 113 route-miles, with 31 locomotives and 1,876 freight cars. RF&P operating revenues totaled $54.4 million in 1989.

—Lawrence R. Duffee

REFERENCES

Griffin, William E., Jr. *One Hundred Fifty Years of History along the Richmond, Fredericksburg and Potomac Railroad.* Richmond, Va.: Richmond, Fredericksburg & Potomac Railroad, 1983.

———. *Richmond, Fredericksburg & Potomac Railroad: The Capitol Cities Route.* Lynchburg, Va.: TLC, 1994.

Rio Grande Southern Railroad

The 3-foot-gauge Rio Grande Southern (RGS), built by narrow-gauge entrepreneur Otto Mears between 1889 and

1891, made a wide loop through the silver-mining area of southwest Colorado from Durango to Ridgway through Dolores, Rico, and Telluride. Built through exceedingly difficult mountain terrain, the RGS was an improbable railroad that never found prosperity. The ending of the silver standard in 1893 brought an expectable drop in silver mining. Carloadings from the mines quickly fell off, and RGS went bankrupt, to be turned over to the Denver & Rio Grande as receiver. The line never did repay its construction costs and never paid a dividend to its stockholders.

For well over half a century RGS continued to operate under D&RG control. In the 1930s and 1940s the road was notable for its homemade Galloping Goose motor cars cobbled together from automobile parts. During World War II the RGS enjoyed a brief traffic bonanza when it transported much of the uranium ore used by the U.S. government. Soon after the war most of the few mines that still used the railroad turned to trucks. There were no formal protests when RGS finally petitioned to shut down. Service ended on December 27, 1951.

In 1951, the year it was abandoned, Rio Grande Southern operated 172 route-miles and 199 track-miles, with 5 locomotives, 5 motor cars, 84 cars, and 60 employees. Its operating revenues were $171,000.

—George H. Drury

REFERENCE

Ferrell, Mallory Hope. *Silver San Juan*. Boulder, Colo.: Pruett, 1973.

Ripley, William Z. (1867–1941)

William Zebina Ripley was an academic economist who was also trained in civil engineering, geography, sociology, and anthropology. Ripley was born on October 13, 1867, in Medford, Massachusetts, and was trained at MIT and at Columbia University, where he obtained a Ph.D. in economics in 1893. He was a professor of sociology and economics at MIT from 1894 to 1901. He joined Harvard University in 1901 as Nathaniel Ropes Professor of Economics and remained in this position until his retirement in 1933. Ripley died in East Edgecomb, Maine, on August 16, 1941.

Ripley was frequently called upon by government leaders to analyze and solve problems related to railroads, shipping, and labor relations. He helped settle a wage dispute between longshoremen and steamship owners in Atlantic ports, completed a major report to Congress on the impact of a new railroad labor law, and contributed analysis and recommendations to the study of a number of other government and business issues. Ripley was also a strong supporter of the small investor, and much of his thinking was reflected in the creation of the Securities and Exchange Commission in 1934.

The Transportation Act of 1920 gave a number of new responsibilities to the Interstate Commerce Commission, which had been established in 1887 as part of the Interstate Commerce Act to provide federal economic regulation of the railroad industry. Among these were the authority to set maximum and minimum rates and to approve the construction of new lines and the abandonment of old ones. The act increased the number of commissioners from 9 to 11. Further, it included a directive to the commission to prepare a plan for consolidating the nation's many railroads into a group of larger systems.

The ICC asked Ripley to prepare a plan for consolidation. The guidelines were that the industry must consist of no more than 30 systems of roughly the same size and financial strength, and that competition among the roads must be preserved. After a year of work on the plan, Ripley proposed that the nation's railroads be divided into 24 systems, and the ICC held preliminary hearings on the plan in 1921. During the hearings some modifications were made, and it was presented as the commission's Tentative Plan.

For nearly two years after the presentation the ICC held formal hearings throughout the country. As these progressed, it became apparent that the interests of specific roads outweighed the mission of creating parity among the nation's railroads required by the Transportation Act of 1920. There were numerous disagreements and debates over many recommendations in the plan, and many of the hearings were inconclusive because the discussion became mired in detail and intractable stalemate. Upon completion of the hearings the ICC took three years to present its recommendation to Congress, which was expecting to receive a Final Plan. Instead, Congress was told not to expect a plan. The ICC concluded that it could not develop and recommend any plan because the issues were too complex and the different viewpoints too contentious.

Congress, however, required the commission to complete and submit a Final Plan. This was done in December 1929. The Final Plan was received favorably by very few, including William Ripley. He fundamentally disagreed with it, indicating that it simply did not fulfill the mission that Congress had intended with the Transportation Act of 1920.

During his career Ripley's writing and research on railroad matters were not always popular. Although he published widely and was considered an authority, the quality of his research was sometimes lacking. He occasionally championed popular versions of events without thoroughly researching and verifying the facts. An example is found in his writing about Edward H. Harriman. When Harriman took control of the Chicago & Alton Railroad in 1900, he made investments that improved the line's profitability, as well as its physical plant. Although Harriman had increased the capitalization of the Chicago & Alton in the process, Ripley wrote that Harriman had committed reckless financial dealings and downright fraud. When challenged by those who knew better, Ripley was hard pressed to support his conclusions. Unfortunately, his response was to ridicule and denounce his critics rather than address the merits of their arguments.

Despite this difficulty, Ripley is remembered primarily for his work on railroad consolidation for the ICC. Although his efforts did not result in the planned reorganization of the railroad industry, they were not completely in vain. As railroad executives and industry planners worked on the many railroad merger plans during the balance of the twentieth century, his work was often used for reference when the alignment of various railroads was considered.

—David C. Lester

REFERENCES

Klein, Maury. *Unfinished Business: The Railroad in American Life.* Hanover, N.H.: Univ. Press of New England, 1994.

Mercer, Lloyd J. "Edward Henry Harriman." In *Railroads in the Nineteenth Century*, ed. Robert L. Frey, 155–164. A volume in *Encyclopedia of American Business History and Biography*, gen. ed. William H. Becker. New York: Bruccoli Clark Layman and Facts on File, 1988.

National Cyclopaedia of American Biography.

Rock Island Line. *See* CHICAGO, ROCK ISLAND & PACIFIC RAILROAD (ROCK ISLAND)

Roebling, John Augustus (1806–1869)

German-American engineer and bridge builder John Augustus Roebling was born in Mühlhausen, Germany, studied at the Royal Polytechnic Institute in Berlin, and came to the United States in 1831. For a time he engaged in farming in Pennsylvania, but as an engineer he became involved in canal building. He developed a wire-rope cable as a substitute for the hemp rope used to pull boats and cars up inclines of the Allegheny Portage Railroad; hemp had proved unsatisfactory on the rugged Alleghenies. Roebling invented and began manufacturing a much thinner wire-rope cable composed of strands of wire.

In the 1840s Roebling established a wire-manufacturing plant at Trenton, New Jersey. It subsequently became a major American industry and brought considerable wealth to the Roebling family. Using his own technology, Roebling

John A. Roebling. —Library of Congress

began designing suspension bridges; the first important one was over the Monongahela River at Pittsburgh. Numerous other bridges followed, including one over the Ohio River at Cincinnati. His greatest early triumph, and perhaps the first truly modem suspension bridge, was the 825-foot single-span leap over the Niagara River near Niagara Falls. This was the first bridge of its kind planned to handle railroad traffic. Thousands of spectators watched in wonder on March 16, 1855, as a heavy freight train began crawling over this bridge. Most expressed disbelief that such a slender-appearing structure could carry the weight of a train. Roebling, of course, knew that his bridge could handle a load many times greater.

Roebling's greatest triumph undoubtedly was his design of the Brooklyn Bridge, built over the East River between Brooklyn and Manhattan. With a central river span of 1,595 feet (total length of bridge, 5,989 feet), the bridge took fourteen years (1869–1883) to build. Although Roebling designed this extremely aesthetic and structurally sound bridge, he did not live to see it built. While surveying at the location of the proposed Brooklyn tower in 1869, he was injured in a minor accident, and his injury later developed into a fatal case of tetanus. He was succeeded as chief engineer by his son Washington Roebling, who saw the bridge through to its completion.

—George H. Douglas

REFERENCE

Steinman, D. B. *The Builders of the Bridge: The Story of John Roebling and His Son.* New York: Harcourt, Brace, 1945.

Rogers, Albert Bowman (1829–1889)

An engineer who spent most of his career in railroad location work, A. B. Rogers early in his career displayed ingenuity for discovering economical locations, a talent that won him the nickname Railway Pathfinder. Born in 1829, Rogers was a native of Orleans, Massachusetts. After studies at both Brown and Yale universities, he earned an engineering degree in 1853. Rogers worked for a time on the Erie Canal before moving west to begin a railroad career. Except for a brief interlude as a major of cavalry during a Dakota Sioux uprising in 1862, Rogers spent the rest of his life in railroad location work.

Rogers worked on the construction of two midwestern lines before joining the engineering staff of the Chicago, Milwaukee & St. Paul in 1861. His reputation in location work brought him to the attention of James J. Hill, then a member of the Canadian Pacific Railway executive committee. Early in 1881 Hill hired Rogers to take charge of all mountain location work for the CPR. That summer Rogers located the CPR main line through the Canadian Rockies in Kicking Horse Pass. In successive trips in the spring of 1881 and the spring and summer of 1882 he searched for a route for the CPR through the rugged Selkirk Mountains of what is now British Columbia. On his third attempt, on July 24, 1882, Rogers discovered the pass that bears his name.

Rogers was noted for his ability to travel light, living off uncooked beans and biscuits. He was a tough and profane man who chewed tobacco incessantly. He drove his men hard and fed them poorly. Most quit as soon as they could, but others admired him greatly and went anywhere with him. Rogers was a driven man, and the challenge of locating the way across the Rockies was a chance at fame, rather than fortune. Hill had told him that a pass would be named for him if he found it, and it was. Instead of cashing the $5,000 bonus check the CPR gave him, he framed it and hung it on the wall.

After completing his work for the CPR, Rogers was hired by Hill again, this time as a locating engineer for the Great Northern. His engineering career came to an end when he was badly injured in a fall from his horse in 1887. He died two years later at the home of his brother in Waterville, Minnesota.

—William D. Middleton

REFERENCE

Dictionary of Canadian Biography.

Russell, Andrew J. (1830–1902)

Andrew J. Russell, who photographed the famous view of the construction engineers holding up a champagne bottle at the golden-spike ceremony at Promontory, Utah, on May 10, 1869, spent three years in the West as a photographer of the transcontinental railroad. Russell covered the joining of the rails at Promontory with Alfred Hart for the Central Pacific and Charles R. Savage of Salt Lake City. When his photos of the "Wedding of the Rails" appeared as woodcuts in *Frank Leslie's Illustrated Newspaper*, Russell wrote: "The great railroad problem of the age is now solved. The continental iron band now permanently unites the distant portions of the Republic and opens up to commerce, navigation, and enterprise the vast unpeopled plains and lofty mountain ranges that divide the East from the West."

Russell made three trips as official photographer for the Union Pacific in 1868 and two in 1869. His extensive series "Union Pacific R.R. Stereoscopic Views" showed construction from Cheyenne, Wyoming Territory, to Promontory, Utah Territory. In 1870 he continued coverage of the Pacific railroad as far as California. His collection of more than 200 large plate and 400 stereo glass negatives is at the Oakland Museum of California.

Russell grew up in Nunda, New York, where his family worked in canal and railroad construction. He taught in the public schools, then left for New York City to open a painting studio. As an army captain during the Civil War he was assigned special duty as a photographer for the U.S. Military Railroad.

After he finished the railroad project in the West, he returned to New York City and joined *Leslie's* as a full-time staff photographer in 1870. Some of his photos are attributed to "our staff photographer," while others are credited to Russell. Most writers attribute to him the photos of Mr. and Mrs. Leslie's highly publicized three-month trip in 1877 by special train to California. Many of the illustrations were republished in Mrs. Leslie's book, *A Pleasure Trip from Gotham to the Golden Gate*. Russell continued at *Leslie's* until 1891, when he applied for a disability pension from the military, retired, and moved to Brooklyn, where he died in 1902.

—John E. Gruber

REFERENCES

Combs, Barry B. *Westward to Promontory: Building the Union Pacific across the Plains and Mountains*. Palo Alto, Calif., and New York: American West with the Oakland Museum, Garland Books, 1969.

Current, Karen. "Building the Railroad: Andrew J. Russell (1830–1902)." In *Photography and the Old West*. New York: Abrams, 1978.

S

Sacramento Northern

One of the most colorful western interurbans was the Sacramento Northern, which extended northward from San Francisco Bay to Sacramento and through the Sacramento Valley to Chico over a 185-mile main line that made it North America's longest interurban. The product of a 1929 consolidation under Western Pacific control of two connecting electric lines, SN was made up of two very dissimilar districts north and south of Sacramento.

Northern Electric, the earlier of the two properties that made up Sacramento Northern, was organized in 1905 to build an electric line from Chico south to Sacramento. Completed only two years later, the line was unusual among interurbans for its choice of a 600-volt DC unprotected third-rail power-distribution system. A more conventional overhead trolley system was installed wherever the line operated through city streets. Construction of a number of branches continued over the next five years.

Northern Electric operated frequent passenger service over its main line, competing with Southern Pacific services between Chico and Sacramento. For travelers en route to or from San Francisco, the railway established joint tariffs for through service using the overnight Sacramento River steamship services of the California Transportation Co. between Sacramento and San Francisco. Freight from the agricultural Sacramento Valley was an important component of its traffic from the beginning, and by 1918 the railway was earning more than half of its revenues from freight.

In 1909 construction began for the first component of what would become the south end of the future SN system. Originally planned to link Oakland with communities lying east of the Contra Costa hills, the Oakland & Antioch soon changed its name to Oakland, Antioch & Eastern and set its sights on Sacramento.

The railway faced two major geographic challenges. To build the line east out of Oakland, the line's engineers decided upon a direct assault on the Contra Costa hills, selecting an alignment that required maximum grades of 4.6 percent and a tunnel over two-thirds of a mile long. Near Pittsburg, California, a half-mile crossing of the upper arm of Suisun Bay was another formidable barrier.

The railroad solved the problem with a "temporary" car-ferry crossing while plans were developed for a high-level bridge 10,000 feet long and 70 feet high that would have cost an estimated $1.5 million. Financing for a work of this magnitude never became available, and the ferry crossing became a permanent feature of the line.

OA&E construction standards were unusually high. Track was good for maximum speeds in excess of 70 mph. Current collection was from a catenary overhead system energized at 1,200 volts DC (later raised to 1,500 volts), and the entire main line was protected by an automatic color-light block signal system.

Operation began in 1913, and passenger service was closely coordinated with that of the Northern Electric. By 1915 the two roads were operating through parlor-observation cars on such limited name trains as the *Sacramento Valley Limited* and the *Meteor* between Oakland and Chico, and by the early 1920s dining service was being provided as well on what ranked as one of North America's longest interurban journeys. At Oakland SN trains operated from the Key System's ferry terminal for its suburban electric service, and San Francisco passengers began or ended their journeys on board the Key System's San Francisco Bay ferries.

Much like Northern Electric, the OA&E developed a significant freight traffic and established interchanges with both connecting electric lines and steam railroads. It was the two roads' freight traffic that attracted the interest of the Western Pacific, which in 1921 first acquired the Northern Electric, which had become the Sacramento Northern Railroad in a 1918 bankruptcy reorganization. The OA&E, which had become the San Francisco–Sacramento Railroad in its own 1920 reorganization, was acquired by WP in 1929, and the two roads consolidated.

Although freight traffic remained relatively strong, passenger traffic fell off badly during the Depression. Together with the Key System and Southern Pacific's interurban electric railroad, SN trains began operating across the new San Francisco–Oakland Bay Bridge to a downtown San Francisco terminal early in 1939. The convenient new terminal had little noticeable effect on SN passenger traffic, and the railroad gave up its through service to Sacramento and Chico in mid-1940. A suburban service to Pittsburg continued for another year, and the company's last local streetcar service was ended at Chico in 1947. Electric freight operation, however, continued over the entire system.

Shortly after the end of World War II SN converted the third-rail north-end lines to diesel operation, and de-electrification of most of the south end was carried out during the 1950s. The last SN electric operation ended at Marysville and Yuba City in 1965. The SN's through route between Oakland and Sacramento was broken in 1954 when the aging car ferry *Ramon* was retired and the Suisun Bay crossing closed. Piecemeal track abandonments elsewhere followed, to be replaced by trackage rights over connecting rail lines. Even after Western Pacific was merged into Union Pacific in 1981, the Sacramento Northern continued to enjoy a separate corporate existence as a UP subsidiary until 1987, when SN too was merged into Union Pacific.

Even in 1969 the Sacramento Northern was disappearing into its parent Western Pacific, and distinctions between the two were blurred; SN's lines were abandoned in favor of trackage rights on parallel routes of WP, Southern Pacific, and Santa Fe. In 1969 Sacramento Northern operated 177 route-miles and 488 track-miles, with 12 locomotives, 227 freight cars, and 24 company service cars. Operating revenues were $3.3 million.

—William D. Middleton

REFERENCE

Swett, Ira L., ed. *Sacramento Northern*. Interurbans Special 26. Los Angeles, Calif.: Interurbans, 1962.

Safety

Railroad safety is not merely the absence of train accidents, for accidents such as collisions and derailments have typically accounted for only a fraction of all casualties (injuries and fatalities) to passengers and employees. Moreover, from the very beginning of railroading, most casualties have occurred not to employees or passengers, but to citizens at grade crossings or to trespassers. Because casualties reflect scale, as well as risk, in the following they are usually expressed relative to some measure of exposure such as passenger-miles, worker-hours, or train-miles.

The evolution of railroad safety mirrors the way Americans have lived, and it is one of the many forces that have contributed to the general rise in longevity. Death by railroad was the first large-scale public experience with the dangers of the Industrial Revolution. By 1907 the death toll came to nearly 12,000 a year. It was the largest single source of violent death—a bit less important than diphtheria as a source of mortality, but far more important than measles, diabetes, venereal diseases, or dysentery. Since then the decline in railroad injuries and fatalities has made an important contribution to improving public health.

The history of safety divides into three broad periods. The first, from the beginning down to about 1900, was characterized by the novelty and unreliability of railroad technology, by the enormous expansion of the rail network, and by the small beginnings of state and federal safety regulation. During these years some forms of safety improved, but others deteriorated. The second period, from 1900 to World War II, saw dramatic improvements in transportation technology, the expansion of safety regulation, and the institutionalization of safety in railroad organizational structures. These resulted in sharp improvements in all forms of railroad safety. In the third, from World War II on, investment in better technology continued to improve rail safety, but until the mid-1970s economic regulation, along with a number of other forces, eroded railroad profitability and adversely affected some forms of safety. After the 1970s increasing federal control over safety regulation, along with decreasing economic regulation that raised profits again, led to improvements in nearly all aspects of rail safety.

The Early Years, 1828–1900

In the beginning, in all countries, the primitive state of technology made railroading dangerous work. And just as nineteenth-century American carriers were accident-prone, so they were also generally less safe for workers, passengers, and others than were European lines. Although companies took great pains to protect passengers from train accidents, they were less likely to be liable in situations where passenger negligence was a contributing factor, so they took fewer precautions to avoid them. Thus in New York State from 1850 through 1852 only about 28 percent of all passenger fatalities occurred in collisions or derailments. Most of the others were at stations, where people were crossing the tracks or getting off and on trains. These sorts of dangers were also greater on American than European railroads and were part of the reason for the comparatively poor safety record of American carriers. Antebellum data from a small number of U.S. states show passenger fatality rates significantly higher than those in Britain, although in both countries safety improved throughout the nineteenth century. Although European stations usually fenced off the tracks, in America they were open, and passengers routinely stepped in front of moving trains. American passenger cars also boarded from the end, and passengers could hop off early or run to catch a train, often with lethal results. In the early years before Ezra Miller's platform (couplings), moving between cars was also highly dangerous. In Britain, by contrast, passengers rode in compartments that boarded from the side, and so moving between cars or running for the platform was less likely.

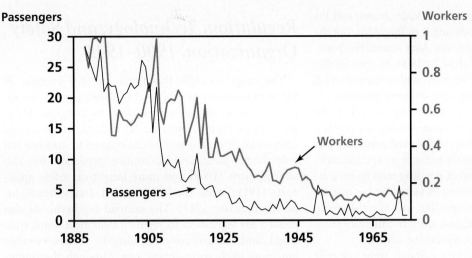

Figure 1. Passenger and Worker Fatality Rates, 1888–1974. Rates are per billion passenger-miles and per million worker-hours.
—Author's calculations.

These and a host of other modifications in practices and equipment reduced passenger risks not only from train accidents but from other dangers as well (Figure 1). Vestibules, introduced in the 1890s, lessened chances that a passenger would be hurt passing between cars. Gates on end platforms appeared about the same time; their main purpose was to prevent no-fare passengers, but they also reduced casualties.

The comparatively dangerous work on American railroads reflected a number of technical and economic differences. American lines were more freight intensive than those in Britain, freight work was more dangerous, and braking and coupling American freight cars were also comparatively riskier. In Britain until the late nineteenth century trains were stopped by a separate brake van. In America longer hauls put a premium on larger cars and trains, which reduced costs. But these required separate brakes on each car, and until the air brake they required men to walk on the tops of cars, where they might fall or hit overhead obstructions. British lines also used buffers and link connections that were less hazardous than the American link-and-pin connections that required workers to go between moving cars.

Worker safety also reflected labor and legal conditions. From roughly 1830 to 1900 the rapid growth of American carriers resulted in rapid employment growth and high labor turnover, both of which diminished worker experience. Since much safety knowledge was company specific and acquired on the job, labor conditions heightened risks. Liability laws made work accidents cheap until the twentieth century, thus dulling companies' concern with safety. Data from a small number of American states suggest antebellum fatality rates of around 3 to 4 per 1,000 workers, while in Britain they averaged less than 2. National data in the 1890s also confirm that American worker risks were comparatively high compared to Britain but declining in both the United States and Britain.

The first nationwide information on causes of work accidents came from the Interstate Commerce Commission (ICC) in 1889, and the next year it collected data for groups of workers. These data (Table 1) reveal that for all workers,

collisions and derailments accounted for only about one-fifth of fatalities. The fatality rate for trainmen (engineers, firemen, conductors, and brakemen) was a staggering 9.62 per 1,000, over half of it resulting from coupling cars or from falls and overhead obstructions.

The carriers and their employees responded to this mounting casualty list in a number of ways. The railroad unions provided accident insurance for their members, while by the 1880s most carriers had some form of medical services, and some even developed hospital associations. Many companies continued the wages of injured workers until they returned to the job, and in 1880 the Baltimore & Ohio became the first line to set up a relief organization. These medical and relief programs served a variety of purposes. To workers they provided care and sometimes financial assistance during injury and illness; and they helped companies retain workers, maintain goodwill, reduce the lure of unionism, and discourage lawsuits.

ICC data also provided the ammunition for a small band of reformers led by Lorenzo Coffin, who, along with the railroad unions, state regulators, and the ICC, mobilized public support to pass the Safety Appliance Act of 1893. The act required companies to equip freights with air brakes and to introduce automatic couplers. This equipment not only

Table 1. Casualties to American Railroad Employees by Occupation and Cause, 1890 (per 1,000 workers)

	Coupling Cars	Riding Cars*	Train Accidents	Other	Total
All Workers					
Fatality Rate	.49	.87	.69	1.22	3.27
Injury Rate	10.48	3.61	3.45	12.36	29.90
Trainmen					
Fatality Rate	1.75	3.54	2.55	1.78	9.62
Injury Rate	40.10	14.18	13.27	19.34	86.89

Source: ICC, *Third Annual Report on the Statistics of Railways of the United States, 1890* (Washington, D.C., 1891).

*Fatalities from falls and hitting overhead obstructions.

improved safety, but also permitted larger trains, and the companies had begun introducing it in the 1880s, but the law may have speeded the process. After several postponements the law finally took effect in 1900; by then fatality rates had declined sharply (Figure 1) and continued to fall as companies improved equipment and work practices.

The law was important for other reasons as well. As the first significant federal regulation governing rail safety, it provided a model that ultimately proved misleading. It encouraged critics of rail safety to focus on specific technologies or practices instead of devising ways to encourage a broader corporate interest in safety. Yet because no other single danger was comparable with the risks from coupling and riding freight cars, early twentieth-century safety regulation had extremely modest effects.

Nineteenth-century American railroads were not only comparatively dangerous to passengers and workers but to others as well, most of whom were killed trespassing or at grade crossings. Massachusetts data for the 1850s and 1860s show that other fatalities per train-mile were six times the level prevalent in Britain. In Europe a guard staffed grade crossings. In America crossings were unguarded except sometimes by a warning sign, and as pedestrian and train traffic rose, so did accidents and fatalities. Unlike European lines, American carriers were also unfenced, and because they were often in better condition than roads, they became highways for common people, while hoboes, who could not afford passenger fares, rode the rods in search of work. In Massachusetts in 1882 fares averaged 2.32 cents per mile, and wages (nationwide) averaged $1.16 a day. Thus a 20-mile round trip cost 40 percent of a day's wages, so hoboes hopped freighters. Towns and cities also grew up around railroads, which often ran down the streets; children played on the tracks or sneaked into yards to steal coal or play, often with deadly results.

Although railroads killed trespassers by the thousands—the annual toll came to 4,346 by 1900—neither they nor public officials took effective action. Because liability rules placed most of the blame on the individuals, these accidents were not very costly to the railroads. And when they evicted and prosecuted trespassers, courts usually failed to convict, and the carriers sometimes faced retaliation. Grade-crossing accidents resulted in more public concern, probably because the victims were not breaking any law. And probably because in the East, at least, many crossings were instituted by railroads, and because the roads predated the railroads, safe crossings were seen as a railroad obligation, not as a matter of public safety. Massachusetts passed the first state law that regulated rail safety in 1834 when it required trains to whistle for crossings. By the 1880s municipalities had begun to require guards at high-density crossings, and states such as Connecticut and Massachusetts were beginning to require grade separation, usually with at least half the costs financed by the railroads. Despite such policies, fatalities at crossings rose relative to train-miles after 1890, amounting to a total of 730 fatalities in 1900.

Regulation, Technology, and Safety Organization, 1900–1945

The surge in traffic that began in 1897 brought all forms of accidents to new heights in 1907, and it also induced a flurry of safety legislation in Congress. Influenced by the Safety Appliance Act of 1893, reformers and railroad labor unions pressured Congress to mandate not only shorter hours and locomotive inspection, but also safer ashpans (1908) and more freight-car safety appliances (1911), while the ICC required electric headlights on locomotives (1917). The railroad brotherhoods also pressed for legislation to regulate clearances, limit train length, and mandate crew size, allegedly to improve safety but more likely to maintain jobs. Although the unions were unsuccessful at the federal level, many states did legislate train crew size. There were also threats of expensive legislation intended to reduce collisions and derailments (see ACCIDENTS). The most important item in this flurry of legislation was the Federal Employers' Liability Act of 1908, which sharply increased the carriers' cost of worker casualties and provided a continuing incentive for employers to improve work safety.

Carriers responded by embracing the Safety First movement, just then beginning in manufacturing. Ralph Richards, claim agent on the Chicago & North Western, introduced Safety First on the railroads in 1910; the American Railway Assn. endorsed it in 1912, and in the next decade, with an assist from the U.S. Railroad Administration in 1918–1919, it swept through the major carriers. In 1920 the ARA took over the work and organized a safety section.

Safety First was an organizational innovation. Carriers that followed Richards's model set up safety committees that included both workers and managers; the immediate focus was to reduce "little accidents" to workers. As one safety agent observed, most injuries had little or nothing to do with efficiency, and so their prevention was no one's job; safety organizations filled that void. But if Richards's focus was on workers, his goal was to reduce all accidents and injuries. "If the little accidents could be stopped the big ones would take care of themselves, thus wiping out the whole accident business on the road," he claimed.

As practiced by the North Western, Safety First was a three-legged stool. The first leg was management: the general manager had to make safety a corporate goal and a management responsibility at all levels. The second leg was financial: the company had to spend money fixing and guarding equipment and cleaning up yards. These investments improved safety. The stool's third leg was worker involvement. Workers knew better than anyone else where the dangers were, and because much railroad work was unsupervised, workers had to be motivated to work safely. Accordingly, companies invested in safer equipment to demonstrate good faith, and they established worker safety committees whose function was to report on unsafe conditions and root out unsafe practices.

Safety First was therefore an effort to reorient corporate goals to include safety, and it relied largely on modifying the behavior of workers and managers. Because safety organizations had to justify their existence, they became a continuing force for reducing accidents, often collaborating with union locals to achieve their goals. The methods included increasingly detailed and better-enforced safety rules, as well as safety contests to motivate workers. The contests probably led to underreporting of injuries, but they really did improve safety, and worker fatality rates declined steadily in the 1920s and 1930s (Figure 1).

Other forces contributed to these gains. Improvements and investments in rail, brakes, and signals reduced casualties from collisions and derailments, while the stabilization of employment after 1920 also yielded safety gains. Turnover and new hiring fell to very low levels, leading to a more experienced, better-trained labor force. The spread of employee retirement and pension plans in the 1920s also helped reduce turnover, thereby contributing to better safety.

The twentieth century brought steady improvements in passenger safety as well (Figure 1), not only because of the decline in collisions and derailments, but because "little accidents" also fell sharply. The casualty rate from station accidents declined both because traffic was shifting to newer, better-designed urban stations and because the rise of electric interurbans and then automobiles cut into the carriers' short-haul traffic. This had the effect of reducing boarding, detraining, and other forms of station accidents relative to passenger-miles. Between 1923 and 1939 the passenger fatality rate declined 50 percent, from 3.4 to 1.7 per billion passenger-miles, and 70 percent of the improvement was from "little accidents."

The steady improvement in worker and passenger safety was matched by sharp reductions in casualties to trespassers that began about World War I (Figure 2). An important difference was that while public policy and corporate behavior were responsible for the former gains, the decline in trespassing fatalities was almost wholly a reflection of market forces. Trespassing resulted because walking the tracks or stealing a ride was a superior means of transport for poor and working-class individuals; trespassing declined as these supporting conditions eroded. Some carriers began publicity campaigns to reduce trespassing, but the major causes were rising incomes, falling fares, and automobility. As daily wages rose and as interurbans and then automobiles provided cheap and convenient transportation, trespassing fell. By the 1920s driving and hitchhiking began to supplant walking the tracks and "riding the rods" on the underframes of freight cars. These long-term trends were briefly reversed by the Great Depression, but as unemployment fell in the 1940s, trespassing deaths again declined.

The one area where safety worsened in the early twentieth century was at grade crossings, thanks to the automobile. From 1890 to 1900 fatalities at crossings rose from 402 to 730, or by 82 percent, as both population and train-miles increased, and they rose another 15 percent to 839 by 1910. Thereafter, even as growth in train mileage slowed, they exploded, rising 114 percent to 1,797 in 1920.

Before the automobile, most crossing accidents had occurred in high-density urban areas. But just as cars enormously expanded mobility, so more cars and roads expanded the list of dangerous crossings. In the nineteenth century the goal of reformers had always been grade separation, which was expensive but economic at high-density crossings. But by World War I the growing number of crossings and accidents led to a new focus on guarding, and the fast, noisy, poorly braked automobile required different forms of guard than were appropriate for a horse-drawn world. And as the number of potentially dangerous crossings increased, they raised the problem of how to allocate scarce funds to separate or guard crossings so as to maximize their safety benefits.

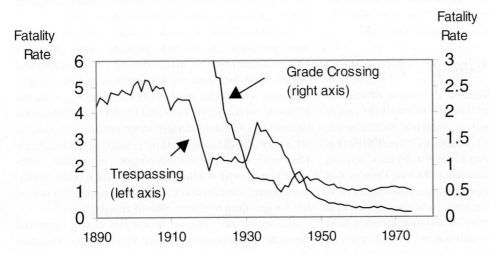

Figure 2. Trespasser and Grade-Crossing Fatality Rates, 1890–1974. Trespassing fatalities per million train-miles and grade-crossing fatalities per million vehicle-miles. —Interstate Commerce Commission and Federal Railroad Administration

To the carriers, the rise in automobile accidents at crossings was a serious concern. Such accidents increasingly led to lawsuits, and hitting a car might cause a costly derailment. Even worse were expensive state and local requirements to guard or separate the rapidly increasing number of crossings. Accordingly, in the 1920s, working individually and through the ARA safety section, the railroads instituted safe-crossing campaigns. These were intended not only to reduce accidents but also to plant the idea that crossing safety was a public good, not simply a railroad problem. To this end, the railroads regularly advertised the number of accidents resulting when automobiles ran into trains rather than the reverse.

Increased automobile travel and road construction in the 1920s also supported the railroads' efforts to transform public attitudes. As train-miles declined while both roads and automobile travel expanded, it became difficult to see crossing safety as simply a railroad obligation. Accordingly, in the 1930s some states began to assume an increasing share of the costs of grade separation, although guarding long remained a railroad obligation. Federal funding also arrived in a big way in 1935 with New Deal public works programs, which separated hundreds of crossings and helped guard others. Greater state and federal involvement also led to more rational analysis of funding allocation. Illinois developed the first model to predict crossing hazards in the mid-1930s.

Despite the increase in vehicle miles traveled, grade-crossing fatalities peaked at 2,568 in 1928 and fell relative to travel from the 1920s on (Figure 2). In part, these gains reflected the abolition and guarding of a comparatively small number of the more than 200,000 grade crossings, as well as improvements in the effectiveness of guards. But the decline also reflected a reduction in train-miles, which came about both because the carriers were losing traffic and because pressures for efficiency led them to increase train size.

World War II temporarily interrupted some of these safety trends. Although accidents to trespassers declined, under the press of heavy traffic, worker and passenger risks increased. Yet even here the increase was modest because the carriers' interwar Safety First work and efficiency gains paid both traffic and safety dividends.

Continuity and Change, 1945–2000

Four broad trends influenced the course of railroad safety in the years between World War II and the end of the twentieth century. These included, first, the continuation of the economic and technological pressures that had steadily been improving safety for decades. Second, the carriers' economic circumstances sharply deteriorated in the late 1950s, and this decline, especially among eastern and midwestern carriers, began to erode some aspects of safety. Third, and in part in response to worsening safety conditions, a major shift toward federalization of

all aspects of railroad safety began in the mid-1960s. The Federal Railroad Administration (FRA) took over safety work from the ICC in 1966, and increasing worries over derailments involving hazardous substances led Congress to pass the Federal Railroad Safety Act of 1970. Along with subsequent acts, this gave the FRA authority over all aspects of railroad safety. Fourth, in the mid-1970s and especially after 1980, economic deregulation began to improve both the carriers' financial health and their safety.

Trespassing casualties fell from World War II down to the late 1960s, both in absolute numbers and relative to train-miles (Figure 2). No doubt most of this gain reflected the continued spread of automobiles, but individual carriers and the Association of American Railroads (AAR) also intensified the publicity campaigns that dated back to before World War I. In the 1950s lines such as the Baltimore & Ohio and Union Pacific developed movies and programs aimed at schoolchildren, and 1972 saw the beginning of Operation Lifesaver, a joint state and railroad venture intended to educate the public and improve and enforce state safety regulations. Yet thereafter there has been little progress, and some writers postulate that many of those who are killed may be suicides.

Between 1945 and the 1960s crossing fatalities declined steadily, both absolutely and relative to vehicle miles traveled (Figures 2 and 3). Up to about 1960 federal policy played only a minor role in these safety gains. The dominant forces were the decline in train-miles resulting from larger cars and trains and lessened demand for rail services, the closing of some crossings, and increasing use of automatic crossing guards, which were still mostly financed by the carriers. Throughout the entire postwar period the carriers, often with state and later federal assistance, continued publicity campaigns intended to encourage crossing safety. In the late 1940s the AAR, working through the National Safety Council, began another careful-crossing campaign, and in the early 1950s individual carriers such as the B&O and the Atlantic Coast Line used radio advertisements and warnings that targeted motorists who ran crossing signals. In the early 1970s Operation Lifesaver initiated a broad campaign against crossing, as well as trespassing, accidents.

The federal role in crossing safety gradually became more pervasive. The interstate highway system (begun in 1956) shifted travel to roads without rail crossings, and large-scale federal funding for abolition and guarding of crossings also began in the 1950s. Beginning with the Highway Safety Act of 1973 and the Surface Transportation Act of 1978, the federal government authorized up to 90 percent funding for crossing protection. During these years both states and the federal government also developed increasingly sophisticated statistical models to estimate hazards that have been employed to develop priorities for guarding or elimination of crossings.

The safety of passenger travel has slowly improved throughout the postwar period (Figures 1 and 4). Fatal-

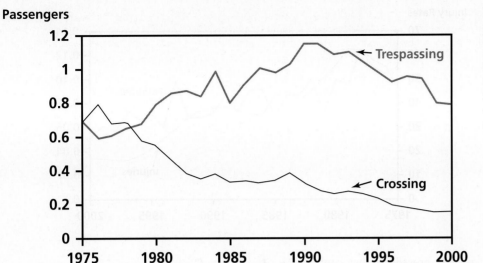

Passengers

ity rates averaged about 2 per billion passenger miles in the immediate postwar years; by the 1990s they were typically less than 1, and injury rates have fallen sharply as well. Some of this improvement reflected the reduction in train accidents, but station accidents have also declined.

The trend in work safety after World War II is complex. From war's end to 1957, safety improved steadily (Figure 1). Fatality rates averaged around 0.2 per million man-hours in the immediate postwar years, and by 1957 they had fallen by half. To a considerable extent this was a by-product of events and policies undertaken for other purposes. Declining employment continued to keep labor turnover at low levels. And sometimes new technology proved to be inherently safer. Diesel locomotives, for example, were introduced to lower costs and raise productivity, but they were also safer than steam locomotives. Similarly, the rising wages of railroad workers encouraged the spread of car retarders in yards, and reduced the need to ride freights in

hump yards, and the increasing use of train and yard communication systems improved the safety of yard work.

Safety gains also reflected the technological and organizational momentum of forces that had been at work for decades. All the large carriers had safety organizations. These continued to emphasize improved supervision and training and the need to follow rules. Working through the AAR Safety Section, they developed and implemented safety codes and pressed for the use of safety equipment such as hard hats, goggles, and safety shoes.

Because work safety had become a corporate goal, all departments evaluated the safety of new machines and new methods of work. Thus although diesels were safer than steam, they were subject to fires, crankcase explosions, and potentially catastrophic wheel failures, so companies instituted procedures to reduce these dangers. As rising wages encouraged mechanization of maintenance-of-way, the new machines introduced new hazards—for example, their noise made it more difficult to hear a train

Injury Rates

Fatality Rates

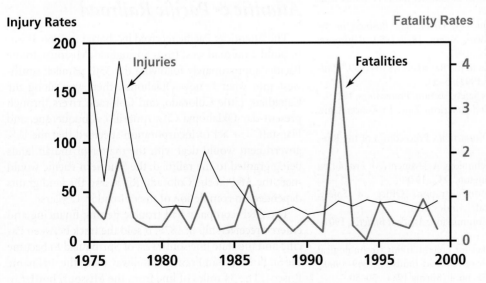

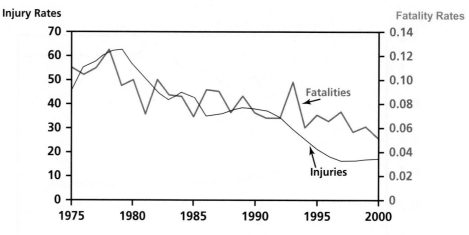

Figure 5. Worker Injury and Fatality Rates, 1975–2000 (per Million Hours Worked). —Federal Railroad Administration

coming—but with proper safety procedures they could improve safety. The new equipment also led to smaller workforces and better supervision while reducing the number of inherently dangerous jobs.

Yet these forces were overwhelmed after the mid-1950s by the impact of the carriers' crumbling financial position; worker safety deteriorated for about two decades until the middle 1970s (Figure 1). Declining profits eroded safety in several ways. Many lines skimped on maintenance of track and equipment, which led to increasing numbers of derailments (*see* ACCIDENTS). Lack of funds also slowed the spread of car retarders and similar devices that reduced injuries and led carriers to keep obsolete freight cars with old, dangerous hand brakes. Finally, some carriers pared their safety programs to cut costs. By the mid-1970s, however, stricter federal safety regulations, along with improving profitability, reversed these forces (Figure 5), and work safety has steadily improved since then.

—**Mark Aldrich**

REFERENCES

Aldrich, Mark. *Death Rode the Rails: American Railroad Accidents and Safety, 1828–1965.* Baltimore: Johns Hopkins University Press, 2006.

———. *Safety First: Technology, Labor, and Business in the Building of American Work Safety, 1870–1939.* Baltimore: Johns Hopkins Univ. Press, 1997.

———. "Safety First Comes to the Railroads, 1910–1939." *Railroad History* 166 (Spring 1992): 5–33.

Assn. of American Railways Safety Section. *Proceedings*, 1921–.

Ely, James W. *Railroads and American Law.* Lawrence: Univ. Press of Kansas, 2001.

National Safety Council. *Transactions*, Proceedings of the Railroad Section, 1912–.

U.S. Congress. Office of Technology Assessment. *An Evaluation of Railroad Safety.* Washington, D.C., 1978.

U.S. Federal Railroad Administration, Office of Safety. http://www.fra.dot.gov/safety/index.html

U.S. Interstate Commerce Commission. *Accident Bulletin*, 1901–1965.

Usselman, Steven. "Air Brakes for Freight Trains: Technological Innovation in the American Railroad Industry, 1869–1900." *Business History Review* 58, no. 1 (Spring 1984): 30–50.

St. Louis–San Francisco Railway

Groundbreaking ceremonies for the Pacific Railroad of Missouri took place at St. Louis on July 4, 1851. Chartered to build west to the Pacific via Jefferson City, it had the honor of operating the first train west of the Mississippi River. It was the nucleus of the Missouri Pacific Railroad. Two years later at Franklin, Missouri (present-day Pacific), 34 miles from St. Louis, ground was broken for the South-West Branch of the Pacific Railroad. The railhead was at Rolla in 1860 when construction stopped because of the Civil War. The State of Missouri took over the South-West Branch in 1866 to separate it from the parent Pacific Railroad. The state then sold it to John C. Frémont, who reorganized the company as the Southwest Pacific Railroad. Frémont defaulted on the payments, and in 1868 the company was again reorganized as the South Pacific Railroad. Construction continued. The line reached Springfield in 1870. That same year the company was consolidated with the Atlantic & Pacific Railroad.

Atlantic & Pacific Railroad

The Atlantic & Pacific received its charter in 1866. It was to build a railroad west from Springfield, Missouri, to the Pacific, approximately following the 35th parallel: southwest into what is now Oklahoma, then west along the Canadian, Little Colorado, and Colorado rivers through present-day Oklahoma City, Amarillo, Albuquerque, and Flagstaff. The act of incorporation specified that the U.S. government would deal with the matter of Indian lands being granted to the railroad, the Southern Pacific would meet the A&P at the Colorado River, and the land grants depended on completion of the railroad in 12 years.

The A&P company had trouble getting financing and entered receivership in 1875. It sold the track between Pacific and the state line southwest of Springfield to become the St. Louis & San Francisco Railway (with the nickname Frisco). The 34 miles of line from the Missouri border to

Vinita, in Indian Territory (now Oklahoma), retained the Atlantic & Pacific name. In 1879 the A&P, the Santa Fe, and the Frisco agreed that the Santa Fe and the Frisco would jointly build and own the A&P west of Albuquerque (the Santa Fe, building west and southwest from Topeka, reached Albuquerque in 1880).

The A&P completed its line from Albuquerque to a junction with the Southern Pacific at Needles, California, in 1883, but the Santa Fe would not allow revenues from the completed portion of the line to finance construction of the line from Albuquerque east to Tulsa. The land grants for that line were rescinded in 1886. A railroad was built over much of the route in the early 1900s by the Rock Island.

St. Louis & San Francisco

In 1882 the St. Louis & San Francisco came under the control of Jay Gould and Collis P. Huntington. Gould's Texas & Pacific was building westward across Texas, and Gould wanted to divert the Frisco, which was aiming toward Texas. The Frisco blossomed under Gould and Huntington. In the early 1880s it extended lines west to Wichita, Kansas, south to Fort Smith, Arkansas, southwest from Vinita to Tulsa, and east from Pacific to St. Louis parallel to the Missouri Pacific. A few years later the Wichita line was extended northwest to Ellsworth, Kansas, and the Fort Smith line southwest to Paris, Texas.

In 1890 the Santa Fe purchased the Frisco, creating for a few years the largest railroad in the United States. The Santa Fe fell into receivership during the panic of 1893 and lost its Frisco holdings. In 1896 a new company, the St. Louis & San Francisco Railroad, was organized to purchase the St. Louis & San Francisco Railway and the portion of the A&P in Indian Territory (the Santa Fe purchased the rest of the A&P, the line from Albuquerque to Needles, in 1898). The new railroad expanded to the southwest (from Tulsa to Oklahoma City and from Sapulpa, near Tulsa, to Denison and Carrolton, Texas), the northwest (two Springfield–Kansas City routes), and the southeast (from Springfield through Memphis to Birmingham, Alabama).

Not long after 1900 Benjamin F. Yoakum got control of the Frisco and added it to his system of railroads, which included the Rock Island, the Chicago & Eastern Illinois, and a chain of railroads between New Orleans, Houston, and Brownsville, Texas. Yoakum's empire fell apart in 1913.

St. Louis–San Francisco

The Frisco went through yet another reorganization, becoming the St. Louis–San Francisco Railway. At that point it was an X-shaped system. One leg of the X ran from St. Louis southwest through Springfield, Missouri, then branched to Fort Smith, Arkansas, and Paris, Texas; through Tulsa to Fort Worth, Brownwood, and Menard,

Texas; and through Tulsa to Oklahoma City and southwest to Quanah, Texas. From Quanah a subsidiary, the Quanah, Acme & Pacific, reached 111 miles west to a connection with the Santa Fe at Floydada, Texas. The other leg of the X ran from Kansas City southeast through Springfield, Missouri, to Memphis, Tennessee, and Birmingham, Alabama. North-south routes connected St. Louis with Memphis and Kansas City with Tulsa. Networks of branches from those routes served southeastern Missouri and southeastern Kansas.

In 1925 Frisco purchased and built a line from Amory, Alabama, to the Gulf of Mexico at Pensacola, Florida, and in 1948 Frisco acquired a second Gulf port, Mobile, Alabama, by purchasing the Alabama, Tennessee & Northern Railroad. The other southern extremity of the system was trimmed back in 1937 when Frisco sold a subsidiary, the Fort Worth & Rio Grande Railway, a line from Fort Worth to Menard, Texas, to the Santa Fe.

In common with many other American railroads, the Frisco was in receivership from 1932 to 1947. The Depression put the Frisco into receivership; wartime traffic helped it out. In 1956 the Frisco further emphasized its presence in the Southeast by buying control of the Central of Georgia Railway, with which it connected at Birmingham, Alabama. The Interstate Commerce Commission refused to approve the purchase, and Frisco sold its interest in the CofG to the Southern Railway.

The Frisco's principal passenger routes were from Kansas City to Memphis, Birmingham, and Jacksonville, Florida, and from St. Louis to Oklahoma and Texas. The

Herald and reporting marks of a Frisco wood-framed boxcar were photographed on the Southern Pacific at San Bernardino, California, in March 1943. —Jack Delano photograph, Office of War Information, Library of Congress (Neg. LC-USW3-21576-E)

road's flagship was the St. Louis–San Antonio *Texas Special* operated jointly with the Missouri-Kansas-Texas—the two roads crossed at Vinita, Oklahoma. In January 1959 Frisco discontinued the north end of the *Texas Special* (St. Louis–Vinita), then began a campaign to end the rest of its passenger service, which it did in 1967. Toward the end of passenger service the four remaining trains—the two St. Louis–Oklahoma City trains and the two Kansas City–Birmingham trains—all met each afternoon at Springfield, Missouri.

In the 1960s the Frisco discussed merger with the Chicago Great Western, with the Santa Fe, with the Southern Railway, and with the Illinois Central and the Gulf, Mobile & Ohio, which were themselves discussing merger. The Chicago, Burlington & Quincy bought a large block of Frisco stock in 1966, and for about ten years nothing was heard about a Frisco merger. In 1977 Burlington Northern (successor to the Chicago, Burlington & Quincy) and the Frisco began discussing merger, which took place on November 21, 1980.

In 1979, the year before its inclusion in Burlington Northern, the St. Louis–San Francisco operated 4,658 route-miles and 6,710 track-miles, with 438 locomotives, 18,395 freight cars, 1,048 company service cars, and 8,270 employees. Freight traffic totaled 16,463.2 million ton-miles in 1979, and foodstuffs (14.6 percent), chemicals (10.8 percent), transportation equipment (10.0 percent), and farm products (9.0 percent) were its principal traffic sources. Frisco operating revenues totaled $388.2 million in 1979, and the railroad achieved a 90.1 percent operating ratio.

—George H. Drury

REFERENCES

Collias, Joe G. *Frisco Power.* Crestwood, Mo.: MM Books, 1984.

Miner, H. Craig. *The St. Louis–San Francisco Transcontinental Railroad.* Lawrence: Univ. Press of Kansas, 1972.

Saunders, Stuart T. (1909–1987)

A key figure in mid-twentieth-century railroading, Stuart Thomas Saunders experienced about the best and the worst that a business career can offer. He served as president and chief executive officer of the Norfolk & Western from 1958 through 1963 and as president of the Pennsylvania Railroad from 1963 through 1968. He is best known, however, for his role in creating, and his brief chairmanship of, the Penn Central Railroad, which was formed in 1968 from the merger of two mighty railroads, the Pennsylvania and the New York Central. The merger went into effect on February 1,

1968, and a little more than two years later Penn Central filed for bankruptcy. Shortly before the bankruptcy filing Saunders, along with two other Penn Central executives, was dismissed by the railroad's board of directors. He spent the rest of his life as an essentially discredited business executive, discredited because of his ineffective leadership and poor judgment displayed during the process of merging the Pennsy and the NYC, as well as during his time as the new corporation's chairman and chief executive officer. Saunders died on February 8, 1987, in Richmond, Virginia.

Saunders was born in McDowall, West Virginia, on July 16, 1909. After a childhood on a dairy farm, he graduated from Roanoke College in 1930, then headed to Harvard Law School, from which he graduated in 1934. Saunders then went to work as a lawyer in Washington, D.C., where he practiced for 13 years. He joined the Norfolk & Western as assistant general counsel in 1947 and worked his way up to presidency of the railroad in 1958. He did not rise through the operational ranks of the railroad, which had been the traditional path to the executive suite for most of the twentieth century, but through the legal and administrative route.

Saunders was known for his ability to convince others of the merits of his positions, and he made some good decisions for the N&W. First, he initiated a major program of bringing diesel locomotives to the railroad, which was particularly tough because of the N&W's allegiance to coal-fired steam locomotives and to the coal industry itself. He also worked to acquire other railroads that would complement and expand the railroad's basic route structure. Saunders completed the mergers with the Virginian Railroad, the New York, Chicago & St. Louis Railroad, also known as the Nickel Plate, and the Wabash Railroad. These roads greatly enhanced the N&W's route structure and strengthened its traffic mix.

The Norfolk & Western, as well as a couple of its newly acquired lines, was controlled, to some extent, by the Pennsylvania Railroad. Seeing his strong success with the N&W, the Pennsy's board of directors asked Saunders to become the new chairman and chief executive officer of that railroad upon the retirement of James Symes in 1963. The attributes that made Saunders successful at the N&W, however, did not work at the Pennsylvania. Although he made several strong strategic decisions for the N&W, he was not actively involved in the railroad's day-to-day operation. The Pennsylvania, however, needed a president who would focus on ensuring that the railroad could successfully operate on a daily basis. It was in bad financial and physical shape and was burdened with a large and unprofitable commuter operation. Upon joining the Pennsy, Saunders focused on consummating the merger with the New York Central and not upon improving the operation of the railroad. A memorable story from his Pennsy days was Saunders's use of a chauffeured limousine for his daily journey to and from the office, while passengers on his railroad's commuter trains endured uncomfortable, perpetually late, and mechanically deficient cars.

In his effort to win the support of organized labor for the Penn Central merger, Saunders negotiated an agreement that offered lifetime job security to all employees of both railroads as of May 20, 1964. Saunders believed that approval of the merger was just a short time away, and that relatively few employees would be affected by this agreement. By the time the merger was finally approved four years later, however, hundreds of people fell under the umbrella of the 1964 agreement, and the new Penn Central had to provide jobs for all of them. Obviously, this dealt a serious blow to the new railroad as it was just getting out of the gate. This was just one of several things Saunders did to achieve the overall goal of getting the merger approved. Others included adding the financially strapped New Haven Railroad to the merger plans, as well as misrepresenting the financial condition of the Pennsylvania during merger negotiations.

Another failing in the preparation for and the execution of the merger was the lack of effort made to modify the thoughts and attitudes of each road's employees. The Pennsy and the Central had been fierce rivals; to expect everyone to come together as a big, happy Penn Central family was unrealistic. The problem extended from the rank and file right up to the executive suite. The team that ran the Penn Central from day one was essentially divided as the Red Team (Pennsylvania Railroad) and the Green Team (New York Central). Furthermore, Saunders did not work well with Alfred E. Perlman, the former president and chief executive officer of the New York Central, who became president and chief operating officer of the Penn Central. In addition to all the other problems shouldered by the new railroad, the inability of its employees to work together was a major impediment to success.

After his termination from the Penn Central, Saunders joined a Richmond securities firm in 1972 as a consultant. During this time his activities around the Penn Central merger were investigated by the Interstate Commerce Commission, the Securities and Exchange Commission, and the U.S. Congress. In order to settle a lawsuit filed by the SEC, Saunders and several other Penn Central executives signed an agreement in 1974 that required them to pay into a settlement fund of $12.6 million.

—David C. Lester

REFERENCES

Daughen, Joseph R., and Peter Binzen. *The Wreck of the Penn Central.* Boston: Little, Brown, 1971.

Saunders, Richard. "Stuart T. Saunders." In *Railroads in the Age of Regulation, 1900–1980,* ed. Keith L. Bryant, Jr., 386–391. A volume in *Encyclopedia of American Business History and Biography,* gen. ed. William H. Becker. New York: Bruccoli Clark Layman and Facts on File, 1988.

Saunders, Richard S. *Merging Lines: American Railroads, 1900–1970.* DeKalb: Northern Illinois Univ. Press, 2001.

Scott, Thomas A. (1823–1881)

Thomas Alexander Scott was born in Fort Loudon, Pennsylvania, on December 28, 1823, one of 11 children of tavernkeeper Thomas Scott and his second wife, Rebecca Douglas. He attended a country school only in the winter months, as was common practice, until he was 10, when his father died. He worked in a general store until he was 17, then moved to Columbia, Pennsylvania, to work for his brother-in-law, Maj. James Patton, who was collector of tolls on the state system of roads and canals. Scott left state employ in 1845 and became involved in private business ventures in Columbia. Between 1847 and 1849 he went back to work for the state as chief clerk in the office of the collector of tolls in Philadelphia. He later became station agent for the Pennsylvania Railroad at Duncansville (Hollidaysburg), Pennsylvania, at the junction and transfer point between the PRR, the state canal line, and the Allegheny Portage Railroad.

Scott impressed his employers at the Pennsylvania. When the railroad line was extended to Pittsburgh in December 1852, he was appointed third assistant superintendent of the division of the railroad west from Altoona; his office was at Pittsburgh. A man of ability, patience, resolve, and charm, Scott rose quickly, and in January 1858 he was named general superintendent of the entire railroad. On March 21, 1860, he was named first vice president.

Scott was involved in the Civil War and gained the title of colonel. He advised President-elect Lincoln not to travel directly to Washington for inauguration, but to slip into the capital secretly in order to avoid assassination. When the war

Thomas A. Scott. —Middleton Collection

began, Secretary of War Simon Cameron summoned Scott to Washington in April 1861 to operate the Northern Central Railroad from Washington to Harrisburg, a key artery for the transportation of materials and military personnel. Scott took with him a young telegraph operator from the Pennsylvania Railroad named Andrew Carnegie. On May 3, 1861, Scott was commissioned colonel of the U.S. Volunteers. The following August he was appointed by Congress to the post of assistant secretary of war to supervise all of the government's transportation lines and railroads. By the time he resigned on June 1, 1862, Scott had provided the foundation for effective transport of the Union armies. He later was called back into government service with a temporary appointment as colonel and assistant quartermaster general on the staff of Maj. Gen. Joseph Hooker for a special job: the movement of 13,000 troops, equipment, artillery, wagons, and horses from Virginia through Nashville to Chattanooga. On other occasions Scott was called upon for advice concerning the use of railroads in the war.

With J. Edgar Thomson as its president, the Pennsylvania Railroad was about to begin its greatest expansion. Through lease and stock ownership the Pennsy gained control of newly built lines from Pittsburgh to Cincinnati, Indianapolis, St. Louis, and Chicago. To link Philadelphia with New York, the Pennsylvania in 1871 leased the United Canal & Railroad Companies of New Jersey. Other leases and purchases extended the PRR to Baltimore and Washington. With Scott as president, the Pennsylvania Co. was organized as a separate firm to manage all lines leased by the Pennsylvania Railroad west of Pittsburgh.

Scott was active in other railroad ventures. In 1871 he played a major role in the PRR's acquisition of a financial interest in the Southern Railway Securities Co., a firm with stakes in railroads south of Richmond, Virginia. Scott felt that an interest in this company might help provide valuable feeder traffic to the Pennsylvania as the South returned to prosperity in the wake of the Civil War. The ploy did not work, however, and the Pennsylvania sold off its holdings in the South by 1881. Another opportunity appeared in the West with the financial problems of the Union Pacific; Scott felt that the then-singular transcontinental route might be brought under control of the Pennsylvania. To that end he was elected president of UP on March 8, 1871; he held the presidency only until March 6, 1872, and sold his UP holdings to Jay Gould.

J. Edgar Thomson died on May 27, 1874, and Scott succeeded him on June 3 as president of the Pennsylvania. Scott had also helped promote other railroad ventures, and from 1872 to 1880 he was president of the Texas & Pacific Railway. Scott suffered a paralytic stroke in 1880. He recovered sufficiently to continue working until June 1, 1880, when he resigned the PRR presidency. One of his final efforts was the building of Broad Street Station at Broad and Market streets in the heart of Philadelphia. Scott died at his home in Darby, Pennsylvania, on May 21, 1881.

—George M. Smerk

REFERENCES

Burgess, George M., and Miles C. Kennedy. *Centennial History of the Pennsylvania Railroad, 1846–1946.* Part 3. Philadelphia: Pennsylvania Railroad, 1949.

Dictionary of American Biography.

Ward, James A. "J. Edgar Thompson and Thomas A. Scott: A Symbiotic Partnership?" *Pennsylvania Magazine of History and Biography* 50 (1976): 37–65.

Seaboard Air Line Railway

The Seaboard Air Line Railway was located between the main lines of two of the three strong railroads of the South, the Atlantic Coast Line and the Southern Railway (the Louisville & Nashville was the third). It competed vigorously with the Atlantic Coast Line for passenger traffic between the Northeast and Florida. ACL had the advantages of double track and a flat route; SAL's curving, sawtooth-profiled route was 36 miles shorter between Richmond and Jacksonville. Seaboard was the more adventurous of the two railroads (it had to be, to compete with ACL). It was ten months ahead of the Coast Line in putting a New York–Florida streamliner on the rails, and Seaboard bought diesels at the same time ACL was buying 4-8-4s (which proved to be grossly unsuitable for fast passenger service). In 1958 the competitors realized that their true competition was not each other but highways and airways. The Interstate Commerce Commission surprised the railroad industry by approving a merger of parallel railroads: ACL and SAL merged on July 1, 1967.

About the time Atlantic Coast Line predecessors were forging a link between Richmond, Virginia, and Weldon, North Carolina, the Portsmouth & Roanoke Railroad was organized to build a railroad between Portsmouth, Virginia, and Weldon, shortcutting a long water journey (Weldon was the limit of navigation on the Roanoke River). The Portsmouth & Roanoke was completed in 1837, but it was not a success, possibly because the only connection at Weldon was back toward Petersburg and Richmond. The railroad was purchased by the Virginia State Board of Public Works, leased to the town of Portsmouth, and reorganized as the Seaboard & Roanoke Railroad. Control of the railroad was acquired in the 1850s by a group of businessmen who also controlled the Richmond & Petersburg and the Richmond, Fredericksburg & Potomac railroads.

In 1840 the Raleigh & Gaston Railroad opened from the North Carolina state capital to a town named Gaston a few miles up the Roanoke River from the present town of that name. The railroad was extended east to Weldon in 1853. During the Civil War both Union and Confederate troops destroyed, rebuilt, and used the Raleigh & Gaston.

Several years after the end of the war, in 1871, the Raleigh & Gaston obtained control of the Raleigh & Augusta Air-

Line Railroad, which was building southwest from Raleigh in as straight a line as possible—an air line or beeline. In 1877 it reached Hamlet, North Carolina, where it connected with the Carolina Central Railroad, which had a line from Wilmington through Charlotte to Shelby, North Carolina.

By the late 1870s the two Raleigh railroads and the Seaboard & Roanoke were controlled by John M. Robinson, president of the Richmond, Fredericksburg & Potomac and the Baltimore Steam Packet Co. (the Old Bay Line), which operated boats on Chesapeake Bay from Baltimore to Norfolk and Portsmouth. In 1881 the Carolina Central also came under Robinson's control. At Charlotte the Seaboard group of railroads connected with the Atlanta & Charlotte Air Line Railway. It was a friendly connection until 1881, when the Atlanta & Charlotte came under the influence of the Richmond & Danville, the forerunner of the Southern Railway. As a result of losing the friendly connection, in 1887 the Seaboard began building the Georgia, Carolina & Northern Railway from Monroe, North Carolina (west of Hamlet and southeast of Charlotte), to Atlanta. Its rails reached Atlanta in 1892.

At the north end of the Seaboard system the Richmond, Petersburg & Carolina Railroad was built from Norlina, North Carolina (on the former Raleigh & Gaston about 35 miles west of Weldon), to Richmond. In 1900 the Richmond, Petersburg & Carolina was renamed the Seaboard Air Line Railway.

Routes in Florida

Seaboard Air Line's ancestor in Florida was the Tallahassee Railroad, which opened a 22-mile line from Tallahassee to the Gulf of Mexico in 1836. The line from Tallahassee to Jacksonville, which was completed in 1860, was built by two railroads that were later combined to become the Florida Central & Western Railroad.

In 1861 the Florida Railroad opened a line from Fernandina, on the Atlantic Coast, southwest to Cedar Key on the Gulf of Mexico. It became the Atlantic, Gulf & West India Transit Co. and later the Florida Transit Railroad ("transit" being used in its older sense). Successive mergers created the Florida Transit & Peninsular Railroad, the Florida Railway & Navigation Co., and the Florida Central & Peninsular Railway. The FC&P extended its rails south to Tampa in 1890 and three years later north to Savannah and a connection with the new South Bound Railroad between Savannah and Columbia, South Carolina. (The FC&P soon acquired the Savannah-Columbia line.)

John Skelton Williams

John Skelton Williams of Richmond, Virginia, in 1896 got control of the Georgia & Alabama Railway, which had opened five years earlier between Montgomery, Alabama, and Lyons, Georgia, just east of Vidalia. Skelton extended the line east 75 miles to Savannah. Williams acquired control of the Seaboard group of railroads in 1898 and the Florida Central & Peninsular in 1899. Construction in 1900 between Columbia and Cheraw, South Carolina, connected the Seaboard railroad with the Florida Central & Peninsular. Skelton proposed building north from Richmond to connect with the Baltimore & Ohio, avoiding the Richmond, Fredericksburg & Potomac, which was controlled by the Atlantic Coast Line and Pennsylvania railroads. The owners of the RF&P first applied pressure, then allowed the Seaboard to sign traffic agreements with the RF&P and the Pennsylvania.

Williams lost his control of the Seaboard in 1903. The railroad continued to expand by building branches and acquiring short lines. Notable additions were a line from Atlanta to Birmingham and a line from Charleston to Savannah that formed part of a freight line with easier grades than the main line between Hamlet and Savannah. The company underwent a brief receivership in 1908 and reorganization in 1915.

The Seaboard acquired several short lines in the agricultural and phosphate-mining area of central Florida, then began building lines south to Fort Myers and Naples and southeast to Miami. About the time those two lines were completed, the Florida land boom collapsed, and the stock market crashed three years later, in 1929. Seaboard entered receivership in 1930.

Streamliners

Seaboard Air Line inaugurated a diesel-powered coach streamliner, the *Silver Meteor*, between New York and Miami and St. Petersburg in 1939, almost a year ahead of competing Atlantic Coast Line's *Champion*. Later that year SAL acquired additional cars so that train frequency could be increased from every six days to daily on the Miami run and every three days to St. Petersburg, and by 1941 the train also carried sleeping cars. In 1947 the *Silver Meteor* was joined by the New York–Miami *Silver Star* and the New York–Atlanta-Birmingham *Silver Comet*. The *Silver Meteor* and *Silver Star* names are still used by Amtrak. Seaboard's best-known train, the *Orange Blossom Special*, was a winter-season all-Pullman train between New York and Miami. Never streamlined, it was eclipsed by the *Silver Meteor* and *Silver Star*, and the 1952–1953 winter season was its last.

The Postwar Era

Government loans and revenues from the busy years of World War II helped Seaboard modernize, notably adding signals or centralized traffic control to many of its lines. The lack of signals had caused several major accidents during the war years.

During the postwar years phosphate rock, used in the production of fertilizers, came to make up 20 percent of Seaboard's freight tonnage, and the road's passenger business remained vigorous. SAL absorbed longtime subsidiary Macon, Dublin & Savannah in 1958 and purchased another Georgia short line, the Gainesville Midland, in 1959.

Merger with the parallel, competing Atlantic Coast Line was proposed in 1958; benefits would stem from elimination of duplicate lines and terminals. The merger, which created the Seaboard Coast Line, took place on July 1, 1967. In recent years parts of Seaboard's main line between Richmond and Jacksonville, shorter than Atlantic Coast Line's but hilly and curving, have been dismantled.

In 1966, its last year before the Seaboard Coast Line merger, the Seaboard Air Line operated a system of 4,122 route-miles and 6,323 track-miles, with 551 locomotives, 414 passenger cars, 28,778 freight cars, 1,003 company service cars, and 11,452 employees. Freight traffic totaled 13,273.2 million ton-miles in 1966, and phosphate rock (13.4 percent), other stone and rock (11.7 percent), and pulpwood (10.7 percent) were the principal commodities carried. Passenger traffic totaled 513,985,999 passenger-miles. Seaboard Air Line operating revenues totaled $188.4 million in 1966.

—George H. Drury

REFERENCES

Langley, Albert M., W. Forrest Beckum, Jr., and C. Ronnie Tidwell. *Seaboard Air Line Railway Album*. North Augusta, S.C.: Union Station, 1988.

Prince, Richard E. *Seaboard Air Line Railway*. Green River, Wyo.: Richard E. Prince, 1969. Rpt. Bloomington: Indiana Univ. Press, 2000.

Seaboard System

Since the early 1970s the holding company Seaboard Coast Line Industries (SCLI) had been using "Family Lines" as its marketing label to cover all its railroad companies—Seaboard Coast Line, Louisville & Nashville, Clinchfield, and the Georgia Railroad and its two associated lines, Atlanta & West Point and Western Railway of Alabama. The Family Lines label and its accompanying equipment paint scheme, a motley combination of stripes and initials, never seemed to present the unified railroad image its management apparently hoped for. External appearances aside, the Family Lines had steadily streamlined its internal management structure and functioned more and more as a single company. Further impetus came on November 1, 1980, when SCLI announced that it had merged with another major rail holding company, the Chessie System, which operated the Baltimore & Ohio, Chesapeake & Ohio, and Western Maryland. The merged holding company was called CSX—temporarily, according to announcements at the time—after Chessie, Seaboard, and the multiplication symbol X, signifying

"merger" and CSX's intention to expand into nonrail ventures.

CSX initially made few visible changes in either of its railroad groups, which continued to operate under their own names and, for the most part, independently. However, a number of management consolidations took place, coordination of trains running between Family Lines and Chessie territory was implemented (particularly for intermodal and coal trains), and plans were laid to coordinate the car and locomotive fleets of the two railroads. In mid-1981 operations of all Family Lines units were consolidated in Jacksonville, Florida. The logical conclusion of these steps came at the end of 1982, when Seaboard Coast Line absorbed the Georgia Railroad and Louisville & Nashville and became Seaboard System effective January 1, 1983. The Clinchfield, A&WP, and WRA were taken into the new company as well.

To some, the new Seaboard System name too strongly suggested the Seaboard Air Line, itself the junior partner in the 1967 SCL merger and certainly not descriptive of a system that reached the Mississippi River, the Gulf of Mexico, and Lake Michigan. But the label was perhaps as simple as could be had from the menagerie of constituent lines. In any case the new railroad replaced it with an image that had a far more "railroady" look and sound; the basic Family Lines colors of French gray with red and yellow accents stayed, but the FL initials-in-a-box logo was replaced with the Seaboard System name and bold new graphics.

Business levels during SBD's existence varied, but the railroad's bottom line was helped by passage of the Staggers Act in 1980, which deregulated most facets of railroad operation. The landmark legislation repealed much of the Interstate Commerce Commission's regulatory authority, giving the carriers more flexibility to merge and set their own rates. Staggers also opened the floodgates for SBD and other railroads to abandon or sell many miles of lightly used track that the ICC had formerly made them keep intact. Ironically, a chief victim of the abandonment frenzy was Seaboard System's namesake, the old Seaboard Air Line. Not only were a number of SAL branches and secondary lines abandoned or sold, but the SAL's main lines were cut in several places as well. Large segments between Petersburg and Raleigh, Savannah and Jacksonville, and Atlanta and Birmingham were taken out of service or pegged for abandonment during the SBD years. There were former ACL lines in each case that roughly paralleled the eliminated mains, and at the time the alternate routes simply seemed redundant. In the years since, with periodic line closures caused by hurricanes and congestion from the present boom in traffic, successor CSX has no doubt often wished that it could summon back the hastily ripped-up rails.

Seaboard System kept up its predecessors' program of physical plant improvements along its nearly 16,000-mile system, including, for example, new piggyback yards in Chicago, Nashville, Atlanta, and Orlando in 1984. Other facilities now deemed redundant, such as the former

Seaboard Air Line West Jacksonville yard, were phased out. The first new power to arrive in SBD colors was an order for EMD's 3,500-hp SD50s in 1983 and 1984. The SD50s were favored power for SBD's frequent unit coal trains. Intermodal, phosphate, grain, and merchandise rounded out the freight picture. SBD also condensed the number of operating divisions, a process helped along by the reduction in mileage from sales and abandonments.

Seaboard System's energetic president was Dick Sanborn, an Atlantic Coast Line alumnus who had also headed the Family Lines since 1982. An admitted railfan, Sanborn gained notice in enthusiast circles for such moves as naming a new perishable piggyback service the *Orange Blossom Special* (honoring the Seaboard Air Line's famous old luxury flyer), running a quartet of F units on business trains, and continuing the popular Santa Claus trains over the former Clinchfield. On the other hand, SBD also brought to an end the former Georgia Railroad mixed trains, a staple of fan affection for many decades. Yet they exited in style, with extra coaches and a former Georgia GP38-2 named for Atlanta railroad historian Franklin M. Garrett.

Officials of CSX's constituent companies had indicated several times in print that they were not anxious to move ahead too quickly with full mergers in light of the notorious problems that Penn Central, for one, had experienced in the 1970s. Nevertheless, the pace of alignments and consolidations between SBD and Chessie continued. For example, both railroads' sales and marketing departments combined in early 1985, followed soon after by consolidation of other management functions. The SBD and Chessie company magazines were combined into *CSX News* in March 1986. And despite an assurance from CSX just after it was formed that the name CSX would never be applied to equipment, a new CSX paint scheme was in fact unveiled the same month.

These were the outward clues that CSX was moving forward toward full absorption of its railroads. On July 1, 1986, Seaboard System became CSX Transportation (CSXT). The next year CSXT merged the remaining CSX railroads, Baltimore & Ohio and Chesapeake & Ohio, completing the unification process CSX Corp. had begun seven years earlier.

In 1986 Seaboard System operated 13,506 route-miles, with 2,093 locomotives, 90,753 freight cars, and 3,845 company service cars.

—Charles Lawrence Goolsby

Seniority

The essence of the social relations and underlying social structure in railroad work is a seniority system. Seniority is an institutionalized age grouping that gives members rights and duties and allocates privilege and power. It is one kind of social linkage, constraining actions and fostering order. It has a charter or rationale, including purpose. Seniority systems provide equitable relationships among individuals and efficient structures within organizations. Across North America, in the webs of rules of railroad industrial relations and encompassing law, *craft seniority* has loomed central in creating and maintaining a bargaining unit of employees represented by a component of a labor union. Indeed, the term *seniority* has traditionally served as a metaphor for railroad employment. Craft seniority provides the foundation of railroad social interactions and norms, including industrial relations and unionism. The supporting federal labor laws for seniority developed first during 1888 in the Arbitration Act for the railroad industry and later furnished models for other industries. It is not surprising that the earliest widespread and substantial web of rules for occupational seniority outside the church, armed services, and government is found in the oldest industry, enormous in cost, colossal in scale, and vast in dispersion—the railroads.

From the broadest perspective, seniority concerns employment. Thus it is valued more than increases in wages or fringe benefits. These gains are worth little if a worker faces job loss at employer whim. Accordingly, the rail unions have expanded the seniority provisions of agreements in bargaining with management. It appears that as seniority increases, so does loyalty to a union, providing the membership solidarity needed for union goals.

Originally, on railroads, seniority was a unilateral (from management) policy *principle*. Later, on most railroads, it became a bilaterally (management-labor) negotiated legal *right*. By *principle* is meant that which belongs to a person or group—apart from law—by a rule adopted as a guide to action. By *right* is meant that which belongs to a person or group by a law or tradition. Right is a just claim of a person or group against others, legally enforceable by the state. It is an interest existing along a continuum, developing at one end into an interest legally constructed by rules defining as property a thing held. Rail seniority rights are only somewhat those defining property. Rail seniority has been exchanged and sold, however.

On North American railroads, then, seniority *principle* comes from a company's policies, and seniority *right* comes from a labor agreement between union bargaining agent and company. The seniority right thus stems from the provisions of work rules in a labor agreement regarding a craft bargaining unit of employees and an employer. Over time, bilateral interpretations of the provisions further shape seniority. When the parties cannot bilaterally interpret, third-party arbitral, court, and congressional interpretations are imposed.

The seniority principle originates in a managerial *grant*—giving it to employees. The earliest known record of seniority principle, in 1870, is in the Brotherhood of Locomotive Engineers (BLE's) *Monthly Journal*. In "A Step in the Right Direction" Charles Wilson, the BLE's grand chief engineer, discussed a general order of Jay Gould, president of the Erie Railway, granting a principle of seniority for various railroad crafts. Gould ordered a list of employees showing date of first employment, occupational position first held, and dates of promotion or other change of position. Gould's managerial "rules and regulations" for seniority guided construction of craft seniority rosters classified by the territory of an operating division or span of a department. Thus, just as seniority on railroads originates in a principle granted by management, so too, the related bounding of crafts stems originally from managerial grants. Rail management desired separated specialized crafts for cost-effectiveness in the market and efficient, safe operations.

The ideas of work rules defining seniority by craft did not explode suddenly into Gould's mind. They were necessarily based on earlier policy and practice. During the second half of the nineteenth century work rules developed regarding railroad seniority. A mature unilateral seniority principle is in Atchison, Topeka & Santa Fe Circular no. 1 of October 20, 1883—a grant labor schedule for conductors, brakemen, and train baggagemen.

Today, most North American railroaders are unionized, and employment is fixed by the terms and conditions of labor agreements. From a unilateral principle, craft seniority evolved into a cardinal right, the underpinning of bilateral labor agreements between rail management and union bargaining agent. The first agreement schedule of record, in 1875, was between the New York Central & Hudson River and a BLE committee. It contains intricate rules on rail craft seniority. After 1900 the craft unions of the engineers, firemen, conductors, and trainmen began standardizing the seniority provisions of agreements. Thus they ushered in concerted bargaining across broad regions of the United States. By the 1910s, as the bilateral work rules including seniority right continued to develop, agreement schedules grew from a page or two into ever-lengthier booklets.

At times, seniority may be a right first constructed and imposed on the employer by a court, arbitrator, or government administrator. Under the federal control of the railroads during World War I, the U.S. Railroad Administration imposed seniority provisions, creating crafts not previously agreed to by the carriers. Although it is customary to speak of work rules as bilateral, between management and labor, on railroads they have long been trilaterally formed, among these two parties and the state.

Seniority as principle can be found in many industries—including railroads—that do not have a union agreement but where management grants seniority to employees. On the Florida East Coast, which had abrogated its standard seniority-bound agreements after a losing strike by rail unions in 1963, management felt that a variety of seniority was necessary. On the Wisconsin Central in 1989, absent a union bargaining agent, management granted unilaterally a procedure that established "a length of service (seniority) list of all employees categorized by departments."

As a right, seniority has at its core a number of formal contractual rules, protecting an employee's interest in work. Fundamental is a rule establishing an employee's seniority date, usually the earliest time of paid work of a designated kind, for example, as a switchman or when promoted to conductor. The rules of the essential roster for seniority include maintaining and posting, periodic updating, and appeal processes and their durations for changing errors. Also found are rules for periodic bulletining and filling of job vacancies, assigning vacation times, and regulating other employee job prerogatives. Seniority determines rank order of persons for receiving prerogatives in such areas as promotion, demotion, furlough, recall, forced assignment, and forced transfer and for choice of prerogatives such as a job's kind, location, time, and rate and number of days of remuneration.

Under seniority rules, the employee who has the longest service in a craft with a railroad receives the greatest protection from layoff and undesired pressures of work and the most desired allocation of job prerogatives. Seniority necessarily favors those with greater length of service over those with less. Overall, in the United States and Canada the matter of the underlying fairness of a seniority system accords with widely held societal values regarding longevity.

On its fundamental level, for an employee, seniority may be considered a variety of fairness and justice that serves as insurance against the risks of market fluctuations that create unemployment. Seniority becomes a store of advantages regarding fellow employees and all those not fellow employees. At least since the policy of Gould, persons "off the street" are added to a seniority roster only when none on it are furloughed.

With regard to social relations, seniority is also an overall protection for an employee against insecurity of employment stemming from the employer's capriciousness, such as displeasure over an action, nepotism, or other discrimination. It protects an employee from managerial arbitrariness in discipline, promotions or demotions, wage increases or decreases, allocation of tasks and work sites, transfer, layoff, recall from layoff, and other circumstances. Without seniority, an employer could dismiss employees not held in esteem. Accordingly, for unionized workers, the consequences of the subjective displeasure of a manager concerning an employee are almost eliminated. A seniority system necessarily limits the employer's ability to have unrestricted control over employees, more so than under other work rules. In its broadest dimension, then, agreement seniority involves some degree of union control of an employer's jobs and work processes on behalf of represented employees. A seniority system lessens uncertainty and unrest in industrial relations.

At the very heart of any bargaining unit must be a mechanism for fairly allocating to unit members jobs and other prerogatives of employment that are part of the unit's jurisdiction. Without such a mechanism of unit stability, strife would result among members and lead to internal chaos in relations with management and nonunit personnel. In short, without this mechanism of social stability, a bargaining unit could not easily be created and, if founded, could rarely endure. The mechanism is seniority rights.

Placing a person on craft seniority list A confers membership for the listee in the corresponding craft bargaining unit. The membership of a particular bargaining unit might be entirely on one seniority roster or could be on two or more such lists, each for a separate jurisdictional territory of the unit. On a railroad, a seniority *territory* for a craft might be limited to a *point* such as a particular facility; it could extend across a *district* such as a stretch of lines, perhaps a superintendent's division; or it might comprise an entire railroad. Over the years, through negotiated and imposed collective bargaining, a tendency has emerged toward larger seniority territories.

Under Section 1, Fifth, the Railway Labor Act differs markedly from the National Labor Relations Act in that the term "employee" is linked with "subordinate officials." That is, first-line supervisors, such as yardmasters, foremen of various kinds, and train dispatchers may form unions and negotiate craft seniority rights. Such linkage is contrary to the usual practice outside railroads.

On railroads the day-to-day administration of the seniority-driven apportioning of job prerogatives is left with the employer, but the process is monitored closely by a concerned general committee of adjustment of a union. If a union member contests the manner of handling a seniority or other grievance, the National Railroad Adjustment Board (NRAB), a public law board, or their superordinated National Mediation Board will not casually overturn the union's actions and views on the matter. Indeed, only arbitrary or grossly unreasonable handling by the union would be a cause for doing so. Once the parties negotiate a seniority clause, its interpretation is largely by the union. All contractually covered employees must abide by what a union bargaining agent in good faith agrees to in the matter of seniority, subject to modification by the internal appeals process within the agent's union.

A distinction is necessary between longevity in employment and seniority from an agreement roster. *Longevity* is the total length of time of a person's employment with an employer, whereas *seniority* is as follows: initiated by a specified first date of service and functionally governed by the rostered rank order of an employee in an agreement-bounded employment group, seniority is a mechanism for regulating social relations in the allocation of scarce prerogatives among employees in the group and for the protection of this advantage against persons outside the group. Seniority rules provide uniform procedures for allocating desired agreement-defined prerogatives from employment and for setting fair priorities among disputed claims concerning the prerogatives within the group.

Lawfully, seniority includes a roster monopoly over designated work. The right of agreement seniority was further defined in this way by the NRAB's First Division (Award No. 1842:132, Caldwell case; Award No. 1843:147, Haileyville case, 1937): "Seniority, in railway service, is a preferential right to perform a certain class of work to the exclusion of all others not holding such seniority in that service. Once established it cannot be arbitrarily destroyed." Thus the webs of evolving law alter the characteristics of seniority rights over time.

Accordingly, those excluded from a bona fide monopolizing right are a class of all persons not in the roster group. As affirmed by the NRAB, no particular class of persons is, by virtue of existence of seniority right, a target for exclusion from performance of right-protected work. Instead, the global class of all not on the governing seniority roster is excluded, without prejudice to any subclass within this universal group. The rights of persons already on a seniority roster may not be diminished by any extra-agreement addition of a new person.

The seniority rights of a worker are conditioned by the wording of the labor agreement that creates them. Because seniority right is contractually based, it can only be modified by agreement between a bargaining agent and management. The right is enforceable only by the terms of the agreement. Because seniority rights issue from an agreement, they do not go beyond the provisions of an extant contract. Employees furloughed from employment have seniority rights only as provided by the contract. When duration of rights is not limited by the contract, furloughed workers retain the rights as long as they are available and able to work. It is not empty talk when a person "hires out" on a railroad and the first thing heard is: "The only thing you will ever have on this railroad is your seniority." It takes years of on-the-job practice, discussion, and reflection to comprehend the words.

—Frederick C. Gamst

REFERENCES

Brotherhood of Locomotive Engineers. *Official Report of Agreements Made between the Officials of the Roads Represented and the Committees Representing the Engineers Employed Thereon, as Reported March 1st, 1892.* Cleveland, Ohio: Cleveland Printing & Publishing, 1892.

Mater, Daniel H. "The Development and Operation of the Railroad Seniority System." *Journal of Business* 13 (1940): 387–419; 14 (1940): 36–67 [the two parts constitute the second of four articles in a series on seniority].

U.S. Interstate Commerce Commission. *Ex Parte 72, In the Matter of Regulation Concerning the Class of Employees & Subordinate Officials to Be Included within the Term "Employee" under the Railway Labor Act, Roadmaster and Supervisors.* 268 I.C.C. 55 (1947).

U.S. Railroad Administration. "Decisions of the Railway Boards of Adjustment, Nos. 1, 2, and 3 to December 31, 1918." *Director General of Railroads Bulletin*, No. 10 (1919).

Shaughnessy, Sir Thomas G. (1853–1923)

Thomas George Shaughnessy was born on October 6, 1853, in Milwaukee, Wisconsin, to Irish immigrant parents. He was educated in the classics and economics at the

Jesuit-run St. Aloysius Academy. In July 1869, at age 15, he began work as a clerk for the Chicago, Milwaukee & St. Paul Railroad. His interest in local politics got him elected as alderman from Milwaukee's Third Ward, and later he became president of the Milwaukee Common Council.

After ten years at the Milwaukee Road, Shaughnessy was still a bookkeeper in the supply department. But a new general superintendent, William C. Van Horne, arrived in 1880, soon recognized Shaughnessy's capabilities, and promoted him to company storekeeper. In 1882 Van Horne was appointed general manager of the fledgling Canadian Pacific Railway (CPR), which was struggling to complete its line across Canada to the Pacific shore. He brought Shaughnessy with him as general purchasing agent. Shaughnessy's rise in the CPR corporate structure was meteoric; he became assistant general manager in 1889, assistant to the president in 1891, and vice president and a member of the board of directors in 1899. Shaughnessy succeeded Van Horne as the third president of CPR in 1899. In 1910 he became chairman of the board, and remained chairman until his death in 1923.

Shaughnessy's first great contribution to the CPR was as a matchless provider of supplies during the 1880s construction phase, before the arrival of government and other financial aid that led up to completion of the railway on November 7, 1885. During Shaughnessy's tenure CPR spent $600 million on capital expenditures, increasing the track mileage from 7,000 to 11,200, double-tracking 70 percent of the western main line, and purchasing an Atlantic shipping fleet to match CPR's Pacific maritime operation. Under Shaughnessy, Canadian Pacific built palatial hotels across Canada, developed real estate holdings in Vancouver, supplemented snow sheds in the Rockies with tunnels, and irrigated vast dry areas in the southwestern area of the prairies. These massive projects gave rise to CPR's audacious slogan "The World's Greatest Travel System."

Shaughnessy's accomplishments did not go unnoticed. In 1901 he was made knight bachelor by King Edward VII. In 1907 Shaughnessy became knight commander of the Royal Victorian Order, and in 1916 he was elevated to the peerage as Baron Shaughnessy, at which point he was addressed as Lord Shaughnessy. He was also honored with doctoral degrees from Trinity College, Dublin, and Dartmouth and McGill universities. He died on December 9, 1923. Today a mountain in the Selkirk Range of British Columbia bears Shaughnessy's name, as does a tunnel opened in 1990 as part of Canadian Pacific's huge Rogers Pass line improvement in the Rockies.

—Jim Shaughnessy

REFERENCES

Berton, Pierre. *The Impossible Railway.* New York: Alfred A. Knopf, 1972.

Gibbon, John Murray. *Steel of Empire.* New York: Bobbs-Merrill, 1935.

Sherman Antitrust Act

The Sherman Antitrust Act of 1890 was passed by the U.S. Congress in response to growing public concern over a wave of corporate mergers in the late nineteenth century. Railroads were instrumental in forging a larger national market. This transportation revolution in turn opened new marketing opportunities and encouraged the growth of large-scale enterprise. New manufacturing technology also contributed to the flood of corporate consolidations. Although these developments could be viewed as the natural result of competition, they awakened latent antimonopoly sentiment. There was widespread fear that large corporations could stifle competition, fix prices, and manipulate market conditions. One early legal device used to facilitate corporate consolidation was the trust arrangement. The stock of several companies within an industry would be delivered to a board of trustees that then controlled the operations of the nominally different businesses. The trust device was later replaced by the use of holding companies, but the term "trust" was widely and loosely applied to various forms of business consolidation.

Railroads were pioneers in the merger movement. Even before the Civil War small railroads began to combine into larger systems. Anxious to preserve competition, a number of states enacted statutes or adopted constitutional provisions that banned the consolidation of railroads with competing or parallel lines. In addition to formal mergers, railroads in the Gilded Age experimented with pooling and price-fixing agreements in an attempt to stabilize volatile markets.

As concern about the emergence of large business corporations mounted, states began to enact antitrust laws. Congress followed suit in 1890, passing the Sherman Antitrust Act by an overwhelming margin in both houses. Affirming the ideals of competition and the free market, the Sherman Act in many respects was quite traditional in outlook. The act was predicated upon the common-law concept that conspiracies in restraint of trade violated public policy. Moreover, the measure did not create an administrative agency such as the Interstate Commerce Commission (ICC) to enforce its provisions. Instead, Congress relied upon enforcement by governmental and private litigation in the federal courts. Specifically, the act declared that "every contract, combination in the form of trust or otherwise, or conspiracy, in restraint of trade or commerce among the several States or with foreign relations, is hereby declared illegal." The statute also made it a crime to monopolize or attempt to monopolize any part of trade or commerce among the states. This vague wording virtually invited the federal courts to play a key role in formulating policy toward corporate mergers. Although scholars have long debated what Congress hoped to achieve with the Sherman Act, it is clear that the statute was not intended to ban all business combinations.

In *United States v. E. C. Knight Co.* (1895), the first case involving the Sherman Act to reach the Supreme Court, the justices accepted the constitutionality of the measure but restricted the reach of congressional power with respect to manufacturing. Writing for the Court, Chief Justice Melville W. Fuller followed the traditional view that manufacturing was local in nature and held that congressional authority under the commerce clause was limited to trade among the states. The *Knight* decision, coupled with the disinclination of the government to vigorously prosecute under the Sherman Act, did much to blunt the enforcement of this measure before 1900. Corporate mergers continued unabated.

Railroads, of course, were clearly engaged in interstate commerce. Still, it was uncertain whether the railroad industry was subject to the Sherman Act. Many felt that the act did not apply to railroads because Congress had already established a separate administrative system of governance for railroads by creating the ICC in 1887. Indeed, with the implicit approval of the ICC, railroads organized traffic associations to maintain uniform rates and eliminate price cutting.

In *United States v. Trans-Missouri Freight Assn.* (1897), however, a sharply divided Supreme Court invalidated a traffic association rate agreement as a violation of the Sherman Act. The majority of the Court, speaking through Justice Rufus W. Peckham, ruled that railroads were covered by the Sherman Antitrust Act. The Court gave a literal interpretation to the Sherman Act as invalidating all combinations in restraint of trade. Observing that many saw competition as the best means to secure proper transportation charges, the Court rejected the railroads' argument that the act outlawed only unreasonable restraints of commerce and that the rate agreement served the public interest. Dissenting, Justice Edward D. White formulated what later became known as the rule of reason in antitrust doctrine. He insisted that the act should be interpreted in light of the traditional common-law distinction between reasonable and unreasonable restraints of trade. He asserted that one purpose behind the Interstate Commerce Act was to foster stability of rates and to eliminate rate wars. It followed that rate agreements among carriers were reasonable and consistent with the objectives of the Interstate Commerce Act. White's dissenting opinion highlighted the tension between the antitrust and administrative approaches to railroad regulation. The Supreme Court reached a similar result in *Joint Traffic Freight Assn. v. United States* (1898), striking down a rate-fixing agreement among a number of carriers. Thus the first combinations condemned under the Sherman Act by the Supreme Court involved agreements among railroads.

Since agreements among competing railroads were illegal, some rail entrepreneurs turned to the holding company as a means of securing stability in setting rates.

At issue in the famous *Northern Securities Co. v. United States* (1904) case was an attempt to bring three major railroad lines operating in the Pacific Northwest under joint control. The carriers organized a holding company to manage transportation in the region. By a 5-4 vote the Supreme Court held that the holding company was a combination in restraint of trade and thus violated the Sherman Act. Concluding that a holding company was engaged in commerce, a plurality of the Court maintained that the act banned all restraints of trade and was not limited simply to unreasonable restraints. The Supreme Court also looked skeptically at the acquisition of a controlling stock interest by one carrier in a competing line. In *United States v. Union Pacific Railroad Co.* (1912) the justices ruled that the purchase by the Union Pacific Railroad Co. of stock in the Southern Pacific Co. constituted a restraint of trade within the meaning of the Sherman Act. The justices emphasized that consolidation of competing railroad systems abridged competition in interstate trade.

Attacks on consolidation in the rail industry did much to shape early antitrust doctrine. But there was an air of unreality about the application of antitrust principles to railroading. Policy makers during the Progressive Era were slow to perceive the basic inconsistency between insistence upon economic competition among railroads and the imposition of administrative control over the industry. They spoke in terms of restoring competition even as they built a regulatory scheme that reduced competition.

In the Transportation Act of 1920 Congress made a number of significant changes in railroad regulatory policy. Congress strengthened the power of the ICC and abandoned the notion of fostering competition. Instead, the Transportation Act sought to encourage consolidation of carriers into a limited number of systems. Not only was ICC approval now required for rail mergers, but such action by the commission conferred immunity from antitrust laws.

The principle of competition embedded in the Sherman Antitrust Act was ill suited to the economic conditions of the rail industry. Although railroad mergers contributed to the political agitation for control of trusts, and many of the early antitrust cases involved carriers, ultimately Congress recognized that the unique nature of railroading required a different approach.

—James W. Ely, Jr.

REFERENCES

Ely, James W., Jr. *Railroads and American Law.* Lawrence: Univ. Press of Kansas, 2001.
Hovenkamp, Herbert. *Enterprise and American Law, 1836–1937.* Cambridge, Mass.: Harvard Univ. Press, 1991.

See also REGULATION.

Shortline and Regional Railroads

Shortline railroads, or local line-haul railroads, have been defined by the Assn. of American Railroads (AAR) since 1986 as firms with less than 350 miles of track and less than $40 million in annual gross operating revenue. More than 500 such carriers operate 20,000 route-miles of track, serve 15,000 rail shippers, and originate or terminate 1.8 million carloads per year. This traffic is principally farm products, chemicals, lumber, paper, and coal; 70 percent of this traffic is either originated or terminated on-line, and the tracks serve principally as feeders for larger carriers. The shortline industry has a total asset value of $1.7 billion and employs approximately 25,000 persons.

Shortline railroads are one of the important building blocks of the North American railroad system. They are as old as the components of the major trunk lines of the nineteenth century and as new as the "rationalizations" of the Class 1 lines since passage of the Staggers Rail Act of 1980. The impetus behind the formation of these local carriers was the same in both instances—to enhance local economic self-interest. The nineteenth century formations were an effort to gain access to wider markets and to stimulate emerging industries. The recent formations have been efforts to retain and expand the remaining rail-dependent industries on marginally profitable local tracks.

The modern formation of shortlines has been strengthened by a series of federal statutes that have sought to diminish railroad regulatory requirements and to encourage local response to track abandonment by major carriers. In 1973 the Regional Rail Regulatory Act (the 3R Act) established the Federal Railroad Administration (FRA), which in turn created the Consolidated Rail Corp. (Conrail). The U.S. Railway Association (USRA) created by Congress developed a Final System Plan that permitted Conrail to abandon 30 percent of its lines while providing funds for the continuation of local rail service. The Rail Revitalization and Regulatory Reform Act (the 4R Act) of 1976 and the Staggers Act of 1980 speeded the process of route rationalization and freed all railroads from many regulatory constraints. Finally, the transfer of railroad regulation from the Interstate Commerce Commission (ICC) to the new Surface Transportation Board (STB) simplified the procedures for structural change within the industry.

The fortunes of a single shortline in northeastern Ohio, the Franklin & Warren, illustrate the role of these lines in the last two centuries. Originally conceived as access for a town bypassed by existing carriers, it was built in the early 1860s. It then became part of the Erie Railroad trunk line from New Jersey to Chicago. In 1992 Conrail filed for abandonment of the track, and local interests were able to retain service in several ways. The rhetoric that supported the formation of both the original shortline and the present shortline is quite similar. The 1860s cry "What is the use for me to build these mills if I can have no railroad connection?" for the disadvantaged Kent, Ohio, sounds very like the 1990s phrase "in a position of economic disadvantage" applied to service to a present-day industry at Ravenna, Ohio.

Modern shortline ownership takes many forms. Some national firms—Rail America, Genesee & Wyoming, Ohio Central System—own and operate a number of disparate tracks. Many regional railroads operate publicly owned shortlines. Entrepreneurs and private investment groups operate still other lines. This diversity illustrates the rather ad hoc nature of shortline formation where the imperative is to maintain service. As one operator put it, "It takes a lot to kill a railroad." Again, the example of the Franklin & Warren is instructive, because it is now owned in part by a transit authority, a public development authority, a shortline, and a Class 1 carrier, and it is operated by two regional rail systems.

Industry statistics illustrate the realities of a segment of the railroad industry that is shaped by the nature of its origins as the low-earning castoff of larger firms. The motive power used is normally of less than 3,000 hp, and 93 percent of the units are more than 20 years old. The freight equipment is also more than 20 years old, and most cars are standard boxcars. The average revenue per carload is less than $300, and the average length of car haul is approximately 35 miles. The trackage used is Class 2 or Class 1 or even Exempted (10 mph) track. Half of the bridges are still wooden, and only 22 percent of grade crossings have automatic safety protection. Tie replacement averages only 60 per track-mile per year.

Contemporary shortlines may be characterized as low-cost operations with a local focus and a personal service orientation. The length of the line may be a couple of miles, or it may be 50 or 60. Shortlines normally employ a nonunion workforce, and job classifications are extremely flexible. Shortlines commonly originate and terminate from only a single Class 1 carrier and act as a middleman between their shipper and the line-haul carrier. Car supply is usually the responsibility of the Class 1, although there are notable exceptions for shortlines that serve the paper, agricultural, and coal industries. Because of their smaller corporate size, shortlines rely on outside vendors and consultants for such functions as civil engineering, traffic development, and legal services.

In contrast to shortlines, regional railroads were defined by AAR in 1986 as those lines with a minimum of 350 miles of track and yearly revenues from $40 million up to the lower level for a Class 1 railroad. Thirty-one such firms in the United States operate a total of 17,000 track-miles and originate or terminate 2.8 million carloads yearly. Regional lines are typically formed from the sale of Class 1 lines' marginally profitable routes, and profit, rather than local access, is the rationale for their creation.

Shortlines face difficulties that are unique to their segment of the industry. Because of the nature of their formation, the track over which they operate may have been undermaintained for years. The rail itself may be of insufficient weight to support heavier modern freight cars. Financing for improvements and maintenance may be dependent on the generosity of various state and federal funding sources. Plant closings are a constant threat, and changes in ownership and in operators are common. Attraction of new customers is problematic because only 5 percent of industrial site searches specify rail service as a requirement.

Both shortlines and regionals typically may face similar constraints imposed by the selling carrier—limited access to terminals, restricted access to other Class 1 carriers, retained trackage or hauling rights, and the revenue stream for retained fiber-optic easements and rights. (In matters of legislative interest, both are represented by the American Short Line and Regional Railroad Assn.) Nonetheless, hope springs eternal in the shortline industry.

—Dan Donaghy

REFERENCES

Donaghy, Dan. "The Other Side of the Tracks: Local Response to a Deregulated Rail Industry." *Economic Development Review* (Summer 1996): 50.

Hungerford, Edward. *Men of Erie.* New York: Random House, 1946.

Signaling

Train Operations

Wayside signals have been a familiar feature of railroads ever since the industry's beginnings. In essence, signals are communication devices designed to inform locomotive engineers of track conditions ahead of the train and tell them how to react to those conditions. Thus they are, first of all, safety devices that help trains avoid collisions, but they are also tools for maximizing the efficiency of both train operations and track use.

The earliest railroads used a variety of simple devices to inform locomotive engineers about track conditions ahead, including a lighted candle in the stationmaster's office window to tell an approaching train that the way ahead was clear, wayside signals with discs or boxes with lanterns, or the use of a flag by day and a lantern by night. Among the first crude signals was a rotating board, introduced in the 1830s and said to have been the first movable signal.

One of the earliest signaling systems used to move trains was a ball signal device in 1832 on the 17-mile New Castle & Frenchtown Railroad. Stations were placed 3 miles apart between New Castle, Delaware, and Frenchtown, Maryland, with a raised white ball to indicate that a train had passed on time, while a black ball indicated that a train had been delayed. A ball at half-mast meant that a train should be prepared to stop at the next station for passengers and freight. The ball at the bottom of the mast meant that the arriving train should stop and wait. The raised ball at the top of the mast, indicating a clear track ahead, was the origin of the railroad term "highball."

Semaphore signals go back to the nineteenth century. These lower-quadrant signals dating from the construction of Boston's South Station in 1899 were still in service in 1980, but would soon be replaced by more modern signals. —Tom Nelligan, *Trains* Magazine Collection

The development of more powerful signal lighting made possible the use of color-light or searchlight signals, which gave good visibility at a long distance. These former Erie searchlight signals were installed at River Junction, New York. —Tommy Kraemer, *Trains* Magazine Collection

One of the first semaphore signals in the United States was installed in 1863 on the Utica & Black Hawk Railroad. This used a single-track line with two semaphore arms mounted on the same mast, one facing in each direction. Three glasses were in a light receptacle; the semaphore arm inclined downward, with a white light at night, indicated "proceed," while a horizontal arm, with two red lights at night, indicated "stop."

Other semaphore signals were soon adopted, and semaphores became the nearly universal standard for the next 80 years. They were of two general types: upper quadrant and lower quadrant. With both types, the "stop" indication is given when the blade is horizontal. The clear—proceed at normal speed—indication is given when the blade rises to the vertical position in an upper-quadrant signal or drops to the near-vertical position in a lower-quadrant signal.

In addition to the mechanism required to raise and lower the blade, the semaphore signal had lights for night operation. Through the early twentieth century almost all railroad signals used a clear white light to indicate a clear signal. A number of collisions were caused by a misread white light, or a colored red signal lens falling out, giving a false "clear" proceed. The Railway Signaling Club in 1895—later the Signal Section of the American Railway Assn. (now part of the Assn. of American Railroads)—set out to standardize signal lenses, changing from clear to green for proceed, yellow for caution, and red for stop.

In 1905 an electrically operated light signal was devel-

The Pennsylvania Railroad used a distinctive position-light signal that employed three yellow lights to provide light positions parallel to those of semaphores. This shows a T-1 locomotive with an eastbound mail and express under the position-light signals nearing the Crestline, Ohio, station. —Ben F. Cutler, *Trains* Magazine Collection

oped on the New York Central and over the next several years by the Long Island Rail Road and the Pennsylvania, using lamps of sufficient wattage, proper lenses, reflectors, and backgrounds. By 1912 medium-range (1,500 feet) color-light signals were developed, and by 1914 the New York, New Haven & Hartford and the Chicago, Milwaukee & St. Paul had installed long-range (3,500 feet) daylight-aspect signals. By 1920 the daylight range of color-light signals had been extended to 4,500 feet. With these powerful lamps and lenses that could be seen long distances, even in bright sunlight, it became feasible to display the signal aspects with lights only, day or night. Since that time light signals have become universal for new and replacement installations.

Two main types of light signals were developed: color-light and searchlight. Color-light signals have separate lamps and color lenses for each aspect, usually red, yellow, and green. Searchlight signals use a single powerful lamp and lens, and the colors are displayed by filters or roundels that are rotated between the lamp and the lens.

Two variations of position-light systems have been used by several roads, in a manner similar to a semaphore signal. One used two colored lenses in red, yellow, and green position to replicate the position of a semaphore. A similarly arranged position-light signal used yellow lights for all indications, with three lights in each of the positions of semaphore locations. The Pennsylvania Railroad and its affiliated lines and the Norfolk & Western were among the principal users of the latter type.

Operation by Timetable and Train Order

Whatever the type of wayside signals adopted by a particular railroad, the signals became integrated or used in conjunction with the railroad's operating system. The earliest railroads had no signals beyond the crude devices mentioned previously. As their traffic grew, they began to operate their trains by timetables that spaced the trains moving in the same direction by providing time intervals between them. On single-track lines the timetables also specified the times and places where trains moving in opposite directions were to meet. The timetables had to be followed strictly.

Operation by timetable alone worked, but only if all trains were on time. If a train was delayed, the entire railroad could be paralyzed, because it was impossible to change the meeting points. That problem was solved on September 22, 1851, when Charles Minot, superintendent of the Erie Railway, used the railroad's new telegraph line to send a message changing the meeting point of two trains. From this first "train-order," the "timetable and train order" system of operation evolved and was rapidly and widely adopted by North American railroads. The train orders were issued by train dispatchers and telegraphed (later, telephoned) to operators at wayside stations, who delivered them to the train crews. To avoid mistakes and misunderstandings, strict rules and procedures were developed. The entire procedure and the format of the orders were standardized.

The timetable and train-order system has served the railroads well for more than a century and a half. "T&TO" and variations of it made possible by modern technology are still in use on thousands of miles of North American railroads, mostly on lines with moderate or light traffic.

Manual and Automatic Block Signals

Another operating system that had early and wide acceptance in North America (and elsewhere) is the manual block system. In this system the railroad is divided into blocks or sections; only one train at a time is allowed to use each block. The boundaries between blocks are marked with block stations, each staffed with an operator, who controls signals that, when set to clear, allow a train to proceed into the block. Before the operator can clear a block signal, he must verify that any train previously granted authority to use the block has moved out of it.

The effectiveness of manual block control on a particular line segment depends on the number of block stations that are open (staffed), and on whether it has distant signals that give train crews advance notice of the block signal indications. Without distant signals, trains must approach each block signal prepared to stop.

The automatic block signal (ABS) system, in which trains set the signals themselves, was a major advance in railroad signaling and an early example of industrial automation. It was made possible in 1872 with the invention by Dr. William Robinson of the track circuit, which continues to be the basis of most railroad signaling.

The basic direct-current track circuit consists of the two rails of the track block, separated from the rails of adjacent blocks by insulated rail joints. The rails are connected to a battery at one end of the block and to a relay at the other end. When there is no train in the block, the electrical circuit is completed and the relay is energized, causing its armature to energize and the associated signal to display a clear indication. When a train enters the block, its wheels and axles short-circuit the system, causing the relay armature to drop and the signal to indicate "stop" (Figure 1).

The track circuit is fail-safe. Not only train wheels, but also any event that interrupts the circuit, such as battery failure or a broken rail, will cause the signal to display a stop indication. This fail-safe principle is incorporated into all signaling "vital" circuits, that is, circuits where malfunctioning equipment could result in unsafe signal indications.

In jointed-rail track the individual rails must be electrically tied together with bond wires. On electrified railroads and urban transit lines, different types of relays and other signaling equipment are required.

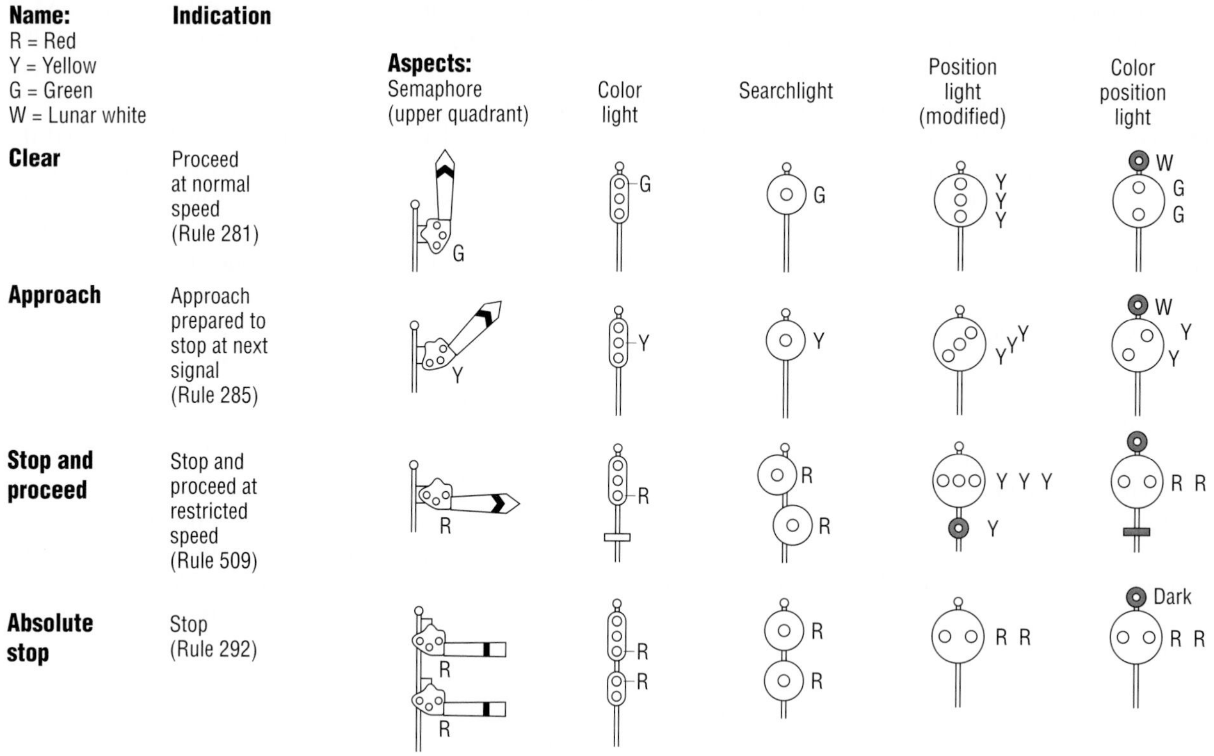

Name:	Indication	Aspects: Semaphore (upper quadrant)	Color light	Searchlight	Position light (modified)	Color position light
R = Red / Y = Yellow / G = Green / W = Lunar white						
Clear	Proceed at normal speed (Rule 281)	G	G	G	Y Y Y	W / G G
Approach	Approach prepared to stop at next signal (Rule 285)	Y	Y	Y	Y Y Y	W / Y Y
Stop and proceed	Stop and proceed at restricted speed (Rule 509)	R	R	R / R	Y Y Y / Y	R R
Absolute stop	Stop (Rule 292)	R / R	R / R	R / R	R R	Dark / R R

Figure 1. Signals of Different Types. —Rick Johnson

A main advantage of ABS is that it allows trains moving in the same direction to be more closely spaced. To permit this, the stop indication is designated as permissive, or stop and proceed at restricted speed; that is, it allows a train, once it has stopped, to move ahead at slow speed, prepared to stop for the train or other obstruction that has caused the red signal. Stop-and-proceed signals are identified with a number plate or staggered light below the signal head or, on semaphore signals, with a pointed blade.

Still another important advance was the absolute permissive block (APB), first put into service in 1911 on the Toronto, Hamilton & Buffalo Railway between Kennear and Vinemount, Ontario. In APB operation, when a train leaves double track and enters single track, all opposing signals are set at the stop aspect for the next siding or double track and any intermediate signals. Thus opposing trains cannot operate into an occupied single track beyond the next available siding or the end of double track.

Cab Signals and Train Control

After World War I steady advances in electrical and electronics technology began to be reflected in railroad signaling and traffic control systems. Several types of automatic train stop systems were developed. Mechanical systems, which use wayside trip devices that trigger a brake valve on the train, are widely used in urban rail transit systems. The trigger acts only if the motorman fails to acknowledge a restrictive signal indication. A similar system, used on some intercity railroads, uses a magnetic device on the locomotive that is triggered by a wayside inductor if the engineer does not respond to a restrictive block signal indication.

More sophisticated and effective are continuous automatic train control (ATC) systems. They use pulsed alternating current (AC) at various frequencies transmitted through the rails to repeat the wayside signal indications in the locomotive and to apply the brakes if necessary to bring the train into compliance with whatever speed the signals require.

Usually, ATC is combined with cab signals, which remotely display the status of wayside signals in the engineer's cab. Cab signals significantly improve safety by allowing the engineer to more easily know the state of a wayside signal. They eliminate visibility problems such as fog or snow, and they allow the engineer to see and act upon changes in signal indications when they occur, instead of having to wait until the wayside signal itself can be seen. This is especially valuable when visibility of a wayside signal might be limited because of an obstruction or curve.

Cab signals were made possible by modulating signal currents in the running rails. Antennae, attached to the locomotive's lead truck and cantilevered in front of its lead axle, receive one of several unique code rates or data words. The antennae are positioned a few inches above the top of the rail. On electrified railroads the signals received from the rails are combined in such a way that the cab signal received by each antenna is added together and thereby increased in value, while the traction-power return currents in each rail are subtracted. This makes it possible to recover the much smaller signal currents in the presence of larger traction-power currents.

Interlocking

As the early railroads began to expand—adding extensions, connections, and new branches, as well as crossing each other at grade—the question of how to expedite traffic safely across these junctions and crossings became acute. The answer was interlocking, developed to prevent a signal operator from clearing a route through the interlocked area when he had already cleared a train to move through the area on a conflicting route. The first American interlocking was the installation of a British Saxby & Farmer plant placed in service in 1870 at a junction of the Bordentown branch of the United New Jersey Canal & Railroad Cos.

Early interlocking plants, many of which were still in use in the 1960s, were entirely mechanical. Large levers in the interlocking machine controlled the switches, signals, and derails through long rods (usually made of pipe). Locking bars made it impossible to operate the levers except in the proper sequence. Before he could clear the signal for a route through the interlocking plant, the operator had to make sure that all signals on conflicting routes were at stop and that derails on the conflicting routes were open.

A major improvement in the mechanical interlocking system was the introduction of electropneumatic control. The switches, signals, and derails were operated by air cylinders that were electrically controlled. A pneumatic interlocking plant was installed at Wellington, Ohio, in 1882. It was just a short step from that to full electrical control of the track and signal equipment in an interlocking plant, and the first all-electric interlocking was installed at a crossing of the Baltimore & Ohio Southwestern and the Cincinnati Northern at Cincinnati.

Advancing technology soon brought increasing automation of interlocking functions. Where two railroads cross in isolated locations, the interlocking can be completely automatic and unattended. When a train enters the interlocked trackage, the interlocking machine automatically clears its route unless a conflicting train movement has already been cleared or is in progress.

Another important advance in interlocking technology was the development of automated route interlocking, especially helpful at busy locations such as passenger-train terminals. The first such installation was in 1937 at Girard Junction, Pennsylvania, where a four-track main line connected with a double-track line. The interlocking included universal crossovers between all four main-line tracks, as well as the double-track line. The operator or dispatcher had a display map of the interlocked trackage. He simply pressed a button at the point where a train or switching movement was to enter the plant and another button at the point where it was to exit. The machine automatically selected and cleared the best available route between those two points. This "entrance-exit" system vastly improved interlocking plant productivity: One operator could handle a busy terminal or junction that typically, with earlier technology, would have required several lever operators and a supervisor.

Other developments included the first installation, in

Signal maintainers look after the electric and electronic infrastructure of the railroad signaling system. A Southern Railway signal maintainer was adjusting an electric switch lock mechanism along the railway's main line at Spartanburg, South Carolina, in August 1982. —John Uckley, *Trains* Magazine Collection

1953, of a Delaware, Lackawanna & Western multiplex code control system at Newark, New Jersey, involving three major electricpneumatic interlockings. Traffic involved 233 through trains and 33 daily switching movements.

Centralized Traffic Control

A logical extension adapted interlocking to the centralized control of traffic on long stretches of main-line track. With centralized traffic control (CTC), the train dispatcher has a control console with a track diagram showing all the main-line switches and signals on a district that may be as short as a few miles or as long as several hundred miles. Lights show the progress of trains across the territory and the position of the signals and switches at each end of each passing track. Levers and pushbuttons enable the dispatcher to route a train into the siding to pass a train moving in the opposite direction or to wait for a faster train moving in the same direction. In effect, the dispatcher controls a small interlocker consisting of the switches and signals at each end of each passing track. Today, levers and pushbuttons have been largely replaced by computer graphics with icons representing signals, turnouts, and other features on the railroad. The dispatcher controls interlockings and signals with a click of a computer mouse.

The first installation of CTC in North America went into service on the New York Central Railroad on a 40-mile segment of track between Toledo and Berwick, Ohio, on July 25, 1927. By about 1930 pulse-code technology had made it possible to control switches and signals over long distances with only two line wires. Subsequently, as railroads acquired microwave radio systems, they used them to transmit CTC control pulses. By 1940 railroads had installed more than 2,400 miles of CTC-controlled territory.

CTC (also known as TCS, for traffic control system) was highly effective, especially on single-track lines carrying heavy traffic. Indeed, it was claimed that a single-track line with CTC has 70 to 75 percent of the capacity of a double-track line with automatic block signals. Installed on critical, congested line segments during World War II between 1941 and 1945, CTC played an important role in keeping the railroads fluid.

During the lean years of the 1960s railroads found that converting double-track lines into CTC-equipped single-track routes could reduce the cost of materials, maintenance, and taxes. In addition, because the trains operated entirely by signal indication, train orders were not required (except very rarely in emergencies), and there was no need for signal or block stations or operators.

By the late 1960s the steady advance of electronic and computer technology had resulted in still more automated signal and train operation functions that permitted a single dispatcher to supervise still longer districts. In an early form of computer-aided dispatching the CTC machine could set the switches and signals for all the trains as they proceeded across the territory, executing meets as needed. The dispatcher had to intervene only in special circumstances. The

system gave him more time to plan train moves to expedite priority traffic, as well as for his record-keeping duties. Also by the late 1960s it had become possible to operate urban rail transit systems and high-speed intercity passenger systems under full-programmed automation.

Train Control and Cab Signals

On January 10, 1922, the ICC ordered the installation of automatic train stop or train control systems in trains over designated divisions. Two basic train control systems developed: (1) Intermittent inductive train stop controls use an inductor located alongside the approach to a wayside signal. If a restrictive signal is displayed from the inductor, the locomotive will automatically apply brakes unless the engineer acknowledges within eight seconds that the train is under control. (2) Continuous inductive train control uses AC track circuits to create inductive fields that are picked up by receiver coils mounted under the front of the locomotive. Any change in a track circuit ahead is detected by the AC track-circuit receiver coils on the locomotive indicating a changed cab signal for the engineer. If the engineer does not acknowledge within eight seconds that the train is under control and reducing speed, the brakes are automatically applied and the train is brought to a complete stop.

An important element in continuous inductive train control was the development of cab signals on the locomotive. An installation by the Pennsylvania Railroad in 1923 was the first application of vacuum tubes outside the communications industry, and the first time a cab signal was used instead of a wayside signal. The PRR installation included a three-speed, continuous train control system over 47 miles of single or double track between Lewiston and Sunbury, Pennsylvania. A miniature cab signal advised of any change when a more restrictive signal was indicated, with an acknowledgment to the engineman.

Improvements in Track-Circuit Design

In the 1960s a new generation of track circuits appeared. Called audio frequency (AF) track circuits because the carrier frequency was well within the range of human hearing, they eliminated the need for most insulated joints on main-line track. Further, on electrified railroads and transit systems, AF track circuits allowed impedance bonds weighing several hundred pounds to be replaced by smaller bonds.

Recall that direct current (DC) requires the running rails to be electrically isolated into blocks by periodically cutting the rail and inserting electrical insulators. To hold these cut rail sections together, overlapping insulated joint bars are attached to both sides of the rails and bolted together via holes drilled into the web of the rail.

Impedance bonds are, simply, balanced inductors configured so that traction-power currents on electrified railroads can return to the substation while simultaneously constraining track signal currents to within each track circuit. Since traction-power return currents are large compared with track signal currents, for reducing energy loss in the form of heat at each bond it is important for the resistance at each bond to be as low as practical.

To achieve a low resistance, the coils in impedance bonds must be large. But impedance increases with frequency, so bonds designed for AF track circuits can be much smaller. In addition, insulated joint failures can also be largely eliminated. Further, because no bolt holes are needed for insulated joints, it is possible to use continuously welded rail. The reduction in bolted track means reduction of the number of potential points for fractures, increasing system safety and track-circuit reliability.

Although high-performance fixed-block passenger rail systems may have up to nine speed commands (compared with perhaps three or four aspects for many freight railroads), the key factor constraining signal performance is block length. Further, a traditional fixed-block signal system must be designed for the longest train with the worst-case braking. Trains with improved braking (for example, trains equipped with electronically controlled pneumatic brakes that can have up to 70 percent shorter braking distances) must be constrained by the worst-case train that might operate on that same track.

If only a few trains per hour are required, block lengths can be long, and this reduces the total number of track circuits required. Conversely, when headway requirements are very short (typical of a subway system), the number of track circuits is relatively large.

Advanced Train Control Systems

While the United States was focusing on advanced track-circuit technology in the late 1960s and early 1970s, signal suppliers in Germany were taking a radically different approach. First appearing on German Federal Railroads in the early 1970s, Linienzugbeeinflussung (LZB) was a revolutionary train control system that did not require track circuits. LZB, which continues to be used in Germany, formed the basis for later variants used around the world. Today, most moving-block systems are known as communications-based train control (CBTC). Most CBTC systems in service today have been developed for rail transit, but work continues on railroad applications of this technology.

In the mid-1980s U.S. and Canadian railroads began to see benefits in migrating away from fixed-block track circuits and started work on a major new detection architecture known as advanced train control system (ATCS), using radio-frequency-based (RF-based) communications in the 900 MHz band. The plan was to build a common infrastructure to safely and seamlessly control freight trains. Key requirements for ATCS included open system interfaces and multiple sources of supply.

Because ATCS was RF based and thus did not use an inductive wire loop in the trackway like LZB, absolute train position needed to be determined via other means. The original ATCS program specified the use of radio-frequency identification (RF-ID) tags attached to crossties at periodic intervals.

Such tags are not new to U.S. railroads. Today, virtually every freight car in North America is equipped with RF-ID tags to identify it as it passes by an ID reader, with such information as road number, owner, equipment type, and trailers or containers. This system is known as Automatic Equipment Identification (AEI). AEI tags are passive. This means that they do not require a battery or other external source of power. When tags pass by an AEI reader, the reader emits RF energy. This RF energy is received by the tag and rectified by a diode that converts the RF energy to DC. This DC is used to power the sensitive electronics in the tag, and it begins to emit a unique identification code pattern that is then received by the same AEI reader.

Although a number of successful pilot programs demonstrated the potential technical viability of full deployment, ATCS was not a commercial success. The principal concern for the railroads was the high cost of the wayside radio infrastructure.

Nevertheless, CBTC applications are still being developed for railroads. The technology for this type of application is known as positive train control (PTC). Most PTC systems are being designed to augment ("overlay") existing track-circuit-based ABS technology. The objectives of PTC are to manage track occupancy, issue movement authorities, track trains and assure safe train separation, enforce limits of operating authority, automatically enforce speeds, monitor and control wayside systems (including grade-crossing warning systems), and enable higher speeds for passenger trains that operate on the same tracks as freight trains.

The North American Joint PTC Project in Illinois on Union Pacific's Joliet and Springfield subdivisions is one of the latest attempts to develop industry-standard PTC architecture that can be used by many railroads. Lockheed Martin contracted with the U.S. Federal Railroad Administration to develop PTC with open-system architecture providing interoperability and compatibility through commercial off-the-shelf (COTS) hardware and software. Lockheed Martin devised a train location system that does not require wayside hardware. It uses Differential GPS (with 10-foot accuracy), inertial sensors (wheel tachometers), and a track database. A color liquid crystal diode (LCD) flat panel with analog and digital readouts provides graphic displays to the locomotive engineer. Sixteen Union Pacific and Amtrak locomotives have been equipped.

A similar undertaking, the Michigan High Speed PTC Project, involves Amtrak, General Electric Transportation–Global Signaling, Norfolk Southern, the Michigan Department of Transportation, and FRA. Installed on Amtrak's former Michigan Central right of way on the

Chicago-Detroit corridor, this system is designed to enable speeds up to 110 mph for passenger trains operating in mixed-traffic territory with freight trains. The technology is Incremental Train Control System (ITCS), which enforces civil speed limits, locomotive/train speed, and temporary speeds through work areas. It provides onboard delivery of movement authorities without the need for engineer interaction and continuously monitors signals, turnouts, and crossings to provide immediate information to locomotives. Signal aspects, turnout positions, and crossing status are relayed to equipped trains every six seconds from wayside interface units. A digital onboard display provides the engineer with "targets" (grade crossings, interlockings, speed restrictions, stop signals) and the distance and time to those targets based on speed and braking calculations.

ITCS is an overlay that can also be applied to dark territory, CTC, or cab-signal territory. It has been in revenue service since April 2000. Amtrak and Norfolk Southern are operating trains under ITCS under full enforcement and continuous train supervision, with Amtrak trains operating at 95 mph. Speeds were planned to be gradually increased to 110 mph.

New Signaling Technologies for Rail Transit

Several Class I railroads have embarked on independent PTC pilot programs, all of which are designed to provide basic PTC functions like speed limit and movement authority enforcement. CSX Transportation was the first, with a system called communications-based train management (CBTM), largely developed internally and supplied by Wabtec Railway Electronics. CBTM is intended for unsignaled territory but has a so-called migration path that would allow it to be deployed as an overlay on CTC territory. BNSF Railway's electronic train management system (ETMS), also supplied by Wabtec, is based on CBTM. A successful pilot program on the railroad's Beardstown (Illinois) Subdivision in 2004–2005, ETMS is being applied to other unsignaled territory, most recently in Texas. CBTM and ETMS are both "non-vital."

Norfolk Southern is taking a different approach to PTC, and is currently developing a vital system for unsignaled territory called optimized train control (OTC), which it planned to deploy on the Piedmont Division (Charleston-Columbia, South Carolina main line) by 2008. Two suppliers are teaming on OTC to develop specifications and perform system integration: Lockheed Martin, system integrator on NAJPTC, and GE Transportation Global Signaling, supplier of NS's Unified Traffic Control System (UTCS) dispatching technology. OTC will not initially provide moving-block operation, but will have the ability to do so if NS decides to go that route. UTCS, which has the ability to perform movement authority conflict checks and resolutions, will provide digital movement authorities

and speed restrictions to OTC-equipped trains, which will be equipped with cab displays. One safety feature NS wants to have is manual-switch position verification.

Currently under way on the Alaska Railroad is a multiphased program to design, develop, and implement a computer-based collision avoidance system (CAS). Utilizing $12 million in Federal Railroad Administration funding, it includes train management and train/wayside communications functions. When fully installed, CAS will utilize Global Positioning System satellites, onboard computers, and early notification warnings on switches to improve train spacing and safety in all areas of operations.

New Jersey's Port Authority Transit Corp. (PATCO) and San Francisco's Bay Area Rapid Transit (BART) were the first automated rapid-transit systems in the United States, and BART was one of the first to use AF track circuits. BART's original train control system was a mix of traditional vital relay-based interlockings and modern aerospace technology. Integrated circuits were used both in BART's train control equipment rooms and in wayside signal equipment. Unfortunately, these efforts to reduce costs by applying aerospace technology in many cases created more problems than they were intended to solve. As a result, when specifications for the Washington Metropolitan Area Transit Authority (WMATA) subway were developed in the early 1970s, they specifically precluded the use of "active electronic equipment on the wayside." WMATA's more conservative design requirements resulted in extensive use of traditional relays and wayside cabling when compared with BART's train control system.

A descendant of LZB known as Seltrac was developed for rail rapid-transit systems. It was first deployed in the mid-1980s in Toronto, Detroit and Vancouver. During the 1986 Vancouver Expo, SkyTrain operated trains on headways as low as 43 seconds. In the early 1990s the San Francisco Municipal Railway overlaid a Seltrac system over its existing manual three-speed fixed-block system. By doing so, Muni was able to double (from 23 to 46) the number of trains per hour it could operate in its Market Street Subway.

Muni was the first major U.S. rail transit system to upgrade to CBTC. Because this first generation of CBTC technology was based upon "near-field inductive loop," it is sometimes referred to as IL-CBTC to distinguish it from a later generation of radio-frequency-based CBTC, which is sometimes referred to as RF-CBTC.

In the early 1990s, as a number of inductive loop CBTC systems began to come on line, NYC Transit undertook a major multiyear, multimillion-dollar worldwide investigation of CBTC technology. Before this, many in the United States believed that CBTC technology was only appropriate for smaller systems, such as people movers at airports. However, NYCT's study concluded that its peers worldwide generally felt that there was considerable merit to deploying CBTC technology and that it was sufficiently safe and mature to be deployed at major rail transit systems. The principal problem was that all current CBTC systems were proprietary.

NYCT believed that inductive loop CBTC was inappropriate for its harsh environment, so it proceeded on a research and development program to develop a CBTC system based upon RF technology. Others such as BART agreed and began a similar R&D program.

But because of its size (722 miles of track and 6,000 subway cars), NYCT was not in a position to allow itself to be tethered to any one signal supplier's CBTC technology. Thus NYCT began a CBTC pilot program on its Canarsie Line in the late 1990s known as a Leader-Follower program. A Leader technology was selected in 1999 to develop core RF-CBTC technology that is to be interoperable and compatible with systems provided by two Followers. This is intended to ensure that NYCT has future multiple sources of supply. NYCT's Canarsie Line CBTC system was placed in revenue service in 2005.

BART and Philadelphia's SEPTA systems are among the other U.S. rail transit properties to deploy RF-CBTC. BART's technology, supplied by GE Transportation, is called Advanced Automatic Train Control (AATC) and is designed for fully automatic train operation. SEPTA uses technology from Bombardier called Flexiblock to maintain safe braking distance between light-rail vehicles and enforce speed restrictions.

Beyond CBTC

One of the significant challenges in building next-generation train control systems is the need to address the problem of rapid obsolescence with advanced technology. Today, for example, RF communications subsystems (the underpinning for CBTC systems) have become obsolete in just a few years, but many railroads and rail transit properties expect signal systems to last 40 or more years. The prospect of replacing older signal systems with new-technology signal systems every few years is neither attractive nor financially viable. Pressure is building for the signal industry to rethink its traditional business model, based upon proprietary technologies and monolithic train control systems, and to rely more on commercial off-the-shelf products and open industry standards.

Another important change is the need to expose key subsystem interfaces. This will allow suppliers to build compatible interoperable equipment and also new equipment with compatible migration paths. Already the railroad industry is seeing new proprietary CBTC radios becoming obsolete in just a few years, while superior open-industry-standard data radios are dropping rapidly in price.

—Robert W. McKnight, Tom Shedd, Thomas D. Sullivan, and William C. Vantuono

REFERENCES

Armstrong, John H. *The Railroad, What It Is, What It Does.* 3rd ed. Omaha, Nebr.: Simmons-Boardman, 1990.

Brignano, Mary, and Hax McCullough. *The Search for Safety: A History of Railroad Signals and the People Who Made Them.* Pittsburgh, Pa.: American Standard, 1981.

General Railway Signal Co. *Elements of Railway Signaling.* Rochester, N.Y., 1979.

Josserand, Peter. *Rights of Trains.* 5th ed. New York: Simmons-Boardman, 1957.

King, Everett E. *Railway Signaling.* New York: McGraw-Hill, 1921.

Phillips, Edmund J., Jr. *Railroad Operation and Railway Signaling.* New York: Simmons-Boardman, 1953.

Shedd, Thomas C. "Railroad Automation." Chap. 9 in *Automation and Society*, ed. Howard Boone Jacobson and Joseph S. Roucek. New York: Philosophical Library, 1959.

———. "Railroads and Locomotives." *Encyclopaedia Britannica,* 15th ed., 1974.

Tuthill, John K. *Transit Engineering: Principles and Practice.* St. Louis: John S. Swift, 1935.

Vantuono, William C. *All about Railroading.* New York: Simmons-Boardman, 2000.

See also ALSTOM SIGNALING (GENERAL RAILWAY SIGNAL CO.); SIGNALING SUPPLIERS; UNION SWITCH & SIGNAL CO.

Signaling Suppliers

Union Switch & Signal and General Railway Signal were long the two giants of railway signaling and control, but there was no shortage of competition from smaller firms. Although these two continue to be major participants, two other firms have now emerged as strong competitors for the railway signaling and control market.

The first of these to reach its present form was Safetran Systems Corp., formed in 1971 from two long-standing predecessor firms, Railroad Accessories Corp. and Marquardt Industrial Products Co. Like many of their predecessors, these two firms, in turn, came from a long history of smaller firms in the industry.

Railroad Accessories was formed in 1920 for signal system work and over the next 20 years acquired more than half a dozen other firms that gave it a complete line of highway-rail crossing systems. Marquardt was more recent, formed to acquire the manufacturing rights for the new constant warning time (CWT) for highway-rail grade crossings developed with Southern Pacific's Arlo C. Krout and the Stanford Research Institute. Soon looking for an expanded line of communications and components, Marquardt acquired three firms active primarily in a variety of voice and control systems.

Merger of the two into Safetran in 1971 formed a new firm with a comprehensive range of signaling and train control products. It was further expanded a year later by the acquisition of Transportation Engineering Services, a signal company, and in 1976 by its acquisition of the Nachod & United States Signal Co. Nachod had been acquired by firms active in signaling, highway-rail grade crossing, and other firms that dated as far back as 1901.

Safetran went international in 1984 through an agreement with Hawker Siddeley, of London, United Kingdom, to market the products of its Westinghouse Brake & Signal Co. Ltd. in the United States and Canada. Although still operated under the Safetran name, the firm was acquired in the early 1990s first by Hawker Siddeley and then by BTR Rail Group.

General Electric Transportation Systems–Global Signaling is the newest of the major firms in signaling and train control. It began operating around 1950 as Harmon Electronics, developing carrier circuits for VHF radios and centralized traffic control (CTC). By 1960 the firm had begun to branch out with electronic track circuits, known as Audio Frequency Trains Actuated Circuits (AFTAC), and then with flashing-light signals, automatic gates, and other signal structures. By 1986 Harmon had acquired Modern Industries, a manufacturer of highway-rail grade-crossing systems.

Significant advances in computer and microprocessor technological development by Harmon included a motion-sensor highway-crossing processor, known as HXP, that gave a minimum 20-second warning for any train approaching a crossing. A centralized, computer-aided system developed by Harmon in the 1980s dispatched rail operations over the entire line. The firm also developed a Vital Harmon Logic Controller (VHLC) that was used extensively in centralized traffic control systems.

The company added the Electric-Pneumatic Corp. and Servo Corp. firms in 1985 and 1986. Electric-Pneumatic had developed a system of track circuits, called Electrocode, that eliminated line wire controls for wayside signals, using instead electronic track circuits. Servo brought into the firm an extensive business in infrared hot-bearing detectors, first developed in 1956 for the Chesapeake & Ohio. More advanced versions had the capability of roller, plain, and inboard bearings and provided an immediate radio train crew warning.

Reflecting its wider range of railroad products, the company changed its name to Harmon Industries in 1996. By 1998 it had acquired a new device that developed computer control to analyze outputs from hot-bearing detectors. The firm acquired the rights to the Hughes Electronic Advanced Automatic Train Control, a highly advanced technology being developed for Bay Area Rapid Transit (BART).

General Electric had been in signaling and train control as early as 1905, but sold its patents and manufacturing rights to Union Switch & Signal Co. GE was back in the business in 1959 with a hot-bearing detector, but again left the field to Harmon Electronics in 1980. GE came back for the third time in 1995, entering a joint venture with Harris Corp., a defense supplier, to develop a train control and computer-aided dispatching system. A year later the joint venture contracted with the Burlington Northern & Santa Fe and the Union Pacific for an 845-mile, three-year test and demonstration project in Washington State. This employed a communications-based safety system with movement authorities via digital radios to a computer-calculated distance to the authorized end of its authority. Braking was automatic if a train did not obey a signal to it at the end of its authorized end point.

GE acquired the Harris firm in 1998, when it bought a developed software for computer-aided dispatching from Train Tracking Co. Two years later GE had acquired the entire Harmon Industries to create a new firm GE Harris Harmon Railway Technology, and by the following year the firm had adopted its present name, General Electric Transportation Systems–Global Signaling. By the end of 2002 the new firm had acquired LaBarge Inc. and its network and cellular system for monitoring warning devices and controls at highway-rail grade crossings.

—Robert W. McKnight

See also ALSTOM SIGNALING (GENERAL RAILWAY SIGNAL CO.); SIGNALING; UNION SWITCH & SIGNAL CO.

Signals and Whistles

Hand, Flag, and Lamp Signals

Communication among a train crew is required in handling the movement of a train, and a clear understanding between the crew members of their intent is essential to safe operation. Today, the ubiquitous radio is the usual form for this communication, but in an earlier time it was customary to use a well-designed set of hand, flag, or lamp signals, as shown in Figure 1.

The color of a signal lamp or flag was normally white; a hand signal could be used as well if necessary. Any object waved violently by anyone on or near the track was treated as a signal to stop. Signals were required to be given from a point where they could be plainly seen and in such a manner that they could not be misunderstood. If there was doubt about the meaning of a signal, or for whom it was intended, it must be regarded as a stop signal. If signals disappeared from view, the movement must be stopped immediately.

Engine Whistle Signals

Signals from a locomotive engineer to train crew members or others are made with a series of prescribed whistle signals. These were made through prescribed short and long sounds, in which "o" represents a short sound, and "—" represents a long sound. Table 1 presents examples of some of the most common whistle signals in use.

Communicating Signals

Signals used between passenger train crews and the locomotive engineer are conveyed by air whistles and a high-

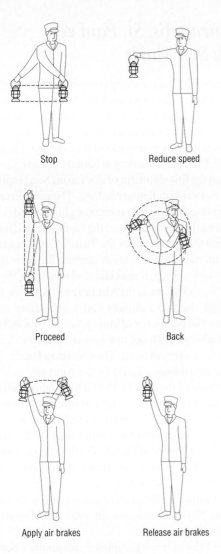

Stop

Reduce speed

Proceed

Back

Apply air brakes

Release air brakes

Figure 1. Hand, Flag, and Lamp Signals. —Rick Johnson

Table 1. Whistle Signals

Sound	Indication
o	Apply brakes. Stop.
— —	Release brakes. Proceed.
— o o o	Flagman protect rear of train.
— — — —	Flagman may return from west or south.
— — — — —	Flagman may return from east or north.
o o	Answer to any signal not otherwise provided for.
o o o	When standing, back up.
o o o o	Call for signals.
— — o —	Approaching public crossings at grade. To be prolonged or repeated until crossing is reached.
———	Approaching stations, junctions, and rail crossings at grade.
— — o	Approaching meeting or waiting points.
o —	Inspect train line for leak or for brakes sticking.
Succession of short sounds	Alarm for persons or livestock on the track.

Table 2. Communication Signals

Sound	Indication
o o	When standing—start.
o o	When running—stop at once.
o o o	When standing—back.
o o o	When running—stop at next passenger station.
o o o o	When standing—apply or release air brakes.
o o o o	When running—reduce speed.
o o o o o	When standing—recall flagmen.
o o o o o	When running—increase speed.
o o o o o o	When running—increase train heat.
o — o	Shut off train heat.
———	When running—brakes sticking; look back for hand signals.

pitched whistle to the engineman, or electric buzzer signals, and express a variety of indications, with "o" representing a short sound and "—" a longer sound (Table 2).

—William D. Middleton

REFERENCE

Josserand, Peter. *Rights of Trains.* 5th ed. New York: Simmons-Boardman, 1957.

Sinclair, Angus (1841–1919)

Angus Sinclair was a rare combination: a man who loved running locomotives, but later turned to publishing as a career. He was born in 1841 in Forfar, Scotland, where his father was a railway employee. Sinclair found his first job as a telegrapher on the Scottish Northeastern Railway. In a few years he became an engine driver. To many young men, dashing across the countryside with one hand on the throttle of a high-wheel locomotive was a thrilling occupation. Sinclair developed a lifelong affection for the iron horse.

About 1870 Sinclair emigrated to the United States. He ran engines on the Erie and then moved west to become an engineer on the Burlington, Cedar Rapids & Northern Railroad. But the fun of engine running began to wear thin as Sinclair matured. He decided to better himself and took an evening class to study chemistry. He combined his experience on the footplate with his new understanding of chemistry to write a few articles on combustion and smoke prevention. An editor with the *American Machinist* noticed one of these articles and liked the clear and engaging writing. In 1883 Sinclair was invited to the New York offices of the magazine and joined the staff.

At the age of 42 he was off on a new and unexpected career. That hardly seemed possible for a middle-aged man with only a grammar-school education. He soon set to work on a book titled *Locomotive Running and Management* that was published in 1885. It was aimed at entry-level workmen who wanted to become locomotive engineers. The little volume was well received and went through 26 editions. Two years after this book appeared, the owners of *American Machinist* decided to start a new magazine called *Locomotive Engineering*. Sinclair was named assistant editor. In 1892 Sinclair and another editor jointly bought the magazine from *American Machinist*. Five years later Sinclair bought out his partner and became the sole owner of the publication. Current technology was the primary focus of the magazine, but space was always found for a short historical piece on steam locomotives. Old-timers were encouraged to submit recollections of pioneering engines and engine builders. Old prints and engravings were reproduced along with the text, and sometimes new art was commissioned to illustrate the articles.

Sinclair was very active in the American Railway Master Mechanics' Assn., serving as the group's secretary from 1887 to 1896. A few years later he took up the position of treasurer. This put him in close contact with all the leading locomotive designers and managers in the nation. He gained access to what was new in the industry, gossip about its leaders, and endless stories about the early years of American steam. Much of this material found its way into his magazine, and as articles appeared in print, others were stimulated to comment or send in more antiquarian notes and accounts.

Sinclair himself became a student of locomotive history, and after years of collecting and publishing on the subject, he decided to produce a book. It was a sizable work of 33 chapters and over 600 pages. When *Development of the Locomotive Engine* appeared in 1907, it filled a void in engineering history. MIT Press printed an annotated edition in 1970. Sinclair also published three other books and was a recognized authority in the area of locomotives. In 1908 Purdue University awarded him an honorary doctor of engineering degree. As he reached his 70th year, however, Sinclair's productivity slowed greatly, but he remained active until his death on January 1, 1919, at his home in Milburn, New Jersey.

—John H. White, Jr.

REFERENCE

White, John H., Jr. Introduction to *Development of the Locomotive Engine*, by Angus Sinclair. New York: A. Sinclair, 1907. Repr., Cambridge, Mass.: MIT Press, 1970.

Soo Line Railroad

The history of the Soo Line is confused by a nickname, Soo Line, that later became a formal name and another name, Wisconsin Central, that disappeared early in the twentieth century and reappeared in 1987 attached to essentially the same route map.

Minneapolis, St. Paul & Sault Ste. Marie

Minneapolis flour-milling companies that sought lower rates to the East incorporated the Minneapolis, Sault Ste. Marie & Atlantic Railway in 1883. Construction began the following year at Cameron, Wisconsin, and as many as 7,000 men were soon at work on the new line. The rails met the Canadian Pacific Railway at Sault Ste. Marie, Ontario, in 1887, and the first shipment of flour from Minneapolis mills moved eastward on January 5, 1888. The new alternative to shipping through Chicago soon brought lower rates for traffic between the Twin Cities and the East Coast and had much to do with the emergence of the Twin Cities as manufacturing, financial, and distribution centers. Between 1884 and 1886 the same entrepreneurs laid steel west from Minneapolis into North Dakota as the Minneapolis & Pacific Railway.

In 1888 the two railroads and a subsidiary company were consolidated as the Minneapolis, St. Paul & Sault Ste. Marie Railway, which became known as the Soo Line from a phonetic spelling of Sault. The Canadian Pacific soon acquired a controlling interest in the company to block expansion toward the west by the Grand Trunk Railway.

During 1891–1893 the Soo built northwest from Hankinson, North Dakota, just west of the Minnesota border, to establish a second connection with Canadian Pacific on the international border at Portal, North Dakota. A period of significant expansion in Wisconsin, Minnesota, and North Dakota followed. Major new routes reached Bismarck, North Dakota, in 1902, a third connection with Canadian Pacific at Noyes, Minnesota, in 1903, and Duluth, Minnesota, in 1909.

In 1913 the railroad completed still another new route, extending westward from Flaxton, just south of Portal, to Whitetail, Montana, that proved to be the Soo Line's westernmost reach. The final expansion of the "old Soo" was its acquisition in 1921 of the Wisconsin & Northern Railroad, a line from Neenah, in the Fox River valley, to Argonne, on the Soo's original line between Minneapolis and Sault Ste. Marie.

Wisconsin Central

The Wisconsin Central Railroad was incorporated in June 1871 to build from Neenah and Menasha, Wisconsin, at the north end of Lake Winnebago, northwest through the forests of northern Wisconsin to Ashland, on the south shore of Lake Superior. The line reached Ashland in 1877, and other WC routes reached Portage, Wisconsin, in 1876, St. Paul, Minnesota, in 1884, and Chicago in 1886. At Chicago the Wisconsin Central teamed up with a predecessor of the Chicago Great Western to build Grand Central Station and operate a short-lived suburban train service; at about that same time the Northern Pacific Railroad briefly leased the WC. The station in time became the property of the Baltimore & Ohio.

WC's growth concluded with construction of a line between Owen and Superior, Wisconsin, in 1908. In 1909 the Minneapolis, St. Paul & Sault Ste. Marie leased the Wisconsin Central, seemingly absorbing it but in actuality maintaining a separate pool of equipment and separate accounts.

Duluth, South Shore & Atlantic

The Duluth, South Shore & Atlantic Railway was assembled in 1887 from several railroads in Michigan's Upper Peninsula. Within a year it came under the financial control of the Canadian Pacific, which was blocking westward expansion of competing railroads. The DSS&A originally reached Superior, Wisconsin, and Duluth, Minnesota, on Northern Pacific rails from Ashland, Wisconsin, but in 1892 extended its own line west to Superior. The DSS&A lost much of its iron-ore business to other railroads in the late 1890s but continued to exist as a carrier of forest products. It was never a strong railroad, and by 1930 it was sharing officers with the Soo Line, also part of the Canadian Pacific family. As early as the 1930s the DSS&A began abandoning the western portion of its line in favor of again operating on Northern Pacific rails. (By the mid-1980s almost nothing remained of the western half of the DSS&A.) In March 1949 the DSS&A emerged from a 12-year bankruptcy and reorganization as the Duluth, South Shore & Atlantic Railroad, this time with its own officers.

Soo Line Railroad

The "old Soo" and its leased and operated Wisconsin Central subsidiary represented the quintessential Granger railroad, hauling cargos of grain and milled flour, iron ore from Minnesota's Gogebic and Cuyuna ranges, and the products of Minnesota, Wisconsin, and Michigan forests. Its passenger trains ran on leisurely schedules. The Soo never entered the streamliner era, and its trains operated to the very end with conventional unstreamlined heavyweight equipment, elderly though well kept. It was never prosperous. Beset by an excess of competition in a region that did not produce much traffic, the Soo had one of the lowest traffic densities among major U.S. railroads, and it struggled against severe winter weather conditions. Depression traffic levels helped send the MStP&SSteM into a 14-year bankruptcy in 1938, and the Wisconsin Central spent a near-record 22 years in receivership, from 1932 to 1954.

In March 1960 MStP&SSteM, WC, and DSS&A made known their intent to combine, an idea that had been floated as far back as the 1930s. Since all three were already subsidiaries of Canadian Pacific and in a sense already partially merged, there were few financial benefits to their combination, which took place on December 30, 1960. The "new Soo" was built upon the corporate structure of the Duluth, South Shore & Atlantic, which then changed its name to Soo Line Railroad.

The Soo Line and the Chicago Great Western considered merger but broke off studies in 1963. In 1982 the Soo acquired the Minneapolis, Northfield & Southern Railway, essentially a terminal line in the Minneapolis area. The Soo was also interested in acquiring the former Rock Island between Northfield, Minnesota, and Kansas City, but lost out to a bid by Chicago & North Western, which had been operating that line for some time.

Recognizing that it would have to grow to remain healthy, the Soo turned its attention to acquiring what remained of the bankrupt Chicago, Milwaukee, St. Paul & Pacific. By early 1985 the Soo (and parent Canadian Pacific) had won control of the Milwaukee and had fully merged it into the Soo Line company by year's end.

The Soo sold most of its lines east of the Twin Cities, including some acquired from the Milwaukee, to the new Wisconsin Central in 1987. Later Canadian Pacific and Soo sold other portions of the former Milwaukee Road to Twin Cities Western and to I&M Rail Link. The only route east of St. Paul that remained on the Soo's map was the former Milwaukee Road main line through La Crosse and Milwaukee to Chicago and Louisville.

For many years Canadian Pacific held a 56 percent interest in the Soo Line. After the Soo acquired the viable sections of the Milwaukee Road, CPR seriously thought about disposing of its stock, but then turned in the opposite direction to acquire full ownership. There still exists a Soo Line Corp., a holding company formed in 1983, but Canadian Pacific has fully absorbed the operations of the Soo Line as its Soo District.

In 1991 Soo Line operated 5,045 route-miles and 7,363 track-miles, with 400 locomotives and 12,965 freight cars. Freight traffic totaled 22.9 billion ton-miles in 1991, and farm products (19.5 percent), chemicals (18.1 percent), coal (9.8 percent), and foodstuffs (8.2 percent) were its principal traffic sources. Soo Line operating revenues totaled $589.2 million in 1991, and the railroad achieved a 95.5 percent operating ratio.

—Jim Scribbins

REFERENCES

Abbey, Wallace W. *The Little Jewel*. Pueblo: Piñon Productions, 1984.

Middleton, William D. "The Soo's Not Sleeping." *Trains* 19, no. 2 (Dec. 1958): 14–26.

Suprey, Leslie V. *Steam Trains of the Soo*. Mora, Minn.: B&W, 1962.

South Carolina Railroad

In the last third of the nineteenth century railroad development in the South would lag behind that in the North, but at the end of 1833 the South Carolina Railroad was the longest railroad anywhere on the planet and the first in North America operated by steam power. By the 1820s Charleston, South Carolina, was no longer the dominant port and trading center of the South. As settlement and cotton production expanded inland to the Piedmont region, the most effective route to the interior became the Savannah River, and the cities of Augusta and Savannah, Georgia, became ports. As a measure to improve Charleston's accessibility to the hinterland and restore its competitive position, an act of the South Carolina state legislature on December 19, 1827, authorized the formation of the South Carolina Canal & Rail-Road Co. The idea of a railroad had been suggested as early as 1821. As the development of railroad technology in England became known, it became evident that a railroad should be built, not a canal.

Financing was difficult. Despite South Carolina's fierce adherence to the principle of state sovereignty, federal aid was sought. The effort was unsuccessful, and the state legislature voted some financial support. In the summer of 1829 Horatio Allen was hired as chief engineer of the project. A civil engineer experienced in canal work, Allen had studied railways in England.

Construction began on January 9, 1830. By the end of the year 6 miles of track had been built. There was considerable experimentation with methods of powering the trains, including sails. A director of the company, Ezra L. Miller, a staunch advocate of steam power, contracted for a locomotive on his own account. Built at the West Point Foundry in New York City, it had a vertical boiler based on Miller's patent. When the locomotive arrived at Charleston on October 23, 1830, it was christened *The Best Friend of Charleston*. Its performance was judged to be eminently satisfactory, and the company purchased it from Miller. After an inauguration on Christmas Day 1830 it began making regular daily trips.

The boiler of the *Best Friend* blew up on June 17, 1831. The explosion was attributed to a fireman who, not understanding the function of the safety valve, tied or held it down to stop the noise of the escaping steam. The running gear of the locomotive was salvaged, and it was rebuilt as the *Phoenix*. A second locomotive, the *West Point*, was ordered after the *Best Friend* had proved itself. It did not perform as well as the *Best Friend*, and Allen did considerable work to improve its boiler.

After the experimental period construction of the remainder of the line proceeded. The road opened to Branchville, 62 miles from Charleston, on November 7, 1832. On October 3, 1833, the entire 136-mile route opened to Hamburg, across the Savannah River from Augusta, Georgia. At the Hamburg end an inclined plane was required for the steep grade down to the river. (At Charleston, the tracks ended at the city limits 2 miles from the docks.)

The railroad's charter allowed it to build a branch to Columbia. That project was given impetus by a proposal to connect Charleston with the Ohio River. The Louisville, Cincinnati & Charleston Railroad was formed, funds were raised, and surveys were made. The project foundered in the early 1840s because of inadequate support outside South Carolina, but the LC&C was able to purchase the South Carolina Railroad in late 1837. The line from Branchville to Columbia opened on June 20, 1842. The two companies merged in 1844 as the South Carolina Railroad Co. The railroad opened a 38-mile branch to Camden from a point on the Columbia branch on November 1, 1848. In the early 1850s the railroad eliminated the inclined plane near Hamburg, bridged the Savannah River to connect with the Georgia Railroad in Augusta, and extended its line to the docks in Charleston.

The railroad was destroyed near the end of the Civil War, when Sherman's forces swept unopposed through South Carolina. The main line to Branchville and the Columbia branch went back into operation in January 1866, and the rest of the main line was restored three months later. The Camden branch returned to operation in May 1867.

The remainder of the century was a period of financial struggle for the company. The panic of 1873 started a steady decline in revenue, culminating in a bankruptcy and reorganization as the South Carolina Railway in 1881. The 1880s produced no turnaround, and another period of receivership starting in 1889 brought an 1894 reorganization as the South Carolina & Georgia Railroad. The Southern Railway leased it in April 1899. The corporate existence of the company ended in 1902.

The Charleston-Branchville-Columbia route remains in service as part of the Norfolk Southern system, as do two short pieces of the Camden branch. Except for a short piece between Aiken and Augusta, the main line has been abandoned west of Branchville.

—Adrian Ettlinger

REFERENCES

Derrick, Samuel Melanchthon. *Centennial History of South Carolina Railroad.* Columbia, S.C.: State Co., 1930.

Gerstner, Franz Anton Ritter von. *Early American Railroads.* Ed. Frederick C. Gamst. Stanford, Calif.: Stanford Univ. Press, 1997 [1842–1843].

White, John H., Jr. *American Locomotives: An Engineering History, 1830–1880.* Baltimore: Johns Hopkins Univ. Press, 1997.

South Shore Line. *See* CHICAGO SOUTH SHORE & SOUTH BEND RAILROAD

Southeastern Pennsylvania Transportation Authority (SEPTA)

The Southeastern Pennsylvania Transportation Authority was formed on February 17, 1964, to bring all the public transportation facilities in Philadelphia and its Pennsylvania suburbs under a single public authority. The city of Philadelphia had begun subsidizing Pennsylvania Railroad (PRR) and Reading Co. commuter rail service within the city limits in 1958 in return for increased service and a flat 30-cent fare. The Passenger Service Improvement Corp. of Philadelphia was created in July 1960 to administer this program, and it also purchased 55 lightweight electric multiple-unit (M.U.) cars and 12 secondhand Budd Rail Diesel Cars for the Reading Co.'s nonelectrified lines. The PSIC also sponsored the electrification of the Reading's line between Newtown Junction and Fox Chase, which opened in September 1966.

To extend subsidized service beyond the city limits, Philadelphia, Bucks, Chester, and Montgomery counties formed the Southeastern Pennsylvania Transportation Compact (SEPACT) in September 1961. Delaware County refused to join. SEPACT conducted three special projects using federal mass-transit funds: service improvements to Levittown on the PRR and to Lansdale and Hatboro on the Reading, a 15-year commuter rail plan, and a crash program in 1965 and 1966 to meet a threatened shutdown of all Reading passenger service.

SEPTA became the managing agent for SEPACT on November 1, 1965, thus bringing Delaware County into the program. Service improvements on the PRR's Paoli, Media/West Chester, and Wilmington lines followed in 1966, and the agency bought 20 new Silverliner III M.U. cars in 1967. SEPTA purchased the Philadelphia Transportation Co.'s subway, trolley, and bus system on September 30, 1968, and the Philadelphia Suburban Transportation Co.'s Red Arrow trolley and bus network on January 29, 1970. With the creation of Amtrak in 1971, SEPTA assumed responsibility for the remaining long-distance Reading trains to Pottsville, Bethlehem, and Newark, New Jersey. SEPTA received 144 Silverliner IV cars in 1974–1976 and extended the Reading's electrification from Hatboro to Warminster in July 1974.

On April 1, 1976, Conrail became the service operator for SEPTA, and the agency became a tenant of Amtrak on its Trenton, Wilmington, and Paoli lines. SEPTA purchased most of its other lines, which had little freight traffic, from Conrail in 1976 and 1979. The former Reading long-distance services beyond the electrified zone were discontinued in the summer of 1981. Conrail exited the commuter business and transferred operations to SEPTA on January 1, 1983. Service on the Wilmington line was cut back to Marcus Hook, Pennsylvania, on January 11, 1983, after the State of Delaware declined to grant a subsidy. Service between Fox Chase and Newtown, Pennsylvania, was discontinued on January 18, 1983, because of deterioration of the Budd cars and the opposition of influential residents.

In 1984 SEPTA completed the Center City Commuter Tunnel to link the former PRR and Reading lines. A new subway-type station at Market East replaced the venerable Reading Terminal, which closed on November 6, 1984. During the 1980s SEPTA was forced to make substantial repairs to badly deteriorated bridges, catenary, and signal systems. To serve the growing western suburbs, service on the Paoli line was extended to Downingtown in March 1985 and to Parkesburg in April 1990, then cut back to Downingtown in 1996 before being extended to a new station at Thorndale in 1999. Rail service was extended to Philadelphia International Airport on April 28, 1985, and a subsidy from Delaware permitted the restoration of service to Wilmington in 1989 and Newark, Delaware, in 1997. Two lightly used lines were abandoned because of poor track conditions, Elywn to West Chester in September 1986 and Cynwyd to Ivy Ridge in October 1986. The purchase of seven five-car push-pull train sets and AEM-7 electric locomotives in 1988 permitted the retirement of the last heavyweight M.U. cars.

More than its counterparts in other old metropolitan areas, SEPTA has been hampered by the relative decline in center-city employment, the increasing importance of suburb-to-suburb commuting, and fringe sprawl at densities too low for transit service. SEPTA's rail and subway routes often lead to places that were the urban center a century ago, but no longer are, and suburbanites can reach the airport, stadiums, museums, and new shopping and entertainment districts just as easily by car except during the traditional rush hours. Reverse commuting of city residents to suburban jobs has grown markedly, but it too is hampered by distance and the need for transfers.

—Christopher T. Baer

REFERENCE

Williams, Gerry. *Trains, Trolleys & Transit: A Guide to Philadelphia Area Rail Transit.* Piscataway, N.J.: Railpace, 1998.

Southern California Regional Rail Authority (Metrolink)

Although the sprawling Southern California conurbation is today the "freeway capital of the world," this vast metropolitan area was originally knit together by the interurban rail services of the great Pacific Electric Railway system. PE survived as a major passenger rail carrier through World War II, but its rail services were rapidly converted to buses as Los Angeles embarked on a major freeway-construction program in the postwar years. The last PE passenger rail line ceased operation in 1961.

Population growth and traffic congestion soon overwhelmed the vaunted freeway system, and exhaust emissions from the region's millions of automobiles became a principal contributor to the worst air quality anywhere in the United States. Even before the last PE rail line shut down, the region had begun to plan for new generations of both urban and commuter rail transit. By the mid-1970s a plan for a Los Angeles–Orange County commuter service had emerged, and a single train of rehabilitated main-line cars operated briefly in the late 1970s. Another attempt came in 1982 when a single daily round trip began operating over Southern Pacific's Coast Line between Los Angeles and Oxnard, in Ventura County, but ended only four months after it began in a funding dispute.

By the late 1980s the region was ready to try again. In 1988 the Los Angeles County Transportation Commission (LACTC) completed planning for an expansive commuter rail system that would operate throughout a five-county area of some 7,000 square miles with a population of 12 million. In 1990 voters in the five counties—Los Angeles, Ventura, San Bernardino, Riverside, and Orange—approved a referendum that expanded a transportation sales tax to help pay for the system. By the end of 1990 LACTC and the five counties had struck a deal with Southern Pacific to buy 175 miles of right of way and other properties in the area. By June 1991 the five counties had plans for an eight-route, 412-mile commuter system and had set up the Southern California Regional Rail Authority (SCRRA) to build the necessary improvements, acquire equipment, and operate the system.

By October 1992 SCRRA was ready to begin service over the first three Metrolink routes, all centered on Los Angeles Union Station. These included a 47-mile Ventura County line to Moorpark, in Ventura County; a 35-mile route over the Antelope Valley line to Santa Clarita; and an initial 32-mile Los Angeles–Pomona segment of a planned 57-mile route to San Bernardino, in Riverside County. The full route to San Bernardino was operating by May 1993, and by June SCRRA was carrying commuters over a fourth, 57-mile route that operated over the Union Pacific main line to Riverside. Service expanded again after the January 1994 Northridge earthquake. As an alternative to the badly damaged freeway system, SCRRA quickly extended its Ventura County route to Oxnard and the Antelope Valley service to Palmdale and Lancaster.

The rest of the planned system was dependent upon the acquisition of property from the Atchison, Topeka & Santa Fe Railway. By mid-1992 the five counties had reached an agreement that gave them 340 miles of Santa Fe right of way or trackage rights. Early in 1994 Metrolink trains began operating an 87-mile Orange County line to Oceanside, in San Diego County. A sixth route, the Inland Empire/Orange County line, opened between San Bernardino and Oceanside via Orange and Santa Ana in 1995, the only Metrolink route not serving Los Angeles Union Station. SCRRA's seventh route, a Los Angeles–Riverside service via Fullerton over Burlington Northern Santa Fe, opened in 2002.

Ongoing improvements to the busy Metrolink system include double- and triple-tracking of much of the network. A planned run-through project at Union Station will provide more direct access for trains operating over the Burlington Northern Santa Fe main line east of Los Angeles. Planned system expansion includes extensions to Santa Paula on the Ventura County line, from San Bernardino to Redlands in San Bernardino County, and from Riverside to Perris and Hemet in Riverside County.

SCRRA's equipment and operating practices are typical of North America's new generation of regional or commuter railroads. Trains of Bombardier bilevel cars and Electro-Motive F59PH diesels, both originally developed for GO Transit service at Toronto, are operated in push-pull service. Like all recent North American commuter services, Metrolink uses a barrier-free, proof-of-payment fare-collection system. Reflecting the population density and automobile orientation of Southern California, the system's stations are typically provided with extensive park-and-ride spaces.

One of the most successful new regional rail systems in North America, Metrolink saw its average daily passenger count grow steadily from a weekday average of 3,000 passengers on its three initial routes to 26,000 daily passengers only five years later. By 2005 the system was operating a fleet of 39 locomotives and 155 bilevel cars over a 512 route-mile system of six routes serving 54 stations, and its 144 daily trains were carrying a weekday average of 41,300 passengers.

—**William D. Middleton**

REFERENCE

Middleton, William D. "California Gets It Together." 1993 Regional Passenger Railroad Planner's Guide. *Railway Age* 193, no. 11 (Nov. 1992): 37–49, 52–56.

Southern Pacific Railroad

"We have bought not only a railroad," Edward H. Harriman exulted in 1901, "but an empire." He was referring to Southern Pacific, "the greatest transportation system in the world," as one of his biographers labeled it. SP's impressive crescent-shaped system stretched from Portland, Oregon, through San Francisco, Los Angeles, Tucson, San Antonio, and Houston to New Orleans (before 1951 it also reached down the west coast of Mexico to Guadalajara). SP also owned the western portion of the first transcontinental railroad from Ogden, Utah, to Oakland, California, plus important secondary lines and branches.

Harriman, of course, was acting to protect his investment in Union Pacific, SP's historic partner on the Overland Route. Unlike UP, which was forced to rely heavily on overhead or bridge traffic, SP boasted a desirable and diversified traffic mix of locally billed business, long average hauls, and high average earnings. "Lacking Southern Pacific," said transportation observer Frank H. Spearman,

"Union Pacific never had been and never could be a great railway."

Harriman's opportunity came after Collis P. Huntington died suddenly on August 13, 1900. Huntington was one of the Big Four (along with Charles Crocker, Mark Hopkins, and Leland Stanford), the men who put together and controlled Central Pacific, the SP predecessor with which UP teamed on the fabled first transcontinental railroad. (There is another Big Four in U.S. railroad history: the Cleveland, Cincinnati, Chicago & St. Louis Railway, part of the New York Central System, nicknamed the Big Four. There should be no confusion as to which Big Four is under discussion.)

Central Pacific derived, in part, from the pioneer Sacramento Valley Railroad. In 1852 the sponsors of this road hired Theodore D. Judah to locate and build a line from Sacramento to Folsom and on to Placerville. The Big Four, not railroaders but businessmen, were recruited four years later when transcontinental aspirations took root in California. These hopes were rewarded after expensive lobbying by many persons, including Judah and the Big Four, when President Abraham Lincoln signed the Pacific Railroad Act in 1862. This legislation authorized Central Pacific (formed by Judah, Crocker, Huntington, Hopkins, and Stanford) to build east from California to meet Union Pacific building west from Iowa.

Progress was slow on the CP-UP project because of the Civil War, among other problems. Theodore Judah became estranged from the other partners over financial matters in 1863 and died later that year; the Big Four thereafter were in complete control. Labor was scarce, construction materials were expensive, and engineering challenges were monumental, but CP finally reached the Nevada border in 1867, still two years and several hundred miles from a junction with UP.

"Done." That astonishingly brief message winged over telegraph wires from windswept Promontory, Utah Territory, on May 10, 1869. Rails finally linked CP with UP to bind East and West with the first cross-country rail line.

Meanwhile, rails began to extend throughout northern California. In 1864 the San Francisco & San Jose Railroad began operation between its namesake cities. In 1865 the owners of the SF&SJ incorporated the Southern Pacific Railroad to build south and east to New Orleans. By 1870 the Southern Pacific and the San Francisco & San Jose were owned by the Big Four. Southern Pacific's first plan was to build southeast from San Jose through the San Andreas Rift Zone, then turn east to cross the mountains and reach California's central valley northwest of Bakersfield. However, the mountains were devoid of any population that might support a railroad, so SP halted construction at Tres Pinos and began building southeast from Lathrop, near Stockton in the San Joaquin Valley. The line was built in the name of the Central Pacific as far as Goshen Junction, where it met the original Southern Pacific survey.

The Central Pacific terminated at Sacramento. To reach San Francisco Bay, the Western Pacific Railroad was built by CP interests from Sacramento south to Stockton, west to the bay, and north to Oakland. In 1876 CP acquired the California Pacific Railroad, which ran from Sacramento southwest to Vallejo. In 1879 Central Pacific opened a line from Port Costa, across the Carquinez Strait from Vallejo, along the shore to Oakland, and soon afterward train ferries entered service between Port Costa and Benicia, just east of Vallejo, creating a shorter route than the Western Pacific (the Western Pacific of the twentieth century, the Western Pacific of George Gould and the Feather River Canyon and the *California Zephyr*, followed much the same route but was a different undertaking entirely).

Time did not permit the Big Four to rest on their laurels. "Done" did not apply to their labors. Indeed, they and the company they headed were deeply in debt; the future frankly looked bleak. Completion of the Suez Canal in the same year drained traffic that the Californians had counted on from Asia, and on-line business in Nevada declined as the silver-mining boom passed into a lengthy recession. Moreover, their home state of California was largely underpopulated and destitute of capital. But the Big Four had little option but to plunge ahead; they were in too deep to get out.

Expansion—piling up more debt but adding appreciable reach—became their watchword. Certainly that was the case for Collis Huntington, who seemed more daring than the others. By 1880 the Big Four owned or controlled lines pointed northward to Oregon, southward along the California coast, and southward through the San Joaquin Valley to Los Angeles. That was for starters. A major new route was pushed eastward from Los Angeles to Yuma by the summer of 1881 and then on to the Rio Grande at El Paso. At Deming, New Mexico, it met the Atchison, Topeka & Santa Fe, forming a second transcontinental route. Additional expansion followed in Texas and Louisiana as in California and Oregon. To all of this was added ferry service on San Francisco Bay and significant waterborne activity elsewhere. Some of these projects and operations were under Central Pacific's flag, but more of them were carried out by much the larger Southern Pacific, of which CP was an integral element. Corporate simplification was deemed necessary in 1884. A new Southern Pacific Co. was formed. The Central Pacific Railroad was reorganized as the Central Pacific Railway and leased its properties to the Southern Pacific.

Southern Pacific was a colossus. Indeed, the Big Four and SP transformed California and a huge block of the West, and they did so in an amazingly brief span of time. Their enterprise opened up astonishing opportunities for the public at large and provided employment for thousands. And, incidentally, each one of the Big Four became wealthy in the process.

Its impressive stature notwithstanding, SP at the turn of the twentieth century needed a constant and growing source of cash to fully develop its franchise. That cash would not come from the Big Four. Hopkins had died in 1878; he was followed in death by Crocker in 1888 and

Stanford in 1893. In 1900, Huntington, the most talented railroader of the bunch, joined them. Stock control of SP passed to Edward H. Harriman shortly thereafter.

Harriman was not one to milk a railroad but instead sought to improve it, knowing that this would ultimately increase earnings. Among the improvements that he instituted were a second track over the Sierra, the Bayshore Cutoff south of San Francisco, avoiding the steep grades of the original SF&SJ route, the Lucin Cutoff across the Great Salt Lake, which reduced the distance between Ogden and Oakland by 44 miles, and automatic block signaling on the main lines.

Harriman did not merge Union Pacific with Southern Pacific, but operated the two in concert as a system. However meritorious from a business point of view, the Harriman system of roads ran afoul of increasingly hostile public sentiment regarding giant enterprise (and Frank Norris's novel *The Octopus* aggravated matters). Legal action by the federal government succeeded in forcing Union Pacific to sell its Southern Pacific stock and required SP to justify its retention of Central Pacific. The federal government's legal harassment of SP did not end until the 1920s and diverted talent and treasure that might otherwise have been advantageously employed by Southern Pacific for new lines and betterment projects. The corporate existence of Central Pacific ended in 1959.

Despite these travails, SP managed to expand by its own construction and by acquisition. In 1926 it opened

Herald and reporting marks of a Southern Pacific wood-framed boxcar were photographed on the railroad at San Bernardino, California, in March 1943. —Jack Delano photograph, Office of War Information, Library of Congress (Neg. LC-USW3-21567-E)

the Natron Cutoff between Eugene and Klamath Falls, Oregon. The line was intended to head off a Great Northern extension, but it became the principal route in Oregon because it had easier grades and curves than the original route through Grants Pass. At the same time SP built a line southeast from Klamath Falls to the Oakland-Ogden route. The Modoc Line served as a shortcut for lumber moving east from Oregon. Both the Natron Cutoff and the Modoc Line were actually Central Pacific properties. SP acquired the El Paso & Southwestern in 1924, essentially double-tracking its route between Tucson, Arizona, and El Paso, and gained control of the St. Louis Southwestern (the Cotton Belt) in 1932.

The earliest parts of the SP system there both dated from 1850: the Buffalo Bayou, Brazos & Colorado Railroad (reorganized in 1870 as the Galveston, Harrisburg & San Antonio Railway) and the New Orleans, Opelousas & Great Western Railroad (which later became Morgan's Louisiana & Texas Railroad). Among the other SP subsidiaries were the Louisiana Western Railroad, the Texas & New Orleans Railroad (into which all the subsidiaries were consolidated in 1934), the Houston & Texas Central Railroad, the Houston, East & West Texas Railway, and the Houston & Shreveport Railroad.

In the 1960s the SP put forth an attitude that was arguably antipassenger. Some said that SP was simply being honest; others said that SP had forgotten about carrying passengers. SP's first streamlined train was the *City of San Francisco*, operated jointly with Union Pacific and Chicago & North Western on the Chicago-Oakland route. It entered service in June 1936. In March 1937 SP inaugurated the *Daylight* on a daytime schedule between San Francisco and Los Angeles. From the early years of the twenty-first century it is hard to imagine the splash the red and orange train made in a world accustomed to dark olive green passenger trains. The *Daylight* was soon joined by the *Noon Daylight*, operating on a noon-to-midevening schedule, and the streamlined *San Joaquin*, running from Los Angeles to Oakland and Sacramento via the San Joaquin Valley. In 1941 the overnight *Lark* between San Francisco and Los Angeles received new streamlined equipment. In 1949 the *Shasta Daylight* began Oakland-Portland service on a new daytime schedule, and in 1950 the overnight Oakland-Portland *Cascade* and the New Orleans–Los Angeles *Sunset Limited* received streamlined equipment. All the new trains had innovative equipment, such as triple-unit articulated dining and lounge cars, and interior decor that reflected the area the trains passed through.

By 1960 jet airliners had taken away SP's first-class passengers, automobiles the coach passengers. SP began discontinuing trains, and by the end of the 1960s each of SP's main routes was served by a single train, most of which passed into Amtrak's hands.

World War II was Southern Pacific's finest hour. Good times continued in the 1950s and 1960s under the effective leadership of Donald J. Russell. Indeed, some observers considered SP the "new standard railroad of the world."

But difficult times followed when critical elements of SP's customer base—fresh fruits and vegetables, lumber, automobile parts—declined or went to other carriers during the 1970s and 1980s. SP's changed fortunes corresponded, ironically, with public policy that finally acknowledged the end of the age of railways and admitted that railroads no longer held dominance in transport. Not surprisingly, then, Harriman's dream of melding Southern Pacific fully with Union Pacific became a reality in 1996.

In 1994, two years before it was purchased by Union Pacific, Southern Pacific operated 13,715 route-miles and 15,167 track-miles, with 2,407 locomotives and 45,050 freight and company service cars. Freight traffic totaled 132.9 billion ton-miles in 1994, and intermodal (32.0 percent), chemicals (15.1 percent), and coal (13.3 percent) were its principal traffic sources. SP operating revenues totaled $3 billion in 1994.

—Don L. Hofsommer

REFERENCES

Hofsommer, Don L. *The Southern Pacific, 1901–1985*. College Station: Texas A&M Univ. Press, 1986.

Orsi, Richard J. *Sunset Limited: The Southern Pacific Railroad and the Development of the American West*. Berkeley, Calif.: Univ. of California Press, 2005.

Southern Railway System

Like many large railroad systems, the Southern Railway System grew by acquiring other railroads. Its components continued to exist with their old names and corporate structures much longer than the subsidiaries of most other railroads. The Southern could trace its history back to the South Carolina Canal & Rail Road Co., chartered in 1828 and by 1857 part of the longest connected system of railroads in the world, reaching from Charleston, South Carolina, to Memphis, Tennessee.

Richmond & Danville and Richmond Terminal

The nucleus of the Southern Railway, however, was the Richmond & Danville Railroad, which opened in 1856 between Richmond and Danville, Virginia, 141 miles. The Richmond & Danville's charter permitted it to control and acquire railroads with which it connected directly. R&D interests established the Richmond & West Point Terminal Railway & Warehouse Co. (the Richmond Terminal) in 1880 to acquire railroads that did not connect with the R&D. Later, in a series of transactions that crowded the dictionary definition of "shenanigan," the R&D's charter was amended, the R&D leased the sub-

sidiary railroads directly, and the Richmond Terminal acquired the Richmond & Danville. In the following paragraphs, "R&D" means either Richmond & Danville or Richmond Terminal, whichever was in charge at the time.

In 1863 the R&D purchased control of the Piedmont Railroad, which was under construction between Danville and Greensboro, North Carolina. In 1871 the R&D extended its reach by leasing the North Carolina Railroad, which had a line from Goldsboro, North Carolina, through Raleigh and Greensboro to Charlotte. The R&D assisted with the construction of the Atlanta & Richmond Air-Line Railroad from Charlotte to Atlanta. In 1881 the R&D leased its successor, the Atlanta & Richmond Air-Line Railway.

At its north end, in 1881 the R&D purchased the Virginia Midland Railway to obtain a route to Washington that was shorter than the dogleg through Richmond. It was built between 1854 and 1874 and had been part of the Baltimore & Ohio and later the property of the State of Virginia. It briefly had one of the most resounding names in the history of railroading: the Washington City, Virginia Midland & Great Southern Railroad.

Five years later, in 1886, the R&D extended itself west from Salisbury, North Carolina, to the Tennessee state line and a connection with the East Tennessee, Virginia & Georgia by leasing the Western North Carolina Railroad. The R&D reached west from Atlanta by leasing the Georgia Pacific Railway in 1889. The Georgia Pacific was intended to connect Atlanta with the Texas & Pacific Railway at Texarkana. It got as far as the Mississippi River at Greenville, Mississippi. The State of Mississippi required that the portion of the line from Columbus, Mississippi, to Greenville remain a separate entity (it received independence as the Columbus & Greenville in 1920).

The East Tennessee, Virginia & Georgia Railroad (ETV&G) was formed in 1869 by the consolidation of two railroads out of Knoxville, Tennessee. The company's main line ran from Bristol, Virginia, through Knoxville to Dalton, Georgia, and Chattanooga, Tennessee. Within a few years lines were built from Dalton southeast through Atlanta to Brunswick, Georgia, and from Dalton southwest to Meridian, Mississippi. The company forged alliances with several other routes—Chattanooga to Memphis, Selma, Alabama, to Mobile, and Lexington, Kentucky, to Louisville—and it came under the control of the Richmond Terminal. By 1890, then, the Richmond Terminal/Richmond & Danville's influence reached from Washington and Richmond southwest through Charlotte, Atlanta, and Birmingham to the Mississippi River at Memphis, Tennessee, and Greenville, Mississippi, to the Gulf Coast at Mobile, and to the Atlantic Coast at Brunswick, Georgia.

Reorganization of the Richmond Terminal

Then hard times struck. The Richmond Terminal and the roads it controlled declared insolvency and entered receivership in 1892. The J. P. Morgan Co., a New York banking and finance company, stepped in and combined and reorganized the Richmond & Danville and the East Tennessee, Virginia & Georgia into the Southern Railway.

The new railroad began operation on July 1, 1894, under the leadership of Samuel Spencer, a close associate of Morgan's. It continued to grow by acquisition, as its predecessors had. Among its early acquisitions were the Georgia, Southern & Florida Railway, which reached from Macon, Georgia, south to Jacksonville and Palatka, Florida, and the Louisville, Evansville & St. Louis Consolidated Railroad, which extended the Lexington-Louisville line west to St. Louis.

Queen & Crescent Route

Running from Cincinnati (the Queen City) to New Orleans (the Crescent City) were five railroads that advertised themselves as the Queen & Crescent Route: the Cincinnati, New Orleans & Texas Pacific (which leased and operated the Cincinnati Southern Railway, which was owned by the City of Cincinnati), the Alabama Great Southern, the New Orleans & Northeastern, the Alabama & Vicksburg, and the Vicksburg, Shreveport & Pacific. These railroads were owned by two British-owned holding companies, control of one of which was acquired by the R&D and the ETV&G in 1890. Ownership and control of these companies was particularly convoluted. The two Vicksburg companies became part of the Illinois Central system in 1927. The other three were firmly in the Southern Railway family by the end of the nineteenth century, and the corporate existence of the Alabama Great Southern and Cincinnati, New Orleans & Texas Pacific continued through most of the twentieth century.

Georgia Southern & Florida

The Georgia Southern & Florida Railway was incorporated in 1895 under Southern Railway control as a reorganization of the Georgia Southern & Florida Railroad, which had been opened in 1890 from Macon, Georgia, through Valdosta, Georgia, to Palatka, Florida. It was intended to be part of a route from Birmingham, Alabama, to Florida that would bypass Atlanta. In 1902 it purchased the Atlantic, Valdosta & Western Railway line from Valdosta, Georgia, to a point near Jacksonville, Florida. Southern acquired control in 1895.

Other Subsidiaries

The Mobile & Ohio was part of the Southern Railway System from 1901 to 1938. It was never especially prosperous, but Southern went so far as to propose merger (it wanted M&O's Gulf-to–St. Louis route). The merger was vetoed by the governor of Mississippi. During the Depression the Southern had sufficient financial difficulty of its own that it was unable to aid the M&O. The expanding Gulf, Mobile & Northern acquired the M&O to form the Gulf, Mobile & Ohio Railroad.

The Southern and the Louisville & Nashville jointly acquired control of the Chicago, Indianapolis & Louisville in 1902 as a route to Chicago. However, Southern and L&N both had faster connections to Chicago on other railroads and were of no help to the CI&L during its hard times in the 1930s and 1940s. Both large roads lost their financial interests in the CI&L's 1946 reorganization.

Despite its coverage of the state of Georgia, the Central of Georgia Railway was for much of its existence part of the Illinois Central system. From 1956 to 1961 it was under the control of the St. Louis–San Francisco, with which it connected at Birmingham. The Interstate Commerce Commission rejected SLSF's proposal to merge with the CofG and approved control by the Southern. That took effect in 1963. A few months later in the same year a 56-mile portion of the Tennessee Railroad was incorporated into the Southern system.

Passenger Service

In 1925 the Southern joined with several other railroads to launch the all-Pullman *Crescent Limited*, a train that became the pride of the system. The train traveled from New York City to New Orleans on a schedule of 37 hours and 50 minutes. North of Washington it was operated by the Pennsylvania Railroad; the West Point Route and the Louisville & Nashville operated it between Atlanta and New Orleans. It was reequipped in 1929 with cars painted two-tone green to echo the green-painted specifically assigned locomotives that pulled the train. The Southern entered the streamliner era in 1941 with two diesel-powered streamliners, the *Southerner* between New York and New Orleans and the *Tennessean* between Washington and Memphis.

In the 1970s the Southern was notable for staying out of Amtrak, continuing to run its remaining few passenger trains and gradually trimming its service to just the Washington-Atlanta–New Orleans *Southern Crescent*. Often the train's primary purpose seemed to be moving company employees between the Southern's offices in Atlanta and Washington. Amtrak took over the operation of the *Southern Crescent* on February 1, 1979.

Presidents of the Southern

For 12 years the Southern Railway System was guided by Samuel Spencer, a close associate of J. P. Morgan. In 1906 Spencer was killed in a collision when the car he was riding was struck in the rear by another train. The Southern entered a period of slow growth over the next decade and a half. Some of the leased railroads were returned to independent operation. In 1915 the Southern began using an advertising slogan that it would use for decades. Vice President L. E. Jeffries drew a circle, tracing around a half dollar. Inside it he drew a second circle, using a quarter. Inside the smaller circle, he placed a simple "SR," and in the space between the two circles, he wrote "The Southern Serves the South."

Just before World War I Southern president Fairfax Harrison established a foreign freight traffic department. Agents were assigned to Mobile and New Orleans in hopes of capitalizing on Southern's strategic location on the Gulf, yet with quick access to Atlantic ports as well. The war postponed the implementation of the foreign freight department, but involved the Southern Railway System in a much broader future development.

In 1937 Ernest Norris took over as CEO from Fairfax Harrison and began a 14-year "turnaround" term; he was the first non-Southerner to hold the position. During Norris's tenure the Southern weathered the Depression, ushered in the diesel era for passenger service, and persevered through World War II. *Forbes* magazine reported the achievements of Norris when it stated, "Ernest Norris, energetic, capable and articulate, president of the Southern Railway System, has made both himself and his road a potent factor in the upbuilding of the South."

In the 1960s, under the guidance of mercurial D. W. Brosnan, the Southern entered into a period of unprecedented growth. Brosnan's research team developed a large covered hopper car for grain and numerous other specialized freight cars. Brosnan increased yard capacities and built new yards in Birmingham and New Orleans. He traveled extensively around the Southern system in a pair of business cars. As ideas came to his mind, he would sketch them on a cocktail napkin, often stopping at the next yard or station to telephone the idea to the mechanical department.

Brosnan could get his designers to focus on solutions rather than excuses. In researching the problem of returning coal-service cars to revenue service more quickly, Brosnan isolated his research team at a resort until they came up with a solution: the world's first unit trains in which aluminum hoppers were dedicated to year-round delivery of one product, coal. An order was placed for 200 of the new cars, and the railroad soon discovered that they did the work of 740 smaller hopper cars.

Southern's best-known and best-loved president was W. Graham Claytor, Jr., who in 1967 succeeded D. W. Brosnan. Claytor was an unabashed railroad enthusiast and a collector of antique toy trains. Under his direction the Southern developed a steam locomotive program that included nine locomotives pulling excursion trains almost every weekend during nine months of the year. The steam program proved to be enormously successful public relations and had the effect of acquainting the public with the railroad and showing how modern railroading had evolved.

Claytor retired from the Southern in 1977 at the mandatory retirement age of 65 and served the federal government as secretary of the navy, acting secretary of transportation, and deputy secretary of defense. In 1982 Claytor returned to railroading as president and chairman of the board of Amtrak.

Innovation

The Southern built a reputation for innovation. In an attempt to lure grain traffic back to the rails from barges, Southern's research team developed a 5,000-cubic-foot covered hopper car (grain had traditionally moved in boxcars, which were difficult to unload). The Big John cars shocked the transportation industry, largely because the Southern proposed cutting rates by 60 percent—the new rates would save farmers and consumers approximately $40 million a year. Howls arose from barge companies and from the Tennessee Valley Authority, which felt that it would lose barge business to the railroads. The Interstate Commerce Commission intervened. Southern's president D. W. Brosnan was the first witness in a hearing that lasted 30 weeks and produced 16,000 pages of testimony and 765 exhibits. The Southern prevailed, and the new rates went into effect. The victory gave the Southern the confidence it needed to handle the ICC in the future, and the perceived invincibility of regulators was forever gone.

The Southern was the first railroad to employ a computer system to relay information from the field to a central processing computer, and in June 1965 the railroad was the first railroad entity to conduct any phase of its operations with computers. The railroad installed a microwave communication system between Atlanta and Washington. Within a decade the system had been expanded to 4,500 path-miles, giving the Southern the most extensive private communication system in the world at the time.

The Southern was also noted for quickly implementing innovations that other railroads had originated but were slow to implement. The Southern waited until other railroads had perfected the product, and it benefited because it did not have to outlay the research and design costs. The railroad pioneered the use of crosstie-removal and replacing equipment. It installed hotbox detectors along its routes and replaced most of its jointed rail with rail welded into quarter-mile lengths.

Merger

To combat the near encirclement of the Southern by the newly formed CSX system, the Southern entered into merger negotiations with the Norfolk & Western Railway. On June 1, 1982, the Norfolk Southern Corp., a new holding company, acquired the Southern and the Norfolk & Western railways. At the end of 1990 the N&W became a subsidiary of the Southern Railway, and the Southern changed its name to Norfolk Southern Railway.

In 1988, shortly before the creation of the new Norfolk Southern Railway, the Southern Railway operated 9,757 route-miles, with 1,416 locomotives, 58,929 freight cars, 2,678 company service cars, and 16,496 employees. Freight traffic totaled 50,627 million ton-miles in 1988, and paper (19.9 percent), chemicals (17.6 percent), and coal (17.3

percent) were its principal traffic sources. Southern operating revenues totaled $1,756.6 million in 1988, and the railroad achieved a 75.7 percent operating ratio.

—Cary Franklin Poole and George H. Drury

REFERENCES

Davis, Burke. *The Southern Railway: Road of the Innovators.* Chapel Hill: Univ. of North Carolina Press, 1985.

Prince, Richard E. *Southern Railway System: Steam Locomotives and Boats.* Salt Lake City: K/P Graphics, 1970.

Special Trains

From their earliest beginnings, trains, both passenger and freight, were called upon to provide a wide range of special-purpose trips. A list of special trains is almost endless in the diversity and imagination of the railroads and their clients.

Sightseeing

One of the most enduring special movements was for recreation and sightseeing excursions. Undoubtedly the earliest of these was the one that opened the first common carrier railroad itself. The pioneer Baltimore & Ohio began operating inaugural trains, still horse powered, over a short section of its line at Baltimore, Maryland, on January 7, 1830, and curious excursionists paid 9 cents for a one-way ticket. Before automobile ownership became common, special excursion trains to view wildflowers in the spring and summer or fall foliage in the fall or just to enjoy the countryside were popular.

Occasionally, excursion service was a railroad's main purpose. Two examples are the mountain sightseeing services still operating to Mt. Washington in New Hampshire and to Pikes Peak in Colorado. The Mt. Washington Cog Railway, which still uses nineteenth-century steam locomotives, has been in operation since 1869, while the Manitou & Pike's Peak Railway has been running since 1891.

Speed Runs

There is a recurring theme of special trains operated to exploit high-speed services. The coast-to-coast journey of the Jarrett & Palmer Special of 1876, less than a decade after completion of the transcontinental railway, ostensibly came about to get actors Lawrence Barrett and C. B. Bishop to San Francisco in time for a June 5 performance of Shakespeare's *Henry V* after a May 31 evening performance in New York. More to the point, however, was the accompanying publicity bonanza. The three-car train specially outfitted for the occasion included a sleeping car, a dining and smoking car, and a baggage car, with extra water and fuel for the locomotive. It operated over the Pennsylvania, Chicago & North Western, Union Pacific, and Central Pacific. Tickets for premium-priced travelers on the train were sold, the *New York Herald* ran special editions, and large crowds waited for the train to pass. The train departed shortly after midnight June 1 and rolled into San Francisco just three and a half days later, in half the time required for the railroad's fastest regularly scheduled trains. It covered 3,313.5 miles in only 84 hours and 17 minutes; its overall average speed was just under 40 mph, with a maximum of 72 mph. The coast-to-coast record stood for 30 years, until E. H. Harriman made the trip in 1906 in 71 hours and 27 minutes.

In July 1905, having made his fortune in gold mining, Walter Scott (better known as Death Valley Scotty) teamed up with the Santa Fe's general passenger agent, who agreed to a price of $5,500 for a special train from Los Angeles to Chicago. The Santa Fe promised Scotty a 46-hour run, almost 12 hours faster than the previous record. With Scotty, his wife, and two publicists on board, the three-car train raced off from Los Angeles' La Grande Station at 1 P.M. on July 9. One engine after another powered the train at each division point, each one bringing the train over its scheduled segment ahead of schedule. In the division to Barstow, California, the train hit a record speed of 96 mph. East of La Junta, Colorado, the train ran over the high plains at an average speed of better than 70 mph. At Dodge City, Kansas, Scotty fired off a telegram to President Theodore Roosevelt: "An American cowboy is coming east on a special train faster than any cowpuncher ever road before. How much shall I break transcontinental record?" The president did not reply.

On its last day of the trip, just east of Galesburg, Illinois, the train marked up three miles of running at 106 mph. It rolled to a stop at Chicago's Dearborn Station at 11:54 A.M., completing the 2,265-mile run in just 44 hours 54 minutes. It would be another 30 years before a train would beat that.

Sometimes urgent news or valuable cargo called for high-speed special runs. In July 1912 the circulation manager for the New York *American* came up with the idea of running a special train from New York to the Democratic National Convention at Baltimore to provide the earliest news from the New York papers of the nomination of the party presidential candidate at Baltimore. The Jersey Central, Reading, and Baltimore & Ohio trains agreed to make the run. As soon as the first 500 copies were run off with the news of Woodrow Wilson's nomination, the train was off at 3:11 A.M., reaching Baltimore at 6:20 A.M., running faster then the crack *Royal Blue* and beating the *American*'s rival New York newspapers by hours.

After the completion of Charles A. Lindbergh's flight to Paris, Washington, D.C., prepared for his triumphal return on June 11, 1927. Eager to get their films of the celebration to New York theaters, most newsreel companies planned to fly them to New York, but the International News Reel Co. figured out a better way—by train. The train would take a little longer, but was fully equipped to process the films, while the other companies would have to wait for processing in New York. The Pennsylvania Railroad furnished a fast steam locomotive and a photo laboratory in the baggage car. The film was ready at 1:14 P.M., and the train set out on what would be a record high-speed run. Traveling at speeds as high as 110 mph, it completed the trip to New York in just 3 hours 7 minutes. Ten completed newsreels were raced to New York movie houses under police escort, and within 15 minutes Broadway theatergoers were watching Lindbergh's triumphant arrival at Washington. It was more than an hour before the rival companies were ready.

Quite different were the fabled silk trains run to Chicago and New York from Far East markets through the West Coast ports. Shipments of silk, both in finished goods and in the form of cocoons of live Asiatic silkworms, fed on mulberry leaves, began to be shipped by ships and trains in the nineteenth century, and by the early twentieth century the trains were special, all-silk high-speed trains. The material was extremely expensive—one shipment of three trains from the West Coast was valued at a million dollars—and the problems of spoilage to the fragile cargo, price fluctuations, and insurance costs made it desirable to get the trains over the road as rapidly as possible. Speed was equally important to the Pacific Ocean liners. On one shipment, for example, the Canadian Pacific's *Empress of Canada* and its railroad connections at Vancouver made the run in only 13 days from Japan to New York. Silk trains typically had preference over everything else and generally ran even faster than the fastest passenger trains. In January 1929, for example, an Overland Route train, carrying almost $1.5 million worth of silk, ran from San Francisco to Chicago—operating over Southern Pacific, Union Pacific, and the Chicago & North Western—in a record 49 hours. The traffic reached its peak in the 1920s, before all-ship travel through the Panama Canal and then the switch to synthetic nylon and rayon.

Special-Purpose Trains

Extra trains were operated for groups of almost every description—business and veterans' organizations, lodges, religious and political groups, and the like—to meetings or special events. Railroad officers and directors were particularly fond of travel over their railroad. The trip west to celebrate the completion of the Union Pacific to the 100th meridian in midprairie Nebraska in October 1864 for UP vice president Thomas C. Durant may well have been a celebration without equal. The UP's arrival there, before any others, gave the company the right, under the Pacific Railroad Act, to continue to build the railroad to meet with the Central Pacific. Durant made the most of it. Invitations to some 300 were issued, including President John-

son and his entire cabinet, all members of the House and Senate, senior military officers, foreign dignitaries in Washington, directors and commissioners of the Union Pacific, board members, stockbrokers, and the like. About 200 accepted, to be carried by train, coach, or steamboat to Omaha. After a governor's ball, the party climbed aboard the special train. There were two locomotives and nine cars, which included a baggage and supply car, a mail car with a refreshment saloon, a cooking stove, four passenger cars, Durant's private car, and the UP's magnificent directors' car.

The first day's running ended at Columbus, Nebraska, where the passengers could spend the night either on the train or in the brilliantly illuminated encampment. Dinner was followed by entertainment—a war dance by a large number of hired Pawnees. The Pawnees returned again to wake the visitors. The next night the train stopped at Fort McPherson to celebrate reaching the 100th meridian. The following morning Jack and Dan Casement and their men laid 800 feet of track, and that evening there was dinner, followed by a fireworks show, musical entertainment, and a phrenologist's show. Next day a monument was erected on the 100th meridian, and the party began the return trip, which featured a large prairie-dog colony at Kearney and an enormous after-dark prairie fire set on the Platte Valley. It was, according to the Union Pacific's Silas Seymour, "the most important and successful celebration of the kind, that has ever been attempted in the world."

A more recent example, in October 1968, was put on by private banker Brown Brothers Harriman & Co., which was celebrating its sesquicentennial by means of an outing with the Union Pacific for the presidents of 44 U.S. corporations and 55 overseas banks and their wives. Operated from Seattle, Washington, to Sun Valley, Idaho, the assembly included a luggage pilot train and two long, immaculately polished trains of lounges, diners, sleepers, and office cars. In a final touch of corporate zeal on the eve of the sesquicentennial, painters had traveled the route, painting everything along the way, from signals, gates, and depots to shanties.

The Shriners have run some big trains. One of the largest events was the 76th annual convention at Los Angeles, California, in June 1950, which handled some 200,000 visitors. A sizable share of the delegates and such assorted paraphernalia as horses and mules, drums, miniature locomotives, trick cars, and the like traveled by trains. In addition to passengers on regular trains, the three railroads—Southern Pacific, Union Pacific, and Santa Fe—handled a total of 80 inbound special trains that brought in visitors from all over the United States and Canada. Many were housed in a "Fez City" and then headed out again by special trains at the end of the convention.

See also CHAPEL CARS; CIRCUSES AND RAILROADS; PRESIDENTIAL CAMPAIGNS AND TRAVEL.

To the Game by Train

Special trains to major athletic events have long been popular. Annual bowl games often bring large crowds for the New Year's Day contests. In 1922, for example, the New Haven carried nearly 57,000 people on 22 special trains to New York for the annual Yale-Harvard game. One of the most notable special-train events was the annual Army-Navy football contest, which has long been held at Philadelphia's Municipal Stadium, conveniently located between West Point and Annapolis. The Philadelphia location also has the advantage of a neighboring freight yard that can be used once a year for arriving and departing special football trains. For the 1951 game at Philadelphia, trains transported some 40,000 passengers to the stadium. The Pennsylvania used 39 locomotives and 377 cars for the occasion, divided between 17 specials from New York and another 12 from Baltimore and Washington. The first special departed just 6 minutes after the end of the game, and the entire fleet was under way in only 1 hour 11 minutes. The Baltimore & Ohio handled another 9 special trains to and from destinations at Baltimore and Washington.

As far back as the mid-1850s special trains for both horses and spectators were popular on race days. Special cars for the racehorses were operated on both regular trains and special trains, and race-day trains ran to a number of racetracks. In 1946 the Pennsylvania ran special trains from Washington, Philadelphia, and Baltimore to Bowie Race Track in Maryland, with a typical race-day train carrying about 2,000 riders, and as many as ten special cars running on a busy Saturday. The biggest train ride to a racetrack, however, was the annual first Saturday in May running of the Kentucky Derby at Churchill Downs at Louisville. First run in 1875, the Derby had special trains as early as 1878. The event probably reached its heaviest rail travel in the 1920s, with about 500 cars moved in 50 special trains. Even as recently as 1965 the Derby was running 350 cars in 30 special trains, and many more extra cars were being handled on regular trains. A different sort of athletic event, with the train passengers as participants instead of spectators, is the ski train, operated from large urban areas to nearby skiing resorts, such as the Denver & Rio Grande's train from Denver to Winter Park, Colorado, just a 2-hour trip away.

Promotion

In the nineteenth and early twentieth centuries U.S. and Canadian railroads were eager to encourage land development and attract settlers in the vast undeveloped areas of the two countries. While the Union Pacific was still being built, immigrants were brought to the land on cheap tickets in a freight car with a cookstove. Some even came from Europe via steamship and train. In the 1870s James J. Hill was bringing whole families from half a world away for only $10. Many prospective farmers first came out from the East by train to look California over and then headed back to gather up their belongings and families.

A football special from Milwaukee unloaded fans on the University of Wisconsin campus in Madison for the October 16, 1954, Wisconsin-Purdue game. —William D. Middleton

Once the new settlers had come, the railroads helped them improve farming practices with special trains. In 1912 the Burlington ran two specials through Nebraska with lectures on improved corn breeding, followed several years later by a special car that visited 27 towns to help potato farmers improve their yield. The Burlington helped set up a special dairy train with lectures on improved milking practice and cattle breeds. In Colorado the railroad ran a special purebred swine and cattle train. Still other programs included poultry specials (see AGRICULTURAL DEVELOPMENT).

It may seem unlikely, but railroads were active proponents of "good roads." They saw improved roads as a benefit that would help extend their tributary areas. Beginning in the late nineteenth century, there was a growing movement to build a system of improved roads, both for their economic benefits and to accommodate the new hobby of bicycling. By 1900 more than 100 national and local organizations promoted road development. One of the most energetic was the National Good Roads Assn., headed by Col. William H. Moore. In 1901 Moore came up with the idea of a traveling show to educate the public on the advantages of improved highways. An early participant was the Illinois Central Railroad. The IC signed up an 11-car special train that included 9 flatcars loaded with road machinery and 2 sleeping cars. It left from Chicago early in April 1901 and traveled all the way to New Orleans, visiting 16 cities in five states by the end of the trip in August. The trip was so successful that Colonel Moore had no trouble bringing in

other railroads. The Lake Shore & Michigan Southern made a trip from Chicago to Buffalo in 1901, and the Pere Marquette ran one in 1902. The most elaborate Good Roads train was operated by the Southern Railway; it began in Alexandria, Virginia, at the end of October 1901 and was on the road for five months, traveling more than 4,000 miles to 18 Good Roads meetings. The last Good Roads train left from St. Paul on the Great Northern in September 1903 on a trip to the Pacific Coast.

Quite often special trains were operated to promote business activities. Locomotive builder Samuel Vauclain, president of the Baldwin Locomotive Works, staged several events featuring his locomotives that were still talked about years later. In 1892 he lined up a fleet of 20 new Vauclain compound Forney-type locomotives being shipped from Philadelphia to the Chicago & South Side elevated line. The 20 new locomotives were shipped in a solid train, pulled by Vauclain's new design of compound 4-6-0s that would then be tested on several midwestern roads. Vauclain got even more publicity 30 years later. With a big order of 2-10-2s for Southern Pacific ready to leave from the Eddystone plant at Philadelphia, he came up with the idea of shipping as many as they could get into a single train and sending it west on the *Prosperity Special*. The new locomotives would help demonstrate business confidence after the 1921 recession. On May 26, 1922, a 20-car train of the big locomotives set out, powered by as many as 7 additional locomotives. Large crowds came down to see the train, and speeches were made by politicians, leaders

Perhaps the most extensive use of the railroad for commercial promotion was the 1936 United Drug Co.'s *Rexall* train, which used the New York Central's 4-8-2 Mohawk locomotive No. 2873. The blue and white train traveled 29,000 miles on a goodwill trip through the United States and Canada. —*Trains* Magazine Collection

of chambers of commerce, and railroad officials. Traveling over the Pennsylvania, the St. Louis Southwestern, and the Southern Pacific, the train had gone 3,740 miles by the time it ended the trip at Los Angeles' Exposition Park on June 30.

The United Drug Co. planned a special train in 1936 to promote its Rexall products. A New York Central 4-8-2, dubbed the *Rexall*, was fitted with a streamlined shroud similar to the *Commodore Vanderbilt*, and 12 blue and white cars were given such names as the *Bisma-Rex* and the *Ad-Vantage* for the occasion. The train departed from Boston on March 29, 1936, to make a 29,000-mile goodwill tour that covered 47 states.

Freedom Trains

An unprecedented 1947 tour of the Freedom Train, transporting some of America's most priceless original documents, including the Declaration of Independence, an early draft of the Constitution, and the Bill of Rights, set out on a yearlong journey that would take it over 33,000 miles in 48 states. A brand new Alco-GE diesel, the *Spirit of 1776*, headed the train, which included specially protected exhibit cars, domicile cars, and a diesel power plant.

An even more ambitious Freedom Train was put together in 1975 to celebrate the U.S. bicentennial on a tour of the 48 contiguous states. Financed by private donations, the trip was preceded in 1974 by the *Preamble Express*, which toured 76 cities in all 48 states to help raise support for the train, which was operated by the Freedom Train Foundation. More than 700 historic artifacts were transported on the train, including the Declaration of Independence, George Washington's copy of the Constitution, and the Emancipation Proclamation. Carrying more than 20 cars, the train had 10 cars for visitors and a variety of support cars, dormitory space, and a power plant. The train was largely operated by a restored and specially decorated Reading Railroad 4-8-4 and a Southern Pacific Daylight 4-8-4. The completed train went on display at Wilmington, Delaware, on April 1, 1975, followed by a 21-month tour that ended at Seattle, Washington, in January 1977.

A similar Canadian excursion was operated over a five-year period that began in mid-1978. The idea for the train, called *Discovery Train* or *Le Découverte*, was similar to that of the Freedom Train, even to use of much of the same equipment, and it was operated by the National Museums of Canada and other supporting foundations or corporations. More than 1,200 historical items and an elaborate display of audiovisual and electronic material moved through 13 cars that displayed the diversity of the Canadian experience. A train of 15 cars was extensively rebuilt for the new train, which began operation from Kingston, Ontario, on July 22, 1978. It operated for the next five years, coast to coast, even including visits to Prince Edward Island and Vancouver Islands, where the train was moved across the water by car ferries and reassembled.

In 1947 the brand-new Alco-GE PA-l diesel *Spirit of 1776*, guarded by a Marine Corps contingent, headed the U.S. Freedom Train on a yearlong, 33,000-mile tour to 48 states. —George Burns, *Trains* Magazine Collection

Celebrating the U.S. bicentennial, another Freedom Train carried a historic exhibit over all 48 contiguous states from April 1975 to January 1977. Powered by the Southern Pacific's celebrated 4-8-4 Daylight locomotive 4449, the red, white, and blue train was ready to depart from Santa Barbara, California, on January 4, 1976. —William D. Middleton

National Leaders

Before the airplane era travel on special trains by U.S. presidents was common (*see* PRESIDENTIAL CAMPAIGNS AND TRAVEL). Sometimes other heads of state traveled by train as well. Members of the United Kingdom's royal family have traveled by train on a number of occasions during visits to Canada, but the most extensive train trip by the king and queen, and the first by a ruling monarch, was the monthlong, nationwide special train for King George VI and Queen Elizabeth in 1939. The six-car special train was painted for the occasion in a deep blue, with window panels finished in aluminum leaf edged with gold. For its westbound journey, a pilot train preceded the royal train. Both were powered by the Canadian Pacific Railway's new semistreamlined 4-6-4 Hudson type. The trains were finished in stainless steel and trimmed in blue and silver, with gilt trimmings. The locomotive of the royal train itself also was fitted with the royal crest. The trip was also an unprecedented run for the CPR's new steam power, for both locomotives ran all the way from Quebec to Vancouver—3,224 miles—without a change of engine. The royal train departed from Quebec on May 18, 1939, and made stops at such points as Montreal, Ottawa, Toronto, Winnipeg, and Banff before finally steaming into Vancouver on May 29.

Canadian National logged another 4,212 miles on its eastward trip, leaving Vancouver on May 31, pulled by a streamlined 4-8-4 locomotive that was capable of operation up to 100 mph. The train was specially decorated in a deep blue, with a royal blue trim, similar to that of the CPR engine, complete with the royal arms. The eastward run included Edmonton, Saskatoon, and Sudbury before a trip via Niagara Falls to the United States at Washington. The last leg of the marathon journey was through the Atlantic Provinces from Fredericktown, New Brunswick, to Halifax, Nova Scotia, on June 15.

Another U.S. royal train was run in 1957 for Queen Elizabeth II and Prince Philip on the final segment of a goodwill tour to the United States. The overnight train ran over the Baltimore & Ohio from Washington, D.C., on October 20, with a 12-car royal train, followed by an 11-car press train. The train followed an unusual routing: it proceeded north from Philadelphia on the Reading, the Lehigh Valley, and finally B&O's State Island Rapid Transit Railway to St. George on Staten Island. This approach to New York was at the queen's request; she had wanted to view the New York skyline over water.

A much different sort of political leader, Soviet premier Nikita Khrushchev, came to ride two special trains during a 13-day state visit to the United States in 1959. Both trains drew enormous crowds desiring a glimpse of the USSR visitor. The first ran over the Pennsylvania between New York and Washington on September 17 with a 15-car train headed by two GG1 electrics. Just ahead was train No. 126, the *Legislator*, running as a pilot train for the

Khrushchev special. A second trip three days later on September 20 took Khrushchev from Los Angeles to San Francisco. The 18-car special operated as a second section of the *Coast Daylight*, just behind the regular train.

—William D. Middleton

REFERENCES

Abbey, Wallace W. "Wild Ride of Death Valley Scotty." *Trains* 13, no. 4 (Feb. 1953): 14–17.

America's Highways, 1776–1976. Washington, D.C.: U.S. Dept. of Transportation, Federal Highway Admin., 1976.

Behr, E. H. "Race Train to Bowie." *Trains* 6, no. 10 (Aug. 1946): 42–45.

Castner, Charles B. "Strange Love Affair between the Rails . . . and a Horse Race." *Trains* 26, no. 9 (May 1966): 20–28.

Comstock, Henry B. "Strange Special." *Railroad* 41, no. 4 (Jan. 1947): 26–35.

Connolly, J. P. "One for the Books." *Trains* 3, no. 12 (Oct. 1943): 17.

Ellis, William F. "Railroaders Want a Runaway." *Trains* 13, no. 3 (Jan. 1953): 16–18.

Gross, Harriet H. "The Land Grant Legend." *Railroad* 55, no. 3 (Aug. 1951): 28–49; 55, no. 4 (Sept. 1951): 64–77; 56, no. 1 (Oct. 1951): 68–79; 56, no. 2 (Nov. 1951): 30–41; 56, no. 3 (Dec. 1951): 40–53.

Hubbard, Freeman. "There Never Was a Signal Set against a Silk Train." *Railroad* 76, no. 6 (Apr. 1965): 13–24.

Kelso, H. L. "Shriners and Streamliners." *Railroad* 53, no. 3 (Dec. 1950): 38–46.

Morgan, David P. "The Train That Raced the Airplanes." *Trains* 12, no. 12 (Oct. 1952): 18–22.

"Nikita Rides the Rails." *Trains* 20, no. 2 (Dec. 1959): 17.

"Royal Train Sets World Record." *Railroad* 29, no. 4 (Sept. 1939): 74–78.

Stewart, E. S. "Whirled across the Continent." *Trains* 15, no. 6 (Apr. 1955): 27–30.

Religion on the Rails

Cardinals Train

Not many railroad movements have been spawned by religion, but there were a few. One of the most notable came about as a result of the Roman Catholic Church's XXVIII International Eucharistic Conference—the first in the United States—in Chicago on June 20–24, 1926. Delegates attended from all over the world.

The New York Central Railroad and the Pullman Co. contributed a seven-car Cardinals Train to take the College of Cardinals and their aides to the conference from Manhattan's Grand Central Station. Pullman had repainted the cars—five sleepers, a club car, and an NYC diner—a dazzling cardinal red with yellow trim at its Calumet, Illinois, shops and renamed them for prominent Catholics and the seminary where the final session took place. An hour before departure on June 16, 10,000 people gathered in Grand Central Station's concourse to applaud the cardinals as they arrived. Michael Cardinal von Faulhaber, archbishop of Munich, Germany, boarded first. Giovanni Cardinal Bonzano, the papal legate from Rome who presided over the

conference, blessed the crowd from the rear platform as the train departed.

Cheering crowds, dignitaries, and marching bands greeted the "red special" throughout its journey. There were 10,000 people at Albany, New York, 30,000 at Syracuse, and 50,000 at Rochester. In between, the passengers enjoyed elegant meals ordered from special menus with red covers and silk ribbons and served by a handpicked crew.

The train traveled the final 44 miles from Porter, Indiana, on Michigan Central tracks, arriving at Illinois Central's Central Station at 9:45 A.M., June 17—five minutes early. George Cardinal Mundelein, Mayor William Dever, and several Chicago city councilmen in morning dress were among the throng of greeters.

After the cardinals returned to New York on June 25–26, the cars' original Pullman green livery and names were restored at Calumet. Pullman said that its expenses for the move were minimal, since the cars all were due for overhauls anyway. The passengers paid neither railroad fares nor Pullman space charges, and their meals also were complimentary. Pullman saw the move as a public relations gesture.

But the Cardinals Train is just part of the story. At least a million people—believed to be the greatest assemblage for a single event up to that moment in world history—were expected to attend the conference at Soldier Field. Chicago's Surface Lines, the Chicago, Aurora & Elgin interurban line, and Samuel Insull's rail properties—Chicago Rapid Transit Co., the Chicago North Shore & Milwaukee Railroad, and the Chicago South Shore & South Bend Railroad—found ways to move the crowds to the stadium each day from their filled-to-capacity hotels, tents in Cook County's forest preserves, sidetracked Pullmans, docked passenger boats, and private homes.

The final session took place at St. Mary of the Lake Seminary near Mundelein, 40 miles north of downtown Chicago. Planners worked for more than a year to determine that rail systems could carry 275,000 of the delegates: 15,000 via the Minneapolis, St. Paul & Sault Ste. Marie Railway to Mundelein; 30,000 via the Chicago, Milwaukee & St. Paul Railroad to Libertyville; 60,000 via the Chicago & North Western Railway Co. to Lake Bluff; and the remaining 170,000 by the Rapid Transit lines and North Shore from the Loop and several other downtown locations via the North Shore's new Skokie Valley Route, which was rushed to completion for the conference. More of the North Shore's cars ran as shuttles on its Lake Bluff–Mundelein branch to carry the 60,000 passengers from the C&NW trains and other delegates riding several five-car North Shore specials from Milwaukee, Wisconsin, and regular North Shore interurbans serving points between Evanston and Lake Forest.

To handle the extra traffic, six eight-car spur tracks were built on a ten-acre site across from the seminary gates, with loading platforms between them. A 9,000-person "stockade" led to fenced-in enclosures to which were admitted just enough people to fill a single train—all orchestrated by officers on a walk bridge over the tracks. Two temporary 350-foot platforms were installed at Lake Bluff to handle the transfers, and a tower went up near the station to direct movements. Three temporary substations were added, one of them on the flatcar that delivered it. Even 450 lights were strung to illuminate the terminals after dark.

Doctors and nurses staffed hospital cars and army field hospital tents at Mundelein and Lake Bluff to meet medical emergencies. First-aid personnel also were located along the route. A temporary lunch stand greeted passengers at Mundelein with 200 staffers and vast stores of supplies, including eight tons of hot dogs, and band concerts and motion pictures were featured at the conclusion of the ceremonies to prevent passengers from trying to load at once.

On June 23, the day before the final Mass, North Shore carried Cardinal Bonzano and his assistants from Chicago's Uptown Station to Mundelein aboard an elaborately decorated five-car Cardinals Special, featuring a parlor-observation car on the rear. A second special hauled other important clerics.

Then, starting in the wee hours of the 24th, Chicago Rapid Transit and the North Shore operated six-car "L" trains out of the Loop, one every two minutes, originating alternately from the Jackson Park and Loomis Street terminals of the South Side "L" lines on four-minute headways. Other trains originated at the Adams Street/South Wabash Avenue station on the Loop and at Howard Street, where the Rapid Transit became the North Shore and the North Shore's Skokie Valley Line and Shore Line diverged. Thirteen eight-car shuttles moved across North Shore's Lake Bluff–Mundelein branch.

For eight hours starting at 5:35 A.M., a loaded electric train arrived at Mundelein on an average of every 40 seconds. By day's end, 225,000 North Shore passengers had arrived at the seminary gates. The number rose to 275,000 on the homebound trips because many who had arrived by other means returned on that line. It was the greatest mass movement in interurban history, and the biggest day's traffic the three-week-old Skokie Valley Route would ever know. The tensest moment came at about 3:30 P.M., when a severe thunderstorm dumped hail and a drenching rain, sending thousands of delegates rushing for the homebound trains. But, in all, 445 trains with 2,785 cars had carried their precious cargos to and from the seminary without a single accident or injury on board and little delay. A Chicago newspaper called the 20-hour daybreak-to-midnight mass movement "a miracle in transportation."

Pilgrim Trains

Another type of religious rail journey was provided by the pilgrim train to shrines such as Ste.-Anne-de-Beaupré, along the St. Lawrence River 21 miles east of Quebec in Canada. This shrine was built in 1658 by shipwrecked French sailors who believed that the saint had saved their lives. The railroad line that opened between the two points in 1889—the Quebec, Montmorency & Charlevoix Railway, which became the Quebec Railway, Light & Power Co. in 1899 and was absorbed by the Canadian National Railways in 1950—became a conduit for pilgrims going to the shrine. First on steam-powered trains and after 1900 in electric interurbans, they came from all over the world to pay homage and pray.

Interestingly, the first passengers to ride the electric cars from Ste.-Anne did so on August 15, 1900, before regular service started, as the result of an accident. Msgr. Nazaire Begin, archbishop of Quebec; the archbishop's secretary; and Msgr. Merry del Val, apostolic delegate to Canada, were returning to Quebec after a religious visit to Ste.-Anne when their carriage broke down. They flagged down an electric car on a test trip and asked the electrician in charge for a ride. He declined at first, but they were persuasive, and he finally agreed to their request.

The biggest day of the year for the QRL&P always fell on July 26, the Catholic feast day of St. Anne. Special trains ran from Quebec on that day—and indeed all summer long—to accommodate the pilgrims. One of the few railroads whose passenger traffic outmatched its freight tonnage, the QRL&P boasted that 240,734 people visited the shrine between November 1, 1912, and October 31, 1913, and 190,054 of them went by rail. The line came to be known among French Canadians as "Chemin de Fer de la Bonne Sainte-Anne" (the Good Saint Anne's Railway).

In 1958 the Canadian National published a lavish brochure about the "Special Tourist Electric Train Service" running to the shrine daily between June 22 and September 2 on the occasion of its 300th anniversary. But by that time improved highways had been built in the area, and only a fraction of the expected patronage materialized. Passenger service was discontinued in its entirety the following year. The shrine, however, still attracts pilgrims.

—Bob Withers

REFERENCES

Dubin, Arthur D. *Some Classic Trains.* Milwaukee, Wis.: Kalmbach, 1964.
"Handling Eucharistic Conference Millions." *Electric Traction,* 1926.
Lavallée, Omer S. A. *Chemin de fer de la bonne Sainte-Anne.* Montreal, Que.: Privately published, ca. 1960.
Middleton, William D. *North Shore: America's Fastest Interurban.* San Marino, Calif.: Golden West Books, 1964.
Route of the Electroliners. Chicago: Central Electric Railfans' Assn., Bulletin 107, 1963.

Speed

For almost a century, until the first airliners came along in the 1920s, the railroad train was the fastest travel conveyance in the world. Passengers on the first steam cars marveled at the speed of their travel, and from the earliest days railroad men always desired to ride faster yet on the rails.

Among the most notable early North American speed runs were special trains, operated at substantially higher speeds than regular scheduled service: the Jarrett & Palmer Special of 1876, which made a coast-to-coast trip from New York to San Francisco at an average speed of just under 40 miles per hour, for example, or the 1905 high-speed journey for Death Valley Scotty between Los Angeles and Chicago, which made the run at an average speed of over 50 mph that would stand as a record for another 30 years (*see* SPECIAL TRAINS). But the real test of high-speed railroading came in regularly scheduled operation. What longtime North American train speed writer Donald M. Steffee called the first "Golden Age" of modern passenger service began in the last decade of the nineteenth century. In August 1888 a series of high-speed runs in Great Britain by the competitors of the East Coast and West Coast lines between London and Edinburgh attracted international attention. One, on an East Coast line, made the 392.5-mile trip in 7 hours 26¾ minutes, with an overall average speed of almost 53 mph.

In August 1888 what was probably the earliest survey of international train speeds was compiled by two English authorities, E. Foxwell and T. C. Farrar. The men surveyed what they called fast or express trains in Great Britain and the United States, using a minimum average speed of 40 mph for start-to-stop times on runs at least 40 miles in length. Minimum average speeds of 29 mph were used for other countries. At this early point Great Britain was well ahead, with a total of 62,904 miles at or above 40 mph, nearly five times the U.S. total of 13,956 miles at 40 mph or better. Railroads in the highly competitive Northeast Corridor accounted for a large share of the fastest running. The Pennsylvania Railroad alone accounted for more than 6,000 miles of running at 40 mph or better, almost half the national total, in its trains between Philadelphia and Jersey City, the ferry terminal for New York. The Central Railroad of New Jersey and the Philadelphia & Reading operated 14 fast expresses between the two cities. The Baltimore & Ohio operated four daily trains between Baltimore and Washington at 53.3 mph, the fastest of all American schedules.

Still other notable U.S. times included routes between New York and Boston that operated at an overall average speed of 39 mph. The summertime-only *Mt. Desert Limited* made the 136.6-mile Portland-to-Bangor (Maine) section of its run in 3 hours 10 minutes, an average schedule of 43.1 mph. This timing was not bettered for almost

A pacesetter for the "first golden era of railroad speed" was the New York Central's *Empire State Express*, launched in 1891. Fitted with enormous 86-inch driving wheels, the remarkable 4-4-0 No. 999 hit a world speed record of 112.5 mph with the *Express* on May 10, 1893. —Library of Congress (Neg. LC-USZ62-71699)

50 years, until the introduction of the Maine Central *Flying Yankee* streamliner.

Much faster trains soon followed. On October 26, 1891, the New York Central & Hudson River launched America's fastest train, the *Empire State Express* between New York and Buffalo. It covered the 440 miles in 8 hours and 40 minutes, with an overall average speed of almost 51 mph. The locomotives for the new train had their driving wheels increased from 70 inches to 78 inches to attain higher speeds, and in one test run the train covered the distance between New York and Buffalo at an average speed of 61.4 mph. Two years later George Henry Daniels, the New York Central's general passenger agent, came up with the idea for a record-breaking high-speed run for the *Empire State Express* that would generate even more publicity for the railroad. A special 4-4-0 locomotive, No. 999, with enormous 86-inch driving wheels was built, and on May 10, 1893, it headed the *Empire State Express* over a straight section of track just west of Batavia, New York, that reached a world-record maximum speed of 112.5 mph.

Other operators of new fast trains included the Baltimore & Ohio, together with the connecting Philadelphia & Reading and the Central Railroad of New Jersey, which ran the *Royal Blue* trains between Jersey City and Washington on a 5-hour schedule, including the ferry connection from Manhattan. In 1892 what was to become the Southern Railway began operating the *Washington & Southwestern Line* between Washington and Atlanta on an 18-hour schedule. The Central of Georgia began operating the *Nancy Hanks* over the 191-mile route between Savannah and Atlanta on a 4-hour schedule that was called the "Fastest Railroad in the South." In the summer of 1897 the Philadelphia & Reading established the first mile-a-minute schedule in the Western Hemisphere, with a train that made the 55.5-mile run between Camden and Atlantic City in 55 minutes. The schedule was later cut to 52 minutes and then 50, and for a few months in 1903–1904 to 49 minutes. In the Midwest the Chicago & North Western touched off a rivalry with its competitors on New Year's Day 1899 with a 10-hour Chicago–St. Paul schedule for the 409-mile route. By the turn of the century the Illinois Central, which in 1888 had taken 35 hours for the Chicago–New Orleans journey, had reduced the running time by almost 10 hours. In 1900 the Chicago, Rock Island & Pacific cut 2 hours from the schedule of its overnight Chicago–Omaha schedule, making the 504-mile run in just 12 hours 5 minutes. The rival Chicago & North Western promptly cut its Chicago–Omaha schedule to 10 minutes less than that of the Rock Island train. For the journey from Chicago to the West Coast the best times in the late 1880s were about 90 hours. By 1902 the Santa Fe's winter season *California Limited* was making the run in only 66 hours between Chicago and Los Angeles.

By the early twentieth century the New York Central and the Pennsylvania began operating some of the most hotly competitive of all American long-distance schedules in the New York–Chicago market. In 1888 the two trains required 24 hours for their fastest runs between New York and Chicago. By 1893 the New York Central had cut the running time between the two cities to just 20 hours for the new *Exposition Flyer*, a summer and fall special run for the 1893 World's Columbian Exposition at Chicago. The *Flyer* was taken off at the end of the exposition, but Daniels retained the idea of a permanent extra-fare, all-Pullman flyer between New York and Chicago that would operate under the record 20-hour schedule.

Daniels's new train, the *20th Century Limited*, began daily service on June 15, 1902, making the 980-mile trip in 20 hours, 4 hours fewer than the railroad's previous first-class train, *The Lake Shore Limited*. The Pennsylvania Railroad countered with its new *Pennsylvania Limited*, which began operating on the same day and an identical timing. In 1905 running time for the *Pennsylvania Limited* was cut to 18 hours, which was promptly met by the *20th Century Limited*. In much later years, with streamlined equipment, the trains were scheduled to make the trip in as little as 16 hours. Similar advances in equipment and operating speeds were made in other important markets.

The first golden era of railroad speed continued through the 1890s and the first decade of the new century. But because of such problems as the burdens of World War I traffic, U.S. Railroad Administration (USRA) oversight during the war, and the deteriorated physical condition and financial problems that followed the war, there was little progress toward new or improved high-speed trains after about 1910. But there were some bright spots. In 1911 the Illinois Central inaugurated the all-Pullman *Panama Limited* between Chicago and New Orleans. The Missouri Pacific's *Sunshine Special* and the competing Missouri-Kansas-Texas's *Texas Special* established fast, deluxe trains between St. Louis and San Antonio. The Katy's *Texas Special*, introduced in 1916, covered 1,037 miles between the two cities in 26 hours, an average overall speed of 40 mph, and was the fastest train in the Southwest. The Chicago & North Western, Union Pacific, and Southern Pacific, which had lengthened the record 63-hour timing of their *Overland Limited* between Chicago and San Francisco before World War I, restored the 63-hour schedule in 1926 and over the next several years further accelerated the schedule to 56 hours. In 1929 the Jersey Central put its fast new all-coach *Blue Comet* in service between New York and Atlantic City, covering the 136 rail miles between Jersey City and Atlantic City in 2 hours 48 minutes, an average speed of almost 50 mph.

The decade after the Wall Street crash of 1929 was a difficult one for passenger trains. Improved highways carrying both intercity buses and private automobiles, as well as a fledgling new air transport system, were growing competitors. In just four years the strengthening road and air competition, combined with the economic downturn, brought a decline of almost 50 percent in railroad passenger traffic from the 1929 traffic level. The railroads' response was an unprecedented investment in innovative new streamlined equipment, radically improved passenger service, and a new golden age of high-speed trains.

The first of these new trains were the Burlington's *Zephyr*, a stainless-steel streamliner powered by a diesel-electric power plant, and the Union Pacific's distillate-powered aluminum streamliner M-10000, *City of Salinas*, both completed in 1934. Unlike anything the public had ever seen before, the new trains attracted enormous publicity as they toured the country. Other streamliners soon followed. In October 1934 the UP's new *City of Portland* ran the 3,248 miles from Los Angeles to New York in 56 hours 55 minutes, the fastest transcontinental rail journey ever made.

UP soon had its new streamliners, *City of Los Angeles* and *City of San Francisco*, in service. The Chicago–San Francisco journey, which had required over 100 hours for the *Overland Flyer* between the two cities in 1888, was reduced to a 63-hour timing before World War I and to 56 hours by the end of the 1920s. With the arrival of *City of San Francisco* in 1936, the running time was cut again, to only 39¾ hours for the 2,263-mile journey, and both *City of Portland* and *City of Los Angeles* were operated on identical 39¾-hour schedules. By 1937 the Santa Fe had matched Union Pacific's Southern California competition with its all-Pullman streamliner *Super Chief*, which made the Chicago–Los Angeles run in 39½ hours.

The Burlington acquired an expanding fleet of *Zephyr*s. Among the most fiercely contested routes were the daytime journeys between Chicago and the Twin Cities. In 1935 the Burlington installed *Twin Zephyr* streamliners between the two cities, the Milwaukee Road built its own streamlined *Hiawatha*s, and the Chicago & North Western operated conventional equipment in a new *400* high-speed service. The streamliners were a phenomenal success, and over the next decade more than two dozen railroads acquired them. Most were equipped with the new diesel-electric locomotives, while others operated with modern steam or electric power.

Before the end of 1936 streamlined trains had entered service from coast to coast, and in October 1936 *Railroad Stories* magazine ran the first tabulation of North America's extraordinary age of high-speed trains. Compiler Donald M. Steffee conducted his annual speed surveys for nearly 40 years, first in *Railroad* and then in *Trains*, with a few final tabulations from the British journal *Railway Gazette*. Instead of surveying train speeds on the basis of overall origin-to-destination journey times, the usual American practice, Steffee followed the British practice of tabulating train speeds on a point-to-point basis, taking an average speed on nonstop runs.

Although North America's new streamlined trains had begun operating scarcely two years before, Steffee's survey showed an already-impressive listing of high-speed trains. As recently as 1930 North American trains had operated only about 1,100 miles at mile-a-minute or better speeds.

By 1936 Steffee's survey found 644 different start-to-stop runs and a total of 40,205 miles running at or above 60 mph averages. The Union Pacific and Santa Fe operated a number of high-speed runs with their new transcontinental streamliners. The Burlington, Milwaukee Road, and Chicago & North Western ran head-to-head in the competitive Chicago–Twin Cities market. The Illinois Central, the Wabash, and the B&O (Alton) scheduled some fast trips on the Chicago–St. Louis corridor. With a total of 9,772 high-speed miles operated by steam or electric power, the Pennsylvania Railroad led U.S. railroads in runs at or above 60 mph. The New York Central followed with 5,609 miles, all by steam power. In New England the New Haven and the Boston & Maine ran a number of fast trips. High-speed trains were absent only in the South.

The fastest American train of all was the Santa Fe's *Super Chief*, which made the 202.4-mile run between La Junta and Dodge City at a start-to-stop average of 83.8 mph. Average speed such as this required top-speed running well in excess of 100 mph. New diesel-electric locomotives powered the largest share of high-speed services, particularly for the higher speeds, but the Milwaukee, the Chicago & North Western, the Pennsylvania, and the Reading also operated a few steam-powered trains that averaged more than 70 mph. The Milwaukee's new *Hiawatha* 4-4-2 locomotives were capable of 120 mph speeds and operated the fastest of all steam trains, with a 75.8 mph average between stops at Sturtevant, Wisconsin, and Deerfield, Illinois. Some of the most remarkable runs, however, were the short high-speed schedules by the electric interurbans of the Chicago North Shore & Milwaukee. Each day the North Shore operated almost 100 start-to-stop runs of 60 mph or more, all of them in runs of less than 30 miles, and the fastest of all North Shore schedules were two trains that covered the 15 miles between stops at Kenosha and Waukegan at an average speed of 76 mph.

By 1941 Steffee's annual survey showed that the new streamliners had more than doubled the mileage of high-speed train operation, with a total of 1,529 separate runs and 85,872 miles of trains operated at 60 mph and above. Additional high-speed trains were added in the Northeast, the Midwest, and the West. New streamlined trains in the Southeast brought fast trains to the Richmond, Fredericksburg & Potomac, Seaboard Air Line, Atlantic Coast Line, and Florida East Coast. Save for a number of fast trains operated across Ontario between Detroit and Buffalo by the Michigan Central, high-speed operation had not yet come to Canada. The fastest American train was now the Burlington, whose *Morning Zephyr* made a start-to-stop 84.0 mph average speed for the 54.6-mile run from East Dubuque, Illinois, to Prairie du Chien, Wisconsin. The Pennsylvania operated a total of almost 29,000 miles at 60 mph or better speeds, and the New York Central was not far behind with more than 20,000 miles of mile-a-minute or better runs. The Santa Fe, the Burlington, and the Union Pacific each operated well over 10,000 miles of fast trains.

The 1941 speed survey proved to be the best one until after the end of World War II. From 1945 until well into the 1950s the railroads purchased hundreds of new diesel-electric locomotives and lightweight streamlined cars that made the next two decades a remarkable era of high-speed service. Even before war's end the railroads had begun to restore some of the high-speed services cut back in the war. In 1945 the total of 81,711 miles of mile-a-minute or better trains was the highest mileage ever except for the record schedules of 1941. Chicago & North Western's *City of Milwaukee 400*, which covered the start-to-stop 15.7 miles between Kenosha and Waukegan at an average of 85.4 mph, was North America's fastest train. Only a year later high-speed running was up by nearly a third to a new total of 108,629 miles. New streamliners brought high-speed service to the Chicago-Florida run and to the Pacific Northwest between Chicago and Seattle.

In the 1949 annual speed survey trains at or above 60 mph reached a total of almost 140,000 miles that would soon double the 1945 level. By 1954 total U.S. and Canadian mile-a-minute runs had reached a record level of 169,474 miles, and a map of high-speed trains reached virtually every point of the U.S. compass. There were predictions of still more growth of high-speed trains to come, but 1954 turned out to be as good as it would ever get. As rail passenger traffic continued to drop, and passenger losses became ever more severe, the number of high-speed trains slowly began to decline as they were cut back or eliminated. A substantial number of those that survived were discontinued with the transfer of intercity rail service to Amtrak in 1971. The United States, once the world leader in high-speed train operation, was challenged by new overseas high-speed routes. And with the opening of Japan's new 130 mph New Tokaido Line in 1964, leadership in high-speed railroads passed outside North America.

But even as North America's nationwide high-speed rail system was disappearing, a new kind of high-speed service was at hand. The High Speed Ground Transportation and Research and Development Act in 1965 led to joint U.S. government and Pennsylvania Railroad funding of a program that would upgrade the existing New York–Washington corridor and build a new Metroliner train capable of 150 mph operation. Although the train had more than the usual share of problems, Metroliner achieved a test speed as high as 164 mph, and when it finally began regular service, start-to-stop average speeds in excess of 90 mph were soon reached. In a separate federal program a high-speed, gas-turbine *TurboTrain* hit a record test run of 170.8 mph in the late 1960s.

Newer electric power had begun to replace the original Metroliner trains in 1980, and dozens of daily Amtrak Northeast Corridor trains were being operated at start-to-stop averages in excess of 90 mph. The upgrading and electrification of the New Haven–Boston corridor and the addition of the Acela Express high-speed trains in 2000 brought high-speed trains that operate start-to-stop schedules that average as much as 100 mph and that are capable of maximum operating speeds up to 150 mph.

—William D. Middleton

REFERENCES

Foxwell, E., and T. C. Farrer. *Express Trains: English and Foreign.* London: Smith, Elder, 1889. Repr., London: Railway Publications, 1964.
Steffee, Donald M. High-speed train surveys in *Railroad Stories* or *Railroad* magazine issues of Apr. 1938, Feb. 1939, Jan. 1940, Jan. 1941, Jan. 1942, Mar. 1943, Mar. 1944, Mar. 1945, Mar. 1946, Apr. 1947, Apr. 1948, Apr. 1949, Apr. 1950, Apr. 1951, and Apr. 1952. Surveys published in *Trains* magazine issues of May 1954, May 1955, May 1956, May 1957, May 1958, May 1959, May 1960, June 1961, June 1962, June 1963, June 1964, June 1965, June 1966, May 1967, June 1968, June 1969, July 1969, Sept. 1970, June 1971, June 1972, and July 1973.
———. "Years for Minutes: A Half Century of Passenger Schedules." *Railroad* 50, no. 4 (Jan. 1950): 10–47.

Sperry Rail Service. *See* RAIL

DEFECTS, DETECTION OF

Spokane, Portland & Seattle Railway

In 1905 the Union Pacific approached Portland, Oregon, from the east along the south bank of the Columbia River. The Southern Pacific came north to Portland along the valley of the Willamette River. The Northern Pacific Railway came southwest from Spokane, Washington, crossed the Columbia River at Pasco, turned northwest toward Seattle and Tacoma, and approached Portland from the north, recrossing the Columbia at Vancouver, Washington. The Great Northern Railway also passed through Spokane and headed directly west for Seattle. The Chicago, Milwaukee & St. Paul was just getting ready to build its extension to the Pacific Northwest.

The Union Pacific and the Southern Pacific were controlled by E. H. Harriman; James J. Hill controlled the Great Northern and the Northern Pacific. Hill wanted a direct route for his railroads to reach Portland, a seaport despite its location 100 miles from the mouth of the Columbia River, a route that did not require a climb from the Columbia River to the summit of the Cascades, a descent to tidewater, and a climb over the divide separating Puget Sound from the Columbia River. He also wanted to invade Oregon, which was pretty much Harriman's territory, and prevent the Chicago, Milwaukee & St. Paul from doing so.

In 1905 the Portland & Seattle Railway was incorporated, financed and jointly owned by the Northern Pacific and the Great Northern. Three years later the name was changed to Spokane, Portland & Seattle (SP&S). The railroad opened between Pasco and Portland along the north bank of the Columbia River that same year, 1908, and from Pasco to Spokane the next year. The railroad acquired Northern Pacific's old line along the Columbia downstream from Portland to Goble and another existing railroad from Goble west to Astoria. At Astoria, passengers to and from San Francisco could connect with the ships of the Great Northern Pacific Steamship Co.

Along the Columbia between Portland and Pasco the SP&S was laid out with easy curves and gentle grades and was considered the fastest railroad in the Northwest (it still is). The line from Pasco to Spokane was equally well laid out but required heavy construction in the form of fills, tunnels, and bridges.

For most of its life the Spokane, Portland & Seattle was a stepchild of its two parents, the Great Northern and the Northern Pacific. The two larger roads seemed to compete with each other in miserliness. The steam locomotives they provided were generally older castoffs. When the U.S. Railroad Administration (USRA) allocated freight and switching locomotives in 1919, Great Northern and Northern Pacific came up with secondhand locomotives for the SP&S and took the new USRA locomotives themselves.

In 1933 the two railroads began managing the SP&S in alternate years and closed most of SP&S's offices and shops. In 1940 SP&S resumed management of its own affairs. In the diesel era SP&S showed its independence by favoring the products of the American Locomotive Co. (Electro-Motive diesels predominated on the rails of Great Northern and Northern Pacific).

SP&S had three subsidiaries. The United Railways Co. was a former electric line that ran west from Portland into logging country. The Oregon Electric Railway began service between Portland and Salem in 1908, was acquired by SP&S in 1910, and extended its line south to Eugene in 1912, in direct competition with Southern Pacific's electrically operated Portland, Eugene & Eastern subsidiary. The Oregon Trunk Railway reached south along the Deschutes River to the high country of central Oregon at Bend. The Oregon Trunk and the Union Pacific battled for occupancy of the canyon of the Deschutes, eventually declaring a truce in the form of trackage rights over parts of each other's line. The SP&S from Spokane to Wishram, Washington, and the Oregon Trunk south to Bend formed a bridge between the Great Northern's main line and an isolated piece of the Great Northern that ran from Bend south through Klamath Falls, Oregon, to Bieber, California, and a connection with the Western Pacific.

Spokane, Portland & Seattle's two owners, Great Northern and Northern Pacific, merged on March 2, 1970, to become Burlington Northern (a merger James J. Hill had planned about 70 years before). SP&S was a part of that merger.

In 1969, its last year before the Burlington Northern merger, Spokane, Portland & Seattle operated 922 route-miles and 1,313 track-miles, with 112 locomotives, 54 passenger cars, 3,216 freight cars, 355 company service cars, and 2,439 employees. SP&S operating revenues totaled $32.2 million in 1969, and the railroad achieved an 82.7 percent operating ratio.

—George H. Drury

REFERENCES

Gaertner, John T. *North Bank Road*. Pullman: Washington State Univ. Press, 1990.
Grande, Walter R. *The Northwest's Own Railway*. Portland, Ore.: Grande Press, 1992.

Sports and the Railroads

The development of U.S. professional sports teams was largely made possible by the availability of extensive and affordable rail passenger transportation. In order to have viable competition among the best teams, it was critical that they have the opportunity to play against each other, which depended on their ability to travel to each other's cities. In order to support their home team while it was on the road, fans also depended on the railroad for intercity transportation. Having the fans of the "away" team in the stands made the games more exciting and fun for fans and players alike.

Baseball first became widely popular during the Civil War, when both Confederate and Union troops enjoyed the game as recreation. It was the first professional sport to benefit from rail travel, which was important to both major- and minor-league teams. Having started in the early 1870s, professional baseball grew as rail passenger service expanded in both extent and quality.

Until the 1950s major-league baseball was confined to the northeastern United States, the location of the large cities that could support major-league teams. All these large cities were linked by rail; the most distant—Boston to St. Louis, for example—could be reached by an overnight journey. City size and railroad travel feasibility defined the major baseball leagues. The minor leagues took root in smaller urban areas but were likewise defined by reasonable travel time. Travel by any means other than rail was not practical for long distances. Night baseball developed in the 1930s, and it was not uncommon for a night game of the Philadelphia Phillies to be suspended so the team could catch the last sleeper train through North Philadelphia Station and meet the Pirates in Pittsburgh for a day game the following afternoon.

The railroad was long an integral part of major-league baseball, transporting the teams to and from their games or, in this case, off to spring training. The 1910 Chicago White Sox posed at Royal Gorge on the Denver & Rio Grande Western Railroad in Colorado. At the far right rear, brandishing a railroad flare, is future National Baseball Hall of Famer Ed Walsh. —National Baseball Hall of Fame and Museum

Life for a baseball player on the sleeping cars was fraught with practical jokes. Babe Ruth, for example, started in the big leagues as a pitcher for the Boston Red Sox. In his first trip in a Pullman berth, his teammates told him that the small hammock made of netting installed in each berth for personal effects was for the use of pitchers to rest their pitching arms; the Babe took the bait, put his left arm in the small hammock, and found it so stiff the next day he could hardly move it.

In the days before air conditioning, travel on even the best trains could be daunting, with heat, smoke, and cinders making travel unpleasant. Minor-league teams also traveled by rail, but often without the benefit of the more costly sleeping cars. For short trips early minor leaguers often traveled by horse-powered means. In the 1920s, when highways were finally paved, the minor-league teams usually traveled by bus; for impecunious teams, the

manager or one of the coaches often drove the bus. Travel by bus is still the usual transport for minor-league baseball teams.

With the rapid growth of western U.S. cities after World War II and the development of reliable air transportation, major-league baseball expanded first to the Midwest and the South. The Philadelphia Athletics moved first to Kansas City and then to Oakland; the Boston Braves moved first to Milwaukee and then to Atlanta. There was heartbreak in Brooklyn when the beloved Dodgers moved to Los Angeles. There was corresponding unhappiness in New York when the Giants moved to San Francisco. Today, major-league teams travel by chartered flight, with luggage and equipment stored in the cargo hold. Charter buses move the teams to hotels and the baseball field.

Professional football and basketball teams also used rail travel, although the development of professional leagues for

In town for one of America's most celebrated annual sporting events, a group of well-dressed and well-off visitors gathered around the solarium car of the just arrived "Texas Millionaires Derby Special" at Louisville Union Station in May 1949. —University of Louisville

these sports trailed baseball by about 70 years. Nonetheless, the availability of rail travel was a significant factor in the growth of these sports as well. Since major-league professional football and basketball did not come along until the 1920s and 1930s and only became really big after the advent of television and reliable air transportation, the charter plane became the early travel norm.

Rail travel had a strong association with college football because fans and players boarded trains for games throughout the country. The vibrant rivalries and bragging rights associated with many collegiate football contests made these trips especially fun. For really important games, colleges chartered special trains. For many years, for example, special trains were chartered on the Monon Railroad to move fans between Bloomington and Lafayette for the Indiana University–Purdue Old Oaken Bucket games. The New Haven Railroad ran special trains to handle the crowds from New Haven and Boston to attend the games of rivals Yale and Harvard. Commuter railroads today often run special trains to handle the fans, or extra cars are added to regularly scheduled services.

Professional golf benefited tremendously from rail travel because tournaments were played at courses around the country. Players like Bobby Jones, Jimmy Demaret, Byron Nelson, and Ben Hogan traveled by train to a tournament site, usually arriving a few days early in order to get in a couple of practice rounds before the tournament. Fans also traveled by rail to watch their favorites compete.

Special trains to football, baseball, and basketball games, particularly the major championships of these sports, have often been the most efficient way to move thousands of fans into and out of a particular sports venue. Horse-racing events, such as the Kentucky Derby, held in Louisville each May, were particularly well served by rail. For many years the Louisville & Nashville (L&N) Railroad handled the bulk of travel to the Derby, running more than 30 special trains, along with several hundred extra cars. The railroad also had a special fleet of baggage cars for transporting horses.

Professional and college sports are a significant component of the American fabric, and the history associated with each sport is vast and rich. Today, commercial aviation handles the majority of travel associated with sports and has enabled the geographic reach of each sport to be well beyond the dreams of its founding fathers. The railroads, however, were responsible for helping the sports industry take root in the United States, an industry that provides goals, competition, and enrichment to the lives of millions of Americans, both young and old.

—David C. Lester

REFERENCES

Castner, Charles B., Robert E. Chapman, and Patrick C. Dorin. *Louisville & Nashville Passenger Trains.* Lynchburg, Va.: TLC, 1999.

Darnell, Tim. *The Crackers: Early Days of Atlanta Baseball.* Athens, Ga.: Hill Street Press, 2003.

Dubin, Arthur D. *More Classic Trains.* Milwaukee, Wis.: Kalmbach, 1974.

Newton, Lewis M. *Rails Remembered.* Vol. 2. Roanoke, Va.: Louis Maitland Newton/Progress Press, 1996.

Sprague, Frank J. (1857–1934)

Frank Julian Sprague was first among the pantheon of inventors who developed electric traction into a commercially feasible system in the late nineteenth century. Born in Milford, Connecticut, in 1857 and brought up by an aunt at North Adams, Massachusetts, Sprague in 1874 won appointment to the U.S. Naval Academy. Developing an intense interest in electricity, Sprague continued his electrical experimentation after graduation, producing a number of inventions and installing various electrical systems on several ships.

In 1882 Sprague attended the British Electrical Exhibition at the Crystal Palace in London, where he was made secretary of the jury testing dynamos and gas engines and produced a voluminous report on the test results, published in full by the Navy Department. While he was there, Sprague often rode London's pioneer steam-powered underground railway and began to think seriously of the application of electric power to railway operation, conceiving the idea of using the tracks and an overhead conductor for power supply.

Sprague left the navy in 1883 to join Thomas Edison as an assistant, but quit only a year later to form the Sprague Electric Railway & Motor Co. and take up the development of his electric railway ideas. He conducted tests with electric power on the Manhattan Railway and with battery-powered streetcars in several cities. In 1887 Sprague won contracts for the electrification of street railways at St. Joseph, Missouri, and Richmond, Virginia. The St. Joseph installation was a modest one, but the Richmond contract called for what was by far the most important street railway electrification yet attempted anywhere. Sprague's successful completion of the work over the next year both made his reputation and launched the electric street railway as a major industry.

Sprague next took up electric operation of elevators, where his work on control systems led to the idea of multiple-unit operation of electric trains that he perfected for Chicago's South Side "L" in 1898. In 1902 he was a member of the Electric Traction Commission that guided electrification of the New York Central's lines into the new Grand Central Terminal at New York, then the greatest railroad electrification project yet undertaken anywhere in the world. Sprague remained a prolific inventor throughout his long life. He developed, among other things, an automatic train control system in 1906, depth charges and fuses for the navy during World War I, and a dual elevator system in 1927. At the time of his death in 1934 the *New York Herald Tribune* ranked Sprague with Thomas Edison and Alexander Graham Bell as a "remarkable trio of American inventors who made notable the closing quarter of the last century. Perhaps no three men in all human history have done more to change the daily lives of humankind."

—**William D. Middleton**

REFERENCE

"Memoir of Frank Julian Sprague." *Proceedings of the American Society of Civil Engineers* 100 (1935): 1736–1741.

Frank Julian Sprague. —Middleton Collection

Staggers Act. *See* REGULATION

Standard Gauge

Gauge is the inside distance between the rails of a railway line. In the United States and in much of the world the standard gauge is 4 feet 8½ inches. In the early days of railway construction a variety of gauges were employed. At first there seemed no need for a standard gauge that would allow the free interchange of cars and locomotives. Early railroads were constructed to serve a very limited market, such as to haul coal to a waterway or cotton and tobacco to a seaport.

In Britain, where railroads were created, the 4-foot 8½-inch gauge was purported to have been selected because that was the gauge of the wheels of Roman chariots.

The platform of a chariot had to be wide enough to hold the driver, and if it was a war or hunting chariot, sufficient space was needed for the bowman or spearman and his weapon. The speculation is that the passage of the Roman chariots produced ruts in the primitive and unpaved roads. It followed that British wainwrights would build carts or wagons that could fit comfortably in the ruts.

Later, construction of the British plateways sought to create a smoother path than was possible with a dirt, gravel, or otherwise unpaved roadway. Because of the lessened friction of the hard-surfaced plates, it was easier and more efficient for heavier loads to be moved. The plates were L-shaped iron castings about 3 feet long that were placed on stone sets or wooden crossties; the plates were set apart at a gauge so that any wagon, cart, or carriage could use the plateway. The plateway was seen as a type of turnpike or toll road; anyone willing to pay the toll could use it.

The revolutionary idea of putting the flange on the wheel instead of on the plate or rail is evidence that the advent of steam locomotion required the exclusive control and operation of the railway line by the railway company; it could not be host to a turnpike with a wide variety of users. It was inefficient for a powerful, fast, and expensive steam locomotive to be trapped behind a horse-drawn wagon. Steam power was used on plateways established in industrial or mining sites. George Stephenson chose the standard plateway gauge of 4 feet 8½ inches for the locomotives and railways he was engaged to develop.

When the railway age began in the United States, a number of locomotives were imported from England; these were made to the 4-foot 8½-inch gauge. Early American locomotive manufacturers adopted the British gauge for many of their early products. As long as railroads were viewed in very local, limited market terms, rather than as part of a network, there could be variations in gauge. Wide gauge was employed in some early construction to permit larger and more powerful locomotives to be used. In the construction of the Great Western Railway of England, engineer Isambard Kingdom Brunel used a gauge of 7 feet, which he felt provided the space for really large and efficient cars and locomotives. Brilliant as he was, Brunel did not see the need to interchange cars with parts of England outside of the west.

Most early U.S. railroads in the Northeast used imported locomotives at first and adopted the standard British gauge. In 1846, seeing the burden and inefficiency of a variety of gauges, the British Parliament established 4 feet 8½ inches as the standard to which all future British railways must be built. But the standard gauge in most of the southern United States was 5 feet. The Erie Railroad was constructed with a 6-foot gauge, as was the Ohio & Mississippi. When interchange between railways of different gauge became necessary, it was carried out by several means. One was the transloading of the goods or the passengers from a car of one railroad to the car of another. Another option was to jack up a car and place it on trucks that would fit the railroad to be used. Both means were slow and labor intensive.

The lack of a standard gauge initially was not the only reason that an integrated railway network was not formed in the United States. Several railways might be built into a city, but in many cases they were not connected physically even if they were of the same gauge. Teamsters enjoyed a good business hauling freight or passengers from one line to another and worked politically to keep the various railway lines from physically joining.

The value of a standard gauge was pointed up by the Civil War. The Confederate states were served by railroads of a wide spectrum of gauges, ranging from 4 feet 10 inches to 5 feet 6 inches and 6 feet; and many railways of the same gauge were not connected. A large reason for the South's defeat was the lack of an integrated railway network for moving troops and supplies. There was far more standardization in the Union states, and troops and supplies were moved with relative ease.

The construction of the Pacific railroad, the first transcontinental, provided a further push for standard gauge. At first it was recommended that it be built to 5-foot gauge, but standard gauge was used in its construction. This had a powerful influence on other railways built in the West; except for narrow-gauge lines built in difficult territory or to save initial expense, standard gauge became the norm.

Gauge variation could be used as a defensive measure. Napoleon swept across Europe and into Russia and down across the Iberian Peninsula. Rulers learned a lesson about holding back an invader. By 1860 the prevailing gauge in Russia was 6 feet, and 5 feet 6 inches was the gauge in Spain and Portugal. The gauge difference hindered but did not stop the Nazi invasion of the Soviet Union.

Local influence, which had led to the gauge variation in the United States, was waning as the Civil War began and was later overtaken by the influence of financiers and other investors, who understood that rail properties could only prosper with the heavy traffic possible on a fully connected, integrated network. The great railway building boom of the 1870s and 1880s further stimulated a push to standardization. By 1880 over 80 percent of the U.S. railway system was built to standard gauge or converted to it. Some rail carriers fudged by employing 4-foot 9-inch gauge, and by using a wide tread on the wheels of cars and locomotives, standard-gauge equipment could be used on 4-foot 10-inch lines. Some railroads installed a third rail to permit rolling stock of several gauges to be used. The decade of the 1880s led the South to convert from 5-foot gauge to standard gauge, in part because of the influence of investors, who saw the economic merits of intersectional transportation. Moreover, the bridges across the Ohio and Mississippi rivers were mainly set to standard gauge; the South could not hold out.

On February 2, 1886, representatives of the broad-gauge southern railways met in Atlanta to plan the move to standard gauge. Over 13,000 miles of line were involved, and it was decided to synchronize the shift. The

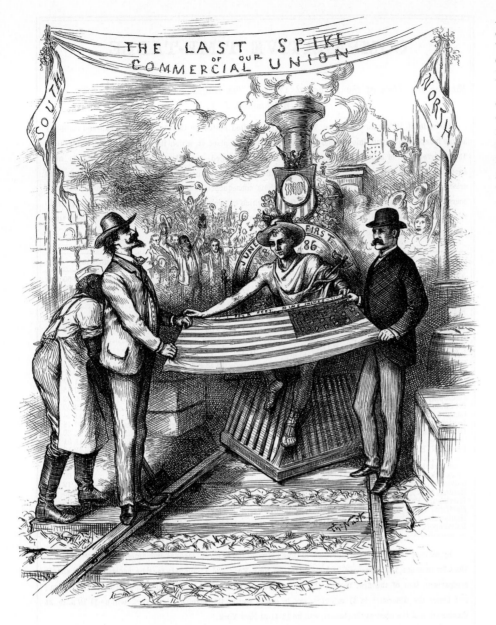

Artist Thomas Nast celebrated what he called "The Last Spike of Our Commercial Union" in the June 5, 1886, *Harper's Weekly,* marking the completion of conversion of more than 9,000 miles of railways in the South from 5-foot broad gauge to 4-foot 8½-inch standard gauge. —Middleton Collection

job was to be accomplished on Monday, May 31, and Tuesday, June 1, 1886. Only one rail needed to be shifted, and in the months preceding the gauge change preparations were carefully made. Ten roads made the change on May 31; the remainder did the job on June 1. On both days the task was carried out between 3:30 A.M. and 4 P.M. After 4 P.M. on June 1, 1886, for all practical purposes the United States had a unified commonly gauged railway network, and with it an integrated economy.

—George M. Smerk

REFERENCES

Frey, Robert L., ed. *Encyclopedia of American Business History and Biography: Railroads in the Nineteenth Century.* New York: Facts on File, 1988.

Holbrook, Stewart H. *The Story of American Railroads.* Chap. 32. New York: Crown, 1947.

Taylor, George Rogers, and Irene D. Neu. *The American Railroad Network, 1861–1890.* Cambridge, Mass.: Harvard Univ. Press, 1956. Repr., Urbana: Univ. of Illinois Press, 2003.

See also NARROW GAUGE.

Standard Time

Time and how to measure it are today paramount in everyday travel all over the globe. This was not always so. The measure of the time it took to get somewhere was not a major issue when travel covered only short distances and the pace of movement was very slow. Rail travel and freight transportation changed the nature of movement and the perception and importance of time. Because of

The lack of standard time in the United States or Canada, and each railroad's practice of basing its time on that of its principal office, created difficulties for the traveler that can readily be imagined. This comparative timetable, included in the first *Official Railway Guide* of June 1868, was an attempt by the guide's editor, Edward Vernon, "to relieve, in some degree, this anomaly in American railroading."
—Middleton Collection

COMPARATIVE TIME-TABLE.

Showing the Time at the Principal Cities of the United States, compared with Noon at Washington, D. C.

There is no "Standard Railroad Time" in the United States or Canada but each railroad company adopts independently the time of its own locality, or of that place at which its principal office is situated. The inconvenience of such a system, if system it can be called, must be apparent to all, but is most annoying to persons strangers to the fact. From this cause many miscalculations and misconnections have arisen, which not unfrequently have been of serious consequence to individuals, and have, as a matter of course, brought into disrepute all Railroad Guides, which of necessity give the local times. In order to relieve, in some degree, this anomaly in American railroading, we present the following table of local time, compared with that of Washington, D. C.:

NOON AT WASHINGTON.		NOON AT WASHINGTON.		NOON AT WASHINGTON.	
Albany, N. Y.	12 14 P.M.	Jackson, Miss.	11 08 A.M.	Petersburg, Va.	11 50 A.M.
Augusta, Ga.	11 41 A.M.	Jefferson, Mo.	11 00 "	Philadelphia, Pa.	12 08 P.M.
Augusta, Me.	12 31 P.M.	Kingston, Can.	12 02 P.M.	Pittsburg, Pa.	11 48 A.M.
Baltimore, Md.	12 02 "	Knoxville, Tenn.	11 33 A.M.	Plattsburg, N. Y.	12 15 P.M.
Beaufort, S. C.	11 47 A.M.	Lancaster, Pa.	12 03 P.M.	Portland, Me.	12 23 "
Boston, Mass.	12 24 P.M.	Lexington, Ky.	11 31 A.M.	Portsmouth, N.H.	12 25 "
Bridgport, Ct.	12 16 "	Little Rock, Ark.	11 00 "	Providence, R. I.	12 23 "
Buffalo, N. Y.	11 53 A.M.	Louisville, Ky.	11 26 "	Quebec, Can.	12 23 "
Burlington, N. J.	12 09 P.M.	Lowell, Mass.	12 23 P.M.	Racine, Wis.	11 18 A.M.
Burlington, Vt.	12 16 "	Lynchburg, Va.	11 51 A.M.	Raleigh, N. C.	11 53 "
Canandaigua.	11 59 A.M.	Middletown, Ct.	12 18 P.M.	Richmond, Va.	11 58 "
Charleston, S. C.	11 49 "	Milledgeville, Ga.	11 35 A.M.	Rochester, N. Y.	11 57 "
Chicago, Ill.	11 18 "	Milwaukee, Wis.	11 17 "	St. Louis, Mo.	11 07 "
Cincinnati, O.	11 31 "	Mobile. Ala.	11 16 "	St. Paul, Min.	10 56 "
Columbia, S. C.	11 44 "	Montpelier, Vt.	12 18 P.M.	Sacramento, Cal.	9 02 "
Columbus, O.	11 36 "	Montreal, Can.	12 14 "	Salem, Mass.	12 26 P.M.
Concord, N. H.	12 23 P.M.	Nashville, Tenn.	11 21 A.M.	Savannah, Ga.	11 44 A.M.
Dayton, O	11 32 A.M.	Natchez, Miss.	11 03 "	Springfield, Mass.	12 18 P.M.
Detroit, Mich.	11 36 "	Newark, N. J.	12 11 P.M.	Tallahassee, Fla.	11 30 A.M.
Dover, Del.	12 06 P.M.	New Bedford,	12 25 "	Toronto, Can.	11 51 "
Dover, N. H.	12 37 "	Newburg, N. Y.	12 12 "	Trenton, N. J.	12 10 P.M.
Eastport, Me.	12 41 "	Newcastle, Del.	12 06 "	Troy, N. Y.	12 14 "
Frankfort, Ky.	11 30 A.M.	New Haven, Ct.	12 17 "	Tuscaloosa, Ala.	11 18 A.M.
Fredericksburg.	11 58 "	New Orleans, La.	11 08 A.M.	Utica, N. Y.	12 08 P.M.
Galveston, Texas.	10 49 "	Newport, R. I.	12 23 P.M.	Vincennes, Ind.	11 19 A.M.
Halifax, N. S.	12 54 P.M.	New York, N.Y.	12 12 "	Wheeling, Va.	11 45 "
Harrisburg, Pa.	12 01 "	Norfolk, Va.	12 03 "	Wilmington, Del.	12 06 P.M.
Hartford, Ct.	12 18 "	Northampton, Ms.	12 18 "	Wilmington, N. C.	11 56 A.M.
Huntsville, Ala.	11 21 A.M.	Norwich, Ct.	12 20 "	Worcester, Mass.	12 21 P.M.
Indianapolis, Ind.	11 26 "	Pensacola, Fla.	11 20 A.M.	York, Pa.	12 02 "

By an easy calculation, the difference in time between the several places abovenamed may be ascertained. Thus, for instance, the difference in time between New York and Cincinnati may be ascertained by simple comparison, that of the first having the Washington noon at 12 12 p. m., and of the latter at 11 31 a. m; and hence the difference is 41 minutes, or, in other words, the noon at New York will be 11 19 a. m. at Cincinnati, and the noon at Cincinnati, will be 12 41 at New York.

the speed possible with the steam locomotive, distances traveled could be greatly increased.

Originally railroads used the time of their home terminal headquarters as the standard time for the entire line. The New York Central used New York City time as the standard upon which the entire railroad operated; the Pennsylvania Railroad used Philadelphia. A disturbing factor was the position of the sun, because there would be a notable difference when the sun's position at noon in New York City was not the same as it was in Buffalo. Worse yet, local communities used noon at their location to set the local time, which could be very different from the time used by the railroad that served the community.

There was a clear need for a regular schedule of trains.

Timetables were at first prepared only for the trainmen; eventually there were public timetables. That did not end the problem of time. A city served by three railroads might find each carrier operating on a different time. As noted earlier, cities used sun time, generally the time when the sun was at its noon high point, to set their clocks. But the sun is not at its high point at the same instant as one moves east or west. The smaller cities in the region would usually adopt the same time as the major city, but that did not help as distance increased and what time it was became problematic.

The use of solar time caused difficulties. When it was 12 noon in Chicago, other cities showed a notable difference. In Pittsburgh it was 12:31, in Cleveland 12:24, in Cincinnati 12:13, in Louisville 12:09, and in Indianapolis

12:07. It was 11:41 in St. Paul, 11:48 in Dubuque, 11:50 in St. Louis, and 11:27 in Omaha. To illustrate the confusion in the 1870s, there were 27 local times in Michigan, 38 in Wisconsin, 27 in Illinois, and 23 in Indiana.

These variations confused passengers, shippers, and railroad employees and were potentially dangerous as railroads increasingly operated fast trains on tight schedules to make the most efficient use of costly rolling stock, locomotives, and fixed facilities. A standard time was clearly needed.

One of the first advocates of standard bands or zones of time was Professor C. F. Dowd, principal of the Temple Grove Seminary for Young Ladies at Saratoga Springs, New York. Dowd wrote to the officials of all the major U.S. railroad companies. He prepared and distributed pamphlets calling for four time belts running north and south across the continent. By 1873 he had received letters from a majority of the railroad executives he had contacted agreeing to the merit of his proposal.

In 1872 superintendents of many railroads met in St. Louis to arrange the passenger schedules for the summer. In the meeting the officials saw the need for cooperation and standards on a number of issues, including time, and they agreed to found a permanent organization. Over the years the organization had several names: Time-Table Convention, General Time Convention, American Railway Assn., and Assn. of American Railroads.

A key figure was William Frederick Allen. He had been the resident engineer for the Camden & Amboy Rail Road. Since 1872 he had been a staff member of *The Official Guide of the Railways and Steam Navigation Lines of the United States*. Allen was elected secretary of the First General Time Convention in 1876. Early in 1883 he submitted a plan to the convention, and it was adopted on October 11, 1883. It was to go into effect on November 18, 1883. There were five time zones in the proposal: Intercolonial (the Canadian Maritime Provinces), Eastern, Central, Mountain, and Pacific. The four time belts that affected the United States were based on the 75th, 100th, 105th, and 120th meridians west of Greenwich. Objections to the idea arose from some quarters, including ministers who felt that the time zones were an affront to God. Newspapers generally approved.

The railroads adopted Standard Time as scheduled on November 18, 1883. They laid out careful plans for the implementation, and the deed was done with few problems. Americans were obliged to adopt railroad time. The attorney general of the United States was displeased (probably because no one had consulted him or any other federal official) and issued an order that no federal department could adopt railroad time until it was authorized by Congress.

It took more than a generation for Congress to act; it was not until March 19, 1918, that the Standard Time Act was passed. The Interstate Commerce Commission was empowered by the act to order the precise boundaries of each time zone and to make changes as needed. After its creation, the Department of Transportation was given the power to make changes and adjustments in the time boundaries.

The standardization of time was conceived and implemented by private railroad companies without an initial role for the national government. It is a good example of an industry setting its own standards.

—George M. Smerk

REFERENCES

Frey, Robert L., ed. *Encyclopedia of American Business History and Biography: Railroads in the Nineteenth Century*. New York: Facts on File, 1988.

Holbrook, Stewart H. *The Story of American Railroads*. Chap. 21. New York: Crown, 1947.

Stanford, Leland (1824–1893)

Leland Stanford was born on March 9, 1824 in Watervliet, New York, the fourth son in a prosperous farm family. He studied law, passed the New York bar, and practiced law first in Albany, New York, and then in Wisconsin. In 1852 he and his new wife moved to California, where Leland joined his three merchant brothers in Sacramento. He soon tried his hand at politics, serving as a justice of the peace and then running unsuccessfully for governor. In 1861 he was again a candidate for governor. The outbreak of the Civil War had split the Democratic Party, and this time he was victorious, serving a two-year term in 1862–1863.

Stanford's political success, such as it was, was due to his personal popularity and to his strong Union and Re-

Leland Stanford. —Library of Congress (Neg. LC-USZ62-34945)

publican convictions; he had not distinguished himself in public service. It can be claimed, however, that his election kept the state in the Union. He was not renominated and held no other public office until 1885, when he arranged for the California legislature to appoint him to the U.S. Senate. Here, as one biographer puts it, he served without distinction but with pleasure until his death.

Stanford's political activities and mercantile career brought him into contact with fellow merchants Collis P. Huntington, Charles Crocker, and Mark Hopkins. He joined with them and engineer Theodore Judah in forming the Central Pacific Railroad in 1861 and served as its president until his death. The actual leader of the Big Four, Collis Huntington, allowed Stanford nominal leadership because of his own preference for obscurity. Stanford was Huntington's equal in ruthlessness and craving for power, but lacked his cunning.

As president of the Central Pacific, Stanford's duties were largely ceremonial. Huntington once remarked that Stanford's share in building the railroad consisted of turning the first shovelful of earth and driving the last spike. Stanford, however, was always convinced that his popularity and political influence were responsible for the success of the enterprise.

The ceremony commemorating the completion of the first transcontinental railroad took place at Promontory Point, Utah, on May 10, 1869. As the nation waited breathlessly for news by telegraph of the completion of the great work, the two locomotives approached the site from west and east, respectively. The tracklaying was completed, and the two final spikes were hammered in by Leland Stanford and Thomas Durant of the Union Pacific. "California Annexes the United States," read a San Francisco newspaper headline when the news reached the West Coast.

In 1870 the Big Four incorporated the Southern Pacific Railroad to build in Southern California and eventually to reach New Orleans. Fourteen years later a holding company, the Southern Pacific Co., merged the Southern Pacific Railroad, Central Pacific, and others into one combine. Stanford was president of the combine from 1885 to 1890, when Collis Huntington, fed up with Stanford's profligacy and particularly with his ascension to a Senate seat that had belonged to Huntington's friend Aaron Sargent, took his place as president and essentially cut off his funds.

In lifestyle Stanford was by far the most ostentatious of the Big Four. He retained the title of governor long after his two-year term in office. His Nob Hill home was palatial. At his ranch near Palo Alto he raised thoroughbred horses on a vast scale and later embarked on a project to create what he hoped would be the world's largest and finest vineyard on 55,000 acres of land in Vina, north of Sacramento. In 1884 the death of their 15-year-old son prompted the Stanfords to found and endow Stanford University in his memory. Leland Stanford died on June 20, 1893, in Palo Alto, California.

—Roberta L. Diehl

REFERENCES

Bain, David Haward. *Empire Express: Building the First Transcontinental Railroad.* New York: Viking, 1999.

Dictionary of American Biography.

Dictionary of National Biography.

Lewis, Oscar. *The Big Four.* New York: Alfred A. Knopf, 1938.

Steam Locomotives

The primary method of propulsion for world railways until the end of World War II was the steam locomotive, a product of the Industrial Revolution that began in England during the early part of the eighteenth century when machines were first designed and constructed to replace the physical effort of men and animals. The most significant machine of the Industrial Revolution was the stationary steam engine, which soon found numerous applications in transportation propulsion. Although the English pioneers of machine design and production were led by their experience and intuition, this field of technology came to be known as mechanical engineering.

Steam locomotives were imported to the United States from English builders beginning in 1829 and quickly became the patterns from which American machinists and mechanics constructed their own devices. Soon it became clear that because of the longer distances and more primitive roadbeds of American railways, their locomotives must be much larger and more robust than those of their British cousins, which were also constrained in height by existing bridges and tunnels. In these early years, however, there was no standard gauge for track in America, and thus early railways along the East Coast were constructed in a variety of widths, ranging from 3 to 5 feet, although the English standard (56.5 inches) was dominant.

Components of a Locomotive

In its simplest form a steam locomotive (ca. 1920) consists of a cylindrical boiler mounted atop a set of wheels of various sizes. The purpose of the boiler is to generate steam while the wheels support the weight, but, more important, to convert the energy of steam into rotation of large driving wheels (or *drivers*). At the rear of the boiler, its end enclosed by the crew cab, is the *firebox* (or *furnace*), in which a fuel is burned to produce hot gas. The boiler itself contains many small tubes through which the hot combustion gas flows, and around which there is water. Hot gas inside each passage heats each steel tube and creates small bubbles of water vapor. Eventually the vapor, being highly buoyant, rises to the *steam dome*, the highest point in the boiler. The steam is now ready to pass through the throttle mechanism into the conversion component of the locomotive.

Meanwhile, after heating the water, the combustion

gases exhaust from the tubes into a chamber at the front of the boiler (smokebox) and, merging with the exhaust steam from the power cylinders, escape through the stack into the atmosphere. The escaping exhaust steam also creates a strong draft that pulls the hot gas from the firebox through the boiler tubes. A large housing on top of the boiler is the *sand dome*. Pipes running downward from this container allow sand to be sprayed onto the rails in front of the drivers. The dusting of sand increases friction on the drivers and prevents them from slipping when the rail is wet or the locomotive is pulling up a steep grade. Above the firebox are safety valves (*pop valves*) that will open if the boiler pressure rises to an unsafe level. Elsewhere atop the boiler is a steam-driven electric generator that supplies power for lights and other needs.

Below each side of the smokebox is a power cylinder containing a large piston that is driven by high-pressure steam from the boiler. The piston produces a reciprocating motion that must be converted into rotating motion of the drivers. This is accomplished by connecting the piston rod to a *crankpin* on the driver by means of the main driving rod (or *main rod*). The crankpins are located slightly off-center so that the reciprocating piston causes the driver to rotate. The front end of the main rod is connected to the piston rod by the *crosshead*. The main driver transmits force to the other drivers through *side rods*.

Controlling the flow of steam into and away from each cylinder is a reciprocating valve located in the upper portion of the power-cylinder housing. The valve motion is modulated by a complicated set of mechanical links known collectively as the *valve gear*. The function of this linkage, normally located outside the drivers, is to control the timing of steam admission into the power cylinder at the beginning of a stroke, as well as its exhaust at the end of the stroke.

Although not apparent when observing a steam locomotive during operation, it is necessary that strokes of the power pistons on each side of the locomotive *not* be synchronized. Thus, when one piston is at the end of its stroke, the other is in midstroke. This requires that the drivers on one side be out of phase from those on the opposite side by 90 degrees (one-quarter rotation). If the strokes were simultaneous, there would be no force to move the drivers in the proper direction at the beginning or end of each stroke. These alternating piston strokes impart a significant (and periodic) sideways oscillation to the engine as it moves.

One of the most important visual features of a steam locomotive is the *wheel arrangement* that largely determines its primary usage. Traditionally, passenger locomotives had large-diameter drivers that suited high-speed operation. In contrast, engines used in main-line freight or yard switching service generally rode on small-diameter drivers that produced more pulling force, but at a slower speed than larger ones.

The number of drivers and supporting wheels was also a function of the locomotive's usage. A set of small wheels in front of (or below) the power cylinders was known as the *leading truck*, whereas those behind the drivers formed the *trailing truck*. In addition to carrying a portion of the engine weight, leading trucks also served to steer the engine around curves at speed. Yard switchers generally had no other support wheels in order to maximize the weight over the drivers and hence the engine's pulling power. Each driving wheel contains *counterweights* to balance the rotating forces produced by side-rod connections on the opposite side of the driver. For the main driver the counterweight must be larger than on the other drivers since it must counterbalance not only the side-rod but also the main-rod connection.

Although there is a labyrinth of piping surrounding the boiler, it is generally unseen because of a layer of insulation (originally wood, later asbestos) covered by a sheet-metal jacket. However, the jacket usually did not cover the lower part of the firebox, where one could observe some of the large rivets and staybolts that hold the firebox together and connect it to the boiler shell.

Another important feature of a steam locomotive was the trailing car (the *tender*) that carried water and fuel. Coal (or oil) was carried in a bunker adjacent to the cab, while water was in the lower and rearward section. Most tenders rode on a pair of four-wheel trucks; larger ones used six-wheel trucks. Some tender designs incorporated a cylindrical tank for water, but the standard configuration was a rectangular "box" design. Switchers were often fitted with sloped-back water tanks for better rearward visibility during switching duties.

Wheel Arrangements

During the first decades of steam locomotion in the mid-1800s, each model of engine was given an individual name, usually to honor some prominent person. Later a group of similar or identical locomotives were given a "class" designation, either by name or by the number of the first engine of that class. Eventually it was realized that the overall performance of a steam locomotive was determined largely by the arrangement of its supporting wheels. Consequently, various types of codes were developed to describe the three groups of wheels mentioned in the previous section. Numerical or alphabetical codes became the most common, and the one devised in 1901 by Frederic Methvane Whyte became the British and American standard. In Europe it was customary to count axles, while the Whyte system counted the number of wheels. The first number of the code identified those wheels in front of the driving wheels; the second was for drivers themselves; and the third number accounted for the wheels behind the drivers. This three-number code became the most useful way of identifying locomotives.

Switching locomotives with no supplementary wheels ranged in size from 0-4-0 to 0-10-0. Freight engines generally carried two leading wheels, while passenger power included four such wheels. Early locomotive designs carried no support wheels behind the drivers, but as engine

Table 1. Summary of Wheel Arrangements

Rigid Frame		
OOO	0-6-0	Six-wheeled switcher
OOOO	0-8-0	Eight-wheeled switcher
o OOO	2-6-0	Mogul
o OOO o	2-6-2	Prairie
o OOOO	2-8-0	Consolidation
o OOOO o	2-8-2	Mikado
o OOOO oo	2-8-4	Berkshire
o OOOOO	2-10-0	Decapod
o OOOOO o	2-10-2	Santa Fe
o OOOOO oo	2-10-4	Texas
oo OO	4-4-0	American
oo OO o	4-4-2	Atlantic
oo OOO	4-6-0	Ten Wheeler
oo OOO o	4-6-2	Pacific
oo OOO oo	4-6-4	Hudson
oo OOOO	4-8-0	Mastodon (12-wheeler)
oo OOOO o	4-8-2	Mountain
oo OOOO oo	4-8-4	Northern
oo OOOOO o	4-10-2	Southern Pacific (compound)
oo OOOOOO o	4-12-2	Union Pacific (compound)

Duplex (Two Sets of Power Cylinders on Rigid Frame)		
oo OO OO oo	4-4-4-4	
oo OO OOO oo	4-4-6-4	
oo OOO OO oo	4-6-4-4	

Articulated Frame		
o OOO OOO o	2-6-6-2	
o OOO OOO oo	2-6-6-4	
o OOO OOO ooo	2-6-6-6	Allegheny
o OOOO OOOO o	2-8-8-2	
o OOOO OOOO oo	2-8-8-4	Yellowstone
o OOOO OOOO OOOO oo	2-8-8-8-4	Triplex
oo OOO OOO oo	4-6-6-4	Challenger
oo OOOO OOOO oo	4-8-8-4	Big Boy

Note: O indicates a driving wheel; o indicates a non-driving wheel.

power increased, the number of trailing wheels increased from two to four in order to support a larger and heavier firebox. Table 1 lists many of the most widely used wheel arrangements and their commonly unofficial names.

As the need arose for more pulling power, locomotive designers added more drivers until the length of the main frame was too large for the curvature of the rails. Thus it became necessary to articulate the frame and employ two separate sets of cylinders and drivers. The corresponding wheel arrangements for these locomotives included four numbers. The first articulated engines in America were large, slow pusher engines with the 0-6-6-0 wheel arrangement, while one of the largest locomotives ever built was a 4-8-8-4. Although attempts were made in the early part of the twentieth century to build locomotives with three sets of drivers, this configuration proved to be impractical at the time and was never duplicated.

English Origins

Credit for perfecting the stationary steam engine is given to James Watt, a Scotsman trained at Glasgow and London as a mathematical instrument maker. With his scientific background, he eschewed the purely empirical approach used in developing previous engines and began a series of experiments to determine the properties of steam, as well as the amount of energy required to evaporate water. These studies led to many inventions and patents related to stationary engines. For over 27 years he was a partner in Boulton & Watt, one of England's largest steam-engine-manufacturing firms, which by 1800 had constructed over 500 engines. After his death in 1819 at age 83, a statue at Westminster Abbey memorialized him as "the father of the steam engine."

During the last decade of the eighteenth century there was much interest in using a steam engine to replace horses as the power source on existing tramways and railways. Richard Trevithick, an engine mechanic who had developed stationary engines with high boiler pressures and later worked for Boulton & Watt, became the leading proponent of using steam power for propulsion. In 1804 he constructed the first steam locomotive to pull a group of freight cars on a track, a 5-ton engine with four 56-inch, rod-connected drivers below a horizontal boiler, which was 6 feet in length and contained one U-shaped flue. Power was transmitted to the drivers by a series of gears; a large flywheel stored rotary momentum of the mechanism.

Although its 10-ton pulling power was satisfactory, the engine could not be used extensively because its weight caused widespread destruction of the cast-iron plates on which it ran. However, Trevithick's attempts, along with those of other locomotive developers, provided a platform for the eventual success of George Stephenson, another practical man with no formal education, but with great instincts as a mechanical designer and later as a businessman. As an enginewright with a large coal company, he became interested in designing better locomotives for mine service. Starting in 1814, he soon completed 16 locomotives for various coal mines owned by his employer. George's son Robert Stephenson also exhibited a keen talent for technical work and was a worthy partner and successor. In 1825 the two opened Robert Stephenson & Co. for the sole purpose of building steam locomotives, the first such company to exist.

Robert's recognition as a leading designer and builder was spotlighted in a competition sponsored by the Liverpool & Manchester Railway in 1829. His *Rocket* design was by far the most successful locomotive tested. With a horizontal 3-foot-diameter boiler running at 50 pounds per square inch (psi), the engine had but one set of drivers (about 4 feet in diameter) plus a pair of trailing wheels. Although it weighed less than 5 tons, it pulled 38 carriages (90 tons weight) at speeds of 12 to 16 mph and, without a load, could sprint as fast as 28 mph, which was a new land speed record.

Steam Locomotion Crosses the Atlantic

The first three locomotives to come to the United States were bought by Horatio Allen, a prominent New

York engineer, for the Delaware & Hudson Canal Co. These were constructed by Foster, Rastrick & Co. of Stourbridge, England in 1828, with the first engine arriving in New York harbor in May 1829. Shipped by canal to Honesdale, Pennsylvania, the *Stourbridge Lion* was handled on its initial run by Allen himself, thus becoming the first steam locomotive to operate over an American railroad. Unfortunately, the engine's 7-ton weight proved to be too large for the track and trestles on the line, and it was relegated to stationary power service.

The arrival of English locomotives also spurred a number of other American entrepreneurs into action. The first was Peter Cooper, a wealthy New York manufacturer and alderman who in 1829 built a 1-ton, 1-horsepower locomotive (*Tom Thumb*) to demonstrate the capabilities of steam power to the board of directors of the Baltimore & Ohio Railroad. It consisted of a vertical boiler mounted on a four-wheel car with a gear drive powering one axle. Its single cylinder was 3.5 inches in diameter with a piston stroke of 14 inches. On August 28, 1830, it pulled a carriage of passengers over B&O tracks, the first steam-powered passenger train on an American railroad.

Less than a year after *Tom Thumb*'s performance the South Carolina Railroad began regular service with a four-wheeled locomotive (*Best Friend of Charleston*) designed by E. L. Miller of Charleston and constructed by the West Point Foundry of New York City. This company also constructed the third and fourth American steam locomotives. The *West Point* was designed by Horatio Allen

and built in 1830 for the South Carolina Railroad, and the *De Witt Clinton* was delivered to the Mohawk & Hudson River Railroad in 1831.

Among the first generation of locomotive builders was Matthias William Baldwin, a former watchmaker turned machinist who had some experience in building stationary steam engines. Although he had constructed a small steam locomotive and carriages for public demonstration at the Philadelphia Museum in 1831, his first revenue machine was built a year later for the Philadelphia, Germantown & Norristown Railroad (later part of the Philadelphia & Reading Railway). It was a four-wheeled engine carrying a 30-inch-diameter, horizontal boiler containing 72 copper tubes (1.5 inches in diameter). In appearance his 5-ton *Old Ironsides* was similar to Robert Stephenson's *Planet* of 1830, with 54-inch driving wheels and 45-inch front wheels. Cylinders were 9.5 inches in diameter, and the piston stroke was 19 inches. His next engine, named *E. L. Miller,* was a 7-ton 4-2-0 using the four-wheeled lead truck originated by John B. Jervis. Its performance was much improved over Baldwin's initial design and prepared the way for his lifelong devotion to the steam locomotive business that later bore his name. Indeed, the quality of workmanship on Baldwin's initial machines quickly propelled his company into the leading position among builders, its prominence demonstrated by the production of 136 engines during the eight years after construction of *Old Ironsides.*

Although later English and European designs were gen-

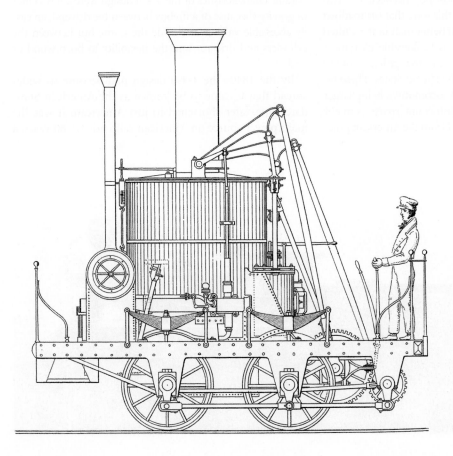

The earliest road locomotives of the Baltimore & Ohio were these unusual four-wheel engines with vertical boilers called Grasshoppers. The name apparently came from the engine's vertical cylinders and rods. The vertical boiler was quickly changed to a horizontal design. This drawing dates to 1838. —David Stevenson, *Civil Engineering in North America* (1838)

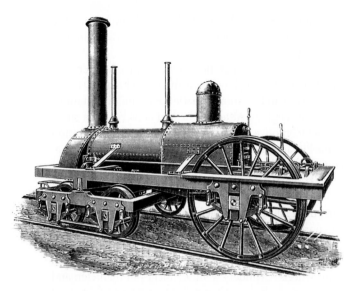

In 1832 John B. Jervis, chief engineer of the Mohawk & Hudson Railroad, designed the six-wheel *Experiment,* which used a four-wheel guiding truck and two driving wheels. Built by the West Point Foundry at New York City, the 7-ton locomotive served for many years. Renamed the *Brother Jonathan,* it was later converted to an eight-wheel locomotive. —James Dredge, *A Record of the Transportation Exhibits at the World's Columbian Exposition of 1893*

erally direct descendants of the early machines, the emergence of American builders highlighted significant differences in locomotive design philosophy between the two groups. The primary reasons for this were that (*a*) roadbed quality in Great Britain was much better than in the United States during these early times, (*b*) allowable clearances were much less in England, and (*c*) the average length of rail lines was many times greater in the United States. These requirements resulted in American locomotives being larger and more rugged than their English counterparts. A major difference in appearance stemmed from the American prac-

tice of mounting large headlights and "cowcatcher" frames (known more properly as *pilots*) on the fronts of locomotives. Mechanically, many early English engines employed cylinders and valve gear situated inside the main frame. This arrangement was seldom used in American locomotives after 1900. Fireboxes on many early steamers used the Bury design, a vertical cylinder with a rounded top (often called a beehive firebox).

Design Evolution before 1900

The foregoing types of motive power were soon shown to be inadequate for the rapidly growing American railroad industry. A breakthrough occurred in 1836 when Henry Campbell of Philadelphia patented a 4-4-0 locomotive as a way to "distribute the weight over rails more completely." He contracted with a local shop to construct the first 4-4-0 in 1837. However, its performance was unsuccessful because its rigid axle mountings did not allow the eight wheels to conform to uneven track contours. Fortunately, by 1838 Joseph Harrison, Jr., another Philadelphia builder, had patented a weight-equalization method for locomotive wheels. It consisted of a series of interconnected, pivoted arms (*equalizer bars*) that allowed each driver to move up or down independently and thus stay in contact with undulating trackage. The resulting three-point suspension for the 4-4-0 included one point on each side between the two drivers and the third at the center of the leading truck. These equalizers gave the locomotive an unusually effective tracking ability. Other favorable characteristics of the 4-4-0 design were a low center of gravity (because of a firebox between the drivers), an easily accessible valve gear (inside the frame but between the cylinders and drivers), and the flexibility to burn wood or coal.

By the 1840s the 4-4-0 design had become so widespread that it came to be known as the American Standard type, later shortened to just American. It was the main power source on American railroads for 60 years, a

Before the end of the 1830s steam locomotive design had evolved into what was often called the American Standard 4-4-0 arrangement, with a four-wheel pilot truck and four driving wheels. The Schenectady Locomotive Works built No. 286 for the Grand Trunk Railway. —Middleton Collection

Locomotive builders often added additional driving wheels to handle heavier trains. Western & Atlantic Railroad No. 54, the *Acworth*, was a ten-wheeler, with a four-wheel lead truck and six driving wheels. —W. E. Mims Collection

period that included the Civil War and completion of the nation's first transcontinental rail route. Indeed, in a reversal of the 1830s period, this wheel arrangement was exported to Britain in the 1870s and became a standard for it, as well as for major European railway systems.

The next wheel arrangement to appear on American rails was the 4-6-0 Ten Wheeler, which was slightly more powerful than the American type while retaining the four-wheel leading truck. It was produced from 1847 until the 1920s. Ironically, the two-wheel leading truck turned out to be difficult to design so as to provide the proper guiding capability on curved track. By 1860, when these two-wheel designs were finally perfected to a stage where they could be applied to locomotives, both the 2-6-0 Mogul and the 2-8-0 Consolidation wheel arrangements were soon in use. The smaller Moguls were produced through 1910, while production of the more popular Consolidation types lasted until the mid-1920s. Both types were used mainly in freight service.

Although locomotive designers during the first generation of American production realized quickly the impor-

tance of leading trucks, there was little concern for trailing wheels to carry larger fireboxes. Most engines through the 1880s carried fireboxes tucked between the last two sets of drivers, and thus their width was limited to about 42 inches, with grate areas of approximately 17 square feet. However, by the turn of the century some locomotives included fireboxes that were raised above the drivers (especially the smaller drivers of freight engines), and thus their widths could be increased to 60 inches.

Although the top of the boiler shell and the crown sheet of the firebox inside the shell were usually cylindrical in shape, a different design was introduced by Alfred Jules Belpaire in 1860. It was characterized by longitudinal bulges on each side near the top, resulting in a flat upper surface. This unusual shape produced both increased structural integrity and a greater surface area for heat transfer. Unfortunately, because of the extra expense of fabricating this complex boiler shell, only two major railroads ever adopted the Belpaire furnace to any extent. The Pennsylvania was by far the most extensive user, with the Great Northern a close second.

Another popular design for heavy freight service was the Consolidation, with a two-wheel lead truck and eight driving wheels. The Chesapeake & Ohio's Consolidation No. 350, built by the Richmond (Virginia) Locomotive and Machine Works, was exhibited at the 1893 World's Columbian Exposition in Chicago. —James Dredge, *A Record of the Transportation Exhibits at the World's Columbian Exposition of 1893*

The use of anthracite coal required a larger firebox. These were often built with a separate forward cab location, often called a camelback or Mother Hubbard design. The fireman remained behind the firebox under a small shelter. Delaware & Hudson camelback 4-4-0 No. 237 was built by Danforth & Cook in 1866 and rebuilt by D&H in 1898. —Jim Shaughnessy Collection

Another exception to the usual design was the Wootten firebox, developed by Philadelphia & Reading general manager John E. Wootten in 1877 specifically to burn anthracite (hard) coal that was found principally in the Lackawanna Valley of northeastern Pennsylvania. Since the amount of heat liberated by hard coal was considerably less than that from the same amount of bituminous (soft) coal, the firebox grate (bottom surface) for burning anthracite needed to be much larger than for a conventional firebox. Thus Wootten furnaces were generally around 90 inches in width.

In most engines with Wootten fireboxes, the engineer's cab was moved to a position in front of the firebox, leaving the fireman in his usual location behind the firebox, laboring beneath a short canopy. The resulting locomotive configurations, known as camelbacks or Mother Hubbards, were built in a wide range of wheel arrangements during the 1890–1910 period, primarily for the Central Railroad of New Jersey, Delaware & Hudson, Delaware, Lackawanna & Western, Erie, Lehigh Valley, and Philadelphia & Reading.

Boiler Safety

There was a distinct downside to the rapid development of the steam engine, and that was the proliferation of poorly constructed boilers. Between 1870 and 1910 the nation experienced over 10,000 explosions, including some 1,400 in the year 1910 alone. After a lengthy study by the American Society of Mechanical Engineers, the ASME Boiler Codes of 1914–1915 gave the nation a set of legally accepted requirements for constructing and testing pressurized boilers. Among these rules was a safety factor of four between the operating pressure and the bursting pressure of the boiler. As a direct consequence of the boiler codes, random explosions (caused by poor construction) virtually disappeared.

To combat locomotive explosions, the Interstate Commerce Commission (ICC) instituted the first *Steam Locomotive Boiler Regulations* in 1911. Unfortunately, most early locomotive explosions were caused by crew error, generally by allowing boiler water levels to drop too low. The firebox

is virtually surrounded by water that prevents its structure from overheating. However, if the water level drops below the *crown sheet* (top) of the firebox, the internal structure is unprotected from the intense fire. Eventually the rear of the firebox would weaken and detach itself from the outer boiler shell. Once any small leak developed in the outer shell, high-pressure water inside would be exposed to atmospheric pressure and would instantly flash into steam, producing a lethal cloud of scalding vapor. These explosions usually caused the rear of the boiler to rise, tear loose from the frame, and project itself end over end to a point well in front of the locomotive. In many instances the locomotive chassis would not even derail during an explosion since all the energy was directed upward.

By 1920 various appliances were available to warn the crew of trouble and prevent an explosion. First, all engines were required to be equipped with two means of determining the water level, gauge cocks and sight glasses (often on both sides of the cab). Second, it became mandatory that there be two means of supplying water to the boiler. This could be either by two injector pumps or one injector and one feedwater pump (used with the feedwater heater). In addition, low-water alarms were patented that emitted a shrill whistle in the cab to warn of unsafe conditions. Another device was a "soft plug" made of brass surrounded by a soft metal alloy. If temperatures reached unsafe levels, a precursor of danger, the soft metal would melt, causing the brass plug to drop and creating a deliberate leak that would drown the fire with jets of water. Usually two or three of these plugs were placed along the top of the crown sheet. Because some explosions were the result of equipment failure, they continued to occur, although rarely, until the last decade of steam power use. The last boiler explosion on an American common carrier was on a compound articulated locomotive in December 1955 on the Norfolk & Western Railway west of Roanoke.

Machinery Details

One of the most complicated assemblies in a steam locomotive was the valve gear. This consisted of a set of in-

Valve-Gear Details

In primitive reciprocating steam locomotives, such as Stephenson's *Rocket*, a valve admits boiler steam into one end of a cylinder, the steam pressure pushes a piston to the other end, and then the steam exhausts at the instant the valve admits steam to the other side of the piston. Boiler steam flows into the cylinder throughout the piston stroke and exhausts while still at boiler pressure and temperature. This rudimentary valve operates out of phase with the piston rod—the valve is in midstroke when the piston is at one or the other end of the cylinder. Such operation discards most of the steam's heat energy up the stack, with low thermal efficiency.

Thermal energy of the steam can be more efficiently turned to mechanical work by using a valve that provides "cutoff" (sealing the steam in the cylinder for much of the piston stroke). This allows the steam pressure and temperature to drop as it pushes the piston. More heat energy is converted into mechanical energy, and both fuel and water are economized.

Much ingenuity was expended during the nineteenth century in devising valves that would operate in this fashion. Matthias Baldwin, for instance, early patented a two-valve system for each cylinder, with one valve controlling only cutoff. But the method that became standard on railroads involved giving the valve "lap," which means a broadening of its sliding surfaces so that they could overlap the cylinder's steam ports. A valve with lap, however, still cannot operate at the correct phase difference to the piston rod since it would be closed just when the cylinder needed an inlet or exhaust of steam. Rather, the valve motion must "lead" the piston rod. This is why the commonly used Stephenson valve gear has two "eccentrics," one providing proper lead for forward running and the other for reverse operation.

Vital to this and most other valve gears are the oscillating link and die blocks (sometimes replaced in gears such as Baker or Southern by lever arrangements that eliminate these costly, wear-prone components). When the die block is at the top or bottom of the link (full forward or full reverse), steam enters the cylinder throughout a large part of the piston stroke. This provides maximum force for starting or climbing steep grades but, as noted, wastes fuel and water. Therefore, as the train gains speed, the engineer reduces valve travel by moving the die block closer to the center of the link. This reduced travel provides earlier cutoff, admitting less steam but letting it expand more within the cylinder, converting more of its heat into work.

Thus the valve gear is not only a reversing mechanism, but actually the main power control of the locomotive. The throttle provides fine control, to keep the drivers from slipping at startup and the like, but is normally run wide open once the train gets up to speed. Most builders, when they decided to mount the valve gear on the outside of the locomotive, found Stephenson's two eccentrics somewhat bulky. They almost unanimously turned to valve gears that used a single cranklike eccentric (Walschaerts, Baker, and others). Since this crank is rigidly positioned at 90 degrees to the drive pin, another means of obtaining lead was needed. Most configurations, in essence, combine the eccentric crank motion with a small component of motion from the crosshead via the combination link (or combining lever). The resulting valve motion is very similar to that produced by the Stephenson mechanism, although each system had its partisans. As noted in the main text, there was also a widespread change around this time from the D-valve to the piston valve. This also involved changing from so-called outside admission to inside admission, requiring slight rearrangement of the valve linkage.

Locomotives with three cylinders (apart from Shays) sometimes employed Gresley conjugated gear, which used a lever system for a third valve whose motion was modulated by the other two. Unless meticulously maintained, Gresley gear caused some inaccuracy in the movement of the third valve. Thus American builders often installed a third complete valve gear instead. The highest development of locomotive valving was, as the main text states, cam-operated poppet valves. These could be individually designed and adjusted to give nearly ideal steam control under the widest variety of conditions. —Dan LeMaire-Bauch

terconnected links that oscillated in a complex pattern so as to modulate a valve that admitted steam into the power cylinder and exhausted it at the proper intervals during the revolution of the drivers. Mechanics often referred to this linkage as "monkey motion" because of its gyrations.

There were six major designs for reciprocating valve gear employed on American locomotives. The Stephenson configuration came to America in 1850 and was widely used until around 1900. A later variation, the Joy design, saw little application. In both of these configurations the links were attached to the main driver axle inside the locomotive main frame, and thus, when repairs or adjustments were needed, workers usually gained access from beneath the locomotive. Eventually this proved to be incompatible with American shop practice, and all later valve gears were attached to the outside of the driving gear.

By far the most popular valve gears were the Walschaerts and Baker designs. Belgian inventor Egide Walschaerts (1820–1901) patented his design in France in 1844. It was brought to America in 1876, but at first found little acceptance. However, between 1900 and 1905 it saw a resurgence in use and remained quite popular until the end of the steam era. The ad-

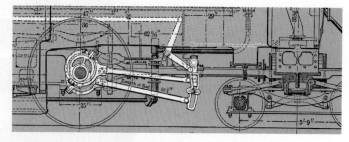

Stephenson valve gear. —© Dan LeMaire-Bauch

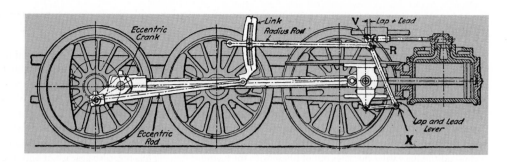

Walschaerts valve gear.
—© Dan LeMaire-Bauch

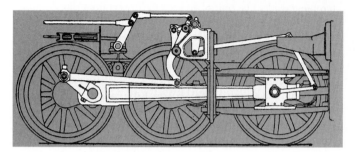

Baker valve gear. —© Dan LeMaire-Bauch

vanced Baker gear was introduced around 1912 and had the unique advantage of avoiding sliding contacts, using only rotating elements connected with pins and bushings. Two other designs, Southern (1917) and Young (1920), were either too expensive or not sufficiently robust to be employed widely.

Along with the refinements in valve gears was an evolution of the valves themselves. Early locomotives used a *slide valve,* an inverted U-shaped block that slid back and forth across the intake and exhaust ports. The slide valve was also called a *D-valve* since its external appearance suggested this

shape. However, as boiler pressures increased, this design was less effective because of the difficulty in effecting a seal between two flat surfaces. Although an improved design was developed around 1866, the *spool valve* (or *piston valve*) did not come into widespread use until 1902. As its name implies, the sliding surface was cylindrical (similar to a power piston), but its cross-sectional contour was similar to a pair of slide valves placed back to back.

Although the outside valve gears differed in design details, they included common functional components. For example, all designs included an *eccentric crank* attached to the main crankpin. This transmitted the rotational position of the drivers to the other valve-gear elements. The *eccentric rod* connected its crank to a pivoting element (*reverse link*), while the *radius rod* connected the pivot point directly to the piston rod. Further modulation of the valve position was required, so a *crosshead link* and *combination link* were also needed.

In the beginning, control of the valve gear was effected via a long rod (*reach rod*) from the cab to the radius rod. This connection allowed the engineer to change direction of travel. He controlled the reach rod with a lever called the *Johnson bar.* When the bar was fixed in a forward po-

A steam locomotive photographed at Big Springs, Texas, in 1940 shows a close-up view of a Baker valve gear.
—Russell Lee photograph, Farm Security Administration, Library of Congress (LC-USF34-35824-D)

sition, the locomotive would move forward, while the opposite occurred if the bar was set in the rearward position. When the engine was operating at speed, it was common for the engineer to set the bar at an intermediate forward setting (called *cutoff*) that produced a shortened time of steam admission and thus allowed for more complete expansion in the cylinder. Usually a cutoff position of 70 to 90 percent of the full forward position was used for maximum performance.

For an emergency stop in the early days when brakes were either weak or nonexistent, many engineers would close the throttle and pull the Johnson bar backward so that steam paths in the valve chambers were reversed; thus the cylinders acted as a "steam brake." By 1913 an air-driven cylinder (*power reverse*) replaced the hand-operated Johnson bar.

Compound Steam Distribution

Parallel to the development of first-generation, single-expansion engines were two other design concepts of note, namely, the compound locomotive and an articulated main frame. Much credit for developing these to a practical level is given to the Swiss-born designer Anatole Mallet (rhymes with ballet), who in 1874 patented a compound locomotive and, 13 years later, built the first articulated engine. Steam distribution is commonly classified as either *simple* or *compound*. In the former design steam is expanded once in a single power cylinder and then exhausted, while in a compound design the steam is first passed through a high-pressure cylinder and then into a larger-diameter low-pressure cylinder before being exhausted. The increased size is required to compensate for the lower average pressure.

The main advantage of any compound design is that it provides more power during the low-pressure portion of the steam expansion between boiler and atmospheric pressures. However, as with any other such improvements, there was a price to pay in the added mechanical complexity, both initially and in maintenance. The general adoption of superheated steam by 1915 diminished the need to extract this additional power in a rigid-frame engine.

When the compound concept came to America in the 1880s, it was directed first toward improving rigid-frame (first-generation) engines. However, this proposal provoked a heated debate among railroad mechanical departments. Some saw significant economic advantages for engines that used steam twice, while others said that the added mechanical complexity was not worth the fuel savings. The Baldwin Locomotive Works came down on the pro side and, using its considerable industrial prowess, promoted and produced these designs for nearly four decades.

Four configurations for compound, rigid-frame locomotives were used on American locomotives. The simplest was Mallet's original design, called a *cross compound*, which carried a high-pressure cylinder on one side and a larger (by 2.5 times) cylinder on the other side that was powered by the exhaust steam. The next design was developed by Samuel M. Vauclain of the Baldwin Works. In 1883 he patented a four-cylinder configuration in which both low- and high-pressure cylinders were located on each side, one above the other. In most cases the smaller-diameter chamber was placed above the low-pressure one. The two piston rods were attached to a common crosshead that was connected to the main driving rod. For an engine with a small driver diameter (less ground clearance), it was necessary to place the smaller cylinder in the lower position. The first Vauclain compound was a 4-4-0 delivered to the B&O in October 1889.

In 1902 the Baldwin Works celebrated its 70th anniversary as Vauclain unveiled his new *balanced compound* design embodied in a 4-6-0, the 20,000th locomotive number to be produced by this company. The word "balanced" referred to the arrangement of the four piston strokes. The two high-pressure cylinders were inside the frame and drove the first axle, which was built with two "cranks" (similar to an automobile crankshaft). The two low-pressure, outside cylinders drove crankpins on the first drivers in the usual manner (with outside crankpins out of phase by 90 degrees). But, in addition, the strokes from the inside pistons were out of phase by 180 degrees from those on the outside of the same drivers. The result of this mechanical timing was that virtually all the rotational forces on the drivers were balanced out. Thus the driving-wheel counterweights could be very small, and there was almost no pounding of the rails.

The final type of rigid-frame dual-expansion engine was the *tandem compound*. In this design both the low- and high-pressure cylinders were on the outside of the frame and were placed one behind the other. This arrangement had the advantage of producing more power with much simpler mechanisms (and thus lower maintenance costs). Although the Brooks Works produced the first workable model on a 2-8-0 for the Great Northern in 1892, it was left to the Santa Fe to push this design toward the mainstream. In the late 1890s the road's Topeka shops built a 4-6-0 express engine and several 2-8-0s for testing. These engines proved to be very efficient, and when the road turned to Baldwin for an entirely new type of locomotive, it specified tandems. Between 1903 and 1917 Baldwin turned out 160 such engines with the 2-10-2 wheel arrangement (Santa Fe type).

When the superheater was introduced around 1910, the additional complexity of compounds was no longer necessary. Thus simple engines could have compound economies without compound maintenance costs. Better yet, superheaters could easily be fitted onto existing engines. The result was that most rigid-frame compounds were soon scrapped or rebuilt as simple engines with superheaters.

Maturing of the Steam Locomotive

Early steam locomotive designs were the result of trial and error. Virtually none of the designers and builders had more than a rudimentary education; they succeeded because of their reasoning ability and their intuition. After the nation's colleges began producing engineers in 1830, there evolved a cadre of scientifically grounded mechanical engineers who were familiar with the fundamental scientific principles on which the steam locomotive was based.

The basic theoretical concept of the steam engine is that of a thermodynamic cycle in which a working fluid (liquid water) is boiled to produce steam (water vapor). The steam contains a high level of both thermal (temperature) and mechanical (pressure) energy. By passing this steam through a piston-cylinder configuration, the energy of the working fluid is converted into a force that can rotate the driving wheels.

Early research in the science of thermodynamics showed that the thermal efficiency of the steam-engine cycle (known as the Rankine cycle) was related to the input and output of energy by the following equation:

net work produced = total heat input × thermal efficiency

From this we see that the efficiency merely expresses the proportion of heat (entering the working fluid inside the boiler) that can be delivered as useful work by rotating the drivers. For a steam locomotive the thermal efficiency is a primary indicator of how much fuel must be burned to produce a given pulling force.

An important feature of steam, discovered in the late nineteenth century, was known as superheating. If a mass of liquid is fully vaporized, one obtains *saturated steam*. However, additional heating of this vapor produces *superheated steam*, which contains considerably more thermal energy at the same pressure. Thus the piston can produce much more thrust when fed by superheated steam, and the cycle efficiency will be increased. The second advantage of using superheated steam is the reduction of moisture inside the cylinder. Steam entering the cylinder expands to a lower temperature and pressure as the piston moves toward the end of a stroke. These changes can cause microscopic droplets of liquid water to condense on the cylinder walls, causing surface degradation that would damage the seal between the cylinder and piston. If the entering steam is superheated, there will much less moisture (and damage) than if the entering vapor is saturated.

During this same time the *feedwater heater* was developed to provide an additional increase in thermal efficiency. Its origin lay in the discovery that some of the *waste heat*, escaping in the hot exhaust gases, could be captured to preheat the water before it entered the boiler, thus reducing the heat needed from the firebox. The steam going into the cylinders would remain unchanged, and thus the work output would not decrease.

The evolutionary improvement in locomotive performance was manifested by increasing the number of drivers, and thereby the pulling force. Clearly each pair of additional drivers increased the frictional surface area in contact with the rails, and thus the ability of the locomotive to pull more. However, early builders found that the engine weight supported by the drivers should be about four times its tractive effort. This was known as the *factor of adhesion*. If its value dropped below four, designers found that the engine would slip easily, indicating insufficient friction between the drivers and the rail.

It is convenient to classify nineteenth-century locomotive designs as *first-generation* engines, characterized by small fireboxes and no trailing wheels. Eventually these designs proved to have a limit in the speed with which they could move trains. After starting, they could keep a train moving at a slow to moderate speed along a level main line, but they would slow or stall, because of an inadequate steam supply, upon encountering a grade or attempting to accelerate. This required a delay while steam pressure was rebuilt or necessitated a helper engine.

Not until the first decades of the twentieth century did the capability for scientific analysis progress to the point where engine performance could be characterized using one basic parameter known as *tractive effort* (more correctly, rated tractive effort). By determining the mechanical work done by the power pistons to move a locomotive through one rotation of its drivers, design engineers were able to obtain a simple formula that showed that the starting tractive effort was proportional to the boiler pressure and volume of the cylinders but inversely proportional to the driver diameter.

It is clear from this formula why driver diameters were quite different for freight and passenger locomotives. Freight locomotives, designed for heavy trains, needed smaller drivers than passenger engines, while the latter needed larger drivers for greater speed. Tractive effort is a computed parameter, and although it approximates the locomotive's starting drawbar pull, it is not identical. The actual force is always less than the rated tractive effort. However, the latter was always reported with other engine specifications and became the most convenient way to compare engine performance at low speed.

Early fireboxes were limited to the width of the locomotive main frame, but designers later realized that this was insufficient. It was learned in the 1910s that the most significant measures of firebox size are the grate area (bottom of the firebox) and the volume. The first parameter determines the surface covered by combustion, while a large volume allows the fire to be hotter and thus maximizes the amount of hot gas flowing through the boiler tubes and superheater flues. Moreover, the amount of water evaporated is related directly to the outside surface area of all boiler tubes (since that is where boiling occurs). This concept is more clearly illustrated by considering the work done by a unit mass of working fluid using equations for the Rankine cycle of thermodynamics. This computation yields the value of mechanical work done per pound (mass) of steam. Power produced by an actual locomotive is found by multiplying the cycle work times the pounds of steam produced by the boiler per unit of time (pounds per hour).

We thus conclude that even if the cycle efficiency is high, the power will be limited if the firebox is too small. It was this realization that led designers to consider locomotives with larger fireboxes supported by trailing trucks. Eventually these longer furnaces also produced a need for mechanical stokers to spray crushed coal into the firebox at much greater rates than any fireman was able to sustain.

Increasing the rate of steam production (steaming rate) by the boiler-firebox was the missing element that, once fully understood in the mid-1920s, produced the pinnacle of American steam locomotive development during the so-called Super-Power era. To understand this concept, we recall from physics that the drawbar (pulling) force produces mechanical work determined by multiplying force times distance. However, the rate of work done is defined as power and is commonly measured by horsepower. It is expressed dimensionally as force times distance divided by time. For a locomotive, it can be determined by multiplying drawbar force by the speed at which the force is generated.

There were a number of ways to characterize the power produced by a locomotive. Two of the most common methods involved direct measurement by dynamometers. The most scientific dynamometer test was conducted inside a stationary laboratory that allowed locomotive performance to be controlled much more closely than while pulling a train. Only three such facilities were ever constructed in the United States, at Purdue University in Indiana, at the University of Illinois, and in the Pennsylvania Railroad's Juniata shops at Altoona, Pennsylvania. Of these, only the latter facility was operated continuously until the end of the steam era. Stationary dynamometer tests yielded a value of the brake horsepower, the amount of power needed to propel the engine, tender, and train.

A more common type of test measured drawbar power with a dynamometer car located between the engine and its train. Such rolling measurement laboratories appeared around 1900 and carried a concentration of equipment for measuring almost two dozen performance variables on a continuous basis. The first dynamometer cars used the deflection of a large compression spring for determining drawbar force, while more modern designs employed a hydraulic system that required only a pressure measurement of the compressed fluid.

To determine drawbar horsepower, we must measure the variation of drawbar force as speed increases. A simple equation then determines drawbar horsepower by multiplying drawbar force (pounds) by speed (mph) and dividing by 375 (a conversion factor for dimensional consistency). Inside the dynamometer car this determination was carried out automatically and continuously, allowing test engineers to monitor the locomotive performance on a real-time basis. As soon as these testing procedures were perfected, it was found that drawbar force decreases as speed increases. Therefore, the product of these two values will always produce a maximum value. In general, freight locomotives generated maximum power at speeds between 30 and 40 mph, while passenger power usually peaked at 65 to 75 mph. The overall goal of designers during steam's final decades was to increase both the horsepower generated and the speed at which the peak horsepower occurred. The first parameter indicated how heavy the train could be, and the second determined how fast it could traverse the main line.

Steam's Second Generation

Considering only those engines used on American railroads, it is not surprising that the 4-4-0 type was the most common, with some 25,000 built, while the 2-8-0 was second at about 21,000. In contrast, the two most popular second-generation engines were the 2-8-2 Mikado (19,500) and the 4-6-2 Pacific (6,000). Clearly their popularity was a reflection of their versatility, for they had the tractive effort to start heavy trains and the steaming capacity (horsepower) to crest main-line grades at speed. Indeed, 2-8-2s could handle passenger trains if necessary, and a few roads used 4-6-2s in freight service on lines with flat profiles. Production numbers for other second-generation engines (4-4-2, 4-8-2, and 2-10-2) were almost the same, about 2,000 each.

The introduction of trailing wheels (attached rigidly to the frame) occurred in 1893 when Baldwin produced a 2-4-2 (Columbia type) for the World's Columbian Exposition in Chicago. Two years later the company delivered a batch of 4-4-2s to the Atlantic Coast Line (hence the name Atlantic). The first Atlantic type with an enlarged firebox and a movable trailing truck was delivered by American Locomotive Co. (Alco) in 1900 to the Chicago & North Western.

Most Atlantic types were produced during the 1900–1906 period and demonstrated clearly the importance of steaming rate to sustaining high speeds on the main line, but eventually long strings of all-steel passenger cars overwhelmed their pulling capability. The zenith of this configuration occurred three decades after its introduction when the Milwaukee Road bought four streamlined, shovel-nosed models for Hiawatha service between Chicago and the Twin Cities. Built by Alco during 1935–1937 with contemporary technology, these oil-burning Hiawatha types had ample grate areas, a 300 psi boiler pressure, and 84-inch drivers. They routinely met or bettered a schedule that called for short sprints of 102 mph with a train of 6 to 9 lightweight cars.

The first decade of the twentieth century saw production begin on three other second-generation machines. The next evolutionary link appeared in 1902 when Missouri Pacific began receiving an order of 4-6-2s from the Brooks Works. This was followed closely by deliveries to the Chesapeake & Ohio (1902) and Santa Fe (1903). During the following two years Pacific-type engines also went to ten other lines from coast to coast. Indeed, an ICC census in 1911 showed that 2,240 Pacifics were in operation, compared with just 670 Mikados.

The 2-8-2 Mikado became one of the most widely used locomotives, mostly in freight service. Great Northern, for example, put almost 300 of them in service over a 20-year period, more than any other steam locomotive type. No. 3233 was an O-4 class 2-8-2 built by Baldwin in 1920. —Paul Eilenberger, Louis R. Saillard Collection

As we review the evolution of the American railroad system in the first three decades of the twentieth century, we see that this period paralleled the development of the Pacific as the premier passenger locomotive. For example, the 1911 census figures reveal that 80 percent of the 6,000 American-built Pacifics had been delivered before 1920, although production continued until 1930. Not surprising, then, is the pervasiveness of the 4-6-2's contributions to the nation's rail service. In terms of geography, it operated in every mainland state, and the named trains it headed formed a pantheon of early American luxury travel.

The next second-generation model to appear was not a beefed up 2-8-0 but a stretched 2-10-0. Santa Fe needed more horsepower for its challenging profiles in the Far West and in 1903 received from Baldwin the first of 250 engines with a 2-10-2 wheel arrangement. Naturally, they were called Santa Fe types. Only a year after these engines went into service, the first American 2-8-2s were deliv-

The 4-6-2 Pacific type was widely used for heavy, fast passenger service. Some 6,000 were built, and they long served as the Pennsylvania Railroad's principal passenger power, with a record ownership of almost 700 4-6-2s. One of the handsomest was the Baltimore & Ohio's class P7, one of 20 built by Baldwin in 1927. No. 5301, a modernized and streamlined P7d version of the class, headed the northbound Cincinnati-Detroit *Cincinnatian* at Dayton, Ohio, in 1955. —J. Parker Lamb

Late in the nineteenth century a new design added a two-wheel trailing truck to a 4-4-0 locomotive, permitting a greatly expanded firebox, and was usually combined with large drivers for high-speed passenger service. Atlantic Coast Line's 4-4-2 No. 163, built by Baldwin in 1895, was the first of the Atlantic class. —W. E. Mims Collection

ered to Northern Pacific. The name Mikado for the 2-8-2 wheel arrangement came about after Baldwin shipped a group of such machines to Japan in 1906. Even though these were not second-generation engines, the Japanese name stuck, although it was not particularly popular during World War II, when some roads began calling their 2-8-2s the MacArthur type.

The final model of second-generation, rigid-frame locomotives to appear was the 4-8-2 Mountain type, delivered to C&O by Alco in 1911. Their initial usage was for heavy passenger trains between Charlottesville and Clifton Forge, where they were able to replace double-headed Pacifics. On many roads the 4-8-2 was also used for high-speed freight service. Both Illinois Central and Frisco used their company shops to rebuild low-speed 2-10-2s into higher-horsepower 4-8-2s with 70-inch drivers, while the 50 engines of New York Central's L4 Class (known as Mohawks), built by Lima in 1942–1943 with 72-inch drivers, could take full advantage of the NYC's "water-level" profiles.

With steaming rates increasing because of larger fireboxes carried by trailing trucks, designers soon realized that there was sufficient power available at low speed to add a small booster engine to drive the trailing axle. This idea was conceived by New York Central's progressive mechanical department while attempting to enhance the starting tractive effort of the road's K-11 Pacifics. It devised a small, fully enclosed, two-cylinder steam engine that drove a pinion (small gear), which was connected via an intermediate gear (idler) to the trailing axle. As soon as the train speed reached 10 or 15 mph, the booster was cut off, the idler gear retracted, and the locomotive began operating in its usual mode. The additional starting tractive effort was usually between 10,000 and 15,000 pounds. These booster engines were used until the end of the steam era to assist high-speed locomotives in starting heavy trains.

Second-generation locomotives were at the epicenter of the nation's only attempt to create a government-controlled railway system. After America's entry into World War I, the U.S. Railroad Administration (USRA) organized a centralized program of review and improvement of the nation's freight-hauling ability, which was limited by the number of modern locomotives. The cornerstone of this program was a group of USRA locomotive designs that were agreed to, somewhat reluctantly, by representatives of the railroad mechanical departments.

The final menu from which individual roads could choose new locomotives included two switchers, four rigid-frame engines, and two compound articulateds. A total of 1,830 USRA engines were constructed by the three major builders between 1917 and 1919. These were spread among the wheel arrangements in this order: Mikado types, 46.9 percent; 6- and 8-wheeled switchers, 23.5 percent; Santa Fe types, 14.7 percent; 12- and 16-wheeled articulateds, 6 percent; Pacific types, 5.5 percent; and Mountain types, 3.4 percent. Although these engines were generally rugged and reliable, for many wealthy and progressive roads the second-generation designs were treated with some disdain as representing the status quo of locomotive technology. On the other hand, many lines that initially chafed under the revolutionary concept of "one size fits all" later duplicated and improved these designs once government control ended on March 1, 1920.

Articulated Configurations

Mallet's concept of a jointed main frame with two sets of drivers was married to the idea of compounding from the beginning. In this design the rear driving gear, attached rigidly to the boiler, included high-pressure power cylinders, while the pivoted front drivers, which moved on a sliding surface beneath the boiler, used exhaust steam and thus needed larger cylinders. The first American application of Mallet's design concept was an 0-6-6-0 built by Alco in 1904 for the B&O. Without leading or trailing trucks, these were powerful but slow-speed engines for hump-yard and pusher service. Within five years a slightly larger 0-8-8-0 design was built for both the B&O and the Erie railroads. The first mainline Mallets were 2-8-8-0s that were built until about 1915, at which time there were some 80 in service.

The first Mallet with a large firebox appeared in 1906 when Baldwin delivered a prototype 2-6-6-2 to the Great Northern. Its tractive effort was 59,500 pounds, and its job

The compound articulated locomotive was first tried in the United States by the B&O in 1904. The Norfolk & Western made further advances. Over more than 40 years the railroad built 227 of its Y-class 2-8-8-2 compound articulateds, culminating in its final 1952 Y6b version, a locomotive that could produce 5,600 drawbar horsepower at 25 mph. No. 2137 is a 1936–1940 version of the Y6 built in N&W shops. —Norfolk & Western, Middleton Collection

was to replace twin Consolidation types on Cascade grades and curves. GN's favorable response to its performance was reflected in the production models that featured a larger boiler diameter (from 7 feet to 8 feet), larger cylinders and grate area, and a 20 percent increase in tractive effort (to 71,600 pounds). Weighing in at some 355,000 pounds, these were the heaviest American locomotives built to that date.

The second production articulated compound was also a 2-6-6-2. In 1911 Alco produced 25 such engines for the Chesapeake & Ohio. In parallel to the GN, these engines were a replacement for double-headed 2-8-0s on the mountainous Hinton Division. By 1923 the road was operating 120 similar engines of five different designs. One of the significant features of these and most later Mallet compounds was that the engineer could start his train with the engine operating in a "simple" mode (i.e., high-pressure steam to all cylinders). Once he was moving, the engineer closed a diverter valve and allowed the locomotive to revert to compound operation. Virtually all articulated locomotives of this early period were "drag engines," used mainly in slow-speed service as pushers or helpers. Their usual role was to provide tractive effort in hilly terrain, not to speed along on the flat profiles. Eventually over 3,000 articulateds were built in the United States, the majority of which were Mallet compounds.

During the 1910s there were attempts to push the Mallet articulated to new limits of power. By far the most audacious approach came in 1913 when the Erie Railroad mechanical department decided to order a triplex compound from Baldwin. The idea was to put a "tractor engine" beneath the tender of a 2-8-8-0 to produce a 2-8-8-8-4 wheel arrangement containing six cylinders of identical size. In operation, each of the high-pressure, center cylinders exhausted to a pair of the low-pressure cylinders. Exhaust from the third set of drivers exited from an exhaust stack at the rear of the tender.

In its first test the prototype, named *Matt Shay*, lugged a 250-car train (17,900 tons and 1.6 miles long) up a slight grade (0.09 percent) and around a 5-degree curve. But soon it became clear that this mammoth machine, with its impressive 160,000-pound starting tractive effort, had such a low steaming rate that it could not attain a speed of more than 10 to 15 mph, and even that would not last very long. Despite its shortcomings, Erie received two more triplexes in 1916, assigning the three to pusher service around Susquehanna. Triplexes for the Virginian Railway met a similar fate. With our present understanding, we can see clearly why such experimental articulated engines had virtually no chance of succeeding. Neither their total evaporative surface nor the firebox volume could produce the necessary steam-generation rate demanded by the six power cylinders.

The Pinnacle of American Steam

Somewhat surprisingly, the intuition and design concepts needed for American locomotives to reach their pinnacle came from neither of the nation's two largest builders, but from the smallest and youngest, Lima Locomotive Works. This company had been reorganized in 1915 and soon brought in a new design group composed of leading engineers from other builders, especially Alco. Led by a forward thinker named William Woodard, the Lima engineering staff began serious work during World War I on the future of the American steam locomotive. An overview report by Lima in May 1921 exposed Woodard's conclusion that engines had reached their physical limitations because of clearances and weight restrictions, and that only internal changes such as large and efficient fireboxes, and appliances such as superheaters and feedwater heaters, represented possible improvements.

Eventually Lima put forth some successful proposals to the New York Central, which in the early 1920s was focusing its efforts toward improvements to the road's two workhorses, the H-7 Mikados and L-1 Mohawks (4-8-2). Soon NYC asked the Ohio company to take the lead in re-working the smaller of the two engines. Construction of the improved 2-8-2, designated the H-10 class, began in late 1921, and it left the plant in early 1922 as Michigan Central No. 8000. Since one of Woodard's goals was to demonstrate how the main-line performance of an existing locomotive could be enhanced, the H-10's starting tractive effort was only slightly larger than that of the H-7. However, on the main line No. 8000 was able to haul more using less fuel. In one impressive test the H-10 pulled an unusually long train consisting of 138 cars (9,254 tons) between Detroit and Toledo. Its measured drawbar horsepower was as much as 35 percent greater than that of the H-7, and its boiler efficiency was far superior to any previously attained on a locomotive. The NYC motive-power people were ecstatic, calling the 8000 a "wonder engine," and, after only six weeks of testing, ordered 75 duplicates plus the prototype itself.

Once the H-10 was completed, Lima turned its attention to building a new high-horsepower locomotive from the ground up. Using the H-10 as a starting point, it added an even larger firebox that was supported for the first time on a four-wheel trailing truck. When completed in January 1925, the new engine, numbered 1 and classed as A-1, was lettered for NYC's Boston & Albany Railroad, which operated a line across the Berkshire Mountains of western New England.

Lima Order 1070   Placed 7/29/24   Rd. No. 1   C/n 6883   Cost: $ 72,350   Shipped: Feb 14, 1925
First 2-8-4 "Berkshire" type locomotive built and first "Super Power" locomotive incorporating design improvements.

LIMA LOCOMOTIVE WORKS, INCORPORATED
LIMA, OHIO

Class: 284—S—385

Road No. 1

Built for LIMA LOCOMOTIVE WORKS, Incorporated

GAUGE OF TRACK	DRIVING WHEEL DIAMETER	FUEL KIND	CYLINDERS		BOILER		FIREBOX	
			DIAMETER	STROKE	DIAMETER	PRESSURE	LENGTH	WIDTH
4'-8½''	63''	SOFT COAL	28''	30''	88''	240 LBS.	150⅛''	96¼''

WHEEL BASE			TRACTIVE POWER		FACTOR OF ADHESION	TUBES & FLUES		
DRIVING	ENGINE	ENGINE AND TENDER	MAIN CYLINDERS	WITH BOOSTER		NUMBER	DIAMETER	LENGTH
16'-6''	41'-8''	82'-6''	69400 LBS. AT 60% CUT-OFF	82600	3.58	90 204	2¼'' 3½''	20'-0''

AVERAGE WEIGHT IN WORKING ORDER, POUNDS				GRATE AREA SQ. FT.	HEATING SURFACES, SQUARE FEET				
ON DRIVERS	TRUCK	TRAILER	TOTAL ENGINE	TENDER LOADED		TUBES & FLUES	FIREBOX	ARCH TUBES	TOTAL	SUPER-HEATER
248200	35500	101300	385000	275000	100	4773	284	53	5110	2111

Tender, Type 12 Wheel   Capacity, Water 15000 Gallons   Fuel, 18 Tons

Lima's demonstration A-1 class 2-8-4, developed in the 1920s, featured a much-enlarged firebox. This new Berkshire design demonstrated remarkable operating performance and efficiency, and the A-1 soon joined a Boston & Albany 2-8-4 collection that would reach 45 locomotives within the next few years. —Eric Hirsimaki Collection

Lima Order 1080   Placed 7/18/25   Rd. Nos. 600-609   c/n 6959-6968   Cost: $ 100,489   Shipped: Nov-Dec 1925

LIMA LOCOMOTIVE WORKS, INCORPORATED
LIMA, OHIO

Class: 2104 S 448   Road No. 600

Built for THE TEXAS & PACIFIC RY. CO.

GAUGE OF TRACK	DRIVING WHEEL DIAMETER	FUEL KIND	CYLINDERS		BOILER		FIREBOX	
			DIAMETER	STROKE	DIAMETER	PRESSURE	LENGTH	WIDTH
4'-8½"	63"	OIL	29"	32"	86½"	250 LBS.	150⅙"	96¼"

WHEEL BASE			TRACTIVE POWER		FACTOR OF ADHESION	TUBES AND FLUES		
DRIVING	ENGINE	ENGINE AND TENDER	MAIN CYLINDERS	WITH BOOSTER		NUMBER	DIAMETER	LENGTH
22'-0"	46'-8"	86'-8"	83000	96000	3.61	82 / 184	2¼" / 3½"	21'-6"

AVERAGE WEIGHT IN WORKING ORDER, POUNDS					GRATE AREA SQ. FT.	HEATING SURFACES, SQUARE FEET				
ON DRIVERS	TRUCK	TRAILER	TOTAL ENGINE	TENDER LOADED		TUBES AND FLUES	FIREBOX	SYPHONS	TOTAL	SUPER-HEATER
300000	41800	106200	448000	275200	100	4640	375	98	5113	2100

Tender, Type 12 Wheel   Capacity, Water 14000 Gallons   Fuel, 5000 Gals.

An enlarged version of the A-1 for the Texas & Pacific added another pair of driving wheels. Delivered late in 1925, these Class I-1A Texas-type 2-10-4s were able to develop a maximum of 4,200 hp and demonstrated radical improvements in performance and efficiency. An initial 10 units delivered in 1925 were soon followed by another 60 locomotives. —Eric Hirsimaki Collection

The new 2-8-4 quickly proved its capabilities on the 60-mile stretch of mountainous track between Selkirk, New York, and Washington, Massachusetts. One of the most impressive test runs by the A-1 was on April 14, when it left Selkirk eastbound with a 54-car train (2,296 tons). Approximately 45 minutes earlier an H-10 with 46 cars (1,691 tons) had also left eastbound. To almost everyone's surprise, the 2-8-4 and its train began gaining on the earlier train, and at Chatham, New York, the two trains were abreast on parallel tracks before the A-1 pulled ahead. Twenty miles further east the 2-8-4 was 10 minutes ahead of the H-10.

The A-1 had handled 36 percent more tonnage and taken 57 minutes less time for the trip to North Adams Junction. Measurements showed that the 2-8-4 had an average boiler efficiency of 80.5 percent and a maximum drawbar horsepower of 3,890. Both the water-use rate and the corresponding coal rate were new records of efficiency. This outstanding performance was soon headlined by every publication in the industry and was the main topic of conversation at meetings of railroad associations. Woodard's design concepts now became the new standards for all builders. The A-1's name, first suggested as the Lima type, finally became Berkshire in honor of the line on which it proved itself and would later operate as a B&A engine.

The hoopla surrounding the A-1's initial performance on the New York Central soon came to the attention of the Texas & Pacific Railway, which in 1924 was searching for new power to replace an aging fleet of 44 Santa Fe types (2-10-2). Early in 1925 it approached Lima about an elongated A-1, with five sets of drivers, an idea that the builder had already been considering. With the impressive performance of the A-1 in mind, the railroad quickly settled on an order of 10 2-10-4s, to be known as Class I-1A. These engines would include almost all the features of the 2-8-4, and thus the design and assembly were relatively straightforward. Both its weight and total tractive effort were about 16 percent higher than corresponding values for the A-1. However, it produced a maximum horsepower of 4,200, which was 8 percent higher. Likewise, when the new engines were delivered in late 1925 (only five months after the order), their performance on the undulating profiles of T&P's 600-mile line between Fort Worth and El Paso was as surprising as that of the A-1 some nine months earlier.

Christened the Texas type, the 2-10-4s outperformed T&P's 2-10-2s in every category. Average tonnage was up by 44 percent, average speed increased by 33 percent, fuel oil used was down by 43 percent, and maintenance cost per mile was down 29 percent per month. Figures like these persuaded the T&P to purchase 60 more of these monster machines over the following five years.

1020   STEAM LOCOMOTIVES

We now understand that the 20 months between June 1922 and February 1925 were a watershed period in the evolution of the steam locomotive. Using two new wheel arrangements, Lima had produced the first of a new type of locomotive that would be the prototype for the final two decades of American steam development. Within months of the publication of test data for the A-1 and I-1A, the two larger builders were turning their considerable economic and technical muscle toward production of these new designs.

The period between production of the T&P 2-10-4 in 1925 and the stock market crash of 1929 saw a flood of new locomotive designs using four-wheel trailing trucks to support jumbo-sized fireboxes. Two more models hit the rails during the first two years after the name Super-Power was coined. Alco's progressive engineering team was quickest out of the chute with a 4-8-4 delivered to the Northern Pacific in 1926, and close behind was a 4-6-4 for New York Central in 1927.

Workhorses of the New Era

The pioneer A-2 Class 4-8-4 for the NP was built with an unusually large grate area (115 square feet) to better burn lignite, a low grade of coal plentiful in the West. Baldwin's first 4-8-4 was the S-1 Class delivered to the

Chicago & North Western in 1929. Also in that year Alco began delivering the first of Rock Island's R-67 Class. Later CRI&P received 20 larger 4-8-4s, giving this Granger road the second-largest fleet of this wheel arrangement (behind only Southern Pacific). The Northern type (for Northern Pacific) eventually became the standard engine of the Super-Power era, just as the 4-4-0 was in the beginning decades, followed by the 2-8-0 and the 2-8-2. Thirty-one railroads purchased over 900 engines of this type, produced from 70 different designs.

The year 1930 saw the 4-8-4 break new ground in another area besides its horsepower. The Timken Roller Bearing Co. of Canton, Ohio, had experienced considerable difficulties in getting roads to substitute its products for older, friction bearings, even after extensive tests in the 1920s. Unable to obtain permission from any railroad or builder to allow a demonstration of its bearings on a large main-line locomotive, Timken purchased in 1929 a stock 4-8-4 from Alco. Officially designated TRBX 1111, but known informally as the *Four Aces*, it began a nationwide tour that consistently impressed railroads with its operating capabilities and the general public with its unusual characteristics.

In 21 months of roaming the main-lines of 13 roads, the *Four Aces* ran off 119,600 miles between Portland, Maine, and Seattle with no bearing problems. Even after the na-

| Lima Order 1158 | Placed 3/13/41 | Rd. No.s 4450-4456
4457, 4458* | c/n 7848-7854
7855, 7856 | Cost: $ 192,873
209,339 | Shipped: Mar-Apr 1942
Jun, Apr 1942 |

* equipped with roller bearings

LIMA LOCOMOTIVE WORKS, INCORPORATED
LIMA, OHIO

Class: 484-S-475
R. R. Class: GS-4
Built for SOUTHERN PACIFIC LINES
Road No. 4454

GAUGE OF TRACK	DRIVING WHEEL DIAMETER	FUEL KIND	CYLINDERS		BOILER		FIREBOX	
			DIAMETER	STROKE	DIAMETER	PRESSURE	LENGTH	WIDTH
4'-8½"	80"	OIL	25½"	32"	86" O.D.	300 LBS.	127¼"	102¼"

WHEEL BASE			TRACTIVE POWER		FACTOR OF ADHESION	TUBES AND FLUES		
DRIVING	ENGINE	ENGINE AND TENDER	MAIN CYLINDERS	WITH BOOSTER		NUMBER	DIAMETER	LENGTH
21'-6"	47'-8"	96' 3"	64760	77760	4.28	49 198	2¼" 3½"	21'-6"

AVERAGE WEIGHT IN WORKING ORDER, POUNDS						GRATE AREA SQ. FT.	HEATING SURFACES, SQUARE FEET				
ON DRIVERS	TRUCK	TRAILER		TOTAL ENGINE	TENDER ⅔ LOAD		TUBES	FLUES	FIREBOX & COMB. CHAM	TOTAL	SUPER-HEATER
		FRONT AXLE	REAR AXLE								
275700	81300	56000	62000	475000	313730	90.4	617	3885	385	4887	2086

Tender, Type 12 Wheel   Capacity, Water 23300 Gallons   Fuel, 5880 Gals.

Other builders followed Lima's lead with two new locomotive wheel arrangements that would become a standard for modern heavy passenger or fast freight steam power. The most widely used was the 4-8-4 Northern. Southern Pacific had the most, with 81 locomotives, and its Lima-built Northerns for SP's *Daylight* trains were considered the handsomest of all. No. 4454, completed by Lima in 1942, was one of two equipped with roller bearings. —Eric Hirsimaki Collection

tional tour, lingering effects of the Depression slowed the incorporation of roller bearings, and only three lines ordered any installations by 1934. After 1936, however, the majority of new locomotives, slated for long-distance, high-speed service, included roller bearings, at least for drivers and truck axles.

The 4-6-4 Type

A problem that faced the New York Central and many other roads in the late 1920s was that their Pacific designs had reached their zenith. Despite improvements, these sturdy engines could no longer cope with the weight of all-steel coaches and sleepers, including two diners and a lounge car on premier trains. Their steaming capacity was insufficient to hold high-speed, long-distance schedules.

On January 1, 1926, Paul W. Kiefer became NYC's chief engineer for motive power and rolling stock and immediately set about designing a new type of passenger locomotive. Kiefer was fully aware of Lima's success with the B&A Berkshire design, and so he began to consider how to employ the principles of this new Super-Power concept. Quickly the NYC decided to stick with its familiar six-coupled driving gear because it would also help keep down weight and cost (both initial and maintenance).

The final design specs that went to Alco included a large firebox volume along with 79-inch drivers and trail-ing truck booster. Construction of No. 5200, known as the J-1a Class, proceeded at a rapid pace, illustrating the longtime cooperation between the builder and its primary customer. The 4-6-4's boiler arrived at the erecting-shop floor on January 28, 1927, and only 17 days later Alco formally passed the new machine over to NYC president Patrick E. Crowley, who, in a unique ceremony for the nation, christened it the Hudson type.

The first Hudson turned out to be a lot more than handsome in appearance. During its first trials the 5200 was able to sustain a speed of 75 mph with a train of 26 steel coaches that weighed 1,700 tons, with a peak of 4,300 hp at 69 mph. In comparison with the road's Pacifics, the J-1a produced a 16 percent increase in starting tractive effort (without booster) over NYC's most advanced 4-6-2. A smaller-drivered version of the Hudson, the J-2a, was produced by Alco in 1928 for the hilly Boston & Albany line. The final production series was the J-3 version, with a 16 percent smaller cylinder volume than the J-1 but a slightly higher boiler pressure, which kept the starting tractive effort essentially the same. Total production of NYC Hudsons was 275 engines between 1927 and 1938.

Super-Power Articulateds

The desire to move from compounds to simple, articulated locomotives was mainly a matter of efficiency (fuel

Second only to the Northerns for Super-Power passenger locomotives were the 4-6-4 Hudsons. New York Central bought 275 of them over a ten-year period beginning in 1927, and they were used in heavy, fast passenger service almost everywhere on the railroad. Once shrouded in the memorable streamlined design of Henry Dreyfuss, New York Central class J3a Hudson No. 5452 is seen here in its twilight years of service in 1955 at Dayton, Ohio, on a run between Cincinnati and Cleveland. —J. Parker Lamb

Super-Power technology brought forth a number of new high-performance designs that combined the large and efficient boilers and fireboxes with a better understanding of the dynamic forces involved. Largest of all were 18 Yellowstone-type 2-8-8-4 articulateds built by Baldwin in 1941 and 1943 for the Duluth, Missabe & Iron Range. Class M4 locomotive No. 228 prepared to depart Fraser, Minnesota, with a load of 190 cars of iron ore—a gross train weight of about 18,000 tons—for Duluth in 1959. —William D. Middleton

economy). The massive front cylinders of the Mallets were very heavy and thus required robust side rodding that made balancing difficult, and their use of low-pressure steam made them less efficient. A simple engine required much smaller cylinders, pistons, and other moving parts on the lead engine. The idea of a true, simple articulated engine materialized in 1912, only a year after C&O received its first Mallet compounds, when the Pennsylvania Railroad received a 2-8-8-2 from Alco. Seven years later PRR's Juniata shops in Altoona built the first of its 2-8-8-0s, which provided a starting tractive effort of 135,000 pounds. Chesapeake & Ohio received 25 simple 2-8-8-2s from Alco in 1924 and another 20 from Baldwin in 1926.

In the beginning all articulateds were confined to low-speed service because there was little understanding of ways to control the lateral motion of the front engine, caused by dynamic loads from the alternating piston strokes. Moreover, in common with early two-wheel leading trucks, the front engine did not provide enough guid-ing force when the locomotive was negotiating a curve at speed. By the end of the 1930s both the lateral-motion and guidance problems were solved, and articulateds became high-speed main-line machines.

The first simple articulateds of the Super-Power age were produced in 1928 when Alco began delivering a batch of 2-8-8-4s to the Northern Pacific, a railroad that seemed to relish pushing the envelope of locomotive design. The road named these locomotives Yellowstone types; like its pioneering Northern types, they carried unusually large fireboxes. The 2-8-8-4's grate area of 182 square feet was never exceeded, and its starting tractive effort of 153,400 pounds (including 13,400 from a trailing truck booster) was the largest ever for a simple articulated. For a number of years these were the world's largest locomotives.

In the wake of the leanest Depression years, the financial picture brightened a bit in 1934, and railroads once again started ordering Super-Power machines. Consequently, engineering design innovations came forth at a rapid pace between 1935 and the beginning of World War II. Although diesel-powered passenger trains appeared in the mid-1930s, steam power, especially Super-Power locomotives, still ruled American main lines.

By far the most unconventional American articulated made its appearance long before Lima's pioneering Berkshire. Southern Pacific's cab-forward design grew out of the need for better crew-cab ventilation on the road's line over the Sierra Nevada. The numerous tunnels and snow sheds produced an extremely harsh environment when conventional articulateds were used. The first cab-forward Mallet compounds were turned out by Baldwin in 1909 in a 2-8-8-2 wheel arrangement and were an immediate success. From its original group of 15 engines, its fleet grew to 47 with 12 engines in 1911 and another 20 in 1913. All of these were eventually rebuilt as simple engines.

The first 10 of the Super-Power cab-forwards arrived from Baldwin in 1928. In the ensuing 16 years the Southern Pacific built a roster of 195 of these "backward-running" Yellowstones, the largest fleet of engines from the same base design in the Super-Power era. The final engine of this order (1944) was SP's last new steam locomotive. Counting the earlier compounds that were rebuilt as simple engines, the total number of cab forwards was 256, spread over three wheel arrangements, including a dozen 4-6-6-2s that had originally been bought for passenger service as 2-6-6-2s.

A moderate number of 2-8-8-4s were built just before or during World War II. Lima constructed 12 Yellowstone engines for Southern Pacific in 1939. These were similar to the famous cab-forwards, but since they burned New Mexico coal, they were of conventional design and were also the heaviest steam locomotives ever owned by the SP. The Duluth, Missabe & Iron Range's mammoth M-3 Class (8 engines) were constructed by Baldwin in 1941, and 10 similar M-4s came from Eddystone in 1943. It should be noted that these engines used Super-Power concepts to optimize drawbar pull rather than horsepower since the DM&IR hauled only one commodity at low speed.

Baldwin's first production of simple articulateds occurred in 1935 when it rolled out two batches of 2-6-6-4 engines for the Pittsburgh & West Virginia and the Seaboard Air Line. The three P&WV locomotives, with Belpaire fireboxes and 63-inch drivers, pioneered this wheel arrangement, and their strong performance resulted in 4 similar engines two years later. In contrast, the 10 SAL locomotives ran on 69-inch drivers and were designed as dual-purpose engines, although they were used almost exclusively on freight trains.

Although not an extremely popular configuration, the 2-6-6-4 gained widespread attention as a result of Norfolk & Western's innovative Class A design unveiled in 1936. It was the first attempt by N&W's Roanoke shops to design and construct a modern locomotive from the ground up. Using the latest technology, the Class A employed a one-piece cast-steel main frame with integral cylinders (developed only recently by General Steel Castings), roller bearings on all axles, and the advanced lubri-cation methods developed by the Nathan Co. The Class As had mechanical lubrication at 238 points and pressurized lube at 98 locations.

The first of 10 new 70-inch-drivered Class As rolled out of the shops in late May 1936 and, just as Lima's pioneering A-1 had done 11 years earlier, immediately set new records for efficiency and low maintenance. Dynamometer tests showed that its massive boiler-firebox could produce 6,300 drawbar horsepower at 45 mph, and that it could sustain a 6,000-hp rating between 32 and 57 mph. It could even move a passenger train comfortably at speeds up to 70 mph. A total of 43 Class As were built, the last 5 during 1949–1950. These were distinguished by the large rodding that housed roller bearings.

One of the most widely used simple articulated designs was conceived in the early 1930s when Union Pacific vice president Otto Jabelman began studying his road's needs for larger locomotives. His engineering staff soon sketched a layout for a new wheel arrangement, the 4-6-6-4, and sent it to Alco in early 1936. Both the builder and the railroad knew that the secret to success would be good weight balance (to keep the front drivers from slipping), as well as controlling the lateral oscillations of the front engine. Fortunately, Alco was able to design an improved suspension system, just as had been required to make the early 4-4-0s usable. Following usual Super-Power practice, the builder also used lightweight main and side rods and crankpins. Upon arrival from Alco in late 1936, the new high-speed articulateds, named the Challenger type, became the premier power on the Sherman Hill line.

The last-built and most modern Mallet compound did not appear until 1936 and was in some respects a Super-Power design. Norfolk & Western's traffic base required the movement of high-tonnage trains at moderate speeds over very difficult terrain. The road was quite happy with the performance of its Y-5 Class 2-8-8-2 compounds that had evolved during 1930–1933 from the original USRA design. Rather than switch to a simple engine, the road decided to concentrate on upgrading the Y-5 to include the advanced features from the Class A design such as cast-steel main frames, roller bearings, and lubrication.

The first of 25 Y-6s were produced in 1936 with 57-inch drivers and a boiler pressure of 300 psi, a combination that yielded a starting tractive effort of 152,000 pounds (simple) or 127,000 (compound). Tests proved that at 25 mph the Y-6 would produce 5,500 drawbar horsepower, while its top speed was 50 mph. A final production of 30 Y-6bs appeared between 1949 and 1952. These N&W designs, the only Mallets produced in America after 1935, had taken this nineteenth-century concept about as far up the ladder of technology as was possible in the mid-twentieth century.

Steam Power's Golden Age

During the design evolution described so far, steam locomotive technology had nearly reached the pinnacle that was to be manifested during the 15 years beginning around 1935. By this time all three builders had refined their designs and were adept at constructing efficient steam engines in a variety of sizes. The appearance of stronger metals and new fabrication methods (e.g., welding and casting) had brought about even higher levels of performance and efficiency. Railroad-company shops in Altoona, Pennsylvania (PRR), and Roanoke, Virginia (N&W), possessed capabilities equal to those of the three major builders in being able to design and construct locomotives from the ground up. This peaking in technical capability of railroad locomotion could not have occurred at a more advantageous time in the nation's history. Without knowing it, railroads were preparing for the unimaginable transportation crisis that would be created by World War II.

Notable rigid-frame locomotives to appear in the six years before World War II included the famous Daylight 4-8-4s of the Southern Pacific (Lima), N&W's finely engineered J-Class 4-8-4 (Roanoke), and 4-6-4s for New Haven (Baldwin), New York Central (Alco), Milwaukee Road (Alco), and Santa Fe (Baldwin). In addition, many Berkshire and Texas types were produced for heavy freight service, including over 100 2-8-4s for the Erie (Lima) and a group of heavy 2-10-4s for Santa Fe and Kansas City Southern. These were based largely on an extremely successful design produced by Lima in 1930 for the C&O. Its T-1 Class virtually rewrote the book on moving heavy coal traffic to midwestern industrial centers.

On the eve of the war in late 1941, two unique locomotive designs appeared on the American scene. Their subsequent performance still stands as a pinnacle of achievement in the steam era. Rolling out of Alco's Schenectady works were 20 large engines with a 4-8-8-4 configuration, while Lima unveiled 10 copies of its 2-6-6-6 design. The Alco engine was christened Big Boy by the Union Pacific, which intended it as a replacement for its Challengers on heavy trains across the Continental Divide between Cheyenne and Ogden. The Lima engine went to the Chesapeake & Ohio and served as a replacement for Mallet compounds and 2-10-4s on heavy trains moving from the coalfields to the Great Lakes.

The father of the Big Boy design was the same Otto Jabelman who had led the design of the Challenger. In this case the road asked him to start with the Challenger and make an even bigger engine with more speed (80 mph) and more pulling capability, a seemingly impossible task given the difficulty of minimizing oscillations and vibrations of the eight-wheeled front engine. However, Alco was able to develop an improved suspension that made the huge engine quite rigid on tangent track yet able to glide around curves with a restrained movement, free of dangerous oscillations. More than its sheer size, this was the most significant technical advance embodied in the 4-8-8-4.

With 68-inch drivers, a 300 psi boiler, and a 19-foot-long firebox with a 150-square-foot grate, the 4-8-8-4 could lug 100-car trains over Sherman Hill at 35 mph, while tonnage was still at a respectable 4,200 on a 1.4 percent grade at a speed of 20 mph. Its weight of 772,200 pounds was the largest ever published for a locomotive anywhere. When it was running wide open, the Big Boy consumed 22 tons of coal per hour, along with 100,000 pounds of water, and at 41 mph showed a peak drawbar horsepower of 6,290 (essentially the same as an N&W Class A). The last five Big Boys were built during 1944.

Beginning with its inaugural deadheaded trip in September 1941 from Schenectady to Omaha (via NYC and C&NW), the first Big Boy (No. 4000) was a magnet for local press coverage, inspiring some 520 newspaper articles in 45 states. The title "biggest locomotive" was the recurrent theme of the writers, who also used this occasion to congratulate the nation for its technological success, clearly symbolized in this powerful machine. With the encouragement of Union Pacific, along with their outstanding performance on a highly visible line, the 25 Big Boys became a national symbol as "America's Greatest Locomotive."

Although technically and operationally equivalent to UP's premier engine, Lima's 2-6-6-6 Allegheny type did not garner nearly as much attention. While it performed extremely well, there is considerable evidence that the C&O was not interested in maximizing the use of the engine in main-line service or publicizing its capabilities. Two years after delivery Lima was allowed to run some dynamometer tests, and on one occasion an Allegheny produced nearly 7,500 drawbar horsepower at a speed of 46 mph with a train of 14,075 tons. This level of power was over 1,000 hp greater than that from similar tests of either Big Boy or the N&W Class A.

In early 1942 wartime conditions began controlling American industry, and the government formed the War Production Board in an attempt to maximize efficiency. As it applied to locomotive manufacture, the WPB's concept of efficiency involved allocating certain types of locomotives to each builder. Although doubtless helpful to the war effort, this action also changed the industrial landscape both immediately and for a decade after the war's end. In a number of instances prewar locomotive designs were pulled out of storage files and used to produce new engines quickly. Although allocation of steam engines was the major effort of the WPB, it also restricted the relatively new diesel-electric power to certain builders (and limited the number of models they could build).

Among the most notable wartime Northerns were those of Santa Fe and Union Pacific, both built with 80-inch drivers and large tenders for long-distance runs. The AT&SF's magnificent 2900s were built by Baldwin in 1943–1944. Because of the shortage of high-strength steels, side rods and other parts used a lower-grade metal. To achieve the necessary strength, the substitute parts were larger and weighed considerably more than they should have, making these 30 locomotives, at 510,150 pounds, the heaviest 4-8-4s ever built (almost 8 tons heavier than the road's 3765 series).

Lima Order 1162   Placed 10/22/41   Rd. No. 1610-1619   c/n 7882-7892   Cost: $ 274,552   Shipped: Sep-Oct 1942

LIMA LOCOMOTIVE WORKS, INCORPORATED
LIMA, OHIO

Class: 2666-S-725   Built for CHESAPEAKE & OHIO RY. CO.   Road No. 1610

GAUGE OF TRACK	DRIVING WHEEL DIAMETER	FUEL KIND	CYLINDERS		BOILER		FIREBOX	
			DIAMETER	STROKE	DIAMETER	PRESSURE	LENGTH	WIDTH
4'-8½"	67"	SOFT COAL	22½"	33"	109"	260 LBS.	180"	108½"

WHEEL BASE			MAXIMUM TRACTIVE POWER	FACTOR OF ADHESION	TUBES AND FLUES		
DRIVING	ENGINE	ENGINE AND TENDER			NUMBER	DIAMETER	LENGTH
34'-8"	62'-6"	112'-11"	110200	4.27	48 278	2¼" 3½"	23'-0"

AVERAGE WEIGHT IN WORKING ORDER, POUNDS					GRATE AREA SQ. FT.	HEATING SURFACES, SQUARE FEET				
ON DRIVERS	TRUCK	TRAILER	TOTAL ENGINE	TENDER ⅔ LOAD		TUBES AND FLUES	SYPHONS	FIREBOX & COMB. CHAM.	TOTAL	SUPER-HEATER
471000	64500	189000	724500	341600	135.2	6478	162	600	7240	3186

Tender, Type 14 Wheel   Capacity, Water 25000 Gallons   Fuel 25 Tons

A new articulated wheel arrangement of the Super-Power era was the Chesapeake & Ohio's 2-6-6-6 Allegheny locomotive. Looking for an ability to haul coal through the Allegheny Mountains with the highest possible steaming rate, the C&O settled on an enormous firebox that required a six-wheel trailing truck. C&O liked the performance of the Alleghenies, first delivered in 1942, and acquired a total of 60, and the Virginian bought another 8. —Eric Hirsimaki Collection

To minimize fuel and water stops over the 1,765-mile run between Kansas City and Los Angeles, the 4-8-4s pulled a gigantic 55-foot tender (total capacity of 31,500 gallons of fuel and water) carried on two eight-wheel trucks. A major external feature of the wartime engines was their side rods that were tapered in each direction from the second (main) driver. They also featured mechanically operated stack extensions that lifted smoke in high-speed operation.

Another notable 4-8-4 of the postwar period was the New York Central's Niagara, constructed in 1945–1946. Designed by the same team that produced the Hudsons, the S-Class was the pinnacle of excellence in NYC's devotion to continual increases in steam-generation capability and overall thermal efficiency along with decreases in the weight per horsepower. The Niagara's mechanical efficiency was increased by the use of roller bearings, along with lightweight rodding and improved counterbalancing. Niagaras were known for their durability; one engine ran 700 miles a day to chalk up 228,849 miles in 11 months before its initial shopping.

The midsize Berkshire type was also very popular during the war. In particular, those roads controlled by the Van Sweringens (C&O, Erie, Nickel Plate, and Pere Marquette) became heavy users of these workhorse engines, with nearly 350 purchases, mostly from Lima. Louisville & Nashville, one of the few southern roads to purchase engines with four-wheel trailing trucks, wanted to buy 4-8-4s, but its South Louisville shops would not accommodate such long engines, so instead it began building a fleet of 2-8-4s with 15 Baldwin locomotives in 1942 and 1944. The last order for 22 Berkshires went to Lima, and they were completed in 1949.

In retrospect, it seems entirely appropriate that the machine that started the Super-Power era brought down the curtain on all steam locomotive production at the two companies responsible for 88 percent of all 2-8-4s built. After the delivery of seven Pittsburgh & Lake Erie Berkshires in the summer of 1948, the famous Schenectady erecting shops were soon modified to build other forms of motive power. In fact, with its tender shop already dismantled, Alco contracted with Lima to construct tenders for this final order. A year later, in May 1949, the Ohio company's 71-year steam-engine production ended with the shipment of No. 779, the last of the Nickel Plate machines.

During World War II the 2-10-4 was not a big seller. For many railroads it had become a midrange engine, since most could use Northerns and Berkshires when speed was important, while simple articulateds satisfied the need for extra power. Despite this, two of the nation's largest lines acquired virtually all the production during this period. In the late 1930s Santa Fe had ordered 10 large, coal-burning 2-10-4s from Baldwin. They performed so well that the road ordered 25 more in 1943. These were oil burners that used the same 16-wheeled tender mentioned earlier in connection with the 2900-class 4-8-4s. The 5011-class locomotives were legendary in their pulling capability, developing 5,600 drawbar horsepower at 40 mph. Fittingly, they represented Santa Fe's final order for steam power and did not retire until 1957.

Another WPB decision gave the Pennsylvania Railroad one of its most reliable engines, and one of the few not conceived in its shops at Altoona. When PRR asked for permission in 1943 to design an entirely new 2-10-4, the WPB decided that the road must use an existing C&O design (Lima-built T-1 Class from 1930). Despite the lack of the PRR's usual Belpaire firebox, its J-1 Class 2-10-4s were powerful machines, with 70-inch drivers and 110,100 pounds of tractive effort (including 15,000 from a trailing truck booster). Altoona shops turned out a total of 125 of these workhorse machines between 1943 and 1944.

Super-Power Production

A total of 3,078 engines were produced during the Super-Power period, with Alco barely edging out Baldwin for the lead. Alco produced the most Hudsons, Challengers, and Big Boys, while Lima constructed the most Berkshire, Texas, and Allegheny types. Baldwin led in Northerns and Yellowstones. The most popular wheel arrangement by far was the Northern, followed by Berkshire, Hudson, and Texas types, while Yellowstones barely edged out Challengers for the top spot in simple articulateds, mainly because of the inclusion of SP's largest cab-forwards in the former category. Northerns and Berkshires were also one-two in the number of roads ordering, with Hudsons coming in third. It is not surprising that, as the originator of the Super-Power concept, Lima's share of total production was 23 percent, considerably larger (by 6 percent) than its general market share.

Another interesting statistic is that only four roads purchased over one-third of the total production, with New York Central at 365 leading Southern Pacific (281), C&O (220), and Pennsylvania (205). We also note two aspects of the final production of conventional steam locomotives. While both Alco (1948) and Lima (1949) closed out their production with orders for Berkshires, for NYC and Nickel Plate, respectively, the oldest company, Baldwin, concluded its domestic steam business with a 1949 order for C&O 2-6-6-2 Mallets to be used on coal-mine branches. At the time this was a questionable decision for a coal hauler that was already buying diesels for much of its main-line freight traffic. Just as surprising were the Roanoke shops' final products in 1953, a group of 0-8-0 switchers based on a C&O design.

American steam's finest hour began with the introduction of 2-8-4 super-power machines by Lima in 1925. This engine and its successors put history's stamp on the American steam locomotive as one of technology's greatest achievements. A quantitative summary of this period is presented in Table 2, which lists the total production of locomotives by type and by builder. We see that Alco pro-

Table 2. Summary of Super-Power Locomotives

Type	Alco	Baldwin	Lima	Railroad Shops	Total	Railroads's Using
4-6-4	289*	75	14	27	405	15
4-8-4	330	383*	96	108	917	31
2-8-4	166	75	368*	—	609	17
2-10-4	20	106	141*	125	392	9
2-6-6-4	—	17	—	43*	60	3
2-6-6-6	—	—	68*	—	68	2
2-8-8-4	1	254*	12	—	267	4
4-6-6-4	225*	27	—	—	252	9
4-8-8-4	25*	—	—	—	25	1
Duplex	—	28	—	55	83	3
TOTAL	1,056	965	699	358	3,078	

Source: Hirsimaki, 1986.

Note: * indicates largest producer of type.

duced the most Hudsons, Challengers, and Big Boys, while Lima constructed the most Berkshire, Texas, and Allegheny types. Baldwin led in Northerns and Yellowstones. As noted earlier, Northerns were by far the most popular wheel arrangement followed by Berkshire, Hudson, and Texas types, while Yellowstones barely edged out Challengers for the top spot in simple articulateds, due mainly to the inclusion of SP's largest cab-forwards in the former category. Northerns and Berkshires were also one-two in the number of roads ordering, with Hudson's coming in third. It is not surprising that, as the originator of super-power concept, Lima's share of total production was 23 percent, considerably larger (by 6 percent) than its general market share.

Final Improvements

Throughout the later part of the Super-Power era designers came to realize that these locomotives suffered from two major limitations, both due to the ever-increasing need for more main-line speed. First, controlling the flow of steam through the valves and the power cylinders became ever more inefficient at high speed, and second, the pounding and destruction of the roadbed by large drivers could not be eliminated.

During the last years of steam locomotive production, designers tried out many ideas for getting steam into and out of the power cylinders in a precise way during high-speed operation, but none was completely successful. These failures confirmed that a reciprocating machine has an upper limit on speed that is due to inertia of the large moving parts (piston valves and valve gear). The result was that the steam did not enter or exit the power cylinder with the proper timing, and thus the power produced in each stroke was diminished.

The most obvious solutions envisioned by designers were to reduce the mass (and inertia) of the piston valve and also to replace the inertia-laden valve-gear linkage with a smaller, but functionally equivalent, control system. Eventually they turned to the design used for automotive engines. The *poppet valve* is a thin, precisely machined disk that is attached to a push rod (tappet) and activated by a mechanical cam. When enlarged to 6 inches in diameter with foot-long tappets, the poppet valve became the heart of a locomotive valve-gear system that could provide a more precise timing of all events associated with steam passage through the cylinder.

The first American installation (of an Italian design) was in 1928 when B&O rebuilt one of its heavy Pacifics for an unsuccessful trial period that lasted only a year. The primary American effort to develop a reliable poppet-valve control began in 1937 at Franklin Railway Supply; this system was eventually installed on a Pennsylvania K4 Pacific. During its first series of road tests in the fall of 1939, the engine performed brilliantly. Dynamometer-car data displayed an increase of 24 percent in drawbar horsepower at 60 mph (compared with a conventional valve gear) and a whopping 60 percent increase at 80 mph. Later tests at the Altoona test lab confirmed these results. However, further progress was put on hold until after World War II.

The second area of concern to designers in the late 1930s was the failure of the latest methods of balancing drivers. Consequently, roadbed damage from unbalanced drivers continued to be a major problem. Recognizing that the most significant unbalanced forces came from the main rod, side rods, and valve gear, Baldwin had proposed a possible solution to the B&O in 1932. It consisted of splitting a 4-8-4 into two separately driven four-wheeled engines, thus producing a rigid-frame 4-4-4-4 configuration known as a *duplex drive*. This reduced the size of the rods and valve gear and consequently the unbalanced loads and track wear.

Although the B&O initially rejected Baldwin's design, the road later decided to pursue this approach and rolled out a 4-4-4-4, the *George H. Emerson*, from its Mt. Claire Shops in May 1937. In an effort to minimize the long wheelbase, designers had used opposed pistons, with one set of power cylinders near the cab. But, like many other proposals for new steam locomotives, this one was quashed by the railroad's management, which called a halt to further steam development.

Soon the duplex concept was picked up by the Pennsylvania Railroad, which prided itself on designing and building its own locomotives at Altoona. In 1939 it turned out a streamlined, duplex passenger engine of monumental proportions. With a 6-4-4-6 wheel arrangement, it weighed over 300 tons, ran on 84-inch drivers, and was capable of generating 6,000 hp, enough to move a 1,200-ton train at 100 mph. Even though it proved to be both fast and powerful, in many ways it was too big for everyday work and extremely slippery. During the war years its fancy skirt was stripped away to facilitate maintenance, and eventually the engine was scrapped after a short 10-year operating career.

Not surprisingly, Baldwin engineers had not been strong supporters of either the B&O or PRR duplex designs and in 1939 persuaded their company to build its own design as a rolling salesman. Before starting construction, however, the company's sales staff scurried around to court potential buyers. Finally, in July 1940 the Pennsylvania signed up for two 4-4-4-4s to be called Class T-1. These engines were designed to pull 11 80-ton cars at 100 mph and contained lateral-motion pedestals on the first and third drivers to allow passage through 17-degree curves. The 80-inch-drivered T-1s weighed about the same as a large Northern. The first T-1 was delivered in late April 1942 and the second one a month later. Soon they were making a strong showing on trains in the Harrisburg-Chicago passenger pool.

After 120,000 miles of service one of the T-1s, sent to the Altoona dynamometer lab in April 1944, exhibited a maximum of 6,100 drawbar horsepower. Sensing that it had the steam equivalent of the highly successful GG1 electric locomotive, the road ordered 50 more T-1s in 1944, splitting the order between Baldwin and Altoona. Unfortunately for supporters of steam power, only two years after the last T-1 was delivered in August 1946, PRR announced that it was dieselizing all passenger service west of Harrisburg and buying freight diesels as well.

In parallel with the T-1's development, Baldwin and PRR also crafted a duplex engine for freight service. Wanting five sets of drivers on the rail within the shortest wheelbase, they designed the experimental Q-1, like B&O's *Emerson*, with opposed power cylinders. A single prototype, with a 4-6-4-4 configuration, was built in 1942 for testing. However, the Pennsylvania was not completely satisfied with the Q-1 and ordered a Q-2 model in 1944. On this engine the power cylinders were conventionally located. Carrying the six-wheeled engine in the rear, this 4-4-6-4 engine performed brilliantly at the Altoona test lab, producing almost 8,000 indicated horsepower at 57 mph. Soon Altoona was at work on an order of 25 more Q-2s that were completed in 1945. Both the T-1 and the Q-2 designs, which in many respects represented the highest technical level of the American steam locomotive, gave a good account of themselves during short operating careers that helped bring down the curtain on the American steam epoch. Had they been produced two or three years earlier, their story might have had a different ending.

Steam-Turbine Prime Movers

In the late 1940s most lines capitulated completely to diesel-electric motive power, but there were three roads on which this switch constituted nothing less than an assault on their corporate identity. Each had over a century of tradition of hauling large amounts of coal behind coal-burning locomotives. Before releasing their grip on steam-power technology, these three wanted to investigate one more option, the steam turbine.

They turned to a concept that had been introduced in 1938 on a streamlined locomotive built for Union Pacific by General Electric. As a major builder of electric locomotives and electric power plant equipment, the GE steam-turbine design incorporated an electric propulsion system driven by a turbine similar to those in electric power plants. The engine included a water-tube, oil-fired boiler that supplied steam at 1500 psi. Unlike traditional railroad practice, the boiler used distilled water that was condensed after use exactly as in a power plant, and it featured dynamic braking, as would a diesel-electric. The complete locomotive was composed of two identical 2,500-hp, 90-foot-long units, each of which was enclosed in a streamlined carbody similar to Union Pacific's M1003 passenger diesels built in 1936 by GM's Electro-Motive Division. Each unit, containing boiler, turbine, generators, condensers, and water tank, was powered by six traction motors in a 2-C+C-2 wheel arrangement. Although they were given extensive trial runs on the Union Pacific and later on the Great Northern and New York Central, no orders were forthcoming, and the locomotive was scrapped. It is clear that these experimental units were too far ahead of contemporary railroad technology.

The Pennsylvania was the first to try steam turbines in the 1940s when it ordered a large engine from Baldwin in 1944 that contained two rotary machines built by Westinghouse Electric & Manufacturing Co. At first glance, Class S-2 No. 6200 resembled a conventional PRR locomotive with Belpaire firebox (310 psi), four 68-inch drivers connected by side rods, and a large 14-wheel tender. But instead of power cylinders above the lead truck of its long 6-8-6 platform, it contained two circular housings on the main frame between the second and third drivers. The larger housing was on the right side and contained an impulse-type turbine (6,500 hp) that was connected to the main driver by a set of gears (much like an electric lo-

Several efforts were made to develop a coal-fired geared steam-turbine-drive locomotive. Probably the most successful was the Norfolk & Western's steam-turbine-electric No. 2300, which was delivered by the Baldwin-Lima-Hamilton Corp., with a Babcock & Wilcox water-tube boiler in 1953. Twelve traction motors were mounted on a C-C+C-C arrangement. Performance tests were remarkable, but in the end N&W decided not to order any more, and diesel-electrics came along soon afterward. The 2300, the *Jawn Henry*, pulled a long train of loaded coal hoppers headed east through Christiansburg, Virginia. —Norfolk & Western, Middleton Collection

comotive). This provided power for forward motion, while a similar 1,500-hp turbine (for backup movements) sat on the left side of the engine. The S-2 weighed 580,000 pounds and had a tractive effort of 70,500 pounds.

Although it worked well on the main line, the S-2 was incompatible with the variable speed requirements of a railroad. For example, just as inertial effects limit reciprocating machines at high speeds, turbines operate best at very high rpm, and their rotary inertia resists attempts to change speeds rapidly. Consequently, the S-2 was in the shop frequently and was finally stored for a while before being scrapped in 1949.

While this PRR experiment was in progress, the C&O decided to investigate a significantly different design in 1947. It ordered three turbine locomotives from Baldwin and Westinghouse Electric that, like the GE experiment of 1938, used reaction-type turbines that produced 6,000 hp to drive four 1,000 kw generators that fed eight traction motors. These hefty locomotives weighed 857,000 pounds (without tender) and had a starting tractive effort of 98,000 pounds. They were built on 100-foot-long main frames with an asymmetrical wheel arrangement (2-D+2-D-2) that reflected the interior loading. The forward part of the locomotive carried a 29-ton coal bunker, while the remainder was taken up with a rearward-facing, conventional boiler that supplied steam at 310 psi. The cab was placed between the coal and the firebox, while the trailing tender carried only water. All of the machinery was shrouded with a streamlined cowling that featured an unusual forward-slanting nose fairing. Since the design of these hybrid locomotives was at the edge of postwar technology, it is not surprising that there were many problems with the C&O engine.

Only a year after production ended at its Roanoke shops in 1953, the N&W received a prototype turbine engine from the now Baldwin-Lima-Hamilton Corp. Like the C&O machines, it was 106 feet long (plus a 55-foot water tender), carried 20 tons of coal in a large bunker at the front, used a reaction turbine to drive DC generators, and weighed 1 million pounds with tender. But it was an entirely different machine mechanically. First, it contained a Babcock & Wilcox water-tube firebox that produced 600 psi steam. It also used a more conventional support configuration that included 12 traction motors in a C-C+C-C arrangement. It was also quite different in overall appearance. With its hulk covered with a boxy, black N&W shroud, it was a strong contrast to the highly contoured and brightly painted C&O turbines.

On the locomotive roster it was carried as No. 2300 with the classification of TE-1 (for turbine electric), but in everyday work it was known as *Jawn Henry*, a mythical icon of hard labor on the railroad. And like the other turbine-powered locomotives, it could pull heavy trains economically, even outperforming the Y-6b on coal trains while using less fuel. For example, on one dynamometer test its starting drawbar force measurement was 224,000 pounds. However, *Jawn Henry*'s problems were much the same as those of the other two designs, namely, high ini-

tial cost, high maintenance expense, and even its length (too long for turntables). Despite these potential pitfalls, the road's operating department wanted to keep testing this type of locomotive and even prepared a proposal to the board of directors in 1956 to purchase five more TE-1s. Although there were some strong steam advocates in N&W's management, the road ultimately decided against this move. However, even after N&W began ordering diesels in 1955, the TE-1 labored on for two more years before being retired, thus ending American railroading's 11-year flirtation with steam turbines.

Special-Service Locomotives

The evolution of American steam power also includes a large group of engines that were designed for narrowly defined sectors of operation, among which were suburban commuter service, general industrial support, and lumber industry use. Street traffic in Chicago and New York City forced the construction of elevated commuter lines between 1870 and 1890. Before their electrification around 1900, the motive power was provided by hundreds of small tank engines based on the design of Matthias N. Forney and constructed by a number of eastern builders. The common wheel arrangement was 0-4-4-T, with a total weight of about 20 tons. Their short wheelbase allowed them to navigate the sharp curves of downtown routes, and their power was sufficient to haul the light trains of that period. As the railroads' suburban services began to expand outward 20 to 40 miles from city centers, larger power was needed for commuter trains. Typical designs during this period included a 2-6-2T for the Chicago & Western Indiana (Rogers, 1904), a 2-4-4T for NYC (Alco, 1909), and a 4-6-6T for the Boston & Albany (Alco, 1928). Weights of these engines ranged from 70 tons for the NYC engine to 176 tons for the B&A locomotive, which was the largest suburban steam power ever built. Most of these engines carried water and fuel behind the cab, but a few were side-tank models.

The term "industrial locomotive" is generally applied to small power used within large plants and extensive construction sites. Before 1920 (when trucks were introduced) thousands of these "standard contractor engines" were constructed in stock lots by virtually all builders. They were simple and rugged machines, with four or six wheels (0-4-0T or 0-6-0T) and saddle or side tanks, and could be fitted to run on a wide variety of track gauges. In some industries it was common to use small power that had much lower heights than normal switching locomotives to accommodate close clearances inside plant buildings. Another specialty type of industrial locomotive was based in plants where there was a fire hazard. Termed "fireless" engines, they had no firebox but merely a tank that accepted steam (up to 250 psi) supplied by a local source. A reducing valve kept the pressure entering the cylinders to about 50 psi.

America's logging industry offered many opportunities

for locomotive builders, but there were also numerous design challenges. Most of the operating difficulties were a result of the poorly constructed and often-temporary trackage that navigated curvatures of 30 to 40 degrees and gradients of up to 10 percent. Moreover, locomotives needed to operate easily in both directions, and light axle loadings were required because of the crude track. Although some traditional rod-drive engines were used on more permanent lines, they were often tenderless models with wheel arrangements as large as 2-10-2T and even 2-6-6-2T.

However, the three most popular designs were radically different from conventional side-rod locomotives. These were "geared" engines and rode on two or three two-axle trucks that gave them virtually the same turning radius as a freight car, whereas their gear ratios assured that tractive force could be generated on steep grades. Although all three used conventional boilers and onboard tenders, each had a unique and complicated drive train. The oldest design, patented in the 1870s by Michigan lumberman Ephraim Shay, used an asymmetric layout in which the boiler was offset from the centerline of the main frame in order to accommodate three vertical-power pistons near the center of the engine (on the engineer's side). The pistons drove a horizontal crankshaft (parallel to the rails) that was connected by line shafts and universal joints to bevel-gear connections on the rim of each wheel.

Soon after Shay, assisted by local mechanics, had completed the prototype engine, he approached the nearby Lima Machine Works for assistance in rebuilding it for more rugged use. With Lima's help the Shay design became immensely popular in the logging industry, and Lima became the sole producer of these engines until the original patents expired in the 1920s. They were built for many track gauges and in varying sizes, from the early two-truck models weighing about 6 tons to the largest one, a 191-ton, three-truck model for Kansas City Southern in 1913. The final model was a 160-ton machine for the Western Maryland. These latter two railroads used them on steep coal spurs in mountainous territory. After the 1920s the Willamette Iron & Steel Co. of Portland, Oregon, began producing large Shays needed by western loggers and forced Lima to improve its designs to include superheaters, piston valves, cast-steel trucks, and other modern features. These larger models were usually called Pacific Coast Shays.

The second most popular gear-drive locomotive was the Climax design, introduced in 1888 by the Climax Manufacturing Co. of Corry, Pennsylvania. Although it carried a conventional power cylinder on each side, each was placed above the main frame and oriented at a 30-degree angle in order to drive a transverse crankshaft below the boiler. Power was then transferred to each axle by line shafts and gearing below the frame. A total of 1,050 Climaxes were produced before the company ceased operation in 1928.

The final lumber engine to appear was invented by Charles Heisler in the 1890s. His layout involved twin power cylinders in a V configuration with one cylinder on each side of the boiler. The two pistons drove a longitudinal crankshaft beneath the center of the boiler that was connected by shafts and universal joints to one axle of each truck. The remaining axle on each truck was powered by a side rod. Heislers generally used only two trucks that included small drivers of conventional design. The Stearns Manufacturing Co. of Erie, Pennsylvania, produced 625 Heislers between 1894 and 1941.

—J. Parker Lamb

REFERENCES

Alexander, Edwin P. *The Pennsylvania Railroad: A Pictorial History.* New York: Bonanza Books, 1967.

Baldwin Locomotive Works. *Catalog of Locomotives.* New York: Rand-McNally, 1915. Repr., Ocean, N.J.: Specialty Press, ca. 1970.

Brown, John K. *The Baldwin Locomotive Works, 1831–1915.* Baltimore: Johns Hopkins Univ. Press, 1995.

Bruce, Alfred W. *The Steam Locomotive in America: Its Development in the Twentieth Century.* New York: W. W. Norton, 1952.

Dunscomb, Guy L. *A Century of Southern Pacific Steam Locomotives, 1862–1962.* Modesto, Calif.: Guy L. Dunscomb, 1963.

Hirsimaki, Eric F. *Lima: The History.* Edmonds, Wash.: Hundman, 1986.

Huddleston, Eugene L. *Uncle Sam's Locomotives.* Bloomington: Indiana Univ. Press, 2002.

Huddleston, Eugene L., and T. L. Dixon. *The Allegheny: Lima's Finest.* Edmonds, Wash.: Hundman, 1984.

Johnson, Ralph P. *The Steam Locomotive.* New York: Simmons-Boardman, 1942.

Kiefer, Paul W. *A Practical Evaluation of Railroad Motive Power.* New York: Simmons-Boardman, 1949.

Lamb, J. Parker. *Perfecting the American Steam Locomotive.* Bloomington: Indiana Univ. Press, 2003.

Westcott, Linn H., ed. *Model Railroader Cyclopedia.* Vol. 1, *Steam Locomotives.* Milwaukee, Wis.: Kalmbach, 1960.

White, John H. *American Locomotives: An Engineering History, 1830–1880.* Baltimore: Johns Hopkins Univ. Press, 1997.

———. *A Short History of American Locomotive Builders in the Steam Era.* Washington, D.C.: Bass, 1982.

Yoder, Jacob H., and George B. Warren. *Locomotive Valves and Valve Gears.* New York: Van Nostrand, 1917.

See also LOCOMOTIVE TESTING.

Stephenson, George (1781–1848)

Often called the father of railroading, George Stephenson was born at Wylam, eight miles from Newcastle, England. His father was a mechanic who operated a Newcomen atmospheric steam engine at the collieries of Newcastle. He received virtually no schooling, but later taught himself to read and write. At the age of 8 he was helping his father at

George Stephenson. —Middleton Collection

the mines and learned everything he could about existing steam engines. By age 19 Stephenson was operating an engine himself at several collieries. As a young man he moved to the town of Killingworth, also near Newcastle, where there were active pits; this was his home for many years. He became enginewright (chief mechanic) there in 1812, and by this time he was known in the vicinity as the man to see about engines.

By 1814 Stephenson had made his first steam-blast locomotive. It moved a load of 30 tons up an incline at 4 miles per hour. He had also married and had a son, Robert (born in 1803). Stephenson saw to it that Robert had a good formal education at a private academy in Newcastle. Every evening when his son came home, father and son studied mathematics and physics together.

The early Newcomen engines then in use were mostly for drawing water out of mines, but Stephenson was one of the first to see that a steam engine could be used for hauling coal over land and to market. He bent his energies to this work and made constant improvements over the first Trevithick engine designed to run on a railroad track. Between 1810 and 1820 a number of other people were working on steam locomotives, but Stephenson's genius in this area was becoming widely recognized. He was a virtuoso tinkerer and, independent of Sir Humphry Davy, invented a miner's safety lamp.

In 1821 Stephenson was appointed engineer of the proposed Stockton & Darlington Railroad, which would become the first public railroad in the world. This was to be primarily another coal-carrying line on a slightly

larger scale, but Stephenson persuaded the proprietors to scrap the idea of using a plateway and instead employed an edge railway of 4-foot 8-inch gauge (½ inch being added later to reduce friction). He also convinced them that locomotives were preferable to horses (no easy task). The line was opened on September 27, 1825, perhaps the true beginning of the railroad age.

By this time Stephenson, unlike many other engineers of the day, was thinking far into the future. He envisioned railroads as a new form of transportation: common carriers, not just coal roads. Naturally he perceived the need for better locomotives. He also was the first to perceive that if the railroad idea was to work, a wholly new field of engineering would have to be invented. A railroad line could not be useful if it had to go up hill and down dale; it would need a specially prepared right of way, and this would require cuts and fills, bridges, tunnels, and new techniques for passing bogs and other poor terrain. While Robert Stephenson was working on improved locomotive design, George addressed these new issues of civil engineering and convinced business and government leaders of their importance.

As a result of his success with the Stockton & Darlington, Stephenson was appointed chief engineer of another and much larger line, the Liverpool & Manchester. Here he encountered political issues, land claims, and still more difficult terrain. Although Stephenson knew that only steam locomotives would be right for this enterprise, he once again had to fight the horse traction enthusiasts.

A man of charisma and character, Stephenson eventually overcame most of these difficulties. His son Robert was working to create a much-advanced locomotive for the line, and it was proposed to have a competition for the best locomotive of the day. In the famous Rainhill trials of October 1829, the Stephenson-designed *Rocket*, with tubular boilers, was chosen as the most effective locomotive then in existence (in competition with several other locomotive builders), and the line was opened in a grand ceremony on September 15, 1830. This was without a doubt the first railroad in the modern sense, a purpose-built double-track line of malleable iron rails designed to transport both passengers and freight with steam traction. Stephenson predicted at this time that a vast network of railroads would cover the entire British Isles; that this was the most efficient means of transportation yet devised. He believed that it would be cheaper for a man to ride in a steam train than to walk.

Recent historians have carped over some of Stephenson's achievements and failures (there were some), but, like the conductor of a symphony orchestra, he brought all the ingredients of the railroad together through the force of his personality, technical skills, and foresight. And there were many years of railroad achievement ahead. Stephenson died as one of the most famous men in England in spite of his humble origins. Ralph Waldo Emerson met Stephenson on one of his trips to England and declared that it was worth crossing the Atlantic

Ocean just to meet a great man, "one who had the lives of many men in him."

—George H. Douglas

REFERENCES

Rolt, L. T. C. *The Railway Revolution: George and Robert Stephenson.* New York: St. Martin's Press, 1962.
Smiles, Samuel. *The Life of George Stephenson and of His Son, Robert Stephenson; Comprising Also a History of the Invention and Introduction of the Railway Locomotive.* New York: Harper & Brothers, 1868.

Stephenson, Robert (1803–1859)

Robert Stephenson received the full benefit of being the only son of railroad pioneer George Stephenson. The elder Stephenson, without formal learning, insisted that his son receive the best education and enrolled him at Bruce's Academy at Newcastle-upon-Tyne. Even as a teenager, young Stephenson was intimately involved with all of his father's endeavors. At the age of 20 he was put in charge of the first works anywhere in the world dedicated to building railway locomotives—Robert Stephenson & Co. of Newcastle. He was intimately involved with the design and construction of all of the early and famous Stephenson locomotives, and it has never been easy to determine which advancements were the work of the father and which of the son.

In 1825 George Stephenson received approval to construct the Stockton & Darlington, the first public railway to convey freight and passengers by steam locomotion. Robert took over many of the responsibilities for engine design, while his father attended to laying out the line and dealing with the public and the line's proprietors. Robert was also involved in surveying the much more extensive railroad line, the Liverpool & Manchester (built between 1824 and 1830), the first railroad conceived in the modern sense. During these years Robert Stephenson was perhaps more responsible than his father for making steady improvements in locomotive design, leading up to the Rainhill trials of 1829, held to determine the best locomotive for the Liverpool & Manchester. The Stephenson-designed *Rocket* won this contest, and Stephenson-built locomotives paved the way for the advanced steam locomotives as they would come to be known.

By the 1830s Robert Stephenson was a major figure in his own right. He was named chief engineer of the London & Birmingham Railroad in 1833 and subsequently was called upon to build other railroads in England and South America. In time he became most famous as a bridge and tunnel builder in England. Among his many

Robert Stephenson. —Science Museum, London

great achievements was the six-arch iron bridge over the Tyne River, using the newly invented steam hammer to drive his foundations. In 1854 he designed the Victoria Bridge in Montreal, Canada, for the Grand Trunk Railway (now the Canadian National), the longest bridge in the world at the time.

At the time of his death in 1859 Robert Stephenson, along with Isambard Kingdom Brunel, was the most famous railroad engineer in the world. He was president of both the Institution of Civil Engineers and the Institution of Mechanical Engineers. He is buried in Westminster Abbey.

—George H. Douglas

REFERENCES

Rolt, L. T. C. *The Railway Revolution: George and Robert Stephenson.* New York: St. Martin's Press, 1962.
Smiles, Samuel. *The Life of George Stephenson and of His Son, Robert Stephenson; Comprising Also a History of the Invention and Introduction of the Railway Locomotive.* New York: Harper & Brothers, 1868.

Stevens, Col. John (1749–1838)

Steamboat and railroad pioneer John Stevens has often been called the father of American railroading. Born in New York to a well-to-do landowning family of New Jersey, he graduated from Kings College (now Columbia University) in 1768. Stevens served with distinction in the

Revolutionary War and soon afterward formed a partnership with Nicholas Roosevelt, who had built a foundry in what today is Belleville, New Jersey. Roosevelt and Stevens experimented with several different designs of steamboats and operated them on the Passaic and Hudson rivers. Stevens's hope was to operate steamboat service across the Hudson between New Jersey and New York. He managed to inaugurate such a service but ran into difficulties with competitors Robert Fulton and Robert Livingston, who had obtained a monopoly for such traffic from the State of New York. This monopoly was declared unconstitutional by the U.S. Supreme Court in 1824, but in the meantime Stevens had to remove his most advanced craft to the Delaware River. This boat, the *Phoenix,* made its way onto the Atlantic Ocean in 1809 as the first steamboat ever to sail in ocean waters.

Thwarted by the Fulton-Livingston monopoly, Stevens turned his attention to another form of transportation: the railroad. Even as late as 1810 there was little knowledge of or interest in railroads in the United States, although there had been much activity in England. In 1811 Stevens wrote a tract titled *Documents to Prove the Superior Advantages of Railway and Steam Carriages over Canal Navigation.* This was the first book written anywhere in the world on the subject of railroads. Few people were moved by his arguments in 1811, but Stevens, a perpetual gadfly, pushed the idea whenever and wherever he could. In 1815 he applied to the State of New Jersey for a charter to build a railroad. The charter was in fact granted—the first ever for an American railroad—but Stevens was still far enough ahead of his time that no capital could be raised for the venture.

Stevens had to bide his time for another decade on the railroad issue, but he kept up his advocacy. Turnpikes were the rage in these years, and Stevens for a time became president of the Bergen Turnpike Co. Still, he remained convinced that the railroad was the optimum form of transportation for the vast inland areas of the United States.

A decade later Stevens was prepared for a new push that would change the history of American transportation. By this time he had made the first survey of a railroad route in America, across central New Jersey between New York and Philadelphia, the busiest travel corridor in the country. But first he needed to prove that steam locomotion by rail was possible. Accordingly, in 1825 he built a circular track on his estate in Hoboken, New Jersey, and constructed for it a 16-foot "steam wagon" with a vertical boiler. He ran this beast around and around the circular track, a demonstration that frightened nearby spectators. Although the steam wagon was little more than a toy by the standards of just a couple of decades later, it was the first steam locomotive ever to run on a rail in the United States.

By this time Stevens was 76 and not in a position to fulfill his dream of a railroad across New Jersey. But he did live to see the construction of this railroad, the Camden & Amboy, planned and executed by his sons Robert and Edwin. Stevens was there on November 12, 1831, for the first day of operation with the English-made locomotive *John Bull* at Bordentown, New Jersey.

Stevens could be described as one of America's great visionaries. He predicted that bridges and tunnels would cross the Hudson River, and that New York would build an elevated railroad. But he was more than a visionary— he became a prime mover for railroads. Although he did not live to see America crisscrossed by a vast network of railroads, he knew that it was coming, and he knew it before anyone else.

—George H. Douglas

REFERENCE

Turnbull, Archibald Douglas. *John Stevens, an American Record.* New York: American Society of Mechanical Engineers, 1928.

Stevens, John F. (1853–1943)

Born on a farm near West Gardiner, Maine, John Frank Stevens was educated in public schools and the State Normal School. Despite the lack of any formal training, he began an engineering career in the Minneapolis city engineer's office in 1874. He took up railroad work two years later, when he moved to Texas to conduct location surveys for the projected Sabine Pass & Northwestern, followed by similar assignments with other companies.

During 1882–1885 Stevens worked in location and construction for the Canadian Pacific, then took charge of the construction of two lines for the Chicago, Milwaukee & St. Paul and supervised the building of the Duluth, South Shore & Atlantic's line from Sault Ste. Marie, Michigan, to Duluth, Minnesota. In 1889 Stevens went to work for the Great Northern, leading to his best-known achievement, the location of a favorable route across the Rocky Mountains at Marias Pass in Montana. In December 1889, accompanied only by an Indian guide, Stevens set out on snowshoes through deep snow to locate a crossing of the Continental Divide that was the lowest and best of all in the northwestern United States. Stevens went on to head the final location and construction work for the GN's Pacific extension across Washington. He located a route across the Cascade Mountains through the pass that was later named in his honor. He was appointed GN's chief engineer in 1895 and became chief engineer and general manager in 1902. He moved to a similar post with the Rock Island during 1903–1905.

In June 1905 Stevens took up one of the most challenging assignments of his career when President Theodore Roosevelt appointed him chief engineer of the Panama Canal. Stevens ran the canal project the way he had the Great Northern: he got the work going in good order and led the fight for a locked rather than a sea-level canal. But for reasons that he never made clear, Stevens abruptly resigned in 1907 and soon returned to railroad work.

After serving for two years as a vice president of the New Haven, Stevens joined James J. Hill once again to head the Spokane, Portland & Seattle and its subsidiaries. In 1917 he was appointed by President Woodrow Wilson to head a U.S. railroad commission to restore the railroad system in Russia and then became president of a technical board created to oversee reorganization of the railways in Siberia and Manchuria. Returning to the United States in 1923, he was a consultant to the Great Northern in planning the new Cascade Tunnel. He was 90 years old when he died at his home in Pinehurst, North Carolina, in 1943.

—William D. Middleton

REFERENCES

Brimlow, George F., ed. "Marias Pass Explorer, John F. Stevens." *Montana Magazine of History*, Summer 1953, 39–44.
Dictionary of American Biography.
Martin, Albro. *James J. Hill and the Opening of the Northwest.* New York: Oxford Univ. Press, 1976.
National Cyclopaedia of American Biography.

Sunday Service Restrictions

During the initial years of rail service in the United States, train operations tended to be concentrated in New England and the Northeast, a region where advocates of proper Sunday observance (Sabbatarians) had long been vocal in their opposition to unnecessary activity on the Lord's Day. State and local laws dating from colonial times forbade all types of labor and amusements on Sundays. During the nineteenth century it was common for lawmakers to seek to restrict railroad operations.

Because it was easy for passenger trains in geographically compact New England to complete their scheduled journeys within the space of a single day, railroads typically trimmed service on Sundays, apparently without creating major hardships for travelers or shippers. Printed railway guides from the 1850s do not indicate clearly which passenger trains operated on Sundays, but without doubt the Northeast led the nation in restricting railroad operations on the Lord's Day.

The argument for some Sabbatarians was whether any trains should operate, and whether railroad workers should be required to take an enforced day of rest. A variety of "blue laws" attempted to impose those convictions on society generally. A particularly outspoken proponent of proper Sunday observance by railroads was William E. Dodge, a wealthy New York City merchant and a member of the boards of several major railroads. In 1857 the pious Dodge abruptly resigned from the board of the Erie Railroad, one of the nation's largest at the time, after he split with fellow directors over whether the company should run its trains on Sundays. Subsequent events only strengthened his convictions. Barely two years after Dodge sold his Erie stock at a good price, the railroad failed financially.

A similar scenario played out on the New Jersey Central Railroad, where Dodge served as a director for 15 years. Before he resigned from the board, he protested to fellow directors that they should place a flag on all their locomotives bearing the legend, "We break God's Law for a dividend." He sold his stock for $116 to $118 a share. Two years later the New Jersey Central sank into bankruptcy, and its common stock sold for a lowly 10 cents a share. To his dying day in 1883, Dodge continued to protest "Sunday Railway Desecration."

West of the Mississippi River, where the space that separated major population centers was typically many times greater, it was impractical for transportation providers to halt service for one day out of seven. When the overland stagecoaches commenced service between St. Louis and Memphis and San Francisco in the late 1850s, they ran day and night for as long as four weeks. Any passengers who wished to observe a proper Sunday by remaining behind a day at a stage station could reboard the next coach only if seats were unoccupied. Sometimes during periods of heavy travel that meant being stranded for several days in an isolated and uncomfortable hotel. A similar problem occurred when railroads commenced overland service across the West. They simply could not halt their long-distance passenger trains during the hours of the Lord's Day. There was, in fact, much less pressure from Sabbatarians on the railroads of the West than on those of the Northeast and South. Even in the Northeast the proper way for a railroad to observe Sunday became much less an issue by the dawn of the twentieth century, after which the secularization of American life grew much more noticeable.

—Carlos Arnaldo Schwantes

REFERENCES

Ely, James W., Jr. *Railroads and American Law.* Lawrence: Univ. Press of Kansas, 2001.
Fuller, Wayne E. *Morality and the Mail in Nineteenth-Century America.* Urbana: Univ. of Illinois Press, 2003.

Surface Transportation Board

The Surface Transportation Board (STB) was created by the Interstate Commerce Commission Termination Act of 1995. The ICC passed into history on December 31, 1995, and the STB began its work on January 1, 1996. The STB is not an independent regulatory commission, as was the ICC. Nevertheless, the STB is established as an independent adjudicatory body that is housed in the U.S.

Department of Transportation for administrative purposes. The ICC never had fewer than 5 commissioners and had as many as 11 at its peak; the Surface Transportation Board was established with three board members and may operate with just one board member present.

The passage of the ICC Termination Act represented another important change in federal regulatory policy toward transportation. Economic deregulation began in 1978 with the deregulation of the airline industry and continued with the Staggers Act in 1980, which partially deregulated the railroad industry, and the Motor Carrier Act of 1980, which did the same for interstate motor carriers. The nature of regulation of the water carriers was such that there was never more than minimal regulatory effort. Regulation of pipelines had been transferred to the Federal Energy Regulatory Commission in 1978. The ICC Termination Act also ended virtually all economic regulation of interstate motor carrier transportation.

The primary work of the STB is the oversight of interstate surface transportation and is focused mainly on the railroads. The STB has jurisdiction over railroad rate issues and service matters. A major STB role concerns the restructuring of railroads, including mergers, line sales, construction of new lines, and the abandonment of existing rail lines. The STB also deals with labor problems arising from restructuring of the railroads. On a limited basis, it is involved in rate matters concerning motor carriers, household goods movers, and ocean shipping firms in noncontiguous parts of the nation. The STB is also authorized to work on pipeline matters not regulated by the Federal Energy Regulatory Commission and may become involved in certain structural, financial, and operational matters of intercity bus services. Railroad mergers have taken up a large portion of the STB's time since its creation.

Like its predecessor, the work of the STB is carried out through administrative law proceedings. The Office of Proceedings develops the formal legal record in cases brought before the STB by means of hearings, statements from involved and affected parties, and other fact-gathering activities. It makes recommendations to the STB board on possible solutions to problems brought to the STB and assists in preparing and implementing STB decisions.

The Office of the General Counsel is charged with defending STB decisions in federal court. Under the Hobbs Act, the STB has independent litigating authority, similar to that of the ICC. The STB's Office of Compliance and Enforcement has oversight over the operational aspects of carriers that fall under the jurisdiction of the STB; it also has relationships with the public on matters relating to tariffs and the Rail Consumer Assistance Program.

The Office of Economics, Environmental Analysis, and Administration has broad responsibilities. These include economic, cost, financial, engineering, and environmental analyses of matters that come before the STB. A major role is administrative support, which includes human relations management, computer systems, and space management.

Finally, the Office of Congressional and Public Services is the main connection of the STB board with the public and with legislators. Press and congressional reaction to STB decisions and public concerns about the STB and its decisions also fall under the purview of this office.

The STB is administratively related to the Department of Transportation, but is independent in its actions. The ICC Termination Act sought to reduce the cost of providing what economic regulation of transportation, primarily rail transportation, would remain in effect. The U.S. DOT provides the general administrative functions necessary for the STB, such as payroll, personnel, equal employment opportunity matters, and such work as administration of the Freedom of Information Act. The need for a separate bureaucracy is eliminated by placing the STB under the DOT umbrella. There also is a degree of budgetary independence. The STB sends its budget directly to Congress at the same time it is transmitted to the DOT.

For funding, the STB is on a recurring authorization cycle. The STB must be reauthorized periodically, in contrast with the permanent authorization of the ICC. In addition to the funds from the federal budget, the STB also collects filing and user fees from its clients. At the beginning of the twenty-first century the STB budget was in the range of $18 million to $20 million annually. The STB had a staff of approximately 200.

In its work the STB has jurisdiction over rates, classifications, rules, practices, services, acquisitions, railroad facilities, and the abandonment of lines. For the motor carrier industry, the STB is involved with tariffs for movers of household goods and trade with noncontiguous parts of the United States, such as Hawaii and Alaska. Undercharge and overcharge claims are filed with the STB. Under the STB, motor carriers retain immunity from antitrust action in carrying out the practices of collective ratemaking. Freight forwarders and transportation brokers are required to register with the STB. The largest impact of the STB on the transportation and business communities has been its rulings on matters of merger and acquisition of railroads. It has usually acted quickly in comparison with the ICC. The takeover of the Southern Pacific by the Union Pacific was decided in less than two years. The proposed merger of the Burlington Northern & Santa Fe with the Canadian National resulted in the STB declaring a moratorium on large-scale mergers for a lengthy time.

—George M. Smerk

REFERENCES

Coyle, John J., Edward J. Bardi, and Robert A. Novack. *Transportation*. 5th ed. Chap. 2. Cincinnati, Ohio: South-Western, 1999.

Spychalski, John C. "From ICC to STB: Continuing Vestiges of U.S. Surface Transportation Regulation." *Journal of Transport Economics and Policy* 71, no. 1 (Jan. 1997): 131–136.

Switching and Terminal Railroads

Rail carriers identified as switching and terminal railroads have played supporting roles in the North American railway industry since the nineteenth century. They serve limited areas, such as a city, a greater metropolitan area, an ocean or river port, or an industrial district. Their basic purpose is the performance of origination, termination, and interchange functions for line-haul railroads with which they connect. A railroad classified within the overall category of "switching and terminal" can, on the basis of its dominant operational orientation, be subclassified as a switching railroad, a terminal railroad, or a comprehensive terminal railroad.

A switching railroad exists primarily to move freight to and from private sidings for manufacturing, warehousing, and other commercial installations. Some switching railroads serve sidetracks within public facilities such as coastal, river, and Great Lakes ports. To provide access to rail service for shippers and consignees who lack private sidings, a switching railroad may maintain public delivery or team tracks at which freight can be transloaded between railcars and motor trucks.

Switching railroads can be owned by line-haul railroads, manufacturing or warehousing companies, private stevedoring firms, government-sponsored quasi-private entities such as port authorities, or municipal governments. A prominent example of the latter is the New Orleans Public Belt Railroad (NOPB), founded (in 1904), owned, and operated by the City of New Orleans through the Public Belt Railroad Commission.

The NOPB was conceived to provide switching service without discrimination in price and quality "to all who require and can use it." Its more than 100 miles of track along the New Orleans waterfront and adjacent sites connect public wharves, private industries, and public delivery tracks with one another and with all line-haul railroads that serve the city. NOPB thus serves as a neutral carrier, providing shippers and consignees within its service area, and its line-haul connectors, with a broader range of rail transport access than could be provided individually by line-haul carriers.

In 1935 NOPB added toll-bridge service to its switching business base when it completed and opened the 4.4-mile-long (including approaches) Huey P. Long Bridge spanning the Mississippi River. The new bridge provided a double-track railroad crossing, paralleled on each side by two highway lanes and a pedestrian walk. It replaced costly and time-consuming ferry services, on which all rail and road traffic crossing the river at New Orleans had previously been forced to rely.

Historically, passenger traffic was the dominant focus among terminal railroads. From the inception of rail transport in North America until the assumption of most intercity passenger service by Amtrak and VIA Rail Canada more than 14 decades later, passenger operations were conducted by individual railway companies. With a few early exceptions (notably in Chicago), this initially resulted in the construction and operation of separate passenger stations and supporting terminal facilities in communities served by more than one rail carrier.

Such individualism began to erode in the face of burgeoning growth in passenger traffic through the nineteenth century and into the first two decades of the twentieth century, along with rising urban population, congestion and land costs, and related civic and political forces. The need for expansion of terminal capacity stemming from these conditions induced the establishment of union passenger stations in many cities. Union station users included carriers that competed heavily with one another, as well as those that exchanged interline passengers. Prominent examples included Los Angeles Union Passenger Terminal (Southern Pacific, Atchison, Topeka & Santa Fe, and Union Pacific), Toronto Union Station (Canadian Pacific and Canadian National), and the Washington Terminal Co. (WTC), owner of Washington (D.C.) Union Station. The WTC, founded in 1903 as a jointly owned subsidiary of the rival Baltimore & Ohio and Pennsylvania railroads, also served the Richmond, Fredericksburg & Potomac, the Chesapeake & Ohio, and the Southern as tenants.

The business focus of a comprehensive terminal railroad encompasses services offered by both switching and terminal railroads. A leading contemporary example is the Belt Railway Co. of Chicago (BRC). It originates and terminates through freight trains for line-haul railroads and interchanges freight between them at its Clearing Yard on the southwest edge of Chicago, where it also operates locomotive- and freight-car-servicing facilities. Additionally, it accommodates interyard freight transfer movements for line-haul railroads and switches more than 100 private industries and a rail-to-water coal transloading facility along its main-line trackage, which brackets the southern and western sides of Chicago. Two rivals, the Indiana Harbor Belt Railroad (IHB) and the Elgin, Joliet & Eastern Railway (EJ&E), also operate belt lines that partly encircle Chicago and intersect with line-haul railroads entering the city. The EJ&E's main line reaches east to Gary, Indiana, where the company operates its primary classification yard and serves U.S. Steel's Gary Works. In addition to moving rail traffic into and out of the steel works, the EJ&E provides it with intra-plant switching service.

Important comprehensive terminal railroads in other localities include the Terminal Railroad Assn. of St. Louis (TRRA) and the Houston Belt & Terminal Railway Co. Both provide freight interchange and industrial switching service for their line-haul connectors. In the past, both also owned and maintained the union passenger stations in their namesake cities. Ownership of two bridges spanning the Mississippi River between St. Louis, Missouri, and East St. Louis, Illinois, used by trains of both the TRRA and line-haul carriers entering St. Louis from the east, is another function of the TRRA.

The purchase (1997) and subsequent operational split-up (1999) of the Consolidated Rail Corp. (Conrail) by Norfolk Southern (NS) and CSX was accompanied by the establishment of a comprehensive terminal railroad bearing the Conrail name and owned jointly by NS and CSX. Its purpose is to provide shippers in the New York–New Jersey area with neutral (in price and quality) access to line-haul services of NS and CSX. The conditions underlying the appearance of this relatively new terminal system and its elder peers suggest that the comprehensive terminal railroad will continue to play a role in the American freight railroad industry as long as localities for origination and termination of significant volumes of traffic continue to be served by two or more line-haul carriers, and as long as the number of carriers in the industry remains sufficient to require interchange of large quantities of traffic at key gateways.

—John C. Spychalski

REFERENCE

Campbell, G. M. "Why We Have Terminal Railroads." *Trains* 9, no. 3 (Jan. 1949): 28–30.

Symes, James Miller (1897–1976)

Pennsylvania Railroad executive James Miller Symes was born in Glen Osborne, Pennsylvania, near Pittsburgh. In 1916, having completed a secretarial course at the Carnegie Institute of Technology, he joined the PRR as a clerk and car tracer. On September 27, 1919, he married Fern Elizabeth Dick, also a PRR clerk. In 1920 he became chief statistician for the Pennsylvania's Lake Division in Cleveland. After two years he entered the operating department as division freight movement director. He rose quickly through the ranks to become Lake Division train movement director, then general manager of passenger transportation for the Western Region in Chicago. In 1929 he was transferred in that same capacity to the Eastern Region in Philadelphia, but went back to the freight side in 1934 as chief of freight transportation for the entire PRR system. As freight chief, he represented the PRR on the Eastman Commission, a federal panel charged with encouraging voluntary reduction of the nation's overbuilt rail network. In 1935 he took a leave of absence from the Pennsylvania to serve as the Assn. of American Railroads' vice president for operations and maintenance.

In 1939 Symes returned to the PRR's Western Region as general manager and later became regional vice president.

In 1947 he was promoted to vice president of operations. He clashed with other operating executives when he proposed replacing the railroad's 4,100 steam locomotives with diesels at a cost of $400 million. Pennsylvania president Martin Clement backed his plan, however, which was implemented during the ensuing decade. The economies of dieselization could not prevent a decline in the railroad's financial condition. Obsolete rolling stock, a physical plant exhausted by wartime demands, competition from highway and air transportation, money-losing passenger trains, and a shrinking industrial base in the Northeast were only a few of the railroad's troubles.

Symes became vice president in 1949 and executive vice president in 1952 and succeeded Walter Franklin as PRR president in 1954. As president, he developed a three-pronged approach to stemming the company's financial losses and building new traffic.

First, he introduced a modernization program that featured construction of two world-class facilities: a huge automated classification yard at Conway, near Pittsburgh, and the Samuel Rea Car Shop at Hollidaysburg, Pennsylvania. The program also included the adoption of truck-trailer-on-flatcar shipments, putting the Pennsylvania in the forefront of intermodalism. But Symes was unable to overcome his company's preference for paying dividends to bolster its stock price instead of directing surplus earnings toward improvements, a policy that seriously compromised his modernization goals.

Second, he sought federal regulatory reform. He testified repeatedly that if railroads were not given freedom to set rates, and if government subsidies continued to favor highway users and airlines, railroad bankruptcy and government ownership were inevitable. His warnings were largely ignored.

Third, returning to ideas he first studied as a member of the Eastman Commission, Symes advocated railroad consolidation, contending that mergers would eliminate duplicate services and facilities and reduce labor costs. For the PRR, he proposed in 1957 a merger with archrival New York Central. The two lines served the same northeastern and midwestern industrial base, were beset by heavy long-haul and commuter passenger-train losses, operated numerous parallel lines with duplicate facilities, and were experiencing serious financial problems. Within two years the stockholders of both companies approved the merger, and hearings began before the Interstate Commerce Commission.

In 1959 Symes was named to the newly created post of chairman of the board and guided the merger discussions until his retirement on September 30, 1963, shortly before the ICC approved the consolidation. He served as a PRR director through five years of litigation that followed the ICC's decision and an additional year as a director of the new Penn Central Transportation Co., formed on February 1, 1968. Penn Central failed to produce the results that he had forecast. When it declared bankruptcy in June 1970, PC became the largest business failure in American history up to that time. The fiasco finally persuaded Congress to deregulate railroads in order to make them more competitive with other transport modes. Penn Central was folded into the federally backed Consolidated Rail Corp., which eventually posted impressive earnings, as Symes had predicted it would, if given freedom of the marketplace. Thirty years of railroad consolidation since Penn Central proved that his thinking was theoretically sound; he simply chose the wrong partner for the PRR. The Pennsylvania and New York Central were too similar. Their merger magnified their problems and diluted their strengths. Symes died in Feasterville, Pennsylvania, in 1976.

—Michael Bezilla

REFERENCES

Churella, Albert. "'The Company Could Not Take Complete Advantage of Its Bigness': Managerial Culture and the Pennsylvania Railroad's 1955 Corporate Reorganization." *Business and Economic History On-Line* 3 (2005). http://www.thebhc.org/publications/BEHonline/2005/churella.pdf

Daughen, Joseph R., and Peter Binzen. *The Wreck of the Penn Central*. Boston: Little, Brown, 1971.

"The Future . . . What Jim Symes Is Doing About It." *Railway Age*, Sept. 14, 1954.

Maurer, Herrymon. "New Signals for the Pennsy." *Fortune*, Nov. 1955.

Obituaries in *Philadelphia Inquirer*, Aug. 4, 1976; and *New York Times*, Aug. 5, 1976.

Salsbury, Stephen. *No Way to Run a Railroad*. New York: McGraw-Hill, 1982.

Note: Documents relating to Symes's service as a PRR regional and system executive are scattered throughout the Pennsylvania Railroad collections at the Pennsylvania State Archives in Harrisburg; the Hagley Museum and Library in Greenville, Del.; and to a lesser extent the PRR Central Region records at Pennsylvania State University's Historical Collections and Labor Archives.

T

Tariffs. *See* RATES AND RATE

ASSOCIATIONS

Taxation

For much of their history railroads were the dominant mode of transportation. Among competing transportation modes they had by far the largest proportion of fixed plant; it could neither be moved nor abandoned. Thus they were vulnerable to property taxes. As long as they were the dominant overland carrier, the railroads were able to absorb these often-discriminatory state and local property taxes, but the situation changed when trucks became vigorous competitors.

Trucks and water carriers, of course, use an infrastructure built and maintained at taxpayer expense. Yet their user fees and fuel taxes do not cover their proportionate share of the cost of building and maintaining highways or navigational facilities. As a result, railroads have lost market share: in 1929 they carried 75 percent of the nation's intercity freight, but they now haul little more than 40 percent. In this competitive environment state and local property tax discrimination against railroads grew from being an annoyance to a crushing burden.

Because railroad operating property extended beyond individual taxing jurisdictions, most states provided for the assessment of such property by a centralized state agency. Other commercial and industrial taxpayers were assessed locally, and their property was listed at something less than the legal assessment ratio. Centrally assessed railroad taxpayers, however, enjoyed no such latitude and were annually overassessed by the states in spite of state laws requiring uniform treatment. Assessment requires four major steps: determination of the value of the carrier as a unit, allocation of system value to the state, equalization of the state allocation with local assessments, and determination of the amount of equalized assessment assignable to the local taxing district.

In such a highly subjective system state tax discrimination against railroad property was unchecked. Consequently, railroads paid 9.3 percent of the assessed value of their property in property tax payments, while other similarly situated property paid a normal maximum of 3 percent or 4 percent. For example, Minnesota chose to levy a property tax on docks, but only one set of docks in the state fit the statutory criteria, those owned by the railroad. By law California could reassess property only upon sale, but raised the property tax assessment on railroad property because the railroad intended to sell it at some time in the future. An Alabama business license fee was levied on only one kind of business: railroads. South Dakota taxed railroad personal property, but exempted 75 percent of comparable property. Iowa exempted 95 percent of comparable property.

If the railroad wished to contest the assessment, it had to pay the tax in full, file a refund claim, and pursue its appeal administratively before it could get to state court. Such appeals were usually heard by the very state officials who had established the discriminatory tax assessment and were fraught with procedural hazards and delays. Decisions were virtually always adverse to the railroad.

After exhausting its administrative appeal, the railroad could sue in state court. However, an elected state court judge quickly realized that granting tax relief to a railroad would increase taxes on his constituents. He also realized this was not a winning campaign theme.

More important, state laws often require the challenging taxpayer to prove either fraud or malfeasance in the state's property tax assessment or that it was arbitrary and capricious in order to obtain relief. Proof frequently had to be by clear and convincing evidence rather than by a preponderance. Given the vast subjectivity of the state property tax assessment process, these obstacles proved impossible for a railroad to overcome.

In the rare case where the railroad prevailed in state court, it might not get its cash back. Relief could be given in the form of a credit against future taxes. If cash was recovered, it was often refunded without interest or at a submarket rate.

Unfortunately, the smothering federal regulation of railroading did not include oversight power to remedy state property tax discrimination. On the contrary, federal law specifically barred access to federal courts for state tax claims.

As several large railroads lurched into bankruptcy in the 1960s, Congress conducted hearings on the railroads' financial problems that culminated in the Doyle Report. The Senate Commerce Committee concluded that the property tax discrimination practiced against the railroads was so pervasive and complex that it could not be rectified. The committee recommended that Congress exempt all railroad right-of-way property from state property taxes. The committee viewed this as a twofold solution: first as a means of redressing the competitive imbalance between railroads and trucks (privately funded infrastructure versus publicly funded infrastructure) and second as a way of eliminating property tax discrimination against the railroads.

Exemption of railroad property from state and local property taxation, however, was not politically feasible, so the railroads had to settle for Section 306 of the Railroad Revitalization and Regulatory Reform Act of 1976, 49 U.S.C. § 11503, Pub. L. 94-210, 90 Stat. 31 (1976) (hereinafter cited as the 4R Act). Section 306 was designed to allow railroads to be taxed like other commercial and industrial taxpayers; property tax discrimination against railroads was deemed to be contrary to federal transportation policy. "[A]ssessment ratios or taxation rates imposed on railroad property which differ significantly from the ratios or rates imposed on other commercial and industrial property are prohibited as burdens on interstate commerce" (*Burlington Northern R.R. v. Oklahoma Tax Commission*, 481 U.S. 454, 457 [1987], hereinafter cited as *BN*). Federal courts were empowered to hear railroad tax discrimination complaints and to enjoin the discriminatory tax. The statute also established a quantitative measure to determine whether discrimination existed. Finally, Section 306(1)(d) prohibited the "imposition of any other tax which results in discriminatory treatment of a . . . railroad." This catchall provision effectively barred states from devising new taxes in lieu of property taxes on railroads.

Despite the congressional mandate of the 4R Act, the states did not reform their property tax regimes. Twenty-three states joined Oklahoma in its futile opposition to Section 306 before the U.S. Supreme Court (*BN*). For the past two decades railroads have been compelled to sue virtually every state in order to obtain relief; they have won the overwhelming majority of cases.

The Congress correctly concluded that the long-term solution to state tax discrimination against railroads is to exempt railroad right-of-way property from all state property taxes. This solution would also partially rectify the competitive imbalance created by taxpayer-subsidized infrastructures provided to the trucks, airlines, and barges.

—Daniel J. Westerbeck

REFERENCE

Report of the Senate Committee on Interstate and Foreign Commerce on National Transportation Policy. 87th Cong., 1st sess., 1969. S. Rep. 445. Also known as the Doyle Report.

Terminal Railroad Assn. of St. Louis (TRRA)

The opening of the St. Louis Bridge (now known as the Eads Bridge) across the Mississippi River at St. Louis in 1874 established St. Louis as a major gateway between the railroads east and west of the Mississippi. The new bridge, however, got off to a bad start. The railroads on the Illinois side lacked authority to operate in Missouri, and for almost a year freight and passengers continued to cross the river by ferry. The bridge company and the St. Louis Tunnel Co., which had completed a tunnel under downtown St. Louis to link the bridge with the city's rail lines, then formed two new terminal subsidiaries, both named Union Railway & Transit (of St. Louis and of Illinois) to build the tracks, establish the terminals, and operate the trains required to link the railroads in Illinois and Missouri. Another company, the Union Depot Co. of St. Louis, was organized to establish a new union depot for all passenger trains originating or terminating in St. Louis.

In 1889 Jay Gould, who then controlled both the Wabash and the Missouri Pacific, negotiated an agreement among six of the railroads serving St. Louis to form the jointly owned Terminal Railroad Association of St. Louis (TRRA), which then took control of the bridge, tunnel, terminal, and union depot companies. Four years later TRRA gained control of the rival Merchants Bridge, which had been completed in 1890 to circumvent the Eads Bridge monopoly. In 1894 TRRA completed the splendid new St. Louis Union Station, designed by architect Theodore C. Link, to replace the outmoded Union Depot. The station was the largest in North America in terms of the number of tracks on a single level (32 under the arched trainshed; 10 more tracks were later added in an annex to the west).

TRRA's historic Eads Bridge safely carried rail traffic across the Mississippi for a full century, until the structure proved unable to handle the trilevel auto racks and 125-ton-capacity cars of modern practice. The bridge was closed to rail traffic in 1974 (it continued to carry highway traffic on its upper deck). Eads Bridge was just what was needed, however, for a new regional light-rail line, and in 1989 TRRA transferred ownership of the structure to the City of St. Louis in exchange for the MacArthur Bridge. New track was laid, and in July 1993 MetroLink light-rail trains of the Missouri-Illinois Bi-State Development Agency began using the bridge.

Amtrak used St. Louis Union Station until 1978, when it moved to a temporary building nearby. Handsomely restored and adapted, Union Station and its trainshed became a hotel, restaurant, and shopping complex.

Five of the current six largest North American railroads are TRRA's owners: Burlington Northern & Santa Fe, Canadian National (which inherited Illinois Central's share), CSX Transportation, Norfolk Southern, and Union Pacific. TRRA today operates some 230 miles of track providing connections with the main-line carriers and serving local industries.

—George H. Drury

REFERENCE

Grant, H. Roger, Don L. Hofsommer, and Osmund Overby. *St. Louis Union Station: A Place for People, a Place for Trains.* St. Louis, Mo.: St. Louis Mercantile Library, 1994.

Texas & Pacific Railway

With the nation still reveling in the completion of its first transcontinental rail line via Ogden, Utah, Congress gave a charter to another group of backers who aspired to construct a southern route to the Pacific. The 1872 charter for the Texas & Pacific Railway approved a routing from Marshall, Texas, through El Paso to San Diego and required 100 consecutive miles of construction by 1882. The T&P hired former Union Pacific executive Grenville Dodge as chief engineer, and his crews began work at three points in early 1873. Within 10 months 250 miles of line had been completed, including Longview-Dallas, Paris-Sherman, and Marshall-Texarkana. These segments connected with lines that had been built before the Civil War between Waskom and Marshall and between Jefferson and Paris, giving the new T&P a strong network in northeast Texas.

But these successes were abruptly halted by the panic of 1873, which forced the construction company into receivership in 1875. One of its last projects was a bridge over the Trinity River in Dallas that enabled T&P to handle the massive amount of livestock traffic originating on the many ranches to the west. Nearby Fort Worth, a major livestock-marketing center, became increasingly dissatisfied with the lack of a T&P connection. Finally, in frustration with the cash-strapped railroad, an organization of farmers and stockmen graded the 30-mile stretch between the two cities and laid down ties, allowing the first T&P train to enter "Cowtown, Texas," in July 1876.

For a number of years the western terminus of the railroad remained at Fort Worth because of a lack of financial backing. However, the T&P was growing rapidly as a transportation enterprise because of its strategic importance in northeast Texas and its connections through Texarkana and Shreveport to major cities such as St. Louis, New Orleans, and Atlanta. It is ironic that the city of Fort Worth, which had to pay to get into the T&P family, eventually became the road's headquarters city, as well as an operating and shop hub for the entire Texas railroad network.

Enter Jay Gould

Although T&P's board of directors included some well-connected business and political leaders and was headed by President Thomas Scott, a former executive of the Pennsylvania Railroad, the road was unable to secure any federal assistance in building across western Texas to California. However, in January 1880 the road's prospects changed abruptly with the seating of two new directors, Jay Gould and his associate Russell Sage. Gould had just completed acquisition of the Missouri Pacific system and was looking for new opportunities. When Scott decided to sell his T&P holdings a year later, they were acquired by Gould, who became president of the railroad and immediately formulated an ambitious expansion plan. The T&P fit perfectly into his Missouri Pacific system, whose St. Louis, Iron Mountain & Southern connected with the T&P at Texarkana. One of his first moves was to build a line connecting Fort Worth with Sherman, giving the T&P a second route to Texarkana, as well as a direct connection at Denison with the recently completed Missouri, Kansas & Texas, which Gould had acquired in 1880.

In the meantime Gould commissioned Dodge to begin an all-out effort to lay rails through the vast and nearly uninhabited desert of western Texas. Commencing in mid-1880, construction crews reached Big Spring (267 miles from Fort Worth) in April 1881 and Sierra Blanca (522 miles) on December 16, 1881. However, at the latter village Gould's dream of a transcontinental railroad evaporated when it ran up against Collis P. Huntington, another railroad tycoon as determined and ruthless as himself. Huntington's eastward construction crews had passed through Sierra Blanca some three weeks earlier (November 25, 1881) en route to the last-spike ceremony of the Sunset Route, held at the Pecos River bridge, west of Del Rio, in January 1883. When it became clear that Huntington was winning the race for a transcontinental line, a series of court battles ensued, followed by nefarious delaying tactics (including sabotage) by each construction crew, and finally by personal negotiation between the two principals. Gould would have settled for joint ownership of the 90 miles west of Sierra Blanca, but Huntington was unwilling to budge and was eventually victorious in the courts. Thus, although T&P maintained yards and other trackage within El Paso, it operated trains west of Sierra Blanca though a trackage rights agreement that continued in effect until the 1996 takeover of Southern Pacific by Union Pacific.

After completing his line to the west, Gould turned eastward and completed T&P's own line between Waskom and Shreveport. More important, he pushed on to New Orleans by acquiring some shortlines and constructing connecting segments. The New Orleans–Dallas–El Paso route constituted the geographic limits of the T&P, although the Marshall-Texarkana stretch was probably the busiest segment since it was used by both east-west and north-south traffic from connecting MoPac lines.

Gould's reckless management of his railroad empire during perilous financial times caused his holdings to crumble in the mid-1880s. One by one his roads entered receivership: Wabash (1884), T&P (1885), MK&T (1888), and International & Great Northern (1889). He was able to maintain MoPac control of only two, T&P and I&GN (eastern and southern Texas lines). This is not surprising since they were the most critical to MoPac operations. The T&P connection was tightened during a 1923 reorganization in which T&P issued preferred stock to MoPac in exchange for mortgage bonds, giving the parent company over 50 percent of common stock and all the preferred stock. Thus, even though its operations were thoroughly integrated with those of its parent, T&P continued to be a semiautonomous subsidiary. Shielded by a state law that required all railroads operating in Texas to have a general office within the state, the T&P exhibited "Texas pride" with its own motive-power department, its own shops (at Marshall and Fort Worth), and its own identity on rolling stock. The earliest rendition of the T&P herald was a stylized diamond with the names of its four major terminal cities outside the slanted sides (Texarkana, El Paso, Shreveport, and New Orleans).

T&P was blessed by the discovery of oil at both ends of the Lone Star State. The massive eastern Texas fields around Ranger were opened in 1918, and a few years later the Permian Basin of western Texas (near Midland and Odessa) began producing. During World War II the T&P was one of the major originators of tank-car trains headed to the two coasts.

Locomotives

T&P's independent-minded motive-power department holds the distinction of originating the second of Lima's so-called Super-Power steam locomotives of the mid-1920s. Its I-1 Class 2-10-4 design, first produced in 1925 to pull heavy tonnage over the mountains of western Texas, was named the Texas type. Eventually the road acquired 70 of these large engines—almost 20 percent of its 1929 roster of 372 locomotives. Styling was also important to the T&P motive-power people. The road's larger steamers generally carried English-type capped stacks along with Elesco feedwater heaters on their smokeboxes adorned with a diamond herald and, when needed, air-pump shields on the pilot beam (also trimmed with the herald). Most passenger power sparkled with blue boiler jackets accented with white striping on tender sides and running-board skirts.

Along with its parent, T&P began dieselizing just after the war, primarily with Electro-Motive locomotives: switchers in 1946, E7 passenger units in 1947, and F7 freight cabs in 1949. Paint schemes for cab units were similar to those of MoPac (blue and white), whereas light orange with black trim was used initially on yard and road switcher units. Eventually (1960s) the solid blue colors of MoPac prevailed even though the diamond herald was still applied to T&P-owned units until trust certificates expired.

Missouri Pacific Purchase and Ownership

In 1956 MoPac began systematic purchases of T&P stock with a goal of 80 percent ownership that would allow consolidated tax returns for the two companies. Ironically, one of the last large blocks of stock acquired was 12,000 shares from the estate of Frank Gould, grandson of the flamboyant tycoon. By 1957 MoPac owned 77 percent of T&P, and there was talk of official merger, but a cautious management, fearful of a negative public perception, decided not to pursue it. However, in 1976 the semi-independent status of the Texas & Pacific was finally brought to an end after a 30-year legal battle for recapitalization of the MoPac system's holding company. In the end, the new Missouri Pacific Corp. absorbed its three major railroads, MoPac, T&P, and Chicago & Eastern Illinois.

In another large slice of irony, the Fort Worth–Sierra Blanca line actually became a key segment in one of the nation's premier transcontinental routes in 1996 when the Union Pacific, after swallowing up Missouri Pacific and Western Pacific, also merged with the Southern Pacific. The former T&P line between Texarkana and El Paso is some 200 miles shorter than the route that uses former Cotton Belt and SP track.

In 1975, its last year before being merged by Missouri Pacific, Texas & Pacific operated 2,139 route-miles and 3,069 track-miles, with 153 locomotives, 13,366 freight cars, 263 company service cars, and 3,368 employees. Freight traffic totaled 7,066.9 million ton-miles in 1975, and chemicals (22.7 percent), transportation equipment (10.9 percent), and foodstuffs (10.9 percent) were its principal traffic sources. Texas & Pacific operating revenues totaled $150.2 million in 1975, and the railroad achieved a 77.7 percent operating ratio.

—J. Parker Lamb

REFERENCE

Reed, S. G. *A History of the Texas Railroads.* Houston, Tex.: St. Clair, 1941.

Texas Electric Railway

The first interurban electric railway in Texas and the first segment of what would become the Texas Electric Railway began operation between Denison and Sherman, Texas, in 1901. Chartered in 1900, the 10-mile Denison & Sherman Railway grew through construction and merger into the premier interurban line in the Southwest. Within a year of the line's opening, Dallas and Fort Worth were connected by interurban as well, and a rush to connect the remainder of the major communities in north central Texas by interurban was soon under way.

Leading the development of the Texas Electric was Dallas-area public utilities entrepreneur J. F. Strickland, who incorporated the Texas Traction Co. in 1906 and began building a 65-mile line north from Dallas to Sherman, reaching a connection with the Denison & Sherman on July 1, 1908, and completing what was then the longest interurban in the Southwest. Within a year Strickland had gained control of the D&S and merged it into Texas Traction in 1911.

Strickland had a sometimes rival, other times partner, in the form of the Stone & Webster Engineering Co., which was building from Dallas to Waxahachie, a distance of 28 miles. The company had been consulting engineers for Texas Traction and was also responsible for the completion of the interurban line from Dallas to Fort Worth and another line south from Fort Worth to Cleburne. Work on the Waxahachie line, the Dallas Southern Traction Co., began in January 1912; by September of that year the rails had reached Waxahachie. The Strickland interests had also begun construction of a line south from Dallas through Waxahachie to Waco, but within a month of its opening had purchased the Dallas Southern for $1 million.

Strickland reorganized the Dallas Southern as the Southern Traction Co. and continued building. The line opened all the way to Waco, 97 miles from Dallas, on October 1, 1913. Less than a month later a second new line began operating over a 52-mile route between Dallas and Corsicana, center of a cotton- and oil-producing area. In 1916 a handsome new seven-track interurban terminal opened in Dallas, serving the trains of the Dallas–Fort Worth interurban, as well as the Strickland lines.

A merger of Texas Traction and Southern Traction, effective on January 1, 1917, created the Texas Electric Railway. With 250 miles of route it was one of the largest electric interurbans in the country and the largest in the Southwest. To develop new revenues, the TE established an express service in and around the downtown Dallas business district and inaugurated Railway Post Office service between Dallas and Denison. Freight service was always important to the Texas Electric. For the first two decades of operation freight was handled by box motor cars and special interurban trailers, but in the late 1920s the company set out to develop interline freight service with steam railroads, establishing interchange points in 1928 with both the Missouri-Kansas-Texas and the Missouri Pacific.

Faced with increasing road competition, Texas Electric passenger revenues had begun to fall off by the late 1920s. By January 1931 the railroad had entered receivership, but fought to restore profitable operation with a series of cost-cutting measures, including the introduction of one-man operation. A further setback came in 1934 in an adverse decision by the Interstate Commerce Commission. Because 54 percent of the line's revenue came from freight, the ICC determined that TE was, in effect, a conventional railroad and not an interurban and therefore was subject to the more costly Railway Labor Act and the Railroad Retirement Act. Nevertheless, the company was able to end its operating losses and emerged from receivership in 1936.

However, the interurban scene around Dallas and Fort Worth was rapidly changing. By 1934 the Dallas–Fort Worth line and two other interurbans had ended operation, leaving Texas Electric alone in the big Dallas interurban terminal. After running up losses for more than five consecutive years on its weakest line, the 52-mile Corsicana route, Texas Electric applied for abandonment in 1940, and the line closed early in 1941.

The TE experienced a resurgence of passenger and freight traffic during World War II, but traffic dropped again at the end of the war. Three serious accidents in the immediate postwar period did not help the situation: a rear-end collision near Lancaster on March 14, 1946, and two head-on collisions, one near Denison on September 29, 1946, and the other at Kirkland siding on the north side of Dallas on April 10, 1948. There were no fatalities in any of these mishaps, although the third injured a motorman and 30 passengers. All three accidents severely damaged the cars involved, as well as the Texas Electric's safety reputation.

Among recommendations issued by the ICC in the aftermath of these accidents was one that the line install a modern block signal system. But Texas Electric stockholders, anticipating expensive lawsuits and further operating losses, voted instead on April 20, 1948, to seek permission to abandon all rail operations and convert the Waco line to bus operations. The ICC consented, and the last Texas Electric passenger run came on the evening of December 31, 1948, while the last rail operation, a freight train, ran on September 10, 1949.

In 1947 Texas Electric operated 174 route-miles and 199 track-miles, with 26 passenger cars, 31 express and baggage cars, 22 company service cars, 3 locomotives, and 225 employees. Operating revenues for 1947 were $1.2 million, but the net result for the year was a deficit of $286,000.

—Cary Franklin Poole

REFERENCES

Myers, Johnnie J. *Texas Electric Railway.* Chicago: Central Electric Railfans' Assn., 1982.

Varney, Rod, and the Texas ERA. *Texas Electric Album.* Glendale, Calif.: Interurbans, 1975.

Theater

The first appearance of a railroad train in a stage play was undoubtedly in a British farce, *The Railroad Station*, by T. E. Wilkes (1840). In this play a train appeared to move as seen through windows at the back of the stage. Apparently, though, in Victorian times the British did not develop a vogue for railroad drama, except insofar as it involved devious financial schemes.

But the railroad and steam locomotives were inherently melodramatic, something that did not go unnoticed in the United States. The last quarter of the nineteenth century was the age of melodrama in the American theater, and the best-known playwrights used trains and railroad settings in melodramatic and often-hair-raising situations. One of the most successful of all such melodramas (occasionally revived in recent times) was *Under the Gaslight,* written by Augustin Daly and first performed in 1867. For this play the stage carpenters outdid themselves, creating on the stage actual track, a switchman's shanty, a siding track, and off to one side a railroad depot. More important, at a crucial moment there appeared a faux locomotive with smoke, lights, bells, and whistles. In the play's denouement a silk-hatted villain twirling a waxed mustache ties the hero to the railroad tracks, then slinks off into the underbrush to await the arrival of the midnight express. With the train approaching, the pure and innocent heroine craftily pulls a switch to send the train onto the siding. The hero is saved. Undoubtedly few in the audience bothered to ask at this dramatic moment how it was that a Victorian maiden knew enough about railroad technology to operate a railroad switch, but so effective was the scene that it has been engraved in the American imagination.

In the next several decades the railroad made numerous other theatrical appearances. The year 1892 was remarkable for having as many as three railroad melodramas on the American stage: *The Limited Mail, A Mile a Minute,* and *The Midnight Special.* This was the year of planning for the great Columbian Exposition in Chicago, and railroads were in the forefront of the popular imagi-nation, much like the space program in the 1960s. Speed was the order of the day, and in the spring of 1893 the *Empire State Express,* led by Engine 999, achieved a speed of 112 mph in upstate New York. Nothing on earth had moved this fast before.

A great master of the melodramatic art in these years was Lincoln J. Carter, whose play *The Fast Mail* was a big hit both on Broadway and on the road. The play offered not one but two night mail trains and much heart-stopping action. Another thrilling drama of Carter's was *The Bride Special.* In this play the heroine, daughter of a railroad executive, plans to elope but is pirated away by her father on a private railway car. The hero gives chase in a commandeered switch engine and lifts his inamorata onto his locomotive from the back of the special's observation platform.

One of the best of the early stage melodramas played an important role in American cultural history. A. H. Wood's *The Great Express Robbery* so impressed Thomas Alva Edison that he persuaded Edwin S. Porter, one of the photographers in his early cinema company, to film an abbreviated version of this play in what has been called the first motion picture in the modern sense. This was *The Great Train Robbery,* filmed in 1903 (*see* CINEMA AND RAILROADS). Melodramas of this kind continued to reign for another generation. One particularly successful play was *The Ninety and Nine* (1902), which dealt with an engineer having to drive his engine through the great Hinckley fire in Minnesota, an actual event of the previous decade. Another melodrama, slightly reminiscent of *Under the Gaslight,* was *Home Sweet Home,* which featured several railroad scenes.

The railroad got a starring role in the Broadway play *On the Twentieth Century* in 1976. A mockup of New York Central's streamlined Hudson was complete even to imitation steam from the engine's cylinders. —Martha Swope, *Trains* Magazine Collection

As the twentieth century moved on, other types of drama came to the fore—sometimes comedy, sometimes mystery. Successful plays of various types continued until the 1930s. Among them were George M. Cohan's *Forty Five Minutes from Broadway*, which has a good depot scene, *Mrs. Wiggs of the Cabbage Patch, The Traveling Salesman, A Stubborn Cinderella*, and *Honeymoon Express*, in which Al Jolson played a Pullman porter. *The Ghost Train*, a British confection, both mystery and comedy, was successful both here and abroad. It was three times made into a movie. Some plays took place inside railroad or Pullman cars. One such was Rachel Crothers's *A Little Journey*. Another highly successful play with scenes inside a Pullman car was *Twentieth Century* (1933), by Ben Hecht and Charles MacArthur. Only the second half of the play was set on board the *20th Century Limited*, but the scenes there, farcical and witty, are among the most polished ever written involving railroad ambiance. The play was immediately made into a movie, giving John Barrymore one of the most successful film roles of his career.

After the early 1930s the railroad had few successes on the American stage. The year 1937 saw a dramatization of *Casey Jones*, well liked by many railfans and apparently quite competent with lots of authentic railroad atmosphere, but a flop on Broadway, as was *Heavenly Express* (1940), a variant of the ghost-train story. After this the railroad mostly disappeared from the American stage, probably in part because the dramatic possibilities were so much greater in the cinema. On the other hand, Hecht and MacArthur's *Twentieth Century* was revived in 1951 with Gloria Swanson in the female lead. Certainly that play's charm and wit had not faded by that time.

—George H. Douglas

REFERENCE

Holbrook, Stewart H. *The Story of American Railroads*. New York: Crown, 1947.

Theatrical Touring Companies

For the greater part of American history the acting profession was an itinerant one. Today, nearly all major actors and actresses can center their lives around Hollywood or New York. No such possibility existed until well into the twentieth century. To act meant to travel, and for nearly a century almost all this travel was by rail.

Even before the Civil War, when the rail network was incomplete, few acting companies could stay in one place. Some form of traveling was required. Some of this travel was by wagon, and where rivers were available, boat travel was the easiest way to go. Indeed, the first "show boat" began plying the waters as early as about 1817, when Noah Miller Ludlow ran a flatboat with a shelter down the Cumberland and Ohio rivers. Until after the Civil War nearly all theatrical companies were what were called "stock companies." A group of actors, functioning as a unit, would perform a series of plays, with a given actor playing many parts. The possibilities of production were determined by the size and ability of the troupe. But the stock companies were not precisely like the so-called residential companies of today that might perform only in a particular community. If a company was based in Columbus, Ohio, for example, it would invariably go on the road to other nearby communities—sometimes for one-night stands, sometimes for a run of plays.

As the railroad network was completed, this changed. Something like a star system spread throughout the land, and major actors were able to visit large areas of the country, where their very presence assured sold-out houses. They also invariably brought with them more professional players. The ability to get around by train assured principal actors a good living. Of course, travel in those days was not easy. There were interminable delays, washouts, and derailments. Hotels were often poor and unreliable; meals in unknown dining rooms could be execrable. Touring, or trouping, as theater people usually called it, could be emotionally draining as well. Many actors hated to tour. But it was a fact of life.

Edwin Booth, the greatest American actor of his day, perhaps of all time, was a melancholy man, and trouping weighed heavily on him. Hoping to plant himself and his company permanently, he built an ornate and modern theater in New York in 1869, but this did not relieve him of the obligation to go on the road. On the other hand, by the 1880s he had the luxury of a private railroad car with a bed in an alcove, a sitting room, a piano, and a bookcase. Even so, touring caused him unease and trepidation.

No matter how big the star, there was no possibility of avoiding the road during the nineteenth century. Over 3,000 theaters were built in the United States between the Civil War and the turn of the century, and the demand to fill them was relentless. Between the Civil War and 1880 railroad mileage increased from 35,000 to more than 90,000 miles, and by 1910 to 240,000. Even though New York was a theatrical mecca by this time, it was not possible to remain there year-round. Actors had to go on the road.

But conditions of travel were not good. Journeymen actors, if they found employment at all, were expected to pay their own travel expenses; only stars of the first rank were able to afford Pullman accommodations whenever they were available. Most performers went by day coach. A century ago actors did not receive contracts; they were not even paid for rehearsals. Occasionally they had to provide their own costumes. And things did not improve when local theaters became part of large chains. In the 1890s a monopolistic entity known only as the Syndicate, controlled by a group of rapacious producers including Charles Frohman, Mark Klaw, and Abraham Erlanger, got a viselike grip on the theatrical world that was every bit as tenacious as that of Rockefeller's on oil. This group was eventually bested by another controlled by the brothers Shubert, supposedly more benign, but actually every bit as grasping and suffocating. These collusive organizations squeezed out all the old stock companies and completely controlled theatrical bookings. They insisted on exclusive representation, so that theaters that had once been independent were forced to accept the shows, actors, show dates, and prices dictated by the syndicates.

The life of thespians became so intolerable under these monopolies that an effort was made to unionize performers. This effort resulted in the creation of the Actors Equity Association, founded in 1913. For a few years Actors Equity made no inroads against the syndicates, but by the early 1920s things improved somewhat in that actors received contracts stipulating wages, severance pay, and working conditions. Travel arrangements followed, but only slowly. By the mid-1920s the Equity had contracts assuring that journeymen actors, chorus members, and the like were entitled to Pullman sleeping accommodations for any train that left after 10 P.M. But the arrangement called for open-section sleeping—two to a lower berth and one to an upper. Needless to say, major stars had been and continued to be rewarded by more luxurious accommodations.

Theatrical touring, however, had been in decline since about 1910. In 1900 there were 339 companies on tour in the United States, by 1915 there were 124, by 1925 there were 75, and by 1935 only 22. A great many things account for this decline. The coming of the movies was surely one of the most serious. Theater owners discovered that they could enjoy more lucrative earnings by converting their houses to movie palaces. Another was the rapid rise of cheaper vaudeville shows. Ticket prices for so-called legitimate theater rose. At the turn of the century ordinary seats were 25 to 50 cents (some were only 10 or 15 cents), the best seats perhaps $1.50. By 1925 the very cheapest seats were $1.25. The automobile also entered the mix, allowing people in smaller communities to drive to larger cities where they could see higher-quality shows. But many theatrical people blamed the railroad for rapidly rising costs of transportation. Both railroad passenger and freight rates rose precipitously during World War I.

During the 1920s the number of theatrical companies dropped off drastically. For the most part the theater retreated to the safety of New York. There was some revival of the old stock-company idea; there were important new community theaters in places such as Cleveland and Minneapolis. There was also a new and healthy "little theater" movement. Road travel continued for a small number of major productions. Invariably after the 1920s, if a show was a smash hit in New York, the company would set out on a blue-ribbon tour, often involving the employment of special trains for carrying the whole cast plus scenery and costumes. Accordingly, for the road shows that continued in these times, travel conditions were much improved.

Katharine Cornell, the "first lady" of the stage in the 1930s, went on a national tour in the dark Depression year of 1934 with her hit play *The Barretts of Wimpole Street,* taking with her a first-rate troupe that covered 74 cities and 16,000 miles. They traveled in a special train; all had sleeping accommodations. Cornell had her own private car. This same year saw several similar grand tours by rail. Helen Hayes was on the road with her impersonation of *Mary of Scotland,* and George M. Cohan with Eugene O'Neill's only comedy, *Ah, Wilderness!* Of course, these major tours involved only a few hundred actors, not the thousands who were on the road 30 years earlier.

Cecil B. DeMille, who began in the theater and later became a major film director, praised touring. "Playing on the road was not easy, but it gave one a feeling of and for America." Ethel Barrymore felt the same way. As a young actress at the end of the nineteenth century, traveling with her famous uncle, John Drew, Barrymore remarked, "I loved seeing America and I wanted to see it all." Her younger brother John, on the other hand, hated touring and refused to do it after reaching stardom. Content with staying in New York, he also escaped to the movies as soon as he could. Many other actors sought similar relief from "the road."

One of the reasons for the decline of touring was the rise of competing forms of entertainment that could be booked in theaters around the country. Even before the movies there was vaudeville, which offered cheap entertainment for the masses. Vaudeville was organized into a series of short acts (no long plays), usually involving trained animals, dancing girls, magicians, jugglers, blackfaced singers, sports stars, and stand-up comedians. There rapidly arose a tightly controlled vaudeville circuit run by B. F. Keith and Edward F. Albee, who were, if anything, even more niggardly in their treatment of performers than the Shubert brothers. Vaudeville shows involved individual acts, so performers shuffled around the country, staying always in the dreariest hotels. Needless to say, except for a few stars who could afford to buy Pullman space, vaudeville performers traveled almost exclusively in day coaches. Vaudeville died very rapidly after 1930, but many of its struggling performers reached the big time through radio, including Bob Hope, Jack Benny, Fred Allen, Ed Wynn, Eddie Cantor, and George Burns and Gracie Allen. Others rode a wave to the top in the movies.

During these same years there were other forms of itinerant entertainment, all of which invariably used railroad transportation, but nicely filled hundreds of idle theaters or "opera houses." There was burlesque (equally organized by two overpowering syndicates), there were Wild West shows, and there were tabloid shows, or tabs, as they were called—reduced versions of Broadway shows. One of the most popular tab shows for decades was a scaled-down *Uncle Tom's Cabin,* often performed in tents. There were also numerous other tent shows in these years, and these offered the cheapest form of entertainment known at the time.

Two allied phenomena of the time were lyceum and

Chautauqua. Lyceum was originally a lecture circuit dedicated to educational ends, but during the early twentieth century some entertainment and occasional short theatrical interludes were added. Chautauqua was a summer adult education program founded by the Methodist Episcopal Church at Lake Chautauqua in western New York in 1874. Out of it there developed around 1904 a Chautauqua circuit that retained an educational function not unlike lyceum, but added such entertainment as animal acts, yodelers, and bell ringers to promote a carnival atmosphere. Not infrequently it also presented sentimental plays or skits. Chautauqua spread widely, especially in the Midwest, where the programs were often put on in tents.

A symbiotic relationship developed between the Chautauqua organizers and the interurbans. Chautauquas frequently set up their tents or lodges in parks or picnic groves near interurban railroad rights of way. Brief trolley rides (usually costing a nickel) transported the audience to these "centers of learning." Chautauqua grew big in the time of the trolleys and faded with them as well. Today the Chautauqua circuit is long gone, but the original assembly on Lake Chautauqua still exists.

It is clear that the world of popular live theatrical entertainment was exceedingly rich in the United States in the first few decades of the twentieth century. Americans everywhere, even in remote areas far from the metropolitan corridor, were served superlatively by live entertainers and invariably held them in high affection. And one cannot help but point out that the show went on because the railroad was there. Nearly all of these performers arrived at their destinations by railroad train, and the railroads seldom let them down.

—George H. Douglas

REFERENCES

Lewis, Philip C. *Trouping: How the Show Came to Town.* New York: Harper & Row, 1973.
Wilmeth, Don B., and Christopher Bigsby, eds. *The Cambridge History of American Theatre, 1870–1945.* Vol. 2, 1870–1945. New York: Cambridge Univ. Press, 1999.

Thomas, Philip Evan
(1776–1861)

Philip Thomas was a Baltimore businessman who developed a solid vision of the possibilities of railroads. Born in Montgomery County, Maryland, on November 11, 1776, he was the third son of Evan and Rachel (Hopkins) Thomas. Young Philip decided to seek his career in Baltimore, and in 1800 he started his own hardware business there. The following year he married Elizabeth George of Kent County, Maryland.

Thomas quickly rose in Baltimore business circles. He became president of the Mechanics Bank and a leading promoter of the city. At that time city leaders were increasingly concerned about Baltimore's economic position and its connection with what was then called the Ohio Country to the west. The National Road had been Baltimore's link with development in the Ohio and Mississippi River valleys. Trade with western settlements had helped make it the third-largest city in the United States by 1827.

However, New York's Erie Canal, which opened in 1825, and the ongoing projects of the Pennsylvania System of Public Works threatened Baltimore's prominence. These projects promised to divert trade from the west to New York City and to Philadelphia by cutting the cost and increasing the speed of transportation from the developing western territories to the Eastern Seaboard. Maryland and Virginia joined together to revive the Chesapeake & Ohio canal project that would link Georgetown, near the nation's capital, with the Youghiogheny River near Pittsburgh and the beginning of the Ohio River. Philip Thomas was made a commissioner for the State of Maryland in the canal project, but soon became convinced that a canal would do little for Baltimore even if it were practical to construct it over the backbone of the Appalachians.

Coming across an account of the construction and operation of the Stockton & Darlington Railroad in England, he began to research railroads as a practical means of transportation. In February 1827, with colleague George Brown, Thomas called a meeting of businessmen to explain the superiority of railways over canals. He later called a second meeting to consider a railway as a means of reviving Baltimore's faltering trade with the west. Thomas was made chairman of a committee to devise definitive plans for such a transportation venture. The charter for a railroad from Maryland was approved on February 28, 1827. The incorporation of the Baltimore & Ohio Railroad took place on April 24, 1827. Thomas was made a director and first president of the Baltimore & Ohio.

Philip Thomas faced many problems in his presidency. Railroads were new, and many questions had to be answered. Other obstacles included the hostility of the directors of the Chesapeake & Ohio Canal, delayed payment of the subscriptions of Baltimoreans backing the railroad project, and conflict concerning the route the railroad would take on its way west. Also alarming was the unexpected cost of excavation for the first few miles of line to the west of Baltimore.

By the time Thomas resigned as president of the railroad in 1836, many of the mechanical problems had been solved or were on their way to solution. The B&O had reached the strategic city of Harpers Ferry, West Virginia. The great stone arch bridge at Relay, Maryland, a major early railway engineering triumph, was named the Thomas Viaduct in his honor. Thomas died on September 1, 1861, while visiting a daughter in Yonkers, New York.

—George M. Smerk

REFERENCES

Dictionary of American Biography.

Hungerford, Edward. *The Story of the Baltimore & Ohio Railroad, 1827–1927.* Vol. 1. New York: G. P. Putnam's Sons, 1928.

Thomson, J. Edgar (1808–1874)

John Edgar Thomson was the third president of the Pennsylvania Railroad and guided it through its major period of growth from a system of 250 route-miles to over 6,000. An innovator in railroad management structure and technique, he set the pattern for many other railroad managers who followed him.

Thomson was born on February 10, 1808, the son of a surveyor, and was trained in that profession in his youth. He played a small role in an early component of the Pennsylvania Railroad by participating at age 20 in the preliminary surveys for the Philadelphia & Columbia Railroad, which later became part of the main line of the PRR. He also took part in the origin of another later PRR component, the Camden & Amboy, by working in 1830 as an assistant engineer in charge of part of the original survey.

After spending some time in Europe in 1831–1832 to broaden his knowledge to cover steam locomotive mechanical engineering, as well as civil engineering, he returned to the United States and worked on various projects in the Philadelphia area. By 1834 his reputation for sound and mature judgment was such that he was offered the position of chief engineer for the Georgia Railroad, then chartered but not yet surveyed. He tackled the job of surveying and constructing the railroad with relentless energy and in 1836 persuaded the stockholders to adopt steam rather than horsepower.

After the financial panic of 1837 economic conditions gradually worsened in the South, and Thomson's persistence in pushing financial resources to the limit to speed completion of the railroad had by 1841 caused friction with a fiscally conservative faction among the stockholders, nearly resulting in his ouster. He eventually won the internal political battle and stayed on to complete the construction in 1845. He is credited with having coined the name Atlanta for the terminal point of the railroad, where it linked up with the state-built Western & Atlantic.

The exact date of the termination of his employment by the Georgia Railroad cannot be pinpointed, but after construction was completed, he found that he was more interested in building than in operating railroads. In 1847 Thomson accepted the job of chief engineer for the Pennsylvania Railroad, although he continued a part-time association with the Georgia until as late as 1852, at which time he became president of the PRR.

John Edgar Thomson. —Middleton Collection

The Pennsylvania Railroad was originally chartered to extend from Harrisburg to Pittsburgh, paralleling the canal portion of the state's Main Line of Public Works, which included the Allegheny Portage Railroad over the summit. Thomson's first task was to locate and build that railroad. He decided initially to include the Allegheny Portage in the route until the PRR's line over the mountains could be completed. As the work progressed, after a couple of years inadequate funding became a source of frustration for Thomson, just as it had been in Georgia. He did not have enough money to pursue the project at a reasonable pace. The initial policy had been to raise all funds by the sale of stock, but by 1851 Thomson was vigorously advocating the sale of bonds. His position led stockholders to elect a new board of directors, which in turn elected Thomson president of the company on February 3, 1852.

The first task as Thomson entered his presidency was the matter of finance, and within three months a stockholders' resolution was overwhelmingly passed authorizing a bond issue. Completion of the first initially projected railroad soon followed, as December 1852 saw the completion of the route with the Allegheny Portage as its central link. The complete through line, including the Summit Tunnel, opened for traffic on February 15, 1854. Purchase of the Main Line of Public Works in 1857 gave the Pennsylvania control of the entire route between Philadelphia and Pittsburgh.

This expanded operation became unwieldy under the centralized management common in the early railroad industry. To address the lack of efficiency and to solve some financial issues, Thomson reorganized the company into a structure that became a model for the industry. He broke down train operations into operating divisions, an approach that had originated two years previously on the Erie Railroad. He also borrowed a departmental structure from the Baltimore & Ohio. These steps created the first line and staff organizational structure in the American corporate realm.

Connection to the west had become a priority, and the Pennsylvania had invested in two of the three railroads consolidated in 1856 as the Pittsburgh, Fort Wayne & Chicago. To accelerate completion of this route, Thomson in January 1858 assumed the position of chief engineer of the railroad and then briefly served as its president.

By 1858 Thomson had created the foundation for the greater Pennsylvania Railroad. During his presidency the PRR grew to near its eventual full geographic extent, reaching from the Hudson River to Chicago and St. Louis. Moreover, PRR stock paid annual dividends never less than 6 percent and some years as high as 10 percent. Toward the end of his life Thomson suffered occasionally from heart trouble, and he died on May 27, 1874, his death probably hastened by the problems of dealing with the consequences of the financial panic of 1873.

—Adrian Ettlinger

REFERENCES

Burgess, George H., and Miles C. Kennedy. *Centennial History of the Pennsylvania Railroad Company, 1846–1946*. Philadelphia: Pennsylvania Railroad, 1949.

Ward, James A. "J. Edgar Thomson and the Georgia Railroad." *Railroad History*, no. 134 (1976): 4–33.

———. *J. Edgar Thomson, Master of the Pennsylvania*. Westport, Conn.: Greenwood Press, 1980.

TOFC/COFC. *See* INTERMODAL

FREIGHT

Tonopah & Goldfield Railroad

The discovery of rich silver ore in 1900 created the city of Tonopah, revitalized the state of Nevada, and sparked railroad construction across the state. Starting near Mina, Nevada, the narrow-gauge Tonopah Railroad built a line to Tonopah in July 1904. A year later, when the former Carson & Colorado Railroad (by then part of the Southern Pacific) through Mina was converted to standard gauge, the Tonopah Railroad also widened its gauge.

The Goldfield Railroad, which opened in 1905 from near Tonopah south to Goldfield, had a very short in-dependent life before consolidation with the Tonopah Railroad in November 1905 to form The Tonopah & Goldfield Railroad, which operated a total of 113 route-miles. The same interests formed the Bullfrog Goldfield Railroad to build 83 miles southeast to Beatty, reaching there on April 18, 1907, and nearby Rhyolite two months later.

Shortly thereafter mining activity in the area began to shrink. The Tonopah & Goldfield survived through World War II on traffic to an Army Air Force base at Tonopah. After the war traffic disappeared almost entirely, and the railroad was officially abandoned on October 15, 1947.

In 1941 Tonopah & Goldfield operated 102 route-miles and 110 track-miles, with 4 locomotives, 6 passenger cars, 50 freight cars, 17 company service cars, and 53 employees. Freight traffic totaled 2.7 million ton-miles in 1941; passenger traffic totaled 12,176 passenger-miles. Operating revenues totaled $134,193 in 1941, and the railroad achieved a 95.5 percent operating ratio.

—David F. Myrick

REFERENCE

Myrick, David F. *Railroads of Nevada and Eastern California*. Vols. 1–2. Reno: Univ. of Nevada Press, 1962, 1990.

Tonopah & Tidewater Railroad

F. M. "Borax" Smith wanted to build a railroad to his borax mines in Death Valley and onward to Tonopah, Nevada. He began construction at Las Vegas in spring 1905, but after J. Ross Clark decided to build from that point, Smith moved his operations to Ludlow, California, and resumed work in the summer of 1905. In October 1907 the T&T arrived at Gold Center, near Beatty, 168 miles from Ludlow, and, by 2 miles of trackage rights over the Bullfrog Goldfield Railroad, gained access to Rhyolite. In 1914 a subsidiary, the Death Valley Railroad, commenced building a 20-mile narrow-gauge line from Death Valley Junction to Ryan. It operated until 1931. In 1918, upon abandonment of the Las Vegas & Tonopah Railroad, the T&T took over operation of the Bullfrog Goldfield Railroad and operated it until 1928. The T&T ceased operation in 1940, and its track was dismantled in 1942.

In 1939 the Tonopah & Tidewater operated 143 route-miles and 154 track-miles, with 5 locomotives, 5 passenger cars, 29 freight cars, 9 company service cars, and 63 employees. Operating revenues totaled $98,000 in 1939, with an operating ratio in the neighborhood of 150 percent.

—David F. Myrick

REFERENCE

Myrick, David F. *Railroads of Nevada and Eastern California*. Vols. 1–2. Reno: Univ. of Nevada Press, 1962, 1990.

Toronto, Hamilton & Buffalo Railway

The Toronto, Hamilton & Buffalo (TH&B) was incorporated in 1884 to give the Canadian Pacific Railway access to industries at Hamilton, Ontario, and to U.S. railroads at Buffalo, New York. The TH&B built a 38-mile line from Hamilton to a connection with the Michigan Central at Welland, Ontario.

In 1895 the TH&B was bought by four railroads: Canadian Pacific, New York Central, Michigan Central, and Canada Southern (the last two were part of the New York Central System). The TH&B became primarily a Toronto extension of the NYC.

Canadian Pacific acquired trackage rights on the Grand Trunk (a predecessor of Canadian National Railways) from a point near Hamilton to Toronto, obviating the need for TH&B to build its own track to Toronto. In the early 1900s CPR, TH&B, and Michigan Central agreed to pool crews and locomotives between Buffalo and Toronto. NYC's 73 percent ownership of the TH&B passed to Penn Central. Canadian Pacific purchased Penn Central's interest in 1977 and absorbed the TH&B at the beginning of 1987.

—George H. Drury

REFERENCE

Helm, Norman. *In the Shadow of Giants*. Erin, Ont.: Boston Mills Press, 1978.

Track Gauge. *See* NARROW GAUGE;

STANDARD GAUGE

Track Location and Construction. *See* CIVIL ENGINEERING

Trade Publications

Freight and Passenger Railroads

From the nineteenth century through well into the twentieth, railway trade magazines proliferated in the United States. By the late 1990s only three remained: *Railway Age*, founded in 1876 but with a lineage that can be traced to 1832; *Railway Track & Structures*, a magazine devoted strictly to railway engineering; and *Progressive Railroading*, founded in 1957.

Railway Age is believed to be the world's oldest continuously published trade publication. The Railway Age Publishing Co. was founded by George S. Bangs, Charles F. Hatch, and E. H. Talbott in Chicago in June 1876. Bangs had been superintendent of the U.S. Railway Mail Service; besides founding *Railway Age*, his claim to fame was establishment of fast mail trains. Bangs, the first editor of *Railway Age*, wrote in the first issue: "If we shall succeed in producing a railway journal comprehensive without diffusiveness, practical without dryness, solid without heaviness, and of value both to those who build and operate our railroads, and those who use them, we shall feel assured of abundant success." Thus *Railway Age* was geared more to the business aspects of railroad management than to technical matters. It is the product of mergers and acquisitions that began when its earliest ancestor, the *American Rail-Road Journal*, began publication in 1832. The most important of these mergers was the acquisition of *Railway Age* by its main competitor, the *Railroad Gazette*, in 1908. (Before this merger, in September 1891, *Railway Age* had merged with the *Northwestern Railroader*, founded in Minneapolis in April 1887 by Harry P. Robinson. The magazine was called the *Railway Age & Northwestern Railroader*; in May 1901 it reverted to the *Railway Age*.)

The *Railroad Gazette* was founded as the *Western Railroad Gazette* in November 1856 at the Chicago Tribune as a publicly circulated periodical. Its self-described purpose was "to detail, for the public benefit and convenience, statistics and reliable information" on railways. In 1870 the publication was purchased by W. N. Kellog, who changed its name to the *Railroad Gazette*. In 1871, after most of its assets were destroyed in the Chicago fire, the *Railroad Gazette* was acquired by Silas W. Dunning and Mathias N. Forney, who moved it to New York City and began transforming it into a business publication focused heavily on technical subjects.

Dunning was joint owner and editor until 1887; it was his ambition to establish a journal that would influence railroad practice and legislation. Co-owner Forney, a mechanical engineer, was the magazine's engineering and mechanical editor until 1883. He is credited with positioning the *Railroad Gazette* as a key influence in the campaign to establish standard bolt threads in the United States. Forney was also a founder of the American Society of Mechanical Engineers (ASME) and the Master Car Builders Association, which eventually was folded into the Association of American Railroads.

Henry G. Prout, a civil engineer who is credited with influencing the U.S. Senate to select Panama, not Nicaragua, as the site of a canal linking the Atlantic and Pacific oceans (today's Panama Canal), became editor of the *Railroad Gazette* in 1887. He retired from the magazine in 1903 to become vice president and general manager of Union Switch & Signal Co. Prout was succeeded by William H. Boardman, who had joined the *Gazette* in 1869 and had become owner and president in 1887 after acquiring the holdings of Dunning and Forney.

Boardman and E. A. Simmons, the *Gazette*'s vice president for advertising, purchased the *Railway Age* in June 1908 for $265,000 and established the Simmons-Boardman Publishing Corp. Until January 1910 the surviving magazine was known as the *Railroad Age Gazette*; it then became the *Railway Age Gazette* before reverting simply to *Railway Age* in January 1918. In January 1927 *Railway Age* absorbed the *Railway Review*, which had been founded by Willard A. Smith in May 1868 as *Chicago Railway Review*. In 1954 a controlling interest in Simmons-Boardman was sold to a group of employee investors led by Arthur J. McGinnis, Sr., and James G. Lyne; Lyne had been appointed editor of *Railway Age* and president of the company in 1950. Simmons-Boardman is now a subsidiary of the McGinnis Corp., whose chairman is Arthur J. McGinnis, Jr. The most recent merger involving *Railway Age* occurred in 1992, when Simmons-Boardman acquired *Modern Railroads*, which had been established in 1946, and folded it into *Railway Age*.

Railway Age at one time was the world's biggest periodical in sheer physical size, with single issues containing as much as 400 or more editorial and advertising pages. The editors traveled in the magazine's own business car, the first built by Pullman for a nonrailroad company. *Railway Age* was a weekly publication until early 1970. At that time, when the industry was in the early stages of what was to become a long period of consolidation and industry suppliers were becoming fewer in number, the magazine began publishing biweekly. *Railway Age* has been published in its present monthly form since 1983.

For many years, along with the weekly *Railway Age*, there were several monthly or semimonthly technical publications devoted to specific industry disciplines. Most were eventually folded into *Railway Age*.

Railway Locomotives & Cars was founded in January 1832 as the *American Rail-Road Journal* (*Railway Age*'s earliest ancestor) with the purpose of stimulating public interest in the then-newest mode of transportation, railways. In 1849 its editorial focus shifted to railway financing and the interests of investors. In 1886, when Mathias Forney took over as editor and publisher (three years after selling his interest in the *Railroad Gazette* to William Boardman), the publication became the *American Engineer & Railroad Journal*. When Simmons-Boardman Publishing acquired it in 1911, it became *Railway Mechanical Engineer*, then finally *Railway Locomotives & Cars*. It was last published in 1975.

Railway System Controls, founded in 1907 as *Railway Signal Engineer*, was purchased by Simmons-Boardman in 1910. It later became *Railway Signaling & Communications* (it was discontinued in 1975 but was resurrected as an electronic newsletter distributed by email in 2005). Other publications of this type included *Railway Pur-*

chases & Stores, last published in 1967; *Railway Electrical Engineer*, last published in 1942; and *Railway Freight Traffic*, last published in 1958. The only surviving print publication of this type is *Railway Track & Structures*, which was founded as *Railway Engineering & Maintenance* in 1904.

Railway Age was for many years a magazine devoted strictly to freight and main-line passenger (intercity and commuter) railroads. The magazine's editors did not consider rail transit (subways, interurbans, light rail) part of the industry. That changed in 1963, when the first issue of *Railway Age* devoted to rail transit was published.

Railway Age was widely credited with helping the U.S. railway industry win three monumental battles: against government ownership, which had wide support in the early 1920s and again in the 1960s; against federal regulation that paralyzed the entrepreneurial spirit, drove many railroads into bankruptcy, and came close to pulling down the whole industry; and against anachronistic work rules that penalized railroad labor in lost jobs and railroad management in lost productivity. Among several business publication "firsts" credited to *Railway Age* or its predecessors are the following: In the 1880s it was the first periodical to operate a permanent exhibition center for advertisers, at Chicago's Grand Pacific Hotel. In 1909 it was the first periodical of any kind to define and use the term "public relations." It was the first U.S. weekly business periodical to publish daily editions during industry conventions. It was the first technical publication serving a single industry to use photoengravings and the first to use color on editorial pages (1881) and advertising pages (Westinghouse Air Brake Co., 1896). In 1916 it was the first single-industry weekly to open an editorial office in Washington, D.C., and put a full-time staff editor in charge. *Railway Age*'s Washington editor in the 1930s was the only trade writer with full White House accreditation.

James G. Lyne in 1955 was accused of steering the industry toward socialism by suggesting that railroads needed to be indemnified by government for the huge losses they incurred operating commuter trains for "the public convenience and necessity." The president of the Illinois Central threatened to boycott *Railway Age* and ordered his purchasing people not to buy any product advertised in its pages. Interestingly, it was this railroad, under new management, that was among the first to line up for federal aid when it became available in the 1960s through the U.S. Department of Transportation.

Electric Railways

Specialized business publications covering electric railways have been around since the late 1880s, when this form of transportation was established. While originally devoted to urban street railways, these journals later also covered the development of interurban electric passenger and freight railways and of electrified main-line railroads.

The first of these was the *Street Railway Journal*, established in 1884 as a technical publication. In 1908 it became the *Electric Railway Journal* when it merged with *Electric Railway Review*, which had been founded in 1891 as *Street Railway Review*. From 1932 until it ceased publication in 1942, the publication was known as the *Transit Journal*. Special issues were published for the annual conventions of the American Street Railway Assn.

Street Railway Gazette was founded in 1886. It later became *Electric Railway Gazette* before merging with *Electrical World* in 1896. The *Interurban Railway Journal* was established in 1905 and became *Electric Traction Weekly* the following year. In 1912 it became *Electric Traction*, then *Mass Transportation*. Publication ceased in 1960. The two principal current publications that cover both rail and bus transit are *Mass Transit,* established in 1974, and *Metro* magazine, established in 1975.

—William C. Vantuono

Traffic Categories and Trends

Freight traffic categories and quantities are affected by a number of forces. The state of the national economy at any given time affects the total volume of traffic. In a booming economy there will be an abundance of goods to move to serve that economy.

Population size is another prime factor that determines the volume of goods that must be transported by rail or other means to meet demand. Changes in population in the United States have generally seen secular growth trends with occasional booms. Large families were needed when the United States was predominantly agricultural. Population growth eased during the transition to a manufacturing economy. In times of economic distress, such as the Great Depression, it moderated. The famous baby boom after World War II saw a sharp increase in population, the impact of which has been felt for many years.

The population's location affects the demand for goods and the need to transport them to and from given places. From the colonial period onward, for many years the bulk of the U.S. population lived in the Northeast. Aided by railroads and other means of transportation, population growth spread westward to the mountains and then the Pacific shore. The Southeast was less heavily populated than the Northeast. It was at first dominated by agriculture and an expansive use of land; not until well into the twentieth century did it develop its strong manufacturing component. The eventual southward growth and movement of population was greatly aided by air conditioning.

A final factor that affects traffic is the birth of new products and changes in patterns of demand. Railroads had developed a healthy business in transporting wagons and buggies from manufacturing centers to distant customers. The automobile and truck destroyed the wagon and buggy business, but replaced it with the movement of auto parts and the shipment of assembled motor vehicles. New products, such as television in the 1940s and 1950s, created a whole new source of freight traffic.

Among the earliest commodities to use the new railroads were coal and bulk goods. Some railroads were built mainly to move coal. Coal is still the typical base of traffic for railroads nationwide, although it is now used for electrical generation rather than for home heating and for the steam engines that powered factories, as was true initially. In some instances the role of the carriers in the early days of railroading was to move coal or some other bulk commodity, such as gravel and crushed stone, to a canal or waterway for movement to the relevant market.

Since the U.S. economy was mainly based on agriculture until after the Civil War, farm goods dominated rail traffic for many years. Cotton and tobacco were important components of freight traffic in the South before industry migrated to the area south of the Ohio River and east of the Mississippi River. Both coal and agricultural goods moved to the cities and towns and eventually to processing centers mainly located in the northern United States.

Westward expansion shifted population and changed some of the focus of demand. It set up the pattern of raw materials and supplies moving to eastern processing centers and the processed products of early manufacturing industries moving west and south to supply the needs of those who produced the raw materials. Midwestern population growth initially encouraged building of rail lines to serve that population. Later, railroads' expansion beyond the Mississippi River acted as a magnet to shift population growth to the West.

The Civil War interrupted development and saw the movement of freight to supply the needs of the Union and Confederate armies. The war also helped determine the future of the Northeast as the manufacturing center of the United States for most of the next century. Goods were made in the Northeast that in earlier days had been imported. Economic effort and innovation were also devoted to the making of new products, such as steel. Also at this time the timber resources of the Midwest, principally in Michigan and Wisconsin, were exploited to supply the need for homes and businesses.

The end of the nineteenth century saw an enormous increase in the production of manufactured goods and the growth of such midwestern manufacturing centers as Toledo, Cleveland, Detroit, Chicago, and St. Louis, as well as places farther west. The movement of raw materials and supplies to these new centers complemented eastern industrial expansion in New England and Pennsylvania.

The cattle industry boomed to meet the demands of city folks in the Midwest and East. At first the herds were driven from grazing areas in the arid portions of Texas and the middle prairies to railheads in Kansas, Oklahoma, and Texas. Live cattle were moved in large numbers to the meatpacking centers. The invention of the refrigerator car helped the meatpacking industry grow in Chicago, Omaha, and cities in Iowa. Fresh meats and packinghouse products were shipped to eastern consumption centers. The refrigerator car also spurred the movement of other perishables, such as fruit and vegetables from the South and Southwest and eventually from the Far West, to midwestern and eastern tables.

The demand for goods in smaller quantities for both business and consumers led to demand for less-than-carload (LCL) lots of traffic. Local trains delivered relatively small shipments to freight houses in smaller cities and towns and then for distribution by wagon to the customers. The express services and LCL also served the rapid evolution of the mail-order business at the end of the century. The demand for farm machinery also built another source of significant railroad traffic. So did an increased use of paper and paper products by popular newspapers, magazines, and other publications.

The petroleum industry began its growth in the 1870s, with the demand for petroleum-based products for lighting of homes and businesses. As petroleum-based lubricants replaced tallow, that sector of the oil business expanded. Toward the end of the century and later the use of petroleum as a fuel contributed to the demand.

The railroads during most of the nineteenth century were the only practical and economic means of transporting goods long distances or moving bulk goods for almost any distance. They enjoyed a transportation monopoly. In some parts of the United States there was competition from water transportation, but it was limited to places along navigable rivers. Traffic growth was interrupted from time to time by economic downturns.

Twentieth-century freight traffic was dominated by the key factors of population and economic growth and the concurrent stimulation of demand for transportation. The century experienced continued growth of small shipments via express and LCL, and new products entered the market. Automobile parts and the movement of assembled automobiles and trucks became a large element of transportation demand. Tractors were added to the mix of farm machinery finding its way onto the rails. This was also the time of the development of consumer-oriented electrical appliances ranging from fans to washing machines, radios, and refrigerators.

Two wars greatly influenced rail traffic. World War I created a demand for war materiel, and World War II engendered unprecedented demand for military goods and supplies ranging from uniforms to tanks, foodstuffs, and ammunition. At the same time, during World War II the production of civilian goods, such as automobiles and appliances, was either halted or severely limited.

Significant competition arose to eliminate the railroads' monopoly in the movement of freight. Automobiles and trucks were an early threat to railroad traffic of both passengers and freight. Federal aid to highways began in 1916, progressed through the 1920s, and was a focus of federal policy, as well as state and local efforts, in the Depression days in an attempt to reduce unemployment and improve the transportation infrastructure. The entire nation was linked by paved roads by 1950, and plans were in place for the interstate highway system that would abet the explosive growth of the motor carrier industry. The U.S. Army Corps of Engineers began large-scale programs of publicly financed waterway improvements in the 1920s. The motor carriers diverted higher-value, lighter-weight traffic from the rails, while the growing water carrier industry tempted shippers of low-value bulk commodities to move their goods by very low-cost water transportation. In the 1920s the construction of welded, high-pressure pipelines diverted petroleum business from the rails. The century had started with the railroads as the dominant means of moving freight and passengers. By 1950 the railroads were moving a declining proportion of the nation's business and faced increasing competition.

The latter part of the twentieth century was not a good time for the railroads. The low point was reached in the 1960s and 1970s. Some parts of the previous traffic mix almost disappeared. The meatpacking industry moved close to the feedlots, and rail haulage of live cattle to packing houses was gone by the 1980s. Perishable traffic also eroded. Refrigerated trucks were more nimble than refrigerator cars and could deliver meat and other perishables directly to the market without the intermediary of warehouses or produce auctions at carside in city markets.

A freight innovation that had its roots in the 1920s and 1930s developed as a prime source of railroad freight traffic. This was the movement of highway trailers by rail, known as piggyback or trailer-on-flatcar (TOFC). Motor carriers discovered that it was cheaper to use rail service to move their trailers over long distances than to pay drivers to deliver via highways. Containers, pushed strongly by the maritime shipping industry, became the surprise star of railroad freight movement; by the end of the century mile-long trains of containers were common sights along the rail right of way.

Innovative ideas of pricing and service born in the 1950s came to dominate much rail freight business. One of these was the unit train. The notion started with freight rates based on multiple carloads of traffic; rates on 5 to 15 cars of a single commodity, moving from one origin point to one destination, became common in the 1960s. Soon this was expanded to rates and minimum weights that required an entire trainload. Grain moved in giant covered hopper cars from large-scale elevators to destinations in trains of 10,000 tons or more. The same thing happened to the movement of coal. Individual carload shipments of grain and coal are a thing of the past. Railroads are now wholesalers of freight movement.

As the twenty-first century began, all transportation modes were experiencing greatly increased demand for their services. This will likely continue as long as the economy stays strong. The railroads may no longer have a monopoly of transportation, but they are significant players in goods movement, moving larger quantities than ever before.

—George M. Smerk

Train Control

American railroads in their primitive stage of development soon began organizing their train movements by timetable schedules. On single-track lines, which accounted for most of the then-modest mileage, this method was ineffective, to say the least. Opposing trains were scheduled to meet at stations where passing sidings were available, but in those days of breakdown-prone equipment and uneven track, roadbed delays were endemic, and gridlock often ensued. If a train arrived at a meeting point and the opposing train was nowhere in sight, it simply waited, having no information as to the whereabouts or condition of the other train. When delays were lengthy, more trains were affected, and the timetable became a shambles. Fortunately, by mid-nineteenth century, just before the heyday of railroad construction, the telegraph evolved into an effective means of communication, enabling the railroads to advance to the next phase of controlling train movement.

Timetable and Train-Order Operations

With railroad-installed telegraph lines proliferating along the rails, information and instructions could be transmitted via Morse code between stations and to and from dispatchers' offices. The objective was not only to increase the capacity of main-line tracks (greater flexibility, reduced delays), but also to accomplish this with a high degree of safety (collisions avoided). At first, each railroad went its own way in establishing rules to attain these ends. Over time, train frequency increased, so rules multiplied and became more complex. This raised the risk of misunderstandings and consequent mishaps. Realizing the need for greater uniformity and clarity, in 1889 the railroads collectively assembled their top operating people at what was known as the General Time Convention. Out of this came the first Standard Code, officially titled *Uniform Train Rules and Rules for the Movement of Trains by Telegraphic Orders*. The convention established a process for periodic revision of the code to account for changing conditions—more trains, lines with two or more main tracks, introduction of the telephone, and so on. (The convention was also the basis for the later formation of the industry's trade organization, now the Assn. of American Railroads, or AAR.)

The Standard Code starts off with the basics, such as

"Obedience to the rules is essential to safety" and "Employees whose duties are prescribed by these rules must provide themselves with a copy." It follows with a series of definitions in alphabetical order; for instance, a train is "an engine or more than one engine coupled, with or without cars, displaying markers." In railroad usage *markers* referred early on to oil lamps hung on the ends of engines, passenger cars, and cabooses, which evolved into today's built-in electric lights on passenger cars and end-of-train devices on cabooseless freight trains. (The presumption: no markers, train not complete, part of it left behind, main track possibly blocked.) After the definitions come the operating rules, beginning with coverage of subjects such as timetables, hand, flag, and lamp signals, engine whistle signals, communicating signals on passenger trains, and display of headlights and markers. Subsections follow dealing with superiority of trains, movement of trains and engines, movement by train orders, and forms of train orders. Block signal rules and interlocking rules are next, each in a separate section. Later, with the introduction of centralized traffic control, a section was added to cover that subject.

With the advent of communication systems that permitted transmission of train orders came a major change in train-movement authority, with, as indicated, a body of rules to govern all its ramifications. The emphasis was on safety, and the byword was clarity, the enemy of ambiguity. Before train orders the timetable could make a train superior to, that is, give it precedence over, another train in two ways: class or direction. First-class trains were superior to second-class, second to third, and so on, and trains running in the direction specified were superior to opposing trains of the same class. These distinctions determined which train was required to take siding at meeting points. Train orders, on the other hand, conferred superiority by right, and right was superior to class or direction. This priority put the dispatcher, as the issuer of train orders, in the driver's seat. He could take away superiority by class or direction, if by doing so he could run his territory more efficiently. Also, if business warranted, he could create extra trains not authorized by timetable schedules, taking care to arrange their meets with opposing extras. Extras took sidings for regular trains, those authorized by timetable schedule, as required by rules (unless made superior to them by train order). The dispatcher could change meeting points, annul a schedule, add sections to scheduled trains, or direct a regular train to run late on its schedule. Given such authority, he was able to make better use of his railroad, thereby increasing track capacity.

To issue and deliver train orders, the sending dispatcher and receiving operators at stations had to be familiar with a host of exacting procedures. These covered transmission formats for station names, engine numbers, and time, along with proper addresses, recording by dispatchers, repeating by operators, authorized abbreviations, and many other subjects. Various train-order forms were prescribed, each covering a specific movement or set of circumstances, or similar movements over single versus two or more main tracks.

The introduction of timetable and train-order operations, with the concomitant increase in train frequency, put a premium on proper observance of Rule 99, which sets forth flagging requirements. Although operators at train-order offices were required to space trains running in the same direction 10 minutes apart and did so by means of their train-order signal and a clearance form, there was no guarantee that the preceding train had not stopped for some reason a few miles beyond the spacing office. In that event, Rule 99, properly observed, would avert a collision. The rule reads, in part: "When a train stops under circumstances in which it may be overtaken by another train, the flagman must go back immediately with flagman's signals a sufficient distance to insure full protection, placing two torpedoes and, when necessary, in addition, displaying lighted fusees." Further, "When a train is moving under circumstances in which it may be overtaken by another train, the flagman must drop lighted fusees at proper intervals." (A fusee is a flare that burns for 10 minutes; a torpedo, when placed on a rail and run over, explodes to provide an instant alert.) The language of Rule 99—"under circumstances," "sufficient distance," "proper intervals"—leaves a great deal to the judgment of the flagman. He must size up the situation—maximum authorized speed in the area, ascending or descending grade for following trains, curved or tangent track, day or night, clear or foggy, and so on. It has been said that probably more wrecks have resulted from failure to comply with Rule 99 than from any other single cause. In deference to countless flagmen, however, many wrecks have undoubtedly been prevented by their faithful observance of this important rule. (This and other rules cited are from the Standard Code; the code stipulates, "Where proper safeguards are provided, railroads may modify or add to these rules to suit their requirements.")

Manual Block System

A block is defined as "a length of track of defined limits, the use of which by trains and engines is governed by block signals." Building on that definition, a manual block system is "a series of consecutive blocks, governed by block signals operated manually, upon information by telegraph, telephone, or other means of communication." A manual block system could readily be established in timetable and train-order territory; the train-order offices doubled as block stations, and the operators manning them took on the additional duties of block operators. The system worked as follows: as a train approached a station, the operator there checked the block record, and if the block in advance was clear of trains, requested a block for the train from the block operator at the block station in advance. That operator replied, "OK, blocking for [train]." The requesting operator would then display a clear signal indication to the approaching train, and when it entered the block, would re-

port it to the next block station in advance. When it passed the station, that event was reported to the next block station in the rear, provided the markers were properly displayed.

The primary contribution of a manual block system was to safety, because train separation was converted from time (10 minutes) to space (length of blocks). Flagging requirements were retained, but the consequences of inadequate flagging were less catastrophic. (A train other than a passenger train was permitted to enter a block occupied by a train other than a passenger train at a speed not exceeding 15 mph by means of a *permissive* signal indication, to cover exigencies such as breakdowns.) A manual block system could also confer an operating advantage; track conditions permitting, when it was introduced in timetable and train-order territory, it raised maximum authorized speed from 59 mph for passenger and 49 mph for freight to 79 mph by federal rule. This, of course, was in recognition of its safety feature.

This method of running trains has, however, become a victim of progress. Block operators, along with their stations and signals, are now relics of the past, and the manual block systems they controlled have been replaced by more efficient ways of managing traffic flow.

Automatic Block System

The automatic block system is defined as "a series of consecutive blocks governed by block signals activated by a train, or engine, or by certain conditions affecting the use of a block." The inclusion of the words "certain conditions" covers events such as a switch left open, broken rail, or washout. The change from manually controlled to train-actuated signals was made possible by the track circuit, an 1872 invention that featured low-voltage direct current fed into the rails from line-side batteries. As a train enters a block, which is electrically isolated by insulated rail joints at both ends, its wheels shunt the current and thereby cause a contact to open. The consequent interruption of current flow results in a change in signal aspect from green to red. A key element of this arrangement is that it is fail-safe; interruption of power due to battery failure, broken rail, insulation breakdown, or lightning strike opens the contact, and the signals go to red.

The operative language for an automatic block system is found in Rule 251: "On portions of the railroad, and on designated tracks so specified in the timetable, trains will run with reference to other trains in the same direction by block signals whose indications will supersede the superiority of trains." One result was a significant reduction in train orders in double-track territory, where the current of traffic was established in one direction on each main track (similar to an interstate highway). Another was a decline in the importance of Rule 99 as railroads eliminated the requirement for rear-end flagging where protection was provided by automatic block signals.

As automatic block systems replaced manual block systems in the early 1900s, the random spacing between open block stations gave way to signal spacing to accommodate the key objectives of expediting train movements and providing safe stopping distances. The simplest signal sequence behind a stopped train or other obstruction is two-block, three-indication; the signals go from *clear* (maximum authorized speed) to *approach* (30 mph) to *stop*. With one-mile spacing, this can result in speed reduction to 30 mph nearly two miles behind a stopped train when its rear car, standing just back of a signal, is barely occupying the second block ahead of a following train. To reduce excess train spacing while still maintaining safe stopping distances, three-block, four-indication and, less frequently, four-block, five-indication sequences were established. These sequences with their shortened signal spacing enable train speeds to be reduced more gradually over the same distance, cutting down excess spacing versus two-block sequences with mile-long blocks. In the many decades since the installation of automatic block systems, train speeds have increased significantly and train tonnages and train lengths dramatically, with consequent lengthening of safe stopping distances. Quicker-acting air brakes have helped, as has the availability of dynamic braking on diesel-electric locomotives. Otherwise, rather than respacing signals, railroads have adjusted maximum authorized speeds for trains on the basis of such factors as train length and tons per operative air brake.

In automatic block system territory the stop indication referred to earlier requires a train to come to a stop and then permits it to proceed at restricted speed (never more than 15 mph, and it must be able to stop within half the range of vision). A number plate on the signal mast commonly identifies such stop and proceed indications. Exceptions to the stopping requirement may be found on ascending grades, where at automatic block signals marked with the letters G (grade) or P (permissive), stop and proceed indications may be passed at restricted speed without stopping by trains whose locomotives are pulling their maximum rated tonnage. This is intended to avoid the disruptive consequences of stalling on the grade. (Interlocking signals at junctions, railroad crossings, movable bridges, and similar sites displaying a stop indication require a train to remain stopped until a proceed indication is received—i.e., stop and stay.)

Automatic block signaling, by bringing about a substantial increase in track capacity while at the same time providing a higher level of safety, was a major step forward in railroad operations. With the subsequent introduction of centralized traffic control, automatic block systems in their pure form now account for only 15 percent of U.S. track mileage. This is a misleading statistic, however, since their signals are an integral part of nearly every CTC installation.

Centralized Traffic Control

Well into the twentieth century signal engineers found a way to use the track circuit to its fullest extent by developing a technology that enabled trains to move in both directions on single track by signal indication only. Implementation of this breakthrough was initially minimal—a short operator-controlled installation in northern Ohio was the first in 1927, but then the Great Depression intervened and a 15-year hiatus followed. Thereafter, installations proceeded until CTC became paramount, as will be noted in more detail later.

The applicable Standard Code language is found in Rule 261: "On portions of the railroad, and on designated tracks so specified in the timetable, trains will be governed by block signals whose indications will supersede the superiority of trains for both opposing and following movements on the same track." For movement authority, installation of CTC immediately eliminated the use of train orders except for those related to track conditions, which were issued on a Form Z. The latter was subsequently discontinued, and now this subject is dealt with in dispatcher's bulletins transmitted to crews via computer at on-duty points. Operator-controlled CTC installations were prevalent on some railroads for a time, often as a result of labor agreements, but now the dispatchers are in virtually complete command. Typically, they have at their disposal a series of controlled points, consisting of interlockings at vital locations such as crossovers between two or more main tracks, switches at both ends of passing sidings and yards, diverging routes at junctions, and railroad crossings at grade. When the variable distances between these controlled points are long enough to warrant, the intervening segments are divided into blocks governed by automatic block signals that both expedite and protect against following movements. The CTC system prevents the dispatcher from displaying proceed signal indications to opposing trains on the same track between controlled points. For hand-operated switches at auxiliary tracks outside controlled points, alternate arrangements are in effect. When it is desirable to have trains clear the main track at such locations, the switches are equipped with electric locks. Reentering the main track requires activation of a timing mechanism on the lock that sets the protecting signals at their most restrictive indication. After expiration of an interval of three to eight minutes (depending on the length of track circuits), the switch can be opened. Under the alternate arrangement, trains must occupy the main track while using the switches, which are listed in the timetable as nonclearing.

Extensive applications of CTC have occurred in three phases. The first phase was during World War II, primarily on single-track lines in the West. Traffic surges on many of these lines threatened gridlock as stressed dispatchers coped with reams of train orders. The second and much longer phase began about 10 years later in a period of declining traffic, both passenger and freight. Then, installation of CTC enabled major eastern trunk lines to rid themselves of excess track capacity, reducing from four tracks with automatic block systems to two with CTC in the most blatant circumstances, and from two to one oth-

Centralized traffic control (CTC) gave all switches and signals under CTC territory central control over train movements, providing a significant increase in capacity. This was a new CTC system completed on the Nickel Plate Railroad late in 1942. —*Trains* Magazine Collection

erwise. A subsequent wave of mergers created additional overcapacity and extended this phase. The third phase began when traffic rebounded after passage of the Staggers Act (deregulation) in 1980 and, concurrently, when flows of low-sulfur coal out of the Powder River Basin in Wyoming overwhelmed affected routes. Here CTC provided the necessary increases in capacity by replacing automatic block systems on both single and double track and by installation on new main tracks. Otherwise, CTC with its flexibility on multitracked main lines has helped ease the strain during maintenance windows when a main track is taken out of service for rehabilitation or upgrading. To sum up, although only 40 percent of U.S. track-miles are equipped with CTC, it predominates on virtually all high-density routes and thus expedites the movement of some 75 to 80 percent of the traffic.

Track-Warrant Control

With the demise of train orders, the most common form of train movement authority in single-track automatic block signal and nonsignaled territory is the track-warrant, issued and repeated back via radio. The format is as follows: at the top are spaces for track-warrant number, date, train addressed, and location; next is a list of items numbered sequentially, each worded to fit specific commands or time limits given by dispatchers to train crews, and each supplied with a box following its number

to be checked if the item applies; and at the bottom are spaces for the dispatcher's OK and name (after correct repetition by the receiving crew member), the time the warrant limits were cleared, and by whom reported clear. The number of items included per warrant varies by railroad, but all contain those essential to train movement. Track-warrant limits can be stations, mileposts, or elsewhere. A meet is not established in so many words; rather, at a given siding, one train is ordered to "hold main track" at last-named point and the other to "clear main track" at last-named point, the last-named point being the limit of movement authority for both. In that regard, once the authority granted by the warrant has been used, or its time limit has expired, further authority must be issued on a new warrant.

One major railroad does it differently. In something of a throwback to manual block systems, it divides its single-track automatic block signal and nonsignaled territories into blocks whose limits are identified by signs bearing their names. Its movement authority is likewise recorded on a form, at the top of which is an address to an engine by number on a specific subdivision. The body of the form is divided vertically into nine columns, each labeled at the top. Left to right, the labels call for the following information: "copied by [crew member]," "block name," "type of block [clear, occupied, and so on]," "direction," "relieved from flagging [yes or no]," "time authorized," "authorized by dispatcher," "released by," and "time released." Unlike track warrants, this form can accommodate numerous grants of authority, because it has 18 blank horizontal columns. Also, it relies entirely on the dispatcher's bulletin for information and restrictions concerning track conditions. (Track warrants cover those to some degree.) Grants of authority, recorded one block per horizontal column, are confined to the named blocks.

Much of the track mileage governed by these kinds of forms is nonsignaled and light density, often occupied by just 1 train at a time: the ubiquitous local freight. In single-track automatic block signal territory, density can vary from moderate to fairly heavy; counts of up to 20 trains per day are found, in such cases requiring a nimble dispatcher to cope with the volume of warrants generated. In a few instances relief has been afforded by installation of CTC islands, controlled sidings between intervals of nonsignaled or automatic block signal territory; track warrants provide movement authority between and through these places.

—Jeremy Taylor

REFERENCES

Armstrong, John H. *The Railroad, What It Is, What It Does: The Introduction to Railroading.* 4th ed. Omaha, Nebr.: Simmons-Boardman, 1998.
Josserand, Peter. *Rights of Trains.* 5th ed. New York: Simmons-Boardman, 1957.

See also SIGNALING.

Train Movement

Making Up the Train

If an originating yard (Yard A) is a major freight classification facility, cars for its destination yard (Yard B) are going to arrive there mixed in with cars for other destinations in numerous trains from a variety of origin points. If Yard B is also an important facility, there will be a daily train from the two yards, so cars for the Yard B destination will begin to arrive at the originating Yard A not long after the departure of the previous train for the Yard B destination or over a period of up to 24 hours.

As trains to be classified at Yard A approach it, they pass a trackside device known as a "reader" that by means of a radio signal obtains information from "data tags," computer circuits located in plastic boxes attached to the car sides. The car types, owners' initials, and numbers thus retrieved are sent to a central computer, permitting customer service personnel to advise shippers and receivers of the location of cargos as they progress toward their destinations. After these inbound trains stop in the originating

yards' receiving yard, the compressed air is manually discharged by a bleed valve from the air-brake systems on each car (a few hand brakes are applied to keep the trains from rolling after the air brakes are thus released). A thorough mechanical inspection is made of each car; any defects noted are identified as those that can be repaired in the yard with no delay versus those that must be diverted to the originating yard's car shop (e.g., for wheel replacement), usually involving a one-day delay.

A switch list for each train is generated by the central computer and sent to the originating yard. As each train is classified (sorted) in accordance with its switch list, cars for the destination yard are sent into a track in the classification yard designated for that destination. A yard supervisor determines when the last car to be included in the next Yard B destination train has been switched and advises central headquarters that the train has been closed out. Cars for the Yard B destination are then moved from the classification yard to the departure yard. (At some facilities trains depart from classification tracks.) Air hoses between cars are coupled by the carmen, the air line from the stationary air compressor located in the yard is connected to the head car, and the train is "charged," that is, its air-brake system filled with compressed air. Brakes are applied, each car is checked for proper brake application, air pressure is restored, and each car is checked for brake release. (This is the yard air test, performed by car department personnel.) The chief train dispatcher responsible for trains leaving the originating Yard A plans the departure time for the Yard B destination train, notifying the originating yard locomotive and car departments and the crew dispatcher at central headquarters. They in turn advise whether that time is acceptable, or if not, when locomotive, train, and/or crew will be available. The train is then ordered accordingly. (If the destination train is considered to be one of mid- to high-priority status, under normal circumstances planned departure time and order time will coincide.)

Train Crew Responsibilities before Departure

First, the crew dispatcher at central headquarters will advise the train crew assignment by train symbol and time ordered. For crews in "pool" service, the vast majority, this summons can come at any time of day. Leaving home, the typical two-man crew of conductor and engineer will each bring a grip containing company materials covering responsibilities and eventualities with which crew members must be thoroughly familiar. Essential items are the employee timetable that includes the portion of the railroad over which the train will run, operations and safety rulebooks, air-brake regulations, instructions for special equipment handling, and a hazardous-materials guidebook, plus, in most cases, some food.

Arriving more or less simultaneously at the originating yard's crew reporting location, conductor and engineer will go over together documents provided there that relate specifically to their assignment. From a printer reserved for its transmission comes the dispatcher's bulletin, sent from the dispatcher's office to the yard not more than 30 minutes before ordering time. This contains bulletins advising of conditions to be encountered en route not found in the timetable, such as maintenance crews working, temporary speed restrictions, or bad footing trackside, each pinpointed by milepost location.

From central headquarters via another printer comes the work order, a detailed explanation of the transportation function the subject train is expected to perform, in this case the straightforward mission of moving the entire train between originating and terminating yards. (For other trains, there could be multiple functions involving not only cars to be moved from origin to destination but also others to be set off and/or picked up at intermediate points.) The work order includes a train consist, a car-by-car list showing position in train, initials and number, load or empty, type of car, weight to nearest ton, and contents. It also includes a page to be completed and signed by the conductor, then faxed to central headquarters from destination, certifying that the specified transportation function(s) were accomplished. For exceptions (for instance, a defective car left at an intermediate point), there is a covering procedure. Attached to the work order in the same printout from central headquarters comes the train documentation, a three-part advisory.

First up is the tonnage graph, another train consist that shows cumulative train tonnage and train length and highlights by diagramming the location of heavy loads; the special format is for the benefit of the engineer, to assist him in handling the train. Second is the restricted and special-handling list, which calls attention to high and/or wide cars, if any, their position in the train, and associated restrictions, such as wide loads not to be passed by trains on adjacent tracks. The third relates to commodities classified as hazardous materials; this part can be a short statement that there are no hazardous materials or a multipage advisory mandated by the Federal Railroad Administration. Included for each hazardous-materials load, as well as empty tank cars whose previous load was hazardous, is the following information: location of hazardous-materials ("hazmat") cars in train, identification code numbers for contents (placarded on the cars), inherent-risk letter codes (flammable, explosive, and so on), and car-by-car detail giving contents, hazards involved, addresses of shippers and receivers, and emergency telephone numbers. Last, there is detail for each hazmat regarding form (liquid, gas, and so on), risks of exposure, circulation propensities in the event of leakage, and instructions for containment measures.

After digesting these documents (collectively, the "job briefing"), the crew may be required to call a supervisor (yardmaster or trainmaster) for a safety message—typically, the safety rule of the day, plus an account of any recent safety-related incidents and the lessons to be learned from them. The conductor will then ascertain from the yardmaster the track on which the train is located, and from the engine house the numbers of the locomotive units assigned. After removing essential items from lockers—radio, lantern, foul-weather gear if needed—the crew proceeds to the engine-ready tracks to take charge of the locomotive consist, most often two or three diesel-electric units in multiple control. A check is made for on-board supplies such as drinking water, ice, spare air hose, wrench, and fusees (railroad terminology for flares). Permission is obtained from the engine-house foreman to move the locomotive, and a route through the yard to the head end of the train is received from the yardmaster. The conductor couples the locomotive to the head car, connects the air hoses, and walks back past six cars, releasing any applied hand brakes and looking out for hazardous materials (not permitted within six cars of the locomotive). A train brake test is made: the engineer applies the brakes, and a car inspector at the rear of the train checks the rear car for brake application; if this is okay, the engineer is instructed to release the brakes, and the rear car is checked for brake release. The car inspector hangs an end-of-train device (EOT) on the rear coupler, connects it to the air hose on the car, and activates it, advising the engineer by radio or hand or lantern signal. The latter then dials the EOT number on the receiving unit in the locomotive cab, establishing communication between head and rear end. By means of the EOT, the engineer will be informed (1) of the air pressure at the rear of the train, (2) that the warning light on the EOT is illuminated, and (3) when, after starting the train, the slack has run out and the rear car begins to move. The train is now ready for departure.

Before the run to the terminating Yard B begins, a qualification involving some of the events described needs to be made. At most major yards located astride main lines there will be a number of "run-through" trains that do not enter or depart from the yard. Instead, they stop on the main track, change crews, and depart with no change in locomotives or cars. Typically, these trains will be intermodal (trailers and containers with mixed cargos mounted on specially equipped flatcars), vehicle (automobiles and trucks carried in enclosed bilevel and trilevel cars), and unit (single-commodity, single-shipper, single-receiver trains, most often carrying coal in open-top cars or grain products in covered hopper cars). Occasionally, too, a train of mixed freight, similar to an origination and termination Yard A–to–Yard B train, will run through major yards at intermediate points along its route. For a crew called at Yard A for a run-through train, the chain of events through the safety briefing remains the same. Thereafter, that crew is instead driven by van to the run-through locomotive on the main track to relieve the inbound crew.

Under Way: Factors That Influence Movement

The yardmaster has approved a route out of the yard, the dispatcher has lined the switches and cleared the signals to the main line, the engineer has opened the throttle, and the train is being timed out of the originating yard. Once on the main track, the engineer, punching the odometer to zero and using the train-length figure shown on the tonnage graph, estimates when the rear car has exited the yard, then applies full power in an effort to achieve maximum authorized speed as indicated in the timetable. Whether this is possible depends to a large extent on the ratio of locomotive horsepower to train tonnage. Lavish motive-power allotments up to 4 hp per ton are reserved for intermodal trains running on highly competitive schedules and permitted speeds of 60 to 70 mph. This train of lesser status is more likely to be at 2 to 2½ hp per ton at best, enough perhaps to occasionally reach its permitted speeds of 50 to 55 mph. (At around $2 million per diesel-electric unit, railroads are not wont to overinvest in motive power.) Sustained grades, however modest, are inevitably a deterrent to progress; a mixed train such as this one is apt to gross between 5,000 and 10,000 tons. Weather can interfere; a moderate headwind can create a significant drag on 100 or so cars. Then there are slow orders, which apply in defined areas and serve to reduce maximum authorized speed. These can either be permanent, carried in the timetable (because of curves, bridges, urban areas, and the like), or temporary, announced in dispatcher's bulletins (usually for maintenance work, occasionally for roadbed deficiencies).

To mitigate the adverse effect of these factors, the railroad must be kept free of congestion, and the best guarantee of fluidity is a modern control system (in the hands of a skilled dispatcher, of course). That system is centralized traffic control (CTC), the savior of many hard-pressed lines during World War II, greatly refined since, and now the installation of choice on virtually all heavy-density routes in the United States. In CTC territory, signal indications govern the movement of trains in both directions on main tracks and also on auxiliary tracks designated in the timetable as controlled sidings. Commonly, the dispatcher governs movements between two or more main tracks, to and from controlled sidings, at crossings with other railroads and junctions, and in and out of yards. This is done by manipulation of switches and signals at locations known as controlled points. Depending on such variables as train frequency, length of controlled sidings, and presence of severe grades, controlled points may be within a mile of one another or separated by 20 or more miles. When so separated, the intervening segments, while still in CTC territory, are usually subdivided into blocks of a mile or more in length, movements into which are governed by automatic block signals—that is, not dispatcher controlled, but activated by the passage of trains. Trains following one another between controlled points are thus kept apart. (The CTC system will not permit the dispatcher to display proceed signal indications to opposing trains on the same track between controlled points.)

Under Way: Inside the Locomotive Cab

In carrying out their mission to move their train toward its destination as expeditiously as possible consistent with safety, what activities engage the conductor and engineer in the climate-controlled, sound-insulated command post they occupy on a modern locomotive? Commensurate with the assumption that they are in CTC territory, they must keep a vigilant watch for signal indications governing their train and must call out these indications by name to each other. They may also be required to send a radio message to trains in the vicinity, identifying their train and advising signal indication and location. On some railroads the conductor is supplied with a form on which the following must be recorded: track occupied, signal location, signal indication, speed, and time (sometimes only for indications other than proceed). Of course, the engineer must reduce speed for restrictive signal indications and also for the aforementioned slow orders. This can be accomplished in two ways: by applying the train's air brakes or by use of the dynamic brake on the locomotive, and sometimes by a combination of the two. (Dynamic braking forces are created when the polarity is reversed on the electric motors that drive the locomotive wheels, turning them into generators; the current thus built up is dissipated as heat via fan-cooled grids.) If a stop signal is encountered, and no apparent reason is observed, after stopping, a member of the crew must contact the dispatcher. In well-populated areas the engineer will be kept busy sounding the horn for road crossings. When their train meets or is passed by other trains on adjacent tracks, both crew members will watch for abnormal conditions and, if any are spotted, will alert the other crews via radio. If no trouble is detected, the familiar "all black" message will be given. (No dust clouds, spark showers, fire, or smoke, no problem.) On curves the engineer or conductor will look back at the train to make sure that all is well within sight distance.

Under Way: Technology for Safety

There are three systems in general usage that provide either added accident protection or investigative support in the event of trouble. Two are installed on locomotives and the third alongside the tracks. Aboard locomotives there is a device to ensure that the engineer does not doze off or to alert the conductor if he or she should lose consciousness.

This will only be activated if a time interval elapses during which the device detects no control manipulation of any kind on the part of the engineer (e.g., sounding the horn, adjusting the throttle setting, or applying the brakes). The greater the train speed, the shorter the time interval. Once the device is activated, a sequence of events takes place: a flashing light is illuminated in full view of the engineer, then a tone of escalating volume is sounded. Again, the greater the speed, the more quickly the sequence evolves. If alerted, the engineer can reset the device by striking a small lever or pressing a button on the control console. If there is no response, the device will trigger a full-service application of the air brakes, and the train will be brought to a stop. The conductor, aroused by the alarms, could of course take action to prevent the brake application and if necessary take temporary control of the train. The other onboard device is an event-recorder, a mechanism required by law on any locomotive that will be operated at more than 30 mph over public grade crossings—in effect, all locomotive units to be run in leading position in main-line service. This device records in real time a sequence of vital information such as speed, sounding of horn, ringing of bell, power and dynamic brake settings, and brake applications. The picture thus presented would clearly be of use in a train-vehicle collision at a highway crossing, a contest in which the motorist is almost always the loser. The record is also useful to railroad supervisors checking on observance of speed limits and train handling. The third device referred to, situated at trackside at roughly 20-mile intervals, is a combination of hotbox and dragging-equipment detectors. (These functions can be separated in different locations, and there are detectors for other conditions, but this particular installation is typical.) The term "hotbox" is derived from the now-vanished situation that developed when the lubrication surrounding a friction wheel bearing, enclosed in a journal box at the end of an axle, dried out; the bearing then overheated, and a grease fire, sometimes spectacular, flamed up in the box. With the conversion from friction to roller bearings, this all-too-frequent occurrence disappeared, but roller bearings do fail occasionally, hence this detector with its heat sensor. The dragging-equipment detector consists of paddles that when rocked by contact trigger a warning response. When either of these conditions is detected, the train crew is alerted via a synthesized voice on radio that advises which of the two defective conditions is involved, how many axles from the head end must be counted to pinpoint the trouble spot, and which side of the train to examine. The train is stopped, and the conductor, after consulting the consist and counting axles, walks back to investigate. Suffice it to say that if the defect (assuming there is one—false alarms do occur) exceeds the rather limited opportunity to take corrective action, the offending car must be set off on the closest suitable sidetrack for attention by the car department. The delay can be substantial, but a derailment saved avoids what could be a major tieup, damaged or destroyed equipment and cargo, and extensive cleanup operations, all at great expense to the railroad.

Arrival at the Terminating Yard B

As the train nears Yard B, the dispatcher checks with yard supervision to see if it is going to be taken right in or held out until a clear track is available. If there is to be a "holdout" of some duration, the dispatcher will position it clear of the main track to avoid delay to other trains. The crew sometimes has a stake in this, too—the last controlled siding short of the yard into which it will likely be diverted may be bisected by a highway crossing that the train when stopped will block. So, to avoid a citation under the state's 10-minute antiblocking law, the crossing will have to be "cut"—that is, the conductor will have to uncouple the train back of the crossing and have the engineer pull ahead until the highway is cleared. Then, when the train is ready to depart, he will have to recouple, and the engineer, with the help of the EOT device, will have to test the air-brake system to be sure it is operative at the rear of the train. In short, cutting a long train for whatever reason is often a tedious process. The supervisors at the receiving yard have been made aware that holdouts are frowned upon; thus this train will likely be yarded promptly. The dispatcher lines the switches and displays the signals at the entry controlled point. The conductor radios the yardmaster to ascertain the track upon which the train is to be yarded. When the train is stopped, before uncoupling the locomotive, the conductor will apply the hand brakes on a specified number of cars on the head end to prevent the train from rolling after the air brakes are released preparatory to switching. The yardmaster is contacted again for permission to move the locomotive to the engine-servicing facility, where it is left in a location designated by the engine-house foreman. The engineer, before disembarking, fills out a report on the performance of the locomotive, indicating defects, if any, and leaves it in a holder aboard the locomotive for mechanical department personnel to check out. In the crew room the conductor fills out and faxes the "mission accomplished" page of the work order to the customer service department at central headquarters. As the person in charge, the conductor enters into a computer a time slip for both crew members for use by the payroll department in calculating wages due for service performed. The time-slip information includes time off-duty, which serves two purposes: it sets the starting time of the minimum eight-hour off-duty period required by federal law, and, in pool service, it places this crew at the bottom of the list of Yard A crews off-duty at Yard B.

Paperwork completed, the crew will be taxied at railroad expense to a motel designated as the "R and R" facility for train service employees away from home at Yard B. They will get their rest there, then await a call for a train back to Yard A and home.

—Jeremy Taylor

REFERENCES

Armstrong, John H. *The Railroad, What It Is, What It Does: The Introduction to Railroading.* 4th ed. Omaha, Nebr.: Simmons-Boardman, 1998.

Josserand, Peter. *Rights of Trains.* 5th ed. New York: Simmons-Boardman, 1957.

Training of Railroad Workers

Carriers and unions alike wanted bright, conscientious, and courteous men operating the trains. Members of four unions, the Brotherhood of Locomotive Engineers (BLE), the Brotherhood of Locomotive Firemen and Enginemen (BLF&E), the Brotherhood of Railroad Trainmen (BRT), and the Order of Railroad Conductors (ORC), known collectively as the operating or independent brotherhoods, dominated the running of trains. The operating brotherhoods, unlike other organized railroad labor, did not belong to the American Federation of Labor. These unions emphasized safety, sobriety and, following a trend of the late nineteenth century, professionalism. By World War I the operating brotherhoods had succeeded in implanting a keen sense of professional responsibility in their members and had secured contracts with most large carriers. Men in the train service were among the nation's elite industrial workers. According to one operative whose career encompassed more than half a century from 1873 to 1930, a conductor or an engineer had about as much prestige as an airmail pilot of the 1930s. To be sure, incompetent men still operated trains, but they were less in evidence.

The workaday world of railroaders has changed immensely since the industry's beginnings. Employment requirements have become more stringent. In the nineteenth century, when industry officials considered qualifications, they often spoke in vague moralistic terms: employees should be "sober," "prompt," and "honest" and "exhibit gentlemanly behavior towards passengers." One exacting standard that carriers upheld except in extreme situations was dismissal for violation of Rule G, which forbade alcohol consumption on the job. Joel Seidman, historian of the BRT, wrote, "Prior to World War I all that was required in the way of educational background was an ability to read and write, for which a fourth grade education might suffice." By the 1950s many railroads required high-school graduation whenever the state labor market permitted.

In the middle of the nineteenth century carriers decentralized their hiring procedure. Delegating hiring to local officials reminded operatives from where authority emanated. Local officials were required to follow increasingly stringent regulations. Job candidates often had to fill out a multipage application, undergo a complete physical examination, and answer questions concerning their education and work experience. Some applications also contained a section that dealt with prior injuries, as well as the current physical examination. Still, in the nineteenth century family and personal connections were often the most important factors in gaining employment, but this practice declined to some degree over time.

A characteristic of early careers in railroading was fluidity. Early accounts of railroad work are filled with reminiscences of frequent job changes, known as booming, and of great flexibility in job classification. Men often had experience switching, braking, firing, and conducting. Obviously, formal education was not as important as practical experience. By the twentieth century both carriers and unions had become more systematic and bureaucratized, job classifications had become more rigid, and their educational requirements had become more stringent.

Hiring procedures evolved over the preceding decades, and bureaucratic procedures developed that allowed carriers to employ the most qualified applicants. By the twentieth century a fairly set pattern of work and education had emerged. Carriers expected that train service operatives be literate. Firemen's and engineers' jobs required technical knowledge of numerous engines, which could only be gained by experience. Well into the twentieth century most of the men who occupied these positions were native born, white, and Protestant, as were the railroad managers. Career paths were governed by a rigid seniority system. One consequence was that firemen and engineers, especially in the passenger service, which were the industry's plum assignments, were often older. In the 1920s a fireman often worked 10 years or more before being promoted.

By the 1950s the average fireman was in his 40s, while his partner in the cab was on the average nearly 60. The seniority system ensured years and often decades of on-the-job training. Although the route to a conductor's job was perhaps not quite as long, brakemen and switchmen by the twentieth century often worked for years before they could expect to be promoted.

Firing was physically one of the most demanding jobs in the industry. Firemen were responsible for shoveling as much as 10 or 20 tons of coal into the firebox, or for making sure that the mechanical stoker was operating properly. On many roads, to move to the "right side of the cab," a fireman had to pass a series of exams. If he could not, he would not be retained as long as qualified men were available. The BLF&E booklet *Feeding the Iron Hog* notes that requirements of carriers varied, but outlined the criteria of one major railroad. After six months a fireman took an exam consisting of more than 200 questions ranging from general rules to the operation of air brakes. Six months later he took a second exam dealing with firing and fuel economy and answered additional questions concerning air brakes. At the end of the second year he took another test that dealt with firing and air brakes. The final exam incorporated nearly 1,000 questions. Additionally, firemen and engineers had to acquaint themselves with a variety of locomotives, 44 under the Whyte system of classification. Firemen and engineers often operated several types of engines over the course of a typical week.

The usual entry-level position for future conductors was either as a switchman or a brakeman. They had to pass a rigorous physical exam and then participate in a training program that by the mid-twentieth century usually lasted several days. Its purpose was to acquaint them with signals, safety requirements, working rules, and company regulations. Exams were given after the operative had accumulated three years of service or 72,000 miles. If he failed, he could retake the test in 90 days. A second failure usually resulted in termination. If he passed, he could be promoted to conductor. However, as with firemen, some refused promotion because it meant a loss of seniority, which meant that they often worked fewer hours on less desirable assignments.

By the last decade of the twentieth century training requirements had become much more standardized, partly because of federal regulation, but also because the union, now (since 2004) the Brotherhood of Locomotive Engineers & Trainmen (BLET), created an education department in 1991. According to the BLET website prospective engineers must be at least 21 years of age, must be in good physical condition with good eyesight and hearing, and must have completed an engineer training program.

Today engineers usually enter the industry as conductors or brakemen and, like their predecessors, learn on the job. However, formalized training is now an important component—some of it through the union or through technical colleges. According to the BLET website, nationwide 12 colleges offer associate degrees or certification programs in railroad operation technology. The National Academy of Railroad Sciences also offers training and certification programs. The curriculum for engineer's training includes train-handling methods, air-brake operation, locomotive and freight-car mechanics and electronics, and hazardous-materials management. Other courses cover current safety principles, operating rules, and Federal Railroad Administration (FRA) regulations. The FRA requires that all locomotive engineers be trained, tested, and recertified every three years. Some of the training is conducted on simulators, which allow trainees to practice skills that match their job requirements.

—Jon R. Huibregtse

REFERENCES

Feeding the Iron Hog: The Life and Work of a Locomotive Fireman. Cleveland: Brotherhood of Locomotive Firemen and Enginemen, 1927.

French, Chauncey Del. *Railroadman.* New York: Macmillan, 1938.

Licht, Walter. *Working for the Railroad: The Organization of Work in the Nineteenth Century.* Princeton, N.J.: Princeton Univ. Press, 1983.

Richardson, Reed C. *The Locomotive Engineer, 1863–1963: A Century of Railway Labor Relations and Work Rules.* Ann Arbor: Univ. of Michigan, 1963.

Seidman, Joel. *The Brotherhood of Railroad Trainmen: The Internal Political Life of a National Union.* New York: John Wiley & Sons, 1962.

Transportation Act of 1920.

See REGULATION

Transportation Act of 1958.

See REGULATION

Trevithick, Richard, Jr. (1771–1833)

Pioneering steam-engine builder Richard Trevithick, Jr., was born on April 13, 1771, in the parish of Illogan in Cornwall, England. For centuries mining flourished in Cornwall, where the pursuit of tin and later copper was the principal enterprise. As the mines grew deeper, water flooding the shafts became a serious problem. It was in Cornwall that steam technology was employed on a large scale to pump out the water. At first relatively primitive Savery engines were used, later Newcomen engines. These soon were superseded by more sophisticated Boulton & Watt engines. All of these employed low-pressure steam.

Richard Trevithick, Sr., was a Cornish mine captain, responsible for operating a mine, hiring the miners, and acquiring the needed machinery. Following in his father's footsteps, Richard, Jr., was fascinated by mining and the steam engines that ran the pumps. He proved to be a natural engineer, with vision and energy and a talent for solving practical problems. At age 15 Richard, Jr., was named engineer of several mines, proof of his prowess with things mechanical.

A major problem for the mine captains was the inefficiency of the low-pressure steam engines then in use in Cornwall and elsewhere. Unfortunately, the Boulton & Watt patents made it virtually impossible to make any modifications or improvements without running afoul of the manufacturer's solicitors. Yet Trevithick was attracted to the use of high-pressure steam, and when the Boulton & Watt patents terminated in 1800, he pursued the development of new engines, including a portable, high-pressure version that could be easily moved. Working with

Andrew Vivian and Davies Gilbert, Trevithick fashioned a steam carriage that could be used for transportation and also to move the steam engine to places where power was required. A patent on the steam carriage was awarded to Trevithick on March 26, 1802. The carriage worked in test runs, but investors were not attracted.

Then an opportunity arose. Samuel Homfray of the Penydarran Iron Works at Merthyr Tydfil contacted Trevithick to see if a locomotive could be designed and produced to move cars along a plateway line constructed parallel to the highly congested Glamorganshire Canal. Homfray believed that a locomotive could move a train of trams along the plateway and bypass the canal. He had a 500-guinea wager with one of his competitors that the proposed locomotive could move 10 tons of iron from Merthyr Tydfil to Abercynon and return with the empty train.

Trevithick constructed a vehicle strange-looking by modern standards. It was a combination of a stout boiler, cog wheels, an awkward drive-rod mechanism, and a huge flywheel. The Penydarran locomotive proved up to the task; on February 13, 1804, it successfully pulled the cars along the plateway. It was the world's first steam-powered railway. Unfortunately, the plateway was not up to the task; many of the cast-iron plates broke under the locomotive's weight. There were more trials and more broken plates, and the locomotive was soon disassembled. The steam engine was used for many years to power a hammer.

Trevithick tried several means of promoting his steam locomotive, but until the technology of the rails or plateways improved, the locomotive was a dead end. Two decades later George Stephenson and others used Trevithick's ideas to develop steam locomotives with practical capabilities.

Despite his ingenuity, real financial success eluded Trevithick. He designed other steam-powered devices and worked in Central and South America on a series of mining ventures. He died on April 22, 1833; his widow had the pleasure of seeing his ideas come to fruition in the hands of others. Richard Trevithick, Jr., built the first steam locomotive and showed the path of progress that would eventually lead to the modern railway.

—George M. Smerk

REFERENCES

Burton, Anthony. *Richard Trevithick: Giant of Steam.* London: Aurum Press, 2000.

Nock, O. S. *Locomotion: A World Survey of Railway Traction.* New York: Charles Scribner's Sons, 1975.

Tunnels. *See* CIVIL ENGINEERING

U

Union Pacific Railroad

The early days of the Union Pacific and the history and construction of the first transcontinental railroad are discussed in the entry on the Pacific railroad. The three decades that followed the driving of the golden spike on May 10, 1869, were not good years for the Union Pacific, not only because of overextension, debt owed to the federal government, and the Crédit Mobilier scandal, but because the railroad served undeveloped territory that provided little traffic and little revenue.

Even so, during those years the Union Pacific expanded, largely through subsidiaries Oregon Short Line and Oregon Railway & Navigation Co., with lines from Ogden, Utah, to Butte, Montana, from Granger, Wyoming, northwest to Portland, Oregon, and from Salt Lake City southwest to Uvada, near the Utah-Nevada state line. In 1880 UP merged the Kansas Pacific Railway, which had begun operation from Kansas City to Denver ten years earlier, and the Denver Pacific, which connected Denver with the UP main line at Cheyenne. In the 1870s and 1880s UP acquired and built a group of lines that would become the Colorado & Southern Railway; the Union Pacific system even reached southeast from Denver into Texas for a few years.

The Union Pacific entered receivership in 1893 and was purchased at a public auction in 1897 by Edward H. Harriman. He soon added to it the Southern Pacific, Central Pacific, Illinois Central, Chicago & Alton, a half interest in the Los Angeles & Salt Lake, and the Central of Georgia. Harriman was not one to squeeze quick profits out of a railroad but believed instead that a railroad would yield greater income if it were well managed and its physical plant was in good condition. Harriman's improvement program for UP included double track from Omaha to Granger, Wyoming, and a new line over Sherman Hill between Cheyenne and Laramie.

The Los Angeles & Salt Lake Railroad was completed from Los Angeles to a connection with the OSL at Uvada in 1905, but because of severe flooding in Nevada and Utah, through operation did not begin until 1912. The Salt Lake City–Uvada portion of the OSL was transferred to the LA&SL, and the LA&SL became part of the Union Pacific system.

In 1912 the federal government broke up the Harriman system. Despite the separation, though, close cooperation continued between Union Pacific and Southern Pacific. A 1924 agreement that permitted Southern Pacific to control Central Pacific required SP to solicit traffic to move via the Union Pacific.

The map of the Union Pacific remained substantially the same from about 1900 to about 1980: main lines from Omaha through Ogden to Los Angeles, Granger, Wyoming, to Portland (thence to Seattle by trackage rights, mostly on Northern Pacific), and Kansas City–Denver-Cheyenne, secondary main lines from Hinkle, Oregon, northeast to Spokane and from Ogden north to Butte, Montana, and branch lines all over its system—the networks were particularly dense in Nebraska, Idaho, and eastern Washington. The double-track line of the Chicago & North Western carried UP freight and passenger trains 500 miles east from Omaha to Chicago. Although UP's principal business was moving heavy freight trains long distances across the West, it also operated fleets of yellow passenger trains, and its dining-car service was at least the equal of Santa Fe's much-touted Fred Harvey service.

The Depression of the 1930s was at its worst when two western railroads, Union Pacific and the Chicago, Burlington & Quincy, designed and ordered internal-combustion-powered streamlined trains for local service. Union Pacific's M-10000 was built by Pullman-Standard and was powered by a spark-ignition distillate engine built by the Electro-Motive Corp., a subsidiary of General Motors. The train consisted of three permanently connected units: a power car with a Railway Post Office apartment and a baggage compartment, a coach, and a buffet-coach—the buffet kitchen was tucked into the windowless rounded rear of the car. The train was completed in February 1934 and brought UP the honor of owning the first streamliner; Burlington's *Zephyr*, which rolled out of the Budd plant two months later, was the first diesel-powered streamlined train. M-10000 toured the country, creating excitement everywhere it went. Within two years Union Pacific operated a fleet of long-distance streamliners between Chicago and Portland, San Francisco, and Los Angeles. M-10000 was configured for short-distance service. UP served very few short-distance markets; for a few years M-10000 ran

Perhaps no streamlined train so beguiled the American public as did the early Union Pacific Streamliners, with their wondrously shaped noses, front-end grilles, portholes, and brilliant Armour yellow colors. In this pre–World War II photograph the *City of San Francisco* and two of its City Streamliner companions have just arrived from the West at Chicago's Northwestern Station.
—Louis A. Marre Collection, *Trains* Magazine Collection

between Kansas City and Salina, Kansas, as the *City of Salina*. It was scrapped in the early 1940s.

In 1955, with hardly any advance notice, UP shifted its streamliners to the Milwaukee Road between Chicago and Omaha. Eight years later it petitioned to merge the Rock Island, mostly for its Chicago-Omaha line. The Union Pacific–Rock Island merger case excited most of the railroads in the West and Midwest, and the proceedings went on for 12 years, by which time the Rock Island had deteriorated to the point that Union Pacific no longer wanted it.

Meanwhile, the Burlington Northern was created from four large railroads. BN was not a surprise to the industry, since the railroads involved had been affiliated for more than 60 years. Then Burlington Northern swallowed the Frisco, and Union Pacific saw that in order to survive, it would also have to grow by merger. In 1980 UP announced that it was acquiring Missouri Pacific and Western Pacific. The announcement constituted a major realignment of the railroads in the western United States. Missouri Pacific and Western Pacific had traditionally been part of the Gould system, as was the Denver & Rio Grande Western, which connected MoPac and WP. In addition, D&RGW and WP had long been associated with the Burlington, at least for passenger-train operation. Union Pacific acquired Missouri Pacific and Western Pacific on December 22, 1982, more than doubling its size. The name Pacific Rail Systems was used briefly by the enlarged UP, but it was soon dropped.

In 1987 the Union Pacific merged several longtime subsidiaries: Los Angeles & Salt Lake, Oregon Short Line, Oregon-Washington Railroad & Navigation Co., St. Joseph & Grand Island, Spokane International, and Yakima Valley Transportation Co., plus Western Pacific and its two subsidiaries, Sacramento Northern and Tidewater Southern. On May 16, 1988, the Interstate Commerce Commission approved the purchase of the Missouri-Kansas-Texas by the Missouri Pacific Railroad. UP absorbed the Katy's operations on August 12, 1988, acquiring the shortest route from Kansas City to Texas. At the same time UP had been buying Chicago & North Western stock. On April 24, 1995, UP merged Chicago & North Western. The merger went poorly: more employees than anticipated accepted UP's buyout offer, creating shortages of train crews.

Southern Pacific and Santa Fe announced their merger proposal in May 1980, called it off four months later, and revived it in 1983. The ICC rejected the proposal in 1986 and rejected the appeal in 1987. Rebounding from the ICC's rejection, Santa Fe paired up with Burlington Northern and Southern Pacific with Denver & Rio Grande Western. Southern Pacific's financial condition became perilous, and SP (which included D&RGW) saw that it had to merge with a stronger railroad. Union Pacific was the only one left.

On September 11, 1996, UP announced that it would acquire Southern Pacific. UP assured shippers and regulatory agencies that problems of the magnitude experienced when UP acquired C&NW would not happen during the SP merger. As matters fell out, the problems were several times worse and continued much longer.

In 2005 UP operated a system of 32,426 route-miles and 52,667 track miles, with 8,226 locomotives, 106,473 freight cars, 5,041 work and other cars, and 49,747 employees. Freight traffic totaled over 9.5 million carloads and 1,043.9 billion revenue ton-miles in 2005, and its principal traffic sources were agricultural products (15 percent), automotive (10 percent), chemicals (14 percent), energy (20 percent), industrial products (22 percent), and intermodal traffic (19 percent). UP operating revenues totaled $13,578 million in 2005, with $11,783 million in operating expenses, and the railroad achieved an 86.8 percent operating ratio.

—George H. Drury

REFERENCE

Klein, Maury. *Union Pacific.* Vols. 1–2. Garden City, N.Y.: Doubleday, 1987, 1989.

Union Switch & Signal Co.

One of the oldest names in railway signaling and still active in the field, Union Switch & Signal Co. (US&S) was founded by George Westinghouse, known for his invention of the air brake for railroad motive power and rolling stock. Among his several hundred patents, Westinghouse held 13 on signaling equipment and 3 on telegraph systems.

The first step toward formation of US&S came in March 1881, when Westinghouse bought a controlling interest in the Union Electric Signal Co., which a year earlier had bought the telegraph patents of the Electric Railway Signal Co. Shortly after acquiring Union Electric Signal, Westinghouse and his partners bought International Switch & Signal Co., which gave them rights to manufacture switches, signals, and telegraph equipment. The two companies were then merged to form the Union Switch & Signal Co.

The new company's primary product was automatic block signaling systems using track circuits, but its product line was soon expanded through acquisitions. By November 1881 US&S was installing Saxby & Farmer mechanical interlocking systems. In 1887 US&S bought the patent rights, materials, and machinery of the mechanical interlocking business of the Pennsylvania Steel Co. At this time it moved its offices and manufacturing facilities from Pittsburgh, Pennsylvania, to neighboring Swissvale.

By 1894 the US&S catalog listed such products as Saxby & Farmer mechanical and electropneumatic interlocking systems, switches, signals, derails, relays, track circuits, electric locks, lightning arresters, indicators, switch stands, and pushbutton operating machines for interlocking. Expansion continued in 1898 with the purchase of National Switch & Signal Co., a manufacturer of mechanical and electrical interlocking systems and manual block signals that had been formed in the early 1880s. A few years earlier, in 1895, National had acquired the Johnson Railroad Signal Co., which was formed in 1888 to manufacture interlocking equipment and block signals.

From its beginnings, the company was a leader in the development of railway signaling systems. In 1881, for example, US&S installed the first interlocking of the hydraulic type at Wellington, Ohio, for a crossing of the Wheeling & Lake Erie and the Cleveland, Cincinnati, Chicago & St. Louis. In 1898 Union's patented one-arm, two-position lower-quadrant semaphore automatic block signal was first used on the Santa Fe Railway. This had a direct-current electric motor, housed in a case that formed the base of the mast, with the up-and-down rod inside the mast.

A new type of interlocking was installed in 1904 on the Lake Shore & Michigan Southern at Millbury Junction, Ohio. One of its special features was the generation of alternating current for signal and switch indication by the use of a special commutator effective only when the motor idled after the movement of the switch or signal was completed. In the same year J. B. Struble, a US&S engineer and inventor of the alternating-current system of automatic block signaling, had developed the new system to meet the demands of high-speed trains. Ordinary direct-current track circuits applied to steam roads were not satisfactory for this service, since the running rails were used as return conductors for the motor current. This would incorrectly affect the operation of the track relays and the signal. To solve this problem, it was necessary to employ a current for the track circuit that would not have the characteristic of direct current to operate selectively upon the track relay. The use of alternating current made it possible to do this by inducing another current in a circuit brought within a magnetic field—a property not possessed by direct current—allowing the use of a track relay of the induction type.

L. V. Lewis, the "father of industrial electronics," as his US&S engineering colleagues knew him, proved in 1923 that vacuum tubes could be used to provide a continuous inductive train control and cab-signal system. Soon afterward the Interstate Commerce Commission ordered the installation of train control on the Pennsylvania Railroad for the purposes of test and development. The PRR put in a US&S three-speed, continuous train control on 49 miles of single or double track between Lewistown and Sunbury, Pennsylvania. The new installation opened on July 11, 1923. It was the first use of vacuum tubes outside the communications industry and the first use of a cab signal instead of wayside signals.

In 1926 US&S introduced its copper oxide rectifier, which converted alternating current into direct current. By 1933 a team of US&S engineers developed a system of coded track circuits for electrified territory. Alternating-current track-circuit energy was superimposed upon

A well-maintained double-track line on the Boston & Maine, fully signalized with a modern system supplied by Union Switch & Signal Co.
—*Trains* Magazine Collection

steady-energy track circuits. The AC in the track circuit was interrupted at fixed frequencies according to track conditions ahead. The number of interruptions per minute was the code rate, and it determined what signal indication would be displayed in the locomotive cab. A pair of receivers was located ahead of the front wheels on the locomotive. An amplifier unit amplified the current picked up by the receivers and operated decoding equipment. Thus the track circuit was "translated" into the languages or frequencies needed to communicate safety messages to the enginemen.

In March 1933 the first installation of coded track circuits for three- and four-indication wayside and cab signaling in electrified territory was made between Zoo and Arsenal, Philadelphia, Pennsylvania, on the Pennsylvania Railroad. This installation used 100 Hz coded alternating current. A year later the Pennsylvania installed US&S coded track circuits in steam territory between Lewistown and Mt. Union, Pennsylvania, on 20 miles of four-track main line, with an average track-circuit length of about a mile. Coded DC was used to provide for three- and four-indication wayside signals. Cab-signal energy was coded AC at 100 Hz.

In 1952 US&S developed the first completely automatic switching system for the Milwaukee Road at its Air Line Yard in Milwaukee, Wisconsin, combining it with automatic retarder speed control. In 1953 the Delaware, Lackawanna & Western made the first installation of Union's multiplex code control systems, involving the consolidation of three major electropneumatic interlocking systems. The three plants located in Newark, New Jersey, han-

dled 233 through trains and 33 drilling moves daily. This new high-speed code control system transmitted 25 controls and 50 indications concurrently per second, and its capacity could be expanded in multiples of 25 controls and 50 indications. More recently, in 1985, Conrail put into service its US&S microprocessor-controlled interlocking at Esplen Junction, near Pittsburgh, Pennsylvania, which involves a five-track junction.

The combination of other competitors in the signaling field into mergers with US&S and the firm's aggressive marketing of its services made it—along with its primary competitor, General Railway Signal—a leader in the field. Early in 1917 the Union Switch & Signal Co. was merged with the Westinghouse Air Brake Co., although the US&S name was retained. Even before the merger the *Railway Age Gazette* announced that US&S, General Railway Signal Co., Federal Signal Co., and Hall Switch & Signal Co. had entered into a cross-licensing agreement to enable the several companies to make use of the patents, applications for patents, and inventions owned by all of them. After some three decades of such practices, during which US&S and General Railway Signal had acquired some 90 percent of the business, the Federal Trade Commission issued consent decree orders against them in 1964, accusing them of fixing and maintaining prices and terms and conditions of sale, agreeing to divide markets and customers, and monopolizing the sale of signaling and control equipment. Although the two firms never admitted any wrongdoing, they agreed to halt the unfair practices and price discrimination cited by the FTC.

Over the next several decades US&S changed its name

several times. After being made a division of Westing-house Air Brake Co. in 1951, in 1967 it was renamed the Signal & Communications Division of WABCO. In 1968 American Standard Inc. purchased the stock of Westing-house Air Brake Co., and in 1972 the Signal & Communications Division of WABCO returned to its original name of Union Switch & Signal Division of WABCO. Still another change came in 1988, when the Ansaldo Group of Genoa, Italy, acquired Union Switch & Signal Division of WABCO from American Standard Inc., but retained the familiar US&S name.

—Robert W. McKnight

REFERENCE

Solomon, Brian. *Railroad Signaling*. St. Paul, Minn.: MBI Books, 2003.

See also ALSTOM SIGNALING (GENERAL RAILWAY SIGNAL CO.); SIGNALING; SIGNALING SUPPLIERS.

Unions. *See* LABOR

Unit Trains

Unit trains are dedicated trains containing one commodity that typically moves from one shipper at one location to one receiver at another location. Such a dedicated trainset operates efficiently by avoiding intermediate switching at terminals and local switching at origin and destination. Unit trains are generally made up of equipment committed to that particular movement and are usually moved by assigned locomotives. In the case of trains moving over more than one railroad, run-through power is usually provided to minimize any delays to the trains.

These dedicated trainsets have become vital to the North American rail industry. Unit trains maximize operational efficiencies by optimizing use of equipment, physical plant, and labor. By eliminating costly local and intermediate switching, the unit train becomes an efficient way to move large volumes over long distances. Moreover, bypassing yards and intermediate terminals allows unit trains to move on faster, more reliable schedules than would otherwise be possible.

Almost from their inception, railroads have looked for ways to become more efficient. The earliest freight cars were little more than wagons on iron wheels, and many served the function of unit trains—though not by that name—in being dedicated to moving a single commod-

ity, like coal, from mines to water transport. An early reference to what would now be called a unit train is found in a letter written by the vice president and general manager of the Crystal River Railroad in March 1901. He talks of using 20 cars "to take coal from a mine, which we have been opening up, down to our coke ovens, 12 miles away. At the lower end they are dumped in a bin, and we have dumped eight cars in 10 minutes, using only the train crew to dump them, and without uncoupling from the engine." References such as this demonstrate that the development of unit trains was an evolutionary process that started far earlier than the mid-twentieth century.

The Southern Railway is generally credited with running the first modern unit train, which began delivering coal to the Southern Electric Generating Co. plant on January 21, 1960. By the mid-1960s unit trains were moving 27 percent of U.S. coal.

Typical unit trains today move large volumes of commodities between a single origin and destination. Their most extensive use is in the movement of coal, where the vast majority of product moves from mines to electrical generation stations. In 2000 U.S. railroads moved almost 7 million carloads of coal, or about 757.8 million tons, nearly all of it in unit trains. This was approximately 43.6 percent of the total tons carried by railroads in 2000.

Railroads now commonly use freight cars that can hold more than 110 tons of lading. The combined gross weight of lading and freight car is often as much as 286,000 pounds. By reducing the proportion of tare weight to the lading itself, railroads can haul more freight for a given unit of output, again increasing efficiency.

In the past, electric utilities typically furnished the rolling stock for these trains. Because of the regulated environment in which they operate, electric utilities often acquire the freight cars. Since the utilities are able to put the invested capital into their rate base, owning cars allows them to earn a return on that investment. In a few cases,

A southbound Burlington Northern Santa Fe unit coal train at Boise City, Oklahoma, in March 2004. —George Drury

such as trains operated for Detroit Edison, the utility also purchased the locomotives, but this is the exception.

Other commodities that rely extensively on unit-train deliveries include grain from large elevators to grain-processing facilities, food-production plants, or export markets. The intensive use of unit trains for grain shipment has had a profound effect on the marketing of grain. The improved distribution of grain through unit-train deliveries has reduced shipping costs considerably. Because unit trains usually require an originating elevator to be able to load a train in less than 24 hours, however, only those facilities that can do so get the benefit of much lower rail rates. Consequently, many small elevators have not been able to remain competitive and have either closed or turned to truck delivery to nearby terminal elevators.

Unit trains are sometimes used to move petroleum in dedicated trains of tank cars with interconnecting hoses, allowing large quantities of product to move either between shipping points and refineries or between refineries. These tank trains are often found where inadequate pipeline capacity exists, or where new markets are developing.

CSX moves a unit train of orange juice in boxcars twice a week from Tropicana's production plant near Bradenton, Florida, to a distribution center in Kearney, New Jersey. Boxcars are furnished by the shipper and are operated by CSX as a dedicated train on an expedited schedule. The aggregate industry also takes advantage of unit-train economics. Many railroads move unit trains of sand, gravel, or other aggregate material to users such as ready-mix plants. The shipper often provides the equipment, consisting of open-top hopper cars.

Unit trains have allowed U.S. railroads to become more efficient by eliminating intermediate switching and maximizing the use of locomotives and rolling stock. These efficiencies have translated into lower rates for customers that have in turn allowed railroads to begin to increase market share of traffic moving in many markets.

—Thomas G. Hoback

REFERENCE

Starr, John T., Jr. *Evolution of the Unit Train, 1960–1969.* Chicago: Univ. of Chicago, Department of Geography, 1976.

U.S. Railroad Administration

The takeover of American railroads by the federal government during World War I was a departure from the standard of privately owned and operated railroads in the nation. Often misunderstood, the U.S. Railroad Administration (USRA) had its roots in the problems that faced the railroad industry in the early twenieth century. The war thrust an additional burden upon the U.S. railroads when they were virtually the intercity transportation system of the nation. At the time of World War I there was no highly developed highway transportation system and no developed inland water transportation service. There were no airlines and no network of high-pressure crude and product petroleum pipelines. The railroads were absolutely critical.

There was some precedent for federal government takeover of the railroads. During the Civil War President Lincoln exercised his authority to take over railroads that were needed by the Union forces in the conflict. In the case of World War I, the other belligerent powers had taken over their privately owned railway lines in order to form a unified system.

Perhaps the most important reason for creation of the USRA was the condition of the American railroads at the time. The Interstate Commerce Commission and Congress failed to understand the financial problems of the railroads and their need for sufficient revenue to make the capital investments required to meet the growing demands of traffic in a growing economy. The first decade of the twentieth century had seen economic regulation of railroads increase without concomitant increases in understanding the serious need for more investment. Retained earnings to purchase equipment or make other investments were sparse, and the profitability of the carriers was not always sufficient to readily attract capital in the private money market. The railroads needed more and more powerful locomotives and additional rolling stock with the capacity to move heavier loads. Double- and triple-tracking was needed on some lines, along with modern signal systems to increase safety while helping add capacity to a rail infrastructure that was not fully capable of handling the business thrust upon it under wartime conditions.

There were other problems. The Adamson 8-Hour Day Act prevented the rail carriers from using employees as intensively as they had in the past; this act improved working conditions and safety, but the 16-hour limit on work in one stretch limited how much the railroad workforce could accomplish. Worse, railroad pay had lagged behind that of other industries for some years, and when the United States entered the war, defense and other enterprises offered higher wages and attracted experienced railroad employees into other lines of work.

The government had given some consideration to the notion that transportation might be a problem if the nation went to war. The Army Appropriation Act of August 29, 1916, made provision for the creation of the Council of National Defense consisting of six cabinet officers. The council was authorized to appoint an advisory commission of representative individuals from the business world to mobilize the economic resources of the nation for national defense in time of war. The respected Daniel Willard, president of the Baltimore & Ohio Railroad, was selected for the Advisory Commission because of his expertise in transportation. At Willard's recommendation the American Railway Assn. (the railroad trade organization) created the Committee on National Defense, which came into being on February 16, 1917. The committee met with the secretary of war and other officials and officers of the War Department on March 1, 1917, to begin planning for the cooperation of the railway companies with the military.

The Council of National Defense called on Daniel Willard to encourage the railroads to organize in a fashion that would expedite the movement of freight. Even before a declaration of war, freight traffic had built up in 1915 and 1916 as American industry began to supply the Allied powers in the conflict. The rails became crowded with freight. Worsening the problem of an increase in traffic was the fact that coordinating rail freight moving to East Coast ports with the ships coming to take away the freight was very difficult. The ports were soon blockaded with freight cars waiting to be unloaded, and there were reports of cars backed up in yards and sidings as far west as Pittsburgh. When war was finally declared, it was expected that the congestion and backup of traffic would only grow worse. Willard called a conference of railroad executives in Washington on April 11, 1917, and 700 railroad presidents and other railway officers attended. In the discussion the idea of a free-flowing continental railroad system was developed, with the aim of moving traffic to help in a wartime situation.

To help carry out the idea, the Railroads' War Board was created with an executive committee of five. Its main job was to improve coordination of the nation's railway companies. The War Board had no legal authority to achieve the desired coordination, but instead relied on voluntary action.

The United States declared war against the Central Powers on April 6, 1917. The railroads understood that their capacity was limited and the capital investments that would offer the needed capacity would take too long to come to fruition in the near future of a wartime of unknown length. To help face the eventual capital needs, the U.S. railroads approached the ICC seeking a 15 percent rate increase, which was denied. A small rate increase was permitted in Eastern Territory. The commission took the position that the railroads were profitable and, in coming to that position, relied on statistics for 1916, which had been a good year financially. The ICC paid no attention to the traffic growth and congestion tendencies that had already begun to appear and would only grow worse with war actually at hand.

Almost immediately matters grew worse; clearly the continental railway system was not being formed. Congestion increased as it became clear that railroad managers could not overcome the practices of many years; they could not forfeit their competitive advantage on a voluntary basis. For the most part, they could not bring

themselves to divert freight to another carrier that had the necessary capacity. The ICC was authorized to control car service (disposition of equipment and routing of freight), and on August 10, 1917, Congress enacted a Priority Law under which the president could order priorities on movements of freight deemed essential by the chief executive. A number of federal agencies issued priority tags with little or no coordination. At one point in the middle of 1917 it was estimated that 85 percent of freight carried a priority tag, meaning that in reality there were no priorities. To help straighten out the priority problems, Judge Robert Lovett, chairman of the executive committee of the Union Pacific Railroad, was named director of priority shipments on August 18; matters improved slightly for a time, but soon congestion again worsened. By December 1917 the rail situation was clearly near crisis stage. On December 1, 1917, the ICC in a special report to Congress recommended that the president assume control of the railroads and operate them for the duration of the war. Congress should also act to remove legal obstacles to unified railroad operations, especially the antitrust laws. Furthermore, the commission recommended that the federal government give whatever financial assistance was needed to help the railroads meet U.S. needs.

As Christmas approached, Willard met with President Wilson at the White House and discussed the ICC recommendations. On December 26, 1917, Wilson issued a decree taking over the U.S. railroads. The presidential order became effective at noon on December 28, 1917, and the U.S. Railroad Administration was established, with William Gibbs McAdoo as director general. McAdoo was President Wilson's secretary of the Treasury and was also the president's son-in-law. He had worked on Wall Street and had an excellent knowledge of financial matters. McAdoo also had experience with railroads; he had built the first tunnels under the Hudson River for the Hudson & Manhattan Railroad that linked Newark, Jersey City, and Hoboken with both midtown Manhattan and the area near the Battery, which in time became the site of the World Trade Center.

Under McAdoo's direction, the USRA divided the nation into three operating regions. A federal manager was appointed for each railroad in place of the railroad's president. All Class 1 steam railroads were taken into the USRA fold; some shortline railroads were not included. The USRA ordered managers to disregard the railroads' history of individualism and direct freight via routes with the necessary capacity. The aim of the USRA was often misunderstood. It was not to operate the railroads as a profitable enterprise; rather, it was to move freight and military personnel in an efficient and effective manner to help in the war effort.

More legislation was needed to handle the details and the problems that quickly arose. On March 21, 1918, Congress passed the Railroad Control Act. The act guaranteed each of the railroads involved in the USRA an annual payment that was not to exceed the particular carrier's average net operating income for the three years ending June 30, 1917. The law authorized the U.S. president to determine the amount and come to an agreement with each railroad on the specific sum, and if a problem of just compensation arose, it was to be submitted to boards of referees; if the decision was unsatisfactory, the rail carrier could make an appeal to the U.S. Court of Claims. The federal government, through the USRA, was to provide for all maintenance, repairs, and renewals of the properties it was managing. When the war was over, the railroad properties were to be returned in good repair and as completely equipped as at the beginning of federal control. The U.S. government was to be reimbursed by the railroads for all the additions and improvements that could not be justly charged to the government. A revolving fund of $500 million was established to finance the operation of the railroads and to pay the cost of federal control. There was a role for the ICC. The president, through the USRA, was to initiate all charges, regulations, classifications, and other traffic and rate-related matters and file them with the ICC. The matters had to be handled immediately because of the wartime circumstances; to this end the ICC forfeited its rate-suspension powers.

Soon into the game the USRA made important changes to increase efficiency and effectiveness. The railways were to make joint use of terminals, repair shops, and all physical facilities. The USRA took over the direction and routing of freight traffic to move freight to facilities not being fully used. To free up human and material resources, duplicate passenger trains were eliminated and timetables were consolidated; duplicate ticket offices were closed.

The USRA took a long-range view. When the war began in 1914, it was not expected to last long. But the brutal trench warfare in France dragged on, and by the time the United States joined the Allied forces in 1917, there were some ideas circulated that the war might last as long as 1930. To provide capacity for a long war, the USRA, working with its own staff of mechanical engineers and the staffs of the locomotive and car builders, as well as the railway operating companies, developed a series of standard locomotive and freight-car designs. Standardization was expected to permit greater efficiency in production and maintenance. The locomotive designs were excellent and, with some modifications, formed the basis for many of the locomotives produced for the remainder of the steam era.

The USRA believed that more transportation capacity was needed for a long-term war and acted to make improvements in the inland waterway system. This was the job of the Division of Inland Waterways. Although little was actually carried out during the war, the actions began the program of federal improvements to the inland waterways through construction of locks and dams and dredging and marking river channels. Later this function

moved to the U.S. Army Corps of Engineers, which then created the Federal Barge Line in the 1920s to demonstrate that inland water transportation was practical and could be taken over by the private sector.

In a major change in policy, the USRA pursued collective bargaining with all railway employees, not just the few skilled employees who had enjoyed collective bargaining for some years. The USRA early on created the Railway Wage Commission. In May 1918 Director General McAdoo ordered a wage increase, retroactive to January 1, 1918. The Board of Railroad Wages and Working Conditions was established to consider the needs and claims of different classes of railroad workers, to make adjustments to maintain fairness and labor peace, and to make recommendations for wage policy to the director general. The eight-hour day was made standard in the railroad industry by the USRA.

Soon after getting under way, the USRA staff found that railway pay was not competitive and that the railroads needed an increase in rates to provide necessary revenue. On May 25, 1918, McAdoo ordered a 25 percent raise in all class and commodity rates. Passenger fares, which averaged a little over 2 cents per mile, were raised to 3 cents per mile, commuter fares were raised 10 percent, and Pullman fares were also boosted. Discounted import and export freight rates were eliminated, and higher minimum rates on both carload and less-than-carload freight shipments were implemented. At the same time the administration was sensitive to the rate structures that had been laboriously worked out over many years between the railroads, the shippers, and certain geographic areas; the USRA sought to maintain as well as possible the integrity of those agreements. Regional and district rate committees were established, which included representatives of shippers as well as railroads; for the duration of the war the committees replaced the railroad rate associations.

Although often criticized, the USRA was successful in forming a unified railway system that reduced the congestion threatening the war effort. When the federal operation ceased after 26 months, it appeared that an operating deficit of $900 million had been incurred. McAdoo resigned from his post soon after the November 11, 1918, Armistice, and Walker D. Hines, assistant director general and former chairman of the board of the Atchison, Topeka & Santa Fe Railway, became director general. Hines had the unenviable job of working out the various problems in the absence of the sense of wartime necessity. The return of the railroads to private ownership and operation was covered by the Esch-Cummins Act, usually called the Transportation Act of 1920. The return to private rail ownership took place on March 1, 1920.

The USRA played an important and successful role in wartime. An understanding of railroad problems was clarified, and the gaffes, blunders, and mistakes of previous federal policies were noted; the act of 1920 sought, however clumsily and with much misdirection, to correct the problems of the past.

—George M. Smerk

REFERENCES

Ely, James W., Jr. *Railroads and American Law.* Chap. 11. Lawrence: Univ. Press of Kansas, 2001.

Godfrey, Aaron Austin. *Government Operation of the Railroads 1918–1920: Its Necessity, Success, and Consequences.* Austin, Tex.: San Felipe Press, 1974.

Johnson, Emory R., and Thurman W. Van Metre. *Principles of Railroad Transportation.* Chap. 28. New York: D. Appleton, 1924.

Lieb, Robert C. *Transportation: The Domestic System.* Chap. 11. Reston, Va.: Reston, 1981.

Martin, Albro. *Enterprise Denied: Origins of the Decline of American Railroads, 1897–1917.* Chap. 11. New York: Columbia Univ. Press, 1971.

See also REGULATION.

V

Valuation of U.S. Railroads

A valuation of all railroad property was not proposed until after the formation of the Interstate Commerce Commission (ICC) in 1887. The Act to Regulate Commerce authorized the ICC to require annual reports from the carriers, which would show the cost and value of the carriers' property, franchises, and equipment. The railroads then in existence had been built over a long period of years, and many mergers and reorganizations had taken place. Also, many additions had been made to the properties paid for out of income. The lack of standardized accounting regulations made it difficult to contrast items on balance-sheet statements of different carriers, and regulatory commissions had no knowledge of the property represented by securities that were sought to be issued. The states of New Jersey, Texas, Wisconsin, Minnesota, Nebraska, and Kansas had made appraisals of railroad property for guidance in approving security issues, imposing taxation, and testing reasonableness of rates, but these were the only ones.

In 1898 the U.S. Supreme Court in *Smyth vs. Ames* stated, "The basis of . . . calculations as to reasonableness of rates to be charged must be the fair value of the property being used . . . to ascertain that value, [and] the original cost of construction . . . permanent improvements . . . value of bonds and stock . . . probable earning capacity . . . are to be given such weight as may be just and right." In 1905 the Department of Commerce and Labor, Bureau of the Census, made a report of the commercial value of railroad property by capitalizing the net earnings of each railway and railway system. In 1910 Congress passed an act setting up the Railroad Securities Commission to investigate questions pertaining to the issuance of railroad stocks and bonds. In 1903 and every year thereafter until 1913 the ICC urged a physical valuation of railroad property. Because of this and other factors, Congress passed the Railroad Valuation Act (Section 19a of the Act to Regulate Commerce, approved on March 1, 1913).

The act required the ICC to ascertain the value of all property owned and used by every common carrier and authorized the commission to set up staffs to accomplish this. It was required to make an inventory in detail of each carrier, with the original cost to date, the cost of reproduction new, the reproduction cost less depreciation, and an analysis of methods by which these costs were obtained. There were other requirements as well. The carriers were required to cooperate with the ICC at their own expense. A tentative valuation was to be made, and any protests could be made within 30 days. Provision was made to perpetuate the valuation. Reproduction costs were to be based on 1914 prices that were taken to be an average of prices from 1905 to 1910. This entailed a work of great magnitude and detail.

The carriers furnished maps, profiles, contracts, engineer reports, and other documents and provided engineers as pilots to show the ICC field parties properties owned and used by them. They formed the Presidents' Conference Committee and subcommittees to deal with the ICC rules, methods, and principles in determining values. They also looked at what the ICC was not doing, in particular the original cost of the properties and this reproduction, which by ICC methods was a replacement cost, not a reproduction cost. One example was the ICC's assumption that all railroads in existence at date of valuation were in existence at the date of the railroad line's original construction, thus reducing the valuation cost of transportation of men and materials, a major factor in nineteenth-century railroad construction.

The field inventories were divided into engineering sections (six groups), land section, and accounting section. These inventories were begun by 1915 and concluded about 1919. Thousands of engineers, accountants, and others were employed in the work. Tentative valuations were presented to the carriers, and differences were adjusted in some cases but not in others. After years of conferences and protests the ICC issued the last final valuations in 1934. There were 1,046 valuations representing 274,032 miles of main tracks.

The "value for rate making purposes" as stated by the ICC was $16.2 billion as of the dates of valuation. Noncarrier lands, rights, and working capital made this $17.2 billion. Total railway capital in the hands of the public was calculated by the ICC as $16.3 billion. Thus the property investment accounts that had been bitterly attacked by the ICC at every opportunity were supported by the ICC's own valuation of the properties. But the result was a loss of interest by the antirailroad foes in Congress, and funds to perpetuate the valuations as required by the 1913 act were hard to come by for a number of years.

To keep the valuations current, the ICC set up a system of accounting based on 25 "Valuation Orders" and many directives. This was generally referred to as "betterment accounting," wherein the track structure, grading, tunnel bores, and a few other items were treated differently from similar items in other industries. Thus if a carrier "bettered" its track by laying heavier rails, only the excess weight over the old rails was capitalized, and the balance was expensed. Replaced ties were expensed, as were ballast and the labor for these items. This system required carriers to maintain two sets of accounting books, one for ICC purposes and one for other purposes such as federal taxation. Internal Revenue Service (IRS) rules allowed taxpayers to use original cost or 1913 cost, whichever was higher, and carriers had to restate retirement costs in order to claim larger costs involved in their older properties. Detailed record keeping was required, ICC examiners were placed in the larger railroads to oversee these records, and many reports to the ICC were mandated. The larger railroads set up separate valuation departments to handle this work, including personnel in the field divisions.

The cost of all this was enormous for the times. From the inception of the work in 1913 to June 30, 1950, the cost to the government was $58 million, and to the carriers, $162 million, which equated to $230 and $650, respectively, per mile of road.

The ICC generally tried to keep valuations as low as possible. This action prompted much litigation by the carriers as to methods and principles, and cases sometimes went all the way to the U.S. Supreme Court. The Transportation Act of 1920 set up a new rule that allowed the ICC to prescribe rates allowing a return of 5½ to 6 percent on carrier property held for transportation purposes. This led to "recapture" proceedings and more litigation. Recapture was repealed in 1933.

After World War II funds to support the ICC valuations decreased, and by the 1950s the number of examiners at the larger railroads was greatly reduced. Competition from airlines and trucks made significant inroads on carriers' earnings, with the result that valuations of railroad property played a smaller and smaller part in ratemaking. The reports required by the ICC also were modified from time to time, reflecting these changes.

The system of valuation accounting described here was materially altered in the late 1980s. Betterment accounting was replaced by "standard" or depreciation accounting for all railroad properties (except some items such as land), as recommended by the Financial Accounting Standards Board (FASB). This allowed the carriers to reduce most of the bookkeeping involved with two sets of books and brought railroad accounting into the mainstream of industrial financial review.

—Lynn Farrar

REFERENCE

Moore, Bowman H. *The Federal Valuation of the Railroads in the United States.* Repr., Bulletin 503, American Railway Engineering Assn. (AREA, now AREMA), Sept.–Oct. 1952.

Van Depoele, Charles J. (1846–1892)

Belgian-born Charles Joseph Van Depoele was one of the principal developers of the electric street railway as a commercially successful technology. Born in Lichtervelde, Belgium, in 1846, he was educated in Belgium and France. Van Depoele showed a strong interest in physics and electricity at an early age, successfully generating electric light from batteries at the age of 15. Van Depoele emigrated to the United States in 1868 to establish a successful church-furniture-manufacturing business at Detroit while continuing his electrical studies and experiments.

As early as 1870 Van Depoele was demonstrating an electrical arc lighting system, and within a few years he first showed his ideas for electric traction. In 1877 he turned his furniture business over to his father, who had followed him to the United States, and devoted himself entirely to his electrical work. The Van Depoele Electric Light Co. was formed in 1880, and a year later he established an electrical manufacturing company. By 1881 Van Depoele was lighting the streets of Chicago with power from a generator of his own invention. He began operating an experimental electric railway at Chicago early in 1883, followed later in the year by a demonstration at the Chicago Inter-State Industrial Exposition at which an electric car drew its power from an overhead wire.

Van Depoele's electric railway ideas gained wide recognition from demonstrations at the Toronto Industrial Exhibition in 1884 and again in 1885. During the first year a mile-long Van Depoele electric railway powered from an underground conduit transported as many as 200 passengers a trip and reached a speed of 30 mph. An improved version the following year carried as many as 250 passengers a trip and over 10,000 people a day, this time powered from an overhead wire by what was probably the first use of a trolley pole. Later patented by Van Depoele, the device drew current from the wire by an underrunning wheel mounted on a pivoted beam held in place against the wire by spring tension.

Van Depoele's success at Toronto soon led to contracts for some of North America's first electric street railways. The first of these opened late in 1885 in South Bend, Indiana; by the end of 1886 eight Van Depoele lines had been installed in the United States and Canada, including a 15-mile installation at Montgomery, Alabama, that was the first all-electric street railway system anywhere in North America.

In 1888 Van Depoele sold his patents and business to the Thomson-Houston Electric Co. of Lynn, Massachusetts, and joined the firm's engineering staff. He remained with Thomson-Houston until his untimely death in 1892. Altogether he had patented some 250 electrical inventions, and patents for nearly 50 more were approved and assigned to Thomson-Houston after his death. In addition to electric railways, this prodigious output included patents concerned with electric lighting, motors, generators, and mining equipment. Two of the most important were his patents for the underrunning trolley pole and the carbon commutator brush for electric motors.

—William D. Middleton

REFERENCES

A Century of Progress: The General Electric Story. Schenectady, N.Y.: Hall of History Fdn., 1981.
Dictionary of American Biography.
National Cyclopaedia of American Biography.
Stevens, John R., ed. *Pioneers of Electric Railroading: Their Story in Words and Pictures.* New York: Electric Railroaders' Assn., 1991.

William C. Van Horne. —Canadian Pacific Railway, *Trains* Magazine Collection

Van Horne, William Cornelius (1843–1915)

William Cornelius Van Horne was born in a log house along the La Porte Road near Chelsea, Illinois, in 1843 and rose to become not only one of North America's great railway builders, but a pillar of Canadian confederation. Indeed, Van Horne's role in the construction and successful completion of the Canadian Pacific Railway secured him a place in history as one of the most important non-political fathers of Canadian confederation, as well as an eventual knighthood.

The death of his father, Cornelius Covenhoven Van Horne, forced young William to take on odd jobs at the age of 11. As a telegraph messenger, he learned the basics of telegraphy, a skill that would serve him well when expulsion from school at age 14 prompted Van Horne to seek full-time employment on the Illinois Central Railroad.

Van Horne took naturally to railroading, rising quickly through the ranks, from car checker on the Michigan Central to ticket agent, and to division superintendent on the Chicago & Alton. Promoted by 1872 to general superintendent of C&A's recently acquired St. Louis, Kansas City & Northern, Van Horne helped reverse the fortunes of the troubled line. With the line's sale in 1874, he moved on to perform similar feats on the Southern Minnesota as its general manager and then as president. By 1878 his credentials included superintendent of the Chicago & Alton as well.

In 1880 Van Horne was appointed general manager of the Chicago, Milwaukee & St. Paul Railroad, but his tenure there was brief. Van Horne's abilities had attracted the attention of St. Paul–based shipping, coal, and railway magnate James J. Hill, who had much bigger things in mind for the talented young executive.

Hill, whose St. Paul, Minneapolis & Manitoba stretched from the Twin Cities to a connection with the fledgling Canadian Pacific Railway at St. Vincent on the Minnesota-Manitoba border, was part of a syndicate contracted by the Canadian government to complete the CPR to the Pacific Coast. Canadian born, Hill had a vested interest in the completion of the CPR's line to the Pacific, not for any allegiance to the country of his birth, but because he saw the Canadian transcontinental as a vital western outlet for his St. Paul, Minneapolis & Manitoba. Furthermore, if Hill could convince the Canadian government that construction of a railway along the rugged north shore of Lake Superior was impractical, if not impossible, his "Manitoba Road" offered an obvious southerly alternative to route traffic around the Great Lakes to eastern Canada.

In the fall of 1881, with construction of the CPR progressing at a less-than-satisfactory pace, Hill courted Van Horne to take over the position of general manager of the Canadian Pacific Railway. The two men made an inspection tour of the CPR lines east and west of Winnipeg in October 1881. Van Horne was impressed with what he saw, swayed by the offer of a $15,000 salary (reportedly the highest ever offered a railroader at the time), and seduced by the challenge of building a railway that many deemed impossible. He was appointed general manager and took office on January 2, 1882, at Winnipeg, Manitoba.

Van Horne brought other talent with him on his move north. John M. Egan, who had worked for Van Horne on the Southern Minnesota Railroad, accompanied him to serve as general superintendent of the CPR. Thomas G. Shaughnessy, employed as general storekeeper on the Chicago, Milwaukee & St. Paul, followed Van Horne to Canada in October 1882. He ultimately rose to the presidency of the CPR (succeeding Van Horne in 1899) and became chairman of the board in 1910.

In Van Horne, Hill saw a man "best equipped mentally for the job, and in every other way as well." He also saw a potential ally in his campaign to dissuade the government from its intention to build the CPR along the north shore of Lake Superior. The proposed railway along Lake Superior's rugged north shore was characterized by Van Horne as "200 miles of engineering impossibilities." History is unclear on whether Van Horne stood with Hill on the hotly controversial matter of the Superior route. However, when the Canadian government proved immovable on the issue of the Superior line, as well as an all-Canadian route for the CPR, Hill had had enough. He resigned from the Canadian Pacific board on May 3, 1883, and set to building his own transcontinental line across the United States: the Great Northern. Van Horne, meanwhile, set about achieving the impossible: carving the CPR into the Precambrian rock of Lake Superior's north shore and completing the promised railway to the Pacific.

Van Horne and Hill became archrivals as each oversaw transcontinental railways on opposite sides of the 49th parallel. Two and a half years after Hill's resignation, Van Horne and a small group of track workers and CPR officials looked on as Donald A. Smith drove the last spike (a plain iron one, as Van Horne had decreed) at Craigellachie, British Columbia, on November 7, 1885.

Completion of the CPR fulfilled the promises of confederation and united the young nation, but for Van Horne, it was just the beginning. Promoted to president in 1888, Van Horne was instrumental in nationwide expansion of the CPR with construction of branch lines and new main lines in the west, as well as in Ontario, Quebec, and the Maritime Provinces. Van Horne also championed immigration, colonization, and agricultural programs on the prairies, as well as the development of tourism, particularly in the Rockies, where the CPR built resorts and still-legendary hotels at Banff and Lake Louise. He also played a key role in making the CPR a global transportation system with the formation of Canadian Pacific Steamships, establishing Pacific routes to the Orient, as well as transatlantic services to Europe. Under Van Horne, Canadian Pacific grew from a near-bankrupt railway many said could never be completed to not only a transcontinental network of main and branch lines, but a powerful transportation and communication conglomer-

ate with domestic and international steamship services and telegraph and express services, as well as hotel operations and tourism businesses worldwide.

With the title of knight commander of the Order of St. Michael and St. George, bestowed by Queen Victoria in May 1894, Van Horne continued to serve as president of Canadian Pacific until June 12, 1899, when, at age 56, health concerns, including bronchitis, forced him to spend increasing time in warmer climates. He continued as chairman of the board of directors until 1910.

After handing the presidency of Canadian Pacific over to Thomas Shaughnessy in 1899, Van Horne redirected his energies with involvement in the electrification of Canadian street railways, as well as projects in England, Latin America, and South America. It was in Cuba, however, that Van Horne found his next major challenge.

Drawn to the Caribbean island in part, at least, by his participation in a consortium concerned with electrifying the mule-drawn tramways of Havana, Van Horne quickly discovered a greater opportunity during a visit to Cuba in January 1900. The absence of a railway linking major Cuban cities, ports, and the few disconnected lines already in existence on the island played to Van Horne's greatest strengths. Within months a new consortium had been formed, and the Cuba Co.—incorporated in New Jersey with Van Horne as its president—had been established to create a railway that would at last span the island.

The Cuba Co., renamed the Cuba Railroad Co. by 1902, spiked down 360 miles of new railway between Santiago, at the eastern extreme of the island, through Camagüey to a connection with the United Railroads of Havana at Santa Clara. With the completion of the new line, travel time between Camagüey and Havana was reduced from a three-day journey by steamship to just 15 hours by train. The railroad established its headquarters, main shops, and a resort hotel in Camagüey, while Van Horne built a personal estate and experimental farm nearby.

As president of the new venture, Van Horne used his experience with the CPR well, and the Cuba Railroad Co., much like the Canadian Pacific, was much more than a railway. With company-owned sugar plantations and mills, hotels, port facilities, and mining and lumber interests, the Cuba Railroad was like a Caribbean microcosm of the CPR. Just as he had in western Canada, Van Horne helped promote and develop agricultural programs, colonization, and settlement in Cuba. Branch lines were built to open new areas to farming and commerce, and in a joint venture with the United Fruit Co. the railroad built a new port on the shore of Nipe Bay at Antilla.

Cuba was Van Horne's last hurrah. By late 1913 the tireless, hard-driving, cigar-smoking, poker-playing legend was fighting the effects of rheumatism. Despite his declining health, Van Horne remained active until his death in Montreal, Quebec, on September 11, 1915. After funeral services in Montreal, his body was conveyed by a special CPR funeral train from Windsor Station in Montreal to Joliet, Illinois, where he was buried in Oakwood Cemetery.

—Greg McDonnell

REFERENCES

Berton, Pierre. *The Last Spike: The Great Railway, 1881–1885.* Toronto: McClelland & Stewart, 1971.
Dictionary of Canadian Biography.
Gibbon, John Murray. *Steel of Empire.* Indianapolis: Bobbs-Merrill, 1935.
Knowles, Valerie. *From Telegrapher to Titan: The Life of William C. Van Horne.* Toronto: Dundurn Press, 2004.
Lavallée, Omer. *Van Horne's Road.* Montreal: Railfare Enterprises, 1974.
1952: 50 Anos de Progreso Ferroviario. Ferrocarriles Consolidados de Cuba, 1952.

See also CANADIAN PACIFIC RAILWAY; CUBAN RAILROADS.

M. J. Van Sweringen. —From the collection of the Shaker Historical Society, Nord Library, Shaker Heights, Ohio

Van Sweringen, O. P. (1879–1936), and Van Sweringen, M. J. (1881–1935)

Tightly bonded bachelor brothers O. P. and M. J. Van Sweringen began as obscure Cleveland suburban real estate promoters and by 1930 controlled the country's largest railroad system, reaching from the Atlantic to the Rockies and from Ontario to the Mexican border. Often called "the Vans" by outsiders and "O. P." and "M. J." by their associates, the brothers first won notice by acquiring in 1907 a large suburban tract to develop as an innovative planned community called Shaker Heights Village. Essential to their plan was a high-speed rapid-transit line to Cleveland's downtown heart, the Public Square. At the Square they also developed plans for a complex combining railroad and rapid-transit terminals with offices, retail facilities, and a hotel.

In the process they formed a close friendship with New York Central president Alfred H. Smith, who subsequently helped them build their rapid-transit line and union railroad terminal (which included the landmark Terminal Tower building), and who put them into the railroad business. Bowing to antitrust pressures, Smith sold them the NYC-controlled Nickel Plate Road in 1916 and gave them an NYC executive, John J. Bernet, to run it.

After their success in upgrading the Nickel Plate, the brothers (under Smith's guidance) expanded the NKP in 1922 by acquiring and merging the Lake Erie & Western and Toledo, St. Louis & Western (Clover Leaf Route). Beginning with their Nickel Plate purchase, they also became masters at highly leveraged holding-company fi-

nancing and took this method to spectacular heights during the 1920s.

Working swiftly and almost silently, the brothers gathered in other eastern rail systems and by 1924 not only had an expanded Nickel Plate, but also controlled the Chesapeake & Ohio, Pere Marquette, and Erie. Taken together, the Van Sweringen lines now ranked as the fourth major eastern rail system. Following their established pattern, they financed their acquisitions through a progressively more complex array of leveraged holding companies that allowed them direct personal control with minimum cash outlay.

For various reasons, however, the Vans were never able to merge their railroads into a single unit. As an interim step, they created the Alleghany Corp. in 1929 as a master holding company to control their railroads and promptly used it to double the system's size by acquiring the Missouri Pacific–Texas & Pacific system and the Chicago & Eastern Illinois. Their MoPac control, in turn, also gave them a half interest in the Denver & Rio Grande Western and the potential for eventually achieving a coast-to-coast system.

But just as these railroads were being brought into the fold in 1930, the Depression struck. The MoPac and C&EI declared bankruptcy in 1933, and the precarious Van Sweringen holding-company structure began to col-

O. P. Van Sweringen. —From the collection of the Shaker Historical Society, Nord Library, Shaker Heights, Ohio

Vanderbilt, Cornelius (1794–1877)

Steamship and railroad promoter and financier Cornelius Vanderbilt was born on Staten Island to a poor Dutch family. He left school at the age of 11 and began hanging around the New York waterfront. With a $100 loan from his mother he bought a flat-bottomed sailing boat that allowed him to enter the growing ferry business in New York Harbor. Through industry, foresight, and guile he eventually became a major player in the steamboat industry as it developed early in the nineteenth century, although he waged a long and bitter fight with Robert Livingston, who held a licensed monopoly from the state to operate steam ferries. Vanderbilt learned early that there were no obstacles in law or society that could not be overcome by craft and ingenuity.

Between the 1820s and the Civil War Vanderbilt's maritime business made him a wealthy man. He owned a number of vessels that plied the waters off the East Coast of the United States and later Central America. When gold was discovered in California in 1849, he began steamship service to San Francisco, obtaining a monopoly on portage over Lake Nicaragua. By 1854 he initiated stubborn competition with the Cunard Line for transatlantic business. Vanderbilt's successes had long since earned him the sobriquet Commodore, a half-facetious title that stuck with him throughout his life.

Around this time Vanderbilt began investing in rail-

lapse. But the brothers proved adept at staving off disaster, immeasurably aided by the financially strong coal-hauling Chesapeake & Ohio. Their entire empire remained technically intact (although heavily mortgaged) until 1935, when their New York bankers refused to refinance a large and critical loan. The brothers solved this problem, too, by setting up the Midamerica Corp. with the help of Indiana millionaire George Ball. Midamerica took over the Van Sweringen empire under an agreement to keep the brothers in control.

This coup, coupled with gradually improving business, seemed to promise recovery and more expansion. But five years of constant stress had taken too great a toll. Both brothers died of heart failure within a year of each other—M.J. on December 12, 1935, and O.P. while on a train on November 23, 1936.

—Herbert H. Harwood, Jr.

REFERENCES

Haberman, Ian. *The Van Sweringens of Cleveland.* Cleveland, Ohio: Western Reserve Historical Society, 1979.

Harwood, Herbert H., Jr. *Invisible Giants: The Empires of Cleveland's Van Sweringen Brothers.* Bloomington: Indiana Univ. Press, 2003.

"Commodore" Cornelius Vanderbilt. —Signal Corps, Brady Collection, National Archives

roads. He maneuvered a controlling interest in the New York & Harlem Railroad by 1857, the Hudson River Railroad in 1865, and the New York Central Railroad (then pushing west to the Great Lakes from Albany) in 1867. These he then consolidated into a vast system with the aim of eventually moving on to Chicago, a feat established by acquiring control of the Michigan Central and the Lake Shore & Michigan Southern railroads.

For a time in the 1860s Vanderbilt struggled with the Erie's principals, Daniel Drew, Jay Gould, and Jim Fisk, for control of the Erie Railroad. These enterprising rogues outsmarted Vanderbilt by printing watered stock, but in outsmarting Vanderbilt the Erie ring, as it was called, did nearly irreparable damage to the Erie and to their own finances.

Vanderbilt was poorly educated and unlettered, but he was an intelligent, resourceful, and farsighted railroad manager. Unlike other "robber barons" of his time, he believed that railroads needed to be well run if they were to be popular. He not only offered excellent service, but also built an elegant terminal in New York for his customers, the first Grand Central Depot.

When he died in 1877, Vanderbilt was something of a folk hero and remains one of the major figures of American railroading. He was also the richest man in the country at the time of his death—the first American to leave a fortune of $100 million, nearly all of it to his son William, with the result that the New York Central remained a Vanderbilt road for many years.

—George H. Douglas

REFERENCE

Andrews, Wayne. *The Vanderbilt Legend: The Story of the Vanderbilt Family, 1794–1940.* New York: Harcourt, Brace, 1941.

See also NEW YORK CENTRAL SYSTEM.

Vanderbilt, William Henry (1821–1885)

Railroad executive and financier and son of Cornelius Vanderbilt, William Henry Vanderbilt grew up in New York, attended Columbia College Grammar School, and, at the age of 17, worked in a ship chandler's shop. Under his father's watchful eye he entered a banking house, but later joined the family railroad ventures. In 1857 he was appointed receiver of the struggling Staten Island Railroad and stabilized its finances. After his father acquired the New York & Harlem Railroad and later the New York & Hudson River Railroad in the 1860s, William served as vice president of both roads. The younger Vanderbilt was intimately involved in the acquisition of the New York Central and its eventual merger with the two earlier roads.

By the late 1860s, with his father well into his 70s, William

William H. Vanderbilt. —Penn Central Co.

was virtually running the New York Central. At his recommendation it acquired control of the Lake Shore & Michigan Southern and the Michigan Central, giving the New York Central through routes to Chicago. When Commodore Vanderbilt died in 1877, William inherited almost his entire fortune and became president of the New York Central and related lines. In the early 1880s he began acquisition of other lines, including the Chicago & North Western, the Nickel Plate, and the Cleveland, Cincinnati, Chicago & St. Louis Railway—the Big Four (which became part of the New York Central System).

By and large an able and highly successful railroad manager, Vanderbilt greatly increased his family fortune. Somewhat more civic minded than his father, he donated a large sum of money to establish Vanderbilt University in Nashville, Tennessee. He donated an even larger sum to the Columbia University College of Physicians and Surgeons.

Cartoonists of the 1880s tended to caricature Vanderbilt as a rotund and bloated capitalist, something of an exaggeration. Historians have made much of his most famous quote, "The public be damned." This was not a general statement but an expletive uttered to two newspaper reporters who burst in on him while he was eating breakfast in his private railway car.

—George H. Douglas

REFERENCE

Andrews, Wayne. *The Vanderbilt Legend: The Story of the Vanderbilt Family, 1794–1940.* New York: Harcourt, Brace, 1941.

Vauclain, Samuel M. (1856–1940)

Samuel Matthews Vauclain was born in Philadelphia in 1856, the son of a Pennsylvania Railroad roundhouse foreman. The young Vauclain came to Altoona as a baby and grew into adulthood there. In June 1872, at age 16, he joined the PRR at Altoona as an apprentice in the railroad's shops. He completed his apprenticeship in 1877. Vauclain entered the shops with a good basic education, strong curiosity, and some trade skills. He was a hard worker, willing to attempt untried techniques and to commit to completing jobs under pressure. He married Annie Kearney of Altoona in April 1879.

In 1881, during his tenure as a PRR shop foreman, Vauclain was attached to Baldwin Locomotive Works at Philadelphia as an inspector of locomotives being built for the PRR. In July 1883 Vauclain accepted the position of superintendent of the Baldwin 17th Street tender shop. He was associated with Baldwin for the rest of his life. Vauclain attracted responsibility and extensively reorganized and modernized Baldwin shops as they came under his purview, rising to superintendent of equipment and then general superintendent by 1886.

Vauclain's contributions to Baldwin were technical, as well as managerial. His patents for forging wrought-iron wheels were used by the subsidiary Standard Steel Works. By 1889 Vauclain had developed and patented a laterally symmetrical four-cylinder compound design that Baldwin applied to thousands of locomotives between 1890 and 1905. Vauclain's compound locomotive was commercially very successful. By 1905 he was applying a smokebox superheater of his design to some locomotives. Firetube superheaters, as pioneered by Wilhelm Schmidt of Germany, rapidly superseded Vauclain's smokebox superheater.

By 1905 Baldwin was outgrowing the Philadelphia works. Starting in 1906, Vauclain drove an expansion into an extensive site at Eddystone, just southwest of Philadelphia. By 1912 Eddystone was used to erect large locomotives, and it did munitions work during the war. Accessible to three railroads and near the Delaware River, Eddystone was an ideal site for a heavy manufacturer with significant international business. During the 1920s all of Baldwin's manufacturing moved to Eddystone. The Broad Street site closed in 1928.

Vauclain rose through management at Baldwin, becoming a partner in 1896, vice president in 1911, and president in 1919. In 1929, at age 73, Vauclain retired as president of Baldwin, but continued to serve as chairman and director.

Vauclain was an intuitive engineer and inventor of significant accomplishment. With his active mind and relentless capacity for hard work, and with the mechanical and economic resources of Baldwin behind him, Vauclain tried his ideas in prototype. His lack of analytical training, then typical of American engineers, meant that many of his ideas needed extensive development. Some were dead ends.

Vauclain's uncompromising personality, combined with his railroad shop training, high skill, imagination, intelligence, and capacity and enthusiasm for work, made him an extremely effective manager. In spite of being a strongly cyclical business with consequent hiring and layoff episodes, Vauclain's Baldwin became a preferred place of employment for skilled workmen around Philadelphia. Vauclain instituted Baldwin's contract manufacturing system, double shifts for efficient use of capital equipment, and standardization of individual parts and complete locomotives to the extent allowed by constraints and individualities of the locomotive market.

As works superintendent and president, Vauclain was responsible not only for the shops' operation but also for the company's reputation, for the performance in the field of Baldwin products, and for solicitation of business. Vauclain occasionally went to imaginative lengths to troubleshoot locomotives on customers' railroads under difficult conditions. He would even accept a salable commodity—Romanian oil in one case—in order to book an order during difficult times. Vauclain's position as a Baldwin partner and his familiarity with his business let him quote firm prices and delivery dates immediately, face-to-face with customers.

Shortly before World War I Baldwin was reorganized from a partnership to a public stock corporation. Baldwin's market had long been worldwide, and Vauclain supported and expanded export business. During the war, before American involvement, Vauclain made several difficult trips to Europe to solicit business for Baldwin, Midvale Steel, and Remington Arms. After the war Vauclain reorganized and staffed Baldwin's foreign sales organizations, traveling worldwide for Baldwin and often working at the highest levels of national governments.

Vauclain's accomplishments, associations, affiliations, and, in his later years, honors were vast. For services during the war he received in 1919 the civilian Distinguished Service Medal. He was made cavalier of the Legion of Honor of France in 1919 and councilor of the Order of the Crown of Italy in 1920. He received an honorary doctorate of science from the University of Pennsylvania and a doctorate of laws from Villanova University. He served as a director of 12 major corporations, manager of four hospitals, and president and trustee of a fifth. Samuel M. Vauclain died in 1940, at age 83, at his home at Rosemont, near Philadelphia.

—Thomas L. De Fazio

REFERENCES

Brown, John K. *The Baldwin Locomotive Works, 1831–1915.* Baltimore: Johns Hopkins Univ. Press, 1995.

Custer, Edgar A. Stories of Custer's apprenticeship to Vauclain at Altoona (1877–1878), working with Vauclain developing the Vauclain compound (1888), and Vauclain's hiring of Harry Burrell [*sic*; the correct name is Harry G. Burall] (1888), adapted from *No Royal Road* (New York: H. C. Kinsey & Co., 1937), in *Workin' on the Railroad*, ed. Richard Reinhardt. New York: Weathervane Books, 1970.

McShane, Charles L. *The Locomotive up to Date.* Chicago: Griffin & Winters, 1923.

Sinclair, Angus. *Development of the Locomotive Engine.* Ed. John H. White, Jr. Cambridge, Mass.: MIT Press, 1970.

Vauclain, Samuel M., with Earl Chapin May. *Steaming Up!* (autobiography). New York: Brewer & Warren, 1930.

Westing, Fred. *The Locomotives that Baldwin Built* (including Anonymous, *History of the Baldwin Locomotive Works, 1831–1923* in facsimile). New York: Bonanza Books, 1966.

Villard, Henry (1835–1900)

A noted financier and builder, Henry Villard was for a time one of the great American railroad builders of the late nineteenth century. The son of a prominent family from Speyer, Rhenish Bavaria, Villard was born Heinrich Hilgard. He attended a military school at Phalsbourg in Lorraine and other schools in Germany. At age 18 he decided to emigrate to the United States, where he adopted the name Villard after one of his Phalsbourg classmates.

Villard moved west to Illinois, where he studied law, sold books, and tried a small-town newspaper. He settled on journalism and for the next decade reported on the 1857 Lincoln-Douglas debates, developed a personal friendship with Abraham Lincoln, and accompanied Lincoln on his way to the presidency in 1861. His work as a journalist continued throughout the Civil War.

After 1871 ill health caused Villard to return to Germany for four years. There he became involved with the German bondholders of the Oregon & California Railroad. As a representative of the bondholders, he later traveled to Oregon to plan the railroad's future policies. Villard developed a plan for cooperation involving the Oregon & California, the Oregon Central Railroad, and the Oregon Steamship Co., becoming the president of both the O&C and the steamship company in 1876. A similar bondholder committee in 1874 linked Villard with the faltering Kansas Pacific Railway, where he won a major financial success in battles with financier Jay Gould.

In the Pacific Northwest Villard had developed plans for a railway empire, and in 1879 he began work on the Oregon Railway & Navigation Co. to build a line along the Columbia River as an outlet for a future transcontinental railroad. In the fall of 1880, however, a major infusion of capital to the Northern Pacific had given that railroad the ability to build all the way to Puget Sound on its own, without any need to involve Villard. Fearing that the new competitor would depress his own stock, Villard decided that he would have to take control of the NP himself—a formidable financial undertaking.

Villard achieved his goal with a remarkable arrangement. Knowing that he would have to keep NP backers unaware of what he was doing, he quietly bought shares of NP stock through 1880 and into 1881. Having gone as far as he could by himself, he then set out a daring procedure called the "blind pool." A confidential proposal to 55 friends in high finance offered subscription to an $8 million fund, soon followed by another $12 million, without the fund's purpose or any pledge being offered except Villard's own name. His reputation was all that was necessary, and he soon took control of the NP and became its president in September 1881. At the same time, the Oregon & Transcontinental was established to coordinate the work of the Oregon & California, the NP, and the Oregon Improvement Co., a natural resource development company. By 1883 the Northern Pacific had completed the railroad's transcontinental route, and Villard was described as perhaps the most important railway developer in the United States.

It proved to be a short-lived triumph. Villard's rapid construction of the NP far exceeded its income, and he was forced to resign the NP presidency in 1884. Again in poor health, Villard went back to Germany for another two years, returning to New York as an agent for the Deutsche Bank to save the capital of the Oregon & Transcontinental. By 1888 he was back on the board of the NP and later became chairman of the board until his involvement in railroads ended in 1893.

Villard had plenty of other irons in the fire. He was always a financier. In 1881 he acquired control of the influential *New York Evening Post*. In 1879 he could see the possibilities of electricity and became an influential backer of the young Thomas A. Edison, at one point encouraging Edison's development of electric railways. By 1889 Villard had joined with J. P. Morgan to combine two German electrical companies with Edison's interests to create a huge multinational electrical conglomerate, the Edison General Electric Co. Villard was the new company's first president.

Within a few years Villard was working to merge Edison General Electric with the rival firm of Thomson-Houston. J. P. Morgan also got into the act, and by the time the new firm, General Electric Co., was formed in 1892, both Thomas Edison and Henry Villard had been forced out. Largely withdrawn from active financial activities after 1893, Henry Villard died at his home at Dobbs Ferry, New York, in 1900.

—William D. Middleton

REFERENCE

de Borchgrave, Alexandra Villard, and John Cullen. *Villard: The Life and Times of an American Titan.* New York: Doubleday, 2001.

Virginia & Truckee Railroad

The discovery of workable gold and silver deposits in Nevada's Comstock Lode in the 1860s called for a railroad from newly established Virginia City to mills along the Carson River. In March 1868 the Virginia & Truckee Railroad (V&T) was incorporated. Its line from Carson City reached Virginia City in January 1870, and a line from Carson City north to a connection with the Central Pacific at Reno opened in August 1872.

As mining began to decline in the 1880s, the railroad declined with it. The V&T began to derive more of its revenue from agricultural commodities than from products of mines. It paid its last dividend in 1924 and entered receivership in 1938. Somehow the line soldiered on with its antiquated locomotives and rolling stock, some of which dated from the line's nineteenth-century origins. Lucius Beebe discovered the V&T in the mid-1940s and soon made it an object of veneration. Veneration pays no bills, though, and the V&T was abandoned on May 31, 1950.

In 1949 the Virginia & Truckee operated 46 route-miles and 56 track-miles, with 3 locomotives. Operating revenues for the previous year, 1948, were $152,037, and the operating ratio was 119.7 percent.

—George H. Drury

REFERENCES

Beebe, Lucius, and Charles Clegg. *Steamcars to the Comstock.* Berkeley, Calif.: Howell-North, 1957.

Wurm, Ted, and Harre Demoro. *The Silver Short Line.* Glendale, Calif.: Trans-Anglo Books, 1983.

Virginian Railway

The Virginian Railway was created by one man, Henry Huttleston Rogers, and had one purpose, to carry coal from mines in West Virginia to tidewater at Norfolk. It began with the Deepwater Railway, which was to build a rail line south from Deepwater, West Virginia, on the Chesapeake & Ohio 30 miles southeast of Charleston. By 1902 Rogers, vice president of Standard Oil, had purchased an interest in the 4-mile railroad. Neither the Chesapeake & Ohio nor the Norfolk & Western would agree with the Deepwater Railway on freight rates, so Rogers decided to build his own railroad to Norfolk. He had the charter of the Deepwater Railway amended to permit it to go to the Virginia state line, approximately 100 miles away, and he organized the Tidewater Railway to build another 324 miles from the state line to Norfolk, Virginia.

The name of the Tidewater Railway was changed to Virginian Railway in March 1907; in the next month it acquired the property of the Deepwater Railway. The railroad was completed from Deepwater to Norfolk in early 1909. From Roanoke to Norfolk the line had a continual gradual descent. West of Roanoke lay the Blue Ridge Mountains. There were ascending grades in both directions; the worst eastbound grade was 2 percent from Elmore to Clarks Gap, West Virginia.

The Virginian's singleness of purpose was reflected in its equipment. Although other coal haulers used hopper cars that could carry 50 tons, the Virginian had a fleet of 12-wheel, 120-ton gondolas. The Virginian's first Mallets, 2-6-6-0s, came in 1909. Within less than ten years the Virginian operated 2-8-8-2s and 2-10-10-2s and acquired an experimental 2-8-8-8-4 that could not generate enough steam for its cylinders. The Virginian electrified its line over the mountains between Roanoke, Virginia, and Mullens, West Virginia, in the 1920s in order to move heavier trains and move them faster.

The Norfolk & Western envied the Virginian's easy run from Roanoke to Norfolk and arranged to lease the Virginian in 1925, but the Interstate Commerce Commission refused approval. The Pennsylvania, New York Central, and Chesapeake & Ohio also tried to merge, lease, or otherwise acquire the Virginian.

The Virginian's passenger service consisted of all-stops local trains: a daytime train west of Roanoke and night and day trains between Roanoke and Norfolk. By 1933 the only luxury cars on those trains, a Norfolk-Roanoke sleeper and a Roanoke–Huntington, West Virginia, parlor car, had been discontinued, as had the Norfolk-Roanoke night train. The Virginian's last passenger trains, daytime locals between Roanoke and Norfolk, made their last runs on January 29, 1956.

By 1948 the side-rod electrics of the Virginian's electrification were showing their age. The Virginian began replacing them in 1948 with four two-unit streamlined locomotives. In 1956 and 1957 the remaining side-rod electrics were replaced by a dozen electric locomotives that were essentially diesel road switchers with ignitron rectifiers instead of diesel engines and generators. About the same time the Virginian replaced its steam locomotives with diesels.

The Norfolk & Western and the Virginian reconsidered merger. This time the ICC approved it, and the two railroads merged on December 1, 1959. The Virginian's modernized and reequipped electrification was not to endure much longer. Norfolk & Western took advantage of the best grades and established a one-way traffic flow, with only eastbound traffic using the former Virginian electrified line. Electrified operation ceased in June 1962 (the nearly new rectifier locomotives were sold to the New Haven and later worked for Penn Central and Conrail).

In 1958, the year before it was merged by the Norfolk & Western, the Virginian Railway operated 608 route-miles and 1,092 track-miles, with 120 locomotives, 17,143 freight cars, 184 company service cars, and 2,730 employees. Freight traffic totaled 5,942.9 million ton-miles in 1957, and bituminous coal constituted 86 percent of its traffic. Virginian operating revenues were $49.7 million in 1958, and the railroad achieved a 51.1 percent operating ratio.

—George H. Drury

REFERENCE

Reid, H. *The Virginian Railway.* Milwaukee, Wis.: Kalmbach, 1961.

W

Wabash Railway

The Wabash Railway ran west from Buffalo, New York, across southern Ontario (by trackage rights on Canadian National Railways) to Detroit and then on to Chicago, St. Louis, and Kansas City. The Wabash also served Toledo, Ohio, as well as portions of Indiana and central and eastern Illinois; branches reached across northern Missouri and Iowa to Des Moines and Council Bluffs. After the Norfolk & Western merged with the Nickel Plate in the early 1960s, the N&W gained control of the Wabash. Norfolk Southern operates the heart of the old Wabash, the Detroit–St. Louis–Kansas City route and the Decatur, Illinois–Moberly, Missouri, cutoff.

The earliest predecessor of the Wabash was the Northern Cross Railroad, which was chartered in 1837 to build a line from Quincy, Illinois, east to the Indiana border. The Northern Cross was the first steam railroad west of the Allegheny Mountains and was later acquired by the Great Western of Illinois, which eventually became part of the Wabash. In 1851 the North Missouri Railroad was chartered to build a line from St. Louis to the Iowa state line. The line reached Ottumwa, Iowa, in 1870. The North Missouri acquired a branch line to Brunswick, Missouri, in the 1860s. It was extended to Kansas City in 1868 and from Brunswick to Council Bluffs, Iowa, in 1879. The North Missouri was reorganized as the St. Louis, Kansas City & Northern Railroad in 1872.

In 1853 the Toledo & Illinois was organized to build a line from Toledo, Ohio, to the Indiana state line. That same year the Lake Erie, Wabash & St. Louis was organized to continue the line of the Toledo & Illinois across Indiana to the Indiana-Illinois state line at Attica, Indiana. It was built along the route of the Wabash & Erie Canal in Indiana. In 1856 the Toledo & Illinois was merged with the Lake Erie, Wabash & St. Louis to form the Toledo, Wabash & Western Railroad, which was reorganized as the Toledo & Wabash Railway in 1858.

Jay Gould entered the picture in 1879 when he acquired control of both the Toledo & Wabash and the St. Louis, Kansas City & Northern. He merged these two roads to form the Wabash, St. Louis & Pacific Railroad. After ten years that saw both growth and receivership, the system was again reorganized in 1889 as the Wabash Railroad. The Wabash acquired trackage rights on the Grand Trunk across the southern portion of Ontario along Lake Erie in order to reach Buffalo. The road connected to the Grand Trunk by a car float across the Detroit River between Detroit and Windsor, Ontario. In 1902 a line from Butler to New Haven, Indiana, opened, enabling trains between Detroit and St. Louis to be routed through Fort Wayne instead of on the old route along the Eel River. The Wabash system was extended to Pittsburgh in 1904 through trackage rights on the Wheeling & Lake Erie and the Wabash Pittsburgh Terminal. In 1911, however, the railroad entered receivership again, and the extension to Pittsburgh was eliminated. The road emerged from receivership in 1915 and was reorganized as the Wabash Railway.

The Wabash gained control of the Ann Arbor Railroad in 1925. The Ann Arbor operated a 292-mile line from Toledo to Frankfort, Michigan, and connected with the Wabash at Milan, Michigan, near Detroit. The Ann Arbor operated several car-ferry routes across Lake Michigan to several points in Wisconsin, enabling shippers to route traffic to the Northwest without the delays of going through Chicago.

In 1928 the Pennsylvania Co., a subsidiary of the Pennsylvania Railroad, acquired control of the Wabash. This was a defensive move on the part of the Pennsylvania, in response to an alliance between the Wabash and the Delaware & Hudson, which had joined forces to purchase the Lehigh Valley Railroad as part of a plan to organize a new rail system in the East. Pennsy's involvement began when it invested in the proposed organization, whereupon the Delaware & Hudson terminated its involvement in the plan, leaving the Pennsylvania in control of both the Wabash and the Lehigh Valley. The Wabash entered receivership in 1931 and emerged ten years later, reorganized as the Wabash Railroad Co.

The Pennsylvania's control of the Wabash lasted until 1964, when the winds of change were blowing through the railroad industry. The Pennsylvania and the New York Central were planning to merge, and neither party was interested in retaining any portion of the Wabash, except for the Ann Arbor, which was sold to the Detroit, Toledo & Ironton, another road controlled by the Pennsylvania, in 1963. Meanwhile, the Norfolk & Western was planning its merger with the Nickel Plate and decided to include the Wabash in the merger, which occurred on October 16, 1964.

By the 1960s Wabash's main-line passenger service consisted of two daytime trains each way between St. Louis and Chicago and between St. Louis and Kansas City, a day train and a night train between St. Louis and Detroit, and a night train between St. Louis and Council Bluffs. The star of the Chicago–St. Louis run was the streamlined *Blue Bird*, which carried dome cars (even if the Illinois prairie did not merit them). One of the St. Louis–Kansas City trains was Union Pacific's *City of St. Louis*, which carried cars to Los Angeles and San Francisco. The St. Louis–Detroit day train had a legendary name, *Wabash Cannon Ball*, but the train was named for the 1950s folksong, rather than vice versa.

The traffic base of the Wabash reflected the industrial economy of its service territory. Although it carried a wide variety of manufactured goods, traffic from the automobile industry provided the greatest portion of its revenue. Indeed, in the early 1960s the Ford Motor Co. alone accounted for 25 percent of revenue, with Chrysler providing approximately 15 percent. The road's direct line from Detroit to Kansas City made it an attractive choice for automotive traffic managers. As a bridge carrier, the Wabash also carried significant amounts of grain, perishables, and other general freight.

During the 20 years before its acquisition by the Norfolk & Western, the Wabash was generally considered to be a well-managed railroad. The road's physical plant was in excellent shape, permitting passenger-train speeds of up to 79 mph and freight-train speeds of 60 mph. The service offered to freight customers and passengers was highly regarded by the business community and the traveling public. However, the Wabash faced very tough competition from many railroads in its service territory, and although it was profitable every year between its emergence from receivership in 1941 and its absorption by the Norfolk & Western in 1964, the road was never a financial powerhouse.

In 1963, its last year before the Norfolk & Western merger, the Wabash operated 2,422 route-miles and 4,306 track-miles, with 307 locomotives, 101 passenger cars, 15,028 freight cars, 644 company service cars, and 7,790 employees. Freight traffic totaled 7,698.0 million ton-miles in 1963, and manufactured goods constituted almost 60 percent of Wabash's freight traffic. Passenger traffic totaled 107.6 million passenger-miles. Wabash operating revenues totaled $124 million in 1963, and the railroad achieved a 75.6 percent operating ratio.

—David C. Lester

REFERENCES

Heimburger, Donald J. *Wabash*. 2nd ed. River Forest, Ill.: Heimburger House, 1984.

Striplin, E. F. "Pat." *The Norfolk & Western: A History*. Roanoke, Va.: Norfolk & Western Ry., 1981.

Wagner, Webster (1817–1882)

Webster Wagner was an early sleeping-car operator who managed to survive Pullman's monopoly of that business because of his association with Cornelius Vanderbilt, master of the mighty New York Central System. Wagner was born on October 2, 1817, in Palatine, New York, into a farming family of German descent. As a young man he engaged in wagon and furniture making, but the business failed, and in 1843 he became a railroad station agent. He observed the misery of nighttime railway travel and in common with several other railroad men decided to enter the sleeping-car trade. In May 1858 he was given a contract to operate Woodruff-style sleepers over the New York Central between Albany and Buffalo. Within two years Wagner had 10 cars in service and expanded his operation to the Hudson River Railroad. In 1866 he and his partner organized the New York Central Sleeping Car Co. with a capital limit of $80,000. The modest former station agent was on his way to a fortune.

Just as Wagner's prospects for success were growing, Cornelius Vanderbilt plunged into the railroad business. Vanderbilt soon had control of the New York Central and Hudson River railroads and cast a covetous eye toward the west. His plan was to seize control of enough lines to reach Chicago and even beyond.

Vanderbilt had little patience with contractors and wanted to control every phase of the business over his lines. Wagner had the personal skills to ingratiate himself with the crusty old commodore and was able to retain the sleeping-car contract. Indeed, his business grew as Vanderbilt bought control of the Lake Shore & Michigan Southern, the Michigan Central, and other trunk lines. Wagner happily expanded his sleeping-car fleet to 200 cars. By 1870 the capital stock was increased to $600,000. A few years earlier Wagner introduced elegant parlor cars, so that first-class passengers might enjoy deluxe daytime travel—for an extra fare, of course.

George Pullman was displeased at Wagner's success and instituted a patent infringement lawsuit against the Vanderbilt-sponsored operation that raged on for years. Pullman ultimately lost the case, but sought other ways to punish the Vanderbilts for supporting such a powerful rival in the sleeping-car business. Pullman was an enthusiastic supporter of the New York, West Shore & Buffalo Railroad, established in the 1880s to throttle the NYC monopoly along the Hudson River. This scheme, too, failed to accomplish its intended purpose.

Meanwhile, Wagner entered politics and was handily elected to the New York State Assembly. In 1872 he became a state senator and remained in that chamber for another decade. His personal income was approaching $1 million per year. The Vanderbilts were no doubt pleased to have one of their loyal lieutenants comfortably settled inside the state house. But Wagner's good fortune ran out in his 65th year—he was killed on one of his own drawing-room cars in a rear-end collision at Spuyten Duyvil, New York, on the evening of January 13, 1882.

The sleeping-car company survived the death of its founder. After a few interim managers, a Vanderbilt son-in-law, Dr. William S. Webb, was made president of the firm. Webb attempted to enlarge the operation and sought to expand beyond the Vanderbilt lines. But Pullman was too well established to be unseated even in a small way. By the late 1890s it was clear that it was time to sell the business. The Pullman Co. made a generous offer, and the Wagner Palace Car Co. expired in 1899.

—John H. White, Jr.

REFERENCES

Dictionary of American Biography.
White, John H., Jr. The American Railroad Passenger Car. Baltimore: Johns Hopkins Univ. Press, 1978.

Washington Terminal Co.

In the last part of the nineteenth century railroading in the nation's capital was for the most part in the hands of the Baltimore & Ohio, which got there first in 1835, and two subsidiaries of the Pennsylvania Railroad, the Baltimore & Potomac and the Washington Southern. The B&P, which reached Washington in 1872, was Pennsy's answer to B&O's monopoly. It was chartered to build straight south from Baltimore to the Potomac River at Popes Creek, Maryland, but could also build branches up to 20 miles in length. A 19-mile branch from Bowie put the Baltimore & Potomac in Washington, with an overall distance from Baltimore that was the same as the Baltimore & Ohio's mileage. Moreover, Congress authorized the Pennsylvania to continue its line through Washington and across the Potomac to connect with railroads in Virginia.

The railroads were right in the middle of things in Washington. The Baltimore & Ohio station was at New Jersey Avenue and C Street N.W., two blocks from the Capitol. The Pennsylvania station was at 6th Street and Constitution Avenue, the location of today's National Gallery of Art. An act of Congress in 1901 incorporated the Washington Terminal Co., owned by the Baltimore & Ohio; a 1903 act authorized a union station and put the Washington Terminal under the joint ownership of the B&O and the Philadelphia, Baltimore & Washington, a PRR subsidiary that had taken over the B&P in 1902. It eased the organizational task that the Pennsylvania had recently purchased a controlling interest in the B&O.

Washington Union Station, an elegant Beaux Arts–style building designed by Daniel Burnham, opened in 1907. It was (and is) a combination stub and through station. B&O and Pennsy trains used the 20 stub tracks at street level, and trains of the Richmond, Fredericksburg & Potomac, the Chesapeake & Ohio, and the Southern Railway used the 9 lower-level tracks, which led to a new tunnel under Capitol Hill. Most of those trains operated to and from New York over the Pennsylvania Railroad, either as entire trains or as through cars.

Passenger traffic dwindled in the 1970s, and it was proposed that the station be converted to a visitor center. While construction dragged on, Amtrak passengers and a growing number of commuters picked their way through the rubble and walked great distances to their trains. Eventually all concerned had had enough. In 1988 the building was restored to its former function, and large portions of it became an elegant, upscale shopping and restaurant center.

B&O's ownership of the Washington Terminal Co. passed to Chessie System, Pennsylvania's to Amtrak. Amtrak assumed sole ownership on September 1, 1984. Washington Union Station now serves Amtrak, Maryland Rail Commuter (MARC), and Virginia Railway Express trains and is one of the principal stops on the Washington subway system.

In 1978 Washington Terminal operated 29 track-miles, with 8 locomotives and 8 company service cars. Operating revenues for 1978 were $81,220, and the road achieved a 12.9 percent operating ratio.

—George H. Drury

REFERENCE

Highsmith, Carol M., and Ted Landphair. Union Station: A Decorative History of Washington's Grand Terminal. Washington, D.C.: Chelsea, 1988.

Water Transportation

The role and importance of domestic water transportation have varied greatly over the course of American history. Before the railroad era freight and passenger traffic moved principally by coastal shipping and on the nation's rivers and canals and the Great Lakes. In the 1850s the technological superiority of the railroads, rapid growth of the nation's rail network, and aggressive competitive practices by railroad managers started a prolonged decline in domestic water transportation that lasted well into the twentieth century.

After World War I large-scale federal investment in waterway improvements and more efficient technology stimulated a revival that accelerated significantly after World War II. Low-priced water transportation attracted commercial and industrial development along inland rivers and presented serious competition for the nation's railroads that has continued to the present day.

Pre–Civil War Dominance

Water transport was the dominant mode of transportation in colonial America and during the first half of the nineteenth century. Most of the nation's population lived in seaboard states, and the long Atlantic coastline with dozens of harbors suitable for sailing vessels of the day provided the chief highway for the movement of passengers and freight. Goods produced at interior locations typically moved by rivers to coastal ports for shipment to other states or abroad. Moreover, many early turnpike, canal, and railroad projects along the Atlantic Coast were designed to reinforce and strengthen commercial ties between specific tidewater ports and their hinterlands. Examples included the Middlesex Canal from the Merrimack River to Boston Harbor, the Lancaster Turnpike westward from Philadelphia, the Baltimore & Ohio, the James River & Kanawha Canal, and the Charleston & Hamburg Railroad.

Settlement of the trans-Appalachian region was profoundly influenced by water transportation. The Ohio-Mississippi river system with its numerous tributaries provided excellent access into the future heartland of the nation, as well as an outlet for its produce. Cincinnati, St. Louis, and New Orleans served as initial destinations for many settlers and key locations for the distribution of manufactured goods and collection and shipment of agricultural commodities.

Initially, trans-Appalachian river transportation was rudimentary in nature, and traffic moved almost solely downstream. "Vessels" consisted of crude rafts and flatboats that typically were broken up and sold for lumber at the end of their journey. Depending on river conditions, flatboats from western Pennsylvania required four to six weeks to float some 1,900 miles downstream to New Orleans. Despite navigation hazards and other limitations, this simple technology did provide economical transportation for commerce that could not bear the cost of long-distance land carriage. Upstream transportation was a different matter. The journey was so laborious, costly, and time consuming that traffic was limited to occasional keelboats and barges with small quantities of badly needed, high-value freight. An upriver trip from New Orleans to Pittsburgh required four months or more.

The introduction of the steamboat revolutionized transportation on U.S. rivers, lakes, and bays. After experimental work by several inventors, in 1807 Robert Fulton demonstrated the commercial feasibility of the steamboat on the Hudson River, and two years later Col. John Stevens was similarly successful on the Delaware River. The first voyage of a steamboat from Pittsburgh to New Orleans occurred during the winter of 1811–1812, and the first complete upstream voyage was accomplished in 1815. The end of the War of 1812, rapid progress in hull and engine design, and the end of legal efforts by the Robert R. Livingston–Robert Fulton group to retain lucrative monopoly privileges opened the way for rapid expansion of steamboat service throughout the Ohio-Mississippi system.

Early steamboats on eastern rivers and bays and the Great Lakes were deep-draft vessels designed primarily for passenger service. This design was poorly suited for western rivers with their sharp fluctuations in depth, shifting channels, and serious navigation hazards, particularly piles of lumber floating downstream and huge uprooted tree stumps (snags) that could easily tear the bottom out of a boat. Steamboat accidents were common on western rivers, and more than 40 percent of the losses were due to snags or similar obstructions. Henry Miller Shreve, a gifted river navigator, adapted existing steamboat technology to a distinctive new design that quickly became the standard for western rivers. The Mississippi steamboat was a shallow-draft, flat-bottomed vessel with a high superstructure for passengers and freight, boilers, and engine gear mounted on deck, and paddlewheels for propulsion and control. Shreve also led a lengthy campaign to remove snags from western rivers and designed a specialized boat for this purpose.

The period 1830–1850 was the golden age of western steamboats. The lower Ohio River and the Mississippi River below Cairo carried the heaviest traffic, but the most revolutionary change was in upriver travel and trade. Steamboats made two-way traffic practical and economical throughout the western river system. Prices of manufactured articles needed by settlers dropped significantly, and prices of agricultural products shipped from the region improved. However, because the volume of products exported from the region far exceeded upriver traffic, flatboats remained important in moving produce to downstream markets. Flatboat arrivals at New Orleans increased from 598 in 1814 to a peak of 2,792 in 1846–1847 and then declined sharply to 541 in 1856–1857. Meanwhile, the number of western steamboats increased from 69 in 1820 to 727 in 1855.

In the prerailroad era the Erie Canal and the Great Lakes provided the second great trans-Appalachian artery. The 363-mile-long Erie Canal, completed in 1825, linked the Hudson River valley and the port of New York with Buffalo on Lake Erie and the Great Lakes region beyond. Despite limitations imposed by winter weather, the Erie Canal was a resounding success. Large numbers of immigrants used the route to move west, and for the first time western frontier products could be shipped directly east. The Erie's success led to the construction of other canals in the seaboard states and the Old Northwest. Some were designed to bring upcountry agricultural products and coal to coastal cities and ports. Others provided convenient shortcuts between population centers, connected important bays and rivers, and served as feeders to river and lake transportation.

The most ambitious project was the Pennsylvania

Main Line system, completed in 1834. It linked Philadelphia with the Ohio River basin and sought to keep Philadelphia competitive with New York City in trans-Appalachian trade. This was a daunting task because goods valued at nearly $10 million were shipped west on the Erie Canal in 1836. By 1853 this figure exceeded $94 million. Draft animals pulled canal boats, but steamboats came into use in shallow, narrow areas of the Great Lakes in the 1820s, especially on Lake Erie. After Canada opened the Welland Canal in 1829 connecting Lake Erie and Lake Ontario, steam navigation increased on Lake Ontario. However, on the open waters of the Great Lakes, as on the ocean, sailing ships held their own against steam-powered vessels for decades to come.

The Long Decline

Domestic transportation and trade flows changed frequently during the first half of the nineteenth century. Steamboat technology and the construction of canals, turnpikes, and plank roads reduced transportation costs and intensified competition between established commercial centers and existing transport routes and their new rivals. Early railroads were an additional factor in this fast-changing competitive situation, but their scattered location, limited distance, and rudimentary technology did not initially threaten water transportation.

Competitive circumstances changed rapidly during the 1850s. Total railroad mileage trebled from nearly 9,000 miles in 1850 to more than 30,000 miles in 1860. Many previously scattered segments were connected, and new routes developed. Construction was particularly extensive in the Old Northwest, and four long-distance trunk lines reached Chicago and St. Louis. Steamboat freight rates remained lower than railroad rates, but railroad routes were often shorter and faster, and improvements in rail technology gradually brought lower railroad freight rates. Commerce increasingly moved along an east-west axis, with immigrants and manufactured goods flowing west from seaboard states and the rich output of farms, forests, and mines moving east.

Some canals succumbed quickly to the competitive advantages of rail transportation, which also included fewer weather interruptions and the ability to serve areas with both main lines and branches. Coastal shipping and western steamboats also were affected by railroad competition, but the most disruptive force on those routes was the Civil War. The Union naval blockade of South Atlantic and Gulf Coast ports and military operations on western rivers brought commercial traffic in those waters to a virtual standstill. After Appomattox neither route ever fully recovered.

In the late nineteenth century water transportation continued to decline as a competitive force in the nation's transport system. Conversely, the railroad industry, the new dominant mode, continued to increase its total mileage, establish multiple routes between major cities,

blanket most states with branch lines, and improve industry technology. However, the railroads were not content to rely on their inherent advantages. Managers aggressively used a variety of techniques to nullify the effectiveness of water competition where it still existed.

For example, by 1909 the railroads had acquired almost one-third of the remaining canal mileage in the country (632 of 1,991 miles). They showed little interest in maintaining or using these properties. In other cases, such as the Erie Canal, railroads gained control of terminals, established their own line of canal boats, and refused to interchange freight with independent boat operators. Similar techniques were used against independent steamboat operators on rivers and at coastal ports such as Los Angeles, which handled a large volume of lumber and other inbound freight. Railroads also frequently used rate wars, including rates below cost, to stifle water competition.

The traffic decline on the nation's inland waterways was sharp and severe. For example, in 1880 the Erie Canal carried 4.6 million tons between Buffalo and New York, approximately 18 percent of total traffic. In 1906 the Erie carried 2.4 million tons, only 3 percent of total traffic. Meanwhile, the New York Central and Erie railroads carried 78.7 million tons. In 1880 some 65 percent of the cotton arriving at New Orleans came by river; in 1910 the percentage was only 10 percent. Traffic on the upper Mississippi River declined 85 percent, and total receipts and shipments at St. Louis dropped 90 percent between 1880 and 1910. Only the Ohio River, with its heavy industrial development, avoided a total collapse.

Great Lakes traffic continued to flourish between the Civil War and World War I with large shipments of iron ore, limestone, coal, lumber, and agricultural commodities. Lake Superior was unable to participate extensively in Great Lakes shipping activity until 1855, when the State of Michigan completed a canal between Lake Huron and Lake Superior at Sault Ste. Marie. Railroads gradually established passenger and car ferries across Lake Michigan to facilitate traffic between eastern and western lines, and passenger and package freight vessels also operated on the lakes. The initial success of the Great Lakes as a transportation artery stemmed from their role in the east-west flow of commerce that developed before the Civil War. Subsequent growth was based on large inbound shipments of lumber for midwestern cities and raw materials for the iron and steel industry, plus outbound shipments of agricultural commodities. By 1910 the Great Lakes fleet was larger than the fleet of every foreign nation except Great Britain and Germany.

Revival and Rivalry

Public interest in waterways resurfaced around the turn of the century as merchants and other groups sought relief from prevailing railroad rates and practices. In 1905, after a successful referendum, the State of New York began work on the New York State Barge Canal, a modern replacement for the historic but outmoded Erie Canal. The project, which included side canals to Lakes Ontario, Champlain, Cayuga, and Seneca, made extensive use of natural lakes and rivers and was completed in 1918. By 1924 the original estimated cost of $101 million had increased to nearly $231 million.

Federal appropriations for rivers and harbors began in 1824 and occurred annually after the Civil War. However, it was not until the Rivers and Harbors Act of 1902 that Congress replaced piecemeal waterway appropriations with a formal process for reviewing proposed waterway improvements. Regional and national meetings to promote interest in water transportation became more frequent, and in 1907 President Theodore Roosevelt appointed the Inland Waterways Commission to study the potential for waterway transportation and make recommendations. Not surprisingly, the commission and its successors recommended further federal aid for waterways.

The first significant commitment occurred in 1911 when Congress authorized a multiyear project to canalize the Ohio River. The project was completed in 1929. In 1930 a similar commitment was made to establish a 9-foot-deep channel on the upper Mississippi River from near St. Louis to St. Paul–Minneapolis. The establishment of reliable navigation channels on these major river systems, including tributaries such as the Missouri, Tennessee, and Arkansas rivers, created attractive opportunities for barge companies to handle large volumes of liquid and dry bulk commodities. In addition, until 1980 barge operators could use the inland waterways system without charge. Since 1980 water carriers have paid gradually increasing diesel fuel taxes.

As the twentieth century progressed, federal funding for waterway improvements became increasingly multipurpose in nature. Flood control, conservation, recreation, electric power generation, and regional economic development were integrated with navigation into huge multipurpose river basin projects costing hundreds of millions of dollars. Moreover, after World War II annual waterway expenditures by state and local governments typically equaled or exceeded federal expenditures.

The inherently low-cost structure of barge transportation, coupled with zero or minimal user charges for the right of way, presented an almost insurmountable problem for railroads operating in water-competitive markets. Traffic on rivers and canals grew steadily from 9 billion ton-miles in 1929 to 416 billion ton-miles in 1997. In terms of market share, this was an increase from 1.5 percent to 11.5 percent of intercity freight ton-miles. Federal rate regulation was not an important competitive factor in the industry because most barge operations involved private or exempt traffic. The principal waterway commodities were petroleum and petroleum products, coal, agricultural commodities, and a wide variety of construction materials.

Renewed national interest in waterways and construction of the Panama Canal caused many parties to fear that the economic benefits of these developments would be nullified by anticompetitive railroad practices. To foreclose such actions, Congress passed the Panama Canal Act of 1912, which sought to end railroad control of competing water carriers and flatly prohibited railroad control of any shipping line using the Panama Canal. Except in unusual circumstances, railroads could not "own, lease, operate, control, or have any interest whatsoever . . . in any common carrier by water or any vessel with which

Federal and local government waterways improvements made modern barge services a major competitor to railroads for heavy bulk traffic. The towboat *Orco* moved a long string of coal barges down the Ohio River at Sewickley, Pennsylvania, in December 1981. —William Metzger, *Trains* Magazine Collection

the railroad does or may compete for traffic." Railroads were forced to give up control of steamship lines on the Great Lakes and other routes and were precluded from a serious role in water transportation for decades to come.

The Panama Canal opened in 1914 but did not play an important role in intercoastal traffic until the early 1920s because American-flag vessels were in short supply during World War I. When rich petroleum deposits were discovered in the Los Angeles basin, production quickly outpaced local refining capacity, and a parade of tankers used the Panama Canal to carry crude to eastern refineries. A similar oil boom in Texas and Louisiana a few years earlier and the rapid growth of demand for gasoline, home heating oil, and other petroleum products led to heavy tanker traffic from Gulf Coast ports to East Coast refineries and distribution centers.

As soon as the United States entered World War II, German submarines made coastal shipping, especially tankers, a priority strategic target. The results were devastating. Shipping losses along the Atlantic and Gulf coasts were extremely high until mid-1943, and East Coast petroleum supplies plummeted. Petroleum traffic was shifted onto the railroads, which performed superbly despite equipment shortages. Large-diameter long-distance pipelines also were built to move crude oil, petroleum products, and natural gas from production areas to northern refineries and markets. Coastal shipping never fully recovered after the war. Maritime labor costs and disputes handcuffed general cargo traffic (even after the advent of containerization), and petroleum traffic shifted increasingly to pipelines and barges. Oil pipeline traffic grew rapidly from 4.4 percent of intercity freight ton-miles in 1929 to a peak of 23.6 percent in 1980 and then receded slightly.

Great Lakes traffic increased from 97 billion ton-miles in 1929 to a peak of 119 billion during World War II and averaged 100 billion ton-miles annually during the second half of the century. However, in the U.S. intercity freight market as a whole, Great Lakes traffic declined from 16.0 percent in 1929 to only 2.6 percent in 1997. Several factors contributed to this sharp drop. Iron-ore deposits were slowly depleted, large integrated steel producers lost market share to domestic minimills and imported steel, regional forest resources were diminished, and shipments of midwestern agricultural commodities shifted increasingly to Gulf Coast and Pacific Coast terminals. Railroads used unit trains and relatively low freight rates to compete vigorously for this long-distance traffic.

The railroad industry and its allies also lobbied diligently for many years to block joint U.S.-Canadian development of the St. Lawrence Seaway. Plans included huge hydroelectric dams, recreational facilities, and a 27-foot-deep navigation channel from the Atlantic Ocean into the Great Lakes. Opposition by the railroads, the Appalachian coal industry, and East Coast shipping interests finally collapsed in the early 1950s when Canada decided to proceed alone. Rather than be left out, the U.S. government joined the project and helped the Canadians develop the

seaway and its important resources. The deepwater route to America's "fourth seacoast" was opened in 1959, but overseas traffic ultimately proved disappointing. The changing economics of ocean shipping (especially larger vessels and containerization), slow passage through the 27-mile-long Welland Canal, seaway tolls, and harsh winter weather collectively posed serious constraints on long-term traffic growth. But Seaway competition did help keep down shipping costs; freight rates were usually lower during the months that the Seaway was open. The St. Lawrence Seaway was an impressive project and was especially important to Canadian interests, but it did not revolutionize the competitive relationship between water carriers and railroads in the United States.

—Richard W. Barsness

REFERENCES

Big Load Afloat. Washington, D.C.: American Waterways Operators, 1965.

Faulkner, Harold U. *The Decline of Laissez Faire, 1897–1917.* New York: Holt, Rinehart & Winston, 1951.

Harper, Donald V. *Transportation in America: Users, Carriers, Government.* Englewood Cliffs, N.J.: Prentice-Hall, 1978.

Lieb, Robert C. *Transportation.* 4th ed. Houston, Tex.: Dame, 1994.

Railroad Facts. Washington, D.C.: Assn. of American Railroads, 1998.

Taylor, George Rogers. *The Transportation Revolution, 1815–1860.* New York: Rinehart, 1951.

Waterloo, Cedar Falls & Northern Railroad

Many electric interurban railroads, either because of construction standards that precluded the interchange of standard freight cars or the unwillingness of steam lines, were unable to operate as a part of the larger railroad network. A notable exception to this was in Iowa, where several major interurban lines operated as an integral part of the steam railroad system and even evolved into diesel-powered shortlines after electric operation ended.

Among the most important of these was the Waterloo, Cedar Falls & Northern, organized by three brothers, Louis S., Claude D., and Joseph F. Cass. The oldest part of the WCF&N was built as the Waterloo & Cedar Falls Rapid Transit Co., which opened an 8-mile route between Waterloo and Cedar Falls in 1897. A second line, completed in 1903, added a 22-mile route north from Waterloo to Waverly. The company changed its name to Waterloo, Cedar Falls & Northern Railway in 1904. The railroad reached its full extent in 1914 when it completed a 64-mile line south from Waterloo to Cedar Rapids. WCF&N passenger equipment was typical interurban rolling stock, with handsome parlor-buffet-observation cars operated between Waterloo and Cedar Rapids. The entire line was able to operate steam railroad equipment in interchange service with light electric locomotives.

A key to the WCF&N's success was the development of a belt line around Waterloo that served industrial users and connecting steam lines. At one time the WCF&N took in enough revenue to rank it as a Class 1 carrier, and, like the nearby Fort Dodge Line, it was taken over by the U.S. Railroad Administration (USRA) during World War I.

Electric interurban passenger operation ended in 1956, but a local streetcar line between Waterloo and Cedar Rapids lasted until 1958. The Waterloo Railroad was organized under the joint ownership of the Rock Island and the Illinois Central and purchased the railroad properties of the WCF&N on July 1, 1956, and electric freight operation ended in 1958. Portions of the line were later abandoned, and what survived was merged into the Illinois Central.

In 1955 Waterloo, Cedar Falls & Northern operated 98 route-miles and 129 track-miles, with 10 locomotives, 2 passenger cars, 28 freight cars, 67 company service cars, and 230 employees. WCF&N operating revenues were $1.8 million.

—William D. Middleton

REFERENCES

Carlson, Norman, ed. *Iowa Trolleys*. Chicago: Central Electric Railfans' Assn., Bulletin 114, 1975.

Donovan, Frank P., Jr. "Interurbans in Iowa." *Palimpsest* 35, no. 5 (May 1954): 177–212.

West Point Route. *See* ATLANTA & WEST POINT RAIL ROAD

Western Maryland Railway

The Western Maryland Railway dates from May 1852, when the Baltimore, Carroll & Frederick Rail Road Co. was chartered by the Maryland General Assembly to build west from the Baltimore area toward Hagerstown. By August 1859, when the line opened between Relay House and Owings Mills, the assembly had passed an act renaming it the Western Maryland Rail Road.

In 1872 the Western Maryland finally reached Hagerstown. The next year it opened to Williamsport, Maryland, where it made a (temporarily) important connection with the Chesapeake & Ohio Canal. Two years after that a significant era began when John Mifflin Hood was

elected president of the railroad. When he took over, the WM had just 90 miles of line, from Fulton Station on the outskirts of Baltimore to Williamsport. When he resigned in 1902, the railroad had 270 route-miles that reached Hanover, York, Gettysburg, Chambersburg, and Shippensburg, Pennsylvania, and Cherry Run, West Virginia.

For half a century after its chartering in 1852, the Western Maryland had been financed largely by the City of Baltimore through stock subscriptions, loans, and loan guarantees, with the railroad's indebtedness to the city reaching $9 million. In 1902 that changed dramatically when Baltimore's WM holdings were sold to the Fuller Sydicate, which represented George Gould, who wanted to make the WM the eastern end of a transcontinental rail system that would include the Wheeling & Lake Erie, Wabash, Missouri Pacific, and Denver & Rio Grande, all of which the syndicate already controlled.

Gould's syndicate promised to repay the WM's indebtedness to the city, build a tidewater terminal in Baltimore, and extend the railroad west from Big Pool to Cumberland. There it would connect with the West Virginia Central & Pittsburg Railway, which had been chartered in 1866 as the Potomac & Piedmont Coal & Railroad Co. and had been acquired in 1902 by the Gould group. The tidewater terminal, Port Covington, at Winans Cove on the Middle Branch of the Patapsco River, opened in September 1904. By that time construction of the Cumberland Extension had been under way for more than a year. Because its entire route lay within the Potomac River valley, construction challenges might have seemed few. However, because the Chesapeake & Ohio Canal, Baltimore & Ohio Railroad, and National Turnpike had already built through the valley, taking the best routes, WM's surveyors had no choice but to use what was left, which required 23 bridges and five tunnels totaling more than 2 miles.

WM had two distinct personalities: coal hauler and fast freight carrier. Hauling coal was an activity that centered primarily on Elkins, West Virginia, the heart of the West Virginia Central system, which included the Piedmont & Cumberland Railway, the Coal & Iron Railway (extending to Durbin and a junction with the Chesapeake & Ohio Railway), and the Belington & Beaver Creek Railroad. Coal was gathered from these lines and, later, from the Greenbrier, Cheat & Elk Railroad and the Chafee Branch, then forwarded northeast to Cumberland, WM's operating hub. This required hoisting coal trains up Black Fork Grade, 10 miles of unrelieved 3.05 percent grade in remote Blackwater Canyon. Helper locomotives—typically both midtrain and rear-end—were necessary in diesel days, as well as in the steam era.

Gould's transcontinental empire was destroyed by two expensive railroad-construction projects: the Wabash Pittsburgh Terminal Railway to connect the Wheeling & Lake Erie with the city of Pittsburgh and the Western Pacific Railway from Salt Lake City to Oakland, California. The Western Maryland Rail Road entered receivership on

March 6, 1908, and emerged on January 1, 1910, as the Western Maryland Railway.

Two years later WM opened its Connellsville Extension, an 86-mile line west from Cumberland, Maryland, to connections with the Pittsburgh & Lake Erie at Connellsville, Pennsylvania. The Connellsville Extension was always called the New Line, even long after it ceased being new. The New Line eventually became an important link in the six-railroad Alphabet Route that carried freight between the Midwest and the Northeast: the Nickel Plate, Wheeling & Lake Erie, Pittsburgh & West Virginia (which reached Connellsville in 1931), Western Maryland, Reading, and Central Railroad of New Jersey. Clerks who wrote out the routing on waybills as "NKP-W&LE-P&WV-WM-RDG-CNJ" coined the term "Alphabet Route." Their coinage stuck; in fact, it was formalized with the introduction in 1955 of the name Alpha Jets for fast freights on that route.

WM never became part of a transcontinental system, but it thrived not only as a coal hauler but also as a bridge route forwarding "overhead" traffic—freight that both originated and terminated off-line. WM called itself the Fast Freight Line and introduced a "fireball" herald on its ultimate fast freight steam power, a dozen 4-6-6-4s delivered by Baldwin in 1940. Through the steam era WM progressed from ever-mightier 2-8-0s (not supplanted on the coal lines until dieselization) through 2-10-0s and 2-8-8-2 Mallets to the Challengers. The dozen 4-8-4s delivered by Baldwin in 1947 for fast freight service were WM's newest steam power. They were called Potomacs, not Northerns. Many of Western Maryland's first-generation diesel locomotives lasted until the railroad's demise.

The passenger trade was never very important to the WM, which discontinued its last accommodation trains, which were supported in large part by mail revenue, in the 1950s. The last passenger-only run, a Cumberland-Elkins local, died in January 1958; a Durban-Elkins mixed train soldiered on for 15 months more.

WM's demise came about through no fault of its own—it was a first-rate railroad right to the end—but because of redundancy in the face of control by Chesapeake & Ohio and Baltimore & Ohio, which the Interstate Commerce Commission approved in 1967. Substantial operational changes occurred in 1973, and in 1975 the ICC approved abandonment of much of the WM trackage that paralleled the B&O. Today fragments of the Western Maryland survive as parts of CSX.

In 1982, the year before it was merged by Baltimore & Ohio, Western Maryland operated 1,152 route-miles and 1,940 track-miles, with 109 locomotives, 6,836 freight cars, 145 company service cars, and 994 employees. Freight traffic totaled 1,626.6 million ton-miles in 1982, and coal constituted more than 70 percent of WM's traffic. WM operating revenues totaled $86.4 million in 1982, and the railroad achieved a 77.9 percent operating ratio.

—Karl Zimmermann

REFERENCE

Cook, Roger, and Karl Zimmermann. *The Western Maryland Railway: Fireballs and Black Diamonds.* San Diego, Calif.: Howell-North, 1981.

Western Pacific Railroad

By the 1890s the Denver & Rio Grande was part of the railroad empire of Jay Gould and his son George. D&RG connected several eastern railroads at Denver and Pueblo, Colorado, with the Southern Pacific at Ogden, Utah. Harriman control of both SP and Union Pacific (which also connected with SP at Ogden) effectively closed the Ogden gateway to through traffic to and from the D&RG. The Gould interests needed to extend their system to the Pacific, or it would wither from lack of traffic.

Arthur W. Keddie was a surveyor who had championed a rail route over Beckwourth Pass as the best possible over the rugged Sierra Nevada range. He had been laughed out of the offices of the Big Four, builders of the Central Pacific over Donner Pass at grades exceeding 2 percent and an elevation over 7,000 feet. On December 1, 1902, Keddie and Walter Bartnett formed the Stockton & Beckwith [*sic*] Pass Railroad. Bartnett met with George Gould, who saw that the new railroad could become the western extension he needed and agreed to back the project, though his participation was kept secret for two years. The Western Pacific Railroad was created on March 3, 1903, to build a rail line from San Francisco to Salt Lake City through the Feather River Canyon and over Beckwourth Pass, at 5,003 feet the lowest crossing of the Sierra Nevada.

The new railroad's first obstacle was the Southern Pacific, which claimed right to the Western Pacific name because an early Central Pacific subsidiary, completed in 1869 from Sacramento to Oakland via Altamont Pass, had used it. Bartnett and the Gould interests threatened mandamus proceedings, and SP quietly withdrew its objections.

Early planning and surveying were done quietly to keep Southern Pacific from creating further roadblocks. Not until the spring of 1905 did Gould publicly announce his paternity of the Western Pacific and sign construction contracts. Construction progressed rapidly westward from Salt Lake City. In 1908 the WP established mixed-train service from Salt Lake City to Shafter, Nevada, the junction with the Nevada Northern Railway. Western Pacific's bondholders had mandated a maximum grade of 1 percent and a maximum curve of 10 degrees. It was not difficult to keep the grade to 1 percent in the Feather River Canyon, but the grade and curvature requirements necessitated a complete circle, Williams Loop, between Massack and Spring Garden, California, and an impressive horseshoe curve called Arnold Loop over Silver Zone Pass east of Shafter.

Tracklaying from the west started with the driving of

the first spike at Third and Union streets in Oakland on January 2, 1906. Track crews from east and west met on the bridge over Spanish Creek at Keddie on November 1, 1909. Track foreman Leonardo de Tomasso did the honors. No magnums of champagne were broached; the only spectators were four women.

Western Pacific's early years were slim, because it had virtually no branches to feed traffic to the main line. Moreover, competitor Southern Pacific pretty much controlled the West. It was quipped at the time that the capitol of the state of California was not at Sacramento but in Southern Pacific's general office building in San Francisco. The traffic surge of World War I saved the fledgling railroad.

Passenger service had started on August 22, 1910, with a pair of through trains, the *Atlantic Limited* and the *Pacific Limited,* and two pairs of local trains operating between San Francisco and Oroville and between San Francisco and Stockton. Passage across San Francisco Bay was on the ferry *Edward T. Jeffery,* named for WP's first president.

After World War I passenger service was cut back to one train a day, the *Scenic Limited.* Service remained at one train until 1939, when the San Francisco Golden Gate International Exposition opened. The *Scenic Limited* was renamed *Exposition Flyer* and became a Chicago–San Francisco train, and a local train, the *Feather River Express,* was added to the timetable running between San Francisco and Portola.

In early years Western Pacific shared its president, Edward T. Jeffery, with the Denver & Rio Grande. In 1915 both railroads were forced into receivership because of the WP's construction cost, which was twice the estimate. The Western Pacific Railway was sold at auction on the steps of the Oakland station on June 28, 1916, and the Western Pacific Railroad took over the property.

The new company began to acquire and build branches and feeder lines in California. In 1917 WP purchased control of the Tidewater Southern Railway, which reached from Stockton to Manteca, Modesto, and Turlock. In 1921 the WP acquired the Sacramento Northern Railroad, an electric interurban line between Sacramento and Chico, and a few years later bought control of another interurban, the San Francisco–Sacramento Railroad (the former Oakland, Antioch & Eastern). At the end of 1928 the SN acquired all the properties of the SF-S, creating a single electric railroad between Oakland and Chico. The electric railways gave Western Pacific a much greater presence in the agricultural heart of California's Central Valley.

Meanwhile, in 1926 Arthur Curtiss James, probably the last of the great railroad financiers, sold his interests in the El Paso & Southwestern to Southern Pacific and purchased control of Western Pacific, adding it to his large holdings in Great Northern, Northern Pacific, and Chicago, Burlington & Quincy. James proposed several new lines: extension of the Tidewater Southern to Fresno (ve-

toed by regulatory commissions), acquisition of the Petaluma & Santa Rosa Railroad (ditto), extension to San Francisco via San Jose (approved but killed by the economic climate of the Great Depression), and a line north from Keddie to Bieber, California, to connect with the Great Northern (completed on November 10, 1931). Great Northern and Western Pacific contemplated extending the *Empire Builder,* GN's premier train, to San Francisco, but the Depression kept it from happening.

WP entered reorganization in 1935 and with Reconstruction Finance Corp. funds replaced 85-pound rail with 112-pound in the Feather River Canyon, purchased 10 4-8-2 passenger locomotives from the Florida East Coast, and modernized and air-conditioned its passenger cars. It installed centralized traffic control, starting in the Feather River Canyon and extending it by 1949 to the entire railroad, except for the track paired with Southern Pacific between Winnemucca and Wells, Nevada.

At the end of World War II WP was in the best physical and financial condition in its history. It faced two decisions: how to replace an aging fleet of locomotives and whether to stay in the passenger business. By the end of 1951 most of WP's steam locomotives had been replaced with diesels, and dieselization was complete in mid-1953. Remaining in the passenger business would require new or modernized passenger cars to compete with Southern Pacific, which paralleled the WP and ran faster, more frequent trains. The *Exposition Flyer* of 1939, operated jointly by the Chicago, Burlington & Quincy, Denver & Rio Grande Western, and Western Pacific, had been surprisingly successful. The three railroads teamed up to operate the *California Zephyr,* inaugurated on March 20, 1949. Instead of speed, the emphasis was on the scenery—the train was scheduled through the Rockies and the Feather River Canyon by day, and it carried five Vista-Domes.

The WP enjoyed prosperity in the 1950s, but the Interstate Highway Act of 1958 had the effect of shifting passengers and perishable freight to automobiles and trucks. In 1961 Southern Pacific entered a hostile bid to take over WP. Western Pacific encouraged the Santa Fe to enter the fray and present a competing bid. Union Pacific, to protect itself, purchased 10 percent of Western Pacific's stock. The Interstate Commerce Commission said no to both Southern Pacific and Santa Fe.

WP continued to be successful in the 1970s but encountered increasing difficulty remaining a small, independent railroad. Southern Pacific had turned its attention to the Denver & Rio Grande Western, so Union Pacific increased the amount of traffic it interchanged with WP at Salt Lake City and proposed merger, which took effect on December 22, 1982.

Today the former Western Pacific is still physically complete. After Union Pacific merged with Southern Pacific, the Inside Gateway route was redundant and was sold to Burlington Northern & Santa Fe, continuing the through freight connections to and from the Pacific Northwest. Passenger trains operate on former WP rails between Stockton and Niles Junction (Altamont Commuter Express) and between Winnemucca and Salt Lake City (Amtrak's *California Zephyr*).

In 1978 (figures for later years are unavailable) Western Pacific operated 1,483 route-miles and 2,391 track-miles, with 142 locomotives, 6,024 freight cars, 219 company service cars, and 2,908 employees. Freight traffic totaled 5,122.8 million ton-miles in 1978, and foodstuffs (39.1 percent) and transportation equipment (14.9 percent) were its principal traffic sources. WP operating revenues totaled $144.2 million in 1978, and the railroad achieved a 93.1 percent operating ratio.

—Arthur L. Lloyd

REFERENCES

Kneiss, Gilbert H. "Fifty Candles for Western Pacific." In *Mileposts.* San Francisco: Western Pacific Railroad. Republished in *Trains & Travel* Magazine (*Trains* Magazine) 13, no. 9 (July 1953): 50–58 and 13, no. 10 (August 1953): 48–57.
Myrick, David F. *Western Pacific: The Last Transcontinental Railroad.* Golden, Colo.: Colorado Railroad Museum, 2006.

See also PACIFIC RAILROAD.

Western Railroad

The Western Railroad was the most ambitious railroad-construction project of its time. When it was completed, it extended 157 miles from Worcester, Massachusetts, west to Albany, New York, and was the longest and most expensive railroad yet built by a single U.S. company.

The directors of the Boston & Worcester Railroad decided in 1833, even before their line opened, that an extension to the Hudson River was the natural next step. They obtained a charter on March 15, 1833. The cost of building the railroad was estimated at $4 million, and financing proved difficult. Eventually the Commonwealth of Massachusetts chipped in with a $1 million loan. Construction did not start until the winter of 1836–1837. Operation commenced between Worcester and Springfield, the first segment of the line to be completed, on October 1, 1839.

There was considerable uncertainty about the New York portion of the line. The Castleton & West Stockbridge Railroad was chartered in 1834, but no action was taken. The company was rechartered as the Albany & West Stockbridge in 1836, but the project continued to lag, although the City of Albany was authorized to invest funds in it.

In the meantime, the Hudson & Berkshire Railroad was chartered in 1835 and opened a railroad from Hudson, New York, to West Stockbridge, Massachusetts, on December 1, 1838. The line was constructed at minimum cost, with flimsy track, sharp curves, and stiff grades. It gave the Western the prospect of a connection to the Hudson River, albeit of doubtful adequacy and at Hudson rather than Albany. The Western was unable to reach agreement with the Hudson & Berkshire for relocation and improvement of its line. Instead, it leased the still-unbuilt Albany & West Stockbridge in 1840.

The Western built both eastward from the Massachusetts–New York state line and westward from West Springfield. The line was completed from the state line east to Pittsfield in May 1841, and by October 1841 the Connecticut River had been bridged at Springfield and there was a continuous rail route from Boston to Hudson, New York, via the Hudson & Berkshire.

The Western undertook to construct the Albany & West Stockbridge with the aid of a further loan from the City of Albany. It opened in 1842 between the state line and Greenbush, New York, across the Hudson River from Albany. (The Hudson River was not bridged at Albany until 1866.)

The Western had motive-power requirements in common with only one other early railroad, the Baltimore & Ohio. As a consequence, in 1841 and 1842 manager George W. Whistler ordered several 0-8-0 vertical-boilered Crab-type locomotives from Ross Winans. Although a dozen Mud Digger 0-8-0s, similar except for horizontal boilers, built by Winans for the B&O soon afterward proved successful, the design was a failure on the Western, and all were disposed of by 1850. A number of innovations in locomotive design appeared on the Western because of the inventiveness of Wilson Eddy, who started with the Western as locomotive-shop foreman in 1840 and became master mechanic in 1850.

In the 1840s the Western's routes played a part in travel from both Albany and Boston to New York City. In winter when the Hudson was frozen, the fastest route to New York City—far faster than the slow stage along the bank of the Hudson River—was by the Western Railroad to State Line, the Housatonic Railroad south to Bridgeport, Connecticut, and boat to New York. The principal route from Boston to New York was over the Western to Springfield, south through Hartford to New Haven, and on to New York. The route via Springfield remained the main route between Boston and New York into the 1880s.

The Western soon became a profitable operation. It began to double-track its line in the late 1840s. In 1854 it acquired the Hudson & Berkshire, which was proving to be a valuable link to the Hudson River for coal traffic. The portion of the Hudson & Berkshire east of Chatham, New York, closely paralleled the Western's own line and was soon abandoned.

Despite the Western's common roots with the Boston & Worcester, the managements of the two railroads squabbled repeatedly about the division of revenues from through traffic. After five years of maneuvering the two roads merged in October 1867 as the Boston & Albany Railroad. The B&A remained independent until it was leased to the New York Central in 1900.

Today the Western's route remains the principal route for freight traffic between New England and the west. It is currently operated by CSX and is also used by Amtrak.

—Adrian Ettlinger

REFERENCE

Salsbury, Stephen. *The State, the Investor, and the Railroad: The Boston & Albany, 1825–1867.* Cambridge, Mass.: Harvard Univ. Press, 1967.

Western Railway of Alabama.

See Atlanta & West Point Rail Road

George Westinghouse. —Westinghouse Electric Corp.

Westinghouse, George (1846–1914)

Born at Central Bridge, New York, George Westinghouse was the eighth of ten children. His father was a developer and manufacturer of agricultural implements at Schenectady, New York, and the young Westinghouse seems to have grown up with an aptitude for machinery and inventions. Westinghouse served in both the Union army and navy, from which he was mustered out in 1865 as an acting third assistant engineer. He briefly attended Union College at Schenectady, but soon returned to work at his father's shop.

Early Westinghouse inventions included patents for a rotary steam engine, a device for putting derailed freight cars on the track, and a railroad frog. When still only 22, Westinghouse in 1868–1869 developed one of the most important advances in railway technology, the first workable design for compressed-air braking. Westinghouse is often credited with invention of the air-brake. This is an overstatement, for there had been much earlier air-brake designs by both British and American inventors. But what Westinghouse did was to put all of the components together to provide the first practicable set of air-brake equipment, employing a steam-driven air pump and reservoir on the locomotive, a three-way cock operated by the engineer, a brake pipe and connections running throughout the train, and a cylinder and piston assembly on each car to set the brakes. The first train operated successfully with the Westinghouse system at Pittsburgh in December 1868. Westinghouse obtained the first of many patents on the system in April 1869 and by July had formed the new Westinghouse Air Brake Co. to build and market it.

The Westinghouse air brake was quickly adopted for passenger trains, but its use for freight trains was another matter, and it was almost 30 years before it was in universal use in North America. The original Westinghouse air brake, which operated on straight air pressure, had some shortcomings, however. It had no built-in safety features, and it required a long time to activate in a long train, with heavy slack action and slow release. Westinghouse corrected these problems with the development of the automatic air brake in 1872, using an arrangement of triple valves and an auxiliary air reservoir on each car that would automatically set the brakes with a reduction in air pressure. Other improvements followed, and the firm still operates as part of the Wabtec Corp.

George Westinghouse was an innovative and wide-ranging inventor who, perhaps equally important, was able to see the potential in others' inventions and to develop them into useful products. Seeking other uses for compressed-air equipment, Westinghouse developed a pneumatic system of interlocking signals operated by air pressure with electric signals and in 1881 formed the Union Switch & Signal Co. to develop and manufacture all types of railway signaling. It is still active today. In 1888 he invented the friction draft gear, which helped reduce the shocks and strains of starting and stopping long trains. The Pennsylvania Railroad's Alexander Cassatt once called it more important than the air brake itself.

Westinghouse's interest in electricity, which evolved from his signaling efforts, soon broadened to all areas of electric power. Joining with his younger brother Henry Herman Westinghouse, in 1885 he acquired the alternating-current developments of Lucien Gaulard of France and John Dixon Gibbs from England and hired such electrical pioneers as

Nikola Tesla, William Stanley, and Benjamin G. Lamme to develop AC electrification. He formed the Westinghouse Electric & Manufacturing Co. at Pittsburgh in 1886. Proponents of direct-current electrification were convinced that AC electrification was dangerous to life, and the controversy went on for over a decade before Westinghouse's AC successes settled the matter. In 1893 Westinghouse contracted to supply electric power to the World's Columbian Exposition at Chicago, and in 1895 he completed AC power plants that generated 15,000 hp from the Niagara River. Westinghouse pioneered the use of AC power for railroads, most notably with the 1907 electrification of the New York, New Haven & Hartford out of New York.

In 1883 Westinghouse became interested in the use of natural gas, soon developed some 38 patents in gas distribution, and acquired the Philadelphia Co., a natural gas company. In 1880 he began developing high-speed steam engines with his brother Herman, in 1895 gas engines of high capacity, and in 1896 he acquired the American rights to and made improvements on the Parsons steam turbine. His last invention was an air spring for automobiles and trucks in 1912.

George Westinghouse, a man of extraordinary energy and remarkable foresight, founded one of the world's greatest manufacturing companies. In 1888 he began to build in Turtle Creek Valley at Wilmerding, east of Pittsburgh, a model factory and model town based upon industrial plants abroad. It became the site for his largest manufacturing plants. At various times Westinghouse controlled over 40 corporations, including subsidiary firms in Canada and Europe. The combined capitalization of all these companies was about $200 million, and they employed over 50,000 persons. In the course of 48 years Westinghouse took out some 400 patents.

In the financial panic of 1907 the electrical and machine companies were thrown into bankruptcy, and Westinghouse lost control. After reorganization in 1908 he came back as president, but with very limited powers. He gave up work with the companies in 1911 but continued with other projects. He became ill late in 1913 and died in New York in March 1914.

—William D. Middleton

REFERENCES

Leupp, Francis E. *George Westinghouse: His Life and Achievements.* Boston: Little, Brown, 1918.

Prout, Henry G. *A Life of George Westinghouse.* London: Benn Brothers, 1922.

Westinghouse Air Brake Co.

Two significant events occurred in 1869 that spawned a new age of railroad travel in North America. In May of that year the final spike was driven securing the last section of track at Promontory Summit, Utah, connecting the Union Pacific and Central Pacific railroads to form the first transcontinental railroad. Another event, however, that occurred a month earlier and half a continent away proved to be an even larger contribution.

Until that time the biggest problem facing the railroad industry was how to slow down and stop a moving train. The average train consist at the time was made up of a steam-driven locomotive followed by a tender and two to four trailing cars. When the engineer wanted to stop the train, he would blow a whistle in the locomotive cab, signaling the brakemen riding in the trailing cars to jump from car to car, turning the handbrake crank to tighten the chains connected to a series of fulcrums and levers used to force a brake beam and brake shoes against the wheels of each car.

That antiquated and hazardous procedure was about to change in April 1869 when George Westinghouse installed the first practicable set of air-brake equipment on regular service on a train known as the Steubenville accommodation, owned by the Pittsburgh, Columbus & St. Louis Railroad (also known as the Panhandle Railroad). The train, which consisted of the locomotive, tender, and three passenger cars, operated between the Pennsylvania Railroad Union Station in Pittsburgh, Pennsylvania, and Steubenville, Ohio, a distance of 65 miles. This original air-brake equipment, known as the straight air brake, consisted of an air pump (compressor) installed in the locomotive driven by steam taken from the locomotive boiler. The compressed air is forced to a pressure of 80 pounds per square inch into a reservoir fastened under the footplate of the engine. Air is piped from this reservoir to one opening of a three-way cock located near the engineer's seat. Another pipe, called the brake pipe, is connected to a second opening in the three-way cock, is extended down beneath the tender, and runs throughout the length of the train. A cylinder and piston assembly is bolted to the underframe of each car. The piston is connected to a brake lever that is used to force the brake shoes against the wheels when air is applied to the cylinder through a branch pipe connected to the brake pipe. A strong spring forces the piston away from the wheel when the brakes are released by expelling air from the brake cylinder through the three-way cock. Flexible hoses that have malleable iron couplings provided with cutoff valves join the pipes from car to car. The valves are forced open when the couplings are united, providing a free passageway from the three-way cock through the entire length of the train to the last coupling where the cutoff valve is in the closed position, preventing the air from escaping the system.

To apply the brakes on a moving train, the engineer moves the handle of the three-way cock to open the flow of air from the reservoir through the brake pipe and into the brake cylinder on each car, forcing the pistons out to apply the brake shoes to the wheels of each car almost instantaneously on a short four- to five-car train. The speed and force of the brake application is limited only by the amount of pressure carried in the reservoir. To release the brakes, the engineer moves the three-way cock to the exhaust position, which closes the communication between the brake pipe and reservoir and opens a communication from the brake pipe to the atmosphere, discharging the air from the cylinders, which permits the spring force to take over and push the brake shoes back from the wheels.

The equipment for this first air brake was designed by George Westinghouse and manufactured at a foundry and machine shop owned by a business associate, Ralph Bagaley, who accompanied Westinghouse on the eventful trial run. Daniel Tate, a veteran of the Panhandle Railroad, was the locomotive engineer. A dramatic incident during this trip immediately established the importance of the air brake. Soon after the train left Union Station and traversed through the Panhandle Tunnel, the speed increased to nearly 30 miles per hour as it approached a crossing at Third Avenue. A drayman in a horse-driven cart began crossing the tracks. The engineer instinctively pulled the cord to blow the whistle, but this only startled the horse, and it stopped in the center of the tracks. Tate then reached for the lever of the brake handle and made the first practical emergency brake application on record. The speed of the train slackened at once, and the train came to a complete stop within four feet of the crossing.

Soon after this trial run the Westinghouse Air Brake Co. was formed in July 1869. The first few sets of brake equipment were manufactured in Bagaley's machine shop before the operations, which included an updated foundry, machine shop, and blacksmith shop, moved to the corner of Liberty and 25th Street, Pittsburgh, in 1870. Within a year the company employed 105 men and had a production capacity of 18 sets of car equipment and 4 sets of locomotive equipment per day.

The straight air brake was notable for its simplicity, but it had two major shortcomings. First, it had no built-in safety features. In case of a train break-in-two with the brakes released, no power brake was available on the rear section. When the system was first designed, George Westinghouse had developed the clutch type of "glad-hand" hose coupling that included a check valve that would close in case of an undesired train parting. This would retain any pressure in the system as long as the brakes had been applied at the time the separation occurred. If the brakes were in the released position (as when going uphill), hand brakes would have to be applied promptly in order to prevent the rear section from rolling back down the hill. The second shortcoming was the time required to get the brakes applied and released on long trains (over 6 to 10 cars). Slack action was harsh on long trains, and brake applications and release were sluggish. Since all the air to fill the brake cylinders on each car had to flow back through the brake pipe from the locomotive, the brakes would apply hard on the locomotive and first 2 or 3 cars before much brake was ap-

plied to the cars on the rear. Thus the cars on the rear would actually run into the cars on the front, which had the brakes fully applied. The reverse would be true during a brake release, because the locomotive and cars in the front would release while the brakes on the rear of the train hung on, causing slack to run out.

To alleviate these problems, George Westinghouse perfected the first automatic air brake in 1872 (Figure 1). This new brake arrangement added a triple valve and auxiliary reservoir to each car. The engineer would charge the system by applying air through the brake-pipe that ran the length of the train and permitted air to pass through the triple valve and into the auxiliary reservoir on each car. To make a brake application, the engineer would make a reduction in the brake-pipe pressure, which would cause the triple valve on each car to close off brake-cylinder exhaust and allow air to flow directly from the auxiliary reservoirs into the brake cylinders. This system had two advantages over the original straight air brake. It improved the transmission time for setting the brakes on the entire length of the train, which led to increased train lengths. Whereas the straight air brake was used mostly on passenger trains limited to 5 or 6 cars, the automatic air brake operated much faster on longer trains and made handling 25 to 30 freight cars a practical matter. The other advantage of the automatic brake was its built-in safety factor. If the train were to break in two, or if a brake-pipe hose ruptured, the auxiliary reservoir on each car would recognize the drop in brake-pipe pressure as a signal to apply the brake on both sections of the train.

The success of the automatic air brake was so great that the manufacturing plant in Pittsburgh could no longer keep up with demand, so in 1881 George Westinghouse moved his operation to a larger facility in the town of Allegheny (now known as the North Side of Pittsburgh). The new plant provided 125,000 square feet of floor space and had the capacity to produce 100 sets of brake equipment per day. By that time the Westinghouse air brake had been introduced to Europe, and Westinghouse Air Brake Co. manufacturing plants were operational in Sevran, France, and London, England. In 1884 a Westinghouse Air Brake plant opened in Hanover, Germany.

In 1888 Westinghouse introduced the Quick Action Automatic Brake, which added an emergency brake feature and used a revamped triple valve with larger parts and passages (later to be known as the H Triple Valve) in combination with a larger-diameter brake pipe (1-¼ inches instead of 1 inch). In 1889 the Master Car Builders Assn., the forerunner of the Assn. of American Railroads (AAR), voted the Quick Action Automatic Air Brake the standard for all interchange cars. From the time of the first straight air brake in 1869 until the introduction of the Quick Action Automatic Air Brake 20 years later, the capacity of typical freight trains increased tenfold from 5 to 10 cars hauling 150 to 250 tons to 50 cars hauling 1,500 to 2,500 tons. Train speeds also doubled, from 10 to 12 mph to 25 mph. Although many new developments and

Figure 1. The "Westinghouse" Plain Automatic Air Brake, 1872

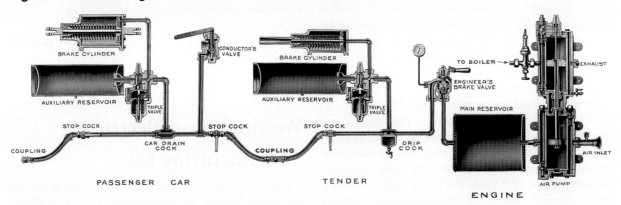

THE "WESTINGHOUSE" PLAIN AUTOMATIC AIR BRAKE 1872.

Air is compressed to 80 psi by the air pump, which is driven by steam taken from the locomotive boiler and stored in the locomotive main reservoir. The engineer charges the system by applying air into the brake pipe, which branches through one opening in the triple valve and through a second opening into the auxiliary reservoir on each car. A third opening in the triple valve leads to the brake cylinder. The triple valve is designed so that when air is applied from the main reservoir through the brake pipe, the auxiliary reservoir on each car will be charged with the same pressure, while at the same time an opening is made from the brake cylinder to the atmosphere. The brakes are in the released position when the system is charged. To apply the brakes, the engineer makes a *reduction* in the brake-pipe pressure. This causes the triple valve to shift, closing the opening from the auxiliary reservoir to the brake pipe and from the brake cylinder to the atmosphere and at the same time opening a direct passage from the auxiliary reservoir to the brake cylinders, applying the brakes with the full force of the pressure in the reservoir. A conductor's valve is installed on each passenger car, which enables the conductor or brakeman to discharge air from the system and apply the brakes on the entire train. The brakes would also be applied automatically if the train were to break in two or if a brake hose burst or otherwise became uncoupled. Drip cocks and drain cocks are installed under the tender and following cars to help prevent any moisture from entering the triple valves. —WABCO

refinements were made to air-brake control valves throughout the next century, the basic principle of applying brakes by making reductions in brake-pipe pressure remains unchanged.

In 1890 the Westinghouse Air Brake Co. completed construction of a new manufacturing facility on a tract of land situated near the Pennsylvania Railroad tracks, 14 miles east of Pittsburgh. The new facility eventually included a foundry, machine shops, a blacksmith shop, a rubber plant, and assembly areas and had the capacity to produce 1,000 complete sets of standard freight brake equipment per day. George Westinghouse purchased an aggregate 500 acres of land surrounding the plant and worked closely with area developers who proceeded to build the borough of Wilmerding around the plant. The Westinghouse Air Brake Co. (later known as WABCO) financed the construction of hundreds of affordable houses in the new borough that were sold to employees through interest-free payroll deductions. Today, the manufacturing facility for WABCO Locomotive Products Division and the corporate headquarters for Wabtec Corp. (successor to Westinghouse Air Brake Co.) remain on the same site, and most of the original company houses are still standing.

George Westinghouse died on March 12, 1914, but his legacy lived on, and his company continued to prosper. Throughout the twentieth century, nearly every major

breakthrough in railroad air-brake technology was engineered and developed by WABCO. In 1932 WABCO introduced the AB Freight Brake Control Valve, which featured separate service and emergency portions affixed to a pipe bracket. The new system featured improved quick-service functions that produced much faster transmission times. This made it possible for trains to haul 150 fully loaded cars safely and efficiently at higher speeds. The AB control valve was the industry standard for more than 30 years, until WABCO introduced the ABD control valve in 1962, the ABDW valve in 1974, and the ABDX/ABDXL valves in 1989. Each of these valves led to significant improvements in overall train performance and air-brake reliability.

In 1994 WABCO purchased Pulse Electronics, an industry leader in the field of locomotive event recorders and end-of-train devices, to form a research and development venture for design and manufacture of electronic-oriented air-brake components and equipment. The new railway electronics group (now known as Wabtec Railway Electronics) began development of a cable-based electronically controlled pneumatic (ECP) brake system. One of the first ECP systems developed by Wabtec Railway Electronics was placed in operation on long, heavy-haul coal trains operated by Spoornet in South Africa in 2000.

Though cable-based ECP braking is the most significant change in railway braking since the invention of the first automatic brake 130 years earlier, the basic principles are fairly simple. A two-conductor cable is installed throughout the full length of the train. This is used to deliver power to a car-control device (CCD) installed on each car using a 230-volt DC power supply in the locomotives, as well as two-way data communications, using a powerline transceiver.

Brake commands are broadcast over the cable in data form from the lead locomotive and are acted upon simultaneously by each CCD. Pneumatics are still used as the "muscle" for brake application, using conventional reservoirs and brake cylinders. The brake pipe becomes a supply line when in the ECP mode and is not reduced to signal brake commands as with conventional pneumatic systems, although conventional means of initiating an emergency brake application are still available through rapid brake-pipe reduction. The ECP cable and communications capabilities are used both to send commands to each car and to receive status information. This allows the lead locomotive to monitor total train health and performance.

The development of the ECP brake culminated what would become the final chapter in the 130-year history of the Westinghouse Air Brake Co. and the first chapter in the history of a new company. In November 1999 WABCO merged with MotivePower Industries to form a new entity known as Wabtec Corp. As of January 1, 2004, Wabtec maintained facilities in more than 30 locations in North America and 12 more in Europe, Asia, and Australia, covering a diverse product line ranging from rubber gaskets to new state-of-the-art commuter locomotives.

—George J. Belchick

Westinghouse Electric & Manufacturing Co.

From the formative years of electric traction in the late nineteenth century, the Westinghouse Electric & Manufacturing Co. and its rivals at General Electric ranked as the two principal builders for railroad electrification. George Westinghouse had come into railway work as a young man. He was only 23 when he patented the first practical air-brake system in 1869 and formed the Westinghouse Air Brake Co. He then went on to a diverse range of new technology and business developments. A younger brother, Herman Westinghouse, had gone into the electrical business in 1880, developing an improved design for high-speed DC generators. George Westinghouse soon became interested in the technology himself, originally for the possibilities of railway signal installation, and his earliest work was done with Union Switch & Signal, the signaling company he formed in 1881.

Westinghouse almost always worked in partnership with the Baldwin Locomotive Works. The two firms formed their relationship in 1895 to build this early test locomotive, which operated in both AC and DC equipment on test runs at East Pittsburgh, Pennsylvania. —Chaney Collection, Smithsonian Institution (Neg. 20281)

Westinghouse soon began a broader interest in electrification, developing DC generators for lighting systems. Almost immediately, however, he recognized the disadvantage of DC and began to consider the use of AC. In 1883 two European inventors, the French electrician Lucien Gaulard and the English inventor John Dixon Gibbs, had demonstrated the use of AC current, using what they called transformers. Westinghouse's firm did some further testing and development of the AC system, and in 1886 Westinghouse had bought the U.S. patents from Gaulard and Gibbs and rapidly began the development of AC electrification. Early in 1886 Westinghouse completed the formation of the Westinghouse Electric & Manufacturing Co. (WEMCo), taking over all the electrical patents. Westinghouse brought to the new firm such electrical talent as Austrian-born inventor Nikola Tesla and electrical engineers William Stanley and Benjamin G. Lamme. About the same time that the electrical firm was set up, the Union Switch & Signal Co. was moving to a new plant at Swissvale, Pennsylvania, and the new WEMCo firm moved into the old US&S plant at Garrison Alley in Pittsburgh, Pennsylvania.

Westinghouse's development of AC was initially devoted to power system and lighting development, and before the end of 1886 the first commercial AC plant was in operation at Buffalo, New York. In 1890 a commission at Niagara Falls had begun to develop plans for large AC plants from the power of falling water. Westinghouse won the contract, and by 1895 the company had in successful operation plants that produced 15,000 horsepower.

Westinghouse began to look at railroad electrification in the late 1880s. There were some experiments with AC power, but this was not yet practical for railroad use, and Westinghouse would have to be satisfied with DC power. By late 1889 the street railway business was beginning its rapid growth. Westinghouse had decided to enter the field and soon became a major competitor for a full line of traction motors, control systems, and other electrical supplies.

Westinghouse was rapidly growing, and late in 1894 the company moved to an expansive new plant at East Pittsburgh. WEMCo was active, too, in developing a number of overseas subsidiary companies, creating firms in several European countries, Canada, and Australia.

Despite his heavy involvement in DC railways, George Westinghouse continued to believe in the superiority of AC traction. In 1895, beginning a long-standing relationship between Westinghouse and the Baldwin Locomotive Works, an experimental electric locomotive was built with its mechanical components by Baldwin and the electrical installation by Westinghouse. Equipped for trial operations with single-phase and three-phase AC, as well as DC power, the unit operated for more than a decade at Westinghouse's East Pittsburgh plant. By the early 1900s AC traction had developed into a practical system, and a number of AC electric interurban railways, one as early as 1904, were equipped with Westinghouse equipment.

By this time Westinghouse was ready to take on mainline electrification with AC power. The several major electrifications thus far had all been built with low-voltage—about 600-volt DC—systems operated by a third rail.

Westinghouse began developing its high-voltage, single-phase AC electrification soon after the beginning of the twentieth century and built the first single-phase American locomotive in 1904. Tested at the company's East Pittsburgh plant, the 126-ton No. 9 could exert a drawbar pull of 97,000 pounds. Westinghouse used traction-motor armatures on quills surrounding the axles, an arrangement similar to that used by the company's pioneering single-phase electrification for the New Haven the following year. —Industrial Photo Service

Westinghouse built more than 500 main-line electric locomotives, most of them jointly with Baldwin, with three-quarters of these going to just two railroads, the New Haven and the Pennsylvania. Between 1932 and 1935 the Pennsylvania bought 54 of these Baldwin-Westinghouse P-5a electrics. The mechanical portions of the locomotive had been completed at Baldwin, and it would now go to Westinghouse for its electric equipment. —H. L. Broadbelt Collection

They worked reasonably well in relatively short distances, but the high power demands and line losses made them ill suited for long-distance installations.

The first main-line WEMCo electrification was installed on the extremely heavy suburban and long-distance service of the New Haven out of New York, using an 11,000-volt, single-phase, 25-cycle system. It worked well, and the railroad expansion was extended all the way to New Haven, Connecticut, by 1914. Over a ten-year period the New Haven acquired over 100 electric locomotives, all built in the usual Baldwin-Westinghouse arrangement. Other AC installation followed. The Grand Trunk Railway's St. Clair Tunnel was opened in 1908, the Boston & Maine's Hoosac Tunnel in 1911, and the Pennsylvania Railroad and Norfolk & Western in 1915.

The electrification of the Norfolk & Western in West Virginia was a pioneer North American application of electric power to the heavy traffic of a long mountain grade. Each of the initial 12 two-unit electrics supplied by Baldwin-Westinghouse weighed 300 tons and developed an hourly rating of 3,200 hp, the largest electric locomotives yet built. Westinghouse had built the locomotives with what was called a phase-splitting arrangement, permitting the simpler single-phase power supply to be used with a three-phase motor that would provide superior performance for the extremely heavy coal traffic. This arrangement also provided a superior arrangement for regenerative braking.

Although George Westinghouse believed that AC was the preferable system, he built equipment for DC systems as well. In 1896 Westinghouse engineered a general exchange of licenses between his company and General Electric that gave each other access to all their railway patents. WEMCo built all the original DC electric locomotives for

the Pennsylvania Railroad's New York terminal electrification and built for a number of other DC electrifications as well. Westinghouse usually teamed with Baldwin for the mechanical components, although there is at least one example—for the Virginian Railway—where the mechanical work was done by Alco, and the mechanical work for a majority of locomotives for the Pennsylvania was built by the company's own shops, with electrical installation by Westinghouse. By the early 1940s Westinghouse had built over 500 main-line units for North American railroads, with hundreds more for overseas markets. The major electrifications of New Haven and the Pennsylvania alone accounted for three-quarters of total Westinghouse North American main-line electrics. By the end of World War II Westinghouse had supplied two-thirds of the locomotives for North America's largest electrification—the Pennsylvania—and had built the electrical equipment for more than half of the Pennsylvania's celebrated 139 GG1 electrics built during 1934–1943.

In addition to its main-line electrics, Baldwin-Westinghouse was a principal supplier of the light electric locomotives—usually not more than 50 to 60 tons—used by interurban electric railways. From the beginning of the twentieth century until the market dried up at the end of the 1920s, the team built nearly 200 of the light electrics.

After World War II Westinghouse moved into an important new development for railroad electrification. As far back as 1913 Westinghouse, together with a test car supplied by the Pennsylvania and the New Haven, had operated a mercury-vapor rectifier unit to convert single-phase power to 600-volt DC power. At that early stage, however, the rectifier units then available proved unable to withstand the rigors of railroad service. With the improved ignitron rectifiers developed during World War II, Westinghouse was again ready to test the technology and in 1949 built a trial installation on a Pennsylvania Railroad multiple-unit (M.U.) car.

The new equipment worked well, and the ignitron-rectifier technology offered significant economies over the existing AC traction motors. During 1951–1952 Westinghouse supplied two similar two-unit locomotives that were equipped with ignitron rectifiers that permitted their operation in standard DC-traction motors. The performance of the new WEMCo design offered substantial improvements and performance over that of the AC commutator power previously used by the Pennsylvania, although the prototype units presented some maintenance costs and reliability problems.

In any event, despite the potential advantages, the Pennsylvania was not yet ready to take on any new locomotive orders. The future for other electrifications looked bleak as well. Although many had anticipated further expansion of electrification after World War II, nothing had ever happened. The lack of any new orders from the Pennsylvania, as well as the failure of any new electrifications to develop, made the electric locomotive market a dwindling one. In 1954 Westinghouse had decided to withdraw from the heavy electric field.

Although it had ended orders for electric locomotives, Westinghouse continued as an electrical supplier both for diesel-electric locomotives built by other companies and for electric M.U. cars, including the new ignitron-rectifier technology. In 1954 the New Haven, for example, ordered 100 M.U. cars that were equipped with Westinghouse ignitron-rectifier and other electrical equipment, the first production orders anywhere in the North American

market. Other M.U. car orders followed, such as a portion of the traction equipment for the Pennsylvania's Metroliner high-speed trains of the late 1960s, but Westinghouse's status as a major builder of electric locomotives had ended.

As well as its commanding position on railroad electrification, Westinghouse was also an early developer of diesel-electric motive power. The first development of internal combustion power came in the form of gas-electric or gas-mechanical railcars beginning early in the twentieth century. General Electric gas-electric and McKeen mechanical-drive cars were two of the most successful, together with a host of less successful builders. Early diesel-electrics were too heavy for railroad use, but a British firm, William Beardmore Co., developed a much lighter design for World War I airships, which was then adapted for railcar use on the London Midland & Scottish in 1922. Canadian National was interested in the new cars and ordered 10 Beardmore diesel engines for rail car use. CN would complete the assemblies, with separate contracts for carbodies and the electrical equipment. Electrical equipment was to be supplied from British Thomson-Houston for 7 small CN cars, while in 1925 Westinghouse was to supply the electrical equipment for 2 larger, 320-hp cars that were to be driven by a diesel-battery car. It soon became apparent that diesel-battery would not work, and WEMCo was then asked to redesign the cars for diesel-electric drive.

Westinghouse made a number of improvements to the engine, and the new cars worked well. WEMCo became increasingly interested in the possibilities for the Beardmore engine. The CN was pursuing more railcar designs and was planning a much larger diesel-electric locomotive. Before the end of 1925 Westinghouse had formed a

Westinghouse moved into an important new electrification technology with experiments in ignitron rectifiers soon after World War II, first with a test of the technology in a modified electrified commuter car and then with two pairs of experimental ignitron-rectifier units built for the Pennsylvania Railroad in 1951–1952. One is seen eastbound at Thorndale, Pennsylvania, in May 1952. —John E. Pickett

Westinghouse entered the diesel-electric locomotive field in 1925, when it contracted to supply the electrical equipment for a two-unit Canadian National locomotive powered by diesels built by the British firm William Beardmore Co. The unit was a success and remained in service for almost 20 years. Westinghouse went on to develop electrical equipment for railcars and then its own line of diesel-electrics, powered by the Beardmore engine, before it decided to leave the diesel-electric business in 1936. —*Trains* Magazine Collection

new engineering department and had reached a sales and production agreement with Beardmore. Engines were shipped from Britain through 1930, after which Westinghouse was building a revised and larger design of the Westinghouse-Beardmore engine itself. The earliest construction was for diesel-electric cars, and over the next decade Westinghouse and Beardmore diesel-electric car construction totaled 36 diesel-electric cars.

Almost as soon as Westinghouse got into the railcar business, it had begun the development of diesel-electric units. Using the same 300 hp engine used on the railcar, Westinghouse put together a semipermanently coupled pair of four-wheel switching units that were extensively tested by Westinghouse before being sold to the Long Island Rail Road. Soon afterward Canadian National went ahead with a two-unit diesel of 1,330 hp on each engine. The Beardmore units were supplied directly from Britain and the carbody was built in Canada, but the electrical components were designed by Westinghouse and built in the Canadian Westinghouse plant.

At the same time Westinghouse began to develop its own diesel-electrics, with all but a few units using Baldwin mechanical components, while the diesels and electric equipment came from Westinghouse. The earliest units were built in a box-cab arrangement, but Westinghouse had soon shifted to a better-visibility design. Some had end cabs like typical switchers of later years, while others had a center-cab arrangement. Single-engine diesels ranged from 300 to 530 hp, while most of the twin-engine units ranged as high as 1,600 hp. By 1937 Westinghouse had built 29 diesel-electrics. They acquitted themselves well, but the project had never met the development costs, and in 1936 the company had decided to end production, not long before the diesel-electric would revolutionize the railroads.

In addition to its long-running experience with mainline electrification and its much shorter venture into diesel-electric power, Westinghouse made one more try for the railroad locomotive market. A test unit completed in 1950 was a gas-turbine-electric locomotive, powered with a gas-turbine unit that had originally been developed in 1945 by Westinghouse for stationary power plants. Two gas turbines and electrical generator units were housed in the 230-ton locomotive and were mounted on four power trucks. Rated at 4,000 hp in a single unit, it could do the same job as a two-unit diesel of that period and was rated at a maximum safe speed of 100 mph. Nicknamed the *Blue Goose*, the locomotive spent the next several years in test runs over a wide variety of operating conditions. Although it performed well, the fuel usage also promised high operating costs. In the end there were no takers, and the unit was cut up for scrap several years later. The gas-turbine locomotive program was ended.

Westinghouse continued to supply traction motors and other electrical equipment. In 1962 Westinghouse began an innovative automated rail transit program, known originally as Transit Expressway, that successfully developed airport transportation and an urban transit system at Miami. As the Westinghouse organization broke apart, the transit division went into partnership with and then full ownership of AEG Transportation Systems and subsequently became a part of Bombardier Transportation. Other electric portions of the Westinghouse firm were sold to the Siemens electrical firm and other companies. The storied plant at East Pittsburgh is closed.

—William D. Middleton

REFERENCES

Hamley, David H. "These People Made a Good Locomotive." *Trains* 30, no. 2 (Dec. 1969): 28–43.

Leupp, Francis E. *George Westinghouse: His Life and Achievements.* Boston: Little, Brown, 1918.

Morgan, David P. "The Thrifty Glutton." *Trains & Travel* 13, no. 3 (Jan. 1953): 25–28.

Prout, Henry G. *A Life of George Westinghouse.* London: Benn Brothers, 1922.

See also LOCOMOTIVE BUILDERS.

Whistler, George W. (1800–1849)

George Washington Whistler was one of the early railroad engineers educated at the U.S. Military Academy. Named for the first president, he was born in 1800 at the army post of Fort Wayne, in what is now Indiana, where his father was commandant. Whistler was appointed to West Point in 1814. For several years after his graduation in 1819 the young lieutenant taught at the academy and conducted topographical surveys of the international boundary between Lake Superior and Lake of the Woods.

Whistler's railroad engineering career began in 1828 when he was assigned to assist in the location and construction of the Baltimore & Ohio. Together with fellow West Pointer William G. McNeill and engineer Jonathan Knight, Whistler went to Europe to study railroads and their equipment and returned to supervise construction of the B&O's first mile of track. McNeill and Whistler were next assigned to locate the Baltimore & Susquehanna, now part of Amtrak's Northeast Corridor. The two then moved on to do similar work for the Patterson & Hudson in New Jersey, which later became part of the Erie, and the Providence & Stonington in Rhode Island, now also part of Amtrak's Northeast Corridor. Whistler resigned from the army in 1833 to spend several years with the Proprietors of the Locks and Canals on the Merrimack River at Lowell, Massachusetts, where, among other things, he built several locomotives. He returned to railroad location work in 1836 with his appointment to the Western Railroad of Massachusetts and served also for a short time on the New York, Providence & Boston in 1837.

His extraordinary achievements in the construction of the Western Railroad across the Berkshires of western Massachusetts brought Whistler to the attention of the government of Russia, where Tsar Nicholas I had decided to link Moscow and St. Petersburg with a railroad. In 1842 he accepted an invitation to plan and build this great railway of more than 400 miles. Whistler spent six difficult years in Russia, and the great railroad was nearly complete when he was stricken with cholera and died at St. Petersburg, cutting short the career of one of the best early American railroad engineers.

After the death of his first wife in 1827, Whistler married Anna Matilda McNeill, the sister of his longtime professional colleague, in 1831. Among their five sons was the painter James Abbott McNeill Whistler, whose celebrated 1872 painting of his mother has become one of the best-known works of American art.

—William D. Middleton

REFERENCES

Angevine, Robert G. *The Railroad and the State: War, Politics, and Technology in Nineteenth-Century America.* Stanford, Calif.: Stanford Univ. Press, 2004.
Dictionary of American Biography.
Fisher, Charles E. "Whistler's Railroad." *Bulletin of the Railway & Locomotive Historical Society* 69 (1947): 8–100.
Harlow, Alvin F. "George Washington Whistler." *Trains* 8, no. 6 (April 1948): 14–18.
———. *Steelways of New England.* New York: Creative Age Press, 1946.

White Pass & Yukon Railway

A result of the Klondike gold rush of 1898, the White Pass & Yukon Railway (WP&YR) was built in only 26 months from Skagway, Alaska, over the 110 miles to Whitehorse, Yukon. It was completed on July 29, 1900, and regular service commenced on August 15, by which time the gold fields were practically exhausted. The line was laid on a 3-foot gauge and climbs almost 3,000 feet in the first 20 miles out of Skagway. Because of the rugged country through which the line was laid, the WP&YR is an international historic civil engineering landmark.

The line struggled on into the 1940s, supplying the small population in and around the Yukon's capital. The entry of the United States into World War II in December 1941 led to a tenfold increase in traffic on the line as the Alaska Highway was constructed. The Military Railway Service took over the line until the end of hostilities. After the war there was a mining boom in the Yukon, and the railway hauled in supplies and took out lead, zinc, and silver ore mined in the area at Faro, Mayo, and Clinton Creek. The railway introduced special-sized containers to enable speedy transshipment between trucks, trains, and ships. Unfortunately, in 1982, after the collapse in ore

George Washington Whistler. —Smithsonian Institution

prices, the last of the mines closed and the railway was shut down. The railway reopened in 1988 for special trains carrying tourists off the cruise liners that call at Skagway, which have become a booming business. These trains usually operate over the first 40 miles to Bennett, British Columbia, but trains are occasionally operated over the line as far as Carcross, Yukon Territory.

In 1980 the White Pass & Yukon Corp. operated 111 route-miles of railroad, with 20 locomotives, 34 passenger cars, 399 freight cars, and 36 company service cars. The revenue figures reported include pipeline, truck, and marine operations; railroad figures were not separated out. The tourist service carried a record 430,037 passengers in 2005, operating with 19 diesel-electric and 2 steam locomotives and 70 passenger cars.

—Donald M. Bain

REFERENCES

Cohen, Stan. *The White Pass and Yukon Route.* Missoula, Mont.: Pictorial Histories, 1980.

Zimmerman, Karl. "White Pass' New Gold." *Trains* 65, no. 5 (May 2006): 30–39.

Wilgus, William J. (1865–1949)

A largely self-made civil engineer, William John Wilgus was born in Buffalo, New York, in 1865. He graduated from high school there and then studied for two years under Marsden Davey, a Buffalo civil engineer. His formal education ended at the age of 20 with the completion of a Cornell University correspondence course in drafting. Wilgus then began a distinguished career in railroad civil engineering, first as a surveyor and draftsman for the Minnesota & Northwestern, a Chicago Great Western predecessor, where he quickly worked his way up to division engineer.

After doing location work and managing construction for several other midwestern lines, Wilgus returned east to join the New York Central & Hudson River in 1893 and rose rapidly through the engineering ranks. By 1898 he was the railroad's engineer of maintenance-of-way, responsible for an extensive rehabilitation of the entire system to accommodate heavier motive power. Only a year later he was named its chief engineer. Over the next several years he planned the electrification of the Central's lines entering New York City and the new Grand Central Terminal that would represent his greatest achievements.

In 1905 Wilgus was named chairman of a board of engineers to guide the work of constructing the Detroit River Tunnel between Detroit and Windsor, Ontario, for the subsidiary Michigan Central. He developed an innovative "trench and tube" concept for development of the tunnel under which prefabricated sections of tunnel were floated into position and sunk into a trench dredged in the floor of the river. The method saved an estimated $2 million for the project and became one of the most commonly used methods of underwater tunneling.

Wilgus left the New York Central several years later to practice as a consulting engineer. As a U.S. Army colonel, he served as director of military railways in the American Expeditionary Force during World War I. Shortly after the war, as chairman of a board of engineers studying a New York–New Jersey crossing of the Hudson River, he had an early role in the planning of the Holland Tunnel at New York. Rich with honors, he died at Claremont, New Hampshire, at the age of 83.

—William D. Middleton

REFERENCE

National Cyclopaedia of American Biography.

Willard, Daniel (1861–1942)

Daniel Willard was one of the most admired railroaders during the first half of the twentieth century. Beginning his career as a section hand on the Vermont Central in 1879, Willard moved into increasingly responsible positions with several railroads until he was appointed president of the Baltimore & Ohio in 1910, where he spent the remainder of his railroad career. He served as president of the B&O for 29 years and as chairman of the board for a little over a year. During his time at the B&O Willard made his mark on railroad history through his excellent performance as a railroad president, as well as his understanding of and good relationship with railroad labor. Having spent many years as a workingman himself, Willard possessed keen insight into the needs and interests of the rank and file, and this enabled him to negotiate contracts and resolve labor disputes in ways that nearly everyone found acceptable.

Born in North Hartland, Vermont, in 1861, Willard was a bright and focused child who grew up on his family's farm in Vermont. After completing high school in 1878, he entered the Massachusetts State Agricultural College. He had to drop out, however, after only six months because of problems with his vision. Shortly after moving back to the family farm, Willard began working on the Vermont Central and stayed with the railroad for several months. Between 1879 and 1884 he worked for the Connecticut & Passumpsic Rivers Railroad as both a fireman and a locomotive engineer, along with the Lake Shore & Michigan Southern as a locomotive engineer. In 1884 Willard joined the Minneapolis, Sault Ste. Marie & Atlantic Railway, also known as the Soo Line, and served in a variety of positions there, including division superintendent. From 1899 to 1910 Willard held management

Daniel Willard. —Library of Congress (Neg. LC-USZ62-21538)

positions with the B&O, the Erie, and the Burlington. In 1910 he was named president of the Baltimore & Ohio.

When Willard returned to the B&O as president, it was still in the process of recovering from a three-year period of receivership that had ended in 1898. Although the recovery had been going well, the entire U.S. rail system was experiencing a tremendous increase in traffic as the economy worked its way out of a serious downturn that had begun in the 1890s. Significant improvements to the railroad had been made after it had come out of bankruptcy, but much remained to be done, and shippers and travelers were not happy with the quality of service offered by the B&O.

To address the situation, Willard aggressively continued the improvements to the railroad. He invested heavily in the repair and upgrade of nearly every aspect of the railroad's physical plant and purchased new locomotives, freight cars, and passenger cars. He focused on improving the quality of both freight and passenger service throughout the system. Further, Willard did what all good railroad presidents do—he traveled the railroad extensively to inspect the lines and meet the employees.

Indeed, Daniel Willard's approach to mentoring and managing the railroad's employees is perhaps his greatest legacy. The goal of Willard's approach in this area was not only to promote a family environment among everyone who worked for the company, but also to tap into their capabilities by soliciting suggestions for improvement in the way the railroad's daily business was conducted. Having management and labor working together on developing

better ways to do business, Willard believed, would result in a stronger company. In 1923 Willard introduced the Cooperative Plan, which formalized the program for employees to offer their ideas for improvement. The program proved successful, and it was expanded to other locations on the B&O. In a sense, Willard's efforts were a precursor to the improvement initiatives implemented by corporate America in the 1980s and 1990s, a key element of which is providing everyone in the company, regardless of position, the opportunity to contribute ideas for the betterment of operations. In addition to his focus on private-sector railroading, Willard also contributed to a national effort during World War I. For a little over a year, while president of the B&O, he served on a commission that advised the Council of National Defense, created by the Wilson administration in 1916 in an attempt to provide better organization and control to the U.S. economy as it was gearing up for war. During Willard's service on the commission, the United States entered the war on April 6, 1917. Fearing a possible takeover by the federal government, Willard worked with other railroad presidents to create the Railway War Board, the mission of which was to provide coordinated management of the nation's railroads as they bore the increasing burden of traffic generated by the war economy. The board's efforts were not adequate, though; the federal government took over operation of the railroads on December 28, 1917 (*see* U.S. RAILROAD ADMINISTRATION).

After a full and successful career Daniel Willard, like many dedicated businessmen, found it difficult to think of leaving his job for retirement. Shortly after his 80th birthday, however, Willard believed that it was time for him to step down from the presidency of the B&O, and he was elected chairman of the board on June 1, 1941. After having served as chairman for only 13 months, Willard became ill and died on July 6, 1942.

Willard's career provides useful lessons to those in leadership positions in the railroad industry, as well as in other businesses. The years Willard spent working with the nuts and bolts of railroading gave him valuable experience that he put to use upon arriving in the executive suite. Not only did he have keen insight into the perspective of rail labor, he also thoroughly understood the operation of the railroad industry. He was able to blend this understanding with the unique knowledge and experience required of those in railroad management to make effective decisions in the president's office.

—David C. Lester

REFERENCES

Brinkley, Alan. *The Unfinished Nation: A Concise History of the American People.* 2nd ed. New York: Knopf, 1997.

Stover, John F. "Daniel Willard." In *Railroads in the Age of Regulation, 1900–1980,* ed. Keith L. Bryant, Jr., 478–487. A volume in *Encyclopedia of American Business History & Biography,* gen. ed. William H. Becker. New York: Bruccoli Clark Layman and Facts on File, 1988.

Vrooman, David M. *Daniel Willard and Progressive Management on the Baltimore & Ohio Railroad.* Columbus: Ohio State Univ. Press, 1991.

REFERENCES

Brown, John K. *The Baldwin Locomotive Works, 1831–1915: A Study in American Industrial Practice.* Baltimore: Johns Hopkins Univ. Press, 1995.

Wilson, William Bender. *General Superintendents of the Pennsylvania Railroad Division, Pennsylvania Railroad Co.* Philadelphia: Kensington Press, 1900.

Williams, Edward H. (1824–1899)

Physician and railway official Edward Higginson Williams was born in Woodstock, Vermont, on June 1, 1824. He showed an early aptitude for mathematics and received his education at home and in Montreal. Before reaching adulthood he visited Michigan and accompanied the engineering corps of the Michigan Central Railroad until he suffered severe attacks of asthma. Williams's doctors decided that his illness precluded an engineering career with its rigorous fieldwork, so Williams enrolled at the Vermont Medical College, from which he graduated in 1846. After another brief stint with the Michigan Central he established a medical practice, first at Proctorsville, Vermont, and later at Northfield.

Williams gained considerable medical fame in September 1848 when he was the first to treat Phineas Gage, a foreman on the Rutland & Burlington Railroad at Cavendish, Vermont, who had a 3-foot tamping bar blown clear through his skull in a freak blasting accident. Williams did not, however, conduct the follow-up study that established this case as a landmark of brain science. As a doctor, Williams was never far from the local railroads, and with his recovery from asthma he returned to his first career choice.

As a civil engineer, Williams moved frequently. Starting on the Plattsburgh & Montreal in 1851, he soon moved back to the Michigan Central, the Michigan Southern, and early lines in Illinois and Wisconsin. He then moved into operations, becoming superintendent of the Chicago & North Western's Galena Division in 1864. On January 1, 1866, he became general superintendent of the Pennsylvania Railroad and served until April 1, 1870, when he resigned and was replaced by Alexander J. Cassatt.

Williams capitalized on his peripatetic career by becoming a partner in the Baldwin Locomotive Works. His PRR assistant John H. Converse accompanied him as his confidential secretary and became a Baldwin partner in 1873. Williams joined Baldwin at a time when it was expanding and the individual partners were assuming specialized duties. Williams took charge of sales, using his many contacts at his former employers. When domestic sales collapsed after the panic of 1873, Williams took the lead in expanding export sales to Russia, Latin America, Asia, and Australia. After nearly 30 years at Baldwin, Williams died of heart disease at Santa Barbara, California, on December 21, 1899.

—**Christopher T. Baer**

Winans, Ross (1796–1877)

A farmer-mechanic who made a sizable fortune in the locomotive business, Ross Winans was born in Vernon, New Jersey, on October 17, 1796, to a family of Dutch descent. He gained an interest in mechanics after reading a book on the subject. This new involvement led in June 1821 to a patent for a plow.

Winans continued to farm and might have remained an obscure worker of the land save for a visit to Baltimore in 1828 to sell horses to the newly formed Baltimore & Ohio Railroad. He was 32 at the time, but decided to change careers and devote himself to the improvement of railway machines. He devised a clever plan for a low-friction wheel bearing that attracted considerable attention as far away as England. The bearing worked well at the demonstration stage but failed in regular service. Undeterred, Winans continued his research. He was made an assistant engineer in the B&O's mechanical department and became involved in locomotive and car design in 1831.

Many biographers have claimed that Winans invented the eight-wheel or double-truck railroad car at this time. It is true that he acquired a patent for a vehicle of this type in October 1834, but the idea was hardly original. Many other mechanics already were building and testing eight-wheel cars. Yet Winans persisted in pursuing his claim and engaged in a series of lawsuits that won him many enemies in the railroad industry. The U.S. Supreme Court ruled against Winans early in 1859, ending his 20-year war against U.S. railroads.

Years before the eight-wheel-car case heated up, Winans was busy developing his locomotive business. He formed a partnership with George Gillingham in 1835 and took over the B&O's Mt. Clare shops in Baltimore for the repair and manufacture of railway engines. They built engines not just for the parent company but for other railroads as well. In 1837 they opened their own shop next door to Mt. Clare. Gillingham died in 1840, and Winans went on alone to improve and enlarge the peculiar vertical-boiler Grasshopper style of locomotive. Within a year he produced an eight-wheel version and in 1842 sold several to the Western Railroad (Massachusetts).

These machines were not satisfactory, so Winans modified the design with a horizontal boiler. In 1848 he introduced his famous Camel locomotive, so called because of the very large steam dome as well as the engine cab atop the forward end of the boiler. They were crude and ungainly in appearance, but were among the first American engines to burn coal successfully. Winans sold over 100 Camels to the B&O over the next decade. The Philadelphia & Reading was another large purchaser of the Winans Camel.

In 1856 Winans and Henry Tyson, master of machinery for the B&O, argued over the merits of the Camel locomotive. The debate went public via published pamphlets that contained very strong language and a clear difference of opinion. This controversy largely ended Winans's career as a major locomotive builder. His shop closed by the early 1860s and was leased to another firm.

In the opening months of the Civil War Winans made apparent his sympathy with the cause of the South. As a member of the Maryland legislature, he made his anti-Union feelings public, only to be arrested and charged with high treason. There was talk of hanging, but after a short time Winans was released, only to be arrested and released again. Winans and his family took an extended European tour to avoid future situations of this nature.

After the war Winans and his son Thomas spent considerable time and money trying to perfect their design for a strange oceangoing vessel known as the cigar ship. It was circular in cross section and tapered to a point at both ends. One or more full-size prototypes were built, but the project failed to attract acceptance.

Winans spent his retirement pursuing many interests that included public charities. He operated a soup kitchen near his house that fed 4,000 needy people a day. He built a large public housing project and developed a plan to improve a small river that ran through the city, known as Jones Falls. More pamphlets appeared as Winans gave vent to his strong-minded opinions. The largest of these was a religious tract titled *One Religion, Many Creeds*. With a personal estate reportedly worth $20 million, Winans could indulge his various passions. The millionaire engineer and inventor died in his 81st year on April 11, 1877, in Baltimore.

—John H. White, Jr.

REFERENCES

Dictionary of American Biography.
New York Times, April 12, 1877.

Wisconsin Central Ltd.

In 1985 the Soo Line Railroad acquired what remained of the Chicago, Milwaukee, St. Paul & Pacific (the Milwaukee Road). The Soo concentrated its Chicago–Twin Cities traffic on the shorter, faster former Milwaukee Road line and in February 1986 created an internal subsidiary, Lake States Transportation Division, to operate most of the company's routes lying east and north of the former Milwaukee Road main line—in large measure former Wisconsin Central routes.

Burdened with a network of light-density lines and traditional work rules, Lake States was seen as unprofitable by the Soo Line. Moreover, the railroad was short of cash; the Milwaukee Road acquisition had been more expensive than the Soo Line had anticipated. The Lake States lines were put up for sale.

Edward A. Burkhardt, formerly a Chicago & North Western executive, and Thomas F. Power, Jr., formerly with the Milwaukee Road, incorporated Wisconsin Central Transportation Corp. (WCTC) in 1987 to purchase the Lake States lines; they would be operated by a subsidiary, Wisconsin Central Ltd. Operations began on October 11, 1987, over 2,047 route-miles of track purchased from the Soo Line for $122 million. Wisconsin Central's major routes reached from Chicago to Superior, Wisconsin, and to Minneapolis; from Fond du Lac to Neenah and Green Bay, Wisconsin; and from Green Bay to Escanaba, Michigan, and Sault Ste. Marie, Ontario. Wisconsin Central derived much of its traffic base from Wisconsin's paper industry and quickly became known for its personalized customer service. Traffic and profits grew quickly. The company also tapped into the iron-ore market, cooperating with several other railroads to move trains of taconite ore from Minnesota's Mesabi Range to steel mills around the United States.

Originally privately held, WCTC went public on May 22, 1991. The company soon expanded. In 1991 and 1992 it purchased both the Soo Line and Chicago & North Western routes into Superior, Wisconsin, for $22.3 million and combined the best portions of the two lines. In 1993 the company acquired the Fox River Valley and Green Bay & Western railroads for $67.7 million, adding 479 miles of railroad to the system and giving it increased access to the lucrative paper traffic in Wisconsin's Fox River valley.

In January 1995 Wisconsin Central paid $19.4 million to buy the 321-mile Algoma Central Railway, which provided freight and passenger service between Sault Ste. Marie and Hearst, Ontario, including popular tourist passenger trains to Agawa Canyon. In 1997 Wisconsin Central paid $88.6 million to Union Pacific to acquire 198 route-miles of former Chicago & North Western track from Green Bay to Ishpeming and Iron Mountain, Michigan, including the ore docks at Escanaba and access to two mines near Ishpeming. Another subsidiary, the Sault Ste. Marie Bridge Co., was used to acquire these lines. By the end of 1999 Wisconsin Central's North American operations comprised approximately 2,855 route-miles, 2,230 employees, 244 locomotives, and 13,900 cars.

Wisconsin Central also expanded overseas. In 1993 WCTC became the operating partner in the privatization of New Zealand's government-owned railway and ferry company. WCTC recovered its $22 million initial investment in 1995, and the company became publicly traded in 1996. Beginning in late 1995, the English, Welsh & Scottish Railway (EWS) was formed over a two-year period through acquisitions of five properties of British Rail, the former government-owned railway in the United Kingdom. In November 1997 WCTC led a consortium that acquired the stock of Tasrail Pty. Ltd., a government-owned company that provided rail service on 360 miles of track in Tasmania, an island state of Australia.

In 1995 Wisconsin Central signed an agreement with Chicago's Regional Transportation Authority (Metra) to operate commuter trains between Chicago and Antioch, Illinois. As part of the agreement, Metra funded extensive track improvements, including four additional passing sidings, new signals, and centralized traffic control. Speed limits were raised to 60 mph for passenger and intermodal trains and 50 mph for freights. Commuter service began on August 19, 1996. Metra planned to make the Wisconsin Central line double track by 2005. In 1998 the railroad signed a 20-year haulage agreement with Canadian National Railways under which it hauled CN trains 461 miles between Superior and Chicago.

Meanwhile, with no more expansions in the offing and overseas properties not performing as expected, WCTC's stock, once the darling of Wall Street, began a sharp decline. Despite being named 1999 Railroader of the Year by *Railway Age* magazine, Burkhardt was removed from his position by WCTC's board of directors in the summer of 1999 and replaced by Power. The new management worked in vain to shore up the stock price. In 2000 Burkhardt attempted a proxy fight to regain control of the company, an effort that failed on a close vote. On January 30, 2001, the new management announced that it had made a deal to sell all of Wisconsin Central Transportation Corp.'s common stock to Canadian National Railways. After necessary approvals from U.S. and Canadian regulators, Wisconsin Central was merged into CN on October 9, 2001.

In 2000 the Wisconsin Central operated a total of 2,528 route-miles of line, with 244 locomotives, 13,164 freight cars, and 2,180 employees. Freight revenues totaled $314,669,000, with $279,100,000 in operating expenses, for an 89 percent operating ratio.

—Steve Glischinski

REFERENCE

Dobnick, Otto P., and Steve Glischinski. *Wisconsin Central: Railroad Success Story.* Waukesha, Wis.: Kalmbach, 1997.

Women in Railroading

Women have a long history of involvement with the railroad industry. From the industry's beginnings,

women have worked as coach and depot cleaners, Harvey girls serving food in trackside restaurants, and hostesses aboard passenger trains. A few women have held positions in management or as designers of railroad equipment, and one woman, Mary Elizabeth Jane Colter, designed depots and trackside hotels throughout the Southwest. Women worked most directly with railroad operations in the capacity of telegrapher or clerk, but were generally excluded from the operating crafts and skilled maintenance crafts. This exclusion relaxed somewhat during the two world wars. The return of male workers, however, saw renewed discrimination. It was not until the 1970s that women benefited from civil rights legislation giving them full access to all railroad occupations.

The watershed change in occupations and opportunities available to women in the railroad industry occurred in the 1970s as women entered the operating crafts in train and engine service. Women entered these craft unions for the first time as full members with seniority protection, retirement benefits, and Federal Employees Liability Act (FELA) protection.

The history of this breakthrough is the history of civil rights legislation and activism after World War II. Title VII of the Civil Rights Act of 1964 prohibited discrimination on the basis of race, color, religion, sex, and national origin. Employers could discriminate in employment on the basis of sex only if there was a "bona fide occupational qualification" that all members of an excluded group lacked. Examples would be the occupations of wet nurse or sperm donor. This legislation conflicted with previous protective labor laws designed to restrict the nature of work women as a class could perform, such as restrictions on how much weight they could lift and how long they could work. Legal challenges to the railroads' labor practices followed, with the result that all the crafts had to open their doors to qualified women, as they had earlier to races other than white. The conflicting "protective" state labor laws had to be overturned. State protective labor laws date to *Muller v. Oregon* in 1908, and more than 40 states subsequently adopted such protective laws.

The history of federal protective laws relating to women in the railroad industry dates to World War I, when the federal government took control of the railroads from December 1917 to March 1920. Women were recruited for jobs other than clerks or telegraphers, such as common laborers, office, shop, and roundhouse cleaners, passenger conductors, dockworkers, electric lift operators, and helpers in the skilled crafts. The federal bureau created to supervise women in the workforce, the Women's Service Section, soon recommended "protective" restrictions on their performance, with the result that they could not perform all aspects of their craft and were easily displaced when male workers returned from the war. The restrictions caused certain classes of women workers, such as common laborers, to lose their railroad jobs immediately. Loss of these jobs led to pay cuts of 50

percent for most of the women laborers who found subsequent nonrailroad employment. After the war most crafts wrote similar "protective" provisions into their bylaws, effectively restricting entry for women. Restrictions on the type of work women could perform remained in place during their second wartime recruitment in World War II.

Women were excluded from the operating craft unions in both wars, except in passenger service as temporary conductors without union membership. Toward the end of World War II some women passenger brakemen agitated to get the New York Lodge of the Brotherhood of Railroad Trainmen to amend its constitution to delete the "white male" membership requirement and give women equal right of recall, the right to hold regular jobs, and the right to receive equal pay for equal work. Their local victory underscored a pervasive problem. Both railroad management and unions had long cooperated to exclude both women and racial minorities from elite railroad jobs. The Big Four unions—the Brotherhoods of Engineers, Trainmen, Firemen, and Conductors—typically defined their membership in exclusionary terms of race and gender. Only white men could be members. The unions chose to fight efforts for seniority rights for black firemen and brakemen and continued this attitude until civil rights legislation forced them to open shop. Black, Mexican American, and Asian males were first admitted to previously white unions, and women were next in line in the 1970s when the feminist movement provided the impetus to mount legal challenges, thus enabling women to enter so-called nontraditional jobs.

Why was the ability to work in the operating department necessary to full employment opportunity on the railroad? Operating department experience is necessary for promotion to positions such as conductor, engineer, yardmaster, trainmaster, road foreman of engines, and superintendent. Even the son of a railroad owner would typically start as a switchman to learn the business from the ground up. Maggie Silver, who inherited the Hoosac Tunnel & Wilmington Railroad in 1977 and subsequently owned seven railroad shortlines, regretted not being able to learn "all aspects of the business early in life." Working in the operating department also meant that women were allowed access to every part of the physical plant. They had to use the locker rooms and bathrooms, company away-from-home housing, and restroom facilities on engines and cabooses. Their presence in these previously all-male spaces caused the whole atmosphere in the freight yard to change. Nudie pinups came down. Separate bathrooms were put in. Railroad language had to be cleaned up. Poorly maintained equipment that could be operated only by brute force had to be serviced. Not all these changes were welcomed by management or by operating employees. Resistance to changes in ambiance still accounts for much of the harassment women have to deal with as operating employees. The changes women brought to the workplace, however, were only part of broader changes taking place, such as federally mandated random drug testing, the radical reduction of crew size, technological advances such as radios, end-of-train devices, power switches, and computerized reporting and data retrieval, and the reduction of supporting crafts such as clerks, maintenance-of-way workers, special agents, and roundhouse workers. By 1984 Southern Pacific trains were running with two operating personnel, an engineer and a conductor, instead of five—three brakemen, a conductor, and an engineer. Some crews now consist of one trainman operating a remote-control engine. The conductor or foreman now performs much of the reporting work previously done by clerks. Under the onslaught of such changes in the craft, the presence of women soon became a minor threat. Women were among the last brakemen to be hired by the railroads in the 1970s and maintained a minimal presence until hiring resumed again in the 1990s.

Attrition in the number of employees working for the railroad proved to be a problem for women beginning their careers in the 1970s. Typically, a railroader had to endure several years of being furloughed before he could expect to work year-round. Then, low seniority brought more years of extra-board work before a person could expect to hold a regular job with somewhat predictable hours. Because women entered the crafts as crew size was being reduced drastically, they could rarely gain the seniority to have a secure job. The co-author of the present entry, Linda Niemann, was the baby on the Southern Pacific brakemen's extra board in Watsonville Junction, California, for 18 years. Similar situations led many women operating employees to exercise their seniority to relocate over and over again to follow the work. This practice was known as "booming." Many train service women also elected to switch crafts to engine service, where work was steadier for them. Engine service was also perceived as being more suitable for women because it did not require as much physical strength.

Women trainmen on the Long Island Rail Road looked over general orders at the crew dispatcher's office in 1943. —Library of Congress (Neg. LC-USW3-34170-C)

Amtrak took over passenger service in the United States in 1971, but continued to use operating personnel from the railroads that owned the track it ran over until 1983. Since these positions were bid by seniority, it was rare for women to hold them, although they often worked them off an extra board. Since 1983, phasing in different regions over a five-year period, Amtrak has hired its own operating personnel, freeing those jobs up for newly hired women. When Linda Niemann worked as a conductor for Amtrak in 1986, onboard personnel often commented that she was making railroad history by holding that position.

Consistent with their entry into operating jobs in the 1970s, women are currently represented in management as yardmasters, road foremen, and trainmasters. With antidiscrimination legislation in place, it would not be unreasonable to predict that women will eventually be represented in all railroad positions if they are willing to pay their dues to get there.

If women could not hold secure work in operating, what railroad occupations were available to them before the 1970s? Even in wartime most women working for railroads had clerical jobs, including stenographer, accountant, telephone operator, freight rate analyst, ticket seller, and routing handler. Other jobs held by a smaller percentage of women were telegraph operator, coach cleaner, and passenger-service hostess or onboard nurse (a position technically part of the passenger train's operating crew). Of course, as the 1900 census documents, women have always been represented in every railroad occupation. Their presence has simply not been officially acknowledged or recorded. Some women dressed as men to circumvent discrimination. Others performed a variety of jobs without belonging to a union. Before the U.S. Railroad Administration's (USRA) control of the railroads during World War I, there was little industry-wide uniformity in labor practices. It should also be mentioned that race played a role in what jobs a woman could hold. Black women were relegated to the most laborious jobs, and work crews were segregated by race.

In the 1860s the previously all-male Order of Railroad Telegraphers admitted women into its union. Women's entrance into this occupation constituted a major breakthrough in employment opportunity. A telegrapher's job was one of significant responsibility and a departure from the domestic model of women's work. The 1900 census lists, out of 9,000 women working in the railroad industry, 7,229 working as railroad telegraphers. It was a telegrapher and station agent, Leah Rosenfeld, who, in 1968, played a significant role in overturning "women's protective laws" through her suit in California against the Southern Pacific. Stockton Municipal Court judge Rolleen McIlwrath wrote, "The . . . decision not only impacted favorably upon all women in the California labor force but also created a substantial benefit for all women through the United States." The U.S. district court decided that California's Industrial Labor Code, which regulated the hours, wages, and working conditions for women and minors in the transportation industry, was in conflict with Title VII of the 1964 Civil Rights Act.

Northern Pacific stewardess-nurse Marilyn Sanden chatted with passengers in the buffet-lounge car of the westbound *North Coast Limited* en route from Chicago to Puget Sound in April 1959. —William D. Middleton

Rosenfeld's employment with the Southern Pacific Railroad dated to 1944, when she hired on during World War II. During the ensuing decade she worked as a telegraph operator, clerk, and station agent. When a position opened for agent/telegrapher at Saugus, California, in 1955, Rosenfeld applied. Although she had ten years more seniority than the successful applicant, Rosenfeld was turned down because she was female. Southern Pacific based its decision on California's labor codes 1171 through 1256 and 1350 that limited women to lifting no more than 25 pounds or working longer than eight hours. She reminded the railroad in a telegram on January 4, 1955, that the railroads operated under a federal statute, the Railway Labor Act, that made no distinction between male and female employees and that federal law takes precedence over state law. After several more attempts to secure better-paying jobs with her seniority entitlement and getting turned down, she again requested that her Transportation-Communication Employees Union (TCEU) take steps "to protect the rights of its feminine members and endeavor either to have the state laws modified to exempt employees in transportation industries or secure an interpretation of the Railway Labor Act holding that the words 'all employees' means all employees." Nothing was done, and Rosenfeld continued to apply for promotions to better-paying jobs.

On March 21, 1966, Rosenfeld was summarily turned down for still another job because she was female. This time Title VII of the Civil Rights Act of 1964 had given her additional ammunition. Not to be put off any longer, she sent a telegram to the chairman of the Equal Employment Opportunity Commission (EEOC), Franklin D. Roosevelt, Jr., after the commission had posted a notice at work that any person who believed that he or she had been discriminated against by an employer should contact it. But again she hit a stumbling block over a year later when the EEOC decided not to make a determination, advising Rosenfeld of her right to bring suit under the act within 30 days. Her only recourse was to take legal action. On August 30, 1968, Rosenfeld's attorneys filed a lawsuit against Southern Pacific Railroad and the TCEU in the U.S. District Court of Central California. On September 10, 1968, the court threw out the case against the TCEU, but added to the suit the State of California's Department of Industrial Relations and Industrial Welfare Commission as interested parties. After presenting significant amounts of documentation, Rosenfeld prevailed, and on November 25, 1968, a judgment for her against Southern Pacific and the State of California was settled. Leah Rosenfeld was awarded no back pay—only attorney's legal fees. She continued to work for Southern Pacific and got her promotions until she retired in 1974. After several futile appeals by the railroad in regard to payment of court expenses, the case was closed in 1975. Her attorney, Hermione K. Brown, wrote, "In view of the developments of the past decade, you must realize that you were a pioneer in the battle for sex equality and that

you made legal history. You should be proud of what you have done." In a 1987 interview Rosenfeld said, "My main goal was for fairness in the work place and I fought for it." During her suit she was ostracized by other women employees for "rocking the boat," but her persistence opened the doors for employment of choice for future generations of women.

Although women have always worked in some capacity for the nation's railroads, it was not until the 1970s, after legal challenges, that they were admitted with full employment opportunities into all railroad occupations. Initially, women had to overcome the force of custom, which dictated stereotypes about women's capacities, ambitions, and proper place in society. As society has redefined women's roles, women's right to full employment opportunity does not seem as revolutionary as it once did. Women still face prejudice in nontraditional employment, but as more women choose to enter railroad operating crafts and advance through the seniority system, the crafts themselves will necessarily change as a result of the inclusion of women workers.

—Shirley Burman and Linda Grant Niemann

REFERENCES

Cooper, Patricia. "Cherished Classifications: Bathrooms and the Construction of Gender/Race on the Pennsylvania Railroad during World War II." *Feminist Studies*, Spring 1999.

Greenwald, Maurine Weiner. *Women, War, and Work: The Impact of World War I on Women Workers in the United States.* Westport, Conn.: Greenwood Press, 1980.

Knowles, Jocelyn W. "The Lady Brakemen." *American Heritage* 46, no. 4 (July–Aug. 1995): 72.

Levinson, Nancy Smiler, and Shirley Burman. *She's Been Working on the Railroad.* New York: Dutton, 1997.

Niemann, Linda. *On the Rails.* San Francisco: Cleis Press, 1994 (formerly *Boomer: Railroad Memoirs*).

Niemann, Linda, and Lina Bertucci. *Railroad Voices.* Stanford, Calif.: Stanford Univ. Press, 1998.

Woodruff, Theodore T. (1811–1892)

An inventor and railroad-car builder important to the introduction of the sleeping car, Theodore T. Woodruff was born near Watertown, New York, to a farming family in April 1811. After a limited education he was apprenticed to a local wagon maker and learned about mechanics as a pattern maker. Little more is known of his early career, but by 1855 he was master car builder for the Terre Haute, Alton & St. Louis Railroad.

Woodruff was attracted to improving the comfort of railroad night travel. Many other mechanics had attempted to introduce sleeping cars earlier, but the need was not great because most railroad trips were short in the industry's early years. By the mid-1850s, however, it was possible to travel for hundreds of miles over a single railroad. Weary passengers would detrain and spend the night in a hotel, but less prosperous travelers would suffer on through in their coach seat.

Woodruff devised a collapsible bed that could be converted from a seat during the day. In fact, he devised a scheme for a three-level set of berths. The THA&StL's chief engineer, Orville W. Childs (1803–1870), encouraged Woodruff to perfect his ideas and helped him obtain two patents. In 1857 Childs also helped Woodruff find backers to build a test car. The prototype worked so well that more cars were built for service on the Illinois Central, the Galena & Chicago Union, and several other lines. The first big contract of Woodruff's own company was made in 1858 with the Pennsylvania Railroad. The cars were owned and operated by Woodruff's firm and ran over various railroads, with the revenue shared by both parties.

By December 1862 Woodruff and his several partners decided to incorporate as the Central Transportation Co., with headquarters in Philadelphia. The capital stock was limited to $200,000, and O. W. Childs was named president. A competitor, sugar baron E. C. Knight, joined the new company. More luxurious cars now could be produced with fancy interiors and heat. The age of the palace car had begun. It was necessary to boost the capital limit to $2 million in 1865. A year later 88 Woodruff cars were running.

Yet although the business prospered and paid large dividends, Woodruff retired for reasons never explained. Perhaps he was simply ready to quit, or maybe he was no longer really necessary. Perhaps he was not particularly adept at managing CTC affairs. Whatever the cause, Woodruff was gone by 1864. Six years later George Pullman leased Woodruff's former enterprise, which proved a major step toward the consolidation of the sleeping-car business. Andrew Carnegie invested in the Woodruff enterprise at its beginning, while he was still a minor employee of the Pennsylvania Railroad. It proved to be one of his best decisions. But Carnegie grew impatient with the elderly and conservative managers at CTC and helped Pullman take over the business.

Woodruff moved to Mansfield, Ohio, but grew weary of retirement and bought an ironworks in Norristown, Pennsylvania, in 1870. The financial hard times after the panic of 1873 ruined the business, and Woodruff was bankrupt two years later. He lost everything and was forced to live with his daughter. He never lost hope, however, and worked to restore his fortune by promoting a number of patented inventions. While on a business trip to promote a screw propeller, the aged mechanic was run down and killed by a train at Gloucester, New Jersey, on May 2, 1892.

—John H. White, Jr.

REFERENCES

National Cyclopaedia of American Biography.
Wall, Joseph F. *Andrew Carnegie.* New York: Oxford Univ. Press, 1970.
White, John H., Jr. *The American Railroad Passenger Car.* Baltimore: Johns Hopkins Univ. Press, 1978.

Wootten, John E. (1823–1898)

Inventor and engineer John Eastburn Wootten was born in Philadelphia on September 22, 1823. As a boy, he was apprenticed to the Baldwin Locomotive Works and in July 1845 became foreman of the Pottstown shops of the Philadelphia & Reading Railroad, on which he spent his entire career. Promotions followed, and in 1866 the talented James Millholland chose Wootten to succeed him as engineer of machinery at the Reading shops. He became general superintendent in 1873 and was elevated to the new post of general manager in 1877.

Although he eventually directed all phases of railroad operations, Wootten is best remembered as a mechanical engineer, continuing the work of Millholland in developing anthracite-burning locomotives for the Reading. The coal-breaking process produced huge quantities of very small pieces that were dumped as waste at the breakers. Wootten devised a way of using this hitherto-useless by-product as locomotive fuel. The solution lay in creating a very wide, thin fire with a low draft to keep the coal from being drawn out the stack. Wootten elevated the firebox above the drivers, so that its width was limited only by external clearance. A combustion chamber, separated from the firebox by a bridge wall, extended forward into the boiler. The first locomotive with a Wootten boiler, 4-6-0 No. 408, left the Reading shops in January 1877. A sister, No. 412, built a year later, was exhibited at Paris and tested on French and Italian railways.

Originally Wootten had mounted the cab on top of the wide firebox, but for the European tests, the cab was moved forward astride the boiler, and this became the general practice. Wootten engines were called camelbacks because of their humped profile, or Mother Hubbards from the resemblance of the firebox to the wide loose dress of the same name. By 1883, 171 Reading camelbacks had effected an annual fuel saving of $378,000.

Wootten boilers were applied to fast passenger locomotives and to 2-8-0s for drag freights. Camelbacks became the dominant form of power on all the anthracite roads in the Middle Atlantic states. Around 1914 railroads began fitting conventional cabs on the back of Wootten fireboxes, and the Reading continued to use a modified Wootten boiler until the end of steam. Wootten retired in 1886 and died in Philadelphia on December 16, 1898.

—Christopher T. Baer

REFERENCES

A Century of Reading Company Motive Power. Philadelphia: Reading, 1941.

Holton, James L. "John Wootten: Locomotive Pioneer." *Historical Review of Berks County* 44 (1979): 97–107.

See also READING CO.

Workers' Housing

American railroads did not, as a rule, provide housing for their workers. Rather, they subsidized it in various ways. In this they followed the practice in Great Britain. A major exception in both countries was housing for agents at small-town, suburban, or rural stations, and that was generally provided in the station building itself. Accommodations for railroad workers often depended on the type of work. Construction or maintenance-of-way crews from the very early days of railroading in North America slept in bunk cars. Train crews after about 1875 often stayed at Railroad YMCAs.

The first railroad workers' housing consisted of primitive shanties built by the laborers themselves from the materials at hand. In 1830 British visitor James Boardman saw some of the "temporary wooden cabins" put up by the construction workers at Vinegar Hill near Relay, Maryland, as the Baltimore & Ohio Railroad got under way: "Every hovel had its swarm of children, its barrel of superfine flour, flitch of bacon, and stone bottle of the 'creature,' and the interstices were filled up with pigs and poultry" (Boardman 1833, 262). Boardman noted that another collection of windowless huts with flour-barrel chimneys was called Dublin.

A few years later and a few miles farther on, when the B&O's Thomas Viaduct was being built, the laborers, carpenters, and masons lived in the local taverns and boardinghouses, in dozens of shanties nearby, or in four railroad "house cars" that moved from place to place along the line. These bunk cars, which grew into two-story behemoths in the West, became common sights at the end of the tracks as the railroads spread across the United States and into Canada and Mexico (where bunk cars are still in use). They preceded the notorious camps known as "Hell on Wheels": wood and canvas communities of whiskey dealers, gamblers, and prostitutes who traced the railroads' progress and set up shop at likely locations. Sometimes the tent communities were replaced by more substantial settlements when the camp followers moved on.

Railroad lines were divided into divisions and sections: "section housing" was later developed for track gangs that maintained a particular section of railroad track. These housing units were often prefabricated and deliverable by rail and could be dismantled and moved elsewhere when no longer needed. Section housing was commonly assembled in multiunit groups.

Mexican construction crews working for the Southern Pacific Railroad in the San Gorgonio Pass near San Bernardino, California, in the early 1900s stayed in "campo trains" of wooden boxcars converted to living quarters. When towns sprang up in the pass, the railroad workers lived in section housing: six railroad families in attached two-room cottages in each community. (This housing was torn down in the 1960s.) In 1969 workers on Mexico's Chihuahua-Pacific Railway, completed in 1961, lived with their families in converted steel freight cars along the line, an engineering marvel that crosses the Sierra Madre from Topolobampo to Ciudad Juárez and Ojinaga with 39 bridges and 86 tunnels.

There were also company-built section houses for maintenance-of-way foremen. One of these, designed by H. Jacob for the Chesapeake & Ohio Railway, was a two-story frame Stick-style house with a rear extension. It contained four rooms: a kitchen, dining room, and parlor on the ground floor and a bedroom above. Railroad structures at remote but important points on the line that were manned, such as signals, junctions, and bridges, often had a dwelling attached.

The small stations and other railroad buildings that housed railroad workers could be pretty basic, even near highly populated areas, and quite rustic in the hinterlands. The station at Bladensburg, Maryland, halfway between Baltimore and Washington, D.C., on the B&O's Washington Branch, in 1872 was a two-story, two-bay brick building with a flat roof and a wooden front porch. If the agent lived on the second floor, his lodgings must have been spartan. The bridge man and his family at the B&O's Tray Run Viaduct in the Cheat River Valley near Rowlesburg, West Virginia, that same year occupied a simple board cabin with a pitched roof and a white picket fence. His pay would have been minimal, but the spectacular scenery was free.

The agent's living space in a small station usually consisted of a suite of rooms located over the waiting room, freight or baggage room, and agent's office downstairs. Sometimes the station building served as a dormitory for track workers or engine crews. That was evidently the case at the B&O Railroad's well-known station at Point of Rocks, Maryland, where several of the second-floor rooms were labeled "dormitory" on the plans.

Like their British counterparts, U.S. railroads customarily planned and laid out towns, but left the construction, ownership, and rental of housing to others. One example is Brunswick, Maryland, a division point on the B&O Railroad's main line between Baltimore and Cumberland, Maryland. It was a village of 300 named Berlin when the B&O selected the site in 1890 to build the largest freight classification yards on its system. The yards eventually stretched for 7.5 miles along the Potomac River flats between Point of Rocks and Harpers Ferry. The town changed its name to Brunswick (there was already

A typical wood-frame Canadian National station occupied its busy Montmorency Subdivision at Montmorency Falls, Quebec, where the operator issued train orders, handled CN telegrams and cables, and sold tickets for the CN's Quebec interurban, while his wife took care of the wash in the second floor of the station (*bottom*). —William D. Middleton

another Berlin, Maryland). The B&O built a roundhouse to repair locomotives, other yard facilities, and a Railroad YMCA (hotel) to house crews laying over. It also laid out lots for houses. Private contractors built most of the 41 cottages constructed for B&O employees at an average cost of a little over $1,000 each. They were designed, from eight different sets of plans, by E. Francis Baldwin, the B&O's architect and the designer of the 1892 Brunswick station. In 20 years Brunswick had a population of 5,000, its present size. (The yards have been reduced, and the roundhouse and other facilities have been demolished, but there is an active MARC rail commuter station.) Brunswick was a railroad town, but not a company town. The B&O Railroad, as Brunswick's largest employer, was paternalistic, but it did not own the stores and houses, as the company owners did in isolated American mill towns or mining towns. The railroad could fire troublesome workers, but it could not evict them from their homes.

The most important single supplier of housing for railroad workers (primarily train crews) in North America was the Railroad YMCA. The Young Men's Christian Assn., founded in London in 1844, later decided to provide housing facilities. The first Railroad YMCA in America was established in 1872. Railroad companies often donated buildings and equipment, and the YMCA staffed the facilities. Because railroad lines were expanding rapidly during this period, the housing program spread quickly. In 1903 the YMCA made it available to miners and lumbermen. The Railroad YMCA buildings appeared in a range of sizes, styles, and materials depending on the era and locale. The programs, however, were basically the same: clean baths and showers and sleeping rooms, meals in the lunchroom or cafeteria, libraries, and recreation (usually cards, pool, or table tennis).

In 1880 the Atchison, Topeka & Santa Fe Railway donated a two-story brick building for a Railroad YMCA in Emporia, Kansas, and contributed $1,200 annually for its operation as a "home for employees who were without home privileges." Some Railroad YMCAs even fielded sports teams. The Pennsylvania Railroad's YMCA in Philadelphia began operations in 1894 in an extensive, three-story Gothic Revival building with a large tower and conical roof at 41st Street and Westminster Avenue. Its football team, the Railroaders, made up of employees who were former college players, took on area colleges such as Franklin and Marshall, Villanova, and Bucknell— not too successfully, it seems, although their games were written up regularly in the press.

The B&O Railroad's Brunswick, Maryland, YMCA, "a huge barn-like yellow frame structure" by the side of the tracks, had 88 rooms. Its 30,000 annual overnight guests increased the local population by a third, and "its porches, recreation room and cafeteria serve as a daily meeting place for trainmen." (Brunswick ceased being a CSX railroad division point in 1988, and the building was demolished.) The handsome Neoclassical Revival Railroad YMCA in Richmond, Virginia, at 1548 East Main Street (1907), adjacent to the restored and reactivated Main Street Station, has recently been converted to a bar-restaurant and 30 apartments. In the first quarter of the twentieth century Theodore C. Link, architect of Union Station in St. Louis, designed the Railroad YMCA in Douglas, Arizona, in a Spanish Colonial Revival style. It is now a private sports facility.

Alburgh, Vermont, near the Canadian border, had a very unusual Railroad YMCA. After the previous Railroad workers' residence burned, the Rutland Railroad in 1925 bought an attractive Greek Revival mansion near the station, turned it into a Railroad YMCA, and operated it as a department of the company. Railroad and union officials both served on the board. The building was open 24 hours a day, had a staff of four, and could sleep 18. Membership was $5. A bed cost 35 cents; a meal was 40 cents. (The building was destroyed by fire.) Railroad YMCAs were still being built as late as the 1950s.

The first Canadian Railroad YMCA building was built in Toronto in 1890; by 1920 there were 15 such facilities. "The YMCA offered alternative pastimes such as reading and Bible studies to railway workers who otherwise were limited to visiting saloons during their leisure hours" (YMCA Canada).

—James D. Dilts

REFERENCES

Boardman, James. "A Citizen of the World." In *America and the Americans.* London, 1833, 262.
YMCA Canada. www.ymca.ca/downloads/themes/railroad

World War I and the Railroads

When Europe went to war in August 1914, U.S. railroads were in trouble. Rates were at all-time lows, and the Interstate Commerce Commission was hostile to the carriers' revenue needs despite operating cost increases of more than 30 percent since 1900. Deferred maintenance was common. One-sixth of the nation's route mileage was in trusteeship or receivership. Average rates of return on investment failed to cover the cost of capital.

Export traffic boomed as American industry and agriculture aided the British and French with equipment, munitions, fuel, and food. By November 1916 estimates of freight-car shortages exceeded 100,000 as exports and surging coal demand created serious capacity problems. Conditions deteriorated further as blizzards fouled operations in the East and Midwest. After Germany resumed unrestricted submarine warfare in January 1917, owners held vessels in port to avoid exposing valuable ships and cargos to U-boat torpedoes. With ship loadings dramatically curtailed, yards and routes near East Coast ports became clogged with traffic. Chaos ensued.

On February 5, 1917, 30 railroads imposed a virtual embargo on rail shipments to eastern ports. Quotas were set for the return of empty cars in order to clear overflowing midwestern grain elevators. The situation remained critical, and Samuel Rea, president of the Pennsylvania Railroad, told the ICC on March 22 that "the condition of the railroads today presents a menace to the country." Meanwhile, the army was adding manpower, growing from a peacetime force of only 213,000 to 3.7 million soldiers by war's end. Dozens of new training camps were needed, and railroads would deliver both the construction materials and soldiers.

The United States declared war on April 6, 1917. Five days later the nation's leading railroad executives met in Washington to create the Railroads' War Board (RWB). The five-member group, chaired by Southern Railway president Fairfax Harrison, suspended car-service rules, took charge of freight-car distribution, and created pools to facilitate coal movements. Conditions gradually improved. Between April and July rail ton-miles increased by 15 percent, and average trainloads rose from 705 to 782 tons. The shortage of freight cars, as high as 150,000 in the spring, was cut in half by late summer. Given that the RWB lacked authority to supersede federal and state regulatory agencies, its performance was more than creditable.

Events of autumn 1917 soon dashed any optimism. With European food demand at record levels, American farmers produced bumper crops. Labor disputes interfered with operations and added to operating costs. Cold weather and industrial needs spurred coal demand. Compounding the railroads' woes were ill-advised actions by federal officials who were attempting to impose their own priorities. The U.S. Shipping Board developed a system of "preference tags" intended to give priority over all other shipments to carloads so designated by its staff. Railroads were swamped with preference tags, and at one point the Pennsylvania Railroad noted that 85 percent of the traffic on its Pittsburgh division carried these documents. When the federal government decided to erect a major shipyard at Hog Island on the Delaware River near Philadelphia, priority was given to delivery of its construction materials, even though no unloading facilities had yet been established. At one point carloads of Hog Island–bound freight were backed up for 11 miles on the rail approaches to the proposed shipyard.

With car shortages again reaching the prior winter's levels, it was apparent that more drastic federal intervention was imminent. A provision of the Army Appropriations Act of 1916 empowered the president to take control of any transportation system during a wartime emergency. During the early months of the war President Woodrow Wilson had resisted doing so. By December 1917, with bitter winter weather once again snarling rail lines, industry leaders reconciled themselves to federal control, although many of them believed that this action was unnecessary.

USRA

President Wilson announced that federal operation of the railways would commence on December 28, 1917. In an address seven days later he pledged "as little disturbance of the present operations and personnel of the railways as possible." Treasury Secretary William Gibbs McAdoo, the president's son-in-law, was placed in charge of the U.S. Railroad Administration (USRA) with the title of director general of railways. Implementing legislation took the form of the Railroad Control Act of March 21, 1918. Individual railroads were to receive an annual rental payment from the government that equaled their average net operating income for the 1914–1917 period. The act also committed the government to return the lines to private control after the war in a condition roughly equivalent to that which existed at the time of the federal takeover.

McAdoo moved quickly. His first order revoked all governmental preference orders, directed railroads to move traffic by the most convenient and expeditious routes, placed embargoes on some eastern lines against all freight other than food, fuel, and munitions, and ordered the discontinuance of 400 passenger trains. USRA also mandated sharp increases in freight rates and demurrage charges. It can be argued that McAdoo's greatest achievement resulted from his ability to impose by administrative fiat changes that in peacetime would have required individual railroads to engage in prolonged and convoluted proceedings before the ICC and state regulatory commissions.

McAdoo was assisted at USRA by a cadre of veteran railroad executives, including his assistant, Walker D. Hines, chairman of the board of the Atchison, Topeka & Santa Fe. (Hines would succeed McAdoo as director general at war's end.) Three regional directors—for route systems in the East, South, and West—coordinated rail operations. A senior executive of each railroad, often its chief operating officer, became a federal employee and continued to supervise his former company, although answerable to USRA. Each railroad's proposed capital expenditures required the agency's approval.

Higher demurrage charges discouraged the inefficient use of freight cars as temporary warehouses by shippers and receivers. Coal movements were restructured to ensure that coal delivered to factories and utilities originated from mines within the same region, a process known as "zoning." Operations at major terminal yards were consolidated, and centralized purchasing of some supplies and equipment was implemented.

In order to bring more efficiency to the acquisition of locomotives and rolling stock, the agency devised standards for equipment design. Each category of freight car was to be built to a single specification. Twelve classes of locomotives were resolved upon. During the 26 months of federal control USRA ordered 100,000 freight cars and 1,930 locomotives.

Wartime inflation had severely cut the buying power of railroad workers. The inflation rate since 1915 had been double the rate of pay increases. But USRA's actions on wages and work rules brought widespread criticism from railroad executives. USRA raised the average annual wage from $1,004 in 1917 to $1,820 in 1920, when the companies were released from federal control. Another effect was to exchange the practice of company-by-company bargaining for national wage agreements. Labor costs rose from 40 to 55 percent of railroad operating revenues. McAdoo also set uniform national work rules that railroads were unable to roll back after the war. USRA critics contend that its actions contributed to what later would be termed "featherbedding."

Although rail travelers were inconvenienced, wartime curtailments of service and passenger amenities did not produce hardship. The trains eliminated by USRA usually were in city pairs in which several carriers provided multiple daily runs. A few "name trains" disappeared temporarily, including the Pennsylvania's flagship *Broadway Limited*. More significant was the diversion of sleeping-car equipment and coaches to the movement of troops. During the first 11 months of 1918 railroads transported nearly 6.5 million armed forces personnel, an average of more than 20,000 daily. Dining-car service was eliminated on some short-distance runs, and limited menus with "meatless days" appeared on those that remained as part of a national food-conservation effort. USRA banned advertising by rail companies. Travel during peak periods was discouraged. Passengers flocked to train stations anyway. Total passenger-miles traveled by both intercity riders and commuters had totaled 32 billion in 1915 and 35.2 billion in 1916. The passenger-mile total surpassed 40 billion in 1917 and reached 43.2 billion the next year.

Analysts are divided in their opinions of USRA's performance. The agency was credited with alleviating the worst equipment shortages and traffic bottlenecks, largely because of its ability to override the procedures of the ICC, the U.S. Shipping Board, and state regulatory commissions. Its equipment-standardization effort was judged less successful because the conflict ended before much of the equipment built under the new designs actually was delivered. Traffic volumes in 1918 were only 2 percent higher than 1917's total under RWB coordination. The sharpest criticism was directed at the agency's wage increases and work-rule decisions. However, the carriers would have been forced to raise pay significantly to avoid mass employee defections during a period of extreme labor shortages and runaway inflation. Federal control ultimately cost the federal government $1.12 billion.

The nation had been ill prepared to marshal its economic, industrial, and transportation resources for conflict on so vast a scale. Fortunately, it was a relatively brief conflict in terms of U.S. involvement. USRA's faults were duplicated throughout the management of U.S. participation in World War I.

Return to Private Control

McAdoo, who stepped down after the Armistice, recommended that the railroads remain federalized for another five years. Rail labor organizations endorsed permanent nationalization. Voters and politicians had little sympathy for public ownership, and Congress enacted the Transportation Act of 1920, which returned the carriers to their shareholders on March 1, 1920, although the income guarantee was extended until September 1. Railroad leaders complained that their property was returned in inferior condition and eventually settled for compensation of $204 million. Federal control proved costly to the carriers' economic health. The industry's operating ratio (a standard measure of operating productivity), which had stood at an acceptable 70 percent in 1917, rose to an alarming 94 percent in 1919.

Military Rail Operations

To serve the American Expeditionary Force (AEF) upon its arrival in France, the War Department created nine regiments of railroad personnel, with 1,080 persons per regiment, to provide transportation from ports of debarkation to front-line supply depots. Brigadier General William W. Atterbury, former vice president of the Pennsylvania Railroad, commanded these units, which drew many key personnel from railroad companies.

The logistical tasks were enormous. By September 1918 more than 1.6 million army personnel were serving with the AEF. The railroad regiments ran trains, built new lines, expanded rail facilities at French ports, and established shops to repair and build rolling stock.

—William J. Watt

REFERENCES

Godfrey, Aaron A. *Government Operation of the Railroads, 1918–1920: Its Necessity, Success, and Consequences.* Austin, Tex.: San Felipe Press, 1974.

Stover, John F. *American Railroads.* Chicago: Univ. of Chicago Press, 1961.

World War II and the Railroads

Confronting daunting challenges and unprecedented demand, America's railroads delivered an impressive performance during World War II. Many factors accounted for productivity that eclipsed the industry's earlier experience in 1917 and 1918. Extensive main-line double-tracking had been carried out during the intervening years and heavier rail had been installed. Automatic block signals controlled 66,000 miles of route, up from 39,000 miles 20 years earlier. Centralized traffic control (CTC) systems functioned on 2,163 route-miles in 1941, which permitted increased throughput. CTC was installed on another 4,332 miles by war's end. Almost as important, basic arrangements for coordination between the military and the railroads were in place 16 months before the attack on Pearl Harbor. Finally, railroad managers did not want to endure another federal takeover.

The transportation requirements were staggering. In addition to hauling armed forces personnel and equipment for global war, railroads took on burdens resulting from deep cuts in highway traffic due to gasoline rationing and the near disappearance of new automobile tires for civilian use. Meanwhile, more than 15 million Americans relocated to new cities as workers moved to defense jobs and families followed servicemen to duty stations.

Military Transportation Requirements

From December 1941 through August 1945 railroads carried 90 percent of military freight and 97 percent of military passengers. Freight traffic accelerated in 1941 with the flow of Lend-Lease Act armaments aid to Britain. National Guard and Reserve units were activated beginning in the autumn of 1940, and these personnel, together with a torrent of draftees, traveled by rail in 1941 to training centers.

World War I traffic had centered on movements from the eastern half of the United States to Atlantic coastal ports. The conflict against Japan created heavy demands upon the less dense western rail network, and officials worried throughout the war that key routes to California ports would be overwhelmed. That did not happen because railroads and the government cooperated to keep traffic flowing nationwide.

The Assn. of American Railroads' Car Service Division had the authority to suspend rules on freight-car use, transfer equipment among carriers, and order embargoes to alleviate congestion. During the summer of 1940 a military transportation section within the army's Office of the Quartermaster General had reached agreements with the railroads to coordinate military movements. Each railroad created an office to provide liaison for troop movements. Ten days after the United States declared war on Japan, military responsibilities were placed in the Office of Defense Transportation (ODT), which exercised broad powers over all surface transport within the country.

Troop movements were irregular in nature, often came at odd times, required special equipment, and frequently involved origins and destinations in remote areas. Hospital cars needed special handling, as did the transportation of prisoners of war. During the war nearly 114,000 special

War for the United States was only 11 days old when the U.S. Army's 35th Division boarded trains for departure from Camp Robinson, Arkansas, on December 18, 1941. —U.S. Army Signal Corps, *Trains* Magazine Collection

After German submarines forced cancellation of oil deliveries from U.S. coastal tankers, the railroads moved more than a million gallons of oil daily to the East in solid tank-car trains. This is an eastbound Baltimore & Ohio tank-car train in November 1942. —Library of Congress (Neg. LC-USE6-D-006784)

troop trains moved 43.7 million armed forces personnel—about 1 million per month. To ease the pressure on dining cars, railroads provided empty baggage cars in which military kitchen equipment was placed. Twenty-five percent of railroad coaches and 50 percent of sleeping cars were allocated to exclusive military use, and in 1943 the War Department placed orders for 1,200 military sleeping cars and 400 kitchen cars.

Freight traffic moving on War Department bills of lading amounted to 5 percent of total railroad freight tonnage in 1942 and escalated to 12 percent in early 1945. Explosives required special handling and security procedures. ODT also needed open-top freight cars, which were in short supply. Twelve thousand railroad police guarded key rail facilities against sabotage and other security risks. Branch lines were built to new military posts, and ODT expanded storage tracks at coastal ports. Friction between ODT and railroad managers occasionally developed as the carriers attempted to balance the army's and the navy's obvious priorities against the intense demand for civilian passenger service and commercial freight.

Freight Transportation Performance

No severe or prolonged car shortages developed, despite an increase in overall railroad freight traffic from 292 billion ton-miles in 1938 to 477 billion in 1941 and to a wartime high of 740 billion in 1944. Average daily car shortages in 1917 had totaled 113,000. The worst shortage in World War II—10,000 cars daily—was posted in 1945. Although the freight-car fleet was 20 percent smaller than in 1917, average capacity per car had increased from 41 tons to 50 tons. The locomotive fleet had

shrunk by one-third during the same period, but the greater pulling power of 1941's locomotives compensated for the smaller numbers. Although both ODT and railroad managers battled to secure additional equipment, the freight-car fleet expanded by only 3 percent during the war, and locomotives by 4 percent. Too many conflicting priorities existed for the use of steel and other critical materials for the railroads' needs to be fully met.

With the merchant oil tanker fleet a prime target for German U-boat torpedoes in 1942, severe shortages developed at East Coast refineries. Railroads were called upon to deliver crude petroleum and refined products by tank car. In order to augment its fleet, the Baltimore & Ohio fitted wooden tanks lined with thin steel sheeting into conventional boxcars. At the wartime peak in 1943 railroads delivered 900,000 barrels of oil daily. The Pennsylvania Railroad reported that petroleum shipments constituted about one-fifth of its total freight car-miles.

Shortages of key materials and components caused railroad managers to scramble to find substitutes for aluminum, tin, and rubber. Damaged freight cars were salvaged with welded patches of new metal. Outdated equipment was cannibalized for useful parts. Worn-out air-brake gaskets were boiled in water to restore them to their original shape. Crews walked yards and main lines to reclaim spikes, tie plates, and scrap metal.

Civilian Passenger Traffic

Entering the war with a smaller passenger-car fleet—soon cut even more drastically by the diversion of coaches and sleepers to military use—railroads were inundated with riders for whom the automobile had ceased to be an option for intercity and commuter travel. Passenger depots were jammed and often chaotic. People who could not find seats in stations or on trains stood for hours or perched upon their luggage. With its territory garnering new defense plants, the Southern Pacific reported a 374 percent ridership increase in the first six months of 1942 versus the same period in 1940—and the company had eliminated 27 daily trains during the war's early months. Club and observation cars were eliminated, or their seats were reserved for paying passengers and overflow dining space.

Peak holiday travel periods added to the strain. The Pennsylvania Railroad placed advertisements in December 1942 warning passengers to expect standing-room-only service, urging them to avoid weekends, and asking that luggage be limited to one suitcase. On Easter weekend

U.S. and Canadian railroads transported intense wartime passenger traffic. This was a typical wartime weekend scene at the Pennsylvania Railroad's Penn Station, which carried the heaviest traffic in its history.
—Associated Press, *Trains* Magazine Collection

Railroads heavily promoted the wartime drive to buy war bonds and stamps. Chicago & Eastern Illinois's coach 444 was resplendently repainted in red, white, and blue in 1942 in the effort to sell war bonds.
—*Trains* Magazine Collection

in 1942 the Pennsylvania had been swamped with more than 100,000 passengers per day on trains in its New York–Washington corridor. The worst holiday jams occurred in December 1945 as officials strove to return service personnel home in time for Christmas. More than 15,000 people packed Chicago's Union Station on December 21. The next day the New York Central temporarily stopped selling tickets on eastbound trains out of Chicago. The NYC reported great difficulty collecting tickets on board its trains because aisles were crammed with standees.

Traditional operating practices were altered. Schedules for long-distance trains were lengthened because efforts to sustain prewar running times would have interfered with priority military traffic. Equipment formerly dedicated to an individual train was pooled at major hubs to enhance flexibility in its use. Terminal dwell times were reduced by placing car cleaners aboard trains to carry out their work en route.

Dining service was adjusted to reflect the crush of riders and the realities of food shortages. Box lunches were available on some trains, and menus were leaner. Meat often was served only at dinner, and coffee—limited to one cup—was available only at breakfast. Embellishments such as jelly and cranberry sauce disappeared. However, many long-distance travelers spent much of their journeys standing in lines to enter dining cars. In 1945 ODT ordered the discontinuance of passenger trains with an occupancy below 35 percent, and in July 1945 the agency commandeered additional sleeping cars to accommodate an onrush of service personnel returning from Europe.

Passenger statistics for the war years are astounding. In 1940 total passenger-miles for intercity and commuter rail service had amounted to 23.8 billion. The volume boomed to 53.7 billion in 1942, 87.9 billion in 1943, and 95.6 billion in 1944 before falling off slightly to 91.8 billion in the war's final year.

Labor Shortages and Other Problems

U.S. railroads lost 315,000 employees to the military during World War II, but frantic efforts to recruit and train replacements resulted in a workforce expansion from 1.14 million in 1941 to 1.42 million by 1944. Retirees were called back. The Illinois Central trained thousands of teenagers. More than 100,000 women were recruited as car cleaners, shop workers, telegraphers, track workers, ticket takers, tower operators, railroad police, and clerks. Through an arrangement with the Mexican government, 125,000 temporary workers from that country were imported to serve on track-maintenance gangs.

Unhappy with the level of government-approved wage increases during a period of wartime inflation, rail labor threatened a national strike in December 1943. To avoid a shutdown, President Franklin Roosevelt ordered the army to take over the railroads on December 27, 1943, but government supervision lasted only until January 18, 1944, when all unions had reached agreements. The president's order had little practical effect upon day-to-day railroad operations.

The U.S. Army's Military Railway Service, largely staffed with railroad workers, operated wartime trains in such diverse points as Alaska, North Africa, Europe, Iran, and the Philippines. Pulled by an American-built 2-8-0, this hospital train boarded wounded on the Italian front at Riardo, Italy, during World War II. —*Trains* Magazine Collection

Wartime profits allowed the carriers to reduce their funded debt by roughly 20 percent, but wartime wage increases of 33 percent were much higher than the overall economy's 19 percent inflation rate. Railroads were unable to achieve rate increases sufficient to offset either of those cost impacts. Equipment and infrastructure had been heavily punished by overuse and badly needed replacement, yet industry executives worried that reduced peacetime traffic levels would fail to generate revenues adequate to pay for overdue modernization. Passengers had been irritated by wartime travel conditions. With consumer savings at record levels in 1945, many Americans placed new automobiles high on their wish lists for postwar purchases.

Military Railway Service

As it had done during the Civil War and World War I, the army deployed railway units to provide transportation in overseas combat areas. Railway battalions had functioned as part of the peacetime Army Reserve. Under the command of Maj. Gen. Carl R. Gray, the Military Railway Service (MRS) expanded to 38 operating battalions and six shop battalions, with total personnel of 43,000 and nearly all officers and enlisted personnel recruited from the ranks of U.S. railroads. Railroad companies supervised the training of these units, which were deployed in Europe, North Africa, and Asia to run trains, build and maintain track, and service and repair locomotives and freight cars.

As Allied offensives reclaimed territory, MRS officials confronted railway lines that often had been heavily damaged by retreating enemy forces. Compounding their problems were chronic shortages of replacement equipment and maintenance materials, along with serious problems at coastal ports. Port snarls impaired the delivery of freight and materials that MRS needed for its own use. Restoration of the rail system of northern France began soon after the June 1944 Normandy invasion, and the French railroads remained under military control until early 1945. By October 1944, MRS operated nearly 4,700 miles of track in France and Belgium, and about 30 freight trains shuttled daily from coastal ports to the Paris region. In November of that year about 50 percent of the freight tonnage supporting the combat zone moved by rail to forward-area supply depots.

—William J. Watt

REFERENCES

Stover, John F. *American Railroads*. Chicago: Univ. of Chicago Press, 1961.

Wardlow, Chester. *The United States Army in World War II: The Transportation Corps*. Vols. 1–2. Washington, D.C.: Department of the Army, 1951, 1956.

Y

YMCA, Railroad Department

The Young Men's Christian Association (YMCA) was founded in London in 1844 by Sir George Williams. Its Railroad Department was not organized until April 14, 1872, in Cleveland, Ohio, by station agent George Myers and Henry W. Stager, a young railroad worker. At their peak, nearly 180 Railroad Ys provided a safe, wholesome home for thousands of railroad men across America, a place where they could find clean beds, good food, reading material, healthy physical activity, and spiritual guidance.

In the 1800s, particularly before the formation of rail unions, "life on the rails was cheap." Crews suffered long hours, unfit food, and infested beds. As a rule, the only place where they were welcome during waking hours was a saloon. Many train wrecks could be linked directly to excessive duty and unhealthy rest periods when "booze, gambling, wenching, and brawling" were favorite pastimes. As a result, thousands of railroaders were killed or maimed, and the general public was endangered.

Stager was motivated by a story he heard at a busy depot about the body of a man killed in the performance of duty carried through the crowd. A curious passerby inquired, "Who is it?" and the callous answer came, "Only a railroad man." Stager never forgot. His feeling was that the best way to give railroad men a better reputation in the public mind was by providing decent living quarters for them.

Along with the Cleveland beginning, the Lake Shore & Michigan Southern Railway and the Chicago, Rock Island & Pacific cooperated with the Chicago YMCA, opening a room next to the LaSalle Street station. An 1872 *Chicago Tribune* article described the new endeavor as so "attractive by its literature and surroundings that the employees of the road will be unable to resist the temptation to accept the frequent use of its benefits and spend their leisure hours in the improvement of their minds, and keep out of saloons, gambling dens and other places of bad resort."

Railroad YMCA work was not limited to the United States; in fact, there is some evidence that the second railroad association established in 1872 was in Stratford, Ontario. By 1909 new buildings in Canada were still being opened, such as the one in Kenora, Ontario, costing $35,000.

Among the early supporters of the Railroad YMCA was Cornelius Vanderbilt, grandson of the Commodore, who in 1897 contributed $215,000 for the erection of an association building in New York City. Along with his financial support, he stressed the necessity for a maximum of autonomy for railroad associations. He saw that the policy of corporate gifts from the railroads could create problems, especially during times of labor disputes when the issue became whether the railroad associations that were supported by the management could still serve striking workers. Related was the criticism that since the Railroad Y was primarily a Christian movement, and since railroad employees were of all creeds and of no creed, railroads should not contribute to its existence. An example of the cooperation between the associations and railroad management occurred in Knoxville, Tennessee, in 1913, when the railroad men of the association raised $15,000 for a new building, while the Southern Railway contributed a desirable site worth $10,000 and $15,000 in cash.

In spite of some problems concerning corporate involvement, railroad management generally praised the work of the Railroad YMCA. In 1910 W. C. Brown, president of the New York Central, described the impact of the associations on service. He said that the Y, with its wholesome meals, its baths and quiet rest rooms, and its library and gymnasium, offered a home to homeless men where every influence was elevating, where the surroundings were calculated to make them better men, as well as safer and more efficient employees. It was emphasized that the most perfect system of signals that can be devised is of no avail if for any reason the signal is disregarded. The general manager of the Pittsburg & Lake Erie Railroad called the Railroad Y "one of the greatest factors for safety first on American railroads."

By 1895 a restaurant had become an important feature of a well-appointed railroad association. A typical menu might include pork and beans, coffee and pie, Irish stew, ham sandwiches, oatmeal, and four fried eggs—each item for 5 cents. A complete meal of beefsteak, liver and bacon,

B. & O. Y. M. C. A., S. Cumberland, Md.

YMCA hotels like this one at a Baltimore & Ohio division point provided wholesome accommodations for railroad men between their runs over the railroad. —James C. Dilts Collection

or veal and pork chops, along with potatoes, bread and butter, pie, and a drink, cost just 20 cents.

In a time when bathing facilities were rarely found in the average home, the Railroad YMCAs that had baths were very popular. The association branch in Chicago in 1879 made quite a feature of this service. An entire basement of the association was devoted to a barber shop, dressing rooms, and bathing facilities.

Although bargain meals and free baths were available at the Railroad Ys, billiards, card playing, and dancing usually were not. One Philadelphia association had learned by experience what happened when these activities were introduced into their program. "Whilst a prayer meeting was going forward in the first story young men were playing checkers in the second."

Among the earliest religious activities of the railroad associations were the gospel trains, usually composed of a Christian engineer, fireman, conductor, and brakeman, all men of outstanding character and fervor, gifted with simple and homely speech. Services were conducted in churches and railroad association buildings. The gospel trains visited railroad communities where no railroad association existed, promoting interest and sometimes organization of a Y branch. The service was simplicity itself— singing of old-time hymns, scripture, and prayer, followed by thrilling recitals of personal experiences. Then would come an invitation to the audience "to entrain with the gospel crew as the train sped on toward the City of God."

The problem of Sunday work on the railroads dominated many association gatherings. One delegate, a train conductor, stated that when he was asked to break the commandment and labor on the Sabbath Day, he said, "That's the day God calls me off the railroad." Another delegate blamed Sunday work on the merchants who demanded that their wares be delivered on Sunday.

When the U.S. government took over control of all railroads and operated them as a single unified system during World War I, there was concern about the future of the Railroad YMCA facilities. Even after a direct appeal to William G. McAdoo, director general of railways, there was no promise of continued support. Then Carl R. Gray, a friend of the Railroad Assn., became the operating head of the unified Government Railways and made it possible for the Railroad Ys to continue their work.

During World War I the Railroad YMCA contributed to the war effort by traveling on troop trains and providing the men with writing paper, postage stamps, checkerboards, and other such conveniences. Classes in French were conducted, and hundreds of Protestant and Catholic New Testaments and Jewish prayer books were distributed. Many times the last meal a serviceman ate before boarding his ship was provided by a Railroad Y. Similar services were offered in World War II. By 1927 the membership of the Railroad Y had exceeded 145,000, but as a result of improved living conditions and companies building their own crew quarters, such as the Santa Fe's Fred Harvey system of hotels and restaurants, the Railroad Ys began to experience fading participation.

In 1943 one Railroad Y, nestled in the bosom of the Cumberland Mountains, 84 miles north of Chattanooga, Tennessee, had become legendary. The Babahatchie Y, once a historic inn, was dwarfed by the lofty peaks of Walden's Ridge. It faced the Cincinnati Southern Railway tracks and had the river at its back. Before it became a Railroad Y, H. G. Monroe, a brakeman on the Southern Railway reported in *Railroad Magazine* in February 1943, it had been a wild hotel and saloon, "drunken brawls were common, red-eye flowed like water," and a railroader could lose his full month's pay and wager his last cent on a toss of the dice. In 1906 the railroad management invited the YMCA to enter the field, and the old inn was renovated. More than 12,000 meals a month were served in its spacious and well-equipped dining room, and railroaders enjoyed the comfortable facilities and religious opportunities. Although the inn was damaged by fire in 1941, the Cincinnati Southern continued to operate the Babahatchie Y for several more decades. The last Railroad YMCA building was closed about 1970, but the impact of its witness changed the moral climate of railroaders and the direction of railroad safety.

—Wilma Rugh Taylor

REFERENCES

Moore, John F. *The Story of the Railroad "Y."* New York: Association Press, 1930.
Railroad Men: A Monthly Publication Devoted to the Railroad Service, Feb. 1910.
YMCA of the USA Archives. Univ. of Minnesota Libraries, St. Paul.

Young, Robert R. (1897–1958)

Described by some as a gifted visionary and by others as a misguided maverick, investor, and stock speculator, Robert R. Young shook up the railroad industry in the late 1940s and early 1950s. His successful 1954 bid to control the New York Central was one of the great Wall Street

Robert R. Young. —New York Central Railroad, *Trains* Magazine Collection

battles of the era, and his penchant for publicity presaged corporate "raiders" of the 1970s and 1980s.

Young was born on February 14, 1897, in Canadian, Texas, a dusty Panhandle town where his father was a banker. His mother, Mary, died when he was 10, after which he was sent to Indiana's Culver Military Academy. After graduating in 1914, he attended the University of Virginia but dropped out in his sophomore year.

Young's first job was as a powder cutter at an E. I. du Pont powder plant in Carney's Point, New Jersey. He soon won a promotion to the du Pont Corp.'s treasurer's office, where he had a chance to demonstrate his financial acumen. Meanwhile, he married Anita Ten Eyck O'Keeffe, sister of the noted American painter Georgia O'Keeffe. The couple soon had a daughter.

The future speculator left du Pont by 1920 and began his securities career by investing a $5,000 inheritance. Young ended up losing all the money, but his interest in Wall Street and the stock market was sealed. He joined General Motors in 1922 and became assistant treasurer of the automaker in 1928. He subsequently went to work for GM chairman John J. Roskob, handling the executive's finances while Roskob worked in Democratic politics. But the pair had a falling-out when Roskob disagreed with Young's prediction of a stock market crash. When Black Friday came in October 1929, Young made a fortune selling short.

In 1931 Young formed a stock brokerage partnership and bought a seat on the New York Stock Exchange. An inheritance after his father's death in 1927 included a controlling interest in the First National Bank back in Canadian; Young sold the bank in 1939 but kept close ties to his hometown.

By 1941 Young was making waves in railroading after his purchase of a controlling interest in the Alleghany Corp., a bankrupt railroading holding company formerly owned by the Van Sweringen brothers of Cleveland. Young became chairman of the Chesapeake & Ohio Railway and used the position to promote his own industry agenda, which included disparate initiatives ranging from lightweight passenger-train equipment and steam-turbine locomotives to mergers and sweeping management reform. A frequent target was banking interests that Young said exercised excessive influence over railroads.

Young next took his crusade to a larger arena: the fight for control of the New York Central. Facing a difficult foe in the form of old-line New York financial interests and NYC management led by William White, the diminutive but street-savvy Young waged a tough proxy fight that extended over several years. A measure of Young's high public profile is *Time* magazine's 1948 description of him as "Bantam Bob, who crows louder than any other bird in the railroad yard."

Young finally won his proxy fight in 1954 and appointed reformer Alfred E. Perlman as NYC president. The pair began to radically change the hidebound Central, cutting operating costs and shedding massive amounts of fixed plant. The railroad's profits grew ac-

A Hog Can Cross America Without Changing Trains—But YOU Can't!

The Chesapeake & Ohio and the Nickel Plate Road again propose to give humans a break!

Railroad advertising probably never attracted more notice than did Robert R. Young's 1946 proposal for through passenger service between eastern and western roads using the C&O and Nickel Plate lines he then controlled. A few other lines later did add some through sleeping-car schedules. —Chesapeake & Ohio Railway–Nickel Plate Railroad

It's hard to believe, but it's true.

If you want to ship a hog from coast to coast, he can make the entire trip without changing cars. You can't. It is impossible for you to pass through Chicago, St. Louis, or New Orleans without breaking your trip!

There is an invisible barrier down the middle of the United States which you cannot cross without inconvenience, lost time, and trouble.

560,000 Victims in 1945!

If you want to board a sleeper on one coast and ride through to the other, you must make double Pullman reservations, pack and transfer your baggage, often change stations, and wait around for connections.

It's the same sad story if you make a relatively short trip. You can't cross that mysterious line! To go from Fort Wayne to Milwaukee or from Cleveland to Des Moines, you must also stop and change trains.

Last year alone, more than 560,000 people were forced to make annoying, time-wasting stopovers at the phantom Chinese wall which splits America in half!

End the Secrecy!

Why should travel be less convenient for people than it is for pigs? Why should Americans be denied the benefits of through train service? No one has yet been able to explain it.

Canada has this service . . . with a choice of two routes. Canada isn't split down the middle. Why should we be? No reasonable answer has yet been given. Passengers still have to stop off at Chicago, St. Louis, and New Orleans— although they can ride right through other important rail centers.

It's time to pry the lid off this mystery. It's time for action to end this inconvenience to the public . . . NOW!

Many railroads could cooperate to provide this needed through service. To date, the Chesapeake & Ohio and the Nickel Plate ALONE have made a public offer to do so.

How about it!

Once more we would like to go on record with this specific proposal:

The Chesapeake & Ohio, whose western passenger terminus is Cincinnati, stands ready now to join with any combination of other railroads to set up connecting transcontinental and intermediate service through Chicago and St. Louis, on practical schedules and routes.

The Nickel Plate Road, which runs to Chicago and St. Louis, also stands ready now to join with any combination of roads to set up the same kind of connecting service through these two cities.

Through railroad service can't be blocked forever. The public wants it. It's bound to come. Again, we invite the support of the public, of railroad people and railroad investors—for this vitally needed improvement in rail transportation!

Chesapeake & Ohio Railway · Nickel Plate Road

Terminal Tower, Cleveland 1, Ohio

---

cordingly in the first year, and Central common stock climbed from 23½ to 49½. But progress soon slowed as the economy dipped and passenger losses mounted. NYC stock fell to 13¼. Young committed suicide in his Palm Beach, Florida mansion on January 25, 1958.

—Kevin P. Keefe

REFERENCES

".00006% Isn't Enough." *Time*, May 24, 1948.
"Birthday for Bob." *Time*, June 6, 1955.
Morgan, David P. "Robert R. Young, 1897–1958" (obituary). *Trains* 18, no. 6 (April 1958): 6.
University of Texas–Austin. *Handbook of Texas Online.* www.tsha.utexas.edu/handbook/online

Appendix A

A Statistical Abstract of North American Railroads

William D. Middleton III

It is a truism that, outside of baseball, statistics are rarely collected and compiled until well after their significance has been recognized. This is certainly the case with statistics on the operation of railroads in the United States, Canada, or Mexico. There are few readily available data for the first several decades (1830–1890) of their existence, and they are spotty and often of questionable accuracy. Beginning with the 1890s, data are increasingly available, and their quality improves. However, they are plagued with problems ranging from changing definitions (particularly changes in the definition of Class 1 railroads; *see* CLASSIFICATION), the pooling of data from different classes of railroads, and changes in recording standards to changes in the industry itself (such as the commodities shipped and the units in which the statistics are reported), not to mention social and political changes (such as the Mexican Revolution) that obviated the context in which the statistics were recorded and reported in the first place. Many lines of inquiry had to be abandoned during the course of this study because the data were not consistently recorded throughout the period. Other data had to be summarized very roughly because of changes in reporting units, and there are occasional gaps.

These problems (and Mark Twain's famous witticism: "There are three kinds of lies: lies, damned lies, and statistics") notwithstanding, the data provide us with powerful insights into the evolution of the industry over its approximately 170 years of development. This appendix presents the history of North American railroading through its operating statistics. The three cases presented here, the railroads of the United States, Canada, and Mexico, all represent distinct historical trajectories in differing circumstances. The differences between them can help us better understand the factors involved in and the forces affecting the development of the railroads.

A Note on the Data

The data were compiled from a variety of sources, including the annual reports of the Assn. of American Railroads, the Railway Assn. of Canada, and Ferrocarriles Nacionales de Mexico; governmental institutions, including the Interstate Commerce Commission and Bureau of Transportation Statistics in the United States, the Dominion Bureau of Statistics, Canada, and the Minister of Supply and Services in Canada; the Instituto Nacional de Estadísticas, Geografía e Informática, the Secrataría de Comunicaciones y Transportes of Mexico; and compendiums of historical data from each of the three countries. Metric units have been converted to standard units.

The tables present data from selected years (generally every ten years, but occasionally from the best available or from particular years of interest). These are for the specific year, not averages for the decade. * denotes no data; nd denotes data not found, but probably exist; and other symbols are explained with the tables. The graphs present the annual data. Gaps in the data sequence are extrapolated (straight line) between the two closest known data points.

U.S. Railroads

Railroading in the United States began with the completion of the first 23 miles of the Baltimore & Ohio Railroad in 1830 and from this modest beginning rapidly grew into a continental colossus. Within two decades the United States had laid as much track as the rest of the world combined, and by 1869 railroads spanned the continent. Their growth continued into the second decade of the twentieth century, when they reached a high-water mark of over 1,200 railroads operating over 250,000 miles of line. From this point numbers dwindled steadily: in terms of miles of track, number of locomotives, and number of cars, the physical plant of today's railroad infrastructure is equivalent to what it was in 1880 (Table 1,

Figures 1–3). The decline represents the elimination of excess capacity (the railroads overbuilt during the boom years), the impact of competition by other modes of transport, and the introduction of new, more efficient technologies that required less physical plant (discussed later).

The traffic volume of today's railroads measured in tons of freight originated has risen only modestly from the post–World War II low, while traffic measured in ton-miles is about twice the volume of the peak years of World War II (with a physical plant roughly half the size), an almost exponential growth. This is due in part to the greater capacity of both locomotives and freight cars, as well as longer hauls (Table 2, Figure 4). The increase in intermodal shipping over the past 20 years appears to play a

Table 1. Railroad Plant and Personnel, United States

Year	Track Mileage	Line Mileage	Line Mileage Added/Lost	Total Locomotives	Steam Locomotives	Diesel Locomotives	Electric Locomotives	Freight Cars	Passenger Cars	Employees
1830	*	23	*	*	*	*	*	*	*	*
1840	*	2,818	2,795	*	*	*	*	*	*	*
1850	*	9,021	6,203	*	*	*	*	*	*	*
1860	*	30,626	21,605	*	*	*	*	*	*	*
1870	*	52,922	22,296	*	*	*	*	*	*	*
1880	115,647	92,147	39,225	17,949	*	*	*	539,255	12,789	*
1890	208,152	163,359	71,212	31,812	*	*	*	1,061,952	21,664	749,000
1900	258,784	193,346	29,987	37,663	*	*	*	1,365,531	34,713	1,018,000
1910	351,767	240,293	46,947	60,019	*	*	*	2,148,478	47,179	1,699,000
1920	406,580	252,845	12,552	68,942	68,554		388	2,388,424	56,102	2,022,832
1930	429,883	249,052	−3,793	60,189	59,406	77	663	2,322,267	53,584	1,517,000
1940	405,975	233,670	−15,382	44,333	42,410	967	900	1,684,171	38,308	1,026,848
1950	396,380	223,779	−9,891	42,951	26,680	15,396	827	1,745,778	37,359	1,237,000
1960	358,520	217,552	−6,227	29,031	261	28,278	492	1,658,292	28,305	780,494
1970	336,332	206,265	−11,287	27,077	13	26,796	268	1,423,921	11,177	566,282
1980	270,263	164,822	−41,443	28,396	12	28,243	141	1,168,114	**	458,994
1990	200,074	119,758	−45,064	18,835	**	18,835	**	658,902	**	216,000
2000	168,535	99,250	−20,508	20,028	**	20,028	**	560,154	**	168,000

**AAR reports zero for these categories.

Figure 1. Line and Track Mileage, U.S. Railroads

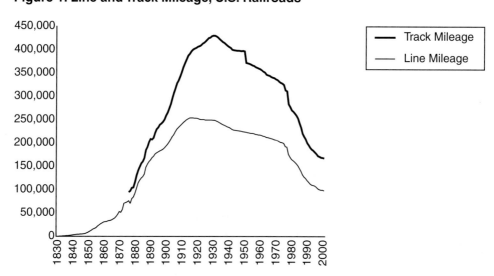

Figure 2. Locomotives by Type, U.S. Railroads

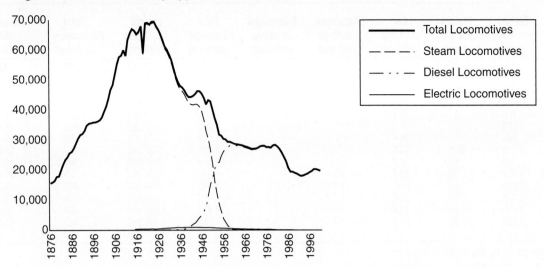

Figure 3. Equipment, Freight and Passenger Cars, U.S. Railroads

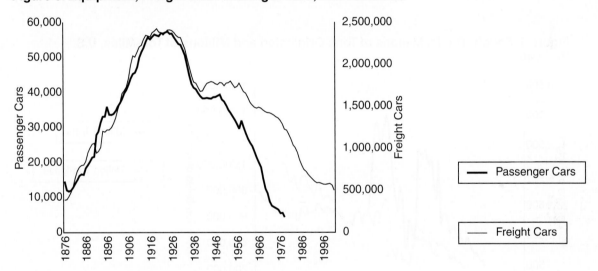

significant role in greater haul length (intermodal loading and ton-miles of traffic are very stongly correlated). Rail passenger traffic has declined precipitously since the peak of World War II, although the numbers (both passengers and passenger-miles) have been climbing steadily since their postwar low in the early 1970s (Table 2, Figure 5). Much of the recent growth is due to increased commuter traffic, but even Amtrak ridership has increased in recent years. It also is interesting to note the spikes in railroad traffic for both freight and passengers during the world wars. These traffic spikes show not only the important role played by the railroads in the war effort, but also the magnitude of the economic impact that these wars had on the U.S. economy.

The commodities that railroads carry have changed substantially over time, along with the trade and industries of the United States, so that tracking them in a meaningful way is difficult. Both reporting units and commodity categories are different, so that the data presented here had to be rather unsatisfactorily summarized (Tables 3A–3C). The most significant patterns visible here are the abandonment of both animals and animal products (which included livestock for part of the period) and the less-than-carload (LCL) categories, as well as the decline in importance of forest products and mine products.

Although railroads are carrying nearly twice the traffic (as measured in ton-miles of freight) of the previous high during World War II, their share of commercial traffic has declined from nearly three-quarters in 1930 to less than half the total in 2000 (Tables 4A–4B and Figure 6). Much of this decline is due to the growth of truck traffic, but pipelines and inland waterways also have increased their share. Unsurprisingly, passenger traffic experiences a

Table 2. Railroad Traffic, United States

Year	Freight per Train (tons)	Freight per Car (tons)	Car Loadings (millions)	Piggyback Loadings (millions)	Intermodal Loadings (millions)	Total Tonnage (millions)	Freight Ton-Miles (millions)	Total Passengers** (millions)	Passenger-Miles* (millions)
1882	*	*	*	*	*	*	39,302	289	7,688
1890	*	*	*	*	*	*	79,193	520	12,522
1900	*	*	*	*	*	583	141,597	577	16,038
1910	*	*	*	*	*	1,026	255,017	972	32,338
1920[a]	708	*	45.1	*	*	2,260	367,161	1,235	46,849
1930[b]	784	*	45.9	*	*	1,220	447,322	708	26,876
1940	849	*	36.4	*	*	1,843	333,438	453	23,762
1944[c]	1,139	50.8	43.0	*	*	2,824	737,246	910	95,549
1950	nd	nd	38.9	*	*	1,354	591,550	488	31,790
1960	1,453	55	30.4	0.6	*	1,241	572,309	326	21,258
1970	1,820	67	27.2	1.3	2.4	1,485	764,809	284	10,740
1980	2,175	79	22.6	1.7	3.1	1,492	918,621	300	10,995
1990	2,755	88	21.4	nd	6.2	1,425	1,033,969	348	12,095
2000	2,923	93	27.8	nd	9.2	1,738	1,465,960	335	14,900

[a]1920 is the pre–World War II peak for passenger-miles.

[b]1930 is the pre–World War II peak for freight ton-miles.

[c]1944 is the World War II peak for freight ton-miles and the all-time peak for passenger-miles.

**Passenger data from 1990 and 2000 are from Amtrak and APTA.

Figure 4. Freight Traffic, Millions of Tons Originated and Millions of Ton-Miles, U.S. Railroads

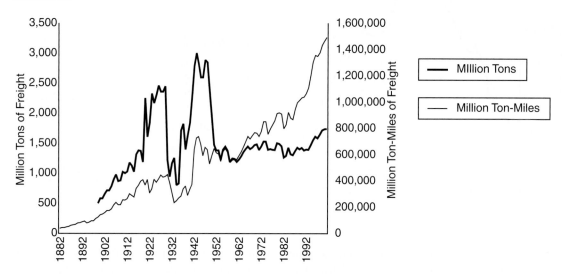

much more dramatic decline. Ignoring automobiles (which throughout this period always constitute at least 80 percent of the total), railroad passenger traffic has declined from almost 80 percent to just over 3 percent of the total (Tables 5A–5B and Figure 7). Again, setting automobiles aside, the growth of airline travel is entirely responsible for this decline.

Railroad finance is complex, and its complexity is compounded by the inconsistency of the data over the reporting period. Therefore, only basic data are reported here. The strongest pattern is the steady increase of most categories through the sequence, with jumps for the two world wars (Table 6). Ratios, however, can

somewhat compensate for the effect of inflation. Two interesting relationships are the percentage of total revenue that is devoted to covering operating expenses and that contributed by passenger traffic (Figure 8). The percentage of revenue, while rising and falling over the short term, shows a clear trend for increase to the present: clearly, railroads are operating on a thinner margin. Other patterns include the very sharp jump (representing a drop in profitability) that begins in 1917 when the U.S. government took over the railroads and the sharp drop (representing a jump in profitability) corresponding to World War II, during which the railroads were not taken over by the government. Finally,

Figure 5. Passenger Traffic, Millions of Passengers and Millions of Passenger-Miles, U.S. Railroads

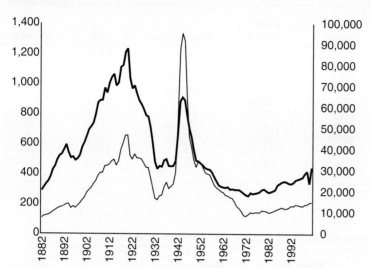

Table 3A. Commodities Shipped, United States (millions of tons)

Year	Total	Agriculture	Animals and Products	Mine Products	Forest Products	Manufactured	LCL	Miscellaneous*
1911	866	82	23	484	79	163	35	*
1920	1,256	111	27	712	101	252	53	*
1930	1,154	111	23	643	69	278	30	*
1940	1,009	89	15	570	58	262	15	*
1950	1,354	129	14	747	79	374	11	*

*There is no miscellaneous category reported for this period.

Table 3B. Commodities Shipped, United States (millions of carloads)

Year	Total	Agriculture	Animals and Products**	Mine Products	Forest Products	Manufactured	LCL	Miscellaneous
1960	30.4	2.8	.2	7.9	2.0	***	1.8	15.7
1970	27.2	4.6	*	10.5	3.2	5.0	0.05	3.8
1980	22.6	3.6	*	9.7	2.5	4.0	0.01	2.7
1990	21.4	3.0	*	8.2	1.4	4.1	0.00	4.7
2000	27.8	2.8	*	9.1	1.3	5.6	0.00	8.9

**Animals and animal products are not reported separately for this period.

***Manufactured is not reported separately for this period.

there is another sharp increase in the percentage beginning during the 1970s, which corresponds to the precarious situation that preceded the implementation of the Staggers Act of 1980. The percentage of revenue contributed by passenger traffic shows a clear decline during the reporting period, with a brief jump during World War II, from nearly a third of revenue to only a few percent at the time Amtrak took over. Interestingly, the two relationships appear to be negatively correlated: as the cost of running the railroads increased, it became increasingly difficult to make a profit from passenger rail service.

Table 3C. Commodities Shipped, U.S. Railroads, Percentage of Total (tons, 1911–1950/carloads, 1960–2000)

Year	Agriculture	Animals and Products	Mine Products	Forest Products	Manufactured	LCL	Miscellaneous
1911	9.44%	2.64%	55.85%	9.16%	18.86%	4.06%	*
1920	8.83%	2.12%	56.73%	8.03%	20.06%	4.24%	*
1930	9.60%	2.01%	55.72%	6.02%	24.09%	2.57%	*
1940	8.80%	1.53%	56.49%	5.77%	25.96%	1.46%	*
1950	9.54%	1.06%	55.15%	5.82%	27.63%	0.80%	*
1960	9.15%	0.85%	26.05%	6.41%	*	5.94%	51.60%
1970	16.90%	*	38.72%	11.91%	18.46%	0.17%	13.83%
1980	15.99%	*	43.10%	11.20%	17.77%	0.05%	11.88%
1990	14.00%	*	38.13%	6.50%	19.21%	0.00%	22.15%
2000	10.14%	*	32.87%	4.61%	20.23%	0.00%	32.15%

Table 4A. Commercial Traffic, Freight, United States (millions of ton-miles)

Year	Rail	Great Lakes	Rivers and Canals	Motor Trucks	Oil Pipelines	Air Carriers
1930	389,648	77,366	9,087	20,345	27,900	4
1940	379,161	87,593	22,412	51,003	67,270	14
1950	596,940	111,687	51,657	172,860	129,175	318
1960	579,130	99,468	120,785	285,483	228,626	778
1970	776,000	117,000	190,000	400,000	415,000	3,400
1980	932,000	113,000	307,000	565,000	575,000	5,000
1990	1,080,000	81,000	380,000	735,000	585,000	10,000
2000	1,534,000	97,000	409,000	1,074,000	617,000	16,000

Table 4B. Commercial Traffic, Freight, United States, Percentage of Total (millions of ton-miles)

Year	Rail	Great Lakes	Rivers and Canals	Motor Trucks	Oil Pipelines	Air Carriers
1930	74.3%	14.8%	1.7%	3.9%	5.3%	0.0%
1940	62.4%	14.4%	3.7%	8.4%	11.1%	0.0%
1950	56.2%	10.5%	4.9%	16.3%	12.2%	0.0%
1960	44.1%	7.6%	9.2%	21.7%	17.4%	0.1%
1970	40.8%	6.2%	10.0%	21.0%	21.8%	0.2%
1980	37.3%	4.5%	12.3%	22.6%	23.0%	0.2%
1990	37.6%	2.8%	13.2%	25.6%	20.4%	0.3%
2000	41.0%	2.6%	10.9%	28.7%	16.5%	0.4%

Figure 6. Commercial Traffic, Freight, by Mode, Percentage of Total, U.S. Railroads

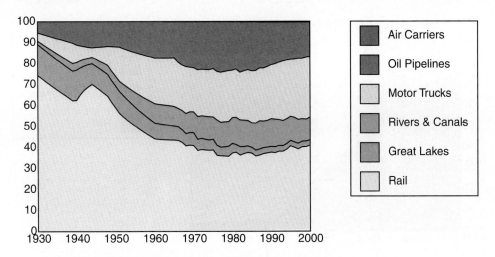

Table 5A. Commercial Traffic, Passengers, United States (millions of passenger-miles)

Year**	Rail	Inland Waterways	Buses	Air Carriers	Automobile
1930	29,276	2,800	7,100	73	160,900
1940	24,766	1,317	11,613	1,041	nd
1950	32,481	1,190	26,436	10,072	402,843
1960	21,574	2,688	19,896	33,958	706,079
1970	11,000	4,000	25,000	114,000	1,026,000
1980	11,400	4,000	26,900	202,000	1,263,400
1988	12,800	0	23,100	334,200	1,586,000

**AAR ceased reporting passenger commercial traffic after 1988.

Table 5B. Commercial Traffic, Passengers, United States, Percentage of Total (millions of passenger-miles)

Year**	Rail	Inland Waterways	Buses	Air Carriers	Automobile
1930	14.6%	1.4%	3.5%	0.0%	80.4%
1940	63.9%	3.4%	30.0%	2.7%	nd
1950	6.9%	0.3%	5.6%	2.1%	85.2%
1960	2.8%	0.3%	2.5%	4.3%	90.0%
1970	0.9%	0.3%	2.1%	9.7%	86.9%
1980	0.8%	0.3%	1.8%	13.4%	83.8%
1988	0.7%	0.0%	1.2%	17.1%	81.1%

**AAR ceased reporting passenger commercial traffic after 1988.

Figure 7. Commercial Traffic, Passengers, by Mode, Percentage of Total, U.S. Railroads (automobiles excluded)

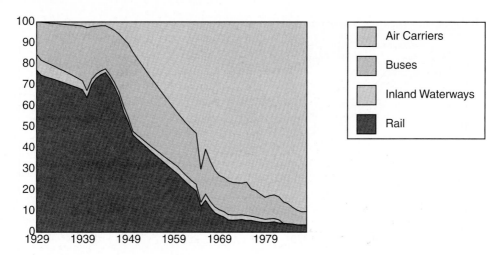

Table 6. Revenue and Expenses, United States (millions of dollars)

Year**	Operating Expenses	Payroll	Total Revenue	Net Earnings	Freight Revenue	Passenger Revenue
1851	*	*	40	*	*	*
1855	43	*	84	*	*	*
1861	*	*	130	*	*	*
1863	*	*	190	*	*	*
1867	229	*	334	105	*	*
1871	*	*	403	142	294	109
1880	*	*	614	256	468	148
1885	499	*	765	266	510	201
1890	*	*	1,052	342	735	272
1900	961	577	1,487	481	1,049	324
1910	1,882	1,144	2,812	805	1,926	629
1920	5,828	3,682	6,178	12	4,421	1,305
1930	3,994	2,551	5,281	874	4,145	731
1940	3,089	1,964	4,297	691	3,537	417
1950	7,135	4,594	9,473	1,055	7,817	813
1960	7,565	4,894	9,514	584	8,025	640
1970	9,660	5,711	11,992	486	10,922	420
1980	26,250	11,318	28,103	1,339	26,200	807
1990	24,652	8,654	28,370	2,648	27,471	nd
2000	29,040	9,623	34,102	3,924	33,083	nd

**Reporting before 1900 is irregular. The table shows the best available data, 1850–1900.

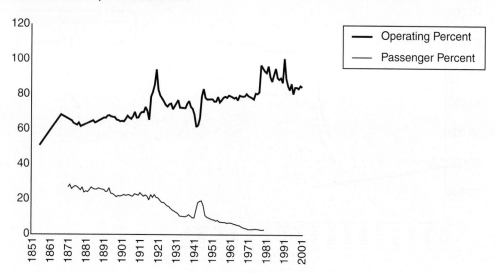

Figure 8. Operating Expenses and Passenger Revenue as a Percentage of Total Revenue, U.S. Railroads

Railroads in Canada

Canada's first railroad, the Champlain & St. Lawrence, began service in 1836. Many others soon followed. The first Canadian transcontinental railroad was inaugurated in 1885. A significant difference between Canadian and U.S. railroads is the degree of government involvement in their development. From the formation of the dominion in 1867, the Canadian government took an active role in the development and management of some of Canada's railroads.

Canadian railroads show a developmental pattern similar to that of U.S. railroads. There is a rapid buildup of the physical plant, although neither as rapid nor as large as in the United States. Then there is an eventual decline, although it starts later and is not as dramatic (Table 7, Figures 9–11). Also as in the United States, the decline represents a combination of factors (competition with other modes, overdevelopment, and increased efficiency); most interesting is the much lesser degree of overbuilding. This is probably due to the greater level of governmental involvement (with some exceptions), as opposed to the unrestrained capitalist competition of U.S. railroads.

Traffic patterns in Canada are a bit different also (apart from the lower overall volume). Although freight traffic (both tons originated and ton-miles) has climbed steadily, the impact of the world wars is much less pronounced; it

Table 7. Railroad Plant and Personnel, Canada

Year	Track Mileage	Line Mileage	Total Locomotives	Steam Locomotives**	Diesel Locomotives	Electric Locomotives	Freight Cars	Passenger Cars	Employees
1836		16							
1840		16							
1850		66							
1860		2,065							
1870		2,617							
1880		6,858	1,157				24,079	879	
1890		13,151	1,771				49,356	1,493	
1900		17,657	2,282				64,979	2,166	
1910	31,429	24,730	4,079	4,079			119,713	4,320	123,768
1920	51,174	38,805	6,030	6,014		16	224,489	6,557	185,177
1930	56,585	42,047	5,451	5,414		37	215,027	7,346	158,500
1940	56,533	42,565	4,308	4,272		36	160,697	6,267	122,300
1950	57,997	42,979	4,655	4,272	350	33	175,597	6,338	171,200
1960	59,193	44,029	3,752	403	3,308	41	191,553	5,119	145,100
1970	59,629	43,983	3,417	0	3,399	18	188,737	2,801	116,053
1980	57,884	41,581	4,167	0	4,153	14	179,139	1,580	nd
1990	nd	35,299	3,434	0	nd	nd	119,125	539	6,5637
2000	nd	28,889	3,115	0	nd	nd	104,000	450	41,118

**Sources report 0 steam locomotives after 1960.

Figure 9. Line and Track Mileage, Canada

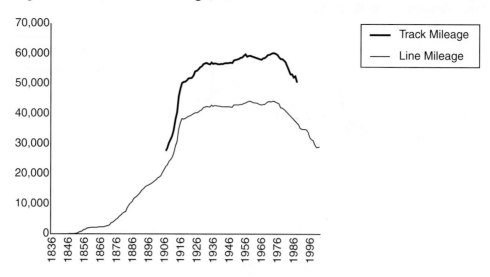

Figure 10. Equipment, Locomotives by Type, Canada

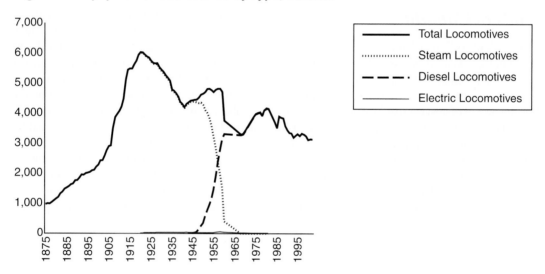

Figure 11. Equipment, Freight and Passenger Cars, Canada

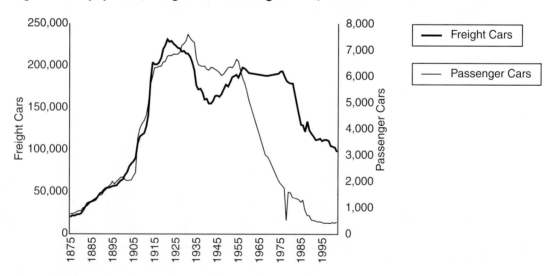

seems that instead of wartime peaks, there was a Depression-era drop between the wars. The correlation between tons of freight originated and ton-miles of freight also is much stronger, which suggests that unlike the United States, haul length has not increased with respect to the tons of freight originated. The passenger traffic pattern, on the other hand, more closely resembles that of the United States (again, apart from the lower overall volume). The biggest factors affecting passenger traffic were the wartime booms and the postwar decline (Table 8, Figures 12–13).

Unfortunately, the reporting on commodities shipped on Canadian railroads was highly variable throughout the reporting period; consistent data were only found for the period 1875–1970 (after which there are substantial gaps and changing recording units). Products of mines were not separately listed until the beginning of the twentieth century, while firewood (here summarized under forest

products) was a separate category up to the beginning of the twentieth century. Animal and agricultural products both decline in significance throughout the recording period (Table 9, Figure 14). No consistent data on the volume of commercial traffic were collected.

The revenue and expense data show a similar, if somewhat more precarious, situation to that in the United States (Table 10, Figure 15). For most of the reporting period the percentage of revenue used to cover operating expenses is above 80 percent and frequently above 90 percent. There is an abrupt spike in the percentage during World War I and a drop during World War II, although neither is as pronounced. Also similar is the percentage of total revenue contributed by passenger traffic over time. At the beginning of the reporting period passenger revenue is over a third of the total, but from this high point it declines steadily, with only a slight jump during World War II, to its present insignificant levels.

Table 8. Railroad Traffic, Canada

Year	Millions of Tons Originated	Millions of Ton-Miles	Millions of Passengers	Millions of Passenger-Miles
1875	6	*	5	*
1880	10	*	6	*
1890	21	*	13	*
1900	36	*	22	*
1910	75	15,712	36	2,467
1920	127	31,894	51	3,523
1930	115	29,605	35	2,423
1940	110	37,898	22	2,177
1950	164	55,538	31	2,816
1960	179	65,445	20	2,264
1970	261	108,171	24	2,270
1980	nd	nd	nd	nd
1990	211	160,000	4	839
2000	328	221,000	4	954

Figure 12. Freight Traffic, Millions of Tons Originated and Millions of Ton-Miles, Canada

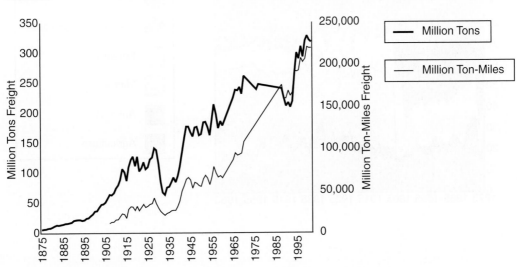

Figure 13. Passenger Traffic, Millions of Passengers and Millions of Passenger-Miles, Canada

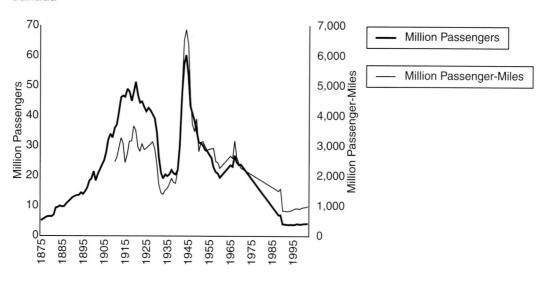

Table 9. Commodities Shipped, Canada (tons)

Year	Agriculture	Animals	Mines	Forest	Manufacture and Miscellaneous	LCL
1875	692,000	157,000		816,000	1,171,000	
1880	1,922,000	154,000		1,065,000	3,221,000	
1890	4,220,000	872,000		3,986,000	11,588,000	
1900	6,482,000	861,000		6,930,000	21,673,000	
1910	12,891,000	2,765,000	26,152,000	13,070,000	19,605,000	
1920	23,306,000	3,801,000	45,077,000	22,280,000	27,825,000	
1930	19,664,000	2,520,000	35,695,000	12,379,000	32,471,000	
1940	19,870,000	2,357,000	36,822,000	10,876,000	28,024,000	
1950	24,376,000	2,302,000	55,748,000	15,830,000	45,961,000	
1960	26,666,000	1,695,000	65,541,000	14,960,000	48,286,000	
1970	24,449,824	1,109,576	85,875,023	22,865,373	73,135,456	160,196

Figure 14. Commodities Shipped, Percentage of Total, Canada

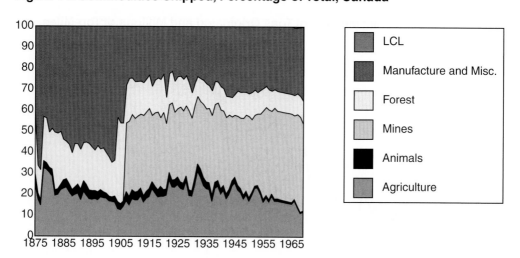

Table 10. Income and Operating Expense, Canada (Canadian dollars)

Year	Operating Expenses	Payroll	Total Revenue	Net Earnings	Freight Revenue	Passenger Revenue
1875	15	0	20	4	12	6
1880	17	0	24	7	16	7
1890	33	0	47	14	30	14
1900	48	0	71	23	46	19
1910	120	67	174	54	116	46
1920	478	291	492	14	341	103
1930	381	249	454	74	323	67
1940	335	197	429	94	334	43
1950	834	477	959	125	769	79
1960	1,051	632	1,152	101	993	69
1970	1,574	929	1,680	106	1,429	64
1980	5,003	0	5,334	331	0	0
1990	6,215	2,708	6,396	181	5,816	151
2000	6,455	2,498	8,031	1,576	7,231	323

Figure 15. Operating Expenses and Passenger Revenue as a Percentage of Total Revenue, Canada

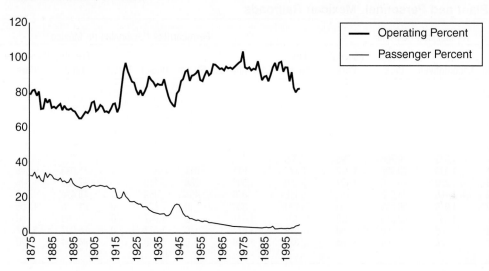

Railroads in Mexico

The concession for the first railway in Mexico was granted in 1837, but it took another three and a half decades, with the turmoil of foreign invasion (by both the United States and France) and additional concessions, before service between Veracruz and Mexico City was finally inaugurated in 1873. Subsequently, additional regional railroads were inaugurated, servicing various parts of Mexico and connecting the Gulf and Pacific coasts. In 1937 nationalization and integration of the railroads under Ferrocarriles Nacionales de México was initiated, a process that continued until 1986, at which point Ferrocarriles Nacionales de México controlled nearly all the railroads in Mexico. Finally, in 1995 the Mexican Constitution was amended to allow the privatization of the railroads, and Ferrocarriles Nacionales de México was disbanded.

Data on Mexican railways from the end of the nineteenth century and the first three decades of the twentieth century are sketchy at best—not surprisingly, considering that the Mexican Revolution (1910–1920) caused considerable disruption to the country. However, beginning in the 1930s, especially with the creation of Ferrocarriles Nacionales de México, their quality and consistency greatly improve.

The data on physical plant show that Mexican railroads never developed any significant overcapacity and continue to be much smaller in all measures than their northern counterparts (Table 11, Figures 16–18). Hardly any line mileage has been abandoned, and much of the abandonment has been offset by new construction. The number of locomotives and freight cars has dropped slightly in the last decade, but this is in stark contrast to the patterns for the United States and Canada, where the

Table 11. Plant and Personnel, Mexican Railroads

	All Mexican Railroads				Ferrocarriles Nacionales de México							
Year	Line Mileage	Locomotives	Freight Cars	Passenger Cars	Line Mileage	Locomotives	Steam	Diesel	Electric	Freight Cars	Passenger Cars	Employees
1873	334	*	*	*	*	*	*	*	*	*	*	*
1880	597	*	*	*	*	*	*	*	*	*	*	*
1890	5,915	*	*	*	*	*	*	*	*	*	*	*
1900	8,246	*	*	*	*	*	*	*	*	*	*	*
1910	12,244	*	*	*	*	*	*	*	*	*	*	*
1921	12,639	*	*	*	*	*	*	*	*	*	*	*
1930	14,474	1,623	20,268	899	7,085	*	*	*	*	*	*	45,561
1940	14,247	1,333	20,302	1,222	7,277	911	911	*	*	15,039	695	44,464
1950	14,466	1,229	20,756	1,127	8,259	1,006	888	118		17,329	648	57,993
1960	14,489	1,158	23,570	785	8,118	876	407	459	10	18,424	680	53,983
1970	15,170	1,075	26,856	nd	8,729	830	0	821	9	21,178	1,006	58,880
1980	15,816	1,635	48,613	813	12,401	1,647	0	1,647	0	nd	nd	78,838
1990	nd	nd	nd	nd	12,618	1,677	0	1,677	0	46,602	1,427	83,290
2000	nd	nd	nd	nd	12,826	1,446	0	1,446	0	34,764	220	15,184

Figure 16. Line Mileage, Mexico

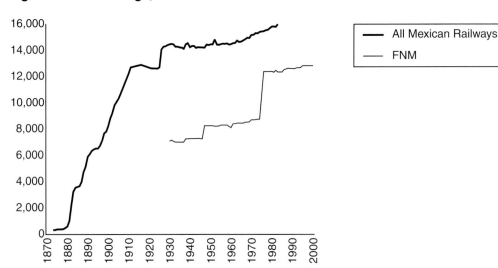

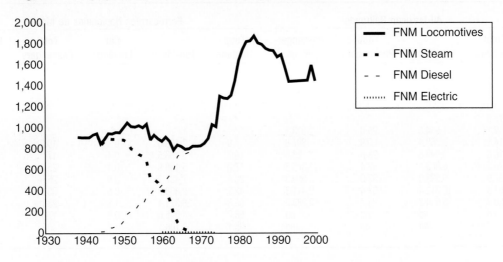

Figure 17. Equipment, Locomotives by Type, Mexico

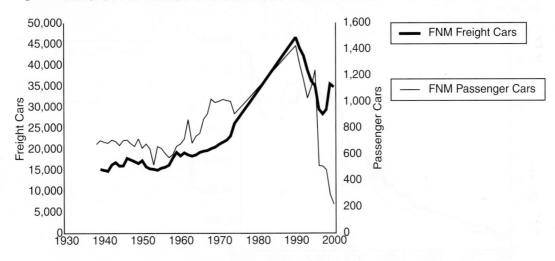

Figure 18. Equipment, Freight and Passenger Cars, Mexico

numbers of locomotives and freight cars have been in decline since the second decade of the twentieth century. Even the pattern for passenger cars is distinct, although it ultimately has the same result; their numbers had been growing fairly steadily until the 1990s, then abruptly dropped (reflecting the almost complete abandonment of passenger service after privatization). The recent drop in the numbers of locomotives and cars is almost certainly the result of consolidation after the privatization of Ferrocarriles Nacionales de México. A final major difference between Mexican railroads and their northern counterparts is the number of employees; unlike the United States and Canada, where the number of railroad employees has declined steadily since the second decade of the twentieth century, the number of employees of Mexican railroads continued to grow until the 1990s. Then, with privatization, employee numbers were slashed by over 80 percent. This is closely equivalent to the proportionate drop from the high points for the

United States and Canada to their present levels, suggesting that in a single decade Mexican railroads adopted labor management practices that were developed over an 80-year period in the north.

Traffic data for Mexican railroads also differ, although, in the end, results are essentially the same (Table 12, Figures 19–20). Overall, freight traffic (measured in both tons originated and ton-miles) has steadily increased, with only one drop during the 1980s, from which it rapidly rebounded after privatization. Passenger traffic (measured in both passengers and passenger-miles) fluctuated considerably between 1940 and the 1960s, but was generally increasing. It then suffered a sharp drop, but quickly rebounded, particularly in terms of passenger-miles. Although actual passengers began a terminal decline in the early 1980s, passenger-miles continued to increase into the late 1980s, suggesting that average trip length must have increased considerably. This was probably due to a shift

Table 12. Traffic, Mexican Railroads (millions of units)

| Year | All Mexican Railroads | | | | Ferrocarriles Nacionales de México | | | | |
	Total Tonnage	Ton-Miles	Total Passengers	Passenger-Miles	Total Tonnage	Ton-Miles	Car Loadings	Total Passengers	Passenger-Miles
1873	0.2	*	*	*	*	*	*	*	*
1880	0.3	*	*	*	*	*	*	*	*
1890	3.0	*	*	*	*	*	*	*	*
1900	8.3	*	*	*	*	*	*	*	*
1909	15.9	*	*	*	*	*	*	*	*
1921	9.1	1,554.5	25.0	1,323.3	*	*	*	*	*
1930	14.3	2,768.4	20.9	897.8	7.9	2,103.0	0.3	10.2	560.4
1940	16.6	3,948.8	28.0	1,153.8	10.7	3,163.5	0.4	17.2	745.3
1950	25.3	6,803.1	32.4	1,875.3	17.0	5,108.9	0.4	25.3	1,378.0
1960	37.9	9,593.0	32.6	2,559.3	26.4	7,437.1	0.5	26.9	1,932.8
1970	51.6	15,812.4	37.4	2,811.3	42.2	12,398.2	0.6	33.2	2,129.8
1980	80.3	28,654.2	23.7	3,283.5	66.8	28,311.1	1.2	23.7	3,282.9
1990	nd	nd	nd	nd	56.2	24,945.6	0.9	17.1	3,308.3
2000	nd	nd	nd	nd	85.1	33,108.1	nd	0.3	50.8

Figure 19. Freight Traffic, Millions of Tons Originated and Millions of Ton-Miles, Mexico

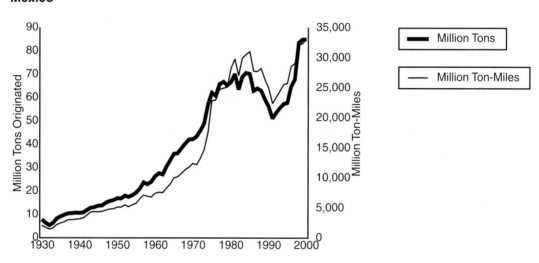

Figure 20. Passenger Traffic, Millions of Passengers and Millions of Passenger-Miles, Mexico

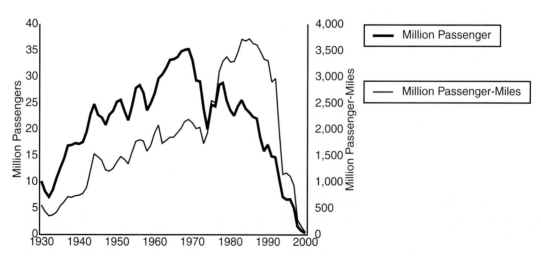

in passenger service away from short-haul to more intercity service. Nevertheless, the all-but-total abandonment of passenger service after privatization brought the era of passenger rail in Mexico to an end (although this process had already begun under Ferrocarriles Nacionales de México).

The commodities shipped by Mexican railways gradually came to be dominated by industrial goods, which constitute nearly half the present total (Tables 13A–13B,

Figure 21). All other categories with the exception of agricultural products (which have consistently constituted between 20 and 30 percent of the total) have steadily declined in their overall proportion of the total (although minerals, petroleum, and inorganic goods have all increased in actual volume by at least a factor of four). Consistent data on overall commercial traffic and on railroad expenses and revenue could not be found, so they are not reported here.

Table 13A. Commodities, Ferrocarriles Nacionales de México (millions of tons)

Year	Agricultural	Animals and Products	Minerals	Petroleum and Derivatives	Inorganic	Industrial	LCL
1938	3.0	0.3	2.0	1.3	1.2	0.8	0.6
1940	2.9	0.3	2.1	1.4	1.4	1.0	0.6
1950	4.2	0.2	4.0	2.7	2.6	2.0	0.4
1960	5.3	0.1	6.4	4.1	4.0	5.7	0.1
1970	8.3	0.2	11.1	5.3	5.8	11.0	0.1
1980	14.1	0.2	15.7	5.2	7.8	22.3	0.0
1990	12.7	0.2	9.9	4.0	7.0	21.9	0.0
2000	23.1	0.3	9.9	4.4	5.5	37.5	0.0

Table 13B. Commodities, Ferrocarriles Nacionales de México, Percentage of Total (short tons)

Year	Agriculture	Animals and Products	Minerals	Petroleum	Inorganic	Industrial	LCL
1938	29.89%	2.68%	19.89%	13.30%	12.49%	8.49%	5.96%
1940	27.58%	2.76%	20.68%	13.95%	13.47%	9.42%	5.40%
1950	25.17%	1.31%	23.76%	16.03%	15.47%	12.20%	2.09%
1960	20.26%	0.57%	24.50%	15.52%	15.37%	21.84%	0.43%
1970	19.63%	0.50%	26.19%	12.54%	13.75%	26.08%	0.25%
1980	21.21%	0.33%	23.58%	7.75%	11.69%	33.53%	0.00%
1990	22.56%	0.39%	17.67%	7.15%	12.44%	39.02%	0.00%
2000	28.38%	0.38%	12.16%	5.40%	6.76%	45.94%	0.00%

Figure 21. Commodities Shipped, Percentage of Total, Mexico

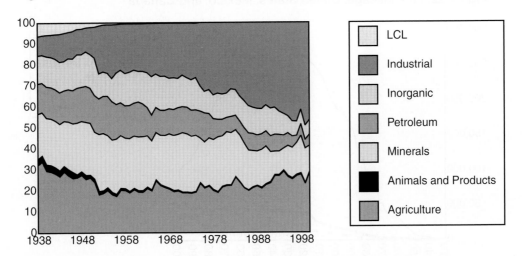

Discussion

Many factors affect the development and survival of a national rail network: land area to be covered, population density, the nature of the economy, availability of capital for infrastructure development, the cost of infrastructure development, competition from other modes of transportation, and degree of governmental regulation and/or involvement, to name just a few. When one compares the United States, Canada, and Mexico, U.S. railroads dwarf the others by at least a factor of five (Figure 22).

Conditions in the United States during the last two-thirds of the nineteenth century were extremely favorable for the development of a large national rail network. It was a large country with a relatively high population density (compared with Canada, for instance). It had an expanding, industrializing, competitive, capitalist economy with available capital. There was very little competition from other modes of transportation (canals). Finally, there was no direct involvement by the government, and consequently no centralized planning (although government regulation, which was a factor, can certainly be viewed as a restraining force). As a result, the United States developed a tremendous excess capacity in its railroad infrastructure in an atmosphere reminiscent of the "irrational exuberance" characteristic of a financial bubble (so described by Alan Greenspan in 1996).

In part, this excess capacity can be seen as a consequence of the railroads' dominant position in the nineteenth-century transportation network. Nearly every demographic center, every point of origin, and every major destination for freight had to be within easy travel distance of a railroad (with the modest exception of centers integrated with the marine transport network, although the two were not mutually exclusive) if it was to participate in the national economy. But the excess capacity went beyond merely providing comprehensive cover-

age: competing railroads built multiple, redundant routes, with the consequence that some parts of the country were covered with a veritable spiderweb of railroad tracks.

If competing modes of overland transport had not developed, the network's excess capacity might have been sustainable, although it would certainly have depressed the overall profitability of the rail system. But in the face of growing competition from private automobiles, buses, airliners, and, most important, trucks, the excess capacity was highly unsustainable. As a result, the national rail network began an extended process of decline in the second decade of the twentieth century, and even now, almost 90 years later, the decline may not be complete.

Neither Canada nor Mexico could have built such a large rail network, nor would they have needed to. Canada's population density is too low, and Mexico's land area too small. However, other factors prevented the same process from happening on a smaller scale. In Canada, although the same capitalist forces were at work, the early involvement of the government in the railroads' development contributed a degree of central planning that helped reduce redundancy in the network, so the post-boom decline was not as serious. Mexico, for its part, was still in the grips of a feudal-colonial economy for much of the nineteenth century, the effects of which it is still recovering from. Mexico's economy lacked the capital for industrial development, and this limited the development of railroads to the extent that they may not yet have reached their full potential.

In the United States the prolonged decline of the railroad industry and the struggle for survival of the most competitive have done incalculable harm to the industry (that is, beyond the decline itself). Many companies struggled for years to survive, only to ultimately fail or merge with rivals. Their failure in turn harmed the survivors by forcing them to undergo years or decades of

Figure 22. Line Mileage, United States, Mexico, and Canada

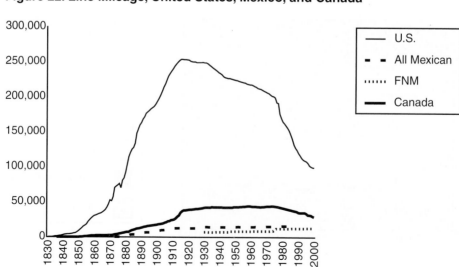

needless competition to outlast their doomed rivals. A great deal of potential productivity was wasted in this lengthy bout of economic Darwinism. In an article in *Trains* George W. Hilton makes the point that some railroads were not worth saving for this reason (January 1971). He uses the example of the North Western, whose physical plant was so hopelessly redundant that he believed that it should either be abandoned or sold off to more viable railroads. The North Western was finally absorbed by the Union Pacific in 1995.

Although this battle for survival left many casualties, it also resulted in some impressive innovations. New and enhanced technologies have played an important role in the railroads' survival by contributing to the efficiency of operations. A good example is the process of dieselization, which began shortly after the decline started. In less than two decades U.S. railroads converted from nearly all steam locomotives to nearly all diesel (Figure 23). The process started slightly later in Canada and Mexico, but was accomplished with the same rapidity. Another factor that has improved efficiency is the increasing capacity of both locomotives (to haul more and larger cars) and freight cars (to hold more freight) (Figure 24). At the same time, the fuel efficiency of locomotives (in terms of ton-miles of freight per unit of fuel consumed) has markedly increased: today's locomotives are twice as efficient as they were only four decades ago (Figure 25). Finally, although this is not directly apparent in the data, we must also consider the mechanization of time- and labor-intensive tasks, particularly the loading and unloading of cars: the less time and labor spent putting trains together and taking them apart, the more time this infrastructure can spend generating revenue.

Although the preceding factors can be thought of as

Figure 23. Dieselization, Percentage of Fleet Dieselized, United States, Mexico, and Canada

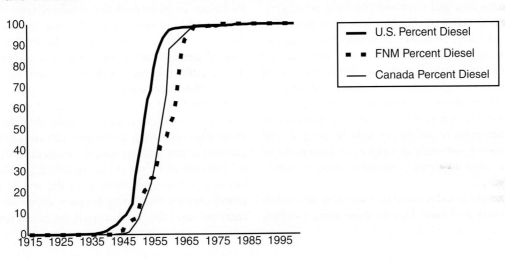

Figure 24. Freight Capacity, Tons of Freight per Train and per Car, U.S. Railroads

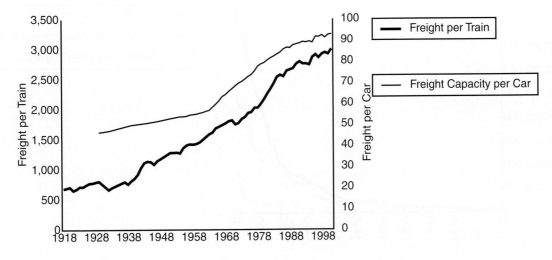

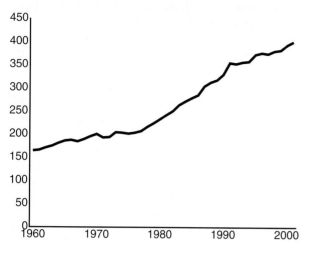

mechanical contributions to efficiency, producing linear increase, improvements in the management of both physical plant and labor through communications and information technology and improved planning, scheduling, and personnel management contribute even more. The efficiency of labor, measured in terms of ton-miles of freight per employee, increased at a very slow rate for most of the twentieth century, but in the last several decades for the United States and Canada, and since the 1990s in Mexico, the increase has been exponential (Figure 26). The efficiency of the physical plant, measured in terms of ton-miles of freight per mile of line (and the same is true for ton-miles of freight per locomotive or freight car), also shows an exponential increase in efficiency (Figure 27).

By any measure, today's railroads are more productive than they have ever been. Despite these gains, however, they are making less money than they ever have on their primary service: freight transport. The data on revenue and expense have one obvious, clear, dominant trend: over time, the numbers go up. This is largely, although not necessarily entirely, due to inflation. We can compensate for the declining value of the dollar over time by using an index to convert the actual dollars (actual dollar amounts from any given year in a sequence) to their equivalent in dollars for a specific reference year (chained dollars). This is analogous to using a conversion factor to compare the value of international currencies in terms of a reference currency. This is far from perfect (indices are typically based on consumer goods rather than industrial materials and services), and it gets more equivocal the further back in time one goes. Furthermore, it does not take into account differences in the real cost of goods, which can change over time: an example would be pocket calculators, which are both relatively and absolutely cheaper today than they were when they were first introduced because of economies of scale in their production that are available today. Nevertheless, while not perfect, the index should give us an idea of at least the order of magnitude of the change in the profitability of railroads over time.

Railroads' net earnings for the past 120 years show a great deal of fluctuation in actual dollars, but a general upward trend. Chained 2000 dollars (converting actual dollars in the sequence to their equivalent value in 2000 dollars), however, show that, although more profitable today than they have been for the past few decades, railroads are still making less money today than they have for about nine out of ten of the past 120 years (Figure 28). Looking at this another way, if we calculate the revenue per ton-mile of freight (in actual dollars), we find that it has changed relatively little since the end of the nineteenth century, fluctuating between about one and two cents per ton-mile. If we convert the actual revenue per

Figure 26. Employee Efficiency, Ton-Miles per Employee, United States, Canada, and Mexico

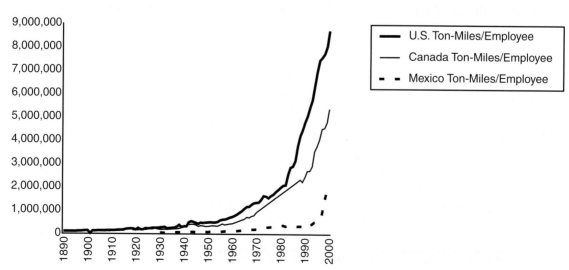

Figure 27. Infrastructure Efficiency, Millions of Ton-Miles per Mile of Line, United States, Canada, and Mexico

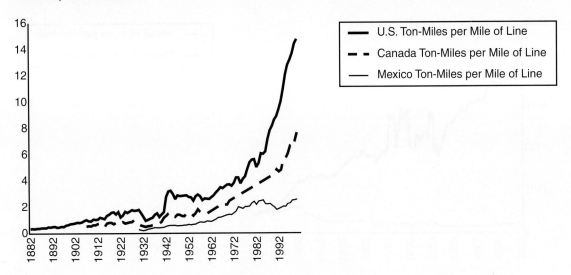

Figure 28. Profitability, Actual Earnings (net revenue), Millions of Dollars, and Inflation-Adjusted Earnings (chained 2000 dollars), U.S. Railroads

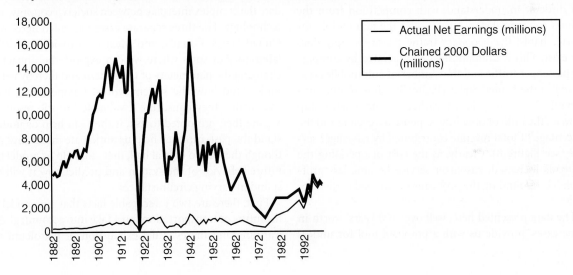

ton-mile to the value of money in the year 2000 (chained 2000 dollars) using McCusker's index, we see that, relative to the value of money in 2000, revenue per ton-mile has been steadily declining throughout the period. In terms of today's dollars, railroads today are making about a tenth of what they did 100 years ago per ton-mile (Figure 29). Although this comparison is inexact, it is clear and dramatic enough that we can conclude that there has been a serious decline in railroad income. Clearly, with the revenue ton-mile (the railroads' bread and butter, so to speak) so unremunerative, the vastly enhanced efficiency of operations is a vital necessity.

A final element of the decline of the railroad is the nearly total abandonment of passenger service in the United States, Canada, and Mexico. In the United States

and Canada passenger service made a significant contribution to revenue (about one-third) at the end of the nineteenth century and still 20 percent by the end of the second decade of the twentieth. By the third decade of the twentieth century, however, passenger revenue began to decline, despite a brief jump during World War II, to an insignificant percentage. Ridership figures tell a somewhat different story. In both the United States and Canada there was a postwar slump: in Canada this continued to the present, but in the United States ridership figures have been climbing steadily, albeit modestly, since the early 1970s. Again, the majority of this increase is due to commuter traffic, but even Amtrak is experiencing increased ridership. We saw that with freight, the railroads' key to survival was essentially to take advantage of

Figure 29. Income, Actual Revenue per Ton-Mile, Dollars, and Inflation-Adjusted Revenue per Ton-Mile (chained 2000 dollars), U.S. Railroads

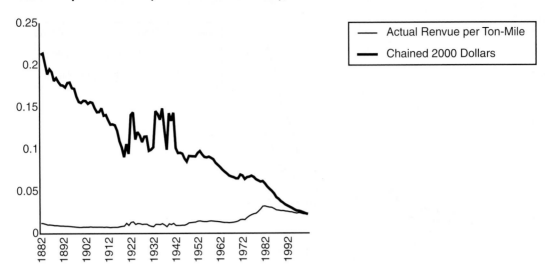

— Actual Renvue per Ton-Mile
— Chained 2000 Dollars

economies of scale made possible by greater efficiency. This has not been possible with passenger traffic, and it is not difficult to understand, with competition from the airlines for long-distance travel and the automobile for shorter hauls; the necessary traffic density simply does not exist. This is dramatically demonstrated by comparing passenger traffic and the number of automobiles registered in the United States (Figure 30). But another important factor, mentioned earlier, is the relationship between the ratio of operating expense to revenue and the percentage of total revenue contributed by passenger service (see Figure 8). Clearly, as the cost of operating the railroads increased, passenger service became less profitable, compounding the problems mentioned earlier.

The data presented here, well over 100 years' worth in some cases, provide us with a powerful tool for under-

standing the development of railroads in North America. In their aggregate, the annual operating statistics elucidate the complex interplay between society, economy, and technology. The three separate cases presented here—the United States, Canada, and Mexico—provide us with a laboratory of sorts where we can explore the impact of changing the parameters of the system and thereby better understand how the system works. I hope that I have shown that they constitute a valuable historic resource. We are then prompted to ask, if they can help us understand the past, can they help us anticipate the future? Although there is no crystal ball, they can help us model the future behavior of the system and predict how it will respond in varying circumstances.

First, there are two inescapable facts that any model of the future of transportation must take into account: global warming and the eventual exhaustion of petroleum re-

Figure 30. Automobile Ownership versus Rail Ridership, United States

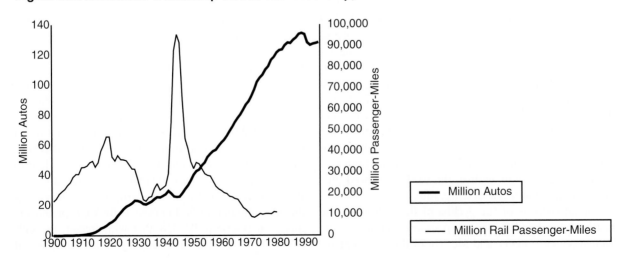

— Million Autos
— Million Rail Passenger-Miles

serves. Many still resist the acceptance of these issues, but the international scientific community has left no doubt.

In light of these facts (and without them as well), railroads will continue to play a vital role in freight transportation. The incredible levels of efficiency, particularly fuel efficiency, that they have developed in the past several decades will be increasingly advantageous to them as fuel prices rise: railroads can carry more freight per unit of fuel. Even should cheap alternative fuels be developed in the near future, railroads will still be the most economic option for high-bulk, long-distance transport. The same argument holds for greenhouse-gas emissions: more freight carried per unit of fuel also means more freight carried per unit of greenhouse gas. Even if cheap alternative fuels are developed, greenhouse-gas emissions will continue to be a critical issue.

Although the efficiency of the railroad industry is to its advantage, the narrow profitability of the industry perhaps places it in a somewhat more vulnerable position than its rivals. Rising fuel costs will further narrow the railroads' profit margin, at least in part because of the fact that while the railroads are solely responsible for the maintenance of their infrastructure, their major competitor, commercial trucking, pays only a fraction of the cost for the maintenance of the infrastructure on which it relies. Given the importance of the railroads to the national economy and their contribution to fuel economy and reduced greenhouse-gas emissions, it would behoove the government to reduce the burden placed on them, either through tax credits or direct support something on the order of what the trucking industry enjoys.

A final point to consider on the future of the railroads is passenger rail. Although many argue today that it is a thing of the past and that the remaining services are underused, ridership figures show that this is not the case. Passenger rail traffic is on the rise: in terms of the number of passengers, it is higher today than it has been for the past 50 years; in terms of passenger-miles, it is higher today than it has been for the past 40 years. If, as suggested earlier, some of the burden of maintaining the rail infrastructure were lifted, it is easily conceivable that passenger service could once again be a remunerative proposition, and if they can profit from it, the railroads would likely once again turn to passenger service.

Appendix B
Maps

Tony Howe

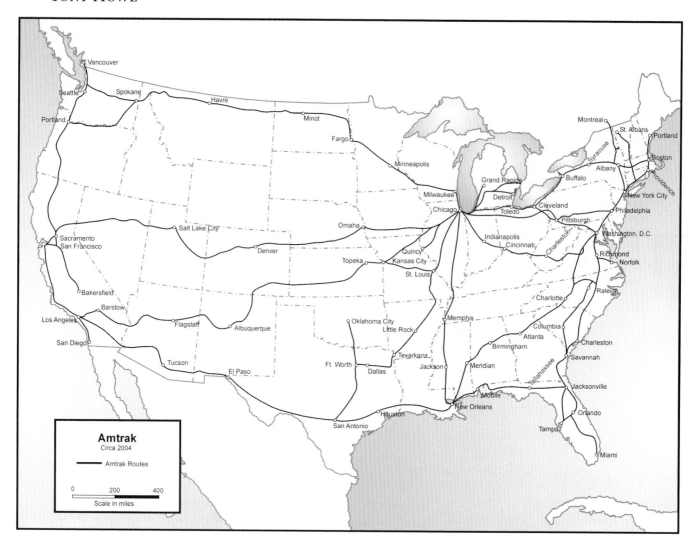

Amtrak
Circa 2004

— Amtrak Routes

0   200   400
Scale in miles

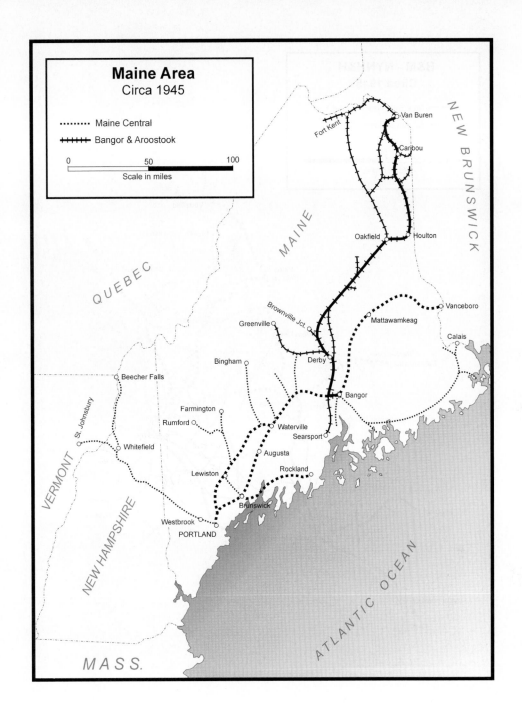

Maine Area
Circa 1945

· · · · · · Maine Central
+++++++ Bangor & Aroostook

0   50   100
Scale in miles

QUEBEC

MAINE

NEW BRUNSWICK

Fort Kent

Van Buren

Caribou

Oakfield   Houlton

Vanceboro

Brownville Jct.   Mattawamkeag

Greenville

Calais

Bingham   Derby

Beecher Falls

St. Johnsbury   Bangor

VERMONT   Farmington   Waterville   Searsport

Rumford

Whitefield   Augusta

Lewiston   Rockland

NEW HAMPSHIRE   Brunswick

Westbrook

PORTLAND

ATLANTIC OCEAN

MASS.

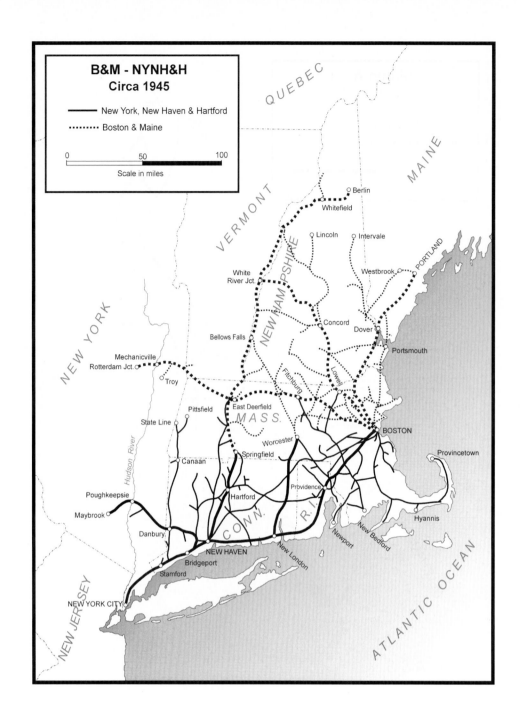

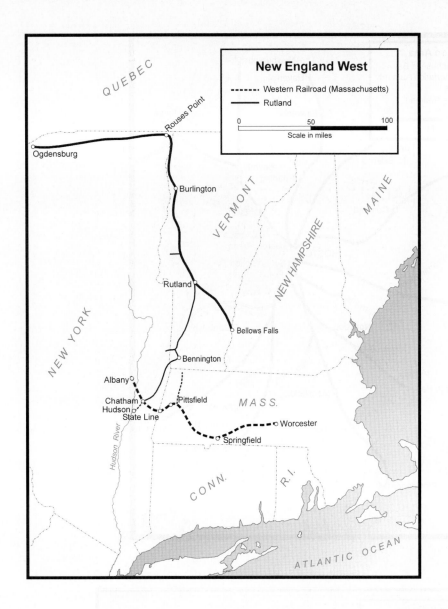

New England West

- - - - - Western Railroad (Massachusetts)
———— Rutland

0   50   100
Scale in miles

QUEBEC

Rouses Point

Ogdensburg

Burlington

VERMONT

NEW HAMPSHIRE

MAINE

NEW YORK

Rutland

Bellows Falls

Bennington

Albany

Chatham
Hudson
State Line

Pittsfield

MASS.

Worcester

Springfield

Hudson River

CONN.

R. I.

ATLANTIC OCEAN

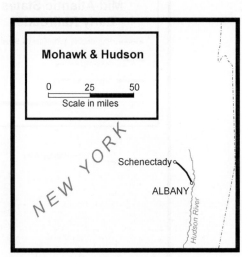

Mohawk & Hudson

0   25   50
Scale in miles

NEW YORK

Schenectady

ALBANY

Hudson River

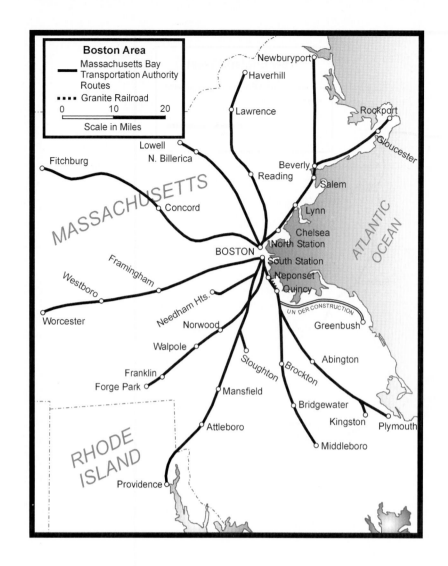

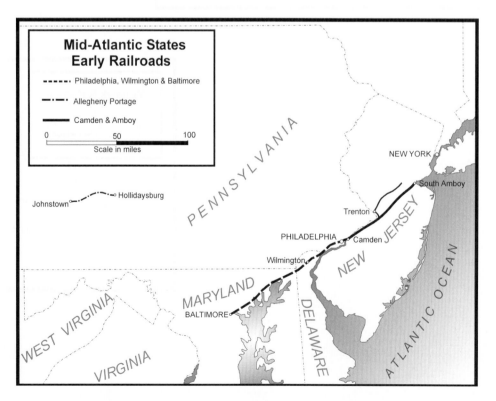

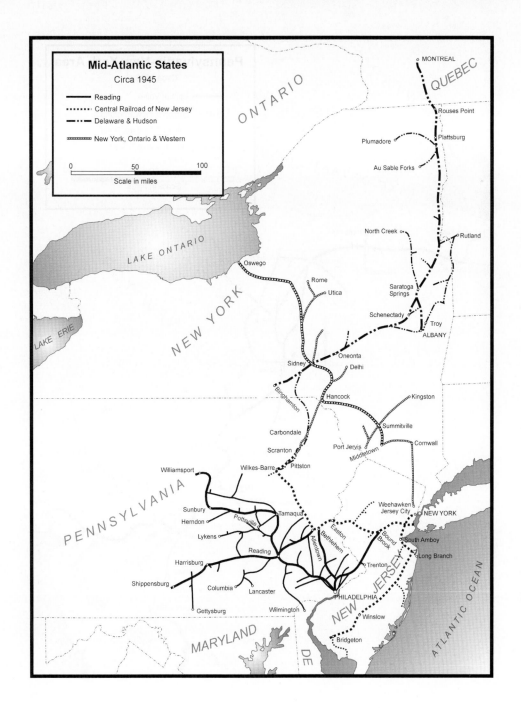

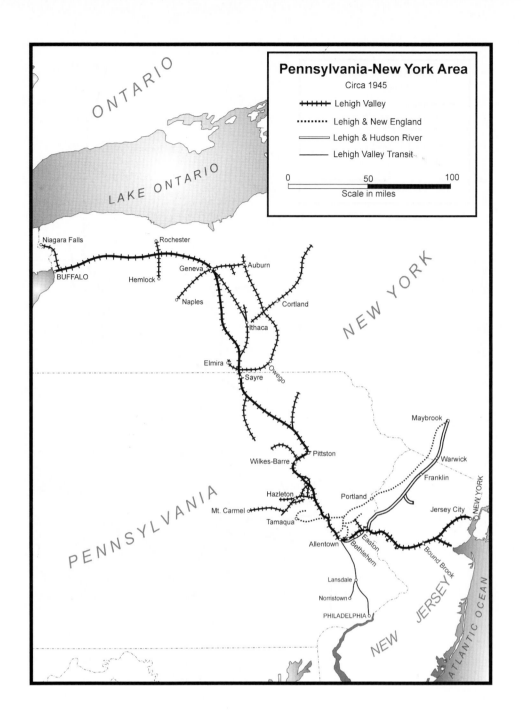

Pennsylvania-New York Area
Circa 1945

├┼┼┼┤ Lehigh Valley
········ Lehigh & New England
═══ Lehigh & Hudson River
─── Lehigh Valley Transit

0   50   100
Scale in miles

ONTARIO

LAKE ONTARIO

NEW YORK

Niagara Falls   Rochester
BUFFALO   Hemlock   Geneva   Auburn
                              Cortland
          Naples
                    Ithaca
       Elmira   Owego
            Sayre
                              Maybrook
                    Pittston   Warwick
     Wilkes-Barre   Franklin
          Hazleton   Portland
Mt. Carmel   Jersey City   NEW YORK
     Tamaqua   Allentown   Easton   Bound Brook
                         Bethlehem
PENNSYLVANIA
               Lansdale
          Norristown   NEW JERSEY
       PHILADELPHIA

ATLANTIC OCEAN

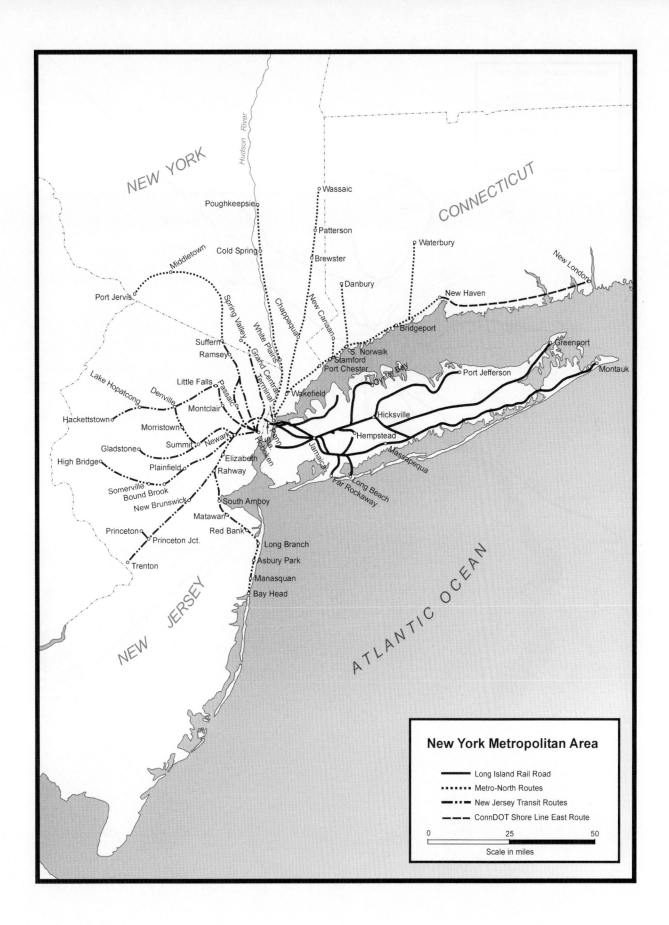

New York Metropolitan Area

———	Long Island Rail Road
·······	Metro-North Routes
–·–·–	New Jersey Transit Routes
– – –	ConnDOT Shore Line East Route

0   25   50
Scale in miles

Labels visible on map:

NEW YORK

CONNECTICUT

Hudson River

Wassaic
Poughkeepsie
Patterson
Middletown
Cold Spring
Brewster
Waterbury
Port Jervis
Danbury
New London
New Haven
New Canaan
Chappaqua
Spring Valley
White Plains
Bridgeport
Suffern
Grand Central Terminal
S. Norwalk
Stamford
Ramsey
Port Chester
Greenport
Lake Hopatcong
Little Falls
Oyster Bay
Passaic
Wakefield
Port Jefferson
Montauk
Denville
Montclair
Hicksville
Hackettstown
Morristown
Hempstead
Summit
Newark
Penn Sta.
High Bridge
Gladstone
Elizabeth
Hoboken
Jamaica
Massapequa
Plainfield
Rahway
Somerville
Bound Brook
Long Beach
New Brunswick
South Amboy
Far Rockaway
Princeton
Matawan
Princeton Jct.
Red Bank
Trenton
Long Branch
Asbury Park
Manasquan
Bay Head

NEW JERSEY

ATLANTIC OCEAN

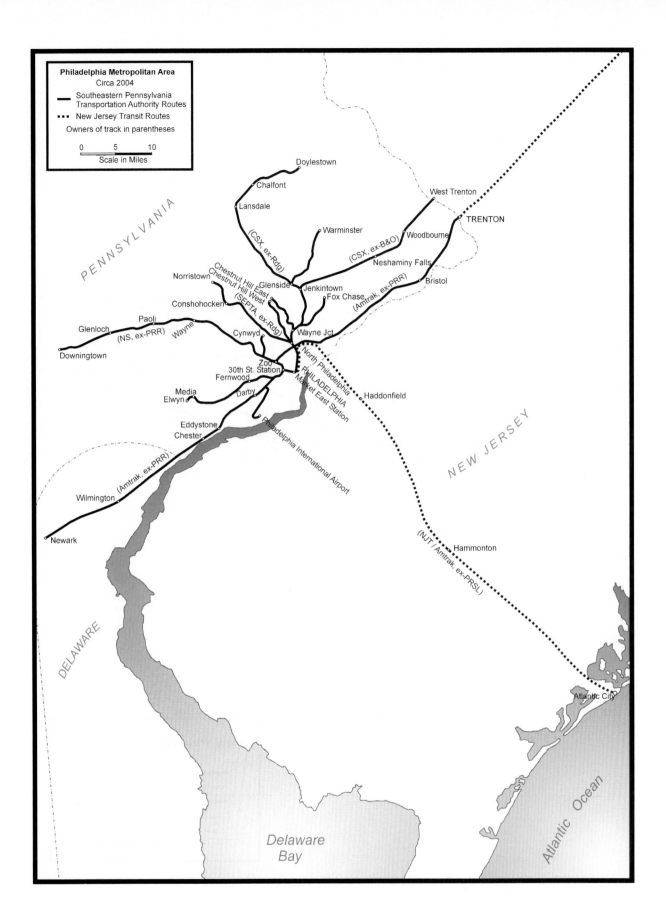

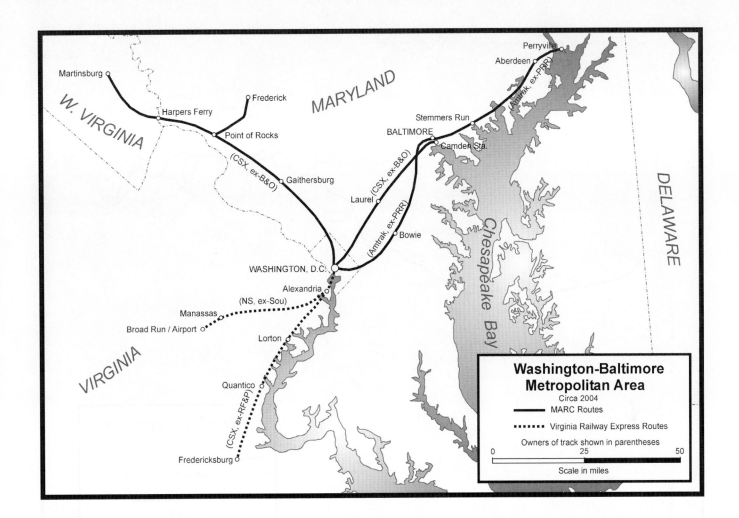

Martinsburg

W. VIRGINIA

Harpers Ferry

Frederick

MARYLAND

Perryville

Aberdeen

(Amtrak, ex-PRR)

Point of Rocks

Stemmers Run

BALTIMORE

Camden Sta.

(CSX, ex-B&O)

Gaithersburg

(CSX, ex-B&O)

Laurel

(Amtrak, ex-PRR)

Bowie

DELAWARE

Chesapeake Bay

WASHINGTON, D.C.

Alexandria

(NS, ex-Sou)

Manassas

Broad Run / Airport

Lorton

VIRGINIA

Quantico

(CSX, ex-RF&P)

Fredericksburg

Washington-Baltimore Metropolitan Area

Circa 2004

——— MARC Routes

▪▪▪▪▪ Virginia Railway Express Routes

Owners of track shown in parentheses

0   25   50

Scale in miles

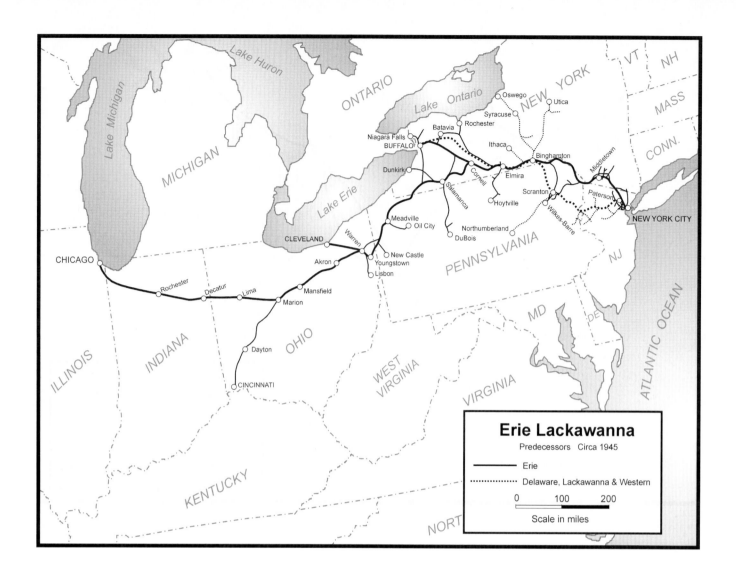

Erie Lackawanna

Predecessors Circa 1945

— Erie

···· Delaware, Lackawanna & Western

Scale in miles

0   100   200

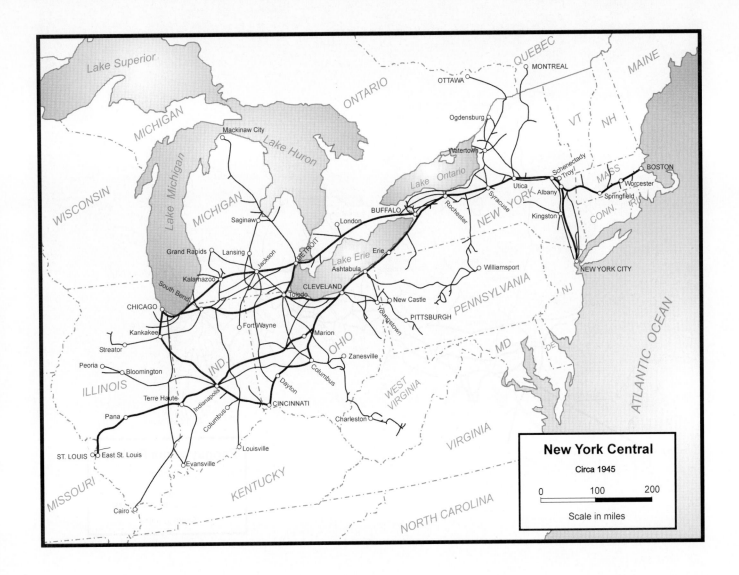

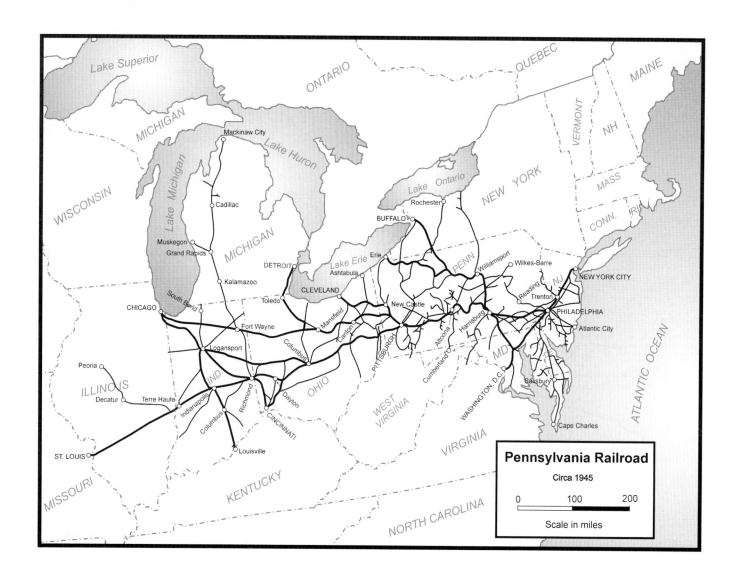

Pennsylvania Railroad

Circa 1945

| 0 | 100 | 200 |

Scale in miles

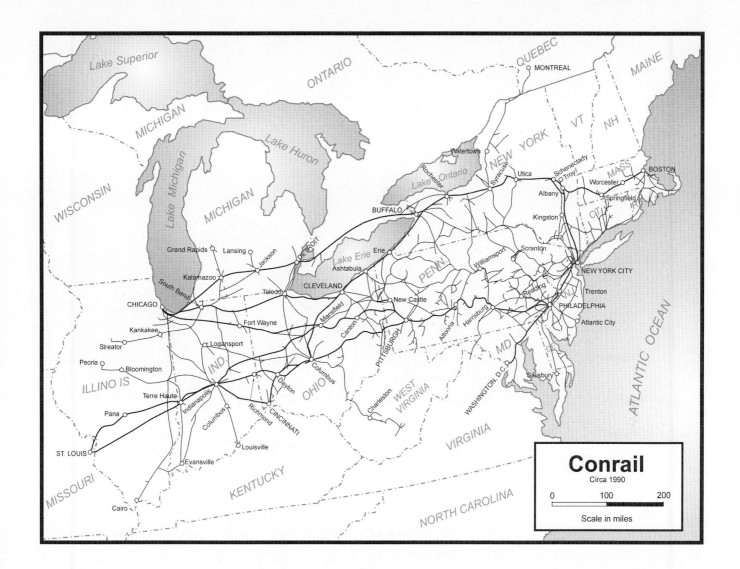

Conrail
Circa 1990

0   100   200

Scale in miles

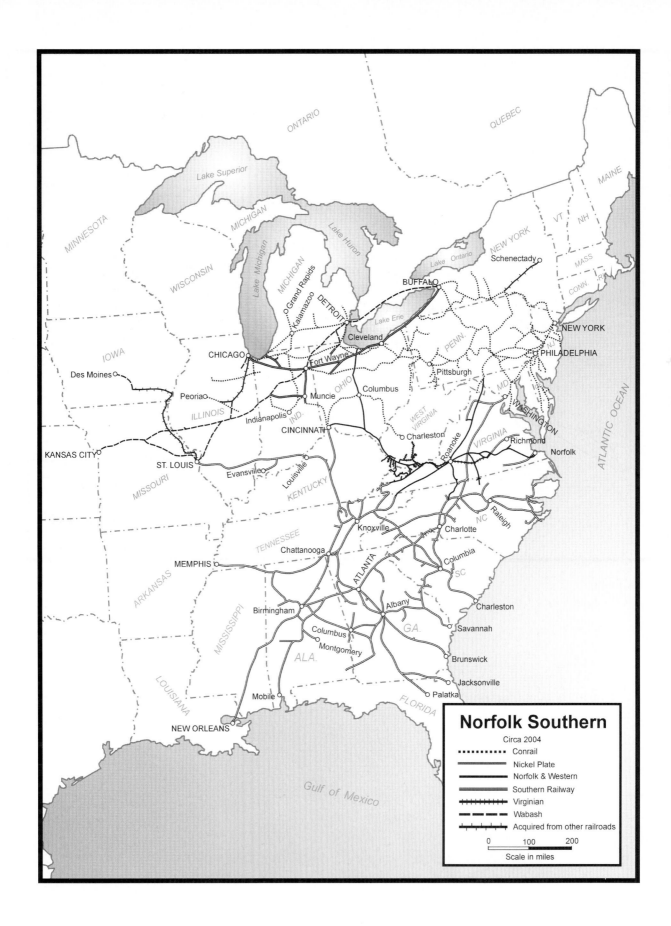

Norfolk Southern

Circa 2004

.... Conrail

.... Nickel Plate

——— Norfolk & Western

═══ Southern Railway

++++++ Virginian

– – – Wabash

++++ Acquired from other railroads

0   100   200

Scale in miles

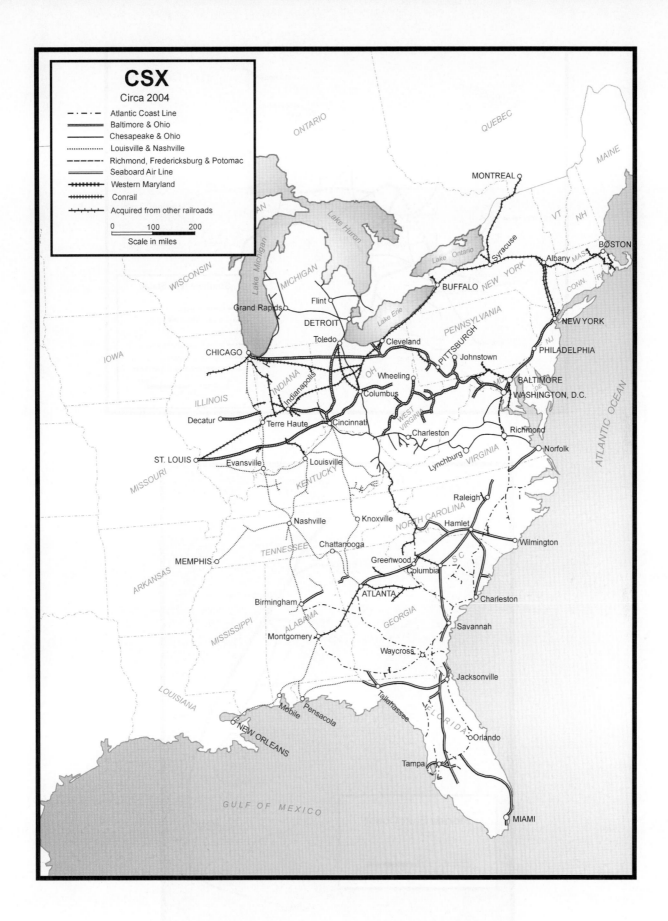

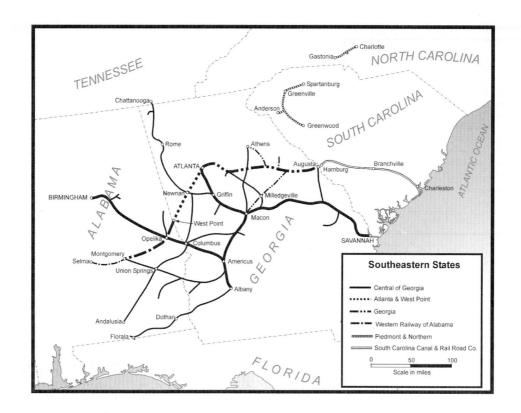

Southeastern States

— Central of Georgia
··· Atlanta & West Point
—··— Georgia
—·—· Western Railway of Alabama
···· Piedmont & Northern
═ South Carolina Canal & Rail Road Co.

0   50   100
Scale in miles

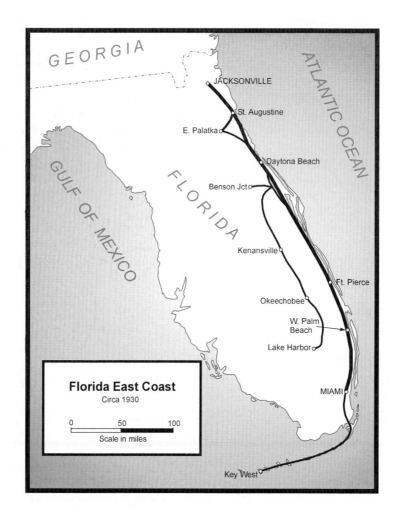

Florida East Coast
Circa 1930

0   50   100
Scale in miles

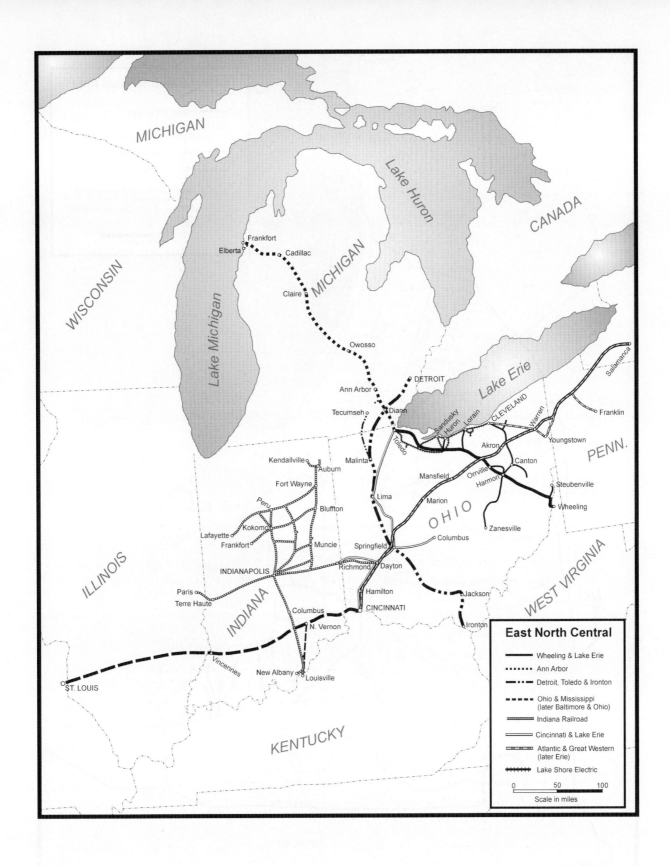

East North Central

- ———— Wheeling & Lake Erie
- ·········· Ann Arbor
- —··—··— Detroit, Toledo & Ironton
- – – – – Ohio & Mississippi (later Baltimore & Ohio)
- ▭▭▭▭▭ Indiana Railroad
- ══════ Cincinnati & Lake Erie
- ▭█▭█▭ Atlantic & Great Western (later Erie)
- ┼┼┼┼┼ Lake Shore Electric

0 — 50 — 100
Scale in miles

MICHIGAN

Lake Huron

CANADA

WISCONSIN

Frankfort
Elberta
Cadillac

Claire

MICHIGAN

Lake Michigan

Owosso

DETROIT

Lake Erie

Ann Arbor

Tecumseh
Diann

Salamanca

Franklin

Sandusky
Huron
Lorain
CLEVELAND
Warren

Youngstown

PENN.

Malinta

Toledo

Lima

Akron

Canton

Steubenville

Mansfield
Orrville
Harmon

Wheeling

Kendallville
Auburn

Fort Wayne

Peru
Bluffton

Marion

OHIO

Zanesville

Lafayette
Kokomo
Frankfort
Muncie

Springfield

Columbus

WEST VIRGINIA

INDIANAPOLIS

Richmond
Dayton

Paris
Terre Haute

Hamilton

Jackson

Columbus

CINCINNATI

Vincennes

N. Vernon

Ironton

ILLINOIS

INDIANA

New Albany
Louisville

ST. LOUIS

KENTUCKY

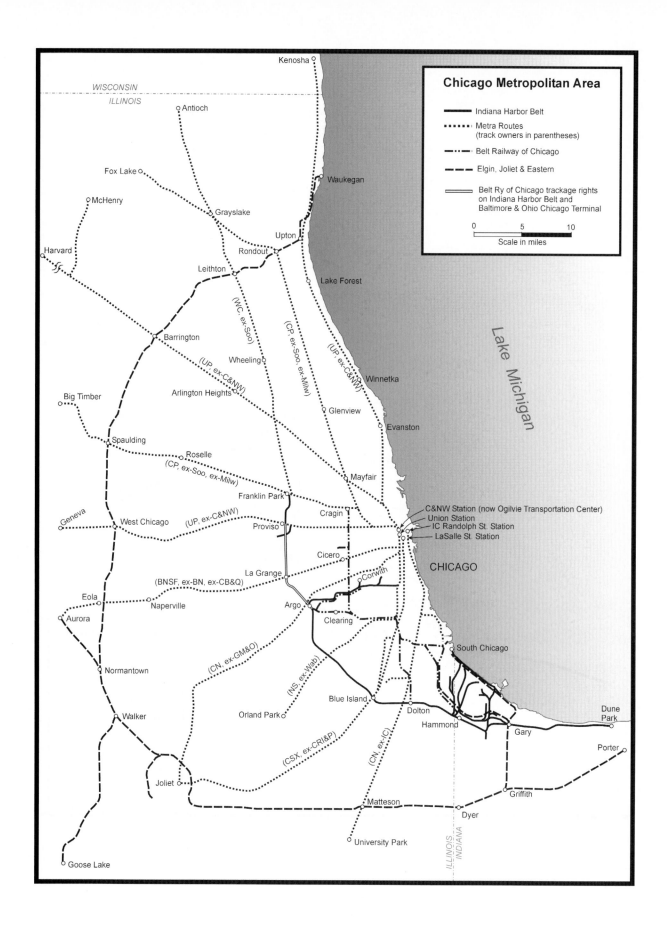

Chicago Metropolitan Area

- —— Indiana Harbor Belt
- ······ Metra Routes
  (track owners in parentheses)
- —·—·— Belt Railway of Chicago
- — — — Elgin, Joliet & Eastern
- ═══ Belt Ry of Chicago trackage rights
  on Indiana Harbor Belt and
  Baltimore & Ohio Chicago Terminal

Scale in miles
0   5   10

Lake Michigan

WISCONSIN
ILLINOIS

Kenosha

Antioch

Fox Lake

McHenry

Grayslake

Waukegan

Harvard

Leithton

Upton

Rondout

Lake Forest

(WC, ex-Soo)

Barrington

Wheeling

(CP, ex-Soo, ex-Milw)

(UP, ex-C&NW)

Winnetka

Big Timber

Arlington Heights

(UP, ex-C&NW)

Glenview

Evanston

Spaulding

Roselle

(CP, ex-Soo, ex-Milw)

Mayfair

Franklin Park

C&NW Station (now Ogilvie Transportation Center)
Union Station
IC Randolph St. Station
LaSalle St. Station

Cragin

Geneva

West Chicago

(UP, ex-C&NW)

Proviso

Cicero

CHICAGO

La Grange

Corwith

(BNSF, ex-BN, ex-CB&Q)

Eola

Naperville

Argo

Clearing

Aurora

South Chicago

Normantown

(CN, ex-GM&O)

Blue Island

(NS, ex-Wab)

Dolton

Dune
Park

Walker

Orland Park

Hammond

Gary

Porter

(CSX, ex-CRI&P)

(CN, ex-IC)

Griffith

Joliet

Matteson

Dyer

ILLINOIS
INDIANA

University Park

Goose Lake

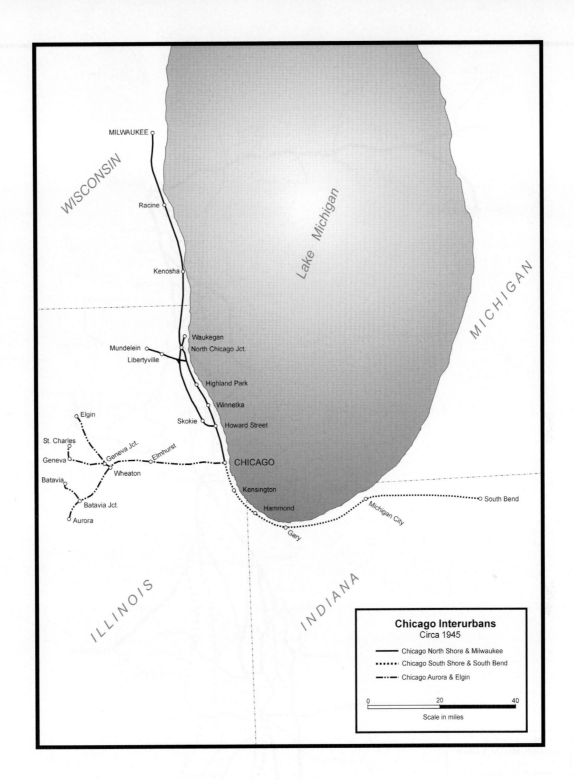

MILWAUKEE

WISCONSIN

Racine

Lake Michigan

Kenosha

MICHIGAN

Waukegan
Mundelein   North Chicago Jct.
Libertyville

Highland Park

Winnetka

Elgin

Skokie   Howard Street

St. Charles
Geneva Jct.
Geneva   Elmhurst   CHICAGO

Wheaton
Batavia

Kensington
Batavia Jct.   Hammond   South Bend
Aurora   Michigan City

Gary

ILLINOIS

INDIANA

Chicago Interurbans
Circa 1945

——— Chicago North Shore & Milwaukee
········· Chicago South Shore & South Bend
—··—··— Chicago Aurora & Elgin

0   20   40
Scale in miles

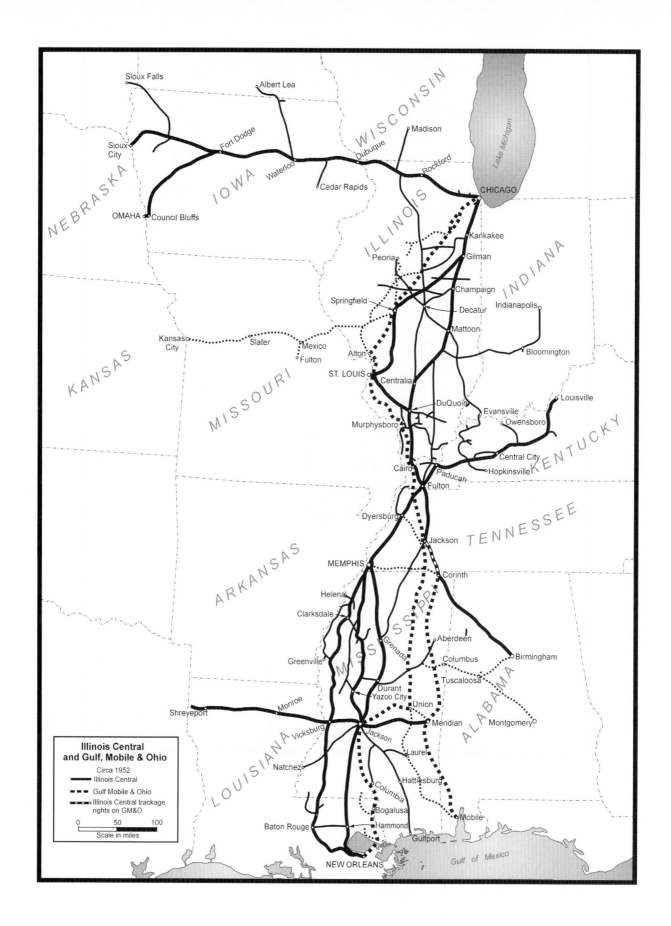

**Illinois Central
and Gulf, Mobile & Ohio**

Circa 1952

———— Illinois Central

- - - - Gulf Mobile & Ohio

━•━•━ Illinois Central trackage
rights on GM&O

0   50   100

Scale in miles

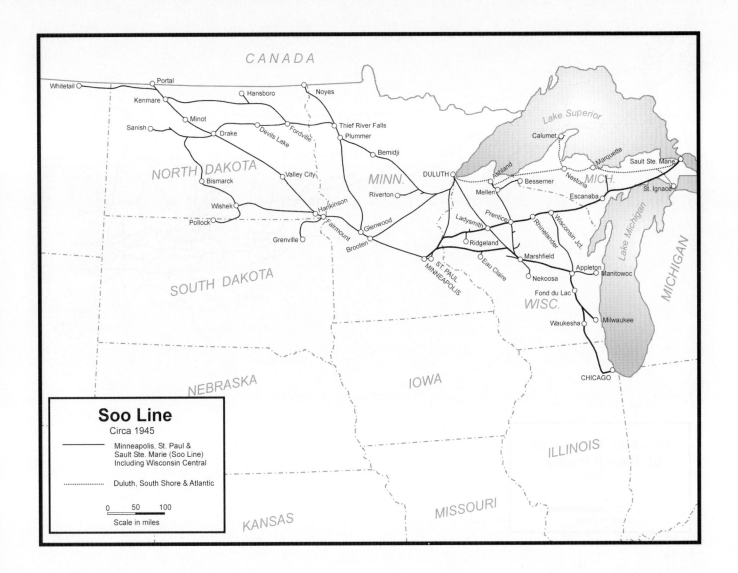

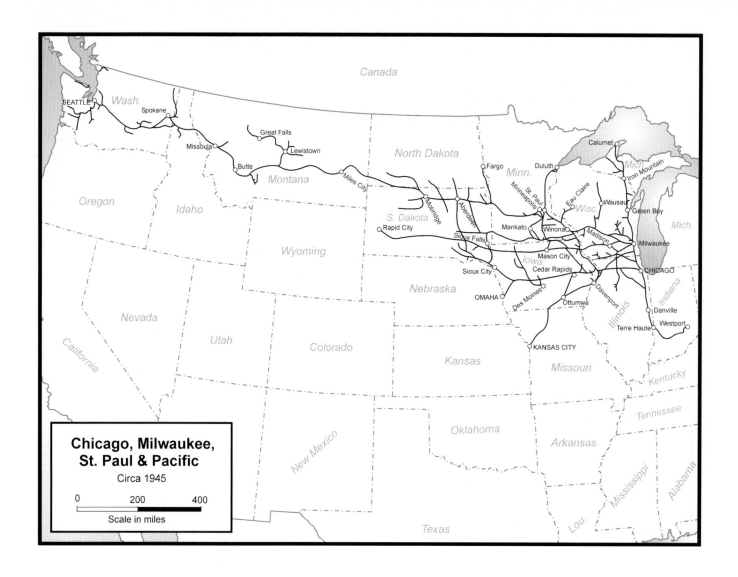

Chicago, Milwaukee, St. Paul & Pacific

Circa 1945

0   200   400

Scale in miles

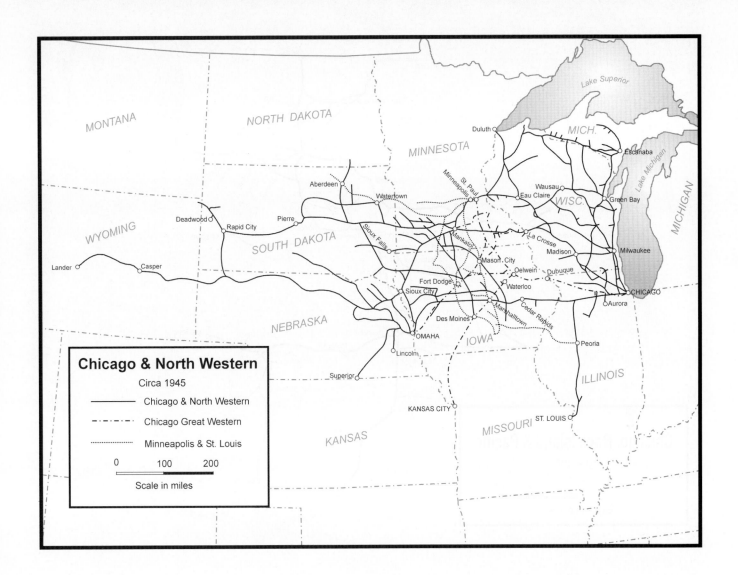

Chicago & North Western

Circa 1945

—————— Chicago & North Western

—·—·—·— Chicago Great Western

················ Minneapolis & St. Louis

```
0        100       200
Scale in miles
```

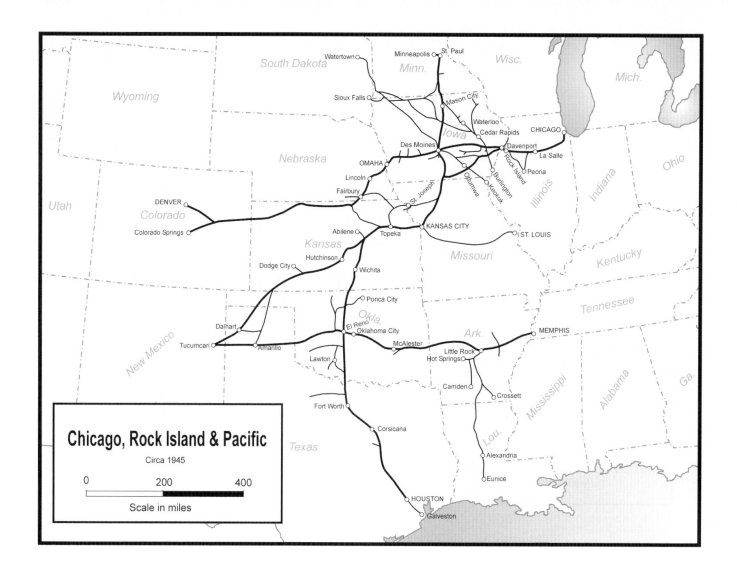

Chicago, Rock Island & Pacific

Circa 1945

0   200   400

Scale in miles

Duluth, Missabe & Iron Range

Circa 1945

0   50   100

Scale in miles

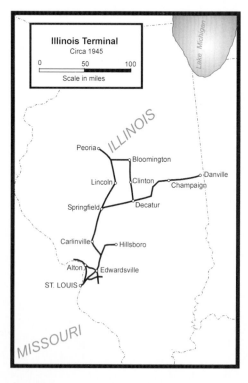

Illinois Terminal

Circa 1945

0   50   100

Scale in miles

1178   APPENDIX B

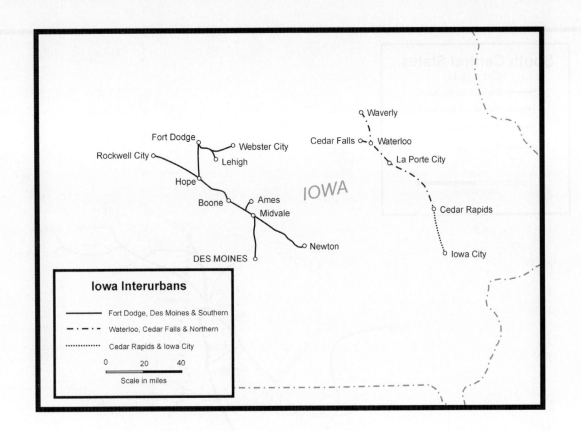

Iowa Interurbans

Waverly
Cedar Falls — Waterloo
La Porte City
Cedar Rapids
Iowa City

Fort Dodge — Webster City
Rockwell City — Lehigh
Hope
Boone — Ames
Midvale
Newton
DES MOINES

IOWA

— Fort Dodge, Des Moines & Southern
—·—· Waterloo, Cedar Falls & Northern
········ Cedar Rapids & Iowa City

0   20   40
Scale in miles

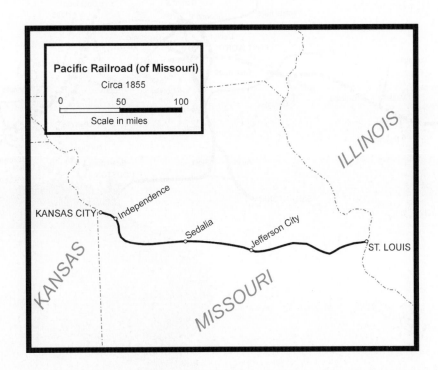

Pacific Railroad (of Missouri)

Circa 1855

0   50   100
Scale in miles

ILLINOIS

KANSAS CITY — Independence
Sedalia
Jefferson City
ST. LOUIS

KANSAS

MISSOURI

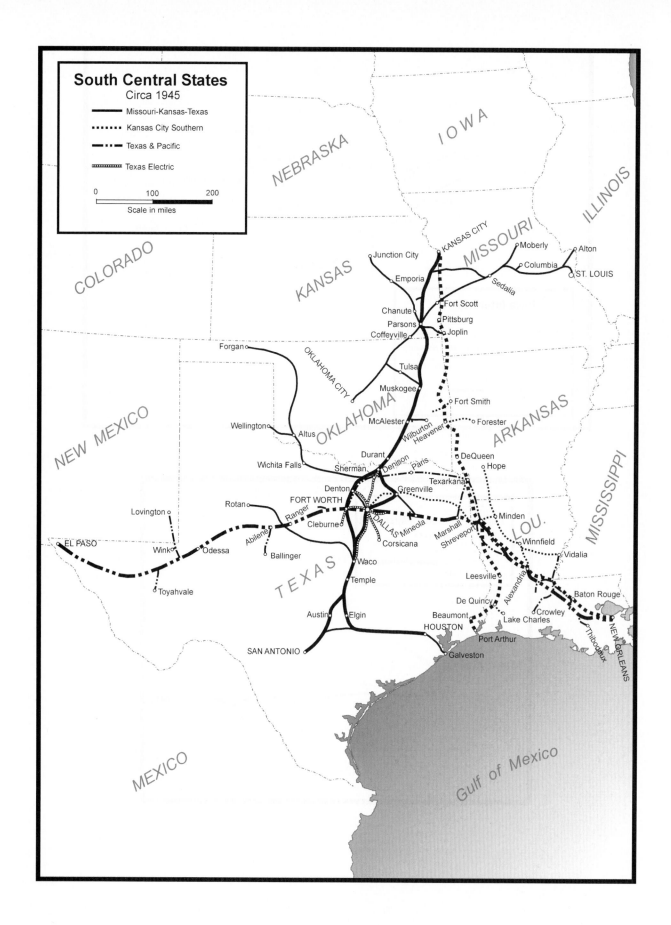

South Central States
Circa 1945

Missouri-Kansas-Texas
Kansas City Southern
Texas & Pacific
Texas Electric

0   100   200
Scale in miles

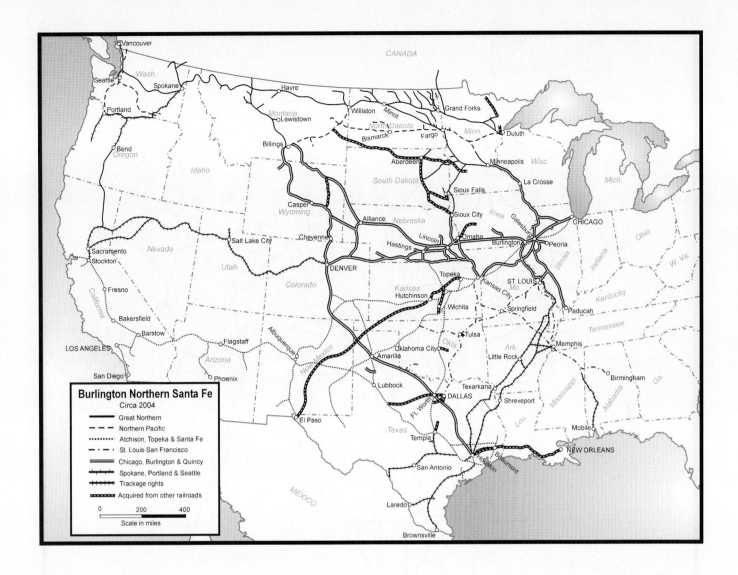

Burlington Northern Santa Fe
Circa 2004

————	Great Northern
– – – –	Northern Pacific
··········	Atchison, Topeka & Santa Fe
–·–·–·–	St. Louis-San Francisco
≡≡≡≡	Chicago, Burlington & Quincy
┼┼┼┼	Spokane, Portland & Seattle
+++++	Trackage rights
▓▓▓▓	Acquired from other railroads

0   200   400

Scale in miles

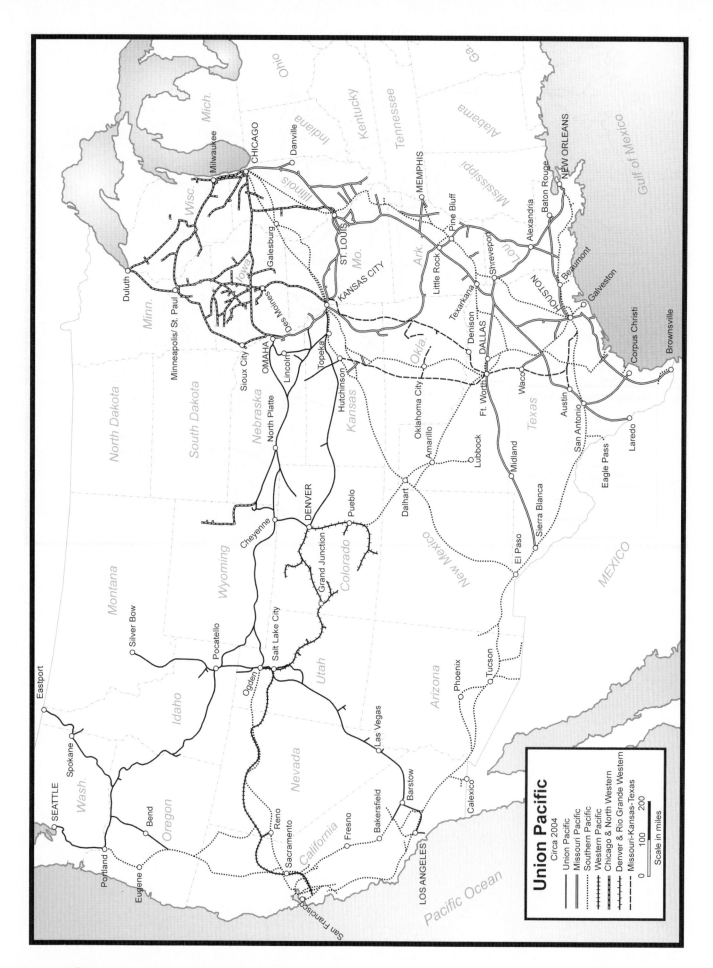

Union Pacific
Circa 2004

- Union Pacific
- Missouri Pacific
- Southern Pacific
- Western Pacific
- Chicago & North Western
- Denver & Rio Grande Western
- Missouri-Kansas-Texas

Scale in miles
0   100   200

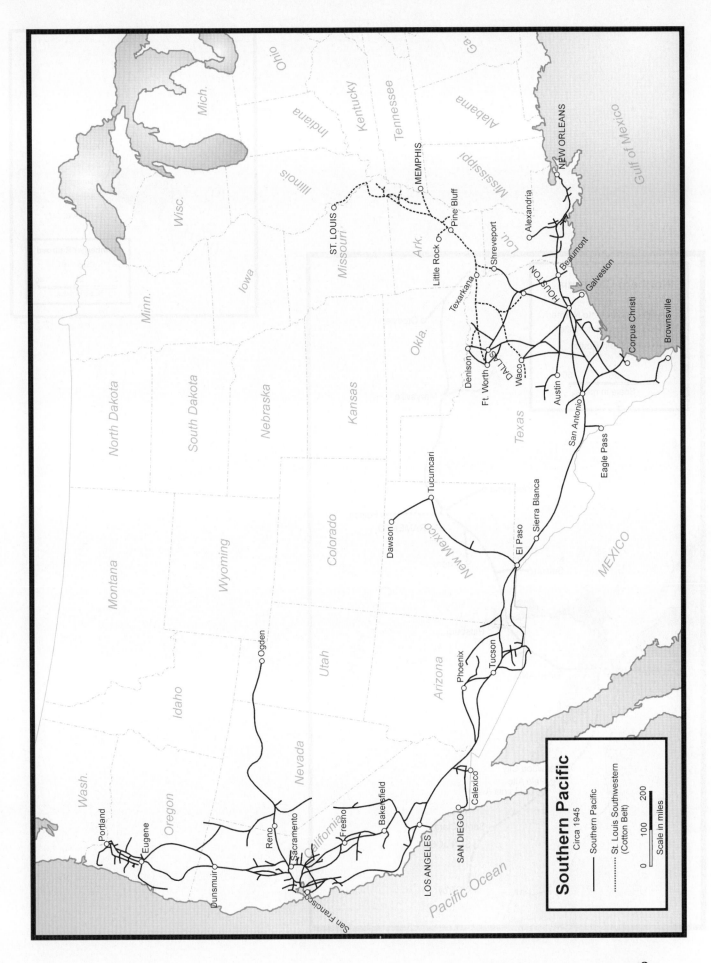

Southern Pacific

Circa 1945

—— Southern Pacific

········ St. Louis Southwestern
(Cotton Belt)

Scale in miles

0   100   200

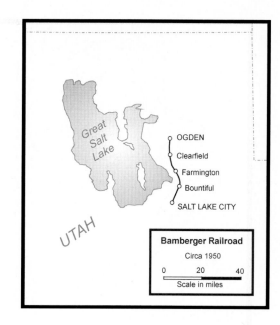

Great
Salt
Lake

OGDEN
Clearfield
Farmington
Bountiful
SALT LAKE CITY

UTAH

Bamberger Railroad

Circa 1950

0   20   40
Scale in miles

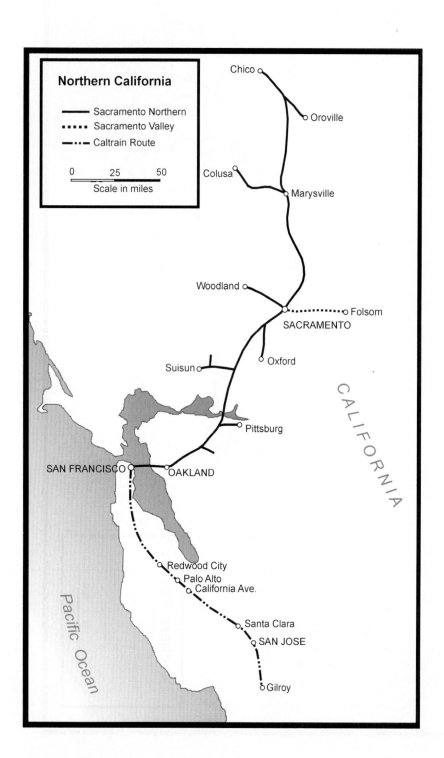

Chico

Oroville

Northern California

——— Sacramento Northern
▪▪▪▪▪ Sacramento Valley
—▪▪— Caltrain Route

0   25   50
Scale in miles

Colusa

Marysville

Woodland

Folsom

SACRAMENTO

Oxford

Suisun

CALIFORNIA

Pittsburg

SAN FRANCISCO   OAKLAND

Pacific Ocean

Redwood City
Palo Alto
California Ave.

Santa Clara

SAN JOSE

Gilroy

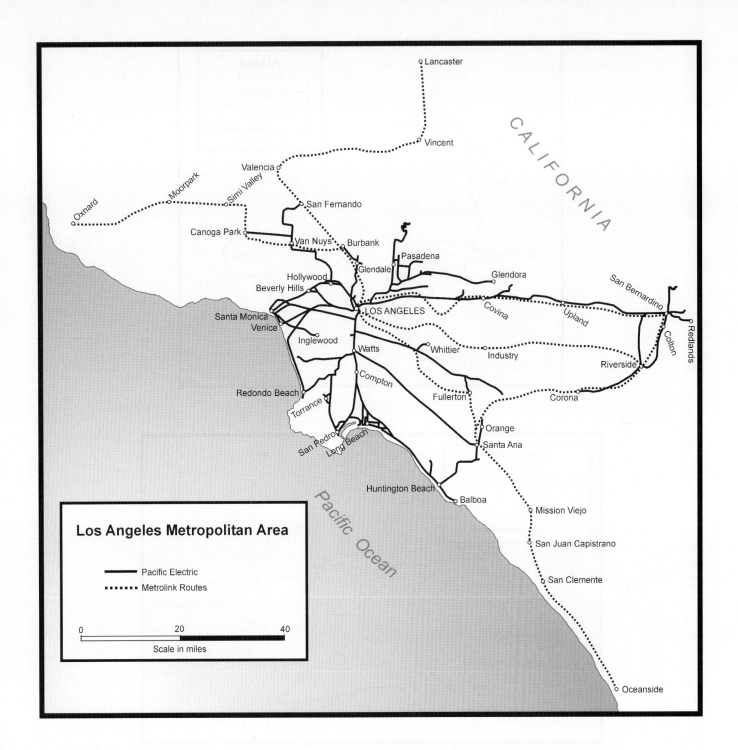

Los Angeles Metropolitan Area

— Pacific Electric
····· Metrolink Routes

0   20   40
Scale in miles

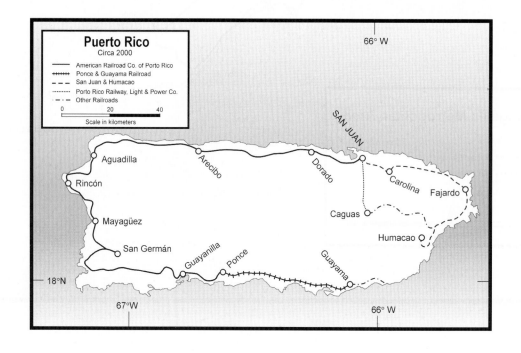

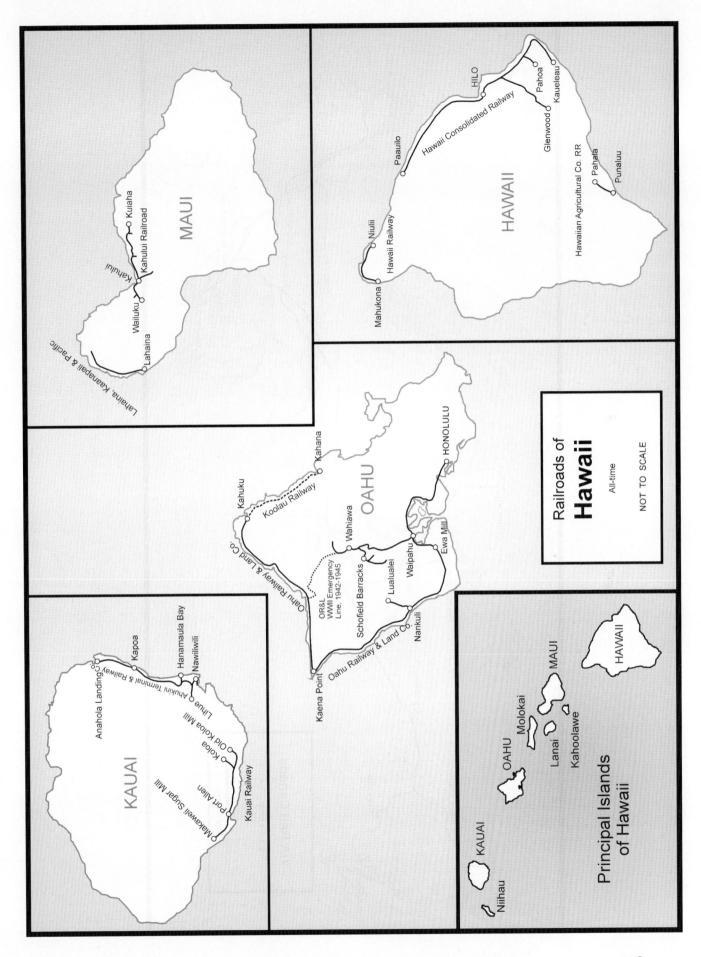

MAUI

Kuiaha

Kahului Railroad

Kahului

Wailuku

Lahaina

Lahaina, Kaanapali & Pacific

HAWAII

HILO

Pahoa

Kaueleau

Glenwood

Hawaii Consolidated Railway

Paauilo

Hawaiian Agricultural Co. RR

Pahala

Punaluu

Niulii

Hawaii Railway

Mahukona

Kahana

Kahuku

OAHU

HONOLULU

Koolau Railway

Wahiawa

Oahu Railway & Land Co.

OR&L
WWII Emergency
Line, 1942-1945

Schofield Barracks

Lualualei

Waipahu

Ewa Mill

Nankuli

Oahu Railway & Land Co.

Kaena Point

Railroads of

Hawaii

All-time

NOT TO SCALE

KAUAI

Anahola Landing

Kapoa

Hanamaula Bay

Nawiliwili

Ahukini Terminal & Railway Co.

Lihue

Koloa Mill

Old Koloa Mill

Makawell Sugar Mill

Port Allen

Kauai Railway

Niihau

KAUAI

OAHU

Molokai

MAUI

Lanai

Kahoolawe

HAWAII

**Principal Islands
of Hawaii**

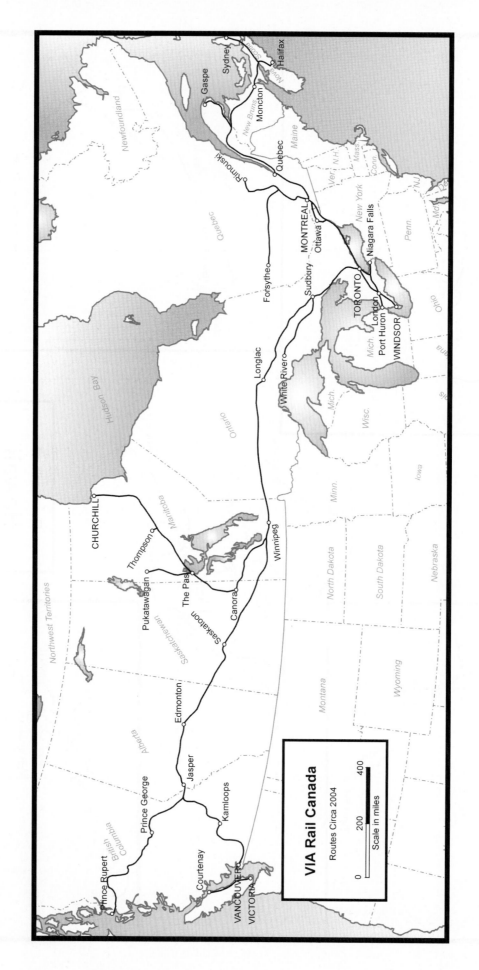

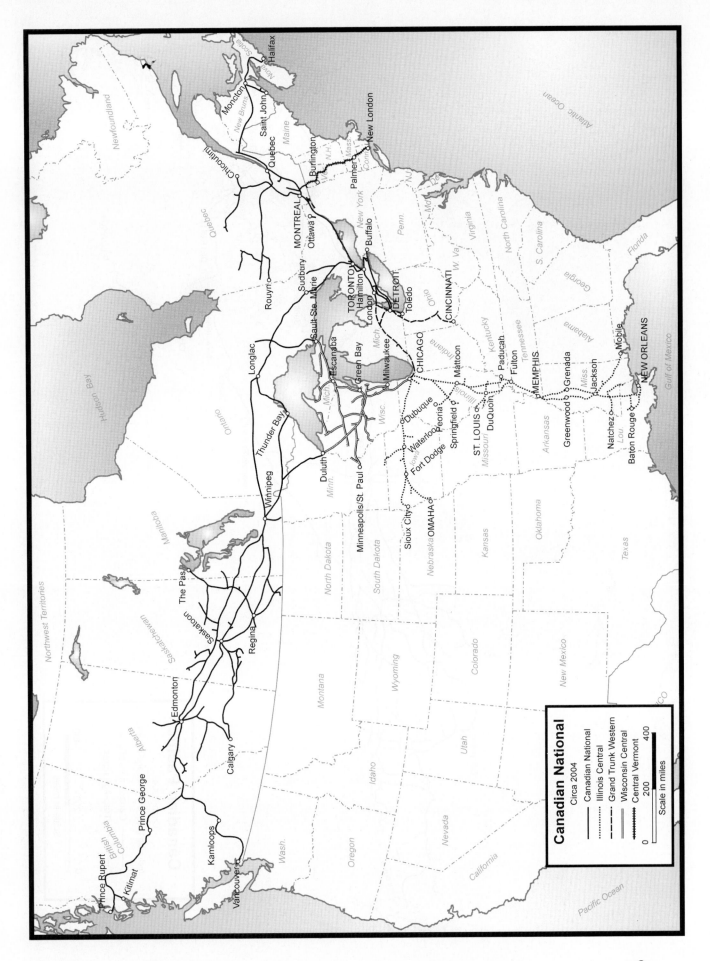

Canadian National

Circa 2004

Canadian National
Illinois Central
Grand Trunk Western
Wisconsin Central
Central Vermont

Scale in miles

0   200   400

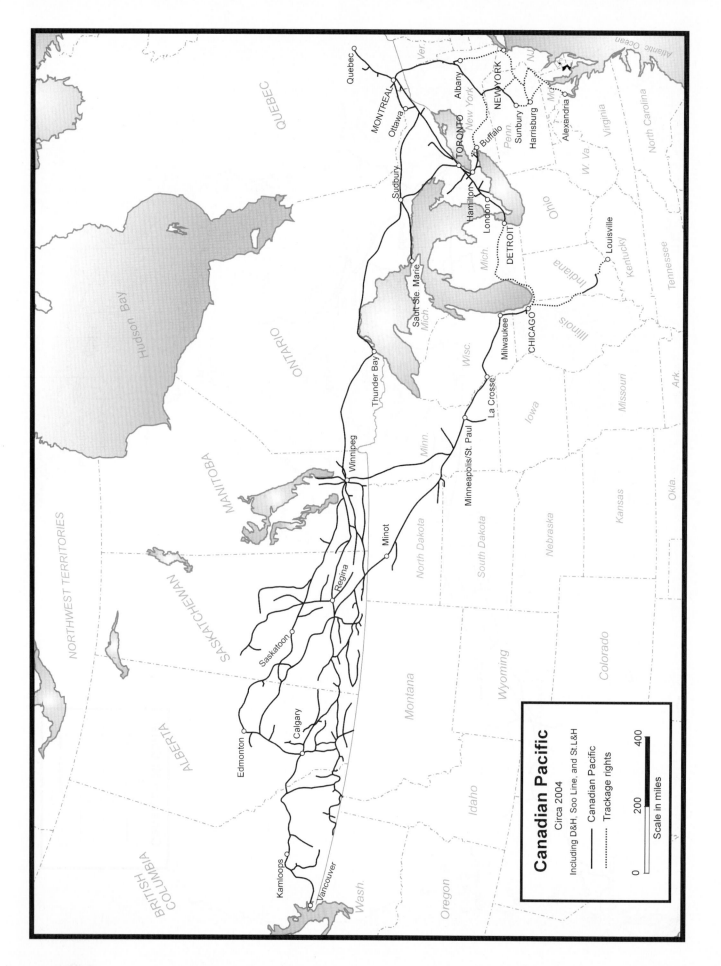

Canadian Pacific

Circa 2004

Including D&H, Soo Line, and St.L&H

—— Canadian Pacific

········· Trackage rights

Scale in miles

0   200   400

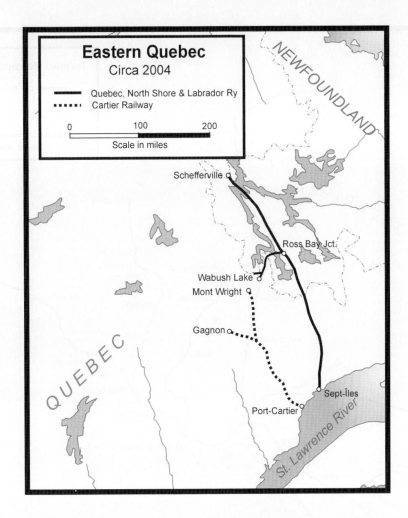

Eastern Quebec
Circa 2004

——— Quebec, North Shore & Labrador Ry
•••••• Cartier Railway

0   100   200
Scale in miles

NEWFOUNDLAND

QUEBEC

Schefferville

Ross Bay Jct.

Wabush Lake
Mont Wright

Gagnon

Port-Cartier
Sept-Îles

St. Lawrence River

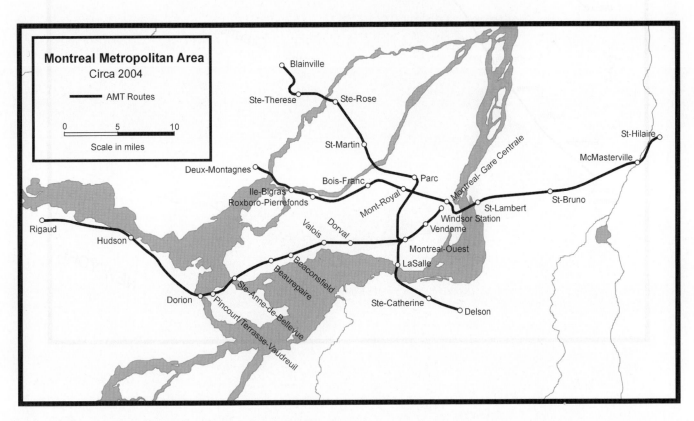

Montreal Metropolitan Area
Circa 2004

——— AMT Routes

0   5   10
Scale in miles

Blainville

Ste-Therese   Ste-Rose

St-Martin

St-Hilaire

Deux-Montagnes

McMasterville

Bois-Franc   Parc

Montreal- Gare Centrale

Ile-Bigras
Roxboro-Pierrefonds

Mont-Royal

St-Bruno

St-Lambert

Valois   Dorval

Windsor Station
Vendome

Rigaud

Hudson

Montreal-Ouest

Beaconsfield

LaSalle

Dorion

Beaurepaire

Ste-Anne-de-Bellevue

Pincourt/Terrasse-Vaudreuil

Ste-Catherine

Delson

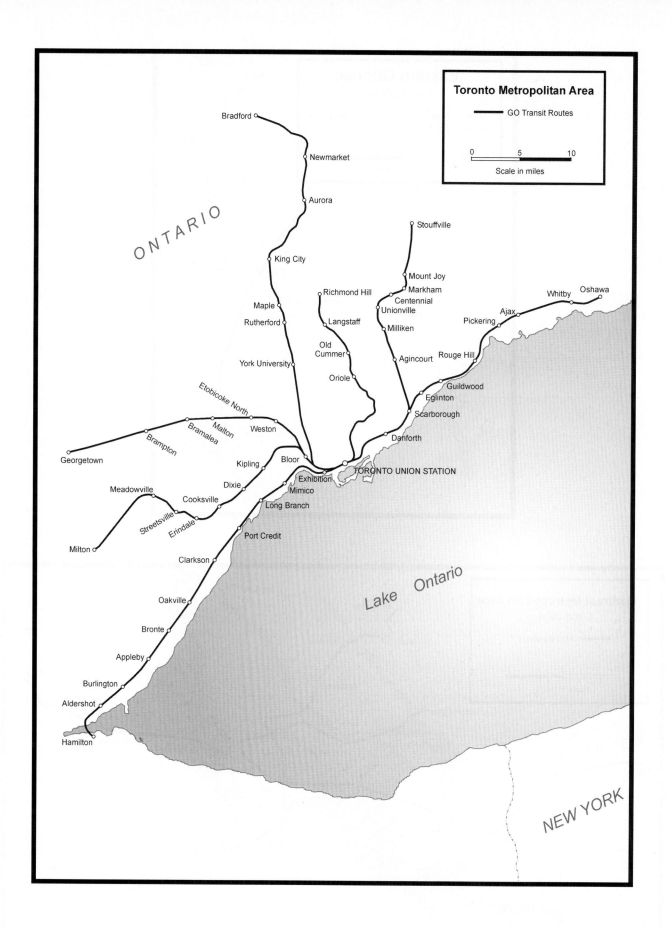

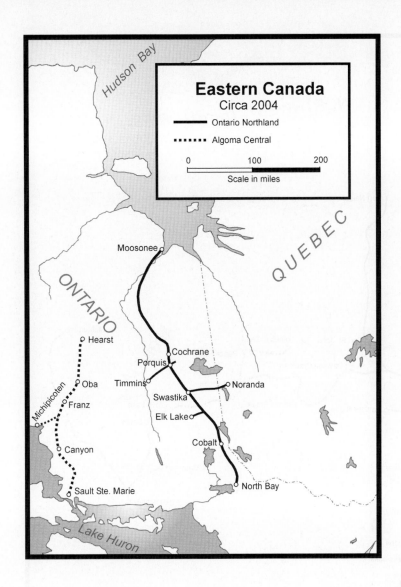

Eastern Canada
Circa 2004

——— Ontario Northland
▪▪▪▪▪ Algoma Central

0   100   200
Scale in miles

Hudson Bay

QUEBEC

ONTARIO

Moosonee

Hearst

Cochrane

Porquis

Oba

Timmins

Noranda

Franz

Swastika

Michipicoten

Elk Lake

Canyon

Cobalt

Sault Ste. Marie

North Bay

Lake Huron

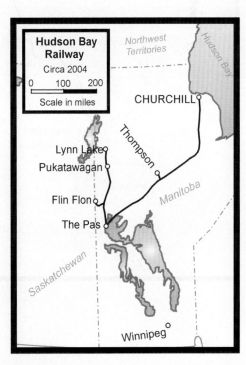

Hudson Bay Railway
Circa 2004

0   100   200
Scale in miles

Northwest Territories

Hudson Bay

CHURCHILL

Thompson

Lynn Lake

Pukatawagan

Manitoba

Flin Flon

The Pas

Saskatchewan

Winnipeg

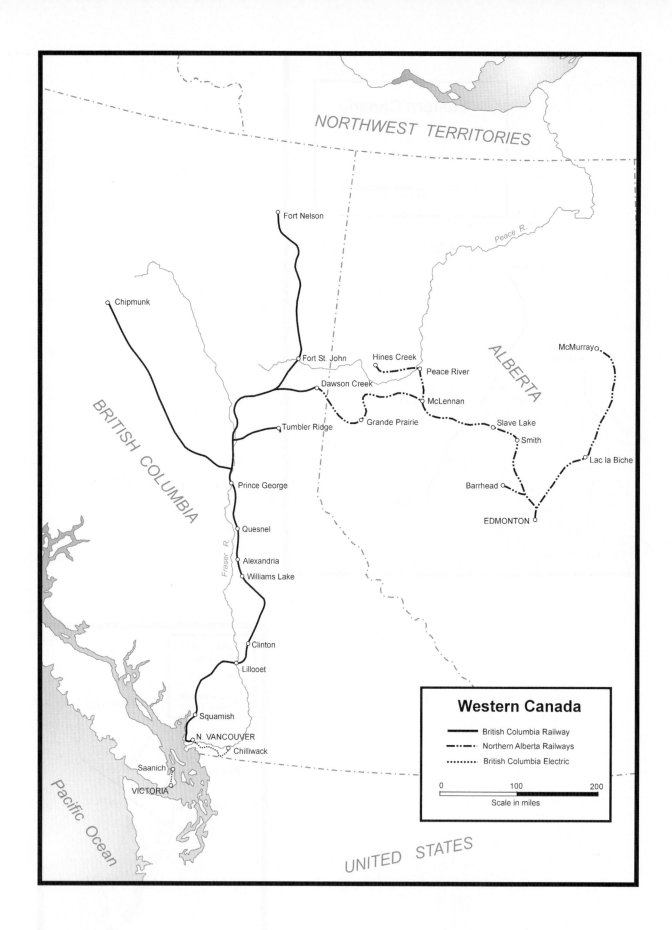

Western Canada

— British Columbia Railway
—·—·— Northern Alberta Railways
········· British Columbia Electric

| 0 | 100 | 200 |

Scale in miles

NORTHWEST TERRITORIES

ALBERTA

BRITISH COLUMBIA

Pacific Ocean

UNITED STATES

Peace R.

Fraser R.

Fort Nelson

Chipmunk

Fort St. John

Hines Creek

Peace River

Dawson Creek

McLennan

Grande Prairie

Slave Lake

McMurray

Tumbler Ridge

Smith

Lac la Biche

Prince George

Barrhead

EDMONTON

Quesnel

Alexandria

Williams Lake

Clinton

Lillooet

Squamish

N. VANCOUVER

Chilliwack

Saanich

VICTORIA

1194   APPENDIX B

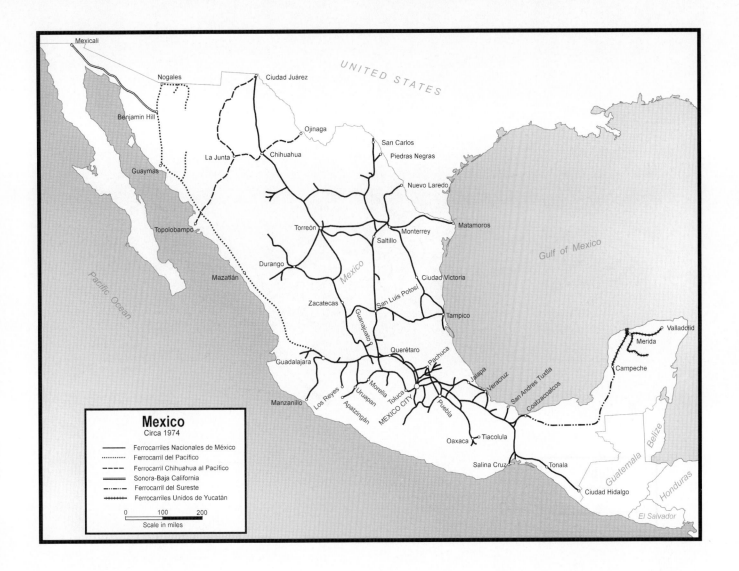

Mexico
Circa 1974

——————	Ferrocarriles Nacionales de México
··············	Ferrocarril del Pacífico
– – – – –	Ferrocarril Chihuahua al Pacífico
══════	Sonora-Baja California
—·—·—·	Ferrocarril del Sureste
++++++++	Ferrocarriles Unidos de Yucatán

0   100   200
Scale in miles

Mexicali

Nogales

Ciudad Juárez

Benjamin Hill

San Carlos

Ojinaga

Piedras Negras

Guaymas

La Junta

Chihuahua

Nuevo Laredo

Topolobampo

Torreón

Monterrey

Matamoros

Saltillo

Durango

Mazatlán

Ciudad Victoria

Zacatecas

San Luis Potosí

Tampico

Guanajuato

Querétaro

Guadalajara

Pachuca

Valladolid

Merida

Campeche

Jalapa

Veracruz

San Andres Tuxtla

Coatzacoalcos

Los Reyes

Morella

Uruapan

Toluca

MEXICO CITY

Puebla

Manzanillo

Apatzingán

Oaxaca

Tlacolula

Salina Cruz

Tonala

Ciudad Hidalgo

UNITED STATES

Mexico

Pacific Ocean

Gulf of Mexico

Guatemala

Belize

Honduras

El Salvador

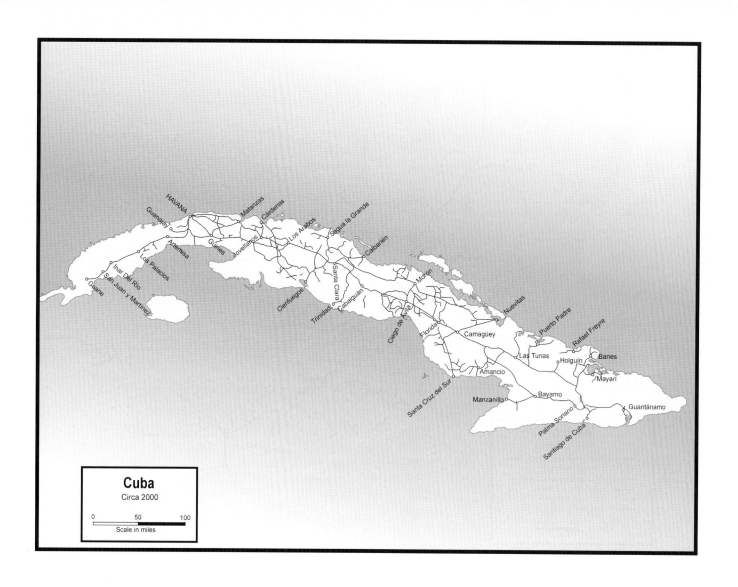

Cuba

Circa 2000

0   50   100
Scale in miles

Appendix C
Glossary of Railroad Terms

John C. Spychalski

Successive generations of personnel in the railroad industry and in rail-related industries and agencies have coined an abundance of specialized terms relating to rail operations, technology, business practices and processes, job titles, and regulation. Some of these terms have endured since the early phases of the industry. Others have emerged and prevailed through one or several eras and then disappeared from common usage as conditions and practices changed. Many of the terms are formal or proper in nature, but some constitute slang. Many have achieved industry- and company-wide usage, while others have been unique to particular rail carriers and/or to specific departments or functional areas within carriers. Adding to these complicating conditions, some similar or almost identical operating practices, types of equipment, and other objects of reference are (or have been) identi-fied by more than one term, sometimes even by different employees of the same railway. In a few instances differences in spelling of the same term exist, such as "gage" versus "gauge" in reference to the distance between the heads of the running rails on a rail track.

These conditions make the compilation of an all-inclusive and totally incontrovertible railroad glossary an impossible task. The terms presented in this glossary were selected on the basis of the appendix editor's judgment of their relative universality, durability, and utility as reference aids in the study of historical, as well as contemporary, railway subject matter. A final note: definitive attribution of authorship and identification of precise time of entry into usage for almost all railway terms is virtually impossible. The terms presented here therefore have been judged as "lying within the public domain of the railway world."

A end of car   The end opposite that on which the hand brake is mounted.

AAR   Assn. of American Railroads. The major trade association for large railroads in the United States, Canada, and Mexico. Represents rail industry interests to federal government legislators and agencies. Provides mechanisms for setting equipment standards and procedures and disseminating information of industry-wide importance. Two subsidiaries provide technological support services.

absolute block   A block that must not be occupied by more than one train.

absolute permissive block   An automatic block signal system in which a train will cause the head block signal governing opposing train movements to display a stop signal while permitting signals for following movements to display other than a stop signal.

ACI   Automatic car identification. Electronic system used to provide automated identification of cars in a train by owner, number, and equipment classification when read by a wayside scanner. See also **AEI**.

AEI   Automatic Equipment Identification. An electronic automatic car-scanning system for tracking and tracing cars. The system requires a transponder mounted on diagonally opposite corners of a railcar or other type of equipment to respond to radio-frequency interrogation. See also **ACI**.

air brake   The general term used to describe the compressed-air braking system used on North American railways.

air-brake hose   The flexible connection between the brake pipes of cars or locomotives.

air-flow indicator   An instrument in the locomotive cab that indicates the rate of flow of air pressure through the automatic brake valve to the brake pipe.

alertor   A device that detects the frequency of the engineer's movements and initiates an air brake application when the required frequency of these movements is not maintained. See also **deadman control**.

alley   (Slang) A clear track for movement through a yard.

all-room sleeper   A sleeping car with all beds or berths located in private rooms.

angle cock   Manually operated valve at ends of cars and locomotives for opening or closing the flow of air through connections between brake pipes. See **air-brake hose**.

approach signal   A fixed signal preceding a stop signal.

AREA   American Railway Engineering Assn. See **AREMA**.

AREMA   American Railway Engineering and Maintenance-of-Way Assn. Formed in 1997 by an amalgamation of the AREA, the AAR's Communications and Signals Division, the Roadmasters and Maintenance-of-Way Assn. of America, and the American Railway Bridge and Building Assn. Develops and advances knowledge and recommended practices for the design, construction, and maintenance of railway infrastructure.

arrival notice   A notice, furnished to consignee, of the arrival of a freight shipment.

ash cat   (Slang) Steam locomotive fireman.

ASLRRA   American Short Line and Regional Railroad Assn. The primary trade association for fulfilling common needs of shortline and regional railroads. Provides information to members and represents interests of its membership in relations with large railroads and with federal legislators and agencies.

assigned car A railroad-owned or controlled car that has been placed in dedicated service to a specific customer.

ATC Automatic train control. A speed-control system that provides continuous signaling information and enforces speed limits. See also **LSL**.

ATS Automatic train stop. A system that enforces acknowledgment of restrictive signals and automatically applies the train and locomotive brakes if this acknowledgment is not made.

automatic air brake A braking system that draws air from the atmosphere and stores it under pressure. A reduction in brake-pipe pressure, regardless of how it is made (bleeding of air by use of a valve or by a break in the train line) automatically applies the brakes. An increase of brake-pipe pressure causes the brakes to release.

automatic block signal A block signal that is activated either by track circuit or in conjunction with interlocking or controlled point circuits. This block signal automatically indicates block (specific segment of track) occupancy.

automatic block signal system (ABS) A block signal system in which the use of each block is governed by an automatic block signal, cab signal, or both.

automatic block signaling A system in which signals are operated automatically by a train, a broken rail, an open switch, or a car standing on a turnout fouling the main track.

automobile car A car specially designed for transporting automobiles. It may be a type of boxcar (pre-1960 era) or a bilevel or trilevel flatcar usually called an automobile rack car (post-1960 era).

automobile parts car A boxcar specially fitted for transporting automobile parts in racks without packing.

automobile rack car Flatcar with steel racks for transporting fully assembled automobiles. Racks have either two or three levels, are equipped with tie-down devices, and are cushioned for vertical and horizontal shocks. Early designs with open tops and sides have been supplanted by fully enclosed designs.

average agreement An agreement in which a customer accrues credits and debits for demurrage charges. The customer is then billed monthly.

B&B See **bridges and buildings**.

B end of car The end on which the hand brake is located.

B unit A diesel locomotive unit without a cab and without a complete set of operating controls. B units are usually equipped with a minimum of controls (hostler controls) for independent operation at engine terminals.

back haul 1. To move a shipment back over part of the route that it has traveled. Usually the result of mishandling the car. 2. A marketing strategy to generate additional revenue by acquiring loads for cars that normally would have to be returned to their home road or to the point of origin of a front-haul shipment as empties.

back shop Facility for rebuilding and heavy repair of locomotives.

backup air signal A warning whistle that can be operated at the rear of the train when backing up. Air for its operation is taken from the train line.

bad order Designates a car as defective and in need of repair.

baggage car Car for haulage of passengers' checked luggage and often also express and mail traffic in the consist of a passenger train.

ballast Granular or aggregate material (crushed stone, gravel, cinders, or the like) placed on the roadbed to hold track in line. Ballast preferably consists of hard particles easily handled in tamping that distribute the load imposed by train movements, drain well, and resist plant growth.

ballast car A car for carrying ballast for repair and construction work, usually a gondola or hopper.

ballast tamper A machine for compacting ballast under the ties.

bat out, batting them out (Slang) Switching cars, especially by "kicking" movements. See **kick**; **switching**.

bay-window caboose See **side-bay caboose**.

belt line A railroad that generally operates only within or around a metropolitan area.

bl (Slang) See **bilevel**.

big hole (Slang) Emergency position of the air-brake valve. Also used as an expression to stop as quickly as possible. See **emergency application**.

big ox (Slang) Conductor.

bilevel A two-level freight car used to transport automobiles or light trucks.

bill of lading Contract tendered to the railroad by a customer for transportation services authorized by a tariff. Used to prepare a waybill.

billed weight The weight of a freight shipment (lading) shown on a waybill and freight bill.

billet car A low-side gondola car built of steel throughout for transportation of hot steel billets.

billing repair card The card furnished to the car owner when repair is done on a foreign car.

blanket waybill One waybill produced for a multiple-car shipment. The waybill is associated with the lead car, while the other cars are listed in the body of the waybill for the lead car.

bleed a car To drain the air from a car's reservoir by pulling a rod on the side of the car. Bleeding removes air brakes, but not the hand brakes, allowing the car to roll freely.

block 1. A length of track with defined limits on which train movements are governed by block signals, block-limit signals, or cab signals. 2. A group of cars classified for movement to the same destination.

block operator   A person who follows a train dispatcher's instructions for aligning signals and switches on tracks within a block.

block signal   A fixed signal (hand signal or verbal block indication in the absence of a fixed signal) at the entrance of a block to govern use of that block.

block signal system   A method of governing the movement of trains into or within one or more blocks by the use of signals.

block station   A place provided for governance of the movement of trains by block signals or other means.

blocking   Wood or metal supports to keep shipments in place in or on cars.

blocking device   A lever, plug, ring, or other method of control that restricts the operation of a switch or signal.

blue flag   A blue light, flag, or sign placed on a track or equipment that signifies that employees are working on, under, or between equipment on that track.

board   A list of employees available for service. See also **extra board**.

boarding car   See **camp car**.

body bolster   See **bolster**.

bogie   1. (Slang) The chassis or running gear of a highway semitrailer on which a container is hauled. 2. Alternative term for truck on a car or locomotive. See **truck**.

BOL   See **bill of lading**.

bolster   A cross-member on the underside of a carbody and in the center of a truck, through which the weight is transmitted. The bolsters carry the body and truck center plates. The body bolster rests on the truck bolster, and they are connected by a center pin mounted on the truck bolster.

book of rules classes   Annual classes held for operating department personnel at which they review and are instructed in the safe operating practices and procedures required by the transportation department.

boomer   (Slang) Worker who moves from one railway employer to another relatively frequently.

bottle car   A car used for transporting molten metal.

bouncer   (Slang) Caboose, usually short four-wheel type. See **caboose**.

bowl   The fan-shaped tracks at the bottom of a hump used to receive cars that are being classified.

box or boxcar   An enclosed railcar used for transporting lading that must be protected from the weather. Generally the lading is packaged or palletized, but can be bulk.

bracing   See **blocking**.

brain or brains   Slang term for conductor.

brain box   (Slang) See **caboose**.

brake club   Three-foot-long hickory stick used by freight trainmen to tighten hand brakes.

brake footboard   See **brake step**.

brake pawl   A small, specially shaped steel piece pivoted to engage the teeth of a brake ratchet wheel to prevent turning backward and thus releasing the brakes.

brake pipe   The air-brake piping of a car or locomotive that acts as a supply pipe for the reservoirs. When all brake pipes on the cars are joined, the entire pipeline comprises what is commonly called the train line.

brake ratchet   A round metal forging attached to the brake wheel shaft that has teeth that the pawl engages, thus preventing the wheel and shaft from turning backward.

brake shaft   A shaft on which a chain is wound and by which the power of a hand brake is applied to the wheels.

brake shoe   Friction material shaped to fit the tread of the wheel when the brakes are applied.

brake slug   A locomotive, without diesel engine or traction motors, used as additional braking (in conjunction with another locomotive) for hump or yard operations.

brake step   A small shelf or ledge on the end of a freight car on which the brakeman stands when applying the hand brake.

brake wheel   A wheel attached to the upper end of the brake shaft that is manually turned to apply hand brakes.

brakeman   Train service employee who assists with train and yard operations.

brass collar or brass hat   Any railroad official.

brass pounder   (Slang, obsolete) A railway telegrapher.

bridge carrier   A railway that serves primarily as a connecting carrier between two or more other railways, rather than as a traffic-originating or terminating carrier.

bridge warning   See **telltale**.

bridges and buildings   Department responsible for the maintenance of railway buildings and bridges.

broad gauge   A distance between the heads of the rails greater than 4 feet 9 inches. See also **gauge of track; narrow gauge; standard gauge**.

Budd RDC, or Budd car   See **RDC**.

buggy   (Slang) Caboose.

bulk freight   Freight not in packages or containers.

bulkhead   Movable partition that divides a car into sections or compartments.

bulkhead flat   A flatcar with bulkheads at each end of the car, used for shipments of wood, wallboard, and similar materials.

bull   (Slang) Railway police officer.

bulletin order   An order that contains items affecting the movement of trains and is issued by authority and over the signature of the superintendent.

bump   (Slang) Displace a junior person (one with less seniority) from an existing position.

bumping post   A braced post or block placed at the end of a stub track to prevent rolling cars from going off the ends of the rails.

business car   See **office car**.

C&S   See **communications and signals**.

cab   The space in the locomotive unit that contains the operating controls and provides shelter and seats for crew members.

cab signal   A signal (located in the engine control compartment) that indicates a condition affecting the movement of a train and is used in conjunction with interlocking signals and with or in lieu of block signals.

cabin car   Formal term for caboose on the former Pennsylvania Railroad.

caboose   A car usually attached to the rear of freight trains for accommodation of the conductor and trainmen (as office and quarters) while in transit. (Generally, cabooses have been replaced by the end-of-train telemetry device, and the conductor rides in the locomotive cab.) Also formally termed "cabin car" and "van" on a few railroads and referred to by approximately 25 slang terms, including (most commonly) way car, hack, shanty, crummy, crum box, brain box, buggy, bouncer, and chariot.

CACD   Computer-assisted crew dispatching. A system designed to provide information for filling crews on scheduled and nonscheduled trains and for monitoring individual train and engine employees' work records and qualifications.

call board   (Obsolete) A chalk board listing crew members, engine numbers, and train numbers, on view in a division office.

caller   An employee who notifies train and engine crews and other employees to report for duty.

camelback   (Obsolete) 1. A steam locomotive with a cab atop the boiler (rare). 2. See **Mother Hubbard**.

camp car   A term commonly applied to a car used as a place of lodging for workmen.

cap   (Slang) Track torpedo.

capacity   The normal load in pounds, cubic feet, or gallons that the car is designed to carry. These figures are stenciled on the car.

car distributor   An individual who is assigned the responsibility of distributing empty freight cars.

car dumper   A device for quick unloading of bulk materials such as coal or grain. After being clamped to the rail, the car is tilted or rolled over to discharge the lading.

car float   A large, flat-bottomed vessel equipped with tracks on which railroad cars are moved over inland waterways or across harbors.

car hire   See **per diem**.

car inspector   Person who works for the mechanical department and has the responsibility to identify cars in need of repair.

car knocker   (Slang) Car Inspector.

car lining   Material placed on the walls of a car to protect the lading.

car seal   See **seals**.

car stop   A device for stopping motion of a car by engaging the wheels, as distinguished from a bumping post that arrests motion upon contact with the coupler of a car.

car toad   (Slang) Car inspector or carman.

card board   Sometimes called a **tack board**. A small board, secured to the outside of a freight car, on which are tacked cards giving shipping directions or warning of dangerous lading or other conditions.

carload   1. A one-car shipment of freight from one consignor to one consignee at one time on one day. 2. The quantity of freight required for the application of a carload rate.

carload rate   A rate applicable to a carload quantity of freight.

carman   Person who inspects and performs repairs on cars. Overlaps with car inspector.

car-mile   The movement of a car the distance of one mile. A term used in statistical data.

cash customer   A consignee who must pay any freight charges assessed against an inbound shipment before delivery of the car.

CATD   Computer-assisted train dispatching. 1. An automated train-tracking system that receives a signal when a train passes over a pressure-sensitive switch physically attached to a track and electronically transmits the "pass" time to the TMS. 2. Control of train movements by a dispatcher with the aid of computer-based tools for optimization of the use of track capacity and movement of trains.

catenary   On electric railways, the term describing the overhead conductor of electricity that is contacted by the pantograph or trolley pole (current collector), and the related support structure for supplying electricity to propel trains (traction current).

center pin   A large steel pin that passes through the center plates on the body bolster and truck bolster. The truck turns about the pin, and stress is taken by the center plates.

center plate   One of a pair of plates that fit one into the other and support the carbody on the trucks allowing them to turn freely under the car.

center sill   The center, longitudinal member of the underframe of a car that forms the backbone of the underframe and transmits most of the buffing shocks from one end of the car to the other.

center-beam car   A bulkhead flatcar equipped with a girder or truss extending the full length of the car between the end bulkheads. It is used for transporting finished, packaged lumber.

center-dump car   A car that discharges its entire load between the rails.

chair car   1. See **parlor car**. 2. Passenger car for accommodation of coach passengers, equipped with seating offering above-average comfort level.

chariot   (Slang) Caboose.

cinder dick   (Slang) Railway police officer.

circus loading   A means of loading highway trailers onto flatcars by moving them over the ends of the cars.

class rate   A rate based on an assigned class rating (a percentage of first class) published in the uniform freight classification.

classification signals   (Obsolete) Lights and flags displayed on both sides of the front of a train to denote an extra train (white lights, flags) or that a train is being followed by another section of the same scheduled train (green lights, flags).

classification yard   A yard where cars are grouped according to their destination and made ready for proper train movement.

cleaning in transit   The stopping of shipments, such as peanuts, to be cleaned at a point short of their final destination.

clearance   The limiting dimensions of height and width for all cars in tunnels, station platforms, and other structures.

clearance car   A car for measuring maximum vertical and horizontal clearance limits within bridges and tunnels, beneath overpasses, and against structures and other trackside fixtures.

cleat   A strip of wood or metal used to afford additional strength to prevent warping or to hold lading in position.

CLM   Car location message. System and service that allows customers to inquire (from their own computer terminals) on the last reported move or status of cars owned, leased, or assigned to them.

CMC   Car management center. Locations on a railroad from which car management personnel monitor and supply car requirements for customers.

CMS   Connection monitoring system. A computerized system designed to track the progress of train and block movement to ensure that schedules are maintained and traffic moves in the best possible way.

coal car   A car for carrying coal; usually a hopper car or high-side gondola.

coal train   A unit train that carries only carloads of coal.

COBAN   Coil steel and banana cars. Car-use report that identifies the location and/or status of cars on the system. Originally created to keep track of gondolas used for coil-steel lading and carloads of bananas.

COFC   Acronym for container-on-flatcar intermodal service or equipment.

coil-steel car   A gondola specially fitted to haul coil steel.

coke rack   A slatted frame or box applied above the sides and ends of gondola or hopper cars to increase the cubic capacity for the purpose of carrying coke or other freight in which the bulk is large relative to the weight.

coke train   A unit train that carries only carloads of coke.

collect   A term used in waybilling to indicate that the freight charges will be paid at the destination point of the shipment.

combination rate   A rate made by combining two or more rates published in different tariffs.

combine   Passenger car containing a baggage-express and a passenger compartment.

commodity rate   A rate applicable to carriage of a specific commodity between certain specified points.

communications and signals   Department responsible for the maintenance of train communications and the track signaling system.

compartment tank car   A tank car with the tank divided into several sections for the purpose of carrying different commodities in a single shipment.

compartmentizer car   A boxcar equipped with movable bulkheads that can be used to divide the car into separate sections.

computer-assisted train dispatching   See **CATD**.

concealed damage   Damage to the contents of a package that is in good order externally.

conductor   Train service employee in charge of the train or yard crew.

conflicting routes   Two or more routes over which movements cannot be made simultaneously because of the possibility of collision.

connecting carrier   A railroad that has a direct physical connection with another or forms a connecting link between two or more railroads.

consignee   Person or company to whom a shipment is destined.

consignee marks   A symbol placed on packages for export, generally consisting of a square, triangle, diamond, circle, cross, or the like, with designed letters and/or numbers for the purpose of identification.

consignor   Person or firm from whom a shipment originates. Also called shipper.

consist   1. A list of all the cars in a train in standing order (from engine to caboose/marker). 2. All the cars in a train.

consolidator   A person or company that contracts with individual shippers and consolidates shipments into one or more trailers, containers, or railcars.

constructive placement   When, because of some disability on the part of the consignor or consignee, a car cannot be placed for loading or unloading, it is considered as being under constructive placement and subject to demurrage rules and charges, the same as if it were actually placed.

container car   A flatcar or open-top car, such as a gondola, on which containers of freight are loaded.

continuous seals   A term denoting that the seals on a car remained intact during the movement of the car from point of origin to destination, or, if the seals were broken in transit, that this was done by proper authority and without opportunity for loss to occur before new seals were applied. See also **seals**.

control or driving trailer   An unpowered passenger car operated in train with self-propelled electric or diesel M.U. cars and equipped with controls and other appliances on one or both ends to permit its operation as the lead car in a train of such cars. See **M.U.**

controlled point A place designated in the timetable where signals are remotely controlled.

controlled siding A siding whose use is governed by signals under the control of a train dispatcher or operator.

cornered A term used when a car has been struck by another car because it was not in the clear. See **in the clear**.

coupler An appliance for connecting cars or locomotives together. Government regulations require that these must couple automatically by impact and must be uncoupled without going between the cars.

coupler centering device An arrangement for maintaining the coupler normally in the center line of draft but allowing it to move to either side when a car is rounding a curve while coupled to another car.

coupler knuckle lock The block that drops into position when the knuckle closes and holds it in place, preventing uncoupling.

coupler lock lifter The part of the mechanism inside the coupler head that is moved by the uncoupling rod and, in moving, lifts the knuckle lock so that the knuckle can open.

covered gondola Gondola that has been equipped with some form of removable cover that can be placed over the lading to protect it from weather exposure in transit. Used primarily for loading sheet steel in coils or bundles without the necessity of packing.

covered hopper car A hopper car with a permanent roof, roof hatches, and bottom openings for unloading. Used for carrying cement or other bulk commodities.

CP See **constructive placement**; **controlled point**.

crane A railcar (or highway equipment) equipped with a boom and other mechanisms used to rerail cars.

crew General term used to describe the individuals working together as a unit, such as train crew.

crib That portion of ballast between two adjacent ties.

cripple (Slang) See **bad order**.

crossing (Track) A structure used where one track crosses another at grade and consisting of four connected frogs.

crossing watchman Person who uses handheld stop sign, lantern, and/or flag to stop road traffic at rail grade crossings of streets and highways when a train approaches and occupies the crossing.

crossover A combination of two switches (turnouts) connecting two adjacent tracks. This combination provides a means for movement to cross from one track to another.

crosstie The transverse member of the track structure to which the rails are fastened to provide proper gauge and to cushion, distribute, and transmit the stresses of traffic through the ballast to the roadbed. In North America, usually made of wood, sometimes made of concrete, steel, or plastic.

crum box (Slang) Caboose.

crummy (Slang) Caboose.

CSD Car service directive. A method for effecting equipment control and use for specific customers or lading.

CTC Centralized traffic control. A system of railroad operation under which train movements are authorized by block signal indications for both opposing and following movement on the same track. Signals (and, in most instances, switches) are remotely controlled by a dispatcher. Also called traffic control system (TCS).

cubic capacity The carrying capacity of a car according to measurement in cubic feet.

cupola A small structure built on top of a caboose roof to afford a means of lookout for the train crew.

current of traffic The assigned direction for movement on a main track as specified in the timetable.

cushion underframe A term commonly used to designate an appliance within the framework of a railcar designed to prevent the shocks and impact stresses from damaging the car structure or its lading. See also **center sill**.

cut 1. To uncouple a car. 2. A group of cars coupled together. 3. That part of the right of way that is excavated out of a hill or mountain instead of running up and over or being tunneled through.

cut lever See **uncoupling lever**.

cut the board (Slang) To reduce the number of people on the extra board. See **extra board**.

cutout cock A valve that, when closed, will bypass (cut out) the air-brake system for that car.

damage-free car Car equipped with interior lading restraint devices to decrease the possibility of damage to lading during movement.

dangerous Term applied to any shipment of a hazardous commodity.

dead rail A second set of rails over a scale used when cars are not being weighed. It provides a bypass around the set of rails connected to the weighing mechanism. See **scale track**.

deadhead 1. Any person riding a train (freight or passenger) who is not part of the crew and does not pay for passage. 2. Employees (generally train crews) receiving pay for, and being transported from one terminal to another to perform, or after having performed, work.

deadman 1. A buried timber, log, or beam designed as an anchorage to which a guy wire or cable is fastened to support a structure, such as a wood or steel column, derrick, or mast. 2. (Slang) See **deadman control**.

deadman control A foot pedal or brake valve that must be kept in a depressed position while the locomotive is operating. A release from this depressed position initiates an air-brake application after a short time delay.

deck 1. Floor of a flatcar or gondola. 2. Floor of a steam locomotive cab.

deep-well flatcar See **depressed-center flatcar**.

defect card receptacle A small metal container, placed underneath the car for protection from the weather, in which cards identifying defects are placed.

delayer (Slang) Train dispatcher.

delivering carrier   The railroad that delivers a shipment to the consignee.

demurrage   A tariff application designed to limit the amount of time a customer has a car for loading or unloading. It includes a schedule of charges assessed against the customer when a car is held in excess of the allotted free time.

departure yard   That section of a railroad yard used to group cars on tracks from which trains are made up and depart.

depressed-center flatcar   A flatcar on which the section of the floor between the trucks is depressed to permit loading of high shipments within overhead clearance limits. Also called a deep-well flatcar.

derail   A track safety device designed to guide a car off the rails at a selected spot as a means of protection against collisions or other accidents; commonly used on spurs or sidings to prevent cars from fouling the main line.

destination   1. The place to which a shipment is consigned. 2. The termination point for a train crew.

detention   1. Term applied to tariff charges applicable (in addition to regular demurrage) to certain cars. 2. Charges assessed for the use of a railroad-owned or controlled trailer/container when off railroad property.

DF car   See **damage-free car**.

diamond   See **crossing**.

diaphragm   A canvas or rubber shield used to provide an enclosed passageway between two coupled railcars.

diesel terminal   Location where locomotives are fueled, inspected, and given light repairs.

diesel-electric locomotive   A locomotive in which the diesel engine drives an electric generator or alternator that in turn supplies electricity to traction motors that are geared to the driving axles.

dining car   Passenger car for full meal service; typically contains food-preparation facilities (galley) and dining area.

dinky   (Slang) 1. A small engine used for switching around roundhouses or shops. 2. A commuter or short-haul passenger train.

distant signal   A fixed signal used to govern the approach of a train to a home signal.

distributed power   Locomotives located in two or more locations in a long train, usually controlled by radio.

diversion   Term and charges applied to shipments that have their destination or consignee changed before being moved to their final destination, and provided the change does not require a back-haul.

division   1. On some railroads, a designated part of the railroad's system assigned to the supervision of a division superintendent.   2. The apportionment, by carriers, of revenue received from a shipment moved over more than one rail carrier.

division notice   Notice issued by authority and over the signature of the superintendent that contains instructions that do not affect the movement of trains.

dog catcher   (Slang) A relief crew for a train that has stopped because its initial crew members reached the limits of their allowed hours of service time under the federal hours-of-service law.

dog law   (Slang) See **hog law**.

dogs got 'em   (Slang) Phrase used to indicate that members of a crew reached the limit of their active hours-of-service time under the federal hours-of-service law.

dome car   Also Vista-Dome car and Astra Dome car. Passenger car with glass-enclosed upper level for viewing of scenery. The lower level may contain either coach seats, parlor-car seats, or lounge facilities.

doodlebug   (Slang) See **gas-electric car**.

dormitory car   A passenger car with sleeping accommodations for onboard service personal, such as dining-car staff.

double   1. Two consecutive tours of duty, or two tours within a 24-hour period. 2. Putting a train together when part of a train is on one track and the balance is on another.

double the hill   (Slang) Uncoupling of a train into two or more parts for separate movement of each part to surmount a grade too steep for the pulling power of the locomotive in relation to the total weight of the entire train.

double-deck   (Stock car) A car with a second floor (often made removable) halfway between the ordinary floor and the roof to increase the carrying capacity of the car for small livestock, such as pigs and sheep.

double-stack train   A train of specially equipped flatcars (or well cars) on which intermodal containers are stacked two-high.

draft gear   The unit that forms the connection between the coupler rigging and the center sill. The purpose of this unit is to receive the shocks incidental to train movements and coupling cars and so cushion the force of impact.

drag   (Slang)1. A heavy train, usually carrying coal, ore, or stone. 2. A group of cars for movement from one point to another within a terminal. 3. A train of empties.

dragging-equipment detector   A sensor between and alongside the rails to detect dragging equipment on cars and engines.

draw head   1. The head of an automatic coupler, exclusive of the knuckle, knuckle pin, and lock. 2. (Obsolete) The head of a link-and-pin coupler into which the link is inserted and secured with a pin. See **link-and-pin**.

drawbar   1. The wrench-shaped piece of metal into which the knuckle of a coupler fits. The heaviest component of a coupler. 2. A steel bar used to connect two cars, two diesel locomotive units, or a steam locomotive and tender, in lieu of a conventional coupler.

drill   The handling or switching of cars in freight yards.

drill track   A track connecting with the ladder track, over which engines and cars move back and forth in switching.

drone   A locomotive unit without its own controls used in conjunction with one or more other locomotives. See also **radio-controlled engine**.

drop   Switching movement in which cars are cut off from an engine and allowed to roll free into a track in order to reverse the position of the cars in relation to the engine.

drop brake shaft   A brake shaft for flatcars that normally extends above the floor, but can be dropped down should conditions of lading require.

drop-bottom car   A gondola with a level floor, equipped with a number of drop doors in the floor of the car for discharging the load.

drop-end gondola   A gondola with end doors that can be lowered against the car floor when the car is used for shipping long material that extends over more than one car.

drop-frame trailer   A truck trailer, similar to a moving van, that has a portion of its floor lowered to a point below the top of the wheels.

dual-control switch   A power-operated switch also equipped for hand operation.

dump car   A car from which the load is discharged either through doors or by tipping the carbody.

dunnage   The material used to protect or support freight in or on cars, such as bracings, false floors, or racks.

dynamic braking   A means of braking on a locomotive by using the traction motors as generators and dissipating this power through resistors. Used to reduce the speed of the train separately from the air brakes.

eagle eye   (Slang) Locomotive engineer.

easy sign   (Slang) A hand signal indicating that the train is to move slowly.

electric locomotive   A locomotive that receives electric power from an overhead contact wire or third rail and uses the power to drive electric traction motors connected by gears to the driving axles.

electrically locked switch   A hand-operated switch equipped with an electrically controlled device that restricts the movement of the switch.

embargo   An order prohibiting the acceptance and/or handling of freight at certain points or via certain routes because of emergencies, congestion, strikes, or other disruptions.

emergency application   A quick heavy reduction of brake-pipe pressure made when a train must be stopped in the minimum distance possible. An emergency application may also occur when a brake pipe is broken, or when air hoses between cars are disconnected with angle cocks open.

emergency brake valve   A valve for applying the train brakes in an emergency. It is connected to the brake pipe by a branch pipe and operated by releasing brake-pipe air to the atmosphere.

emergency rate   A freight rate established to meet some immediate and pressing need, without due regard to the usual rate factors.

employees timetable   See **timetable**.

empty-car bill   Waybill used to move ordinary empty cars from one station to another.

end door   A door in the end of a car. In some boxcars so equipped, this door is used for loading and unloading long material that cannot be handled through the side door.

engine   A locomotive unit propelled by any form of energy or a combination of such units operated from a single control and used in either train or yard service.

engineer or locomotive engineer   The driver or operator of a locomotive.

engineman   See **engineer**.

EOT or EOTD   End-of-train telemetry device. A portable device attached to the rear coupler of a train that is capable of monitoring air pressure in the air-brake system, train integrity, and condition of the battery powering the device, and transmitting this information by radio signal to the locomotive cab, where it is displayed. It includes a flashing marker light and rear-of-train emergency brake application capability. This device has replaced most uses of cabooses. Also referred to as a sense and transmit unit (STU).

equipment register   Official guide listing all railroad and privately owned rail and intermodal equipment.

excessive-dimension car   See **high and wide car**.

exchange bill of lading   A bill of lading issued in exchange for another bill of lading.

express-train caboose   (Obsolete) A caboose with high-speed trucks for accommodation of the conductor and brakeman at the rear of a mail and express train. See also **rider coach**.

extra board   A list of employees available for service or "on call," who do not have regularly scheduled work assignments.

extra train   A train not represented on and authorized to move by the timetable.

fabrication in transit   The stopping of steel or other products at a point located between the points of origin and destination for further process of manufacture, for example, steel beams to be fabricated as bridge girders.

facing movement   The movement of a train over the points of a switch that face in a direction opposite to that in which the train is moving.

FAK   Freight all kinds. A term used to indicate that the lading of a boxcar or an intermodal trailer or container load is mixed, that is, includes two or more types of commodities.

Federal Railroad Administration   See **FRA**.

feeding in transit   The stopping of shipments of livestock at a point located between the points of shipment origin and destination to be fed and watered.

field man   Brakeman or switchman who works the position farthest from the engine.

fifth wheel   The supporting plate and pivot mounted on the rear of the frame of a truck tractor. It engages the kingpin mounted on the underside of the forward end of a truck trailer (and also of a chassis for highway movement of an intermodal container).

fireman   (Obsolete) Person who rides on a locomotive and assists the engineer in the operation of the train (and, on a steam locomotive, is responsible for maintaining the flow of fuel into the locomotive's firebox and related tasks necessary for production of steam).

first trick   Term designating the working hours between 6:30 A.M. and 3:59 P.M.

fixed signal   A signal of fixed location that affects the movement of a train.

fixed stanchion   A nonmovable, vertical support device on a flatcar on which the front end of a trailer rests and in which the kingpin of the trailer is locked while it is being transported on a flatcar. See also **knock-down stanchion**.

flag stop or flag station   A station at which passenger trains stop when signaled.

flagman   (Obsolete) 1. Brakeman who was primarily responsible for assisting with the operations of the train and protecting the rear end of a train in an emergency. 2. Person who worked at a crossing of rail tracks and signaled approaching trains to either stop or proceed, or operated crossing gates, to prevent rail-crossing accidents.

flammable   Term used to indicate a commodity that can easily be ignited. Railcars and intermodal trailers and containers carrying these commodities must carry prescribed placards.

flammable liquids   Liquids that are highly flammable. Railcars and intermodal trailers and containers carrying these liquids must carry prescribed placards.

flatcar   1. An open car without sides, ends, or top, used principally for hauling lumber, heavy machinery, structural steel, and other large-sized shipments. 2. The same type of car, although usually of greater length, used for hauling intermodal trailers and containers.

flat spots   Term used to indicate flattened areas on the tread of the wheels of a car or locomotive. Generally caused when a car or locomotive has been dragged on the rails (as in applying the brakes and skidding).

flat switch   Switching of cars in a yard not equipped with a man-made hill or "hump" to provide gravity-assisted movement of cars.

flat wheel   A car wheel that has flat spots on the tread. See also **flat spots**.

flexi-flo   Term used to indicate a type of intermodal shipment. Usually applied to covered hoppers whose lading is to be transferred under air pressure from a railcar to a highway truck trailer.

flimsy   (Slang, obsolete) Copy of train order on thin paper. See **train order**.

float bridge   A bridge-type structure capable of vertical movement on its waterside end used to connect car floats and railcar-ferry ships with rail landings.

float train   A train that is transported across a body of water on barges.

floatage   The floating or transfer of railroad cars across water, and the charge for such service.

floating load   A load in which the lading is consolidated into a single unit. The movement of the unit over the floor of the car permits the dissipation of impact shocks. No blocking or braking devices are used to dissipate of bar impact shocks between the unitized lading and the ends of the car.

following section   An additional section of a train scheduled in the timetable, running closely behind the first section or another multiple section of the same train.

foreign car   Any car not owned by the particular railroad on which it is running.

Form D   Written instructions set forth in a prescribed format governing operation of trains, track cars, and other types of equipment on a designated section of railroad.

FRA   Federal Railroad Administration. Agency within the U.S. Department of Transportation responsible for ensuring that all railroads comply with safe and statutory operating principles and for administering other rail-related federal government-sponsored programs.

free time   The time allowed by a rail carrier to customers to load or unload freight, after which demurrage and/or detention charges will accrue.

freight all kinds   See **FAK**.

freight bill   A statement given to a customer identifying the charges assessed for transportation.

freight charge   The charge assessed for transporting freight.

freight claims   Claims from shippers arising as a result of damage to or loss of commodities transported in rail service.

freight classification   See **uniform freight classification**.

freight forwarder   A person or firm engaged in the business of shipping and distributing less-than-carload freight.

freight house   (Obsolete) The station facility of a railway for receiving and delivering freight, particularly shipments of less-than-carload size.

frog   1. A track structure used at the intersection of two running rails to provide support for wheels and passageways for their flanges, thus permitting wheels on either rail to cross to the other. 2. An implement for rerailing car wheels.

full-service application   An application of the air brakes resulting from a reduction in brake-pipe pressure at a service rate until maximum brake-cylinder pressure is developed.

fusee   Red flare used for flagging purposes.

gallery car   A passenger car normally used in commuter or suburban service that contains a main seating area on the lower level and an upper-deck level with an open aisleway through the center. The aisleway gives a "gallery" appearance to the car interior.

gandy dancer   (Slang) Track (maintenance-of-way) worker.

gantlet or gauntlet   A segment of rail line within which two tracks overlap to permit passage through a narrow structure or area such as a bridge or tunnel.

gantry crane   A stilted traveling crane supported on a bridge or trestle. Trestle bents are constructed on wheels so the whole structure travels on a track laid on the ground or floor.

gas-electric car   (Obsolete) Self-propelled passenger car, usually also containing a baggage-express and an RPO compartment. Some models were built with only baggage-express and RPO compartments and were normally paired with an unpowered (trailer) passenger coach. It was powered by a gasoline-engine-driven generator that fed electricity to traction motors geared to axles. In later years many were converted from gasoline to diesel power.

gateway   A point at which freight moving from one territory to another is interchanged between railroads.

gauge of track   The distance between the heads of the rails, measured at a point ⅝ inch below the top of rails. See **broad gauge**; **narrow gauge**; **standard gauge**.

GBL   Government bill of lading. See **bill of lading**.

general order   Order (issued by authority and over the signature of the designated official) that contains changes in rules, revisions to the timetable, and/or other instructions.

general-service car   Box car, gondola car, or flatcar without special equipment and not designed for a specific commodity or shipper.

gladhand   Metal coupling piece on the end of an air hose.

goat   (Slang) Switch engine.

gondola car   A freight car with sides and ends, but without a top covering. Gondola cars are sometimes distinguished as high-side, low-side, drop-end, drop-bottom, and general-service.

grab iron   Steel bar attached to cars and engines as a handhold.

grain door   A partition placed across the inside of the regular door of a boxcar to prevent loss of grain by leaking.

graveyard shift   See **third trick**.

gross ton-mile   The movement of a ton of transportation equipment and contents one mile.

gross weight   The combined weight of a car, the material used for packing, and the lading or contents.

grounded or grounding   Term used to indicate that a trailer or container has been removed from a railcar.

guard rail   1. Auxiliary rails between the running rails on bridges, in tunnels, or near other hazardous site conditions to prevent derailed engines and cars from leaving the roadbed before exiting the danger site. 2. A short, heavily braced rail or steel fitting opposite a frog to prevent wheels from striking the frog point and/or taking the wrong route.

gun   (Slang) Track torpedo.

hack   (Slang) See **caboose**.

hand brake   The brake apparatus used to manually apply the brakes on a car or locomotive.

hauler   (Slang) Engine assigned to pull train from origin to destination, as distinguished from a helper or pusher engine added for a portion of the train's trip.

hazardous materials   Term used to identify dangerous contents in a car.

hazmat   Acronym for hazardous-materials shipments.

head block   The fixed signal at the entrance to a segment of absolute permissive block territory, indicated by a block-limit signal.

head end   1. Beginning or forward portion of any train. 2. (Slang) The locomotive or control-cab car positioned at the front of a train.

head man   Brakeman responsible for work done in connection with the forward section of the train.

head pin   (Slang) Head man.

head shack   (Slang) See **brakeman**; **head man**.

head tapper   (Slang, obsolete) See **telltale**.

head-end traffic   (Slang) Mail and express traffic, commonly (but not always) handled in cars coupled immediately behind the locomotive at the head end of a passenger train.

heater car   An insulated boxcar equipped with heating apparatus for the protection of perishables.

heavy OK   Term used to indicate that repairs (of more than 51 man-hours) have been completed for a car that was classified as a heavy repair.

heavy repair   Term used to indicate that a car is in need of repairs requiring more than 51 man-hours to complete.

heavy-repair shop   Facility where heavy repairs are performed.

held-for-billing   Term used to designate a car in the yard for which there is no waybill or forwarding instructions.

helper engine   A locomotive placed at the front, middle, or rear of a train to assist in movement of the train over a heavy grade. Diesel-electric and electric helper locomotives can be either manned or remotely controlled from the head unit.

hi-cube car   See **hy-cube car**.

high and wide car   Car of excessive dimensions that must be handled with special care and attention to clearances in tunnels, on bridges, and with other line-side fixtures.

high iron   (Slang) Main-line or high-speed track or a set of such tracks.

high rail   1. The outer or elevated rail of a curved track. 2. The inspection of a section of railroad using a highway vehicle equipped with rail wheels.

highball (Slang) Signal to proceed at maximum authorized speed.

high-side gondola A gondola car with sides and ends over 36 inches high.

hog (Slang) Locomotive.

hog law (Slang) The federal statute that provides that all train and engine crews must be relieved of duty after 12 hours of continuous service.

hogger (Slang) Locomotive engineer.

hoghead (Slang) Locomotive engineer.

hold track A track on which cars awaiting disposition are held.

hole (Slang) Passing track enabling one train to pass another.

home A location where a car is on the tracks of its owner.

home car A car on the tracks of its owner.

home junction A junction with the road that owns the car.

home road The owning road of a railroad car.

home route The return route of a foreign empty car to the owning road.

home signal A fixed signal that governs the entrance to an interlocking or controlled point.

hook (Slang) A crane used in wreck train service. Also called big hook or wrecker.

hopper An open-top car with one or more pockets (hoppers) opening on the underside of the car to permit quick unloading of bulk commodities.

hostler An employee who operates light engines in designated engine-house territory.

hostler's control A simplified throttle provided to move the B unit of a diesel locomotive not equipped with a regular engineer's control.

hotbox (Slang) An overheated journal caused by excessive friction between bearing and journal resulting from lack of lubricant or entry of foreign matter into bearing surfaces.

hotbox detector A wayside infrared sensing instrument used to identify overheated journal bearings.

hump A man-made hill in a classification yard used to separate cars from each other by gravity.

hump rider (Obsolete) Term for a brakeman who rides uncoupled, switched cars and applies the hand brake to stop the car.

hy-cube car A boxcar of approximately 86-foot length and 10,000-cubic-foot capacity designed for hauling automobile body stampings and other low-density freight.

ICC See **Interstate Commerce Commission**.

ICC Termination Act of 1995 See **Interstate Commerce Act**.

ICL Instant car location message. Any number of on-line inquiries providing car movement, status, or historical data.

idler car An unloaded flatcar or gondola used to protect overhanging loads or used between cars loaded with long material.

impact register, dutch clock (Slang) An appliance placed in a freight car with a shipment that is both a time clock and a measuring device to record the amount of shock the car received en route.

in the clear A car (or train) is in the clear when it has passed over a switch and frog so far that another car (or train) can pass without collision.

in the hole (Slang) In a siding.

in-bond shipment An import or export shipment that has not been cleared by federal customs officials.

inbound train A train arriving at or moving toward a yard.

independent brake valve A brake valve used to operate the locomotive brakes independently of the train brakes.

indication The information conveyed by a signal.

industrial carrier A short railroad owned or controlled by one or more of the principal industries served by it.

industrial interchange Interchange of cars from one railroad to another that takes place within the confines of a customer's plant.

industrial line See **industrial carrier**.

industrial road See **industrial carrier**.

inflammable liquids Liquids that give off vapors that become combustible at a certain temperature.

in-gate Term used to indicate that a trailer or container has been brought into an intermodal terminal or transfer facility site by a drayman.

initial carrier The railroad on which a shipment originates.

inland carrier A transportation line that hauls export or import traffic between ports and inland points.

insulated rail joint A rail joint that arrests the flow of electric current from rail to rail, as at the end of a track circuit, by means of nonconductors separating rail ends and other metal parts.

interchange The exchange of cars between railroads at specified junction points.

interchange point The location where cars are transferred from one road to another.

interchange track A track on which freight is delivered by one railroad to another.

interline Traffic moving between one or more railroads.

interline freight Freight moving from point of origin to destination over the lines of two or more railroads.

interline waybill A waybill that covers the movement of freight over two or more railroads.

interlocking At a point where two or more rail routes meet or cross, or where movements are made between different tracks on a multiple-track line, an arrangement of signals and signal appliances interconnected so that their movement must succeed each other in a pre-arranged sequence, thus assuring that clear or proceed signals cannot be displayed simultaneously on conflicting routes.

interlocking, automatic An interlocking at which signals and related appliances governing movements function automatically upon the approach of a train, rather than by manual control.

interlocking limits The tracks between the opposing home signals of an interlocking.

interlocking signals The fixed signals of an interlocking.

intermediate carrier A railroad over which a shipment moves but is the road neither of origin nor of destination.

intermediate clause A clause or basis contained in a tariff to provide for rates to a point not named therein, but which is intermediate to points that are named.

intermediate pickup Location or activity between the origin and destination of a train where cars are added to the train.

intermodal 1. Movement of freight in containers or truck trailers by more than one mode of transport. 2. Movement of commodities by a combination of two or more modes of transport, with transloading of the commodities themselves (i.e., not in containers or trailers) between the vehicles and vessels of the different modes.

interplant switch The movement of a car from one industrial plant to another industrial plant.

Interstate Commerce Act An act of Congress that regulates the practices, rates, and rules of transportation lines engaged in handling interstate traffic, superseded by the ICC Termination Act of 1995.

Interstate Commerce Commission U.S. government body that regulated railroads between 1887 and 1995. Replaced by the Surface Transportation Board in 1996.

intraplant switch The movement of cars from one track or spot to another within the yard(s) of a single industrial plant.

iron (Slang) Rail or rails.

ISC Inter system communication. Electronic transfer of data from one computer to another.

joint (Slang) A coupling between two cars.

joint agent A person who has authority to transact business for two or more railroads.

joint bar A steel bar used to fasten together the ends of rails; sometimes called a splice bar or a fishplate.

joint rate A rate applicable to movement of a shipment over the lines of two or more carriers, made by agreement and published in a single tariff under proper concurrence of all railroads or other carriers over which the rate applies.

journal The end of the wheel axle that moves in the bearings.

journal bearing A combination of rollers and races or a block of metal (usually brass or bronze) in contact with

the journal, on which the load rests. In car construction the term, when unqualified, means a car-axle journal bearing. See also **roller bearing**.

journal box The metal housing that encloses the journal of a car axle, the journal bearing, and the wedge, and that holds the oil and lubricating device for lubricating the journal.

journal box lubricator A device for supplying oil to a car journal bearing.

journal brass See **journal bearing**.

juice jack, juice hog (Slang) Electric locomotive.

jumper A flexible cable composed of one or more conductors of electric current, insulated from one another and covered with suitable material to resist abrasion, used to connect electrically the controller circuits between locomotives.

junction Location where the tracks of one railroad intersect with the tracks of another railroad, and cars can be interchanged.

junction point 1. A point at which a branch-line track connects with a main-line track. 2. A location at which two or more railroads interchange cars over connecting tracks. 3. A point of connection between two main lines.

keeper See **latch**.

kick (Slang) The act of pushing one or more cars (uncoupled) at a speed sufficient to allow free forward movement (when uncoupled) into selected tracks.

knock-down stanchion A movable, vertical support device on which the front end of a trailer rests while being transported on a flatcar. See also **fifth wheel**; **fixed stanchion**.

known damage Damage to a shipment discovered before or at the time of delivery of the shipment.

knuckle The rotating coupling hook by which coupling is effected when it is locked.

knuckle pin The pin holding the knuckle in the jaws of the coupler. Sometimes called pivot pin.

knuckle thrower A device that throws the knuckle of a car coupler open when the uncoupling lever is operated.

ladder The main track of a yard from which individual tracks branch.

lading Freight or cargo making up a shipment.

land-bridge Term that designates containerized traffic that originates overseas, then moves across the United States by rail, and is next forwarded to its destination overseas. An example: Japan to Seattle, Washington, by ship; Seattle to South Kearny, New Jersey, by rail; South Kearny to England by ship.

latch A device for catching and holding the lever of a switch stand in position.

lateral motion The motion that takes place crosswise of the track, of all car parts except the wheels and axles.

lawful rate   A rate published in conformity with the provisions of the regulatory law and that does not violate any other provisions of such law.

LCL   Less-than-carload. Term applied to a shipment that does not fill a car.

lead   See **lead track**.

lead track   A yard track from which the ladder track and other tracks branch. It usually connects either end of a yard with the main track.

less-than-carload   See **LCL**.

less-than-carload rate   A rate applicable to a less-than-carload shipment.

light engine   A locomotive, or two or more locomotive units coupled together, moving without caboose or cars attached.

light repair   A car with a defect requiring less than 50 man-hours to repair.

light weight   The weight of any empty freight car.

lighter   (Largely obsolete) A flat-bottomed boat usually used in harbors to move freight between a waterside rail terminal and either a ship or another terminal in the harbor area.

lighterage limits   The limits of the area within which freight is handled by lighters or barges under certain lightering charges, rules, and regulations.

lightering   The hauling of freight on lighters or barges.

limited speed   For passenger trains, not exceeding 45 miles per hour; for freight trains, not exceeding 40 miles per hour.

line haul   The movement of freight over the tracks of a railroad between terminals or from one town or city to another town or city (not a switching service).

line-haul switching   The movement of cars within yard or switching limits of a station, preceding or following a line-haul move.

link-and-pin   (Obsolete) An old (nineteenth-century) type of coupler employing a single link attached to each drawhead by a vertical pin inserted manually when coupling.

lite OK   Term applied to a light-repair car that has been fixed.

livestock car   A special freight car for handling of livestock, equipped with slatted sides to permit inflow of fresh air.

livestock waybill   A special waybill used for shipments of livestock showing feeding and watering instructions.

LMS   Locomotive management system. Computer-based tool for providing information used in managing use and maintenance of locomotive fleets.

load limit   The maximum load, in pounds or kilograms, that a car is designed to carry.

local   1. Road freight train that performs industry switching. 2. A passenger train that receives and discharges passengers at all or a large number of passenger stations between its origin and destination terminals.

local rate   The rate for a shipment originating and terminating on a single railroad.

local waybill   A waybill covering the movement of freight over a single railroad.

locomotive   See **engine**.

long ton   A 2,200-pound ton.

long-and-short-haul clause   (Obsolete) Section 4 of the Interstate Commerce Act, which prohibited railroads from charging more for a shorter than for a longer haul over the same route, except by special permission of the Interstate Commerce Commission.

lookout   See **cupola**.

lounge car   Passenger car equipped with light food- and beverage-serving facilities and, typically, a mixture of seating arranged for scenery viewing and conversation.

low rail   The inner rail of a track on a curve that is maintained at grade, while the opposite or outer rail is elevated.

low-side gondola   A gondola car with sides and ends 36 inches high or less.

LRC   Locomotive remote control. Electronic system for control of locomotives by an employee located outside a locomotive control cab. Remote-control "packs" typically are suspended from a strap or harness sling over the operation employee's shoulders and attached to his or her belt.

LSL   Locomotive speed limits. A speed-control system used in conjunction with cab-signal systems that visually and audibly warns the locomotive operator if an overspeed condition exists and automatically applies the train and locomotive brakes if the operator fails to correct the overspeed within a predetermined braking profile. See also **ATC**.

LTL   Less-than-trailer or Less-than-truck load. Term applied to a shipment that does not fill a trailer or container.

M of E   Maintenance of equipment. Mechanical department in a railroad responsible for the repair and maintenance of rolling stock.

M of W   Maintenance-of-way. Department in a railroad that repairs, replaces, and maintains track, structures and other physical plant components.

mail and express train   Train dedicated exclusively to haulage of mail and express traffic, typically operated at passenger-train speed.

mail storage car   A baggage car or boxcar equipped for high-speed operation in passenger trains and mail and express trains, used to carry full-carload consignments of U.S. mail.

main   See **main track**.

main iron   (Slang) Main track.

main line   Primary rail line over which trains operate between terminals. It excludes sidings and yard and industry tracks.

main reservoir   A tank on an engine for storing the main compressed-air supply, so called in distinction from the auxiliary reservoirs under each car.

main track   A track (designated by the timetable) extending through and between stations upon which train movements are authorized by block system or interlocking rules.

maintenance of equipment   See **M of E.**

maintenance-of-way   See **M of W.**

make a joint   (Slang) To couple cars.

make the air   (Slang) Hook up the air hoses and cut the air into them by turning the angle cock on the end of a car.

manifest   A complete description and list of the contents of a shipment.

manifest train   A scheduled freight train, usually consisting of single-carload and multiple-carload consignments of numerous different types of commodities.

manual block system   A block system in which the use of each block is governed by a Form D, a track warrant, or block signal indications set manually by a block operator.

mark off   1. Report as not available for duty. 2. The act of filling out a railway employee's time slip with the time released from duty.

mark up   Report as available for duty.

marked capacity   The carrying capacity of a car as marked or stenciled on the car.

marker   A reflector, flag, lamp, or other highly visible marking device, in the red-orange-amber color range, affixed to the rear of a train to indicate that the train is complete.

maximum rate   The highest rate that may be charged for a shipment.

meat rack   (Obsolete) The supports near the ceiling of a refrigerator car from which meat is suspended. Also called beef rail.

mechanical car   See **refrigerator car.**

medium speed   Not exceeding 30 miles per hour.

memo waybill   Memorandum waybill. A waybill used when the agent does not have sufficient information to determine the freight charges. It contains adequate information to enable yards to properly handle the car.

memorandum bill of lading   The duplicate copy of a bill of lading.

merchandise car   A car containing several less-than-carload shipments.

mileage allowance   An allowance based on distance made by railroads to owners of privately owned freight cars.

mileage rate   Rates applicable according to distance.

mill gondola   An extra-long gondola car for carrying items of great length such as structural steel.

milling-in-transit   The stopping of grain, lumber, or other commodities for the purpose of milling or other processing at a point located between the origin and destination of a shipment.

mini-land-bridge   The movement of a containerized shipment (that originated overseas) across the United States via rail to its destination.

minimum charge   The lowest charge for which a shipment will be handled.

minimum rate   The lowest rate that may be charged.

minimum weight   The minimum weight applied to a shipment (usually LCL or LTL) on which the charges are based.

mixed carload   A carload of different articles in a single consignment.

mixed train   A train carrying both freight and passengers.

MOOW   Moved or move on own wheels.

Mother Hubbard   (Obsolete) A steam locomotive with a cab positioned astride the boiler, ahead of the firebox.

motive power   Alternative term for engine or locomotive, both singular and plural.

motorman   Operator of electric-powered rail equipment. See **engineer.**

movable stanchion   See **knock-down stanchion.**

M.U.   Multiple unit. Operation of two or more locomotive units or self-propelled passenger cars coupled together and controlled from the locomotive unit or car positioned at the head end of the train.

mudhop   (Slang) A yard clerk.

multilevel car   See **automobile rack car.**

muzzle-loader   (Slang) A hand-fired steam engine.

narrow gauge   A distance between the heads of the rails less than 4 feet 8 inches.

NEC   1. Not elsewhere classified. Term applied in tariff publications for articles generic in nature and not specifically identified. 2. Northeast Corridor. Amtrak-controlled intercity passenger-service territory generally between Washington, D.C., and Boston via Philadelphia and New York City and west to Harrisburg, Pennsylvania. Commuter passenger railroads and freight railroads also operate on trackage rights in this territory. (A segment of the NEC in Connecticut is owned by the Connecticut Department of Transportation.)

nested   Packed one within another.

net ton-mile   The movement of a net ton of freight one mile.

net weight   The weight of the lading of a shipment minus the dunnage allowance. Used in calculating the freight charge.

news butcher   (Obsolete) A man or often a young boy who sold newspapers, magazines, and food items to on-board coach-service passengers.

no bill   A car without forwarding instructions or an associated waybill.

NOIBN   Not indexed by name.

nonagency station   A station that does not have an agent. Also called a closed station.

NORAC   Northeast Operating Rules Advisory Committee. A committee representing several northeastern U.S. railroads that has developed a set of operating rules common to all these railroads.

normal speed   The maximum authorized speed shown in the timetable.

NOS   Not otherwise shown. See **NEC**.

observation car   A passenger car equipped with large windows at the rear for viewing of the railroad right of way and adjacent scenery. Older models featured brass-railed open-air observation platforms at the rear, on which passengers could sit or stand.

office car   Passenger car used by railway officials for inspection trips over the railroad and for other railway business purposes.

old head   (Slang) Railroad employee with a lot of seniority.

on the ground   (Slang) On the ties, not on the rails; a derailed train.

on the point   (Slang) To ride on the leading end of a car or engine to protect the movement.

op   (Slang) A railway telegrapher or station or tower operator.

open and prepay, open and shut   Publication that lists all the stations in the United States, Mexico, and Canada to which rail shipments can be made. It also indicates the railroad that switches each station and any limitations applying to service (e.g., team track only or height restrictions).

operating ratio   The ratio of railway operating expenses to railway operating revenue.

operating timetable   See **timetable**. For employees' use.

opposing signals   Signals that govern movements in opposite directions on the same track.

orc   (Slang) Conductor. Derived from former railway labor organization, Order of Railway Conductors.

order board   (Obsolete) A signal controlled by an operator at a station or tower indicating that the operator had written train orders to deliver to the train or trains for which the signal was set.

order-notify   A shipment for which the consignee must provide proof of payment (for the value of the contents) before the railroad will deliver the car. Proof of payment is either by surrendering the original bill of lading stamped by a bank or providing proof of a bond for 125 percent of the value of the lading.

ore car   An open-top hopper or gondola car that is custom designed to carry a particular type of metallic ore. Typically of shorter-than-normal length because of the high density of most ores.

ore train   A unit train that contains only carloads of ore.

origin or origin station   The point at which a car is loaded or a train begins.

OS   On-sheet. Train dispatcher's term used to identify the reported location of a train and the time that the train passed that location. The dispatcher (under now largely obsolete practice) entered the time on a preprinted train sheet. The entries on the sheet for each train provided a record of the progress of each train across the division or territory under the dispatcher's control.

OS & D   See **over, short & damage**.

out-gate   Term applied to indicate that a trailer or container has been taken off railroad property by a drayman.

outlawed   (Slang) See **dogs got 'em**.

outturn weight   Term used to indicate that the weight of a shipment will be provided at destination by the shipper or consignee.

over, short & damage   Term used to refer to freight claims.

overhead   Term for overheard wire system and structure on an electric railroad. See **catenary**.

overhead traffic   Freight traffic received from, and delivered to, connecting carriers. See **bridge carrier**.

package car   A car containing several less-than-carload shipments.

package freight   Merchandise shipped in less-than-carload quantities.

packer   A large, motorized device, operated by a driver, used to lift trailers and containers onto or off flatcars.

palace car   (Obsolete) Car for first-class passenger traffic. See **parlor car; sleeping car**.

pantograph   A device (located on top of electric locomotives and self-propelled electric passenger cars) that collects electric power from an overhead contact wire by means of a sliding contact shoe.

paper rate   A published rate under which no traffic moves.

parlor car   A passenger car with deluxe seating for accommodating passengers paying first-class fares for daytime travel.

parlor-buffet car   A passenger car equipped with both first-class deluxe seating and facilities for preparing and serving beverages and small food items.

parlor-dining car   A passenger car containing a first-class deluxe seating section, a dining section, and a galley (kitchen) for food preparation.

participating carrier   A railroad that is a party, under concurrence, to a tariff issued by another railroad or by a tariff-publishing agent.

pawl   A pivoted bar on a car brake wheel adapted to fall into the notches or teeth of a wheel as it rotates in one direction and to restrain it from backward motion. See **brake ratchet, brake pawl**.

P.D. car   1. Permanent dunnage car. A boxcar equipped

with dunnage. 2. Pressure-differential car. A type of covered hopper in which air pressure is used to unload the contents.

per diem   A charge made by one railroad against another for the use of its cars. The charge is based on a fixed rate per day.

perishable   Term used to describe commodities easily spoiled or damaged because of weather or delay in transit, usually foodstuffs.

permanent dunnage car   See **P.D. car.**

pickle car   (Obsolete) A specially equipped car for transporting pickles in bulk in brine.

pig   (Slang) TOFC shipment, or to use TOFC service for movement of a shipment.

piggyback   The transportation of truck trailers on railroad flatcars. See **TOFC.**

pilot   1. An employee assigned to a train or track car when the engineer or driver is not qualified on the physical characteristics or rules of the railroad or portion of the railroad over which the movement is made. 2. A fixture on the lower portion of the front of an engine to deflect objects that could cause a derailment. Sometimes called a cowcatcher.

pin puller   (Slang) A trainman who uncouples the cars while switching by lifting the coupler pin with the uncoupling lever located on each end of a car.

piston travel   The amount of air-brake cylinder piston movement when forced outward as the air brakes are applied.

pivot pin   See **knuckle pin.**

placard   Paper, plastic, or metal forms (containing various designs, names, or numbers) that are attached to the sides and ends of cars, trailers, and containers when the lading is classified as hazardous.

plug door   A door on refrigerator cars or boxcars that is flush with the side of the car when closed. To open, it is swung out and rolled to one side. Also called sliding flush door.

plugged   Term used to indicate that a track is full.

point of origin   The station at which a shipment is received by the railroad from the shipper.

pool cars   Specially equipped cars of different ownerships assigned to a specific company or location.

pop valve   (Slang) See **safety valve.**

port of entry   A port at which foreign goods are admitted into the receiving country.

post/posting   On-the-job training.

poultry car   (Obsolete) A specially equipped boxcar with screened sides for transport of live poultry, with a space in the center of the car for an attendant to provide in-transit care for the poultry.

prepaid   A term denoting that transportation charges have been or are to be paid at the origin point of shipment.

prepaid station   A station to which the transportation

charges on shipments must be prepaid, generally a non-agency station.

prepay station   See **prepaid station.**

prior rights   Term used to indicate that members of a craft have priority over jobs held on former railroads acquired by mergers or consolidations.

prior-prior rights   See **prior rights.** (More than one merger applies.)

private car   A car owned by a nonrailroad or nonrailroad-controlled entity, either freight or passenger.

private siding   A side track owned or leased by an individual or firm.

pro number   "Pro" is an abbreviation of the word "progressive." A pro number is usually applied by the agent on freight bills, waybills, and similar documents for control purposes as part of the accounting procedure.

programmer   Person who assigns trailers and containers to railcar space on intermodal trains.

proportional rate   A rate specifically published to be used only as a factor in making a combination through rate. A rate published from New York to Chicago to apply only on traffic destined to points beyond Chicago would be a proportional rate.

P/T line   Term used to describe a detail line for a demurrage record. "P" means that the car is on a private track, whereas "T" is a team track.

PTC   Positive train control. Technology for controlling train movements designed to keep trains separated from one another on the basis of their velocities rather than by the fixed block method.

public timetable   Publication for use by the general public containing schedules of passenger-train services and information relating to those services.

publishing agent   A person authorized by transportation lines to publish tariffs of rates, rules, and regulations for their account.

pull the pin   (Slang) 1. Uncouple a car by pulling up the coupling pin. 2. An expression meaning to resign or leave a railway job.

Pullman   (Obsolete) 1. Name of company that owned and/or staffed almost all sleeping cars, some parlor cars, and some buffet and dining cars between the late nineteenth century and the 1960s. 2. A sleeping car.

pusher   An extra engine at the rear of a train used to assist a train in climbing a grade. See **helper engine; snapper.**

push-pull train   A passenger train with a locomotive on one end and a car equipped with a control cab on the other end.

qualification   Certification of train and engine employees indicating that they are familiar with and may operate on certain sections of the railroad.

RAC   The Railway Assn. of Canada. Provides information on the Canadian railway industry to the public, government, and industry, promotes the commercial viability and safe operation of the Canadian railway industry, and represents the rail industry to government officials.

rack car See **automobile rack car**.

radio-controlled engine An unmanned engine situated within the train separated by cars from the lead unit, but controlled from it by radio signals.

rail 1. A rolled-steel structural shape used to form the track for railway vehicles. 2. (Slang) A railway employee.

rail bond An electrical conductor for bridging joints between rails for the purpose of carrying electrical current as part of a track block signal circuit and/or the negative side of the traction current system on an electrified railway.

rail detector car A railcar, usually self-propelled, used for inspection for internal defects in rails.

rail joint A fastening designed to unite abutting ends of rails.

Railway Labor Act A federal statute act providing for adjustment of disputes between railroads and employees.

Railway Post Office car See **RPO car**.

rate scale A table of rates graduated according to distance or zones.

RDC Rail Diesel Car. Self-propelled multiple-unit car manufactured by the Budd Co. beginning in 1949, in four models: RDC-1, straight passenger car; RDC-2, combination passenger and baggage-express car; RDC-3, combination passenger, baggage-express, and RPO car; RDC-4, combination baggage-express and RPO car. Powered by under-floor diesel engines connected to drive axles by torque converters. See **M.U.; RPO car**.

RDU Receive and display unit. That portion of an end-of-train telemetry system mounted in the locomotive cab that displays information to the operator regarding air pressure, motion, and battery condition. See **EOT**.

rear of signal The side of the signal from which the indication is received, that is, before reaching the signal.

rear shack (Slang) Brakeman responsible for work performed on the rear portion of a train. See **brakeman**.

rebill A term applied to a shipment for which the owner of the freight has requested a change of the destination of the car, and the car has arrived at the destination indicated on the original waybill. This is a chargeable service provided by the railroad.

receiving track A yard track on which arriving trains are usually set.

receiving yard A section of a yard in which one or more receiving tracks are located.

reconsignment A service extended by the railroad to the owner of the freight (shipper, consignee) permitting a change to the waybill in the name of the shipper, consignee, destination, route, or other instructions to effect delivery of the car, providing no back haul is involved, after the original destination is reached.

red board (Slang) 1. A fixed signal to stop. 2. An order

board signal displaying red. 3. A block signal displaying red. See also **block signal; order board**.

reefer (Slang) See **refrigerator car**.

refining in transit Stopping a shipment of sugar, oil, or some other commodity at a point between its origin and destination for the lading to be refined.

refrigeration charge A fixed charge for refrigeration from origin to destination or a portion of the trip.

refrigerator car A car with insulated walls, floor, and roof for carrying commodities that need cooling in transit. There are two major types: those that depend upon ice or ice and salt for cooling (obsolete) and those that are cooled by mechanical refrigerating equipment or by a cryogenic method.

regular train A train authorized by a timetable schedule.

relay train A train with one or more blocks of cars that remain intact through one or more crew-change points.

release cock See **release valve**.

release rod A small iron rod generally located at the side of a car for the purpose of operating the air-brake release valve.

release valve A valve attached to the auxiliary reservoir for reducing the air pressure when the locomotive is detached from the train so as to release the brakes.

reload Term used to designate a car (inbound load) that is unloaded and then reloaded by that same customer for an outbound move.

remote unit See **radio-controlled engine**.

repair track Also RIP or Repair-in-place track. A track designated for use to repair cars, usually cars that are in service under load or empty but needed for loading, that cannot be moved in road service without having defects repaired.

reservoir A cylindrical container for the storage of air under pressure. Main reservoirs of large capacity are located in locomotives and under all motor cars that have air compressors; auxiliary and emergency reservoirs are located under the cars.

restricted speed Control of movement to permit stopping within one-half the range of vision, short of a train, cars, obstruction, switch improperly lined, derail set in the derailing position, broken rail, and any signal requiring a stop, but not exceeding 15 miles per hour within interlocking limits and 20 miles per hour outside interlocking limits. Speed applies to entire movement.

retaining valve A small manually operated valve located near the brake wheel on a freight car for retaining part of the brake-cylinder pressure, to aid in retarding the acceleration of a train when descending long grades.

retarder A metal grip adjacent to the rails, usually operated by compressed air or electric motors, for regulating the speed of a car by pressure on the wheels while the car is rolling down a hump incline.

revenue waybill A waybill showing the amount of charges due on a shipment.

reverse lever The lever that controls the direction of motion of the locomotive by reversing the traction-motor field connections on diesel-electric and electric locomotives, and by reversing the inflow and outflow of steam into the cylinders on a steam locomotive.

ribbon rail   Term used to describe rail that has been welded together at the joints.

rider coach   Passenger coach used in lieu of a caboose at the rear of mail and express trains to provide accommodation for the conductor and brakeman. See also **express-train caboose**.

right of way   The property owned by a railroad over which tracks have been or may be laid.

RIP   (Slang) 1. Repair in place. 2. Car in need of repair.

RIP track   See **repair track**.

road bed   The foundation on which the track and ballast rest.

road foreman   Company official who supervises locomotive engineers.

road haul   See **line haul**.

roadmaster   Official in charge of track maintenance within a designated area.

roll-by   (Slang) Making a check of cars as they pass.

roller bearing   The general term applied to a group of journal bearings that depend upon the action of a set of rollers to reduce rotational friction.

roundhouse   Building of circular or semicircular form used to house engines while they are being serviced or repaired.

route   1. The course or direction that a shipment will move. 2. To designate the course or direction a shipment will move.

RPO car   (Obsolete) Railway Post Office car, in which mail was sorted en route by U.S. Postal Service employees. RPO cars typically were operated near the head end of a passenger train.

rubber interchange   The exchange of an intermodal shipment between railroads using a drayage company to move the trailers/containers via highway.

Rule G   A railroad operating rule that prohibits the possession or use of intoxicants, narcotics, or controlled substances while on duty.

rump rail   A side slat on a single-deck stock car made heavier than the usual slats. It is placed about four feet above the floor to resist movement of cattle against the car sides.

run through a switch   To move through a switch in the trailing point direction without lining it for the movement, bending the switch points.

running gear   A general term applied to and including the wheels, axles, springs, axle boxes, frames, and other carrying parts of a truck or locomotive.

running repair   A repair made to a car on an ordinary track or in a train that has not yet reached its destination.

running track   1. A designated track on which movements

may be made by signal indication or at restricted speed under the authority of the employee designated in the timetable. Sometimes used for movement through or around a yard, subject to prescribed signals and rules or special instructions. 2. A track reserved for movement through a yard.

safety valve   Pressure-relief valve on the boiler of a steam locomotive to permit the release of steam in excess of the rated capacity of the boiler.

sand house   Structure for drying and storage of locomotive sand.

sand house talk   (Slang) Railroad employee gossip.

sanders   Devices operated by air for applying sand to the rail in front of the driving wheels of the engine.

sanding tower   Structure for filling locomotive sandboxes.

scale house   Structure erected to house the weight-recording mechanism used in weighing freight cars.

scale test car   A car (of exact weight) for testing the accuracy of track scales.

scale track   A track that contains a scale for cars needing to be weighed.

schedule   That part of a timetable that prescribes direction, number, frequency, and times for movement of scheduled trains.

SCO   Special car order. Rules established by AAR to provide the shortest route-miles return of empty equipment to its owner.

seals   Metal strips or bolts designed for onetime use, applied to the hasp of closed freight-car doors. They are used to indicate whether or not the contents have been tampered with while in transit. They are stamped with a name, initial, and/or number for identification.

second trick   Term designating the working hours between 2:30 P.M. and midnight.

self-aligning coupler   A coupler that has a tapered shank rather than a straight shank to prevent the jackknifing of cars or locomotive units operating in multiple.

service application   A reduction of air pressure in the brake pipe at a rate that will produce an application of the locomotive and train brakes and a gradual speed reduction.

serving yard   A yard auxiliary to a major yard where cars are grouped before delivery to customers or after being received from customers.

shack   (Slang) Brakeman.

shanty   1. Small building erected along right of way to provide shelter for railroad employees. 2. (Slang) Caboose.

shift   1. Term used to indicate a daily tour of duty. 2. Switch cars.

shifting   See **switching**.

shipment in bond   See **in-bond shipment**.

shipper   Person or firm from whom a shipment originates. Also called consignor.

shipper's export declaration   A form required by the Treasury Department and filled out by a shipper showing the value, weight, consignee, destination, and other necessary information about shipments to be exported.

shipper's load and count   A term denoting that the contents of a car were loaded and counted by the shipper and not checked or verified by the railroad.

shipper's load and tally   See **shipper's load and count**.

shipper's weight agreement   See **weight agreement**.

shipping order   Shipping instructions to the railroad for forwarding all goods; usually the second copy of the bill of lading.

shop   Term applied to a structure where building, rebuilding, and repairing of cars, locomotives, and other railroad equipment are performed.

short ton   Two thousand pounds.

side track   A track adjacent to the main track for purposes other than for meeting and passing trains.

side-bay caboose   A caboose car having side-bay windows instead of a cupola. This permits the train crew to look along the side of a train, especially when rounding curves, for detection of hotboxes or other trouble.

siding   A track adjacent to a main or a secondary track for meeting or passing trains.

signal aspect   The appearance of a fixed signal conveying an indication as viewed from the direction of an approaching train; the appearance of a cab signal conveying an indication as viewed by an observer in the engine control compartment.

signal indication   The information conveyed by the aspect of a signal.

signboard   Information stenciled on the side of a car pertaining to empty-car movement instructions.

single track   A main track upon which trains are operated in both directions.

sinker   (Slang) See **control or driving trailer; trailer**.

skate   A metal skid placed on rail in a hump yard to stop cars from running out of a yard or beyond a safety point.

SL & C   See **shipper's load and count**.

SL & T   shipper's load and tally. See **shipper's load and count**.

slack   Unrestrained free movement in the coupling device between the cars in a train, and in the draft gear of each car.

slave unit   See **radio-controlled engine**.

sleeper   See **crosstie; sleeping car**.

sleeping car   A passenger car equipped with beds and lavatory fixtures for overnight travel. Historically, first-class rail fare plus an accommodation charge applied to sleeping-car service.

slip switch   A combination of a shallow-angle crossing of two tracks and a switch connection either on one side of the angled crossing (single slip) or on both sides (double slip).

slow board   A signal indication to proceed at reduced speed.

slow speed   Not exceeding 15 miles per hour.

slug   A locomotive, without a diesel engine, but equipped with traction motors, taking electrical power from another unit.

snapper   Alternative term for pusher engine on the former Pennsylvania Railroad. See **pusher**.

solid track   (Slang) Track full of cars.

special equipment   Freight cars designed to carry specific commodities, with special devices to protect and/or aid in handling shipments.

Sperry Car   See **rail detector car**.

spine car   A car consisting primarily of a center sill and several structural cross-members, and sometimes a short length of floor or deck at one end, for carrying intermodal containers and (in some instances) trailers. Unlike a flatcar, it does not have a full-length and full-width floor.

splice bar   See **joint bar**.

spot   To place a car in a designated position or specific location, usually for loading or unloading, such as at a warehouse door.

spot for air   To position the cars in the yard so as to use a central compressed-air supply to charge the brake system.

spot system   A system in which cars and locomotives undergoing repairs are classified as to the types of repair tasks needed and then moved progressively from one spot to another for the performance of particular tasks.

spotter   Inspector or "company spy" who checks on employees' honesty.

spotting   The placing of a car where required to be accessible for loading or unloading.

spring switch   A switch equipped with a spring mechanism arranged to restore the switch points to normal position after having been passed through by a trailing movement.

spur   See **spur track**.

spur track   A stub track extending from a main or other track.

Staggers Act   Law passed in 1980 that removed much of the government regulation of business practices, such as the pricing of service, in the rail industry.

stanchion   Vertical fixture with a fifth-wheel-like head used to support and lock in one end of a trailer while loaded on a flatcar. See **fifth wheel**.

standard gauge   A distance of 4 feet 8½ inches between the heads of the rails. See also **Broad Gauge; Gauge of Track; Narrow Gauge**.

standard rate   A rate established via direct routes from one point to another.

standard route   The line or lines that maintain standard rates for movement of freight shipments.

standing order   The actual order of cars in a train from the engine to the last car.

star marker   A type of flashing-light marker used to designate the rear of a train. Manufactured without telemetry capability.

station   1. Location (in most cases the name of a city) at which there is a siding and rail shipments can originate or terminate. 2. A place designated in the timetable by name at which a train may stop for traffic or enter or leave the main track, or from which fixed signals are operated.

station agent   An employee who transacted freight and/or passenger business at a station.

status message   A computer-generated message used to indicate a change of the condition of a car.

stock car   See **livestock car**.

stopping in transit   The holding of a shipment by the carrier on order of the owner after the transportation movement has started and before it is completed.

storage in transit   The stopping of freight at a point located between the point of origin and destination to be stored and forwarded at a later date.

storage track   A track on which cars are placed when not in service.

stretch   An order to the engineer to pull on a cut of cars to see if they are coupled.

string   (Slang) Two or more freight cars coupled together as a string of cars.

STU   Sense and transmit unit. See **EOT**.

stub track   A track connected to another with a switch at one end only; a dead-end track.

superior train   A train that has precedence over another train.

supplement   A publication that contains additions to and/or changes in a tariff.

SWA   Shipper's weight agreement. See **weight agreement**.

switch   1. A track structure fixture with movable rails (switch points) that provides a connection between two lines of track to permit cars or trains to pass from one track to the other track. 2. To move cars from one place to another within a defined territory such as an industry, a yard, or a terminal.

switch delivery   Term applied when a car is interchanged from one railroad to another for direct delivery to patron. The receiving road is paid a switching rate in lieu of a portion of the road-haul freight charges since it does not transport the shipment outside the switching limits.

switch engine   A locomotive used for switching cars in yards and terminals. Sometimes termed switcher.

switch heater   A device for melting snow and ice at track switches.

switch list   A list of freight cars in track standing order showing cars by initial, number, and type of car and stating where cars are to be switched as required by local practice.

switch lock   A fastener, usually a spring padlock, used to secure the switch or derail stand in place.

switch order   An order to move a car from one place to another within switching limits.

switch stand   A device by which the points of a switch are thrown (moved) and locked, and their position is indicated. It consists essentially of a base, spindle, lever, and connecting rod and is usually furnished with a banner signal (and sometimes a lamp) to indicate the direction of movement for which the switch is set.

switch target   A visual day signal fixed on the spindle of a switch stand, or the circular flaring collar fitted around the switch's lamp lens and painted a distinctive color to indicate the position of the switch.

switch tender   Train service employee responsible for aligning tracks for engine and car movements by throwing switches.

switchback   Track constructed in a series of zigzag or see-saw segments in mountainous terrain to reduce rate of climb or descent.

switching   The movement of cars from one place to another within a terminal, a yard, or an industry.

switching limits   A geographic area within a metropolitan district defined as a terminal. Traffic moved entirely within that area by a rail carrier is entitled to a "switch delivery" rate and not a portion of the road haul.

switchman   A yard brakeman.

tallow pot   (Slang) Steam locomotive fireman.

tamper   A power-driven machine for compacting ballast under ties.

tank car   A car used for carrying liquids, such as oil, molasses, vinegar, or acid.

tank dome   A vertical cylinder attached to the top of a tank car. It permits the tank proper to be filled to full cubic capacity, which would be impossible if there were no allowance for expansion into the dome of the liquid lading being carried.

tap line   (Slang) A short railroad usually owned or controlled by the industries it serves and "tapping" (connecting with) a trunk line.

tare weight   1. The weight of any empty freight car. 2. The weight of a container and the material used for packing.

tariff   A published document (either paper or electronic) containing information relative to a carrier's rates, rules, and regulations for providing transportation service.

TCS   See **CTC**.

team track   A track on which cars are placed for the use of the public in loading or unloading freight.

telltale   (Obsolete) A device consisting of long strips hanging over a track at the approach to a low-overhead bridge, tunnel, or other overhead obstruction, used to warn trainmen riding the top of a train to lower themselves below the obstruction. Use of this device ended when the practice of riding on top of moving equipment was prohibited.

tender   Car coupled to a steam locomotive that carries the locomotive's fuel and water supply.

terminal   1. A railroad facility used for handling freight and/or passengers and for the receiving, classifying, assembling, and dispatching of trains. 2. Point where train and engine employees originate and/or terminate their tour of duty. 3. A designated area within a metropolitan area where one or more rail yards exist.

terminal carrier   The railroad that makes delivery of a shipment at its destination.

terminal charge   A charge made for services performed at terminals.

test weight car   See **scale test car**.

third rail   An electric conductor rail located parallel to one of the running rails from which power is collected by means of a sliding contact shoe attached to the truck of an electric locomotive or an electric-powered M.U. car (usually passenger).

third trick   Term designating the working hours between 10:30 P.M. and 7:59 A.M.

third-rail shoe   A metallic sliding contact mounted on the truck of an electric locomotive or an electric M.U. car for collecting current from a third rail located alongside the running rails. Positive contact between shoe and rail is maintained by gravity, a spring, or pneumatic pressure.

through rate   A rate applicable from point of origin to destination. A through rate may be either a joint rate or a combination of two or more local rates.

through train   A train that does not stop at all stations on its route.

tie   See **crosstie**.

tie 'em down   (Slang) Apply hand brake of cars to prevent them from rolling free.

tie on   (Slang) Couple cars or a locomotive to a train.

tie plate   A steel plate interposed between the bottom of a rail and the top of a tie to provide a safe bearing area on the tie. The top of the plate contains a shoulder to restrain outward movement of the rail.

tie up   (Slang) Terminate the run of a train and go off duty.

timetable   A printed booklet that contains schedules and special instructions that govern the movement of trains.

TMS   Transportation monitoring system. Computerized system for ordering, moving, and controlling the movement of trains.

TOFC   Acronym for "trailer-on-flatcar" intermodal service or equipment.

tool train   (Slang) Wreck train used for clearing up derailments.

torpedo   See **track torpedo**.

tower   Building of sufficient height erected along the right of way to permit maximum viewing and containing instruments for control of train movements. May house yardmaster, trainmaster, or block operator.

tracer   1. A request to trace a shipment for the purpose of expediting its movement or establishing delivery. 2. A request for an answer to a communication.

track   The space between the rails and space of not less than 4 feet outside each rail.

track car   Equipment, other than trains, operated on track for inspection or maintenance that may not operate signals.

track check   See **switch list**.

track circuit   An electrical circuit that includes the rails and the wheels of the train. Used for controlling signal devices.

track geometry car   A car equipped with instruments to measure track-structure alignment conditions.

track pan   (Obsolete) A trough between the running rails from which a steam locomotive could take water while running by means of a scoop attached to the bottom of the locomotive's tender.

track speed   The maximum authorized speed for a specified segment of traffic for particular classes or types of trains.

track structure   Railroad track in its entirety, including rail, ties, tie plates, spikes and other types of fasteners, joint bars, ballast, and subgrade.

track torpedo   Noisemaking explosive device, strapped to head of rail. Detonation by wheels of locomotive provides a warning signal to engine crew to stop. Used as a supplement or stand-alone alternative to flag and lantern stop signals. Becoming obsolete because of soundproof cabs in newer models of diesel-electric locomotives.

track warrant   System for governing operation of trains, track cars, and other equipment on a designated section of railroad. Similar to Form D system.

trackage right   Right obtained by one railroad to operate its trains on trackage of another railroad.

tractor   Motorized vehicle used to haul trailers or containers on the highway.

traffic control system   See **CTC**.

trailer   1. Unpowered passenger car, with or without control equipment, operated in train with electric or diesel-powered M.U. cars. See **control or driving trailer M.U.** 2. Highway semitrailer or truck trailer.

trailing movement   The movement of a train over the points of a switch that face in the direction in which the train is moving.

trailing-point switch   A switch whose points face away from approaching traffic.

train   A locomotive with or without cars.

train dispatcher   The employee responsible for the movement of trains within a specific section or division of a rail carrier's system.

train line   The complete line of air-brake pipes in a train. These lines include the rigid piping secured under the cars and the flexible connections between cars and the locomotive.

train order   (Obsolete) Written order issued by a train dispatcher governing movement of a train. Replaced by Form D and track-warrant systems.

train standing order   See **standing order**.

trainmaster   Company official in charge of a portion of a division and its train operations.

train-mile   The movement of a train one mile.

transship   To transfer goods from one transportation line to another, particularly from a rail to a water carrier or vice versa.

tri   (Slang) See **trilevel car**.

trick   (Slang) Shift or hours of duty.

trilevel car   A three-level freight car used for transporting automobiles.

trimmer   Yard crew used to switch cars at the outer end of the bowl tracks in a hump yard.

triple load   A shipment that requires the use of two carrying cars with an idler car between them (or one carrying car with idlers at each end).

trolley pole   A device located on the roof of an electric locomotive or self-propelled electric car that collects electric power from an overhead contact wire by means of either a sliding shoe or a rotating wheel.

truck   A general term for the complete wheel and passenger assembly that supports the body of a car, diesel-electric, or electric locomotive at each end. Most steam locomotives, except those designed as switch engines, also are equipped with a truck located in front of the drive (powered) wheels and often also at the rear of the drive wheels.

truck bolster   See **bolster**.

trunk line   A transportation line that operates over an extensive territory.

turnout   See **switch**, 1.

UDE   Undesired emergency. Emergency brake application on a train for which no apparent cause can be determined.

UMLER   Universal Machine Language Equipment Register. Electronic registration system for cars and locomotives moved in interchange.

unassigned car   A car, usually with some interior loading devices, that is not assigned to a particular industry or commodity.

unclaimed freight   Freight that has not been called for by the consignee or owner.

uncoupling lever or uncoupling rod   A rod with a bent handle forming a lever, usually attached to the end sill, by which the lock of the automatic coupler is opened and the cars uncoupled without going between them.

uniform demurrage rules   Schedules that provide rules and charges for demurrage that are, in general, used throughout the United States.

uniform freight classification   A listing of articles (commodities) showing their assigned class rating (a percentage of first class) to be used in determining freight rates, together with governing rules and regulations.

unit train   A train with a fixed, coupled consist of cars, all loaded with the same commodity, that is operated continuously in shuttle service under load from origin, delivered intact at destination, and returning (usually) for reloading at the same origin.

UOR   Unusual occurrence reports. A reporting system where rail accidents or unusual occurrences and delays to train movement can be reported and inquired on.

van   See **caboose**. Term distinctive to railways in Canada and to U.S. subsidiaries of Canadian railway companies.

varnish   (Slang) Passenger train.

ventilated boxcar   Similar to an ordinary boxcar, but arranged for ventilation and suitable for the transportation of produce or other foodstuffs not needing refrigeration.

washout   1. Section of track destroyed by flooding. 2. (Slang) Signal to stop quickly.

water trough   (Obsolete) See **track pan**.

way car   1. (Slang) See **caboose**. 2. (Obsolete) Boxcar in a local or way freight train used for hauling LCL freight.

way freight   See **local**.

waybill   1. The document covering a freight shipment and showing the forwarding (originating) and receiving stations, the name of consignor and consignee, the car initials and number, the routing, the description and weight of the commodity, instructions for special services required (if any), the rate, total charges, advances and the waybill reference for previous services, and the amount prepaid (if any). 2. (Slang) To prepare a waybill.

waybill release   An activity that terminates the waybill cycle and triggers the generation of a freight bill.

wayside signal   A fixed signal located along the track right of way.

weight agreement   An agreement between shipper and carrier, usually following a series of weighing tests, under which the carrier accepts shipper's goods at certain agreed weights.

welded rail   See **ribbon rail**.

well car   See **depressed-center flatcar**.

wheel flange   The projection edge or rim on the circumference of a car wheel for keeping it on the rail.

wheel report   A list of a train in standing order used by a conductor to record activity times and exceptions.

whistle stop   (Slang) A small town not normally served by most trains.

white lead or white leaded   (Slang) Holding of out-of-service locomotives in dead or long-term storage.

white-hat　(Slang) Any railroad official.

whiteline　Term used to designate that a car or engine can no longer be used safely in transportation service and/or has been withdrawn from service. Historically, a white line would be painted through the number of such a car or engine.

white-shirt　(Slang) Any railroad official.

wood check　See **switch list**.

woodchip hopper　Open-top gondola or hopper car of high cubic capacity used to transport woodchips.

work order　Computer-generated form for use by freight conductor showing required industry switching and listing all cars involved (to be delivered, picked up, shifted, and so on).

work train　A train that serves the maintenance-of-way department in track repair and in other infrastructure construction, rebuilding, and maintenance tasks.

wye　A triangular arrangement of tracks on which cars, locomotives, and trains may be turned to reverse direction.

yard　A system of tracks used for making up trains and storing cars. Movements in a yard must be made at restricted speed, subject to applicable rules and special instructions.

yard dwell　The average duration, measured in hours, that cars spend in a specific operating terminal or yard.

yard engine　See **switch engine**.

yard goat　(Slang) See **switch engine**.

yard limits　Boundary points between yard and nonyard trackage.

yard train　A train that moves from one yard to another within a terminal.

yarding in transit　Unloading, storing, sorting, or other handling of forest products before the shipment reaches its final destination.

yardmaster　Person responsible for control of train and engine operations within a yard.

Zulu car　(Slang, obsolete) Boxcar used to carry immigrants and their belongings.

Appendix D

130 Most Notable Railroad Books

A List by the Editors of Railroad History

To shoehorn the many books written about North American railroads into a list of 130 superior titles required some limitations at the outset. The editors of *Railroad History* looked for books that made an original contribution to the understanding of railroading and that set high standards in both scholarship and writing. We also made a conscious attempt to include books published across the time spectrum of the industry. Finally, we avoided books of railroad fiction and books that were primarily pictorial albums or hobbyist in nature.

Even with these limitations, our initial list came to more than 250 titles, which we whittled down to 13 categories of 10 books each. The usual caveats of list making apply, foremost that some popular and appealing books fell by the wayside. On the other hand, we hope

that the volumes cited highlight the range of historical material available about the most ubiquitous and important artifact of the Industrial Revolution. We doubly hope that some neglected and out-of-print books regain their rightful place on the shelves of historians and enthusiasts.

Railroad History is the twice-yearly journal of the Railway & Locomotive Historical Society, published since 1921. The panel members, all of them noted railroad scholars in their own right, were Gregory P. Ames, Dan Cupper, James D. Dilts, George H. Drury, Don L. Hofsommer, Tony Reevy, Mark Reutter (chair), J. W. Swanberg, and John H. White, Jr.

—Mark Reutter
Editor, *Railroad History*

GENERAL HISTORY

Thomas C. Clarke, et al. *The American Railway: Its Construction, Development, Management, and Appliances.* New York: Charles Scribner's Sons, 1892.

Seymour Dunbar. *A History of Travel in America, Showing the Development of Travel and Transportation from the Crude Methods of the Canoe and the Dog-Sled to the Highly Organized Railway Systems of the Present.* Vols. 3 and 4. Indianapolis: Bobbs-Merrill, 1915.

Henry M. Flint. *The Railroads of the United States: Their History and Statistics.* Philadelphia: John E. Potter, 1868. Repr., New York: Arno Press, 1976.

Robert Selph Henry. *This Fascinating Railroad Business.* Indianapolis: Bobbs-Merrill, 1942.

Stewart H. Holbrook. *The Story of American Railroads.* New York: Crown Publishers, 1947.

Oliver Jensen. *The American Heritage History of Railroads in America.* New York: American Heritage Publishing, 1975.

Balthasar H. Meyer. Caroline E. MacGill, et al. *History of Transportation in the United States before 1860.* Carnegie Institution, 1917.

J. Luther Ringwalt. *Development of Transportation Systems in the United States.* N.p.: Self-published, 1888.

Richard Saunders, Jr. *Merging Lines: American Railroads, 1900–1970,* and *Main Lines: Rebirth of the North American Railroads, 1970–2002.* DeKalb: Northern Illinois University Press, 2001 and 2003.

Slason Thompson. *A Short History of American Railways, Covering Ten Decades.* N.p.: D. Appleton, 1925.

MAJOR RAILROAD LINES

Keith L. Bryant. *History of the Atchison, Topeka and Santa Fe Railway.* New York: Macmillan, 1974.

George H. Burgess and Miles C. Kennedy. *Centennial History of the Pennsylvania Railroad Company, 1846–1946.* Philadelphia: Pennsylvania Railroad Company, 1949.

Carlton J. Corliss. *Main Line of Mid-America: The Story of the Illinois Central.* New York: Creative Age Press, 1950.

James D. Dilts. *The Great Road: The Building of the Baltimore and Ohio, the Nation's First Railroad, 1828–1853.* Stanford, Calif.: Stanford University Press, 1993.

Alvin F. Harlow. *The Road of the Century: The Story of the New York Central.* New York: Creative Age Press, 1947.

Don L. Hofsommer. *The Southern Pacific, 1901–1985.* College Station: Texas A&M University Press, 1986.

Maury Klein. *Union Pacific: Birth of a Railroad, 1862–1893,* and *The Rebirth, 1894–1969.* (2 vols.) Garden City, N.Y.: Doubleday, 1987 and 1989.

Edward H. Mott. *Between the Ocean and the Lakes: The Story of Erie.* New York: John S. Collins, 1901.

Richard C. Overton. *Burlington Route: A History of the Burlington Lines.* New York: Alfred A. Knopf, 1965.

George R. Stevens. *Canadian National Railways.* (2 vols.) Toronto: Clarke, Irwin, 1960.

OTHER RAILROADS AND SHORTLINES

Robert G. Athearn. *Rebel of the Rockies: A History of the Denver and Rio Grande Western Railroad.* New Haven, Conn.: Yale University Press, 1962.

George Pierce Baker. *The Formation of the New England Railroad Systems.* Cambridge, Mass.: Harvard University Press, 1937.

Lucius Beebe. *Mixed Train Daily: A Book of Short-Line Railroads.* New York: E. P. Dutton, 1947.

Jules I. Bogen. *The Anthracite Railroads: A Study in American Railroad Enterprise.* New York: Ronald Press, 1927.

A Century of Progress: History of the Delaware & Hudson Company, 1823–1923. Albany, N.Y.: Delaware & Hudson, 1925.

August Derleth. *The Milwaukee Road: Its First Hundred Years.* New York: Creative Age Press, 1948. Repr., Iowa City: University of Iowa Press, 2002.

George W. Hilton. *The Ma & Pa: A History of the Maryland &*

Pennsylvania Railroad. Berkeley, Calif.: Howell-North Books, 1963 and 1980. Repr., Baltimore: Johns Hopkins University Press, 2000.

Roy Minter. *The White Pass: Gateway to the Klondike.* Fairbanks: University of Alaska Press, 1987.

John A. Rehor. *The Nickel Plate Story.* Milwaukee, Wis.: Kalmbach Books, 1965.

Thomas T. Taber and Thomas T. Taber III. *The Delaware, Lackawanna & Western Railroad in the Twentieth Century.* (3 vols.) N.p.: Self-published, 1980–1982.

BIOGRAPHIES OF EXECUTIVES

Thomas C. Cochran. *Railroad Leaders, 1845–1890: The Business Mind in Action.* Cambridge, Mass.: Harvard University Press, 1953.

Herbert H. Harwood, Jr. *Invisible Giants: The Empires of Cleveland's Van Sweringen Brothers.* Bloomington: Indiana University Press, 2003.

Stanley P. Hirshson. *Grenville M. Dodge: Soldier, Politician, Railroad Pioneer.* Bloomington: Indiana University Press, 1967.

Maury Klein. *The Life and Legend of Jay Gould.* Baltimore: Johns Hopkins University Press, 1986.

Wheaton J. Lane. *Commodore Vanderbilt: An Epic of the Steam Age.* New York: Alfred A. Knopf, 1942. Repr., New York: Johnson Reprint, 1973.

John L. Larson. *Bonds of Enterprise: John Murray Forbes and Western Development in America's Railway Age.* Cambridge, Mass.: Harvard University Press, 1984.

Oscar Lewis. *The Big Four: The Story of Huntington, Stanford, Hopkins, and Crocker, and of the Building of the Central Pacific.* New York: Alfred A. Knopf, 1938.

Albro Martin. *James J. Hill and the Opening of the Northwest.* New York: Oxford University Press, 1976.

James A. Ward. *J. Edgar Thomson, Master of the Pennsylvania.* Westport, Conn.: Greenwood Press, 1980.

Robin W. Winks. *Frederick Billings: A Life.* New York: Oxford University Press, 1991.

LOCOMOTIVES AND CARS

John K. Brown. *The Baldwin Locomotive Works, 1831–1915: A Study in American Industrial Practice.* Baltimore: Johns Hopkins University Press, 1995.

William H. Brown. *The History of the First Locomotives in America: From Original Documents and the Testimony of Living Witnesses.* New York: D. Appleton, 1871.

Alfred Bruce. *The Steam Locomotive in America: Its Development in the Twentieth Century.* New York: W. W. Norton, 1952.

Zerah Colburn, et al. *Locomotive Engineering and the Mechanism of Railways.* London: William Collins, 1871.

M. N. Forney, et al. *Catechism of the Locomotive.* New York: Railway Age Gazette, 1873, 1889, and 1911.

John Kirkland. *Dawn of the Diesel Age* and *The Diesel Builders.* (3 vols.) Glendale, Calif.: Interurban Press, 1983, 1985, and 1989.

J. G. A. Meyer. *Modern Locomotive Construction.* New York: John Wiley & Sons, 1892.

William Voss. *Railway Car Construction.* New York: R. M. Van Arsdale, 1892.

John H. White, Jr. *The American Railroad Freight Car: From the Wood-Car Era to the Coming of Steel.* Baltimore: Johns Hopkins University Press, 1993.

———. *The American Railroad Passenger Car.* Baltimore: Johns Hopkins University Press, 1978.

RIGHT OF WAY AND STRUCTURES

Walter G. Berg. *Buildings and Structures of American Railroads.* New York: John Wiley & Sons, 1893.

W. M. Camp. *Notes on Track: Construction and Maintenance.* N.p.: Self-published, 1903.

Carl W. Condit. *The Port of New York: A History of the Rail and Terminal System.* (2 vols.) Chicago: University of Chicago Press, 1980–1981.

John A. Droege. *Freight Terminals and Trains* and *Passenger Terminals and Trains.* (2 vols.) New York: McGraw-Hill, 1912 and 1916; the latter volume repr., Milwaukee, Wis.: Kalmbach Books, 1969.

Carroll L. V. Meeks. *The Railroad Station: An Architectural History.* New Haven, Conn.: Yale University Press, 1956.

William D. Middleton. *Landmarks on the Iron Road: Two Centuries of North American Railroad Engineering.* Bloomington: Indiana University Press, 1999.

Janet G. Potter. *Great American Railroad Stations.* New York: John Wiley, 1996.

Edward E. R. Russell. *Railway Track and Track Work.* New York: McGraw-Hill, 1897, 1900, 1908, and 1926.

Walter L. Webb. *The Economics of Railroad Construction.* New York: John Wiley & Sons, 1906 and 1915.

Arthur M. Wellington. *The Economic Theory of the Location of Railways.* New York: John Wiley & Sons, 1887, 1898, and 1906.

DEVELOPMENT OF THE NORTH AMERICAN SYSTEM

David Haward Bain. *Empire Express: Building the First Transcontinental Railroad.* New York: Viking, 1999.

Pierre Berton. *The National Dream; The Last Spike.* Abridged. Toronto: McClelland & Stewart, 1974. See also the individual volumes. Toronto: McClelland and Stewart, 1970 and 1971.

Albert Fishlow. *American Railroads and the Transformation of the Antebellum Economy.* Cambridge, Mass.: Harvard Univ. Press, 1965.

Franz Anton Ritter von Gerstner, *Early American Railroads.* Ed. Frederick C. Gamst. Stanford, CA: Stanford University Press, 1997 [1842–1843].

George W. Hilton. *American Narrow Gauge Railroads.* Stanford, Calif.: Stanford University Press, 1990.

Carlos J. Schwantes. *Railroad Signatures across the Pacific Northwest.* Seattle: University of Washington Press, 1993.

Frank H. Spearman. *The Strategy of Great Railroads.* New York: Charles Scribner's Sons, 1904.

John F. Stover. *The Railroads of the South, 1865–1900.* Chapel Hill: University of North Carolina Press, 1955.

George Rogers Taylor and Irene D. Neu. *The American Railroad Network, 1861–1890.* Cambridge, Mass.: Harvard University Press, 1956. Repr., Urbana: University of Illinois Press, 2003.

James E. Vance, Jr. *The North American Railroad: Its Origin, Evolution, and Geography.* Baltimore: Johns Hopkins Univ. Press, 1995.

TRAVELING BY TRAIN

Charles Dickens, et al. (edited by H. Roger Grant). *We Took the Train.* DeKalb: Northern Illinois University Press, 1990.

Arthur D. Dubin. *Some Classic Trains.* Milwaukee, Wis.: Kalmbach Books, 1964.

Fred W. Frailey. *Twilight of the Great Trains.* Waukesha, Wis.: Kalmbach, Books, 1998.

Bruce A. MacGregor and Ted Benson. *Portrait of a Silver Lady:*

The Train They Called the California Zephyr. Boulder, Colo.: Pruett Publishing, 1977.

David P. Morgan. *Confessions of a Train-Watcher.* Ed. George H. Drury. Waukesha, Wis.: Kalmbach Books, 1997.

Archie Robertson. *Slow Train to Yesterday: A Last Glance at the Local.* Boston: Houghton Mifflin, 1945.

Wolfgang Schivelbusch. *The Railway Journey: Trains and Travel in the 19th Century.* New York: Urizen Books, 1986.

Robert B. Shaw. *Down Brakes: A History of Railroad Accidents, Safety Precautions, and Operating Practices in the United States of America.* London: P. R. Macmillan, 1961.

Rogers E. M. Whitaker and Tony Hiss. *All Aboard with E. M. Frimbo, World's Greatest Railroad Buff.* New York: Grossman Publishers, 1974.

Bob Withers. *The President Travels by Train: Politics and Pullmans.* Lynchburg, Va.: TLC Publishing, 1996.

RAILROAD ECONOMICS, FINANCE, AND GOVERNMENT REGULATION

Charles Francis Adams, Jr. *A Chapter of Erie.* Boston: Fields, Osgood, 1869.

Frederick A. Cleveland and Fred Wilbur Powell. *Railroad Promotion and Capitalization in the United States.* New York: Longmans, Green, 1909.

Joseph R. Daughen and Peter Binzen. *The Wreck of the Penn Central.* Boston: Little, Brown, 1971.

Carter Goodrich. *Government Promotion of American Canals and Railroads, 1800–1890.* New York: Columbia University Press, 1960.

Julius Grodinsky. *The Iowa Pool: A Study in Railroad Competition, 1870–84.* Chicago: University of Chicago Press, 1950.

Ari Hoogenboom and Olive Hoogenboom. *A History of the ICC: From Panacea to Palliative.* New York: W. W. Norton, 1976.

Gabriel Kolko. *Railroads and Regulation, 1877–1916.* Princeton, N.J.: Princeton University Press, 1965.

Joseph T. Lambie. *From Mine to Market: The History of Coal Transportation on the Norfolk & Western Railway.* New York: New York Univ. Press, 1954.

Albro Martin. *Enterprise Denied: Origins of the Decline of American Railroads, 1897–1917.* New York: Columbia Univ. Press, 1971.

George H. Miller. *Railroads and the Granger Laws.* Madison: University of Wisconsin Press, 1971.

RAILROAD LABOR

Eric Arnesen. *Brotherhoods of Color: Black Railroad Workers and the Struggle for Equality.* Cambridge, Mass.: Harvard Univ. Press, 2001.

Nimrod J. Bell (edited by James A. Ward). *Southern Railroad Man: Conductor N. J. Bell's Recollections of the Civil War Era.* DeKalb: Northern Illinois Univ. Press, 1994.

Charles P. Brown (edited by H. Roger Grant). *Brownie the Boomer: The Life of Charles P. Brown, an American Railroader.* DeKalb: Northern Illinois University Press, 1991.

W. Fred Cottrell. *The Railroader.* Stanford, CA: Stanford Univ. Press, 1940.

James H. Ducker. *Men of the Steel Rails: Workers on the Atchison, Topeka & Santa Fe Railroad, 1869–1900.* Lincoln: University of Nebraska Press, 1983.

Feeding the Iron Hog: The Life and Work of a Locomotive Fireman. Cleveland: Brotherhood of Locomotive Firemen and Enginemen, 1927.

Stuart Leuthner. *The Railroaders.* New York: Random House, 1983.

Walter Licht. *Working for the Railroad.* Princeton, N.J.: Princeton University Press, 1983.

John W. Orr. *Set Up Running: The Life of a Pennsylvania Railroad Engineman, 1904–1949.* University Park: Pennsylvania State University Press, 2001.

Richard Reinhardt. *Workin' on the Railroad.* New York: Weathervane Books, 1970.

RAILROADS IN SOCIETY

Lucius Beebe and Charles Clegg. *Hear the Train Blow.* New York: E. P. Dutton, 1952.

Benjamin A. Botkin and Alvin F. Harlow, eds., *A Treasury of Railroad Folklore.* New York: Crown Publishers, 1953.

Norm Cohen. *Long Steel Rail: The Railroad in American Folksong.* Urbana: University of Illinois Press, 1981 and 2000.

Frank P. Donovan. *The Railroad in Literature.* Boston: Railway & Locomotive Historical Society, 1940.

Freeman Hubbard. *Railroad Avenue: Great Stories and Legends of American Railroading.* New York: McGraw-Hill, 1945. Repr., San Marino, Calif.: Golden West Books, 1964.

Gustavus Myers. *History of the Great American Fortunes.* Vols. 2 and 3. Chicago: Charles H. Kerr, 1908–1910. Repr., New York: Modern Library, 1936, 1964.

Joseph P. Schwieterman. *When the Railroad Leaves Town: American Communities in the Age of Rail Line Abandonment.* (2 vols.) Kirksville, Mo.: Truman State University Press, 2001, 2004.

John R. Stilgoe. *Metropolitan Corridor: Railroads and the American Scene.* New Haven, Conn.: Yale University Press, 1983.

Allen W. Trelease. *The North Carolina Railroad, 1849–1871, and the Modernization of North Carolina.* Chapel Hill: University of North Carolina Press, 1991.

James A. Ward. *Railroads and the Character of America, 1820–1887.* Knoxville: University of Tennessee Press, 1986.

RAILROAD DESIGN AND IMAGE

E. P. Alexander. *Collector's Book of the Locomotive.* N.p.: Bramhall House, 1966.

Don Ball, Jr., and Rogers E. M. Whitaker. *Decade of the Trains: The 1940s.* Boston: New York Graphic Society, 1977.

Ranulph Bye. *The Vanishing Depot.* Wynnewood, Pa.: Livingston Publishing, 1973.

Dan Cupper. *Crossroads of Commerce: The Pennsylvania Railroad Calendar Art of Grif Teller.* N.p.: Great Eastern Publishing, 1992. Repr., Mechanicsburg, Pa.: Stackpole Press, 2003.

O. Winston Link, photographs, with text by Tim Hensley and afterword by Thomas H. Garver. *Steam, Steel & Stars: America's Last Steam Railroad.* New York: Harry N. Abrams, 1987.

Brad S. Lomazzi. *Railroad Timetables, Travel Brochures and Posters.* Spencertown, N.Y.: Golden Hill Press, 1995.

William H. Rau. (edited by John C. Van Horne with Eileen E. Drelick). *Traveling the Pennsylvania Railroad.* Philadelphia: University of Pennsylvania Press, 2002.

Robert C. Reed. *The Streamline Era.* San Marino, Calif.: Golden West Books, 1975.

Ted Rose. *In the Traces: Railroad Paintings of Ted Rose.* Bloomington: Indiana University Press, 2000.

Michael E. Zega and John E. Gruber. *Travel by Train: The American Railroad Poster, 1870–1950.* Bloomington: Indiana Univ. Press, 2002.

REFERENCE BOOKS

John H. Armstrong. *The Railroad, What It Is, What It Does: The Introduction to Railroading*. Omaha, Nebr.: Simmons-Boardman, 1978, 1982, 1990, and 1997.

Car Builders' Dictionary. This guide to railcar construction with drawings and photographs was started in 1879 by M. N. Forney and revised and reissued in 1884, 1895, 1903, 1906, 1909, 1912, 1916, and 1919. The title changed in the 1922 edition to *Car Builders' Cyclopedia of American Practice*, and new editions were issued by Simmons-Boardman in 1925, 1928, 1931, 1937, 1940, 1943, 1946, 1949, 1953, 1957, and 1961. It was combined with *Locomotive Cyclopedia* in 1966 (see below), and the series ended in 1997.

George H. Drury. *Guide to North American Steam Locomotives*. Waukesha, Wis.: Kalmbach Books, 1993. Also see Drury, *The Historical Guide to North American Railroads* (1985, 1991, and 2000) and *The Train-Watcher's Guide to North American Railroads* (1984 and 1992).

William D. Edson. *Railroad Names: A Directory of Common Carrier Railroads Operating in the United States, 1826–1982*. N.p.: Self-published, 1984.

Edward A. Lewis. *American Shortline Railway Guide*. N.p.: Self-published, 1973, 1978; Milwaukee, Wis.: Kalmbach Books, 1986, 1991, and 1996.

Locomotive Dictionary. First edition in 1906 by George L. Fowler. New editions in 1909, 1912, 1916, and 1919. Title changed in 1922 edition to *Locomotive Cyclopedia of American Practice*, and new editions issued by Simmons-Boardman in 1925, 1927, 1930, 1938, 1941, 1944, 1947, 1950–1952, and 1956. Title changed in 1966 to *Car and Locomotive Cyclopedia*, and new editions in 1970, 1974, 1980, 1984, and 1997.

Official Guide of the Railways. A monthly master listing of passenger timetables in North America, Cuba, and Puerto Rico from 1868 (called *Travelers' Official Railway Guide* between 1868 and 1899) through 1973. Published bimonthly to present with listings of national and regional freight carriers in North America.

Poor's Manual of Railroads of the United States. N.p.: Poor's Publishing Co. A yearly financial survey of railroad companies (1868–1924) started by Henry Varnum Poor. It absorbed *Moody's Manual of Railroads and Corporation Securities* (1900–1919), started by John Moody.

Railroad Facts. Published yearly since 1924, first by the Western Railways' Committee on Public Relations and later by the Association of American Railroads. *A Yearbook of Railroad Information*, with similar data, was published between 1929 and 1966 by the Eastern Railroad Presidents Conference Committee on Public Relations.

Railroads in the Nineteenth Century, Robert L. Frey, editor, and *Railroads in the Age of Regulation, 1900–1980*, Keith Bryant, editor. Both volumes part of *Encyclopedia of American Business History and Biography*. New York: Facts on File Publications, 1988.

Contributors

MARK ALDRICH is a professor of economics at Smith College. He has written extensively on railroad safety for *Railroad History* and other publications and in his recent book, *Death Rode the Rails.*

CHRISTOPHER T. BAER is assistant curator of manuscripts and archives at the Harley Museum and Library at Wilmington, Delaware. He was the principal author of *The Trail of the Blue Comet*, which received the Railway & Locomotive Historical Society's (R&LHS) 1997 Hilton Book Award.

DONALD M. BAIN was born and raised in Scotland before coming to Canada as a geologist. He has published almost 100 works, largely on Canadian railroads, as well as on such topics as Greyhound coaches, Canadian Pacific Air Lines, and Calgary transit.

RICHARD W. BARSNESS teaches in the business school and served as dean at Lehigh University. He was previously with Northwestern University. He has served as president of the Business History Conference and the Lexington Group in Transportation History.

GEORGE J. BELCHICK spent more than 40 years in manufacturing and marketing communications at Wabtec Corp. and is currently a marketing communications consultant.

MICHAEL BEZILLA is author of *Electric Traction on the Pennsylvania Railroad, 1895–1968*, and co-author of a book on the railroad's P5 electrics, and he has written numerous articles and essays on the PRR and central Pennsylvania.

R. CLIFFORD BLACK IV is a former high-school English teacher who has been a spokesman for Amtrak since 1981.

JOHN H. BROADLEY is a law graduate of the University of California at Berkeley. He began his legal work in government practice and moved into railroad legal work in 1976, working on Conrail bankruptcy negotiations. He later served as counsel to the Federal Railroad Administration and then to the Interstate Commerce Commission. He became a partner in private practice in 1984, specializing in transportation matters, and in 2000 formed his own firm in transportation law and litigation.

JOHN K. "JACK" BROWN teaches American industrial history at the University of Virginia and is author of *The Baldwin Locomotive Works, 1831–1915*, which won the R&LHS's 1996 Hilton Book Award.

KEITH L. BRYANT, JR., is professor of history emeritus at the University of Akron. His many publications include a history of the Santa Fe and a biography of railroad builder Arthur E. Stilwell. He received the R&LHS's 1990 Hilton Book Award for his editing of the *Encyclopedia of American Business History and Biography: Railroads in the Age of Regulation* and the R&LHS's David P. Morgan Articles Award in 1998 for a 1996 article in *Railroad History.*

SHIRLEY BURMAN is a railroad women's historian, a photographer, and curator for the exhibit Women and the American Railroad.

ANNE CALHOUN served as librarian for the Baltimore & Ohio Railroad Museum for more than 20 years and is now a library associate at Baltimore's Enoch Pratt Free Library.

NORMAN CARLSON is the retired managing partner of Arthur Anderson's transportation industry practice and is a member of the Business Advisory Committee of the Transportation Center at Northwestern University. He has written or edited 18 books on railroads and edits the quarterly *First & Fastest* of the Shore Line Interurban Historical Society.

MANUEL DIAZ CEBALLOS is a railroad historian and freelance consultant in urban restoration and design and planning of exhibits and expositions at Cienfuegos, Cuba.

ALBERT J. CHURELLA teaches business history at Southern Polytechnic State University and has written extensively on railroad history. His book *From Steam to Diesel* analyzed the transition between the two technologies. He is currently working on a complete history of the Pennsylvania Railroad.

NORM COHEN is the author of a number of books on American folk music, including *Folk Music: A Regional Exploration* and *Long Steel Rail: The Railroad in American Folksong*, as well as many articles, and has annotated or edited a number of albums. He teaches both chemistry and traditional American folk music at the Portland, Oregon, Community College.

BRIAN J. CUDAHY was a professor of philosophy and is retired from the U.S. Department of Transportation. He has written widely in the fields of both urban mass transit and maritime history. The most popular of his books has been *Under the Sidewalks of New York*, a history of the subway in his native city.

CHRISTOPHER P. D'AMATO is a lifelong rail enthusiast and for the last 25 years has been with Carstens Publications as an editor for *Railroad Model Craftsman.*

THOMAS L. DE FAZIO is a mechanical engineer who has taught at the Florida Institute of Technology and has done extensive design work in inertial navigation systems, robotics, and other technologies, with an avocation interest in steam railroading.

DAVID J. DEBOER has wide experience in transportation, including work in airlines, assignments with the Federal Railroad Administration and the Interstate Commerce Commission, and marketing and operation positions with the New York Central and Southern Pacific, and was one of the founders of Greenbrier Intermodal. He used his long experience in intermodal to author *Piggyback and Containers: A History of Rail Intermodal on America's Steel Highway.*

ROBERTA L. DIEHL retired in 2002 after more than 25 years with Indiana University Press, serving in a variety of capacities, most recently as sponsoring editor of railroad books.

JAMES D. DILTS is a railroad and architectural historian and the author of several books on these subjects, including *The Great Road: The Building of the Baltimore and Ohio, the Nation's First Railroad, 1828–1853*, which won the R&LHS's 1994 Hilton Book Award.

THOMAS W. DIXON, JR., is the publisher of TLC Railroad Books. He is also the founder and president of the Chesapeake & Ohio Historical Society and the author of numerous articles and books, among them *Chesapeake &*

Ohio for Progress: The C&O at Mid-20th Century, 1948–1963. He was one of the authors for an update of Charles W. Turner's landmark 1956 history, *Chessie's Road.*

LUIS V. DOMINGUEZ is a professor of international business at Florida Atlantic University and is researching Cuba's railroad history through the middle of the twentieth century.

DAN DONAGHY is chairman of an Ohio bank and has spent some 15 years in local economic development, which has often led to dealing with the problems of rail-dependent industries and an awareness of the importance of shortlines.

GEOFFREY H. DOUGHTY has been a safety director for railroads under Guilford ownership and is currently a safety consultant. He is the author of more than 16 articles and books on passenger-train history, including several recent volumes on the New Haven.

GEORGE H. DOUGLAS is a professor of English at the University of Illinois, specializing in American literature and studies. He is the author of several books on railroad subjects, including *Rail City: Chicago USA* and *All Aboard: The Railroad in American Life.*

GEORGE H. DRURY was with Kalmbach Publishing Co. for almost 25 years, serving as the librarian of *Trains* and *Model Railroader* magazines, a books editor, and the author of four volumes of Kalmbach's well-known railroad reference series. He is now a freelance writer and travel guide.

LAWRENCE R. DUFFEE lives in Fredericksburg, Virginia, and has a particular interest in the railroads of the Civil War and the South. He writes for the local newspaper and does book reviews for *Railroad History.*

DONALD DUKE has been active for more than 40 years as the publisher of Golden West Books, concentrating on railroad Americana. He has written several books and has edited and researched more than 140 titles. He won the R&LHS's 2003 Gerald M. Best Senior Achievement Award.

JAMES W. ELY, JR., is a professor of law and history at Vanderbilt University and is author of *Railroads and American Law.*

ADRIAN ETTLINGER is an electrical engineer, now retired from a career in software engineering, with a lifelong interest in railroads. He is webmaster for the Railway & Locomotive Historical Society.

BILL FAHRENWALD has been writing about transportation subjects since he began work as a *Railway Age* associate editor more than 25 years ago. He is currently a communications consultant with major logistics and supply-chain companies.

LYNN D. FARRAR developed his knowledge of railroad valuation from his long-time position, now retired, as a valuation engineer for the Southern Pacific.

WILLIAM HENRY FLAYHART III teaches at Delaware State University. His books include *The American Line (1871–1902)* and *Majesty at Sea: The Four Stackers*, with John H. Schaum, Jr.

JIM FULLER joined the Missouri Pacific Railroad in 1971, where he had a leading role in the initial proposal to the FRA and development of the M. Pac's car-scheduling project, and has subsequently been involved in the design and implementation of the Union Pacific's performance-measuring system.

ROBERT E. GALLAMORE is the director of the Transportation Center and teaches in the management school at Northwestern University. His earlier work includes assignments in positive train control at the Transportation Technology Center, strategic analysis for the Union Pacific, and federal assignments with the Federal Railroad Administration, Urban Mass Transportation Administration, and U.S. Railway Assn. His extensive publications include works on railroad mergers and transportation economics.

FREDERICK C. GAMST is professor of industrial and organizational anthropology emeritus at the University of Massachusetts, Boston, and adjunct professor of anthropology at the University of Wyoming. He has written numerous articles and technical reports on the railroad industry.

STEVE GLISCHINSKI is a freelance writer and photographer based in St. Paul, Minnesota. He is a regular correspondent for *Trains* magazine and is the author of five books on railroad topics.

CHARLES LAWRENCE GOOLSBY, a social policy analyst in Washington, D.C., grew up along the main line of the Atlanta, Birmingham & Coast. He has been a long-time student of the AB&C and its successor, the Atlantic Coast Line, and is a charter member of the ACL & SAL Historical Society. He is the author of books on ACL passenger service and the AB&C and is completing a third, on Seaboard Air Line's passenger service.

H. ROGER GRANT teaches history at Clemson University and is the author or editor of two dozen books. His most recent titles include *Follow the Flag*, a history of the Wabash Railroad, and *The Railroad: The Life Story of a Technology*. He won the R&LHS's annual Hilton Book Award in 1999 for *The North Western* and the 2005 Gerald M. Best Senior Achievement Award.

JOHN E. GRUBER is a freelance railroad writer and photographer and president of the Center for Railroad Photography & Art. His extensive publications include editorial work for *Classic Trains*, *Trains*, and *Vintage Rails*, and he is co-author of the book *Travel by Rail*. His imaginative and dramatic photography received the 1994 Stindt Award for Photography from the R&LHS.

RICHARD GRUBER is a heavy-equipment operator, track inspector, and conductor for the Wisconsin & Southern Railroad and a freelance photographer.

W. L. GWYER is retired from 37 years in operation positions with both eastern and western railroads, most recently with Burlington Northern Santa Fe. His operating experience includes work on the Penn Central's standing rules committee.

THOMAS HALEY has an MBA from Indiana University and has worked at CSX. He is currently assistant vice president for network and capital planning at Union Pacific.

JOHN HANKEY is a scholar in railroad history who has worked in various capacities at the Baltimore & Ohio from brakeman to curator of the B&O Museum. He presently works in cultural resource planning and management and writes for *Trains*, *Classic Trains*, and other publications.

PETER A. HANSEN is a writer and rail museum consultant. He is a frequent contributor to *Trains* and *Classic Trains* magazines on historical and modern industry topics.

SCOTT A. HARTLEY is a Connecticut native and a long-time enthusiast of the New Haven railroad. He has written eight books about northeastern railroads, including *New Haven Railroad: The Final Decades*.

HERBERT H. HARWOOD, JR., served for 30 years as an officer in the finance and marketing departments of the Chesapeake & Ohio, Baltimore & Ohio, and Chessie railroads. His writings on railroad history include extensive articles and 11 books, among them *Invisible Giants: The Empires of Cleveland's Van Sweringen Brothers* and *Impossible Challenge II*, a history of the building of the Baltimore & Ohio. In 1992 he received the Railroad History Senior Achievement Award for his writing, photography, and preservation efforts, and *Invisible Giants* was given the Railroad History Book Award in 2004.

CORNELIUS W. HAUCK is a longtime enthusiast of shortline and narrow-gauge railroads. A cofounder of the Colorado Railroad Museum at Golden in 1958, he edits the museum's *Colorado Rail Annual* series.

DENNIS C. HENRY teaches and is chair of the physics department at Gustavus Adolphus College. He did signal circuit design for the Northern Pacific in his college years and has been a research consultant for Burlington Northern on gravity retarder yards. Other research consulting has included work on transportation control systems, magnetic materials, and electromagnetic interference.

ERIC HIRSIMAKI has written extensively on railroad and Great Lakes shipping topics. His books include a history of the Lima Locomotive Works, as well as several histories of the Nickel Plate Railroad.

THOMAS G. HOBACK studied transportation and economics, and his early experience included marketing work on Western Pacific and a job as director of coal marketing for Illinois Central Gulf. In 1986 he founded the Indiana Rail Road, a spinoff from an ICG regional line, on which innovative technology and marketing savvy generated an eightfold traffic growth. He is an active member of the Railway & Locomotive Historical Society, the Lexington Group, and the Indiana Historical Society (IHS) and was a cofounder of the IHS's Midwest Railroad Research Center.

DON L. HOFSOMMER teaches history at St. Cloud State University and has written extensively in the field of American railroad history. His many books have included histories of the Minneapolis & St. Louis, the Great Northern, and the Iowa Central Railway; his book on the Southern Pacific received the 1988 Hilton Book Award of the R&LHS, and he received the R&LHS's 1995 Gerald M. Best Senior Achievement Award.

LAVAHN G. HOH teaches drama at the University of Virginia, specializing in theater technology with a special emphasis on the circus. His publications and presentations include several television programs on the circus, encyclopedia entries, and the book *Step Right Up! The Adventure of Circus in America*, with co-author William H. Rough.

KEVIN J. HOLLAND is a Toronto-based writer and editor specializing in transportation topics. He has written numerous articles and more than a dozen books, including *Berkshires of the Nickel Plate Road* and *The SteamLiners*.

CHARLES W. HOPPE has worked in a variety of management positions in transit and railroad consulting worldwide. He served with the Baltimore & Ohio, was president of the Long Island Rail Road from 1990 to 1994, and was vice president for operations and facilities planning at the U.S. Railway Assn. during the planning for formation of Conrail.

F. H. "JOE" HOWARD began his engineering career as a draftsman and roundhouse foreman (all in steam power) at Canadian Pacific, spent 10 years at Electro-Motive's London, Ontario, plant, and helped build and then operate Canadian National's ship-rail intermodal terminal at Halifax, Nova Scotia. He has written for *Trains* and other journals. He died in 2006.

TONY HOWE, who prepared the maps for the *Encyclopedia*, is a computer illustrator and railroad artist. His primary interest is in the railroads of Mississippi, Alabama, and Louisiana, with a particular focus on shortlines and logging railroads.

JON R. HUIBREGTSE is an associate professor of history at Framingham State University, where he teaches twentieth-century American history. His research studies railroad labor in the interwar years.

RICK JOHNSON, who prepared illustrations for the *Encyclopedia*, is the illustration supervisor at Kalmbach Publishing Co. and is active in the publication *The SOO* of the Soo Line Historical and Technical Society.

BOB JOHNSTON writes frequently on rail transportation, with over 100 news stories and topical features for *Trains* and *Classic Trains*, and co-authored the book *The Art of the Streamliner*.

EDWARD S. KAMINSKI is both a district sales manager and company historian for ACF Industries. His several books on railroad freight cars include *American Car & Foundry Company: A Centennial History, 1899–1999*.

KEVIN P. KEEFE studied journalism at Michigan State University and worked for newspapers in Michigan and Wisconsin before joining *Trains* magazine. He was editor of *Trains* from 1992 to 2000 and is now vice president, editorial, at Kalmbach Publishing Co.

JOHN A. KIRCHNER teaches geography and transportation at California State University, Los Angeles, and is a former trainman and clerk at the Santa Fe. The railroads of Latin America have been a major focus of his research, reflected by a number of articles and books on the topic.

MAURY KLEIN teaches history at the University of Rhode Island and is the author of 13 books, among them definitive biographies of Jay Gould and Edward H. Harriman and a two-volume history of the Union Pacific, which won the 1989 Hilton Book Award of the R&LHS.

THOMAS O. KLOEHN is a lawyer who developed extensive research on and understanding of railroad foreclosures through a 16-year period representing the Green Bay & Western Railroad and its officers and directors against the holders of Class B debentures issued by GB&W in 1896 as the culmination of three successive nineteenth-century federal equity foreclosure reorganizations.

EDWIN R. KRAFT is a systems engineer with experience in finance, planning, and information technology. He has worked at several railroads and in network analysis for Amtrak mail and express. He is now a consultant developing rail-costing models. He wrote an in-depth profile of the railroad freight yard in the June and July 2002 *Trains*.

J. PARKER LAMB taught mechanical engineering at the University of Texas and has written extensively on railroad topics and photographed trains for more than half a century. His recent books include *Perfecting the American Steam Locomotive* and *Evolution of the American Diesel Locomotive*. In 1991 he received the Stindt Railroad Photography Award from the Railway & Locomotive Historical Society.

JOHN LAURITZ LARSON teaches history at Purdue University and is the author of books on western development in America's railway age and national public works and early popular government in the United States, including the recent *Internal Improvement: National Public Works and the Promise of Popular Government in the Early United States*. His current research interests are in the environmental and cultural history of the colonial era.

DAN LEMAIRE-BAUCH maintains a longtime interest in all forms of rail transportation, particularly reciprocating steam power. His extensive list of publications includes works on computing and the Erie-Lackawanna ferry.

DAVID C. LESTER is a consultant in health care software and an independent transportation historian specializing in railroads and commercial aviation. He is the editor of the Railway & Locomotive Historical Society's quarterly newsletter.

LLOYD D. LEWIS has served in public relations and other departments for CSX Transportation and predecessors, as a reporter and editor for daily newspapers, and as a schoolteacher. His four books include three devoted to the Virginian Railway.

ARTHUR L. LLOYD is a longtime railroad enthusiast whose railroad work includes long assignments with the San Francisco & Napa Valley Railroad, Western Pacific, and Amtrak. He is currently a board member for the Bay Area's Caltrain commuter rail service.

MITCHELL A. MARKOVITZ has spent more than 30 years in railroad train service and as a distinguished railroad artist. His art studies included work at the American Academy of Art and the Chicago Academy of Fine Art, and his work has appeared in books, magazines, and in dramatic railroad poster art.

LOUIS A. MARRE teaches at the University of Dayton and is the author of a dozen books on railroad topics, including *The Diesel Locomotive: The First 50 Years* and several editions of the popular *Diesel Spotters Guide*.

GREG MCDONNELL is a professional firefighter and a longtime columnist and writer for *Trains* and other railroad publications. He edits Boston Mills Press's Master of Railway Photography series and is the author of nine books, including the recent *Canadian Pacific: Stand Fast, Craigellachie!* He was awarded the 2005 Stindt Award for Photography from the R&LHS.

ROBERT W. MCKNIGHT is a railway signaling historian and an electrical engineer with long experience as an editor for *Railway Signaling & Communications* and the *Signalman's Journal* and as manager of communications and signal engineering for the Assn. of American Railroads.

LLOYD J. MERCER teaches economics at the University of California at Santa Barbara. His books include *Railroads and Land Grant Policy: A Study of Government Intervention* and *E. H. Harriman: Master Railroader*.

WILLIAM D. MIDDLETON has spent over 50 years as a U.S. Navy officer, university manager, and civil engineer. He has also long been active as a writer of over 20 books and many hundreds of articles on rail transportation, engineering, and travel topics. He received the R&LHS's senior achievement award in 1984, and its Stindt Award for Photography in 2006.

WILLIAM D. MIDDLETON III is a Rochester Institute of Technology archaeologist, with field experience in Central America, Turkey, and China, and was codirector of an excavation at the Pullman plant in Chicago.

DAVID F. MYRICK served for a number of years as a financial officer with the Southern Pacific Co. and is a prolific and widely recognized writer. The majority of his dozen books are focused on western railroad history, with three additional titles planned.

ERIC A. NEUBAUER is a chemical engineer who has pursued a long interest in railroad freight cars. He has published numerous articles and drawings of freight cars for model magazines and has written some two dozen books on freight cars.

LINDA GRANT NIEMANN followed a 20-year career as a Southern Pacific trainman with her current teaching career in creative writing at Kennesaw State University. She writes for *Railroad History* and *Trains*, and her books include *Boomer: Railroad Memoirs* (later republished as *On the Rails*) and *Railroad Voices*, a text and photographic collaboration with Lina Bertucci.

DENNIS S. NORDIN teaches history at Mississippi State University. He has published and lectured widely on such topics as the history and development of agriculture. His books include *Rich Harvest: A History of the Grange, 1867–1900* and, with Roy V. Scott, *From Prairie Farmer to Entrepreneur.*

DON PHILLIPS's interest in railroads began with a mid-1940s encounter with the Atlanta, Birmingham & Coast station at Talladega, Alabama, and soon expanded to include all types of transportation. This led to his more than 40-year career as a newspaper journalist, currently with the *International Herald Tribune.* His widely read monthly column for *Trains* has appeared for almost 30 years.

CARY FRANKLIN POOLE has worked in university administration for over 20 years and is now the dean of students at Texas Wesleyan University. His railroad writings have included a regional railroad history of North Carolina, a study of the Santa Fe's CF7 program, and a history of the Edwards Railway Motor Car Co.

DOUG RIDDELL studied communication and spent a decade in radio and television broadcasting before fulfilling his life's ambition to become a locomotive engineer with the Seaboard Coast Line and then Amtrak. With 30 years of seniority, he frequently finds himself working the *Silver Star* and *Capitol Limited.* He has written extensively about his railroad experiences for *Passenger Train Journal, Trains,* and other publications.

ALFRED RUNTE is an architectural historian and a specialist in the national parks. He has written extensively on this subject, and his books include *National Parks: The American Experience* and the popular *Trains of Discovery.*

G. WILLIAM "BILL" SCHAFER is a career railroader with more than 30 years at the Southern Railway and Norfolk Southern and is now NS's director of corporate affairs. He is also a founder of the Southern Railway Historical Assn.

CARLOS ARNALDO SCHWANTES is a professor of transportation studies and the West at the University of Missouri at St. Louis and has written extensively on western transportation. His 14 books include *Railroad Signatures across the Pacific Northwest,* which won the 1995 annual Hilton Book Award of the R&LHS.

JIM SCRIBBINS spent 40 years with the Milwaukee Road in the passenger department and then in freight sales and public relations work. He has written numerous articles for *Trains* and other publications and has authored five books, among them *The Milwaukee Road, 1928–1985.*

JIM SHAUGHNESSY is a civil engineer with a lifelong interest in railroads. His railroad photographs rank among the very best of the last half of the twentieth century; he received the annual R&LHS Stindt Award for Photography in 1987. His books include histories of the Delaware & Hudson and Rutland railroads.

TOM SHEDD was a contributing editor for several railroad trade journals and edited *Modern Railroads* for almost 25 years. He also completed work for a number of encyclopedias, including the *Encyclopaedia Britannica*'s "Railroads and Locomotives" article.

GEORGE M. SMERK taught transportation at Indiana University for more than 40 years, directed the Institute for Urban Transportation for 36 years, and was director of transportation on the Bloomington campus for 11 years. He has written extensively on urban transportation, including a longtime column for *Railroad & Railfan* magazine. The most recent of his five books is *The Federal Role in Urban Mass Transportation.*

BRIAN SOLOMON studied photographic illustration and has gained a wide reputation for his dramatic railroad photographs. He has become a prolific railroad writer as well for *Trains* and many other publications, spent several years as an editor for *Pacific Rail News,* and now works as a freelance writer and photographer. His more than two dozen books include titles on railroad maintenance equipment and signaling and the Burlington Northern Santa Fe Railway.

JOHN C. SPYCHALSKI is professor of supply-chain management in the business college at Pennsylvania State University. His research and teaching include rail transport-related economic, managerial, and public policy issues.

THOMAS D. SULLIVAN studied electrical engineering and computer science and was widely recognized for his work in railroad signaling and communications. In recent years he developed advanced signaling systems for both the San Francisco and New York City transit systems. He did consulting work until his death in June 2005.

J. W. SWANBERG studied at Trinity College. His railroad career spanned almost 40 years, from a fireman's job on the New Haven to lead trainmaster at Metro-North, as well as service as a naval aviator. He has written extensively for *Trains, Railroad History,* and many other publications. His *New Haven Power: 1838–1968* provides a comprehensive account of all forms of New Haven motive power.

JEREMY TAYLOR has had long experience in railroad operations, beginning as a New York Central transportation trainee in 1952. This was followed by general manager posts on New York Central's Southern Division and the Penn Central's Southern and New Haven regions, and as vice president of operations for the Long Island Rail Road.

WILMA RUGH TAYLOR is a retired schoolteacher and journalist who has studied the extensive work of the church in developing a mission to railroad people and workers. Her books include *This Train Is Bound for Glory: The Story of America's Chapel Cars* and *Gospel Tracks through Texas: The Mission of Chapel Car Good Will.*

ROBERT E. TUZIK has spent more than 30 years in railroads, beginning as a Santa Fe switchman and later becoming a yardmaster and operating supervisor. He served as editor of *Railway Track & Structures* and as engineering editor for *Railway Age* before heading a railroad supply company. He now is president of a supply industry marketing and editorial company and publishes *Interface, the Journal of Wheel/Rail Interaction.*

WILLIAM C. VANTUONO studied theater arts, speech, and public media and writes regularly for the North American railroad industry as editor of the leading trade publication *Railway Age.* His recent book *All about Railroading* is designed to inform young adults about railroads.

WILLIAM J. WATT is a retired writer and transportation consultant and a former Federal Railroad Administration policy administrator who has also chaired the state of Indiana's transportation coordinating board and transportation finance authority. He has written extensively on railroad topics.

GEORGE C. WERNER studied business and completed a long career in corporate planning for Exxon, USA. He also pursued a long avocational career in railroads, specializing in Texas railroads. He has written extensively for *Trains* and other publications and wrote or edited more than 300 railroad entries for *The New Handbook of Texas.*

DANIEL J. WESTERBECK is a retired vice president and general tax counsel for Burlington Northern Santa Fe who was instrumental in mitigating many railroad tax cases under the 4R Act after 1980. He was also codeveloper of the reform of the Railroad Retirement Tax Act of 2002 that allowed the investment of railroad retirement funds in equities.

JOHN H. WHITE, JR., is the emeritus curator of transportation at the Smithsonian Institution and now teaches at Miami University in Oxford, Ohio. A frequent writer on early railroad topics for *Railroad History* and many other journals, he is the author of 13 books on railway operations, locomotives, and car-building technology. Particularly notable are his works on railroad passenger and freight cars and American locomotives of the nineteenth century. He received the R&LHS's senior achievement award in 1982.

W. THOMAS WHITE has served as the first curator of the James J. Hill and Louis W. Hill manuscript collections at the James J. Hill Library in St. Paul since they were opened to researchers in 1982. His writings on the history of business, labor, and politics in the American Northwest have appeared in a variety of publications.

BOB WITHERS is both a reporter for a daily newspaper and a Baptist pastor. He has written for several railroad magazines and is author of the book *The President Travels by Train.*

MICHAEL E. ZEGA has written extensively about railroad history, marketing, art, and design for *Vintage Rails, Classic Trains,* and other publications. His series of articles in *Classic Trains* in 2000–2001 won the 2002 annual David P. Morgan Articles Award of the R&LHS. He was the author, jointly with John E. Gruber, of the recent book *Travel by Train: The American Railroad Poster, 1870–1950.*

Index

air transportation, 17, 65, **107–109**, 521; Bombardier aircraft manufacture, 174; decline in passenger traffic, 1134; Department of Transportation challenges, 358; deregulation of, 358, 924; professional sports, 997

air-conditioned cars and trains, 21, 165, 534, 821, 824, 829–830

Airline Deregulation Act of 1978, 358, 924

Airport Express, 819

Airslide covered hopper cars, 202–203, 468

Alabama & Vicksburg Railroad, 532, 982

Alabama Great Southern Railroad, 982

Alabama Midland Railroad, 155, 927

Alameda Corridor, California, 498

Alaska, route map of, *1186*

Alaska Central Railroad, 110

Alaska Northern Railway, 110

Alaska Railroad (ARR), **109–110**, 908, *1186*

Albany & Schenectady Railroad, 712. *See also* Mohawk & Hudson Rail Road

Albany & Susquehanna Railroad (A&S), 353

Albany & West Stockbridge Railroad, 1095

The Albany Depot (Howells), 594

Albee, Edward F., 1047

Alberta & Great Waterways Railway, 754

Albion Mines Railway, 194

Alco. *See* American Locomotive Co.

alcohol availability during Prohibition, 18–19

Aldene Plan, 213

Alexandria & Washington Railroad (A&W), 939

Alger, Horatio, 597

Algoma Central & Hudson Bay Railway, **110**, 908, *1193*

Algoma Central Railway, 1109

Algoma Eastern Railway, 110

alignment of track, 252, 657

All Red Route, 679

Allan, Hugh, 678

Allan Steamship Co., 678

all-door boxcars, 62

Allegheny Corp., 1079, 1128

Allegheny Mountains pass (Pennsylvania Railroad), 248

Allegheny Portage Railroad, **110–112**, 628, 863, 1049; inclined-plane railways, 537–538; route map, 1158

allegories, railroad, 722–723

Allen, Horatio, 112, **112–113**, 976, 1006–1007

Allen, Richard N., 845

Allen, Samuel G., 119, 295

Allen, W. E., 781

Allen, William Frederick, 1003

alloy steels. See steel manufacture

Allport, James, 882

Alpert, George, 744

Alpha Jets, 1093

alphabet communities, 32

Alphabet Route, 1093

Alstom Signaling (General Railway Signal Co.), **113–114**, 175, 430, 971, 1069; AEI program, *see* automatic equipment identification

alternate power-transmission system, 587

alternating current. *See* AC electrification

alternative discipline agreement, 784

alternative piston strokes, 1005

Alton. *See* Chicago & Alton Railroad

Altoona plant, Pennsylvania Railroad, 204, 900

aluminothermic welding, 652

aluminum: bridge designs, 259; freight cars, 457, 457; passenger cars, 883

American Car & Foundry (AC&F), **114–116**, 201, 202, 204, 468, 833, 835–836; Charles, Missouri plant, 115; Cuba Railroad, 348

American Civil War. *See* Civil War

American Engineering Association (AREA), 614

American Federation of Labor (AFL), 576, 579

American Flyer streamliners, 830

American Guide, 776

American Line, 678

American literature, railroads in, 593

American Locomotive Co. (Alco), 16, **116–122**, 159, 486–488, 588, 590, 600–603, 645; 2-10-10-2s, 117; Alco class HR-4-2-6-7-2, *699*; Alco demonstrator 4-6-2 No. 50000, 117; Big Boy (4-8-8-4) engines, *119*, 119, 1006, 1025, 1027; Cooke Locomotive and Machine Works merger, 600; diesel locomotives, 161, 426; diesel-electric locomotives, *118*, 369–370; GE-Alco locomotives, 488, 601–602; Mexican railways, 699; Montreal Locomotive Works, acquisition of, 173; plant acquisitions and mergers, 600; production for Canadian National, 199; Schenectady Locomotive Works, *116*, 600; Super-Power production, 1027

American Machinist (periodical), 973–974

American President Lines (APL), 77

American Public Transportation Association, 686

American Railroad Co. of Puerto Rico, 879, *1186*

American Rail-Road Journal, 873, 1051, 1052

American Railway Association (ARA), 149

American Railway Engineering and Maintenance-of-Way Association (AREMA), 645, 647

American Railway Engineering Association (AREA), 642

American Railway Express Co., 634, 911

American Railway Guide, 775–776

American Railway Signal Co., 113

American Railway Union (ARU), 9, 351, 504, 576–579; Pullman strike (1894), 9, 351, 379, 504, 577–579, 876, 880–881, 886

American Short Line and Regional Railroad Association (ASLRRA), **122**

American Steamship Co., American-flag, 678

American Telegraph Co., 336

Ames, Oakes, **122–123**, 334, 713, 797, 806–807

Ames, Oliver, **123**, 713, 797, 806–807

Ames Monument, 713

AMF Beaird, Inc., 206

Amfleet coaches, *80*, 184, 738

Ammann, Othmar H., 593

Amtech Corp., 430

Amtrak. *See* National Railroad Passenger Corp. (Amtrak)

Amtrak Service Workers Council (ASWC), 436

anchors, rail, 646

Anderson, Frank, 101

Andrews, James J., 124–125, 716

Andrews, Samuel, 450

Andrews's Raid, **124–125**

Androscoggin & Kennebec Railroad, 638

Angel of Resurrection monument, *716*, 717

Angels Flight Incline, Los Angeles, 538

angle bars, 52

Angola Horror (1867), 91, *91*

Ann Arbor Railroad, **125–126**, 1085; DT&I purchase of, 360; railcar ferry services, 667; route map, *1171*

annual reports, ICC collection of, 1075

annual revenue classifications, 278–279

anthracite coal, 292, 351, 353, 607, 1010, 1115; NYO&W mining, 745

anticipation classification, 283–286

antitrust issues, 13, 307, 504, 756, 914, 916, 960–961; Charles Sanger Mellen and New Haven, 693, 720, 743; Electro-Motive Corporation, 426; Northern Securities Co., 756; Pullman companies, 883–884

APB signaling system, 113, 966

appealing disciplinary decisions, 784

Appleton, Victor, 598

Appleton's *Railroad and Steam Navigation Guide*, 775, 777

approach signal, 1057

aquarium cars, 446–449

Arbitration Act of 1888, 957

arch bridges, 253–254, 257, 258, 261–262. *See also entries at* bridge

arch-bar trucks, freight cars, 461, 464

architecture, 24–25, 48–49, **126–143**; Boston commuter services, 309; buildings, types of, 126–128, 133–135; historic preservation, 36; history of, 133–135; non-U.S., 142–143; public image, 29; railroad suburbs and towns, 130; signature styles, 130–132; workers' housing, 1116–1118. *See also specific buildings by name*

argot (and nicknames), 31–32, **144–145**

Arkansas, Louisiana & Southern Railway (AL&S), 572

Arkansas River canalization, 1090

Armour & Co., 162

Armstrong, George B., 637

armstrong levers, 773

Army Appropriation Act of 1916, 1071, 1119

Army management model, 662

Army-Navy football contests, 986

Arnaud Railway, 889

Arnold Loop (Western Pacific), 1093

Around the World in Eighty Days, 242
Arreola, Juan José, 698
Arrival of a Train at the Ciotat Station, 239
art, 33–35, **145–149**. *See also* literary
    works; music; photographers
Arthur Kill bridge (Elizabeth), 259
articulated configurations, 1006; com-
    pound articulateds, 117, 662,
    1017–1019, 1082; compound articulat-
    eds, Vauclain, 160, 1013; five-platform,
    553; freight cars, 454–455, *467*, 467,
    554; lightweight sleeping cars, 831;
    semipermanently coupled passenger
    cars, 830, 840–842; super-power,
    1022–1024
artifacts, railroading, 874. *See also* collec-
    tors of railroad paraphernalia
Artists' Excursion, B&O (1858), 33,
    145–146, *146*
As the Centuries Pass in the Night, 148
ash disposal, 608
Ashcan school of art, 33
Ashland Oil, 639
Ashtabula, 667
Ashtabula collapse (1876), 90, 94, 256
"Asleep at the Switch" (song), 723
ASME Boiler Codes, 1010
asphalt underlayments, hot-mix, 641
assessment (tax), 1040–1041
asset accounts, 97
assistant conductors, 760
Association of American Railroads (AAR)
    (also: American Railway Association),
    149–150, 458, 463, 496, 705; car-type
    codes, 463; Committee on National
    Defense, 1072; heavy-haul load impact
    studies, 517; railroad classification,
    278–279; Track Loading Vehicle
    (TLV), 650; Transportation Technol-
    ogy Center (TTCI), 444, 517, 640–641;
    William Wallace Atterbury, 157
Association of Colored Railway Trainmen
    and Locomotive Firemen, 435
Association of Railway Executives
    (ARE), 149
Astor, John Jacob, 222, 482
Astrom Transport, 323–324
Atchison, Topeka & Santa Fe Railroad
    (Santa Fe), 7, 13, **150–153**, 571, *616*,
    814–815; Argentine Yard, 173; B&RG
    competition, 355; Burlington North-
    ern merger, *see* BNSF Railway; Canyon
    Diablo crossing, *49*; *Chief*, 853; Cor-
    with Yard, *289*; diesel shops, *620*;
    Emerson Harrington, 545; encourag-
    ing colonization, 302–304; Frederick
    H. Harvey, 513–514; Grand Canyon
    National Park monopoly, 735; Hi-
    Level passenger cars, 840; Kansas City,
    Mexico & Orient Railroad (Orient),
    acquisition of, 572; labor unrest, 545;
    marketing campaigns, 680, 682, 684;
    Metrolink system, 978; MOW laborers
    at work maintaining rails, *654*; passen-
    ger ferry services, 676; railcar ferry ser-
    vices, 669; Railroad YMCA (Emporia),
    1118; Railway Exchange (Chicago),
    129; route map, *1181*; seniority prin-

ciple, 958; Southern Pacific merger,
    153, 172, 1067; speed runs, 984; *Super
    Chief*, 151–152, *152*, 182, 853, 994
athletic events, trains to, 986
Atlanta, Birmingham & Coast
    Railroad, 156
Atlanta, Valdosta & Western Railway, 982
Atlanta & Charlotte Air Line Railway, 955
Atlanta & La Grange Rail Road, 154
Atlanta & Pacific Railroad (A&P),
    950–951
Atlanta & Richmond Air-Line
    Railroad, 981
Atlanta & West Point Rail Road, 32,
    153–154, 211–212; Civil War destruc-
    tion, 278; J. Edgar Thomson, 1049;
    race strike, 435; route map, *1170*
Atlantic, Gulf & West India Transit
    Co., 955
Atlantic & Great Western Railroad. *See*
    Erie Railroad
Atlantic & Gulf Railroad, 155
Atlantic & Pacific Railroad, 151, 582
Atlantic & St. Lawrence (A&StL). *See*
    Maine Central Railroad
Atlantic Coast Line Railroad (ACL), 153,
    154, **155–156**, 344; CC&O, lease of,
    292; *Florida Special*, 156, 851, 904;
    route map, *1169*; Seaboard Air Line
    and, 954–956
Atlantic Limited, 1094
Atlantic Railway, 337
Atlantic Refining consent decree
    (1942), 872
attendants (occupation), 764–765
Atterbury, William Wallace, **156–157**, *157*,
    182, 682; military rail operations
    (World War I), 1120
Atwood, Charles B., 136
audio frequency track circuits, 968–969
Aurora, Elgin & Chicago Railway, 234
Austin, William, 160
Austin-Western Co., 162
automated hump yards, 282
automated rail transit program, 1104
automated route interlocking, 967
automated tie renewal, 654, 656
automated warning systems, 497–498
automatic air brakes, *822*, 1096, 1098
automatic block signaling (ABS), 53, 59,
    93, 113, 965–966, 1056–1057,
    1120–1121. *See also* Union Switch
    & Signal Co.
automatic car identification (ACI), 430
automatic couplers, 9–10, 458–459, 566
automatic dump cars, 203
automatic equipment identification
    (AEI), 61, 329, 340, 430, 969
automatic equipment management
    (AEM), 430
automatic interlocking function, 967
automatic Janney coupler, 842
Automatic Pneumatic Railway Signal
    Co., 113
automatic switching systems, 1069
automatic train control (ATC), 59, 93,
    966. *See also* classification yards
automobiles. *See* motor vehicles

automotive laborers, 770
auxiliary generators, 622
auxiliary motors, 622
auxiliary water tenders, 604
Averell, Mary, 511
aviation. *See* air transportation
Avila Camacho, Manuel, 878
axle-hung arrangement. *See* gear-drive
    locomotives
axles, steel, 45
Aydelott, Gale, 73
Azobe hardwood ties, 643
Aztec Eagle (Aguila Azteca), 700

B7 snowmobile (Bombardier), 173
Babahatchie YMCA, 1127–1128
Babbage, Charles, 608
"baby railroad," 728, 732
Back Bay Station (Boston), 138
back-shop layout, 618–620
Bacon, Charles, 243
Baer, George F., 918
Bagaley, Ralph, 1098
baggage handling, *28*, *765*, 765, 847
Bailey Brothers circus, 244–246
Bailey Yard, 285
Bainer, H. M., 102
Baker valve gear design, 1011–1012, *1012*
balance sheet accounts, 98, 895
balanced compound engines, 1013
balancing drivers, 1028
Baldwin, E. Francis, 133–134, 1118
Baldwin, Gilbert S. *See Free Railroad
    Guide*
Baldwin, Matthias W., 6, **158–159**, *158*,
    159–160, 187, 600, 820, 1007, 1011
Baldwin, William M., 718
Baldwin Locomotive Works, 119, 158,
    159–163, 588, 590–591, 599–601, 820;
    Alco, competition with, 116–117; busi-
    ness promotion activities, 987; Charles
    Thomas Parry, 820; diesel locomotives,
    161, 426 (*see also* Centipede diesels);
    diesel-electric locomotives, 370–373;
    Eddystone plant, *159*, 159, 160–161,
    372, 1082; Edward H. Williams, 1108;
    electric locomotives, 409; geared
    steam locomotives, 587; George
    Burnham, Sr., 160, 187; John E. Woot-
    ten, 1115; Lima-Hamilton merger,
    603 (*see also* Baldwin-Lima-Hamilton
    Corp.); Mexican railways, 699; rack
    railways, 296; relationship with
    Westinghouse, 601, 1100–1102;
    Samuel M. Vauclain, 1082; Super-
    Power production, 1027; Ten Wheeler
    (4-6-0) engine, *160*, 1009, 1013;
    Westinghouse, collaboration with, 601,
    1100–1103; Whitcomb Locomotive
    Works, 603
Baldwin-Lima-Hamilton Corp. (B-L-H),
    162, 590, 603, 836
Ball, George, 1080
ball signal device, 963
ballads, narrative railroad, 725–726
ballast, 641, 643
ballast cleaning, 658, 661
ballast regulators, 659, *660*

ballast tamping, 657
ballast undercutting/cleaning, 658, 661
ballasted bridge decks, 266–267
balloon sheds, 136
balloon-track formation, 282, 287
Baltimore, Carroll & Frederick Rail Road
    Co., 1092
Baltimore & Liverpool Steamship Co.,
    677–678
Baltimore & Ohio Railroad (B&O), 4–6, 9,
    12–13, **163–166**, 489, 574, 865; Albert
    Fink, 445–446; architecture, 129,
    133–134, *134*; Artists' Excursion
    (1858), 33, 145–146, *146*; B&O Trans-
    portation Museum, 874; Benjamin H.
    Latrobe, Jr., 584; C&A, acquisition
    of, 510; C&O merger, *see* Chessie Sys-
    tem; *Capitol Limited*, 165, 853; "The
    Carollton March," 722; Carrollton
    Viaduct, 163, 253; CH&D, acquisition
    of, 223; charter, 540; Chicago Termi-
    nal, 164; during Civil War, 274, 483;
    coal dumpers, *293*; commuter services,
    314; construction, 1105; as CSX prede-
    cessor, 344, 345; Daniel Willard, 528,
    1106–1107; double-truck passenger
    cars, 820; electrification, *409*, 409, 420;
    Fair of the Iron Horse (1927), 528,
    874; fish cars, 446; Grasshopper loco-
    motives, 163, *1007*, 1108; great rail-
    road strike of 1877, *577*; inclined-
    plane railways, 536, 538;
    incorporation, 1048; Jervis Langdon,
    Jr., 583; John W. Garrett, 483, 677;
    Joseph Gladding Pangborn, 817–818,
    874; Leonor F. Loree, 630; as major
    railroad, 437–438; maximum grade
    determination, 248; *Messenger of Agri-
    cultural Development*, 102; Olive W.
    Dennis, 354–355; Pennsylvania Rail-
    road, rivalry with, 483; physicians, em-
    ployment of, 691; porters (sleeping
    car), *855*; pot hopper cars, 456; PRR
    rivalry with, 865, 870; railcar ferry ser-
    vices, 668; railroad police force, 339;
    Railroad YMCAs, 1118, 1127; Republic
    wreck (1887), 92, 94; role in preserva-
    tion, 874; Ross Winans, 163, 181, 820,
    1095, 1108–1109; route map, *1169*;
    Royal Blue Line, 164, 166, 213; stream-
    liners, 832; Thomas Viaduct, *147*, 163,
    253, 584, 712–713, 1048, 1116; *Tom
    Thumb*, 5, 163, 336, 614, *1007*; train
    speed, 992–993 (*see also* speed);
    transatlantic steamship lines, 677–678;
    Washington Terminal Co., 1087;
    William Prescott Smith, 874; workers'
    housing, 1116–1118
Baltimore & Potomac Railroad (B&P),
    1087
Baltimore & Susquehanna Railroad, 133,
    1105
Baltimore Belt Line, 164
Baltimore Steam Packet Co., 955
Baltimore trusses, 254, 446
Baltimore-area routes, *1163*
Bamberger Railroad, **166**, *1184*
Bandeen, Robert A., 499

bands of time (time zones), 8, 1003
Bangor & Aroostook Railroad (BAR), **167**
Bangor & Katahdin Iron Works
    Railway, 167
Bangor & Piscataquis Railroad, 167
Bangs, George S., *635*, 1051
banking privileges, 540
Bankruptcy Act of 1898, Section 77,
    929–930, 938
Baptist chapel cars, 215–216
bar cars, 309
Bar Harbor Express. See Mt. Desert Limited
Bar Harbor resort, 904
Barabe, Buck (fictional), 170
barge operation. *See* canals; water trans-
    portation
Barlow, Samuel, 792
Barlow, William H., 135
Barnes, Al G., 245
Barney & Smith Car Co., 215–216
barney pusher system, 534
Barnum, John, 71, 73
Barnum, P. T., 243
Barnum & Bailey Circus, 245–247
Barnum circus, 243–244
Barrett, Lawrence, 984
Barrett, Nathan F., 885
Barriger, John W., III, 149, **167–169**, *168*,
    177, 223, 230, 235, 710, 868
Bartlett, W. H., *147*
Bartnett, Water, 1093
Barzun, Jacques, 596
bascule bridges, 259, 266–267
baseball, 996–998
basketball, 997–998
Batterman's *American Railway Guide*,
    775–776
Baumgardner, Newton L., 107
Bay Area Rapid Transit (BART), 322,
    970–971
BC Rail, **169**; electrification, 421; route
    map, *1194*
Beach, Alfred Ely, 271
Beach Hydraulic Tunneling Shields, *271*
bearing defects, detecting, 430–431
Beaver Tail Point (sleeping car), 833
Bedwell, Harry, 34, **169–170**, 598
Beebe, Lucius, **170–171**, 596, 715
Beggs, Eugene, 909
Beggs, James, 71
Begin, Nazaire, 991
Beissel, Minnie L., *25*
Bel Geddes, Norman, 830
Belen Cutoff, 151
Belington & Beaver Creek Railroad, 1092
Bell, Edwin, 291
Bellefontaine Railway, 776
Belpaire, Alfred Jules, 1009
Belpaire firebox, 1009
Belt Railway of Chicago (BRC), **171**, 231,
    1037; Clearing Yard, 171, 280; route
    map, *1172*
Beman, Solon S., 134, 885
Bentley, Edward M., 408, 484
Benton, Thomas Hart, 793, 807, 808
bents, 261
Bergen Turnpike Co., 1034
Berkshire Hills pass, 248

Berlin, Irving, *725*
Bernays, Edward L., 878
Bernet, John J., 741, 1079
Berwind, Edward J., 348
Besler steam train (1936), 832
Bessemer, Henry, 48, 256
Bessemer & Lake Erie Railroad, 667, 782
Bessemer process (steel), 45, 48, 256
The Best Friend of Charleston, 5, 112, 976,
    1007; Charleston explosion (1831),
    87–88, 976
BethGon Coalporter, 202
Bethlehem Steel Corp., 201–202
betterment accounting, 97, 1076
Bhn (Brinell hardness), 645
BHP Iron Ore Railroad, 517
Biddle, Nicholas, 918
bidirectional passenger trains, 832
bidirectional self-propelled rail cars,
    837, 839
bids (applications for employment),
    767–768
Bierce, Ambrose, 596
Big Four. *See* Cleveland, Cincinnati,
    Chicago & St. Louis Railway
Big Four brotherhoods, 576–579
Big Inch pipeline, 872
Big John cars, 62, 69, 983
Big John case, 69, 180, 338, 983
bilevel automobile carriers, *467*
bilevel commuter cars, 322
bilevel passenger cars, 839–840
Billings, Frederick, 755
bimodal equipment, 455. *See also* inter-
    modal transportation
bipolar gearless passenger locomotives, *416*
Bishop, C. B., 984
Bisma-Rex, 988
black employees and passengers, 434–436,
    913. *See also* racial discrimination and
    segregation
Black Maria locomotive, 120
black operating employees, 435
Black Worker (*Messenger*) magazine, 913
blacklisting of strikers, 578–579
blacksmiths and blacksmith-welders, 68,
    766; shops, 615
Blair, John I., 387, 506
Blair, Montgomery, 637
Blenkinsop, John, 296
block lengths, train control and, 969
block operators, 771
block signals, 113; accident prevention
    regulations, 92–93, 95; automatic
    (ABS), 53, 59, 93, 113, 965–966,
    1056–1057, 1120–1121 (*see also* Union
    Switch & Signal Co.); manual, 394,
    965, 1056
blocking theory, 283–285
blocks (grouping of cars), 279
blower aspiration (internal
    combustion), 363
Blue Bird, 1086
Blue China pattern (B&O), 355
Blue Comet, 993
Blue Corner, 213
Blue Cut, Missouri, 341

Blue Goose, 1104
blue laws, 1035
Blue Ridge Tunnel, 269, 272
blue-flag rule, 782
blues songs, railroad, 723
BNSF Railway (Burlington Northern & Santa Fe Railway), 85, 153, **171–173**, 186; BN and Santa Fe merger, 171–172, 187; Canadian National, co-ordination with, 191; CN Rail, failed merger with, 200; coal mining, 295; route map, *1181. See also* Atchison, Topeka & Santa Fe Railroad; Burlington Northern Railroad
board membership, interlocking. *See* communities of interest
Board of Railroad Wages and Working Conditions, 1073
Boardman, James, 1116
Boardman, William H., 1052
boats: ferryboats, 309, 666–677, 1094; flatboats, 1088; steamboats, *see* steamboats and steamships. *See also* water transportation
Bob Elson aboard the Century, 890
boiler and flue maintenance, 615, 617. *See also* railroad shops
boiler shops, 615
boilermakers, 68, *766*, 766
boilers on steam locomotives, 605, 1010
Bollman trusses (Wendell Bollman), 254
bolsters, 459–461
Bombardier, **173–176**, 201, 203, 601, 840, 842; Comet cars, 740; commuter cars, 322–323; MLW, acquisition of, 601 (*see also* Montreal Locomotive Works); Pullman cars and, 884; push-pull coaches, 721; Westinghouse organization ownership, 1104
Bombardier, Joseph-Armand, 173
Bond, Milton J., 626
bonds, railroad, 936–938
Bonner Railwagon trailer-on-flatcar (TOFC) intermodal service, 580
Bonzano, Giovanni Cardinal, 990–991
books, children's, 598
books on railroads, 874–876, 909, 1220–1223. *See also specific books by title*
The Boomer: A Story of the Rails (novel), 170, 598
Boomer, L. T., 145
booming, 1112
boosters (classification yards), 286
Bordentown Monument, 714
boring mills, 617
Boston, Hoosac Tunnel & Western Railroad, 176–177
Boston, Revere Beach & Lynn Railroad, 417; electrification, 420; passenger ferry, 675–676
Boston & Albany Railroad (B&A), 177, 1095; commuter services, 310, 684; station architecture, *132*
Boston & Lowell Railroad, 39, 176; Charles River drawbridge, 259, 555; commuter services, 309
Boston & Maine Railroad (B&M), 167, **176–178**, 214, 639; commuter services,

310, 324, 684; electrification, 414, 420; Hoosac Tunnel, *see* Hoosac Tunnel; New Haven gained gained control of, 743; Patrick B. McGinnis, 690; route map, *1156*
Boston & Providence Railroad: commuter services, 309; Neponset River viaduct, 253
Boston & Worcester Railroad, 528, 539, 684, 1095; commuter services, 308–309
Boston area: commuter services, 309; route map, *1158*
Boston Elevated Railway, 684
Boulton & Watt, 1006, 1064
Bouscaren, Louis F. G., 256, 268
box caisson, 268
box girder bridges, 265–266
box-anchor, rail, 646
boxcars, 203, 462–464, *463*
boycotts. *See* Pullman strike (1894)
Boyd, Alan S., 77, 357
Bozo Texino, *525*
Brady, James Buchanan "Diamond Jim," **178**
Braitmayer, Otto E., 325–326
brake horsepower measurements, 1015
"Brakeman's Blues" (song), 35
brakemen, *50, 760,* 760, 945, 1064; African American, 435; slang terms for, 144; union for, 576
brakes, 52, 460, 843–844, 1096–1100; automatic air brakes, *822,* 1096, 1098; compressed-air braking, 1096 (*see also* Westinghouse Air Brake Co.); ECP braking, 64, 1099–1100; electric locomotives, 407; Johnson bar, 1013; passenger cars, 821–823, *822,* 843–844; in response to engineer inactivity, 1061–1062; safety, 945 (*see also* safety); testing, 1060
Branch, G. R., 391
Brandeis, Louis D., 402, 546
branding, 681, 690, 850–851
Brandon, Homer, 766
Brave and Bold (magazine), *597*
breast (bridge abutment), 267
Bressler, Richard M., 186, 665
Brett, Harold, 148
Breyfogle, William L., 223
bridge and building (B&B), 759; blacksmith-welders, 68, 766; carpenters, 767; foremen, 770; iron workers and welders, 770; steel erectors, 774
bridge decks, 266–267
bridge rail, 41
bridge tenders, 766
bridge trains, 630
"The Bridge Was Burned at Chatsworth" (song), 723
bridges (railroad), 8, 48, 55–56, 90–91, 490, 555–556, 711; accidents, 90–91 (*see also entries at* accidents); cantilever truss, 711; construction and design, 515, 555, 625, 628; forms and types of, 261–269; history, 253–261; Howe truss, 528; occupations of, *see* bridge and building; STRACNET

report, 300; Theodore Cooper, 256, 268, 337; timber in, 625. *See also* civil engineering; *specific bridges by name*
Bridget (ferry), 669
Brinegar, Claude, 73
Brinell hardness (Bhn), 645
British Columbia Electric Railway (BCE), **178–179**, 560, *1194*
British Columbia Railway. *See* BC Rail
British railways, 3–4
British standard gauge, 1000
broad gauge railroads, 531, 638, 640, 727; Lehigh & Hudson River Railway, 584; Missouri Pacific (MoPac), 707
Broad Street Station (Philadelphia), 136, *137*
Broad Street Station (Richmond), 939
The Broad Way of Commerce, 148
broadcast stations, 771
Broadway Limited, 58, 65, 242, 851, 1120
Broady, Steve, 723
Brooklyn & Jamaica Railroad, 311
Brooklyn Bridge, 941
Brooklyn Rapid Transit Co., 314
Brooks, James, 222, 334
Brooks, John W., 452, 569
Brooks Locomotive Works, 600
Broomsedge Glasgow, 595
Brosnan, Dennis William, II, 69, **179–180**, 338, 665, 983
Brother Jonathan, 1008
brotherhoods, 576; Brotherhood of Locomotive Engineers (BLE), 576, 580; Brotherhood of Locomotive Engineers & Trainmen (BLET), 1064; Brotherhood of Locomotive Firemen & Enginemen, 435–436, 576; Brotherhood of Railroad Trainmen (BRT), 436, 576; Brotherhood of Sleeping Car Porters (BSCP), 436, 876, 913; Brotherhood of the Footboard, 576
Brown, George R., 783, 1048
Brown, Hermione K., 1114
Brown, J. Purdy, 242
Brown, Ken, 218
Brown, Rollo Walter 4, 596
Brown, Virginia Mae, 76
Brown, W. C., 1126
Brown, William H., 135
Brown Brothers Harriman & Co., 985
Brown demerit system, 783–784
Brown v. Board of Education (1954), 435
Browne, Kenneth, 835
Brunel, Isambard Kingdom, **180–181**, 270–271, 1000
Brunswick & Birmingham Railroad, *823*
Brunswick & Western Railroad, 155
Bryan, William Jennings, 13, 523, 572, 876
Bryant, Gridley, **181**, 502
Brynner, Witter, 596
Buchanan, James, 256, 794
Buchanan, William, 397, 572
Buchholz, C. W., 136
Buchi, Alfred, 120
Buckhout, Isaac C., 135
Budd, Edward Gowen, 181
Budd, John M., 185, 230, 505
Budd, Ralph, 16, 221, 425, 505, 509, 602

Budd Co. (Edward G. Budd Manufacturing Co.), **181–184**, 201, 425, 831, 837–838; *Crusader*, 312, 832, 919; economy sleeping cars, *838*; production for Canadian railways, 199; RDC, *see* Rail Diesel Car
Budd Wheel Corp., 182
Buell, Don Carlos, 124, 277
Buffalo, Rochester & Pittsburgh Railroad, 165, 345
Buffalo & Susquehanna Railroad, 165
Buffalo Bayou, Brazos & Colorado Railroad, 980
buffet, smoking and library coach car, *851*
building architecture. *See* architecture
building occupations, 759
bulk traffic, 786
bulk-commodity terminals, 474–478
Bullet cars, *561*
Bullfrog Goldfield Railroad, 1050
bump-along system, 283
bumps (job changes), 768
bums, 526. *See also* hoboes
bunk cars, 1116
Bunker Hill Monument, 502
Burchfield, Charles, 33
Burdakin, John H., 499
Bureau for the Safe Transportation of Explosives and Other Dangerous Articles, 93
Bureau of Public Roads, 359
bureaucratic management style, 664–665
burial societies, 576
Burke, James, 73
Burkhardt, Edward A., 1109, 1110
Burlington, Cedar Rapids & Northern Railroad, 228; Angus Sinclair, 973
Burlington & Missouri River Railroad, 32
Burlington Northern & Santa Fe Railway. *See* BNSF Railway
Burlington Northern Railroad (BN), **184–187**, 440–441, 505, 523, 1067; C&S Railway, control of, 306 (*see also* Colorado & Southern Railway); coal mining, 295; communities of interest, 307; Frisco merger, 153, 186, 952 (*see also* Burlington Northern & Santa Fe Railway); immigrants as colonists, encouraging, 304; Latah Creek canyon crossing, 261; Louis Wilson Menk, 693–694; merger, 694; Northern Pacific Railroad merged by, 757; oceangoing railcar ferry services, 671; unit coal train, *1070*; *Zephyr, see* Zephyr. *See also* Burlington Northern & Santa Fe Railway
Burlington Route. *See* Chicago, Burlington & Quincy Railroad
Burlington–Rock Island Railroad (B-RI), 306–307
Burnettizing, 642
Burnham, D. H., & Co., 129
Burnham, Daniel, 1087
Burnham, George, Jr., 187
Burnham, George, Sr., 160, **187**
Burr, William H., 256
Burro crane threading new rail, *652*
bus service, 518–521, 542–543, 790

Busch, Adolphus, 361
Bush, Lincoln, 136, 352
Butler, William L., 238
Butte, Anaconda & Pacific Railroad (BA&P), 415, 421
Byers, M. L., 283
bypass blocking, 285

C30-7A engines, *74*
C40–8 diesel engines, 378
cab signals, 93, 966–968
cable-based ECP braking, 64, 1099–1100
cables, hoisting, 534–535
cable-stayed bridges, 263
caboose cars, 19, 46, 204, 453–454, 462, 469, 470; cleaners (occupation), 766
cage wagons, 243
caisson disease, 256
Cajon Pass, *251*
calendar, railroad, 681
calendars (art), 148–149
Calgary & Edmonton Railway, 196
Calhoun, John C., 2, 793
California Department of Transportation (Caltrans), 861
California Development Co., 389–390
California Limited, 993
California Northern Railroad, 758
California Pacific Railroad, 979
California resorts, 902
California Zephyr, 65, 221, 356, 761, 856, 979, 1094. *See also* Exposition Flyer
call letters (broadcast stations), 771
Caltrain. *See* Peninsula Corridor Joint Powers Board (Caltrain)
Calvert Station (Baltimore), 133
Cambria Incline, Johnstown, Pennsylvania, 538
Cambria Iron Co., 202
Cambria Steel Co., 202
Camden & Amboy Rail Road, 43, *88*, **188–189**, 213, 1034; Bordentown Monument, 714; Isaac Dripps, 397; J. Edgar Thomson, 1049; route map, *1158. See also* John Bull
Camden Station (Baltimore), 133
Camden Warehouse (B&O, Baltimore), 129
Camel locomotives, 163, 1108–1109
camelback engines (Wootten boilers), 353, *619, 1010,* 1010, 1115
Cameron, Simon, 954
Camilo Cienfuegos Devision, 349
Camino de Hierro (Iron Road), 167, 346
Caminos de Hierro de la Habana, 347
campaign trains, 876–878
Campbell, Henry B., 515, 1008
Campbell Bros. Circus, 245
"Campbell's Wedding Race," 170
campo trains, 1116
Canada Air Line, 189
Canada Atlantic Railway, 189
Canada Car Co., 202
The Canadian, 192, 199
Canadian Car & Foundry Co., 174, 202
Canadian Government Railways, 198
Canadian Locomotive Co. (CanLoCo), 198, 601

Canadian National Canadian Pacific Act of 1933, 198
Canadian national parks, 735
Canadian National Railways (CN), 15, 167, **189–191**, 198–201, 440, 735, *1189;* AMT, agreement with, 694–695; Canadian Pacific, competition with, 198; Central Vermont Railway, 214; commuter services, 319; diesel-electric motive power, 1103–1104; GTW, becoming part of, 499; IC, acquisition of (1988), 499, 533; Montmorency Falls station, *1117;* national leaders, trains for, 989; Northern Alberta Railways acquisition, 754; oceangoing railcar ferry services, 670; railcar ferry services, 668; scheduled operating plans, 285; Union Station (Toronto), 142, 1037; Wisconsin Central, acquisition of, 499, 1110
Canadian Northern Railway, 189–190; electrification, 56, 417, 421
Canadian Pacific Ocean Services Ltd., 679
Canadian Pacific Railway (CPR), *12,* 15, 142, 167, 189, **191–193**, 195, 197, 199–201, 754; Albert B. Rogers, 942; AMT, service agreement with, 694–695; artist invitations to Rockies, 146; Banff Springs Hotel, 735; Canadian National, competition with, 198; commuter services, 319; completion of, 1077–1078; *Continental Limited,* 853; D&H, purchase of, 354; dome cars (passenger cars), *834;* geography, impact on, 489, 491; *Imperial Limited,* 851; Kicking Horse Pass, 195, 249–250, *250,* 272; Lethbridge Viaduct, *258;* Macdonald Tunnel, 273; merge into Canadian National Railways, 190; Montreal station, *142;* Mount Macdonald Tunnel, 192, 200, 272; MOW tie gang, *656;* railcar ferry services, 667, 668, 670, 672; Rogers Pass, 196, *250,* 942; route map, *1190;* Selkirk Mountains pass, 248, 942; sleeping car, *303;* St. Lawrence River bridge (Montreal), 258, 260; Soo Line, *see* Soo Line Railroad; statues and monuments, 714, 717; Thomas G. Shaughnessy, 960; Toronto, Hamilton & Buffalo Railway, 1051; transoceanic steamship services, 678–680, *679;* Van Horne, *see* Van Horne, William Cornelius
Canadian Pacific Steamships Ltd., 679, 1078
Canadian Rail, 907
Canadian railcar ferry services, 670–671, 672, *672*
Canadian railroad charters, 541
Canadian Railroad Historical Association, 907
Canadian railways, 15, 1148; commuter services, 694–695; freedom train, 988; interurban development, 560; locomotive builders, 601; national railway system, 197–198; package delivery, 634; RAC (Railway Association of Canada), 907; Railroad YMCA (Toronto), 1118;

statistics on, 1139–1143; train architecture, 142–143; U.S. railways vs., 1139
Canadian Railways, **193–201**
Canadian Shield, 489
canals, 2–3, 37, 863–864, 1090; Asa Packer, 813; improvements to, 555–558. *See also specific canals by name*; water transportation
Candy, John, 242
Cannon Ball, 314
cantilever-truss bridges, 257–258, 264–265, 711
Canton Co., 336
Canton Viaduct, 253, 260
Canyon Diablo crossing, *49*
capacity analysis, 787, 1149
capital assets and asset accounts, 97, 439, 894
Capitol Limited, 165, 853
Captain Edward Richardson (railcar barge), 672
car builders, **201–206**
car classification. *See* classification yards
car ferries. *See* marine operations
car floats, 478, 666–667, *668*, 672, *673*. *See also* marine operations
car foremen, 770
car knockers, *767*
car naming system, Pullman's, 883
car scheduling, **206–207**
Caracas Railroad, 349
carbon-black cars, 205, 468
car-control device (CCD), 1100
card punch. *See* keypunch machines
Cárdenas, Lázaro, 698
Cardinals Train, 990–991
careers. *See* employees; occupations
Carey, Matthew, 557
Carlisle & Finch, 909
carload trolley freight service, 580
Carlyle, Thomas, 593
carmen, 766–767
Carnegie (Pullman car), 882
Carnegie, Andrew, **207–208**, 383, 881, 954
Carnegie Steel, 208, 429
Carnes, Ira, 588
Carnes, John, 587–588
Carolina, Clinchfield & Ohio Railway, 156, 292
Carolina & Northwestern, 752
Carolina Central Railroad, 955
carpenters, 544, 767
Carranza, Venustiano, 698
carriage cars, 463
Carroll, Charles, 163
"The Carrollton March" (song), 722
Carrollton Viaduct, 163, 253
cars (road). *See* motor vehicles
cars (track). *See* specific types of cars by name
Carter, Lincoln J., 1045
Cartier Railway, **208**, *1191*
Cartlidge, Charles H., 711
Cartopper, Herzog Contracting Corp., 654, 656
Cascade, 980

Cascade Tunnel, 55, 272, 273, 404, 410, 490–491, 1035; electrification, 414–415, 421
Case, J. I., 553
Case Sleeping Car Co., 824
Casement, Dan, 804–805
Casement, Jack, 804–805
Casement, John S., **208–210**, *209*, 337
Casement's rolling train, *805*
"Casey Jones" (song), 35, 568–569, 723
Casey Jones (stage play), 1046
Cass brothers, 1091
Cassandre, A. M., 148
Cassatt, Alexander Johnston, 156, *210*, **210–211**, 629, 1096; statue at Pennsylvania Station (New York), 714
Cassidy, Butch (Robert Leroy Parker), 341
cast iron wheels, 821
cast steel freight cars, 458
cast-iron rails, fish-bellied, 643
Castleton & West Stockbridge Railroad, 1095
cast-steel truck frames and wheels, 821
casually identifiable costs, 895–896
casualties, 87, 944. *See also entries at* accidents
catalogs, mail order, 637
catenary construction, 405
catenary electricians, 769
Cathcard, Andrew, 296
The Cathedral Car of North Dakota: Church of the Advent, 215, 216
Catholic chapel cars, 216
cattle cars, 462, 469, *469–470. See also* livestock
Cedar Rapids & Iowa City Railway (CR&IC), **211**, *1179*
celebration trains, 985
"The Celestial Railroad" (Hawthorne), 722
cement bridges, 258–259, 261, 262
cement cars, 468
Center City Commuter Tunnel, 321, 977
Center Flow covered hopper cars, 468
Center for Railroad Photography and Art, 876
center sills, 459–460
center-heading tunneling, 270
center-pivoted swing bridges, 259, 266
Centipede diesels, 161–162, *162, 372*
The Central. *See* New York Central System
Central Electric Railfans' Association, 907–908
Central of Georgia Railway (CofG), **211–212**, 438, 982; bought by Southern Railway, 951; Edward Henry Harriman, 532; *Nancy Hawks*, 993; route map, *1170*
Central Ohio Railroad, 164
Central Pacific Railroad, 7, *9*, 10, 570, 575; building of, 343; Collis Potter Huntington, 529; commuter services, 319; construction of Southern Pacific, 979–980 (*see also* Southern Pacific Railroad); Donner Pass, 55, 248; geography, impact on, 490; hospitals, 691; Johns Hopkins, 527; joining UP at Promontory, Utah, *806; Jupiter* (loco-

motive), 806–807; leadership and organization, 796–797; Leland Stanford, *see* Stanford, Leland; monument to Theodore Dehone Judah, 715; Pacific Railroad Act of 1862, 7, 511, 540, 591–592, 795–796, 979; passenger ferry services, 674, 676; Pullman cars, 881; railcar ferry services, 669; transpacific steamship services, 679; William Hood, 526–527. *See also* Pacific Railroad
Central Rail Road & Canal Co., 211
Central Railroad Co. of New Jersey (CNJ), **212–214**, 918; barney pusher system, 537; commuter services, 312; passenger ferry services, *676*, 676–677; route map, *1159*; train speed, 992–993
central storehouse, 888
Central Transportation Co. (CTC), 880, 881, 1115
Central Vermont Railway (CV), 189, **214–215**; locomotive fueling, *605*; route map, *1189*
centralized purchasing, 888
centralized traffic control (CTC), 16, 59–62, *60*, 95, 113–114, 567, 781, 968, 1057–1058, *1058*, 1060, 1121; computerization, 329; CSX, 345; introduction of, 393–394. *See also* dispatchers
centralized traffic departments, 663
Century Limited, 993
CEO, railroad company, 664–665
certificates of value, 933
certification of employees, 785
Chaffey, George, 389
chain of command, 663
Chair Car, 147
chair car attendants, 764–765
chair lifts, 512
chair-style joints, 52
Chambly Canal, 193–194
Champerico & Northern Railroad, 507
Champion, 156, 955
Champlain & St. Lawrence Railroad, 194
Chandler, Alfred D., 426
change, management slow to accept, 664–665
channeling and wedging, 269
Chaparra Railroad, 349
Chapel Car Emmanuel, 215, 217
chapel cars, **215–217**
Chaplin, Charlie, 242
Chapman, Allen, 34, 598
Chapter 77, Bankruptcy Act of 1898, 929–930, 938
Chapters of Erie, 99
charging air brakes, 1059
Charles River Bridge, 259, 555
Charleston & Hamburg Railroad, 435, 1088
Charleston & Savannah Railroad, 155
Charleston & Western Carolina Railroad (C&WC), 155, 212
Charlotte & South Carolina Railroad, 278
Charlton, George J., 681
"The Charming Young Widow I Met in the Train" (song), 723
charter grants, 539–541, 920

Cincinnati Southern Railroad: Babahatchie YMCA, 1127–1128; Kentucky River bridge, 258, 260
Cincinnatian, 355, *1016*
cinema and railroads, **239–242**, 1047
circuses and railroads, **242–247**, *244, 246,* 551. *See also* entertainment tours
The City from Greenwich Village, 147
city inclines, 538–539
City of Midland (railcar ferry), 667, *668*
City of New York (steamship), 678
City of Paris (steamship), 678
City of Portland, 831
City streamliners, 226; *City of Denver,* 59; *City of Los Angeles,* 994; *City of Miami,* 156; *City of Milwaukee 400,* 995; *City of Portland,* 994; *City of Salinas,* 994, 1067; *City of St. Louis,* 1086; *City of San Francisco,* 21, 94, 980, 994
Civil Aeronautics Act of 1938, 108
Civil Aeronautics Board (CAB), 109
civil engineering, **247–274**, 898–899; bridges, *see entries at* bridges; employees of, 759; gauge, *see* track gauge; standard gauge; grade, curvature, cut and fill, 250–253; internal improvements, 554–559, 628; location and construction, 247–250; tunneling, *see entries at* tunnels
civil rights, 1110, 1113
Civil Rights Act of 1964, 436, 1110, 1114
Civil War, 7, 22, 1053; Andrews's Raid, *124–125,* 124–125; L&N, destruction of, 631; lack of standard gauge, 1000; railroad development and, 489; Richmond, Fredericksburg & Potomac Railroad, 939
Civil War railroads, **274–278**
civilian traffic. *See* passenger service, effects of world wars
claim agents, 767
Clair, J. C., 101
Clark, Eli P., 790
Clark, J. Ross, 583, 1050
Clark, Lewis Gaylord, 792
Clark, W. A., 583
Clark, William, 791
Clark Car Co., 203
Clarke, Thomas C., 256
Clark's Summit–Hallstead Cutoff, 352
clasp retarders, 281
Class 1 railroads, 644, 648, 651, 654
Class 3 repairs, 618–620
class rate system, 915
classification, **278–279**
classification signals, 780
classification systems, 461–463; electric locomotives, 405–406; locomotive identification codes, 1005–1006; railroads, 278–279; truck configurations, 362
classification yards, 60, 114, **279–291**; blocking theory, 283–285; humping, 287–291; location of, 279–280; modern and future practice, 285–287; types of, 280–283
Clay Belt, 778
Claytor, W. Graham, Jr., 79, 338, 665, 983
Clayton Antitrust Act of 1914, 426

Clean Air Act of 1970, 186, 294–295
cleaning locomotives, *623,* 661, *771. See also* maintenance
clear signal, 1057
Clearing Yard, 171, 280
Clegg, Charles M., 170, 596, 715
Clement, Martin W., 182, 623
clerestory roofs, 821
Clergue, Francis H., 298
clergy passes, **291**
clerical roles for women, 1111–1113
clerks, 767–769, *768*
Cleveland, Cincinnati, Chicago & St. Louis Railway (Big Four), 230, 527, 529–530, 570, 746–747, 979; Melville E. Ingalls, 218; Ohio River bridge (Louisville), 256–257, 260; Vanderbilt acquisition of, 1081
Cleveland, Columbus, Cincinnati & Indianapolis Railroad, 208, 439
Cleveland, Grover, 351, 503–504, 576
Cleveland, Lorain & Wheeling Railroad, 164
Cleveland Union Terminal, 129–130, 421; electrification, 420
client-server networks, 330
Clifton Suspension Bridge, 180
Climax gear-drive locomotives, 627, *730,* 1031
Clinchfield Railroad, 156, **292**
C-liners. *See* Consolidation engines
Clinton, DeWitt, 556
Clinton, William Jefferson, 513
club cars, 309, 1123
clubs, railroading, 874–876
Clyde Beatty Circus, 246–247
coach attendants, 764–765
coach class (airlines), 109
coach cleaners, 769
coach passengers, 46, *46, 850*
coach streamliners, 632
Coal & Iron Railway, 1092
coal and railroads, 38, **292–295**, *293–294,* 607–608, 632, 1053, 1054, *1070;* coal delivery and storage, 607; coaling station architecture, 128; piers, 471, 474–475; railroad costs, 898; transporting equipment, 465, 474
coal hoppers, *465*
coaling plants, 607
coaling stations, 615
coaling towers, *605*
Coast Daylight, 990
Coast Starlight, 80
coastal shipping. *See* water transportation
Coatsworth, John, 698
code 30 (telegraph), 771
code 31 (telegraph), 771
code control systems, 1069
Code of Federal Regulations (CFR), 98
Code of Standard Train Rules, 781
coded track circuits, 59, 1068–1069
codes for locomotive identification, 1005–1006
codes for truck configurations, 362
Cody, Buffalo Bill, 805
Coe, Simeon, 27
cofferdams, 256, 268

Coffin, J. S., **295–296**
Coffin, Lorenzo, 566, 945
cog, rack, or mountain railways, **296–299**
Cohan, George M., 1046, 1047
coke transporting equipment, 465
Cold War railroads, **299–300**
Cole, Edwin, 733
Cole, Francis J., 117
Cole, Thomas, 145
Coleman, William T., 73, 74
Coleman Cutoff, 151
collective bargaining, 576–580
collective ratemaking, 916
collectors of railroad paraphernalia, 35, 908
college football, 986, 998
Collingwood shops, 545
Collins, Gary, 73
collisions. *See entries at* accident
Colo, Iowa, 32
Colonie Shops, D&H, 631
colonization of the West, **300–305**
Colorado & Southern Railway (C&S), 202, 220–221, **305–307**
Colorado Central Railroad, 305–306, 728
Colorado Midland Railroad, 151
Colorado Springs & Cripple Creek District Railway (CS&CCD), 306
Colorado's narrow gauge railways, *732*
color-light signals, 965, *966,* 972
Colter, Mary Elizabeth Jane, 130–132, 514, 1110
Colton, Simon, 187
Columbia Railroad, 111
Columbia University locomotive test plant, 611
Columbian, 165, 355
Columbus, Chicago & Indiana Central Railroad, 439
Combination Crossing Gate and Signal Protective Means, 496
combination layout, back-shop, 618
combination link (steam locomotive), 1012
combination stations, 24
Comet (bidirectional streamliner), 830, 832
commercial air transportation, 17, 65, 107–109, 521; Bombardier aircraft manufacture, 174; decline in passenger traffic, 1134; Department of Transportation challenges, 358; deregulation of, 358, 924; professional sports, 997
commercial bus service, 518–519
commercial traffic statistics. *See* traffic categories and quantities
Commission Division Act of 1917, 923
Committee on National Defense, 1072
commodity rates, 898, 915
commodity shipping, 7, 1053–1054; hazardous materials, 1060; oil (petroleum), *see* oil transport; statistics on, 1133, 1135–1136, 1141–1142; during World War II, 1122. *See also specific commodities by name*
Commodore Vanderbilt, 988
common law, 920–921

Corbett, Scott, 553
Corbin, Austin, 629
Corliss steam engine, 885
Corn Belt, 100
Cornell, Katharine, 1047
Cornell, Paul, 315
Cornell, Thomas, 353
corner casting, 554
corporate advertising, 682
corporate charters. *See* charter grants
corporate communications, 878–879
corporate identification and image, 680, 690, 924; Amtrak, 738; NYNH&H, 738
corporate offices, 129
corruption and graft, 558, 602; fares and ticketing, 851–852; Pacific Railroad, 797–799, 806–807. *See also* scandals
Corwith Yard, *289*
Costa Rican railroads, **337–338**
costs, railroad, 894–898. *See also* expense statistics; profitability statistics
Côte d'Azur Pullman, 148
cottages, employee (B&O), 1118
Cotton Belt. *See* St. Louis Southwestern Railroad
cotton shipping, 1053
Couch, Harvey, 573
Council of National Defense, 1072
counterweights (steam locomotives), 1005
country fairs, to attract colonists, 304
Country Life Commission, 101
Coup, W. C., 243
couplers, 458–459, 566
couplings, 458
Coutan, Jules, 139
covered hopper cars, 62, *464*
Covington & Ohio Railway, 217
cowcatcher frames (pilots), 41, *44*, 397, 1008; riding, 21
Cowen, Joshua Lionel, 909
Cox, Barbara B., *326*
CP Rail, 193, 200–201
cradle system, river landing inclines, 674
Craft, C. William, Jr., 71
craft seniority, 957–959
Crane, Hart, 596
Crane, L. Stanley, 180, 332, **338–339**, 612
Crane, Stephen, 595
cranes, 621, 625; crane-equipped barges, 672; ferry loading and unloading, 617; gantry, *see* gantry cranes
Cranford (passenger ferry), *676*
crankpin (steam locomotives), 1005
crankshaft revolutions, 363
Crawford, William, 482
Crawfordsville & Wabash Railroad, 222
Crayon, Porte (David Hunter Strother), 146
Creamer, William G., 843
Crédit Mobilier, 10, 123, 334, 400, 797, 806–807
Creel, Enrique, 571
creosote-treated timber ties, 642
Crerar, John, 881
Crescent Limited, 632, 982
Crest of the Continent (book), 565
Cret, Paul Philippe, 132, 182, 831
crew callers, 767
crew dispatching clerks, 767

crew facilities. *See also* railroad shops
crew housing, 1116–1118. *See also* living space; YMCA, Railroad Department
crews. *See* employees
cribs, 641
crime, **339–343**; antitrust, *see* Sherman Antitrust Act; railroad policemen, 145, 338–340; train robberies, 340–342
Cripe, Alan, 835–836, 840
Cripple Creek, 306
Crocker, Charles, **343**, *343*, 527, 529, 570, 795, 797, 799, 802, 1004
Crocker, Edwin Bryant, 527, 795, 797, 806
Cropsey, Jasper Francis, 145
cross compound engines, 1013
cross-buck "Railroad Crossing" sign, 497–498
Crosser, Robert, 906
crosshead (steam locomotives), 1005
crosshead link (steam locomotive), 1012
crossing diamonds, 646
crossing gates, 495–498
crossing safety. *See* grade crossings
crossties, 641–643; automated tie renewal, 654, 656; concrete, 84; wooden, 40–41
Crostwait, William L., 388
Crothers, Rachel, 1046
Croton Aqueduct, 112
Crowley, Patrick E., 1022
crown (arches), 261
Crown, Henry, 228–229
crown sheet (steam locomotives), 1010
Crow's Nest Pass Agreement of 1897, 200
Crowsnest Line (Canadian Pacific), 197
Crozet, Claudius, 217
Cruger, Alfred, 346–347
cruise trains, 856–857, 908
crummy. *See* caboose cars
Crusader, 312, 832, 919
CSX, 85, 166, 218–219, **343–346**, 633, 956–957; Conrail purchase, 85–86, 332, 333, 339, 345; Indiana Rail Road ownership, 542; railcar ferry services, 668; route map, *1169*; rulebook for, 782; unit trains of orange juice, 1071. *See also* Baltimore & Ohio Railroad; Seaboard System
CSX-Sea-Land Intermodal (CSLI), 345
Cuba Northern Railways, 348
Cuba Railroad Co., 347–349, 396, 1078
Cuban Central Railways, 347
Cuban railroads, **346–350**; route map, *1196*; William Cornelius Van Horne, 347–348, 1078
Cullom Committee, 921
Culter, C. W., 291
cultural geography, 489–492
Cumberland Road. *See* National Road
Cumberland Valley Railroad, 864
Cumbres & Toltec Scenic Railroad, 908
Cummins, Albert E., 928–929
Cummins Engine Co., 603
current, alternating. *See* AC electrification
current, direct. *See* DC electrification
current collection, 405
current tax accounting, 98
Currier, Nathaniel, 33

Curtis, Jonathan, 791
Curtiss JN-4 "Jennies" aircraft, 108
curvature (route), 250–252; compensated grade, 251–252; rail maintenance, 651
The Curve, 147
cushioned underframes, 459–460
cut and fill (track alignment), 252, 657
cut spikes, 646
cutaway beds (in roomettes), 832–833
cutoff (Johnson bar), 1013
cutoff time (car scheduling), 206
cutoffs, specific: Belen Cutoff, 151; Clark's Summit–Hallstead Cutoff, 352; Coleman Cutoff, 151; Dotsero Cutoff, 356; Lackawanna Cutoff, 55; Lucin Cutoff bridge, 55, 260; Magnolia Cutoff, 164; Natron Cutoff, 980; New Jersey Cutoff, 352; Palmdale-Colton Cutoff, 62; Perry Cutoff, 155; Summit Cutoff, 55
cutting trains, 1062
cutwater piers, 267
Cyclone. *See* Mt. Desert Limited

D car (New York Central), 397
Daft, Leo, 408
daily railroad operation. *See* operating practices
dairy train, 987
Dakota, Minnesota & Eastern Railroad, 295
Dakota & Great Southern Railroad, 515
Dale Creek Bridge, 490
Dallas Area Rapid Transit (DART), 324
Dallas Southern Railroad, 1044
Dalton brothers, 341
Daly, Augustin, 1045
damage control officers, 878
damage-free boxcars, 62
Dan Castello Circus, 243
Dan Rice, Howes & Robinson, 243
Daniels, George Henry, 681, 993
data input terminals, 327–328
data on North American railroads. *See* statistics on North American railroads
data tags (for tracking trains), 1059
The Daughter of a Magnate, 239
Davenport, Charles, 842
Davenport, Thomas, 407–408
Davenport (Iowa) Locomotive Works, 603
Davey, Marsden, 1106
Davidson, Robert, 408
Davies, James, 72
Davin, John W., 742
Davis, Champion McDowell, 155
Davis, Jefferson, 227, 689, 793
Davis, John, 688
Davis, W. A., 637
Davis Grasshoppers (locomotive), 537
Dawn in Pennsylvania, 147
Day Express, 384, *384–385*
Daylight, 58, 66, 853, 980
daylight-aspect signals, 965
Dayliners, 199
Dayton & Western Railroad, 239
DC electrification, 404, 407, 411, 865, 1101, 1102; AC power vs., 484–485, 559, 561–562; conversion from AC, *see* rectifiers. *See also* electrification

DC series motors, 364, 407
DD1 electric locomotives, 410
DD35 booster units, 377
DD40X booster units, 378
de Herrera, José Joaquín, 695
De La Vergne Engine Co., *371*
de Tomaso, Leonardo, 1094
De Witt Clinton, 614, 1007
dead blocks, 459
Dearborn Street Station (Chicago), 140
death by railroad. *See* casualties; *entries at* accident
Death Valley Railroad, 1050
Death Valley Scotty, 207, 208, 210, *953, 953–954,* 1042
DeBoer, David, 75
Debs, Eugene V., 9, **351,** 504, 577–579
DeButts, Harry A., 77, 179–180, *327*
decision support software, 329
deck trusses, 255, 263
decking, 21
decline in passenger traffic, 51, 53, 58, 737–738, 1134, 1151. *See also* statistics on North American railroads; traffic categories and trends
decor, passenger cars, 821, *822,* 827
dedicated trainsets. *See* unit trains
deep head-hardened rails, 645
Deepwater Railway, 1084
defect inspection, 648–651, 891–894
deferment classification, 283–284
deferred tax accounting, 97–98
DeHavilland DH-4 aircraft, 108
del Val, Merry, 991
Delano, Jack, 473
Delaware, Lackawanna & Western Railroad (DL&W), 213, **351–353,** 438, 674–675; commuter services, 312, *313,* 320; electrification, 56, 352–353, 417, 420; Erie Railroad merger, 331, 352–353, 432, 434, 440; Hoboken Terminal (New Jersey), 136, 352, 740; line relocations, 55; route map, *1164;* Tunkhannock Viaduct, *55,* 55–56, 259, 260, 352
Delaware, Lehigh, Schuylkill & Susquehanna Railroad, 813
Delaware & Cobb's Gap Railway, 351–352
Delaware & Hudson Canal Co., 112, 177, 353, 568; route map, *1190; Stourbridge Lion,* 112, 353, 568, 899, 1007
Delaware & Hudson Railroad (D&H), 200, 331–332, **353–354;** Colonie Shops, 631; Horatio Allen, *112,* 112–113, 976, 1006–1007; inclined-plane railways, 538; Leonor F. Loree, 630–631; strike of 1922, 631; Wabash, alliance with, 1085
Delaware River Viaduct, 352
delays, 847, 851–852, 1055. *See also* train control
Dellinger, E. S., 34, 598
Delmonico, 827, 881
demerits for compliance failure, 783–784
DeMille, Cecil B., 241, 1047
Democratic Republicans, 482
demographics, freight traffic and, 1053

demonstration train (educating farmers), 102
demurrage charges, 1119
Den Stone's Original Railroad Circus, 243
Denali (Mount McKinley) National Park, 737
Denison, George, 709
Denison & Sherman Railway (D&S), 1043–1044
Dennis, Olive W., **354–355**
Denver, Leadville & Gunnison Railroad, 306
Denver, South Park & Pacific Railroad (DSP&P), 305
Denver, Texas & Forth Worth Railroad, 305–306
Denver, Texas & Gulf Railroad, 305–306
Denver & Interurban Railroad (D&I), 306
Denver & New Orleans Railroad, 305, 306
Denver & Rio Grande Western Railroad (D&RGW), 166, 305, **355–356,** *732,* 814–815, 868–869, 1067, 1092, 1093; Burnham diesel shop, 621; *California Zephyr,* 65, 221, 356, 761, 856, 979, 1094 (*see also Exposition Flyer*); Denver & Salt Lake merger, 440; Krauss-Maffei A.G. locomotives, 603; narrow gauge, 728, *729;* rotary snowplow at work, *649;* route map, *1182;* Tennessee Pass, 249, 355
Denver & Salt Lake Railroad, 355–356, 440
Denver Pacific Railroad, 1066
Denver Zephyr, 182, 221
Department of Transportation (DOT), **356–359,** 738, 1036
departmental structures, 662–665
departments, railroad, 759. *See also* occupations
departure responsibilities, 1059–1060
departure yards, 282, 283
Depew, Chauncey M., *359,* **359–360**
depot parks, 29–30
depots. *See* stations and terminals
depreciation accounting, 97–98, 894–895
depressed-center flatcars, 466
derailments. *See entries at* accident
Deramus, William N., III, 235, 710
Dereco, 751
deregulation of airline industry, 359
deregulation of railroad industry, 71, 82–83, 152, 444–445, 521–522, 548, 567, 924. *See also* government regulations; *entries at* privatization; Staggers Act
Derious, Edward, 243
derrick lighters (barges), 672
Des Moines & Central Iowa Railroad, 233
Des Moines Northern & Western Railroad, 225
Desert Storm, 147
designs, passenger car, 823, 826
Despatch Shops, Inc., 203
detecting equipment faults. *See* equipment identification and fault detection
detector cars, 650
Detroit, Grand Rapids & Western Railroad, 866

Detroit, Toledo & Ironton Railroad (DT&I), 126, 191, **360–361,** 411; route map, *1171*
Detroit River Tunnel (Ontario), 272–273, 421, 668
Detroit Southern Railroad, 360
development, impact of geography, 489–492
Development of the Locomotive Engine, 974
Dewey, Thomas E., 877
Dewhurst, D. H., 339
Dexter, Samuel, 791–792
Dey, Peter, 400, 797, 803
diagonals (trusses), 263
Diaz, Porfirio, 695, 698
Dickens, Charles, 593
Dickinson, Emily, 596
Dickson Manufacturing Co., 600
Die Baltimore-Ohio Eisenbahn über das Allegheny-Gebirg, 493
die blocks, 1011
Die innern Communicationen der Vereinigten Staaten von Nordamerica, 492–493
Diesel, Rudolf, 16, **361,** 368, 601
diesel cycle engine, 363
diesel fueling, 608
diesel locomotives, 362–364, 442, 486, 509, 548, 575, 601, 867; 30–7A engines, 378; 241 engines, 120–121; 244 engine, 120–121; 251 engines, 121; *400* streamliners, 32, 58, 232, 994; 567-series engines, 363, 426; 645-series engines, 363–364; 710-series engines, 363–364, 428; A Class 2-6-6-4 engines, 1024; A-1 class 2-8-4 engines, 56, *1019,* 1019–1020, *1020;* A-2 class 4-8-4 engines, 1021; Alco manufacture of, 120–121; Baldwin Locomotive Works, 161, 426 (*see also* Centipede diesels); building, 602; coolant, 608; Dash-2 engines, 428; Dash-7 engines, 488; Dash-8 engines, 378, 381, 428, 488; deregulation effects, 83; Electro-Motive Corporation (EMC), 488, 603; engine shutdowns, 608; fueling, *607,* 608; George D. Whitcomb Co., 603; IT freight service, 534; maintenance and repair, *620,* 620–622; opposed-piston (OP), 374–375, 442; slang terms for, 144; steam locomotives vs., 548; testing, 612
diesel multiple-unit (DMU) cars, 324
diesel pollutants, 382–383, 612
diesel shops, 615
diesel-electric locomotives, 21, 57, 61–63, *68,* 186, 198, 346, **361–383,** 486–489, 508, 545, 575, 590, 601; Canadian National Railways, 1103–1104; commuter cars, 324; control systems, 486; derivatives of, 376–377; electrical details, 364; electricians, 769; electrification and, 379–382, 419; Electro-Motive Corporation (EMC), 364–367; environmental influences, 382–383; Erie Railroad, *488;* first-generation, 364–374; as industry savior, 67–68; machinists, 770; remotely operated

units, 378–379; Rudolf Diesel, *see* Diesel, Rudolf; second-generation, 375–376; steam turbines vs., 1028–1030; switch engines, 442. *See also* electric locomotives

diesel-hydraulic locomotives, 377, 590, 836

dieselization, 16, 590, 1043, 1149; Electro-Motive Division (EMD), 366, 368; Erie Railroad, 434; PEC freight service, 791

Dietzel, Oscar and Maggie, 717

Difco, Inc., 206

"Different Trains" (song), 725

Differential Steel Car, 206

differentiation in pricing, 897

Dillingham, Benjamin F., 515

Dilworth, Richard M., 364, 424

dining cars and on-board dining, 19, *47*, 514, 823–824, 827, 827–828, *848, 848–849, 855*, 881; black employees, 436, 913; dining noted in timetables, 776; employees of, 765; World War I effects, 1120; World War II effects, 1122, 1124

dinner trains, 908

Dinsmore's *American Railway Guide*, 775–776

direct current. *See* DC electrification

direct expenses, 895

direct train control (DTC), 782

directional authority, 780

directorates, interlocking. *See* communities of interest

disasters and railroads, **383–392**; Florida Keys Hurricane (1935), 391; Galveston Hurricane (1900), 387; Hinckley Firestorm (1894), 386; Imperial Valley Flood (1904–1907), 388–391; Johnstown Flood (1889), 383–386; Tehachapi Earthquake (1952), 392

disasters, train. *See entries at* accident

disc drives, 327

disc (plate) wheels, 46

discipline, 783–785

disconnects (car type), 625, *626*

Discovery Train, 988

discrimination: racial, 21, 24, 435, 436, 851, 1113 (*see also* ethnicity); rate discrimination, 914, 921, 925–927 (*see also* Elkins Act of 1903; Hepburn Act of 1906); tax assessments, *see* taxation; women, 1110, 1113

dispatchers, 49, **392–395**, *393*, 767, *774*, 774; centralized, *see* centralized traffic control; operations testing, 783; radio, 782; responsibilities, 1061, 1062

distillate fuel, 363

distribution of electric current, 405

ditch diggers, 661

Divide in Pipestone Pass, 249

divisible costs, 895–896

Division of Inland Waterways, 1073

divisional structures, 662

Dix, John Adams, 399

Dixie Flagler, 156, 230

Dixie Flyer, 230, *561*

Dixie Land, 67

Dixie Limited, 230

Dixie Mail, 230

Dixie Route, 230

Dixon, John E., 295

DMU (diesel multiple-unit) cars, 324

Dod, Ezra Mitchell, 347

Dodge, Grenville M., *395*, **395–396**, 400, 591, *593*, 795, 803–804, 806–807, 1042; portraits of, *717*

Dodge, John and Horace, 182

Dodge, William E., 351, 1035

dog spikes, 646

Doggett's *Railroad Guide and Gazetteer*, 775

Dombey and Son (Dickens), 593

dome car (passenger car), 833

The Dominion, 199

Dominion Car & Foundry, 202

Dominion Steel & Coal Co., 202

Donahue, Peter, 757

Donner Pass, 55, 248

doodlebugs, *365*, 838

Dorchester, 194

dormitories. *See* workers' housing

Dos Passos, John, 596

dot-and-dash (Morse code), 770

Dotsero Cutoff, 356

double signaling system, 870

double-deck passenger cars. *See* gallery cars

double-ended ferryboat, 675–676

double-ended side-wheeler railcar ferries, 671

double-room passenger cars, 828

double-shoulder tie plates, 642

double-slip switches, 645

double-stack container cars, *77*, 554

double-truck cars, 453, *484*, 516, 820–821, *821*, 1108

Douglas, Stephen A., 28, 300, 793–794

Douglas DC-3 aircraft, 108

Dover station (Delaware), 133

Dowd, C. F., 1003

Downs, Tom, 79

Dowty yards (Dowty retarders), 281, 286

Doyle Report, 1041

DPUs (distributed power units), 378–379

draft components, 458–460

draft gear, 458–460, 842

draft sills, 459–460

drag engines, 1018

dragging-equipment detectors, 84, 430–431, 1062

drainage concerns, 647, 658

Drake, Edwin L., 871

drawbar power, 1015

drawbridges, 259

drawbridges (draw spans), 266–267

Drayton-Acworth Royal Commission, 198

Dred Scott v. Sandford (1857), 435

Dreiser, Theodore, 352, 594

Dresden (steamer), 361

Drew, Daniel, 11, 99, **396**, 433, 449, 494, 1081

Drexel, Anthony, 586

Dreyfuss, Henry, 132, 830, 832

drilling tunnels. *See* tunnels

Dripps, Isaac, 188, **396–397**

drive systems (electric locomotives), 406–407

drivers (steam locomotives), 1004, 1014, 1028

drop tables, 617, 621

drovers, 769

DTC (direct train control), 782

dual gauge railroads, *732*

dual platforms, 688

dual-power locomotives, 324, 744

Dudley, Charles B., 545

Dudley, Plimmon H., **397–398**, 608–609

Duke, James Buchanan, 870

Duke Power Co., 870–871

Duluth, Missabe & Iron Range Railway (DM&IR), 161, 398, **398–399**; ACI, *see* automatic car identification; automatic equipment identification (AEI), 430; route map, *1178*

Duluth, Missabe & Northern Railway (DM&N), 398, *475*

Duluth, South Shore & Atlantic Railroad (DSS&A), 975, 1034; route map, *1175*

Duluth, Winnipeg & Pacific Railway, 189

Duluth & Iron Range Rail Road (D&IR), 398

Duluth Limited, 386, 387

Dumaine, Frederic C., Jr., 354, 744

Dumaine, Frederic C., Sr., 743–744

Dunkirk Engineering Works, 627

Dunn, Tom, 387

Dunning, Silas W., 1051

duplex engines, *612*, 1006, 1027, 1028

duplex sleeper cars, Pullman Co., 839

DuPont, Alfred I., 451

Durant, Thomas Clark, **399–400**, 797, 803, 806–807, 985, 1004

Duryea, Otho, 842

Duryea cushioned underframes, 459

Dustin, Alan, 177

D-valves (slide valves), 1012

dwell times, 787

dynagraph, *609*

dynamic braking, 68, 1061

dynamic track stabilizers, 658

dynamometer cars, 608–610, *609–610*, 1015. *See also* engines and locomotives, testing; locomotive testing

E. & T. Fairbanks Co., 442

E. D. Kingsley, 174

E. G. Budd Manufacturing Co., 16

E. L. Miller, 1007

Eads, James Buchanan, 256, 337, **401–402**

Eads Bridge (St. Louis Bridge), 256, 257, 260, 402, 1041

Eagles (MoPac passenger trains), 623, 708–709

Eames, Frederick W., 844

Earl, Harley, 835–836

earnings statistics, 1150–1152

earthquake at Tehachapi (1952), 392

easement curves, 252

East Coast Champion, 156

East Conemaugh yard (Pennsylvania), 383–384

East Side Access project, Long Island Rail Road, 630

East Side Railway, 559

East Tennessee, Virginia & Georgia Railroad (ETV&G), 277, 981–982
Eastern Canada routes, *1193*
Eastern Car Co., 202
Eastern Illinois & Mississippi River Railroad, 230
Eastern Minnesota Railroad, 386
Eastern Railroad, 176; Revere wreck (1871), 88, 94
Eastern Railway Association, 397
Eastland, James, 95
Eastman, Joseph B., 16, 149, *402*, **402–403**, 930
Eastman heater cars, 465
eccentrics (steam locomotives), 1011, 1012
economic costs, 895
economic geography, 489–492
Economic Recovery Act of 1981, 36
economic regulation. *See entries at* government regulations
economies of scale, 887, 897
economy class (airlines), 109
economy sleeping cars, *838*
ECP braking, 64, 1099–1100
Eddystone plant (Baldwin Locomotive Works), 159, *159*, 160–161, 372, 1082
Edenborn, William, 573
edge rail, 40
Edgewood Cutoff line on IC, 532
Edinger, F. S., 389
Edison, Bill, 75
Edison, Thomas Alva, 239, 353, **403–404**, 408, 483, 549, 999, 1045, 1083
Edison General Electric Co. *See* General Electric Co.
Edison Illuminating Co., 403
Edison Storage Battery Co., 403
education. *See* training of railroad workers
educational train (farmer training), 102
Edward G. Budd Manufacturing Co. *See* Budd Co.
Edward T. Jeffery (ferry), 1094
EEOC (Equal Employment Opportunity Commission), 1114
efficiency, need for, 16, 438, 785–788; deregulation effects, 83; historic growth in efficiency, 1150; World War I, 1119
Effie Afton (steamboat), 227, 591
Egan, John M., 1078
Eidlitz, Cyrus L. W., 140
1896 London Memorandum, 504
eight-hour day, 579
8-Hour Day Act, 14, 579, 928, 1071
eight-wheeled switchers, 41, 43–45, 453–454, 1005, 1006, 1017, 1095; patent for, 1108
Eisenhower, Dwight David, 479–480, 737, 878; presidential rail travel, 876, 878
Eisenhower, Mamie, 481
El Capitan, 184
El Fuerte span, 699
El Guardajujas (*The Switchman*), 698
El Paso & Southwestern Railroad, 1094
El Tapatio, 700
elastic rail fasteners, 646–647

electric flash butt welding, 644, 651
electric headlights, 946
electric locomotives, 484, 485, 601; Alco manufacture of, 120; Charles J. Van Depoele, 408, 484, 559, 1076–1077; classification system, 405–406; fueling, *607*; Pennsylvania Railroad electrification, 157; testing, 608–612. *See also* diesel-electric locomotives
electric motive power, 484–489, 534
electric multiple-unit cars (M.U.), 485–486, 629–630
electric passenger locomotives, *487*
Electric Railroaders Association, 907
Electric Railway Co., 404
Electric Railway Gazette (periodical), 1053
Electric Railway Journal (periodical), 1053
Electric Railway Signal Co., 1068
electric railways, 452, 484; Indiana Railroad, 542–543; interurban, *see* interurban electric railways; New Haven, 743; trade publications, 1052–1053. *See also* electrification
electric traction, 484
Electric Traction Commission, 999
Electric Traction Weekly (periodical), 1053
electrical appliance shipping, 1054
electrical engineering, 900
electrical shops, 615
electrical signals, 964–965
electric-drive internal combustion locomotive, 486
electricians, *769*, 769
electricity, Westinghouse interest in, 1096–1097. *See also* Westinghouse Electric & Manufacturing Co.
Electric-Pneumatic Corp., 972
electrification, 54, 56, 61, 63, **404–423**, 452, 483, 484, 601, 870–871, 1100–1102; *list of principal electrifications*, 420–421; AC vs. DC power, 484–485, 559, 561–562 (*see also* AC electrification; DC electrification); commuter services, 417, 531; competing technologies, 412–413; Delaware, Lackawanna & Western Railroad, 352–353; diesel-electric motive power, impact on, 485; early development, 407–409; east coast (map), *413*; Edison inventions and ideas, 403–404; Frank J. Sprague, *see* Sprague, Frank J.; GE, *see* General Electric Co.; IC's suburban service, 532; modern practice, 418–423; New York Central terminals, *54*, 409–412, 420, 484, 747, 999, 1106; Norfolk & Western Railroad, 750; northeast (map), *414*; Pacific northwest (map), *416*; Pennsylvania Railroad, 16, 56, 410, 417–421, 865, 1102; pioneer electrifications, 409; technology of, 404–407; train speeds, 995; tunnels and mountains, 413–417; Westinghouse, *see* Westinghouse Electric & Manufacturing Co.
electrification plants, 404–405
Electroliner streamliners, *562*, 908
Electro-Motive Division, General Motors Corp., 16, 57, 67–68, 120–121, 161,

221, **423–429**, 487–488, 601–603, 744, 1043; 567-series engines, 363, 426; 645-series engines, 363–364; commuter cars, 323–324; competition with GE, 603; diesel-electric locomotives, 364–367, *365*; diesel locomotives, 488, 603; FT freight locomotives, 362, *366*, 366, 426; self-propelled railcars, 602. *See also* General Motors
electronic train management system (ETMS), 970
electronically controlled pneumatic brakes. *See* ECP braking
electronics technicians, 769–770
electropneumatic interlocking control, 967
elephant transport (circuses), 245–246, *246*
elevated trains, 484; in cinema, 242; "L" trains, 234; steam locomotives, 1030
elevation (route), 247
elevators, grain, 471, 500, 617
Elgin, Joliet & Eastern Railway (EJ&E), 322, *429*, 1037; route map, *1172*
Elizabeth (passenger ferry), *676*
Elizabeth & Somerville Railroad, 212–213
Elizabeth City & Norfolk Railroad, 751
Elkhorn Tunnel, 415, *415*, 750
Elkins, William L., 315
Elkins Act of 1903, 13, 21, 210, 872, 922, 924–927
Ellicott's Mills depot (Maryland), 24
Ellis, Edward Sylvester, 597
Ellis, John, 600
Elmira (passenger ferry), *675*
Elson, Bob, 890
Elvin, Albert G., 295
emergency brakes. *See* automatic air brakes
Emergency Railroad Transportation Act. *See* Rail Transportation Act of 1933
Emergency Transportation Act of 1933, 930
Emerson (George H.), 1028
Emerson, Harrington, 545
Emerson, Ralph Waldo, 452, 594, 1032–1033
eminent domain, power of, 540
emissions from diesel engines, 382–383, 612
Emmanuel, 215, 216
Empire Builder, 185, 221, 1094. *See also* Hill, James J.
Empire State Express (stage play), 1045
Empire State Express (train), 22, 148, 398, 851, *992*, 993
employee timetables. *See* timetables
employees, 9, 18–19, 21, 437; certification, 785; crew size legislation, 84, 946; discipline, 783–785; effects on community, 30–31; efficiency growth, 1150; ethnicity, *see* ethnicity; housing, 1116–1118 (*see also* living space; YMCA, Railroad Department); labor conditions, 945, 946; labor organizations, 576–580; labor relations, 576–580, 759; labor-management conflicts, 576–580, 631, 698 (*see also* strikes); medical coverage

and screening, 691–693; mentoring by Daniel Willard (B&O), 1107; numbers of, 16, 1132, 1139, 1144; pensions, 905–906; preserving heritage, 874–876; at railroad shops, 545–548; religion, *see* religion; resource planning, 788; responsibilities before train departures, 1059–1060; safety of, *see entries at* accident; safety; seniority, 957–959, 1063, 1112; signals between, 972; slang terms, 144–145; strikes, *see* strikes; testing for compliance, 783; training, *see* training of railroad workers; unions for, *see* labor unions; wartime wage increases, 1120, 1124; women, *see* women in railroading; World War II labor shortages, 1124–1125. *See also* occupations

Empresa Sidera Mecánica (SIME), 349
Empress of Britain (steamship), *679*, 679
Empress of Canada, 985
Empress of Ireland (steamship), 679
empty-load brake, 460
enclosed vestibule passenger cars, 821–823, 882
Endicott, William, Jr., 32
end-of-car cushioning, 459
end-of-train device (EOT), 780, 1060
enforcement of operating rules, 783–785. *See also* operating practices
engine control system. *See* train control
engine crews. *See* employees
engine foremen. *See* foremen
engine house architecture, 128–129. *See also* workers' housing
engine service employees, 759, 1112. *See also* occupations
engine testing. *See* engines and locomotives, testing
engine watchmen, 770, 775
engine whistle signals. *See* whistles
engineering, civil. *See* civil engineering
engineering departments, 759
engineering laborers, 770
engineers, 9, *50*, 761–762, *762–763*; ethnicity of, *see* ethnicity; fatality rate, 945; job requirements, 1063–1064; responsibilities of, 1061–1062; slang terms for, 144
enginemen, 761; fatality rate, 945. *See also* engineers
engines and locomotives, 41–42, 442–443, 598–623; articulated, *see* articulated configurations; camelback engines (Wootten boilers), 353, *1010*, 1010, 1115; compound, *see* compound articulateds; conventional rod, 626; design, 599, 662; diesel, *see* diesel locomotives; diesel-electric, *see* diesel-electric locomotives; diesel-hydraulic locomotives, 590; electric, *see entries at* electric; electric drive internal combustion, 486; electrification, *see* electrification; Erie-builts, 442–443; fireless engines, 588, 1030; fueling, *604–607*, 604–608; gasoline-mechanical, 588, 603; gas-turbine-electric, 486 (*see also* gas-turbine locomotives); gauge, *see* track

gauge; geared, *see* steam locomotives, geared; identification codes, *see* identification codes for locomotives; internal combustion, *see* internal combustion power; lumber engines and lumbering, 62, 624–628, 1030–1031; maintenance and repair work, *see* maintenance; railroad shops; passenger service, *see* passenger service; preserving the heritage, 874–876; requirements planning, 787–788; safety, *see* safety; standardization in manufacturing, 599, 601–602; statistics, 1132–1133; steam, *see* steam locomotives; switchers, *see* switchers and switching systems; swiveling truck, 712; testing, *607*, 608–613; Texas & Pacific Railway, 1043; Train Master, 443; truck configuration codes, *see* codes for truck configurations; Whyte coding system, 1005–1006. *See also entries at* locomotive; *specific locomotives or locomotive models by name*; steam locomotives
Englewood Yard, *284*
English, Welsh & Scottish Railway (EWS), 1110
Enola Yard, 280, *288*
Ensign Manufacturing Co., 201
entertainment tours, 247, 853–854, 856–857; opera, 778–780; theater, 1044–1046; theater touring companies, 1046–1048. *See also* circuses and railroads
enthusiasts, 35, 874–876, 907–911
eNtrance-eXit machine, 114
entrance-exit system, 967
Environmental Protection Agency (EPA), 382, 612
Episcopal chapel cars, 215, 216
Equal Employment Opportunity Commission (EEOC), 1114
equalizer bars, 1008
equipment: automated tie renewal, 654, 656; automatic identification (AEI), 61, 329, 340, 430, 969; commuter, 322–323; heavy-haul loads, 517; intermodal transportation, 454–455, 479, 551–554; maintenance shops, 543–548 (*see also* railroad shops); mobile flash butt welders, 651; operating resources, 785–786; passenger service improvements, 820–830, 846–857; rail grinding, 651; track grading and construction, 640; track maintenance machinery, 84
equipment identification and fault detection, **429–432**
equity reorganization. *See* reorganization and receivership
The Erie. *See* New York & Erie Railroad
Erie Canal, *3*, 3–5, 37, 163, 219, *556*, 556–557, 581, 712, 863, 1048, 1088–1090; railroad control over, 1089
Erie Lackawanna Railroad (EL), 331, 353, **432–433**, 751; *Elmira* (passenger ferry), *675*; route map, *1164*
Erie plant (GE), *487*
Erie Railroad, *14*, 147, 337, **433–434**; Angus Sinclair, 973; battle for control

(Great Erie War), 433, 494; construction of, by George W. Whistler, 1105; Daniel Willard, 1107; diesel-electric locomotives, *488*; DL&W merger, 331, 352–353, 432, 434, 440; passenger ferry services, *675*, 677; route map, *1164*, *1171*; Sunday service restrictions, 1035; Van Sweringen acquisition, 433–434, 1079; Vanderbilt involvement in, 11, 433, 494, 1081
The Erie Train Boy, 597
Erie-builts, 442–443
Erlanger, Abraham, 1046
error detection procedures, 663
error management, 663
Escandón brothers, 695–696
Esch-Cummins Act. *See* Transportation Act of 1920
E-series passenger locomotives, 425–426
Esquaimalt & Nanaimo Railway, 198
essays, 596
etchings. *See* art
ethnicity, 30–31, **434–437**
Eucharistic Congress at Chicago (1926), 883
European & North American Railway (E&NA), 167, 194–195, 638–639
Evangel, 215, 216
Evans, John, 305
Evans, Oliver, **437**
Evansville & Illinois Railroad, 230
Evansville & Indianapolis Railroad, 230
Evansville & Richmond Railroad, 230
Evansville & Terre Haute Railroad (E&TH), 230
Evansville Belt Railway, 230
Evansville Railways, 669
event recorders, 1062
evolution of major railroads, **437–441**
Ewart, Peter, 148
excavation, 252, 657. *See also* tunnels
exciter generators, 622
excursion trains, 22, 145–146, *304*, 849, 853–854, 856–857, 875. *See also* sightseeing trains
executive departments, 759
exempt employees, 759
exemptions from economic regulation, 934
exemptions from property taxes, 540, 1041
exhibitions, railroad, 874
Expediting Act of 1903, 925
expendables, 888
expenditures, highway industry, 359. *See also* road improvements
expense statistics, 894, 1134–1135, 1138–1139, 1141, 1143, 1150–1152. *See also* railroad costs
Experiment (locomotive), 568, 712, *1008*
explorers of the American West, 791
explosions, boilers, 1010
explosives, 93, 799
Exposition Flyer, 356, 993, 1094. *See also California Zephyr*
expositions, railroad, 874
Express (railcar ferry), 669

Illinois Terminal Railroad, **533–534**; route map, *1178*
Illinois Traction System (ITS), 533, 563; Illinois Terminal Co. merger, 533
illustrations. *See* art
immigrants, attracting as colonists, 302–304
impedance bonds, 968–969
Imperial Limited, 851
Imperial Valley Flood (1904–1907), 388–391
import of railroad technology, 38–39, 1006–1008
improvements, passenger service, 820–830, 846–856
impurities in water, 605
"In the Baggage Coach Ahead" (song), 725–726
"In the Pines" (song), 35
In the Traces (Rose), 149
incense burning, 876
inclined-plane railways, 42, **534–539**, 625, 628, 712; Allegheny Portage Railroad, 863; at Mount Pisgah, *536*; river landings, 674
Incofer (Instituto Costarricense de Ferrocarriles), 337
incomes. *See* wages
incorporation laws and charters, **539–541**, 920
Increase the Crop per Acre, 102
incremental train control system (ITCS), 970
indenture, 936
independent brotherhoods, 1063
independent car builders, 543–544, 546
Indian tribes, relations with, 802, 804
Indiana Block Coal Railroad, 230
Indiana Columbus & Eastern Railroad, 238
Indiana Harbor Belt Railroad (IHB), 282, 1037; route map, *1172*
Indiana interurban electric railways, 542–543
Indiana Rail Road, **541–542**
Indiana Railroad (IR), 239, **542–543**; route map, *1171*
Indianapolis, Delphi & Chicago Railway, 222
Indianapolis Southern Railroad, 541
Indian-Pacific, 184
indictments, anti-trust. *See* Mellen, Charles S.
indivisibility of cost, 896
induction testing, 892
inductive train controls, 968, 970
industrial designers, 623–624, 830
industrial engineers, 545
industrial growth, 491
industrial locomotives, 1030
industrial material-handling equipment, 552–554
industrial shop practice, **543–548**
Industrial Workers of the World (IWW), 351, 579
infinite blocking, 282
inflation, wartime, 1120, 1124
information technology. *See* computerization

infrastructure: efficiency growth, 1151; excess capacity in, 1148; heavy-haul loads, impact on, 517; improvements, 554–559, 628; non-railroad, public, 554–558; resources for, 785–787
Ingalls, Melville E., 218
Ingersoll, Ernest, 565
Ingersoll-Rand Co. (IR), 16, 368–369, 487, 601
Ingram, John, 71, 168
initial reconnaissance (for railroad location), 41, 247–248
injured workers, relief for, 945
injuries. *See* casualties
Inland Waterways Commission, 1090
Inman, Arthur Crew, 596
Inman & International Steamship Co., 678
Inman Line, British-flag, 678
Inness, George, 33, 145
innocent until proven guilty, 784
inserters, spike, 660
inserters, tie, 660
Inside Gateway, 173
inside hostlers, 761
inspection cars, 470
inspection of railroads, 87, *767*; Locomotive Inspection Act of 1911, 92; slang terms, 145
inspections, track. *See* rail defects, detection of
institutional advertising, 682
Instituto Costarricense de Ferrocarriles (Incofer), 337
instrumentals, railroad, 725
instrumentmen, 770
Insull, Samuel, 98, 234, 236, 237, 542–543, **548–549**, *549*, 564
insurance, 631, 692, 759
Inter-California Railroad, 389
intercity service. *See* entries at interurban
Intercolonial Railway (ICR), 189, 190, 195, 198
interior design, passenger cars, 821, *822*, 827
interlocking board membership. *See* communities of interest
interlocking signaling systems, 394, 1068–1069, 1096
interlocking systems, 967
intermittent inductive train controls, 968
intermodal clerks, 768–769
intermodal freight, *455*, 467, 479, **549–554**, *550–553*, 816
Intermodal Surface Transportation Efficiency Act of 1991 (ISTEA), 498, 687
intermodal transportation, 69, 75–78, *76*, 83, 357, 549–554; equipment, 454–455, 479, 551–554; Flexi-Van container systems, 748; piggyback, *550–551*; rolling stock, *553*; steamships, 554; terminals, 471, 472, 479; Travellift, 553
internal combustion power, 54, 56–58, 486, 1103–1104; invention of, *see* Diesel, Rudolf
internal improvements, **554–559**, 628
Internal Revenue Service (IRS) accounting regulations, 97

International & Great Northern Railroad, 707
International Bridge, 189
International Brotherhood of Redcaps (IBR), 436
International Business Machines Corp., 326–327
International Car Co., 204
International Eucharistic Conference (1926), 990
International Limited, 198
International Mercantile Marine (IMM), 678
International Navigation Co. (INC), 678
International New Brunswick Railway, 167
International Pneumatic Railway Signal Co., 113
International Power Co., 361, 575
international railcar ferry services, 670–671
International Railways of Central America, 508
international steamship services, 677–680
International Switch & Signal Co., 1068
Internet, 330. *See also* computerization
Interstate Commerce Act of 1887. *See* Act to Regulate Commerce of 1887
Interstate Commerce Act of 1903, 12, 924–927, 961; Part II, 520; revisions (1958), 737–738
Interstate Commerce Commission (ICC), 12, 15–16, 67, 506, 520, 922, 924–932, 1071–1073; accident statistics and prevention, 91–93; antitrust concerns and, 961; creation of, 96; Elkins Act of 1903, 924–925 (*see also* Elkins Act of 1903); Emergency Transportation Act of 1933, 930; freight rates, 583; Hepburn Act of 1906, 926–927 (*see also* Hepburn Act of 1906); ICC Termination Act of 1985, 1036; intermodalism, 75–76, 551; Joseph B. Eastman, 16, 149, *402*, 402–403, 930; merger plan of 1929, 585; New Haven investigation, 693, 720; Piedmont & Northern Railway case, 871; *Pipe Line Cases*, 872; railroad classification, *see* classification systems; railroad valuation, 1075–1076; rate regulation, 682; safety regulations, *see* safety; Santa Fe requests, denied, 152; *Steam Locomotive Boiler Regulations*, 1010; trucking, federal regulation of, 520; work accident data, 945. *See also* regulation
Interstate Highway Act of 1956, 61
Interstate Public Service Co., *561*
interurban electric railways, 59, **559–564**, 587, 687, 854–856, 994, 1091–1092; Baldwin-Westinghouse, trains from, 1102; Chautauqua program, 1048; General Electric Co., 484; Henry E. Huntington, 530; Pacific Electric Railway, 790–791; Piedmont & Northern Railway, 870–871; Samuel Insull, 549; track gauge, 560–561; trends, 859. *See also* commuter services; *specific railroads by name*

knuckle couplers. *See* automatic couplers
Knudsen Motor Co., 370
Koolau Railway, 516
Koppel Industrial Car & Equipment Co., 205
Korean War railroads, 299–300
Kraft, Nikolai, 493
Kraus-Maffei Company, 377
Krauss-Maffei A.G., 603
Krebs, Robert D., 153, 172
Krollmann, Gustav, 148
Krout, Arlo C., 496
Kruttschnitt, Julius, 92, **574–575**, 665, 783
K-trusses, 254, 263
Kuehn, Loeb, 504
Kuhler, Otto, 147, *370*, 830, 832
Kuntz, Peter, 216

L. S. Brach Co., 496
"The L&N Rag" (song), 35
"L" trains (Chicago Transit Authority), 234
L-97 order, 426, 427, 602
La Bête Humaine (Zola), 595
La Crosse & Milwaukee Rail Road, 224
La Follette, Robert M., 579
La Gare Saint-Lazare, 146
La Grange factory (EMC), 425, *425–426*, 428–429
labor, **576–580**. *See also* employees
Labor (union newspaper), 579
labor conditions, 945, 946
labor laws (women), 1110
labor organizations, 576–580
labor policies to reduce accidents, 92
labor relations, 576–580, 759, 820
labor unions, 76, 576–580, 945, 946, 1063; crew size, 84; impact of, 548; pensions, 905; representation of black employees, 435–436; seniority and, 958–959; women in railroading, 1111
laborers, 770; ethnicity, *see* ethnicity; preserving the heritage, 874–876; songs about, 724. *See also* employees
labor-management conflicts, 576–580, 631, 698, 880–881. *See also* strikes
Labrador. *See* Quebec North Shore & Labrador Railway
Lachine Canal, 193–194
Lackawanna (Railroad). *See* Delaware, Lackawanna & Western Railroad
Lackawanna Cutoff, 55
Lackawanna Limited, 352
Lackawanna Steel, 202
The Lackawanna Valley, 33, 145
Ladd, Alan, 597
Ladies in Waiting, 147
ladies' sitting room car, *853*
Lafayette, 240
Lake Cities, 352
Lake Erie, Wabash & St. Louis Railroad, 1085
Lake Erie & Western Railway (LE&W), 741, 1079
Lake Erie water traffic, 1088–1089
Lake Ontario water traffic, 1088–1089
Lake Shore & Michigan Southern Railroad: Ashtabula collapse (1876), 90, 94, 256; Chicago YMCA, cooperation

with, 1126; Daniel Willard, 1106; Millbury Junction interlocking, 1068; Vanderbilt control of, 1081
Lake Shore Electric Railway (LSE), 239, **580**
The Lake Shore Limited, 993
Lake Shore Line, 208
Lake Shore Railroad, Angola derailment (1867), *91*, 91
Lake Superior water traffic, 1089
Lamme, Benjamin G., 1097, 1101
LaMotte, L. H., *327*
lamp signals, 972–973, 1055
Lancaster Turnpike, 37, 1088
land, taking by eminent domain, 540
land cruises, 856–857
land development promotion trains, 986–988
Land Grant Act of 1862, 301
land grants, 6–7, 99, 300, **581–582**, 709, 796; Pacific Railroad, 796
Langdon, Jervis, Jr., 229, **583**
Lange, John, 76
Lanigan, Jack, 553
lap, valve, 1011
lap orders, 394
large freight cars, 516–518
Lark, 980
Las Vegas & Tonopah Railroad, **583**, 1050
Last Spike monument, 714, *715*
Latah Creek canyon crossing, 261
lateral travel (on tracks), 661
lathes, 617
Lathrop, Gilbert A., 598
Latrobe, Benjamin H., Jr., 445, **583–584**
lattice-truss bridges, 254
Laurentian, 353–354
Laurie, Annie, 388
Laurier, Wilfrid, 190, 197
law departments, 759
layouts, railroad shops, 618–622
Le chemin de fer, 146
Le Découverte, 988
leading truck (steam locomotives), 1005
Learned, Edward, 697
leasing railroads, 307. *See also specific railroads by name*
Leavenworth, Pawnee & Western Railroad, 795–796
Lebanon & Northern Railroad, *729*
Ledbetter, Huddie, 724
Lee, Robert E., 275, 278
Lee, William States, 870
legacies, 32–36, 722–723
Legislator, 989
Lehigh & Hudson River Railway (L&HR), **584**, *1159*
Lehigh & New England Railroad (L&NE), **584–585**, *1159*
Lehigh & Susquehanna Railroad (L&S), 213
Lehigh & Wilkes-Barre Coal Co., 213
Lehigh Car, Wheel & Axle Works, 201
Lehigh Valley Railroad, 201, 213, **585–586**, 813; Manchester wreck (1911), 92, 94, 891; Pennsylvania Railroad purchase of, 1085; route map, *1159*

Lehigh Valley Transit Co., **586–587**
Lemp, Hermann, 361, 364, 367–368, 424, 486
Lendabarker, James, 227
Lend-Lease Act of 1941, 16, 1121
length, rail, 644
Leonard (railcar ferry), 672
Leslie, Florence, 19
Leslie's (periodical), 942
less-than-carload (LCL) services, 59, 472–474, *473*, 518, *550*, 580, 1054, 1133; railcar ferry services for, 672
Lethbridge Viaduct, *258*
LeTourneau units, *552*, 553
level cylinders, 44
Lew, Ivy, 878
Lewis, Arthur, 73
Lewis, Drew, 172
Lewis, L. V., 1068
Lewis, Meriwether, 791
Lewis, Oscar, 527, 596
Lewis, Richard, 79
Lewis, Roger, 738
Lewis, Sinclair, 595
lexicon of train talk. *See* argot (and nicknames)
Lexington & Big Sandy Railroad, 217
Lexington & Ohio Railroad, 537
liability for safety, 944–946
Liberty Bell Limited (LVT trains), 587
Lidgerwoods, 625
"Life's Railroad to Heaven" (allegory), 722–723
lift bridges, 266–267
lift equipment, 553
lifting devices, 617
Liggett's Gap Railway, 351
Light Rapid Comfortable (LRC) trainsets, 174, 842
light signals (classification), 780, 782, 1055
lighters (barges), 672
lighting, car, 45–46, 51, 821, 824–826
"The Lightning Express" (song), 35
light-rail transit, 687
lightweight streamliners, 833, 883
lignite fuel, steam locomotives, 607
Lima Locomotive Works, 56, 117–118, 119, 162, 295, **587–591**, *588*, 600, 626–627, 1006, 1019–1021, 1025, *1026*, 1027; diesel-electric locomotives, *371*, 373–374; General Machinery Corp merger, 603; J. S. Coffin, 295–296; Shay gear-drive locomotives, 587, 600, 626–627, *627*, 1031; Super-Power production, 1027
Lima Machine Works. *See* Lima Locomotive Works
Lima Shay locomotives. *See* Shay gear-drive locomotives
Lima-Hamilton Corp., 590, 590–591
Limantour, José Ives, 698
Lima-Toledo Railroad, 238
lime cars, 467
The Limited Mail (stage play), 1045
Lincoln, Abraham, 227, 336, 395, 479, 515, *591*, **591**, *592*, 754, 791, 794, 795, 803,

Mackenzie, William, 196, 197
MacLeish, Archibald, 596
Macon & Western Railroad, 154
Madero, Francisco, 698
Madigan, Myers & Barton's Railroad Circus & Amphitheatre, 243
Madison & Indianapolis Railroad (M&I), 296
magazines, railroading, 874–876; *Messenger* (*Black Worker*), 913. *See also specific magazines by name*; trade publications
magic wear rate, 651
magnates, 439–440
magnetic induction testing, 892
Magnolia Cutoff, 164
Magor Car Corp., 203, 348, 457
mail and express delivery, rail-based, **634–636**, *635*, 790; decline in, 738. *See also* U.S. Railway Post Office
mail order, **637–638**, 1054
Main Line of Public Works, 39, 42, 111, 1049; Johnstown Flood (1889), 383–386
main rod (steam locomotives), 1005
Main Street Incline (Cincinnati), 538–539
Main Street Station (Richmond), 134
Maine area, routes of, *1155*
Maine Central Railroad (MEC), 167, 177, **638–639**, 874; New Haven gained control of, 743; Portland Terminal Co., subsidiary of, 638
main-line electrification, 601
main-line excursions, 875.
main-line grades, 534
main-line switches, 645
maintainers (occupation), 765
maintenance: accounting regulations, 97; AC-traction motors, 382; diesel locomotives, *620*, 620–622; facilities, locomotive, *see* railroad shops; general repairs, 618–619; grade crossings, 647; heavy-load operation, impact on, 517; operations testing, 783; repair and maintenance facilities, 128; steam locomotives, 615–616, 615–620, *616*; track, *see* maintenance-of-way; wheels, 615–616. *See also* railroad shops
maintenance-of-way (MOW), 63, **639–659**, 759; construction, 641–648; definition, 648; discipline, 784; equipment and machinery, 470, *648*, 648–654, *651–653*, 656, 659–661; equipment laborers, 770; grade crossings, 647; housing for workers, 1116; inspection, 648–650; maintenance and renewal, 84, 470, 644, 651–659, *654–655*, 661; purchases for, 888; track inspection, 648–659
maintenance-of-way machinery, **659–661**
major-league baseball, 996–998
making up the train, 1059
Mallet, Anatole, 54, **661–662**, 1013, 1017–1018
Mallet locomotives, compound, 625–626
Maltrata Incline, 248
management information services (MIS), 759
management structure and practice, **662–665**, 820

managerial accounting, 894
Manassas Gap Railroad, 164
Manchester wreck (1911), 92, 94, 891
Manhattan terminal (Pennsylvania Railroad), *57*
manifest traffic, 786
Manistique & Lake Superior Railroad, 126
Manitoba. *See* St. Paul, Minneapolis & Manitoba Railroad
Manitoba Road, 1077
Manitou & Pike's Peak Railroad, *298*, 984. *See also* Peak Cog Railway
Manitowoc (railcar ferry), 668
Mann, Donald, 196, 197
Mann, William D., **665–666**, 882
Mann Boudoir Car Co., 666
Mann-Elkins Act of 1910, 13, 927
Manning, Maxwell & Moore, 178
Mansfield, Josie, 450
manual block system, 394, 965, 1056
manual brakes, freight cars, 460. *See also* brakes
Manual of Industrial and Miscellaneous Securities (Moody), 718
Manual of the Railroads of the United States, 873
manufactured goods, shipping, 1053
manufacturers of locomotives. *See* locomotive builders
Manypenny, George W., 793
Maple Leaf System, 31, 234
maps, series of, *1154–1196*
Marbury, William, 708–709
Marias Pass, 249, 1034
Marietta & Cincinnati Railroad, 163, 438
marine cranes. *See* gantry cranes
marine employees, 770
marine operations, **666–680**; car floats, 478, 666–667, *668*, 672, *673*; oceangoing steamship services, 677–680; passenger ferry services, 674–677; railcar ferry services, 666–674. *See also* water transportation
Mark IV RoadRailer, 455
Mark V RoadRailer, 455
markers at train ends, 780, 1055
market monopolies. *See* monopolies
market share. *See* traffic categories and trends
marketing and promotion, **680–684**, 759, 850–852; branding, 681, 690, 850–851; national parks, *734–735*; as role of station agent, 681; Yellowstone National Park and Union Pacific Railroad, *734*. *See also* advertising
Marquardt Industrial Products Co., 971
Marquette and Bessemer No. 2, 667
Marsh, Reginald, 33, 147
Marsh, Sylvester, 297
Marshall Pass, 356
Martha Washington, 354–355
Martin, John, 757
Martin, Steve, 242
Martins Creek Viaduct, 352
Martland, Carl, 517
Mary of Scotland (stage play), 1047
Maryland & Pennsylvania Railroad (Ma & Pa), **684**

Maryland II (railcar ferry), 669
Maryland Rail Commuter (MARC), 322, 323; route map, *1163*
Masich, Bill, 77
Mason, David, 158
Mason Machine Works, 600
masonry arch bridges, 253–254, 257, 258, 261–262. *See also entries at* bridge
masons, 767
mass merchandising by mail, 637
Mass Transit (periodical), 1053
Mass Transportation (periodical), 1053
Massachusetts Bay Commuter Railroad Co., 685
Massachusetts Bay Transportation Authority (MBTA), 308, *308*, 320, 322, 323, **684–685**; route map, *1158*
Massachusetts Board of Railroad Commissioners, 99
Massachusetts Central Railroad, 176–177
mass-transit legislation and programs, **685–688**. *See also* public transportation
master car builders, 544
Master Car Builders Association (MCB), 48, 149, 842, 1098; automatic couplers, 459; mechanical designations, 463; quality control testing, 545
master mechanics, 544
Master Mechanics Association, 545
master retarders, 285, 287
master test section (humping), 287
Matanzas Railroad, 347
materials, ballast, 641
materials management, 759
Mather, Stephen T., 736
Matt Shay, 1018
Matter, Hergbert, 690
Matthews, Brander, 596
Mauch Chunk Railway, 535, 539, 820
maximum grade. *See* grade of route
May, Ren G. *See* Berlin, Irving
MBTA. *See* Massachusetts Bay Transportation Authority
McAdoo, William Gibbs, 15–16, 688, **688–689**, 928, 1072, 1073, 1127; USRA management during World War I, 1119–1120
McCallum, Daniel C., 275, 663
McCarthy, Wilson, 355
McCartney, John, 133
McClellan, George B., **689**
McClellan, James, 71, 72, 73, 85
McCormick, Cyrus, 398
McCoy, Charlie, 725
McCrea, James, 714
McGee, Homer E., 506–507
McGee, Weldon, 507
McGinnis, Arthur J., Sr., 1052
McGinnis, Lucille, 690
McGinnis, Patrick B., **689–690**, *690*, 743–744, 752
McGowen, Jack, 386
McGregor Western Railway, 224
McIlwrath, Rolleen, 1113
McIntosh & Seymour Corp. (M&S), 369
McKee, Fuller & Co., 201
McKeen, William R., 838
McKeen railcars, 181–182, 838

McKim, Mead & White, 138
McKinley, William B., 523, 533, 756
McKinley Bridge (St. Louis), 711
McLean, Malcolm, 69, 554
McLeod, Archibald, 586, 918
McNair Pullman sleeping car, *829*
McNeill, William Gibbs, 574, 1105
McQueen, Walter, 600
Meadows Maintenance Complex, 740
Mears, Otto, 939
meat. *See* livestock
mechanical departments, 759
mechanical engineering, 899–900
mechanical retarders, 282
mechanics (employees), 770–771
media relations, 878–879. *See also* corporate identification and image; public image
Medicare Act (1965), *692*
medicine, **691–693**
Meeks, Carroll L. V., 56
Mehegan, Mary Theresa, 523
Meigs, Henry, 337
Mellen, Charles S., **693**, 720, 743
Mellen, George K., 693
Mellen, Hanna M. (Sanger), 693
Mellon, Timothy, 177
Melnikov, Pavel P., 493
Memorial of the Central Pacific Railroad Company of California, 795
Memphis & Charlestown Railroad, 277
Memphis & Ohio Railroad, 277
Mencken, August, 596
Mencken, H. L., 360, 596
Menk, Louis Wilson, 171, 185, 221, **693–694**; "Menk the Fink" buttons, 694
Menlo Park, New York, 312
Mennonite farmers, 302
merchandising, 637
Merchants Bridge, 1041
Merchants Despatch Transportation Corp., 203
Merchants Limited, 849
Mercury (streamliner), 832
mercury-arc rectifiers, 405, 407, 1103
mergers. *See* consolidation of railroads
Merritt brothers of Duluth, 398
Merwin, Samuel, 597
Mesabi Range, 398
Messenger (*Black Worker*) magazine, 913
Messenger of Agricultural Development, 102
Messenger of Peace, 215–216
messengers, 634, 764; express messengers, 26, 634, 765; Railway Express Agency, 911–912. *See also* U.S. Railway Post Office
metal bridges, 254–257. *See also* entries at bridge
metallurgical cleanliness, 645
Meteor, 943
meter-gauge railroad, 507
Metra. *See* Northeast Illinois Regional Commuter Railroad Corp. (Metra)
Metro (periodical), 1053
Metroliners, 63, 78, *79*, 840, 862
Metrolink. *See* Southern California Regional Rail Authority (Metrolink)
Metro-North Routes, New York City, *1161*
Metropolitan Coach Lines, 790

Metropolitan Opera Co. of New York, 778–780
metropolitan stations, architecture of, 127, 136–138
Metropolitan Transit Authority of Massachusetts (MTA), 684
Metropolitan Transportation Agency (Agence métropolitaine de transport, AMT), 322, **694–695**; route map, *1191*
Metropolitan Transportation Authority (MTA), 630, 721–722
Mexican American employees, 434
Mexican Central Railway, 15, 703
Mexican National Railways (Ferrocarriles Nacionales de México), 15, 143, 440, 696–698, 703, 808, 1144–1145; electrification, 56, 421, 422; Maltrata Incline, 248; privatization, 704–705; route map, *1195*; William Jackson Palmer, 636–697, 815
Mexican railroads, general history, **695–703**; fictitious, 702; privatization, 701–702; revolution of 1910, 698, 701. *See also* Mexico and Mexican railways
Mexican railroads, nationalization, **703–704**
Mexican railroads, privatization, **704–706**
Mexican Railway Co. Ltd., *696*
Mexicanization, 698–699
Mexico and Mexican railways, 15, 695–703, 1148; architecture, 143; Bombardier operations, 175; concessions, 541; consolidation (1908), 698; fictitious, 702; general history, 695–702; nationalization of, 703–704; privatization, 701–702, 704–706; revolution of 1910, 698, 701; route map, *1195*; statistics, 1144–1147; tourist trains, 908. *See also specific railroads by name*
Mexico North-Western Railroad, 571
Michelin Co., 182
Michigan Central Railroad, 222, 452, 569; Edward H. Williams, 1108; electrification, 414, 420; James Frederick Joy, 569; NYC merger, 746; railcar ferry services, 668; Vanderbilt control of, 1081
Michigan Central Station, 129, 140, *141*; Detroit River tunnel (Ontario), 272–273, 421, 668
Michigan High Speed PTC Project, 969–970
Michigan Interstate Railroad, 126
Michigan Northern Railroad, 126
Michigan Southern & Northern Indiana Railroad, 437
Michigan Southern Railroad, 568, 1108
microprocessor-controlled interlocking, 1069
Mid South Rail Corp., 573
Midamerica Corp., 1080
Mid-Atlantic states routes, *1158–1159*
Middle Western Utilities, 549
Middlesex Canal, 1088
Midland Railroad, 135, 882
"The Midnight Special" (song), 723
The Midnight Special (stage play), 1045
Midvale Steel Car & Ordinance, 201–202
Mi-Jack, 553, 816

A Mile a Minute (stage play), 1045
mileage statistics, 1132, 1139–1140, 1144–1145, 1148
Military Railway Service (MRS), 1105, *1124*, 1124, 1125
military transportation, 16–17, 22, *1121*; during World War I, 1120–1122; during World War II, 1121–1122
milk runs, 765
Mill Mountain Incline, Roanoke, Virginia, 539
Millbrae station (San Francisco), 861
Miller, Ezra L., 88, 842, 976, 1007
Miller, Joaquin, 596
Millholland, James, 454, 1115
milling machines, 617
Mills, Darius Ogden, 319
Mills, Robert, 791
Milwaukee, Lake Shore & Western Railroad, 231
Milwaukee & Prairie du Chien Railway, 224
Milwaukee & St. Paul Railway, 224
Milwaukee & Waukesha Rail Road, 224
Milwaukee Road. *See* Chicago, Milwaukee, St. Paul & Pacific Railroad
Milwaukee Road 1802 (FM switcher), 443
mineral mining, encouraging, 304
Mineta, Norman Y., 81
miniatures. *See* model railroading
mining, encouraging, 304
Minneapolis, Northfield & Southern Railway, 975
Minneapolis, St. Paul & Sault Ste. Marie Railroad (MStP&SSteM), 974. *See also* Soo Line Railroad
Minneapolis & St. Louis Railway (M&StL), **706–707**, *1177*
Minnesota & Northwestern Railroad, 234, 1106
Minnesota Central Railway, 224
minor-league sports, 997
Minot, Charles, 22, 392, 780, 965–966; monument to, 718
Minturn, Charles, 757
Missabe. *See* Duluth, Missabe & Iron Range Railway
Mississippi & Missouri Railroad Co. (M&M), 227–228, 399
Mississippi Central Railway, 531
Mississippi River: Memphis bridge, 258; Rock Island bridge, 259; St. Louis bridge, *see* Eads Bridge; water traffic, 669, 1088–1090
Missouri Pacific Railroad (MoPac), 328, 566–567, 671, **707–709**, 950, 1042, 1092; C&EI merger, 230–231; car scheduling, development of, 206; computerization (1959), 328; Downing Bland Jenks, 230, 566–567, *567*, 708–709; *Eagle* streamliner, 623; railroad hospital, 30; route map, *1182*; soil conservation efforts, 103; *Sunshine Special*, 993; Texas & Pacific, purchase of, 1042–1043; Union Pacific acquisition of, 567, 709, 1067; Van Sweringen ownership, 230, 1079; William Marbury, 708–709. *See also* Pacific Railroad of Missouri

Missouri River bridge (Glasgow), 256
Missouri River canalization, 1090
Missouri-Kansas-Texas Railroad (Katy), **709–711**, 1042, 1067; route map, *1180, 1182; Texas Special*, 952, 993
Mitchel, O. M., 124
Mitchell, Alexander, 224, 225
mixed gauge railroads, *732*
mixed trains, 21
"mixing centers," 479
Mobile, Jackson & Kansas City Railroad, 509
Mobile & Ohio Railroad (M&O), 438, 508–510, 531, 982
mobile flash butt welders, 651
model farms, 102
Model Railroader magazine, 35
model railroading, 35, 907, 909–911
Model 60 gasoline-powered motor cars, 115
model town, 880, 882, 884–887
Modern Railroads (periodical), 1052
Modjeski, Ralph (Rudolphe Modrzejewski), **711–712**
Modoc Line, 980
modulus, track, 640–641
Moffat, David, 355–356
Moffat Tunnel, 273, 356
Mohawk & Hudson Rail Road (M&H), 112, **712**, 746; Benjamin Wright, 568; *Experiment*, 568; inclined-plane railways, 536; route map, *1157*
money pools, 914
monolithic concrete ties, 642
Monon. *See* Chicago, Indianapolis & Louisville Railway (Monon Railroad)
Monongahela Incline (Pittsburgh), 538
monopolies, 920; B&O, 865; Charles Sanger Mellen, 693; charter grants, 539–540; diesel locomotive market, 602; EMD, 602–603; Glacier National Park (Great Northern), 735; Grand Canyon National Park (Santa Fe), 735; Hill-Morgan alliance, 755–756; Maine Central Railroad, 638; North Atlantic steamship lines, 678; Northern Securities Co., 720, 756; Pullman Co. sleeper cars, 881; Standard Oil Co., 871; Yellowstone National Park (Northern Pacific), 734–735
Monroe, H. G., 1127
Montezuma (locomotive), *728, 730*
Montgomery & Eufala Railroad, 211
Montgomery Rail Road, 154
Montgomery Ward, 637–638
Montreal, Quebec (city): Canadian Pacific station, *142*; commuter services, 319, 695; route maps, *1191*
Montreal & Lachine Railroad, 194
Montreal Limited, 353–354
Montreal Locomotive Works (MLW), 122, 173–174, 199, 370, 601
Montrealer, 214
monuments, **712–718**
Monzani, Willoughby, 254
Moody, John, **718**
Moore, Charles A., 178
Moore, William H., 440, 987

Moran, Thomas, 145–146, 565
Morgan, David P., 612
Morgan, J. P., 12, 223, 429, 504, 523, 574, 586, 677, 678, 693, **718–720**, *719*, 743, 871, 1083; communities of interest, 307; Erie Railroad, 433; Hill-Morgan alliance, 755–756; NYC-PRR rivalry, settled by, 746; rail empire, 440; Southern Railway System, 982
Morgan, Linda, 85–86
Morgan, Lloyd, Sr., 247
Morgan Improvement Co., 334
Morgan's Louisiana & Texas Railroad, 980
Morison, George Shattuck, 258, 711
Morning Zephyr, 994
Morris & Essex Railroad (M&E), 309, 312, 352
Morrison-Knudsen, 603
Morse, Charles Hosmer, 442
Morse, Samuel F. B., **720–721**
Morse code, 770
mortgages, 936–937
Moseley, Spencer D., 912
Mosso brothers, 695
Mother Hubbards (camelback engines), 353, *1010*, 1010, 1115
motion pictures. *See* cinema and railroads
motion sensors, 496
motive power, 484–489
Motor Carrier Act of 1935, 520
Motor Carrier Act of 1980, 924, 1036
motor cars, 590, 603; Galloping Goose motor cars, 940; Model 60, 115
motor coach services, 790
Motor Transit Lines, 790
motor trucks, 518, *519*, 521–522
motor vehicles, 58, 61, 65, 518; accidents at grade crossings, 947–948; car ownership, growth in, 1152; federal expenditures for highways, 359; as freight, 463–464, *467*, 467, 479; national parks, 736–737; parts shipping, 1053, 1054; perishable foodstuffs transport, 107; regulation of, 923; roads, *see* road improvements; trilevel automobile carrier, 62, *467*; trucking, *see* trucking industry; World War I effects, 492, 518; World War II effects, 518–522, *519*
Motorailers, 115
motorbuses, 518
motor-generator locomotives, 407
Mount Clare shops, 129, 1108
Mt. Desert Limited, 904, 992
Mount Lowe Incline (Los Angeles), 539
Mount Macdonald Tunnel, 192, 200, 272
Mount Manitou Incline, Colorado, 538
Mount Pisgah inclined-plan system, *536*
Mount Rainier National Park, 734
Mount Royal Tunnel, 319, 417
Mount Tom Incline (Massachusetts), 539
Mount Vernon Car & Manufacturing Co., 203, 205
Mount Washington Cog Railway, 297, *297*, 984
mountains, 490–491; climbing lines, *see* rack railways; list of mountain passes, 248

movable bridges, 259
"movable cities," 805
movable-point frogs, 64
movies. *See* cinema and railroads
"Mr. Clean" (nickname), 567, 708. *See also* Jenks, Downing B.
Mrs. Wiggs of the Cabbage Patch (stage play), 1046
MTA Metro-North Railroad, **721–722**
Muhlenberg, John, 437
Muir, John, 734
Mullan Pass, 249
Muller v. Oregon (1908), 1110
multilevel gallery cars. *See* gallery cars
multiple unit control, 559
multiple-unit cars, 406, 1103; commuter services technology, 323, 417
Mumford, F. B., 101
Municipal Bridge, 256
Municipal Loan Act of 1852, 194
Munn v. Illinois (1877), 12, 501, 920
Murchison, Kenneth M., 136, 352
Murphy, Anthony, 124
Murphy, Harry C., 221, 694
Murray, Dougal & Co., 201
Murray, Matthew, 39, 296
Murray, Oscar G., 164
museums, railroad, 874, 875, 908; B&O Transportation Museum, 874
music, 35, 598, **722–726**, *724, 725. See also* art
MX missiles, transport of, 300
My Antonia (Cather), 595
My Little Chickadee (film), 242
Myers, George, 1126

Nachod & United States Signal Co., 971
Nagelmackers, Georges, 666, 882
Nahatlatch River bridge, 254, *254*
names for towns, 32
naming trains, 681, 849–851, 853, 856; Pullman cars, 883
Nancy Hawks, 993
Nandua (railcar ferry barge), 671
Napa Valley Wine Train, 908
narrow gauge, 516, 640, 703, **727–733**, 757, 814–816, 879; IRCA, 508, 697; locomotives, *729–732*; Mexican, 696–697; Panama Railroad, 815–816; photography, 565. *See also specific railroads by name*; standard gauge
Narrow Passage Creek bridge, *276*
Nash, Charles, 182
Nashville, Chattanooga & St. Louis Railway (NC&StL), 156, 344, **733–734**; Louisville & Nashville merger, 440; Nashville collisions (1918), 22, 93, 94
Nashville & Chattanooga Railroad (N&C), 733
Nast, Thomas, *14*
Natchez (steamboat), *558*
National Association of General Passenger and Ticket Agents, 776
National Association of Railroad Enthusiasts, *908*
National Association of Railroad Passengers (NARP), 738
National Civic Union, 576

National General Ticket Agents Association, 776
National Good Roads Association, 987
National Historic Preservation Act (1966), 36
A National Institution, 148
National Irrigation Association, 100
national leaders, travel by, 989–990. *See also* presidential campaigns and travel
National Narrow Gauge Convention (1872), 728
national parks, 681, **734–737**
National Railroad Passenger Act (1970), 738; revision (1998), 739
National Railroad Passenger Corp. (Amtrak), 63–64, 71, *80*, 331, 444–445, 488, **737–739**, 816–817; Acela service, 64, 81, 175, 422, *422*, 842, 995; *Adirondack*, 354; advertising, 684; Amfleet coaches, *80*, 184, 738; attempts to dissolve, 79–81; commuter services, 685, 862; electrification, 420; formation of, 78–80, 357, 932, 1105; high-speed operation, 498; long-distance passenger service, 862–863; Northeast Corridor, 78, 81, 184, 188–189, 738–739, 862; railroad police force, 340; route map, *1154*; SEPTA (Philadelphia) and, 977; *Sunset Limited* accident (1993), 94, 96; Superliners (bilevel), 840; track geometry cars, 650; TurboTrain, *see* Turbo-Train; women employees, 1113
national railroad strike (1877), 483
National Railway Bulletin, 907
National Railway Historical Society, 35, 875
National Railways of Mexico (NdeM). *See* Mexican National Railways
National Register of Historic Places, 875
National Road, 2, 1048
National Steel Car Corp., Ltd., 203, 203–204
National Switch & Signal Co., 1068
National System of Interstate and Defense Highways, 737
national time system. *See* Standard Time
National Transcontinental Railway (NTR), 167, 190, 197; railcar ferry services, 670, 672; T&NO, relationship with, 778
National Transcontinental Railway Act of 1903, 197
National Transportation Act of 1987, 907
National Transportation Safety Board (NTSB), 95
National Traveler's Aid Society, 26, *27*
nationalization of Mexican railroads, 703
nationalization of railways, 13, 15, 440, 579
Native Americans, railroads' effect on, 492
Natron Cutoff, 980
natural aspiration (internal combustion), 363
natural disasters, 383–392; Florida Keys Hurricane (1935), 391; Galveston Hurricane (1900), 387; Hinckley Firestorm (1894), 386; Imperial Valley Flood (1904–1907), 388–391; Johnstown

Flood (1889), 383–386; Tehachapi Earthquake (1952), 392
natural gas, Westinghouse interest in, 1097
Nautilus (fish car), 448–449
Nautilus II (fish car), 449
Navajo employees, 434
Neal, Charles E., 758
Nebraska Zephyr, 356, 908
Nebraskan agricultural development, 99
Neponset River viaduct, 253
net earnings statistics, 1134–1135, 1150–1152; World War II effects, 1125
New Albany & Salem Rail Road (NA&S), 222
New England Central Railroad, 214–215
New England transportation: New Haven control over, 743; route map, *1156*, *1158*
New Haven. *See* New York, New Haven & Hartford Railroad
New Haven & New London Railroad, 666
New Jersey Cutoff, 352
New Jersey Department of Transportation, 739
New Jersey Railroad: commuter services, 309, 311, 312; Sunday service restrictions, 1035
New Jersey Southern Railroad, 213
New Jersey Transit, 213, **739–741**; route maps, *1161–1162*
New Line (Western Maryland), 1093
new markets in passenger service, 858–859
New Orleans, Jackson & Great Northern Railroad (NOJ&GN), 531
New Orleans, Mobile & Chicago Railroad, 509
New Orleans, Opelousas & Great Western Railroad, 980
New Orleans, Texas & Mexico (NOT&M), 707
New Orleans & Northeastern Railroad, 982
New Orleans Great Northern (NOGN), 509
New Orleans Public Belt Railroad (NOPB), 1037
New Orleans Special, 569
New Portage Railroad, 111
new responsibilities, impact on management structures, 663–664
"New River Train" (song), 35
"The New Steel Trail," *724*
New Track Construction (NTC) machines, 656
New York, Chicago & St. Louis Railroad (Nickel Plate Road), 218, **741–742**, 1079, 1129; CTC system, *1058*; John J. Bernet, 741; Norfolk & Western merger, 440, 749, 952, 1085–1086; route map, *1168*; Vanderbilt acquisition of, 439, 1081
New York, Lake Erie & Western Railroad, 433. *See also* Erie Railroad
New York, New Haven & Hartford Railroad (New Haven), 70–71, 168, 177, 211, 311, 689–690, **742–745**; Charles Sanger Mellen, 693, 743; commuter

services, 309–310, *310*, 323–324, 684; electrification, 414, 420, 1097, 1102; John F. Stevens, 1035; L&NE merger, 585; *Merchants Limited*, 849; monopolistic practices, 720; Norwalk disaster (1853), 87, 94; passenger ferry services, 677; route map, *1156*; streamliners, *833*; transfer bridges, 672, 674; Twenty Questions case, 551; Yale-Harvard game train, 986
New York, Ontario & Western Railway, 331, **745–746**; route map, *1159*
New York, Philadelphia & Norfolk Railroad, 210, 670–671
New York, Providence & Boston Railroad, 1105
New York, Susquehanna & Western Railroad, 313
New York, West Shore & Buffalo Railroad, 746, 1086
New York & Erie Railroad, 113, 135, 433; commuter services, 312–313; as major railroad, 437; monument to Charles Minot, 718; Starrucca Viaduct, *148*, *253*, 253
New York & Harlem Railroad, 311, 1081
New York & Long Branch Railroad (NY&LB), 213, 312, *605*
New York & New England Railroad, 668
New York & New Jersey Railroad, 688
New York & Oswego Midland Railroad (NY&OM), 745
New York Central & Hudson River Railroad (NYC&HR), 746
New York Central Sleeping Car Co., 1086
New York Central System, 166, 168, 177, 203, 712, 741, **746–749**; 4-6-4 Hudsons, 56; *20th Century Limited*, 21, 56, 58, 147, 148, 247, *682*, 747, *748*, *829*, 851, 869, 993, 1046; agricultural development activities, 102; Alfred E. Perlman, 869; bus operations, 519; Chauncey M. Depew, 359–360; during Civil War, 274; coal dumpers, *293*; communities of interest, 13, 307, 439–440; commuter services, 311–312, 318; electrification, *54*, 409–412, 420, 484, 747, 999, 1106; *Empire State Express* (train), 22, 148, 398, 851, *992*, 993; establishment as major railroad, 437–439; *Exposition Flyer*, 356, 993, 1094 (*see also California Zephyr*); Grand Central, *see* Grand Central Terminal (New York); intermodal transport, 550; *The Lake Shore Limited*, 993; LCL services, 550; Little Falls derailment (1940), 94; marketing campaigns, 680, 682; *Mercury* streamliner, 832; merger with Pennsylvania, *see* Penn Central Railroad; MOW car to verify clearances, 648; New York Central 1550, 120; Northern (4-8-4) engines, 353; passenger ferry services, 686; Pennsylvania Railroad, conflict, 719; Plimmon H. Dudley, 397; PRR, rivalry with, 678, 746; Robert R. Young control of, 1128–1129; route map, *1165*; Super-Power steam locomotives,

Oakland, Antioch & Eastern Railroad (OA&E), 943, 1094
Oberender, Herman, 240
Obregón, Alvaro, 698
observation cars, 834, *834*, *854*, 1123
Occident elevator (Duluth), *477*
Occidental and Oriental Steamship Co., 679
occupations, **759–775**; nonoperating employees, 764–775; operating employees, 760–764; railroad departments, 759; women, *see* women in railroading. *See also specific occupations by name*
oceangoing railcar ferry services, 670–671
oceangoing steamship services, 677–680
Ocos Railway (Ferrocarril Ocos), 507
The Octopus (novel), 13, 529, 595, *596*, 980
Of Time and the River (Wolfe), 595
Office of Defense Transportation (ODT), 1121–1122
Office of the Secretary of Transportation (OST), 357
Official Guide of the Railways, 35–36, **775–777**, *776*, 908, *1002*, 1003
The Official Railway Equipment Register, 463
Official Territory (rate territory), 915
off-track equipment, use of, 868
Ogdensburg & Lake Champlain Railway (O&LC), 214, 874
Ohio & Indiana Railroad, 438
Ohio & Mississippi Railroad, 163, 438; George Brinton McClellan, 689; route map, *1171*; train robberies, 340
Ohio & Pennsylvania Railroad, 438, 864
Ohio Electric Railway, 238
Ohio River, *1090*; bridge over (Cincinnati), 255; bridge over (Louisville), 256; bridge over (Metropolis), 256–257, 260; bridge over (Sciotoville), 48, 258, 260; canalization, 1090; railcar ferry services, 669; traffic on, 1088
Ohio River & Charlestown Railroad, 292
Ohio River Railroad, 164
Ohio Southern Railroad, 360
oil fuel, steam locomotives, 607
oil pipelines, 871–873
oil transport, 871–872, 1054, *1122*; coastal, 1091; unit trains, 1071
Oil Transportation Association, 871
O'Keeffe, Anita Ten Eyck, 1128
Old Colony Railroad, 309–310, 502, 629, 743
Old Faithful Inn, 903
Old Ironsides, 159, 187, 1007
Old Point Comfort resort, 904
old-age pensions, 905–906
Olmstead, Frederick Law, 132, *132*, 136, 141, 309, 318
Olympian Hiawatha, 226, 443
Omaha Road. *See* Chicago, St. Paul, Minneapolis & Omaha Railway
omnibus drivers, 26
omnibus injunctions, federal (1894), 576
"On the Atchison, Topeka and the Santa Fe" (song), 514

On the Twentieth Century (stage play), *1045*
On Time, 149
Onderdonk, Andrew, 195
O'Neal, A. Daniel, 77
O'Neill, Eugene, 1047
on-line data input terminals, 327–328
Ontario No. 1 (railcar ferry), 668
Ontario No. 2 (railcar ferry), 668
Ontario Northland Railway (ON), **778**, *1193*; tourist trains, 908
on-the-job accidents, 691
open bridge decks, 266
open caisson, 268
open stock cars, *103*
open-decked railcar ferries, 671
Opening of the Wilderness, 145
opera and the railroads, **778–780**. *See also* entertainment tours
opera houses, 1047
operating brotherhoods, 1063
operating costs, 894
operating departments, 759, 1112
operating employees, 759–764; African American, 435; women, 1112–1113. *See also* occupations
operating expense statistics, 894, 1134–1135, 1138–1139, 1141, 1143, 1150–1152. *See also* railroad costs
operating practices, 37–52, 516–517, 821–830, 846–857; commuter railroads, 321–322; management structure, 663; monopolistic practices, 920; promoting efficiency, 680; timeline (1820 to 1850), 39–43; timeline (1850 to 1870), 43–49; timeline (1870 to 1900), 50–52; timeline (1900 to today), 53–64
operating property, taxes on, 540, 1040
operating resources, list of, 785–786
operating rules and enforcement, **780–785**. *See also* government regulations
Operation Lifesaver, Inc., 340, 498
operational problems, passenger service, 847, 850, 852
operations planning and analysis, **785–789**
operations research, 329
operations testing, 783
operators (agents), 766, *771–773*, 887–888; express messengers, 26, 634, 765 (*see also* U.S. Railway Post Office); living space in terminals, 24–25, 1116; Railway Express Agency, 911–912
operators (block), 771
operators (telegraphers), 770, 1113
operators (towermen), 771–773, *772–773*
opportunity cost, 895
opposed-piston (OP) diesel engines, 374–375, 442
optimized train control (OTC), 970
Orange & Alexandria Railroad, 164
Orange Blossom Special, 156, 853, 955, 957
oranges and orange juice, 105, 1071
Orco (towboat), *1090*
Order of Railroad Telegraphers, 1111–1113

Order of Railway Conductors and Brakemen, 576
Oregon & California Railroad, 1083
Oregon & Transcontinental Railroad, 1083
Oregon Central Railroad, 1083
Oregon Electric Railway, 996
Oregon Railway & Navigation Co., 1083
Oregon Short Line (OSL), 1066, 1067
Oregon Steamship Co., 1083
Oregon Trail, 831
Oregon Trunk Railway, 996
Oregon-Washington Railroad & Navigation Co., 1067
organizational structures, 662–665
organizations, railroading, 874–876. *See also specific organizations by name*
organized labor, 576–580
organized tours, 22
Orient. *See* Kansas City, Mexico & Orient Railroad
"Orient Express" mysteries, 242
Oriental Limited, 851
originating yards, departures from, 1059–1060
Oriol, Lucas de, 835
orphan trains, **789**
Orris, Don, 77
Ortner Freight Car Co., 205
Orukter Amphibolos (dredge), 437
Osborn, C. R., 833
Osborne, Richard B., 254
O-scale models, 909
Osgood Bradley Car Co., 883
OSs (copy operators), 393
Oswald, F. Jordan, 659
Otis Elevating Railway incline, 539
Otto cycle engine, 363
Our Hospitality, 241
out-of-face tamping, ballast, 657
outside hostlers, 761
outsourcing: maintenance and repair work, 623; refrigerator car operation, 105–106
overbuilding of railroad systems, 492
overhead carrier systems, 474
overhead costs, 895
overhead distribution of current, 405
The Overland Limited, 20–21, *682*, 851, 993
Overland Trail, 831
Owen, Albert Kimsey, 571
Owen, Chandler, 913
Owen, Robert Dale, 792

PA-1 model engines, *371*
Paccar, Inc., 204
Pacific Car & Foundry Co., 204
Pacific Coast Shays, 1031
Pacific Electric Railway (PE), 337, 421, **790–791**, 977; route map, *1185*
Pacific Express, 256
Pacific Fruit Express Co. (PFE), 105–106
Pacific Great Eastern Railway (PGE), 169. *See also* BC Rail
Pacific Iron Works, 601
Pacific Limited, 1094
Pacific Mail Steamship Co., 679

Andrew Carnegie, *see* Carnegie, Andrew; Angel of Resurrection monument (30th Street Station), 717; Army-Navy football contest trains, 986; B&O, competition with, 164, 865, 870; Baltimore & Ohio Railroad, rivalry with, 483; Broad Street Station, 136, *137*; *Broadway Limited*, 58, 65, 242, 851, 1120; bus operations, 519; car production, 204; Cassatt, *see* Cassatt, Alexander Johnston; during Civil War, 274; Class PD standard coach, *825*; communities of interest, 13, 307, 439–440; commuter services, 312, 314–315, 318, 321, 417, 977 (*see also* Southeastern Pennsylvania Transportation Authority); competitive initiatives, 682; *Congressional Limited* derailment (1943), 94; Cuyahoga Falls collision (1940), 94; dining cars, twin-unit, 624; Edward H. Williams, 1108; electric locomotives, fueling, *607*; electrification, 16, 56, 410, 417–421, 865, 1102; Enola Yard, 280, *288*; establishment as major railroad, 437–439; Fleet of Modernism of 1938, passenger trains, 623; George B. Roberts, 315, 917; GG-1 electric locomotive, 623; gravity switching, 281–282; great railroad strike of 1877, 576–577; Henry H. Houston, 315; Herman Haupt, 515; Horseshoe Curve, 249; Hudson River tunnel (New York), 272; *Increase the Crop per Acre*, 102; intermodal transport, 552; J. Edgar Thomson, *see* Thomson, J. Edgar; James Miller Symes, 70, 1038–1039; Jersey City trainshed, 135; L. Stanley Crane, *see* Crane, L. Stanley; locomotive test plant, 611, *612*; locomotives, builder, 543; Main Line of Public Works, 39, 42, 111, 383–386, 1049; merger with New York Central, *see* Penn Central Railroad; Mount Union derailment (1910), 92, 94; *New York–Chicago Limited*, 851; NYC, merger to form Penn Central Railroad, 744; NYC, rivalry and merger, 678, 719, 746; passenger ferry services, 674–677; passenger traffic, 858–859; *Pennsylvania Limited*, 993; Pennsylvania Station (Pittsburgh), 129; railcar ferry services, 667, 669, 672; Railroad YMCA (Philadelphia), 1118; Raymond Loewy, 623; Reading Co., competition with, 918; Reading Terminal, 129, 136, 314; recreation cars, 624; regional management structure, established, 663; role in preservation, 874; route map, *1166*; Samuel M. Vauclain, 160–161, 370–371, 602, 987, 1013, 1082; Samuel Rea, 917; signaling system, *964*; steamship lines, transatlantic, 678; steel passenger cars, *826*; Stuart T. Saunders, 952; Thomas A. Scott, 953; vacuum tubes testing, 1068; Virginian Railway, interest in, 1084; Wabash, acquisition of, 1085; wall calendars, 148–149; Washington Terminal Co., 1087; William Wallace Atterbury, 156–157, *157*, 182, 682, 1120; Woodruff sleeping cars, 1115; World War II effects, 1123–1124. *See also* Camden & Amboy Rail Road

Pennsylvania Special, 56

Pennsylvania Station (New York City), 57, 136, 211, 312, 314, 623, 629, 740, 865; demolition of, 875; statues, 714; World War II weekend traffic, *1123*

Pennsylvania Station (Pittsburgh), 129

Pennsylvania truss, 254, 446

Pennsylvania-area routes, *1160*, *1162*

Penobscot & Kennebec Railroad, 638

Penoles Mining Co., 299

pension plans, 631

pensions, 905–906

Penydarran Iron Works, 1065

Peoria & Eastern Railway, *609*

percent grade. *See* grade of route

Pere Marquette Railway, 217, 218, 230, **866–867**; Chesapeake & Ohio merger, 440; *Pere Marquette 12* (railcar ferry), 671; railcar ferry services, 667–668, 671; Van Sweringen ownership, 230, 1079

performing arts and the railroads. *See* cinema and railroads; music; *entries at* opera; radio and television; theater; theatrical touring companies

Perkins, Charles E., 452, **867–868**

Perkins, James Handasyd, 867

Perkins, Sarah Hart (Elliott), 867

Perkins, Thomas H., 502

Perlman, Alfred E., 70, 71, 168, 394, 665, 748, *868*, **868–869**, 953, 1128

Perry Cutoff, 155

Pershing, John J., 157

personnel departments, 759

personnel statistics, 16, 1132, 1139, 1144

Petersburg Railroad, 155

Petit truss, 446

petroleum shipments, 871, 1054; coastal, 1091; unit trains, 1071; during World War II, 1122

Pettibone-Mulliken Speed Swing, *651*

Pevler, Herman, 432

Philadelphia, 480

Philadelphia, Baltimore & Washington Railroad, 865, 1087

Philadelphia, Germantown & Norristown Railroad: commuter services, 314; *Old Ironsides*, 159, 187, 1007

Philadelphia, Wilmington & Baltimore Railroad (PW&B), 164, 229, 315, 827–828, 865, **869–870**; commuter tickets, 309; route map, *1158*; *Susquehanna* (railcar ferry), 666

Philadelphia & Columbia Railroad, 1049

Philadelphia & Reading Railroad, 43, 177, 202, 213, 917–918; Black Rock tunnel, 269; J. P. Morgan, 719; John E. Wootten, 1115; reorganizations, 719; train speed, 993. *See also* Reading Co.

Philadelphia commuter railroads, 314–315

Philadelphia Museum, 159

Phillips, Henry W., 597

Phillips Pipe Line Co., 872

Phillips-Judson Company, 22

Phoebe Snow, 352

Phoenix (steamboat), 1034

phosphate cars, covered, 468

photographers: Andrew J. Russell, 942; O. Winston Link, 750; William Henry Jackson, 565. *See also* art

physical geography. *See* geography and railroad development

physicians, employment of, 691

The Picturesque B&O, 817

piecework, 544, 545–547

Piedmont & Northern Railway, **870–871**, *1170*

Piedmont Railroad, 981

Piedmont Traction Co., 870

Pierce, Franklin, 793

piers, bridge, 267

piggyback service, 62, 75, 235, 236, 550, 550–551, 553, 1054; circus transport, 244. *See also* intermodal freight

Piggypacker, 553

Pigs Eye Yard, *289–290*

Pike, Zebulon, 791

Pikes Peak Line, 298–299, 908

pilgrim trains, 990–991

pilot train, 876

pilots (cowcatcher frames), 41, *44*, 1008; invention of, 397; riding, 21

pilots (employees), 764

pin pullers, 764

Pinkerton, Allan, 339

Pinsch, Julius, 826

pin-turning machines, 618

Pioneer, 827, 881

Pioneer III designs, 184

Pioneer Zephyr, 183, *183*, 221, *365*

Pipe Line Cases, 872

pipelines, **871–873**

piston asynchronization, 1005

piston valves (spool valves), 1012

Pitcairn family, 315

pits, ash, 608

Pittsburgh, 491

Pittsburgh, Bessemer & Lake Erie Railroad, 204–205

Pittsburgh, Cincinnati & St. Louis Railway, 864–865

Pittsburgh, Cincinnati, Chicago & St. Louis Railroad, 865

Pittsburgh, Columbus & St. Louis Railroad, 1097

Pittsburgh, Fort Wayne & Chicago Railroad (PFW&C), 274, 439, 1050; Isaac Dripps, 397; John Bloomfield Jervis, 568

Pittsburgh & Lake Erie Railroad (P&LE), 165, 168

Pittsburgh & Steubenville Railroad, 864

Pittsburgh & Western Railroad, 164

Plain Automatic Air Brake, 1069, 1097–1099

Plamer, William J., 717

Plan Sexenal (1935–1940), 698

planers, 617–618

Planes, Trains and Automobiles, 242

Planet, 1007

planned industrial communities, 880, 882, 884–887

planning and development departments, 759

Plant, Henry, 155

Plant System, 155

Plasser American Corp., 659–660

Plassman, Ernest, 714

plastic ties, composite, 643

plastics, fiber-reinforced, 457

plate girder bridges, 258, 265

plate (disc) wheels, 46

plateway, 1000

platform cars. *See* flatcars

platform floats, 672

platform scale, 442

platform trucks, 473

platforms, moving, 474

Plattsburgh & Montreal Railroad, 1108

plays, 594

Plumb Plan, 440, 579

Plumbe, Glenn E., 928

Plumbe, John, 792

Plummer, J. C., 384

Plymouth Locomotive Works, 603

plywood-sheathed boxcars, 456

pneumatic brakes, 1099–1100

pneumatic caisson, 60, 256, 268

pneumatic interlocking plants, 967

Pneumatic Railway Signal Co., 113

pneumatic shield method, 526

Pocahontas Coalfields, Norfolk & Western, 750

Pocket Edition of the Official Railway Guide, 777

Pocket List of Railroad Officials, 777

Pocono (4-8-4) engines, 353

poetry, 34

poets, 596

Point of Rocks station (Maryland), 133–134, *134*, 1116

Polar Bear Express, 778, 908

policemen, railroad, 145, 338–340

poling yards, 281

political corruption, 540

political geography, 489–492

political impact of railroads, 491–492

political leaders, travel by, 989–990

Ponce & Guayam Railroad, 879, *1186*

Pontchartrain Railroad, 435

Pony Express, 634

pony trusses, 263

pool agreements, 681

pooling arrangements, 681

Poor, Henry Varnum, 718, **873**

Pope, John Russell. *See* Alexandria & Washington Railroad

Pope Pius XI, 480

poppet valves, 1028

Poppy, 242

popular literature, 596–598

population dispersion and shifts, 492

population size, freight traffic and, 1053

Port Arthur, Texas, 572

Port Authority Trans-Hudson (PATH), 313

Port Royal & Augusta Railroad, 212

Portec, Inc., 205

Porter, Edwin S., *34*, 239

Porter, Henry H., 398

porter-brakemen, 764

porters (sleeping car), 19, 765, *855*, 881; black employees, 436, 913; Brotherhood of Sleeping Car Porters (BSCP), 436, 876, 913

Portland, Saco & Portsmouth (PS&P), 176

Portland & Kennebec Railroad, 638

Portland & Ogdensburg Railroad, 638–639, **874**; Saco River bridge (Maine), *255*

Portland & Seattle Railway, 996. *See also* Spokane, Portland & Seattle Railway

Portland Locomotive Works (Maine), 600

Portland Terminal Co. (Maine), 638

Portsmouth & Roanoke Rail Road, 344, 954. *See also* Portsmouth & Roanoke Rail Road

position-light signals, 965, *966*

positive train control (PTC), 84, 969–970

post and stringer trestles, 253

Post Cereal Company, 33

post roads, 634

postage stamp, "Casey" Jones, 715

postal service. *See* U.S. Railway Post Office

posters (advertising), 148, 681

postmaster generals, 634, 637

pot hopper cars, 456

Potomac & Piedmont Coal & Railroad Co. *See* West Virginia Central & Pittsburgh Railway

Potomac Yard (Washington, D.C.), 280

Potter Law, 501

poultry (stock) cars, 469

Powder River Basin, 233, 295

Power, Thomas F., Jr., 1109

power brakes, 93

power hand brakes, freight cars, 460

power of electric locomotives, 406

power sawing metal, 617

power sources, railroad shops, 545

power strokes (internal combustion engines), 363

power supply for electrification, 405

power tamping tools, 659–660

power trucks, *485*, 622

A Practical Plan for Building the Pacific Railroad, 794

Prairie Oil & Gas, 871

Pratt, Thomas W., 254

Pratt, Zadock, 792

Pratt trusses, 254, 263, 625

Preamble Express, 988

preblocking. *See* blocking theory

preference tags, 1119

preliminary route surveys. *See* surveying railroad location

Preliminary System Plan, 72, 73

premier passenger trains, 747, 849. *See also* luxury accommodations

premium traffic, 786

Presbrey, Frank, 681

Prescott, C. H., 32

preservation, 36, **874–876**

preservationists, 736

President, 827

presidential campaigns and travel, **876–878**, 989

Presidents' Conference Committee, 1075

press offices, 878–879

Pressed Steel Car Co., 201, 203, 204–205

pressed-steel freight cars, 456

pressed-steel railway car seats, 181

presses, mechanical, 618

pressure-differential cars, 468

prestressing, 261

Price, Bruce, 132, 142

price competition, end of, 682

pricing, 896–897, 915

primary RCOs, 764

Primghar, Iowa, 32

Prince Edward Island, 195

Prince Plan, 168, 440

principle of seniority. *See* seniority

prints. *See* art

private automobile travel, 518

private club cars, 309, 1123

private detectives, 339

private funding of railroads, 581

privatization of Mexican railroads, 701–702, 704–705

privatization of Mexican railways, 1145–1147

Procor Ltd., 206

produce. *See* fruit and vegetable transport

product identification, 681

production of locomotives. *See* locomotive builders; statistics on North American railroads

Professional Air Traffic Controllers Organization (PATCO), 358

professional sports. *See* sports and the railroads

profile grinding, 651

profitability statistics, 1134–1135, 1150–1152; World War II effects, 1125

Progress (passenger car), 831

Progressive Era regulations, 13–15

Progressive Railroading (periodical), 1051

progressive system of car repair, 547

Prohibition, 18–19

projects vs. routine maintenance (accounting), 97

promoting settlers, 986–988. *See also* land grants

promotion. *See* marketing and promotion

property taxes, 540, 1040

Prospectus for Change in the Freight Rail Industry (1978), 444

Prosperity Special, 987

prostitution, 22

Prout, Henry G., 1051

Providence & Stonington Railroad, 1105

Proviso Yard (C&NW), *473*

Prussian State Railways, 361

public affairs, 878–879

Public Broadcasting System (PBS), 890, 909

public image, 29, 924. *See also* corporate identification and image

public investment, 919

public land grants. *See* land grants

public relations, **878–879**

public transportation, 320, 685, 739–741

Railroad Safety Act of 1970: FRA Track Safety Standards, 656–657; track quality, FRA jurisdiction, 650

railroad shops, 127, 128, *612*, 613, 614–622; diesel locomotives, *620*, 620–622; industrial practice, 543–548; Meadows Maintenance Complex (NJ Transit), 740–741; outsourcing, 623, 658–659, 661; productivity, 545–547; resource planning, 788; roundhouses and turntables, 613–614; safety, 547; track maintenance, *see* maintenance-of-way (MOW). *See also* maintenance

The Railroad Station (stage play), 1044

railroad stations. *See* stations and terminals

Railroad Stories. See Railroad Magazine

railroad strikes. *See* strikes

railroad suburbs and towns, 7, 30, 68, 130, 858; Chicago, 315 (*see also entries at* Chicago); depots in, 27; names of, 32; slang terms, 145; town names, 32

Railroad Sunset, 147

railroad terminals. *See* stations and terminals

Railroad Train, 147

railroad valuation, 1075–1076

Railroad Valuation Act of 1913, 14, 1075

railroad writers, 596–598

Railroad YMCAs. *See* YMCA, Railroad Department

railroaders. *See* occupations

railroading heritage, 817, 874–876

railroad-operated passenger ferry services, 674–677

railroads, impact on: Civil War, 489; energy sources, changes in, 492; geography, 491–492; globalization of manufacturing, 492; highway development, 492; industry dispersion, 492; motor vehicle transportation, 492, 518–522; overbuilding, 492; Panama Canal, 492; population dispersion, 492; trucking industry, 492, 518–522; World War I, 518, *519*; World War II, 520

Railroads' War Board (RWB), 1072, 1119

railrogues, 10

rails (employees), 759

rails (track). *See* track and track technology

Rails-to-Trails Conservancy, 36

RailTex, Inc., 214–215

rail-truck competition, 518–522

Railvans, 455, 553

The Railway (Manet), 146

Railway Act of Canada, 340

Railway Adjustment Board, 782

Railway Age (periodical), 1051–1052

Railway & Locomotive Historical Society (R&LHS), 875, 907

Railway Association of Canada (RAC), **907**

Railway Clauses Consolidation Act of 1851, 541

Railway Electrical Engineer (periodical), 1052

Railway Employees Department (RED), 579

Railway Engineering & Maintenance (periodical), 1052

railway enthusiasts, 35, 874–876, **907–911**

Railway Exchange, Chicago, 129

Railway Express Agency (REA), 552, 634–635, **911–912**; American Railway Express Co. becomes, 634

Railway Guide, 777

Railway Labor Act of 1926, 16, 579, 759, 784, 959, 1114

Railway Locomotives & Cars (periodical), 1052

Railway Mail Service, 634–636; competition from trucks, buses, and airlines, 634–635

railway mail service employees, 765

Railway Mechanical Engineer (periodical), 1052

Railway Post Office. *See* U.S. Railway Post Office

Railway Purchases & Stores (periodical), 1052

railway signaling. *See* signaling

Railway Signaling & Communications (periodical), 1052

Railway Signaling Club, 964

Railway System Controls (periodical), 1052

"Railway to Heaven" (allegory), 722

"Railway to Hell" (allegory), 722

Railway Track & Structures (periodical), 1051, 1052

railway trade magazines. *See* trade publications

Railway Wage Commission, 1073

Railway War Board, 1107

railways, elevated, 484

Rain, Steam and Speed—The Great Western Railway, 146

Rainhill trials, 1032

Raleigh & Augusta Air-Line Railroad, 954–955

Raleigh & Gaston Railroad, 954–955

Ralph railroad stories, 34

Ralston, William, 319

Ralston Steel Car Co., 205

Ramon (passenger & railcar ferry), 669

ramp loaders, 773

ramped diamond crossings, 646

ranching, encouraging, 304. *See also* livestock

Rand McNally & Co.'s *Western Railway Guide*, 777

Randolph, A. Philip, 436, 876, **913**

Randolph, Epes, 389

Randolph Street terminal (Chicago), 317

Rankin, W. I., 871

Rankine cycle, 1014–1015

Raritan & Delaware Bay Railroad, 213

rate agreements, 914

rate clerks, 769

rated tractive effort. *See* traction motors

rates and rate associations, 500–501, 506, **913–917**; discrimination and regulation, 914, 920–921, 925–927, 933, 934 (*see also* Elkins Act of 1903; Hepburn Act of 1906; Staggers Act); farmer complaints, 920; rate territories, 915

Raton Pass, 355

The Rattler, 147

Rau, William H., 33

Ray, George J., 352

Raymond, Walter, 902

Rea, Samuel, 157, **917**, 1119; statue at Pennsylvania Station (New York), 714

reach rod (steam locomotive), 1012

readers (for tracking trains), 1059

Reading Co., 12–13, 417, **917–919**; commuter services, 314, 315, 977; *Crusader*, 312, 832, 919; electrification, 56, 420; Graver's Station (Philadelphia), 141; passenger ferry services, 675–676; route map, *1159. See also* Philadelphia & Reading Railroad

Reading Terminal, Philadelphia, 129, 136, 314

Regan, Ronald, *81*

real estate departments, 759

Realco, 552

Reamer, Robert C., 735

rear brakeman, 760

rear-loading railcar ferries, 671

rebating, 681, 924n

Rebel streamliner, 115

recapture of property, 1076

receivership, 935–938

receiving yards, 282

reciprocity in purchasing, 887–888

reconnaissance (for railroad location), 41, 247–248

Reconstruction Finance Corp. (RFC), 16, 168, 223, 868

recruitment of senior executives, 665

rectifiers, 61, 404, 407, 419, 865, 1103; ignitron rectifiers, 61, 380–381, 405, 407, 1103, *1104*; mercury-arc rectifiers, 405, 407, 1103

redcaps, 436

Redfield, William C., 791

Reed, Charles, 139, 747

Reed, John S., 152, 153

Reed & Stem, 138–139

reefers. *See* refrigerator cars

Reeves, Samuel, 256

references for additional reading, 1220–1223; *Manual of the Railroads of the United States*, 873

refined oil products. *See* oil transport

reflective targets, switch, 645

refrigerator cars, 62, 103–107, *104*, 462, 464–465, 1054; ice dock men, 770

refueling. *See* locomotive fueling

regenerative braking, 407

Regiomontono (The Mountain Region), 700

Regional Rail Reorganization Act (3R Act), 72, 74, 331, 357, 444, 933, 962. *See also* regulation

regional railroads, 279, 962–963

Regional Transportation Authority (RTA), 753

regulation, **919–935**; Act to Regulate Commerce, 921–922; Elkins Act of 1903, 922, 924–927; Hepburn Act of 1906, 922, 925–927; Interstate Commerce Commission, 922–924; Mann-Elkins Act of 1910, 927;

regulatory reform, 932–935; Transportation Act of 1920, 927–931; Transportation Act of 1958, 931–932. *See also* government regulations

Reid, Gil, 33

reinforced-concrete arch bridges, 259, 261, 262

Reistrup, Paul, 79

Relay, Maryland, viaduct monument, 712–713

relief organizations for injured workers, 945

religion: gospel trains, 1127; influence of railroad workers, 30–31; special trains, 990–991; Sunday service restrictions, 1035; YMCA sponsorship, 1126

remote control operation, 378–379, 764

remote-control operators (RCOs), 764

Renaissance cars, 842

Reno, 241

RENPA (Railroad Employees National Pension Association), 905

Rensselaer & Saratoga Railroad, 353

Rentschler, George A., 590

Rentschler, Walter A., 590

reorganization and receivership, 444–445, 719, **935–938**. *See also* consolidation of railroads

repair and maintenance facilities. *See* maintenance; railroad shops

Report of the Secretary of the Treasury on the Subject of Public Roads and Canals (1808), 482

repositioning crews, 788

representation, union, 576

Republic, Ohio, wreck (1887), 92, 94

resilient rail fasteners, 646

resistance, testing train, 608

resort hotels, 514, 681, 900–904; Montezuma (resort hotel), 514, 903

resource decisions. *See entries at* operations planning and analysis

responsibility with authority, delegating, 663

restaurants in stations, 26, 513–514. *See also* railroad hotels and resorts

restraint of trade. *See* Sherman Antitrust Act

restricted and special-handling lists, 1060

restrictive signal indications, 966

restructuring the railroads. *See* deregulation of railroad industry

retarders (classification yards), 60, 281–282, 285–288, *289*; gravity yards (gravity switching), 39, 281–282, 290, 353, 535

retiring rooms, 849

retraining. *See* training of railroad workers

revenue adequacy levels, 933–934

revenue classifications, 278–279

revenue statistics, 1134–1135, 1138, 1141, 1143, 1150–1152; passengers and passenger service, 858–859

reverse commuting, 321

reverse curves, 252

reverse links (steam locomotives), 1012

revolution, Mexico, 698

revolution of 1910 (Mexico), 698

Rexall train, *987*, 988

RF-based train control, 969, 971

RF-CBTC systems, 971

Rhodes Curry Co., 202

Rice, Edmund, 335, 502

Richards, Ralph, 946

Richardson, Henry Hobson, 132, *132*, 309, 713

Richmond, Fredericksburg & Potomac Railroad (RF&P), 345, **938–939**, 955; Civil War destruction, 939; CSX acquisition of, 280; route map, *1169*

Richmond, Petersburg & Carolina. *See* Seaboard Air Line Railway

Richmond & Allegheny Railroad, 217–218

Richmond & Danville Railroad (R&D), 212, 955, 981

Richmond & Petersburg Railroad, 155

Richmond Basin (Virginia), 292

Richmond Locomotive and Machine Works, 600

Richmond Terminal, 13, 981–982

Rideau Canal, 193–194

rider humps, 282

ridership. *See entries at* passenger

riding the blinds, 21

riding the rods, 21, 947

right of seniority. *See* seniority

Rights of Trains, 781

rights of way, rail, 581–582

rigid frame engines, 1006, 1013, 1014

Riley, James Whitcomb, 596

rim-bearing swing bridges, 266

Ringling Brothers, 245–247

Rio Grande Southern Railroad (RGS), *731*, **939–940**

Rio Grande Western Railroad, 306, 814–815

Rio Grande Zephyr, 356

Ripley, Edward P., 151

Ripley, William Z., 334, 440, 929, **940–941**

River in the Catskills, 145

river landing inclines, 674

River Line (Southern New Jersey), 189

river systems. *See* water transportation

Rivers and Harbors Act of 1902, 1090

riveted construction, 458

riveting, 617

Roach, Hal, 241, 242

Road Gang (highway lobby), 359

road improvements, 17, 61, 555–556, 1054; assistance to farmers, 103; encouraging, 987; federal expenditures for highways, 359

road locomotives, 161

Road of Anthracite. *See* Delaware, Lackawanna & Western Railroad

road switcher locomotives. *See* switchers and switching systems

roadbeds, 252, 640, 657; maintenance cars, 470

Roadrailer, 218

Road-Railer service, 701

RoadRailers, 554

roadside trolley intercity lines, 560

roadway, primary, 641

roadway workers, 773

robber barons, 11, 494, 512

robberies. *See* train robberies

Robert Fulton, 614

Robert Garret & Sons, 482–483

Robert Stephenson & Co., 1006

Roberts, George B., 315, 917

Robinson, Edwin Arlington, 596

Robinson, Harry P., 342, 1051

Robinson, John M., 955

Rock Island Bridge Co., Hurd v., 591

Rock Island Line. *See* Chicago, Rock Island & Pacific Railroad

"Rock Island Line" (song), 724

Rockefeller, Andrews & Flagler (RA&F), 450

Rockefeller, John D., 398, 450–451, 510, 871, 921

Rockefeller, Percival, 348

Rockefeller, William, 504, 523, 756

Rocket, 39, 227, 228, 247, *857*, 1006, 1032, 1033

Rocket Freight Service, 228

Rockville Bridge, near Harrisburg, 148

Rocky Mount yard, 280

Rocky Mountain Railtours, 908

Rocky Mountains pass, 248

Rocla Concrete Tie, 643

rod locomotives, 626

Rodgers, Jimmie, 35

rodmen, 770

Roebling, John Augustus, 526, **941**. *See also* Niagara River bridge

Roebuck, Alvah C., 637

Roff, J. A., 723

Roger Williams, 837

Rogers, Albert Bowman, 192, 195–196, **942**

Rogers, Charles J., 243

Rogers, Henry H., 504, 1084

Rogers Locomotive Works, 600

Rogers Pass, 196, *250*, 942

rolled (edge) rail, 40

roller bearings, freight car, 461

rolling resistance, 291

Rollins, James, 795

roomette cars, 832–833, *838*

Roosevelt, Franklin D., 402–403, 479–480, 513, 883, 1124; presidential rail travel, 876–878

Roosevelt, Nicholas, 1034

Roosevelt, Theodore, 13, 101, 307, 390, 436, *480*, 504, 693, 720, 756, *926*; presidential rail travel, 876

Root, James, 386

Rose, Ted, 33, 149

Rosenfeld, Leah, 1113–1114

Rosenwald, Julius, 637

Roskob, John J., 1128

Rossiter, Thomas Pritchard, 145

rotary snowplow, *649*

rotary-dump equipment, 474

roundhouse architecture, 128–129. *See also* workers' housing

roundhouse foremen, 770

roundhouses, 543, 613–614

Rouse, Ervin, 725

route I-95, 556

route maps, series of, *1154–1196*

"The Route of Phoebe Snow" slogan, 352

speed runs, 64, 984–985
"speeder" cars, 442
Speedy, 242
Spencer, Samuel, 614, 719, 982; statue
    of, 717
Spencer Shops, 614–615
Speno International, 893
Speno Rail Services, 661
Sperry, Elmer A., 93, 650, 891–892
Sperry Rail Service. *See* rail defects,
    detection of
spike pullers and inserters, 660
spikes, 646
spiral curves, 252
spiral retarders, 286
spiral routes (to maintain low grades), 249
Spiral Tunnels, 196
Spirit of 1776, 987
"The Spiritual Railway" (allegory), 722
spoilage. *See* refrigerator cars
Spokane, Portland & Seattle Railway, 171,
    995–996; John F. Stevens, 1035; route
    map, *1181*; united into Burlington
    Northern, 185, 222
Spokane International Railroad, 1067
spokespersons, 878
sports and the railroads, 986, **996–998**;
    horse racing, 986, 998
Sportsman, 218
spot tamping, ballast, 657
Sprague, Frank J., 404, *408*, 408–409, 484,
    559, **999**
Sprague, Lucian C., 706
Sprague Electric Railway & Motor Co.,
    483–484
spread trucks, 44
spreadsheet programs (software), 330
springers (arches), 261–262
Sprint project, 77
SPV2000 car (Budd), 324
S-scale models, 910
SST (Supersonic Transport) program, 358
Stager, Henry W., 1126
Staggers Act (Staggers Rail Act of 1980),
    77, 82–83, 95, 97, 122, 329, 332, 358,
    444, 567, 924, 934, 956, 962, 1036,
    1058. *See also* deregulation of railroad
    industry; regulation
stainless steel, 182, 457; welding, 831
Stampede Pass (Stampede Tunnel), 172,
    249, 490
Standard Code, 782, 1055–1057
standard gauge, 5, 8, 516, 531, 584–585,
    638, 640, 703, 727, **999–1001**; Canada,
    196; conversation from narrow gauge,
    730; Mexico, 696–698; MoPac, begin-
    ning in 1869, 707; opposition to, 489.
    See also narrow gauge
standard light electric locomotives, 485
Standard Oil Co., 450–451, 871–872,
    921, 926
Standard Oil of New Jersey (SONJ), 872
Standard Railroad of the South. *See* At-
    lantic Coast Line Railroad
standard refrigeration (before refrigerator
    cars), 105
Standard Steel Car Co., 883
Standard Tank Car Co., 202

Standard Time, 8, **1001–1003**; General
    Time Convention, 149, 1055; *Official
    Guide of the Railways*, 776; Standard
    Time Act of 1918, 1003. *See also*
    timetables
standards: Advisory Mechanical Commit-
    tee, 741; grade-crossing warnings,
    497–498; manufacturing, 601–602;
    track, 650 (*see also* standard gauge);
    track construction, 642, 644, 645
Stanford, Leland, 343, 527, 529, 570,
    795–796, 798, 800, 807, **1003–1004**
Stanlaus, Penrhyn, 352
Stanley, William, 1097, 1101
Stanton, Edwin M., 275
Staple Bend Tunnel, 111, 269
Starbuck, W. H., 32
Starling, David, 816
Starrucca House, 133
Starrucca Viaduct, *148*, 253, *253*
Starrucca Viaduct, Pennsylvania
    (painting), 145, 147
state fairs, to attract colonists, 304
state funding vs. federal funding, 581
state public works, 554–558
state regulation. *See* government
    regulations
Staten Island Ferry, 677
Staten Island Railroad, 417, 1081
Staten Island Rapid Transit Railway,
    164, 677
state-owned railroads, 540
station agents. *See* agents
station call letters, 771
station floats, 672
station masters, 773
stationary dynamometer tests, 1015
stationary engineers, 773–774
stationary test plants, 611
stations, broadcast, 771
stations and terminals, 850; agents' living
    space, 24–25, 1116; architecture,
    48–49, 126–128, 133–135, 138–141;
    capacity analysis, 787; Chicago, 819; in
    cinema, 242; commuter services and,
    309 (*see also* commuter services);
    electrification, *see* electrification; for
    freight, *see* freight terminals; images
    of, *302–303*; intermodal transporta-
    tion, 471, 472, 479; for locomotive
    servicing, *see* railroad shops; passenger
    casualties, 944–945, 947; for passenger
    service, *see* passenger service; preserv-
    ing the heritage, 874–876; public image,
    29; social history and impact, 23–27;
    steam locomotive terminal design,
    613; transfer service between, 818–819;
    unruly and rude employees, 850.
    *See also specific stations or terminals by
    name*
statistics on North American railroads,
    1131–1153; Canadian railways,
    1139–1143; decline in passenger traf-
    fic, 51, 53, 58, 737–738, 1134, 1151;
    market share, 521; Mexican railways,
    1144–1147; passengers and passenger
    service, 858–861; U.S. railways, 38,
    1132–1138

Statue of Liberty dedication address, 360
statues, railroad, 714, 717
statutory regulation. *See* government
    regulations
steam dome, 1004
steam heating, 51, 821, 824, 829–830
Steam Locomotive Boiler Regulations, 1010
steam locomotive design, 54, 1008–1021;
    articulated configurations, 1017–1019;
    final improvements, 1027–1028;
    second-generation, 1015–1017; super-
    power articulateds, 1022–1024; valve
    gear (steam locomotives), 44, 1005,
    1010–1013, 1027–1028
steam locomotive maintenance and repair,
    615–620, *616*. *See also* maintenance;
    railroad shops
steam locomotives, 3, 508, 568,
    1004–1031, 1010–1013; boiler safety,
    1010; components of, 1004; com-
    pound steam distribution, 1013; diesel
    locomotives vs., 548 (*see also entries at*
    diesel); early, 194, 568, 1006–1008;
    firemen, *see* firemen; flanged wheels,
    1000; fueling, *604–607*, 604–608;
    geared, 587, 600, 626–627, *730*; golden
    age of, 1024–1027; obsolescence of, 68
    (*see also* diesel-electric locomotives);
    Richard Trevithick, Jr., 437, 1006,
    1064–1065; roundhouses, *see* round-
    houses; slang terms for, 144; special
    service, 1030–1031; steam turbines,
    1028–1030; streamliners, *see* stream-
    liners; Super-Power, *see* Super-Power
    concept; testing, 608–612; water sup-
    plies, 604; wheel arrangements, 1005;
    World War II, impact on, 602. *See also
    Baldwin Locomotive Works; specific lo-
    comotives by name or designation*
steam locomotives, specific: Allegheny
    (2-6-6-6) engines, 1006, 1025, *1026*,
    1027; American Standard (4-4-0)
    engines, *44*, 53, 160, 1006, *1008*, 1008,
    1013; Atlantic (4-4-2) engines, 53,
    1015, *1017*; Berkshire (2-8-4) engines,
    56, 1006, *1019*, 1019–1020, *1020*,
    1025–1027, 1027; cab forward (4-8-8-2)
    engines, 161, 1023, 1024; camelback
    engines (Wootten boilers), 353, *619*,
    1010, *1010*, 1115; Challenger (4-6-6-4)
    engines, *58*; Columba (2-4-2) engines,
    1015; Consolidation engines, 44, 53,
    160, 443, *619*, 699, *729*, 1006, 1009,
    1009, 1013, 1015; Decapod (2-10-0)
    engines, 1006; Grasshopper locomo-
    tives, 163, *1007*, 1108; Hudson (4-6-4)
    engines, 119, 198, 1006, 1022, *1022*,
    1025, 1027, *1045*; Mastodon (4-8-0)
    engines, 1006; Mikado (2-8-2) en-
    gines, 54, 161, 162, *616*, *729*, 1006,
    1015–1017, *1016*, 1019; Mogul (2-6-0)
    engines, *729*, 1006, 1009; Mohawk
    (4-8-2) engines, 1017, 1019; Mountain
    (4-8-2) engines, 54, 117, 1006, 1015,
    1017; Niagara (4-8-4) engines, 56, 119,
    614, 1026; Pacific (4-6-2) engines, 54,
    117, 1006, 1015–1016, *1016*; Prairie
    (2-6-2) engines, 1006; Santa Fe (2-10-2)

steam locomotives (*continued*)
  engines, 54, 1006, 1013, 1015, 1016;
  Ten Wheeler (4-6-0) engine, *160*, 1009,
  1013; Texas (2-10-4) engines, 56, 1006,
  1020, 1025–1027, 1043; Triplex (2-8-8-
  8-4) engines, 1006, 1018; Yellowstone
  (2-8-8-4) engines, 161, 399, 1006,
  1023, 1023, 1027
Steam Passenger Service Directory, 875
steam wagon, 1034
steamboats and steamships, 3, 38, 858,
  1088, 1091; as ferries, 674–677 (*see also*
  ferry services); intermodal transport,
  554; international lines, 677–680; specific vessels, *see specific ships or boats by
  name;* Stevens, Col. John, 1033–1034.
  See also water transportation
steam-powered logging equipment, 625
Steamtown National Historic Site, 875
Stearns, Isaac Ingalls, 32
steel arches, 262
steel axles, 45
steel box girders, 261
steel erectors, 774
steel freight cars, 456–460, *463*
steel manufacture and industry, 54,
  256, 261; Bessemer process (steel), 45,
  48, 256
steel passenger cars, 826–828, 882–883
steel rails, 8, 10, 48, 645; Plimmon H.
  Dudley, 397–398; stress measurement
  (stremmatograph), 397
steel shipments during World War II, 1122
steel shoulders, 642–643
steel tie plates, 642
steel ties, 643
Steele v. Louisville & Nashville R.R.
  (1944), 435
steeple-cab locomotives, *562*
Steffee, Donald M., 994
Stephen, George, 192, 195, 503, 523, 755
Stephenson, George, 3, 39, 640, 791, 1000,
  1006, **1031–1033**
Stephenson, Robert, 255, 261, 346–347,
  526, 614, 791, 1006, 1032, **1033**
Stephenson valve gear design, 1011
Sterlins, Walley (fictional), 170
Stern, Allen, 139
Stern, George, 75–76
stern-loading railcar ferries, 671
Steubenville accommodation, 1097
Stevens, Brooks, 834
Stevens, Col. John, 188, 296, **1033–1034**,
  1088
Stevens, Isaac I., 754
Stevens, John F., 717, **1034–1035**
Stevens, Robert L., 5, 188, 347, 643–644
Stevens, Simon, 697
Stevens Pass, 249, *422*, 1034
Stevenson, Burton Egbert, 597–598
stewards. *See* dining cars and on-board
  dining
Stewart, Alexander T., 314
stick lighters (barges), 672
Stickney, A. B., 27, 171, 234–235
stiffness, track, 640–641
Stilgoe, John R., 594
Stillman, James, 504

Stilwell, Arthur E., 571–573, 699
stock cars, 462, 469
stock companies, 1046
Stockton & Beckwith Pass Railroad, 1093
Stockton & Darlington Railway, 4, 39,
  1032, 1033, 1048
Stone, Amasa, Jr., 528
Stone, Livingston, 446
Stone & Madigan Circus, 243
Stone & Webster Engineering Co., 1044
stone bridges, 253. *See also entries at*
  bridge
stop signal, 1057
storage yards, 478
"storage-in-transit" yards, 478
storehouses, supply, 888
Storey, William Benson, 151
stories, railroad, 596–598
storm damage, NWP (1964), 757–758
Stotesbury, Edward T., 315
Stourbridge Lion, 112, 353, 568, 899, 1007
Stover, John F., 858
Stowell, Charles, 91
straight air brake, 1097–1099; automatic,
  1069
straight-line system of car repair, 547
strain gauge, 612
strap, cast-iron, 643
strap rail, 40
strategic planning and analysis. *See* operations testing
Strategic Rail Corridor Network (STRAC-
  NET), 300
Stratemeyer, Edward, 598
Streamliner, 58
streamliners, 21, 58, 65–66, 156, 362, 830,
  830–833, *833*, 866, 883, 994, *1067*; *400*
  streamliners, 32, 58, 232, 994; coach,
  632; Electroliner, *562*; *Hiawatha*, 58,
  226, 830, 994, 1015; M-10000 streamliners, 58, 362, 425, 1066–1067;
  Seaboard Air Line, 955
Street Railway Journal (periodical),
  1052–1053
streetcar service, 542–543, 560
stremmatograph, 397
stress analysis in trusses, 255
Strickland, J. F., 1043–1044
Strickland, William, 39
strikes: American Railway Union (1894),
  504; blacklisting of strikers, 578–579;
  BLE strike against CB&Q (1988), 577;
  construction workers (1869), 806;
  D&H strike (1922), 631; GN shopmen
  (1922), 505; great railroad strike
  (1877), 576–577; Harriman Lines
  strike (1911–1915), 579; Homestead
  strike (1892), 210; LSE freight-service
  employees (1937), 580; national railroad strike (1877), 483; Pennsylvania
  Railroad strike (1877), 210; Pullman
  strike (1894), 9, 351, 379, 504,
  577–579, 876, 880–881, 886; shopmen's strike (1922), 579, 756; Switchmen's Union strike (1892), *578*
stringer-tracks, 643
strings, rail, 644
Strong, Daniel W., 794

Strong, William Barstow, 151
Strother, David Hunter (Porte Crayon), 146
Stroupe, Carolyn, *67*
Struble, J. B., 1068
stub (head) stations, 127, 136
A Stubborn Cinderella (stage play), 1046
Studebaker Corp., 121
students, 764
Sturdy, John Rhodes, 34
Sturges, Preston, 525
S-Type roomettes, 832–833
subballast, 641
subgrade, 640
submarines, vulnerability to, 1091,
  1118–1119, 1122
subscription club cars, 309. *See also* club
  cars
substructure, track, 640–641
substructures, bridge, 267
Suburban Station, Pennsylvania
  Railroad, 321
suburbs: commuter services and, 309,
  311–312, 321 (*see also* commuter ser-
  vices); electrification, 417. *See also* rail-
  road suburbs and towns
subways: in cinema, 242; GE, 484
Sud Pacífico de Mexico. *See* Southern
  Pacific of Mexico Railroad
Suez Canal, 979
Suisun Bay, California, 669
Sullivan, Thomas, 386
Sullivan's Travels (movie), 525
Summit Cutoff, 55
Summit House (Mt. Holyoke), 539
Sundance Kid (Harry Longabaugh), 341
Sunday service restrictions, **1035**
Sunrise of Sherman Hill, 147
Sunrise Special, 314
Sunset Limited, 980; Mobile accident
  (1993), 94, 96
Sunshine Special, 993
Super Chief, 151–152, *152*, 182, 853, 994
Super Continental, 199
Super Domes, 833
super railroading doctrine, 168
Superb, 480
superchargers, 363
supercolliers, 294, *294*
superelevation, 252
superheaters, 1013, 1014, 1082
Superliner cars, *80*, 739, 840
Super-Power concept, 56, 117–119, *118*,
  589–590, 600, 1015, 1022–1024, *1023*,
  1027; Texas & Pacific Railway, 1043
Supersonic Transport (SST) program, 358
supplies, railroad, 803, 887; storage of,
  887–888
support blocking, 283–284
Surface Transportation Board (STB), 278,
  1035–1036. *See also* Interstate Commerce Commission
surgeons, 774
surveying railroad location, 41, 247, 540;
  Pacific Railroad, 793, 811–812
suspension bridges, 257, 263, 265
suspension for compliance failure,
  783–784
suspension trusses, 254–255, 446

suspensions of record, 784–785
Susquehanna (railcar ferry), 666
swamps, 489, 490
Swan, Henry, 355
Swanson, Gloria, 1046
Sweet, Blanche, 239
Swift, Gustavus, 103
Swift, Tom (fictional), *598*
swing brakemen, 760
swing bridges, 259, 266–267
swing-motion trucks, 461
switch frogs, 52
switch ladder, 645
switch lists, 1059
Switchback gravity line, 535
switchbacks, 249, 625
switchers and switching systems, 120, 279,
    442–443, 590, 602, 645, 1037–1038;
    automatic, 1069; Baldwin Locomotive
    Works, 162; classification yards, *see*
    classification yards; push-pull train
    operation, 63, 322–323
switching and terminal railroads,
    1037–1038
switchmen, *764*, 764, 1064; African
    American, 435; slang terms for, 144;
    union strike (1892), *578*
swivel lead trucks, 568
Symes, James Miller, 70, **1038–1039**
Syndicate, 1046–1047

T-1 Class 4-4-4-4 engines, 1028
T&TO signaling, 965
tabloid shows, 1047
Tabulating Machine Co., 325–326
Tacón, Miguel, 347
taconite, 186
tactical assignment. *See* operations
    planning and analysis
Taft, Robert, 877
Taft, William Howard, 13, 190, 927
Tafts tunnel (Connecticut), 269
Talbott, E. H., 1051
Talcott, Andrew H., 696
Talgo, 115, 835, 842
Tallahassee Railroad, 435, 955
tampers, 659–660
tamping, 657, 659–660
Tanana Valley Railroad, 110
tandem compound engines, 1013
tangent retarders, 286
tangential-geometry turnouts, 645
tank cars, 46, 202–203, 206, 456, 462, 464,
    468, *469*, 469, 871–872
Tank Cars, 147
tapes, magnetic, 327
target-shooting yards, 281, 287–289
tariffs, 915. *See also* rates and rate
    associations
Tate, Daniel, 1098
Taunton Locomotive Manufacturing
    Co., 600
tax accounting practices, 98
taxation, **1040–1041**; avoiding sales tax,
    887–888; exemptions from, 540, 1041;
    Tax Reform Act of 1976, 36
taxi drivers, 26
Taylor, B. F., 28

Taylor, Frederick Winslow, 545–546
Taylor, Moses, 506
Taylor Machine Works, 553
Taylor Switch & Signal Co., 113
Taylorites, 545
Teague, Walter Dorwin, 830
team tracks, 472
Teasdale, Sara, 596
technology: air transportation, 108, 109;
    automatic equipment identification
    (AEI), 61, 329, 340, 430, 969; bridges,
    see entries at bridge; computerized op-
    erations and control systems, 567; as
    dangerous, 944, 947, 949–950 (*see also
    entries at* accidents); electrification,
    404–407 (*see also* electrification); im-
    pact on management, 664; import of,
    38–39, 1006–1008; mergers and con-
    solidations, 960; operations testing,
    783; rail defect detection, 891–894; re-
    frigerator cars, 103, 106–107; remote
    control operation, 379, 764; rise in,
    594; for safety, 1061–1062 (*see also*
    safety); signaling, *see* signaling; tele-
    graph, *see* telegraph technology
technology timeline, 37–52; 1820 to 1850,
    39–43; 1850 to 1870, 43–49; 1870 to
    1900, 50–52; 1900 to present, 53–64
Ted Bates & Co., 738
Tefft, Thomas, 133
Tehachapi Earthquake (1952), 392
Tehachapi Loop, 249, 526
Tehachapi Mountains pass, 248
Tehuantepec Ship Railroad, 402
telegraph technology, 8, 25–26, 207–208;
    invention of, 403, 720; orders by, *see*
    train orders; telegraphers (operators),
    770, 1113. *See also* dispatchers
telephones for dispatching, 393
Telfener, Georgia, 32
Teller, Grif, 148–149
Teller, Henry, 728
Tellier, Paul, 191, 200
Temiskaming & Northern Ontario Rail-
    way (T&NO), 778
tender pusher system, 534–535
tenders, 607, 1005
Tennessean, 982
Tennessee Central, 344
Tennessee Pass (Denver & Rio Grande),
    249, 355
Tennessee River canalization, 1090
tent communities, 1116
tent shows, 1047
Ten-Wheeler, Clinchfield Railroad, 292
Terminal Information Process System
    (TIPS), 329
Terminal Railroad Association of St. Louis
    (TRRA), 1037–1038, **1041–1042**
terminal railroads, **1037–1038**
terminals. *See* stations and terminals
terminating yard arrivals, 1062
Terre Haute, Alton & St. Louis Railroad
    (THA&StL), 1114–1115
Terre Haute & Indianapolis Railroad
    (TH&I), 439
Territorial Enterprise, 170
territories, seniority, 959

Tesla, Nikola, 1097, 1101
test cars, 608–612
test plants, locomotive, 611
testing brakes, 1060
testing employees for compliance, 783
testing facilities, 444, 517, 609–611
testing rails for detects, 648–651,
    891–894
test-to-failure bridge testing, 256
Texarkana & Fort Smith Railroad, 572
Texas, 124–125
Texas & New Orleans Railroad (T&NO),
    674, 778, 980
Texas & Pacific Railway (T&P),
    1042–1043; Grenville M. Dodge, 396;
    Jay Gould, *see* Gould, Jay; locomotives,
    1043; railcar ferry services, 672; route
    map, *1180*; Thomas A. Scott, 954;
    transfer bridges, 674
Texas Co., 871
Texas Electric Railway (TE), **1043–1044**,
    1180
Texas Millionaires Derby Special, *998*
Texas railroads, headquarter require-
    ments, 306
Texas Special, 952, 993
Texas Traction Co., 1043
Texas-Mexican Railroad, 573, 697
Thames River tunnels, 270–271
theater, **1044–1046**. *See also entries at* opera
Theatre Train (Wabash Railway), 22
theatrical touring companies, **1046–1048**.
    See also entertainment tours
thermite welding, 644, 645, 652
thermodynamics of steam engines, 1014
Theroux, Paul, 596
third-rail systems, 405, 411, 484, 747;
    electric locomotives for, 410
thirty-inch gauge railroads, 516
Thomas, Philip Evan, 584, **1048–1049**
Thomas Cook Overseas Timetable, 777
Thomas Viaduct, *147*, 163, 253, 584,
    712–713, 1048, 1116
Thompson, Frank, 210
Thompson, J. G., 678
Thomson, J. Edgar, 154, 207, 208, 515,
    663, 814, 863–864, 954, **1049–1050**
Thomson-Houston Electric Co., 1077,
    1103. *See also* General Electric Co.
Thoreau, Henry David, 593–594
Thorne, George R., 637
Thornton, Henry Worth, 190–191,
    198, 891
Thrall Car Manufacturing Co., 205, 206
3R Act (Regional Rail Reorganization
    Act), 331, 357, 444, 933, 962
3-2 seating, 322–323
three-cylinder locomotives, 117–118
three-foot gauge railroads, 507,
    515–516, 728
three-hinged arches, 262
three-phase electrification, 404
three-truck freight cars, 454
through trusses, 127, 263
throughput. *See* efficiency, need for
Thunder Bay plant (Bombardier),
    174–175
Thunderhawk, 226

ticketing and fare collection, 847, 851–852; commuter rail services, 308, 321; free passes, 681, 682, 847; portable ticket booths, 688; scalping tickets, 851; ticketless riders, *see* hoboes; unscrupulous agents, 851–852. *See also entries at* fare

Tidewater Railway, 1084

Tidewater Southern Railroad, 1067, 1094

tie down clerks, 769

tie machines, 660

tie maintenance and renewal, 654–656

Tie Masters, *656*

tie plates, 642

Tier One environmental regulations, 383

Tier 2 EPA standards, 612

ties, 641–643; automated tie renewal, 654, 656; concrete, 84; wooden, 40–41

Tigrett, Isaac B., 509, 510

Tilden, Samuel J., 540

Tillman, Charles D., 722

timber bridges, 253–254, 259, 261. *See also entries at* bridge

timber harvesting, 624–625

timber shed, interior, *803*

timber ties, 641–642, 656

timber trusses, 625

Time Exposure (book), 565

time slips, 1062

time standardization. *See* Standard Time

time zones, 8, 1003

timekeepers, 774

timeliness. *See* delays

timetables, 776, 780, 847, 851, 852, 1055–1056; Mexican Railway Co., Ltd., *696*; operations planning and analysis, 785–789; signal operation by, 965. *See also* delays; *The Official Guide of the Railways*; rulebooks; schedules; Standard Time

Timken Roller Bearing Co., 1021

tinplate trains, 909

tipple, 474

tire replacement, 619

tobacco shipping, 1053

Tocqueville, Alexis de, 35

TOFC/COFC. *See* container-on-flatcar (COFC) services; intermodal freight; trailer-on-flatcar (TOFC) services

toilets, enclosed, 184, 849

Toledo, Peoria, & Western Railroad disaster (1887), 90

Toledo, St. Louis & Western Railroad, 1079

Toledo & Illinois Railroad, 1085

Toledo & Wabash Railway, 1085

toll bridges. *See entries at* bridge

toll roads, 111, 920, 1000

Tom Swift and His Electric Locomotive (book), 598, *598*

Tom Thumb, 5, 163, 336, 614, 1007

tonnage graphs, 1060

Tonopah & Goldfield Railroad, **1050**

Tonopah & Tidewater Railroad (T&T), **1050**

tools, shop, 544, 617–618

top-down management style, 663

topographic route surveys. *See* surveying railroad location

Toronto, Hamilton & Buffalo Railway (TH&B), **1051**

Toronto, Ontario, route maps, *1192*. *See also* Greater Toronto Transit Authority (GO Transit)

Toronto Union Station, 142, 1037

total loading (bridges), 261

Total Operations Process System (TOPS), 329

Toucey, John M., 178

touring entertainment. *See* entertainment tours

tourism, 849, 851–854, 856–857, 875; railroad tours, 735

Tower, Charlemagne, 398

tower architecture, 128

tower operators, slang terms for, 145

tower skidders, 625

towermen, 771–773, *772–773*

Town, Ithiel, 254

town names, 32

towns. *See* railroad suburbs and towns

toy trains, 35, 909–911

traceable costs, 895–896

track and time system, 395

track and track technology, 39–40, 52, 84; FRA standards, 646, 650, 656–657; gauge, *see* track gauge; grading, *see* grade of route; heavy-haul loads, impact on, 517; location and construction, *see* civil engineering; maintenance and wear, 84, 470, 661 (*see also* maintenance-of-way); pear rail, *40*, 41, 644; rail garrisons, 300; rail grinders, 661; rail grinding, 651; rail hardness, 645; rail heater, *652*; rail joints, 644; rail length, 644; rail pads, 647; rail sidings, 472; rail strings, 644; rail threading equipment at work, *651*; rail warming machines, 660; rail-profile grinding, 651, 661; steel, *see* steel rails; testing and inspection, 608, 648–651, 891–894; T-rail shape, *see* T-rails. *See also* technology; ties; track construction

track bed, 640–641

track circuit crossing warning devices, 496

track construction, 640–648; alignment, 252, 657; gauge, *see* track gauge; grade, *see* grade of route; grade crossings, *see* grade crossings; rails, 643–645, 651; T-rails, *see* T-rails; UP track workers, *804*. *See also* track and track technology

track footage, 787

track foremen, 770

track gauge, 5, 632, 638–640; broad, *see* broad gauge; converting track to another gauge, 727; interurban electric railways, 560–561; logging railroads, 625; narrow, *see* narrow gauge; standard, *see* standard gauge

track geometry cars (TGC), 648–650, *649*

track indicator device, 397

track laborers, 770

track lining, 657

Track Loading Vehicle (TLV), 650

track location and construction. *See* civil engineering

track mileage statistics, 1132, 1139–1140, 1144–1145, 1148

track modulus, 640–641

track pans, 604, *605*

track standards, FRA, 650

track stiffness, 641

track tamping, 659–660

track warrants, 394, 782, 783, 1058–1059

track-circuit design, 965, 968–969

tracking systems. *See* train control

trackmen, 774

Tracks Ahead (television series), 909

trackside water tanks, 604

traction motors, 54, 382, 407, 484, 1014; maintenance, 622; measuring tractive force, 608

tractor shipments, 1054

tractor-trailer system, 474

Tracy, Tom, *431*

trade publications, 907–908, **1051–1053**; model railroading, 911. *See also* popular literature

trade restraint. *See* Sherman Antitrust Act

trade-offs, 786

trades workers, 544

traffic associations, 914–915

traffic categories and trends, 53, 66, **1053–1055**; accidents and, 91–92, 94–95; agricultural, encouraging, 99–107; decline in passenger traffic, 51, 53, 58, 737–738, 1134, 1151; passenger service, 858–861; river system transportation, 1088; statistics on, 1133–1134, 1136–1138, 1141–1142, 1151–1152; by transportation mode, 521; World War II effects, 61, 1054, 1118–1120, 1122. *See also* volume statistics

traffic control. *See* train control

traffic departments, 759

traffic pools, 914

Trailer Train (TTX), 552

trailer-on-flatcar (TOFC) services, 62, 75, 235, 236, 550, 550–551, 553, 1054; circus transport, 244

trailers for intermodal use, 550–553

trailing truck (steam locomotives), 1005

T-rails, 5, 40–41, 188, 643–644

trails for compliance failure, 784

The Train (film), 242

Train, George Francis, 797, 803

train accidents. *See entries at* accident

The Train Boy (Alger), 597

train cars. *See specific types of cars by name*

Train Collectors Association, 35

train control, 64, 486, 567, 663, 708, 966–971, **1055–1059**; ABS (automatic block signaling), 53, 59, 93, 113, 965–966, 1056–1057, 1120–1121 (*see also* Union Switch & Signal Co.); accident prevention regulations, 93, 95; car scheduling, 206–207; centralized, *see* centralized traffic control; direct (DTC), 782; manual block system, 394, 965, 1056; orders, *see* train orders;

positive (PTC), 84; timetables, *see* timetables; track-warrant control, 782

train dispatchers. *See* dispatchers

train heritage, preserving, 874–876

Train Master, 443

train movement, **1059–1063**. *See also* train control

train museums. *See* museums, railroad

Train of Tomorrow, 833

train orders, 49, 393–394, 718, 780–782, 965–966, 968, 1055–1056

train robberies, 340–342, *341*

train safety. *See* safety

train service employees, 759; discipline, 784; women, 1112. *See also* employees; occupations

train sheets, 393

train speed. *See* speed

train stations. *See* stations and terminals

train tamping, ballast, 657, 658

"Train Whistle Blues" (song), 35

train wreck songs, 723

Train X (passenger cars), 218, 835–836, 840–842

train-end markers, 780

train-ferry services, 59, 135–136

training of engineers, 899

training of farmers, 102

training of railroad workers, 785, **1063–1064**

trainmen, 9, 18–19, 760, 764; fatality rate, 945; women as, *1112*, 1113

Trains (magazine), 35, 598, 907

trains, social impact of, 18–23

Trains Unlimited (television series), 909

Trains Unlimited Tours, 908

trainshed architecture, 126–128, 135–138

tramps, 526, 723. *See also* hoboes

tramways, 194

Trans-Alaska Pipeline System (TAPS), 872

Transamerica, 552

transatlantic steamship lines, railroad operated, 677–680

Transbay Tube, 273

transcontinental railroads, 504, 529, 754–757, 808; building of, 640; Theodore Dehone Judah and, 570. *See also* Pacific Railroad

transfer bridges, 672, 674

transfer car float, 672

transfer houses, 473

transfer tables, 614

transformers (electric), 405

Transit Expressway, 1104

Transit Journal (periodical), 1053

transpacific steamship lines, railroad operated, 677–680

transport yards, 478

Transportacíon Ferroviaria Mexicana (TFM), 573, 701

Transportation Act of 1920, 15–16, 67, 93, 97, 440, 923, 927–931, 940, 961, 1073, 1076, 1120; communities of interest, 307. *See also* government regulations; regulation

Transportation Act of 1940, 357

Transportation Act of 1958, 686, 931–932. *See also* government regulations; regulation

Transportation Communication International Union (TCU), 436

Transportation Control System (TCS). *See* train control

transportation departments, 759

Transportation Engineering Services, 971

Transportation Equity Act for the 21st Century (TEA 21) of 1997, 687

transportation funding, 581

transportation improvements, 555

transportation legislation. *See entries at* government regulations

transportation planning, 482

Transportation Technology Center (TTCI), 444, 517, 646

Transportation Test Center (TTC), 150

Transportation-Communication Employees Union (TCEU), 1114

transposing rails in curves, 651

transverse fissures, 92, 891

transverse layout, back-shop, 618

Travel (poem), 34

Traveler's Aid office. *See* National Traveler's Aid Society

Travelers Office Guide of the United States and Canada, 776

Travelers' Ready Reference Guide, 777

The Traveling Salesman (stage play), 1046

Travellift, 553

Trenton Locomotive Works, 202, 203, 397

trespasser fatalities, 944, 946, 947, 949

trestles, 261, 625

Trevithick, Richard, Jr., 437, 1006, **1064–1065**

Trevithick engines, 1006, 1032

triangular sorting, 286

trilevel automobile carriers, 62, *467*

trim crews, 283

Trinity & Brazos Valley Railway (T&BV), 220, 306

Trinity Industries, 201, 203, 205–206

Trinity River Bridge (Dallas), 1042

trip plans. *See* car scheduling

trolley freight service, 580

trolley museums, 875

Trollope, 593

troop transport. *See* military transportation

Troy & Boston Railroad, 176–177

Troy & Greenfield Railroad, 176–177, 337; Hoosac Tunnel, *see* Hoosac Tunnel

trucking industry, 518, 518–522; effects on rail traffic, 492; Indiana Railroad, 543; intermodal use, 550–553. *See also* motor vehicles

Trucking Industry Regulatory Reform Act of 1994, 924

trucks (freight car), 453–455, 461, 464, 467; maintenance (*see also* maintenance; railroad shops)

Truesdale, William H., 352

Truman, Harry S, 876–877

Truman Bridge, 226

trunk lines, 6–8; railroad hotels and resorts, 900–901. *See also specific trunk lines by name*

trusses, 254–258, 262–265, 446, 528, 625; Howe trusses, 254, 264, 528. *See also entries at* bridge

TTC (Transportation Test Center), 150

TTX, 552

tube rattlers, 618

tubular bridges, 255

tug-barge railcar ferry services, 666–674

tugboats, 672

Tully, John, 526

tumble-down passenger car design (Loewy), 624

Tunkhannock Viaduct, *55*, 55–56, 259, 260, 352

tunnels (railroad), 56, *270*, 489, 489–490, 629–630; electrification, *see* electrification; engineering of, 269–273; loop or spiral routes, 249; pneumatic shield method, 526; STRACNET report, 300. *See also* civil engineering; *specific tunnels by name*

Tuohy, Walter, 218

turbine electric engines, 667, 1030

turbine-powered trains, 840–842, 855–856

turbochargers, 376, 377

TurboTrain, 218, 840–842, 862, 995

Turner, J. M. W., 146

turnouts, 645–646

turnover, employee, 947

turnpikes, 2, 37. *See also* road improvements

turntables, 613–614

Tuscola & Saginaw Bay Railroad (T&SB), 126

Twain, Mark, 595

TWC (track-warrant control), 782

12-wheeled freight cars, 454

Twentieth Century (stage play), 1046

The Twentieth Century (train), 242

20th Century Limited, 21, 56, 58, 147, 148, 247, *682*, 747, *748*, *829*, 851, 869, 993, 1046

Twenty Questions case, 551

Twin Zephyr, 221, *857*, 994

two-cycle diesel engines, 442

two-foot gauge railroads, 639, 727, 732

two-hinged arches, 262

Twohy Brothers Co., 204

two-level passenger cars, 839–840

two-stroke cycles (internal combustion engines), 363

two-stroke diesel engines (GM), 621–622

two-valve system (steam locomotives), 1011

two-wheel trailing trucks, 160

typists (clerks), 769

Tyson, Henry, 1109

ultralightweights, 834–836

ultrasonic rail testing, 650, 892–894

Uncle Tom's Cabin (tent show), 1047

Under the Gaslight (stage play), 1045

undercutting, ballast, 661

underframes: freight cars, 456, 458–460; passenger cars, 826

underwater tunneling, 270–271

Underwood, Frederick, 433

unfettered competition, 681

Vee configurations, 363
vegetable and fruit transport, 105, *106*
vegetation control, 658
vehicle transportation, 518–522
ventilation, passenger cars, 821, 824. *See also* air-conditioned cars and trains
ventilation in engine houses, 128
ventilator cars, 463
Veracruz to San Juan River Railway (Ferrocarril de Veracruz al Rio de San Juan), 695
Vermilion Range, 398
Vermont & Canada Railroad, 214
Vermont & Massachusetts Railroad, 176
Vermont Central Railroad, 874, 1106
Vernon, Edward, 776–777, *1002*
vertical alignment of track, 252, 657
vertical curve, 252
vertical lift bridges, 259
vertical-plane couplers, 842
vessels. *See* ships, specific; water transportation
vestibule passenger cars, enclosed, 821–823, *825*, 882
vestibules, 51, 945
VIA Rail, 63–64, 199; Renaissance cars, 842; route map, *1188*
Viaduct on Baltimore and Washington Railroad, 147
viaducts. *See entries at* bridge
Vicksburg, Shreveport & Pacific Railroad (VS&T), 572, 982; IC acquisition, 532; *Natchez* (steamboat), *558*
Vicksburg, Shreveport & Texas Railway, 572
Victoria, Queen, 526
Victoria Bridge, 189, 255, 1033
videotapes, 890–891, 908–909
Vietnam War railroads, 300
Viking, 759
Villa, Francisco "Pancho," 157, 698
Villard, Henry, 403, 409, 483, 755, **1083**
violations of operating rules, 783–785. *See also* operating practices
Virginia & Truckee Railroad (V&T), **1083–1084**
Virginia Central Railway, 217; Blue Ridge Tunnel, 269, 272
Virginia City, 170
Virginia Hot Springs resort, 904
Virginia Midland Railway, 164, 981
Virginia Railway Express, 322, 323; route map, *1163*
Virginia resorts, 904
Virginian Railway, 443, **1084**; electrification, 56, 415, 420, 421; Norfolk & Western merger, 69–70, 952, 1084; route map, *1168*
Vista-Dome cars, 184, 221, 684, 736–737, *837*
Vital Harmon Logic Controller (VHLC), 972
Vivian, Andrew, 1065
Vogt, Axel S., 611
Volpe, John, 71, 79
volume statistics, 1132, 1139–1140, 1144–1145. *See also* traffic categories and trends

voussoirs (arches), 261–262
Vulcan Iron works, 601
VUR-505 rail inspection car, 893

W. B. Flint (steamship), 196, 678
W. W. Cole New York & New Orleans Circus, 244
Wabash, St. Louis & Pacific Railroad, 921, 1085
Wabash & Erie Canal, 1085
Wabash Cannon Ball, 1086
"Wabash Cannon Ball" (song), 35, 723
Wabash 400 engines, *373*
Wabash National Corp., 455
Wabash Pittsburgh Terminal Railway, 1085, 1092
Wabash Railway, 12, 23, 126, 569, 889, 938, **1085–1086**, 1092; commuter services, 318; DT&I, purchase of, 360; hospital, *692*; James Frederick Joy, 569; railcar ferry services, 668; route map, *1168*; Theatre Train, 22
Wabtec Corp. *See* Westinghouse Air Brake Co.
Wadley, William, 154, 212
wages: relief for injured workers, 945; wartime increases in, 1120, 1124
Wagner, Robert, 905–906
Wagner, Webster, **1086–1087**
Wagner Act (1935), 579
Wagner Palace Car Co., 824
Wagner Tractor, 553
wagon shows, 242–243
Wagons-Lits (sleeper cars), 666, 882
Waite, Morrison R., 501
waiters (dining cars), 765
"Waiting for a Train" (song), 35
waiting rooms in stations, 24, 127, 140; Pennsylvania Station (New York City), *57*
Walker, Will (fireman), 391
Walker, William David, 215
walking tracks, 947
Wall, George L., 588
wall calendars, 148–149
Wall Street, 312
Walschaerts, Eddie, 1011
Walschaerts valve gear design, 1011–1012, *1012*
Walsh, Margaret, 518
Walters, William T., 155
Wanamaker, John, 637
war dead, monuments to, 717
War Emergency Pipeline, 872
War Production Board (WPB), 120, 1025, 1027; General Limitation Order L-97, 426, 427, 602
Ward, Aaron Montgomery, 637
warehouse architecture, 129–130
Warman, Cy, 597
warning systems: computerized, 497–498; at grade crossings, 495, *495–498*, *496*; warning gates, *497*. *See also* safety
warrants, 782
Warren, Earl, 185
Warren, James, 254
Warren, Whitney, 747
Warren & Wetmore, 139, 142

Warren City Tank & Boiler Works, 202
Warren trusses, 254, 263
Warrington, George, 81
Washburne, William, 540
washing locomotives, *623*, 661, *771*. *See also* maintenance
Washington, D.C. area routes, *1163*
Washington, George, 3, 557
Washington & Southwestern Line, 993
Washington Terminal Co., **1087**
Washington (D.C.) Union Station, 164, 1037, 1087
waste heat, using, 1014
watchmen, 770, 775
water availability, 605
water exhaust, 604–605
Water Level Route, 248–249
water service, 759, 775
water supply, 604–606
water tanks and towers, 128, *604*
water transportation, 3, 17, 37–38, 58, 489, 1054, **1087–1091**; barge operation, 672; car floats, 478, 666–667, *668*, 672, *673*; ferryboats, 309, 666–677, 1094 (*see also* ferry-rail services); flatboats, 1088; Great Lakes traffic, 666–668, 1088, 1089, 1091; oceangoing steamship services, 677–680; passenger ferry services, 674–677; railcar ferry, *see* railcar ferry services; regulation of, 923; specific vessels, *see* ships, specific; World War II and coastal shipping, 1091, 1122. *See also* canals
water treatment, 605
waterfront freight terminals, 478
Waterloo, Cedar Falls & Northern Railroad (WCF&N), **1091–1092**, *1179*
waterspout and coaling tower, *605*
Watkin, Edward, 194
Watkins, Hays, 74, 218
Watt, James, 899
Watts, May, 36
waybill entry operator, *328*
waycar. *See* caboose cars
wayside signaling, 780, 783, 963. *See also* signaling
wear, track, 661
wear plates, concrete ties, 647
web members (trusses), 263
websites, 330. *See also* Internet
Webb, Simeon, 569, 715
Webb, William S., 1087
"Wedding of the Rails" (photo series), 942
weed control, 658
Weeden Manufacturing Co., 909
weed-spraying, 658
weight, rail, 644
Weinman, Adolph A., 714
welders, 770
welding, 261, 458, 468, 617, 644, 651–652, 654, 831
welfare capitalism, 547
well flatcars, 466
Welland Canal, 1089, 1091
Wellington, A. M., 697
Wells, Fargo & Co., 342
Wells, Reuben, 296
Wells Fargo (film), 240

work songs, railroad, 724–725
workers. *See* employees
"Workers' Administration" (Mexico), 698
workers' housing, **1116–1118.** *See also* living space; YMCA, Railroad Department
work-related injuries, 691
World War I, 15–16; effects on rail traffic, 870, 1054 (*see also specific railroads by name*; traffic categories and quantities); motor trucks, 518, *519*; women in railroading, 1110–1111
World War I and the railroads, **1118–1120**
World War II, 16–17, 60–61, 65; effects on coastal shipping, 1091; effects on manufacturing, 602; effects on rail traffic, 61, 520, 1054 (*see also specific railroads by name*; traffic categories and trends); gauge variation as defensive measure, 1000; motor vehicle transportation, 520; Nickel Plate Road, 742; women in railroading, 1111
World War II and the railroads, **1120–1125**
"The World's Rail Way" (exhibit), 874
World's Railways (Pangborn), 817
worldwide transportation, 677–680
Worthington Corp., 121
"The Wreck of Old 97" (song), 35, 723
wreck songs, train, 723
wreck trains, 470
wrecks. *See entries at* accident
Wright, Benjamin, Jr., 112, 346, 346–347, 568
Wright, Frank Lloyd, 138
Wrightsville & Tennille Railroad, 212

writers, 593, 593–598; Hungerford, Edward, 528–529. *See also* literary works; *specific writers by name*; theater
written orders. *See* train orders
wrought iron pipelines, 871
wrought iron T-rails, 643–644
Wyeth, N. C., 148

X forms (train orders), 782
Xplorer, 836
XTRA Corp., 552

Y class 2-8-8-2 engines, 1024
Y forms (train orders), 782
Yakima Valley Transportation Co., 1067
Yale-Harvard game train, 986, 998
yard air tests, 1059
yard blocks, 206
yard checks, 429
yard clerks, 769
yard conductor, 764
yard departures and arrivals, 1059–1060, 1062
yard facility architecture, 128–129
yard service employees, 759. *See also* occupations
yardmasters, *775*, 775; responsibilities of, 1060, 1062; slang terms for, 145; women as, 1113
yardmen, 9, 764
Yazoo & Mississippi Valley Railroad, 531
yellow dog contracts, 579
The Yellow Mail (movie), 239, 597
Yellowhead Pass, 189, 195, 196, 197
Yellowstone National Park, *734*, *734*, 903

YMCA, Railroad Department, 30, 1118, **1126–1128**
Yoakum, Benjamin F., 230, 951
Yonah, 124
Yosemite National Park, 734
Yosemite Valley Railroad, 735
You Can't Go Home Again (Wolfe), 595
Young, Brigham, 800
Young, Robert R., 218, 219, 553, 708, 747–748, 832, 834–835, 840, 869, *1128*, **1128–1129**
"The Young American" (essay), 594
Young Men's Christian Association (YMCA), 30, 1118, 1126–1128
The Young Mill-wright and Miller's Guide, 437
The Young Train Dispatcher (Stevenson), 597–598
The Young Trainmaster (Stevenson), 598
Young valve gear design, 1012
Younger brothers, 341

Zapata, Emiliano, 698
Zephyr, 16, 57–58, 177, 182–183, 221, 362, 425, 830, 853, 994, 1066; *Afternoon Zephyr*, 185; *California Zephyr*, 65, 221, 356, 761, 856, 979, 1094 (*see also Exposition Flyer*); *Denver Zephyr*, 182, 221; *Morning Zephyr*, 994; *Nebraska Zephyr*, 356, 908; *Pioneer Zephyr*, 183, *183*, 221, *365*; *Rio Grande Zephyr*, 356; *Twin Zephyr*, 221, *857*, 994
Ziegler, Ronald, 78
Zola, Emile, 595
zones of time, 8, 1003
Z-scale models, 910